CAR CARE GUIDE

2000 EDITION

Chek-Chart Publications

320 Soquel Way
Sunnyvale, CA 94086

Car Care Guide
Copyright © 2000 by Chek-Chart Publications

International Standard Book Number: 1-57932-377-4

This edition was created electronically using QuarkXPress® on the Macintosh G4. Diagrams were prepared using Adobe Illustrator™ and Streamline™.

Printed in the United States of America.

Chek-Chart Publications

320 Soquel Way
Sunnyvale, CA 94086
408-739-2435
"Chek" us out on the web at www.chekchart.com.

Executive Editor
Roger Fennema

Editor
Robert W. Colver

Researchers/Writers
Arnold Czarnecki
Robert S.M. Mason
Mark Polomik

Production Artist
Dave Douglass

Production Coordinator
Maria Glidden

DISCLAIMER & TECHNICAL CONCERNS

The publisher has made every reasonable effort to ensure that the material in this book is as accurate and up-to-date as possible. However, neither Chek-Chart nor any of its related companies can be held responsible for mistakes or omissions, or for changes in procedures or specifications by equipment manufacturers or suppliers.

Information in this book supersedes any printed in earlier issues.

Address your technical questions to:
Chek-Chart, Engineering Dept., 320 Soquel Way, Sunnyvale, CA 94086
(408) 739-2435

ACKNOWLEDGEMENTS

In producing this Guide, Chek-Chart has relied on the cooperation and assistance of the manufacturers whose products are included in the text. Without the help of the many marketing, engineering, service, and publications departments involved, this work would not have been possible.

Read This First!

The *Car Care Guide* is designed to provide essential service information for all domestic cars, light trucks, and most imports. It is a complete directory of service and maintenance specifications that you, the technician, will need to properly care for your customers' vehicles in accordance with vehicle manufacturers' service recommendations.

The *Car Care Guide* can be one of the most useful tools available, providing you take a few minutes to learn how to use it. This brief introduction to the *Guide* will show you:
• How to locate information
• How the *Guide* is arranged
• How to use the *Guide* to sell service.

How to Locate Information

The key to finding information in this *Guide* lies in the two-part index. You will notice that shaded tabs are visible on the edge of each page when you close the book. These tabs correspond to the index page at the front of the book. Lubrication and preventive maintenance information in the first half of this book are keyed to the gray tabs, and underhood service information and specifications in the second half of this book are keyed to the black tabs, all arranged alphabetically by vehicle manufacturer.

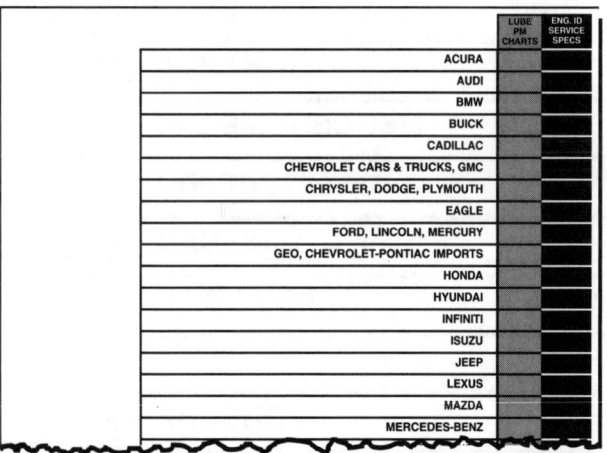

As an alternative, you can use another index located on pages VI through VII. This index is an alphabetical listing by model and year, with corresponding page numbers for lubrication charts and underhood service charts.

MODEL/YEAR		SERVICE DIAGRAMS	LUBE PM	ENG. ID TUNE-UP
Reatta	1989-91	17	17-22	253
Regency	1997-99	186	186-191	414
Regal	1989-99	17	17-22	253
Reliant	1989	50	50-81	291
Riviera	1989-99	17	17-22	253
Roadmaster	1991-96	17	17-22	253
RX-7	1989-95	152	152-163	381

How the *Guide* Is Arranged

So that you can quickly find the information you need, your *Car Care Guide* is divided into three sections:

• **Lubrication and Maintenance Information**, which includes lube and maintenance instructions, lubrication diagrams and specifications, and preventive maintenance schedules
• **Underhood Service Information**, which includes underhood service instructions, diagrams, and specifications.
• **Capacities; Tire and Wheel Data; Tables**, which include cooling and air conditioning system capacities, cooling system air bleed locations, wheel and tire specifications, and wheel-nut torque values
• **Appendix A-G**, provides line-art drawings for testing and adjustment as indicated throughout the Underhood Service Information section

Lubrication and Maintenance Information

The first section of the *Car Care Guide*, shows you how to use the Guide and discusses lubricants and their properties.

Following this section are Lubrication and Preventive Maintenance (Lube/PM) charts for domestic cars, light trucks, and popular imports. Chassis and engine diagrams show service lubrication points. Tables on the pages following these diagrams list lubricant capacities and recommen-

TURBOCHARGED ENGINES
EVERY 3 MO/3 MI–5 KM
Crankcase . . . . change oil

Oil filter . . . . replace
Initial service, then every other oil change

EVERY 6 MONTHS
Brake master cylinder . . check level **HB**

Clutch free pedal travel . . . check/adjust
Front wheel drive models, every 5 mi (8 km)

Power Steering Reservoir ..check level **PS**

dations, which are abbreviated on the charts. Use the "Key To Lubricants" to determine what the abbreviations mean. For example, HB stands for Hydraulic Brake Fluid, SAE J1703 or DOT-3 or -4, as indicated on the Key.

An important feature of the Lube/PM charts is the factory maintenance schedule for each vehicle. These charts list the services required at specific time or mileage intervals by the manufacturers. A table containing lubrication information for less popular makes completes the lubrication section of your *Guide*.

Underhood Service Information

The last section of the *Guide*, which is keyed to the black tabs, includes the specifications and instructions you need to perform underhood service on 1989-00 domestic cars, light trucks, and most imports. This section begins with instructions related to the underhood service specifications. Refer to these guidelines whenever how-to questions arise:

- General Information
- Electrical and Ignition Systems
- Fuel Systems
- Engine Mechanical
- Engine Computer Systems.

Following these instructions are Underhood Service Specifications, which are arranged alphabetically by vehicle manufacturer. Information in this section includes: engine identification information, cylinder numbering, firing order, and timing mark diagrams, followed by specifications necessary to perform underhood service.

Using the Specification Tables

To use the specification tables properly, you must determine which engine is in the vehicle you are servicing. Turn to the appropriate manufacturer's section, and locate the Engine Identification table. Use the vehicle identification number (VIN) on the vehicle and our table to identify the following:

- Model year of the car
- Engine code location
- Engine code
- Engine displacement, type of fuel system, and horsepower.

Once you know exactly which engine you are working on, using the diagrams and charts is simple. Following the engine codes are diagrams showing cylinder numbering sequences, firing order, and timing marks for each engine listed. Then complete specifications and notes required to test and diagnose engine electrical, ignition, fuel, mechanical, and computer systems are listed.

Throughout this section you will see references to the Appendix for testing and adjustment diagrams. These pictures will help clarify what the specifications mean.

Capacites & Tires

Following the lubrication section are tables listing cooling system capacities, fuel tank capacities, and air conditioning system capacities, cooling system air bleed locations, and tire pressures, sizes, and wheel-nut torques for cars, light trucks, and vans.

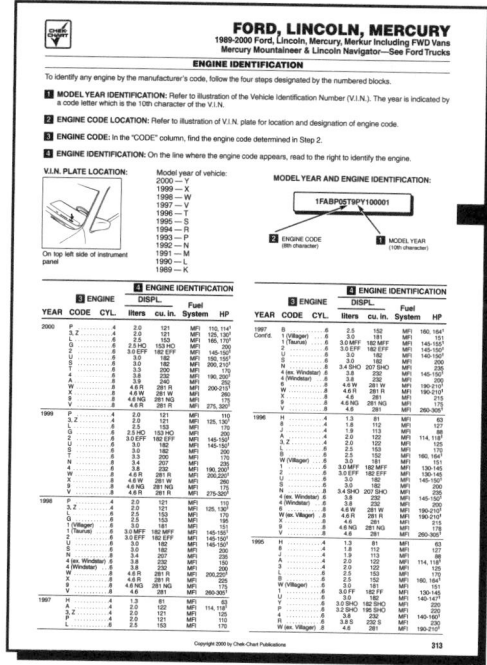

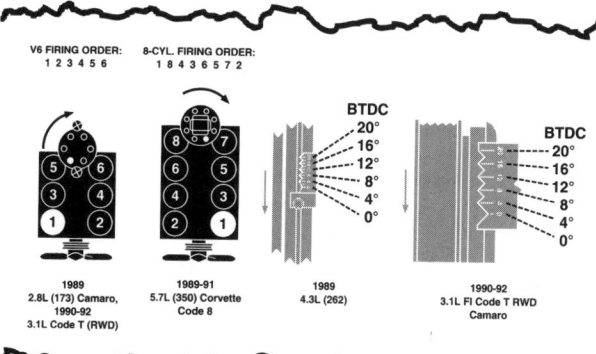

How to Use the *Guide* to Sell Service

Your *Car Care Guide* can help increase profits every time you service a car because it provides you and your customer with the manufacturer's recommended services and service intervals required to properly maintain a vehicle. Many customers will simply get an annual tune-up and lube job, or they will bring in their cars for service when they "think" it is time. Others will wait until the vehicle is not operating properly before having it serviced. Very few customers consistently have their cars serviced according to the factory recommendations.

You can do your customers a favor by using the *Car Care Guide* to point out the factory-recommended services. For the customer it is better service—for you it is greater profit. Once you make a habit of using the *Guide* in this way, you will find it easy to sell more service because the *Guide* will do it for you. The 1998 *Car Care Guide* is the best tool you have to increase the quality and profitability of your business.

INDEX

MODEL/YEAR	SERVICE DIAGRAMS	LUBE PM	ENG. ID TUNE-UP
PASSENGER CARS			
A4, A4 Quattro . . . 1992-99	7	7-12	242
A6, A6 Quattro . . . 1995-99	7	7-12	242
A8 1996-00	7	7-12	242
Accent 1995-00	127	127-130	358
Acclaim 1989-96	50	50-81	291
Accord 1989-96	123	123-126	352
Alero 1998-00	186	186-191	414
Achieva 1992-98	186	186-191	414
Allanté 1989-93	23	23-27	262
Altima 1993-00	178	178-185	406
Aries 1989	50	50-81	291
Aspire 1994-97	87	87-115	315
Aurora 1995-99	186	186-191	414
Avalon 1995-00	211	211-221	455
Avenger 1996-00	50	50-81	291
Axxess 1990-92	178	178-185	406
Beetle 1998-99	222	222-226	466
Beretta 1989-96	28	28-49	268
Bonneville 1989-00	192	192-197	423
Boxter 1997-00	198	198-202	436
Breeze 1996-00	50	50-81	291
Brougham 1990-96	23	23-27	262
C70 1998-99	227	227-230	472
C220, C230, C280 . 1994-98	164	164-169	390
Cabrio 1995-99	222	222-226	466
Cabriolet (Audi) . . . 1994-98	7	7-12	242
Cabriolet (V.W.) . . 1989-93	222	222-226	466
Calais 1989-91	186	186-191	414
Camaro 1989-00	28	28-49	268
Camry 1989-00	211	211-221	455
Capri 1989-94	87	87-115	315
Caprice 1989-99	28	28-49	268
Caravelle 1989	50	50-81	291
Caravelle Salon . . . 1989	50	50-81	291
Catera 1997-00	23	23-27	262
Cavalier 1989-00	28	28-49	268
Celebrity 1989-90	28	28-49	268
Celica 1989-00	211	211-221	455
Century 1989-00	17	17-22	253
Charade 1989-92	—	231-234	—
Ciera 1989-96	186	186-191	414
Cimarron 1989	23	23-27	262
Cirrus 1995-00	50	50-81	291
Civic 1989-00	123	123-126	352
Colony Park 1989-91	87	87-115	315
Colt 1989-96	50	50-81	291
Colt Vista 1989-94	50	50-81	291
Concorde 1993-99	50	50-81	291
Conquest 1989	50	50-81	291
Continental 1989-00	87	87-115	315
Contour 1995-00	87	87-115	315
Cordia 1989	170	170-177	397
Corolla 1989-99	211	211-221	455
Corrado 1990-94	222	222-226	466
Corsica 1989-96	28	28-49	268
Corvette 1989-00	28	28-49	268
Cougar 1989-00	87	87-115	315
Country Squire wagon 1989-91	87	87-115	315
Coupe GT (Audi) . . 1989	7	7-12	242
Coupe Quattro . . . 1990-92	7	7-12	242
Cressida 1989-92	211	211-221	455
Crown Victoria . . . 1989-00	87	87-115	315
CR-V 1997-99	123	123-126	352
CRX 1989-91	123	123-126	352
Custom Cruiser wagon 1989-92	186	186-191	414
Cutlass Calais . . . 1989-92	186	186-191	414
Cutlass Ciera . . . 1989-96	186	186-191	414
Cutlass Cruiser wagon 1989-96	186	186-191	414
Cutlass Supreme . . 1989-99	186	186-191	414
Daytona 1989-93	50	50-81	291
Del Sol 1993-97	123	123-126	352
Delta 88 1989	186	186-191	414
DeVille 1989-00	23	23-27	262
Diamante 1992-00	170	170-177	397
Diplomat 1989	50	50-81	291
DL (Subaru) 1989	208	208-210	449
DL (Volvo) 1989	227	227-230	472
Dynasty 1989-93	50	50-81	291
E320, E420, E500 . 1994-98	164	164-169	390
Echo 2000	211	211-221	455
Eclipse 1990-00	170	170-177	397
Eighty-Eight 1989-99	186	186-191	414
Elantra 1992-00	127	127-130	358
Eldorado 1989-00	23	23-27	262
Electra 1989-90	17	17-22	253
Escort 1989-00	87	87-115	315
Esteem 1995-97	—	231-234	—
ES250 1990-91	211	211-221	455
ES300 1992-00	211	211-221	455
Estate Wagon 1989-96	17	17-22	253
Excel 1989-94	127	127-130	358
Expo, Expo LRV . . 1992-98	170	170-177	397
Festiva 1989-93	87	87-115	315
Firebird 1989-00	192	192-197	423
Firefly 1989-00	192	192-197	423
Fleetwood 1989-92	23	23-27	262
Focus 2000	87	87-115	315
Forester 1998	208	208-210	449
Fox 1989-93	222	222-226	466
Galant 1989-00	170	170-177	397
GL (Subaru) 1989	208	208-210	449
GL (Volvo) 1989	227	227-230	472
Golf 1989-00	222	222-226	466
Gran Fury 1989	50	50-81	291
Grand Am 1989-00	192	192-197	423
Grand Marquis . . . 1989-00	87	87-115	315
Grand Prix 1989-00	192	192-197	423
GS300 1993-00	211	211-221	455
GS400 1998-00	211	211-221	455
GTI 1989-00	222	222-226	466
G20 1992-00	131	131-132	364
Horizon 1989-90	50	50-81	291
I-Mark 1989	133	133-139	367
Impala 1994-00	28	28-49	268
Imperial 1991-93	50	50-81	291
Impreza 1993-00	208	208-210	449
Impulse 1989-92	133	133-139	367
Integra 1989-00	4	4-6	237
Intrepid 1993-00	50	50-81	291
Intrigue 1998-00	186	186-191	414
I30 1995-00	131	131-132	364
Jetta 1989-99	222	222-226	466
Justy 1989-94	208	208-210	449
J30 1993-97	131	131-132	364
Lancer 1989	50	50-81	291
Lanos 1998-00	—	231-234	—
Laser 1989-94	50	50-81	291
LeBaron 1989-95	50	50-81	291
LeBaron GTS . . . 1989	50	50-81	291
Legacy 1990-00	208	208-210	449
Legend 1989-90	4	4-6	237
Leganza 1998-00	—	231-234	—
LeMans 1989-93	192	192-197	423
LeSabre 1989-00	17	17-22	253
LHS 1994-00	50	50-81	291
Loyale 1990-96	208	208-210	449
LS 2000	87	87-115	315
LS400 1990-99	148	148-151	377
Lumina (car) 1990-00	28	28-49	268
Malibu 1997-00	28	28-49	268
Mark VII 1989-93	87	87-115	315
Mark VIII 1993-97	87	87-115	315
Maxima 1989-00	178	178-185	406

MODEL/YEAR	SERVICE DIAGRAMS	LUBE PM	ENG. ID TUNE-UP
Metro 1989-00	116	116-122	346
Miata 1990-00	152	152-163	381
Micra 1989-91	178	178-185	406
Millenia 1995-00	152	152-163	381
Mirage 1989-00	170	170-177	397
Monaco 1990-92	82	82-86	310
Monte Carlo 1995-00	28	28-49	268
MR2 1989-95	211	211-221	455
Mustang 1989-00	87	87-115	315
Mystique 1995-00	87	87-115	315
M Coupe, Roadster . 1999	13	13-16	248
MX-3 1992-95	152	152-163	381
MX-6 1989-97	152	152-163	381
M3 1989-99	13	13-16	248
M5 1989-93	13	13-16	248
M6 1989	13	13-16	248
M30 1990-93	131	131-132	364
Neon 1995-00	50	50-81	291
New Yorker 1989-98	50	50-81	291
Ninety Eight 1989-96	186	186-191	414
Nubira 1998-00	—	231-234	—
NSX 1991-00	—	231-234	—
NX 1991-96	178	178-185	406
Oasis 1995-99	123	123-126	352
Odyssey 1995-99	123	123-126	352
Omni 1989-90	50	50-81	291
Optima 1989-91	192	192-197	423
Outback 1996-00	208	208-210	449
Park Avenue 1989-00	17	17-22	253
Paseo 1992-97	211	211-221	455
Passat 1989-99	222	222-226	466
Precidia 1992-95	152	1502-163	381
Precis 1989-94	127	127-130	358
Prelude 1989-91	123	123-126	352
Premier 1989-92	82	82-86	310
Previa 1991-97	211	211-221	455
Prizm 1989-00	211	211-221	455
Probe 1989-97	87	87-115	315
Protegé 1990-00	152	152-163	381
Prowler 1998-00	50	50-81	291
Pulsar 1989-90	178	178-185	406
Q45 1990-00	131	131-132	364
Reatta 1989-91	17	17-22	253
Regency 1997-99	186	186-191	414
Regal 1989-99	17	17-22	253
Reliant 1989	50	50-81	291
Riviera 1989-99	17	17-22	253
Roadmaster 1991-96	17	17-22	253
RX-7 1989-95	152	152-163	381
RX300 1999	148	148-151	377
S4, S6 1993-95	7	7-12	242
S70 1998-00	227	227-230	472
S80 1999	227	227-230	472
S90 1998	227	227-230	472
S350, S420, S500, S600 . . . 1994-99	164	164-169	390
Sable 1989-00	87	87-115	315
Saturn, S Series . . 1991-00	206	206-207	446
Saturn, L Series . . . 2000	206	206-207	446
Scirocco 1989-91	222	222-226	465
Scoupe 1991-96	127	127-130	358
SC300 1992-00	148	148-149	377
SC400 1992-00	148	148-149	377
Sebring ex. Convertible 1995-00	50	50-81	291
Sebring Convertible . 1996-00	50	50-81	291
Sentra 1989-99	178	178-185	406
Sephia 1993-00	—	231-234	—
Serenia 1992-95	152	152-163	381
Seville 1989-00	23	23-27	262
Shadow 1989-94	50	50-81	291
Skyhawk 1989	17	17-22	253
Skylark 1989-98	17	17-22	253

MODEL/YEAR	SERVICE DIAGRAMS	LUBE PM	ENG. ID TUNE-UP
SL320, SL500, SL600 1994-99	164	164-169	390
Solara 1999-00	211	211-221	455
Sonata 1989-00	127	127-130	358
Spectrum 1989	133	133-139	367
Spider 1989-94	—	231-234	—
Spirit 1989-95	50	50-81	291
Sprint 1989	116	116-122	346
Stanza 1989-92	178	178-185	397
Stealth 1991-96	50	50-81	291
Storm 1990-94	133	133-139	367
Stratus 1995-00	50	50-81	291
Stylus 1990-93	133	133-139	367
Summit 1989-96	82	82-86	310
Sunbird 1989-94	192	192-197	423
Sundance 1989-94	50	50-81	291
Sunfire (Pontiac) . . 1995-00	192	192-197	423
Supra 1989-98	211	211-221	455
SVX 1992-97	208	208-210	449
Swift 1989-97	—	231-234	—
Talon 1990-98	82	82-86	310
Taurus 1989-00	87	87-115	315
Tempest 1989-91	192	192-197	423
Tempo 1989-94	87	87-115	315
Tercel 1989-99	211	211-221	455
Thunderbird 1989-98	87	87-115	315
Tiburon 1997-00	127	127-130	358
Topaz 1989-94	87	87-115	315
Toronado 1989-92	186	186-191	414
Town Car 1989-00	87	87-115	315
Town & Country . . . 1989-00	50	50-81	291
Tracer 1989-99	87	87-115	315
Trans AM 1989-92	192	192-197	423
Troféo 1989-93	186	186-191	414
TT 1999	7	7-12	242
V70 1998-99	227	227-230	472
V90 1998	227	227-230	472
Vigor 1992-95	4	4-6	237
Viper 1995-00	—	231-234	—
Vision 1993-97	50	50-81	291
Vista 1989-94	82	82-86	310
V8 Quattro 1989-94	7	7-12	242
XJ6 1989-99	—	231-234	—
XJ12 1994-99	—	231-234	—
XJS 1989-97	—	231-234	—
XT Coupe 1989-91	208	208-210	449
Z3 1996-99	13	13-16	248
2.2CL, 2.3L, 3.0CL . 1997-00	4	4-6	237
2.5TL 1995-98	4	4-6	237
3.2TL 1995-00	4	4-6	237
3.5RL 1996-00	4	4-6	237
9-3 1998-00	203	203-205	441
9-5 1998-00	203	203-205	441
80, 80 Quattro . . . 1989-92	7	7-12	242
90, 90 Quattro . . . 1989-95	7	7-12	242
100, 100 Quattro . . 1989-95	7	7-12	242
164 (Alfa Romeo) . . 1991-95	—	231-234	—
190 Series (M.B.) . . 1989-93	164	164-169	390
200, 200 Quattro . . 1989-91	7	7-12	242
200SX 1989-98	178	178-785	406
240 Series (Volvo) . 1989-95	227	227-230	472
240SX 1989-98	178	178-785	406
260 Series (M.B.) . . 1989	164	164-169	390
300 Series (M.B.) . . 1989-93	164	164-169	390
300M 1999-00	50	50-81	290
300ZX (Nissan) . . . 1989-96	178	178-185	406
318i 1989-99	13	13-16	248
323 1998-99	152	152-163	381
325e, 325i 1989-95	13	13-16	248
328i, is 1996-99	13	13-16	248
400 Series (M.B.) . . 1989-93	164	164-169	390
405 1989-92	—	231-234	—
420 Series (M.B.) . . 1989-91	164	164-169	390

INDEX

MODEL/YEAR	SERVICE DIAGRAMS	LUBE PM	ENG. ID TUNE-UP
500 Series (M.B.) . . 1989-93	164	164-169	390
524td, 525, 528e . . 1989-95	13	13-16	248
528 1997-99	13	13-16	248
530i, 540i 1994-95	13	13-16	248
540 1997-99	13	13-16	248
533i, 535i 1989-92	13	13-16	248
560 Series (M.B.) . . 1989-91	164	164-169	390
600 Series (M.B.) . . 1992-93	164	164-169	390
626 1989-00	152	152-163	381
635CSi 1989	13	13-16	248
700 Series (Volvo) . 1989-92	227	227-230	472
735i, 740i, iL, 750i, iL 1989-99	13	13-16	248
825, 827 (Sterling) . 1989-91	—	231-234	—
840, 850 (BMW) . . 1991-97	13	13-16	248
850 (Volvo) 1993-97	227	227-230	472
900 (Saab) 1989-97	203	203-205	441
900 Series (Volvo) . 1991-97	227	227-230	472
911, 924, 944, 928, 968 1989-00	198	198-202	436
929 1989-95	152	152-163	381
3000GT 1991-99	170	170-177	397
6000 (Pontiac) . . . 1989-91	192	192-197	423
9000 1989-97	148	148-151	377

LIGHT TRUCKS, VANS, UTILITY VEHICLES

MODEL/YEAR	SERVICE DIAGRAMS	LUBE PM	ENG. ID TUNE-UP
Aerostar. 1989-97	87	87-115	315
Amigo 1991-00	133	133-139	367
Astro 1989-00	28	28-49	268
Blazer (full size) . . . 1989-94	28	28-49	268
Bravada. 1991-00	28	28-49	268
Bronco 1989-96	87	87-115	315
Bronco II 1989-90	87	87-115	315
B2200. 1989-93	152	152-163	381
B2300, B2500. . . . 1994-00	87	87-115	315
B2600. 1989-93	152	152-163	381
B3000, B4000. . . . 1994-00	87	87-115	315
Caravan. 1989-00	50	50-81	291
Cherokee 1989-00	140	140-147	373
Chevrolet:			
C, K1500, 2500, 3500 1989-00	28	28-49	268
G10, 20, 30 . . . 1989-96	28	28-49	268
G1500, 2500, 3500 1996-00	28	28-49	268
R10, 20, 30 1989	28	28-49	268
R1500, 2500, 3500 1989-91	28	28-49	268
S10, S Blazer . . . 1989-00	28	28-49	268
V10, 20, 30 1989	28	28-49	268
V1500, 2500, 3500 1989-91	28	28-49	268
Comanche 1989-93	140	140-147	373
CR-V 1997-00	123	123-126	352
Dakota 1989-00	50	50-81	291
Denali 1999-00	28	28-49	268
Dodge:			
B150, B250, B350 1989-00	50	50-81	291
1500, 2500, 3500 Pickups 1994-00	50	50-81	291
D150, 250, 350 . . 1989-93	50	50-81	291
W150, 250, 350 . . 1989-93	50	50-81	291
Durango. 1998-00	50	50-81	291
Envoy 1999-00	28	28-49	268
Escalade 1999-00	23	23-27	262
EuroVan. 1993-00	222	222-226	466
Expedition. 1997-00	87	87-115	315
Explorer. 1991-00	87	87-115	315
Ford:			
E, F150, 250, 350 . 1989-00	87	87-115	315
Frontier 1998-00	178	178-185	406
Forester 1999	208	208-210	449
GMC:			
C, K1500, 2500, 3500 1989-00	28	28-49	268
G1500, 2500, 3500 1989-00	28	28-49	268
R1500, 2500, 3500 . 1989-91	28	28-49	268
S15, Sonoma, S Jimmy. 1989-00	28	28-49	268

MODEL/YEAR	SERVICE DIAGRAMS	LUBE PM	ENG. ID TUNE-UP
V1500, 2500, 3500 . 1989-91	28	28-49	268
Grand Cherokee . . 1993-00	140	140-147	373
Grand Wagoneer . . 1989-93	140	140-147	373
Hombre 1989-00	28	28-49	268
Hummer. 1996-97	—	231-234	—
Isuzu Pickup 1989-95	131	131-139	367
Jimmy (full size). . . 1989-91	28	28-49	268
Land Cruiser 1989-97	—	231-234	—
1998-00	211	211-221	455
Land Rover 1994-00	—	231-234	—
Lumina APV, Minivan 1990-96	28	28-49	268
LX450. 1996-97	—	231-234	—
LX470. 1998-00	211	211-221	455
Mini Ram Van 1989-93	50	50-81	291
Mitsubishi Pickup . . 1989-96	170	170-177	397
Mitsubishi Van . . . 1989-90	170	170-177	397
Montana 1999-00	192	192-197	423
Montero. 1989-00	170	170-177	397
Montero Sport. . . . 1997-00	170	170-177	397
Mountaineer 1996-00	87	87-115	315
MPV. 1989-98	152	152-163	381
Navajo 1991-94	87	87-115	315
Nissan Pickup. . . . 1989-97	178	178-185	406
Passport 1994-00	133	133-139	367
Pathfinder. 1989-99	178	178-185	406
Previa 1991-97	211	211-221	455
Quest 1993-00	178	178-185	406
QX4 1996-00	178	178-185	406
Raider 1989	170	170-177	397
Ramcharger. 1989-93	50	50-81	291
Ram 50 1989-93	50	50-81	291
Range Rover 1989-99	—	231-234	—
Ranger 1989-00	87	87-115	406
RAV 4 1996-00	211	211-221	455
Rocky. 1990-92	—	231-234	—
Rodeo. 1991-00	133	133-139	367
RX300 1998-00	148	148-151	377
Safari 1989-00	28	28-49	268
Samurai. 1989-95	—	231-234	—
Sidekick 1989-97	—	231-234	—
Sienna 1998-00	211	211-221	455
Silhouette 1990-00	28	28-49	268
SLX 1996-99	133	133-139	367
Sportage 1994-00	—	231-234	—
Suburban 1989-00	28	28-49	268
Suburban LT 2000	28	28-49	268
Sunrunner. 1993-99	116	116-126	346
Syclone 1991-93	28	28-49	268
T100 1993-98	211	211-221	455
Tacoma 1995-00	211	211-221	455
Tahoe 1995-00	28	28-49	268
Town and Country. . 1989-00	50	50-81	291
Toyota Pickup. . . . 1989-95	211	211-221	455
Toyota Van 1989	211	211-221	455
Tracker 1989-00	116	116-122	346
Trans Sport 1990-98	28	28-49	268
Trooper 1989-00	133	133-139	367
Tundra 2000	211	211-221	455
Vanagon 1989-91	222	222-226	466
Vehicross 1999-00	133	133-139	367
Venture 1997-00	28	28-49	268
Villager 1993-00	87	87-115	315
Voyager 1989-00	50	50-81	291
Wagoneer. 1989-90	140	140-147	373
Windstar 1995-00	87	87-115	315
Wrangler 1989-00	140	140-147	373
X90 1996-97	—	231-234	—
Xterra 2000	178	178-185	406
YJ 1989-99	140	140-147	373
Yukon 1991-00	28	28-49	268

Introduction

WARRANTY SERVICE REQUIREMENTS

Most automakers warrant their new models for a specific mileage or period of time from the date of delivery. Some items, such as tires and batteries, are not usually covered by the vehicle warranty, but instead are covered under separate warranties provided by the component manufacturers. The length of the basic vehicle warranty coverage varies from one automaker to the next. Some manufacturers offer extended protection on certain components, and others offer longer warranty coverage at an extra charge. Federal law requires, however, that the emission control systems and related components of all passenger cars and light-duty trucks be warranted for 5 years or 50,000 miles (80,000 km), whichever comes first. According to the 1990 Clean Air Act, this warranty period will be modified at a later time.

To keep warranties in effect, all manufacturers require vehicle owners to service their vehicles at specific intervals. Severe service intervals listed are performed in addition to normal service. The service charts in this manual detail the services required to protect both the basic vehicle warranty and the emission control system warranty. Follow the instructions on each manufacturer's maintenance chart to determine the services required to maintain the warranty. Always provide your customers an itemized work order that clearly shows the date and mileage when required services were performed.

LUBRICANTS

ENGINE OILS

Engine oil is identified in two ways: by the American Petroleum Institute (API) Service Classification and by the Society of Automotive Engineers (SAE) Viscosity Number. Manufacturers' recommendations for both classification and viscosity are shown on the service charts.

API SERVICE CLASSIFICATIONS

The API Service Classifications rate engine oils on their ability to lubricate, resist oxidation, prevent high- and low-temperature engine deposits, and protect the engine from rust and corrosion. The Service Classifications are two-letter codes beginning with either an "S" or a "C." The "S" prefix designates oils formulated for gasoline engine service. The "C" prefix designates oils formulated for diesel engine service.

There are a total of nine "S" classifications (SA through SJ) and eight "C" classifications (CA through CG-4). However, only six of the seventeen classifications are used in modern gasoline and diesel engines.

API Service SG

SG-rated oils are recommended for gasoline engines in passenger cars and trucks made in 1989 and later. Oils developed for SG service provide protection against oxidation, rust, corrosion, and engine deposits formed by high temperatures better than oils with the SF Service Classifications. You may substitute SG-rated oil for SF- or SE-rated oils.

API Service SH

SH-rated oils are recommended for gasoline engines in passenger cars and trucks made in 1993 and later. Oils developed for SH service provide superior deposit control and reduce oxidation, engine wear, rust buildup, and corrosion better than oils with the SG service classification. You may use oils meeting API Service Classification SH where SF or SG oils are recommended.

API Service SJ

SJ-rated oils are recommended for gasoline engines in passenger cars and trucks made in 1996 and later. These oils resist oxidation and wear better than oils with the SH classification. SJ-rated oils also protect against engine deposits, rust, and corrosion. Oils meeting API Service Classification SJ may be used where SG or SH oils are recommended.

API Service CC

CC-rated oils are recommended for some naturally aspirated, turbocharged, or supercharged diesel engines operated in moderate or severe conditions, and some heavy-duty gasoline engines. This type of oil was introduced in 1961, and protects against deposits formed by high temperatures and bearing corrosion in diesel engines. It also protects against rust, corrosion, and low-temperature deposits in gasoline engines.

API Service CD

CD-rated oils are recommended for some naturally aspirated, turbocharged, or supercharged diesel engines where highly effective control of wear and deposits is important. It is also recommended when using fuels of a wide quality range, including high sulfur fuels. This type of oil was introduced in 1955, and protects against bearing corrosion and deposits formed by high temperatures in diesel engines.

API Service CD-II

CD-II–rated oils offer the same protection as CD-rated oils, with additional protective properties for use in heavy-duty two-stroke diesel engines. Vehicles requiring the use of CD-II–rated oils are not covered in this manual.

API Service CE

CE-rated oils are recommended for turbocharged or supercharged heavy-duty diesel engines made in 1983 and later. This oil is specially designed for vehicles that are operated under both low-speed/high-load and high-speed/high-load conditions. You may substitute CE-rated oil for CC- or CD-rated oils.

API Service CF-4

CF-4 oils provide improved performance over CE oils in control of oil consumption and piston deposits. These oils are designed for high-speed, four-stroke diesel engines, particularly those used in heavy-duty, on-highway trucks. Introduced late in 1990, CF-4 oils are required in some vehicles to meet 1991 EPA emission regulations, and may be used where CC, CD, or CE oils are specified.

API Service CG-4

CG-4, designed for four stroke diesel engines, provide improved performance over CF-4 oils. CG-4 oils are required to meet 1994 emission standards. They may be used where CC, CD, CE, or CF-4 oils are specified.

Some oils are identified with dual API Service Classifications separated by a slash, for example, SG/CC, SG/CD, SH/CG-4, or SJ/CG-4. These oils meet the requirements of both Service Classifications, and you can use them in any engine that calls for one or the other. Many manufacturers specify oils that meet both "S" and "C" Service Classifications. This is particularly true for heavy-duty and turbocharged engines. If the manufacturer recommends an oil with a dual Service Classification, do not use an oil that meets only a single classification, as this may void the engine warranty.

SAE VISCOSITY GRADES

The SAE Viscosity Grade is a number that corresponds to an oil's resistance to flow. Typical oil Viscosity Grade numbers are 5W, 10W, 15W, 20W, 20, 30, 40, and 50. If the Viscosity Grade number is low, the oil is thin and flows easily. If the number is high, the oil is thick and has a greater resistance to flow. A "W" after the viscosity grade indicates that the oil viscosity is measured at low temperatures and is intended for use in cold-weather operation.

Oil viscosity is greatly affected by temperature. When an oil is cold, its viscosity increases, and it does not flow easily. If you use a high-viscosity oil in low-temperature conditions, heavily loaded engine parts will not receive oil until the engine warms and the oil thins. When an oil is hot, it thins out and flows easily. If you use a low-viscosity oil in an engine that runs at extremely high temperatures, the oil film between critical engine parts will thin and may break down. This allows moving parts to touch, resulting in rapid wear and possible engine damage.

In the past, manufacturers recommended single-grade oils. However, you must change single-grade oils with respect to the changing seasonal temperatures. Low-viscosity oils are required in winter, while high-viscosity oils are needed in summer. Today, single-grade oils are rec-

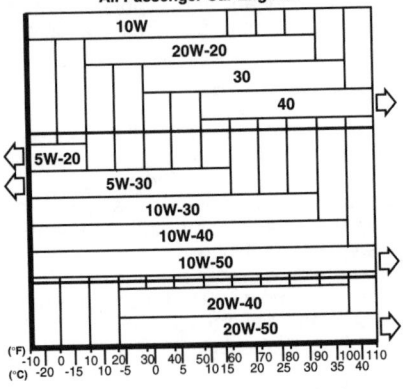

OIL VISCOSITY RECOMMENDATIONS
All Passenger Car Engines

10W
20W-20
30
40
5W-20
5W-30
10W-30
10W-40
10W-50
20W-40
20W-50

(°F) -10 0 10 20 30 40 50 60 70 80 90 100 110
(°C) -20 -15 -10 -5 0 5 10 15 20 25 30 35 40

This chart shows oil viscosity recommendations based on ambient temperature.

ommended primarily for heavy-duty and diesel engines.

Modern oils have dual Viscosity Grade numbers separated by a dash, such as 5W-30, 10W-30, 15W-40, or 20W-50. These multigrade oils meet the low- and high-temperature specifications for both viscosities of oil indicated. Additives called "viscosity index improvers" cause oils to flow well at low temperatures, yet still resist thinning at high temperatures. You can use multigrade oils in passenger vehicles throughout the year.

Most automakers do not recommend using low-viscosity multigrade (nor single-grade) oils for sustained high-speed driving, trailer towing, or other circumstances where the engine is placed under constant, heavy load. Check the service charts for the recommended grade of oil you should use for various temperatures and driving conditions.

ENERGY-CONSERVING OILS

In addition to Service Classification and Viscosity Grade, some oils are designated as Energy-Conserving or Energy-Conserving II by the API. These oils are specially formulated to reduce internal engine friction, and thus improve fuel economy by 1.5 or 2.7 percent respectively. Energy-Conserving oils usually have friction-reducing additives and a relatively low viscosity.

ENGINE OIL IDENTIFICATION

The API uses the Engine Service Classification Symbol, or "doughnut," on oil containers to help you identify oil types. The API Service Classification is in the upper half of the symbol, the SAE Viscosity Grade is in the center of the symbol, and the words "Energy Conserving" or "Energy Conserving II" are in the lower half of the symbol if the oil is formulated to meet "Energy Conserving" requirements. Always make sure that the oil quality information on the API "doughnut" meets the vehicle manufacturer's

specifications. For some vehicles, you will need special oil that has requirements beyond the API oil classifications. Always check the manufacturer's specifications.

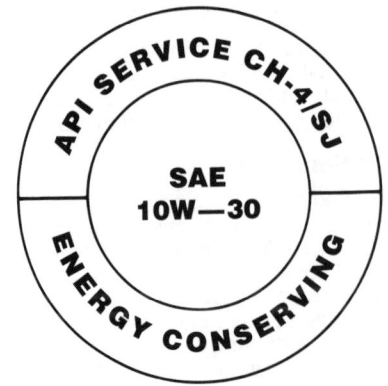

The API engine service classification symbol, or "doughnut," has the information needed to identify engine oils.

Beginning in 1993, oil quality can be further identified by the use of a new "starburst" symbol. This symbol indicates that the oil has been certified by the International Lubricant Standardization & Approval Committee (ILSAC) as the correct type for gasoline engines in passenger cars and light trucks. To qualify for the starburst symbol, oils must meet the Energy Conserving II requirements. Therefore, only multiviscosity oils with SAE 0W, 5W, and 10W, such as 5W-30 and 10W-30, will qualify.

The starburst identifies Energy Conserving II oils suitable for light-duty gasoline engine use. In the Car Care Guide, *these oils are indicated in the* Key to Lubricants *tables by the symbol - API★.*

ENGINE COOLANT

All vehicle manufacturers recommend ethylene glycol antifreeze because it prevents engine freeze-up in winter, raises the boiling point of the coolant in summer, and protects the cooling system from rust and corrosion. In modern vehicles with aluminum cooling system components, you must use a quality coolant that contains the proper anti-corrosion additives.

Most vehicle manufacturers recommend a 50/50 mixture of coolant and water, which provides antifreeze protection

down to approximately -30°F (-34°C). Higher concentrations, up to 67 percent coolant, lower the freezing point even further, but beyond 67-percent concentration, the freezing point rises sharply. High concentrations of coolant additives also will cause the coolant to gel, which inhibits cooling system effectiveness. Always top up a cooling system with a 50/50 mixture of water and coolant. Be sure the coolant meets the vehicle manufacturer's specifications.

POWER STEERING FLUID

Power steering fluid is hydraulic oil that is designed to be compatible with rubber hoses and seals in the power steering system. It resists thinning and breakdown at high temperatures, and usually contains an additive to maintain good flow at temperatures as low as -20° to 40°F (-29° to 4°C).

Some automakers recommend special power steering fluids, although others specify Automatic Transmission Fluid (ATF). Always use the type of fluid recommended by the vehicle manufacturer, as shown on the service charts. Never mix different types of fluid, and never use anything but the specified fluid. Use of the wrong fluid can destroy rubber seals and hoses and cause system failure.

AUTOMATIC TRANSMISSION FLUID (ATF)

Although ATF is used in some manual transmissions, its primary application is in automatic transmissions. Manufacturers specify one of two basic ATF types: those that are friction-modified, and those that are not. The differences between friction-modified and unmodified fluids are chemically complex, but the essential factor is that friction-modified fluids contain additives that make them more slippery under certain operating conditions.

DEXRON®-IIE and DEXRON®-III, used in most modern automatic transmissions, MERCON® and MERCON® V used in most late-model Ford transmissions, and MOPAR ATF+3® and ATF+4® used in DaimlerChrysler automatics with locking torque converters, are friction-modified fluids. If you use an unmodified fluid in a transmission that requires friction modified fluid, harsh shift action will be the most noticeable result. Although this will be objectionable to the customer, it will probably not cause any long-term damage.

Type F fluid, used in early Ford automatic transmissions and some recent automatics from other manufacturers, is an unmodified fluid. If you use a friction-modified fluid in a transmission requiring unmodified fluid, slow shift action and increased slippage will result. Over time, increased heat and wear will cause premature transmission failure.

Many manufacturers require special automatic transmission fluids to accommodate particular transmission designs. In some cases, the recommended fluid for a transmission changes from one model year to

the next because of internal modifications. Always consult the service charts to obtain the proper fluid for the transmission you are servicing.

GEAR OILS

Gear oils are used in many transmissions and other drivetrain components. As with motor oils, both the API and SAE have established rating systems for gear oils. The API Service Classifications run from GL-1 through GL-5. The most common gear oils for late-model cars and light trucks are GL-4 and GL-5. They contain Extreme Pressure (EP) additives, which lubricate the hypoid final drive gears. To avoid synchronizer damage, some transmissions use a special GL-4 with non-reactive EP additives. Some manufacturers use special gear oils that are not classified under the API system. These are designated HP, EP, and GLS on the service charts. See the Key to Lubricants for a description of these gear oils.

The SAE Viscosity Grades for gear oils are similar to those for engine oils. Some examples are 75W, 80W, 80, 90, and 140. Although higher numbers are assigned to gear oils, the oils are not necessarily higher in viscosity than engine oils. As with engine oils, gear oil viscosity grades are measured at both high and low temperatures, and are available in multigrade designations such as 75W-90 and 80W-90.

Special gear oil is often required for limited-slip differentials. Some vehicle manufacturers recommend that you mix an additive with the gear oil. If this is required, you will find the information on the service charts.

VEHICLE HOISTING

Recommended lift points for vehicles are shown as black squares (■) on the chassis diagrams. Position the lift adapters carefully to distribute the vehicle weight evenly. When lifting a vehicle, raise the hoist slowly until it just contacts the chassis. Then double-check the lift adapters to be sure they are secure and that the vehicle does not shift when you raise it. Make sure that the lift does not hit brake lines, fuel lines, wiring harnesses, or exhaust system components.

CAUTION: Take special care when removing wheels, brake drums, the fuel tank, or other components at the rear of FWD vehicles. Because most of the powertrain weight on these vehicles is located above (or in front of) the front axle centerline, any significant reduction in weight at the rear may cause the car to tip forward on the hoist.

CHASSIS AND WHEEL BEARING GREASE

All greases are made from oils and a thickening agent to ensure that the lubricant clings to the surfaces where it is needed. Manufacturers frequently specify different types of greases for the chassis and wheel

bearings. Some greases meet the specifications for both and are called multi-purpose greases. Greases may be classified in two ways: by their National Lubricating Grease Institute (NLGI) number, and by the type of thickening agent used.

The NLGI number designates the viscosity or consistency of a grease—the higher the number, the thicker the grease. The NLGI number is only a means of comparison. It is not a measure of quality or performance. Typically, wheel bearing greases and most chassis greases have an NLGI #2 consistency number.

Greases are thickened with soaps made of calcium, sodium, lithium, or aluminum. The type and amount of soap determine the melting point, appearance, texture, and water resistance of a grease. Most manufacturers today recommend grease made with a lithium-based thickener; these greases have a fairly high melting point and offer good water resistance.

A new NLGI grease classification system was introduced in 1990. Under the new system, greases must pass performance tests and are given a designator, as in the API service classifications for oils. Greases passing all requirements in one or more of the categories display the approved NLGI label on the package. The classifications are "GC" for wheel bearing grease, "LB" for chassis grease, and "GC-LB" for greases that can be used for both applications.

This label reflects the NLGI grease classification system that was introduced in 1990.

Greases also contain additives that improve their performance, such as molybdenum disulfide or "moly," which improves the antiwear and antiseize properties of a grease. To increase the load-carrying ability under extreme pressure, EP additives are sometimes used.

Never mix different types of greases, they are not all compatible with each other. When you lubricate chassis fittings or repack wheel bearings, always use greases that meet the vehicle manufacturer's specifications.

BRAKE FLUIDS

Brake fluid transmits the force that enables the brakes to stop the car. If the brake fluid level is low or if air enters the hydraulic system, partial or complete brake failure will result. The same is true if inferior fluid, fluid of the wrong type, or contaminated fluid is used. Always use brake fluid that meets the vehicle manufacturer's specifications.

There are two ways of identifying brake fluids: by their type and by their Department of Transportation (DOT) grade number. Brake fluids can be made of three different materials: polyglycol, silicone, and Hydraulic System Mineral Oil (HSMO). The fluid type identifies the basic ingredient in the fluid. There are also three DOT grades of fluid: DOT 3, DOT 4, and DOT 5. The DOT grade numbers are performance standards established by the government. The higher the number, the more stringent the standard.

Polyglycol brake fluid is the most common type. All current polyglycol fluids are DOT 3 or DOT 4 grade. Most domestic automakers specify polyglycol DOT 3 fluids. Ford Motor Company cars use a heavy-duty DOT 3 fluid with an extra high boiling point. Many import automakers specify DOT 4 polyglycol fluid.

CAUTION: Polyglycol brake fluid is a strong solvent that dissolves paint on contact. This type of fluid also has a strong natural attraction for water, which reduces its boiling point. Avoid spillage, and always store unused polyglycol brake fluid in a tightly sealed container.

Silicone brake fluids are the only type that meet all of the DOT 5 specifications. Silicone fluid has an extremely high boiling point, is not a solvent, and does not absorb moisture. Despite this, silicone fluid is not used as original equipment in mass production cars at this time. Silicone fluid is compatible with polyglycol fluid, but the two types do not actually blend together. For this reason, do not mix silicone and polyglycol brake fluids.

ACURA
1989-2000 All Models except NSX
SLX—See Isuzu

CHEK-CHART

AAIDP-1

AAIDP-1

SERVICE LOCATIONS — ENGINE AND CHASSIS

HOOD RELEASE: Inside

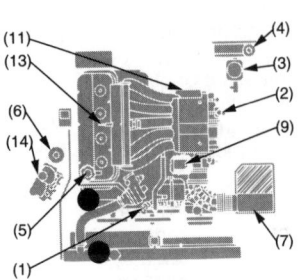

1989-00 Integra

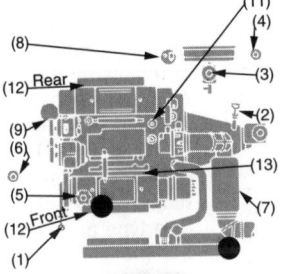

1992-98 Vigor, 2.5TL

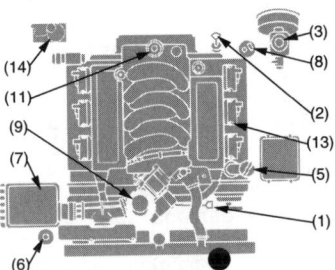

1989-90 Legend

1991-95 Legend 1996-98 3.2TL 1996-99 3.5RL

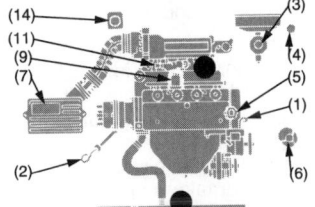

1997-99 2.2CL, 2.3CL

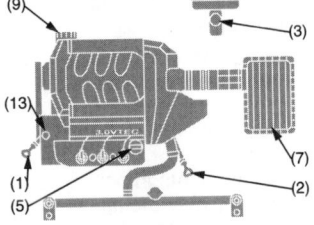

1997-00 3.0CL 1999-00 3.2TL

(1) Crankcase dipstick
(2) Transmission dipstick
(3) Brake fluid reservoir
(4) Clutch fluid reservoir
(5) Oil fill cap
(6) Power steering reservoir
(7) Air filter

(8) Fuel filter
(9) Oil filter
(10) PCV filter
(11) EGR valve
(12) Oxygen sensor
(13) PCV valve
(14) ABS fluid reservoir

0 FITTINGS 0 PLUGS

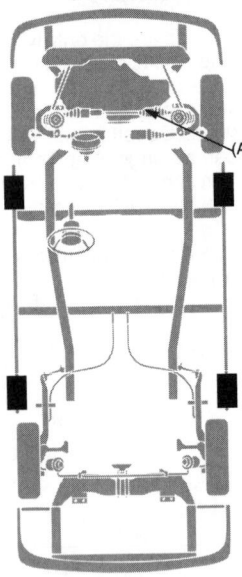

1989-00 Integra 1997-00 2.2CL, 2.3CL, 3.0CL 1999-00 3.2TL

0 FITTINGS 0 PLUGS

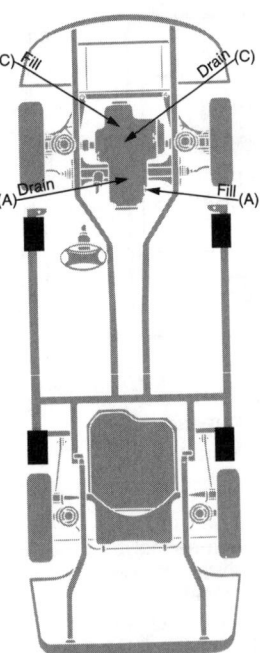

1992-98 Vigor, 2.5TL, 3.2TL

0 FITTINGS 0 PLUGS

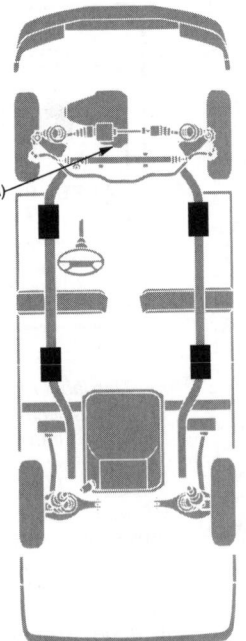

1989-90 Legend

0 FITTINGS 0 PLUGS

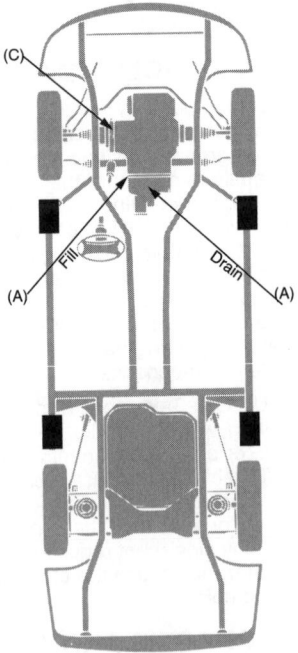

1991-95 Legend 1996-00 3.5RL

● Cooling system drain

■ Lift adapter position

(A) Manual transmission/transaxle, drain & fill

(B) Transfer case, NOT USED

(C) Transaxle, final drive, drain & fill

(D) Differential, NOT USED

4

SERVICE AT TIME OR MILEAGE — WHICHEVER OCCURS FIRST

AAIPM1   AAIPM1

Perform the following maintenance services at the intervals indicated to keep both the vehicle and emission warranties in effect.

MI—MILES IN THOUSANDS
KM—KILOMETERS IN THOUSANDS

EVERY 6 MO/7.5 MI—12 KM
Front brake pads 1989-94 . . . . . . inspect
Crankcase . . . . .change oil
1996, every 12 months
Clutch release arm travel . . . . . . .check
1990-93 Integra
Oil filter, 1989-95 . . . . .replace

EVERY 7.5 MI—12 KM
Tires . . . . .rotate

EVERY 12 MO/15 MI—24 KM
Air conditioner filter . . . . .replace
1992-94 Legend
Brake system . . . . .inspect
Inspect calipers, hoses, lines & rear pads. 1995-96, inspect front pads
Check thickness of rotors
Driveshaft boots 1995-96 . . . . . . .inspect
Exhaust system . . . . .inspect
Fuel lines & connections
1995-96 . . . . .inspect
Front wheel alignment
1989-94 . . . . .inspect/adjust
Suspension mounting bolts
1989-94 . . . . .inspect
Clutch release arm travel . . . . . . .check
1989 Integra
Oil filter, 1996 . . . . .replace
Parking brake adjustment . . . . .inspect
1995-96
Power steering
1989-94 . . . . .check level PS
Inspect power steering system
Valve clearance . . . . .adjust
1989-94 Integra & 1992 Vigor

AT FIRST 12 MO/15 MI—24 KM;
THEN EVERY 24 MO/30 MI—48 KM
Parking brake adjustment
1989-94 . . . . .check
Steering system . . . . .inspect

EVERY 24 MO/30 MI—48 KM
Anti-lock brake system, 1989-94 . .inspect
Ex. 1989-90 Integra
Brake fluid . . . . .replace HB
Also change ABS fluid HB
Final drive . . . . .change lubricant
Vigor, 2.5TL, 3.2TL, 3.5RL, 1991-95 Legend
Fuel lines & connections
1989-94 . . . . .inspect
Transaxle, automatic . . .change lubricant
Ex. 1995 2.5TL & 1996 all
Transaxle, manual . . . .change lubricant
Air cleaner element . . . . .replace
Cooling system hoses &
connections . . . . .inspect
Initial service at 36 mo/45 mi (72 km)
Drive belt(s) . . . . .inspect/adjust
Spark plugs . . . . .replace
Ex. 1991-95 Legend, Integra GSR, 3.2TL, 3.5RL
Valve clearance . . . . .adjust
1995-96 Integra, 2.5TL

AT 36 MO/45 MI—72 KM;
THEN EVERY 24 MO/30 MI—48 KM
Cooling system . . . . .change coolant EC

EVERY 48 MO/60 MI—96 KM
Anti-lock brake system high
pressure hose . . . . .replace
Ex. 1989-90 Integra
Catalytic converter heat shield . . .inspect
Crankcase emission control
system . . . . .inspect
Check PCV valve & blowby filter
Distributor cap & rotor . . . . .inspect
Inspect ignition wires
EGR system, 1989-92
as equipped . . . . .inspect
Evaporative control system,
1989-92 . . . . .inspect
Fuel filter . . . . .replace
Check fuel hoses
Idle speed . . . . .inspect
Check 1989-92 CO level
Ignition timing 1989-92 . . . .check/adjust
Ignition timing control
system . . . . .inspect
1989-91 Integra, 1989-90 Legend
Secondary air supply . . . . .inspect
1989-90 Legend

EVERY 72 MO/60 MI—96 KM
Spark plugs . . . . .replace
1991-96 Legend, Integra GSR & 3.2TL, 3.5RL

1990 LEGEND, 1991-96 ALL,
EVERY 72 MO/90 MI—144 KM
Transaxle, automatic . . . . .change fluid
1995 2.5TL, 1996 all
Timing belt . . . . .replace
Water pump . . . . .inspect

AT 120 MONTHS
Air bag system . . . . .inspect

SEVERE SERVICE
Air cleaner element—Clean every 12 mo/ 15 mi (24 km)

Brake discs, caliper and pads—Inspect every 6 mo/7.5 mi (12 km)

Crankcase—Change oil & filter every: 1989-90, 3 mo/3 mi (5 km); 1991-94 All, 1995-96 Integra, 3 mo/3.75 mi (6 km); 1995-96 Vigor, 2.5TL, Legend 3.2TL, 6 mo/3.75 mi (6 km)

Final drive—1991-96 Legend, Vigor, 2.5TL, 3.2TL, 3.5RL, change lubricant every 12 mo/15 mi (24 km)

Power steering system—Inspect every 6 mo/7.5 mi (12 km)

Timing belt—1995-96 replace every 60 mi (96 km), also inspect water pump

Transaxle—1991-95 Legend, 1992-94 Vigor, change fluid every 12 mo/15 mi (24 km) when towing a trailer; 1995 2.5TL & 1996 all, change fluid every 24 mo/30 mi (48 km)

Suspension, steering driveshaft boots—1995-96, inspect every 6 mo/ 7.5 mi (12 km)

KEY TO LUBRICANTS
See other Acura chart

CRANKCASE . . . . .SJ, GF-1

CAPACITY, Refill:	Liters	Qt
Integra:		
1.6L, 1.8L ex. VTEC	3.5	3.7
1.7L, 1.8L VTEC	3.7	3.9
Legend: 1989-90	4.0	4.2
1991-93	4.5	4.8
1994-95	4.0	4.2
Vigor, 2.5TL, 3.2TL	4.0	4.2
3.5RL	4.3	4.5

Capacity shown does not include filter. When replacing filter, additional oil may be needed

Ex. 1991-93 Integra w/1.7L engine
Above 20°F (−7°C) .10W-30
All temperatures . . . . .5W-30[1]

1991-93 Integra w/1.7L engine
Above −3°F (−20°C) . . . . .10W-30[1]
Below 32°F (0°C) 5W-30
[1] Preferred

TRANSAXLE, Automatic
1989-95 . . . . .AF2, SLF
1996 . . . . .SLF

CAPACITY, Initial Refill[2]:	Liters	Qt
Integra: 1989	2.4	2.5
1990-93	3.0	3.2
1994-96	2.7	2.9
Legend	3.2	3.4
Vigor	2.5	2.6
2.5TL	2.7	2.9
3.2TL	3.0	3.2
3.5RL	3.0	3.2

[2] With engine at operating temperature, shift transmission through all gears. Turn engine off and check fluid level within one minute

TRANSAXLE, Manual
1989-95 .SG, GLS
Above 15°F (−10°C), 30, 1989-92
Above −5°F (−20°C), 20W-40, 1989-92
All temperatures 10W-30, 10W-40
1996 . . . . .GLS

CAPACITY, Refill:	Liters	Pt
Integra: 1989	2.3	4.8
1990-95	2.1	4.4
1996	2.2	4.6
Legend: 5-speed	2.2	4.6
6-speed	2.3	4.8
Vigor	1.8	3.8

FINAL DRIVE
1991-96 Legend, Vigor,
2.5TL, 3.2TL, 3.5RL GL-4, GL-5
Above 0°F (−18°C), 90; below 0°F (−18°C), 80W-90

CAPACITY, Refill:	Liters	Pt
Vigor & 2.5TL, w/MT & AT	0.9	2.0
1991-95 Legend w/MT & AT	1.0	2.2
3.2TL, 3.5RL	1.1	2.3

5

ACURA
1997-2000 Integra, 2.2CL, 2.3CL, 2.5TL, 3.0CL, 3.2TL, 3.5 RL, SLX—See Isuzu Trooper

SERVICE AT TIME OR MILEAGE — WHICHEVER OCCURS FIRST

Perform the following maintenance services at the intervals indicated to keep both the vehicle and emission warranties in effect.

MI—MILES IN THOUSANDS
KM—KILOMETERS IN THOUSANDS

EVERY 12 MO/7.5 MI—12 KM
Crankcase . . . . .change oil

EVERY 7.5 MI—12 KM
Tires . . . . .rotate

EVERY 12 MO/15 MI—24 KM
Brake & clutch fluid . . . . .check level **HB**

Brake system . . . . .inspect
Inspect calipers, hoses, lines
Inspect front and rear pads
Check thickness of rotors

Cooling system, hoses &
    connections . . . . .inspect

Driveshaft boots . . . . .inspect

Exhaust system . . . . .inspect

Fuel lines & connections . . . . . .inspect

Oil filter . . . . .replace

Parking brake adjustment . . . . .inspect

Steering system . . . . .inspect
Includes tie rod ends, steering gearbox, hoses & boots

Suspension . . . . .inspect

Transmission, manual &
    automatic . . . . .check level

Power steering . . . . . . .check level **PS**

EVERY 24 MO/30 MI—48 KM
Air cleaner element . . . . .replace

Cabin air filter . . . . .replace
1996-00 3.5RL
1999-00 3.2TL

Drive belt(s) . . . . .inspect/adjust

Spark plugs . . . . .replace
Integra Ex. VTEC, 2.2 CL, 2.5TL

Valve clearance . . . . .adjust
Integra, 2.2CL, 2.5TL

AT 36 MO/45 MI—72 KM;
THEN EVERY 24 MO/30 MI—48 KM
Cooling system . . . . .change coolant **EC**

EVERY 36 MO/45 MI—72 KM
Brake fluid . . . . .replace **HB**
Also change ABS fluid **HB**

AT 48 MO/60 MI—96 KM;
THEN EVERY 24 MO/30 MI—48 KM
Final drive . . . . .change lubricant
2.5TL, 3.2TL, 3.5RL

EVERY 48 MO/60 MI—96 KM
Distributor cap & rotor, 2.2CL . . .inspect
Inspect ignition wires

Idle speed, 2.2CL . . . . .inspect

EVERY 72 MO/60 MI—96KM
Spark plugs . . . . .replace
Integra VTEC

EVERY 72 MO/90 MI—144 KM
Transmission, automatic &
    manual . . . . .change fluid

Timing belt, 2.2CL . . . . .replace
Also replace balancer belt

Water pump, 2.2CL . . . . .inspect

EVERY 84 MO/105 MI—168 KM
Idle speed . . . . .inspect
All ex. 2.2CL

Spark plugs . . . . .replace
2.3CL, 3.0CL, 3.2TL, 3.5RL, 3.2TL

Timing belt . . . . .replace
All ex. 2.2CL

Valve clearance . . . . .inspect
1990-00 3.2TL only. Adjust only if noisy

Water pump . . . . .inspect
All ex. 2.2CL

AT 120 MONTHS
Air bag system . . . . .inspect

SERVICE AS REQUIRED
Valve clearance . . . . .adjust
2.3CL. Only if noisy

SEVERE SERVICE & CANADIAN MODELS
Air cleaner element—Clean every 12 mo/ 15 mi (24 km)

Brake discs, caliper and pads—Inspect every 6 mo/7.5 mi (12 km)

Cabin air—3.5RL & 1999-00 3.2TL, replace every 15 mi (24 km)

Crankcase—Change oil & filter every 6 mo/3.75 mi (6 km)

Final drive—2.5TL, 3.2TL, 3.5RL, change lubricant at first 24mo/30 mi (48 km), then every 12 mo/15 mi (24 km)

Locks & hinges—Lubricate every 12 mo/15 mi (24 km)

Power steering system—Inspect every 6 mo/7.5 mi (12 km)

Transaxle—Change fluid every 24 mo/30 mi (48 km)

Suspension, steering, driveshaft boots —Inspect every 6 mo/ 7.5 mi (12 km)

Light & controls, vehicle underbody—Inspect every 12 mo/15 mi (24 km)

KEY TO LUBRICANTS

EC	Ethylene Glycol Coolant
GF-1	Motor Oil, API Service GF-1
GL-4	Gear Oil, API Service GL-4
GL-5	Gear Oil, API Service GL-5
GLS	Gear Lubricant, Special Honda Genuine MTF
HB	Hydraulic Brake Fluid, DOT 3 or 4
PS	Power Steering Fluid Honda Power Steering Fluid, Type V Part No. 08206-9002PE
SJ	Motor Oil, API Service SJ
SLF	Special Lubricant Fluid Honda Premium Formula Automatic Transmission Fluid

CRANKCASE . . . . .SJ, GF-1

CAPACITY, Refill:	Liters	Qt
Integra: 1.8L ex. VTEC	3.5	3.7
1.8L VTEC	3.7	3.9
2.2CL, 2.3CL, 3.0CL	4.0	4.2
2.5TL, 3.2TL	4.0	4.2
3.5RL	4.3	4.5

Capacity shown does not include filter. When replacing filter, additional oil may be needed
Above 20°F (−7°C) 10W-30
All temperatures . . . . .5W-30[1]
1 Preferred

TRANSAXLE, Automatic . . . . .SLF

CAPACITY, Initial Refill[2]:	Liters	Qt
Integra	2.7	2.9
2.2CL	2.4	2.5
2.3CL	3.2	3.4
2.5TL	2.7	2.9
3.0CL	2.9	3.1
3.2TL	3.0	3.2
3.5RL	3.0	3.2

2 With engine at operating temperature, shift transmission through all gears. Turn engine off and check fluid level within one minute

TRANSAXLE, Manual . . . . .GLS

CAPACITY, Refill:	Liters	Pt
Integra	2.2	4.6
2.2CL, 2.3CL	1.9	4.0
3.5RL	2.6	5.4

FINAL DRIVE
2.5TL, 3.2TL, 3.5RL GL-4, GL-5
Above 0°F (−18°C), 90; below 0°F (−18°C), 80W-90

CAPACITY, Refill:	Liters	Pt
2.5TL, w/MT & AT	0.9	2.0
3.2TL, 1997-98	1.1	2.3
3.5RL	1.1	2.3

HOOD RELEASE: Inside

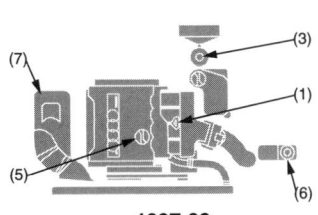

**1997-99
A4
4-cyl. 1.8L Turbo**

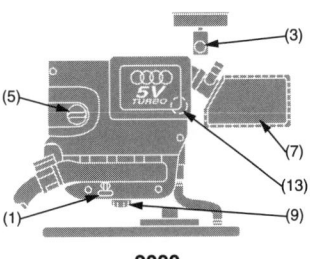

**2000
TT
4-cyl. 1.8L Turbo**

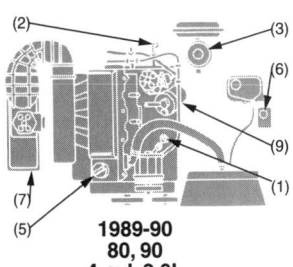

**1989-90
80, 90
4-cyl. 2.0L**

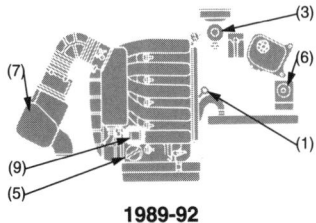

**1989-92
80, 90, 100
5-cyl. 2.3L SOHC**

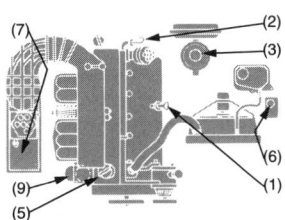

**1990-92
Coupe, 80, 90
5-cyl. 2.3L DOHC
Non-Turbo**

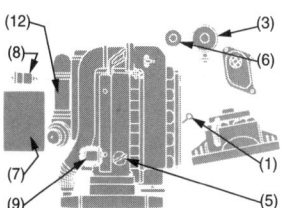

**1991-92 Coupe, 80, 90 5-cyl. 2.3L
DOHC Turbo
1992-95 S4, S6 5-cyl. 2.2L Turbo**

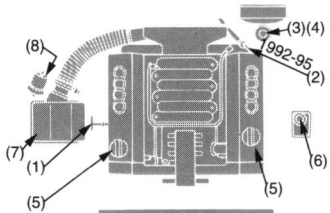

**1992-99
90, 100, A4, A6, Cabriolet,
Sport 90
V6 2.8L**

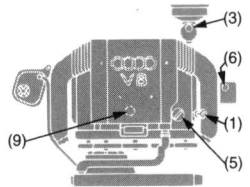

**1990-99
V8 Quattro, A8
V8 3.6L, 3.7L, 4.2L**

(1) Crankcase dipstick
(2) Transmission dipstick, 1989-95
(3) Brake fluid reservoir
(4) Clutch fluid reservoir
(5) Oil fill cap
(6) Power steering reservoir
(7) Air filter

(8) Fuel filter
(9) Oil filter
(10) PCV filter
(11) EGR valve
(12) Oxygen sensor
(13) PCV valve

SERVICE LOCATIONS — ENGINE AND CHASSIS

AIIDP-2   AIIDP-2

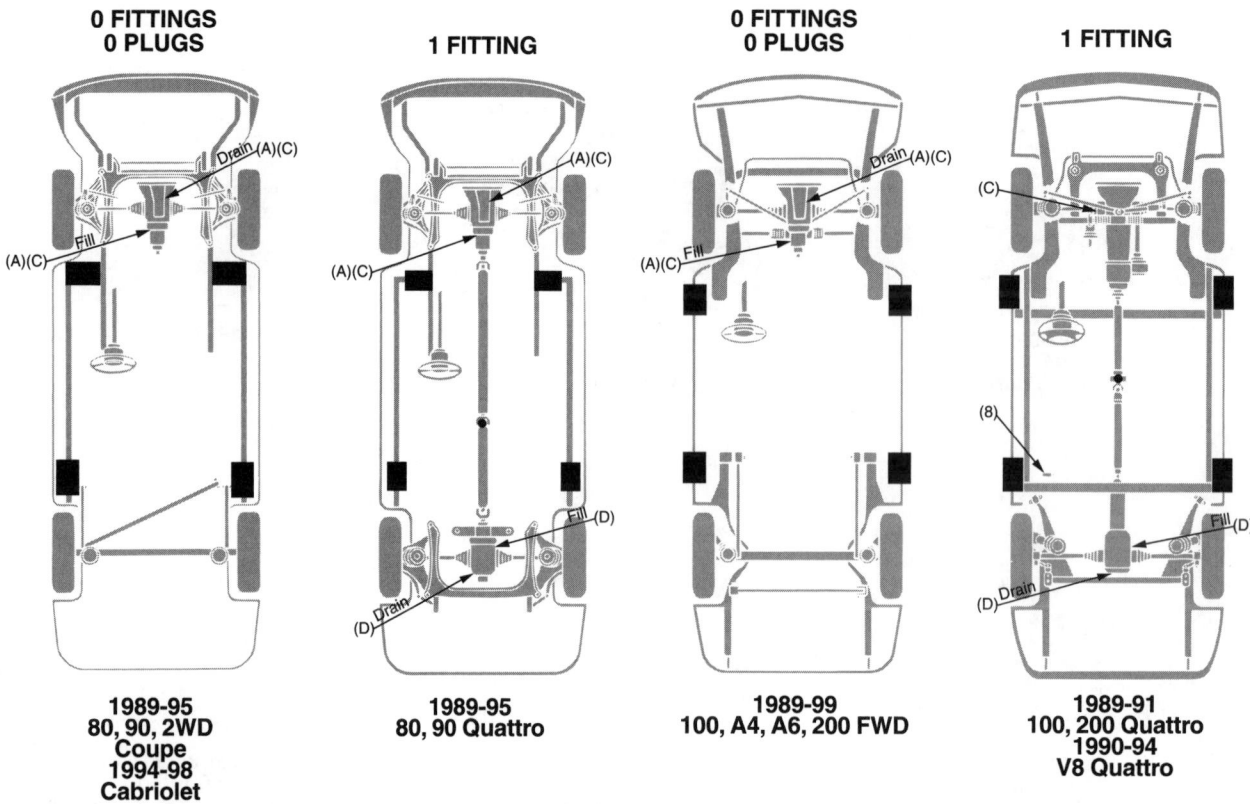

**0 FITTINGS
0 PLUGS**

1 FITTING

**0 FITTINGS
0 PLUGS**

1 FITTING

**1989-95
80, 90, 2WD
Coupe
1994-98
Cabriolet**

**1989-95
80, 90 Quattro**

**1989-99
100, A4, A6, 200 FWD**

**1989-91
100, 200 Quattro
1990-94
V8 Quattro**

**0 FITTINGS
0 PLUGS**

**0 FITTINGS
0 PLUGS**

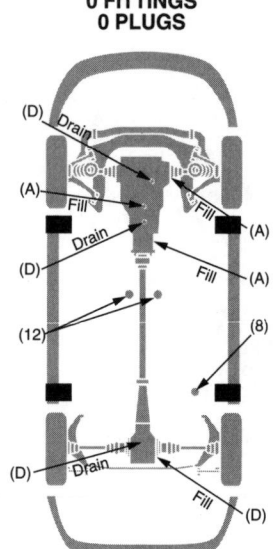

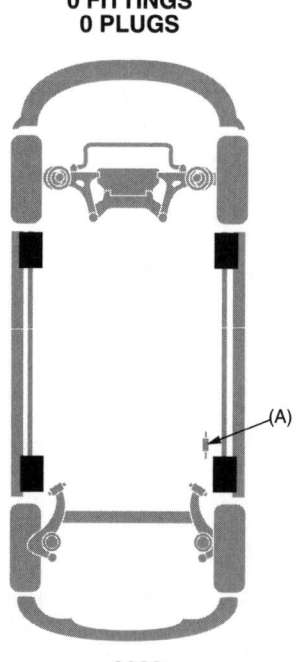

(A) Manual transmission/transaxle,
      drain & fill

(B) Transfer case, NOT USED

(C) Automatic transaxle, final drive,
      drain & fill

(D) Differential, drain & fill

(12) Oxygen sensor

■ Lift adapter position

● Fitting

**1992-99
100, A4, A6, A8 Quattro**

**2000
TT**

CAUTION: On front wheel drive vehicles, the center of gravity is farther forward than on rear wheel drive vehicles. When removing major components from the rear of the vehicle while it is on a hoist, the vehicle must be supported in a manner to prevent it from tipping forward.

SERVICE AT TIME OR MILEAGE — WHICHEVER OCCURS FIRST

AllPM3   AllPM3

Perform the following maintenance services at the intervals indicated to keep the vehicle warranties in effect.

W SERVICE TO MAINTAIN EMISSION WARRANTY

MI—MILES IN THOUSANDS
KM—KILOMETERS IN THOUSANDS

EVERY 6 MO/7.5 MI—12 KM
Brake master cylinder,
1990 . . . . .check level **HB**

Cooling system,
1989-90 . . . . .check level **EC**

Hydraulic system/power
steering . . . . .check level **SLF**

W Crankcase . . . . .change oil

W Crankcase oil filter . . . . .replace
At initial service only

Windshield washers . . . . .fill

Automatic shift
lock, 1990-91 . . . . .check

EVERY 12 MO/15 MI—24 KM
Brake system . . . . .inspect/adjust
Check for damage & leaks, check pad thickness, check
& adjust pedal travel, check pressure regulator, adjust
hand brake.

Drive shaft boots . . . . .inspect

W Exhaust system . . . . .inspect

Final drive, automatic . . . . . .check level

Transaxle, automatic . . . . . .check level
Level check not required for V8 Quattro

Transaxle, manual . . . . .check level

Differential w/3-spd. AT . . . . .check level

Wheels & tires . . . . .inspect

Battery . . . . .check level

Brake master cylinder . . .check level **HB**

Cooling system, 1991 . . .check level **EC**

W Crankcase oil filter . . . . .replace

W Idle speed, ex. Turbo . . . . . .check/adjust
Not required for Calif. warranty

On-board
diagnostic system . . . . .check/clear

Electrical equipment . . . . .inspect

Sunroof rails . . . . . .clean/lubricate **SLS**

EVERY 24 MONTHS
Brakes . . . . .change fluid **HB**
Check operation of warning light switch.

EVERY 24 MO/30 MI—48 KM
Automatic transmission,
w/V8 . . . . .change fluid
Clean pan & strainer, replace gasket.

Front axle . . . . .inspect
Check ball joint & tie rod dust seals, check tie rods.

Differential w/4-spd. AT . . . . .check level

Driveshaft, Quattro 4WD . . .lubricate **LM**

W Air filter element . . . . .replace

W Drive belts . . . . .check/adjust

W Spark plugs . . . . .replace

W Timing belt, V8 . . . . .check/adjust

EVERY 60 MI—96 KM
Oxygen sensor . . . . .replace

Timing belt, V8 1990-91 . . . . . .replace

1991
EVERY 24 MO/90 MI—144 KM
Engine coolant, V8 . . . . .replace **EC**

1990-91
EVERY 72 MONTHS
Tires . . . . .replace

SEVERE SERVICE
Crankcase—Change oil and filter at half
of recommended interval

Air Filter—Replace at 12 mo/15 mi (24 km)

KEY TO LUBRICANTS

AE	ESSO Type LT71141 Fluid Automatic Transmission Fluid Audi Part No. G052162A1 or A2.
AF2	DEXRON®-II Automatic Transmission Fluid
EC	Ethylene Glycol Coolant Mix with water to desired freeze protection: Green in color. If red in color use only VW Part No. G012A8DA1.
GF-2	Motor Oil, Meeting ILSAC GF-2
GL-4	Gear Oil, API Service GL-4
GL-5	Gear Oil, API Service GL-5
HB	Hydraulic Brake Fluid, DOT 4
LM	Lithium Grease
MO	Motor Oil
SH	Motor Oil, API Service SH
SJ	Motor Oil, API Service SJ
SLF	Special Lubricant—Fluid Hydraulic system, power steering, Audi Part No. G002 000
SLS	Silicone Lubricant-Spray

CRANKCASE . . . .**SH**

CAPACITY, Refill:	Liters	Qt
4-cyl. 2.0L:		
80, 90	2.5	2.6
5-cyl. 2.2L, 2.3L:		
80, 90	3.0	3.2
100, 200	4.0	4.2
1990-91 Coupe Quattro	4.0	4.2
V8 3.6L:		
1990-91 V8	8.0[1]	8.5[1]

Capacity shown is without filter. When replacing filter, additional oil may be needed.

[1] Capacity shown includes filter, add specified amount, run engine to operating temperature. Recheck level and correct as necessary.

Above 68°F (20°C)	.40
32° to 86°F (0° to 30°C)	.30
Above 14°F (-10°C)	20W-40, 20W-50
14° to 50°F (-10° to 10°C)	20W-20
Below 25°F (-4°C)	10W
Above 5°F (-15°C)	15W-40, 15W-50
0° to 60°F (-18° to 16°C)	10W-30, 10W-40
Below 14°F (-10°C)	5W-20, 5W-30

TRANSMISSION, Automatic . . . . .**AE, AF2**
Verify fluid installed before topping off. **AE** is yellow in color.
Does not include final drive or center differential

CAPACITY, Initial Refill[2]:	Liters	Qt
80, 90	3.0	3.2
100, 200	3.0	3.2
V8	3.8[3]	4.0[3]

[2] With engine at operating temperature, shift transmission through all gears. Check fluid level in PARK and add fluid as needed.

[3] Vehicle is not equipped with a transmission dipstick, special tools and procedure required, see manufacturer's service literature.

TRANSAXLE,
Manual . . . . .Synthetic 75W-90 **GL-4**[4]
Includes final drive & center differential
[4] Audi Part Number G005000 or G052911A

CAPACITY, Refill:	Liters	Pt
Coupe, 80, 90, 100 2WD	2.4	5.0
Coupe, 90, 100 4WD	2.9	6.0
200 2WD	2.6	5.4
200 4WD: To 9-12-88	2.2	4.6
From 9-13-88	2.6	5.4

FINAL DRIVE, Auto. Trans.
All Models . . . . . .Synthetic 75W-90 **GL-4**[5]
[5] Audi Part Number G052145A2 or G005000

CAPACITY, Refill:	Liters	Pt
80, 90	0.8	1.6
100, 200	1.0	2.2
V8	0.5	1.0

REAR DIFFERENTIAL **90W GL-5**

CAPACITY, Refill:	Liters	Pt
Coupe, 90	0.8	1.6
100, 200, V8	1.7	3.6

SERVICE AT TIME OR MILEAGE — WHICHEVER OCCURS FIRST

Perform the following maintenance services at the intervals indicated to keep the vehicle warranties in effect.

W   SERVICE TO MAINTAIN EMISSION WARRANTY

MI—MILES IN THOUSANDS
KM—KILOMETERS IN THOUSANDS

EVERY 6 MO/7.5 MI—12 KM
Hydraulic system/power
steering . . . . .check level **SLF**

W Crankcase . . . . .change oil

W Crankcase oil filter . . . . .replace
At initial service only

Windshield washers, wipers . . .check/fill

Automatic shift lock . . . . .check
Check operation including park/neutral safety switch

Cooling system . . . . . . .check level **EC**
CAUTION: If coolant is red in color, never mix with any other coolant or engine damage will occur.

Brake master cylinder . . .check level **HB**

Wheels & tires . . . . .rotate
At first interval only

Plenum chamber water
drain valve, A6 wagon only . . . . .check
Replace if dirty

EVERY 12 MO/15 MI—24 KM
Brake system . . . . .inspect/adjust
Check for damage & leaks, check pad thickness, check & adjust pedal travel, check pressure regulator, adjust hand brake

Drive shaft boots . . . . .inspect

W Exhaust system . . . . .inspect

Final drive, automatic . . . . . .check level

Transaxle, automatic . . . . . . .check level
Level check not required for V8 Quattro

Transaxle, manual . . . . .check level

Differential w/3-spd. AT . . . . .check level

Wheels & tires . . . . .inspect
Check pressure including spare

Battery . . . . .check level

Brake master cylinder . . .check level **HB**

W Crankcase oil filter . . . . .replace

W Idle speed, ex. Turbo . . . . .check/adjust
Not required for Calif. warranty

On-board diagnostic
system . . . . .check/clear

Electrical equipment . . . . .inspect

Headlights . . . . .adjust

Sunroof rails . . . . . .clean/lubricate **SLS**

Vehicle . . . . .road test

Body . . . . .lubricate **MO**
Door check straps

Roof frame, guides, lock . . .lubricate **LM**
Cabriolet

EVERY 24 MONTHS
Brakes . . . . .change fluid **HB**
Check operation of warning light switch

EVERY 24 MO/30 MI—48 KM
Automatic transmission,
w/V8 . . . . .change fluid
Clean pan & strainer, replace gasket

Front suspension . . . . .inspect
Check ball joint & tie rod dust seals, check tie rods

Differential w/4-spd. AT . . . . .check level

Driveshaft, Quattro 4WD . . .lubricate **LM**

Dust & pollen filter . . . . .replace

W Air filter element . . . . .replace

W Drive belts . . . . .check/adjust

W Spark plugs . . . . .replace
Except platinum

W Timing belt, V8 . . . . .check/adjust

EVERY 36 MO
Engine coolant, V8 1995 . . . . .replace **EC**
CAUTION: If coolant is red in color never mix with any other coolant or engine damage will occur.

EVERY 48 MO/45 MI—72 KM
Generator drive belt . . . . .replace
Except V8

Transmission,
automatic 1994-95 . . . . . .change fluid
Except 1995 Cabriolet, 90 w/01N
Except A8

EVERY 36 MO/60 MI—96 KM
Oxygen sensor . . . . .replace

Ribbed V-belt, V6. . . . . .replace
1994

Spark plugs . . . . .replace
1995. Platinum tipped only

1992-94
EVERY 24 MO/60 MI—96 KM
Engine coolant, V8 . . . . .replace **EC**
CAUTION: If coolant is red in color, never mix with any other cooland or engine damage will occur.

EVERY 90 MI—144 KM
Timing belt . . . . .replace
5-cyl., V8

Ribbed V-belt . . . . .replace
1995, All except V8

EVERY 72 MONTHS
Tires .replace

SEVERE SERVICE
Crankcase—Change oil and filter at half of recommended interval, 3 mo/3.75 mi (6 km)

Air Filter—Replace at 12 mo/15 mi (24 km)

Automatic Transmission—Change fluid every 30 mi (48 km), clean pan & strainer, replace pan gasket

KEY TO LUBRICANTS
See other Audi chart

CRANKCASE . . . .**SH**

CAPACITY, Refill:	Liters	Qt
5-cyl. 2.2L, 2.3L: 1992-94 S4 . . .	4.5	4.8
1995 S6	4.5	4.7
V6 2.8L: A6,		
Cabriolet, 90, 100	5.0	5.3
V8 4.2L		
V8 Quattro	7.5	8.0

Capacity shown includes filter; add specified amount, run engine to operating temperature. Recheck level and correct as necessary.

1994-95 100, S4 Quattro, V8 Quattro, A6, S6, Cabriolet
Energy Conserving Oil:
All temperatures 5W-30, 5W-40,
10W-30, 10W-40

Except Energy Conserving Oil:
All temperatures 5W-50, 10W-50,10W-60
Below 59°F (15°C) 5W-30, 5W-40,
10W-30, 10W-40
Above 5°F (-15°C) 15W-40, 15W-50,
20W-40, 20W-50

Others
Above 68°F (20°C) 40
32° to 86°F (0° to 30°C) 30
Above 14°F (-10°C) 20W-40, 20W-50
14° to 50°F (-10° to 10°C) 20W-20
Below 25°F (-4°C) 10W
Above 5°F (-15°C) 15W-40, 15W-50
0° to 60°F (-18° to 16°C) 1992 . . . . .10W-30,
10W-40
5° to 80°F (-15° to 25°C) 1993-95 . . .10W-30,
10W-40
Below 14°F (-10°C) 1992 . . . . .5W-20[2], 5W-30
Below 80°F (25°C) 1993-95 . . . . .5W-30
2 5W-20 not recommended for 1992 models

TRANSMISSION, Automatic
Does not include final drive or center differential. Do not use DEXRON-III. In applications where **AF2**, **AE** is recommended, verify fluid installed before topping off. **AE** is yellow in color.
1992-94 All . . . .**AE, AF2**
1995 Cabriolet, 90 w/01N . . . .**AE**
All others . . . .**AE, AF2**
ESSO LT71141, Audi Part Number: G052162A1 or A2

CAPACITY, Initial Refill[3]:	Liters	Qt
1992-94 Cabriolet, 80, 90	3.0	3.2
w/01F:		
100 Quattro, A6 Quattro	2.7	2.9
1995 Cabriolet, 90 w/01N	5.4	5.7
100	3.0	3.2
V8 Quattro	3.8[4]	4.0[4]

3 With engine at operating temperature, shift transmission through all gears. Check fluid level in PARK and add fluid as needed

4 Vehicle is not equipped with a transmission dipstick, special tools and procedure required, see manufacturer's service literature

TRANSAXLE,
Manual . . . . . .Synthetic 75W-90 **GL-4**[5, 6]
Includes final drive & center differential
5 Audi Part Number G005000 or G052911A or G052145A1 or A2
6 S4 add .1 ltr. Audi Part No. G009 000 01 additive

CAPACITY, Refill:	Liters	Pt
90, 100 2WD	2.4	5.0
90, 100 4WD	2.9	6.0
S4	2.6	5.5

FINAL DRIVE, Man. Trans **90W GL-5**

CAPACITY, Refill:	Liters	Pt
90 Quattro	1.3	2.7
100 Quattro	1.7	3.6
S4	1.5	3.2

FINAL DRIVE, Auto. Trans.
All Models . . . . . .Synthetic 75W-90 **GL-4**[7]
7 Audi Part Number G052145A2 or G005000

CAPACITY, Refill:	Liters	Pt
90	1.0	2.2
100	1.0	2.2
V8 Quattro	0.5	1.0
Cabriolet	1.0	2.1
A6	0.7	1.4

TRANSFER CASE . . . . .Synthetic
75W-90 **GL-4**[8]
All ex. V8 w/auto. trans.
8 Audi Part Number G052145A2 or G005000

CAPACITY, Refill:	Liters	Pt
01F: 100 Quattro,		
A6 Quattro, 90	1.0	2.2

REAR DIFFERENTIAL **90W GL-5**

CAPACITY, Refill:	Liters	Pt
90	0.8	1.6
100, V8 Quattro	1.7	3.6
A6	1.7	3.6

SERVICE AT TIME OR MILEAGE — WHICHEVER OCCURS FIRST

AIIPM5

AIIPM4

Perform the following maintenance services at the intervals indicated to keep the vehicle warranties in effect.
W SERVICE TO MAINTAIN EMISSION WARRANTY

MI—MILES IN THOUSANDS
KM—KILOMETERS IN THOUSANDS

TURBO ENGINE
EVERY 5 MI—8 KM

OTHERS
EVERY 6 MO/7.5 MI—12 KM
Hydraulic system/power
   steering . . . . .check level **SLF**

W Crankcase . . . . .change oil

W Crankcase oil filter . . . . .replace
At initial service only

Windshield washers, wipers . . .check/fill

Service interval display . . . . .reset

Automatic shift lock . . . . .check
Check operation including park/neutral safety switch.

Cooling system . . . . . . .check level **EC**
CAUTION: If coolant is red in color, never mix with any
other coolant or engine damage will occur.

Manual Transmission . . . . .check
Check shift linkage & clutch for interlock operation.

Brake master cylinder . . .check level **HB**

Wheels & tires . . . . .rotate
At first interval only

Plenum chamber water
   drain valve, A6 wagon only . . . . .check
Replace if dirty.

TURBO ENGINE
EVERY 10MI—16KM
OTHERS:
EVERY 12 MO/15 MI—24 KM
Brake system . . . . .inspect/adjust
Check for damage & leaks, check pad thickness, check
& adjust pedal travel, check pressure regulator, adjust
hand brake.

Drive shaft boots . . . . .inspect

W Exhaust system . . . . .inspect

Final drive, automatic . . . . . .check level

Transaxle, automatic . . . . . .check level
Level check not required for V8.

Transaxle, manual . . . . .check level

Differential w/3-spd. AT . . . . .check level

Wheels & tires . . . . .inspect
Check pressure including spare.

Battery . . . . .check level

Brake master cylinder . . .check level **HB**

W Crankcase oil filter . . . . .replace

W Idle speed, ex. Turbo . . . . .check/adjust
Not required for Calif. warranty

On-board   diagnostic
   system . . . . .check/clear

Electrical equipment . . . . .inspect

Headlights . . . . .adjust

Sunroof rails . . . . . .clean/lubricate **SLS**

Vehicle . . . . .road test

Body . . . . .lubricate **MO**
Door check straps.

Roof frame, guides, lock . . .lubricate **LM**
Cabriolet

EVERY 24 MONTHS
Brakes . . . . .change fluid **HB**
Check operation of warning light switch.

TURBO ENGINE
EVERY 20MI—32K
OTHERS:
EVERY 24 MO/30 MI—48 KM
Automatic transmission,
   w/V8 . . . . change fluid
Clean pan & strainer, replace gasket.

Front suspension . . . . .inspect
Check ball joint & tie rod dust seals, check tie rods.

Differential w/4-spd. AT . . . .check level

Driveshaft, Quattro 4WD . . .lubricate **LM**

Dust & pollen filter . . . . .replace

W Air filter element . . . . .replace

W Drive belts . . . . .check/adjust

W Spark plugs . . . . .replace
Except platinum

W Timing belt, V8 . . . . .check/adjust

EVERY 36 MO
Engine coolant, V8 1996 . . . . .replace **EC**
Caution: If coolant is red in color, never mix with any other
coolant or engine damage will occur.

EVERY 48 MO/45 MI—72 KM
Generator drive belt . . . . .replace
Except V8

Transmission, automatic . . .change fluid
Except A4, A8, AG4

EVERY 36 MO/60 MI—96 KM
Oxygen sensor . . . . .replace

Spark plugs . . . . .replace
Platinum-tipped only

EVERY 90 MI—144 KM
Timing belt . . . . .replace
5-cyl., V8

Ribbed V-belt . . . . .replace
All except V8

EVERY 72 MONTHS
Tires . . . . .replace

SEVERE SERVICE
Crankcase—Change oil and filter at half
of recommended interval, 3 mo/3.75 mi
(6 km)

Air Filter—Replace at 12 mo/15 mi (24 km)

Automatic Transmission—Change fluid
every 30 mi (48km), clean pan & strainer,
replace pan gasket

KEY TO LUBRICANTS
See other Audi chart

CRANKCASE . . . . .SH, GF-2

CAPACITY, Refill:	Liters	Qt
4-cyl. 1.8L	4.0	4.2
5-cyl. 2.2L, 2.3L	4.5	4.8
2.8L, A6	5.0	5.3
V8 3.7L, 4.2L	7.5	8.0

Capacity shown includes filter, add specified amount, run
engine to operating temperature. Recheck level and correct as necessary.

A4, A6, A8, Cabriolet
Energy Conserving Oil:
All temperatures 5W-30, 5W-40,
                            10W-30, 10W-40

Except Energy Conserving Oil:
All temperatures 5W-50, 10W-50,10W-60
Below 59°F (15°C) 5W-30, 5W-40,
                            10W-30, 10W-40
Above 5°F (-15°C) 15W-40, 15W-50,
                            20W-40, 20W-50

Others 1996
Above 68°F (20°C) 40
32° to 86°F (0° to 30°C) 30
Above 14°F (-10°C) 20W-40, 20W-50
14° to 50°F (-10° to 10°C) 20W-20
Below 25°F (-4°C) .10W
Above 5°F (-15°C) 15W-40, 15W-50
5° to 80°F (-15° to 25°C) 1996 . . . . .10W-30,
                            10W-40
Below 80°F (25°C) 1996 . . . . .5W-30

TRANSMISSION, Automatic
All . . . .**AE**
ESSO LT71141, Audi Part Number: G052162A1 or A2

CAPACITY, Initial Refill[3]:	Liters	Qt
1996 w/01F:		
A6 Quattro	2.7	2.9
Cabriolet, w/01N	5.4	5.7
A4	2.6	2.8
A6 1996	2.7	2.9
1997	2.6	2.7
A8 1997	2.6[4]	2.7[4]

3 With engine at operating temperature, shift transmission
  through all gears. Check fluid level in PARK and add fluid
  as needed.
4 Vehicle is not equipped with a transmission dipstick,
  special tools and procedure required, see manufacturer's service literature.

TRANSAXLE,
  Manual . . . . . . .Synthetic 75W-90 **GL-4**[5]
Includes front drive & transfer case
5 Audi Part Number G005000 or G052911A or G052145A1
  or A2

CAPACITY, Refill:	Liters	Pt
A4 2WD	2.3	4.8
A4 4WD	2.8	5.8
A6	2.2	4.7

FINAL DRIVE, Auto. Trans.
All Models . . . . . .Synthetic 75W-90 **GL-4**[7]
7 Audi Part Number G052145A2 or G005000

CAPACITY, Refill:	Liters	Pt
Cabriolet	1.0	2.1
A4	0.8	1.6
A6	0.7	1.4
A8 1997	0.7	1.6

TRANSFER CASE
  Synthetic . . . . .75W-90 **GL-4**[8]
All ex. V8 w/auto. trans.
8 Audi Part Number G052145A2 or G005000

CAPACITY, Refill:	Liters	Pt
01F:A6 Quattro, ...	1.0	2.2

REAR DIFFERENTIAL 90W GL-5

CAPACITY, Refill:	Liters	Pt
A4	1.9	4.0
A6	1.7	3.6

AUDI
1998-99 All Models

CHEK-CHART

Perform the following maintenance services at the intervals indicated to keep the vehicle warranties in effect.
W SERVICE TO MAINTAIN EMISSION WARRANTY

MI—MILES IN THOUSANDS
KM—KILOMETERS IN THOUSANDS

TURBO ENGINE
EVERY 5 MI—8 KM
OTHERS
EVERY 6 MO/7.5 MI—12 KM

Hydraulic system/power
 steering . . . . .check level **SLF**

W Crankcase . . . . .change oil

W Crankcase oil filter . . . . .replace
At initial service only

Windshield washers, wipers . . .check/fill

Service interval display . . . . .reset

Automatic shift lock . . . . .check
Check operation including park/neutral safety switch.

Cooling system . . . . . . .check level **EC**
CAUTION: If coolant is red in color, never mix with any
other coolant or engine damage will occur.

Brake master cylinder . . .check level **HB**

Wheels & tires . . . . .rotate
At first interval only

Plenum chamber water
 drain valve, ...check
A6 wagon, Avant only. Replace if dirty.

TURBO ENGINE
EVERY 10MI—16KM
OTHERS:
EVERY 12 MO/15 MI—24 KM

Brake system . . . . .inspect/adjust
Check for damage & leaks, check pad thickness, check
& adjust pedal travel, check pressure regulator, adjust
hand brake.

Drive shaft boots . . . . .inspect

W Exhaust system . . . . .inspect

Final drive, automatic . . . . . .check level

Transaxle, automatic . . . . . . .check level
Level check not required for V8.

Transaxle, manual . . . . .check level

Differential . . . . .check level

Wheels & tires . . . . .inspect
Check pressure including spare.

Battery . . . . .check level

W Crankcase oil filter . . . . .replace

On-board   diagnostic
 system . . . . .check/clear

Electrical equipment . . . . .inspect

Dust & pollen filter . . . . .replace
A4, A6, A8

Headlights . . . . .adjust

Vehicle . . . . .road test

Body . . . . .lubricate **MO**
Door check straps.

Roof frame, guides, lock . . .lubricate **LM**
Cabriolet & sunroofs

EVERY 24 MONTHS
Brakes . . . . .change fluid **HB**
Check operation of warning light switch.

TURBO ENGINE
EVERY 20MI—32KM
OTHERS:
EVERY 24 MO/30 MI—48 KM

Front suspension . . . . .inspect
Check ball joint & tie rod dust seals, check tie rods.

W Air filter element . . . . .replace

W Spark plugs . . . . .replace

1998
EVERY 48 MO/45 MI—72 KM

Transmission, automatic . . .change fluid
Except A4, A8, AG4

EVERY 75 MI—120 KM

Timing belt, 1999 . . . . .replace
V6 5V & V8 engines

Timing belt tensioner roller,
 1999 V6 5V . . . . .replace

EVERY 80 MI—120 KM

Ribbed V-belt . . . . .replace
1999 1.8L Turbo A4

EVERY 90 MI—144 KM

Timing belt, 1998 . . . . .replace
Except 4-cyl. turbo

Ribbed V-belt, 1998 . . . . .replace

EVERY 72 MONTHS

Tires . . . . .replace
Regardless of tread depth

EVERY 168 MONTHS

Airbags . . . . .replace

SEVERE SERVICE

Crankcase—Change oil and filter at half
of recommended interval.

Air Filter—Replace at 12 mo/15 mi (24 km).

Automatic Transmission—Change fluid
every 30 mi (48km), clean pan & strainer, replace pan gasket.

KEY TO LUBRICANTS
See other Audi chart

CRANKCASE . . . . .SH, SJ, GF-2

CAPACITY, Refill:	Liters	Qt
4-cyl. 1.8L A4	3.5	3.7
4-cyl. 1.8L TT	4.5	4.8
6-cyl. 2.8L Cabriolet	5.0	5.3
2.8L A4	5.2	5.5
2.8L A6	6.0	6.3
V8 3.7L, 4.2L A8	7.5	8.0

Capacity shown includes filter; add specified amount, run
engine to operating temperature. Recheck level and correct as necessary.

A4, A6, A8, Cabriolet
Energy Conserving Oil:
All temperatures 5W-30, 5W-40,
10W-30, 10W-40

Except Energy Conserving Oil:
All temperatures 5W-50, 10W-50,10W-60
Below 59°F (15°C) 5W-30, 5W-40,
10W-30, 10W-40
Above 5°F (-15°C) 15W-40, 15W-50,
20W-40, 20W-50

TRANSMISSION, Automatic . . . . .AE
ESSO LT71141, Audi Part Number: G052162A1 or A2

CAPACITY, Initial Refill[3]:	Liters	Qt
Cabriolet, w/01N	5.4	5.7
A4	2.6	2.8
A6	2.6	2.7
A8	3.6[4]	3.7[4]

3 With engine at operating temperature, shift transmission
through all gears. Check fluid level in PARK and add fluid
as needed.
4 Vehicle is not equipped with a transmission dipstick,
special tools and procedure required, see manufacturer's service literature.

TRANSAXLE,
Manual . . . . . . .Synthetic 75W-90 GL-4[5]
Includes final drive & transfer case
5 Audi Part Number G005000 or G052911A or G052145A1
or A2

CAPACITY, Refill:	Liters	Pt
A4 2WD	2.3	4.8
A4 4WD	2.8	5.8
TT	2.0	4.2

TRANSFER
CASE . . . . .Synthetic 75W-90 GL-4[8]
All ex. V8 w/auto. trans.
8 Audi Part Number G052145A2 or G005000

CAPACITY, Refill:	Liters	Pt
A6	0.8	1.7

REAR DIFFERENTIAL 90W GL-5

CAPACITY, Refill:	Liters	Pt
A4	1.9	4.0
A6	1.5	3.2

FINAL DRIVE, Auto. Trans.
All Models . . . . . .Synthetic 75W-90 GL-4[7]
7 Audi Part Number G052145A2 or G005000

CAPACITY, Refill:	Liters	Pt
Cabriolet	1.0	2.1
A4	0.8	1.6
A6	0.8	1.7
A8	0.7	1.6

BMW
1989-99 All Models

SERVICE LOCATIONS — ENGINE AND CHASSIS

HOOD RELEASE: Inside

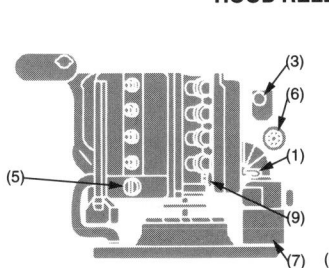

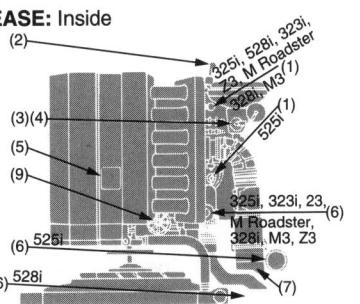

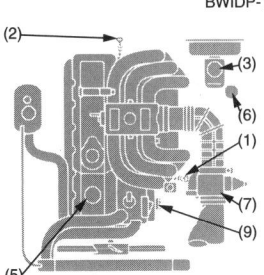

1990-99
318, Z3
4-cyl. 1796cc, 1895cc DOHC
1997 3161
4-cyl. 1596cc

1989-91
M3
4-cyl. 2302cc DOHC

1991-99
3-Series, Z3, 525i, 528i
6-cyl. 1991cc, 2494cc DOHC
2793cc, 2990cc
1997-99 M Roadster, M Coupe, M3
6-cyl. 3152cc

1989-92
325-Series, 525i
6-cyl. 2494cc SOHC

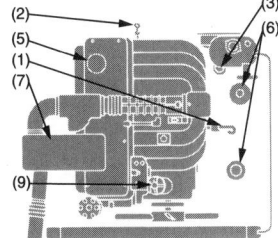

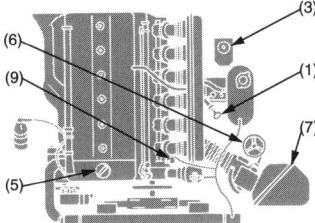

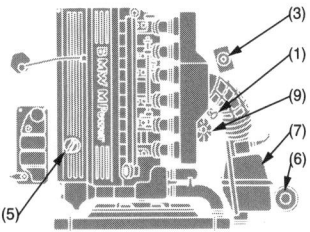

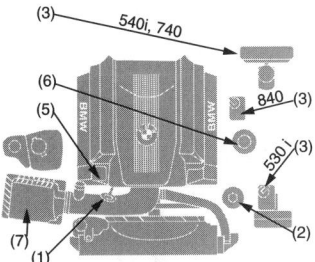

1989-93
535, 635Cs, 735, L6
6-cyl. 3428cc

1989
M5, M6
6-cyl. 3453cc DOHC

1990-93
M5
6-cyl. 3453cc DOHC, 3535cc

1993-99
530i
V8 2997cc
540i, 740, 840
V8 3982cc
V8 4398cc

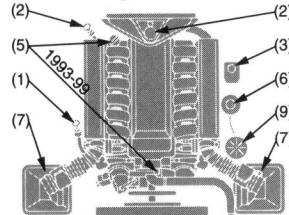

1989-99
750, 850
V12 4988cc,
5379cc, 5576cc

(1) Crankcase dipstick
(2) Transmission dipstick
(3) Brake fluid reservoir
(4) Clutch fluid reservoir
(5) Oil fill cap
(6) Power steering reservoir/
    self-leveling suspension or
    Hydroboost reservoir

(7) Air filter
(8) Fuel filter
(9) Oil filter
(10) PCV filter
(11) EGR valve
(12) Oxygen sensor
(13) PCV valve

(A) Manual transmission/transaxle,
    drain & fill
(B) Transfer case, 325iX only
(C) Automatic transaxle final drive,
    NOT USED
(D) Differential, drain & fill

■ Lift adapter position

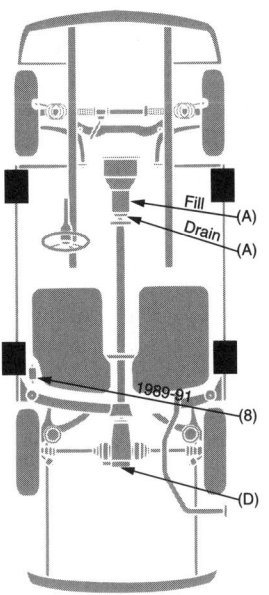

1989-99
3-Series

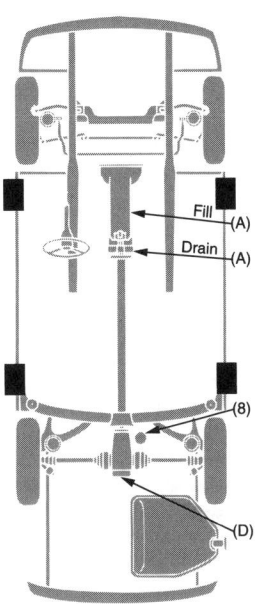

1989
6-Series

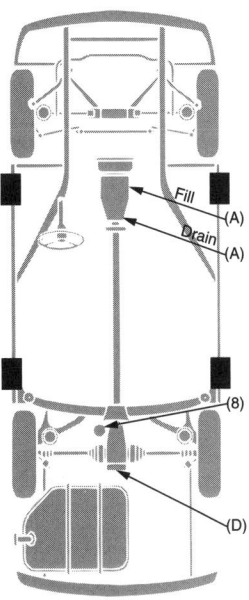

1989-98
5-Series,
7-Series, 8-Seris

13

SERVICE AT TIME OR MILEAGE — WHICHEVER OCCURS FIRST

BWIPM2   BWIPM2

Perform the following maintenance services at the intervals indicated to keep the vehicle warranties in effect.

W   SERVICE TO MAINTAIN EMISSION WARRANTY

MI—MILES IN THOUSANDS
KM—KILOMETERS IN THOUSANDS

1989-91 INDICATED LUBRICATION SERVICE

Brakes .inspect
Check thickness of pads & rotors, check condition of hoses, lines & fittings, check operation of hand brake

W Crankcase . . . . .change oil

W Oil filter .replace

Steering . . . . .inspect/adjust
Check tightness of steering box, joint disc & threaded connections. Adjust free play

Wheels & tires . . . . .inspect
Including spare tire

Brake master cylinder . . .check level **HB**

Clutch master cylinder . . .check level **HB**

Lighting . . . . .inspect
Check all lighting, aim headlights as necessary

Power steering . . . . .check level **AF3**
Ex. models with self-leveling suspension
On models with Hydroboost, use **SLF**, then pump brake pedal several times to discharge accumulator before checking level

Power steering w/self-
leveling suspension . . .check level **PS**

Seat belts . . . . .inspect

Windshield wipers . . . . .inspect
Check condition of blades, aim washers, fill

Service indicator . . . . .reset
Special tool required

1989-90 EVERY 12 MONTHS

Brakes . . . . .change fluid **HB**

INDICATED INSPECTION SERVICE I

Exhaust system . . . . .inspect/tighten

Final drive . . . . .check level

Hand brake . . . . .inspect/adjust
Check shoes & cables for wear, adjust & lube

Suspension . . . . .inspect
Check condition of axle joints, tie rods & linkage

Transmission,
automatic . . . . .change fluid **AF3**
Replace strainer & gasket, do not repeat at inspection service II

Transmission, manual . . . . .check level

Air conditioner . . . . .check/tighten
Tighten compressor mounts, check operation & charge

Battery . . . . .check/fill

Cooling system . . . . .inspect/fill **EC**

Engine diagnostic
system . . . . .access codes

Fuel injectors . . . . .clean
Clean carbon from intake valves as necessary

Microfilter, interior air . . . . .replace
Does not apply to all models

Throttle linkage . . . . .lubricate **LM**

W Valve clearance . . . . .check/adjust
Ex. 1.8L DOHC, 2.5L DOHC & V12 engines

Door, hood, trunk
hinges . . . . .tighten/lubricate **MO**

Door, hood, trunk latches . .lubricate **LM**

Fuel tank, lines, cap . . . . .inspect
Clean filter screen on fuel pickup

Sunroof . . . . .lubricate

Service indicator . . . . .reset
Special tool required

EVERY 24 MONTHS

Brakes, 1991 . . . . .change fluid **HB**

Cooling system . . . . .replace coolant **EC**

INDICATED INSPECTION SERVICE II

Clutch .inspect

Drive shaft & axles . . . . .inspect
Inspect flexible couplings & constant velocity joint boots

Final drive . . . . .change lubricant
Includes front differential on 325ix

W Fuel filter . . . . .replace
Not required for Calif. warranty

Front wheel bearings . .check/adjust **WB**

Transfer case, 325ix . . .change lubricant

Transmission, manual . .change lubricant

W Air filter element . . . . .replace

Air intake dust separators, 850i . . .clean

Automatic skid & traction
control filter . . . . .replace
1991 735i, 750iL & 850i if equipped

W Drive belts . . . . .inspect/adjust
Replace belts on 1991 M5. Not required for Calif. warranty

W Spark plugs . . . . .replace

Timing belt, 2.5L . . . . . . .inspect/adjust
Replace belt every second service

Service indicator . . . . .reset
Special tool required

EVERY 36 MONTHS

Air bag system . . . . .inspect
Visually check system components

EVERY 50 MI—80 KM

W Oxygen sensor . . . . .replace

KEY TO LUBRICANTS
See other BMW chart

CRANKCASE . . . . .SF, SG
DOHC engines:
All temperatures 15W-40, 15W-50
SOHC engines:
68° to 122°F (20° to 50°C)	40
32° to 86°F (0° to 30°C)	30
14° to 122°F (-10° to 50°C)	. . . . .20W-50
-4° to 104°F (-20° to 40°C)	. . . . .15W-50
-4° to 86°F (-20° to 30°C)	. . . . .15W-40
-4° to 50°F (-20° to 10°C)	20
-22° to 68°F (-30° to 20°C)	. . . . .10W-50
-22° to 50°F (-30° to 10°C) 1989	. . . . .10W-40
-22° to 60°F (-30° to 16°C) 1990-91	. . .10W-40
-22° to 41F° (-30° to 5°C)	. . . . .10W-30
-40° to 23°F (-40° to -5°C)	. . . . .5W-30
-40° to 14°F (-40° to -10°C)	. . . . .5W-20

CAPACITY, Refill:	Liters	Qt
1989-90 535i, 635CSi, 735i	5.0	5.3
1989-90 M3	4.0	4.2
M5, M6	5.0	5.3
1989-91 325i	4.0	4.2
750iL	6.5	6.8
1989-90 525i	4.0	4.2
1990-91 318i	4.3	4.5
1991 525i, 535i, M5, 735i	5.0	5.3
1991 850i	6.5	6.8

Capacity shown is without filter. When replacing filter, additional oil may be needed
Additional oil may be needed if oil cooler is drained

TRANSMISSION, Automatic AF3
CAPACITY, Initial Refill[1]:	Liters	Qt
1989-90 All	3.0	3.2
1991 325i, 525i, 535i	3.0	3.2
1991 735i	3.0	3.2
1991 750iL	3.5	3.7
1991 850i	3.5	3.7

1 With engine at operating temperature, shift transmission through all gears. Check level in PARK and add fluid as needed

TRANSMISSION, Manual
Inspect for color coded fluid identification label, usually affixed to passenger side of the transmission bellhousing. Verify fluid installed before topping up or refilling transmission
GREEN LABEL[2] . . . . .GLS
RED LABEL[2] AF3
NO LABEL[3] . . . . .80W GL-4[4]

2 Units that are factory filled with **AF** or **GLS** are fitted with 17mm external hex head drain and fill plugs
3 Units that are factory filled with **GL-4** are fitted with 17mm internal hex (Allen) head drain and fill plugs
4 May use 20, 30, or 40 **SG** to improve shift effort

CAPACITY, Refill:	Liters	Pt
1989-90 M5	1.3	2.7
1989 635CSi, M6	1.3	2.7
1989-90 325i, 525i, 535i	1.3	2.7
1989-91 M3	1.2	2.5
735i	1.3	2.7
1991 318i, 318iS	1.2	2.4
1991 525i	1.0	2.2
1991 325i, 535i, M5	1.3	2.7
1991 850i	2.3	4.8

TRANSFER CASE AF3
CAPACITY, Refill:	Liters	Pt
325iX	0.5	1.0

DIFFERENTIAL 90 GL-5
CAPACITY, Refill:	Liters	Pt
Rear:		
1989-90 635CSi, M6	1.9	4.0
1989-91 535i, M5, 735i	1.9	4.0
1989-91 750iL	1.9	4.0
M3, 325i, 525i	1.7	3.6
1990-91 318i	0.9	1.9
1991 850i	1.9	4.0
Front:		
1989-91 325ix	0.7	1.4

SERVICE AT TIME OR MILEAGE — WHICHEVER OCCURS FIRST

BWIPM3   BWIPM3

Perform the following maintenance services at the intervals indicated to keep the vehicle warranties in effect.
W   SERVICE TO MAINTAIN EMISSION WARRANTY

MI—MILES IN THOUSANDS
KM—KILOMETERS IN THOUSANDS

EVERY 12 MONTHS
Brake master cylinder . . . . .inspect

Headlights/foglights . . . . . . .check/adjust

Steering .check

INDICATED ENGINE OIL SERVICE
W Crankcase . . . . .change oil
At least once a year

W Oil filter .replace
At least once a year

Service indicator . . . . .reset
Special tool required

Rear axle, 318i, 325i,
  750iL, 850Ci . . . . . . .change lubricant
At first service interval only

INDICATED INSPECTION SERVICE I

Brakes .inspect
Check thickness of pads & rotors, check condition of hoses, lines & fittings, check operation of hand brake

Steering . . . . .inspect/adjust
Check tightness of steering box, joint disc & threaded connections. Adjust free play

Wheels & tires . . . . .inspect
Including spare tire

Front wheel bearings . .check/repack **WB**

Brake master cylinder . . .check level **HB**

Clutch master cylinder . . .check level **HB**

Lighting .inspect
Check all lighting, aim headlights as necessary

Power steering . . . . . . .check level **AF3**
Ex. models with self-leveling suspension
On models with Hydroboost use **SLF**, then pump brake pedal several times to discharge accumulator before checking level

Power steering w/self-
  leveling suspension . . .check level **PS**

Seat belts . . . . .inspect

Windshield wipers . . . . .inspect
Check condition of blades, aim washers, fill

Exhaust system . . . . . . .inspect/tighten

Rear axle . . . . .check level

Suspension . . . . .inspect
Check condition of axle joints, tie rods & linkage

Transmission . . . . .check level

Air conditioner . . . . .check/tighten
Tighten compressor mounts, check operation & charge

Battery . . . . .check/fill

Cooling system . . . . .inspect/fill **EC**

Engine diagnostic
  system . . . . .access codes

Microfilter, interior air . . . . .replace
Does not apply to all models

Throttle linkage . . . . .lubricate **LM**

W Valve clearance . . . . .check/adjust
Ex. 1.8L DOHC, 2.5L DOHC & V12 engines

Door, hood, trunk
  hinges . . . . .tighten/lubricate **MO**

Door, hood, trunk latches . . .lubricate **LM**

Fuel tank, lines, cap . . . . .inspect
Clean filter screen on fuel pickup

Sunroof . . . . .lubricate

Service indicator . . . . .reset
Special tool required

EVERY 24 MONTHS
Brakes . . . . .change fluid **HB**

Cooling system . . . . .replace coolant **EC**

INDICATED INSPECTION SERVICE II

Clutch .inspect
At every second service

Drive shaft & axles . . . . .inspect
Inspect flexible couplings & constant velocity joint boots

Rear axle . . . . .change lubricant
Includes front differential on 325ix

W Fuel filter . . . . .replace
Not required for Calif. warranty

Transmission,
  automatic . . . . .change fluid **AF3**

W Air filter element . . . . .replace

Air intake dust separators,
  850i . . . . .clean

Automatic skid & traction
  control filter . . . . .replace
735, 750, 850 if equipped

W Drive belts . . . . .inspect/adjust
Not required for Calif. warranty

W Spark plugs . . . . .replace

Timing belt, 2.5L . . . . . . .inspect/adjust
Replace belt every second service, or 50,000 miles

Service indicator . . . . .reset
Special tool required

EVERY 36 MONTHS
Air bag system . . . . .inspect
Visually check system components

EVERY 50 MI—80 KM
W Oxygen sensor, 325iC . . . . .replace

EVERY 60 MI—96 KM
W Oxygen sensor, 318i, 535i,
  M5, All 7 & 8 Series . . . . .replace

EVERY 100 MI—161 KM
W Oxygen sensor, 325i, 525i/iT . . . .replace

KEY TO LUBRICANTS

AE	ESSO Type LT71141 fluid
AF3	DEXRON® III Automatic Transmission Fluid
EC	Ethylene Glycol Coolant Mix 50% with water
GL-4	Gear Oil, API Service GL-4
GL-5	Gear Oil, API Service GL-5
GLS	Gear Lubricant, Special Mobil SHC 630, synthetic lubricant
HB	Hydraulic Brake Fluid, DOT 4
LM	Lithium Multipurpose Grease
MO	Motor Oil
PS	Pentosin CHF 11S
SF	Motor Oil, API Service SF
SG	Motor Oil, API Service SG
SLF	Special Lubricant, Fluid BMW Part No. 81 22 9 407 549 Shell LA 2634
WB	Wheel Bearing Grease

CRANKCASE . . . .**SF, SG**

Temperature	Grade
14° to 122°F (-10° to 50°C)	20W-50
-4° to 104°F (-20° to 40°C)	15W-50
-4° to 86°F (-20° to 30°C)	15W-40
-4° to 50°F (-20° to 10°C)	20
-22° to 68°F (-30° to 20°C)	10W-50
-22° to 60°F (-30° to 16°C)	10W-40
-22° to 41°F (-30° to 5°C)	10W-30
-40° to 23°F (-40° to -5°C)	5W-30
-40° to 14°F (-40° to -10°C)	5W-20

CAPACITY, Refill:	Liters	Qt
318i	4.3	4.5
325i	5.8	6.1
525i, 535i, M5	5.7[1]	6.1[1]
735i	5.0	5.3
750iL	6.5	6.8
850Ci	7.5[1]	7.9[1]
850i	6.5	6.8

Capacity shown is without filter. When replacing filter, additional oil may be needed
Additional oil may be needed if oil cooler is drained
[1] Includes filter

TRANSMISSION, Automatic **AF3**

CAPACITY, Initial Refill[2]:	Liters	Qt
318i, 325i, 525i, 535i	3.0	3.2
735i	3.0	3.2
750iL	3.5	3.7
850i	3.5	3.7

[2] With engine at operating temperature, shift transmission through all gears. Check level in PARK and add fluid as needed

TRANSMISSION, Manual
Inspect for color coded fluid identification label, usually affixed to passenger side of the transmission bellhousing. Verify fluid installed before topping up or refilling transmission

GREEN LABEL[3]	**GLS**
RED LABEL[3]	**AF3**
NO LABEL[4]	**80W GL-4**[5]

[3] Units that are factory filled with AF or GLS are fitted with 17mm external hex head drain and fill plugs
[4] Units that are factory filled with GL-4 are fitted with 17mm internal hex (Allen) head drain and fill plugs
[5] May use 20, 30, or 40 SG to improve shift effort

CAPACITY, Refill:	Liters	Pt
318i, 325i	1.1	2.4
535i, M5	1.3	2.7
525i	1.0	2.2
735i	1.3	2.7
850i	2.3	4.8

DIFFERENTIAL . . . .**.90 GL-5**

CAPACITY, Refill:	Liters	Pt
318i	1.1	2.4
M3, 325i, 325i	1.7	3.6
535i, M5, 735i	1.9	4.0
750iL	1.9	4.0
850i	1.9	4.0

SERVICE AT TIME OR MILEAGE — WHICHEVER OCCURS FIRST

BWIPM4   BWIPM4

Perform the following maintenance services at the intervals indicated to keep the vehicle warranties in effect.

W   SERVICE TO MAINTAIN EMISSION WARRANTY

MI—MILES IN THOUSANDS
KM—KILOMETERS IN THOUSANDS

EVERY 12 MONTHS
Brake master cylinder . . . . .inspect

Headlights/foglights . . . . . . .check/adjust

Steering . . . . .check

Alarm remote control battery . . . .replace
1995-99 5, 7 & 8 Series

INDICATED ENGINE OIL SERVICE
W Crankcase . . . . .change oil
At least once a year

W Oil filter . . . . .replace
At least once a year

Service indicator . . . . .reset
Rear axle, 1993-94, 318i/iS,
  325i/iS, 740i/iL, 750iL, 850Ci
  1995-99 All . . . . .change lubricant
1998 built from 5/97–8/97 7-series only
At first service interval only

INDICATED INSPECTION
SERVICE I
Alarm remote control battery . . . .replace
1995-99 5, 7, 8 Series

Brakes . . . . .inspect
Check thickness of pads & rotors, check condition of
hoses, lines & fittings, check operation of parking brake

Steering . . . . .inspect/adjust
Check tightness of steering box, joint disc & threaded
connections. Adjust free play

Wheels & tires . . . . .inspect
Including spare tire

Front wheel bearings . .check/repack **WB**

Brake master cylinder . . .check level **HB**
1997-99 5-Series: low level indicated by dash light

Clutch master cylinder . . .check level **HB**
1997-99 5-Series: low level indicated by dash light

Lighting . . . . .inspect

Power steering . . . . . . .check level **AF3**
Ex. models with self-leveling suspension
On models with Hydroboost use **SLF**, then pump brake
pedal several times to discharge accumulator before
checking level

Power steering w/self-
  leveling suspension . . .check level **PS**

Seat belts . . . . .inspect

Windshield wipers & washers . . .inspect
Front & Rear

Exhaust system . . . . .inspect/tighten

Rear axle . . . . .check level

Suspension . . . . .inspect
Check condition of axle joints, tie rods & linkage

Transmission . . . . .check level

Air conditioner . . . . .check/tighten
Also, heater & defroster.
Tighten compressor mounts, check operation & charge

Battery . . . . .check/fill

Cooling system . . . . .inspect/fill **EC**

Roll-over protection system . . . .activate
1995-99 318i, 325i, 328

Engine diagnostic
  system . . . . .access codes

Airbags . . . . .check

Microfilters, interior air . . . . . .replace
Some models have two

Throttle linkage . . . . .lubricate **LM**

W Valve clearance . . . . .check/adjust
Ex. 1.8L DOHC, 2.5L DOHC & V12 engines

Door, hood, trunk
  hinges . . . . .tighten/lubricate **MO**

Door, hood, trunk latches . . .lubricate **LM**

Fuel tank, lines, cap . . . . .inspect
Clean filter screen on fuel pickup

Service indicator . . . . .reset

EVERY 24 MONTHS
Brakes . . . . .change fluid **HB**

Cooling system . . . . .replace coolant **EC**
1993-94

INDICATED INSPECTION
SERVICE II
Clutch . . . . .inspect
At every second service
Ex. 1997-99 540i

Drive shaft & axles . . . . .inspect
Inspect flexible couplings & constant velocity joint boots

Rear axle . . . . .change lubricant
1995-99 Every other service
Includes front differential on 325ix

W Fuel filter . . . . .replace
Ex. 1995 3-Series, 1996 7&8 Series
Not required for Calif. warranty

Transmission,
  automatic . . . . .change fluid **AF3**
Ex. 1995 540i, 7 & 8 Series, 1996-99 All lifetime fill
3-series, 530i, 540i

Transmission, manual . .change lubricant
1993 535i, M5 1995: 850csi
At every second service: 1993 318i/iS, 325i/iS, 525i/iT,
850Ci

W Air filter element . . . . .replace

Air intake dust separators,
  840 & 850, 1993-97 . . . . .clean

Automatic skid & traction
  control filter . . . . .replace
740, 750, 850 if equipped

W Drive belts 1993-94 . . . . . .inspect/adjust
1993 M5 3.5L (S38) recommend drive belt change

W Spark plugs . . . . .replace

Timing belt, 2.5L . . . . . . .inspect/adjust
Replace belt every second service, or 50,000 miles

Service indicator . . . . .reset

EVERY 36 MONTHS
Air bag system . . . . .inspect

Cooling system . . . . .replace coolant **EC**
1995-99

EVERY 50 MI—80 KM
W Oxygen sensor, 325iC . . . . .replace

EVERY 60 MI—96 KM
W Oxygen sensor, 318i/iS, 535i,
  M5, All 7 & 8 Series . . . . .replace

EVERY 72 MONTHS
Tires, 1999 . . . . .replace
Including spare

EVERY 100 MI—161 KM
W Oxygen sensor, 1993-94 325i/iS, 525i/iT
1995-99 All . . . . .replace

EVERY 120 MONTHS
Tires, 1993-98 . . . . .replace
Including spare

KEY TO LUBRICANTS
See other BMW chart

CRANKCASE . . . . . . .SG, SG/CD, SG/CE, SH, SH/CD, SH/CE

1993-95: 14° to 122°F (-10° to 50°C) 20W-50
  -4° to 104°F (-20° to 40°C) 15W-50
  -4° to 86°F (-20° to 30°C) 15W-40
  -22° to 60°F (-30° to 16°C) 10W-40
  -22° to 41°F (-30° to 5°C) 10W-30
  -40° to 23°F (-40° to -5°C) 5W-30
  -40° to 14°F (-40° to -10°C) 5W-20
1996-98: 15° to 86°F (-10° to 30°C) 15W-40
  -5° to 68°F (-20° to 20°C) 10W-40
  -5° to 50°F (-20° to 10°C) 10W-30
  -40° to 50°F (-40° to 10°C) 5W-30
  -40° to 32°F (-40° to 0°C) 5W-20
1999: 15° to 86°F (-10° to 30°C) 15W-40
  -25° to 50°F (10° to -30°C) 5W-30

CAPACITY, Refill:	Liters	Qt
Includes filter		
318-Series: 1993	5.0	5.3
1994	4.5	4.7
1995-99	4.9	5.2
320, 323, 325, 328-Series	6.5	6.9
525i, 535i	5.7	6.1
528i, 2.8L 1997-99	6.5	7.0
530i, 540i	7.5	8.0
740, 840-Series	7.5	7.9
750, 850-Series: 1993-94	7.5	7.9
1995-99	8.0	8.5
M3 1995-97	6.5	6.9
M3 1998-99	6.0	6.3
M5	5.7	6.1
Z3 1996-97	4.5	4.7
Z3 1998-99 1.9L	5.0	5.3
1998-99 2.8L	6.5	6.9
M Roadster & Coupe 1998 3.2L	5.5	5.8

Additional oil may be needed if oil cooler is drained

TRANSMISSION, Automatic
1993-97 3-Series ex. M3	AF3
1998-99 3-Series ex. M3	SLF
1995-99 M3	AE
1993-97 525, 528	AF3
1994-95 530, 540	SLF
1997-99 530, 540	AE
1998-99 5-Series ex. 540	SLF
1993-99 740	AE
1995-99 750, 850	SLF
1994-95 840	SLF
1996-97 840	AE

CAPACITY, Initial Refill[2]:	Liters	Qt
1993-99 3-Series	3.0	3.2
1995-99 Z3	3.0	3.2
1995-99 M3	3.0	3.2
1993-99 525, 530, 535, M5	3.0	3.2
1993-99 540	5.5	5.8
1993-99 740	5.5	5.8
1993-95 750	3.5	3.7
1996-99 750	3.0	3.2
1993-95 850	3.5	3.7

2 With engine at operating temperature, shift transmission
through all gears. Check level in PARK and add fluid as
needed

TRANSMISSION, Manual AF3
CAPACITY, Refill:	Liters	Pt
318, 320, 325	1.1	2.4
328	1.2	2.6
M3	1.2	2.6
Z3	1.0	2.0
535i, M5	1.3	2.7
525i	1.2	2.5
530i, 540i	1.2	2.6
840Ci, 850Ci, 850CSi	2.3	4.8

DIFFERENTIAL
1993-96 7, 8-Series	GLS[3]
1994-96 5-Series	GLS[3]
1995-96 M3	GLS[3]
1996 3-Series	GLS[3]
1997-99 All	GLS[3]
All Others	90 GL-5

3 BMW Synthetic Final Drive Oil or Castrol SAF-XO BMW
Part No. 83 22 9 407 768 with multiple limited-slip SAFX-
LS. BMW Part No. 83 22 9 407 803

CAPACITY, Refill:	Liters	Pt
318i, 320	1.1	2.4
328	1.4	3.0
325, 525i, 530i	1.7	3.6
M3 1993-96	1.7	3.6
M3 1997-99	1.4	3.0
Z3	1.0	2.0
M Roadster & Coupe	1.4	3.0
535i, 540i, M5	1.9	4.0
740, 750: 1993-94	1.9	4.0
1995-99	1.6	3.4
840, 850	1.9	4.0

SERVICE LOCATIONS—ENGINE AND CHASSIS

HOOD RELEASE: Inside

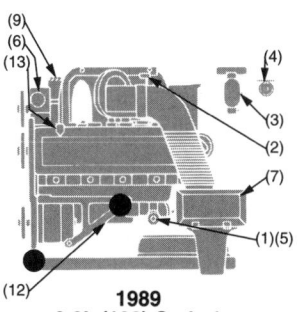

1989
2.0L (122) Code 1

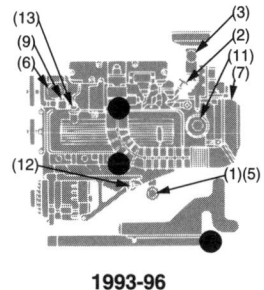

1993-96
2.2L Code 4

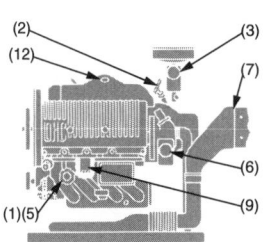

1992-94
2.3L SOHC Code 3
Skylark

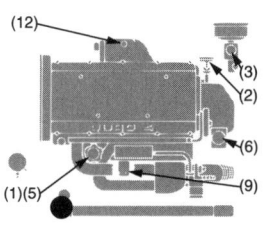

1989-91 2.3L Code D
1995 2.3L Code D

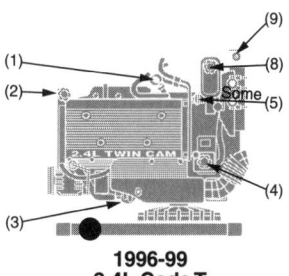

1996-99
2.4L Code T

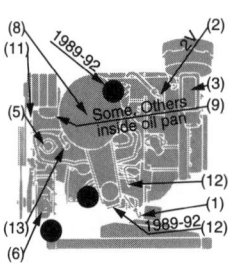

1989-92
2.5L (151)
(2V shown)
Code 5, R, U
Air induction
system varies.

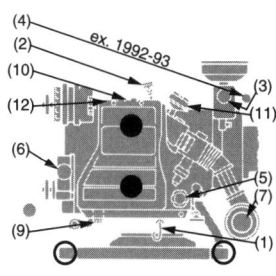

1989
2.8L (173) Code W
1989-93
3.1L Code T Regal

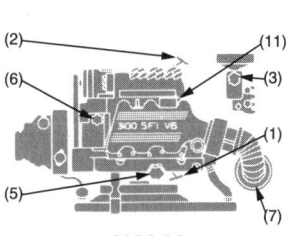

1994-00
3.1L Code M, J
Century, Regal, Skylark

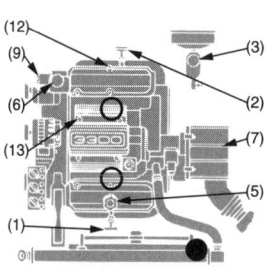

1989-93
3.3L Code N
Century, Skylark

(1) Crankcase dipstick	(8) Fuel filter
(2) Transmission dipstick	(9) Oil filter
(3) Brake fluid reservoir	(10) PCV filter
(4) Clutch fluid reservoir	(11) EGR valve
(5) Oil fill cap	(12) Oxygen sensor
(6) Power steering reservoir	(13) PCV valve
(7) Air filter	

● Cooling system drain   ○ Cooling system drain, some models

SERVICE LOCATIONS—ENGINE AND CHASSIS

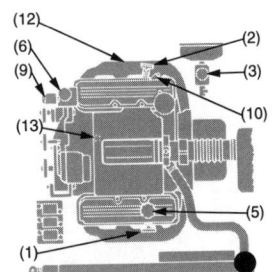

1989-91 3.8L (231) Code C
Electra, LeSabre, Reatta, Riviera

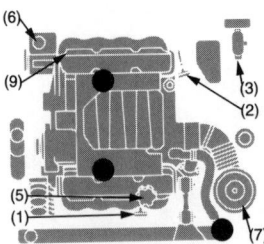

1990-00 3.8L Code L, K
Electra, LeSabre, Park Ave.,
Reatta, Regal, Riviera

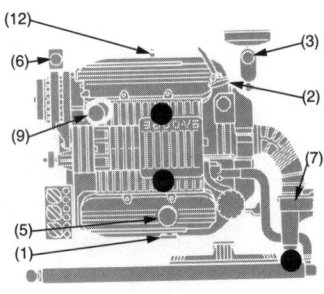

**1992-00
3.8L Code 1
Supercharged**

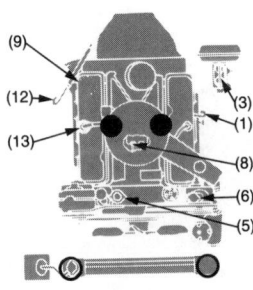

**1989-90
5.0L (307)**

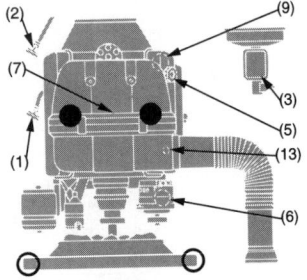

**1991-92 5.0L Code E
1991-93 5.7L Code 7
Roadmaster**

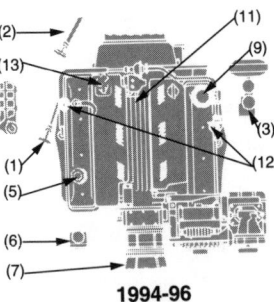

**1994-96
5.7L Code P
Roadmaster**

(1) Crankcase dipstick
(2) Transmission dipstick
(3) Brake fluid reservoir
(4) Clutch fluid reservoir
(5) Oil fill cap
(6) Power steering reservoir
(7) Air filter

(8) Fuel filter
(9) Oil filter
(10) PCV filter
(11) EGR valve
(12) Oxygen sensor
(13) PCV valve

● Cooling system drain   ○ Cooling system drain, some models

SERVICE LOCATIONS—ENGINE AND CHASSIS

4 FITTINGS

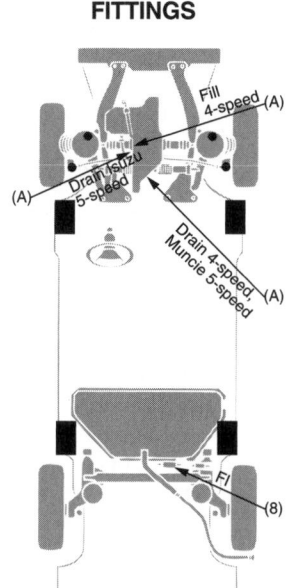

Fill 4-speed (A)
Drain Isuzu 5-speed
(A)
Drain 4-speed, Muncie 5-speed (A)
FI (8)

1989 Skyhawk FWD, 1989-98 Skylark

4 FITTINGS

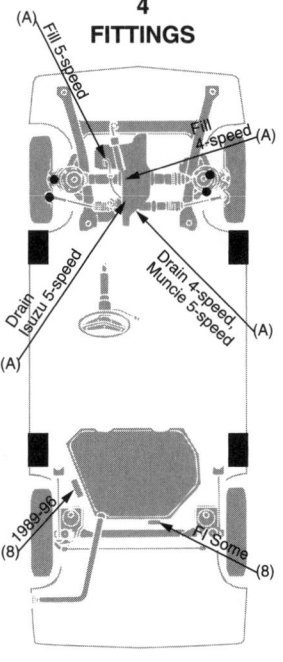

(A) Fill 5-speed
Fill 4-speed (A)
Drain Isuzu 5-speed
(A)
Drain 4-speed, Muncie 5-speed (A)
1989-96 (8)
FI Some (8)

1989-96 Century

0-4 FITTINGS

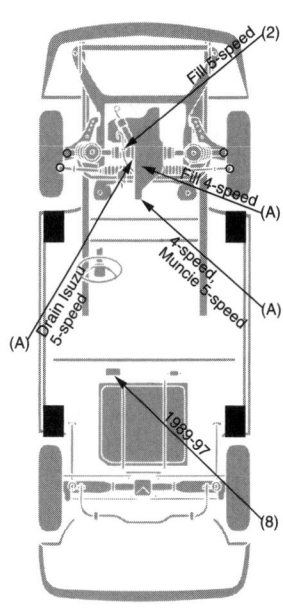

(2)
Fill 5-speed
Fill 4-speed (A)
4-speed, Muncie 5-speed (A)
Drain Isuzu 5-speed (A)
1989-97
(8)

1989-00 Regal, 1997-00 Century

4 FITTINGS

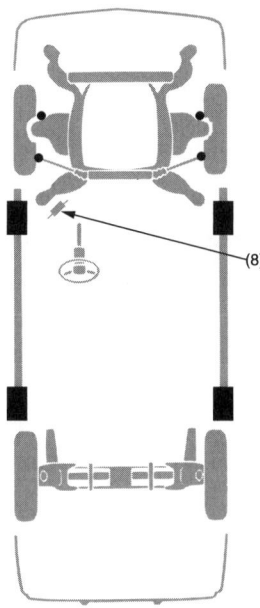

(8)

1989-93 Riviera, 1989-91 Reatta

11 FITTINGS

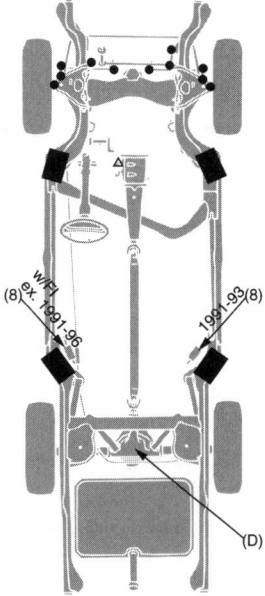

w/ex. 1991-96 (8)
1991-93 (8)
(D)

1989-90 Estate Wagon, 1991-96 Roadmaster

8 FITTINGS

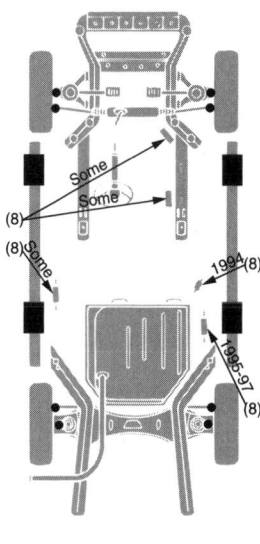

Some
Some
(8)
(8) Some
1994 (8)
1989-97

1989-91 Electra, 1989-99 LeSabre, 1992-00 Park Avenue

△ Plug, some models
• Fitting
○ Fitting, some models
■ Lift adapter position

(A) Manual transmission/transaxle, drain & fill
(B) Transfer case, NOT USED
(C) Automatic transaxle final drive, drain & fill
(D) Differential, drain & fill
(2) Transmission dipstick
(8) Fuel filter

CAUTION: On front wheel drive vehicles, the center of gravity is farther forward than on rear wheel drive vehicles. When removing major components from the rear of the vehicle while it is on a hoist, the vehicle must be supported in a manner to prevent it from tipping forward.

BUICK
1989-91 All Models

BKPM12   BKPM12

Perform the following maintenance services at the intervals indicated to keep the vehicle warranties in effect.
W   SERVICE TO MAINTAIN EMISSION WARRANTY

MI—MILES IN THOUSANDS
KM—KILOMETERS IN THOUSANDS

EVERY 6 MONTHS
Brake master cylinder . . .check level **HB**

Clutch master cylinder . . .check level **HB**

Power steering
   reservoir . . . . .check level **PS**

FIRST 7.5 MI—12 KM
W Carburetor or throttle body mounting
    bolts . . . . .torque
Ex. 2.3L

W Engine idle speed . . . . .adjust
Without Idle Speed or Idle Air Control

Diff., Limited-Slip . . . . .change lubricant
As equipped

Tires . . . . .inspect/rotate
Initial service, then every 15 mi (24 km). Check brake linings.

W Choke & hoses . . . . .check/clean
As equipped

EVERY 12 MO/7.5 MI—12 KM
Brake system . . . . .inspect
Check hydraulic system for leaks. Inspect linings.

W Crankcase . . . . .change oil

W Oil filter . . . . .replace
3.8L turbocharged, at every oil change; all others at first oil change, then at every other oil change, but at least every 12 months

Differential . . . . .check level

Exhaust system . . . . .inspect

Suspension &
   steering linkage . . . . . **4-11 fittings LB**

Parking brake cable guides . . . . .coat **LB**
Check adjustment

Shift linkage . . . . .coat **LB**
With floor shift, coat contact faces

Suspension & steering . . . . .inspect
Also inspect front drive axle boots and seals

Transaxle or transmission . . check level

Drive belts 1989 . . . . .inspect/adjust
Ex. vacuum/air pump belts

Throttle linkage . . . . .inspect
Check for damage or binding

Body . . . . .lubricate

EVERY 12 MONTHS
W Cooling system . . . . . . .inspect hoses &
                    tighten clamps
Wash radiator filler neck & cap; pressure-test system. Clean exterior of radiator core and air-conditioning condenser. Inspect coolant, service as required.

EVERY 24 MO/30 MI—50 KM
W Cooling system . . . .change coolant **EC**
Flush system. Use 50% concentration for −34°F (−37°C) protection.

W Drive belts . . . . .inspect/adjust
1990-91

W Vacuum/air pump belts . . . .inspect/adjust
1989 as equipped

EVERY 36 MO/30 MI—50 KM
Air cleaner element 1989-90 . . . .replace

PCV filter 1989-90 . . . . .replace
As equipped

W EGR system 1989-90 . . . . .clean/inspect
Engine codes H, R, U, Y, 1, 7

EVERY 30 MI—50 KM
W Air cleaner element . . . . .replace
1991

W Fuel tank, cap & lines . . . . .inspect

Choke & hoses . . . . .check/clean
As equipped

Front wheel bearings, ex.
   front wheel drive . . . . .clean/repack **GC**
Service at mileage intervals or at each brake reline, whichever comes first. Tighten spindle nut to 12 ft-lb while turning wheel. Back off nut & retighten finger tight. End play, .001"-.005". Loosen nut just enough so that hole in spindle lines up with slot in nut. (Not more than 1/2 flat.)

W EGR system . . . . .clean/inspect
1991 engine codes E, R, U

W Distributor cap . . . . .inspect
Except distributorless ignition
Inspect distributor cap, clean or replace

W Ignition timing . . . . .adjust
Except distributorless ignition

W Ignition wires . . . . .inspect/clean
As equipped

PCV filter . . . . .replace
1991

W PCV system . . . . .inspect
1989-91 All

W Spark plugs . . . . .replace

W Thermostatic air cleaner . . . . . . .inspect
As equipped

EVERY 100 MI—160 KM
Transaxle or trans., auto . . . .change fluid
Replace filter

SEVERE SERVICE
W **Carburetor or throttle body**—Torque mounting bolts & adjust idle speed at 6 mi (10 km). Inspect carburetor choke & hoses at 6 mi (10 km), then every 30 mi (50 km).

W **Crankcase**—Change oil and oil filter every 3 mo/3 mi (5 km)

Suspension & steering linkage—Lubricate every other oil change

Front wheel bearings—RWD, repack every 15 mi (24 km) or at each brake service, whichever comes first

Tires—Inspect/rotate at 6 mi (10 km), then every 15 mi (24 km)

Transaxle or transmission, automatic—Change fluid & filter every 15 mi (24 km)

Differential—Change lubricant every 7.5 mi (12 km) when towing a trailer

KEY TO LUBRICANTS

AF3	DEXRON®-III Automatic Transmission Fluid
API ★	Motor Oil certified by the American Petroleum Institute (Starburst Symbol)
EC	Ethylene Glycol Coolant GM Spec. 1825M
GC	Wheel Bearing Grease NLGI Category GC
GL-5	Gear Oil, API Service GL-5
GL-5★	Special Lubricant for Limited-Slip Differential GM Part No. 1052271 plus additive GM Part No. 1052358
GLS	Gear Lubricant, Special
HB	Hydraulic Brake Fluid, DOT 3
LB	Chassis Grease, NLGI Category LB
PS	Power Steering Fluid
SG	Motor Oil, API Service SG Use Energy Conserving II Oils
SH	Motor Oil, API Service SH Use Energy Conserving II Oils

CRANKCASE . . . . .SG, SH, API ★

CAPACITY, Refill:	Liters	Qt
1989-91	3.8	4.0

Capacity shown is without filter. When replacing filter, additional oil may be needed.

1990 3.8L V6 Code L;
1991 3.3L V6, 3.8L V6:
Above 40°F (4°C) . . . . .30[1]
Above 0°F (−18°C) . . . . .10W-30[2]
Below 60°F (16°C) 5W-30

1989-91
All others:
Above 40°F (4°C) . . . . .30[1]
Above 0°F (−18°C) 10W-30
All temperatures . . . . .5W-30[2]

1 Use only if other specified grades are unavailable
2 Preferred

TRANSMISSION/TRANSAXLE,
  Automatic **AF3**

CAPACITY, Initial Refill[3]:	Liters	Qt
125 C (3T40)	3.8	4.0
200 C	3.3	3.5
440-T4 (4T60)	5.7	6.0
700-R4 (4L60)	4.7	5.0
Others	2.8	3.0

3 With the engine at operating temperature, shift transmission through all gears. Let engine slow idle in PARK for 3 minutes or more. Check fluid level and add fluid as needed.

TRANSAXLE, Manual . . . . .GLS

CAPACITY, Refill:	Liters	Pt
All	1.9	4.0

DIFFERENTIAL
Standard . . . . .80W-90[6] GL-5
Limited-Slip . . . . .80W-90[6] GL-5★
6 1989-90, for vehicles normally operated in Canada, 80W only

CAPACITY, Refill:	Liters	Pt
7½" ring gear	1.7	3.5
8½", 8¾" ring gear	2.0	4.3

LIMITED-SLIP IDENTIFICATION:
Tag under rear cover-attaching bolt

SERVICE AT TIME OR MILEAGE—WHICHEVER OCCURS FIRST

BKPM13   BKPM13

Perform the following maintenance services at the intervals indicated to keep the vehicle warranties in effect.
W   SERVICE TO MAINTAIN EMISSION WARRANTY

MI—MILES IN THOUSANDS
KM—KILOMETERS IN THOUSANDS

EVERY 6 MONTHS

Brake master cylinder . . .check level **HB**

Clutch master cylinder . . .check level **HB**

Power steering reservoir   .check level **PS**

W Throttle linkage . . . . .inspect
Check for damage or binding

Brake system . . . . .inspect
Check hydraulic system, disc pads, drum linings

W Exhaust system . . . . .inspect

Suspension . . . . .inspect
Also inspect front drive axle boots and seals

Transaxle or
transmission . . . . .check level

FIRST 7.5 MI—12 KM

W Throttle body mounting
bolts . . . . .torque
1992 Codes E, R, 7. 1993 Code 7

Diff., Limited-Slip . . . . .change lubricant
As equipped

Tires . . . . .inspect/rotate
Initial service, then every 15 mi (24 km). Check brake
linings.

EVERY 12 MO/7.5 MI—12 KM

W Crankcase . . . . .change oil
Or sooner if indicated by the Oil Life Monitor

W Oil filter .replace
1992-94, at first oil change, then every other oil change.
1995, every oil change.

Differential . . . . .check level

Suspension &
steering linkage . . . . . .**0-11 fittings LB**

Parking brake cable guides and
underbody contact points . . . . .coat **LB**
Check adjustment

Shift linkage . . . . .coat **LB**
With floor shift, coat contact faces

Body .lubricate

EVERY 12 MONTHS

W Cooling system . . . . . . .inspect hoses &
tighten clamps
Wash radiator filler neck & cap; pressure-test system.
Clean exterior of radiator core and air-conditioning
condenser. Inspect coolant, service as required.

EVERY 24 MO/30 MI—50 KM

W Cooling system . . . . .change coolant **EC**
Flush system. Use 50% concentration for −34°F (−37°C)
protection and add two sealant pellets (GM Part No.
3634621).

W Drive belts . . . . .inspect/adjust
1992-93

EVERY 36 MO/30 MI—50 KM

Supercharger 1992-95 . . . . .check level
3.8L code 1 engine
Use Synthetic 5W-30 oil. GM Part Number 12345982.

EVERY 30 MI—50 KM

W Air cleaner element . . . . .replace

W Fuel tank, cap & lines . . . . .inspect

Front wheel bearings
RWD . . . . .inspect/repack **GC**
Service at mileage intervals or at each brake reline,
whichever comes first. Tighten spindle nut to 12 ft-lb
while turning wheel. Back off nut & retighten finger tight.
End play, .001"-.005". Loosen nut just enough so that
hole in spindle lines up with slot in nut. (Not more than ½
flat.)

W EGR system . . . . .clean/inspect
1992 engine codes E, R, 7
1993 engine codes 4, 7
1994-95 engine code 4

W Distributor cap 1992-93 Code 7 . .inspect
Inspect distributor cap, clean or replace.

W Ignition timing 1992-93 Code 7 . . .adjust

W Ignition wires . . . . .inspect/clean
As equipped

PCV filter . . . . .replace
1992-93
Use API **SG, SH** oil.

W Spark plugs ex. 1994-95 V8 . . . . .replace

W Thermostatic air cleaner . . . . . . .inspect
As equipped
Use API **SG, SH**, oil

EVERY 100 MI—160 KM

Spark Plugs 1994-95 V8 . . . . . . .replace

Transaxle or
trans., auto. 1992-94 . . . . .change fluid
Replace filter

SEVERE SERVICE

W **Throttle body**—Torque mounting bolts at
6 mi (10 km).

W **Crankcase**—Change oil and oil filter every
3 mo/3 mi (5 km)

Suspension & steering linkage—Lubricate
every other oil change

Front wheel bearings—RWD, inspect/
repack every 15 mi (24 km) or at each
brake service, whichever comes first

Tires—Inspect/rotate at 6 mi (10 km), then
every 12 mi (20 km)

Transaxle or transmission, automatic—
Change fluid & filter every: 1992-94, 15 mi
(24 km); 1995, 50 mi (80 km)

Differential—Change lubricant every 7.5
mi (12 km) when towing a trailer

KEY TO LUBRICANTS

AF3   DEXRON® -III
Automatic Transmission Fluid

API★   Motor Oil certified by the American
Petroleum Institute (Starburst
Symbol)

EC   Ethylene Glycol Coolant
For 1995 only: Replace green coolant with green
coolant; replace orange coolant (DEX-COOL®)
with orange coolant. Do not mix.

GC   Wheel Bearing Grease, NLGI
Category GC

GL-5   Gear Oil, API Service GL-5

GL-5★   Special Lubricant for Limited-Slip
Differential

GLS   Gear Lubricant, Special

HB   Hydraulic Brake Fluid, DOT 3

LB   Chassis Grease, NLGI Category LB

PS   Power Steering Fluid
GM Part No. 1052884

SH   Motor Oil, API Service SH
Use Energy Conserving II Oils

CRANKCASE

1992-94 . . . . **SH, API★**
1995 . . . .**API★**

CAPACITY, Initial Refill:	Liters	Qt
5.7L Code 7, P	4.7	5.0

Capacity shown is with filter. Check level after adding oil.

	Liters	Qt
All others	3.8	4.0

Capacity shown is without filter. When replacing filter,
additional oil may be needed.

3.3L V6, 3.8L V6, 1992 5.7L V8 Code 7, Code P
Above 40°F (4°C) . . . . .30[1]
Above 0°F (−18°C) . . . . .10W-30[2]
Below 60°F (16°C) .5W-30

All others:
Above 40°F (4°C) . . . . .30[1]
Above 0°F (−18°C) 10W-30
All temperatures . . . . .5W-30 [2]

[1] Use only if other specified grades are unavailable. Use
API **SG, SH** oil.
[2] Preferred.

TRANSMISSION/TRANSAXLE,
Automatic **AF3**

CAPACITY, Initial Refill[3]:	Liters	Qt
125 C (3T40)	3.8	4.0
440-T4 (4T60)	5.7	6.0
4T60E	6.6	7.0
700-R4 (4L60)	4.7	5.0

[3] With the engine at operating temperature, shift transmission
through all gears. Let engine slow idle in PARK for 3 minutes or more. Check fluid level and add fluid as needed.

TRANSAXLE, Manual . . . .**GLS**

CAPACITY, Refill:	Liters	Pt
5-speed Isuzu[4]	1.9	4.0
5-speed Muncie[5]	1.9	4.0

[4] Has a 7-bolt aluminum end cap
[5] Has a 9-bolt steel end cap

DIFFERENTIAL

Standard 80W-90 **GL-5**
Limited-Slip . . . . .80W-90 **GL-5★**

CAPACITY, Refill:	Liters	Pt
7½" ring gear	1.7	3.5
8½", 8¾" ring gear	2.0	4.3

LIMITED-SLIP IDENTIFICATION:
Tag under rear cover-attaching bolt

BUICK
1996-2000 All Models

SERVICE AT TIME OR MILEAGE—WHICHEVER OCCURS FIRST

Perform the following maintenance services at the intervals indicated to keep the vehicle warranties in effect.

W   SERVICE TO MAINTAIN EMISSION WARRANTY

MI—MILES IN THOUSANDS
KM—KILOMETERS IN THOUSANDS

EVERY MONTH
Tires . . . . .check pressure

EVERY 6 MONTHS
Brake master cylinder   . . .check level **HB**

Power steering reservoir   .check level **PS**

Throttle linkage . . . . .inspect
Check for damage or binding. Do not lubricate.

Brake system . . . . .inspect
Check hydraulic system, disc pads, drum linings, hoses and lines. Check parking brake adjustment.

Caliper pins, knuckle brake pad
abutments . . . . .check/lubricate
When operating in a corrosive environment or every other tire change, or as necessary 1997-98, LeSabre, Skylark

Exhaust system . . . . .inspect

RWD differential, 1996 . . . . .check level

Steering linkage & suspension . . .inspect
Also inspect front drive axle boots and seals

W Cooling system . . . . . . .inspect hoses &
tighten clamps

Transaxle or
transmission . . . . .check level

EVERY 3.0 MI—5.0 KM
Crankcase . . . . .change oil & filter
Dusty conditions, or sooner if indicated by oil life monitor

FIRST 7.5 MI—12 KM
RWD diff., Limited-Slip . . .change lubricant
As equipped

Tires, 1996 . . . . .inspect/rotate
Initial service, then every 15 mi (24 km). Check brake linings.

EVERY 7.5 MI—12 KM
Tires, 1997-00 . . . . .inspect/rotate

EVERY 12 MO/7.5 MI—12 KM
W Crankcase . . . . .change oil & filter
Or sooner if indicated by the Oil Life Monitor. Reset Oil Life Monitor.

Hood & door hinges . . . . .lubricate
Multipurpose lubricant, GM part No. 12346241

Hood latch assembly . . . . .lubricate **LB**

Suspension &
steering linkage . . . . .0-11 fittings **LB**
Except 1998-00 Century and Regal

Parking brake cable guides and
underbody contact points,
linkage points . . . . .coat **LB**

Transmission/transaxle
shift linkage . . . . .lubricate **LB**

EVERY 12 MONTHS
Body . . . . .lubricate

Underbody . . . . .flush
Every spring

EVERY 15 MI—25 KM
Passenger compartment
air filter . . . . .replace
1997-99 Century, Park Ave., Regal
2000 All
For dusty conditions, replace as needed

EVERY 30 MI—50 KM
W Air cleaner element . . . . .replace

W Fuel tank, cap & gasket, lines . . .inspect

Front wheel bearings
RWD, 1996 . . . . . .inspect/repack **GC**
Service at mileage intervals or at each brake reline, whichever comes first. Tighten spindle nut to 12 ft-lb while turning wheel. Back off nut & retighten finger tight. End play, .001"-.005". Loosen nut just enough that hole in spindle lines up with slot in nut. (Not more than ½ flat.)

W EGR system, 1996 . . . . . .clean/inspect
Code 4 engine

EVERY 36 MO/30 MI—50 KM
Supercharger . . . . .check level
3.8L code 1 engine
Use synthetic 5W-30 oil. GM Part Number 12345982

EVERY 60 MI—100 KM
W Drive Belt . . . . .inspect

EVERY 100 MI—160 KM
W Spark Plugs . . . . .replace

W Spark Plug Wires . . . . .inspect

1999-00 EVERY 100 MI—160 KM
Transaxle or transmission,
automatic . . . . .change fluid & filter
If automatic has not been serviced for the past 100 mi (160 km)

1996, EVERY 60 MO/100 MI—160 KM
1997-00, EVERY 60 MO/150 MI—240 KM
W Cooling System . . . . .change coolant **EC**
Flush system. Use 50% concentration for –34°F (–37°C) protection. 1996-97, add 2 sealant pellets (GM Part No. 3634621).

SEVERE SERVICE
W **Crankcase**—Change oil and oil filter every 3 mo/3 mi (5 km), or sooner if indicated by the Oil Life Monitor

Air distribution filter—replace every 12 mi (20 km), 1997 Century

Passenger compartment air filter—replace every 12 mi (20 km), 1997-00

W **Air cleaner filter**—Dusty conditions, replace if necessary every 15 mi (24 km)

Suspension & steering linkage—Lubricate every other oil change, except 1998-00 Century and Regal

Front wheel bearings—RWD, 1996 inspect/ repack every 15 mi (24 km) or at each brake service, whichever comes first

Tires—Inspect/rotate at: 1996, 6 mi (10 km), then every 12 mi (20 km); 1997-98 except 1998 Century and Regal, every 6 mi (10 km); 1999 Riviera and 1999-00 Park Ave., LeSabre, every 6 mi (10 km)

Transaxle or transmission, automatic—Change fluid & filter every 50 mi (80 km) when in either: heavy city traffic at temperatures regularly above 90°F (32°C); hilly terrain; taxi, police, delivery, trailer towing service; car top carrier use

RWD differential—1996 all, change lubricant every 6 mi (10 km) when towing a trailer

RWD differential—1996 limited-slip, change lubricant at first 6 mi (10 km)

KEY TO LUBRICANTS

AF3	DEXRON® -III Automatic Transmission Fluid
API★	Motor Oil certified by the American Petroleum Institute (Starburst Symbol)
EC	Ethylene Glycol Coolant GM DEX-COOL® or Havoline® DEX-COOL®
GC	Wheel Bearing Grease, NLGI Category GC
GL-5	Gear Oil, API Service GL-5 GM Part No 1052271
GL-5★	Special Lubricant for Limited-Slip Differential GM Part No 1052271 plus 4 oz. limited-slip additive GM 1052358 when fluid is changed
HB	Hydraulic Brake Fluid, DOT 3 Delco Supreme 11, GM Part No. 12377967
LB	Chassis Grease, NLGI Category LB or GC-LB
MO	Motor Oil
PS	Power Steering Fluid GM Part No. 1052884, 1-pint GM Part No. 1050017, 1-qt

CRANKCASE . . . . .API★

CAPACITY, Initial Refill:	Liters	Qt
2.4L	3.8	4.0
3.1L	4.3	4.5
3.8L	4.3	4.5

Capacity shown is with filter. Recheck oil level after filling.

3.8L V6 Codes 1, K
Above 0°F (–18°C) . . . . .10W-30[1]
Below 60°F (16°C) 5W-30
All others:
Above 0°F (–18°C) 10W-30
All temperatures . . . . .5W-30 [1]
1 Preferred

TRANSMISSION/TRANSAXLE,
Automatic AF3

CAPACITY, Initial Refill[2]:	Liters	Qt
1996-99		
3T40	3.8	4.0
4T60E, 4T65-E	7.0	7.4
4L60E, 1996	4.7	5.0
2000		
Century, Regal	7.0	7.4
LeSabre, Park Ave.	5.7	6.0

2 With the engine at operating temperature, shift transmission through all gears. Let engine slow idle in PARK for 3 minutes or more. Check fluid level and add fluid as needed.

DIFFERENTIAL
Standard, 1996 . . . . .80W-90 **GL-5**
Limited-Slip, 1996 . . . . . . .80W-90 **GL-5★**

CAPACITY, Refill:	Liters	Pt
7⅝" ring gear	1.7	3.5
8½" ring gear	2.0	4.2

LIMITED-SLIP IDENTIFICATION:
Tag under rear cover-attaching bolt

SERVICE LOCATIONS — ENGINE AND CHASSIS

HOOD RELEASE: Inside

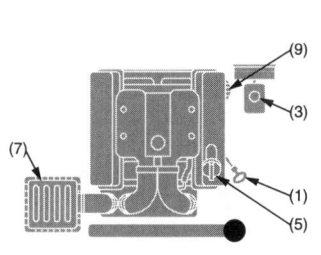

1998-00
3.0L Code R
Catera

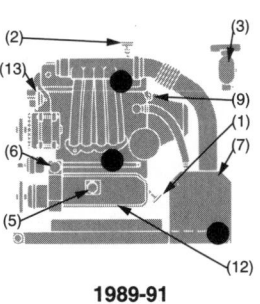

1989-91
4.5L Allanté

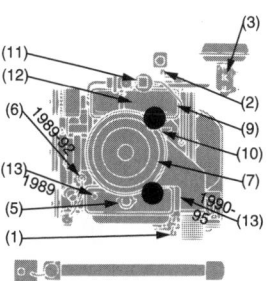

1989-92
4.1L (250), 4.5L (273)
1991-95 4.9L Code B

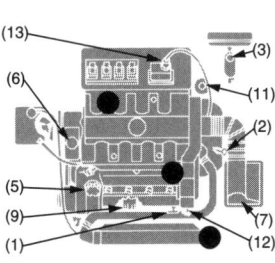

1993-00 4.6 Code Y, 9

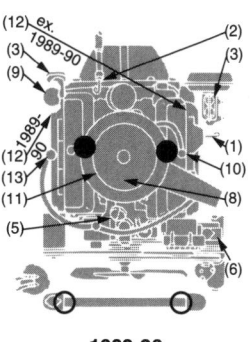

1989-90
5.0L (307)

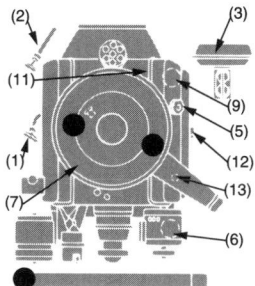

1990-93 5.7L Brougham,
RWD Fleetwood
1991-92 5.0L Brougham

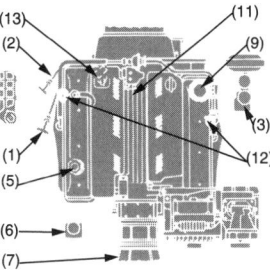

1994-96 5.7L Code P
RWD Fleetwood

(1) Crankcase dipstick	(8) Fuel filter
(2) Transmission dipstick	(9) Oil filter
(3) Brake fluid reservoir	(10) PCV filter
(4) Clutch fluid reservoir	(11) EGR valve
(5) Oil fill cap	(12) Oxygen sensor
(6) Power steering reservoir	(13) PCV valve
(7) Air filter	

● Cooling system drain   ○ Cooling system drain, some models

23

CADILLAC
1989-2000 All Models ex. Escalade

SERVICE LOCATIONS — ENGINE AND CHASSIS

0 FITTINGS
0 PLUGS

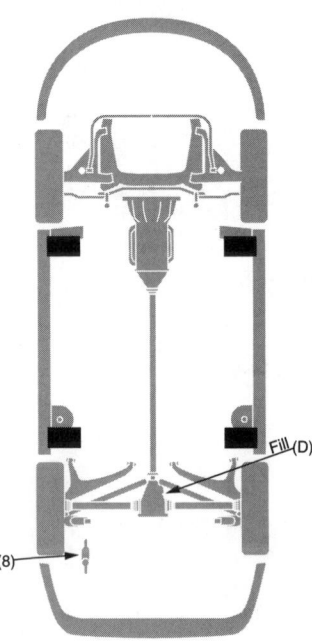

Fill (D)

(8)

1997-00
Catera

4 FITTINGS

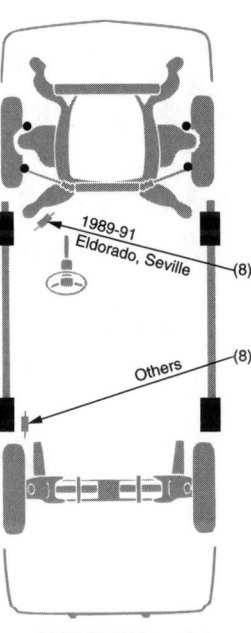

1989-91
Eldorado, Seville
(8)

Others
(8)

(8)

1989-00 Eldorado
1989-00 Seville
1989-97 Allanté

6-8 FITTINGS

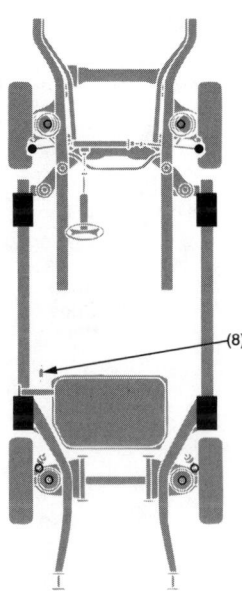

(8)

(8)

1989-93
FWD DeVille,
Fleetwood
1994-00
Concours, DeVille

11 FITTINGS

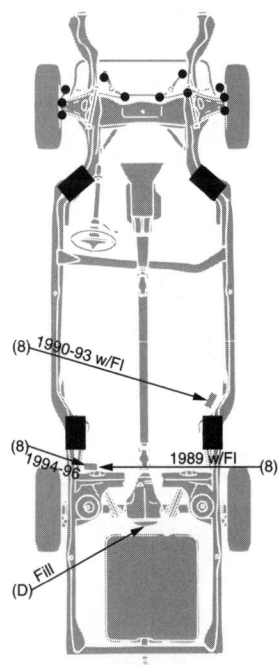

(8) 1990-93 w/FI

(8) 1994-96
1989 w/FI (8)

Fill
(D)

LIFTING CAUTION
Do not use frame contact
hoist on Commercial or 75
Series. Do not use bumper
jack on Commercial.

All RWD

(A) Manual transmission/transaxle,
    drain, & fill

(B) Transfer case, NOT USED

(C) Automatic transaxle final drive,
    NOT USED

(D) Differential, drain, & fill

(2) Transmission dipstick

(8) Fuel filter

■ Lift adapter position

• Fitting

○ Fitting, some models

CAUTION: On front wheel drive vehicles, the center of gravity is farther forward than on rear wheel drive vehicles. When removing major
components from the rear of the vehicle while it is on a hoist, the vehicle must be supported in a manner to prevent it from tipping forward.

SERVICE AT TIME OR MILEAGE — WHICHEVER OCCURS FIRST

CCPM9   CCPM9

Perform the following maintenance services at the intervals indicated to keep the vehicle warranties in effect.

W   SERVICE TO MAINTAIN EMISSION WARRANTY

MI—MILES IN THOUSANDS
KM—KILOMETERS IN THOUSANDS

FIRST 7.5 MI–12.5 KM

W Choke & hoses ex. FI . . . . . .check/clean

W Engine idle speeds ex. FI . . .check/adjust

W Carburetor or throttle
    body mounting . . . . .torque

Tires . . . . .inspect/rotate
Then every 15 mi (24 km)

EVERY 6 MONTHS

Power steering
    reservoir . . . . .check level **PS**

Brake master cylinder . .check level **HB**
Also Cimarron hydraulic clutch

Cooling system . . . . . . .check level **EC**
At each fuel stop

EVERY 12 MO/7.5 MI–12.5 KM

Brake system . . . . .inspect
Check disc brake pads; replace when ⅛" thick. Inspect brake hoses & lines, check drum brake lining & parking brake adjustment.

W Crankcase . . . . .change oil
Check level at each fuel stop

Final Drive/Differential . . . . . .check level
Ex. models with transverse engine

Front suspension &
    steering linkage . . . . . .**4-11 fittings LB**
Inspect steering linkage & suspension, also inspect front drive axle boots & seals

Parking brake cable guides . . . . .coat **LB**

Transmission/transaxle
    shift linkage . . . . .lubricate **MO**

Drive belts . . . . .inspect/adjust
1989 ex. AIR pump & vacuum pump

Exhaust system . . . . .inspect

W Oil filter .replace
At first oil change, then every other but at least every 12 months

Transaxle/transmission . . . . .check level

Body hinges . . . . .lubricate **MO**
Flush underbody every spring

EVERY 12 MONTHS

W Cooling system . .inspect & tighten hoses
Wash radiator filler neck & cap; pressure test system. Clean exterior of radiator core & air conditioning condenser

EVERY 24 MO/30 MI–50 KM

W Cooling system . . . . .change coolant **EC**
Flush system, then use 50% concentration for −34°F (−37°C) protection. 4.1L, 4.5L, 4.9L engines, cooling system additive, GM Part No. 3634621 must be used.

W Drive belts . . . . .inspect/adjust
1989 air pump & vacuum pump only. 1990 all.

EVERY 30 MI–50 KM

Front wheel bearings, rear
    wheel drive cars . . . . .clean/repack **GC**
Or at time of front brake relining. Torque, 12 ft-lb. Back off to 0; tighten nut finger tight & replace cotter pin.

W Air cleaner valve . . . . .check

W Choke & hoses ex. FI . . . . .check

W Fuel cap, tank, lines . . . . .inspect

W Ignition timing . . . . .check/adjust

W PCV valve & hoses . . . . .inspect

W Spark plugs . . . . .replace

W Spark plug wires . . . . .clean/inspect

EVERY 36 MO/30 MI–50 KM

W Air cleaner element . . . . .replace
Ex. 2.0L eng.

W A.I.R. filter 1989-90 . . . . .replace

W EGR system . . . . .check/clean

W PCV filter . . . . .replace

EVERY 100 MI–160 KM

Transaxle/transmission,
    automatic . . . . .change fluid
Replace sump filter

SEVERE SERVICE

W **Carburetor or TBI**—Torque mounting bolts. Adjust idle speed (ex. with FI) at first 6 mi (10 km), also check carburetor choke & hoses.

Crankcase—Change oil & filter every 3 mo/3 mi (5 km)

Final Drive/Differential—Change lubricant (ex. models with transverse engine) every 7.5 mi (12.5 km) when towing a trailer

Front suspension & steering linkage, parking brake cable guides, transmission or transaxle shift linkage, body hinges—Lubricate every 6 mo/6 mi (10 km)

Front wheel bearings—Rear wheel drive cars, clean/repack with **GC** every 15 mi (25 km)

Tires—Rotate at first 6 mi (10 km)

Transaxle or transmission, automatic—Change fluid & filter every 15 mi (24 km). Clean sump or replace filter.

KEY TO LUBRICANTS

AF3	DEXRON®-III Automatic Transmission Fluid
API★	Motor Oil certified by the American Petroleum Institute (Starburst Symbol)
EC	Ethylene Glycol Coolant
GC	Wheel Bearing Grease, NLGI Category GC
GL-5	Gear Oil, API Service GL-5
GL-5★	Special Lubricant for Limited-Slip Differentials
GLS	Gear Lubricant, Special
HB	Hydraulic Brake Fluid, DOT 3
LB	Chassis Grease, NLGI Category LB
MO	Motor Oil
PS	Power Steering Fluid
SH	Motor Oil, API Service SH
WB	Wheel Bearing Grease

CRANKCASE . . . . .SH, API★

CAPACITY, Refill:	Liters	Qt
4.1L, 4.5L Allanté	5.7	6.0
All other FWD 4.1L, 4.5L, 4.9L eng.	4.7	5.0
Others	3.8	4.0

Capacity shown is without filter. When replacing filter, additional oil may be needed.

Above 40°F (4°C)	30
Above 0°F (−18°C)	. . . . .10W-30[1]
Below 100°F (38°C) Cimarron & 1989 5.0L	. . . . .5W-30[2]
Below 60°F (16°C) ex. Cimarron & 1989 5.0L	. . . . .5W-30

[1] Preferred ex. Cimarron & 1989 5.0L
[2] Preferred in Cimarron & 1989 5.0L

TRANSMISSION/TRANSAXLE, Automatic .AF3

CAPACITY, Initial Refill[3]:	Liters	Qt
Allanté	7.6	8.0
Cimarron	3.8	4.0
1989-90 Eldorado, Seville & 1989-90 FWD DeVille, Fleetwood	6.2	6.5
Others	5.0	5.3

[3] With the engine at operating temperature, shift transmission through all gears. Let engine slow idle in PARK for at least 3 minutes. Check fluid level and add fluid as needed.

TRANSAXLE, Manual . . . . .GLS

CAPACITY, Refill:	Liters	Pt
4-speed	2.8	6.0
5-speed Isuzu[4]	2.6	5.4
5-speed Muncie[5]	1.9	4.0

[4] Has 7-bolt aluminum end cap
[5] Has 9-bolt steel end cap

DIFFERENTIAL/FINAL DRIVE
RWD Only

Standard	. . . . .80W, 80W-90[6] GL-5
Limited-Slip	. . . . .80W, 80W-90 GL-5★

[6] For vehicles normally operated in Canada, 80W only

CAPACITY, Refill:	Liters	Pt
1989-90 RWD w/2.73 & 2.93:1 ratio	1.7	3.5
All other RWD	2.0	4.3

CADILLAC
1991-95 All Gasoline Models

Perform the following maintenance services at the intervals indicated to keep the vehicle warranties in effect

W   SERVICE TO MAINTAIN EMISSION WARRANTY

MI—MILES IN THOUSANDS
KM—KILOMETERS IN THOUSANDS

EVERY 6 MONTHS

Power steering
reservoir . . . . .check level **PS**

Brake master cylinder . . .check level **HB**

Brake system . . . . .inspect
Check disc brake pads; replace when ⅛" thick. Check brake hoses & lines, check drum brake lining & parking brake adjustment.

RWD differential . . . . .check level

Steering linkage & suspension . . .inspect

Drive axle boots & seals . . . . . . .inspect
Ex. RWD

Exhaust system . . . . .inspect

Throttle linkage . . . . .inspect
Check for damage or binding

Cooling system . . . . . . .check level **EC**
At each fuel stop

Restraint system . . . . .check
1994-95

FIRST 7.5 MI–12 KM

Throttle body mounting bolts . . . . .torque

Tires . . . . .inspect/rotate
Initial service, then every 15 mi (24 km) or as necessary

Diff. limited-slip . . . . . . .change lubricant

EVERY 12 MO/7.5 MI–12.5 KM

W Crankcase . . . . .change oil
Or sooner if indicated by Oil Life Indicator
Check level at each fuel stop

Front suspension &
steering linkage . . . . . **4-11 fittings LB**

Parking brake cable guides, underbody
contact points, linkage points . . .coat **LB**

Transmission/transaxle
shift linkage . . . . .lubricate **MO**

W Oil filter .replace
1991-93, at first oil change, then every other but at least every 12 months. 1994-95, every oil change.

Transaxle/transmission . . . . .check level
Check for leaks

Body .lubricate
Flush underbody every spring

EVERY 12 MONTHS

W Cooling system . . . . . . .inspect hoses &
tighten clamps
Wash radiator filler neck & cap; pressure-test system. Clean exterior of radiator core & air-conditioning condenser.

EVERY 24 MO/30 MI–50 KM

W Cooling system . . . . .change coolant **EC**
Flush system, then use 50% concentration for –34°F (–37°C) protection and add specified number of sealant pellets (GM Part No. 3634621): 4.5L Code 8, 3; 4.6L Codes 9 and Y, 3; 4.9L Code B, 6; 5.0L Code E, 2; 5.7L Code P, 2

W Drive belts . . . . .inspect/adjust
Replace as needed

EVERY 30 MI–50 KM

W Air cleaner element . . . . .replace

W A.I.R. filter . . . . .replace

Front wheel bearings, rear
wheel drive cars . . . .clean/repack **GC**
Or at time of front brake relining. Torque, 12 ft-lb. Back off to "just loose" position; tighten nut finger tight & replace cotter pin.

W EGR system . . . . .check/clean

W Fuel cap, tank, lines . . . . .inspect

W Ignition timing . . . . .check/adjust
1991-93 all, 1994-95 4.9L Code B

W PCV filter . . . . .replace
If equipped

W PCV valve & hoses 1991 . . . . . . .inspect

W Spark plugs . . . . .replace
1991 all, 1992 Brougham

W Spark plug wires . . . . .clean/inspect

W Throttle body . . . . .inspect

EVERY 100 MI–160 KM

Spark plugs, 1992-95 ex. 1992
Brougham . . . . .replace

Transaxle/transmission,
automatic 1991-94 . . . . . .change fluid
Or when indicated by a "change transmission fluid" message (4T80E), whichever occurs first. 4T80E, replace scavenging screens; others, replace filter.

SEVERE SERVICE

Crankcase—Change oil & filter every 3 mo/3 mi (5 km) or sooner if indicated by Oil Life Indicator

RWD differential—Change lubricant every 7.5 mi (12.5 km) when towing a trailer. For 1993 models, also change lubricant at first 1.0 mi (1.6 km).

Front suspension & steering linkage, parking brake cable guides, underbody contact points, linkage points, transmission or transaxle shift linkage, body hinges—Lubricate every 6 mo/6 mi (10 km)

Front wheel bearings—Rear wheel drive car, clean/repack with **GC** every 15 mi (25 km) or at every brake service, whichever comes first

Tires—Rotate at first 6 mi (10 km) then every 15 mi (24 km)

Transaxle or transmission, automatic—Change fluid & filter ex. 4T80E every: 1991-94, 15 mi (24 km); 1995, 50 mi (83 km); or when indicated by a "change transmission fluid" message (4T80E), whichever occurs first

KEY TO LUBRICANTS

AF3	DEXRON®-III Automatic Transmission Fluid
API★	Motor Oil certified by the American Petroleum Institute (Starburst Symbol)
EC	Ethylene Glycol Coolant For 1995 only: Replace green coolant with green coolant; replace orange coolant (DEX-COOL®) with orange coolant. Do not mix.
GC	Wheel Bearing Grease, NLGI Category GC
GL-5	Gear Oil, API Service GL-5
GLS	Gear Lubricant, Special
HB	Hydraulic Brake Fluid, DOT 3
LB	Chassis Grease, NLGI Category LB
MO	Motor Oil
PS	Power Steering Fluid GM Part No. 1052884
SH	Motor Oil, API Service SH

CRANKCASE

1991-94 . . . . .SH, API★
1995 . . . . .API★

CAPACITY, Refill:	Liters	Qt
Allanté 4.5L Code 8	5.7	6.0
4.6L Code Y, 9	6.6	7.0
Code B	4.7	5.0
RWD 5.7L Code 7, P	3.8	4.0

Capacity shown is without filter. When replacing filter, additional oil may be needed.

Above 40°F (4°C) ex. 4.9L Code B . . . . .30[1]
Above 40°F (4°C) 4.9L Code B . . . . .30[2]
Above 0°F (-18°C) . . . . .10W-30[3]
Below 60°F (16°C) ex. 1993-95 RWD . . . . .5W-30[4]
All temperatures 1993-95 RWD . . . . .5W-30[4]

[1] Use only if other specified grades are unavailable. Use API SH oil.
[2] Use API SH oil.
[3] Preferred FWD.
[4] Preferred RWD.

TRANSMISSION/TRANSAXLE,

Automatic AF3

CAPACITY, Initial Refill[5]:	Liters	Qt
4T80E	10.4[6]	11.0[6]
Allanté 1991-92	6.2	6.5
4T60E	6.6	7.0
Other FWD	5.7	6.0
All RWD	4.7	5.0

[5] With the engine at operating temperature, shift transmission through all gears. Let engine slow idle in PARK for at least 3 minutes. Check fluid level and add fluid as needed.
[6] Both pan and drain plug removed.

DIFFERENTIAL

Standard . . . . .80W-90[7] GL-5
Locking . . . . .80W-90[7] GL-5
Limousines
Limited-Slip . . . . .80W-90[7] GL-5
Add limited slip additive GM Part No. 1052358
[7] For vehicles normally operated in Canada, 80W

CAPACITY, Refill:	Liters	Pt
RWD	2.0	4.3

SERVICE AT TIME OR MILEAGE — WHICHEVER OCCURS FIRST

CCPM12   CCPM12

Perform the following maintenance services at the intervals indicated to keep the vehicle warranties in effect.

W   SERVICE TO MAINTAIN EMISSION WARRANTY

MI—MILES IN THOUSANDS
KM—KILOMETERS IN THOUSANDS

FIRST 5 MI—8 KM
THEN EVERY 10 MI—16 KM
Tires, Catera . . . . .rotate

FIRST 3 MO/5 MI—8 KM
THEN EVERY 12 MO/10 MI—16 KM
W Crankcase, Catera . . . .change oil & filter

EVERY MONTH
Tires . . . . .check pressure

EVERY 6 MONTHS
Power steering
reservoir . . . . .check level **PS**

Brake master cylinder . . .check level **HB**

Brake system . . . . .inspect
Check disc brake pads; replace when ⅛" thick. Check brake hoses & lines, check drum (RWD only ex. Catera), brake lining & parking brake adjustment.

RWD differential, 1996 . . . . .check level

Steering linkage & suspension . . .inspect

Drive axle boots & seals , ...inspect
Ex. RWD

Exhaust system . . . . .inspect

Throttle linkage . . . . .inspect
Check for damage or binding. Do not lubricate.

W Cooling system . . . . . . .inspect hoses &
tighten clamps

Restraint system . . . . .check

Transaxle/transmission . . . .check level
Check for leaks

FIRST 7.5 MI—12 KM
Differential,
limited-slip, 1996 . . . . .change lubricant

EVERY 7.5 MI—12 KM
Tires, ex. Catera . . . . .inspect/rotate

EVERY 12 MO/7.5 MI—12.5 KM
W Crankcase, 1996-99
ex. Catera . . . . .change oil & filter
Or sooner if indicated by Oil Life Indicator. Reset indicator at oil change.

EVERY 7.5 MI—12.5 KM
Front suspension &
steering linkage . . . . .**0-11 fittings LB**
1996-97, ex. Catera
1998-99 Seville professional

Rear suspension . . . . .lubricate **LB**
1996-97, ex. Catera
1998-99 Seville

Parking brake cable guides, underbody
contact points, linkage points . . .coat **LB**
1996-97, ex. Catera
1998-99 Seville

Transmission/transaxle
shift linkage . . . . .lubricate **MO**

EVERY 12 MO/10 MI—16 KM
W Crankcase, 2000
ex. Catera . . . . .change oil & filter

EVERY 12 MONTHS
Body . . . . .lubricate
Flush underbody every spring

EVERY 15 MI—25 KM
Air filter . . . . .replace
Catera, 1999-00 Seville, 2000 DeVille
Passenger compartment

1996, FIRST 15 MI—24 KM
THEN EVERY 30 MI—48 KM
1997-00, EVERY 30 MI—48 KM
W Throttle body, 4.6L . . . . .inspect
Bore & valve plates for deposits

EVERY 30 MI—50 KM
W Air cleaner element . . . . .replace

Passenger compartment air filter . . .replace
1998-99 Seville

Front wheel bearings, rear-wheel
drive vehicles, 1996 . .clean/repack **GC**
Or at time of front brake relining. Torque, 12 ft-lb. Back off to "just loose" position; tighten nut finger tight & replace cotter pin.

W Fuel cap & gasket, tank, lines . . .inspect

Differential, Catera . . . . .check level

EVERY 60 MI—100 KM
W Drive belts . . . . .inspect
Ex. Catera

Drive belt, Catera . . . . .inspect
Then at 75,000 mi. (120,000 km), and every 10,000 mi. (16,000 km) thereafter

Camshaft timing belt, Catera . . . .replace
1996-00, when started at least once in temperatures below −20°F (−28°C) without use of coolant heater. 1998-00, reset cold start counter.

EVERY 100 MI—160 KM
W Spark plug wires . . . . .clean/inspect
1996-99

W Spark plugs . . . . .replace

Camshaft timing belt, Catera . . . .replace
1996-00, When not started in temperatures below −20°F (−28°C), or when started below -20°F (-28°C) while using an engine coolant heater.

1996, EVERY 60 MO/100 MI—160 KM
1997-00, EVERY 60 MO/150 MI—240 KM
W Cooling system . . . . . .change coolant **EC**
Flush system, then use 50% concentration for −34°F (−37°C) protection and add the following number of sealant pellets (GM Part No. 3634621): 1996-97, 4.6L, 3; 5.7L, 2; 3.0L, 2. 1998, 4.0L & 4.6L, 3.

EVERY 96 MONTHS
Camshaft timing belt . . . . .Catera
1998-00, when not started in temperatures below −20°F (−28°C) without use of coolant heater.

SERVICE AS REQUIRED
Transaxle . . . . .change fluid
1998-00 ex. Catera, when "change transmission fluid" message is displayed.

SEVERE SERVICE
Crankcase, including dusty conditions—
Change oil & filter every: Catera, 3 mo/5 mi (8 km); others, 3 mo/3 mi (5 km) or sooner if indicated by Oil Life Indicator

Air Cleaner, dusty conditions—Inspect/ replace every 15 mi (25 km)

RWD differential—Ex. Catera, change lubricant every 7.5 mi (12.5 km) when towing a trailer

Front wheel bearings—RWD Ex. Catera, clean/repack with **GC** every 15 mi (25 km) or at every brake service, whichever comes first when used in livery, daily rental or trailer towing

Transaxle or transmission, automatic—
Change fluid, & filter every 50 mi (83 km) when operating under any of the following: heavy city traffic regularly above 90°F (32°C); hilly or mountainous terrain; high performance conditions; trailer towing conditions/or when indicated by a "change transmission fluid" message, whichever occurs first.

KEY TO LUBRICANTS

AF3	DEXRON®-III Automatic Transmission Fluid
API★	Motor Oil certified by the American Petroleum Institute (Starburst Symbol)
EC	Ethylene Glycol Coolant GM DEX-COOL® or Havoline® DEX-COOL®
GC	Wheel Bearing Grease, NLGI Category GC
GL-5	Gear Oil, API Service GL-5 80W-90 GL-5 meeting GM spec. 9985290, GM Part No. 12345777, or equivalent
HB	Hydraulic Brake Fluid, DOT 3
LB	Chassis Grease, NLGI Category LB
MO	Motor Oil
PS	Power Steering Fluid GM Part No. 1052884

CRANKCASE . . . . .API★
CAPACITY, Refill:

	Liters	Qt
3.0L	5.8	6.1
4.6L	7.1	7.5
5.7L	3.8	4.0

Capacity shown is with filter. Add oil as necessary

Above 0°F (-18°C) . . . . .10W-30[1]
Below 60°F (16°C) 3.0L, 4.6L 5W-30
All temperatures 5.7L . . . . .5W-30[2]
[1] Preferred 3.0L, 4.6L
[2] Preferred 5.7L

TRANSMISSION/TRANSAXLE,
Automatic .AF3
CAPACITY, Initial Refill[3]:

	Liters	Qt
4T80E	10.4[4]	11.0[4]
RWD ex. Catera	4.7	5.0
Catera	6.6	7.0

[3] With the engine at operating temperature, shift transmission through all gears. Let engine slow idle in PARK for at least 3 minutes. Check fluid level and add fluid as needed.
[4] Remove drain plug in case after pan removal. Replace scavenging screens.

DIFFERENTIAL
Standard 80W-90 **GL-5**
Locking 80W-90 **GL-5**
Limousines
Limited-Slip 80W-90 **GL-5**
Add limited-slip additive GM Part No. 1052358
CAPACITY, Refill:

	Liters	Pt
RWD, limousine	2.6	5.5
RWD, others except Catera	2.0	4.3

HOOD RELEASE: Inside

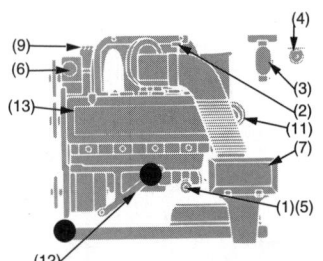

1989-91 2.0L (122) Code 1
1990-91 2.2L Code G
Cavalier, Corsica, Beretta

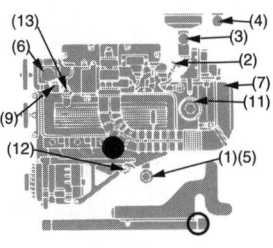

1992-00
2.2L Code 4

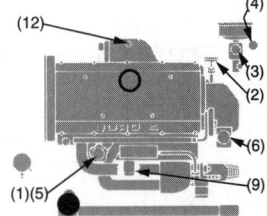

1990-94 2.3L Code A
1995 2.3L Code D
1996-00 2.4L Code T

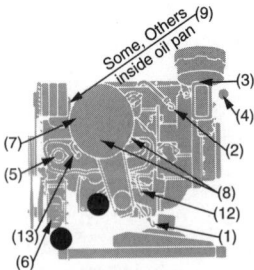

1989-92
2.5L (151) Code 2, 5, R
Air induction
system varies

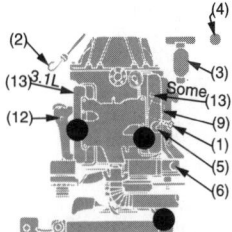

1989-97 2.8L FI Code S
1990-92 3.1L FI Code T
Camaro

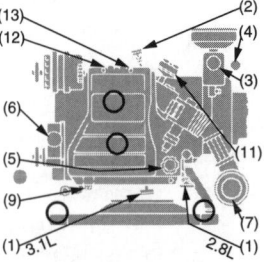

1989 2.8L (173) Code W
1990-94 3.1L Code T

1994-99
3.1L Code M
1999-00
3.1L Code J

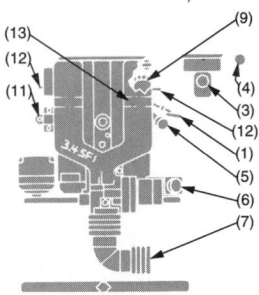

1993-95
3.4L Code S
Camaro

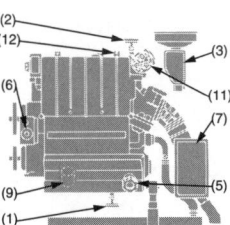

1991-97
3.4L DOHC Code X
Lumina

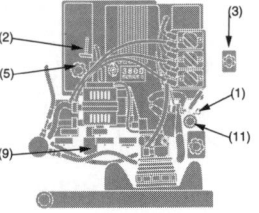

1995-98
3.8L Code K
Camaro

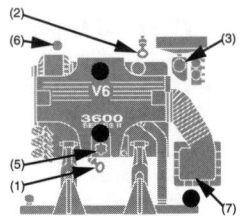

1998-00
3.8L Code K
Lumina, Monte Carlo

(1)	Crankcase dipstick	(8)	Fuel filter
(2)	Transmission dipstick	(9)	Oil filter
(3)	Brake fluid reservoir	(10)	PCV filter
(4)	Clutch fluid reservoir	(11)	EGR valve
(5)	Oil fill cap	(12)	Oxygen sensor
(6)	Power steering reservoir	(13)	PCV valve
(7)	Air filter		

● Cooling system drain   ○ Cooling system drain, some models

CHEK-CHART

CHEVROLET
1989-2000 All Models Except Lumina APV, Venture

SERVICE LOCATIONS — ENGINE AND CHASSIS

CTDP-2

CTDP-2

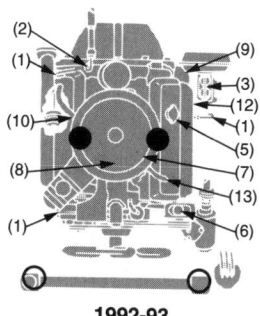

1992-93
4.3L Code Z

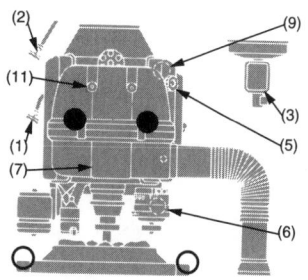

1989-90 5.0L (305) FI Code E
Camaro, Caprice
1989-90 5.7L Code 7
Caprice Police

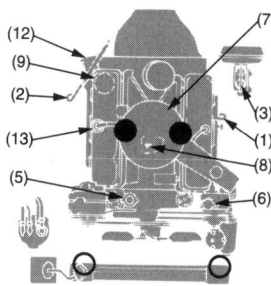

1991-93 5.0L Code E
1991-93 5.7L Code 7

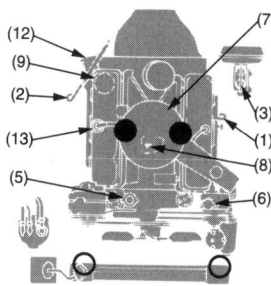

1989-90
5.0L (307) Code Y

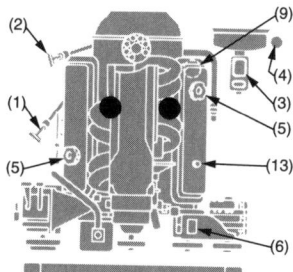

1989-92
5.0L (350) FI Camaro
5.7L (350) Code 8
Camaro, Corvette

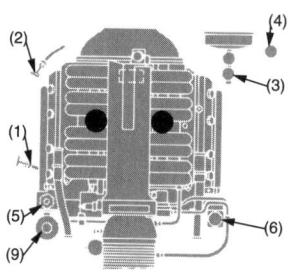

1989-95
5.7L Code J
Corvette

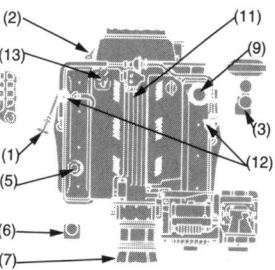

1992-97
5.7L Code P, 5
Corvette, Camaro, Caprice
1994-1996
4.3L V8 Code W
Caprice

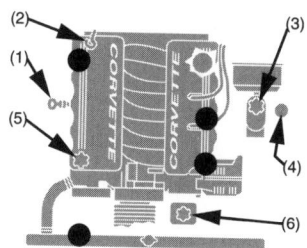

1997-00
Code G
Corvette, Camaro

4
FITTINGS

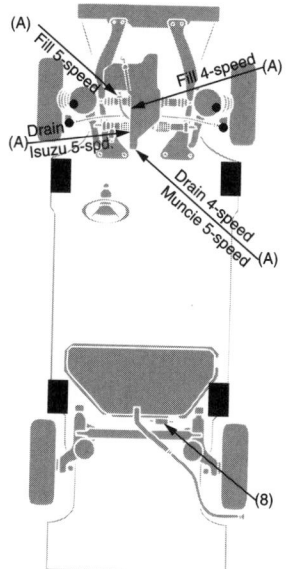

Fill 5-speed (A)
Fill 4-speed (A)
(A) Drain
(A) Isuzu 5-spd.
Drain 4-speed
Muncie 5-speed (A)
(A)

(8)

1996-99
Beretta, Corsica
1989-00
Cavalier

● Cooling system drain

○ Cooling system drain, some

■ Lift adapter position

• Fitting

○ Fitting, some models

(A) Manual transmission/transaxle,
    drain & fill

(B) Transfer case, NOT USED

(C) Automatic transaxle final drive,
    NOT USED

(D) Differential, drain & fill

SERVICE LOCATIONS — ENGINE AND CHASSIS

CTDP-3

CTDP-3

4 FITTINGS

Fill 5-speed
Fill 4-speed (A)
(A)
Drain 4-speed
Muncie 5-speed
Drain Isuzu 5-speed
(A)
(A)
1989-90
Others
(8)

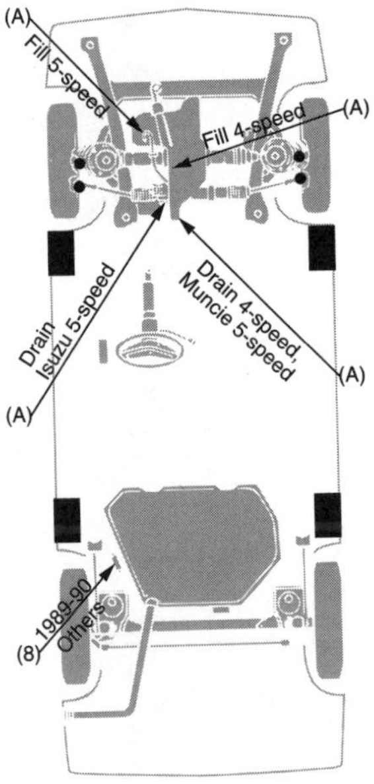

1989-90 Celebrity

**0 FITTINGS
0 PLUGS**

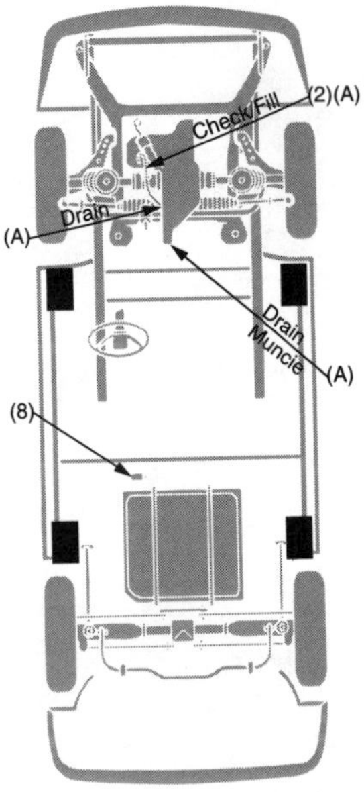

Check/Fill
(2)(A)
(A) Drain
Drain Muncie
(A)
(8)

**1996-00 Monte Carlo
1990-00 Lumina
ex. APV**

**0 FITTINGS
0 PLUGS**

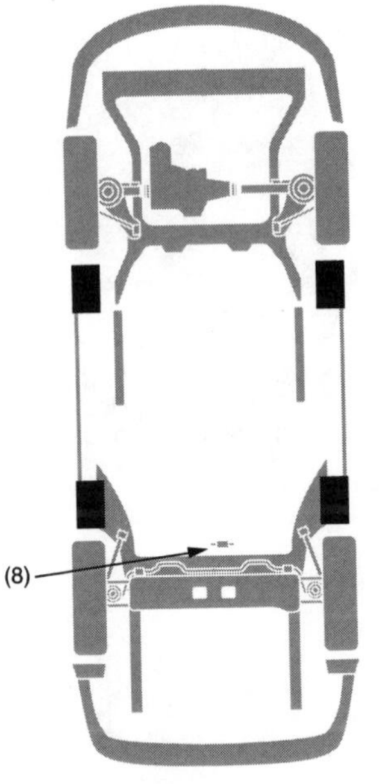

(8)
(8)

1997-00 Malibu

7-10 FITTINGS

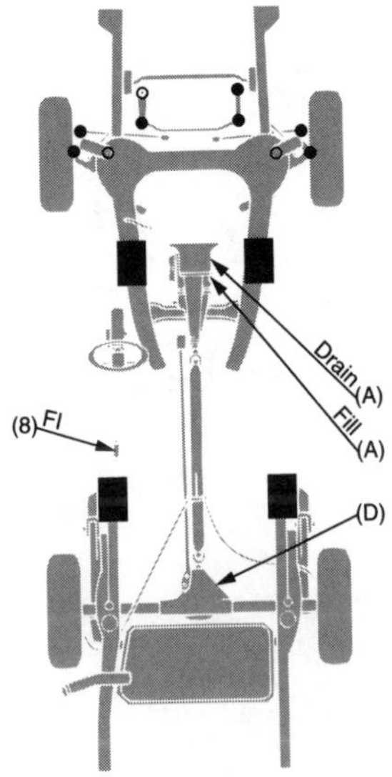

Drain (A)
Fill (A)
(8) Fl
(D)

1989-92 Camaro

(A) Manual transmission/transaxle, drain & fill

(B) Transfer case, NOT USED

(C) Automatic transaxle final drive, NOT USED

(D) Differential, drain & fill

(2) Transmission dipstick

(8) Fuel filter

**2 FITTINGS
0 PLUGS**

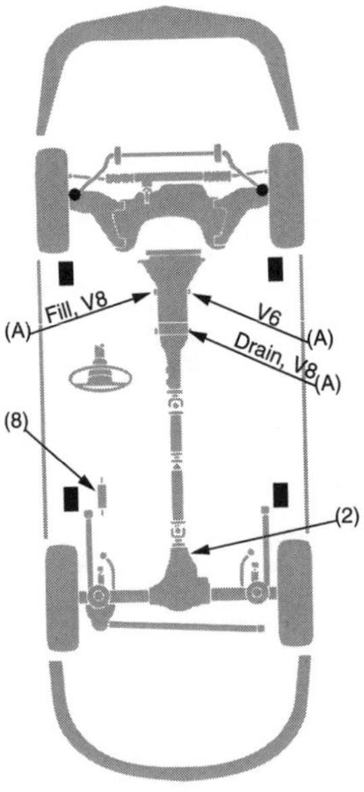

(A) Fill, V8
V6 (A)
Drain, V8 (A)
(8)
(2)

1993-00 Camaro

6-8 FITTINGS

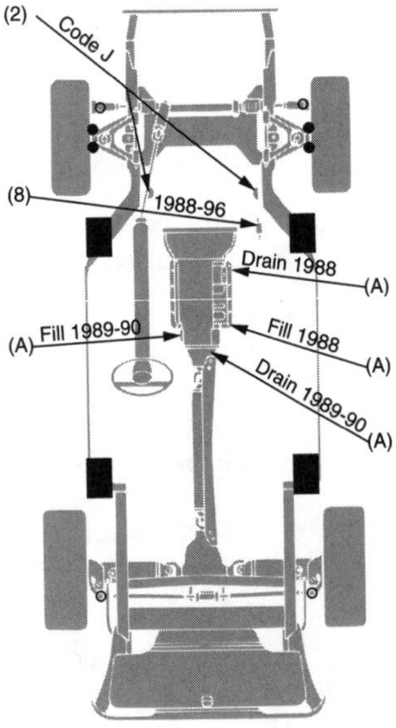

(2)
Code J
(2)
(8) 1988-96
Drain 1988
(A)
(A) Fill 1989-90 Fill 1988
Drain 1989-90 (A)
(A)

1989-96 Corvette

**0 FITTINGS
0 PLUGS**

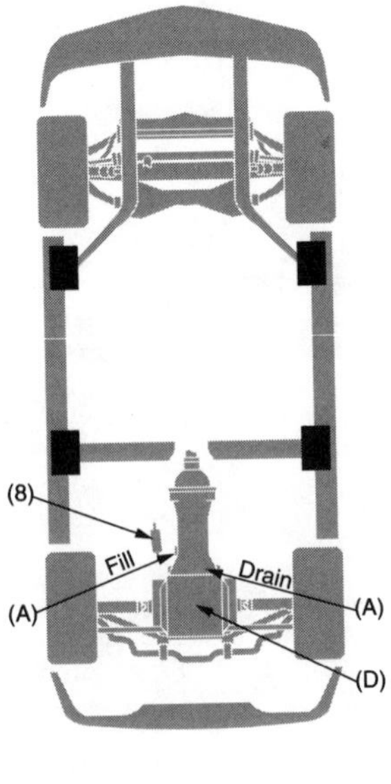

(8)
Fill Drain
(A) (A)
(D)

1997-00 Corvette

**11-13 FITTINGS
0-1 PLUGS**

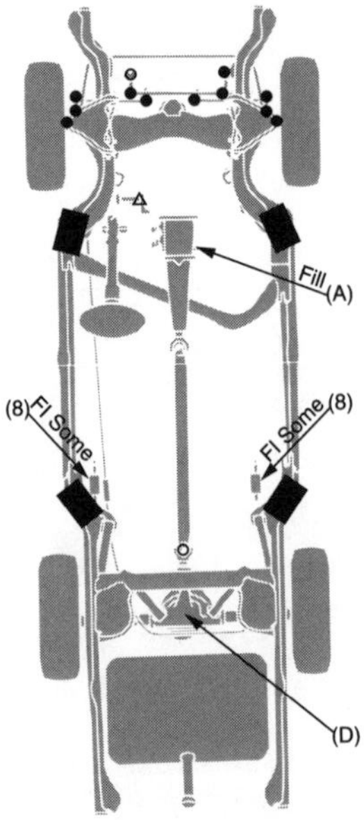

Fill (A)
(8) Fl Some
Fl Some (8)
(D)

**Caprice, Monte Carlo,
El Camino, Impala, Malibu**

CAUTION: On front wheel drive vehicles, the center of gravity is farther forward than on rear wheel drive vehicles. When removing major components from the rear of the vehicle while it is on a hoist, the vehicle must be supported in a manner to prevent it from tipping forward.

■ Lift adapter position △ Plug, some models • Fitting ○ Fitting, some models

SERVICE AT TIME OR MILEAGE — WHICHEVER OCCURS FIRST

CTPM11   CTPM11

Perform the following maintenance services at the intervals indicated to keep the vehicle warranties in effect

W   SERVICE TO MAINTAIN EMISSION WARRANTY

MI—MILES IN THOUSANDS
KM—KILOMETERS IN THOUSANDS

EVERY 6 MONTHS
Brake master cylinder . . .check level **HB**

Clutch master cylinder . . .check level **HB**

Power steering
reservoir . . . . .check level **PS**

FIRST 7.5 MI—12 KM
W Carburetor or throttle body mounting
bolts ex. 2.3L . . . . .torque

W Choke & hoses . . . . .check/clean
As equipped

Diff., Limited-Slip . . . . .change lubricant

Tires . . . . .rotate
Initial service, then every 15 mi (24 km)

EVERY 12 MO/7.5 MI—12 KM
W Crankcase . . . . .change oil

W Oil filter . . . . .replace
At first oil change, then every other or 12 months

Brake system . . . . .inspect
Check hydraulic system for leaks. Inspect drum brake linings and disc pads.

RWD differential . . . . .check level

Exhaust system . . . . .inspect

Suspension &
steering linkage . . . . . .**0-11 fittings LB**

Parking brake cable guides . . . . .coat **LB**
Check adjustment

Shift linkage . . . . .coat **LB**
With floor shift, coat contact faces

Suspension & steering . . . . .inspect
Also inspect FWD drive axle boots and seals

Transaxle or transmission . . .check level

Drive belts 1989 . . . . .inspect/adjust

W Throttle linkage . . . . .inspect
Check for damage or binding

Body . . . . .lubricate

EVERY 12 MONTHS
W Cooling system . . . . . . .inspect hoses &
tighten clamps
Wash radiator filler neck and cap; pressure test system. Clean exterior of radiator core and air conditioning condenser. Inspect coolant and service as needed.

EVERY 24 MO/30 MI—50 KM
W Cooling system . . . . .change coolant **EC**
Flush system, then use 50% concentration for -34°F (-37°C) protection

W Drive belts . . . . .inspect/adjust
1989 vacuum/air pump. 1990 all.

EVERY 36 MO/30 MI—50 KM
W Air cleaner element 1989 . . . . . .replace

W EGR system 1989 . . . . . . .clean/inspect
Engine V.I.N. codes E, J, R, Y, 1, 7

W Crankcase inlet air filter . . . . . . .replace
As equipped

EVERY 30 MI—50 KM
Front wheel bearings ex. front wheel
drive & Corvette . . . .clean/repack **GC**
Service at mileage interval or at each brake reline, whichever comes first. Tighten spindle nut to 12 ft lb while turning wheel. Back off nut & retighten finger tight. Loosen nut just enough that hole in spindle lines up with slot in nut (not more than ½ flat). End play, .001"-.005".

W Choke & hoses . . . . .check/clean
As equipped

W Air cleaner element 1990 . . . . . .replace
Also replace PCV filter, as equipped

W EGR system 1990 . . . . . . .clean/inspect
Engine codes E, G (2.2L), J, R, Y, 7

W Fuel cap, tank, and lines . . . . . .inspect

W Distributor cap . . . . .inspect
Except distributorless ignition

W Ignition timing . . . . .adjust
Except distributorless ignition

W Ignition wires . . . . .inspect/clean
Some models

W PCV valve . . . . .inspect
Some models. Blow out or replace hoses.

W Spark plugs . . . . .replace

W Thermostatic air cleaner . . . . . . .inspect
Some models

EVERY 100 MI—160 KM
Transaxle or trans., auto. . . .change fluid
Replace filter

SEVERE SERVICE
W Carburetor or throttle body—Ex. 2.3L,
torque mounting bolts at 6 mi (10 km), also inspect carburetor choke & hoses

W Crankcase—Change oil: Every 3 mo/3 mi
(5 km); change filter every oil change

Differential—Change lubricant every 7.5
mi (12 km) when towing a trailer

Front suspension & steering linkage—
Lubricate every other oil change

Front wheel bearings—RWD ex. Corvette,
repack every 15 mi (24 km) or every brake service, whichever comes first

Tires—Rotate first 6 mi (9 km), then every
15 mi (24 km)

Transaxle or transmission, automatic—
Change fluid & filter every 15 mi (24 km)

KEY TO LUBRICANTS

AF3	DEXRON®III Automatic Transmission Fluid
API★	Motor Oil certified by the American Petroleum Institute (Starburst Symbol)
EC	Ethylene Glycol Coolant
GC	Wheel Bearing Grease, NLGI Category GC
GLS	Gear Lubricant, Special
GL-5	Gear Oil, API Service GL-5
GL-5★	Special Lubricant for Limited-Slip Differential
HB	Hydraulic Brake Fluid, DOT 3
LB	Chassis Grease, NLGI Category LB
PS	Power Steering Fluid
SG	Motor Oil, API Service SG Use Energy Conserving II Oils
SH	Motor Oil, API Service SH Use Energy Conserving II Oils

CRANKCASE . . . . .SG, SH, API★
CAPACITY, Refill:

	Liters	Qt
1990 Corvette Code J	7.1	7.6
Others	3.8	4.0

Capacity shown is without filter. When replacing filter, additional oil may be needed.

Corvette 5.7L Code J:
Above 40°F (4°C) . . . . .30[1]
Above 0°F (-18°C) . . . . .10W-30[2]
Below 60°F (16°C) 5W-30

Others:
Above 40°F (4°C) . . . . .30[1]
Above 0°F (-18°C) 10W-30
All temperatures . . . . .5W-30[2]

[1] Use only if other specified grades are unavailable
[2] Preferred

TRANSMISSION/TRANSAXLE, Automatic .AF3
CAPACITY, Initial Refill[3]:

	Liters	Qt
125 (3T40)	3.8	4.0
180 (3L30)	3.3	3.5
200C	3.3	3.5
200-4R	4.8	5.0
440-T4 (4T60)	5.7	6.0
700-R4 (4L60)	4.7	5.0
4T60E	7.6	7.4

[3] With the engine at operating temperature, shift transmission through all gears. Let engine slow idle in PARK for 3 minutes or more. Check fluid level and add fluid as needed.

TRANSMISSION/TRANSAXLE, Manual
FWD . . . . .GLS
RWD: Corvette . . . . .GLS
Camaro AF3
CAPACITY, Refill:

	Liters	Pt
FWD: 4-speed	2.8	6.0
5-speed Isuzu[4]	1.9	4.0
5-speed Muncie[5] Celebrity	1.9	4.0
5-speed Muncie[5], others	2.1	5.0
RWD: Corvette	2.1	4.4
Camaro	2.8	6.0

[4] Has 7-bolt aluminum end cap
[5] Has 9-bolt steel end cap

DIFFERENTIAL
Standard . . . . .80W-90[6] GL-5
Limited-Slip . . . . .80W-90[6] GL-5★
[6] For vehicles normally operated in Canada, 80W only
CAPACITY, Refill:

	Liters	Pt
Camaro	1.7	3.6
Caprice, Monte Carlo 8½" ring gear	1.9	4.3
Corvette	1.5	3.3

LIMITED-SLIP IDENTIFICATION:
Tag under rear cover-attaching bolt

CHEVROLET
1991-95 All FWD Models Except Geo, Lumina APV, Nova, Spectrum, Sprint, Venture

SERVICE AT TIME OR MILEAGE — WHICHEVER OCCURS FIRST

CTPM12   CTPM12

Perform the following maintenance services at the intervals indicated to keep the vehicle warranties in effect.

W   SERVICE TO MAINTAIN EMISSION WARRANTY

MI—MILES IN THOUSANDS
KM—KILOMETERS IN THOUSANDS

EVERY 3 MO/3 MI—5 KM
W Crankcase . . . . .change oil & filter
Variable fuel engine only

EVERY 6 MONTHS
Brake master cylinder . . .check level **HB**

Clutch master cylinder . . .check level **HB**

Power steering
reservoir . . . . .check level **PS**

W Throttle linkage 1992-95 . . . . . . .inspect
Check for damage or binding

Brake system 1992-95 . . . . .inspect
Check hydraulic system, disc pads, drum linings

Exhaust system 1992-95 . . . . . .inspect

Suspension & steering linkage
1992-95 . . . . .inspect
Also inspect front drive axle boots & seals

Transaxle, manual 1992-95 . .check level

FIRST 7.5 MI—12 KM
W Throttle body mounting bolts . . . . .torque
Code E,G,R,Z,7 engines

Tires . . . . .rotate
Initial service, then every 15 mi (24 km) or as necessary.
Check brake linings.

EVERY 12 MO/7.5 MI—12 KM
W Crankcase . . . . .change oil

W Oil filter . . . . .replace
1991-94 at first oil change, then every other oil change or
every 12 months. 1995, every oil change.

Brake system . . . . .inspect
Check hydraulic system for leaks. Inspect disc pads &
drum brake linings.

Exhaust system 1991 . . . . .inspect

Suspension & steering
linkage . . . . .lubricate fittings **LB**

Suspension & steering linkage
1991 . . . . .inspect

Parking brake cable guides and
underbody contact points . . . . .coat **LB**
Check adjustment

Shift linkage . . . . .coat **LB**
With floor shift, coat contact faces

Drive axle boots & seals 1991 . . .inspect

Transaxle . . . . . .inspect fluid/check level

Throttle linkage 1991 . . . . .inspect
Check for damage or binding

Body . . . . .lubricate

EVERY 12 MONTHS
W Cooling system . . . . . . .inspect hoses &
tighten clamps

EVERY 15 MI—24 KM
W Fuel filter . . . . .change
Variable fuel engine only

EVERY 24 MO/30 MI—50 KM
W Cooling system . . . . .change coolant **EC**
Flush system. Use 50% concentration for -34°F (-37°C)
protection. For 1993 Cavalier, Corsica, Beretta, add 2
pellets.*
*GM coolant sealer Part No. 3634621.

W Drive belts . . . . .inspect/adjust

EVERY 30 MI—50 KM
W Air cleaner element . . . . .replace

Crankcase ventilation filter . . . . . .replace
As equipped

W EGR system . . . . .clean/inspect
Engine vin codes E, G, R, T, X, 4

W Distributor cap . . . . .inspect
Except distributorless ignition

W Fuel cap, tank, and lines . . . . . .inspect

W Ignition timing . . . . .adjust
Except distributorless ignition

W Ignition wires . . . . .inspect/clean
Ex. 2.3L engine

W PCV system . . . . .inspect
1991-93 some

W Spark plugs . . . . .replace
Ex. 2.2L with platinum plugs

W Thermostatic air cleaner . . . . . . .inspect
1991 some models

EVERY 60 MI—100 KM
W PCV system . . . . .inspect
1993 some

FIRST 60 MI—100 KM;
THEN EVERY 15 MI—25 KM
W Camshaft timing belt . . . . .inspect
3.4L Code X engine

EVERY 100 MI—160 KM
Transaxle, auto. 1991-94 . . .change fluid
Replace filter

W Spark plugs . . . . .replace
2.2L with platinum plugs

SEVERE SERVICE
W **Throttle body**—Code E,G,R,Z,7 engines,
torque mounting bolts at 6 mi (10 km)

W **Crankcase**—Change oil and oil filter every
3 mo/3 mi (5 km)

**Chassis, suspension & steering link-
age**—Lubricate every other oil change

Tires—Rotate first 6 mi (9 km), then every
15 mi (24 km). Check brakes.

Transaxle, automatic—Change fluid & filter every: 1992-94, 15 mi (24 km); 1995, 50
mi (80 km)

KEY TO LUBRICANTS

AF3   DEXRON®-III
Automatic Transmission Fluid

API★   Motor Oil certified by the American
Petroleum Institute (Starburst Symbol)

EC   Ethylene Glycol Coolant
For 1995: Replace green coolant with green
coolant; replace orange coolant (DEX-COOL®)
with orange coolant

GC   Wheel Bearing Grease, NLGI
Category GC

GLS   Gear Lubricant, Special

HB   Hydraulic Brake Fluid, DOT 3

LB   Chassis Grease, NLGI Category LB

PS   Power Steering Fluid

SG   Motor Oil, API Service SG
Use Energy Conserving II Oil

SH   Motor Oil, API Service SH
Use Energy Conserving II Oil

CRANKCASE
1991-94 . . . . .SG[1], SH[1], API★
1995 . . . . .API★

CAPACITY, Refill:	Liters	Qt
1991-95 3.4L Code X	4.8	5.0
Others	3.8	4.0

Capacity shown is without filter. When replacing filter, additional oil may be needed.

Variable Fuel engine
All temperatures . . . . .10W-30[1]
Others:
Above 40°F (4°C) . . . . .30[2]
Above 0°F (-18°C) 10W-30
All temperatures . . . . .5W-30[3]

1 1993, variable fuel engine oil must meet GM spec. 4717M.
For emergency use only 10W-30 **SG, SH, GF-1** oil and un-
leaded gasoline. Replace oil & oil filter as soon as possible with GM spec. 4717M oil.
2 Use only if other specified grades are unavailable. Use API
SG, SH oil.
3 Preferred.

TRANSMISSION/TRANSAXLE,
Automatic **AF3**

CAPACITY, Initial Refill[4]:	Liters	Qt
125 (3T40)	3.8	4.0
4T40E[5]	7.0	7.4
440-T4, (4T60)	5.7	6.0
4T60E	6.6	7.0

4 All except 4T40E. With the engine at operating temperature, shift transmission through all gears. Let engine slow
idle in PARK for 3 minutes or more. Check fluid level and
add fluid as needed.
5 Has no fluid level indicator.

TRANSAXLE, Manual . . . . .GLS

CAPACITY, Refill:	Liters	Pt
FWD: 4-speed	2.8	6.0
5-speed Isuzu[6]	1.9	4.0
5-speed Muncie[7], Celebrity	1.9	4.0
5-speed Muncie[7], others . . .	2.1	5.0

6 Has 7-bolt aluminum end cap
7 Has 9-bolt steel end cap

32   Copyright 2000 by Chek-Chart Publications

SERVICE AT TIME OR MILEAGE — WHICHEVER OCCURS FIRST

CTPM13   CTPM13

Perform the following maintenance services at the intervals indicated to keep the vehicle warranties in effect.
W   SERVICE TO MAINTAIN EMISSION WARRANTY

MI—MILES IN THOUSANDS
KM—KILOMETERS IN THOUSANDS

EVERY 6 MONTHS
Brake master cylinder . . .check level **HB**

Clutch master cylinder . . .check level **HB**
1993-95 Camaro, Corvette use part no. 12345347 or Castrol TLXC88

Power steering reservoir . . .check level **PS**

W Throttle linkage 1992-95 . . . . . . .inspect
Check for damage or binding

Brake system 1992-95 . . . . .inspect
Check hydraulic system, disc pads, drum linings

Exhaust system 1992-95 . . . . . .inspect

Suspension, 1992-95 . . . . .inspect

Transmission, manual
1992-95 . . . . .check level

FIRST 7.5 MI—12 KM
W Throttle body mounting bolts . . . . .torque
1991-93, some

Diff., Limited-Slip . . . . . .change lubricant
Except Corvette

Tires . . . . .rotate
Initial service, then every 15 mi (24 km). Check brake linings. Camaro, Corvette: certain tire/wheel systems cannot be rotated.

EVERY 12 MO/7.5 MI—12 KM
W Crankcase . . . . .change oil
Or sooner when indicated by the Oil Life Monitor

W Oil filter . . . . .replace
1991-94, at first oil change, then every other. 1995, every oil change.

Brake system 1991 . . . . .inspect
Check hydraulic system for leaks. Inspect disc pads & drum brake linings.

Differential . . . . .check level

Exhaust system 1991 . . . . .inspect

Suspension & steering
linkage . . . . .lubricate **fittings LB**

Suspension & steering linkage
1991 .inspect

Parking brake cable guides,
under body contact points . . . .coat **LB**
Check adjustment

Shift linkage . . . . .coat **LB**
With floor shift, coat contact faces
Also inspect drive axle boots and seals

Transmission . . . . .check level

Throttle linkage 1991 . . . . .inspect

Body .lubricate

EVERY 12 MONTHS
W Cooling system . . . . .inspect hoses &
tighten clamps

EVERY 24 MO/30 MI—50 KM
W Cooling system . . . . .change coolant **EC**
Flush system. Use 50% concentration for -34°F (-37°C) protection. 1992-95 Corvette Code P engine, add 6 pellets.*
*GM coolant sealer Part No. 3634621.

W Drive belts . . . . .inspect/adjust

EVERY 30 MI—50 KM
Front wheel bearings ex. Corvette,
1993-95 Camaro . . . .clean/repack **GC**
Service at mileage interval or at each brake reline, whichever comes first. Tighten spindle nut to 12 ft lb while turning wheel. Back off nut & retighten finger tight. Loosen nut just enough that hole in spindle lines up with slot in nut (not more than ½ flat). End play, .001"-.005".

W Air cleaner element . . . . .replace

W Crankcase ventilation filter . . . . .replace
Some models

EGR system . . . . .clean/inspect
Engine vin codes E, Z, 7, 8

W Distributor cap . . . . .inspect
Except distributorless ignition

W Fuel cap, tank, and lines . . . . . .inspect

W Ignition timing . . . . .adjust
Except distributorless ignition

W Ignition wires . . . . .inspect/clean

W PCV system . . . . .inspect
Some

W Spark plugs . . . . .replace
Except 1993-95 code J, and 1992-95 code P, 1994-95 code W

W Thermostatic air cleaner . . . . . . .inspect
1991-92 some models

EVERY 100 MI—160 KM
W Spark plugs . . . . .replace
1993-95 code J, and 1992-95 code P, 1994-95 code W

Trans., auto. . . . . .change fluid
1991-94 all, Camaro, Corvette
Replace filter

SEVERE SERVICE
W Throttle body—1991-93 some, torque mounting bolts at 6 mi (10 km)

W Crankcase—Change oil and filter every 3 mo/3 mi (5 km).

Chassis, suspension and steering linkage—Lubricate every other oil change

Differential—Ex. Corvette, change lubricant every 7.5 mi (12 km) when towing a trailer

Front wheel bearings—Ex. Corvette, 1993-95 Camaro, repack every 15 mi (24 km) or every brake service, whichever comes first

Tires—Rotate first 6 mi (9 km), then every 15 mi (24 km) or as necessary. Check brakes.

Transmission, automatic—Change fluid & filter every 15 mi (24 km)

KEY TO LUBRICANTS

AF3   DEXRON®-III
Automatic Transmission Fluid

API★ Motor Oil certified by the American Petroleum Institute (Starburst Symbol)

EC   Ethylene Glycol Coolant
For 1995: Replace green coolant with green coolant; replace orange coolant with orange coolant

GC   Wheel Bearing Grease, NLGI Category GC

GLS Gear Lubricant, Special

GL-5 Gear Oil, API Service GL-5
1994-95 Camaro, 1993-95 Corvette, GM Part No. 12345977 or 80W-90 **GL-5** meeting GM spec. 9985182. Others, GM Part No. 1052271 or 80W-90 **GL-5**

GL-5★ Special Lubricant for Limited-Slip Differential
1994-95 Camaro, 1993-95 Corvette, GM Part No. 12345977 plus 4 oz. additive[1] or 80W-90 **GL-5** meeting GM spec. 9985082; all others, GM Part No. 1052271 plus 4 oz. additive[1]
[1] GM Part No. 1052358

HB   Hydraulic Brake Fluid, DOT 3

LB   Chassis Grease, NLGI Category LB

PS   Power Steering Fluid
1992-95 Corvette: GM Part No. 12345866, others GM Part No. 1052884

SG   Motor Oil, API Service SG
Use Energy Conserving II Oil

SH   Motor Oil, API Service SH
Use Energy Conserving II Oil

CRANKCASE
1991-94 . . . . .SG[2], SH[2], API★
1995 . . . . .API★

CAPACITY, Refill:	Liters	Qt
Corvette Code J	7.2	7.6
Others	3.8	4.0

Capacity shown is without filter. When replacing filter, additional oil may be needed.

1993-95 Corvette engines
1992 Corvette code P engine:
Above 0°F (-18°C) . . . . .10W-30[2]
All temperatures . . . . .5W-30[2,3]
1991-92 Corvette 5.7L Code J, 3.8L Code K:
Above 40°F (4°C) . . . . .30[4]
Above 0°F (-18°C) . . . . .10W-30[3]
Below 60°F (16°C) 5W-30
Others:
Above 40°F (4°C) . . . . .30[4]
Above 0°F (-18°C) 10W-30
All temperatures . . . . .5W-30[3]
[2] 1993-95 Corvette and 1992 Corvette code P engine oil must also meet GM spec 4718M.
[3] Preferred.
[4] Used only if other specified grades are unavailable. Use API **SG, SH** oil.

TRANSMISSION, Automatic **AF3**

CAPACITY, Initial Refill[5]:	Liters	Qt
700-R4 (4L60)	4.7	5.0
4L60E	6.6	7.0

[5] With the engine at operating temperature, shift transmission through all gears. Let engine slow idle in PARK for 3 minutes or more. Check fluid level and add fluid as needed.

TRANSMISSION, Manual
Corvette . . . .**GLS**
Camaro **AF3**

CAPACITY, Refill:	Liters	Pt
Corvette	2.1	4.4
Camaro 5-speed	2.8	6.0
Camaro 6-speed, 1993-94	3.8	8.1

DIFFERENTIAL
Standard 80W-90 **GL-5**
Limited-Slip . . . . .80W-90 **GL-5★**

CAPACITY, Refill:	Liters	Pt
Camaro	1.7	3.5
Caprice 7½" ring gear	1.7	3.5
Caprice 8½" ring gear	2.0	4.3
Corvette	1.5	3.3

LIMITED-SLIP IDENTIFICATION:
Tag under rear cover-attaching bolt

CHEVROLET
1996-2000 All FWD Models Except: Geo, Lumina APV, 1998-99 Metro, Prizm, Venture

---

SERVICE AT TIME OR MILEAGE — WHICHEVER OCCURS FIRST

CTPM14   CTPM14

Perform the following maintenance services at the intervals indicated to keep the vehicle warranties in effect.
W   SERVICE TO MAINTAIN EMISSION WARRANTY

MI—MILES IN THOUSANDS
KM—KILOMETERS IN THOUSANDS

EVERY MONTH
Tires . . . . .check pressure

EVERY 6 MONTHS
Brake master cylinder . . .check level **HB**

Clutch reservoir . . . . . . .check level **HB**
Part No. 12345347 preferred

W Cooling system . . . . . . .inspect hoses &
tighten clamps

Power steering
reservoir . . . . .check level **PS**

W Throttle linkage . . . . .inspect
Check for damage or binding. Do not lubricate

Brake system . . . . .inspect
Check hydraulic system, disc pads, drum linings, hoses
& lines

Caliper pins, knuckle brake pad
abutments . . . . .check/lubricate
When operating in a corrosive environment
Or every other tire change, or as necessary
1997-00 Cavalier

Exhaust system . . . . .inspect

Suspension & steering linkage . . .inspect
Also inspect front drive axle boots & seals

Transaxle . . . . .check level
Ex. 4T40E

FIRST 7.5 MI—12 KM
Tires, 1996 . . . . .rotate
Initial service, then every 15 mi (24 km) or as necessary.
Check brake linings.

EVERY 7.5 MI—12 KM
Tires, 1997-00 . . . . .rotate
Check brake linings

EVERY 12 MO/7.5 MI—12 KM
W Crankcase . . . . .change oil & filter
Or sooner if indicated by Oil Life Monitor

Suspension & steering
linkage . . . . .lubricate **fittings LB**
As equipped

Parking brake cable guides and
underbody contact points . . . . .coat **LB**

Shift linkage . . . . .coat **LB**
With floor shift, coat contact faces

EVERY 12 MONTHS
Body .lubricate

Underbody . . . . .flush
Every spring

EVERY 30 MI—50 KM
W Air cleaner element . . . . .replace

Crankcase ventilation filter . . . . . .replace
As equipped

W EGR system . . . . .clean/inspect
1996-98 2.2L Code 4 engine

W Fuel cap & gasket, tank,
and lines . . . . .inspect

EVERY 60 MI—100 KM
W Drive belts . . . . .inspect/adjust

FIRST 60 MI—100 KM;
THEN EVERY 15 MI—25 KM
W Camshaft timing belt . . . . .inspect
1996-97 3.4L Code X engine

1996
EVERY 60 MO/100 MI—160 KM
1997-00
EVERY 60 MO/150 MI—240 KM
W Cooling system . . . . .change coolant **EC**
Flush system. Use 50% concentration for –34°F (–37°C)
protection. 1996-97, add 2 GM coolant sealer Part No.
3634621. If silicated coolant is used, change every
24 mo/30 mi—50 km.

EVERY 100 MI—160 KM
W Spark plug wires . . . . .inspect
Except 2.4L Code T engine

W Spark plugs . . . . .replace

Transmission,
automatic . . . . .change fluid & filter
1999-00 Lumina, Monte Carlo
2000 Impala

SEVERE SERVICE
W **Air cleaner element**, dusty conditions—
Replace if necessary every 15 mi (24km)

W **Crankcase**—Change oil and oil filter every
3 mo/3 mi (5 km) or sooner if indicated by
oil life monitor

**Chassis, suspension & steering
linkage**—Lubricate every other oil change

As equipped

Tires—Rotate: 1996, first 6 mi (9 km), then
every 12 mi (20 km); 1997 all and
1998-00 Cavalier, Malibu, every 6 mi
(9 km). Check brakes.

Transaxle, automatic—Change fluid & filter every 50 mi (80 km) when in either:
heavy city traffic at temperatures regularly
above 90°F (32°C); hilly terrain; taxi, police, delivery, trailer towing service; car top
carrier use

KEY TO LUBRICANTS

AF3	DEXRON®-III Automatic Transmission Fluid
API★	Motor Oil certified by the American Petroleum Institute (Starburst Symbol)
EC	Ethylene Glycol Coolant GM DEX-COOL® or Havoline® DEX-COOL®
GLS	Gear Lubricant, Special GM Part No. 12345349
GL-5	Gear Oil, API Service GL-5
HB	Hydraulic Brake Fluid, DOT 3 GM Part No. 12377967
LB	Chassis Grease, NLGI Category LB
PS	Power Steering Fluid GM Part No. 1052884

CRANKCASE . . . .**API★**

CAPACITY, Refill:	Liters	Qt
3.1L Code J	4.3	4.5
3.4L Code E, 2000	4.3	4.5
3.4L Code X	5.2	5.5
3.8L	4.3	4.5
Others	3.8	4.0

Capacities include filter change

3.4L Code X, 3.8L
Above 0°F (-18°C) . . . . .10W-30[1]
Below 60°F (16°C) 5W-30
Others
Above 0°F (-18°C) 10W-30
All temperatures . . . . .5W-30[1]
1 Preferred

TRANSMISSION/TRANSAXLE,
   Automatic **AF3**

CAPACITY, Initial Refill[2]:	Liters	Qt
125 (3T40)	3.8	4.0
4T40E[3]	6.5	6.9
440-T4, (4T60)	5.7	6.0
4T60E	6.7	7.0
4T65E	7.0	7.4

2 With the engine at operating temperature, shift transmission through all gears. Let engine slow idle in PARK for 3
minutes or more. Check fluid level and add fluid as needed. Do not overfill.
3 Has no fluid level indicator. Not owner serviceable.

TRANSAXLE, Manual
1996-99 . . . .**GLS**
GM Part No. 12345349
2000 . . . .**AF3**

CAPACITY, Refill:	Liters	Pt
All	1.9	4.0

SERVICE AT TIME OR MILEAGE — WHICHEVER OCCURS FIRST

CTPM15   CTPM15

Perform the following maintenance services at the intervals indicated to keep the vehicle warranties in effect.
W   SERVICE TO MAINTAIN EMISSION WARRANTY

MI—MILES IN THOUSANDS
KM—KILOMETERS IN THOUSANDS

EVERY MONTH
Tires . . . . .check pressure

EVERY 6 MONTHS
Brake master cylinder . . .check level **HB**

Clutch fluid reservoir . . . .check level **HB**
Part No. 12345347 preferred

Power steering reservoir . . .check level **PS**

W Throttle linkage . . . . .inspect
Check for damage or binding. Do not lubricate.

W Cooling system . . . . .inspect hoses & tighten clamps

Brake system . . . . .inspect
Check hydraulic system, disc pads, drum linings, hoses, & lines

Exhaust system . . . . .inspect

Steering linkage & suspension . . .inspect

Transmission . . . . .check level

FIRST 7.5 MI—12 KM
Diff., all ex. Corvette . . .change lubricant

Tires, 1996 Caprice and Camaro . . .rotate
Initial service, then every 15 mi (24 km). Check brake linings. Camaro, special rotation pattern may apply unidirectionally.

EVERY 12 MO/7.5 MI—12 KM
W Crankcase . . . . .change oil & filter
Or sooner when indicated by the Oil Life Monitor Ex. 1997-00 Corvette

Differential . . . . .check level

Suspension & steering linkage . . . . .lubricate **fittings LB**
As equipped

Parking brake cable guides, under body contact points . . . .coat **LB**
Check adjustment

Shift linkage . . . . .coat **LB**
With floor shift, coat contact faces
Also inspect drive axle boots and seals

EVERY 7.5 MI—12 KM
Tires, 1997-00 Camaro . . . . .inspect/rotate
Special rotation pattern may apply

EVERY 12MO/10MI—16 KM
W Crankcase . . . . .change oil and filter
Or sooner if indicated by the oil life monitor 1997-00 Corvette

EVERY 12 MONTHS
Body . . . . .lubricate

Underbody . . . . .flush
Every spring

EVERY 30 MI—50 KM
Front wheel bearings, Caprice, 1996 . . . . . .clean/repack **GC**
Service at mileage interval or at each brake reline, whichever comes first. Tighten spindle nut to 12 ft lb while turning wheel. Back off nut & retighten finger tight. Loosen nut just enough so that hole in spindle lines up with slot in nut (not more than ½ flat). End play, .001"-.005".

W Air cleaner element . . . . .replace

W Crankcase ventilation filter . . . . . .replace
Some models

W Fuel cap & gasket, tank, and lines, 1996-99 . . . . .inspect

EVERY 50 MI—80 KM
Transmission automatic . . . . . . .change fluid & filter
1999-00 Camaro

EVERY 60 MI—100 KM
W Drive belts . . . . .inspect/adjust

1996
EVERY 60 MO/100 MI—160 KM
1997-00
EVERY 60 MO/150 MI—240 KM
W Cooling system . . . . .change coolant **EC**
Flush system. Use 50% concentration for −34°F (−37°C) protection. 1996-97: Corvette, add 6 GM coolant sealer Part No. 3634621; 1996-97 others, and 1998 Camaro V6, add 2. If silicated coolant is used, change every 24 mo/30 mi—50 km

EVERY 100 MI—160 KM
W Spark plug wires . . . . .inspect

W Spark plugs . . . . .replace

Transmission automatic. . . . . . . .change fluid & filter
1996-98 Camaro, 1996 and 1998-00 Corvette

SEVERE SERVICE
W Air cleaner element, dusty conditions—Replace if necessary every: 1997-98 Corvette, 10 mi (16 km); others, 15 mi (24 km).

W Crankcase—Change oil and filter every 3 mo/3 mi (5 km) or sooner when indicated by the Oil Life Monitor, or when driving in dusty conditions.

Chassis, suspension and steering linkage—Lubricate every other oil change
As equipped

Differential Standard & Limited Slip—Ex. Corvette, change lubricant every 7.5 mi (12 km) when towing a trailer

Front wheel bearings—1996 Caprice, repack every 15 mi (24 km) or every brake service, whichever comes first

Tires—Ex. Corvette: 1996, rotate first 6 mi (9 km), then every 15 mi (24 km); 1997-00, check every 6 to 8 mi (10 to 13 km); or as necessary. Check brakes.

Transmission, automatic—Change fluid & filter every: 15 mi (24 km) for 1996-00 Camaro and 1996 Corvette; 50 mi (80 km) for others when in either: heavy city traffic at temperatures regularly above 90°F (32°C); hilly terrain; taxi, police, delivery, trailer towing service; car top carrier use

KEY TO LUBRICANTS

AF3 DEXRON®-III Automatic Transmission Fluid

API★ Motor Oil certified by the American Petroleum Institute (Starburst Symbol)

EC Ethylene Glycol Coolant GM DEX-COOL® or Havoline® DEX-COOL®

GC Wheel Bearing Grease, NLGI Category GC

GLS Gear Lubricant, Special

GL-5 Gear Oil, API Service GL-5
1996-97 Camaro, GM Part No. 12345977 or 80W-90 meeting GM Spec. 9985182. 1998-00 Camaro, GM Part No. 12378261 or 75W-90 synthetic meeting GM Spec. 9986115. 1996 Caprice, GM Part No. 1052271.

GL-5★ Special Lubricant for Limited-Slip Differential
1996-97 Camaro and 1996-98 Corvette, GM Part No. 12345977 or 80W-90 meeting GM Spec. 9985182, plus 4 oz. GM Part No. 1052358. 1998-00 Camaro and 1999-00 Corvette, GM Part No. 12378261 or 75W-90 synthetic meeting GM Spec. 9986115, plus 4 oz. GM Part No. 1052358. Caprice, GM Part No. 1052271 plus 4 oz. GM Part No. 1052358.

HB Hydraulic Brake Fluid, DOT 3
Brake system: Delco Supreme 11®, GM Part No. 12377967
Clutch system: GM Part No. 12345347

LB Chassis Grease, NLGI Category LB

PS Power Steering Fluid
Corvette 1996-98, GM Part No. 12345866 (synthetic), others, GM Part No. 1052884

CRANKCASE . . . . .API★

CAPACITY, Refill:	Liters	Qt
3.8L	4.3	4.5
5.7L Code G, Corvette	6.1	6.5
5.7L Code G, Camaro	5.2	5.5
5.7L Code P	4.7	5.0

Capacity shown is with filter. Recheck oil level after filling.

Corvette engines:
Above 0°F (-18°C) . . . . .10W-30[2]
All temperatures . . . . .5W-30[2,3]
3.8L Code K:
Above 0°F (-18°C) . . . . .10W-30[3]
Below 60°F (16°C) 5W-30
Others:
Above 0°F (-18°C) 10W-30
All temperatures . . . . .5W-30[3]
[2] Engine oil must also meet GM spec 4718M. API★ oil not meeting GM Spec 4718M may be used for top off only.
[3] Preferred.

TRANSMISSION, Automatic AF3

CAPACITY, Initial Refill[4]:	Liters	Qt
All	4.7	5.0

[4] With the engine at operating temperature, shift transmission through all gears. Let engine slow idle in PARK for 3 minutes or more. Check fluid level and add fluid as needed. Do not overfill.

TRANSMISSION, Manual
Corvette, 1996 . . . . .GLS[5]
Camaro all; Corvette, 1997-00 . . . . . .AF3

CAPACITY, Refill:	Liters	Pt
Corvette, 1996	2.1	4.4
Corvette, 1997-00, overhaul	3.8	8.2
Camaro 5-speed	3.2	6.8
Camaro 6-speed	3.8	8.0

[5] GM Part 1052931

DIFFERENTIAL
Standard GL-5
Limited-Slip .GL-5★

CAPACITY, Refill:	Liters	Pt
Camaro	1.7	3.5
Caprice 7½" ring gear	1.7	3.5
Caprice 8½" ring gear	2.0	4.3
Corvette	1.6	3.3

LIMITED-SLIP IDENTIFICATION:
Tag under rear cover-attaching bolt

CHEVROLET, GMC TRUCKS

1989-2000 All Models Includes Chevrolet Lumina APV/Minivan & Venture, Cadillac Escalade Oldsmobile Bravada & Silhouette, Pontiac Trans Sport & Montana, Isuzu Hombre

SERVICE LOCATIONS — ENGINE AND CHASSIS

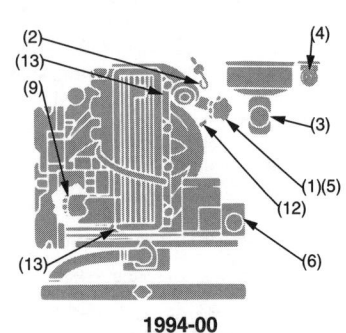

**1994-00
2.2L Code 4**

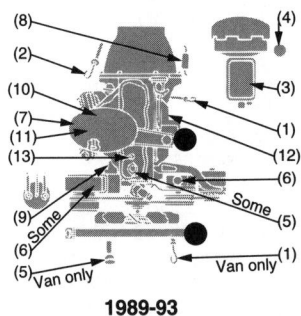

**1989-93
2.5L (151)**

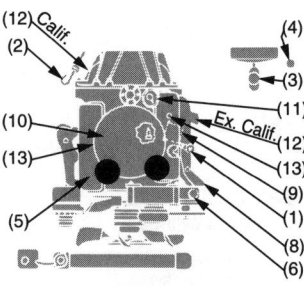

**1989-93
2.8L (173)
S Series**

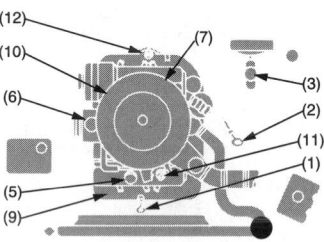

**1990-95
3.1L FI Code D
Lumina APV/Minivan, Silhouette,
Trans Sport**

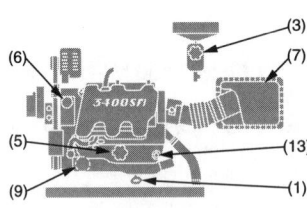

**1996-00
3.4L Code E
Lumina APV/Minivan, Venture
Silhouette, Trans Sport**

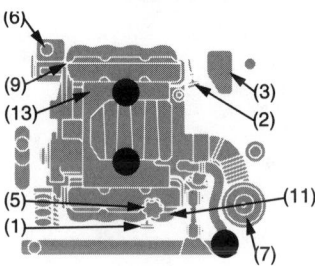

**1992-95
3.8L Code L
Lumina APV/Minivan
Silhouette, Trans Sport**

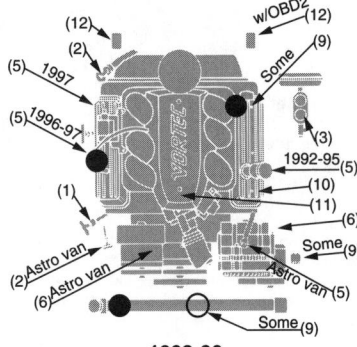

**1992-00
4.3L HO CPI Code W**

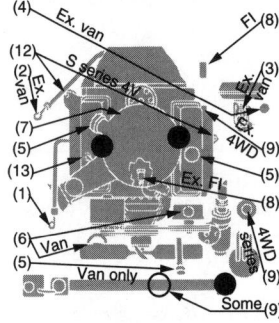

**1989-96 4.3L FI Code Z
1996-00 4.3 FI Code X
Air induction system varies**

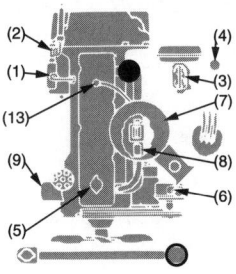

**1989-91 4.8L (292)
Code T**

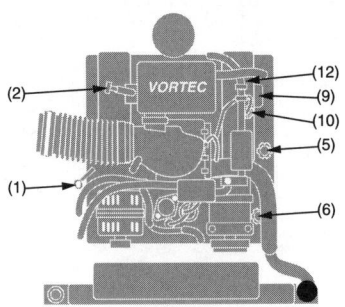

**1996-00
5.0L Code M
5.7L Code R**

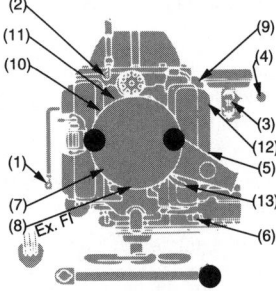

**1996-98
5.0L (305), 5.7L (350)
C,K,R,V
Blazer, Jimmy**

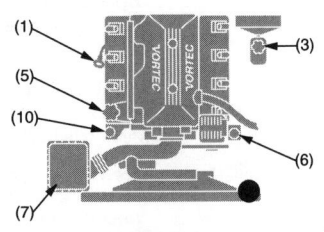

**1999-00
4.8L Code V
5.3L Code T
6.0L Code U**

(1) Crankcase dipstick
(2) Transmission dipstick
(3) Brake fluid reservoir
(4) Clutch fluid reservoir
(5) Oil fill cap
(6) Power steering reservoir
(7) Air filter
(8) Fuel filter
(9) Oil filter
(10) PCV filter
(11) EGR valve
(12) Oxygen sensor
(13) PCV valve

● Cooling system drain   ○ Cooling system drain, some models   • Fitting

CHEVROLET, GMC TRUCKS
1989-2000 All Models Includes Chevrolet Lumina APV/Minivan, Venture,
Oldsmobile Bravada & Silhouette, Pontiac Montana, Trans Sport, Isuzu Hombre

SERVICE LOCATIONS — ENGINE AND CHASSIS

CTTDP-2   CTTDP-2

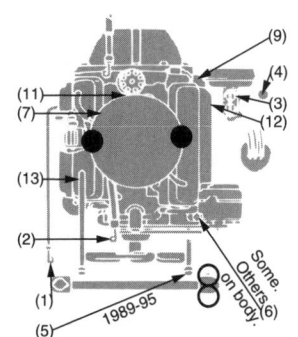

5.0L (305) G Series (4V shown)
5.7L (350) P Series (4V shown)

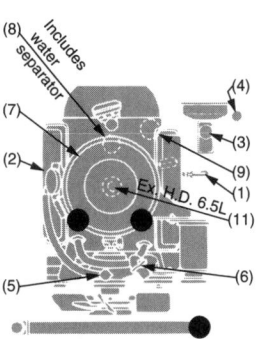

1989-93 6.2L Diesel
1992-00 6.5L Diesel
Air induction system varies

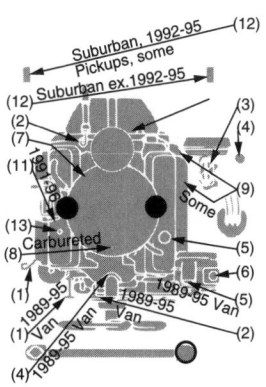

7.4L (454) (4V shown)

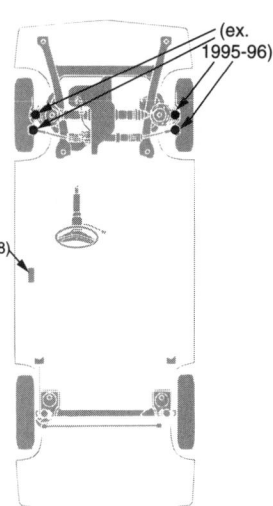

1990-96
Lumina APV/Minivan,
Silhouette,
Trans Sport

(1) Crankcase dipstick
(2) Transmission dipstick
(3) Brake fluid reservoir
(4) Clutch fluid reservoir
(5) Oil fill cap
(6) Power steering reservoir
(7) Air filter

(8) Fuel filter
(9) Oil filter
(10) PCV filter
(11) EGR valve
(12) Oxygen sensor
(13) PCV valve

0 FITTINGS
0 PLUGS

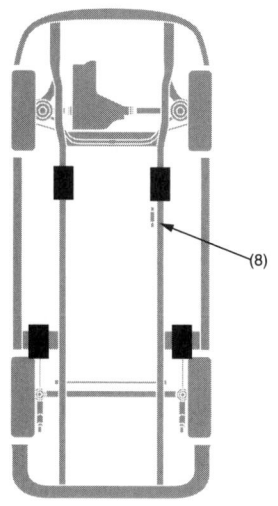

1997-00
Montana, Silhouette, Trans
Sport, Venture

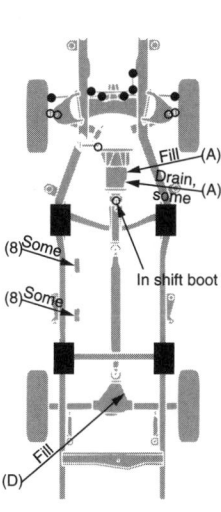

2-WHEEL DRIVE

S10, S15,
S-Blazer, Jimmy,
Sonoma
1996-00 Isuzu Hombre

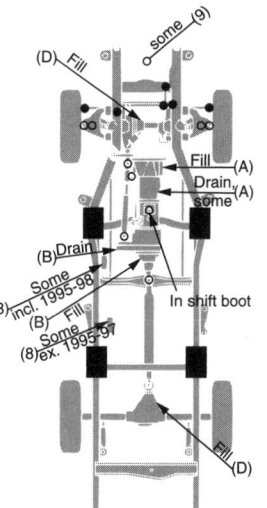

4-WHEEL DRIVE

S10, S15,
S-Blazer, Jimmy, Sonoma,
Syclone, Typhoon
1991-00 Bravada
1996-00 Isuzu Hombre

2-WHEEL DRIVE

1989-00
Astro, Safari

Late 1996-00
G-Van

(A) Manual transmission/transaxle,
   drain & fill

(B) Transfer case, drain & fill

(C) Automatic transaxle final drive,
   NOT USED

(D) Differential, drain & fill

■ Lift adapter position

● Cooling system drain   ○ Cooling system drain, some models   ∘ Fitting, some models   • Fitting

CHEVROLET, GMC TRUCKS
1989-2000 All Models Includes Chevrolet Lumina APV/Minivan, Venture, Oldsmobile Bravada & Silhouette, Pontiac Trans Sport, Isuzu Hombre

SERVICE LOCATIONS — ENGINE AND CHASSIS

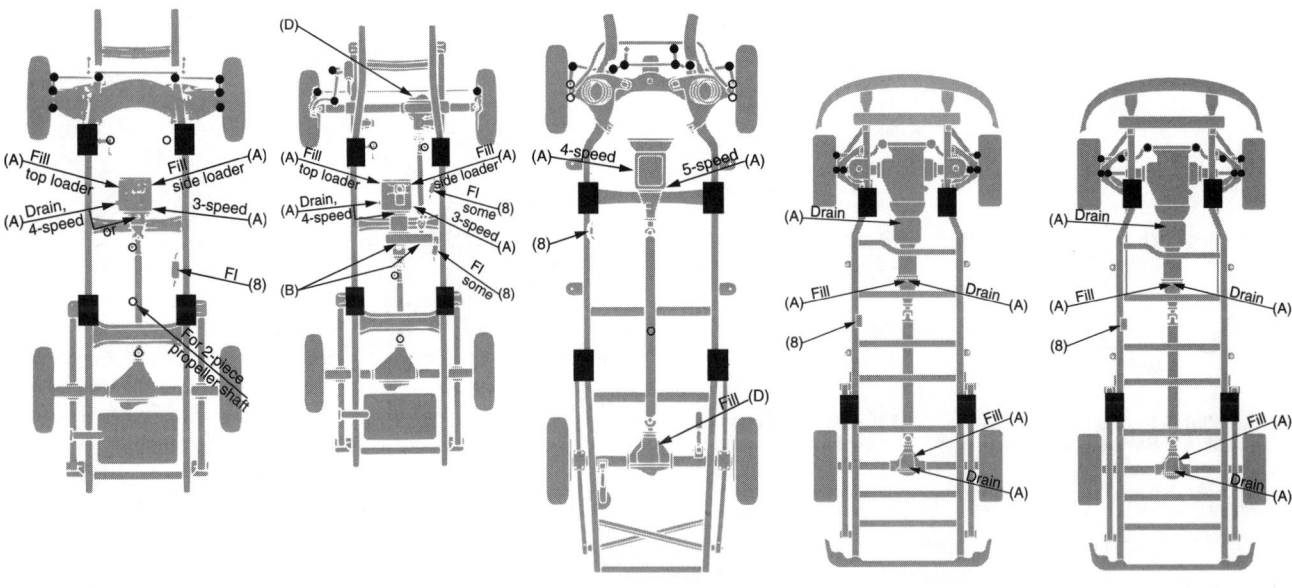

2-WHEEL DRIVE

R-10, -20, -30
1989-91
R-1500, -2500, -3500

4-WHEEL DRIVE

V-10, -20, -30
1989-91
V-1500, -2500, -3500

**1999
C-1500 Extended Cab
Short Box**
1989-98
C-1500, -2500, -3500
1999-00
C-2500, -3500
1992-00
K Blazer, Jimmy;
Tahoe, Yukon, Denali,
Escalade

**1999-00
GMT 800
2WD Sierra, Silverado**

**1999-00
GMT 800
4WD Sierra, Silverado**

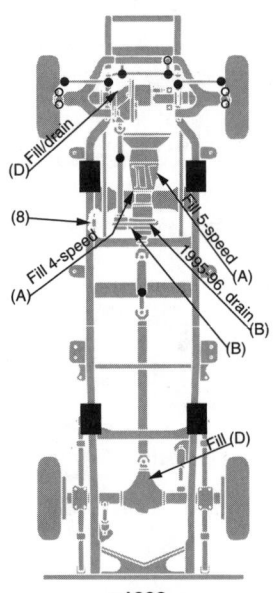

**1999
K-1500 Extended Cab
Short Box**
1989-98
K-1500, -2500, -3500
1999-00
K-2500, -3500
1992-00
K Blazer, Jimmy; Tahoe,
Yukon, Denali, Escalade

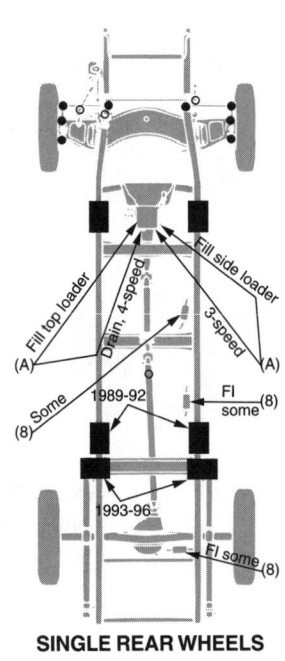

SINGLE REAR WHEELS

Others

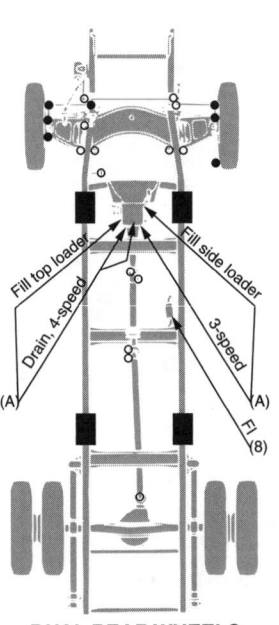

DUAL REAR WHEELS

1989-90

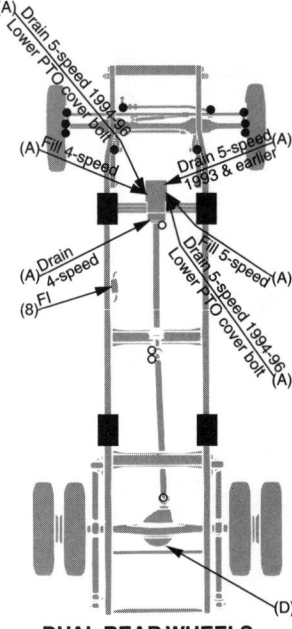

DUAL REAR WHEELS

1991-00

SERVICE AT TIME OR MILEAGE — WHICHEVER OCCURS FIRST

CTTPM24   CTTPM24

Perform the following maintenance services at the intervals indicated to keep the vehicle warranties in effect.

W   SERVICE TO MAINTAIN EMISSION WARRANTY

MI—MILES IN THOUSANDS
KM—KILOMETERS IN THOUSANDS

EVERY 6 MONTHS
Brake master cylinder . . .check level **HB**

Clutch fluid reservoir . . . .check level **HB**

Power steering
reservoir . . . . .check level **PS**

FIRST 12 MO/7.5 MI—12.5 KM
Throttle body mounting bolts . . . . .torque
4.3L engine code Z

Differential, rear locking . .change lubricant

Tires . . . . .check/rotate
Initially, then every 15 mi (25 km) or as necessary

EVERY 12 MO/7.5 MI—12 KM
Brakes & power
steering . . . . .inspect hoses/pads
Inspect drum brake lining, check parking brake

W Crankcase . . . . .change oil

W Oil filter .replace
At first oil change, then every 15 mi (24 km), but at least
every 12 months

Differential, front & rear . . . .check level

Engine drive belts . . . . . .inspect/adjust

Exhaust system . . . . .inspect

Fittings . . . . .lubricate **LB**

Parking brake cable guides . . . . .coat **LB**

Propeller shaft spline . . . . .lubricate **SLG**
1990 Astro and Safari: 2WD/auto. trans. powertrain
equipped with one-piece propshaft only

Propeller shafts . . . . .lubricate **LB**
Front axle propshaft spline, rear driveline, center splines

Shift linkage . . . . .coat **LB**
With floor shift, coat lever contact faces

Suspension & steering . . . . .inspect

Throttle linkage . . . . .inspect
Check for damage or binding

Transfer case . . . . .check level
Check vent hose

Transmission, automatic . . . .check level

Universal CV joint, 4WD . . . . .**fitting LB**

W Cooling system . . . . . . .check level **EC**

Body . . . . .lubricate
Flush underbody every spring

EVERY 12 MONTHS
W Cooling system . . . . .inspect hoses,
tighten clamps
Wash radiator filler neck & cap; pressure test system.
Clean exterior of radiator core & air-conditioning
condenser. Service coolant as needed.

EVERY 30 MI—48 KM
Clutch fork ball stud . . . . . .lubricate **GC**
Some, lubricate sparingly

Clutch cross shaft . . . . .lubricate
Vehicles without hydraulic clutch

Front wheel bearings,
2WD . . . . .clean/repack **GC**
Tighten spindle nut to 12 ft-lb while turning wheel forward.
Adjust spindle nut to "just loose" position by hand. Back
off until the hole in spindle aligns with slot. Do not back off
more than ¼ turn.

W Air cleaner element . . . . .replace

W ECS canister & hoses ex. Calif. . .inspect

EFE system . . . . .check

W EGR system . . . . .inspect

Eng. shield & insulation . . . . . . .inspect

W Spark plugs . . . . .replace

Transmission,
automatic . . . . .change fluid
Replace filter

EVERY 24 MO/30 MI—48 KM
W Cooling system . . . . .change coolant **EC**
Flush system; inspect hoses, tighten clamps. Use 50%
mixture for −34°F (−37°C) protection

EVERY 60 MI—100 KM
Distributor cap . . . . .inspect

W EVRV system . . . . .check

W Fuel filter . . . . .replace

W PCV system . . . . .check
Some models

W Fuel tank, cap, lines . . . . .inspect

W Ignition timing . . . . .check

W Spark plug wires . . . . .inspect

W Engine drive belts . . . . . .inspect/replace

SEVERE SERVICE

Crankcase—Change oil and filter every
3 mi (5 km). Also lubricate chassis.

Differential—Check lubricant every 3 mi
(5 km). Change fluid at least every 15 mi
(24 km).

Front wheel bearings—2WD only, repack
every 15 mi (24 km) or whenever brakes are
relined

W Fuel filter and spark plugs—Replace
every 30 mi (50 km)

Tires—Inspect, rotate at 6 mi (10 km), then
every 15 mi (25 km)

Transmission, automatic—Change fluid
and filter every 15 mi (24 km)

KEY TO LUBRICANTS

AF3 DEXRON®-III Automatic Transmission Fluid

API★ Motor Oil certified by the American Petroleum Institute (Starburst Symbol)

EC Ethylene Glycol Coolant
GM Spec. No. 6038-M

GC Wheel Bearing Grease, NLGI Category GC

GL-5 Gear Oil, API Service GL-5

GLS Special Gear Lubricant
GM Part No. 12345349

HB Hydraulic Brake Fluid, DOT 3

LB Chassis Grease, NLGI Category LB

PS Power Steering Fluid
GM Part No. 1052884; Canada, 992646

SG Motor Oil, API Service SG

SH Motor Oil, API Service SH

SLG Special Lubricant—Grease
GM Part No. 12345879; GM Spec. 9985830

CRANKCASE . . . . .SG, SH, API★

CAPACITY, Refill:

	Liters	Qt
4-cyl. 2.5L	2.8	3.0
Others	3.8	4.0

Capacity shown is without filter. When replacing filter, additional oil may be needed.

1989-90
Above 40°F (4°C) . . . . .30[1]
Above 0°F (−18°C) . . . . .10W-30[2]
All temperatures . . . . .5W-30[2]
[1] May be used when other recommended viscosities are unavailable
[2] Preferred

TRANSMISSION, Automatic AF3

CAPACITY, Initial Refill[3]:

	Liters	Qt
180C 3L30	2.8	3.0
700-R4 4L60	4.7	5.0

[3] With the engine at operating temperature, shift transmission through all gears. Check fluid level in PARK and add fluid as needed

TRANSMISSION, Manual
Astro, Safari AF3
S-Series 5-speed sectional case
(NV3500) . . . . .GLS
S-Series, others AF3

CAPACITY, Initial Fill:

	Liters	Pt
Astro, Safari:		
5-speed	2.0	4.4
S-Series:		
4-speed w/top load	2.0	4.2
5-speed top cover: 1989-90	2.0	4.2
5-speed sectional case	1.9	4.0

TRANSFER CASE AF3

CAPACITY, Refill:

	Liters	Pt
NP207	2.2	4.6
NP231, NP233	1.0	2.2
BW4472 (Full Time)	1.4	3.0

DIFFERENTIAL
Standard & locking . . . .80W, 80W-90[4] GL-5
[4] For vehicles normally operated in Canada, 80W only

CAPACITY, Refill:

	Liters	Pt
Front, Astro, Safari	1.7	3.5
Front S-Series	1.2	2.6
Rear	1.95	3.95

SERVICE AT TIME OR MILEAGE — WHICHEVER OCCURS FIRST

CTTPM19   CTTPM19

Perform the following maintenance services at the intervals indicated to keep the vehicle warranties in effect.

W   SERVICE TO MAINTAIN EMISSION WARRANTY

Includes: 1989, C & K Series with 5.7L, 7.4L engines and over 8500 GVWR. R & V Series with 5.7L, 7.4L 4V engines and over 8500 GVWR. G Series with 5.7L engine and over 10,000 GVWR; and all P-Series.

MI—MILES IN THOUSANDS
KM—KILOMETERS IN THOUSANDS

FIRST 6 MO/24 MI—40 KM

W Engine idle speed . . . . .adjust
Carbureted engines only

EVERY 6 MONTHS

Brake master cylinder . . .check level **HB**

Clutch pedal free play . . . . .check/adjust
Ex. hydraulic

Clutch fluid reservoir . . . . .check level **HB**

Power steering or hydro-boost
reservoir . . . . .check level **PS**

Transmission . . . . .check level

EVERY 7.5 MI—12 KM

Tires . . . . .inspect/rotate
Then every 15 mi/24 km

EVERY 12 MO/6 MI—10 KM

Brakes & power
steering . . . . .inspect hoses/pads
Inspect drum brake lining, check parking brake

W Crankcase . . . . .change oil

W Oil filter . . . . .replace
At first oil change, then every other, but at least every 12 months

Locking differentials . . . .change lubricant
One-time service at mileage only

Differentials . . . . .check level

Engine drive belts . . . . . .inspect/adjust

W Exhaust system . . . . .inspect

Parking brake cable guides . . . .coat **LB**

Shift linkage . . . . .coat **LB**
With floor shift, coat lever contact faces

Front suspension & steering . .lubricate **LB**

Throttle linkage . . . . .inspect
Check for damage or binding

Transfer case . . . . .check level
Check vent hose

Transmission . . . . .check level

Propeller shaft . . . . .lubricate **LB**
Lubricate U-joints/splines

Universal CV joint, 4WD . . . . .**fitting LB**

Body . . . . .lubricate
Flush underbody every spring

EVERY 12 MONTHS

W Cooling system . . . . .inspect hoses,
tighten clamps
Wash radiator filler neck & cap; pressure test system. Clean exterior of radiator core & air conditioning condenser.

EVERY 12 MO/12 MI—19.2 KM

W Accessory drive belts . . . . .inspect

W Thermostatically controlled fan . . . . .test

W Throttle return control system
& hoses . . . . .check/inspect

EVERY 12 MI—19.2 KM

Engine shield & insulation . . . . . .inspect

W Manifold heat valve . . . . .check **MH**

W Spark plugs . . . . .replace

EVERY 24 MO/24 MI—38.4 KM

W Air intake system . . . . . .check for leaks

W Carb. to manifold bolts . . . . .torque

W Cooling system . . . . .change coolant **EC**
Flush system, inspect hoses. Mix 56/44 water to **EC** for –20°F (–29°C) protection; 50/50 for Canada or cold climates

W EFE system . . . . .check **MH**

W Fuel cap, tank & lines . . . . .inspect

W ECS canister & hoses . . . . .inspect

W Idle mixture 6-cyl. 292 eng. . . . . .adjust
California only

EVERY 24 MI—38.4 KM

Standard differential . . .change lubricant

Transmission, automatic . . . .change fluid
Replace filter

W EGR system . . . . .check

W Fuel filter . . . . .replace

W Ignition timing some models . . . . .adjust
Inspect distributor cap and rotor; clean or replace

W Air cleaner element . . . . .replace

W A.I.R., and PCV filters . . . . .replace
If equipped

W Idle speed . . . . .adjust

Front wheel bearings,
2WD . . . . .clean/repack **GC**
Tighten spindle nut to 12 ft-lb, while turning wheel forward. Adjust spindle nut to "just loose" position by hand. Back spindle nut until hole in spindle aligns with slot. Do not back off more than ¼ turn.

EVERY 30 MI—50 KM

Clutch cross shaft . . . . . .0-1 fitting **LB**
Some models

Clutch fork ball stud . . . . . .lubricate **GC**
Some models—lubricate sparingly

W Vacuum advance system
& hoses . . . . .inspect

EVERY 48 MO/48 MI—76.8 KM

Engine governor . . . . .inspect/test

EVERY 60 MI—100 KM

Engine drive belts . . . . . .inspect/replace

Idle mixture 6-cyl. . . . . .adjust

W Choke & hoses . . . . .inspect
As equipped

W Vacuum advance system . . . . . . .inspect
As equipped

W Ignition wires . . . . .clean/inspect

W PCV system . . . . .inspect

SEVERE SERVICE

W **Crankcase**—Change oil every 3 mi (5 km). Change filter every oil change.

Differential—Check lubricant every 3 mi (5 km). Change fluid at least every 15 mi (24 km).

EFE system—Check at 3 mi (5 km), then at 12 mi (19.2 km), then at every 12 mi (19.2 km)

W **Engine idle speed**—Check/adjust every 12 mi (19.2 km)

Fittings—Lubricate every 3 mi (5 km)

Front wheel bearings—Repack every 12 mi (19.2 km)

W **Fuel filter**—Replace every 12 mi (19.2 km)

Tires—Inspect & rotate first 6 mi (10 km), then every 15 mi (24 km)

Transmission, automatic—Change fluid and filter every 12 mi (19.2 km)

KEY TO LUBRICANTS

AF3	DEXRON®-III Automatic Transmission Fluid
API★	Motor Oil certified by the American Petroleum Institute (Starburst Symbol)
EC	Ethylene Glycol Coolant GM Spec. No. 6038-M
GC	Wheel Bearing Grease, NLGI Category GC
GL-5	Gear Oil, API Service GL-5
GLS	Special Gear Lubricant GM Part No. 12345349
HB	Hydraulic Brake Fluid, DOT 3
LB	Chassis Grease, NLGI Category LB
MH	Manifold Heat Valve Solvent
PS	Power Steering Fluid GM Part No. 1052884; Canada, 992646
SG	Motor Oil, API Service SG
SH	Motor Oil, API Service SH

CRANKCASE . . . . .SG, SH, API★

CAPACITY, Refill:	Liters	Qt
6-cyl. 292 eng.	4.7	5.0
6-cyl. 4.3L	3.8	4.0
8-cyl. 350	3.8	4.0
8-cyl. 454 4V	5.7	6.0
8-cyl. 454 others	4.8	5.0

Capacity shown is without filter. When replacing filter, additional oil may be needed.

Above 40°F (4°C) . . . . .30[1]
Above 0°F (–18°C) . . . . .10W-30[2]
Below 60°F (16°C) 5W-30

1 May be used when other recommended viscosities are unavailable
2 Preferred

TRANSMISSION, Automatic AF3

CAPACITY, Initial Refill[3]:	Liters	Qt
400 (3L80)	4.1	4.3
700-R4 (4L60)	4.7	5.0

3 With the engine at operating temperature, shift transmission through all gears. Let engine slow idle in PARK for 3 minutes or more. Check fluid level and add fluid as needed.

TRANSMISSION, Manual

4-speed:
Top shift, iron case . . . . .GLS
GM Part No. 12345577

Side shift, side load AF3

CAPACITY, Refill:	Liters	Pt
4-speed:		
Top shift, iron case	4.0	8.4
Side shift, side load	4.0	8.4
Top shift, aluminum case	1.8	3.8

TRANSFER CASE AF3

CAPACITY, Refill:	Liters	Pt
NP205	2.4[4]	5.0[4]
NP208	4.8	10.8
NP231	1.2	2.5
NP241	2.1	4.5
BW1370	1.5	3.1

To identify, see tag on case
4 Fill to one inch (25 mm) of fill plug

DIFFERENTIAL

Conventional
& locking . . . . .80W, 80W-90[5] GL-5

5 For vehicles normally operated in Canada, 80W only

CAPACITY, Refill:	Liters	Pt
Front: K-30/35	2.1	4.6
V-30/35	2.8	6.0
Rear: Chev. 8½" ring gear	2.0	4.6
Chev. 9½" ring gear	2.6	5.5
Dana 9¾" ring gear	2.8	6.0
Dana 10½" ring gear	3.4	7.2
Rockwell 12" ring gear	6.6	14.0

CHEVROLET, GMC TRUCKS
1989-91 C, G, K, P, R, V Series
All Light Duty Gasoline Models

SERVICE AT TIME OR MILEAGE — WHICHEVER OCCURS FIRST

CTTPM20   CTTPM20

Perform the following maintenance services at the intervals indicated to keep the vehicle warranties in effect.
W   SERVICE TO MAINTAIN EMISSION WARRANTY

1989: All 2.5L, 2.8L, 4.3L, 5.0L; 5.7L under 8501 GVWR ex. G-Van 5.7L under 10001 GVWR G-Van; 7.4L TBI.
1990-91: All 2.5L, 2.8L, 5.0L; 4.3L ex. P-model; 5.7L (ex. G 31303, and P-model) under 8501 GVWR, 7.4L 454 SuperSport.

MI—MILES IN THOUSANDS
KM—KILOMETERS IN THOUSANDS

EVERY 6 MONTHS

Brake master cylinder . . .check level **HB**

Clutch pedal free play . . . . .check/adjust
Ex. hydraulic

Clutch fluid reservoir . . . . .check level **HB**

Engine drive belts . . . . . . .inspect/adjust
1991

Power steering or hydro-boost
reservoir . . . . .check level **PS**

Accelerator control system . . . . . .inspect

Exhaust system, 1991 . . . . .inspect

Differentials, 1991 . . . . .check level

Transfer case, 1991 . . . . . . .check level

FIRST 12 MO/7.5 MI—12.5 KM
Differential, locking . . . . .change fluid

EVERY 12 MO/7.5 MI—12 KM
Brakes & power
steering . . . . .inspect hoses/pads
Inspect drum brake lining, check parking brake

W Crankcase . . . . .change oil

Engine drive belts . . . . . . .inspect/adjust

W Oil filter . . . . .replace
At first oil change, then every other oil change, but at least every 12 months

Differential, front & rear . . . .check level
1989-90

W Exhaust system . . . . .inspect
1989-90

W Choke & hoses . . . . .check/clean
1989-90 some

Parking brake cable guides . . . . .coat **LB**

Propeller shaft spline . . . .lubricate **SLG**
1990-91, 2WD/auto. trans. powertrain equipped with one-piece propshaft only

Propeller shafts . . . . .lubricate **LB**
Front axle propshaft spline, rear driveline, center splines

Shift linkage . . . . .coat **LB**
With floor shift, coat lever contact faces

Front suspension & steering . .lubricate **LB**

Throttle linkage, 1989-90 . . . . . . .inspect
Check for damage or binding

Tires . . . . .check/rotate
Then every 15 mi (24 km)

Transfer case, 1989-90 . . . . .check level
Check vent hose

Transmission, automatic . . . .check level

Universal CV joint, 4WD . . . . .**fitting LB**

W Cooling system . . . . . . .check level **EC**
Check concentration

Engine drive belts . . . . .check

Body . . . . .lubricate
Flush underbody every spring

EVERY 12 MONTHS

W Cooling system . . . . .inspect hoses,
tighten clamps
Wash radiator filler neck & cap; pressure test system. Clean exterior or radiator core & air conditioning condenser. Service coolant as needed.

EVERY 30 MI—48 KM

Clutch fork ball stud . . . . . .lubricate **GC**
Some models—lubricate sparingly

Front wheel bearings,
2WD . . . . .clean/repack **GC**
Tighten spindle nut to 12 ft-lb while turning wheel forward by hand. Adjust spindle nut to "just loose" position by hand. Then back off spindle nut until hole in spindle aligns with slot in nut. Do not back off nut more than 1/4 turn.

Transmission,
automatic . . . . .change filter & fluid

W Air cleaner element . . . . .replace

W PCV, and A.I.R. filters . . . . .replace
Some

W ECS canister & hoses
ex. Calif. . . . . .inspect

EGR system . . . . .inspect

W Spark plugs . . . . .replace

W Vacuum advance system . . . . . .inspect
Service every 15 mi (24 km) thereafter

EVERY 24 MO/30 MI—48 KM

W Cooling system . . . . .change coolant **EC**
Flush system; inspect hoses. Use 50% concentration for −34°F (−37°C) protection.

EVERY 60 MI—100 KM

W Engine drive belts . . . . . . .inspect/adjust

W Engine idle speed . . . . . .inspect/replace

W Engine timing . . . . .check
Some. Inspect cap & rotor

W EVRV . . . . .inspect

W Fuel filter . . . . .replace
1989-91

W Fuel tank, cap & lines . . . . .inspect

W PCV system . . . . .inspect

W Ignition wires . . . . .inspect

SEVERE SERVICE

W Crankcase—Change oil and filter every 3 mi (5 km). Also lubricate chassis.

W Differential—Check lubricant every 3 mi (5 km). Change lubricant fluid at least every 15 mi (24 km).

Front wheel bearings—Repack every 15 mi (24 km) or whenever brakes are relined

W Fuel filter—Replace every 30 mi (50 km)
1989-91

W Fuel tank, cap & lines—Inspect every 30 mi (50 km)

W Transmission, automatic—Change fluid and filter every 15 mi (24 km)

Tires—Inspect & rotate tires first 6 mi (10 km), then every 15 mi (24 km)

KEY TO LUBRICANTS
See other Chevrolet/GMC Truck charts

CRANKCASE . . . . . . .SG, SH, GF-1, GF-2

CAPACITY, Refill:	Liters	Qt
7.4L 4V	5.7	6.0
7.4L others 1989-90	4.8	5.0
7.4L 1991	5.7	6.0
All others	3.8	4.0

Capacity shown is without filter. When replacing filter, additional oil may be needed.

7.4L:
Above 40°F (4°C) . . . . .30[1]
Above 0°F (−18°C) . . . . .10W-30[2]
Below 60°F (16°C) 5W-30
Others:
Above 40°F (4°C) . . . . .30[1]
Above 0°F (−18°C) 10W-30
All temperatures . . . . .5W-30[2]

[1] May be used only when other recommended viscosities are not available
[2] Preferred

TRANSMISSION, Automatic AF3

CAPACITY, Initial Refill[3]:	Liters	Qt
400 (3L80)	4.1	4.3
475 (3L80-HD)	4.1	4.3
700-R4 (4L60), 4L80E	4.7	5.0

[3] With the engine at operating temperature, shift transmission through all gears. Let engine slow idle in PARK for 3 minutes or more. Check fluid level and add fluid as needed.

TRANSMISSION, Manual
4-speed:
Top shift, iron case . . . .**GLS**
GM Part No. 12345577
Side shift, side load, 1989-90 . . . . . .**AF3**
GM Part No. 1052931
5-speed: Sectional case . . . .**GLS**
GM Part No. 12345349 or
GM Part No. 1052931
Top cover, 1991 . . . .**GLS**
GM Part No. 12345871

CAPACITY, Refill:	Liters	Pt
4-speed: Top shift, iron case	4.0	8.4
Side shift, side load	4.0	8.4
Top shift, aluminum case	1.8	3.8
5-speed: Sectional case	1.9	4.0
Top cover	3.8	8.0

TRANSFER CASE AF3

CAPACITY, Refill:	Liters	Pt
NP205	2.4[4]	5.0[4]
NP208	4.8	10.0
NP231	1.0	2.2
NP241	2.1	4.5
BW1370, 4401	1.5	3.1
BW4470	3.1	6.5

To identify, see tag on case
[4] Fill to within one inch (25 mm) of fill plug

DIFFERENTIAL
Conventional &
locking . . . . .80W, 80W-90[5] GL-5
[5] 1989-90, for vehicles normally operated in Canada, 80W only

CAPACITY, Refill:	Liters	Pt
Front:		
K-10/15, -20/25	1.7	3.6
K-30/35	2.1	4.6
V-10/15, -20/25 1989	1.9	4.0
V-30/35 1989	2.8	6.0
V-10/15, -20/25 1990-91	1.7	3.6
V-30/35, 1990-91	2.1	4.6
Rear:		
Chev. 8½" ring gear	2.0	4.2
Chev. 9½" ring gear	2.6	5.5
Dana 9¾" ring gear	2.6	5.5
10½" ring gear:		
Chev.	3.4	7.2
Dana	2.6	5.5
Rockwell 12" ring gear	6.6	14.0

CHEVROLET, GMC TRUCKS
1989-95 All Diesel Models

Perform the following maintenance services at the intervals indicated to keep the vehicle warranties in effect.

W   SERVICE TO MAINTAIN EMISSION WARRANTY

MI—MILES IN THOUSANDS
KM—KILOMETERS IN THOUSANDS

FIRST 12 MO/5 MI—8 KM
Locking differentials . . . .change lubricant

FIRST 5 MI—8 KM
W Engine idle speed . . . . . . .check/adjust
1989-93 all, 1994-95 code Y

Differential, Dana 70/80 . . .change lubricant

Tires . . . . .inspect/rotate
1990-95, initial service, then every 10 mi (16 km)

FIRST 25 MI—40 KM
EGR system 1989-92 . . . . .check
Then at 45 mi (72 km), 60 mi (96 km), then every 15 mi (40 km)

EVERY 3 MI—5 KM
King pins and bushings . . . .lubricate **LB**
1991-95, C3500 w/I-beam axle. Do not lube at temperature below 10°F (-12°C).

EVERY 6 MONTHS
Brake master cylinder . . .check level **HB**
1989

Power steering . . . . .check level **PS**
1989

Suspension/steering . . . . .inspect
W Exhaust system . . . . .inspect
Clutch system . . . . .check/adjust

1989-95, EVERY 12 MO/5 MI—8 KM
Brake system . . . . .inspect
Pads, drum linings, hoses, check parking brake

Brake master cylinder . . .check level **HB**
1990-95

Power steering . . . . .check level **PS**
1990-95

Differentials . . . . .check level
Mileage only

W Crankcase & oil filter . . . . .replace
Drive belts . . . . .inspect/adjust
Except serpentine

Propeller shaft spline . . . .lubricate **SLG**
1990-95, 2WD/auto. trans. powertrain equipped with one-piece propshaft only

Propeller shafts . . . . .lubricate **LB**
Front axle propshaft spline, rear driveline, center splines

Parking brake cable guides . .lubricate **LB**
Park brake cams . . . . .lubricate **LB**
Motor home 16,000 GVW chassis

Front suspension & steering . .lubricate **LB**
Do not lube ball joints at temperatures below 10°F (-12°C). Use low pressure grease gun.

Transfer case . . . . .check level
Transmission, automatic . . . .check level
Transmission, manual . . . . . .check level
Transmission, manual
  W/OD . . . . .lubricate shifter **LB**
Sideloaded transmission with grease fitting

Throttle linkage . . . . .inspect

EVERY 10 MI—16 KM
Air intake system . . . . .inspect
Underhood shields &
  insulation . . . . .check condition

EVERY 12 MO/10 MI—16 KM
Thermostatically controlled
  fan . . . . .check operation

EVERY 12 MONTHS
W Cooling system . . . . . . .inspect hoses &
                         tighten clamps
Wash radiator filler neck & cap; pressure-test system. Clean exterior of radiator core.

EVERY 15 MI—24 KM
W Air cleaner element . . . . .replace
Ex. code C

EVERY 24 MO/30 MI—40 KM
W Cooling system . . . . .change coolant **EC**
Flush system, inspect hoses. Replace hoses if checked, swollen or rotted. Use 50% concentration for -34°F (-37°C) protection.

EVERY 24 MO/100 MI—160 KM
Drive axle, Dana 70/80 . .change lubricant

EVERY 24 MI—40 KM
Transmission,
  automatic . . . . .change fluid
1989-94 models over 8600 lb GVW

EVERY 30 MI—48 KM
W Engine idle speed . . . . . . .check/adjust
1989-93 all, 1994-95 code Y

Clutch fork ball stud . . . .**GC**
Some models—lubricate sparingly

Transmission,
  automatic . . . . .change fluid
1989-94 models under 8600 GVWR

Front wheel bearings
  2WD . . . . .clean/repack **GC**
Tighten spindle nut to 12 ft-lb while turning wheel forward. Adjust spindle nut to "just loose" position by hand. Back off nut until hole in spindle aligns with slot. Do not back off more than 1/4 turn.

W Air cleaner element code C eng. . . . .replace
W Crankcase ventilation system . . . .inspect
1989-94, inspect rubber fittings, hoses & regulator

W Fuel filter . . . . .replace

EVERY 60 MI—96 KM
W Exhaust pressure regulator
  valve . . . . .check operation
W EGR system . . . . .check
1993-95 as equipped

W CDRV system . . . . .check
W Drive belts . . . . .inspect/replace
Serpentine

EVERY 100 MI—160KM
Accelerator cable, 1994-95 . . . . .replace
Code F engine

SEVERE SERVICE
W **Crankcase**—Change oil & filter every 3 mo/2.5 mi (4 km)
Chassis—Lubricate every 2.5 mi (4 km)
King pins and bushings, I-beam axle—Lubricate every 1.5 mi (2.5 km)
Differential—Change lubricant every 15 mi (24 km); more often for heavy-duty or off-road service. HD 3500 with extreme overload/tow and extended high speeds, change fluid every 3 mi (4.8 km) or use 75W-140 synthetic and change every 30 mi (50 km). Dana, 70/80 series, change fluid every 6 mo/25 mi (42 km)
W **Fittings**—Lubricate every 3 mo/2.5 mi (4 km)
Tires—Inspect & rotate first 6 mi (10 km), then every 15 mi (25 km)
Transmission, automatic—Change fluid and filter every: 1989-94 models over 8600 GVW, 12 mi (19 km); 1989-94 models under 8600 GVW, 15 mi (24 km); 1995 models, 50 mi (80 km) when GVWR is over 8,500 lb or in either: heavy city traffic at temperatures regularly above 90°F (32°C); hilly terrain; taxi, police, delivery, trailer towing service
Transfer case—Change fluid every 30 mi (50 km)
Front wheel bearings—2WD, repack every 15 mi (24 km)

KEY TO LUBRICANTS
See other Chevrolet/GMC Truck charts

CRANKCASE . . . . .CG-4, CF-4, CE

CAPACITY, Refill[1]:	Liters	Qt
6.2L, 6.5L	6.6	7.0

1 Includes filter. After refill level must be checked.

1989
Above 32°F (0°C)	.30[2]
Above 0°F (-18°C)	.15W-40
Below 60°F (16°C)	.10W-30

1990-95
Above 0°F (-18°C)	.15W-40[2]
Above 32°F (0°C)	.30
Below 60°F (16°C), 1990-93	.10W-30
Below 32°F (0°C), 1994-95	.10W-30

2 Preferred

TRANSMISSION, Automatic AF3

CAPACITY, Initial Refill[3]:	Liters	Qt
350	3.3	3.5
400 (3L80)	4.1	4.3
700-R4 (4L60), 4L60E, 4L80E . .	4.7	5.0

3 Add specified quantity. With the engine at operating temperature, shift transmission through all gears. Let engine slow idle in PARK for 3 minutes or more. Check fluid level and add fluid as needed.

TRANSMISSION, Manual
4-speed:
  Top shift, iron case 1989-91 . . . .**GLS**
GM Part No. 12345577
  Side shift, side load 1989 . . . .**AF3**
5-speed:
  Sectional case (NV3500) 1994-95 . . .**GLS**
GM Part No. 12345349
  Top cover (NV4500)
    1991-95 . . . . . . .synthetic 75W-90 **GL-4**
GM Part No. 12346190

CAPACITY, Refill:	Liters	Pt
4-speed: Top shift, iron case	4.0	8.4
Side shift, side load	4.0	8.4
5-speed:		
Sectional case 1994-95	1.9[4]	4.0[4]
Top cover	3.8	8.0

4 Approximate; fill to level of fill plug

TRANSFER CASE AF3
CAPACITY, Refill:	Liters	Pt
NP205	2.4[5]	5.0[5]
NP208	4.8	10.0
NP241	2.1	4.5
BW1370, 4401	1.5	3.1
BW4470	3.1	6.5

To identify, see tag on case
5 Fill to within one inch (25 mm) below fill plug

DIFFERENTIAL
Standard & locking . . . . . . .80W-90[6] **GL-5**
6 1989-90, for vehicles normally operated in Canada, 80W only

CAPACITY, Refill:	Liters	Pt
Front:		
K-10/15, -20/25, 1989-95	1.7	3.6
K-30/35, 1989-95	2.1	4.6
V-10/15, -20/25, 1989	1.9	4.0
V-30/35, 1989	2.8	6.0
V-10/15-20/25, 1990-91	1.7	3.6
V-30/35, 1990-91	2.1	4.6
Rear:		
Chev. 8½" ring gear	2.0	4.2
Chev. 9½" ring gear	2.6	5.5
Chev. 10½" ring gear	3.4	7.2
Dana 9¾" ring gear	2.6	5.5
Dana 10½" ring gear	2.6	5.5
Dana 11" ring gear	4.0	8.2
Rockwell 12" ring gear	6.6	14.0

CHEVROLET, OLDSMOBILE, PONTIAC TRUCKS

1990-2000 Chevrolet Venture, Lumina APV; Oldsmobile Silhouette; Pontiac Montana, Trans Sport

Perform the following maintenance services at the intervals indicated to keep the vehicle warranties in effect.

W   SERVICE TO MAINTAIN EMISSION WARRANTY

MI—MILES IN THOUSANDS
KM—KILOMETERS IN THOUSANDS

FIRST 7.5 MI—12.5 KM

W T.B.I. mounting bolts/nuts . . . . . . .torque
1990-93 3.1L engine code D

Tires, 1990-94 . . . . .check/rotate
Then every 15 mi (24 km)

EVERY 7.5 MI—12.5 KM

Tires, 1995-00 . . . . .check/rotate

EVERY 6 MONTHS

Brake master cylinder . . .check level **HB**

W Cooling system . . . . . . .inspect hoses &
tighten clamps

Power steering
reservoir . . . . .check level **PS**

Throttle linkage . . . . .inspect
Do not lubricate cables

Power steering . . . . .inspect hoses

Transaxle, 1996-00 . . . . . . .check level
Or at oil change

Suspension, steering . . . . .inspect

Exhaust system . . . . .inspect

Brake systems, 2000 . . . . .inspect
Hoses, pads, drum linings, parking brake

Front drive axle boots . . . . .inspect

EVERY 12 MO/7.5 MI—12 KM

W Crankcase . . . . .change oil
1990-99, all; 2000, or sooner if indicated by the Oil Life
System

W Oil filter . . . . .replace
1990-94, at first oil change, then every other, but at least
every 12 months. 1995-00, every oil change.

Front suspension . . . .**4 fittings LB**
1990-94

Parking brake cable guides and
underbody contact points . . . . .coat **LB**
Do not lubricate brake cables

Brake systems, 1990-99 . . . . . . .inspect
Hoses, pads, drum brake linings, parking brake
Mileage only

Shift linkage . . . . .lubricate **MO**

Transaxle, automatic . . . . . . .check level

W Cooling system . . . . . . .check level **EC**

Body pivot points . . . . .lubricate
Flush underbody every spring

1997-00 EVERY 15 MI—25 KM

Passenger compartment
air filter . . . . .replace

EVERY 30 MI—48 KM

W Fuel tank, cap & lines . . . . .inspect
1990-92

W Fuel filter . . . . .replace
1990-91

W Crankcase air filter . . . . .replace
1992

W Ignition timing, 1992 3.1L . . . . . . .check
Inspect distributor cap & spark plug wires

EGR system . . . . .inspect
1992 3.1L engine Code D

W Spark plugs . . . . .replace
1990-95

W Air cleaner element . . . . .replace

W Air cleaner system . . . . .inspect
3.1L engine Code D

EVERY 24 MO/30 MI—48 KM

W Cooling system,
1990-95 . . . . .change coolant **EC**
Flush system. Inspect hoses, tighten clamps. Wash
radiator filler neck & cap; pressure test system. Clean
exterior of radiator core & air-conditioning condenser.
Use 50% concentration for −34°F (−37°C) protection.

EVERY 60 MO/60 MI—100 KM

W EGR system . . . . .inspect
1993-95 3.1L engine Code D

W Fuel tank, cap & lines . . . . .inspect
1993-99

W Ignition timing, 1993-95
3.1L Code D . . . . .check
Inspect distributor cap & ign. wires; clean or replace

EVERY 60 MI—100 KM

W Engine drive belts . . . . . . .inspect/adjust

W EVRV system . . . . .check
1990-91 3.1L engine code D

W PCV system . . . . .check
1990-92

W Spark plug wires . . . . .inspect
1990-95

EVERY 100 MI—160 KM

W Spark plugs . . . . .replace
1996-00

W Spark plug wires . . . . .inspect
1996-00

Transaxle, automatic,
1990-94 . . . . .change fluid & filter

1996
EVERY 60 MO/100 MI—160 KM
1997-00
EVERY 60 MO/150 MI—240 KM

W Cooling system . . . . .change coolant **EC**
Flush system. Use 50% concentration for −34°F (−37°C)
protection. Add 2 pellets (1996) or 3 pellets (1997) (GM
coolant sealer Part No. 3634621).
Note: 1996-00, if silicated coolant is used, change every
24 mo/30 mi (50 km).

EVERY 100 MI—160 KM

Transaxle, 1999-00 . .change fluid & filter

SEVERE SERVICE

W Crankcase—Change oil and filter every
3 mo/3 mi (5 km)

Passenger compartment air filter—
1997-99, replace every 12 mi (20 km);
2000, inspect

W Air cleaner filter—Inspect every 15 mi
(25 km)

W T.B.I. mounting bolts—1990-93 3.1L
engine, torque at 6 mi (10 km)

Brake system—1997-99, inspect every
6 mi (10 km)

Chassis—Lubricate: 1990-94 every 12 mo/
3 mi (5 km); 1995-99, every 6 mo/6 mi
(10 km)

Tires—Inspect, rotate first 6 mi (10 km)
then: 1990-94, every 15 mi (24 km);
1995-96, every 12 mi (20 km); 1997-99,
every 6 mi (10 km)

Transaxle, automatic—Change fluid and
filter every: 1990-94, 15 mi (24 km);
1995-00, 50 mi (80 km) when in either:
heavy city traffic at temperatures regularly
above 90°F (32°C); hilly terrain; taxi, police, delivery, trailer towing service

KEY TO LUBRICANTS

AF3   DEXRON®-III Automatic
Transmission Fluid

API★   Motor Oil certified by the American
Petroleum Institute (Starburst
Symbol)

EC   Ethylene Glycol Coolant
1990-94, use only green coolant
1995, replace green coolant with green coolant;
replace orange coolant with orange coolant
1996-99 use GM DEX-COOL® or Havoline®
DEX-COOL®

HB   Hydraulic Brake Fluid, DOT 3
GM Part No. 12377967 or equivalent

LB   Chassis Grease, NLGI Category LB

MO   Motor Oil

PS   Power Steering Fluid
GM Part No. 1052884. For cold climates: GM
Part No. 12345866. (Complete system flush
required prior to use of this fluid)

SG   Motor Oil, API Service SG
Use Energy Conserving II Oils

SH   Motor Oil, API Service SH
Use Energy Conserving II Oils

CRANKCASE

1990-94 . . . . .SG, SH, API★
1995-00 . . . . .API★

CAPACITY, Refill:	Liters	Qt
3.4L	4.3	4.5
3.1L, 3.8L	3.8	4.0

Capacity shown is with filter. Additional oil may be needed.

3.1L VIN Code D, 3.4L Code E
Above 40°F (4°C) . . . . .30[1]
Above 0°F (−18°C) 10W-30
All temperatures . . . . .5W-30[2]
3.8L VIN code L
Above 40°F (4°C) . . . . .30[1]
Above 0°F (−18°C) . . . . .10W-30[2]
Below 60°F (16°C) 5W-30

[1] 1990-95, may be used when other recommended viscosities are unavailable. Use API **SH** oil.
[2] Preferred.

TRANSMISSION/TRANSAXLE,

Automatic **AF3**

CAPACITY, Initial Refill[3]:	Liters	Qt
3T40 (3-speed)	3.8	4.0
4T60-E (4-speed), 1996	6.6	7.0
4T60-E (4-speed), 1997-98	7.5	8.0
4T65-E, 1999-00	7.5	8.0

[3] With the engine at operating temperature, shift transmission through all gears. Let engine slow idle in PARK
for 3 minutes or more. Check fluid level and add fluid
as needed.

SERVICE AT TIME OR MILEAGE — WHICHEVER OCCURS FIRST

CTTPM23   CTTPM23

Perform the following maintenance services at the intervals indicated to keep the vehicle warranties in effect.

W SERVICE TO MAINTAIN EMISSION WARRANTY

1990, 4.3L P-models, all models with 5.7L, over 8500 GVWR, 7.4L all except 454 Super Sport; 1991, 4.3L P-models, 5.7 P-models, high cube, and cutaway van, 4.3L in forward control chassis and other models over 9500 GVWR, 5.7L in models over 8500 GVWR, 7.4L all except 454 Super Sport. 1992, 4.8L, 7.4L, and 5.7L over 8500 GVW. 1993-95 over 8500 GVW 4.3L, 5.7L, and 7.4L.

MI—MILES IN THOUSANDS
KM—KILOMETERS IN THOUSANDS

EVERY 6 MONTHS
Brake master cylinder . . .check level **HB**
Clutch pedal free travel . . . .check/adjust
Clutch reservoir . . . . .check level **HB**
GM Part No. 12345347 preferred
Suspension/steering . . . . .inspect
W Exhaust system . . . . .inspect
Power steering or hydro-boost
    reservoir . . . . .check level **PS**
Transmission, automatic . . . .check level

EVERY 3 MI—5 KM
King pins and bushings . . . .lubricate **LB**
1991-95 C3500 w/I-beam axle. Do not lube at temperatures below 10°F (−12°C).

FIRST 6 MI—10 KM
Tires . . . . .inspect/rotate
Then every 12 mi (20 km)
Differential . . . . .change lubricant
Locking, and Dana 70/80 series

EVERY 12 MO/6 MI—10 KM
Brakes & power steering . . . . .inspect
Pads, drum brake lining, check parking brake
W Crankcase . . . . .change oil
W Oil filter . . . . .replace
1990-94, at first oil change, then every other, but at least every 12 months 1995, every oil change.
W Differentials, front and rear . . .check level
Mileage only
W Engine drive belts . . . . . .inspect/adjust
Except serpentine
Parking brake cable guides . . . . .coat **LB**
Shift linkage . . . . .coat **LB**
With floor shift, coat lever contact faces
Front suspension & steering . .lubricate **LB**
Do not lube ball joints or king pin bushings at temperatures below 10°F (−12°C).
Throttle linkage . . . . .inspect
Check for damage or binding
Transfer case . . . . .check level
Transmission, manual . . . . . .check level
Park brake cam . . . . .lubricate **LB**
Motorhome 1600 lb GVWR chassis
Propeller shaft spline . . . . .lubricate **SLG**
2WD/auto. trans. powertrain equipped with one-piece propshaft only
Propeller shafts . . . . .lubricate **LB**
Front axle propshaft spline, rear driveline, center splines
Universal CV joint, 4WD . . . . . .fitting **LB**
Body . . . . .lubricate
Flush underbody every spring

EVERY 12 MO/12 MI—19.2 KM
W Thermostatically controlled fan . . . . .test
W Throttle return control system
    & hoses . . . . .check/inspect

EVERY 12 MI/19.2 KM
Eng. shields & insulation . . . . .inspect
W Engine belt, serpentine . . . . . . .inspect
W Manifold heat valve . . . . .check **MH**
W Spark plugs . . . . .replace
1990 engines using leaded fuel

EVERY 24 MO/24 MI—38.4 KM
Cooling system . . . . .change coolant **EC**
Flush system, inspect hoses, tighten clamps. Use 50% concentration for −34°F (−37°C) protection. Add 2 pellets of GM Part No. 3634621.
W EGR system, 1990 . . . . .check
W ECS canister & hoses . . . . .inspect

EVERY 24 MO/100 MI—160 KM
Drive axle, Dana 70/80 . . . .change lube

EVERY 24 MI—38.4 KM
Front wheel bearings,
    2WD . . . . .clean/repack **GC**
Tighten spindle nut to 12 ft-lb while turning wheel forward. Adjust spindle nut to "just loose" position by hand. Back spindle nut until hole in spindle aligns with slot. Do not back off more than 1/4 turn.
W Air intake system . . . . . .check for leaks
1992-95
Fuel tank cap & lines, 1990-91 . . .inspect
W Fuel filter . . . . .replace
W Ignition timing, some models . . . . .adjust
Inspect distributor cap and rotor; clean or replace
Standard differential . . .change lubricant
Transmission,
    automatic . . . . . . .change filter & fluid
W PCV filter, 1990-91 . . . . .replace
W Engine idle speed, 1990-91 . . . .adjust
W Thermostatically controlled
    air cleaner . . . . .inspect
1992-95 some
W Air cleaner elements . . . . .replace

EVERY 27 MI—45 KM
W Spark plugs, 1991-95 . . . . .replace

EVERY 30 MI—50 KM
Clutch fork ball stud . . . . . .lubricate **GC**
Some models—lubricate sparingly

EVERY 48 MO/48 MI—76.8 KM
Engine governor . . . . .inspect/test

EVERY 60 MI—100 KM
W Ignition wires . . . . .clean/inspect
W EGR system, 1991-95 . . . . .inspect
W EVRV . . . . .inspect
Some 1992-95
W Fuel cap, tank & lines, 1992-95 . .inspect
W PCV system, 1990-91 . . . . .inspect
W Evaporative control system . . . . .inspect
1992-95

SEVERE SERVICE
W **Crankcase**—Change oil & filter every 3 mi (5 km)

Differential—Check lubricant every 3 mi (5 km). Change fluid at least every 15 mi (24 km). HD 3500 with extreme overload/tow and extended time periods over 45 mph (72 kph), change fluid every 3 mi (4.8 km) or use 75W-140 synthetic and change every 30 mi (50 km). Dana 70/80 Series, change fluid every 6 mo or 25 mi (42 km)

EFE system—Check at 3 mi (5 km), then at 12 mi (19.2 km), then at every 12 mi (19.2 km)

Fuel tank, cap & lines—Inspect every 30 mi (48 km)

Chassis—Lubricate every 3 mi (5 km)

King pins and bushings—1991-95 C3500 w/I beam axle, lubricate every 1.5 mi (2.5 km)

Front wheel bearings—Repack every 12 mi (19.2 km)

W **Fuel filter**—Replace every 12 mi (19.2 km)

Tires—Inspect & rotate first 6 mi (10 km) then every 12 mi (20 km)

Transmission, automatic—Change fluid and filter every 12 mi (19.2 km)

KEY TO LUBRICANTS
See other Chevrolet/GMC Truck charts

CRANKCASE

	Liters	Qt
1990-94 . . . . .SH, SG, API★		
1995 . . . . .API★		
CAPACITY, Refill:	**Liters**	**Qt**
4.3L: 1990-91	4.8	5.0
1992-95	4.3	4.5
5.7L: 1990	4.8	5.0
1991-95	4.8[1,2]	5.0[1,2]
7.4L: 1990 P-chassis	6.6	7.0
1990 Others	5.7	6.0
1991	6.6	7.0
1992-95	6.6[2]	7.0[2]

Capicity shown is with filter change
1 Add 1 qt. (0.9L) additional for CNG, or large crankcase option
2 Add 1 qt. (0.9L) additional for C3500HD installation
Above 40°F (4°C) . . . . .30[3]
Above 0°F (−18°C) . . . . .10W-30[4]
Below 60°F (16°C) 5W-30
3 May be used when other recommended viscosities are unavailable
4 Preferred

TRANSMISSION, Automatic AF3

CAPACITY, Initial Refill[5]:	**Liters**	**Qt**
350	3.3	3.5
400 (3L80)	4.1	4.3
475 (3L80-HD)	4.1	4.3
700-R4 (4L60), 4L60E, 4L80E . . .	4.7	5.0

5 With the engine at operating temperature, shift transmission through all gears. Let engine slow idle in PARK for 3 minutes or more. Check fluid level and add fluid as needed.

TRANSMISSION, Manual
4-speed:
    Top shift, iron case, 1990-91 . . . . . . .GLS
    GM Part No. 12345577
5-speed: Sectional case (NV3500) . . . .GLS
    GM Part No. 12345349, 1989-95; or
    GM Part No. 1052931, 1989-91
Top cover, (NV4500)
    1991-95 . . . . .Synthetic 75W-90 GL-4
    GM Part No. 12346190

CAPACITY:	**Liters**	**Pt**
4-speed: Top shift, iron case	4.0	8.4
5-speed: Sectional case	1.9[6]	4.0[6]
Top cover	3.8	8.0

6 Approximate, fill to level of fill plug

TRANSFER CASE AF3

CAPACITY, Refill:	**Liters**	**Pt**
NP205	2.4[7]	5.0[7]
NP241	2.1	4.5
BW1370, 4401	1.5	3.1
BW4470	3.1	6.5

To identify, see tag on case
7 Fill to one inch (25 mm) of fill plug

DIFFERENTIAL
Standard . . . . .80W-90[8] GL-5
8 1990, for vehicles normally operated in Canada, 80W only

CAPACITY, Refill:	**Liters**	**Pt**
Front	2.1	4.6
Rear:		
Chev. 8½" ring gear	2.0	4.2
Chev. 9½" ring gear	2.6	5.5
Dana 9¾" ring gear	2.8	6.0
Dana 10½" ring gear	3.4	7.2
Dana 11" ring gear	4.0	8.2
Rockwell 12" ring gear	6.6	14.0

CHEVROLET, GMC TRUCKS
1992-95 C, G, K Series
All Light Duty Gasoline Models

SERVICE AT TIME OR MILEAGE — WHICHEVER OCCURS FIRST

CTTPM25   CTTPM25

Perform the following maintenance services at the intervals indicated to keep the vehicle warranties in effect.

W   SERVICE TO MAINTAIN EMISSION WARRANTY
1992 4.3L ex. P-Model, 5.0L, 5.7L under 8501 GVWR, 7.4L SuperSport. 1993 4.3L, 5.0L, 5.7L under 8501 GVWR.

MI—MILES IN THOUSANDS
KM—KILOMETERS IN THOUSANDS

EVERY 6 MONTHS

TBI throttle lever stud . . . . .lubricate **MO**

Brake master cylinder . . .check level **HB**

Clutch pedal free travel . . . .check/adjust

Suspension, steering . . . . .inspect

W Exhaust system . . . . .inspect

Transfer case . . . . .check level

Power steering/hydro-boost
reservoir . . . . .check level **PS**

FIRST 7.5 MI—12.5 KM
Differential, locking . . . . . . .change fluid

FIRST 7.5 MI—12.5 KM
THEN EVERY 15 MI—25 KM
Tires . . . . .inspect/rotate

EVERY 12 MO/7.5 MI—12 KM
Brakes & power
steering . . . . .inspect hoses/pads
Inspect disc brake pads and drum brake lining, check parking brake

W Crankcase . . . . .change oil

W Oil filter . . . . .replace
1992-94 at first oil change, then every other oil change, but at least every 12 months. 1995, every oil change.

W Differential, front & rear . . . . .check level
Mileage only

W Engine drive belts . . . . . .inspect/adjust

Exhaust system . . . . .inspect

Parking brake cable guides . . . .coat **LB**

Propeller shaft spline . . . .lubricate **SLG**
2WD/auto. trans. powertrain equipped with one-piece propshaft only

Propeller shafts . . . . .lubricate **LB**
Front axle propshaft spline, rear driveline, center splines

Shift linkage . . . . .coat **LB**
With floor shift, coat lever contact faces

Front suspension &
steering . . . . .lubricate **LB**
Do not lube ball joints, king pin bushings below 10°F (−12°C)

Throttle linkage . . . . .inspect
Check for damage or binding

Transfer case . . . . .check level
Check vent hose

W Transmission, automatic . . . .check level

Universal CV joint, 4WD . . . . .**fitting LB**

W Cooling system . . . . . . .check level **EC**

Body . . . . .lubricate
Flush underbody every spring

EVERY 30 MI—48 KM
Clutch fork ball stud and
cross shaft . . . . .lubricate **GC**
Some models—lubricate sparingly

Front wheel bearings,
2WD . . . . .clean/repack **GC**
Tighten spindle nut to 12 ft-lb while turning wheel forward by hand. Adjust spindle nut to "just loose" position by hand. Then back off spindle nut until hole in spindle aligns with slot in nut. Do not back off nut more than ¼ turn.

Transmission, automatic
1992-94 . . . . .change filter & fluid

W Air cleaner element . . . . .replace

W PCV filter . . . . .replace
If equipped

W ECS canister & hoses
ex. Calif. . . . . .inspect

W Spark plugs . . . . .replace

EVERY 24 MO/30 MI—48 KM
W Cooling system . . . . .change coolant **EC**
Flush system; inspect hoses, tighten clamps. Wash radiator filler neck & cap; pressure test system. Clean exterior or radiator core & air conditioning condenser. Use 50% concentration for −34°F (−37°C) protection.

EVERY 60 MI—100 KM
W Engine drive belts,
Serpentine . . . . .inspect

W Engine timing . . . . .check
Some. Inspect cap & rotor.

W EGR or EVRV system . . . . .inspect
As equipped

W Fuel filter . . . . .replace

W Fuel tank, cap & lines . . . . .inspect

W Ignition wires . . . . .inspect

SEVERE SERVICE
W Crankcase—Change oil and filter every 3 mi (5 km). Also lubricate chassis.

W Differential—Check lubricant every 3 mi (5 km). Change lubricant fluid at least every 15 mi (24 km).

Front wheel bearings—2WD, repack every 15 mi (24 km) or whenever brakes are relined

W Fuel filter—Replace every 30 mi (50 km)

W Fuel tank, cap & lines—Inspect every 30 mi (50 km)

Transmission, automatic—Change fluid and filter every: 1992-94, 15 mi (24 km); 1995, 50 mi (80 km) when in either: heavy city traffic at temperatures regularly above 90°F (32°C); hilly terrain; taxi, police, delivery, trailer towing service

Tires—Inspect & rotate tires first 6 mi (10 km) then every 12 mi (20 km)

KEY TO LUBRICANTS

AF3	DEXRON®-III Automatic Transmission Fluid
API★	Motor Oil certified by the American Petroleum Institute (Starburst Symbol)
EC	Ethylene Glycol Coolant 1995, replace green coolant with green coolant; replace orange coolant with orange coolant
GC	Wheel Bearing Grease, NLGI Category GC
GLS	Gear Lubricant, Special GM Part No. 12345349
GL-5	Gear Oil, API Service GL-5
HB	Hydraulic Brake Fluid, DOT 3
LB	Chassis Grease, NLGI Category LB
PS	Power Steering Fluid GM Part No. 1052884
SG	Motor Oil, API Service SG Use Energy Conserving II Oils
SH	Motor Oil, API Service SH Use Energy Conserving II Oils
SLG	Special Lubricant—Grease GM Part No. 12345879, GM Spec. 9985830

CRANKCASE
1992-94 . . . . .SG, SH, API★
1995 . . . . .API★

CAPACITY, Refill:	Liters	Qt
4.3L	4.3	4.5
5.0L, 5.7L	4.8	5.0
7.4L	6.5	7.0

Capacity shown is with filter. For 5.7L engine, add 1.0 qt (0.9L) for either natural gas, or 5.0 qt (4.8L) crankcase option.

Above 40°F (4°C) .30[1]
Above 0°F (−18°C) 10W-30
All temperatures . . . . .5W-30[2]

[1] May be used only when other recommended viscosities are not available. Use API **SH** oil.
[2] Preferred.

TRANSMISSION, Automatic AF3

CAPACITY, Initial Refill[3]:	Liters	Qt
400 (3L80)	4.1	4.3
475 (3L80-HD)	4.1	4.3
700-R4 (4L60), 4L60E, 4L80E . .	4.7	5.0

[3] With the engine at operating temperature, shift transmission through all gears. Let engine slow idle in PARK for 3 minutes or more. Check fluid level and add fluid as needed.

TRANSMISSION, Manual
NV3500 (Sectional case) . . . .**GLS**
GM Part No. 12345349

NV4500
(Top cover) . . . . .Synthetic 75W-90 **GL-4**
GM Part No. 12346190

CAPACITY, Refill:	Liters	Pt
Sectional case	1.9[4]	4.0[4]
Top cover	3.8	8.0

[4] Approximate, fill to level of fill plug

TRANSFER CASE (4x4) AF3

CAPACITY, Refill:	Liters	Pt
NP231	1.0	2.2
NP241	2.1	4.5
BW1370, 4401	1.5	3.1
BW4470	3.1	6.5

To identify, see tag on case

DIFFERENTIAL
Conventional & locking 80W-90 **GL-5**
GM Part No. 1052071

CAPACITY, Refill:	Liters	Pt
Front:		
K-10/15, -20/25	1.7	3.6
K-30/35	2.1	4.6
Rear:		
Chev. 8½" ring gear	2.0	4.2
Chev. 9½" ring gear	2.6	5.5
Dana 9¾" ring gear	2.6	5.5
Chev. 10½" ring gear	3.4	7.2
Dana 10½" ring gear	2.6	5.5
Dana 11" ring gear	4.0	8.2
Rockwell 12" ring gear	6.6	14.0

SERVICE AT TIME OR MILEAGE — WHICHEVER OCCURS FIRST

CTTPM26   CTTPM26

Perform the following maintenance services at the intervals indicated to keep the vehicle warranties in effect.

W   SERVICE TO MAINTAIN EMISSION WARRANTY

MI—MILES IN THOUSANDS
KM—KILOMETERS IN THOUSANDS

SYCLONE, TYPHOON, EVERY 3 MO/2.5 MI—4 KM

W Crankcase . . . . .oil change
Change oil filter at each oil change

Chassis . . . . .lubricate **LB**

SYCLONE, TYPHOON, FIRST 6 MI—10 KM

Tires . . . . .check/rotate
Initially, then every 15 mi (25 km) or as necessary

FIRST 12 MO/7.5 MI—12.5 KM

Throttle body mounting bolts . . . . .torque
4.3L engine code Z

Differential, rear locking . . .change lubricant

Tires ex.; Syclone,
Typhoon . . . . .check/rotate
Initially, then every 15 mi (25 km) or as necessary

EVERY 6 MONTHS

Brake master cylinder . . .check level **HB**

Clutch system . . . . .check level **HB**

Power steering
reservoir . . . . .check level **PS**

Accelerator control system . . . . . .inspect

Exhaust system . . . . .inspect

Differentials, 1991-94 . . . . . . .check level

EVERY 7.5 MI—12.5 KM

Differentials, 1995 . . . . .check level

U-joints, axle seals, 1995 . . . . . . .check

EVERY 12 MO/7.5 MI—12 KM

Brakes & power
steering . . . . .inspect hoses/pads
Inspect drum brake lining, check parking brake

W Crankcase . . . . .change oil

W Oil filter . . . . .replace
1991-94, at first oil change, then every 15 mi (24 km),
but at least every 12 months. 1995 every oil change

Engine drive belts . . . . .inspect/adjust

Fittings . . . . .lubricate **LB**

Parking brake cable guides . . . . .coat **LB**

Propeller shaft spline . . .lubricate **SLG**
Astro and Safari: 2WD/auto. trans. powertrain equipped
with one-piece propshaft only

Propeller shafts . . . . .lubricate **LB**
Front axle propshaft spline, rear driveline, center splines

Shift linkage . . . . .coat **LB**
With floor shift, coat lever contact faces

Suspension & steering . . . . .inspect

Transfer case . . . . .check level
Check vent hose

Transmission, automatic . . . .check level

Universal CV joint, 4WD . . . . .**fitting LB**

Double cardan joint . . . . .lubricate **LB**
Syclone, Typhoon

W Cooling system . . . . . . .check level **EC**

Body . . . . .lubricate
Flush underbody every spring

EVERY 15 MI—24 KM

Transmission,
automatic . . . . .change fluid
Replace filter
Syclone, Typhoon

EVERY 30 MI—48 KM

Clutch fork ball stud . . . . . .lubricate **GC**
4.3L engine, lubricate sparingly

Clutch cross shaft . . . . .lubricate
Vehicles without hydraulic clutch

W Fuel filter 1992-95 . . . . .replace

W Fuel tank, cap & lines
1992-94 . . . . .inspect

Front wheel bearings,
2WD . . . . .clean/repack **GC**
Tighten spindle nut to 12 ft-lb while turning wheel
forward. Adjust spindle nut to "just loose" position by
hand. Back off until the hole in spindle aligns with slot. Do
not back off more than 1/4 turn.

W Air cleaner element . . . . .replace

W ECS canister & hoses ex. Calif. . .inspect

EFE system . . . . .check

W EGR system . . . . .inspect

Eng. shield & insulation . . . . . . .inspect

W Spark plugs . . . . .replace

Transmission,
automatic 1991-94 . . . . . . .change fluid
Replace filter

EVERY 24 MO/30 MI—48 KM

W Cooling system . . . . .change coolant **EC**
Flush system; inspect hoses, tighten clamps. Use 50%
mixture for −34°F (−37°C) protection. 1991-94: wash
radiator filler neck & cap; pressure test system. Clean
exterior of radiator core & air conditioning condenser.

Charge air
cooling system . . . .change coolant **EC**
Syclone, Typhoon only

EVERY 60 MI—100 KM

W EVRV system 1991-92 . . . . .check

W Fuel filter 1991 . . . . .replace

W PCV system . . . . .check
Some models

W Fuel tank, cap, lines 1991-95 . . . .inspect

W Ignition timing . . . . .check

W Spark plug wires . . . . .inspect

W Engine drive belts . . . . .inspect/replace

EVERY 100 MI—160 KM

W Spark plugs, 1995 2.2L . . . . . . .replace

SEVERE SERVICE

Crankcase—Change oil and filter every
3 mi (5 km). Also lubricate chassis.

Differential—Check lubricant every 3 mi
(5 km). Change fluid at least every 15 mi
(24 km).

Front wheel bearings—2WD only, repack
every 15 mi (24 km) or whenever brakes are
relined

W **Fuel filter and spark plugs**—Ex. 1995
2.2L engine, replace every 30 mi (50 km)

Tires—Inspect, rotate at 6 mi (10 km), then
every 15 mi (25 km)

Transfer case—1990-94, change fluid
every 30 mi (50 km); 1995, off-road use,
may need more frequent lubrication

Transmission, automatic—Change fluid
and filter every: 1991-94, 15 mi (24 km);
1995, 50 mi (80 km) when in either: heavy
city traffic at temperatures regularly above
90°F (32°C); hilly terrain; taxi, police, delivery, trailer towing service

KEY TO LUBRICANTS

AF3	DEXRON® -III, Automatic Transmission Fluid
API★	Motor Oil certified by the American Petroleum Institute (Starburst Symbol)
EC	Ethylene Glycol Coolant
For 1995, replace green coolant with green coolant, replace orange coolant with orange coolant
GC	Wheel Bearing Grease, NLGI Category GC
GL-5	Gear Oil, API Service GL-5
GLS	Special Gear Lubricant
GM Part No. 12345349
HB	Hydraulic Brake Fluid, DOT 3
LB	Chassis Grease, NLGI Category LB
PS	Power Steering Fluid
GM Part No. 1052884 Canada, 992646
SG	Motor Oil, API Service SG
SH	Motor Oil, API Service SH
SLG	Special Lubricant—Grease
GM Part No. 12345879, GM Spec. 9985830

CRANKCASE

1991-94 . . . . .SG, SH, API★
1995 . . . . .API★
Note: 1992-93 Syclone, Typhoon oil must be Mobil 1 synthetic or equivalent

CAPACITY, Refill:	Liters	Qt
4-cyl. 2.5L	2.8	3.0
Others	3.8	4.0

Capacity shown is without filter. When replacing filter, additional oil may be needed.

1991-95 except Syclone, Typhoon:
Above 40°F (4°C) . . . . .30[1]
Above 0°F (−18°C) 10W-30
All temperatures . . . . .5W-30[2]

1992-93 Syclone, Typhoon:
All temperatures 10W-30
[1] May be used when other recommended viscosities are-
unavailable. Use API **SH** oil.
[2] Preferred.

TRANSMISSION, Automatic AF3

CAPACITY, Initial Refill[3]:	Liters	Qt
700-R4 4L60, 4L60E	4.7	5.0

[3] With the engine at operating temperature, shift transmission through all gears. Check fluid level in PARK and add
fluid as needed.

TRANSMISSION, Manual

Astro, Safari AF3
S-Series 5-speed sectional case
(NV3500) . . . . .GLS
S-Series, BW T5 . . . . .AF3

CAPACITY, Initial Fill:	Liters	Pt
4-speed w/top load	2.0	4.2
5-speed top cover: 1992-95 . . .	2.8	5.9
1991	2.0	4.2
5-speed sectional case	1.9	4.0

TRANSFER CASE AF3

CAPACITY, Refill:	Liters	Pt
All	1.2	2.6

DIFFERENTIAL

Standard & locking 80W-90 **GL-5**

CAPACITY, Refill:	Liters	Pt
Astro, Safari: Front	1.2	2.6
Rear	1.9	4.0
S-Series, Bravada: Front		
7¼", AWD	1.2	2.6
Rear		
7⅝"	1.9	4.0
8½", 9½"	[4]	[4]

[4] Fill to ⅜" (9.5 mm) below fill plug hole

CHEVROLET, GMC TRUCKS
1996-2000 C, G, K, P Gasoline Models

SERVICE AT TIME OR MILEAGE — WHICHEVER OCCURS FIRST

CTTPM27   CTTPM27

Perform the following maintenance services at the intervals indicated to keep the vehicle warranties in effect.
W SERVICE TO MAINTAIN EMISSION WARRANTY

MI—MILES IN THOUSANDS
KM—KILOMETERS IN THOUSANDS

EVERY 6 MONTHS
Air filter . . . . . .check restriction indicator

Brake system . . . . .inspect
Pads, drum linings, lines, hoses, parking brake

W Cooling system . . . . .inspect hoses &
tighten clamps

Clutch reservoir . . . . . . .check level HB
GM Part No. 12345347 preferred

Brake master cylinder . . .check level HB

Clutch pedal free travel . . . .check/adjust

Suspension/steering . . . . .inspect

Exhaust system . . . . .inspect

Throttle linkage . . . . .inspect
Check for damage or binding. Do not lube cables.

Transmission, manual . . . . . .check level

Transmission, automatic . . . .check level

CV joints & seals . . . . .check

EVERY 3 MI—5 KM
King pins and bushings . . . .lubricate LB
I-beam axle. Do not lube at temperatures below 10°F (−12°C).

EVERY 7.5 MI—12.5 KM
W Differentials, front and rear . . .check level
Tires . . . . .inspect/rotate

EVERY 12 MO/7.5 MI—12.5 KM
W Crankcase . . . . .change oil & filter
All ex. 1999 Sierra/Silverado. 1999-00 Sierra/Silverado: Mileage only or sooner if indicated by Oil Life Monitor.

Power steering . . . . .check level PS

Parking brake cable guides . . . .coat LB

Shift linkage . . . . .coat LB
With floor shift, coat lever contact faces

Front suspension &
steering . . . . .lubricate LB
Do not lube ball joints or king pin bushings at temperatures below 10°F (−12°C)

Transfer case . . . . .check level

Park brake cam . . . . .lubricate LB
Motorhome 1600 lb GVWR chassis

Propeller shaft spline . . . .lubricate SLG
2WD/auto. trans. powertrain equipped with one-piece propshaft

Propeller shafts . . . . .lubricate LB
Front axle propshaft spline, rear driveline, center splines

Universal CV joint, 4WD . . . . .fitting LB

Body . . . . .lubricate
Ex. 1997-00 G-van door hinges
Flush underbody every spring

EVERY 12 MO/15 MI—25 KM
W Thermostatically controlled fan . . . . .test

EVERY 12 MI—19.2 KM
Eng. shields & insulation . . . . . .inspect
GVWR above 8,500 only

EVERY 15 MI—25 KM
Passenger compartment
air filter . . . . .replace
1999-00 Sierra, Silverado, as equipped

EVERY 30 MI—50 KM
Air filter . . . . .replace
P-models
Clutch fork ball stud
and cross shaft . . . . .lubricate GC
Some models—lubricate sparingly
Front wheel bearings,
2WD . . . . .clean/repack GC
Or at brake reline, whichever occurs first
W Fuel filter . . . . .replace

EVERY 50 MI—80 KM
Transmission, auto . . . . . . .change fluid
P-models

EVERY 60 MI—100 KM
W EGR system . . . . .inspect
Drive belt, accessory . . . . .inspect
W Fuel cap, tank & lines . . . . .inspect
W PCV system . . . . .inspect
W Evaporative control system . . . .inspect

EVERY 100 MI—166 KM
W Spark plug wires . . . . .inspect
W Spark plugs . . . . .replace
W PCV valve . . . . .inspect
Transmission, auto . . . . . . .change fluid
1998-00

1996
EVERY 60 MO/100 MI—160 KM
1997-00
EVERY 60 MO/150 MI—240 KM
Cooling system . . . . .change coolant EC
Flush system, inspect hoses, tighten clamps. Use 50% concentration for −34°F (−37°C) protection. 1996-97, add 2 pellets GM Part No. 3634621
Note: If silicated coolant is used, change every 24 mo/ 30 mi (50 km).

EVERY 150 MI—240 KM
Transmission,
manual,1999-00 . . . . .change fluid
Sierra/Silverado with 4.3L or 4.8L engine

EVERY 200 MI—321 KM
Transmission,
manual,1999-00 . . . . .change fluid
Sierra/Silverado with 6.0L engine

SEVERE SERVICE
Air filter, P-model—Inspect every 15 mi (25 km)
W **Crankcase**—Change oil & filter every 3 mi (5 km)
W **Differentials**—Check lubricant every oil change. HD 3500 operating for extended time periods over 45 mph (72 kph), change fluid every 30 mi (50 km)
Chassis—Lubricate every 3 mo/3 mi (5 km)
King pins and bushings, I-beam axle—Lubricate every 1.5 mi (2.5 km)
Front wheel bearings ex. 1999-00 GMT 800—Repack every15 mi (24 km)
W **Fuel filter**—Replace every 12 mi (19.2 km)
Tires—Inspect & rotate every 6 mi (10 km)
Transfer Case—Off road use, may need more frequent lubrication
Transmission, automatic—Change fluid and filter every 50 mi (80 km) or when in either: heavy city traffic at temperatures regularly above 90°F (32°C); hilly terrain; taxi, police, delivery, trailer towing service; car top carrier use

KEY TO LUBRICANTS
AF3	DEXRON®-III Automatic Transmission Fluid
API★	Motor Oil certified by the American Petroleum Institute (Starburst Symbol)
EC	Ethylene Glycol Coolant GM DEX-COOL®, or Havoline® DEX-COOL®
GC	Wheel Bearing Grease, NLGI #2 Category GC or GC-LB
GL-5	Gear Oil, API Service GL-5
GLS	Special Gear Lubricant GM Part No. 12345349
HB	Hydraulic Brake Fluid, DOT 3 Delco Supreme II® GM Part No. 12377967
LB	Chassis Grease, NLGI Category LB
PS	Power Steering Fluid GM Part No. 1052884
SLF	Automatic Transfer Case Fluid Beginning with models produced starting late June, 1999, use only Part No. 12378508 which is colored blue. Other models should also use Part No. 12378508. Mixing of blue fluid with the old red Autotrac fluid Part No. 12378396 for top off is permitted.
SLG	Special Lubricant—Grease GM Part No. 12345879, GM Spec. 9985830

CRANKCASE . . . . .API★

CAPACITY, Refill:	Liters	Qt
4.3L	4.3	4.5
4.8L	5.7	6.0
5.0L	4.8	5.0
5.3L	5.7	6.0
5.7L	4.8[1]	5.0[1]
6.0L V8	5.7	6.0
7.4L, 1996-97	6.5[1]	7.0[1]
7.4L, 1998	6.3	6.6
7.4L, 1999-00	5.7	6.0

Capacity shown is with filter change
1 Add 1 qt. (0.9L) additional for: CNG; large crankcase option; C3500HD installation
All temperatures . . . . .5W-30[2]
Above 0°F (−18°C) 10W-30
2 Preferred

TRANSMISSION, Automatic AF3
CAPACITY, Initial Refill[3]:	Liters	Qt
4L60E, 4L80E	4.7	5.0

3 With the engine at operating temperature, shift transmission through all gears. Check fluid level in PARK and add fluid as needed.

TRANSMISSION, Manual
NV3500 (Sectional case) . . . . .GLS
5-speed without low gear. GM Part No. 12345349
NV4500 (Top Cover) . . . . .Synthetic 75W-90 GL-4
5-speed with low gear
GM Part No. 12346190 or equivalent

CAPACITY, Refill:	Liters	Pt
Sectional case	2.0[4]	4.4[4]
Top cover	3.8	8.0

4 Approximate, fill to level of fill plug

TRANSFER CASE
Manual AF3
Automatic .SLF

CAPACITY, Refill:	Liters	Pt
NV241, 243	2.1	4.5
BW4401	1.5	3.1
BW4470	3.1	6.5
NV236, 246	2.1	4.5

To identify, see tag on case

DIFFERENTIAL
C3500 HD
w/Dana 11" . . . . .Synthetic 75W-140 GL-5
GM Part No. 12346140
All others
1999-00 GMT800 . . . . . .Synthetic 75W-90 GL-5
Part No. 12378261
2000 GMT400 . . . . .Synthetic 75W-90 GL-5
Part No. 12378261
1999 GMT400 . . . . .80W-90 GL-5
Part No. 1052271
All others 80W-90 GL-5
GM Part No. 1052271
Use synthetic 75W-90 GM Part No. 12345836 in front differential when excessive effort is required to shift into 4WD.

CAPACITY, Refill:	Liters	Pt
Front: K1, K2	1.7	3.5
K3	2.1	4.5
Rear: American Axle		
8½", 8⅝" ring gear	2.0	4.2
9½" ring gear	2.6	5.5
10½" ring gear	3.1	6.5
Dana 11" ring gear	4.0	8.2

SERVICE AT TIME OR MILEAGE — WHICHEVER OCCURS FIRST

CTTPM28   CTTPM28

Perform the following maintenance services at the intervals indicated to keep the vehicle warranties in effect.
W   SERVICE TO MAINTAIN EMISSION WARRANTY

MI—MILES IN THOUSANDS
KM—KILOMETERS IN THOUSANDS

FIRST ENGINE OIL CHANGE
Locking differentials . . . .change lubricant

FIRST 5 MI—8 KM
Tires . . . . .inspect/rotate
Initial service, then every 10 mi (16 km)

EVERY 5 MI—8 KM
Differentials . . . . .check level
CV joints & seals . . . . .check

EVERY 6 MONTHS
Air filter . . . . .check/replace
Ex. G-van, check air cleaner filter restriction indicator on engine

Brake system . . . . .inspect
Pads, drum linings, hoses, check parking brake

Clutch system . . . . .check/adjust

Exhaust system . . . . .inspect

Suspension/steering . . . . .inspect

Transmission, manual . . . . .check level

Clutch reservoir . . . . .check level **HB**
GM Part No. 12345347 preferred

W Cooling system . . . . . . .inspect hoses & tighten clamps

Throttle linkage . . . . .inspect

Transmission, automatic . . . .check level

EVERY 12 MO/5 MI—8 KM
Brake master cylinder . . .check level **HB**

W Crankcase . . . . .change oil & filter

Power steering . . . . .check level **PS**

Front suspension & steering . .lubricate **LB**
Do not lube ball joints or king pin bushings below 10°F (−12°C)

Parking brake cable guides . .lubricate **LB**

Park brake cams . . . . .lubricate **LB**
Motor home 16,000 GVW chassis

Propeller shaft spline . . . . .lubricate **SLG**
2WD/auto. trans. powertrain equipped with one-piece propshaft

Propeller shafts . . . . .lubricate **LB**
4WD: Front axle propshaft spline, rear driveline, center splines

Transfer case . . . . .check level

Body . . . . .lubricate
Ex. 1997-00 G-van door hinges

EVERY 10 MI—16 KM
Air intake system . . . . .inspect

Engine shields & insulation . . . . .check condition

EVERY 12 MO/10 MI—16 KM
Thermostatically controlled fan . . . . .check operation

EVERY 30 MI—48 KM
Clutch fork ball stud . . . .**GC**
Some models—lubricate sparingly

Front wheel bearings
  2WD . . . . .clean/repack **GC**
Tighten spindle nut to 12 ft-lb while turning wheel forward. Adjust spindle nut to "just loose" position by hand. Back off nut until hole in spindle aligns with slot. Do not back off more than 1/4 turn

W Air cleaner element. . . . . .replace
G-van

W Fuel filter . . . . .replace

EVERY 50 MI—80 KM
Transmission,
  automatic, 1998-00 . . . . .change
                   fluid and filter

EVERY 60 MI—96 KM
W CDRV system . . . . .check

W Drive belts . . . . .inspect/replace

W EGR system . . . . .check
As equipped ex. Code F engines

W Exhaust pressure regulator valve . . . . .check operation

1996
EVERY 60 MO/100 MI—160KM
1997-00
EVERY 60 MO/150 MI—240 KM
Cooling system . . . . .change coolant **EC**
Flush system, inspect hoses. Replace hoses if checked, swollen or rotted. Use 50% concentration for −34°F (−37°C) protection. 1996-97, add 2 coolant sealer pellets, GM Part No. 3634621 **Note:** If silicated coolant is used, change every 24 mo/30 mi (50 km)

SEVERE SERVICE
W Air cleaner—Van, inspect when in dusty conditions; every 15 mi (24 km) or sooner in extremely dusty conditions

Fuel cap—When in dustry conditions, re-place every 25 mi (40 km)

W Crankcase—Change oil & filter every 3 mo/2.5 mi (4 km)

Chassis—Lubricate every oil change

Differentials—Check lubricant every: 1996-97, 5 mi (8 km); 1998-00, 2.5 mi (4 km). When trailer towing or in dusty con-ditions, change lubricant every 15 mi (24 km). HD 3500 operating for extended time periods over 45 mph (72 kph), change fluid every 30 mi (48 km)

W Fittings—Lubricate every 3 mo/2.5 mi (4 km)

Front wheel bearings, 2WD—Repack every 15 mi (24 km)

King pins and bushings, I-beam axle—lubricate every 1.5 mi (2.5 km)

Tires—Inspect & rotate every 7.5 mi (12 km)

Transfer case—Off road use may need more frequent lubrication

Transmission, automatic—1996-97, Change fluid and filter every 50 mi (80 km) when GVWR is over 8,600 lb or in either: heavy city traffic at temperatures regularly above 90°F (32°C); hilly terrain; taxi, po-lice, delivery, trailer towing service

KEY TO LUBRICANTS

AF3	DEXRON®-III Automatic Transmission Fluid
CF-4	Motor Oil, API Service CF-4
CG-4	Motor Oil, API Service CG-4
EC	Ethylene Glycol Coolant GM DEX-COOL®, or Havoline® DEX-COOL®
GC	Wheel Bearing Grease, NLGI No. 2, Category GC
GLS	Special Gear Lubricant GM Part No. 12345349
GL-5	Gear Oil, API Service GL-5
HB	Hydraulic Brake Fluid, DOT 3 Delco Supreme II® GM Part No. 12377967
LB	Chassis Grease, NLGI No. 2, Category LB or GC-LB
PS	Power Steering Fluid GM Part No. 1052884
SH	Motor Oil, API Service SH Use Energy Conserving II Oils
SLG	Special Lubricant—Grease GM Part No. 1235879, Spec. 9985830
SLF	Automatic Transfer Case Fluid GM Part No. 12378396

CRANKCASE . . . . .CG-4[1], SH/CF-4

CAPACITY, Refill[2]:	Liters	Qt
6.5L 1996-97	6.5	7.0
6.5L 1998-00	7.6	8.0
Above 0°F (-18°C) . . . . .15W-40[3]		
Above 32°F (0°C) 30		
Below 32°F (0°C) 10W-30		

1 1998-00, required; 1996-97 preferred.
2 Includes filter. After refill level must be checked.
3 Preferred.

TRANSMISSION, Automatic AF3

CAPACITY, Initial Refill[4]:	Liters	Qt
4L60, 4L60E, 4L80E	4.7	5.0
4L80E, 2000	7.3	7.7

4 Add specified quantity. With the engine at operating tem-perature, shift transmission through all gears. Let engine slow idle in PARK for 3 minutes or more. Check fluid level and add fluid as needed.

TRANSMISSION, Manual
NV3500 (Sectional case) . . . .**GLS**
GM Part No. 12345349
NV4500
(Top cover) . . . . . .Synthetic 75W-90 **GL-4**
GM Part No. 12346190, or equivalent

CAPACITY, Refill:	Liters	Pt
Sectional case	2.0[5]	4.4[5]
Top cover	3.8	8.0

5 Approximate, fill to level of fill plug

TRANSFER CASE, Manual
NV236, 246 . . . .**SLF**
Others **AF3**

CAPACITY, Refill:	Liters	Pt
NV241, 243	2.1	4.5
BW4401	3.1	6.5
BW4470	3.1	6.5
NV236, 246	2.3	4.9

To identify, see tag on case

DIFFERENTIAL
C3500 HD
  w/Dana 11" . . . . .Synthetic 75W-140 **GL-5**
GM Part No. 12346140
All Others
2000 GMT400 . . . . .Synthetic 75W-90 **GL-5**
Part No. 12378261
1999 GMT400 . . . . .80W-90 **GL-5**
Part No. 1052271
All Others 80W-90 **GL-5**
GM Part No. 1052271 preferred
Use synthetic 75W-90 GM Part No. 12345836 in front dif-ferential when Excessive effort is required to shift into 4WD.

CAPACITY, Refill:	Liters	Pt
Front: K1, K2	1.7	3.5
K3 1996-97	2.1	4.5
K3 1998	1.9	3.9
Rear: American Axle:		
8½", 8⅝" ring gear	2.0	4.2
9½" ring gear	2.6	5.5
10½" ring gear	3.1	6.5
Dana 11" ring gear	4.0	8.2

CHEVROLET, GMC TRUCKS
1996-2000 S-Series, Astro, Safari
Oldsmobile Bravada, Isuzu Hombre

SERVICE AT TIME OR MILEAGE — WHICHEVER OCCURS FIRST

CTTPM29   CTTPM29

Perform the following maintenance services at the intervals indicated to keep the vehicle warranties in effect.
W   SERVICE TO MAINTAIN EMISSION WARRANTY

MI—MILES IN THOUSANDS
KM—KILOMETERS IN THOUSANDS

FIRST 7.5 MI—12.5 KM
Tires, 1996 . . . . .check/rotate
Initially, then every 15 mi (25 km) or as necessary

EVERY 3 MONTHS
Tailgate . . . . .lubricate
All pivot points, use multi-purpose lube

EVERY 3 MO/3 MI—5 KM
Crankcase . . . . .change oil & filter
2.2L Code 5 engine which has used Ethanol Fuel since last oil change

EVERY 6 MONTHS
Brake master cylinder . . .check level **HB**

Clutch fluid reservoir . . . .check level **HB**
Part No. 12345347 preferred

Power steering
   reservoir . . . . .check level **PS**

Throttle linkage . . . . .inspect
Do not lubricate throttle or cruise control cables

Exhaust system . . . . .inspect

Brakes . . . . .inspect hoses/pads
Inspect drum brake lining, check parking brake, brake lines & hoses

EVERY 7.5 MI—12.5 KM
U-joints, axle seals . . . . .check

Tires, 1997-00 . . . . .check/rotate

EVERY 12 MO/7.5 MI—12 KM
W Crankcase . . . . .change oil & filter
Ex. 2.2L Code 5 engine which has used Ethanol Fuel since last oil change

Brake pedal springs . . . . . . .lubricate **LB**

Clutch pedal springs . . . . . . .lubricate **LB**

Fittings . . . . .lubricate **LB**

Parking brake cable guides . . . . .coat **LB**

Propeller shaft spline . . . . .lubricate **SLG**
Astro and Safari: 2WD/auto. trans. powertrain equipped with one-piece propshaft only

Propeller shafts . . . . .lubricate **LB**
Front axle propshaft spline, rear driveline, center splines

Shift linkage . . . . .coat **LB**
With floor shift, coat lever contact faces

Differentials . . . . .check level

Suspension & steering . . . . .inspect

Transfer case shift linkage . . . .**LB**

Transfer case, AWD . . . .**LB**
Lube control lever pivot point

Transfer case . . . . .check level
Check vent hose

Transmission, automatic . . . .check level

W Cooling system . . . . . . .check level **EC**

Body . . . . .lubricate
Flush underbody every spring

EVERY 30 MI—48 KM
W Air cleaner element . . . . .replace

W Fuel filter . . . . .replace

Front wheel bearings,
   2WD . . . . .clean/repack **GC**
Tighten spindle nut to 12 ft-lb while turning wheel forward. Adjust spindle nut to finger tight. Back off until the hole in spindle aligns with slot. Do not back off more than ½ flat.

Transmission,
   automatic . . . . .change fluid and filter
1996-97 Astro and Safari

EVERY 50 MI—80 KM
Transmission,
   automatic . . . . .change fluid and filter
1998-00

EVERY 60 MI—100 KM
W Engine drive belts . . . . . .inspect/replace

W Fuel tank, cap, lines, 1996-99 . . .inspect

EVERY 100 MI—160 KM
W Spark plugs . . . . .replace

W Spark plug wires . . . . .inspect

W PCV system . . . . .inspect

1996
EVERY 60 MO/100 MI—160 KM
1997-00
EVERY 60 MO/150 MI—240 KM
W Cooling system . . . . .change coolant **EC**
Flush system; inspect hoses, tighten clamps. Use 50% (1995-97) mixture for −34°F (−37°C) protection. Add 2 pellets Part No. 3634621. If silicated coolant is used, change coolant every 24 mo/30 mi (50 km).

SEVERE SERVICE
Crankcase—Change oil and filter every 3 mi (5 km). Also lubricate chassis.

Air Cleaner—Dusty conditions, replace every 15 mi (24 km)

Differential—Check lubricant every oil change.

Front wheel bearings—2WD only, repack every 15 mi (24 km) or whenever brakes are relined

Tires—Inspect, rotate at: 1996, 6 mi (10 km), then every 15 mi (25 km); 1997-00, every 6 mi (10 km)

Transmission, automatic—Change fluid and filter every 15 mi (24 km) when operating in either heavy city traffic at temperatures regularly above 90°F (32°C), hilly terrain, taxi, police, delivery, or trailer towing service

---

KEY TO LUBRICANTS

AF3   Automatic Transmission Fluid DEXRON®-III

API★   Motor Oil certified by the American Petroleum Institute (Starburst Symbol)

EC   Ethylene Glycol Coolant GM DEX-COOL®, or Havoline® DEX-COOL®

GC   Wheel Bearing Grease, NLGI #2 Category GC or GC-LB

GL-5   Gear Oil, API Service GL-5

GLS   Special Gear Lubricant NV1500, GM Part No. 12377916 NV3500, GM Part No. 12345349

HB   Hydraulic Brake Fluid, DOT 3 GM Part No. 12377967 or equivalent

LB   Chassis Grease, NLGI Category LB

PS   Power Steering Fluid GM Part No. 1052884

SLF   Automatic Transfer Case Fluid Beginning with models produced starting late June, 1999, use only Part No. 12378508 which is colored blue. Other models should also use Part No. 12378508. Mixing of blue fluid with the old red Autotrac fluid Part No. 12378396 for top off is permitted.

SLG   Special Lubricant—Grease GM Part No. 12345879, GM Spec. 9985830

CRANKCASE . . . .**API★**

CAPACITY, Refill:	Liters	Qt
All	4.3	4.5

Includes filter. Level must be checked after refill.
Above 0°F (−18°C) 10W-30
All temperatures . . . . .5W-30[1]
[1] Preferred

TRANSMISSION, Automatic **AF3**

CAPACITY, Initial Refill[2]:	Liters	Qt
4L40E, 4L60E	4.7	5.0

[2] With the engine at operating temperature, shift transmission through all gears. Check fluid level in PARK and add fluid as needed.

TRANSMISSION, Manual

NV1500, 4-cyl.. . . . .**GLS**
GM Part No. 12377916
NV3500, V6. . . . .**GLS**
GM Part No. 12345349

CAPACITY, Initial Fill:	Liters	Pt
NV1500	2.7	5.8
NV3500	2.0	4.4

TRANSFER CASE

Manual **AF3**
Automatic . . . .**SLF**

CAPACITY, Refill:	Liters	Pt
NV 231, 233	1.2	2.6
BW 4472	1.2	2.6
NV 136, 236, 246	2.3	4.9

DIFFERENTIAL

Standard & locking 80W-90 **GL-5**
GM Part No. 1052271 preferred

CAPACITY, Refill:	Liters	Pt
Front	1.2	2.6
Rear Astro and Safari	1.7	3.5
Others	1.9	4.0

CHRYSLER, DODGE, PLYMOUTH

1989-2000 All Models including FWD Vans
Except Colt, Colt Vista, Conquest, Laser (1990-94), Stealth, Sebring Coupe, Avenger, Viper, Prowler

SERVICE LOCATIONS — ENGINE AND CHASSIS

HOOD RELEASE: Inside

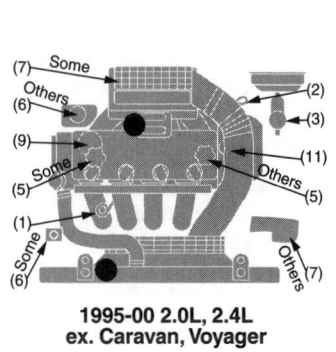

1995-00 2.0L, 2.4L
ex. Caravan, Voyager

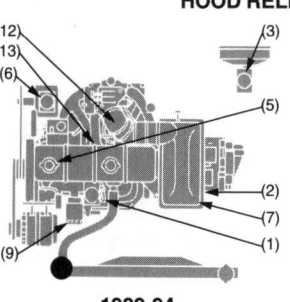

1989-94
2.2L (135) FI

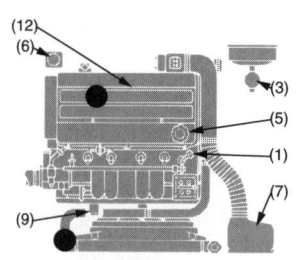

1989-93 2.2L 16V Turbo

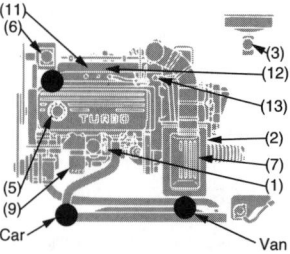

1989-92
2.2L (135) & 2.5L Turbo
ex. 16V

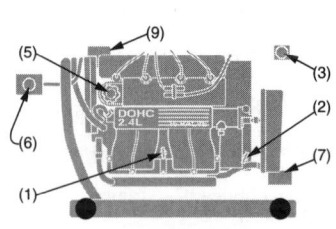

1996-00 2.4L
Caravan, Voyager

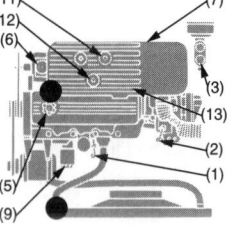

1989-95
2.5L (153) 4-cyl.

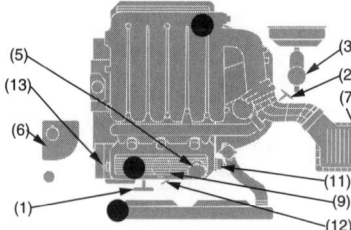

1995-00
2.5L V6

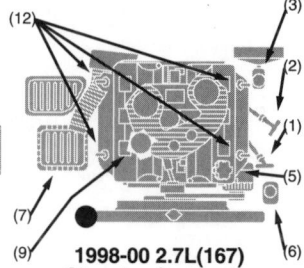

1998-00 2.7L(167)
Chrysler Concorde,
Dodge Intrepid

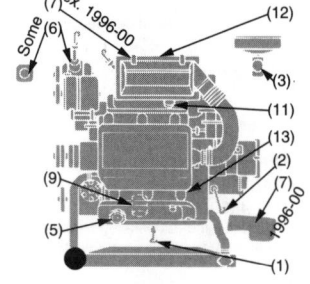

1989-00
3.0L (182)

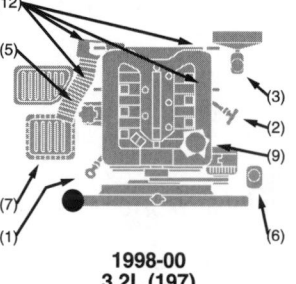

1998-00
3.2L (197)
1999-00 3.5L

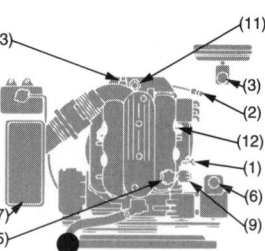

1993-97 3.3L
Concorde, Intrepid,
New Yorker

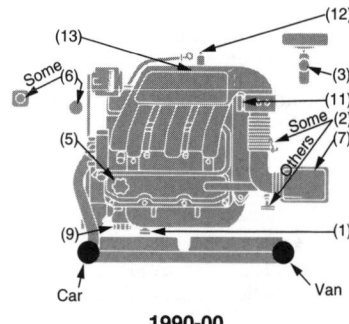

1990-00
Other 3.3L, 3.8L

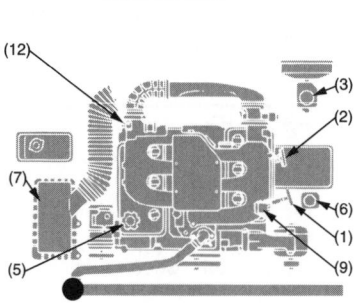

1993-97 3.5L

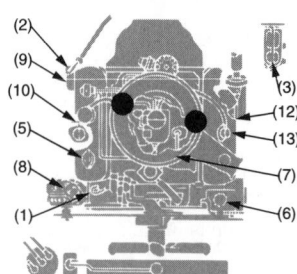

1989
5.2L (318)

(1) Crankcase dipstick	(5) Oil fill cap	(10) PCV filter
(2) Transmission dipstick	(6) Power steering reservoir	(11) EGR valve
(3) Brake fluid reservoir	(7) Air filter	(12) Oxygen sensor
(4) Clutch fluid reservoir	(8) Fuel filter	(13) PCV valve
	(9) Oil filter	

● Cooling system drain   ○ Cooling system drain, some models

CHRYSLER, DODGE, PLYMOUTH
1989-2000 All Models including FWD Vans
Except Colt, Colt Vista, Conquest, Laser (1990-94), Stealth, Sebring Coupe, Avenger, Viper, Prowler

SERVICE LOCATIONS — ENGINE AND CHASSIS

CRDP-2

CRDP-2

0-2 FITTINGS

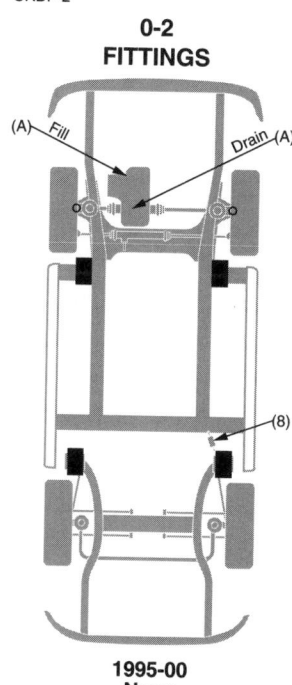

(A) Fill

Drain (A)

(8)

**1995-00
Neon**

2-4 FITTINGS

(A) Fill

FI & Turbo (8)

**Dodge: Omni,
FWD Charger, De Tomaso
Plymouth: Horizon,
Turismo**

4 FITTINGS

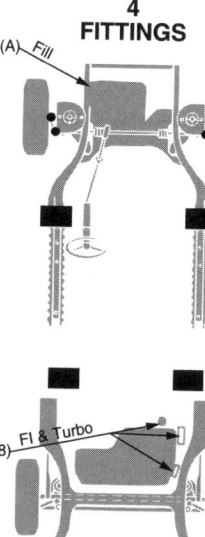

(A) Fill

(8) FI & Turbo

**Chrysler: Laser, FWD LeBaron,
Limousine, E Class, Maserati TC,
FWD New Yorker
Dodge: Aries, 600, Daytona,
Dynasty, Lancer, Shadow, Spirit
Plymouth: Acclaim, Reliant,
FWD Caravelle, Sundance
FWD Imperial**

0-4 FITTINGS

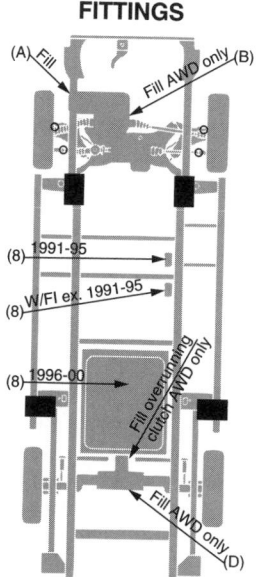

(A) Fill

Fill AWD only (B)

(8) 1991-95

(8) W/FI ex. 1991-95

(8) 1996-00

Fill overrunning clutch AWD only

Fill AWD only (D)

**Mini Ram Van,
Caravan, Voyager
1990-00 Chrysler
Town & Country**

4 FITTINGS

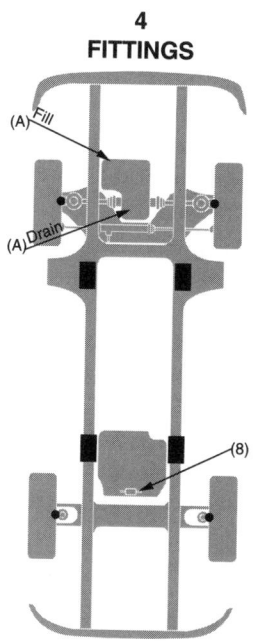

(A) Fill

(A) Drain

(8)

**1995-00
Cirrus, Stratus
1996-00 Breeze,
Sebring Convertible**

0-2 FITTINGS 0 PLUGS

(D) Drain

Fill (D)

1993-97

1993-97

1998-00

Others

(8)

1998-99

**1993-00
Concorde, Intrepid,
New Yorker, LHS
1999-00 300M**

0 FITTINGS 0 PLUGS

(C) Fill

Fill

Drain (A)(C)

(A)

(8)

**1990-92
Dodge Monaco**

9-10 FITTINGS

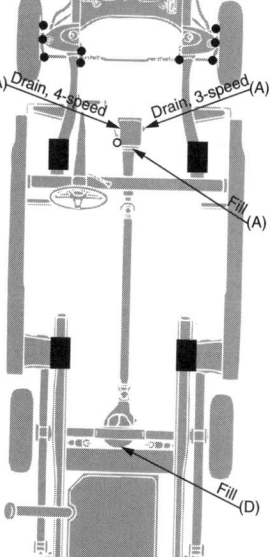

(A) Drain, 4-speed

Drain, 3-speed (A)

Fill (A)

Fill (D)

**1989
RWD New Yorker, 5th Ave.
Dodge: Diplomat
Plymouth:
RWD Caravelle Salon,
Gran Fury**

(A) Manual transmission/transaxle, drain & fill

(B) Transfer case, drain & fill

(8) Fuel filter

(C) Automatic transaxle final drive, drain & fill

(D) Differential, drain & fill

○ Fitting, some models

● Fitting

■ Lift adapter position

CAUTION: On front wheel drive vehicles, the center of gravity is further forward than on rear wheel drive vehicles. When removing major components from the rear of the vehicle while it is on a hoist, the vehicle must be supported in a manner to prevent it from tipping forward.

SERVICE AT TIME OR MILEAGE — WHICHEVER OCCURS FIRST

CRPM11   CRPM11

Dodge Monaco, see Eagle/Renault
W   SERVICE TO MAINTAIN EMISSION WARRANTY

MI—MILES IN THOUSANDS
KM—KILOMETERS IN THOUSANDS

TURBO ENGINE,
EVERY 6 MO/7.5 MI—12 KM

Crankcase . . . . .change oil
Every 3 mo/3 mi (4.8 km) if following oil is not used:
SG/CD

Oil filter . . . . .replace
Every other oil change ex. if mileage is less than 7.5 mi
(12 km) each 12 mo, replace every oil change

EVERY 12 MONTHS

Air conditioning system . . . . .inspect

Cooling system . . . . .inspect

Throttle linkage, V8 . . . . . . .lubricate **LB**

EVERY 12 MO/7.5 MI—12 KM

Brake, fuel & power
  steering hoses . . . . .check

Crankcase ex. Turbo eng. . . . .change oil

Differential . . . . .check for leaks

Exhaust system . . . . .inspect

Front suspension &
  steering linkage . . . . .inspect

Oil filter ex. Turbo eng. . . . . . . .replace
Every other oil change ex. if mileage is less than 7.5 mi
(12 km) each 12 mo, replace every oil change

CV & universal joints & boots . . . .inspect

Brake master cylinder . . .check level **HB**

Power steering reservoir .check level **PS**

Transmission, automatic . . . .check level

Transaxle, manual . . . . .check level

EVERY 15 MI—24 KM

W Drive belts . . . . .inspect/adjust
Do not adjust auto-tension belt. RWD: Check air pump
belts, required for California warranty every 30 mi (48 km)

EGR system, V8 . . . . .inspect
Clean passages

EVERY 22.5 MI—36 KM

Brake linings . . . . .inspect
Replace disc pads when 1/32" above rivet head or
backing plate

Wheel bearings: Front for RWD
  Rear for FWD . . . . .inspect **GC**
Clean and repack whenever brake drums or rotors are
removed. To adjust, torque 20-25 ft lb; back off nut 1/4
turn then finger tighten nut & install lock nut with pin. End
play, .001"-.003"

EVERY 30 MI—48 KM

W Air cleaner element . . . . .replace
FWD Vans only

W Carburetor choke shaft, fast idle cam
  & pivot pin, V8 . . . . .clean **PC**

W PCV filter . . . . .replace
FWD Vans only

W Spark plugs . . . . .replace

EVERY 36 MO/30 MI—48 KM

Front suspension & steering
  linkage . . . . .4-9 fittings **LB**
Fill until grease flows out. Do not rupture seals

FIRST 36 MO/52.5 MI—84 KM;
THEN EVERY 24 MO/30 MI—48 KM

Cooling system . . . .change coolant **EC**
Flush system

EVERY 52.5 MI—84 KM

Air cleaner element . . . . .replace
Ex. vans

Crankcase inlet air
  cleaner RWD . . . . .clean/oil

FWD VANS: EVERY 60 MI—96 KM

EGR valve & tube . . . . .replace
At mileage or every 60 mo or when indicated by
emissions maintenance reminder light if equipped. Also
clean passages every 60 mi (96 km)

Ignition cables . . . . .replace

Distributor cap & rotor . . . . .replace
Check distributor

Ignition timing . . . . .check/adjust

PCV valve . . . . .replace
When indicated by emissions maintenance reminder light
if equipped

Timing belt 3.0L eng. . . . . .check/replace
Thereafter every 30 mi (48 km)

Vacuum operated
  emission components . . . . . . .inspect

FWD VANS: EVERY 75 MI—120 KM

Alternator brushes . . . . .replace

EVERY 82.5 MI—132 KM

Oxygen sensor . . . . .replace
Or when indicated by emissions maintenance reminder
light if equipped

SERVICE AS REQUIRED

Clutch cable FWD . . . . . . .lubricate **LB**

Tires . . . . .inspect/rotate

Transmission linkage FWD . .lubricate **LB**

Fuel filter . . . . .replace

PCV system . . . . .inspect

Locks & hinges . . . . .lubricate

SEVERE SERVICE

Brake lining—Inspect every 9 mi (14 km)

Crankcase—Change oil: Highway, police,
taxi, limousine, when not operating at sustained high speed driving when above
90°F (32°C), every 6 mo/5 mi (8 km); all
others, every 3 mo/3 mi (4.8 km). Replace
filter every second oil change

Rear differential—Change lubricant every
36 mi (57.6 km)

Front suspension ball joints—FWD, inspect every 3 mo/3 mi (4.8 km); others, lubricate every 18 mo/15 mi (24 km)

Front wheel bearings—Ex. FWD, clean
and repack every 9 mi (14 km) or whenever brake rotors are removed

Steering linkage—Lubricate every 18
mo/15 mi (24 km)

Rear wheel bearings—FWD, clean or
repack every 9 mi (14 km), or whenever
rear brake drums are removed

Transmission, automatic—Change fluid
every 15 mi (24 km). Replace filter & adjust
bands at each drain

Transaxle, manual—Change lubricant
and clean magnet every 15 mi (24 km)

CV & universal joints—Inspect every 3
mo/3 mi (4.8 km)

Air cleaner element—Inspect every 15 mi
(24 km)

KEY TO LUBRICANTS

AF2	DEXRON®-II ATF
AP3	MOPAR ATF+3®
CD	Motor Oil, API Service CD
EC	Ethylene Glycol Coolant Mix 50% to 70% with water
GC	Wheel Bearing Grease, NLGI Classification GC
GL-5	Gear Oil, API Service GL-5
GL-5★	Special Lubricant for Sure-Grip Differential Chrysler Part No. 4318059 plus 4 oz. Part No. 4318060
HB	Hydraulic Brake Fluid, DOT 3
LB	Chassis Grease, NLGI Classification LB
PC	Carburetor Cleaner
PS	Power Steering Fluid
SG	Motor Oil, API Service SG

CRANKCASE . . . . .SG, SG/CD[1]
[1] Preferred with Turbo engine

CAPACITY, Refill:	Liters	Qt
All	3.8	4.0

Capacity shown is without filter. When replacing filter, additional oil may be needed

Above 20°F (−7°C) 10W-30, 15W-40, 30
20° to 80°F (−7° to 27°C) 20W-20
Above 10°F (−12°C) 15W-40
Above 0°F (−18°C) 10W-30
Below 100°F (38°C) . . . . .5W-30[2]
[2] Not recommended in Turbo or 4-cyl. Vans; above 32°F
(0°C) or in all 5.2L-4V engines at any temperature
5.2L-4V engines used for maximum performance service:
40, 30, or 20W-40, 20W-50 providing cold starting is satis-
factory

TRANSMISSION/TRANSAXLE,
Automatic AP3

CAPACITY, Initial Refill[4]:	Liters	Qt
All	3.8	4.0

[4] With the engine at operating temperature, shift transmission through all gears. Check fluid level in PARK and add
fluid as needed

TRANSAXLE, Manual

Horizon, Omni AF2, AP3
Ex. Horizon,
  Omni . . . . .5W-30 SG, SG/CD

CAPACITY, Refill:	Liters	Pt
5-speed A525	2.1	4.6
5-speed A520, A523, A543, A555, A568, A569	2.3	4.8

REAR DIFFERENTIAL

Standard GL-5
Sure-Grip . . . . .90 GL-5★
Above −10°F (−23°C), 90, 80W-90, 85W-90; −30°
to −10°F (−34° to −23°C), 80W, 80W-90, 85W-90;
below −30°F (−34°C), 75W

CAPACITY, Refill:	Liters	Pt
7¼" ring gear w/2½" dia. axle tube[5]	1.2	2.5
8¼" ring gear w/3" dia. axle tube[5]	2.1	4.5

[5] Measured adjacent to differential

CHRYSLER, DODGE, PLYMOUTH
1990 All Models Including FWD Vans
Except Colt, Laser, Monaco, Vista, Ram 50

SERVICE AT TIME OR MILEAGE — WHICHEVER OCCURS FIRST

CRPM12   CRPM12

Dodge Monaco, see Eagle/Renault
W   SERVICE TO MAINTAIN EMISSION WARRANTY

MI—MILES IN THOUSANDS
KM—KILOMETERS IN THOUSANDS

TURBO ENGINE
EVERY 6 MO/7.5 MI—12 KM
Crankcase . . . . .change oil

Oil filter . . . . .replace
Every other oil change ex. if mileage is less than 7.5 mi
(12 km) each 12 mo, replace every oil change

EVERY 12 MONTHS
Air conditioning system . . . . .inspect

Cooling system . . . . .inspect

EVERY 12 MO/7.5 MI—12 KM
Brake, fuel & power
    steering hoses . . . . .check

Crankcase ex. Turbo . . . . . . .change oil

Exhaust system . . . . .inspect

Front suspension & steering
    linkage . . . . .inspect

Oil Filter ex. Turbo . . . . .replace
Every other oil change ex. if mileage is less than 7.5 mi
(12 km) each 12 mo, replace every oil change

Transaxle, manual . . . . .check level

CV joint boots . . . . .inspect

Brake master cylinder . . .check level **HB**

Power steering reservoir .check level **PS**

Transmission, automatic . . . .check level

EVERY 15 MI—24 KM
W Drive belts . . . . .inspect/adjust
Do not adjust auto-tension type

EVERY 22.5 MI—36 KM
Brake linings . . . . .inspect
Replace disc pads when 1/32" above rivet head or
backing plate

Rear wheel bearings . . . . . . .inspect **GC**
Clean and repack whenever brake drums or rotors are
removed. To adjust, torque 20-25 ft lbs; back off nut 1/4
turn then finger tighten nut & install lock nut with pin. End
play, .001"-.003"

EVERY 30 MI—48 KM
W Air cleaner element . . . . .replace
FWD Vans only

W PCV filter . . . . .replace
FWD Vans only

W Spark plugs . . . . .replace

EVERY 36 MO/30 MI—48 KM
Front suspension & steering
    linkage . . . .**2-4 fittings LB**
Fill until grease flows out. Do not rupture seals

FIRST 36 MO/52.5 MI—84 KM;
THEN EVERY 24 MO/30 MI—48 KM
Cooling system . . . . .change coolant **EC**
Flush system

EVERY 52.5 MI—84 KM
W Air cleaner element ex. Vans . . . .replace

W Crankcase inlet air filter
    ex. Vans . . . . .clean/oil

FWD VANS
EVERY 60 MI—96 KM
Drive belts . . . . .replace

EGR valve & tube . . . . .replace
Or when indicated by emissions maintenance reminder
light if equipped. Also clean passages

Ignition cables . . . . .replace

Distributor cap & rotor ex. 3.3L . .replace

Ignition timing ex. 3.3L . . . . .check/adjust

PCV valve . . . . .replace
Or when indicated by emissions maintenance reminder
light if equipped

Timing belt 3.0L . . . . .check/replace
Thereafter every 30 mi (48 km)

Vacuum operated emission
    components . . . . .inspect

EVERY 82.5 MI—132 KM
Oxygen sensor . . . . .replace
Or when indicated by emissions maintenance reminder
light if equipped.

SERVICE AS REQUIRED
Clutch cable FWD . . . . . . .lubricate **LB**

Tires . . . . .inspect/rotate

Transmission linkage . . . . .lubricate **LB**
With manual transmission, remove shift unit and replace
grommets, bushings & clip when lubricating

Fuel filter . . . . .replace

PCV system . . . . .inspect

Locks & hinges . . . . .lubricate

SEVERE SERVICE
Brake linings—Inspect every 9 mi (14 km)

Crankcase—Change oil: Highway, police, taxi, limousine, when not operating at sustained high speed driving above 90°F (32°C), every 6 mo/5 mi (8 km); all others, every 3 mo/3 mi (4.8 km). Replace filter every second oil change

CV joints & front suspension ball joints—Inspect every 3 mo/3 mi (4.8 km)

4WD overrunning clutch and rear carrier—Change fluid every 22.5 mi (36 km)

4WD power transfer unit—Change fluid every 12 mi (29 km)

Rear wheel bearings—Clean or repack every 9 mi (14 km), or whenever rear brake drums are removed

Steerage linkage—Lubricate every 18 mo/15 mi (24 km)

Transaxle, manual—Change lubricant and clean magnet every 15 mi (24 km)

Transmission, automatic—Change fluid every 15 mi (24 km). Replace filter & adjust bands at each drain

Air cleaner element—Inspect every 15 mi (24 km)

KEY TO LUBRICANTS

AF2	DEXRON®-II ATF
AP3	MOPAR ATF+3®
CD	Motor Oil, API Service CD
EC	Ethylene Glycol Coolant Mix 50% to 70% with water
GC	Wheel Bearing Grease, NLGI Classification GC
GL-5	Gear Oil, API Service GL-5 Chrysler Part No. 4318059 plus 4 oz. Part No. 4318060
HB	Hydraulic Brake Fluid, DOT 3
LB	Chassis Grease, NLGI Classification LB
MA	MERCON® Automatic Transmission Fluid
MH	Manifold Heat Valve Solvent
PS	Power Steering Fluid
SF	Motor Oil, API Service SF
SG	Motor Oil, API Service SG

CRANKCASE . . . .**SG, SG/CD[1]**
[1] Preferred with Turbo engine

CAPACITY, Refill:	Liters	Qt
All	3.8	4.0

Capacity shown is without filter. When replacing filter, additional oil may be needed

All eng. above 0°F (–18°C) . . . . .10W-30[2]
2.5L Van & Turbo below 32°F (0°C) . . . . . .5W-30[3]
Non-Turbo ex. 2.5L Van
    below 100°F (38°C) 5W-30

[2] Preferred in all Turbo, 2.5L Van
[3] Preferred in all non-Turbo ex. 2.5L Van

TRANSMISSION/TRANSAXLE,
    Automatic **AP3**

CAPACITY, Initial Refill[5]:	Liters	Qt
All	3.8	4.0

[5] With the engine at operating temperature, shift transmission through all gears. Check fluid level in PARK and add fluid as needed

TRANSAXLE, Manual
Horizon, Omni **AF2, AP3**
All Others . . . . .5W-30 **SG, SG/CD**

CAPACITY, Refill:	Liters	Pt
5-speed A525	2.1	4.6
5-speed A520, A523, A543, A555, A568, A569	2.3	4.8

CHRYSLER, DODGE, PLYMOUTH
1991-92 All Models Including FWD Vans
Except Colt, Laser, Monaco, Stealth, Vista

SERVICE AT TIME OR MILEAGE — WHICHEVER OCCURS FIRST

Dodge Monaco, see Eagle/Renault
W   SERVICE TO MAINTAIN EMISSION WARRANTY

MI—MILES IN THOUSANDS
KM—KILOMETERS IN THOUSANDS

EVERY 6 MO/7.5 MI—12 KM
Crankcase . . . . .change oil

Oil Filter . . . . .replace
Every other oil change ex. if mileage is less than 7.5 mi
(12 km) each 12 mo, replace every oil change

EVERY 12 MONTHS
Air conditioning system . . . . .inspect

Cooling system ex. Vans . . . . . . .inspect

EVERY 12 MO/7.5 MI—12 KM
CV joint boots . . . . .inspect

Exhaust system . . . . .inspect

Front suspension & steering
linkage . . . . .inspect

Tires . . . . .inspect/rotate
At mileage interval only

Transaxle, manual . . . . .check level

Brake, fuel & power steering
hoses .check

Brake master cylinder . . .check level **HB**

Cooling system Vans . . . . .inspect

Power steering reservoir   .check level **PS**

Transmission, automatic . . . .check level

EVERY 15 MI—24 KM
W Drive belts . . . . .inspect/adjust
Do not adjust serpentine type

EVERY 22.5 MI—36 KM
Brake linings . . . . .inspect
Replace disc pads when 1/32" above rivet head or
backing plate

Rear wheel bearings . . . . . . .inspect **GC**
Clean and repack whenever brake drums or rotors are
removed. To adjust, torque 20-25 ft lbs; back off nut 1/4
turn then finger tighten nut & install lock nut with pin. End
play, .001"-.003"

EVERY 30 MO/30 MI—48 KM
W Air cleaner element ex. Vans . . . .replace

W Crankcase inlet air filter . . . . . . .clean/oil
Ex. Vans, as equipped

EVERY 30 MI—48 KM
W Air cleaner element . . . . .replace
FWD Vans only

W PCV filter . . . . .replace
FWD Vans only

W Spark plugs . . . . .replace

EVERY 36 MO/30 MI—48 KM
Front suspension & steering
linkage . . . . .2-4 fittings **LB**
Fill until grease flows out. Do not rupture seals

Airbag system . . . . .inspect

FIRST 36 MO/52.5 MI—84 KM;
THEN EVERY 24MO/30 MI—48 KM
Cooling system . . . .change coolant **EC**
Flush system

FWD VANS
EVERY 60 MI—96 KM
Distributor cap & rotor
ex. 3.3L, 3.8L . . . . .replace
Check distributor

Drive belts . . . . .replace
Replace serpentine belts only as needed. If not replaced
at this interval inspect every 30 mi (48 km) thereafter

EGR valve & tube 1991 . . . . . . .replace
Or when indicated by emissions maintenance reminder
light if equipped. Also clean passages

Ignition cables . . . . .replace

Ignition timing ex.
3.3L, 3.8L . . . . .check/adjust

PCV valve . . . . .replace
Or when indicated by emissions maintenance reminder
light if equipped.

Timing belt 3.0L . . . . .check/replace
Thereafter every 30 mi (48 km)

Vacuum operated emission
components . . . . .inspect

EVERY 82.5 MI—132 KM
Oxygen sensor . . . . .replace
Or when indicated by emissions maintenance reminder
light if equipped

SERVICE AS REQUIRED
Brake system . . . . .inspect

Clutch cable FWD . . . . . . .lubricate **LB**

Transmission linkage . . . . .lubricate **LB**

Fuel filter . . . . .replace

PCV system . . . . .inspect

Locks & hinges . . . . .lubricate

SEVERE SERVICE
Brake linings—Inspect every 9 mi (14 km)

Crankcase—Change oil: Highway, police,
taxi, limousine, when not operating at sustained high speed driving above 90°F
(32°C), every 6 mo/5 mi (8 km); all others,
every 3 mo/3 mi (4.8 km). Replace filter
every second oil change

**CV joints & front suspension ball
joints**—Inspect every 3 mo/3 mi (4.8 km)

**AWD overrunning clutch and rear
carrier**—Change fluid every 22.5 mi
(36 km)

AWD power transfer unit—Change fluid
every 15 mi (24 km)

Rear wheel bearings—Clean or repack
every 9 mi (14 km), or whenever rear brake
drums are removed

Steerage linkage—Lubricate every 18 mo/
15 mi (24 km)

Transaxle, manual—Change lubricant
and clean magnet every 15 mi (24 km)

Transmission, automatic—Change fluid
every 15 mi (24 km). Replace filter & adjust
bands at each drain

Air cleaner element—Inspect every 15 mi
(24 km)

KEY TO LUBRICANTS

AF2	DEXRON®-II ATF
AP3	MOPAR ATF+3®
CD	Motor Oil, API Service CD
EC	Ethylene Glycol Coolant Mix 50% to 70% with water
GC	Wheel Bearing Grease, NLGI Classification GC
GL-5	Gear Oil, API Service GL-5 Chrysler Part No. 4318059 plus 4 oz. Part No. 4318060
HB	Hydraulic Brake Fluid, DOT 3
LB	Chassis Grease, NLGI Classification LB
MA	MERCON® Automatic Transmission Fluid
MH	Manifold Heat Valve Solvent
PS	Power Steering Fluid
SF	Motor Oil, API Service SF
SG	Motor Oil, API Service SG

CRANKCASE . . . . .SG, SG/CD[1]
[1] SG/CD required for Turbo engine

CAPACITY, Refill:	Liters	Qt
All	3.8	4.0

Capacity shown is without filter. When replacing filter, additional oil may be needed

All eng. above 0°F (−18°C) . . . . .10W-30[2]
2.5L Van & Turbo below 32°F (0°C) . . . . .5W-30[3]
Non-Turbo ex. 2.5L Van
below 100°F (38°C) 5W-30
[2] Preferred in all Turbo, 2.5L Van
[3] Preferred in all non-Turbo ex. 2.5L Van

TRANSMISSION/TRANSAXLE,
Automatic AP3

CAPACITY, Initial Refill[5]:	Liters	Qt
All	3.8	4.0

[5] With the engine at operating temperature, shift transmission through all gears. Check fluid level in PARK and add
fluid as needed

TRANSAXLE,
Manual . . . . .5W-30 **SG, SG/CD**

CAPACITY, Refill:	Liters	Pt
5-speed A525	2.1	4.6
5-speed A520, A523, A543, A555, A568, A569	2.3	4.8

AWD MINI VAN
Power Transfer Unit &
Rear Carrier Assembly 80W-90 **GL-5**
Overrunning Clutch AP3

CAPACITY, Refill:	Liters	Pt
Power Transfer Unit	1.15	2.4
Rear Carrier	1.9	4.0
Overrunning Clutch	0.4	0.8

CHRYSLER, DODGE, PLYMOUTH
1993-97 All Models Including FWD Vans & Eagle Vision
Except Colt, Laser, Stealth, Viper, Vista, Prowler, Sebring Coupe & Avenger

SERVICE AT TIME OR MILEAGE — WHICHEVER OCCURS FIRST

MI—MILES IN THOUSANDS
KM—KILOMETERS IN THOUSANDS

1995-97, EVERY MONTH
Battery . . . . .clean/inspect
Radiator .inspect
1996-97 FWD vans only, check rubber seals on each side (proper fit required)
Cooling reservoir . . . . .check level
Brake master cylinder . . .check level **HB**
Power steering reservoir . .check level **PS**
Transmission, automatic . . . .check level

FLEXIBLE FUEL MODELS:
EVERY 6 MO/5 MI—8 KM
OTHERS:
EVERY 6 MO/7.5 MI—12 KM
Crankcase . . . . .change oil
Oil Filter . . . . .replace
1995-97 2.0L, 2.4L engines, at oil change. All others every second oil change
CV joint boots . . . . .inspect
Exhaust system . . . . .inspect
Front suspension & steering
  linkage . . . . .inspect
Tires . . . . .inspect/rotate
1993, at mileage interval only
Transaxle, manual . . . . .check level
Brake & power steering hoses . . . .check
Brake master cylinder . . .check level **HB**
Cooling system . . . . .inspect
Power steering reservoir . .check level **PS**
Transmission, automatic . . . .check level

EVERY 12 MONTHS
Air conditioning system . . . . .inspect
Coolant concentration (1995-97) . .check

EVERY 12 MO/15 MI—24 KM
W Drive belts . . . . .inspect/adjust
Ex. with automatic tensioner
Automatic seat belt track . . . . .lubricate
1993-95, if equipped

EVERY 22.5 MI—36 KM
Brake linings . . . . .inspect
Replace disc pads when 1/32" above rivet head or backing plate
Rear wheel bearings . . . . . .inspect **GC**
1995 LeBaron, Spirit, Acclaim & FWD Vans only. Clean and repack whenever brake drums or rotors are removed. To adjust, torque 20-25 ft lbs; back off nut 1/4 turn then finger tighten nut & install locknut with pin. End play, .001"-.003"

EVERY 24 MO/30 MI—48 KM
W Air cleaner element . . . . .replace
W PCV filter (1993-95) . . . . .replace
If equipped
W Spark plugs . . . . .replace
Ex. 2.5L V-6 & 1996-97 FWD Van 3.3L, 3.8L
Timing belt . . . . .inspect
1994 3.0L van only. Replace as needed

1993, EVERY 36 MO/30 MI—48 KM
1994-97, EVERY 24 MO/30 MI—48 KM
Front suspension ball joints & steering
  linkage . . . . .2-4 fittings **LB**
Fill until grease flows out. Do not rupture seals

FIRST 36 MO/52.5 MI—84 KM;
THEN EVERY 24 MO/30 MI—48 KM
Cooling system . . . . .change coolant **EC**
Flush system. Add 1 Mopar stop leak nugget part no. 4318005

EVERY 48 MO/60 MI—96 KM
Distributor cap & rotor Vans
  ex. 3.3L, 3.8L . . . . .replace
Drive belts . . . . .replace
Ex. with automatic tensioner

Drive belts . . . . .inspect
Models with automatic tensioner. Inspect every 30 mi (48 km) thereafter if belts are not replaced
W Ignition cables . . . . .replace
Ex. 1996-97 2.5L v6 & FWD Van 3.3L, 3.8L
Ignition timing ex.3.3L, 3.8L; 1995, 2.5L & 3.0L FWD vans only . . . . . .check/adjust
W PCV valve . . . . .inspect
Replace as needed. Inspect every 30 mi (48 km) thereafter if valve is not replaced
Timing belt 3.0L
  ex. 1994 Vans . . . . .check/replace
Thereafter every 30 mi (48 km) if not replaced
Vacuum operated emission
  components Vans . . . . .replace

EVERY 90 MI—144 KM
Timing belt 4-cyl. (1995, 2.5L) . . .replace

EVERY 100 MI—160 KM
W Spark plugs (1995-97) . . . . .replace
2.5L V6 & FWD Van 3.3L, 3.8L
W Ignition cables (1996-97) . . . . . .replace
2.5L V6 & FWD Van 3.3L, 3.8L only

EVERY 105 MI—168 KM
W Timing belt (1995-97) . . . . .replace
2.0L, 2.4L, & 3.2L only except 2.4L FWD vans
W Spark plugs (1995-97) . . . . .replace
2.7L & 3.2L only

EVERY 120 MI—192 KM
W Timing belt (1995-97) . . . . .replace
2.4L FWD vans only

SERVICE AS REQUIRED
Brake system . . . . .inspect
Clutch cable FWD . . . . . . .lubricate **LB**
Transmission linkage . . . . .lubricate **LB**
With manual transmission, remove shift unit & replace grommets, bushings & clip when lubricating
Fuel filter . . . . .replace
Locks & hinges . . . . .lubricate

SEVERE SERVICE
Brake & power steering hoses, exhaust & cooling system—1995-97: Inspect/check every 3 mi (4.8 km)
Brake linings—Inspect every 9 mi (14 km)
Crankcase—Change oil: Highway, police, taxi, limousine, when not operating at sustained high speed driving above 90°F (32°C), every 6 mo/5 mi (8 km); all others, every 3 mo/3 mi (4.8 km). Replace filter every second oil change, ex. 1995-97 2.0L, 2.4L engines, replace filter at all oil changes
CV joints & front suspension ball joints—Inspect every 3 mo/3 mi (4.8 km)
AWD overrunning clutch and rear carrier—Change fluid every 22.5 mi (36 km)
AWD power transfer unit—Change fluid every 15 mi (24 km)
Steerage linkage—Lubricate every 18 mo/15 mi (24 km)
Transmission, automatic—Change fluid every 15 mi (24 km). Replace filter & adjust bands (if equipped)
Transmission, manual—Check level every 3 mi (4.8 km)
Air cleaner element—Inspect every 15 mi (24 km)
PCV valve—Replace as required every 30 mi (48 km)
W Spark plugs & ignition cables—1996-97: Replace every 75 mi (120 km) 2.5L V-6 & FWD van 3.3L, 3.8L only
Final drive differential—(Only vehicles w/longitudinal engine). Change fluid every 15 mi (24 km)
Tires—1995: Rotate every 3 mi (4.8 km), vehicles w/longitudinal engine). Every 6 mi (10 km) vehicles w/transverse engine. 1996-97: Rotate every 6 mi. (10 km)

KEY TO LUBRICANTS

AP3	MOPAR ATF+3®
API★	Motor Oil certified by the American Petroleum Institute (Starburst Symbol)
CD	Motor Oil, API Service CD
EC	Ethylene Glycol Coolant Mix 50% to 70% with water
GC	Wheel Bearing Grease, NLGI Classification GC
GL-5	Gear Oil, API Service GL-5
GLS	Mopar Manual Transmission Fluid Meeting M.S. 9417
HB	Hydraulic Brake Fluid, DOT 3
LB	Chassis Grease, NLGI Classification LB (1995-97: No. 2 EP)
PS	Power Steering Fluid
SG	Motor Oil, API Service SG

CRANKCASE . . .SG, SG/CD[1,2], SH[2], API★[2]
[1] Preferred with Turbo engine. SG/CD required for 1993 Turbo eng.
[2] Flexible fuel engine oil must meet Chrysler Standard MS-9214

CAPACITY, Refill:	Liters	Qt
2.4L (including filter)	4.7	5.0
3.3L, Concorde, Intrepid, Vision .	4.3	4.5
3.5L, All	4.8	5.0
All others	3.8	4.0

Capacity shown is without filter unless otherwise noted. When replacing filter, additional oil may be needed
All eng. above 0°F (−18°C) . . . . .10W-30[3]
1993-94 2.5L Van, 3.5L & Turbo
  below 32°F (0°C) . . . . .5W-30[4]
1993-94 Non-Turbo ex. 2.5L Van
  below 100°F (38°C) 5W-30
1995-97 Below 32°F (O°C) 5W-30
1995-97 Below 90°F (32C) . . . . .5W-30[5]
[3] Preferred in all Turbo, 2.5L Van & 3.5L
[4] Preferred in all non-Turbo ex. 2.5L Van
[5] Not recommended for 3.5L engine or 1995 FWD van 2.5L engine above 32°F (0°C). For these applications: above 0°F (-18°C), 10W-30 preferred.

TRANSMISSION/TRANSAXLE,
Automatic **AP3**
All w/longitudinal eng., does not include final drive

CAPACITY, Initial Refill[7]:	Liters	Qt
All w/transverse engine	3.8	4.0
All w/longitudinal engine	4.2	4.5

[7] With the engine at operating temperature, shift transmission through all gears. Check fluid level in PARK and add fluid as needed

TRANSAXLE, Manual
NVT 350 (A578) . . . .**GLS**
Others . . . . .5W-30 SG, SG/CD

CAPACITY, Refill:	Liters	Pt
5-speed NV T350 (A578)	2.1	4.4
5-speed A525	2.1	4.6
5-speed A520, A523, A543, A555, A568, A569	2.3	4.8

FINAL DRIVE
All w/longitudinal
  engine 75W-90 **GL-5**

CAPACITY, Refill:	Liters	Pt
All	0.9	2.0

AWD MINI VAN
Power Transfer Unit &
  Rear Carrier Assembly 80W-90 **GL-5**
Overrunning Clutch **AP3**

CAPACITY, Refill:	Liters	Pt
Power Transfer Unit	1.15	2.4
Rear Carrier	1.9	4.0
Overrunning Clutch	0.4	0.8

CHEK-CHART

SERVICE AT TIME OR MILEAGE — WHICHEVER OCCURS FIRST

CRPM16   CRPM16

W SERVICE TO MAINTAIN EMISSION WARRANTY

Note: 3.3L FWD van flexible fuel models follow SEVERE SERVICE schedule when using E 85 (ethanol) fuel.

MI—MILES IN THOUSANDS
KM—KILOMETERS IN THOUSANDS

EVERY MONTH
Battery . . . . .clean/inspect
FWD vans & Neon only
Radiator . . . . .inspect
FWD vans only, check rubber seals on each side (proper fit required)
Cooling reservoir . . . . .check level
Brake master cylinder . . .check level **HB**
Power steering
    reservoir . . . . .check level **PS**
All models, ex. FWD vans use MS-9933, Part No. 05010304AA. All others use MS-5931, Part No. 04883077.
Transmission, automatic . . . .check level

EVERY 6 MO/7.5 MI—12 KM
Crankcase . . . . .change oil
Oil filter . . . . .replace
2.0L, 2.4L engines at oil change. All others every second oil change
W Air cleaner element 1999 . . . . . .inspect
2.7L, 3.2L & 3.5L only
CV joint boots . . . . .inspect
Exhaust system . . . . .inspect
Front suspension & steering
    linkage . . . . .inspect
Tires . . . . .inspect/rotate
At mileage interval only
Transaxle, manual . . . . .check level
Brake & power steering hoses . . . .check
Cooling system . . . . .inspect

EVERY 12 MONTHS
Air conditioning system . . . . .inspect
Coolant concentration . . . . .check

EVERY 12 MO/15 MI—24 KM
Drive belts . . . . .inspect/adjust
Ex. with automatic tensioner

EVERY 22.5 MI—36 KM
Brake linings & rotors . . . . .inspect
Replace disc pads when 1/32" above rivet head or backing plate

EVERY 24 MO/30 MI—48 KM
W Air cleaner element . . . . .replace
W Spark plugs . . . . .replace
2.0L, 2.4L & 3.0L only
Suspension ball joints & steering
    linkage . . . . .inspect/lubricate **LB**
0-4 fittings. Fill until grease flows out. Do not rupture seals
Transaxle, automatic . . . . . .change fluid
At mileage
Vehicle with AP3 fluid only. Service w/AP3
Note: Change fluid in 1999 Cirrus/Stratus/ Breeze built before 9-7-98 & service w/AP4. AP4 fluid has no normal service change interval.

FIRST 36 MO/52.5 MI—84 KM;
THEN EVERY 24 MO/30 MI—48 KM
Cooling system . . . . .change coolant **EC**
Flush system. Except 2.7L, 3.2L, 3.5L

EVERY 48 MO/60 MI—96 KM
Drive belts . . . . .replace
2.0L, 2.4L, 2.5L (Ex. FWD Van 2.4L)
Drive belts . . . . .inspect
Models with automatic tensioner. Inspect every 15 mi (24 km) thereafter if belts are not replaced
W Ignition cables . . . . .replace
Ex. 2.5L V6 & FWD Van 3.3L, 3.8L
PCV valve . . . . .inspect
Replace as needed. Inspect every 30 mi (48 km) thereafter if valve is not replaced
W Ignition Timing . . . . .check
1999 2.5L V-6 only

W Timing belt 3.0L . . . . .check/replace
Thereafter every 30 mi (48 km) if not replaced

EVERY 100 MI—160 KM
W Timing belt . . . . .replace
1999 2.7L, 3.2L, 3.5L, ex. Calif.
W Spark plugs . . . . .replace
2.7L, 3.2L, 3.5L, 2.5L V6 & FWD Van 3.3L, 3.8L
W Ignition cables . . . . .replace
2.7L, 3.2L, 3.5L, 2.5L V6 & FWD Van 3.3L, 3.8L only

EVERY 60 MO/100 MI—160 KM
Cooling system . . . . .drain/flush/refill **EC**
2.7L, 3.2L, 3.5L only. Use Mopar® Extended Life Coolant (orange in color). Do not mix w/green coolant

EVERY 105 MI—168 KM
W Timing belt . . . . .replace
1998-99 2.0L, 2.4L, 1998 3.2L
Except 2.4L FWD vans
1999 2.7L, 3.2L, 3.5L Calif. only

EVERY 120 MI—192 KM
W Timing belt . . . . .replace
2.4L FWD vans only

SERVICE AS REQUIRED
Brake system . . . . .inspect
Fuel filter . . . . .replace
Locks & hinges . . . . .lubricate

SEVERE SERVICE
Brake & power steering hoses, exhaust & cooling system—Inspect/check every 3 mi (4.8 km)
Brake linings—Inspect every 9 mi (14 km)
Crankcase—Change oil every 3 mo/3 mi (4.8 km). Replace filter every second oil change ex. 2.0L, 2.4L engines, replace filter at oil change
CV joints & front suspension ball joints—Inspect every 3 mo/3 mi (4.8 km)
AWD overrunning clutch and rear carrier—Change fluid every 21 mi (34 km)
AWD power transfer unit—Change fluid every 15 mi (24 km)
Transaxle, automatic—Change fluid every 15 mi (24 km) where **AP3** is recommended/used. Every 48 mi (77km) where **AP4** is recommended. (Note: 1999 Cirrus/Stratus/Breeze built before 9-7-98 have AP3 installed. Service those models w/**AP4**). Replace filter & adjust bands (if equipped)—Check level every 3 mi (4.8 km)
Transaxle, manual—Check level every 3 mi (4.8 km)
W **Air cleaner element**—Inspect every 15 mi (24 km) ex. 2.7L, 3.2L & 3.5L inspect every 3 mi (4.8 km), replace every 15 mi (24 km)
PCV valve—Replace as required every 30 mi (4.8 km)
W **Spark plugs & ignition cables**—replace every 75 mi (120 km) 2.5L V-6 & FWD van 3.3L, 3.8L only
Final drive differential—(Only vehicles w/longitudinal engine). Change fluid every 15 mi (24 km)
Tires—Rotate every 6 mi (10 km)
Power steering—(Concorde, Intrepid, LHS, 300M only). Change fluid every 30 mi (48 km). Use MS-9933, Part No. 05010304AA.

KEY TO LUBRICANTS

AP3	MOPAR ATF+3®
AP4	MOPAR ATF+4®
API★	Motor Oil certified by the American Petroleum Institute (Starburst Symbol)
EC	Ethylene Glycol Coolant Mix 50% to 70% with water
GC	Wheel Bearing Grease, NLGI Classification GC
GL-5	Gear Oil, API Service GL-5
GLS	Mopar Manual Transmission Fluid Meeting M.S. 9417
HB	Hydraulic Brake Fluid, DOT 3
LB	Chassis Grease, NLGI Classification No. 2 EP LB
PS	Power Steering Fluid

CRANKCASE . . . . .API★[1]
[1] Flexible fuel engine oil must meet Chrysler Standard MS-9214.

CAPACITY, Refill:	Liters	Qt
2.4L (incl. filter)	4.7	5.0
2.7L	4.3	4.5
3.2L, 3.5L	4.3	4.5
All others	3.8	4.0

Capacity shown is without filter unless otherwise noted. When replacing filter, additional oil may be needed.
Below 32°F (0°C) 5W-30
Below 100°F (38°C) . . . . .5W-30[2]
Above 0°F (−18°C) 10W-30
[2] Not recommended for 3.2L/3.5L engine above 32°F (0°C). For these applications: above 0°F (−18°C) 10W-30 preferred.

TRANSMISSION/TRANSAXLE,
Automatic
1999 Cirrus, Stratus, Breeze, Concorde, Intrepid, LHS, 300M **AP4**
All others **AP3**
All w/longitudinal eng., does not include final drive

CAPACITY, Initial Refill[3]:	Liters	Qt
All w/transverse engine	3.8	4.0
All w/longitudinal engine	4.2	4.5

[3] With the engine at operating temperature, shift transmission through all gears. Check fluid level in PARK and add fluid as needed.

TRANSAXLE,
Manual NV T350 (A578) . . . .**GLS**

CAPACITY, Refill:	Liters	Pt
All	2.1	4.4

FINAL DRIVE
All w/longitudinal
    engine 75W-90 **GL-5**

CAPACITY, Refill:	Liters	Pt
All	0.9	2.0

AWD MINI VAN
Power Transfer Unit &
    Rear Carrier Assembly 80W-90 **GL-5**
Overrunning Clutch **AP3**

CAPACITY, Refill:	Liters	Pt
Power Transfer Unit	1.15	2.4
Rear Carrier	1.9	4.0
Overrunning Clutch	0.4	0.8

SERVICE AT TIME OR MILEAGE — WHICHEVER OCCURS FIRST

CRPM17   CRPM17

W   SERVICE TO MAINTAIN EMISSION WARRANTY

Note: 3.3L FWD van flexible fuel models follow SEVERE SERVICE schedule when using E 85 (ethanol) fuel.

MI—MILES IN THOUSANDS
KM—KILOMETERS IN THOUSANDS

EVERY MONTH

Battery . . . . .clean/inspect
FWD vans & Neon only

Radiator . . . . .inspect
FWD vans only, check rubber seals on each side (proper fit required)

Cooling reservoir . . . . .check level

Brake master cylinder . . .check level **HB**

Power steering
reservoir . . . . .check level **PS**
All models, ex. FWD Vans use MS-9933, Part No. 05010304AA. All others use MS-5931, Part No. 04883077.

Transmission, automatic . . . .check level

EVERY 6 MO/7.5 MI—12 KM

Crankcase . . . . .change oil

Oil filter .replace

W Air cleaner element . . . . .inspect
2.7L, 3.2L & 3.5L only

CV joint boots . . . . .inspect

Exhaust system . . . . .inspect

Front suspension & steering
linkage .inspect

Tires . . . . .inspect/rotate
At mileage interval only

Transaxle, manual . . . . .check level

Brake & power steering hoses . . . .check

Cooling system . . . . .inspect

EVERY 12 MONTHS

Air conditioning system . . . . .inspect

Coolant concentration . . . . .check

EVERY 12 MO/15 MI—24 KM

Drive belts . . . . .inspect/adjust
Ex. with automatic tensioner

EVERY 22.5 MI—36 KM

Brake linings & rotors . . . . .inspect
Replace disc pads when 1/32" above rivet head or backing plate

EVERY 24 MO/30 MI—48 KM

W Air cleaner element . . . . .replace

W Spark plugs . . . . .replace
2.0L, 2.4L & 3.0L only

Suspension ball joints & steering
linkage . . . . .inspect/lubricate **LB**
0-4 fittings. Fill until grease flows out. Do not rupture seals

Transaxle, automatic . . . . .change fluid
Some early production models w/AP3 installed only. See dipstick & TSB 21-16-99. 2000 FWD Vans using AP3 may be serviced w/AP4. See TSB 21-18-99

Transaxle, automatic . . . . .adjust bands
FWD Vans w/3 speed only

FIRST 36 MO/52.5 MI—84 KM;
THEN EVERY 24MO/30 MI—48 KM

Cooling system . . . . . .change coolant **EC**
Flush system. Except 2.7L, 3.2L, 3.5L & FWD Vans

EVERY 48 MO/60 MI—96 KM

Drive belts . . . . .replace
2.0L, 2.4L, 2.5L (Ex. FWD Van 2.4L)

Drive belts . . . . .inspect
Models with automatic tensioner. Inspect every 15 mi (24 km) thereafter if belts are not replaced

W Ignition cables . . . . .replace
Ex. 2.5L V6 & FWD Van 3.3L, 3.8L

PCV valve . . . . .inspect
Replace as needed. Inspect every 30 mi (48 km) thereafter if valve is not replaced

W Timing belt 3.0L . . . . .check/replace
Thereafter every 30 mi (48 km) if not replaced

EVERY 100 MI—160 KM

W Timing belt . . . . .replace
2.0L, 2.4L (ex. FWD Vans), 2.7L, 3.2L, 3.5L, ex. Calif.

Transaxle, Automatic . . . . . .change fluid
Replace filter except Neon

W Spark plugs . . . . .replace
2.7L, 3.2L, 3.5L, 2.5L V6 & FWD Van 3.3L, 3.8L

W Ignition cables . . . . .replace
2.7L, 3.2L, 3.5L, 2.5L V6 & FWD Van 3.3L, 3.8L only

EVERY 60 MO/100 MI—160 KM

Cooling system . . . . .drain/flush/refill **EC**
2.7L, 3.2L, 3.5L & FWD Vans only. Use Mopar® Extended Life Coolant (orange in color). Do not mix w/green coolant

EVERY 105 MI—168 KM

W Timing belt . . . . .replace
2.0L, 2.4L (ex. FWD Vans), 2.7L, 3.2L, 3.5L Calif. only

EVERY 120 MI—192 KM

W Timing belt . . . . .replace
2.4L FWD vans only

SERVICE AS REQUIRED

Brake system . . . . .inspect

Fuel filter . . . . .replace

Locks & hinges . . . . .lubricate

Steering shaft seal . . . . .lubricate
FWD Vans only

SEVERE SERVICE

Brake & power steering hoses, exhaust & cooling system—Inspect/check every 3 mi (4.8 km)

Brake linings—Inspect every 9 mi (14 km)

Crankcase—Change oil every 3 mo/3 mi (4.8 km). Replace filter every oil change

CV joints & front suspension ball joints—Inspect every 3 mo/3 mi (4.8 km)

AWD overrunning clutch and rear carrier—Change fluid every 21 mi (34 km)

AWD power transfer unit—Change fluid every 15 mi (24 km)

Transaxle, automatic—Adjust bands on FWD Vans w/3 speed every 15 mi (24 km). Change fluid in all transaxles every 48 mi (77 km). Except some early production models w/AP3 installed, change fluid every 15 mi (24 km). dee sipstick & TSB 21-16-99. Replace filter & adjust bands (if equipped)—Check level every 3 mi (4.8 km)

Transaxle, manual—Check level every 3 mi (4.8 km)

W **Air cleaner element**—Inspect every 15 mi (24 km) ex. 2.7L, 3.2L & 3.5L inspect every 3 mi (4.8 km), replace every 15 mi (24 km)

PCV valve—Replace as required every 30 mi (4.8 km)

W **Spark plugs & ignition cables**—replace every 75 mi (120 km) 2.5L V-6 & FWD van 3.3L, 3.8L only

Final drive differential—(Only vehicles w/longitudinal engine). Change fluid every 15 mi (24 km)

Tires—Rotate every 6 mi (10 km)

Power steering—(Concorde, Intrepid, LHS, 300M only). Change fluid every 30 mi (48 km). Use **MS-9933**, Part No. 05010304AA.

KEY TO LUBRICANTS

AP3	MOPAR ATF+3®
AP4	MOPAR ATF+4®
API★	Motor Oil certified by the American Petroleum Institute (Starburst Symbol)
EC	Ethylene Glycol Coolant Mix 50% to 70% with water
GC	Wheel Bearing Grease, NLGI Classification GC
GL-5	Gear Oil, API Service GL-5
GLS	Mopar Manual Transmission Fluid Meeting M.S. 9417
HB	Hydraulic Brake Fluid, DOT 3
LB	Chassis Grease, NLGI Classification No. 2 EP LB
PS	Power Steering Fluid

CRANKCASE . . . . .API★[1]

[1] Flexible fuel engine oil must meet Chrysler Standard MS-9214.

CAPACITY, Refill:	Liters	Qt
2.4L, 2.7L, 3.2L, 3.5L	4.7	5.0
All others	4.3	4.5

Capacity shown includes filter

Below 32°F (0°C) 5W-30
Below 100°F (38°C) . . . . .5W-30[2]
Above 0°F (−18°C) 10W-30

[2] Not recommended for 3.2L/3.5L engine above 32°F (0°C). For these applications: above 0°F (−18°C) 10W-30 preferred.

TRANSMISSION/TRANSAXLE, Automatic

All *AP4

*Some early production models have AP3 installed. See dipstick & TSB 21-16-99. 2000 FWD Vans using AP3 may be serviced w/AP4. See TSB 21-18-99

All w/longitudinal eng., does not include final drive

CAPACITY, Initial Refill[3]:	Liters	Qt
All w/transverse engine	3.8	4.0
All w/longitudinal engine	4.2	4.5

[3] With the engine at operating temperature, shift transmission through all gears. Check fluid level in PARK and add fluid as needed.

TRANSAXLE,

Manual NV T350 (A578) . . . .**GLS**

CAPACITY, Refill:	Liters	Pt
All	2.1	4.4

FINAL DRIVE

All w/longitudinal
engine 75W-90 **GL-5**

CAPACITY, Refill:	Liters	Pt
All	0.7[4]	1.6[4]

[4] 42LE transaxles built after 7-26-99 fill to ⅜" (9mm) below fill hole.

AWD MINI VAN

Power Transfer Unit &
Rear Carrier Assembly 80W-90 **GL-5**

Overrunning Clutch **AP3**

CAPACITY, Refill:	Liters	Pt
Power Transfer Unit	1.15	2.4
Rear Carrier	1.9	4.0
Overrunning Clutch	0.4	0.8

HOOD RELEASE: Inside

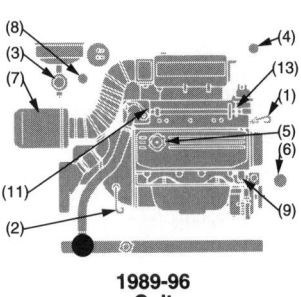

**1989-96
Colt
1.5L FI**

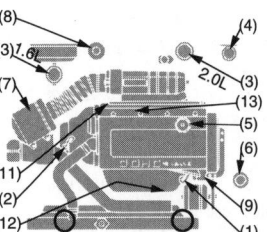

**1989-90
1.6L DOHC
Colt ex. Wagon
1990-94
2.0L Laser DOHC**

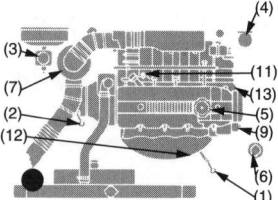

**1989-90
1.8L FI Colt Wagon
1990-94
1.8L Laser**

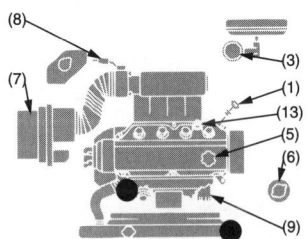

**1992-96
Colt, Colt Wagon/Vista
1.8L**

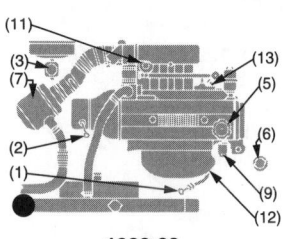

**1989-92
2.0L FI Vista**

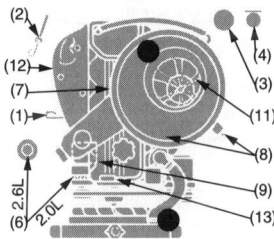

**1989
2.0L 2V & 2.6L 2V
Ram 50, Raider**

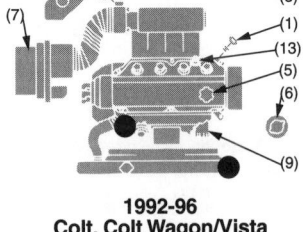

**1995-99
2.0L DOHC
Code Y
Sebring Coupe, Avenger**

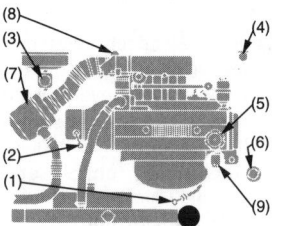

**1993-96
Colt Wagon/Vista
2.4L**

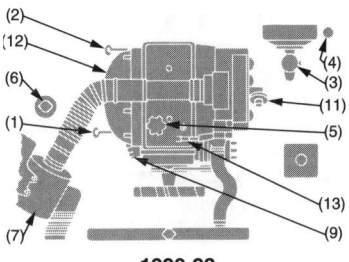

**1990-93
2.4L Ram 50**

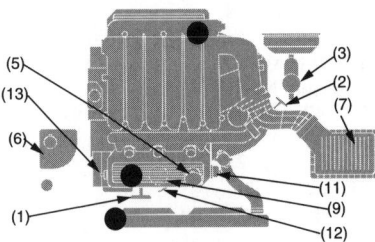

**1995-00
2.5L V6
Sebring Coupe, Avenger**

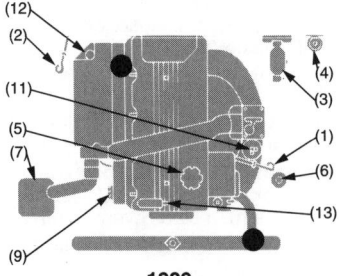

**1989
2.6L Turbo
Conquest**

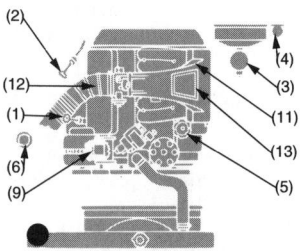

**1989-93
3.0L FI
Ram 50, Raider**

(1) Crankcase dipstick
(2) Transmission dipstick
(3) Brake fluid reservoir
(4) Clutch fluid reservoir

(5) Oil fill cap
(6) Power steering reservoir
(7) Air filter
(8) Fuel filter
(9) Oil filter

(10) PCV filter
(11) EGR valve
(12) Oxygen sensor
(13) PCV valve

● Cooling system drain   ○ Cooling system drain, some models

CHRYSLER, DODGE, PLYMOUTH
1989-2000 Colt, Colt Vista, Conquest, Raider, Ram 50
Laser (1990-94), Stealth, Sebring Coupe, Avenger

SERVICE LOCATIONS — ENGINE AND CHASSIS

CRIDP-2   CRIDP-2

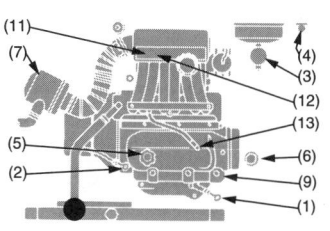

**1991-96
3.0L SOHC
Stealth**

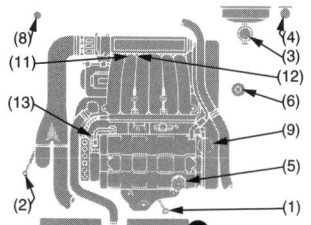

**1991-96
3.0L DOHC
Stealth**

(1) Crankcase dipstick
(2) Transmission dipstick
(3) Brake fluid reservoir
(4) Clutch fluid reservoir
(5) Oil fill cap
(6) Power steering reservoir
(7) Air filter
(8) Fuel filter
(9) Oil filter
(10) PCV filter
(11) EGR valve
(12) Oxygen sensor
(13) PCV valve

● Cooling system drain

○ Cooling system drain, some models

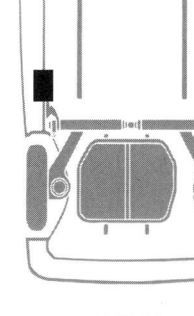

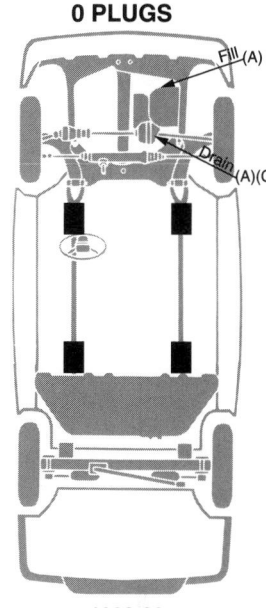

**0 FITTINGS
0 PLUGS**

**1989-92
Colt ex. Wagon**

**0 FITTINGS
0 PLUGS**

**1989-90
Colt Wagon**

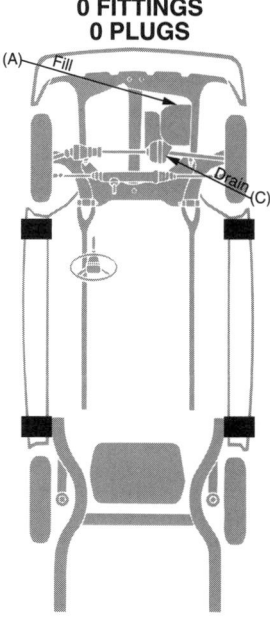

**0 FITTINGS
0 PLUGS**

**1993-96
Colt**

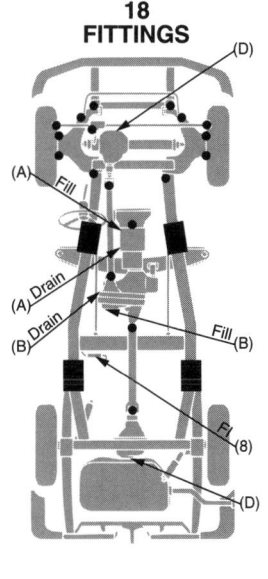

**18
FITTINGS**

**1989
Raider**

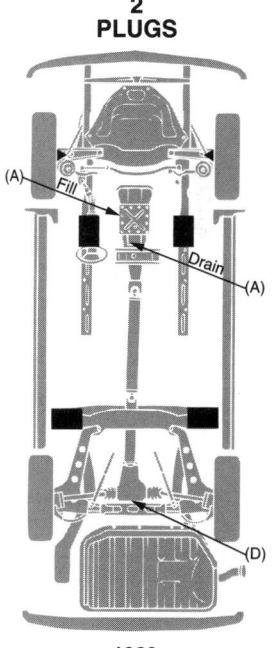

**2
PLUGS**

**1989
Conquest**

CAUTION: On front wheel drive vehicles, the center of gravity is farther forward than on rear wheel drive vehicles. When removing major components from the rear of the vehicle while it is on a hoist, the vehicle must be supported in a manner to prevent it from tipping forward.

■ Lift adapter position ▲ Plug
• Fitting ○ Fitting, some models

(A) Manual transmission/transaxle, drain & fill
(B) Transfer case, drain & fill
(8) Fuel filter
(C) Automatic transaxle final drive, drain & fill
(D) Differential, drain & fill

CHRYSLER, DODGE, PLYMOUTH

1989-2000 Colt, Colt Vista, Conquest, Raider, Ram 50
Laser (1990-94), Stealth, Sebring Coupe, Avenger

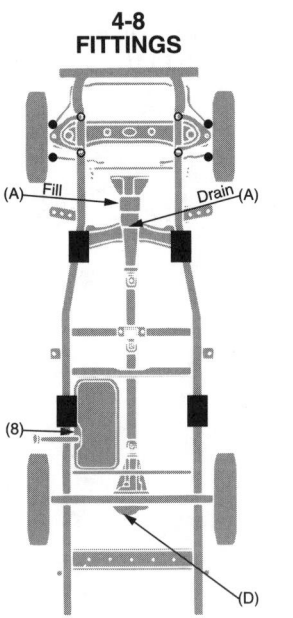

2WD Ram 50, Raider

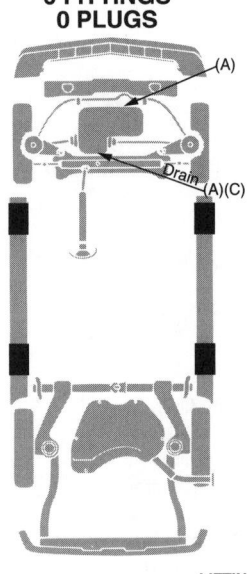

**1989-91
2WD
Colt Vista**

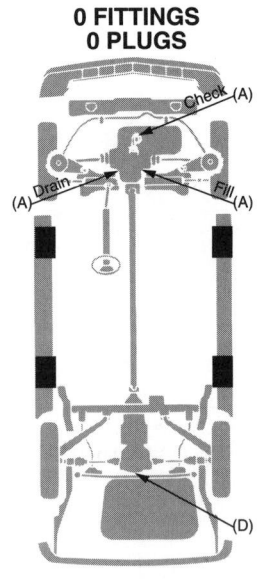

**1989-91
4WD
Colt Vista**

4-8 FITTINGS

9-17 FITTINGS

0 FITTINGS 0 PLUGS

0 FITTINGS 0 PLUGS

4WD Ram 50, Raider

LIFTING CAUTION
When lifting vehicle, ensure that hoist pads are lifted enough to gain adequate clearance between hoist arms and vehicle components.

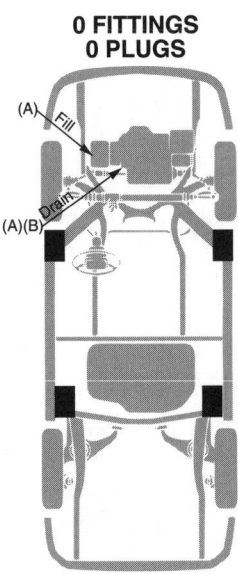

0 FITTINGS 0 PLUGS

**1992-96
2WD
Colt Wagon/Vista**

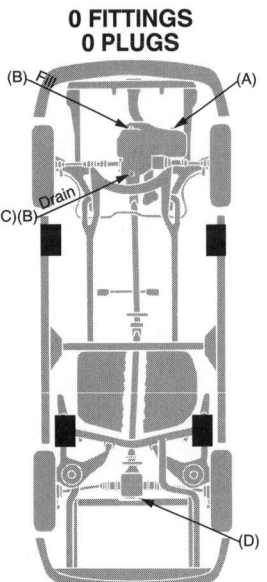

0 FITTINGS 0 PLUGS

**1992-96
4WD
Colt Wagon/Vista**

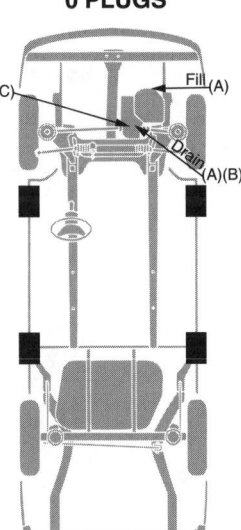

0 FITTINGS 0 PLUGS

**Stealth, Sebring Coupe, Avenger,
1990-94 Laser 2WD**

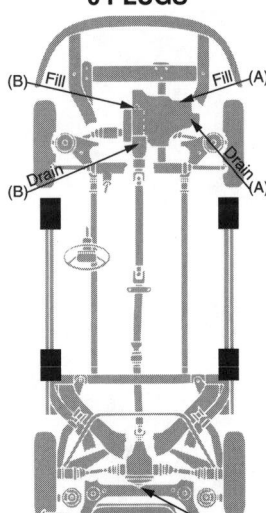

0 FITTINGS 0 PLUGS

**Stealth,
1990-94 Laser 4WD**

CAUTION: On front wheel drive vehicles, the center of gravity is farther forward than on rear wheel drive vehicles. When removing major components from the rear of the vehicle while it is on a hoist, the vehicle must be supported in a manner to prevent it from tipping forward.

■ Lift adapter position

(A) Manual transmission/transaxle, drain & fill

(B) Transfer case, drain & fill

(C) Automatic transaxle final drive, drain & fill

(D) Differential, drain & fill

SERVICE AT TIME OR MILEAGE — WHICHEVER OCCURS FIRST

CRIPM11   CRIPM11

W SERVICE TO MAINTAIN EMISSION WARRANTY

MI—MILES IN THOUSANDS
KM—KILOMETERS IN THOUSANDS

TURBO ENGINES:
EVERY 6 MO/5 MI—8 KM

Crankcase . . . . .change oil

Oil filter .replace
Every second oil change

EVERY 12 MO/7.5 MI—12 KM
Brake & clutch
   fluid reservoir . . . . .check level **HB**

Crankcase ex. turbo . . . . . . .change oil

Oil filter ex. turbo . . . . .replace
At every second change, but at least every 12 months

Power steering fluid . . . . . . .check **AF2**

EVERY 12 MO/15 MI—24 KM
Brake hoses . . . . .check

Disc brake pads . . . . .inspect

Driveshaft boots . . . . .inspect

Transaxle, automatic . . . . . . .check level

EVERY 15 MI—24 KM
W Valve clearance . . . . .inspect/adjust
Adjust only when specifications are on emission label

EVERY 24 MO/30 MI—48 KM
Ball joint, steering linkage seals &
   FWD steering . . . . .inspect

Exhaust system . . . . .inspect

Front wheel bearings
   RWD . . . . .clean/repack **GC**
Inspect for leaks. Inspect & repack whenever rotors are removed

Rear drum brake lining
   & wheel cylinders . . . . .inspect

Rear wheel bearings FWD
   ex. w/disc brakes . . . .clean/repack **GC**
Inspect for leaks. Repack whenever drums are removed

Coolant . . . . .drain/flush/refill **EC**

EVERY 30 MI—48 KM
Differential . . . . .check level
Limited-Slip, change oil

Transaxle, automatic FWD . .change fluid
Change filter & adjust bands

Transmission/Transaxle,
   manual . . . . .check level

W Air cleaner filter . . . . .replace

W Drive belt . . . . .replace
Water pump & alternator only. Not required for 1989-90 emission warranty

W Spark plugs . . . . .replace
Ex. Stealth DOHC

EVERY 60 MO/50 MI—80 KM
EGR valve, 4WD Vista . . . . .replace

W Fuel lines, connections,
   fill cap & tank . . . . .check

W Fuel & fuel vapor hoses . . .check/replace

4WD VISTA:
EVERY 60 MO/60 MI—96 KM
Distributor cap & rotor, 1991 . . . . .inspect

W Evaporative control system . . . .inspect

W Ignition wires . . . . .check/replace

W Vacuum hoses . . . . .replace

W Vacuum control system
   solenoid valve air filter
   1989 ex. Calif. . . . . .replace

EVERY 60 MI—96 KM
W Crankcase emission
   system . . . . .check/clean
4WD Vista

Spark plugs . . . . .replace
Stealth DOHC only

Timing belts . . . . .replace
Also replace the balancer belt when equipped

4WD VISTA: EVERY 80 MI—128 KM
W Oxygen sensor . . . . .check/replace

4WD VISTA: EVERY 100 MI—160 KM
W Evaporative canister . . . . .replace

SEVERE SERVICE
W **Air cleaner filter & brake system**—Service more frequently

W **Crankcase**—Change oil every 3 mo/3 mi (4.8 km) & filter every second oil change

Transmission, automatic, rear wheel drive—Change fluid, filter, & adjust bands every 30 mi (48 km)

Transfer case, 4WD Vista & 4WD Colt manual transaxle—Change lubricant every 30 mi (48 km)

W **Spark plugs**—Replace every 15 mi (24 km)

KEY TO LUBRICANTS

AF2	DEXRON®-II Automatic Transmission Fluid
AP3	MOPAR ATF+3®
CD	Motor Oil, API Service CD
EC	Ethylene Glycol Coolant Mix 50% to 70% with water
GC	Wheel Bearing Grease NLGI Category GC
GL-4	Gear Oil, API Service GL-4
GL-5	Gear Oil, API Service GL-5
GL-5★	Special Lubricant for Limited-Slip Differentials
HB	Hydraulic Brake Fluid, DOT 3
PC	Carburetor Cleaner
SG	Motor Oil, API Service SG

CRANKCASE . . . . .SG, SG/CD

CAPACITY, Refill:	Liters	Qt
1.5L Colt	3.0	3.2
1.6L	4.0	4.2
1.8L, 2.0L ex. DOHC . . .	3.5	3.8
2.0L DOHC	4.0	4.2
2.6L	4.3	4.6
3.0L	4.0	4.2

Capacity shown is without filter or oil cooler. When replacing filter, additional oil may be needed

Turbo Models
Above 32°F (0°C) 20W-20, 20W-40
Above −10°F (−23°C) 10W-30
Below 60°F (16°C) 5W-30

All Other Models
Above 32°F (0°C) 20W-20, 20W-40, 20W-50
Above −10°F (−23°C) 10W-30,
                                                  10W-40, 10W-50
Below 60°F (16°C) . . . . . .5W-20[1], 5W-30, 5W-40
1 Not recommended for sustained high-speed driving

TRANSMISSION/TRANSAXLE,
   Automatic
1989 . . . .**AF2, AP3**
1990-91 . . . .**AP3**

CAPACITY, Initial Refill[2]:	Liters	Qt
Conquest	5.0	5.3
Stealth	4.5	4.0
Others	4.0	4.2

2 With the engine at operating temperature, shift transmission through all gears. Check fluid level in NEUTRAL and add fluid as needed

TRANSMISSION/TRANSAXLE, Manual
RWD 80W, 75W-85W **GL-4**
FWD 75W-85W **GL-4**

CAPACITY, Refill:	Liters	Pt
5-speed RWD	2.3	4.8
Colt ex. wagon: 4-speed	1.7	3.6
5-speed	1.8	3.8
Turbo	2.1	4.4
Colt wagon: 1.5L	1.8	3.8
1.8L	2.2	4.6
Vista: 2WD	2.5	5.2
4WD	2.1	4.4
Laser	1.8	3.8
Turbo	2.2	4.6
Stealth: 2WD	2.3	4.8
4WD	2.4	5.0

TRANSFER
   CASE 80W, 75W-85W **GL-4**

CAPACITY, Refill:	Liters	Pt
Vista 4WD	0.7	1.5
Colt 4WD	0.5	1.1
Stealth 4WD	0.3	0.6

DIFFERENTIAL
Limited-Slip . . . .**GL-5★**
Standard **GL-5**
Above −10°F (-23°C), 90, 85W-90, 80W-90; −30° to −10°F (−34° to −23°C), 80W, 80W-90; below −30°F (−34°C), 75W

CAPACITY, Refill:	Liters	Pt
Conquest	1.3	2.8
Vista 4WD	0.8	1.7
Colt, Stealth	1.1	2.3

61

SERVICE AT TIME OR MILEAGE — WHICHEVER OCCURS FIRST

CRIPM13   CRIPM13

W   SERVICE TO MAINTAIN EMISSION WARRANTY

MI—MILES IN THOUSANDS
KM—KILOMETERS IN THOUSANDS

TURBO ENGINES:
EVERY 6 MO/5 MI—8 KM
Crankcase . . . . .change oil

Oil filter . . . . .replace
Every second oil change

EVERY 12 MO/7.5 MI—12 KM
Brake & clutch
  fluid reservoir . . . . .check level **HB**

Crankcase ex. turbo . . . . . . .change oil

Oil filter ex. turbo . . . . .replace
At every second change, but at least every 12 months

Power steering fluid . . . . . . .check **AF2**

EVERY 12 MO/15 MI—24 KM
Brake hoses . . . . .check

Disc brake pads . . . . .inspect

Driveshaft boots . . . . .inspect

Transaxle, automatic . . . . . . .check level

EVERY 15 MI—24 KM
W Valve clearance . . . . .inspect/adjust
Adjust only when specifications are on emission label

EVERY 24 MO/30 MI—48 KM
Ball joint, steering linkage
  seals & steering . . . . .inspect

Exhaust system . . . . .inspect

Rear drum brake lining
  & wheel cylinders . . . . .inspect

Rear wheel bearings
  ex. w/disc brakes . . . .clean/repack **GC**
Inspect for leaks. Repack whenever drums are removed

Coolant . . . . .drain/flush/refill **EC**

W Fuel hoses . . . . .inspect

EVERY 30 MI—48 KM
Differential . . . . .check level
4WD, rear ex. limited-slip

Differential, limited-slip . . . . .change fluid

Transaxle, automatic . . . . .change fluid
Change filter & adjust bands

Transmission/Transaxle,
  manual . . . . .check level
Also check transfer case

W Air cleaner filter . . . . .replace

W Drive belt . . . . .check/replace
Water pump & alternator only

W Spark plugs . . . . .replace
Ex. with platinum plugs

EVERY 60 MO/50 MI—80 KM
W Fuel lines, connections, fill cap
  & tank, 1992 . . . . .check

EVERY 60 MO/60 MI—96 KM
W Distributor Cap & rotor
  1993-94 Colt, Vista . . . . .check
Calif. only

W Evaporative control system
  1993-94 Colt, Vista . . . . .inspect
Calif. only

W Fuel lines, connections,
  fill cap & tank, 1993-94 . . . . . . .check

W Ignition wires 1993-94
  Colt, Vista . . . . .replace
Calif. only

EVERY 60 MI—96 KM
Spark plugs . . . . .replace

Timing belts . . . . .replace
Also replace the balancer belt when equipped

EVERY 120 MONTHS
Airbag system . . . . .inspect
As equipped

SERVICE AS REQUIRED
Locks & hinges . . . . .lubricate **LB**

Transaxle linkage . . . . .lubricate **LB**

Parking brake cable . . . . . .lubricate **LB**

SEVERE SERVICE
W Air cleaner filter, PCV system & brake
system—Service more frequently

W **Crankcase**—Change oil every 3 mo/3 mi
(4.8 km) & filter every second oil change

W **Spark plugs**—Replace every 15 mi (24 km)

KEY TO LUBRICANTS
AF2	DEXRON®-II Automatic Transmission Fluid
AP3	MOPAR ATF+3®
CD	Motor Oil, API Service CD
EC	Ethylene Glycol Coolant Mix 50% to 70% with water
GC	Wheel Bearing Grease NLGI Category GC
GL-4	Gear Oil, API Service GL-4
GL-5	Gear Oil, API Service GL-5
GL-5★	Special Lubricant for Limited-Slip Differentials
HB	Hydraulic Brake Fluid, DOT 3
LB	Chassis Grease, NLGI Category LB
PC	Carburetor Cleaner
SG	Motor Oil, API Service SG

CRANKCASE . . . . .SG, SG/CD
CAPACITY, Refill:	Liters	Qt
1.5L Colt	3.0	3.2
1.8L, 2.0L ex. DOHC	3.5	3.8
2.0L DOHC	4.0	4.2
2.4L: 1992	3.5	3.8
1993-94	4.0	4.2
3.0L	4.0	4.2

Capacity shown is without filter or oil cooler. When replacing filter, additional oil may be needed.

Turbo Models
Above 32°F (0°C) 20W-40
Above −10°F (−23°C) 10W-30
Below 60°F (16°C) 5W-30
All Other Models
Above 32°F (0°C) 20W-40, 20W-50
Above −10°F (−23°C) . .10W-30, 10W-40, 10W-50
All 1992 & 1993 Laser
  below 60°F (16°C) . . . . .5W-20[1], 5W-30, 5W-40
1993 ex. Laser
  below 100°F (38°C) 5W-30, 5W-40
All 1994 below 100°F (38°C) 5W-30, 5W-40
1 Not recommended for sustained high-speed driving

TRANSMISSION/TRANSAXLE,
Automatic AP3
CAPACITY, Initial Refill[2]:	Liters	Qt
1993-94 Colt, Vista: 2WD	6.1[3]	6.4[3]
4WD	6.5[3]	6.9[3]
1992-94 Stealth	4.5	4.8
Others	4.0	4.2

2 With the engine at operating temperature, shift transmission through all gears. Check fluid level in NEUTRAL and add fluid as needed
3 Total or dry fill shown, use less fluid when refilling

TRANSMISSION/TRANSAXLE,
Manual 75W-85W, 75W-90 GL-4
CAPACITY, Refill:	Liters	Pt
Colt: 4-speed	1.7	3.6
5-speed	1.8	3.8
Turbo	2.1	4.4
Vista: 1.8L	1.8	3.8
2.4L	2.3	4.8
Laser	1.8	3.8
Turbo	2.3	4.8
Stealth: 2WD	2.3	4.8
4WD	2.4	5.0

TRANSFER
CASE 75W-85W, 75W-90 GL-4
CAPACITY, Refill:	Liters	Pt
Laser, Vista 4WD	0.6	1.2
Stealth: 1991-93 5-speed	0.3[4]	0.6[4]
1993-94 6-speed	0.6	1.2

4 Fill no higher than 7/16-1/2" below fill hole

DIFFERENTIAL
Limited-Slip . . . . .GL-5★
Standard GL-5
Above −10°F (−23°C), 90, 85W-90, 80W-90; −30°F to −10°F (−34° to −23°C), 80W, 80W-90; below −30°F (−34°C), 75W
CAPACITY, Refill:	Liters	Pt
Laser, Vista 4WD	0.7	1.5
Stealth	1.1	2.3

CHRYSLER, DODGE, PLYMOUTH
1995-2000 Colt, Colt Wagon, Stealth, Sebring Coupe, Avenger

SERVICE AT TIME OR MILEAGE — WHICHEVER OCCURS FIRST

CRIPM14   CRIPM14

W   SERVICE TO MAINTAIN EMISSION WARRANTY

MI—MILES IN THOUSANDS
KM—KILOMETERS IN THOUSANDS

TURBO ENGINES:
EVERY 6 MO/5 MI—8 KM
2.0L ENGINES:
EVERY 6 MO/7.5 MI—12 KM
OTHER ENGINES:
EVERY 12 MO/7.5 MI—12 KM
Crankcase . . . . .change oil

Oil filter . . . . .replace
Every second oil change, but at least every 12 months

Brake & clutch
fluid reservoir . . . . .check level **HB**

Power steering fluid . . . . . . .check **AF2**
May also use AP3

Tires . . . . .rotate
2000 models

EVERY 12 MO/15 MI—24 KM
Brake hoses . . . . .check

Disc brake pads . . . . .inspect

Driveshaft boots . . . . .inspect

Transaxle, automatic . . . . . .check level

EVERY 15 MI—24 KM
W Valve clearance . . . . .inspect/adjust
1.5L & 1.8L only

EVERY 24 MO/30 MI—48 KM
Ball joint, steering linkage
seals & steering . . . . .inspect

Exhaust system . . . . .inspect

Rear drum brake lining
& wheel cylinders . . . . .inspect

Coolant . . . . .drain/flush/refill **EC**

W Fuel hoses . . . . .inspect

EVERY 30 MI—48 KM
Differential . . . . .check level
4WD, rear

Differential . . . . .change fluid
1995 Stealth

Transaxle, automatic . . . . .change fluid
(Ex. Sebring, Avenger) Change filter if damaged or contaminated

Transaxle, automatic . . . . .change fluid
1999 Sebring, Avenger w/2.0L

Transmission/Transaxle,
manual . . . . .check level
Also check transfer case

W Air cleaner filter . . . . .replace

W Drive belt . . . . .check/replace
Water pump, power steering pump & alternator only

W Spark plugs . . . . .replace
Ex. with platinum plugs

EVERY 60 MO/60 MI—96 KM
W Distributor Cap & rotor . . . . .check
Ex. 2.0L & Federal Stealth

W Evaporative control system . . . . .inspect
Ex. Federal Stealth

W Fuel lines, connections,
fill cap & tank . . . . .check
Ex. Federal Stealth

W Ignition wires . . . . .replace
Ex. Federal Stealth

EVERY 60 MI—96 KM
W Spark plugs . . . . .replace
Platinum plugs ex. 1996-00 2.5L V-6

Timing belts . . . . .replace
1995-00 Recommended but not required for California
1998-00 Recommended but not required for Connecticut & Massachusetts

EVERY 100 MI—160 KM
Timing belt . . . . .replace
Not required if belt was replaced previously

W Spark plugs . . . . .replace
1996-00 2.5L V-6

EVERY 120 MONTHS
Airbag system . . . . .inspect
As equipped

SERVICE AS REQUIRED
Locks & hinges . . . . .lubricate **LB**

Transaxle linkage . . . . .lubricate **LB**

Parking brake cable . . . . . .lubricate **LB**

SEVERE SERVICE
W **Air cleaner filter**—Replace every 15 mi (24 km)

Disc brake pads—Inspect every 6 mo/ 6 mi (9.6 km)

Rear drum brake system—Inspect every 12 mo/15 mi (24 km)

Transaxle, automatic—Sebring, Avenger, change fluid every 15 mi (24 km). 2000 models—Change filter every 30 mi (48 km)

Transaxle, manual & transfer case—ex. 1995-96 Sebring, Avenger, change fluid every 30 mi (48 km)

W **Crankcase**—Change oil every 3 mo/3 mi (4.8 km) & filter every second oil change

W **Spark plugs**—Replace every 15 mi (24 km)

KEY TO LUBRICANTS
AF2	DEXRON®-II Automatic Transmission Fluid
AP3	MOPAR ATF+3®
API★	Motor Oil certified by the American Petroleum Institute (Starburst Symbol)
CD	Motor Oil, API Service CD
EC	Ethylene Glycol Coolant Mix 50% to 70% with water
GLS	Gear Lubricant, Special Mopar Manual Trans. Fluid Part No. 04874465 meeting MS 9417
GL-4	Gear Oil, API Service GL-4
GL-5	Gear Oil, API Service GL-5
GL-5★	Special Lubricant for Limited-Slip Differentials
HB	Hydraulic Brake Fluid, DOT 3
LB	Chassis Grease, NLGI Category LB
SJ	Motor Oil, API Service SJ

CRANKCASE . . . . .SJ, SJ/CD, API★
CAPACITY, Refill:	Liters	Qt
1.5L Colt	3.0	3.2
1.8L	3.5	3.8
2.0L, 2.5L	3.8	4.0
2.4L	4.0	4.2
3.0L	4.0	4.2

Capacity shown is without filter or oil cooler. When replacing filter, additional oil may be needed

Turbo Models
Above 32°F (0°C) 20W-40
Above −10°F (−23°C) 10W-30
Below 60°F (16°C) 5W-30
2.0L
Above −10°F (−23°C) 10W-30
Below 100°F (38°C) . . . . .5W-30[1]
Others
Above 0°F (−18°C) 10W-30
Below 100°F (38°C) . . . . .5W-30[1]
[1] Preferred

TRANSMISSION/TRANSAXLE,
Automatic AP3
CAPACITY, Initial Refill[2]:	Liters	Qt
Colt: 2WD	6.1[3]	6.4[3]
4WD	6.5[3]	6.9[3]
Stealth	4.5	4.8
Sebring, Avenger	3.8	4.0

[2] With the engine at operating temperature, shift transmission through all gears. Check fluid level in NEUTRAL and add fluid as needed
[3] Total or dry fill shown, use less fluid when refilling

TRANSMISSION/TRANSAXLE,
Manual
Sebring, Avenger . . . . .GLS
Others 75W-85W, 75W-90 **GL-4**
CAPACITY, Refill:	Liters	Pt
Colt:	1.8	3.8
Colt Wagon: 1.8L	1.8	3.8
2.4L	2.3	4.8
Sebring, Avenger	2.0	4.2
Stealth: 2WD	2.3	4.8
4WD	2.4	5.0

TRANSFER
CASE 75W-85W, 75W-90 **GL-4**
CAPACITY, Refill:	Liters	Pt
Colt Wagon, Stealth	0.6	1.2

DIFFERENTIAL
Limited-Slip . . . . .GL-5★
Standard .GL-5
Above −10°F (−23°C), 90, 85W-90, 80W-90; −10° to −10°F (−34° to −23°C), 80W, 80W-90; below −30°F (−34°C), 75W
CAPACITY, Refill:	Liters	Pt
Colt Wagon 4WD	0.7	1.5
Stealth	1.1	2.3

Copyright 2000 by Chek-Chart Publications

63

DODGE, PLYMOUTH
1989 Raider, Ram 50

SERVICE AT TIME OR MILEAGE — WHICHEVER OCCURS FIRST

W   SERVICE TO MAINTAIN EMISSION WARRANTY

MI—MILES IN THOUSANDS
KM—KILOMETERS IN THOUSANDS

EVERY 12 MO/7.5 MI—12 KM
Brake & clutch
fluid reservoir . . . . .check level **HB**

W Crankcase . . . . .change oil

W Oil filter . . . . .replace
At every second change, but at least every 12 months

Power steering fluid . . . . . . .check **AF2**

EVERY 12 MO/15 MI—24 KM
Automatic transmission . . . . .check level

Disc brake pads . . . . .inspect
Also check hoses

Exhaust system . . . . .inspect

Ball joints w/fittings . . . . . . .lubricate **LB**

EVERY 15 MI—24 KM
W Idle speed . . . . .check/adjust
Not required for California

W Valve clearance . . . . .inspect/adjust
Required when specifications are on emission label.
Adjust jet valve only on 2.0L & 2.6L engines

EVERY 24 MO/30 MI—48 KM
Drum brakes . . . . .inspect
Linings, wheel cylinders

Front wheel bearings . .clean/repack **GC**

Coolant . . . . .drain/flush/refill **EC**

Drive shaft joints . . . . .lubricate **LB**

Ball joint, steering linkage
seals, driveshaft joints . . . . .inspect

EVERY 30 MI—48 KM
Differentials . . . . .check level
Limited-Slip, change oil

Transmission, automatic . . . .change fluid
4WD only

Transmission, manual . . . . .check level
Also check transfer case

W Air cleaner filter . . . . .replace

W Carburetor choke & linkage . . . .clean **PC**

Drive belt . . . . .replace
Water pump & alternator only

W Spark plugs . . . . .replace

EGR valve ex. Calif. & 3.0L . . . . .replace
At mileage interval only

W Fuel filter . . . . .replace

W Fuel lines, connections, fill cap
& tank . . . . .check

W Fuel, water, & fuel
vapor hoses . . . . .check/replace

EVERY 60 MO/60 MI—96 KM
W Distributor cap, rotor & advance
system ex. California . . . . .check

W Evaporative control system
ex. Calif. . . . . .inspect

W Hot intake air control valve
ex. Calif. . . . . .check

W Ignition wires . . . . .check/replace

W Vacuum hoses . . . . .replace
Includes secondary air hoses & crankcase ventilation
hoses

W Vacuum control system solenoid
valve air filter ex. Calif. . . . . . .replace

EVERY 60 MI—96 KM
Timing belts . . . . .replace
Ex. 2.6L engine

EVERY 80 MI—128 KM
W Crankcase emission
control system . . . . .check/clean

W Oxygen sensor,
ex. Calif. . . . . .replace

EVERY 100 MI—160 KM
W Evaporative canister . . . . .replace

SEVERE SERVICE
W **Air cleaner filter, PCV system & brake
system**—Service more frequently

W **Crankcase**—Change oil every 3 mo/3 mi
(4.8 km) & filter every second oil change

Transmission 2WD, automatic—Change
fluid & filter every 30 mi (48 km)

Transfer case, manual transmission—
Change lubricant every 30 mi (48 km)

W **Spark plugs**—Replace every 15 mi (24 km)

KEY TO LUBRICANTS

AF2	DEXRON®-II Automatic Transmission Fluid
AP3	MOPAR ATF+3®
CD	Motor Oil, API Service CD
EC	Ethylene Glycol Coolant Mix 50% to 70% with water
GC	Wheel Bearing Grease NLGI Category GC
GL-4	Gear Oil, API Service GL-4
GL-5	Gear Oil, API Service GL-5
GL-5★	Special Lubricant for Limited-Slip Differentials
HB	Hydraulic Brake Fluid, DOT 3
LB	Chassis Grease, NLGI Category LB
PC	Carburetor Cleaner
SG	Motor Oil, API Service SG

CRANKCASE . . . . .SG, SG/CD

CAPACITY, Refill:	Liters	Qt
2.0L	3.9	4.0
2.6L Pickup: 4WD	4.5	4.7
2WD	3.8	4.0
4WD Raider	4.5	4.8
3.0L Raider	4.3	4.5

Capacity shown is without filter. When replacing filter, additional oil may be needed
Above 32°F (0°C) 20W-20, 20W-40, 20W-50
Above −10°F (−23°C) . .10W-30, 10W-40, 10W-50
Below 60°F (16°C) . . . . . .5W-20[1], 5W-30, 5W-40
1 Not recommended for sustained high-speed driving

TRANSMISSION, Automatic AF2, AP3

CAPACITY, Initial Refill[2]:	Liters	Qt
All models	5.0	5.3

2 With the engine at operating temperature, shift transmission through all gears. Check fluid level in NEUTRAL and add fluid as needed

TRANSMISSION, Manual 80W, 75W-85W GL-4

CAPACITY, Refill:	Liters	Pt
5-speed	2.3	4.8

TRANSFER CASE 80W, 75W-85W GL-4

CAPACITY, Refill:	Liters	Pt
All models	2.2	4.6

DIFFERENTIAL
Limited-Slip . . . . .GL-5★
Standard GL-4, GL-5
Above −10°F (−23°C), 90, 85W-90, 80W-90; −30° to −10°F (−34° to −23°C), 80W, 80W-90; below −30°F (−34°C), 75W

CAPACITY, Refill:	Liters	Pt
Front	1.1	2.3
Rear, Pickup: All	1.5	3.2
Rear, Raider: w/2.6L eng.	1.8	3.8
w/3.0L eng.	2.6	5.5

LIMITED-SLIP IDENTIFICATION:
Lift rear of vehicle, turn one wheel and the other will turn in the same direction

SERVICE AT TIME OR MILEAGE — WHICHEVER OCCURS FIRST

CRIPM12   CRIPM12

W   SERVICE TO MAINTAIN EMISSION WARRANTY

MI—MILES IN THOUSANDS
KM—KILOMETERS IN THOUSANDS

EVERY 12 MO/7.5 MI—12 KM
Brake & clutch
  fluid reservoir . . . . .check level **HB**

Crankcase . . . . .change oil

Oil filter .replace
At every second change, but at least every 12 months

Power steering fluid . . . . . . .check **AF2**

EVERY 12 MO/15 MI—24 KM
Automatic transmission . . . .check level

Driveshaft boots . . . . .inspect

Ball joints
  w/fittings 1990-91 . . . . . . .lubricate **LB**

EVERY 24 MO/30 MI—48 KM
Drum brakes . . . . .inspect
Linings, wheel cylinders

Exhaust system . . . . .inspect

Front wheel bearings
  1990 . . . . .clean/repack **GC**
Inspect for leaks. Inspect & repack whenever rotors are
removed

Coolant . . . . .drain/flush/refill **EC**

Driveshaft joints . . . . .lubricate **LB**

W Fuel hoses 1991-93 . . . . .check

Ball joints
  w/fittings, 1992-93 . . . . . .lubricate **LB**
Ball joint & steering linkage
  seals .inspect

EVERY 30 MI—48 KM
Differential . . . . .check level
Limited-Slip, change oil

Transmission, automatic . . . .change fluid
4WD only. Also change AT transfer case fluid

Transmission, manual . . . . .check level
Also check transfer case

W Air cleaner filter . . . . .replace

Drive belt . . . . .replace
Water pump & alternator only

W Spark plugs 1990-92 . . . . .replace

EVERY 60 MO/50 MI—80 KM
EGR valve ex. Calif. . . . . .replace

W Fuel lines, connections, fill cap
  & tank 1990-92 . . . . .check

W Fuel & fuel
  vapor hoses 1990 . . . . . .check/replace

EVERY 60 MO/60 MI—96 KM
W Distributor cap & rotor,
  1990-91 ex. Calif. . . . . .check

W Evaporative control system,
  1990-92 ex. Calif. . . . . .inspect

Fuel line, connections,
  fill cap & tank, 1993 . . . . .check

W Hot intake air control valve,
  1990-91 ex. Calif. . . . . .check

W Ignition wires Calif. . . . . . . .check/replace

W Vacuum hoses 1990-91 . . . . . . .replace
Includes secondary air hoses & crankcase ventilation
hoses

EVERY 60 MI—96 KM
W Spark plugs 1993 . . . . .replace

Timing belts . . . . .replace

EVERY 80 MI—128 KM
W Crankcase emission
  system, 1990-92 . . . . .check/clean

W Oxygen sensor, 1990-92 . . . . . .replace

EVERY 100 MI—160 KM
EGR valve, 1993 4-cyl. ex. Calif. . .replace

Crankcase emission
  system, 1993 . . . . .check/clean

Evaporative canister . . . . .replace
Ex. 1993 Calif.

SEVERE SERVICE
**W Air cleaner filter, PCV system & brake
system**—Service more frequently

W Crankcase—Change oil every 3 mo/3 mi
(4.8 km) & filter every second oil change

Transmission 2WD, automatic—Change
fluid & filter every 30 mi (48 km)

Transfer case, manual transmission—
Change lubricant every 30 mi (48 km)

W Spark plugs—Replace every 15 mi (24 km)

KEY TO LUBRICANTS

AF2	DEXRON®-II Automatic Transmission Fluid
AP3	MOPAR ATF+3®
CD	Motor Oil, API Service CD
EC	Ethylene Glycol Coolant Mix 50% to 70% with water
GC	Wheel Bearing Grease NLGI Category GC
GL-4	Gear Oil, API Service GL-4
GL-5	Gear Oil, API Service GL-5
GL-5★	Special Lubricant for Limited-Slip Differentials
HB	Hydraulic Brake Fluid, DOT 3
LB	Chassis Grease, NLGI Category LB
PC	Carburetor Cleaner
SG	Motor Oil, API Service SG

CRANKCASE . . . . .SG, SG/CD

CAPACITY, Refill:	Liters	Qt
2.4L: 2WD, 1990-92	3.5	3.7
2WD, 1993	4.5	4.7
4WD	4.5	4.7
3.0L	4.3	4.5

Capacity shown is without filter. When replacing filter, additional oil may be needed
Above 32°F (0°C) 20W-40, 20W-50
Above −10°F (−23°C) . .10W-30, 10W-40, 10W-50
Below 60°F (16°C)[1] 5W-30, 5W-40
1 1993 Below 100°F (38°C)

TRANSMISSION, Automatic AP3

CAPACITY, Initial Refill[2]:	Liters	Qt
All models	1.9	2.0

2 With the engine at operating temperature, shift transmission through all gears. Check fluid level in NEUTRAL and add fluid as needed

TRANSMISSION,
Manual . . .80W, 75W-85W, 75W-90 **GL-4**

CAPACITY, Refill:	Liters	Pt
5-speed	2.3	4.8

TRANSFER
CASE 80W, 75W-85W, 75W-90 **GL-4**

CAPACITY, Refill:	Liters	Pt
All models	2.2	4.6

DIFFERENTIAL
Limited-Slip . . . .**GL-5★**
Standard **GL-4, GL-5**
Above −10°F (−23°C), 90, 85W-90, 80W-90; −30°
to −10°F (−34° to −23°C), 80W, 80W-90; below
−30°F (−34°C), 75W

CAPACITY, Refill:	Liters	Pt
Front: 2.4L	1.1	2.3
3.0L	2.6	5.5
Rear: 2.4L	1.5	3.2
3.0L	2.6	5.5

LIMITED-SLIP IDENTIFICATION:
Lift rear of vehicle, turn one wheel and the other will turn in the same direction

65

SERVICE LOCATIONS — ENGINE AND CHASSIS

DETDP-1   DETDP-1

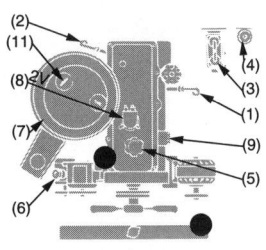

1989-95
4-cyl. 2.2L, 2.5L
Dakota

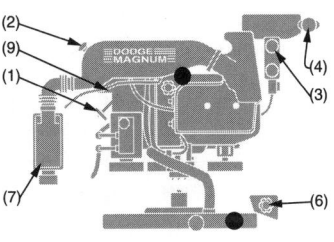

1996
2.5L Dakota

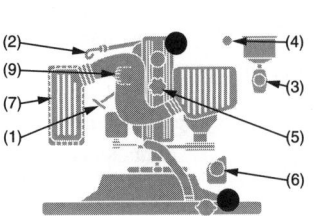

1997-00
2.5L Dakota

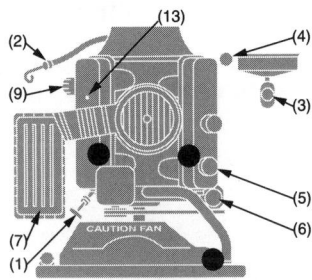

1997-00
3.9L Dakota/Durango
5.2L, 5.9L
Dakota/Durango
2000 3.9L, 5.2L, 5.9L
Ram Pickup

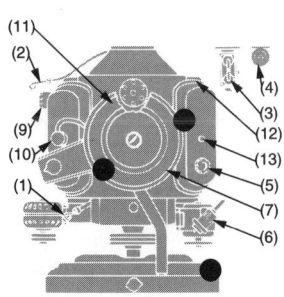

1989-99
V6 3.9L
ex. 1997-99 Dakota,
Durango

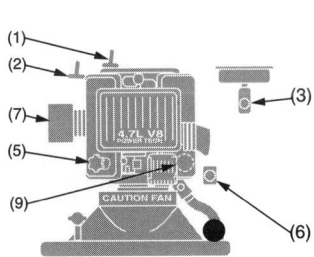

2000
4.7L (287)

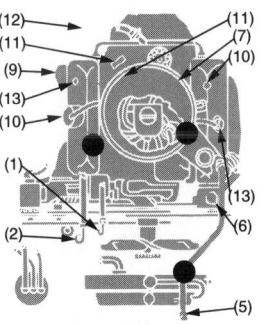

V8 5.2L, 5.9L
B Series

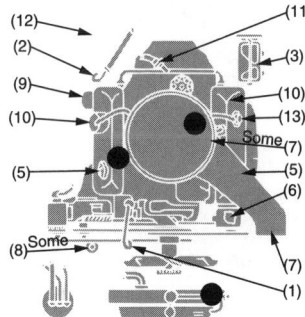

1989-93
V8 5.2L, 5.9L
ex. B Series

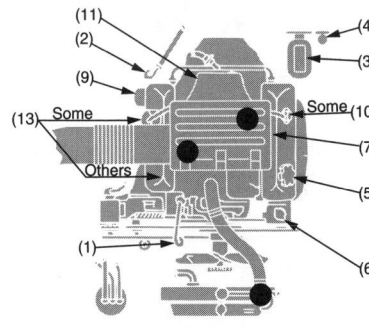

1994-99
V8 5.2L, 5.9L
ex. B Series & 1997-99
Dakota, Durango

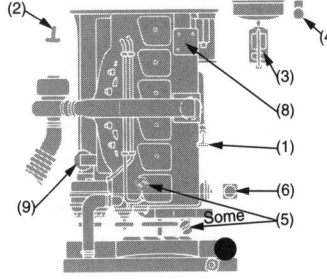

1989-00
6-cyl. 5.9L Diesel

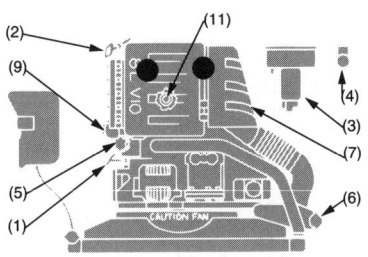

1994-00
V10 8.0L

● Cooling system drain

(1) Crankcase dipstick
(2) Transmission dipstick
(3) Brake fluid reservoir
(4) Clutch fluid reservoir
(5) Oil fill cap
(6) Power steering reservoir
(7) Air filter

(8) Fuel filter
(9) Oil filter
(10) PCV filter
(11) EGR valve
(12) Oxygen sensor
(13) PCV valve

DODGE TRUCKS
1989-2000 All Models Except Raider, Ram 50

SERVICE LOCATIONS — ENGINE AND CHASSIS

DETDP-2   DETDP-2

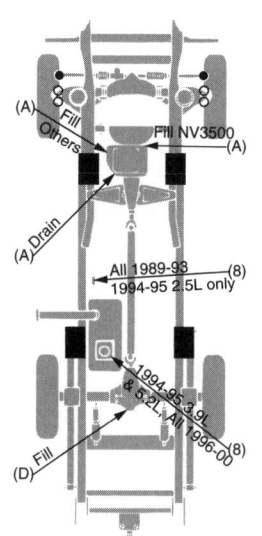

**2-Wheel Drive
Dakota
Durango**

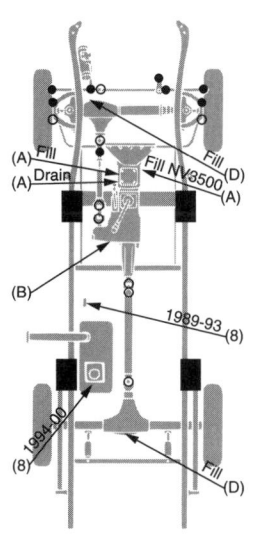

**4-Wheel Drive
Dakota
Durango**

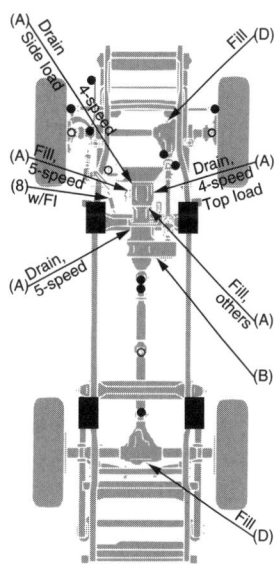

**1989-93
4-Wheel Drive
W Series**

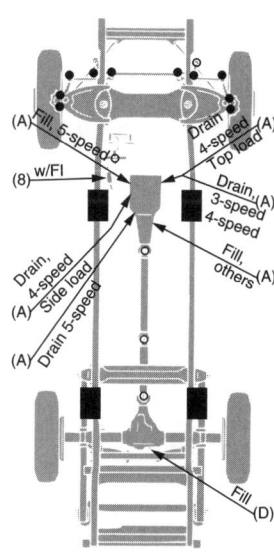

**1989-93
2-Wheel Drive
D Series**

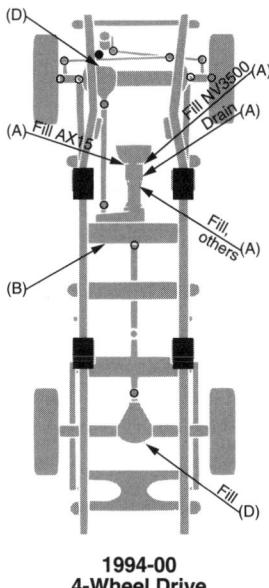

**1994-00
4-Wheel Drive
Ram Pickup**

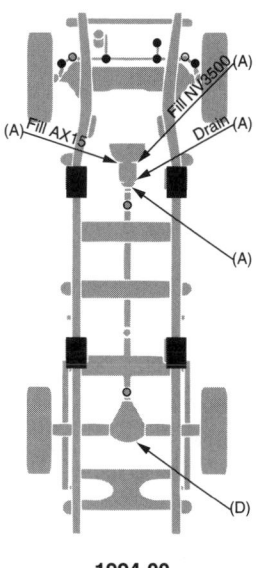

**1994-00
2-Wheel Drive
Ram Pickup**

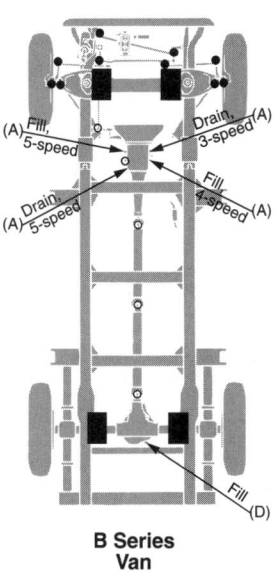

**B Series
Van
Ram Van/Wagon**

■ Lift adapter position	• Fitting	(A) Manual transmission/transaxle, drain & fill	(C) Automatic transaxle final drive, NOT USED
	○ Fitting, some models	(B) Transfer case, drain & fill	(D) Differential, drain & fill

DODGE TRUCKS
1989 All Rear Wheel & 4-Wheel
Light Duty Gasoline Emission Models Except Raider & Ram 50

CHEK-CHART

SERVICE AT TIME OR MILEAGE — WHICHEVER OCCURS FIRST

DETPM16   DETPM16

W   SERVICE TO MAINTAIN EMISSION WARRANTY

8,500 & under GVWR & all GVWR for B-Series Vans & Wagons. GVWR is found on Safety Certification Label on left
door lock pillar. 1989: models with emission & hose routing label on underside of the hood. See passenger car
charts for front-wheel drive vans

MI—MILES IN THOUSANDS
KM—KILOMETERS IN THOUSANDS

EVERY 6 MO/7.5 MI—12 KM
Steering linkage
& propeller shafts, 4WD . . .lubricate **LB**

EVERY 12 MO/7.5 MI—12 KM
Brake hoses . . . . .inspect

W Crankcase . . . . .change oil
Replace oil filter at every other oil change but at least
every 12 months

Differential . . . . .check for leaks

Exhaust system . . . . .inspect

Suspension ball joints, seals,
U-joints (sealed) 2WD . . . . . . .inspect

Transfer case . . . . .check level

Transmission, manual . . . . . .check level

Brake & clutch
master cylinder . . . . . .check level **HB**

Power steering reservoir .check level **PS**

Transmission, automatic . . . .check level
Fluid warm, engine idling, in NEUTRAL

Body, brake & clutch
actuating mechanisms . . .lubricate **MO**

EVERY 12 MONTHS
Air conditioning system . . . . .inspect

Cooling system . . . . .inspect

EVERY 12 MO/15 MI—24 KM
Brake booster bellcrank
pivot B-350 series . . . . . .lubricate **MO**

W Drive belts . . . . .inspect/adjust
Not required for Calif. warranty

Front wheel bearings
4WD ex. Dakota . . . . .inspect **GC**
At mileage interval or when replacing disc pads.
With 44F-BJ & 60F front differentials, clean & repack
needle bearings

AT FIRST 7.5 MI—12 KM
THEN EVERY 15 MI—24 KM
Tires . . . . .rotate

EVERY 24 MO/22.5 MI—36 KM
Steering linkage, 2WD . . . .lubricate **LB**

Front suspension ball joints . .lubricate **LB**

Parking brake ratio
lever pivot . . . . .lubricate **LB**

Propeller shafts, 2WD . . . .lubricate **LB**
With fittings, ex. Dakota

Transmission linkage . . . .**fitting LB**
4-speed OD only, while in reverse, engine off

EVERY 22.5 MI—36 KM
Brake linings . . . . .inspect

Front wheel bearings, 2WD . .inspect **GC**
Also inspect at brake inspection or servicing; lubricate
rear wheel bearings whenever axles are removed.
Clean/repack front wheel bearings when replacing disc
pads ex. Dakota, clean/repack when brake rotors are
resurfaced

AT FIRST 36 MO/52.5 MI—84 KM
THEN EVERY 24 MO/30 MI—48 KM
Cooling system . . . . .change coolant **EC**

EVERY 30 MI—48 KM
W Air cleaner element . . . . .replace
Clean air filter wrapper if equipped

W PCV filter . . . . .replace
If equipped

W Spark plugs . . . . .replace

EVERY 37.5 MI—60 KM
Transfer case . . . . .change lubricant

Transmission, automatic . . . .change fluid
Not required for Ram Wagon. Replace filter & adjust
bands

Transmission, manual . .change lubricant

Crankcase inlet air cleaner
ex. 4-cyl. . . . . .clean/oil

EGR Valve & Tube . . . . .replace
Clean passages

Idle speed . . . . .adjust
Vehicles w/carburetor only

Ignition cables, distributor cap
& rotor . . . . .replace

Ignition timing . . . . .check

Manifold heat valve
if equipped . . . . . .check/lubricate **MH**

PCV valve . . . . .replace

Vacuum operated emission
components . . . . .replace

EVERY 75 MI—120 KM
Alternator brushes . . . . .replace

EVERY 82.5 MI—132 KM
Oxygen sensor . . . . .replace

SERVICE AS REQUIRED
Rear wheel bearings,
Dana axle . . . . .inspect **GC**
Repack as required or whenever axles are removed or
Dana axle brakes are serviced, repack

Transfer case linkage . . . . .lubricate
NP205 lubricate with **MO**
NP207, NP208, NP241 lubricate with **LB**

Vacuum & fuel rubber hoses . . . . .check

Fuel filter . . . . .replace

SEVERE SERVICE
W Crankcase—Drain every 3 mo/3 mi (4.8
km). Every 50 hours for 4WD used for
off-road driving

Drive line fittings—Lubricate every 3 mo/
3 mi (4.8 km). Inspect 4WD front wheel
bearings every 1 mi (1.6 km) for off-road
use. Lubricate daily if operating in water

Transmission, automatic—Change fluid
every 12 mi (19 km). Replace filter & adjust
bands

Transmission, manual—Change lubricant every 18 mi (29 km)

KEY TO LUBRICANTS
AF2	DEXRON®-II ATF
AP3	MOPAR ATF+3®
CD	Motor Oil, API Service CD
EC	Ethylene Glycol Coolant
	Mix with water to desired freeze protection
GC	Wheel Bearing Grease, NLGI Classification GC
GL-4	Gear Oil, API Service GL-4
GL-5	Gear Oil, API Service GL-5
GL-5★	Special Lubricant for Anti-Spin, Limited-Slip, Powr-Loc, Sure-Grip or Trac-Loc Differential
HB	Hydraulic Brake Fluid, DOT 3
LB	Chassis Grease, NLGI Classification LB
MH	Manifold Heat Valve Solvent
MO	Motor Oil
PC	Carburetor Cleaner
PS	Power Steering Fluid
SG	Motor Oil, API Service SG

CRANKCASE . . . . .SG, SG/CD
CAPACITY, Refill:	Liters	Qt
All	3.8	4.0

Capacity shown is without filter. When replacing filter, additional oil may be needed

Above 20°F (-7°C) 10W-30, 15W-40, 30
Above 10°F (-12°C) 15W-40
Above 0°F (-18°C) 10W-30
Below 32°F (0°C) 5W-30

TRANSMISSION, Automatic AP3
CAPACITY, Initial Refill[2]:	Liters	Qt
All models	3.8	4.0

2 With the engine at operating temperature, shift transmission through all gears. Check fluid level in NEUTRAL and
add fluid as needed

TRANSMISSION, Manual
A833 OD .AP3, AF2
75W, 75W-80, 80W-90, 85W-90, 90 GL-5 may also
be used
NP435 . . . . .GL-5, SG, SG/CD
SG, SG/CD: Above 32°F (0°C), 50; below 32°F
(0°C), 30
GL-5: Above 90°F (32°C), 140; above -10°F
(-23°C), 90; below -10°F (-23°C), 80W
NP2500 . . . . .10W-30 SG, SG/CD
Use AP3 below 32°F (0°C) to improve shift efforts

CAPACITY, Refill:	Liters	Pt
NP435	3.3	7.0
NP2500	1.9	4.0
A833 OD	3.5	7.5

TRANSFER CASE
NP205 . . . . .GL-5, SG, SG/CD
SG, SG/CD: Above 32°F (0°C), 50; below 32°F
(0°C), 30
GL-5: Above 90°F (32°C), 140; above -10°F (-3°C),
90; below -10°F (-23°C), 80W
NP207, 208, 231, 241 . . . . .AP3, AF2

CAPACITY, Refill:	Liters	Pt
NP205, NP207	2.1	4.5
NP208	2.8	6.0
NP231	1.2	2.5
NP241	2.2	4.6

DIFFERENTIAL
Above 90°F (32°C), 140, 80W-140, 85W-140;
above -10°F (-23°C), 90, 80W-90, 80W-140,
85W-140; below -10°F (-23°C), 75W, 80W, 75W-90,
80W-140

Standard & all Dana, Spicer GL-5
Anti-Spin, Limited-Slip, Powr-Loc, Sure-Grip,
Trac-Loc ex. Dana, Spicer . . . . .GL-5★
All with limited slip add one container of Mopar Trac-Loc
additive

CAPACITY, Refill:	Liters	Pt
Front: 4-wheel drive Dakota	1.2	2.6
Spicer 60F axle	3.1	6.5
Others	2.7	5.6
Rear	1.4	3.0
Dana 60, 60 HD	2.8	6.0
Dana 70	3.3	7.0
Others	2.1	4.5

ANTI-SPIN, LIMITED-SLIP, POWR-LOC, SURE-GRIP OR TRAC-LOC IDENTIFICATION:
Lift both rear wheels off ground, turn one wheel & other will
rotate in same direction

DODGE TRUCKS
1989-92 All Gasoline Heavy Duty Emission Models

SERVICE AT TIME OR MILEAGE — WHICHEVER OCCURS FIRST

DETPM19   DETPM19

W   SERVICE TO MAINTAIN EMISSION WARRANTY
Heavy duty models have emission control label on the air cleaner and hose routing label on underside of the hood.

MI—MILES IN THOUSANDS
KM—KILOMETERS IN THOUSANDS

EVERY 6 MO/6 MI—9.6 KM
2WD, 4WD propeller shaft,
steering linkage &
1991-92 suspension . . . . .lubricate **LB**

1989-90, EVERY 12 MO/6 MI—9.6 KM
1991-92, EVERY 6 MO/6 MI—9.6 KM
Brake hoses . . . . .inspect
Crankcase 1989-90 . . . . .change oil
Change oil filter every other oil change but at least every 12 months
Differential . . . . .check for leaks
Exhaust system . . . . .inspect
Front axle drive joint
& pivot bearings . . . . .lubricate
With Spicer 60F axle
Suspension ball joints, seals,
U-joints (sealed) 2WD . . . . .inspect
Transfer case . . . . .check level
Transmission, manual . . . . . .check level
Air intake & air injection system . .inspect
Brake & clutch
master cylinder . . . . . . .check level **HB**
Power steering reservoir . . .check level **PS**
CB & MB 350 require Hydroboost Power Steering Fluid
PS★
Transmission, automatic . . . .check level
Fluid warm, engine idling, in NEUTRAL
Body, brake & clutch
actuating mechanisms . . . . . . .lubricate

EVERY 12 MONTHS
Air conditioning system . . . . .inspect
Cooling system . . . . .inspect

EVERY 12 MO/12 MI—19 KM
Front wheel bearings
4WD . . . . .inspect **GC**
At mileage interval only or when replacing disc pads.
With 44F-BJ & 60F front differentials, clean & repack
front spindle needle bearings

AT FIRST 7.5 MI—12 KM
THEN EVERY 15 MI—24 KM
Tires . . . . .rotate

EVERY 18 MI—29 KM
W Drive belts . . . . .inspect/adjust

EVERY 24 MI—38 KM
Propeller shafts, 2WD . . . . . . .lubricate
2WD steering linkage
& suspension, 1989-90 . . .lubricate **LB**
Air cleaner element . . . . .replace
W Air pump filter . . . . .replace
Brake linings . . . . .inspect
Front wheel bearings, 2WD . .inspect **GC**
Also inspect at brake inspection or servicing; lubricate
rear wheel bearings whenever axles are removed.
Clean/repack front wheel bearings when replacing disc
pads
Transmission, automatic . . . .change fluid
Not required for Ram Wagon. Replace filter & adjust
bands

Crankcase inlet air cleaner . . . .clean/oil

AT FIRST 36 MO/54 MI—84 KM
THEN EVERY 24 MO/30 MI—48 KM
Cooling system . . . . .change coolant **EC**

EVERY 30 MI—48 KM
W Spark plugs . . . . .replace

EVERY 36 MI—58 KM
Transfer case . . . . .change lubricant
Transmission,
manual, gasoline . . . . .change lubricant

EVERY 54 MI—85 KM
Drive belts, V type 1989-91 . . . . .replace

EVERY 60 MI—96 KM
Battery . . . . .replace
EGR valve . . . . .replace
Also clean passages. Or as indicated by emissions
maintenance light
Ignition cables, distributor cap
& rotor . . . . .replace
Ignition timing . . . . .check/adjust
PCV valve . . . . .replace
Or as indicated by emissions maintenance light
Vacuum operated
emission components . . . . . . .replace
Or as indicated by emissions maintenance light
Manifold heat valve . . . . . . .lubricate **MH**

EVERY 78 MI—125 KM
Alternator brushes, 1989 . . . . . .replace

EVERY 82.5 MI—132 KM
Oxygen sensor . . . . .replace
Or as indicated by emissions maintenance light

SERVICE AS REQUIRED
W Drive belts 1992 . . . . .replace
W Fuel filter . . . . .replace
Rear wheel bearings . . . . . .inspect **GC**
Repack as required or whenever axles are removed or
Dana axle brakes are serviced, repack
Transfer case linkage . . . . .lubricate
NP205, **MO**; NP208 & NP241, **LB**

SEVERE SERVICE
Crankcase—Drain every 3 mo/3 mi (4.8 km). Every 50 hours for 4WD used for off-road driving

Differential—1990-92, change fluid every 12 mi (19 km) when frequent trailer towing. Axle fluid should be changed when axle is submerged in water

Drive line fittings—Lubricate every 3 mo/3 mi (4.8 km), every 1 mi (1.6 km), includes front wheel bearing inspection for off-road use. Lubricate daily if operating in water

Transmission, automatic—Change fluid every 12 mi (19 km). Replace filter & adjust bands

Transmission, manual—Change lubricant every 18 mi (29 km)

KEY TO LUBRICANTS
See inside front cover

CRANKCASE . . . . .SG, SG/CD

CAPACITY, Refill:	Liters	Qt
All	3.8	4.0

Capacity shown is without filter. When replacing filter, additional oil may be needed
Above 20°F (-7°C), 1989 30
Above 10°F (-12°C), 1989 . . . . .15W-40
Above 0°F (-18°C) 10W-30
Below 32°F (0°C) 5W-30

TRANSMISSION, Automatic AP3

CAPACITY, Initial Refill[2]:	Liters	Qt
All models	3.8	4.0

2 With the engine at operating temperature, shift transmission through all gears. Check fluid level in NEUTRAL and add fluid as needed

TRANSMISSION, Manual
AX-15 . . . . .75W-90 **GL-5**
A833 OD **AP3, AF2**
75W, 75W-80, 80W-90, 85W-90, 90 **GL-5** may be used
NP435 . . . .**GL-5, SG, SG/CD**
SF/CC, SF/CD, SG, SG/CD: Above 32°F (0°C), 50;
below 32°F (0°C), 30
GL-5: Above 90°F (32°C), 140; above -10°F
(-23°C), 90; below -10°F (-23°C), 80W
NV4500 . . . . .Synthetic 75W-90 **GL-4**[3]
3 Part No. 4874459

CAPACITY, Refill:	Liters	Pt
NP435	3.3	7.0
AX-15	3.1	6.6
NV4500	3.8	8.0
A833 OD	3.5	7.5

TRANSFER CASE
NP205: . . . .**GL-5, SG, SG/CD**
SG, SG/CD: Above 32°F (0°C), 50; below 32°F
(0°C), 30
GL-5: Above 90°F (32°C), 140; above -10°F
(-23°C), 90; below -10°F (-23°C), 80W
NP207, 208, 241 . . . .**AP3, AF2**

CAPACITY, Refill:	Liters	Pt
NP205, NP207	2.1	4.5
NP208	2.8	6.0
NP241	2.2	4.6

DIFFERENTIAL
Above 90°F (32°C), 140, 80W-140, 85W-140;
above -10°F (-23°C), 90, 80W-90, 80W-140,
85W-140; below -10°F (-23°C), 75W, 80W, 75W-90,
80W-140
Standard & all Dana/Spicer **GL-5**
Anti-Spin, Limited-Slip, Powr-Loc,
Sure-Grip, Trac-Loc
ex. Dana/Spicer . . . .**GL-5★**
All with limited slip add one container of Mopar Trac-Loc
additive

CAPACITY, Refill[4]:	Liters	Pt
Front: 4-wheel drive		
Spicer 60F	3.1	6.5
Others	2.7	5.6
Rear: Dana 60, 60 HD	2.8	6.0
Dana 70	3.3	7.0
Others	2.1	4.5

4 1992 Dana axles, lubricant level must be ½-1" (12-24 mm)
below fill plug opening

DETPM18   DETPM18

W   SERVICE TO MAINTAIN EMISSION WARRANTY

KEY TO LUBRICANTS
See inside front cover

MI—MILES IN THOUSANDS
KM—KILOMETERS IN THOUSANDS

EVERY 6 MO/6 MI—9.6 KM
Brake hoses . . . . .inspect
1994

Exhaust system . . . . .inspect

W Air filter, 1989-93 . . . . .clean/inspect
Also inspect air inlet pipe

Fittings 4WD . . . . .lubricate **LB**
Includes front wheel bearings; remove wheels to reach
fitting if equipped

Suspension ball joints, seals,
  U-joints (sealed) 4WD . . . . . . .inspect

Steering linkage, suspension
  & 4WD propeller shafts . . .lubricate **LB**
Also slip splines

Crankcase . . . . .change oil & filter

Engine coolant, hoses, clamps . . .inspect
1994

Tires . . . . .rotate

EVERY 12 MONTHS
Air conditioning system . . . . .inspect

EVERY 12 MO/12 MI—19 KM
Front wheel bearings 2WD . .inspect **GC**
Also inspect at brake inspection or servicing; lubricate
rear wheel bearings whenever axles are removed.
Clean/repack front wheel bearings when replacing disc
pads

Drive belts . . . . .inspect/adjust

Engine coolant, hoses & clamps . . .inspect
1989-93

Front wheel bearings
  4WD . . . . .inspect **GC**
At mileage interval only or when replacing disc pads.
With 44F-B5 & 60F front differentials, clean & repack
front spindle needle bearings.

Fuel filter . . . . .replace

Water pump weep hole . . . .clean/inspect
1994

Transmission, automatic . . . .change fluid
Replace filter & adjust bands

EVERY 24 MO/24 MI—38 KM
Brake lining, 1994 . . . . .inspect

Gearshift control, 1994 . . . .lubricate **MO**
Manual transmission only

Air filter, 1989-93 . . . . .replace

Fan hub . . . . .inspect

Cooling system . . . . .change coolant **EC**

Valve clearance . . . . .check/adjust

Engine vibration dampener . . . .inspect

1989-93, EVERY 36 MI—58 KM
1994, EVERY 36 MO/36 MI—58 KM
Transfer case . . . . .change lubricant

Transmission, manual . .change lubricant
1993, every 37.5 mi (60 km)

EVERY 78 MI—125 KM
Alternator brushes, 1989 . . . . . . .replace

SERVICE AS REQUIRED
Differential(s) . . . . .check for leaks

Transfer case . . . . .check level

Transmission, manual . . . . .check level

Air filter, 1994 . . . . .replace

Brake & clutch
  master cylinder . . . . . .check level **HB**

Power steering reservoir . .check level **PS**

Transmission, automatic . . . .check level
Fluid warm, engine idling, in NEUTRAL

Body, brake & clutch
  actuating mechanisms . . . . . . .lubricate

Rear wheel bearings . . . . . . .inspect **GC**
Repack as required or whenever axles are removed or
Dana axle brakes are serviced, repack

Underhood plastic &
  rubber components . . . . .inspect

Brake linings, 1989-93 . . . . .inspect

SEVERE SERVICE
Crankcase—Change oil and filter every:
1989-93, 3 mo/3 mi (4.8 km). 1994, 5 mi
(8 km) or 200 hours

Differential—Change lubricant every 12 mi
(19 km). Axle fluid should be changed
when axle is submerged in water

Drive line fittings—Lubricate every 3 mo/
3 mi (4.8 km) ex. W-350, every 1 mi
(1.6 km), includes front wheel bearing inspection for off-road use. Lubricate daily if
operating in water

Suspension ball joints—Lubricate every
engine oil change

Transmission, manual—Change lubricant every 18 mi (29 km)

CRANKCASE . . . .**CE, SG/CE**

CAPACITY, Refill:	Liters	Qt
1989-93	10.4	11.0
1994	9.5	10.0

Capacity shown is without filter. When replacing filter, fill it
with oil before installing. Run engine and check dipstick, additional oil may be needed

Above 10°F (-12°C) 15W-40
0°to 10°F (-18° to -12°C) 10W-30
-10° to 0°F (-23° to -18°C) . . . . .10W-30[1]
Below 0°F (-18°C) . . . . .5W-30 synthetic
[1] With block heater

TRANSMISSION, Automatic **AP3**

CAPACITY, Initial Refill[3]:	Liters	Qt
1989-93	3.8	4.0
1994	14.6[4]	15.4[4]

[3] With the engine at operating temperature, shift transmission through all gears. Check fluid level in NEUTRAL and
add fluid as needed
[4] Dry or total fill

TRANSMISSION, Manual
G-360, 1989-94 . . . . . . .5W-30 **SG, SG/CD**
NV4500, 1994 . . .Synthetic 75W-85, **GL-4**[5]
[5] Part No. 4874459

CAPACITY, Refill:	Liters	Pt
Getrag G-360	3.3	7.0
NV4500, 1994	3.8	8.0

TRANSFER CASE
NP205, 1989-93 . . . .**GL-5, SG, SG/CD**
NP241, 1994 . . . .**AP3, AF2**
SG, SG/CD: Above 32°F (0°C), 50; below 32°F
(0°C), 30
GL-5: Above 90°F (32°C), 140; above -10°F
(-23°C), 90; below -10°F (-23°C), 80W

CAPACITY, Refill:	Liters	Pt
NP205	2.1	4.5
NP241	3.1	6.53

PTO ADAPTER **AP3, AF2**

CAPACITY, Refill:	Liters	Pt
NV-021	2.1	4.6

DIFFERENTIAL
Above 90°F (32°C), 140, 80W-140, 85W-140;
above -10°F (-23°C), 90, 80W-90, 80W-140,
85W-140; below -10°F (-23°C), 75W, 80W, 75W-90,
80W-140
Standard & all Dana/Spicer **GL-5**
Anti-Spin, Limited-Slip, Powr-Loc,
  Sure-Grip, Trac-Loc
  ex. Dana/Spicer . . . .**GL-5★**
All with limited slip, add one container of Mopar Trac-Loc
additive

CAPACITY, Refill[6]:	Liters	Pt
Front: Spicer 60F	3.1	6.5
Dana 60, 1994	3.0	6.3
Others	2.7	5.6
Rear: Dana 60, 60 HD	2.8	6.0
Dana 70: 1989-93	3.3	7.0
1994	3.2	6.7
Dana 80	3.3	6.8
Others	2.1	4.5

[6] 1994, lubricant level in axle must be ¼-¾" (6-17 mm)
below fill plug opening. 1992-93 Dana axles, lubricant level
in axle must be ½-1" (12-24 mm) below fill plug opening

CHEK-CHART

DODGE TRUCKS
1990-92 All Rear-Wheel & 4-Wheel
Light Duty Gasoline Emission Models Except Raider & Ram 50

SERVICE AT TIME OR MILEAGE — WHICHEVER OCCURS FIRST

DETPM20   DETPM20

W   SERVICE TO MAINTAIN EMISSION WARRANTY

8,500 & under GVWR & all GVWR for B-Series Vans & Wagons. GVWR is found on underside of the hood. See passenger car charts for front-wheel drive vans

MI—MILES IN THOUSANDS
KM—KILOMETERS IN THOUSANDS

EVERY 6 MO/7.5 MI—12 KM
Propeller shafts
& steering linkage, 4WD   . .lubricate **LB**

1990, EVERY 12 MO/7.5 MI—12 KM
1991-92, EVERY 6 MO/7.5 MI—12 KM
Brake hoses . . . . .inspect

W Crankcase . . . . .change oil
Replace oil filter at every other oil change but at least every 12 months

Differential . . . . .check for leaks

W Engine coolant, hoses
& clamps . . . . .check
At mileage only

Exhaust system . . . . .inspect

Suspension ball joints, seals,
U-joints (sealed) 2WD . . . . .inspect

Transfer case . . . . .check level

Transmission, manual . . . . .check level

Brake & clutch
master cylinder . . . . . . .check level **HB**

Power steering reservoir .check level **PS**

Transmission, automatic . . . .check level
Fluid warm, engine idling, in NEUTRAL

Body, brake & clutch
actuating mechanisms . . .lubricate **MO**

EVERY 12 MONTHS
Air conditioning system . . . . .inspect
Cooling system . . . . .inspect

EVERY 12 MO/15 MI—24 KM
Brake booster bellcrank
pivot B-350 series . . . . . .lubricate **MO**

W Drive belts V6, V8 . . . . . .inspect/adjust
Not required for Calif. warranty

Front wheel bearings
4WD ex. Dakota . . . . .inspect **GC**
At mileage interval only or when replacing disc pads. With 44F-BJ & 60F front differentials, clean & repack needle bearings

Steering linkage 1991-92 . . .lubricate **LB**
2WD

FIRST 7.5 MI—12 KM;
THEN EVERY 15 MI—24 KM
Tires . . . . .rotate

EVERY 24 MO/22.5 MI—36 KM
Front suspension ball joints .lubricate **LB**
Parking brake ratio
lever pivot . . . . .lubricate **LB**
Transmission linkage . . . .**fitting LB**
OD only, while in reverse, engine off

EVERY 22.5 MI—36 KM
Brake linings . . . . .inspect
Front wheel bearings 2WD   . .inspect **GC**
Also inspect at brake inspection or servicing; lubricate rear wheel bearings whenever axles are removed. Clean/repack front wheel bearings when replacing disc pads ex. Dakota, clean/repack when brake rotors are resurfaced

Propeller shafts, 2WD . . . . .lubricate **LB**

AT FIRST 36 MO/52.5 MI—84 KM;
THEN EVERY 24 MO/30 MI—48 KM
Cooling system . . . . .change coolant **EC**
Also flush system at first 36 mo/52.5 mi (84 km), then every 24 mo/30 mi (48 km). 1993 add two Mopar Stop Leak Nuggets Part No. 4318005

EVERY 30 MI—48 KM
W Air cleaner element . . . . .replace
Clean air filter wrapper if equipped

W Drive belts 4-cyl. . . . . . . .inspect/adjust

W PCV filter . . . . .replace
If equipped

W Spark plugs . . . . .replace

EVERY 37.5 MI—60 KM
Transfer case . . . . .change lubricant

Transmission, automatic . . . .change fluid
Not required for Ram Wagon. Replace filter & adjust bands

Transmission, manual . .change lubricant

EVERY 60 MI—96 KM
Battery . . . . .replace

Crankcase inlet
air cleaner ex. 4-cyl. . . . . . . .clean/oil

Drive belts (V-Type) . . . . .replace

EGR Valve & Tube . . . . .replace
Clean passages

Ignition cables,
distributor cap & rotor . . . . . . .replace

Ignition timing . . . . .check
1990-91 All. 1992 5.9L

Manifold heat
valve if equipped . . .check/lubricate **MH**

PCV valve . . . . .replace

Vacuum operated
emission components . . . . . . .replace

EVERY 82.5 MI—132 KM
Oxygen sensor . . . . .replace

SERVICE AS REQUIRED
Fuel filter . . . . .replace

Rear wheel bearings,
Dana axle . . . . .inspect **GC**
Repack as required or whenever axles are removed or Dana axle brakes are serviced, repack

Transfer case linkage . . . . .lubricate
NP205 lubricate with **MO**
NP207, NP208, NP241 lubricate with **LB**

Vacuum & fuel rubber hoses . . . . .check

SEVERE SERVICE
W **Crankcase**—Drain every 3 mo/3 mi (4.8 km). Every 50 hours for 4WD used for off-road driving

Differential—change fluid every 12 mi (19 km) when frequent trailer towing. Axle fluid should be changed when axle is submerged in water

Drive line fittings—Lubricate every 3 mo/3 mi (4.8 km). Inspect 4WD front wheel bearings every 1 mi (1.6 km) for off-road use. Lubricate daily if operating in water

Suspension ball joints—Lubricate every engine oil change

Transmission, automatic—Change fluid every 12 mi (19 km). Replace filter & adjust bands

Transmission, manual—Change lubricant every 18 mi (29 km)

KEY TO LUBRICANTS
AF2	DEXRON®-II ATF
AP3	MOPAR ATF+3®
CD	Motor Oil, API Service CD
EC	Ethylene Glycol Coolant
	Mix with water to desired freeze protection
GC	Wheel Bearing Grease, NLGI Classification GC
GL-4	Gear Oil, API Service GL-4
GL-5	Gear Oil, API Service GL-5
GL-5★	Special Lubricant for Anti-Spin, Limited-Slip, Powr-Loc, Sure-Grip or Trac-Loc Differential
HB	Hydraulic Brake Fluid, DOT 3
LB	Chassis Grease, NLGI Classification LB
MH	Manifold Heat Valve Solvent
MO	Motor Oil
PC	Carburetor Cleaner
PS	Power Steering Fluid
SG	Motor Oil, API Service SG

CRANKCASE . . . . .SG, SG/CD

CAPACITY, Refill:	Liters	Qt
All	3.8	4.0

Capacity shown is without filter. When replacing filter, additional oil may be added.
Above 0°F (-18°C) 10W-30
Below 32°F (0°C) 5W-30

TRANSMISSION, Automatic AP3

CAPACITY, Initial Refill[2]:	Liters	Qt
All models	3.8	4.0

2 With the engine at operating temperature, shift transmission through all gears. Check fluid level in NEUTRAL and add fluid as needed

TRANSMISSION, Manual
AX-15 . . . . .75W-90 **GL-5**
A833 OD **AP3, AF2**
75W, 75W-80, 80W-90, 85W-90, 90 **GL-5** may also be used
NP435 . . . . **GL-5, SG, SG/CD**
SG, SG/CD: Above 32°F (0°C), 50; below 32°F (0°C), 30
GL-5: Above 90°F (32°C), 140; above -10°F (-23°C), 90; below -10°F (-23°C), 80W
NP2500 . . . . .10W-30 **SG, SG/CD**
Use **AP3** below 32°F (0°C) to improve shift efforts
NV4500 . . . . .Synthetic 75W-85 **GL-4**[3]
3 Part No. 4874459

CAPACITY, Refill:	Liters	Pt
NP435	3.3	7.0
NP2500	1.9	4.0
AX-15	3.1	6.6
NV4500	3.8	8.0
A833 OD	3.5	7.5

TRANSFER CASE
NP205 . . . . **GL-5, SG, SG/CD**
SG, SG/CD: Above 32°F (0°C), 50; below 32°F (0°C), 30
GL-5: Above 90°F (32°C), 140; above -10°F (-23°C), 90; below -10°F (-23°C), 80W
NP207, 208, 231, 241 . . . .**AP3, AF2**

CAPACITY, Refill:	Liters	Pt
NP205, NP207	2.1	4.5
NP208	2.8	6.0
NP231: 1990-91	1.2	2.5
1992	1.0	2.2
NP241	2.2	4.6

DIFFERENTIAL
Above 90°F (32°C), 140, 80W-140, 85W-140; above -10°F (-23°C), 90, 80W-90, 80W-140, 85W-90; below -10°F (-23°C), 75W, 80W, 75W-90, 80W-140
Standard & all Dana, Spicer **GL-5**
Anti-Spin, Limited-Slip, Powr-Loc, Sure-Grip,
Trac-Loc ex. Dana, Spicer . . . . . .**GL-5★**
All with limited slip add one container of Mopar Trac-Loc additive

CAPACITY, Refill[4]:	Liters	Pt
Front: 4-wheel drive		
Dakota	1.2	2.6
Spicer 60F axle	3.1	6.5
Others	2.7	5.6
Rear	1.4	3.0
Dana 60, 60 HD	2.8	6.0
Dana 70	3.3	7.0
Others	2.1	4.5

4 1992 Dana axles, lubricant level must be ½-1" (12-24 mm) below fill plug opening

DODGE TRUCKS
1993 All Gasoline Heavy Duty Emission Models

SERVICE AT TIME OR MILEAGE — WHICHEVER OCCURS FIRST

DETPM21   DETPM21

W SERVICE TO MAINTAIN EMISSION WARRANTY
Heavy duty models have emission control label on the air cleaner and hose routing label on underside of the hood.

MI—MILES IN THOUSANDS
KM—KILOMETERS IN THOUSANDS

EVERY 6 MO/6 MI—9.6 KM
Brake hoses . . . . .inspect

Crankcase . . . . .change oil
Change oil filter every other oil change but at least every 12 months

Differential . . . . .check for leaks

Engine coolant, hoses, clamps . . .inspect
At mileage interval only

Steering linkage, suspension
   ball joints . . . . .lubricate **LB**

Exhaust system . . . . .inspect

Suspension ball joints, seals,
   U-joints (sealed) 2WD . . . . . . .inspect

Transfer case . . . . .check level

Transmission, manual . . . . .check level

Air intake & air injection system . .inspect

Brake master cylinder . . .check level **HB**

Power steering reservoir . . check level **PS**
CB & MB 350 require Hydroboost Power Steering Fluid **PS★**

Transmission, automatic . . . .check level
Fluid warm, engine idling, in NEUTRAL

EVERY 12 MONTHS
Air conditioning system . . . . .inspect

EVERY 12 MO/12 MI—19 KM
Front wheel bearings
   4WD . . . . .inspect **GC**
At mileage interval only or when replacing disc pads. With 44F-BJ & 60F front differentials, clean & repack front spindle needle bearings

EVERY 22.5 MI—36 KM
Brake linings . . . . .inspect

EVERY 24 MO/24 MI—38 KM
Propeller shafts, 4WD . . . . .lubricate **LB**
And slip splines

Air cleaner element . . . . .replace

W Air pump filter . . . . .replace

Front wheel bearings, 2WD . .inspect **GC**
At mileage interval only. Also inspect at brake inspection or servicing; lubricate rear wheel bearings whenever axles are removed. Clean/repack front wheel bearings when replacing disc pads

Transmission, automatic . . . .change fluid
At mileage interval only. Replace filter & adjust bands

Crankcase inlet air cleaner . . . .clean/oil

AT FIRST 36 MO/54 MI—84 KM
THEN EVERY 24 MO/30 MI—48 KM
Cooling system . . . . .change coolant **EC**
Add two Mopar Stop Leak Nuggets Part No. 4318005

EVERY 30 MI—48 KM
W Spark plugs . . . . .replace

EVERY 37.5 MI—60 KM
Transfer case . . . . .change lubricant

Transmission, manual . .change lubricant

EVERY 60 MO/60 MI—96 KM
Battery . . . . .replace

EGR valve . . . . .replace
Also clean passages. Or as indicated by emissions maintenance light

Ignition cables, distributor cap
   & rotor . . . . .replace

PCV valve . . . . .replace
Or as indicated by emissions maintenance light

EVERY 84 MO/84 MI—135 KM
Oxygen sensor . . . . .replace
Or as indicated by emissions maintenance light

SERVICE AS REQUIRED
W Drive belts . . . . .inspect

EGR system . . . . .inspect

W Fuel filter . . . . .replace

Rear wheel bearings,
   Dana axles . . . . .inspect **GC**
Repack as required or whenever axles are removed or Dana axle brakes are serviced, repack

Transfer case linkage . . . . .lubricate
NP205, **MO**; NP208 & NP241, **LB**

SEVERE SERVICE
Crankcase—Drain every 3 mo/3 mi (4.8 km). Every 50 hours for 4WD used for off-road driving

Differential—Change fluid every 12 mi (19 km) when frequent trailer towing. Axle fluid should be changed when axel is submerged in water

Drive line fittings—Lubricate every 3 mo/ 3 mi (4.8 km), every 1 mi (1.6 km), includes front wheel bearing inspection for off-road use. Lubricate daily if operating in water

Suspension ball joints—Lubricate every engine oil change

Transmission, automatic—Change fluid every 12 mi (19 km). Replace filter & adjust bands

Transmission, manual—Change lubricant every 18 mi (29 km)

KEY TO LUBRICANTS
See inside front cover

CRANKCASE . . . . .SG, SG/CD
CAPACITY, Refill:	Liters	Qt
All	3.8	4.0

Capacity shown is without filter. When replacing filter, additional oil may be needed
Above 0°F (-18°C) 10W-30
Below 32°F (0°C) 5W-30

TRANSMISSION, Automatic AP3
CAPACITY, Initial Refill[2]:	Liters	Qt
All models	3.8	4.0

2 With the engine at operating temperature, shift transmission through all gears. Check fluid level in NEUTRAL and add fluid as needed

TRANSMISSION, Manual
AX-15 . . . . .75W-90 **GL-5**
A833 OD **AP3, AF2**
75W, 75W-80, 80W-90, 85W-90, 90 **GL-5** may be used
NP435 . . . .**GL-5, SG, SG/CD**
SF/CC, SF/CD, SG, SG/CD: Above 32°F (0°C), 50; below 32°F (0°C), 30
GL-5: Above 90°F (32°C), 140; above -10°F (-23°C), 90; below -10°F (-23°C), 80W
NV4500 . . . . .Synthetic 75W-85 **GL-4**[3]
3 Part No. 4874459
CAPACITY, Refill:	Liters	Pt
NP435	3.3	7.0
AX-15	3.1	6.6
NV4500	3.8	8.0
A833 OD	3.5	7.5

TRANSFER CASE
NP205: . . . .**GL-5, SG, SG/CD**
SG, SG/CD: Above 32°F (0°C), 50; below 32°F (0°C), 30
GL-5: Above 90°F (32°C), 140; above -10°F (-23°C), 90; below -10°F (-23°C), 80W
NP207, 208, 241 . . . .**AP3, AF2**
CAPACITY, Refill:	Liters	Pt
NP205, NP207	2.1	4.5
NP208	2.8	6.0
NP241	2.2	4.6

DIFFERENTIAL
Above 90°F (32°C), 140, 80W-140, 85W-140; above -10°F (-23°C), 90, 80W-90, 80W-140, 85W-140; below -10°F (-23°C), 75W, 80W, 75W-90, 80W-140
Standard & all Dana/Spicer **GL-5**
Anti-Spin, Limited-Slip, Powr-Loc,
   Sure-Grip, Trac-Loc
   ex. Dana/Spicer . . . .**GL-5★**
All with limited slip add one container of Mopar Trac-Loc additive
CAPACITY, Refill[4]:	Liters	Pt
Front: 4-wheel drive		
Spicer 60F	3.1	6.5
Others	2.7	5.6
Rear: Dana 60, 60 HD	2.8	6.0
Dana 70	3.3	7.0
Others	2.1	4.5

4 Dana axles, lubricant level must be ½-1" (12-24 mm) below fill plug opening

DODGE TRUCKS
1993 All Rear-Wheel & 4-Wheel
Light Duty Gasoline Emission Models Except Raider & Ram 50

SERVICE AT TIME OR MILEAGE — WHICHEVER OCCURS FIRST

W   SERVICE TO MAINTAIN EMISSION WARRANTY

8,500 & under GVWR & all GVWR for B-Series Vans & Wagons. GVWR is found on underside of the hood. See passenger car charts for front wheel drive vans.

MI—MILES IN THOUSANDS
KM—KILOMETERS IN THOUSANDS

EVERY 6 MO/7.5 MI—12 KM

Exhaust system . . . . .inspect

Crankcase . . . . .change oil
Replace oil filter at every other oil change but at least every 12 months

Steering linkage &
   propeller shafts, 4WD . . . .lubricate **LB**

Differential . . . . .check for leaks

W Engine coolant, hoses
   & clamps . . . . .check
At mileage only

Propeller shaft joints,
   4WD Dakota . . . . .lubricate **LB**
At mileage interval only

Steering & suspension . . . . .inspect

Transfer case . . . . .check level

Transmission, manual . . . . . .check level

Transmission, automatic . . . .check level
Fluid warm, engine idling, in NEUTRAL

EVERY 12 MONTHS

Air conditioning system . . . . .inspect
Also check drive belt tension

EVERY 12 MO/15 MI—24 KM

Front wheel bearings
   4WD ex. Dakota . . . . .inspect **GC**
At mileage interval only or when replacing disc pads. With 44F-BJ & 60F front differentials, clean & repack needle bearings

EVERY 12 MI—19 KM

Tires . . . . .rotate

EVERY 24 MO/22.5 MI—36 KM

Front suspension ball joints . . .lubricate **LB**
Also inspect brake hoses

Parking brake ratio
   lever pivot . . . . .lubricate **LB**

Propeller shaft splines,
   4WD Dakota . . . . .lubricate **LB**
At mileage interval only

Propeller shaft joints . . . . . .lubricate **LB**
With fittings. ex. Dakota

Transmission linkage . . . .**fitting LB**
Ex. Dakota. 4-speed OD only, while in reverse, engine off

EVERY 22.5 MI—36 KM

Brake linings . . . . .inspect
Also inspect brake hoses

Front wheel bearings 2WD
   & 4WD Dakota . . . . .inspect **GC**
Also inspect at brake inspection or servicing; lubricate rear wheel bearings whenever axles are removed. Clean/repack front wheel bearings when replacing disc pads ex. Dakota, clean/repack when brake rotors are resurfaced

EVERY 30 MI—48 KM

W Air cleaner element . . . . .replace
Clean air filter wrapper if equipped

W Spark plugs . . . . .replace

EVERY 37.5 MI—60 KM

Transfer case . . . . .change lubricant

Transmission, automatic . . . .change fluid
Not required for Ram Wagon. Replace filter

Transmission, manual . .change lubricant

AT FIRST 36 MO/52.5 MI—84 KM
THEN EVERY 24 MO/30 MI—48 KM

Cooling system . . . . .change coolant **EC**
Also flush system. Add two Mopar Stop Leak Nuggets Part No. 4318005

EVERY 60 MI—96 KM

Ignition wires . . . . .replace

PCV valve . . . . .replace

SERVICE AS REQUIRED

W Drive belts . . . . .inspect/adjust

Brake & clutch
   master cylinder . . . . . . .check level **HB**

Fuel filter . . . . .replace

Power steering reservoir .check level **PS**

Body, brake & clutch
   actuating mechanisms . . .lubricate **MO**

Rear wheel bearings,
   Dana axle . . . . .inspect **GC**
Repack as required or whenever axles are removed or Dana axle brakes are serviced, repack

Brake booster
   bellcrank pivot B-series . . .lubricate **MO**

Transfer case linkage . . . . .lubricate
NP205 lubricate with **MO**
NP207, NP208, NP241 lubricate with **LB**

SEVERE SERVICE

Air cleaner element—Inspect every 15 mi (24 km)

W Crankcase—Drain every 3 mo/3 mi (4.8 km). Every 50 hours for 4WD used for off-road driving

Differential— change fluid every 12 mi (19 km) when frequent trailer towing. Axle fluid should be changed when axle is submerged in water

Drive line fittings—Lubricate every 3 mo/ 3 mi (4.8 km). Inspect 4WD front wheel bearings every 1 mi (1.6 km) for off-road use. Lubricate daily if operating in water

Transmission, automatic—Change fluid every 12 mi (19 km). Replace filter

Transmission, manual—Change lubricant every 18 mi (29 km)

KEY TO LUBRICANTS

AF2	DEXRON®-II ATF
AP3	MOPAR ATF+3®
CD	Motor Oil, API Service CD
EC	Ethylene Glycol Coolant Mix with water to desired freeze protection
GC	Wheel Bearing Grease, NLGI Classification GC
GL-4	Gear Oil, API Service GL-4
GL-5	Gear Oil, API Service GL-5
GL-5★	Special Lubricant for Anti-Spin, Limited-Slip, Powr-Loc, Sure-Grip or Trac-Loc Differential
HB	Hydraulic Brake Fluid, DOT 3
LB	Chassis Grease, NLGI Classification LB
MH	Manifold Heat Valve Solvent
MO	Motor Oil
PC	Carburetor Cleaner
PS	Power Steering Fluid
SG	Motor Oil, API Service SG

CRANKCASE . . . . .SG, SG/CD

CAPACITY, Refill:	Liters	Qt
All	3.8	4.0

Capacity shown is without filter. When replacing filter, additional oil may be needed
Above 0°F (-18°C) 10W-30
Below 32°F (0°C) 5W-30

TRANSMISSION, Automatic AP3

CAPACITY, Initial Refill[2]:	Liters	Qt
All models	3.8	4.0

2 With the engine at operating temperature, shift transmission through all gears. Check fluid level in NEUTRAL and add fluid as needed

TRANSMISSION, Manual

AX-15 . . . . .75W-90 **GL-5**
A833 OD **AP3, AF2**
75W, 75W-80, 80W-90, 85W-90, 90 **GL-5** may also be used
NP435 . . . .**GL-5, SG, SG/CD**
SG, SG/CD: Above 32°F (0°C), 50; below 32°F (0°C), 30
GL-5: Above 90°F (32°C), 140; above -10°F (-23°C), 90; below -10°F (-23°C), 80W
NP2500 . . . . .10W-30 **SG, SG/CD**
Use **AP3** below 32°F (0°C) to improve shift efforts
NV4500 . . . . .Synthetic 75W-85 **GL-4**[3]
3 Part No. 4874459

CAPACITY, Refill:	Liters	Pt
NP435	3.3	7.0
NP2500	1.9	4.0
AX-15	3.1	6.6
NV4500	3.8	8.0
A833 OD	3.5	7.5

TRANSFER CASE

NP205 . . . .**GL-5, SG, SG/CD**
SG, SG/CD: Above 32°F (0°C), 50; below 32°F (0°C), 30
GL-5: Above 90°F (32°C), 140; above -10°F (-23°C), 90; below -10°F (-23°C), 80W
NP207, 208, 231, 241 . . . .**AP3, AF2**

CAPACITY, Refill:	Liters	Pt
NP205, NP207	2.1	4.5
NP208	2.8	6.0
NP231	1.0	2.2
NP241	2.2	4.6

DIFFERENTIAL

Above 90°F (32°C), 140, 80W-140, 85W-140; above -10°F (-23°C), 90, 80W-90, 80W-140, 85W-140; below -10°F (-23°C), 75W, 80W, 75W-90, 80W-140
Standard & all Dana, Spicer **GL-5**
Anti-Spin, Limited-Slip, Powr-Loc, Sure-Grip, Trac-Loc ex. Dana, Spicer . . . .**GL-5★**
All with limited slip add one container of Mopar Trac-Loc additive

CAPACITY, Refill[4]:	Liters	Pt
Front: 4-wheel drive		
Dakota	1.2	2.6
Spicer 60F axle	3.1	6.5
Others	2.7	5.6
Rear	1.4	3.0
Dana 60, 60 HD	2.8	6.0
Dana 70	3.3	7.0
Others	2.1	4.5

4 Dana axles, lubricant level must be ½-1" (12-24 km) below fill plug opening

SERVICE AT TIME OR MILEAGE — WHICHEVER OCCURS FIRST

DETPM22   DETPM22

W   SERVICE TO MAINTAIN EMISSION WARRANTY
Heavy duty models have emission control label on the air cleaner and hose routing label on underside of the hood.

MI—MILES IN THOUSANDS
KM—KILOMETERS IN THOUSANDS

EVERY 6 MO/6 MI—9.6 KM
Brake hoses . . . . .inspect

Crankcase . . . . .change oil
8.0L change oil filter every oil change. All others every second oil change

Differential . . . . .check for leaks

Exhaust system . . . . .inspect

Engine coolant, hoses, clamps . . .inspect

Steering linkage, suspension
    & 4WD propeller shafts . . .lubricate LB
Also lubricate slip splines

Suspension ball joints, seals,
    U-joints (sealed) 2WD . . . . . . .inspect

Front axle drive joint
    & pivot bearings . . . . .lubricate LB

Tires . . . . .rotate

Transfer case . . . . .check level

Transmission, manual . . . . .check level

Brake master cylinder . . .check level HB

Power steering
    reservoir . . . . .check level PS
CB & MB 350 require Hydroboost Power Steering Fluid PS★

Transmission, automatic . . . .check level
Fluid warm, engine idling, in NEUTRAL

EVERY 12 MONTHS
Air conditioning system . . . . .inspect

EVERY 12 MO/12 MI—19 KM
Front wheel bearings
    4WD . . . . .inspect GC
At mileage interval only or when replacing disc pads

Cooling system . . . . .inspect

EVERY 24 MO/24 MI—38 KM
W Air cleaner element . . . . .replace

W Air pump filter . . . . .replace

Front wheel bearings, 2WD . . inspect GC
Also inspect at brake inspection or servicing; lubricate rear wheel bearings whenever axles are removed. Clean/repack front wheel bearings when replacing disc pads

Transmission, automatic . . . .change fluid
Replace filter & adjust bands

Crankcase inlet air cleaner . . . .clean/oil

EVERY 54 MO/54 MI—85 KM
Cooling system . . . . .change coolant EC

EVERY 30 MO/30 MI—48 KM
W Spark plugs . . . . .replace

EVERY 36 MO/36 MI—58 KM
Transfer case . . . . .change lubricant

Transmission, manual . .change lubricant

EVERY 60 MO/60 MI—96 KM
Battery . . . . .replace

EGR valve . . . . .replace
Also clean passages. Or as indicated by emissions maintenance light

Ignition cables . . . . .replace

PCV valve . . . . .replace
Or as indicated by emissions maintenance light

EVERY 82.5 MI—133 KM
Oxygen sensor . . . . .replace
5.9L only or as indicated by emissions maintenance light

SERVICE AS REQUIRED
W Drive belts . . . . .inspect

EGR system . . . . .inspect

W Fuel filter . . . . .replace

Rear wheel bearings,
    Dana axles . . . . .inspect GC
Repack as required or whenever axles are removed or Dana axle brakes are serviced, repack

Transfer case linkage . . . . .lubricate LB

SEVERE SERVICE
Crankcase—Drain every 3 mo/3 mi (4.8 km). Every 50 hours for 4WD used for off-road driving

Differential—Change lubricant every 12 mi (19 km). Axle fluid should be changed when axle is submerged in water

Drive line fittings—Lubricate every 3 mo/ 3 mi (4.8 km), every 1 mi (1.6 km), includes front wheel bearing inspection for off-road use. Lubricate daily if operating in water

Suspension ball joints—Lubricate every engine oil change

Transmission, automatic—Change fluid every 12 mi (19 km). Replace filter & adjust bands

Transmission, manual—Change lubricant every 18 mi (29 km)

KEY TO LUBRICANTS
AF2	DEXRON®-II ATF
AP3	MOPAR ATF+3®
CD	Motor Oil, API Service CD
EC	Ethylene Glycol Coolant
	Mix with water to desired freeze protection
GC	Wheel Bearing Grease, NLGI Classification GC
GL-4	Gear Oil, API Service GL-4
GL-5	Gear Oil, API Service GL-5
GL-5★	Special Lubricant for Anti-Spin, Limited-Slip, Powr-Loc, Sure-Grip or Trac-Loc Differential
HB	Hydraulic Brake Fluid, DOT 3
LB	Chassis Grease, NLGI Classification LB
MH	Manifold Heat Valve Solvent
MO	Motor Oil
PC	Carburetor Cleaner
PS	Power Steering Fluid
SG	Motor Oil, API Service SG

CRANKCASE . . . . .SG, SG/CD
CAPACITY, Refill:	Liters	Qt
8.0L (includes filter)	6.6	7.0
All others	3.8	4.0

Capacity shown is without filter. When replacing filter, additional oil may be needed
Above 0°F (-18°C) 10W-30
Below 32°F (0°C) 5W-30

TRANSMISSION, Automatic AP3
CAPACITY, Initial Refill[2]:	Liters	Qt
46RH	4.9	5.7
47RH	14.6[3]	15.4[3]

2 With the engine at operating temperature, shift transmission through all gears. Check fluid level in NEUTRAL and add fluid as needed
3 Dry or total fill

TRANSMISSION, Manual
NV4500 . . . . .Synthetic 75W-85 GL-4[4]
4 Part No. 4874459
CAPACITY, Refill:	Liters	Pt
NV4500	3.8	8.0

TRANSFER CASE
NP241 . . . . .AP3, AF2
CAPACITY, Refill:	Liters	Pt
NP241	2.2	4.6
NP241 HD	3.1	6.5

PTO ADAPTER AP3, AF2
CAPACITY, Refill:	Liters	Pt
NV021	2.1	4.6

DIFFERENTIAL
Above 90°F (32°C), 140, 80W-140, 85W-140; above -10°F (-23°C), 90, 80W-90, 80W-140, 85W-140; below -10°F (-23°C), 75W, 80W, 75W-90, 80W-140
Standard & all Dana/Spicer GL-5
Anti-Spin, Limited-Slip, Powr-Loc,
    Sure-Grip, Trac-Loc
    ex. Dana/Spicer . . . . .GL-5★
All with limited slip add one container of Mopar Trac-Loc additive
CAPACITY, Refill[5]:	Liters	Pt
Front: 4-wheel drive		
Dana 60	3.0	6.3
Rear: Dana 60	3.0	6.3
Dana 70	3.2	6.7
Dana 80	3.3	6.8

5 Lubricant level in axle must be ¼"-¾" (6-17 mm) below fill plug opening.

DODGE TRUCKS
1994 All Rear-Wheel & 4-Wheel
Light Duty Gasoline Emission Models Except Raider & Ram 50

SERVICE AT TIME OR MILEAGE — WHICHEVER OCCURS FIRST

DETPM24   DETPM24

W   SERVICE TO MAINTAIN EMISSION WARRANTY

8,500 & under GVWR & all GVWR for B-Series Vans & Wagons. GVWR is found on underside of the hood. See passenger car charts for front-wheel drive vans.

MI—MILES IN THOUSANDS
KM—KILOMETERS IN THOUSANDS

EVERY 6 MO/7.5 MI—12 KM

Exhaust system . . . . .inspect

Crankcase . . . . .change oil
Replace oil filter at every other oil change but at least every 12 months

Steering linkage . . . .inspect/lubricate **LB**
Ex. B-Series

Differential . . . . .check for leaks

W Engine coolant, hoses
   & clamps . . . . .check

Propeller shaft U joints,
   & slip splines 4WD . . . . . . .lubricate **LB**
Ex. Dakota slip splines

Universal joints, B-Series . . .lubricate **LB**
As equipped

Tires . . . . .rotate

Brake & fuel hoses . . . . .inspect

Transfer case . . . . .check level

Transmission, manual . . . . .check level

Transmission, automatic . . . .check level
Fluid warm, engine idling, in NEUTRAL

EVERY 12 MONTHS
Air conditioning system . . . . .inspect

EVERY 12 MO/15 MI—24 KM
Brake booster
   Bellcrank pivot, B-Series . .lubricate **MO**
At mileage only

Steering linkage,
   B-Series . . . . .inspect/lubricate **LB**

Front wheel bearings
   4WD ex. Dakota . . . . .inspect **GC**

EVERY 18 MO/22.5 MI—36 KM
Front suspension
   ball joints . . . . .lubricate **LB**

Gearshift control . . . . .lubricate **MO**
Manual transmission Ram truck only

Parking brake ratio
   lever pivot . . . . .lubricate **LB**
Ram truck only

Propeller shaft splines,
   4WD Dakota . . . . .lubricate **LB**
At mileage interval only

Brake linings . . . . .inspect

Front wheel bearings . . . . . .inspect **GC**
All 2WD & 4WD Dakotas. Also inspect at brake inspection or servicing; lubricate rear wheel bearings whenever axles are removed. Clean/repack front wheel bearings when replacing disc pads ex. Dakota, clean/repack when brake rotors are resurfaced

EVERY 24 MO/30 MI—48 KM
W Air cleaner element . . . . .replace
Clean air filter wrapper if equipped

W Drive belt . . . . .check/adjust
2.5L only

W Spark plugs . . . . .replace

EVERY 30 MO/37.5 MI—60 KM
Transfer case . . . . .change lubricant

Transmission, automatic . . . .change fluid
Adjust bands & replace filter

Transmission, manual . .change lubricant

AT FIRST 36 MO/52.5 MI—84 KM
THEN EVERY 24 MO/30 MI—48 KM
Cooling system . . . . .change coolant **EC**
Also flush system

EVERY 48 MO/60 MI—96 KM
W Ignition wires . . . . .replace

PCV valve . . . . .check/replace

EVERY 96 MO/120 MI—193 KM
W Fuel filter . . . . .replace

SERVICE AS REQUIRED
W Drive belts . . . . .inspect/adjust

Brake & clutch
   master cylinder . . . . . . .check level **HB**

Fuel filter . . . . .replace

Power steering reservoir .check level **PS**

Body, brake & clutch
   actuating mechanisms . . .lubricate **MO**

Rear wheel bearings,
   Dana axle . . . . .inspect **GC**
Repack as required or whenever axles are removed or Dana axle brakes are serviced, repack

Transfer case linkage . . . . .lubricate **LB**

SEVERE SERVICE
Air cleaner element—Inspect every 15 mi (24 km)

W Crankcase—Drain every 3 mo/3 mi (4.8 km). Every 50 hours for 4WD used for off-road driving

Differential—Change lubricant every 12 mi (19 km). Axle fluid should be changed when axle is submerged in water

Drive line fittings—Lubricate every 3 mo/ 3 mi (4.8 km). Inspect 4WD front wheel bearings every 1 mi (1.6 km) for off-road use. Lubricate daily if operating in water

Transmission, automatic—Change fluid every 12 mi (19 km). Replace filter and adjust bands

Transmission, manual—Change lubricant every 18 mi (29 km)

KEY TO LUBRICANTS

AF2	DEXRON®-II ATF
AP3	MOPAR ATF+3®
CD	Motor Oil, API Service CD
EC	Ethylene Glycol Coolant
	Mix with water to desired freeze protection
GC	Wheel Bearing Grease, NLGI Classification GC
GLS	Mopar Manual Trans. fluid meeting MS 9224 specification
GL-4	Gear Oil, API Service GL-4
GL-5	Gear Oil, API Service GL-5
GL-5★	Special Lubricant for Anti-Spin, Limited-Slip, Powr-Loc, Sure-Grip or Trac-Loc Differential
HB	Hydraulic Brake Fluid, DOT 3
LB	Chassis Grease, NLGI Classification LB
MH	Manifold Heat Valve Solvent
MO	Motor Oil
PC	Carburetor Cleaner
PS	Power Steering Fluid
SG	Motor Oil, API Service SG

CRANKCASE . . . . .SG, SG/CD

CAPACITY, Refill:	Liters	Qt
All models	3.8	4.0

Capacity shown is without filter. When replacing filter, additional oil may be needed
Above 0°F (-18°C) 10W-30
Below 32°F (0°C) 5W-30

TRANSMISSION, Automatic AP3

CAPACITY, Initial Refill[2]:	Liters	Qt
47RH	14.6[3]	15.4[3]
46RH	4.9	5.7
All others	4.4	5.2

2 With the engine at operating temperature, shift transmission through all gears. Check fluid level in NEUTRAL and add fluid as needed
3 Dry fill

TRANSMISSION, Manual

NV3500	. . . . .GLS
AX-15	. . . . .75W-90 **GL-5**
NV4500	. . . . .Synthetic 75W-85 **GL-4**[4]

4 Part No. 4874459

CAPACITY, Refill:	Liters	Pt
AX-15	3.1	6.6
NV3500	2.0	4.2
NV4500	3.8	8.0

TRANSFER CASE

NP231, 241	. . . . .AP3, AF2

CAPACITY, Refill:	Liters	Pt
NP231	1.2	2.5
NP241	2.2	4.6

DIFFERENTIAL
Above 90°F (32°C), 140, 80W-140, 85W-140; above -10°F (-23°C), 90, 80W-90, 80W-140, 85W-140; below -10°F (-23°C), 75W, 80W, 75W-90, 80W-140

Standard & all Dana, Spicer **GL-5**
Anti-Spin, Limited-Slip, Powr-Loc,
   Sure-Grip, Trac-Loc
   ex. Dana, Spicer . . . .**GL-5★**
All with limited slip add one container of Mopar Trac-Loc additive

CAPACITY, Refill[5]:	Liters	Pt
Front: 4-wheel drive 7¼"	1.4	3.0
Dana 44	2.7	5.6
Dana 60	3.0	6.3
Rear: 7¼"	1.4	3.0
8¼"	2.1	4.4
9¼"	2.2	4.7
Dana 60	3.0	6.3

5 Lubricant level in axle must be ¼-¾" (6-17 mm) below fill plug opening.

DODGE TRUCKS
1995-98 Diesel Models

W   SERVICE TO MAINTAIN EMISSION WARRANTY

KEY TO LUBRICANTS
See inside front cover

MI—MILES IN THOUSANDS
KM—KILOMETERS IN THOUSANDS

EVERY MONTH
Battery . . . . .clean/inspect

Brake master cylinder   . . .check level **HB**

Power steering
  reservoir . . . . .check level **PS**
Part No. 04883077

Coolant reservoir . . . . . . .check level **EC**
Also check rubber seals on each side of radiator (proper fit required)

Transmission, automatic   . . . .check level
Fluid warm, engine idling, in NEUTRAL

Tires . . . . .check

Clutch fluid reservoir, 1995 . . . .check **HB**

Fuel filter . . . . .drain water

W Air filter .check
Check filter minder restriction gauge on air filter housing. Replace filter as needed

EVERY 6 MO/6 MI—9.6 KM
Brake hoses . . . . .inspect

Brake shoes, rear 1998 . . . . .adjust

Exhaust system . . . . .inspect

Front suspension . . . . .inspect

Steering linkage, suspension & 4WD
  propeller shafts . . . .lubricate **GC-LB**
When equipped with fittings

Crankcase . . . . .change oil & filter

Engine coolant, hoses, clamps . . .inspect

Tires . . . . .rotate
At mileage only

Transfer case . . . . .check level

Transmission, manual . . . . .check level

Differential . . . . .check for leaks

EVERY 12 MONTHS
Air conditioning system . . . . .inspect

Coolant concentration . . . . .check

EVERY 12 MO/12 MI—19 KM
Fuel filter . . . . .replace
Also clean strainer

Water pump weep hole . . . .clean/inspect

EVERY 18 MI—29 KM
Drive belts . . . . .inspect
Replace as needed

Brake linings . . . . .inspect

Front wheel bearings,
  2WD, 1995-97 . . . . .inspect EP **GC-LB**
Clean and repack as needed

Fan hub, 1995-97 . . . . .inspect

EVERY 24 MO/24 MI—38 KM
Front wheel bearings,
2WD, 1998 . . . . .inspect EP **GC-LB**
Clean and repack as needed
Fan hub, 1998 . . . . .inspect
Transmission, automatic . . . .change fluid
Replace filter & adjust bands

Valve clearance . . . . .check/adjust

Engine vibration dampener . . . . .inspect

EVERY 36 MO/36 MI—58 KM
Transfer case . . . . .change lubricant

FIRST 36 MO/48 MI—77 KM
THEN EVERY 24 MO/30 MI—48 KM
Cooling system . . . . .change coolant **EC**
Also flush system

EVERY 48 MO/48 MI—77 KM
W Intake air temp. sensor . . . .clean/inspect
1998 Calif. models only.
Replace as needed.

SERVICE AS REQUIRED
Charge air cooler (inter-cooler) . . . .check
Check hoses & clamps

Transfer case shift
  lever pivot . . . . .lubricate **GC-LB**
Lubricate linkage w/**MO**

Clutch pedal linkage   . . .lubricate **GC-LB**

Body, brake & clutch
  actuating mechanisms . . . . . . .lubricate

Rear wheel bearings   . . . .inspect **GC-LB**
Repack as required or whenever axles are removed or Dana axle brakes are serviced, repack

Underhood plastic &
  rubber components . . . . .inspect

SEVERE SERVICE
Brake hoses, exhaust, cooling system—Inspect every 3 mi (4.8 km)

Steering linkage—Lubricate every 3 mi (4.8 km) or daily if operating in water

Crankcase—Change oil and filter every: 3 mo/3 mi (4.8 km)

Transmission, automatic—Change fluid every 12 mi (19 km). Replace filter & adjust bands

Differential—Change lubricant every 12 mi (19 km). Axle fluid should be changed when axle is submerged in water

Brake linings—Inspect every 12 mi (19 km)

Fuel filter—1997-98, replace every 6 mi (10 km). Also clean strainer

Brake shoes (rear)—1998, adjust every 3 mi (4.8 km).

CRANKCASE CG-4

CAPACITY, Refill:	Liters	Qt
5.9L	9.5	10.0

Capacity shown is without filter. When replacing filter, fill it with oil before installing. Run engine and check dipstick, additional oil may be needed. Must let oil settle for 5 minutes before checking

Above 10°F (-12°C)	15W-40
0° to 30°F (-18° to -1°C)	10W-30
-10° to 0°F (-23° to -18°C)	10W-30[1]
Below 0°F (-18°C)	5W-30 synthetic

1 With block heater

TRANSMISSION, Automatic AP3

CAPACITY, Initial Refill[3]:	Liters	Qt
All: 1995	1.9	2.0
1996-98	3.8	4.0

3 With the engine at operating temperature, shift transmission through all gears. Check fluid level in NEUTRAL and add fluid as needed

TRANSMISSION, Manual
NV4500 . . . . .Synthetic 75W-85 **GL-4**[4]
4 Part No. 4874459

CAPACITY, Refill:	Liters	Pt
NV4500	3.8	8.0

TRANSFER CASE
All . . . . .AP3, AF2, AF3, MA

CAPACITY, Refill:	Liters	Pt
NP241 HD, NV241 HD	3.1	6.5
NV241 HD w/PTO	4.9	9.0

PTO ADAPTER . . . . . .AP3, AF2, AF3, MA

CAPACITY, Refill:	Liters	Pt
NV-021	2.1	4.6

DIFFERENTIAL
1997-98 Dana -60 (248), -70 (267), rear:
Standard	90 GL-5
Limited-Slip	90 GL-5★
Others: Standard	80W-90 GL-5
Limited-Slip	80W-90 GL-5★

1995-96
Above 90°F (32°C), 140, 80W-140, 85W-140; above -10°F (-23°C), 90, 80W-90, 80W-140, 85W-140; below -10°F (-23°C), 75W, 80W, 75W-90, 80W-140
Standard & all Dana/Spicer **GL-5**
Anti-Spin, Limited-Slip, Powr-Loc,
  Sure-Grip, Trac-Loc
  ex. Dana/Spicer . . . .**GL-5★**
Rear axles with limited slip include 5% friction modifier additive. Part No. 4318060

CAPACITY, Refill[5]:	Liters	Pt
Front: Dana 60 (248), 1995	3.0	6.3
1996-98	3.6	7.6
Rear: Dana 60 (248) 2WD	3.0	6.3
4WD	3.4	7.3
Dana 70 (267) 2WD	3.3	7.0
4WD	3.6	7.8
Dana 80 (286) 2WD	3.2	6.8
4WD	4.8	10.1

5 Lubricant level in axle must be 1/4-3/4" (6-17 mm) below fill plug opening

SERVICE AT TIME OR MILEAGE — WHICHEVER OCCURS FIRST

DETPM26   DETPM26

W   SERVICE TO MAINTAIN EMISSION WARRANTY
Includes all Ram Truck 3500 models & all models equipped with 8.0L V-10 engine.

MI—MILES IN THOUSANDS
KM—KILOMETERS IN THOUSANDS

EVERY MONTH
Battery . . . . .clean/inspect

Brake master cylinder . . .check level **HB**

Power steering
   reservoir . . . . .check level **PS**
Part No. 04883077

Coolant reservoir . . . . . .check level **EC**
Also check rubber seals on each side of radiator (proper fit required)

Transmission, automatic . . . .check level
Fluid warm, engine idling, in NEUTRAL

Tires . . . . .check

Clutch fluid reservoir (1995) . . .check **HB**

EVERY 6 MO/6 MI—9.6 KM
Brake hoses . . . . .inspect

Brake shoes, rear 1998-99 . . . . . .adjust

Crankcase . . . . .change oil
8.0L change oil filter every oil change. All others every second oil change

Differential . . . . .check for leaks

Exhaust system . . . . .inspect

Engine coolant, hoses, clamps . . .inspect

Steering linkage, suspension & 4WD
   propeller shafts . . . . .lubricate **GC-LB**
When equipped with fittings

Front suspension . . . . .inspect

Tires . . . . .rotate
At mileage only

Transfer case . . . . .check level

Transmission, manual . . . . .check level

EVERY 12 MONTHS
Air conditioning system . . . . .inspect

Coolant concentration . . . . .check

EVERY 12 MO/12 MI—19 KM
Air cleaner element (1999) . . . . . .inspect
8.0L V-10 only ex. Calif. models

EVERY 18 MI—29 KM
Brake linings . . . . .inspect

Front wheel bearings . .inspect EP **GC-LB**
Clean and repack as needed

EVERY 24 MO/24 MI—38 KM
W Air cleaner element . . . . .replace
Ex. 1996-99 Calif. 8.0L V-10

W Air pump filter (as equipped) . . . .replace
Ex. 1996-99 Calif. 8.0L V-10

Front suspension
   ball joints (1995) . . . .lubricate **GC-LB**

Transmission, automatic . . . .change fluid
Replace filter & adjust bands

Crankcase inlet air cleaner . . . . .clean/oil
5.9L

EVERY 30 MO/30 MI—48 KM
W Spark plugs . . . . .replace

W Air cleaner element (1996-99) . . .replace
Calif. 8.0L V10 only

EVERY 36 MO/36 MI—58 KM
Transfer case . . . . .change lubricant

FIRST 36 MO/48 MI—77 KM
THEN EVERY 24 MO/30 MI—48 KM
Cooling system . . . . .change coolant **EC**
Also flush system. Add two Mopar Stop Leak Nuggets Part No. 4318005

EVERY 60 MO/60 MI—96 KM
Battery (1995-96) . . . . .replace

W Distributor cap & rotor . . . . .replace
(5.9L only)

EGR valve . . . . .replace
1995 8.0L & 5.9L
1996-98 5.9L only
Also clean passages. Or as indicated by emissions maintenance light

W Ignition cables . . . . .replace

W PCV valve 5.9L . . . . .replace
Or as indicated by emissions maintenance light

EVERY 82.5 MI—133 KM
Oxygen sensor . . . . .replace
5.9L only or as indicated by emissions maintenance light

SERVICE AS REQUIRED
W Drive belts . . . . .inspect

Clutch pedal linkage . . .lubricate **GC-LB**

EGR system . . . . .inspect

W Fuel filter . . . . .replace

Rear wheel bearings,
   Dana axles . . . . .inspect **GC-LB**
Repack as required or whenever axles are removed or Dana axle brakes are serviced, repack

Parking brake
   mechanism . . . . .lubricate **GC-LB**

Transfer case shift
   lever pivot . . . . .lubricate **GC-LB**
Lubricate linkage w/**MO**

SEVERE SERVICE
Brake hoses, exhaust, cooling system—Inspect every 3 mi (4.8 km)

Steering linkage—Lubricate every 3 mi (4.8 km) or daily if operating in water

Crankcase—Drain every 3 mo/3 mi (4.8 km) or every 50 hours for off-road 4WD use. 8.0L, change oil filter every oil change. All others, every second oil change

Differential—Change lubricant every 12 mi (19 km). Axle fluid should be changed when axle is submerged in water

W **Air cleaner element & air pump filters**—Inspect every 12 mi (19 km)

Crankcase inlet air cleaner—1995, clean oil (5.9L) every 12 mi (19 km)

Brake linings—Inspect every 12 mi (19 km)

Brake shoes (rear)—1998-99, adjust every 3 mi (4.8 km)

Front wheel bearings—1998-99, (ex. Calif. models w/8.0L V-10.) Inspect 4WD every 6 mi (10 km) Inspect 2WD every 9 mi (14 km)

Transfer Case—1999, (ex. Calif. models w/8.0L V-10) change fluid every 18 mi (29 km)

EGR Valve—1999, 5.9L as equipped. Replace every 60 mi (96 km). Also clean passages. Or as indicated by emmision maintenance light.

PCV valve—5.9L inspect every 30 mi (48 km)

Transmission, automatic—Change fluid every 12 mi (19 km). Replace filter & adjust bands

KEY TO LUBRICANTS
See inside front cover

CRANKCASE . . . . .API★

CAPACITY:	Liters	Qt
8.0L (includes filter)	6.6	7.0
5.2L, 5.9L	4.2	4.5

Capacity shown is without filter. When replacing filter, additional oil may be needed

Above 0°F (-18°C) . . . . .10W-30 Preferred
Below 32°F (0°C) 5W-30

TRANSMISSION, Automatic AP3

CAPACITY, Initial Refill[2]:	Liters	Qt
All: 1995	1.9	2.0
1996-99	3.8	4.0

2 With the engine at operating temperature, shift transmission through all gears. Check fluid level in NEUTRAL and add fluid as needed

TRANSMISSION, Manual

NV4500 . . . . .Synthetic 75W-85 **GL-4**[3]
3 Part No. 4874459

NV5600 . . . .**GLS**

CAPACITY, Refill:	Liters	Pt
NV4500	3.8	8.0
NV5600	4.5	9.5

TRANSFER CASE

All . . . .**AP3, AF2, AF3, MA**

CAPACITY, Refill:	Liters	Pt
NP241 (1995)	2.2	4.6
NV241 (1996-99)	2.7	5.0
NP241 HD, NV241 HD	3.1	6.5
NV241 HD w/PTO	4.9	9.0

PTO ADAPTER . . . . . .**AP3, AF2, AF3, MA**

CAPACITY, Refill:	Liters	Pt
NV021	2.1	4.6

DIFFERENTIAL

1997-99 Dana -60 (248), -70 (267), rear:
   Standard 90 **GL-5**
   Limited-Slip . . . . .90 **GL-5**★
Others: Standard 80W-90 **GL-5**
   Limited-Slip . . . . .80W-90 **GL-5**★

1995-96:
Above 90°F (32°C), 140, 80W-140, 85W-140; above -10°F (-23°C), 90, 80W-90, 80W-140, 85W-140; below -10°F (-23°C), 75W, 80W, 75W-90, 80W-140

Standard & all Dana/Spicer **GL-5**

Anti-Spin, Limited-Slip, Powr-Loc,
   Sure-Grip, Trac-Loc
   ex. Dana/Spicer . . . .**GL-5**★
Rear axles with limited slip include 5% friction modifier additive. Part No. 4318060

CAPACITY, Refill[4]:	Liters	Pt
Front: 4-wheel drive		
Dana 60 (248), 1995	3.0	6.3
1996-99	3.6	7.6
Rear: Dana 60 (248) 2WD	3.0	6.3
4WD	3.4	7.3
Dana 70 (267) 2WD	3.3	7.0
4WD	3.6	7.8
Dana 80 (286) 2WD	3.2	6.8
4WD	4.8	10.1

4 Lubricant level in axle must be ¼"-¾" (6-17 mm) below fill plug opening

DODGE TRUCKS
1995-99 All Rear-Wheel & 4-Wheel
Light Duty Gasoline Emission Models

DETPM27   DETPM27

W SERVICE TO MAINTAIN EMISSION WARRANTY

Includes B-Series, Dakota, Durango, Ram 1500 & 2500 model trucks ex. those equipped with 8.0L V-10 engine, see medium & heavy duty chart. See passenger car charts for front wheel drive vans.

MI—MILES IN THOUSANDS
KM—KILOMETERS IN THOUSANDS

EVERY MONTH

Battery . . . . .clean/inspect
Brake master cylinder . . .check level **HB**
Power steering reservoir .check level **PS**
Part No. 04883077
Coolant reservoir . . . . . . .check level **EC**
Also check rubber seals on each side of radiator (proper fit required)
Transmission, automatic . . . .check level
Fluid warm, engine idling, in NEUTRAL
Tires . . . . .check
Clutch fluid reservoir . . . .check level **HB**
1995

EVERY 6 MO/7.5 MI—12 KM

Brake shoes, rear . . . . .adjust
1998-99 Ram Truck only
Exhaust system . . . . .inspect
Crankcase . . . . .change oil
Replace oil filter at every other oil change but at least every 12 months
Steering
   linkage . . . . .inspect/lubricate **GC-LB**
Ex. B-Series & 2WD Dakota/Durango
Differential . . . . .check for leaks
Engine coolant, hoses & clamps . .check
Propeller shaft U joints,
  & slip splines 4WD . . .lubricate **GC-LB**
When equipped with fittings.
Front suspension &
   steering linkage . . . . .inspect
Suspension Arm Bushings,
   B-Series . . . . .inspect
Tires . . . . .rotate
At mileage only
Brake, power
   steering & fuel hoses . . . . .inspect
Transfer case . . . . .check level
Transmission, manual . . . . . .check level

EVERY 12 MONTHS

Air conditioning system . . . . .inspect
Coolant concentration . . . . .check

EVERY 12 MO/15 MI—24 KM

Brake booster
  Bellcrank pivot, B-Series . .lubricate **MO**
3500 only
Steering linkage, B-Series & 2WD
  Dakota/Durango . .inspect/lubricate **GC-LB**

EVERY 18 MO/22.5 MI—36 KM

Front suspension
  ball joints . . . . .lubricate **GC-LB**
B-series, Durango & Dakota
Brake linings . . . . .inspect
Front wheel bearings . . . . .inspect
1998-99 Dakota, Durango
Front wheel bearings
  2WD . . . . .inspect EP **GC-LB**
Ex. 1997-99 Dakota/Durango (inspect only), others clean & repack as needed. Also inspect at brake inspection or servicing; lubricate rear wheel bearings whenever axles are removed. Clean/repack front wheel bearings when replacing disc pads or whenever brake rotors are removed

EVERY 24 MO/30 MI—48 KM

W Air cleaner element . . . . .replace
Clean air filter wrapper if equipped
W Drive belt, 1995 . . . . .check/adjust
2.5L only

W Spark plugs . . . . .replace

EVERY 30 MO/37.5 MI—60 KM

Transfer case . . . . .change lubricant
Transmission, automatic . . . .change fluid
Ex. B-Series
Adjust bands & replace filter
Transmission, manual . .change lubricant
Dakota w/ AX-15 only

AT FIRST 36 MO/52.5 MI—84 KM
THEN EVERY 24 MO/30 MI—48 KM

Cooling system . . . . .change coolant **EC**
Also flush system. Add two Mopar Stop Leak Nuggets Part No. 4318005

EVERY 48 MO/60 MI—96 KM

W Ignition wires . . . . .replace
PCV valve . . . . .check/replace
Ex. 1996-99 2.5L
Crankcase inlet air cleaner . . . .clean/oil
1995 Ex. B-Series & 2.5L
1996 3.9L & 5.2L Dakota
Drive belts . . . . .inspect
Models with automatic tensioner. Inspect every 15 mi (24 km) thereafter if belts are not replaced.
Drive belts, 1995 . . . . .replace
B-Series automatic tensioning belts & 2.5L only
Fuel filter, 1995 . . . . .replace
B-Series & 2.5L Dakota (Federal only)

SERVICE AS REQUIRED

W Drive belts . . . . .inspect/adjust
Clutch pedal linkage . . .lubricate **GC-LB**
Fuel filter . . . . .replace
Body, brake & clutch
  actuating mechanisms . .lubricate **MO**
Rear wheel bearings,
  Dana axle . . . . .inspect **GC-LB**
Repack as required or whenever axles are removed or Dana axle brakes are serviced, repack
Transfer case shift
  lever pivot . . . . .lubricate **GC-LB**
Lubricate linkage w/MO

SEVERE SERVICE

W Air cleaner element—Inspect every 15 mi (24 km)
Crankcase—Drain every 3 mo/3 mi (4.8 km) or every 50 hours for off-road 4WD use. Change filter every second oil change
Differential—Change lubricant every 12 mi (19 km). Axle fluid should be changed when axle is submerged in water
Brake linings—Inspect every 12 mi (19 km)
Brake shoes, rear—(1998-99 Ram Truck) adjust every 3 mi (4.8 km)
PCV valve—Inspect every 30 mi (48 km)
Ball joints—(Dakota, 1998 Durango & 1997-98 B-Series) lubricate every 12 mi (19 km)
Brake hoses, exhaust, cooling system—Inspect every 3 mi (4.8 km)
Tires—Rotate every 6 mi (10 km)
Steering linkage—Lubricate every 3 mi (4.8 km) or daily if operating in water
Transmission, automatic—Change fluid every 12 mi (19 km). Replace filter and adjust bands
Transmission, manual—Change lubricant every 18 mi (29 km). Dakota w/AX-15 only

KEY TO LUBRICANTS
See inside front cover

CRANKCASE . . . . .API★

CAPACITY, Refill:	Liters	Qt
2.5L	3.8	4.0
3.9L	3.3	3.5
5.2L, 5.9L	4.2	4.5

Capacity shown is without filter. When replacing filter, additional oil may be needed
Above 0°F (-18°C) . . . . .10W-30 Preferred
Below 32°F (0°C) 5W-30

TRANSMISSION, Automatic AP3

CAPACITY, Initial Refill[2]:	Liters	Qt
1995: Ram Truck 1500-2500 . . .	1.9	2.0
Others	1.4	1.5
1996-99 All	3.8	4.0

2 With the engine at operating temperature, shift transmission through all gears. Check fluid level in NEUTRAL and add fluid as needed

TRANSMISSION, Manual

NV1500, NV3500 . . . . .GLS[5]
AX-15 1995-97 . . . . .75W-90 GL-5
1998-99 . . . . .75W-90 GL-3*
* Part No. 04897622AA
NV4500 . . . . .Synthetic 75W-85 GL-4[3]
3 Part No. 4874459
5 NV1500, include 0.2 pt. (0.1L) friction modifier

CAPACITY, Refill:	Liters	Pt
AX-15	3.1	6.6
NV1500	2.2	4.7
NV3500	2.0	4.2
NV4500	3.8	8.0

TRANSFER CASE

All . . . . .AP3, AF3, AF2, MA

CAPACITY, Refill:	Liters	Pt
NP231, NV231 HD	1.2	2.5
NP241 (1995)	2.2	4.6
NV241 (1996-99)	2.7	5.0
NV242	1.3	2.9

DIFFERENTIAL

1998-99 8¼" & 9¼" rear:
  Standard 75W-90 **GL-5**
  Limited-Slip . . . . .75W-90 **GL-5★**
1997-99 Dana 60 (248) rear:
  Standard 90 **GL-5**
  Limited-Slip . . . . .90 **GL-5★**
Others: Standard 80W-90 **GL-5**
  Limited-Slip . . . . .80W-90 **GL-5★**
1995-96
Above 90°F (32°C), 140, 80W-140, 85W-140; above -10°F (-23°C), 90, 80W-90, 80W-140, 85W-140; below -10°F (-23°C), 75W, 80W, 75W-90, 80W-140
Standard & all Dana, Spicer **GL-5**
Anti-Spin, Limited-Slip, Powr-Loc, Sure-Grip,
  Trac-Loc ex. Dana, Spicer . . . . . .**GL-5★**
Rear axles with limited slip include 5% friction modifier additive. Part No. 4318060

CAPACITY, Refill[4]:	Liters	Pt
Front: 4-wheel drive 7¼"	1.4	3.0
Model 194 FIA	1.4	3.0
Dana 44 (216), 1995	2.7	5.6
1996-98	3.2	6.8
1999	2.3	4.8
Dana 60 (248), 1995	3.0	6.3
1996-99	3.6	7.6
Rear: 7¼"	1.4	3.0
8¼"	2.1	4.4
9¼"	2.2	4.7
Dana 60 (248) 2WD	3.0	6.3
4WD	3.4	7.3

4 Lubricant level in axle must be ¼-¾" (6-17 mm) below fill plug opening.

DODGE TRUCKS
2000 All Gasoline Medium & Heavy Duty Emission Models

SERVICE AT TIME OR MILEAGE — WHICHEVER OCCURS FIRST

DETPM28   **W SERVICE TO MAINTAIN EMISSION WARRANTY**   DETPM28

Includes all Ram Truck 3500 models & all models equipped with 8.0L V-10 engine.

MI—MILES IN THOUSANDS
KM—KILOMETERS IN THOUSANDS

EVERY MONTH
Battery . . . . .clean/inspect

Brake master cylinder . . .check level **HB**

Power steering
reservoir . . . . .check level **PS**
Part No. 04883077

Coolant reservoir . . . . . .check level **EC**
Also check rubber seals on each side of radiator (proper fit required)

Transmission, automatic . . . .check level
Fluid warm, engine idling, in NEUTRAL

Tires .check

EVERY 6 MO/6 MI—9.6 KM
Brake hoses . . . . .inspect

Brake shoes, rear . . . . .adjust

Crankcase . . . . .change oil

Oil filter . . . . .replace

Differential . . . . .check for leaks

Exhaust system . . . . .inspect

Engine coolant, hoses, clamps . . .inspect

Steering linkage, suspension & 4WD
propeller shafts . . . . .lubricate **GC-LB**
When equipped with fittings

Front suspension . . . . .inspect

Tires .rotate
At mileage only

Transfer case . . . . .check level

Transmission, manual . . . .check level

EVERY 12 MONTHS
Air conditioning system . . . . .inspect

Coolant concentration . . . . .check

EVERY 12 MO/12 MI—19 KM
Air cleaner element . . . . .inspect
8.0L V-10 only ex. Calif. models

EVERY 18 MI—29 KM
Brake linings . . . . .inspect

Front wheel bearings . .inspect EP **GC-LB**
Clean and repack as needed

EVERY 24 MO/24 MI—38 KM
W Air cleaner element . . . . .replace
Ex. Calif. 8.0L V-10

W Air pump filter (as equipped) . . . .replace
Ex. Calif. 8.0L V-10

Transmission, automatic . . . .change fluid
Replace filter & adjust bands

Crankcase inlet air cleaner . . . . .clean/oil
5.9L

EVERY 30 MO/30 MI—48 KM
W Spark plugs . . . . .replace

W Air cleaner element . . . . .replace
Calif. 8.0L V10 only

EVERY 36 MO/36 MI—58 KM
Transfer case . . . . .change lubricant

FIRST 36 MO/48 MI—77 KM
THEN EVERY 24 MO/30 MI—48 KM
Cooling system . . . . .change coolant **EC**
Also flush system

EVERY 60 MO/60 MI—96 KM
W Distributor cap & rotor . . . . .replace
(5.9L only)

W Ignition cables . . . . .replace

W PCV valve 5.9L . . . . .replace
Or as indicated by emissions maintenance light

EVERY 82.5 MI—133 KM
Oxygen sensor . . . . .replace
5.9L only or as indicated by emissions maintenance light

SERVICE AS REQUIRED
W Drive belts . . . . .inspect

Clutch pedal linkage . . .lubricate **GC-LB**

EGR system . . . . .inspect

W Fuel filter . . . . .replace

Rear wheel bearings,
Dana axles . . . . .inspect **GC-LB**
Repack as required or whenever axles are removed or Dana axle brakes are serviced, repack

Parking brake
mechanism . . . . .lubricate **GC-LB**

Transfer case shift
lever pivot . . . . .lubricate **GC-LB**
Lubricate linkage w/**MO**

SEVERE SERVICE
Brake hoses, exhaust, cooling system—Inspect every 3 mi (4.8 km)

Steering linkage—Lubricate every 3 mi (4.8 km) or daily if operating in water

Crankcase—Drain every 3 mo/3 mi (4.8 km) or every 50 hours for off-road 4WD. Change oil filter every oil change

Differential—Change lubricant every 12 mi (19 km). Axle fluid should be changed when axle is submerged in water

W Air cleaner element & air pump filters—Inspect every 12 mi (19 km)

Brake linings—Inspect every 12 mi (19 km)

Brake shoes (rear)—Adjust every 3 mi (4.8 km)

Front wheel bearings—(ex. Calif. models w/8.0L V-10.) Inspect 4WD every 6 mi (10 km) Inspect 2WD every 9 mi (14 km)

Transfer Case—(ex. Calif. models w/8.0L V-10) change fluid every 18 mi (29 km)

EGR Valve—5.9L as equipped. Replace every 60 mi (96 km). Also clean passages. Or as indicated by emmission maintenance light.

PCV valve—5.9L inspect every 30 mi (48 km)

Transmission, automatic—Change fluid every 12 mi (19 km). Replace filter & adjust bands

KEY TO LUBRICANTS
See inside front cover

CRANKCASE . . . . .API★

CAPACITY, Refill:	Liters	Qt
8.0L	6.6	7.0
5.2L, 5.9L	4.7	5.0

Capacity shown includes filter. When replacing filter, additional oil may be needed

Above 0°F (-18°C) . . . . .10W-30 Preferred
Below 100°F (38°C) 5W-30

TRANSMISSION, Automatic AP3

CAPACITY, Initial Refill[2]:	Liters	Qt
All	3.8	4.0

2 With the engine at operating temperature, shift transmission through all gears. Check fluid level in NEUTRAL and add fluid as needed

TRANSMISSION, Manual

NV4500 . . . . .Synthetic 75W-85 **GL-4**[3]
3 Part No. 4874459
NV5600 . . . .**GLS**

CAPACITY, Refill:	Liters	Pt
NV4500	3.8	8.0
NV5600	4.5	9.5

TRANSFER CASE

All AP3, AF3

CAPACITY, Refill:	Liters	Pt
NV241	2.7	5.0
NV241 HD	3.1	6.5
NV241 HD w/PTO	4.9	9.0

PTO ADAPTER AP3, AF3

CAPACITY, Refill:	Liters	Pt
NV021	2.1	4.6

DIFFERENTIAL

Dana -60 (248), -70 (267), rear:
Standard 90 **GL-5**
Limited-Slip . . . . .90 **GL-5**★
Others: Standard 80W-90 **GL-5**
Limited-Slip . . . . . .80W-90 **GL-5**★
Rear axles with limited slip include 5% friction modifier additive. Part No. 4318060

CAPACITY, Refill[4]:	Liters	Pt
Front: 4-wheel drive		
Dana 60 (248)	4.0	8.5
Rear: Dana 60 (248) 2WD	3.0	6.3
4WD	3.4	7.3
Dana 70 (267) 2WD	3.3	7.0
4WD	3.6	7.8
Dana 80 (286) 2WD	3.2	6.8
4WD	4.8	10.1

4 Lubricant level in axle must be ¼"-¾" (6-17 mm) below fill plug opening

SERVICE AT TIME OR MILEAGE — WHICHEVER OCCURS FIRST

DETPM29

DETPM29

W   SERVICE TO MAINTAIN EMISSION WARRANTY

MI—MILES IN THOUSANDS
KM—KILOMETERS IN THOUSANDS

EVERY FUEL STOP
Fuel filter . . . . .drain water

Crankcase oil . . . . .check level

EVERY MONTH
Battery . . . . .clean/inspect

Brake master cylinder . . .check level **HB**

Power steering
  reservoir . . . . .check level **PS**
Part No. 04883077

Coolant reservoir . . . . . .check level **EC**

Transmission, automatic . . . .check level
Fluid warm, engine idling, in NEUTRAL

Tires . . . . .check

W Air filter . . . . .check
Check filter minder restriction gauge on air filter housing.
Replace filter as needed

EVERY 6 MO/7.5 MI—12 KM
Brake hoses . . . . .inspect

Brake shoes, rear . . . . .adjust

Exhaust system . . . . .inspect

Front suspension . . . . .inspect

Steering linkage, suspension & 4WD
  propeller shafts . . . . .lubricate **GC-LB**
When equipped with fittings

Crankcase . . . . .change oil & filter
Or every 200 hours

Engine coolant, hoses, clamps . . .inspect

Tires . . . . .rotate
At mileage only

Transfer case . . . . .check level

Transmission, manual . . . . . .check level

Differential . . . . .check for leaks

EVERY 12 MONTHS
Air conditioning system . . . . .inspect

Coolant concentration . . . . .check

EVERY 12 MO/15 MI—24 KM
Fuel filter . . . . .replace
Also clean strainer

Water pump weep hole . . . .clean/inspect

EVERY 22.5 MI—36 KM
Drive belts . . . . .inspect
Replace as needed

Brake linings . . . . .inspect

EVERY 24 MO/30 MI—48 KM
Front wheel bearings,
  2WD . . . . .inspect EP **GC-LB**
Clean and repack as needed

Fan hub . . . . .inspect
Transmission, automatic . . . .change fluid
Replace filter & adjust bands

Engine vibration dampener . . . . .inspect

EVERY 36 MO/45 MI—72 KM
Transfer case . . . . .change lubricant

FIRST 36 MO/45 MI—72 KM
THEN EVERY 24 MO/30 MI—48 KM
Cooling system . . . . .change coolant **EC**
Also flush system

EVERY 150 MO/150 MI—241 KM
Valve clearance . . . . .check/adjust

SERVICE AS REQUIRED
Charge air cooler (inter-cooler) . . . .check
Check hoses & clamps

Transfer case shift
  lever pivot . . . . .lubricate **GC-LB**
Lubricate linkage w/**MO**

Clutch pedal linkage . . .lubricate **GC-LB**

Body, brake & clutch
  actuating mechanisms . . . . . .lubricate

Rear wheel bearings . . . .inspect **GC-LB**
Repack as required or whenever axles are removed or
Dana axle brakes are serviced, repack

Underhood plastic &
  rubber components . . . . .inspect

SEVERE SERVICE
**Brake hoses, exhaust, cooling
system**—Inspect every 3.75 mi (6 km)

Steering linkage—Lubricate every 3.75
mi (6 km) or daily if operating in water

Crankcase—Change oil and filter every:
3 mo/3.75 mi (6 km)

Transmission, automatic—Change fluid
every 15 mi (24 km). Replace filter & adjust
bands

Differential—Change lubricant every 15 mi
(24 km). Axle fluid should be changed
when axle is submerged in water

Valve clearance—Check/adjust every 135
mi (216 km)

Brake linings—Inspect every 15 mi (24
km)

Fuel filter—replace every 7.5 mi (12 km).
Also clean strainer.

Brake shoes (rear)—adjust every 3.75 mi
(6 km).

KEY TO LUBRICANTS
See inside front cover

CRANKCASE **CG-4**

CAPACITY, Refill:	Liters	Qt
5.9L	9.5	10.0

Capacity shown is without filter. When replacing filter, fill it
with oil before installing. Run engine and check dipstick, additional oil may be needed. Must let oil settle for 5 minutes
before checking

Above 10°F (-12°C) 15W-40
0° to 30°F (-18° to -1°C) 10W-30
-10° to 0°F (-23° to -18°C) . . . . .10W-30[1]
Below 20°F (-7°C) . . . . .5W-30 synthetic
1 With block heater

TRANSMISSION, Automatic **AP3**

CAPACITY, Initial Refill[3]:	Liters	Qt
All	3.8	4.0

3 With the engine at operating temperature, shift transmission through all gears. Check fluid level in NEUTRAL and
add fluid as needed

TRANSMISSION, Manual
NV4500 . . . . .Synthetic 75W-85 **GL-4**[4]
4 Part No. 4874459
NV5600 . . . .**GLS**

CAPACITY, Refill:	Liters	Pt
NV4500	3.8	8.0
NV5600	4.5	9.5

TRANSFER CASE
All **AP3, AF3**

CAPACITY, Refill:	Liters	Pt
NV241 HD	3.1	6.5
NV241 HD w/PTO	4.9	9.0

PTO ADAPTER **AP3, AF3**

CAPACITY, Refill:	Liters	Pt
NV-021	2.1	4.6

DIFFERENTIAL
Dana -60 (248), -70 (267), rear:
  Standard 90 **GL-5**
  Limited-Slip . . . . .90 **GL-5★**
Others: Standard 80W-90 **GL-5**
  Limited-Slip . . . . .80W-90 **GL-5★**
Rear axles with limited slip include 6.5% friction modifier ad-
ditive. Part No. 4318060

CAPACITY, Refill[5]:	Liters	Pt
Front: Dana 60 (248): 1999	3.6	7.6
2000	4.0	8.5
Rear: Dana 60 (248) 2WD	3.0	6.3
4WD	3.4	7.3
Dana 70 (267) 2WD	3.3	7.0
4WD	3.6	7.8
Dana 80 (286) 2WD	3.2	6.9
4WD	4.8	10.1

5 Lubricant level in axle must be ¼-¾" (6-17 mm) below fill
plug opening

SERVICE AT TIME OR MILEAGE — WHICHEVER OCCURS FIRST

DETPM30   DETPM30

W   SERVICE TO MAINTAIN EMISSION WARRANTY

Includes Ram Van/Wagon, Dakota, Durango, Ram 1500 & 2500 model trucks ex. those equipped with 8.0L V-10 engine, see medium & heavy duty chart. See passenger car charts for front wheel drive vans.

MI—MILES IN THOUSANDS
KM—KILOMETERS IN THOUSANDS

EVERY MONTH

Battery . . . . .clean/inspect

Brake master cylinder . . .check level **HB**

Power steering reservoir .check level **PS**
Part No. 04883077

Coolant reservoir . . . . . .check level **EC**

Transmission, automatic . . . .check level
Fluid warm, engine idling, in NEUTRAL

Tires . . . . .check

EVERY 6 MO/7.5 MI—12 KM

Brake shoes, rear . . . . .adjust
Ram Truck only

Exhaust system . . . . .inspect

Crankcase . . . . .change oil

Oil filter . . . . .replace

Steering
   linkage . . . . .inspect/lubricate **GC-LB**
Ex. Ram Van/Wagon & 2WD Dakota/Durango

Differential . . . . .check for leaks

Engine coolant, hoses & clamps . .check

Front suspension &
   steering linkage . . . . .inspect

Tires . . . . .rotate
At mileage only

Brake hoses . . . . .inspect

Transfer case . . . . .check level

Transmission, manual . . . . .check level

EVERY 12 MONTHS

Air conditioning system . . . . .inspect

Coolant concentration . . . . .check

EVERY 12 MO/15 MI—24 KM

Brake booster
   Bellcrank pivot . . . . .lubricate **MO**
Ram Van/Wagon 3500 only

Steering linkage . .inspect/lubricate **GC-LB**
Ram Van/Wagon only

EVERY 18 MO/22.5 MI—36 KM

Front suspension
   ball joints . . . . .lubricate **GC-LB**
Ram Van/Wagon & Ram Truck

Brake linings . . . . .inspect

Front wheel bearings . . . . .inspect
Dakota, Durango

Front wheel bearings
   2WD . . . . .inspect EP **GC-LB**
Ex. Dakota/Durango (inspect only), others clean & repack as needed. Also inspect at brake inspection or servicing; lubricate rear wheel bearings whenever axles are removed. Clean/repack front wheel bearings when replacing disc pads or whenever brake rotors are removed

EVERY 24 MO/30 MI—48 KM

W Air cleaner element . . . . .replace
Clean air filter wrapper if equipped

Drive belt . . . . .check/adjust
2.5L only

W Spark plugs . . . . .replace

Transmission, automatic . . . .change fluid
Dakota/Durango w/4.7L only
Replace filter

EVERY 30 MO/37.5 MI—60 KM

Transfer case . . . . .change lubricant

Transmission, automatic . . . .change fluid
Ex. Dakota/Durango w/4.7L
Adjust bands & replace filter

AT FIRST 36 MO/52.5 MI—84 KM
THEN EVERY 24 MO/30 MI—48 KM

Cooling system . . . . .change coolant **EC**
Also flush system

EVERY 48 MO/60 MI—96 KM

W Ignition wires . . . . .replace
Ex. 4.7L

PCV valve . . . . .check/replace
Ex. 2.5L

Drive belts . . . . .inspect
Models with automatic tensioner. Inspect every 15 mi (24 km) thereafter if belts are not replaced.

SERVICE AS REQUIRED

W Drive belts . . . . .inspect/adjust

Clutch pedal linkage . . .lubricate **GC-LB**

Fuel filter . . . . .replace

Body, brake & clutch
   actuating mechanisms . . .lubricate **MO**

Rear wheel bearings,
   Dana axle . . . . .inspect **GC-LB**
Repack as required or whenever axles are removed or Dana axle brakes are serviced, repack

Transfer case shift
   lever pivot . . . . .lubricate **GC-LB**
Lubricate linkage w/MO

SEVERE SERVICE

W Air cleaner element—Inspect every 15 mi (24 km)

Crankcase—Drain every 3 mo/3 mi (4.8 km) or every 50 hours for off-road 4WD use. Change filter every oil change

Differential—Change lubricant every 12 mi (19 km). Axle fluid should be changed when axle is submerged in water

Brake linings—Inspect every 12 mi (19 km)

Brake shoes, rear—(Ram Truck) adjust every 3 mi (4.8 km)

PCV valve—Inspect every 30 mi (48 km)

Brake hoses, exhaust, cooling system—Inspect every 3 mi (4.8 km)

Tires—Rotate every 6 mi (10 km)

Steering linkage—Lubricate every 3 mi (4.8 km) or daily if operating in water

Transmission, automatic—Change fluid every 12 mi (19 km). Replace filter and adjust bands (as equipped)

KEY TO LUBRICANTS
See inside front cover

CRANKCASE . . . . .API★

CAPACITY, Refill:	Liters	Qt
2.5L, 3.9L	4.3	4.5
4.7L	5.7	6.0
5.2L, 5.9L	4.7	5.0

Capacity shown includes filter. When replacing filter, additional oil may be needed

4.7L V8
Above 0°F (-18°C) 10W-30
Below 100°F (38°C) . . . . .5W-30 Preferred

Others:
Above 0°F (-18°C) . . . . .10W-30 Preferred
Below 100°F (38°C) 5W-30

TRANSMISSION, Automatic AP3

CAPACITY, Initial Refill[2]:	Liters	Qt
45RFE[6]	4.7	5.0
Others	3.8	4.0

2 With the engine at operating temperature, shift transmission through all gears. Check fluid level in NEUTRAL and add fluid as needed
6 DTC's may be set, reset with the DRBIII®, if necessary

TRANSMISSION, Manual
NV1500, NV3500 . . . .**GLS[5]**
NV4500 . . . . .Synthetic 75W-85 **GL-4[3]**
3 Part No. 4874459
5 NV1500, include 0.2 pt. (0.1L) friction modifier

CAPACITY, Refill:	Liters	Pt
NV1500	2.2	4.7
NV3500	2.0	4.2
NV4500	3.8	8.0

TRANSFER CASE
All **AP3, AF3**

CAPACITY, Refill:	Liters	Pt
NV231 HD	1.2	2.5
NV241	2.7	5.0
NV242	1.3	2.9

DIFFERENTIAL
8¼" & 9¼" rear:
   Standard 75W-90 **GL-5**
   Limited-Slip . . . . .75W-90 **GL-5★**
Dana 60 (248) rear:
   Standard 90 **GL-5**
   Limited-Slip . . . . .90 **GL-5★**
Others: Standard 80W-90 **GL-5**
   Limited-Slip . . . . .80W-90 **GL-5★**
Rear axles with limited slip include 5% friction modifier additive. Part No. 4318060

CAPACITY, Refill[4]:	Liters	Pt
Front: Dakota/Durango		
C205F	1.7	3.5
Dana 44 (216)	2.3	4.8
Dana 60 (248)	4.0	8.5
Rear: 7¼"	1.4	3.0
8¼"	2.1	4.4
9¼"	2.2	4.7
Dana 60 (248) 2WD	3.0	6.3
4WD	3.4	7.3

4 Lubricant level in axle must be ¼-¾" (6-17 mm) below fill plug opening.

SERVICE LOCATIONS — ENGINE AND CHASSIS

HOOD RELEASE: Inside

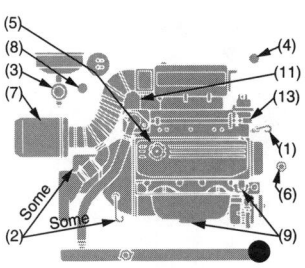

1989-96
1.5L Summit

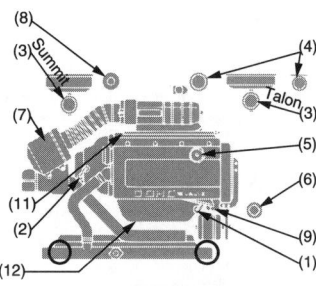

1989-90
1.6L DOHC Summit
1990-98
2.0L DOHC Talon ex. Code Y

(1) Crankcase dipstick
(2) Transmission dipstick
(3) Brake fluid reservoir
(4) Clutch fluid reservoir
(5) Oil fill cap
(6) Power steering reservoir
(7) Air filter
(8) Fuel filter
(9) Oil filter
(10) PCV filter
(11) EGR valve
(12) Oxygen sensor
(13) PCV valve

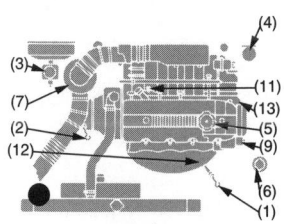

1990-94
1.8L Talon

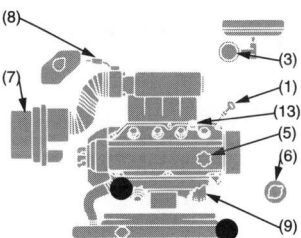

1992-96
1.8L Summit, Summit
Wagon

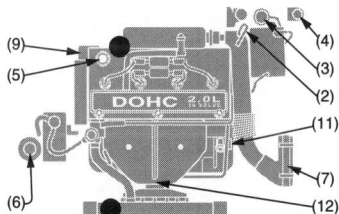

1995-98
2.0L DOHC
Code Y Talon

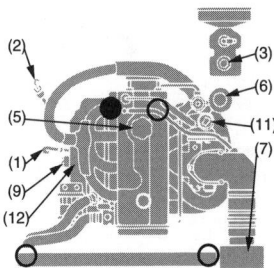

1989
2.2L Medallion

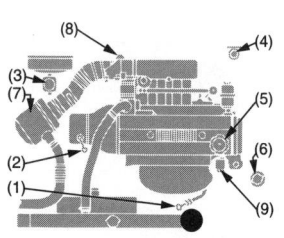

1993-96
2.4L Summit Wagon

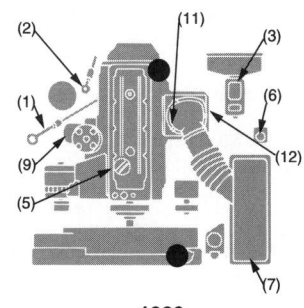

1989
2.5L Premier

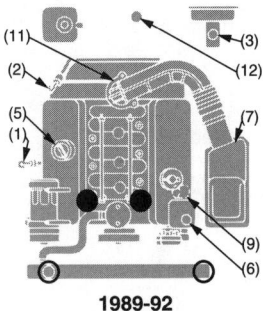

1989-92
3.0L Premier

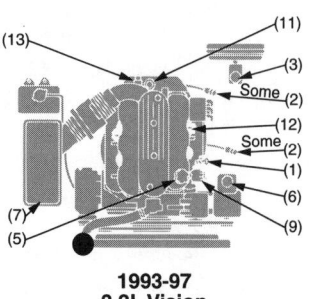

1993-97
3.3L Vision

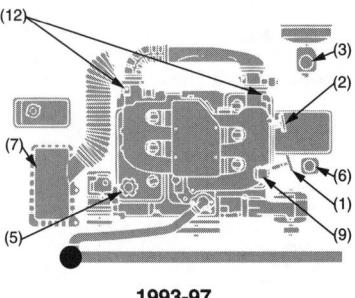

1993-97
3.5L Vision

● Cooling system drain   ○ Cooling system drain, some models

SERVICE LOCATIONS — ENGINE AND CHASSIS

EEIDP-2   EEIDP-2

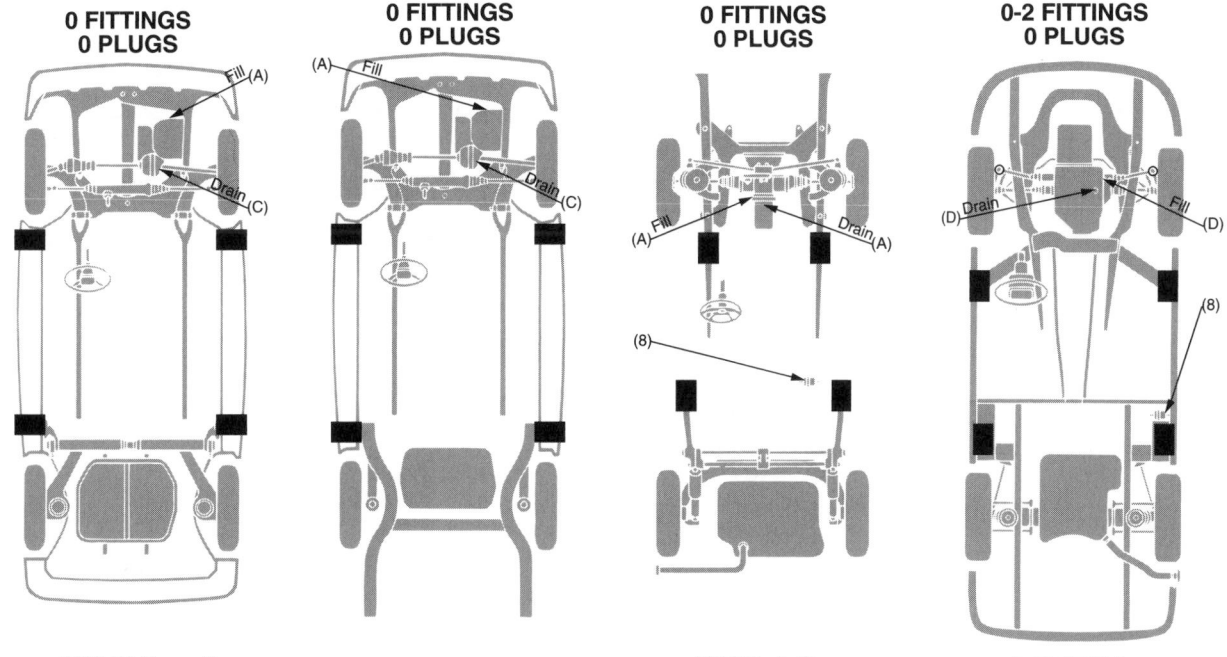

0 FITTINGS 0 PLUGS — 1989-92 Summit

0 FITTINGS 0 PLUGS — 1993-96 Summit

0 FITTINGS 0 PLUGS — 1989 Medallion

0-2 FITTINGS 0 PLUGS — 1993-97 Vision

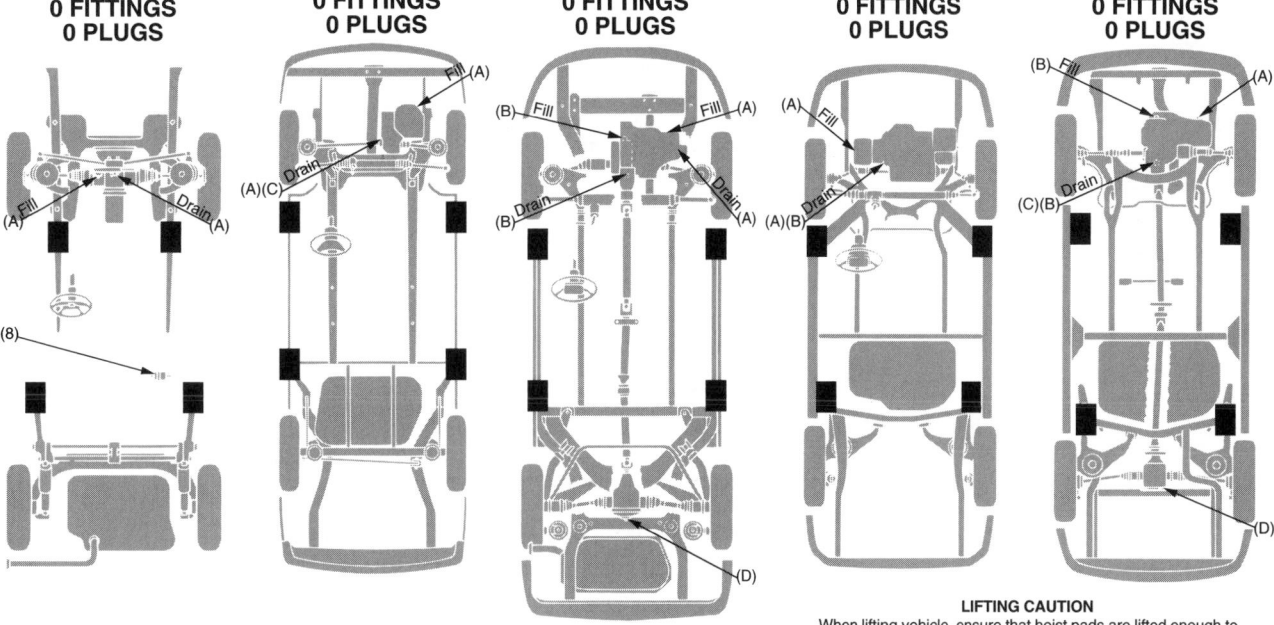

0 FITTINGS 0 PLUGS — 1989-92 Premier

0 FITTINGS 0 PLUGS — 1990-98 Talon 2WD

0 FITTINGS 0 PLUGS — 1990-98 Talon 4WD

0 FITTINGS 0 PLUGS — 1992-96 Summit Wagon 2WD

0 FITTINGS 0 PLUGS — 1992-96 Summit Wagon 4WD

LIFTING CAUTION
When lifting vehicle, ensure that hoist pads are lifted enough to gain adequate clearance between hoist arms and vehicle components.

(A) Manual transmission/transaxle, drain & fill
(B) Transfer case, drain & fill
(C) Automatic transaxle final drive, drain & fill
(D) Differential, drain & fill
(8) Fuel filter   ■ Lift adapter position   • Fitting

CAUTION: On front wheel drive vehicles, the center of gravity is farther forward than on rear wheel drive vehicles. When removing major components from the rear of the vehicle while it is on a hoist, the vehicle must be supported in a manner to prevent it from tipping forward.

EAGLE
1989-92 Medallion, Premier; Dodge Monaco

W   SERVICE TO MAINTAIN EMISSION WARRANTY

MI—MILES IN THOUSANDS
KM—KILOMETERS IN THOUSANDS

1989,
EVERY 7.5 MI—12 KM
1990-92,
EVERY 6 MO/7.5 MI—12 KM

W Crankcase . . . . .change oil

W Oil filter .replace
Premier, Monaco, every oil change. Medallion at first oil
change, then every other

Exhaust system . . . . .inspect

Transaxle, automatic . . . . . . .check level
With engine at operating temperature and at slow idle,
move shift lever through all gear ranges, then check fluid
level when lever is in PARK. Use dipstick side marked
hot. Add fluid as needed
For cold fluid (preferred method), use dipstick side
marked "COLD" (60°-100°F [16°-38°C])

Hoses & connectors,
1989 . . . . .inspect/tighten
Check vacuum hoses, and cooling, fuel, brake, and
power steering systems

Drive belts . . . . .inspect
Medallion 2.2L eng.

Driveshaft boots . . . . .inspect
At mileage interval only

Transaxle, manual . . . . .check level

Suspension, steering . . . . .inspect

Tires . . . . .inspect
At mileage interval only. Check pressure & wear

Battery, 1989 . . . . .clean terminals
Check voltage, fluid level. Inspect case & tiedowns

Brake fluid reservoir . . . . .check level **HB**

Brake, power steering & fuel
hoses, 1990-92 . . . . .check

Clutch, Medallion . . . . .adjust
Pull up clutch (against the stop) to activate self adjuster

Hydraulic clutch . . . . . . .check level **HB**

Cooling system . . . . . . .check level **EC**

Power steering
reservoir . . . . .check level **PS**

EVERY 12 MO
Air conditioning system . . . . .inspect

Cooling system . . . . .inspect

EVERY 15 MI—24 KM
W Drive belts, 3.0L . . . . .inspect

1989, EVERY 15 MI—24 KM
1990-92,
EVERY 12 MO/22 MI—36 KM
Brake linings . . . . .inspect

1989, EVERY 22.5 MI—36 KM
1990-92,
EVERY 12 MO/22.5 MI—36 KM
Rear wheel
bearings . . . . . . .inspect/lubricate **GC**

EVERY 30 MI—48 KM
W Spark plugs . . . . .replace

1989,
EVERY 22.5 MO/22.5 MI—36 KM
1990-92,
EVERY 36 MO/30 MI—48 KM
Ball joints & tie
rod ends . . . . .inspect/lube **LB**

EVERY 30 MO/30 MI—48 KM
Cooling system . . . . .change coolant **EC**
Initial service, then at the beginning of each winter
season

Body, 1989 . . . . .lubricate 10W **MO**
Door hinges & latches as needed. Inspect wiring & hose
routings

Differential . . . . .check level
1989 Premier

W Fuel filter, 1989 . . . . .replace

Ignition system, 1989 . . . . .inspect
Distributor cap, rotor, wires

Transaxle, automatic . . . . . .change fluid
Clean/change filter

Transaxle, manual,
1989 . . . . .change lubricant

W Air cleaner element . . . . .replace

Drive belts, 2.5L . . . . .inspect

Evaporative emission control
system, 1989 . . . . .inspect

Valves 2.2L eng. . . . . .adjust

SERVICE AS REQUIRED
Crankcase emission control
system, 1990-92 . . . . .inspect

Fuel filter, 1990-92 . . . . .replace

Body, 1990-92 . . . . .lubricate

SEVERE SERVICE
Crankcase—Change oil every 3 mo/3 mi
(4.8 km); change oil filter at first, then every
other oil change.

Universal joints & ball joints—inspect
every oil change

Tie rod ends—Lubricate every 18 mo/
15 mi (24 km)

Brake linings, and rear wheel bearings—
Inspect every 9 mi (14.4 km)

Engine air filter—Inspect every 15 mi
(24 km)

Automatic transaxle—Change fluid, filter,
and adjust bands every 15 mi (24 km)

KEY TO LUBRICANTS

AF2	DEXRON®-II Automatic Transmission Fluid
CD	Motor Oil, API Service CD
EC	Ethylene Glycol Coolant With ALUGARD 340-2™. Mix 50/50 with distilled water
GC	Wheel Bearing Grease, NLGI Category GC
GLS	Gear Lubricant, Special Mopar Part No. 82200945
GL-5	Gear Oil, API Service GL-5
HB	Hydraulic Brake Fluid, DOT 3
LB	Chassis Grease, NLGI Category LB
MA	MERCON® Automatic Transmission Fluid
MO	Motor Oil
PS	Power Steering Fluid Jeep/Eagle: Premier, 8982 200 946; Medallion, 8993342
SG	Motor Oil, API Service SG

CRANKCASE
Medallion . . . .**SG**
Premier, Monaco . . . .**SG, SG/CD**

CAPACITY, Refill:	Liters	Qt
Includes filter:		
2.2L Medallion	5.0	5.3
2.5L Premier	4.7	5.0
3.0L Premier, Monaco	5.7	6.0

1989
Above 30°F (−1°C) 20W-40, 20W-50
Above 0°F (−18°C) 10W-30
Below 60°F (16°C) 5W-30
1990-92
Above 0°F (−18°C) 10W-30
Below 60°F (16°C) . . . . .5W-30[1]
1 Preferred when temperatures consistently fall below
10°F (−12°C)

TRANSAXLE, Automatic
Premier final drive serviced separately
Medallion; Premier, Monaco . . . .**MA**

CAPACITY, Initial Refill[2]:	Liters	Qt
Medallion	2.5	2.7
Premier, Monaco	2.6	2.8

2 With the engine at operating temperature, shift transmission through all gears. Check fluid level in PARK and add
fluid as needed

TRANSAXLE, Manual 75W-90 **GL-5**

CAPACITY, Refill:	Liters	Pt
Medallion	2.3	5.0
Premier	3.4	7.0

FINAL DRIVE
Premier, Monaco w/Auto. Trans. . . . . . .**GLS**

CAPACITY, Refill:	Liters	Pt
4-cyl. Premier	0.9	1.8
6-cyl. Premier, Monaco	0.7	1.3

SERVICE AT TIME OR MILEAGE — WHICHEVER OCCURS FIRST

EEIPM2   EEIPM2

W   SERVICE TO MAINTAIN EMISSION WARRANTY

MI—MILES IN THOUSANDS
KM—KILOMETERS IN THOUSANDS

TURBO ENGINES:
EVERY 6 MO/5 MI—8 KM
Crankcase . . . . .change oil

Oil filter .replace
Every second oil change

EVERY 12 MO/7.5 MI—12 KM
Brake and clutch fluid
   reservoir . . . . .check level **HB**

Crankcase ex. turbo . . . . . . .change oil

Oil filter ex. turbo . . . . .replace
At every second change, but at least every 12 months

Power steering fluid . . . . . . .check **AF2**

EVERY 12 MO/15 MI—24 KM
Disc brake pads . . . . .inspect
Also check hoses

Driveshaft boots . . . . .inspect

Transaxle, automatic . . . . . .check level

EVERY 15 MI—24 KM
W Valve clearance . . . . . . .inspect/replace
Adjust only when specifications are on emission label

EVERY 24 MO/30 MI—48 KM
Ball joint, steering linkage seals &
   FWD steering . . . . .inspect

Drum brakes . . . . .inspect
Lining, wheel cylinders

Exhaust system . . . . .check

W Fuel hoses 1991-94 . . . . .check

Rear wheel bearings FWD
   ex. w/disc brakes . . . .clean/repack **GC**
Inspect for leaks. Repack whenever drums are removed

Coolant . . . . .drain/flush/refill **EC**

EVERY 30 MI—48 KM
Differential, Limited-Slip . . . .change fluid

Differential 4WD, rear . . . . . .check level
Ex. Limited-Slip

Transaxle, automatic . . . . . .change fluid
Change filter

Transaxle, manual . . . . .check level
Also check 4WD transfer case fluid level

W Air cleaner filter . . . . .replace

Drive belt . . . . .inspect
Water pump & alternator only

W Spark plugs . . . . .replace
Ex. with platinum plugs

EVERY 60 MO/50 MI—80 KM
W Fuel lines, connections, fill cap
   & tank 1989-92 . . . . .check

W Fuel, & fuel vapor
   hoses . . . . .check/replace

EVERY 60 MO/60 MI—96 KM
W Distributor cap & rotor 1993-94 Calif.
   Summit, Summit Wagon . . . . . . .check

W Evaporative control system 1993-94 Calif.
   Summit, Summit Wagon . . . . .inspect

Fuel lines, connections, fill cap
   & tank, 1993-94 . . . . .check

W Ignition wires 1993-94 Calif.
   Summit, Summit Wagon . . . . .replace

EVERY 60 MI—96 KM
Spark plugs . . . . .replace
Platinum tip only

Timing belts . . . . .replace
Also replace the balancer belt when equipped

EVERY 120 MONTHS
Air bag system . . . . .inspect
As equipped

1994, SERVICE AS REQUIRED
Locks & hinges . . . . .lubricate

Transaxle linkage . . . . .lubricate **LB**

Parking brake cable . . . . . .lubricate **LB**

SEVERE SERVICE
W **Air cleaner filter & brake system**—Service
more frequently

W **Crankcase**—Change oil every 3 mo/3 mi
(4.8 km) & filter every second oil change

W **Spark plugs**—Replace every 15 mi (24 km)

KEY TO LUBRICANTS

AF2	DEXRON®-II Automatic Transmission Fluid
AP3	MOPAR ATF+3®
CD	Motor Oil, API Service CD
EC	Ethylene Glycol Coolant Mix 50% to 70% with water
GC	Wheel Bearing Grease
GL-4	Gear Oil, API Service GL-4
GL-5	Gear Oil, API Service GL-5
GL-5★	Special Lubricant for Limited-Slip Differentials
HB	Hydraulic Brake Fluid, DOT 3
LB	Chassis Grease, NLGI Classification LB
SG	Motor Oil, API Service SG

CRANKCASE . . . . .SG, SG/CD

CAPACITY, Refill:	Liters	Qt
1.5L	3.0	3.2
1.8L	3.5	3.7
2.0L	4.0	4.2
2.4L: 1992	3.5	3.7
1993-94	4.0	4.2

Capacity shown is without filter or oil cooler. When replacing filter, additional oil may be needed

Turbo Models
Above 32°F (0°C) 20W-40
Above −10°F (−23°C) 10W-30
Below 60°F (16°C) 5W-30

All Other Models
Above 32°F (0°C) 20W-40, 20W-50
Above −10°F (−23°C) 10W-30,
                            10W-40, 10W-50

All 1989-92 & 1993 Talon
   below 60°F (16°C) . . . . .5W-20[1], 5W-30, 5W-40
1993 ex. Talon below 100°F (38°C) 5W-30,
                                       5W-40
All 1994 Below 100F° (38°C) 5W-30, 5W-40
1 Not recommended for sustained high-speed driving

TRANSAXLE Automatic AP3

CAPACITY, Initial Refill[2]:	Liters	Qt
1993-94 Summit: 2WD	6.1[3]	6.5[3]
4WD	6.5[3]	6.9[3]
All others	4.0	4.2

2 With the engine at operating temperature, shift transmission through all gears. Check fluid level in Neutral and add fluid as needed
3 Total or dry fill shown, use less fluid when refilling

TRANSAXLE Manual
1989-91 . . . . .75W-85W **GL-4**
1992-94 . . . . . . .75W-85W, 75W-90 **GL-4**

CAPACITY, Refill:	Liters	Pt
Summit & Talon		
FWD non-Turbo	1.8	3.7
Talon 4WD Turbo	2.3	4.8
Summit Wagon 1.8L FWD	1.8	3.8
Summit Wagon		
2.4L FWD & 4WD	2.3	4.8

TRANSFER CASE 75W-85W,
                                 75W-90 **GL-4**

CAPACITY, Refill:	Liters	Pt
Talon 4WD, Summit Wagon AWD	0.6	1.3

DIFFERENTIAL
Limited-Slip . . . .**GL-5★**
Standard **GL-5**
Above −10°F (−23°C), 90, 85W-90, 80W-90; −30°
to −10°F (−34° to −23°C), 80W, 80W-90; below
−30°F (−34°C), 75W

CAPACITY, Refill:	Liters	Pt
All models	0.7	1.5

LIMITED-SLIP IDENTIFICATION:
Lift rear of vehicle, turn one wheel and the other will turn in the same direction

EAGLE
1995-98 Summit, Summit Wagon, Talon
Vision—See Chrysler, Dodge, Plymouth

SERVICE AT TIME OR MILEAGE — WHICHEVER OCCURS FIRST

W   SERVICE TO MAINTAIN EMISSION WARRANTY

MI—MILES IN THOUSANDS
KM—KILOMETERS IN THOUSANDS

TURBO ENGINES:
EVERY 6 MO/5 MI—8 KM
TALON NON-TURBO ENGINES:
EVERY 6 MO/7.5 MI—12 KM
OTHER ENGINES:
EVERY 12 MO/7.5 MI—12 KM
Crankcase . . . . .change oil

Oil filter .replace
Every second oil change, but at least every 12 months

Brake and clutch fluid
    reservoir . . . . .check level **HB**

Power steering fluid . . . . . . .check **AF2**
May also use **AP3**

EVERY 12 MO/15 MI—24 KM
Disc brake pads . . . . .inspect
Also check hoses

Driveshaft boots . . . . .inspect

Transaxle, automatic . . . . . . .check level

EVERY 15 MI—24 KM
W Valve clearance . . . . .inspect/adjust
1.5L & 1.8L only

EVERY 24 MO/30 MI—48 KM
Ball joint, steering linkage seals &
    FWD steering . . . . .inspect

Drum brakes . . . . .inspect
Lining, wheel cylinders

Exhaust system . . . . .check

W Fuel hoses . . . . .check

Coolant . . . . .drain/flush/refill **EC**

EVERY 30 MI—48 KM
Differential 4WD, rear . . . . . . .check level

Transaxle, automatic
    1995-96 . . . . .change fluid
Change filter ex. Talon w/ non turbo

Transaxle, manual . . . . .check level
Also check 4WD transfer case fluid level

W Air cleaner filter . . . . .replace

Drive belt . . . . .inspect
Water pump, power steering pump & alternator only

W Spark plugs . . . . .replace

EVERY 60 MO/60 MI—96 KM
W Distributor cap & rotor
    Summit Wagon & Summit . . . . . .check

W Evaporative control system . . . . .inspect

W Fuel lines, connections, fill cap
    & tank . . . . .check

W Ignition wires . . . . .replace

EVERY 60 MI—96 KM
Timing belts . . . . .replace
1995-98 Recommended but not required for California.
1998 Recommended but not required for Connecticut &
Massachusetts.

EVERY 100 MI—160 KM
Timing belt . . . . .replace
Not required if belt was replaced previously.

EVERY 120 MONTHS
Air bag system . . . . .inspect
As equipped

SERVICE AS REQUIRED
Locks & hinges . . . . .lubricate

Transaxle linkage . . . . .lubricate **LB**

Parking brake cable . . . . . .lubricate **LB**

SEVERE SERVICE
W Air cleaner filter—Replace every 15 mi
(24 km)

Disc brake pads—Inspect every 6 mo/
6 mi (9.6 km)

Rear drum brake system—Inspect every
12 mo/15 mi (24 km)

Transaxle, automatic—1995-98 Talon
w/non turbo, change fluid every 15 mi (24
km); 1997-98 Talon w/turbo, change fluid
every 30 mi (48 km)

Transaxle, manual & transfer case—ex.
Talon w/non-turbo, change fluid every 30
mi (48 km)

Crankcase—Change oil every 3 mo/3 mi
(4.8 km) & filter every second oil change

W Spark plugs—Replace every 15 mi (24 km)

KEY TO LUBRICANTS

AF2	DEXRON®-II Automatic Transmission Fluid
AP3	MOPAR ATF+3®
API★	Motor Oil certified by the American Petroleum Institute (Starburst Symbol)
CD	Motor Oil, API Service CD
EC	Ethylene Glycol Coolant Mix 50% to 70% with water
GLS	Mopar Manual Trans. Fluid Part No. 04874465 meeting MS9417
GL-4	Gear Oil, API Service GL-4
GL-5	Gear Oil, API Service GL-5
GL-5★	Special Lubricant for Limited-Slip Differentials
HB	Hydraulic Brake Fluid, DOT 3
LB	Chassis Grease, NLGI Classification LB
SJ	Motor Oil, API Service SJ

CRANKCASE . . . . .SJ, SJ/CD, API★

CAPACITY, Refill:	Liters	Qt
1.5L	3.0	3.2
1.8L	3.5	3.7
2.0L turbo	4.0	4.2
2.0L ex. turbo	3.8	4.0
2.4L	4.0	4.2

Capacity shown is without filter or oil cooler. When replacing
filter, additional oil may be needed

Turbo Models
Above 32°F (0°C) 20W-40
Above −10°F (−23°C) 10W-30
Below 60°F (16°C) 5W-30
All Other Models
Above 0°F (−18°C) 10W-30
Below 100°F (38°C) . . . . .5W-30[1]
1 Preferred

TRANSAXLE Automatic AP3

CAPACITY, Initial Refill[2]:	Liters	Qt
Summit: 2WD	6.1[3]	6.5[3]
4WD	6.5[3]	6.9[3]
Talon w/o-turbo	3.8	4.0
w/turbo	6.7[3]	7.1[3]

2 With the engine at operating temperature, shift transmission through all gears. Check fluid level in Neutral (ex.
Talon w/o-turbo, check in PARK) and add fluid as
needed
3 Total or dry fill shown, use less fluid when refilling

TRANSAXLE Manual
Talon w/o Turbo . . . .**GLS**
Others 75W-85W, 75W-90 **GL-4**

CAPACITY, Refill:	Liters	Pt
Summit Wagon 1.8L FWD & Summit	1.8	3.8
Summit Wagon 2.4L FWD & 4WD	2.3	4.8
Talon FWD	2.0	4.2
AWD	2.2	4.6

TRANSFER CASE 75W-85W, 75W-90 **GL-4**

CAPACITY, Refill:	Liters	Pt
Summit Wagon AWD	0.6	1.3
Talon AWD	0.5	1.1

DIFFERENTIAL
Limited-Slip . . . .**GL-5★**
Standard **GL-5**
Above −10°F (−23°C), 90, 85W-90, 80W-90; −30°
to −10°F (−34° to −23°C), 80W, 80W-90; below
−30°F (−34°C), 75W

CAPACITY, Refill:	Liters	Pt
Summit Wagon AWD	0.7	1.5
Talon AWD	0.8	1.8

FORD, LINCOLN, MERCURY
1989-2000 All Models Including FWD Vans
Except Mountaineer & Navigator—See FORD TRUCKS

SERVICE LOCATIONS — ENGINE AND CHASSIS

HOOD RELEASE: Inside

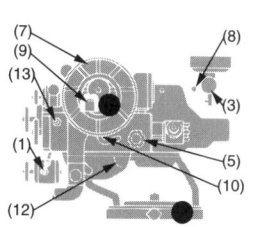

**1989
1.3L (79) 2V
Festiva**

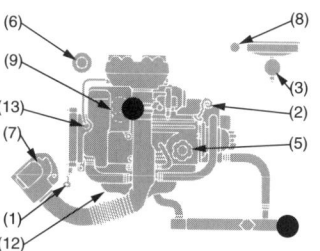

**1989-97
1.3L FI
Festiva, Aspire**

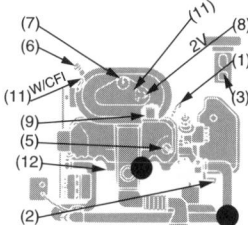

**1.9L (113) 2V, CFI
Escort, Lynx, EXP, LN7**

(1) Crankcase dipstick
(2) Transmission dipstick
(3) Brake fluid reservoir
(4) Clutch fluid reservoir
(5) Oil fill cap
(6) Power steering reservoir
(7) Air filter
(8) Fuel filter
(9) Oil filter
(10) PCV filter
(11) EGR valve
(12) Oxygen sensor
(13) PCV valve

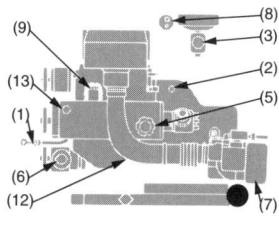

**1989
1.6L (98) EFI
Tracer**

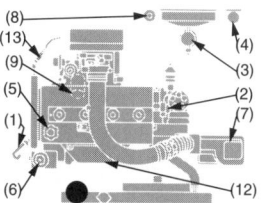

**1991-94
1.6L ex. Turbo
Capri**

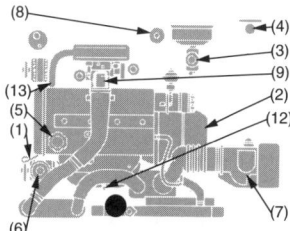

**1991-94
1.6L Turbo
Capri**

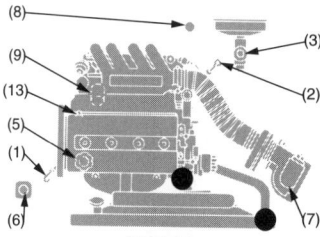

**1991-96
1.8L DOHC
Escort, Tracer**

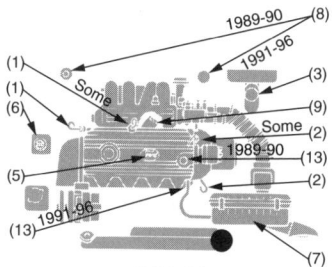

**1989-96
1.9L (116) EFI
Escort, Lynx, EXP, Tracer**

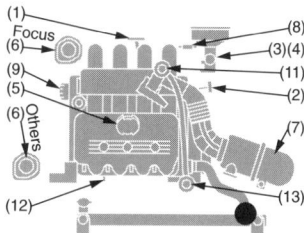

**1997-00
2.0L ex. Zetec
Focus, Escort, Tracer
ex. Escort ZX2 Coupe**

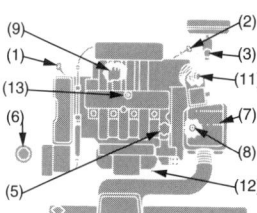

**1993-97
2.0L (122)
Probe**

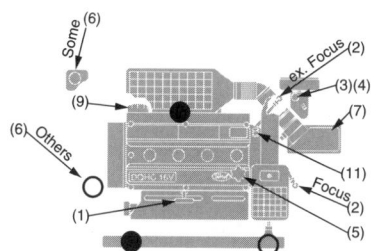

**1995-00
2.0L DOHC Zetec
Contour, Mystique, Cougar
1998-00
Escort ZX2 Coupe
2000 Focus**

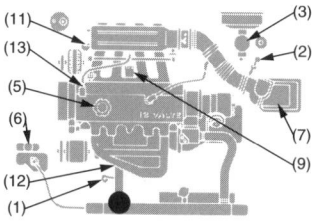

**1989-92
2.2L EFI
Probe**

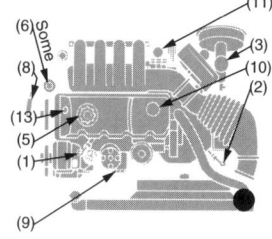

**1989-94
2.3L (140) Tempo, Topaz**

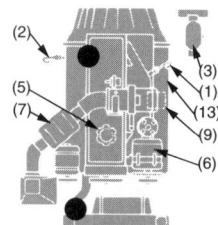

**1989-93
2.3L (140) EFI RWD**

● Cooling system drain   ○ Cooling system drain, some models

FORD, LINCOLN, MERCURY
1989-2000 All Models Including FWD Vans
Except Mountaineer & Navigator—See FORD TRUCKS

SERVICE LOCATIONS — ENGINE AND CHASSIS

HOOD RELEASE: Inside

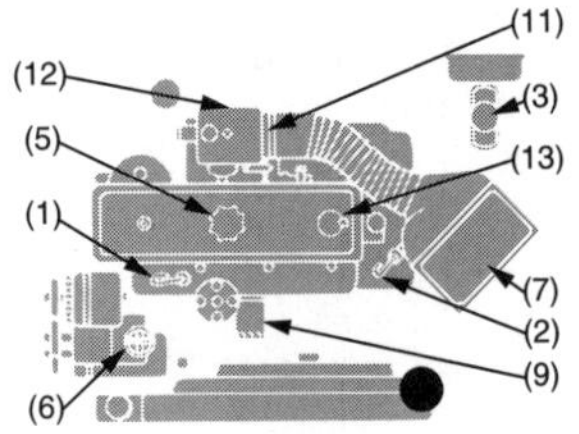

**1989-91
2.5L (153)
Taurus, Sable**

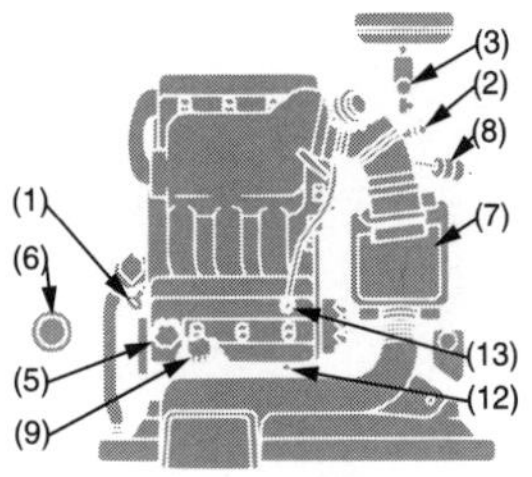

**1993-97
2.5L (152)
Probe**

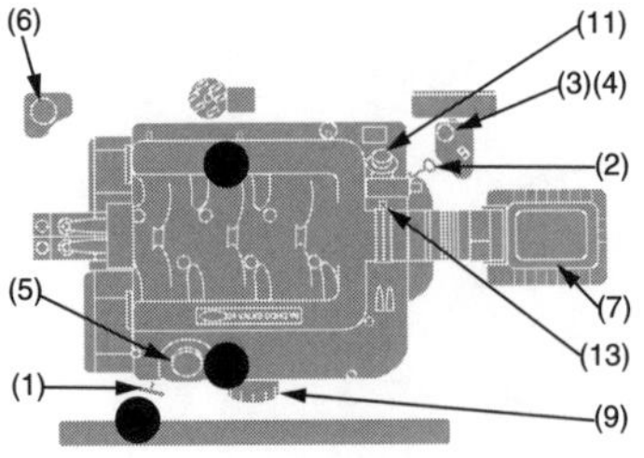

**1995-00
2.5L DOHC
Contour, Mystique, Cougar**

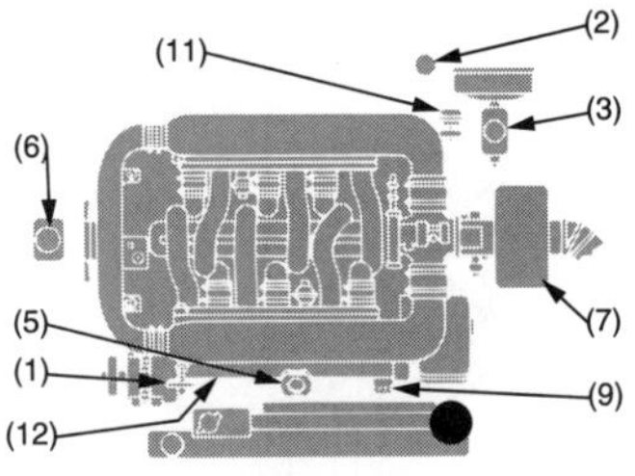

**1989-95
3.0L, 3.2L DOHC-SHO
Taurus**

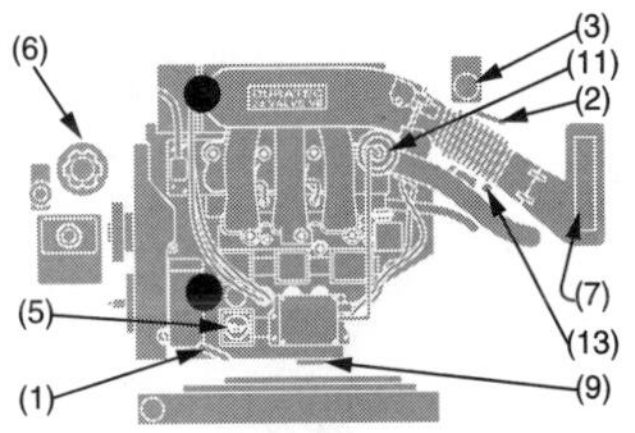

**1996-00
3.0L Duratec FWD
DOHC**

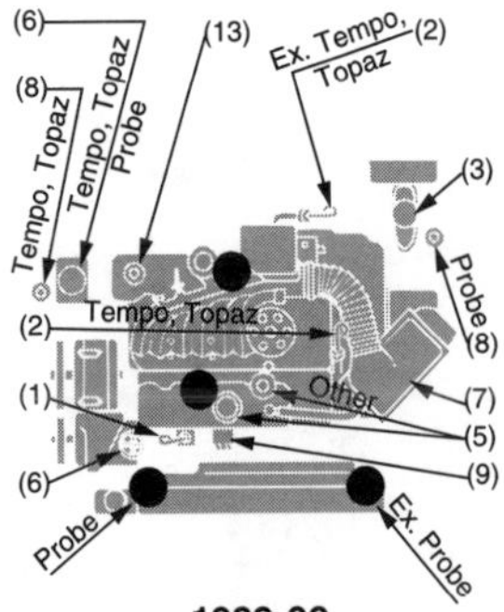

**1989-00
3.0L (182) Vulcan FWD ex.
DOHC, SHO, & Villager**

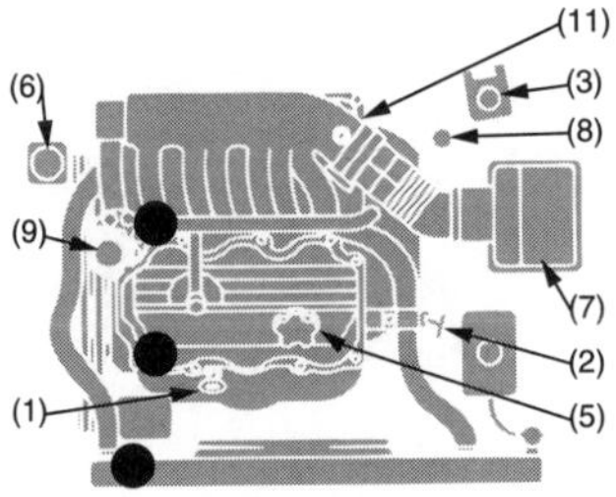

**1993-00
3.0L (181) & 3.3L (200)
Villager**

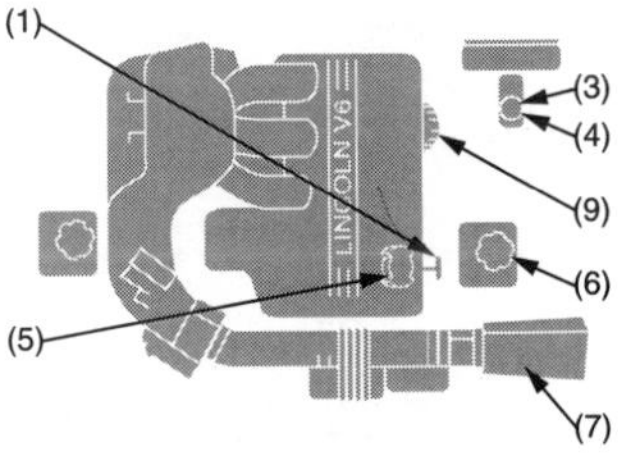

**2000
3.0L Lincoln LS**

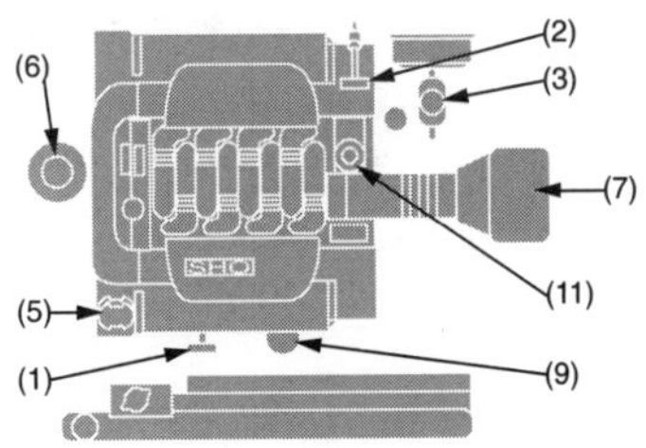

**1996-99
3.4L SHO**

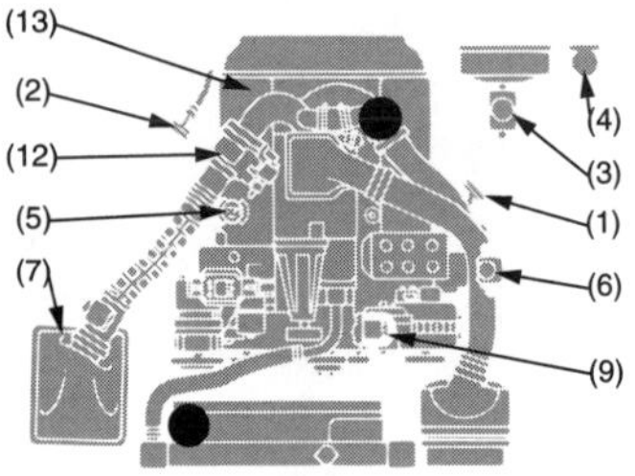

**1989-95
3.8L Supercharged
Thunderbird, Cougar**

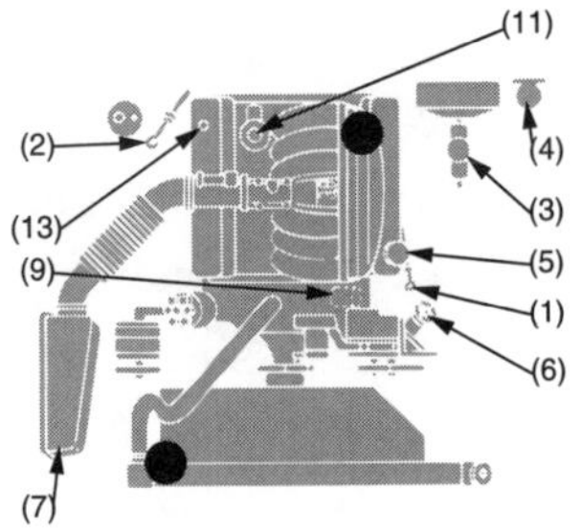

**1989-00 3.8L (232) RWD
ex. Supercharged
Thunderbird, Cougar**

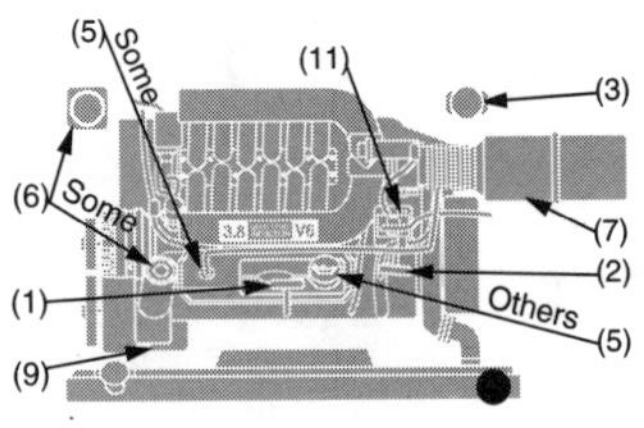

**1996-00
3.8L (232)
Windstar**

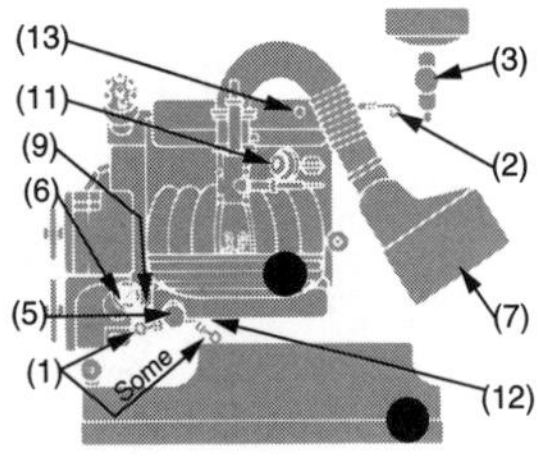

**1989-95
3.8L (232) FWD**

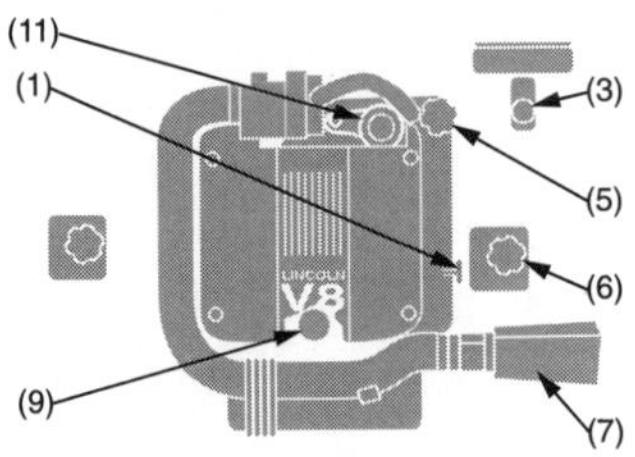

**2000
3.9L Lincoln LS**

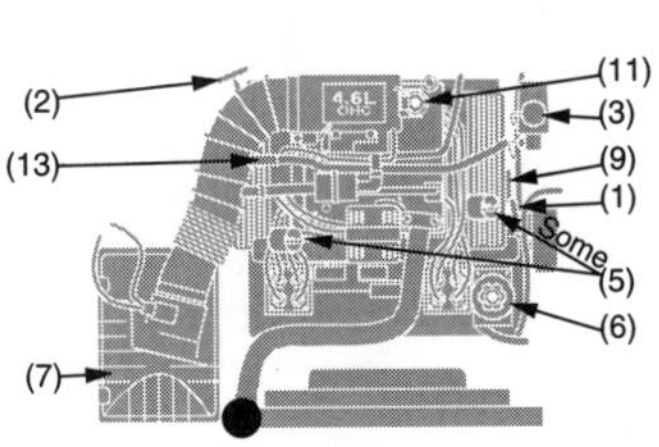

**1996-00
4.6L SOHC
Mustang, Thunderbird
1996-97
Cougar**

● Cooling system drain   ○ Cooling system drain, some models

FORD, LINCOLN, MERCURY
1989-2000 All Models Including FWD Vans
Except Mountaineer & Navigator—See FORD TRUCKS

SERVICE LOCATIONS — ENGINE AND CHASSIS

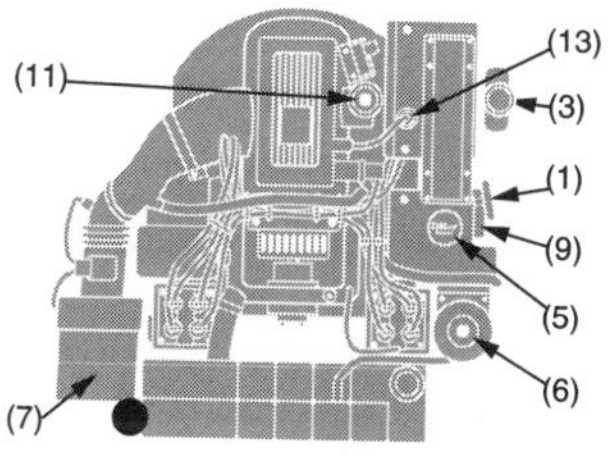

**1996-00
4.6L DOHC
Mustang Cobra**

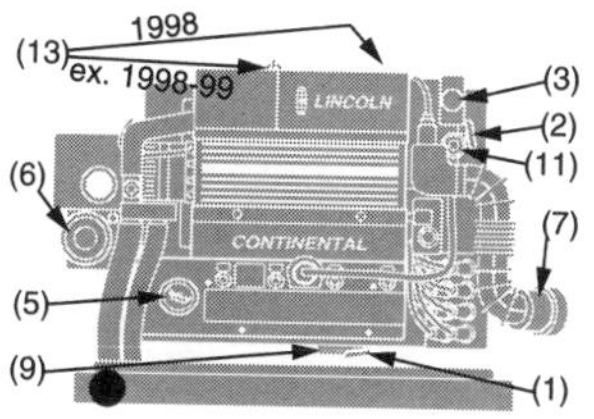

**1995-00
4.6L
Continental**

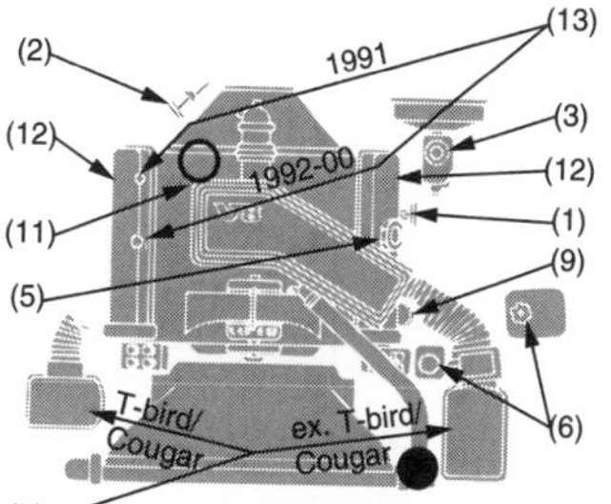

**1991-00
4.6L ex. Mark VIII,
1996-00 Mustang, Thunderbird,
Cougar & 1995-00 Continental**

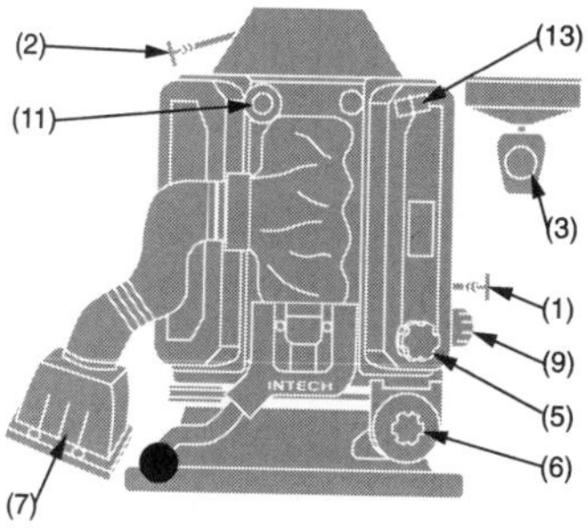

T-bird/
Cougar

ex. T-bird/
Cougar

1998

ex. 1998-99

1991

1992-00

**1997-98
4.6L Mark VIII**

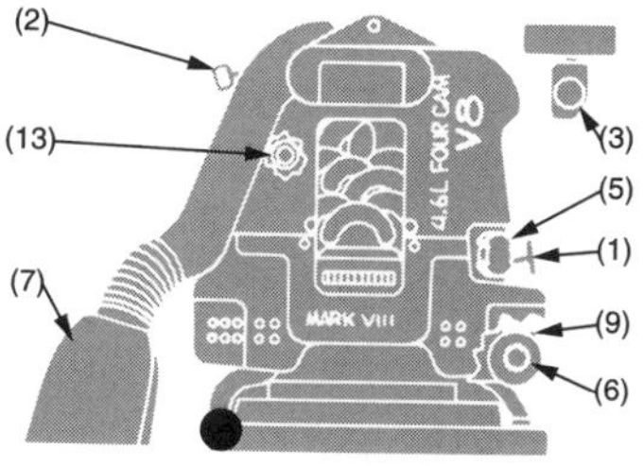

**1993-96
4.6L
Mark VIII**

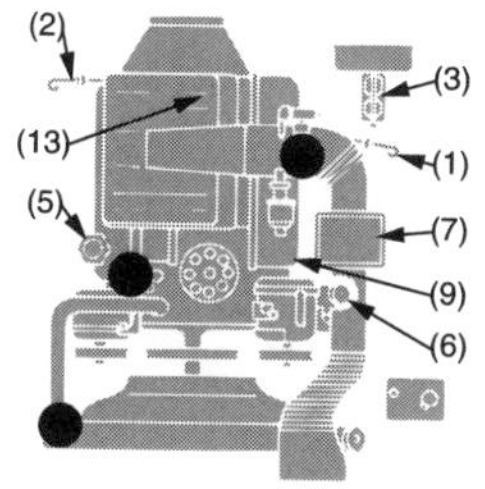

**1989-92
5.0L (302) Lincoln
Town Car, Crown Victoria
Grand Marquis**

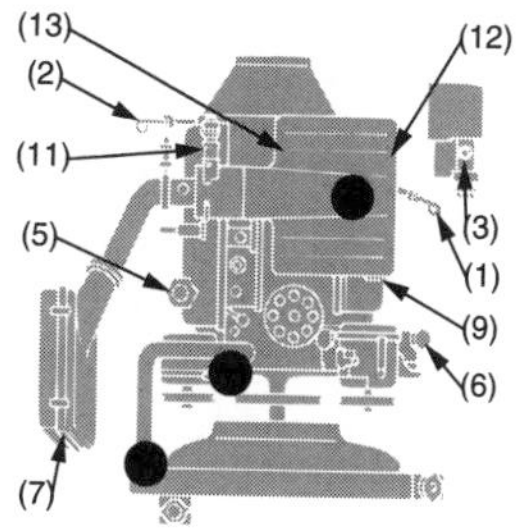

**1989-95 5.0L (302)
All Others**

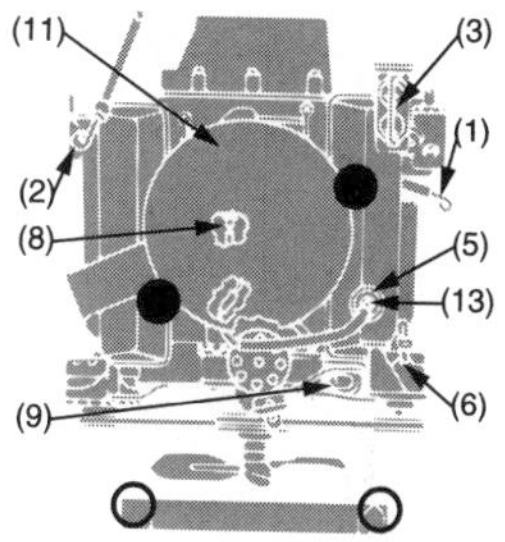

**1989-91
5.8L (351)**

**0 FITTINGS
0 PLUGS**

**0 FITTINGS
0 PLUGS**

**0 FITTINGS
0 PLUGS**

**0 FITTINGS
0 PLUGS**

(1) Crankcase dipstick
(2) Transmission dipstick
(3) Brake fluid reservoir
(4) Clutch fluid reservoir
(5) Oil fill cap
(6) Power steering reservoir
(7) Air filter
(8) Fuel filter
(9) Oil filter
(10) PCV filter
(11) EGR valve
(12) Oxygen sensor
(13) PCV valve

○ Cooling system drain, some models

● Cooling system drain

(A) Drain

(A) Check/Fill

(A) Fill

(A) Fill

(A) Drain

(A) Check/Fill

(D) Fill

Aspire

Festiva

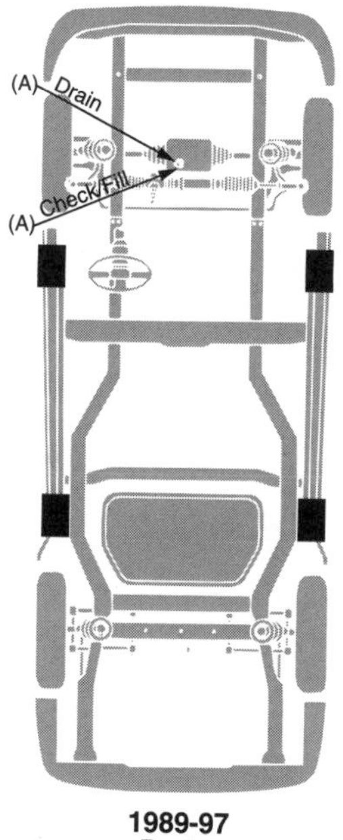

**1989-97
Probe**

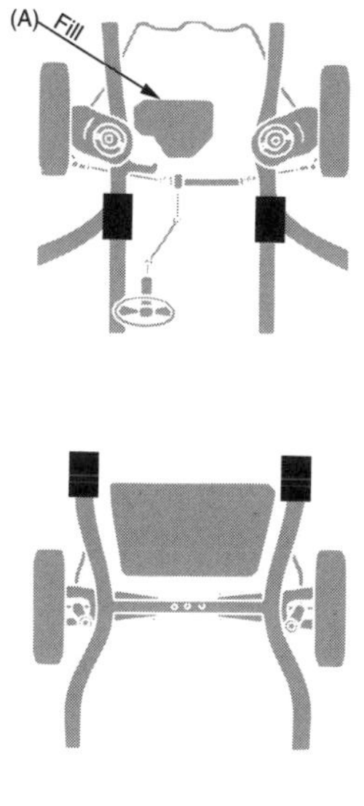

**1989-90
Escort, Lynx, EXP, LN7
1989-94
Tempo, Topaz 2WD**

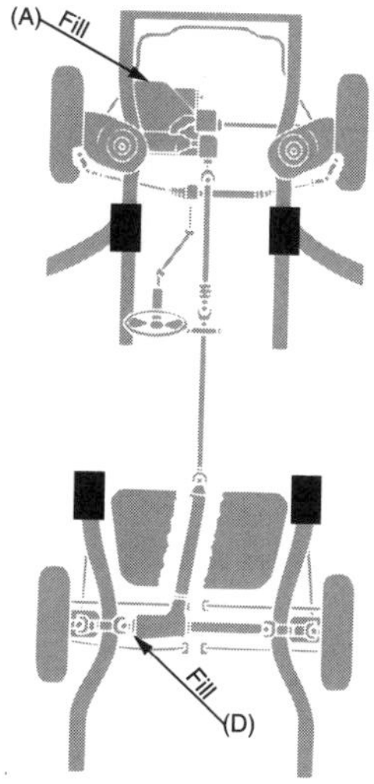

**1989-94
Tempo, Topaz 4WD**

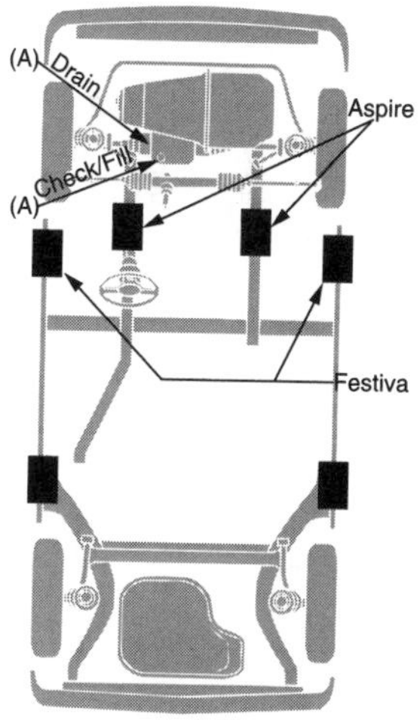

**1989-93
Festiva
1994-97 Aspire**

LIFTING CAUTION Never lift car with bumper jack

CAUTION: On front wheel drive vehicles, the center of gravity is farther forward than on rear wheel drive vehicles. When removing major components from the rear of the vehicle while it is on a hoist, the vehicle must be supported in a manner to prevent it from tipping forward.

■ Lift adapter position

△ Plug, some models

○ Fitting, some models

(A) Manual transmission/transaxle, drain & fill

(B) Transfer case, NOT USED

(C) Automatic transaxle final drive, NOT USED

(D) Differential, drain & fill

SERVICE LOCATIONS — ENGINE AND CHASSIS

FDDP-4   FDDP-4

0 FITTINGS 0 PLUGS

(A) Check/Fill
(A) Drain

2000 Focus
1991-00
Capri, Escort
1989-99 Tracer
1998-00
Escort ZX2 Coupe

0 FITTINGS 0 PLUGS

(A) Fill
(A) Drain

1995-00
Contour, Mystique
1999-00 Cougar

0 FITTINGS 0 PLUGS

1993-00
Villager

0 FITTINGS 0 PLUGS

AIR SUSPENSION
Turn air suspension off
(switch located in jack storage area)
before jacking or hoisting vehicle

(8)

1995-00
Windstar

2 FITTINGS, POLICE
0 FITTINGS, OTHERS
0 PLUGS

(A) Fill

AIR SUSPENSION
Turn air suspension off
(switch located in trunk)
before jacking or hoisting vehicle

(8)

Wagon
Ex. wagon

Sable, Taurus
1989-00 Continental

0 FITTINGS 0 PLUGS

(2)(A)

(D) Fill

Lincoln LS

0-2 FITTINGS 0-2 PLUGS

Type RUG, RAD (A)
Type ET 4-speed
5-speed ex. T5
(A) 4-speed
T5 5-speed (A)

AIR SUSPENSION
Turn air suspension off
(switch located in trunk on left side)
before jacking or hoisting vehicle

(8) Others
Some (8)

(D) Fill

Mustang
Mark VII

0-4 FITTINGS 0-5 PLUGS

AIR SUSPENSION
Turn air suspension off
(switch located in trunk on right side)
before jacking or hoisting vehicle

1991-97 Town Car (8)
1992-97 Grand Marquis,
Crown Victoria, Touring Sedan
W/EFI
Others (8)

(D) Fill

Crown Victoria &
Grand Marquis
Lincoln Town Car

0-2 FITTINGS 0-2 PLUGS

(A)

(8)

AIR SUSPENSION
Turn air suspension off
(switch located in trunk on left side)
before jacking or hoisting vehicle

(D) Fill

Thunderbird,
Cougar (1989-97),
Mark VIII (1993-98)

(A) Manual transmission/
    transaxle, drain & fill

(B) Transfer case, NOT USED

(C) Automatic transaxle final
    drive, NOT USED

(D) Differential, drain & fill

(2) Automatic transmission,
    drain & fill

(8) Fuel Filter

CAUTION: On front wheel drive vehicles, the center of gravity is farther forward than on rear wheel drive vehicles. When removing major components from the rear of the vehicle while it is on a hoist, the vehicle must be supported in a manner to prevent it from tipping forward.

■ Lift adapter position   △ Plug, some models   ○ Fitting, some models   ▲ Plug

SERVICE AT TIME OR MILEAGE — WHICHEVER OCCURS FIRST

FDPM19   FDPM19

Perform the following maintenance services at the intervals indicated to keep the vehicle warranties in effect.
W   SERVICE TO MAINTAIN EMISSION WARRANTY

MI—MILES IN THOUSANDS
KM—KILOMETERS IN THOUSANDS

EVERY MONTH
Cooling system . . . . .check level **EC**

EVERY 6 MONTHS
Exhaust system . . . . .inspect

Accessory drive belts . . . . .inspect
Festiva, Tracer only

Radiator, heater & AC hoses . . . .inspect

FIRST 7.5 MI—12 KM
Tires . . . . .rotate
At this interval, then every 15 mi (24 km)

EVERY 12 MONTHS
Air conditioning system . . . . .inspect

Brake master cyl. . . . . .check level **HBH**

W Cooling system . . . . .inspect
Also hoses and clamps

Power steering reservoir . .check level **FA**

Transmission/Transaxle controls
& linkage . . . . .lubricate **LM**

Transmission/Transaxle,
manual . . . . .check level

Body hinges . . . . .lubricate **MO**

TURBO & SUPERCHARGED ENGINE, EVERY 6 MO/5 MI—8 KM
OTHERS, EVERY 6 MO/7.5 MI—12 KM
W Crankcase oil & filter . . . . .replace
Or when indicated by vehicle maintenance monitor, whichever occurs first

EVERY 15 MI—24 KM
Clutch pedal freeplay . . . . . .check/adjust
Festiva

Front disc brakes . . . . .inspect
Festiva, Probe, Tracer.
Also inspect brake lines & connections

Front suspension &
steering linkage . . . . . .fittings/plugs **LM**
RWD only

W Valve clearance 1.3L 2V . . . . .adjust

W Idle speed 1.3L . . . . .check

Choke linkage &
shaft 1.3L 2V . . . . .clean/inspect

PCV valve 5.0L . . . . .replace
Replace 1990 crankcase ventilation filter

Spark plugs . . . . .check/clean
Festiva only

Spark plugs . . . . .replace
Turbo eng. only

AT FIRST 15 MI—24KM; THEN EVERY 30 MI—48 KM
Body & chassis nuts & bolts . . . .tighten
Festiva, Probe, Tracer

EVERY 24 MO/24 MI—38.4 KM
Battery fluid
1990 3.0L SHO . . . . .check level

EVERY 30 MI—48 KM
Brake system ex. Festiva,
Probe, Tracer . . . . .inspect
Inspect hoses & replace lining when 1/32" from rivet head ex. disc pads when 1/8" thick

Driveshaft boots . . . . .inspect
Festiva, Probe, Tracer

Exhaust system heat shields . . . .inspect

Front suspension . . .**0-4 fittings/plugs LM**
1.3L, 1.6L eng. inspect ball joints, driveshaft boots & fuel lines

Rear drum brakes . . . . .inspect
Festiva, Probe, Tracer

Steering & suspension . . . . .inspect
Festiva, Probe, Tracer

W Accessory drive belts . . . . .inspect/adjust

W Air cleaner element . . . . .replace

W Choke system, 5.8L . . . . . . .clean/check

W Crankcase emission filter . . . . . .replace
Not required for 1.3L, 1.6L, 3.0L engine

W Fuel filter 1.3L 2V . . . . .replace

Fuel lines . . . . .inspect
Festiva, Tracer, Probe

W Spark plugs (ex. platinum) . . . . . .replace

Supercharger fluid
1990 3.8L . . . . .check level **SLF**

Wheel bearings ex. Festiva,
Tracer, Probe . . . . . .inspect/repack **LM**
Non-driving wheels only

EVERY 36 MO/30 MI—48 KM
W Cooling system . . . . .change coolant **EC**

EVERY 45 MI—72 KM
Transaxle, shaft boots . . . . .inspect
Festiva, Tracer

EVERY 60 MI—96 KM
Fuel filter 1.3L, 1.6L,
2.2L & Probe 3.0L . . . . .replace

Spark plugs (platinum) . . . . .replace

Timing belt 1.3L, 1.6L, 2.2L . . . .replace

Wheel bearings Festiva, Tracer
front & rear . . . . .lubricate **LM**

SERVICE AS REQUIRED
Steering mechanism . . . . .inspect

Fluid leaks on pavement . . . . . . .check

SEVERE SERVICE
W Crankcase—Change oil & filter every
3 mo/3 mi (4.8 km)

Transmission/Transaxle, automatic—
Change fluid every 30 mi (48 km)

W Air cleaner element—Replace as required

Tires—1989-90, rotate at first 6 mi (9.6 km),
then every 15 mi (24 km)

KEY TO LUBRICANTS

API★	Motor oil certified by the American Petroleum Institute (Starburst symbol)
EC	Ethylene Glycol Coolant Mix 50/50 with water or at least to -20°F (-29°C) protection
FA	Automatic Transmission Fluid, Type F
HBH	Hydraulic Brake Fluid, Extra Heavy-Duty
HP	Hypoid Gear Oil Ford Part No. E0AZ-19580A
HP★	Hypoid Gear Oil for Traction-Lok Differential Ford Part No. E0AZ-19580A
LM	Lithium Grease, with Polyethylene & Molybdenum Disulfide
MA	MERCON® Automatic Transmission Fluid
MO	Motor Oil
SLF	Special Lubricant -Fluid Synthetic Supercharger Fluid 3.8L, Spec No. ESE-M99C115-A Part No. E9SZ-19577-A

CRANKCASE . . . . .5W-30 **API★**

CAPACITY, Refill:	Liters	Qt
1.3L	3.0	3.2
1.6L (incl. filter)	3.3	3.5
1.9L	3.3	3.5
2.2L	3.9	4.1
2.3L, 2.5L, 3.0L SHO (incl. filter)	4.7	5.0
3.0L ex. SHO & Probe, 3.8L FWD (incl. filter)	4.3	4.5
3.0L Probe, 3.8L RWD, 5.0L, 5.8L	3.8	4.0

8-cyl. engines have 2 oil drain plugs. Add 0.45 liter (0.5 qt) for Police oil cooler
Capacity shown is without filter. When replacing filter, additional oil may be needed

TRANSMISSION/TRANSAXLE, Automatic . . . . .MA

CAPACITY, Total Fill:	Liters	Qt
AXOD, AXODE	12.2	12.8
4WD Tempo, Topaz	9.5	10.0
Taurus ex. O.D.	7.4	8.0
Festiva	2.8[3]	3.0[3]
Tracer	5.7	6.0
Others, FWD	7.9	8.3
All RWD	2.8[3]	3.0[3]

3 Initial Refill: With the engine at operating temperature, shift transmission through all gears. Check fluid level in PARK and add fluid as needed. With AOD, AODE transmission, drain torque converter.

TRANSMISSION/TRANSAXLE, Manual . . . . .MA

CAPACITY, Refill:	Liters	Pt
Festiva	2.5	5.2
Probe ex. Turbo	3.4	7.2
Probe w/Turbo	3.7	7.8
1989 Tracer	3.2	6.8
All others, FWD	2.9	6.2
Mustang	2.6	5.5
Thunderbird, Cougar	3.0	6.4

DIFFERENTIAL
Standard . . . . .90 **HP**
Tempo, Topaz 4WD . . . . .90 **HP★**
Traction-Lok .90 **HP★**

CAPACITY, Refill:	Liters	Pt
7.5" ring gear:		
Thunderbird/Cougar	1.4	3.0
Others	1.5	3.25
8.8" ring gear:		
Thunderbird/Cougar	1.5	3.25
Others	1.8	3.75
Tempo, Topaz 4WD	0.6	1.3

FORD, LINCOLN, MERCURY
1991-92 All Models

FDPM20   FDPM20

Perform the following maintenance services at the intervals indicated to keep the vehicle warranties in effect.

W   SERVICE TO MAINTAIN EMISSION WARRANTY

MI—MILES IN THOUSANDS
KM—KILOMETERS IN THOUSANDS

EVERY MONTH
Cooling system . . . . . . .check level **EC**

EVERY 6 MONTHS
Exhaust system . . . . .inspect

Radiator, heater & AC hoses . . . .inspect

EVERY 12 MONTHS
Air conditioning system . . . . .inspect

Brake master cyl. . . . . .check level **HBH**

W Cooling system . . . . .inspect
Also hoses and clamps

Power steering reservoir . .check level **FA**

Transmission/Transaxle controls
   & linkage . . . . .lubricate **LM**

Transmission/Transaxle,
   manual . . . . .check level

Body hinges . . . . .lubricate **MO**

SUPERCHARGED ENGINE,
EVERY 6 MO/5 MI—8 KM
OTHERS,
EVERY 6 MO/7.5 MI—12 KM
W Crankcase oil & filter . . . . .replace
Or when indicated by vehicle maintenance monitor,
whichever occurs first

AT FIRST 7.5 MI—12 KM;
THEN AT EVERY 15 MI—24 KM
Tires .rotate
At 7.5 mi (12 km). Then every 15 mi (24 km)
thereafter.
Lug nut torque 80-105 ft lb

EVERY 15 MI—24 KM
Brake lines & connections . . . . .inspect
Capri, Escort, Festiva, Probe, Tracer

Disc brake pads & rotors . . . . . .inspect
Capri, Probe

Front suspension &
   steering linkage . . . . .lubricate **LM**
RWD as equipped with fittings

W Idle speed 1.3L, 1.6L . . . . .check

W Spark plugs Turbo . . . . .replace

W PCV valve, 5.0L . . . . .replace
Replace crankcase ventilation filter

AT FIRST 15 MI—24 KM;
THEN EVERY 30 MI—48 KM
Body & chassis nuts & bolts . . . . .tighten
Capri, Escort, Festiva, Probe, Tracer

EVERY 22.5 MI—36 KM
Battery fluid 3.0L SHO . . . . . .check level

EVERY 30 MI—48 KM
Brake system . . . . .inspect
Ex. Capri, Probe. Inspect hoses & replace lining when
1/32" from rivet head ex. disc pads when 1/8" thick

Driveshaft boots . . . . .inspect
Capri, Escort, Festiva, Probe, Tracer

Exhaust system heat shields . . . .inspect

Rear drum brakes . . . . .inspect
Capri, Probe

W Accessory drive belts . . . . .inspect/adjust

W Air cleaner element . . . . .replace

Clutch pedal freeplay . . . .inspect/adjust
Ex. Taurus, Tempo, Topaz

W Crankcase emission filter . . . . . . .replace
Not required for 1.3L, 1.6L, 1.8L, 3.0L engine

Fuel lines . . . . .inspect
Capri, Festiva, Probe

W Spark plugs (ex. platinum) . . . . . .replace

W Supercharger fluid 3.8L .check level **SLF**

Wheel bearings,
   ex. Festiva . . . . . . .inspect/repack **LM**
Non-driving wheels only. Not required for sealed
bearings

EVERY 36 MO/30 MI—48 KM
W Cooling system . . . . .change coolant **EC**

EVERY 45 MI—72 KM
Transaxle shift linkage boots . . . .inspect
Festiva only

EVERY 60 MI—96 KM
Front & rear wheel bearings . .lubricate **LM**
Festiva only

W Fuel filter 1.3L, 1.6L, & Probe . . .replace

W Spark plugs (platinum) . . . . .replace

W Timing belt . . . . .replace
Belt driven overhead cam engine ex. 1.9L, 2.3L

W Valve lash 3.0L, 3.2L SHO . . . . . .adjust

EVERY 100 MI—160 KM
Rear axle, RWD . . . . . .change lubricant

SEVERE SERVICE
W Crankcase—Change oil & filter every
3 mo/3 mi (4.8 km)

Transmission/Transaxle, automatic—
Change fluid every 30 mi (48 km)

W Air cleaner element—Replace as required

Tires—Rotate at first 6 mi (9.6 km), then
every 15 mi (24 km)

KEY TO LUBRICANTS
See other Ford, Lincoln, Mercury charts

CRANKCASE . . . . .5W-30 API★		
CAPACITY, Refill:	**Liters**	**Qt**
1.3L	3.0	3.2
1.6L	3.0	3.2
1.8L	3.6	3.8
1.9L	3.3	3.5
2.2L	3.9	4.1
2.3L, 2.5L, 3.0L SHO, 3.2L SHO, 4.6L Code W (incl. filter)	4.7	5.0
3.0L ex. SHO, Probe, 3.8L FWD (incl. filter)	4.3	4.5
3.0L Probe, 3.8L RWD, 5.0L, 5.8L	3.8	4.0

5.0L, 5.8L engines have 2 oil drain plugs. Add 0.45 liter
(0.5 qt) for Police oil cooler
Capacity shown is without filter. When replacing filter, additional oil may be needed

TRANSMISSION/TRANSAXLE,
Automatic
1992 AODE/4R70W **MA5**
Others . . . .**MA**

CAPACITY, Total Fill:	**Liters**	**Qt**
AXOD	12.2	12.8
AXODE, AXODEW	11.8	12.5
4WD Tempo, Topaz	9.5	10.0
Taurus ex. O.D.	7.4	8.0
Festiva	2.8⁵	3.0⁵
Capri	5.7	6.0
Probe	6.8	7.2
Escort & Tracer	5.8	6.1
Others, FWD	7.9	8.3
All RWD	2.8⁵	3.0⁵

5 Initial Refill: With the engine at operating temperature, shift
transmission through all gears. Check fluid level in PARK
and add fluid as needed. With AOD, AODE, or 4R70W
transmission, drain torque converter.

TRANSMISSION/TRANSAXLE,
Manual . . . .**MA**

CAPACITY, Refill:	**Liters**	**Pt**
Festiva	2.5	5.2
Probe ex. Turbo	3.4	7.2
Probe w/Turbo	3.7	7.8
Capri	3.2	6.8
Escort, Tracer: 1.9L	2.7	5.6
1.8L	3.3	7.1
Mustang	2.6	5.5
Thunderbird, Cougar	3.0	6.4
All others, FWD	2.9	6.2

DIFFERENTIAL
Standard . . . . .90 **HP**
1991 Tempo, Topaz 4WD . . . . .90 **HP★**
Traction-Lok . . . . .90 **HP★**

CAPACITY, Refill:	**Liters**	**Pt**
7.5" ring gear:		
Thunderbird/Cougar	1.4	3.0
Others	1.5	3.25
8.8" ring gear:		
Thunderbird/Cougar	1.5	3.25
Others	1.8	3.75
Tempo, Topaz 4WD	0.6	1.3

SERVICE AT TIME OR MILEAGE — WHICHEVER OCCURS FIRST

FDPM21   FDPM21

Perform the following maintenance services at the intervals indicated to keep the vehicle warranties in effect.
W SERVICE TO MAINTAIN EMISSION WARRANTY

MI—MILES IN THOUSANDS
KM—KILOMETERS IN THOUSANDS

EVERY MONTH
Cooling system . . . . . . .check level **EC**

EVERY 6 MONTHS
Exhaust system . . . . .inspect

Radiator, heater & AC hoses . . . .inspect

EVERY 12 MONTHS
Air conditioning system . . . . .inspect

Brake master cyl. . . . .check level **HBH**

W Cooling system . . . . .inspect
Also hoses and clamps

Power steering reservoir . .check level **FA**

Transmission/Transaxle controls
  & linkage . . . . .lubricate **LM**

Transmission/Transaxle,
  manual . . . . .check level

Body hinges . . . . .lubricate **MO**

SUPERCHARGED ENGINE, EVERY 6 MO/5 MI—8 KM
OTHERS, EVERY 6 MO/7.5 MI—12 KM
W Crankcase oil & filter . . . . .replace
Or when indicated by vehicle maintenance monitor, whichever occurs first

Clutch pedal freeplay, Mustang . . .check

AT FIRST 7.5 MI—12 KM; THEN EVERY 15 MI—24 KM
Tires . . . . .rotate

EVERY 15 MI—24 KM
Brake system, Capri . . . . .inspect
Inspect hoses and replace lining when 1/32" from rivet head ex. disc pads when 1/8" thick

Front suspension &
  steering linkage . . . . .fittings/plugs **LM**
RWD only

W Spark plugs Turbo . . . . .replace

EVERY 22.5 MI—36 KM
Battery fluid 3.0L & 3.2L SHO . .check level

EVERY 30 MI—48 KM
Brake system ex. Capri . . . . . . .inspect
Inspect hoses & replace lining when 1/32" from rivet head ex. disc pads when 1/8" thick

Exhaust system heat shields . . . .inspect

Driveshaft boots . . . . .inspect
Capri, Escort, Festiva, Probe, Tracer

Steering & suspension . . . . .inspect
Capri, Escort, Festiva, Probe, Tracer

W Air cleaner element . . . . .replace

Clutch master cylinder . . .check level **HB**
Cougar, Thunderbird

W Crankcase emission filter . . . . . .replace
1.9L, 2.3L HSC, 5.0L only

W Accessory drive belts . . . .inspect/adjust
1.3L, 1.6L, 1.8L, 1.9L, Probe & Villager only

Clutch pedal freeplay . . . . . .check/adjust
Capri, Escort, Festiva, Probe, Tracer

Fuel lines & hoses . . . . .inspect
Capri, Festiva, Probe

W Idle speed Festiva, Capri, Probe . .check

W Spark plugs (ex. platinum) . . . . .replace

W Supercharger fluid
    3.8L . . . . .check level **SLF**

Wheel bearings ex.
    Festiva, Villager . . . .inspect/repack **LM**
Non-driving wheels only. Not required for sealed bearings

Body & chassis nuts & bolts . . . .inspect
Capri, Escort, Festiva, Probe, Tracer

EVERY 36 MO/30 MI—48 KM
W Cooling system . . . . .change coolant **EC**

EVERY 60 MI—96 KM
Front & rear wheel
    bearings . . . . .lubricate **LM**
Festiva only

W Accessory drive belts . . . .inspect/adjust

W Fuel filter 1.3L, 1.6L, & Probe . . .replace

W Fuel filter, flex. fuel models . . . . .replace

W PCV valve, as equipped . . . . . . .replace

W Spark plugs (platinum) . . . . .replace

W Timing belt . . . . .replace
Belt driven overhead cam engine ex. 1.9L, 2.3L

W Valve lash 3.0L, 3.2L SHO . . . . . .adjust

EVERY 100 MI—160 KM
Rear axle, RWD . . . . . .change lubricant

SEVERE SERVICE
W Crankcase—Change oil & filter every 3 mo/3 mi (4.8 km)

Disc brake pads—Festiva & Probe, inspect every 15 mi (24 km)

Transmission/Transaxle, automatic—Change fluid every 30 mi (48 km)

W Air cleaner element—Replace as required

Body & chassis nuts & bolts—Inspect every 15 mi (24 km)

Tires—Rotate at first 6 mi (9.6 km), then every 15 mi (24 km)

KEY TO LUBRICANTS
See other Ford, Lincoln, Mercury charts

CRANKCASE . . . . .5W-30 API★		
CAPACITY, Refill:	Liters	Qt
1.3L	3.0	3.2
1.6L	3.0	3.2
1.8L	3.6	3.8
1.9L, 2.0L	3.3	3.5
2.3L, 3.0L SHO, 3.2L SHO,		
4.6L Code W (incl. filter)	4.7	5.0
3.0L ex. SHO, Villager,		
3.8L FWD (incl. filter)	4.3	4.5
2.5L Probe	3.7	3.9
3.8L RWD, 5.0L	3.8	4.0
3.0L Villager	3.5	3.7
4.6L Code V (incl. filter)	5.7	6.0

4.6L Code V, 5.0L, engines have 2 oil drain plugs. Add 0.45 liter (0.5 qt) for Police oil cooler
Capacity shown is without filter. When replacing filter, additional oil may be needed

TRANSMISSION/TRANSAXLE, Automatic

AODE/4R70W .MA5		
Others . . . . .MA		
CAPACITY, Total Fill:	Liters	Qt
AXOD	12.2	12.8
AXODE, AXODEW	11.8	12.5
4R70W	11.8	12.5
Taurus ex. O.D.	7.4	8.0
Festiva	2.8³	3.0³
Capri	5.7	6.0
Probe	8.8	9.3
Escort & Tracer	5.8	6.1
Villager	8.3	8.7
Others, FWD	7.9	8.3
All RWD	2.8³	3.0³

3 Initial Refill: With the engine at operating temperature, shift transmission through all gears. Check fluid level in PARK and add fluid as needed. With AOD, AODE, or 4R70W transmission, drain torque converter.

TRANSMISSION/TRANSAXLE, Manual

Probe 75W-90 **GL-4**		
All others . . . . .MA		
CAPACITY, Refill:	Liters	Pt
Festiva	2.5	5.2
Probe	2.7	5.6
Capri	3.2	6.8
Escort, Tracer w/1.9L	2.7	5.6
Escort, Tracer w/1.8L	3.3	7.1
Mustang	2.6	5.5
Thunderbird, Cougar	3.0	6.4
All others, FWD	2.9	6.2

DIFFERENTIAL

Standard . . . . .90 **HP**		
Traction-Lok . . . . .90 **HP★**		
CAPACITY, Refill:	Liters	Pt
7.5" ring gear:		
Thunderbird/Cougar	1.4	3.0
Others	1.5	3.25
8.8" ring gear:		
Mark VIII	1.4	3.0
Thunderbird/Cougar	1.5	3.25
Others	1.8	3.75

FORD, LINCOLN, MERCURY
1994 All Models

Perform the following maintenance services at the intervals indicated to keep the vehicle warranties in effect.
W   SERVICE TO MAINTAIN EMISSION WARRANTY

MI—MILES IN THOUSANDS
KM—KILOMETERS IN THOUSANDS

EVERY MONTH
Cooling system . . . . . . .check level **EC**

EVERY 6 MONTHS
Exhaust system . . . . .inspect
Radiator, heater & AC hoses . . . .inspect

EVERY 12 MONTHS
Air conditioning system . . . . .inspect
Brake master cyl. . . . . .check level **HBH**
W Cooling system . . . . .inspect
Also hoses, clamps & coolant strength. Except Escort, Tracer & Probe

Power steering reservoir . .check level **FA**
Transmission/Transaxle controls
& linkage . . . . .lubricate **LM**
Transmission/Transaxle,
manual . . . . .check level
Body hinges . . . . .lubricate **MO**

EVERY 6 MO/5 MI—8 KM
W Crankcase oil & filter . . . . .replace
Or when indicated by vehicle maintenance monitor, whichever occurs first

EVERY 5 MI—8 KM
Clutch pedal freeplay,
Mustang . . . . .check/adjust

AT FIRST 5 MI—8 KM;
THEN EVERY 10 MI—16 KM
Tires . . . . .rotate

EVERY 12 MO/15 MI—24 KM
W Cooling system Escort,
Tracer 1.9L . . . . .inspect
Also hoses, clamps & coolant strength

EVERY 15 MI—24 KM
Brake system, Capri . . . . .inspect
Inspect hoses and replace lining when 1/32" from rivet head ex. disc pads when 1/8" thick

Front suspension &
steering linkage . . . . . .fittings/plugs **LM**
RWD only. Except Town Car
W Spark plugs Capri Turbo . . . . . . .replace

EVERY 22.5 MI—36 KM
Battery fluid
3.0L & 3.2L SHO . . . . .check level

EVERY 30 MI—48 KM
Brake system ex. Capri . . . . . . .inspect
Inspect hoses & replace lining when 1/32" from rivet head ex. disc pads when 1/8," thick

Exhaust system heat shields . . .inspect
Driveshaft boots . . . . .inspect
Aspire, Capri, Escort, Probe, Tracer
Steering & suspension . . . . .inspect
Aspire, Capri, Escort, Probe, Tracer
Front suspension
& steering linkage . . .fittings/plugs **LM**
Town Car only
Seat belt retractors & anchors . . .inspect
Capri only
W Air cleaner element . . . . .replace
Clutch master cylinder . .check level **HB**
W Crankcase emission filter . . . . . .replace
1.9L, 2.3L HSC, 5.0L only

W Accessory drive belts . . . .inspect/adjust
1.3L, 1.6L, 1.8L, 1.9L, Probe & Villager
Clutch pedal freeplay . . . . .check/adjust
Aspire, Capri, Escort, Tracer
Fuel lines & hoses . . . . .inspect
Capri, Probe & 1.8L
W Idle speed Aspire, Capri, Probe . . .check
W Spark plugs (ex. platinum) . . . . . .replace
W Supercharger fluid 3.8L .check level **SLF**
Wheel bearings Capri,
Tempo, Topaz only . .inspect/repack **LM**
Non-driving wheels only. Not required for sealed bearings
Body & chassis nuts & bolts . . . . .inspect
Aspire, Capri, Escort, Probe, Tracer

EVERY 36 MO/30 MI—48 KM
W Cooling system . . . . .change coolant **EC**
W Cooling system Probe & 1.8L . . . .inspect
Also hoses, clamps and coolant strength

EVERY 60 MI—96 KM
Evaporative fuel hose & tube . . . .inspect
Aspire, Probe only
W Accessory drive belts . . . . .inspect/adjust
W Fuel filter 1.3L, 1.6L,
1.8L & Probe . . . . .replace
Ignition timing . . . . .check/adjust
Aspire only
W PCV valve, as equipped . . . . . . .replace
W Spark plugs (platinum) . . . . .replace
W Timing belt . . . . .replace
Non-Calif. Probe & 1.8L only

EVERY 90 MI—145 KM
Timing belt . . . . .inspect
Calif. Probe only

EVERY 100 MI—160 KM
W Timing belt . . . . .replace
3.0L & 3.2L SHO only
W Valve lash 3.0L, 3.2L SHO . . . . . .adjust
Rear axle, RWD . . . . . .change lubricant

EVERY 105 MI—169 KM
W Timing belt . . . . .replace
Villager, Capri & Calif. Probe only

EVERY 120 MI—193 KM
W Transmission/Transaxle
automatic . . . . .change fluid/filter
Except Escort, Tracer, Probe, Capri, Aspire, Villager

SERVICE AS REQUIRED
Fuel filter flex. fuel models . . . . . .replace
Cooling system . . . . .replace
Hoses & clamps

SEVERE SERVICE
W **Crankcase**—Change oil & filter every 3 mo/ 3 mi (4.8 km)
Disc brake pads—Probe, inspect every 15 mi (24 km)
Transmission/Transaxle, automatic—Change fluid every 30 mi (48 km)
W **Air cleaner element**—Replace as required
Body & chassis nuts & bolts—Inspect every 15 mi (24 km)
Tires—Rotate at first 6 mi (9.6 km), then every 9 mi (14 km)

KEY TO LUBRICANTS
See other Ford, Lincoln, Mercury charts

CRANKCASE . . . .*5W-30 API★
*Methanol flexible fuel oil must meet Ford Spec. M2C909-A2 Part No. X0-10W-30-FFV

CAPACITY, Refill:	Liters	Qt
1.3L	3.1	3.3
1.6L	3.0	3.2
1.8L	3.6	3.8
1.9L, 2.0L	3.3	3.5
2.3L, 3.0L SHO, 3.2L SHO, 4.6L Code W (incl. filter)	4.7	5.0
3.0L ex. SHO, Villager, 3.8L FWD (incl. filter)	4.3	4.5
2.5L Probe	3.7	3.9
3.8L RWD, 5.0L	3.8	4.0
3.0L Villager	3.5	3.7
4.6L Code V (incl. filter)	5.7	6.0

5.0L engines have 2 oil drain plugs. Add 0.45 liter (0.5 qt) for Police oil cooler
Capacity shown is without filter. When replacing filter, additional oil may be needed

TRANSMISSION/TRANSAXLE, Automatic
AODE/4R70W **MA5**
Others . . . .**MA**

CAPACITY, Total Fill:	Liters	Qt
4R70W	11.8	12.5
AX4S	11.6	12.3
AODE ex. Mustang	12.9	13.6
Mustang AODE	11.8	12.5
Villager	8.3	8.7
Tempo, Topaz	8.1	8.6
Capri	6.8	7.2
Probe, Aspire	2.8[3]	3.0[3]
Escort & Tracer	3.9[3]	4.1[3]

3 Initial Refill: With the engine at operating temperature, shift transmission through all gears. Check fluid level in PARK and add fluid as needed. With AOD, AODE, or 4R70W transmission, drain torque converter.

TRANSMISSION/TRANSAXLE, Manual
Probe, Capri ex. Turbo 75W-90 **GL-4**
All others . . . .**MA**

CAPACITY, Refill:	Liters	Pt
Aspire	2.5	5.2
Probe	2.7	5.8
Capri	3.2	6.8
Escort & Tracer: 1.9L	2.7	5.6
1.8L	3.2	6.7
Mustang	2.6	5.5
Thunderbird, Cougar	3.0	6.4
All others, FWD	2.9	6.2

DIFFERENTIAL
Standard . . . . .90 **HP**
Traction-Lok . . . . .90 **HP★**

CAPACITY, Refill:	Liters	Pt
7.5" ring gear: Thunderbird/Cougar	1.4	3.0
Others	1.5	3.25
8.8" ring gear: Mark VIII	1.4	3.0
Thunderbird/Cougar	1.5	3.25
Others	1.8	3.75

SERVICE AT TIME OR MILEAGE — WHICHEVER OCCURS FIRST

FDPM23   FDPM23

Perform the following maintenance services at the intervals indicated to keep the vehicle warranties in effect.

W   SERVICE TO MAINTAIN EMISSION WARRANTY

MI—MILES IN THOUSANDS
KM—KILOMETERS IN THOUSANDS
FIRST 0.5 MI—0.8 KM
Wheel lug nuts . . . . .torque
Windstar only

EVERY MONTH
Cooling system . . . . . . .check level **EC**

EVERY 6 MONTHS
Power steering reservoir . .check level **FA**
Exhaust system . . . . .inspect
Radiator, heater & AC hoses . . . .inspect
Driveshaft boots . . . . .inspect
All FWD ex Aspire, Escort, Tracer, Probe, Villager

EVERY 12 MONTHS
Air conditioning system . . . . .inspect
Battery . . . . .clean inspect
Brake master cyl. . . . . .check level **HBH**
W Cooling system . . . . .inspect
Also hoses & clamps

Transmission/Transaxle controls
& linkage . . . . .lubricate **LM**
Transmission/Transaxle,
manual . . . . .check level
Body hinges . . . . .lubricate **MO**

EVERY 6 MO/5 MI—8 KM
W Crankcase oil & filter . . . . .replace
Or when indicated by vehicle maintenance monitor, whichever occurs first

EVERY 5 MI—8 KM
Clutch pedal freeplay,
Mustang . . . . .check/adjust
Adjust by lifting pedal

AT FIRST 5 MI—8 KM;
THEN EVERY 10 MI—16 KM
Tires . . . . .rotate
Also check/adjust air pressure
Wheel lug nuts . . . . .torque

EVERY 12 MO/15 MI—24 KM
W Cooling system
All ex. 1.3L, 1.8L & Probe . . . . .inspect
Also hoses, clamps & coolant strength

EVERY 15 MI—24 KM
Passenger compartment
air filter . . . . .replace
Continental only
Front suspension &
steering linkage . . . . . .fittings/plugs **LM**
RWD only. Except Town Car

EVERY 20 MI—32 KM
Passenger compartment
air filter . . . . .replace
Contour, Mystique only

EVERY 24 MO/25 MI—40 KM
Battery fluid 3.0L & 3.2L SHO check level

EVERY 30 MI—48 KM
Brake system . . . . .inspect
Inspect hoses & replace lining when 1/32" from rivet head ex. disc pads when 1/8," thick
Transmission, Transaxle,
automatic . . . . .change fluid **MA**
Exhaust system heat shields . . . .inspect
Driveshaft boots . . . . .inspect
Aspire, Escort, Probe, Tracer
Steering & suspension . . . . .inspect
Aspire, Escort, Probe, Tracer
Front suspension
& steering linkage . . . .fittings/plugs **LM**
Town Car only
W Air cleaner element . . . . .replace
Clutch master cylinder . . .check level **HB**
Thunderbird S.C. only
W Crankcase emission filter . . . . . . .replace
1.9L & 5.0L only
W Accessory drive belts . . . .inspect/adjust
1.3L, Probe & Villager

Clutch pedal freeplay . . . . . .check/adjust
Aspire, Escort, Tracer
Fuel lines & hoses . . . . .inspect
1.3L, Probe & 1.8L
W Idle speed Aspire, 1.8L Probe . . . .check
W Spark plugs (ex. platinum) . . . . . .replace
Body & chassis nuts & bolts . . . . .inspect
Aspire, Escort, Probe, Tracer

EVERY 36 MO/30 MI—48 KM
W Cooling system . . . . .change coolant **EC**
1.3L, 1.8L, Probe only
W Cooling system . . . . .inspect
1.3L, 1.8L & Probe only
Also hoses, clamps and coolant strength

FIRST 48 MO/50 MI—80 KM THEN
EVERY 36 MO/ 30 MI—48KM
W Cooling system . . . . .change coolant **EC**
All ex. 1.3L, 1.8L, Probe

EVERY 60 MI—96 KM
Wheel bearings, Aspire . . . . . . .repack
W Supercharger fluid 3.8L . .check level **SLF**
Evaporative fuel hose & tube . . . .inspect
Aspire, Probe & 1.8L only
W Accessory drive belts . . . . .inspect/adjust
W Fuel filter 1.3L, 1.8L & Probe . . . .replace
Ignition timing . . . . .check/adjust
Aspire only
W PCV valve, as equipped . . . . . . .replace
W Spark plugs (platinum) . . . . .replace
ex. (2.5L Contour, Mystique), Mark VIII, 3.0L Windstar & Continental
W Timing belt . . . . .replace
Probe, 1.8L, 1.3L—ex. Calif. models

EVERY 90 MI—145 KM
Timing belt . . . . .inspect
Probe, 1.8L, 1.3L—Calif. models only.

EVERY 100 MI—160 KM
W Timing belt . . . . .replace
3.0L & 3.2L SHO only
W Spark plugs . . . . .replace
2.5L Contour & Mystique, Mark VIII, 3.0L Windstar & Continental only
W Valve lash 3.0L, 3.2L SHO . . . . . .adjust
Rear axle, RWD . . . . . . .change lubricant
Axle lubricant should be changed if axle is submerged in water

EVERY 105 MI—169 KM
W Timing belt . . . . .replace
Villager& (Calif. Probe, 1.3L, 1.8L)

SERVICE AS REQUIRED
Wheel lug nuts . . . . .re-torque
Windstar only. 0.5 mi (0.8 km) after lug nuts are loosened
Fuel filter . . . . .replace
Air cleaner element . . . . .replace
Cooling system . . . . .replace
Hoses & clamps

SEVERE SERVICE
W **Crankcase**—Change oil & filter every 3 mo/3 mi (4.8 km)
W **Spark plugs**—(2.5L Contour, Mystique) Mark VIII, 3.0L Windstar & Continental replace every 60 mi (100 km)
Steering linkage—Town Car, lubricate every 15 mi (25 km)
Disc brake pads & rotors—Inspect every 15 mi (24 km) Aspire, Escort, Tracer & Probe only
Transmission/Transaxle, automatic—Change fluid every 21 mi (35 km)
W **Air cleaner element**—Inspect every 15 mi (25 km) 1.3L, 1.8L & Probe only
Body & chassis nuts & bolts—Inspect every 15 mi (24 km) Probe, Aspire, Escort, Tracer only

KEY TO LUBRICANTS
See other Ford, Lincoln, Mercury charts

CRANKCASE . . . .*5W-30 **API**★
*Methanol flexible fuel oil must meet Ford Spec. M2C909-A2
Part No. X0-10W-30-FFV

CAPACITY, Refill:[1]	Liters	Qt
1.3L (w/o filter)	3.1	3.3
1.8L (w/o filter)	3.6	3.8
1.9L (w/o filter)	3.3	3.5
2.0L Probe	3.5	3.7
2.0L ex. Probe	4.3	4.5
3.0L SHO, 3.2L SHO, 3.0L ex. SHO, Villager, 3.8L FWD	4.3	4.5
2.5L Probe	4.0	4.2
2.5L ex. Probe	5.5	5.8
3.8L RWD, 5.0L	4.7	5.0
3.0L Villager (w/o filter)	3.5	3.7
4.6L Mark VIII, Continental	5.7	6.0
Other 4.6L	4.7	5.0

5.0L engines have 2 oil drain plugs. Add 0.45 liter (0.5 qt) for Police oil cooler
1 Capacities include filter ex. when noted

TRANSMISSION/TRANSAXLE,
Automatic
AODE/4R70W **MA5**
Others . . . .**MA**

CAPACITY, Total Fill:	Liters	Qt
4R70W ex. Mark VIII	12.9	13.6
Mark VIII 4R70W	11.8	12.5
Mustang AODE	12.9	13.6
Villager	8.3	8.7
Probe w/2.0L	8.3	8.8
w/2.5L	8.8	9.3
Taurus, Sable, Windstar	11.6	12.3
Continental	12.6	13.3
Contour, Mystique	4.7[4]	5.0[4]
Aspire	2.8[4]	3.0[4]
Escort & Tracer	3.9[4]	4.1[4]

4 Initial Refill: With the engine at operating temperature, shift transmission through all gears. Check fluid level in PARK and add fluid as needed. With AOD, AODE, or 4R70W transmission, drain torque converter.

TRANSMISSION/TRANSAXLE,
Manual
Probe, ...75W-90 **GL-4**
All others **MA5**

CAPACITY, Refill:	Liters	Pt
Aspire	2.5	5.2
Probe	2.7	5.8
Escort & Tracer: 1.9L	2.7	5.6
1.8L	3.2	6.7
Mustang, Contour, Mystique	2.6	5.5
Thunderbird, Cougar	3.0	6.4
All others, FWD	2.9	6.2

5 Contour, Mystique—When replacing fluid add 52 ml (1.8 oz) additive, Spec. No. WSP-M2C196-A. Part No. F3TZ-19B456-MA

DIFFERENTIAL
Standard 80W-90 **GL-5**
Traction-Lok . . . . .80W-90 **GL-5**★

CAPACITY, Refill:	Liters	Pt
7.5" ring gear:		
Thunderbird/Cougar	1.4	3.0
Others	1.5[6]	3.25[6]
8.8" ring gear: Mark VIII	1.4	3.0
Thunderbird/Cougar	1.5	3.25
Others	1.8[6]	3.75[6]

6 Fill 1/2" to 9/16" below bottom of fill hole

FORD, LINCOLN, MERCURY
1996-98 All RWD Models
Except Mountaineer & Navigator—See Ford Trucks

CHEK-CHART

FDPM24   FDPM24

Perform the following maintenance services at the intervals indicated to keep the vehicle warranties in effect.

W   SERVICE TO MAINTAIN EMISSION WARRANTY

MI—MILES IN THOUSANDS
KM—KILOMETERS IN THOUSANDS

EVERY MONTH
Cooling system . . . . .check level **EC**
Fluid leaks on pavement . . . . . .inspect

EVERY 6 MONTHS
Exhaust system . . . . .inspect
Radiator, heater & AC hoses . . . .inspect
Power steering reservoir . .check level **MA**
Parking brake system . . . . .inspect
Driveshaft boots . . . . .inspect
As equipped

EVERY 12 MONTHS
Air conditioning system . . . . .inspect
Battery . . . . .clean inspect
Brake master cyl. . . . . .check level **HBH**
Cooling system . . . . .inspect
Also hoses & clamps

Transmission controls
& linkage . . . . .lubricate **LM**
Transmission, manual . . . . .check level
Body hinges & latches . . . .lubricate **SLS**

EVERY 6 MO/5 MI—8 KM
W Crankcase oil & filter . . . . .replace
Or when indicated by vehicle maintenance monitor,
whichever occurs first

EVERY 5 MI—8 KM
Clutch pedal freeplay,
Mustang . . . . .check/adjust
Adjust by lifting pedal

Coalescent filter 1996-97 . . . . .drain
Natural Gas 4.6L only

AT FIRST 5 MI—8 KM;
THEN EVERY 10 MI—16 KM
Tires .rotate
Also check/adjust air pressure

EVERY 12 MO/15 MI—24 KM
W Cooling system . . . . .inspect
Also hoses, clamps & coolant strength

Front suspension &
steering linkage . . . . . .fittings/plugs **LM**
Except 1996-97 Town Car
Also lubricate steering stops

EVERY 25 MI—40 KM
Fuel filter (Natural Gas 4.6L) . . . .replace
1996-97 only
Also replace O-ring seal

EVERY 30 MI—48 KM
Brake system . . . . .inspect
Inspect hoses & replace lining when 1/32" from rivet head
ex. disc pads when 1/8," thick

Transmission,
automatic . . . . .change fluid
Exhaust system heat shields . . . .inspect
Front suspension
& steering linkage . . . .fittings/plugs **LM**
1996-97 Town Car only
Also lubricate steering stops

W Air cleaner element . . . . .replace
Replace every 30 mo/30 mi (48 km)

W Spark plugs, 1996 . . . . .replace

Natural Gas 4.6L only

FIRST 48 MO/50 MI—80 KM THEN
EVERY 36 MO/ 30 MI—48KM
W Cooling system . . . . .change coolant **EC**

EVERY 60 MI—96 KM
W Spark plugs, 1997-98 . . . . .replace
Natural Gas 4.6L only

W Accessory drive belts . . . .inspect/adjust
At mileage, then every 30 mi (48 km) after initial service.
Ex. 1997 Mark VIII & Mustang Cobra
1998: 3.8L & 4.6L Natural Gas only

W PCV valve . . . . .replace
1996: Except, Mark VIII
1997: Except, Mark VIII, Town Car & 3.8L
1998: Except, Mark VIII & 3.8L

EVERY 100 MI—160 KM
W Spark plugs . . . . .replace
All ex. Natural Gas 4.6L

W Accessory drive belts . . . . .inspect/adjust
At mileage, then every 20 mi (32 km) after initial service
1997 Mark VIII & Mustang Cobra
1998: All except 3.8L & 4.6L Natural Gas

Rear axle . . . . .change lubricant
(Mineral-based oil only) Axle lubricant should be changed
if axle is submerged in water

W PCV valve . . . . .replace
1996: Mark VIII only
1997: Mark VIII, Town Car & 3.8L only
1998: Mark VIII & 3.8L only

EVERY 120 MI—190 KM
Coalescent filter . . . . .drain
1998 Natural Gas 4.6L only

Fuel filter (Natural Gas 4.6L) . . . .replace
1998 only. Also replace O-ring seal

SERVICE AS REQUIRED
Fuel filter . . . . .replace
Air cleaner element . . . . .replace
Cooling system . . . . .replace
Hoses & clamps

SEVERE SERVICE
W Accesory drive belts—Inspect/adjust initially at 60 mi (96 km), then every 30 mi (48 km)

Clutch pedal freeplay—Mustang, adjust by lifting pedal every 3 mi (4.8 km)

Coalescent filter—1996-97 Natural Gas 4.6L, drain every 3 mi (4.8 km)

W **Crankcase**—Change oil & filter every 3 mo/3 mi (4.8 km)

W **PCV valve**—1997-98 Mark VIII & 1997 Town Car, replace every 90 mi (150 km)

Rear axle—1997-98, change lubricant every 3 mi (4.8 km) (mineral-based oil). Waive interval where synthetic 75W-140 GL-5 gear oil is used Part No. FITZ-19580-B. Axle lubricant should be changed if axle is submerged in water

W **Spark plugs**—1998 Natural Gas 4.6L, replace every 36 mi (60 km). All gasoline engines, replace every 60 mi (100 km)

Steering linkage—Town Car, lubricate every 15 mi (25 km). Also lubricate steering stops

Transmission, automatic—Change fluid every 21 mi (35 km)

KEY TO LUBRICANTS

API★   Motor oil certified by the American Petroleum Institute (Starburst symbol)

EC   Ethylene Glycol Coolant
Mix 50/50 with water at least to -34°F (-37°C) protection

FA   Automatic Transmission Fluid, Type F

GL-4   Gear Oil, API Service GL-4

GL-5   Gear Oil, API Service GL-5

GL-5★ GL-5 Gear Oil with additive for Traction-Lok Differentials

HBH   Hydraulic Brake Fluid, Extra Heavy-Duty

LM   Lithium Grease, with Polyethylene

MA   MERCON® Automatic Transmission Fluid

MA5   MERCON® Automatic Transmission Fluid
Ford Part No. XT-5-QM

SLS   Special Lubricant—Spray
Ford Part No. D0AZ-19584-A

CRANKCASE . . . . .5W-30 **API★**
CAPACITY, Refill:[1]

	Liters	Qt
3.8L RWD	4.7	5.0
4.6L DOHC, 4V, Mark VIII,		
Mustang, Cobra	5.7	6.0
4.6L SOHC, 2V	4.7	5.0

Add 0.45 liter (0.5 qt) for Police oil cooler
1 Capacities include filter

TRANSMISSION, Automatic **MA5***
*Part No. XT-5-QM. Do not use MERCON®
CAPACITY, Initial Refill[2]:

	Liters	Qt
1997-98 Mark VIII	4.7	5.0
1998 Town Car	4.7	5.0
All others	6.1	6.5

2 With the engine at operating temperature, shift transmission through all gears. Check fluid level in PARK and add fluid as needed. Note: Torque converter must be drained

TRANSMISSION, Manual
All . . . .**MA**
CAPACITY, Refill:

	Liters	Pt
Mustang w/3.8L	2.6	5.5
w/4.6L	3.1	6.6

DIFFERENTIAL
Standard 80W-90 **GL-5**
Traction-Lok . . . . .80W-90 **GL-5★**
CAPACITY, Refill:

	Liters	Pt
7.5" ring gear:		
Thunderbird/Cougar	1.4	3.0
Others	1.5[3]	3.25[3]
8.8" ring gear: Mark VIII	1.4[3]	3.0[3]
Thunderbird/Cougar	1.5	3.25
Others	1.8[3]	3.75[3]

3 Fill 1/4" to 9/16" below bottom of fill hole

FORD, LINCOLN, MERCURY

1996-98 All FWD Models
Including FWD Vans

SERVICE AT TIME OR MILEAGE — WHICHEVER OCCURS FIRST

Perform the following maintenance services at the intervals indicated to keep the vehicle warranties in effect.

W SERVICE TO MAINTAIN EMISSION WARRANTY

MI—MILES IN THOUSANDS
KM—KILOMETERS IN THOUSANDS

FIRST 0.5 MI—0.8 KM
Wheel lug nuts . . . . .torque
Windstar only

EVERY MONTH
Cooling system . . . . . . .check level **EC**
Fluid leaks on pavement . . . . . . .inspect

EVERY 6 MONTHS
Power steering reservoir . . . . .check level
1998: Windstar use **FA**, other FWD use **MA**
1997: Contour, Mystique, Taurus, Sable & Continental use **MA**, other FWD use **FA**
1996: Taurus, Sable & Continental use **MA**, other FWD use **FA**
Parking brake system . . . . .inspect
Accessory drive belts . . . . .inspect
Aspire only
Exhaust system . . . . .inspect
Clutch reservoir . . . . . . .check level **HBH**
Radiator, heater & AC hoses . . . .inspect
Driveshaft boots . . . . .inspect
1996-97: All FWD ex. Aspire, Escort, Tracer, Probe, Villager
1998: All FWD ex. Villager

EVERY 12 MONTHS
Air conditioning system . . . . .inspect
Battery . . . . .clean inspect
Brake master cyl. . . . . .check level **HBH**
W Cooling system . . . . .inspect
Also hoses & clamps
Transaxle, automatic . . . . . . .check level
Probe, Aspire
Transaxle controls
& linkage . . . . .lubricate **LM**
Transaxle, manual . . . . .check level
Body hinges & latches . . . .lubricate **SLS**

EVERY 6 MO/5 MI—8 KM
W Crankcase oil & filter . . . . .replace
Or when indicated by vehicle maintenance monitor, whichever occurs first

AT FIRST 5 MI—8 KM;
THEN EVERY 10 MI—16 KM
Tires . . . . .rotate
Also check/adjust air pressure
Wheel lug nuts . . . . .torque

EVERY 10 MI—16 KM
Brake system . . . . .inspect
Contour, Mystique only

EVERY 12 MO/15 MI—24 KM
W Cooling system
All ex. 1.3L, 1.8L & Probe . . . . .inspect
Also hoses, clamps & coolant strength

EVERY 15 MI—24 KM
Transaxle, auto. Villager . . . . .check level
Inspect fluid
Passenger compartment
air filter (cabin air filter) . . . . . . .replace
1996: Continental only
1997: Continental, Taurus, Sable, Contour, Mystique only
1998: Continental, Taurus, Sable only

EVERY 20 MI—32 KM
Passenger compartment
air filter (cabin air filter) . . . . . . .replace
1996: Taurus, Sable, Contour, Mystique only
1998: Contour, Mystique only

EVERY 30 MI—48 KM
Brake system
ex. Contour, Mystique . . . . . . .inspect
Inspect hoses & replace lining when 1/32" from rivet head ex. disc pads when 1/8" thick
Transaxle, automatic . . . . . .change fluid
2.5L Probe, Continental, Taurus, Windstar only

Exhaust system heat shields . . . .inspect
Driveshaft boots . . . . .inspect
Aspire, Escort, Probe, Tracer
Steering & suspension . . . . .inspect
Aspire, Escort, Probe, Tracer
W Air cleaner element . . . . .replace
Replace every 30 mo/30 mi (48 km)
W Crankcase emission filter, 1996 . .replace
1.9L & 2.0L Contour, Mystique
W Accessory drive belts . . . .inspect/adjust
1.3L, 1.8L, Probe & Villager
Clutch pedal freeplay . . . . . .check/adjust
Aspire, Escort, Tracer
Fuel lines & hoses . . . . .inspect
1.3L, Probe & 1.8L
W Idle speed Aspire, 1.8L & Probe . . .check
W Spark plugs . . . . .replace
1.3L, 1.8L, Probe, Villager & 3.0L Flexible Fuel
Body & chassis nuts & bolts . . . .inspect
Aspire, Escort, Probe, Tracer

EVERY 36 MO/30 MI—48 KM
W Cooling system . . . . .inspect
1.3L, 1.8L & Probe only
Also hoses, clamps and coolant strength

FIRST 48 MO/50 MI—80 KM THEN
EVERY 36 MO/ 30 MI—48KM
W Cooling system . . . . . .change coolant **EC**

EVERY 60 MI—96 KM
Wheel bearings, Aspire . . . . . .repack **LM**
W Evaporative fuel hose & tube . . . .inspect
Aspire, Probe & 1.8L only
W Accessory drive belts . . . .inspect/adjust
At mileage, then every 30 mi (48 km) after initial service
Except 1998 4.6L, 3.4L SHO, (3.0L Vulcan, Taurus, Sable)
W Fuel filter 1.3L 1.8L & Probe . . . .replace
Recommended but not required for Calif. models
Ignition timing . . . . .check/adjust
Aspire only
W PCV valve, as equipped . . . . . . .replace
1996: Except 3.8L Windstar, 3.0L Duratec
1997: Except 3.8L Windstar, 3.0L Duratec, 4.6L, Contour, Mystique
1998: 3.0L Windstar, Escort, Tracer only
W Spark plugs, 1996 . . . . .replace
1.9L & (2.0L Contour, Mystique)
W Timing belt . . . . .replace
Probe, 1.8L, 1.3L—ex. Calif. models

EVERY 90 MI—145 KM
Timing belt . . . . .inspect
Probe, 1.8L, 1.3L—Calif. models only

EVERY 100 MI—160 KM
W Spark plugs (platinum) . . . . .replace
1996-98: Sable, Windstar, Continental, 2.5L Duratec, Taurus ex. Flexible Fuel
1997-98: Contour, Mystique, Escort, Tracer
W PCV valve . . . . .replace
1996-98: 3.8L Windstar, 3.0L Duratec
1997-98: 4.6L, Contour, Mystique
1998: Taurus, Sable
W Valve lash 3.4L SHO . . . . . .check/adjust
W Accessory drive belts . . . .inspect/adjust
At mileage, then every 20 mi (32 km) after initial service
1998: 4.6L, Taurus, Sable ex. Duratec

EVERY 105 MI—169 KM
W Timing belt . . . . .replace
Villager & (Calif. Probe, 1.3L, 1.8L)

EVERY 120 MI—192 KM
W Fuel filter 1.3L, 1.8L & Probe . . . .replace
Calif. models only

SERVICE AS REQUIRED
Wheel lug nuts . . . . .re-torque
Windstar only. 0.5 mi (0.8 km) after lug nuts are loosened
Fuel filter . . . . .replace
Air cleaner element . . . . .replace
Cooling system . . . . .replace
Hoses & clamps

KEY TO LUBRICANTS
See other Ford, Lincoln, Mercury charts

CRANKCASE . . . . .5W-30 API★[1]		
CAPACITY, Refill:[2]	**Liters**	**Qt**
1.3L	3.4	3.6
1.8L, 1.9L, 2.0L Escort, ex. ZX2, Tracer	3.8	4.0
2.0L Probe	3.5	3.7
2.0L Contour, Mystique, Escort ZX2	4.3	4.5
3.0L ex. Duratec & Villager, 3.8L . .	4.3	4.5
3.0L Duratec	5.2	5.5
3.0L Villager	4.0	4.2
2.5L Probe	4.0	4.2
2.5L ex. Probe	5.5	5.8
3.4L SHO	6.1	6.5
4.6L Continental	5.7	6.0

1 Methanol flexible fuel oil must meet Ford Spec. M2C909-A2 Part No. X0-10W-30-FFV
2 Capacities include filter

TRANSMISSION/TRANSAXLE,
Automatic
1996-97 . . . . **MA**
1998: Villager, Escort, Tracer, Contour, Mystique . . . .**MA**
Other FWD **MA5***
*Except 1998 Windstar built before 9/9/97 use MA

CAPACITY, Total Fill:	Liters	Qt
Villager	8.3	8.7
Probe w/2.0L	8.3	8.8
w/2.5L	8.8	9.3
Taurus, Sable w/AX4S	11.6	12.3
w/AX4N	12.7	13.4
Windstar	11.6	12.3
Continental	13.0	13.7
Contour, Mystique	3.7[3]	4.0[3]
Aspire	2.8[3]	3.0[3]
Escort & Tracer	3.9[3]	4.1[3]

3 Initial Refill: With the engine at operating temperature, shift transmission through all gears. Check fluid level in PARK and add fluid as needed

TRANSMISSION/TRANSAXLE,
Manual
Probe 75W-90 **GL-4**
All others **MA4**

CAPACITY, Refill:	Liters	Pt
Aspire	2.5	5.2
Probe	2.7	5.8
Escort & Tracer: 1.9L (1996) . . .	2.7	5.6
1.8L (1996)	3.2	6.7
w/2.0L (1997-98)	3.4	7.1
Contour, Mystique	2.6	5.5

4 Contour, Mystique 1996-97—When replacing fluid add 52 ml (1.8 oz) additive, Spec. No. WSP-M2C196-A Part No. F3TZ-19B456-MA

SEVERE SERVICE
W Crankcase—Change oil & filter every 3 mo/3 mi (4.8 km)
W Spark plugs—(2.5L Contour, Mystique), 3.0L Vulcan, 3.4L SHO, Windstar & Continental replace every 60 mi (100 km)
Brake linings—Taurus, Sable, inspect every 12 mi (20 km)
Disc brake pads & rotors—Inspect every 15 mi (24 km) Aspire, Escort, Tracer & Probe only
Transaxle, automatic—Change fluid every 21 mi (35 km) ex. Contour, Mystique, Villager, 2.0L Probe, Aspire, Escort, Tracer
Transaxle, automatic—(Contour, Mystique, 2.0L Probe & Villager), change fluid every 30 mi (50 km)
W Air cleaner element—Inspect every 15 mi (25 km) 1.3L, 1.8L & Probe only
Body & chassis nuts & bolts—Inspect every 15 mi (24 km) Probe, Aspire, Escort, Tracer only

FORD, LINCOLN, MERCURY
1999-2000 All RWD Models
Except Mountaineer & Navigator—See Ford Trucks

SERVICE AT TIME OR MILEAGE — WHICHEVER OCCURS FIRST

FDPM   FDPM

Perform the following maintenance services at the intervals indicated to keep the vehicle warranties in effect.

W   SERVICE TO MAINTAIN EMISSION WARRANTY

MI—MILES IN THOUSANDS
KM—KILOMETERS IN THOUSANDS

EVERY MONTH
Tires . . . . .check
Check air pressure & wear

Engine oil . . . . .check level

EVERY 6 MONTHS
Power steering . . . . .check level **MA**
Parking brake system . . . . .inspect
Warning lights . . . . .check
Brake, ABS, air bag, safety belt
Cooling System . . . . . . .check level **EC**
Also check coolant strength. Do not mix orange with green coolant
Battery . . . . .clean/inspect
Clutch reservoir . . . . . .check level **HBH**
Body hinges & latches . . . .lubricate **SLS**

EVERY 6 MO/5 MI—8 KM
Crankcase oil & filter . . . . .replace

EVERY 5 MI—8 KM
Clutch pedal freeplay,
  Mustang . . . . .check/adjust
Adjust by lifting pedal
Tires . . . . .rotate

EVERY 12 MONTHS
Air-conditioning system . . . . . . .inspect

EVERY 12 MO/15 MI—24 KM
Cabin air filter . . . . .replace
As equipped

EVERY 15 MI—24 KM
Transmission, automatic . . . .check level
Inspect fluid except Lincoln LS
Brake System. . . . . .inspect
Including brake lines & hoses
Cooling System . . . . .inspect
Suspension &
  steering linkage . . . . .inspect

EVERY 30 MI—48 KM
Exhaust system & heat shields . . .inspect
Air cleaner element . . . . .replace
Fuel filter . . . . .replace
Transmission, automatic . . . .change fluid
Except Lincoln LS
Compressed gas fuel tanks . . . . .inspect
Natural Gas Vehicles only

EVERY 36 MI—60 KM
Spark plugs . . . . .replace
Natural Gas Vehicles only

AT FIRST 45 MI—72 KM;
THEN EVERY 30 MI—48 KM
Cooling system . . . . .change coolant EC
Green coolant only. Do not use orange coolant

EVERY 100 MI—160 KM
Accessory drive belts . . . . .inspect
PCV valve . . . . .replace
Spark plugs . . . . .replace
Except Natural Gas Vehicles
Differential, rear . . . . .change lubricant
Police & Taxi applications with mineral-based oil installed

EVERY 120 MI—192 KM
Coalescent filter . . . . .drain bowl
Replace filter
Natural Gas Vehicles only

EVERY 150 MI—240 KM
Differential, 2000 . . . . . .change lubricant
Mineral-based lubricant only

EVERY 180 MONTHS
Compressed gas fuel tanks . . . . .replace
Natural Gas Vehicles only

SERVICE AS REQUIRED
Hydraulic engine cooling fan . . . . . .**MA**
Lincoln LS only
Brake reservoir . . . . . .check level **HBH**
Differential . . . . .check level
Only if evidence of a leak
Differential . . . . .check oil
Only when submerged in water
Transmission, manual . . . .change fluid
U-joints . . . . .inspect/lubricate **LM**
As equipped w/fittings
Cabin air filter . . . . .replace
As equipped
Air cleaner element . . . . .replace

SEVERE SERVICE
Crankcase—Change oil & filter every 3 mo/3 mi (4.8 km)

Brake system—Inspect every 5 mi (8 km)

Differential—Change lubricant every 3 mo/3mi (4.8 km) (mineral-based oil) during extended trailer towing above 70°F (21°C) and extended wide open throttle above 45 mph. Waive interval where synthetic 75W-140 GL-5 gear oil is used Part No. F1TZ-19580-B.

Fuel filter—Replace every 15 mi (24 km)

Spark plugs—Replace every 60 mi (96 km)

Transmission, automatic—Change fluid every 30 mi (48 km)

KEY TO LUBRICANTS
API★	Motor oil certified by the American Petroleum Institute (Starburst symbol)
EC	Ethylene Glycol Coolant Mix 50/50 with water at least to -34°F (-37°C) protection
FA	Automatic Transmission Fluid, Type F
GL-4	Gear Oil, API Service GL-4
GL-5	Gear Oil, API Service GL-5
GL-5★	GL-5 Gear Oil with additive for Traction-Lok Differentials
HBH	Hydraulic Brake Fluid, Extra Heavy-Duty
LM	Lithium Grease, with Polyethylene
MA	MERCON® Automatic Transmission Fluid
MA5	MERCON® V Automatic Transmission Fluid
SLS	Special Lubricant—Spray Ford Part No. D0AZ-19584-A

CRANKCASE . . . . .5W-30 **API★**

CAPACITY, Refill:[1]	Liters	Qt
3.0L, 3.9L	5.7	6.0
3.8L RWD	4.7	5.0
4.6L DOHC, 4V	5.7	6.0
4.6L SOHC, 2V	4.7	5.0

Add 0.45 liter (0.5 qt) for Police oil cooler
1 Capacities include filter

TRANSMISSION,
  Automatic **MA5***
*Part No. XT-5-QM. Do not use MERCON®

CAPACITY, Initial Refill:[2]	Liters	Qt
Lincoln LS	11.2[3]	11.9[3]
4R70W	4.7	5.0

2 With the engine at operating temperature, shift transmission through all gears. Check fluid level in PARK and add fluid as needed. Note: Torque converter must be drained
3 Total fill, fill to bottom of fill plug

TRANSMISSION, Manual
All . . . .**MA**

CAPACITY, Refill:	Liters	Pt
Lincoln LS	1.1	2.3
Mustang w/3.8L	2.6	5.5
w/4.6L	3.1	6.6

DIFFERENTIAL
Town Car limousine
*Synthetic . . . . .75W-140 **GL-5★**
Lincoln LS . . . . . . *Synthetic 75W-140 **GL-5**
*Part No. F1TZ-19580-B
All others:
Standard 80W-90 **GL-5**
Traction-Lok . . . . .80W-90 **GL-5★**

CAPACITY, Refill:	Liters	Pt
Lincoln LS	1.4[4]	3.0[4]
7.5" ring gear:	1.5[4]	3.25[4]
8.8" ring gear:	1.8[4]	3.75[4]
Town Car limousine	2.2[4]	4.75[4]

4 Fill ¼" to 9/16" below bottom of fill hole

SERVICE AT TIME OR MILEAGE — WHICHEVER OCCURS FIRST

FDPM   FDPM

Perform the following maintenance services at the intervals indicated to keep the vehicle warranties in effect.
W   SERVICE TO MAINTAIN EMISSION WARRANTY

MI—MILES IN THOUSANDS
KM—KILOMETERS IN THOUSANDS

EVERY MONTH
Tires . . . . .check
Check air pressure & wear

Engine oil . . . . .check level

EVERY 6 MONTHS
Power steering . . . . .check level **MA**
Parking brake system . . . . .inspect
Warning lights . . . . .check
Brake, ABS, air bag, safety belt
Cooling System . . . . . . .check level **EC**
Also check coolant strength. Do not mix orange with green coolant
Battery . . . . .clean/inspect
Clutch reservoir . . . . .check level **HBH***
*Focus, use Super DOT 4 Spec. No. ESD-M6C57-A
Body hinges & latches . . . .lubricate **SLS**

EVERY 6 MO/5 MI—8 KM
Crankcase oil & filter . . . . .replace

EVERY 5 MI—8 KM
Tires . . . . .rotate

EVERY 12 MONTHS
Air-conditioning system . . . . . . .inspect

EVERY 12 MO/15 MI—24 KM
Cabin air filter . . . . .replace
As equipped

EVERY 15 MI—24 KM
Transmission, automatic . . . .check level
Inspect fluid
Brake System. . . . . .inspect
Including brake lines & hoses
Cooling system . . . . .inspect
Suspension &
steering linkage . . . . .inspect

EVERY 30 MI—48 KM
Exhaust System heat shields . . . .inspect
Air cleaner element . . . . .replace
Fuel filter . . . . .replace
Accessory drive belts . . . . .inspect
Villager only
Transaxle, automatic . . . . .change fluid
AX4S, AX4N, 4F27E only

AT FIRST 45 MI—72 KM; THEN EVERY 30 MI—48 KM
Cooling system . . . . .change coolant **EC**
Green coolant only. Do not use orange coolant
All models except Cougar

EVERY 60 MI—96 KM
PCV valve, 1999 4 cyl. . . . . .replace

EVERY 100 MI—160 KM
Accessory drive belts . . . . .inspect
Except Villager
PCV valve . . . . .replace
Except 1999 4 cyl, engines
Spark plugs . . . . .replace

EVERY 105 MI—169 KM
Timing belt . . . . .replace
Villager only

EVERY 120 MI—192 KM
Timing belt 2.0L . . . . .inspect

EVERY 150 MI—240 KM
Cooling system,
Cougar . . . . .change coolant **EC**
Orange coolant only. Do not mix orange with green coolant

Transaxle, automatic 2000 . .change fluid
All except AX4S, AX4N, 4F27E

SERVICE AS REQUIRED
Brake reservoir . . . . .check level **HBH***
*Focus use Super DOT 4 w/manual transaxle Spec. No. ESD-M6C57-A
Transmission, manual . . . .change fluid
U-joints . . . . .inspect/lubricate **LM**
As equipped w/fittings
CV-joints . . . . .inspect/lubricate **CV**
Cabin air filter . . . . .replace
As equipped
Air cleaner element . . . . .replace

SEVERE SERVICE
Crankcase—Change oil & filter every 3 mo/3 mi (4.8 km)
Brake system—Inspect every 5 mi (8 km)
Fuel filter—Replace every 15 mi (24 km)
Spark plugs—Replace every 60 mi (96 km)
Transaxle auto.—Change fluid every 30 mi (48 km)

KEY TO LUBRICANTS
API★ Motor oil certified by the American Petroleum Institute (Starburst symbol)

CV Constant Velocity Joint Grease
Part No. E43Z-19590-A

EC Ethylene Glycol Coolant
Mix 50/50 with water at least to -34°F (-37°C) protection

HBH Hydraulic Brake Fluid, Extra Heavy-Duty

LM Lithium Grease, with Polyethylene

MA MERCON® Automatic Transmission Fluid

MA5 MERCON® V Automatic Transmission Fluid

SLF Synthetic Manual Transmission Fluid Part No. XT-M5-QS

SLS Special Lubricant—Spray
Ford Part No. D0AZ-19584-A

CRANKCASE . . . . .5W-30 API★

CAPACITY, Refill:[1]	Liters	Qt
2.0L SPI	3.8	4.0
2.0L Zetec	4.3	4.5
3.0L Vulcan	4.3	4.5
3.0L Duratec	5.2	5.5
3.3L Villager	4.0	4.2
2.5L	5.5	5.8
3.4L SHO	6.1	6.5
3.8L	4.7	5.0
4.6L Continental	5.7	6.0

1 Capacities include filter

TRANSMISSION/TRANSAXLE, Automatic
Villager, Escort, Tracer, Contour,
Mystique,Cougar . . . .**MA**
Other FWD **MA5***
*Part No. XT5-QM. Do not use MERCON®

CAPACITY, Total Fill:	Liters	Qt
Focus	6.6	6.9
Villager	8.3	8.7
Taurus, Sable w/AX4S	11.6	12.3
w/AX4N	12.7	13.4
Windstar	11.6	12.3
Continental	13.0	13.7
Contour, Mystique, Cougar	3.7[2]	4.0[2]
Escort & Tracer	3.9[2]	4.1[2]

2 Initial Refill: With the engine at operating temperature, shift transmission through all gears. Check fluid level in PARK and add fluid as needed

TRANSMISSION/TRANSAXLE, Manual
Focus w/IB5 (2.0L SPI) . . . .**SLF**
Others . . . .**MA**[3]

CAPACITY, Refill:	Liters	Pt
Focus w/IB5 (2.0L SPI)	2.3[4]	4.9[4]
w/MTX 75 (2.0L Zetec)	1.9	4.0
Escort & Tracer	3.4	7.1
Contour, Mystique, Cougar	2.6	5.5

3 1999 Cougar—When replacing fluid add 52 ml (1.8 oz) additive, Part No. EZL-401
4 Fill to 5mm below fill hole

FORD TRUCKS

1989-2000 All Models Including Mercury Mountaineer & Lincoln Navigator
Except FWD Vans—See Ford, Lincoln, Mercury
Includes Mazda Navajo & B Series Trucks

SERVICE LOCATIONS — ENGINE AND CHASSIS

(1) Crankcase dipstick
(2) Transmission dipstick
(3) Brake fluid reservoir
(4) Clutch fluid reservoir
(5) Oil fill cap
(6) Power steering reservoir
(7) Air filter
(8) Fuel filter
(9) Oil filter
(10) PCV filter
(11) EGR valve
(12) Oxygen sensor
(13) PCV valve

1989-97
2.3L (140) EFI
1998-00 2.5L (152)

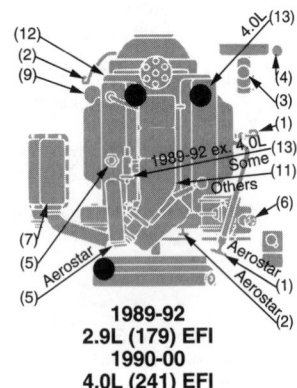

1989-92
2.9L (179) EFI
1990-00
4.0L (241) EFI
ex. SOHC

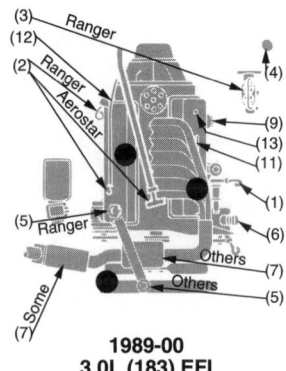

1989-00
3.0L (183) EFI

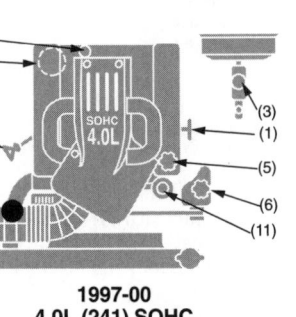

1997-00
4.0L (241) SOHC
Explorer, Mountaineer

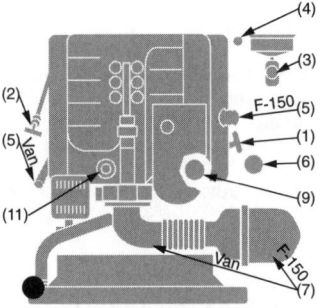

1997-00
4.2L (256)

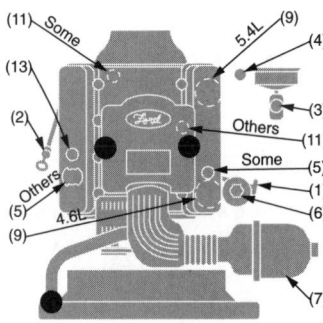

1997-00
4.6L (281), 5.4L (330)
ex. Econoline,
Club Wagon, Super Duty F-Series,
Excursion

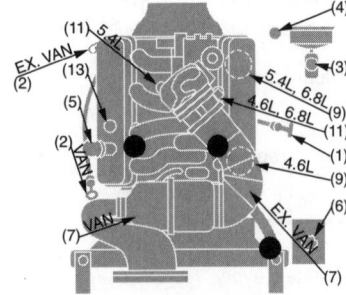

1997-00
4.6L, 5.4L, 6.8L
Econoline, Club Wagon
1999-00 5.4L, 6.8L
Super Duty F-Series, Excursion

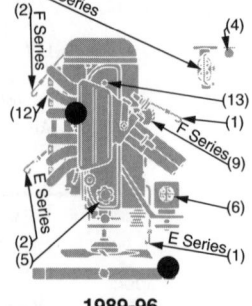

1989-96
4.9L (300) EFI

● Cooling system drain   ○ Cooling system drain, some models

FORD TRUCKS
1989-2000 All Models Including Mercury Mountaineer & Lincoln Navigator
Except FWD Vans—See Ford, Lincoln, Mercury
Includes Mazda Navajo & B Series Trucks

SERVICE LOCATIONS — ENGINE AND CHASSIS

FDTDP-2   FDTDP-2

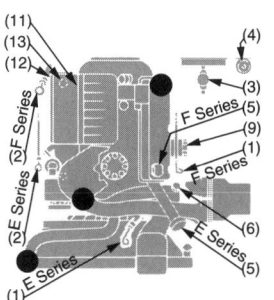

1989-98
5.0L (302) EFI,
5.8L (351) EFI
ex. Explorer, Mountaineer

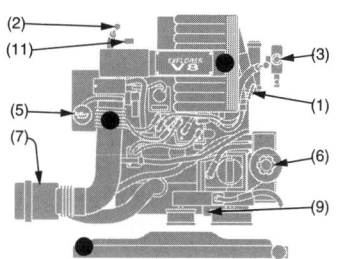

1996-00
5.0L (302)
Explorer,
Mountaineer

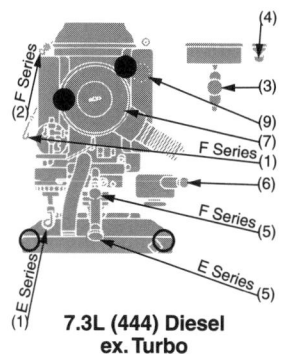

7.3L (444) Diesel
ex. Turbo

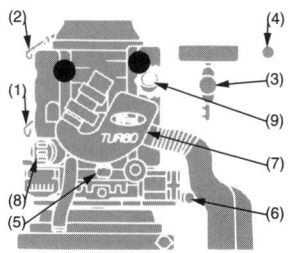

1993-94
7.3L (444)
Indirect Injection
Turbo Diesel

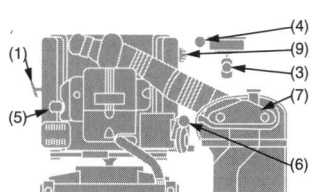

1994-00
7.3L (444)
Direct Injection
Turbo Diesel

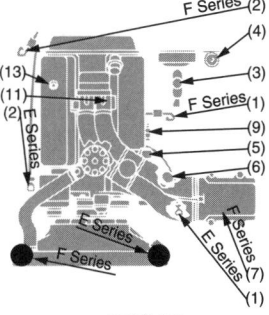

1989-98
7.5L (460) EFI

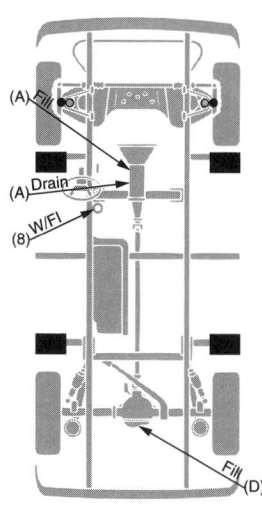

Aerostar
2-Wheel Drive

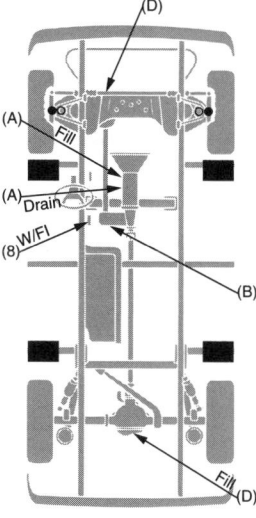

Aerostar
4-Wheel Drive

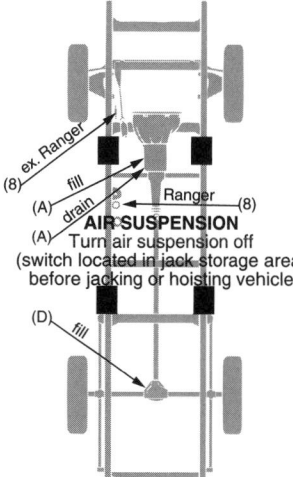

1998-00 Ranger
1995-00 Explorer
1997-00 Mountaineer
2-Wheel Drive

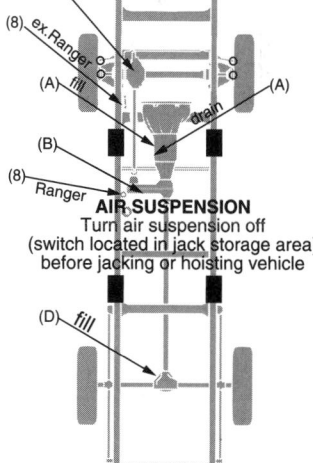

1998-00 Ranger
1995-00 Explorer
1997-00 Mountaineer
4-Wheel Drive, All Wheel Drive

■ Lift adapter position

● Fitting

○ Fitting, some models

(A) Manual transmission/transaxle, drain & fill

(B) Transfer case, drain & fill

(C) Automatic transaxle final drive, NOT USED

(D) Differential, drain & fill

(8) Fuel filter

FORD TRUCKS

**1989-2000 All Models Including Mercury Mountaineer & Lincoln Navigator
Except FWD Vans—See Ford, Lincoln, Mercury
Includes Mazda Navajo & B Series Trucks**

SERVICE LOCATIONS — ENGINE AND CHASSIS

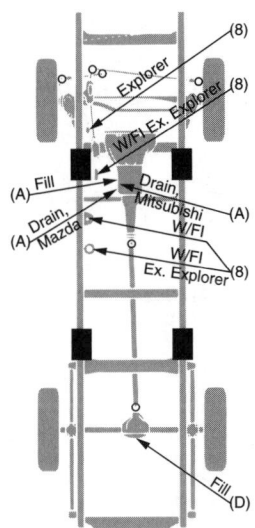

**1989-97 Ranger, Bronco II,
1991-94 Explorer
2-Wheel Drive**

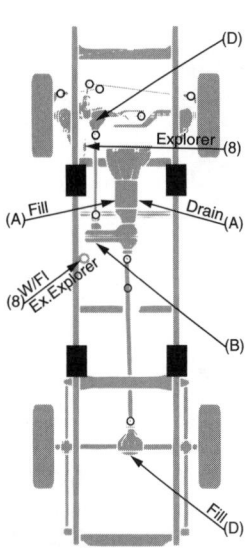

**1989-97 Ranger, Bronco II,
1991-94 Explorer
4-Wheel Drive**

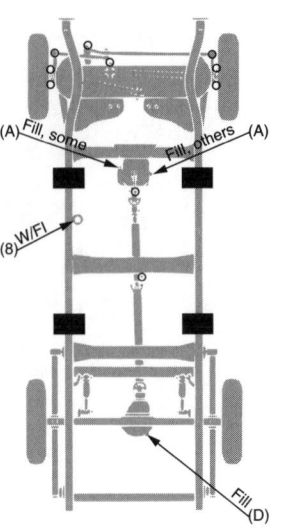

**E Series
(Econoline,
Club Wagon)**

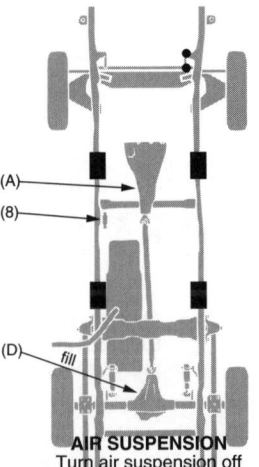

AIR SUSPENSION
Turn air suspension off
(switch located behind access panel
underneath passenger side dashboard)
before jacking or hoisting vehicle

**1997-00 Expedition, Navigator,
1997-00 F-150, -250 (ex. HD)
2-Wheel Drive**

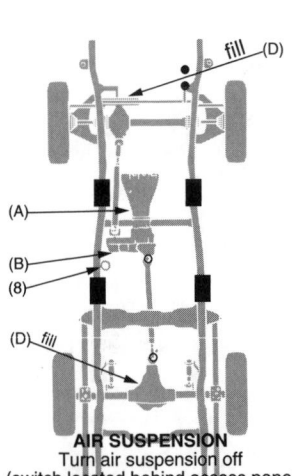

AIR SUSPENSION
Turn air suspension off
(switch located behind access panel
underneath passenger side dashboard)
before jacking or hoisting vehicle

**1997-00 Expedition, Navigator,
1997-00 F-150, -250 (ex. HD)
4-Wheel Drive**

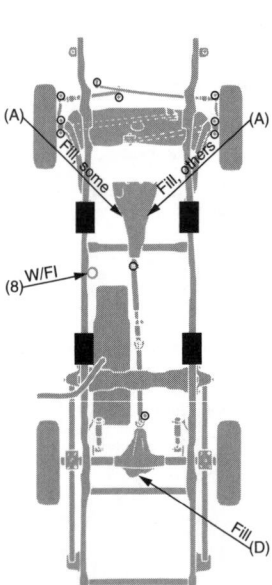

**1997-00 F-250 HD
1989-96 F-150, -250
1989-00 F-350, -450, -550,
Excursion
2-Wheel Drive**

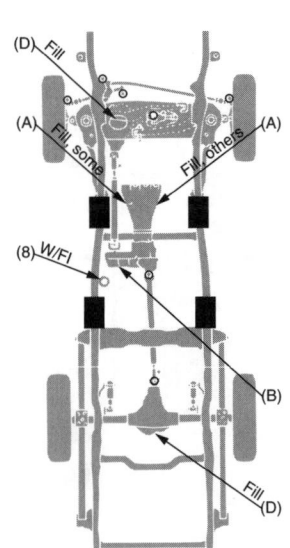

**1989-96
Bronco, F-150
4-Wheel Drive**

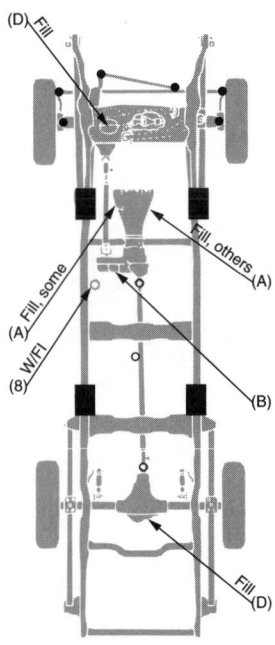

**1997-00 F-250 HD
1989-96 F-250
1989-00 F-350, -450, -550,
Excursion
4-Wheel Drive**

■ Lift adapter position

● Fitting

○ Fitting, some models

(A) Manual transmission/transaxle,
 drain & fill

(B) Transfer case, drain & fill

(C) Automatic transaxle final drive,
 NOT USED

(D) Differential, drain & fill

(8) Fuel filter

SERVICE AT TIME OR MILEAGE — WHICHEVER OCCURS FIRST

FDTPM20   FDTPM20

Perform the following maintenance services at the intervals indicated to keep the vehicle warranties in effect.

W   SERVICE TO MAINTAIN EMISSION WARRANTY

MI—MILES IN THOUSANDS
KM—KILOMETERS IN THOUSANDS

EVERY 6 MO/7.5 MI—12 KM
Automatic transmission
external controls . . . . . . .lubricate **LM**
At mileage interval only

Clutch reservoir . . . . . .check level **HBH**

W Crankcase . . . . .change oil

Fittings . . . . .lubricate **LM**
At mileage only
Ex. 4WD front axle driveshaft U-joints, slip splines & yoke

Driveshaft U-joints &
slip yoke . . . . .lubricate **HG**
4WD front axle only. At mileage only

W Oil filter . . . . .replace

Power steering . . . . .check level **FA**

Tires . . . . .rotate
At mileage, then every 15 mi (24 km) after initial service

Wheel lug nuts . . . . .torque
At mileage only

EVERY 12 MONTHS
Body . . . . .lubricate **SLS**

W Cooling system . . . . .inspect **EC**
Hoses, clamps. Replace coolant if necessary

Transmission, transfer case
& differential(s) . . . . .check level

EVERY 15 MI—24 KM
Disc brake system . . . . .inspect
Ranger, Aerostar, Bronco II

Disc brake caliper
slide rails . . . . .lubricate **BL**

E & F Series, Bronco
transfer case linkage . . . . .lubricate **LM**
Shift lever pivot bolt & control rod connecting pins.
F-series only

EVERY 36 MO/30 MI—48 KM
W Cooling
system . . . . .change coolant **EC**

EVERY 30 MI—48 KM
Brake system . . . . .inspect
E & F Series, Bronco
Lubricate disc brake caliper slide rails **BL**. Check all
brake lines & lining

Drum brake system . . . . .inspect

Front wheel bearings,
slip yoke & spindle
needle bearings . .inspect/lubricate **HG**
4WD front axle only

Exhaust system . . . . .inspect

Front hubs 4×4 . . . . .inspect **LS**
Inspect spindle needle & thrust bearings **LM** ex. 1989.
With automatic hub locks, inspect lubricant in drag
sleeve; special lubricant required

Front wheel
bearings . . . . . . .inspect/lubricate **LM**
2WD only

Parking brake system . . . . .inspect

W Air cleaner element . . . . .replace

Brake master cylinder . .check level **HBH**

W Carburetor hang-on
devices 2.0L . . . . .inspect
Clean choke linkages & external controls ex. FI

W Crankcase emission filter . . . . . .replace
Ex. 2.3L, 2.9L, 3.0L

Drive belts . . . . .inspect/adjust

W Spark plugs (ex. platinum) . . . . .replace

Throttle ball stud . . . . .lubricate **LM**

Transfer case front output
& axle shafts . . . . .lubricate **LM**

EVERY 60 MI—96 KM
Transfer case . . . . .change fluid

Idle speed control air bypass valve
(if equipped) . . . . .check/clean

EGR valve 2.0L . . . . .replace

Ignition wires . . . . .replace

Manual transmission . . . . .change oil
Except Aerostar, Bronco II, Ranger & Mazda R2 trans.

PCV valve . . . . .replace

Spark plugs (platinum) . . . . .replace

Thermactor hoses & clamps ex.
2.3L, 2.9L & 3.0L . . . . .check

SERVICE AS REQUIRED
Parking brake linkage
pivots & clevises . . . . . . .lubricate **LM**

Manual steering gear . . . .check level **LS**

Fluid leaks on pavement . . . . . .inspect

SEVERE SERVICE
W Crankcase—Change oil & filter every
3 mo/3 mi (4.8 km)

Differentials, transfer case & all trans-
missions—Check level daily when operating in water (if water has entered, change
lubricant)

Front wheel bearing lubricant, 4×4 front
spindle needle bearing & hub lock lu-
bricant, disc & drum brake compo-
nents—Inspect every 1 mi (1.6 km) or
daily if operating in mud or water

Fittings, front hub bearings & disc
brake caliper slide rails—Lubricate every
1 mi (1.6 km) or daily when operating in
mud or water

Transmission, automatic—Change fluid
every 30 mi (48 km). Lubricate external
controls every 1 mi (1.6 km)

W **Spark plugs**—Check, clean & regap:
Aerostar every 30 mi (48 km); others,
every 15 mi (24 km)

KEY TO LUBRICANTS
See other Ford Truck charts

CRANKCASE . . . . .5W-30 API★

CAPACITY, Refill:	Liters	Qt
2.3L, 2.9L, 3.0L, 4.0L	3.8	4.0
Others	4.7	5.0

Capacity shown is without filter. When replacing filter, additional oil may be needed

TRANSMISSION, Automatic . . . .**MA**

CAPACITY, Initial Refill[3]:	Liters	Qt
C-6 (shallow pan)	4.7	5.0
C-6 (deep pan)	5.6	6.0
Others	2.8	3.0

3 With the engine at operating temperature, shift transmission through all gears. Check fluid level in PARK and add
fluid as needed

TRANSMISSION, Manual
4-speed . . . . .80W **EP**
5-speed Mitsubishi[4] . . . . .80W **EP**
5-speed, All others . . . .**MA**

4 Used in some Ranger & Bronco II and identified by drain
plug located in middle of pan

CAPACITY, Refill:	Liters	Pt
4-speed ex. OD	3.3	7.0
W/OD	2.1	4.5
5-speed (Mazda)		
R1 Aerostar, Ranger, Bronco II, Explorer . . .	2.6	5.6
R2 Bronco, Econoline, F-series	3.6	7.6
5-speed S5-42 ZF Bronco, Econoline, F-series	3.2	6.8
5-speed (Mitsubishi) Ranger, Bronco II	2.3	4.8

TRANSFER CASE . . . .**MA**

CAPACITY, Refill:	Liters	Pt
Warner 1345	3.0	6.5
Warner 1350 Ranger, Bronco II .	1.4	3.0
Warner 1354 Ranger, Bronco II, Explorer	1.2	2.5
Warner 1356	1.9	4.0

DIFFERENTIAL
Standard .90 **HP**
Limited-Slip . . . . .90 **HP**★

CAPACITY, Refill:	Liters	Pt
Front:		
Dana 28 Ranger, Bronco II	0.5	1.0
Dana 35 Ranger, Bronco II, Explorer	1.7	3.5
Dana 44	1.7	3.6
Dana 50	1.8	3.8
Dana 60	2.8	5.8
Rear:		
Aerostar w/Ford 7.5" ring gear .	1.7[5]	3.5[5]
Aerostar w/Dana	1.2	2.5
Bronco II	2.6	5.5
Ranger w/7.5" ring gear	2.4[5]	5.0[5]
Ranger w/8.8" ring gear	2.6[5]	5.5[5]
Other Ford		
w/8.8" ring gear[6]	2.6	5.5
w/10¼" ring gear[6]	3.5	7.5
Dana 60 & 61 ex. 60-IU	2.8	6.0
Dana 60-IU	3.0	6.3
Dana 70 ex. HD	3.1	6.5
70 HD	3.5	7.4
Dana 80	3.9	8.3

5 Fill no higher than ¼" to 9/16" below fill plug
6 8.8" & 10¼" have removable cover

LIMITED-SLIP OR TRACTION-LOK
IDENTIFICATION:
Label on door lock pillar has letter and number

FORD TRUCKS
1989 All Diesel Models

SERVICE AT TIME OR MILEAGE — WHICHEVER OCCURS FIRST

Perform the following maintenance services at the intervals indicated to keep the vehicle warranties in effect.
W   **SERVICE TO MAINTAIN EMISSION WARRANTY**

MI—MILES IN THOUSANDS
KM—KILOMETERS IN THOUSANDS

EVERY MONTH
W Cooling system . . . . .check level

FIRST 5 MI—8 KM;
THEN EVERY 15 MI—24 KM
W Curb idle speed . . . . .check
W Fuel injector pump . . . . .inspect
Clean & lubricate face cam
W Idle return spring & throttle . . . . . .check
   Tires . . . . .rotate

EVERY 6 MO/5 MI—8 KM
Automatic transmission external
   controls . . . . .lubricate **LM**
At mileage only
Clutch lever pivots . . . . . . .lubricate **LM**
At mileage only
Clutch reservoir . . . . . . .check level **HBH**
At mileage only
W Crankcase . . . . .change oil
   Fittings . . . . .lubricate **LM**
At mileage only
Ex. 4WD front axle driveshaft U-joints, slip splines & yoke
Driveshaft U-joints &
   slip yoke . . . . .lubricate **HG**
4WD front axle only
At mileage only
W Oil filter . . . . .replace
   Power steering . . . . .check level **FA**
W Fuel/water separator . . . . .drain
At mileage only
More frequently if dash light illuminates
   Steering linkage . . . . . . .lubricate **LM**
When equipped with fittings
   Wheel lug nuts . . . . .torque

EVERY 12 MONTHS
   Body . . . . .lubricate **SLS**
W Cooling system . . . . .inspect **EC**
Hoses, clamps. Replace coolant if necessary
   Transmission, transfer case
   & differential . . . . .check level

EVERY 15 MI—24 KM
Disc brake caliper slide rails . .lubricate **BL**
Inspect brake system lining, lines & hoses
Parking brake fluid
   F-Super Duty . . . . .check level **MA**
Unit located behind transmission
Parking brake system . . . . .inspect
Transfer case linkage . . . . .lubricate **LM**
Shift lever pivot bolt & control rod connecting pins

EVERY 36 MO/30 MI—48 KM
W Cooling
   system . . . . .change coolant **EC**

EVERY 30 MI—48 KM
Brake system . . . . .inspect
Lubricate disc brake caliper rails **BL**. Check all brake lines & lining
Exhaust system . . . . .inspect
W Drive belts . . . . .inspect/adjust

Front hubs 4×4 . . . . . .clean/repack **LM**
With automatic hub locks, inspect lubricant in drag sleeve; special lubricant required
Front wheel bearings,
   slip yoke & spindle
   needle bearings . .inspect lubricate **HG**
4WD front axle only
Front wheel bearings . . .clean/repack **LM**
2WD only
Transfer case
   output & axle shafts . . . . .lubricate **LM**
W Air cleaner element . . . . .replace
W Air induction system & hoses . . . .inspect
   Brake master cylinder . .check level **HBH**
W Throttle ball stud . . . . .lubricate **LM**

EVERY 60 MI—96 KM
Manual transmission . . . . . . .change oil
HD M50D (S5-42 ZF) & 4 speed only
Transfer case . . . . .change fluid
Fuel filter . . . . .replace

SERVICE AS REQUIRED
Parking brake linkage
   pivots & clevises . . . . . . .lubricate **LM**
Manual steering gear . . . .check level **LS**
Fluid leaks on pavement . . . . . .inspect

SEVERE SERVICE
W **Crankcase**—Change oil & filter every 3 mo/2.5 mi (4 km)

Differentials, transfer case & all transmissions—Check level daily when operating in water (if water has entered, change lubricant)

Differential—Rear F-Super Duty E & F-250, -350, change lubricant every 30 mi (48 km). For extended trailer towing above 70°F (21°C) and extended wide open throttle above 45 mph, change lubricant every 3 mo/3 mi (4.8 km). Where 75W-140 synthetic gear oil, Spec. No. WSLM2C192-A Part No. F1TZ-19580-B is used, above intervals are every 100 mi (160 km) & 30 mi (48 km), respectively.

Front wheel bearing lubricant, 4×4 front spindle needle bearing & hub lock lubricant, disc & drum brake components—Inspect every 1 mi (1.6 km) or daily if operating in mud or water

Fittings & front hub bearings, clutch release lever pivot & disc brake caliper slide rails—Lubricate every 1 mi (1.6 km) or daily when operating in mud or water

Transmission, automatic—Change fluid every 30 mi (48 km)

Transmission, manual HD M50D (S5-42-ZF)—Change fluid every 30 mi (48 km)

KEY TO LUBRICANTS

BL	Self-adjusting Brake Lubricant
CH-4	Motor Oil, API Service CH-4
EC	Ethylene Glycol Coolant Mix 50/50 with water at least to –20°F (–29°C) protection
EP	Extreme Pressure Gear Lubricant
FA	Automatic Transmission Fluid, Type F
HBH	Hydraulic Brake Fluid, Extra Heavy-Duty
HG	High Temperature Grease Ford Spec. No. ESA-MIC198-A Part No. E8TZ-19590-A
HP	Hypoid Gear Oil
HP★	Hypoid Gear Oil for Limited-Slip or Traction-Lok Differential
LM	Lithium Grease, with Polyethylene
LS	Steering Gear Lubricant
MA	MERCON® Automatic Transmission Fluid
SH	Motor Oil, API Service SH
SJ	Motor Oil, API Service SJ
SLS	Special Lubricant—Spray Ford Part No. D7AZ-19584-A

CRANKCASE CH-4/SH, CH-4/SJ

CAPACITY, Refill:	Liters	Qt
All models (incl. filter)	9.3	10.0
Above 32°F (0°C) .30[1]		
Above 0°F (–18°C) 15W-40		
Below 90°F (32°C) . . . . .10W-30[2]		

[1] Preferred above 32°F (0°C)
[2] Preferred below 32°F (0°C)

TRANSMISSION, Automatic . . . . .MA

CAPACITY, Initial Refill[3]:	Liters	Qt
C-6	4.7	5.0

[3] With the engine at operating temperature, shift transmission through all gears. Check fluid level in PARK and add fluid as needed

TRANSMISSION, Manual

4-speed . . . . .80W **EP**		
5-speed . . . .**MA**		

CAPACITY, Refill:	Liters	Pt
4-speed ex. OD	3.3	7.0
W/OD	2.1	4.5
5-speed (Mazda trans.) R2	3.6	7.6
5-speed S5-42 ZF	3.2	6.8
5-speed (Mitsubishi trans.)	2.3	4.8

TRANSFER CASE . . . . .MA

CAPACITY, Refill:	Liters	Pt
Warner 1345	3.0	6.5
Warner 1356	1.9	4.0

DIFFERENTIAL

Standard . . . . .90 **HP**		
Limited-Slip . . . . .90 **HP★**		

CAPACITY, Refill:	Liters	Pt
Front:		
Dana 44	1.7	3.6
Dana 50	1.8	3.8
Dana 60	2.8	6.0
Rear:		
Ford w/8.8" ring gear[4]	2.6	5.5
w/10¼" ring gear[4]	3.5	7.5
Dana 60 & 61 ex. 60-IU	2.8	6.0
Dana 60-IU	3.0	6.3
Dana 70 ex. HD	3.1	6.5
70 HD	3.5	7.4
Dana 80	3.9	8.3

[4] 8.8" & 10¼" have removable rear cover

LIMITED-SLIP OR TRACTION-LOK IDENTIFICATION:
Label on door lock pillar shows letter & number

SERVICE AT TIME OR MILEAGE — WHICHEVER OCCURS FIRST

FDTPM22   FDTPM22

Perform the following maintenance services at the intervals indicated to keep the vehicle warranties in effect.
W   SERVICE TO MAINTAIN EMISSION WARRANTY

MI—MILES IN THOUSANDS
KM—KILOMETERS IN THOUSANDS

EVERY 6 MO/5 MI—8 KM
Automatic transmission external
  controls . . . . .lubricate **LM**
At mileage interval only

Clutch release lever
  7.5L F-series . . . . .lubricate **LM**

Clutch reservoir . . . . . . .check level **HBH**
At mileage only

W Crankcase . . . . .change oil

Fittings . . . . .lubricate **LM**
At mileage only
Ex. 4WD front axle driveshaft U-joints, slip splines & yoke

Driveshaft U-joints &
  slip yoke, 1989-91 . . . . . .lubricate **HG**
4WD front axle only
At mileage only

W Oil filter . . . . .replace

Power steering . . . . .check level **FA**

Tires .rotate
At mileage, then every 15 mi (24 km) after initial service

Wheel lug nuts . . . . .torque
At mileage only

EVERY 12 MONTHS
Body . . . . .lubricate **SLS**

W Cooling system . . . . .inspect **EC**
Hoses, clamps. Replace coolant if necessary

Transmission, transfer case
  & differential . . . . .check level

EVERY 15 MI—24 KM
Disc brake system, 1989-90 . . . . .inspect
Lubricate caliper slide rails **BL**

Drive belts . . . . .inspect/adjust

Parking brake system . . . . .inspect

Transfer case linkage . . . . .lubricate **LM**
Shift lever pivot bolt & control rod connecting pins

EVERY 36 MO/30 MI—48 KM
W Cooling system . . . . change coolant **EC**

EVERY 30 MI—48 KM
Drum brakes . . . . .inspect
Also check hoses & lines

Exhaust system . . . . .inspect

Front hubs 4×4 . . . . .inspect **LS**
With automatic hub locks, inspect lubricant in drag sleeve; special lubricant required

Front wheel
  bearings . . . . .inspect/lubricate **LM**
2WD only

Front wheel bearings,
  slip yoke & spindle
  needle bearings . .inspect/lubricate **HG**
4WD front axle only

Transfer case, 1991 . . . .change lubricant

W Air cleaner element . . . . .replace

W Crankcase emission filter . . . . . . .replace

Parking brake fluid
  F-super duty . . . . .check level **MA**
Unit located behind transmission

W Spark plugs . . . . .replace

Transfer case front output
  & axle slip shafts . . . . . . .lubricate **LM**

Throttle ball stud . . . . .lubricate **LM**

EVERY 60 MI—96 KM
Transfer case, 1989-90 . . . .change fluid

Idle speed control air
  bypass valve . . . . .clean

Ignition wires . . . . .replace

Manual transmission . . . . . . .change oil
HD M50D (S5-42 ZF) & 4 speed only

PCV valve . . . . .replace

Throttle body, 1990-91 . . . . .check/clean

Thermactor hoses & clamps . . . . . .check

SERVICE AS REQUIRED
Parking brake linkage
  pivots & clevises . . . . .lubricate **LM**

Manual steering gear . . . .check level **LS**

Fluid leaks on pavement . . . . . .inspect

SEVERE SERVICE
W **Crankcase**—Change oil & filter every
3 mo/3 mi (4.8 km)

**Differentials, transfer case & all trans-
missions**—Check level daily when operating in water (if water has entered, change
lubricant)

Differential—Rear F-Super Duty E &
F-250, -350, change lubricant every 30 mi
(48 km). For extended trailer towing above
70°F (21°C) and extended wide open throttle above 45 mph, change lubricant every
3 mo/3 mi (4.8 km). Where 75W-140 synthetic gear oil, Spec. No. WSLM2C192-A
Part No. F1TZ-19580-B is used, above intervals are every 100 mi (160 km) & 30 mi
(48 km), respectively

**Front wheel bearing lubricant, 4×4 front
spindle needle bearing & hub lock lubricant, disc & drum brake components**—Inspect every 1 mi (1.6 km) or
daily if operating in mud or water

**Fittings, front hub bearings, clutch re-
lease lever pivot 7.5L engine & disc
brake caliper slide rails**—Lubricate every
1 mi (1.6 km) or daily when operating in
mud or water

Transmission, automatic—Change fluid
every 30 mi (48 km). Lubricate external
controls every 1 mi (1.6 km)

**Transmission, manual HD M50D
(S5-42 ZF)**—Change fluid every 30 mi
(48 km)

W **Spark plugs**—Check, clean & regap:
every 15 mi (24 km)

KEY TO LUBRICANTS

API★	Motor oil certified by the American Petroleum Institute (Starburst symbol)
BL	Self-adjusting Brake Lubricant
EC	Ethylene Glycol Coolant Mix 50/50 with water at least to −20°F (−29°C) protection
EP	Extreme Pressure Gear Lubricant
FA	Automatic Transmission Fluid, Type F
HBH	Hydraulic Brake Fluid, Extra Heavy-Duty
HG	High Temperature Grease Ford Spec No. ESA-MIC198-A Part No. E8TZ-19590-A
HP	Hypoid Gear Oil Ford Part No. EOAZ-19580-A
HP★	Hypoid Gear Oil for Limited-Slip or Traction-Lok Differential
LM	Lithium Grease, with Polyethylene
LS	Steering Gear Lubricant
MA	MERCON® Automatic Transmission Fluid
MH	Manifold Heat Valve Solvent
SLS	Special Lubricant—Spray Ford Part No. D0AZ-19584-A

CRANKCASE . . . . .5W-30 **API★**

CAPACITY, Refill:	Liters	Qt
All models	4.7	5.0

Capacity shown is without filter. When replacing filter, additional oil may be needed

TRANSMISSION, Automatic . . . .**MA**

CAPACITY, Initial Refill[2]	Liters	Qt
C-6 (deep pan)	5.6	6.0
C-6 (shallow pan)	4.7	5.0
Others	2.8	3.0

[2] With the engine at operating temperature shift transmission through all gears. Check fluid level in PARK and add
fluid as needed

TRANSMISSION, Manual

4-speed . . . . .80W **EP**
5-speed . . . .**MA**

CAPACITY, Refill:	Liters	Pt
4-speed ex. OD	3.3	7.0
W/OD	2.1	4.5
5-speed (Mazda) R2	3.6	7.6
5-speed S5-42 ZF	3.2	6.8

TRANSFER CASE . . . .**MA**

CAPACITY, Refill:	Liters	Pt
Warner 1345	3.0	6.5
Warner 1356	1.9	4.0

DIFFERENTIAL

Standard . . . . .90 **HP**
Limited-Slip . . . . .90 **HP★**

CAPACITY, Refill:	Liters	Pt
Front:		
Dana 44	1.7	3.6
Dana 50	1.8	3.8
Dana 60	2.8	6.0
Rear:		
Ford w/8.8" ring gear[3]	2.6	5.5
w/10¼" ring gear[3]	3.5	7.5
Dana 60 & 61 ex. 60-IU	2.8	6.0
Dana 60-IU	3.0	6.3
Dana 70 ex. HD	3.1	6.5
70 HD	3.5	7.4
Dana 80	3.9	8.3

[3] 8.8" & 10¼" have removable cover

**LIMITED-SLIP OR TRACTION-LOK
IDENTIFICATION:**
Label on door lock pillar shows letter and number

Copyright 2000 by Chek-Chart Publications

FORD TRUCKS
1990-93 All Gasoline Models Under 8500 GVWR
Includes Mazda Navajo

SERVICE AT TIME OR MILEAGE — WHICHEVER OCCURS FIRST

FDTPM23   FDTPM23

Perform the following maintenance services at the intervals indicated to keep the vehicle warranties in effect.
W   SERVICE TO MAINTAIN EMISSION WARRANTY

MI—MILES IN THOUSANDS
KM—KILOMETERS IN THOUSANDS

EVERY 6 MO/7.5 MI—12 KM
Automatic transmission
external controls . . . . . . .lubricate **LM**
At mileage interval only. 1992-93, also check fluid level
Clutch reservoir . . . . . . .check level **HBH**
W Crankcase . . . . .change oil
Fittings . . . . .lubricate **LM**
At mileage only
Ex. 4WD front axle driveshaft U-joint, slip splines & yoke
Driveshaft U-joints &
slip yoke . . . . .lubricate **HG**
4WD front axle only
At mileage only
Manual transmission, 1993 . .check level
At first 7.5 mi (12 km). Aerostar, Explorer, Ranger
W Oil filter .replace
Power steering . . . . .check level **FA**
Tires . . . . .rotate
At mileage, then every 15 mi (24 km) after initial service
Wheel lug nuts . . . . .torque
At mileage only

EVERY 12 MONTHS
Body . . . . .lubricate **SLS**
W Cooling system . . . . .inspect **EC**
Hoses, clamps. Replace coolant if necessary
Transmission, transfer case
& differential(s) . . . . .check level

EVERY 15 MI—24 KM
Disc brake caliper
slide rails . . . . .lubricate **BL**
Also lubricate 1992-93 E & F Series, Bronco knuckle top & bottom inner pad slots. Inspect disc brake system
Drum brake system . . . . .inspect
Also check hoses & lines
W Fuel filter 1993 E & F series . . . . .replace
Frame mounted under driver area
Parking brake system . . . . .inspect
Transfer case linkage . . . . .lubricate **LM**
Shift lever pivot bolt & control rod connecting pins. F-series only

EVERY 36 MO/30 MI—48 KM
W Cooling system . . . . .change coolant **EC**

EVERY 30 MI—48 KM
Front hubs 4×4 . . . . .inspect **LS**
With automatic hub locks, inspect lubricant in drag sleeve; special lubricant required
Front wheel bearings, slip yoke & spindle
needle bearings, ...inspect/lubricate **HG**
4WD front axle only
Front wheel
bearings 2WD . . . .inspect/lubricate **LM**
W Air cleaner element . . . . .replace
Brake master cylinder . .check level **HBH**
W Crankcase emission filter . . . . . .replace
Ex. 2.3L, 2.9L, Ranger 4.0L
W Spark plugs (ex. platinum) . . . . .replace
Throttle & kickdown
lever ball stud . . . . .lubricate **LM**
Transfer case front
output & axle shafts . . . . .lubricate **LM**

EVERY 60 MI—96 KM
Exhaust system . . . . .inspect
Transfer case . . . . .change fluid
Drive belts . . . . .inspect/adjust
Idle speed control air bypass valve
(if equipped), 1990-91 . . . .check/clean
Ignition wires, 1990-91 . . . . . . .replace

Manual transmission . . . . . . .change oil
Except Aerostar, Bronco II, Explorer, Ranger & Mazda R2 trans.
However, for 1993 Aerostar, Explorer & Ranger, inspect the fluid, change if dark brown or black in color
PCV valve . . . . .replace
Spark plugs (platinum) . . . . .replace
Thermactor hoses & clamps ex.
2.3L, 2.9L & 3.0L . . . . .check
Throttle body, 1990-91 . . . . .check/clean

1991-93 EVERY 100 MI—160 KM
Differential (rear) . . . . . .change lubricant

SERVICE AS REQUIRED
Parking brake linkage
pivots & clevises . . . . . . .lubricate **LM**
Manual steering gear . . . .check level **LS**
Fluid leaks on pavement . . . . . .inspect

SEVERE SERVICE
W Crankcase—Change oil & filter every 3 mo/3 mi (4.8 km)
Differentials, transfer case & all transmissions—Check level daily when operating in water (if water has entered, change lubricant)
Differential—Rear; for extended trailer towing above 70°F (21°C) and extended wide open throttle above 45 mph change lubricant every 3 mo/3 mi (4.8 km). Where 75W-140 synthetic gear oil, Spec. No. WSL-M2C192-A, Part No. F1TZ19580-B is used, change every 30 mi (48 km)
Front wheel bearing lubricant, 4x4 front spindle needle bearing & hub lock lubricant, disc & drum brake components—Inspect every 1 mi (1.6 km) or daily if operating in mud or water
Fittings, front hub bearings & disc brake caliper slide rails—Lubricate every 1 mi (1.6 km) or daily when operating in mud or water
Transmission, automatic—Change fluid every 30 mi (48 km). Lubricate external controls every 1 mi (1.6 km)
W Spark plugs—1990-91, check, clean & regap: Aerostar every 30 mi (48 km); others, every 15 mi (24 km)

CAPACITY, Refill:	Liters	Pt
Rear:		
Aerostar w/Ford 7.5" ring gear . .	1.7[8]	3.5[8]
Aerostar w/Ford 8.8" ring gear . .	2.4[8]	5.0[8]
Aerostar w/Dana	1.2	2.5
Bronco II	2.6	5.5
Ranger w/7.5" ring gear	2.4[8]	5.0[8]
Ranger w/8.8" ring gear	2.4[8]	5.0[8]
Other Ford w/8.8" ring gear[9] . . .	2.6	5.5
w/10¼" ring gear[9]	3.5	7.5
Dana 60 & 61 ex. 60-IU	2.8	6.0
Dana 60-IU	3.0[10]	6.3[10]
Dana 70 ex. HD	3.1[10]	6.5[10]
70 HD	3.5[10]	7.4[10]
Dana 80	3.9[10]	8.3[10]

7 With auto-locking hubs
8 Fill no higher than ¼" to 9/16" below fill plug
9 8.8" & 10¼" have removable cover
10 1993 fill ¼" to ¾" below fill hole

LIMITED-SLIP OR TRACTION-LOK IDENTIFICATION:
Label on door lock pillar has letter and number

KEY TO LUBRICANTS
See other Ford Truck charts

CRANKCASE . . . . .5W-30 API★

CAPACITY, Refill:	Liters	Qt
1992-93 3.0L	3.3	3.5
2.3L, 2.9L, 4.0L, 1990-91 3.0L . .	3.8	4.0
Others	4.7	5.0

Capacity shown is without filter. When replacing filter, additional oil may be needed

TRANSMISSION, Automatic . . . . .MA

CAPACITY, Initial Refill[3]:	Liters	Qt
C-6 (shallow pan)	4.7	5.0
C-6 (deep pan)	5.6	6.0
E40D	8.0	8.5
4R70W	12.9[4]	13.6[4]
Others	2.8	3.0

3 With the engine at operating temperature, shift transmission through all gears. Check fluid level in PARK and add fluid as needed
4 Dry fill

TRANSMISSION, Manual
4-speed: 1990-91 . . . . .80W **EP**
1992-93 . . . . .MA
5-speed Mitsubishi[5] . . . . .80W **EP**
5-speed, All others . . . . .MA
5 Used in some Ranger, Explorer & Bronco II and identified by drain plug located in middle of pan

CAPACITY, Refill:	Liters	Pt
4-speed ex. OD	3.3	7.0
W/OD	2.1	4.5
5-speed (Mazda) R1 Aerostar,		
Ranger, Bronco II, Explorer . . .	2.6	5.6
R2 Bronco, Econoline,		
F-series	3.6	7.6
5-speed S5-42 ZF Bronco,		
Econoline, F-series	3.2	6.8
5-speed (Mitsubishi)		
Ranger, Explorer, Bronco II . . .	2.3	4.8

TRANSFER CASE . . . . .MA

CAPACITY, Refill:	Liters	Pt
Warner 1345	3.0	6.5
Warner 1350 Ranger, Bronco II . .	1.4	3.0
Warner 1354 Ranger, Bronco II,		
Explorer	1.2	2.5
Warner 1356	1.9	4.0
Spicer TC28 Aerostar	2.1[6]	4.5[6]

6 (1993) Fill to ⅛" - ¼" below fill plug

DIFFERENTIAL
Aerostar, front . . . . .MA
1992-93 Bronco, F150,
F250, front . . . . .75W-90 **GL-5★**
Bronco II, Explorer,
Ranger, front[7] 75W-90 **GL-5**
All others: Standard . . . . .90 **HP**
Limited-Slip . . . . .90 **HP★**

CAPACITY, Refill:	Liters	Pt
Front:		
Dana 28 Ranger, Bronco II	0.5	1.0
Dana 28-2 Aerostar	1.0	2.2
Dana 35 Ranger, Bronco II,		
Explorer	1.7	3.5
Dana 44	1.7	3.6
Dana 50	1.8	3.8
Dana 60	2.8	5.8

SERVICE AT TIME OR MILEAGE — WHICHEVER OCCURS FIRST

FDTPM24   FDTPM24

Perform the following maintenance services at the intervals indicated to keep the vehicle warranties in effect.

W   SERVICE TO MAINTAIN EMISSION WARRANTY

MI—MILES IN THOUSANDS
KM—KILOMETERS IN THOUSANDS

EVERY MONTH
W Cooling system . . . . .check level
FIRST 12 MO/5 MI—8 KM;
THEN EVERY 12 MO/15 MI—24 KM
W Curb idle speed . . . . .check
W Fuel injector pump, 1990-91 . . . . .inspect
Clean & lubricate face cam
At mileage only
W Idle return spring & throttle . . . . . . .check
Tires . . . . .rotate
At mileage only

EVERY 6 MO/5 MI—8 KM
Automatic transmission external
   controls . . . . .lubricate LM
At mileage only
Clutch lever pivots . . . . . . .lubricate LM
At mileage only
Clutch reservoir . . . . . .check level HBH
At mileage only
W Crankcase . . . . .change oil
Fittings . . . . .lubricate LM
At mileage only
Ex. 4WD front axle driveshaft U-joints, slip splines & yoke
Driveshaft U-joints &
   slip yoke . . . . .lubricate HG
4WD front axle only
At mileage only
W Oil filter . . . . .replace
Power steering . . . . .check level FA
W Fuel/water separator . . . . .drain
At mileage only
More frequently if dash light illuminates
Steering linkage . . . . .lubricate LM
When equipped with fittings
Wheel lug nuts . . . . .torque

EVERY 12 MONTHS
Body . . . . .lubricate SLS
W Cooling system . . . . .inspect EC
Hoses, clamps. Replace coolant if necessary
1994 If coolant is replaced add 2 pints of coolant additive
FW-15
Transmission, transfer case
   & differential . . . . .check level

1994 EVERY 18 MO/15 MI—24 KM
W Coolant additive . . . . .install
Add 8 to 10 ounces of coolant additvie FW-15 to the
cooling system

EVERY 15 MI—24 KM
Disc brake caliper slide rails &
   knuckle top & bottom
   inner pad slots . . . . .lubricate BL
Inspect brake system lining, lines & hoses
Drum brake system, 1992-94 . . . .inspect
Also check hoses & lines
Parking brake fluid
   F-Super Duty . . . . . . .check level MA
Unit located behind transmission
Parking brake system . . . . .inspect
Transfer case linkage . . . . .lubricate LM
Shift lever pivot bolt & control rod connecting pins

EVERY 36 MO/30 MI—48 KM
W Cooling
   system . . . . .change coolant EC
1994 Add 2 pints of coolant additive FW-15

EVERY 30 MI—48 KM
Drum brake system, 1990-91 . . . .inspect
Check all brake lines & lining
Exhaust system, 1994 . . . . . . .inspect
Engine & body noise shields 1994 inspect
W Drive belts . . . . .inspect/adjust
Adjustment not required for 1993-94 models

Front hubs 4×4 . . . . . .clean/repack LM
With automatic hub locks, inspect lubricant in drag
sleeve; special lubricant required
Front wheel bearings,
   slip yoke & spindle needle
   bearings . . . . . . .inspect/lubricate HG
4WD front axle only
Front wheel bearings . . .clean/repack LM
2WD only
Transfer case . . . . .change fluid
1991-93 HD models
Transfer case
   output & axle shafts . . . . .lubricate LM
W Air cleaner element . . . . .replace
W Air induction system & hoses . . . .inspect
Brake master cylinder . .check level HBH
Throttle ball stud . . . . .lubricate LM

EVERY 60 MI—96 KM
Engine & body
   noise shields, 1990-93 . . . . . . .inspect
Exhaust systems, 1990-93 . . . . . .inspect
Manual transmission . . . . . . .change oil
HD M50D (S5-42 ZF) & 4 speed only
Transfer case . . . . .change fluid
1990 All. 1991-93 LD models
1994 All
Fuel filter . . . . .replace
More frequently if dash light illuminates

EVERY 100 MI—160 KM
Differential (rear) . . . . . . change lubricant
SERVICE AS REQUIRED
Parking brake linkage
   pivots & clevises . . . . . . .lubricate LM
Manual steering gear . . .check level LS
Fluid leaks on pavement . . . . . .inspect

SEVERE SERVICE
W **Crankcase**—Change oil & filter every
3 mo/2.5 mi (4 km)

Differentials, transfer case & all transmissions—Check level daily when operating in water (if water has entered, change lubricant)

Differential—Rear F-Super Duty E & F-250, -350, change lubricant every 30 mi (48 km). For extended trailer towing above 70°F (21°C) and extended wide open throttle above 45 mph change lubricant every 3 mo/3 mi (4.8 km). Where 75W-140 synthetic gear oil, Spec. No. WSLM2C192-A, Part No. F1TZ-19580-B is used, above intervals are every 100 mi (160 km) & 30 mi (48 km), respectively

Front wheel bearing lubricant, 4×4 front spindle needle bearing & hub lock lubricant, disc & drum brake components—Inspect every 1 mi (1.6 km) (1990-93) or daily (all years) if operating in mud or water

Fittings & front hub bearings, clutch release lever pivot & disc brake caliper slide rails—Lubricate every 1 mi (1.6 km) (1990-93) or daily (all years) when operating in mud or water

Transmission, automatic—Change fluid every: 1990-93, 30 mi (48 km); 1994, 24 mi (39 km)

Transmission, manual HD M50D (S5-42-ZF)—Change fluid every 30 mi (48 km)

KEY TO LUBRICANTS
BL	Self-adjusting Brake Lubricant
CH-4	Motor Oil, API Service CH-4
EC	Ethylene Glycol Coolant Mix 50/50 with water at least to −20°F (−29°C) protection
EP	Extreme Pressure Gear Lubricant
FA	Automatic Transmission Fluid, Type F
GL-5★	Special Gear Oil for Limited-Slip Differentials
HBH	Hydraulic Brake Fluid, Extra Heavy-Duty
HG	High Temperature Grease Ford Spec. No. ESA-MIC 198-A Part No. E8TZ-19590-A
HP	Hypoid Gear Oil
HP★	Hypoid Gear Oil for Limited-Slip or Traction-Lok Differential
LM	Lithium Grease, with Polyethylene
LS	Steering Gear Lubricant
MA	MERCON® Automatic Transmission Fluid
SH	Motor Oil, API Service SH
SJ	Motor Oil, API Service SJ
SLS	Special Lubricant—Spray Ford Part No. D0AZ-19584-A

CRANKCASE CH-4/SH, CH-4/SJ
CAPACITY, Refill:	Liters	Qt
1994 7.3L Code F	13.2	14.0
Others	9.3	10.0

Capacity shown includes filter change
1990-93:
   Above 32°F (0°C) . . . . .30[1]
   Above 0°F (−18°C) 15W-40
   Below 90°F (32°C) 10W-30
1994: Above 32°F (0°C) . . . . .30[1]
   Below 90°F (32°C) . . . . .15W-40[2,3]
[1] Preferred above 32°F (0°C)
[2] Preferred below 32°F (0°C)
[3] Substitute 15W-40 SG/CD when 15W-40 CF-4/SG is not available below 32°F (0°C)

TRANSMISSION, Automatic . . . . .MA
CAPACITY, Initial Refill[4]:	Liters	Qt
C-6 (shallow pan)	4.7	5.0
C-6 (deep pan)	5.6	6.0
E40D 1990-93	8.0	8.5
1994	6.1	6.5

[4] With the engine at operating temperature, shift transmission through all gears. Check fluid level in PARK and add fluid as needed

TRANSMISSION, Manual
4-speed: 1991-90 . . . . .80W EP
1992-93 .MA
5-speed . . . . .MA
1994 S5-42 ZF
   w/7.3L Code F . . . . .Synthetic MA[5]
[5] Only vehicles with engines built after 2/2/94 Use Spec. No. ESR-M2C163-A2 Part No. E6AZ-19582-B
Others . . . . .MA
CAPACITY, Refill:	Liters	Pt
4-speed ex. OD	3.3	7.0
W/OD	2.1	4.5
5-speed (Mazda trans.) R2	3.6	7.6
5-speed S5-42 ZF	3.2	6.8
Other 5-speed	3.5	7.4

TRANSFER CASE . . . . .MA
CAPACITY, Refill:	Liters	Pt
Warner 1345	3.0	6.5
Warner 1356	1.9[6]	4.0[6]

[6] Add additional 3.9L (8.2 pt) if equipped with PTO

DIFFERENTIAL
1992-94 F250, front . . . . . .75W-90 GL-5★
All others:
   Standard . . . . .90 HP
   Limited-Slip . . . . .90 HP★
CAPACITY, Refill:	Liters	Pt
Front: Dana 44	1.7	3.6
Dana 50	1.8	3.8
Dana 60	2.8	6.0
Rear: Ford w/8.8" ring gear[7]	2.6	5.5
w/10¼" ring gear[7]	3.5	7.5
Dana 60 & 61 ex. 60-IU . . .	2.8	6.0
Dana 60-IU	3.0[8]	6.3[8]
Dana 70 ex. HD	3.1[8]	6.5[8]
70 HD	3.5[8]	7.4[8]
Dana 80	3.9[8]	8.3[8]

[7] 8.8" & 10¼" have removable rear cover
[8] 1994-93 fill ¼" to ¾" below fill hole

LIMITED-SLIP OR TRACTION-LOK IDENTIFICATION:
Label on door lock pillar shows letter & number

SERVICE AT TIME OR MILEAGE — WHICHEVER OCCURS FIRST

FDTPM25   FDTPM25

Perform the following maintenance services at the intervals indicated to keep the vehicle warranties in effect.
W   SERVICE TO MAINTAIN EMISSION WARRANTY

MI—MILES IN THOUSANDS
KM—KILOMETERS IN THOUSANDS

EVERY 6 MO/5 MI—8 KM
Automatic transmission external
  controls . . . . .lubricate **LM**
At mileage interval only

Clutch release lever
  7.5L F-series . . . . .lubricate **LM**

Clutch reservoir . . . . . . .check level **HBH**
At mileage only

W Crankcase . . . . .change oil

Fittings . . . . .lubricate **LM**
At mileage only
Ex. 4WD front axle driveshaft U-joints, slip splines & yoke

Driveshaft U-joints &
  slip yoke . . . . .lubricate **HG**
4WD front axle only
At mileage only

W Oil filter . . . . .replace

Power steering . . . . .check level **FA**

Tires .rotate
At mileage, then every 15 mi (24 km) after initial service

Wheel lug nuts . . . . .torque
At mileage only

EVERY 12 MONTHS
Body . . . . .lubricate **SLS**

W Cooling system . . . . .inspect **EC**
Hoses, clamps. Replace coolant if necessary

Transmission, transfer case
  & differential . . . . .check level

EVERY 15 MI—24 KM
Brake system . . . . .inspect
Lubricate disc brake caliper slide rails **BL**. Check all
brake lines & lining

Parking brake system . . . . .inspect

Transfer case . . . . .change lubricant

Drum brake system . . . . .inspect
Also check hoses & lines

Drive belts . . . . .inspect/adjust

W Fuel filter, 1993 . . . . .replace
Frame mounted under driver area

Parking brake fluid
  F-Super Duty . . . . .check level **MA**
Unit located behind transmission

Transfer case linkage . . . . .lubricate **LM**
Shift lever pivot bolt & control rod connecting pins

EVERY 36 MO/30 MI—48 KM
W Cooling
  system . . . . .change coolant **EC**

EVERY 30 MI—48 KM
Front hubs 4×4 . . . . .inspect **LS**
With automatic hub locks, inspect lubricant in drag
sleeve; special lubricant required

Front wheel bearings,
  slip yoke & spindle needle
  bearings . . . . . . .inspect/lubricate **HG**
4WD front axle only

Front wheel
  bearings 2WD . . . .inspect/lubricate **LM**

W Air cleaner element . . . . .replace

W Crankcase emission filter . . . . . .replace
Also known as crankcase ventilation filter for 1992

W Spark plugs . . . . .replace

Transfer case front output
  & axle slip shafts . . . . . . .lubricate **LM**

Throttle & kickdown cable
  ball studs . . . . .lubricate **LM**

EVERY 60 MI—96 KM
Exhaust system . . . . .inspect

Idle speed control air
  bypass valve . . . . .clean

Ignition wires . . . . .replace

Manual transmission . . . . . . .change oil
HD M50D (S5-42 ZF) & 4 speed only

PCV valve . . . . .replace

Thermactor hoses & clamps . . . . . .check
1993 called Secondary air injection

EVERY 100 MI—160 KM
Differential (rear) . . . . . .change lubricant

SERVICE AS REQUIRED
Parking brake linkage
  pivots & clevises . . . . . . .lubricate **LM**

Manual steering gear . . . .check level **LS**

Fluid leaks on pavement . . . . . .inspect

SEVERE SERVICE
W Crankcase—Change oil & filter every
3 mo/3 mi (4.8 km)

**Differentials, transfer case & all trans-
missions**—Check level daily when operating in water (if water has entered, change
lubricant)

Differential—Rear F-Super Duty E &
F-250, -350, change lubricant every 30 mi
(48 km). For extended trailer towing above
70°F (21°C) and extended wide open throttle above 45 mph change lubricant every
3 mo/3 mi (4.8 km). Where 75W-140 synthetic gear oil, Spec. No. WSL-M2C192-A,
Part No. F1TZ-19580-B is used, above intervals are every 100 mi (160 km) & 30 mi
(48 km), respectively

**Front wheel bearing lubricant, 4×4 front
spindle needle bearing & hub lock lubricant, disc & drum brake components**—Inspect every 1 mi (1.6 km) or
daily if operating in mud or water

**Fittings, front hub bearings, clutch re-
lease lever pivot 7.5L engine & disc
brake caliper slide rails**—Lubricate every
1 mi (1.6 km) or daily when operating in
mud or water

Transmission, automatic—Change fluid
every 30 mi (48 km). Lubricate external
controls every 1 mi (1.6 km)

**Transmission, manual HD M50D (S5-42
ZF)**—Change fluid every 30 mi (48 km)

KEY TO LUBRICANTS
API★	Motor oil certified by the American Petroleum Institute (Starburst symbol)
BL	Self-adjusting Brake Lubricant
EC	Ethylene Glycol Coolant Mix 50/50 with water at least to –20°F (–29°C) protection
EP	Extreme Pressure Gear Lubricant Ford Part No. D8DZ-10C547-A
FA	Automatic Transmission Fluid, Type F
GL-5★	Special Gear Oil for Limited-Slip Differentials
HBH	Hydraulic Brake Fluid, Extra Heavy-Duty
HG	High Temperature Grease Ford Spec. No. ESA-MIC198-A Part. No. E8TZ-19590-A
HP	Hypoid Gear Oil Ford Part No. EOAZ-19580-A
HP★	Hypoid Gear Oil for Limited-Slip or Traction-Lok Differential
LM	Lithium Grease, with Polyethylene
LS	Steering Gear Lubricant
MA	MERCON® Automatic Transmission Fluid
MH	Manifold Heat Valve Solvent
SLS	Special Lubricant—Spray Ford Part No. D0AZ-19584-A

CRANKCASE . . . . .5W-30 **API★**
CAPACITY, Refill:	Liters	Qt
All models	4.7	5.0

Capacity shown is without filter. When replacing filter, additional oil may be needed

TRANSMISSION, Automatic . . . .**MA**
CAPACITY, Initial Refill[2]:	Liters	Qt
C-6 (deep pan)	5.6	6.0
C-6 (shallow pan)	4.7	5.0
E40D	8.0	8.5
Others	2.8	3.0

2 With the engine at operating temperature shift transmission through all gears. Check fluid level in PARK and add
fluid as needed

TRANSMISSION, Manual . . . .**MA**
CAPACITY, Refill:	Liters	Pt
4-speed ex. OD	3.3	7.0
W/OD	2.1	4.5
5-speed (Mazda) R2	3.6	7.6
5-speed S5-42 ZF	3.2	6.8

TRANSFER CASE . . . .**MA**
CAPACITY, Refill:	Liters	Pt
Warner 1345	3.0	6.5
Warner 1356	1.9	4.0

DIFFERENTIAL
F250, front . . . . .75W-90 **GL-5★**

All others:
  Standard . . . . .90 **HP**
  Limited-Slip . . . . .90 **HP★**

CAPACITY, Refill:	Liters	Pt
Front:		
Dana 44	1.7	3.6
Dana 50	1.8	3.8
Dana 60	2.8	6.0
Rear:		
Ford w/8.8" ring gear[3]	2.6	5.5
w/10¼" ring gear[3]	3.5	7.5
Dana 60 & 61 ex. 60-IU	2.8	6.0
Dana 60-IU	3.0[4]	6.3[4]
Dana 70 ex. HD	3.1[4]	6.5[4]
70 HD	3.5[4]	7.4[4]
Dana 80	3.9[4]	8.3[4]

3 8.8" & 10¼" have removable cover
4 1993 fill ¼" to ¾" below fill hole

LIMITED-SLIP OR TRACTION-LOK IDENTIFICATION:
Label on door lock pillar shows letter and number

SERVICE AT TIME OR MILEAGE — WHICHEVER OCCURS FIRST

FDTPM26   FDTPM26

Perform the following maintenance services at the intervals indicated to keep the vehicle warranties in effect.
W   SERVICE TO MAINTAIN EMISSION WARRANTY

MI—MILES IN THOUSANDS
KM—KILOMETERS IN THOUSANDS

FIRST 0.5 MI—0.8 KM
Wheel lug nuts . . . . .torque
Snow plow vehicles 0.1 mi (0.16 km)

EVERY MONTH
Cooling system . . . . . . .check level **EC**
Fluid leaks on pavement . . . . . . .inspect

EVERY 6 MONTHS
Power steering . . . . .check level **FA**
1996 use **MA**
Clutch reservoir . . . . . . .check level **HBH**
Radiator, heater & A/C hoses . . . .inspect
Parking brake system . . . . .inspect
Transmission, automatic . .check level **MA**

EVERY 6 MO/5 MI—8 KM
W Crankcase . . . . .change oil
W Oil filter . . . . .replace

FIRST 5 MI—8 KM;
THEN EVERY 10 MI—16 KM
Automatic transmission
  external controls . . . . . . .lubricate **LM**
Clutch reservoir . . . . . . .check level **HBH**
Fittings . . . . .lubricate **LM**
Ex. 4WD front axle driveshaft U-joints, slip splines & yoke
Driveshaft U-joints &
  slip yoke . . . . .lubricate **HG**
4WD front axle only
Tires . . . . .rotate
Also check/adjust air pressure
Wheel lug nuts . . . . .torque
Exhaust system . . . . .check
Also remove foreign objects trapped in heat shielding

EVERY 12 MONTHS
Differentials, transfer case
  & manual transmission . . . .check level
Body hinges & latches . . . .lubricate **SLS**
W Cooling system . . . . .inspect **EC**
Inspect every 12 mo/15 mi (24 km)
Hoses, clamps. Replace coolant if necessary
Brake master cylinder . .check level **HBH**

EVERY 12 MO/12 MI—20 KM
Battery . . . . .clean/inspect
Check electrolyte level, ex. maintenance free type

EVERY 15 MI—24 KM
Disc brake caliper
  slide rails . . . . .lubricate **BL**
Brake system . . . . .inspect
Also check hoses & lines
Transfer case linkage . . . . .lubricate **LM**
Shift lever pivot bolt & control rod connecting pins
Except Aerostar 4WD

1994 EVERY 36 MO/30 MI—48 KM
W Cooling system . . . . .change coolant **EC**

EVERY 30 MI—48 KM
Front hubs 4×4 . . . . .inspect **LS**
As equipped. With automatic hub locks, inspect lubricant in drag sleeve; special lubricant required
Transmission, automatic,
  1995-96 . . . . .change fluid **MA**
Front wheel bearings,
  slip yoke & spindle needle
  bearings . . . . .inspect/lubricate **HG**
4WD front axle only. Except Aerostar 4WD
Front wheel
  bearings 2WD . . . .inspect/lubricate **LM**

Ball joints
  Aerostar . . . . . . .inspect/lubricate **LM**
Also inspect/lubricate bushings, arms, springs rear jounce bumpers for wear or deterioration
Parking brake system . . . . .inspect
Fuel filter . . . . .replace
W Air cleaner element . . . . .replace
Replace every 30 mo/30 mi (48 km)
Throttle & kickdown
  lever ball stud . . . . .lubricate **LM**

1995-96
FIRST 48 MO/50 MI—80 KM;
THEN EVERY 36 MO/30 MI—48 KM
W Cooling system . . . . .change coolant **EC**

EVERY 60 MI—96 KM
Transfer case . . . . .change fluid
Differential front . . . .change lubricant **MA**
4WD Aerostar only
W Drive belts . . . . .inspect/adjust
At mileage, then every 30 mi (48 km) after initial service
Manual transmission . . . . .change oil
W PCV valve . . . . .replace
W Spark plugs . . . . .replace
1994 2.3L & 4.0L only. 1995 2.3L only. 1996 5.0L only

EVERY 100 MI—160 KM
Differential (rear) . . . . .change lubricant
W Spark plugs . . . . .replace
1994 3.0L only. 1995-96 3.0L & 4.0L. 1996 2.3L

EVERY 120 MI—193 KM
W Crankcase emission filter . . . . . . .replace
1994 Aerostar only
W Timing belt tension . . . . .inspect
2.3L only

SERVICE AS REQUIRED
Parking brake linkage
  pivots & clevises . . . . . . .lubricate **LM**
Manual steering gear . . . .check level **LS**
Wheel lug nuts . . . . .re-torque
0.5 mi (0.8 km) after lug nuts are loosened

SEVERE SERVICE
W **Crankcase**—Change oil & filter every 3 mo/3 mi (4.8 km). When idling for extended periods, every 200 hours
Differentials, transfer case & all transmissions—Check level daily when operating in water (if water has entered, change lubricant)
Fittings—Lubricate every 6 mi (9.5 km) or daily when operating in mud or water deeper than wheel hubs (½ wheel height)
Wheel bearing lubricant, caliper slide rails, 4×4 front spindle needle bearing & hub lock lubricant, disc & drum components—Inspect/lubricate daily when operating in mud or water deeper than wheel hubs (½ wheel height)
W **Spark Plugs**—Change every 60 mi (100 km)
Transmission, automatic—Change fluid: 1994, every 24 mi (39 km); 1995-96, every 21 mi (35 km). Lubricate external controls every 6 mi (9.5 km)
Transmission, manual—Change fluid every 30 mi (48 km)
Air cleaner element—Inspect every 3 mi (4.8 km) in dusty conditions

---

KEY TO LUBRICANTS

API★	Motor oil certified by the American Petroleum Institute (Starburst symbol)
BL	Self-adjusting Brake Lubricant
EC	Ethylene Glycol Coolant Mix 50/50 with water at least to −20°F (−29°C) protection
FA	Automatic Transmission Fluid, Type F
GL-5	Gear Oil, API Service GL-5
GL-5★	Special Gear Oil for Limited-Slip Differentials
HBH	Hydraulic Brake Fluid, Extra Heavy-Duty
HG	High Temperature Grease Ford Spec. No. ESA-MIC198-A Part No. E8TZ-19590-A
HP	Hypoid Gear Oil
HP★	Hypoid Gear Oil for Limited-Slip or Traction-Lok Differential
LM	Lithium Grease, with Polyethylene
LS	Steering Gear Lubricant
MA	MERCON® Automatic Transmission Fluid
SLS	Special Lubricant—Spray Ford Part No. D0AZ-19584-A

CRANKCASE . . . . .5W-30 API★
CAPACITY, Refill:	Liters	Qt
3.0L	4.3	4.5
Others	4.7	5.0

Capacity includes filter change

TRANSMISSION, Automatic . . . . .MA
CAPACITY, Initial Refill[2]:	Liters	Qt
A4LD	2.8	3.0
4R70W	6.1	6.5

2 With the engine at operating temperature, shift transmission through all gears. Check fluid level in PARK and add fluid as needed

TRANSMISSION, Manual
5-speed, M50D . . . . .MA
CAPACITY, Refill:	Liters	Pt
5-speed (Mazda) R1 Aerostar, Ranger, Explorer	2.6	5.6

TRANSFER CASE . . . . .MA
CAPACITY, Refill:	Liters	Pt
Warner 1354 Ranger, Explorer . .	1.2	2.5
Spicer TC28 Aerostar	2.1[3]	4.5[3]
Warner 4405 Explorer	1.4	3.0

3 Fill no higher than ⅛" to ¼" below fill plug

DIFFERENTIAL
Aerostar, front . . . . .MA
Explorer, Ranger, front 75W-90 **GL-5**
All others:
1994: Standard . . . . .90 **HP**
    Limited-Slip . . . . .90 **HP★**
1995-96: Standard 80W-90 **GL-5**
    Limited-slip . . . . .80W-90 **GL-5★**

CAPACITY, Refill:	Liters	Pt
Front:		
Dana 28 Ranger	1.4	3.0
Dana 28-2 Aerostar	1.0	2.2
Dana 35 Ranger, Explorer	1.7	3.5
Rear:		
Aerostar w/Ford 7.5" ring gear . .	1.7[4]	3.5[4]
Aerostar w/8.8" ring gear . .	2.4[4]	5.0[4]
Ranger w/7.5" ring gear . .	2.4[4]	5.0[4]
Ranger w/8.8" ring gear	2.4[4]	5.0[4]
Other Ford w/8.8" ring gear[5]	2.6[4]	5.5[4]

4 Fill no higher than ¼" to 9/16" below fill plug
5 8.8" & 10¼" have removable cover

LIMITED-SLIP OR TRACTION-LOK IDENTIFICATION:
Label on door lock pillar has letter and number

FORD TRUCKS
1994 All Gasoline Model Bronco, E & F Series thru 350 including F-Super Duty

SERVICE AT TIME OR MILEAGE — WHICHEVER OCCURS FIRST

FDTPM27   FDTPM27

Perform the following maintenance services at the intervals indicated to keep the vehicle warranties in effect.

W   SERVICE TO MAINTAIN EMISSION WARRANTY

MI—MILES IN THOUSANDS
KM—KILOMETERS IN THOUSANDS

EVERY 6 MO/5 MI—8 KM
W Crankcase . . . . .change oil
W Oil filter . . . . .replace
Power steering . . . . .check level **FA**
At least twice annually

FIRST 5 MI—8 KM; THEN EVERY 10 MI—16 KM
Automatic transmission external
  controls . . . . .lubricate **LM**
Clutch release lever
  7.5L F-series . . . . .check/lubricate **LM**
At mileage then every 15 mi (24 km)
Clutch reservoir . . . . . . .check level **HBH**
Fittings . . . . .lubricate **LM**
Ex. 4WD front axle driveshaft U-joints, slip splines & yoke
Driveshaft
  U-joints & slip yoke . . . . . .lubricate **HG**
4WD front axle only
Exhaust system . . . . .check
Also remove foreign objects trapped in heat shielding
Tires .rotate
Wheel lug nuts . . . . .torque

EVERY 12 MONTHS
Body . . . . .lubricate **SLS**
W Cooling system . . . . .inspect **EC**
Inspect every 12 mo/15 mi (24 km)
Hoses, clamps. Replace coolant if necessary
Transmission, transfer case
  & differential . . . . .check level
Brake master cylinder . .check level **HBH**

EVERY 15 MI—24 KM
Brake system . . . . .inspect
Lubricate disc brake caliper slide rails **BL**. Check all brake lines & lining
Drum brake system . . . . .inspect
Also check hoses & lines
W Fuel filter . . . . .replace
Frame mounted under driver area
Leaf-spring U-bolt torque . . . . . . .check
F-Super Duty only
Parking brake fluid
  F-Super Duty . . . . . . .check level **MA**
Unit located behind transmission
Transfer case linkage . . . . . .lubricate **LM**
Shift lever pivot bolt & control rod connecting pins

EVERY 36 MO/30 MI—48 KM
W Cooling system . . . . .change coolant **EC**

EVERY 30 MI—48 KM
Parking brake system . . . . .inspect
Front hubs 4×4 . . . . .inspect **LS**
With automatic hub locks, inspect lubricant in drag sleeve; special lubricant required
Front wheel bearings, slip yoke & spindle
  needle bearings . .inspect/lubricate **HG**
4WD front axle only
Front wheel
  bearings 2WD . . . .inspect/lubricate **LM**
W Air cleaner element . . . . .replace
Replace every 30 mo/30 mi (48 km)
W Crankcase emission filter . . . . . . .replace

W Spark plugs . . . . .replace
Transfer case front output
  & axle slip shafts . . . . . . .lubricate **LM**
Throttle & kickdown cable
  ball studs . . . . .lubricate **LM**

EVERY 60 MI—96 KM
W Drive belts . . . . .inspect/adjust
At mileage, then every 30 mi (48 km) after initial service
Transfer case . . . . .change lubricant
Manual transmission . . . . . . .change oil
PCV valve . . . . .replace
Thermactor hoses & clamps . . . . . .check

EVERY 65 MI—104 KM
Clutch release lever
  7.5L E-Series . . . . .check/lubricate **LM**
At mileage then every 30 mi (48 km) after initial service

EVERY 100 MI—160 KM
Differential (rear) . . . . . .change lubricant

SERVICE AS REQUIRED
Parking brake linkage
  pivots & clevises . . . . . . .lubricate **LM**
Manual steering gear . . .check level **LS**
Fluid leaks on pavement . . . . . .inspect

SEVERE SERVICE
W Crankcase—Change oil & filter every 3 mo/3 mi (4.8 km)

Differentials, transfer case & all transmissions—Check level daily when operating in water (if water has entered, change lubricant)

Differential—Rear F-Super Duty, change lubricant every 30 mi (48 km). For extended trailer towing above 70°F (21°C) and extended wide open throttle above 45 mph change lubricant every 3 mo/3 mi (4.8 km). Where 75W-140 synthetic gear oil, Spec. No. WSL-M2C192-A, Part No. F1TZ-19580-B is used, above intervals are every 100 mi (160 km) & 30 mi (48 km), respectively

Fittings—Lubricate every 6 mi (9.5 km) or daily when operating in mud or water deeper than wheel hubs (½ wheel height)

Wheel bearing lubricant, caliper slide rails, 4×4 front spindle needle bearing & hub lock lubricant, disc & drum components—Inspect/lubricate daily when operating in mud or water deeper than wheel hubs (½ wheel height)

Transmission, automatic—Change fluid every 24 mi (39 km). Lubricate external controls every 6 mi (9.5 km)

Transmission, manual—Change fluid every 30 mi (48 km)

Clutch release lever 7.5L E & F Series—Lubricate initially at 3 mi (4.8 km), then every 15 mi (24 km)

KEY TO LUBRICANTS

API★	Motor oil certified by the American Petroleum Institute (Starburst symbol)
BL	Self-adjusting Brake Lubricant
EC	Ethylene Glycol Coolant Mix 50/50 with water at least to −20°F (−29°C) protection
FA	Automatic Transmission Fluid, Type F
GL-5★	Special Gear Oil for Limited-Slip Differentials
HBH	Hydraulic Brake Fluid, Extra Heavy-Duty
HG	High Temperature Grease Ford Spec No. ESA-MIC198-A Part No. E8TZ-19590-A
HP	Hypoid Gear Oil Ford Part No. EOAZ-19580-A
HP★	Hypoid Gear Oil for Limited-Slip or Traction-Lok Differential
LM	Lithium Grease, with Polyethylene
LS	Steering Gear Lubricant
MA	MERCON® Automatic Transmission Fluid
MH	Manifold Heat Valve Solvent
SLS	Special Lubricant—Spray Ford Part No. D0AZ-19584-A

CRANKCASE . . . . 5W-30 API★

CAPACITY, Refill:	Liters	Qt
All models	4.7	5.0

Capacity shown is without filter. When replacing filter, additional oil may be needed

TRANSMISSION, Automatic . . . . .MA

CAPACITY, Initial Refill[2]:	Liters	Qt
C-6 (deep pan)	5.6	6.0
C-6 (shallow pan)	4.7	5.0
E40D	6.1	6.5
4R70W w/4×2	12.9[3]	13.6[3]
w/4×4	13.9[3]	14.6[3]

2 With the engine at operating temperature shift transmission through all gears. Check fluid level in PARK and add fluid as needed
3 Dry fill

TRANSMISSION, Manual

All		.MA
CAPACITY, Refill:	Liters	Pt
M5OD (Mazda R2)	3.6	7.6
5-speed OD S5-42 ZF	3.2	6.8

TRANSFER CASE . . . . .MA

CAPACITY, Refill:	Liters	Pt
Warner 1356	1.9[4]	4.0[4]

4 Add additional 3.9L (8.2 pt) if equipped with PTO

DIFFERENTIAL
Bronco, F150, F250, front . .75W-90 **GL-5★**
F150 Lightning,
  rear . . . . . . .Synthetic 75W-140 **GL-5★***
*Part No. F1TZ-19580-B
All others: Standard . . . . .90 **HP**
  Limited-slip . . . . .90 **HP★**

CAPACITY, Refill:	Liters	Pt
Front:		
Dana 44	1.7	3.6
Dana 50	1.8	3.8
Dana 60	2.8	6.0
Rear:		
Ford w/8.8" ring gear[5]	2.6	5.5
w/10¼" ring gear[5]	3.5	7.5
Dana 60 & 61 ex. 60-IU	2.8	6.0
Dana 60-IU	3.0[6]	6.3[6]
Dana 70 ex. HD	3.1[6]	6.5[6]
70 HD	3.5[6]	7.4[6]
Dana 80	3.9[6]	8.3[6]

5 8.8" & 10¼" have removable cover
6 Fill ¼" to ¾" below fill hole

LIMITED-SLIP OR TRACTION-LOK IDENTIFICATION:
Label on door lock pillar shows letter and number

SERVICE AT TIME OR MILEAGE — WHICHEVER OCCURS FIRST

FDTPM28

FDTPM28

Perform the following maintenance services at the intervals indicated to keep the vehicle warranties in effect.

W   SERVICE TO MAINTAIN EMISSION WARRANTY

MI—MILES IN THOUSANDS
KM—KILOMETERS IN THOUSANDS

FIRST 0.5 MI—0.8 KM
Wheel lug nuts . . . . .torque
Snow plow vehicles 0.1 mi (0.16 km)

EVERY MONTH
Cooling system . . . . .check level **EC**
Fluid leaks on pavement . . . . . .inspect

EVERY 6 MONTHS
Power steering . . . . .check level **FA**
Clutch reservoir . . . . . .check level **HBH**
Radiator, heater
  & A/C hoses . . . . .inspect
Parking brake system . . . . .inspect

EVERY 6 MO/5 MI—8 KM
W Crankcase . . . . .change oil
W Oil filter . . . . .replace
Fuel/Water separator 7.3L Diesel . .drain
At mileage only
More frequently if dash light illuminates

FIRST 5 MI—8 KM;
THEN EVERY 10 MI—16 KM
Automatic transmission external
  controls . . . . .lubricate **LM**
Clutch release lever F-series:
  7.3L diesel & 7.5L . .check/lubricate **LM**
At mileage then every 15 mi (24 km)
Clutch reservoir . . . . .check level **HBH**
Fittings . . . . .lubricate **LM**
Ex. 4WD front axle driveshaft U-joints, slip splines & yoke
Driveshaft U-joints &
  slip yoke . . . . .lubricate **HG**
4WD front axle only
Exhaust system . . . . .check
Also remove foreign objects trapped in heat shielding
Tires .rotate
Also check/adjust air pressure
Wheel lug nuts . . . . .torque

EVERY 12 MONTHS
Body hinges & latches . . . .lubricate **SLS**
Brake master cylinder . .check level **HBH**
Transmission, transfer case
  & differential . . . . .check level

EVERY 12 MO/12 MI—20 KM
Battery . . . . .clean/inspect
Check electrolyte level ex. maintenance free type

EVERY 12 MO/15 MI—24 KM
W Cooling system . . . . .inspect **EC**
Also hoses, clamps & coolant strength. 7.3L Diesel, every 15 mi (24 km) add 8-10 ounces of FW-15 additive

EVERY 15 MI—24 KM
Brake system . . . . .inspect
Lubricate disc brake caliper slide rails **BL**. Check all brake lines & lining
Drum brake system . . . . .inspect
Also check hoses & lines
Fuel filter . . . . .replace
More frequently if dash light illuminates with 7.3L Diesel
Leaf-spring U-bolt torque . . . . . . .check
E & F-Super Duty only
Parking brake fluid
  E & F-Super Duty . . . .check level **MA**
Unit located behind transmission
Transfer case linkage . . . . .lubricate **LM**
Shift lever pivot bolt & control rod connecting pins

1995 7.3L DIESEL
EVERY 36 MO/30 MI—48 KM
W Cooling system . . . . .change coolant **EC**
7.3L Diesel, add 4 pints of FW-15 additive

EVERY 30 MI—48 KM
Parking brake system . . . . .inspect

Front hubs 4×4 . . . . .inspect **LS**
With automatic hub locks, inspect lubricant in drag sleeve; special lubricant required
Transmission, auto. . . . .change fluid **MA**
Ex. C6 & E40D
Front wheel bearings, slip yoke & spindle
  needle bearings . .inspect/lubricate **HG**
4WD front axle only
Front wheel
  bearings 2WD . . . .inspect/lubricate **LM**
W Air cleaner element . . . . .replace
Replace every 30 mo/30 mi (48 km)
7.3L Diesel, replace when indicated by restriction gauge
W Crankcase emission filter . . . . . .replace
When equipped
W Spark plugs, 1995 . . . . .replace
Throttle & kickdown cable
  ball studs . . . . .lubricate **LM**

FIRST 48 MO/50 MI—80 KM;
THEN EVERY 36 MO/30 MI—48 KM
W Cooling system . . . . .change coolant **EC**
1995 Gasoline engines only. 1996 All engines. 7.3L Diesel, add 4 pints of FW-15 additive

EVERY 60 MI—96 KM
W Spark plugs, 1996 . . . . .replace
W Drive belts . . . . .inspect/adjust
At mileage, then every 30 mi (48 km) after initial service
Transfer case . . . . .change lubricant
Manual transmission . . . . .change oil
PCV valve . . . . .replace
Thermactor hoses & clamps . . . . .check

EVERY 100 MI—160 KM
Differential (rear) . . . . . . .change lubricant

SERVICE AS REQUIRED
Parking brake linkage
  pivots & clevises . . . . . . .lubricate **LM**
Parking brake cable . . . . . .lubricate **SP**
Manual steering gear . . . .check level **LS**
Wheel lug nuts . . . . .re-torque
0.5 mi (0.8 km) after lug nuts are loosened

SEVERE SERVICE
W Crankcase—Change oil & filter every 3 mo/3 mi (4.8 km). When idling for extended periods, every 200 hours.
Differentials, transfer case & all transmissions—Check level daily when operating in water (if water has entered, change lubricant)
Differential—Rear E & F-Super Duty, change lubricant every 30 mi (48 km). Where 75W-140 synthetic gear oil, Spec. No. WSL-M2C192-A, Part No. F1TZ-19580-B is used, change every 100 mi (160 km)
Fittings—Lubricate every 6 mi (9.5 km) or daily when operating in mud or water deeper than wheel hubs (1/2 wheel height)
Wheel bearing lubricant, caliper slide rails, 4×4 front spindle needle bearing & hub lock lubricant, disc & drum components—Inspect/lubricate daily when operating in mud or water deeper than wheel hubs (1/2 wheel height)
Transmission, automatic—Change fluid every 21 mi (35 km). Lubricate external controls every 6 mi (9.5 km)
Transmission, manual—Change fluid every 30 mi (48 km)
Clutch release lever—F-Series: 7.3L Diesel & 7.5L, lubricate initially at 3 mi (4.8 km), then every 15 mi (24 km)
Air cleaner element & crankcase emission filter—Inspect every 3 mi (4.8 km) in dusty conditions

KEY TO LUBRICANTS
See other Ford Trucks charts

CRANKCASE
Gasoline . . . . .5W-30 **API★**
Diesel CH-4/SH, CH-4/SJ

CAPACITY, Refill:	Liters	Qt
All gasoline models	4.7	5.0
7.3L Diesel (incl. filter)	13.2	14.0

Capacity shown is without filter. When replacing filter, additional oil may be needed

Diesel:
7.3L:
Above 0°F (−18°C) . . . . .15W-40[1]
−10°F (−23°C) to 90°F (32°C) . . . . .10W-30[2]
Below 50°F (10°C) 5W-30
[1] Preferred above 30°F (−1°C)
[2] Preferred -10° to 30°F (−23° to −1°C)

TRANSMISSION, Automatic . . . .**MA**

CAPACITY, Initial Refill[4]:	Liters	Qt
C-6 (deep pan) w/4×4	5.6	6.0
C-6 (shallow pan) w/4×2	4.7	5.0
E40D	6.1	6.5
4R70W (1996)	6.1	6.5
4R70W w/4×2 (1995)	12.9[5]	13.6[5]
w/4×4 (1995)	13.9[5]	14.6[5]

[4] With the engine at operating temperature shift transmission through all gears. Check fluid level in PARK and add fluid as needed
[5] Dry fill

TRANSMISSION, Manual
S5-42 ZF w/7.3L Diesel . . .Synthetic **MA**[6]
[6] Spec. No. ESR-M2C163-A2
   Part No. E6AZ-19582-B
All others . . . .**MA**

CAPACITY, Refill:	Liters	Pt
M5OD (Mazda R2)	3.6	7.6
5-speed OD S5-42 ZF	3.2	6.8

TRANSFER CASE . . . .**MA**

CAPACITY, Refill:	Liters	Pt
Warner 1356	1.9[7]	4.0[7]

[7] Add additional 3.9L (8.2 pt) if equipped with PTO

DIFFERENTIAL
Bronco, F150, F250, front . .75W-90 **GL-5★**
F150/4.10:1 axle ratio
  & Lightning Pickup,
  rear . . . . . .synthetic 75W-140 **GL-5★***
*Part No. F1TZ-19580-B
Others: Standard 80W-90 **GL-5**
  Limited-slip . . . . .80W-90 **GL-5★**

CAPACITY, Refill:	Liters	Pt
Front:		
Dana 44	1.7	3.6
Dana 50	1.8	3.8
Dana 60	2.8	6.0
Rear:		
Ford w/8.8" ring gear[8]	2.6[9]	5.5[9]
w/10 1/4" ring gear[8]	3.5	7.5
Dana 60-IU	3.0[10]	6.3[10]
Dana 70 ex. HD	3.1[10]	6.5[10]
70 HD	3.5[10]	7.4[10]
Dana 80	3.9[10]	8.3[10]

[8] 8.8" & 10 1/4" have removable cover
[9] Fill 1/4" to 9/16" below fill hole
[10] Fill Dana rear axles 1/4" to 3/4" below fill hole

LIMITED-SLIP OR TRACTION-LOK IDENTIFICATION:
Label on door lock pillar shows letter and number

FORD TRUCKS
1997-98 Aerostar, Explorer, Ranger
Includes Mercury Mountaineer, Mazda B2300, B2500, B3000, B4000

SERVICE AT TIME OR MILEAGE — WHICHEVER OCCURS FIRST

Perform the following maintenance services at the intervals indicated to keep the vehicle warranties in effect.

W   SERVICE TO MAINTAIN EMISSION WARRANTY

MI—MILES IN THOUSANDS
KM—KILOMETERS IN THOUSANDS

FIRST 0.5 MI—0.8 KM
Wheel lug nuts . . . . .torque
Snow plow vehicles 0.1 mi (0.16 km)

EVERY MONTH
Cooling system . . . . .check level **EC**
Fluid leaks on pavement . . . . . . .inspect

EVERY 6 MONTHS
Power steering . . . . .check level **MA**
Clutch reservoir . . . . .check level **HBH**
Radiator, heater & A/C hoses . . . .inspect
Parking brake system . . . . .inspect

EVERY 6 MO/5 MI—8 KM
W Crankcase . . . . .change oil
W Oil filter .replace

FIRST 5 MI—8 KM;
THEN EVERY 10 MI—16 KM
Automatic transmission
external controls . . . . . . .lubricate **LM**
Clutch reservoir . . . . . . .check level **HBH**
Fittings . . . . .lubricate **LM**
Ex. 4WD front axle driveshaft U-joints, slip splines & yoke
Driveshaft U-joints &
slip yoke 1997 . . . . .lubricate **HG**
4WD front axle only
Tires . . . . .rotate
Also check/adjust air pressure
Wheel lug nuts . . . . .torque
Exhaust system . . . . .check
Also remove foreign objects trapped in heat shielding

EVERY 12 MONTHS
Body hinges & latches . . . .lubricate **SLS**
W Cooling system . . . . .inspect **EC**
Inspect every 12 mo/15 mi (24 km)
Hoses, clamps. Replace coolant if necessary
Brake master cylinder . .check level **HBH**
Battery . . . . .clean/inspect
Check electrolyte level, ex. maintenance free type

EVERY 15 MI—24 KM
Disc brake caliper
slide rails . . . . .lubricate **BL**
Brake system . . . . .inspect
Also check hoses & lines
Transfer case linkage 1997 .lubricate **LM**
Shift lever pivot bolt & control rod connecting pins
Except Aerostar 4WD & AWD models

EVERY 30 MI—48 KM
Transfer case 1997 . . . .change fluid **MA**
Front hubs 4×4 1997 . . . . . . .inspect **LS**
Ranger only. With automatic hub locks, inspect lubricant
in drag sleeve; special lubricant required
Transmission,
automatic . . . . .change fluid **MA**
1997 5.0L Explorer & Mountaineer only
1998 All ex. Ranger
Front wheel bearings,
slip yoke & spindle needle
bearings 1997 . . . .inspect/lubricate **HG**
4WD front axle only. Except Aerostar 4WD
Front wheel
bearings 2WD . . . . .inspect/lubricate **LM**
Ball joints
Aerostar . . . . . . .inspect/lubricate **LM**
Also inspect/lubricate bushings, arms, springs rear
jounce bumpers for wear or deterioration
Parking brake system . . . . .inspect

Fuel filter . . . . .replace
ex. 1998 Ranger
Except Calif., recommended but not required
W Air cleaner element . . . . .replace
Replace every 30 mo/30 mi (48 km)
Throttle & kickdown
lever ball stud . . . . .lubricate **LM**

FIRST 48 MO/50 MI—80 KM;
THEN EVERY 36 MO/30 MI—48 KM
W Cooling system . . . . .change coolant **EC**

EVERY 50 MI—80 KM
Fuel filter 1998 Ranger . . . . . . .replace
Except Calif., recommended but not required

EVERY 60 MI—96 KM
Differential front . . . .change lubricant **MA**
4WD Aerostar only
W Drive belts . . . . .inspect/adjust
At mileage, then every 30 mi (48 km) after initial service
Manual transmission . . . . .change oil
W PCV valve . . . . .replace
Transfer Case . . . .1998 change fluid **MA**
W Spark plugs (1998 2.5L) . . . . . . .replace

EVERY 100 MI—160 KM
Differential . . . . .change lubricant
Where non-synthetic is used
W Spark plugs . . . . .replace
ex. 1998 2.5L

EVERY 120 MI—193 KM
W Timing belt tension . . . . .inspect
2.3L & 2.5L only

SERVICE AS REQUIRED
Parking brake linkage
pivots & clevises . . . . . . .lubricate **LM**
Manual steering gear . . . .check level **LS**
Wheel lug nuts . . . . .re-torque
0.5 mi (0.8 km) after lug nuts are loosened

SEVERE SERVICE
W Crankcase—Change oil & filter every
3 mo/3 mi (4.8 km). When idling for extended periods, every 200 hours
Differentials, transfer case & all transmissions—Check level daily when operating in water (if water has entered, change lubricant)
Differentials (1998) Rear,—Where non-synthetic is used change lubricant every 3 mi (4.8 km) or 3 mo. No change interval where synthetic gear oil is used. Front, change lubricant every 100 mi (160 km).
Fittings—Lubricate every 6 mi (9.5 km) or daily when operating in mud or water deeper than wheel hubs (½ wheel height)
Wheel bearing lubricant, caliper slide rails, 4×4 front spindle needle bearing & hub lock lubricant, disc & drum components—Inspect/lubricate daily when operating in mud or water deeper than wheel hubs (½ wheel height)
W **Spark plugs**—Change every 60 mi (100 km)
Transmission, automatic All w/5.0L—Change fluid: every 21 mi (35 km); others every 50 mi (80 km). Lubricate external controls every 6 mi (9.5 km)
Transmission, manual & Transfer case—Change fluid every 30 mi (48 km)
Air cleaner element—Inspect every 3 mi (4.8 km) in dusty conditions

KEY TO LUBRICANTS

API★	Motor oil certified by the American Petroleum Institute (Starburst symbol)
BL	Self-adjusting Brake Lubricant
EC	Ethylene Glycol Coolant Mix 50/50 with water at least to −20°F (−29°C) protection
GL-5	Gear Oil, API Service GL-5
GL-5★	Special Gear Oil for Limited-Slip Differentials
HBH	Hydraulic Brake Fluid, Extra Heavy-Duty
HG	High Temperature Grease Ford Spec. No. ESA-M1C198-A Part No. E8TZ-19590-A
LM	Lithium Grease, with Polyethylene
LS	Steering Gear Lubricant/Automatic Hublock Grease
MA	MERCON® Automatic Transmission Fluid
MA5	MERCON® V Automatic Transmission Fluid
SLS	Special Lubricant—Spray Ford Part No. D0AZ-19584-A

CRANKCASE . . . . .5W-30 **API★**

CAPACITY, Refill:	Liters	Qt
2.5L, 3.0L	4.3	4.5
Others	4.7	5.0

Capacity includes filter change

TRANSMISSION, Automatic
1997: Explorer w/4.0L, Aerostar,
Ranger **MA5***
Others . . . .**MA**
1998: All **MA5***
* Part No. XT-5-QM. Do not use MERCON®

CAPACITY, Initial Refill[3]:	Liters	Qt
4R70W w/5.0L	4.7	5.0
Others (1997)	2.8	3.0
(1998)	3.7	4.0

3 With the engine at operating temperature, shift transmission through all gears. Check fluid level in PARK and add fluid as needed

TRANSMISSION, Manual
5-speed, M50D . . . .**MA**

CAPACITY, Refill:	Liters	Pt
5-speed (Mazda) R1, Ranger, Explorer	2.6	5.6

TRANSFER CASE . . . .**MA**

CAPACITY, Refill:	Liters	Pt
Warner 1354 Ranger	1.2	2.5
Spicer TC28 Aerostar	2.1[4]	4.5[4]
Warner 4405 Explorer, w/4WD	1.4	3.0
Explorer, Mountaineer w/AWD	1.3	2.6

4 Fill no higher than ⅛" to ¼" below fill plug

DIFFERENTIAL
Aerostar, front . . . .**MA**
1997: Explorer, Mountaineer, Ranger,
front 75W-90 **GL-5**
1998 front 80W-90 **GL-5**
Explorer, Mountaineer w/5.0L, 4.0L SOHC,
4.0L w/3.73 or 4.10 axle ratio, rear:
Standard . . . .*Synthetic 75W-140 **GL-5**
Limited-Slip . . .*Synthetic 75W-140 **GL-5★**
*Part No. F1TZ-19580-B
Others: Standard 80W-90 **GL-5**
Limited-slip . . . . .80W-90 **GL-5★**

CAPACITY, Refill:	Liters	Pt
Front:		
Dana 28 Ranger 1997	1.4	3.0
Dana 28-2 Aerostar	1.0	2.2
Dana 35 Ranger, Explorer, Mountaineer	1.7	3.5
Rear:		
Aerostar w/Ford 7.5" ring gear	1.7[5]	3.5[5]
Aerostar w/Ford 8.8" ring gear	2.4[5]	5.0[5]
Ranger w/7.5" ring gear	2.4[5]	5.0[5]
Ranger w/8.8" ring gear	2.4[5]	5.0[5]
Others w/8.8" ring gear	2.6[5]	5.5[5]

5 Fill no higher than ¼" to 9/16" below fill plug

LIMITED-SLIP OR TRACTION-LOK IDENTIFICATION:
Label on door lock pillar has letter and number

CHEK-CHART

FORD TRUCKS
1997-98 All Expedition, E & F Series thru 350 including E & F-Super Duty
Includes Lincoln Navigator, ex. Natural Gas Vehicles

SERVICE AT TIME OR MILEAGE — WHICHEVER OCCURS FIRST

FDTPM30   FDTPM30

Perform the following maintenance services at the intervals indicated to keep the vehicle warranties in effect.
W SERVICE TO MAINTAIN EMISSION WARRANTY

MI—MILES IN THOUSANDS
KM—KILOMETERS IN THOUSANDS

EVERY MONTH
Cooling system . . . . . . .check level EC
Fluid leaks on pavement . . . . . .inspect

EVERY 6 MONTHS
Power steering . . . . . . .check level MA
Clutch reservoir . . . . . . .check level HBH
Radiator, heater & A/C hoses . . . .inspect
Parking brake system . . . . .inspect

EVERY 6 MO/5 MI—8 KM
W Crankcase . . . . .change oil
W Oil filter .replace
Fuel/water separator 7.3L Diesel . . .drain
At mileage only. More frequently if dash light illuminates

FIRST 5 MI—8 KM;
THEN EVERY 10 MI—16 KM
Automatic transmission external
   controls . . . . .lubricate LM
Except Vans
Clutch release lever F-series:
   7.3L Diesel & 7.5L . .check/lubricate LM
At mileage then every 15 mi (24 km)
Clutch reservoir . . . . . . .check level HBH
Fittings . . . . .lubricate LM
Ex. 4WD front axle driveshaft U-joints, slip splines & yoke
Driveshaft U-joints &
   slip yoke . . . . .lubricate HG
4WD front axle only
Exhaust system . . . . .check
Also remove foreign objects trapped in heat shielding
Except Vans. Every 15 mi (24 km)
Tires . . . . .rotate
Also check/adjust air pressure
Wheel lug nuts . . . . .torque

EVERY 12 MONTHS
Body hinges & latches . . . .lubricate SLS
Brake master cylinder . .check level HBH
Battery . . . . .clean/inspect
Check electrolyte level ex. maintenance free type

EVERY 12 MO/15 MI—24 KM
W Cooling system . . . . .inspect EC
Also hoses, clamps & coolant strength. 7.3L Diesel, every 15 mi (24 km) add 8-10 ounces of FW-15 additive

EVERY 15 MI—24 KM
Disc brake system . . . . .inspect
Lubricate disc brake caliper slide rails BL. Check all brake lines & lining
Drum brake system . . . . .inspect
Also check hoses & lines
Fuel filter . . . . .replace
5.8L, 7.5L & 7.3L Diesel only
More frequently if dash light illuminates with 7.3L Diesel
Except Calif., recommended but not required
Leaf-spring U-bolt torque . . . . . . .check
E & F-Super Duty only
Parking brake fluid
   E & F-Super Duty . . . .check level MA
Unit located behind transmission
Transfer case linkage . . . . .lubricate LM
Shift lever pivot bolt & control rod connecting pins F-250 HD, -350 only

EVERY 30 MI—48 KM
Fuel filter . . . . .replace
Except 5.8L, 7.5L, 7.3L Diesel & Calif., recommended but not required
Parking brake system . . . . .inspect
Front hubs 4×4 . . . . .inspect LS
F-250 HD, -350 only. With automatic hub locks, inspect lubricant in drag sleeve; special lubricant required
Transmission, auto. . . . . . . .change fluid
1997 Except Van w/E40D
1998 Except all w/E40D
Front wheel bearings, slip yoke & spindle
   needle bearings . . . .inspect/lubricate HG
F-250 HD, -350 4WD front axle only
Front wheel
   bearings 2WD . . . . . .inspect/lubricate LM
W Air cleaner element . . . . .replace
Replace every 30 mo/30 mi (48 km)
7.3L Diesel, replace when indicated by restriction gauge

W Crankcase emission filter . . . . . .replace
7.5L only
Throttle & kickdown cable
   ball studs . . . . .lubricate LM
5.8L & 7.5L only

FIRST 48 MO/50 MI—80 KM;
THEN EVERY 36 MO/30 MI—48 KM
W Cooling system . . . . . . .change coolant EC
7.3L Diesel, add 4 pints of FW-15 additive

EVERY 60 MI—96 KM
W Spark plugs . . . . .replace
5.8L & 7.5L only
Transfer case . . . . .change lubricant
Manual transmission . . . . .change oil
PCV valve . . . . .replace
Thermactor hoses & clamps . . . . .check
5.8L & 7.5L only

EVERY 100 MI—160 KM
W Accessory drive belts . . . . .inspect
Initially, then every 20 mi (32 km).
W Spark plugs . . . . .replace
Except 5.8L & 7.5L
Differential (rear) . . . . . .change lubricant
where non-synthetic is used

SERVICE AS REQUIRED
Parking brake linkage
   pivots & clevises . . . . . . .lubricate LM
Parking brake cable . . . . . .lubricate SP
Manual steering gear . . . .check level LS

SEVERE SERVICE
W **Crankcase**—Change oil & filter every 3 mo/3 mi (4.8 km). When idling for extended periods, every 200 hours
W **Spark plugs**—Replace every 60 mi (96 km)
W **Drive belts**—Inspect/adjust initially at 60 mi (96 km) then every 30 mi (48 km)
Fuel filter—Replace every 15 mi (24 km). Except Calif. gasoline models, recommended but not required
Differential—1997 Front Expedition, F-150, -250 ex. HD change lubricant every 100 mi (160 km)
Transfer case—Except F-250 HD & -350, change fluid every 30 mi (48 km)
Differentials, transfer case & all transmissions—Check level daily when operating in water (if water has entered, change lubricant)
Differential—1997 Rear E & F-Super Duty, change lubricant every 30 mi (48 km). Where 75W-140 synthetic gear oil, Spec. No. WSL-M2C192-A, Part No. F1TZ-19580-B is used, change every 100 mi (160 km)
1998: Where non-synthetic is used change lubricant every 3 mi (4.8 km) or 3 mo. No change interval where synthetic gear oil is used.
Fittings—Lubricate every 6 mi (9.5 km) or daily when operating in mud or water deeper than wheel hubs (1/2 wheel height)
Wheel bearing lubricant, caliper slide rails, 4×4 front spindle needle bearing & hub lock lubricant, disc & drum components—Inspect/lubricate daily when operating in mud or water deeper than wheel hubs (1/2 wheel height)
Transmission, automatic—Change fluid every 21 mi (35 km). ex. 1998 E40D Lubricate external controls every 6 mi (9.5 km)
Transmission, manual—Change fluid every 30 mi (48 km)
Clutch release lever—F-Series: 7.3L Diesel & 7.5L, lubricate initially at 3 mi (4.8 km), then every 15 mi (24 km)
Air cleaner element & crankcase emission filter—Inspect every 3 mi (4.8 km) in dusty conditions

---

KEY TO LUBRICANTS
See other Ford Trucks charts

CRANKCASE
Gasoline . . . . .5W-30 API★
Diesel CH-4/SH, CH-4/SJ
CAPACITY, Refill:

	Liters	Qt
4.2L, 4.6L, 5.4L, 6.8L (incl. filter)	5.7	6.0
5.8L, 7.5L	4.7	5.0
7.3L (incl. filter)	13.2	14.0

Capacity shown is without filter. When replacing filter, additional oil may be needed. Diesel engines – Must let oil settle for 20 minutes before checking.
Diesel:
7.3L:
   Above 10°F (−12°C) . . . . .15W-40[1]
   −10°F (−23°C) to 90°F (32°C) . . . . . . .10W-30[2]
   Below 50°F (10°C), 1997 . . . . .5W-30
   Below 30°F (-1°C), 1998 . . . . .5W-30
   Below 0°F (-18°C), 1998 . . . . .0W-30
[1] Preferred above 30°F (−1°C)
[2] Preferred −10° to 30°F (−23° to −1°C)

TRANSMISSION, Automatic
1998 4R70W . . . . .MA5[10]
Others . . . . .MA
[10] Part No. XT-5-QM. Do not use MERCON®.
CAPACITY, Initial Refill[4]:

	Liters	Qt
4R70W	4.7	5.0
E40D	6.1	6.5

[4] With the engine at operating temperature shift transmission through all gears. Check fluid level in PARK and add fluid as needed

TRANSMISSION, Manual
S5-42 ZF w/7.3L Diesel . . .Synthetic MA[5]
[5] Spec. No. ESR-M2C163-A2
   Part No. E6AZ-19582-B
All others . . . . .MA
CAPACITY, Refill:

	Liters	Pt
M5OD (Mazda R2)	3.6	7.6
5-speed OD S5-42 ZF	3.2	6.8

TRANSFER CASE . . . . .MA
CAPACITY, Refill:

	Liters	Pt
Warner 1356 & 4406	1.9[6]	4.0[6]

[6] Add additional 3.9L (8.2 pt) if equipped with PTO, F-350 only

DIFFERENTIAL
F-250 HD, front . . . . .75W-90 GL-5★
F-350, front . . . . .80W-90 GL-5★
Others, front 75W-90 GL-5
Ford axles Dana 80 & E-350 w/Dana 4.10 ratio, rear:
   Standard . . . .*Synthetic 75W-140 GL-5
   Limited-slip . . . .*Synthetic 75W-140 GL-5★
*Part No. F1TZ-19580-B
Dana axles ex. Dana 80 & E-350 w/Dana 4.10 ratio, rear:
   Standard 80W-90 GL-5
   Limited-slip . . . . .80W-90 GL-5★
CAPACITY, Refill:

Front:	Liters	Pt
Ford w/8.8" ring gear	1.6	3.5
Dana 50	1.8	3.8
Dana 60	2.8	6.0
Rear:		
Ford w/8.8" & 9¾" ring gear[7]	2.6[8]	5.5[8]
w/10¼" ring gear[7]	3.5	7.5
Dana 60-IU	3.0[9]	6.3[9]
Dana 70 ex. HD	3.1[9]	6.5[9]
70 HD	3.5[9]	7.4[9]
Dana 80	3.9[9]	8.3[9]

[7] 8.8" & 10¼" have removable cover
[8] Fill ¼" to 9/16" below fill hole
[9] Fill Dana rear axles ¼" to ¾" below fill hole

LIMITED-SLIP OR TRACTION-LOK IDENTIFICATION:
Label on door lock pillar shows letter and number

FORD TRUCKS
1999-2000 Ranger, Explorer & Mercury Mountaineer
Includes Mazda B2500, B3000, B4000

SERVICE AT TIME OR MILEAGE — WHICHEVER OCCURS FIRST

Perform the following maintenance services at the intervals indicated to keep the vehicle warranties in effect.
W   SERVICE TO MAINTAIN EMISSION WARRANTY

MI—MILES IN THOUSANDS
KM—KILOMETERS IN THOUSANDS

EVERY MONTH
Tires . . . . .check
Check air pressure & wear

Engine Oil . . . . .check level

EVERY 6 MONTHS
Power Steering . . . . .check level **MA**

Parking brake system . . . . .inspect

Warning lights . . . . .check
Brake, ABS, air bag, safety belt

Cooling System . . . . . . .check level **EC**
Also check coolant strength. Do not mix orange with green coolant

Battery . . . . .clean/inspect

Clutch reservoir . . . . . .check level **HBH**

Body hinges & latches . . . .lubricate **SLS**

EVERY 6 MO/5 MI—8 KM
Crankcase oil & filter . . . . .replace

EVERY 5 MI—8 KM
Tires . . . . .rotate

EVERY 12 MONTHS
Air-conditioning system . . . . . . .inspect

EVERY 12 MO/15 MI—24 KM
Cabin air filter . . . . .replace
As equipped

EVERY 15 MI—24 KM
Transmission, automatic . . . .check level
Inspect fluid

Brake System. . . . . .inspect
Including brake lines & hoses

Cooling system . . . . .inspect
Including hoses & clamps

Suspension &
   steering linkage . . . . .inspect
Including driveshaft

Ball joints 2WD . . . .inspect/lubricate **LM**

Transfer case
   linkage, 1999 . . . . .lubricate **LM**

EVERY 30 MI—48 KM
Exhaust System heat shields . . . .inspect

Air cleaner element . . . . .replace

Fuel filter . . . . .replace

Transmission, automatic . . . .change fluid
4R70W only

Front wheel bearings
   2WD, 1999 . . . . .inspect/adjust

Half-shaft slip yoke, 1999 . . .lubricate **HG**

AT FIRST 45 MI—72 KM;
THEN EVERY 30 MI—48 KM
Cooling system . . . . .change coolant **EC**
Green coolant only. Do not use orange coolant

EVERY 60 MI—96 KM
PCV valve, 4 cyl. . . . . .replace

Front wheel bearings 2WD .lubricate **LM**
2000 models, replace grease seals & adjust bearings

Transmission, manual . . . . .change fluid

Transfer case, 1999 . . . . . . .change fluid

EVERY 100 MI—160 KM
Accessory drive belts . . . . .inspect

PCV valve . . . . .replace
Except 4 cyl, engines

Spark plugs . . . . .replace

Differential, rear . . . . . .change lubricant
Police & Taxi applications with mineral-based oil installed.

EVERY 120 MI—192 KM
Timing belts 2.5L . . . . .inspect

EVERY 150 MI—240 KM
Transmission,
   automatic, 2000 . . . . .change fluid
Except 4R70W

Differential,
   front & rear . . . . .change lubricant
2000 models. Except rear axles w/synthetic lube installed

Transfer case, 2000 . . . . . .change fluid

Front wheel bearings 2WD . . . . .replace
2000 models only. Also replace grease seals, adjust bearings & lubricate w/**LM**

SERVICE AS REQUIRED
Brake reservoir . . . . . .check level **HBH**

Differential . . . . .check level
Only if evidence of a leak

Differential . . . . .change fluid
When submerged in water

Transmission, manual . . . . .change fluid

U-joints . . . . .inspect/lubricate **LM**
As equipped w/fittings

Cabin air filter . . . . .replace
As equipped

Air cleaner element . . . . .replace

SEVERE SERVICE
Crankcase—Change oil & filter every 3 mo/3 mi (4.8 km)

Brake system—Inspect every 5 mi (8 km)

Differential—Change lubricant every 3 mo/3 mi (4.8 km) (mineral-based oil) during extended trailer towing above 70°F (21°C) and extended wide open throttle above 45 mph. Waive interval where synthetic 75W-140 GL-5 gear oil is used Part No. F1TZ-19580-B.

Fuel filter—Replace every 15 mi (24 km)

Spark plugs—Replace every 60 mi (96 km)

Transmission automatic—Change fluid every 30 mi (48 km)

Transfer case—change fluid every 60 MI (96 KM)

Front wheel bearings, 2WD. 2000 models—Lubricate w/**LM** every 30 mi (48 km).
Also replace grease seals & adjust bearings

KEY TO LUBRICANTS

API★	Motor oil certified by the American Petroleum Institute (Starburst symbol)
BL	Self-adjusting Brake Lubricant
EC	Ethylene Glycol Coolant Mix 50/50 with water at least to −20°F (−29°C) protection
GL-5	Gear Oil, API Service GL-5
GL-5★	Special Gear Oil for Limited-Slip Differentials
HBH	Hydraulic Brake Fluid, Extra Heavy-Duty
HG	High Temperature Grease Ford Spec. No. ESA-MIC198-A Part No. E8TZ-19590-A
LM	Lithium Grease, with Polyethylene
LS	Steering Gear Lubricant/Automatic Hublock Grease
MA	MERCON® Automatic Transmission Fluid
MA5	MERCON® V Automatic Transmission Fluid
SLS	Special Lubricant—Spray Ford Part No. D0AZ-19584-A

CRANKCASE . . . . .5W-30 **API★**

CAPACITY, Refill:	Liters	Qt
2.5L, 3.0L	4.3	4.5
Others	4.7	5.0

Capacity includes filter change

TRANSMISSION, Automatic
All **MA5***
* Part No. XT-5-QM. Do not use MERCON®

CAPACITY, Initial Refill[3]:	Liters	Qt
4R70W w/5.0L	4.7	5.0
Others	3.7	4.0

3 With the engine at operating temperature, shift transmission through all gears. Check fluid level in PARK and add fluid as needed

TRANSMISSION, Manual
5-speed, M50D . . . .**MA**

CAPACITY, Refill:	Liters	Pt
5-speed (Mazda) R1, Ranger, Explorer	2.6	5.6

TRANSFER CASE . . . .**MA**

CAPACITY, Refill:	Liters	Pt
Warner 1354 Ranger	1.2	2.5
Warner 4405 Explorer, Mountaineer w/4WD	1.4	3.0
Explorer, Mountaineer w/AWD . .	1.3	2.6

4 Fill no higher than 1/8" to 1/4" below fill plug

DIFFERENTIAL
Front .80W-90 **GL-5**
Explorer, Mountaineer: 1999-00 w/5.0L, 1999 4.0L SOHC, 4.0L w/3.73 or 4.10 axle ratio, 2000 4.0L w/Limited-Slip rear:
   Standard . . . . . . *Synthetic 75W-140 **GL-5**
   Limited-Slip . .*Synthetic 75W-140 **GL-5★**
*Part No. F1TZ-19580-B
Others: Standard 80W-90 **GL-5**
   Limited-slip . . . . .80W-90 **GL-5★**

CAPACITY, Refill:	Liters	Pt
Front:		
Dana 35 Ranger, Explorer, Mountaineer	1.7	3.5
Rear:		
Ranger w/7.5" ring gear	2.4[5]	5.0[5]
Ranger w/8.8" ring gear	2.4[5]	5.0[5]
Others w/8.8" ring gear	2.6[5]	5.5[5]

5 Fill no higher than 1/4" to 9/16" below fill plug

LIMITED-SLIP OR TRACTION-LOK IDENTIFICATION:
Label on door lock pillar has letter and number

SERVICE AT TIME OR MILEAGE — WHICHEVER OCCURS FIRST

FDTPM   FDTPM

Perform the following maintenance services at the intervals indicated to keep the vehicle warranties in effect.

W   SERVICE TO MAINTAIN EMISSION WARRANTY

MI—MILES IN THOUSANDS
KM—KILOMETERS IN THOUSANDS

EVERY MONTH
Tires . . . . .check
Check air pressure & wear
Engine oil . . . . .check level
Fuel/water separator 7.3L Diesel . . .drain
More frequently if dash light illuminates

EVERY 6 MONTHS
Power Steering . . . . .check level **MA**
Parking brake system . . . . .inspect
Warning lights . . . . .check
Brake, ABS, air bag, safety belt
Cooling System . . . . . . .check level **EC**
Also check coolant strength. Do not mix orange with green coolant
Battery . . . . .clean/inspect
Clutch reservoir . . . . . .check level **HBH**
Body hinges & latches . . . .lubricate **SLS**

EVERY 6 MO/5 MI—8 KM
Crankcase oil & filter . . . . .replace

EVERY 5 MI—8 KM
Tires . . . . .rotate
Air filter, 7.3L Diesel . . . . .check
Check filter minder restriction gauge.
Replace filter as needed

EVERY 12 MONTHS
Air-conditioning system . . . . .inspect

EVERY 12 MO/15 MI—24 KM
Cabin air filter . . . . .replace
As equipped

EVERY 15 MI—24 KM
Transmission, automatic . . . .check level
Inspect fluid
Brake System. . . . . .inspect
Including brake lines & hoses
Cooling System . . . . .inspect
Including hoses & clamps. 7.3L Diesel-add 8-10 ounces of FW-15 additive
Suspension &
   steering linkage . . . . .inspect
Including driveshaft
Ball joints 2WD . . . .inspect/lubricate **LM**
Except F-450, -550
Steering linkage . . . .inspect/lubricate **LM**
Fuel filter . . . . .replace
1999 E/F Super Duty gasoline models & all models w/7.3L Diesel only
2000 7.3L Diesel only
Transfer case linkage . . . . .lubricate **LM**
1999 only

EVERY 30 MI—48 KM
Exhaust System heat shields . . . .inspect
Air cleaner element . . . . .replace
Except 1999 7.3L Diesel
Fuel filter . . . . .replace
1999 except E/F Super Duty gasoline models & all models w/ 7.3L Diesel
2000 except 7.3L Diesel
Transmission, automatic . . . .change fluid
1999 4R70W only
2000 4R70W & 4R100
Compressed gas fuel tanks . . . . .inspect
Natural Gas Vehicles only
Front wheel bearings
   2WD, 1999 . . . . .inspect/adjust
Except F-450, -550
Half-shaft slip yoke, 1999 . . .lubricate **HG**
Climate-controlled seat filters . . .replace
2000 Navigator, as equipped

AT FIRST 45 MI—72 KM;
THEN EVERY 30 MI—48 KM
Cooling system . . . .change coolant **EC**
Green coolant only. Do not use orange coolant
7.3L Diesel-add 4 pints of FW-15 additive

EVERY 60 MI—96 KM
Spark plugs . . . . .replace
Natural gas vehicles only
Front wheel bearings 2WD .lubricate **LM**
Except 1999 F-450, -550
2000 replace grease seals & adjust bearings
Transmission, manual . . . . .change fluid
Transfer case, 1999 . . . . . .change fluid

EVERY 100 MI—160 KM
Accessory drive belts . . . . .inspect
PCV valve . . . . .replace
1999 All
2000 models under 6,000 GVW
Spark plugs . . . . .replace
Except Natural gas-vehicles
Differential, rear . . . . . . .change lubricant
Police & Taxi applications with mineral-based oil installed.
Also 2000 F-450, -550 commercial applications

EVERY 120 MI—192 KM
Coalescent filter . . . . .drain bowl
Natural Gas Vehicles only
Replace filter
PCV valve . . . . .replace
2000 models over 6,000 GVW only

EVERY 150 MI—240 KM
Differential,
   front & rear . . . . .change lubricant
2000 models. Except rear axles w/synthetic lube installed
Transfer case, 2000 . . . . . .change fluid
Front wheel bearings 2WD . . . . .replace
2000 models only. Also replace grease seals, adjust bearings & lubrict w/**LM**

EVERY 180 MONTHS
Compressed gas fuel tanks . . . . .inspect
Natural Gas Vehicles only

SERVICE AS REQUIRED
Brake reservoir . . . . . .check level **HBH**
Differential . . . . .check level
Only if evidence of a leak
Differential . . . . .change fluid
When submerged in water
Transmission, manual . . . .change fluid
U-joints . . . . .inspect/lubricate **LM**
As equipped w/fittings
Cabin air filter . . . . .replace
As equipped
Air cleaner element . . . . .replace

SEVERE SERVICE
Crankcase—Change oil & filter every 3 mo/3 mi (4.8 km)

Brake system—Inspect every 5 mi (8 km)

Differential— Change lubricant every 3 mo/3 mi (4.8 km) (mineral-based oil) during extended trailer towing above 70°F (21°C) and extended wide open throttle above 45 mph. Waive interval where synthetic 75W-140 GL-5 gear oil is used Part No. F1TZ-19580-B. Except 2000 F-450, -550 operating near max GVWR, or off road/dusty conditions, change lubricant every 50 mi (80 km)

Fuel filter—Replace every 15 mi (24 km)

Spark plugs—Replace every 60 mi (96 km)

KEY TO LUBRICANTS
See other Ford Trucks charts

CRANKCASE
Gasoline . . . . .5W-30 **API★**
Diesel **CH-4/SH, CH-4/SJ**

CAPACITY, Refill:	Liters	Qt
4.2L, 4.6L, 5.4L, 6.8L	5.7	6.0
7.3L Diesel	14.2	15.0

Capacity shown includes filter change. Diesel engines – Must let oil settle for 20 minutes before checking.
Diesel:
7.3L:
   Above 10°F (−12°C) . . . . .15W-40[1]
   −10°F (−23°C) to 90°F (32°C) . . . . . .10W-30[2]
   Below 30°F (-1°C) 5W-30
   Below 0°F (-18°C) 0W-30
[1] Preferred above 30°F (−1°C)
[2] Preferred −10° to 30°F (−23° to −1°C)

TRANSMISSION, Automatic
4R70W . . . .**MA5**[10]
Others . . . .**MA**
[10] Part No. XT-5-QM. Do not use MERCON®.

CAPACITY, Initial Refill[4]:	Liters	Qt
4R70W	4.7	5.0
4R100	6.1	6.5

[4] With the engine at operating temperature shift transmission through all gears. Check fluid level in PARK and add fluid as needed

TRANSMISSION, Manual
5-speed S5-42 ZF . . . . . . .Synthetic **MA**[5]
[5] Spec. No. ESR-M2C163-A2
Part No. E6AZ-19582-B
All others . . . .**MA**

CAPACITY, Refill:	Liters	Pt
M5OD (Mazda R2)	3.6	7.6
5-speed OD S5-42 ZF	3.2	6.8
6-speed ZF:		
w/o oil cooler	5.5	11.6
w/oil cooler	6.0	12.7

TRANSFER CASE . . . .**MA**

CAPACITY, Refill:	Liters	Pt
NV271	1.9	4.0
Warner 4406	1.9	4.0

DIFFERENTIAL
Front .75W-90 **GL-5**
Ford axles, Dana 80 & 1999 E-350 w/Dana 4.10 ratio, rear:
   Standard . . . .*Synthetic 75W-140 **GL-5**
   Limited-slip . . .*Synthetic 75W-140 **GL-5★**
*Part No. F1TZ-19580-B
Dana axles ex. Dana 80 & 1999 E-350 w/Dana 4.10 ratio, rear:
   Standard 80W-90 **GL-5**
   Limited-slip . . . . .80W-90 **GL-5★**

CAPACITY, Refill:	Liters	Pt
Front:		
Ford w/8.8" ring gear	1.6	3.5
Dana 50	1.8	3.8
Dana 60	2.8	6.0
Rear:		
Ford w/8.8" & 9¾" ring gear[7] . . .	2.6[8]	5.5[8]
w/10¼" ring gear[7]	3.5	7.5
w/10.5" ring gear	3.3	6.9
Dana 60-IU	3.0[9]	6.3[9]
Dana 70 ex. HD	3.1[9]	6.5[9]
70 HD	3.5[9]	7.4[9]
Dana 80	3.9[9]	8.3[9]
Dana 135	11.6	24.5

[7] 8.8" & 10¼" have removable cover
[8] Fill ¼" to 9/16" below fill hole
[9] Fill Dana rear axles ¼" to ¾" below fill hole

LIMITED-SLIP OR TRACTION-LOK IDENTIFICATION:
Label on door lock pillar shows letter and number

Transmission automatic—Change fluid every 30 mi (48 km)

Transfer case—change fluid every 60 MI (96 KM)

Front wheel bearings, 2WD. 2000 models—Lubricate w/**LM** every 30 mi (48 km). Also replace grease seals & adjust bearings

Copyright 2000 by Chek-Chart Publications

GEO-ASUNA, CHEVROLET—PONTIAC

1989-93 Metro, Firefly, Sprint, Prizm, Storm, Sunfire, Tracker, Sunrunner
1994-2000 Metro, Firefly, Prizm, Tracker, sunrunner

SERVICE LOCATIONS — ENGINE AND CHASSIS

HOOD RELEASE: Inside

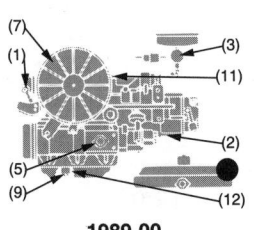

1989-00
1.0L 3-cyl. Metro
Sprint, Firefly

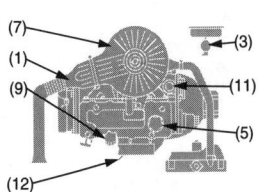

1993-97
1.3L 4-cyl. Metro
1994-97
1.3L 4-cyl. Firefly

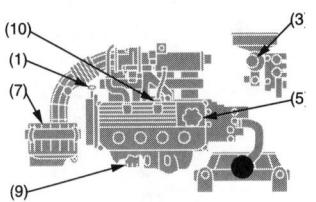

1998-00
1.3L 4-cyl.
Metro

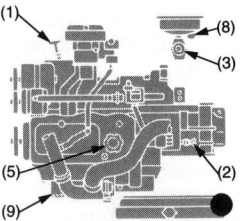

1989-91
Sprint Turbo
Firefly Turbo

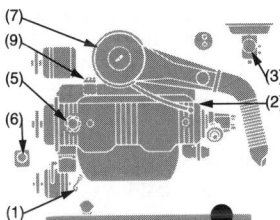

1989
Spectrum, Sunburst 2V

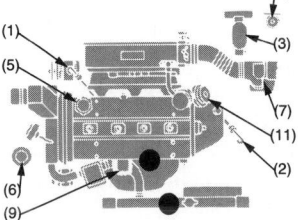

1989-92 1.6L Prizm
Code 5

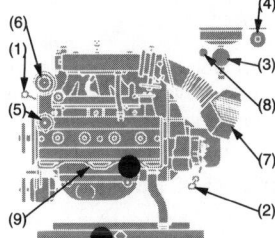

1989-92 1.6L Prizm
Code 6

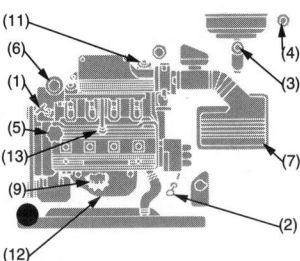

1993-97 Prizm
1.6L Code 6
1.6L Code 8

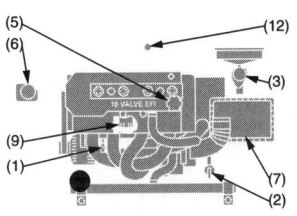

1998-00
Prizm
1.8L Code 8

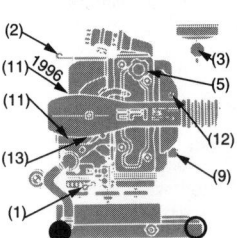

1989-00 1.6L Tracker,
Sunrunner

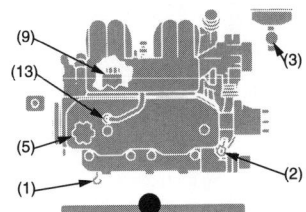

1990-93 1.6L SOCH Code 6
Storm, Sunfire

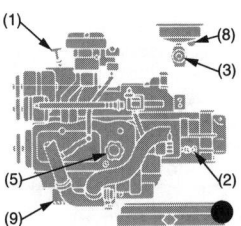

1990-91 1.6L DOHC Code 5
1992-93 1.8L DOHC Code 8
Storm, Sunfire

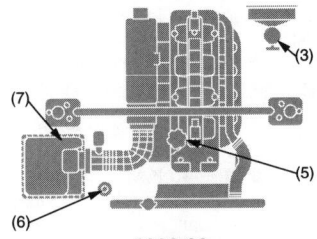

1999-00
2.0L Code C
Tracker

(1) Crankcase dipstick	(8) Fuel filter
(2) Transmission dipstick	(9) Oil filter
(3) Brake fluid reservoir	(10) PCV filter
(4) Clutch fluid reservoir	(11) EGR valve
(5) Oil fill cap	(12) Oxygen sensor
(6) Power steering reservoir	(13) PCV valve
(7) Air filter	

● Cooling system drain   ○ Cooling system drain, some models

GEO-ASUNA, CHEVROLET—PONTIAC

1989-93 Metro, Firefly, Sprint, Prizm, Storm, Sunfire, Tracker, Sunrunner
1994-2000 Metro, Firefly, Prizm, Tracker, Sunrunner

SERVICE LOCATIONS — ENGINE AND CHASSIS

0 FITTINGS
0 PLUGS

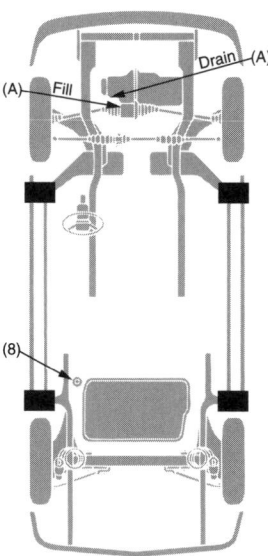

1989-93
Metro, Sprint, Firefly
1994-00
Metro, Firefly

0 FITTINGS
0 PLUGS

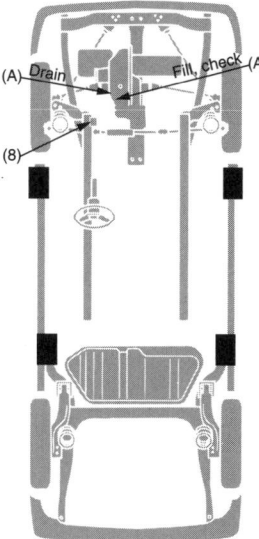

1989-89 Spectrum
1989-93 Storm, Sunfire

0 FITTINGS
0 PLUGS

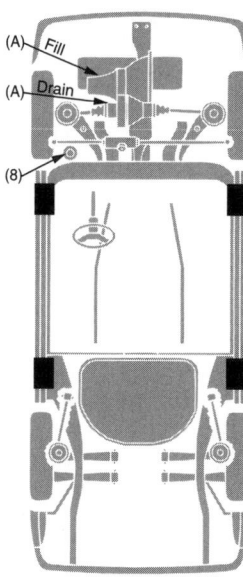

1989-00
Prizm

0 FITTINGS
0 PLUGS

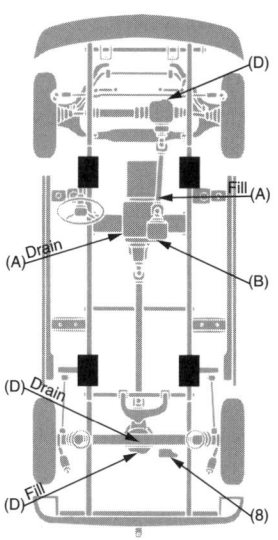

1989-98
Tracker, Sunrunner

(A) Manual transmission/transaxle,
    drain & fill

(B) Transfer case, drain & fill

(C) Automatic transaxle final drive,
    NOT USED

(D) Differential, drain & fill

(8) Fuel filter

CAUTION: On front wheel drive vehicles, the center of gravity is farther forward than on rear wheel drive vehicles. When removing major components from the rear of the vehicle while it is on a hoist, the vehicle must be supported in a manner to prevent it from tipping forward.

■ Lift adapter position

GEO, CHEVROLET—PONTIAC
1989-91 Firefly, Metro, Sprint
1992-98 Firefly, Metro; 1998-2000 Chevy Metro

SERVICE AT TIME OR MILEAGE — WHICHEVER OCCURS FIRST

Perform the following maintenance services at the intervals indicated to keep the vehicle warranties in effect.

W   SERVICE TO MAINTAIN EMISSION WARRANTY

MI—MILES IN THOUSANDS
KM—KILOMETERS IN THOUSANDS

EVERY MONTH
Tires . . . . .check pressure

1991-00, EVERY 6 MONTHS
W Throttle linkage . . . . .inspect
Check for damage or binding

Cooling system . . . . .inspect
Hoses and pipes

Brake system . . . . .inspect

W Exhaust system . . . . .inspect

Suspension . . . . .inspect

Transaxle . . . . .check level

EVERY 6 MONTHS
Brake fluid, 1994-00 . . . . .check level **HB**

Clutch . . . . .check pedal free travel

SPRINT & FIREFLY TURBO, EVERY 12 MO/5 MI—8 KM
W Crankcase . . . . .change oil
Change filter at each oil change

EVERY 7.5 MI—12.5 KM
Tires, 1994-00 . . . . .rotate

FIRST 7.5 MI—12.5 KM; THEN EVERY 15 MI—25 KM
Tires, 1989-93 . . . . .inspect, rotate

W Engine idle speed, 1989 . . .check/adjust

1989 EVERY 12 MO/7.5 MI—12.5 KM
1990-00 EVERY 7.5 MO/7.5 MI—12.5 KM
Brake system, 1989-90 . . . . . . .inspect

Crankcase ex. Turbo . .change oil & filter

Transaxle, 1989-90 . . . . . . .check level

W Exhaust system, 1989-90 . . . . . .inspect

Steering & suspension, 1989-90 . . .inspect
Check boots, seals, & all components

W Throttle linkage, 1989-90 . . . . . . .inspect

EVERY SPRING
Underbody . . . . .flush

EVERY 12 MO/7.5 MI—12.5 KM
Chassis . . . . .lubricate **LB**
Lubricate transaxle shift linkage, hood latch, door latch & hinges, parking brake cable guides, & underbody contact points

1989 EVERY 12 MO/15 MI—25 KM
W Fuel tank, cap & lines . . . . .inspect

Brake fluid . . . . .inspect **HB**

EVERY 15 MO/15 MI—25 KM
W Fuel tank, cap, & lines, 1990-00 . . . . .inspect

Brake fluid, 1990-93 . . . . .check level **HB**

EVERY 15 MI—25 KM
Transaxle, manual, 1989 change lubricant

W Cooling system, 1989-90 . . . . . . .inspect

W Idle speed, 1989 . . . . .check/adjust

Valve lash . . . . .inspect/adjust
1989, 1994 Canadian Metro and Firefly, 1998-99 Metro and Firefly Code 2 engine

EVERY 24 MO/30 MI—50 KM
W Air cleaner, 1989 . . . . .replace element

W Carburetor choke, 1989 . . . . . . .inspect

W Drive belts . . . . .inspect/adjust
1989, 1994-00

W Fuel cut solenoid, 1989 . . . . .inspect

W Cooling system . . . . .change coolant **EC**
Use 50% concentration for –34°F (–37°C) protection
1989-90

W PCV system, 1989 . . . . .inspect

W Pulse air system, 1989 . . . . .inspect

W Spark plug wires, 1989 . . . . .check
Check distributor cap & rotor

EVERY 30 MI—50 KM
W Air cleaner, 1993-00 . . . . .replace

W Cooling system . . . . .change coolant **EC**
Use 50% concentration for –34°F (–7°C) protection
1991-94

W Oxygen sensor, 1989 . . . . .inspect
Check indicator light to assure proper system function

W Fuel filter, 1989 . . . . .replace

W Spark plugs . . . . .replace

EVERY 30 MO/30 MI—50 KM
W Drive belts . . . . .inspect/adjust
1990-93

W Air cleaner, 1990-92 . . . . .replace

W Camshaft timing belt, 1994-96 . . .inspect

W Cooling system . . . . .change coolant **EC**
Use 50% concentration for –34°F (–37°C) protection, 1995-99

Transaxle, manual 1994-00 . . . . .change fluid

W Fuel filter, 1994-95 . . . . .replace

W Ignition Coil Plug Cap . . . . .inspect
1999-00 Code 2 engine

EVERY 45 MO/45 MI—75 KM
Transaxle oil hoses . . . . .replace
1991-95 Metro, 1994-95 Firefly

EVERY 60 MI—96 KM
W Camshaft timing belt, 1997-00 . . .inspect

W Camshaft timing belt, 1992-96 . . .replace

Brake fluid, 1994-00 . . . . .replace **HB**

EVERY 60 MO/60 MI—100 KM
W Wiring harness & connectors . . . .inspect
1989-1999

Spark plug wires . . . . .replace
1990-00

EVERY 100 MI—166 KM
Transaxle, automatic . .change fluid & filter
1989-1994

W Camshaft timing belt, 1997-00 . . . .replace

W Fuel Filter, 1996-00 . . . . .replace

SEVERE SERVICE
W **Air cleaner element, dusty conditions—**
check every 15 mo/15 mi (20 km)

W **Crankcase**—Change oil & filter every 3 mo/3 mi (5 km)

Chassis—Lubricate every 6 mo/6 mi (10 km)

Tires—rotate: every 6 mi (10 km)

Transaxle, manual—Change fluid every 12 mo/12 mi

Transaxle, automatic—Change fluid and filter; 1989-94 every 15 mi (25 km); 1995-00, every 50 mi (83 km)

KEY TO LUBRICANTS

AF3   DEXRON®-III
Automatic Transmission Fluid

API★   Motor Oil certified by the American Petroleum Institute (Starburst Symbol)

EC   Ethylene Glycol Coolant or approved recycled coolant.
GM specification 1825M

GL-4   Gear Oil, API Service GL-4

GL-5   Gear Oil, API Service GL-5

HB   Hydraulic Brake Fluid, DOT 3
GM Part No. 12377967 or equivalent

LB   Chassis Grease, NLGI Category LB, or GC-LB

CRANKCASE . . . . .API★

CAPACITY, Refill:	Liters	Qt
3 cyl. 1989-93 (incl. filter)	3.5	3.7
Others	3.3	3.5

Capacity shown is with filter. Additional oil may be needed. Check level after filling.

Firefly & Sprint Turbo:
Above 40°F (4°C), 1989 . . . . .30[1]
All temperatures . . . . .10W-30[2]

Others:
Above 40°F (4°C), 1989-95 . . . . .30[1]
Above 0°F (–18°C) 10W-30
All temperatures . . . . .5W-30[2]
1997-00, at temperatures below –20°F (–29°C), 5W-30 synthetic, or 0W-30 should be considered

[1] May be used only if other recommended viscosities are not available.
[2] Preferred.

TRANSAXLE, Automatic AF3

CAPACITY, Initial Refill[3]:	Liters	Qt
All	1.5	1.6

[3] With the engine at operating temperature, shift transmission through all gears. Let engine slow idle in PARK for 3 minutes or more. Check fluid level and add fluid as needed.

TRANSAXLE, Manual . . . . Synthetic 75W-90 GL-4[4]

CAPACITY, Refill:	Liters	Pt
All	2.4	5.0

[4] GM Part No. 12346190

GEO—ASUNA, CHEVROLET
1989-93 Spectrum, Storm, Sunfire

SERVICE AT TIME OR MILEAGE — WHICHEVER OCCURS FIRST

GOIPM4

GOIPM4

W SERVICE TO MAINTAIN EMISSION WARRANTY

MI—MILES IN THOUSANDS
KM—KILOMETERS IN THOUSANDS

FIRST 7.5 MI—12.5 KM
Tires . . . . .inspect, rotate

EVERY 12 MO/7.5 MI—12.5 KM
Crankcase . . . . .change oil
Change oil filter at first oil change then every other change but at least every 12 months

Chassis . . . . .lubricate **LB**
Lubricate transaxle shift linkage, hood latch, door latch & hinges, parking brake cable guides, & underbody contact points

Clutch bushing & linkage . . . . . .lubricate

Transaxle . . . . .check level

W Exhaust system . . . . .inspect

Steering & suspension . . . . .inspect
Check boots, seals, & all components

W Throttle linkage . . . . .inspect

EVERY SPRING
Underbody . . . . .flush

EVERY 12 MO/15 MI—25 KM
Brake system . . . . .inspect **HB**

EVERY 15 MI—25 KM
W Valve clearance . . . . .adjust
All SOHC engines

Tires . . . . .inspect/rotate

Cooling system, 1991-93 . . . . . . .inspect

Fuel tank, cap, and lines . . . . . .inspect

EVERY 24 MO/22.5 MI—37.5 KM
Power steering fluid . . . . . . .change **PS**

EVERY 24 MO/30 MI—50 KM
W Cooling system . . . . .change coolant **EC**
Use 50% concentration for −34°F (−37°C) protection

W Drive belts, 1991-93 . . . . .inspect/adjust

EVERY 30 MI—50 KM
Rear wheel bearings . . . . . . .repack **GC**
1989 Spectrum

Transaxle, automatic . . . . . .change fluid

Transaxle, manual . . . . .change lubricant

W Air cleaner . . . . .replace element

W Drive belts, 1989-90 . . . . .inspect/adjust

W Choke, 1989 . . . . .inspect

W Oxygen sensor . . . . .inspect

PCV system . . . . .inspect

W Spark plugs . . . . .replace

EVERY 45 MO/45 MI—75 KM
Power steering hoses . . . . .replace

EVERY 60 MI—96 KM
Timing belt . . . . .replace

W Valve clearance . . . . .adjust
1990-91 DOHC engine

EVERY 100 MI—166 KM
Automatic transmission . . . .change fluid

SEVERE SERVICE
W Crankcase—Change oil every 3 mo/3 mi (5 km); change oil filter at first oil change, then every other change

Chassis—Lubricate every 6 mo/6 mi (10 km)

Transaxle, automatic—Change fluid and clean screen every 15 mi (25 km)

KEY TO LUBRICANTS

AF3   DEXRON®-III Automatic Transmission Fluid

API★   Motor Oil certified by the American Petroleum Institute (Starburst Symbol)

EC   Ethylene Glycol Coolant

GC   Wheel Bearing Grease, NLGI Classification GC

GLS   Special Gear Lubricant GM Part No. 12345349

HB   Hydraulic Brake Fluid, DOT 3

LB   Chassis Grease, NLGI Category LB

PS   Power Steering Fluid GM Part No. 1052884

SG   Motor Oil, API Service SG Use Energy Conserving-II oils

SH   Motor Oil, API Service SH Use Energy Conserving-II oils

CRANKCASE . . . .**SG, SH, API★**

CAPACITY, Refill:	Liters	Qt
Spectrum	2.8	3.0
Storm, Sunfire: SOHC	3.0	3.2
DOHC	3.8	4.0

Capacity shown is without filter. When replacing filter, additional oil may be needed.

1989 Spectrum
Above 40°F (4°C), 1989 . . . . .30[1]
Above 0°F (−18°C) 10W-30
All temperatures . . . . .5W-30[2]

1990-93 Storm, Sunfire
Above 40°F (4°C) . . . . .30[1]
Above 0°F (−18°C) . . . . .10W-30[2]
All temperatures, SOHC . . . . .5W-30[2]
Below 60°F (16°C), DOHC 5W-30

[1] May be used only if other recommended viscosities are not available
[2] 10W-30 preferred in DOHC engines
5W-30 preferred in SOHC engines

TRANSAXLE, Automatic **AF3**

CAPACITY, Initial Refill[3]:	Liters	Qt
Spectrum (Total fill[4])	6.0	6.3
Storm, Sunfire	4.1	4.4

[3] With the engine at operating temperature, shift transmission through all gears. Let engine slow idle in PARK for 3 minutes or more. Check fluid level and add fluid as needed.
[4] Use less fluid when refilling.

TRANSAXLE, Manual . . . .**GLS[5]**

CAPACITY, Refill:	Liters	Pt
All	1.9	4.0

[5] GM Part No. 12345349

SERVICE AT TIME OR MILEAGE — WHICHEVER OCCURS FIRST

GOIPM3

GOIPM3

Perform the following maintenance services at the intervals indicated to keep the vehicle warranties in effect.

W SERVICE TO MAINTAIN EMISSION WARRANTY

MI—MILES IN THOUSANDS
KM—KILOMETERS IN THOUSANDS

EVERY MONTH
Tire inflation . . . . .check

1989-91
FIRST 7.5 MI—12.5 KM;
THEN EVERY 36 MO/30 MI—50 KM
1992-93
FIRST 12 MO/7.5 MI—12.5 KM;
THEN AT 24 MO/15 MI—25 KM;
THEN EVERY 24 MO/15 MI—25 KM
W Engine idle speed . . . . . . .check/adjust

EVERY 6 MONTHS/OIL CHANGE
Clutch & brake fluid . . . . .check level **HB**

Steering & suspension, 1991-94 . . .inspect
Check boots & seals

Brake system . . . . .inspect

Parking brake cable guides . . . . .coat **LB**

Exhaust system, 1991-95 . . . . . .inspect

W Throttle linkage, 1991-95 . . . . . .inspect

Power steering
fluid, 1989-92 . . . . .check level **AF2**
Do not use DEXRON®-III

Power steering
fluid, 1993-95 . . . . . . .check level **AF3**

EVERY 7.5 MI—12.5 KM
Tires . . . . .inspect/rotate

1989
EVERY 12 MO/10 MI—16.7 KM
1990-95
EVERY 12 MO/7.5 MI—12.5 KM
Brake system . . . . .inspect
Inspect hoses & lines for damage/wear
Inspect friction surfaces for wear or cracks. Check for
leaks. Check parking brake adjustment.

W Crankcase . . . . .change oil
All ex. 1991, change oil filter at each oil change
1991 change oil filter at first, then every other oil change

W Accessory drive belt . . . . .inspect
1989-92

Steering & suspension, 1989-90 . . .inspect
Check boots, seals, & all components

Chassis . . . . .lubricate **LB**
Lubricate transaxle shift linkage hood latch, door latch &
hinges, parking brake cable guides, & underbody contact
points

Exhaust system, 1989-90 . . . . . .inspect

Transaxle, 1989-93 . . . . . . .check level

W Throttle linkage, 1989-90 . . .inspect

EVERY SPRING
Underbody . . . . .flush

EVERY 15 MI—25 KM
W Cooling system . . . . .inspect

Transaxle, 1994-95 . . . . . . .check level

EVERY 30 MI—50 KM
W Spark plugs . . . . .replace
1994-95

W Air cleaner . . . . .replace
More often under dusty conditions

EVERY 36 MO/30 MI—50 KM
W Spark plugs . . . . .replace
1989-93 ex. 1990-92 Code 5

W Fuel tank, cap, lines . . . . .inspect

Exhaust system . . . . .inspect

FIRST 36 MO/45 MI—75 KM;
THEN EVERY 24 MO/30 MI—50 KM
W Cooling system . . . . .change coolant **EC**
Flush system, then use 50% concentration for –34°F
(–37°C) protection

1993-94
FIRST 36 MO/ 60 MI—100 KM;
1995
FIRST 72 MO/60 MI—100 KM;
THEN EVERY
12 MO/7.5 MI—12.5 KM
W Accessory drive belt . . . . .inspect

EVERY 72 MO/60 MI—100 KM
W Spark plugs . . . . .replace
1990-92 Code 5

W Vapor canister . . . . .inspect

W Valve clearance . . . . .check/adjust

W Fuel cap gasket . . . . .replace

EVERY 100 MI—166 KM
Automatic transaxle . . . . . . .change fluid
1989-93

Differential, 1989-93 . . . . . . .change fluid
3-speed automatic only

SEVERE SERVICE
W **Air cleaner element**—Every 3 mo/5 mi
(8 km)

Chassis—Lubricate every 6 mo/6 mi
(10 km)

W **Crankcase**—Change oil & filter every
3 mo/3 mi (5 km)

Timing belt—On engines with excessive
idling or driven long distances at slow
speeds, replace every 60 mi (100 km)

**Transaxle, automatic, and 3-speed
automatic final drive**—Change fluid
every 15 mi (25 km) when in either heavy
city traffic at temperatures regularly above
90°F (32°C); hilly terrain; commercial or
trailer towing service

Transaxle, manual—Change fluid every
30 mi (50 km) when trailer towing

KEY TO LUBRICANTS

AF2	DEXRON®-IIE Automatic Transmission Fluid
AF3	DEXRON®-III Automatic Transmission Fluid
API★	Motor Oil certified by the American Petroleum Institute (Starburst Symbol)
EC	Ethylene Glycol Coolant GM Specification 1825M
GL-4	Gear Oil, API Service GL-4
GL-5	Gear Oil, API Service GL-5
HB	Hydraulic Brake Fluid, DOT 3
LB	Chassis grease, NLGI Category LB
SG	Motor Oil, API Service SG Use Energy Conserving-II Oils
SH	Motor Oil, API Service SH Use Energy Conserving-II Oils

CRANKCASE
1989-94 . . . . .SG, SH, API★
1995 . . . . .API★

CAPACITY, Refill:	Liters	Qt
Code 5	3.4	3.6
Code 6	3.1	3.3
Code 8	3.5	3.7

Capacity shown is without filter. When replacing filter, additional oil may be needed.

1989-90
Above 40°F (4°C) . . . . .30[1]
Above 0°F (–18°C) 10W-30
All temperatures . . . . .5W-30[2]
1991-95
Above 40°F (4°C) . . . . .30[1]
Above 0°F (–18°C) . . . . .10W-30[2]
Below 50°F (10°C) 5W-30
[1] May be used only if other recommended viscosities are not
available. Use API **SH** oil.
[2] Preferred.

TRANSAXLE, Automatic AF3
Three-speed final drive serviced separately

CAPACITY, Initial Refill[3]:	Liters	Qt
3-speed	2.5	2.6
4-speed	3.3	3.5

[3] With the engine at operating temperature, shift transmission through all gears. Let engine slow idle in PARK for 3 to 5 minutes. Check fluid level and add fluid as needed.

TRANSAXLE,
Manual . . . . Synthetic 75W-90 **GL-4**[4]

CAPACITY, Refill:	Liters	Pt
All	2.6	5.4

[4] GM Part No. 12346190

FINAL DRIVE
Three-speed AT AF3

CAPACITY, Refill:	Liters	Pt
All	1.4	3.0

SERVICE AT TIME OR MILEAGE — WHICHEVER OCCURS FIRST

GOIPM5   GOIPM5

Perform the following maintenance services at the intervals indicated to keep the vehicle warranties in effect.
W SERVICE TO MAINTAIN EMISSION WARRANTY

MI—MILES IN THOUSANDS
KM—KILOMETERS IN THOUSANDS

EVERY MONTH
Tire inflation . . . . .check

W Air cleaner . . . . .replace
More often under dusty conditions

EVERY 6 MONTHS/OIL CHANGE
Clutch & brake fluid . . . . .check level **HB**
GM Part No. 12345347 preferred

Transaxle, manual . . . . .check level

Steering & suspension . . . . .inspect
Check boots & seals

Brake system . . . . .inspect

Parking brake cable guides . . . . .coat **LB**

Exhaust system . . . . .inspect

W Throttle linkage . . . . .inspect

Power steering
fluid . . . . .check level **AF3**

EVERY 12 MO/7.5 MI—12.5 KM
Tires . . . . .inspect/rotate
Mileage only

W Crankcase . . . . .change oil & filter

Chassis . . . . .lubricate **LB**
Lubricate transaxle shift linkage hood latch, door latch & hinges, parking brake cable guides, & underbody contact points

EVERY SPRING
Underbody . . . . .flush

EVERY 15 MI—25 KM
W Cooling system . . . . .inspect

Transaxle, automatic . . . . . . .check level

EVERY 24 MO/30 MI—50 KM
W Fuel tank, cap, cap gasket
lines, 1997-00 . . . . .inspect

W Cooling system . . . . .change coolant **EC**
Flush system, then use 50% concentration for –34°F (–37°C) protection. Inspect hoses.

EVERY 30 MI—50 KM
W Spark plugs . . . . .replace
1996-99

EVERY 36 MO/30 MI—50 KM
W Fuel tank, cap, lines, 1996 . . . . . .inspect

FIRST 48 MO/60 MI—100 KM; THEN EVERY 12 MO/15 MI—25 KM
W Accessory drive belt . . . . .inspect

EVERY 48 MO/60 MI—100 KM
W Vapor canister . . . . .inspect

W Valve clearance . . . . .check/adjust

EVERY 72 MO/60 MI—100 KM
Timing belt, 1996-97 . . . . .replace

EVERY 120 MI—200 KM
Spark plugs . . . . .replace

SEVERE SERVICE
W **Crankcase**—Change oil & filter every 3 mo/3 mi (5 km)

Chassis—Lubricate every 6 mo/6 mi (10 km)

W **Air cleaner element, dusty conditions**—Inspect every 6 mi (10 km)

Transaxle, automatic—Change fluid and filter every 15 mi (25 km) when in either: heavy city traffic at temperatures regularly above 90°F (32°C); hilly terrain; commercial; or frequent towing of a trailer or using a car top carrier

Tires—Inspect/rotate every 6 mi (10 km)

Transaxle, manual—Change fluid 30 mi (50 km) or 24 months when trailer towing

KEY TO LUBRICANTS

AF3   DEXRON®-III Automatic Transmission Fluid

API★   Motor Oil certified by the American Petroleum Institute (Starburst Symbol)

EC   Ethylene Glycol Coolant
GM Specification 1825M. GM Part No. 1052753

GL-5   Gear Oil, API Service GL-5
GM Part No. 12346190

HB   Hydraulic Brake Fluid, DOT 3
GM Part No. 12377967

LB   Chassis Grease, NLGI #2, Category LB, GC-LB

CRANKCASE . . . . .API★

CAPACITY, Refill:	Liters	Qt
Code 6	2.8	3.0
Code 8, 1996-97	3.5	3.7
Code 8, 1998-00	3.7	3.9

When replacing filter, additional oil may be needed
1.6L Code 6:
Above 0°F (–18°C) . . . . .10W-30[1]
Below 60°F (16°C) 5W-30
1.8L Code 8:
Above 0°F (–18°C) 10W-30
All temperatures . . . . .5W-30[1]
[1] Preferred
1997-00 all, at temperatures below –20°F (–29°C), 5W-30 synthetic, or 0W-30 should be considered

TRANSAXLE, Automatic AF3
3-speed final drive serviced separately

CAPACITY, Initial Refill[2]:	Liters	Qt
3-speed	2.5	2.6
4-speed	3.1[3]	3.3[3]

[2] With the engine at operating temperature, shift transmission through all gears. Let engine slow idle in PARK for 3 to 5 minutes. Check fluid level and add fluid as needed.
[3] Includes differential.

TRANSAXLE,
Manual . . . . Synthetic 75W-90 **GL-5**[4]

CAPACITY, Refill:	Liters	Pt
All	1.9	4.0

[4] GM Part No. 12346190, or equivalent 75W-90 **GL-5**

FINAL DRIVE
3-speed AT .AF3

CAPACITY, Refill:	Liters	Pt
All	1.4	3.0

SERVICE AT TIME OR MILEAGE — WHICHEVER OCCURS FIRST

GOIPM2   GOIPM2

Perform the following maintenance services at the intervals indicated to keep the vehicle warranties in effect.

W   **SERVICE TO MAINTAIN EMISSION WARRANTY**

MI—MILES IN THOUSANDS
KM—KILOMETERS IN THOUSANDS

EVERY 3 MO/7.5 MI—12.5 KM
Locking front hubs . . . . .inspect
1989-98 as equipped

EVERY 6 MO
W Throttle linkage, 1991-00 . . . . . . .inspect
Check for damage or binding
Cooling system . . . . .inspect
Hoses & pipes
Brake system . . . . .inspect
Check hydraulic system, disc pads, drum linings
Exhaust system, 1991-00 . . . . . . .inspect
Steering & suspension, 1991-00 . .inspect
Also inspect front drive axle boots & seals
Transmission, manual, 1997-00 . .check level
Axles, 1993-00 . . . . .check level
Drive belts, 1991 . . . . .check
Clutch . . . . .check pedal free travel

FIRST 7.5 MI—12.5 KM
Manual transmission, differentials &
transfer case . . . . .change fluid
1989-93

EVERY 7.5 MO/7.5 MI—12.5 KM
Clutch & brake fluid . . . . .check level **HB**
W Crankcase . . . . .change oil & filter
Steering & suspension . . . . .inspect
1989-90 check boots, seals, & all components
Power steering system . .check level **AF3**
1990-00
Transmission & transfer case . .check level
Tires . . . . .inspect/rotate
Mileage only

EVERY 12 MO/7.5 MI—12.5 KM
Brake system . . . . .inspect
Check parking brake adjustment
Chassis . . . . .lubricate **LM**
Lubricate transaxle shift linkage, hood latch, door latch &
hinges, parking brake cable guides, & underbody contact
points
W Exhaust system . . . . .inspect
W Throttle linkage, 1989-90 . . . . . . .inspect

EVERY SPRING
Underbody . . . . .flush

EVERY 15 MI—25 KM
Brake system . . . . .inspect
W Cooling system, 1989 . . . . .inspect
W Idle speed . . . . .check/adjust
W Valve clearance . . . . .adjust
1989-98 all, 1999-00 Code 6

EVERY 15 MO/15 MI—24 KM
Air filter, passenger
compartment, 1999-00 . . . . . . .inspect
Propeller shaft & U-joints . . . . . .inspect
Transmission, manual &
transfer case . . . . .change fluid
1993
Front wheel
bearings, 1989-95 . . .inspect/repack **WB**
Or at brake reline

EVERY 24 MO/24 MI—40 KM
W Cooling system . . . . . .change coolant **EC**
1989-90

EVERY 24 MO/30 MI—50 KM
W Drive belts . . . . .check/adjust

EVERY 30 MO/30 MI—50 KM
W Cooling system . . . . . . .change coolant **EC**
1991-00 flush system, then use 50% concentration for
−34°F (−37°C) protection
W Fuel filter . . . . .replace

EVERY 30 MI—50 KM
Transmission, manual . . . . .change fluid
1989-00
Differentials & transfer case . .change fluid
1989-92, 1999-00
Front wheel bearings,
2WD, 1996-00 . . . .inspect/repack **WB**
Or at brake relign
Air filter, passenger
compartment, 1999-00 . . . . . . .replace
W Fuel tank, cap & lines . . . . .inspect
W Air cleaner . . . . .replace element
W PCV filter . . . . .replace
If equipped
Camshaft timing belt . . . . .inspect/adjust
Commencing at 90 mi. 1989-98 all, 1999-00 Code 6
W Spark plugs . . . . .replace

EVERY 45 MO/45 MI—75 KM
Transmission, automatic hoses . .replace
1998-00

EVERY 50 MI—83 KM
Transmission, automatic
hoses . . . . .replace
1989-97
W EGR system . . . . .inspect
1989-95
W PCV valve . . . . .replace

EVERY 60 MI—100 KM
Brake fluid, 1994-00 . . . . . . .replace **HB**
W Camshaft timing belt . . . . .replace
1989-98 all, 1999-00 Code 6
W Distributor cap . . . . .clean/replace
Distributor advance, 1989 . . . . . . .check
W Drive belts, 1989-91 . . . . .replace
W Emission hoses . . . . .inspect
W Fuel tank, cap gasket . . . . .replace
W Ignition timing . . . . .check/adjust
Wiring harness . . . . .inspect

EVERY 60 MO/60 MI—100 KM
W Ignition wires . . . . .replace

EVERY 80 MI—133 KM
W Oxygen sensor, 1989-94 . . . . .replace

EVERY 100 MI—166 KM
Automatic transmission,
1989-94, 1998-00 . . . . . .change fluid
W Catalytic converter . . . . .inspect
1989-94
W ECM sensors . . . . .inspect
W EGR system, 1996 . . . . .inspect
W Fuel injectors . . . . .inspect
W Vapor canister . . . . .replace

SEVERE SERVICE
Air filter, passenger compartment,
1999-00— inspect every 6 mi (10 km)
W **Air cleaner**—Inspect every 15 mi (25 km)
in dusty conditions only
W **Crankcase**—Change oil & filter every
3 mo/3 mi (5 km)
Chassis—Lubricate every 6 mo/6 mi (10 km)
Front wheel bearings 2WD—Repack
every 15 mi (24 km), or at brake reline
Automatic transmission—Change lubricant: 1989-94, every 15 mo/15 mi (24 km);
1995-97, every 50 mi (83 km); 1998-00,
15 mi (24km)
Manual transmission, transfer case &
differentials—Change lubricant every
15 mi (12.5 km)
Tires—Rotate every 6 mi (10 km)
Locking front hubs, 1989-98 as
equipped—Inspect every 3 mo/3 mi (5 km)

KEY TO LUBRICANTS

AF3   DEXRON®-III Automatic
Transmission Fluid

API★   Motor Oil certified by the American
Petroleum Institute (Starburst
Symbol)

EC   Ethylene Glycol Coolant
GM Spec. 1825-M or approved recycled coolant

GL-4   Gear Oil, API Service GL-4
GM Part No. 12346790

GL-5   Gear Oil, API Service GL-5
GM Part No. 12345977

HB   Hydraulic Brake Fluid, DOT 3
Brakes, GM Part No. 12377967
Clutch, GM Part No. 12345347

LM   Lithium Grease with EP

WB   Wheel Bearing Grease
GM Part No. 1051344

CRANKCASE . . . . .API★

CAPACITY, Refill:	Liters	Qt
Always check level after refill.		
2.0L Code C (incl. filter)	5.2	5.5
All others (incl. filter)	4.2	4.5
Above 40°F (4°C), 1989-95 . . . . .30[1]
Above 0°F (−18°C) 10W-30
All temperatures . . . . .5W-30[2]

Temperatures below −20°F (−29°C), 5W-30 synthetic,
or 0W-30 should be considered.
1 May be used only if other viscosities are unavailable. Use
API **SH** oil.
2 Preferred.

TRANSMISSION, Automatic AF3

CAPACITY, Initial Refill[3]:	Liters	Qt
3-speed	2.8	3.0
4-speed	2.5	2.6

3 With the engine at operating temperature, shift transmission through all gears. Let engine slow idle in PARK for
3 minutes or more. Check fluid level and add fluid as
needed.

TRANSMISSION,
Manual . . . . . . .Synthetic 75W-90 **GL-4**[4]

CAPACITY, Refill:	Liters	Pt
4-wheel drive	1.5	3.2
2-wheel drive, 1996	1.7	3.6
1997-00	1.9	2.0

4 GM Part No. 12346190, or equivalent 75W-90 **GL-4**

TRANSFER
CASE . . . . .Synthetic 75W-90 **GL-4**[5]

CAPACITY, Refill:	Liters	Pt
All	1.7	3.6

5 GM Part No. 12346190, or equivalent 75W-90 **GL-4**

DIFFERENTIAL . . . . .80W-90 **GL-5**[6]

CAPACITY, Refill:	Liters	Pt
Front	1.0	2.1
Rear	2.2	4.6

6 GM Part No. 12345977 or equivalent

SERVICE LOCATIONS — ENGINE AND CHASSIS

HOOD RELEASE: Inside

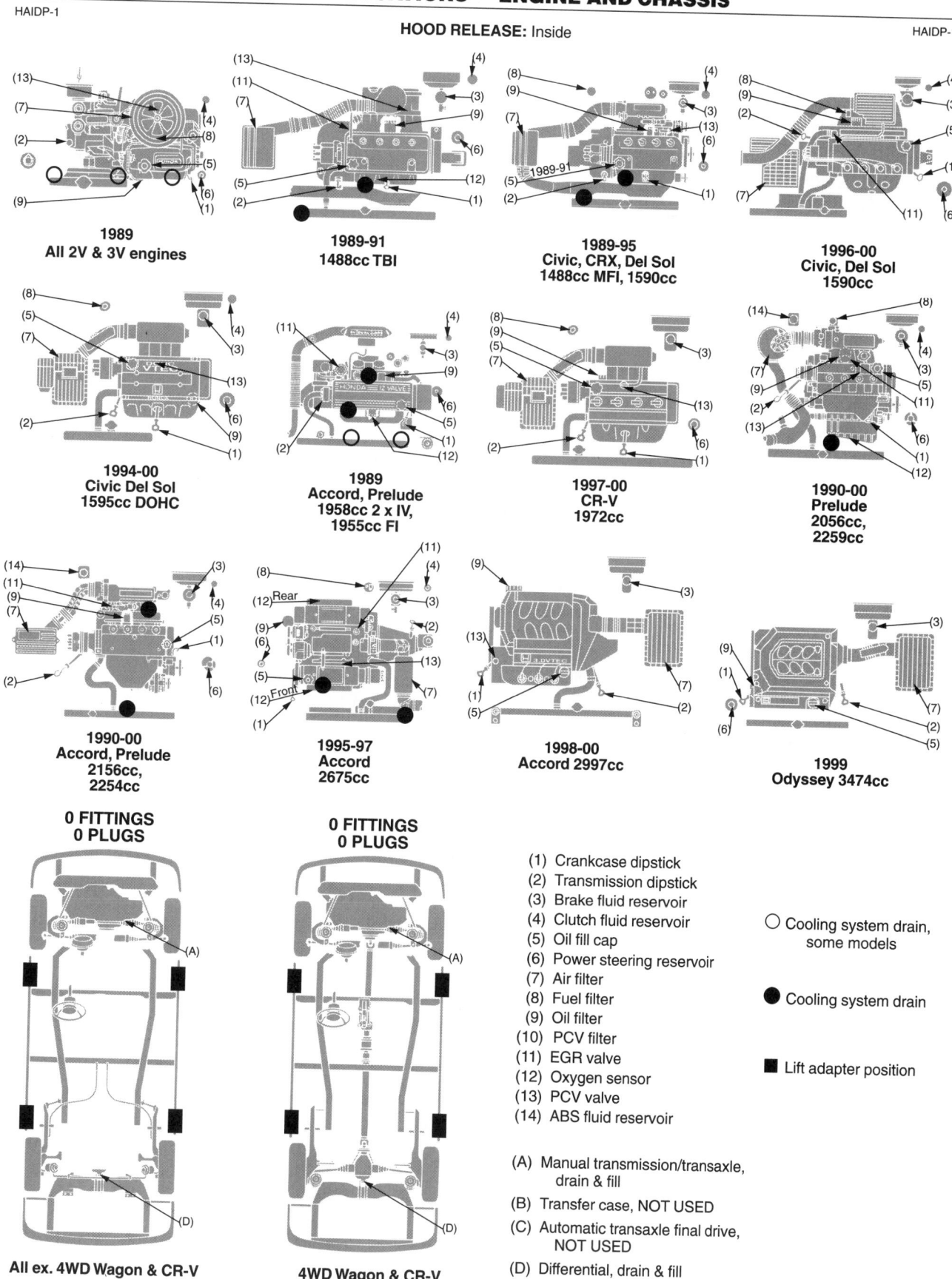

1989
All 2V & 3V engines

1989-91
1488cc TBI

1989-95
Civic, CRX, Del Sol
1488cc MFI, 1590cc

1996-00
Civic, Del Sol
1590cc

1994-00
Civic Del Sol
1595cc DOHC

1989
Accord, Prelude
1958cc 2 x IV,
1955cc FI

1997-00
CR-V
1972cc

1990-00
Prelude
2056cc,
2259cc

1990-00
Accord, Prelude
2156cc,
2254cc

1995-97
Accord
2675cc

1998-00
Accord 2997cc

1999
Odyssey 3474cc

0 FITTINGS
0 PLUGS

0 FITTINGS
0 PLUGS

(1) Crankcase dipstick
(2) Transmission dipstick
(3) Brake fluid reservoir
(4) Clutch fluid reservoir
(5) Oil fill cap
(6) Power steering reservoir
(7) Air filter
(8) Fuel filter
(9) Oil filter
(10) PCV filter
(11) EGR valve
(12) Oxygen sensor
(13) PCV valve
(14) ABS fluid reservoir

(A) Manual transmission/transaxle,
  drain & fill
(B) Transfer case, NOT USED
(C) Automatic transaxle final drive,
  NOT USED
(D) Differential, drain & fill

○ Cooling system drain,
  some models

● Cooling system drain

■ Lift adapter position

All ex. 4WD Wagon & CR-V

4WD Wagon & CR-V

HONDA
1989-91 Civic, CRX, Accord, Prelude

SERVICE AT TIME OR MILEAGE — WHICHEVER OCCURS FIRST

Perform the following maintenance services at the intervals indicated to keep both the vehicle and emission warranties in effect.

MI—MILES IN THOUSANDS
KM—KILOMETERS IN THOUSANDS

SERVICE PERIODICALLY
Brake & clutch fluid
  reservoirs . . . . .check level **HB**

Power steering
  reservoir . . . . .check level **PS**

EVERY 6 MO/7.5 MI—12 KM
Crankcase . . . . .change oil

Front brake pads . . . . .inspect

Oil filter . . . . .replace

EVERY 12 MO/15 MI—24 KM
Brake discs, calipers, hoses,
  lines, fluid . . . . .inspect
1990-91, inspect rear disc brakes

Exhaust system . . . . .inspect

Front wheel alignment . . . .inspect/adjust

Suspension
  mounting bolts . . . . .inspect

Clutch release arm travel . . . . . . .check
1989-90 Civic, CRX, Accord, 1991 Civic

Power steering system . . . . .inspect

Steering & suspension . . . . .inspect
4-wheel steering only

Valve clearance . . . . .adjust

AT FIRST 12 MO/15 MI—24 KM
THEN EVERY 24 MO/30 MI—48 KM
Parking brake . . . . .inspect

Front steering system . . . . .inspect
Ex. 4WS

EVERY 24 MO/30 MI—48 KM
Anti-lock brake
  system operation . . . . .inspect

Brake fluid . . . . .replace **HB**
Inspect rear drum brakes

Cooling system . . . . .change coolant **EC**
Inspect hoses & connections. Initial service at 36 mo/
45 mi (72 km) for coolant change

Drive belt(s) . . . . .inspect/adjust

Fuel lines & connections . . . . . .inspect

Rear differential, 4WD . .change lubricant
1991, initial service at 36 mo/45 mi (72 km)

Transaxle, automatic . . . .change fluid

Transaxle, manual . . . .change lubricant

Air cleaner element . . . . .replace

Choke mechanism ex. FI . . . . . . .clean

Spark plugs . . . . .replace

EVERY 48 MO/60 MI—96 KM
Anti-lock brake system
  high pressure hose . . . . .replace

Catalytic converter heat
  shield . . . . .inspect

Choke ex. FI . . . . .inspect

Crankcase emission
  control system . . . . .inspect
Check PCV valve & blowby filter

Distributor cap & rotor . . . . .inspect

EGR system . . . . .inspect

Evaporative control system . . . .inspect

Fuel filter(s) . . . . .replace
Check fuel lines & connections. Replace carbureted
engine fuel hoses

Idle speed & CO . . . . .inspect
Check idle control & fast idle systems

Ignition timing, control system,
  wiring . . . . .inspect

Intake air temp. control . . . . .inspect
Carbureted engines only

Secondary air supply . . . . .inspect
Carbureted engines only

Throttle control system . . . . .inspect
Carbureted engines only

1990-91,
EVERY 72 MO/90 MI—144 KM
Timing belt . . . . .replace

Water pump . . . . .inspect

SEVERE SERVICE
Clutch freeplay—1989 Accord, 1989-91 Civic, CRX, check every 3 mo/3.75 mi (6 km)

Crankcase—Change oil & filter every: 1989, 3 mo/3 mi (5 km); 1990-91, 3 mo/ 3.75 mi (6 km)

Front & rear brakes, clutch pedal travel—Inspect every 6 mo/7.5 mi (12 km)

Transaxles, automatic & manual—1989-91 Accord, Prelude, change fluid or lubricant every 12 mo/15 mi (24 km) when towing a trailer

KEY TO LUBRICANTS
AF2 DEXRON®-II Automatic
     Transmission Fluid

EC Ethylene Glycol Coolant

GL-5 Gear Oil, API Service GL-5

HB Hydraulic Brake Fluid, DOT 3 or 4

PS Power Steering Fluid
     Honda Power Steering Fluid, Type V Part No.
     08206-9002 PE

SG Motor Oil, API Service SG
     Use Energy Conserving-II oils

CRANKCASE . . . . .SG

CAPACITY, Refill:	Liters	Qt
1989-91 Prelude	3.4	3.6
1990-91 Accord	3.5	3.7
1989-91 Others	3.0	3.2

Capacity shown is without filter. When replacing filter, additional oil may be needed

1989-91
Above 20°F (−7°C) 10W-30
All temperatures . . . . .5W-30[1]
[1] Preferred

TRANSAXLE, Automatic AF2

CAPACITY, Refill[2]:	Liters	Qt
Prelude	2.8	3.0
Civic, CRX: 2WD: 1989-91	2.4	2.5
4WD: 1989-90	2.7	2.9
1991	3.2	3.4
Accord: 1989	3.0	3.2
1990-91	2.4	2.5

[2] With the engine at operating temperature, shift transmission through all gears. Turn engine off and check fluid level within 1 minute

TRANSAXLE, Manual . . . . .SG
Above 20°F (−7°C), 30
Above 0°F (−18°C), 20W-40
All temperatures, 10W-30[3], 10W-40[3]
[3] Preferred

CAPACITY, Refill:	Liters	Pt
1989-91: Civic, CRX, 2WD	1.8	3.8
4WD	2.3	4.8
Prelude	1.9	4.0
Accord, 1989	2.3	4.8
Accord, 1990-91	1.9	4.0

DIFFERENTIAL GL-5
Above 41°F (5°C), 90
Below 41°F (5°C), 80

CAPACITY, Refill:	Liters	Pt
4WD Civic wagon:	0.6	1.2

SERVICE AT TIME OR MILEAGE — WHICHEVER OCCURS FIRST

HAIPM4   HAIPM4

Perform the following maintenance services at the intervals indicated to keep both the vehicle and emission warranties in effect.

MI—MILES IN THOUSANDS
KM—KILOMETERS IN THOUSANDS

SERVICE PERIODICALLY
Brake & clutch fluid
reservoirs . . . . .check level **HB**
Cooling System . . . . . . .check level **EC**
Power steering reservoir .check level **PS**

EVERY 6 MO/7.5 MI—12 KM
Crankcase . . . . .change oil
Oil filter . . . . .replace
Tires, 1995 . . . . .rotate
At mileage interval only

EVERY 12 MO/15 MI—24 KM
Brake calipers, discs, hoses,
lines, fluid . . . . .inspect
Inspect rear disc brakes & 1995-96 linings
Driveshaft boots, 1995 . . . . .inspect
Cooling system, 1995 . . .check level **EC**
Exhaust system . . . . .inspect
Fuel lines & connectors,1995 . . . .inspect
Front wheel alignment . . .inspect/adjust
Power steering
reservoir, 1995 . . . . . . .check level **PS**
Suspension mounting bolts . . . .inspect
Transmission fluid, 1995 . . . .check level
Valve clearance . . . . .adjust
1992-94 All, 1995 Civic CX & VX, Prelude VTEC

AT FIRST 12 MO/15 MI—24 KM
THEN EVERY 24 MO/30 MI—48 KM
Parking brake . . . . .check
Steering system . . . . .inspect

EVERY 24 MO/30 MI—48 KM
Air cleaner element, 1995 . . . . . .replace
At mileage interval only
Anti-lock brake
system operation . . . . .inspect
Brake fluid . . . . .replace **HB**
Inspect rear drum brakes. Also replace ABS fluid **HB**
Cooling system . . . . .change coolant **EC**
Inspect hoses & connections. Initial service at 36 mo/
45 mi (72 km) for coolant change
Parking brake . . . . .check
Steering system . . . . .inspect
Drive belts . . . . .inspect
Fuel lines & connections,
1992-94 . . . . .inspect
Transaxle, automatic . . . . . .change fluid
Transaxle, manual . . . .change lubricant
Air cleaner element . . . . .replace
Spark plugs . . . . .replace
Ex. 1993-95 Prelude 2.2L VTEC
Valve clearance . . . . .adjust
1995 Civic DX & Si, Del Sol, Accord, Odyssey, Prelude
ex. VTEC

AT 36 MO/45 MI—72KM,
THEN EVERY 24MO/30 MI—45 KM
Transaxle, automatic . . . . . .change fluid
Odyssey only

EVERY 48 MO/60 MI—96 KM
Anti-lock brake system
high pressure hose . . . . .replace
Catalytic converter heat
shield . . . . .replace
Crankcase emission control
system . . . . .replace
Check PCV valve & blowby filter
Distributor cap & rotor . . . . .inspect
EGR system . . . . .inspect
1992 as equipped
Evaporative control system . . . . .inspect
1992 only
Fuel filter . . . . .replace
Idle speed . . . . .inspect
Check idle control system. Inspect 1992 CO level
Ignition timing . . . . .inspect
1992 only
Ignition wiring . . . . .inspect

EVERY 72 MO/60 MI—96 KM
Spark plugs . . . . .replace
1993-95 Prelude 2.2L VTEC only

EVERY 72 MO/90 MI—144 KM
Timing belt . . . . .replace
Also replace Odyssey, Prelude balancer belt
Water pump . . . . .inspect

AT 120 MONTHS
Air bag system . . . . .inspect

SEVERE SERVICE
Crankcase—Change oil & filter every: 3 mo/3.75 mi (6 km)

Front & rear brakes, clutch pedal travel & power steering system—Inspect every 6 mo/7.5 mi (12 km)

Power steering system—Inspect every 6 mo/7.5 mi (12 km)

Timing belt—1995 replace and inspect water pump every 60 mi (96 km)

Transaxles, automatic & manual—Accord, Prelude, change fluid or lubricant every: 12 mo/ 15 mi (24 km) when towing a trailer

KEY TO LUBRICANTS

AF2	DEXRON®-II Automatic Transmission Fluid
EC	Ethylene Glycol Coolant
GF-1	Motor Oil, API Service GF-1
GLS	Gear Lubricant, Special Honda MTF Fluid
GL-5	Gear Oil, API Service GL-5
HB	Brake Fluid, DOT 3 or 4
PS	Power Steering Fluid Honda Power Steering Fluid, Type V Part No. 08206-9002 PE
SJ	Motor Oil, API Service SJ Use Energy Conserving-II oils
SLF	Special Lubricant Fluid Honda Premium Formula Automatic Transmission Fluid

CRANKCASE SJ,GF-1

CAPACITY, Refill:	Liters	Qt
Accord	3.5	3.7
VTEC, 1994-97	4.0	4.2
V6	4.0	4.2
Civic & Del Sol	3.0	3.2
B16A2 VTEC	3.7	3.9
Odyssey	3.5	3.7
Prelude: 2.2L	3.5	3.7
2.2L VTEC	4.5	4.8
2.3L	4.0	4.2

Capacity shown is without filter. When replacing filter, additional oil may be needed

Del Sol 1.6L VTEC & Prelude 2.2L VTEC:
Above −2°F (−20°C) . . . . .10W-30[1]
Below 32°F (0°C) .5W-30
All Others:
Above 20°F (−7°C) 10W-30
All temperatures . . . . .5W-30[1]
[1] Preferred

TRANSAXLE, Automatic AF2

CAPACITY, Refill[2]:	Liters	Qt
Accord: 4-cyl.	2.4	2.5
V6	2.7	2.9
Civic, Del Sol	2.7	2.9
Odyssey, Oasis	2.4	2.5
Prelude	2.4	2.5

[2] With the engine at operating temperature, shift transmission through all gears. Turn engine off and check fluid level within 1 minute

TRANSAXLE, Manual . . . . .SG
Above 20°F (−7°C), 1992, 30
Above 0°F (−18°C), 1992, 20W-40
All temperatures, 10W-30[3], 10W-40[3]
[3] Preferred

CAPACITY, Refill:	Liters	Pt
Accord	1.9	4.0
Civic, Del Sol	1.8	3.8
VTEC, 1992-95	2.2	4.6
Prelude	1.9	4.0

HONDA
1996-2000 Accord, Civic, CR-V, Del Sol, Odyssey, Prelude
Includes Isuzu Oasis; Passport—See Isuzu

HAIPM5   HAIPM5

Perform the following maintenance services at the intervals indicated to keep both the vehicle and emission warranties in effect. Canada Models: Maintain the vehicle by following Severe Service intervals.

MI—MILES IN THOUSANDS
KM—KILOMETERS IN THOUSANDS

SERVICE PERIODICALLY
Brake & clutch fluid
  reservoirs . . . . check level **HB**

Cooling System . . . . check level **EC**

Power steering reservoir . check level **PS**

EVERY 12 MO/7.5 MI—12 KM
Crankcase . . . . .change oil

Tires . . . . .rotate
At mileage interval only

EVERY 12 MO/15 MI—24 KM
Brake calipers, discs, hoses,
  lines, fluid . . . . .inspect
Inspect rear disc brakes & 1995-96 linings

Driveshaft boots . . . . .inspect

Cooling system . . . . . . .check level **EC**

Exhaust system . . . . .inspect

Fuel lines & connectors,1996 . . . . .inspect

Front wheel alignment . . . .inspect/adjust

Oil filter . . . . .replace

Power steering
  reservoir . . . . check level **PS**

Suspension mounting bolts . . . . .inspect

Transmission fluid . . . . .check level

EVERY 24 MO/30 MI—48 KM
Air cleaner element . . . . .replace
At mileage interval only

Anti-lock brake
  system operation . . . . .inspect

Cooling system . . . . .change coolant **EC**
Inspect hoses & connections. Initial service at 36 mo/ 45 mi (72 km) for coolant change

Parking brake . . . . .check

Steering system . . . . .inspect

Air cleaner element . . . . .replace

Cabin air filter . . . . .replace
CR-V, 1998-00 Accord

Drive belts . . . . .inspect

Spark plugs . . . . .replace
Ex. 1996 Prelude 2.2L VTEC. 1997-00 Prelude, all. 1998-00 Accord V6, 1999-00 Civic 1595cc & Accord 4-cyl.

Valve clearance . . . . .adjust
Civic, Del Sol, CR-V, initial service only at mileage interval. Odyssey, Oasis, 1997-98 Prelude, adjust only if noisy.

AT 36 MO/45 MI—72KM,
THEN EVERY 24MO/30 MI—45 KM
Transaxle, automatic . . . . . .change fluid
Odyssey, Oasis only

EVERY 36 MO/45 MI—72KM
Brake fluid . . . . .replace **HB**
Also replace ABS fluid **HB**

EVERY 48 MO/60 MI—96 KM
Distributor cap & rotor, 1996 . . . . .inspect

Fuel filter . . . . .replace

Idle speed, 1996 . . . . .inspect
Check idle control system.

Ignition wiring . . . . .inspect

EVERY 72 MO/60 MI—96 KM
Spark plugs . . . . .replace
1996 Prelude 2.2L VTEC only

EVERY 72 MO/90 MI—144 KM
Active torque transfer system
  (ATTS) . . . . .change fluid **SLF**
1997-00 Prelude SH

Differential, rear . . . . .change fluid
CR-V only

Transaxle, automatic ex. CV-T,
  Odyssey, Oasis . . . . .change fluid

Transaxle, manual,
  ex. Odyssey, Oasis . . . . .replace fluid

Timing belt, 1996 . . . . .replace
Also replace Odyssey, Prelude balancer belt

Water pump, 1996 . . . . .inspect

EVERY 84 MO/105 MI—168KM
Idle speed, 1997-00 . . . . .inspect

Spark plugs . . . . .replace
1997-00 Prelude, 1998-00 Accord V6, 1999-00 Civic 1595cc, Odyssey, Accord 4-cyl.

Timing belt, 1997-00 . . . . .replace

Valve clearance . . . . .inspect
1997-00 CR-V, 1999-00 Prelude & Odyssey, 1998-00 Accord 4-cyl. Adjust only if noisy.

Water pump, 1997-00 . . . . .inspect

AT 120 MONTHS
Air bag system, 1996-00 . . . . . . .inspect

SEVERE SERVICE &
1997-00 CANADIAN MODELS
Active torque transfer system (ATTS), Prelude—Change fluid every 24 mo/30 mi (48 km)

Air cleaner element—Change every 12 mo/15 mi (24 km)

Crankcase—Change oil & filter every 6 mo/3.75 mi (6 km)

Differential, CR-V—Change fluid every 48 mo/60 mi (96 km)

Front & rear brakes, clutch pedal travel & power steering system—Inspect every 6 mo/7.5 mi (12 km)

Lights & Controls, vehicle underbody—1997-98, inspect every 12 mo/15 mi (24km)

Power steering system—Inspect every 6 mo/7.5 mi (12 km)

Spark plugs—1999 Civic 1595cc, replace every 24 mo/30 mi (48 km); 2000 Accord, 48 mo/60 mi (96 km)

Timing belt—1996 all, 1998-99 Accord, 1999 Odyssey, replace and inspect water pump every 60 mi (96 km)

Transaxles, automatic & manual—Change fluid or lubricant every 24 mo/ 30 mi (48 km)

KEY TO LUBRICANTS
EC	Ethylene Glycol Coolant
GF-1	Motor Oil, API Service GF-1
GLS	Gear Lubricant, Special Honda MTF Fluid
GL-5	Gear Oil, API Service GL-5
HB	Brake Fluid, DOT 3 or 4
PS	Power Steering Fluid Honda Power Steering Fluid, Type S, V Part No. 08206-9002 PE
SJ	Motor Oil, API Service SJ Use Energy Conserving-II oils
SLF	Special Lubricant Fluid With CVT, Genuine Honda CVT Fluid. All others including ATTS: Honda Premium Formula Automatic Transmission Fluid

CRANKCASE SJ,GF-1
CAPACITY, Refill:	Liters	Qt
Accord: 4 cyl. 1996-97	3.5	3.7
1998-00	4.0	4.2
V6	4.0	4.2
Civic, D16Y7 eng.	3.3	3.5
D16Y5, D16Y8 eng.	3.0	3.2
B16A2 eng.	3.7	3.9
CR-V	3.5	3.7
Del Sol	3.0	3.2
B16A2 eng.	3.7	3.9
Odyssey, Oasis: 1996-97	3.5	3.7
1998-00	4.0	4.2
Prelude: 2.2L	3.5	3.7
2.2L VTEC	4.5	4.8
2.3L	4.0	4.2

Capacity shown is without filter. When replacing filter, additional oil may be needed

Prelude 2.2L VTEC:
Above −2°F (−20°C) . . . . .10W-30[1]
Below 32°F (0°C) 5W-30
CR-V, Prelude, 1998-00 Accord, 1999-00 Odyssey:
Above 15°F (−10°C) 10W-30
Below 95°F (35°) 5W-30
All Others:
Above 20°F (−7°C) 10W-30
All temperatures . . . . .5W-30[1]
1 Preferred

TRANSAXLE, Automatic
With CVT . . . . .SLF
Genuine Honda CVT Fluid
All others .SLF
CAPACITY, Refill[2]:	Liters	Qt
Accord: 4-cyl.	2.4	2.5
V6: 1996-97	2.7	2.9
1998-00	2.9	3.1
Civic, Del Sol	2.7	2.9
with CVT	3.9	4.1
CR-V: 2WD	2.7	2.9
4WD	2.9	3.1
Odyssey, Oasis: 1996-98	2.4	2.5
1999-00	2.9	3.1
Prelude	2.4	2.5

2 With the engine at operating temperature, shift transmission through all gears. Turn engine off and check fluid level within 1 minute

TRANSAXLE, Manual . . . . .GLS
CAPACITY, Refill:	Liters	Pt
Accord	1.9	4.0
Civic, Del Sol	1.8	3.8
VTEC	2.2	4.6
CR-V	1.7	3.6
Prelude	1.9	4.0
VTEC, 1997-00	2.1	4.4

DIFFERENTIAL
CR-V . . . . .SLF
Genuine Honda CVT Fluid
CAPACITY, Refill:	Liters	Pt.
All	1.0	2.2

SERVICE LOCATIONS — ENGINE AND CHASSIS

HOOD RELEASE: Inside

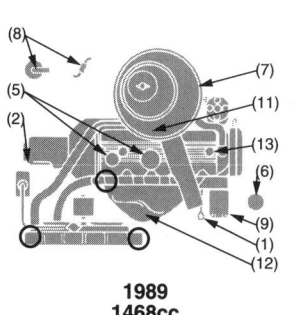

1989
1468cc
Excel

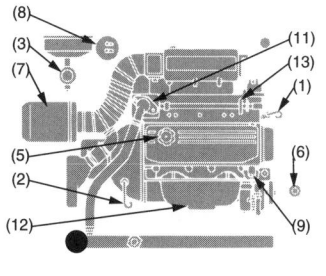

1990-94
1468cc FI
Excel, Scoupe

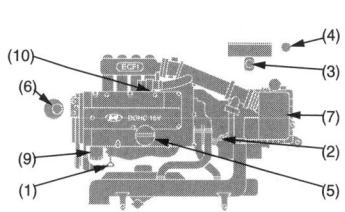

1993-00
1495cc

1996-00
1795cc, 1975cc
Elantra, Tiburon

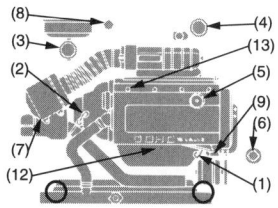

1992-95
1597cc DOHC,
1834cc DOHC, Elantra
1992-98
1997cc DOHC, Sonata

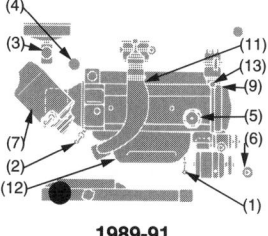

1989-91
2351cc
Sonata

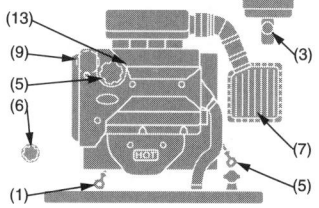

1999-00
2351cc
Sonata

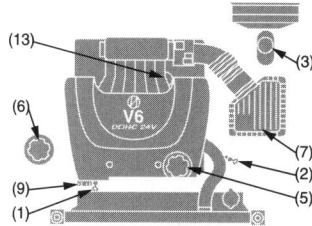

1999-00
V6 2493cc
Sonata

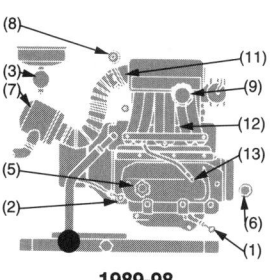

1989-98
V6 2972cc
Sonata

(1) Crankcase dipstick
(2) Transmission dipstick
(3) Brake fluid reservoir
(4) Clutch fluid reservoir
(5) Oil fill cap
(6) Power steering reservoir
(7) Air filter
(8) Fuel filter
(9) Oil filter
(10) PCV filter
(11) EGR valve
(12) Oxygen sensor
(13) PCV valve

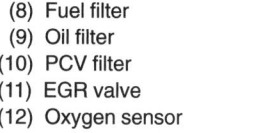

0 FITTINGS
0 PLUGS

Accent, Excel,
Scoupe

0 FITTINGS
0 PLUGS

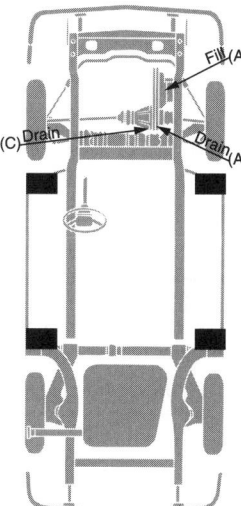

Elantra, Sonata,
Tiburon

■ Lift adapter position   ● Cooling system drain

○ Cooling system drain, some models

(A) Manual transmission/transaxle, drain & fill

(B) Transfer case, NOT USED

(C) Automatic transaxle final drive, drain & fill

(D) Differential, drain & fill

SERVICE AT TIME OR MILEAGE — WHICHEVER OCCURS FIRST

Perform the following maintenance services at the intervals indicated to keep both the vehicle and emission warranties in effect.

MI—MILES IN THOUSANDS
KM—KILOMETERS IN THOUSANDS

EVERY 6 MO/7.5 MI—12 KM
Driveshaft & steering
  boots, Canada . . . . .inspect

Front brakes . . . . .inspect
Calipers, rotors, replace pads when lining is .040 in. thick
or less. Canada, inspect parking brake.

Air cleaner element, Canada . . . .inspect

Choke, Canada . . . . .inspect

Cooling system, Canada . . . . . . .inspect

Crankcase . . . . .change oil

Fuel filter & lines, Canada . . . . .inspect

Transmission, manual,
  Canada . . . . .check level

Oil filter . . . . .replace

Vacuum hoses, Canada . . . . . . .inspect

EVERY 12 MO/15 MI—24 KM
Brake lines & hoses . . . . .inspect
U.S., check fluid level

Drive shafts & CV boots, U.S. . . .inspect

Exhaust system . . . . .inspect

Rear brakes . . . . .inspect
Inspect drums, replace lining when .040 in. or less. Also
check parking brake adjustment.

Steering gear rack,
  linkage, & boots . . . . .inspect

Brake master cylinder . . .check level HB

Cooling system, U.S. . . . . .inspect

Cooling system,
  Canada . . . . .replace coolant EC
Flush system

Drive belts . . . . .inspect

Idle speed . . . . .check/adjust

Power steering . . . . . . .check level AF2

Spark plugs, Canada . . . . .inspect

Throttle positioner . . . . .inspect
Initial service only

Trans., automatic, Canada . . .check level

Valve clearance, 4-cyl. . . . . .adjust
Sonata jet valve only

EVERY 24 MO/30 MI—48 KM
Rear wheel
  bearings . . . . . . .inspect/lubricate LM

Transmission, manual &
  automatic . . . . .change fluid

Air cleaner element . . . . .replace

Brake fluid, U.S. . . . . .replace HB
Canada, inspect level

Choke, U.S. . . . . .inspect

Cooling system,
  U.S. . . . . .replace coolant EC
Flush system

Drive belt . . . . .replace
Alternator only

EGR system, Canada . . . . .inspect

Fuel filter & lines, U.S. . . . . .inspect

Spark plugs . . . . .replace

Timing belt, Canada . . . . .inspect

EVERY 40 MO/50 MI—80 KM
Brake fluid, Canada . . . . .replace

Carbon canister . . . . .replace

EGR system, U.S. . . . . .inspect

Evaporative emission
  control system . . . . .inspect

Fuel filter . . . . .replace

Fuel & vapor hoses . . . . .replace

Ignition timing . . . . .check/adjust
Excel only

Ignition wires, Excel . . . . .replace

Oxygen sensor . . . . .replace

PCV valve . . . . .inspect

Vacuum hoses . . . . .replace

Throttle positioner . . . . .inspect

EVERY 48 MO/60 MI—96 KM
Timing belt . . . . .replace

SEVERE SERVICE
Air cleaner element & U.S. PCV system—
Inspect/replace more frequently

Brake fluid, transmission lubricant—
Canada, replace every 12 mo/15 mi
(24km)

Crankcase—Change oil & filter every
3 mo/3 mi (4.8 km)

Exhaust system—Canada, inspect every
6 mo/7.5 mi (12 km)

Brake pads & linings—Inspect more
often

Spark plugs—U.S., replace every 18 mo/
24 mi (40 km)

**Steering, suspension, driveshafts, &
boots—**U.S., inspect every 6 mo/7.5 mi
(12 km)

KEY TO LUBRICANTS

AF2	DEXRON®-II Automatic Transmission Fluid
AP3	HYUNDAI ATF Automatic Transmission Fluid or MOPAR ATF-PLUS
EC	Ethylene Glycol Coolant
GL-4	Gear Oil, API Service GL-4
HB	Hydraulic Brake Fluid, DOT 3
LM	Lithium Grease, EP
SG	Motor Oil, API Service SG

CRANKCASE .SG

CAPACITY, Refill:	Liters	Qt
Excel, Precis	3.0	3.2
Sonata: 4-cyl.	3.5	3.7
V6	3.7	3.9

Capacity shown is without filter. When replacing filter, additional oil may be needed.
Above 32°F (0°C) 20W-20, 20W-40, 20W-50
Above -10°F (-23°C) . .10W-30, 10W-40, 10W-50
Below 60°F (16°C) . . . . . .5W-20[1], 5W-30, 5W-40
1 Not recommended for sustained high speed driving

TRANSAXLE, Automatic AP3

CAPACITY, Refill[2]:	Liters	Qt
All models	4.0	4.2

2 With the engine at operating temperature, shift transmission through all gears. Check fluid level in NEUTRAL and add fluid as needed.

TRANSAXLE,
  Manual 75W-85W, 75W-90 GL-4

CAPACITY, Refill:	Liters	Pt
Excel, Precis	2.1	4.4
Sonata	2.5	5.4

SERVICE AT TIME OR MILEAGE — WHICHEVER OCCURS FIRST

HIIPM3   HIIPM3

Perform the following maintenance services at the intervals indicated to keep both the vehicle and emission warranties in effect.

MI—MILES IN THOUSANDS
KM—KILOMETERS IN THOUSANDS

U.S., AT FIRST & SECOND
5 MO/7.5 MI—12 KM;
THEN EVERY 10 MO/7.5 MI—12 KM
CANADA,
EVERY 6 MO/7.5 MI—12 KM

Crankcase . . . . .change oil
Turbo, change oil & filter every 6 mo/5 mi (8 km)

Oil filter . . . . .replace

U.S., AT FIRST 10 MO/15 MI—24 KM;
THEN EVERY 20 MO/15 MI—24 KM
CANADA, EVERY 15 MI—24 KM

Brake lines & hoses . . . . .inspect

Drive shafts & CV boots . . . . . . .inspect

Front brakes . . . . .inspect
Calipers, rotors, replace pads when lining is .040 in. thick or less

Brake master cylinder . . .check level **HB**

Cooling system 1990 . . . . .inspect

Fuel lines & connections 1990 . . .inspect

Power steering . . . . . . .check level **AF2**

Power steering system 1990 . . . .inspect

Transaxle, automatic . . . . . .check level

Valve clearance, 1990-94 4-cyl. . . .adjust
Sonata 2.4L, adjust jet valve only

U.S., EVERY 30 MO/30 MI—48 KM
CANADA, EVERY 30 MI—48 KM

Body & chassis nuts and bolts . . . .torque
1995-96 Accent only

Exhaust system . . . . .inspect

Rear brakes . . . . .inspect
Inspect drums, replace lining when .040 in. or less. Also check parking brake adjustment.

Steering gear rack,
    linkage & boots . . . . .inspect

Suspension, 1995-96 . . . . .inspect
Check ball joints and dust covers

Rear wheel bearings . . . . . .inspect **LM**

Transaxle, automatic . . . . . .change fluid

Transaxle, manual . . . . .check level

Air cleaner element . . . . .replace

Brake fluid . . . . .replace **HB**
Canada, at least every 24 months

Cooling system . . . . .replace coolant **EC**
Flush system. Canada, at least every 24 months.

Drive belts . . . . .inspect

Spark plugs . . . . .replace
Ex. 1992-96 V6

Timing belt . . . . .inspect
1990, 1995-96 1.5L

U.S. EVERY 60 MO/52.5 MI—84 KM
CANADA, EVERY 52.5 MI—84 KM

Carbon canister 1990 . . . . .replace

EGR system 1990 . . . . .inspect

Fuel filter . . . . .replace

Fuel & vapor hoses . . . . .replace
1990 All, 1991 Canada only

Fuel lines & connections . . . . . . .inspect
1991 U.S., 1992-94 All

Fuel tank cap . . . . .inspect
1990 All, 1991 Canada only, replace

Ignition timing . . . . .check/adjust
1990 Excel only

Oxygen sensor 1990 . . . . .replace

PCV valve 1990 . . . . .inspect

Vacuum hoses . . . . .replace
1990 All, 1991 Canada only, replace

Vacuum & vapor hoses . . . . . . .inspect
1991 U.S. 1992-94 all

U.S., EVERY 70 MO/60 MI—96 KM
CANADA, EVERY 60 MI—96 KM

Ignition wires 1990 . . . . .inspect

Drive belt 1990 . . . . .replace
Alt. & PS only

Spark plugs . . . . .replace
1992-96 V6

Timing belt . . . . .replace

SEVERE SERVICE

Air cleaner element—Inspect/replace more frequently

Crankcase—Change oil & filter every 3 mo/3 mi (4.8 km)

Brake system—Inspect more often

Spark plugs—Replace every 18 mo/24 mi (40 km)

Steering system, driveshafts, & boots— Inspect every 6 mo/7.5 mi (12 km)

Transaxle, automatic—1994-96, change fluid every 10 mo/15 mi (24 km)

KEY TO LUBRICANTS

AF2	DEXRON®-II Automatic Transmission Fluid
AP3	Hyundai ATF Automatic Transmission Fluid or MOPAR ATF-PLUS
CD	Motor Oil, API Service CD
EC	Ethylene Glycol Coolant
GL-4	Gear Oil, API Service GL-4
HB	Hydraulic Brake Fluid, DOT 3
LM	Lithium Grease, EP
SG	Motor Oil, API Service SG

CRANKCASE . . . . .SG, SG/CD

CAPACITY, Refill:	Liters	Qt
Accent, Excel, Precis	3.0	3.2
Scoupe: 1990-92	3.0	3.2
1993-95	2.9	3.1
Elantra: 1992-95	4.0	4.2
1996	3.7	3.9
Sonata: 2.0L	3.3	3.5
2.4L	3.5	3.7
3.0L	3.7	3.9

Capacity shown is without filter. When replacing filter, additional oil may be needed.

Turbo Models:
Above 32°F (0°C) 20W-20, 20W-40
Above -10°F (-23°C) 10W-30
Extremely cold weather 5W-30

All Other Models:
Above 32°F (0°C) 20W-40, 20W-50
Above -10°F
    (-23°C) 10W-30, 10W-40, 10W-50
Below 60°F (16°C),
    1990-93 . . . . .5W-20[1], 5W-30, 5W-40
Below 60°F (38°C),
    1994 ex. Excel 5W-30, 5W-40
    1995-96, ex. Sonata
Below 60°F (16°C),
    1995-96 Sonata, 1994 Excel . .5W-30, 5W-40

[1] Not recommended for sustained high speed driving

TRANSAXLE, Automatic

1990-95 . . . . .AP3, SLF
1996 . . . . .SLF

CAPACITY, Initial Refill[2]:	Liters	Qt
All models	4.0	4.2

[2] With the engine at operating temperature, shift transmission through all gears. Check fluid level in NEUTRAL and add fluid as needed.

TRANSAXLE,
Manual 75W-85W, 75W-90 GL-4

CAPACITY, Refill:	Liters	Pt
Accent	2.2	4.6
Excel, Precis:		
4-speed	1.7	3.6
5-speed	1.8	3.8
Elantra: 1992-95	1.8	3.8
1996	2.1	4.4
Scoupe: 1990-92		
4-speed	1.7	3.6
5-speed	1.8	3.8
1993-95	2.1	4.4

HYUNDAI
1997-2000 All Models

Perform the following maintenance services at the intervals indicated to keep both the vehicle and emission warranties in effect.

MI—MILES IN THOUSANDS
KM—KILOMETERS IN THOUSANDS

SERVICE PERIODICALLY
Brake & clutch . . . . .check level **HB**

Cooling system . . . . . . .check level **EC**

Power steering
reservoir . . . . .check level **AF2**

Transmission, automatic . . . .check level

1998-00 CANADA,
EVERY 6 MO/6 MI—9 KM
1997 ALL; 1998-00 U.S.,
EVERY 6 MO/7.5 MI—12 KM
Crankcase . . . . .change oil

Oil filter . . . . .replace

Drive belts . . . . .inspect
1998-00 Canada models & 1999-00 V6

Transaxle, automatic . . . . . .check level

EVERY 12 MO/15 MI—24 KM
Brake lines & hoses . . . . .inspect

Cooling system . . . . . . .check level **EC**
1998-00 Canada models

Drive shafts & CV boots . . . . . . .inspect

Exhaust system . . . . .inspect

Front brakes . . . . .inspect
Calipers, rotors, replace pads when lining is .040 in. thick or less

Suspension & steering . . . . .inspect
Includes suspension mounting bolts, linkage, boots, ball joints, seals, & steering gearbox.
Ex. 1998-00 Canada models

Air-conditioning system . . . . . . .inspect
Ex. 1998 Canada models

Transaxle, automatic, 1997-98 .check level

Body . . . . .inspect
1998-00 Canada only. Inspect and lubricate lock, hinges, latches.

EVERY 24 MO/30 MI—48 KM
Fuel lines & connections . . . . . . .inspect
Also inspect fuel filter cap

Power steering system . . . . .inspect
Includes pump, belt, hoses

Rear brakes . . . . .inspect
Inspect drums, replace lining when .040 in. or less. Also check parking brake adjustment.

Suspension & steering . . . . .inspect
1998 Canada. Includes suspension mounting bolts, linkage, boots, ball joints, seals, and steering gearbox.

Transaxle, manual . . . . .check level

Air cleaner element . . . . .replace

Brake fluid . . . . .replace **HB**

Drive belt . . . . .inspect
Ex 1999 V6

Cooling system . . . . .replace coolant **EC**
Flush system

Spark plugs . . . . .replace
Ex. 2.4L & V6

Vapor hoses . . . . .inspect

Cabin air filter . . . . .replace
1999-00 Sonata V6 only

EVERY 30 MO/ 37.5 MI—60 KM
Drive belts . . . . .inspect
Ex. 1998-00 Canada models

Timing belt . . . . .inspect
All ex. 1998-00 Canada Accent, Elantra, Tiburon

EVERY 42 MO/52.5 MI—84 KM
Fuel filter . . . . .replace

Vacuum & ventilation hoses . . . .inspect

EVERY 48 MO/60 MI—100 KM
Drive belt . . . . .replace
Alt. & WP only

Spark plugs . . . . .replace
2.4L & V6

Timing belt . . . . .replace

EVERY 84 MO/105 MI—168 KM
Transaxle,
automatic, 1999-00 . . . . . .change fluid
Also replace filter

SEVERE SERVICE
Air cleaner element—Inspect/replace more frequently

Brake system—Inspect more often

Crankcase—Ex. 1998 Canada, change oil & filter every 3 mo/3 mi (4.8 km)

Driveshafts & CV boots—Inspect every 6 mo/7.5 mi (12 km)

Spark plugs—Replace : 1997-98, every 18 mo/24 mi (40 km). 1999-00, more frequently

Transaxle, automatic—Change fluid: 30 mi (48 km)

KEY TO LUBRICANTS

AF2	DEXRON®-II Automatic Transmission Fluid
CD	Motor Oil, API Service CD
EC	Ethylene Glycol Coolant
GL-4	Gear Oil, API Service GL-4
HB	Hydraulic Brake Fluid, DOT 3
SG	Motor Oil, API Service SG
SLF	Hyundai ATF Automatic Transmission Fluid

CRANKCASE . . . . .SG, SG/CD

CAPACITY, Refill:	Liters	Qt
Accent	3.0	3.2
Elantra	3.7	3.9
Sonata: 2.0L	3.3	3.5
2.4L	3.7	3.9
2.5L	4.2	4.4
3.0L	3.7	3.9
Tiburon	3.7	3.9

Capacity shown is without filter. When replacing filter, additional oil may be needed.
Above 32°F (0°C) 20W-40, 20W-50
Above -10°F (-23°C) . .10W-30, 10W-40, 10W-50
Below 100°F (38°C) 5W-30, 5W-40

TRANSAXLE, Automatic . . . .**SLF**

CAPACITY, Initial Refill[1]:	Liters	Qt
All models	4.0	4.2

1 With the engine at operating temperature, shift transmission through all gears. Check fluid level in NEUTRAL and add fluid as needed.

TRANSAXLE,
Manual 75W-85W, 75W-90 **GL-4**

CAPACITY, Refill:	Liters	Pt
Accent	2.2	4.6
Elantra	2.1	4.4
Sonata: 1997-98	1.8	3.8
1999-00	2.1	4.4
Tiburon	2.1	4.4

SERVICE LOCATIONS — ENGINE AND CHASSIS

HOOD RELEASE: Inside

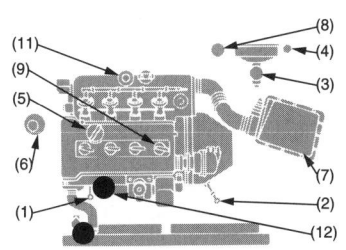

1991-00
1998cc G20

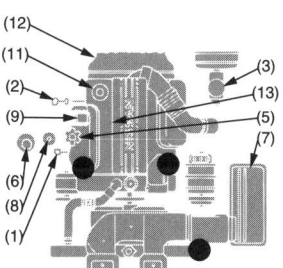

1990-92
2960cc M30

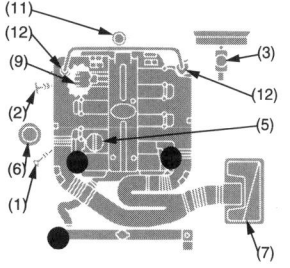

1993-97
2960cc J30

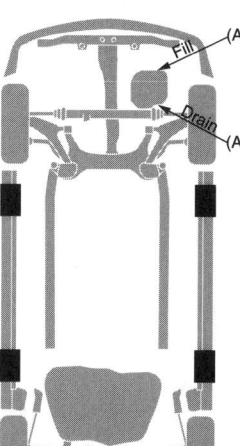

0 FITTINGS
0 PLUGS

1991-00
G20

1995-00
I30
2960cc

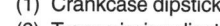

1990-00
4130cc, 4494cc, Q45

(1) Crankcase dipstick
(2) Transmission dipstick
(3) Brake fluid reservoir
(4) Clutch fluid reservoir
(5) Oil fill cap
(6) Power steering reservoir
(7) Air filter
(8) Fuel filter
(9) Oil filter
(10) PCV filter
(11) EGR valve
(12) Oxygen sensor
(13) PCV valve
(14) Active suspension fluid reservoir
(15) Traction control system reservoir
(16) Automatic transmission fluid filter

0 FITTINGS
0 PLUGS

1990-92
M30

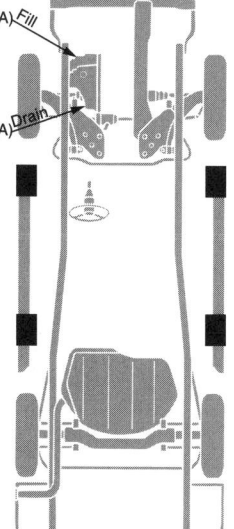

0 FITTINGS
0 PLUGS

1995-00
I30

0 FITTINGS
0 PLUGS

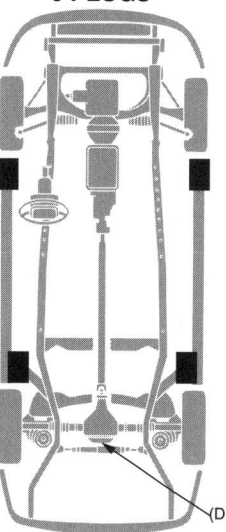

1993-97
J30

0 FITTINGS
0 PLUGS

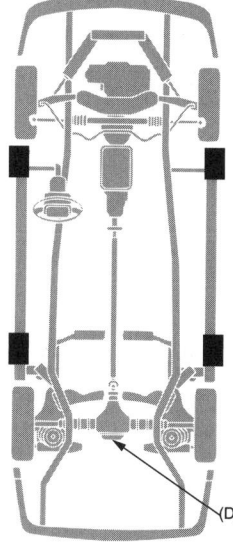

1990-00
Q45

● Cooling system drain

■ Lift adapter position

(A) Manual transmission/transaxle, drain & fill

(B) Transfer case, NOT USED

(C) Automatic transaxle final drive, NOT USED

(D) Differential, drain & fill

131

CHEK-CHART

SERVICE AT TIME OR MILEAGE — WHICHEVER OCCURS FIRST

IIIPM1   IIIPM1

Perform the following maintenance services at the intervals indicated to keep the vehicle warranties in effect.
W   SERVICE TO MAINTAIN EMISSION WARRANTY

MI—MILES IN THOUSANDS
KM—KILOMETERS IN THOUSANDS

SERVICE PERIODICALLY
Brake & clutch master cylinders . . . . .**HB**
Check systems

Cooling system . . . . .inspect

Power steering reservoir . . . .check level
1990-96, **AF2**
1997-00, **AF2, AF3**
Inspect lines & hoses

Traction control fluid
reservoir . . . . .check level **HB**
Q45 as equipped

Body .lubricate
Includes cables, linkages, locks, latches, hinges. Also inspect seat belts

EVERY 6 MO/7.5 MI—12 KM
Battery . . . . .check level

W Crankcase . . . . .change oil

W Oil filter .replace
1990-95 At first oil change, then every other
1996-00 at every oil change

Tires . . . . .rotate
At mileage interval only

EVERY 12 MONTHS
Underbody . . . . .flush/clean

EVERY 12 MO/15 MI—24 KM
Brake system . . . . .inspect
Inspect linings, drums, disc pads, lines & hoses

Differential, RWD . . . . .check level

Drive shaft boots, FWD . . . . . . .inspect

Exhaust system . . . . .inspect
1990-92

Transmission/Transaxle,
manual & automatic . . . . . . .check level

Active suspension
fluid reservoir . . . . . . .check level **SLF**
J30, Q45 As equipped

Automatic speed
control device, 2000 . . . . .inspect
Input vacuum hoses

Cabin air filter . . . . .replace
1996-00 Q45, 1999-00 G20

EVERY 24 MO/30 MI—48 KM
Suspension & steering
linkage . . . . .inspect

Cooling system . . . .change coolant **EC**
1991-97, initial service at 48 mo/60 mi (96 km)

Exhaust system . . . . .inspect
1993-95

W Air cleaner element . . . . .replace
At mileage interval only

Fuel & fuel vapor lines . . . . .inspect

PCV hoses . . . . .inspect
1990-92

W Spark plugs . . . . .replace
Ex. platinum-tipped. At mileage interval only

Super HICAS linkage . . . . .inspect
1990-94 Q45†
1993-97 J30†

EVERY 60 MI—96 KM
Active suspension
fluid reservoir . . . . . .change fluid **SLF**
J30, Q45 As equipped

Drive belts . . . . .inspect
Inspect every 12 mo/15 mi (24 km) thereafter

Spark plugs, 1990-00 . . . . .replace
Platinum-tipped only

W Timing belt . . . . .replace
1990-93 V6 only

EVERY 105 MI—168 KM
Spark plugs, 2000 . . . . .replace
Platinum-tipped only

W Timing belt . . . . .replace
1994-97 J30 only

AT 120 MONTHS
Air bag system . . . . .inspect

SERVICE AS REQUIRED
W Fuel filter . . . . .replace

Valve clearance . . . . .adjust
G20 & I30 only

SEVERE SERVICE
Cabin air filter—1996-99 inspect every 6 mo/7.5 mi (12 km)

W **Crankcase**—Gasoline, change oil & filter every 3 mo/3.75 mi (6 km)

Steering, suspension, locks, hinges, exhaust, brake system, Super HICAS linkage—inspect every 6 mo/ 7.5 mi (12 km)

Transmission, manual & automatic; differential—Change fluid or lubricant every 24 mo/30 mi (48 km) when towing a trailer or driving on rough or muddy roads

KEY TO LUBRICANTS
AF2	Dexron®-II Automatic Transmission Fluid
AF3	Dexron®-III Automatic Transmission Fluid
EC	Ethylene Glycol Coolant
GF-2	Motor Oil, Meeting ILSAC GF-2 (API★)
GL-4	Gear Oil, API Service GL-4
GL-5	Gear Oil, API Service GL-5
HB	Hydraulic Brake Fluid, DOT 3
SJ	Motor Oil, API Service SJ
SLF	Special Lubricant—Fluid
	Nissan Fluid-A Active Suspension

CRANKCASE . . . . .SJ, GF-2
CAPACITY, Refill:	Liters	Qt
G20	3.2	3.4
M30	4.0	4.3
J30	3.9	4.1
I30	3.7	3.9
Q45: 1990-96	5.6	5.9
1997-00	5.0	5.3

Capacity is without filter. When replacing filter, additional oil may be needed
Above 0°F (-18°C) . . . . .10W-30[1], 10W-40
Below 60°F (16°C), 1993-97 J30,
    1990-94 Q45 .5W-30
All temperatures G20, I30, M30 . . . . .5W-30[2]
All temperatures, 1995-00 Q45 . . . . .5W-30
[1] Preferred for J30, Q45
[2] Preferred

TRANSMISSION,
TRANSAXLE, Automatic AF2, AF3
1990-95, use Dexron-II or Nissan branded fluid while vehicle is under warranty, then use Dexron-III
CAPACITY Total Fill[3]:	Liters	Qt
G20	7.0	7.3
I30	9.4	10.0
M30, J30	8.3	8.7
Q45: 1990	8.6	9.1
1991-93	10.2	10.8
1994-00	10.5	11.1

[3] Total (dry) fill shown. Use less fluid when refilling

TRANSAXLE, Manual
1998-00 I30 . . . . .80W-90 **GL-4**
1990-97 All **GL-4**
Above 50°F (10°C), 140; 30° to 100°F (-1° to 38°C), 90; 10° to 85°F (-12° to 29°C), 85W; below 100°F (38°C), 75W-90, 80W-90; below 85°F (29°C), 80W; below 50°F (10°C), 75W
1999-00 G20 . . . . .75W-90 **GL-4**
CAPACITY, Refill:	Liters	Pt
G20	3.6	7.6
I30	4.5	9.5

DIFFERENTIAL GL-5
Above 50°F (10°C), 140; 30° to 100°F (-1° to 38°C), 90; 10° to 85°F (-12° to 29°C), 85W; below 100°F (38°C), 75W-90, 80W-90; below 85°F (29°C), 80W; below 50°F (10°C), 75W
CAPACITY, Refill:	Liters	Pt
M30	1.3	2.5
J30	1.5	3.1
Q45: 1990-94	1.5	3.1
1995-00	1.3	2.5

ISUZU

1989-2000 All Models—Includes Acura SLX & Honda Passport
Hombre—See Chevrolet S10; Oasis—See Honda Odyssey

SERVICE LOCATIONS — ENGINE AND CHASSIS

IUIDP-1   IUIDP-1

HOOD RELEASE: Inside

(1) Crankcase dipstick
(2) Transmission dipstick
(3) Brake fluid reservoir
(4) Clutch fluid reservoir
(5) Oil fill cap
(6) Power steering reservoir
(7) Air filter
(8) Fuel filter
(9) Oil filter
(10) PCV filter
(11) EGR valve
(12) Oxygen sensor
(13) PCV valve

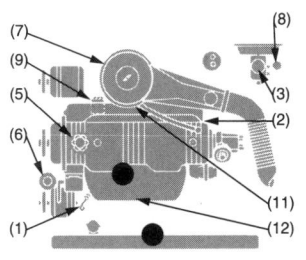

1989
I-Mark
1471cc 2V

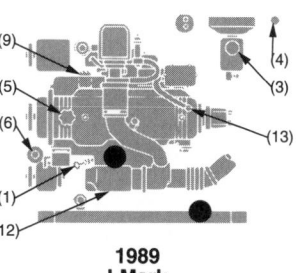

1989
I-Mark
1471cc Turbo

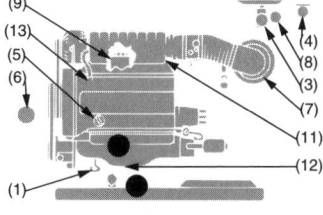

1989-93
I-Mark, Stylus, Impulse FWD
1588cc DOHC,
1809cc DOHC

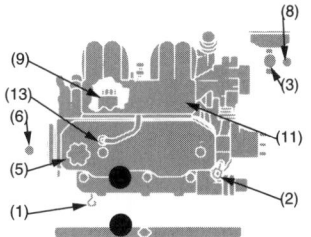

1990-93
Stylus, Impulse
1588cc SOHC

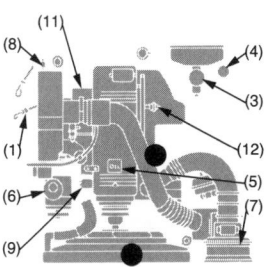

1989
Impulse
1994cc Turbo

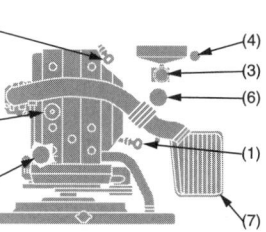

1998-00
Amigo, Rodeo
2198cc

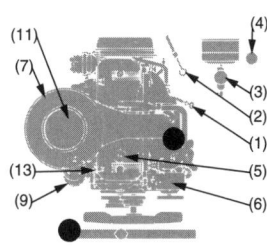

1989-95
Amigo, Pickup, Trooper
2256cc 2V

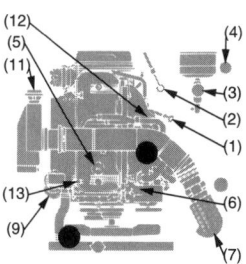

1989-97
Amigo, Pickup, Trooper
Impulse, Rodeo
2256cc FI,
2559cc

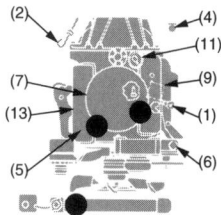

1989-93
Pickup, Trooper,
Rodeo
V6 2.8L, 3.1L

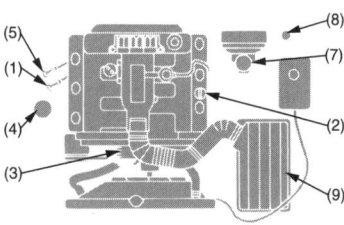

1992-97
Trooper, Rodeo
V6 3.2L

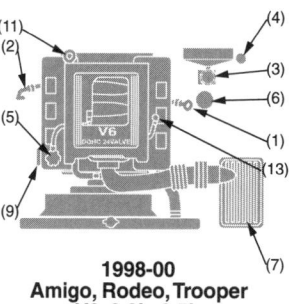

1998-00
Amigo, Rodeo, Trooper
V6, 3.2L, 3.5L

● Cooling system drain   ○ Cooling system drain, some models

ISUZU

1989-2000 All Models—Includes Acura SLX & Honda Passport
Hombre—See Chevrolet S10; Oasis—See Honda Odyssey

SERVICE LOCATIONS — ENGINE AND CHASSIS

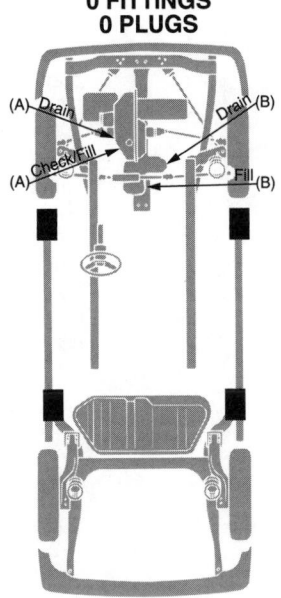

0 FITTINGS
0 PLUGS

(A) Drain   Drain (B)

(A) Check/Fill

(A)   Fill (B)

1989
I-Mark
FWD
1990-93
Stylus, Impulse FWD

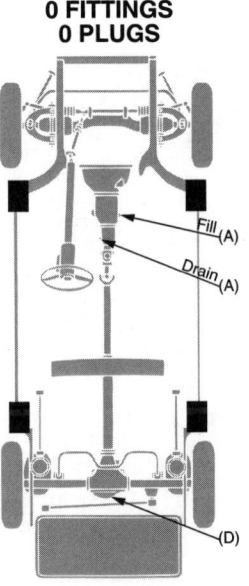

0 FITTINGS
0 PLUGS

Fill (A)

Drain (A)

(D)

1989
Impulse

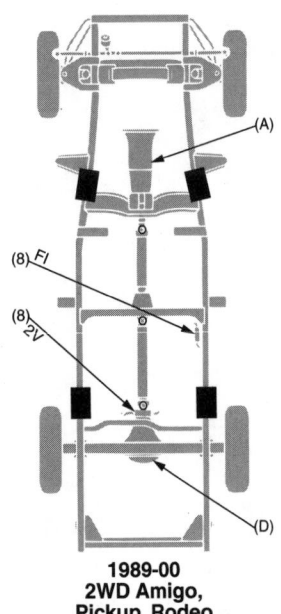

(A)

(8) Fl

(8) 2V

(D)

1989-00
2WD Amigo,
Pickup, Rodeo

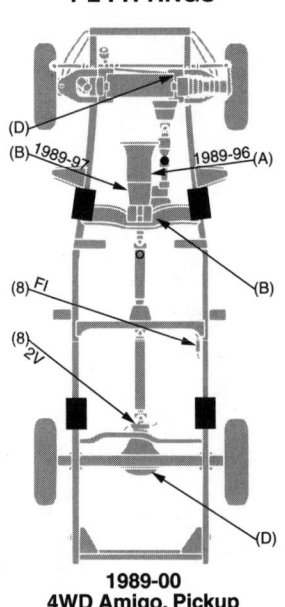

1-2 FITTINGS

(D)

(B) 1989-97   1989-96 (A)

(B)

(8) Fl

(8) 2V

(D)

1989-00
4WD Amigo, Pickup
Trooper, Rodeo, Vehicross

• Fitting   ○ Fitting, some models   ■ Lift adapter position

(A) Manual transmission/transaxle, drain & fill
(B) Transfer case, drain & fill
(C) Automatic transaxle, final drive, NOT USED
(D) Differential, drain & fill

SERVICE AT TIME OR MILEAGE — WHICHEVER OCCURS FIRST

IUIPM1　　　　　　　　　　　　　　　　　　　　IUIPM1

Perform the following maintenance services at the intervals indicated to keep both the vehicle and emission warranties in effect.

MI—MILES IN THOUSANDS
KM—KILOMETERS IN THOUSANDS

EVERY 12 MONTHS
Air conditioning system . . . . .inspect

AT FIRST 7.5 MI—12 KM; THEN EVERY 30 MI—48 KM
Rear differential . . . . . .change lubricant

Transmission, transaxle
  manual . . . . .change lubricant
Initial service for RWD only

EVERY 12 MO/7.5 MI—12 KM
Body . . . . .lubricate
Hinges **MO**, automatic transmission shift linkage & clutch pivot points **MO**, clutch fork joint & cross shaft **LM**, parking brake cables **LM**

Brake line & hoses . . . . .inspect
Impulse, check hydraulic clutch lines & hoses.

Front disc brake pads . . . . .inspect
RWD cars only. Replace when lining is .067 in. or less.

Exhaust system . . . . .inspect
RWD cars only

Propeller shaft flange bolts . . . . . .torque
18-20 ft-lbs

Rear axle . . . . .check level

Steering & suspension . . .lube fittings **LM**
All RWD cars only, also inspect front end components.

Transmission, manual . . . . . .check level

Brake master cyl. . . . . . .check level **HB**

Clutch fluid . . . . .check level **HB**

Coolant . . . . .check level **EC**

Fluid leaks under vehicle . . . . .check

Power steering
  reservoir . . . . .check level **AF2**
Also check system hoses.

Tires & wheels . . . . .inspect
Check for wear, vibrations, air pressure.

Transmission, automatic . . . .check level

Body . . . . .flush
Wash under car every spring.

EVERY 15 MI—24 KM
Valve clearance . . . . .check/adjust
SOHC engines only

EVERY 12 MO/15 MI—24 KM
Fuel tank, cap & lines . . . . .inspect

Rear drum brakes . . . . .inspect
RWD cars only. Replace shoes when lining is .039 in. or less. Check all other hardware & parking brake adjustment.

Brake & clutch pedals . . . . .lubricate **MO**
Also check clutch adjustment.

Brake fluid, Impulse . . . . . . .change **HB**

Cooling system . . . . .inspect
Pressure test system & inspect cap. Check condition of all hoses & tighten hose clamps.

Cruise control, Impulse . .inspect system

Throttle linkage . . . . .check

EVERY 22.5 MI—36 KM
Power steering fluid . . . . . .change **AF2**
I-Mark, Impulse only

EVERY 30 MI—48 KM
Wheel bearings . . . . .repack **WB**
Front on RWD cars, rear on FWD cars

Transmission, transaxle
  automatic . . . . .change fluid
1989 Impulse, initial service at 15 mi (24km)

Air cleaner element . . . . .replace

Spark plugs . . . . .replace

EVERY 24 MO/30 MI—48 KM
Cooling system . . . . .replace coolant **EC**
Flush system

Carb. choke & hoses . . . . .inspect
I-Mark 2V only

Drive belts . . . . .inspect

EVERY 45 MI—72 KM
Power steering hoses . . . . .change
I-Mark only

EVERY 60 MI—96 KM
Timing belt . . . . .replace
1989 only

Valve clearance . . . . .check/adjust
DOHC engine only

SEVERE SERVICE
Crankcase—Change oil every 3 mo/3 mi (4.8 km). Change oil filter every other oil change.

Brake pads & linings—Inspect more often.

Transmission, automatic—Change fluid & filter every 15 mi (24 km).

KEY TO LUBRICANTS
See other Isuzu Charts.

CRANKCASE
Gasoline . . . .**SF, SF/CC, SF/CD**
Diesel . . . .**SF/CC, SF/CD**

CAPACITY, Refill:	Liters	Qt
1471cc	2.8	3.0
1588cc DOHC	3.8	4.0
1949cc,1994cc, 2254cc	3.2	3.4

Gasoline engines, capacity shown is without filter. When replacing filter, additional oil may be needed.
Diesel engine, capacity includes oil filter.

1989:
I-Mark:
Above 40°F (5°C) 30
Above 10°F (-12°C) . . .15W-40, 20W-40, 20W-50
Above 0°F (-18°C) 10W-30
Below 60°F (16°C), Turbo & DOHC 5W-30
All temperatures, ex. Turbo, DOHC 5W-30

Impulse:
Above 77°F (25°C) 40, 50
Above 5°F (-15°C) 15W-40, 20W-40, 20W-50
32°F to 100°F (0° to 38°C) 30
5° to 60°F (-15° to 16°C) 20W
-13° to 100°F (-25° to 38°C) 10W-30
-13° to 32°F (-25° to 0°C) 10W
Below 100°F (38°C) 5W-30

TRANSMISSION/TRANSAXLE,
Automatic **AF3**

CAPACITY, Initial Refill[2]:	Liters	Qt
All models	2.0	2.1

2 With the engine at operating temperature, shift transmission through all gears. Check fluid level in PARK and add fluid as needed.

TRANSMISSION/TRANSAXLE, Manual
I-Mark . . . . .5W-30 **SF**
In areas where temperature is consistently over 90°F (32°C), 15W-40, 20W-40, 20W-50

Impulse . . . . **SF**
Above 90°F (32°C), 40; 0° to 90°F (-18° to 32°C), 30; below 50°F (10°C), 10W-30; all temperatures, 5W-30[3]
3 Preferred

CAPACITY, Refill:	Liters	Pt
I-Mark	1.9	4.0
Impulse: 4-speed	1.3	2.6
5-speed	1.6	3.3

DIFFERENTIAL, RWD Models
Standard **GL-5**
Limited-Slip . . . .**GL-5★**
Above 50°F (10°C), 140; 0° to 90°F (-18° to 32°C), 90; below 50°F (10°C), 80

CAPACITY, Refill:	Liters	Pt
All	1.5	3.2

ISUZU
1990-93 Impulse, Stylus

CHEK-CHART

IUIPM4   IUIPM4

Perform the following maintenance services at the intervals indicated to keep both the vehicle and emission warranties in effect.

MI—MILES IN THOUSANDS
KM—KILOMETERS IN THOUSANDS

TURBO,
EVERY 6 MO/5 MI—8 KM
OTHERS,
EVERY 12 MO/7.5 MI—12 KM
Crankcase . . . . .change oil

Oil filter .replace
At first oil change, then every other

EVERY 12 MO/7.5 MI—12 KM
Body . . . . .lubricate
Hinges **MO**, transaxle shift linkage & clutch pivot points **MO**, clutch fork joint & cross shaft **LM**, parking brake cables **LM**

Rear axle . . . . .check level

Transmission, manual . . . . . .check level

Brake master cylinder . . .check level **HB**

Coolant . . . . .check level **EC**

Fluid leaks under vehicle . . . . . . .check

Power steering
reservoir . . . . .check level **AF2**
Also check system hoses.

Tires & wheels . . . . .inspect
Check for wear, vibrations, air pressure.

Transmission, automatic . . . .check level

Body . . . . .flush
Wash under car every spring.

EVERY 15 MI—24 KM
Valve clearance . . . . .check/adjust
SOHC engines only

EVERY 12 MO/15 MI—24 KM
Fuel tank, cap & lines . . . . .inspect

Cooling system . . . . .inspect
Pressure test system & inspect cap. Check condition of all hoses & tighten hose clamps.

EVERY 24 MO/22.5 MI—36 KM
Power steering fluid . . . . . . .change **AF2**

EVERY 30 MI—48 KM
Transaxle, automatic . . . . . .change fluid

Transaxle, manual . . . . .change lubricant

Transfer case, 4WD . . . .change lubricant

Propeller shaft,
4WD . . . . .check/lubricate **LM**
Tighten flange bolts to 26 ft-lbs (35 Nm).

Rear axle, 4WD . . . . . . .change lubricant

Air cleaner element . . . . .replace

Spark plugs . . . . .replace

EVERY 24 MO/30 MI—48 KM
Cooling system . . . . .replace coolant **EC**
Flush system.

Drive belts . . . . .inspect

EVERY 60 MI—96 KM
Timing belt . . . . .replace

Valve clearance . . . . .check/adjust
1990-91 DOHC engine only

SEVERE SERVICE
Crankcase—Change oil every 3 mo/3 mi (4.8 km). Change oil filter every other oil change.

Brake pads & linings—Inspect more often.

Air cleaner element—Change more frequently.

Transmission, automatic—Change fluid & filter every 15 mi (24 km).

KEY TO LUBRICANTS

AF2	DEXRON®-II Automatic Transmission Fluid
AF3	DEXRON®-III Automatic Transmission Fluid
CC	Motor Oil, API Service CC
CD	Motor Oil, API Service CD
EC	Ethylene Glycol Coolant
GL-5	Gear Oil, API Service GL-5
HB	Hydraulic Brake Fluid DOT 3
LM	Lithium Multipurpose Grease
MO	Motor Oil
SF	Motor Oil, API Service SF
SG	Motor Oil, API Service SG

CRANKCASE . . . . .SG, SG/CC, SG/CD

CAPACITY, Refill:	Liters	Qt
1588cc SOHC	3.0	3.2
1588cc, 1809cc DOHC	3.8	4.0

Capacity shown is without filter. When replacing filter, additional oil may be needed.
Above 40°F (5°C) 30
Above 10°F (-12°C) . . .15W-40, 20W-40, 20W-50
Above 0°F (-18°C) 10W-30
Below 60°F (16°C), DOHC 5W-30
All temperatures, ex. DOHC 5W-30

TRANSAXLE, Automatic AF3

CAPACITY, Initial Refill[1]:	Liters	Qt
All models	2.9	3.0

1 With engine at operating temperature, shift transmission through all gears. Check fluid level in PARK and add fluid as needed.

TRANSAXLE, Manual . . . . .5W-30 SF, SG
In areas where temperature is consistently over 90°F (32°C), 15W-40, 20W-40, 20W-50

CAPACITY, Refill:	Liters	Pt
All	1.9	4.0

TRANSFER CASE 80W-90 GL-5

CAPACITY, Refill:	Liters	Pt
Impulse 4WD	1.3	2.8

REAR DIFFERENTIAL GL-5
Above 50°F (10°C) 140
0° to 90°F (-18° to 32°C) 90
Below 50°F (10°C) .80

CAPACITY, Refill:	Liters	Pt
Impulse 4WD	0.7	1.4

136

SERVICE AT TIME OR MILEAGE — WHICHEVER OCCURS FIRST

IUIPM3   IUIPM3

Perform the following maintenance services at the intervals indicated to keep both the vehicle and emission warranties in effect.

MI—MILES IN THOUSANDS
KM—KILOMETERS IN THOUSANDS

AT FIRST 7.5 MI—12 KM;
THEN AT 60 MI—96 KM;
THEN EVERY 15 MI—24 KM
Engine idle speed . . . . .adjust
4-cyl. only

EVERY 7.5 MI—12 KM
Rear axle . . . . .check level
Rodeo, Passport, Pickup w/V6 only

Throttle body
mounting bolts, 2.8L, 3.1L . . . . .torque

Tires . . . . .rotate

EVERY 6 MO/7.5 MI—12 KM
Accelerator linkage . . . . . . .lubricate MO

Body . . . . .lubricate
Hinges MO, automatic transmission shift linkage & clutch pivot points MO, clutch fork joint & cross shaft LM, parking brake cables LM

Ball joints, Trooper . . . . . . .lubricate LM

Front & rear propeller shafts . . . .lubricate
Sliding yokes, LM; U-joints, Moly LM

EVERY 12 MO/7.5 MI—12 KM
Brake lines & hoses . . . . .inspect

Propeller shaft
flange bolts . . . . .torque
20-25 ft-lbs (30-34 Nm)

Suspension & steering . . . . .inspect
1990-94 Amigo, Pickup only

Crankcase . . . . .change oil

Oil filter . . . . .replace
At first oil change, then every other

Exhaust system . . . . .inspect

Automatic transmission . . . . .check level

Battery fluid level, ex. 2.8L, 3.1L . .check

Brake master cyl. . . . . . . .check level HB

Clutch fluid . . . . .check level HB
When equipped with hydraulic clutch

Coolant . . . . .check level EC

Fluid leaks under vehicle . . . . .check

Starter safety switch . . . . .check

Tires & wheels . . . . .inspect
Check for wear, vibration, air pressure.

AT FIRST 15 MI—24 KM;
THEN AT 30 MI—48 KM;
THEN EVERY 30 MI—48 KM
Differentials, front
& rear . . . . .change lubricant
Except Amigo & pickup w/Saginaw rear axle

Manual transmission . . .change lubricant

Transfer case . . . . .change lubricant
Ex. 4-cyl. w/AT

EVERY 15 MI—24 KM
Valve clearance . . . . .check/adjust
4-cyl. only

EVERY 12 MO/15 MI—24 KM
Drum & disc brake system . . . . .inspect

Brake & clutch pedals . . . .lubricate MO
Also check freeplay.

Cooling system . . . . .inspect
Pressure test system & inspect cap. Check condition of all hoses & tighten hose clamps.

Cruise control . . . . .inspect system
Shift-on-the-fly
gear oil . . . . .check level 75W-90 GL-5
1992-95 Trooper, Rodeo

Throttle linkage . . . . .check

EVERY 30 MI—48 KM
Front wheel bearings . . . . . .repack WB

Air cleaner element . . . . .replace
Also replace 2.8L, 3.1L V6 crankcase filter.

Air cleaner housing 2.8L, 3.1L . . .inspect

Cooling system . . . . .replace coolant EC
Flush system.

Carb. choke & hoses . . . . .inspect

Ignition wires 2.8L, 3.1L . . . . . . .inspect

Power steering fluid . . . . . . .change AF2

Spark plugs . . . . .replace

EVERY 12 MO/30 MI—48 KM
Automatic transmission & transfer case,
4WD w/AT 1989-91
4 cyl. only . . . . .check level

Clutch lines & hose . . . . .inspect
Models with hydraulic clutch only

EVERY 24 MO/30 MI—48 KM
Drive belts . . . . .inspect

Steering gearbox . . . . .check/adjust

EVERY 60 MI—96 KM
Fuel tank, cap & lines . . . . .inspect

Ignition timing 2.8L, 3.1L . . .check/adjust

PCV system 2.8L, 3.1L . . . . . . .inspect

Timing belt . . . . .replace

Radiator core & AC condenser . . . .clean

Spark plug wires . . . . .inspect
1990-95 only

EVERY 90 MI—144 KM
Oxygen sensor . . . . .replace
Ex. 1995 Trooper

SEVERE SERVICE
Crankcase—Change oil every: 4-cyl., 3 mo/3.75 mi (6 km); V6, 3 mo/3 mi (4.8 km). All engines, change oil filter every other oil change

Differential—Amigo, Pickup w/Saginaw rear axle, Rodeo rear axle, 1995 Trooper front & rear axle: change lubricant every 15 mi (24 km)

Transmission, automatic—Change fluid & filter every 20 mi (32 km)

Transfer case—4-cyl. w/AT, change fluid every 20 mi (32 km)

KEY TO LUBRICANTS
See other Isuzu charts.

CRANKCASE . . . . .SG, SG/CC, SG/CD, SH, GF-1

CAPACITY, Refill:	Liters	Qt
2.3L: 1989-91	3.6	3.8
1992-95	3.2	3.4
2.6L: 1989-90	4.5	4.8
1991-95	3.9	4.1
2.8L, 3.1L	3.8	4.0
3.2L	4.7	5.0

Capacity shown is without filter. When replacing filter, additional oil may be needed.

1989-92 ex. 3.2L
Above 40°F (5°C) 30
Above 20°F (-7°C) 20W-20, 20W-40
Above 0°F (-18°C) . . . . .10W-30[1]
0° to 60°F (-18° to 15°C) 10W
Below 60°F (15°C) 5W-30
Below 20°F (-7°C) 5W-20
1 Preferred

1992-95 Trooper:
Above 5°F (-15°C) . . .15W-40, 20W-40, 20W-50
32° to 100°F (0° to 38°C) 30
-13°C to 100°F (-25° to 38°C) 10W-30
5° to 60°F (-15° to 15°C) 20W
-13° to 32°F (-25° to 0°C) 10W
Below 100°F (38°C) 5W-30

1993-95 Amigo, Pickup, Rodeo, Passport:
Above 40°F (4°C) .30
Above 10°F (-12°C) . . .15W-40, 20W-40, 20W-50
Above 0°F (-18°C) 10W-30
All temperatures 5W-30

TRANSMISSION, Automatic AF3

CAPACITY, Initial Refill[2]:	Liters	Qt
2WD	2.5	2.6
4WD, 4-cyl.	4.5	4.8

2 With the engine at operating temperature, shift transmission & 4-cyl. 4WD transfer case through all gears. Check fluid level in PARK and add fluid as needed.

TRANSMISSION, Manual
B.W. T-5 . . . . .AF3
All others . . . . .SG
Above 90°F (32°C) 1989-92 40
Above 90°F (32°C), 1993-95 . . .15W-40, 20W-40, 20W-50
All temperatures . . . . .5W-30[3]
3 Preferred

CAPACITY, Refill:	Liters	Pt
B.W. T-5	2.3	4.8
Others: 2.3L	1.5	3.2
2.6L, 2.8L, 3.1L, 3.2L	3.0	6.2

TRANSFER CASE
W/Manual Transmission . . . . .SG
Above 90°F (32°C), 1989-92 40
Above 90°F (32°C), 1993-95 . . .15W-40, 20W-40, 20W-50
All temperatures . . . . .5W-30[4]
W/Automatic Transmission: 4-cyl. AF3
V6 . . . . .SG
Above 90°F (32°C), 1989-92 40
Above 90°F (32°C), 1993-95 . . .15W-40, 20W-40, 20W-50
All temperatures . . . . .5W-30[4]
4 Preferred

Capacity, Refill:	Liters	Pt
Man. trans	1.5	3.2
Auto. trans.: 4-cyl	0.8	1.6
V6	1.5	3.2

DIFFERENTIAL
1990-95 W/Saginaw
rear axle 80W-90 GL-5
5/95 & later Trooper w/Limited-
Slip Differential . . . . .GL-5★
All others .GL-5
Above 50°F (10°C), 140; 0° to 90°F (-18° to 32°C), 80W-90, 90; below 50°F (10°C), 80W-90

CAPACITY, Refill:	Liters	Pt
Front	1.5	3.2
Rear: 2.3L	1.5	3.2
2.6L, 2.8L, 3.1L, 3.2L	1.8	3.8
All w/Saginaw axle	1.9	4.0

Saginaw axle has removable rear cover without fill plug.

ISUZU
1996-97 Amigo, Rodeo, Trooper, Vehicross; Includes Acura SLX & Honda Passport
Hombre—See Chevrolet S10; Oasis—See Honda Odyssey

SERVICE AT TIME OR MILEAGE — WHICHEVER OCCURS FIRST

IUIPM5   IUIPM5

Perform the following maintenance services at the intervals indicated to keep both the vehicle and emission warranties in effect.

MI—MILES IN THOUSANDS
KM—KILOMETERS IN THOUSANDS

AT FIRST 7.5 MI—12 KM;
THEN AT 60 MI—96 KM;
THEN EVERY 15 MI—24 KM
Engine idle speed 2.6L . . . . .adjust

EVERY 7.5 MI—12 KM
Rear axle . . . . .check level
Rodeo, Passport

Tires . . . . .rotate

EVERY 6 MO/7.5 MI—12 KM
Accelerator linkage . . . . . . .lubricate MO

Power steering
fluid . . . . .check level AF2, AF3

Body . . . . .lubricate
Hinges MO, automatic transmission shift linkage & clutch
pivot points MO, clutch fork joint & cross shaft LM,
parking brake cables LM

Ball joints, Trooper, SLX . . . .lubricate LM

Front & rear
propeller shafts . . . . .lubricate
Sliding yokes, LM; U-joints, Moly LM

EVERY 12 MO/7.5 MI—12 KM
Brake lines & hoses . . . . .inspect

Propeller shaft flange bolts . . . . . .torque
20-25 ft-lbs (30-34 Nm)

Crankcase . . . . .change oil

Oil filter . . . . .replace
At first oil change, then every other

Exhaust system . . . . .inspect

Automatic transmission . . . . .check level

Battery fluid level . . . . .check

Brake master cyl. . . . . . .check level HB

Clutch fluid . . . . .check level HB
When equipped with hydraulic clutch

Coolant . . . . .check level EC

Fluid leaks . . . . .check

Starter safety switch . . . . .check

Tires & wheels . . . . .inspect
Check for wear, vibration, air pressure.

AT FIRST 15 MI—24 KM;
THEN AT 30 MI—48 KM;
THEN EVERY 30 MI—48 KM
Differentials, front
& rear . . . . .change lubricant
Except Saginaw rear axle

Manual transmission . . .change lubricant

Transfer case . . . . .change lubricant

EVERY 15 MI—24 KM
Valve clearance . . . . .check/adjust
4-cyl. 2.6L only

EVERY 12 MO/15 MI—24 KM
Drum & disc brake system . . . . .inspect

Brake & clutch pedals . . . . .lubricate MO
Also check freeplay.

Cooling system . . . . .inspect
Pressure test system & inspect cap. Check condition of
all hoses & tighten hose clamps.

Cruise control . . . . .inspect system

Shift-on-the-fly
gear oil . . . . .check level 75W-90 GL-5

Steering & suspension . . . . .inspect

Throttle linkage . . . . .check

Lock cylinders . . . . .lubricate

EVERY 30 MI—48 KM
Front wheel bearings . . . . . . .repack WB

Air cleaner element . . . . .replace

Cooling system . . . . .replace coolant EC
Flush system.

Power steering fluid . . .change AF2, AF3

Spark plugs . . . . .replace

EVERY 12 MO/30 MI—48 KM
Clutch lines & hose . . . . .inspect
Models with hydraulic clutch only

EVERY 24 MO/30 MI—48 KM
Drive belts . . . . .inspect

Steering gearbox . . . . .check/adjust

EVERY 60 MI—96 KM
Fuel tank, cap & lines . . . . .inspect

Timing belt . . . . .replace

Radiator core & AC condenser . . . .clean

Spark plug wires, 2.6L . . . . .inspect

Valve clearance . . . . .check/adjust

SEVERE SERVICE
Crankcase—Change oil every: 4-cyl., 3 mo/3.75 mi (6 km); V6, 3 mo/3 mi (4.8 km). All engines, change oil filter every other oil change.

Differential—1996 Rodeo, Passport rear axle, 1997 Rodeo, Passport front & rear axle, Trooper, SLX front & rear axle change lubricant every 15 mi (24 km).

Transmission, automatic—Change fluid & filter every 20 mi (32 km).

KEY TO LUBRICANTS
AF2	DEXRON®-II Automatic Transmission Fluid
AF3	DEXRON®-III Automatic Transmission Fluid Power Steering, Dexron-II
EC	Ethylene Glycol Coolant
GF-1	Motor Oil, API Service GF-1
GL-5	Gear Oil, API Service GL-5
GL-5★	Special lubricant for limited-slip differentials
HB	Hydraulic Brake Fluid, DOT 3 or 4
LM	Lithium Multipurpose Grease With Moly where noted
MO	Motor Oil
SG	Motor Oil, API Service SG
SH	Motor Oil, API Service SH
WB	Wheel Bearing Grease

CRANKCASE . . . . .SH, GF-1
CAPACITY, Refill:	Liters	Qt
2.6L	3.9	4.1
3.2L	4.7	5.0

Capacity shown is without filter. When replacing filter, additional oil may be needed.

Trooper, SLX:
Above 5°F (-15°C) 15W-40, 20W-40, 20W-50
32° to 100°F (0° to 38°C) 30
-13°C to 100°F (-25° to 38°C) 10W-30
5° to 60°F (-15° to 15°C) 20W
-13° to 32°F (-25° to 0°C) 10W
Below 100°F (38°C) 5W-30

Amigo, Rodeo, Passport:
Above 40°F (4°C) 30
Above 10°F (-12°C) . . .15W-40, 20W-40, 20W-50
Above 0°F (-18°C) 10W-30
All temperatures 5W-30

TRANSMISSION, Automatic AF3
CAPACITY, Total Refill[1]:	Liters	Qt
All	8.6	9.1

1 Transmission does not have a dipstick.

TRANSMISSION, Manual
B.W. T-5 . . . . .AF3
All others . . . . .SF, SG
Above 90°F (32°C) . . .15W-40, 20W-40, 20W-50
All temperatures . . . . .5W-30[2]
2 Preferred
CAPACITY, Refill:	Liters	Pt
B.W. T-5	2.1	4.6
Others	3.0	6.2

TRANSFER CASE . . . . .SF, SG
Above 90°F (32°C) 15W-40, 20W-40, 20W-50
All temperatures 5W-30
Capacity, Refill:	Liters	Pt
All	1.5	3.2

DIFFERENTIAL
1997 Trooper, SLX; front GL-5
Above 50°F (10°C), 80W-90, 80W-140; below 90°F
(30°C), 75W-90
W/Saginaw rear axle 80W-90 GL-5
All w/Limited-Slip Diff. . . . . .GL-5★
All others .GL-5
Above 50°F (10°C), 140; 0° to 90°F (-18° to 32°C),
80W-90, 90; below 50°F (10°C), 80W-90
CAPACITY, Refill:	Liters	Pt
Front	1.5	3.2
Rear	1.8	3.8
All w/Saginaw axle	1.9	4.0

Saginaw axle has removable rear cover without fill plug.

CHEK-CHART

ISUZU

1998-2000 Amigo, Rodeo, Trooper, Vehicross; Includes Acura SLX & Honda Passport
Hombre—See Chevrolet S10; Oasis—See Honda Odyssey

SERVICE AT TIME OR MILEAGE — WHICHEVER OCCURS FIRST

IUIPM6   IUIPM6

Perform the following maintenance services at the intervals indicated to keep both the vehicle and emission warranties in effect.

MI—MILES IN THOUSANDS
KM—KILOMETERS IN THOUSANDS

EVERY 7.5 MI—12 KM
Tires . . . . .rotate

EVERY 6 MO/7.5 MI—12 KM
Accelerator linkage . . . . . .lubricate **MO**

Power steering
  fluid . . . . .check level **AF2, AF3**

Body .lubricate
Hinges **MO**, automatic transmission shift linkage & clutch pivot points **MO**, clutch fork joint & cross shaft **LM**, parking brake cables **LM**

Front propeller shaft . . . . .lubricate
2.2L double cardan joint only

EVERY 12 MO/7.5 MI—12 KM
Propeller shaft flange bolts . . . . .torque
20-25 ft-lbs (30-34 Nm)

Steering & suspension . . . . .inspect

Crankcase . . . . .change oil

Oil filter . . . . .replace
At every oil change

Exhaust system . . . . .inspect

Automatic transmission . . . . .check level

Battery fluid level, 1998-99 . . . . . . .check

Brake master cyl. . . . . . . .check level **HB**

Clutch fluid . . . . .check level **HB**
When equipped with hydraulic clutch

Coolant . . . . .check level **EC**

Fluid leaks . . . . .check

Starter safety switch . . . . .check

Tires & wheels . . . . .inspect
Check for wear, vibration, air pressure.

AT FIRST 15 MI—24 KM;
THEN AT 30 MI—48 KM;
THEN EVERY 30 MI—48 KM
Differentials, front
  & rear . . . . .change lubricant
Except Saginaw rear axle

Manual transmission . . .change lubricant
ex. 2.2L

Transfer case . . . . .change lubricant
ex. 2.2L & T.O.D. type transfer case

EVERY 6 MO/15 MI—24 KM
Clutch pedal . . . . .lubricate

EVERY 12 MO/15 MI—24 KM
Brake lines & hoses . . . . .inspect

Drum & disc brake system . . . . . .inspect

Cooling system . . . . .inspect
Pressure test system & inspect cap. Check condition of all hoses & tighten hose clamps.

Cruise control . . . . .inspect system

Shift-on-the-fly
  gear oil . . . . .check level 75W-90 **GL-5**

Throttle linkage . . . . .check
1998-99 All, 2000 4-cyl. only

T.O.D. transfer case
  lubricant . . . . . .check level **AF2, AF3**

Lock cylinders . . . . .lubricate

EVERY 30 MI—48 KM
Front wheel bearings . . . . . .repack **WB**

Air cleaner element . . . . .replace

Cooling system . . . . .replace coolant **EC**
Flush system.

Power steering fluid . . .change **AF2, AF3**

EVERY 12 MO/30 MI—48 KM
Clutch lines & hose . . . . .inspect
Models with hydraulic clutch only

EVERY 24 MO/30 MI—48 KM
Drive belts . . . . .inspect

Steering gearbox . . . . .check/adjust

EVERY 60 MI—96 KM
Fuel tank, cap & lines . . . . .inspect

Radiator core & AC condenser . . . .clean

Spark plug wires, 2.2L, 2.6L . . . . .inspect

Valve clearance . . . . .check/adjust
3.2L, 3.5L

EVERY 100 MI—160 KM
Spark plugs . . . . .replace

Timing belt . . . . .replace

SEVERE SERVICE
Crankcase—Change oil every: 4-cyl., 3 mo/3.75 mi (6 km); V6, 3 mo/3 mi (4.8 km). All engines, change oil filter every other oil change.

Differential—Rodeo, Passport front & rear axle, Trooper, SLX front & rear axle change lubricant every 15 mi (24 km).

Power steering fluid—Replace every 30 mi (48 km).

Timing belt—Replace every 75 mi (128 km).

Transmission, automatic—Change fluid & filter every 20 mi (32 km).

KEY TO LUBRICANTS
AF2	DEXRON®-II Automatic Transmission Fluid
AF3	DEXRON®-III Automatic Transmission Fluid Power Steering, Dexron-II
EC	Ethylene Glycol Coolant
GF-1	Motor Oil, API Service GF-1
GL-5	Gear Oil, API Service GL-5
GL-5★	Special lubricant for limited-slip differentials
HB	Hydraulic Brake Fluid, DOT 3 or 4
LM	Lithium Multipurpose Grease With Moly where noted
MO	Motor Oil
SJ	Motor Oil, API Service SJ
WB	Wheel Bearing Grease

CRANKCASE . . . . .SJ, GF-1

CAPACITY, Refill:	Liters	Qt
2.2L	4.2	4.4
3.2L	4.0	4.2
3.5L	4.0	4.2

Capacity shown is without filter. When replacing filter, additional oil may be needed.

Above 40°F (4°C)	.30
Above 10°F (-12°C) . . .15W-40, 20W-40, 20W-50	
Above 0°F (-18°C)	10W-30
All temperatures	5W-30

TRANSMISSION, Automatic AF3

CAPACITY, Total Refill[1]:	Liters	Qt
All	8.6	9.1

1 Transmission does not have a dipstick.

TRANSMISSION, Manual

B.W. T-5 . . . . .AF3
All others . . . . .SF, SG
Above 90°F (32°C) 15W-40, 20W-40, 20W-50
All temperatures . . . . .5W-30[2]
2 Preferred

CAPACITY, Refill:	Liters	Pt
B.W. T-5	2.1	4.6
Trooper, SLX	2.7	5.6
Others	3.0	6.2

TRANSFER CASE

All w/T.O.D. system AF2, AF3
All others . . . . .SF, SG
Above 90°F (32°C) 15W-40, 20W-40, 20W-50
All temperatures 5W-30

Capacity, Refill:	Liters	Pt
Trooper, SLX, Vehicross w/TOD	1.9	4.0
All others	1.5	3.2

DIFFERENTIAL

Front GL-5
Above 50°F (10°C), 80W-90, 80W-140; below 90°F (30°C), 75W-90
W/Saginaw rear axle 80W-90 **GL-5**
All w/Limited-Slip Diff. . . . . .GL-5★
All others, rear GL-5
Above 50°F (10°C), 140; 0° to 90°F (-18° to 32°C), 80W-90, 90; below 50°F (10°C), 80W-90

CAPACITY, Refill:	Liters	Pt
Trooper, SLX: front	1.4	3.0
Rear	3.0	6.4
Vehicross: front	1.4	3.0
Rear	2.2	4.6
All others: front	1.5	3.2
Rear	1.8	3.8
All w/Saginaw axle	1.9	4.0

Saginaw axle has removable rear cover without fill plug.

SERVICE LOCATIONS — ENGINE AND CHASSIS

HOOD RELEASE: Inside & front; some Wrangler models, also release side latches

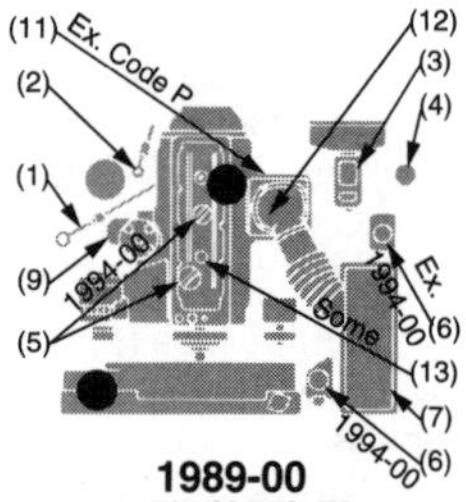

**1989-00
2.5L (150) FI
ex. 1997-00 Wrangler, TJ**

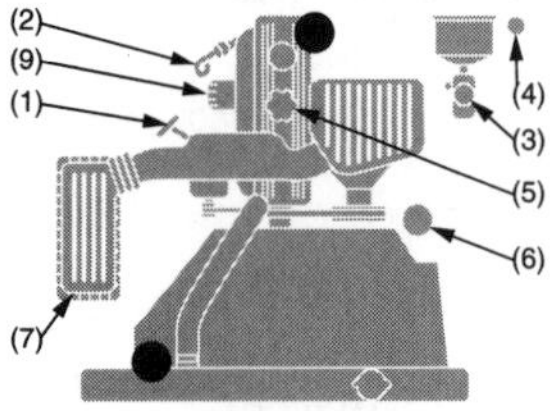

**1997-00
2.5L (150)
Wrangler, TJ**

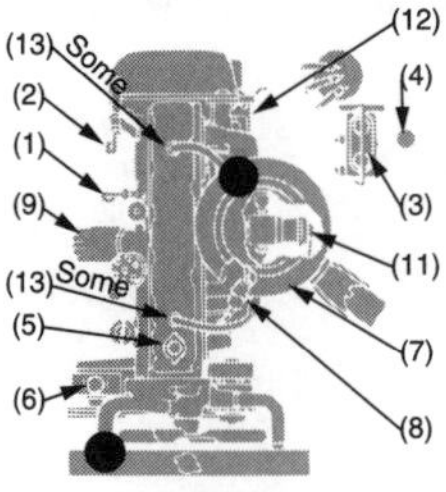

**1989-90
4.2L (258)**

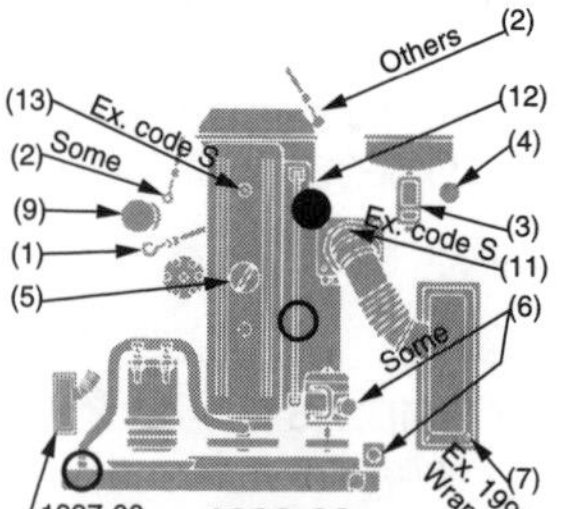

**1989-00
4.0L (242)**

(1) Crankcase dipstick
(2) Transmission dipstick
(3) Brake fluid reservoir
(4) Clutch fluid reservoir
(5) Oil fill cap
(6) Power steering reservoir
(7) Air filter
(8) Fuel filter
(9) Oil filter
(10) PCV filter
(11) EGR valve
(12) Oxygen sensor
(13) PCV valve

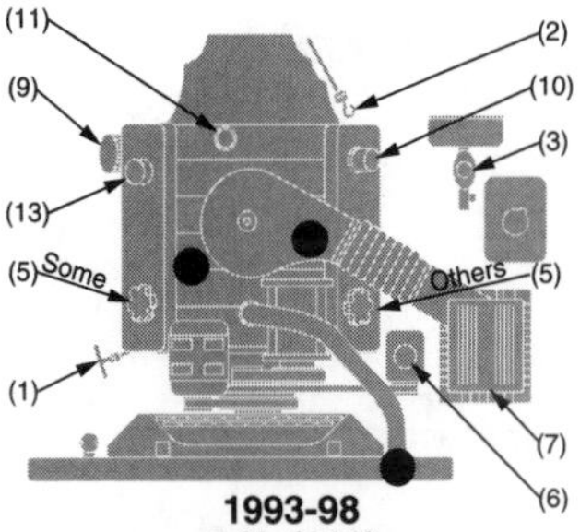

**1993-98
5.2L (318)
1998 5.9L (360)**

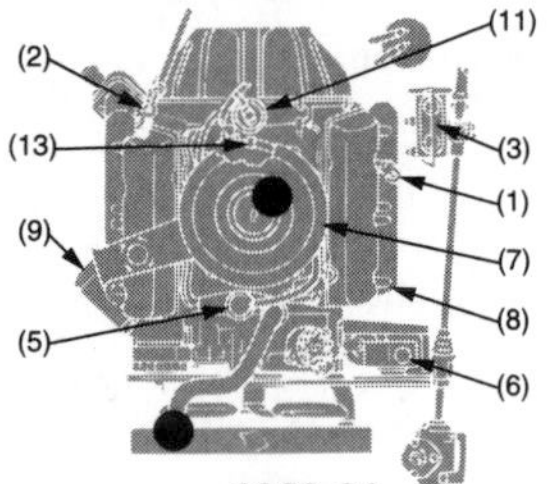

**1989-91
8-cyl.**

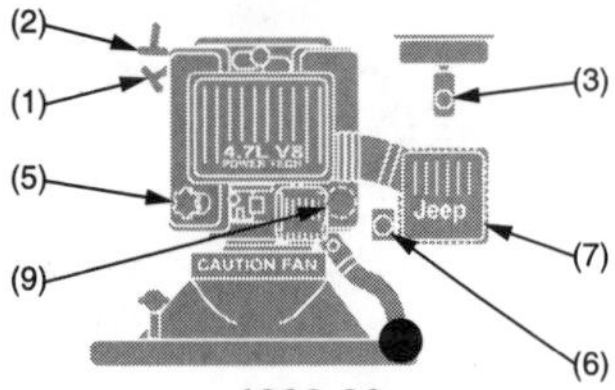

**1999-00
4.7L (287)**

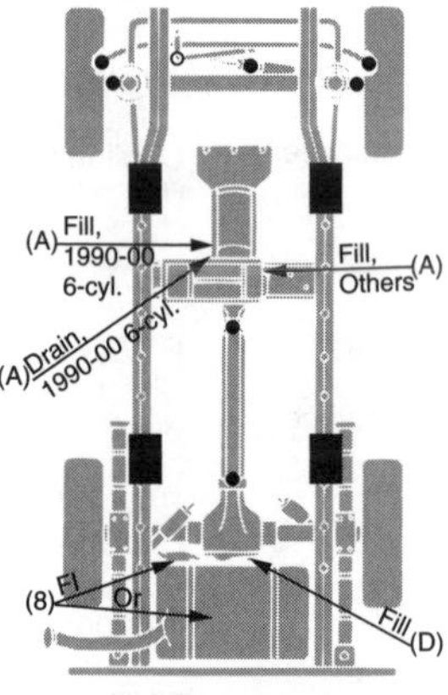

**1989-00
Cherokee 2WD,
Grand Cherokee 2WD**

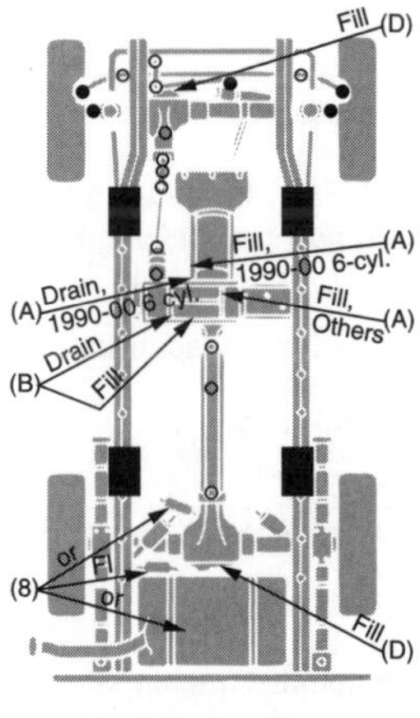

**1989-00 Cherokee 4WD
Wagoneer
1993-98 Grand Cherokee,
Grand Wagoneer
1997-00 Wrangler, TJ**

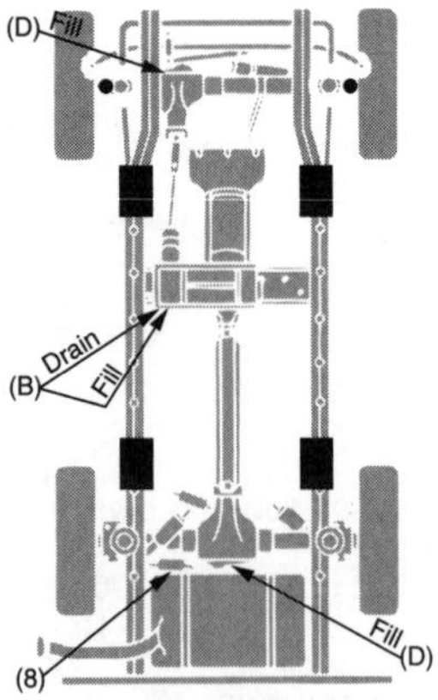

**1999-00
Grand Cherokee**

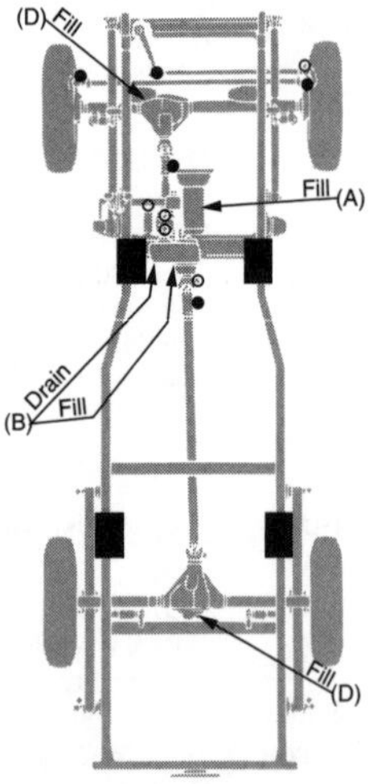

**1989-91
Grand Wagoneer**

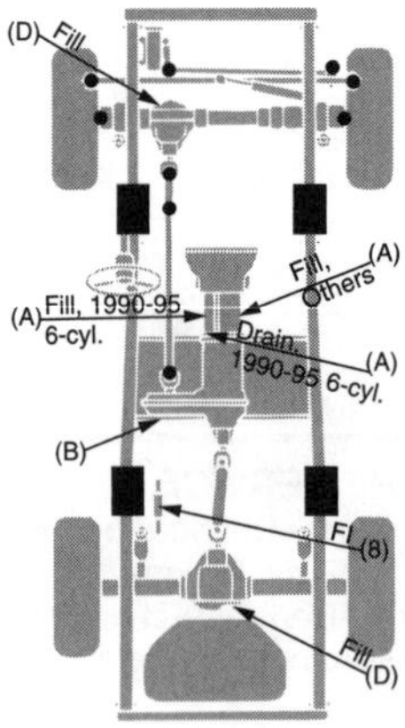

**1989-95
Wrangler**

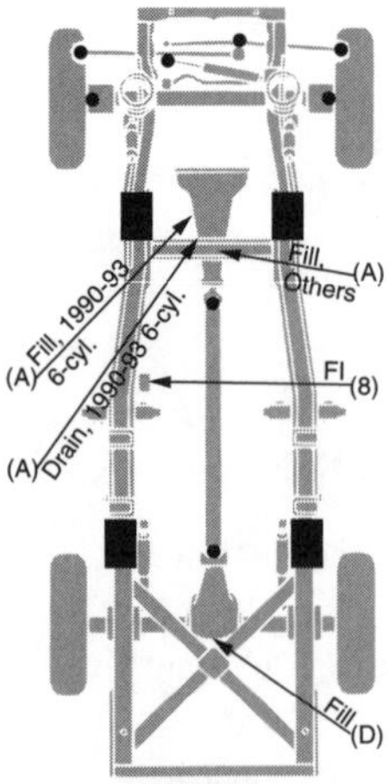

**1989-93
Comanche 2WD**

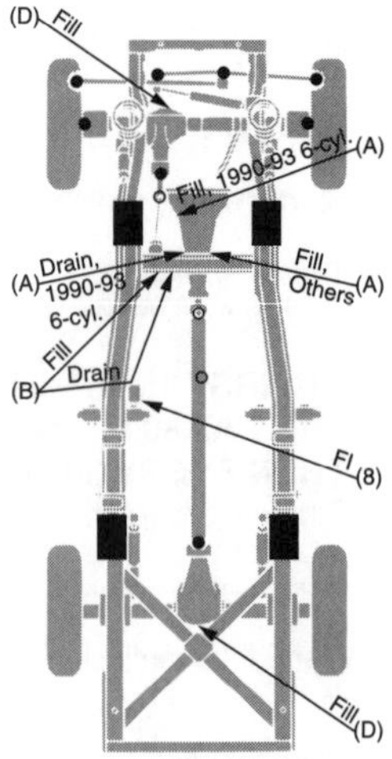

**1989-93
Comanche 4WD**

(A) Manual transmission/transaxle, drain & fill
(B) Transfer case, drain & fill
(C) Automatic transaxle final drive, NOT USED
(D) Differential, drain & fill

○ Cooling system drain, some models   • Fitting   ○ Fitting, some models   ■ Lift adapter position   ● Cooling system drain

SERVICE AT TIME OR MILEAGE — WHICHEVER OCCURS FIRST

JPPM5   JPPM5

W   SERVICE TO MAINTAIN EMISSION WARRANTY

MI—MILES IN THOUSANDS
KM—KILOMETERS IN THOUSANDS

EVERY MONTH
Brake master cylinder . .check level **HBH**

Clutch fluid reservoir . . .check level **HBH**

Cooling system . . . . .check level **EC**

Power steering
reservoir . . . . .check level **PS**

Tires . . . . .check

Transmission, automatic . . . .check level

FIRST 5 MI—8 KM
W Idle speeds . . . . .check/adjust
Wrangler & YJ 6-cyl., Grand Wagoneer

EVERY 7.5 MI—12 KM
W Crankcase . . . . .change oil
Change oil filter every oil change

Differentials . . . . .check level

W Exhaust system . . . . .inspect

Propeller shafts . . . . .lubricate **LB**
U-joint & splines or yokes. Also inspect seals.

Steering gear, manual . . .check level **LB**

Steering linkage . . . . .lubricate **LB**
Inspect seals & components. Lubricate ball joints.

Tires . . . . .rotate

Transfer case . . . . .check level

Transmission, manual . . . . .check level

EVERY 12 MONTHS
Air-conditioning system . . . . .inspect

EVERY 15 MI—24 KM
Air cleaner element . . . . .replace
Calif. Grand Wagoneer

Battery . . . . .check level
Clean terminals, check tiedowns & voltage

W Drive belts . . . . .inspect/adjust
Wrangler & YJ, Grand Wagoneer

EVERY 22.5 MI—36 KM
Cooling system . . . . .change coolant **EC**
Use 50% concentration for -34°F (-37°C) protection

EVERY 30 MI—48 KM
Brakes . . . . .inspect
Front & rear brake linings, master cylinder, calipers,
wheel cylinders. Check general condition of system.

Differentials, front & rear . . . .change fluid

Front wheel bearings . .check/repack **LB**
Grand Wagoneer & all 2WD

W Fuel filter . . . . .replace

W Fuel system, Calif. . . . . .inspect
Check filler cap, tank, lines, hoses & connections

Trans., automatic . . . . .change fluid/filter

Transmission, manual . .change lubricant

Transfer case . . . . .change lubricant

W Air cleaner element . . . . .replace

W Choke system . . . . .clean

Differentials . . . . .check level

Distributor cap & rotor . . . . .inspect
Calif. only

W Drive belts . . . . .inspect/adjust
Comanche, Cherokee, Wagoneer

Fuel cap . . . . .replace
Calif. only

Idle speeds, Calif. . . . . . . .check/adjust
Wrangler & YJ 6-cyl., Grand Wagoneer

W Ignition timing . . . . .check
Calif. 4.2L & 5.9L

W Manifold heat valve 8-cyl. . .lubricate **MH**

W PCV filter . . . . .clean/oil
Wrangler & YJ, Grand Wagoneer

PCV valve . . . . .replace
Calif. Wrangler & YJ, Grand Wagoneer

W Spark plugs . . . . .replace

Thermostatic air cleaner system . . .inspect
Calif. only

Distributor advance . . . . .check
Calif. only

Vacuum hoses, connections . . . .inspect
Calif. only

Body . . . . .lubricate
Hinges, door latches, slides, locks

EVERY 52.5 MI—84.5 KM
W Drive belts . . . . .replace
Ex. California

Fuel cap . . . . .replace
Ex. California

W Idle speeds . . . . .check/adjust
Wrangler & YJ 6-cyl., Grand Wagoneer

W Vacuum hoses . . . . .replace
Ex. California

Ignition timing . . . . .check/adjust
4.2L & 5.9L only, ex. California

W Ignition wires . . . . .replace
Ex. California

W Distributor cap & rotor . . . . .replace
Ex. California

EVERY 60 MI—96 KM
Battery . . . . .replace
Ex. California

EVERY 82 MO/82.5 MI—133 KM
W PCV valve . . . . .replace
Wrangler & YJ, Grand Wagoneer, ex. California

W Oxygen sensor . . . . .replace
Ex. V8

SEVERE SERVICE
Perform scheduled maintenance twice as frequently

KEY TO LUBRICANTS

AF2	DEXRON®-II Automatic Transmission Fluid
AP3	MOPAR ATF+3® Automatic Transmission Fluid
CD	Motor Oil, API Service CD
EC	Ethylene Glycol Coolant
GC	Wheel Bearing Grease, NLGI Category GC
GL-5	Gear Oil, API Service GL-5
HBH	Hydraulic Brake Fluid, Extra Heavy Duty
LB	Chassis Grease, NLGI Category LB
MA	MERCON® Automatic Transmission Fluid
MH	Manifold Heat Valve Solvent
PS	Power Steering Fluid
SG	Motor Oil, API Service SG

CRANKCASE . . . . .SG, SG/CD

CAPACITY, Refill:	Liters	Qt
4-cyl., 8-cyl.	3.8	4.0
6-cyl.	4.7	5.0

Capacity shown is without filter. When replacing filter, additional oil may be needed.

Above 30°F (-1°C) 20W-40, 20W-50
Above 0°F (-18°C) 10W-30, 10W-40
Below 60°F (16°C) 5W-30

TRANSMISSION, Automatic
727, 999 . . . .**AP3**
AW-4 . . . .**MA**

CAPACITY, Initial Refill[3]:	Liters	Qt
All models	3.8	4.0

[3] With the engine at operating temperature, shift transmission through all gears. Check fluid level in PARK (Comanche, Cherokee, Wagoneer) or NEUTRAL (all others) and add fluid as needed.

TRANSMISSION, Manual . . .75W-90 GL-5

CAPACITY, Refill:	Liters	Pt
AX4 2WD[4]	3.7	7.8
AX4 4WD[4]	3.5	7.4
AX5 2WD[4]	3.5	7.4
AX5 4WD[4]	3.3	7.0
B.A.10/5 2WD[5]	2.5	5.2
B.A.10/5 4WD[5]	2.3	4.9

[4] Case has cast iron & aluminum sections
[5] B.A.10 has I.D. plate on passenger side of transmission front case. AX5 has I.D. code stamped next to drain plug

TRANSFER CASE . . . . .MA, AF2

CAPACITY, Refill:	Liters	Pt
Model 229 Grand Wagoneer	2.8	6.0
Model 231: Wrangler, YJ	1.5	3.3
Cherokee, Comanche, Wagoneer	1.0	2.2
Model 242 Cherokee, Wagoneer	1.4	3.0

DIFFERENTIAL
Comanche, Grand Wagoneer
Wrangler, YJ 75W-90 **GL-5**
With trailer tow pkg. 80W-140 **GL-5**
Cherokee 75W-90 **GL-5**
With Class III
hitch . . . . .Synthetic 75W-140 **GL-5**[6]

[6] Mopar synthetic gear oil. Part No. 82200945
All with Limited-Slip differential, add 2 oz. container Mopar Trac-Loc additive. Part No. 4318060

CAPACITY	Liters	Pt
Grand Wagoneer	1.8	3.8
Comanche w/Metric Ton Pkg. . . .	1.4	3.0
Others	1.2	2.5

JEEP
1990-91 All Models

W SERVICE TO MAINTAIN EMISSION WARRANTY

MI—MILES IN THOUSANDS
KM—KILOMETERS IN THOUSANDS

EVERY MONTH
Battery . . . . .clean/inspect
Check electrolyte level ex. maintenance free type

Brake master cylinder . .check level **HBH**

Clutch fluid reservoir . . .check level **HBH**

Cooling system . . . . . . .check level **EC**

Power steering
    reservoir . . . . .check level **PS**

Tires .check

Transmission, automatic . . . .check level

FIRST 5 MO/5 MI—8 KM
W Idle speeds . . . . .check/adjust
Grand Wagoneer & 1990 Wrangler, YJ 6-cyl.

EVERY 6 MO/7.5 MI—12 KM
W Crankcase . . . . .change oil
Change oil filter at each oil change

EVERY 7.5 MI—12 KM
Exhaust system . . . . .inspect

Propeller shafts . . . . . .lubricate **GC-LB**
U-joint & splines or yokes; inspect seals

Steering gear,
    manual . . . . .check level **GC-LB**

Steering linkage,
    ball joints . . . . .lubricate **GC-LB**

Tires .rotate

Transfer case, differentials . . .check level

Transmission, manual . . . . . .check level

EVERY 12 MONTHS
Air-conditioning system . . . . .inspect

EVERY 15 MI—24 KM
Air filter . . . . .replace
California Grand Wagoneer

W Drive belts . . . . .inspect/adjust
Grand Wagoneer & 1990 Wrangler, YJ V-belts

FIRST 36 MO/22.5 MI—36 KM; THEN
EVERY 24 MO/22.5 MI—36 KM
Cooling system . . . . .replace coolant **EC**
Grand Wagoneer only
Use 50% concentration for -34°F (-37°C) protection

EVERY 30 MI—48 KM
Brakes . . . . .inspect
Front & rear brake linings, master cylinder, calipers,
wheel cylinders. Check general condition of system.

Differentials, front & rear . . . .change fluid

Front wheel bearing . .check/repack **GC-LB**
Grand Wagoneer, 2WD Cherokee, 2WD Comanche

W Fuel filter . . . . .replace

W Fuel system,
    Calif. Grand Wagoneer . . . . . .inspect
Check filler cap, tank, lines, hoses & connections

Trans., automatic . . . . .change fluid/filter

Transmission, manual . .change lubricant

Transfer case . . . . .change lubricant

W Air cleaner element . . . . .replace
Ex. Calif. Grand Wagoneer

W Choke system . . . . .clean
As equipped

Distributor cap & rotor . . . . .inspect
Calif. Grand Wagoneer

W Drive belts . . . . .inspect/adjust
Ex. Grand Wagoneer

Idle speeds . . . . .check/adjust
Calif. Grand Wagoneer

Ignition timing . . . . .check
Calif. Grand Wagoneer

Manifold heat valve 8-cyl. . . . .check **MH**

PCV filter, Calif. . . . . .clean/oil
Grand Wagoneer, Wrangler, YJ

PCV hoses . . . . .replace
Calif. Grand Wagoneer

W Spark plugs . . . . .replace

Thermostatic air cleaner . . . . . . .inspect
Calif. Grand Wagoneer

Distributor advance . . . . .check
Calif. Grand Wagoneer

Vacuum hoses, connections . . . . .inspect
Calif. Grand Wagoneer

Body . . . . .lubricate
Hinges, door latches, slides, locks

FIRST 36 MO/52.5 MI—84.5 KM; THEN EVERY 24 MO/30 MI—48 KM
Cooling system . . . .change coolant **EC**
All ex. Grand Wagoneer
Use 50% concentration for -34°F (-37°C) protection

GRAND WAGONEER & 1990 WRANGLER, YJ; EX. CALIF. EVERY 52 MO/52.5 MI—84.5 KM
W Drive belts, Grand Wagoneer . . . .replace

Fuel cap . . . . .replace
Ex. California

Idle speed . . . . .check/adjust
Ex. Calif. models

W Ignition timing . . . . .check
Grand Wagoneer

Vacuum hoses . . . . .replace
Grand Wagoneer

W Ignition wires . . . . .replace
Grand Wagoneer

W Distributor cap & rotor . . . . .replace
Grand Wagoneer

EVERY 60 MI—96 KM
Battery . . . . .replace
Ex. Calif. models

W Distributor cap & rotor . . . . .replace
Ex. Grand Wagoneer & Calif. models

W Drive belts . . . . .replace
Ex. Grand Wagoneer & Calif. models

W Ignition wires . . . . .replace
Ex. Grand Wagoneer & Calif. models

Vacuum hoses . . . . .replace
Ex. Grand Wagoneer & Calif. models

EVERY 82.5 MI—133 KM
W Oxygen sensor . . . . .replace
Ex. Calif. models

PCV valve . . . . .replace
Grand Wagoneer, ex. Calif.

SEVERE SERVICE
Crankcase—Change oil & filter every 1990, 3 mo/3.75 mi (6km); 1991, 3 mo/3 mi (4.8km)

Perform other scheduled maintenance twice as frequently

KEY TO LUBRICANTS

AF2	DEXRON®-II Automatic Transmission Fluid
AP3	MOPAR ATF-3® Automatic Transmission Fluid
CD	Motor Oil, API Service CD
CE	Motor Oil, API Service CE
EC	Ethylene Glycol Coolant
GC	Wheel Bearing Grease, NLGI Category GC
GL-5	Gear Oil, API Service GL-5
HBH	Hydraulic Brake Fluid, Extra Heavy Duty
LB	Chassis Grease, NLGI Category LB
MA	MERCON® Automatic Transmission Fluid
MH	Manifold Heat Valve Solvent
PS	Power Steering Fluid
SG	Motor Oil, API Service SG
WB	Wheel Bearing Lubricant

CRANKCASE . . . . .SG, SG/CD, SG/CE

CAPACITY, Refill:	Liters	Qt
4-cyl.	3.8	4.0
6-cyl.	5.7	6.0
8-cyl.	4.7	5.0

Capacity shown includes filter
Above 0°F (-18°C) 10W-30
Below 60°F (16°C) 5W-30

TRANSMISSION, Automatic
727, 999 . . . .**AP3**
AW-4 . . . .**MA**

CAPACITY, Initial Refill[2]:	Liters	Qt
AW4, 727	4.0	4.3
999	3.8	4.0

2 With the engine at operating temperature, shift transmission through all gears. Check fluid level in PARK (Comanche, Grand Wagoneer) or NEUTRAL (All others) and add fluid as needed.

TRANSMISSION, Manual . . .75W-90 GL-5

CAPACITY, Refill:	Liters	Pt
AX4 2WD	3.7	7.8
AX4 4WD	3.5	7.4
AX5 2WD	3.5	7.4
AX5 4WD	3.3	7.0
AX15 2WD	3.2	6.7
AX15 4WD	3.2	6.8

AX4, AX5 transmissions have drain on bottom of case. AX15 transmission has drain on passenger side of case

TRANSFER CASE . . . . .MA, AF2

CAPACITY, Refill:	Liters	Pt
Model 229 Grand Wagoneer	2.8	6.0
Model 231: Wrangler, YJ	1.5	3.3
Cherokee, Comanche	1.0	2.2
Model 242 Cherokee	1.4	3.0

DIFFERENTIAL
Comanche, Grand Wagoneer,
    Wrangler, YJ 75W-90 **GL-5**
    With trailer tow pkg. 80W-140 **GL-5**
Cherokee 75W-90 **GL-5**
    With Class III
    hitch . . . . Synthetic 75W-140 **GL-5**[3]

3 Mopar synthetic gear oil. Part No. 82200945
All with Limited-Slip differential, add 2 oz. container Mopar Trac-Loc additive. Part No. 4318060

CAPACITY	Liters	Pt
Grand Wagoneer	1.8	3.8
Comanche w/Metric Ton Pkg. . . .	1.4	3.0
Others	1.2	2.5

SERVICE AT TIME OR MILEAGE — WHICHEVER OCCURS FIRST

JPPM7   JPPM7

W   SERVICE TO MAINTAIN EMISSION WARRANTY

MI—MILES IN THOUSANDS
KM—KILOMETERS IN THOUSANDS

EVERY MONTH
Battery . . . . .clean/inspect
Check electrolyte level ex. maintenance free type

Brake master cylinder   . . .check level **HB**

Clutch fluid reservoir   . . . .check level **HB**

Cooling system   . . . . . . .check level **EC**

Power steering
   reservoir . . . . .check level **PS**

Tires . . . . .check

Transmission, automatic   . . . .check level

Front wheel
   bearing . . . . .check/repack **GC-LB**
2WD Cherokee & Comanche

Trans., automatic   . . . . .change fluid/filter

Trans, manual . . . . .change lubricant

Transfer case . . . . .change lubricant

W Air cleaner element . . . . .replace

Drive belts . . . . .inspect/adjust

Fuel filter . . . . .replace

W Spark plugs . . . . .replace

Body . . . . .lubricate
Hinges, door latches, slides, locks

EVERY 6 MO/7.5 MI—12 KM
Crankcase . . . . .change oil
Change oil filter at each oil change

EVERY 7.5 MI—12 KM
Exhaust system . . . . .inspect

Propeller shafts . . . . . .lubricate **GC-LB**
U-joint & splines or yokes; inspect seals

Steering gear,
   manual . . . . .check level **GC-LB**

Steering linkage,
   ball joints . . . . .lubricate **GC-LB**
4X4 only

Tires .rotate

Transfer case, differentials . . .check level

Transmission, manual . . . . .check level

EVERY 12 MONTHS
Air-conditioning system . . . . . . .inspect

EVERY 30 MI—48 KM
Brakes . . . . .inspect
Front & rear brake linings, master cylinder, calipers,
wheel cylinders. Check general condition of system.

Differentials, front & rear . . . .change fluid

FIRST 36 MO/52.5 MI—84.5 KM;
THEN EVERY 24 MO/30 MI—48 KM
W Cooling
   system . . . . .flush, change coolant **EC**
Use 50% concentration for -34°F (-37°C) protection

EVERY 60 MI—96 KM
Battery .replace
Ex. Calif.

W Distributor cap & rotor . . . . .replace
Ex. Calif.

W Drive belts . . . . .replace
Ex. Calif.

W Ignition wires . . . . .replace
Ex. Calif.

Vacuum hoses . . . . .replace
Ex. Calif.

EVERY 82.5 MI—133 KM
W Oxygen sensor . . . . .replace
Ex. California

SEVERE SERVICE
Crankcase—Change oil & filter every
3 mo/3 mi (4.8 km)

Perform other scheduled maintenance
twice as frequently

KEY TO LUBRICANTS

AF2	DEXRON®-II Automatic Transmission Fluid
AP3	MOPAR ATF-3® Automatic Transmission
CD	Motor Oil, API Service CD
CE	Motor Oil, API Service CE
EC	Ethylene Glycol Coolant
GC	Wheel Bearing Grease, NLGI Category GC
GL-5	Gear Oil, API Service GL-5
GL-5★	Special Lubricant for Trac-Lok Differential
HB	Hydraulic Brake Fluid, Dot 3
LB	Chassis Grease, NLGI Category LB
MA	MERCON® Automatic Transmission Fluid
PS	Power Steering Fluid
SG	Motor Oil, API Service SG

CRANKCASE . . . . .SG, SG/CD, SG/CE

CAPACITY, Refill:	Liters	Qt
4-cyl.	3.8	4.0
6-cyl.	5.7	6.0
8-cyl.	4.7	5.0

Capacity shown includes filter
Above 0F° (-18°C) 10W-30
Below 60°F (16°C) 5W-30

TRANSMISSION, Automatic
32RH (Wrangler) 42RE,
   46RH **AP3**
AW-4 . . . .**MA**

CAPACITY, Initial Refill[2]:	Liters	Qt
AW4	4.0	4.3
Others	3.8	4.0

2 With the engine at operating temperature, shift transmission through all gears. Check fluid level in PARK (Commanche), or NEUTRAL (All others) and add fluid as needed.

TRANSMISSION, Manual . . .75W-90 GL-5

CAPACITY, Refill:	Liters	Pt
AX5 2WD	3.5	7.4
AX5 4WD	3.3	7.0
AX15 2WD	3.2	6.7
AX15 4WD	3.2	6.8

AX5 transmission has drain on bottom of case. AX15 transmission has drain on passenger side of case.

TRANSFER CASE . . . . . . .AF2, AP3, MA

CAPACITY, Refill:	Liters	Pt
Model 231 Command-Trac:		
Wrangler, YJ	1.5	3.3
Cherokee, Comanche, Grand Cherokee, Grand Wagoneer	1.0	2.2
Model 242 Select-Trac: Cherokee, Grand Cherokee, Grand Wagoneer	1.4	3.0

DIFFERENTIAL
Comanche, Grand Cherokee,
   Grand Wagoneer,
   Wrangler, YJ 75W-90 **GL-5**
With trailer tow pkg. 80W-140 **GL-5**
Cherokee 75W-90 **GL-5**
Grand Cherokee, Grand Wagoneer,
   Cherokee with Class III
   hitch . . . . .Synthetic 75W-140 **GL-5**[3]
3 Mopar synthetic gear oil. Part No. 82200945
All with Limited-Slip differential, add 2 oz. container Mopar Trac-Loc additive. Part No. 4318060

CAPACITY	Liters	Pt
Grand Cherokee, Grand Wagoneer		
Front	1.4	3.0
Rear	1.2	2.5
Comanche w/Metric Ton Pkg. . .	1.4	3.0
Cherokee 8¼" axle[4]	2.0	4.4
Others	1.2	2.5

4 3" axle shaft tube diameter

JEEP
1993 All Models

W   SERVICE TO MAINTAIN EMISSION WARRANTY

MI—MILES IN THOUSANDS
KM—KILOMETERS IN THOUSANDS

EVERY MONTH
Battery . . . . .clean/inspect
Check electrolyte level ex. maintenance free type

Brake master cylinder . . .check level **HB**

Coolant reservoir . . . . . .check level **EC**
Also check rubber seals on each side of radiator (proper fit required)

Power steering
   reservoir . . . . .check level **PS**

Tires . . . . .check

Transmission, automatic . . . .check level

Clutch fluid reservoir . . . .check level **HB**

EVERY 6 MO/7.5 MI—12 KM
Brake hoses . . . . .inspect

Crankcase . . . . .change oil
Change oil filter at each oil change

Exhaust system . . . . .inspect

Cooling system . . . . . . .check level **EC**
Inspect hoses, tighten clamps, check radiator cap

Propeller shafts . . . . . .lubricate **GC-LB**
At mileage interval only. U-joint & splines or yokes; inspect seals

Steering linkage,
   ball joints, 4WD . . . . .lubricate **GC-LB**

EVERY 6 MO/15 MI—24 KM
Steering linkage,
   ball joints, 2WD . . . . .lubricate **GC-LB**

EVERY 15 MI—24 KM
Battery . . . . .check level

Tires .rotate
Initial service at 7.5 mi (12 km)

EVERY 12 MONTHS
Air-conditioning system . . . . . . .inspect

EVERY 30 MI—48 KM
Differentials, front & rear . . . .change fluid

EVERY 24 MO/30 MI—48 KM
Transmission,
   automatic . . . . .change fluid/filter
At mileage interval only

Transfer case . . . . .change lubricant
At mileage interval only

W Air cleaner element . . . . .replace

Distributor cap & rotor . . . . .replace
Ex. Calif.

Drive belts . . . . .inspect/adjust

W Spark plugs . . . . .replace

EVERY 37.5 MI—60 KM
Trans, manual . . . . . . .change lubricant

FIRST 36 MO/52.5 MI—84.5 KM; THEN EVERY 24 MO/30 MI—48 KM
W Cooling
   system . . . . .flush, change coolant **EC**
Use 50% concentration for -34°F (-37°C) protection

EVERY 48 MO/60 MI—96 KM
W Drive belts . . . . .replace

Fuel filter . . . . .replace

W Ignition wires . . . . .replace

SERVICE AS REQUIRED
Transfer case, differentials . . .check level

Transmission, manual . . . . . .check level

Brakes . . . . .inspect
Front & rear brake linings, master cylinder, calipers, wheel cylinders. Check general condition of system.

Parking brake
   mechanism . . . . .lubricate **GC-LB**

Body .lubricate
Hinges, door latches, slides, locks

Chassis . . . . .inspect
Steering gear & linkage, springs, shocks, tires; check overall steering & suspension condition

SEVERE SERVICE
Crankcase—Change oil & filter every 3 mo/3 mi (4.8 km)

Transmission, automatic—Change fluid every 12 mi (19 km)

Transmission, manual—Change lubricant every 18 mi (29 km)

Differentials—Change fluid every 12 mi (19 km)

Propeller shafts—Lubricate every 3 mi (4.8 km)

Perform other scheduled maintenance twice as frequently

KEY TO LUBRICANTS
AF2	DEXRON®-II Automatic Transmission Fluid
AP3	MOPAR ATF-3® Automatic Transmission
CD	Motor Oil, API Service CD
CE	Motor Oil, API Service CE
EC	Ethylene Glycol Coolant
GC	Wheel Bearing Grease, NLGI Category GC
GL-5	Gear Oil, API Service GL-5
GL-5★	Special Lubricant for Trac-Lok Differential
HB	Hydraulic Brake Fluid, Dot 3
LB	Chassis Grease, NLGI Category LB
MA	MERCON® Automatic Transmission Fluid
PS	Power Steering Fluid
SG	Motor Oil, API Service SG

CRANKCASE . . . . . . .SG, SG/CD, SG/CE
CAPACITY, Refill:	Liters	Qt
4-cyl.	3.8	4.0
6-cyl.	5.7	6.0
8-cyl.	4.7	5.0

Capacity shown includes filter
Above 0°F (-18°C) 10W-30
Below 60°F (16°C) 5W-30

TRANSMISSION, Automatic
32RH (Wrangler) 42RE, 46RH **AP3**
AW-4 . . . .**MA**
CAPACITY, Initial Refill[2]:	Liters	Qt
AW4	4.0	4.3
Others	3.8	4.0

2 With the engine at operating temperature, shift transmission through all gears. Check fluid level in NEUTRAL and add fluid as needed.

TRANSMISSION, Manual . . .75W-90 GL-5
CAPACITY, Refill:	Liters	Pt
AX5 2WD	3.5	7.4
AX5 4WD	3.3	7.0
AX15 2WD	3.2	6.7
AX15 4WD	3.2	6.8

AX5 transmission has drain on bottom of case. AX15 transmission has drain on passenger side of case.

TRANSFER CASE . . . . . . .AF2, AP3, MA
CAPACITY, Refill:	Liters	Pt
Model 231 Command-Trac:		
Wrangler, YJ	1.5	3.3
Cherokee, Comanche, Grand Cherokee, Grand Wagoneer	1.0	2.2
Model 242 Select-Trac:		
Cherokee, Grand Cherokee, Grand Wagoneer	1.4	3.0
Model 249 Quadra-Trac:		
Grand Cherokee		
Grand Wagoneer	1.2	2.5

DIFFERENTIAL
Comanche, Grand Cherokee,
   Grand Wagoneer,
   Cherokee, Wrangler, YJ . .75W-90 **GL-5**
Wrangler, YJ with trailer
   tow pkg. 80W-140 **GL-5**
Grand Cherokee, Grand Wagoneer,
   Cherokee with Class III or IV
   hitch . . . . . . .Synthetic 75W-140 **GL-5**[3]

3 Mopar synthetic gear oil. Part No. 82200945
All with Limited-Slip differential, add 2 oz. container Mopar Trac-Loc additive. Part No. 4318060

CAPACITY	Liters	Pt
Grand Cherokee, Grand Wagoneer Cherokee, Wrangler		
Front	1.4	3.0
Rear	1.2	2.5
Comanche w/Metric Ton Pkg. . . .	1.4	3.0
Cherokee 8¼" axle[4]	2.0	4.4
Others	1.2	2.5

4 3" axle shaft tube diameter

144

SERVICE AT TIME OR MILEAGE — WHICHEVER OCCURS FIRST

JPPM9   JPPM9

W   SERVICE TO MAINTAIN EMISSION WARRANTY

MI—MILES IN THOUSANDS
KM—KILOMETERS IN THOUSANDS

EVERY MONTH
Battery . . . . .clean/inspect
Check electrolyte level ex. maintenance free type

Brake master cylinder . . .check level **HB**

Coolant reservoir . . . . . . .check level **EC**
Also check rubber seals on each side of radiator (proper fit required)

Power steering
   reservoir . . . . .check level **PS**

Tires .check

Transmission, automatic . . . .check level

Clutch fluid reservoir . . . .check level **HB**
Ex. 1996-97

EVERY 6 MO/7.5 MI—12 KM
Brake hoses . . . . .inspect

Crankcase . . . . .change oil
Change oil filter at each oil change

Suspension ball joints,
   1995-97 . . . . .lubricate **GC-LB**

Chassis, 1995-97 . . . . .inspect
After off-road (4WD) use, examine overall steering & suspension condition.

Exhaust system . . . . .inspect

Cooling system . . . . . . .check level **EC**
Inspect hoses, tighten clamps, check radiator cap

Propeller shafts . . . . . .lubricate **GC-LB**
At mileage interval only. U-joint & splines or yokes; inspect seals.

Steering linkage,
   ball joints, 4WD . . . . .lubricate **GC-LB**

Tires .rotate
At mileage only.

EVERY 12 MO/15 MI—24 KM
Battery . . . . .check level

Steering linkage,
   ball joints, 2WD . . . . .lubricate **GC-LB**

EVERY 12 MONTHS
Air-conditioning system . . . . .inspect

EVERY 22.5 MI—36 KM
Brake linings, 1995-97 . . . . .inspect

EVERY 30 MI—48 KM
Differentials,
   front & rear, 1994 . . . . . . .change fluid

EVERY 24 MO/30 MI—48 KM
Transmission,
   automatic . . . . .change fluid/filter

Transfer case . . . . .change lubricant

W Air cleaner element . . . . .replace

Drive belts . . . . .inspect/adjust
1997 all models, 1994-96 all ex. 5.2L V-8

W Spark plugs . . . . .replace

EVERY 30 MO/37.5 MI—60 KM
Trans, manual . . . . . . .change lubricant

1994
FIRST 42 MO/52.5 MI—84.5 KM
1995-97
FIRST 36 MO/52.5 MI—84.5 KM
THEN EVERY 24 MO/30 MI—48 KM
W Cooling
   system . . . . .flush, change coolant **EC**
Use 50% concentration for -34°F (-37°C) protection

EVERY 48 MO/60 MI—96 KM
PCV valve . . . . .check/replace
5.2L only

Distributor cap & rotor, 1994 . . . .replace
Ex. 5.2L

W Drive belts, 1994 . . . . .replace
4.0L only

Fuel filter . . . . .replace
1994, ex. 5.2L & Calif. vehicles
1995-96, Federal only
1997, Calif. Grand Cherokee

W Ignition wires . . . . .replace

SERVICE AS REQUIRED
Transfer case, differentials . . .check level

Transmission, manual . . . . .check level

Brakes, 1994 . . . . .inspect
Front & rear brake linings, master cylinder, calipers, wheel cylinders. Check general condition of system

Body . . . . .lubricate
Hinges, door latches, slides, locks

Chassis . . . . .inspect
Steering gear & linkage, springs, shocks, tires; check overall steering & suspension condition

Parking brake
   mechanism . . . . .lubricate **GC-LB**

Fuel filter . . . . .replace

SEVERE SERVICE
Crankcase—Change oil & filter every 3 mo/3 mi (4.8 km)

Transmission, automatic—Change fluid every 12 mi (19 km)

Transmission, manual—Change lubricant every 18 mi (29 km)

Differentials—Change fluid every 12 mi (19 km)

Propeller shafts & slip splines—Lubricate every 3 mi (4.8 km)

Brake linings—1995-97, inspect every 12 mi (19 km)

PCV valve—(5.2L) Inspect every 30 mi (48 km)

Brake hoses, exhaust, cooling system—Check every 3 mi (4.8 km)

Suspension ball joints—1995-97, lubricate every 3 mi (4.8 km)

Steering linkage 4WD—Lubricate every 3 mi (4.8 km) ex. 1997 Wrangler every 6 mi (9.6 km)

Tires—Rotate every 6 mi (10 km)

W **Air Cleaner element**—Inspect/replace every 15 mi (24 km)

KEY TO LUBRICANTS

AF3	DEXRON®-III Automatic Transmission Fluid
AF2	DEXRON®-II Automatic Transmission Fluid
AP3	MOPAR ATF+3® Automatic Transmission Fluid
API★	Motor Oil certified by the Amercian Petroleum Institute (Starburst Symbol)
EC	Ethylene Glycol Coolant
GC	Wheel Bearing Grease, NLGI Category GC
GL-3	Gear Oil, API Service GL-3
GL-5	Gear Oil, API Service GL-5
GL-5★	Special Lubricant for Trac-Lok Differential
HB	Hydraulic Brake Fluid, Dot 3
LB	Chassis Grease, NLGI No. 2 EP Category LB
MA	MERCON® Automatic Transmission Fluid
PS	MOPAR Power Steering Fluid Meeting MS-5931

CRANKCASE . . . . .API★

CAPACITY, Refill:	Liters	Qt
4-cyl.	3.8	4.0
6-cyl.	5.7	6.0
8-cyl.	4.7	5.0

Capacity shown includes filter
Above 0°F (-18°C) 10W-30
Below 60°F (16°C) 5W-30

TRANSMISSION, Automatic
32RH 30RH (Wrangler) 42RE, 44RE,
  42RH 46RH **AP3**
AW-4 . . . .**MA**

CAPACITY, Initial Refill[2]:	Liters	Qt
All models[3]	3.8	4.0

2 With the engine at operating temperature, shift transmission through all gears. Check fluid level in NEUTRAL and add fluid as needed.

3 Approximate.

TRANSMISSION, Manual
1997 Cherokee 75W-90 **GL-3**
Others 75W-90 **GL-5**

CAPACITY, Refill:	Liters	Pt
AX 4/5 2WD (1995-97)	3.3	7.0
AX 5 4WD (1995-97)	3.2	6.6
AX5 2WD (1994)	3.5	7.4
AX5 4WD (1994)	3.3	7.0
AX15 2WD	3.2	6.7
AX15 4WD	3.2	6.8

AX5 transmission has drain on bottom of case. AX15 transmission has drain on passenger side of case.

TRANSFER CASE . . . . **AP3, AF2, AF3, MA**

CAPACITY, Refill:	Liters	Pt
Model 231 Command-Trac:		
Wrangler, YJ & TJ w/manual . .	1.5	3.3
Cherokee, Grand Cherokee,		
Wrangler, XJ & TJ w/automatic	1.0	2.2
Model 242 Select-Trac:		
Cherokee, Grand Cherokee . . .	1.4	3.0
Model 249 Quadra-Trac:		
Grand Cherokee	1.2	2.5

DIFFERENTIAL
Cherokee, Grand Cherokee,
  Wrangler, YJ, 1994-95 . . . . .75W-90 **GL-5**
     1996-97 . . . . .80W-90 **GL-5**

Wrangler, YJ with trailer
  tow pkg., 1994-95 . . . . .80W-140 **GL-5**

Grand Cherokee, Cherokee with Class III
  or IV hitch & 1997 Wrangler w/trailer
  tow pkg. . . . . .Synthetic 75W-140 **GL-5**[4]

4 Mopar synthetic gear oil. Part No. 82200945
All with Limited-Slip differential, add 5% Mopar Trac-Loc additive. Part No. 4318060

CAPACITY, Refill:[5]	Liters	Pt
Grand Cherokee,		
Cherokee, Wrangler: Front . . .	1.5	3.1
Rear	1.2	2.5
Cherokee 8¼" axle[6]	2.0	4.4

5 Lubricate level in axle must be ½" below fill plug opening.
6 3" axle shaft tube diameter.

SERVICE AT TIME OR MILEAGE — WHICHEVER OCCURS FIRST

JPPM10   JPPM10

W   SERVICE TO MAINTAIN EMISSION WARRANTY

MI—MILES IN THOUSANDS
KM—KILOMETERS IN THOUSANDS

EVERY MONTH
Battery . . . . .clean/inspect
Check electrolyte level ex. maintenance free type

Brake master cylinder . . .check level **HB**

Coolant reservoir . . . . . . .check level **EC**
Also check rubber seals on each side of radiator (proper fit required)

Power steering
 reservoir . . . . .check level **PS**

Tires . . . . .check

Transmission, automatic . . . .check level

EVERY 6 MO/7.5 MI—12 KM
Brake hoses . . . . .inspect

Crankcase . . . . .change oil
Change oil filter at each oil change

Suspension ball joints . .lubricate **GC-LB**

Chassis . . . . .inspect
After off-road (4WD) use, examine overall steering & suspension condition.

Exhaust system . . . . .inspect

Cooling system . . . . . . .check level **EC**
Inspect hoses, tighten clamps, check radiator cap

Propeller shafts . . . . . .lubricate **GC-LB**
At mileage interval only. U-joint & splines or yokes; inspect seals.

Steering linkage,
 ball joints, 4WD . . . . .lubricate **GC-LB**
Ex. Cherokee

Tires . . . . .rotate
At mileage only.

EVERY 12 MO/15 MI—24 KM
Battery . . . . .check level

Steering linkage,
 ball joints . . . . .lubricate **GC-LB**
Grand Cherokee 2WD & Cherokee

EVERY 12 MONTHS
Air-conditioning system . . . . . . .inspect

EVERY 22.5 MI—36 KM
Brake linings . . . . .inspect

EVERY 24 MO/30 MI—48 KM
Transmission,
 automatic . . . . .change fluid/filter
Ex. Wrangler

Transfer case . . . . .change lubricant

W Air cleaner element . . . . .replace

Drive belts . . . . .inspect/adjust

W Spark plugs . . . . .replace

EVERY 30 MO/37.5 MI—60 KM
Trans, manual . . . . .change lubricant
Wrangler only
Trans, automatic . . . . . .change fluid/filter
Wrangler

WRANGLER:
FIRST 36 MO/52.5 MI—84.5 KM
THEN EVERY 36 MO/45 MI—72.5 KM
OTHERS:
FIRST 36 MO/52.5 MI—84.5 KM
THEN EVERY 24 MO/30 MI—48 KM
W Cooling
 system . . . . .flush, change coolant **EC**
Use 50% concentration for -34°F (-37°C) protection

EVERY 48 MO/60 MI—96 KM
PCV valve . . . . .check/replace
5.2L only

Fuel filter . . . . .replace
Calif. Grand Cherokee only

W Ignition wires . . . . .replace

SERVICE AS REQUIRED
Transfer case, differentials . . .check level

Transmission, manual . . . . .check level

Body . . . . .lubricate
Hinges, door latches, slides, locks

Chassis . . . . .inspect
Steering gear & linkage, springs, shocks, tires; check overall steering & suspension condition

Parking brake
 mechanism . . . . .lubricate **GC-LB**

Fuel filter . . . . .replace

SEVERE SERVICE
Crankcase—Change oil & filter every 3 mo/3 mi (4.8 km)

Transmission, automatic—Change fluid & replace filter every 12 mi (19 km)

Transmission, manual—Wrangler: change lubricant every 18 mi (29 km)

Differentials—Change fluid every 12 mi (19 km)

Propeller shafts & slip splines—Lubricate every 3 mi (4.8 km)

Brake linings—inspect every 12 mi (19 km)

PCV valve—(5.2L) Inspect every 30 mi (48 km)

Brake hoses, exhaust, cooling system—Check every 3 mi (4.8 km)

Suspension ball joints—lubricate every 3 mi (4.8 km), ex. Wrangler every 6 mi (9.6 km)

Steering linkage—Lubricate Grand Cherokee 4WD every 3 mi (4.8 km), Wrangler & Cherokee every 6 mi (9.6 km)

Tires—Rotate every 6 mi (10 km)

W **Air Cleaner element**—Inspect/replace every 15 mi (24 km)

Battery—Check level every 7.5 mi (12 km)

KEY TO LUBRICANTS
AF3	DEXRON®-III Automatic Transmission Fluid
AF2	DEXRON®-II
AP3	MOPAR ATF+3®
API★	Motor Oil certified by the American Petroleum Institute (Starburst Symbol)
EC	Ethylene Glycol Coolant
GC	Wheel Bearing Grease, NLGI Category GC
GL-3	Gear Oil, API Service GL-3
GL-5	Gear Oil, API Service GL-5
GL-5★	Special Lubricant for Trac-Lok Differential
HB	Hydraulic Brake Fluid, Dot 3
LB	Chassis Grease, NLGI No. 2 EP Category LB
MA	MERCON® Automatic Transmission Fluid
PS	MOPAR Power Steering Fluid Meeting MS-5931

CRANKCASE . . . . .API★
CAPACITY, Refill:	Liters	Qt
4-cyl.	3.8	4.0
6-cyl.	5.7	6.0
8-cyl.	4.7	5.0

Capacity shown includes filter
Above 0°F (-18°C) 10W-30*
Below 60°F (16°C) 5W-30
*Preferred

TRANSMISSION, Automatic
Cherokee w/4.0L (AW-4) . . . .**MA**
Others **AP3**
CAPACITY, Initial Refill[2]:	Liters	Qt
Cherokee w/4.0L (AW-4)[3]	1.9	2.0
Others[3]	3.8	4.0

2 With the engine at operating temperature, shift transmission through all gears. Check fluid level in NEUTRAL and add fluid as needed.
3 Approximate.

TRANSMISSION, Manual . . .75W-90 **GL-3**
CAPACITY, Refill:	Liters	Pt
AX5 2WD	3.5	7.4
Others	3.2	6.6

AX5 transmission has drain on bottom of case. AX15 transmission has drain on passenger side of case.

TRANSFER CASE . . . .AP3, AF2, AF3, MA
CAPACITY, Refill:	Liters	Pt
Model 231 Command-Trac:		
Wrangler, Cherokee	1.0	2.2
Model 242 Select-Trac:		
Cherokee, Grand Cherokee . . .	1.4	3.0
Model 249 Quadra-Trac:		
Grand Cherokee	1.2	2.5

DIFFERENTIAL
Cherokee 75W-90 **GL-5**
Grand Cherokee,
 Wrangler 80W-90 **GL-5**
Grand Cherokee, Cherokee with Class III
 or IV hitch & Wrangler w/trailer
 tow pkg. . . . . .Synthetic 75W-140 **GL-5**[4]
4 Mopar synthetic gear oil. Part No. 82200945
All with Limited-Slip differential, add 5% Mopar Trac-Loc additive. Part No. 4318060
CAPACITY, Refill:[5]	Liters	Pt
Front: Cherokee	1.5	3.2
Others	1.2	2.5
Rear: 194 RBI	1.7	3.5
Wrangler 216 RBI	1.9	4.0
Cherokee 8¼" axle[6]	2.0	4.4
Grand Cherokee 216 RBA (aluminum)	2.3	4.8

5 Lubricate level in axle must be ½" below fill plug opening.
6 3" axle shaft tube diameter.

SERVICE AT TIME OR MILEAGE — WHICHEVER OCCURS FIRST

JPPM11   JPPM11

W   SERVICE TO MAINTAIN EMISSION WARRANTY

KEY TO LUBRICANTS
See inside front cover

MI—MILES IN THOUSANDS
KM—KILOMETERS IN THOUSANDS

EVERY MONTH
Battery . . . . .clean/inspect
Check electrolyte level ex. maintenance free type

Brake master cylinder   . . .check level **HB**

Coolant reservoir . . . . . . .check level **EC**
Also check rubber seals on each side of radiator (proper fit required)

Power steering
    reservoir . . . . .check level **PS**

Tires . . . . .check

Transmission, automatic . . .check level

EVERY 6 MO/7.5 MI—12 KM
Brake hoses . . . . .inspect

Crankcase . . . . .change oil
Change oil filter at each oil change

Chassis . . . . .inspect
After off-road (4WD) use, examine overall steering & suspension condition.

Exhaust system . . . . .inspect

Cooling system . . . . . . .check level **EC**
Inspect hoses, tighten clamps, check radiator cap

Propeller shafts . . . . . .lubricate **GC-LB**
(When equipped w/fittings) At mileage interval only. U-joint & splines or yokes; inspect seals

Steering linkage, 4WD . .lubricate **GC-LB**
Ex. Grand Cherokee

Tires . . . . .rotate
At mileage only.

EVERY 12 MO/15 MI—24 KM
Battery . . . . .check level

Suspension ball joints . .lubricate **GC-LB**

Steering linkage, 2WD . .lubricate **GC-LB**

EVERY 12 MONTHS
Air-conditioning system . . . . . . .inspect

EVERY 18 MO/22.5 MI—36 KM
Transfer case . . . . .change lubricant
Grand Cherokee w/NV 247 only

EVERY 22.5 MI—36 KM
Brake caliper pins . . . .clean/lubricate **BL**
2000 Grand Cherokee only

Brake linings . . . . .inspect

EVERY 24 MO/30 MI—48 KM
Transmission,
    automatic . . . . .change fluid/filter
1999 All models
2000 Grand Cherokee w/4.7L & Cherokee w/4.0L

Transfer case . . . . .change lubricant
Except Grand Cherokee w/NV 247

W Air cleaner element . . . . .replace

Drive belts . . . . .inspect/adjust
1999 2.5L & 4.0L only
2000 Cherokee & 2.5L Wrangler

W Spark plugs . . . . .replace

EVERY 30 MO/37.5 MI—60 KM
Transmission,
    manual, 1999 . . . . . . .change lubricant

Transmission,
    automatic . . . . .change fluid/filter
2000 ex. Grand Cherokee w/4.7L & Cherokee w/4.0L

FIRST 36 MO/52.5 MI—84.5 KM
THEN EVERY 24 MO/30 MI—48 KM
W Cooling
    system . . . . .flush, change coolant **EC**
Use 50% concentration for -34°F (-37°C) protection

EVERY 48 MO/60 MI—96 KM
Brake fluid . . . . .replace **HB**
2000 Grand Cherokee only

Drive belt, 2000 . . . . . . .inspect/replace
4.0L Grand Cherokee. Inspect every 15 mi (24 km) if belt is not replaced

PCV valve . . . . .check/replace
4.7L V-8 only

Fuel filter, 1999 . . . . .replace
Calif. Grand Cherokee only

W Ignition wires . . . . .replace
Ex. Grand Cherokee

1999
EVERY 72 MO/90 MI—144 KM
2000
EVERY 60 MO/75 MI—120 KM
Drive belt 4.7L V-8 . . . . .inspect/replace
Initially, then every 15 mi (24 km) if belt not replaced

SERVICE AS REQUIRED
Transfer case, differentials . . .check level

Transmission, manual . . . . .check level

Body . . . . .lubricate
Hinges, door latches, slides, locks

Chassis . . . . .inspect
Steering gear & linkage, springs, shocks, tires; check overall steering & suspension condition

Parking brake
    mechanism . . . . .lubricate **GC-LB**

Fuel filter . . . . .replace

SEVERE SERVICE
Crankcase—Change oil & filter every 3 mo/3 mi (4.8 km)

Transmission, automatic—Change fluid & replace filter every 12 mi (19 km)

Transmission, manual—1999 Change lubricant every 18 mi (29 km)

Differentials—Change fluid every 12 mi (19 km)

Propeller shafts & slip splines—Lubricate every 3 mi (4.8 km)
(When equipped w/fittings)

Brake linings—inspect every 12 mi (19 km); 2000 Grand Cherokee lubricate caliper pins w/**BL**

Brake hoses, exhaust, cooling system—Check every 3 mi (4.8 km)

Suspension ball joints—lubricate every 6 mi (9.6 km)

Steering linkage—Lubricate every 3 mi (4.8 km)

Tires—Rotate every 6 mi (10 km)

W **Air Cleaner element**—Inspect/replace every 15 mi (24 km)

Battery—Check level every 7.5 mi (12 km)

CRANKCASE . . . . .API★

CAPACITY, Refill:	Liters	Qt
4-cyl.	3.8	4.0
6-cyl. & 8-cyl.	5.7	6.0

Capacity shown includes filter
8-cyl. (4.7L)
Above 0°F (-18°C) 10W-30
Below 100°F (38°C) 5W-30*
Others:
Above 0°F (-18°C) 10W-30*
Below 60°F (16°C) 1999 . . . . .5W-30
Below 100°F (38°C) 2000 . . . . .5W-30
*Preferred

TRANSMISSION, Automatic
Cherokee w/4.0L (AW-4) . . . .**MA**
Others **AP3**

CAPACITY, Initial Refill[2]:	Liters	Qt
Cherokee w/4.0L (AW-4)[3]	1.9	2.0
Grand Cherokee w/45 RFE[3, 4]	4.7	5.0
Others[3]	3.8	4.0

2 With the engine at operating temperature, shift transmission through all gears. Check fluid level in NEUTRAL and add fluid as needed.
3 Approximate
4 DTC's may be set, reset with the DRB III®, if necessary

TRANSMISSION, Manual
NV 3550 . . . .**GLS**
Others 75W-90 **GL-3**

CAPACITY, Refill:	Liters	Pt
NV 3550	2.3	4.8
AX5 2WD	3.5	7.4
Others	3.2	6.6

AX5 transmission has drain on bottom of case. AX15 transmission has drain on passenger side of case

TRANSFER CASE
NV 247 . . . .**SLF**
Others . . . .**AP3, AF2, AF3, MA**

CAPACITY, Refill:	Liters	Pt
NV 231 Command-Trac:		
Wrangler, Cherokee	1.0	2.2
NV 242 Select-Trac:		
Cherokee, Grand Cherokee . . .	1.4	3.0
NV 247 Quadra-Trac® II:		
Grand Cherokee	1.6	3.4

DIFFERENTIAL
Cherokee 75W-90 **GL-5**
Grand Cherokee,
    Wrangler 80W-90 **GL-5**
Grand Cherokee, Cherokee with Class III
    or IV hitch or Quadra Drive & Wrangler
    w/trailer
    tow pkg. . . . . .Synthetic 75W-140 **GL-5**[4]
4 Mopar synthetic gear oil. Part No. 82200945
All with Limited-Slip differential, & models wirh Quadra Drive (front & rear axle), add 5% Mopar Trac-Loc additive. Part No. 4318060

CAPACITY, Refill:[5]	Liters	Pt
Front: Cherokee	1.5	3.2
Others	1.2	2.5
Rear: 194 RBI	1.7	3.5
Wrangler 216 RBI	1.9	4.0
Cherokee 8¼" axle	2.0	4.4
Grand Cherokee 198 RBI	1.7	3.6
226 RBA	2.3	4.8

5 Lubricate level in axle must be ½" below fill plug opening.

SERVICE LOCATIONS—ENGINE AND CHASSIS

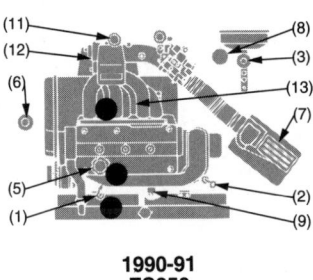

**1990-91
ES250
2507cc**

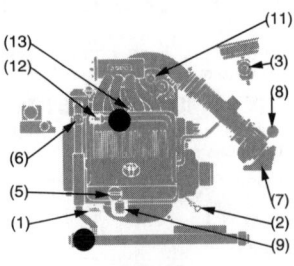

**1992-00
ES300, RX300
2958cc, 2995cc**

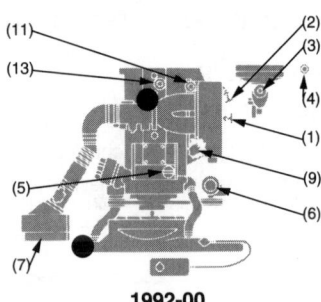

**1992-00
GS300, SC300
2997cc**

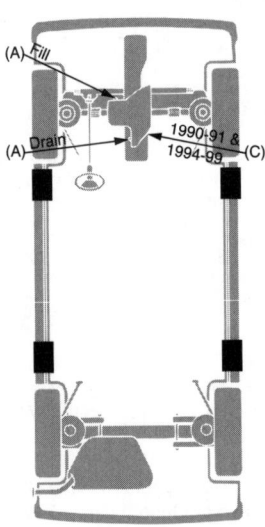

**1990-00
LS400, LX470, SC400
3969cc, 4669cc**

(1) Crankcase dipstick
(2) Transmission dipstick
(3) Brake fluid reservoir
(4) Clutch fluid reservoir
(5) Oil fill cap
(6) Power steering reservoir
(7) Air filter

(8) Fuel filter
(9) Oil filter
(10) PCV filter
(11) EGR valve
(12) Oxygen sensor
(13) PCV valve

● Cooling system drain

**1990-00
ES250, ES300,
RX300**

**1992-00
GS300,
SC300, SC400**

**1990-00
LS400**

■ Lift adapter position

(A) Manual transmission/transaxle, drain & fill

(B) Transfer case, NOT USED

(C) Automatic transaxle final drive, drain & fill

(D) Differential, drain & fill

148

SERVICE AT TIME OR MILEAGE—WHICHEVER OCCURS FIRST

LXIPM1   LXIPM1

Perform the following maintenance services at the intervals indicated to keep the vehicle warranties in effect.
W   SERVICE TO MAINTAIN EMISSION WARRANTY

MI—MILES IN THOUSANDS
KM—KILOMETERS IN THOUSANDS

EVERY 12 MO/7.5 MI—12 KM
Body . . . . .inspect
Check for rust & scratches. Road test and check vehicle integrity.

W Crankcase . . . . .change oil

W Oil filter . . . . .replace

Tires . . . . .rotate

EVERY 24 MO/15 MI—24 KM
Brake system . . . . .check
Fluid level **HB**, disc pads & rotors, drums, linings, booster, parking brake, lines, pipes & hoses

Front suspension . . . . .inspect
Ball joints, dust covers

Differential . . . . .check level

Drive shaft boots FWD . . . . .inspect

Transmission, transaxle,
   manual . . . . .check level

Steering . . . . .inspect
Check linkage & free play

Power steering fluid . . . .check level **AF3**

Transmission, transaxle,
   automatic . . . . .check level

Body . . . . .inspect
Torque nuts & bolts

EVERY 36 MO/30 MI—48 KM
Brake system . . . . .change fluid **HB**

Exhaust system . . . . .inspect

W Air cleaner element . . . . .replace

Fuel lines & hoses . . . . .inspect

FIRST 36 MO/45 MI—72 KM; THEN EVERY 24 MO/30 MI—48 KM
Cooling system . . . . .change coolant **EC**

EVERY 72 MO/60 MI—96 KM
Charcoal canister . . . . .inspect
Check fuel evaporative system, hoses & connections

Drive belts . . . . .inspect
Initial service, inspect every 12 mo/7.5 mi (12 km) thereafter

Fuel cap gasket . . . . .replace

Spark plugs . . . . .replace

W Valve clearance . . . . .adjust

EVERY 120 MONTHS
Air bag system . . . . .inspect
Initial service; then every 24 months

SEVERE SERVICE

W **Crankcase**—Change oil & filter every 6 mo/3.75 mi (6 km)

Exhaust system—Inspect every 24 mo/15 mi (24 km)

Suspension steering & brake components—Inspect every 12 mo/7.5 mi (12 km)

Transmission, transaxle, transfer case & differential—Change fluid or lubricant every 24 mo/15mi (24 km)

W **Air cleaner element**—Inspect every 6 mo/3.75 mi (6 km)

Timing belt—Replace every 60 mi (96 km)

KEY TO LUBRICANTS

AF3	DEXRON®-III Automatic Transmission Fluid
EC	Ethylene Glycol Coolant
	Maintain coolant protection to at least -34°F (-37°C)
GL-4	Gear Oil, API Service GL-4
GL-5	Gear Oil, API Service GL-5
HB	Hydraulic Brake Fluid, DOT 3
SH	Motor Oil, API Service SH
SLF	Special Lubricant Fluid
	Toyota ATF, Type TIV

CRANKCASE . . . .**SH**
CAPACITY, Refill:

	Liters	Qt
ES250	3.7	3.9
ES300: 1992-93	4.1	4.3
1994-95	4.5	4.8
GS300	5.1	5.4
LS400: 1990	4.7	5.0
1991-92	5.0	5.3
1993-95	4.8	5.1
SC300	4.9	5.2
SC400	4.5	4.8

Capacity shown is without filter. When replacing filter, additional oil may be needed.

1990 ES250:
Above 10°F (-12°C) . . .15W-40, 20W-40, 20W-50
Above -10°F (-23°C) . .10W-30, 10W-40, 10W-50
Below 50°F (10°C) 5W-30
1991-93 ES250, ES300:
Above 0°F (-18°C) 10W-30
Below 50°F (10°C) 5W-30
1990-95 LS400
1992-95 SC300, GS300, SC400
1994-95 ES300:
Above 0°F (-18°C) 10W-30
Below 100°F (38°C) . . . . .5W-30[1]
[1] Preferred

TRANSMISSION/TRANSAXLE, Automatic
GS300, LS400, SC400 . . . .**SLF**[2]
[2] ATF Type TIV, Part No. 08886-80105
ES250, ES300, SC300 . . . .**AF3**
Differential is serviced separately in 1990-91 ES250 & 1994-95 ES300

CAPACITY, Initial Refill[3]:

	Liters	Qt
ES250	2.5	2.6
ES300: 1992-93	3.1	3.3
1994-95	3.5	3.7
GS300	1.9	2.0
LS400	2.0	2.1
SC300	1.6	1.7
SC400	1.9	2.0

[3] With the engine at operating temperature, shift transmission through all gears. Check fluid level in PARK and add fluid as needed.

TRANSMISSION/TRANSAXLE, Manual 75W-90, 80W-90 **GL-4, GL-5**
CAPACITY, Refill:

	Liters	Pt
ES250, ES300	4.2	8.8
SC300	2.6	4.8

FINAL DRIVE **AF3**
1990-91 ES250 & 1994-95 ES300
CAPACITY, Refill:

	Liters	Pt
1990-91	1.0	2.2
1994-95	0.9	2.0

DIFFERENTIAL, Rear **GL-5**
Above 0°F (-18°C), 90; below 0°F (-18°C), 80W, 80W-90
CAPACITY, Refill:

	Liters	Pt
GS300, LS400, SC300, SC400	1.3	2.6

Copyright 2000 by Chek-Chart Publications

149

LEXUS
1996-2000 All Models
ex. LX450, LX470, RX300

Perform the following maintenance services at the intervals indicated to keep the vehicle warranties in effect.
W   SERVICE TO MAINTAIN EMISSION WARRANTY

MI—MILES IN THOUSANDS
KM—KILOMETERS IN THOUSANDS

SERVICE PERIODICALLY
Brake & clutch fluid
   reservoir . . . . .check level **HB**

Power steering . . . . . . .check level **AF3**

Transmission, manual . . . . .inspect
Check for leaks

EVERY 6 MO/7.5 MI—12 KM
Cabin air filter, 1996-00 LS400,
   2000 ES300 . . . . .inspect/clean

Crankcase . . . . .change oil

Oil filter . . . . .replace

Tires .rotate
At mileage interval only

EVERY 12 MO/15 MI—24 KM
Ball joints . . . . .inspect
Also check dust covers

Brake system . . . . .inspect

Differential or final drive . . . . .check level
All models, as equipped. Check for leaks.

Drive shaft boots . . . . .inspect
Retorque flange bolts

Exhaust system . . . . .inspect

Rack & pinion assembly . . . . .check
Inspect for leaks

Steering linkage . . . . .inspect

Cabin air filter . . . . .replace
1996-99 LS400, 1998-99 GS300, GS400, 2000 All models

Drive belts . . . . .inspect/adjust
After initial service only

Transmission, automatic . . . .check level
Check for leaks

Body . . . . .inspect

Road test vehicle
Check for proper operation of engine, transmission, brakes, and steering. Check for abnormal noise or vibration.

EVERY 24 MO/30 MI—48 KM
Brake fluid . . . . .replace **HB**

Air cleaner element . . . . .replace

Cooling system . . . . .replace coolant **EC**

Drive belts, 1996 . . . . . . .inspect/adjust
Ex. ribbed belts, initial service only

Fuel lines & connections . . . . . . .inspect

Fuel tank . . . . .inspect
Check vapor vent system & bands. Also check fuel tank cap.

EVERY 48 MO/60 MI—96 KM
Drive belts . . . . .inspect/adjust
Second service for 1996 non-ribbed. Initial service for ribbed.

W Spark plugs . . . . .replace
1996-98 All, 1999-00 GS300, SC300

Valve clearance . . . . .inspect/adjust
Adjust only if noisy

EVERY 72 MO/60 MI—96 KM
Charcoal canister, 1996-98 . . . . . .inspect
Ex. 1998 GS300, GS400

W Spark plugs . . . . .replace
1999 LS400, GS400, SC400, ES300

EVERY 72 MO/90 MI—144 KM
Timing belt . . . . .replace
1996-97 SC400, LS400
1999 ex. ES300
2000 All

EVERY 96 MO/120 MI—192 KM
W Spark plugs . . . . .replace
2000 LS400, GS400, SC400, ES300

EVERY 120 MONTHS
THEN EVERY 24 MONTHS
Air bag system . . . . .inspect

SEVERE SERVICE
Automatic transmission, final drive, differential—Change lubricant every 12 mo/15 mi (24 km)

Brake system—Inspect every 4 mo/5 mi (8 km)

Cabin air filter—LS400 & 2000 ES300, inspect every 4 mo/5 mi (8 km)

Crankcase—Change oil & filter every 4 mo/5 mi (8 km)

Drive shaft boots—Inspect every 4 mo/5 mi (8 km). Also torque flange bolts.

Manual transmission/transaxle—Change lubricant every 24 mo/30 mi (48 km)

Steering linkage & ball joints—Inspect every 4 mo/5 mi (8 km)

Air cleaner element—Inspect every 4 mo/5 mi (8 km)

Body & chassis—Torque nuts and bolts every 4 mo/5 mi (8 km)

Timing belt—Replace every: 1996-97 all, 60 mi (96 km). 1998-99 ES300, 72mo/90mi (144 km).

Road test vehicle—Every 4 mo/5 mi (8 km)

Tires—1997-00, rotate every 4mo/5mi (8 km)

KEY TO LUBRICANTS
AF3   DEXRON®-III Automatic Transmission Fluid

EC   Ethylene Glycol Coolant
Maintain coolant protection to at least -34°F (-37°C)

GL-4   Gear Oil, API Service GL-4

GL-5   Gear Oil, API Service GL-5

HB   Hydraulic Brake Fluid, DOT 3

SJ   Motor Oil, API Service SJ

SLF   Special Lubricant Fluid
Toyota ATF, Type TIV

CRANKCASE . . . . .SJ

CAPACITY, Refill:	Liters	Qt
ES300	4.5	4.8
GS300	5.1	5.4
GS400	4.9	5.2
LS400: 1996-97	4.8	5.1
1998-00	5.3	5.6
SC300	4.9	5.2
SC400	4.5	4.8

Capacity shown is without filter. When replacing filter, additional oil may be needed.
Above 0°F (-18°C) 10W-30
Below 100°F (38°C), 1996-97 . . . . .5W-30[1]
All temperatures, 1998-00 . . . . .5W-30[1]
1 Preferred

TRANSMISSION/TRANSAXLE, Automatic
1996-97: GS300, LS400, SC400 . . . . .**SLF[2]**
ES300, SC300 . . . .**AF3**
1996-98 ES300, final drive is serviced separately
1998-99 All ex. ES300 . . . .**SLF[2]**
   ES300 . . . .**AF3**
2000 All Models . . . .**SLF[2]**
2 ATF Type T IV, Part No. 08886-80105

CAPACITY, Initial Refill[3]:	Liters	Qt
ES300	3.5	3.7
GS300, GS400: 1996-99	1.9	2.0
2000	2.4	2.5
LS400: 1996-97	2.0	2.1
1998-00	1.9	2.0
SC300	1.6	1.7
SC400: 1996-99	1.9	2.0
2000	2.4	2.5

3 With the engine at operating temperature, shift transmission through all gears. Check fluid level in PARK and add fluid as needed.

TRANSMISSION/TRANSAXLE,
Manual 75W-90, 80W-90 **GL-4, GL-5**

CAPACITY, Refill:	Liters	Pt
ES300	4.2	8.8
SC300	2.6	4.8

FINAL DRIVE .AF3

CAPACITY, Refill:	Liters	Pt
1996-98 ES300	0.9	2.0

DIFFERENTIAL, Rear GL-5
Above 0°F (-18°C), 90; below 0°F (-18°C), 80W, 80W-90

CAPACITY, Refill:	Liters	Pt
All	1.3	2.6

SERVICE AT TIME OR MILEAGE—WHICHEVER OCCURS FIRST

LXIPM2   LXIPM2

Perform the following maintenance services at the intervals indicated to keep the vehicle warranties in effect.
W   SERVICE TO MAINTAIN EMISSION WARRANTY

MI—MILES IN THOUSANDS
KM—KILOMETERS IN THOUSANDS

SERVICE PERIODICALLY

Brake & clutch fluid
   reservoir . . . . .check level **HB**

Power steering . . . . . . .check level **AF3**

Transmission, manual . . . . .inspect
Check for leaks

EVERY 6 MO/7.5 MI—12 KM

Cabin air filter . . . . .inspect
LX470 only

Crankcase . . . . .change oil

Oil filter . . . . .replace

Road test vehicle
Check for proper operation of engine, transmission, brakes, and steering. Check for abnormal noise or vibration.

Tires . . . . .rotate
At mileage interval only

EVERY 12 MO/15 MI—24 KM

Ball joints . . . . .inspect
Also check dust covers

Brake system . . . . .inspect

Differential . . . . .check level
All models, as equipped. Check for leaks.

Drive shaft boots . . . . .inspect
Retorque flange bolts

Drive shaft flange
   bolts, RX300 . . . . .retorque

Exhaust system . . . . .inspect

Propellor shaft, LX470 . . . .lubricate **LM**
Also retorque bolts

Rack & pinion assembly or
   steering gearbox . . . . .check
Inspect for leaks

Steering linkage . . . . .inspect

Cabin air filter . . . . .Inspect
LX470, replace

Drive belts . . . . .inspect/adjust
After initial service only

Transmission, automatic . . . .check level
Check for leaks

Body . . . . .inspect

EVERY 24 MO/30 MI—48 KM

Active height control suspension
   and accumulator . . . . .inspect
LX470 only. Check for leaks.

Brake fluid . . . . .replace **HB**

Front drive shaft bushings . .lubricate **LM**

Front wheel bearings,
   LX470 . . . . .replace

Limited-slip differential . .change lubricant
LX470

Air cleaner element . . . . .replace

Cabin air filter, RX300 . . . . .replace

Cooling system . . . . .replace coolant **EC**

Drive belts, 1996 . . . . . . .inspect/adjust
Ex. ribbed belts, initial service only

Fuel lines & connections . . . . . . .inspect

Fuel tank . . . . .inspect
Check vapor vent system & bands. Also check fuel tank cap.

EVERY 48 MO/60 MI—96 KM

Active height control
   suspension fluid . . . . .replace **SLF**
LX470

Drive belts . . . . .inspect/adjust
Second service for 1996 non-ribbed. Initial service for ribbed.

W Spark plugs . . . . .replace
1996-98

Valve clearance . . . . .inspect/adjust
Adjust only if noisy

EVERY 72 MO/90 MI—144 KM

W Spark plugs . . . . .replace
1999

Timing belt . . . . .replace
1998-00 LX470

2000, EVERY 96 MO/120 MI—192 KM
W Spark plugs . . . . .replace

EVERY 120 MONTHS
THEN EVERY 24 MONTHS
Air bag system . . . . .inspect

SEVERE SERVICE
Automatic transmission, differential—
Change lubricant every 12 mo/15 mi (24 km)

Brake system—Inspect every 4 mo/5 mi (8 km)

Cabin air filter—inspect every 4 mo/5 mi (8 km); 2000 RX300, replace every 18 mo/22.5 mi (36 km)

Crankcase—Change oil & filter every 4 mo/5 mi (8 km)

Drive shaft boots—Inspect every 4 mo/5 mi (8 km). Also torque RX300 flange bolts.

Steering linkage & ball joints—Inspect every 4 mo/5 mi (8 km)

Transfer case—Change lubricant every 24 mo/30 mi (48 km); 2000 RX300, change lubricant every 12 mo/15 mi (24 km) when towing a trailer or using a car top carrier

Air cleaner element—Inspect every 4 mo/5 mi (8 km)

Body & chassis—Torque nuts and bolts every 4 mo/5 mi (8 km)

Timing belt—Replace every 72mo/90mi (144 km) 1999-00 RX300 only

Road test vehicle—Every 4 mo/5 mi (8 km)

Tires—1997-00, rotate every 4mo/5mi (8 km)

KEY TO LUBRICANTS

AF3	DEXRON®-III Automatic Transmission Fluid
EC	Ethylene Glycol Coolant Maintain coolant protection to at least -34°F (-37°C)
GL-4	Gear Oil, API Service GL-4
GL-5	Gear Oil, API Service GL-5
GL-5★	Gear Oil, API Service GL-5 Plus additive for limited slip
HB	Hydraulic Brake Fluid, DOT 3
SG	Motor Oil, API Service SG
SJ	Motor Oil, API Service SJ
SLF	Special Lubricant Fluid Transmission, Toyota ATF, Type TIV Suspension, Toyota Suspension Fluid, AHC

CRANKCASE . . . . .SH, SJ

CAPACITY, Refill:	Liters	Qt
RX300	4.5	4.8
LX470	6.4	6.8

Capacity shown is without filter. When replacing filter, additional oil may be needed.

Above 0°F (-18°C) 10W-30
All temperatures . . . . .5W-30[1]
1 Preferred

TRANSMISSION/TRANSAXLE, Automatic
RX300 . . . . .SLF[2]
2 ATF Type TIV, Part No. 08886-80105
LX470 . . . . .AF3

CAPACITY, Initial Refill[3]:	Liters	Qt
RX300: 2WD	3.1	3.3
4WD	3.9	4.1
LX470	1.9	2.0

3 With the engine at operating temperature, shift transmission through all gears. Check fluid level in PARK and add fluid as needed.

TRANSFER CASE
RX300 . . . . .GL-5
Above 0°F (-18°C), 90; below 0°F (-18°C), 80W, 80W-90
LX470 . . . . .75W-90 **GL-5**

CAPACITY, Refill:	Liters	Pt
RX300	0.9	2.0
LX470	1.3	2.8

DIFFERENTIAL
LX470: Standard GL-5
   Limited-slip . . . . .GL-5★
RX300 . . . . .GL-5
Above 0°F (-18°C), 90; below 0°F (-18°C), 80W, 80W-90

CAPACITY, Refill:	Liters	Pt
RX300	0.9	2.0
LX470: Front	1.7	3.6
Rear	3.2	6.8
w/L.S.D.	3.3	7.0

MAZDA

1989-2000 All Models
1991-2000 Navajo, B2300, B2500, B3000, B4000 — See Ford Trucks

SERVICE LOCATIONS — ENGINE AND CHASSIS

HOOD RELEASE: Inside

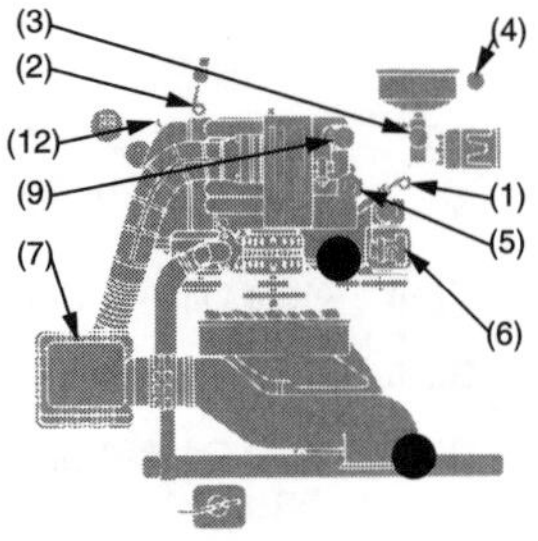

1989-91
RX-7
1308cc FI ex.
Turbo

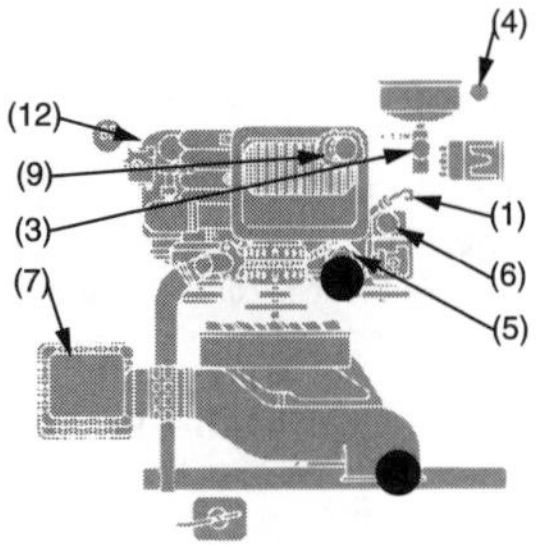

1989-91
RX-7
1308cc Turbo

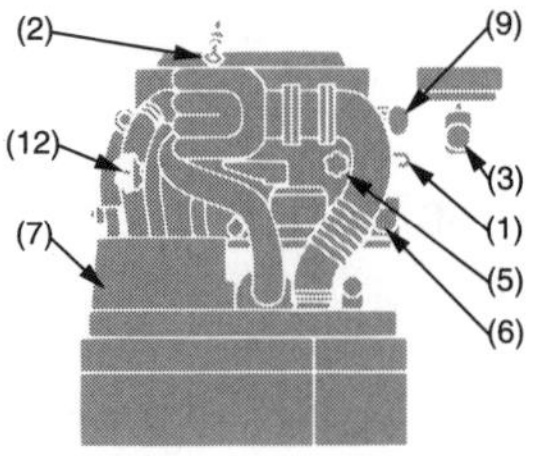

1993-95
RX-7
1308cc

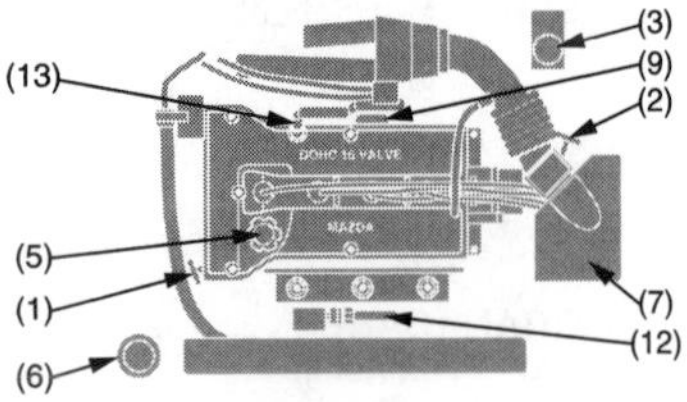

1995-00
Protegé
1489cc, 1596cc

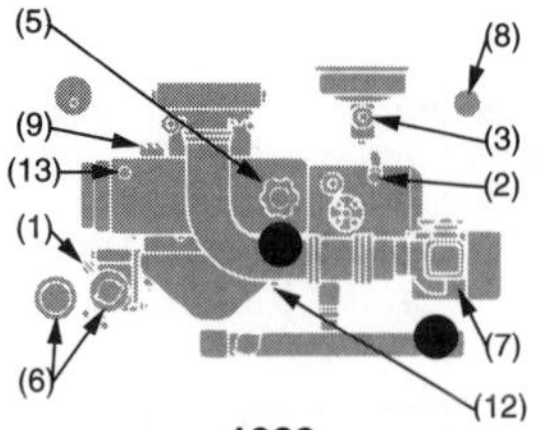

1989
323, Protegé
1597cc ex. Turbo

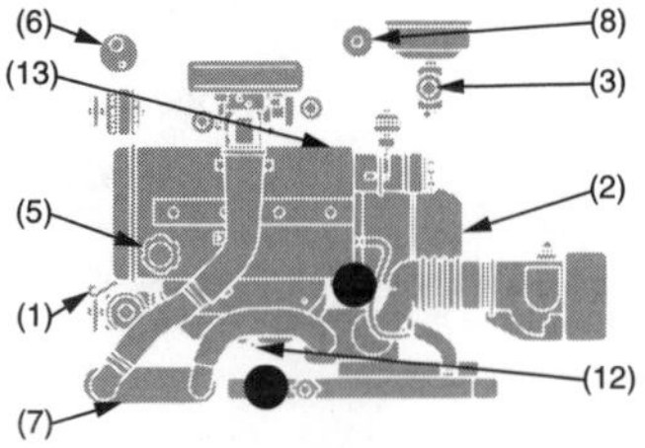

1989
323
1597cc Turbo

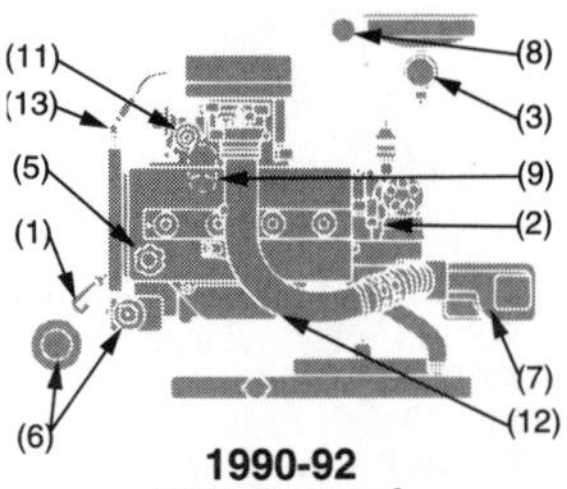

1990-92
323, Protegé
1597cc DOHC

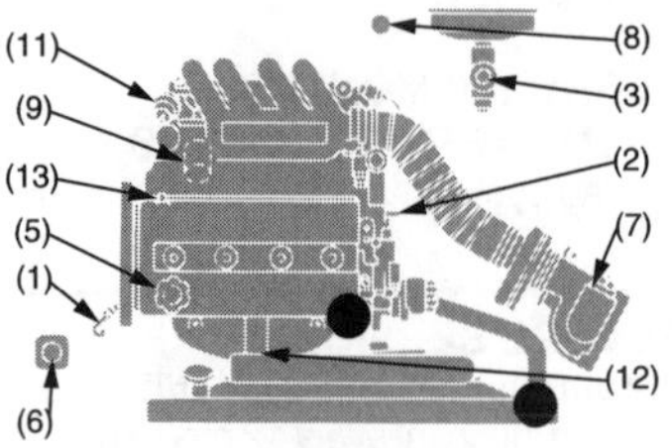

1990-00
323, Protegé, MX-3, Precidia
1597cc, 1839cc

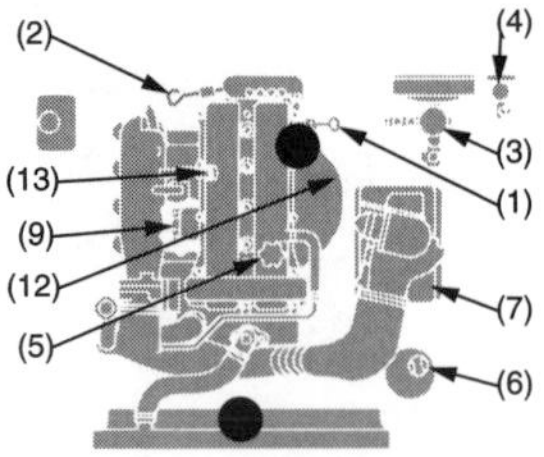

1990-00
MX-5 Miata
1597cc, 1839cc DOHC

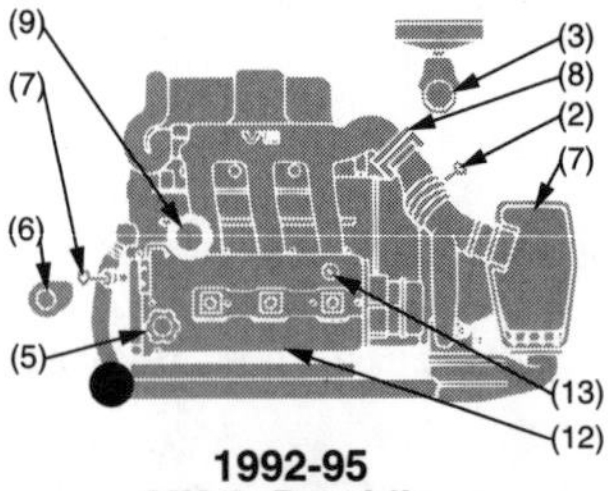

1992-95
MX-3, Precidia
V6, 1844cc

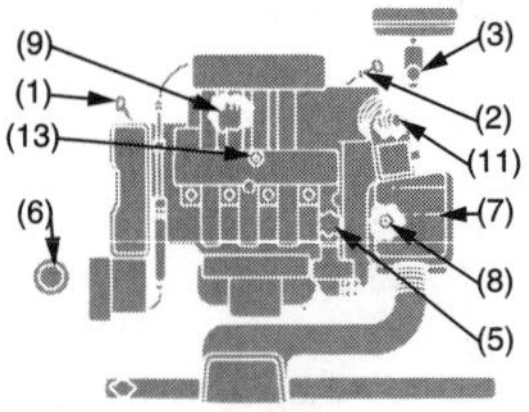

1993-98
626, MX-6
1991cc

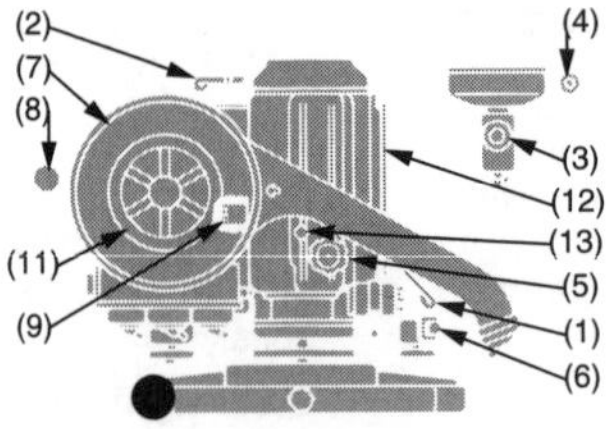

1989-93
B2200
2184cc 2V

(1) Crankcase dipstick
(2) Transmission dipstick
(3) Brake fluid reservoir
(4) Clutch fluid reservoir
(5) Oil fill cap
(6) Power steering reservoir
(7) Air filter
(8) Fuel filter
(9) Oil filter
(10) PCV filter
(11) EGR valve
(12) Oxygen sensor
(13) PCV valve

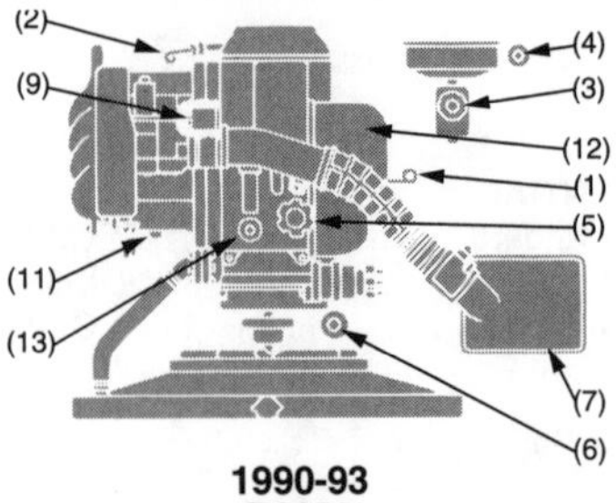

1990-93
B2200
2184cc FI

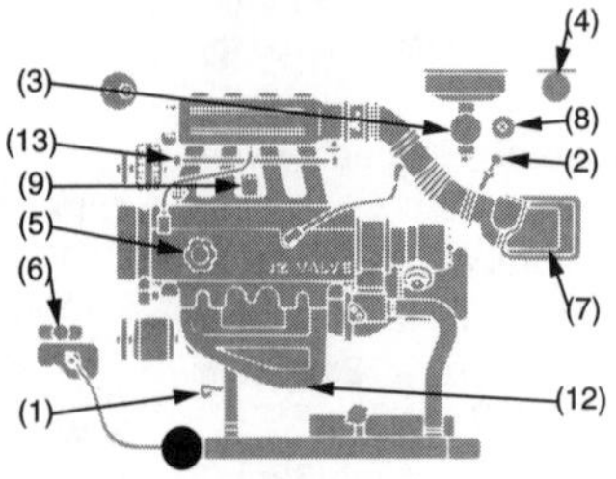

1989-92
626, MX-6
2184cc

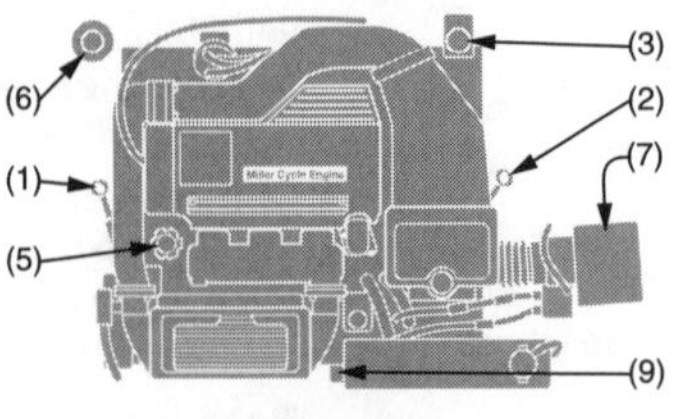

1995-00
2254cc
Millenia

● Cooling system drain

HOOD RELEASE: Inside

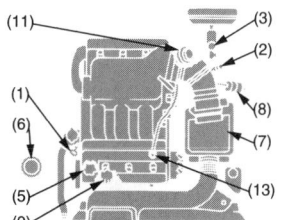

1993-00
626, MX-6, Millenia, MPV
2497cc

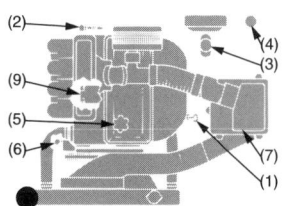

1989-95
B2600, MPV
2606cc

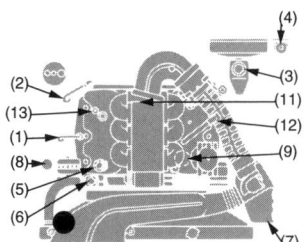

1989-97
929, MPV
2954cc SOHC

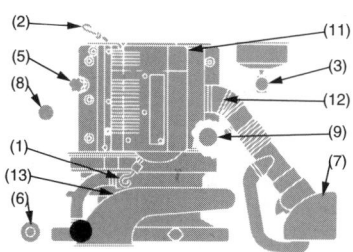

1990-96
929
2954cc DOHC

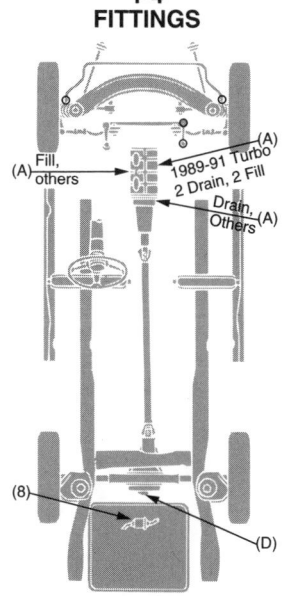

1-4
FITTINGS

1989-91
RX-7

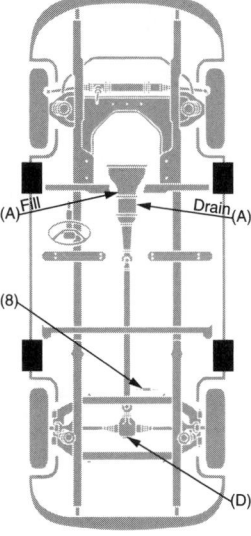

0 FITTINGS
0 PLUGS

1990-00
MX-5 Miata

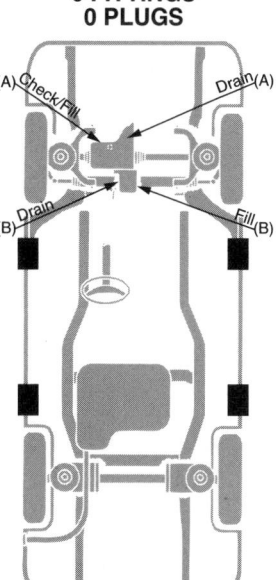

0 FITTINGS
0 PLUGS

1989-00
323, Protegé, MX-3

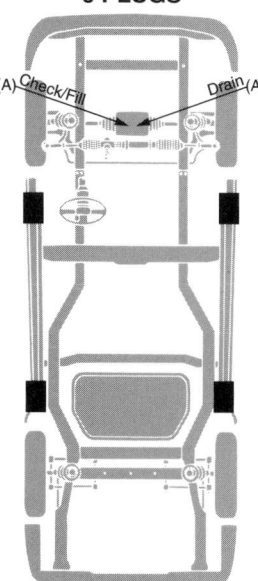

0 FITTINGS
0 PLUGS

1989-99
626 MX-6

CAUTION: On front-wheel drive vehicles, the center of gravity is farther forward than on rear-wheel drive vehicles. When removing major components from the rear of the vehicle while it is on a hoist, the vehicle must be supported in a manner to prevent it from tipping forward.

(A) Manual transmission/transaxle, drain & fill

(B) Transfer case, drain & fill

(C) Automatic transaxle final drive, NOT USED

(D) Differential, drain & fill

(8) Fuel filter

■ Lift adapter position

● Cooling system drain

○ Fitting, some models

SERVICE LOCATIONS — ENGINE AND CHASSIS

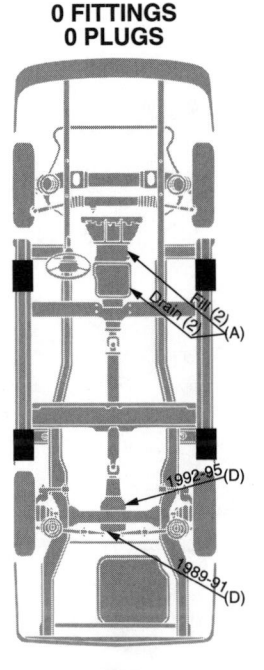

0 FITTINGS
0 PLUGS

1989-95
929

0 FITTINGS
0 PLUGS

1995-00
Millenia

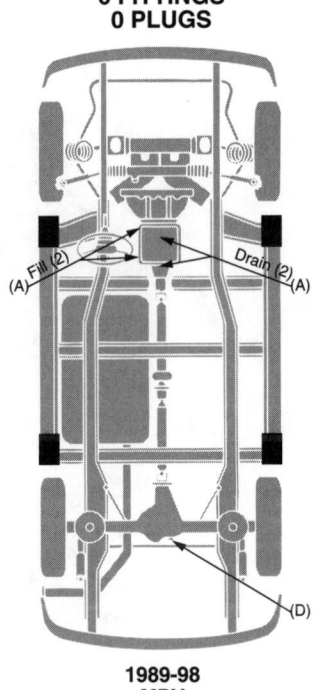

0 FITTINGS
0 PLUGS

1989-98
MPV

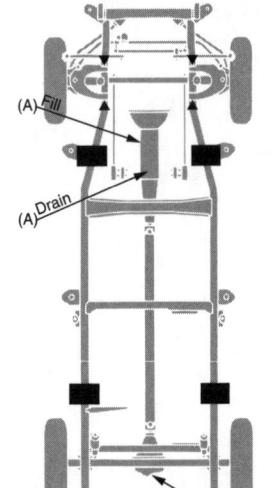

0 FITTINGS
4 PLUGS

1989-93
2WD Pickup

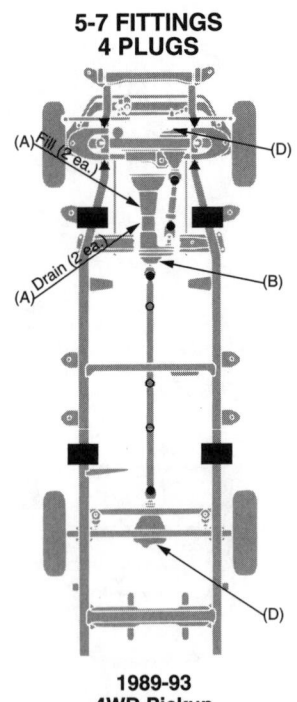

5-7 FITTINGS
4 PLUGS

1989-93
4WD Pickup

CAUTION: On front-wheel drive vehicles, the center of gravity is farther forward than on rear-wheel drive vehicles. When removing major components from the rear of the vehicle while it is on a hoist, the vehicle must be supported in a manner to prevent it from tipping forward.

(A) Manual transmission/transaxle, drain & fill

(B) Transfer case, drain & fill

(C) Automatic transaxle final drive, NOT USED

(D) Differential, drain & fill

(8) Fuel filter

■ Lift adapter position

▲ Plug

• Fitting

○ Fitting, some models

SERVICE AT TIME OR MILEAGE — WHICHEVER OCCURS FIRST

MAIPM1   MAIPM1

Perform the following maintenance services at the intervals indicated to keep both the vehicle and emission warranties in effect.

MI—MILES IN THOUSANDS
KM—KILOMETERS IN THOUSANDS

EVERY MONTH
Drive belts . . . . .check tension

Brake pedal &
  parking brake . . . . .check freeplay

TURBO, EVERY 5 MO/5 MI—8 KM
Crankcase . . . . .change oil

Oil filter . . . . .replace

EVERY 7.5 MO/7.5 MI—12 KM
Crankcase ex. Turbo . . . . .change oil
Change oil filter every other oil change

AT EACH FUEL STOP
Brake & clutch
  reservoirs . . . . .check level HB

EVERY 6 MONTHS
Power steering
  reservoir . . . . .check level AF2, MA

Automatic transmission . . . . .check level

1989-91, EVERY 12 MONTHS
A/C system . . . . .inspect

Power brake booster . . . . .inspect

EVERY 15 MO/15 MI—24 KM
Choke system . . . . .inspect

Cooling system . . . . .inspect
Clutch fluid & freeplay

Engine oil level
  warning system . . . . .inspect

Idle speed . . . . .check/adjust
Check dashpot & throttle opener with A/C for binding

Power steering reservoir . .check level FA
AF2 may be used

Spark plugs . . . . .inspect
Ex. Calif.

Body & chassis nuts,

EVERY 30 MO/30 MI—48 KM
Brake fluid . . . . .replace HB

Brake system, 1989-91 . . . . . . .inspect

Driveshaft boots . . . . .inspect

Exhaust system heat shields . . . .inspect

Front wheel bearings . . . . .LM
Adjust preload to .9-2.2 lb (.4-1 kg) on spring scale attached to wheel bolt

Front suspension ball joints . . . .inspect

Steering system . . . . .inspect

Toe control hub and control
  link . . . . .inspect

Air cleaner element . . . . .replace

Cooling level warning
  system . . . . .inspect

Cooling system . . . . .change coolant EC

Drive belts . . . . .inspect
Ex. air pump

Fuel lines . . . . .inspect

Spark plugs . . . . .replace

Body & chassis nuts,
  bolts, 1989-91 . . . . .torque

EVERY 60 MO/60 MI—96 KM
Differential . . . . .change lubricant

Fuel filter . . . . .replace

Transmission, manual . .change lubricant

SERVICE AS REQUIRED
Starting assist
  system . . . . .inspect seasonally
To replenish fluid, add a mixture of 90% EC and 10% water to system reservoir

SEVERE SERVICE
Disk brakes—Inspect every 15 mo/15 mi (24 km)

Body & chassis nuts and bolts—Tighten every 15 mo/15 mi (24 km)

Crankcase—Change oil & filter: ex. Turbo, 5 mo/5 mi (8 km); Turbo, 3 mo/3 mi (5 km)

Differential—Change lubricant every 30 mo/30 mi (48 km)

Transmission, manual—Change lubricant every 30 mo/30 mi (48 km)

Air cleaner element—Inspect & change more frequently in very dusty or sandy areas

KEY TO LUBRICANTS

AF2	DEXRON®-II, Automatic Transmission Fluid
EC	Ethylene Glycol Coolant
FA	Automatic Transmission Fluid, Type F
GL-4	Gear Oil, API Service GL-4
GL-5	Gear Oil, API Service GL-5
GL-5★	Special Lubricant for Limited-Slip Differential
HB	Hydraulic Brake Fluid, DOT 3 or 4
LM	Lithium Grease, with Moly
MA	MERCON®, Automatic Transmission Fluid
SG	Motor Oil, API Service SG

CRANKCASE .SG
CAPACITY, Refill:	Liters	Qt
RX-7 FI	4.4	4.7

Capacity shown is without filter. When replacing filter, additional oil may be needed

1989-90:
Above 15°F (–9°C) 20W-40, 20W-50
Above –15°F (–26°C) 10W-40, 10W-50
–15° to 85°F (–26° to 29°C) 10W-30
Below 32°F (0°C) 5W-30
1991:
Above: –15°F (–25°C) 10W-30
Below 32°F (0°C) 5W-30

TRANSMISSION, Automatic . . . .AF2, MA
CAPACITY, Initial Refill[1]:	Liters	Qt
All	4.0[1]	4.2[1]

1 With the engine at operating temperature, shift transmission through all gears. Check fluid level in PARK and add fluid as needed.

TRANSMISSION, Manual
Above 50°F (10°C), may use 80W-90
CAPACITY, Refill:	Liters	Pt
All	2.5	5.2

DIFFERENTIAL
Standard GL-5
Above 0°F (–18°C), 90; below 0°F (–18°C), 80W
Limited-Slip . . . . .90 GL-5★
CAPACITY, Refill:	Liters	Pt
All	1.3	2.8
Turbo	1.4	3.0

MAZDA
1989-90 Miata, Protegé, 323, 626, MX-6, 929

SERVICE AT TIME OR MILEAGE — WHICHEVER OCCURS FIRST

Perform the following maintenance services at the intervals indicated to keep both the vehicle and emission warranties in effect.

MI—MILES IN THOUSANDS
KM—KILOMETERS IN THOUSANDS

AT EACH FUEL STOP
Brake & clutch
 reservoirs . . . . .check level **HB**

EVERY MONTH
Brake pedal
 & parking brake . . . . . . .check freeplay

Drive belts . . . . .check tension

TURBO ENGINES,
EVERY 5 MO/5 MI—8 KM
Crankcase . . . . .change oil

Oil filter . . . . .replace

EVERY 6 MONTHS
Transmission, automatic . . . .check level

Power steering fluid
 reservoir . . . . . . .check level **AF2,MA**

EVERY 7.5 MO/7.5 MI—12 KM
Crankcase, gasoline . . . . . . .change oil
Ex. Turbo

Oil filter . . . . .replace

EVERY 12 MONTHS
Air conditioning system . . . . .inspect

Power brake unit . . . . .inspect

EVERY 15 MO/15 MI—24 KM
Cooling system . . . . .inspect

EVERY 30 MO/30 MI—48 KM
Body & chassis
 nuts & bolts . . . . .torque

Brake system . . . . .inspect
Check linings, hoses & lines, connections

Cooling system . . . . .change coolant **EC**

Driveshaft boots . . . . .inspect

Exhaust system heat shield . . . . .inspect

Steering & suspension system . . .inspect
Front & 4-wheel steering rear. Replace solenoid valve oil filter on 4-wheel steering models

Air cleaner element . . . . .replace

Cooling system, 1990 . . . . .inspect

Drive belts . . . . .inspect/adjust

Fuel lines . . . . .inspect

Idle speed . . . . .check/adjust
Ex. 626, MX-6

Spark plugs . . . . .replace

EVERY 60 MO/60 MI—96 KM
Manual transmission . . .change lubricant
Miata, 929 only

Transfer case oil . . . . .change lubricant
323, Protegé 4WD

Rear axle . . . . .change lubricant

Fuel filter . . . . .replace

Timing belt . . . . .replace
At mileage interval only

SEVERE SERVICE
Air cleaner element & cooling system—Inspect every 15 mo/15 mi (24 km)

Body & chassis nuts and bolts—Torque every 15 mo/15 mi (24 km)

Crankcase—Change oil & filter: ex. Turbo, 5 mo/5 mi (8 km); Turbo, 3 mo/3 mi (5 km)

Disc brakes—Inspect every 15 mo/ 15 mi (24 km)

Manual transmission (RWD), transfer case, rear axle—Change lubricant every 30 mo/30 mi (48 km)

KEY TO LUBRICANTS
See other Mazda charts

CRANKCASE .SG

CAPACITY, Refill:	Liters	Qt
323: 4-cyl.	3.0	3.2
Turbo	3.2	3.4
V6	3.7	3.9
Protegé	3.6	3.8
Miata	3.2	3.4
626, MX-6	3.9	4.1
929	4.5	4.8

Capacity shown is without filter. When replacing filter, additional oil may be needed.

Above 85°F (29°C)	.40
Above 15°F (−9°C) 20W-40, 20W-50	
Above −15°F (−25°C) 10W-40, 10W-50	
32° to 105°F (0° to 39°C)	.30
15° to 65°F (−9° to 20°C) 20W-20	
−15° to 85°F (−25° to 29°C) 10W-30	
Below 32°F (0°C) 5W-30	
Below −5°F (−20°C) 5W-20	

TRANSMISSION/TRANSAXLE,
 Automatic . . . . .AF2, MA

CAPACITY, Total Fill:	Liters	Qt
323, Protegé	6.3	6.7
626, MX-6	6.8	7.2
Miata, 929[1]	4.0	4.2

[1] Initial refill shown. With engine at operating temperature, shift transmission through all gears. Check fluid level in PARK and add fluid as needed.

TRANSMISSION/TRANSAXLE, Manual
Refer to lubricant specifications label under hood to determine proper fluid
Verify fluid installed before topping up or refilling transaxle

323, Protegé:
1990:
 SOHC . .**AF2,MA, FA**, 75W-90 **GL-4, GL-5**
Above 0°F (−18°C), 80W-90 **GL-4, GL-5**
 DOHC . . . .**AF2,MA, FA**
Above 0°F (−18°C), 80W-90 **GL-4, GL-5**
1989: 2WD . . . .**AF2,MA, FA**
May also use 80W-90, 90 **GL-4, GL-5**
 4WD **AF2,MA**
626, MX-6 . . . .**AF2,MA**
Above 0°F (−18°C), 80W-90, 90 **GL-4, GL-5**
Miata, 929 . . . . .75W-90 **GL-4, GL-5**
Above 50F° (10°C), 80W-90

CAPACITY, Total Refill:	Liters	Pt
323, Protegé:		
1990: SOHC	2.7	5.6
DOHC	3.4	7.1
1989:		
2WD ex. Turbo	3.2	6.8
4WD	3.6	7.6
Turbo	3.4	7.1
Miata	2.0	4.2
626, MX-6, ex. Turbo	3.4	7.2
Turbo	3.7	7.8
929	2.5	5.2

TRANSFER CASE
323, Protegé **GL-5**
Above 0°F (−18°C), 90; below 0°F (−18°C), 80W
All others **GL-4, GL-5**
All temperatures, 75W-90; above 50°F (10°C), 80W-90

CAPACITY, Refill:	Liters	Pt
323, Protegé 4WD	0.5	1.1

DIFFERENTIAL GL-5
Above 0°F (−18°C), 90; below 0°F (−18°C), 80W

CAPACITY, Refill:	Liters	Pt
323, Protegé 4WD, Miata	0.7	1.4
929	1.3	2.8

SERVICE AT TIME OR MILEAGE — WHICHEVER OCCURS FIRST

MAIPM8   MAIPM8

Perform the following maintenance services at the intervals indicated to keep both the vehicle and emission warranties in effect.

MI—MILES IN THOUSANDS
KM—KILOMETERS IN THOUSANDS

AT EACH FUEL STOP
Brake &
  clutch reservoirs ......check level **HB**

EVERY MONTH
Brake pedal
  & parking brake ....check freeplay

Drive belts ....check tension

TURBO ENGINES,
EVERY 5 MO/5 MI—8 KM
Crankcase ....change oil

Oil filter ....replace

EVERY 6 MONTHS
Transmission, automatic ....check level

Power steering fluid
  reservoir ....check level **AF2,MA**

EVERY 7.5 MO/7.5 MI—12 KM
Body, 1992-93 ....lubricate
Hinges, locks

Crankcase, gasoline ....change oil
Ex. Turbo

Oil filter ....replace

EVERY 12 MONTHS
Air-conditioning system ....inspect

EVERY 30 MO/30 MI—48 KM
Body & chassis nuts
  & bolts ....inspect/torque

Brake system ....inspect
Check linings, hoses & lines, connections

Clutch ....check freeplay
323, Protegé only

Cooling system .....change coolant **EC**
Also inspect system

Driveshaft boots ....inspect

Exhaust system heat shield .....inspect

Steering & suspension system ...inspect

Air cleaner element ....replace

Drive belts ....inspect

Fuel lines ....inspect

Idle speed ....check/adjust
Ex. 1991-92 626, MX-6

Spark plugs ....replace

EVERY 60 MO/60 MI—96 KM
Manual transmission ...change lubricant
Miata, 929 only

Transfer case oil .....change lubricant
323, Protegé 4WD

Rear axle ....change lubricant

Fuel filter ....replace

PCV hoses ....inspect
1993 1.6L

Timing belt ....replace
At mileage interval only. 1993 California 323 1.6L, inspect only. Also inspect again at 90 mi/144 km.

EVERY 105 MI—168 KM
Fuel hoses, California ....replace
1993 323, Miata

Timing belt, California ....replace
1993 323, Miata

SEVERE SERVICE
Air cleaner element & cooling system— Inspect every 15 mo/15 mi (24 km)

Body & chassis nuts and bolts—Torque every 15 mo/15 mi (24 km)

Crankcase—Change oil & filter: ex. Turbo, 5 mo/5 mi (8 km); Turbo, 3 mo/3 mi (5 km)

Disc brakes—Inspect every 15 mo/15 mi (24 km)

Manual transmission (RWD), transfer case, rear axle—Change lubricant every 30 mo/30 mi (48 km)

KEY TO LUBRICANTS

AF2,MA	DEXRON®-II, Automatic Transmission Fluid
EC	Ethylene Glycol Coolant
FA	Automatic Transmission Fluid, Type F
GF-1	Motor Oil, API Service GF-1
GL-4	Gear Oil, API Service GL-4
GL-5	Gear Oil, API Service GL-5
GL-5★	Special Lubricant for Limited-Slip Differential
HB	Hydraulic Brake Fluid, DOT 3 or 4
LM	Lithium Grease, with Moly
MA	MERCON®, Automatic Transmission Fluid
SG	Motor Oil, API Service SG
SH	Motor Oil, API Service SH

CRANKCASE ....SG, SH; GF-1

CAPACITY, Refill:	Liters	Qt
323, 4-cyl.	3.0	3.2
Turbo	3.2	3.4
MX-3, Precidia: 4-cyl.	3.2	3.4
V6	3.7	3.9
Protegé	3.6	3.8
Miata	3.2	3.4
626, MX-6: 1993 2.0L	3.3	3.5
1991-92 2.2L ...	3.9	4.1
1993 2.5L	3.7	3.9
929, Serenia	4.5	4.8

Capacity shown is without filter. When replacing filter, additional oil may be needed.
Above −15°F (−25°C) 10W-30
Below 32°F (0°C) 5W-30

TRANSMISSION/TRANSAXLE,
Automatic AF2,MA

CAPACITY, Total Fill:	Liters	Qt
323, Protegé	6.3	6.7
MX-3, Precidia: 4-cyl.	6.3	6.7
V6	5.8	6.1
626, MX-6: 1991-92	6.8	7.2
1993	8.8	9.3
Miata, 929, Serenia[1]	4.0	4.2

[1] Initial refill shown. With engine at operating temperature, shift transmission through all gears. Check fluid level in PARK and add fluid as needed.

TRANSMISSION/TRANSAXLE, Manual
Refer to lubricant specifications label under hood to determine proper fluid
Verify fluid installed before topping up or refilling transaxle

323, Protegé:
1991-92: 2WD SOHC 75W-90 **GL-4**
  DOHC ....**AF2,MA, FA**
Above 0°F (−18°C), 80W-90 **GL-4**
  4WD 75W-90 **GL-4, AF2,MA**
1993: SOHC 75W-90 **GL-4, GL-5**
Above 0°F (−18°C), 80W-90 **GL-4, GL-5**
Below 0°F (−18°C), **AF2, MA**
  DOHC ..**AF2,MA, FA,** 75W-80 **GL-4, GL-5**
Above 0°F (−18°C), 80W-90 **GL-4, GL-5**
MX-3, Precidia 75W-90 **GL-4, GL-5**
May also use 80W-90 **GL-4, GL-5** above 0°F (−18°C); or **AF2,MA** below 0°F (−18°C)
626, MX-6: 1991-92 **AF2,MA,** 75W-90 **GL-4, GL-5**
Above 0°F (−18°C), 80W-90, 90 **GL-4, GL-5**
1993 ....75W-90 **GL-4, GL-5**
Above 50°F (10°C), 80W-90
Miata, 929, Serenia ...75W-90 **GL-4, GL-5**
Above 50F (10°C), 80W-90

CAPACITY, Total Refill:	Liters	Pt
323, Protegé: SOHC	2.7	5.6
DOHC	3.4	7.1
MX-3, Precidia	2.7	5.6
Miata	2.0	4.2
626, MX-6: 1991-92 ex. Turbo ..	3.4	7.2
Turbo	3.7	7.8
1993	2.7	5.6
929, Serenia	2.5	5.2

TRANSFER CASE GL-5
Above 0°F (−18°C), 90; below 0°F (−18°C), 80W

CAPACITY, Refill:	Liters	Pt
Protegé 4WD	0.5	1.1

DIFFERENTIAL GL-5
Above 0°F (−18°C), 90; below 0°F (−18°C), 80W

CAPACITY, Refill:	Liters	Pt
Miata	0.7	1.4
Protegé 4WD	0.7	1.4
929, Serenia	1.3	2.8

CHEK-CHART

SERVICE AT TIME OR MILEAGE — WHICHEVER OCCURS FIRST

MAIPM9

MAIPM9

Perform the following maintenance services at the intervals indicated to keep both the vehicle and emission warranties in effect.

MI—MILES IN THOUSANDS
KM—KILOMETERS IN THOUSANDS

AT EACH FUEL STOP
Brake &
clutch reservoirs, U.S. . .check level **HB**
Canada, check level every 5 mo/5 mi (8 km)

EVERY MONTH
Brake pedal
& parking brake . . . . . . .check freeplay

Drive belts . . . . .check tension

EVERY 6 MONTHS
Transmission,
automatic, U.S. . . . . .check level
Canada, inspect every 5 mo/5 mi (8 km)

Power steering fluid
reservoir, U.S. . . . .check level **AF2,MA**
Canada, inspect every 5 mo/5 mi (8 km)

CANADA, EVERY 5 MO/5 MI—8 KM
U.S., EVERY 6 MO/7.5 MI—12 KM
Body, ex. Millenia . . . . .lubricate
Hinges, locks

Body, Millenia . . . . .inspect
Inspect paint, check for corrosion

Coolant, Canada . . . . .inspect

Crankcase . . . . .change oil
Ex. Turbo

Differential, Canada . . . . .check level

Drive belts, Canada . . . . .inspect

Oil filter . . . . .replace

Exterior lights, Canada . . . . .inspect

EVERY 12 MONTHS
Air-conditioning system, 1994 . . .inspect

CANADA, EVERY 15 MO/15 MI—24 KM
Air cleaner element . . . . .inspect

Idle speed . . . . .inspect

Cooling system . . . . .inspect

Disc brake system . . . . .inspect

Body & chassis
nuts & bolts . . . . .inspect/torque

Tires .rotate

CANADA, EVERY 30 MO/30 MI—48 KM
U.S., EVERY 24 MO/30 MI—48 KM
Air conditioning system . . . . .inspect
1995-99

Body & chassis nuts
& bolts, U.S. . . . . .inspect/torque

Brake system . . . . .inspect
U.S., check linings, hoses & lines, connections. Canada, inspect lines & hoses.

Clutch . . . . .check freeplay
Protegé only

Cooling system,
1994-95 . . . . .change coolant **EC**

Cooling system, U.S. . . . . .inspect

Driveshaft boots . . . . .inspect

Differential, Canada . . . .change lubricant

Exhaust system heat shield . . . . .inspect

Transmission, manual &
automatic, Canada . . .change lubricant

Steering & suspension system . . .inspect

Air cleaner element . . . . .replace

Drive belts, U.S. . . . . .inspect

Fuel filter, Canada . . . . .replace

Fuel lines . . . . .inspect

Idle speed, U.S. . . . . .check/adjust

Spark plugs . . . . .replace
Ex. 2.3L Millenia

1999 626, AT FIRST 60 MO/105 MI —168 KM
ALL OTHERS: AT FIRST 36 MO/45 MI—72 KM;
THEN EVERY 24 MO/30 MI—48 KM
Cooling system,
1996-99 . . . . .change coolant **EC**
Also inspect system

CANADA, EVERY 60 MO/60 MI—96 KM
U.S., EVERY 48 MO/60 MI—96 KM
Manual transmission,
U.S. . . . . .change lubricant
Miata only

Rear axle, U.S. . . . . . .change lubricant

Fuel filter, U.S. . . . . .replace

PCV hoses . . . . .inspect
1994 1.6L & 1.8L Protegé, 1995-99 All

PCV valve, Canada . . . . .inspect

Spark plugs . . . . .replace
2.3L Millenia & 1998-00 2.5L 626 only

Timing belt . . . . .replace
At mileage interval only. California & 1998-99 N.E. states models, inspect only. Also inspect again at 90 mi/144 km

Valve clearance . . . . .check/adjust
1995-96 1.5L Protegé & 2.3L Millenia only. Also all 1998-99 models

EVERY 105 MI—168 KM
Drive belts . . . . .replace
1995-00 2.3L Millenia only

Fuel hoses 1994-97, California . .replace

Timing belt, California
& 1998-99 N.E. states . . . . . . .replace

SEVERE SERVICE
U.S. Models Only

Air cleaner element & cooling system—Inspect every 12 mo/15 mi (24 km)

Body—Lubricate every 4 mo/5 mi (8 km)

Body & chassis nuts and bolts—Torque every 12 mo/15 mi (24 km)

Crankcase—Change oil & filter every 4 mo/5 mi (8 km)

Disc brakes—Inspect every 12 mo/15 mi (24 km)

Manual transmission (RWD), rear axle—Change lubricant every 24 mo/30 mi (48 km)

KEY TO LUBRICANTS
AF2	DEXRON®-II, Automatic Transmission Fluid
EC	Ethylene Glycol Coolant
FA	Automatic Transmission Fluid, Type F
GF-2	Motor Oil, API Service GF-2
GL-4	Gear Oil, API Service GL-4
GL-5	Gear Oil, API Service GL-5
GL-5★	Special Lubricant for Limited-Slip Differential
HB	Hydraulic Brake Fluid, DOT 3 or 4
LM	Lithium Grease, with Moly
MA	MERCON®, Automatic Transmission Fluid
SJ	Motor Oil, API Service SJ

CRANKCASE . . . . .SJ, GF-2
CAPACITY, Refill:	Liters	Qt
323,4-cyl.	3.0	3.2
MX-3, Precidia: 4-cyl.	3.2	3.4
V6	3.7	3.9
Protegé 1994	3.6	3.8
1995-99 1.5L, 1.6L	3.2	3.4
1.8L	3.6	3.8
Miata	3.6	3.8
Millenia: 2.3L	3.8	4.0
2.5L	3.7	3.9
626, MX-6: 2.0L	3.3	3.5
2.5L	3.7	3.9
929, Serenia	4.5	4.8

Capacity shown is without filter. When replacing filter, additional oil may be needed.
Above −13°F (−25°C) 10W-30
Below 32°F (0°C) 5W-30

TRANSMISSION/TRANSAXLE, Automatic
2.0L 626, MX-6 . . . .**MA**
All others . . . .**AF2, MA**
CAPACITY, Total Fill:	Liters	Qt
323, Protegé 1994	6.3	6.7
1995-98	5.4	5.7
1999	7.2	7.6
MX-3, Precidia: 1994 4-cyl.	6.3	6.7
V6	5.8	6.1
1995-96	4.9	5.2
626, MX-6 1994-95	8.8	9.3
1996-97	8.0	8.5
1998-99 2.0L	8.7	9.2
2.5L	8.0	8.5
Miata, 929, Serenia[1]	4.0	4.2
Millenia 1995-96: 2.3L	8.0	8.5
2.5L	8.8	9.3
1997-98: 2.3L	7.4	7.8
2.5L	8.0	8.4

[1] Initial refill shown. With engine at operating temperature, shift transmission through all gears. Check fluid level in PARK and add fluid as needed.

TRANSMISSION/TRANSAXLE, Manual
Refer to lubricant specifications label under hood to determine proper fluid. (Discontinued after Feb. 1994.)
Verify fluid installed before topping up or refilling transaxle.
323, Protegé:
1994: SOHC 75W-90 **GL-4, GL-5**
Above 0°F (−18°C), 80W-90 **GL-4, GL-5**
Below 0°F (−18°C), **AF2, MA**
DOHC .**AF2, MA, FA**, 75W-80 **GL-4, GL-5**
Above 0°F (−18°C), 80W-90 **GL-4, GL-5**
1995-99 . . . . .75W-90 **GL-4, GL-5**
MX-3, Precidia 75W-90 **GL-4, GL-5**
1994, may also use 80W-90 **GL-4, GL-5** above 0°F (−18°C); or **AF** below 0°F (−18°C)
626, MX-6 . . . . .75W-90 **GL-4, GL-5**
Above 50°F (10°C), 80W-90
Miata, 929, Serenia . . .75W-90 **GL-4, GL-5**
Above 50°F (10°C), 80W

CAPACITY, Total Refill:	Liters	Pt
323, Protegé: 1994 SOHC	2.7	5.6
DOHC	3.4	7.1
1995-99	2.7	5.6
MX-3, Precidia	2.7	5.6
Miata	2.0	4.2
626, MX-6	2.7	5.6
929, Serenia	2.5	5.2

DIFFERENTIAL GL-5
Above 0°F (−18°C), 90; below 0°F (−18°C), 80W
CAPACITY, Refill:	Liters	Pt
Miata	1.0	2.1
929, Serenia	1.3	2.8

SERVICE AT TIME OR MILEAGE — WHICHEVER OCCURS FIRST

MAIPM11

MAIPM11

Perform the following maintenance services at the intervals indicated to keep both the vehicle and emission warranty in effect.

MI—MILES IN THOUSANDS
KM—KILOMETERS IN THOUSANDS

AT EACH FUEL STOP
Brake &
  clutch reservoirs. . . . . . .check level **HB**

Coolant . . . . .check level EC

Engine oil . . . . .check level

EVERY MONTH
Tire pressure . . . . .check

EVERY 6 MONTHS
Transmission,
  automatic . . . . .check level

Power steering fluid
  reservoir . . . . . . .check level **AF2,MA**

EVERY 6 MO/7.5 MI—12 KM
Body, ex. Millenia . . . . .lubricate
Hinges, locks

Body, Millenia . . . . .inspect
Inspect paint, check for corrosion

Crankcase . . . . .change oil

Oil filter . . . . .replace

EVERY 12 MO/12 MI—20 KM
Cabin air filter . . . . .replace
626 only

EVERY 12 MO/15 MI—24 KM
AC compressor & refrigerant . . . .inspect

EVERY 24 MO/30 MI—48 KM
Body & chassis nuts
  & bolts . . . . .inspect/torque

Brake system . . . . .inspect
Check linings, hoses & lines, connections

Cooling system . . . . .inspect

Driveshaft boots . . . . .inspect

Exhaust system heat shield . . . .inspect

Steering & suspension system . . .inspect

Air cleaner element . . . . .replace

Drive belts . . . . .inspect
Check tension

Fuel lines & hoses . . . . .inspect

Idle speed . . . . .check/adjust

Spark plugs . . . . .replace
Ex. 2.3L Millenia

626,
AT FIRST 60 MO/105 MI —168 KM
ALL OTHERS:
AT FIRST 36 MO/45 MI—72 KM;
ALL,
THEN EVERY 24 MO/30 MI—48 KM
Cooling system . . . . .change coolant **EC**

EVERY 48 MO/60 MI—96 KM
Manual transmission . . .change lubricant
Miata only

Rear axle . . . . .change lubricant
Miata only

Fuel filter . . . . .replace

PCV hoses . . . . .inspect

Spark plugs . . . . .replace
2.3L Millenia & 2.5L 626 only

Timing belt . . . . .replace
At mileage interval only. California & N.E. states models, inspect only. Also inspect again at 90 mi/144 km

Valve clearance . . . . .check/adjust

EVERY 105 MI—168 KM
Drive belts . . . . .replace
2.3L Millenia only

Timing belt, California
  & N.E. states . . . . .replace

SEVERE SERVICE & ALL CANADIAN MODELS
Air cleaner element—Inspect every 12 mo/15 mi (24 km)

Body—Lubricate every 4 mo/5 mi (8 km)

Body & chassis nuts and bolts—Torque every 12 mo/15 mi (24 km)

Crankcase—Change oil & filter every 4 mo/5 mi (8 km)

Disc brakes—Inspect every 12 mo/15 mi (24 km)

Fluid levels—Inspect coolant, power steering, clutch and brake systems every 4 mo/5 mi (8 km)

Manual transmission (RWD), rear axle—Change lubricant every 24 mo/30 mi (48 km)

Tire inflation pressute & wear—Inspect every 4 mo/5 mi (8 km)

Vehicle lighting system—Inspect every 4 mo/5 mi (8 km)

KEY TO LUBRICANTS

AF2	DEXRON®-II, Automatic Transmission Fluid
EC	Ethylene Glycol Coolant
GF-1	Motor Oil, API Service GF-1
GL-4	Gear Oil, API Service GL-4
GL-5	Gear Oil, API Service GL-5
HB	Hydraulic Brake Fluid, DOT 3 or 4
LM	Lithium Grease, with Moly
MA	MERCON®, Automatic Transmission Fluid
SJ	Motor Oil, API Service SJ

CRANKCASE . . . . .SJ, API★

CAPACITY, Refill:	Liters	Qt
Protegé: 1.6L	2.7	2.9
1.8L	3.3	3.5
Miata	3.6	3.8
Millenia: 2.3L	3.8	4.0
2.5L	3.7	3.9
626, 2.0L	3.3	3.5
2.5L	3.7	3.9

Capacity shown is without filter. When replacing filter, additional oil may be needed.
Above −13°F (−25°C) 10W-30
Below 32°F (0°C) 5W-30

TRANSMISSION/TRANSAXLE, Automatic
2.0L 626 . . . .**MA**
All others . . . .**AF2, MA**

CAPACITY, Total Fill:	Liters	Qt
Protegé	7.2	7.6
626 2.0L	8.7	9.2
2.5L	8.0	8.5
Miata 4.0	4.2	
Millenia	7.4	7.8
2.5L	8.0	8.4

1 Initial refill shown. With engine at operating temperature, shift transmission through all gears. Check fluid level in PARK and add fluid as needed.

TRANSMISSION/TRANSAXLE, Manual
Protegé, 626, Millenia . .75W-90 **GL-4, GL-5**
Miata 75W-90 **GL-4, GL-5**

CAPACITY, Total Refill:	Liters	Pt
Protegé	2.7	5.6
Miata: 5-speed	2.0	4.2
6-speed	1.8	3.8
626	2.7	5.6

DIFFERENTIAL GL-5
Above 0°F (−18°C), 90; below 0°F (−18°C), 80W

CAPACITY, Refill:	Liters	Pt
Miata	1.0	2.1

MAZDA
1992-95 RX-7

MAIPM7   MAIPM7

Perform the following maintenance services at the intervals indicated to keep both the vehicle and emission warranties in effect.

MI—MILES IN THOUSANDS
KM—KILOMETERS IN THOUSANDS

AT EACH FUEL STOP
Brake & clutch
   reservoirs . . . . .check level **HB**

EVERY 5 MO/5 MI—8 KM
Crankcase . . . . .change oil

Oil filter . . . . .replace

1992-93
EVERY 7.5 MO/7.5 MI—12 KM
1994-95
EVERY 6 MO/7.5 MI—12 KM
Locks & hinges . . . . .lubricate

EVERY 6 MONTHS
Power steering
   reservoir . . . . . . .check level **AF2, MA**

Transmission, automatic . . . .check level

EVERY 12 MONTHS
A/C system, 1992-94 . . . . .inspect

1992-93
EVERY 15 MO/15 MI—24 KM
1994-95
EVERY 12 MO/15 MI—24 KM
Cooling system . . . . .inspect

Cooling level warning
   system . . . . .inspect

Engine oil level
   warning system . . . . .inspect

Idle speed . . . . .check/adjust

1992-93
EVERY 30 MO/30 MI—48 KM
1994-95
EVERY 24 MO/30 MI—48 KM
Brake system . . . . .inspect

Driveshaft boots . . . . .inspect

Exhaust system heat shields . . . .inspect

Steering linkage & suspension . . .inspect

Air cleaner element . . . . .replace

Cooling system . . . .change coolant **EC**

Drive belts . . . . .inspect/adjust

Fuel lines . . . . .inspect

Spark plugs . . . . .replace

Body & chassis nuts, bolts . . . . . . .torque

1992-93
EVERY 60 MO/60 MI—96 KM
1994-95
EVERY 48 MO/60 MI—96 KM
Differential . . . . .change lubricant

Fuel filter . . . . .replace

Transmission, manual . .change lubricant

SEVERE SERVICE
Brake fluid—Replace every: 1992-93, 30 mo/30 mi (48 km); 1994-95, 24 mo/ 30 mi (48 km)

Brake system—Inspect every: 1992-93, 15 mo/15 mi (24 km); 1994-95, 12 mo/ 15 mi (24 km)

Crankcase—Change oil & filter every 3 mo/3 mi (5 km)

Differential—Change lubricant every: 1992-93, 30 mo/30 mi (48 km); 1994-95, 24 mo/30 mi (48 km)

Locks & hinges—Lubricate every 1992-93, 5 mo/5 mi (8 km); 1994-95, 4 mo/5 mi (8 km)

Transmission, manual—Change lubricant every: 1992-93, 30 mo/30 mi (48 km); 1994-95, 24 mo/30 mi (48 km)

KEY TO LUBRICANTS

AF2	DEXRON®-II, Automatic Transmission Fluid
EC	Ethylene Glycol Coolant
GF-1	Motor Oil, API Service GF-1
GL-4	Gear Oil, API Service GL-4
GL-5	Gear Oil, API Service GL-5
HB	Hydraulic Brake Fluid, DOT 3 or 4
MA	MERCON®, Automatic Transmission Fluid
SG	Motor Oil, API Service SG

CRANKCASE . . . .**SG, GF-1**

CAPACITY, Refill:	Liters	Qt
1992-93	3.3	3.5
1994-95	3.6	3.8

Capacity shown is without filter. When replacing filter, additional oil may be needed.
Above −15°F (−25°C) 10W-30
Below 32°F (0°C) 5W-30

TRANSMISSION, Automatic . . . .**AF2, MA**

CAPACITY, Initial Refill[1]:	Liters	Qt
All	4.0[1]	4.2[1]

[1] With the engine at operating temperature, shift transmission through all gears. Check fluid level in PARK and add fluid as needed.

TRANSMISSION,
  Manual **75W-90 GL-4, GL-5**
Above 50°F (10°C), may use 80W-90

CAPACITY, Refill:	Liters	Pt
All	2.5	5.2

DIFFERENTIAL
Standard **GL-5**
Above 0°F (−18°C), 90; below 0°F (−18°C), 80W

CAPACITY, Refill:	Liters	Pt
All	1.3	2.8

SERVICE AT TIME OR MILEAGE — WHICHEVER OCCURS FIRST

MAIPM6   MAIPM6

Perform the following maintenance services at the intervals indicated to keep both the vehicle and emission warranties in effect.

MI—MILES IN THOUSANDS
KM—KILOMETERS IN THOUSANDS

AT EACH FUEL STOP
Brake & clutch reservoirs . .check level **HB**

EVERY MONTH
Drive belts . . . . .check/adjust

EVERY 6 MONTHS
Power steering
   reservoir . . . . .check level **AF**

Transmission, automatic . . . .check level

EVERY 7.5 MO/7.5 MI—12 KM
Body, 1992-93 . . . . .lubricate
Hinges, locks

Crankcase . . . . .change oil

Oil filter .replace

EVERY 12 MONTHS
Air conditioning system . . . . .inspect

EVERY 15 MO/15 MI—24 KM
Choke, B2200 2V . . . . .clean/inspect

Cooling system, MPV . . . . .inspect

Idle speed . . . . .check/adjust
B2200 2V also inspect idle switch
Initial service for B2600, MPV

Power brake unit & hoses . . . . .inspect

Propeller shaft, 4WD . . . . .lubricate **LM**

EVERY 30 MO/30 MI—48 KM
Body & chassis nuts & bolts . . . . .torque

Brake system . . . . .change fluid **HB**

Brake system . . . . .inspect

Driveshaft boots, 4WD . . . . .inspect

Steering & suspension,
   ex. MPV . . . . .lubricate **LM**
Wheel bearings; upper arm shaft

Steering gearbox
   oil, ex. MPV . . . . .check 90 **GL-4**

Steering & suspension system . . .inspect

Air cleaner element . . . . .replace

Cooling system . . . . .change coolant **EC**

Drive belts . . . . .inspect/adjust

Exhaust system heat shield . . . .inspect

Fuel filter, B2200 . . . . .replace

Fuel lines & hoses . . . . .inspect

Idle speed, B2600, MPV . . .check/adjust
Initial service at 15 mo/15 mi (24 km)

Spark plugs . . . . .replace

EVERY 60 MO/60 MI—96 KM
Differentials . . . . .change lubricant

Transfer case . . . . .change lubricant

Transmission, automatic . . . .change fluid
B Series

Transmission, manual . .change lubricant

EGR valve, B2200 2V . . . . .replace
At mileage interval only

Emission systems vacuum hoses . .replace
B2200, B2600, 1993 B2200 w/FI & MPV, inspect only,
replace at 105 mi (168 km)

Fuel filter, B2600, MPV . . . . . . .replace

High altitude compensator
   air filter, 2.2L 2V . . . . .replace

Ignition timing . . . . .check/adjust

PCV valve . . . . .inspect

Timing belt, B2200 & MPV V6 . . .replace
At mileage interval only. 1993 B2200 w/FI, inspect only
and also at 90 mi (144 km).

EVERY 80 MI—128 KM
Emission systems vacuum
   hoses . . . . .replace
MPV

Oxygen sensor . . . . .replace

EVERY 105 MI—168 KM
Fuel hoses . . . . .replace
1992-93 B2200 w/FI

Timing belt . . . . .replace
1993 B2200 w/FI

SEVERE SERVICE
Air cleaner element—Inspect every 15 mo/15 mi (24 km)

Body & chassis nuts and bolts—Torque every 15 mo/15 mi (24 km)

Crankcase—Change oil & filter every 5 mo/5 mi (8 km). 1992-93, also lubricate locks & hinges

Front disc brakes—Inspect every 15 mo/ 15 mi (24 km)

Transmissions, transfer case, differentials—Change fluid or lubricant every 30 mo/30 mi (48 km)

KEY TO LUBRICANTS

AF2	DEXRON®-II, Automatic Transmission Fluid
CC	Motor Oil, API Service CC
CD	Motor Oil, API Service CD
EC	Ethylene Glycol Coolant
FA	Automatic Transmission Fluid, Type F
GF-1	Motor Oil, API Service GF-1
GL-4	Gear Oil, API Service GL-4
GL-5	Gear Oil, API Service GL-5
HB	Hydraulic Brake Fluid, DOT 3 or 4
LM	Lithium Grease, with Moly
MA	MERCON®, Automatic Transmission Fluid
SG	Motor Oil, API Service SG
SH	Motor Oil, API Service SH

CRANKCASE . . . . .SG, SH; GF-1

CAPACITY, Refill:	Liters	Qt
2.2L	3.9	4.1
2.6L, 3.0L	4.5	4.8

Capacity shown is without filter. When replacing filter, additional oil may be needed.

1989-90:
Above 85°F (29°C) .40
Above 15°F (–9°C) 20W-40, 20W-50
Above –15°F (–25°C) 10W-40, 10W-50
32° to 105°F (0° to 39°C) 30
15° to 65°F (–9° to 20°C) 20W-20
–15° to 85°F (–25° to 29°C) 10W-30
Below 32°F (0°C) 5W-30
Below –5°F (–20°C) 5W-20
1991-93:
Above –15°F (–25°C) 10W-30
Below 32°F (0°C) 5W-30

TRANSMISSION, Automatic . . .AF2, MA3

CAPACITY, Initial Refill[1]:	Liters	Qt
All	4.0	4.2

1 With the engine at operating temperature, shift transmission through all gears. Check fluid level in PARK and add fluid as needed.

TRANSMISSION, Manual GL-4, GL-5
All temperatures, 75W-90; above 50°F (10°C), 80W-90

CAPACITY, Refill:	Liters	Pt
B2200: 4-speed	1.7	3.6
5-speed	2.0	4.2
B2600: 2WD	2.8	6.0
4WD	3.2	6.8
MPV	2.5	5.2

TRANSFER CASE GL-4, GL-5
All temperatures, 75W-90; above 32°F (0°C), 80W-90

CAPACITY, Refill:	Liters	Pt
B2600	2.0	4.2
MPV	1.5	3.2

DIFFERENTIAL GL-5
Above 0°F (–18°C), 90; below 0°F (–18°C), 80W

CAPACITY, Refill:	Liters	Pt
B2200	1.2	2.6
B2600: Front	1.5	3.2
Rear: 2WD	1.3	2.8
4WD	1.7	3.6
MPV: Front	1.7	3.6
Rear	1.5	3.2

MAZDA
1994-98 MPV
Navajo & B2300, B2500, B3000, B4000—See Ford Trucks

SERVICE AT TIME OR MILEAGE — WHICHEVER OCCURS FIRST

MAIPM10   MAIPM10

Perform the following maintenance services at the intervals indicated to keep both the vehicle and emission warranties in effect.

MI—MILES IN THOUSANDS
KM—KILOMETERS IN THOUSANDS

AT EACH FUEL STOP
Brake & clutch reservoirs . .check level **HB**
Canada, every 5 mo/5 mi (8 km)

EVERY MONTH
Drive belts . . . . .check/adjust

EVERY 6 MONTHS
Power steering
   reservoir . . . . . . .check level **AF2, MA**
Canada, every 5 mo/5 mi (8 km)

Transmission, automatic . . . .check level
Canada, every 5 mo/5 mi (8 km). Also check transfer case and differentials.

CANADA, EVERY 5 MO/5 MI—8 KM
U.S., EVERY 6 MO/7.5 MI—12 KM
Body . . . . .lubricate
Hinges, locks

Coolant, Canada . . . . .inspect **EC**

Crankcase . . . . .change oil

Drive belts, Canada . . . . .inspect/adjust

Oil filter .replace

Exterior lights, Canada . . . . .inspect

EVERY 12 MONTHS
Air-conditioning system, 1994 . . .inspect

CANADA,
EVERY 15 MO/15 MI—24 KM
U.S., EVERY 12 MO/15 MI—24 KM
Disc brakes, Canada . . . . .inspect

Air cleaner element, Canada . . . .inspect

Air-conditioning system, 1995-98 . . .inspect

Cooling system, Canada . . . . . .inspect

Idle speed . . . . .check/adjust
Initial service U.S. only

Power brake unit & hoses . . . . . .inspect

Propeller shaft,
   1994-95 4WD . . . . .lubricate **LM**

Tires, Canada . . . . .rotate

CANADA,
EVERY 30 MO/30 MI—48 KM
U.S, EVERY 24 MO/30 MI—48 KM
Body & chassis nuts & bolts . . . .torque

Brake system . . . . .change fluid **HB**

Brake system . . . . .inspect
U.S., pad linings, lines & hoses; Canada, lines & hoses only

Differentials, Canada . . .change lubricant

Driveshaft boots, 4WD . . . . .inspect

Steering & suspension system . . .inspect

Transfer case,
   Canada . . . . .change lubricant

Transmission, manual &
   automatic, Canada . . .change lubricant

Air cleaner element . . . . .replace

Cooling system,
   1994-95 . . . . .change coolant **EC**

Cooling system, U.S. . . . . .inspect

Drive belts, U.S. . . . . .inspect/adjust

Exhaust system heat shield . . . . .inspect

Fuel filter, Canada . . . . .replace

Fuel lines & hoses . . . . .inspect

Idle speed, U.S. . . . . .check/adjust
Initial service at 15 mo/15 mi (24 km)

Spark plugs . . . . .replace

AT FIRST 36 MO/45 MI—72 KM;
THEN EVERY 24 MO/30 MI—48 KM
Cooling system . . . . .change coolant **EC**

CANADA,
EVERY 60 MO/60 MI—96 KM
U.S., EVERY 48 MO/60 MI—96 KM
Differentials, U.S. . . . . . .change lubricant

Transfer case, U.S. . . . .change lubricant

Transmission,
   automatic, U.S. . . . . .change fluid

Transmission, manual . .change lubricant

Emission systems
   vacuum hoses . . . . .inspect

Fuel filter, U.S. . . . . .replace

Ignition timing . . . . .check/adjust

PCV valve . . . . .inspect

Timing belt, MPV V6 . . . . .replace
At mileage interval. California, inspect only. Inspect again at 90 mi (144 km)

EVERY 80 MI—128 KM
Emission systems vacuum
   hoses . . . . .replace
MPV

Oxygen sensor, 1994-95 . . . . . .replace

EVERY 105 MI—168 KM
Fuel hoses . . . . .replace
1994-97 California only

Timing belt . . . . .replace
California only

SEVERE SERVICE
U.S. Models Only

Air cleaner element—Inspect every 12 mo/ 15 mi (24 km)

Body & chassis nuts and bolts—Torque every 12 mo/15 mi (24 km)

Crankcase—Change oil & filter every 4 mo/5 mi (8 km). Also lubricate locks & hinges

Front disc brakes—Inspect every 12 mo/ 15 mi (24 km)

Transmissions, transfer case, differentials—Change fluid or lubricant every 24 mo/30 mi (48 km)

KEY TO LUBRICANTS

AF2	DEXRON®-II, Automatic Transmission Fluid
CC	Motor Oil, API Service CC
CD	Motor Oil, API Service CD
EC	Ethylene Glycol Coolant
GF-1	Motor Oil, API Service GF-1
GL-4	Gear Oil, API Service GL-4
GL-5	Gear Oil, API Service GL-5
HB	Hydraulic Brake Fluid, DOT 3 or 4
LM	Lithium Grease, with Moly
MA	MERCON®, Automatic Transmission Fluid
SH	Motor Oil, API Service SH
SJ	Motor Oil, API Service SJ

CRANKCASE . . . . .SH, SJ; GF-1, GF-2

CAPACITY, Refill:	Liters	Qt
2.6L, 3.0L	4.5	4.8

Capacity shown is without filter. When replacing filter, additional oil may be needed
Above −15°F (−25°C) 10W-30
Below 32°F (0°C) 5W-30

TRANSMISSION, Automatic . . . .AF2, MA

CAPACITY, Initial Refill[1]:	Liters	Qt
All	4.0	4.2

1 With the engine at operating temperature, shift transmission through all gears. Check fluid level in PARK and add fluid as needed.

TRANSMISSION, Manual GL-4, GL-5

All temperatures, 75W-90; above 50°F (10°C), 80W-90

CAPACITY, Refill:	Liters	Pt
MPV	2.5	5.2

TRANSFER CASE GL-4, GL-5

All temperatures, 75W-90; above 32°F (0°C), 80W-90

CAPACITY, Refill:	Liters	Pt
MPV	1.5	3.2

DIFFERENTIAL GL-5

Above 0°F (−18°C), 90; below 0°F (−18°C), 80W

CAPACITY, Refill:	Liters	Pt
MPV: Front	1.7	3.6
Rear	1.5	3.2

SERVICE AT TIME OR MILEAGE — WHICHEVER OCCURS FIRST

MAIPM12   MAIPM12

Perform the following maintenance services at the intervals indicated to keep both the vehicle and emission warranties in effect.

MI—MILES IN THOUSANDS
KM—KILOMETERS IN THOUSANDS

AT EACH FUEL STOP
Brake reservoirs . . . . .check level **HB**

Coolant . . . . .check level **EC**

Engine oil . . . . .check level

EVERY MONTH
Tire pressure . . . . .check

EVERY 6 MONTHS
Power steering
   reservoir . . . . . . .check level **AF2, MA**

Transmission, automatic . . . .check level

EVERY 6 MO/7.5 MI—12 KM
Body . . . . .lubricate
Hinges, locks

Crankcase . . . . .change oil

Oil filter .replace

EVERY 12 MO/12 MI — 20 KM
Cabin air filter . . . . .replace

EVERY 12 MO/15 MI—24 KM
Air-conditioning system . . . . .inspect

EVERY 24 MO/30 MI—48 KM
Body & chassis nuts & bolts . . . . .torque

Brake system . . . . .change fluid **HB**

Brake system . . . . .inspect
Pad linings, lines & hoses

Steering & suspension system . . .inspect

Air cleaner element . . . . .replace

Cooling system . . . . .inspect

Drive belts . . . . .inspect/adjust

Exhaust system heat shield . . . . .inspect

Fuel lines & hoses . . . . .inspect

AT FIRST 36 MO/45 MI—72 KM; THEN EVERY 24 MO/30 MI—48 KM
Cooling system . . . . .change coolant **EC**

EVERY 48 MO/60 MI—96 KM
Emission systems
   vacuum hoses . . . . .inspect

PCV valve . . . . .inspect

Spark plugs . . . . .replace
At mileage interval only

SEVERE SERVICE & ALL CANADIAN MODELS
Air cleaner element—Inspect every 12 mo/ 15 mi (24 km)

Body & chassis nuts and bolts—Torque every 12 mo/15 mi (24 km)

Crankcase—Change oil & filter every 4 mo/5 mi (8 km). Also lubricate locks & hinges & inspect lighting system

Front disc brakes—Inspect every 12 mo/ 15 mi (24 km)

Tire inflation and wear—Inspect every 4 mo/5 mi (8 km)

Vehicle fluid levels—Check coolant power steering every 4 mo/5 mi (8 km)

KEY TO LUBRICANTS

AF2	DEXRON®-II, Automatic Transmission Fluid
CC	Motor Oil, API Service CC
CD	Motor Oil, API Service CD
EC	Ethylene Glycol Coolant
GF-2	Motor Oil, API Service GF-2
GL-4	Gear Oil, API Service GL-4
GL-5	Gear Oil, API Service GL-5
HB	Hydraulic Brake Fluid, DOT 3 or 4
LM	Lithium Grease, with Moly
MA	MERCON®, Automatic Transmission Fluid
SJ	Motor Oil, API Service SJ

CRANKCASE . . . . .SJ, GF-2, API★

CAPACITY, Refill:	Liters	Qt
2.5L	4.7	5.0

Capacity shown is without filter. When replacing filter, additional oil may be needed

All temperatures 5W-30

TRANSMISSION, Automatic . . . .AF2, MA

CAPACITY, Total Fill:	Liters	Qt
All	8.0	8.4

SERVICE LOCATIONS — ENGINE AND CHASSIS

MZIDP-1   MZIDP-1

HOOD RELEASE: Inside

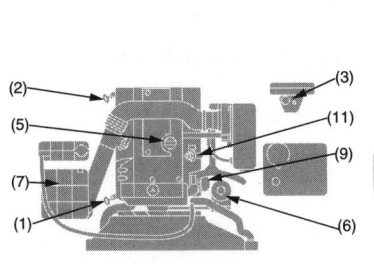

**1994-96
4-cyl. 2199cc C-220
1998-99
4-cyl. 2295cc Supercharged
C230, SLK230**

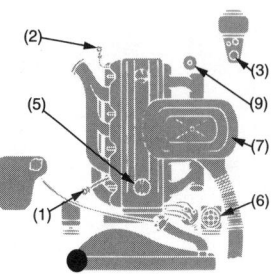

**4-cyl. 2299cc
1991-93 190E**

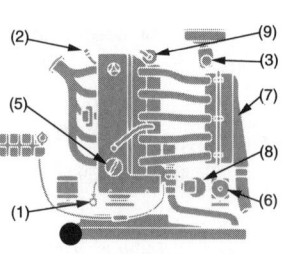

**5-cyl. 2497cc Diesel
1989 190D**

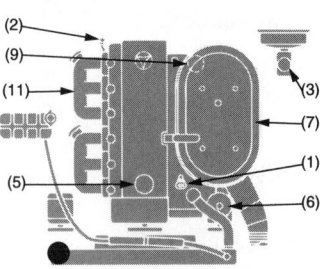

**6-cyl. 2599cc, 2960cc Gas
1989-93 190 2.6L
1989 260E
1989-93 300E**

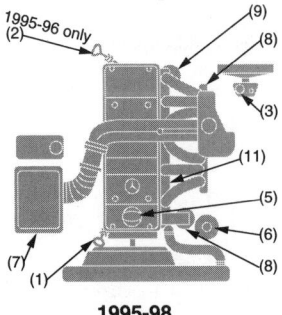

**1995-98
6-cyl. 2996cc Diesel
E300**

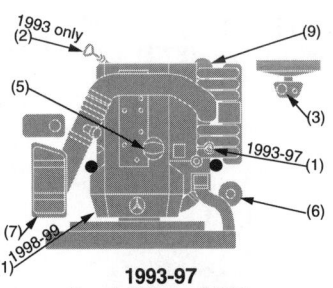

**1993-97
6-cyl. 2799cc C280,
6-cyl. 3199cc
1994-99
CLK320, ES20, ML320, S320, SL320
1995-97
6-cyl. 3606cc C36AMG**

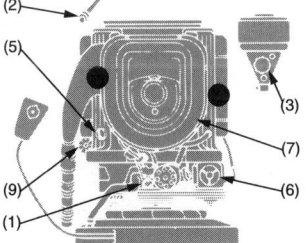

**V8 4196cc
4973cc, 5547cc
1989 All w/V8
1989-91 420SEL, 560SEC, SEL**

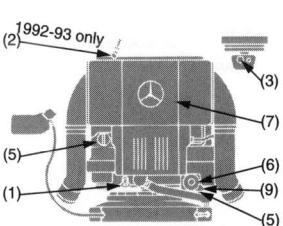

**V8 4196cc
1992-93 400E, 400SEL
1994-98 E420, S420**

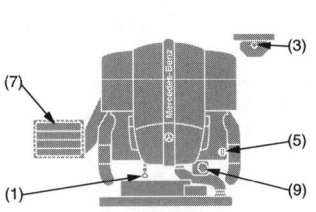

**1999
V8 4265cc, 4366cc, 4966cc
E430, ML430, SL500**

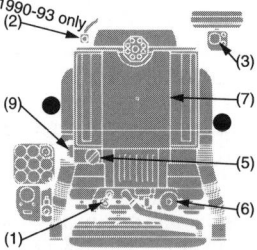

**V8 4973cc DOHC
1990-93 500: E, SEC, SEL, SL
1994-98, CL500, E500, S500, SL500**

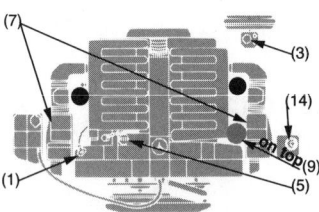

**V12 5987cc
1992-93 600SEC, 600SEL, 600SL
1996-99 CL600, S600, SL600**

(1) Crankcase dipstick
(2) Transmission dipstick
(3) Brake fluid reservoir
(4) Clutch fluid reservoir
(5) Oil fill cap
(6) Power steering reservoir
(7) Air filter

(8) Fuel filter
(9) Oil filter
(10) PCV filter
(11) EGR valve
(12) Oxygen sensor
(13) PCV valve
(14) Hydropneumatic
     suspension reservoir

● Cooling system drain

SERVICE LOCATIONS — ENGINE AND CHASSIS

MZIDP-2   MZIDP-2

0 FITTINGS
0 PLUGS

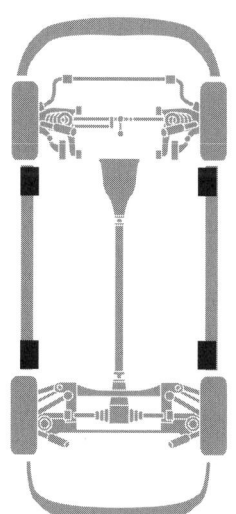

1994-99
170, 202, 208 Chassis:
SLK230, C220, C230, C280,
CLK320,
1996-99 124 Chassis: E300,
E320, E420, E500, C36 AMG

0 FITTINGS
0 PLUGS

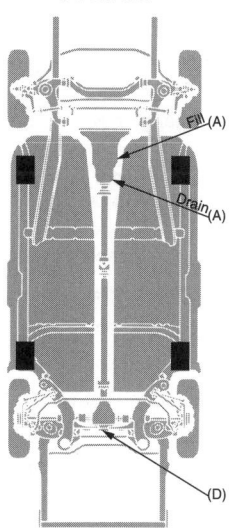

1989-93 201 Chassis:
190D, 190E;
1989-97 124 Chassis:
260E, 300CE, 300D, 300E,
300TE, 400E, 500E
E300, E320, E420, E500

0 FITTINGS
0 PLUGS

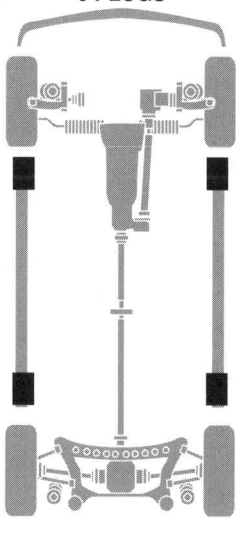

1998-99 210 Chassis:
4WD Version Shown
E300, E320, E420

0 FITTINGS
0 PLUGS

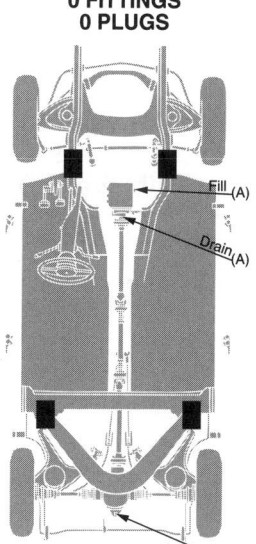

1989 107 Chassis:
560SL

0 FITTINGS
0 PLUGS

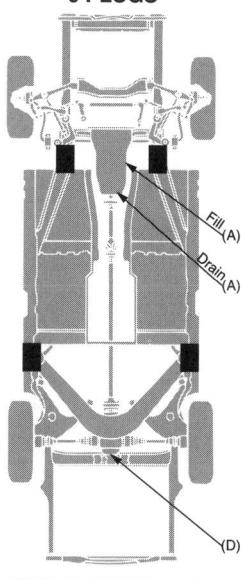

1989-91 126 Chassis:
300SD, 300SE, 300SEL, 420SEL,
560SEC, 560SEL

0 FITTINGS
0 PLUGS

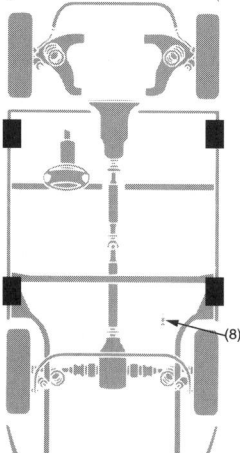

1990-99 129 Chassis:
300SL, 500SL
SL320, SL500, SL600

0 FITTINGS
0 PLUGS

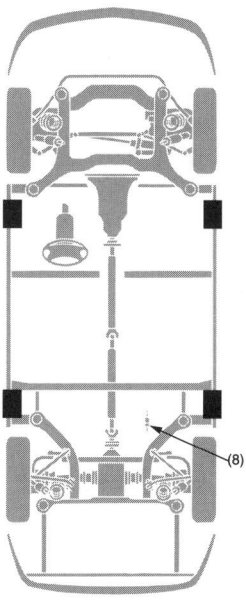

1992-99 140 Chassis:
300SE, 300SD, 400SEL,
500SEC, 500SEL, 600SEC, 600SEL
S320, S350, S420, S500, S600

0 FITTINGS
0 PLUGS

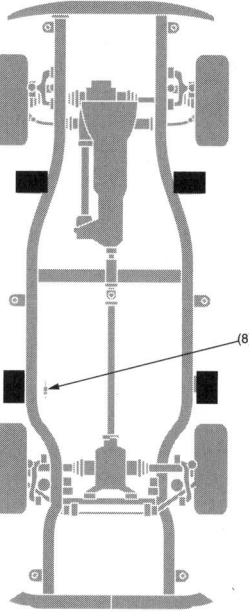

1998-99 163 Chassis:
ML320, ML430

(A) Manual transmission/transaxle, drain & fill

(B) Transfer case, NOT USED

(C) Automatic transaxle final drive, NOT USED

(D) Differential, drain & fill

■ Lift adapter position

(8) Fuel filter

SERVICE AT TIME OR MILEAGE — WHICHEVER OCCURS FIRST

MZIPM1   MZIPM1

W SERVICE TO MAINTAIN EMISSION WARRANTY
Except 1998-99 models with FSS - Flexible Service System

MI—MILES IN THOUSANDS
KM—KILOMETERS IN THOUSANDS

1992-93
300SD, EVERY 7.5 MI—12 KM
ALL OTHERS, EVERY 5 MI—8 KM
1994-97
EVERY 12 MO/7.5 MI—12 KM

W Crankcase . . . . .change oil
At least once a year if year-round multigrade oil is used. Otherwise, at least every spring & fall

W Oil filter .replace
At least once a year if year-round multigrade oil is used. Otherwise, at least every spring & fall

W Transmission,
   manual, 1989 . . . . . . .change lubricant
One time service only

W Engine control
   linkage . . . . .inspect/lubricate **SLF**

Battery, 1989 . . . . .check level

EVERY 24 MO/15 MI—24 KM
Brake system . . . . .inspect
Clean brake discs & pads, road test system. Adjust parking brake at first interval only

Differential . . . . .check level

Front axle, steering
   linkage & boots . . . . .inspect

Steering . . . . .check free play
Inspect linkage & retorque mounting bolts

Tires & wheels . . . . .inspect
Dismount to inspect, rotate if necessary. Retorque after 60-300 mi (97-482 km). Check pressure including spare

W Transmission, manual . . . . .check level

W Air filter element, 1989 . . . .inspect/clean

Brake & clutch reservoir . .check level **HB**

Battery . . . . .check level

W Cooling system . . . . .check level **EC**
Check degree of antifreeze protection

Drive belts . . . . .inspect/adjust

W Fuel system . . . . .inspect
Check fuel tank, lines

Injection timing, 1990-94 . . .check/adjust
At first service interval only

Level control 300SD . . . . .check level **SLF**

Power steering reservoir . . .check level **PS**
Inspect condition of lines & hoses

W Transmission, automatic . . . .check level
1989-96 ex. 5-speed

Windshield & headlight washers . . . . . .fill

Windshield wipers . . . . .replace

Body . . . . .lubricate **LM**

Air conditioner . . . . .inspect
Check operation and Freon® charge

Electrical equipment . . . . .inspect

Seat belts . . . . .inspect

Tape deck head . . . . .clean

Heating & ventilation . . . . .change filter

EVERY 30 MI—48 KM
Propeller shaft . . . . .check flex discs

W Transmission,
   automatic, ex. 5-speed . . .change fluid
Replace internal filter

Steering, 1992-97 . . . . . .check freeplay
Inspect linkage & retorque mounting bolts except 140, 210 chassis

W Air filter element, 1989-96 . . . . . .replace

Clutch plate . . . . .check wear

W Fuel filter, 1989-96 . . . . .replace

W Fuel prefilter, 1989-96 . . . . .replace

W Injection pump timing . . . . .check/adjust
One time service only

W Idle speed, 1989 . . . . .check/adjust

Parking brake cables . . . . .inspect
Check for free operation of cables

Air recirculation filter . . . . .replace
1992-93 300SD only

EVERY 45 MI—72 KM
Heating & ventilation filter . . . . .replace
1994 S Series only

Activated charcoal pre-filter . . . . .replace

EVERY 24 MONTHS
Preferably in the spring
Brake system . . . . .change fluid **HB**

Body water drains . . . . .clean

Chassis & body . . . . .inspect
Check for damage & corrosion

Sunroof rails, 1989-95 . . . . .lubricate **LM**

EVERY 36 MONTHS
W Engine coolant . . . . .replace **EC**

Sunroof rails, 1996-97 . . . . .lubricate **LM**

EVERY 60 MI—96 KM
Activated charcoal filter . . . . .replace
1989-93

W Air filter element, 1997 . . . . .replace

W Fuel filter, 1997 . . . . .replace

W Fuel prefilter, 1997 . . . . .replace

EVERY 48 MO/75 MI—120 KM
Activated charcoal filter . . . . .replace
1994 S Series only

SEVERE SERVICE
Crankcase—Change oil & filter every: 1989-92, 2.5 mi (4 km); 1993-94, 3.75 mi (6 km)

Transmission, automatic—1989-96 ex. 5-speed, change fluid every 15 mi (24 km). Change filter every 30 mi (48 km)

Air filter element—Clean/replace, every 15 mi (24 km) or as needed

Tires—Inspect every 7.5 mi (12 km)

KEY TO LUBRICANTS[1]
AF3	DEXRON III Automatic Transmission Fluid
CE	Motor Oil, API Service CE
CF-4	Motor Oil, API Service CF-4
CG-4	Motor Oil, API Service CG-4
EC	Ethylene Glycol Coolant Mix with water to desired freeze protection Mercedes-Benz Part No. Q1030002
GLS	Gear Lubricant, Special Mercedes-Benz Part No. 000 989 26 03
GL-5	Gear Oil, API Service GL-5
GL-5★	Special Lubricant for Limited-Slip Differential Mercedes-Benz Part No. 000 583 09 04
HB	Hydraulic Brake Fluid, Extra Heavy-Duty DOT 4 Plus
LM	Lithium Multipurpose Grease
PS	Power Steering Fluid Mercedes-Benz Part No. 000 989 88 03
SH	Motor Oil, API Service SH
SJ	Motor Oil, API Service SJ
SLF	Special Lubricant—Fluid Level Control: Part No. 000 989 91 03 10 Auto. Trans.: Part No. 001 989 21 03 10

1 Note: Use only Mercedes-Benz approved fluids

CRANKCASE . . . . . . .CE, CF-4, CG-4, SH
CAPACITY, Refill[2]:	Liters	Qt
5-cyl.: 1989 2.5L	7.0	7.4
1990-91 2.5L	7.5	7.9
1992-93 2.5L	7.0	7.4
6-cyl.:		
1990-95 3.5L	8.0	8.5
1995-99 3.0L	7.0	7.4

2 All capacities shown include filter. On models with oil cooler, additional oil may be needed when cooler is drained. Wait 5 minutes after refilling or turning off engine to check oil level. **Caution:** When using pressure fed oil hose to fill engine, point nozzle toward timing chain cover.
All temperatures 5W-40, 5W-50
Above 5°F (-15°C) 15W-40, 15W-50
Above -4°F (-20°C) . . .10W-40, 10W-50, 10W-30
-4° to 50°F (-20° to 10°C) 10W-30
Below 25°F (-5°C) 5W-30

TRANSMISSION, Automatic
1996-99 5-speed . . . .**SLF**
W5A580 model 722.6
1989-96 All Others **AF3**
CAPACITY, Initial Refill[3]:	Liters	Qt
1989 190D	5.5	5.8
1990-93 300D	5.5	5.8
1992-93 300SD	6.2	6.6
1990-91 350SD, 350SDL	6.2	6.6
1994-95 S350 Turbo Diesel	6.2	6.6
1995-97 E300	6.0	6.3
1998 E300	7.1	7.5
1999 E300	8.0	8.5

3 With engine at operating temperature, shift transmission through all gears. Check fluid level in PARK and add fluid as needed. No dipstick on 1996-97 5-speed models.

DIFFERENTIAL
Standard 85W-90, 90 **GL-5**
Limited-Slip . . . . .90 **GL-5★**
CAPACITY, Refill:	Liters	Pt
190 Series	0.7	1.4
1990 350 SDL	1.1	2.4
1991-93 300SD, SDL	1.3	2.8
1990-93 300D	1.1	2.4
1994-95 S350 Turbo Diesel	1.3	2.8
1995-99 E300	1.1	2.4

LIMITED-SLIP IDENTIFICATION:
Metal plate on rear of differential, near fill plug

SERVICE AT TIME OR MILEAGE — WHICHEVER OCCURS FIRST

MZIPM2   MZIPM2

W   SERVICE TO MAINTAIN EMISSION WARRANTY

MI—MILES IN THOUSANDS
KM—KILOMETERS IN THOUSANDS

EVERY 7.5 MI—12 KM
W Crankcase ....change oil
At least once a year if year-round multigrade oil is used.
Otherwise, at least every spring & fall

W Oil filter ....replace
At least once a year if year-round multigrade oil is used.
Otherwise, at least every spring & fall

W Engine control
linkage ....inspect/lubricate **SLF**
At least twice a year

Rear engine mount ....check/adjust
4MATIC models only, at first interval only

Battery ....check level

EVERY 24 MO/15 MI—24 KM
Brake system ....inspect
Clean brake discs & pads, road test system. Adjust
parking brake ex. 140 chassis, at initial service only

Clutch control ....inspect

Differential ....check level
1990-91 4MATIC models, check front differential level

Front axle, steering
linkage & boots ....inspect

Steering ....check free play
Retorque mounting bolts

Tires & wheels ....inspect
Dismount to inspect, rotate and correct pressure if
necessary

W Transmission, manual .....check level

Transfer case ....check level
1990-91 4MATIC models

Brake & clutch reservoir ..check level **HB**

W Cooling system ....check level **EC**
Check degree of antifreeze protection

Drive belts ....inspect/adjust

Spark plugs ....inspect
Replace as necessary

W Fuel system ....inspect
Check fuel tank, lines

Level control ....check level **SLF**

Power steering reservoir ...check level **PS**
Inspect condition of lines & hoses

W Transmission, automatic ....check level

Windshield washers ....check/fill

Body ....lubricate **LM**

Climate control system ....inspect
Check operation and refrigerant charge

Convertible top, 1990-91 ......inspect
Check level of hydraulic system, check operation of
locking lug

Electrical equipment ....inspect

Heating & ventilation filter .....replace
1990-91 300SL, 500SL only

Seat belts ....inspect

Tape deck head ....clean

EVERY 30 MI—48 KM
Propeller shaft ....check flex discs

W Transmission, automatic ....change fluid
Replace internal filter

W Air filter element ....replace
Replace air pump filter element if equipped

Clutch disc ....check wear

Parking brake cables ....inspect
Check for free operation of cables

W Spark plugs ....replace

EVERY 60 MI—96 KM
W Fuel filter ....replace

W Oxygen sensor, 1989-90 ......replace
One-time service only

EVERY 24 MONTHS
Preferably in the spring
Brake system ....change fluid **HB**

Body water drains ....clean

Chassis & body ....inspect
Check for damage & corrosion

Sunroof rails ....lubricate **LM**

EVERY 36 MONTHS
W Engine coolant ....replace **EC**

SEVERE SERVICE
Crankcase—Change oil & filter every
3.75 mi (6 km)

Tires—Inspect every 7.5 mi (12 km)

Transmission, automatic—Change fluid
every 15 mi (24 km). Change filter every
30 mi (48 km)

Air filter element—Clean/replace every
15 mi (24 km) or as needed

KEY TO LUBRICANTS[1]

AF3	DEXRON® III Automatic Transmission Fluid
CC	Motor Oil, API Service CC
CD	Motor Oil, API Service CD
EC	Ethylene Glycol Coolant Mix with water to desired freeze protection Mercedes-Benz Part No. Q1030002
GLS	Gear Lubricant, Special Mercedes-Benz Part No. 000 989 26 03
GL-5	Gear Oil, API Service GL-5
GL-5★	Special Lubricant for Limited-Slip Differential Rear: Mercedes-Benz Part No. 000 583 09 04 Front: Mercedes-Benz Part No. 001 989 05 03
HB	Hydraulic Brake Fluid, Extra Heavy-Duty DOT 4 Plus
LM	Lithium Multipurpose Grease
PS	Power Steering Fluid Mercedes-Benz Part No. 000 989 88 03
SF	Motor Oil, API Service SF
SG	Motor Oil, API Service SG
SH	Motor Oil, API Service SH
SLF	Special Lubricant—Fluid Engine Control Linkage, Level Control: Part No. 000 989 91 03 10 Auto Trans.: Part No. 001 989 21 03 10

1 Note: Use only Mercedes-Benz approved fluids

CRANKCASE .....SG, SF/CC, SF/CD, SH

CAPACITY, Refill[2]:	Liters	Qt
4-cyl.:		
1991 190E	5.0	5.3
6-cyl.:		
1989 3.0L	6.0	6.3
2.6L	6.0	6.3
1990-91 3.0L SOHC ex. 4MATIC	6.0	6.3
3.0L SOHC 4MATIC	6.5	6.9
3.0L DOHC	7.5	7.9
8-cyl.:		
All models	8.0	8.5

2 All capacities shown include filter. On models with oil cooler, additional oil may be needed when cooler is drained

All temperatures 5W-40, 5W-50
Above 5°F (-15°C) 15W-40, 15W-50
Above -4°F (-20°C) ...10W-40, 10W-50, 10W-60
-4° to 50°F (-20° to 10°C) 10W-30
Below 25°F (-5°C) 5W-30

TRANSMISSION, Automatic AF3

CAPACITY, Initial Refill[3]:	Liters	Qt
All w/V8 engine	7.7	8.1
190E, 260E, 300E 2.6L	6.0	6.3
300 Series ex. SL, 2.6L	6.2	6.6
1990-91 300SL	6.0	6.3

3 Add specified quantity. With engine at operating temperature, shift transmission through all gears. Check fluid level in PARK and add fluid as needed

TRANSMISSION, Manual ....GLS

CAPACITY, Refill:	Liters	Pt
All ex. 300SL	1.5	3.2
1990-91 300SL	1.6	3.4

TRANSFER CASE ....AF

CAPACITY, Refill:	Liters	Pt
1990-91 300E 4MATIC	0.7	1.4

DIFFERENTIAL

Front ....85W-90, 90 **GL-5**[4]
4 Mercedes-Benz Part No. 001 989 05 03

Rear:
Standard 85W-90, 90 **GL-5**
Limited-Slip ....90 **GL-5★**

CAPACITY, Refill:	Liters	Pt
Front: 1990-91 300E 4MATIC ...	1.0	2.2
Rear: All w/V8 engine	1.3	2.8
1989 190E	0.7	1.4
300 Series ex. SL	1.1	2.3
1989-90 260E	1.1	2.3
1990-91 190E	1.1	2.3
300SL	1.3	2.8

LIMITED-SLIP IDENTIFICATION:
Metal plate on rear of differential, near fill plug

SERVICE AT TIME OR MILEAGE — WHICHEVER OCCURS FIRST

MZIPM3

MZIPM3

W   SERVICE TO MAINTAIN EMISSION WARRANTY

MI—MILES IN THOUSANDS
KM—KILOMETERS IN THOUSANDS

EVERY 12 MO/7.5 MI—12 KM
W Crankcase . . . . .change oil

W Oil filter . . . . .replace

W Transmission, manual . .change lubricant
One-time service only

W Engine control
linkage . . . . .inspect/lubricate **SLF**
At least twice a year

EVERY 24 MO/15 MI—24 KM
Brake system . . . . .inspect
Clean brake discs & pads, road test system. Adjust parking brake ex. S series, at initial service only

Clutch control . . . . .inspect

Differential . . . . .check level
4MATIC models, also check front differential level

Front axle, steering
linkage & boots . . . . .inspect

Tires & wheels . . . . .inspect
Dismount to inspect, rotate and correct pressure if necessary. Retorque after 60-300 mi (97-482 km)

W Transmission, manual . . . . . .check level

Transfer case . . . . .check level

Brake & clutch reservoir . .check level **HB**

Battery . . . . .check level

W Cooling system . . . . . . .check level **EC**
Check degree of antifreeze protection

Drive belts . . . . .inspect/adjust

Spark plugs . . . . .inspect

W Fuel system . . . . .inspect

Level control . . . . .check level **SLF**
For ADS Adaptive Damping System

Power steering reservoir . . .check level **PS**
Inspect condition of lines & hoses

W Transmission, automatic . . . .check level
Ex. 5-speed

W Windshield washers . . . . .check/fill

Windshield wipers . . . . .replace

Body . . . . .lubricate **LM**

Climate control system . . . . .inspect

Convertible top . . . . .inspect
Check level of hydraulic system, check operation of locking lug

Electrical equipment . . . . .inspect

Interior heating & ventilation dust
filter C & S Series . . . . .replace

Underhood heating & ventilation dust
filter .replace
S & SL Series w/o activated charcoal filter

Seat belts . . . . .inspect

Tape deck head . . . . .clean

EVERY 30 MI—48 KM
Propeller shaft . . . . .check flex discs

Steering gear . . . . .tighten
Retorque mounting bolts ex. E & S Series

W Transmission, automatic . . . .change fluid
Replace internal filter. Ex. 5-speed

W Air filter element . . . . .replace
Replace air pump filter element if equipped

Clutch disc . . . . .check wear

Parking brake cables . . . . .inspect

W Spark plugs . . . . .replace

EVERY 24 MO/45 MI—72 KM
Underhood dust filter w/activated charcoal
pre-filter S Series . . . . .replace

Interior activated charcoal filter . .replace
E Series

Interior recirculated air filter . . . . .replace
S Series

EVERY 60 MI—96 KM
Fuel filter . . . . .replace

W Oxygen sensor . . . . .replace
One-time service only

EVERY 24 MONTHS
Preferably in the spring
Brake system . . . . .change fluid **HB**

Body water drains . . . . .clean

Chassis & body . . . . .inspect

Sunroof rails . . . . .lubricate **LM**

EVERY 36 MONTHS
W Engine coolant . . . . .replace **EC**

SEVERE SERVICE
Crankcase—Change oil & filter every 3.75 mi (6 km)

Tires—Inspect every 7.5 mi (12 km)

Transmission, automatic—Ex. 5-speed, change fluid every 15 mi (24 km). Change filter every 30 mi (48 km)

Air filter element—Clean/replace every 15 mi (24 km) or as needed

KEY TO LUBRICANTS
See other Mercedes-Benz charts

CRANKCASE . . . . .SG/CC, SG/CD, SH, SJ

CAPACITY, Refill[1]:	Liters	Qt
4-cyl.:		
190E	5.0	5.3
2199cc	6.2	6.6
2295cc ex supercharged	6.2	6.5
6-cyl.:		
2.6L	6.0	6.3
2.8L	7.5	7.9
3.0L SOHC ex. 4MATIC	6.0	6.3
3.0L SOHC 4MATIC	6.5	6.9
3.0L DOHC	7.5	7.9
3.2L	7.5	7.9
8-cyl.:		
All	8.0	8.5
12-cyl:		
600SEC, SEL	10.0	10.7
1993 600SL	11.0	11.6

1 All capacities shown include filter. On models with oil cooler, additional oil may be needed when cooler is drained. Wait 5 minutes after refilling or turning off engine to check oil level. V12 with oil filter on top: use wrench Part No. 103589020900.

All temperatures 5W-40, 5W-50
Above 5°F (-15°C) 15W-40, 15W-50
Above -4°F (-20°C) . . .10W-40, 10W-50, 10W-60
-4° to 50°F (-20° to 10°C) 10W-30
Below 25°F (-5°C) 5W-30

TRANSMISSION, Automatic
All AF3

CAPACITY, Initial Refill[2]:	Liters	Qt
190E 2.6L	6.0	6.3
260E 2.6L, 2.8L	6.0	6.3
300E 2.6L, 2.8L	6.0	6.3
300SE, SL	6.0	6.3
300 Series Others	6.2	6.6
600SEC, SEL, SL	7.7	8.1

2 With engine at operating temperature, shift transmission through all gears. Check fluid level in PARK and add fluid as needed. No dipstick on 1996 and later 5-speed models.

TRANSMISSION, Manual . . . . .GLS
CAPACITY, Refill:	Liters	Pt
190 Series	1.5	3.2
300SL	1.6	3.4

TRANSFER CASE AF3
CAPACITY, Refill:	Liters	Pt
300E, TE 4MATIC	0.7	1.4

DIFFERENTIAL
Front . . . . .85W-90, 90 **GL-5**[4]
Rear:
   Standard 85W-90, 90 **GL-5**
   Limited-Slip . . . . .90 **GL-5★**
4 Mercedes-Benz Part No. 001 989 05 03

CAPACITY, Refill:	Liters	Pt
Front: 300E, TE 4MATIC	1.0	2.2
Rear: 190E	1.1	2.3
300CE, SE, SL	1.3	2.8
300 Series ex. CE, SE, SL	1.1	2.3
400SE	1.4	3.0
400SEL w/V8 engine	1.3	2.8
500SEC, SEL	1.4	3.0
600SEC, SEL	1.4	3.0
600SL	1.3	2.8

LIMITED-SLIP IDENTIFICATION:
Metal plate on rear of differential, near fill plug

SERVICE AT TIME OR MILEAGE — WHICHEVER OCCURS FIRST

MZIPM4   MZIPM4

W   SERVICE TO MAINTAIN EMISSION WARRANTY
Except 1998-99 models with FSS - Flexible Service System

MI—MILES IN THOUSANDS
KM—KILOMETERS IN THOUSANDS

EVERY 12 MO/7.5 MI—12 KM
W Crankcase . . . . .change oil
W Oil filter .replace
W Transmission, manual . .change lubricant
One-time service only
W Engine control
   linkage . . . . .inspect/lubricate **SLF**
At least twice a year

EVERY 24 MO/15 MI—24 KM
Brake system . . . . .inspect
Clean brake discs & pads, road test system. Adjust parking brake ex. S series, at initial service only
Clutch control . . . . .inspect
Differential . . . . .check level
4MATIC models, also check front differential level
Front axle, steering
   linkage & boots . . . . .inspect
Tires & wheels . . . . .inspect
Dismount to inspect, rotate and correct pressure if necessary. Retorque after 60-300 mi (97-482 km)
W Transmission, manual . . . . .check level
Transfer case . . . . .check level
Brake & clutch reservoir . .check level **HB**
Battery . . . . .check level
W Cooling system . . . . . . .check level **EC**
Check degree of antifreeze protection
Drive belts . . . . .inspect/adjust
Spark plugs . . . . .inspect
W Fuel system . . . . .inspect
Level control . . . . .check level **SLF**
For ADS Adaptive Damping System
Power steering reservoir . . .check level **PS**
Inspect condition of lines & hoses
W Transmission, automatic . . . .check level
1994-96 ex. 5-speed
W Windshield washers . . . . .check/fill
Windshield wipers . . . . .replace
Body . . . . .lubricate **LM**
Climate control system . . . . .inspect
Convertible top . . . . .inspect
Check level of hydraulic system, check operation of locking lug
Electrical equipment . . . . .inspect
Interior heating & ventilation dust
   filter C & S Series . . . . .replace
Underhood heating & ventilation dust
   filter .replace
S & SL Series w/o activated charcoal filter
Seat belts . . . . .inspect
Tape deck head . . . . .clean

EVERY 30 MI—48 KM
Propeller shaft . . . . .check flex discs
Steering gear . . . . .tighten
Retorque mounting bolts ex. E & S Series
W Transmission, automatic . . . .change fluid
Replace internal filter. 1994-96 ex. 5-speed
W Air filter element, 1994-96 . . . . .replace
Replace air pump filter element if equipped
Clutch disc . . . . .check wear
Parking brake cables . . . . .inspect
W Spark plugs . . . . .replace

EVERY 24 MO/45 MI—72 KM
Underhood dust filter w/activated charcoal
   pre-filter S Series . . . . .replace
Interior activated charcoal filter . .replace
E Series
Interior recirculated air filter . . . .replace
S Series

EVERY 60 MI—96 KM
Fuel filter . . . . .replace
W Oxygen sensor . . . . .replace
One-time service only
W Air filter element, 1997 . . . . .replace

EVERY 48 MO/75 MI—120 KM
Underhood activated charcoal filter . .replace
1994-97 S Series only

EVERY 24 MONTHS
Preferably in the spring
Brake system . . . . .change fluid **HB**
Body water drains . . . . .clean
Chassis & body . . . . .inspect
Sunroof rails, 1994-95 . . . . .lubricate **LM**

EVERY 36 MONTHS
W Engine coolant . . . . .replace **EC**
Sunroof rails, 1996-97 . . . . .lubricate **LM**

SEVERE SERVICE
Crankcase—Change oil & filter every 3.75 mi (6 km)
Tires—Inspect every 7.5 mi (12 km)
Transmission, automatic—1994-96 ex. 5-speed, change fluid every 15 mi (24 km). Change filter every 30 mi (48 km)
Air filter element—Clean/replace every 15 mi (24 km) or as needed

KEY TO LUBRICANTS
See other Mercedes-Benz charts

CRANKCASE . . . . . .SG/CC, SG/CD, SH, SJ

CAPACITY, Refill[1]:	Liters	Qt
4-cyl.:		
2199cc: 1994-95	6.2	6.6
1996	5.5	5.8
1994-98 2295cc ex supercharged	6.2	6.5
1998 2295cc Supercharged . . .	5.6	5.9
1999 2295cc Supercharged	5.8	6.1
6-cyl.:		
2.6L	6.0	6.3
2.8L: 1994-95	7.5	7.9
1996-97	7.0	7.4
1998-99	8.0	8.5
3.0L SOHC ex. 4MATIC	6.0	6.3
3.0L SOHC 4MATIC	6.5	6.9
3.0L DOHC	7.5	7.9
3.2L: 1994-95	7.5	7.9
1996-98	7.0	7.4
1999	8.0	8.5
3.6L: 1995	7.5	7.9
1996-97	7.0	7.4
8-cyl.:		
C43 AMG 4265cc	7.5	7.9
E55 AMG 5499cc	7.5	8.0
All other models	8.0	8.5
12-cyl.:		
1998 CL600	10.0	10.7
1994-96 SL600	11.0	11.6
1997-99 SL600	10.0	10.7
1995-98 S600	10.0	10.7

1 All capacities shown include filter. On models with oil cooler, additional oil may be needed when cooler is drained. Wait 5 minutes after refilling or turning off engine to check oil level. V12 with oil filter on top: use wrench Part No. 103589020900.

All temperatures 5W-40, 5W-50	
Above 5°F (-15°C) 15W-40, 15W-50	
Above -4°F (-20°C) . . .10W-40, 10W-50, 10W-60	
-4° to 50°F (-20° to 10°C) 10W-30	
Below 25°F (-5°C) 5W-30	

TRANSMISSION, Automatic
1996-99 5-speed . . . .**SLF**
W5A580 model 722.6
1994-96 All others **AF3**

CAPACITY, Initial Refill[2]:	Liters	Qt
1994-96 C220, C280	5.5	5.8
1997-98 C230	7.5[3]	7.9[3]
1999 C230, C280	8.0[3]	8.5[3]
1997-98 C280	7.5[3]	7.9[3]
1996 C36 AMG	6.2	6.6
1997 C36 AMG	9.4[3]	9.9[3]
1998-99 C43 AMG	9.4[3]	9.9[3]
1998-99 CL500, CL600	9.4[3]	9.9[3]
1998 CLK320	6.2	6.6
1999 CLK320	8.0[3]	8.5[3]
1999 CLK430	9.1[3]	9.6[3]
1994-97 E320	6.2	6.6
1998 E320	7.5[3]	7.9[3]
1999 E320	8.0[3]	8.5[3]
1993-96 E420	7.7	8.2
1997 E420	9.4[3]	9.9[3]
1998-99 E430, E55 AMG	9.4[3]	9.9[3]
1998-99 ML320	7.5[3]	7.9[3]
1999 ML430	9.4[3]	9.9[3]
1998-99 S320, SL320	6.0	6.3
1993-96 S420, S500, S600 . . .	7.7	8.1
1997-98 S420, S500, S600, . . .	9.4[3]	9.9[3]
1993-96 SL500, SL600	7.7	8.1
1997-98 SL500, SL600	9.4[3]	9.9[3]
1999 SLK 230	8.0[3]	8.5[3]
1999 SL500, SL600	9.1[3]	9.6[3]
1998 SLK 230	7.1[3]	7.5[3]

2 With engine at operating temperature, shift transmission through all gears. Check fluid level in PARK and add fluid as needed. No dipstick on 1996 and later 5-speed models.
3 Total fill, add less fluid when refilling.

TRANSMISSION, Manual . . . . .GLS

CAPACITY, Refill:	Liters	Pt
SLK 230	1.5	3.2

TRANSFER CASE AF3

CAPACITY, Refill:	Liters	Pt
ML320, ML430	1.0	2.2
E320	1.0	2.2

DIFFERENTIAL
Front . . . . .85W-90, 90 **GL-5**[4]
Rear:
   Standard 85W-90, 90 **GL-5**
   Limited-Slip . . . . .90 **GL-5★**
4 Mercedes-Benz Part No. 001 989 05 03

CAPACITY, Refill:	Liters	Pt
Front 320	0.5	1.0
C220, C280: 1994-95	1.1	2.4
1996	0.7	1.4
C230	1.1	2.4
1997-99 C280	1.1	2.4
C36 AMG, C43 AMG	1.3	2.8
CL500, CL600	1.4	3.0
CLK320, CLK430	1.3	2.8

CAPACITY, Refill:	Liters	Pt
E320 Coupe, Cabriolet	1.3	2.8
E320 Sedan: 1994-96	1.1	2.4
1997-99	1.3	2.8
E320 Wagon	1.3	2.8
E420, E430, E500, E55	1.3	2.8
ML320, ML430 front	1.1	2.4
rear	1.5	3.2
S320, S420	1.3	2.8
S500	1.4	3.0
1993-96 SL320, SL500, SL600 . .	1.3	2.8
1997 SL320	1.3	2.8
1997-98 SL500, SL600	1.4	3.0
1998-99 SLK230	1.3	2.8

LIMITED-SLIP IDENTIFICATION:
Metal plate on rear of differential, near fill plug

SERVICE LOCATIONS — ENGINE AND CHASSIS

HOOD RELEASE: Inside

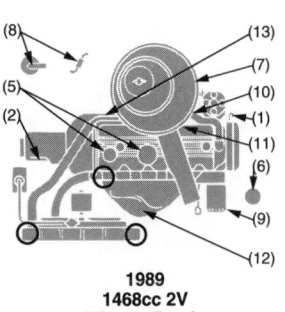

1989
1468cc 2V
Mirage, Precis

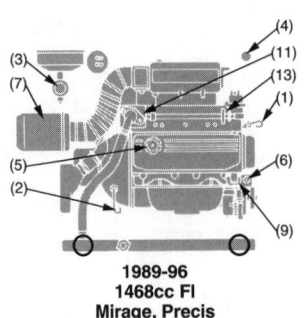

1989-96
1468cc FI
Mirage, Precis

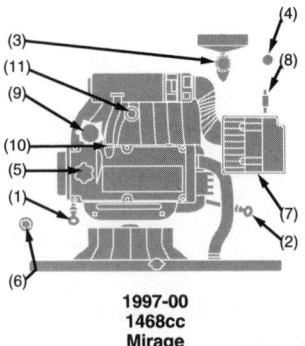

1997-00
1468cc
Mirage

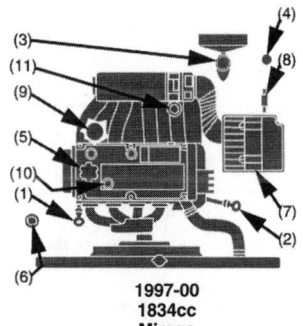

1997-00
1834cc
Mirage

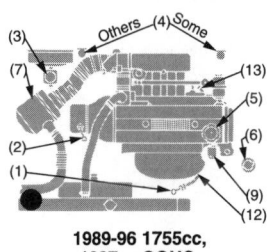

1989-96 1755cc,
1997cc SOHC,
2350cc 8-valve
Galant, Eclipse, Expo

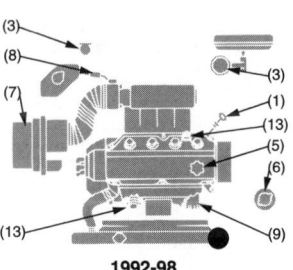

1992-98
1834cc, 2350cc 16-valve
Mirage, Expo, Galant

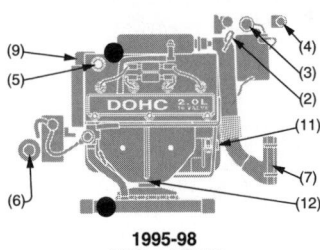

1995-98
1966cc DOHC
Eclipse

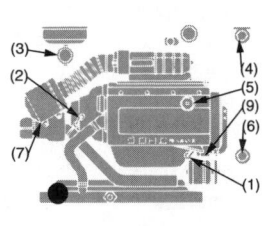

1989-98
1597cc DOHC Turbo,
1997cc DOHC, 2350cc DOHC
Galant, Eclipse, Mirage

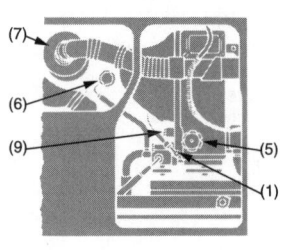

1989-90
2350cc
Van

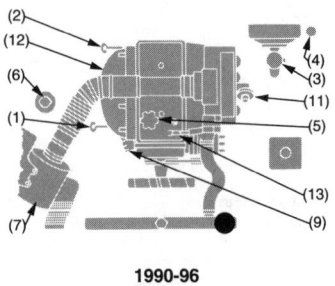

1990-96
2350cc
Pickup

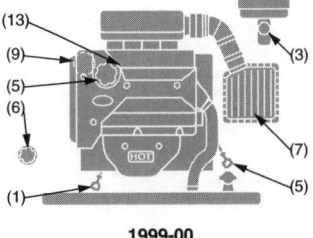

1999-00
2350cc Galant,
Eclipse

(1) Crankcase dipstick
(2) Transmission dipstick
(3) Brake fluid reservoir
(4) Clutch fluid reservoir
(5) Oil fill cap
(6) Power steering reservoir
(7) Air filter
(8) Fuel filter
(9) Oil filter
(10) PCV filter
(11) EGR valve
(12) Oxygen sensor
(13) PCV valve

● Cooling system drain   ○ Cooling system drain,
                                   some models

SERVICE LOCATIONS — ENGINE AND CHASSIS

HOOD RELEASE: Inside

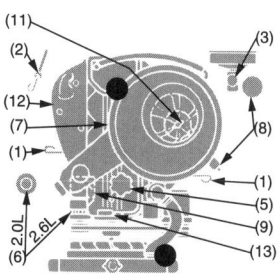

1989
1997cc, 2555cc
Pickup, Montero

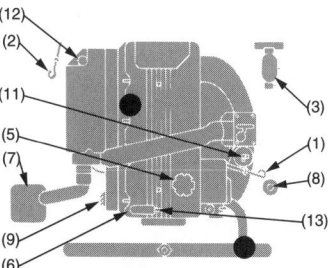

1989
2555cc Turbo
Conquest

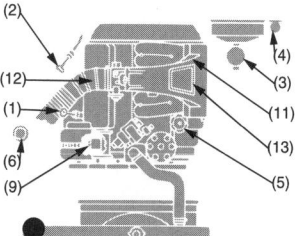

1989-00
2972cc
Montero, Pickup, Montero Sport

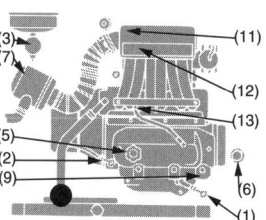

1989-99
2972cc SOHC
Sigma, 300GT, Diamante

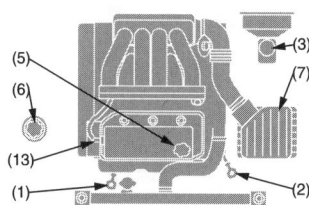

1999-00
2972cc Galant,
Eclipse

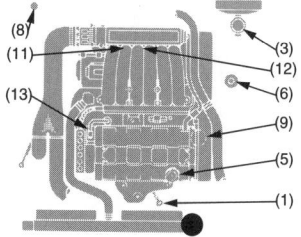

1991-00
2972cc DOHC, 3000GT
3497cc DOHC, Diamante

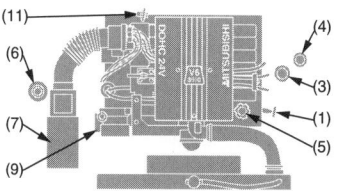

1994-00
3496cc Montero, Montero Sport

(1) Crankcase dipstick
(2) Transmission dipstick
(3) Brake fluid reservoir
(4) Clutch fluid reservoir
(5) Oil fill cap
(6) Power steering reservoir
(7) Air filter
(8) Fuel filter
(9) Oil filter
(10) PCV filter
(11) EGR valve
(12) Oxygen sensor
(13) PCV valve

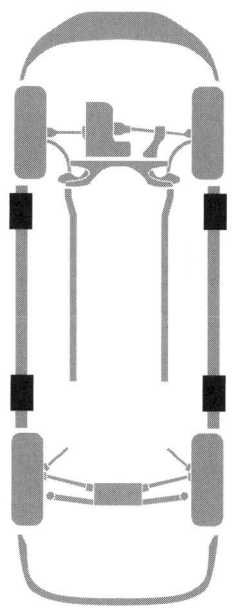

0 FITTINGS
0 PLUGS

1999-00 Galant
2000 Eclipse

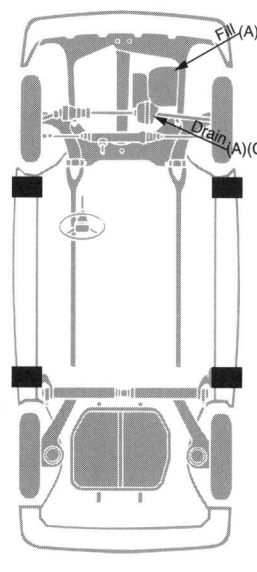

0 FITTINGS
0 PLUGS

1989-97 Mirage
1989-94 Precis

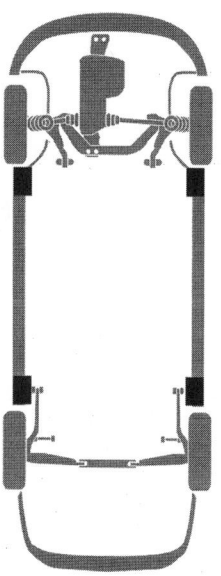

0 FITTINGS
0 PLUGS

1997-00
Mirage

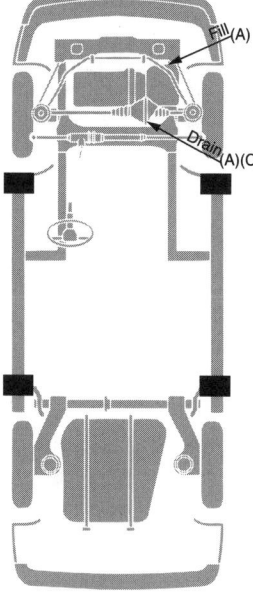

0 FITTINGS
0 PLUGS

1992-00
Diamante

■ Lift adapter position

• Fitting   ○ Fitting, some models

▲ Plug   △ Plug, some models

● Cooling system drain

○ Cooling system drain, some models

(A) Manual transmission/transaxle, drain & fill
(B) Transfer case, drain & fill
(C) Automatic transaxle final drive, drain & fill

(D) Differential, drain & fill
(8) Fuel filter

MITSUBISHI
1989-2000 All Models

SERVICE LOCATIONS — ENGINE AND CHASSIS

0 FITTINGS
0 PLUGS

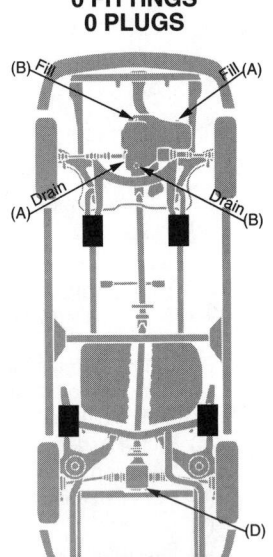

(B) Fill   Fill (A)
(A) Drain   Drain (B)

(D)

1992-95 Expo
4WD version shown

0 FITTINGS
0 PLUGS

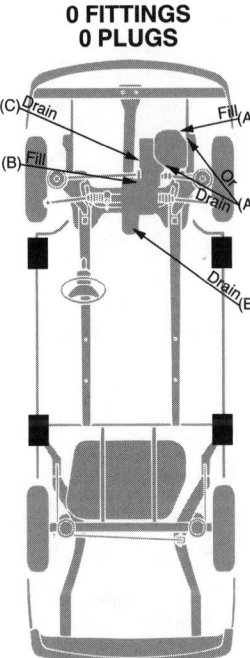

(C) Drain   Fill (A)
(B) Fill   (A)
                  Drain
                  Drain (B)

1989-98 Galant
1989-91 Sigma
1990-99 Eclipse
1991-99 3000GT

4-7
FITTINGS
0-4
PLUGS

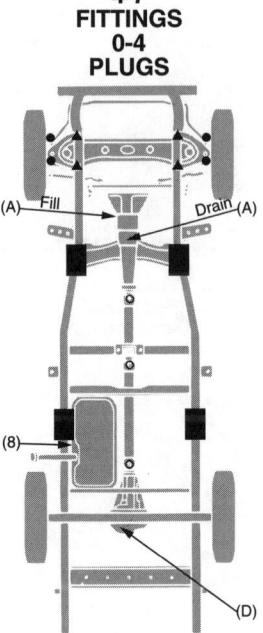

(A) Fill   Drain (A)

(8)

(D)

1989-00
2-Wheel Drive Pickup
& Montero Sport

8-17
FITTINGS

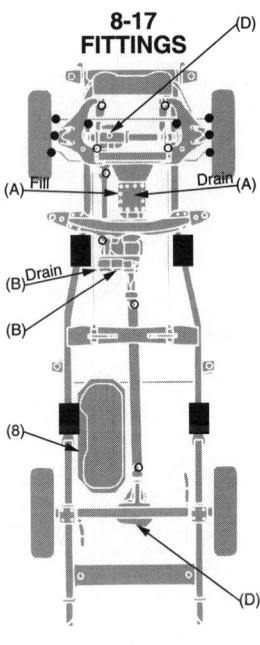

(D)

(A) Fill   Drain (A)

(B) Drain
(B)

(8)

(D)

1989-00
4-Wheel Drive Pickup
& Montero Sport

12-17
FITTINGS

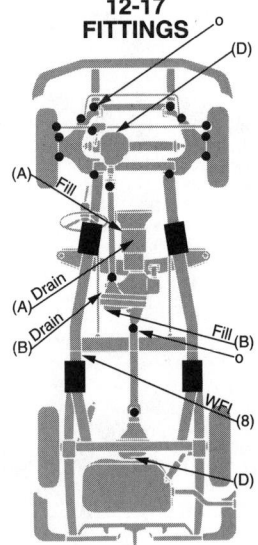

o
(D)

(A) Fill

(A) Drain
(B) Drain   Fill (B)
                 o

                 WFl
                 (8)

                 (D)

1989-99
Montero

2
PLUGS

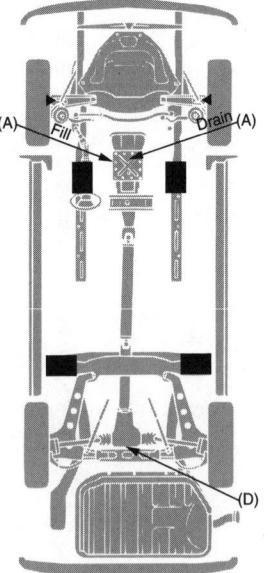

(A) Fill   Drain (A)

(D)

1989
Starion

2 FITTINGS
2 PLUGS

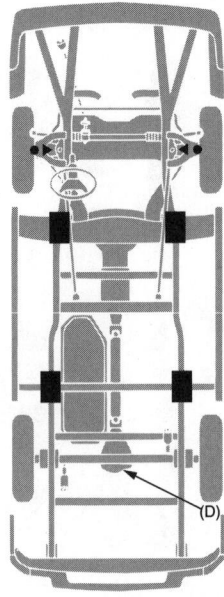

(D)

1989-90
Van

■ Lift adapter position

• Fitting   ○ Fitting, some models

▲ Plug   △ Plug, some models

(A) Manual transmission/transaxle,
    drain & fill

(B) Transfer case, drain & fill

(C) Automatic transaxle final drive,
    drain & fill

(D) Differential, drain & fill

(8) Fuel filter

MITSUBISHI
1989-94 All Models ex. Pickup, Montero
Precis—See Hyundai Excel

SERVICE AT TIME OR MILEAGE — WHICHEVER OCCURS FIRST

MIIPM7   MIIPM7

W   SERVICE TO MAINTAIN EMISSION WARRANTY

MI—MILES IN THOUSANDS
KM—KILOMETERS IN THOUSANDS

TURBO ENGINES
EVERY 6 MO/5 MI—8 KM
Crankcase . . . . .change oil

Oil filter .replace
At second oil change, then every other

EVERY 12 MO/7.5 MI—12 KM
Brake & clutch
  fluid reservoir . . . . .check level **HB**

Crankcase ex. Turbo . . . . . . .change oil

Oil filter ex. Turbo . . . . .replace
Every second oil change, but at least every 12 months

Power steering fluid . . . . . . .check **AF2**

EVERY 12 MO/15 MI—24 KM
Disc brake pads . . . . .inspect
Also check brake hoses

Driveshaft boots . . . . .inspect

Transaxle, automatic . . . . . . .check level

EVERY 15 MI—24 KM
W Valve clearance . . . . .inspect/adjust
1.5L & 1992-93 1.8L Expo only. 1989 others, as equipped, adjust jet valve only on models with hydraulic lifters.

EVERY 24 MO/30 MI—48 KM
Ball joint, steering linkage seals &
  FWD steering . . . . .inspect

Drum brakes . . . . .inspect
Linings, wheel cylinders

Exhaust system . . . . .inspect

Front wheel bearings
  RWD cars . . . . .clean/repack **LM**
Inspect for leaks. Inspect & repack whenever rotors are removed.

Rear wheel bearings FWD cars,
  ex. w/disc brakes . . . .clean/repack **LM**
Inspect for leaks. Repack whenever drums are removed.

Coolant . . . . .drain/flush/refill **EC**

W Fuel hoses 1991-94 . . . . .inspect

EVERY 30 MI—48 KM
Differential,
  RWD or 4WD rear . . . . . . .check level
With Limited-Slip, change lubricant

Transaxle, automatic FWD . .change fluid
Change filter

DIFFERENTIAL
Limited-Slip, RWD . . . .**GL-5★**
Others **GL-5**
Above -10°F (-23°C), 90, 85W-90, 80W-90; -30° to -10°F (-34° to -23°C), 80W, 80W-90; below -30°F (-34°C), 75W

Transmission/Transaxle,
  manual . . . . .check level
Also check 4WD transfer case fluid level

W Air cleaner filter . . . . .replace

Drive belt . . . . .inspect
Waterpump & alternator only

W Spark plugs . . . . .replace
Ex. 3.0L DOHC

EVERY 60 MO/50 MI—80 KM
W Fuel system 1989-92 . . . . .inspect
Tank, lines, connections, cap

W Fuel, & fuel
  vapor hoses 1989-90 . . .check/replace

EVERY 60 MI—96 KM
W Spark plugs . . . . .replace
3.0L DOHC

Timing & balancer belt . . . . .replace
As equipped. 1994 Calif. models, replacement recommended but not required

1993 CALIF. MIRAGE,
EXPO MODELS
1994 MIRAGE, EXPO, GALANT;
CALIF. DIAMANTE & 3000GT
EVERY 60 MO/60 MI—96 KM
W Distributor cap & rotor . . . . .inspect
SOHC engines only

W Evaporative emissions
  control system . . . . .inspect

W Ignition wires . . . . .replace

Fuel system . . . . .inspect
Tank, lines, connections & cap

EVERY 120 MONTHS
Air bag system . . . . .inspect

SEVERE SERVICE
W Air cleaner filter—Service more frequently

Brake system—Inspect more frequently

Crankcase—Change oil every 3 mo/3 mi (4.8 km) & filter every second oil change

Spark plugs—Replace every 15 mi (24 km)

Transmission, automatic—1989 RWD, change fluid every 30 mi (48 km)

CAPACITY, Refill:	Liters	Pt
Starion	1.3	2.8
4WD Galant, Expo	0.7	1.5
4WD Eclipse	0.7	1.5
4WD 3000GT	1.1	2.3

KEY TO LUBRICANTS
See other Mitsubishi charts

CRANKCASE . . . . .SG, SG/CD; GF-1[1]
[1] Preferred

CAPACITY, Refill:	Liters	Qt
1.5L	3.0	3.2
1.6L	4.0	4.2
1.8L, 2.0L SOHC	3.5	3.7
2.0L DOHC	4.0	4.2
2.4L: 8 valve	3.5	3.7
16 valve	4.0	4.2
2.6L	4.3	4.6
3.0L	4.0	4.2

Capacity shown is without filter. When replacing filter, additional oil may be needed.

Turbo Models
Above 32°F (0°C), 1989-92 . . . . .20W-20
Above 32°F (0°C) 20W-40
Above -10°F (-23°C) 10W-30
Below 60°F (16°C) . . . . .5W-30[2]
[2] Preferred below 60°F (16°C) when temperatures drop below -10°F (-23°C)

All Other Models
Above 32°F (0°C), 1989-92 . . . . .20W-20
Above 32°F (0°C) 20W-40, 20W-50
Above -10°F (-23°C) . .10W-30, 10W-40, 10W-50
Below 60°F (16°C), 1989-92 . . . . .5W-20[3],
                              5W-30, 5W-40
Below 100°F (38°C), 1993-94 . . . . .5W-30, 5W-40
[3] Not recommended for sustained high-speed driving

TRANSMISSION/TRANSAXLE,
  Automatic . . . . .AP3, SLF

CAPACITY, Initial Refill[4]:	Liters	Qt
Starion	5.0	5.3
3000GT, Diamante	4.5	4.8
1993-94: Mirage	6.0[5]	6.3[5]
Expo FWD	6.1[5]	6.4[5]
4WD	6.5[5]	6.9[5]
1994 Galant: SOHC	6.3[5]	6.7[5]
DOHC	7.9[5]	8.4
All others	4.0	4.2

[4] With the engine at operating temperature, shift transmission through all gears. Check fluid level in NEUTRAL and add fluid as needed.
[5] Total or dry fill shown, use less fluid when refilling.

TRANSMISSION/TRANSAXLE, Manual
Starion 80W, 75W-85W, **GL-4**
Others, 1989-91 . . . . .75W-85W **GL-4**
  1992-94 . . . . . . .75W-90, 75W-85W **GL-4**

CAPACITY, Refill:	Liters	Pt
Mirage: 4-speed	1.7	3.6
5-speed	1.8	3.8
Sigma	2.5	5.2
Galant, 1989-93: SOHC	1.8	3.8
DOHC	2.3	4.8
Eclipse: SOHC	1.8	3.8
DOHC	2.3	4.8
3000GT: 2WD	2.3	4.8
4WD	2.4	5.0
Expo: FWD, 1.8L	1.8	3.8
2.4L	2.3	4.8
4WD	2.3	4.8
Starion	2.3	4.8

TRANSFER CASE
1989-91 . . . . .75W-85W **GL-4, GL-5**
1992-94 . . .75W-90, 75W-85W **GL-4, GL-5**

CAPACITY, Refill:	Liters	Pt
4WD Galant, Expo	0.6	1.2
4WD Eclipse	0.6	1.2
4WD: 3000GT 1991-92	0.3[6]	0.6[6]
1993-94	0.3	0.6

[6] 1991-92, fill no higher than ½ inch (13 mm) below fill hole

MITSUBISHI
1995-2000 All Models ex. Pickup, Montero

SERVICE AT TIME OR MILEAGE — WHICHEVER OCCURS FIRST

W   SERVICE TO MAINTAIN EMISSION WARRANTY   MIIPM8

MI—MILES IN THOUSANDS
KM—KILOMETERS IN THOUSANDS

TURBO ENGINES
EVERY 6 MO/5 MI—8 KM
Crankcase . . . . .change oil

Oil filter .replace
At second oil change, then every other

EVERY 12 MO/7.5 MI—12 KM
Brake & clutch
 fluid reservoir . . . . .check level **HB**

Cabin air filter . . . . .replace
2000 Galant

Crankcase ex. Turbo . . . . . . .change oil

Oil filter ex. Turbo . . . . .replace
Every second oil change, but at least every 12 months

Power steering fluid . . . . .check
1995-99 **AF2**
2000 **PS**

Tires, 2000 . . . . .rotate

EVERY 12 MO/15 MI—24 KM
Disc brake pads . . . . .inspect
Also check brake hoses

Driveshaft boots . . . . .inspect

Transaxle, automatic . . . . . . .check level

EVERY 15 MI—24 KM
W Valve clearance . . . . .inspect/adjust
1995-97 1.5L & 1.8L only.

EVERY 24 MO/30 MI—48 KM
Ball joint, steering linkage seals &
 FWD steering . . . . .inspect

Drum brakes . . . . .inspect
Linings, wheel cylinders

Exhaust system . . . . .inspect

Front wheel bearings
 RWD cars . . . . .clean/repack **LM**
Inspect for leaks. Inspect & repack whenever rotors are removed.

Rear wheel bearings FWD cars,
 ex. w/disc brakes . . . .clean/repack **LM**
Inspect for leaks. Repack whenever drums are removed.

Coolant . . . . .drain/flush/refill **EC**

W Fuel hoses . . . . .inspect

EVERY 30 MI—48 KM
Differential, 4WD rear . . . . . .check level
With Limited-Slip, change lubricant

Transaxle, automatic FWD,
 1995-96 . . . . .change fluid
Change filter

Transmission/Transaxle,
 manual . . . . .check level
Also check 4WD transfer case fluid level

W Air cleaner filter . . . . .replace

Drive belt . . . . .inspect
Waterpump, alternator, power steering only

W Spark plugs . . . . .replace
Ex. 3.0L DOHC & platinum tipped

EVERY 60 MI—96 KM
W Spark plugs . . . . .replace
3.0L DOHC & platinum tipped

Timing & balancer belt . . . . .replace
As equipped. Calif. models, replacement recommended but not required.

EVERY 60 MO/60 MI—96 KM
W Distributor cap & rotor . . . . .inspect
SOHC engines only

W Evaporative emissions
 control system . . . . .inspect

W Ignition wires . . . . .replace

Fuel system . . . . .inspect
Tank, lines, connections & cap

EVERY 100 MI—160 KM
Timing belt . . . . .replace
Only if belt was not replaced at 60 mi (96 km)

EVERY 120 MONTHS
Air bag system . . . . .inspect

SEVERE SERVICE
W Air cleaner filter—Replace every 15 mi (24 km)

Brake system—Inspect disc pads every 6 mo/6 mi (9.6 km); inspect drum brakes every 15 mi (24 km)

Crankcase—Change oil every 3 mo/3 mi (4.8 km) & filter every second oil change

Spark plugs—Replace every 15 mi (24 km)

Transmission, automatic—1995-96 Eclipse ex. Turbo, change fluid every 15 mi (24 km); 1997-00 all, change fluid & filter every 30 mi (48 km). 1997-00 Mirage, 2000 Diamante. Mirage change external filter

Tires, 2000—Rotate every 6 mo/6 mi (9.6 km)

Transaxle, manual & transfer case—Ex. 2.0L non-turbo, change lubricant every 30 mi (48 km)

KEY TO LUBRICANTS
See other Mitsubishi charts

CRANKCASE: . . . . .SJ, SJ/CD; API★

CAPACITY, Refill:	Liters	Qt
1.5L	3.0	3.2
1.8L	3.5	3.7
2.0L DOHC (1996cc)	3.8	4.0
2.0L DOHC (1997cc)	4.0	4.2
2.4L	4.0	4.2
3.0L, 3.5L	4.0	4.2

Capacity shown is without filter. When replacing filter, additional oil may be needed.

Turbo Models
Above 0°F (-18°C) 20W-40
Above -10°F (-23°C) 10W-30
Below 60°F (16°C) . . . . .5W-30[2]
2 Preferred below 60°F (16°C) when temperatures drop below -10°F (-23°C)

Other Models
Above 0°F (-18°C) 10W-30
Below 100°F (38°C) 5W-30

TRANSMISSION/TRANSAXLE,
Automatic
1995-96 . . . . .AP3, SLF
1997-00 . . . . .SLF

CAPACITY, Initial Refill[3]:	Liters	Qt
Mirage: 1995-96	6.0[4]	6.3[4]
1997-00	3.5	3.7
Expo: FWD	6.1[4]	6.4[4]
4WD	6.5[4]	6.9[4]
Galant: 1995-97	6.0[4]	6.3[4]
1998	2.5	2.6
1999-00	2.0	2.1
Eclipse 2.0L ex. Turbo	3.8	4.0
Turbo: 1995-97	6.7[4]	7.1[4]
1998-99	2.5	2.6
Eclipse 2.4L, 3.0L: 1995-97 . . .	6.1[4]	6.4[4]
1998-00	2.5	2.6
Diamante, 3000GT: 1995-97	7.5[4]	7.9[4]
1998-00	3.0	3.2

3 With the engine at operating temperature, shift transmission through all gears. Check fluid level in NEUTRAL and add fluid as needed.
4 Total or dry fill shown, use less fluid when refilling.

TRANSMISSION/TRANSAXLE, Manual
1995-99 Eclipse, 2.0L non-Turbo . . . . .**GLS**
Texaco MTX Fluid FM
Others 75W-90, 75W-85W **GL-4**

CAPACITY, Refill:	Liters	Pt
Mirage: 1995-96: 4-speed	1.7	3.6
5-speed	1.8	3.8
1997-00: 1.5L	2.1	4.4
1.8L	2.2	4.6
Galant	2.2	4.6
Eclipse 1995-99: ex Turbo	2.0	4.2
Turbo	2.2	4.6
2000: 2.4L	2.2	4.8
3.0L	2.8	6.0
3000GT: 2WD	2.3	4.8
4WD	2.4	5.0
Expo: FWD, 1.8L	1.8	3.8
2.4L	2.3	4.8
4WD	2.3	4.8

TRANSFER
CASE 75W-90, 75W-85W **GL-4, GL-5**

CAPACITY, Refill:	Liters	Pt
4WD Expo	0.6	1.2
4WD Eclipse	0.5	1.0
3000GT	0.3	0.6

DIFFERENTIAL GL-5
Above -10°F (-23°C), 90, 85W-90, 80W-90; -30° to -10°F (-34° to -23°C), 80W, 80W-90; below -30°F (-34°C), 75W

CAPACITY, Refill:	Liters	Pt
4WD Expo	0.7	1.5
4WD Eclipse	0.9	1.9
4WD 3000GT	1.1	2.3

SERVICE AT TIME OR MILEAGE — WHICHEVER OCCURS FIRST

MIIPM3 MIIPM3

W   SERVICE TO MAINTAIN EMISSION WARRANTY

KEY TO LUBRICANTS
See other Mitsubishi charts

MI—MILES IN THOUSANDS
KM—KILOMETERS IN THOUSANDS

EVERY 12 MO/7.5 MI—12 KM
Brake & clutch
   fluid reservoir . . . . .check level **HB**

Crankcase . . . . .change oil

Oil filter .replace
At second oil change then every other

Power steering fluid . . . .check level **AF2**

EVERY 12 MO/15 MI—24 KM
Disc brake pads . . . . .inspect
Also check hoses

Exhaust system . . . . .inspect

Ball joints . . . . .lubricate **LM**
With fittings only

Cooling system . . . . .inspect
Service as required

Transmission, automatic . . . .check level

EVERY 15 MI—24 KM
W Idle speed . . . . .check/adjust

W Valve clearance, 4-cyl . . . .inspect/adjust
Gasoline jet valve only

EVERY 24 MO/30 MI—48 KM
Ball joints, steering linkage seals &
   drive shaft boots . . . . .inspect

Drive shaft joints . . . . .lubricate **LM**

Drum brakes . . . . .inspect
Linings, wheel cylinders

Front wheel bearings . . .clean/repack **LM**

Coolant . . . . .drain/flush/refill

EVERY 30 MI—48 KM
Differential(s) . . . . .check level

Limited-Slip differential . . . . .change oil

Transmission, automatic . . . .change fluid
4WD only

Transmission, manual &
   transfer case . . . . .check level

W Air filter . . . . .replace

W Choke & linkage . . . . .clean **PC**

Drive belt . . . . .replace
Water pump & alternator only

W Spark plugs . . . . .replace

EVERY 48 MO/60 MI—96 KM
Brake system . . . . .change fluid **HB**
Also change hydraulic clutch fluid

EVERY 60 MO/50 MI—80 KM
W Distributor . . . . .check
Ex. Calif. At 60 mo/60 mi (96 km)

EGR valve, 4-cyl. ex. Calif . . . . .replace
At mileage interval only. Also clean sub EGR valve

W Evaporative control system . . . .inspect
At mileage interval only.

W Fuel filter ex. Van . . . . .replace
Check fuel system cap, tank, lines, & connections

W Fuel, water, & fuel
   vapor hoses . . . . .check/replace

W Hot air control valve, 2V ex. Calif . .check
At 60 mo/60 mi (96 km)

W Ignition wires . . . . .check/replace
At 60 mo/60 mi (96 km)

W Vacuum control system solenoid
   valve filter . . . . .replace
At 60 mo/60 mi (96 km)

W Vacuum hoses . . . . .replace
Includes secondary air hoses and crankcase vent hoses.
At 60 mo/60 mi (96 km)

EVERY 60 MI—96 KM
Timing belt . . . . .replace
As equipped

EVERY 80 MI—128 KM
Crankcase emission
   control system . . . . . . .check/clean **PC**

Oxygen sensor, ex. Calif . . . . .replace

EVERY 100 MI—160 KM
Evaporative system canister . . . .replace
Ex. Calif.

SEVERE SERVICE

W Air cleaner filter, PCV system & brake
  system—Service more frequently

W Crankcase—Change oil every 3 mo/3 mi
(4.8 km) & filter every second oil change.

2WD transmission, 2WD automatic—
Change fluid, filter every 30 mi (48 km)

Transmission, manual & transfer case—
Change lubricant every 30 mi (48 km)

W Spark plugs—Replace every 15 mi (24 km)

CRANKCASE . . . . .SF, SF/CC

CAPACITY, Refill:	Liters	Qt
2WD:		
2.0L Pickup	3.8	4.0
2.6L	4.0	4.2
4WD:		
2.6L	4.5	4.8
V6 Montero	4.3	4.5

Capacity shown is without filter. When replacing filter, additional oil may be needed.
Above 32°F (0°C) 20W-20, 20W-40, 20W-50
Above -10°F (-23°C) . .10W-30, 10W-40, 10W-50
Below 60°F (16°C) . . . . .5W-20[1], 5W-30, 5W-40
1 Not recommended for sustained high-speed driving

TRANSMISSION, Automatic . . . .AP3, SLF

CAPACITY, Initial Refill[2]:	Liters	Qt
All models	4.7	5.0

2 With the engine at operating temperature, shift transmission through all gears. Check fluid level in NEUTRAL and add fluid as needed.

TRANSMISSION, Manual
2WD 75W-85W **GL-4**
4WD 80W, 75W-85W **GL-4**
Montero, when changing oil, add one bottle of fraction modifier, Mitsubishi Part No. ME581050 transmission

CAPACITY, Refill:	Liters	Pt
4-speed	2.1	4.4
5-speed: 2WD	2.3	4.8
4WD	2.2	4.6

TRANSFER CASE . . .80W, 75W-85W **GL-4**

CAPACITY, Refill:	Liters	Pt
All models	2.2	4.6

DIFFERENTIALS
Limited-Slip . . . .**GL-5★**
Standard: Pickup, Montero **GL-4, GL-5**
Van **GL-5**
Above -10°F (-23°C), 90, 85W-90, 80W-90; -30° to -10°F (-34° to -23°C), 80W, 80W-90; below -30°F (-34°C), 75W

CAPACITY, Refill:	Liters	Pt
Pickup, Montero: Front	2.2	4.6
Rear, 4-cyl. Pickup	1.5	3.2
Rear, 4-cyl. Montero	1.8	3.8
Rear, V6	2.6	5.4
Van	1.5	3.2

SERVICE AT TIME OR MILEAGE — WHICHEVER OCCURS FIRST

MIIPM6   MIIPM6

W   SERVICE TO MAINTAIN EMISSION WARRANTY

MI—MILES IN THOUSANDS
KM—KILOMETERS IN THOUSANDS

EVERY 12 MO/7.5 MI—12 KM
Brake & clutch
  fluid reservoir . . . . .check level **HB**

Crankcase . . . . .change oil

Oil filter .replace
Every second oil change, but at least every 12 months

Power steering fluid . . . . . . .check **AF2**

EVERY 12 MO/15 MI—24 KM
Disc brake pads . . . . .inspect
Also inspect brake hoses

Ball joints 1990-91 . . . . . . .lubricate **LM**
With fittings only

Drive shaft boots . . . . .inspect

Transmission, automatic . . . .check level

EVERY 15 MI—24 KM
W Idle speed, 2.6L . . . . .check/adjust

W Jet valve clearance
  2.6L . . . . .inspect/adjust

EVERY 24 MO/30 MI—48 KM
Ball joints, ...lubricate **LM**
With fittings only

Ball joint & steering linkage seals . .inspect

Drum brakes . . . . .inspect
Linings, wheel cylinders

Drive shaft joints . . . . .lubricate **LM**

Exhaust system . . . . .inspect

Front wheel bearings,
  1990 . . . . .clean/repack **LM**
Inspect for leaks. Inspect & repack whenever rotors are removed

Coolant . . . . .drain/flush/refill **EC**

W Fuel hoses . . . . .check

EVERY 30 MI—48 KM
Differential(s) . . . . .check level
Ex. Limited Slip

Limited-Slip differential . . .change lubricant

Transmission, automatic &
  transfer case, 4WD . . .change lubricant

Transmission, manual &
  transfer case . . . . .check level

W Air cleaner filter . . . . .replace

W Choke & linkage 2.6L . . . . .clean **PC**

Drive belt . . . . .replace
Water pump & alternator only

W Spark plugs . . . . .replace

EVERY 60 MO/50 MI—80 KM
W EGR valve 4-cyl. ex. Calif. . . . . . .replace
At mileage interval only. 2.6L, also clean sub-EGR valve

W Fuel filter, 2.6L . . . . .replace

W Fuel tank, lines,
  connections, cap . . . . .inspect

W Fuel, & fuel
  vapor hoses . . . . .check/replace
1990 only

EVERY 60 MO/60 MI—96 KM
W Crankcase ventilation, vacuum,
  water hoses . . . . .replace
1990-91 only

W Distributor cap & rotor . . . . .inspect
Ex. Calif.

W Evaporative emissions
  control system . . . . .inspect
Ex. Calif.

W Ignition wires ex. Calif. . . . . .replace

W Intake air temperature control
  system, 1990-91 ex. Calif. . . . . .inspect

W Vacuum control system solenoid valve
  air filter, 2.6L ex. Calif. . . . . .replace

EVERY 60 MI—96 KM
Timing belt . . . . .replace

EVERY 80 MI—128 KM
W Crankcase emission control system,
  ex. Calif. . . . . .check clean **PC**

W Oxygen sensor ex. Calif. . . . . . . .replace

EVERY 100 MI—160 KM
W Canister ex. Calif. . . . . .replace

SEVERE SERVICE
W **Air cleaner filter**—Service more frequently

Brake system—Inspect more frequently.
Inspect drum brakes every 15 mi (24 km)

W **Crankcase**—Change oil every 3 mo/3 mi
(4.8 km) & filter every second oil change

PCV system—Inspect more frequently

W **Spark plugs**—Replace every 15 mi (24 km)

Transmission, 2WD automatic—Change
fluid every 30 mi (48 km)

Transmission, manual & transfer case—
Pickup, Montero, change lubricant every
30 mi (48 km)

KEY TO LUBRICANTS
See other Mitsubishi charts

CRANKCASE . . . . .SG, SG/CD; GF-1[1]
[1] Preferred

CAPACITY, Refill:	Liters	Qt
2.4L	3.5	3.7
2.6L	4.5	4.8
3.0L	4.3	4.5

Capacity shown is without filter. When replacing filter, additional oil may be needed.

Above 32°F (0°C) 20W-20
Above 32°F (0°C) 20W-40, 20W-50
Above -10°F (-23°C) . .10W-30, 10W-40, 10W-50
Below 60°F (16°C) . . . . .5W-20[2],
                        5W-30, 5W-40

[2] Not recommended for sustained high-speed driving

TRANSMISSION, Automatic . . . .AP3, SLF

CAPACITY, Initial Refill[3]:	Liters	Qt
Pickup	1.9	2.0
Montero, Van: 1990-91	4.7	5.0
1992	5.0	5.3
Montero Sport	2.2	2.3

[3] With the engine at operating temperature, shift transmission through all gears. Check fluid level in NEUTRAL and add fluid as needed.

TRANSMISSION, Manual
1990-91 . . . . .80W, 75W-85W **GL-4**
1992 . . . . .75W-90, 75W-85W **GL-4**
1990-91 4WD w/V6, when changing oil add one bottle of friction modifier, Mitsubishi Part No. ME581050 to transmission

CAPACITY, Refill:	Liters	Pt
Montero, Pickup 4-cyl.	2.2	4.6
V6	2.3	4.8
Montero Sport	2.3	4.8

TRANSFER CASE
1990-91 . . . . .80W, 75W-85W **GL-4**
1992 . . . . .75W-90, 75W-85W **GL-4**

CAPACITY, Refill:	Liters	Pt
All	2.2	4.6

DIFFERENTIALS
Limited-Slip . . . .**GL-5★**
Standard **GL-5**
Above -10°F (-23°C), 90, 85W-90, 80W-90; -30° to -10°F
(-34° to -23°C), 80W, 80W-90; below -30°F (-34°C), 75W

CAPACITY, Refill:	Liters	Pt
Front:		
Pickup: 1990	2.2	4.6
1991-92	1.1	2.3
Montero: 1990-91	1.1	2.3
1992	1.2	2.5
Rear:		
Pickup: 2WD	1.5	3.2
4WD	2.6	5.4
Montero: 4-cyl.:	1.8	3.8
V6 3.0L	2.6	5.4
Van	1.5	3.2

SERVICE AT TIME OR MILEAGE — WHICHEVER OCCURS FIRST

MIIPM7   MIIPM7

W   SERVICE TO MAINTAIN EMISSION WARRANTY

MI—MILES IN THOUSANDS
KM—KILOMETERS IN THOUSANDS

EVERY 12 MO/7.5 MI—12 KM
Brake & clutch
 fluid reservoir . . . . check level **HB**

Crankcase . . . . .change oil

Oil filter . . . . .replace
Every second oil change, but at least every 12 months

Power steering fluid . . . . . . .check **AF2**

Tires, 2000 . . . . .rotate

EVERY 12 MO/15 MI—24 KM
Disc brake pads . . . . .inspect
Also inspect brake hoses

Drive shaft boots . . . . .inspect

Transmission, automatic . . . .check level

EVERY 24 MO/30 MI—48 KM
Ball joints, ...lubricate **LM**
With fittings only

Ball joint & steering linkage seals . .inspect

Drum brakes . . . . .inspect
Linings, wheel cylinders

Drive shaft joints . . . . .lubricate **LM**

Exhaust system . . . . .inspect

Coolant . . . . .drain/flush/refill **EC**

W Fuel hoses . . . . .check

EVERY 30 MI—48 KM
Differential(s) . . . . .check level
Ex. Limited Slip

Limited-Slip differential . . .change lubricant

Transmission,
 automatic . . . . .change lubricant
1993-99 4WD only

Transmission, manual &
 transfer case . . . . .check level

Transfer case . . . . .change lubricant

W Air cleaner filter . . . . .replace

Drive belt . . . . .replace
Water pump & alternator only

W Spark plugs . . . . .replace
Ex. Iridium type

EVERY 60 MO/60 MI—96 KM
W Distributor cap & rotor . . . . .inspect

W Evaporative emissions
 control system . . . . .inspect

W Fuel, lines, connections, fill cap,
 & tank .inspect

W Ignition wires ex. Calif. . . . . .replace

EVERY 60 MI—96 KM
W Spark plugs . . . . .replace
Iridium type only

Timing belt . . . . .replace
1995-00 Calif., Massachusetts, Connecticut models,
replacement recommended but not required.

EVERY 100 MI—160 KM
W Canister ex. Calif., 1993-95 . . . . .replace

W Crankcase emission control
 system 1993-94 . . . . . .check/clean **PC**

EGR valve, 4-cyl.
 ex. Calif., 1993-96 . . . . .replace

Timing Belt, 1995-00 . . . . .replace
Only if belt was not replaced at 60 mi (96 km)

SEVERE SERVICE
W Air cleaner filter—1993-94, service more
frequently. 1995-98, replace every 15 mi
(24 km)

Brake system—1993-94, inspect more
frequently. 1995-00 inspect disc brake
pads every 6 mo/6 mi (9.6 km); inspect
drum brakes every 15 mi (24 km)

W Crankcase—Change oil every 3 mo/3 mi
(4.8 km) & filter every second oil change

PCV system—1993-94, inspect more frequently. 1995-97, check and clean every 60
mi (96 km)

W Spark plugs—Replace every 15 mi (24 km)

**Transmission, 1993-99 2WD automatic
& 2000 all**—Change fluid every 30 mi
(48 km)

Tires, 2000—Rotate every 6 mo/6 mi
(9.6 km)

Transmission, manual & transfer case—
Pickup, Montero, change lubricant every
30 mi (48 km)

KEY TO LUBRICANTS
See other Mitsubishi charts

CRANKCASE . . . . .SJ, SJ/CD; API★
1 Preferred

CAPACITY, Refill:	Liters	Qt
2.4L: 1993-96	3.5	3.7
1997-00	4.0	4.2
3.0L	4.3	4.5
3.5L	4.3	4.5

Capacity shown is without filter. When replacing filter, addi-
tional oil may be needed.
1993-94
Above 32°F (0°C) 20W-40, 20W-50
Above -10°F (-23°C) . .10W-30, 10W-40, 10W-50
Below 100°F (38°C) 5W-30, 5W-40
2 Not recommended for sustained high-speed driving
1995-00
Above 0°F (-18°C) 10W-30
Below 100°F (38°C) 5W-30

TRANSMISSION, Automatic
1993-96 .AP3, SLF
1997-98 . . . . .AF2
1999-00 Montero AF2
 Montero Sport . . . . .SLF

CAPACITY, Initial Refill[3]:	Liters	Qt
Montero	5.0	5.3
Pickup	1.9	2.0
Montero Sport	2.2	2.3

3 With the engine at operating temperature, shift transmission through all gears. Check fluid level in NEUTRAL and
add fluid as needed.

TRANSMISSION, Manual 75W-90,
                                        75W-85W **GL-4**

CAPACITY, Refill:	Liters	Pt
Montero, Pickup 4-cyl.	2.2	4.6
V6: 1993-96	2.3	4.8
1997-00	3.2	6.6
Montero Sport	2.3	4.8

TRANSFER CASE 75W-90,
                                        75W-85W **GL-4**

CAPACITY, Refill:	Liters	Pt
1994-00 w/elect AT	2.5	5.2
All other models	2.2	4.6

DIFFERENTIALS
Limited-Slip . . . .**GL-5★**
Standard **GL-5**
Above -10°F (-23°C), 90, 85W-90, 80W-90; -30° to -10°F
(-34° to -23°C), 80W, 80W-90; below -30°F (-34°C), 75W

CAPACITY, Refill:	Liters	Pt
Front:		
Pickup 1993-96	1.1	2.3
Montero: 1993-96	1.2	2.5
1997-00	1.1	2.3
Rear:		
Pickup: 2WD	1.5	3.2
4WD	2.6	5.4
Montero: 4-cyl.: 1993-96 . . .	1.8	3.8
1997-00	1.5	3.2
V6: 3.0L	2.6	5.4
3.5L	3.2	6.6

HOOD RELEASE: Inside

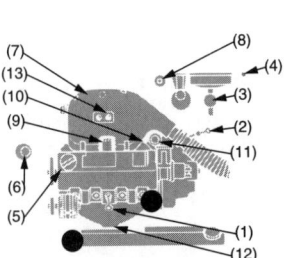

1989-90
Sentra, Pulsar ex. DOHC
1597cc TBI

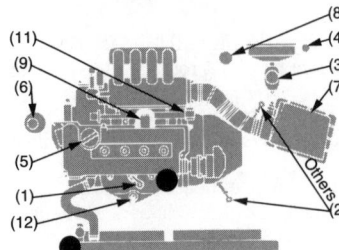

1991-99
1597cc Sentra, NX, 200SX

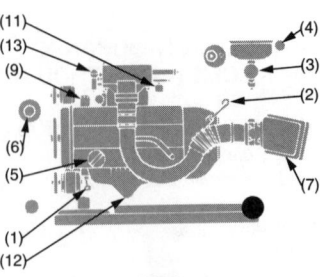

1989
Pulsar
1598cc, 1809cc DOHC

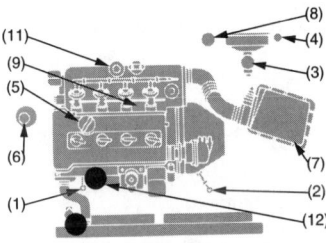

1991-99
1998cc Sentra, NX, 200SX

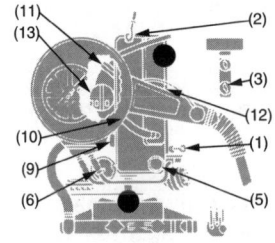

1989
Pickup, Pathfinder
1952cc, 2187cc, 2389cc

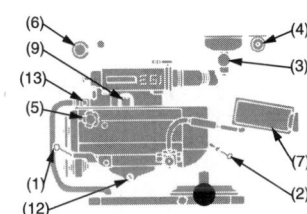

1989
Stanza ex. Wagon
1974cc MFI

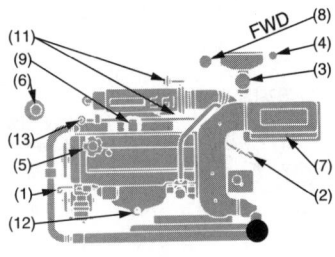

1989
Stanza Wagon
1974cc MFI

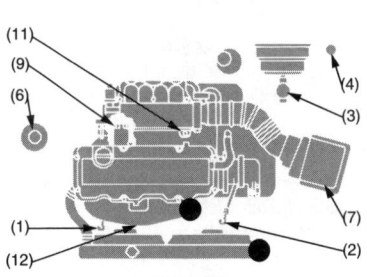

1990-92
Axxess, Stanza
2389cc

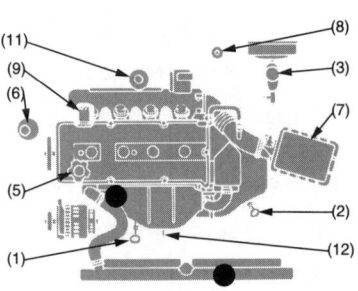

1993-00
2389cc DOHC
Altima

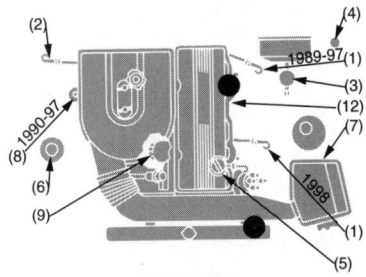

1990-00
Frontier, Pickup, Pathfinder, Xterra
2389cc

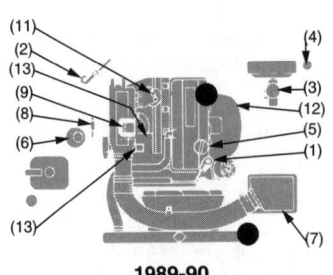

1989-90
240SX
2389cc

(1) Crankcase dipstick
(2) Transmission dipstick
(3) Brake fluid reservoir
(4) Clutch fluid reservoir
(5) Oil fill cap
(6) Power steering reservoir
(7) Air filter
(8) Fuel filter
(9) Oil filter
(10) PCV filter (11) EGR valve
(12) Oxygen sensor
(13) PCV valve

● Cooling system drain   ○ Cooling system drain, some models

SERVICE LOCATIONS — ENGINE AND CHASSIS

HOOD RELEASE: Inside

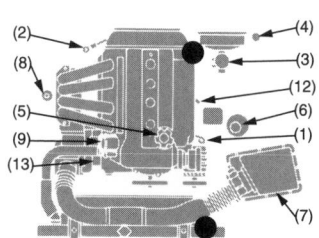

**1991-98
240SX
2389cc DOHC**

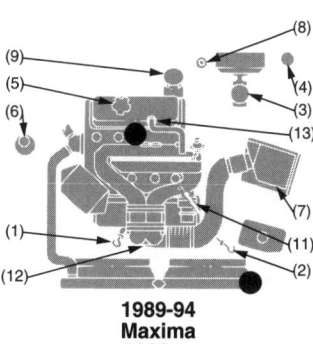

**1989-94
Maxima
2960cc
SOHC**

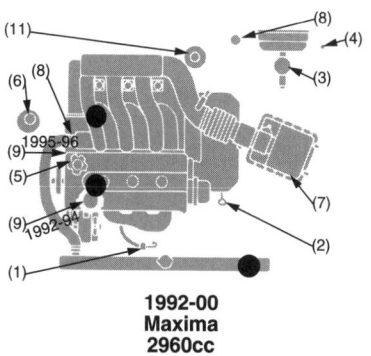

**1992-00
Maxima
2960cc
DOHC, 2988cc**

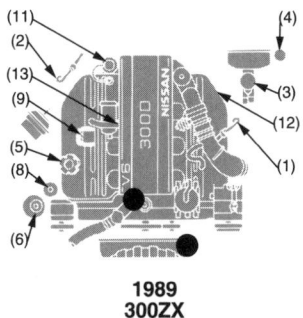

**1989
300ZX
2960cc**

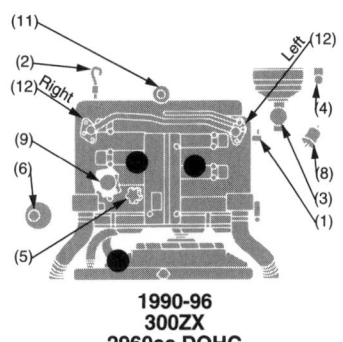

**1990-96
300ZX
2960cc DOHC**

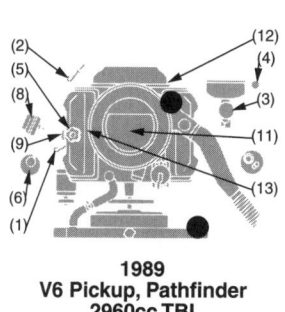

**1989
V6 Pickup, Pathfinder
2960cc TBI**

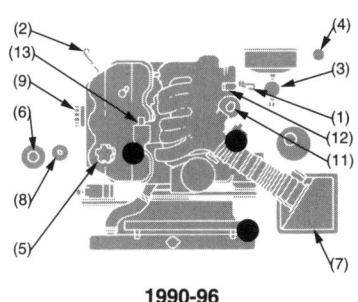

**1990-96
Pickup, Pathfinder
2960cc MFI**

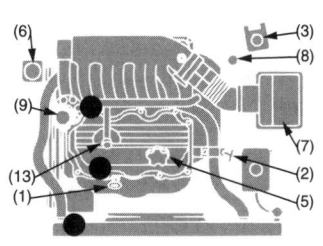

**1993-00
Quest
2960cc, 3275cc MFI**

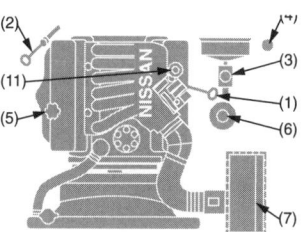

**1996-00
Pathfinder, Frontier, Xterra
3275cc**

● Cooling system drain   ○ Cooling system drain, some models

NISSAN
1989-99 All Models
Includes Infiniti QX4

SERVICE LOCATIONS — ENGINE AND CHASSIS

DNIDP-3

DNIDP-3

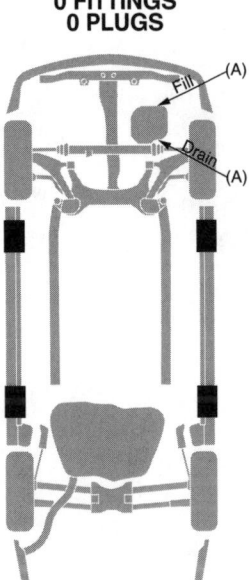

1989-90
Sentra, Pulsar, NX

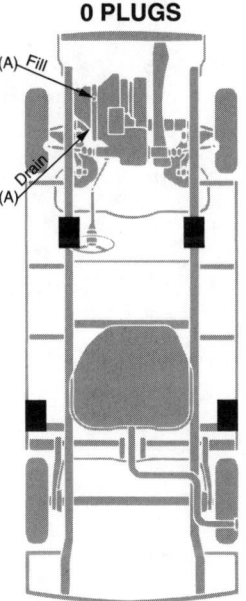

1991-99
Sentra, NX, 200SX

1989
Stanza Wagon, Multi 2WD

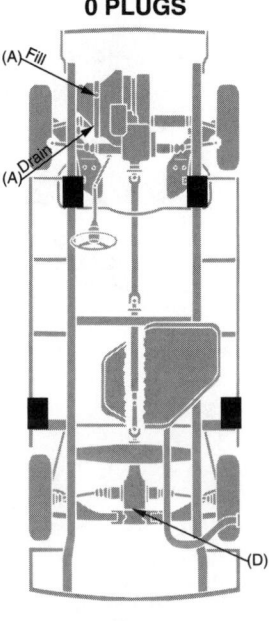

1989
Stanza Wagon 4WD

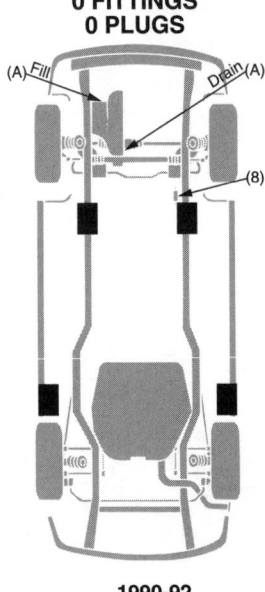

1990-92
Axxess
2WD

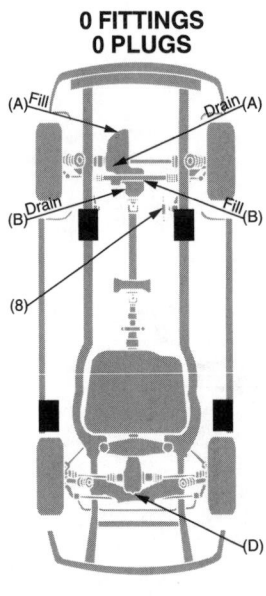

1990-92
Axxess
4WD

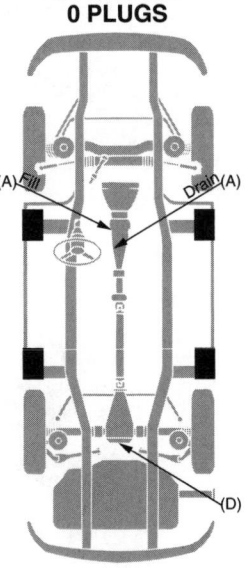

1989-98
240SX

(A) Manual transmission/transaxle,
   drain & fill

(B) Transfer case, drain & fill

(C) Automatic transaxle final drive,
   NOT USED

(D) Differential, drain & fill

(8) Fuel filter

CAUTION: On front wheel drive vehicles, the center of gravity is farther forward than on rear wheel drive vehicles. When removing major components from the rear of the vehicle while it is on a hoist, the vehicle must be supported in a manner to prevent it from tipping forward.

■ Lift adapter position   ▲ Plug   △ Plug, some models

0 FITTINGS
0 PLUGS

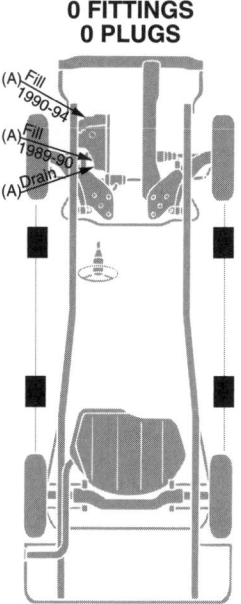

(A) Fill 1990-94
(A) Fill 1989-90
(A) Drain

1989-00
Maxima,
1989-92 Stanza
1993-00 Altima

0 FITTINGS
0 PLUGS

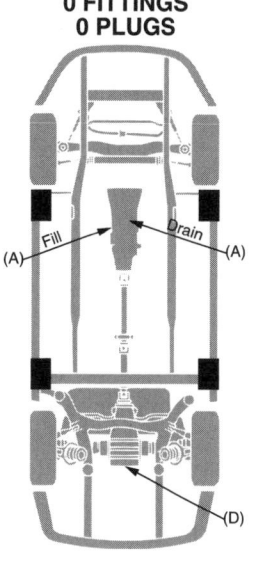

Fill Turbo (A)
(A) Fill ex. Turbo
Drain (A)

1989
300ZX

0 FITTINGS
0 PLUGS

(A) Fill   Drain (A)

(D)

1990-96
300ZX

0 FITTINGS
0 PLUGS

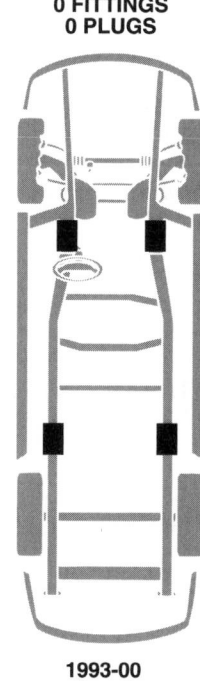

1993-00
Quest

0 FITTINGS
4 PLUGS

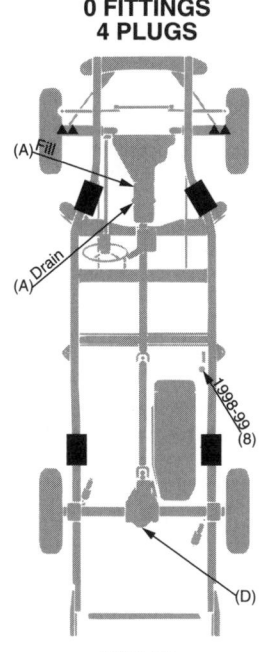

(A) Fill
(A) Drain
1998-99 (8)
(D)

1989-00
2WD Pickup, Frontier, Xterra
1989-95
2WD Pathfinder

1 FITTINGS
4 PLUGS

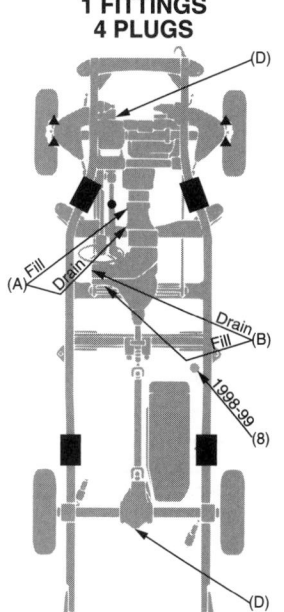

(D)
(A) Fill
Drain
Drain (B)
Fill (B)
1998-99 (8)
(D)

1989-00
4WD Pickup, Frontier, Xterra
1989-95
4WD Pathfinder

1 FITTING, 4WD
6 FITTINGS, 2WD

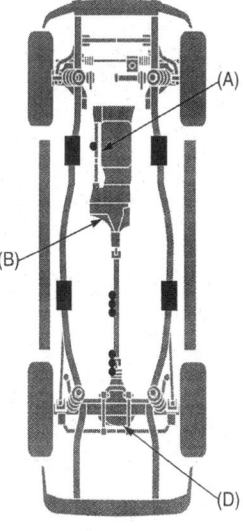

(A)
(B)
(D)

1996-00
Pathfinder, Xterra

CAUTION: On front wheel drive vehicles, the center of gravity is farther forward than on rear wheel drive vehicles. When removing major components from the rear of the vehicle while it is on a hoist, the vehicle must be supported in a manner to prevent it from tipping forward.

■ Lift adapter position   ▲ Plug   △ Plug, some models   • Fitting   ○ Fitting, some models

NISSAN
1989-90 All Models except Pickup, Pathfinder

Perform the following maintenance services at the intervals indicated to keep the vehicle warranties in effect.
W   SERVICE TO MAINTAIN EMISSION WARRANTY

MI—MILES IN THOUSANDS
KM—KILOMETERS IN THOUSANDS

SERVICE PERIODICALLY
Transmission, auto . . . . .check level

Brake & clutch master cylinders . . . . .**HB**

Power steering reservoir .check level **AF3**
Inspect lines & hoses

TURBO ENGINE,
EVERY 6 MO/5 MI—8 KM
W Crankcase . . . . .change oil

W Oil filter .replace
At first oil change then every other

EVERY 6 MO/7.5 MI—12 KM
W Crankcase . . . . .change oil
Ex. Turbo

W Oil filter ex. Turbo . . . . .replace
At first oil change then every other

Tires . . . . .rotate
At mileage interval only

EVERY 12 MONTHS
Underbody . . . . .flush/clean

EVERY 12 MO/15 MI—24 KM
Brake system . . . . .inspect
Inspect linings, drums, disc pads, lines & hoses

Differential . . . . .check level

Driveshaft boots, FWD . . . . .inspect

Exhaust systems . . . . .inspect

Transfer case . . . . .check level

Transmission/Transaxle,
  manual & automatic . . . . . .check level

EVERY 24 MO/30 MI—48 KM
Suspension & steering
  linkage . . . . .inspect

Cooling system . . . . .change coolant **EC**

Differential, 300ZX . . . .change lubricant

W Air cleaner element . . . . .replace
At mileage interval only

Fuel & fuel vapor lines . . . . .inspect

Idle speed . . . . .check/adjust
1989 300ZX ex. Turbo

W Spark plugs . . . . .replace
Ex. platinum tipped. At mileage interval only

Super HICAS linkage . . . . .inspect
1990 240SX, 300ZX Turbo with active suspension

EVERY 36 MONTHS
Ignition wires 1989 . . . . .inspect

EVERY 48 MO/60 MI—96 KM
Drive belts . . . . .inspect
Inspect every 12 mo/15 mi (24 km) thereafter

EVERY 60 MI—96 KM
Spark plugs . . . . .replace
Platinum tipped only

W Timing belt . . . . .replace
V6 only

AT 120 MONTHS
Air bag system . . . . .inspect

SERVICE AS REQUIRED
W Fuel filter . . . . .replace

PCV filter . . . . .replace

W Valve clearance 1.6L . . . . .adjust

SEVERE SERVICE
Air filter—Inspect more frequently

W **Crankcase**—Change oil & filter every:
1989, 3 mo/3 mi (5 km); 1990, 3 mo/
3.75 mi (6 km)

**Steering, suspension, driveshaft boots;
1990 4WD, driveshaft, exhaust, brake
system**—Inspect every 6 mo/7.5 mi (12 km)

**Transmission, manual & automatic; dif-
ferential, transfer case**—Change fluid or
lubricant every 24 mo/30 mi (48 km) when
towing a trailer or driving on rough or
muddy roads

KEY TO LUBRICANTS
See other Nissan charts

CRANKCASE . . . . .SG
CAPACITY, Refill:	Liters	Qt
Sentra, Pulsar: 1.6L	2.8	3.0
1.8L DOHC	3.4	3.6
2.0L	3.2	3.4
Stanza, Axxess	3.1	3.3
Maxima	3.5	3.7
Micra	2.6	2.8
300ZX: 1989	3.6	3.8
1990	3.7	3.9
Turbo	4.1	4.3
240SX	3.2	3.4

Capacity is without filter. When replacing filter, additional oil may be needed
Above 50°F (10°C) 20W-40, 20W-50
Above 0°F (-18°C) . . . . .10W-30[1], 10W-40
1989 All; 1990 Axxess, Stanza;
300ZX:
Below 60°F (16°C) 5W-30
1990 Others:
All temperatures . . . . .5W-30[2]
[1] Preferred for all 1989, 1990 Stanza, Axxess, & 300ZX
[2] Preferred

TRANSMISSION,
TRANSAXLE, Automatic AF3
CAPACITY Refill[3]:	Liters	Qt
Sentra, Pulsar, NX	6.3	6.6
4-speed	7.0	7.3
Micra	6.0	6.3
Axxess, Stanza, Maxima SOHC .	7.4	7.8
Maxima DOHC	9.4	10.0
240SX	8.3	8.7
300ZX: 1989	7.0	7.4
1990	7.7	8.1

[3] Total (dry) fill shown

TRANSMISSION,
TRANSAXLE, Manual GL-4
Above 50°F (10°C), 140; 30° to 100°F (-1° to 38°C),
90; 10° to 85°F (-12° to 29°C), 85W; below 100°F
(38°C), 75W-90*, 80W-90*; below 85°F (29°C),
80W; below 50°F (10°C), 75W
* 75W-90 preferred, RWD 80W-90 preferred, FWD MT and
all differentials and transfer case

CAPACITY, Refill:	Liters	Pt
Sentra, Pulsar, NX:		
SOHC: 4-speed	2.7	5.8
5-speed	2.8	6.0
DOHC	4.7	10.0
Micra: 1989	2.6	5.5
1990	2.9	6.2
Stanza, Axxess, Maxima	4.7	10.0
240SX	2.4	5.1
300ZX: 1989	2.0	4.2
Turbo	2.4	5.1
1990	2.8	6.0

TRANSFER CASE GL-5
Viscosities, see Transmission/Transaxle, Manual
CAPACITY, Refill:	Liters	Pt
Sentra 4WD	1.1	2.3
Axxess 4WD	1.6	3.5

DIFFERENTIAL
Limited-Slip 80W-90 **GL-5**
90 may be used above 0°F (-18°C)
Standard **GL-5**
Viscosities, see Transmission/Transaxle, Manual
CAPACITY, Refill:	Liters	Pt
300ZX: 1989	1.3	2.8
1990	1.5	3.1
Turbo	1.8	3.8
240SX	1.8	3.8
Sentra 4WD	1.0	2.1
Axxess 4WD	1.0	2.1

CHEK-CHART

SERVICE AT TIME OR MILEAGE — WHICHEVER OCCURS FIRST

DNIPM11   DNIPM11

Perform the following maintenance services at the intervals indicated to keep the vehicle warranties in effect.
W SERVICE TO MAINTAIN EMISSION WARRANTY

MI—MILES IN THOUSANDS
KM—KILOMETERS IN THOUSANDS

SERVICE PERIODICALLY
Transmission, automatic . . . .check level

Brake & clutch master cylinders . . . . .**HB**
Check systems

Power steering reservoir . . . .check level
1991-96 ex. Quest, **AF2**
1997-00 ex. Quest, **AF2, AF3**
1993-00 Quest, **FA**. Inspect lines & hoses

TURBO ENGINE,
EVERY 6 MO/5 MI—8 KM
W Crankcase . . . . .change oil

W Oil filter . . . . .replace
1991-95, At first oil change then every other
1996-00, At every oil change

EVERY 6 MO/7.5 MI—12 KM
W Crankcase . . . . .change oil
Ex. Turbo

W Oil filter ex. Turbo . . . . .replace
1991-95, At first oil change then every other
1996-00, At every oil change

Tires . . . . .rotate
At mileage interval only

EVERY 12 MONTHS
Underbody . . . . .flush/clean

EVERY 12 MO/15 MI—24 KM
Brake system . . . . .inspect
Inspect linings, drums, disc pads, lines & hoses

Differential . . . . .check level

Driveshaft boots, FWD . . . . .inspect

Exhaust system . . . . .inspect

Transfer case . . . . .check level

Transmission/Transaxle,
  manual & automatic . . . . . .check level

Automatic speed
  control device, 2000 . . . . .inspect
Inspect vacuum hoses

Cabin air filter . . . . .replace
1999-00 Quest

EVERY 24 MO/30 MI—48 KM
Suspension & steering
  linkage . . . . .inspect

Cooling system
  ex. 1999-00 Quest .change coolant **EC**
Initial service at 48 mo/60 mi (96 km)

W Air cleaner element . . . . .replace
At mileage interval only

Fuel & fuel vapor lines . . . . .inspect

Idle speed . . . . .inspect
Sentra, NX, 200SX 1.6L

W Spark plugs . . . . .replace
Ex. platinum tipped. At mileage interval only

Super HICAS linkage . . . . .inspect
240SX, 300ZX Turbo with active suspension

EVERY 36 MO/30 MI—48 KM
Cooling system . . . . .change coolant **EC**
1999-00 Quest only

EVERY 48 MO/60 MI—96 KM
Drive belts . . . . .inspect
Inspect every 12 mo/15 mi (24 km) thereafter

W Spark plugs, 1991-99 . . . . .replace
Platinum tipped only ex. 1999 Quest. At mileage interval only

W Timing belt . . . . .replace
At mileage interval only
1991-93 All V6
1994 V6 Maxima ex. DOHC & 300ZX Turbo
1995-96 300ZX Turbo

EVERY 105 MI—168 KM
W Spark plugs . . . . .replace
2000, all models & 1999 Quest

W Timing belt . . . . .replace
1994-96 300ZX ex. Turbo, 1994-00 Quest

AT 120 MONTHS
Air bag system . . . . .inspect

SERVICE AS REQUIRED
W Fuel filter . . . . .replace

W Valve clearance, 1991-99 1.6L Sentra,
200SX, NX, 240SX; 1993-94 Altima;
1995-00 Maxima, 2000 Altima . . . .adjust

SEVERE SERVICE
Cabin air filter—1999 Quest, replace every 6 mo/7.5 mi (12 km); 2000 Quest, replace more frequently

W **Crankcase**—Change oil & filter every: Turbo, 3 mo/3 mi (5 km); all others, 3 mo/3.75 mi (6 km)

Steering, suspension, exhaust, brake system—Inspect every 6 mo/7.5 mi (12 km)

Transmission, manual & automatic; differential, transfer case—Change fluid or lubricant every 24 mo/30 mi (48 km) when towing a trailer or driving on rough or muddy roads

KEY TO LUBRICANTS
See other Nissan charts

CRANKCASE . . . . .SJ, GF-2

CAPACITY, Refill:	Liters	Qt
Micra	2.6	2.8
Sentra, NX, 200SX 1.6L	2.8	3.0
2.0L	3.2	3.4
Altima: 1993-97	3.5	3.7
1998-00	3.2	3.4
Stanza, Axxess	3.1	3.3
Maxima: 1991-94: SOHC	3.5	3.7
DOHC	3.4	3.6
1995-00	3.7	3.9
Quest	3.6	3.8
240SX: 1991	3.2	3.4
1992-98	3.5	3.7
300ZX	3.0	3.2

Capacity is without filter. When replacing filter, additional oil may be needed

Above 50°F (10°C), 1991-92 . . .20W-40, 20W-50
Above 0°F (-18°C), 1991-95 . . . . .10W-40
Above 0°F (-18°C) . . . . .10W-30[1]
Below 60°F (16°C), 300ZX 5W-30
All temperatures, Others . . . . .5W-30[2]
[1] Preferred for 300ZX
[2] Preferred

TRANSMISSION,
TRANSAXLE, Automatic AF2, AF3
1991-95, use Dexron-II or Nissan branded fluid until vehicle is out of warranty, then Dexron-III may be used

CAPACITY Refill[3]:	Liters	Qt
Sentra, NX, 200SX	6.3	6.6
4-speed	7.0	7.3
Micra	6.0	6.3
Axxess, Stanza, Maxima SOHC	7.4	7.8
Maxima DOHC, Altima, Quest	9.4	10.0
240SX: 3-speed	7.5	7.9
4-speed	8.3	8.7
300ZX	7.7	8.1

[3] Total (dry) fill shown

TRANSMISSION/TRANSAXLE, Manual
1998-00 Sentra, 200SX, Altima,
  Maxima 80W-90 **GL-4**
All others **GL-4**
Above 50°F (10°C), 140; 30° to 100°F (-1° to 38°C),
90; 10° to 85°F (-12° to 29°C), 85W; below 100°F
(38°C), 75W-90*, 80W-90*; below 85°F (29°C),
80W; below 50°F (10°C), 75W
* 75W-90 preferred, RWD
80W-90 preferred, FWD

CAPACITY, Refill:	Liters	Pt
Sentra, NX, 200SX:		
4-speed	2.8	6.0
5-speed: 1.6L	2.9	6.2
2.0L	3.6	7.6
Micra	2.9	6.2
Stanza, Axxess, Maxima SOHC, Altima	4.7	10.0
Maxima DOHC 1993-94	4.4	9.4
Maxima 1995-00	4.5	9.6
240SX	2.4	5.1
300ZX	2.8	6.0

TRANSFER CASE GL-5
Viscosities, see Transmission/Transaxle, Manual

CAPACITY, Refill:	Liters	Pt
Axxess 4WD	1.6	3.5

DIFFERENTIAL
Limited-Slip 80W-90 **GL-5**
90 may be used above 0°F (-18°C)
Standard **GL-5**
Viscosities, see Transmission/Transaxle, Manual

CAPACITY, Refill:	Liters	Pt
300ZX: 1991-94	1.5	3.1
1995-96	1.3	2.5
Turbo	1.8	3.8
240SX	1.3	2.5
w/Limited-Slip	1.5	3.1
Axxess 4WD	1.0	2.1

CHEK-CHART

SERVICE AT TIME OR MILEAGE — WHICHEVER OCCURS FIRST

DNIPM10   DNIPM10

Perform the following maintenance services at the intervals indicated to keep the vehicle warranties in effect.
W   SERVICE TO MAINTAIN EMISSION WARRANTY

MI—MILES IN THOUSANDS
KM—KILOMETERS IN THOUSANDS

SERVICE PERIODICALLY
Brake & clutch master
cylinders . . . . .check level **HB**

Power steering
reservoir . . . . .check level **AF3**

Transmission, automatic . . . .check level

EVERY 6 MO/7.5 MI—12 KM
W Crankcase . . . . .change oil

W Oil filter . . . . .replace
At first oil change, then every other

Tires . . . . .rotate
At mileage interval only

EVERY 12 MONTHS
Underbody . . . . .flush/clean

EVERY 12 MO/15 MI—24 KM
Brake system . . . . .inspect
At mileage interval only. Inspect lines & hoses, linings,
drums & disc pads

Differential, transfer case . . . .check level

Exhaust system . . . . .inspect

Front suspension, steering linkage
& driveshaft boots . . . . .inspect

Front wheel bearings . . . . . .inspect **LM**
Pickup 4WD

Power steering lines
& hoses . . . . .inspect

Transmission, manual . . . . .check level

Rubber hoses . . . . .inspect

W Valve clearance . . . . .adjust
4-cyl.

EVERY 36 MONTHS
Ignition wires . . . . .inspect

EVERY 24 MO/30 MI—48 KM
Cooling system . . . .change coolant **EC**

Front wheel bearings . . . . .inspect **LM**
4WD, repack **LM**

Limited-Slip differential   . .change lubricant

W Air cleaner element . . . . .replace
At mileage interval only

Auto temp control
air cleaner . . . . .inspect
At mileage interval only

W Drive belts . . . . .inspect

Fuel & fuel vapor lines . . . . .inspect

Idle speed . . . . .inspect

W PCV filter . . . . .replace
At mileage interval only

W Spark plugs . . . . .replace
At mileage interval only

EVERY 48 MO/60 MI—96 KM
Steering, suspension &
ball joints . . . . .inspect

EVERY 60 MI—96 KM
W Spark plugs . . . . .replace
Platinum tipped only

W Timing belt, V6 . . . . .replace

SERVICE AS REQUIRED
W Fuel filter . . . . .replace

SEVERE SERVICE
W Crankcase—Change oil & filter every:
3 mo/3 mi (5 km)

Limited-Slip differential—Change lubricant
every 12 mo/15 mi (24 km) when towing a
trailer or driving on muddy roads

Steering, suspension, locks, hinges, exhaust, brake system—Inspect every 6 mo/
7.5 mi (12 km)

Transmission, manual & automatic;
transfer case, differential—Change fluid
or lubricant every 24 mo/30 mi (48 km)
when towing a trailer or driving on rough or
muddy roads

4WD front hubs—Replace grease every
3 mo/3 mi (5 km) when operating in water

KEY TO LUBRICANTS
AF3	Dexron®-III Automatic Transmission Fluid.
CD	Motor Oil, API Service CD
EC	Ethylene Glycol Coolant Mix with water to desired freeze protection
GL-4	Gear Oil, API Service GL-4
GL-5	Gear Oil, API Service GL-5
GL-5★	Special Lubricant for Limited-Slip Differentials
HB	Hydraulic Brake Fluid, DOT 3
LM	Lithium Grease, No. 2
SG	Motor Oil, API Service SG

CRANKCASE
Gasoline engine . . . .**SG**

CAPACITY, Refill:	Liters	Qt
Pickup, Pathfinder:		
4-cyl.: 2WD	3.3	3.5
4WD	3.8	4.0
V6: 2WD	3.6	3.8
4WD	3.0	3.2

Capacity shown is without filter. When replacing filter, additional oil may be needed

Above 50°F (10°C) 20W-40, 20W-50
Above 0°F (-18°C) . . . . .10W-30[1], 10W-40
Below 60°F (16°C) 5W-30

TRANSMISSION, Automatic **AF3**

CAPACITY, Total Fill[2]:	Liters	Qt
Pickup, Pathfinder:		
2WD	7.0	7.4
4WD	8.5	9.0

2 Total (dry) fill shown. Use less fluid when refilling

TRANSMISSION, Manual **GL-4**
Above 50°F (10°C), 140; 30° to 100°F (-1° to 38°C),
90; 10° to 85°F (-12° to 29°C), 85W; below 100°F
(38°C), 75W-90*, 80W-90†; below 85°F (29°C),
80W; below 50°F (10°C), 75W
* Preferred in MT
† Preferred in differential & transfer case

CAPACITY, Refill:	Liters	Pt
Pickup, Pathfinder:		
4-cyl.: 2WD	2.0	4.2
4WD	4.0	8.4
V6: 2WD	2.4	5.0
4WD	3.6	7.6

TRANSFER CASE **GL-4**
See Transmission, Manual for viscosity

CAPACITY, Refill:	Liters	Pt
All	2.2	4.8

DIFFERENTIAL
Limited-Slip . . . . .80W-90 **GL-5★**
90 may be used above 0°F (-18°C)
Standard **GL-5**
See Transmission, Manual for viscosity

CAPACITY, Refill:	Liters	Pt
Pickup, Pathfinder:		
Front: 4-cyl.	1.3	2.8
V6	1.5	3.2
Rear: 4-cyl.: 2WD	1.5	3.2
4WD	1.3	2.8
V6	2.8	5.9

SERVICE AT TIME OR MILEAGE — WHICHEVER OCCURS FIRST

DNIPM12   DNIPM12

Perform the following maintenance services at the intervals indicated to keep the vehicle warranties in effect.

W   SERVICE TO MAINTAIN EMISSION WARRANTY

MI—MILES IN THOUSANDS
KM—KILOMETERS IN THOUSANDS

SERVICE PERIODICALLY
Brake & clutch master
   cylinders . . . . .check level **HB**

Power steering reservoir . . . . .check level
1991-96, **AF2**
1997-00, **AF2, AF3**

Transmission, automatic . . . .check level

EVERY 6 MO/7.5 MI—12 KM
W Crankcase . . . . .change oil

W Oil filter . . . . .replace
1990-95, At first oil change, then every other
1996-00, At every oil change

Tires . . . . .rotate
At mileage interval only

EVERY 12 MONTHS
Underbody . . . . .flush/clean

EVERY 12 MO/15 MI—24 KM
Brake system . . . . .inspect
Inspect lines & hoses, linings, drums & disc pads

Differential, transfer case . .check level

Driveshaft boots, 4WD . . . . . . .inspect
1996-98 Pathfinder, lubricate propeller shaft **LM**

Exhaust system . . . . .inspect

Front wheel bearings . . . . . .inspect **LM**
4WD only

Transmission, manual . . . .check level

EVERY 24 MO/30 MI—48 KM
Cooling system . . . . .change coolant **EC**
1991-00, initial service at 48 mo/60 mi (96 km)

Front suspension &
   steering linkage . . . . .inspect

Front wheel bearings, 2WD . . .inspect **LM**

Front wheel bearings, 4WD . . .repack **LM**
Also repack free-running hubs

Limited-Slip differential . .change lubricant

W Air cleaner element . . . . .replace
At mileage interval only

W Drive belts . . . . .inspect

Fuel & fuel vapor lines . . . . . . .inspect

W PCV filter, 4 cyl. . . . . .replace
At mileage interval only

W Spark plugs . . . . .replace
Ex. platinum tipped

EVERY 48 MO/60 MI—96 KM
W Spark plugs, 1990-99 . . . . .replace
Platinum tipped only. At mileage interval only

Steering and suspension,
   ball joints . . . . .inspect

Transmission, manual . .change lubricant
Frontier & Xterra only

1990-93, EVERY 60 MI—96 KM
W Timing belt, V6 . . . . .replace

1994-00, EVERY 105 MI—168 KM
W Spark plugs, 2000 . . . . .replace
Platinum tipped only

W Timing belt, V6 . . . . .replace

AT 120 MONTHS
Air bag system . . . . .inspect

SERVICE AS REQUIRED
W Fuel filter . . . . .replace

Valve clearance . . . . .check/adjust
1998-00 4 cyl.

SEVERE SERVICE
Air induction valve filter—4-cyl., replace
every 30 mi (48 km)

W **Crankcase**—Change oil & filter every
3 mo/3.75 mi (6 km)

**Driveshaft boots and propeller
shaft**—4WD, inspect every 6 mo/7.5 mi
(12 km)

Propeller shaft—1996-98 Pathfinder, lubricate every 6 mo/7.5 mi (12 km) or daily
if operating in water

**Steering, suspension, exhaust, brake
system**—Inspect every 6 mo/7.5 mi (12 km)

**Transmission, manual & automatic;
transfer case, differential**—Change fluid
or lubricant every 24 mo/30 mi (48 km)
when towing a trailer or driving on rough or
muddy roads

KEY TO LUBRICANTS
AF2	Dexron®-II Automatic Transmission Fluid
AF3	Dexron®-III Automatic Transmission Fluid
CD	Motor Oil, API Service CD
CO	Cod Liver Oil
EC	Ethylene Glycol Coolant
	Mix with water to desired freeze protection
GF-1	Motor Oil, API Service GF-1
GL-4	Gear Oil, API Service GL-4
GL-5	Gear Oil, API Service GL-5
GL-5★	Special Lubricant for Limited-Slip
	Differentials
HB	Hydraulic Brake Fluid, DOT 3
LM	Lithium Grease, No. 2
SG	Motor Oil, API Service SG

CRANKCASE . . . . .SG, SH, GF-1

CAPACITY, Refill:	Liters	Qt
Frontier, Xterra: 4-cyl. 2WD	3.3	3.5
4WD	3.7	3.9
V6	3.0	3.2
Pickup, Pathfinder: 4-cyl. 2WD . .	3.5	3.7
4WD	3.8	4.0
V6 3.0L: 2WD	3.6	3.8
4WD	3.0	3.2
V6 3.3L	3.4	3.6

Capacity shown is without filter. When replacing filter, addi-
tional oil may be needed
Above 50°F (10°C), 1990-92 . . .20W-40, 20W-50
Above 0°F (-18°C) 10W-30, 10W-40
All temperatures . . . . .5W-30[1]
[1] Preferred

TRANSMISSION, Automatic AF2, AF3
1991-95, use Dexron-II or Nissan branded fluid until vehicle
is out of warranty, then use Dexron-III.

CAPACITY, Total Fill[2]:	Liters	Qt
Pickup, Pathfinder:		
4-cyl., V6 3.0L 2WD	7.9	8.3
4WD	8.5	9.0
V6 3.3L 2WD	8.3	8.8
4WD	8.5	9.0
Frontier, Xterra	7.9	8.3

[2] Total (dry) fill shown. Use less fluid when refilling

TRANSMISSION, Manual
1990-97 . . . .**GL-4**
Above 50°F (10°C), 140; 30° to 100°F (-1° to 38°C),
90; 10° to 85°F (-12° to 29°C), 85W; below 100°F
(38°C), 75W-90*; below 85°F (29°C), 80W-90†; below
80°F; below 50°F (10°C), 75W
1998-00 . . . . .75W-90 **GL-4**
* Preferred in MT
† Preferred in differential

CAPACITY, Refill:	Liters	Pt
4-cyl: 2WD	2.0	4.2
4WD: 1990-95	4.0	8.4
1996-00	4.9	10.4
V6 3.0L: 2WD	2.4	5.0
4WD	3.6	7.6
V6 3.3L: 2WD	2.4	5.1
4WD	5.1	10.8

TRANSFER CASE **AF3**

CAPACITY, Refill:	Liters	Pt
Pickup, Pathfinder, Frontier	2.2	4.8
QX4	3.0	6.4

DIFFERENTIAL
Limited-Slip . . . . .80W-90 **GL-5★**
90 may be used above 0°F (-18°C)
Standard **GL-5**
See Transmission, Manual for viscosity

CAPACITY, Refill:	Liters	Pt
Frontier, Xterra: 2WD: AT	1.5	3.2
MT, std. cab	1.5	3.2
MT, ext. cab	1.3	2.8
4WD: Front	1.3	2.8
Rear	1.3	2.8
Pickup, Pathfinder: 4-cyl. & V6 3.0L:		
Front: 4-cyl.	1.3	2.8
V6	1.5	3.2
Rear: 4-cyl.: 2WD	1.5	3.2
4WD	1.3	2.8
V6	2.8	5.9
V6 3.3L: Front	2.1	4.4
Rear	2.8	5.9

HOOD RELEASE: Inside

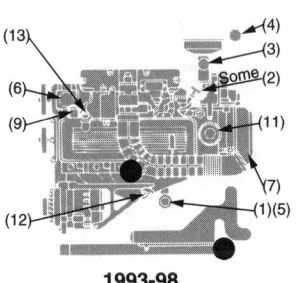

1993-98
2.2L Code 4

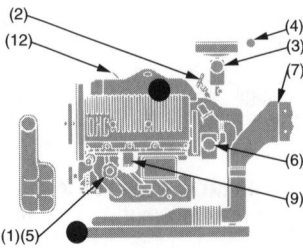

1992-94
2.3L SOHC Code 3

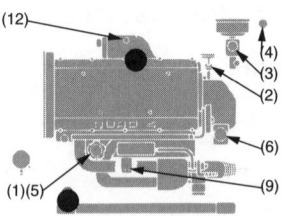

1989-95 2.3L DOHC Code D
1989-94 2.3L DOHC Code A

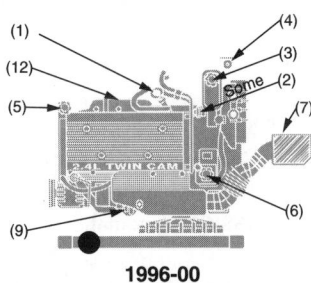

1996-00
2.4L Code T

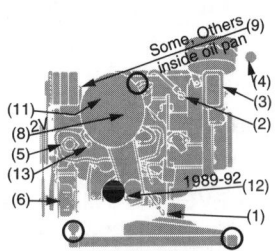

1989-92
2.5L (151) Omega,
Ciera, Calais
Code R, U, 5
Air induction
system varies

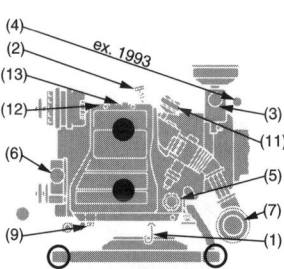

2.8L Code W
1989 Ciera, Cutlass Supreme
3.1L Code T
1989 Cutlass Supreme
1990-93 Ciera, Cutlass Supreme

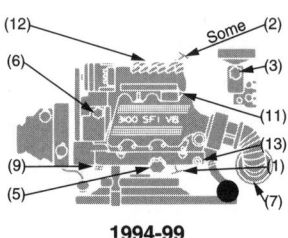

1994-99
3.1L Code M
1999 3.1L Code J

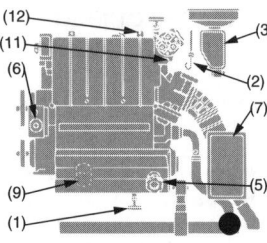

1991-97
3.4L DOHC Code X
Cutlass Supreme

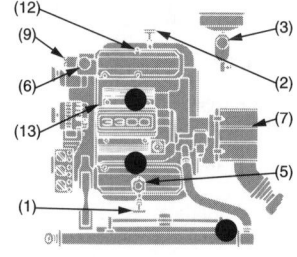

1989-93
3.3L Code N
Achieva, Ciera, Calais,
Cutlass Cruiser

(1) Crankcase dipstick	(8) Fuel filter
(2) Transmission dipstick	(9) Oil filter
(3) Brake fluid reservoir	(10) PCV filter
(4) Clutch fluid reservoir	(11) EGR valve
(5) Oil fill cap	(12) Oxygen sensor
(6) Power steering reservoir	(13) PCV valve
(7) Air filter	

● Cooling system drain   ○ Cooling system drain, some models

SERVICE LOCATIONS — ENGINE AND CHASSIS

HOOD RELEASE: Inside

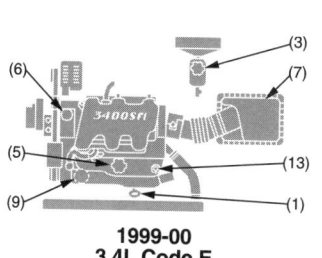

**1999-00
3.4L Code E**

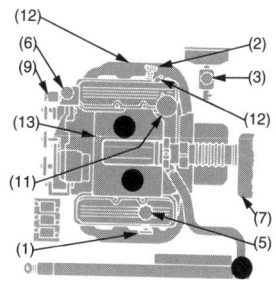

**1989-91 3.8L Code C
Ninety Eight, 88,
Toronado**

**1991-94 3.8L Code L
1995-97 3.8L Code K**

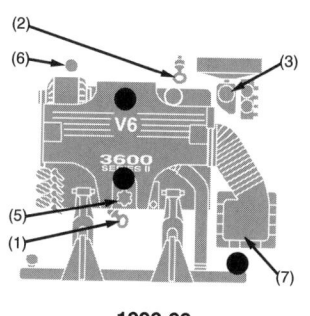

**1998-99
3.8L Code K**

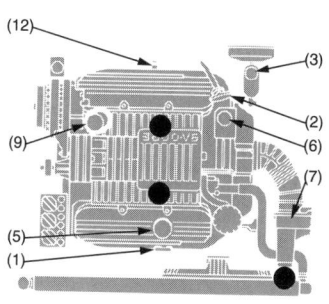

**1992-99
3.8L Code 1
Supercharged**

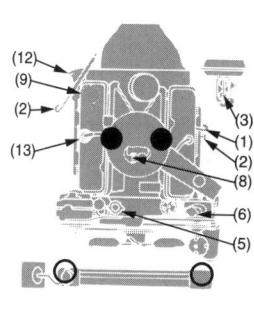

**5.0L (307)
ex. Toronado**

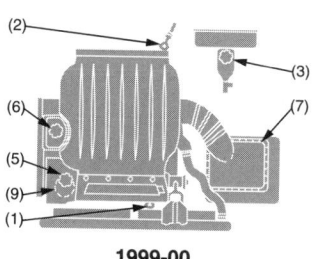

**1999-00
3.5L Code H**

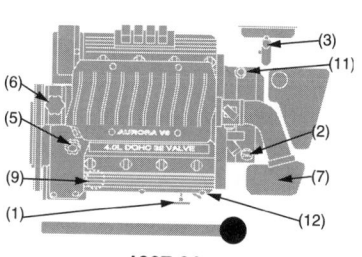

**1997-01
4.0L Code C
Aurora**

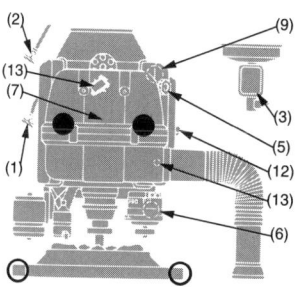

**1991-92 5.0L Code E
5.7L Code 7
Custom Cruiser**

● Cooling system drain   ○ Cooling system drain, some models

SERVICE LOCATIONS — ENGINE AND CHASSIS

OEDP-3   OEDP-3

4 FITTINGS

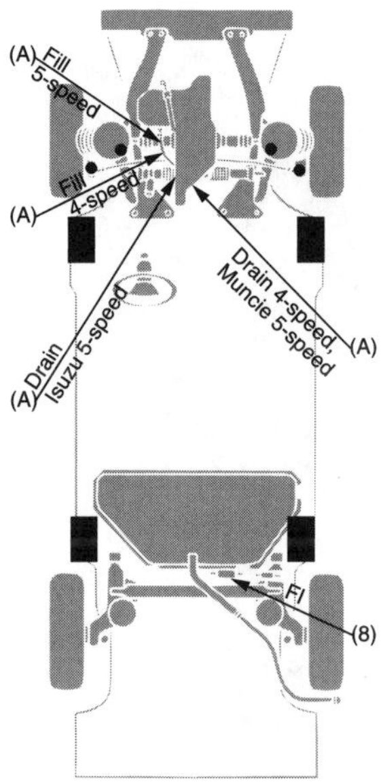

Fill 5-speed
(A) Fill 5-speed
(A) Fill 4-speed
(A) Fill 4-speed
Drain 4-speed, Muncie 5-speed
(A) Drain Isuzu 5-speed
(A) Drain Isuzu 5-speed (A)
FI
(8)

**1989-91 Calais
1992-98 Achieva**

4 FITTINGS

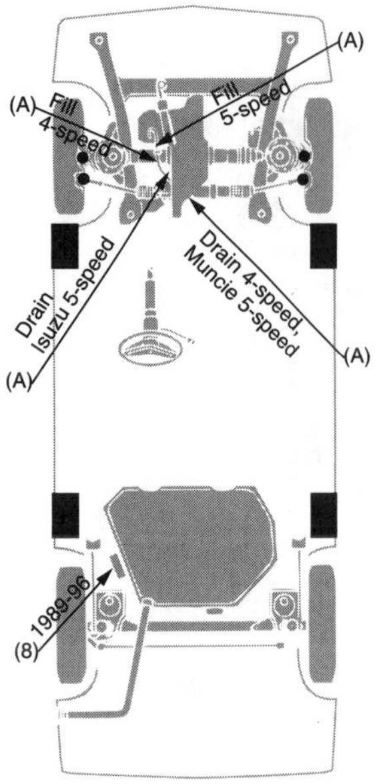

(A) Fill 5-speed
(A) Fill 4-speed
Drain Isuzu 5-speed
Drain 4-speed, Muncie 5-speed
(A)
(A)
1989-96
(8)

**1989-96 Cutlass Cruiser,
Cutlass Ciera**

8 FITTINGS

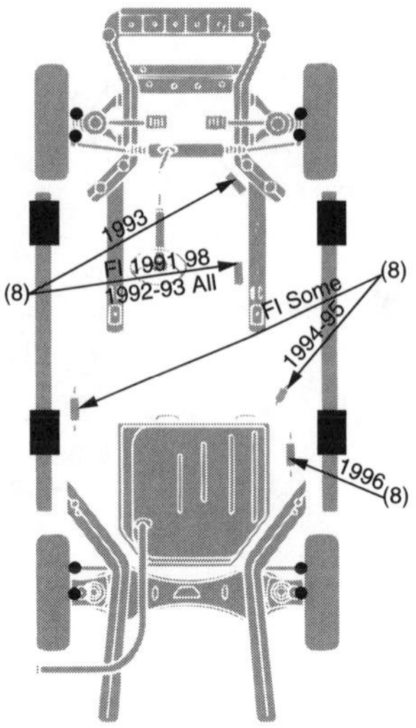

1993
FI 1991-98
1992-93 All
(8)
(8)
FI Some
1994-95
1996 (8)

**1989-97 98
1989-99 88, LSS**

6-8 FITTINGS 0 PLUGS

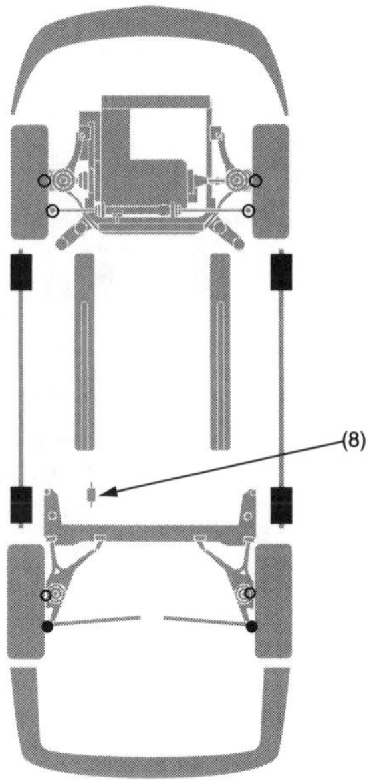

(8)

**1995-01
Aurora
1998-99 Regency**

4 FITTINGS

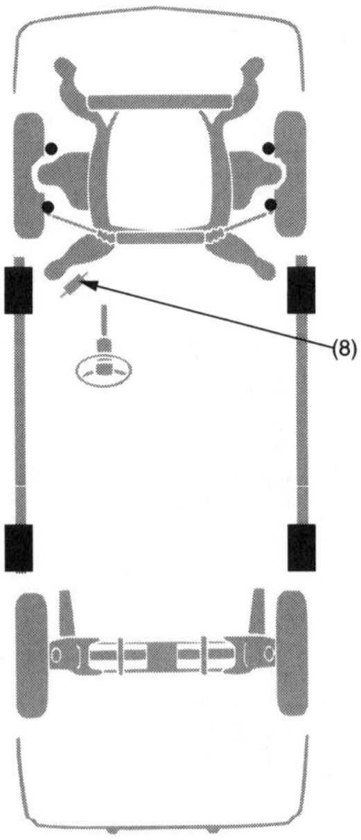

(8)

**1989-93
Toronado, Troféo**

0-4 FITTINGS

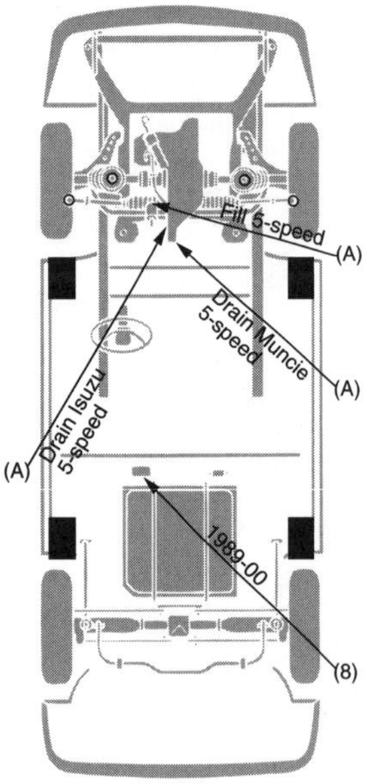

Fill 5-speed
(A)
Drain Muncie 5-speed
(A)
(A) Drain Isuzu 5-speed
1989-00
(8)

**1989-97
Cutlass Supreme
1998-00
Intrigue**

0 FITTINGS 0 PLUGS

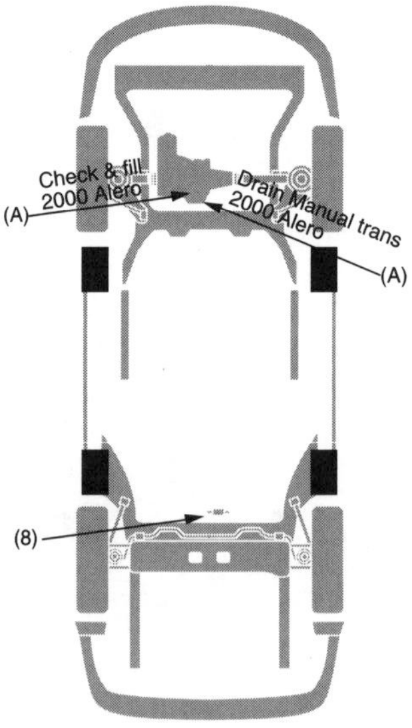

Check & fill 2000 Alero
Drain Manual trans 2000 Alero
(A)
(A)
(8)

**1997-99
Cutlass
1999-00
Alero**

11 FITTINGS 0-1 PLUGS

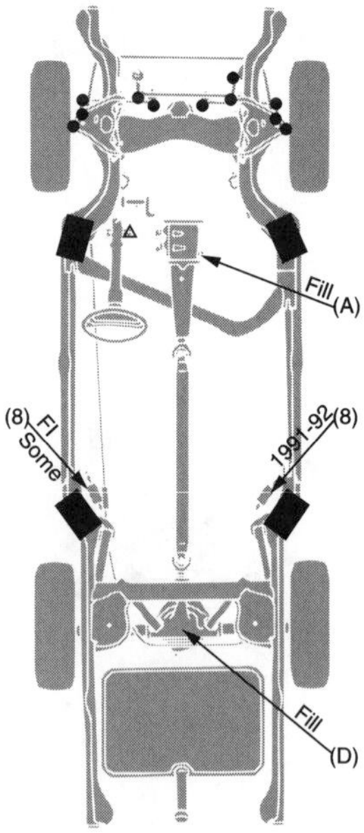

Fill (A)
(8) FI Some
1991-92 (8)
Fill (D)

**1989-92
Custom Cruiser**

(A) Manual transmission/transaxle, drain & fill
(B) Transfer case, NOT USED
(C) Automatic transaxle final drive, drain & fill
(D) Differential, drain & fill
(2) Transmission dipstick
(8) Fuel filter

CAUTION: On front wheel drive vehicles, the center of gravity is farther forward than on rear wheel drive vehicles. When removing major components from the rear of the vehicle while it is on a hoist, the vehicle must be supported in a manner to prevent it from tipping forward.

■ Lift adapter position   ▲ Plug   △ Plug, some models   • Fitting   ○ Fitting, some models

SERVICE AT TIME OR MILEAGE — WHICHEVER OCCURS FIRST

OEPM13   OEPM13

Perform the following maintenance services at the intervals indicated to keep the vehicle warranties in effect.
W   SERVICE TO MAINTAIN EMISSION WARRANTY

MI—MILES IN THOUSANDS
KM—KILOMETERS IN THOUSANDS

EVERY 6 MONTHS
Brake master cylinder . . .check level **HB**

Clutch master cylinder . . .check level **HB**

Power steering reservoir .check level **PS**

FIRST 7.5 MI—12 KM
W Carburetor or throttle body mounting
  bolts, ex. 2.3L . . . . .torque

W Choke & hoses . . . . .check/clean
As equipped

W Engine idle speed . . . . .adjust
Without Idle Speed or Idle Air Control

Diff., Limited-Slip . . . . . .change lubricant
As equipped

Tires . . . . .rotate
Initial service, then every 15 mi (24 km). Check brake
linings.

EVERY 12 MO/7.5 MI—12 KM
Brake system . . . . .inspect
Check hydraulic system, disc pads, drum brake linings

W Crankcase . . . . .change oil

Drive belts . . . . .inspect/adjust

W Oil filter .replace
First oil change, then every other, but at least every 12
months

Differential . . . . .check level
As equipped

Exhaust system . . . . .inspect

Suspension &
  steering linkage . . . . . **4-11 fittings LB**

Parking brake cable guides . . . . .coat **LB**
Check adjustment

Shift linkage . . . . .coat **LB**
With floor shift, coat contact faces

Suspension & steering . . . . .inspect
Also inspect front drive axle boots and seals

Transaxle or transmission . . .check level

W Throttle linkage . . . . .inspect
Check for damage or binding

Body . . . . .lubricate

EVERY 12 MONTHS
W Cooling
  system . . . . . . .inspect & tighten hoses
Wash radiator filler neck & cap; pressure-test system.
Clean exterior of radiator core and air-conditioning
condenser. Inspect coolant, service as needed.

EVERY 24 MO/30 MI—50 KM
W Air pump drive belts . . . . . .inspect/adjust

W Cooling system . . . . .change coolant **EC**
Flush system. Use 50% concentration for −34°F (−37°C)
protection.

EVERY 36 MO/30 MI—50 KM
W Air cleaner element . . . . .replace

W PCV inlet filter . . . . .replace
As equipped

W EGR system . . . . .clean/inspect
Engine codes R, U, Y

EVERY 30 MI—50 KM
Front-wheel bearings ex.
  front-wheel drive . . . . .clean/repack **GC**
Service at mileage interval or at each brake reline,
whichever comes first. Tighten spindle nut to 12 ft lb
while turning wheel. Back off nut & retighten finger tight.
Loosen nut just enough that hole in spindle lines up with
slot in nut. (Not more than ½" flat.) End play, .001"-.005".

W Choke & hoses . . . . .check/clean
As equipped

W Distributor cap . . . . .inspect
Except distributorless ignition

W Fuel tank, cap & lines . . . . .inspect

W Ignition timing . . . . .adjust
Except distributorless ignition

Ignition wires . . . . .inspect/clean
As equipped

PCV system . . . . .inspect
Some models blow out or replace hoses

W Spark plugs . . . . .replace

W Thermostatic air cleaner . . . . . . .inspect
As equipped

EVERY 100 MI—160 KM
Transaxle or trans., auto. . . .change fluid
Replace filter

SEVERE SERVICE
W **Carburetor or throttle body**—Except
2.3L engine, torque mounting bolts & adjust idle speed at 6 mi (10 km). Inspect carburetor choke & hoses at 6 mi (10 km),
then every 30 mi (50 km).

W **Crankcase**—Change oil every 3 mo/3 mi
(5 km). Change filter at each oil change.

Front suspension & steering linkage—
Lubricate every other oil change

Front wheel bearings—RWD, repack
every 15 mi (24 km) or at every brake service, whichever comes first

Tires—Inspect/rotate at 6 mi (10 km), then
every 15 mi (24 km)

Transaxle or transmission, automatic—
Change fluid & filter every 15 mi (24 km)

Differential—Change lubricant every 7.5
mi (12 km) when towing a trailer

KEY TO LUBRICANTS

AF3	DEXRON®-III Automatic Transmission Fluid
API★	Motor Oil certified by the American Petroleum Institute (Starburst Symbol)
EC	Ethylene Glycol Coolant
GC	Wheel Bearing Grease, NLGI Category GC
GL-5	Gear Oil, API Service GL-5
GL-5★	Special Lubricant for Limited-Slip Differential
GLS	Gear Lubricant, Special
HB	Hydraulic Brake Fluid, DOT 3
LB	Chassis Grease, NLGI Category LB
PS	Power Steering Fluid
SG	Motor Oil, API Service SG — Use Energy Conserving II Oils
SH	Motor Oil, API Service SH — Use Energy Conserving II Oils

CRANKCASE . . . .**SG, SH, API★**

CAPACITY, Refill:	Liters	Qt
All	3.8	4.0
Above 40°F (4°C) . . . . .30[1]		
Above 0°F (−18°C) 10W-30		
All temperatures . . . . .5W-30[2]		

1 Use only if other specified grades are unavailable
2 Preferred

TRANSMISSION/TRANSAXLE,
  Automatic **AF3**

CAPACITY, Initial Refill[3]:	Liters	Qt
125 (3T40)	3.8	4.0
200C	3.3	3.5
200-4R	3.3	3.5
440-T4 (4T60, 4T60E)	5.7	6.0
700-R4 (4L60)	4.7	5.0

3 With engine at operating temperature, shift transmission
  through all gears. Let engine slow idle in PARK for 3 minutes or more. Check fluid level and add fluid as needed.

TRANSAXLE, Manual . . . .**GLS**

CAPACITY, Refill:	Liters	Pt
All	1.9	4.0

DIFFERENTIAL
Standard . . . . .80W-90[4] **GL-5**
Limited-Slip . . . . .80W-90[4] **GL-5★**

4 For vehicles normally operated in Canada, 80W

CAPACITY, Refill:	Liters	Pt
7½" ring gear	1.7	3.5
8½", 8¾" ring gear	2.0	4.3

LIMITED-SLIP IDENTIFICATION:
Tag under rear cover-attaching bolt

SERVICE AT TIME OR MILEAGE — WHICHEVER OCCURS FIRST

OEPM14   OEPM14

Perform the following maintenance services at the intervals indicated to keep the vehicle warranties in effect.

W SERVICE TO MAINTAIN EMISSION WARRANTY

MI—MILES IN THOUSANDS
KM—KILOMETERS IN THOUSANDS

EVERY 6 MONTHS
Brake master cylinder . . .check level **HB**
Clutch master cylinder . . .check level **HB**
Power steering reservoir .check level **PS**
W Throttle linkage 1992-95 . . . . . . .inspect
   Check for damage or binding
Brake system 1992-95 . . . . .inspect
   Check brake system, disc pads, drum linings
Exhaust system 1992-95 . . . . . .inspect
Suspension 1992-95 . . . . .inspect
   Also inspect front drive axle boots & seals

FIRST 7.5 MI—12 KM
W Carburetor or throttle body
   mounting bolts . . . . .torque
   Engine Codes: 1990, D, R, U, Y; 1991, D, E, R; 1992,
   E, R, U, 7
W Choke & hoses . . . . .check/clean
   As equipped
Diff., Limited-Slip . . . . . .change lubricant
   As equipped
Tires . . . . .rotate
   Initial service, then every 15 mi (24 km). Check brake
   linings.

FIRST 15 MI—25 KM;
THEN EVERY 30 MI—50 KM
Throttle body bore & plate . . . . . . .clean
   4.0L Code C engine

EVERY 12 MO/7.5 MI—12 KM
Brake system 1990-91 . . . . .inspect
   Check hydraulic system for leaks. Inspect brake linings
W Crankcase . . . . .change oil
   Or sooner if indicated by the Engine Oil Change Indicator
W Oil filter . . . . .replace
   1990-94 at first oil change, then every other, but at least
   every 12 months. 1995 every oil change.
Differential . . . . .check level
   As equipped
Exhaust system 1990-91 . . . . . . .inspect
Suspension &
   steering linkage . . . . . .0-11 fittings **LB**
Parking brake cable guides and
   underbody contact points . . . . .coat **LB**
   Check adjustment
Shift linkage . . . . .coat **LB**
   With floor shift, coat contact faces
Suspension & steering 1990-91 . .inspect
   Also inspect front drive axle boots and seals
Transaxle or transmission . . .check level
Throttle linkage 1990-91 . . . . . . .inspect
   Check for damage or binding
Body . . . . .lubricate

EVERY 12 MONTHS
W Cooling system . . . . . . .inspect hoses &
                         tighten clamps
   Wash radiator filler neck & cap; pressure-test system.
   Clean exterior of radiator core and air-conditioning
   condenser. Inspect coolant, service as needed.

EVERY 24 MO/30 MI—50 KM
W Drive belts . . . . .inspect/adjust
W Cooling system . . . . . . .change coolant **EC**
   Flush system. Use 50% concentration for −34°F (−37°C)
   protection. Add 2 sealant pellets (GM Part No. 3634621).

EVERY 36 MO/30 MI—50 KM
W Air cleaner element . . . . .replace
   1990
PCV filter . . . . .replace
   1990 as equipped

W EGR system . . . . .clean/inspect
   1990 engine codes R, U, Y
Supercharger 1992-95 . . . . .check level
   3.8L code 1 engine
   Use synthetic 5W-30 oil. GM Part Number 12345982

EVERY 30 MI—50 KM
Front-wheel bearings ex.
   front-wheel drive . . . . .clean/repack **GC**
   Service at mileage interval or at each brake reline,
   whichever comes first. Tighten spindle nut to 12 ft lb
   while turning wheel. Back off nut & retighten finger tight.
   Loosen nut just enough that hole in spindle lines up with
   slot in nut. (Not more than ½ flat.) End play, .001"-.005".
W Air cleaner element . . . . .replace
   1991-95
W EGR system . . . . .clean/inspect
   1991-92 engine codes E, R, U, 7
   1993-94 engine codes 4, X
   1995 engine code 4
   Choke & hoses . . . . .check/clean
   As equipped
W Distributor cap . . . . .inspect
   Except distributorless ignition
W Fuel tank, cap & lines . . . . .inspect
W Ignition timing . . . . .adjust
   Except distributorless ignition
W Ignition wires . . . . .inspect/clean
   As equipped
PCV filter . . . . .replace
   1991-94 as equipped
W PCV system . . . . .inspect
   1990-92 some
W Spark plugs . . . . .replace
   Ex. 1994 Code 4, 1995 Codes C,D,4
W Thermostatic air cleaner . . . . . . .inspect
   As equipped

EVERY 60 MI—100 KM
W PCV system . . . . .inspect
   1993 some

FIRST 60 MI—100 KM;
THEN EVERY 15 MI—25 KM
W Camshaft timing belt . . . . .inspect
   3.4L code X engine

EVERY 100 MI—160 KM
Transaxle or trans., auto.
   1990-94 . . . . .change fluid
   Replace filter
Spark plugs . . . . .replace
   1994 Code 4, 1995 Codes C,D,4

SEVERE SERVICE
W **Carburetor or throttle body**—Torque
   mounting bolts & adjust idle speed at 6 mi
   (10 km). Inspect carburetor choke & hoses
   at 6 mi (10 km), then every 30 mi (50 km).
W **Crankcase**—Change oil every 3 mo/3 mi
   (5 km) or sooner if indicated by the Engine
   Oil-Change Indicator. Change filter at each
   oil change.
Front suspension & steering linkage—
   Lubricate every other oil change
Front wheel bearings—RWD, repack
   every 15 mi (24 km) or at every brake service, whichever comes first
Tires—Inspect/rotate at 6 mi (10 km), then
   every 12 mi (20 km)
Transaxle or transmission, automatic—
   Change fluid & filter every: 1990-94, 15 mi
   (24 km); 1995, 50 mi (80 km)
Differential—Change lubricant every 7.5
   mi (12 km) when towing a trailer

KEY TO LUBRICANTS

AF3 DEXRON®-III Automatic
       Transmission Fluid

API★ Motor Oil certified by the American
       Petroleum Institute (Starburst
       Symbol)

EC Ethylene Glycol Coolant
       For 1995: Replace green coolant with green
       coolant; replace orange coolant (DEX-COOL®)
       with orange coolant

GC Wheel Bearing Grease, NLGI
       Category GC

GL-5 Gear Oil, API Service GL-5

GL-5★ Special Lubricant for Limited-Slip
       Differential

GLS Gear Lubricant, Special

HB Hydraulic Brake Fluid, DOT 3

LB Chassis Grease, NLGI Category LB

PS Power Steering Fluid

SG Motor Oil, API Service SG

SH Motor Oil, API Service SH

CRANKCASE . . . .**API★**

CAPACITY, Refill:	Liters	Qt
V6 3.4L	4.7	5.0
V8 4.0L	6.6	7.0
Others	3.8	4.0

Capacity shown is without filter. When replacing filter, additional oil may be needed.

1991-93 3.3L, 1991-95 3.8L, 4.0L:
Above 40°F (4°C) . . . . .30[1]
Above 0°F (−18°C) . . . . .10W-30[2]
Below 60°F (16°C) 5W-30

1990 All; 1991-95 others
Above 40°F (4°C) . . . . .30[1]
Above 0°F (−18°C) 10W-30
All temperatures . . . . .5W-30[2]
[1] Use only if other specified grades are unavailable. USE
   API SG, SH oil.
[2] Preferred.

TRANSMISSION/TRANSAXLE,
  Automatic **AF3**

CAPACITY, Initial Refill[3]:	Liters	Qt
125 (3T40)	3.8	4.0
200-4R	3.3	3.5
440-T4 (4T60)	5.7	6.0
4T60E	6.6	7.0
4T80E	10.4[4]	11.0[4]
700-R4 (4L60)	4.7	5.0

[3] With engine at operating temperature, shift transmission
   through all gears. Let engine slow idle in PARK for 3 minutes or more. Check fluid level and add fluid as needed.
[4] Both pan and drain plug removed.

TRANSAXLE, Manual . . . .**GLS**

CAPACITY, Refill:	Liters	Pt
Front-wheel drive		
4-speed	2.8	6.0
5-speed	1.9	4.0

DIFFERENTIAL
Standard . . . . .80W-90[5] **GL-5**
Limited-Slip . . . . .80W-90[5] **GL-5★**
[5] 1990, for vehicles normally operated in Canada, 80W only

CAPACITY, Refill:	Liters	Pt
7½" ring gear	1.7	3.5
8½", 8¾" ring gear	2.0	4.3

SERVICE AT TIME OR MILEAGE — WHICHEVER OCCURS FIRST

OEPM15   OEPM15

Perform the following maintenance services at the intervals indicated to keep the vehicle warranties in effect.
W   SERVICE TO MAINTAIN EMISSION WARRANTY

MI—MILES IN THOUSANDS
KM—KILOMETERS IN THOUSANDS

EVERY MONTH
Tires . . . . .check pressure

EVERY 6 MONT HS
Brake master cylinder . . .check level **HB**

Clutch master cylinder . . .check level **HB**
GM Part No. 12345347 preferred

Power steering reservoir .check level **PS**

W Cooling system . . . . .inspect hoses &
tighten clamps

Transaxle or transmission . . .check level
As equipped with dipstick

W Throttle linkage . . . . .inspect
Check for damage or binding. Do not lubricate.

Caliper pins, knuckle brake pad
abutments . . . . .check/lubricate
When operating in a corrosive environment.
Or every other tire change, or as necessary.
1997-99, Eighty-Eight, LSS, Regency
1997-98 Achieva

Brake system . . . . .inspect
Check hydraulic system, disc pads, drum linings, hoses
& lines

Exhaust system . . . . .inspect

Steering linkage & suspension . . .inspect
Also inspect front drive axle boots & seals

1996, FIRST 7.5 MI—12 KM
THEN EVERY 15 MI—24 KM
1997-00, EVERY 7.5 MI—12 KM
Tires . . . . .inspect/rotate
Check brake linings

FIRST 15 MI—25 KM;
THEN EVERY 30 MI—50 KM
Throttle body bore & plate . . . . . . .clean
4.0L Code C engine

EVERY 12 MO/7.5 MI—12 KM
W Crankcase . . . . .change oil & filter
Or sooner if indicated by the oil life monitor. Reset oil life
monitor.

Hood & door hinges . . . . .lubricate
Multipurpose lubricant, GM part no. 12346241

Hood latch assembly . . . . . .lubricate **LB**

Suspension &
steering linkage . . . . . .0-11 fittings **LB**
Ex. 1998 Aurora and Intrigue

Parking brake cable guides and
underbody contact points,
linkage points . . . . .coat **LB**

Shift linkage . . . . .coat **LB**
With floor shift, coat contact faces

EVERY 12 MONTHS
Body .lubricate

Underbody . . . . .flush
Every spring

EVERY 36 MO/30 MI—50 KM
Supercharger . . . . .check level
3.8L code 1 engine
GM Part Number 12345982

EVERY 30 MI—50 KM
W Air cleaner element . . . . .replace

W EGR system, 1996 . . . . . . .clean/inspect
Code 4 engine

W Fuel tank, cap & gaskets
& lines, 1996-99 . . . . .inspect

EVERY 60 MI—100 KM
W Drive belts . . . . .inspect/adjust

FIRST 60 MI—100 KM;
THEN EVERY 15 MI—25 KM
W Camshaft timing belt . . . . .inspect
1996-97, 3.4L code X engine

EVERY 100 MI—160 KM
W Spark plug wires . . . . .inspect
As equipped

W Spark plugs . . . . .replace

1996
EVERY 60 MO/100 MI—160 KM
1997-00
EVERY 60 MO/150 MI—240 KM
W Cooling system . . . . .change coolant **EC**
Flush system. Use 50% concentration for −34°F (−37°C)
protection. 1996-97, add 2 sealant pellets GM Part No.
3634621. 1998-99, 3.1L & 3.8L, 4.0L, 3 pellets
When using coolant other than DEX-COOL, change
coolant every 30,000 mi (50,000 km) or 24 months

EVERY 100 MI—160 KM
Transaxle, Automatic . . .change fluid & filter
1999 Eighty-Eight, LSS

SERVICE AS REQUIRED
Transaxle, automatic,
1999 Aurora . . . . .change fluid & filter
When CHANGE TRANS FLUID msg. appears on the
Driver Information Center

SEVERE SERVICE
W Air cleaner element, dusty conditions—
Replace if necessary every 15 mi (24 km)

W Crankcase—Change oil & filter every 3
mo/3 mi (5 km) or sooner if indicated by the
oil life monitor

Front suspension & steering linkage—
Ex. 1998-99 Aurora and Intrigue—
Lubricate every other oil change

Tires—Inspect/rotate at: 1996, 6 mi (10
km), then every 12 mi (20 km); 1997-98 ex.
1998-99 Aurora and Intrigue, every 6 mi
(10 km)

Transaxle, automatic—Change fluid & filter every 50 mi (80 km) when in either:
heavy city traffic at temperatures regularly
above 90°F (32°C); hilly terrain; taxi, police, delivery, trailer towing service; car top
carrier use

KEY TO LUBRICANTS

AF3	DEXRON®-III Automatic Transmission Fluid
API★	Motor Oil certified by the American Petroleum Institute (Starburst Symbol)
EC	Ethylene Glycol Coolant GM DEX-COOL® or Havoline DEX-COOL®
GLS	Gear Lubricant, Special
HB	Hydraulic Brake Fluid, DOT 3 Delco Supreme II GM Part No. 12377967
LB	Chassis Grease, NLGI Category LB
PS	Power Steering Fluid GM Part No. 1052884

CRANKCASE . . . . .API★
CAPACITY, Refill:

	Liters	Qt
3.1L	4.3	4.5
3.4L	4.3	4.5
3.8L	4.3	4.5
4.0L	6.6	7.0
Others	3.8	4.0

Capacity shown is with filter. Recheck oil level after filling.
3.8L, 4.0L:
Above 0°F (−18°C) . . . . .10W-30[1]
Below 60°F (16°C) 5W-30
Others:
Above 0°F (−18°C) 10W-30
All temperatures . . . . .5W-30[1]
[1] Preferred

TRANSMISSION/TRANSAXLE,
Automatic .AF3
CAPACITY, Initial Refill[2]:

	Liters	Qt
3T40	3.8	4.0
4T40E	6.5	6.8
4T45E	6.5	6.8
4T60E, 4T65E	7.0	7.4
4T80E	10.4[3]	11.0[3]

[2] With engine at operating temperature, shift transmission through all gears. Let engine slow idle in PARK for 3 minutes or more. Check fluid level and add fluid as needed. Do not overfill.
[3] Requires drain plug removal.

TRANSAXLE, Manual
1996-99 . . . . .GLS
GM Part No. 12345349
2000 . . . . .AF3
CAPACITY, Refill:

	Liters	Pt
All	1.9	4.0

SERVICE LOCATIONS — ENGINE AND CHASSIS

HOOD RELEASE: Inside

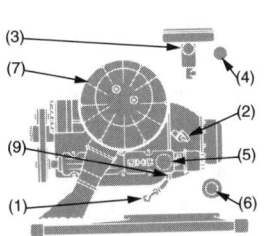

**1989-93
1.6L Code 6
LeMans**

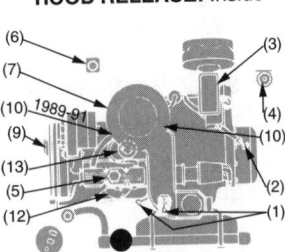

**1989-91
2.0L (122) OHC Code K**

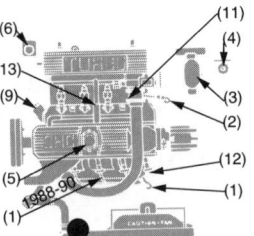

**1989-90
2.0L (122) Turbo OHC Code M**

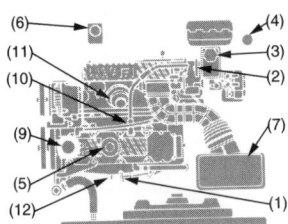

**1992-94
2.0L Code H
LeMans, Sunbird**

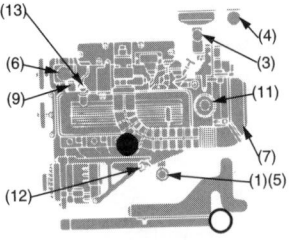

**1995-00
2.2L Code 4
Sunfire**

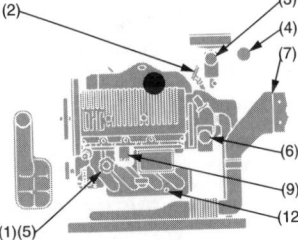

**1992-94
2.3L SOHC Code 3
Grand Am**

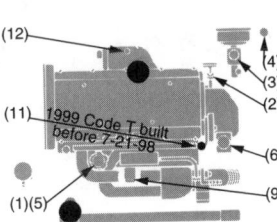

**1989-94
2.3L DOHC Code A, D
1995 2.3L Code D
1996-00 2.4L Code T**

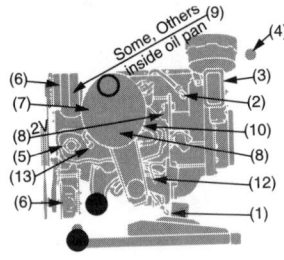

**1989-91
2.5L Phoenix, 6000
Fiero, Grand Am
Code R, U, 5
Air induction
system varies**

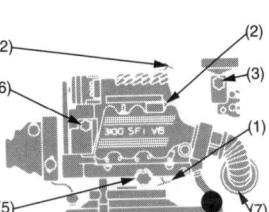

**1994-99
3.1L Code M
2000
3.1L Code J**

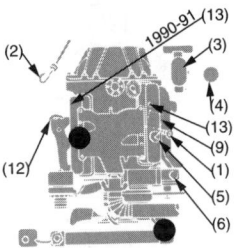

**1989-92
2.8L FI Code S,
3.1L FI Code T
Firebird**

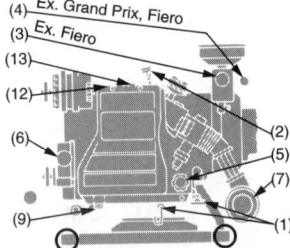

**1989 2.8L Code W, 9
6000, Grand Prix, Fiero
1989-94 3.1L (186) Code T**

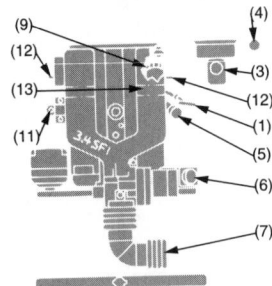

**1993-94
3.4L Code S
Firebird**

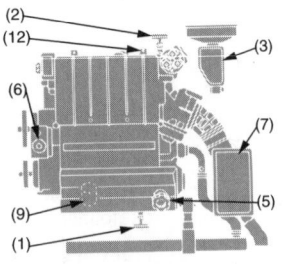

**1992-93
3.3L Code N
Grand Am, 6000**

**1991-96
3.4L DOHC Code X
Grand Prix**

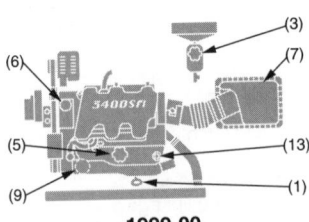

**1999-00
3.4L Code E**

(1) Crankcase dipstick
(2) Transmission dipstick
(3) Brake fluid reservoir
(4) Clutch fluid reservoir

(5) Oil fill cap
(6) Power steering reservoir
(7) Air filter
(8) Fuel filter
(9) Oil filter

(10) PCV filter
(11) EGR valve
(12) Oxygen sensor
(13) PCV valve

● Cooling system drain   ○ Cooling system drain, some models

192

SERVICE LOCATIONS — ENGINE AND CHASSIS

PCDP-2

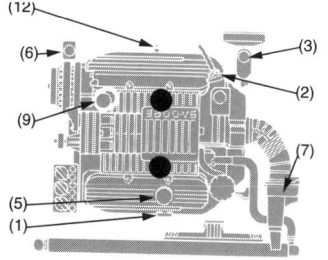

**1992-00
3.8L FI Code 1
Bonneville**

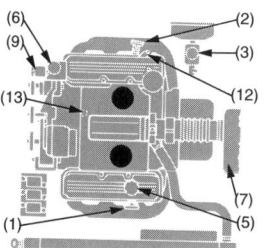

**1989-90
3.8L Code C
Bonneville**

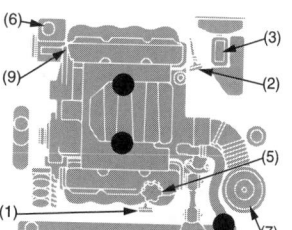

**1991-94 3.8L Code L
Bonneville
1995-97 3.8L Code K**

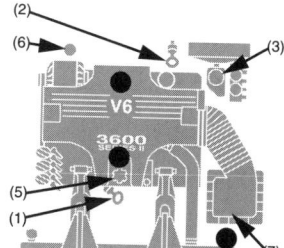

**1998-00
3.8L Code K
Bonneville**

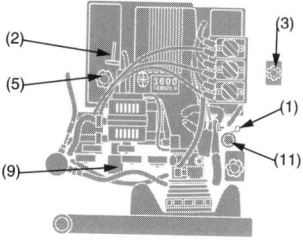

**1995-00
3.8L Code K
Firebird**

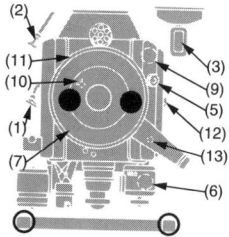

**1989-92
5.0L (305) FI Code E
Firebird
Air Induction
system varies**

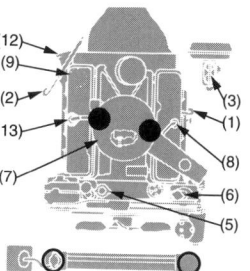

**1989
5.0L (307) Code Y
Parisienne, Safari**

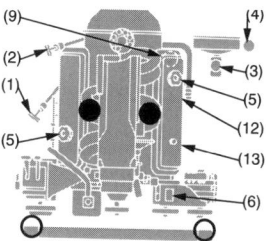

**1989-92 5.0L (350) FI
Code F
1989-91 5.7L (350) FI
Code 8
Firebird**

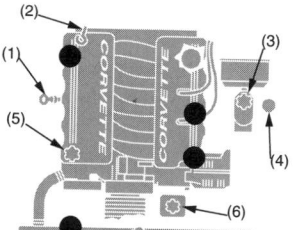

**1997-99
Code G
Firebird**

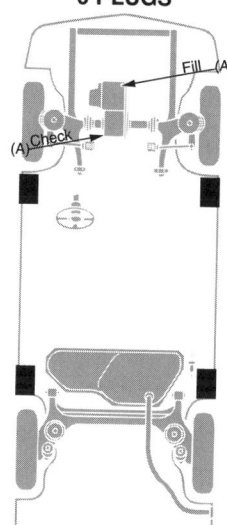

**0 FITTINGS
0 PLUGS**

**1989-93 LeMans,
Optima**

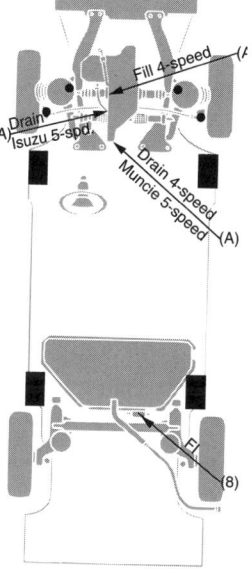

**4
FITTINGS**

**1995-00 Sunfire
1989-94 2000 Sunbird
1989-98 Grand Am
1989-91 Tempest**

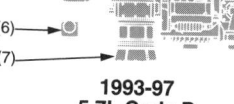

**1993-97
5.7L Code P
Firebird**

○ Cooling system drain, some models ● Cooling system drain ■ Lift adapter position • Fitting

SERVICE LOCATIONS — ENGINE AND CHASSIS

0 FITTINGS
0 PLUGS

(8)

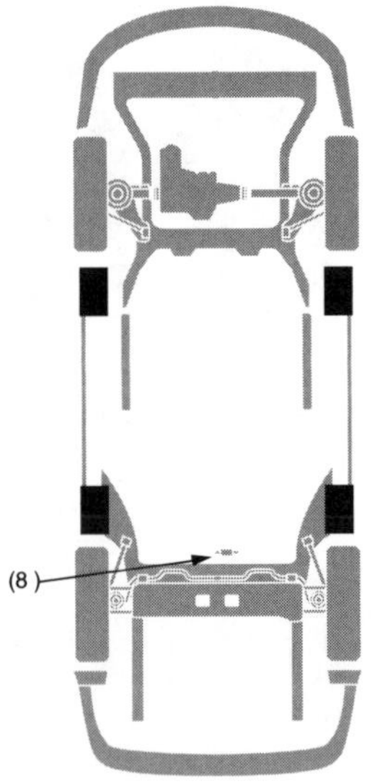

1999-00
Grand Am

4
FITTINGS

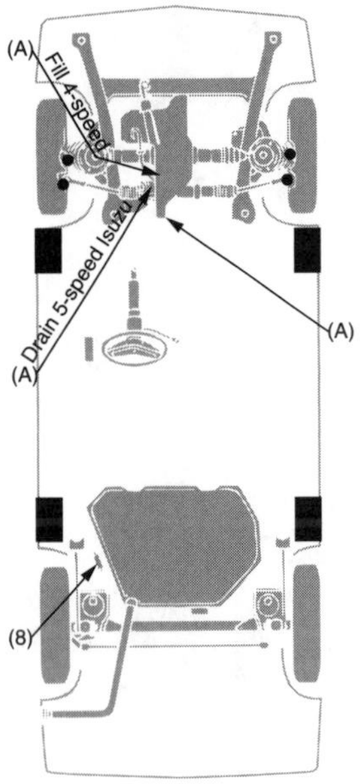

(A) Fill 4-speed
Drain 5-speed Isuzu
(A)
(A)
(8)

1989-91
6000

8
FITTINGS

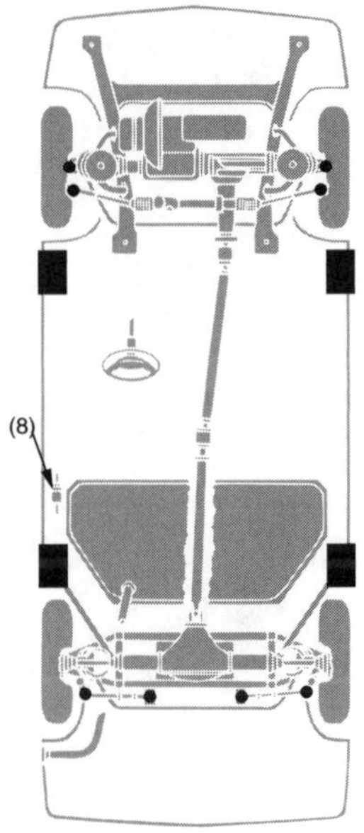

(8)

1989-90
6000 4WD

0 FITTINGS
0 PLUGS

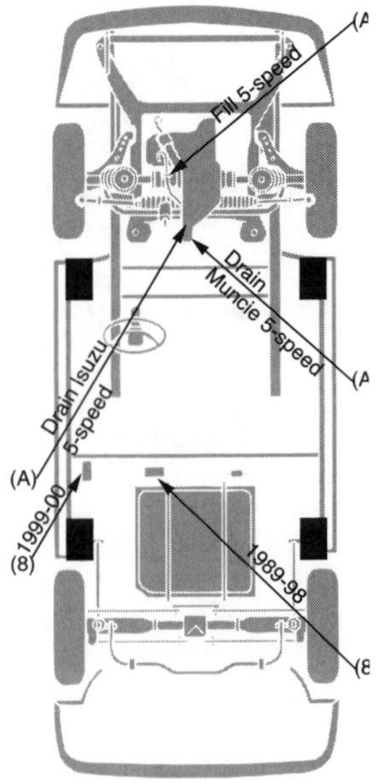

(A)
Fill 5-speed
Drain Muncie 5-speed
(A)
Drain Isuzu 5-speed
(A)
1999-00
(8)
1989-98
(8)

1989-00
Grand Prix

8
FITTINGS

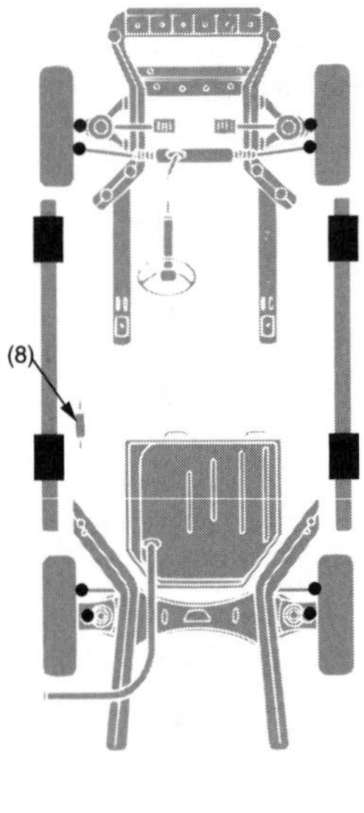

(8)

1989-00
Bonneville

9-11
FITTINGS

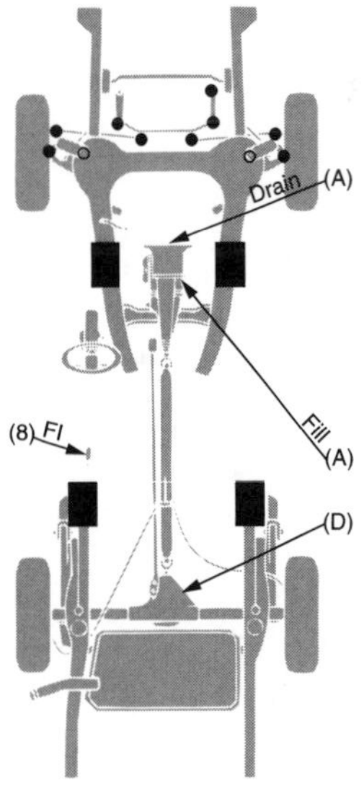

Drain (A)
Fill (A)
(8) FI
(D)

1989-92
Firebird

0-2 FITTINGS
0 PLUGS

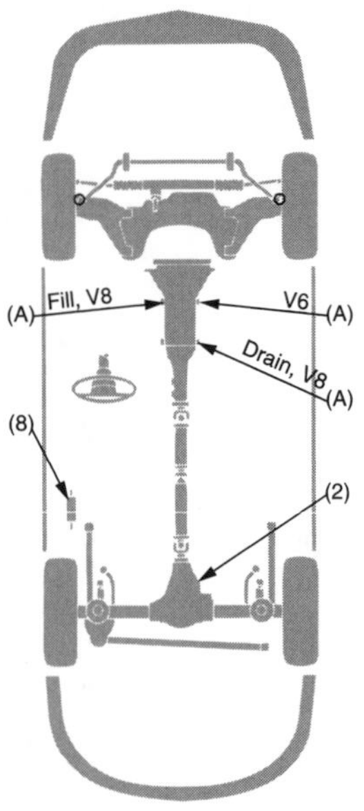

(A) Fill, V8   V6 (A)
Drain, V8 (A)
(8)
(2)

1993-00
Firebird

11-12
FITTINGS
0-1
PLUG

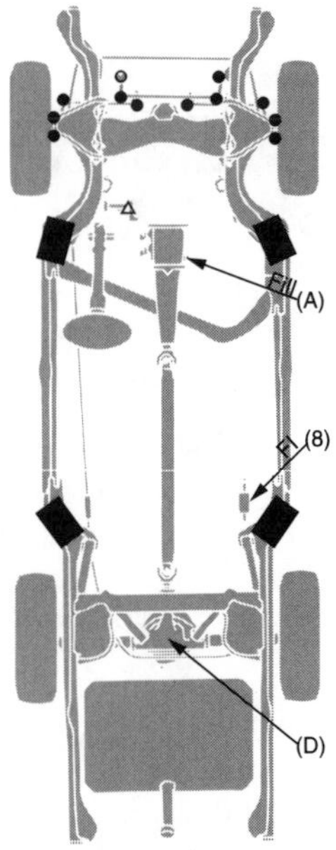

Fill (A)
FI (8)
(D)

1989-90 Safari
Station Wagon

CAUTION: On front wheel drive vehicles, the center of gravity is farther forward than on rear wheel drive vehicles. When removing major components from the rear of the vehicle while it is on a hoist, the vehicle must be supported in a manner to prevent it from tipping forward.

▲ Plug   △ Plug, some models
○ Fitting, some models

(A) Manual transmission/transaxle, drain & fill
(B) Transfer case, NOT USED

(C) Automatic transaxle final drive, NOT USED
(D) Differential, drain & fill

(2) Transmission dipstick
(8) Fuel filter

SERVICE AT TIME OR MILEAGE — WHICHEVER OCCURS FIRST

PCPM12   PCPM12

Perform the following maintenance services at the intervals indicated to keep the vehicle warranties in effect.
W   SERVICE TO MAINTAIN EMISSION WARRANTY

MI—MILES IN THOUSANDS
KM—KILOMETERS IN THOUSANDS

TURBOCHARGED ENGINES, EVERY 3 MO/3 MI—5 KM
W Crankcase . . . . .change oil

W Oil filter . . . . .replace

EVERY 6 MONTHS
Brake master cylinder . . .check level **HB**

Clutch master cylinder . . .check level **HB**

Power steering
   reservoir . . . . .check level **PS**

FIRST 7.5 MI—12 KM
W Carburetor or throttle body
   mounting bolts . . . . .torque

W Choke & hoses . . . . .check/clean
As equipped

W Engine idle speed . . . . .adjust
Ex. engines with Idle Speed or Idle Air Control

Diff., Limited-Slip . . . . .change lubricant
As equipped

Tires . . . . .inspect/rotate
Initial service then every 15 mi (24 km). Check brake linings. Firebird, certain tire/wheel systems cannot be rotated

EVERY 12 MO/7.5 MI—12 KM
Brake system . . . . .inspect
Check hydraulic system for leaks. Inspect disc pads, drum linings. LeMans, Optima, free reservoir cap breather hole from obstructions

W Crankcase ex. Turbo . . . . . . .change oil

W Oil filter ex. Turbo . . . . .replace
First oil change, then every other, or 12 months

Differential . . . . .check level

Exhaust system . . . . .inspect

Suspension &
   steering linkage . . . . . **4-11 fittings LB**
Initial service at mileage interval

Parking brake cable guides . . . .coat **LB**
Check adjustment

Shift linkage . . . . .coat **LB**
With floor shift, coat contact faces

Suspension & steering . . . . .inspect
Also inspect drive axle boots and seals

Transaxle or transmission . . .check level

W Drive belts . . . . .inspect/adjust
1989 ex. vacuum/air pump belts

Throttle linkage . . . . .inspect
Check for damage or binding

Body . . . . .lubricate

EVERY 12 MONTHS
W Cooling system . . . . .inspect hoses
                & tighten clamps
Wash radiator filler neck and cap; pressure test system. Clean exterior of radiator core and air conditioning condenser

EVERY 24 MO/30 MI—50 KM
W Cooling system . . . . .change coolant **EC**
Flush system, then use 50% concentration for −34°F (−37°C) protection

W Drive belts . . . . .inspect/adjust
1990-91

Vacuum/air pump belts . . .inspect/adjust
1989 as equipped

EVERY 36 MO/30 MI—50 KM
W Air cleaner element, 1989-90 . . . .replace

W PCV filter, 1989-90 . . . . .replace
As equipped

W EGR system . . . . .clean/inspect
1989-90 engine VIN codes U, Y,7,9

Fuel micro filter . . . . .replace
LeMans, Optima only

EVERY 30 MI—50 KM
Front wheel bearings ex.
   front-wheel drive . . . . .clean/repack **GC**
Service at mileage interval or at each brake reline, whichever comes first. Tighten spindle nut to 12 ft-lb while turning wheel. Back off & retighten finger tight. Loosen nut just enough that either hole in spindle lines up with slot in nut. (Not more than ½ flat)

W Air cleaner element, 1991 . . . . .replace

W Crankcase air filter, 1991 . . . . . .replace
As equipped

EGR system . . . . .clean/inspect
1991 engine VIN codes E, K, R, U, X, 6

W Choke & hoses . . . . .check/clean
As equipped

W Distributor cap . . . . .inspect
Except distributorless ignition

W Fuel cap, tank, and lines . . . . . .inspect

W Ignition timing . . . . .adjust
Except distributorless ignition

W Ignition wires . . . . .inspect/clean
As equipped

W PCV system . . . . .inspect
1989-91 some

W Spark plugs . . . . .replace

W Thermostatic air cleaner . . . . . . .inspect
As equipped

EVERY 60 MI—100 KM
W PCV system . . . . .inspect

EVERY 100 MI—160 KM
Transaxle or trans., auto. . . .change fluid
Replace filter

SEVERE SERVICE
W **Carburetor or throttle body**—Torque mounting bolts & adjust idle speed at 6 mi (10 km), also inspect carburetor choke & hoses

W **Crankcase**—Change oil & oil filter every 3 mo/3 mi (5 km)

Differential—Change lubricant every 7.5 mi (12 km) when towing a trailer

Suspension & steering linkage—Lubricate every other oil change

Front wheel bearings RWD—Repack every 15 mi (24 km) or at every brake service, whichever comes first

Tires—Rotate at 6 mi (10 km), then every 15 mi (24 km)

Transaxle or transmission, automatic—Change fluid & filter every 15 mi (24 km)

KEY TO LUBRICANTS

AF3	DEXRON®-III Automatic Transmission Fluid
API★	Motor Oil certified by the American Petroleum Institute (Starburst Symbol)
EC	Ethylene Glycol Coolant
GC	Wheel Bearing Grease, NLGI Category GC
GLS	Gear Lubricant, Special LeMans GM Part No. 12345371 Others GM Part No. 12345349
GL-5	Gear Oil, API Service GL-5
GL-5★	Special Lubricant for Limited-Slip Differential GM Part No. 1052271 plus additive GM Part No. 1052358
HB	Hydraulic Brake Fluid, DOT 3
LB	Chassis Grease, NLGI Category LB
PS	Power Steering Fluid
SG	Motor Oil, API Service SG Use Energy Conserving-II oils
SH	Motor Oil, API Service SH Use Energy Conserving-II oils

CRANCKASE . . . . .SG, SH, API★

CAPACITY, Refill:	Liters	Qt
3.4L DOHC	4.7	5.0
Others	3.8	4.0

Capacity shown is without filter. When replacing filter, additional oil may be needed

4-cyl. 2.0L Turbo:
Above 40°F (4°C) . . . . .30[1]
All temperatures . . . . .10W-30[2]

1990 Sunbird Turbo, Grand Prix Turbo
1991 3.1L V6 Turbo, V6 3.3L, 3.8L
Above 40°F (4°C) . . . . .30[1]
Above 0°F (−18°C) . . . . .10W-30[2]
Below 60°F (16°C) 5W-30

Others:
Above 40°F (4°C) . . . . .30[1]
Above 0°F (−18°C) 10W-30
All temperatures . . . . .5W-30[2]

[1] Use only if other specified grades are unavailable
[2] Preferred

TRANSMISSION/TRANSAXLE, Automatic AF3

CAPACITY, Initial Refill[3]:	Liters	Qt
125 (3T40)	3.8	4.0
200C	3.3	3.5
440-T4 (4T60)	5.8	6.0
4T60E	6.6	7.0
700-R4 (4L60)	4.7	5.0
LeMans	3.8	4.0

[3] With the engine at operating temperature, shift transmission through all gears. Let engine slow idle in PARK for 3 minutes or more. Check fluid level and add fluid as needed.

TRANSMISSION/TRANSAXLE, Manual
FWD . . . . .GLS
RWD, Firebird AF3

CAPACITY, Refill:	Liters	Pt
FWD: 4-speed	2.8	6.0
5-speed, Isuzu[4] 1989-91	1.9	4.0
5-speed, Muncie[5]:		
6000, Fiero	1.9	4.0
Others	2.1	4.4
LeMans, Optima:		
4-speed	1.6	3.5
5-speed (1.6L engine)	1.6	3.5
5-speed (2.0L engine)	2.1	4.5
RWD, Firebird:	2.8	6.0

[4] Has 7-bolt aluminum end cap
[5] Has 9-bolt steel end cap

DIFFERENTIAL
Standard . . . . .80W-90[6] **GL-5**
Limited-Slip . . . . .80W-90[6] **GL-5 ★**
[6] 1989-90, for vehicles normally operated in Canada, 80W only

CAPACITY, Refill:	Liters	Pt
Safari: 8½" ring gear	1.9	4.0
8¾" ring gear	2.4	5.4
6000, 4WD rear	1.8	3.8
Others	1.7	3.5

LIMITED-SLIP IDENTIFICATION:
Tag under rear cover-attaching bolt

PONTIAC
1992-95 All Models Except Firefly, Trans Sport

SERVICE AT TIME OR MILEAGE — WHICHEVER OCCURS FIRST

Perform the following maintenance services at the intervals indicated to keep the vehicle warranties in effect.

W　SERVICE TO MAINTAIN EMISSION WARRANTY

MI—MILES IN THOUSANDS
KM—KILOMETERS IN THOUSANDS

EVERY 6 MONTHS
Brake master cylinder . . .check level **HB**

Clutch master cylinder . . . . .check level
Use Part No. 12345347 or Castrol TLXC88

Power steering reservoir .check level **PS**

W Throttle linkage . . . . .inspect
Check for damage or binding

Brake system . . . . .inspect
Check hydraulic system, disc pads, drum linings

Exhaust system . . . . .inspect

Suspension . . . . .inspect
Also inspect front drive axle boots & seals

Differential . . . . .check level

Transaxle or transmission,
manual . . . . .check level

FIRST 7.5 MI—12 KM
W Throttle body mounting
bolts, 1992 Code E . . . . .torque

Diff., Limited-Slip . . . . . .change lubricant
As equipped

Tires . . . . .inspect/rotate
Initial service then every 15 mi (24 km). Check brake linings. Firebird, certain tire/wheel cannot be rotated

EVERY 12 MO/7.5 MI—12 KM
W Crankcase . . . . .change oil
Or sooner when indicated by the Oil Life Monitor

W Oil filter . . . . .replace
1992-94 at first oil change then every other, or 12 months. 1995, every oil change

Suspension &
steering linkage . . . . . .**0-11 fittings LB**

Parking brake cable guides and
underbody contact points . . . . .coat **LB**
Check adjustment

Shift linkage . . . . .coat **LB**
With floor shift, coat contact faces

Transaxle or transmission . . .check level

Body .lubricate

EVERY 12 MONTHS
W Cooling system . . . . .inspect hoses
& tighten clamps
Wash radiator filler neck and cap; pressure test system. Clean exterior of radiator core and air conditioning condenser

EVERY 24 MO/30 MI—50 KM
W Cooling system . . . . .change coolant **EC**
Flush system, then use 50% concentration for −34°F (−37°C) protection. For 1993 Grand AM 2.3L & 3.3L, and 1993 Sunbird engines add 2 pellets*. For 1993 3.3L engine add 3 pellets
* GM sealer Part No. 3634621

W Drive belts . . . . .inspect/adjust

EVERY 36 MO/30 MI—50 KM
Fuel micro filter . . . . .replace
LeMans, Optima only

Supercharger . . . . .check level
3.8L Code 1 engine. Use synthetic 5W-30 oil. GM Part No. 12345982

EVERY 30 MI—50 KM
Front wheel bearings,
1992 Firebird . . . . . .clean/repack **GC**
Service at mileage interval or at each brake reline, whichever comes first. Tighten spindle nut to 12 ft-lb while turning wheel. Back off & retighten finger tight. Loosen nut just enough that either hole in spindle lines up with slot in nut. (Not more than ½ flat)

W Air cleaner element . . . . .replace

W Crankcase air filter . . . . .replace
As equipped

W EGR system . . . . .clean/inspect
1992-93 engine VIN codes E, H, N, T, X, 1; 1994 engine VIN codes H, X; 1995 Code 4

W Distributor cap . . . . .inspect
Except distributorless ignition

W Fuel cap, tank, and lines . . . . . . .inspect

W Ignition timing . . . . .adjust
Except distributorless ignition

W Ignition wires . . . . .inspect/clean
As equipped

W PCV system . . . . .inspect
1992 some

W Spark plugs . . . . .replace
Ex. 1993-95 5.7L Code P

W Thermostatic air cleaner . . . . . . .inspect
As equipped

FIRST 60 MI—100 KM;
THEN EVERY 15 MI—25 KM
W Camshaft timing belt . . . . .inspect
3.4L Code X engine

EVERY 60 MI—100 KM
W PCV system . . . . .inspect
1993 some

EVERY 100 MI—160 KM
W Spark plugs . . . . .replace
1993-95 5.7L Code P only

Transaxle or trans., auto. . . .change fluid
1992-94 all, and 1995 Firebird
Replace filter

SEVERE SERVICE
W Throttle body —1992 Code E, torque mounting bolts at 6 mi (10 km)

W Crankcase—Change oil & oil filter every 3 mo/3 mi (5 km)

Differential—Change lubricant every 7.5 mi (12 km) when towing a trailer

Suspension & steering linkage—Lubricate every other oil change

Front wheel bearings—1992 Firebird, repack every 15 mi (24 km) or at every brake service, whichever comes first

Tires—Rotate at 6 mi (10 km), then every 12 mi (20 km)

Transaxle or transmission, automatic—Change fluid & filter every: 1992-94 all and 1995 Firebird, 15 mi (24 km); 1995 others, 50 mi (80 km)

KEY TO LUBRICANTS
AF3　DEXRON®-III Automatic Transmission Fluid

API★　Motor Oil certified by the American Petroleum Institute (Starburst Symbol)

EC　Ethylene Glycol Coolant
For 1995: Replace green coolant with green coolant; replace orange coolant (DEX-COOL®) with orange coolant

GC　Wheel Bearing Grease, NLGI Category GC

GLS　Gear Lubricant, Special
LeMans GM Part No. 12345371
Others GM Part No. 12345349

GL-5　Gear Oil, API Service GL-5
1992-93 GM Part No. 1052271
1994-95 GM Part No. 12345977

GL-5★　Special Lubricant for Limited-Slip Differential
1994-95 GM Part No. 12345977 plus 2 oz. GM Part No. 1052358. 1992-93, GM Part No. 1052271 plus 4 oz. GM Part No. 1052358.

HB　Hydraulic Brake Fluid, DOT 3

LB　Chassis Grease, NLGI Category LB

PS　Power Steering Fluid
GM Part No. 1052884

SG　Motor Oil, API Service SG
Use Energy Conserving-II oils

SH　Motor Oil, API Service SH
Use Energy Conserving-II oils

CRANKCASE
1992-94 . . . . .SG, SH, API★
1995 . . . . .API★

CAPACITY, Refill:	Liters	Qt
3.4L DOHC	4.7	5.0
Others	3.8	4.0

Capacity shown is without filter. When replacing filter, additional oil may be needed

1992-94 V6 3.3L, 3.8L
Above 40°F (4°C) . . . . .30[1]
Above 0°F (−18°C) . . . . .10W-30[2]
Below 60°F (16°C) 5W-30

Others:
Above 40°F (4°C) . . . . .30[1]
Above 0°F (−18°C) 10W-30
All temperatures . . . . .5W-30[2]

[1] Use only if other specified grades are unavailable. Use API SG, SH oil
[2] Preferred

TRANSMISSION/TRANSAXLE,
Automatic .AF3

CAPACITY, Initial Refill[3]:	Liters	Qt
125 (3T40)	3.8	4.0
4T40E[4]	7.0	7.4
440-T4 (4T60)	5.8	6.0
4T60E	6.6	7.0
700-R4 (4L60)	4.7	5.0
LeMans, Optima	3.8	4.0

[3] All except 4T40E, with the engine at operating temperature, shift transmission through all gears. Let engine slow idle in PARK for 3 minutes or more. Check fluid level and add fluid as needed
[4] Has no fluid level indicator

TRANSMISSION/TRANSAXLE, Manual
FWD . . . . .GLS
RWD, Firebird AF3

CAPACITY, Refill:	Liters	Pt
FWD: Isuzu[5]	1.9	4.0
Muncie[6]	2.1	4.4

[5] Has 7-bolt aluminum end cap
[6] Has 9-bolt steel end cap

LeMans, Optima:		
4-speed	1.6	3.5
5-speed (1.6L engine)	1.6	3.5
5-speed (2.0L engine)	2.1	4.5
RWD, Firebird:		
1992-95 5-speed	2.8	6.0
1993-95 6-speed	3.8	8.1

DIFFERENTIAL
Standard 80W-90 **GL-5**
Limited-Slip . . . . .80W-90 **GL-5 ★**

CAPACITY, Refill:	Liters	Pt
Firebird	1.7	3.5

LIMITED-SLIP IDENTIFICATION:
Tag under rear cover-attaching bolt

SERVICE AT TIME OR MILEAGE — WHICHEVER OCCURS FIRST

PCPM14   PCPM14

Perform the following maintenance services at the intervals indicated to keep the vehicle warranties in effect.
W   SERVICE TO MAINTAIN EMISSION WARRANTY

MI—MILES IN THOUSANDS
KM—KILOMETERS IN THOUSANDS

EVERY MONTH
Tires . . . . .check pressure

EVERY 6 MONTHS
Brake master cylinder . . .check level **HB**

Clutch fluid reservoir . . . .check level **HB**
Part No. 12345347 preferred

Power steering
   reservoir . . . . .check level **PS**

W Throttle linkage . . . . .inspect
Check for damage or binding. Do not lubricate

W Cooling System . . . . .inspect hoses
& tighten clamps

Brake system . . . . .inspect
Check hydraulic system, disc pads, drum linings, hoses
& lines

Caliper pins, knuckle brake pad
   abutments . . . . .check/lubricate
When operating in a corrosive environment
Or every other tire change, or as necessary
1997-98, Bonneville, Grand Am, Sunfire
1999 Bonneville, Sunfire
2000 Sunfire

Exhaust system . . . . .inspect

Steering linkage & suspension . . .inspect
Also inspect front drive axle boots & seals

Differential, Firebird . . . . . . .check level

Transaxle or transmission,
   manual . . . . .check level

FIRST 7.5 MI—12 KM
Diff. all, Firebird . . . . . . .change lubricant

Tires, 1996 . . . . .inspect/rotate
Initial service here every 15 mi (24 km). Check brake linings. Mileage only. Firebird, certain tire wheel systems
require special rotation pattern

EVERY 7.5 MI—12 KM
Tires, 1997-00 . . . . .inspect/rotate
Unusual wear requires rotation as soon as possible.
Firebird may require special rotation pattern.

EVERY 12 MO/7.5 MI—12 KM
W Crankcase . . . . .change oil & filter
Or sooner when indicated by the oil life monitor

Suspension &
   steering linkage . . . . . .0-11 fittings **LB**

Parking brake cable guides and
   underbody contact points . . . . .coat **LB**
Check adjustment

Shift linkage . . . . .coat **LB**
With floor shift, coat contact faces

EVERY 12 MONTHS
Body .lubricate

Underbody . . . . .flush
Every Spring

EVERY 36 MO/30 MI—50 KM
Supercharger . . . . .check level
3.8L Code 1 engine. Use synthetic 5W-30 oil. GM Part
No. 12345982

EVERY 30 MI—50 KM
W Air cleaner element . . . . .replace

W Crankcase air filter . . . . .replace
As equipped

W EGR system . . . . .clean/inspect
Code 4 engine

W Fuel cap & gasket, tank,
   and lines, 1996-99 . . . . .inspect

FIRST 60 MI—100 KM;
THEN EVERY 15 MI—25 KM
W Camshaft timing belt . . . . .inspect
3.4L Code X engine

EVERY 60 MI—100 KM
W Drive belts . . . . .inspect

EVERY 100 MI—160 KM
W Spark plugs . . . . .replace

W Ignition wires . . . . .inspect/clean
As equipped

Transmission,
   automatic . . . . . . .change fluid & filter
1996-00 Firebird; 1999-00 Bonneville, Grand Am, Grand
Prix

1996
EVERY 60 MO/100 MI—160 KM
1997-00
EVERY 60 MO/150 MI—240 KM
W Cooling System . . . . .change coolant **EC**
Flush system, then use 50% concentration for −34°F
(−37°C) protection. 1996-97: add 2 sealant pellets GM
Part No. 3634621

SEVERE SERVICE
W Crankcase —Change oil & oil filter every 3
mo/3 mi (5 km) or sooner when indicated
by the oil life monitor

W Air cleaner element, dusty conditions—
Replace if necessary every 15 mi (24km)

Limited Slip, Differential/Standard—
Firebird, change lubricant every 7.5 mi
(12 km) when towing a trailer

Suspension & steering linkage—
Lubricate every other oil change

Tires—Rotate: 1996, at 6 mi (10 km), then
every 12 mi (20 km); 1997-00, Bonneville
and Sunfire, every 6 mi (10 km)

Transaxle or transmission, automatic—
Change fluid & filter every: 15 mi (24 km)
for 1996-00 Firebird and 50 mi (80 km) for
others when in either: heavy city traffic at
temperatures regularly above 90°F (32°C);
hilly terrain; taxi, police, delivery, trailer
towing service; car top carrier use

KEY TO LUBRICANTS
AF3	DEXRON®-III Automatic Transmission Fluid
API★	Motor Oil certified by the American Petroleum Institute (Starburst Symbol)
EC	Ethylene Glycol Coolant GM DEX-COOL® or Havoline® DEX-COOL®
GLS	Gear Lubricant, Special GM Part No. 12345349
GL-5	Gear Oil, API Service GL-5 1996-97 Firebird, GM Part No. 12345977 or 80W-90 meeting GM Spec. 9985182. 1998-00 Firebird, GM Part No. 12378261 or 75W-90 synthetic meeting GM Spec. 9986115.
GL-5★	Special Lubricant for Limited-Slip Differential 1996-97 Firebird, GM Part No. 12345977 or 80W-90 meeting GM Spec. 9985182, plus 4 oz. additive GM Part No. 1052358. 1998-00 Firebird, GM Part No. 12378261 or 75W-90 synthetic meeting GM Spec. 9986115, plus 4 oz. additive GM Part No. 1052358.
HB	Hydraulic Brake Fluid, DOT 3 Delco Supreme 11, GM Part No. 12377967
LB	Chassis Grease, NLGI Category LB
PS	Power Steering Fluid GM Part No. 1052884

CRANKCASE . . . . .API★
CAPACITY, Refill:	Liters	Qt
2.2L, 2.4L	3.8	4.0
3.1L 1996-99 Code M	4.5	4.7
3.1L 2000 Code J	4.3	4.5
3.4L DOHC, 1996	4.8	5.0
3.4L, 1999-00	4.3	4.5
3.8L	4.3	4.5
5.7L, 1996-97	4.7	5.0
5.7L, 1998-00	5.2	5.5

3.4L Code X, 3.8L:
Above 0°F (−18°C) . . . . .10W-30[1]
Below 60°F (16°C) 5W-30
Others:
Above 0°F (−18°C) 10W-30
All temperatures . . . . .5W-30[1]
[1] Preferred

TRANSMISSION/TRANSAXLE,
Automatic AF3
CAPACITY, Initial Refill[2]:	Liters	Qt
3T40	3.8	4.0
4T40E[3]	6.5	6.9
4T60E	6.7	7.0
4T65E	7.0	7.4
4L60E, 4L65E	4.7	5.0

[2] All except 4T40E, with the engine at operating temperature,
shift transmission through all gears. Let engine slow idle in
PARK for 3 minutes or more. Check fluid level and add fluid
as needed. Do not overfill
[3] Has no fluid level indicator. Not owner serviceable.

TRANSMISSION/TRANSAXLE, Manual
FWD, 1996-99 . . . . .GLS
FWD, 2000 . . . . .AF3
RWD, Firebird AF3
CAPACITY, Refill:	Liters	Pt
FWD	1.9	4.0
RWD, Firebird:		
5-speed	3.2	6.8
6-speed	3.8	8.0

DIFFERENTIAL
Standard 80W-90 **GL-5**
Limited-Slip . . . . .80W-90 **GL-5 ★**
CAPACITY, Refill:	Liters	Pt
Firebird	1.7	3.5

SERVICE LOCATIONS — ENGINE AND CHASSIS

HOOD RELEASE: Inside

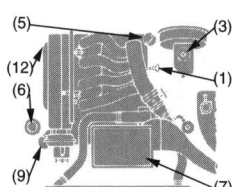

**1989
944
4-cyl. 2479cc Turbo**

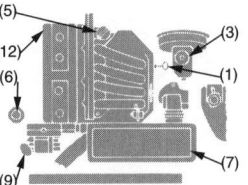

**1989
944
4-cyl. 2681cc DOHC
1989-95
944, 968
4-cyl. 2990cc DOHC**

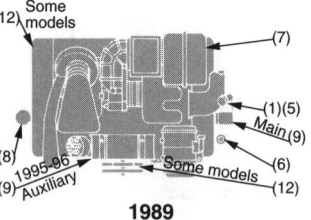

**1989
911
6-cyl. 3164cc
1989-98
911
6-cyl. 3600cc**

(1) Crankcase dipstick
(2) Transmission dipstick
(3) Brake fluid reservoir
(4) Clutch fluid reservoir
(5) Oil fill cap
(6) Power steering reservoir
(7) Air filter

(8) Fuel filter
(9) Oil filter
(10) PCV filter
(11) EGR valve
(12) Oxygen sensor
(13) PCV valve

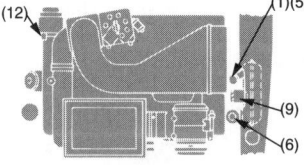

**1989, 1991-92
911
6-cyl. 3299cc Turbo**

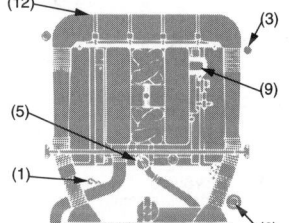

**1989-91
928
V8 4957cc
(DOHC version shown)**

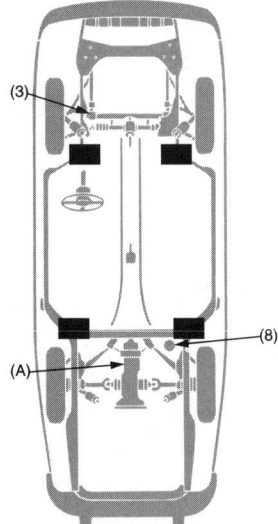

**0 FITTINGS
0 PLUGS**

**1989
911, 911 Turbo
1990-98
911 Carrera 2
1994-98
911 Turbo 3.6,
911 Speedster**

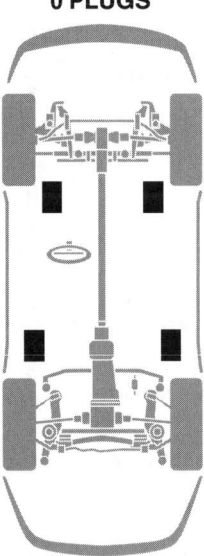

**0 FITTINGS
0 PLUGS**

**1990-98
911 Carrera 4**

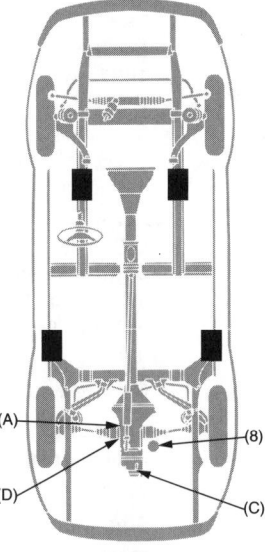

**0 FITTINGS
0 PLUGS**

**1989
944, 944S, 944 Turbo
1990-91
944S2
1992-95
968**

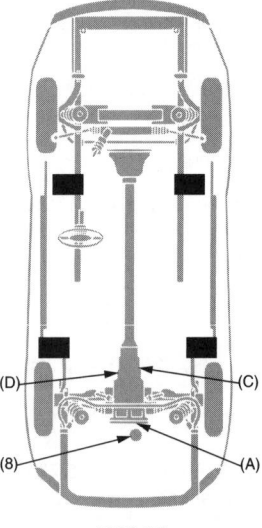

**0 FITTINGS
0 PLUGS**

**1989-95
928GT, 928GTS,
928S, 928S/4**

(A) Manual transmission/transaxle,
    drain & fill
(B) Transfer case, NOT USED

(C) Automatic transmission, check
(D) Differential, drain & fill

■ Lift adapter position

SERVICE AT TIME OR MILEAGE — WHICHEVER OCCURS FIRST

PEIPM1   PEIPM1

1989-98 only. Perform the following maintenance services at the intervals indicated to keep both the vehicle and emission warranties in effect.

MI—MILES IN THOUSANDS
KM—KILOMETERS IN THOUSANDS

EVERY 7.5 MI—12 KM
Crankcase ....change oil
1989 Turbo only

Oil filter ....replace
1989 Turbo only

EVERY 12 MO/15 MI—24 KM
Clutch pedal free play .....check/adjust

Crankcase ....change oil
Inspect for leakage

Oil filter (two), 1989-93 ....replace

Driveshaft boots ....inspect

Exhaust system ....inspect
Turbo: check tightness of reactors, turbocharger, and wastegate

Front axle, steering
  & suspension ....inspect
Check tightness of components & condition of rubber boots & bushings

Front differential ....check level

Transaxle ....check level
Inspect for leakage

Accelerator linkage ....inspect
Check for smooth operation and full throttle opening, lubricate as necessary

Air filter element ....check

Battery ....check level

Boost pressure safety switch ....check
Turbo only

Brake fluid reservoir ..check level HBH

Clutch hydraulic cylinders ....inspect

Crankcase ventilation system ....inspect
Check hoses & connections, clean filter where applicable

Drive belts, 1995-96 ....check

Fuel lines & hoses ....inspect

Fuel pump safety switch ....check
Turbo only 1989-93

Ignition circuits 1 & 2 ....check
Use system tester 928

Intake air hoses ....inspect

Onboard diagnostic
  system ....check/clear

Power steering,
to 3-25-96 ....check level AF3, PS
Ex. 1996 Turbo

Power steering
from 3-25-96 ....check level PS

Power steering & clutch .....inspect PS
1996-97 Turbo. Inspect steering pump drive belt

Resonance flap ....check

Varioram system ....check
Ex. turbo

Valve clearance, 1989-94 ..check/adjust

Windshield & headlight
  washers ....check level

Body ....check/lubricate
Check operation of all locks & hinges, lubricate door hinges & check rods

Cooling system ....inspect

Brake system ....inspect
Check pad wear, condition of lines & hoses, check parking brake

Electrical equipment ....inspect
Check operation of lights, horns, buzzers, wipers, switches, instruments & power accessories

Interior air filter, 1994-98 ......replace

Handbrake ....check/adjust

Headlights ....check/adjust

Seat belts ....inspect
Check condition and operation

Tires ....inspect/adjust
Check tread wear & inflation pressure, including spare

Weatherstrips ....clean/lubricate
Remove residue & coat with talcum powder, glycerine, or other suitable rubber lubricant

Wheel bearings, front .....check/adjust
1989 only

Wheel bearings, rear .....check/adjust
Turbo & turbo look only 1989-94

EVERY 24 MONTHS
Brake fluid ....replace HBH
1989-92, 1997-98 only

EVERY 30 MI—48 KM
Transmission, automatic .change fluid & filter

Oil filters (two), 1994-98 ....replace

Air filter element ....replace
Replace air pump filter where applicable

Drive belts ....check/adjust

Ignition timing ....check/adjust
1989 Turbo only

Oxygen sensor, 1990-93 ......replace

Spark plugs ....replace

EVERY 36 MONTHS
Brake fluid ....replace HBH
1993-96 only Type 200 fluid

FIRST & SECOND 48 MONTHS; THEN EVERY 24 MONTHS
Air bag system ....inspect

EVERY 60 MI—96 KM
Multi-rib belt ....replace

Front differential ......change lubricant

Final drive, automatic
  transmission ....change lubricant
1989-97

Manual transaxle ......change lubricant
1989-97

Fuel filter ....replace

Oxygen sensor ....replace
1989 only

EVERY 72 MONTHS
Tires ....replace
Including spare

EVERY 90 MI—144 KM
Manual transaxle 1998 ...change lubricant

Automatic transaxle
  1998 ....change fluid and filter

Final drive 1998,
automatic transmission ...change lubricant

SEVERE SERVICE
Crankcase—Change oil and filters more frequently

Air filter—Check/replace every 15 mi (24 km)

Battery—Check level more frequently

Brakes—Inspect more frequently

Clutch—Check/adjust more frequently

Tires—Inspect more frequently

KEY TO LUBRICANTS

AF3	DEXRON® III Automatic Transmission Fluid
CD	Motor Oil, API Service CD
GF-1	Motor Oil, API Service GF-1
GL-5	Gear Oil, API Service GL-5
HBH	Hydraulic Brake Fluid, Extra Heavy Duty, DOT 4 Type 200
PS	Power Steering Fluid Pentosin CHF 11S
SF	Motor Oil, API Service SF
SG	Motor Oil, API Service SG
SH	Motor Oil, API Service SH

CRANKCASE
1989-93 ....SF, SF/CD, SG, SG/CD
1994-99 ....SH, GF-1

CAPACITY, Refill[1]:	Liters	Qt
1989-98	9.4	10.0
1999	8.7	9.2

[1] Air cooled: Fill the oil reservoir with 6.1 liters (6.5 quarts). Run the engine at idle and add another 3.0 liters (3.2 quarts). With engine warm and running, check the reservoir dipstick. **DO NOT FILL TO MAX** level. Oil level must be between the MIN and MAX gradients. Includes filter. Draining time is 20 minutes.

3164cc, 3299cc:
Above 14°F (-10°C) 20W-50
Above 5°F (-15°C) 15W-40, 15W-50
-4° to 95°F (-20° to 35°C) 10W-40, 10W-50
-13° to 68°F (-25° to 20°C) 10W-30
-22° to 32°F (-30° to 0°C) 5W-30
Below 14°F (-10°C) 5W-20

3600cc:
Mineral base oils:
Above 50°F (10°C), 1989-96 ...15W-40, 20W-40, 20W-50, 40
Below 50°F (10°C) 15W-40, 10W-40, 10W-30
Below 14°F (-10°C) 10W-30, 5W-30
Synthetic base oils, preferred:
All temperatures, 1989-95 .....10W-40, 15W-50
Above 50°F (10°C), 1996-98 ...10W-40, 15W-40, 15W-50
Below 50°F (10°C), 1989-96 ...10W-40, 10W-30, 5W-30
Below 50°F (10°C), 1993 ....5W-40
Below 14°F (-10°C) 1997-98 ...10W-40, 10W-30, 5W-30

TRANSMISSION, Automatic AF3
Final drive serviced separately

CAPACITY, Initial Refill[2]:	Liters	Qt
1990-98 911 Carrera 2	2.8	3.0
1999 911 Carrera (dryfill)	9.5	10.0

[2] With engine at operating temperature, shift transmission through all gears. Check fluid level in PARK and add fluid as needed.

TRANSAXLE, Manual ...75W-90, 90 GL-5

CAPACITY, Refill:	Liters	Pt
1989 911	3.0	6.4
Turbo	3.7	7.8
1989-98 Carrera 4	3.8	8.0
1990-98 Carrera 2	3.6	7.6
1996-98 Turbo	4.3	9.0
1999 All	2.7	5.7

FINAL DRIVE,
Rear w/AT 75W-90, 90 GL-5

CAPACITY, Refill:	Liters	Pt
1990-99 911 Carrera 2 & 4	0.9	1.9

FRONT DIFFERENTIAL ...75W-90 GL-5

CAPACITY, Refill:	Liters	Pt
1989-94 4WD	1.2	2.6
1995-96 4WD	0.5	1.1
1997-98 4WD	0.6	1.2

199

SERVICE AT TIME OR MILEAGE — WHICHEVER OCCURS FIRST

Perform the following maintenance services at the intervals indicated to keep both the vehicle and emission warranties in effect.

MI—MILES IN THOUSANDS
KM—KILOMETERS IN THOUSANDS

1989 944 TURBO, EVERY 7.5 MI—12 KM

Crankcase . . . . .change oil
Check for leaks

Oil filter . . . . .replace

EVERY 12 MO/15 MI—24 KM

Crankcase . . . . .change oil
Check for leaks

Oil filter . . . . .replace

Driveshaft boots . . . . .inspect

Exhaust system . . . . .inspect

Final drive, automatic
transmission . . . . .check level
Check for leaks

Front axle & steering . . . . .inspect
Check tightness of components & condition of rubber
boots & bushings

Throttle linkage . . . . .inspect
Check for smooth operation and full throttle opening;
lubricate as necessary

Transaxle, manual . . . . .check level
Check for leaks

Transmission, automatic . . . .check level
Check by viewing level in clear plastic reservoir mounted
on the transmission case. Level must be between the
MIN & MAX markings with engine idling at operating
temperature. Check for leaks

Battery . . . . .check level

Brake fluid reservoir . . .check level HBH

Camshaft &
balance shaft belts . . . . . .check/adjust

Cooling system . . . . .inspect
Check tightness of hoses, clean radiator, check level EC

Crankcase ventilation
system . . . . .check/tighten
1989-91 only

Fuel lines & hoses . . . . .inspect

Headlight retractors . . . . .lubricate

Intake air hoses . . . . .inspect

Power steering . . . . . . .check level AF3

Windshield & headlight
washers . . . . .check level/aim

Brake & clutch pedal
free play . . . . .check/adjust

Brake system . . . . .inspect
Check pad wear, condition of lines & hoses

Body . . . . .check/lubricate
Check operation and lubricate all locks, hinges & check
rods

Diagnostic system . . . . .check/clear

Heating & ventilation filter . . . . . .replace
1994-95 only

Electrical equipment . . . . .inspect
Check operation of lights, horns, buzzers, wipers,
switches, instruments & power accessories

Handbrake . . . . .check/adjust

Headlights . . . . .check/adjust

Weatherstrips . . . . .clean/lubricate
Remove residue & coat with talcum powder, glycerine,
or other suitable rubber lubricant

Wheel bearings, front . . . . .check/adjust

Seat belts . . . . .inspect
Check condition and operation

Tires .inspect
Check tread wear & inflation pressure

EVERY 24 MONTHS

Brake fluid, 1992 . . . . . . .replace HBH

Engine coolant . . . . .replace EC

EVERY 30 MI—48 KM

Transmission, automatic . . . .change fluid

Air filter element . . . . .replace

Drive belts . . . . .check/adjust

Spark plugs . . . . .replace

EVERY 36 MONTHS

Brake fluid . . . . .replace HBH
1993-94 only. Type 200.

EVERY 45 MI—72 KM

Camshaft belt, 1989-92 . . . . . . .replace
Check & adjust tension after 2.5 mi (4 km)

EVERY 60 MI—96 KM

Transaxle, manual . . . . .change lubricant

Final drive, automatic
transmission . . . . . . .change lubricant

Fuel filter . . . . .replace

Camshaft belt, 1993-95 . . . . . . .replace
Check & adjust tension after 2.5 mi (4 km)

Oxygen sensor . . . . .replace
1989 only

FIRST & SECOND 48 MONTHS; THEN EVERY 24 MONTHS

Air bag system . . . . .inspect

EVERY 72 MONTHS

Tires .replace
Including spare

SEVERE SERVICE

Crankcase—Change oil and filter more frequently

Cooling system—Inspect more frequently

Air filter—Check/replace more frequently

Battery—Check level more frequently

Brakes—Inspect more frequently

Clutch—Check/adjust more frequently

Tires—Inspect more frequently

KEY TO LUBRICANTS

AF3	DEXRON® III Automatic Transmission Fluid
CC	Motor Oil, API Service CC
CD	Motor Oil, API Service CD
EC	Engine Coolant, Phosphate-free Ethylene Glycol Mix with water to obtain proper protection level
GL-4	Gear Oil, API Service GL-4
GL-5	Gear Oil, API Service GL-5
HBH	Hydraulic Brake Fluid, Extra Heavy Duty, DOT 4
SF	Motor Oil, API Service SF
SG	Motor Oil, API Service SG

CRANKCASE . . . . .SF, SF/CD, SG, SG/CD

CAPACITY, Refill[1]:	Liters	Qt
1989-91 944	5.7[2]	6.0[2]
1992-94 968	6.1	6.5
1995 968	7.0	7.4

1 Capacity shown includes filter
2 When refilling, remove dipstick to provide adequate venting

Mineral base oils:
Above 60°F (16°C)	.40
32° to 86°F (0° to 30°C)	.30
14° to 50°F (-10° to 10°C)	.20, 20W-20
Above 14°F (-10°C)	20W-40, 20W-50
Above 5°F (-15°C)	15W-40
-4° to 95°F (-20° to 35°C)	10W-40
-13° to 68°F (-25° to 20°C)	10W-30
-22° to 32°F (-30° to 0°C)	10W, 5W-30
Below 14°F (-10°C)	5W-20

Synthetic base oils:
32° to 105°F (0° to 42°C)	10W-30, 10W-40, 10W-50
All temperatures	5W-30, 5W-40, 5W-50

TRANSMISSION, Automatic AF3

Final drive serviced separately

CAPACITY, Initial Refill[3]:	Liters	Qt
All	2.8	3.0

3 With engine at operating temperature, shift transmission through all gears. Check fluid level in PARK and add fluid as needed

TRANSAXLE, Manual

1989-90	.80W GL-4
1991	.80W GL-4, 75W-90 GL-5
1992-95	.75W-90 GL-5

CAPACITY, Refill:	Liters	Pt
1989-91	2.0[4]	4.2[4]
1992-95	2.8	5.8

4 Proper level may be ¼ in (6mm) below the fill plug, measure quantity and **do not overfill**

FINAL DRIVE, w/AT 75W-90 GL-5

CAPACITY, Refill:	Liters	Pt
1989-91	1.0	2.1
1992-95	0.6	1.2

SERVICE AT TIME OR MILEAGE — WHICHEVER OCCURS FIRST

PEIPM3   PEIPM3

Perform the following maintenance services at the intervals indicated to keep both the vehicle and emission warranties in effect.

MI—MILES IN THOUSANDS
KM—KILOMETERS IN THOUSANDS

AT FIRST 2.5 MI—4 KM
Camshaft drive belt,
1989-93 . . . . .check/adjust

EVERY 12 MO/15 MI—24 KM
Clutch . . . . .inspect
Check disc for wear, check slave cylinder for leaks

Crankcase . . . . .change oil
Check for leaks

Oil filter .replace

Driveshaft boots . . . . .inspect

Exhaust system . . . . .inspect

Final drive, automatic
transmission . . . . .check level
Check for leaks

Front axle & steering . . . . .inspect
Check tightness of components & condition of rubber boots & bushings

Transaxle, manual . . . . .check level
Check for leaks

Transmission, automatic . . . .check level
Check by viewing level in clear plastic reservoir mounted on the transmission case. Level must be between the MIN & MAX markings with engine idling at operating temperature. Check for leaks

Battery . . . . .check/level

Brake fluid reservoir . . .check level HBH

Camshaft timing belt . . . . . .check/adjust

Cooling system . . . . .inspect
Check tightness of hoses, clean radiator, check level EC

Crankcase ventilation system . . . .inspect

Fuel lines & hoses . . . . .inspect

Intake air hoses . . . . .inspect

Power steering . . . . . . .check level AF3
1990-95 check condition of drive belt

Throttle linkage . . . . .inspect
Check for smooth operation and full throttle opening; lubricate as necessary

Windshield & headlight
washers . . . . .check level/aim

Brake & clutch pedal
free play . . . . .check/adjust

Brake system . . . . .inspect
Check pad wear, condition of lines & hoses

Body . . . . .check/lubricate
Check operation and lubricate all locks, hinges and check rods

Diagnosis system . . . . .check/clear

Electrical equipment . . . . .inspect
Check operation of lights, horns, buzzers, wipers, switches, instruments & power accessories

Handbrake . . . . .check/adjust

Headlights . . . . .check/adjust

Limited-slip differential
regulator, 1990-95 . . .check level HBH

Seat belts, 1990-95 . . . . .inspect
Check condition and operation

Tires . . . . .inspect
Check tread wear & inflation pressure, 1990-95 check condition and operation of pressure warning system

Weatherstrips . . . . .clean/lubricate
Remove residue & oat with talcum powder, glycerine, or other suitable rubber lubricant

Wheel bearings, front . . . . .check/adjust

Heating & ventilation filter . . . . .replace
1994-95 only

EVERY 24 MONTHS
Brake fluid, 1989-92 . . . . . .replace HBH

Engine coolant . . . . .replace EC

Limited-slip differential
regulator fluid, 1990-95 . . .replace HBH

1989-93 EVERY 24 MI—40 KM
Transmission, automatic . . . .change fluid

Air filter element . . . . .replace
Replace air pump filter where applicable

Drive belts . . . . .check/adjust
Includes camshaft & balance shaft belts

Drive belt tensioner . . . . . .check/fill SF

Oxygen sensor . . . . .replace

Spark plugs . . . . .replace

1994-95 EVERY 30 MI—48 KM
Air filter element . . . . .replace
Replace air pump filter where applicable

Drive belts . . . . .check/adjust
Includes camshaft & balance shaft belts

Drive belt tensioner . . . . . .check/fill SF

Spark plugs . . . . .replace

EVERY 36 MONTHS
Brake fluid . . . . .inspect HBH
1993-95 only. Type 200.

FIRST & SECOND 48 MONTHS;
THEN EVERY 24 MONTHS
Air bag system . . . . .inspect

EVERY 60 MI—96 KM
Camshaft drive belt . . . . .replace
Check tension after 2.5 MI—4 KM

Final drive, automatic
transmission . . . . . . .change lubricant

Transaxle, manual . . . . .change lubricant

Fuel filter . . . . .replace

Oxygen sensor . . . . .replace
1989 only

EVERY 72 MONTHS
Tires . . . . .replace
Including spare

SEVERE SERVICE
Crankcase—Change oil and filter more frequently

Cooling system—Inspect more frequently

Air filter—Check/replace more frequently

Battery—Check level more frequently

Brakes—Inspect more frequently

Clutch—Check/adjust more frequently

Tires—Inspect more frequently

KEY TO LUBRICANTS

AF3 DEXRON® III Automatic Transmission Fluid

EC Engine Coolant, Phosphate-free Ethylene Glycol
Mix with water to obtain proper protection level

GL-5 Gear Oil, API Service GL-5

HBH Hydraulic Brake Fluid, Extra Heavy Duty, DOT 4 Type 200

SF Motor Oil, API Service SF

SG Motor Oil, API Service SG

CRANKCASE . . . . .SF, SG

CAPACITY, Refill:	Liters	Qt
All models	7.1	7.5

Capacity shown is without filter. When replacing filter, additional oil may be needed
Mineral base oils:
Above 60°F (16°C) 40
32° to 86°F (0° to 30°C) 30
14° to 50°F (-10° to 10°C) 20, 20W-20
Above 14°F (-10°C) 20W-40, 20W-50
Above 5°F (-15°C) 15W-40, 15W-50
32° to 100°F (0° to 38°C) 10W-40
-13° to 68°F (-25° to 20°C) 10W-30
-22° to 32°F (-30° to 0°C) 10W, 5W-30
Below 14°F (-10°C) 5W-20
Synthetic base oils:
32° to 105°F (0° to 42°C) 10W-30, 10W-40,
10W-50
All temperatures 5W-30, 5W-40, 5W-50

TRANSMISSION, Automatic AF3
Final drive serviced separately

CAPACITY, Initial Refill[1]:	Liters	Qt
1989-92	5.7	6.0
1993-95	7.6	8.0

1 With engine at operating temperature, shift transmission through all gears. Check fluid level in PARK and add fluid as needed

TRANSAXLE, Manual 75W-90 **GL-5**

CAPACITY, Refill:	Liters	Pt
1989-92	4.4	9.4
1993-95	4.7	10.0

FINAL DRIVE, w/AT 75W-90 **GL-5**

CAPACITY, Refill:	Liters	Pt
1989-92	2.8	6.0
1993-95	1.9	4.0

PORSCHE
1997-99 Boxster

SERVICE AT TIME OR MILEAGE — WHICHEVER OCCURS FIRST

Perform the following maintenance services at the intervals indicated to keep both the vehicle and emission warranties in effect.

MI—MILES IN THOUSANDS
KM—KILOMETERS IN THOUSANDS

EVERY 12 MO/15 MI—24 KM

Clutch pedal free play . . . . .check/adjust

Crankcase . . . . .change oil
Inspect for leakage

Cooling system . . . . .inspect
Service as required

Driveshaft boots . . . . .inspect

Front axle, steering
  & suspension . . . . .inspect
Check tightness of components & condition of rubber boots & bushings

Transaxle . . . . .check level
Inspect for leakage

Air filter element . . . . .check

Brake fluid reservoir . . .check level **HBH**

Onboard diagnostic system . .check/clear

Power steering . . . . .check level **PS**

Windshield & headlight
  washers . . . . .check level

Body . . . . .check/lubricate
Check operation of all locks & hinges, lubricate door hinges & check rods

Brake system . . . . .inspect
Check pad wear, condition of lines & hoses, check parking brake

Electrical equipment . . . . .inspect
Check operation of lights, horns, buzzers, wipers, switches, instruments & power accessories

Interior air filter . . . . .replace

Headlights . . . . .check/adjust

Tires . . . . .inspect/adjust
Check tread wear & inflation pressure, including spare

EVERY 24 MONTHS

Brake fluid . . . . .replace **HBH**

EVERY 30 MI—48 KM

Oil filters . . . . .replace

Air filter element . . . . .replace

Drive belts . . . . .check/adjust

Spark plugs . . . . .replace

FIRST & SECOND 48 MONTHS; THEN EVERY 24 MONTHS

Air bag system . . . . .inspect

Mounts for engine, transmission
  & drivetrain . . . . .inspect

EVERY 60 MI—96 KM

Drive belts . . . . .replace

Transaxle, manual . . . .change lubricant

Fuel filter . . . . .replace

EVERY 90 MI—144 KM

Manual Transmission . .change lubricant
Requires special tool: 12 point 17mm socket for drain plug. Part No. T14/1-16 TP

Automatic Transmission .change lubricant
Replace filter

Final drive, automatic
  transmission . . . . . . .change lubricant

EVERY 72 MONTHS

Tires . . . . .replace
Including spare

SEVERE SERVICE

Crankcase—Change oil and filter more frequently

Air filter—Check/replace every 15 mi (24 km)

Battery—Check level more frequently

Brakes—Inspect more frequently

Clutch—Check/adjust more frequently

Tires—Inspect more frequently

KEY TO LUBRICANTS

GF-1   Motor Oil, Meeting ILSAC GF-1 (API Starburst)

GL-5   Gear Oil, API Service GL-5

HBH   Hydraulic Brake Fluid, use only Porsche brake fluid

PS   Power Steering Fluid Pentosin CHF 11S

SH   Motor Oil, API Service SH

SLF   Special Lubricant–Fluid
Auto Trans.: Part No. 999 917 547 00
ESSO LT 71141

CRANKCASE . . . .**SH, GF-1**
Synthetics preferred

CAPACITY, Refill:	Liters	Qt
1997-98	8.2	8.7
1999	8.7	9.2

Includes filter
Mineral base oils:
Above 50°F (10°C) 15W-40, 20W-40, 20W-50
Below 50°F (10°C) 15W-40, 10W-40, 10W-30
Below 14°F (-10°C) 10W-30, 5W-30
Synthetic base oils:
Above 50°F (10°C) 10W-40, 15W-40, 15W-50
Below 14°F (-10°C) . . .5W-30, 10W-30, 10W-40

TRANSMISSION, Automatic . . . .**SLF**[4]
Final drive serviced separately
4 Porsche Part No. 999 917 547 00

CAPACITY, Initial Refill[3]:	Liters	Qt
All	3.5	3.7

2 With engine at operating temperature, shift transmission through all gears. Check fluid level in PARK and add fluid as needed

---

TRANSAXLE, Manual . . . . .**75W-90 GL-5**[3]
Includes differential
Requires special tool: 12 point 17mm socket for drain plug. Part No. T14/1-16 TP

CAPACITY, Refill:	Liters	Pt
All	2.2	4.8

3 Porsche Part No. N 052 911 S0 preferred
4 Proper level may be 1/4 in (6mm) below the fill plug, measure quantity and **do not overfill**

FINAL DRIVE, Rear w/AT . . . .**75W-90 GL-5**[4]

CAPACITY, Refill:	Liters	Pt
All	0.8	1.7

4 Porsche Part No. 999 917 545 00 preferred

SERVICE LOCATIONS — ENGINE AND CHASSIS

SBIDP-1

HOOD RELEASE: Inside

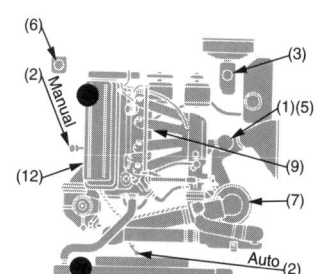

1989-93 900
4-cyl. 1985cc 16-Valve
(Turbo version shown)
1991-93 900
4-cyl. 2119cc

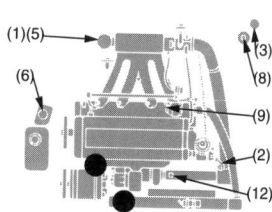

1989-90 9000
4-cyl. 1985cc 16-Valve
(Turbo version shown)

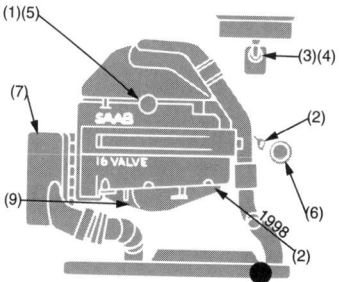

1994-99 900, 9-3
4-cyl. 1985cc Turbo

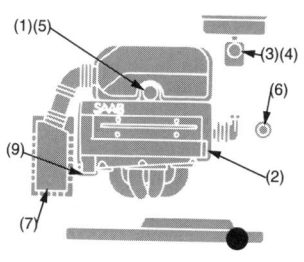

1994-98 900
4-cyl. 2290cc

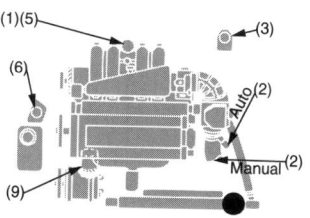

1990-99 9000, 9-5
4-cyl. 2290cc
(Non-Turbo version shown)

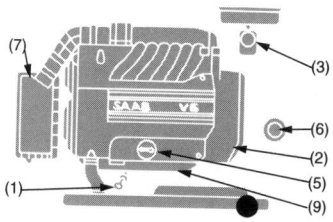

1994-97 900
V6 2498cc

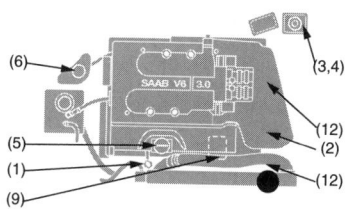

1995-99 9000, 9-5
V6 2962cc

0 FITTINGS
0 PLUGS

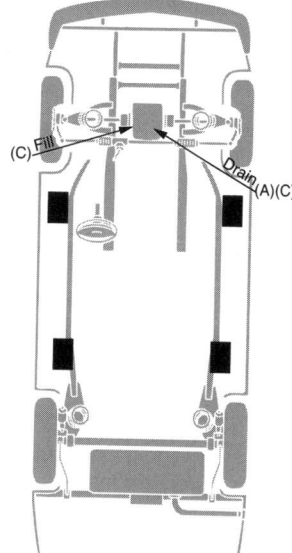

1989-93
900

0 FITTINGS
0 PLUGS

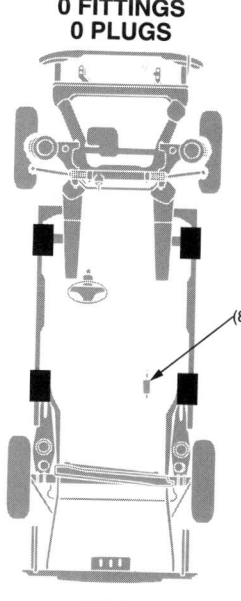

1994-98
900
1989-98
9000
1999
9-3, 9-5

(1) Crankcase dipstick
(2) Transmission dipstick
(3) Brake fluid reservoir
(4) Clutch fluid reservoir
(5) Oil fill cap
(6) Power steering
      reservoir

(7) Air filter
(8) Fuel filter
(9) Oil filter
(10) PCV filter
(11) EGR valve
(12) Oxygen sensor
(13) PCV valve

■ Lift adapter position

● Cooling system drain

(A) Manual transmission/transaxle,
    drain & fill
(B) Transfer case, NOT USED

(C) Automatic transaxle final drive,
    drain & fill
(D) Differential, NOT USED

SERVICE AT TIME OR MILEAGE — WHICHEVER OCCURS FIRST

SBIPM2

SBIPM2

KEY TO LUBRICANTS

W   SERVICE TO MAINTAIN EMISSION WARRANTY

AF3	DEXRON®-III Automatic Transmission Fluid
BL	Brake Lubricant Saab Part No. 30 08 612
CD	Motor Oil, API Service CD
EC	Ethylene Glycol Coolant Mix with water to desired freeze protection
FA	Automatic Transmission Fluid, Type F
GL-4	Gear Oil, API Service GL-4
GL-5	Gear Oil, API Service GL-5
HB	Hydraulic Brake Fluid, Extra Heavy Duty, DOT 4
MO	Motor Oil
PS	Power Steering Fluid Saab Part No. (45) 30 09 800 or GM 1050017
SF	Motor Oil, API Service SF
SG	Motor Oil, API Service SG

MI—MILES IN THOUSANDS
KM—KILOMETERS IN THOUSANDS

EVERY 12 MO/7.5 MI—12.5 KM

W Crankcase . . . . .change oil

W Oil filter . . . . .replace

Brake system . . . . .inspect
Check thickness of brake pads, condition of lines & hoses, tightness of master cylinder & calipers

Chassis .inspect
Check undercarriage for damage, drive shaft boots, ball joint & tie rod dust seals

Exhaust system . . . . .inspect

Final drive . . . . .check level
900 w/automatic transmission only

Transmission, manual . . . . .check level

Transmission, automatic . . . .check level

Battery .inspect
Check level, clean & tighten terminals, lubricate with petroleum jelly

Brake booster . . . . .inspect
Check hoses & connections

Brake/clutch fluid . . . . . .check level **HB**

Cooling system . . . . .inspect **EC**
Check condition & tightness of hoses, level & concentration

Fuel injection system . . . . .inspect
Check hoses, wiring, components & connections for leakage, wear or damage

Power steering . . . . .check level **PS**

Body 1990 . . . . .check/lubricate
Door stops, hinges, latches, locks, sunroof rails

Electrical equipment . . . . .inspect
Check function of all lights, buzzers, heater fan, horn, cooling fans & power accessories

Hand brake . . . . .check/adjust

Tires . . . . .inspect
Check treadwear & inflation pressure, rotate 1989 only

Toe-in . . . . .check/adjust

EVERY 15 MI—25 KM

Cooling system . . . . .change coolant **EC**
If using Saab approved coolant, increase interval to 30 mi (50 km)

1991,
FIRST 24 MO/30 MI—50 KM;
THEN EVERY 12 MONTHS
1989-90, EVERY 30 MI—50 KM

Drive belts . . . . .check/adjust

Ignition wires 1989 . . . . .inspect
Clean & check secondary leads for cuts, burns, or abrasions

EVERY 30 MI—50 KM

Cooling system . . . . .change coolant **EC**
If not using Saab approved coolant, reduce interval to 15 mi (25 km)

1991,
EVERY 24 MO/30 MI—50 KM
1989-90, EVERY 30 MI—50 KM

Brake fluid . . . . .replace **HB**

EVERY 30 MI—50 KM

Brake caliper slides . . . . . .lubricate **BL**

Front suspension . . . . .inspect
Check ball joints & tie rod ends for wear

W Air filter element . . . . .replace

Fuel lines . . . . .inspect

W Fuel filter . . . . .replace

W Overpressure safety switch . . . . .check
Turbocharged engines only. Not required for Calif. warranty

W Oxygen sensor . . . . .replace

W Spark plugs . . . . .replace

Throttle linkage 1989 . . . . .lubricate **MO**

Transmission, automatic . . . .change fluid

Body . . . . .lubricate
Door stops, hinges, latches, locks, sunroof rails, convertible top mechanism

Headlights . . . . .check/adjust

Shock absorbers . . . . .check

Ventilation filter . . . . .replace
9000 all, 900 w/o AC only

Wheel alignment . . . . .check/adjust

1989-90, EVERY 60 MI—100 KM
1991, FIRST 60 MO/60 MI—100 KM;
THEN EVERY 12 MONTHS

W Crankcase ventilation . . . . .inspect
Not required for Calif. warranty

W Evaporative emissions system . . .inspect
Check canister, filler cap, lines, hoses & connections for leaks, damage & tightness
Not required for Calif. warranty

EVERY 60 MI—100 KM

W Charcoal canister . . . . .replace

W Distributor cap & rotor . . . . .replace
Not required for Calif. warrant

W Ignition wires . . . . .inspect
Check resistance of secondary wiring
Not required for Calif. warranty

Ignition timing . . . . .check/adjust
1989 Turbo only, 1991 900 only

W Oxygen sensor . . . . .replace
1989 all engines, lubricate threads with anti-seize compound

SEVERE SERVICE

Crankcase—Change oil & filter at half of specified interval

Spark plugs—Replace every 15 mi (25 km)

Automatic transmission—Change fluid every 15 mi (25 km)

CRANKCASE . . . . .SF/CD, SG[1]

[1] Preferred

CAPACITY, Refill[2]:	Liters	Qt
2.0L DOHC	4.0	4.2
Turbo[3]	4.3	4.5
2.1L	4.0	4.2
2.3L, 1989-90	4.3	4.5
2.3L, 1991	4.7	5.0

[2] Capacity shown includes filter
[3] If oil cooler is drained add 0.5L (0.5 qt)

Above 0°F (-18°C)	10W-30[4]
Below 0°F (-18°C)	5W-30[5]

[4] In extremely hot climates 10W-40, 15W-40, 15W-50 (only if API service classification **SF/CD**, **SG** is met)
[5] Must be fully or semisynthetic oil

TRANSMISSION, Automatic

900 3-speed	.FA
9000 4-speed	.AF3

Does not include 3-speed final drive

CAPACITY, Total Fill[6]	Liters	Qt
900 3-speed	8.0	8.5
9000 4-speed	8.2	8.6

[6] Total capacity including torque converter is shown, when servicing, use less fluid than specified

TRANSAXLE,
Manual . . . . . . .10W-30, 10W-40 **SF**, **SG**[7]

CAPACITY, Refill:	Liters	Pt
All	2.5	5.3

[7] Alternate 900 Series, 75W **GL-4/GL-5**

FINAL DRIVE,
900 w/AT . .10W-30 **SG**, 80W **GL-4**, **GL-5**

CAPACITY, Refill:	Liters	Pt
900	1.3	2.6

SAAB
1992-99 All Models

CHEK-CHART

SERVICE AT TIME OR MILEAGE — WHICHEVER OCCURS FIRST

SBIPM3   SBIPM3

W   SERVICE TO MAINTAIN EMISSION WARRANTY

MI—MILES IN THOUSANDS
KM—KILOMETERS IN THOUSANDS

1999 FIRST 1 MI—1.6 KM;
1992-99 FIRST 5 MI—8 KM;
THEN EVERY 12 MO/10 MI—16 KM

W Crankcase . . . . .change oil
W Oil filter .replace
Brake system . . . . .inspect
Check thickness of brake pads, condition of lines & hoses, tightness of master cylinder & calipers
Chassis . . . . .inspect
Check undercarriage for damage, drive shaft boots, ball joint & tie rod dust seals, retighten suspension mounting points at first interval only
Headlights & foglights,
  1994-99 . . . . .check/adjust
Exhaust system . . . . .inspect
Fuel system,
  1994-99 9000, 9-5 . . . . .inspect
Final drive . . . . .check level
1992-94 900 w/automatic transmission only
Transmission,
  manual, 1992-99 . . . . .check level
Transmission, automatic . . . .check level
9000, 9-5, change fluid & filter at first interval only
Battery . . . . .inspect
Check level, clean & tighten terminals, lubricate with petroleum jelly
Idle speed, 1992-95 . . . . .check
9000 with traction control
Brake booster . . . . .inspect
Check hoses & connections
Brake/clutch fluid . . . . . .check level HB
1993 9000 w/TCS & manual transmission, check with ignition on
Cooling system . . . . .inspect EC
Check condition & tightness of hoses, cap level & concentration
Ventilation air filter 900 . . . . .replace
Drive belts & tensioner . . . . .inspect
Power steering . . . . .check level PS
Windshield wipers & washers . . . .inspect
Electrical equipment . . . . .inspect
Check function of all lights, buzzers, heater fan, horn, cooling fans & power accessories
Parking brake . . . . .check/adjust
Body 900, 9-3, 9-5 . . . . .lubricate
Door stops, hinges, latches, locks, sunroof rails, convertible top mechanism
Airbag system . . . . .check
Also check SRS warning lamp & safety belts
Tires . . . . .inspect
Check treadwear & inflation pressure, rotate front to rear
Check spare pressure

FIRST 30 MI—48 KM;
THEN EVERY 10 MI—16 KM
Shock absorbers, 1994-99 . . . . . .check

EVERY 15 MI—25 KM
Cooling system . . . . .change coolant EC
If using Saab approved coolant; increase interval to 30 mi (50 km)

FIRST 15—MI 24 KM;
THEN EVERY 20 MI—32 KM
Transmission, manual
  1995-98 900 . . . . .check level
Transmission, automatic
  1995-98 900 . . . . .check level

FIRST 24 MO/30 MI 56 KM;
THEN EVERY 24 MO/30 MI—50 KM
Brake fluid . . . . .replace HB

FIRST 36 MO/30 MI—48 KM;
THEN EVERY 36 MO/30 MI—48 KM
Cooling system . . . . .change coolant EC
If not using Saab approved coolant, reduce interval to 15 mi (25 km)

FIRST 30 MI—48 KM;
THEN EVERY 30 MI—48 KM
Front suspension 1992-93 . . . . . .inspect
Check ball joints & tie rod ends for wear
W Air filter element . . . . .replace
Fuel lines 900, 9-3 . . . . .inspect
W Spark plugs . . . . .replace
Camshaft drive belt, V6 . . . . . . .replace
1995-96
Transmission,
  automatic . . . . .change fluid
900, 1992-93 clean filter, 9000 replace filter
Transmission,
  manual, 1999 . . . . .check level
Body 9000 . . . . .lubricate
Door stops, hinges, latches, locks, sunroof rails, convertible top mechanism
Headlights & foglights
  1992-93 . . . . .check/adjust
Shock absorbers 1992-93 . . . . . . .check
Ventilation filter . . . . .replace
9000, 9-3, 9-5
Wheel alignment . . . . .check/adjust
Toe-in only

FIRST 60 MI—96 KM;
THEN EVERY 30 MI—48 KM
W Crankcase ventilation . . . . .inspect
W Evaporative emissions system . . .inspect
Check canister, filler cap, lines, hoses & connections for leaks, damage & tightness
Ignition wires 900 . . . . .inspect

FIRST 60 MI—96 KM;
THEN EVERY 60 MI—96 KM
W Fuel filter . . . . .replace
W Distributor cap & rotor, 900 . . . . .inspect
Drive belts, 9000, 9-3, 9-5 . . . . .replace
Check tensioner
Transmission, automatic . . . .change fluid
1994-98 900, 1999 9-3
Ventilation air absorptive filer . . . .replace
9-5

EVERY 95 MI—152 KM
Camshaft drive belt, V6 . . . . . . .replace
1994 900

SEVERE SERVICE
Crankcase—Change oil & filter at half of specified interval

Air cleaner element—Change more frequently

Spark plugs—Replace every 15 mi (25 km)

Automatic transmission—Change fluid first 20 mi (32 km), then every 30 mi (50 km); 9000, replace filter every 30 mi (50 km)

KEY TO LUBRICANTS

AF3	DEXRON®-III Automatic Transmission Fluid
BL	Brake Lubricant Saab Part No. 30 08 612
CC	Motor Oil, API Service CC
CD	Motor Oil, API Service CD
EC	Ethylene Glycol Coolant Mix with water to desired freeze protection
FA	Automatic Transmission Fluid, Type F
GF-1	Motor Oil API Service GF-1
GL-4	Gear Oil, API Service GL-4
GL-5	Gear Oil, API Service GL-5
HB	Hydraulic Brake Fluid, Extra Heavy Duty, DOT 4
PS	Power Steering Fluid 1992-97 Saab Part No. (45) 30 09 800, 315 161224 or GM 1050017 or Saab 1890 or Texaco 1890 1998-99 CHF 11S Part No. 3032380
SF	Motor Oil, API Service SF
SG	Motor Oil, API Service SG
SH	Motor Oil, API Service SH
SLF	Special Lubricant — Fluid Saab Part No. 8748733

CRANKCASE . . . . .SF/CD, SG, SH[1], GF-1[1]
[1] Preferred

CAPACITY, Refill[2]:	Liters	Qt
2.0L DOHC	4.0	4.2
Turbo[3], 1992-93	4.3	4.5
Turbo, 1994-99	4.0	4.2
2.1L	4.0	4.2
2.3L, 9000	4.7	5.0
Others	4.0	4.2
2.5L	4.5	4.7
3.0L	4.5	4.6
All temperatures	.5W-30[4],	

5W-40[4], 10W-30[5], 10W-40[6]

[2] Capacity shown includes filter
[3] If oil cooler is drained add 0.5L (0.5 qt)
[4] Must be fully or semisynthetic oil
[5] Preferred
[6] In extremely hot climates, 15W-40, 15W-50, 20W-50 (only if API service classification SF/CD, SG, SH, GF-1 is met)

TRANSMISSION, Automatic
1992-93 900 3-speed . . . . .FA
All others AF3
Does not include 3-speed final drive
Do not use synthetic oil

CAPACITY:	Liters	Qt
9-3	3.2[8]	3.4[8]
9-5	3.5[8]	3.7[8]
900 3-speed	8.0[7]	8.5[7]
900 4-speed	3.3[8]	3.4[8]
9000 4-speed	3.0[8]	3.2[8]

[7] Total capacity including torque converter and oil cooler is shown, when refilling, use less fluid than specified
[8] Initial refill capacity

TRANSAXLE, Manual
1992-97 . . . . .10W-30, 10W-40 SF,
                 SF/CC, SF/CD, SG, SH[9], GF-1
1998-99 . . . . .SLF[10]
Saab Part No. 8748733

CAPACITY, Refill:	Liters	Pt
All 1992-93	2.5	5.3
All 1994-99 (Dry fill)	1.8	3.8
All 1999	1.5	3.2

[9] 1992-93 Alternate 900 Series, 75W GL-4/GL-5
[10] May use synthetic AF3 when SLF is not available only for "topping off."

FINAL DRIVE, 1992-93 900
w/AT . . . . . .10W-30 SG, 80W GL-4-GL-5

CAPACITY, Refill:	Liters	Pt
All	1.3	2.6

Copyright 2000 by Chek-Chart Publications

SATURN
1991-2000 All Models

SERVICE AT TIME OR MILEAGE — WHICHEVER OCCURS FIRST

HOOD RELEASE: Inside

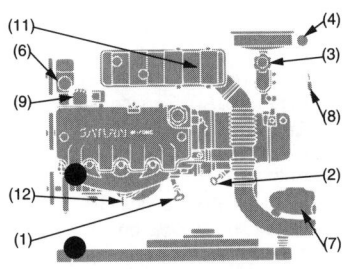

1.9L SOHC
1991-94 Code 9
1995-00 Code 8

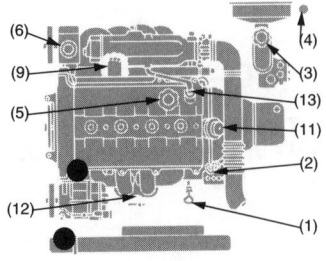

1991-00
1.9L DOHC
Code 7

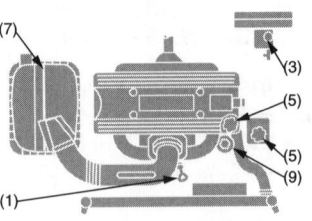

2000
2.2L Code F

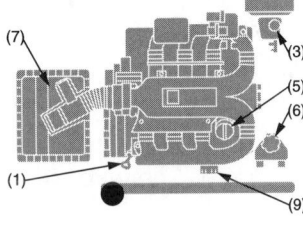

2000
3.0L Code R

(1) Crankcase dipstick
(2) Transmission dipstick
(3) Brake fluid reservoir
(4) Clutch fluid reservoir
(5) Oil fill cap
(6) Power steering reservoir
(7) Air filter
(8) Fuel filter
(9) Oil filter
(10) PCV filter
(11) EGR valve
(12) Oxygen sensor
(13) PCV valve

0 FITTINGS
0 PLUGS

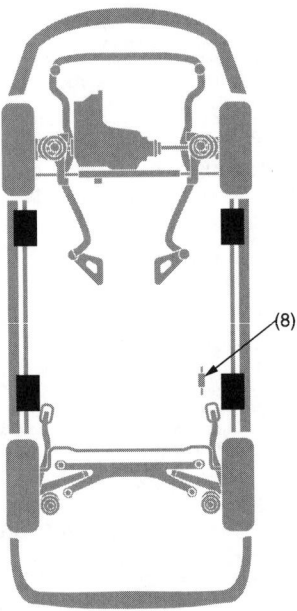

2000
L-Series

0 FITTINGS
0 PLUGS

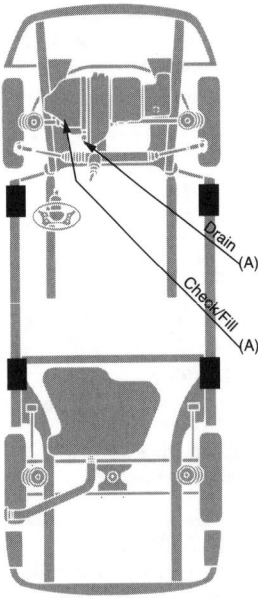

1991-2000
S-Series

(A) Manual transmission/transaxle,
    drain & fill

● Cooling system drain

■ Lift adapter position

CAUTION: On front wheel drive vehicles, the center of gravity is farther forward than on rear wheel drive vehicles. When removing major components from the rear of the vehicle while it is on a hoist, the vehicle must be supported in a manner to prevent it from tipping forward.

SERVICE AT TIME OR MILEAGE — WHICHEVER OCCURS FIRST

SNPM2   SNPM2

Perform the following scheduled maintenance service at the intervals indicated to keep the vehicle warranties in effect.

W   SERVICE TO MAINTAIN EMISSION WARRANTY

MI—MILES IN THOUSANDS
KM—KILOMETERS IN THOUSANDS

FIRST 6 MI—10 KM
Transaxle, manual . . . . . . .change fluid
1991-99

Tires/wheels . . . . .inspect/rotate
Then every 12 mi (20 km)

Brake system . . . . .inspect
Linings, hoses, lines, rotors, drums, calipers
Then every 12 mi—20 km

EVERY 6 MO/6 MI—10 KM
Axle boots . . . . .inspect

W Crankcase, 1991-99 . . .change oil & filter

W Crankcase, 2000 . . . .change oil & filter
Or when the "CHANGE OIL SOON" light comes on

Chassis . . . . .lubricate **MO**
Hood, door hinges, headlight doors, hood latch, rear folding seat, trunk lid hinge. Also, lubricate hood release pawl, door hold-open check link, sunroof track and power passive restraint track with Lubriplate®70.

Exhaust system and shields . . . . .inspect

Parking brake . . . . .inspect

Suspension . . . . .inspect
Axle boots, bushings, ball joint seals

Brake master cylinder . . .check level **HB**

Clutch master cylinder . . .check level **HB**

Power steering . . . . .check level

Shift linkage . . . . .lubricate **LB**

Throttle cable linkage . . . . .inspect

Transaxle, manual,
    and automatic . . . . .check level

EVERY 12 MO
Chassis 1991-92 . . . . .lubricate **MO**
Hood, door hinges, headlight doors, hood latch, rear folding seat, trunk lid hinge. Also, lubricate hood release pawl, door hold-open check link, sunroof track, and power passive restraint track with Lubriplate®70.

EVERY 12 MO/12 MI—20 KM
Passenger compartment
    air filter . . . . .replace
L-Series

EVERY 12 MO/18 MI—30 KM
Cooling system hoses 1992-00 . . .inspect

Drive belts 1992-00 . . . . .inspect

EVERY 30 MI—50 KM
Transaxle,
    automatic, 1991-99 . . . . . .change fluid
1994-99 change filter

W Spark plugs . . . . .replace
S-Series

FIRST 30 MI—50 KM;
THEN EVERY 60 MI—100 KM
Automatic transaxle pressure
    filter . . . . .replace
1991-93

EVERY 24 MO/30 MI—50 KM
Cooling system hoses 1991 . . . . .inspect

Drive belts 1991 . . . . .inspect

EGR system 1991 . . . . .inspect

W Fuel system . . . . .inspect
Tank, pipe/hose, cap

W Vacuum lines & hoses . . . . .inspect

EVERY 36 MO/30 MI—50 KM
W Air cleaner element . . . . .replace

Throttle body, 1995 . . . . .inspect

EVERY 36 MO/36 MI—60 KM
W Cooling system,
    1991-96 . . . . .change coolant **EC**
Replace green coolant with green coolant and add 2 coolant pellets Part No. 21007224; replace orange coolant with orange coolant. Use 50% concentration for -34°F (-37°C) protection

Radiator cap . . . . .check

EVERY 60 MO/100 MI—160 KM
W Cooling system,
    1997-00 . . . . .change coolant **EC**
Use 50% concentration for -34°F (-37°C) protection. Note. Adding/using silicated coolant will require coolant change every 24 mo/30 mi (50 km).

EVERY 48 MO/60 MI—100 KM
Fuel filter . . . . .replace

EVERY 100 MI—160 KM
W Spark plugs, 3.0L engine . . . . . .replace

Timing belt, 3.0L engine . . . . . . .replace

EVERY 150 MI—140 KM
W Spark plugs, 2.2L engine . . . . . .replace

SEVERE SERVICE
W Crankcase—Change oil & oil filter every 3 mo/3 mi (5 km) when operating in: below freezing, dusty, humid weather; police, trailer towing service; or commercial applications.

Transaxle, automatic—Change fluid every 2000 S-Series, 30 mi (50 km); 2000 L-Series, 50 mi (83 km).

KEY TO LUBRICANTS

AF3	DEXRON®-III Automatic Transmission Fluid
API★	Motor Oil certified by the American Petroleum Institute (Starburst Symbol)
EC	Ethylene Glycol Non-Phosphate Coolant
	1991-95, use green coolant. 1996, replace green coolant with green coolant; replace orange coolant (DEX-COOL®) GM Spec. 6277M with orange coolant. 1997-00, DEX-COOL® only
HB	Hydraulic Brake Fluid DOT 3
LB	Chassis Grease, NLGI Category LB
MO	Motor Oil
PS	Power Steering Fluid
	GM Part No. 1052884, or Saturn Part No. 21007583
SG	Motor Oil, API Service SG
	Use Energy Conserving II Oils.
SH	Motor Oil, API Service SH
	Use Energy Conserving II Oils.
SLF	S-Series, Part No. 21005966 L-Series, Part No. 21018899

CRANKCASE
1991-94 . . . . .SG, SH, API★
1995-00 . . . . .API★

CAPACITY, Refill:	Liters	Qt
1.9L	3.8	4.0
2.2L, 3.0L	4.7	5.0

Capacity shown is with filter
Above 40°F (4°C) 1991-95 . . . . .30[1]
Above 0°F (-18°C) 1991-95 . . . . .10W-30
Above 20°F (-7°C) 1996-00 . . . . .10W-30
All temperatures . . . . .5W-30[2]

1 Use only if other viscosities are not available.
2 Preferred.

TRANSAXLE, Automatic AF3

CAPACITY, Initial Refill[3]:	Liters	Qt
1991-93	3.3[4]	3.5[4]
1994-00, S-Series	4.0[4]	4.2[4]
2000, L-Series	6.5	6.9

3 With the engine at operating temperature, shift transmission through all gears. Let engine slow idle in PARK for 3 minutes or more. Check fluid level and add fluid as needed.
4 With pressure filter change.

TRANSAXLE, Manual . . . . .SLF
S-Series may also use AF3

CAPACITY, Refill:	Liters	Pt
S-Series	2.5	5.2
L-Series	1.9	4.0

SERVICE LOCATIONS — ENGINE AND CHASSIS

HOOD RELEASE: Inside

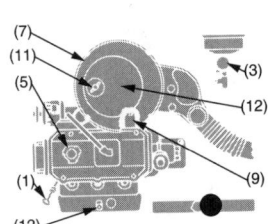

1989-92
3-cyl. 1189cc 2V Justy

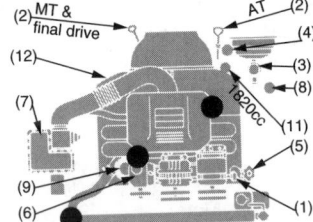

1990-94
3-cyl. 1189cc FI Justy

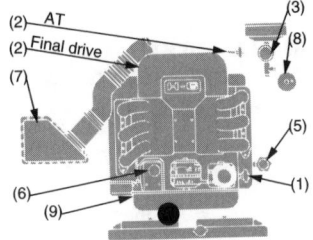

1989-94
4-cyl. 1781cc OHC FI
3 & 4 dr., Wagon, Loyale, XT

1989-90
4-cyl. 1781cc OHC Turbo
3 & 4 dr., Wagon, Loyale, XT

1993-97 4-cyl. 1820cc Impreza
1990-99 4-cyl. 2212cc OHC
Impreza, Legacy
(Non-Turbo version shown)
1996-99
4-cyl. 2457cc Legacy, Forester,
Impreza

1989
6-cyl. 2672cc XT

1992-97
6-cyl. 3318cc SVX

(1) Crankcase dipstick
(2) Transmission dipstick
(3) Brake fluid reservoir
(4) Clutch fluid reservoir
(5) Oil fill cap
(6) Power steering reservoir
(7) Air filter

(8) Fuel filter
(9) Oil filter
(10) PCV filter
(11) EGR valve
(12) Oxygen sensor
(13) PCV valve

(A) Manual transmission/transaxle, drain & fill
(B) Transfer case, NOT USED
(C) Automatic transaxle final drive, drain & fill
(D) Differential, drain & fill

● Cooling system drain   ■ Lift adapter position

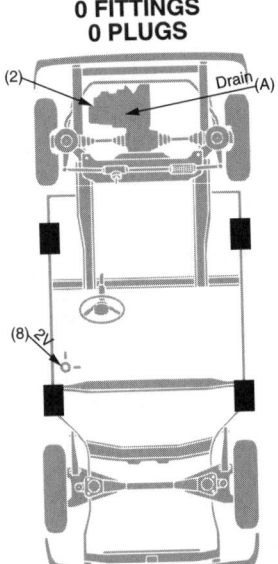

0 FITTINGS
0 PLUGS

1989-94 2WD Justy

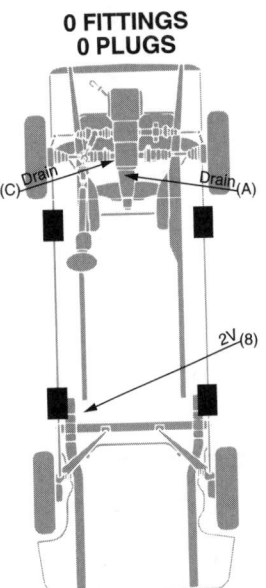

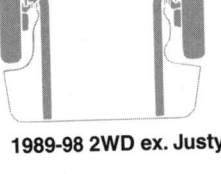

0 FITTINGS
0 PLUGS

1989-98 2WD ex. Justy

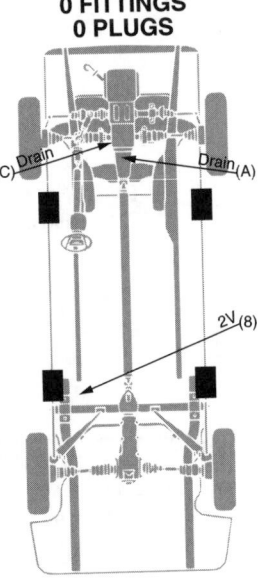

0 FITTINGS
0 PLUGS

1989-99 4WD ex. Justy

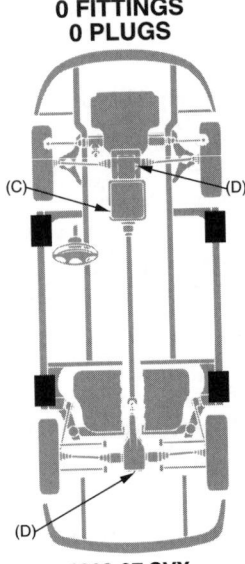

0 FITTINGS
0 PLUGS

1992-97 SVX

CAUTION: On front wheel drive vehicles, the center of gravity is farther forward than on rear wheel drive vehicles. When removing major components from the rear of the vehicle while it is on a hoist, the vehicle must be supported in a manner to prevent it from tipping forward.

SERVICE AT TIME OR MILEAGE — WHICHEVER OCCURS FIRST

SUIPM3   SUIPM3

Perform the following maintenance services at the intervals indicated to keep the vehicle warranties in effect.
W   SERVICE TO MAINTAIN EMISSION WARRANTY

MI—MILES IN THOUSANDS
KM—KILOMETERS IN THOUSANDS

FIRST 3 MO/3 MI—4.8 KM

W Crankcase . . . . .change oil

Oil filter . . . . .replace

EVERY 7.5 MO/7.5 MI—12 KM

W Crankcase . . . . .change oil

W Oil filter . . . . .replace
1989 6-cyl. & 4-cyl. Non-Turbo, initial service, then every other oil change

Brake pads & discs . . . . .inspect
Hatchback

Front & rear axle boots . . . . .inspect
Hatchback

EVERY 15 MO/15 MI—24 KM

Brake system . . . . .inspect
Check pads & discs, & operation of handbrake & servo system. Lubricate park brake lever of front disc caliper

Clutch & hill-holder
   system ex. SVX . . . . . . .inspect/adjust

Suspension & steering . . . . .inspect

W Cooling system . . . . .inspect EC

Power steering . . . . .check level
6-cyl. 2672cc PS, all others AF3

W Valve clearance . . . . .inspect/adjust
Justy engines only

Body . . . . .lubricate MO
Hinges, door locks, hood & trunk lid, pedal assembly

EVERY 30 MO/30 MI—48 KM

Brake drums & lining . . . . .inspect

Brake fluid . . . . .replace HB

Differential, front & rear . . . . . . .inspect

Transmission, automatic . . . .check level

W Air & crankcase filter elements . . .replace

W Choke mechanism . . . . .lubricate

W Cooling system . . . . .change coolant EC
Inspect hoses & connections

Drive belts . . . . .inspect
1990-93 ex. Justy also inspect camshaft belt

W Fuel filter . . . . .replace
Inspect hoses & connections

W Spark plugs . . . . .replace

Headlight aiming . . . . .check/adjust

EVERY 60 MO/60 MI—96 KM

W Drive belts . . . . .replace
Also replace camshaft belt

Wheel bearings
   front & rear . . . . . .inspect/repack WB

EVERY 120 MONTHS
Airbag system . . . . .inspect

SEVERE SERVICE

Crankcase—Change oil every 3 mo/3.75 mi (6 km), change filter at every other oil change

Brake fluid—Replace every 15 mo/15 mi (24 km)

Brake linings—Inspect every 7.5 mo/7.5 mi (12 km)

Differentials, all—Change fluid every 30 mi (48 km)

Front & rear axle boots—Inspect every 7.5 mo/7.5 mi (12 km)

Fuel filter—Replace as needed

Steering & suspension—Inspect every 7.5 mo/7.5 mi (12 km)

Transmission, automatic—Change fluid every 15 mi (24 km)

Transmission, manual all—Change fluid every 30 mi (48 km)

KEY TO LUBRICANTS
See inside cover

CRANKCASE . . . . . .SF, SG, SH, SJ, GF-1

CAPACITY, Refill[1]:	Liters	Qt
3-cyl. 1189cc	2.8	3.0
4-cyl.	3.5	3.7
1781cc	4.0	4.2
1820cc	4.0	4.2
2212cc: 1990-93	4.5	4.8
6-cyl. 2672cc, 1989-91	5.0	5.3
3318cc	6.0	6.3

1 Capacity shown is without filter. When replacing filter, additional oil may be needed.

Warm climate & H.D. applications 30, 40,
          10W-50, 20W-40, 20W-50
-5° to 95°F (-21° to 35°C) 10W-30, 10W-40
Below 32°F (0°C) . . . . .5W-30[2]

2 Not recommended for sustained high-speed driving

TRANSMISSION, Automatic AF3
Does not include front differential.

CAPACITY, Initial Refill[3]:	Liters	Qt
ECVT 2WD	1.8	1.9
4WD	1.9	2.0
All Others	2.5	2.6

3 With engine at operating temperature, shift transmission through all gears. Check fluid level in PARK and add fluid as needed

TRANSAXLE, Manual
Justy . . . . .75W-80 GL-5[4]
All others . . . . .75W-80 GL-5[5]
All Models, Above 30°F (0°C), 90; above -20°F (-30°C), 85W; below 90°F (32°C), 80W.
4 Subaru Part No. K0324F0091
5 Subaru Part No. K032 4AA093

CAPACITY, Refill:	Liters	Pt
Hatchback: 2WD	2.5	5.2
4WD	2.8	6.0
Impreza:		
2WD	2.6	5.4
4WD	4.0	8.4
Justy:		
1989 2WD	2.3	4.8
4WD	3.3	7.0
1990-93 2WD	2.1	4.4
4WD	2.8	6.0
Legacy:		
2WD	3.3	7.0
4WD	3.5	7.4
Loyale:		
2WD	2.6	5.4
4WD	3.3	7.0
Sedan & Wagon:		
1989 2WD	2.6	5.4
1989 4WD	3.3	7.0
XT Coupe:		
4-cyl. 2WD	2.6	5.4
4WD	3.3	7.0
6-cyl. 4WD	3.5	7.4

DIFFERENTIAL,
   Front w/AT 75W-90, 80W-90 GL-5
Above 30°F (0°C), 90; above -20°F (-30°C), 85W; below 90°F (32°C), 80W.

CAPACITY, Refill:	Liters	Pt
Ex. XT-Coupe	1.2	2.6
XT-Coupe	1.4	3.0

DIFFERENTIAL, Rear
Standard 75W-90, 80W-90 GL-5
Above 30°F (0°C), 90; above -20°F (-30°C), 85W; below 90°F (32°C), 80W.
XT w/limited-slip . . . . .GLS

CAPACITY, Refill:	Liters	Pt
All models	0.8	1.6

SUBARU
1994-99 All Models

SUIPM4   SUIPM4

Perform the following maintenance services at the intervals indicated to keep the vehicle warranties in effect.
W   SERVICE TO MAINTAIN EMISSION WARRANTY

MI—MILES IN THOUSANDS
KM—KILOMETERS IN THOUSANDS

FIRST 3 MO/3 MI—4.8 KM
W Crankcase . . . . .change oil

Oil filter .replace

EVERY 7.5 MO/7.5 MI—12 KM
W Crankcase . . . . .change oil

W Oil filter . . . . .replace

Tires . . . . .rotate

EVERY 15 MO/15 MI—24 KM
Brake system . . . . .inspect
Check pads & discs, & operation of handbrake & servo system. Lubricate park brake lever of front disc caliper

Clutch & hill-holder
   system, ex. SVX . . . . . .inspect/adjust

Clutch fluid . . . . .check **HB**

Suspension & steering . . . . .inspect

W Cooling system . . . . .inspect **EC**

Power steering . . . . . . .check level **AF3**

Body . . . . .lubricate **MO**
Hinges, door locks, hood & trunk lid, pedal assembly

EVERY 30 MO/30 MI—48 KM
Brake drums & lining . . . . .inspect

Brake fluid . . . . .replace **HB**

Differential, front & rear . . . . . . .inspect

Transmission . . . . .check/level

W Air & crankcase filter elements . . .replace

W Cooling system . . . . .change coolant **EC**
Inspect hoses and connectors

Drive belts . . . . .inspect

W Fuel filter . . . . .replace
Inspect hoses and connectors

W Spark plugs . . . . .replace
1.2L, 1.8L, 2.2L only 1994-98
1999 All

Headlight aiming . . . . .check/adjust
1994-97

EVERY 60 MO/60 MI—96 KM
Spark plugs . . . . .replace
2.5L & 3.3L only 1994-98

W Drive belts ex. Calif. . . . . .replace
Also replace 2212cc camshaft belt

Wheel bearings front &
   rear . . . . .inspect/repack **WB**

EVERY 105 MO/105 MI— 168 KM
Valve clearance . . . . .inspect/adjust
Adjust only if noisy
Drive belts, Calif. only . . . . .replace
Also replace camshaft belt 2457cc eng.
1999 All, 1994-98

EVERY 120 MONTHS
Airbag system . . . . .inspect

SEVERE SERVICE
Crankcase—Change oil & filter every 3.75 mo/3.75 mi (6 km)

Air filter—Replace every 15 mo/ 15 mi (24 km)

Brake fluid—Replace every 15 mo/15 mi (24 km)

Brake linings—Inspect every 7.5 mo/7.5 mi (12 km)

Differentials, all—Change fluid every 1994-97 30 mo/30 mi (48 km); 1998-99 15 mo/15 mi (24km)

Front & rear axle boots—Inspect every 7.5 mo/7.5 mi (12 km)

Fuel filter—Replace every 15 mo/ 15 mi (24 km)

Spark plugs—Replace every 30 mo/30 mi (48 km) SVX

Fuel hoses & connections—Inspect every 15 mo/15 mi (24 km)

Steering & suspension—Inspect every 7.5 mo/7.5 mi (12 km)

Transmission, automatic—Change fluid every 15 mo/15 mi (24 km)

Transmission, manual all—Change fluid every 1994-97: 30 mo/30 mi (48 km); 1998: 15 mo/15 mi (24 km)

KEY TO LUBRICANTS
See inside cover

CRANKCASE . . . . .SG, SH, SJ, GF-1

CAPACITY, Refill[1]:	Liters	Qt
3-cyl. 1189cc	2.8	3.0
4-cyl.:		
1781cc	4.0	4.2
1820cc	4.0	4.2
2212cc 1994-98	4.0	4.2
2212cc w/filter 1999	4.5	4.8
2457cc 1994-98	4.4	4.7
2457cc w/filter 1999	5.0	5.3
6-cyl.:		
3318cc	6.0	6.3

1 Capacity shown is without filter. When replacing filter, additional oil may be needed.
1994:
Warm climate & H.D. applications 30, 40,
                  10W-50, 20W-40, 20W-50
-5° to 95°F (-21° to 35°C) 10W-30, 10W-40
Below 32°F (0°C) . . . . .5W-30[2]
2 Not recommended for sustained high-speed driving
1995-99:
Warm climate & H.D. applications 30, 40
                  10W-50, 20W-40, 20W-50
Above -13°F (-25°C) 10W-30, 10W-40
Below 32°F (0°C), 1995 . . . . .5W-30[3]
Below 105°F (40°C), 1996-99 . . . . .5W-30[3]
3 Not recommended for sustained high-speed driving

TRANSMISSION, Automatic **AF3**
Does not include final drive.

CAPACITY, Initial Refill[4]:	Liters	Qt
ECVT 2WD	1.8	1.9
4WD	1.9	2.0
Forester (Total Fill)	9.5	10.0
Legacy, Impreza		
1999 (Total Fill)	7.8	8.3
All Others	2.5	2.6

4 With engine at operating temperature, shift transmission through all gears. Check fluid level in PARK and add fluid as needed

TRANSAXLE, Manual
Justy . . . . .75W-80 GL-5[5]
All others . . . . .75W-80, 75W-90 GL-5[6]
All Models, Above 32°F (0°C), 90; above -20°F (-30°C), 85W; below 90°F (32°C), 80W.
All temperatures 75W-90
5 Subaru Part No. K0324F0091
6 Subaru Part No. K0324AA093

CAPACITY, Refill:	Liters	Pt
Forester	3.5	7.4
Impreza:		
2WD 1994-97	2.6	5.5
1998	3.5	7.4
4WD 1994-97	4.0	8.4
1998-99	3.5	7.4
Justy:		
1994 2WD	2.1	4.4
4WD	2.8	6.0
Legacy:		
2WD	3.3	7.0
4WD	3.5	7.4
Loyale:		
2WD	2.6	5.4
4WD	3.3	7.0

FINAL DRIVE,
  Front w/AT 75W-90, 80W-90 **GL-5**
Above 32°F (0°C), 90; above -20°F (-30°C), 85W; below 90°F (32°C), 80W, all temperatures 80W-90.

CAPACITY, Refill:	Liters	Pt
All	1.2	2.6

DIFFERENTIAL,
  Rear 75W-90, 80W-90 **GL-5**
Above 32°F (0°C), 90; above -20°F (-30°C), 85W; below 90°F (32°C), 80W, all temperatures 75W-90.

CAPACITY, Refill:	Liters	Pt
All models	0.8	1.6

SERVICE LOCATIONS — ENGINE AND CHASSIS

TAIDP-2   TAIDP-2

HOOD RELEASE: Inside

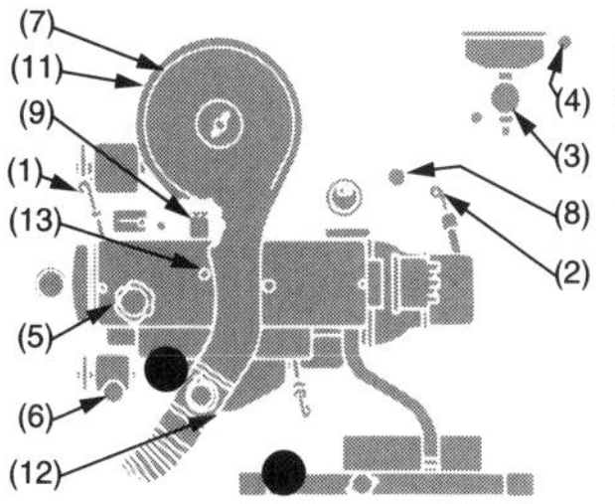

1989-90
Tercel
1456cc 2V

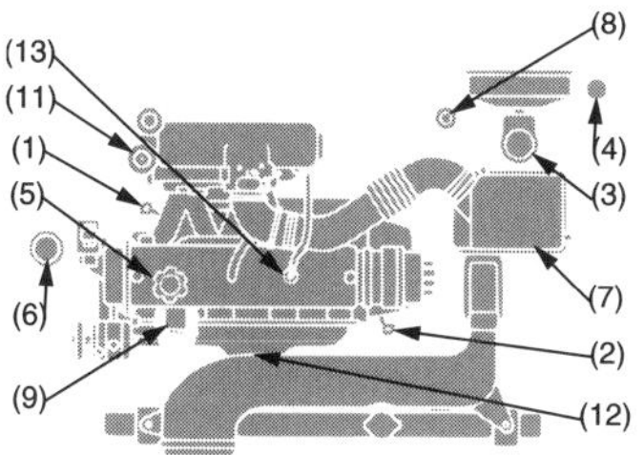

1990-94
Tercel
1456cc FI SOHC

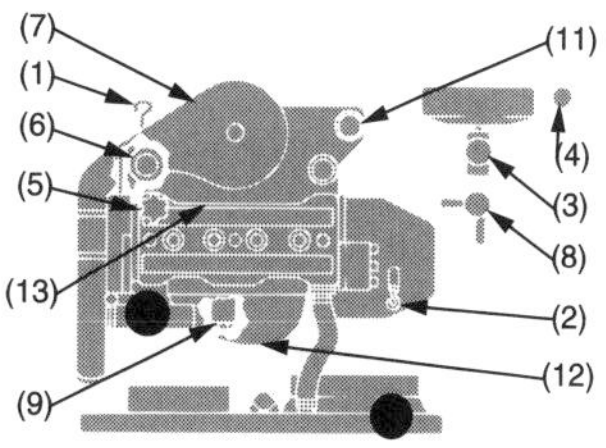

1989
Corolla
1587cc 2V (4A-F)

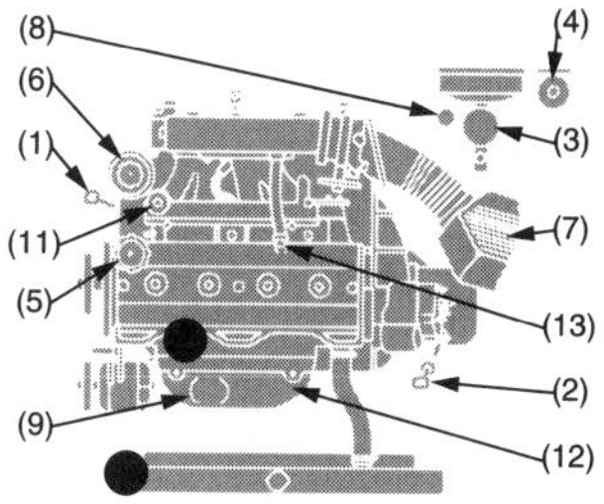

1989-97
Corolla, Celica
1587cc FI (4A-FE)

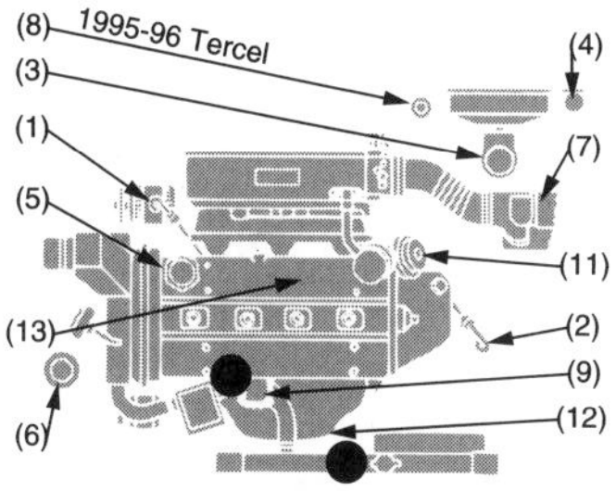

1995-96 Tercel

1989-93
FX16, Corolla
1587cc DOHC (4A-GE)
1992-98 Paseo, Tercel
1497cc FI DOHC

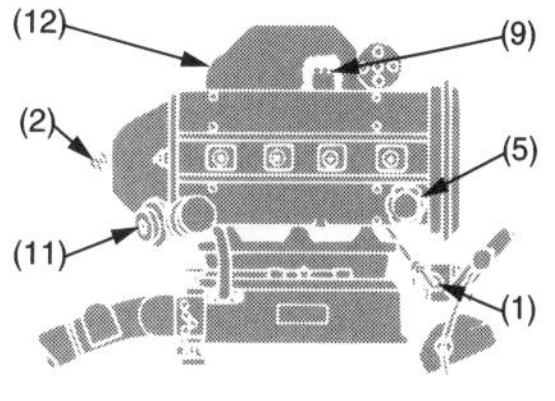

1989-90
MR2
1587cc

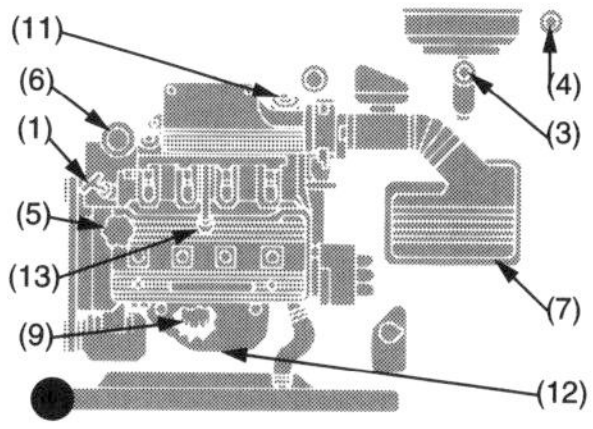

1993-97
Corolla, Celica
1762cc

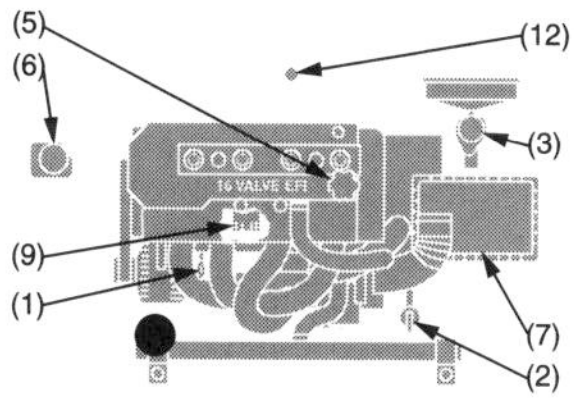

1998-00
Corolla, Celica
1794cc (1ZZ-FE)

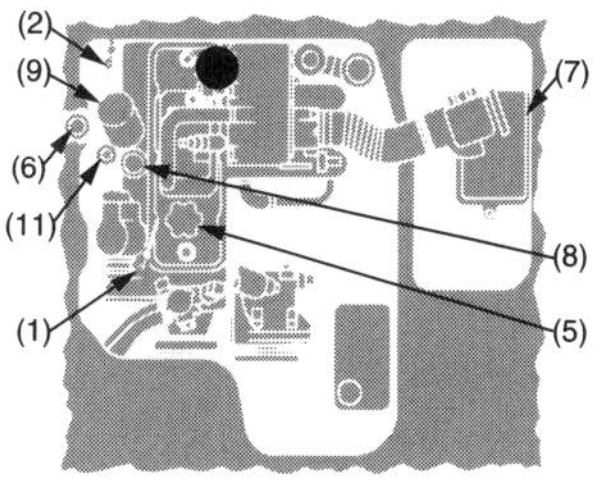

1989
Van
2237cc

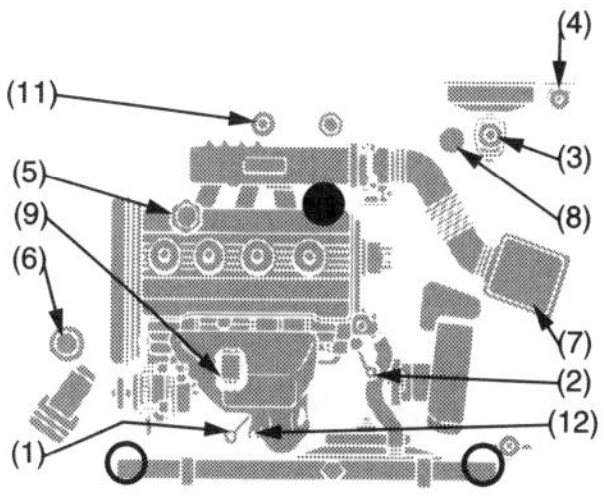

1989-00
Camry, Celica, RAV4, Solara
1998cc DOHC ex. Turbo,
2164cc

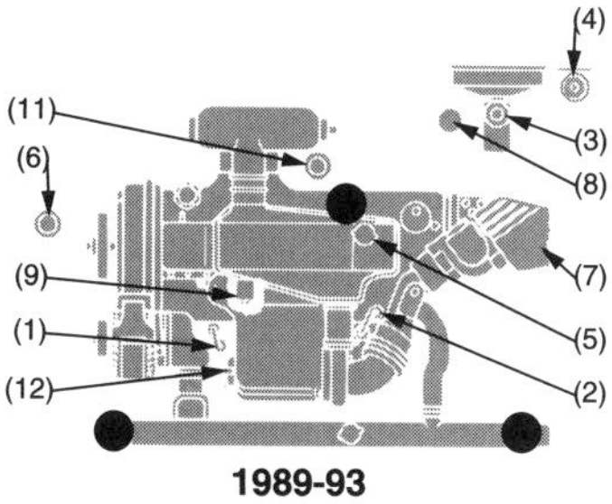

1989-93
Celica
1998cc Turbo

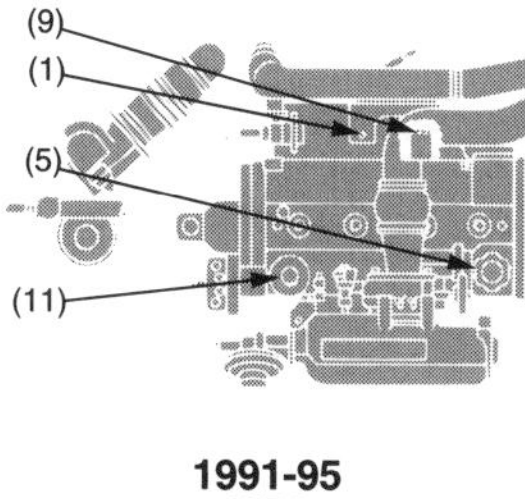

1991-95
MR2
1998cc Turbo

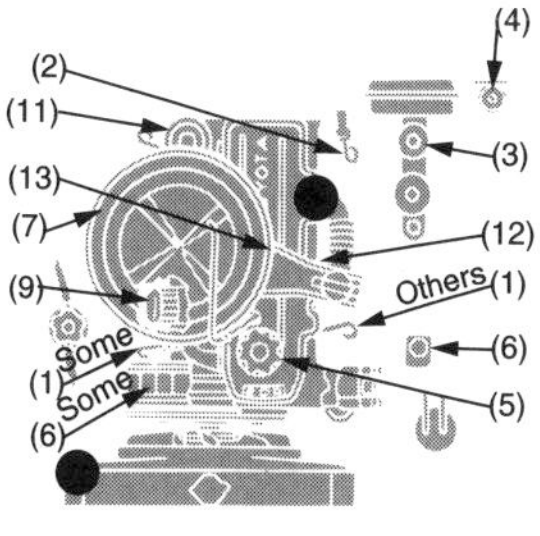

1989-90
Pickup
2366cc 2V

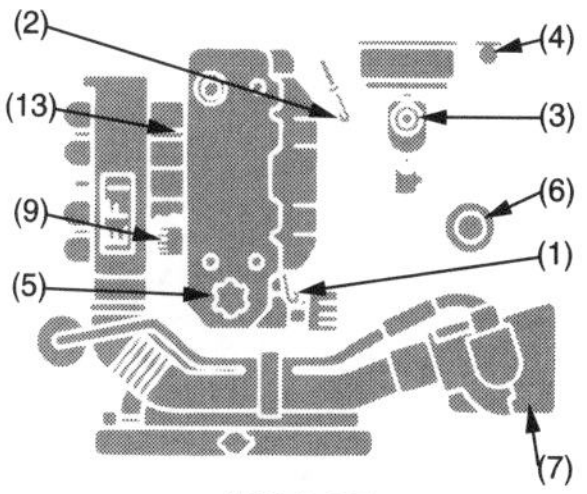

1989-95
Pickup
2366cc FI

(1) Crankcase dipstick
(2) Transmission dipstick
(3) Brake fluid reservoir
(4) Clutch fluid reservoir
(5) Oil fill cap
(6) Power steering reservoir
(7) Air filter

(8) Fuel filter
(9) Oil filter
(10) PCV filter
(11) EGR valve
(12) Oxygen sensor
(13) PCV valve

● Cooling system drain
○ Cooling system drain,
   some models

SERVICE LOCATIONS — ENGINE AND CHASSIS

TAIDP-2   TAIDP-2

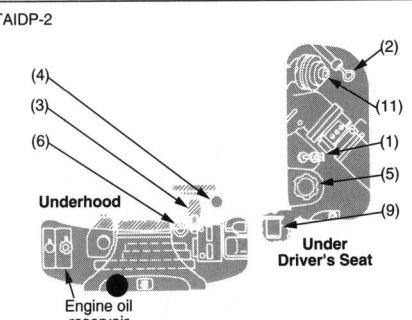

Underhood

Under Driver's Seat

Engine oil reservoir

1991-97 Previa
2438cc

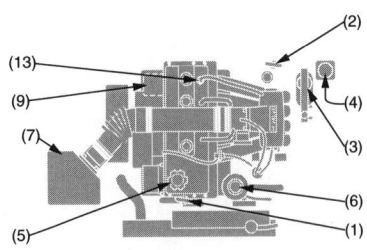

1994-99
Tacoma, T100,
4-Runner
2438cc, 2693cc

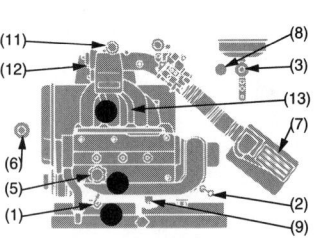

1989-91
Camry
V6 2507cc

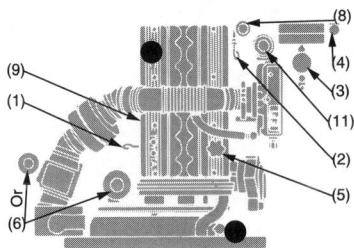

1989-92
Supra, Cressida
6-cyl. 2759cc DOHC, 2960cc

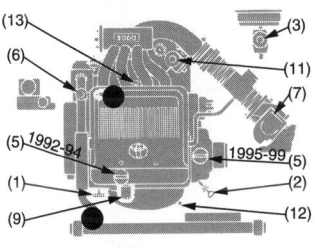

1992-99
Avalon, Camry, Sienna, Solara
V6 2958cc, 2995cc

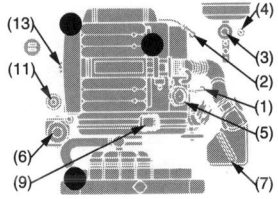

1989-95
Pickup, 4-Runner
V6 2958cc

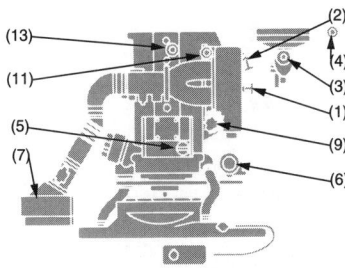

1993-98
Supra
6-cyl. 2997cc Turbo

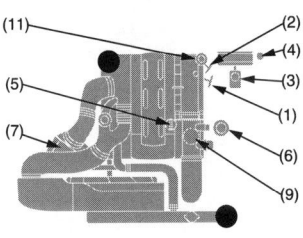

1993-98 Supra
6-cyl. 2997cc ex. Turbo

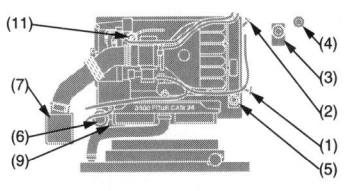

1995-99
T100, Tacoma, Tundra 4-Runner
V6 3378cc

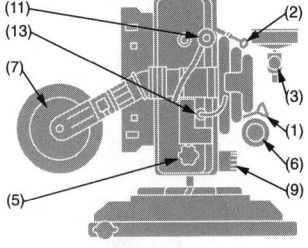

1989-96
Land Cruiser
6-cyl. 3955cc, 4477cc

1998-00
Land Cruiser, Tundra
V8 4669cc

(1) Crankcase dipstick
(2) Transmission dipstick
(3) Brake fluid reservoir
(4) Clutch fluid reservoir
(5) Oil fill cap
(6) Power steering reservoir
(7) Air filter
(8) Fuel filter
(9) Oil filter
(10) PCV filter
(11) EGR valve
(12) Oxygen sensor
(13) PCV valve

● Cooling system drain   ○ Cooling system drain, some models   ■ Lift adapter position

CAUTION: On front wheel drive vehicles, the center of gravity is farther forward than on rear wheel drive vehicles. When removing major components from the rear of the vehicle while it is on a hoist, the vehicle must be supported in a manner to prevent it from tipping forward.

SERVICE LOCATIONS — ENGINE AND CHASSIS

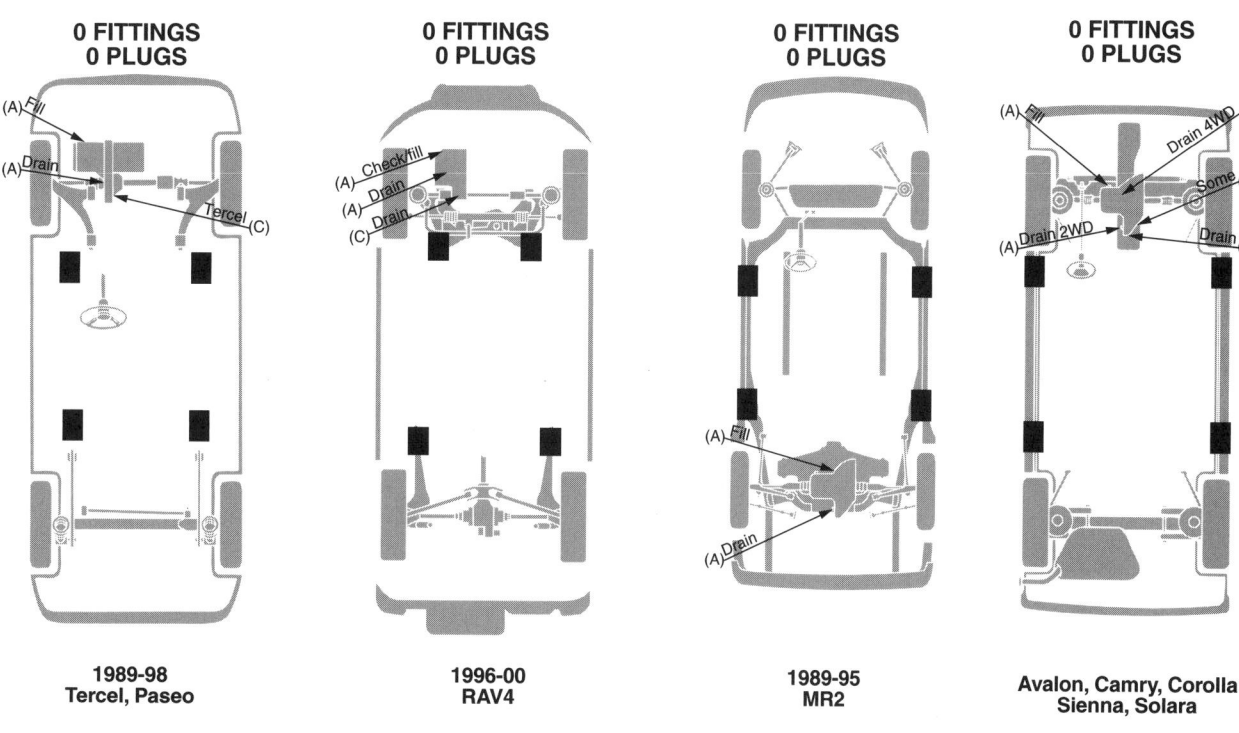

0 FITTINGS 0 PLUGS
1989-98
Tercel, Paseo

0 FITTINGS 0 PLUGS
1996-00
RAV4

0 FITTINGS 0 PLUGS
1989-95
MR2

0 FITTINGS 0 PLUGS
Avalon, Camry, Corolla
Sienna, Solara

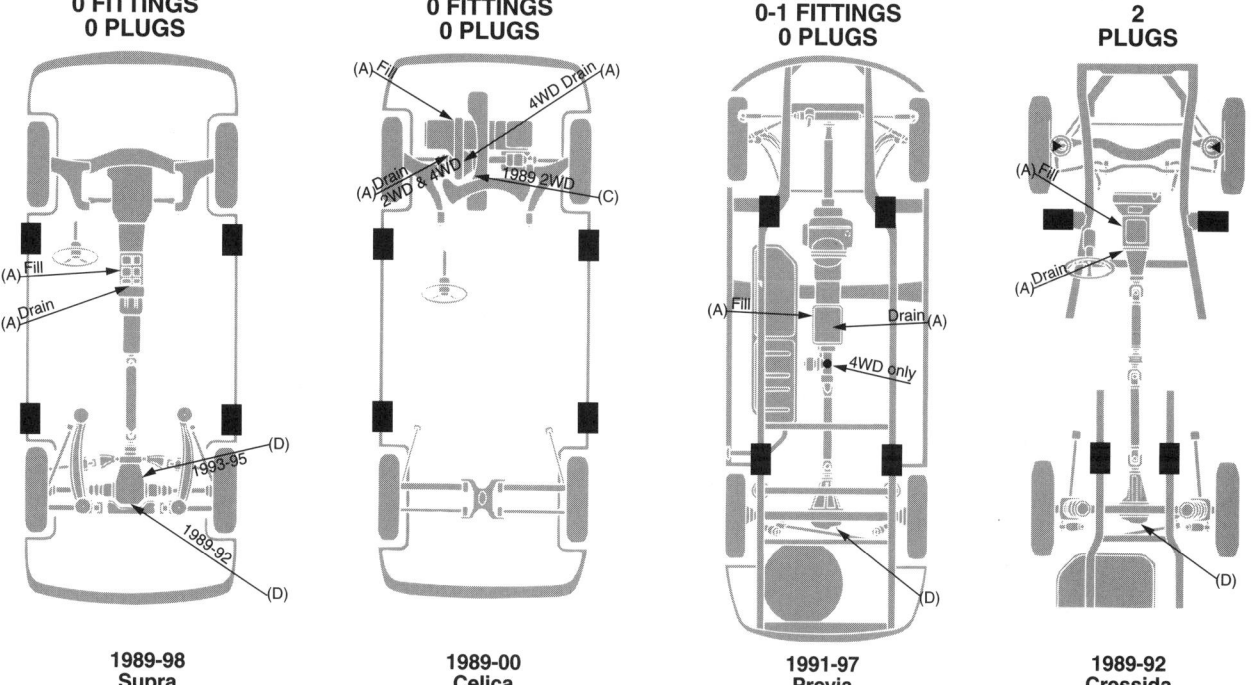

0 FITTINGS 0 PLUGS
1989-98
Supra

0 FITTINGS 0 PLUGS
1989-00
Celica

0-1 FITTINGS 0 PLUGS
1991-97
Previa

2 PLUGS
1989-92
Cressida

CAUTION: On front wheel drive vehicles, the center of gravity is farther forward than on rear wheel drive vehicles. When removing major components from the rear of the vehicle while it is on a hoist, the vehicle must be supported in a manner to prevent it from tipping forward.

HOOD RELEASE: Inside

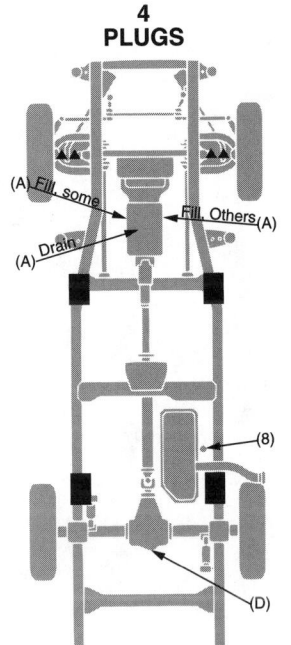

4 PLUGS

(A) *Fill, some*   *Fill, Others* (A)

(A) *Drain*

(8)

(D)

**1989-95
2WD Pickup
1993-98
2WD T100**

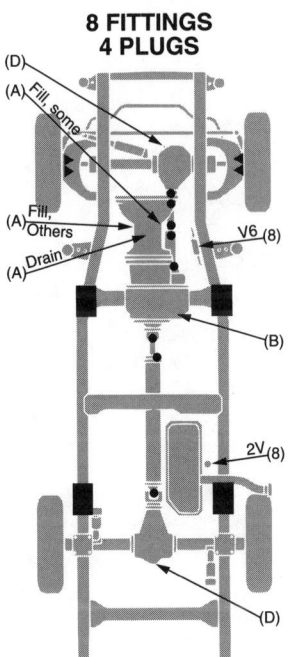

**8 FITTINGS
4 PLUGS**

(D)

(A) *Fill, some*

(A) *Fill, Others*   V6 (8)

(A) *Drain*

(B)

2V (8)

(D)

**1989-95
4WD Pickup, 4-Runner
1993-98
4WD T100**

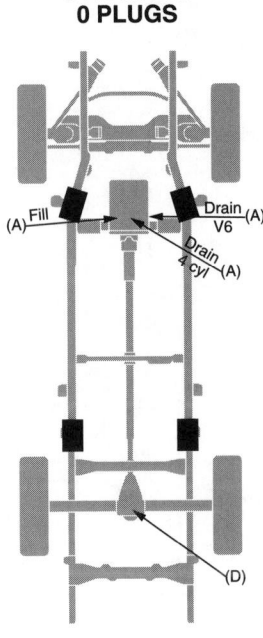

**0 FITTINGS
0 PLUGS**

(A) *Fill*   *Drain* (A)
                           V6

                           *Drain
                           4 cyl* (A)

(D)

**1995-00
2WD Tacoma**

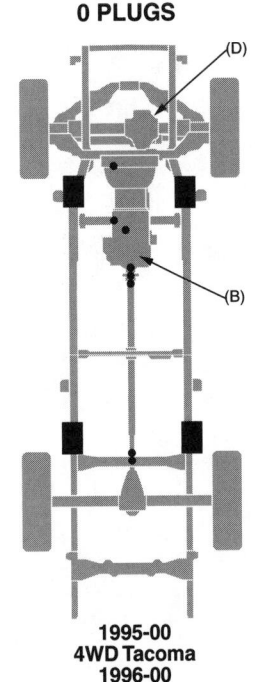

**0 FITTINGS
0 PLUGS**

(D)

(B)

**1995-00
4WD Tacoma
1996-00
4WD 4-Runner**

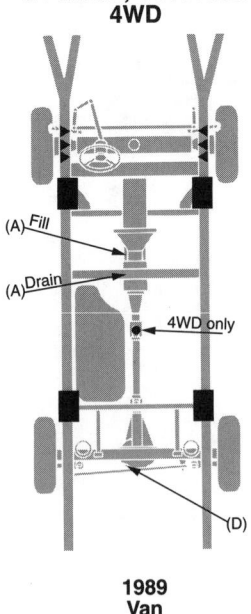

**0 PLUGS, FITTINGS
2WD
6 PLUGS, 1 FITTING
4WD**

(A) *Fill*

(A) *Drain*

4WD only

(D)

**1989
Van**

CAUTION: On front wheel drive vehicles, the center of gravity is farther forward than on rear wheel drive vehicles. When removing major components from the rear of the vehicle while it is on a hoist, the vehicle must be supported in a manner to prevent it from tipping forward.

(A) Manual transmission/transaxle, drain & fill	(C) Automatic transaxle final drive, drain & fill	(8) Fuel filter
(B) Transfer case, drain & fill	(D) Differential, drain & fill	■ Lift adapter position

● Fitting   ○ Fitting, some models

▲ Plug   △ Plug, some models

SERVICE AT TIME OR MILEAGE — WHICHEVER OCCURS FIRST

TAIPM10   TAIPM10

Perform the following maintenance services at the intervals indicated to keep the vehicle warranties in effect.
W   SERVICE TO MAINTAIN EMISSION WARRANTY

MI—MILES IN THOUSANDS
KM—KILOMETERS IN THOUSANDS

SERVICE PERIODICALLY
Brake & clutch
  fluid reservoirs . . . . . . .check level **HB**

Power steering fluid . . . .check level **AF3**

AT FIRST 12 MO/10 MI—16 KM
Idle speed . . . . .adjust
3E, 4A-F & FE engines only

TURBO ENGINES,
EVERY 6 MO/5 MI—8 KM
OTHERS,
EVERY 12 MO/10 MI—16 KM
W Crankcase . . . . .change oil

W Oil filter . . . . .replace
Turbo, every other oil change

EVERY 24 MO/20 MI—32 KM
Brake system . . . . .check
Disc pads & rotors, drums, linings, booster, parking
brake, lines, pipes & hoses

Front suspension . . . . .inspect
Ball joints, dust covers

Differential . . . . .check level

Driveshaft boots FWD . . . . .inspect

Transfer case . . . . .check level

Transmission, transaxle,
  manual . . . . .check level

Steering gearbox . . . . .inspect
Check steering linkage & free play

Transmission, transaxle,
  automatic . . . . .check level

Body . . . . .inspect
Torque nuts & bolts

EVERY 36 MO/30 MI—48 KM
Exhaust system . . . . .inspect

W Air cleaner element . . . . .replace

Fuel lines & connections . . . . . . .inspect

Idle speed 4 cyl. ex. Turbo . .check/adjust
Adjust throttle positioner on carburetted engines. Initial
service only for carburetted engines.

W Spark plugs . . . . .replace
Except platinum tipped

Supercharger MR2 . . . . .check level
Use Toyota Supercharger Oil, Part No. 08885-80108

W Valve clearance . . . . .adjust
Tercel

EVERY 48 MO/40 MI—64 KM
Front wheel bearings, RWD & Rear wheel
  bearings, Tercel . . . . .clean/repack **LM**
Torque to 19-23 ft lb. Back off & retighten finger tight

Limited-Slip differential . . . . .change oil

EVERY 72 MO/60 MI—96 KM
Charcoal canister . . . . .inspect

Cooling system . . . . .change coolant **EC**
Replace coolant every 36 mo/30 mi (48 km) thereafter.
Also replace Celica intercooler coolant

Drive belts . . . . .inspect
Initial service, inspect every 12 mo/10 mi (16 km)

Fuel cap gasket . . . . .replace

Spark plugs . . . . .replace
Platinum tipped only

W Valve clearance . . . . .adjust
All ex. Tercel
Except models with hydraulic lifters

EVERY 120 MONTHS
Air bag system . . . . .inspect
Initial service, then every 24 months

SEVERE SERVICE
W Crankcase—Change oil & filter every:
Turbo, 3 mo/2.5 mi (4 km); Others 6 mo/
5 mi (8 km)

Exhaust system—Inspect every 18 mo/
15 mi (24 km)

**Suspension, driveshaft boots, steering
& brake components**—Inspect every 12
mo/10 mi (16 km)

**Transmission, transaxle, transfer case
& differential**—Change fluid or lubricant
every 24 mo/20 mi (32 km)

W Air cleaner element—Inspect every 6 mo/
5 mi (8 km)

Timing belt—Replace every 60 mi (96 km)

Chassis & body nuts and bolts—Inspect
every 12 mo/10 mi (16 km)

KEY TO LUBRICANTS
See inside front cover

CRANKCASE . . . .**SG**

CAPACITY, Refill:	Liters	Qt
Cressida, Supra	4.1	4.3
Turbo	4.3	4.5
Camry	3.7	3.9
Celica	3.7	3.9
Turbo	3.3	3.5
Tercel	3.0	3.2
Corolla, 4AF, FE	3.0	3.2
4A-GE	3.4	3.6
MR2	3.0	3.2

Capacity shown is without filter. When replacing filter, addi-
tional oil may be needed
Above 10°F (-12°C) . . .15W-40, 20W-40, 20W-50
Above -10°F (-23°C) . .10W-30, 10W-40, 10W-50
Below 50°F (10°C) 5W-30

TRANSMISSION/TRANSAXLE, Automatic
Camry, Corolla 4WD . . . .**SLF¹**
1 ATF Type T
All others **AF3**
Differential is serviced separately in 2WD Camry, Celica,
Corolla 3-speed, and Tercel

CAPACITY, Initial Refill²:	Liters	Qt
MR2	3.3	3.5
Corolla 2WD	2.3	2.4
w/OD or 4WD	3.1	3.3
Supra, Cressida	1.6	1.7
Others	2.5	2.6

2 With the engine at operating temperature, shift transmission through all gears. Check fluid level in PARK and add
fluid as needed

TRANSMISSION/TRANSAXLE, Manual
FWD, includes front differential and 4WD transfer case
Tercel 75W-90, 80W-90 **GL-4, GL-5**
Celica, Camry, Corolla 2WD:
  1.6L 75W-90 **GL-4, GL-5**
  2.0L ex. Turbo, 2.2L **AF3**
  V6 . . . . . . .75W-90, 80W-90 **GL-4, GL-5**
Corolla, Celica, Camry
  4WD 75W-90, 80W-90 **GL-4, GL-5**
May also use 90 above 0°F (-18°C), or 80W below 0°F
(-18°C)
MR2 ex. Supercharged
  Cressida, Supra ex.
  Turbo 75W-90, 80W-90 **GL-4, GL-5**
MR2 Supercharged, Supra Turbo,
  Celica 2WD Turbo 75W-90 **GL-5**

CAPACITY, Refill:	Liters	Pt
Supra, Cressida	2.4	5.2
Turbo	3.0	6.4
MR2	2.6	5.6
Supercharged	4.2	8.8
Camry, Celica, Corolla:		
2WD 4-cyl.	2.6	5.6
2WD V6	4.2	8.8
4WD	5.0	10.6
Tercel, Paseo	2.4	5.0

TRANSFER CASE, 4WD w/AT
Camry, Corolla 75W-90, 80W-90 **GL-5**
May also use 90 above 0°F (-18°C); or 80W below 0°F
(-18°C)

CAPACITY, Refill:	Liters	Pt
Camry, Corolla	0.7	1.4

FINAL DRIVE, FWD w/AT **AF3**
Tercel, Corolla w/3-speed; Camry, Celica 2WD, all V6

CAPACITY, Refill:	Liters	Pt
Camry, Celica: 2WD 4-cyl.	1.6	3.4
V6	1.0	2.2
Corolla, Tercel	1.4	3.0

DIFFERENTIAL, Rear
Limited-Slip . . . .**GL-5★**
Standard **GL-5**
Above 0°F (-18°C), 90; below 0°F (-18°C), 80W, 80W-90

CAPACITY, Refill:	Liters	Pt
Celica, Camry, Corolla:		
4WD rear	1.1	2.4
Supra, Cressida	1.2	2.6

TOYOTA
1990-91 All Models Except Land Cruiser, Pickup, Van, 4-Runner

---

SERVICE AT TIME OR MILEAGE — WHICHEVER OCCURS FIRST

TAIPM12   TAIPM12

Perform the following maintenance services at the intervals indicated to keep the vehicle warranties in effect.

W   SERVICE TO MAINTAIN EMISSION WARRANTY

MI—MILES IN THOUSANDS
KM—KILOMETERS IN THOUSANDS

SERVICE PERIODICALLY
Brake & clutch
fluid reservoirs . . . . . . .check level **HB**

Power steering fluid:
1991 MR2 . . . . .check level **SLF**[1]
All others . . . . .check level **AF3**
1 Toyota Part No. 08886-01206

AT FIRST 12 MO/7.5 MI—12 KM
Idle speed . . . . .adjust
All Tercel & Corolla, Celica w/3E, 4A-FE engines only

TURBO ENGINES,
EVERY 6 MO/5 MI—8 KM
OTHERS,
EVERY 12 MO/7.5 MI—12 KM
W Crankcase . . . . .change oil

W Oil filter .replace
Turbo, every other oil change

EVERY 24 MO/15 MI—24 KM
Brake system . . . . .check
Disc pads & rotors, drums, linings, booster, parking brake, lines, pipes & hoses

Front suspension . . . . .inspect
Ball joints, dust covers

Differential . . . . .check level

Driveshaft boots FWD . . . . .inspect

Transfer case . . . . .check level

Transmission, transaxle,
manual . . . . .check level

Steering gearbox . . . . .inspect
Check steering linkage & free play

Idle speed 1991 4 cyl.
ex. Turbo . . . . .check/adjust

Transmission, transaxle,
automatic . . . . .check level

Body . . . . .inspect
Torque nuts & bolts

EVERY 36 MO/30 MI—48 KM
Exhaust system . . . . .inspect

W Air cleaner element . . . . .replace

Fuel vapor hoses . . . . .inspect
Also check fuel tank bands

Fuel lines & connections . . . . . . .inspect

Idle speed 1990 4 cyl.
ex. Turbo . . . . .check/adjust
Initial service for Tercel, 2V

W Spark plugs . . . . .replace
Except platinum tipped

W Valve clearance . . . . .adjust
Tercel

EVERY 48 MO/30 MI—48 KM
Front wheel bearings, RWD
& Front wheel
bearings, Tercel . . . . .clean/repack **LM**
Torque to 19-23 ft lb. Back off & retighten finger tight. Service rear wheel bearings on cars with FWD

Limited-Slip differential . . . . .change oil

FIRST 36 MO/45 MI—72 KM;
THEN EVERY 24 MO/30 MI—48 KM
Cooling system . . . . .change coolant **EC**

EVERY 72 MO/60 MI—96 KM
Charcoal canister . . . . .inspect

Drive belts . . . . .inspect
Initial service, inspect every 12 mo/7.5 mi (12 km) thereafter

Fuel cap gasket . . . . .replace

Spark plugs . . . . .replace
Platinum tipped only

W Valve clearance . . . . .adjust
All ex. Tercel
Except models with hydraulic lifters

EVERY 120 MONTHS
Air bag system . . . . .inspect
Initial service, then every 24 months

SEVERE SERVICE
W Crankcase—Change oil & filter every:
Turbo, 3 mo/2.5 mi (4 km); others 6 mo/3.75 mi (6 km)

Exhaust system—Inspect every 18 mo/15 mi (24 km)

Suspension, driveshaft boots, steering & brake components—Inspect every 12 mo/7.5 mi (12 km)

Transmission, transaxle, transfer case & differential—Change fluid or lubricant every 24 mo/15 mi (24 km)

W Air cleaner element—Inspect every 6 mo/3.75 mi (6 km)

Timing belt—Replace every 60 mi (96 km)

KEY TO LUBRICANTS
See inside front cover

CRANKCASE . . . .**SG**

CAPACITY, Refill:	Liters	Qt
Cressida, Supra	4.1	4.3
Turbo	4.3	4.5
Camry	3.7	3.9
Celica: 1.6L	3.0	3.2
2.0L, 2.2L	3.7	3.9
Turbo	3.6	3.8
Tercel	2.5	2.7
Corolla, 4AF, FE	2.8	3.0
4A-GE	3.4	3.6
MR2	3.6	3.8
2.2L	3.8	4.0

Capacity shown is without filter. When replacing filter, additional oil may be needed

1990:
Above 10°F (-12°C) . . .15W-40, 20W-40, 20W-50
Above -10°F (-23°C) . .10W-30, 10W-40, 10W-50
Below 50°F (10°C) 5W-30
1991:
Above 0°F (-18°C) 10W-30
Above 0°F (-18°C) 10W-40
Below 50°F (10°C) 5W-30

TRANSMISSION/TRANSAXLE, Automatic
Corolla 4WD,
Camry 4-cyl. 4WD . . . . **SLF**[1]
1 ATF Type T
All others **AF3**
Differential is serviced separately in 2WD Camry, FWD Corolla 3-speed, and Tercel

CAPACITY, Initial Refill[2]:	Liters	Qt
Celica, MR2	3.3	3.5
Corolla 2WD	2.3	2.4
w/OD or 4WD	3.1	3.3
Paseo	3.1	3.3
Camry 4-cyl. 4WD	3.3	3.5
Camry V6: thru 5-15-91	2.5	2.6
from 5-15-91	3.3	3.5
Supra, Cressida	1.6	1.7
Others	2.5	2.6

2 With the engine at operating temperature, shift transmission through all gears. Check fluid level in PARK and add fluid as needed

TRANSMISSION/TRANSAXLE, Manual
FWD, includes front differential and 4WD transfer case
Tercel 75W-90, 80W-90 **GL-4, GL-5**
Celica, Camry, Corolla 2WD:
1.6L 75W-90 **GL-4, GL-5**
2.0L ex. Turbo, 2.2L: 1990 (to 4/90) . .**AF3**
1990-91 (from 4/90) 75W-90 **GL-5**
V6 . . . . . . .75W-90, 80W-90 **GL-4, GL-5**
Corolla, Celica, Camry
4WD 75W-90, 80W-90 **GL-4, GL-5**
May also use 90 above 0°F (-18°C), or 80W below 0°F (-18°C)
Cressida, Supra ex.
Turbo 75W-90, 80W-90 **GL-4, GL-5**
Supra Turbo,
Celica 2WD Turbo 75W-90 **GL-5**
MR2 .75W-90 **GL-5**

CAPACITY, Refill:	Liters	Pt
Supra, Cressida	2.4	5.2
Turbo	3.0	6.4
MR2	2.6	5.6
Turbo	4.2	8.8
Camry, Celica, Corolla:		
2WD 4-cyl.	2.6	5.6
2WD V6	4.2	8.8
4WD	5.0	10.6
Tercel, Paseo	2.4	5.0

TRANSFER CASE, 4WD w/AT
Camry, Corolla 75W-90, 80W-90 **GL-5**
May also use 90 above 0°F (-18°C); or 80W below 0°F (-18°C)

CAPACITY, Refill:	Liters	Pt
Camry, Corolla	0.7	1.4

FINAL DRIVE, FWD w/AT **AF3**
Tercel, Corolla w/3-speed; Camry, all V6 thru 5/15/91 & 2WD 4-cyl.

CAPACITY, Refill:	Liters	Pt
Camry: 2WD 4-cyl.	1.6	3.4
V6 thru 5/15/91	1.0	2.2
Corolla, Tercel	1.4	3.0

DIFFERENTIAL, Rear
Limited-Slip . . . .**GL-5★**
Standard **GL-5**
Above 0°F (-18°C), 90; below 0°F (-18°C), 80W, 80W-90

CAPACITY, Refill:	Liters	Pt
Celica, Camry, Corolla: 4WD rear	1.1	2.4
Supra, Cressida	1.2	2.6

Copyright 2000 by Chek-Chart Publications

SERVICE AT TIME OR MILEAGE — WHICHEVER OCCURS FIRST

TAIPM13

TAIPM13

Perform the following maintenance services at the intervals indicated to keep the vehicle warranties in effect.

W   SERVICE TO MAINTAIN EMISSION WARRANTY

MI—MILES IN THOUSANDS
KM—KILOMETERS IN THOUSANDS

SERVICE PERIODICALLY

Brake & clutch
fluid reservoirs . . . . .check level **HB**

Power steering fluid:
MR2 . . . . .check level **SLF**[1]
All others . . . . .check level **AF3**
[1] Toyota Part No. 08886-01206

AT FIRST 12 MO/7.5 MI—12 KM

Idle speed, 1992-94 . . . . .adjust
3E, 4A-FE engines only

TURBO ENGINES,
EVERY 6 MO/5 MI—8 KM
OTHERS,
EVERY 12 MO/7.5 MI—12 KM

W Crankcase . . . . .change oil

W Oil filter .replace
Turbo, every other oil change

EVERY 24 MO/15 MI—24 KM

Brake system . . . . .check
Disc pads & rotors, drums, linings, booster, parking
brake, lines, pipes & hoses

Front suspension . . . . .inspect
Ball joints, dust covers

Differential . . . . .check level

Driveshaft boots FWD & 4WD . . .inspect

Transfer case . . . . .check level

Transmission, transaxle,
manual . . . . .check level

Steering gearbox . . . . .inspect
Check steering linkage & free play

Idle speed, 1992-94 . . . . . .check/adjust
3E, 4A-FE engines only

Transmission, transaxle,
automatic . . . . .check level

Body . . . . .inspect
Torque nuts & bolts

EVERY 36 MO/30 MI—48 KM

Exhaust system . . . . .inspect

W Air cleaner element . . . . .replace

Fuel lines & connections . . . . . . .inspect

Fuel vapor hoses . . . . .inspect
Check fuel tank bands

W Spark plugs . . . . .replace
Except platinum tipped

W Valve clearance . . . . .adjust
1992-94 Tercel

EVERY 48 MO/30 MI—48 KM

Front wheel bearings, RWD
& Front wheel bearings,
Paseo, Tercel . . . . . .clean/repack **LM**
Torque to 19-23 ft lb. Back off & retighten finger tight
Service rear wheel bearings on cars with FWD

Limited-Slip differential . . . . .change oil
RWD Models

FIRST 36 MO/45 MI—72 KM;
THEN EVERY 24 MO/30 MI—48 KM

Cooling system . . . . .change coolant **EC**

EVERY 72 MO/60 MI—96 KM

Charcoal canister . . . . .inspect

Drive belts . . . . .inspect
Initial service, inspect every: 12 mo/7.5 mi (12 km)
thereafter

Fuel cap gasket . . . . .replace

Spark plugs . . . . .replace
Platinum tipped only

W Valve clearance . . . . .adjust
All ex. 1992-94 Tercel
Except models with hydraulic lifters

EVERY 120 MONTHS

Air bag system . . . . .inspect
Initial service, then every 24 mo

SEVERE SERVICE

W Crankcase—Change oil & filter every:
Turbo, 3 mo/2.5 mi (4 km); Others, 6 mo/
3.75 mi (6 km)

Exhaust system—Inspect every 18 mo/
15 mi (24 km)

**Suspension, driveshaft boots, steering
& brake components**—Inspect every
12 mo/7.5 mi (12 km)

**Transmission, transaxle, transfer case
& differential**—Change fluid or lubricant
every 24 mo/15mi (24 km)

W **Air cleaner element**—Inspect every 6 mo/
3.75 mi (6 km)

Chassis & body nuts and bolts—Tighten
every 6 mo/7.5 mi (12 km)

Timing belt—Replace every 60 mi (96 km)

KEY TO LUBRICANTS
See inside front cover

CRANKCASE . . . .**SH, GF-1**

CAPACITY, Refill:	Liters	Qt
Cressida, Supra, 1992	4.1	4.3
Turbo	4.3	4.5
Supra, 1993-95	4.9	5.2
Turbo	4.7	5.0
Camry, Avalon		
3.0L: 1992-93	3.4	3.6
1994-95	4.1	4.3
	4.5	4.8
Celica: 1.6L	3.0	3.2
1.8L	3.5	3.7
2.0L, 2.2L	3.7	3.9
Turbo	3.6	3.8
Tercel, Paseo	2.5	2.7
Corolla: 1.6L	2.8	3.0
1.8L	3.5	3.7
MR2: 2.0L	3.6	3.8
2.2L	3.8	4.0

Capacity shown is without filter. When replacing filter, additional oil may be needed

1993-95 Supra Turbo:
Above -20°F (-29°C) 10W-30
1994-95 Camry V6 & Avalon
1993-95 Supra ex. Turbo:
Above 0°F (-18°C) 10W-30
Below 100°F (38°C) . . . . .5W-30[1]
1992-95 Others:
Above 0°F (-18°C) 10W-30
Below 50°F (10°C) 5W-30
[1] Preferred

TRANSMISSION/TRANSAXLE, Automatic
Corolla 4WD, 1993-95 Supra Turbo . . .**SLF**[2]
[2] ATF Type T, Corolla;
ATF Type TII, Supra
All others **AF3**
Differential is serviced separately in Avalon, Camry 4-cyl. &
1994-95 V6, Corolla & Tercel 3-speed and 1994-95 Celica 2.2L

CAPACITY, Initial Refill[3]:	Liters	Qt
Avalon, Camry V6: 1992-93 . .	2.9	3.1
1994-95	3.5	3.7
Celica, MR2	3.3	3.5
2.2L, 1994-95: Celica	1.6	1.7
MR2	2.6	2.7
Corolla: 3-speed	2.3	2.4
4-speed	3.1	3.3
Supra, 1992; Cressida	1.6	1.7
Supra, 1993-95	1.6	1.7
Turbo	1.9	2.0
Tercel, Paseo: 3-speed	2.5	2.6
4-speed	3.1	3.3
Others	2.5	2.6

[3] With the engine at operating temperature, shift transmission through all gears. Check fluid level in PARK and add fluid as needed

TRANSMISSION/TRANSAXLE, Manual
FWD, includes front differential and 4WD transfer case
Tercel, Paseo 75W-90 **GL-4, GL-5**
Celica, Camry, Corolla 2WD:
1.6L, 1.8L 75W-90 **GL-4, GL-5**
2.0L ex. Turbo, 2.2L 75W-90 **GL-5**
V6 . . . . .75W-90, 80W-90 **GL-4, GL-5**
Corolla, Celica
4WD 75W-90, 80W-90 **GL-4, GL-5**
May also use 90 above 0°F (-18°C), or 80W below 0°F
(-18°C)
MR2, Cressida, Supra ex.
Turbo 75W-90 **GL-4, GL-5**
MR2 Turbo, 1992 Supra Turbo,
Celica 2WD Turbo 75W-90 **GL-5**
Supra Turbo, 1993-95 . . . .**GLS**

CAPACITY, Refill:	Liters	Pt
Supra, 1992; Cressida	2.4	5.2
Turbo	3.0	6.4
Supra, 1993-95	2.6	5.4
Turbo	1.8	3.8
MR2	2.6	5.6
Turbo ex. Limited-Slip	4.2	8.8
Turbo, Limited-Slip	3.9	8.2
Camry, Celica, Corolla:		
2WD 4-cyl.	2.6	5.6
From 5/95	1.9	4.0
2WD V6	4.2	8.8
4WD	5.0	10.6
Tercel, Paseo	2.4	5.0
From 5/95	1.9	4.0

DIFFERENTIAL, Rear
Limited-Slip . . . .**GL-5★**
Standard **GL-5**
Above 0°F (-18°C), 90; below 0°F (-18°C), 80W,
80W-90

CAPACITY, Refill:	Liters	Pt
Celica, Camry, Corolla: 4WD rear	1.1	2.4
Supra, 1992; Cressida	1.2	2.6
Supra, 1993-95	1.4	2.9

TRANSFER CASE, 4WD w/AT
Corolla 75W-90, 80W-90 **GL-5**
May also use 90 above 0°F (-18°C); or 80W below 0°F
(-18°C)

CAPACITY, Refill:	Liters	Pt
Corolla	0.7	1.4

FINAL DRIVE, FWD w/AT **AF3**
Tercel, Corolla w/3-speed; Avalon, Camry
4-cyl., 1994-95 V6 & Celica 1994-95 2.2L

CAPACITY, Refill:	Liters	Pt
Camry, Avalon, 4-cyl.	1.6	3.4
V6, 1994-95	0.9	2.0
Corolla, Tercel	1.4	3.0
Celica, 1994-95 2.2L	1.6	3.4

SERVICE AT TIME OR MILEAGE — WHICHEVER OCCURS FIRST

TAIPM14   TAIPM14

Perform the following maintenance services at the intervals indicated to keep the vehicle warranties in effect.
W   SERVICE TO MAINTAIN EMISSION WARRANTY

MI—MILES IN THOUSANDS
KM—KILOMETERS IN THOUSANDS

SERVICE PERIODICALLY
Brake & clutch
  fluid reservoirs . . . . . . .check level **HB**

Power steering fluid . . . .check level **AF3**

Transmission, manual . . . . .inspect
Check for leaks

EVERY 6 MO/7.5 MI—12 KM
Crankcase . . . . .change oil

Oil filter . . . . .replace

Tires . . . . .rotate
At mileage interval only

EVERY 12 MO/15 MI—24 KM
Ball joints . . . . .inspect
Also check dust covers

Brake system . . . . .inspect

Differential or final drive . . . . .check level
All models, as equipped. Check for leaks

Drive shaft boots . . . . .inspect
1996-98 Sienna, Supra, Camry, Avalon, 1999 Sienna
also, retorque flange bolts

Exhaust system . . . . .inspect

Limited-slip differential . . . . . .check level
Supra only. Check for leaks

Rack & pinion assembly . . . . .check
Check boots & inspect for leaks

Steering linkage . . . . .inspect

Cabin air filter . . . . .replace
2000 Avalon

Transmission,
  automatic, 1996-99 . . . . . . .check level
Check for leaks

EVERY 24 MO/30 MI—48 KM
Limited-slip
  differential . . . . .change lubricant
1996-97 Supra only

Front wheel bearings . . . . .repack
Tercel, Paseo only

Air cleaner element . . . . .replace

Cooling system . . . . .replace coolant **EC**

Drive belts . . . . .inspect
1998-99 ex V-ribbed

Fuel lines & connections . . . . . . .inspect

Fuel tank . . . . .inspect
Check vapor vent system & bands. Also check fuel
tank cap

W Spark plugs . . . . .replace
Standard spark plugs; 1996-99 Tercel, Paseo, Corolla,
Celica 1.8L, 2000 Echo

EVERY 48 MO/60 MI—96 KM
Limited-slip differential . .change lubricant
1998 Supra only

Charcoal canister . . . . .inspect
1998-99 Paseo, Tercel, Avalon, Sienna, V6 Camry &
Solara: California, Massachusetts, and New York only
2000 Sierra, California, Massachusetts, New York

Drive belts . . . . .inspect/adjust
Initial service then every 12 mo/15 mi (24 km) thereafter
1996-97, 2000 All Models
1998-99 V-ribbed only

W Spark plugs . . . . .replace
1996-99 all, Platinum tipped only
2000 Avalon, Camry, Solara, Sienna

Valve clearance . . . . .inspect/adjust
Adjust only if noisy

EVERY 72 MO/60 MI—96 KM
Charcoal canister, 1996-97 . . . . .inspect

EVERY 72 MO/90 MI—144 KM
Timing belt . . . . .replace
1998 Supra ex. Turbo 1999, all modes ex. Corolla
2000 All models ex. Corolla & Celica

EVERY 96 MO/120 MI—192 KM
W Spark plugs . . . . .replace
2000 Corolla, Celica only

EVERY 120 MONTHS
THEN EVERY 24 MONTHS
Air bag system . . . . .inspect

SEVERE SERVICE
Automatic transmission: 1996-99—
Change fluid every 12 mo/15 mi (24 km)

Automatic transmission: 2000 Avalon,
Camry, Solara, Corolla—Inspect fluid level
and check for leaks every 12 mo/15 mi (24
km); replace every 24 mo/30 mi (48 km)

Automatic transmission: 2000 Sienna,
Celica—Change fluid every 48 mo/60 mi
(96 km)

Brake system—Inspect every 4 mo/5 mi
(8 km)

Crankcase—Change oil & filter every: ex
Turbo, 4 mo/5 mi (8 km); Turbo, 2.5 mi
(4 km). Change Turbo oil filter every other
oil change

Differential or final drive—Change
lubricant every 12 mo/15 mi (24 km)

Drive shaft boots—Inspect every 4 mo/
5 mi (8 km). 1996-98 All & 1999 Sienna,
torque flange bolts

Manual transmission or transaxle—
Change lubricant every 24 mo/30 mi (48 km)

Steering linkage & ball joints—Inspect
every 4 mo/5 mi (8 km)

Air cleaner element—Inspect every 4 mo/
5 mi (8 km)

Body & chassis—Torque nuts and bolts
every 4 mo/5 mi (8 km)

Timing belt—Replace every: 1996-97, 60
mi (96 km); 1998 ex. Corolla, 72 mo/90 mi
(144 km)

Tires—1997-00, rotate every 4mo/5mi
(8 km)

KEY TO LUBRICANTS
See inside front cover
CRANKCASE . . . .**SJ, GF-1**

CAPACITY, Refill:	Liters	Qt
Avalon, Camry, Solara: 4-cyl. . . .	3.4	3.6
V6	4.5	4.8
Celica: 1.8L	3.5	3.7
H.O., 2000	4.2	4.5
2.0L, 2.2L	3.7	3.9
Turbo	3.6	3.8
Corolla: 1.6L	2.8	3.0
1.8L	3.5	3.7
Echo	3.4	3.6
Sienna	4.5	4.8
Supra	4.9	5.2
Turbo	4.7	5.0
Tercel, Paseo	2.5	2.7

Capacity shown is without filter. When replacing filter, additional oil may be needed

1996 Supra Turbo:
Above -20°F (-29°C) 10W-30
1996 Camry V6, Avalon, Corolla, Supra ex. Turbo;
1997-00, All ex. Supra Turbo:
Above 0°F (-18°C) 10W-30
Below 100°F (38°C) 1997 . . . . .5W-30[1]
All Temperatures, 1998-00 . . . . .5W-30[1]
1996 Others; 1997-98 Supra Turbo:
Above 0°F (-18°C) 10W-30
Below 50°F (10°C) 5W-30
1 Preferred

TRANSMISSION/TRANSAXLE, Automatic
1998 Supra, all; 1996-97 Supra Turbo . .**SLF**[2]
2 ATF Type T-IV
2000 Echo, Celica . . . .**SLF**[2]
All others **AF3**
Differential is serviced separately in: 1996-98 Avalon, Camry,
Corolla, Sienna, Tercel 3-speed and Celica 2.2L; 1999 Camry
& Solara 4-cyl., Corolla & Tercel 3-speed, Sienna

CAPACITY, Initial Refill[3]:	Liters	Qt
Avalon, Camry, Solara: 4-cyl. . . .	2.5	2.6
V6 1996-98	3.5	3.7
1999-00	4.8	5.0
Celica: 1.8L, 1996-99	3.3	3.5
2000	2.1	2.2
H.O.	4.0	4.2
2.2L: 1996	1.6	1.7
1997-99	2.5	2.6
Corolla: 3-speed	2.3	2.4
4-speed	3.1	3.3
Sienna	3.5	3.7
Supra	1.6	1.7
Turbo	1.9	2.0
Tercel, Paseo: 3-speed	2.5	2.6
4-speed	3.1	3.3

3 With the engine at operating temperature, shift transmission through all gears. Check fluid level in PARK and add fluid as needed

TRANSMISSION/TRANSAXLE, Manual
FWD, includes front differential and 4WD transfer case
Tercel, Paseo, Echo . . .75W-90 **GL-4, GL-5**
Celica, Camry, Corolla .75W-90 **GL-4, GL-5**
Supra ex. Turbo 75W-90 **GL-4, GL-5**
Supra Turbo . . . .**GLS**

CAPACITY, Refill:	Liters	Pt
Supra	2.6	5.4
Turbo	1.8	3.8
Camry, Solara: 4-cyl.: 1996-97 . .	2.6	5.6
1998-00	2.2	4.6
V6	4.2	8.8
Celica: 1.8L	1.9	4.0
H.O., 2000	2.3	4.8
2.2L 1996-97	2.6	5.6
1998-99	2.2	4.6
Corolla	1.9	4.0
Echo	1.9	4.0
Tercel, Paseo	1.9	4.0

DIFFERENTIAL, Rear
Limited-Slip . . . .**GL-5★**
Standard **GL-5**
Above 0°F (-18°C), 90; below 0°F (-18°C), 80W, 80W-90

CAPACITY, Refill:	Liters	Pt
Supra	1.4	2.9

FINAL DRIVE, FWD w/AT **AF3**
Tercel, Corolla w/3-speed; Avalon & Camry ex. 1999-00 V6,
Sienna, & Celica 2.2L

CAPACITY, Refill:	Liters	Pt
Avalon, Camry, Solara, 4-cyl. . . .	1.6	3.4
V6, 1996-98	0.9	2.0
Corolla, Tercel	1.4	3.0
Celica, 2.2L	1.6	3.4
Sienna	0.9	2.0

SERVICE AT TIME OR MILEAGE — WHICHEVER OCCURS FIRST

TAIPM9   TAIPM9

Perform the following maintenance services at the intervals indicated to keep the vehicle warranties in effect.

W   SERVICE TO MAINTAIN EMISSION WARRANTY

MI—MILES IN THOUSANDS
KM—KILOMETERS IN THOUSANDS

SERVICE PERIODICALLY
Brake & clutch
   fluid reservoirs . . . . . . .check level **HB**

Power steering fluid . . . .check level **AF3**

FIRST 12 MO/7.5 MI—12 KM
Idle speed . . . . .check/adjust

EVERY 12 MO/10 MI—16 KM
W Crankcase . . . . .change oil

W Oil filter .replace

4WD, EVERY 18 MO/15 MI—24 KM
2WD, PICKUPS & ALL VANS
EVERY 24 MO/20 MI—32 KM
Brake system . . . . .check
Disc pads & rotors, drums, linings, booster, parking brake, lines, pipes & hoses

Driveshaft boots 4WD . . . . .inspect

Propeller shaft 4WD . . . . . .lubricate **LM**

Transfer case . . . . .check level

Transmission, manual . . . . .check level

Front suspension . . . . .inspect
Ball joints, dust covers. 4WD van, lubricate control arms, **LM**

Steering gear box . . . . .inspect
Check linkage & free play

Transmission, automatic . . . .check level

Body . . . . .inspect
Torque nuts & bolts

EVERY 36 MO/30 MI—48 KM
Exhaust system . . . . .inspect

W Air cleaner element . . . . .replace

Drive belts . . . . .inspect
Initial service

Fuel lines & connections . . . . . . .inspect

W Idle speeds . . . . .check/adjust
2V, initial service only. Adjust throttle positioner on carburetted engines

Spark plugs . . . . .replace
Ex. Van

W Valve clearance . . . . .adjust
4-cyl. ex. Van

4WD, EVERY 36 MO/30 MI—48 KM
2WD PICKUP & ALL VANS,
EVERY 48 MO/40 MI—64 KM
Front wheel bearings . . .clean/repack **LM**
Torque to 19-23 ft lb. Back off & retighten finger tight

EVERY 72 MO/60 MI—96 KM
Charcoal canister Calif. . . . . . . .inspect
Check fuel evaporative system, hoses & connections

Cooling system . . . . .change coolant **EC**
Replace coolant every 36 mo/30 mi (48 km) thereafter

Drive belts . . . . .inspect
Second service, inspect every 12 mo/10 mi (16 km) thereafter

Fuel cap gasket . . . . .replace

Spark plugs . . . . .replace
Platinum tipped only

Valve clearance . . . . .adjust
V6 engine

AT 80 MI—126 KM
Oxygen sensor . . . . .replace

SEVERE SERVICE
W Crankcase—Change oil & filter every 6 mo/5 mi (8 km)

Exhaust system—Inspect every 18 mo/ 15 mi (24 km)

Propeller shaft—4WD lubricate every 12 mo/7.5 mi (12 km)

Steering, suspension & brake components—Inspect every 12 mo/10 mi (16 km)

Transmission, transfer case & differential fluid or lubricant—Change every 24 mo/20 mi (32 km)

W Air cleaner element—Inspect every 6 mo/ 5 mi (8 km)

Timing belt—Replace every 60 mi (96 km)

Control arms—4WD Van lubricate every 12 mo/10 mi (16 km)

KEY TO LUBRICANTS
See inside front cover

CRANKCASE . . . .**SG**

CAPACITY, Refill:	Liters	Qt
Pickup, 4-Runner 4-cyl.	3.8	4.0
V6: 2WD	4.0	4.2
4WD	4.2	4.4
Van	3.0	3.2

Capacity shown is without filter. When replacing filter, additional oil may be needed

Above 10°F (-12°C) . . .15W-40, 20W-40, 20W-50
Above -10°F (-23°C) . .10W-30, 10W-40, 10W-50
Below 50°F (10°C) 5W-30

TRANSMISSION, Automatic **AF3**

CAPACITY, Initial Refill[1]:	Liters	Qt
Pickup w/OD	4.5	4.8
Others	2.4	2.5

1 With the engine at operating temperature, shift transmission through all gears. Check fluid level in PARK and add fluid as needed

TRANSMISSION, Manual
W series
   trans. 80W-90, 75W-90 **GL-4, GL-5**
Others 75W-90 **GL-4, GL-5**

CAPACITY, Refill:	Liters	Pt
4-Runner	3.0	6.4
Van	2.3	5.0
4WD	2.6	5.4
Pickup, 2WD:		
G40, W46, W55	2.4	5.0
G57	2.2	4.6
R150	3.0	6.4
4WD: W56, R150	3.0	6.4
G58	3.9	8.2

TRANSFER CASE
Pickup, 4-Runner w/MT;
  Van . . . . . . .75W-90[2], 80W-90 **GL-4, GL-5**
2 1989 V6 and Van; 75W-90 preferred
Pickup, 4-Runner w/AT **AF3**

CAPACITY, Refill:	Liters	Pt
Pickup, 4-Runner		
MT: w/W56 trans.	1.6	3.4
w/G56, R150 trans.	1.1	2.4
AT	0.8	1.6
Van	1.2	2.6

DIFFERENTIAL
4WD Pickup, 4-Runner w/Auto.
  Disc. Diff. 75W-90 **GL-5**
Others **GL-5**
Above 0°F (-18°C), 90; below 0°F (-18°C), 80W-90

CAPACITY, Refill:	Liters	Pt
Van	1.5	3.1
4WD front	1.3	2.4
4WD rear	1.9	3.7
Pickup, 4-Runner:		
2WD: 7.5" ring gear	1.4	2.8
8.0" ring gear	1.8	3.8
4WD: Front	1.6	3.4
w/Auto. Disc. Diff.	1.9	4.0
Rear: Turbo, V6	2.4	5.0
Others	2.2	4.6

SERVICE AT TIME OR MILEAGE — WHICHEVER OCCURS FIRST

TAIPM11   TAIPM11

Perform the following maintenance services at the intervals indicated to keep the vehicle warranties in effect.
W   SERVICE TO MAINTAIN EMISSION WARRANTY

MI—MILES IN THOUSANDS
KM—KILOMETERS IN THOUSANDS

SERVICE PERIODICALLY
Brake & clutch
    fluid reservoirs . . . . . . .check level **HB**

Power steering fluid . . . .check level **AF3**

FIRST 12 MO/7.5 MI—12 KM
Idle speed . . . . .check/adjust
1990-95 FI ex. Tacoma

EVERY 12 MO/7.5 MI—12 KM
W Crankcase . . . . .change oil

W Oil filter .replace

EVERY 24 MO/15 MI—24 KM
Brake system . . . . .check
Disc pads & rotors, drums, linings, booster, parking
brake, lines, pipes & hoses

Differentials . . . . .check level

Driveshaft boots 4WD . . . . .inspect

Propeller shaft 4WD . . . . . .lubricate **LM**

Transfer case . . . . .check level

Transmission, manual . . . . .check level

Front suspension . . . . .inspect
Ball joints, dust covers

Steering gearbox . . . . .inspect
Check linkage & free play

Transmission, automatic . . . .check level

Idle speed 1991-95 . . . . . .check/adjust
Ex. Previa & Tacoma

Body . . . . .inspect
Torque nuts & bolts

EVERY 36 MO/30 MI—48 KM
Exhaust system . . . . .inspect

W Air cleaner element . . . . .replace

Drive belts . . . . .inspect
Pickup, 4-Runner, Tacoma, T-100, initial service

Fuel lines & connections . . . . . .inspect
Also inspect fuel vapor hoses and fuel tank bands

Idle speeds 1990 . . . . .check/adjust
2V, initial service only. Adjust throttle positioner on
carburetted engines

Spark plugs . . . . .replace
Ex. Previa

Supercharge oil level . . . . . .inspect **SLF**
Previa only

CAPACITY, Refill:	Liters	Pt
Pickup, 4-Runner: MT:		
w/W56 trans.	1.6	3.4
w/G56, R150 trans.	1.1	2.4
AT	0.8	1.6
Previa	1.3	2.8
Tacoma	1.0	2.2
T100	1.1	2.4

DIFFERENTIAL
4WD Pickup, 4-Runner, T100, Tacoma
    w/Auto. Disc. Diff. 75W-90 **GL-5**
Others **GL-5**
Above 0°F (-18°C), 90; below 0°F (-18°C), 80W,
80W-90

Models with Automatic Disconnecting Differential do not have
locking hubs

W Valve clearance . . . . .adjust
1990-95 4-cyl. Pickup, 4-Runner

AT FIRST 36 MO/45 MI—72 KM
THEN, EVERY 24 MO/30 MI—48 KM
Cooling system . . . . .change coolant **EC**

PICKUP, 4-RUNNER, T100:
2WD, EVERY 48 MO/30 MI—48 KM
4WD, EVERY 36 MO/30 MI—48 KM
Front wheel bearings . . .clean/repack **LM**
2WD Torque to 19-23 ft lb. Back off & retighten finger
tight. Also lubricate driveshaft bushing
4WD, also lubricate thrust bearing

EVERY 72 MO/60 MI—96 KM
Charcoal canister, Calif. . . . . .inspect

Drive belts . . . . .inspect
Inspect every 12 mo/7.5 mi (12 km) thereafter

Fuel cap gasket . . . . .replace

W Spark plugs . . . . .replace
Previa only

Valve clearance . . . . .adjust
Previa & V6 engine; 1995 Tacoma

AT 80 MI—126 KM
Oxygen sensor . . . . .replace
Ex. Calif.

EVERY 120 MONTHS
THEN, EVERY 24 MONTHS
Air bag system . . . . .inspect
As equipped

SEVERE SERVICE
W **Crankcase**—Change oil & filter every 6
mo/3.75 mi (6 km)

Exhaust system—Inspect every 24 mo/
15 mi (24 km)

Propeller shaft—4WD lubricate every
12 mo/7.5 mi (12 km)

**Suspension, steering, brake compo-
nents & 4WD driveshaft boots**—Inspect
every 12 mo/7.5 mi (12 km)

**Transmission, transfer case & differential
fluid or lubricant**—Change every 24 mo/
15 mi (24 km)

W **Air cleaner element**—Inspect every 6 mo/
3.75 mi (6 km)

Timing belt—V6 replace every 60 mi
(96 km)

CAPACITY, Refill:	Liters	Pt
Pickup, 4-Runner: 2WD:		
7.5" RG	1.4	2.8
8.0" RG: 2 pinion	1.8	3.8
4 pinion	2.2	4.6
4WD: Front	1.6	3.4
w/Auto. Disc. Diff.	1.9	4.0
Rear: 4-cyl.	2.2	4.6
V6	2.4	5.0
Previa: Front	1.1	2.2
Rear	1.5	3.2
Tacoma: Front	1.1	2.3
w/A.D.D.	1.2	2.4
Rear: 2.4L	1.4	2.8
2.7L, 3.4L	2.5	5.2
w/LSD	2.6	5.6
4WD, X-long	2.1	4.2
T100: 2WD	2.0	4.2
4WD: Front	1.6	3.4
w/Auto. Disc. Diff. . . .	1.9	4.0
Rear	2.0	4.0

KEY TO LUBRICANTS
See inside front cover

CRANKCASE . . . . .SG, SH

CAPACITY, Refill:	Liters	Qt
Pickup, 4-Runner: 4-cyl.	3.8	4.0
V6: 2WD	4.0	4.2
4WD	4.2	4.4
Previa	5.5	5.8
Oil tank (underhood)	2.0	2.1
Tacoma: 4-cyl., 2WD	4.8	5.1
4WD	4.7	5.0
V6, 2WD	5.1	5.4
4WD	4.9	5.2
T100: 4-cyl.	4.8	5.1
T100, 1993-94 V6: 2WD	5.1	5.4
4WD	4.2	4.4
1995 V6	4.7	5.0

Capacity shown is without filter. When replacing filter, addi-
tional oil may be needed
1990:
Above 10°F (-12°C) . . .15W-40, 20W-40, 20W-50
Above -10°F (-23°C) . . .10W-30, 10W-40, 10W-50
Below 50°F (10°C) 5W-30
1991-95:
Above 0°F (-18°C) 10W-30
Above 0°F (-18°C), 1991 . . . . .10W-40
Below 100°F (38°C),
    Supercharged Previa 5W-30
Below 50°F (10°C) Others 5W-30

TRANSMISSION, Automatic AF3

CAPACITY, Initial Refill[1]:	Liters	Qt
Pickup, 4-Runner 2WD: 4-cyl. . . .	2.4	2.5
V6	1.6	1.7
4WD: 4-cyl. 1990-93	1.6	1.7
1994-95	2.0	2.1
V6	4.5	4.8
Previa	2.4	2.5
Supercharged	1.6	1.7
Tacoma: 4-cyl.	2.4	2.5
V6 2WD	1.6	1.7
V6 4WD	2.0	2.2
T100: 1993-94 All	2.0	2.2
1995 2WD	1.6	1.7
4WD	2.0	2.2

1 With the engine at operating temperature, shift transmission through all gears. Check fluid level in PARK and add
fluid as needed

TRANSMISSION, Manual
1990-93:
W series
    trans. 80W-90, 75W-90 **GL-4, GL-5**
Others 75W-90 **GL-4, GL-5**
1994-95:
W series trans. 80W-90, 75W-90 **GL-4**
Others 75W-90 **GL-4**

CAPACITY, Refill:	Liters	Pt
Pickup, 4-Runner 2WD:		
G40, W46, W55	2.4	5.0
G57	2.2	4.6
R150: to 4/94	3.0	6.4
from 5/94	2.6	5.4
4WD: W56	3.0	6.4
G58	3.9	8.2
R150: to 5/94	3.0	6.2
from 6/94	2.2	4.6
Previa: 2WD	2.2	4.6
4WD	2.6	5.4
Tacoma: 4-cyl., 2WD	2.6	5.4
4WD	2.5	5.2
V6, 2WD	2.6	5.4
4WD	2.2	4.6
T100: 4-cyl.	2.6	5.4
V6: 1993-5/94	3.0	6.4
6/94-1995 2WD	2.6	5.4
6/94-1995 4WD	2.2	4.6

TRANSFER CASE
Pickup, 4-Runner, T100:
    W/MT, all 75W-90 **GL-4, GL-5**
    W/AT: 4-cyl. 75W-90 **GL-4, GL-5**
    V6 . . . .**AF3**
Previa, Tacoma 75W-90 **GL-4, GL-5**

SERVICE AT TIME OR MILEAGE — WHICHEVER OCCURS FIRST

TAIPM15   TAIPM15

Perform the following maintenance services at the intervals indicated to keep the vehicle warranties in effect.

W   **SERVICE TO MAINTAIN EMISSION WARRANTY**

MI—MILES IN THOUSANDS
KM—KILOMETERS IN THOUSANDS

SERVICE PERIODICALLY

Brake & clutch
    fluid reservoirs . . . . . . .check level **HB**
Power steering fluid . . . .check level **AF3**
Transmission, manual . . . . .inspect
Check for leaks

EVERY 6 MO/7.5 MI—12 KM

Crankcase . . . . .change oil
Oil filter .replace
Tires . . . . .rotate
At mileage interval only

EVERY 12 MO/15 MI—24 KM

Ball joints . . . . .inspect
Also check dust covers
Brake system . . . . .inspect
Differentials . . . . .check level
Check for leaks
Drive shaft . . . . .lubricate **LM**
4WD ex. RAV 4
Drive shaft boots . . . . .inspect
All 4WD & 2WD RAV 4
Drive shaft bolt . . . . .retorque
All ex. 2WD RAV 4
Exhaust system . . . . .inspect
Limited-slip differential . . . . .check level
Check for leaks
Steering gearbox . . . . .check
Inspect for leaks
Steering linkage & boots . . . . . .inspect
Transfer case, 1996-99 . . . .check level
Check for leaks
Transmission, automatic . . . .check level
All 1996-99 & 2000 Tundra also check for leaks

EVERY 24 MO/30 MI—48 KM

Drive shaft bushing . . . . .lubricate **LM**
4WD ex. Previa & Tacoma w/Auto. Disc. Diff.
Front wheel bearings . . . . . .repack **LM**
Tacoma ex. Auto. Disc. Diff., & 4-Runner only
Limited-slip differential RAV 4
   & Land Cruiser . . . . . .change lubricant
1998-00 RAV 4, inspect only
Air cleaner element . . . . .replace
Cooling system . . . . .replace coolant **EC**
Drive belts . . . . .inspect/adjust
1998-99 ex. V-ribbed
Fuel lines & connections . . . . . .inspect
Fuel tank . . . . .inspect
Check vapor vent system & bands. Also check fuel
tank cap
W Spark plugs . . . . .replace
Standard spark plugs, Tacoma, Tundra & 4-Runner only
Supercharger fluid level,
   Previa . . . . .inspect **SLF**
Use Toyota Supercharger fluid

EVERY 48 MO/60 MI—96 KM

Limited-slip
   differential RAV 4 . . . .change lubricant
Transfer case, 2000 . . . . .check level
Check for leaks

CAPACITY, Refill:	Liters	Pt
RAV 4	0.9	2.0
T100: Front	1.9	4.0
Rear: 1996	2.4	5.0
1997-98 2WD	2.8	6.0
4WD	3.0	6.2

Drive belts . . . . .inspect/adjust
Initial service only then every 12 mo/15 mi (24 km)
thereafter
1996-97 & 2000 all. 1998-99 V-ribbed only
W Spark plugs . . . . .replace
All ex. Tacoma & 4-Runner w/standard plugs & Land
Cruiser
Valve clearance . . . . .inspect/adjust
Adjust only if noisy

EVERY 72 MO/60 MI—96 KM

Charcoal canister, 1996-97 . . . . .inspect

EVERY 72 MO/90 MI—144 KM

Spark plugs . . . . .replace
Land Cruiser only
Wheel bearings and drive
   shaft bearings . . . . .lubricate **LM**
2000 Land Cruiser only

EVERY 120 MONTHS
THEN EVERY 24 MONTHS

Air bag system . . . . .inspect

SEVERE SERVICE

Automatic transmission: 1996-99 All &
2000 Tundra—Change lubricant every 12
mo/15 mi (24 km). Inspect daily if
operated off-road in sand, mud, or water
Automatic transmission: 2000 ex.
Tundra—Inspect for leaks and fluid level
every 12 mo/15 mi (24 km). Change fluid
every 24 mo/30 mi (48 km)
Brake system—Inspect every 4 mo/5 mi
(8 km). Inspect daily if operated off-road
in sand, mud, or water
Crankcase—Change oil & filter every
4 mo/5 mi (8 km)
Differentials—Change lubricant every 12
mo/15 mi (24 km). Inspect daily if operated
off-road in sand, mud, or water
Drive shaft—All 4WD ex. RAV 4, lubricate
every 4 mo/5 mi (8km). Lubricate daily if
operated off-road in sand, mud, or water
Manual transmission—Change lubricant
every 24 mo/30 mi (48 km)
Drive shaft boots—Inspect every 4 mo/
5 mi (8km). Also torque flange bolts
Steering linkage & ball joints—Inspect
every 4 mo/5 mi (8 km). Inspect daily if
operated off-road in sand, mud, or water
Transfer case—Change lubricant every:
1996, 12 mo/15 mi (24km); 1997-99, 24
mo/30 mi (48km)
Wheel bearings—Inspect daily if operated
off-road in sand, mud, or water
Air cleaner element—Inspect every 4 mo/
5 mi (8 km). Inspect daily if operated off-
road in sand, mud, or water
Body & chassis—Torque nuts and bolts
every 4 mo/5 mi (8 km)
Timing belt—Replace every: 1996-97 ex.
Previa & 2.7L eng., 60 mi (96 km); 1998-00
ex. Tacoma & 4-Runner 4-cyl., 72mo/90 mi
(144 km)
Tires—1997-00, rotate every 4 mo/5 mi
(8 km)

CAPACITY, Refill:	Liters	Pt
Land Cruiser: Front	1.7	3.6
Rear	3.2	6.8
w/limited-slip	3.3	7.0
Tundra: Front	1.2	2.4
Rear, 2WD	3.8	8.0
Rear, 4WD	3.5	7.4

KEY TO LUBRICANTS
See inside front cover

CRANKCASE . . . . .SJ, GF-1

CAPACITY, Refill:	Liters	Qt
Tacoma, 4-Runner: 4-cyl. 2WD . .	4.8	5.1
4WD	4.7	5.0
V6: 2WD	5.1	5.4
4WD	4.9	5.2
Previa	5.5	5.8
Oil tank (underhood)	2.0	2.1
RAV 4	3.9	4.1
T100: 4-cyl.	5.0	5.3
V6: 2WD	4.9	5.2
4WD	4.4	4.7
Land Cruiser	6.4	6.8
Tundra: V6	4.9	5.2
V8	5.7	6.0

Capacity shown is without filter. When replacing filter, additional oil may be needed

Above 0°F (-18°C) 10W-30
Below 100°F (38°C), 1996-97 . . . . .5W-30
All temperatures, 1998-00 . . . . .5W-30

TRANSMISSION, Automatic
RAV 4, 4WD . . . . .SLF[1]
1 ATF Type T
All others AF3

CAPACITY, Initial Refill[2]:	Liters	Qt
Tacoma, 4-Runner: 4-cyl. 2WD . .	2.4	2.5
4WD	2.0	2.1
V6: 2WD	1.6	1.7
4WD	2.0	2.2
Previa	2.4	2.5
Supercharged	1.6	1.7
RAV 4	3.3	3.5
T100: 2WD	1.6	1.7
4WD	2.0	2.2
Land Cruiser	3.5	3.7
Tundra	2.0	2.1

2 With the engine at operating temperature, shift transmission through all gears. Check fluid level in PARK and add
fluid as needed

TRANSMISSION, Manual
RAV 4, 4WD 75W-90 **GL-5**
All others 75W-90 **GL-4, GL-5**

CAPACITY, Refill:	Liters	Pt
Tacoma, 4-Runner: 4-cyl.: 2WD . .	2.6	5.4
4WD	2.5	5.2
V6: 2WD	2.6	5.4
4WD	2.2	4.6
Previa: 2WD	2.2	4.6
4WD	2.6	5.4
RAV 4: 2WD	3.9	8.2
4WD	5.0	10.6
T100: 2WD	2.6	5.4
4WD	2.2	4.6
Tundra: 2WD	2.6	5.4
4WD	2.2	4.6

TRANSFER CASE 75W-90 **GL-4, GL-5**
RAV 4, applies to models w/AT only

CAPACITY, Refill:	Liters	Pt
Tacoma, 4-Runner	1.0	2.2
Electronic type	1.2	2.6
Previa	1.3	2.8
RAV 4	0.7	1.4
T100	1.1	2.4
Land Cruiser	1.3	2.8
Tundra	1.0	2.2

DIFFERENTIAL
RAV 4, applies to 4WD models only
4WD Tacoma, 4-Runner, T100, Tundra
   w/Auto. Disc. Diff. 75W-90 **GL-5**
Land Cruiser w/limited-slip . . . .**GL-5★**
Others **GL-5**
Above 0°F (-18°C), 90; below 0°F (-18°C), 80W,
80W-90
Models with Automatic Disconnecting Differential do not
have locking hubs

CAPACITY, Refill:	Liters	Pt
Tacoma, 4-Runner: Front	1.1	2.3
w/A.D.D.	1.2	2.4
Rear, 2.4L	1.4	2.8
2.7L, 3.4L	2.8	5.8
w/locking diff.	3.0	6.2
4WD, X-long	2.1	4.2
w/locking diff.	3.0	6.2
Previa: Front	1.1	2.2
Rear	1.5	3.2

SERVICE LOCATIONS — ENGINE AND CHASSIS

HOOD RELEASE: Vanagon, push button on rear lid, others, inside

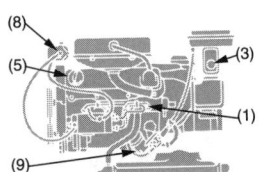

1990-92
4-cyl. 1588cc Diesel
Jetta

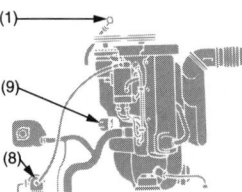

1989-91
4-cyl. 1588cc Diesel

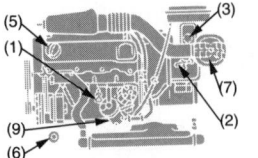

1989-91
4-cyl. 1780cc
Jetta, Scirocco

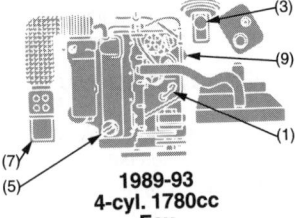

1989-93
4-cyl. 1780cc
Fox

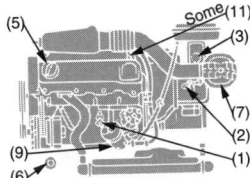

1989-91
4-cyl. 1780cc Golf, GTI
Jetta, Scirocco

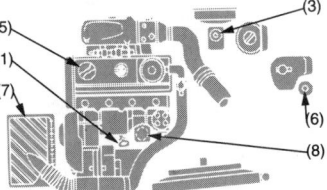

1989-91
4-cyl. 1780cc Supercharged
Corrado

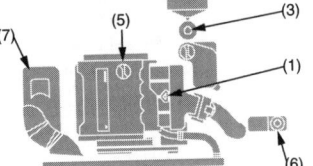

1998
4-cyl. 1781cc
Passat

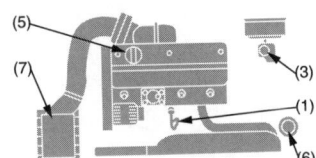

1993-98
4-cyl. 1895cc Diesel
Golf, Jetta, Passat

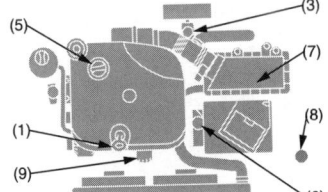

1998-99
4-cyl. 1896cc Diesel
1999
4-cyl. 1781cc Gas Turbo
New Beetle

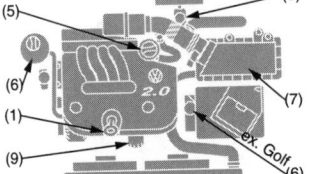

1998-99
4-cyl. 1984cc New Beetle
1999
Jetta, Golf

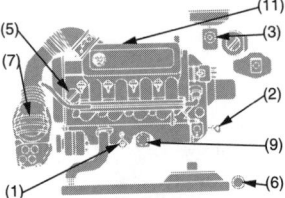

1990-92
4-cyl. 1984cc
Passat

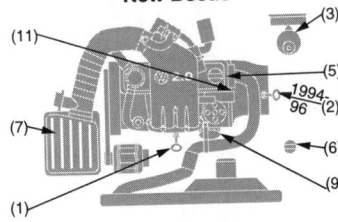

1994-99
4-cyl. 1984cc
Golf, Jetta, Cabrio, Passat
1999
Cabrio

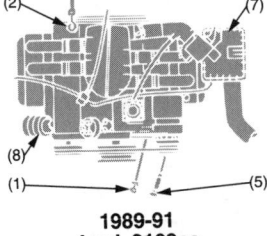

1989-91
4-cyl. 2109cc
Vanagon

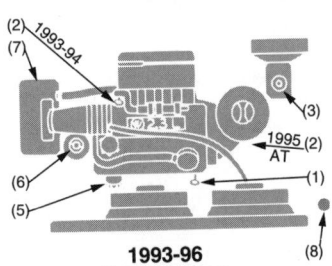

1993-96
5-cyl. 2461cc
EuroVan

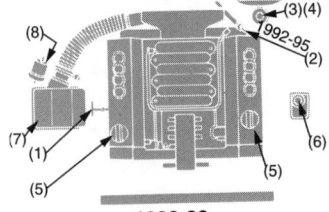

1998-99
V6 2771cc
Passat

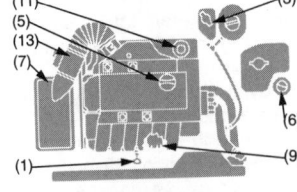

1992-99
V6 2792cc
Corrado, Golf, GTI,
Jetta, Passat

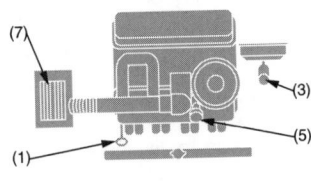

1996-99
V6 2792cc
EuroVan

(1) Crankcase dipstick	(6) Power steering reservoir	(11) EGR valve
(2) Transmission dipstick	(7) Air filter	(12) Oxygen sensor
(3) Brake fluid reservoir	(8) Fuel filter/water separator	(13) PCV valve
(4) Clutch fluid reservoir	(9) Oil filter	
(5) Oil fill cap	(10) PCV filter	

SERVICE LOCATIONS — ENGINE AND CHASSIS

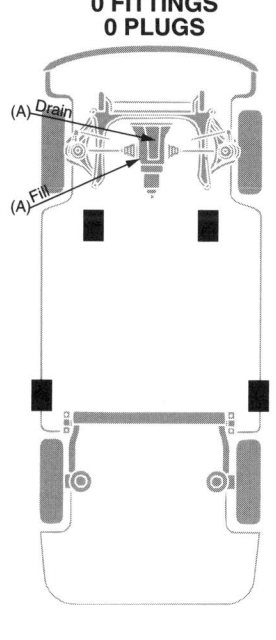

0 FITTINGS
0 PLUGS

(A) Drain
(A) Fill

1989-93
Fox

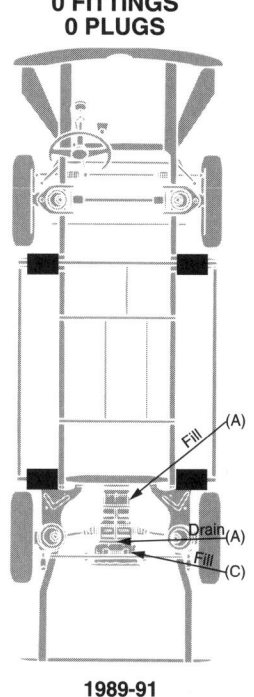

0 FITTINGS
0 PLUGS

Fill (A)
Drain (A)
Fill (C)

1989-91
Vanagon

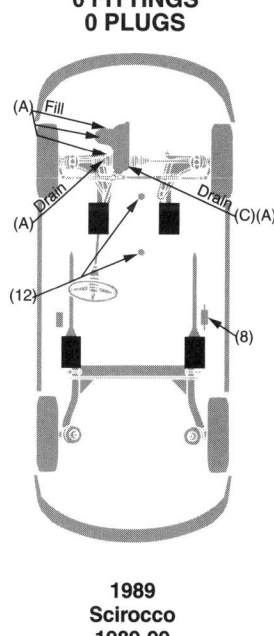

0 FITTINGS
0 PLUGS

(A) Fill
(A) Drain
Drain (C)(A)
(12)
(8)

1989
Scirocco
1989-99
Jetta, Golf
1998-99
New Beetle

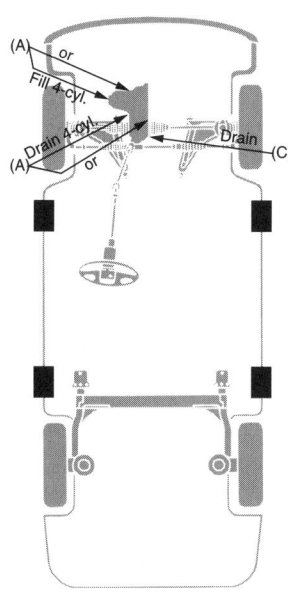

0 FITTINGS
0 PLUGS

(A) or
Fill 4-cyl.
Drain 4-cyl.
(A) or
Drain (C)

1990-94
Corrado
1990-97
Passat

0 FITTINGS
0 PLUGS

Drain (A)(C)
(A)(C) Fill

1998-99
Passat

CAUTION: On front wheel drive vehicles, the center of gravity is farther forward than on rear wheel drive vehicles. When removing major components from the rear of the vehicle while it is on a hoist, the vehicle must be supported in a manner to prevent it from tipping forward.

■ Lift adapter position

(8) Fuel filter

(A) Manual transmission/transaxle, drain & fill

(B) Transfer case, NOT USED

(C) Automatic transaxle final drive, drain & fill

(12) Oxygen sensor

VOLKSWAGEN
1989 All Water-Cooled Gasoline Models

SERVICE AT TIME OR MILEAGE — WHICHEVER OCCURS FIRST

VNIPM2 VNIPM2

W SERVICE TO MAINTAIN EMISSION WARRANTY

MI—MILES IN THOUSANDS
KM—KILOMETERS IN THOUSANDS

EVERY 6 MO/7.5 MI—12 KM
Brake system . . . . .inspect
Vanagon only. Check for damage or leaks. Check pad thickness

W Crankcase . . . . .change oil

W Cooling system . . . . . . .check level EC

W Oil filter . . . . .replace
Initial service only

Clutch . . . . .check/adjust
Ex. Vanagon, initial service only

EVERY 12 MO/15 MI—24 KM
Axle boots . . . . .inspect

W Brake system . . . . .inspect HB
Check fluid level, lining & pad thickness. Where applicable, check operation of pressure regulator

Clutch . . . . .check/adjust
Ex. Scirocco 16V, Vanagon

W Exhaust system . . . . .inspect

W Fuel tank, lines, hoses
& connections . . . . .inspect

Final drive, automatic . . . . . . .check level

W Oil filter . . . . .replace

Transaxle . . . . .check level

W Air cleaner element . . . . .clean
Ex. Vanagon

Battery . . . . .check level

W Compression . . . . .check
Ex. Vanagon

Headlights . . . . .adjust

W Idle speed & CO . . . . . . .check/adjust
Not required for Calif. warranty. 1989 FI engines, check idle speed only

On-board diagnosis
system . . . . .check/clear

Power steering . . . . . . .check level AF2
All from 4-89 ex. Vanagon PS, others AF2

Transmission, automatic . . . .check level
Check final drive for leaks

Door hinges & checks . . . . .lubricate MO

Lights, accessories . . . . .inspect

Sunroof rails . . . . . .clean/lubricate SLS

Supplemental restraint
system . . . . .inspect

Tires & wheels . . . . .inspect

EVERY 24 MONTHS
Brake fluid . . . . .replace HB
Check operation of warning light switch; check brake pressure regulator where applicable

EVERY 24 MO/30 MI—48 KM
Front axle & steering system
boots & seals . . . . .inspect

W Air cleaner element . . . . .replace

W Drive belts . . . . .inspect/adjust

W Spark plugs . . . . .replace

Valve cover gaskets . . . . .replace
Vanagon only

EVERY 60 MI—90 KM
Fuel filter . . . . .replace
Scirocco

Oxygen sensor . . . . .replace
All ex. Vanagon & Canada
Reset mileage counter where applicable

EVERY 90 MI—144 KM
Oxygen sensor . . . . .replace
Vanagon ex. Canada

SEVERE SERVICE
Crankcase—Change oil more frequently

Air cleaner element—Replace more frequently

Transmission, automatic—change fluid every 30 mi (48 km)

KEY TO LUBRICANTS
AE	ESSO type LT71141 Fluid VW Part No. G052162A2, A1
AF2	DEXRON®-II Automatic Transmission Fluid
CC	Motor Oil, API Service CC
CD	Motor Oil, API Service CD
CF-4	Motor Oil, API Service CF-4
CG-4	Motor Oil, API Service CG-4
EC	Ethylene Glycol Coolant: Green in color. If red in color, only use VW Part No. G012A8DA1
GL-4	Gear Oil, API Service GL-4
GL-5	Gear Oil, API Service GL-5
HB	Hydraulic Brake Fluid, DOT 4
MO	Motor Oil
PS	Power Steering Fluid VW Part No. G002000, G002012
SG	Motor Oil, API Service SG
SH	Motor Oil, API Service SH
SLS	Silicone Spray

CRANKCASE . . . . .SG
CAPACITY, Refill:	Liters	Qt
4-cyl. engines:		
Vanagon	3.8	4.2
Fox	3.0	3.2
All others	3.5	3.7

Capacity shown is without filter. When replacing filter, additional oil may be needed
68° to 104°F (20° to 40°C) 40
32° to 86°F (0° to 30°C) 30
14° to 50°F (-10° to 10°C) 20W-20
14° to 86°F (-10° to 30°C) 20W-40, 20W-50
5° to 30°F (-15° to 30°C) 15W-40, 15W-50
-4° to 50°F (-20° to 10°C) 10W-30, 10W-40
-4° to 23°F (-20° to -5°C) 10W
-22° to 14°F (-30° to -10°C) 5W-20, 5W-30

TRANSMISSION, Automatic . . . . .AE, AF2
Final drive serviced separately
Verify fluid installed before topping off. AE is yellow in color
CAPACITY, Initial Refill[1]:	Liters	Qt
All models	3.0	3.2

[1] With engine at operating temperature, shift transmission through all gears. Check level in PARK and add fluid as needed

TRANSAXLE, Manual
Vanagon 80W, 80W-90 GL-4
All others . . . . .75W-90 GL-4[2]
[2] Synthetic gear oil, VW Part No. G005000, if not available 80W GL-4 may be used
CAPACITY, Refill:	Liters	Pt
Fox	1.6	3.4
Vanagon	2.5[3]	5.6[3]
Others: 4-speed	1.4	3.2
5-speed	1.9	4.2

[3] Correct oil level will be approximately 5/8 inch (15 mm) below the bottom of the fill plug opening

FINAL DRIVE 90 GL-5
CAPACITY, Refill:	Liters	Pt
All FWD w/AT	0.8	1.6
Vanagon	1.2	2.6

VOLKSWAGEN
1989-99 All Diesel Models

SERVICE AT TIME OR MILEAGE — WHICHEVER OCCURS FIRST

VNIPM3   VNIPM3

W SERVICE TO MAINTAIN EMISSION WARRANTY

MI—MILES IN THOUSANDS
KM—KILOMETERS IN THOUSANDS

FIRST 6 MO/5MI—8 KM
Crankcase . . . . .change oil

Oil filter . . . . .replace

Fuel filter . . . . .drain water

Timing belt 1.9L . . . . .check
Passat 1995-97, Jetta, Beetle & Passat 1998-99

1989-96 EVERY 6 MO/7.5 MI—12 KM
1997-99 EVERY 12 MO/10 MI—15KM
W Crankcase . . . . .change oil

Service reminder light . . . . .reset
1993-95

Clutch free play . . . . .check/adjust
Initial service only
1993-97

Fuel filter . . . . .drain water

Windshield wiper/washer . . . . . . .check

Automatic shiftlock &
park/neutral switch . . . . .check/adjust
1993-99

Tires . . . . .rotate
Rotate front to rear, check pressure
1993-99

W Oil filter . . . . .replace
At initial service only

Hood lock . . . . .check/lubricate
Canada only 1993-95

Timing belt Beetle, Jetta,
Passat 1.9L . . . . .check
1995-99

Brake system . . . . .inspect
Check pad thickness

1989-96 EVERY 12 MO/15 MI—24 KM
1997-99 EVERY 12 MO/20 MI—30 KM
Brake system . . . . .inspect HB
Check fluid level with ignition switched on & after waiting
for one minute, lining & pad thickness. Where applicable,
check operation of pressure regulator

Clutch pedal free play . . . .check/adjust

W Exhaust system . . . . .inspect

Final drive, auto. trans. . . . . . .check level

Front axle . . . . .inspect

Oil filter . . . . .replace
Models with raised bead on filter sealing surface should
have filter torqued to a minimum of 24 Nm (18 ft lb) after
3-5 minutes of varied speed engine operation

Transaxle . . . . .check level

W Cooling system . . . . . . .check level EC
Green coolant used through late 1996. Late 1996 and
later use red coolant. CAUTION: Never mix with any
other coolant or engine damage will occur.

Belts . . . . .inspect/adjust

Fuel filter . . . . .replace, drain water

Idle speed . . . . .check/adjust

Windshield wiper/washer . . . . . . .check

Axle boots . . . . .inspect

Onboard diagnosis
system . . . . .check/clear

Power steering . . . . .check level PS

Battery . . . . .check level

Transmission, automatic . . . .check level

Door hinges & checks . . . . .lubricate MO

Sunroof . . . . .clean/lubricate SLS

Supplemental restraint
system . . . . .inspect

Interior air filter . . . . .replace
1993-99

Tires & wheels . . . . .inspect
Rotate front to rear
Check pressure including spare

W PCV hoses . . . . .inspect

EVERY 24 MONTHS
Brake fluid . . . . .replace HB
Check operation of warning light switch

Air bag .check
1989-97 After first 72 months. 1998-99 After first 96
months.

1989-96
EVERY 24 MO/30 MI—45 KM
1997-99
EVERY 24 MO/40 MI—60 KM
Steering system boots & seals . . .inspect

W Air cleaner element . . . . .replace

Interior air filter . . . . .replace

Drive belts . . . . .inspect/adjust

W Fuel filter . . . . .replace

Idle speed . . . . .check/adjust

W Timing belt . . . . .check/adjust

Timing belt & tensioner, 1998-99 . .replace

Transmission, auto, 1997-99 . .change fluid
Ex. 1998 AG4

1ST & 2ND 48 MONTHS
Airbag .check

EVERY 60 MI—90 KM
Timing belt & tensioner, 1997-99 . .replace
Ex. 2.8L

Ribbed V-belt . . . . .check/adjust

Transmission, auto. . . . . . . .change fluid
1998-99 Beetle

EVERY 72 MONTHS
Tires . . . . .replace
Regardless of mileage

EVERY 80 MI—120 KM
V-belt 1998-99 . . . . .replace

SEVERE SERVICE
Crankcase—Change oil more frequently

Air cleaner element—Replace more
frequently

Transmission, automatic—Change fluid
every 30 mi (48 km)

KEY TO LUBRICANTS

AE	ESSO type LT71141 Fluid VW Part No. G052162A2, A1
AF2	DEXRON®-II Automatic Transmission Fluid
CC	Motor Oil, API Service CC
CD	Motor Oil, API Service CD
CF-4	Motor Oil, API Service CF-4
CG-4	Motor Oil, API Service CG-4
EC	Ethylene Glycol Coolant: Green in color. If red in color, only use VW Part No. G012A8DA1
GL-4	Gear Oil, API Service GL-4
GL-5	Gear Oil, API Service GL-5
HB	Hydraulic Brake Fluid, DOT 4
MO	Motor Oil
PS	Power Steering Fluid VW Part No. G002000, G002012
SG	Motor Oil, API Service SG
SH	Motor Oil, API Service SH
SLS	Silicone Spray

CRANKCASE
Diesel engines . . . . .CC, CD
Turbo Diesel engines . . . . .CD, CF-4, CG-4

CAPACITY, Refill:	Liters	Qt
1989-98 Golf, Jetta	4.0	4.2
1999 Golf, Jetta w/filter	4.5	4.7
1993 EuroVan	4.0	4.2
1996-98 Passat (incl. filter)	4.4	4.5
1995-97 EuroVan (incl. filter) . . .	5.5	6.0
1998-99 New Beetle (incl. filter) .	4.5	4.7

1989-95:
Above 68°F (20°C) 40
32° to 86°F (0° to 30°C) 30
Below 23°F (-5°C) 10W
14° to 50°F (-10° to 10°C) 20W-20
Above 14°F (-10°C) 20W-40, 20W-50
Above 5°F (-15°C) 15W-40, 15W-50
Below 60°F (15°C) 10W-30, 10W-40

1996-99:
All temperatures 5W-50, 10W-50, 10W-60
Above 5°F (-15°C) 15W-40, 15W-50,
20W-40, 20W-50
Below 60°F (15°C) 5W-30, 5W-40,
10W-30, 10W-40

Energy conserving oils
All temperatures 1993-99 . . . . . . .5W-30,SW-40,
10W-30, 10W-40

TRANSMISSION, Automatic
1995 w/0IM, 0IP . . . . .AE
1989-95 All others . . . . .AF2, AE
1996-99 All .AE
Final drive serviced separately

CAPACITY, Initial Refill[1]:	Liters	Qt
All models	3.0	3.2

1 Add specified quantity. With engine at operating temperature, 1993-97 w/096 transmission temperature must be
140°F (60°C), shift transmission through all gears. Check
level in PARK and add fluid as needed. Some 1995-97
models do not have a dipstick

TRANSAXLE,
Manual . . . . .Synthetic 75W-90 **GL-4**

CAPACITY, Refill:	Liters	Pt
Golf, Jetta: 4-speed	1.5	3.2
5-speed	2.0	4.2

FINAL DRIVE
1989-95 . . . . .90 **GL-5**
1995-97 w/0IM . . . .**AE**
1996-99 others . . . . . .[3]Synthetic 75W-90 **GL-4**
3 VW Part No. G0005000, G052145A1, G052145A2

CAPACITY, Refill:	Liters	Pt
All FWD w/AT	0.8	1.6
Vanagon w/AT	1.2	2.6

VOLKSWAGEN
1990-99 All Gasoline Models

SERVICE AT TIME OR MILEAGE — WHICHEVER OCCURS FIRST

W   SERVICE TO MAINTAIN EMISSION WARRANTY

MI—MILES IN THOUSANDS
KM—KILOMETERS IN THOUSANDS

1998-99 EVERY 6 MO/5 MI—8 KM
Passat 1.8L turbo, 2.8L
1997-99 OTHERS
FIRST 6 MO/5 MI—8 KM
Crankcase . . . . .change oil

Oil filter .replace

1990-96
EVERY 6 MO/7.5 MI—12 KM
1997-99
EVERY 12 MO/10 MI—15 KM
Brake system . . . . .inspect
Check for damage or leaks. Check pad thickness

W Crankcase . . . . .change oil

W Oil filter . . . . .replace
Initial service only 1990-96

Service reminder light . . . . .reset
1993-95

Clutch . . . . .check/adjust
Ex. Vanagon, initial service only

Automatic shiftlock &
  park/neutral switch . . . . . .check/adjust
1993-99

Tires & wheels . . . . .inspect/rotate
Rotate front to rear, check pressure, including spare

Windshield wiper/washer . . . . . . .check

Hood lock . . . . .check/lubricate
Canada only 1993-95

Interior air filter . . . . .replace
1999 EuroVan

1990-96
EVERY 12 MO/15 MI—24 KM
1997-99 EVERY 12 MO/20 MI—30 KM
Axle boots . . . . .inspect

W Brake system . . . . .inspect **HB**
Check fluid level with ignition switch on & after waiting
for one minute, lining & pad thickness. Where applicable,
check operation of pressure regulator

Clutch . . . . .check/adjust
Ex. Vanagon

W Exhaust system . . . . .inspect

Final drive, automatic . . . . . .check level

W Oil filter . . . . .replace

Transaxle . . . . .check level

Spark plugs . . . . .replace
1998-99 2.0L Beetle

W Cooling system . . . . . . .check level **EC**
Green coolant used through late 1996. Late 1996 and
later use red coolant. CAUTION: Never mix with any
other coolant or engine damage will occur.

Windshield wiper/washer . . . . . . .check

W Idle speed & CO 1990-97 . . . . . . .check
Not required for Calif. warranty

Onboard diagnosis
  system . . . . .check/clear

Power steering . . . . .check level **PS**

Battery . . . . .check level

Timing belt . . . . .check/adjust

Transmission, automatic . . . .check level
Check final drive for leaks
W/OIM replace seal on plug after each inspection

Door hinges & checks . . . . .lubricate **MO**

Lights, accessories . . . . .inspect

Sunroof rails . . . . . . .clean/lubricate **SLS**

Supplemental restraint
  system . . . . .inspect

Tires & wheels . . . . .inspect
Rotate front to rear, check pressure, including spare

Interior air filter . . . . .replace
1993-99 Ex. EuroVan

EVERY 24 MONTHS
Brake fluid . . . . .replace **HB**
Check operation of warning light switch; check brake
pressure regulator where applicable

Air bag .check
1990-97 After first 72 months, 1998-99 after first 96
months

1997-99 EVERY 30 MI—45 KM
Spark plugs . . . . .replace
2.0L engine ex. Beetle

1990-96
EVERY 24 MO/30 MI—45 KM,
1997-99 EVERY 24 MO/40 MI—60 KM
Transmission, auto., 1997-99 . .change fluid
Ex. AG4 1998-99

Steering system boots & seals . . .inspect

W Air cleaner element . . . . .replace

Interior air filter . . . . .replace

W Drive belts . . . . .inspect/adjust

W Spark plugs . . . . .replace
Ex. 1997-99 2.0L engine

EVERY 60 MI—90 KM
Oxygen sensor 1990-97 . . . . . . .replace
Ex. Vanagon & Canada
Reset mileage counter where applicable

Timing belt & tensioner 1990-97 . . .replace
16-valve engines

Ribbed V-belt . . . . .check/adjust
1998 Beetle

1ST & 2ND 48 MONTHS
Air bag .check

EVERY 72 MONTHS
Tires . . . . .replace
Regardless of mileage

EVERY 80 MI—120 KM
V-Belt, 1998-99 turbo . . . . .replace

Timing belt & tensioner . . . . .replace
1998 V6 Passat

Timing belt & tensioner 1990-97 . . .replace
16-valve engines

EVERY 90 MI—144 KM
Oxygen sensor 1990-91 . . . . . . .replace
Vanagon ex. Canada

EVERY 105 MI—160 KM
Timing belt & tensioner . . . . . . .replace
1999 All V6 & 1.8L Turbo

SEVERE SERVICE
Crankcase—Change oil more frequently

Air cleaner element—Replace more
frequently

Transmission, automatic—Change fluid
every 30 mi (48 km)

KEY TO LUBRICANTS
See other Volkswagen chart

CRANKCASE . . . .**SF, SG, SH, SJ**

CAPACITY, Refill:	Liters	Qt
4-cyl. engines: Vanagon	3.8	4.2
Fox	3.0	3.2
All others 1990-99	3.5	3.7
5-cyl. engines: EuroVan	5.0	5.3
V6 engines: All 1990-98	5.0	5.3
Jetta, Passat, 1999 w/filter . . .	6.1	6.4
All others 1999 w/filter	5.4	5.7

Capacity shown is without filter. When replacing filter, additional oil may be needed

Above 68°F (20°C)	.40
32° to 86°F (0° to 30°C)	.30
Below 23°F (-5°C)	10W
14° to 50°F (-10° to 10°C)	20W-20
Above 14°F (-10°C) 20W-40, 20W-50	
Above 14°F (-10°C) 1998 . . . .15W-40, 15W-50	
Above 5°F (-15°C) 1990-92 . . . .15W-40, 15W-50	
Above 5°F (-15°C) 1993-97 . . . .15W-40, 15W-50,	
	20W-40, 20W-50
-4° to 60°F (-20° to 15°C), 1990-93 . . . .10W-30,	
	10W-40
Below 14°F (-10°C), 1990-91 . . . .5W-20, 5W-30	
5° to 78°F (-15° to 25°C) 1992-94 . . .10W-30,	
	10W-40
Below 60°F (15°C) 1995 . . . .5W-30, 10W-30	
Below 78°F (25°C), 1992-94 . . . . . . .5W-30	
All temperatures, 1993-99 . . . . .5W-50, 10W-50,	
	10W-60
Below 60°F (15°C) 1996-99 . . . .5W-30, 5W-40,	
	10W-30, 10W-40

Energy-conserving oils
All temperatures 1993-99 . . . . .5W-30, SW-40,
10W-30, 10W-40

TRANSMISSION, Automatic
1995 w/0IM, 0IP . . . .**AE**
1990-95 All others . . . .**AF2, AE**
1996-99 All . . . .**AE**
Final drive serviced separately

CAPACITY, Initial Refill[1]:	Liters	Qt
EuroVan	3.5	3.7
Passat 1998-99 1.8L Turbo	2.6	2.7
Passat 1998-99 2.8L	3.5	3.7
All other models	3.0	3.2

[1] Add specified quantity. With engine at operating temperature, 1993-98 w/096 transmission temperature must be 140°F (60°C), shift transmission through all gears. Check level in PARK and add fluid as needed. Some 1995-97 models do not have a dipstick

TRANSAXLE,
Manual . . . . .Synthetic 75W-90 **GL-4**[2]
[2] VW Part No. G005000, G052911A, if not available 80W
GL-4 may be used

CAPACITY, Refill:	Liters	Pt
Corrado, Passat, 1990-95	2.0	4.2
Passat 1996-99	2.2	4.8
EuroVan	3.0	6.3
Fox	1.6	3.4
Vanagon	4.5[3]	9.2[3]
Others: 4-speed	1.4	3.2
5-speed	2.0	4.2

[3] Correct oil level will be approximately 5/8 inch (15 mm)
below the bottom of the fill plug opening

DIFFERENTIAL
Passat, Vanagon . .Synthetic 75W-90 **GL-4**[2]
[2] VW Part No. G005000

CAPACITY, Refill:	Liters	Pt
Passat	0.7	1.5
Vanagon	1.5	3.2

FINAL DRIVE, w/AT
1990-92: Corrado,
  Passat, Vanagon .Synthetic 75W-90 **GL-4**[4]
All others, 1990-92 . . . . .90 **GL-5**
1993-94 All . . . . . .Synthetic 75W-90 **GL-4**[4]
1995-97 w/0IM . . . .**AE**
1995 Passat ex. 0IM 90 **GL-5**
1996-99 Others . .Synthetic 75W-90 **GL-4**[4]
[4] VW Part No. G052145A1, G052145A2, G0005000

CAPACITY, Refill:	Liters	Pt
All FWD w/AT	0.8	1.6
Vanagon	1.2	2.6
EuroVan	1.1	2.4

SERVICE LOCATIONS — ENGINE AND CHASSIS

VOIDP-1   VOIDP-1

HOOD RELEASE: Inside

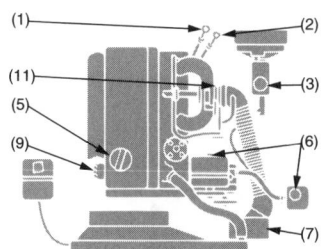

**1989-95
240, 7-Series, 940
4-cyl. 2316cc Non-Turbo**

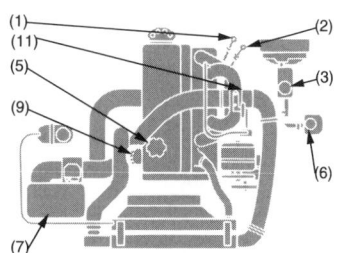

**1989-95
7-Series, 940
4-cyl. 2316cc Turbo**

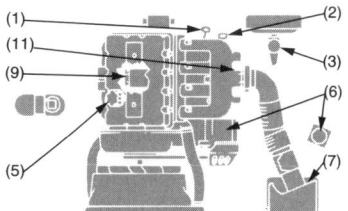

**1989-94
240, 7-Series, 940
4-cyl. 2316cc DOHC**

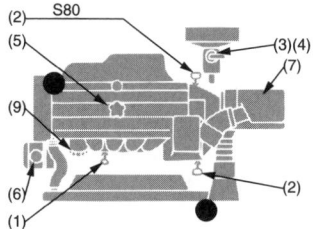

**1993-99
850, C, S & V70
5-cyl. 2435cc
1994-99
850 C, S & V70
5-cyl. 2319cc Turbo
1999
S80
6-cyl. 2783cc, 2922cc**

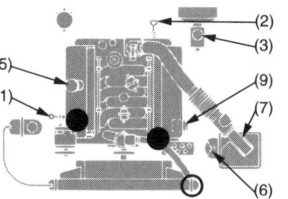

**1989-90
760, 780
6-cyl. 2849cc**

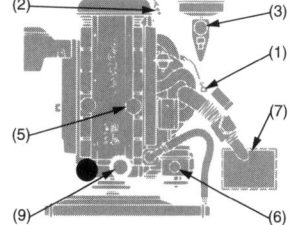

**1995-96
960
6-cyl. 2473cc
1992-98
960, S90, V90
6-cyl. 2922cc DOHC**

(1) Crankcase dipstick
(2) Transmission dipstick
(3) Brake fluid reservoir
(4) Clutch fluid reservoir
(5) Oil fill cap
(6) Power steering reservoir
(7) Air filter
(8) Fuel filter
(9) Oil filter
(10) PCV filter
(11) EGR valve
(12) Oxygen sensor
(13) PCV valve

**0 FITTINGS
0 PLUGS**

**0 FITTINGS
0 PLUGS**

**0 FITTINGS
0 PLUGS**

**0 FITTINGS
0 PLUGS**

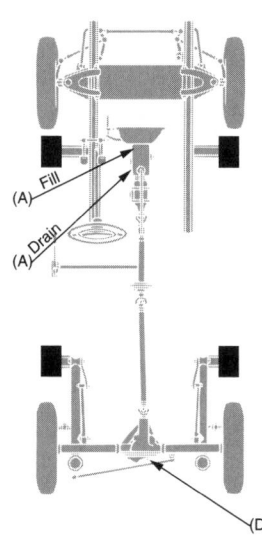

**1989-93
240 Series**

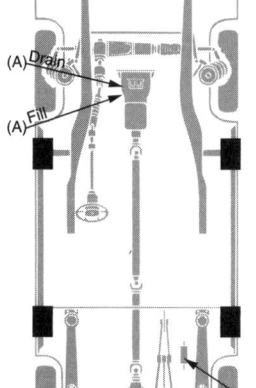

**1989-98
740, 760, 780, 900 Series
S90, V90**

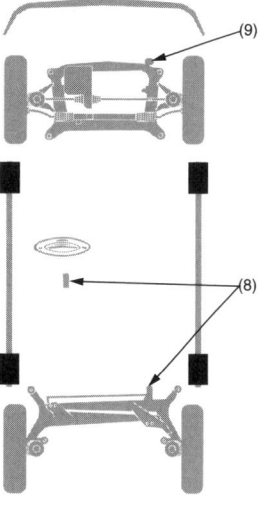

**1993-99
FWD 850 Series
C70, S70, S80, V70**

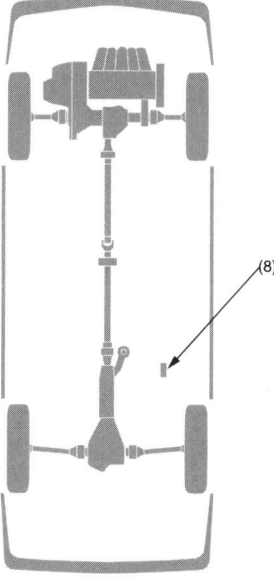

**1997-99
4WD 850 Series
4WD V70**

● Cooling system drain   ○ Cooling system drain, some models   ■ Lift adapter position

(A) Manual transmission/transaxle,   (B) Transfer case, NOT USED   (C) Automatic transaxle final drive,   (D) Differential, drain & fill
     drain & fill   NOT USED

VOLVO
1989-91 All Models

VOIPM4   VOIPM4

Perform the following maintenance services at the intervals indicated to keep the vehicle warranties in effect.
W   SERVICE TO MAINTAIN EMISSION WARRANTY

MI—MILES IN THOUSANDS
KM—KILOMETERS IN THOUSANDS

EVERY 6 MO/5 MI—8 KM
Brake master cylinder . . .check level **HB**

Brake pads, 1991 . . . . .inspect

W Crankcase . . . . .change oil
At least every 6 mo, reset service indicator

Timing belt . . . . .adjust
Initial service only

Differential, 1989-90 . . . . .check level
Ex. 1989 models w/Regina Bendix injection, 1990 700
Series

W Oil filter . . . . .replace
At least every 6 mo

Tires . . . . .inspect
Check pressure, tread depth & wear pattern including
spare

Transmission, manual . . . . . .check level
1989-90 ex. 1989 models w/Regina Bendix injection,
1990 700 Series

Power antenna . . . . .lubricate

Power steering . . . . .check level **FA**

Transmission, automatic . . . .check level

Windshield washers . . . . .check/fill

EVERY 12 MO/10 MI—16 KM
Brake system . . . . .inspect/adjust
Check thickness of pads & linings, check condition of
hoses & lines, check power booster, check parking brake
cables & adjust

Clutch pedal free play . . . . .check

Differential . . . . .check level
1989 models w/Regina Bendix injection, 1990 700 Series
only

Drive shaft, U-joints . . . . .inspect

Exhaust system . . . . .inspect

Front suspension & steering linkage
240 Series . . . . .inspect

Rear suspension 240 Series . . . . .check

Shock absorbers 240 Series . . . .inspect

Steering gear 240 Series . . . . . .inspect

Suspension components
700, 900 series . . . . .retorque
One time service only. Control arm inner mount, 85 Nm
(63 ft-lbs); control arm strut inner mount with 14 mm
hex, 85 Nm (63 ft-lbs), with 19 mm hex, 140 Nm
(103 ft-lbs); control arm strut outer mount, 95 Nm
(70 ft-lbs); steering rack, 44 Nm, (32 ft-lbs); rear axle
clamps, 45 Nm (33 ft-lbs)

Transmission, manual . . . . .check level
1989 models w/Regina Bendix injection & 1990 700
Series only

Turbo to exhaust nuts . . . . .retorque

Wheel bearings
240 Series . . . . .inspect/adjust

Battery . . . . .check level

Coolant . . . . .check level

Cooling system . . . . .pressure test

Fuel lines & hoses . . . . .inspect

Kickdown cable . . . . .check/adjust

Body . . . . .lubricate

Electrical equipment . . . . .inspect

Service indicator . . . . .reset

Windshield wipers . . . . .inspect

EVERY 24 MO/20 MI—32 KM
Automatic transmission . . . .replace fluid
Ex. models with AW30-40 transmission

Shock absorbers . . . . .inspect

Steering gear . . . . .inspect

PCV flame guard, 1989-90 . . . . . .clean
4-cyl. non-turbo engine only

EVERY 36 MO/30 MI—48 KM
W Air filter element . . . . .replace

Brake fluid . . . . .replace **HB**
At least every 24 months

W Cooling system . . . . .change coolant **EC**
At least every 24 months

W Drive belts . . . . .check/adjust

Drive shaft center support . . . . . .inspect

Front suspension
& steering . . . . .inspect
1991 740, 940 retorque

Rear suspension 700, 900 Series . .inspect

W Spark plugs . . . . .replace

W Valve clearance . . . . .check/adjust

Wheel bearings . . . . .inspect/adjust

EVERY 60 MO/50 MI—80 KM
Balance shaft belt DOHC . . . . . . .replace

Timing belt, 4-cyl. . . . . .replace
Readjust after 5 mi (8 km)

EVERY 72 MO/60 MI—96 KM
W Fuel filter . . . . .replace

W EGR system, 1991 . . . . . .inspect/clean

W PCV system . . . . .inspect/clean

SEVERE SERVICE
Crankcase—Change oil & filter every 3 mo

Spark plugs—Replace: 240 every 10 mi
(16 km), 740 every 15 mi (24 km)

Brake fluid—Replace every 15 mi (24 km)

KEY TO LUBRICANTS

AF3	DEXRON®-III Automatic Transmission Fluid
CC	Motor Oil, API Service CC
CD	Motor Oil, API Service CD
EC	Ethylene Glycol Coolant Mix 50/50 with water
FA	Automatic Transmission Fluid, Type F
GF-1	Motor Oil, API Service GF-1 (★)
GL-5	Gear Oil, API Service GL-5
GL-5★	Gear Oil for Limited-Slip Differential
GLS	Special Gear Lubricant Volvo Part No. 1161423-7, 1161324-7
HBH	Hydraulic Brake Fluid Volvo DOT 4+
MA3	MERCON®-III Automatic Transmission Fluid
SF	Motor Oil, API Service SF
SG	Motor Oil, API Service SG
SH	Motor Oil, API Service SH

CRANKCASE
1989-90 . . . . .SF, SF/CC,
SF/CD, SG
1991 . . . . .SG, SG/CD

CAPACITY, Refill:	Liters	Qt
4-cyl. 2.3L, SOHC	3.4	3.6
4-cyl. 2.3L, DOHC	3.5	3.7
V6 2.8L	5.5	5.8

Capacity shown is without filter. When replacing filter, additional oil may be needed. On models with oil cooler, additional oil may be needed if cooler is drained

Above 0°F (-18°C) 15W-40
-4° to 104°F (-20° to 40°C) 10W-30*
Below 68°F (20°C) 5W-30*
*Preferred

TRANSMISSION, Automatic AF3

CAPACITY, Initial Refill[1]:	Liters	Qt
AW70, AW71, AW72	3.4	3.6
ZF4HP22	2.0	2.2

1 With engine at operating temperature, shift transmission through all gears. Check fluid level in PARK and add oil as needed

TRANSMISSION, Manual
1989-90 . . . . .FA
1991 . . . . .FA, MA

CAPACITY, Refill:	Liters	Pt
1989-90: M46 4-speed w/OD . . .	2.3	4.8
M47 5-speed	1.6	3.2
1991 M46 4-speed w/OD	2.6	5.6

DIFFERENTIAL
Standard GL-5
Eaton Automatic Lock GL-5
Dana Limited-Slip . . . . .GL-5★
GL-5 plus Volvo additive Part No. 1161129-0
Above 14°F (-10°C), 90; below 14°F (-10°C) 80W

CAPACITY, Refill:	Liters	Pt
Type 1030	1.3	2.8
Type 1031, 1041	1.6	3.4
Type 1035, 1045	1.4	3.0

SERVICE AT TIME OR MILEAGE — WHICHEVER OCCURS FIRST

VOIPM5   VOIPM5

Perform the following maintenance services at the intervals indicated to keep the vehicle warranties in effect.
W   SERVICE TO MAINTAIN EMISSION WARRANTY

MI—MILES IN THOUSANDS
KM—KILOMETERS IN THOUSANDS

TURBO EVERY 12 MO/5 MI—8 KM
6-CYL 2.9L FIRST 12 MO/5 MI—8KM

W Crankcase . . . . .change oil
W Oil filter . . . . .replace
Turbo to exhaust nuts . . . . .retorque
850 Turbo initial service only
Timing belt . . . . .adjust
1994 B230 FT w/o EGR, initial service only
1993 B230 FT w/EGR, initial service only
1992 B234F, initial service only
Transmission, automatic . . . .check level
Coolant . . . . .check level
Brake master cylinder . .check level **HBH**
Power steering . . . . .check level **FA**

EVERY 12 MO/10 MI—16 KM
W Crankcase ex. Turbo . . . . . . .change oil
At least every 6 months, reset service indicator
W Oil filter ex. Turbo . . . . .replace
Brake system . . . . .inspect/adjust
Check thickness of pads & linings, check condition of hoses & lines, check power booster, check parking brake cables & adjust
Clutch pedal free play . . . . .check
Differential . . . . .check level
Drive shaft, U-joints . . . . .inspect
Exhaust system . . . . .inspect
Front & rear suspension & steering
   linkage 240 series . . . . .inspect
Suspension components
   700, 900 series . . . . .retorque
One time service only. Control arm inner mount, 85 Nm (63 ft-lbs); control arm strut inner mount with 14 mm hex, 85 Nm (63 ft-lbs), with 19 mm hex, 140 Nm (103 ft-lbs); control arm strut outer mount, 95 Nm (70 ft-lbs); steering rack, 44 Nm, (32 ft-lbs); rear axle clamps, 45 Nm (33 ft -lbs)
Steering, suspension 850 . . . . . . .check
After initial 60 mi
Transmission ex. Turbo . . . .check level
Wheel bearings 240 Series . .inspect/adjust
Battery . . . . .check level
Brake master cylinder
   ex. Turbo . . . . .check level **HBH**
Coolant ex. Turbo . . . . .check level
Cooling system . . . . .pressure test
Fuel lines & hoses . . . . .inspect
Kickdown cable . . . . .check/adjust
Not required for 960 models
Power antenna . . . . .inspect/clean
Power steering ex. Turbo . .check level **FA**
Timing belt, 4-cyl. . . . . .check/adjust
At first service interval only B230F, B230FD 1993-94, B230FT w/EGR 1994
Body .lubricate
Electrical equipment . . . . .inspect
Service indicator . . . . .reset
Tires . . . . .rotate
Check pressure, tread depth & wear pattern
Windshield wipers & washers . . . .inspect

EVERY 24 MO/20 MI—32 KM
Automatic transmission . . . .replace fluid
Ex. models with AW30-40 transmission
Brake fluid . . . . .replace **HBH**
At least every 30 mi—48 km
Battery . . . . .check charge
Shock absorbers . . . . .inspect
700, 900 retorque at first service interval only
Drive shaft center support . . . . .inspect
Steering gear . . . . .inspect
W Timing belt, 960,
   6-cyl. 2.9L 1992 . . . . .replace
Belt tensioner, lubricate. Inspect for label on timing belt cover signifying that Torsion Damper is installed, if so service at 30 mi (48 km). Do not exceed by more than 2,500 mi (4 000 km) First interval only.
EGR valve . . . . .clean
After initial 60 mi—96 km service
Body, 1992-93 . . . . .inspect
Visually check for corrosion
Wheel bearings . . . . .inspect/adjust

EVERY 36 MO/30 MI—48 KM
W Air filter element . . . . .replace
Engine & control module box
W Cooling system . . . . .change coolant **EC**
At least every 24 months
W Drive belts . . . . .check/adjust
Lubricate belt tensioner
Front & rear suspension,
   & steering, 740, 940 . . . . .inspect
Timing belt, 960,
   6-cyl. 2.9L 1992-93 . . . . .replace
After initial 40 mi service 1992
Belt tensioner, lubricate. Inspect for label on timing belt cover, if label is not attached and Torsion Damper has not been installed, service at 20 mi (32 km). Do not exceed by more than 2,500 mi (4 000 km)
W Spark plugs . . . . .replace
W Valve clearance . . . . .check/adjust

AT 40 MI—64 KM
Torsion Damper, 960,
   6-cyl. 2.9L 1992-93 . . . . .install
Inspect for label on timing belt cover, if label is attached and Torsion Damper has already been installed, service is not needed. Do not exceed by more than 2,500 mi (4 000 km)

EVERY 60 MO/50 MI—80 KM
Balance shaft belt DOHC . . . . . .replace
Timing belt . . . . .replace
1994 6-cyl. 2.9L. All 1992-94 B230F, (B5254S(F) 850 5-cyl. 2.4L, 1993. Readjust 4-cyl. after 10 mi (16 km)
Lubricate 5-cyl. belt tensioner
Timing belt . . . . .replace
1994 B230FT w/o EGR, readjust after 5 mi (8 km)
1993 B230FT w/EGR, readjust after 5 mi (8 km)
1992 B234F readjust after 5 mi (8 km)

EVERY 72 MO/60 MI—96 KM
Drive belts, 960, 850 . . . . .replace
W Fuel filter . . . . .replace
W EGR system ex.
   B230FD Turbo . . . . .inspect/clean
Clean every 20 mi—32 km thereafter
Rear suspension & shocks,
   850 Series . . . . .inspect
W PCV system . . . . .inspect/clean
Rubber hoses check, replace if needed

KEY TO LUBRICANTS
See other Volvo chart

CRANKCASE . . . . . .SG, SG/CD, SH; GF-1

CAPACITY, Refill:	Liters	Qt
4-cyl. 2.3L, SOHC	3.4	3.6
4-cyl. 2.3L, DOHC	3.5	3.7
5-cyl. 2.3L Turbo, 2.4L	5.0	5.3
6-cyl. 2.5L	5.2	5.5
6-cyl. 2.9L	5.2	5.5

Capacity shown is without filter. When replacing filter, additional oil may be needed. On models with oil cooler, additional oil may be needed if cooler is drained

Above 0°F (-18°C)	15W-40
-4° to 104°F (-20° to 40°C)	10W-30*
Below 68°F (20°C)	5W-30*
Below 104°F (40°C)	5W-40
*Preferred

TRANSMISSION/TRANSAXLE, Automatic

1993-94 850	AF3, MA
All others	AF3

CAPACITY, Initial Refill[1]:	Liters	Qt
850 AW50-42LE	3.0	3.3
940, 960: ZF4HP22	2.0	2.2
AW70, AW71, AW72	3.9	4.1
AW30-34	3.0	3.2
AW40, AW43	3.0	3.2

1 With engine at operating temperature, shift transmission through all gears. Check fluid level in PARK and add oil as needed

TRANSMISSION/TRANSAXLE, Manual

All ex. 850	FA, MA
850	GLS

CAPACITY, Refill:	Liters	Pt
1992-93 M47 5-speed	1.5	3.2
M46 4-speed w/OD	2.6	5.6
1993-94 850 5-speed, all	2.1	4.4

DIFFERENTIAL

Standard	GL-5
Eaton Automatic Lock	GL-5
Dana Limited-Slip	GL-5★

GL-5 plus Volvo additive Part No. 1161129-0
Above 14°F (-10°C), 80W-90, 90; below 14°F (-10°C) 80W

CAPACITY, Refill:	Liters	Pt
850: Transfer Case	2.1	4.4
Differential	1.4	3.0
Others: Type 1030, 1992	1.3	2.8
Type 1031	1.8	3.7
Type 1041	1.6	3.4
Type 1035 1992, 1045	1.4	3.0

EVERY 100 MI—160 KM
Timing belt . . . . .replace
B230 FD: 1993-94, B230FT w/EGR 1994
Readjust after 10 mi (16 km)
EGR system . . . . .inspect/clean
B230FD Turbo

SEVERE SERVICE
Crankcase—Change oil & filter: w/o Turbo every 6 mo, 5 mi (8 km), w/Turbo every 6 mo, 3 mi (5 km)
Spark plugs—Replace: 240 1992 every 10 mi (16 km), 240 1993, 850, 940, 960, 740 every 15 mi (24 km)
Air cleaner filter—Replace more frequently
Brake fluid—Replace every 12 mo/15 mi (24 km)

VOLVO
1995-99 All Models

Perform the following maintenance services at the intervals indicated to keep the vehicle warranties in effect.
W   SERVICE TO MAINTAIN EMISSION WARRANTY

MI—MILES IN THOUSANDS
KM—KILOMETERS IN THOUSANDS

1995-98
TURBO EVERY 12 MO/5 MI—8 KM
1995-98
6-CYL 2.9L FIRST 12 MO/5 MI—8KM

W Crankcase . . . . .change oil

W Oil filter . . . . .replace

Turbo to exhaust nuts . . . . .retorque
850 Turbo initial service only

Transmission, automatic . . . .check level

Coolant . . . . .check level

Brake master cylinder . .check level **HBH**

Power steering . . . . .check level **FA**

1995-98
EVERY 12 MO/10 MI—16 KM
1999
EVERY 12 MO/7.5 MI—2 KM

W Crankcase . . . . .change oil
Reset service indicator

W Oil filter . . . . .replace

Brake system . . . . .inspect/adjust
Check thickness of pads & linings, check condition of
hoses & lines, check power booster, check parking brake
cables & adjust

Clutch pedal free play . . . . .check

Differential . . . . .check level

Drive shaft, U-joints, boots . . . . .inspect

Exhaust system . . . . .inspect

Front link arm stops . . . . .lubricate
850, All 1998

Suspension components
    900 series . . . . .retorque
One time service only. Control arm inner mount, 85 Nm
(63 ft-lbs); control arm strut inner mount with 14 mm
hex, 85 Nm (63 ft-lbs), with 19 mm hex, 140 Nm
(103 ft-lbs); control arm strut outer mount, 95 Nm
(70 ft-lbs); steering rack, 44 Nm, (32 ft-lbs); rear axle
clamps, 45 Nm (33 ft -lbs)

Steering, suspension . . . . .check
After initial 40 mi

Transmission . . . . .check level

Battery . . . . .check level
Check charge

Brake master cylinder . .check level **HBH**

Coolant . . . . .check level

Cooling system . . . . .pressure test
1995-97

Fuel lines & hoses . . . . .inspect

Kickdown cable 1995-97 . . .check/adjust
Not required for 960 models

Power antenna . . . . .inspect/clean

Power steering . . . . .check level **FA**

Timing belt, 4-cyl. . . . . . . .check/adjust
At first service interval only B230FD 1995, B230FT
w/EGR 1995

Body .lubricate

Electrical equipment . . . . .inspect

Headlights, wiper & washer . . . . . .check

Service indicator . . . . .reset

Tires (As needed) . . . . .rotate
Check pressure, including spare, tread depth & wear
pattern

Windshield wipers & washers . . . .inspect

Sunroof 1998-99 . . . . .lubricate

EVERY 24 MO/20 MI—32 KM

Interior air filter . . . . .replace

Brake fluid . . . . .replace **HBH**
At least every 30 mi—48 km

Battery 1995-97 . . . . .check charge

Shock absorbers . . . . .inspect
900 retorque at first service interval only

Drive shaft center support . . . . .inspect

Steering gear . . . . .inspect

EGR valve 1995-97 . . . . .clean
After initial 60 mi—96 km service

Drive belts, 940 1995 . . . . .check/adjust

Wheel bearings 1995-97 . .inspect/adjust

EVERY 36 MO/30 MI—48 KM

W Air filter element . . . . .replace
Engine & control module box

W Cooling system . . . . . . .change coolant **EC**
At least every 24 months, 1995-97

W Drive belts . . . . .check/adjust
Lubricate belt tensioner 1995-96

Front & rear suspension,
    & steering, 940 . . . . .inspect

W Spark plugs . . . . .replace

W Valve clearance . . . . .check/adjust
1995-97

PCV system . . . . .clean
1999

EVERY 45 MI—72 KM

Automatic transmission . . .replace fluid
940 1995

EVERY 60 MO/50 MI—80 KM

Balance shaft belt DOHC . . . . . .replace
1995-97

EVERY 72 MO/60 MI—96 KM

Drive belts, 960, 850, All 1997-99 replace

W Fuel filter 1995-96 . . . . .replace
Ex.1995 850 & 940

W EGR system ex.
    B230FD Turbo . . . . .inspect/clean
Clean every 20 mi—32 km thereafter, 1995-97

Rear suspension & shocks,
    850 Series . . . . .inspect

W PCV system 1995-98 . . . . .inspect/clean
Rubber hoses check, replace if needed
Clean every 40 mi - 64 km thereafter

EVERY 70 MI—112 KM

Timing belt, 850, 1995-98 . . . . .replace

Timing belt, 960, 1995-98 . . . . .replace

EVERY 100 MI—160 KM

Timing belt . . . . .replace
1995, B230FT w/EGR 1995
Readjust after 10 mi (16 km)

EGR system . . . . .inspect/clean
1995-96 850 & 960

Fuel filter 1998 . . . . .replace

EVERY 168 MO/105 MI—168 KM

Fuel filter, 1997-99 . . . . .replace

Timing belt & tensioner . . . . . .replace
1999

KEY TO LUBRICANTS
See other Volvo chart

CRANKCASE . . .SG, SG/CD, SH; SJ, GF-1

CAPACITY, Refill:	Liters	Qt
4-cyl. 2.3L, DOHC	3.5	3.7
5-cyl. 2.3L Turbo, 2.4L: 1995-97 . .	5.0	5.3
1998-99 Inc. filter	5.8	6.1
6-cyl. 2.5L	5.2	5.5
6-cyl. 2.8L Inc. filter	7.5	8.0
6-cyl. 2.9L 1995-98	5.2	5.5
1999 Inc. filter	6.9	7.3

Capacity shown is without filter. When replacing filter, additional oil may be needed. On models with oil cooler, additional oil may be needed if cooler is drained

Above 0°F (-18°C) 1995-97	15W-40
-4° to 104°F (-20° to 40°C)	10W-30*
Below 68°F (20°C) 1995-97	5W-30*
Below 86°F (30°C) 1998-99	5W-30*
Below 104°F (40°C)	5W-40

*Preferred

TRANSMISSION/TRANSAXLE, Automatic

850, 960; 70, 90 Series . . . .**AF3, MA**
940, S80 . . . .**AF3**

CAPACITY, Initial Refill[1]:	Liters	Qt
850; C, S, V70 AW50-42	3.0	3.3
960; S, V90: AW30-34	3.0	3.2
AW40, AW43	3.0	3.2

1 With engine at operating temperature, shift transmission through all gears. Check fluid level in PARK and add oil as needed

TRANSAXLE, Manual

850: FWD . . . .**GLS**
    4WD . . . . .Synthetic 5W-30 **SH**
C, S & V70 . . . .**GLS**

CAPACITY, Refill:	Liters	Pt
850 5-speed, all	2.1	4.4
C, S & V70 5-speed all	2.1	4.4

DIFFERENTIAL

S & V90 . . . . .80W-90 **GL-5**
850 4WD: Transfer Case 80W **GL-5**
    Final Drive 80W **GL-5**
Others: Standard **GL-5**
    Eaton Automatic Lock **GL-5**
    Dana Limited-Slip . . . .**GL-5★**
GL-5 plus Volvo additive Part No. 1161129-0
Above 14°F (-10°C), 80W-90, 90; below 14°F
(-10°C) 80W

CAPACITY, Refill:	Liters	Pt
850: Transfer Case	2.1	4.4
Differential	1.4	3.0
940: Type 1031	1.8	3.7
Type 1041	1.6	3.4
Type 1035	1.6	3.4
960 Sedan, 1995	1.3	2.8
Wagon, 1995	1.7	3.6
960 All, 1996-97	1.3	2.8
S & V90	1.3	2.8

SEVERE SERVICE

Crankcase—Change oil & filter: every 6 mo, 5 mi (8 km), 6 mo, 3 mi (5 km)

Air cleaner filter—Replace more frequently

Spark plugs—Replace every 15 mi (24 km)

Brake fluid—Replace every 12 mo/15 mi (24 km)

Interior air filter—Replace more frequently

Automatic transmission—Change every 52.5 mi if towing

MODEL — CAPACITY — LUBRICANT

ACURA—1991-00 NSX
CRANKCASE . . . . .SJ, GF-1

CAPACITY, Refill:	Liters	Qt
NSX (incl. filter)	5.0	5.3

   Above -4°F (-20°C), 10W-30
   Below 32°F (0°C), 5W-30

TRANSAXLE, Automatic

1900-96 . . . . .SLF		
1995-91 . . . . .AF2,SLF		

Use Dexron-II, do not use Dexron-III

CAPACITY, Initial Refill*:	Liters	Qt
NSX	2.9	3.1

* With engine at operating temperature, shift transmission through all gears. Turn engine off and check fluid level within one minute

TRANSAXLE, Manual

1900-96 . . . . .GLS		
1995-91 . . . . .10W-30, 10W-40 SG		

CAPACITY, Refill:	Liters	Pt
NSX	2.7	5.8

ALFA ROMEO
CRANKCASE

1989-90 . . . . .10W-50, 15W-50 SF		
1991-95 . . . . .10W-40 SG		

CAPACITY, Refill:	Liters	Qt
1989-94 4-cyl.	6.6	7.1
V6	7.0	7.4
1995 All V6	6.5	6.9

Capacity is without filter. When replacing filter, additional oil may be needed

TRANSMISSION, Automatic AF3

CAPACITY, Initial Refill*:	Liters	Qt
1989 Milano	1.7	1.8
1991-94 Spider	1.6	1.7
1991-95 164	5.0	5.4

* With the engine at operating temperature, shift transmission through all gears. Check fluid level in PARK and add fluid as needed

TRANSMISSION/TRANSAXLE, Manual

164 . . . . .AF3		
All Others 80W-90 GL-5		

CAPACITY, Refill:	Liters	Pt
1989-94 Spider	1.9	3.8
1989 Milano	2.4	4.8
1991-95 164	1.8	3.8

DIFFERENTIAL

164 . . . . .AF3		
All Others 80W-90 GL-5		

CAPACITY, Refill:	Liters	Pt
1989-94 All	1.4	3.0

AM GENERAL
Hummer
CRANKCASE

Diesel CG-4		
Gasoline CF-4/CD		

CAPACITY, Refill[1]:	Liters	Qt
Gasoline, 1996	6.1	6.5
Gasoline, 1996 including oil cooler	6.8	7.3
Diesel, 1996-00	7.6	8.0

[1] Includes oil filter. Diesel engine oil must be warm when checking level

Gasoline, 1996
   Above 32°F (0°C), 30
   Above 0°F (-18°C), 10W-30
   Below 60°F (16°C), 5W-30

Diesel, 1996-00
   Above 32°F (0°C), 30
   Above 0°F (-18°C), 15W-40[2]
   Below 60°F (16°C), 10W-30

[2] Preferred

MODEL — CAPACITY — LUBRICANT

AM GENERAL Continued
Hummer Continued
TRANSMISSION AF3

CAPACITY, Refill[3]:	Liters	Qt
1996-98	7.6	8.0
1999-00	7.3	7.7

[3] With the engine at operating temperature, shift transmission through all gears. Let engine slow idle in PARK for 3 minutes or more. Check fluid level and add fluid as needed

TRANSFER CASE AF3

CAPACITY, Refill:	Liters	Qt
All	3.3	3.5

DIFFERENTIAL 80W-90 GL-5

CAPACITY, Refill:	Liters	Pt
Front & rear	1.9	4.0

HUBS, geared 80W-90 GL-5

CAPACITY, Refill:	Liters	Pt
All	0.5	1.0

DAEWOO
CRANKCASE . . . . .SH, SJ, GF-2

CAPACITY, Refill:	Liters	Qt
Lanos	3.8	4.0
Nubira	3.9	4.1
Leganza	4.0	4.2

Includes filter
   Above 0°F (-20°C), 10W-50
   All temperatures. 5W-30

TRANSAXLE, Automatic AF3

CAPACITY, Total Fill:	Liters	Qt
Lanos, Nubira	11.5	12.0
Leganza	7.0	7.5

TRANSAXLE, Manual 75W, 80W, GL-4

CAPACITY, Refill:	Liters	Pt
All	1.8	3.8

Power Steering AF2, AF3

DAIHATSU
CRANKCASE . . . . .SF, SF/CC, SG

CAPACITY, Refill:	Liters	Qt
1989-92 993cc.	2.7	2.9
1989-92 1295cc, 1589cc	3.3	3.5

Capacity is without filter. When replacing filter, additional oil may be needed
   Above 10°F (-12°C), 15W-40, 20W-40, 20W-50
   Above 0°F (-18°C), 10W-30, 10W-40, 10W-50
   Below 50°F (10°C), 5W-30

TRANSMISSION/TRANSAXLE, Automatic AF2

CAPACITY, Initial Refill*:	Liters	Qt
1989-92	1.5	1.6

* With engine at operating temperature, shift transmission through all gears. Check fluid level in PARK and add fluid as needed

TRANSMISSION/TRANSAXLE, Manual 75W-85, 75W-90 GL-4

CAPACITY, Refill:	Liters	Pt
1989-92 Charade	2.4	4.5
1990-92 Rocky	1.7	3.8

TRANSFER CASE 75W-85, 75W-90 GL-4

CAPACITY, Refill:	Liters	Pt
1990-92 Rocky: Part time	1.4	3.0
Full time	1.7	3.8

DIFFERENTIAL

Standard 80W-90, 90 GL-5		
Limited-slip .80W-90, 90 GL-5★		

CAPACITY, Refill:	Liters	Pt
Rocky: Front	0.9	2.0
Rear	2.0	4.2

LUBRICATION FOR OTHER MAKES/MODELS

DODGE
1993-00 Viper
CRANKCASE

1997-00 ....*Synthetic **API★**
* Meeting MS-9615 (full synthetic)

1993-96 ....**API★**

CAPACITY, Refill:	Liters	Qt
8.0L: 2000	9.0	9.5
1997-99	7.5	8.0
1993-96	8.5	9.0

Capacity is without filter. When replacing filter, additional oil may be needed

Above 0°F (-18°C), 15W-30 Preferred

Below 32°F (0°C), 5W-30

TRANSMISSION, Manual

1994-00 w/T56 ....*Synthetic 75W-85 **GL-4**
* Part No. 04874459. Some models may be filled with **AF3**. Do not mix gear oil with **ATF**.

1993 ....**AF-3**

CAPACITY, Refill:	Liters	Qt
All	3.8	4.0

* With engine at operating temperature, shift transmission through all gears. Check fluid level in PARK and add fluid as needed

DIFFERENTIAL ....*Synthetic 75W-140 **GL-5★**
* Part No. 04874469 plus 4 oz (120 ml) of additive Part No. 04318060.

CAPACITY, Refill:	Liters	Pt
1999-00	1.8	3.9
1993-98	1.4	3.0

Power Steering ....**PS**
1999-00 models use Part no. 05010304AA meeting MS 9933, others use Part no. 04883077 meeting MS 5931.

Brake & Clutch Reservoir:

1999-00 ....**HBH**

1993-98 ....**HB**

Grease Fittings ....**LB**

JAGUAR
CRANKCASE ....**SG, SG/CD, SH, SJ, GF-2**

CAPACITY, Refill:	Liters	Qt
1989-96 V12	10.0	10.5
1989-97 6-cyl.	8.0	8.5
1998-99 V8 XJ8: w/o oil cooler	6.5	6.9
w/ oil cooler	7.5	7.9
V8 XK8	6.5	6.9
2000 V6	5.7	6.0
V8 S-type	6.5	6.9

Capacity includes filter

1989:
Above 14°F (-10°C), 10W-40, 10W-50, 15W-50, 20W-40, 20W-50
-4° to 50°F (-20° to 10°C), 10W-30, 10W-40, 10W-50
Below 14°F (-10°C), 5W-20, 5W-30

1990-92:
Above 14°F (-10°C), 15W-40, 15W-50, 20W-40, 20W-50
Above -4°F (-20°C), 10W-60
-4° to 105°F (-20° to 40°C), 10W-30, 10W-40, 10W-50
Below 14°F (-10°C), 5W-20, 5W-30, 5W-40
All temperatures, 5W-50

1993-97:
Above 32°F (0°C), 15W-40, 15W-50, 20W-40, 20W-50
Above -4°F (-20°C), 10W-60
-4° to 105°F (-20° to 40°C), 10W-30, 10W-40, 10W-50
Above -25°F (-30°C), 5W-50
Below 105°F (40°C), 5W-40
Below 52°F (10°C), 5W-30
Below 15°F (-10°C), 5W-20

1998-99:
13° to 127°F (-10° to 50°C), 15W-40
-5° to 127°F (-20° to 50°C), 10W-30
-24° to 127°F (-30° to 50°C), 5W-30

2000:
58° to 123°F (15° to 50°C), 15W-30, 10W-40
-25° to 123°F (-30° to 50°C), 0W-30, 5W-30, 0W-40, 5W-40

JAGUAR Continued
TRANSMISSION, Automatic

1989-92: Borg Warner ....**FA**
Hydra-Matic, ZF **AF3**

1993-96 All **AF3**

1997-99 Models w/o S/C ....(5HP24) **AE**
w/ S/C (W5A580) ....**SLF**

CAPACITY, Initial Refill:	Liters	Qt
1989 XJ6, Vanden Plas (Total fill)	8.0	8.4
1989-93 XJS (Total fill)	9.1	9.5
1990-94 6-cyl. 4.0L	4.3	4.5
1994-96 12-cyl. 6.0L	7.3	7.7
1995-97 6-cyl. 4.0L w/o supercharger	4.3	4.5
1995-97 6-cyl. 4.0L supercharged	7.3	7.7
1997 V8 XK8 (Total fill)	10.0	10.6
1998 XJ8 w/o oil cooler	9.4	10.0
1998 XJ8 w/ oil cooler	10.0	10.6

TRANSMISSION, Manual **AF3**

CAPACITY, Refill:	Liters	Pt
1993-95 All	1.4	3.0

DIFFERENTIAL

1989-92 ....**.90 GL-5**
Powr-Lok ....**.90 GL-5★**

1993-97 ....**.80W-90, 90 GL-5**
Powr-Lok ....**.80W-90, 90 GL-5★**

CAPACITY, Refill:	Liters	Pt
1989-95 XJS	1.6	3.4
All 4-door models ex. XJ12	2.1	4.4
1994 XJ12	1.3	2.8
1996-97 XJ6, XJ12	2.1	4.4
1996 XJS	1.3	2.8

KIA
1993-00 All Models
CRANKCASE ....**SJ**

CAPACITY, Refill:	Liters	Qt
Sephia: 1993-94 1.6L SOHC	3.0	3.2
1995-00 1.6L DOHC	3.2	3.4
1.8L	3.6	3.8
Sportage (w/filter)	4.2	4.4

1993-97 Sephia
1994-00 Sportage
Above 85°F (29°C), 40
Above 15°F (-9°C), 20W-40, 20W-50
Above -15°F (-25°C), 10W-40, 10W-50
32° to 105°F (0° to 39°C), 30
15° to 65°F (-9° to 20°C), 20W-20
-15° to 85°F (-25° to 29°C), 10W-30
Below 32°F (0°C), 5W-30
Below -5°F (-20°C), 5W-20

1998-00 Sephia
-10° to 90°F (-22° to 30°C), 10W-30
Below 32°F (0°C), 5W-30

TRANSAXLE/TRANSMISSION, Automatic **AF3**
Sportage, use Dexron-II

CAPACITY:	Liters	Qt
Sephia (total fill): 1993-94	6.3	6.7
1995-00 1.6L	5.8	6.1
1.8L	5.0	5.3
Sportage (initial fill)	2.5	2.7

TRANSAXLE/TRANSMISSION, Manual

1998-00 Sephia **80W-90 GL-4, GL-5**
All others **75W-90 GL-4, GL-5**

CAPACITY, Refill:	Liters	Pt
Sephia	2.7	5.6
Sportage: 2WD	1.6	3.4
4WD	1.2	2.6

TRANSFER CASE **75W-90 GL-4, GL-5**

CAPACITY, Refill:	Liters	Pt
Sportage: 1994-98	1.3	2.8
1999-00	1.7	3.6

MODEL — CAPACITY — LUBRICANT

KIA Continued
2000-93 All Models Continued
DIFFERENTIAL 80W-90, 90 **GL-5**
CAPACITY, Refill:

	Liters	Pt
Sportage: 1995-96 front & rear	1.3	2.8
1997-00, front	1.2	2.6
rear	1.5	3.2

POWER STEERING **AF2, AF3**

LAND ROVER
CRANKCASE . . . .**SG, SH, SJ**
CAPACITY, Refill:

	Liters	Qt
1989-91 Range Rover	5.7	6.0
1992-94 Range Rover	6.7	7.1
1994-97 Defender 90	6.5	7.1
1995 Range Rover ex. County	4.9	5.1
County	5.7	6.0
1995-98 Discovery	5.7	6.0
1996-98 Range Rover 3.9L & 4.6L	4.9	5.1
1999 Range Rover	5.6	6.0

Capacity includes filter
    Above 60°F (15°C), 25W-40, 25W-50
    Above 32°F (0°C), 20W-40, 20W-50
    Above 14°F (-10°C), 15W-40, 15W-50, 1989-96
    Above 14°F (-10°C), 10W-40, 10W-50, 10W-60, 1997-99
    Below 14°F (-10°C), 5W-20, 5W-30, 5W-40, 1989-94
    Below 95°F (35°C), 5W-30, 1995-99
    Below 122°F (50°C), 5W-40, 5W-50, 1995-99
    Above -4°F (-20°C), 10W-40, 10W-50, 1989-96
    Above -4°F (-20°C), 10W-60, 1995-96
    -4° to 50°F (-20° to 10°C), 10W-30, 1989-94
    14° to 95°F (-20° to 35°C), 10W-30, 1995-99

TRANSMISSION, Automatic **AF3**
CAPACITY, Total Fill:

	Liters	Qt
1989-99 Range Rover	9.8*	10.0*
1995 Discovery	9.8*	10.0*
1996-99 Discovery	9.1	9.5

*Dry or total fill shown, use less fluid when refilling

TRANSMISSION, Manual
1996-98 Discovery . . . .**FA, AF3**
1997 All others . . . .**FA, AF3**
1989-96 All others . . . .**FA**
CAPACITY, Total Fill:

	Liters	Pt
1994-98 Defender 90	2.7	5.6
1995-98 Discovery	2.7	5.6

TRANSFER CASE
1989-99 Range Rover **AF3**
1994-98 Defender 90 . . . . .80W-90, 80W **EP**
1999 Discovery . . . . .Synthetic 75W-90 **GL-5**
1995-98 Discovery . . . . .80W, 80W-90 **EP**
    Above 14°F (-10°C) 90, below 68°F (25°C), 80W
CAPACITY, Refill:

	Liters	Pt
1989-94 Range Rover	1.7	3.6
1995-99 Range Rover	2.3	4.8
1994-97 Defender 90	2.3	4.8
1995-99 Discovery	2.3	4.8

DIFFERENTIALS
1989-98 .80W-90, 80W, 90 **EP**
    Above 14°F (-10°C) 90, below 68°F (25°C), 80W
1999 . . . . .Synthetic 75W-90 **GL-5**
CAPACITY, Refill:

	Liters	Pt
1989-99 Range Rover, Front & Rear	1.7	3.6
1994-97 Defender 90: Front	1.7	3.6
Rear	2.2	4.8
1995-99 Discovery Front & Rear	1.7	3.6

MODEL — CAPACITY — LUBRICANT

PEUGEOT
CRANKCASE . . . .**SF/CC, SF/CD, SG**
CAPACITY, Refill:

	Liters	Qt
1989-91 2155cc Turbo	5.0	5.3
1989 2849cc	6.0	6.3
1989-91 1905cc SOHC	5.0	5.3
1905cc DOHC	5.3	5.6

    All temperatures, 10W-40, 10W-50
    Above 32°F (0°C), Turbo, 10W-30

TRANSMISSION, Automatic **AF2**
CAPACITY, Initial Refill*:

	Liters	Qt
1989-91 2155cc Turbo	2.6	2.8
1989 2849cc	2.6	2.8
1989-91 2165cc	2.6	2.8
1989-91 1905cc	2.4	2.5

* With engine at operating temperature, shift transmission through all gears. Turn engine off and check fluid level within one minute

TRANSMISSION, Manual
1989-91 505 Models .10W-40 **SF**
1989-91 405 Models 75W-80 **GL-5**
CAPACITY, Refill:

	Liters	Pt
505 Models	1.6	3.4
405 Models	2.0	4.2

DIFFERENTIAL .80W-90 **GL-5★**
CAPACITY, Refill:

	Liters	Pt
505 Models	1.6	3.3

PLYMOUTH
1997-00 Prowler
CRANKCASE . . . .**API★**
CAPACITY, Refill:

	Liters	Qt
3.5L	4.8	5.0

Capacity is without filter. When replacing filter, additional oil may be needed
    Above 0°F (-18°C) 10W-30 Preferred
    Below 32°F (0°C), 5W-30

TRANSMISSION, Automatic
1999-00 . . . .**AP4**
1997 . . . .**AP3**
CAPACITY, Initial Refill*:

	Liters	Qt
1997-99	3.8	4.0

* With engine at operating temperature, shift transmission through all gears. Check fluid level in PARK and add fluid as needed

DIFFERENTIAL 75W-90 **GL-5**
CAPACITY, Refill:

	Liters	Qt
2000	0.7[1]	1.6[1]
1997-99	0.9	2.0

1 42LE transaxles built after 7-26-99 only. Fill to 3/8" (9mm) below fill hole.

Power Steering . . . .**PS**
    1999-00 models use Part No. 05010304AA meeting MS 9933, 1997 models use Part No. 04883077 meeting MS 5931
Brake Reservoir . . . .**HB**
    1999 models use DOT 4
Grease Fittings . . . .**LB**

STERLING
CRANKCASE . . . .**SG**
CAPACITY, Refill:

	Liters	Qt
All	4.5	4.8

Capacity includes filter
1989-91:
    Above 20°F (-8°C) 10W-30
    All temperatures, 5W-30*
* Preferred

TRANSAXLE, Automatic . . . .**SLF**
Sterling Automatic Transmission Fluid
CAPACITY, Initial Refill*:

	Liters	Qt
All	3.2	3.4

* With engine at operating temperature, shift transmission through all gears. Turn engine off and check fluid level within one minute

TRANSAXLE, Manual
1989-91 . . . . .5W-30 **SF, SF/CD**
CAPACITY, Refill:

	Liters	Pt
All	2.2	4.6

LUBRICATION FOR OTHER MAKES/MODELS

SUZUKI

CRANKCASE . . . .**SG, SH, GF-1**

CAPACITY, Refill:	Liters	Qt
1989-97 Samurai	3.5	3.7
Sidekick.	4.0	4.2
Swift	3.1	3.3
1995-97 Esteem	3.1	3.3

Capacity is without filter. When replacing filter, additional oil may be needed

1989-92 Swift:
Above 0°F (-18°C), 10W-30
All temperatures, 5W-30*
* Preferred, especially below 32°F (0°C)

1989-97 Samurai, Sidekick, X90, 1993-97 Esteem, Swift:
Above 14°F (-10°C), 20W-50
Above 0°F (-18°C), 15W-40, 15W-50
Above -4°F (-20°C), 10W-40, 10W-50
-4° to 86°F (-20° to 30°C), 10W-30
Below 50°F (10°C), 1993-97 Swift GT, Sidekick, X90, 5W-30
Below 86°F (30°C), Others, 5W-30

Forsa:
Above 40°F (4°C), 30
Above 20°F (-7°C), 20W-20
Above 10°F (-12°C), 15W-40
Above 0°F (-18°C), 10W-30
Below 100°F (38°C), 5W-30

TRANSMISSION/TRANSAXLE, Automatic **AF3**

CAPACITY, Initial Refill*:	Liters	Qt
Esteem	2.5	2.6
Sidekick, X90: 3-speed	2.8	3.0
4-speed	2.5	5.2
Swift	0.8	0.8
Forsa	1.5	1.6

* With the engine at operating temperature, shift transmission through all gears. Check fluid level in PARK and add fluid as needed

TRANSMISSION/TRANSAXLE, Manual
Samurai, Sidekick, Swift, X90 . . . . .75W-85, 75W-90* **GL-4**
Above 5°F (-15°C), 80W-90
Forsa 75W-85, 80W, 80W-90, 90 **GL-4**
* Preferred

CAPACITY, Refill:	Liters	Pt
1989-95 Samurai	1.3	2.7
1989-97 Sidekick, X90: 2WD	1.9	4.0
4WD	1.5	3.2
Swift.	2.4	4.9
1995-97 Esteem	2.4	4.9

TRANSFER CASE
Samurai, Sidekick, X90 . . . . .75W-85, 75W-90* **GL-4**
Above 5°F (-15°C), 80W-90
* Preferred

CAPACITY, Refill:	Liters	Pt
1989-95 Samurai	0.8	1.7
1989-97 Sidekick, X90 4WD.	1.7	3.6
1994-97 2WD	2.2	4.6

DIFFERENTIAL
Samurai, Sidekick, X90 . . . . .75W-85, 75W-90 **GL-5**
Above 5°F (-15°C), 80W-90

SUZUKI Continued

CAPACITY, Refill:	Liters	Pt
1989 Samurai: Front	1.7	3.6
Rear	1.5	3.2
1989-97 Sidekick, X90: Front	1.0	2.1
Rear	2.2	4.6
1990-95 Samurai: Front	2.0	4.2
Rear	1.5	3.2

TOYOTA 1989-97 LAND CRUISER; LEXUS LX450

CRANKCASE . . . .**SG**

CAPACITY, Refill:	Liters	Qt
1989-92	7.0	7.4
1993-97 6-cyl.	6.9	7.3

Capacity is without filter. When replacing filter, additional oil may be needed
1989-90: Above 10°F (-12°C), 15W-40, 20W-40, 20W-50
Above -10°F (-23°C), 10W-30*, 10W-40, 10W-50
Below 50°F (10°C), 5W-30
1991-97: Above 0°F (-18°C), 10W-30
Below 50°F (10°C), 5W-30
1998: All temperatures, 5W-30
Above 0°F (-18°C), 10W-30

TRANSMISSION, Automatic **AF3**

CAPACITY, Initial Refill*:	Liters	Qt
1989	6.0*	6.3*
1995-98	1.9*	2.0*

* With the engine at operating temperature, shift transmission through all gears. Check fluid level in PARK and add fluid as needed

TRANSMISSION, Manual **90 GL-4, GL-5**

CAPACITY, Refill:	Liters	Pt
1987 4-speed	3.5	7.4
5-speed	4.9	10.4

TRANSFER CASE
1989-90 . . . .**90 GL-4, GL-5**
1991-98 . . . .**75W-90 GL-4, GL-5**

CAPACITY, Refill:	Liters	Pt
1989-92	2.2	4.6
1993-98 w/o ABS	1.3	2.8
w/ABS	1.7	3.6
1998	1.3	2.8

DIFFERENTIAL
Standard **GL-5**
Limited-slip . . . .**GL-5★**
Above 0°F (-18°C), 90; below 0°F (-18°C), 80W-90

CAPACITY, Refill:	Liters	Pt
1989-90 Front	3.0	6.4
Rear	2.5	5.2
1991-92 Front & Rear	2.8	5.8
1993-97 Front: w/o locking diff.	2.8	5.8
w/locking diff.	2.6	5.4
Rear	3.3	6.8
1998 Front	1.7	3.6
Rear: w/o locking diff.	3.3	7.0
w/locking diff.	3.2	6.8

THIS SECTION CONTAINS:

- ## UNDERHOOD SERVICE INFORMATION

These include the specifications and instructions you need to perform underhood service on 1989-00 domestic cars, light trucks, and most imports.

Information in this section includes: engine identification information, cylinder numbering, firing order, and timing mark diagrams, followed by specifications necessary to perform underhood service.

ENGINE IDENTIFICATION

To identify any engine by the manufacturer's code, follow the four steps designated by the numbered blocks.

1 MODEL YEAR IDENTIFICATION:

10th character of V.I.N.

2000—Y	1999—X	1998—W
1997—V	1996—T	1995—S
1994—R	1993—P	1992—N
1991—M	1990—L	1989—K

2 ENGINE CODE LOCATION:

Integra, first five characters of engine number, located on flange under the distributor.

Legend, RL first five characters of engine number, located on timing chain cover below engine oil fill cap or below thermostat housing.

Vigor, TL first five characters of engine number, located on bell housing by starter.

V.I.N.
PLATE LOCATION:
Left side of hood support member. Also top left side of instrument panel.

3 ENGINE / 4 ENGINE IDENTIFICATION

YEAR	CODE	CYL.	liters	cc	Fuel System	HP
1999-00	B18C1	4	1.8	1797	MFI	170
	B18B1	4	1.8	1834	MFI	140
	F23A1	4	2.3	2254	MFI	152
	C30A1	6	3.0	2977	MFI	252
	J30A1	6	3.0	2997	MFI	200
	C32A1	6	3.2	3179	MFI	290
	J32A1	6	3.2	3210	MFI	230
	C35A1	6	3.5	3474	MFI	210
1997-98	B18C1	4	1.8	1797	MFI	170
	B18B1	4	1.8	1834	MFI	142
	F22B1	4	2.2	2165	MFI	145
	F23A1	4	2.3	2254	MFI	152
	G25A4	5	2.5	2451	MFI	176
	C30A1	6	3.0	2977	MFI	230
	J30A1	6	3.0	2997	MFI	200
	C32A1	6	3.2	3179	MFI	290
	C32A6	6	3.2	3206	MFI	230
	C35A1	6	3.5	3474	MFI	210
1996	B18C1	4	1.8	1797	MFI	170
	B18B1	4	1.8	1834	MFI	142
	G25A4	5	2.5	2451	MFI	176
	C30A1	6	3.0	2977	MFI	230
	C32A1	6	3.2	3179	MFI	290
	C32A6	6	3.2	3206	MFI	230
	C35A1	6	3.5	3474	MFI	210
1995	B18C1	4	1.8	1797	MFI	170
	B18B1	4	1.8	1834	MFI	142
	G25A4	5	2.5	2451	MFI	176

3 ENGINE / 4 ENGINE IDENTIFICATION

YEAR	CODE	CYL.	liters	cc	Fuel System	HP
1995 Cont'd	C30A1	6	3.0	2977	MFI	230
	C32A1	6	3.2	3179	MFI	290
	C32A6	6	3.2	3206	MFI	230
1994	B18C1	4	1.8	1797	MFI	170
	B18B1	4	1.8	1834	MFI	142
	G25A1	5	2.5	2451	MFI	176
	C30A1	6	3.0	2977	MFI	252, 270
	C32A1	6	3.2	3206	MFI	200, 230
1993	B17A1	4	1.7	1678	MFI	160
	B18A1	4	1.8	1834	MFI	140
	G25A1	5	2.5	2451	MFI	176
	C30A1	6	3.0	2977	MFI	252, 270
	C32A1	6	3.2	3206	MFI	200
1992	B17A1	4	1.7	1678	MFI	160
	B18A1	4	1.8	1834	MFI	140
	G25A1	5	2.5	2451	MFI	176
	C30A1	6	3.0	2977	MFI	252, 270
	C32A1	6	3.2	3206	MFI	200
1991	B17A1	4	1.7	1678	MFI	160
	B18A1	4	1.8	1834	MFI	130
	C30A1	6	3.0	2977	MFI	252, 270
	C32A1	6	3.2	3206	MFI	200
1990	B18A1	4	1.8	1834	MFI	130
	C27A1	6	2.7	2675	MFI	160
1989	D16A1	4	1.6	1590	MFI	118
	C27A1	6	2.7	2675	MFI	161

MFI—Multiport Fuel Injection

UNDERHOOD SERVICE SPECIFICATIONS

AAITU1

CYLINDER NUMBERING SEQUENCE

AAITU1

4-CYL. FIRING ORDER: 1 3 4 2

5-CYL. FIRING ORDER: 1 2 4 5 3

V6 FIRING ORDER: 1 4 2 5 3 6

— Front of car —

1989 1590cc Integra	**1990-00** 1678cc, 1797cc, 1834cc Integra	**1997-00** 2165cc 2.2CL, 2.3CL	**1992-98** 2451cc Vigor, 2.5TL	**1989-90** 2494cc, 2675cc Legend	**1991-00** 2977cc, 3179cc, NSX 3206cc Legend, 3.2TL 3494cc 3.5RL

TIMING MARK

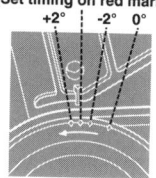

(Set timing on red mark)
+2° -2° 0°

1989-00
1590cc, 1678cc,
1797cc, 1834cc Integra
1997-00
2165cc 2.2CL, 2.3CL

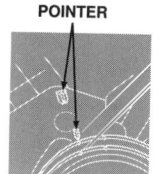

POINTER

1992-98
2451cc
Vigor, 2.5TL

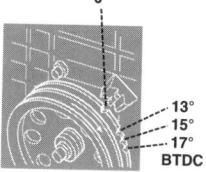

0°
13°
15°
17°
BTDC

1989-00
2494cc, 2675cc,
3206cc, 3474cc Legend,
3.2TL, 3.5RL,
2977cc, 3179cc NSX

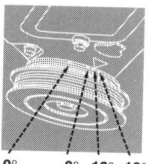

BTDC
0° 8° 10° 12°

1998-99
2977cc, 3.0CL

AAITU2

ELECTRICAL AND IGNITION SYSTEMS

BATTERY

BCI equivalent shown, size may vary from original equipment. Check clearance before replacing, holddown may need to be modified.

Model	Year	STANDARD BCI Group No.	STANDARD Crank. Perf.	OPTIONAL BCI Group No.	OPTIONAL Crank. Perf.
Integra	1989	45	410	—	—
	1990-93	25	435	—	—
	1994-00	51R	405	—	—
Legend	1989	24F	580	—	—
	1990	24F	585	—	—
	1991-95	24	585	—	—
NSX	1991-94	24F	550	—	—
w/MT	1995-99	35	435	—	—
w/AT	1995-99	24F	585	—	—
Vigor	1992-94	24F	550	—	—
2.2CL	1997	24F	550	—	—
2.3CL	1998-00	35	455	24F	550
2.5TL	1995-98	35	440	—	—
3.0CL	1997-99	24	550	—	—
3.2TL	1996-98	25	440	—	—
3.5RL	1996-99	24	550	—	—

GENERATOR

Application	Year	Rated Output	Test Output (amps & eng. rpm)
1590cc	1989	65	40-50 @ 2000
1678cc	1991-93	80	40 min. @ 2000
1797cc, 1834cc	1990-91	70	74-85 @ 2000
	1992-93	80	40 min. @ 2000
	1994-97	90	60 min. @ 2000
	1998-00	85, 90	70 @2000
2165cc	1997	90	75 @ 2000
2254cc	1998-00	90	75 @ 2000
2451cc	1992	100	78 min. @ 2000
	1993-94	100	55 min. @ 2000
	1995-98	100	75 @ 2000
2675cc	1989-90	70	74-85 @ 2000
2977cc, 3179cc	1991-92	110	102 @ 2000
	1993-94	110	40 min. @ 2000
	1995-99	120	85 @ 2000
2997cc	1997-00	100	75 @ 2000
3206cc, 3474cc	1993-99	110	60 min. @ 2000
3210cc	1999-00	105	75 @ 2000

REGULATOR

Application	Year	Test Temp. (deg. F/C)	Voltage Setting
All	1989-00	—	13.5-15.1

STARTER

Engine	Year	Cranking Voltage (min. volts)	Max. Ampere Draw @ Cranking Speed
All	1989-90	8.0	350
1678cc, 1834cc	1991-93	8.0	350
1797cc, 1834cc	1994-95	8.0	360
1797cc, 1834cc: 1.2 kw	1996-00	8.0	270 max.
1.4 kw	1996-00	8.0	360 max.
2165cc, 2254cc		8.5	350 max.
2451cc: 1.6 kw	1992-94	8.0	350
2.0 kw	1992-94	8.0	400
	1995-98	8.5	380 max
2451cc	1995-96	8.5	380
2977cc, 3179cc	1991-00	8.5	350
3206cc	1996-98	8.0	450 max
3474cc	1996-00	8.0	400 max

SPARK PLUGS

Engine	Year	Gap (inches)	Gap (mm)	Torque (ft-lb)
1590cc, 1834cc	1989-00	.039-.043	1.0-1.1	13
1678cc	1991-94	.051	1.3	13
1797cc	1994-00	.047-.051	1.2-1.3	13
2165cc, 2254cc	1997-99	.039-.043	1.0-1.1	13
2451cc	1992-94	.043	1.1	13
	1995-98	.039-.043	1.0-1.1	13
2675cc	1989-90	.039-.043	1.0-1.1	16
2977cc, 3179cc	1991-00	.039-.043	1.0-1.1	13
3206cc, 3210cc, 3474cc	1996-00	.039-.043	1.0-1.1	13

IGNITION COIL

Resistance (ohms @ 70°F or 21°C)

Engine	Year	Windings	Resistance (ohms)
1590cc	1989	Primary	.3-.5
		Secondary	9440-14,160
1678cc	1991-93	Primary	0.6-0.8
		Secondary	9760-14,640
1797cc, 1834cc	1994-00	Primary	0.6-0.8
		Secondary	12,800-19,200
1834cc	1990-93	Primary	.6-.8
		Secondary	9760-14,640
2165cc, 2259cc	1997-00	Primary	.45-.55
		Secondary	16,800-25,000
2451cc	1992-98	Primary	0.3-0.5[3]
		Secondary	10,800-16,200[3]
2675cc	1989	Primary	.3-.4
		Secondary	9040-13,560[1]
2675cc	1990	Primary	.35-.42
		Secondary	16,000-24,000[1]
2977cc, 3179cc	1991-98	Primary	0.9-1.1[2]
2997cc	1997-00	Primary	.34-.42
		Secondary	17,100-20,900
3206cc, 3494cc	1989-96	Primary	0.9-1.1[2]
3210cc	1999-00	Primary	.34-.42
		Secondary	17,100-20,900
3474cc	1996-00	Primary	0.9-1.1

1 Measured between upper right side cavity terminal and secondary terminal.
2 Measured between two electrical leads of each coil.
3 Primary resistance measured between upper right and lower left terminal (under lock) of ignition coil. Secondary resistance measured between upper right and high voltage terminal.

BASE TIMING

At slow idle and Before Top Dead Center, unless otherwise specified.

1989 1590cc, remove the main fuse box cover and jumper terminals Br and Br/Bl.

1989 V6, 1990-00 All: Connect a jumper between the terminals of the 2-pin light grey or blue timing connector under dash.

1989-94 2451cc, 2675cc, 2977cc, 3206cc, access the ignition timing adjuster in the control box under hood. Turn the screw on the unit to adjust timing. Rivets must be drilled from timing adjuster mounting to gain access to screw.

1995-98 2451cc, 2977cc, 3206cc, connect inductive clamp to loop wire by ignitor.

1995-00 2451cc, 2977cc, 3179cc, 3206cc, 3474cc, if timing is not correct, replace ECM.

Engine	Year	Man. Trans. (degrees)	Auto. Trans. (degrees)
1590cc	1989	12±2	12±2
1678cc	1991-93	16±2	16±2
1797cc	1994-00	16±2	16±2
1834cc	1990-00	16±2	16±2
2165cc	1997	15±2	15±2
2254cc	1998-00	12±2	12±2
2451cc	1992-98	15±2	15±2
2675cc	1989-90	15±2	15±2
2977cc, 3179cc	1991-00	15±2	15±2
2997cc	1997-00	—	10±2
3206cc	1996-98	—	15±2
3210cc	1999	—	10±2
3474cc	1996-00	—	15±2

UNDERHOOD SERVICE SPECIFICATIONS

AAITU3

AAITU3

DISTRIBUTOR PICKUP

Engine	Year	Resistance (ohms)
1590cc: Pickup coil	1989	350-550
Crankshaft position sensor	1989	700-1000
1678cc, 1797cc, 1834cc[1]: TDC sensor	1990-95	350-700
	1996-97	500-1000
Camshaft position sensor	1990-95	350-700
	1996-00	500-1000
Crankshaft position sensor	1990-95	350-700
	1996-00	500-1000
2675cc Cylinder sensor	1989-90	500-1000

1 Measured between each of three pairs of terminals on distributor connector.

FUEL SYSTEM

FUEL SYSTEM PRESSURE

Engine	Year	Pressure PSI[1]	Pressure PSI[2]	Fuel Pump PSI
All	1989-90	36-41	35-37	64-85
1678cc	1991-93	48-56	39-46	64-85
1797cc	1994-00	47-55	38-46	—
1834cc	1991-93	41-48	32-39	64-85
	1994-97	40-47	31-36	—
	1998-00	40-47	36-43	—
2165cc	1997	38-46	30-37	—
2254cc	1998-00	47-54	38-46	—
2451cc	1992-98	43-50	33-41	64-85
2977cc, 3179cc	1991-00	46-53	36-44	64-85
2997cc	1997-00	41-48	37-44	—
3206cc	1991-92	38-46	31-37	64-85
	1993	35-41	29-35	64-85
	1994-95	44-51	36-43	—
	1996-98	38-45	28-35	—
3210cc	1999-00	41-48	37-44	—
3474cc	1996-00	43-50	35-42	—

1 With vacuum hose to fuel pressure regulator disconnected.
2 With vacuum hose to fuel pressure regulator connected.

IDLE SPEED W/COMPUTER CONTROL

1990-00 All Canadian Models: Pull up on parking brake lever.

1590cc, 1678cc, 1797cc, 1834cc, 2451cc: With engine idling, disconnect the IAC connector. Adjust speed to specified setting value. Reconnect ISC and remove "Hazard" or "Backup" fuse for 10 seconds minimum. Check that idle speed is at specified checking value. Fast idle is not adjustable. Turn on headlights and rear window defroster. Verify that Electrical load speed-up is at specified value. Turn on A/C, blower on high, verify that A/C speed-up speed is at specified value.

2675cc: Check engine speed at idle against specified checking value. If yellow LED on ECM under passenger section is blinking, turn idle screw 1/4 turn clockwise. If yellow LED is on but not blinking, turn idle screw 1/4 turn counterclockwise. Check yellow LED again after 30 seconds and repeat procedure until it is off.

1991-00 2977cc, 3179cc, 1991-92 3206cc: Disconnect the IAC connector and adjust speed to specified setting value. Reconnect ISC and verify that speed is at specified checking value.

1993-95 3206cc: Connect an inductive clamp around loop wire on ignition control module. Check idle speed. Connect the Service Check connector with a jumper wire. Inspect ECM. If yellow LED is blinking, turn idle screw clockwise 1/4 turn. Wait 30 seconds and repeat until LED is off. If yellow LED is on, turn idle screw 1/4 turn counterclockwise. Wait 30 seconds and repeat until LED is off.

1995-98 2451cc, 1996-00 3206cc, 3494cc, 1997-00 2165cc, 2254cc; Disconnect IAC electrical connector and EVAP purge control solenoid valve. Adjust speed to specified value. Reconnect IAC and remove, then replace HAZARD, BACKUP or CLOCK fuse to clear ECM. Check that idle is at specified value. All ex. 2254cc and 3494cc, turn on headlights, and rear window defroster. Verify that Elect. Speed-up is at specified value. Turn on A/C and verify that A/C Speed up is at specified value.

1997-00 2997cc, 3210cc: Set idle to specified value.

IDLE SPEED W/COMPUTER CONTROL Continued

Engine	Year	Transmission	Checking Speed	Setting Speed	Fast Idle (Cold)
1590cc	1989	MT	700-800	500-600	1250-2250
Elect. & A/C Speed-up	1989	MT	700-800		
1590cc	1989	AT	650-750 N	500-600 N	1250-2250 N
Elect. & A/C Speed-up	1989	AT	700-800 N	—	
1678cc	1991-93	MT	750-850	550-650	1000-2000
Elect. & A/C Speed-up	1991-93	MT	750-850		
1797cc	1994	MT	700-800	430-530	1400-1800
Elect. Speed-up	1994	MT	800-900		
A/C Speed-up	1994	MT	700-800		
1797cc	1994	AT	700-800 N	430-530 N	1400-1800 N
Elect. Speed-up	1994	AT	800-900 N		
A/C Speed-up	1994	AT	700-800 N		
1797cc	1995-97	MT	700-800	430-530	1400-1800
Elect. Speed-up	1995-97	MT	700-800		
A/C Speed-up	1995-97	MT	800-900		
1797cc GSR	1998-00	MT	700-800	430-530	1400-1800
Elect.Speed-up	1998-00	MT	700-800		
A/C Speed-up	1998-00	MT	800-900		
1797cc Type R	1998-00	MT	750-850	600-700	1400-1800
Elect. Speed-up	1998-00	MT	750-850		
A/C Speed-up	1998-00	MT	1000-1100		
1834cc	1990-91	MT	700-800	600-700	1000-1800
Elect. & A/C Speed-up	1990-91	MT	700-800	—	—
1834cc	1990-91	AT	700-800 N	600-700 N	1000-1800 N
Elect. & A/C Speed-up	1990-91	AT	700-800 N		
1834cc	1992-93	MT	700-800	550-650	1000-2000
Elect. & A/C Speed-up	1992-93	MT	700-800		
1834cc	1992-93	AT	700-800 N	550-650 N	1000-2000 N
Elect. & A/C Speed-up	1992-93	AT	700-800 N		
1834cc	1994	MT	700-800	430-530	1400-1800
Elect. Speed-up	1994	MT	770-870		
A/C Speed-up	1994	MT	800-900		
1834cc	1994	AT	700-800 N	430-530 N	1400-1800 N
Elect. Speed-up	1994	AT	790-890 N		
A/C Speed-up	1994	AT	700-800 N		
1834cc	1995-00	MT	700-800	430-530	1400-1800
Elect. Speed-up	1995-00	MT	700-800		
A/C Speed-up	1995-00	MT	770-870		
1834cc	1995-00	AT	700-800 N	430-530 N	1400-1800 N
Elect. Speed-up	1995-00	AT	700-800 N		
A/C Speed-up	1995-00	AT	790-890 N		
2165cc	1997	MT	650-750	500-600	1200-1600
Elect. & A/C Speed-up	1997	MT	720-820		
2165cc	1997	AT	650-750 N	500-600 N	1200-1600 N
Elect. & A/C Speed-up	1997	AT	720-820 N		
2254cc	1998-00	MT	720-820	650-750	1100-1500
		AT	720-820N	650-750N	1100-1500 N
2451cc	1992-98	MT	650-750	500-600	1000-1400
Elect. & A/C Speed-up	1992-98	MT	720-820		
2451cc	1992-98	AT	650-750 N	500-600 N	1000-1400 N
Elect. & A/C Speed-up	1992-98	AT	720-820 N		
2675cc	1989-90	MT	630-730	—	1100-1900
	1989-90	AT	630-730 N	—	1100-1900 N
2977cc, 3179cc	1991-94	MT	750-850	500-600	1100-1900
	1991-94	AT	700-800 N	500-600 N	1100-1900 N
	1995-00	MT	750-850	550-650	1100-1900
	1995-00	AT	730-830 N	550-650 N	1100-1900 N
2997cc	1997-99	AT	—	700-800N	900-1300 N
3206cc	1991-92	MT	600-700	450-550	1300-1700
	1991-92	AT	550-650 P	450-550 N	1300-1700 N
3206cc: Coupe	1993	MT	630-730[1]	—	1300-1700
	1993	AT	580-680N[1]	—	1300-1700 N
Sedan	1993	MT	600-700[1]	—	1300-1700
	1993	AT	550-650N[1]	—	1300-1700 N
3206cc: L, LS Sedan	1994-95	MT	600-700[1]	—	1300-1700
	1994-95	AT	550-650 N[1]	—	1300-1700 N
GS Sedan, Cape	1994-95	MT	630-730[1]	—	1300-1700
	1994-95	AT	580-680 N[1]	—	1300-1700
3206cc	1996-98	AT	590-690N	430-530N	1100-1500 N
Elect.& A/C Speed-up	1996-98	AT	600-700N		
3210cc	1999-00	AT	—	600-700N	900-1300 N
3474cc	1996-00	AT	600-700 N	430-530 N	1100-1500 N

1 With headlights and heater blower, or AC turned on. Idle speed should be maintained.

ACURA
1989-2000 All Models
SLX—See Isuzu

CHEK-CHART

UNDERHOOD SERVICE SPECIFICATIONS

AAITU4

AAITU4

ENGINE MECHANICAL

TIGHTENING TORQUES

Some fasteners are tightened in more than one step.

TORQUE FOOT-POUNDS/NEWTON METERS

Engine	Year	Cylinder Head	Intake Manifold	Exhaust Manifold	Crankshaft Pulley	Water Pump
1590cc	1989	22/30, 48/66	16/22	23/32	83/115	9/12
1678cc, 1797cc, 1834cc	1990-00	22/30, 63/85	17/23	23/32	87/120	9/12
2165cc	1997	29/39, 51/69, 72/98	16/22	23/31	181/245	9/12
2254cc	1998-00	22/29 +90°[2]	16/22	23/31	181/245	9/12
2451cc	1992-98	29/39, 51/69, 72/98	16/22	23/32	181/250	9/12
2675cc	1989-90	29/40, 56/78	16/22	25/34	123/170	9/12, small 16/22, large
2977, 3206cc	1991-00	29/40, 56/78	16/22	25/34	174/240	9/12, small 16/22, large
2997cc	1997-00	29/39, 51/69, 72/98	16/22	23/31	181/250	9/12
3179cc	1995-00	29/40, 71/96	16/22	28/30	181/250	9/12, small 16/22, large
3206cc	1996-98	56/76[3]	16/22	22/30	181/250	9/12, small 16/22, large
3474cc	1996-98	56/76[1]	16/22	23/31	181/245	9/12, small 16/22, large

1 Over 2-3 steps.
2 When using new bolts, turn an additional 90°.
3 Over several steps.

VALVE CLEARANCE

Engine cold.
Measured between camshaft and rocker arm.

Engine	Year	Intake (inches)	Intake (mm)	Exhaust (inches)	Exhaust (mm)
1590cc	1989	.005-.006	.13-.17	.006-.007	.15-.19
1678cc	1991-93	.006-.007	.15-.19	.007-.008	.17-.21
1797cc	1994-00	.006-.007	.15-.19	.007-.008	.17-.21
1834cc	1990-91	.006-.007	.15-.19	.007-.008	.17-.21
1834cc	1992-00	.003-.005	.08-.12	.006-.008	.16-.20
2165cc, 2254cc	1997-00	.009-.011	.24-.28	.011-.013	.28-.32
2451cc	1992-98	.009-.011	.24-.28	.011-.013	.28-.32
2977cc, 3179cc	1991-00	.006-.007	.15-.19	.007-.008	.17-.21
2997cc	1997-00	.008-.009	.20-.24	.011-.013	.28-.32

COMPRESSION PRESSURE

Engine	Year	PSI	Maximum Variation PSI
1590cc	1989	134-192	28
1678cc, 1834cc	1990-93	135-185	28
1797cc	1994-00	135-270	28
1834cc	1994-00	140-199	28
2165cc	1997	135-178	28
2254cc	1998-00	135-242	28
2451cc	1992-94	135-206	28
	1995-98	135-228	28
2675cc	1989-90	142-171	28
2977cc, 3179cc	1991-00	142-199	28
3206cc, 3474cc	1991-00	142-199	28
3210cc	1999-00	135-206	28

BELT TENSION

Deflection method: Deflection midway between pulleys with an applied load of 22 pounds on longest belt segment.

Engine	Year	Generator	Power Steering	Air Cond.
1590cc (inches)	1989	1/4-3/8	3/4-7/8	1/4-3/8
(mm)	1989	7-10	18-22	7-10
1834cc (inches)	1990-91	5/16-7/16	1/4-5/16	1/4-3/8
(mm)	1990-91	8.5-10.5	6-8	7-9
2451cc (inches)	1992-94	—	1/4-13/32	1/4-13/32
(mm)	1992-94	—	6-9	6-9
2494cc, 2675cc (inches)	1989-90	3/4-7/8	1/4-5/16	1/4-3/8
(mm)	1989-90	18-22	19-24	7-10
2977cc (inches)	1991-93	—	—	7/32-5/16
(mm)	1991-93	—	—	5.5-7.5
2977cc (inches)	1994	1/2-9/16	—	3/8-1/2
(mm)	1994	12-14	—	10-12
3206cc (inches)	1991-93	—	7/16-1/2	5/16-7/16
(mm)	1991-93	—	11.5-13.5	8-10

Strand Tension Method

Engine	Year	Generator	Power Steering	Air Cond.
1678cc, 1834cc: New	1991-93	155-200	150-175	—
Used	1991-93	78-110	77-99	—
1797cc, 1834cc: New	1994-99	155-200	170-200	170-200
Used	1994-99	78-110	80-120	88-120
2165cc: New	1997	210-254	170-200	210-254
Used	1997	99-130	88-120	99-130
2451cc: New	1992-95	155-200	—	—
Used	1992-95	78-110	—	—
2451cc: New	1995-98	187-231	187-231	170-200
Used	1995-98	88-121	88-121	88-121
2977cc, 3206cc: New	1991-93	176-200	—	—
Used	1991-93	88-121	—	—
2977cc: New	1995-96	198-243	—	154-198
Used	1995-96	99-143	—	77-121
3206cc: New	1994-95	165-198	154-198	176-220
Used	1994-95	77-121	77-121	88-120
3206cc: New	1996-98	176-220	154-200	157-231
Used	1996-98	88-132	77-120	88-132
3474cc: New	1996-00	180-220	155-200	210-243
Used	1996-00	88-130	77-121	100-143

ENGINE COMPUTER SYSTEM

DIAGNOSTIC TROUBLE CODES

1989-90 turn ignition on and move passenger seat fully rearward to observe LED flashing light on the ECM (Integra, Legend Sedan) or pull down carpet on passenger side under dash (Legend Coupe). The codes will be displayed by the number of times the light flashes followed by a brief pause between cycles. Remove "Hazard" fuse at battery + terminal (4-cyl.) or "Alternator Sense" fuse in the underhood relay box (V6) for ten seconds minimum to erase codes.

1991-00 jumper the two terminals of the Service Check connector under dash on passenger side. Codes will be displayed on Check Engine lamp. Remove ECM fuse to erase codes.

OBD-II compliant systems still allow code retrieval through the MIL.

LED on or off steadily, ECM

Code 1 Oxygen sensor or circuit (4-cyl., 5-cyl.)
Code 1 Left or front oxygen sensor (V6)
Code 2 Right or rear oxygen sensor (V6)
Codes 3, 5 Manifold absolute pressure sensor or circuit
Code 4 Crankshaft position sensor #1
Code 6 Engine coolant temperature sensor or circuit
Code 7 Throttle position sensor or circuit
Code 8 TDC sensor or circuit
Code 9 Cylinder position sensor or circuit
Code 10 Intake air temperature sensor or circuit
Code 12 EGR control system
Code 13 Barometric pressure sensor or circuit
Code 14 Idle air control system
Code 15 Ignition output signal
Code 16 Fuel injector
Code 17 Vehicle speed sensor or circuit
Code 18 Ignition timing adjustment
Code 19 Lock up control solenoid valve
Code 20 Electric load

ACURA
1989-2000 All Models
SLX—See Isuzu

UNDERHOOD SERVICE SPECIFICATIONS

AAITU5

AAITU5

DIAGNOSTIC TROUBLE CODES Continued

Code 21 Front VTEC solenoid valve (NSX)
Code 21 Front spool solenoid valve (others)
Code 22 Front VTEC pressure switch (NSX)
Code 22 Front valve timing oil pressure switch (others)
Code 23 Front knock sensor (Front on NSX, Vigor)
Code 30 AT FI signal A
Code 31 AT FI signal B
Code 35 TC standby signal
Code 36 TC FC signal
Code 41 Front oxygen sensor heater
Code 42 Rear oxygen sensor heater (3.0L)
Code 43 Fuel supply system (4-cyl.)
Code 43 Front fuel supply system (V6)
Code 44 Rear fuel supply system (V6)
Code 45 Front fuel metering system
Code 46 Rear fuel metering system
Code 47 Fuel pump
Code 50 Mass air flow sensor
Code 51 Rear VTEC solenoid valve
Code 52 Rear VTEC pressure switch
Code 53 Rear knock sensor
Code 54 Crankshaft position Sensor B
Code 59 No. 1 cylinder position
Code 61 Primary oxygen sensor slow response
Code 63 Secondary oxygen sensor slow response
Code 65 Secondary oxygen sensor heater
Code 67 Catalyst efficiency low
Code 70 Transaxle problem
Code 71 Cylinder 1 misfire
Code 72 Cylinder 2 misfire
Code 73 Cylinder 3 misfire
Code 74 Cylinder 4 misfire
Code 75 Cylinder 5 misfire
Code 76 Cylinder 6 misfire (6-cyl.)
Code 76 Random misfire (ex. 6-cyl.)
Code 79 Spark plug voltage detection circuit
Code 80 EGR flow insufficient
Code 86 Engine coolant out of range
Code 90 EVAP system leak
Code 92 EVAP system purge

SENSORS, INPUT
TEMPERATURE SENSORS

Engine	Year	Sensor	Resistance Ohms @ deg. F/C
All	1989-00	Coolant, Intake Air	15,000-20,000 @ -4/-20 5000-7000 @ 32/0 2000-4000 @ 68/20 900-1200 @ 104/40 300-400 @ 176/80 100-300 @ 248/120

MANIFOLD ABSOLUTE AND BAROMETRIC PRESSURE SENSORS
5 volts reference.

Engine	Year	Voltage @ In Hg./@Pa
All	1989-00	2.7-2.9 @ 0/0 2.3-2.5 @ 5/17 1.8-2.0 @ 10/34 1.4-1.6 @ 15/51 0.9-1.1 @ 20/68

SENSORS, INPUT Continued
CRANKSHAFT, TDC, & CAMSHAFT POSITION SENSORS

Engine	Year	Resistance (Ohms)
1797cc, 1834cc Crankshaft	1996-00	1600-3200
2165cc, 2254cc: Camshaft	1997-99	1850-2450
Crankshaft	1997-99	1850-2450
2451cc	1992-94	650-850
2451cc: Camshaft	1995-98	500-1000[v1]
Crankshaft	1995-98	800-1500[v1]
2977cc	1991-00	650-850[v1]
2997cc: Camshaft	1997-00	1850-2450
Crankshaft	1997-00	1850-2450
3206cc	1991-95	650-850

[v1] 3 sensors

THROTTLE POSITION SENSOR

Engine	Year	Voltage Idle	WOT
1590cc	1989	0.5	4.5
1797cc, 1834cc	1994-95	0.5	4.0
	1996-00	0.5	4.5
1834cc	1990-91	0.3	4.5
2165cc, 2254cc	1997-00	0.5	4.5
2494cc, 2675cc	1989-90	0.5	4.0
2451cc	1994-98	0.5	4.5
2977cc, 3179cc	1991-00	0.5	4.8
2997cc	1997-00	0.5	4.5
3206cc	1994-95	0.2-0.5	4.5
	1996-98	0.5	4.5
3474cc	1996-00	0.5	4.5
All others	1991-93	0.2-0.5	4.5

ACTUATORS, OUTPUT
IDLE SPEED CONTROL

Engine	Year	Resistance (ohms)
All	1989-90	8-15

FUEL INJECTORS

Engine	Year	Resistance (ohms)	Temperature (deg. F/C)
All	1989-91	1.5-2.5	—
1678cc, 1797cc, 1834cc	1992-95	10-13	—
2451cc, 2977cc, 3206cc	1992-95	1.5-2.5	—

ENGINE IDENTIFICATION

To identify any engine by the manufacturer's code, follow the steps designated by the numbered blocks.

1 MODEL YEAR IDENTIFICATION:

Refer to illustration of the Vehicle Identification number (V.I.N.): The year is indicated by a code letter which is the 10th character of the V.I.N.

3 ENGINE CODE:

In the "CODE" Column, find the engine code.

4 ENGINE IDENTIFICATION:

On the line where the engine code appears, read to the right to identify the engine.

V.I.N. PLATE LOCATION: Top of instrument panel or windshield pillar visible through windshield on driver's side.

1 MODEL YEAR IDENTIFICATION:

10th character of V.I.N.

1999—X	1998—W	1997—V
1996—T	1995—S	1994—R
1993—P	1992—N	1991—M
1990—L	1989—K	

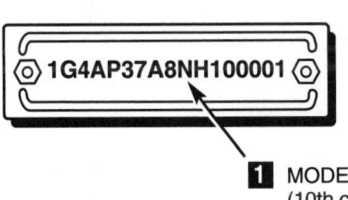

1 MODEL YEAR (10th character)

2 ENGINE CODE LOCATION:

Prefix to engine number:

Code 3B engines — Stamped on side of engine block, passenger's side rear.

Code AAH, ABZ, AEW, AHA, AFC engines — Stamped on right side of engine block between the cylinder head and power steering pump.

All other engines — Stamped on side of engine block below number 2 and 3 spark/glow plugs.

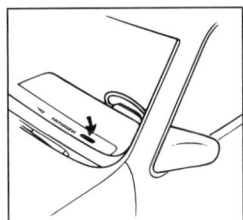

4 ENGINE IDENTIFICATION

YEAR	3 ENGINE CODE	CYL.	DISPL. liters	cc	Fuel System	HP
1999	AEB	4	1.8T	1781T	M	150
	AHA	6	2.8	2771	M	190
	—	6	2.8	2771	M	200
	AEW	8	3.7	3697	M	230
	ABZ	8	4.2	4172	M	300
1998	AEB	4	1.8T	1781T	M	150
	AAH	6	2.8	2771	M	172
	AHA	6	2.8	2771	M	190, 200
	—	6	2.8	2771	M	200
	AEW	8	3.7	3697	M	230
	ABZ	8	4.2	4172	M	300
1997	AEB	4	1.8T	1781T	M	150
	AAH	6	2.8	2771	M	172
	AHA	6	2.8	2771	M	190, 200
	AEW	8	3.7	3697	M	230
	ABZ	8	4.2	4172	M	300
1996	AEB	4	1.8T	1781T	M	150
	AAH	6	2.8	2771	M	172
	AHA	6	2.8	2771	M	190
1995	AAN	5	2.2 T	2226 T	M	227
	AAH, AFC	6	2.8	2771	M	174
1994	AAN	5	2.2 T	2226 T	M	227
	AAH, AFC	6	2.8	2771	M	172
	ABH	8	4.2	4172	M	276

4 ENGINE IDENTIFICATION

YEAR	3 ENGINE CODE	CYL.	DISPL. liters	cc	Fuel System	HP
1993	AAN	5	2.2 T	2226 T	M	227
	AAH, AFC	6	2.8	2771	M	172
	ABH	8	4.2	4172	M	276
1992	AAN	5	2.2 T	2226 T	—	227
	NG	5	2.3	2309	CIS-E	130
	7A	5	2.3	2309	AFC	164
	AAH, AFC	6	2.8	2771	M	172
	PT	8	4.2	4172	M	276
1991	MC	5	2.2 T	2226 T	CIS	157
	3B	5	2.2 T	2226 T	M	217
	NF, NG	5	2.3	2309	CIS-E	130
	7A	5	2.3	2309	AFC	164
	PT	8	3.6	3562	M	240
1990	3A	4	2.0	1984	CIS-E	108
	MC	5	2.2 T	2226 T	CIS	157
	NF, NG	5	2.3	2309	CIS-E	130
	7A	5	2.3	2309	AFC	164
	PT	8	3.6	3562	M	240
1989	3A	4	2.0	1984	CIS-E	108
	MC	5	2.2 T	2226 T	CIS	157
	NF, NG	5	2.3	2309	CIS-E	130

AFC—Air Flow Control. **CIS—Continuous Injection System.**
CIS-E—CIS Electronic. **M—Motronic.** **T—Turbo.**

UNDERHOOD SERVICE SPECIFICATIONS

AIITU1   AIITU1

CYLINDER NUMBERING SEQUENCE

4-CYL. FIRING ORDER: 1 3 4 2

5-CYL. FIRING ORDER: 1 2 4 5 3

V6 FIRING ORDER: 1 4 3 6 2 5

V8 FIRING ORDER: 1 5 4 8 6 3 7 2

 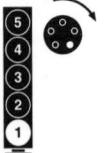  

— Front of car —

1989-90 All 4-cyl. Gasoline, 80, 90	1989-96 All 5-cyl. Gasoline	1992-99 V6 2.8L, 90, 100, A4, A6, Cabriolet	1990-99 V8 3.6L, 3.7L, 4.2L

UNDERHOOD SERVICE SPECIFICATIONS

AIITU2   AIITU2

TIMING MARK

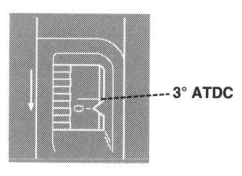

1989-90
2.0L w/MT,
80, 90

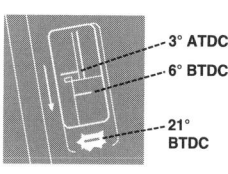

1989-90
2.0L w/AT,
80, 90

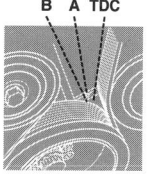

1989-96
2.2L, 2.3L

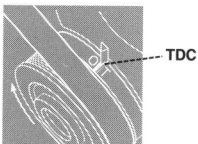

1993-99
V6 2.8L,
90, 100, A4, A6, Cabriolet

1990-99
V8 3.6L, 3.7L, 4.2L
A8, V8

ELECTRICAL AND IGNITION SYSTEMS

BATTERY

BCI equivalent shown, size may vary from original equipment. Check clearance before replacing, holddown may need to be modified.

Engine/Model	Year	STANDARD BCI Group No.	STANDARD Crank. Perf.	OPTIONAL BCI Group No.	OPTIONAL Crank. Perf.
1781cc	1996-97	48	540	—	—
	1998-99	94R	640	—	—
1984cc	1989-90	41	500	—	—
2226cc	1989-91	41[1]	500	—	—
	1993-95	41	650	—	—
2309cc: 80, 90	1989	41	500	—	—
100, 200	1989	41[1]	500	—	—
Coupe Quattro	1990-92	41[1]	650	—	—
2309cc 80	1990-92	41	575	41	650
90	1990-92	41	650	—	—
100	1990-92	41[1]	575	41	650
200	1990-92	41[1]	650	—	—
2771cc A6	1999	48[1]	570	—	—
A4	1999	48	570	—	—
A6	1992-98	41	650	—	—
A4	1997	48	540	—	—
A4	1998	94R	640	—	—
3562cc V8	1990	41[1]	650	—	—
3562cc	1991	49[1]	720	—	—
3697cc	1997-98	49[1]	850	—	—
4172cc V8 Quattro	1991-94	41[1]	720	—	—
4172cc	1997-99	49[1]	850	—	—

1 Battery is vented to outside of vehicle.

GENERATOR

Engine	Year	Rated Output	Test Output (amps @ rpm)
1781cc	1997-99	90	—
1984cc	1989-90	90	74 @ 3000
2226cc	1989-90	90	74 @ 3000
2226cc Turbo	1991-96	110	95 @ 3000
2309cc	1989-92	110	95 @ 3000
2771cc	1992-99	120	—
3562cc	1990-93	110	95 @ 3000
3697cc	1997-99	120	—
4172cc	1992-94	110	95 @ 3000
	1997-99	150	—

REGULATOR

Application	Year	Test Temp. (deg. F/C)	Voltage Setting
All	1989-93	Normal	13.5-14.5

STARTER

Engine	Year	Cranking Voltage (min. volts)
All	1989-93	8.0

SPARK PLUGS

Engine	Year	Gap (inches)	Gap (mm)	Torque (ft-lb)
1984cc	1989	.028-.035	.70-.90	14
2226cc				
Turbo, Code MC	1989-91	.024-.031	.60-.80	14
DOHC Turbo, Code 3B	1991	.020-.028	.50-.70	22
DOHC Turbo, Code AAN	1992	.024-.028	.60-.70	22
	1993-95	.020-.028	.50-.70	22
DOHC Turbo, Code ANN	1994	.020-.028	.50-.70	22
2309cc	1989-91	.028-.035	.70-.90	14
2771cc	1992-93	.028-.035	.70-.90	15
	1994-99	.035-.043	.90-1.10	22
3562cc	1990-91	.028-.035	.70-.90	22
4172cc	1992-94	.028-.035	.70-.90	22

1. 8   98   .031-.035

IGNITION COIL

Engine	Year	Windings	Resistance (ohms)
All ex. Code 7A	1989-91	Primary	0.50-1.50
		Secondary	5000-9000
Code 7A	1990-91	Primary	0.0-1.0
		Secondary	6500-8500
V6 2.8L	1992-99	Primary	0.5-1.2
		Secondary	9000-14,000

BASE TIMING

Set timing Before Top Dead Center, unless otherwise specified.

All Engines: Connect tachometer and timing light; check idle speed, observe timing mark.

Engines w/ISS (Idle Speed Stabilizer): Disconnect plugs from stabilizer and connect them together.

Engine	Year	Man. Trans. (degrees) @ Idle	Auto. Trans. (degrees) @ Idle
1984cc	1989-90	6± 2	6± 2
2226cc Turbo	1989-94	0[1]	0[1]
2309cc SOHC	1989-91	15± 2	15± 2
DOHC	1990-91	0[1]	0[1]
2771cc	1992-94	0[1]	0[1]
3562cc, 4172cc	1990-94	—	0[1]

1 Checking figure only, timing is non-adjustable.

FUEL SYSTEM

FUEL PRESSURE PROCEDURE
AFC System:
1. Connect appropriate pressure gauge to test port of fuel rail and open gauge valve.
2. Bridge diagnostic connector A, terminal 1 negative (-) with diagnostic connector B, terminal 1. Energize fuel pump, listen for pump to run and remove jumper after a minimum of 4 seconds, read system pressure.

UNDERHOOD SERVICE SPECIFICATIONS

FUEL PRESSURE PROCEDURE Continued

CIS Systems:
1. With engine at operating temperature, connect appropriate pressure gauge between fuel distributor and warm-up regulator.
2. Set gauge valve to open position, start engine and run at idle, allow pressure to stabilize, read control pressure.
3. Set gauge valve to closed position, allow pressure to stabilize, read system pressure.
4. Set gauge to open position, switch off ignition, after 10 minutes read residual pressure.

CIS-E Systems:
1. With engine at operating temperature, connect appropriate pressure gauge between cold start line and lower chamber test fittings of the fuel distributor.
2. Disconnect electrical connector from the differential pressure regulator.
3. Set gauge valve to open position, remove fuel pump relay and bridge terminals to energize pump, allow pressure to stabilize, read system pressure.
4. Set gauge valve to closed position, energize fuel pump, read differential pressure.
5. Set gauge valve to open position, energize fuel pump for 30 seconds, after 10 minutes read residual pressure.

Motronic Systems:
1. Connect appropriate pressure gauge to test port of fuel rail.
2. Disconnect vacuum hose from pressure regulator, start engine and run at idle, allow pressure to stabilize and take reading.
3. Reconnect vacuum to pressure regulator and check gauge reading.
4. Switch ignition off, after 10 minutes read residual pressure.

FUEL PRESSURE: AFC, MOTRONIC

Engine	Year	W/o vacuum PSI	W/vacuum PSI	Residual Pressure PSI
			System Pressure	
2226cc	1991	43-46	35-39	36-40
	1992-95	58-61	—	49-54
2309cc	1990-91	—	55-61	46
2771cc	1992-99	55-61	48-54	32-44
3562cc	1990-91	58-62	49-54	43-50
3697cc	1997	61	52	44
4172cc	1992-93	58-62	49-54	43-50
	1997-99	61	52	44

FUEL PRESSURE: CIS, CIS-E

Engine	System	Year	System PSI	Differential PSI	Residual PSI
			Pressure		
1984cc	CIS-E	1989-90	88-96	81-91	48
2309cc	CIS-E	1989-91	89-94	81-90	51

IDLE SPEED

All Engines: Must be at operating temperature, all electrical equipment switched off, cooling fan not running. If equipped with idle speed boost valve, pinch off hose to valve.

1989-91 2226cc Turbo Code MC: Disconnect crankcase breather hoses and plug outlets on valve cover, remove plug from EVAP canister vent pipe at intake boot.

All Other Engines: Disconnect crankcase breather hoses, remove plug from fitting of EVAP canister vent hose.

Engine	Year	Manual Transmission	Automatic Transmission
1984cc	1989-90	780-900[1]	780-900 N[1]
2226cc			
SOHC Turbo	1989-91	750-850	670-770 N
DOHC Turbo	1991-95	770-830[1]	770-830 N[1]
2309cc Code NF	1989-91	670-770[1]	670-770 N[1]
Code NG	1989-92	720-860[1]	720-860 N[1]
DOHC	1990-92	750-850[1]	750-850 N[1]
2771cc	1992-94	700-800[1]	700-800 N[1]
	1995-99	650-750[1]	650-750[1]
3562cc	1990-91	—	660-720 N[1]
3697cc	1997	—	680-760[1]
4172cc	1992-94	—	660-720 N[1]
	1997-99	—	720-800[1]

1 Not Adjustable (checking value only).

IDLE MIXTURE

Engine	Year	Idle CO%
1984cc	1989	0.3-1.2
2226cc		
SOHC Turbo	1989-91	0.3-1.2
DOHC Turbo	1991-95	0.5-0.9
2309cc Code NF	1989-91	0.3-1.2
Code NG	1989	0.6-1.0
DOHC	1990-91	0.5-1.0
2771cc	1992-95	0.3-1.2
3562cc	1990-91	0.5-0.9
4172cc	1992	0.5-0.9

1 Oxygen sensor disconnected.

ENGINE MECHANICAL

TIGHTENING TORQUES

Engine	Year	Cylinder Head	Intake Manifold	Exhaust Manifold	Crankshaft Pulley	Water Pump
		TORQUE FOOT-POUNDS/NEWTON METERS				
4-cyl. 1.8L	1996-99	44/60	—	—	—	15/20
2nd stage[1]		+180°				
4-cyl. 2.0L	1989	44/60	6mm bolt 7/10 8mm bolt 18/25	18/25	15/20	15/20
2nd stage[1]		+180°				
5-cyl. 2.2L:						
SOHC Turbo	1989-91	44/60	—	26/35	258/350[2]	15/20
2nd stage[1]		+180°				
DOHC Turbo	1991	30/40 44/60	18/25	26/35	258/350[2]	16/22
2nd stage						
3rd stage[1]		+180°				
	1992-95	30/40 44/60 +180°	15/20	18/25	—	—
5-cyl. 2.3L:						
SOHC	1989-91	44/60	15/20	18/25	258/350[2]	15/20
2nd stage[1]		+180°				
DOHC	1990-91	29/40 44/60	15/20	18/25	15/20	15/20
2nd stage						
3rd stage[1]		+180°				
V6 2.8L	1992-95	44/60	15/20	15/20	258/350[2] 295/400	7/10
2nd stage[1]		+180°				
V6 2.8L	1996-99	44/60	7/10	18/25	148/200	7/10
2nd stage[1]		+180°			+180°	
V8 3.6L	1990-91	30/40 44/60	11/15	18/25	258/350[2]	7/10
2nd stage						
3rd stage		+180°				
V8 3.7L, 4.2L	1997-99	30/40 44/60	15/20	18/25	258/350[2] 332/450[3]	—
2nd stage						
3rd stage		+180°[1]				

1 Two at 90° is permissible, must be in one even motion.
2 Valid only when using special extension, Audi Part No. 2079.
3 Without using special extension.

COMPRESSION PRESSURE
At cranking speed, engine temperature normalized, throttle open.

Engine	Year	PSI @ RPM	Maximum Variation PSI
1781cc	1996-99	145-189/102 min.	44
1984cc	1989	152-196	44
2226cc SOHC Turbo	1989-91	123-144	44
DOHC Turbo	1991	131-189	44
2309cc SOHC	1989-91	160-172	44
2771cc	1992-93	160-232	44
	1994-99	131-203/109 min.	44
3562cc	1990-91	145-190	44
3697cc, 4172cc	1997-99	145-220	44

UNDERHOOD SERVICE SPECIFICATIONS

BELT TENSION

Deflection method: Measured at midpoint of longest belt segment.

Engine	Year	Generator	Power Steering	Air Cond.
All (inches)	1989-91	1/8-1/4	1/8-1/4	1/8-1/4
All (mm)	1989-91	2-5	2-5	2-5

SERPENTINE BELT DIAGRAMS

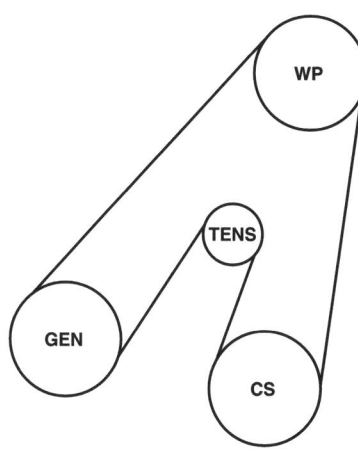

1992-98 V6 2.8L
w/o AC

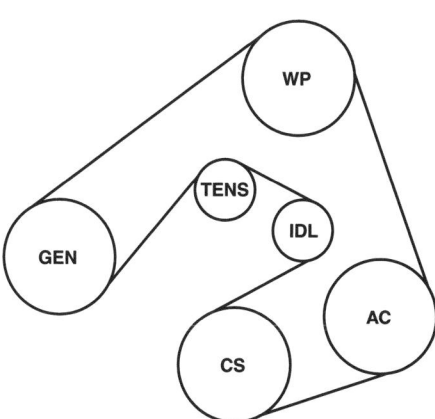

1992-98 V6 2.8L
w/AC

ENGINE COMPUTER SYSTEM

DIAGNOSTIC TROUBLE CODES

All Models:
Drive car at least 5 minutes and leave running at idle, Turbo engines must exceed 3000 rpm and 17 psi of boost. For a no-start condition, crank engine over for a minimum of 6 seconds and leave ignition switched on.

1984cc 1989-90:
1. Connect tester, Audi Part No. US1115, between test lead (next to fuel distributor) and positive battery terminal, codes displayed by tester.
2. Install spare fuse in top of fuel pump relay for 4 seconds.
3. Repeat step 2 to access additional codes, leave fuse in place 10 seconds to erase memory.

DIAGNOSTIC TROUBLE CODES Continued

2226cc SOHC Turbo w/1 knock sensor 1989-91:
1. Connect tester, Audi Part No. US1115, between positive (+) cavity of diagnostic terminal A (light color) and cavity of terminal B (dark color). Codes displayed by tester, California models flash ENGINE light on dash.
2. Momentarily (4 seconds) connect jump wire between negative (-) cavity of diagnostic terminal A and terminal B.
3. Repeat step 2 for additional codes.

2226cc SOHC Turbo w/2 knock sensors 1990-91:
1. Connect tester, Audi Part No. US1115, between positive diagnostic terminals 1 and 3, codes displayed by tester, California models flash ENGINE light on dash.
2. Momentarily (4 seconds) connect jump wire between diagnostic terminals 2 and 1.
3. Repeat step 2 for additional codes.

5-cyl. 2309cc DOHC, V8 3562cc 1990-91:
1. With test equipment connected to access diagnostic codes, switch ignition on without starting engine.
2. Momentarily connect jump wire (5-cyl., 4 seconds; V8, 10 seconds) to begin sequence.
3. Codes will be displayed on light and component activated.
4. Check for component function, then repeat step 2 to continue sequence.

2226cc DOHC Turbo 1991-94:
1. Special test equipment, Audi Part No. VAG1551, required.

2309cc 1989-91:
1. Connect tester, Audi Part No. US1115, between positive (+) cavity of diagnostic terminal A (light color) and cavity of terminal B (dark color). Codes displayed by tester, California models flash ENGINE light on dash.
2. Momentarily (4 seconds) connect jump wire between negative (-) cavity of diagnostic terminal A and terminal B.
3. Repeat step 2 for additional codes, or to erase memory after code 0000.

V6 2771cc 1992-95:
1. Special test equipment, Audi Part No. VAG1551, required.

V8 3562cc 1990-91:
1. Bridge upper cavities of diagnostic terminals 1 & 4 with test light, Audi special tool No. US1115.
2. Crank engine for 5 seconds and leave the ignition switched on.
3. Momentarily (4 seconds) connect jump wire between the lower cavities of diagnostic terminals 1 & 2.
4. Test light flashes codes, California models flash ENGINE light on dash.
5. Repeat step 3 for additional codes, or to erase memory after code 0000.

Code	Application	Definition
1111	ECM	Defective unit or circuit
1119	Trans. range	Defective wiring or circuit
1213	Vehicle Speed Sensor	Transmission sensor or circuit
1231	Vehicle Speed Sensor	Transmission sensor or circuit
2111	RPM Sensor	Defective sensor or circuit
2112	Timing Sensor	Defective sensor or circuit
2113	RPM Sensor	No signal from hall sender
2114	Distributor	Ignition out of adjustment
2114	Hall Reference	Check, camshaft timing out of phase
2121	Idle Switch	Defective switch or circuit
2122	Hall Sender	Defective sender or circuit
2123	Throttle Position Switch	Defective switch or circuit
2132	Control Unit	No signal from ignition to injection
2141	Knock Control	Excessive detonation signal
2142	Knock Control	No signal, defective sensor or circuit
2143	Knock Control	Detonation from sensor No. 2 cyl. 4, 5
2144	Knock Control	Defective sensor No. 2 or circuit
2212	Throttle Valve	Sensor voltage out of range
2214	RPM Signal	Idle speed too high
2214	RPM	Engine over-revved
2221	Vacuum Control	No vacuum to control unit
2222	Pressure Sensor	Defective control unit pressure sensor
2222	Manifold Vacuum	Defective vacuum line, wastegate valve, turbocharger
2223	Altitude Sensor	Defective sensor or circuit
2224	Manifold Pressure	Turbo control circuit, overboost
2224	Boost Pressure	Air leak, wastegate valve defective, vacuum leak, pressure sensor defective
2231	Air Mass Sensor	Defective sensor or circuit
2231	Idle Control	Idle speed outside control limits
2231	Idle Stabilizer	Air leak, defective valve or circuit
2232	Mass Airflow Sensor	No signal, defective sensor or circuit
2233	Mass Airflow Sensor	Reference voltage high
2233	Reference Voltage	No reference signal to control units

AUDI
1989-99

CHEK-CHART

UNDERHOOD SERVICE SPECIFICATIONS

AIITU5

AIITU5

DIAGNOSTIC TROUBLE CODES Continued

Code	Application	Definition
2234	ECM	Supply voltage low
2234	System Voltage	System voltage out of range
2242	CO Sensor	Sensor voltage low
2312	Engine Coolant Temperature	No signal, defective sensor or circuit
2314	Signal Wire	Short circuit to ground between TCM & ECM
2314	Transmission	Defective engine to transmission circuit
2322	Intake Air Temperature	No signal, defective sensor or circuit
2324	Mass Airflow Sensor	Defective sensor or circuit
2331	Oxygen Ratio	Defect in ignition or air/fuel system
2332	Oxygen Sensor II	Short or open circuit
2341	Oxygen Sensor	System operating outside control limits
2342	Oxygen Sensor	No signal, defective sensor or circuit
2343	Fuel Mixture	System running too lean
2344	Fuel Mixture	System running too rich
2411	EGR System	System malfunction, California only
2413	Mixture Control	System running too rich
2413	Fuel Pressure	System pressure too low
3424	Fault Lamp	System not operating
3424	Warning Lamp	Defective circuit, California only
4312	EGR System	System malfunction, except California
4332	Ignition Circuit	Open or short to positive or ground
4343	EVAP Canister Purge	Defective solenoid or circuit
4411	Fuel Injector	Check 1 & 5 injectors and circuit
4412	Fuel Injector	Check 2 & 7 injectors and circuit
4413	Fuel Injector	Check 3 & 6 injectors and circuit
4413	Fuel Injector #3	Defective injector or circuit
4414	Fuel Injector	Check 4 & 8 injectors and circuit
4421	Fuel Injector #5	Defective injector or circuit
4422	Fuel Injector #6	Defective injector or circuit
4423	Injector No. 7	Wide open throttle and listen or feel for pulse
4424	Injector No. 8	Wide open throttle and listen or feel for pulse
4431	Idle Stabilizer	Defective stabilizer or circuit (Idle Air Control)
4433	Fuel Pump	Listen for pump to run (5-cyl. only)
4442	Wastegate	Defective frequency valve or circuit
4442	Boost Pressure	Short circuit
4443	Canister Purge	Listen for solenoid to cycle on and off
4444	No Faults	Stored memory clear
0000	End Diagnosis	No additional stored codes
16486	MAF Sensor	Mass Air Flow sensor signal too low: air leak, air filter plugged, defective circuit
16487	MAF Sensor	Mass Air Flow sensor signal too high: short to positive in wiring
16500	Coolant Temperature	Defective or damp circuit
16501	Coolant Temperature	Short to ground in wiring. Signal low
16502	Coolant Temperature	Signal too high. Short to positive or break in wiring
16504	TP Sensor	Defective switch
16505	TP Sensor	Air leak or moisture in harness
16506	TP Sensor	Signal too low, break in wiring, short to ground
16507	TP Sensor	Signal too high, break in wiring, short to ground
16514	Oxygen Sensor	Corrosion or dampness in harness or connectors
16516	Oxygen Sensor	Voltage too high. Short to positive, spark plug failure, connectors, ignition wires, defective sensor
16518	Oxygen Sensor	Break in wiring, defective sensor
16520	Oxygen Sensor	Bank 1-Sensor 2 Malfunction
16521	Oxygen Sensor	Bank 1-Sensor 2 Low Voltage
16522	Oxygen Sensor	Bank 1-Sensor 2 High Voltage
16524	Oxygen Sensor	Bank 1-Sensor 2 No Activity Detected
16534	Oxygen Sensor	Moisture in harness connector
16536	Oxygen Sensor	Voltage too high. Short to positive, defective sensor, defective spark plugs, connectors, wires
16537	Oxygen Sensor	Bank 2-Sensor 1 Slow Response
16538	Oxygen Sensor	Break in wiring, defective sensor
16539	Oxygen Sensor	Bank 2-Sensor 1 Malfunction
16540	Oxygen Sensor	Bank 2-Sensor 2 Malfunction
16541	Oxygen Sensor	Bank 2-Sensor 2 Low Voltage
16542	Oxygen Sensor	Bank 2-Sensor 2 High Voltage

DIAGNOSTIC TROUBLE CODES Continued

Code	Application	Definition
16554	Fuel System	Air leak in manifold. Fuel in engine oil. MAF sensor false signal. Burning oil
16555	Fuel System	Too lean. Air leak to MAF sensor, exhaust system air leak before oxygen sensor, fuel pump quality low, fuel filter plugged, fuel pressure regulator faulty, or EVAP purge sticks
16556	Fuel System	Too rich. Faulty pressure regulator, injector not closing
16557	Fuel System	Manifold air leak, oil thinning due to fuel contamination, MAF sensor faulty, faulty piston causing oil burning
16558	Fuel System	Too lean. Air leak to MAF sensor, exhaust system air leak ahead of heated oxygen sensor, defective fuel pump or pressure regulator, plugged fuel filter, sticking EVAP canister purge regulator valve
16559	Fuel System	Too rich. Faulty pressure regulator, injector does not close
16706	Engine Speed Sensor	Short to ground or defective sensor
16711	Knock Sensor	Corrosion/dampness in harness connector, defective wiring, short to ground or positive, faulty sensor
16716	Knock Sensor	Corrosion/dampness in harness connector, defective wiring, short to ground or positive, faulty shielding sensor
16721	Crankcase Sensor	Signal too low, faulty ground, defective wiring, short to ground, faulty sensor
16785	EGR	Throughput too low, defective vacuum hose, sticking mechanical valve for EGR
16786	EGR	Throughput too high, sticking or leaking mechanical valve for EGR
16804	Catalyst system	Bank 1-Efficiency Below Threshold
16885	Speed Sensor	Faulty wiring or sensor
16955	Cruise/Brake Switch	(A) Circ. Malfunction
16989	Control Module	Defective module
17509	Oxygen Sensor	Bank 1. Air leak to MAF sensor, exhaust system air leak ahead of oxygen sensor, defective wires, EVAP canister purge regulator valve sticks, plugged fuel filter, faulty fuel pressure regulator, low fuel supply quantity, faulty oxygen sensor
17514	Oxygen Sensor	Bank 2. Air leak to MAF sensor, exhaust system air leak ahead of oxygen sensor, defective wires, EVAP canister purge regulator valve sticks, plugged fuel filter, faulty fuel pressure regulator, low fuel supply quantity, faulty oxygen sensor
17609-14	Fuel Injection	Cylinders 1-6. Short to ground, voltage supply or injector fault
17621-26	Fuel Injection	Cylinders 1-6. Short to positive, faulty injector or input for injector
17733-38	Knock Control	Cylinders 1-6. Defective wiring, fuel quality below 95 RON, knock control module in ECM faulty, engine damaged, sub-assemblies loose
17747	Crankcase Posit/Engine Speed Sensor	3-pin harness connectors transposed
17748	Crankcase/Camshaft Signal	V-belt off track
17749, 51, 53	Ignition Output 1-3	Short to ground, faulty ignition coil power output stage
17799	Camshaft Sensor	Bank 2. Short to ground, faulty sensor
17800	Camshaft Sensor	Bank 2. Faulty voltage or ground supply, defective wiring or short to positive, faulty sensor
17801	Ignition Output 1-3	Short to ground, faulty ignition coil power output stage
17808	EGR Valve	Defective wiring or valve, faulty voltage supply for EGR vacuum regulator solenoid valve
17810	EGR Valve	Short to positive, faulty vacuum regulator solenoid valve
17815	EGR Temperature Sensor	Short to ground, faulty sensor

UNDERHOOD SERVICE SPECIFICATIONS

AIITU6

DIAGNOSTIC TROUBLE CODES Continued

Code	Application	Definition
17816	EGR Temperature Sensor	Faulty ground supply or sensor, short to positive
17817	EVAP Canister Purge Regulator Valve	Faulty voltage supply or valve, short to ground
17818	EVAP Canister Purge Regulator Valve	Faulty valve, short to positive
17819	2ndary Air Injection System	Bank 2. Vacuum hose defect, faulty combination valve
17822	2ndary Air Injection System	Bank 2. Leaking combination valve or Bank 2, defective valve
17828	2ndary Control Valve	Short to ground, defective valve or voltage supply
17830	2ndary Control Valve	Short to positive
17831	2ndary Air Injection System	Bank 1. Defetive hose, faulty combination valve or wiring, faulty voltage supply for solenoid valve
17832	2ndary Air Injection System	Bank 1. Leaking combination valve, faulty solenoid valve
17842	2ndary Air Injection System Pump Relay	Short to positive, faulty relay
17844	2ndary Air Injection System Pump Relay	Short to ground, faulty voltage supply or relay
17908	Fuel Pump Relay	Defective wiring or relay
17912	Intake System	Air leak, faulty air control valve, throttle body second stage not closing
17913	TP Switch	Floor mat pressing on gas pedal, throttle adjustment, sticking throttle, defective wiring or switch
17914	TP Switch	Short to ground, damp harness connector, faulty switch
17918	TP Switch	Short to positive, faulty switch
17919	Intake Manifold Change-Over Valve	Defective wiring or valve
17920	Intake Manifold Change-Over Valve	Short to positive
17978	ECM	ECM not adapted
18008	Voltage Supply Terminal	Battery discharged, faulty ground to ECM, discharge while ignition switched off
18020	ECM	Manual transmission coded for automatic or vice versa, not coded for ATC (Automatic Traction Control)

SENSORS, INPUT
TEMPERATURE SENSORS

Engine	Year	Sensor	Resistance Ohms @ deg. F/C
1781cc	1997-99	Coolant	170 @ 176/80
1984cc	1989-90	Coolant	204 @ 217/105 5000-6500 @ 32/0 1500-2000 @ 86/30 500-650 @ 140/60 200-300 @ 194/90
2226cc, all	1989	Coolant	6000 @ -4/-20 1000 @ 68/20 130 @ 176/80
2309cc, all	1989-91	Coolant	5000-6500 @ 32/0 1500-2000 @ 86/30 500-650 @ 140/60 200-300 @ 194/90
2771cc	1992-99	Coolant	2500 @ 68/20 330 @ 176/80
3562cc	1990-91	Coolant	11,000 @ -4/-20 1250 @ 68/20 600 @ 140/60 200 @ 212/100
		Intake Air	420 @ -4/-20 480 @ 68/20 550 @ 140/60 620 @ 212/100

SENSORS, INPUT Continued
MASS AIRFLOW SENSOR

Engine	Year	Resistance Ohms @ Terminals	Voltage @ Terminals
4-cyl. 1.8L	1997-99	1.5@ 2 & 4	9-14.5 @ 1 & 3
2.0L	1989-90	0-0.8 @ 3 & ground	4.35-5.35 @ 1 & 3 0-200 mV @ 2 & 3[1]
5-cyl. 2.3L	1989-91	0-0.8 @ 3 & ground	4.35-5.35 @ 1 & 3 0-200 mV @ 2 & 3[1]
6-cyl. 2.8L	1992-99	0-0.5 @ 2 or 3 & ground	12-14 @ 2 & 3[2] .3-1.1 @ 1 & 2[2] 1.5-3.4 @ 1 & 2[3]
V8 3.6L	1990-91	—	2.5 @ 1 & 3[2] 3-5 @ 1 & 3[3]

1 With sensor plate in closed position.
2 Engine idling or ignition on, engine off.
3 Engine at higher than idle rpm.

CRANKSHAFT POSITION SENSOR

Engine	Year	Resistance (ohms)
2226cc Turbo	1992-95	1000
2771cc	1992-95	1000

THROTTLE POSITION SENSOR

Engine	Year	Resistance Ohms @ Terminals	Throttle Position
5-cyl. DOHC Turbo	1991	1500-2600 @ 1 & 2	closed
		750-1300 @ 2 & 3	closed
		3600 max. @ 2 & 3	open
V6 2.8L	1992-99	1500-2600 @ 1 & 2	closed
		750-1300 @ 2 & 3	closed
		3600 max. @ 2 & 3	open

REFERENCE, RPM AND TIMING SENSORS

Engine	Year	Resistance (ohms)
2226cc	1989-95	1000
2309cc DOHC	1990-91	1000
2771cc	1992-95	1000
3562cc	1990-91	1000

ACTUATORS, OUTPUT
CONTROL PRESSURE REGULATOR

Engine	Year	Resistance (ohms)
2226cc Turbo	1989	14-22

MANIFOLD DIFFERENTIAL PRESSURE REGULATOR

Engine	Year	Resistance (ohms)
1984cc	1989-90	15-25

IDLE AIR CONTROL VALVE

Engine	Year	Resistance (ohms)
2226cc DOHC Turbo	1991	7.5-8.5
2771cc	1992-99	7-11
3562cc	1990-91	7.5-8.5

FUEL INJECTORS

Engine	Year	Resistance (ohms)
2771cc Siemens	1992-99	13.5-14.5
Bosch	1992-99	15-17
3697cc, 4172cc	1997-99	12-20

BMW
1989-99

CHEK-CHART

ENGINE IDENTIFICATION

To identify any engine by the manufacturer's code, follow the four steps designated by the numbered blocks.

1 MODEL YEAR IDENTIFICATION:

Refer to illustration of the Vehicle Identification Number (V.I.N.): The year is indicated by a code letter which is the 10th character of the V.I.N.

3 ENGINE CODE:

In the "CODE" Column, find the engine code.

4 ENGINE IDENTIFICATION:

On the line where the engine code appears, read to the right to identify the engine.

2000 4.9 4941cc 8ev

1 MODEL YEAR IDENTIFICATION:

10th character of V.I.N.

1999—X	1998—W	1997—V
1996—T	1995—S	1994—R
1993—P	1992—N	1991—M
1990—L	1989—K	

1 MODEL YEAR (10th character)

2 ENGINE CODE LOCATION:

Prefix to engine number, stamped on engine block.

V.I.N. PLATE LOCATION:

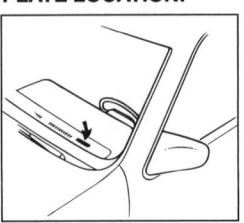

Top of instrument panel, visible through windshield, or right side of heater plenum panel/firewall cover.

4 ENGINE IDENTIFICATION

YEAR	3 ENGINE CODE CYL.	DISPL. liters	cc	Fuel System	HP
1998-99	M44 4	1.9	1895	FI	138
	M52 6	2.5	2494	FI	168
	M52 6	2.8	2793	FI	190
	S52 6	3.2	3152	FI	240
	M62 8	4.4	4398	FI	282
	M73 12	5.4	5379	FI	323
1997	— 4	1.6	1596	FI	102
	M42 4	1.8	1796	FI	138
	M44 4	1.9	1895	FI	138
	M52 6	2.8	2793	FI	190
	S52 6	3.2	3152	FI	240
	M62 8	4.4	4398	FI	282
	M73 12	5.4	5379	FI	323
1996	M42 4	1.8	1796	FI	138
	M44 4	1.9	1895	FI	138
	M52 6	2.8	2793	FI	190
	S50 6	3.0	2990	FI	240
	M60/2 8	4.0	3982	FI	282
	M73 12	5.4	5379	FI	323
1995	M42 4	1.8	1796	FI	138
	M50 6	2.5	2494	FI	189
	S50 6	3.0	2990	FI	240
	M60/1 8	3.0	2997	FI	215
	M60/2 8	4.0	3982	FI	282
	M73 12	5.4	5379	FI	323
	S70 12	5.6	5576	FI	373
1994	M42 4	1.8	1796	FI	138
	M50 6	2.5	2494	FI	189
	M60/1 8	3.0	2997	FI	215
	M60/2 8	4.0	3982	FI	282
	M70 12	5.0	4988	FI	296
	S70 12	5.6	5576	FI	373

3000 4.9

4 ENGINE IDENTIFICATION

YEAR	3 ENGINE CODE CYL.	DISPL. liters	cc	Fuel System	HP
1993	M42 4	1.8	1796	FI	138
	M20 6	2.5	2494	FI	168
	M50 6	2.5	2494	FI	189
	M30 6	3.4	3428	FI	208
	S38, B36 6	3.5	3535	FI	310
	M60/2 8	4.0	3982	FI	282
	M70 12	5.0	4988	FI	296
1992	M42 4	1.8	1796	FI	134
	M20 6	2.5	2494	FI	168
	M50 6	2.5	2494	FI	189
	M30 6	3.5	3428	FI	208
	S38, B36 6	3.5	3535	FI	310
	M70 12	5.0	4988	FI	296
1991	M42 4	1.8	1796	FI	134
	S14 4	2.3	2302	FI	192
	M20 6	2.5	2494	FI	168
	M50 6	2.5	2494	FI	189
	M30 6	3.4	3428	FI	208
	B36 6	3.5	3535	FI	311
	M70 12	5.0	4988	FI	296
1990	S14 4	2.3	2302	FI	192
	M20E 6	2.5	2494	FI	168
	M30E 6	3.4	3428	FI	208
	S38 6	3.5	3453	FI	256
	M70 12	5.0	4988	FI	296
1989	S14 4	2.3	2302	FI	192
	M20E 6	2.5	2494	FI	168
	M30E 6	3.4	3428	FI	208
	S38 6	3.5	3453	FI	256
	M70 12	5.0	4988	FI	296

FI—Fuel Injection.

UNDERHOOD SERVICE SPECIFICATIONS

BWITU1

CYLINDER NUMBERING SEQUENCE

4CYL. FIRING ORDER
1 3 4 2

6-CYL. FIRING ORDER
1 5 3 6 2 4

8-CYL. FIRING ORDER
1 5 4 8 6 3 7 2

12-CYL. FIRING ORDER
1 7 5 11 3 9 6 12 2 8 4 10

1989-99
6-cyl. SOHC
2.5L, 3.0L, 3.4L
3, 5, 6 & 7 Series

— Front of car —

1989-99
V12 5.0L
750 iL, 850i, Ci

BWITU1

TIMING MARK

TDC

1989-93
3.5L
325, M5, M6

248
Copyright 2000 by Chek-Chart Publications

UNDERHOOD SERVICE SPECIFICATIONS

ELECTRICAL AND IGNITION SYSTEMS

BATTERY

BCI equivalent shown, size may vary from original equipment. Check clearance and polarity before replacing, holddown may need to be modified.

Engine/Model	Year	STANDARD BCI Group No.	STANDARD Crank. Perf.	OPTIONAL BCI Group No.	OPTIONAL Crank. Perf.
3 Series conv.	1989	90	500	—	—
ex. conv.	1989	91	650	—	—
3 Series	1990-91	91	650	—	—
318i	1991-92	2	495	—	—
	1993	2	550	—	—
	1992-95	91	650	—	—
318iS, 318Ti	1996-98	91	600	—	—
323i, iS	1998	91	600	—	—
conv.	1998	92¹	575	—	—
	1999	94R	765	—	—
325 conv.	1992-93	91	650	—	—
	1994-95	92¹	575	—	—
ex. conv.	1992-95	92	650	—	—
325i	1989-92	2	495	—	—
325i	1993	2	550	—	—
328 ex. conv.	1996-99	92	650	—	—
conv.	1996-99	92¹	575	—	—
	1999	94R	765	—	—
5 Series ex. 525i	1989-94	93	750	—	—
525i	1989-90	91	650	—	—
	1989-92	2	495	—	—
	1991-96	92	650	—	—
528i	1996-99	49	850	—	—
530i	1995	93	750	—	—
530	1996	93	800	—	—
535i	1989-90	2	740	—	—
540	1996	93	800	—	—
540i	1997-99	49	850	—	—
	1995	93	750	—	—
635CSi	1989	92	650	—	—
635CSi, M6	1989	2	740	—	—
735i, 750iL	1989-92	2	690	—	—
7 Series	1989-94	93	750	—	—
740i	1993	2	740	—	—
740i, iL	1995	95R	800	49	800
740	1996-98	95R	950	—	—
750iL	1993	2	740	—	—
750	1996-98	95R	950	—	—
840	1996	91(2)	600	93	800
8 Series	1990-95	91(2)	650	—	—
840Ci	1996-97	91(2)	600	—	—
850i	1993	2	550	—	—
850Ci, Csi	1995	91(2)	650	93	750
850	1996-97	91(2)	600	93	800
M3	1998-99	92	650	—	—
M5	1989-91	2	740	—	—
	1999	49	950	—	—
M6	1989	93	750	—	—
Z3 1895cc	1996-97	91	600	—	—
2793cc	1996-99	48	650	—	—

1 Vibration proof battery.
2 Special low profile battery, no BCI equivalent.

GENERATOR

Application	Year	Rated Output
1796cc	1991	90
	1992-94	105
	1994-95	80
1895cc	1996-99	80/90
2302cc	1989-91	90
2494cc 323i	1999	80/120
Z3	1999	90
2494cc 325i/iX	1991	95
SOHC	1989-92	80
w/MT	1992-95	80
	1994-95	140
DOHC w/MT	1991	90
w/AT	1991	105
w/AT	1992-95	140
All	1998	80

GENERATOR Continued

Application	Year	Rated Output
2793cc 328i	1999	80/120
Z3	1999	90
528	1999	120
2793cc 328	1996-98	80
528i	1997-98	140
2990cc	1995-96	80
2997cc	1994-95	100
	1994-95	140
3152cc	1997-99	80/115
3428cc ex. 735i	1989-90	90
735i	1989-90	114
3152cc	1997-98	80
3428cc	1991-92	140
535	1993	90
3453cc	1989-90	90
3535cc	1991	140
	1992-93	90
3982cc	1993-96	140
4398cc	1996-98	140
540 Sedan	1999	120
Sportwagen	1999	150
740	1999	150
4988cc	1989-90	114
	1991-94	140
5379cc	1995-98	140
	1999	150
5576cc	1994-95	140

REGULATOR

At 1500 rpm, no load.

Application	Year	Test Temp. (deg. F/C)	Voltage Setting
All	1989-95	68/20	13.5-14.6

STARTER

Engine	Year	Cranking Voltage (min. volts)	Ampere Draw @ Cranking Speed
All 6-cyl.	1989-92	9.0	200

SPARK PLUGS

Engine/Model	Year	Gap (inches)	Gap (mm)	Torque (ft-lb)
M models	1989-98	.024-.028	.60-.70	18-22
All others	1989-98	.028-.032	.70-.80	18-22

IGNITION COIL

Resistance (ohms at 68°F or 20°C)

Engine	Year	Windings	Resistance (ohms)
1796cc	1991-96	Primary	0.40-0.80
		Secondary	—
2302cc	1989-91	Primary	0.37
		Secondary	9000
2494cc SOHC	1989-92	Primary	0.50-0.82
		Secondary	6000-8200
DOHC	1993-96	Primary	0.4-0.8
		Secondary	—
2990cc	1995-96	Primary	0.4-0.8
		Secondary	—
2997cc	1994-95	Primary	0.4-0.8
		Secondary	—
3428cc	1989-92	Primary	0.45-0.55
		Secondary	5400-6600
3453cc	1989-90	Primary	0.37
		Secondary	9000
3982cc	1993-95	Primary	0.4-0.8
		Secondary	—
4988cc	1989-94	Primary	0.45-0.55
		Secondary	5400-6600
5576cc	1994-95	Primary	0.45-0.55
		Secondary	5400-6600

UNDERHOOD SERVICE SPECIFICATIONS

IGNITION PICKUP

Application	Year	Resistance (ohms)	Air Gap (in./mm)
2494cc	1989-92	1000-12000	.012-.028/.30-.70
3428cc	1989-92	1000-12000	.012-.028/.30-.70
4988cc	1989-92	1000-12000	.012-.028/.30-.70

BASE TIMING

Engine warm and distributor vacuum hose(s) disconnected and plugged.

Engine	Year	Man. Trans. (degrees) @ RPM	Auto. Trans. (degrees) @ RPM
1796cc	1991-93	11±3 @ 850[1]	11±3 @ 850[1]
2302cc DOHC	1989-91	0±3 @ 880[1]	—
2494cc SOHC	1989-92	10±5 @ 760[1]	10±5 @ 760[1]
3428cc	1989-92	10±2 @ 800[1]	10±2 @ 800[1]
3453cc DOHC	1989-90	2 @ 840	—

[1] Checking figure only, timing is not adjustable.

FUEL SYSTEM

FUEL PRESSURE

With engine at normal operating temperature and idling.

Engine	Year	Control Pressure PSI	System Pressure PSI
2302cc	1989-91	42-44	40-47
2494cc	1989-92	42-44	40-47
3428cc	1989-92	42-44	40-47
3453cc	1989-90	42-44	40-47
4988cc	1989-92	42-44	40-47

IDLE SPEED

Checking speed given, idle is not adjustable.

Engine	Year	Transmission	Slow Idle	Fast Idle	AC Speed-up
1796cc	1991-93	MT & AT	810-890 N	—	870-960
	1994-97	MT	800-900	—	800-900
		AT	730-830 D	—	780-880 D
1991cc	1994	MT & AT	720-800 N	—	—
2302cc M20	1989-94	MT	830-930 N	—	—
M50	1991-94	MT & AT	640-740 N	—	—
2494cc	1989-93	MT & AT	720-800 N	—	—
	1994-97	MT	800-900	—	690-790
		AT	730-830 D	—	670-770 D
2997cc	1994-97	MT	550-650	—	550-650
		AT	550-650 D	—	550-650 D
3428cc	1989-93	MT & AT	750-850 N	—	—
3453cc M5 to 7-89	1989	MT	840-940 N	—	—
from 7-89	1990	MT	930-1010	—	—
M6	1989	MT	800-900 N	—	—
3535cc	1991-92	MT	930-1010	—	—
	1993	MT	810-970	—	—
3982cc	1994-97	MT	550-650	—	550-650
		AT	550-650 D	—	550-650 D
4988cc	1989-93	AT	650-750 D	—	—
	1994	AT	750-850 D	—	—
5379cc	1995-97	AT	550-650 N	—	550-650 N
5576cc	1994-95	AT	700-800 N	—	—

IDLE MIXTURE

Engine	Year	Idle CO%
1796cc	1991-95	0.2-1.2
1991cc	1994	0.2-1.2
2302cc DOHC	1989-91	0.2-1.2
2494cc	1989-92	0.2-1.2
	1994-95	0.2-1.5
2990cc	1995	0.5-0.9
2997cc	1994-95	0.5-1.5
3428cc	1989-92	0.5-1.5
3453cc DOHC	1989-90	0.6-1.2
3535cc	1991	0.2-1.2
3982cc	1994-95	0.5-1.5
4988cc DOHC	1989-92	0.2-1.2
4988cc	1994	0.4-2.4
5379cc	1995	0.4-1.6
5576cc	1994-95	0.5-0.9

ENGINE MECHANICAL

TIGHTENING TORQUES

Engine	Year	TORQUE FOOT-POUNDS/NEWTON METERS				
		Cylinder Head	Intake Manifold	Exhaust Manifold	Crankshaft Pulley	Water Pump
1796cc DOHC	1991-93	25/35	10-12/13-17	16-18/22-25	217-231/300-320	6mm, 6-7/8-10; 8mm, 15-17/20-24
2nd stage		+90°				
3rd stage		+90°				
1796cc	1994-95	25/35	6mm 7/10	6mm 7/10		6mm 7/10
2nd stage		+90°	7mm 11/15	7mm 11/15		8mm 16/22
3rd stage		+90°	8mm 16/22			
2303cc DOHC	1989-91	36/50	6mm, 6.5-7.0/9-10; 8mm, 14-17/20-24	6mm[3], 6.5-7.0/9-10; 8mm, 16-18/22-25	311-325/430-450	6mm, 6-7/8-10; 8mm, 14-17/20-24
2nd stage		58-80				
3rd stage[1]		72/100				
2494cc SOHC	1989-93	Hex, 29/40 43/60 +20-30°; Torx, 22/30	22-24/30-33	16-18/22-25	283-311/390-430	6mm, 6-7/8-10; 8mm, 14-17/20-24
2nd stage[1]		+90°				
3rd stage[2]		+90°				
2494cc	1994-95	22/30	6mm 7/10	6mm 7/10	302/410	6mm 7/10
2nd stage		+90°	7mm 11/15	7mm 14/20		8mm 16/22
3rd stage		+90°	8mm 16/22			
2990cc	1995	22/30	6mm, 7/10	6mm, 7/10	302/410	6mm
2nd stage[1]		+90°	7mm, 11/15	7mm, 14/20		7/10
3rd stage[2]		+90°	8mm, 16/22			8mm, 16/22
2997cc	1994-95	22/30	6mm, 7/10	6mm, 7/10	73/100	6mm
2nd stage		+80°	7mm, 11/15	7mm	+60°	7/10
3rd stage		+80°	8mm, 16/22	11/15	+60°	8mm
4th stage					+30°	16/22

TIGHTENING TORQUES Continued

TORQUE FOOT-POUNDS/NEWTON METERS

Engine	Year	Cylinder Head	Intake Manifold	Exhaust Manifold	Crankshaft Pulley	Water Pump
3428cc	1989-93	43/60	22-24/	16-18/	311-325/	6mm,
2nd stage[1]		+30-36°	30-33	22-25	430-450	6-7/
3rd stage[2]		+30-40°				8-10;
						8mm,
						14-17/
						20-24
3453cc DOHC	1989-90	36/50	6mm,	6mm[3]	311-325/	6mm,
2nd stage		58-80	6.5-7.0/	6.5-7.0/	430-450	6-7/
3rd stage[1]		72/100	9-10;	9-10;		8-10;
			8mm,	8mm,		8mm,
			14-17/	16-18/		14-17/
			20-24	22-25		20-24
3982cc	1993-95	22/30	6mm	6mm	73/100	6mm
2nd stage		+80°	7/10	7/10	+60°	7/10
3rd stage		+80°	7mm	7mm	+60°	8mm
4th stage			11/15	11/15	+30°	16/22
			8mm			
			16/22			
4988cc	1993-95	22/30	6mm	6mm	73/100	6mm
2nd stage		+120°	7/10	7/10	+60°	7/10
3rd stage			7mm	7mm	+60°	8mm
			11/15	11/15		16/22
			8mm			
			16/22			
4988cc	1989-92	22/30	14-17/	6mm[3],	311-325/	6mm,
2nd stage[1]		+120°	20-24	6.5-7.0/	430-450	6-7/
				9-10;		8-10;
				8mm,		8mm,
				16-18/		14-17/
				22-25		20-24
5379cc	1995	22/30	6mm,	6mm,	73/100	6mm
			7/10	7/10		
2nd stage		+60°	7mm,	7mm	+60°	7/10
			11/15			
3rd stage		+60°	8mm,	11/15	+60°	8mm,
			16/22			16/22
5576cc	1994-95	22/30	6mm,	6mm	73/100	6mm
			7/10			
2nd stage		+90°	7mm,	7/10	+60°	7/10
			11/15			
3rd stage		+90°	8mm,	7mm,	+60°	8mm
			16/22	11/15		16/22

1 Allow cylinder head to settle for 15 minutes before bringing to torque.
2 Run engine to operating temperature, about 25 minutes, before bringing to torque.
3 Retorque after 1200 miles of service.

VALVE CLEARANCE

Engine cold, unless otherwise specified. Maximum coolant temperature; 95°F/ 35°C .

Engine	Year	Intake (inches)	Intake (mm)	Exhaust (inches)	Exhaust (mm)
2302cc DOHC	1989-91	.010-.014	.26-.35	.010-.013	.26-.35
2494cc SOHC	1989-92	.010	.25	.010	.25
3428cc	1989-93	.012	.30	.012	.30
3453cc DOHC	1989-90	.012-.014	.30-.35	.012-.014	.30-.35

COMPRESSION PRESSURE

At cranking speed, engine temperature normalized, throttle open.

Engine	Year	PSI	Maximum Variation Percent[1]
All	1989-95	142-156	60

1 Lowest cylinder pressure must be at least 60% of highest cylinder pressure.

ENGINE COMPUTER SYSTEM

DIAGNOSTIC TROUBLE CODES

1989-91 325i, 325iX: To activate, turn ignition switch to the "ON" position, codes will be displayed as flashes of the "Check Engine" light. Light will stay on continuously when all codes have been displayed. To clear memory, start engine 5 to 10 times.

1989-92 All with Bosch Motronic systems M1.2, M1.3 or M1.7: To activate, turn ignition switch to the "ON" position and depress accelerator pedal 5 times to wide open throttle position. Codes will be displayed as flashes of the "Check Engine" light. To clear memory, use BMW tester or momentarily disconnect multi-pin connector from control unit. For 12-cylinder engines, codes beginning with 1 indicate a fault on the right (cylinders 1-6) bank, codes beginning with 2 indicate a fault on the left (cylinders 7-12) bank, to access codes for left bank, depress accelerator 6 times.

1991-92 All with Bosch Motronic system M3.1: To activate, depress accelerator pedal 5 times to wide open throttle position. Code will be displayed by flashes of the "Check Engine" light. To clear memory, use BMW Tester No. 2013, momentarily disconnect the vehicle battery, or control unit. Memory will automatically clear if vehicle is started 60 times with no repeat of failure.

Code	Indicated Fault
1	Mass airflow sensor
2	Oxygen sensor
3	Engine coolant temperature sensor
4	Idle speed controller
1000, 2000	End of diagnosis
1211, 2211	Control unit
1215, 2215	Mass airflow sensor
1216, 2216	Throttle position sensor
1221, 2221	Oxygen sensor
1222	Oxygen sensor control out of range
1222, 2222	Oxygen sensor regulation
1223, 2223	Engine coolant temperature sensor
1224, 2224	Intake air temperature sensor
1231, 2231	Battery voltage out of range
1232, 2232	Idle switch
1233, 2233	Wide open throttle switch
1251, 2251	Fuel injectors, final stage 1
1252, 2252	Fuel injectors, final stage 2
1253	Fuel injector, cylinder No. 3
1254	Fuel injector, cylinder No. 4
1255	Fuel injector, cylinder No. 5
1256	Fuel injector, cylinder No. 6
1261, 2261	Fuel pump relay
1262	Idle air control valve
1262	Idle speed controller
1263, 2263	EVAP canister purge valve
1264, 2264	Oxygen sensor heating relay
1444, 2444	No faults in memory

SENSORS, INPUT

ENGINE COOLANT TEMPERATURE SENSOR

Engine	Year	Resistance Ohms @ deg. F/C
All w/DME	1989-93	8200-10,500 @ 14/-10
		2200-2700 @ 66-70/19-21
		300-360 @ 174-178/60-63

INTAKE AIR TEMPERATURE SENSOR

Engine	Year	Resistance Ohms @ deg. F/C
All w/DME	1989-93	8200-10,500 @ 14/-10
		2200-2700 @ 66-70/19-21
		760-910 @ 120-124/49-52
		300-360 @ 174-178/60-63

CRANKSHAFT POSITION SENSOR

Engine	Year	Resistance Ohms
All w/DME	1989-92	70-90

BMW
1989-99

SENSORS, INPUT Continued

DME PULSE SENDER

Engine	Year	Resistance Ohms
1796cc	1991-93	480-600
2302cc	1989-91	864-1056
2494cc	1989-92	494-546
2997cc	1994-95	494-546
3428cc	1989-92	486-594
3453cc	1989-90	864-1056
3535cc	1991	950-970
3982cc	1993-95	494-546
4988cc	1989-92	486-594
	1993-94	494-546

THROTTLE POSITION SENSOR

Engine	Year	Resistance Ohms	Throttle Position
1796cc	1991-93	3200-4800	closed
		800-1200	open

ACTUATORS, OUTPUT

IDLE SPEED CONTROLLER

Engine	Year	Resistance Ohms @ Terminals
1796cc	1991-92	6-10
2997cc	1994-95	23 @ 1 & 3
		12 @ 1 & 2, 2 & 3
3982cc	1993-95	23 @ 1 & 3
		12 @ 1 & 2, 2 & 3
All others w/DME	1989-92	40 @ 1 & 3
		20 @ 1 & 2, 2 & 3

FUEL INJECTORS

Engine	Year	Resistance (ohms)
1796cc	1991-93	15-17

BUICK
1989-2000

ENGINE IDENTIFICATION

To identify any engine by the manufacturer's code, follow the four steps designated by the numbered blocks.

1 **MODEL YEAR IDENTIFICATION:** Refer to illustration of the Vehicle Identification Number (V.I.N.). The year is indicated by a code letter which is the 10th character of the V.I.N.

2 **ENGINE CODE LOCATION:** Refer to illustration of V.I.N. plate for location and designation of engine code.

3 **ENGINE CODE:** In the "CODE" column, find the engine code determined in Step 2.

4 **ENGINE IDENTIFICATION:** On the line where the engine code appears, read to the right to identify the engine.

V.I.N. PLATE LOCATION:

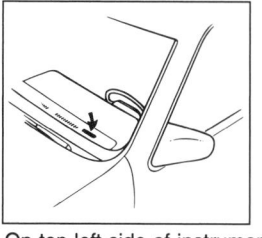

On top left side of instrument panel

Model year of vehicle:

2000 — Y
1999 — X
1998 — W
1997 — V
1996 — T
1995 — S
1994 — R
1993 — P
1992 — N
1991 — M
1990 — L
1989 — K

MODEL YEAR AND ENGINE IDENTIFICATION:

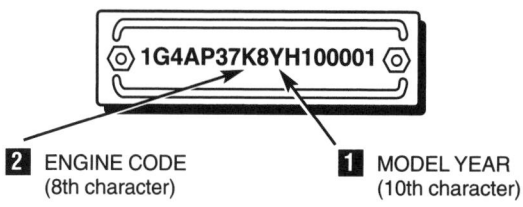

2 ENGINE CODE (8th character)

1 MODEL YEAR (10th character)

YEAR	CODE	CYL.	liters	cu. in.	Fuel System	HP
2000	J	6	3.1	191	MFI	175
	K	6	3.8	231	MFI	200,205
	1	6	3.8	231	MFI	240
1997-99	T	4	2.4	146	MFI	150
	M	6	3.1	191	MFI	155,160[1]
	K	6	3.8	231	MFI	205
	1	6	3.8	231	MFI	240
1996	4	4	2.2	133	MFI	120
	T	4	2.4	146	MFI	150
	M	6	3.1	191	MFI	160
	K	6	3.8	231	MFI	205
	1	6	3.8	231	MFI	240
	P	8	5.7	350	MFI	260
1995	4	4	2.2	133	MFI	120
	D	4	2.3	138	MFI	150
	M	6	3.1	191	MFI	155, 160[1]
	K	6	3.8	231	MFI	205
	L	6	3.8	231	MFI	170
	1	6	3.8	231	MFI	225
	P	8	5.7	350	MFI	260
1994	4	4	2.2	133	MFI	120
	3	4	2.3	138	MFI	115
	M	6	3.1	191	MFI	155, 160[1]
	L	6	3.8	231	MFI	170
	1	6	3.8	231	MFI	225
	P	8	5.7	350	MFI	260
1993	4	4	2.2	133	MFI	110
	3	4	2.3	138	MFI	115
	T	6	3.1	191	MFI	140
	N	6	3.3	204	MFI	160
	L	6	3.8	231	MFI	170
	1	6	3.8	231	MFI	205
	7	8	5.7	350	TBI	180

YEAR	CODE	CYL.	liters	cu. in.	Fuel System	HP
1992	3	4	2.3	138	MFI	120
	R	4	2.5	151	TBI	110
	T	6	3.1	191	MFI	140
	N	6	3.3	204	MFI	160
	1	6	3.8	231	MFI	205
	L	6	3.8	231	MFI	170
	E	8	5.0	305	TBI	170
	7	8	5.7	350	TBI	180
1991	D	4	2.3	138	MFI	160
	R, U	4	2.5	151	TBI	110
	T	6	3.1	191	MFI	140
	N	6	3.3	204	MFI	160
	C	6	3.8	231	MFI	165
	L	6	3.8	231	MFI	170
	E	8	5.0	305	TBI	170
1990	D	4	2.3	138	MFI	160
	R, U	4	2.5	151	TBI	110
	T	6	3.1	191	MFI	135
	N	6	3.3	204	MFI	160
	C	6	3.8	231	MFI	165
	L	6	3.8	231	MFI	170
	Y	8	5.0	307	4V	140
1989	1	4	2.0	122	TBI	90
	D	4	2.3	138	MFI	150
	R	4	2.5	151	TBI	98
	U	4	2.5	151	TBI	110
	W	6	2.8	173	MFI	130
	T	6	3.1	191	MFI	140
	N	6	3.3	204	MFI	160
	C	6	3.8	231	MFI	165
	Y	8	5.0	307	4V	140

TBI—Throttle Body Injection.   **MFI—Multiport Fuel Injection.**
2V—Two Venturi Carburetor.   **4V—Four Venturi Carburetor.**
HO—High Output.   **T—Turbocharged.**   **D—Diesel.**
1 Engine horsepower varies with model installations.

Copyright 2000 by Chek-Chart Publications

253

BUICK
1989-2000

CYLINDER NUMBERING SEQUENCE

4-CYL. FIRING ORDER: 1 3 4 2

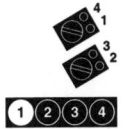

——— Front of car ———

1989 2.0L (122) ex. OHC 1993-96 2.2L Code 4	1989-95 2.3L Code D 1992-94 2.3L Code 3 1996-98 2.4L Code T	1989-92 2.5L (151)

6-CYL. FIRING ORDER 2.8L & 3.1L: 1 2 3 4 5 6; All others: 1 6 5 4 3 2

——— Front of car ———

1989 2.8L (173) Code W 1989-93 3.1L Code T	1994-99 3.1L Code M 2000 3.1L Code J	1989-92 3.3L Code N	1989-91 3.8L Code C 1990-92 3.8L Code L Some	1990-92 Code L Some 1992-00 3.8L Code 1 1993 3.3L Code N 1993-95 3.8L Code L 1995-00 Code K

8-CYL. FIRING ORDER: 1 8 4 3 6 5 7 2

——— Front of car ———

1989-90 5.0L (307)	1991 5.0L Code E 1992-93 5.7L Code 7	1994-96 5.7L Code P

——— TIMING MARK ———

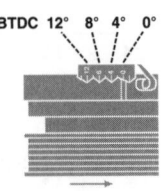
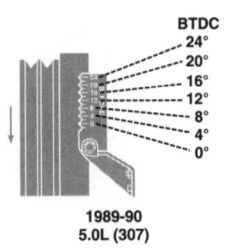

1991 5.0L Code E 1992-93 5.7L Code 7	1989-90 5.0L (307)

CHEK-CHART

UNDERHOOD SERVICE SPECIFICATIONS

BKTU2

BKTU2

ELECTRICAL AND IGNITION SYSTEMS

BATTERY

Engine	Year	STANDARD		OPTIONAL	
		BCI Group No.	Crank. Perf.	BCI Group No.	Crank. Perf.
2.0L (122) MT	1989	75	525	75	630
AT	1989	75	630	75	630
2.2L	1993-96	75	525	—	—
2.3L	1989-93	75	630	—	—
	1994-95	75	600	—	—
2.4L	1996-97	75	600	—	—
2.5L (151)	1989-93	75	630	—	—
3.1L	1989-96	75	525	—	—
Skylark	1994-96	75	600	—	—
3.1L Skylark	1997-98	75	600	—	—
Regal	1997-99	78	600	—	—
Century	1998-00	78	600	—	—
3.3L	1989-92	75	630	—	—
3.3L: Century	1993	75	630	—	—
Skylark	1993	75	600	—	—
3.4L	1994-96	75	690	—	—
3.8L (231) Century, Electra, LeSabre, Park Ave.	1989-93	75	630	78	730
Riviera	1989	75	730	—	—
Reatta	1989	78	770	—	—
Riviera, Reatta	1990-93	78	770	—	—
Regal	1990-93	75	630	—	—
3.8L: LeSabre	1994-95	75	630	78	770
	1996	78	770	—	—
	1997-99	78	690	—	—
Park Ave.	1994-95	78	600	78	770
	1996	78	770	—	—
	1997-00	78	690	78	770
Regal	1994	75	600	—	—
	1995-96	75	690	—	—
	1997-00	78	690	78	770
Riviera	1994-97	76	970	—	—
	1998-99	79	880	—	—
5.0L (307) Estate Wagon	1989	70	525	75	570
5.0L	1990-91	75	525	—	—
5.7L	1991-92	75	525	—	—
5.7L: Sedan	1993-94	75	525	—	—
Wagon	1993	78	690	—	—
	1994	78	770	—	—
5.7L	1995	75	600	—	—
	1996	78	770	—	—

GENERATOR

Year	Rated Output (amps)	Test Output (amps)	Field Current Draw (max. amps)
1989-91	74, 85, 100, 105, 108, 120, 124	1	—
1992-00	100, 105, 124, 140	1	—

1 At moderate engine speed, output must be within 15 amps of rated output.

REGULATOR

Application	Test Temp. (deg. F/C)	Voltage Setting	Field Relay Closing Volts
1989-95	Warm	13.5-16.0	—
1996-00	Warm	13.0-16.0	—

STARTER

Engine	Year	Cranking Voltage (min. volts)	Ampere Draw @ Cranking Speed
All	1989-00	9.0	—

SPARK PLUGS

Engine	Year	Gap (inches)	Gap (mm)	Torque[1] (ft-lb)
1.8L (112), 2.0L (122)	1989	.035	.89	7-15
2.2L	1993	.045	1.14	11
	1994-96	.060	1.52	15
2.3L	1989-94	.035	.89	17
	1995	.060	1.52	17
2.4L	1996-98	.060	1.52	13
2.5L (151)	1989-92	.060	1.52	15
2.8L (173)	1989	.045	1.14	7-15
3.1L	1989-93	.045	1.14	11
	1994-00	.060	1.52	15
3.3L	1989-91	.060	1.52	20
3.3L	1992-93	.060	1.52	11
3.4L	1994-98	.045	1.14	11
3.8L	1989-00	.060	1.52	11
5.0L (305), 5.7L	1989-93	.035	.89	11
5.0L (307)	1989-90	.060	1.52	25
5.7L	1994-96	.050	1.26	15

1 New plugs.

IGNITION COIL
FOR TESTING AND ADJUSTMENT DIAGRAMS, SEE APPENDIX A.

Without distributor, primary resistance measured between the two coil primary power wires on each coil.

Secondary resistance measured across each coil's two towers with coil removed from vehicle.

Application	Year	Resistance (ohms)	
		Primary	Secondary
All w/distributor	1989-92	0-2	6,000-30,000
	1993-95	0.3-0.5	7,000-9,000
2.0L, 2.5L, 2.8L, 3.1L, 3.4L	1989-95	—	5,000-10,000
2.2L	1993-96	—	5,000-8,000
2.3L	1989-95	—	10,000 max.
2.4L	1996-98	—	5,000-8,000
3.0L, 3.8L: Type I coils[1]	1989-92	.5-.9	10,000-13,000
Type II coils[1]	1990-92	.3-.5	5,000-7,000
3.1L, 3.4L	1996-00	—	5,000-7,000
3.3L	1989-92	.5-.9	5,000-8,000
3.3L, 3.8L	1993-95	.5-.9	5,000-8,000
	1996-00	—	5,000-8,000

1 Type I coils, 3 coil towers on each side of coil pack.
Type II coils, 6 coil towers on one side of coil pack.

DISTRIBUTOR PICKUP
FOR TESTING AND ADJUSTMENT DIAGRAMS, SEE APPENDIX B.

Engine	Year	Resistance (ohms)	Air Gap (in./mm)
All	1989-93	500-1500	

BASE TIMING
FOR TESTING AND ADJUSTMENT DIAGRAMS, SEE APPENDIX C.

Set timing at slow idle and Before Top Dead Center, unless otherwise specified.

If "Check Engine" light comes on during procedure, remove ECM fuse to clear.

5.0L (307), ground diagnostic terminal of DLC

5.0L, 5.7L FI, disconnect IC bypass connector (tan/black wire) between distributor and ECU.

All w/o distributor not adjustable.

Engine	Year	Man. Trans. (degrees) @ RPM	Auto. Trans. (degrees) @ RPM
5.0L, 5.7L	1991-93	—	0 @ 500 D
5.0L (307)	1989-90	—	20 @ 1100 P

UNDERHOOD SERVICE SPECIFICATIONS

FUEL SYSTEM

FUEL SYSTEM PRESSURE
FOR TESTING AND ADJUSTMENT DIAGRAMS, SEE APPENDIX D.

All carbureted models, test pump with gauge at carburetor height. On cars equipped with vapor return system, squeeze off return hose to obtain accurate reading.

All models with TBI, pressure measured at fuel inlet of TBI unit.

All models with MFI, pressure measured at fuel rail.

CARBURETED, TBI

Engine	Year	PSI	RPM
2.0L (122) FI	1989	9.0-13.0	idle
		13 min.[1]	idle
2.5L (151) FI	1989-92	9.0-13.0	idle
		13 min.[1]	idle
5.0L, 5.7L	1991-93	9.0-13.0	idle
		13 min.[1]	idle
5.0L (307)	1989-90	5.5-6.5	idle

FUEL INJECTED (MFI)

Engine	Year	Pressure (PSI) Ign. on	Pressure (PSI) Idle	Fuel Pump[1]
2.2L, 2.3L (138), 2.4L	1989-98	40.5-47	30.5-44	47 min.
2.8L (173)	1989	40.5-47	30.5-44	60 min.
3.1L	1989-00	40.5-47	30.5-44	47 min.
3.3L	1989	40-44	32-46	50 min.
3.3L	1990-92	40-47	31-44	47 min.
3.4L	1994-95	40.5-47	30.5-44	47 min.
	1996-97	48-55	38-52	55 min.
3.8L (231) Code C	1989-90	40-47	37-43	75 min.
3.8L Code L, 1	1990-95	40-47	30.5-44	47 min.
3.8L Code K	1995-00	48-55	38-52	55 min.
5.7L	1994-96	40-47	30.5-44	47 min.

1 With fuel return line briefly restricted.

IDLE SPEED W/COMPUTER CONTROL
FOR TESTING AND ADJUSTMENT DIAGRAMS, SEE APPENDIX E.

Midpoint of range given is the preferred setting speed.

Idle speed is adjustable only if a specification is given under "Minimum Speed."

All w/TBI or MFI: When specifications appear in Minimum Speed column, disconnect PCV valve hose and allow engine to draw air for two minutes. Disconnect IAC electrical lead and adjust setting speed to specified value. Others, ground diagnostic lead and turn ignition on for 30 seconds. Remove IAC electrical lead and remove ground from diagnostic connector. Start engine and adjust setting speed to specified value.

All carbureted w/ILC: Disconnect and plug vacuum hoses at EGR and canister purge valves. With engine at operating temperature, remove vacuum hose from ILC and plug. Set maximum speed to specified value by holding hex nut and turning plunger shaft. Reconnect ILC vacuum hose and check that minimum speed is at specified value. To adjust, remove rubber and metal plugs from rear center outlet tube, insert a 3/32" Allen wrench. Remove ILC hose and plug. Connect a remote vacuum source and apply vacuum to the unit. Adjust carb base screw to obtain specified shutdown value.

ALL FUEL INJECTED

Engine	Year	Minimum Speed Man. Trans.	Minimum Speed Auto. Trans.	Checking Speed Man. Trans.	Checking Speed Auto. Trans.
2.0L (122) ex. OHC	1989	450-650	450-650 N	—	—
2.2L	1993	—	—	—	725-875 N
2.3L	1990-92	—	—	—	800 N max.[1]
2.5L (151)	1989-92	550-650	550-650 N	800	800 N max.[1]
2.8L	1989	—	—	—	650-750 D
3.1L	1989-90	—	—	750-950	650-750 D
3.1L	1991-93	—	—	—	700-800 N
3.3L	1989	—	—	—	650-750 N
3.3L Century	1990	—	—	—	650-750 N
3.3L Skylark	1990	—	—	—	675-750 D
3.3L	1991-93	—	—	—	650-750 N
3.4L	1994-95	—	—	650-750	650-750 N
	1996-97	—	—	600-700	600-700 N
3.8L Code C	1989	—	—	—	650-750 N
3.8L Code C	1990-91	—	—	—	650-850 N

IDLE SPEED W/COMPUTER CONTROL Continued
ALL FUEL INJECTED Continued

Engine	Year	Minimum Speed Man. Trans.	Minimum Speed Auto. Trans.	Checking Speed Man. Trans.	Checking Speed Auto. Trans.
3.8L Code K, L	1990-95	—	—	—	650-750 N
	1996-00	—	—	—	600-700 N
5.0L	1991	—	—	—	500-600 D

1 With IAC fully seated.
2 With mass airflow sensor.
3 Speed density system.

ALL CARBURETED

Engine	Year	Trans.	Min. Speed	Max. Speed	Fast	Step of Cam
5.0L (307)	1989-90	AT	450 D	700 D	550 D	Low
Base idle	1989-90	AT	450 D	—		

ENGINE MECHANICAL

TIGHTENING TORQUES
FOR CYLINDER HEAD TORQUE SEQUENCES AND DIAGRAMS, SEE APPENDIX F.

Some fasteners are tightened in more than one step.

Some values are specified in inches.

Engine	Year	TORQUE FOOT-POUNDS/NEWTON METERS Cylinder Head	Intake Manifold	Exhaust Manifold	Crankshaft Pulley	Water Pump
2.0L (122) ex. OHC	1989	73-83/ 99-113[1], 62-70/ 85-95[2]	15-22/ 20-30	6-13/ 8-18	66-89/ 90-120	15-22/ 20-30
2.2L	1993-96	46/63[1], 43/58,[3] +90°	22/30[10]	13/18	77/105	18/25
2.3L	1989-95	[4]	18/25	31/42, nuts	79/100, +90°	106"/12, cover 19/26, others
2.4L	1996-98	[12]	17/24	110"/13	129/178,124"/14, cover +90° 19/26, others	
2.5L	1989-92	18/25, 26/35[8] +90°	25/34	25/43[5,6] 37/50[7]	162/220	25/34
2.8L, 3.1L	1989-93	33/45, +90°	16/22, 23/32	21/28	77/105	7/10
3.1L	1994-99	33/45, +90°	115"/13, lower 18/25, upper	12/16, stud 89"/10, nut	75/102	89"/10
3.3L	1989-90	35/47, +130°[9]	88"/10, lower 22/30, upper	30/41	219/297	8/10
3.3L	1991-93	35/47, +130°[9]	88"/10, lower 22/30, upper	38/52	111/150, +76°	29/39
3.4L	1994	37/50, +90°	18/25	116"/13	37/50[3], 78//105[1]	89"/10
	1995-96	44/60, +90°	18/25	116"/13, nut 13/17, stud	37/50[3] 78/105[1]	97"/12
3.8L	1989-90	35/47, +130°[9]	8/10	41/55	219/297	8/10
3.8L	1991-95	35/47, +130°[9]	[11]	41/55	76/105, +76°	84"/10, short 29/38, long
	1996-00	37/50, +130°[9]	89"/10, upper 11/15, lower	107"/12	110/150, +76°	11/15, +80°

UNDERHOOD SERVICE SPECIFICATIONS

TIGHTENING TORQUES Continued

TORQUE FOOT-POUNDS/NEWTON METERS

Engine	Year	Cylinder Head	Intake Manifold	Exhaust Manifold	Crankshaft Pulley	Water Pump
5.0L, 5.7L	1991-93	68/92	124"/14, 35/47	20/27, studs 36/45, bolts	70/95	30/41
5.0L (307)	1989-90	40/54, +95°, first and last bolts on exhaust manifold side +120°, all others	40/54	25/34	200-310/ 270-400	11/14
5.7L	1994-95	65/88, 35/48	71"/8	25/35	75/102	30/40
	1996	22/30, 2	21"/8, 35/48	30/40	74/100	33/45

1 Long bolts.

2 After turning all bolts to initial value, turn short bolts 55°; medium bolts 65°; long bolts 75°.

3 Short bolts.

4 Tighten bolts 1-8 (long bolts), 30/40. Tighten bolts 9-10 (short bolts), 26/35. Then, turn all bolts 90°.

5 Four outer bolts.

6 Turn last bolt on left (number nine) to 29/40. Then, turn all except number nine 120°, turn number nine 90°.

7 Three inner bolts.

8 Turn last bolt on left (number nine) to 18/25.

9 Tighten four inner bolts an additional 30°.

10 Upper manifold. Lower manifold: studs, 89"/10; nuts, 24/33.

11 1991-92: upper to lower, 21/29; lower to block, 89"/10. 1993-95: upper to lower & lower to block, 11/15.

12 Tighten bolts 1-8, 40/65. Tighten bolts 9-10, 30/40. Then, tighten all bolts 90°.

COMPRESSION PRESSURE

At cranking speed or specified rpm, engine temperature normalized, throttle open.

Engine	Year	PSI	Maximum Variation PSI
All	1989-00	100 min.	1

1 Lowest cylinder pressure must be more than 70% of highest cylinder pressure.

BELT TENSION
All Except With Automatic Tensioner

A belt in operation for 1 minute is considered a used belt.

Use a strand tension gauge. Measurements are in pounds.

Engine	Year	Generator	Power Steering	Air Cond.	Air Pump
Used Belts					
2.3L	1989-93	—	110	—	—
2.5L Code U	1989-94	90	90	90	—
5.0L (307)	1989-90	110	110	110	55
Cogged or 3/8" belt	1989-90	90	—	—	90
New Belts					
2.3L	1989-94	—	110	—	—
2.5L Code U	1989-94	165	180	165	—
5.0L (307)	1989-90	150	165	165	135
Cogged	1989-90	135	—	—	—

All With Automatic Tensioner

If index marks on tensioner are outside the range, replace the belt. If marks are within range and belt tension is below specified value, replace tensioner.

Engine	Year	Tension
2.2L	1993-96	50-70
2.3L, 2.4L	1989-96	50 min.
2.5L Ciera	1989-91	50-70
2.8L	1989	50-70
3.1L	1989-96	50-70
Century, Regal	1996	30-60
3.1L	1997	30-50
3.3L	1989-92	67 min.
3.4L	1996	35-55
3.8L	1989-91	67 min.
	1995-96	50-70
5.0L, 5.7L	1991-93	105-125

SERPENTINE BELT DIAGRAMS

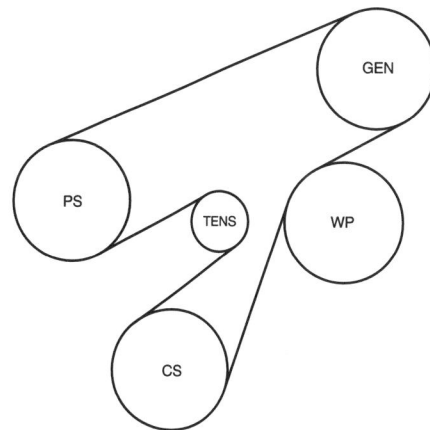

1989-92 2.5L Code R w/o AC

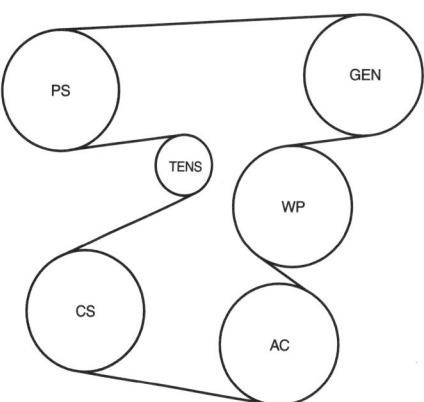

1989-92 2.5L Code R w/AC

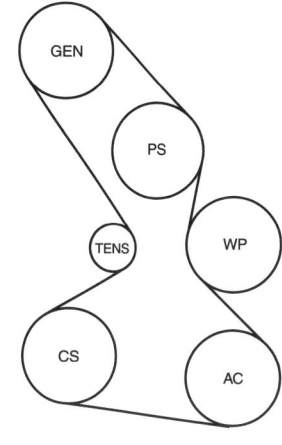

1989-98 2.8L, 3.1L FWD

UNDERHOOD SERVICE SPECIFICATIONS

BKTU5   BKTU5

SERPENTINE BELT DIAGRAMS Continued   **SERPENTINE BELT DIAGRAMS Continued**

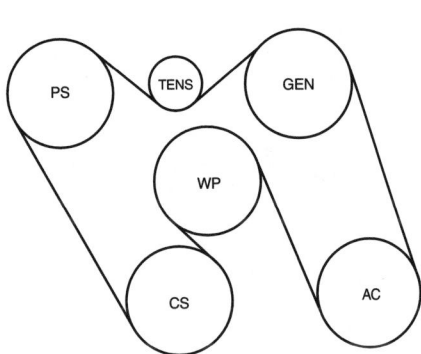

1989-94 3.3L Code N
3.8L Code C, L FWD

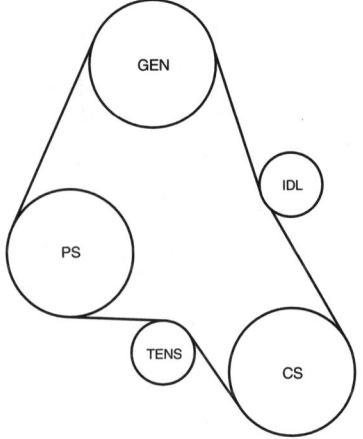

1991-95 3.8L
Supercharged Outer Belt

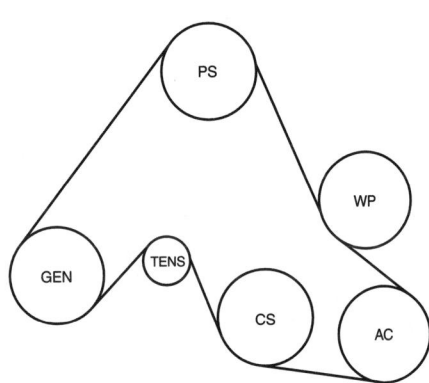

1991-97 3.4L DOHC

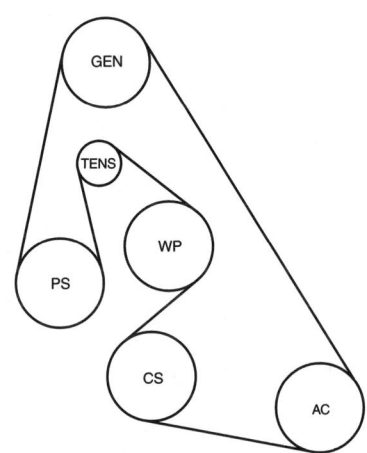

1995-00 3.8L FWD Code K
1995-00 3.8L Supercharged Outer Belt

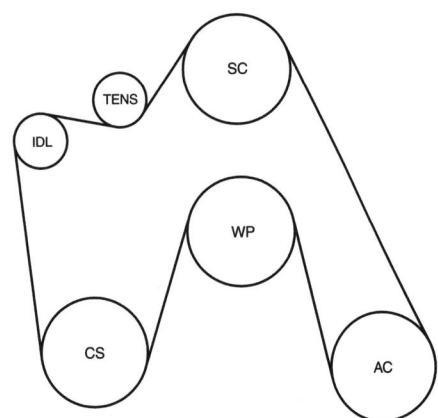

1991-95 3.8L
Supercharged Inner Belt

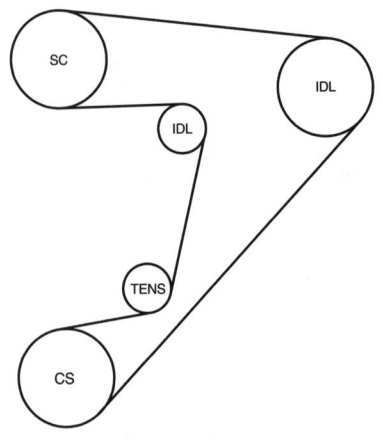

1995-00 3.8L
Supercharged Inner Belt

UNDERHOOD SERVICE SPECIFICATIONS

SERPENTINE BELT DIAGRAMS Continued

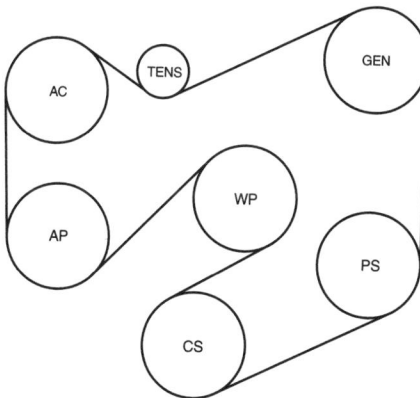

1989-93 5.0L, 5.7L
Code E, 7

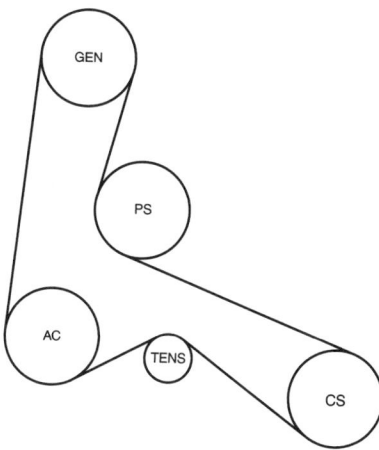

1993-97 5.7L
Code P

ENGINE COMPUTER SYSTEM

DIAGNOSTIC TROUBLE CODES
FOR TESTING AND ADJUSTMENT DIAGRAMS, SEE APPENDIX G.

1989-95

All w/12-pin DLC ex. 1989-90 Riviera, Reatta w/CRT
Connect a jumper between A and B terminals on under dash connector (identified by a slot between the terminals on single-row connectors, or two upper right-hand cavities on two-row connectors). Turn ignition switch on. Code 12 will flash three times, then codes in memory will be displayed. Do not run engine with jumper connected.

Remove ECM fuse for a minimum of ten seconds to clear memory.

1989 Riviera, Reatta w/CRT
To enter diagnostic modes, turn ignition switch on and push "off" and "warm" buttons simultaneously for three seconds and release. Any stored codes will be displayed.

To clear ECM codes, press the "HI" switch after the ECM message is displayed. After accessing the ECM system, continually press the "LO" switch after each message until "CLEAR CODES" is displayed, then press "HI" button. Press the "BI LEVEL" button to exit diagnostics.

The computer system monitors other systems and functions besides ECM trouble codes. See Service Manual for details.

DIAGNOSTIC TROUBLE CODES Continued

1990 Riviera, Reatta
Complicated procedure involved to retrieve code and run self-test modes. See Service Manual for details.

1994-00 All w/16-pin DLC, OBD-II
A Scan tool is required to retrieve codes and code definitions.

1989-93 ex. 1989 Riviera, Reatta w/CRT
1994-95 All w/12-pin DLC
Code 12 No tach reference to ECM
Code 13 Oxygen sensor circuit
Code 14 Coolant sensor circuit shorted
Code 15 Engine coolant sensor circuit open
Code 16 System voltage (high or low)
Code 17 Camshaft sensor circuit error (1993-94 w/SFI)
Code 17 Spark interface circuit (1990-93 others)
Code 18 Cam and crank sensor sync signal (1989-93)
Code 18 Injector circuit (V8)
Code 19 Intermittent 7X reference circuit
Code 21 Throttle position sensor circuit open
Code 22 Throttle position sensor curcuit shorted
Code 23 Open or ground MC solenoid (carbureted)
Code 23 Intake air temperature, circuit open
Code 24 Vehicle speed sensor
Code 25 Intake air temperature, circuit shorted
Code 26 Canister purge solenoid (V8)
Code 26 Quad driver circuit (others)
Code 27 EGR vacuum control solenoid circuit (V8)
Codes 27, 28 Quad driver circuit (others)
Codes 27, 28 Gear switch circuit (3.3L, 3.8L)
Code 28 Transmission range pressure switch (V8)
Code 29 Fourth gear circuit open
Code 29 Secondary air pump circuit
Code 31 EVAP canister purge solenoid (carbureted)
Code 31 Park/neutral switch circuit (1989-91 FI)
Code 31 EGR circuit (1989-90 TBI)
Code 32 Barometric or altitude sensor (carbureted)
Code 32 EGR system failure (FI)
Code 33 MAP, circuit open (FI) or MAF, circuit open (3.3L, 3.8L)
Code 34 MAP, circuit shorted (FI) or MAF, circuit shorted (3.3L, 3.8L)
Code 34 MAP sensor voltage high or low (FI)
Code 35 Idle speed or idle air control circuit
Code 36 24X signal circuit (1993-94 w/SFI)
Code 36 Transaxle shift control (1991)
Code 36 Mass airflow burn off circuit (1989-90)
Code 37 Transmission brake switch error
Code 38 Brake switch circuit (1989-90)
Code 41 Ignition control timing circuit problem (V8)
Code 41 No distributor reference pulses to ECM (carbureted)
Code 41 Cam sensor circuit (3.3L, 3.8L Code 3, C)
Code 41 Cylinder select error (Others, FI)
Code 42 Ignition control or ignition control bypass circuit grounded or open
Code 43 Knock sensor signal
Code 44 Air/fuel mixture lean
Codes 44, 45 Faulty oxygen sensor
Code 45 Air/fuel mixture rich
Code 46 Power steering pressure switch circuit (1989-90)
Code 47 A/C clutch and cruise circuit
Code 47 Knock sensor module missing
Code 48 Misfire
Code 48 Mass airflow sensor circuit
Code 48 Mass airflow sensor circuit
Code 50 System voltage low
Code 51 Faulty PROM or installation
Code 51 EEPROM programming error (V8)
Code 52 CALPAK error
Codes 53, 54, 55 EGR system (1993-95 3.3L, 3.8L)
Code 53 EGR vacuum sensor vacuum incorrect (carbureted)
Code 53 Alternator voltage out of range (MFI others)
Code 54 Fuel pump circuit, low voltage (FI)
Code 54 Shorted MC solenoid or faulty ECM (carbureted)
Code 55 Grounded V-REF, faulty O_2 sensor or ECM
Code 56 Quad driver B circuit
Code 58 PASS key fuel enable circuit (1990-93)
Code 58 Transmission fluid temperature sensor circuit shorted
Code 59 Transmission fluid temperature sensor circuit open
Code 61 Degraded oxygen sensor (ex. 3.8L Code L)
Code 61 Cruise vent solenoid (3.8L Code L)

UNDERHOOD SERVICE SPECIFICATIONS

DIAGNOSTIC TROUBLE CODES Continued

Code 62 Transaxle gear switch (ex. 3.8L Code L)
Code 62 Cruise vac solenoid (3.8L Code L)
Code 63 Cruise system problem (1993-95 3.8L)
Code 63 EGR flow problem, small (1989-90)
Code 64 EGR flow problem, medium (1989-90)
Code 65 EGR flow problem, large (w/CRT only)
Code 65 Fuel injector circuit (ex. CRT & 3.8L Code L)
Code 65 Cruise servo position (3.8L Code L)
Code 65 Fuel injector circuit (others)
Code 66 A/C pressure switch
Code 67 Cruise switches circuit
Code 68 Cruise system problem
Code 69 A/C head pressure switch
Code 70 A/C clutch relay driver (V8)
Code 72 Vehicle speed sensor
Code 73 Transmission pressure control solenoid circuit (V8)
Code 74 Traction control system circuit
Code 75 Transmission system voltage low (V8)
Code 75 Digital EGR #1 solenoid (others)
Code 76 Digital EGR #2 solenoid (others)
Code 77 Cooling fan relay (V8)
Code 77 Digital EGR #3 solenoid (others)
Code 78 Secondary cooling fan relay
Code 79 Transmission fluid over temperature
Code 80 Transmission converter clutch slippage excessive
Code 81 Transmission 2-3 shift
Code 82 Transmission 1-2 shift (V8)
Code 82 Ignition control 3X circuit (others)
Code 83 Reverse inhibit system
Code 84 Transmission 3-2 control
Code 85 Transmission converter clutch locked on (V8)
Code 85 Faulty or incorrect PROM (others)
Code 86 A/D chip error
Code 87 EEPROM error
Code 90 Transmission clutch solenoid circuit error
Code 91 Skip shift lamp circuit
Code 93 Transmission pressure control solenoid
Code 95 Change oil lamp circuit
Code 96 Low oil lamp circuit (Roadmaster)
Code 96 Transmission system voltage low (others)
Code 97 Vehicle speed sensor output circuit
Code 98 Invalid PCM program
Code 99 Invalid PCM program (others)

1989 Reatta, Riviera w/CRT

Code E013 Open oxygen sensor circuit
Code E014 Engine coolant sensor circuit, high temperature
Code E015 Engine coolant sensor circuit, low temperature
Code E016 System voltage out of range
Code E021 TPS, voltage high
Code E022 TPS, voltage low
Code E023 IAT, low temperature
Code E024 Vehicle speed sensor
Code E025 IAT, high temperature
Code E026 Quad driver error
Code E027 Second gear switch circuit
Code E028 Third gear switch circuit
Code E029 Fourth gear switch circuit
Code E031 Park/Neutral switch
Code E034 MAF sensor frequency low
Code E038 Brake switch circuit
Code E039 Torque converter clutch circuit
Code E041 Cam sensor circuit
Code E042 IC or bypass circuit
Code E043 IC system
Code E044 Lean exhaust
Code E045 Rich exhaust
Code E046 Power steering, switch circuit
Code E047 ECM-BCM Data
Code E048 Misfire
Code E063 EGR flow problem, small
Code E064 EGR flow problem, medium
Code E065 EGR flow problem, large

SENSORS, INPUT
TEMPERATURE SENSORS

Engine	Year	Sensor	Resistance Ohms @ deg. F/C
All	1989-90 1989-91	Coolant, Intake Air[1]	13,500 @ 20/-7 7500 @ 40/4 3400 @ 70/20 1800 @ 100/38 450 @ 160/70 185 @ 210/100
All	1991-00 1992-00	Coolant, Intake Air[1]	28,700 @ -4/-20 12,300 @ 23/-5 7200 @ 41/5 3500 @ 68/20 1460 @ 104/40 470 @ 158/70 180 @ 210/100
All	1994-00	Transmission Oil	25,809-28,677 @ -4 (-20) 14,558-16,176 @ 14 (-10) 8481-10,365 @ 0 (32) 3164-3867 @ 68 (20) 1313-1605 @ 104 (40) 420-514 @ 158 (70) 159-195 @ 212 (100) 69-85 @ 266 (130)

1 As equipped, not used on all engines.

MANIFOLD ABSOLUTE, VACUUM, AND BAROMETRIC PRESSURE SENSORS

Engines may use one, or a combination of these sensors. All sensors appear the same. Manifold Absolute Pressure sensors have a vacuum line connected between the unit and manifold vacuum. On Barometric Pressure sensors, the line is not used and the connector is either open or has a filter installed over it. Pressure sensors also have a vacuum line between the sensor and intake manifold and appear only on carbureted models.

Barometric Pressure Sensors: Measure voltage with ignition on and engine off.

Manifold Absolute Pressure Sensors: Measure voltage with ignition on and engine off. Start engine and apply 10 in./250 mm Hg to unit, voltage should be 1.5 volts minimum less.

Pressure Sensors: Measure voltage as indicated.

5 volts reference.

Engine	Year	Sensor	Voltage @ Altitude
All, as equipped	1989-90	Barometric	3.8-5.5 @ 0-1000 3.6-5.3 @ 1000-2000 3.5-5.1 @ 2000-3000 3.3-5.0 @ 3000-4000 3.2-4.8 @ 4000-5000 3.0-4.6 @ 5000-6000 2.9-4.5 @ 6000-7000 2.5-4.3 @ 7000-

MANIFOLD ABSOLUTE, VACUUM, AND BAROMETRIC PRESSURE SENSORS

Engine	Year	Sensor	Voltage @ Condition
All	1989-00	Manifold Absolute	1.0-2.0 @ idle 4.0-4.8 @ WOT

Engine	Year	Sensor	Voltage @ Condition
2.8L 2V, 5.0L 4V	1989-90	Vacuum	.50-.64 @ ign. on 1.7-3.0[1]

1 10 in./250 mm applied to unit.

CRANKSHAFT POSITION SENSORS

Air gap is measured between crankshaft sensor and interrupter rings.
Resistance is measured at room temperature.

Engine	Year	Resistance (ohms)	Air Gap (in./mm)
2.0L ex. OHC, 2.8L, 3.1L, 3.4L	1989-95	900-1200	—
2.2L	1993-95	900-1200	—
2.3L, 2.4L	1989-96	500-900	—
2.5L	1989-92	800-900	—
3.0L, 3.3L, 3.8L w/FI	1989-94	—	.025/.65

UNDERHOOD SERVICE SPECIFICATIONS

SENSORS, INPUT Continued

THROTTLE POSITION SENSOR (TPS)

Verify that minimum idle is at specified value.

Make all checks/adjustments with engine at operating temperature.

Carbureted Models: Remove aluminum plug covering the adjustment screw. Remove the screw and connect a digital voltmeter to the TPS black wire (-) and either of the two other colored wires (+). If voltage is approximately 5 volts, this is the reference voltage source. Connect DVOM to the other wire in this case. Apply thread locking compound to the screw and, with ignition on and engine not running (as applies), quickly adjust screw to obtain specified voltage at indicated condition.

Fuel Injected Models: Disconnect harness connector from TPS. Using three six-inch jumper wires, reconnect harness to TPS. With ignition on and engine not running (as applies), connect a digital voltmeter to black wire (-) and either of the two other colored wires (+). If voltage is approximately 5 volts, this is the reference voltage source. Connect DVOM to the other wire in this case. Check reading against specified value. If TPS is adjustable, loosen the unit retaining screws and rotate the unit to reach specified value.

Engine	Year	TPS Voltage	
		Idle	WOT (approx.)
2.0L ex. OHC	1989	.33-1.33[1]	5.0
2.0L OHC	1989	.20-1.25[1]	5.0
2.2L	1993-95	.33-1.33[1]	4.5 approx.
	1996	.20-.96[1]	4.0-4.7
2.3L	1989	.51	—
	1990-93	.40-.90[1]	4.5 min.
	1994-96	.36-.96[1]	4.0 min.
2.4L	1997	.20-.96[1]	4.0 min.
2.5L (151)	1989-91	.20-1.25[1]	5.0
2.5L	1991-92	.35-1.33[1]	5.0
2.8L (173) FI	1989	.55	
3.1L	1989-95	.29-.98[1]	4.0 approx.
	1996-00	.20-.74[1]	4.0 min.
3.3L	1989-91	.40	4.5 min.
3.3L	1992-93	.20-.74[1]	4.0 min.
3.4L	1994	.28-.98[1]	4.8
	1995-96	.20-.74	4.0 min.
3.8L (231) FI & Turbo	1989-91	.40	5.1
3.8L	1992-00	.20-.70[1]	4.0 min.
5.0L (307)	1989-90	.41[2]	5.0 approx.
5.0L, 5.7L	1991-93	.20-.95[1]	5.0 approx.
	1994-95	.36-.96[1]	4.0 min.
	1996	.30-.90[1]	4.0-4.7

1 Not adjustable.
2 Idle speed or Load compensator (ISC, ILC) retracted.

KNOCK SENSOR

Engine	Year	Resistance (ohms)
2.2L, 2.3L, 2.4L	1994-98	90,000-110,000
3.1L, 3.4L, 3.8L	1992-95	3300-4500
	1996-00	100,000 approx.
5.7L	1994-95	3300-4500
	1996	90,000-110,000

ACTUATORS, OUTPUT

IDLE SPEED CONTROL

All engines with ISC.

Measured between terminals A & B and C & D.

Engine	Year	Resistance (ohms)
All carbureted	1989-90	10 min.
2.8L, 3.1L Century, Regal	1989	.48-.58
3.8L Code C	1989	.48-.58
All others, TBI & MFI	1989	20 min.
2.3L, 2.5L, 3.1L, 3.8L Electra, LeSabre	1990	.40-.80
3.8L Reatta, Riviera	1990	.48-.56
All	1991-00	.40-.80

FUEL INJECTORS

Engine	Year	Resistance (ohms)	Temperature (deg. F/C)
2.0L, 2.5L	1989	1.2 min.	—
	1990-92	1.6 min.	—
2.2L	1993-96	11.8-12.6	68/20
2.3L	1989-95	1.9-2.15	140/60
	1996	1.95-2.30	—
2.4L	1996-98	1.95-2.30	—
2.8L, 3.1L: Regal	1989-92	12.0-12.4[1]	—
Others	1989	8 min.	—
3.1L, 3.4L	1994-00	11.8-12.6	—
3.3L	1989-92	11.8-12.6[1]	68/20
3.8L	1991-95	14.3-14.7	68/20
	1996-00	11.4-12.6	—
5.0L, 5.7L	1991-93	1.2 min.	—
	1994-97	11.8-12.6	—

1 Values for all injectors should be within a range of 0.8 ohms at room temperature.

MIXTURE CONTROL SOLENOID-CARBURETED ENGINES

On some engines, the ECM will be damaged if the resistance of the mixture control solenoid is less than specified.

Engine	Year	Resistance (ohms)
All	1989-90	10 min.

CADILLAC
1989-2000

ENGINE IDENTIFICATION

To identify any engine by the manufacturer's code, follow the four steps designated by the numbered blocks.

1 **MODEL YEAR IDENTIFICATION:** Refer to illustration of the Vehicle Identification Number (V.I.N.). The year is indicated by a code letter which is the 10th character of the V.I.N.

2 **ENGINE CODE LOCATION:** Refer to illustration of V.I.N. plate for location and designation of engine code.

3 **ENGINE CODE:** In the "CODE" column, find the engine code determined in Step 2.

4 **ENGINE IDENTIFICATION:** On the line where the engine code appears, read to the right to identify the engine.

V.I.N. PLATE LOCATION:

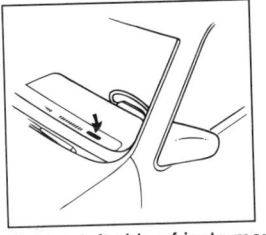

On top left side of instrument panel

Model year of vehicle.

2000 — Y
1999 — X
1998 — W
1997 — V
1996 — T
1995 — S
1994 — R
1993 — P
1992 — N
1991 — M
1990 — L
1989 — K

MODEL YEAR AND ENGINE IDENTIFICATION:

IG6BD69RXY9100001

2 ENGINE CODE (8th character)

1 MODEL YEAR (10th character)

4 ENGINE IDENTIFICATION

YEAR	3 ENGINE CODE	CYL.	DISPL. liters	DISPL. cu. in.	Fuel System	HP
1997-00	R	6	3.0	181	MFI	200
	9	8	4.6	279	MFI	300
	Y	8	4.6	279	MFI	275
1996	9	8	4.6	279	MFI	300
	Y	8	4.6	279	MFI	275
	P	8	5.7	350	MFI	260
1995	9	8	4.6	279	MFI	300
	Y	8	4.6	279	MFI	275
	B	8	4.9	300	MFI	200
	P	8	5.7	350	MFI	260
1994	9	8	4.6	279	MFI	295
	Y	8	4.6	279	MFI	270
	B	8	4.9	300	MFI	200
	P	8	5.7	350	MFI	260
1993	9	8	4.6	279	MFI	295
	Y	8	4.6	279	MFI	270
	B	8	4.9	300	MFI	200
	7	8	5.7	350	TBI	185

4 ENGINE IDENTIFICATION

YEAR	3 ENGINE CODE	CYL.	DISPL. liters	DISPL. cu. in.	Fuel System	HP
1992	8	8	4.5	273	MFI	200
	B	8	4.9	300	MFI	200
	E	8	5.0	305	TBI	170
	7	8	5.7	350	TBI	185
1991	8	8	4.5	273	MFI	200
	B	8	4.9	300	MFI	200
	E	8	5.0	305	TBI	170
	7	8	5.7	350	TBI	180
1990	8	8	4.5	273	MFI	200
	5	8	4.5	273	MFI	180
	Y	8	5.0	307	4V	140
	7	8	5.7	350	TBI	180
1989	5	8	4.5	273	TBI	155
	5	8	4.5	273	MFI	200
	Y	8	5.0	307	4V	140

**D—Diesel. TBI—Throttle Body Injection.
MFI—Multiport Fuel Injection. 2V—Two Venturi Carburetor.
4V—Four Venturi Carburetor.
1 Horsepower varies with model installation.**

UNDERHOOD SERVICE SPECIFICATIONS

CCTU1   CCTU1

CCTU1

CYLINDER NUMBERING SEQUENCE

6-CYL. FIRING ORDER:
3.0L 1 2 3 4 5 6

8-CYL. FIRING ORDER:
4.6L (279) 1 2 7 3 4 5 6 8
All Others 1 8 4 3 6 5 7 2

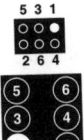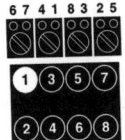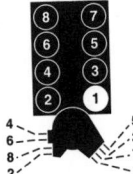

— Front of car —

1997-00 3.0L Code R	1991-95 4.9L (300) FWD	1993-00 4.6L (279)	1989-90 5.0L (307)	1990-93 5.7L (350), 1991-92 5.0L (305)	1994-96 5.7L Code P

262

Copyright 2000 by Chek-Chart Publications

UNDERHOOD SERVICE SPECIFICATIONS

TIMING MARK

No Timing Marks on These Engines

1997-00
3.0L Code R
1993-00 4.6L (279)
1994-96
5.7L Code P

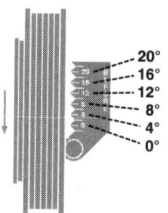

1989-92
4.5L (273),
1991-95
4.9L (300)

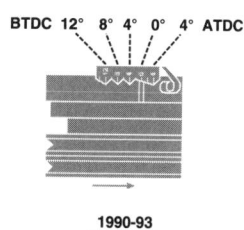

BTDC 12° 8° 4° 0° 4° ATDC

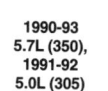

1990-93
5.7L (350),
1991-92
5.0L (305)

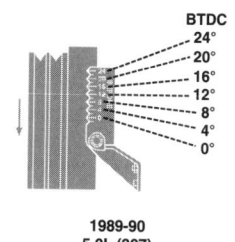

BTDC
24°
20°
16°
12°
8°
4°
0°

1989-90
5.0L (307)

ELECTRICAL AND IGNITION SYSTEMS

BATTERY

		STANDARD		OPTIONAL	
Engine	Year	BCI Group No.	Crank. Perf.	BCI Group No.	Crank. Perf.
3.0L	1997-00	91	600	—	—
4.5L, 4.9L Allanté	1989-92	78	770	—	—
Eldorado, Seville	1989-92	78	770	—	—
DeVille, Fleetwood	1989-92	78	540	78	770
4.6L	1993-97	78	770	—	—
4.6L Seville	1998-00	79	880	—	—
Others	1998-00	78	770	—	—
4.9L	1993	78	540	78	770
Eldorado, Seville	1993	78	770	—	—
4.9L	1994-96	78	770	—	—
5.0L, 5.7L	1989-93	78	730	—	—
5.0L, 5.7L	1993-94	78	690	—	—
	1995-96	78	770	—	—

GENERATOR

Application	Rated Output (amps)	Test Output (amps)
1989-90	78, 100, 120	1
1991-92 Allanté	120	90 @ 1500
Brougham: 5.0L	100	
5.7L	120	
All others	140	
1993-94	140, 144	
1995-96	140	
1997-00 3.0L	140	
4.6L	120	

1 Run engine at moderate speed, output must be within 15 amps of rated output.

REGULATOR

Application	Test Temp. (deg. F/C)	Voltage Setting
1989-00	Warm	13.0-16.0

STARTER

Engine	Year	Cranking Voltage (min. volts)	Ampere Draw @ Cranking Speed
All	1989-99	9.0	—

SPARK PLUGS

Engine	Year	Gap (inches)	Gap (mm)	Torque (ft-lb)
3.0L	1997-00	.035-.043	0.9-1.1	19
V8	1989	.060	1.52	15
V8: 4.5L	1990-92	.060	1.52	11
4.6L	1993-00	.050	1.28	15
4.9L	1991-96	.060	1.52	8-15
5.0L	1990	.060	1.52	25
5.0L	1991-92	.035	.89	22
5.7L	1990-93	.035	.89	22
5.7L	1994-96	.050	1.28	11

IGNITION COIL
Winding resistance (ohms at 80°F or 27°C)
FOR TESTING AND ADJUSTMENT DIAGRAMS, SEE APPENDIX A.

Application	Year	Resistance (ohms)	
		Primary	Secondary
All w/distributor	1989-95	0-2	6,000-30,000
3.0L, 4.6L	1996-00	—	5,000-8,000[1]

1 Without distributor, measured across each coil's two towers with spark plug wires removed.

DISTRIBUTOR PICKUP
FOR TESTING AND ADJUSTMENT DIAGRAMS, SEE APPENDIX B.

Engine	Year	Resistance (ohms)	Air Gap (in./mm)
All w/distributor	1989-96	500-1500	—

BASE TIMING
FOR TESTING AND ADJUSTMENT DIAGRAMS, SEE APPENDIX C.

4.5L (279), 4.9L, 5.0L (307), connect a jumper between terminals A & B of the diagnostic connector.

If "Check Engine" light comes on during this procedure, remove ECM fuse to clear.

Engine	Year	Man. Trans. (degrees) @ RPM	Auto. Trans. (degrees) @ RPM
4.5L (279)	1989	—	10 @ 900 P max.
4.5L, 4.9L	1990-96	—	10[1] @ 800 P max.
4.6L	1993-00	—	10[2]
5.0L (305)	1991	—	0 @ 500 D
5.0L (307)	1989-90	—	20 @ 1100 P
5.7L (350)	1990-93	—	0 @ 500 D

1 4.9L using regular fuel, 6°.
2 Checking figure only, not adjustable.

CADILLAC
1989-2000

FUEL SYSTEM

FUEL SYSTEM PRESSURE
FOR TESTING AND ADJUSTMENT DIAGRAMS, SEE APPENDIX D.

Carbureted models, pinch off fuel return line.

All models with TBI, pressure measured at fuel inlet of TBI unit.

All models with MFI, pressure measured at fuel rail.

Engine	Year	Pressure PSI	RPM
3.0L	1997-00	46-59	ign. on
4.1L (250), 4.5L (279) TBI	1989	9-12	—
4.5L, 4.6L, 4.9L	1990-94	40-50	ign. on
		32-38	idle
	1995	40-50	ign. on
	1996-00	46-59	ign. on
5.0L	1991-92	9-13	idle
		13 min.[1]	idle
5.0L (307)	1989-90	5.5-6.5	idle
5.7L Gas	1990-93	9-13	idle
		13 min.[1]	idle
	1994-96	41-47	ign. on
		31-44	idle

1 Fuel pump pressure with fuel return line briefly restricted.

IDLE SPEED W/COMPUTER CONTROL
FOR TESTING AND ADJUSTMENT DIAGRAMS, SEE APPENDIX E.

Carbureted

1989-90 5.0L (307): Disconnect and plug vacuum hoses at EGR and canister purge valves. With engine at operating temperature, remove vacuum hose from ILC and plug. Set maximum speed to specified value by holding hex nut and turning plunger shaft. Reconnect ILC vacuum hose and check that minimum speed is at specified value. To adjust, remove rubber and metal plugs from rear center outlet tube, insert a ³/₃₂" Allen wrench. Remove ILC hose and plug. Connect a remote vacuum source and apply vacuum to the unit. Adjust carb base screw to obtain specified base value.

Fuel injected

2.0L (122), 2.8L (173) FI: Ground diagnostic lead and turn ignition on for 30 seconds. Remove IAC electrical lead and remove ground from diagnostic connector. Start engine and set minimum speed to specified value.

1989 4.1L (250), 4.5L (279) TBI: With engine at operating temperature, turn engine off and disconnect harness from ISC. Apply 12 volts (+) to third from top of ISC (C), and ground the fourth terminal from top (D) only long enough to retract ISC plunger. Start engine and check minimum speed against specified checking value. If not, set minimum idle to specified value by adjusting base screw.

1989-98 4.1L, 4.5L MFI, 4.6L, 4.9L, 5.7L: With IAC fully retracted, idle should be at specified checking value.

ALL CARBURETED

Engine	Year	Trans.	Min. Speed	Max. Speed	Fast	Step of Cam
5.0L (307)	1989-90	AT	450 D	700 D	550 D	Low
base idle	1989-90	AT	450 D			

ALL FUEL INJECTED

Engine	Year	Transmission	Minimum Speed	Checking Speed
3.0L	1997-00	AT	—	550-675 N
4.5L (279) TBI	1989	AT	525 N	475-550 N
4.5L	1989	AT	500 N	500-600 N
4.5L, 4.9L: Allanté	1990-92	AT	500-600 N	—
Others	1990-92	AT	500-550 N	—
4.6L	1993-94	AT	—	600-800 N
	1995	AT	—	700 N max.
	1996-00	AT	—	550-675 N
4.9L	1993-96	AT	500-550 N	—
5.0L	1991-92	AT	—	500-600 D
5.7L	1990-92	AT	—	500-600 D

ENGINE MECHANICAL

TIGHTENING TORQUES
FOR CYLINDER HEAD TORQUE SEQUENCES AND DIAGRAMS, SEE APPENDIX F.

Some fasteners are tightened in more than one step.

Engine	Year	TORQUE FOOT-POUNDS/NEWTON METERS				
		Cylinder Head	Intake Manifold	Exhaust Manifold	Crankshaft Pulley	Water Pump
3.0L	1997-00	18-25, +90°, +90°, +90°, +15°	15/20	15/20	15/20	18/25
4.5L, 4.9L	1989-94	38/50, 68/90[2]	3	18/25	70/95	5/7, short 30/40, long
	1995-96	30/40, 58/70, 88/110, 5	3	18/25	70/95	5/7, short 30/40, long
4.6L	1993-94	30/40, +70°, +60°, +60°	4/6, +120°	20/25	105/145, +120°	62"/7
	1995-00	30/40, +70°, +60°, +60°	89"/10	18/25	44/60, 73/100, pump +120° 18/25, housing	
5.0L (305)	1990-91	70/95[4]	35/45	26/35	70/95	10/14, short 22/30, long
5.0L (307)	1989-90	40/54, +95°, first and last bolts on exhaust manifold side +120°, all others	40/54	25/34	200-310/ 270-400	11/14
5.7L	1990-93	65/90[4]	35/45	25/35	70/95	22/30
	1994-95	65/88[4]	71/8, 35/48	25/35	75/102	30/40

1 Tighten four center bolts to 15/20. Tighten eight outer bolts to 22/30. Then, tighten all bolts to 22/30.

2 After tightening all bolts to this specification, tighten numbers 1, 3, & 4 (upper row, center three bolts on each head) to 90/120.

3 Tighten four center bolts to 8/12. Tighten eight outer bolts to 12/16. Then, tighten all bolts to 12/16.

4 Over three phases.

5 Tighten 5 upper bolts (by intake manifold) to 96/120. Then, tighten 3 upper center bolts to 104/130.

6 Long bolts.

7 Short bolts.

COMPRESSION PRESSURE
At cranking speed, engine temperature normalized, throttle open.

Engine	Year	PSI	Maximum Variation PSI
3.0L	1997-00	—	1
4.1L, 4.5L, 4.9L	1989-92	140-165	1
	1993-96	140 min.	1
4.6L	1993-00	140-170	1
All others	1989-96	100 min.	1

1 Lowest cylinder pressure must be more than 70% of highest reading cylinder pressure.

BELT TENSION
A belt that has been pretensioned is considered a used belt.

Use a strand tension gauge. Measurements are in pounds.

Engine	Year	Generator	Power Steering	Air Cond.	Air Pump
All w/serpentine	1989-91	70-120[1]	70-120[1]	70-120[1]	—
4.5L, 4.9L	1992-96	120[1]	120[1]	120[1]	—
4.6L	1993-98	65[1]	65[1]	65[1]	—

1 Automatic tensioner operating range. Replace belt if arrow is out of index range.

SERPENTINE BELT DIAGRAMS

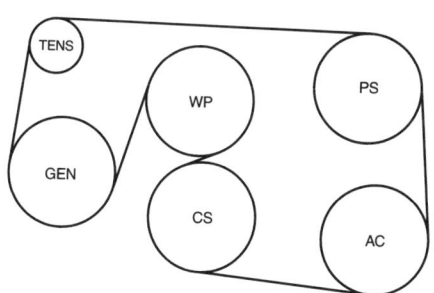

1997-00 3.0L
Catera

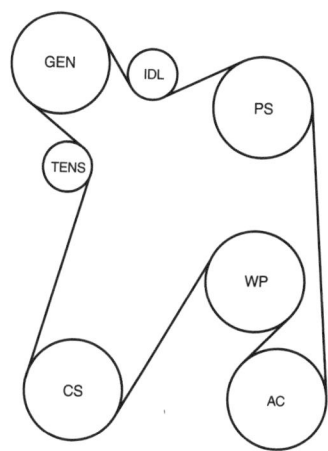

1989-95
4.1L, 4.5L, 4.9L

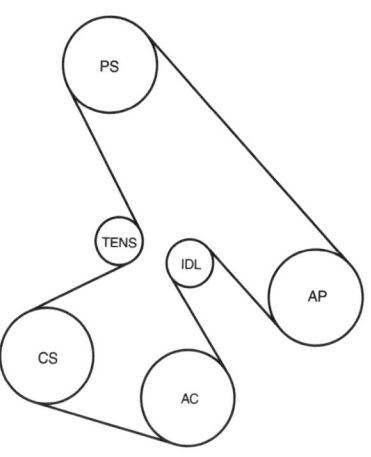

1993-00
4.6L

SERPENTINE BELT DIAGRAMS Continued

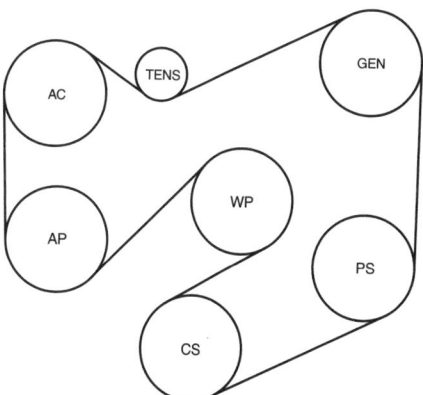

1989-93 5.0L, 5.7L
Code E, F, 7, 8

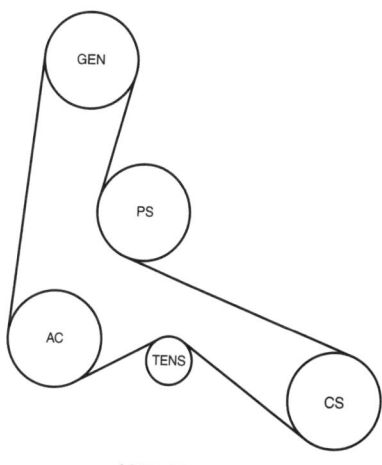

1993-97 5.7L
Code P

ENGINE COMPUTER SYSTEM

DIAGNOSTIC TROUBLE CODES
FOR TESTING AND ADJUSTMENT DIAGRAMS, SEE APPENDIX G.

5.0L, 5.7L
Connect a jumper between A and B terminals on under dash connector (identified by a slot between the terminals or is two upper-right cavities on a two-row connector). Turn ignition on. Code 12 will flash three times, then the codes in memory will be displayed. Remove ECM fuse for a minimum of ten seconds to clear memory.

4.5L, 4.6L, 4.9L
Turn ignition on. Press "OFF" and "WARMER" buttons on Climate Control at the same time. Codes will be displayed on Climate Control indicator or Driver Information Center. Press "Reset" and "Auto" to exit diagnostic mode. Clear codes by pressing "OFF" and "HI" buttons at same time.
Codes will be displayed with either an "E" or "EO" preceding them.

1989-95, complicated procedure required to display BCM codes and "snapshot" parameters. Codes not listed involve transaxle and cruise control. See manufacturer's service data.

1996-00
System w/OBD-II. A Scan tool is needed to retrieve codes.

1989-95 5.0L, 5.7L
Code 12 No tach reference to ECM
Code 13 Oxygen sensor circuit
Code 14 Shorted engine coolant sensor circuit
Code 15 Open engine coolant sensor circuit

CADILLAC
1989-2000

DIAGNOSTIC TROUBLE CODES Continued

Code 21 Throttle position sensor voltage high
Code 22 Throttle position sensor voltage low
Code 23 Open or ground MC solenoid (carbureted)
Code 23 IAT sensor voltage high (FI)
Code 24 Vehicle speed sensor circuit
Code 25 IAT sensor voltage low (FI)
Code 31 EVAP canister purge solenoid
Code 34 MAP or vacuum sensor circuit (carbureted)
Code 35 Idle speed control switch circuit shorted
Code 41 Cylinder select error
Code 42 IC or IC bypass circuit grounded or open
Code 43 Knock sensor signal too long
Code 44 Air/fuel mixture lean
Codes 44 & 45 Faulty oxygen sensor
Code 45 Air/fuel mixture rich
Codes 51 & 52 Faulty PROM or installation
Code 53 Generator voltage high (FI)
Code 53 EGR vacuum valve sensor (carbureted)
Code 54 Shorted MC solenoid or faulty ECM (carbureted)
Code 54 Fuel pump circuit voltage low (FI)
Code 55 Grounded V-REF, faulty oxygen sensor or ECM
Code 61 Degraded oxygen sensor

4.5L, 4.9L

Code 12 No tach signal
Code 13 Oxygen sensor not ready (rear side, 4.6L)
Code 14 Shorted engine coolant sensor circuit
Code 15 Open engine coolant sensor circuit
Code 16 Generator voltage out of range
Code 17 Shorted crankshaft position sensor circuit (TBI)
Code 17 Front oxygen sensor not ready (Allanté)
Code 18 Open crankshaft position sensor circuit
Code 19 Shorted fuel pump circuit
Code 20 Open fuel pump circuit
Code 21 Shorted throttle position sensor circuit
Code 22 Open throttle position sensor circuit
Code 23 IC bypass circuit shorted or open (1989-91)
Code 23 Ignition control circuit (1992-94)
Code 24 Speed sensor circuit problem
Code 25 24× reference signal low (1993-94)
Code 26 Shorted throttle switch circuit
Code 27 Open throttle switch circuit
Code 30 ISC circuit problem (TBI)
Code 30 RPM error (MFI)
Code 31 Shorted MAP sensor circuit
Code 32 Open MAP sensor circuit
Code 33 MAP/Barometric sensor correlation
Code 34 MAP signal out of range
Code 35 Shorted Barometric sensor circuit (1989)
Code 35 Ignition ground voltage out of range (1993-94)
Code 36 Open Barometric sensor circuit (1989)
Code 36 EGR valve pintle out of range (1993-94)
Code 37 Shorted IAT sensor circuit
Code 38 Open IAT sensor circuit
Code 40 Power steering pressure switch circuit
Code 41 Camshaft sensor circuit
Code 42 Front oxygen sensor lean (MFI)
Code 43 Front oxygen sensor rich (MFI)
Code 44 Lean exhaust signal (rear sensor 4.6L, 4.9L)
Code 45 Rich exhaust signal (rear sensor 4.6L, 4.9L)
Code 46 Right to left bank fueling imbalance
Code 47 ECM/BCM data problem
Code 48 EGR system fault
Code 51 PROM error indicator
Code 52 ECM memory reset indicator
Code 53 Distributor or 4× reference signal interrupt
Code 55 TPS misadjusted or out of range
Code 56 Anti-theft system
Code 58 PASS control problem
Code 60 Transmission not in drive
Code 70 Intermittent TPS
Code 71 Intermittent MAP
Code 73 Intermittent coolant sensor
Code 74 Intermittent IAT
Code 75 Intermittent speed sensor
Code 80 TPS idle learn not complete (4.6L)
Code 80 Fuel system rich (others)
Code 81 Cam to 4× reference problem
Code 82 24× reference signal high

DIAGNOSTIC TROUBLE CODES Continued

Code 83 24× reference signal high
Code 85 Idle throttle angle high (4.6L)
Code 85 Throttle body service required (others)
Code 95 Engine stall detected
Code 107 PCM/BCM data link problem
Code 108 PROM checksum mismatch
Code 109 PCM keep alive memory reset
Code 110 Generator L-terminal circuit
Code 112 EEPROM failure
Code 119 Open or shorted fuel injector
Code 131 & 132 Knock sensor failure
Code 137 Loss of ABS/TCS data

SENSORS, INPUT
TEMPERATURE SENSORS

Engine	Year	Sensor	Resistance Ohms @ deg. F/C
All	1989-90	Coolant, Intake Air[1]	13,500 @ 20/-7 7500 @ 40/4 3400 @ 70/20 1800 @ 100/38 450 @ 160/70 185 @ 210/100
All ex. 3.0L	1991-00	Coolant, Intake Air[1]	12,300 @ 23/-5 7280 @ 41/5 3520 @ 68/20 1459 @ 104/40 467 @ 160/70 177 @ 210/100
3.0L	1997-00	Coolant, Intake Air	14,800 @ 0/-18 5200 @ 40/4 2500 @ 70/21 1300 @ 100/38 450 @ 160/70 200 @ 210/100

1 As equipped, not used on all engines.

MANIFOLD ABSOLUTE, VACUUM, AND BAROMETRIC PRESSURE SENSORS
Engines may use one, or a combination of these sensors. All sensors appear the same. Manifold Absolute Pressure sensors have a vacuum line connected between the unit and manifold vacuum. On Barometric Pressure sensors, the line is not used and the connector is either open or has a filter installed over it. Pressure sensors also have a vacuum line between the sensor and intake manifold and appear only on carbureted models.

Barometric Pressure Sensors: Measure voltage with ignition on and engine off.

Manifold Absolute Pressure Sensors: Measure voltage with ignition on and engine off. Start engine and apply 10 in./Hg. (34 kPa) to unit, voltage should be 1.2-2.3 volts less (except 5.0L, 5.7L) or 1.5 volts minimum less (2.0L, 2.8L, 5.0L, 5.7L).

Pressure Sensors: Measure voltage as indicated.
5 volts reference.

Engine	Year	Sensor	Voltage @ in./kPa
4.1L (250), 4.5L, 4.6L, 4.9L	1989-00	Manifold Absolute	0.5-0.9 @ 11-15/37-51 4.5-5.0 @ 28-31/95-105
2.0L, 2.8L, 5.0L, 5.7L	1989-96	Manifold Absolute	1-2 @ idle 4.0-4.8 @ WOT

Engine	Year	Sensor	Voltage @ Altitude
All others, as equipped	1989-90	Barometric, Manifold Absolute	3.8-5.5 @ 0-1000 3.6-5.3 @ 1000-2000 3.5-5.1 @ 2000-3000 3.3-5.0 @ 3000-4000 3.2-4.8 @ 4000-5000 3.0-4.6 @ 5000-6000 2.9-4.5 @ 6000-7000 2.5-4.3 @ 7000

Engine	Year	Sensor	Voltage @ Condition
5.0L 4V	1989-90	Vacuum	.50-.64 @ ign. on 1.7-3.0[1]

1 10 in./Hg. (34 kPa) applied to unit.

UNDERHOOD SERVICE SPECIFICATIONS

SENSORS, INPUT Continued

CRANKSHAFT & CAMSHAFT POSITION SENSORS
Resistance is measured at room temperature.

Engine	Year	Resistance (ohms)
4.6L (camshaft)	1993-95	800-1200
(crankshaft)	1993-95	800-1600

MASS AIRFLOW SENSOR

Engine	Year	Voltage @ Condition
3.0L	1997-00	0.2 min. @ idle 4.8 max. @ ign. on

THROTTLE POSITION SENSOR (TPS)
Verify that minimum idle is at specified value.

Make all checks/adjustments with engine at operating temperature.

1989 All V8 Engines w/FI: With ignition on and engine not running, connect digital voltmeter positive lead to pin A (blue-dark wire) and connect negative lead to pin B (black wire). Check reading against specified value and rotate sensor to adjust.

Engine	Year	TPS Voltage[1] Idle	TPS Voltage WOT
3.0L	1997-00	0.3-0.9[2]	3.3-3.9
4.1L (250), 4.5L (279), 4.9L	1989-96	.50	—
4.6L	1993-95	0.5 min.	4.6-5.4
	1996-00	0.6	4.5-4.96
5.0L	1991-92	.30-1.0[2]	—
5.0L (307)	1989-90	.41[3]	—
5.7L	1990	.20-1.25[2]	—
	1991-93	.30-1.0[2]	—
	1994-95	.30-.90	—

1 ±.10 carbureted engines, ±.05 fuel injected engines.
2 Not adjustable.
3 Idle load compensator retracted.

ACTUATORS, OUTPUT

IDLE SPEED CONTROL

All engines with ISC.

Measured between terminals A & B and C & D.

Engine	Year	Resistance (ohms)
4.1L (250), 4.5L, 4.9L	1989-96	4-100
4.6L	1993-95	4-100
5.0L, 5.7L	1990-93	40-80
5.7L	1994-96	40-80
All others, TBI & MFI	1989	20 min.
All carbureted	1989-90	10 min.

FUEL INJECTORS

Engine	Year	Resistance (ohms)	Temperature (deg. F/C)
4.6L, 4.9L	1991-00	8-25	—
5.0L, 5.7L TBI	1990-93	1.2 min.	—
5.7L	1994-96	11.8-12.6	—

MIXTURE CONTROL SOLENOID-CARBURETED ENGINES
On some engines, the ECM will be damaged if the resistance of the mixture control solenoid is less than specified.

Engine	Year	Resistance (ohms)
5.0L	1989	10 min.
5.0L	1990	20-26

ENGINE IDENTIFICATION

To identify any engine by the manufacturer's code, follow the four steps designated by the numbered blocks.

1 MODEL YEAR IDENTIFICATION: Refer to illustration of the Vehicle Identification Number (V.I.N.). The year is indicated by a code letter which is the 10th character of the V.I.N.

2 ENGINE CODE LOCATION: Refer to illustration of V.I.N. plate for location and designation of engine code.

3 ENGINE CODE: In the "CODE" column, find the engine code determined in Step 2.

4 ENGINE IDENTIFICATION: On the line where the engine code appears, read to the right to identify the engine.

V.I.N. PLATE LOCATION:

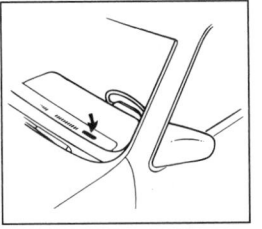

On top left side of instrument panel

Model year of vehicle:

2000 — Y
1999 — X
1998 — W
1997 — V
1996 — T
1995 — S
1994 — R
1993 — P
1992 — N
1991 — M
1990 — L
1989 — K

MODEL YEAR AND ENGINE IDENTIFICATION:

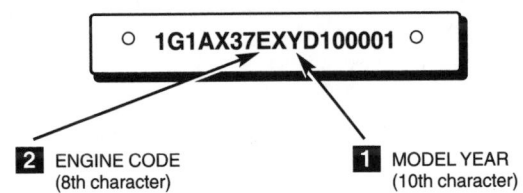

1G1AX37EXYD100001

2 ENGINE CODE (8th character)

1 MODEL YEAR (10th character)

4 ENGINE IDENTIFICATION

YEAR	3 ENGINE CODE	CYL.	DISPL. liters	DISPL. cu. in.	Fuel System	HP
2000	4	4	2.2	133	MFI	115
	T	4	2.4	146	MFI	150
	J	6	3.1	191	MFI	170/175
	E	6	3.4	207	MFI	180
	K	6	3.8	231	MFI	200
	G	8	5.7	350	MFI	305/320
1999	4	4	2.2	133	MFI	115
	T	4	2.4	146	MFI	150
	J	6	3.1	191	MFI	170
	M	6	3.1	191	MFI	150, 160
	K	6	3.8	231	MFI	200
	G	8	5.7	350	MFI	305-345[1]
1998	4	4	2.2	133	MFI	115
	T	4	2.4	146	MFI	150
	M	6	3.1	191	MFI	155, 160[1]
	K	6	3.8	231	MFI	195, 205[1]
	G	8	5.7	346	MFI	305, 345[1]
1997	4	4	2.2	133	MFI	120
	T	4	2.4	146	MFI	150
	M	6	3.1	191	MFI	155, 160[1]
	X	6	3.4	204	MFI	215
	K	6	3.8	231	MFI	195-205[1]
	P	8	5.7	350	MFI	285
	G	8	5.7	346	MFI	340
1996	4	4	2.2	133	MFI	120
	T	4	2.4	146	MFI	150
	M	6	3.1	191	MFI	155, 160[1]
	X	6	3.4	204	MFI	215
	K	6	3.8	231	MFI	200, 205
	W	8	4.3	265	MFI	200
	P	8	5.7	350	MFI	260-300[1]
	5	8	5.7	350	MFI	330
1995	4	4	2.2	133	MFI	120
	D	4	2.3	138	MFI	150
	M	6	3.1	191	MFI	155, 160[1]
	S	6	3.4	204	MFI	160
	X	6	3.4	204	MFI	210
	K	6	3.8	231	MFI	171
	W	8	4.3	265	MFI	200
	P	8	5.7	350	MFI	260, 300[1]
	J	8	5.7	350	MFI	405
1994	4	4	2.2	133	MFI	120
	A	4	2.3	138 HO	MFI	170
	T	6	3.1	191	MFI	140
	M	6	3.1	191	MFI	155, 160[1]
	S	6	3.4	204	MFI	160

4 ENGINE IDENTIFICATION

YEAR	3 ENGINE CODE	CYL.	DISPL. liters	DISPL. cu. in.	Fuel System	HP
1994 Cont'd.	X	6	3.4	204	MFI	210
	W	8	4.3	265	MFI	200
	P	8	5.7	350	MFI	260, 300[1]
	J	8	5.7	350	MFI	405
1993	4	4	2.2	133	MFI	110
	A	4	2.3 HO	138 HO	MFI	175
	T	6	3.1	191	MFI	140
	W	6	3.1 F	191 F	MFI	140
	S	6	3.4	204	MFI	160
	X	6	3.4	204	MFI	200
	Z	6	4.3	262	TBI	145
	E	8	5.0	305	TBI	170
	7	8	5.7	350	TBI	180, 205[1]
	P	8	5.7	350	MFI	300
	J	8	5.7	350	MFI	405
1992	4	4	2.2	133	MFI	110
	A	4	2.3 HO	138 HO	MFI	180
	R	4	2.5	151	TBI	105
	T	6	3.1	191	MFI	140
	X	6	3.4	204	MFI	210
	Z	6	4.3	262	MFI	145
	E	8	5.0	305	TBI	170
	F	8	5.0	305	MFI	130
	7	8	5.7	350	TBI	180
	8	8	5.7	350	MFI	245
	P	8	5.7	350	MFI	300
	J	8	5.7	350	MFI	375
1991	G	4	2.2	133	TBI	95
	A	4	2.3 HO	138 HO	MFI	140
	R	4	2.5	151	TBI	110
	T	6	3.1	191	MFI	140
	X	6	3.4	207	MFI	200, 210[1]
	E	8	5.0	305	TBI	170
	F	8	5.0	305	MFI	205, 230[1]
	J	8	5.7	350	MFI	375
	7	8	5.7	350	TBI	195
	8	8	5.7	350	MFI	245
1990	G	4	2.2	133	TBI	95
	A	4	2.3 HO	138 HO	MFI	180
	R	4	2.5	151	TBI	110
	T	6	3.1	191	MFI	135, 140
	Z	6	4.3	262	TBI	140
	E	8	5.0	305	TBI	170
	F	8	5.0	305	MFI	195, 230[1]
	Y	8	5.0	307	4V	140
	7	8	5.7	350	TBI	240, 245[1]
	8	8	5.7	350	MFI	240, 245[1]
	J	8	5.7	350	MFI	380

ENGINE IDENTIFICATION Continued

YEAR	**3** ENGINE CODE	CYL.	**4** ENGINE IDENTIFICATION DISPL. liters	cu. in.	Fuel System	HP
1989	1	4	2.0	122	TBI	90
	R	4	2.5	151	TBI	110
	W	6	2.8	173	MFI	125-130[1]
	S	6	2.8	173	MFI	135
	Z	6	4.3	262	TBI	140
	E	8	5.0	305	TBI	170
	F	8	5.0	305	MFI	195-230[1]

YEAR	**3** ENGINE CODE	CYL.	**4** ENGINE IDENTIFICATION DISPL. liters	cu. in.	Fuel System	HP
1989	Y	8	5.0	307	4V	140
Cont'd.	7	8	5.7	350	TBI	190
	8	8	5.7	350	MFI	230-245[1]

TBI—Throttle Body Injection.   MFI—Multiport Fuel Injection.
2V—Two Venturi Carburetor.   4V—Four Venturi Carburetor.
D—Diesel.   F—Flexible Fuel.   HO—High Output.
1 Engine horsepower varies with model installation.

UNDERHOOD SERVICE SPECIFICATIONS

CTTU1   CTTU1

CYLINDER NUMBERING SEQUENCE

4-CYL. FIRING ORDER:
1 3 4 2

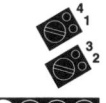

coil on plug

— Front of car —

1989
2.0L (122) Code 1,
1990-91
2.2L Code G,
1992-00
2.2L Code 4

1990-94
2.3L Code A,
1995
2.3L Code D,
1996-00
2.4L Code T

1989-92
2.5L (151)

6-CYL. FIRING ORDER:
2.8L, 3.1L, 3.4L
1 2 3 4 5 6
All Others
1 6 5 4 3 2

8-CYL. FIRING ORDER: 1 8 4 3 6 5 7 2
All except 1997 Corvette Code G

1997-99 Corvette Code G
FIRING ORDER: 1 8 7 2 6 5 4 3

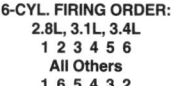

— Front of car —

1989
2.8L (173) ex.
Camaro,
1990-94
3.1L Code T, W

1989
2.8L (173) Camaro,
1990-92
3.1L Code T (RWD)

1994-99
3.1L Code M
1999-00
3.1L Code J

1993-95
3.4L Code S

1991-95
3.4L Code X

1989-90
5.0L (307)

1989-91
5.7L (350) Corvette
Code 8

1989-93
8-cyl. ex.: 5.0L (307),
5.7L (350) Corvette
Code 8, J, P

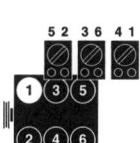
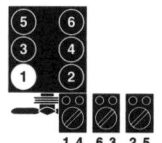
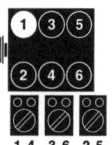

Front of car

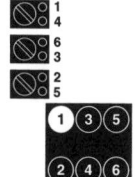
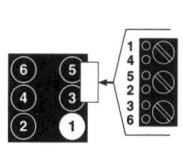
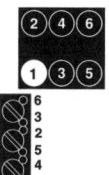

— Front of car —

1996
3.4L Code X

1995-00
3.8L Code K
Camaro

1998-00
3.8L Code K

1989-93
4.3L (262)

1990-95
Corvette
5.7L (350) Code J

1992-96
5.7L Code P, 5
1994-96
4.3L Code W
1997 Code P

1997-00
5.7L Code G

TIMING MARK

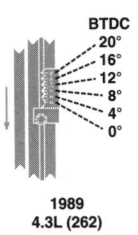

1989
4.3L (262)

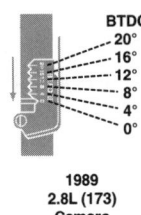

1989
2.8L (173)
Camaro

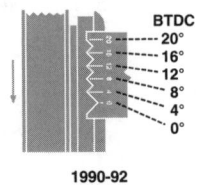

1990-92
3.1L FI Code T RWD
Camaro

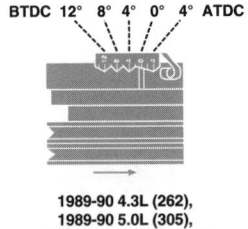

1989-90 4.3L (262),
1989-90 5.0L (305),
1991-93 5.0L Code E, F

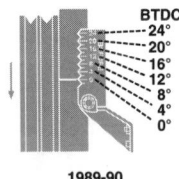

1989-90
5.0L (307)

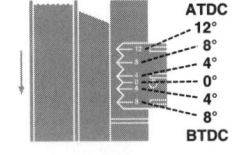

1989-93
5.7L (350) FI
Camaro & Corvette ex.: Code J, P
1989-93
5.7L FI Code 7 (Police)

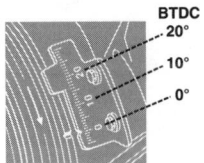

1990-95
5.7L DOHC Code J
Corvette

ELECTRICAL AND IGNITION SYSTEMS

BATTERY

Engine	Year	STANDARD BCI Group No.	STANDARD Crank. Perf.	OPTIONAL BCI Group No.	OPTIONAL Crank. Perf.
2.0L (122) MT	1989	75	525	75	630
2.0L (122) AT	1989	75	630	—	—
2.2L: Cavalier	1990-91	75	630	—	—
Corsica, Beretta: MT	1990-91	75	525	75	630
AT	1990-91	75	630	—	—
2.2L	1992	75	525	75	630
2.2L: Cavalier	1993-00	75	525	—	—
Beretta, Corsica	1993-96	75	525	75	600
2.3L	1989-93	75	630	—	—
	1994-95	75	600	—	—
2.4L	1996-00	75	600	—	—
2.5L (151)	1989-92	75	630	—	—
2.8L: Cavalier	1989	75	630	—	—
Celebrity, Camaro	1989	75	525	75	570
Corsica, Beretta	1989	70	525	75	630
3.1L MFI Cavalier	1990-91	75	630	—	—
Others	1990-91	75	525	75	630
3.1L	1992-93	75	525	—	—
3.1L: Cavalier	1994	75	525	—	—
Beretta, Corsica	1994	75	525	75	600
Lumina	1994	75	525	75	690
3.1L: Beretta, Corsica	1995-96	75	600	—	—
Lumina, Monte Carlo	1995-00	78	600	78	690
3.1L, 3.4L Malibu	1999-00	75	600	—	—
3.4L DOHC	1991-97	75	690	—	—
3.4L Camaro	1993-95	75	525	—	—
3.8L Camaro	1995-00	75	690	—	—
Lumina, Monte Carlo	1997-00	75	690	—	—
4.3L (262)	1989-90	75	630	—	—
	1992-94	78	730	—	—
	1995	78	600	—	—
5.0L (305) 4V, TBI	1989-90	70	525	75	570
5.0L TBI	1992-93	75	525	—	—
5.0L (305) MFI	1989-92	75	525	75	570
5.7L (350) Camaro	1989-92	75	630	—	—
	1993-00	75	525	—	—
5.7L (350) Corvette	1989	75	525	—	—
DOHC	1989	75	630	—	—

BATTERY Continued

Engine	Year	STANDARD BCI Group No.	STANDARD Crank. Perf.	OPTIONAL BCI Group No.	OPTIONAL Crank. Perf.
5.7L Corvette	1990-94	75	525	—	—
DOHC	1990-94	75	690	—	—
5.7L Corvette	1995-00	78	600	—	—
DOHC	1995	78	690	—	—
5.7L (350) Caprice	1989-93	78	730	—	—
	1994	78	770	—	—
	1995	78	600	78	770
	1996	75	525	78	770

GENERATOR

Year	Rated Output (amps)	Test Output (amps)	Field Current Draw (amps)
1989	85, 100, 105, 108, 120	1	—
1990-91	74, 80, 85, 100, 105, 120, 124	1	—
1992-00	80, 100, 105, 124, 140	1	—

1 Output at 2000 rpm must be within 15 amps of rated output.

REGULATOR

Application	Test Temp. (deg. F/C)	Voltage Setting
1989-95	Warm	13.5-16.0
1996-00	Warm	13.0-16.0

STARTER

Engine	Year	Cranking Voltage (min volts)	Ampere Draw @ Cranking Speed
All	1989-00	9.0	—

UNDERHOOD SERVICE SPECIFICATIONS

CTTU3

CTTU3

SPARK PLUGS

Engine	Year	Gap (inches)	Gap (mm)	Torque (ft-lb)
4-cyl.				
1.6L, 2.0L, 2.2L	1989-91	.035	.89	11
2.2L	1992-93	.045	1.14	11
	1994-00	.060	1.52	13
2.3L	1989-94	.035	.89	17
	1995	.060	1.52	17
2.4L	1996-00	.060	1.52	13
2.5L (151)	1989-92	.060	1.52	11
V6				
2.8L (173)	1989	.045	1.14	7-15
3.1L	1990-94	.045	1.14	11
Code M, J	1994-00	.060	1.52	11
3.4L	1991-97	.045	1.14	11
3.8L	1995-00	.060	1.52	11
4.3L (262)	1989-93	.035	.89	11
V8 ex. 5.0L (307)	1989-91	.035	.89	22
5.0L (307)	1989-90	.060	1.52	20
V8: 4.3L	1994-96	.050	1.26	15
5.7L Code P	1992-97	.050	1.26	11
5.7L Code J	1989-95	.050	1.26	11
All Others	1992-93	.035	.89	11
5.7L	1998-00	.060	1.52	11

IGNITION COIL
FOR TESTING AND ADJUSTMENT DIAGRAMS, SEE APPENDIX A.

Winding Resistance (ohms at 75°F or 24°C)

Engine	Year	Windings	Resistance (ohms)
All w/distributor	1989-92	Primary	0-2
		Secondary	6000-30,000
2.0L, 2.5L, 2.8L, 3.1L, 3.4L	1989-95	Secondary	5000-10,000[1]
2.2L	1993	Secondary	5000-10,000[1]
	1994-00	Secondary	5000-8000[1]
2.3L	1989-95	Secondary	10,000 max.[1]
2.4L	1996-00	Secondary	5000-8000
3.1L, 3.4L	1996	Secondary	5000-7000
3.8L	1995-96	Secondary	5000-7000
4.3L, 5.0L, 5.7L TBI	1993	Primary	0.3-0.5
		Secondary	7000-9000
5.7L DOHC	1989-95	Primary	.35-1.45[2]
		Secondary	5000-6500[1]

1 Measured across each coil's towers with coil removed from vehicle.
2 Measured between A terminal of 2-pin connector and each terminal on 4-pin connector.

DISTRIBUTOR PICKUP
FOR TESTING AND ADJUSTMENT DIAGRAMS, SEE APPENDIX B.

Application	Year	Resistance (ohms)	Air Gap (in./mm)
All	1989-93	500-1500	—

BASE TIMING
FOR TESTING AND ADJUSTMENT DIAGRAMS, SEE APPENDIX C.

Set timing at slow idle and Before Top Dead Center, unless otherwise specified.

5.0L (307), ground diagnostic terminal of DLC

All models w/distributor & FI, disconnect timing connector, single wire connector in engine harness between distributor and ECM.

Timing MUST be set to specifications on emission label, if different from setting listed. If "Check Engine" light comes on during procedure, remove ECM fuse to clear.

Engine	Year	Man. Trans. (degrees) @ RPM	Auto. Trans. (degrees) @ RPM
2.8L (173) Camaro	1989	10	10 D
3.1L Camaro	1990-92	10	10 D
4.3L (262)	1989-93	—	0 D
5.0L (305) TBI	1989-93	0	0 D
5.0L (305) MFI	1989-92	6	6 D
5.0L (307)	1989-90	—	20 @ 1100 P
5.7L (350) MFI ex. DOHC	1989-92	6	6 D
5.7L TBI	1989-93	—	0 D

FUEL SYSTEM

FUEL SYSTEM PRESSURE
FOR TESTING AND ADJUSTMENT DIAGRAMS, SEE APPENDIX D.
Carbureted models, pinch off fuel return line.
All models with TBI, pressure measured at fuel inlet of TBI unit.
All models with MFI, pressure measured at fuel rail.

CARBURETED & TBI, DIESEL

Engine	Year	PSI	RPM
4-cyl.			
2.0L (122) 2.2L	1989-93	9.0-13.0	ign. on
		13 min.	idle
2.5L (151) ex. Lumina	1990	9.0-13.0	ign. on
	1989-90	13 min.[1]	idle
2.5L Lumina	1990-92	26-32	idle
6-cyl.			
4.3L (262)	1989-93	9-13	idle
		13 min.[1]	idle
8-cyl.			
5.0L (307, 4V)	1989	5.5-6.5	idle
5.0L (305), 5.7L TBI	1989-93	9-13	ign. on
		13 min.[1]	idle

1 With fuel return line briefly restricted.

GASOLINE MFI

Engine	Year	Pressure (PSI) Ing. On	Pressure (PSI) Idle	Fuel Pump[1]
2.2L, 2.3L, 2.4L	1989-00	40.5-47	30.5-44	47 min.
2.8L (173), 3.1L	1989-00	40.5-47	30.5-44	47 min.
3.1L Flex. fuel	1993-94	48-55	38-52	—
3.4L	1991-95	40.5-47	30.5-44	47 min.
	1996	48-55	38-52	55 min.
	1997-00	41-47	31-44	47 min.
3.8L	1995-96	48-55	38-52	55 min.
4.3L	1994-96	40.5-47	30.5-44	47 min.
5.0L (305)	1989-92	40.5-47	30.5-44	60 min.
5.7L (350) ex. DOHC	1989-00	40.5-47	30.5-44	47 min.
5.7L DOHC	1989-95	48-55	38-52	55 min.

1 With fuel return line briefly restricted.

IDLE SPEED W/COMPUTER CONTROL
FOR TESTING AND ADJUSTMENT DIAGRAMS, SEE APPENDIX E.

Midpoint of range given is the preferred setting speed.

1989-92 All w/FI & TBI when specifications appear in Minimum Speed column:
Ground diagnostic lead and turn ignition on for 30 seconds. Remove IAC electrical lead and remove ground from diagnostic connector. Start engine and set minimum speed to specified value.

All carbureted w/ILC: Disconnect and plug vacuum hoses at EGR and canister purge valves. With engine at operating temperature, remove vacuum hose from ILC and plug. Set maximum speed to specified value by holding hex nut and turning plunger shaft. Reconnect ILC vacuum hose and check to see that minimum speed is at specified value. To adjust, remove rubber and metal plugs from rear center outlet tube, insert a ³/₃₂" Allen wrench. Remove ILC hose and plug. Connect a remote vacuum source and apply vacuum to the unit. Adjust carb base screw to obtain specified shutdown value.

ALL FUEL INJECTED

Engine	Year	Minimum Speed Man. Trans.	Minimum Speed Auto. Trans.	Checking Speed Man. Trans.	Checking Speed Auto. Trans.
2.0L (122)	1989	450-650	450-650 N	—	—
2.2L	1990-91	450-650	450-650 N	—	—
	1992	—	—	525-675	525-675 N
2.2L: Cavalier	1993	—	—	825-975	800-950 N
Beretta, Corsica	1993	—	—	825-975	525-675 N
Lumina	1993	—	—	675-775	675-775 N
2.5L (151)	1989-92	550-650	550-650 N	800[1] max.	800 N[1] max.
2.8L ex. Camaro	1989	—	—	750-950	650-750 D
Camaro	1989	600-700	500-600 D		
3.1L	1990	—	—	750-950	650-750 D
Camaro	1990	—	—	800[1] max.	800 N[1] max.
3.1L ex. SFI & VFV, 3.4L DOHC	1991-93	—	—	800-900	700-800 N

UNDERHOOD SERVICE SPECIFICATIONS

IDLE SPEED W/COMPUTER CONTROL Continued

ALL FUEL INJECTED Continued

Engine	Year	Minimum Speed Man. Trans.	Minimum Speed Auto. Trans.	Checking Speed Man. Trans.	Checking Speed Auto. Trans.
3.4L Camaro	1993	—	—	800[1]	600-700 D
	1994-95	—	—	800[1]	800 N[1]
3.4L DOHC	1994-95	—	—	650-750	650-750 N
	1996-97	—	—	600-700	600-700 N
4.3L (262)	1989	—	400-450 N	—	—
	1990	—	—	—	500-600 D
	1989	400-450	400-450 N	—	—
	1990-91	—	—	600-800	600-800 N
5.0L (305) TBI	1989	400-450	400-450 N	—	—
	1990-92	—	—	550-750	500-600 D
5.7L MFI ex. DOHC	1989	—	400-450 N	—	—
5.7L MFI ex. DOHC	1990-92	—	—	600-800	600-800 N
5.7L TBI	1989	450-500 N	—	—	—
5.7L TBI	1990-92	—	—	—	500-600 D

1 With ISC fully seated.

ALL CARBURETED

Engine	Year	Trans.	Min. Speed	Max. Speed	Fast	Step of Cam
5.0L (307)	1989-90	AT	450 D	700 D	550 D	Low
base idle	1989-90	AT	450 D	—	—	—

ENGINE MECHANICAL

TIGHTENING TORQUES

FOR CYLINDER HEAD TORQUE SEQUENCES AND DIAGRAMS, SEE APPENDIX F.

Some fasteners are tightened in more than one step.

Engine	Year	TORQUE FOOT-POUNDS/NEWTON METERS Cylinder Head	Intake Manifold	Exhaust Manifold	Crankshaft Pulley	Water Pump
2.0L (122)	1989	73-83/ 99-113[1], 62-70/ 85-95[2]	15-22/ 20-30	6-13/ 8-18	66-89/ 90-120	15-22/ 20-30
2.2L	1990	41/55, +45°, +45°, +20°[1], +10°[2]	18/25	10/13	85/115	18/25
2.2L	1991	43/58[2], 46/63[1], +90°	18/25	10/13	77/105	22/30
2.2L	1992-00	43/58[2], 46/63[1], +90°	22/30[10]	115"/13	77/105	22/30[2], 18/25[1]
2.3L	1989-95	[3]	18/25	31/42, nuts 106"/12, studs	74/100, +90°	10/12, cover 19/26, others
2.4L	1996-00	[11]	17/24	110"/113	129/175, +90°	124"/14,cover 19/26, others
2.5L	1989-92	18/25, 26/35[7], +90°	25/34	25/43[4], 37-50[6]	162/220	25/34
2.8L	1989	33/45, +90°	15/20, 24/33	20-30/ 15-22	76/103	7/10, short 18/24, long
3.1L Code M, T ex. Camaro	1990-95	33/45, +90°	15/20, 24/33	21/28	75/102	88"/10
	1996-99	33/45, +90°	18/25, upper 116"/13, lower	12/16	75/102	89"/10
3.1L Camaro	1990-92	40/55, +90°	15/21[8], 19/26[9]	25/34	70/95	88"/10[2], 25/34[1]
3.4L Camaro	1993-95	41/55, +90°	18/25, upper 22/30, lower	18/25	58/79	88"/10[2], 33/45[1]

TIGHTENING TORQUES Continued

Engine	Year	TORQUE FOOT-POUNDS/NEWTON METERS Cylinder Head	Intake Manifold	Exhaust Manifold	Crankshaft Pulley	Water Pump
3.4L DOHC	1991-94	37/50, +90°	18/25	116"/13	37/50[2], 78/105[1]	89"/10
	1995-97	44/60, +90°, +90°, +90°[5]	18/25	116"/13, nut 13/17, stud	37/50[2], 78/105[1]	97"/12
3.8L	1995-00	37/50, +130°[12]	11/15	107"/12	110/150, +76°	11/15, +80°
4.3L, 5.0L, 5.7L ex. Code P, J	1989-93	68/93	124"/14, 35/47	20/27[4], 26/35[6]	70/95	30/40
4.3L	1994-95	65/88	71"/8, 35/48	26/35	75/102	31/42
	1996	22/30, 13, 14	71"/8, 35/48	30/40	74/100	33/45
5.0L (307)	1989-90	40/54 +95°, first and last bolts on exhaust manifold side +120°, all others	40/54	25/34	200-310/ 270-400	11/14[2] 22/30[1]
5.7L ex. DOHC	1989-92	68/93	35/47	20/27[4], 26/35[6]	70/95	30/40
5.7L Code P	1992-95	65/88	71"/8, 35/48	20/35	75/102	88"/10[2] 35/47[1]
	1996	22/30, 13, 15	71"/8, 35/48	30/40	74/100	33/45
	1997	22/30[15]	37/50	30/40	74/100	33/45
5.7L DOHC	1989-95	45/60, 74/100, 118/160	20/26	11/15	148/200	20/26

1 Long bolts.
2 Short bolts. Medium bolts, if equipped, 16/21.
3 Tighten bolts 1-8 (long bolts), 30/40. Tighten bolts 9-10 (short bolts), 26/35. Then, turn all bolts 90°.
4 Four outer bolts.
5 Camaro, Corvette: After tightening all bolts to initial value, turn short bolts 67°. Turn medium and long bolts 80°.
6 Three inner bolts.
7 Turn last bolt on left (number nine) to 18/25.
8 Center two.
9 Others.
10 Upper manifold. Lower manifold: studs, 89"/10; nuts, 24/33.
11 Tighten bolts 1-8, 40/65. Tighten bolts 9-10, 30-40. Then, turn all bolts 90°.
12 Turn four center bolts an additional 30°.
13 Impala, Caprice: After tightening all bolts to initial value, turn short bolts 55°; medium bolts 65°; long bolts 75°.

COMPRESSION PRESSURE

At cranking speed or specified rpm, engine temperature normalized, throttle open.

Engine	Year	PSI	Maximum Variation PSI
All	1989-00	100 min.	[1]

1 Lowest cylinder pressure must be more than 70% of highest cylinder pressure.

BELT TENSION

1989-90: A belt in operation 3 minutes is considered used.

Use a strand tension gauge. Measurements are in pounds.

Engine	Year	Generator	Power Steering	Air Cond.	Air Pump
Used Belts					
2.3L	1989-94	—	110	—	—
5.0L (307)	1989-90	80	90	90	45
Cogged or 3/8" belt	1989-90	55	—	—	70
New Belts					
2.3L	1989-94	—	110	—	—
5.0L (307)	1989-90	160	170	170	80
Cogged or 3/8" belt	1989-90	145	—	—	145

UNDERHOOD SERVICE SPECIFICATIONS

CTTU5

CTTU5

BELT TENSION Continued
All With Automatic Tensioner

If index marks on tensioner are outside the range, replace the belt. If marks are within range, and belt tension is below specified value, replace tensioner.

Engine	Year	Tension
2.0L, 2.2L	1989-92	67-77
2.2L	1993-96	63-77
2.3L, 2.4L	1989-96	50 min.
2.5L	1989-92	50-70
2.8L FWD	1989	50-70
2.8L Camaro	1989	116-142
W/AC	1989	103/127
3.1L FWD	1989-97	50-70
3.1L Camaro	1990	116-142
W/AC	1990	103-127
3.1L Camaro	1991-92	95-140
W/AC	1991-92	85-110
3.4L	1996-97	35-55
4.3L	1992-93	105-125
5.0L, 5.7L	1989-91	99-121
5.0L, 5.7L	1992-93	105-125
5.7L Corvette	1991	60-90
5.7L Corvette	1989-90	120-140

SERPENTINE BELT DIAGRAMS Continued

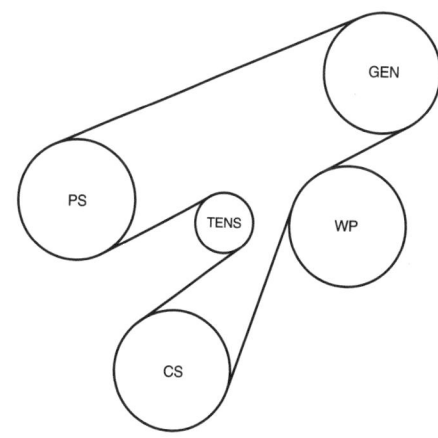

1989-92 2.5L
Code R w/o AC

SERPENTINE BELT DIAGRAMS

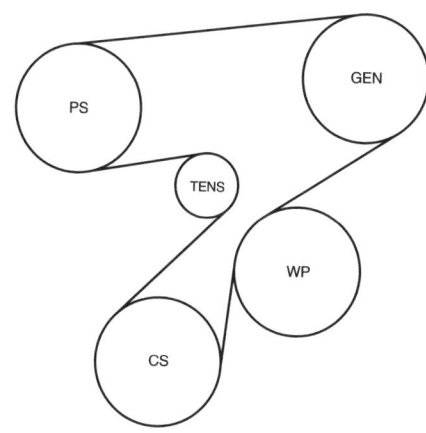

1989 2.0L Code 1
1990-00 2.2L Code G, 4 w/o AC

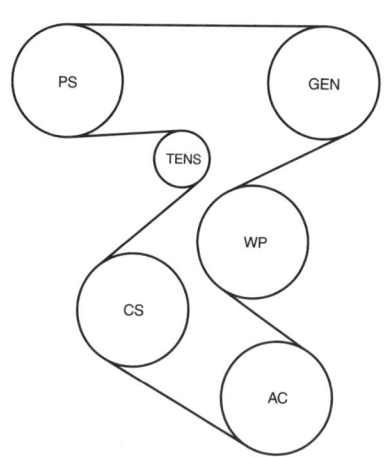

1989 2.0L Code 1
1990-00 2.2L Code G, 4 w/AC

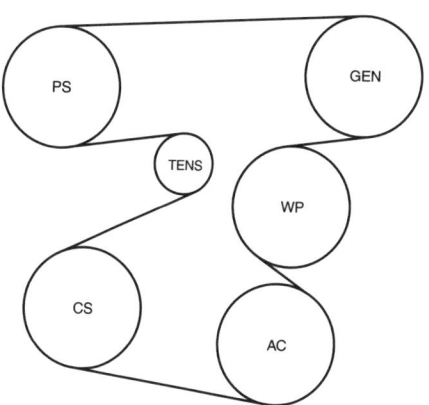

1989-92 2.5L
Code R w/AC

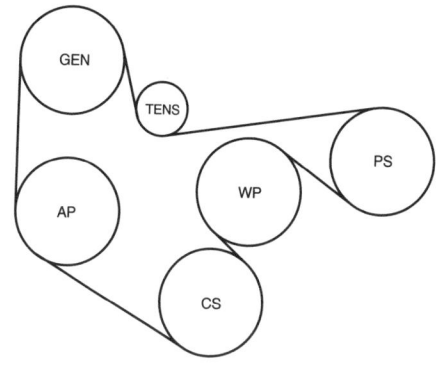

1989 2.8L
Camaro w/MT, w/o AC

273

CHEVROLET
1989-2000 All Models Except Geo, Sprint, Lumina APV, Venture

SERPENTINE BELT DIAGRAMS Continued

SERPENTINE BELT DIAGRAMS Continued

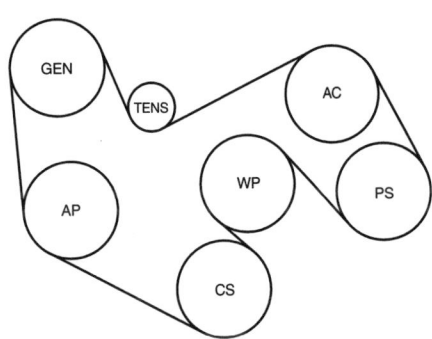

1989 2.8L
Camaro w/AT, w/o AC

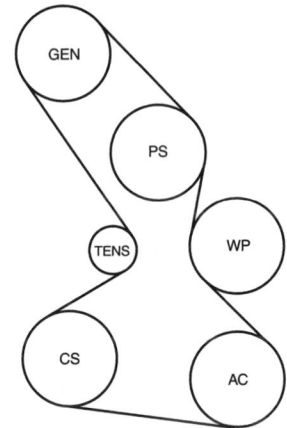

1989-98 2.8L, 3.1L FWD
Code W, T, M, D
1996-00 3.4L

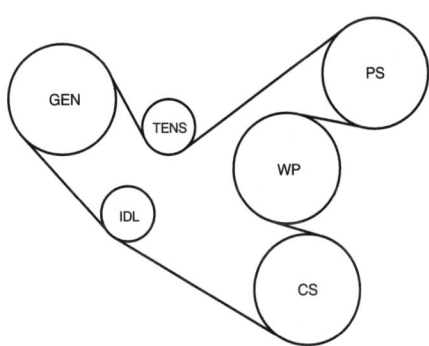

1989 2.8L
Camaro w/MT, w/o AC

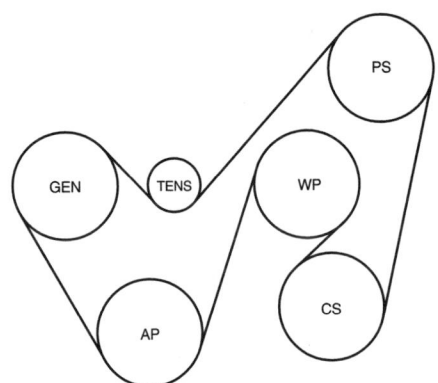

1990-92 3.1L
Camaro w/o AC

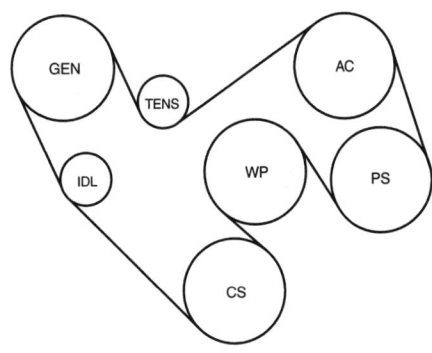

1989
Camaro w/MT & AC

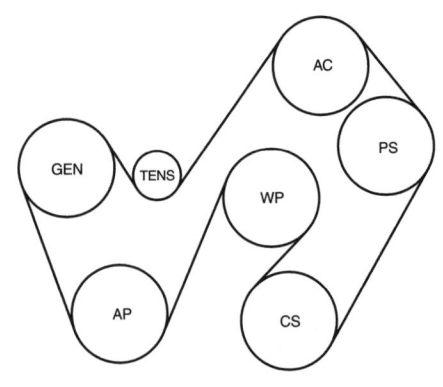

1990-92 3.1L
Camaro w/AC

SERPENTINE BELT DIAGRAMS Continued

SERPENTINE BELT DIAGRAMS Continued

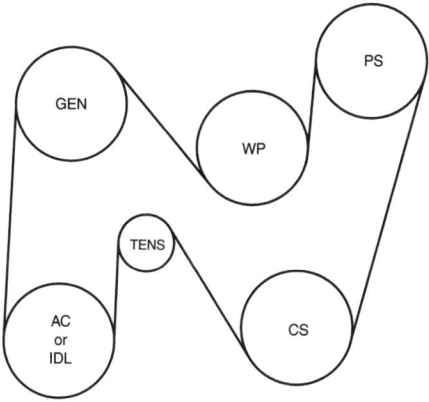

1991-97 3.4L DOHC

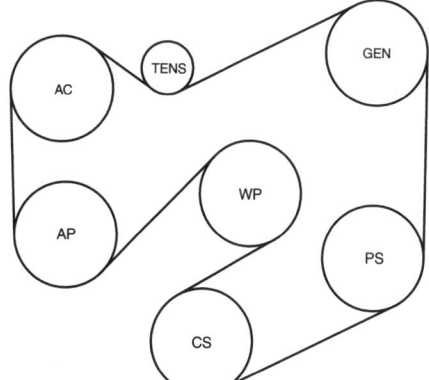

1989-93 5.0L, 5.7L
Code E, F, 7, 8

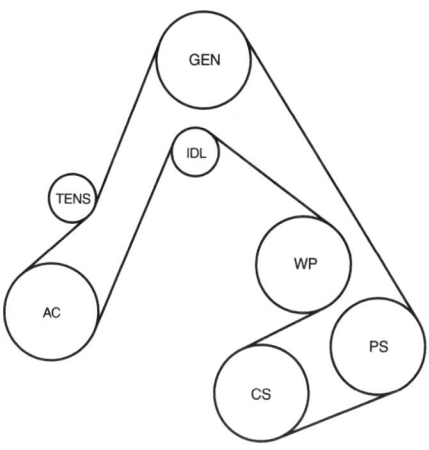

1993-95 3.4L
Camaro

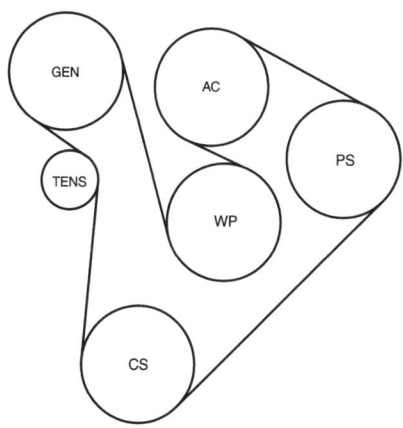

1989-96 5.7L DOHC Code J
Corvette

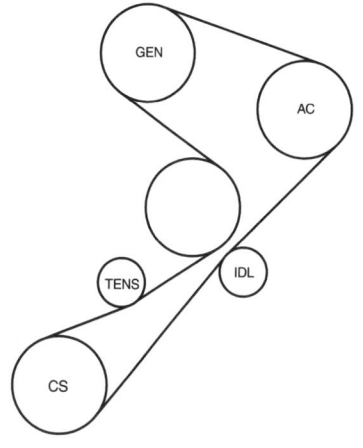

1995-00 3.8L
Camaro

1992-96 5.7L Code P
Corvette

SERPENTINE BELT DIAGRAMS Continued

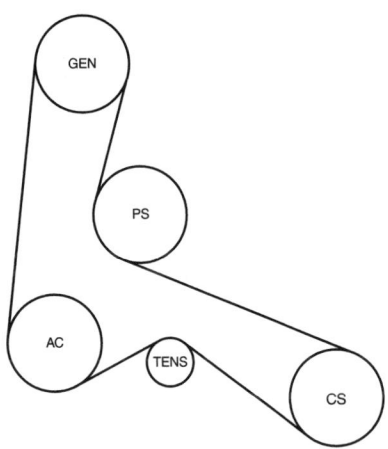

*1993-97 5.7L Code P
ex. Corvette*

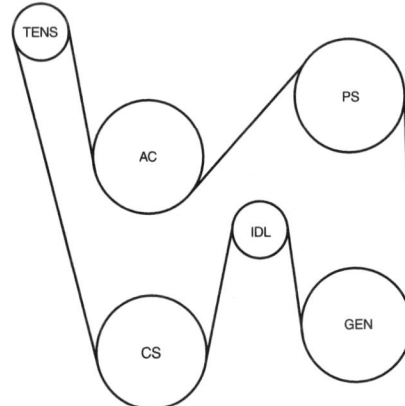

*1997-00 5.7L Code G
Camaro-Outer Belt*

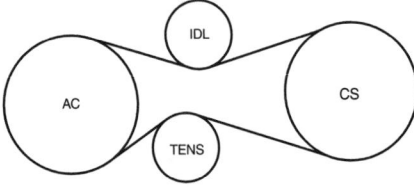

*1997-00 5.7L Code G
Camaro-Inner Belt*

ENGINE COMPUTER SYSTEM

FOR TESTING AND ADJUSTMENT DIAGRAMS, SEE APPENDIX G.
DIAGNOSTIC TROUBLE CODES
See UNDERHOOD SERVICE INSTRUCTIONS at the beginning of this section for test/adjustment diagrams.

1989-95 All w/12-pin DLC:
Connect a jumper between A and B terminals on under dash connector (two upper right-hand cavities of the two row connector). Turn ignition switch on. Code 12 will flash three times, then codes in memory will be displayed. Do not run engine with jumper connected.

Remove the ECM fuse for a minimum of ten seconds to clear memory.

DIAGNOSTIC TROUBLE CODES Continued

1994-00 All w/16-pin DLC, OBD-II:
A Scan tool is required to retrieve codes and code definitions.

1989-95 All w/12-pin DLC:
Code 12 No tach signal to ECM
Code 13 Oxygen sensor circuit
Code 14 Coolant sensor circuit shorted
Code 15 Coolant sensor circuit open
Code 16 Electronic ignition system or Opti-Spark ignition circuit
Code 18 Injector circuit (V8)
Code 19 Intermittent 7X reference circuit
Code 21 Throttle position sensor voltage high, circuit open
Code 22 Throttle position sensor voltage low, circuit shorted
Code 23 Open or grounded MC solenoid (carbureted)
Code 23 Intake air temperature circuit open
Code 24 Vehicle speed sensor circuit
Code 25 Intake air temperature, high temperature indicated
Code 26 Canister purge solenoid (V8)
Code 27 EGR vacuum control solenoid circuit (V8)
Code 28 Transmission range pressure switch (V8)
Codes 26, 27, 28 Quad driver circuit (others)
Code 29 Secondary air pump circuit
Code 31 Camshaft position sensor (FI)
Code 31 EVAP canister purge solenoid (carbureted)
Code 32 Barometric or altitude sensor (carbureted)
Code 32 EGR failure (FI)
Code 32 EGR vacuum control (MFI)
Code 33 MAP, MAF sensor circuit open
Code 34 MAP, MAF sensor circuit shorted
Code 34 Vacuum sensor circuit (carbureted)
Code 35 Idle speed or idle air control circuit
Code 36 MAF burn off circuit (ex. 1990-95 Corvette)
Code 36 Electronic ignition system or Opti-Spark ignition circuit (1990-95 Corvette)
Code 37 Transmission brake switch error
Code 39 Transaxle clutch switch circuit
Code 41 No distributor reference pulses to ECM (1989-90 carbureted)
Code 41 Ignition control timing circuit problem (Camaro V6, all V8)
Code 41 Cylinder select error (1994-95)
Code 42 Ignition control or ignition control bypass circuit grounded or open
Code 43 Knock sensor signal
Code 44 Air/fuel mixture lean (left on Corvette V8)
Codes 44 & 45 Faulty oxygen sensor
Code 45 Air/fuel mixture rich (left on V8 DOHC)
Code 46 No vehicle anti-theft signal
Code 47 Knock sensor module missing
Code 48 Mass air flow sensor circuit
Code 50 System voltage low
Code 51 EEPROM programming error (V8)
Code 51 Faulty PROM, MEM-CAL, ECM or installation (1989-93 others)
Code 51 Faulty or incorrect EPROM (1994-95)
Code 52 Fuel CALPAK (ex. Corvette)
Code 52 Oil temperature sensor (Corvette)
Code 53 EGR vacuum sensor vacuum incorrect (carbureted)
Code 53 Generator voltage out of range (FI ex. 5.0L TBI)
Code 53 Vehicle anti-theft circuit (5.0L TBI)
Code 54 Fuel pump circuit (FI)
Code 54 Faulty MC solenoid or faulty ECM (carbureted)
Code 55 Grounded V-REF, faulty oxygen sensor, ECM (ex. V8 DOHC)
Code 55 Fuel lean monitor (Corvette)
Code 56 Manifold differential pressure sensor circuit
Code 58 Transmission fluid temperature sensor circuit shorted
Code 59 Transmission fluid temperature sensor circuit open
Code 61 Degraded oxygen sensor (ex. Corvette)
Code 61 Secondary part throttle valve system (Corvette)
Code 62 Transaxle switch circuit (ex. Corvette)
Code 62 Engine oil temperature sensor (Corvette)
Code 63 MAP sensor voltage high (ex. Corvette)
Code 63 Right side oxygen sensor, circuit open (Corvette & 1994-95 V8)
Code 64 MAP sensor voltage low (ex. DOHC)
Code 64 Right side oxygen sensor, lean (Corvette & 1994-95 V8)
Code 65 Right side oxygen sensor, rich (Corvette & 1994-95 V8)
Code 65 Fuel injector circuit (others)
Code 66 A/C pressure sensor
Code 67 A/C pressure sensor or clutch circuit (V8 Code P)
Code 68 A/C relay circuit (V8 Code P)
Code 69 A/C clutch circuit (V8 Code P)
Code 70 A/C clutch relay driver (V8)
Code 70 A/C pressure sensor (Camaro V6)
Code 72 Gear selector switch (1989-93)

DIAGNOSTIC TROUBLE CODES Continued

Code 72 Vehicle speed sensor (1994-95)
Code 73 A/C evaporator temperature sensor circuit shorted (Camaro V6)
Code 73 Transmission pressure control solenoid circuit (V8)
Code 74 Traction control system circuit
Code 75 Transmission system voltage low (V8)
Code 75 Digital EGR #1 solenoid (others)
Code 76 Digital EGR #2 solenoid (others)
Code 77 Cooling fan relay (V8)
Code 77 Digital EGR #3 solenoid (others)
Code 78 Secondary cooling fan relay
Code 79 Transmission fluid over temperature
Code 80 Transmission converter clutch slippage excessive
Code 81 Transmission 2-3 shift
Code 82 Transmission 1-2 shift (V8)
Code 82 Ignition control 3X circuit (others)
Code 83 Reverse inhibit system
Code 84 Transmission 3-2 control
Code 85 Transmission converter clutch locked on (V8)
Code 85 Faulty or incorrect PROM (others)
Code 86 A/D chip error
Code 87 EEPROM error
Code 90 Transmission clutch solenoid circuit error
Code 91 Skip shift lamp circuit
Code 93 Vehicle speed sensor output circuit (Camaro V8)
Code 93 Transmission pressure control solenoid (others)
Code 95 Change oil lamp circuit
Code 96 Low oil lamp circuit (Impala, Caprice)
Code 96 Transmission system voltage low (others)
Code 97 Vehicle speed sensor output circuit
Code 98 Invalid PCM program
Code 99 Tach output circuit (Camaro V8)
Code 99 Invalid PCM program (others)

SENSORS, INPUT

TEMPERATURE SENSORS

Engine	Year	Sensor	Resistance Ohms @ deg. F/C
All	1989-90 1989-91	Coolant Intake Air[1]	13,500 @ 20/–7 7500 @ 40/4 3400 @ 70/20 1800 @ 100/38 450 @ 160/70 185 @ 210/100
All	1991-00 1992-00 1992-00	Coolant Intake Air[1] 5.7L Engine Oil	28,700 @ –4/–20 12,300 @ 23/–5 7280 @ 41/5 3500 @ 68/20 1460 @ 104/40 467 @ 158/70 177 @ 212/100
All	1994-00	Transmission Oil[1]	25,809-28,617 @ –4 (–20) 14,558-16,176 @ 14 (–10) 8481-10,365 @ 32 (0) 3164-3867 @ 68 (20) 1308-1609 @ 104 (40) 420-514 @ 158 (70) 159-195 @ 212 (100) 69-85 @ 266 (130)

1 As equipped, not used on all engines. Specifications also apply to V8 DOHC temperature sensor.

MANIFOLD ABSOLUTE, VACUUM, AND BAROMETRIC PRESSURE SENSORS

Engines may use one, or a combination of these sensors. All sensors appear the same. Manifold Absolute Pressure sensors have a vacuum line connected between the unit and manifold vacuum. On Barometric Pressure sensors, the line is not used and the connector is either open or has a filter installed over it. Pressure sensors also have a vacuum line between the sensor and intake manifold and appear only on carbureted models.

Barometric Pressure Sensors: Measure voltage with ignition on and engine off.

Manifold Absolute Pressure Sensors: Measure voltage with ignition on and engine off. Start engine and apply 10 in./Hg. (34 kPa) to unit, voltage should be: 1.5 volts minimum less.

Pressure Sensors: Measure voltage as indicated. 5 volts reference.

SENSORS, INPUT Continued

MANIFOLD ABSOLUTE, VACUUM, AND BAROMETRIC PRESSURE SENSORS Cont.

Engine	Year	Sensor	Voltage @ Altitude/Condition
All, as equipped	1989-90	Barometric	3.8-5.5 @ 0-1000 3.6-5.3 @ 1000-2000 3.5-5.1 @ 2000-3000 3.3-5.0 @ 3000-4000 3.2-4.8 @ 4000-5000 3.0-4.6 @ 5000-6000 2.9-4.5 @ 6000-7000 2.5-4.3 @ 7000

Engine	Year	Sensor	Voltage @ Condition
All, as equipped	1989-00	Manifold Absolute	1.0-2.0 @ idle 4.0-4.8 @ WOT
5.0L 4V	1989-90	Vacuum	.50-.64 @ ign. on 1.7-3.0[1]

1 10 in. Hg. (34 kPa) applied to unit.

CRANKSHAFT POSITION SENSORS
Resistance is measured at room temperature.

Engine	Year	Resistance (ohms)
2.0L, 2.8L, 3.1L, 3.4L	1989-95	900-1200
2.2L	1991-95	900-1200
2.3L, 2.4L	1989-96	500-900
2.5L	1989-92	800-900
5.7L DOHC	1989-95	800-1200

THROTTLE POSITION SENSOR (TPS)
Verify that minimum idle is at specified value.
Make all checks/adjustments with engine at operating temperature.

Carbureted Models: Remove aluminum plug covering the adjustment screw. Remove the screw and connect a digital voltmeter to black wire (-) and either of the other two colored wires (+). If voltage is approximately 5 volts, this is the reference voltage lead. Connect DVOM to other wire in this case. Apply thread locking compound to the screw and with ignition on and engine not running (as applies), quickly adjust screw to obtain specified voltage at indicated condition.

Fuel Injected Models: Disconnect harness connector from TPS. Using three six-inch jumper wires reconnect harness to TPS. With ignition on and engine not running (as applies), connect a digital voltmeter to black wire (-) and either of the other two colored wires (+). If voltage is approximately 5 volts, this is the reference voltage lead. Connect DVOM to other wire in this case. Check reading against specified value. If TPS is adjustable, loosen the unit retaining screws and rotate the unit to reach specified value.

Engine	Year	TPS Voltage[1] Idle	WOT (approx.)
2.0L, 2.2L	1989-94	.33-1.33	4.0 min.
	1995-00	.20-.90	4.0 min.
2.3L	1989-93	.36-.96	4.0 min.
	1994-95	.20-.90	4.5 min.
2.4L	1996-00	.20-.90	4.0 min.
2.5L (151)	1989-92	.20-1.25	4.5
2.8L, 3.1L Camaro	1989	.29-.98	4.8
3.1L	1989	.55	—
	1990-95	.29-.98	4.8
	1996-00	.20-.74	4.0 min.
3.4L DOHC	1991-94	.29-.98	4.8
	1995-97	.20-.74	4.0 min.
3.8L	1995-00	.20-.74	4.0 min.
4.3L (262)	1989-90	.20-1.25	5.0
4.3L	1992	.20-.95	4.0 min.
	1994	.36-.96	4.0 min.
	1995-96	.30-.90	4.0 min.
5.0L (305) MFI	1989	.54	—
5.0L MFI	1990-91	.20-.96	5.0
5.0L MFI	1992	.36-.62	5.0
5.0L TBI	1989	.20-1.25	5.0
5.0L TBI	1990-91	.45-1.25	5.0
5.0L TBI	1992-93	.20-.95	4.0 min.
5.0L MFI	1990-91	.36-.96	4.6
5.0L (307)	1989-90	.41	—
5.7L (350) Corvette, Camaro	1989	.54	—
5.7L MFI	1990	.20-.96	4.6

CHEVROLET
1989-2000 All Models Except Geo, Sprint, Lumina APV, Venture

SENSORS, INPUT Continued
THROTTLE POSITION SENSOR (TPS) Continued

Engine	Year	TPS Voltage[1] Idle	TPS Voltage[1] WOT (approx.)
5.7L MFI	1991	.36-.96	5.0
5.7L Camaro	1992	.36-.62	5.0
Corvette	1992	.30-.90	4.8
5.7L MFI Code P	1993-94	.36-.96	4.0 min.
	1995	.30-.90	4.5 min.
Ex. Camaro	1996	.30-.90	4.0 min.
Camaro	1996	.36-.96	4.0 min.
5.7L Code P	1997-00	.36-.96	4.0 min.
5.7L DOHC	1989-90	.54	5.0
5.7L DOHC	1991-95	.23-59	5.0
5.7L Police	1989	.20-1.25	5.0
5.7L Police	1990-91	.45-1.25	5.0
5.7L TBI	1992-93	.20-.95	4.0 min.

1 ±.10 carbureted, rpm ±.05 fuel injected engines.

KNOCK SENSOR

Engine	Year	Resistance (ohms)
2.2L, 2.3L, 2.4L	1994-00	90,000-110,000
3.1L, 3.4L	1992-95	3300-4500
	1996-00	100,000 approx.
4.3L, 5.7L	1994-95	3300-4500
	1996-00	90,000-110,000

ACTUATORS, OUTPUT
IDLE SPEED CONTROL

All engines with ISC.

Measured between terminals A & B and C & D.

Engine	Year	Resistance (ohms)
2.8L Celebrity	1989	48-58
All Other TBI & MFI	1989	20 min.
All TBI & MFI	1990-00	40-80
DOHC V8	1990	20 min.
All carbureted	1989-90	10 min.

ACTUATORS, OUTPUT Continued
FUEL INJECTORS

Engine	Year	Resistance (ohms)	Temperature (deg. F/C)
2.0L	1989	1.6 min.	—
2.2L	1990-91	1.6 min.	—
	1992-95	11.6-12.4	68/20
	1996-00	11.8-12.6	—
2.3L	1989-93	1.9-2.1	140/68
	1994-95	1.9-2.15	—
2.4L	1996-00	1.9-2.3	—
2.5L	1989	1.2 min.	—
	1990-92	1.6 min.	—
2.8L	1989-89	8 min.	—
3.1L: Lumina	1990-93	12.0-12.4	—
Camaro	1992	11.8-12.6	—
All others	1990-93	8 min.	—
3.1L, 3.4L	1994-00	11.8-12.6	—
3.4L	1992-93	12.0-12.4	—
4.3L	1989-93	1.2 min.	—
	1994-96	11.8-12.6	—
5.0L, 5.7L TBI	1989-93	1.2 min.	—
5.0L, 5.7L MFI	1989-93	10 min.	—
	1994-00	11.8-12.6	—

MIXTURE CONTROL SOLENOID-CARBURETED ENGINES

On some engines, the ECM will be damaged if the resistance of the mixture control solenoid is less than specified.

Engine	Year	Resistance (ohms)
All	1989-90	10 min.

CHEK-CHART

CHEVROLET, GMC TRUCKS
1989-2000 All Models Includes Chevrolet Lumina
APV/Minivan, Venture, Oldsmobile Bravada & Silhouette; Pontiac Trans Sport; Isuzu Hombre

ENGINE IDENTIFICATION

To identify any engine by the manufacturer's code, follow the four steps designated by the numbered blocks.

1 MODEL YEAR IDENTIFICATION: Refer to illustration of the Vehicle Identification Number (V.I.N.). The year is indicated by a code letter which is the 10th character of the V.I.N.

2 ENGINE CODE LOCATION: Refer to illustration of V.I.N. plate for location and designation of engine code.

3 ENGINE CODE: In the "CODE" column, find the engine code determined in Step 2.

4 ENGINE IDENTIFICATION: On the line where the engine code appears, read to the right to identify the engine.

V.I.N. PLATE LOCATION:

All except Forward Control (P) Models — V.I.N. plate is attached to top left of instrument panel and viewed from outside through windshield.

Forward Control (P) Models — V.I.N. plate is attached to front of dash and toe panel.

Model year of vehicle:
2000 — Y
1999 — X
1998 — W
1997 — V
1996 — T
1995 — S
1994 — R
1993 — P
1992 — N
1991 — M
1990 — L
1989 — K

MODEL YEAR AND ENGINE IDENTIFICATION:

1GCEC14E4XF100001

2 ENGINE CODE (8th character)

1 MODEL YEAR (10th character)

4 ENGINE IDENTIFICATION

YEAR	3 ENGINE CODE	CYL.	DISPL. liters	cu. in.	Fuel System	HP
1999-00	4	4	2.2	133	MFI	120
	E	6	3.4	204	MFI	185
	W	6	4.3	262	MFI	180-200[1]
	X	6	4.3	262	MFI	175, 180[1]
	V	8	4.8	293	MFI	255
	M	8	5.0	305	MFI	220-230[1]
	T	8	5.3	325	MFI	270
	R	8	5.7	350	MFI	235-255[1]
	U	8	6.0	368	MFI	300
	F	8	6.5 D	395 D	MFI	195-215[1]
	S	8	6.5 D	395 D	MFI	180-200[1]
	J	8	7.4	454	MFI	290
1998	4	4	2.2	133	MFI	120
	E	6	3.4	204	MFI	180
	W	6	4.3	262	MFI	190-200
	X	6	4.3	262	MFI	175, 180
	M	8	5.0	305	MFI	220-230
	R	8	5.7	350	MFI	235-255
	S	8	6.5 D	395 D	MFI	180
	F	8	6.5 D	395 D	MFI	190
	J	8	7.4	454	MFI	290
1997	4	4	2.2	133	MFI	118
	E	6	3.4	204	MFI	185
	W	6	4.3	262	MFI	190
	X	6	4.3	262	MFI	175, 180
	M	8	5.0	305	MFI	230
	R	8	5.7	350	MFI	245-255
	S	8	6.5 D	395 D	MFI	180
	F	8	6.5 D	395 D	MFI	175, 190
	J	8	7.4	454	MFI	290
1996	4	4	2.2	133	MFI	118
	E	6	3.4	204	MFI	180
	X	6	4.3	262	MFI	170, 180
	W	6	4.3	262	MFI	180-200[1]
	Z	6	4.3	262	MFI	155, 165[1]
	H	8	5.0	305	TBI	175
	M	8	5.0	305	MFI	220
	K	8	5.7	350	TBI	200
	R	8	5.7	350	MFI	250
	F	8	6.5 D	395 D	MFI	190, 200[1]
	P	8	6.5 D	395 D	MFI	155
	S	8	6.5 D	395 D	MFI	180
	Y	8	6.5 D	395 D	MFI	120[2], 160
	J	8	7.4	454	MFI	290
	N	8	7.4	454	TBI	230
1995	4	4	2.2	133	MFI	118
	D	6	3.1	191	TBI	120
	L	6	3.8	231	MFI	170
	Z	6	4.3	262	TBI	155, 165
	W	6	4.3	262	CPI	195, 200
	H	8	5.0	305	TBI	175
	K	8	5.7	350	TBI	180, 200[1]
	P	8	6.5 D	395 D	MFI	155
	Y	8	6.5 D	395 D	MFI	160

4 ENGINE IDENTIFICATION

YEAR	3 ENGINE CODE	CYL.	DISPL. liters	cu. in.	Fuel System	HP
1995 Cont'd.	F	8	6.5 D	395 D	MFI	190
	S	8	6.5 D	395 D	MFI	180
	N	8	7.4	454	TBI	230
1994	4	4	2.2	133	MFI	118
	D	6	3.1	191	TBI	120
	L	6	3.8	231	MFI	170
	Z	6	4.3	262	TBI	155, 165[1]
	W	6	4.3	262	CPI	195, 200[1]
	H	8	5.0	305	TBI	160, 170, 175[1]
	K	8	5.7	350	TBI	190, 195, 210[1]
	P	8	6.5 D	395 D	MFI	155
	Y	8	6.5 D	395 D	MFI	120, 160[1]
	F	8	6.5 D	395 D	MFI	190
	S	8	6.5 D	395 D	MFI	180
	N	8	7.4	454	TBI	230
1993	A	4	2.5	151	TBI	105
	R	6	2.8	173	TBI	125
	D	6	3.1	191	TBI	120
	L	6	3.8	231	MFI	170
	W	6	4.3	262	CPI	195, 200[1]
	Z	6	4.3	262	TBI	155, 165[1]
	Z	6	4.3 T	262 T	MFI	280
	H	8	5.0	305	TBI	160, 170, 175[1]
	K	8	5.7	350	TBI	190
	C	8	6.2 D	379 D	MFI	140, 145[1]
	J	8	6.2 D	379 D	MFI	150, 155, 210[1]
	F	8	6.5 D	379 D	MFI	180, 190[1]
	N	8	7.4	454	TBI	230, 255[1]
1992	A	4	2.5	151	TBI	105
	R	6	2.8	173	TBI	125
	D	6	3.1	191	TBI	120
	L	6	3.8	231	MFI	165
	W	6	4.3	262	CPI	195, 200
	Z	6	4.3	262	TBI	150, 155, 160[1]
	H	8	5.0	305	TBI	170, 175[1]
	K	8	5.7	350	TBI	190, 195, 210[1]
	C	8	6.2 D	379 D	MFI	140, 145
	J	8	6.2 D	379 D	MFI	150, 155
	F	8	6.5 D	379 D	MFI	190
	N	8	7.4	454	TBI	230, 255[1]
1991	A	4	2.5	151	TBI	105
	R	6	2.8	173	TBI	125
	D	6	3.1	191	TBI	120
	Z	6	4.3	262	TBI	150, 155, 160[1]
	B	6	4.3 HO	262 HO	TBI	170
	H	8	5.0	305	TBI	170, 175[1]

ENGINE IDENTIFICATION Continued

4 ENGINE IDENTIFICATION

YEAR	3 ENGINE CODE	CYL.	DISPL. liters	DISPL. cu. in.	Fuel System	HP
1991 Cont'd.	K	8	5.7	350	TBI	190, 195, 210[1]
	J	8	6.2 D	379 D	MFI	150, 155
	C	8	6.2 D	379 D	MFI	140, 145
	N	8	7.4	454	TBI	230, 255
1990	E	4	2.5	151	TBI	94, 96[1]
	R	6	2.8	173	TBI	125
	D	6	3.1	191	TBI	120
	Z	6	4.3	262	TBI	150, 155, 160[1]
	B	6	4.3 HO	262 HO	TBI	175
	H	8	5.0	305	TBI	170, 175[1]
	K	8	5.7	350	TBI	190, 195, 210[1]
	J	8	6.2 D	379 D	MFI	150, 155[1]
	C	8	6.2 D	379 D	MFI	135, 140, 145[1]
	N	8	7.4	454	TBI	230

4 ENGINE IDENTIFICATION

YEAR	3 ENGINE CODE	CYL.	DISPL. liters	DISPL. cu. in.	Fuel System	HP
1989	E	4	2.5	151	TBI	92
	R	6	2.8	173	TBI	125
	Z	6	4.3	262	TBI	150, 160[1]
	T	6	4.8	292	1V	115
	H	8	5.0	305	TBI	170, 175[1]
	K	8	5.7	350	TBI	190, 195, 210[1]
	C	8	6.2 D	379 D	MFI	126, 130[1]
	J	8	6.2 D	379 D	MFI	143, 148[1]
	N	8	7.4	454	TBI	230
	W	8	7.4	454	4V	230

D—Diesel. FI—Fuel Injection. LP—LPG Powered Conversion.
CPI—Central Port Injection. MFI—Multiport Fuel Injection.
TBI—Throttle Body Injection. 1V—One Venturi Carburetor.
2V—Two Venturi Carburetor. 4V—Four Venturi Carburetor.
1 Engine horsepower varies with model installation.
2 Fuel Miser version.

UNDERHOOD SERVICE SPECIFICATIONS

GMTTU1   GMTTU1

CYLINDER NUMBERING SEQUENCE

4-CYL. FIRING ORDER:
1 3 4 2

2.8L, 3.1L, 3.4L V6 FIRING ORDER:
1 2 3 4 5 6

4.3L (262), 3.8L V6 FIRING ORDER:
1 6 5 4 3 2

V8 FIRING ORDER:
GASOLINE
1999
4.8L CODE V, 5.3L CODE T
6.0 CODE U
1 8 7 2 6 5 4 3
OTHERS
1 8 4 3 6 5 7 2

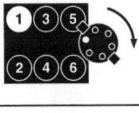
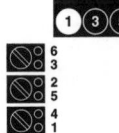
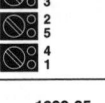

Front of car

1994-00 2.2L	1989-93 2.5L (151)	1989-93 2.8L (173)	1990-95 3.1L	1992-95 3.8L Code L

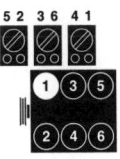
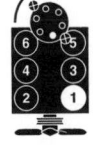
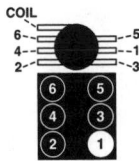

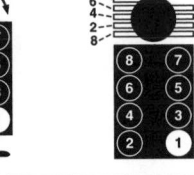

Front of car

1996-00 3.4L Code E	1989-95, 1996 Some, 4.3L (262) FI Code W, Z	1996 4.3L Some 1997-00 4.3L Code W, X	1989-95 All TBI Gasoline	1996-00 All MFI ex. 1999 Codes T, U, V Gasoline	1999-00 4.8L Code V, 5.3L Code T, 6.0 Code U Gasoline

TIMING MARK

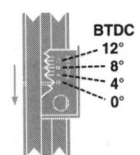
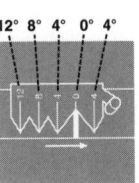
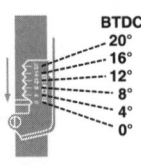
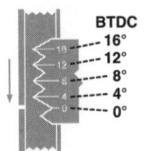
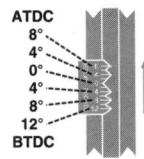

1989-95 4.3L (262) FI ex. G Van, 1989-95 5.0L (305), 5.7L (350)

1989-93 2.5L Code A, E

1989-93 2.8L (173)

1990-95 3.1L Lumina APV/Minivan Silhouette, Trans Sport

1989-95, 1996 Some 4.3L

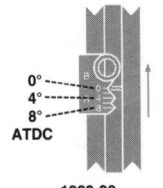
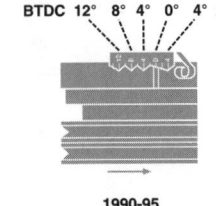

1989-90 4.8L (292)

1989 7.4L (454)

1990-95 7.4L FI Code N Upper & Lower

CHEK-CHART

CHEVROLET, GMC TRUCKS
1989-2000 All Models Includes Chevrolet Lumina
APV/Minivan, Venture, Oldsmobile Bravada & Silhouette; Pontiac Trans Sport; Isuzu Hombre

UNDERHOOD SERVICE SPECIFICATIONS

GMTTU2

GMTTU2

ELECTRICAL AND IGNITION SYSTEMS

BATTERY

		STANDARD		OPTIONAL	
Engine	Year	BCI Group No.	Crank. Perf.	BCI Group No.	Crank. Perf.
4-cyl.					
2.2L	1994	75	525	78	600
	1995-00	75	525	75	690
2.5L (151)	1989-92	75	525	78	630
6-cyl.					
2.8L (173)	1989-92	75	525	78	630
3.1L FWD Vans	1990-96	75	525	—	—
3.4L FWD Vans	1996-00	78	600	—	—
3.8L FWD Vans	1992-95	78	630	—	—
4.1L (250)					
4.3L (262)	1989-90	75	525	78	630
4.3L S Series	1991-93	75	525	78	630
Others	1991-93	78	630	—	—
4.3L S Series	1994	75	525	78	600
Others	1994	78	600	—	—
4.3L S Series	1995-00	75	525	75	690
Others	1995-00	78	600	—	—
V8					
4.8L	1999-00	78	600	—	—
5.0L (305): MT	1989	75	430	78	630
AT	1989	75	525	78	630
5.0L	1990	75	525	78	630
	1991-93	78	630	—	—
	1994-97	78	600	—	—
5.3L	1999-00	78	600	—	—
5.7L (350)	1989-90	75	525	78	630
	1991-93	78	630	—	—
	1994-97	78	600	—	—
6.2L (379) Diesel					
Pickups	1989-92	75	570[1]	—	—
Vans	1989-93	78	540[1]	—	—
6.5L Diesel	1992-93	75	570[1]	—	—
	1994-96	78	770	—	—
	1997-00	78	600[1]	—	—
6.8L	1999-00	78	600	—	—
7.4L (454)	1989-93	78	630	—	—
	1994-98	78	600	—	—

1 Two batteries required.

GENERATOR

Some models, rated output can be verified by stamping on end frame.

Application	Rated Output (amps)	Test Output @2000 rpm (amps)
1989-92	66, 70, 81, 94	1
	85, 100, 105	2
	120, 124	2
1993-95	100, 105, 140	2
1996-97	100, 105, 124, 145	2
1998-00 Astro, Safari	100	70
	105	73
Venture, Silhouette, Trans Sport	105	74
	140	98
All Others	100, 105, 129, 145	2

1 Output at 2000 rpm must be within 10 amps of rated output.
2 Output at 2000 rpm must be within 15 amps of rated output.

REGULATOR

Application	Test Temp. (deg. F/C)	Voltage Setting
1989-95	—	13.5-16.0
1996-00	—	13.0-16.0

STARTER

Engine	Year	Cranking Voltage (min. volts)	Ampere Draw @ Cranking Speed
All	1989-00	9.0	—

SPARK PLUGS

Engine	Year	Gap (inches)	Gap (mm)	Torque (ft-lb)
4-cyl. 2.2L	1994-00	.060	1.52	14
4-cyl. 2.5L (151)	1989-93	.060	1.52	7-15
V6 2.8L, 3.1L	1989-96	.045	1.14	7-15
V6 3.4L	1996-99	.060	1.52	11
V6 3.8L	1992-95	.060	1.52	.20
V6 4.3L TBI	1989-92	.035	.89	7-15
CFI	1992	.035	.89	11
V6 4.3L TBI	1993-96	.035	.89	11
V6 4.3L CFI	1996-00	.060	1.52	14
S Series	1996	.060	1.52	15
	1997-00	.045	1.14	15
6-cyl.	1989	.035	.89	17-27
V8 TBI	1989-96	.035	.89	22
V8 CFI, MFI	1996-00	.060	1.52	14

IGNITION COIL
FOR TESTING AND ADJUSTMENT DIAGRAMS, SEE APPENDIX A.

Winding Resistance (ohms at 75°F or 24°C)

All w/o distributor: Primary resistance measured across each coil's two primary power wires. Secondary resistance measured across companion coil towers with spark plug wires removed.

Engine	Year	Windings	Resistance (ohms)
2.2L, 3.4L	1994-00	Secondary	5000-8000
3.8L Type I[1]	1992	Primary	.50-1.0
		Secondary	10,000-13,000
Type II	1992	Primary	.30-.50
		Secondary	5000-7000
3.8L	1993-95	Primary	.5-.9
		Secondary	5000-8000
All w/distributor	1989-95	Primary	0-2
		Secondary	6000-30,000
	1996	Primary	0.2-0.5
		Secondary	5000-25,000
	1997-00	Primary	0.1
		Secondary	5000-25,000

1 Type I coils have three coil towers on each side.
Type II coils have six coil towers on each side.

IGNITION PICKUP
FOR TESTING AND ADJUSTMENT DIAGRAMS, SEE APPENDIX B.

Engine	Year	Resistance (ohms)	Air Gap (in./mm)
All w/distributor	1989-95	500-1500	—

BASE TIMING
FOR TESTING AND ADJUSTMENT DIAGRAMS, SEE APPENDIX C.

Set timing at slow idle and Before Top Dead Center, unless otherwise specified.

1989-95 all, 1996 w/TBI:

2.5L (151), ground diagnostic connector under dash. Average pulses of cylinders 1 & 4.

2.8L (173), 3.1L TBI, place system in bypass mode, disconnect tan/black wire by ECM in passenger compartment.

All V6 4.3L & V8 w/FI, place system in bypass mode, disconnect tan/black wire single connector. 1989-94 all, 1995 vans, connector is in engine compartment usually by distributor. 1995 pickups, connector is under dash below glove compartment.

All others, disconnect & plug distributor vacuum hose(s).

1996-97 V8 w/CFI, connect a Scan tool and access Cam Retard. Rotate distributor to adjust. Raise idle over 1000 rpm and recheck.

Engine	Year	Man. Trans. (degrees)	Auto. Trans. (degrees)
2.5L (151)	1989-93	8	8 D
2.8L (173)	1989-93	10	10 P
3.1L FWD Vans	1990-96	—	10 D

CHEVROLET, GMC TRUCKS
1989-2000 All Models Includes Chevrolet Lumina, APV/Minivan, Venture, Oldsmobile Bravada & Silhouette; Pontiac Trans Sport; Isuzu Hombre

UNDERHOOD SERVICE SPECIFICATIONS

GMTTU3
GMTTU3

BASE TIMING Continued

Engine	Year	Man. Trans. (degrees)	Auto. Trans. (degrees)
4.3L (262) TBI	1989-96	0	0 P
4.3L CFI	1996-00	1	1
4.8L (292)	1989	8	8
5.0L (305) TBI	1989-96	0	0 P
5.0L CFI	1996-97	0±2	0±2
	1998-99	2	2
5.7L (350) TBI	1989-96	0	0 P
5.7L CFI	1996-97	0±2	0±2
	1998-00	2	2
5.7L (350) 4V	1989	4	4
7.4L (454) 4V & TBI	1989-96	4	4
7.4L CFI	1996-97	0±2	0±2
	1998-00	2	2

1 Timing not adjustable. At TDC rotor blade should be aligned with index mark "6" on distributor housing.

2 Timing not adjustable. At TDC rotor blade should be aligned with index mark "8" on distributor housing.

FUEL SYSTEM

FUEL SYSTEM PRESSURE
FOR TESTING AND ADJUSTMENT DIAGRAMS, SEE APPENDIX D.

Engine	Year	PSI
All carbureted & TBI:		
4-cyl. 2.5L (151)	1989-92	9-13
		13 min.[1]
V6 2.8L (173), 3.1L	1989-96	9-13
		13 min.[1]
V6 4.3L (262) TBI	1989-94	9-13
		13 min.[1]
8-cyl. TBI	1989-93	9-13
		13 min.[1]
8-cyl.: 5.0L, 5.7L	1994-96	9-13
		13 min.[1]
7.4L	1994-96	26-32
8-cyl. Diesel	1989-92	5.5-6.5

1 With fuel return line briefly restricted.

Engine	Year	Pressure Ign. On	Pressure Idle	Pressure Fuel Pump[1]
All MFI:				
2.2L, 3.4L	1994-96	41-47	31-44	47 min.
3.8L	1992-95	40-47	30-44	47 min.
4.3L Turbo	1991-93	38-43	25-30	65 min.
All CFI:				
4.3L	1992-95	55-61	37-43	61 min.
4.3L, 5.0L, 5.7L, 7.4L	1996-00	60-66	50-63	66 min.

1 With fuel return line briefly restricted.

IDLE SPEED W/O COMPUTER CONTROL

Disconnect and plug hoses as indicated on emission label.

Adjust idle to specified rpm by adjusting idle solenoid screw (plunger fully extended) or throttle stop screw.

Air conditioned models equipped with idle speed-up solenoid, turn A/C on, disconnect compressor clutch wire with solenoid fully extended, adjust solenoid to obtain specified rpm. Turn air conditioner off and reconnect compressor wire.

Electrically disconnect idle shutdown solenoid, if so equipped, and adjust idle speed screw or solenoid hex-head screw.

Reconnect hoses, unless specified otherwise on label .

Engine	Year	SLOW Man. Trans.	SLOW Auto. Trans.	FAST Man. Trans.	FAST Auto. Trans.	Step of Cam
4.8L (292)	1989	700	700 N	2400	2400 P, N	High
shutdown idle	1989	450	450 N			
5.7L (350) Heavy-duty[1]	1989	600	700 N	1900	1900 P, N	High
A/C speed-up	1989	800	—			
6.2L (379)	1989-93	650	650 N	800	800 P, N	—

IDLE SPEED W/O COMPUTER CONTROL Continued

Engine	Year	SLOW Man. Trans.	SLOW Auto. Trans.	FAST Man. Trans.	FAST Auto. Trans.	Step of Cam
6.5L: early	1992	650	650 N	—	—	—
late	1992-93	700	700 N	—	—	—
	1994	700	560 N	—	—	—
7.4L 4V	1989	600	700 N	1900	1900 N	High

1 Light-duty emission models: GVW of 8500 lb or less. **Heavy-duty emission models:** GVW of 1801 lb or more.

IDLE SPEED W/COMPUTER CONTROL
FOR TESTING AND ADJUSTMENT DIAGRAMS, SEE APPENDIX E.
1989-90 All; 1991-92 S Series & 7.4L; 1993-96 7.4L TBI: Ground diagnostic terminal (see DIAGNOSTIC TROUBLE CODES), turn ignition on but do not start engine. Wait 30 seconds then disconnect the IAC connector. Remove ground from the diagnostic terminal, start engine and turn throttle stop screw to obtain the specified setting speed.

Checking speed: Allowable variance: 1989-93: ± 100, w/MT; ± 50, w/AT; 1994-98, ± 25 .

Engine	Year	Transmission	Setting Speed	Checking Speed
2.2L	1994-95	MT	—	950
	1994-95	AT	—	890 D
2.5L (151)	1989	MT	550-650	900
2.5L (151): 2WD	1989	AT	450-550 N	800 D
4WD	1989	AT	450-550 N	650 D
2.5L (151) Vans	1989-90	MT	550-650	800
	1989-90	AT	450-550 N	750 D
2.5L S Series	1990	MT	550-650	950
	1990	AT	450-550 N	800 D
2.5L	1991-92	MT	550-650	900
	1991-92	AT	450-550 N	800 D
	1993	MT	—	950
	1993	AT	—	800 D
2.8L (173)	1989-92	MT	650-750	800
2.8L (173)	1989	AT	650-750 N	800 D
2.8L	1993	MT	—	800
3.1L FWD Vans	1990-92	AT	650-750 N	600-700 D
	1993-96	AT	—	600-700 D
3.8L	1992-95	AT	—	650-750 N
4.3L (262)	1989	MT	400-500	500-550
4.3L (262)	1989	AT	350-450 D	500-550 D
S Series	1989	AT	425-525 N	500-550 D
4.3L TBI LD	1990	MT	400-525	550
S Series	1990	MT	400-525	600
4.3L TBI LD	1990	AT	350-450 D	540 D
S Series	1990	AT	425-525 N	500 D
HO Vans	1990	AT	425-525 N	590 D
4.3L TBI LD	1991-92	MT	—	550
S Series	1991-92	MT	400-525	600
4.3L TBI LD	1991-92	AT	—	540 D
	1992	AT	—	525 D
S Series	1991-92	AT	350-450 D	525 D
HO Van	1991-92	AT	—	590 D
4.3L TBI HD	1990	MT	400-525	650
	1990	AT	350-450 N	650 D
4.3L TBI HD	1991-92	MT	—	650
4.3L TBI HD	1991	AT	—	500 D
	1992	AT	—	550 D
4.3L TBI: S Series	1993	MT	—	650
Others	1993	MT	—	600
Astro, Safari	1993	AT	—	540 D
S Series	1993	AT	—	550 D
Others	1993	AT	—	650 D
4.3L TBI: All S Series	1994-95	MT	—	725
S-Blazer, Jimmy	1994	MT	—	700
	1994	AT	—	650 D
Astro, Safari	1994-95	AT	—	540 D
Pickups, G Vans: LD	1994-96	MT	—	550
	1994-96	AT	—	590 D
HD	1994	MT	—	700
	1994	AT	—	650 D
4.3L CFI 4WD Van	1992-93	AT	—	625 D
Others	1992-93	AT	—	550 D
4.3L CFI:	1994-95	MT	—	650
S10, Sonoma	1994-95	AT	—	625 D
S Blazer, S Jimmy	1994-95	AT	—	600 D
Astro, Safari: 2WD	1994-95	AT	—	550 D
4WD	1994-95	AT	—	625 D

CHEK-CHART

CHEVROLET, GMC TRUCKS
1989-2000 All Models Includes Chevrolet Lumina
APV/Minivan, Venture, Oldsmobile Bravada & Silhouette; Pontiac Trans Sport; Isuzu Hombre

UNDERHOOD SERVICE SPECIFICATIONS
GMTTU4

GMTTU4

IDLE SPEED W/COMPUTER CONTROL Continued

Engine	Year	Transmission	Setting Speed	Checking Speed
4.3L CFI: S Series LD	1996-97	MT	—	550
	1996-97	AT	—	590 D
S Series HD	1996-97	MT	—	700
	1996-97	AT	—	650 D
Astro, Safari	1996-97	AT	—	590 D
C, K Series Pickups, Tahoe, Yukon, Suburban	1996-97	MT	—	700
	1996-97	AT	—	600 D
4.3L	1998-00	MT	—	700
		AT	—	600D
5.0L (305)	1989-90	MT	475-525	600
	1989-90	AT	400-450 D	500 D[1]
5.0L	1991-93	MT	—	600
	1991-93	AT	—	500 D
5.0L TBI	1994-95	MT	—	650
	1994-95	AT	—	550 D
5.0L CFI	1996-00	MT	—	700
	1996-00	AT	—	700 D
5.7L (350) LD	1989	MT	475-525	600
5.7L (350) LD	1989	AT	400-450 D	500 D
5.7L LD	1990	MT	475-525	650
	1990	AT	400-450 D	525 D
5.7 LD	1991-92	MT	—	600
	1991-92	AT	—	525 D
5.7L TBI LD	1993-96	MT	—	660
	1993	AT	—	550 D
	1994-96	AT	—	525 D
5.7L (350) HD	1989-90	MT	525-575	650[2]
	1989-90	AT	425-475 D	550 D
5.7L HD	1991-93	MT	—	600
	1994-95	MT	—	590
	1991-95	AT	—	550 D
5.7L CFI	1996-00	MT	—	675
	1996-00	AT	—	550 D
7.4L (454)	1989-93	MT	675-725	800
7.4L (454)	1989	AT	675-725 D	750 D
7.4L	1990-93	AT	600-650 D	750 D
7.4L TBI	1994-99	MT	625	750
	1994-99	AT	625 D	625 D
7.4L CFI	1996-00	MT	—	725
	1996-00	AT	—	600 D

1 1989 C10 Fed. 3-speed AT w/o AIR: 425-475 setting; 550 D checking.
2 G Van or Suburban w/single catalytic converter, 600.

ENGINE MECHANICAL

TIGHTENING TORQUES
FOR TESTING AND ADJUSTMENT DIAGRAMS, SEE APPENDIX F.
Some fasteners are tightened in more than one step.

TORQUE FOOT-POUNDS/NEWTON METERS

Engine	Year	Cylinder Head	Intake Manifold	Exhaust Manifold	Crankshaft Pulley	Water Pump
2.2L	1994-00	43/58[1], 46/63[2], +90°	22/30, upper 24/33, lower	115"/13, nuts 89"/10, studs	77/105	18/25
2.5L	1989-93	18/25, 26/35[6], +90°	25/34	32/43[3], 26/35[5]	162/220	17/23
2.8L	1989-93	40/55, +90°	15/21	25/34	70/95	7/10, short 18/24, long
3.1L	1990-96	41/55, +90°	13/18, 19/26	24/33	70/95	89"/10
3.4L	1996-00	37/50, +90°	18/25, upper 115"/13, lower	12/16	76/103	89"/10
3.8L	1992-95	35/47, +130°[7]	9, 9	38/52	110/150, +76°	84"/10, short 29/39, long

TIGHTENING TORQUES Continued

TORQUE FOOT-POUNDS/NEWTON METERS

Engine	Year	Cylinder Head	Intake Manifold	Exhaust Manifold	Crankshaft Pulley	Water Pump
4.1L (250), 4.8L (292) 4.3L (262)	1989	95/130[8]	38/52	38/52	50/70	15/20
5.0L (305) TBI, 5.7L (350) TBI	1989-96	25/35, 45/60, 65/90	35/48	26/36, center two, 20/28, others	70/95	30/40
4.3L CFI, 5.0L CFI, 5.7L CFI,	1996-00	10	11	11/15, 22/30	74/110	33/45
6.2L (379), 6.5L Diesel	1989-93	20/25, 50/65, +90°	31/42	26/35	85/115	30/40
	1994-95	20/25, 50/65, 50/65, +90°	31/42	26/35	200/270	16/22, short 32/42, long
	1996-97	20/25, 50/75, +90°	31/42	26/35	200/270	16/22, short 32/42, long
7.4L (454) TBI	1989-96	30/40, 60/80, 80/110	30/40	40/50, steel 18/24, iron	85/115	30/40
7.4L CFI	1996-00	30/40, 60/80, 89/120[1], 92/125[2]	10/14, upper 30/40, lower	22/30	110/149	30/40

1 Short bolts.
2 Long bolts.
3 Four outer bolts.
4 Upper: 44"/5, 88"/10
   Lower: 27"/3, 106"/12, 11/15.
5 Three inner bolts.
6 Turn last bolt on left (number nine) to 18/25.
7 Turn four center bolts an additional 30°.
8 Left side, front bolt is tightened to 85/115.
9 1991-92: upper to lower, 21/29; lower to block, 89"/10. 1993-95: upper to lower & lower to block, 11/15.
10 22/30
   +55° short bolts
   +65° med. bolts
   +75° long bolts

COMPRESSION PRESSURE
At cranking speed, engine temperature normalized, throttle open.

Engine	Year	PSI	Maximum Variation PSI
4-cyl.	1989-00	100 min.	1
6-cyl., V6, V8: Gasoline	1989-00	100 min.	1
Diesel	1989-00	380 min.	2

1 Lowest cylinder pressure must be more than 70% of highest cylinder pressure.
2 Lowest cylinder pressure must be more than 80% of highest cylinder pressure at 200 rpm minimum.

BELT TENSION
A belt operated one engine revolution is considered a used belt.

Engine	Year	Generator	Power Steering	Air Cond.	Air Pump
Strand Tension					
USED BELTS					
4.8L (292)	1989	90	90	90	90
V6, V8 Gasoline	1989-91	90	67	90	67
V8 Diesel	1989-93	67	67	90	—
All Serpentine	1989-00	1	1	1	—
NEW BELTS					
4.8L (292)	1989	169	169	169	169
V6, V8 Gasoline	1989-91	135	146	169	146
V8 Diesel	1989-93	146	146	169	—
All Serpentine	1989-00	1	1	1	—

1 Serpentine, w/automatic tensioner.

CHEVROLET, GMC TRUCKS
1989-2000 All Models Includes Chevrolet Lumina
APV/Minivan, Venture, Oldsmobile Bravada & Silhouette; Pontiac Trans Sport; Isuzu Hombre

GMTTU5

SERPENTINE BELT DIAGRAMS

SERPENTINE BELT DIAGRAMS Continued

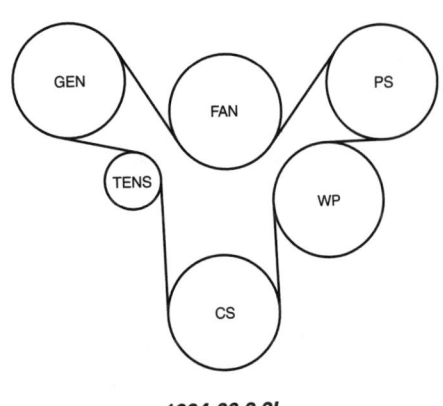

**1994-00 2.2L
w/o AC, w/PS**

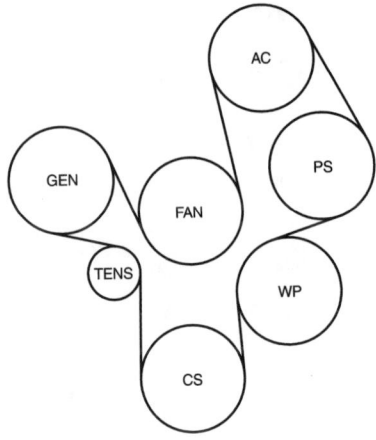

**1994-00 2.2L
w/AC & PS**

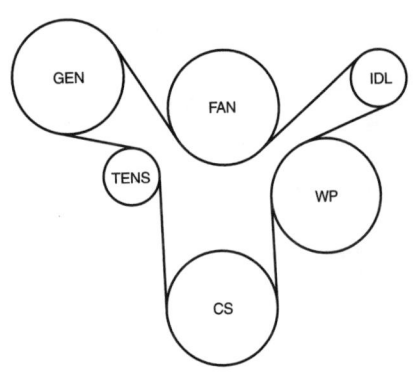

**1994-00 2.2L
w/o AC or PS**

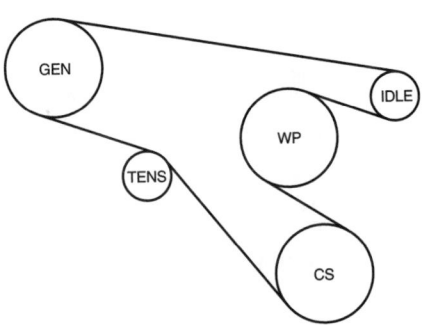

**1989-93 2.5L
w/o AC or PS**

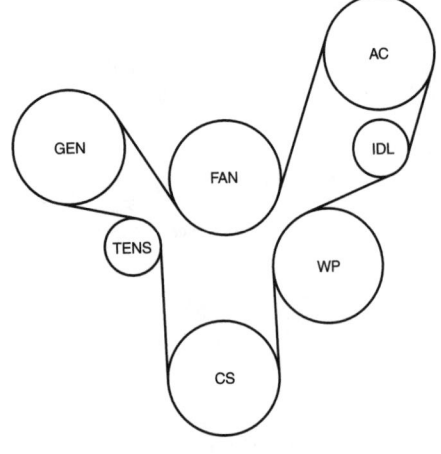

**1994-00 2.2L
w/o AC, w/PS**

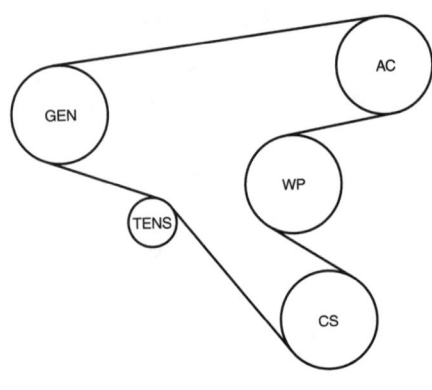

**1989-93 2.5L
w/AC, w/o PS**

CHEK-CHART

CHEVROLET, GMC TRUCKS
1989-2000 All Models Includes Chevrolet Lumina
APV/Minivan, Venture, Oldsmobile Bravada & Silhouette; Pontiac Trans Sport; Isuzu Hombre
UNDERHOOD SERVICE SPECIFICATIONS

GMTTU6

GMTTU6

SERPENTINE BELT DIAGRAMS Continued

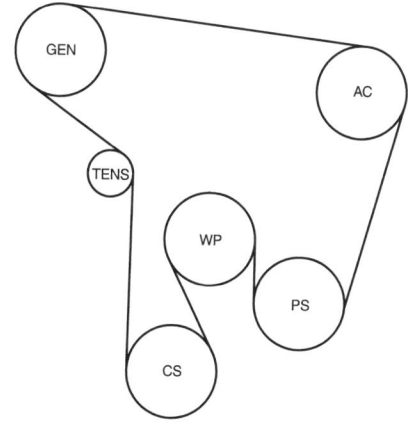

**1989-93 2.5L
w/AC & PS**

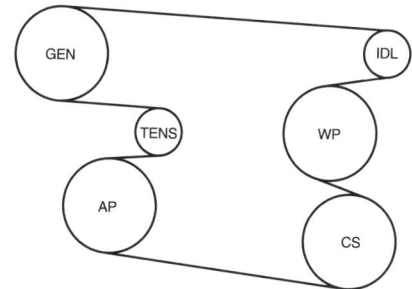

**1989-93 2.8L
w/o AC or PS**

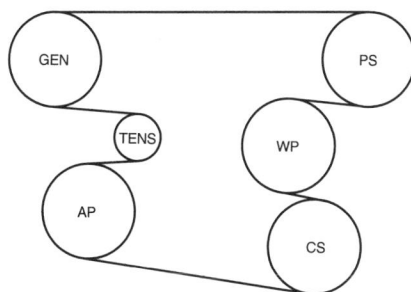

**1989-93 2.8L
w/PS, w/o AC**

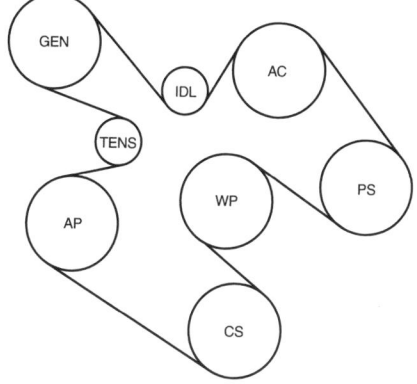

**1989-93 2.8L
w/AC & PS**

SERPENTINE BELT DIAGRAMS Continued

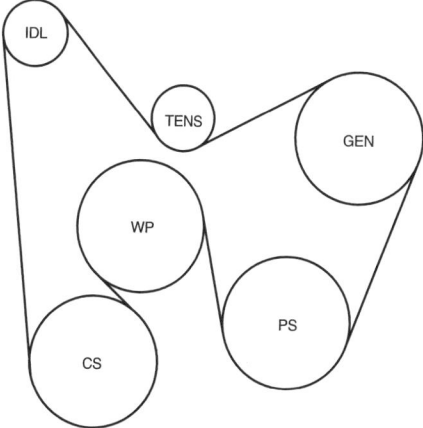

**1989-91 5.7L, 7.4L
R, V Series Pickups, Blazer,
Jimmy, Suburban w/o AC;
1989-97 4.3L Astro, Safari, S Series
Pickups & Blazer, Jimmy w/o AC;
1992-95 4.3L, 5.0L, 5.7L, 7.4L
C, K Series Pickups, Blazer, Yukon,
Suburban w/o AP & AC, w/PS**

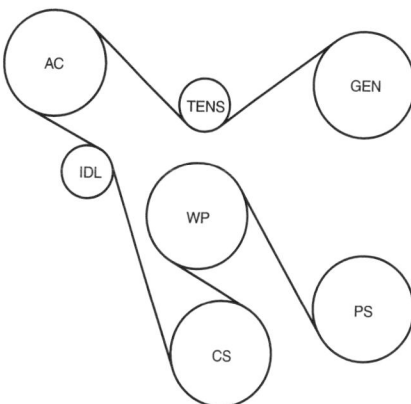

**1989-91 5.7L, 7.4L
R, V Series Pickups, Blazer, Jimmy,
Suburban w/AC;
1989-91 4.3L, 5.0L, 7.4L
G Series Vans w/o AP, w/PS & AC;
1989-97 4.3L Astro, Safari, S Series
Pickups & Blazer, Jimmy w/AC;
1992-95 4.3L, 5.0L, 5.7L
C, K Series Pickups, Blazer, Yukon,
Suburban w/o AP, w/AC & PS;
1992-95 7.4L C & K2500-3500, w/AC**

CHEVROLET, GMC TRUCKS
1989-2000 All Models Includes Chevrolet Lumina
APV/Minivan, Venture, Oldsmobile Bravada & Silhouette; Pontiac Trans Sport; Isuzu Hombre

UNDERHOOD SERVICE SPECIFICATIONS

GMTTU7

SERPENTINE BELT DIAGRAMS Continued

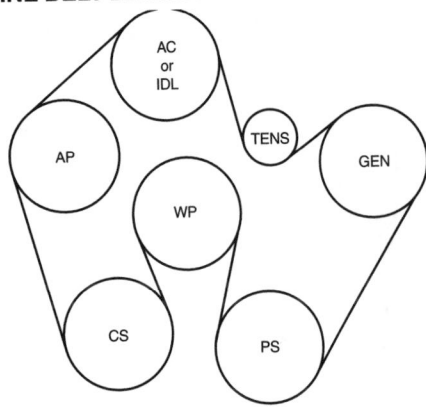

1989-91 4.3L, 5.0L, 7.4L
G Series Vans w/AP, PS & AC—Some
1992-95 4.3L, 5.0L, 5.7L
C, K Series Pickups, Blazer, Yukon,
Suburban w/AP & PS, w/o AC;
1989-91 7.4L
C & K Series Pickups w/o AC

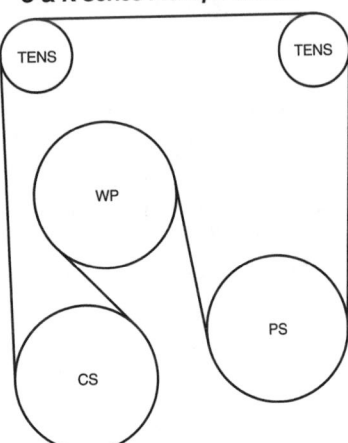

1989 4.3L, 5.0L, 5.7L
C, K Series Pickups w/o AP, w/PS;
1989-91 4.3L, 5.0L, 7.4L
G Series Vans w/o AP, w/PS

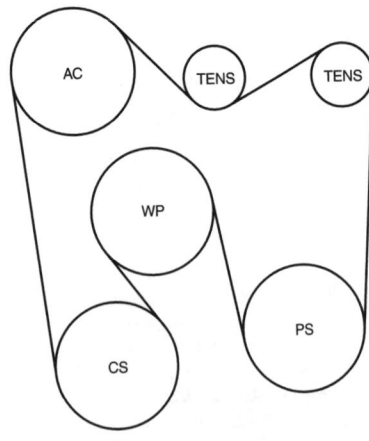

1989 4.3L, 5.0L, 5.7L
C, K Series Pickups w/o PA, w/PS & AC;
1989-91 4.3L, 5.0L, 7.4L
G Series Vans w/o AP, w/PS & AC

SERPENTINE BELT DIAGRAMS Continued

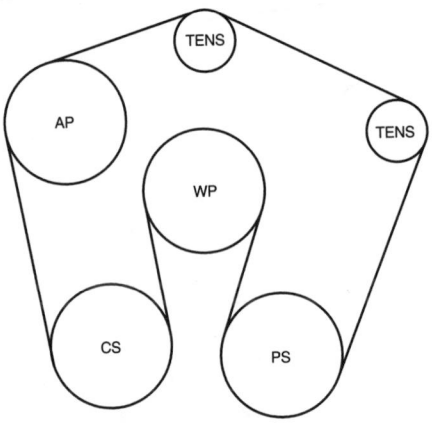

1989 4.3L, 5.0L, 5.7L
C, K Series Pickups w/AP & PS, w/o AC;
1989-91 4.3L, 5.0L, 7.4L
G Series Vans w/AP & PS, w/o AC

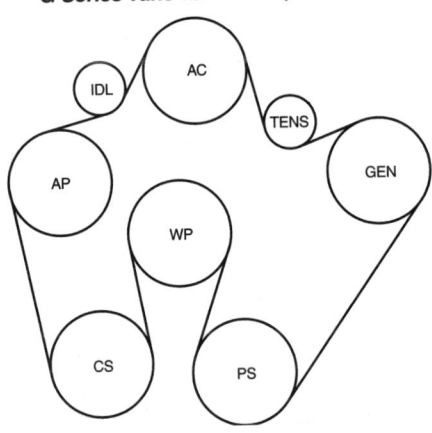

1989 4.3L, 5.0L, 5.7L
C, K Series Pickups w/AP, PS & AC;
1989-91 4.3L, 5.0L, 7.4L
G Series Vans w/AP, PS & AC—Some;
1989-98 C & K Series Pickups w/AC;
1992-95 4.3L, 5.0L, 5.7L
C, K Series Pickups w/AP, PS & AC;
1992-95 7.4L C1500 w/AC

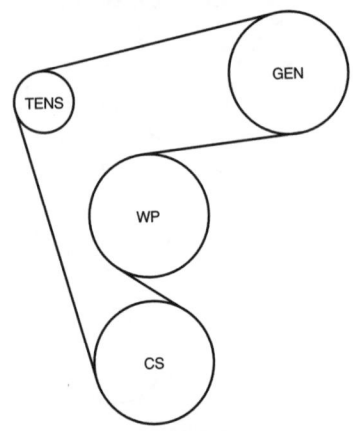

1989-91 4.3L, 5.0L, 7.4L
G Series Vans w/o AP, PS or AC

CHEVROLET, GMC TRUCKS
1989-2000 All Models Includes Chevrolet Lumina
APV/Minivan, Venture, Oldsmobile Bravada & Silhouette; Pontiac Trans Sport; Isuzu Hombre

UNDERHOOD SERVICE SPECIFICATIONS

GMTTU8

GMTTU8

SERPENTINE BELT DIAGRAMS Continued

SERPENTINE BELT DIAGRAMS Continued

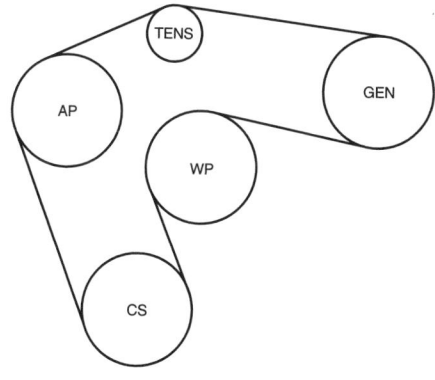

1989-91 4.3L, 5.0L, 7.4L
G Series Vans w/AP, w/o AC or PS

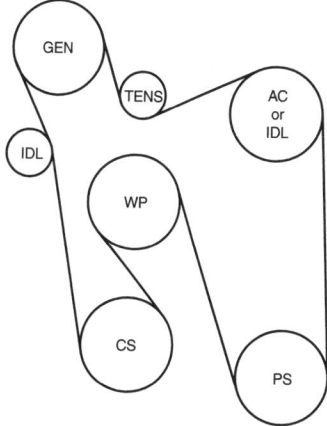

1992-95 6.2L, 6.5L Diesel & 7.4L
G Series Vans

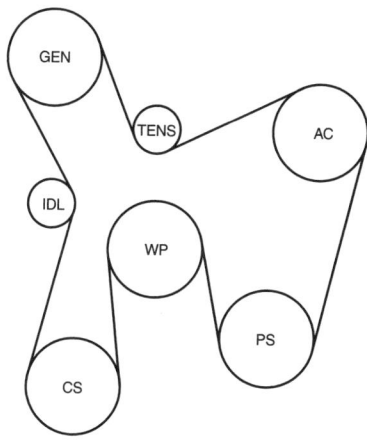

1992-95 4.3L, 5.0L, 5.7L
G Series vans w/AC

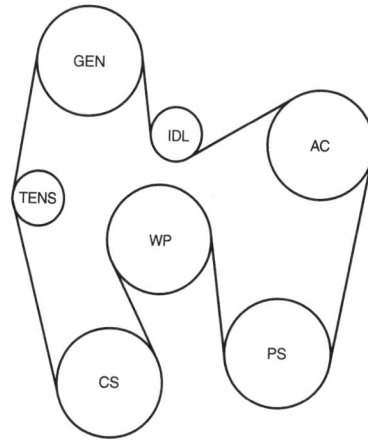

1996-00 4.3L, 5.0L, 5.7L
C, K Series Pickups, Tahoe, Yukon,
Suburban, G Series Vans w/AC

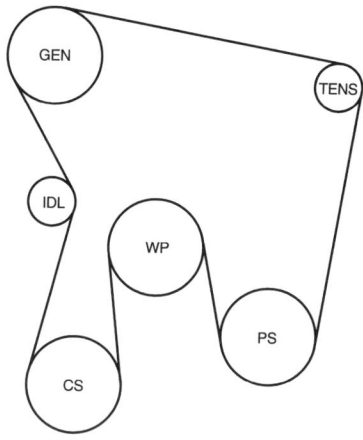

1992-95 4.3L, 5.0L, 5.7L
G Series Vans w/o AC

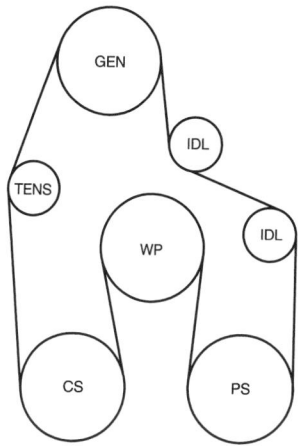

1996-00 4.3L, 5.0L, 5.7L
C, K Series Pickups, Tahoe, Yukon,
Suburban, G Series Vans w/o AC

CHEVROLET, GMC TRUCKS
1989-2000 All Models Includes Chevrolet Lumina
APV/Minivan, Venture, Oldsmobile Bravada & Silhouette; Pontiac Trans Sport; Isuzu Hombre

UNDERHOOD SERVICE SPECIFICATIONS

GMTTU9

CHEK-CHART

GMTTU9

SERPENTINE BELT DIAGRAMS Continued

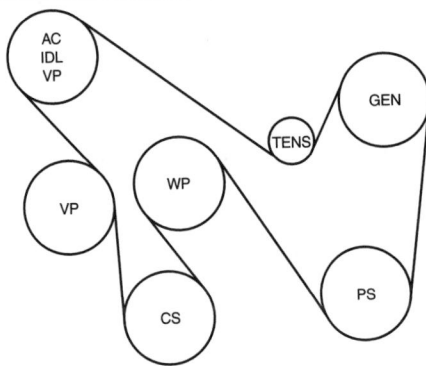

1989-96 6.2L, 6.5L Diesel
All Models w/AC & VP

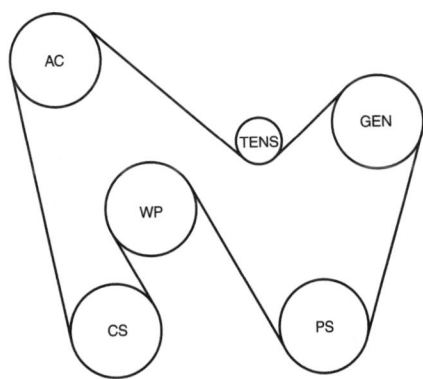

1989-96 6.2L, 6.5L Diesel
All Models w/AC, w/o VP

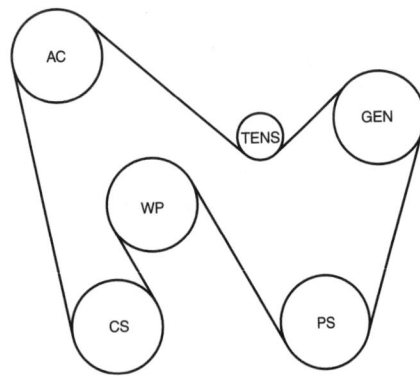

1996-00 6.5L Diesel
All Models w/Single Generator

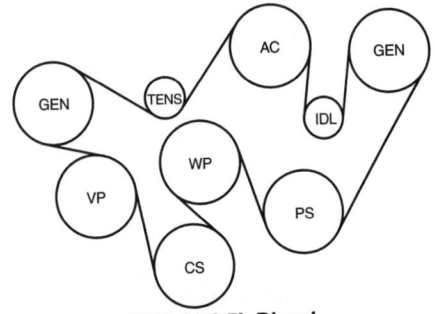

1996-00 6.5L Diesel
All Models w/Dual Generator

SERPENTINE BELT DIAGRAMS Continued

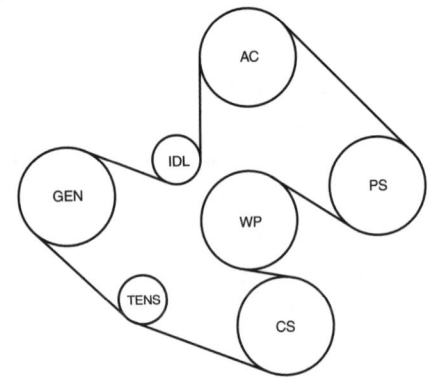

1996-98 7.4L
All Models w/o AP, w/AC

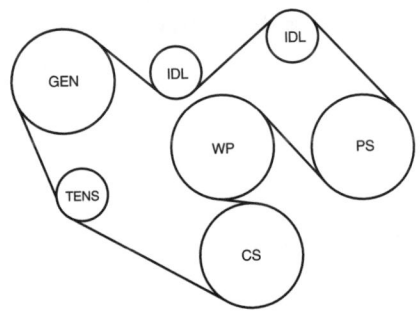

1996-98 7.4L
All Models w/o AP or AC

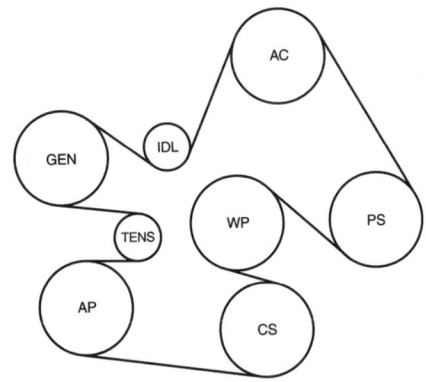

1996-98 7.4L
All Models w/AP & AC

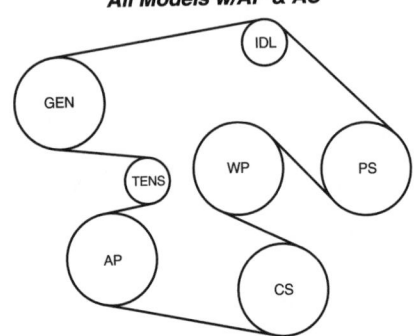

1996-98 7.4L
All Models w/AP, w/o AC

CHEVROLET, GMC TRUCKS
1989-2000 All Models Includes Chevrolet Lumina
APV/Minivan, Venture, Oldsmobile Bravada & Silhouette; Pontiac Trans Sport; Isuzu Hombre

UNDERHOOD SERVICE SPECIFICATIONS

GMTTU10   GMTTU10

ENGINE COMPUTER SYSTEM

DIAGNOSTIC TROUBLE CODES

FOR TESTING AND ADJUSTMENT DIAGRAMS, SEE APPENDIX G.

1989-95: Connect a jumper between A and B terminals on under dash connector (identified by a slot between the terminals, or is two upper right hand cavities on 2-row connector). Turn ignition switch on. Code 12 will flash three times, then codes in memory will be displayed. Do not run engine with jumper connected.

Remove ECM fuse for a minimum of 10 seconds to clear memory.

1996-00: OBD-II system used. Connect a Scan tool and follow manufacturer's instructions to retrieve codes.

Code 12 No tach reference to PCM
Code 13 Oxygen sensor circuit (Gasoline)
Code 13 Engine shutoff solenoid (Diesel)
Code 14 Shorted engine coolant sensor circuit
Code 15 Engine coolant sensor circuit high (V8 Diesel)
Code 15 Open engine coolant sensor circuit (Others)
Code 16 System voltage high or low (1989-92)
Code 16 Vehicle speed signal buffer fault (1994-95)
Code 17 Spark reference circuit (Gasoline)
Code 17 High resolution circuit fault (Diesel)
Code 18 Pump cam reference pulse error
Code 19 Crankshaft position reference error
Code 21 Throttle position sensor circuit, voltage high
Code 22 Throttle position sensor, voltage low
Code 23 Open or ground MC solenoid (carbureted)
Code 23 Intake air temperature sensor temperature low (FI, Gasoline)
Code 23 TPS not calibrated (Diesel)
Code 24 Vehicle speed sensor circuit
Code 25 Intake air temperature sensor temperature high (FI, Gasoline)
Code 25 TPS position 2 circuit high (Diesel)
Code 26 TPS position 2 circuit low (Diesel)
Code 27 TPS position 2 circuit fault
Code 28 Transmission range pressure switch
Code 29 Glow plug relay
Code 31 MAP sensor too low (Diesel)
Code 31 PRNDL switch (FWD Vans)
Code 32 Barometric or altitude sensor (carbureted)
Code 32 EGR vacuum sensor circuit (FI)
Code 33 MAP sensor voltage high
Code 34 MAP or vacuum sensor circuit (carbureted)
Code 34 MAP sensor voltage low (FI, Gasoline)
Code 34 Injection timing stepper motor fault
Code 35 Idle air control switch circuit shorted
Code 36 Transaxle shift problem
Code 37 TCC brake switch stuck on
Code 38 TCC brake switch stuck off (1994-95)
Code 38 TCC brake input circuit (1989-92)
Code 39 Torque converter clutch problem
Code 41 No distributor reference pulses to ECM
Code 41 Camshaft sensor circuit (FWD Vans)
Code 42 IC or IC bypass circuit grounded or open (1989-92)
Code 43 Knock sensor signal
Code 44 Air/fuel mixture lean
Codes 44 & 45 Faulty oxygen sensor
Code 45 Air/fuel mixture rich
Code 51 Faulty PROM or installation
Code 52 Fuel CALPAK
Codes 52 & 53 System voltage high (1994-95 S series)
Code 53 System over voltage (4-cyl.)
Code 53 Faulty PROM (V6, V8 gas)
Code 53 5-volt V-REF overload (V8 Diesel)
Code 54 Shorted MC solenoid or faulty ECM (carbureted)
Code 54 Fuel pump relay (FI)
Code 55 Grounded V-REF, faulty oxygen sensor or ECM
Code 56 Quad drive B circuit problem
Code 58 Transmission fluid temp. sensor circuit shorted
Code 59 Transmission fluid temp. sensor circuit open
Code 61 Cruise vent solenoid circuit
Code 62 Cruise vac solenoid circuit
Code 63 Cruise system problem
Code 66 3-2 control solenoid
Code 67 Torque converter clutch solenoid
Code 69 Torque converter clutch stuck on
Code 72 Vehicle speed sensor circuit loss
Code 73 Pressure control solenoid fault

DIAGNOSTIC TROUBLE CODES Continued

Code 74 Transmission input speed sensor
Code 75 System voltage low
Code 79 Transmission fluid over temp.
Code 81 2-3 shift solenoid circuit
Code 82 1-2 shift solenoid circuit

SENSORS, INPUT
TEMPERATURE SENSORS

Engine	Year	Sensor	Resistance Ohms @ deg. F/C
All	1989-90	Coolant, Intake Air[1]	13,500 @ 20/-7
			7500 @ 40/4
			3400 @ 70/20
			1800 @ 100/38
			450 @ 160/70
			185 @ 210/100
All	1991-00	Coolant, Intake Air[1], Diesel Fuel Temp.	28,700 @ -4/-20
			12,300 @ 23/-5
			7200 @ 41/5
			3500 @ 68/20
			1400 @ 104/40
			467 @ 158/70
			177 @ 210/100
	1996-00	Transmission Oil	25,809-31,545 @ -4/-20
			8481-9423 @ 32/0
			3164-3867 @ 68/20
			1313-1605 @ 104/40
			601-734 @ 140/60
			299-365 @ 176/80
			159-195 @ 212/100

1 As equipped, not used on all engines.

MANIFOLD ABSOLUTE, VACUUM, AND BAROMETRIC PRESSURE SENSORS

Engines may use one, or a combination of these sensors. All sensors appear the same. Manifold Absolute Pressure sensors have a vacuum line connected between the unit and manifold vacuum. On Barometric Pressure sensors, the line is not used and the connector is either open or has a filter installed over it. Pressure sensors also have a vacuum line between the sensor and intake manifold and appear only on carbureted models.

Barometric Pressure Sensors: Measure voltage with ignition on and engine off.

Manifold Absolute Pressure Sensors: Measure voltage with ignition on and engine off. Start engine and apply 10 in./Hg. (34 kPa) to unit, voltage should be 1.5 volts minimum less.

Engine	Year	Sensor	Voltage @ Altitude or Condition
All, as equipped	1989-90	Barometric	3.8-5.5 @ 0-1000
			3.6-5.3 @ 1000-2000
			3.5-5.1 @ 2000-3000
			3.3-5.0 @ 3000-4000
			3.2-4.8 @ 4000-5000
			3.0-4.6 @ 5000-6000
			2.9-4.5 @ 6000-7000
			2.5-4.3 @ 7000-
All	1989-00	Manifold Absolute	1.0-2.0 idle
			4-4.8 WOT

CRANKSHAFT SENSORS
Resistance is measured at room temperature.

Engine	Year	Resistance (ohms)
2.2L	1994-95	800-1200
	1996-97	700-1300

THROTTLE POSITION SENSOR (TPS)
Verify that idle is at specified value.

Make all checks/adjustments with engine at operating temperature.

Carbureted Models: Remove aluminum plug covering the adjustment screw. Remove the screw and connect a digital voltmeter from the TPS center terminal to the bottom terminal. Apply thread locking compound to the screw and with ignition on and engine not running (as applies), quickly adjust screw to obtain specified voltage at indicated condition.

CHEVROLET, GMC TRUCKS
1989-2000 All Models Includes Chevrolet Lumina
APV/Minivan, Venture, Oldsmobile Bravada & Silhouette; Pontiac Trans Sport; Isuzu Hombre

UNDERHOOD SERVICE SPECIFICATIONS

GMTTU12

GMTTU11

SENSORS, INPUT Continued

THROTTLE POSITION SENSOR (TPS) Continued

Fuel Injected Models: Disconnect harness multi-plug from TPS. Using three six-inch jumper wires, reconnect harness to TPS. With ignition on and engine not running, connect a digital voltmeter to terminals A and B of TPS harness. If TPS is adjustable, loosen the unit retaining screws and rotate the unit to obtain the specified value.

Engine	Year	TPS Voltage[1] Idle	WOT
2.2L	1994-95	.45-.85[2]	4.5 min.
	1996-00	.20-.90	4.0 min.
2.5L (151)	1989-91	.20-1.25[2]	—
	1992	.60-1.25[2]	4.5 min.
	1993	.45-1.25[2]	4.5 min.
2.8L (173)	1989-92	.48	—
	1993	.45-1.25[2]	4.5 min.
3.1L FWD Vans	1990-91	.20-1.25	—
3.1L FWD Vans	1992-96	.40-1.25[2]	4.5
3.4L	1996-00	.20-.74	4.0 min.
3.8L	1992	.40	5.1
	1993-95	.20-.74[2]	4.5 min.
4.3L (262) TBI	1989-91	.20-1.25[2]	—
4.3L: MT	1993	.45-1.25[2]	4.5 min.
AT	1993	.35-1.28[2]	4.5 min.
4.3L w/TBI: S Series w/MT	1994-95	.45-.85[2]	4.0
Others	1994-95	.35-1.28[2]	4.0
4.3L w/CFI	1996	.35-.85[2]	4.5 min.
	1997-00	.36-.96[2]	4.0 min.
V8 Gas w/TBI	1989-92	.20-1.25[2]	4.5 min.
V8 Gas w/TBI MT	1993-96	.45-1.25[2]	4.5 min.
AT	1993-96	.35-1.25[2]	4.5 min.
V8 CFI	1996	.35-.85[2]	4.5 min.
	1997-00	.36-.96[2]	4.0 min.
V8 Diesel	1993-95	.35-.95[2]	4.0 min.

1 ±.10.
2 Not adjustable.

KNOCK SENSOR

Engine	Year	Resistance (ohms)
All	1996-00	90,000-110,000

ACTUATORS, OUTPUT

IDLE SPEED CONTROL

All engines with ISC.

Measured between terminals A & B and C & D.

Engine	Year	Resistance (ohms)
All TBI	1989	20 min.
All	1990-00	40-80

MIXTURE CONTROL SOLENOID-CARBURETED ENGINES

On some engines, the ECM will be damaged if the resistance of the mixture control solenoid is less than specified.

Engine	Year	Resistance (ohms)
All	1989	10 min.

FUEL INJECTORS

Engine	Year	Resistance (ohms)	Temperature (deg. F/C)
2.2L MFI	1994-00	11.6-12.4	—
3.4L	1996-00	11.4-12.6	—
3.8L	1992-95	11.6-12.4	—
4.3L Turbo	1991-93	2 min.	—
All TBI	1989	1.2 min.	—
	1990-96	1.3 min.	—

Measured at 50-95°F (10-35°C)

Engine	Year	Volts
V6, V8 CFI	1996-00	5.44-7.53

CHRYSLER, DODGE, PLYMOUTH

1989-2000 Ex. Imported Models, includes Eagle Vision & FWD Vans
(Except Raider, Ram 50, Colt, Conquest, Laser (1990-94), Stealth, Vista, Sebring Coupe, Avenger—See Next Section

---

ENGINE IDENTIFICATION

To identify any engine by the manufacturer's code, follow the four steps designated by the numbered blocks.

1 **MODEL YEAR IDENTIFICATION:** Refer to illustration of the Vehicle Identification Number (V.I.N.). The year is indicated by a code letter which is the 10th character of the V.I.N.

2 **ENGINE CODE LOCATION:** Refer to illustration of V.I.N. plate for location and designation of engine code.

3 **ENGINE CODE:** In the "CODE" column, find the engine code determined in Step 2.

4 **ENGINE IDENTIFICATION:** On the line where the engine code appears, read to the right to identify the engine.

V.I.N. PLATE LOCATION:

On top left side of instrument panel

Model year of vehicle:

2000 — Y
1999 — X
1998 — W
1997 — V
1996 — T
1995 — S
1994 — R
1993 — P
1992 — N
1991 — M
1990 — L
1989 — K

MODEL YEAR AND ENGINE IDENTIFICATION:

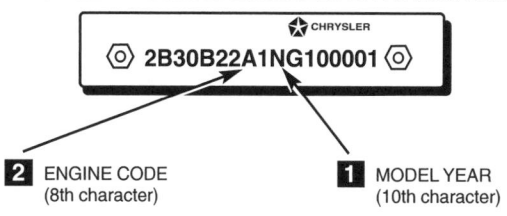

2 ENGINE CODE (8th character)   **1** MODEL YEAR (10th character)

YEAR	CODE	CYL.	liters	cu. in.	Fuel System	HP
2000	C	4	2.0	122	MFI	132
	X, B	4	2.4	148	MFI	150
	H	6	2.5	152	MFI	168
	R (ex. FWD vans)	6	2.7	167	MFI	200, 202[1]
	U, V	6	2.7	167	MFI	200, 202[1]
	3	6	3.0	182	MFI	150
	J	6	3.2	197	MFI	225
	R (FWD vans)	6	3.3	202	MFI	158
	G (FWD vans)	6	3.3 EFF	202 EFF	MFI	158
	G (ex. FWD vans)	6	3.5	214	MFI	242, 253[1]
	L	6	3.8	230	MFI	180
1999	C	4	2.0	122	MFI	132
	Y	4	2.0	122	MFI	150
	X, B	4	2.4	148	MFI	150
	H	6	2.5	152	MFI	168
	R (ex. FWD vans)	6	2.7	167	MFI	200
	3	6	3.0	182	MFI	150
	J	6	3.2	197	MFI	225
	R (FWD vans)	6	3.3	202	MFI	158
	G (FWD vans)	6	3.3 EFF	202 EFF	MFI	N/A
	G (ex. FWD vans)	6	3.5	214	MFI	253
	L	6	3.8	230	MFI	180
1998	C	4	2.0	122	MFI	132
	Y	4	2.0	122	MFI	150
	X, B	4	2.4	148	MFI	150
	H	6	2.5	152	MFI	168
	R (ex. FWD vans)	6	2.7	167	MFI	200
	3	6	3.0	182	MFI	150
	J (ex. FWD vans)	6	3.2	197	MFI	225
	R (FWD vans)	6	3.3	202	MFI	158
	J (FWD vans)	6	3.3 CNG	202 CNG	MFI	N/A
	G	6	3.3 EFF	202 EFF	MFI	N/A
	L	6	3.8	230	MFI	180
1997	C	4	2.0	122	MFI	132
	Y	4	2.0	122	MFI	150
	X, B	4	2.4	148	MFI	150
	H	6	2.5	152	MFI	168
	3	6	3.0	182	MFI	150
	R	6	3.3	202	MFI	158
	T	6	3.3	202	MFI	161
	J	6	3.3 CNG	202 CNG	MFI	N/A
	F	6	3.5	215	MFI	214
	L	6	3.8	230	MFI	166

YEAR	CODE	CYL.	liters	cu. in.	Fuel System	HP
1996	C	4	2.0	122	MFI	132
	Y	4	2.0	122	MFI	150
	X, B	4	2.4	148	MFI	150
	H	6	2.5	152	MFI	164, 168[1]
	3	6	3.0	182	MFI	150
	R	6	3.3	202	MFI	158
	T	6	3.3	202	MFI	161
	J	6	3.3 CNG	202 CNG	MFI	N/A
	F	6	3.5	215	MFI	214
	L	6	3.8	230	MFI	166
1995	C	4	2.0	122	MFI	132
	Y	4	2.0	122	MFI	150
	X	4	2.4	148	MFI	140
	K	4	2.5	153	TBI	100
	H	6	2.5	152	MFI	164
	3	6	3.0	182	MFI	141-142[1]
	R	6	3.3	202	MFI	162
	U	6	3.3 FF	202 FF	MFI	161-167
	T	6	3.3	202	MFI	161
	F	6	3.5	215	MFI	214
	L	6	3.8	230	MFI	162
1994	D	4	2.2	135	TBI	93
	K	4	2.5	153	TBI	100
	V	4	2.5 FF	153 FF	MFI	101-106
	3	6	3.0	182	MFI	141, 142[1]
	R	6	3.3	202	MFI	162
	U	6	3.3 FF	202 FF	MFI	161-167
	T	6	3.3	202	MFI	161
	F	6	3.5	215	MFI	214
	L	6	3.8	230	MFI	162
1993	D	4	2.2	135	TBI	93
	A	4	2.2 T	135 T	MFI	224
	K	4	2.5	153	MFI	100
	3	6	3.0	182	MFI	141
	R	6	3.3	202	MFI	147, 150[1]
	T	6	3.3	202	MFI	153
	F	6	3.5	215	MFI	214
	L	6	3.8	230	MFI	151
1992	D	4	2.2	135	TBI	93
	A	4	2.2 T	135 T	MFI	224
	B	4	2.5	152	TBI	100
	W	4	2.5	152	TBI	100

ENGINE IDENTIFICATION Continued

YEAR	**3** ENGINE CODE	CYL.	**4** ENGINE IDENTIFICATION DISPL. liters	cu. in.	Fuel System	HP
1992 Cont'd.	K 4	4	2.5	152	TBI	100
	J 4	4	2.5 T	152 T	MFI	152
	P 4	4	2.5 T	152 T	MFI	152
	3 6	6	3.0	182	MFI	141, 142[1]
	V 6	6	3.0	182	MFI	141, 142[1]
	U 6	6	3.0	182	MFI	150
	R 6	6	3.3	201	MFI	147, 150[1]
	L 6	6	3.8	230	MFI	150
1991	D 4	4	2.2	135	TBI	122
	A 4	4	2.2 T	135 T	MFI	224
	K 4	4	2.5	152	TBI	100
	J 4	4	2.5 T	152 T	MFI	152
	3 6	6	3.0	182	MFI	141
	R 6	6	3.3	201	MFI	147, 150[1]
	L 6	6	3.8	230	MFI	150
1990	D 4	4	2.2	135	TBI	93
	C 4	4	2.2 T	135 T	MFI	174
	K 4	4	2.5	152	TBI	100

YEAR	**3** ENGINE CODE	CYL.	**4** ENGINE IDENTIFICATION DISPL. liters	cu. in.	Fuel System	HP
1990 Cont'd.	J 4	4	2.5 T	152 T	MFI	150
	3 6	6	3.0	182	MFI	141, 142[1]
	R 6	6	3.3	201	MFI	147, 150[1]
1989	D 4	4	2.2	135	TBI	93
	A 4	4	2.2 T	135 T	MFI	174
	K 4	4	2.5	152	TBI	100
	J 4	4	2.5 T	152 T	MFI	150
	3 6	6	3.0	182	MFI	141
	P, 4 8	8	5.2	318	2V	140
	S 8	8	5.2	318	4V	175

T—Turbocharged.   TBI—Throttle Body Injection.
MFI—Multiport Fuel Injection.   2V—Two Venturi Carburetor.
4V—Four Venturi Carburetor.   FF—Flexible Fuel.
CNG—Compressed Natural Gas.   NA—Not Available.
EFF—Ethanol Flexible Fuel.
1 Engine horsepower varies with model installation.

UNDERHOOD SERVICE SPECIFICATIONS

CRTU1   CRTU1

CYLINDER NUMBERING SEQUENCE
4-CYL. FIRING ORDER: 1 3 4 2

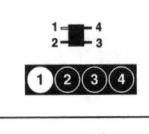

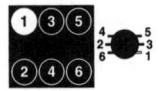

8-CYL. FIRING ORDER:
1 8 4 3 6 5 7 2

— Front of car —

| 1995-00 2.0L, 2.4L | 1989-93 2.2L 16V DOHC Turbo | 2.2L (135) ex. 16V DOHC, 2.5L (153) ex. Code H | 1995-00 2.5L Code H |

V6 FIRING ORDER: 1 2 3 4 5 6

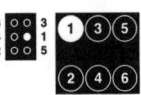

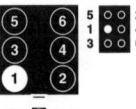

— Front of car —

1989
5.2L (318)

| 1998-00 2.7L, 3.2L 1999-00 3.5L (Coil-on-Plug) | 1989-00 3.0L (182) | 3.3L, 3.8L Ex. 3.3L Code T | 1993-97 3.3L Code T | 1993-97 3.5L |

TIMING MARK

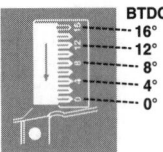

1989-95 2.2L, 2.5L w/AT ex. Code H, 2.2L DOHC Turbo w/MT

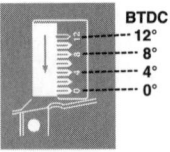

1989 2.2L (135), 2.5L (153) w/MT ex. Code H ex. 2.2L DOHC Turbo

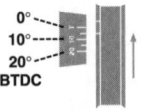

1995-00 2.5L Code H

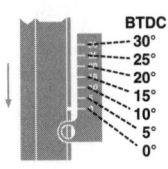

3.0L (182)

No Timing Marks on These Engines

2.0L, 2.4L, 2.7L, 3.2L 3.3L, 3.5L, 3.8L

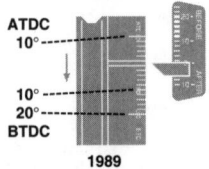

1989 5.2L (318)

CHRYSLER, DODGE, PLYMOUTH
1989-2000 Ex. Imported Models, includes Eagle Vision & FWD Vans

UNDERHOOD SERVICE SPECIFICATIONS

ELECTRICAL AND IGNITION SYSTEMS

BATTERY

Engine	Year	STANDARD BCI Group No.	STANDARD Crank. Perf.	OPTIONAL BCI Group No.	OPTIONAL Crank. Perf.
2.0L Neon	1995-99	58	450	—	—
	2000	26R	450	—	—
Cirrus, Stratus, Breeze, Sebring Convertible	1995-99	75	510	—	—
2.2L (135) TBI	1989-90	34	400	—	—
	1991-95	34	500	—	—
2.2L (135) Turbo	1989-94	34	500	—	—
2.4L ex. Vans	1995-00	75	510	—	—
Vans	1996-00	34	600	—	—
2.5L (153) 4-cyl.	1989-90	34	500	—	—
	1991	34	625	—	—
	1992-95	34	600	—	—
2.5L V6	1995-00	75	510	—	—
2.7L	1998-00	34	500	—	—
3.0L (183)	1989-90	34	500	—	—
3.0L					
Chrysler Models	1991	34	500	—	—
	1991	34	625	—	—
Monaco	1991	34	625	—	—
3.0L	1992-00	34	600	—	—
3.2L	1998-00	34	600	—	—
3.3L	1990-00	34	500	—	—
3.5L	1993-97	34	500	—	—
	1999-00	34	600	—	—
3.8L	1991	34	625	—	—
	1992-97	34	600	—	—
Vans	1992-00	34	500	—	—
5.2L (318)	1989	34	500	34	625

GENERATOR

With 15 volts at alternator and at 1250 rpm unless otherwise specified.

Application	Year	Rated Output (amps)	Test Output (amps @ rpm)
Bosch	1989-91	75	68
	1989-92	90	84-88
	1991-93	90	84-86
Delco (Monaco)	1990-92	85	70 @ 2000
	1990-92	96	78 @ 2000
	1990-92	105	84 @ 2000
Mitsubishi	1990	65	46 @ 2500
	1990	75	53 @ 2500
Nippondenso	1989-94	75	68
4-cyl.	1989-94	90	87
V6	1989-94	90	90
	1989-94	120	98
2.0L, 2.4L	1995	90	63 @ 2500
2.5L	1995	90	63 @ 2500
		110	77 @ 2500
All others: 4-cyl.	1995	90	84 @ 1250
V6	1995	90	86 @ 1250
Neon	1996-99	83	75 @ 2500
	2000	85	75 @ 2500
Cirrus, Breeze, Stratus Sebring Convertible	1996-00	90	74 @ 2500
Vans	1996-00	90	86
		120	98
Intrepid, Vision, Concorde, LHS, New Yorker, 300M	1996-97	90	90 @ 2500
	1998-00	120	105 @ 2500
		130	110 @ 2500

REGULATOR

Application	Test Temp. (deg. F/C)	Voltage Setting
1990-91 Monaco	—	13.5-16.0
1989 Computer regulated	—	—
1990-94 Computer regulated	0-50/-18 to 10	14.5-15.0
1995 Vans, Spirit, Acclaim, LeBaron	50-100/10-38	13.9-14.5
	100-150/38-66	13.8-14
	150-200/66-93	13.8 max.
1995-00 Others		1

1 Measured battery voltage. At 1500 rpm, voltage should be no more than 2.5 volts above battery voltage.

STARTER
Engine at operating temperature.

Engine	Year	Cranking Voltage (min. volts)	Ampere Draw @ Cranking Speed
Monaco	1990-92	9.6	250 max.
Concorde, Intrepid, New Yorker, LHS, Neon	1995-00	9.6	150-280
Cirrus, Breeze, Stratus Sebring Conv.	1995-96	9.6	250 max.
	1997-00	9.6	150-280
All Others	1989-95	9.6	150-220
	1996-00	9.6	150-280

SPARK PLUGS

Engine	Year	Gap (inches)	Gap (mm)	Torque (ft-lb)
2.0L	1995-00	.033-.038	.8-.9	20
2.2L (135), 2.5L (153) (4-cyl.)	1989	.035	.89	20
	1990-95	.033-.038	.8-.9	20
2.4L	1995-00	.048-.053	1.2-1.3	20
2.5L (V6)	1995-00	.038-.043	.9-1.1	20
2.7L	1998-00	.048-.053	1.2-1.3	13
3.0L (183)	1989-00	.039-.043	1.0-1.1	20
3.2L	1998-00	.048-.053	1.2-1.3	13
3.3L, 3.8L	1990-00	.048-.053	1.2-1.3	20
Flex. Fuel	1994-97	.043-.048	1.1-1.2	20
3.5L	1993-95	.048-.053	1.2-1.3	20
	1996-97	.033-.038	.8-.9	20
	1998-00	.048-.053	1.2-1.3	20
5.2L (318)	1989	.03 5	.89	30

IGNITION COIL
FOR TESTING AND ADJUSTMENT DIAGRAMS, SEE APPENDIX A.

Application	Year	Windings	Resistance (ohms)
Models with Distributor: Prestolite	1989-91	Primary	1.34-1.55
		Secondary	9400-11,700
Essex, Echlin	1989-91	Primary	1.34-1.62
		Secondary	9000-12,200
Diamond: Oil filled	1989-91	Primary	1.34-1.55
		Secondary	15,000-19,000
Epoxy	1990-93	Primary	.97-1.18
		Secondary	11,000-15,300
Epoxy	1993	Primary	.95-1.20
		Secondary	8500-15,300
Toyodenso 4-cyl.	1991-93	Primary	.95-1.20
		Secondary	11,300-13,300
2.5L (V6)	1995-98	Primary	0.6-0.8
		Secondary	12,000-18,000
All others	1994-95	Primary	.95-1.20
		Secondary	8500-15,300
Models without Distributor: Diamond: 2.2L Turbo, 3.3L, 3.5L, 3.8L DIS	1990-93	Primary	.52-.63[1]
		Secondary	11,600-15,800[2]
Marshal 3.3L DIS	1990	Primary	.53-.65[1]
		Secondary	7000-9000[2]
Toyodenso, V6	1990-93	Primary	.51-.61[1]
		Secondary	11,500-13,500[2]
2.0L, 2.4L	1995	Primary	.51-.61[1]
		Secondary	11,500-15,300[2]
2.0L Neon, 2.4L Vans	1996-98	Primary	.45-.65[1]
		Secondary	7000-15,800[2]
Steel Towers	1999-00	Primary	.45-.65
		Secondary	11,500-13,500
Copper Towers	1999-00	Primary	.53-.65
		Secondary	10,900-14,700
2.0L Others, 2.4L ex. Vans	1996-00	Primary	.51-.61[1]
		Secondary	11,500-13,500[2]
2.7L, 3.2L, 3.3L, 3.5L, 3.8L	1994-00	Primary	.45-.65[1]
		Secondary	7000-15,800[2]

1 Measured between B+ (upper right) and each of the other three terminals on four wire coil connector.

2 Measured between high voltage terminals of each bank of coils with spark plug wires removed.

CHRYSLER, DODGE, PLYMOUTH
1989-2000 Ex. Imported Models, includes Eagle Vision & FWD Vans

DISTRIBUTOR PICKUP
FOR TESTING AND ADJUSTMENT DIAGRAMS, SEE APPENDIX B.

Application	Resistance (ohms)	Air Gap (in./mm)
Distributor without Hall Effect 1989 6- & 8-cyl. single pickup	150-900	.006/.15
1989 6- & 8-cyl. dual pickups:		
Start	150-900	.006/.15
Run	150-900	.012/.30

BASE TIMING
FOR TESTING AND ADJUSTMENT DIAGRAMS, SEE APPENDIX C.

Set timing at Before Top Dead Center and at slow idle unless otherwise specified.

Disconnect and plug vacuum hoses at distributor or ESC (Electronic Spark Control) unit, as equipped. W/FI, disconnect coolant temperature sensor.

Engine	Year	Man. Trans. (degrees)	Auto. Trans. (degrees)
2.2L (135) TBI	1989-95	12 ± 2	12 ± 2
2.2L (135) Turbo	1989-90	12 ± 2	12 ± 2
2.5L (153) 4-cyl.	1989-95	12 ± 2	12 ± 2
3.0L (183) ex. Monaco	1989-00	12 ± 2	12 ± 2
5.2L (318)	1989	—	16 ± 2

FUEL SYSTEM

FUEL SYSTEM PRESSURE
FOR TESTING AND ADJUSTMENT DIAGRAMS, SEE APPENDIX D.

FI, with vacuum hose connected to fuel pressure regulator.

Engine	Year	Pressure PSI	RPM
4-cyl.			
TBI	1989-91 (early)	13.5-15.5	idle
TBI	1991-95 (late)	38-40	idle
MFI Turbo, Flexible Fuel	1989-94	53-57	idle
MFI	1995	47-51	ign. on
2.0L, 2.4L	1996	48-54	idle
2.0L	1997	48-54	idle
	1998-00	46-50	idle
2.4L	1997	47-51	idle
	1998-00	46-50	idle
6-cyl.			
Transverse engines: 2.5L	1995-97	47-51[1]	idle
		38[2]	idle
3.3L CNG	1995-97	90-140	idle
Flex Fuel	1998-00	50-60	idle
All others	1989-96	46-50	ign. on
	1997-00	43-53	idle
Longitudinal engines			
2.7L, 3.2L	1998-00	44-54	idle
3.3L	1993-97	53-57	ign. on
		44-48	idle
3.5L	1993-97	46-50	ign. on
		37-41	idle
8-cyl.	1998-00	44-54	idle
	1989	5.8-7.3	idle

1 Vacuum hose disconnected from fuel pressure regulator.
2 Vacuum hose connected to fuel pressure regulator.

IDLE SPEED W/O COMPUTER CONTROL
8-cyl.:

Disconnect and plug canister control hose and disconnect oxygen sensor electrical lead.

Disconnect and plug EGR, distributor of SCC vacuum hoses. Air cleaner may be removed but plug the air cleaner vacuum hose and leave the SCC electrical leads connected. Ground carb idle stop switch.

With A/C, turn unit on and disconnect the compressor clutch electrical lead. Set speedup speed to specification. Turn A/C unit off and set idle speed to specification.

Without A/C, set idle speed to specification.

IDLE SPEED W/O COMPUTER CONTROL Continued

Engine	Year	Man. Trans.	Auto. Trans.	SLOW Man. Trans.	SLOW Auto. Trans.	FAST Step of Cam
5.2L (318) 2V	1989	—	630 N	—	1700 N	Second
solenoid	1989		775 N			
5.2L (318) 4V	1989	—	750 N	—	1450 N	Second
solenoid	1989		900 N			

IDLE SPEED W/COMPUTER CONTROL
FOR TESTING AND ADJUSTMENT DIAGRAMS, SEE APPENDIX E.

Idle speed must be within 100 rpm of specification listed.

1989-99 Transverse engines: With TBI, remove PCV valve and install special tool C-5004 (0.125" orifice) into hose. With MFI, disconnect idle purge line from throttle body. Start engine and using Diagnostic Readout Box, access "Minimum Airflow Idle Speed." If checking speed is not within specification range, replace the throttle body.

1993-99 Longitudinal engines: Remove PCV hose from PCV valve and cap the valve. Start engine and using Diagnostic Readout Box, access "Minimum Airflow Idle Speed." If checking speed is not within specified range, replace throttle body.

Engine	Year	Transmission	Checking Speed	Idle Speed	AC Speed-up
2.0L	1995-00	MT	600-1300	—	—
		AT	600-1300 N	—	—
2.2L (135) TBI	1989-90	MT	1100-1300	850	—
	1989-90	AT	1100-1300 N	850 N	—
2.2L TBI	1991-92	MT	1100-1300	—	—
	1991-92	AT	1100-1300 N	—	—
2.2L TBI	1993-95	MT	800-1200	—	—
	1993-95	AT	800-1200 N	—	—
2.2L (135) Turbo	1989	MT	650-900	900	—
	1989	AT	650-900 N	900 N	—
2.2L Turbo	1990	MT	650-1050	950	—
	1990	AT	650-1050 N	900 N	—
2.2L Turbo	1991	MT	550-900	—	—
2.2L Turbo	1992-93	MT	650-1150	—	—
2.4L	1995-00	MT	600-1300	—	—
	1995-00	AT	600-1300 N	—	—
Vans	1996-00	MT	550-875	—	—
		AT	550-875 N	—	—
2.5L (153) TBI	1989-91	MT	1050-1250	850	—
	1989-91	AT	1050-1250 N	850 N	—
2.5L TBI	1992	MT	1050-1250	—	—
	1992	AT	1050-1250 N	—	—
2.5L TBI	1993-95	MT	800-1200	—	—
	1993-95	AT	800-1200 N	—	—
2.5L Turbo	1989	MT	650-900	900	—
	1989	AT	650-900 N	900 N	—
2.5L Turbo	1990-91	MT	650-1200	—	—
	1990-91	AT	650-1200 N	—	—
2.5L Turbo	1992	MT	700-1400	—	—
	1992	AT	700-1400 N	—	—
2.5L Flexible Fuel	1993-94	AT	700-1400 N	—	—
2.5L (V6)	1995-00	MT	500-1100	—	—
	1995-00	AT	500-1100 N	—	—
2.7L	1998-99	AT	350-700N	—	—
	2000		550-1300 N	—	—
3.0L	1989	AT	850-1050 N	700 N	—
Vans	1989	AT	850-1050 N	800 N	—
3.0L	1989-90	MT	750-950	800	—
	1989-90	AT	750-950 N	700 N	—
3.0L ex. Monaco	1991-92	MT	750-950	—	—
	1991-92	AT	750-950 N	—	—
3.0L	1993-99	MT	610-910	—	—
		AT	610-910	—	—
3.2L	1998-99	AT	350-700 N	—	—
	2000		550-1300 N	—	—
3.3L, 3.8L	1990	AT	700-950 N	750 N	—
3.3L, 3.8L	1991-92	AT	700-950 N	—	—
3.3L, 3.8L:					
Transverse engines	1993-98	AT	575-875 N	—	—
Longitudinal engines	1993-97	AT	600-840 N	—	—
3.5L	1993-97	AT	750-1100 N	—	—
	2000		550-1300 N	—	—

ENGINE MECHANICAL

TIGHTENING TORQUES
FOR CYLINDER HEAD TORQUE SEQUENCES AND DIAGRAMS, SEE APPENDIX F.
Some torque values are specified in inches.

TORQUE FOOT-POUNDS/NEWTON METERS

Engine	Year	Cylinder Head	Intake Manifold	Exhaust Manifold	Crankshaft Pulley	Water Pump
2.0L	1995-00	25/34, 50/68, 50/68, +90°	105"/12[4]	200"/23	105/142	105"/12
2.2L (135), 2.5L (153) (4-cyl.)	1989-95	45/61, 65/89, 65/89, +90°[1]	200"/23	200"/23	20/25	250"/28-upper 3 40/54-lower 1
2.4L	1995-00	25/34, 50/68, 50/68, +90°	20/28	200"/23	100/135	105"/12
2.5L (V6)	1995-00	80/108	18/21	33/44	134/182	17/24
2.7L	1998-00	35/47, 55/75, 55/75, +90°	150"/12	200"/23	125/170	105"/12
3.0L (183) ex. Monaco	1989-90	70/95[2]	174"/20	191"/22	110/150	240"/27
3.0L ex. Monaco	1991-96 1997-99	80/108[2] 80/108	174"/20 20/28	200"/22 200"/22	110/150 100/135	23/27 105"/12
3.0L Monaco	1990-92	[2]	11/15	13/18	133/180	20/27
3.2L	1998-00	45/61 65/89, 65/89, +90°	105"/12 M6 250"/28, M8	200"/23	75/102	105"/12
3.3L, 3.8L	1990-00	45/61, 65/89, 65/89, +90°	200"/23,	200"/23	40/54	105"/12
3.5L	1993-00	45/61, 65/89, 65/89, +90°	250"/28	200"/23	85/115	105"/12
5.2L (318)	1989	105/143	40/54	20/27-bolts 15/20-nuts	100/136	30/41

1 Torque should be above 90/122 after this step or replace bolt.
2 Cold.
3 Tighten to 44/60, loosen each bolt individually and retorque to 30/40. Turn an additional 160-200°.
4 DOHC, 250"/28

COMPRESSION PRESSURE
At cranking speed, engine temperature normalized, throttle open.

Engine	Year	PSI	Maximum Variation PSI
4-cyl.:			
2.0L, 2.4L	1995-00	170-225/100 min.	1
Others	1989-96	100 min.	1
V6: 2.5L	1995-00	139-185	14
3.0L ex. Monaco	1989-00	178	14
3.0L Monaco, 3.2L, 3.3L, 3.5L, 3.8L	1990-00	100 min.	1
8-cyl.	1989	100 min.	25

1 Lowest cylinder must be 75% of highest.

BELT TENSION
A belt in operation 15 minutes is considered a used belt.

Engine	Year	Generator	Power Steering or Idler	Air Cond.	Air Pump
Strand Tension					
2.0L Neon new	1995-00	135	135	135	—
used	1995-00	100	100	100	—
2.0L, 2.4L, 2.5L Cirrus, Stratus new	1995-00	150	130	150	—
used	1995-00	80	80	80	—

BELT TENSION Continued

Engine	Year	Generator	Power Steering or Idler	Air Cond.	Air Pump
2.4L Vans new	1996-00	190	140	190	—
used	1996-00	90	90	90	—
2.2L (135) new	1989-95	105	95	95	—
used	1989-95	80	80	80	—
2.5L 4-cyl. new	1989-95	115	105	105	—
used	1989-95	80	80	80	—
2.5L (V6) Cirrus, Stratus new	1995-00	130	150	130	—
used	1995-00	80	80	80	—
V6 2.7L new	1998-00	200[1]	200[1]	200[1]	—
used	1998-00	120[1]	120[1]	120[1]	—
V6 3.0L ex. Monaco new	1989-00	[1]	[1]	125	—
used	1989-00	[1]	[1]	80	—
V6 3.0L Monaco new	1990-91	180-200	180-200	180-200	—
used	1990-91	140-160	140-160	140-160	—
V6 3.2L new	1998-00	140-160[1]	140-160[1]	140-160[1]	—
used	1998-00	120[1]	120[1]	120[1]	—
V6 3.3L ex LH, 3.8L	1990-91	[1]	[1]	[1]	—
3.3L, 3.5L, 3.8L	1990-00	[1]	[1]	[1]	—
6- & 8-cyl. new	1989	120	120	120	120
used	1989	70	70	70	70
Deflection[2]					
2.2L (135) new	1989-90	1/8"	5/16"	5/16"	3/16"
used	1989-90	1/4"	7/16"	7/16"	1/4"
2.5L (153) new	1989-90	1/8"	1/4"	5/16"	3/16"
used	1989-90	1/4"	7/16"	7/16"	1/4"
3.0L (183) ex. Monaco	1989-91	[1]	[1]	1/4"-5/16"	
6- & 8-cyl. all	1989	—	—	—	—

1 Serpentine belt with automatic tensioner.
2 At 10 lb of force on midpoint of belt.

SERPENTINE BELT DIAGRAMS

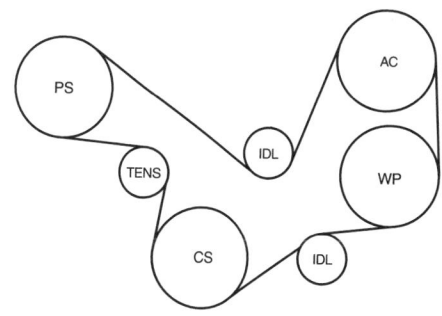

1991-93 2.2L Turbo

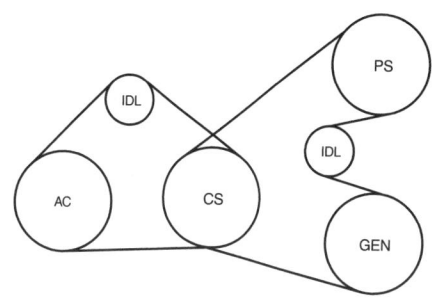

1998-00 2.7L

SERPENTINE BELT DIAGRAMS Continued

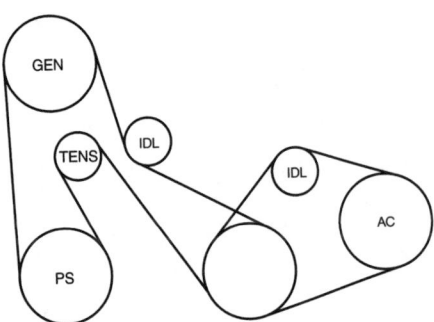

1990-00 3.0L

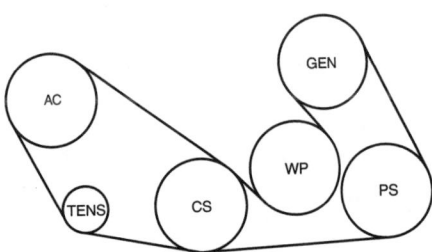

1993-97 3.3L LH

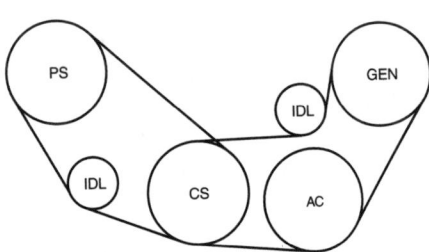

1993-00 3.2L, 3.5L

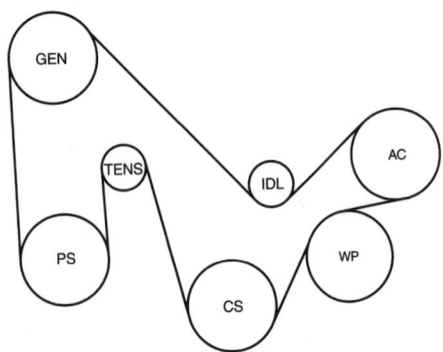

1990-00 3.3L ex. LH, 3.8L

ENGINE COMPUTER SYSTEM

DIAGNOSTIC TROUBLE CODES
FOR TESTING AND ADJUSTMENT DIAGRAMS, SEE APPENIX G.

OBD-II Systems. Codes can still be displayed on MIL.

1989-00: Turn ignition switch on-off-on-off-on and observe POWER LOSS or CHECK ENGINE light on instrument panel.

Code 11 Ignition reference circuit
Code 12 Battery disconnected in last 50 cycles
Code 12 Standby memory (1989-90)
Code 13 MAP sensor vacuum circuit
Code 14 MAP sensor electrical circuit
Code 15 Speed/distance sensor
Code 16 Battery voltage loss (1989)
Code 16 Knock sensor circuit (1993-98)
Code 17 Engine running too cool
Code 21 Oxygen sensor
Code 22 Engine coolant temperature sensor
Code 23 Throttle body temperature sensor (1989-90 TBI)
Code 23 Intake air temperature sensor circuit (1991-98)
Code 24 Throttle position sensor
Code 25 Idle air control circuit
Code 26 Peak injector current not reached (1989-90)
Code 26 Number one injector circuit MFI
Code 27 Fuel injector circuit control
Code 31 EVAP Canister purge solenoid
Code 32 Power loss lamp
Code 33 Air conditioner clutch relay (1989-98)
Code 34 Speed control solenoid driver circuit (1989-98)
Codes 34 & 36 Spare driver circuit
Code 35 Fan control relay circuit
Code 36 Wastegate solenoid circuit
Code 37 Torque converter part throttle unlock solenoid circuit (1989-91)
Code 41 Charging system over voltage (1989)
Code 41 Generator field circuit (1990-98)
Code 42 Automatic shutdown relay circuit
Code 43 Spark interface circuit (1989)
Code 43 Ignition coil primary circuit (1990-98 3.3L)
Code 44 Battery temperature out of range (1990-98)
Code 44 Loss of voltage to logic board (1989)
Code 45 Boost limit exceeded
Code 46 Battery voltage too high
Code 47 Battery voltage too low
Code 53 Internal engine controller fault (1989)
Code 54 Distributor sync pick-up circuit (1989-91)
Code 54 Camshaft sensor signal (1993-98)
Code 55 End of message
Code 61 Baro read solenoid (1989-94)
Code 61 Baro out of range
Code 62 SRI mileage accumulator circuit
Code 63 Fault code error (1989-90)
Code 63 Controller failure, EEPROM write denied (1991-98)
Code 64 Flexible Fuel sensor
Code 64 Variable nozzle turbo solenoid
Code 65 Manifold tuning valve
Code 66 CCD message error
Code 71 5 volt supply too low
Code 72 Catalytic converter efficiency
Code 77 Speed control power relay
Code 88 Start of message

SENSORS, INPUT
TEMPERATURE SENSORS

Engine	Year	Sensor	Resistance Ohms @ deg. F/C
All 4-cyl. FI & V6	1989-00	Coolant, Intake Air[1]	7000-13,000 @ 70/21 700-1000 @ 200/93
	1989-91	Throttle body[2]	5600-14,600 @ 70/21 400-1500 @ 200/93
	1995-97	Fuel[3]	7000-13,000 @ 70/21 700-1000 @ 200/93
5.2L (318)	1989	Intake Air	6000 min. @ 70/21 2500 max. @ 200/93

1 As equipped.
2 1989-91 early TBI only.
3 CNG models only.

CHRYSLER, DODGE, PLYMOUTH
1989-2000 Ex. Imported Models, includes Eagle Vision & FWD Vans

UNDERHOOD SERVICE SPECIFICATIONS

SENSORS, INPUT Continued

MANIFOLD ABSOLUTE PRESSURE SENSORS

Engine	Year	Voltage Change	Voltage @ Condition
All	1995-00	—	4-5 @ ign. on
		—	1.5-2.1 @ idle

THROTTLE POSITION SENSORS

Engine	Year	TPS (voltage) Idle	WOT
2.0L	1995	0.5	3.7
2.0L Neon	1996-00	.35-1.20	3.1-4.0
Others	1996-00	0.6 min.	4.5 max.
2.2L (135) FI, 2.5L (153)	1989	0.5-1.5	3.5
2.2L, 2.5L TBI	1993-95	1.0	4.0
2.4L	1995	0.5	3.7
2.4L Vans	1996	0.4 min.	3.8 max.
	1997-00	.38-1.20	3.1-4.4
Others	1996-00	0.6 min.	4.5 max.
2.5L	1995	0.5	3.7
	1996-00	0.6 min.	4.5 max.
2.2L Turbo	1993	0.5	4.0
2.5L Flexible Fuel	1993-94	1.0	4.0
2.7L	1998-00	.38-1.20	3.1-4.4
3.2L	1998-00	.38-1.20	3.1-4.4
3.0L	1993-94	0.5	3.5
	1995-96	0.5	3.7
	1997-00	.38-1.20	3.1-4.4
3.3L, 3.8L Transverse engine	1993-94	0.5	3.5
	1995-96	0.5	3.7
	1997-99	.38-1.20	3.1-4.4
Longitudinal engine	1993-97	0.6 min.	4.5 max.
3.5L	1993-00	0.6 min.	4.5 max.

ACTUATORS, OUTPUT
FUEL INJECTORS

Engine	Year	Resistance (ohms)	Temperature (deg. F/C)
2.0L, 2.4L	1995-00	12 approx.	68/20
2.2L, 2.5L TBI	1989-95	1.3	—
2.2L, 2.5L Turbo	1989-93	2.4	—
2.5L Flex Fuel	1993-94	2.4	—
2.5L (V6)	1995-00	12 approx.	68/20
2.7L, 3.2L	1998-00	12 approx.	68/20
3.0L	1989-91	2.4	—
	1992-95	14.5	—
	1996-97	12 approx.	68/20
	1996-00	12 approx.	68/20

ACTUATORS, OUTPUT Continued

FUEL INJECTORS Continued

Engine	Year	Resistance (ohms)	Temperature (deg. F/C)
3.3L, 3.8L Transverse engine	1990-91	2.4	—
	1992-95	14.5	—
	1996-99	12 approx.	68/20
CNG	1995	4.2-5.0	—
3.3L Longitudinal engine	1993-97	12 approx.	68/20
3.5L	1993-97	12 approx.	68/20

1 FWD Vans, 1.3.

IDLE SPEED SOLENOID
Avenger, Sebring: Measure resistance between terminals 1 & 4, then 2 & 3 of IAC.

Engine	Year	Resistance (ohms)
5.2L (318)	1989	15-35

COMPUTER TIMING ADVANCE
Specifications are in addition to basic timing.
Perform all tests with engine at operating temperature.
1989-95: With FI, increase engine speed to 2000 RPM and check advance.

Engine	Year	Transmission	Computer Number	Time (minutes)	Advance
2.2L (135) TBI	1989	MT	All	0	22-30
	1989	AT	All	0	29-37
2.2L TBI	1990-95	MT	All	0	17-25
	1990-95	AT	All	0	12-20
2.2L (135) Turbo II	1989	MT & AT	All	0	36-44
2.2L Turbo	1990	MT & AT	All	0	29-37
2.5L (153) Vans	1989	MT	All	0	24-32
	1989	AT	All	0	29-37
2.5L (153) Others	1989	MT	All	0	24-32
2.5L (153) Others	1989	AT	All	0	26-34
2.5L TBI	1990-94	MT & AT	All	0	17-25
2.5L Turbo	1990-92	MT	All	0	21-29
	1990-92	AT	All	0	26-34
2.5L Flex. Fuel	1993-94	AT	All	—	14-22
3.0L (183)	1990-95	MT	All	0	30-38
	1990-95	AT	All	0	34-42
3.3L	1990-91	AT	All	0	24-32
California	1990-91	AT	All	0	33-41
5.2L (318) 2V	1989	AT	All	0	42-50
5.2L (318) 4V	1989	AT	All	0	34-4

ENGINE IDENTIFICATION

To identify any engine by the manufacturer's code, follow the four steps designated by the numbered blocks.

V.I.N.
PLATE LOCATION:

Left side of instrument panel, visible through windshield.

1 MODEL YEAR IDENTIFICATION:

10th character of V.I.N.

2000—Y	1999—X	1998—W
1997—V	1996—T	1995—S
1994—R	1993—P	1992—N
1991—M	1990—L	1989—K

2 ENGINE CODE LOCATION:

8th character of V.I.N.

4 ENGINE IDENTIFICATION

YEAR	3 ENGINE CODE CYL.	DISPL. liters	cc	Fuel System	HP
2000	N 6	2.5	2497	MFI	156, 163[1]
1999	Y 4	2.0	1996	MFI	140
	N 6	2.5	2497	MFI	156, 163[1]
1997-98	Y 4	2.0	1996	MFI	140
	N 6	2.5	2497	MFI	163
1996	A 4	1.5	1468	MFI	92
	C 4	1.8	1834	MFI	113, 119[1]
	Y 4	2.0	1996	MFI	140
	G 4	2.4	2350	MFI	136
	N 6	2.5	2497	MFI	163
	H 6	3.0	2972	MFI	164
	J 6	3.0	2972	MFI	222
	K 6	3.0 T	2972 T	MFI	320
1995	A 4	1.5	1468	MFI	92
	C 4	1.8	1834	MFI	113, 119[1]
	Y 4	2.0	1996	MFI	140
	G 4	2.4	2350	MFI	136
	N 6	2.5	2497	MFI	155
	H 6	3.0	2972	MFI	164
	J 6	3.0	2972	MFI	222
	K 6	3.0 T	2972 T	MFI	320
1994	A 4	1.5	1468	MFI	92
	B 4	1.8	1755	MFI	92
	C 4	1.8	1834	MFI	113
	E 4	2.0	1997	MFI	135
	F 4	2.0 T	1997 T	MFI	180, 195[1]
	G 4	2.4	2350	MFI	136
	H 6	3.0	2972	MFI	164
	J 6	3.0	2972	MFI	222
	K 6	3.0 T	2972 T	MFI	320
1993	A 4	1.5	1468	MFI	92
	B 4	1.8	1755	MFI	92
	C 4	1.8	1834	MFI	113
	E 4	2.0	1997	MFI	135
	F 4	2.0 T	1997 T	MFI	190
	G 4	2.4	2350	MFI	116, 136[1]
	H 6	3.0	2972	MFI	164
	J 6	3.0	2972	MFI	222
	K 6	3.0 T	2972 T	MFI	300
	N 6	3.0	2972	MFI	151

4 ENGINE IDENTIFICATION

YEAR	3 ENGINE CODE CYL.	DISPL. liters	cc	Fuel System	HP
1992	A 4	1.5	1468	MFI	92
	D 4	1.8	1834	MFI	113
	T 4	1.8	1755	MFI	92
	R 4	2.0	1997	MFI	135
	U 4	2.0 T	1997 T	MFI	195
	W 4	2.4	2350	MFI	116
	S 6	3.0	2972	MFI	164
	B 6	3.0	2972	MFI	222
	C 6	3.0 T	2972 T	MFI	300
1991	A 4	1.5	1468	MFI	92
	T 4	1.8	1755	MFI	92
	V 4	2.0	1997	MFI	96
	R 4	2.0	1997	MFI	135
	U 4	2.0 T	1997 T	MFI	190, 195[1]
	W 4	2.4	2350	MFI	107
	S 6	3.0	2972	MFI	164
	B 6	3.0	2972	MFI	222
	C 6	3.0 T	2972 T	MFI	300
1990	X 4	1.5	1468	MFI	75, 81[1]
	Y 4	1.6	1597	MFI	123
	T 4	1.8	1755	MFI	87, 92[1]
	V 4	2.0	1997	MFI	96
	R 4	2.0	1997	MFI	135
	U 4	2.0 T	1997 T	MFI	190, 195[1]
	V 4	2.0	1997	MFI	96
	W 4	2.4	2350	MFI	107
	S 6	3.0	2972	MFI	143
1989	X 4	1.5	1468	MFI	75, 81[1]
	Y 4	1.6	1597	MFI	113
	Z 4	1.6 T	1597 T	MFI	135
	T 4	1.8	1755	MFI	87
	V 4	2.0	1997	MFI	99
	D 4	2.0	1997	2V	90
	E 4	2.6	2555	2V	109
	N 4	2.6 T	2555 T	TBI	188
	S 6	3.0	2972	MFI	143

1 Engine horsepower varies with model installation.
T—Turbo.   2V—Two Venturi Carburetor.
TBI—Throttle Body Injection.   MFI—Multiport Fuel Injection.

UNDERHOOD SERVICE SPECIFICATIONS

CYLINDER NUMBERING SEQUENCE
FIRING ORDER: 4-CYL. 1 3 4 2

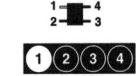

— Front of car —

1989-90 1.4L, 1.5L	1991-96 1.5L	1989-90 1.6L Turbo, 1990-94 2.0L DOHC	1992-96 1.8L Colt & Vista	1989 2.0L-2V FWD	1995-99 2.0L Sebring, Avenger

CHRYSLER, DODGE, PLYMOUTH
1989-2000 Colt, Conquest, Laser (1990-94),
Raider, Ram 50, Stealth, Vista, Sebring Coupe, Avenger
Sebring Convertible—See Previous Section

UNDERHOOD SERVICE SPECIFICATIONS

CYLINDER NUMBERING SEQUENCE

FIRING ORDER: 4-CYL. 1 3 4 2

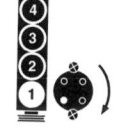

— Front of car —

1989-94 1.8L Laser, 2.0L FI ex. DOHC & RWD
2.0L RWD, 2.6L
1992 2.4L Vista
1993-96 2.4L Colt Wagon/Vista
2.4L Ram 50

6-CYL. 1 2 3 4 5 6

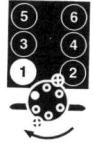
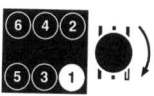
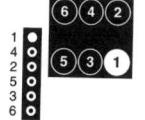
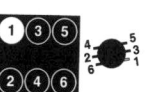

— Front of car —

3.0L ex. Stealth
1991-96 Stealth 3.0L SOHC
1991-96 Stealth 3.0L DOHC
1995-00 2.5L Sebring, Avenger

— TIMING MARK —

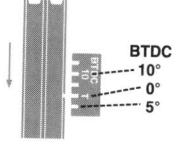

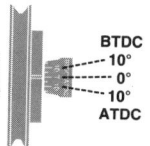

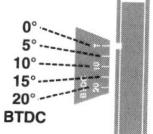

1.5L
1.6L FWD Turbo, 2.0L Vista, 1.8L, 2.0L DOHC ex. Code Y, 2.4L
1.6L RWD, 2.0L ex. DOHC Vista & Code Y, 2.6L
3.0L ex. Stealth
1995-00 2.5L 1991-96 3.0L Stealth
No Timing Marks on These Engines
1995-99 2.0L Code Y Sebring, Avenger

ELECTRICAL AND IGNITION SYSTEMS

BATTERY
BCI equivalent shown, size may vary from original equipment. Check clearance before replacing, holddown may need to be modified.

Engine	Year	STANDARD BCI Group No.	STANDARD Crank. Perf.	OPTIONAL BCI Group No.	OPTIONAL Crank. Perf.
1468cc, 1597cc	1989	25	375	25	420
1468cc, 1597cc ex. Turbo	1990	25	355	—	—
1468cc	1991-92	25	350	25	430
Canada	1991-92	25	430	—	—
1468cc	1993-96	51	430	—	—
1597cc Turbo	1990	45	435	—	—
1755cc Colt Wagon	1989-90	45	435	—	—
1755cc Laser	1990	86	430	—	—
1755cc Laser: U.S.	1991	86	430	—	—
Canada	1991	86	525	—	—
1755cc Laser: U.S.	1992-94	86	430	—	—
Canada MT	1992-94	86	430	—	—
Canada AT	1992-94	86	525	—	—
1834cc Vista, Wagon:					
U.S.	1992-94	25	355	—	—
Canada	1992-94	24	420	—	—
1834cc Colt ex. Wagon	1993-96	51	430	—	—
1834cc Wagon	1995-96	24	580	—	—
1996cc MT	1995-98	86	430	—	—
AT	1995-98	86	525	—	—

BATTERY Continued

Engine	Year	STANDARD BCI Group No.	STANDARD Crank. Perf.	OPTIONAL BCI Group No.	OPTIONAL Crank. Perf.
1997cc Vista	1989	45	435	25	420
Canada	1989	25	420	—	—
1997cc Laser	1990	86	430	—	—
	1991	86	525	—	—
1997cc Laser: U.S.	1992-94	86	430	—	—
Canada	1992-94	86	525	—	—
2350cc Pickup	1990-92	51	430	24	585
Canada	1990-92	24	490	24	585
2350cc Pickup	1993	25	430	24	490
Canada	1993	24	490	—	—
2350cc Vista, Wagons:					
U.S.	1992-94	24	420	—	—
Canada	1992-94	24	580	—	—
2350cc Wagon	1995-96	24	580	—	—
2497cc	1995-00	86	525	—	—
2555cc Pickup, Raider	1989	45	435	24	585
2555cc Conquest	1989	25	420	—	—
2972cc Raider	1989	24	490	—	—
2972cc Pickup	1990-91	24	490	24	585
2972cc Stealth	1991-93	24	490	—	—
	1994-96	25	520	—	—

CHRYSLER, DODGE, PLYMOUTH

1989-2000 Colt, Conquest, Laser (1990-94), Raider, Ram 50, Stealth, Vista, Sebring Coupe, Avenger

UNDERHOOD SERVICE SPECIFICATIONS

GENERATOR

Engine	Year	Rated Output (amps)	Test Output (amps @ eng. rpm)
1468cc 2V MT	1989	60	42 @ 2500
AT	1989	65	45 @ 2500
1468cc FI	1989	75	52 @ 2500
	1990-94	65	46 @ 2500
		75	53 @ 2500
	1995-96	70	49 @ 2500
1597cc U.S.	1989-90	75	52 @ 2500
Canada	1989-90	65	45 @ 2500
1755cc Colt wagon	1989-90	75	52 @ 2500
1755cc, 1997cc Laser	1990-94	65	46 @ 2500
		75	53 @ 2500
		90	63 @ 2500
1834cc Wagons	1992-96	60	42 @ 2500
		65	46 @ 2500
1834cc Colt	1993-94	65	46 @ 2500
		70	49 @ 2500
	1995-96	75	53 @ 2500
1996cc, 2497cc	1995-00	90	63 @ 2500
		110	77 @ 2500
1997cc, 2555cc Pickup	1989	45	31 @ 2500
		60	42 @ 2500
1997cc Vista	1989-91	65	45 @ 2500
Canada	1990-91	75	52 @ 2500
2350cc Pickup	1990-93	40	28 @ 2500
		45	31 @ 2500
		60	42 @ 2500
2350cc Vista, Wagon	1992-96	75	53 @ 2500
2555cc Conquest	1989	65	45 @ 2500
2555cc Raider	1989	50	35 @ 2500
2972cc Raider	1989	75	52 @ 2500
2972cc Pickup	1990-93	65	45 @ 2500
2972cc Stealth SOHC	1991-96	90	63 @ 2500
	1996	95	66 @ 2500
DOHC	1991-96	110	77 @ 2500

REGULATOR

Application	Test Temp. (deg. F/C)	Voltage Setting
1995-00 Avenger, Sebring	-4/-20	14.07-15.07
	32/0	13.89-14.89
	68/20	13.58-14.58
	104/40	13.15-14.15
	144/162	12.84-13.84
1989-96 Others	-4/-20	14.2-15.4
	68/20	13.9-15.9
	140/60	13.4-14.6
	175/80	13.1-14.5

SPARK PLUGS

Engine	Year	Gap (inches)	Gap (mm)	Torque (ft-lb)
1996cc	1995-99	.048-.053	1.2-1.3	20
1997cc Turbo	1989-94	.028-.031	.70-.80	15-21
All Others	1989-99	.039-.043	1.0-1.1	15-21

IGNITION COIL
FOR TESTING AND ADJUSTMENT DIAGRAMS, SEE APPENDIX A.

Engine	Year	Windings	Resistance (ohms)
1468cc FI, 1755cc Wagon	1989-90	Primary	.72-.88
		Secondary	10,300-13,900
1468cc	1991-96	Primary	0.9-1.2
		Secondary	20,000-29,000
1597cc, 1755cc Laser	1989-90	Primary	.77-.95
		Secondary	10,300-13,900

IGNITION COIL Continued

Engine	Year	Windings	Resistance (ohms)
1755cc Laser	1990-94	Primary	0.9-1.2
		Secondary	19,000-27,000
1834cc	1992-96	Primary	0.9-1.2
		Secondary	20,000-29,000
1996cc	1995-99	Primary	.51-.61[3]
		Secondary	11,500-13,500[4]
1997cc Vista	1989-91	Primary	.72-.88
		Secondary	10,900-13,300
1997cc, 2555cc Pickup	1989	Primary	1.1-1.3
		Secondary	22,100-29,900
1997cc Laser	1990-91	Primary[1]	.77-.95
		Secondary[1]	10,300-13,900
	1992-94	Primary	.70-.86
		Secondary	11,300-15,300
2350cc	1990-92	Primary	.72-.88
		Secondary	10,300-13,900
2350cc Truck	1993	Primary	.72-.88
		Secondary	10,300-13,900
2350cc Vista, Wagons	1993-96	Primary	0.9-1.2
		Secondary	20,000-27,000
2497cc	1995-00	Primary	0.6-0.8
		Secondary	12,000-18,000
2555cc Raider	1989	Primary	1.1-1.3
		Secondary	14,500-19,500
2555cc Conquest	1989	Primary	1.12-1.38
		Secondary	9400-12,700
2972cc SOHC	1989-96	Primary	.72-.88
		Secondary	10,300-13,900
2972cc DOHC	1991-96	Primary	.67-.81[2]
		Secondary	11,300-15,300[2]

1 Primary windings measured between terminals 2 & 1 and 2 & 4 of 4-terminal connector. Secondary windings measured between high voltage terminals of coil towers 1 & 4 and 2 & 3.

2 Primary windings measured between terminals 1 & 3, 2 & 3, and 4 & 3 of 4-terminal connector. Secondary winds measured between each pair of coil high tension terminals with spark plug wires removed.

3 Measured between B+ (upper right hand) and each of the other three terminals on the four wire coil connector.

4 Measured between the high voltage terminals on each bank of coils with the spark plug wires removed.

DISTRIBUTOR PICKUP
FOR TESTING AND ADJUSTMENT DIAGRAMS, SEE APPENDIX B.

Application	Year	Resistance (ohms)	Air Gap (in./mm)
Pickup			
w/Mitsubishi distr.	1989	—	.031/.80
w/Nippon-Denso distr.; Vista	1989	130-190	.008-.015/.2-.4
Conquest	1989	920-1120	—

IGNITION RESISTOR

Engine	Year	Type	Resistance (ohms)	Temperature (deg. F/C)
All 2V as equipped	1989	Unit	1.20-1.50	68/20

BASE TIMING
FOR TESTING AND ADJUSTMENT DIAGRAMS, SEE APPENDIX C.
Set timing at slow idle and Before Top Dead Center, unless otherwise specified.

1989-96 Models, ex. Avenger, Sebring, w/electronic advance distributor: Remove cap from timing adjustment connector and ground the terminal. When ungrounded, timing should be at "Check" specification.

1996 Manufacturer prefers that distributor not be rotated.

Engine	Year	Man. Trans. (degrees) @ RPM	Auto. Trans. (degrees) @ RPM
1468cc FI: Set	1989-94	5±2	5±2
Check	1989-93	10±2	10±2
High Altitude	1989-91	15±2	15±2
Check	1994-95	5±7[1]	5±7[1]

CHRYSLER, DODGE, PLYMOUTH
1989-2000 Colt, Conquest, Laser (1990-94), Raider, Ram 50, Stealth, Vista, Sebring Coupe, Avenger

UNDERHOOD SERVICE SPECIFICATIONS

CRITU4   CRITU4

BASE TIMING Continued

Engine	Year	Man. Trans. (degrees) @ RPM	Auto. Trans. (degrees) @ RPM
1468cc	1996	5±3	5±3
Check	1996	15±7[1]	15±7[1]
1597cc: Set	1989-90	5±2	5±2
Check, ex. Wagon	1989-90	8±2[1]	8±2[1]
Check, Wagon	1989	15±2[1]	15±2[1]
1755cc Colt Wagon: Set	1989-90	5±2	5±2
Check	1989-90	15±2[1]	15±2[1]
1755cc Laser: Set	1990-94	5±2	5±2
Check	1990-94	10±2	10±2
1834cc: Set	1992-95	5±2	5±2
Check	1992-93	5±2	5±2
Check	1994-95	5±7[1]	5±7[1]
1834cc	1996	5±3	5±3
Check	1996	15±7[1]	15±7[1]
1996cc	1995-99	10[2]	10[2]
1997cc Vista: Set	1989-91	5±2	5±2
Check	1989-91	10±2	10±2
High Altitude	1989-91	15±2	15±2
1997cc Pickup	1989	8±2	8±2
1997cc Laser: Set	1990-94	5±2	5±2
Check	1990-94	8±2	8±2
2350cc: Set	1990-94	5±2	5±2
Check	1990-93	8±2[1]	8±2[1]
Check	1994-95	10±7[1]	10±7[1]
2350cc	1996	5±3	5±3
Check	1996	15±7[1]	15±7[1]
2497cc	1995-00	12[2]	12[2]
2555cc 2V	1989	7±2	7±2
2555cc FI	1989	10±2	10±2
2972cc: Set	1989-93	5±2	5±2
Check	1989	10±2	10±2
Check	1990-93	15±2	15±2
2972cc SOHC: Set	1994	5±2	5±2
Check	1994	15±7	15±7
2972cc DOHC: Set	1994-96	5±3[2]	5±3[2]
Check	1994-96	15±7[1]	15±7[1]

1 At high altitudes, timing will be advanced further.
2 Not adjustable.

DISTRIBUTOR TIMING ADVANCE
Engine degrees at engine rpm, no load, in addition to basic timing setting. Mechanical advance distributors only.

Engine	Trans-mission	Year	Distributor Number	Degrees @ 2500 RPM Total	Degrees @ 2500 RPM Centrifugal
1997cc Pickup	MT & AT	1989	MD110418	25.8-33.8	7.8-11.8
	MT & AT	1989	MD110419, 40	28.8-36.8	7.8-11.8
	MT & AT	1989	MD125103	25.8-33.8	7.8-11.8
2555cc Turbo	MT & AT	1989	T4T63373	31.7-39.7	10.7-14.7
2555cc Pickup	MT & AT	1989	T3T65572	22.8-30.8	4.8-8.8
	MT & AT	1989	T3T65476	22.8-30.8	4.8-8.8
2555cc Raider	MT & AT	1989	T3T65571	25.8-33.8	4.8-8.8
	MT & AT	1989	T3T65474	22.8-30.8	4.8-8.8

1 Retard, 16-20 degrees @ 17.5 inches hg.

FUEL SYSTEM

FUEL SYSTEM PRESSURE
FOR TESTING AND ADJUSTMENT DIAGRAMS, SEE APPENDIX D.

Engine	Year	Pressure PSI	Pressure RPM
Carbureted & TBI:			
1597cc, 2555cc TBI	1989	35-38	idle

FUEL SYSTEM PRESSURE Continued

Engine	Year	Pressure @ Idle PSI[1]	Pressure @ Idle PSI[2]
Fuel Injected (MFI)			
1468cc FI	1989-96	47-50	38
1597cc	1989-90	47-50	38
1755cc, 1834cc	1989-96	47-50	38
1996cc	1995-97	48-54	—
	1998-99	47-50	—
1997cc	1989-94	47-50	38
Turbo	1990-91	36-38	27
Turbo MT	1992-94	36-38	27
Turbo AT	1992-94	41-46	33
2350cc	1990-96	47-50	38
2497cc	1995-00	47-51	—
2972cc	1989-96	47-50	38
Turbo	1991-96	43-45	34
Pickup	1992-93	47-53	38

1 Pressure regulator vacuum hose disconnected.
2 Pressure regulator vacuum hose connected.

IDLE SPEED W/O COMPUTER CONTROL
Midpoint of range given is the preferred setting.

All 2V: Adjust throttle stop screw or idle speed screw to obtain specified idle rpm. With choke fully closed, adjust fast idle to specified rpm by adjusting fast idle screw under throttle lever.

Midpoint of range given is the preferred setting.

Engine	Year	SLOW Man. Trans.	SLOW Auto. Trans.	FAST Man. Trans.	FAST Auto. Trans.	Step of Cam
1997cc Pickup	1989	650-850	650-850 N	2500	2450 N	2nd High
A/C speed-up	1989	850-950	850-950 N			
2555cc Truck	1989	700-900	700-900 N	2350	2300 N	2nd High
A/C speed-up	1989	850-950	850-950 N			
2555cc Raider	1989	700-900	700-900 N	2350	2300 N	2nd High
A/C speed-up	1989	900-950	900-950 N			

IDLE SPEED W/COMPUTER CONTROL
FOR TESTING AND ADJUSTMENT DIAGRAMS, SEE APPENDIX E.
Midpoint of range given is the preferred setting speed.

1993 1468cc;
1994 1997cc, 1989-93 1597cc, 1834cc, 1997cc, 2350cc Wagons, 2972cc: Ground ignition timing connector and terminal 10 of self diagnostic connector.
1989-93 Others;
1994 1755cc: Turn ignition to ON position for more than 15 seconds. Turn switch off and disconnect ISC servo harness connector. Ground red wire on computer side of ISC connector (1989 2555cc Turbo only). Start engine and adjust speed to specified value.
1994-96 1468cc, 1834cc, 2350cc, 2972cc; 1995 2972cc: Ground ignition timing connector and terminal 1 (upper left) of the self diagnostic connector. Set idle to specified setting speed.
1995-99 Avenger, Sebring: Connect a Scan Tool and check idle against specified value.
All Models: Turn A/C on and verify that speed-up speed is at specified value.

Engine	Year	Trans-mission	Setting Speed	Checking Speed	AC Speed-up
1468cc ex. Wagon	1989-92	MT	700-800	650-850	850
		AT	700-800 N	650-850 N	700 D
1468cc, 1755cc Wagon	1989-90	MT	700	600-800	850
		AT	700 N	600-800 N	650 D
1468cc	1993-96	MT	700-800	650-850	800-900
		AT	700-800 N	650-850 N	800-900 N
1597cc	1989-90	MT	750	650-850	850
		AT	750 N	650-850 N	700 D
1755cc Laser	1990-94	MT	600-800	650-750	850
		AT	600-800 N	650-750 N	650 D

CRITU5   CRITU5

IDLE SPEED W/COMPUTER CONTROL Continued

Engine	Year	Trans-mission	Setting Speed	Checking Speed	AC Speed-up
1834cc Vista,					
Colt Wagon	1992-94	MT	650-750	650-850	830
		AT	650-750 N	650-850 N	830 N
California	1993-94	MT	650-750	600-800	830
		AT	650-750 N	600-800 N	830 N
1834cc Colt	1993-94	MT	650-750	650-850	850
		AT	650-750 N	650-850 N	850 N
1834cc	1995-96	MT	650-750	600-800	800-900
		AT	650-750 N	600-800 N	800-900 N
1996cc	1995	MT	—	600-800	—
		AT	—	600-800N	—
	1996-99	MT	—	700-900	750-950
		AT	—	700-900N	750-950N
1997cc Vista	1989-90	MT & AT	700 N	600-800 N	900 N
	1991	MT	650-750	600-800	900
		AT	650-750 N	600-800 N	600 D
1997cc Laser	1990-94	MT	700-800	650-850	850
		AT	700-800 N	650-850	650 D
2350cc Pickup	1990-93	MT	700-800	650-850	900
		AT	700-800 N	650-850 N	700 D
2350cc Vista, Wagons	1992-94	MT	700-800	650-850	850
		AT	700-800 N	650-850 N	850 N
2350cc	1995-96	MT	700-800	650-850	800-900
		AT	700-800 N	650-850 N	800-900 N
2497cc	1995-00	AT	—	650-850N	650-850N
2555cc Turbo	1989	MT	850	750-950	1000
		AT	850 N	750-950 N	750 D
2972cc	1989-96	MT	650-750	600-800	900
		AT	650-750 N	600-800 N	650 D[1]

1 Truck, 900 N

ENGINE MECHANICAL

TIGHTENING TORQUES
FOR CYLINDER HEAD TORQUE SEQUENCES AND DIAGRAMS, SEE APPENDIX F.

| Engine | Year | TORQUE FOOT-POUNDS/NEWTON METERS | | | | |
		Cylinder Head	Intake Manifold	Exhaust Manifold	Crankshaft Pulley	Water Pump
1468cc	1989-92	51-54/ 69-74	12-14/ 16-19	12-14/ 16-19	9-11/ 12-15	9-11/ 12-15[1]
1468cc	1993-96	53/73	13/18	13/18 10/13[2]	62/85	10/14[1]
1597cc	1989-90	65-72/ 90-100	11-14/ 15-19[2]	18-22/ 25-30	14-22/ 20-30	9-11/ 12-15[1]
1755cc Colt Wagon	1989-90	51-54/ 70-75	15-22/ 21-31	18-22/ 25-30	11-13/ 15-16	9-11/ 12-15[1]
1755cc Laser	1990-94	51-54/ 70-75	11-14/ 15-20	11-14/ 15-20	11-13/ 15-18	9-11/ 12-15
1834cc	1992-96	54/75[3], 14/20, +90°, +90°	14/20	22/30	134/185	18/24
1996cc	1995-99	[7]	105"/12	200"/23	105/42	17/24[2] 30/41[8]
1997cc	1989-90	65-72/ 90-100	11-14/ 15-19	11-14/ 15-19	15-21/ 20-30	9-11/ 12-15[1]
	1990-92	65-72/ 100-110	11-14/ 15-20[4]	11-14/ 15-20	14-22/ 20-30	9-11/ 12-15[1]
	1993-94	58/78[3], 14/20, +90°, +90°	11-14/ 15-20[4]	18-22/ 25-30	15-21/ 20-30	9-11/ 12-15[1]
2350cc Pickup	1990-92	65-72/ 90-100	11-14/ 15-20	11-14/ 15-20	15-21/ 20-30	9-11/ 12-15[1]
	1993	58-80[3], 14/20, +90°, +90°	11-14/ 15-20	11-14/ 15-20	15-21/ 20-30	9-11/ 12-15[1]

TIGHTENING TORQUES Continued

| Engine | Year | TORQUE FOOT-POUNDS/NEWTON METERS | | | | |
		Cylinder Head	Intake Manifold	Exhaust Manifold	Crankshaft Pulley	Water Pump
2350cc Wagons	1992	76-83/ 105-115	13/18	13/18	18/25	10/14
	1993-96	54-75[3], 14/20, +90°, +90°	13/18	22/30	18/25	10/14
2497cc	1995-00	80/108	18/21	22/30	134/182	9/12
2555cc	1989	65-72/ 90-100[5]	11-14/ 15-19	11-14/ 15-19	80-95/ 110-130	9-11/ 12-15
2972cc Pickup, Raider	1989-93	65-72/ 90-100	11-14/ 15-19	11-15/ 15-21	109-115/ 150-160	9-11/ 12-15[1]
2972cc Stealth SOHC, DOHC	1991-96	80/110	13/18	13/18	108-116/ 150-160	17/24
DOHC Turbo	1991-96	90/125	13/18	33/45[6]	130-137/ 180-190	17/24

1 Short bolts, long bolts, 14-20/20-27.
2 Short bolts.
3 Then loosen all bolts.
4 Long bolts, 22-30/30-42.
5 Small bolts forward of cam gear, 11-15/15-22.
6 Turbo, 13/18.
7 Short bolts: Long bolts:
   20/28,   24/33,
   20/28,   48/67,
   20/28,   48/67,
   +90°   +90°
8 Long bolts

VALVE CLEARANCE
Engine hot.

Engine	Year	Intake (inches)	Intake (mm)	Exhaust (inches)	Exhaust (mm)
All ex. Diesel[1]	1989	.006	.15	.010	.25
Jet valve	1989	.010	.25	—	—
1468cc, 1755cc	1990	.006	.15	.010	.25
1468cc	1991-92	.006	.15	.010	.25
	1993-96	.008	.20	.010	.25
1834cc	1992-96	.008	.20	.012	.30

1 1989 2.0L & 2.6L except jet valve have hydraulic lifters.

COMPRESSION PRESSURE
At cranking speed (250-400 rpm), engine temperature normalized, throttle open.

Engine	Year	PSI	Maximum Variation PSI
1468cc	1989-96	137 min.	14
1597cc	1989-90	171 min.	14
Turbo	1989-90	149 min.	14
1755cc Wagon	1989-90	137 min.	14
1755cc Laser	1990-94	131 min.	14
1834cc	1992-94	142 min.	14
	1995-96	151 min.	14
1996cc	1995-99	170-225/100 min.	1
1997cc Laser	1990-91	137 min.	14
Turbo	1990-91	114 min.	14
1997cc Laser	1992-94	145 min.	14
Turbo	1992-94	121 min.	14
2350cc	1990-92	119 min.	14
2350cc Truck	1993	127 min.	14

CHRYSLER, DODGE, PLYMOUTH
1989-2000 Colt, Conquest, Laser (1990-94), Raider, Ram 50, Stealth, Vista, Sebring Coupe, Avenger

UNDERHOOD SERVICE SPECIFICATIONS

CRITU6   CRITU6

COMPRESSION PRESSURE Continued

Engine	Year	PSI	Maximum Variation PSI
2350cc Wagon	1993-96	139 min.	14
2497cc	1995-00	135-189	14
California	1998-00	154-202	14
2555cc Conquest	1989	97 min.	14
	1989	119 min.	14
2972cc Pickup, Raider	1989-91	119 min.	14
	1993	127 min.	14
2972cc Stealth			
SOHC	1991-96	127 min.	14
DOHC	1991-96	139 min.	14
Turbo	1991-96	115 min.	14

1 Lowest cylinder must be 75% of highest.

BELT TENSION
With 22 lbs. of force applied at midpoint of belt.

Engine	Year	Generator	Power Steering	Air Cond.	Air Pump
Deflection method:					
1997cc Pickup					
(inches)	1989	1/4-3/8	7/32-3/8	1/4-11/32	1/4-3/8
(mm)	1989	7-10	7-10	6-9	7-10
2555cc Pickup					
(inches)	1989	1/4-3/8	3/8-7/16	11/16-13/16	1/4-3/8
(mm)	1989	7-10	9-12	17-20	7-20
2555cc Raider					
(inches)	1989	11/32-3/8	11/32-3/8	11/16-1/2	11/32-3/8
(mm)	1989	9-12	9-12	17-20	9-12
2555cc Conquest					
(inches)	1989	1/4-3/8	11/32-1/2	1/4-3/8	—
(mm)	1989	7-10	9-12	7-10	—
2350cc Pickup (inches)	1990-93	7/32-3/8	1/4-5/16	5/16-3/8	—
(mm)	1990-93	7-10	6-9	8-10	—
2972cc DOHC	1991-95	5/32-3/16	13/32-7/16	5/32-3/16	—
(mm)	1991-95	9-5	9-11	4-5	—
Strand Tension method:					
NEW					
1468cc FI	1989-96	110-155	110-190	80-95	—
1597cc	1989-92	110-155	110-155	80-95	—
1755cc, 1997cc	1989-95	110-155	110-155	104-126	—
1834cc: PS w/o A/C	1992-96	110-155	145-190	—	—
PS w/AC	1992-96	110-155	165-175	165-175	—
1996cc	1995-99	110-160	110-160	137-159	—
2350cc Vista	1995-94	110-155	110-155	120-145	—
2497cc	1995-00	145-187	145-187	110-132	—
2972cc SOHC	1989-96	110-155	110-155	104-126	—
2972cc DOHC	1992-96	145-200	145-200	110-155	—
USED					
1468cc FI	1989-96	90	65-110	55-70	—
1597cc	1989-92	90	90	55-70	—
1755cc, 1997cc	1989-95	55-110	55-110	71-88	—
1834cc: PS w/o A/C	1992-96	55-110	90-130	—	—
PS w/A/C	1992-96	55-110	110-140	110-140	—
1996cc	1995-99	90-100	90-110	93-115	—
1997cc	1995-96	55-110	55-110	57-75	—
2350cc Vista	1992-96	55-110	75-100	75-100	—
2497cc	1995-00	110-120	110-120	66-88	—
2972cc SOHC	1989-96	55-110	55-110	71-86	—
2972cc DOHC	1992-96	110-130	110-130	80-90	—

ENGINE COMPUTER SYSTEM

DIAGNOSTIC TROUBLE CODES
FOR TESTING AND ADJUSTMENT DIAGRAMS, SEE APPENDIX G.
1989-93 All w/FI
1994-95 Laser
Access connector in glove box or under dash on passenger side (early models) or by driver side kick panel by fuse block (late models). Connect an analog voltmeter to upper right cavity (+) and lower left (-). Turn ignition switch on. Codes will be displayed as pulses of voltmeter needle. Disconnect battery negative cable to erase codes.

DIAGNOSTIC TROUBLE CODES Continued
1994-95 Colt ex. Wagon:
Access connector by fuse block. Connect an analog voltmeter (+) to terminal 25 (upper left) of twelve terminal male connector and (-) to terminal 4 or 5 (upper middle two) of 16 terminal female connector. Turn ignition on. Codes will be displayed as sweeps of the voltmeter needle. Disconnect battery negative terminal to erase codes.

1994-95 Colt Wagon, Expo, Stealth:
Ground terminal 1 (upper left) of 16 terminal connector under dash. Turn ignition on. Codes will be displayed on CHECK ENGINE light. Disconnect battery negative terminal to erase codes.

1996-99 OBD-II system used. Connect a Scan tool and follow manufacturers' instructions to retrieve codes.

1989 1597cc Turbo;
      2555cc Turbo:
Code 1 Oxygen sensor and/or computer
Code 2 Ignition signal
Code 3 Airflow sensor
Code 4 Pressure sensor
Code 5 Throttle position sensor
Code 6 ISC motor position sensor
Code 7 Engine coolant temperature sensor
Code 8 Vehicle speed sensor
Vista:
Code 1 Oxygen sensor
Code 2 Crankshaft position sensor
Code 3 Airflow sensor
Code 4 Barometric pressure sensor
Code 5 Throttle position sensor
Code 6 ISC motor position sensor
Code 7 Engine temperature sensor
Code 8 TDC sensor
1989-95 All w/FI;
Continuous Flashing System normal
Code 11 Oxygen sensor (front)
Code 12 Volume airflow sensor
Code 13 Intake air temperature sensor
Code 14 TPS
Code 15 Idle air control motor position sensor
Code 21 Engine coolant temperature sensor
Code 22 Crankshaft position sensor
Code 23 Camshaft position sensor
Code 24 Vehicle speed sensor
Code 25 Barometric pressure sensor
Code 31 Knock sensor
Code 32 MAP sensor
Code 36 Ignition timing adjustment
Code 39 Oxygen sensor (rear)
Code 41 Injector
Code 42 Fuel pump
Code 43 EGR
Code 44 Ignition coil power transistor, (cyl. 1 & 4) (V6)
Code 52 Ignition coil power transistor, (cyl. 2 & 5) (V6)
Code 53 Ignition coil power transistor, (cyl. 3 & 6) (V6)
Code 55 Idle air control valve position sensor
Code 59 Heated oxygen sensor
Code 61 Transaxle and ECM interlink
Code 62 Warm-up valve position sensor
One Long Sweep, PCM

SENSORS, INPUT
TEMPERATURE SENSORS

Engine	Year	Sensor	Resistance Ohms @ deg. F/C
Avenger, Sebring	1995-00	Coolant	9000-11,000 @ 77/25
		Intake Air	600-800 @ 212/100
All others	1989-96	Coolant	5100-6500 @ 32/0
			2100-2700 @ 68/20
			900-1300 @ 104/40
			260-360 @ 176/80
1468cc FI, 597cc DOHC, 1755cc, 1997cc FI, 2350cc, 2555cc Turbo, 2972cc	1989-95	Intake Air[1]	5300-6700 @ 32/0
			2300-3000 @ 68/20
			300-420 @ 176/80

1 Measured between terminals 4 & 6 or 6 & 8 (bottom left and right) of airflow sensor.
2 Sensor on air intake pipe.
3 Sensor on air cleaner housing.

CHRYSLER, DODGE, PLYMOUTH

1989-2000 Colt, Conquest, Laser (1990-94), Raider, Ram 50, Stealth, Vista , Sebring Coupe, Avenger

UNDERHOOD SERVICE SPECIFICATIONS

SENSORS, INPUT Continued

PRESSURE SENSORS

Engine	Year	Sensor	Voltage @ in. Hg./kPa
1997cc FI, 2555cc Turbo	1989	Barometric	.79 @ 2.8/9 1.84 @ 7/24 4.00 @ 14.2/48
1468cc	1993-96	MAP	0.9-1.5 idle

THROTTLE POSITION SENSOR (TPS)

All FI: Insert digital voltmeter probes along GW lead (+) and B lead (-) or GB lead (-) on TPS connector. With ignition switch on and engine not running, check reading against specification. Rotate unit to adjust.

All 2V: Connect digital voltmeter probes between two adjacent TPS bottom terminals. With ignition on and engine not running, check reading against specifications. Turn TPS linkage screw to adjust.

Model	Year	TPS Voltage	WOT
Avenger, Sebring	1995-00	0.4 min.	3.8 max.
Colt FI, Conquest	1989-92	.48-.52	—
Colt	1993-96	0.3-1.0[1]	4.5-5.5
Vista	1989-91	.48-.52	—
	1992-93	.3-1.0[1]	4.5-5.5
	1994	0.4[1]	4.5-5.5
Laser	1990-94	.48-.52	4.5-5.5
Pickup, Raider 4-cyl.	1989	.25	—
Pickup 4-cyl.	1990-93	.48-.52	—
California	1993	.3-1.0[1]	—
Raider, Pickup, Stealth V6	1989-96	.4-1.0[1]	4.5-5.5

1 Not adjustable

IDLE AIR CONTROL VALVE POSITION SENSOR

Engine	Year	Resistance (ohms)
1468cc FI, 1755cc	1989-94	4000-6000
1997cc FI, 2350cc, 2555cc Turbo	1989-93	4000-6000

Engine	Year	Frequency (Hz) Idle	Frequency (Hz) 2000 rpm
1755cc	1993-94	25-40	67-88
1834cc	1993-95	23-49	51-91
	1996	20-46	68-108
1997cc	1993-94	25-50	70-90
Turbo	1993-94	25-50	60-85
2350cc Truck	1993	40-60	85-105
2350cc Wagons	1993-96	18-44	43-83
2972cc Truck	1993	25-45	70-90
2350cc Stealth	1993-96	21-47	57-97
DOHC	1993-96	22-48	50-90
DOHC Turbo	1993-96	22-48	68-108

ACTUATORS, OUTPUT

IDLE AIR CONTROL SOLENOID

At 68°F (20°C).

1989 2555cc Turbo, 2972cc: Measured between two upper terminals.

1995-97 1996cc, 2497cc: Measured between two center and then outer left and right terminals of 4-terminal connecto

Engine	Year	Resistance (ohms)
1468cc FI, 1755cc, 1834cc	1989-96	5-35
1996cc, 2497cc	1995-00	38-52
1997cc FI SOHC, 2350cc	1989-96	5-35
2555cc Turbo	1989	5-35
1997cc DOHC, 2972cc	1989-96	28-33[1]

1 Measured between middle and either left or right cavities in both rows of 6-terminal ISC connector.

FUEL INJECTORS

Engine	Year	Resistance (ohms)	Temperature (deg. F/C)
Avenger, Sebring: 4-cyl.	1995-00	11-15	—
V6	1995-00	13-16	—
All others ex. Turbo	1989-96	13-16	68/20
Turbo	1989-96	2-3	68/20

MIXTURE CONTROL SOLENOID

Carbureted engines.

Engine	Year	Resistance (ohms)
1468cc, 1997cc, 2555cc	1989	54-66

COMPUTER TIMING ADVANCE

With engine at operating temperature, check advance at idle and 2000 rpm.

Engine	Year	Advance (Degrees) Idle	Advance (Degrees) 2000 rpm
1468cc	1993-95	2-18	20-40
	1996	2-18	25-45
1755cc	1993-94	8-12	26-34
1834cc Colt	1993-95	0-13	20-40
1834cc Wagons	1993-95	0-13	10-30
1834cc	1996	0-13	22-42
1997cc	1993-94	5-15	33-41
Turbo	1993-94	5-15	30-40
2350cc Wagons	1993-96	2-18	24-44
2972cc Stealth	1993-96	7-23	13-39
DOHC	1993-96	7-23	30-50
DOHC Turbo	1993-96	7-23	23-43

ENGINE IDENTIFICATION

To identify any engine by the manufacturer's code, follow the four steps designated by the numbered blocks.

1 **MODEL YEAR IDENTIFICATION:** Refer to illustration of the Vehicle Identification Number (V.I.N.). The year is indicated by a code letter which is the 10th character of the V.I.N.

2 **ENGINE CODE LOCATION:** Refer to illustration of V.I.N. plate for location and designation of engine code.

3 **ENGINE CODE:** In the "CODE" column, find the engine code determined in Step 2.

4 **ENGINE IDENTIFICATION:** On the line where the engine code appears, read to the right to identify the engine.

V.I.N.
PLATE LOCATION:

Models 100-350
Left front door lock face or pillar.

V.I.N. also on top left side of instrument panel.

Model year of vehicle:

2000—Y	1999—X	1998—W
1997—V	1996—T	1995—S
1994—R	1993—P	1992—N
1991—M	1990—L	1989—K

MODEL YEAR AND ENGINE IDENTIFICATION:

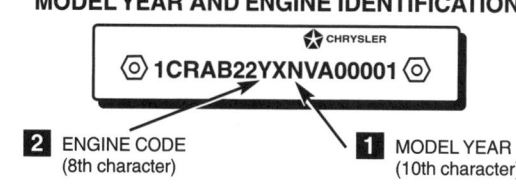

2 ENGINE CODE (8th character)

1 MODEL YEAR (10th character)

4 ENGINE IDENTIFICATION

YEAR	3 ENGINE CODE	CYL.	DISPL. liters	DISPL. cu. in.	Fuel System	HP
2000	P	4	2.5	151	MFI	120
	X	6	3.9	238	MFI	175
	N	8	4.7	287	MFI	235
	Y	8	5.2	318	MFI	225, 230[1]
	T	8	5.2 CNG	318 CNG	MFI	200
	Z, 5	8	5.9	360	MFI	245, 250[1]
	6, 7	6	5.9 TD	359 TD	MFI	215, 235[1]
	W	10	8.0	488	MFI	305, 310[1]
1999	P	4	2.5	151	MFI	120
	X	6	3.9	238	MFI	175
	Y	8	5.2	318	MFI	230
	T	8	5.2 CNG	318 CNG	MFI	200
	Z, 5	8	5.9	360	MFI	245, 250[1]
	6,	6	5.9 TD	359 TD	MFI	215, 230[1]
	W	10	8.0	488	MFI	300
1998	P	4	2.5	151	MFI	120
	X	6	3.9	238	MFI	175
	Y	8	5.2	318	MFI	230
	T	8	5.2 CNG	318 CNG	MFI	N/A
	Z, 5	8	5.9	360	MFI	245, 250[1]
	D, 6, K	6	5.9 TD	359 TD	MFI	180, 215[1]
	W	10	8.0	488	MFI	300
1997	P	4	2.5	151	MFI	120
	X	6	3.9	238	MFI	175
	Y	8	5.2	318	MFI	220-230[1]
	T	8	5.2 CNG	318 CNG	MFI	200
	Z, 5	8	5.9	360	MFI	235, 245[1]
	D	6	5.9 TD	359 TD	MFI	180, 215[1]
	W	10	8.0	488	MFI	295, 300[1]
1996	P	4	2.5	151	MFI	120
	X	6	3.9	238	MFI	170, 175[1]
	Y	8	5.2	318	MFI	220
	T	8	5.2 CNG	318 CNG	MFI	200
	Z, 5	8	5.9	360	MFI	230
	C	6	5.9 TD	359 TD	MFI	180, 215[1]
	W	10	8.0	488	MFI	300
1995	G	4	2.5	152	TBI	99
	X	6	3.9	238	MFI	170, 175[1]
	Y	8	5.2	318	MFI	220
	Z, 5	8	5.9	360	MFI	230
	C	6	5.9 TD	359 TD	MFI	160, 175[1]
	W	10	8.0	488	MFI	300

4 ENGINE IDENTIFICATION

YEAR	3 ENGINE CODE	CYL.	DISPL. liters	DISPL. cu. in.	Fuel System	HP
1994	K	4	2.5	152	TBI	99
	X	6	3.9	238	MFI	175
	Y	8	5.2	318	MFI	220
	Z, A	8	5.9	360	MFI	230
	5	8	5.9	360	MFI	230
	C	6	5.9 TD	359 TD	MFI	160, 175[1]
	W	10	8.0	488	MFI	300
1993	K	4	2.5	152	TBI	99
	X	6	3.9	238	MFI	180
	Y	8	5.2	318	MFI	230
	Z	8	5.9	360	MFI	230
	5	8	5.9	360	MFI	230
	8	6	5.9 TD	359 TD	MFI	160
1992	K	4	2.5	152	TBI	99
	X	6	3.9	238	MFI	180
	Y	8	5.2	318	MFI	230
	Z	8	5.9	360	TBI	190
	5	8	5.9	360	TBI	205
	8	6	5.9 TD	359 TD	MFI	160
1991	K	4	2.5	152	TBI	100
	X	6	3.9	238	TBI	125
	Y	8	5.2	318	TBI	165, 170[1]
	Z	8	5.9	360	TBI	190
	5	8	5.9	360	TBI	205
	8	6	5.9 TD	359 TD	MFI	160
1990	K	4	2.5	152	TBI	100
	X	6	3.9	238	TBI	125
	Y	8	5.2	318	TBI	170
	Z	8	5.9	360	TBI	190
	5	8	5.9	360	TBI	205
	8	6	5.9 TD	359 TD	MFI	160
1989	K	4	2.5	152	TBI	100
	X	6	3.9	238	TBI	125
	Y	8	5.2	318	TBI	170
	5, W	8	5.9	360	TBI	180-193[1]
	8	8	5.9 TD	359 TD	MFI	160

TD—Turbo Diesel.   **TBI**—Throttle Body Injection.
CNG—Compressed Natural Gas. **MFI**—Multiport Fuel Injection.
2V—Two Venturi Carburetor. **4V**—Four Venturi Carburetor.
N/A— Not Available. 1 Engine horsepower varies with model installation.

UNDERHOOD SERVICE SPECIFICATIONS

CRTTU1 ... CRTTU1

CYLINDER NUMBERING SEQUENCE

FIRING ORDER: **4-CYL.** 1 3 4 2   **V6-CYL.** 1 6 5 4 3 2   **8-CYL.** 1 8 4 3 6 5 7 2   **10-CYL.** 1 10 9 4 3 6 5 8 7 2

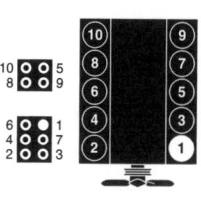

Front of car

| 1989-95 2.5L (152) | 1996-00 2.5L (151) | 1989-96 3.9L (238) | 1997-00 3.9 (238) | 2000 4.7L (287) (coil-on-plug) | 1989-92 5.2L (318), 5.9L (360) | 1993-00 5.2L (318), 5.9L (360) | 1994-00 8.0L (488) |

DODGE TRUCKS
1989-2000 All Rear Wheel & 4-Wheel Drive Models
Raider, Ram 50—See Chrysler, Dodge, Plymouth

UNDERHOOD SERVICE SPECIFICATIONS

TIMING MARK

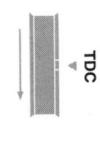

1996-00
2.5L (151)

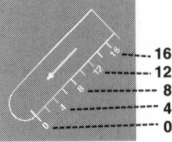

1989-95 2.5L (152)
Viewed at upper left front
side of flywheel housing

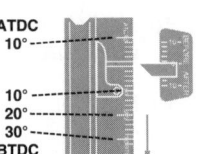

1989-93
3.9L (238)

4.7L (287)

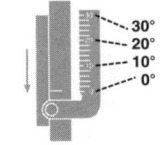

1989-93
5.2L (318), 5.9L (360)
(When viewed from
under hood)

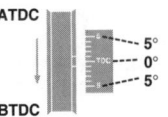

1989-93
5.2L (318),
5.9L (360) Some
(When viewed from under vehicle)

1994-00
3.9L (238)
5.2L (318)
5.9L (360)

No Timing
Marks on These
Engines

8.0L (488)

ELECTRICAL AND IGNITION SYSTEMS

BATTERY

Engine	Year	STANDARD BCI Group No.	STANDARD Crank. Perf.	OPTIONAL BCI Group No.	OPTIONAL Crank. Perf.
All ex. Dakota	1989-91	34	500	34	625
Diesel	1989-91	30H	1025	—	—
Ramcharger	1992-93	34	600	34	685
B, D, W Series	1992-93	27	600	27	810
Diesel	1992-93	30H	1025	—	—
All	1989-91	34	500	34	625
	1992-93	27	600	27	810
	1994-00	27	600	27	750
V10, Diesel	1994-00	27	750	—	—

GENERATOR

1989-95 Test output is measured at 1250 rpm with 15 volts at the alternator.
1996-00 Test output is measured at 2500 rpm with 15 volts at the alternator.

Application	Year	Rated Output	Test Output
All (1989-96 models):			
Bosch: 75HS	1989-90	75	30
90HS	1989	90	75
Nippondenso: 75HS	1989-90	75	68
90HS	1989-90	90	87
120HS	1989-90	120	98
Nippondenso: 75HS	1991-96	75	75
90HS	1991-96	90	90
120HS	1991-96	120	120
Chrysler: 90RS	1989	90	87
120RS	1989	120	98
All	1997-00	117	90
		136	120

REGULATOR

Year	Test Temp. (deg. F/C)	Voltage Setting
1989	—	1
1990-91	—	12.9-15.0[1]

1 Regulated by computer.

STARTER

Engine at operating temperature.

Application	Year	Cranking Voltage (min. volts)	Ampere Draw @ Cranking Speed
All: Gasoline	1989-92	9.6	150-220
Diesel	1989-92	8.0	450-550

STARTER Continued

Application	Year	Cranking Voltage (min. volts)	Ampere Draw @ Cranking Speed
All: Gasoline	1993	9.6	125-200
Diesel	1993	8.0	450-550
Dakota	1994-95	9.6	125-200
Pickups, Vans: Gas	1994-00	9.6	125-250
Diesel	1994-00	8.0	450-700
Dakota: 4-cyl.	1996	9.6	130
V6, V8	1996	9.6	125-200
Dakota, Durango: Mitsubishi	1997-00	9.6	130
Nippondenso	1997-00	9.6	125-250

SPARK PLUGS

Engine	Year	Gap (inches)	Gap (mm)	Torque (ft-lb)
2.5L	1989-95	.035	.89	20
	1996-00	.035	.89	30
3.9L, 5.2L	1997-00	.040	1.01	30
5.9L	1998-00	.040	1.01	30
8.0L	1994-00	.045	1.14	30
All Others	1989-97	.035	.89	30

IGNITION COIL

FOR TESTING AND ADJUSTMENT DIAGRAMS, SEE APPENDIX A.

Resistance (ohms at 70° to 80°F or 21° to 27°C)

Engine	Year	Windings	Resistance (ohms)
All oil filled coils:			
Essex, UTC	1989-92	Primary	1.34-1.55
		Secondary	9000-12,200
Prestolite	1989-92	Primary	1.34-1.55
		Secondary	9400-11,700
All oil filled coils:			
Diamond	1989-92	Primary	1.34-1.55
		Secondary	15,000-19,000
All epoxy type coil: 4-cyl., V6, V8			
Diamond	1991-00	Primary	.96-1.18
		Secondary	11,300-15,300
Toyodenso	1991-00	Primary	.95-1.20
		Secondary	11,300-13,300
V10	1994-00	Primary	.53-.65
		Secondary	10,900-14,700

DODGE TRUCKS
1989-2000 All Rear Wheel & 4-Wheel Drive Models

UNDERHOOD SERVICE SPECIFICATIONS

CRTTU3

CRTTU3

BASE TIMING
FOR TESTING AND ADJUSTMENT DIAGRAMS, SEE APPENDIX C.

1989-91 All, 1992-95 2.5L, 1992 5.9L: Disconnect coolant temperature sensor.
1992-99 3.9L, 5.2L, 1993-99 5.9L: Timing is not adjustable. Set timing marks to TDC and verify that rotor blade is aligned with notch on switch plate.

Engine	Year	Man. Trans. (degrees)	Auto. Trans. (degrees)
2.5L	1989-95	12±2	—
3.9L	1989-91	10±2	10±2
	1992-98	TDC[3]	TDC[3]
5.2L	1989-91	10±2	10±2
	1992-99	TDC[3]	TDC[3]
5.9L	1989-92	10±2	10±2
	1993-99	TDC[3]	TDC[3]

1 Light-duty cycle: GVW of 8500 or less; **Heavy-duty cycle**: GVW of 8501 lb or more.
2 Timing may be readjusted to 3° if detonation is occurring.
3 Not adjustable.

FUEL SYSTEM

FUEL SYSTEM PRESSURE
FOR TESTING AND ADJUSTMENT DIAGRAMS, SEE APPENDIX D.

Engine	Year	Pressure PSI	Pressure RPM
All TBI			
2.5L (135)	1989-95	13.5-15.5	idle
3.9L, 5.2L, 5.9L	1989-91	13.5-15.5	idle

Engine	Year	Pressure PSI[1]	Pressure PSI[2]	Fuel Pump
Fuel injected: 4-cyl.	1996-00	44-54	—	54 min.
3.9L, 5.2L	1992-93	31 approx.	39-41 approx.	75
3.9L, 5.2L, 8.0L	1994-95	35-45	—	45 min.
	1996-00	44-54	—	54 min.
5.9L: Gas	1993-95	35-45[3]	—	45 min.
	1996-00	44-54	—	54 min.
Diesel	1995-99	25 min.	—	—
CNG	1997-98	190-140	—	—
	1999-00	110-125	—	—

1 Vacuum hose connected to fuel pressure regulator.
2 Vacuum hose disconnected from fuel pressure regulator.
3 System pressure, does not have vacuum controlled regulator.

IDLE SPEED W/O COMPUTER CONTROL

5.9L Diesel: Set idle to specified value with A/C on. Push throttle to floor and check or set max. speed.

Engine	Year	SLOW Man. Trans.	SLOW Auto. Trans.	FAST Man. Trans.	FAST Auto. Trans.	Step of Cam
5.9L Diesel	1989-93	750	700 N	—	—	—
Max. Speed	1989-93	2875	2875 N	—	—	—
5.9L Diesel	1994-96	780	750-800 D	—	—	—

1 Light-duty cycle: GVW of 8500 lb or less.

IDLE SPEED W/COMPUTER CONTROL
FOR TESTING AND ADJUSTMENT DIAGRAMS, SEE APPENDIX E.

1989-91 V6, V8, 1992 5.9L: Run engine for two minutes and shut off. After 60 seconds, disconnect ISC and coolant temp. sensor connectors. Adjust extension screw on ISC.
1989-99 4-cyl., 1994-99 V6, V8: Connect DRB-II to "check engine" connector. Disconnect PCV valve and install special tool (0.125" orifice, 4-cyl.) or 0.185" (V6, V8) to PCV hose. Start engine and switch DRB to "Min. Airflow Idle Spd." If minimum throttle body airflow is not correct, throttle body must be replaced.

Engine	Year	Setting Speed	Idle Speed	Checking Speed
2.5L	1989-90	—	850	1050-1250
2.5L	1991-95	—	—	1050-1250
3.9L Dakota	1989	2500-2600 (N)	750 (N)	—

IDLE SPEED W/COMPUTER CONTROL Continued

Engine	Year	Setting Speed	Idle Speed	Checking Speed
3.9L	1989	2500-2600 (N)	750 (N)	—
3.9L	1990-91	2500-2600 (N)	—	—
3.9L	1994-00	—	—	500-900 (N)
5.2L	1989	2750-2850 (N)	700 (N)	—
5.2L	1990-91	2750-2850 (N)	—	—
5.2L	1994-00	—	—	500-900 (N)
5.9L LD	1989	2750-2850 (N)	800 (N)	—
High Altitude	1989	2750-2850 (N)	750 (N)	—
HD	1989	2750-2850 (N)	800 (N)	—
5.9L	1990-92	2750-2850 (N)	—	—
5.9L	1994-00	—	—	500-900 (N)

ENGINE MECHANICAL

TIGHTENING TORQUES
FOR CYLINDER HEAD TORQUE SEQUENCES AND DIAGRAMS, SEE APPENDIX F.

Some fasteners are tightened in more than one step.
Some torques are specified in inches.

Engine	Year	TORQUE FOOT-POUNDS/NEWTON METERS Cylinder Head	Intake Manifold	Exhaust Manifold	Crankshaft Pulley	Water Pump
2.5L (153)	1989-95	45/61, 65/89, 65/89, +90°[1]	200"/23	200"/23	50/68	21/28-upper 40/54-lower
2.5L	1996-97	50/68, 110/143	3	25/34	135/183	30/41
	1998-00	110/149[4]	25/31	22/31	80/108	23/31
3.9L (238)	1989-91	50/68, 105/43	45/61	20/27-bolts 15/20-nuts	135/181	30/41
3.9L	1992-00	50/68, 105/143	72"/8, 12/16	25/36	135/181	30/40
5.2L, 5.9L	1989-91	50/68, 105/43	40/54	20/27-bolts 15/20-nuts	100/136	30/41
5.2L	1992-00	50/68, 105/143	72"/8, 12/16	25/34	135/181	30/40
5.9L	1992	50/68, 105/143	25/34, 40/54	15/20-nuts 20/27-bolts	135/183	30/40
5.9L	1993-99	50/68, 105/143	72"/18, 12/16	25/34	135/181	30/40
5.9L Diesel	1989-92	29/40, 62/85, 93/126	—	32/43	92/125	18/24
5.9L Diesel 12V	1993-98	66/90, 2	—	32/43	135/183	30/41
5.9L Diesel 24V	1998-00	59/80, 77/105, 77/105, +90	—	32/43	—	18/24
8.0L	1994-00	43/58, 105/143	16/22, upper 40/54, lower	16/22	135/183	30/41

1 Torque should be above 90/122 after this step or replace bolt.
2 Then tighten long bolts only to 89/120. Then turn all bolts 90°.
3 Tighten center upper bolt to 30/41. Tighten all others to 23/31.
4. Bolt #11, 100/135

COMPRESSION PRESSURE
At cranking speed, engine temperature normalized, throttle open.

Engine	Year	PSI	Maximum Variation PSI
All Gasoline	1989-00	100 min.	25

BELT TENSION
1990-91 Dakota V8, 1992-97 3.9L, 5.2L & 1993-97 all, use automatic tensioner. Replace belt if index marks are outside of window on tensioner.

UNDERHOOD SERVICE SPECIFICATIONS

BELT TENSION Continued

Engine	Year	Generator	Power Steering	Air Cond.	Air Pump
Strand Tension method:					
NEW					
All	1989	100-140	100-140	100-140	100-140
All ex. Dakota V8	1990-91	100-140	100-140	100-140	100-140
2.5L	1996-00	160	120	160	—
USED					
All	1989	60-90	60-90	60-90	60-90
All ex. Dakota V8	1990-91	60-90	60-90	60-90	60-90
2.5L	1996-00	80	80	80	—

SERPENTINE BELT DIAGRAMS

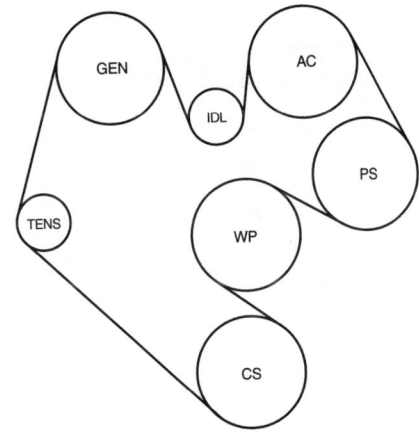

1992-00 3.9L, 5.2L, 5.9L LD w/AC

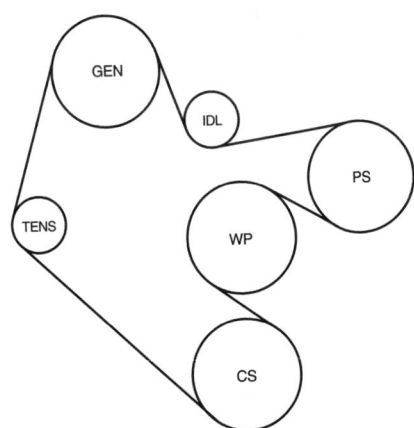

1992-00 3.9L, 5.2L, 5.9L LD w/o AC

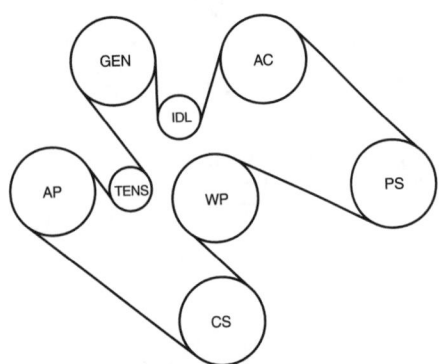

1993-00 5.9L HD, 8.0L w/AC

SERPENTINE BELT DIAGRAMS Continued

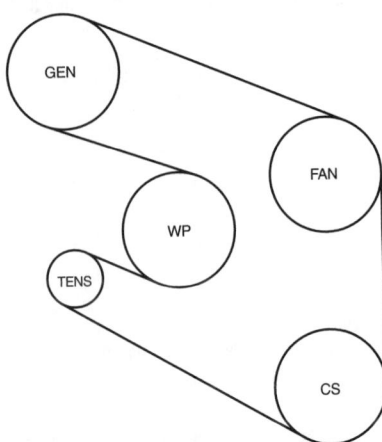

1989-00 5.9L Diesel w/o AC

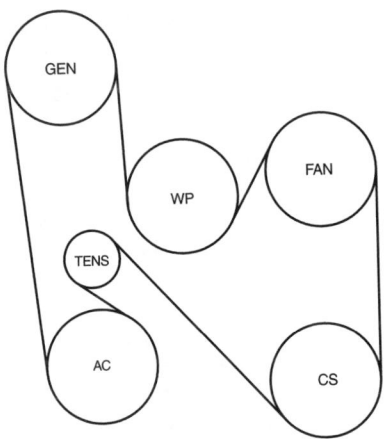

1989-00 5.9L Diesel w/AC

VALVE CLEARANCE
Engine cold.

Engine	Year	Intake (inches)	Intake (mm)	Exhaust (inches)	Exhaust (mm)
5.9L Diesel	1989-96	.010	.25	.020	.50

ENGINE COMPUTER SYSTEM

DIAGNOSTIC TROUBLE CODES
FOR TESTING AND ADJUSTMENT DIAGRAMS, SEE APPENDIX G.

All w/FI: Turn ignition switch on-off-on-off-on and observe. Check Engine light.
OBD-II System. Codes can still be displayed on MIL.
Code 11 Engine not cranked since battery disconnected
Code 12 Battery disconnected in last 50 cycles
Code 12 Standby memory circuit
Code 13 MAP sensor vacuum circuit
Code 14 MAP sensor electrical circuit
Code 15 Speed/distance sensor circuit
Code 16 Battery voltage sense loss
Code 17 Engine running too cool
Code 21 Oxygen sensor circuit
Code 22 Engine coolant temperature sensor circuit
Code 23 Throttle body temperature circuit (1989-93 TBI)
Code 23 Intake air temperature sensor (1993-98 MFI)

UNDERHOOD SERVICE SPECIFICATIONS

DIAGNOSTIC TROUBLE CODES Continued

Code 24 Throttle position sensor circuit
Code 25 Idle air control circuit
Code 26 Peak injector current not reached
Code 27 Fuel injector control problem
Code 31 EVAP Canister purge solenoid circuit
Code 32 EGR diagnostics
Code 33 Air conditioner WOT relay circuit
Code 34 Speed control solenoid driver circuit
Code 35 Radiator for relay (4-cyl.)
Code 35 Idle switch (V6, V8)
Code 36 Air switching solenoid
Code 37 Torque converter lock-up solenoid
Code 41 Charging system over voltage
Code 42 Automatic shutdown relay circuit
Code 43 Ignition coil control (1989-91)
Code 43 Cylinder misfire (1996-98)
Code 44 Loss of F2 to logic board (1989-91)
Code 44 Battery temperature sensor (1994-98)
Code 45 Automatic transmission overdrive circuit
Code 46 Battery over voltage
Code 47 Battery under voltage
Code 51 Oxygen sensor lean
Code 52 Oxygen sensor rich
Code 53 Engine controller fault (1989-98)
Code 54 No cam signal at PCM
Code 55 End of message
Code 62 SRI mileage accumulator
Code 63 PCM failure, EEPROM write denied
Code 64 Catalytic converter efficiency
Code 65 Power steering switch failure
Code 71 Auxiliary 5 volt supply output too low
Code 72 Catalytic converter efficiency
Code 77 Speed control power relay
Code 88 Start of message

SENSORS, INPUT

TEMPERATURE SENSORS

Engine	Year	Sensor	Resistance Ohms @ deg. F/C
All TBI	1989-92	Coolant	7000-13,000 @ 70/21
			700-1000 @ 200/93
		Throttle body (ex. V6)	5600-14,600 @ 70/21
			400-1500 @ 200/93
All MFI	1992-00	Coolant, Intake air, Transmission temp.	29,330-35,990 @ 32/0
			11,370-13,610 @ 68/20
			4900-5750 @ 104/40
			2310-2670 @ 176/80
			640-720 @ 212/100
			370-410 @ 248/210

SENSORS, INPUT Continued

MANIFOLD ABSOLUTE PRESSURE SENSOR
All Models with TBI.

1989-91 Apply 5 in. Hg. (17 kPa) to unit and record output voltage. Apply 20" (500mm) Hg to unit, the difference in voltage should be 2.3-2.9.

Engine	Year	Voltage	
		Idle	Ign. On
All MFI	1992-99	1.5-2.1	4.0-5.0

THROTTLE POSITION SENSOR
All with TBI.

Engine	Year	Voltage	
		Idle	WOT
All	1989-91	0.5-1.5	4.0
2.5L	1992-95	1.0	5.0
	1996	0.2 min	4.8 max
	1997-98	.35-.90	4.5 max
	1999-00	.26-.95	4.5max
3.9L, 5.2L	1992-96	0.2 min	4.8 max
	1997-98	.35-.90	4.5 max
	1999-00	.26-.95	4.5max
5.9L	1992	0.5-1.5	4.0
5.9L Gas	1993-96	0.2 min	4.8 max
	1997-00	.35-.90	4.5 max
5.9L Diesel	1993-96	1.0	2.25-2.75
8.0L	1994-96	0.2 min.	4.8 max
	1997-98	.35-.90	4.5 max
	1999-00	.26-.95	4.5max

ACTUATORS, OUTPUT

FUEL INJECTORS

Engine	Year	Resistance (ohms)	Temperature (deg. F/C)
2.5L	1996-97	13.3-15.7	68/20
	1998-00	10.8-13.2	68/20
3.9L	1992-97	13.3-15.7	68/20
	1998-00	10.8-13.2	68/20
5.2L	1992-97	13.3-15.7	68/20
	1998-00	10.8-13.2	68/20
5.9L	1993-97	13.3-15.7	68/20
	1998-00	10.8-13.2	68/20
8.0L	1994-97	13.3-15.7	68/20
	1998-00	10.8-13.2	68/20

COMPUTER TIMING ADVANCE
All specifications are in addition to basic timing.
Perform tests with engine at operating temperature.

Engine	Year	Transmission	Computer Number	Advance
2.5L	1989-90	MT & AT	All	24-32
3.9L (238) Dakota	1989-90	MT & AT	All	31-39

EAGLE

1989-98 Medallion, Premier, Summit, Talon, Vista
Eagle Vision — See Chrysler, Dodge, Plymouth

ENGINE IDENTIFICATION

To identify any engine by the manufacturer's code, follow the four steps designated by the numbered blocks.

V.I.N.
PLATE LOCATION:

Top left side of instrument panel, visible through windshield

1 MODEL YEAR IDENTIFICATION:

10th character of V.I.N.
1998—W	1997—V	1996—T
1995—S	1994—R	1993—P
1992—N	1991—M	1990—L
1989—K		

2 ENGINE CODE LOCATION:

8th character of V.I.N.

4 ENGINE IDENTIFICATION

YEAR	3 ENGINE CODE	CYL.	DISPL. liters	cc	Fuel System	HP
1997-98	Y	4	2.0	1996	MFI	140
	F	4	2.0 T	1997 T	MFI	205, 210[1]
1995-96	A	4	1.5	1468	MFI	92
	C	4	1.8	1834	MFI	113, 119[1]
	Y	4	2.0	1996	MFI	140
	F	4	2.0 T	1997 T	MFI	205, 210[1]
	G	4	2.4	2350	MFI	136
1994	A	4	1.5	1468	MFI	92
	B	4	1.8	1755	MFI	92
	C	4	1.8	1834	MFI	113
	E	4	2.0	1997	MFI	135
	F	4	2.0 T	1997 T	MFI	180, 195[1]
	G	4	2.4	2350	MFI	136
1993	A	4	1.5	1468	MFI	92
	B	4	1.8	1755	MFI	92
	C	4	1.8	1834	MFI	113
	E	4	2.0	1997	MFI	135
	F	4	2.0 T	1997	MFI	195
	G	4	2.4	2350	MFI	136
1992	A	4	1.5	1468	MFI	92
	D	4	1.8	1797	MFI	113
1992	R	4	2.0	1997	MFI	135

4 ENGINE IDENTIFICATION

YEAR	3 ENGINE CODE	CYL.	DISPL. liters	cc	Fuel System	HP
Cont'd.	U	4	2.0 T	1997	MFI	195
	W	4	2.4	2396	MFI	116
	U	6	3.0	2970	MFI	150
1991	A	4	1.5	1468	MFI	92
	R	4	2.0	1997	MFI	135
	U	4	2.0 T	1997	MFI	190, 195[1]
	U	6	3.0	2970	MFI	150
1990	X	4	1.5	1468	MFI	81
	Y	4	1.6	1597	MFI	113
	R	4	2.0	1997	MFI	135
	U	4	2.0 T	1997	MFI	190
	U	6	3.0	2970	MFI	150
1989	X	4	1.5	1468	MFI	81
	Y	4	1.6	1597	MFI	113
	F	4	2.2	2165	MFI	103
	Z	4	2.5	2460	TBI	111
	U	6	3.0	2970	MFI	150

T—Turbo.   MFI—Multiport Fuel Injection.
1—Engine horsepower varies with model installation.
TBI—Throttle Body Injection.

UNDERHOOD SERVICE SPECIFICATIONS

EETU1

EETU1

CYLINDER NUMBERING SEQUENCE

4-CYL. FIRING ORDER: 1 3 4 2

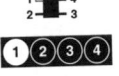

Front of car

| 1989-90 1.5L | 1991-96 1.5L | 1989-90 1.6L, 1990-94 Talon 2.0L | 1.8 Talon | 1995-98 2.0L Talon Turbo Code F | 1995-98 Code Y 2.0L Talon ex. Turbo |

V6 FIRING ORDER: 1 6 3 5 2 4

Front of car

| 1992-96 1.8L Summit | 1989-90 Premier 2.5L | 1989 Medallion 2.2L | 1992 2.4L | 1993-96 2.4L | 1989-92 Premier 3.0L |

Direct ignition

Distributor ignition

TIMING MARK

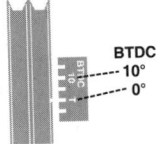
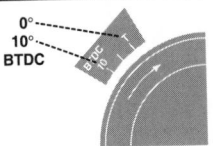
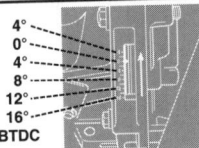

| 1.5L, 1.8L | 1992-98 2.4L, Talon 2.0L ex. Code Y | 1995-98 2.0L Talon Code Y | 2.2L |

No Timing Marks on Engine

EAGLE
1989-98 Medallion, Premier, Summit, Talon, Vista
Eagle Vision — See Chrysler, Dodge, Plymouth

UNDERHOOD SERVICE SPECIFICATIONS

EETU2

EETU2

ELECTRICAL AND IGNITION SYSTEMS

BATTERY

BCI equivalent shown, size may vary from original equipment. Check clearance before replacing, holddown may need to be modified.

Engine	Year	STANDARD BCI Group No.	STANDARD Crank. Perf.	OPTIONAL BCI Group No.	OPTIONAL Crank. Perf.
1.5L, 1.6L Summit	1989-90	45	435	—	—
1.5L, 1.6L Summit	1991-92	25	35	25	430
1.5L Summit	1993-96	51	430	—	—
1.8L Summit	1993-96	51	430	—	—
1.8L Summit Wagon	1992-94	25	355	—	—
Canada	1992-94	24	420	—	—
	1995-96	24	580	—	—
1.8L Talon: U.S.	1990-91	86	430	—	—
Canada	1990-91	86	525	—	—
1.8L Talon: U.S.	1992-94	86	430	—	—
Canada: MT	1992-94	86	430	—	—
AT	1992-94	86	525	—	—
2.0L Talon	1990	86	430	—	—
2.0L Talon	1991	86	525	—	—
2.0L Talon: U.S.	1992-94	86	430	—	—
Canada	1992-94	86	525	—	—
2.0L Talon	1995-98	86	430	—	—
Turbo	1995-98	86	430	86	525
2.0L Vista	1989-91	25	420	—	—
2.2L Medallion	1989	34	375	58	400
2.4L Summit Wagon	1992-96	24	420	—	—
Canada	1992-96	24	580	—	—
2.5L, 3.0L Premier	1989-92	34	500	—	—

GENERATOR

Application	Year	Rated Output (amps)	Test Output (amps)
Medallion	1989	75	61 @ 1200
		90	76 @ 1200
Premier	1989-90	85, 96, 100, 105	1
Premier	1991-92	96	78 @ 2000
Summit	1989-92	65	46 @ 2500
		75	53 @ 2500
		90	63 @ 2500
Summit: 1.5L	1993-94	75	52 @ 2500
1.8L	1993-94	65	46 @ 2500
	1993-94	70	49 @ 2500
Summit	1995-96	70	49 @ 2500
Summit Wagon:			
1.8L	1992-96	60	42 @ 2500
	1992-93	65	46 @ 2500
2.4L	1992-96	75	53 @ 2500
Talon	1990-94	65	46 @ 2500
		75	53 @ 2500
		90	63 @ 2500
	1995-98	90	63 @ 2500
Turbo	1995-98	75	53 @ 2500
		90	63 @ 2500
Vista	1989-91	65	46 @ 2500
		75	53 @ 2500

1 Output at 2000 rpm must be within 15 amps of rated output.

REGULATOR

Application	Test Temp. (deg. F/C)	Voltage Setting
1989 Medallion	175/80	13.0-14.1
1989-91 Premier	—	13.5-16.0
1989-98 Summit, Talon, Vista	-4/-20	14.2-15.4
	68/20	13.9-14.9
	140/60	13.4-14.6
	175/80	13.1-14.5
1995-98 Talon ex. Turbo	-4/-20	14.3-15.3
	68/20	14.1-15.1
	140/60	13.6-14.6
	176/80	13.4-14.4

STARTER

Engine	Year	Cranking Voltage (min. volts)	Ampere Draw @ Cranking Speed
Medallion	1989	9.6	160
Premier	1989-92	9.6	130

SPARK PLUGS

Engine	Year	Gap (inches)	Gap (mm)	Torque (ft-lb)
1.5L, 1.6L	1989-96	.039-.043	1.0-1.1	15-21
1.8L	1990-96	.039-.043	1.0-1.1	15-21
2.0L ex. Turbo	1990-94	.039-.043	1.0-1.1	15-21
	1995-98	.048-.053	1.2-1.4	15-22
2.0L Turbo	1990-98	.028-.031	0.7-0.8	15-21
2.2L	1989	.036	.90	11
2.4L	1993-96	.039-.043	1.0-1.1	15-21
2.5L	1989	.036	.90	28
3.0L	1989-92	.035	.90	11

IGNITION COIL

FOR TESTING AND ADJUSTMENT DIAGRAMS, SEE APPENDIX A.
Resistance (ohms @ 70°F or 21°C)

2.0L & 1991 3.0L (late): Primary windings measured between B+ terminal (upper right on connector) and each of the other three terminals. Secondary resistance measured at each coil's high voltage terminals with spark plug wires removed.

Engine	Year	Resistance Windings	(ohms)
1.5L	1989-90	Primary	.72-.86
		Secondary	10,300-13,900
1.5L	1991-96	Primary	0.9-1.2
		Secondary	20,000-29,000
1.6L	1989-90	Primary	.77-.95
		Secondary	10,300-13,900
1.8L Summit Wagon	1992-96	Primary	0.9-1.2
		Secondary	20,000-29,000
1.8L Talon	1990-94	Primary	0.9-1.2
		Secondary	19,000-27,000
2.0L Talon	1990-91	Primary	.72-.95
		Secondary	10,300-13,900
	1992-94	Primary	.70-.86
		Secondary	11,300-15,300
2.0L Talon	1995-97	Primary	.51-.61
		Secondary	11,500-13,500
Turbo	1995-98	Primary	.70-.86
		Secondary	11,300-15,300
2.0L Vista	1989-91	Primary	.72-.88
		Secondary	10,900-13,300
2.2L, 2.5L, 3.0L (early)	1989-90	Primary	0.5-1.0
		Secondary	4500-5000
2.4L	1992	Primary	.72-.88
		Secondary	10,300-13,900
	1993-96	Primary	0.9-1.2
		Secondary	20,000-29,000

BASE TIMING

FOR TESTING AND ADJUSTMENT DIAGRAMS, SEE APPENDIX C.
Set timing at Before Top Dead Center at idle speed or less.

1.5L, 1.6L, 1.8L, 2.0L, 2.4L: Ground ignition timing connector (on fender skirt or firewall). When ungrounded, timing should be at "Check" value.
1996: Manufacturer prefers that distributor not be turned.

Engine	Year	Man. Trans. (degrees)	Auto. Trans. (degrees)
1.5L: Set	1989-95	5±2	5±2
Check	1989-93	10±2	10±2
Check	1994-95	10±7	10±7
1.5L: Set	1996	5±3	5±3
Check	1996	5±7[1]	5±7[1]
1.6L: Set	1989-90	5±2	5±2
Check	1989-90	8±2	8±2
1.8L Summit: Set	1992-96	5±2	5±2
Check	1992-93	5±2	5±2
Check	1994-95	5±7	5±7
1.8L Talon: Set	1990-94	5±2	5±2
Check	1990-94	10±2	10±2
1.8L: Set	1996	5±3	5±3
Check	1996	5±7[1]	5±7[1]

1989-98 Medallion, Premier, Summit, Talon, Vista
Eagle Vision — See Chrysler, Dodge, Plymouth

UNDERHOOD SERVICE SPECIFICATIONS

BASE TIMING Continued

Engine	Year	Man. Trans. (degrees)	Auto. Trans. (degrees)
2.0L Talon: Set	1990-94	5±2	5±2
Check	1990-94	8±2	8±2
2.0L Talon	1995-98	12[2]	12[2]
Turbo: Check	1995-98	5±3[2]	5±3[2]
Set	1995-98	8±7[1]	8±7[1]
2.0L Vista: Set	1989-91	5±2	5±2
Check	1989-91	10±2	10±2
2.4L: Set	1992-95	5±2	5±2
Check	1992-93	8±2	8±2
Check	1994-95	10±7	10±7
Check	1996	5±3	5±3
2.4L: Set	1996	5±7[1]	5±7[1]
Check	1996		

1 At high altitudes, ignition will be advanced further.
2 Not adjustable.

FUEL SYSTEM

FOR TESTING AND ADJUSTMENT DIAGRAMS, SEE APPENDIX D.

FUEL SYSTEM PRESSURE

CARBURETED & TBI

Engine	Year	PSI	RPM
2.5L	1989	14-15	idle

MFI

Engine	Year	Pressure @ Idle PSI[1]	PSI[2]
1.5L, 1.6L, 1.8L, 2.0L ex. Turbo, 2.4L	1989-98	47-53	38
2.0L ex. Turbo	1995-98	47-50	—
2.0L Turbo MT	1990-94	36-38	27
2.0L Turbo AT	1992-94	41-46	33
2.0L Turbo	1995-97	42-45	33
2.2L	1989	—	33-39
3.0L (early)	1989-91	—	28-30
3.0L (late)	1991-92	—	43

1 Pressure regulator vacuum disconnected.
2 Pressure regulator vacuum connected.

IDLE SPEED W/COMPUTER CONTROL

FOR TESTING AND ADJUSTMENT DIAGRAMS, SEE APPENDIX E.

1995-98 2.0L ex. Turbo:
Remove PVC valve from PCV hose and install special tool (.0125" orifice) into the hose. Connect a Scan tool and access Minimum Idle speed. If checking speeed is not 500-1100 (N), replace the throttle body.

1994-96 1.5L, 1.8L ex. Talon: Ground the ignition timing connector and terminal 1 (upper left) of the 16 terminal self-test connector under dash. Set idle to specified setting speed. Turn A/C on and verify that speed increases to specified value.

1989-93 1.5L, 1.6L; 1.8L Talon:
1994 1.8L Talon: Turn ignition on for more than 15 seconds and turn off. Disconnect ISC and start engine. Set to specified value. Reconnect ISC and turn A/C on, verify that speed increases to specified value.

1989-93 1.8L ex. Talon, 2.0L, 2.4L:
1994 2.0L Talon, 1995-98 2.0L Turbo Talon: Ground ignition timing connector and terminal 10 of the self-diagnostic connector. Set speed to specified value. Reinstate connections and verify the speed increases to specified value with A/C on.

1989 2.5L: Fully extend ISC with tool #7086 and adjust to specified value.

1991-92 3.0L (late): Connect DRB-II and select base idle mode. Verify that idle is at specified checking speed. Replace throttle body if outside range.

Engine	Year	Transmission	Setting Speed	Checking Speed	AC Speed-up
1.5L, 1.6L	1989-92	MT	700-800	650-850	850
		AT	700-800 N	650-850 N	850 N
1.5L Summit	1993-96	MT	750-850	650-850	800-1000
		AT	750-850 N	650-850 N	800-1000 N
1.8L Summit	1993-94	MT	650-750	650-850	850
		AT	650-750 N	650-850 N	850 N
1.8L Summit Wagon	1992-94	MT	650-750	650-850	830
		AT	650-750 N	650-850 N	830 N
California	1993-94	MT	650-750	600-800	830
		AT	650-750 N	600-800 N	830 N

IDLE SPEED W/COMPUTER CONT7ROL Continued

Engine	Year	Transmission	Setting Speed	Checking Speed	AC Speed-up
1.8L	1995-96	MT	650-750	600-800	800-900
		AT	650-750 N	600-800 N	800-900 N
1.8L Talon	1990-94	MT	650-750	600-800	850
		AT	650-750 N	600-800 N	650 D
2.0L Talon	1990-94	MT	700-800	650-850	850
		AT	700-800 N	650-850 N	650 D
2.0L Talon	1995-98	MT	—	700-900	750-950
		AT	—	700-900 N	750-950 N
Turbo	1995-98	MT	700-800	650-850	750-950
		AT	700-800 N	650-850 N	750-950 N
2.0L Vista	1989-91	MT	650-750	600-800	900
		AT	650-750 N	600-800 N	600 D
2.4L	1992-94	MT	650-750	650-850	850
		AT	650-750 N	650-850 N	850 N
	1995-96	MT	700-800	650-850	800-900
		AT	700-800 N	650-850 N	800-900 N
2.5L	1989	MT	3500	750-800	—
		AT	3500 N	750-800 N	—
3.0L (late)	1991-92	AT	—	565-665 D	—

ENGINE MECHANICAL

TIGHTENING TORQUES

FOR CYLINDER HEAD TORQUE SEQUENCES AND DIAGRAMS, SEE APPENDIX F.
1.5L, 1.6L, 1.8L, 2.0L, 2.4L cylinder head bolts are tightened with engine cold.

Engine	Year	TORQUE FOOT-POUNDS/NEWTON METERS Cylinder Head	Intake Manifold	Exhaust Manifold	Crankshaft Pulley	Water Pump
1.5L	1989-92	51-54/ 69-74	12-14/ 16-19	12-14/ 16-19	9-11/ 12-15	9-11/ 12-15[1] 14-20/ 20-27[2]
1.5L	1993-96	53/73	13/18	13/18	62/85[2] 10/13[1]	10-14[1] 19/24[2]
1.6L, 2.0L	1989-92	65-72/ 90-100	11-14/ 15-19[1] 22-30/ 30-42[2]	18-22/ 25-30	14-22/ 22-30	9-11/ 12-15[1] 14-20/ 20-27[2]
1.8L Talon	1989-94	51-54/ 69-74	12-14/ 16-19	12-14/ 16-19	9-11/ 12-15	9-11/ 12-15[1] 14-20/ 20-27[2]
1.8L Summit	1992-96	54/75[3] 14/20, +90°+90°	14/20	22/30	134/185	18/24
2.0L	1993-94	58/78[3], 14/20, +90°, +90°	11-14/ 15-20[1] 22-30/ 30-42[2]	11-14/ 15-20	15-21/ 20-30	9-11/ 12-15[1] 14-20/ 20-27[2]
2.0L ex. Turbo	1995-98	6	17/23	17/23	105/142	9-12
Turbo	1995-98	58/80[3], 15/20, +90°+90°	26/36	22/29	18/25	9-14 12-15
2.2L	1985-89	69/93	—	—	96/130	—
2.4L	1992	76-83/ 105-115	13/18	13/18	18/25	10/14
2.4L	1993-96	58/80[3] 14/20, +90°, +90°	13/18	22/30	18/25	10/14
2.5L	1989	110/149[4]	23/31	23/31	80/108	13/18
3.0L	1989-91	5	11/15	13/18	125/170	20/27

1 Short bolts.
2 Long bolts.
3 Then back off completely.
4 Tighten bolt number eight (first bolt, right front side) to 100/136.
5 Engines built before code 89616 (1989-90), tighten to 45/61. Back off and retighten to 15/19 and then turn 105°. Run engine for 15 minutes, let cool for six hours and tighten an additional 45°. Engines built from code 89616 (1990-91), tighten to 45/61. Back off and retighten to 30/40 then turn 160-200°.
6 Tighten short bolts to 20/27, three times. Then turn 90°. Tighten long bolts to: 25/33, 50/67, 50/67, then turn 90°.

EAGLE
1989-98 Medallion, Premier, Summit, Talon, Vista
Eagle Vision — See Chrysler, Dodge, Plymouth

UNDERHOOD SERVICE SPECIFICATIONS

VALVE CLEARANCE
Engine hot.

Engine	Year	Intake (inches)	Intake (mm)	Exhaust (inches)	Exhaust (mm)
1.5L	1989-92	.006	.15	.010	.25
1.5L	1993-96	.008	.20	.010	.25
1.8L Wagon	1992-96	.008	.20	.012	.30

COMPRESSION PRESSURE
At cranking speed, engine warm, throttle open.

Engine	Year	PSI	Maximum Variation PSI
1.5L	1989-96	137 min.	14
1.6L	1989-90	171 min.	14
1.8L Talon	1990-94	131 min.	14
	1995-96	151 min.	14
1.8L Summit	1992-96	142 min.	14
2.0L Vista	1989-91	119 min.	14
2.0L ex. Vista	1990-91	137 min.	14
2.0L	1992-94	145 min.	14
	1995-98	170-225/100 min.	1
2.0L Turbo	1990-91	114 min.	14
2.0L Turbo	1992-94	121 min.	14
	1995-97	133-178	14
2.4L	1992	119 min.	14
2.4L	1993-96	139 min.	14
2.5L	1989	155-185	30
3.0L	1990-92	—	1

1 Lowest cylinder pressure must be 75% of highest.

BELT TENSION
Use a strand tension gauge. Measurements are in pounds.

Engine	Year	Generator	Power Steering	Air Cond.
Strand Tension method				
NEW BELTS:				
1.5L, 1.8L Talon	1989-96	110-155	110-155	105-125
1.6L, 2.0L	1989-94	110-155	110-155	80-95
1.8L Summit	1992-96	110-155	145-190	165-175
2.0L ex. Turbo	1995-98	110-160	110-160	110-160
Turbo	1995-98	110-155	110-155	86-99
2.2L	1989	65-85	65-85	65-85
Serpentine	1989	140-160	140-160	140-160
2.4L	1992-96	110-155	110-154	120-145
2.5L, 3.0L	1989-92	180-200	180-200	180-200
USED BELTS:				
1.5L, 1.8L Talon	1989-96	90	90	70-90
1.6L, 2.0L	1989-94	55-110	55-110	55-70
1.8L Summit	1992-96	90	90-130	110-140
2.0L ex. Turbo	1995-98	90-110	93-115	93-115
Turbo	1995-98	55-110	55-110	57-75
2.2L	1989	65-85	65-85	65-85
Serpentine	1989	140-160	140-160	140-160
2.4L	1992-96	55-110	77-99	75-110
2.5L, 3.0L	1989-92	140-160	140-160	140-160

ENGINE COMPUTER SYSTEM

FOR TESTING AND ADJUSTMENT DIAGRAMS, SEE APPENDIX G.

DIAGNOSTIC TROUBLE CODES

1996 All. 1995-98 Talon:
OBD-II system used. Connect a Scan tool and follow manufacturers' instructions to retrieve codes.

1994-95 Summit ex. Wagon
Access connector by fuse block. Connect an analog voltmeter (+) to terminal 25 (upper left) of 12 terminal male connector and (-) to terminal 4 or 5 (upper middle two) of 16 terminal female connector. Turn ignition on. Codes will be displayed as sweeps of the voltmeter needle. Disconnect battery negative terminal to erase codes.

1994-95 Summit Wagon
Ground terminal 1 (upper left) of 16 terminal connector under dash. Turn ignition on. Codes will be displayed on CHECK ENGINE light. Disconnect battery negative terminal to erase codes.

DIAGNOSTIC TROUBLE CODES Continued

1994 Talon
1989-93 Summit, Talon, Vista
Access connector in or under glove box or by fuse block. Connect an analog voltmeter to upper right (+) and lower left (-) cavity. Turn ignition on, codes will be displayed as sweeps of voltmeter needle. Disconnect battery to erase codes.

1991-92 Premier (late)
Turn ignition switch on-off-on-off-on. Codes will be displayed on Check Engine light.

1989-95 Summit, Talon, Vista
Code 11 Oxygen sensor (front)
Code 12 Volume airflow sensor
Code 13 Intake air temperature sensor
Code 14 Throttle position sensor
Code 15 Idle air control position sensor
Code 21 Engine coolant temperature sensor
Code 22 Crankshaft position sensor
Code 23 Camshaft position sensor
Code 24 Vehicle speed sensor
Code 25 Barometric pressure sensor
Code 31 Knock sensor
Code 32 MAP sensor
Code 36 Ignition timing adjustment
Code 39 Oxygen sensor (front on Turbo)
Code 41 Injector
Code 42 Fuel pump
Code 43 EGR
Code 44 Ignition coil power circuit
Code 55 Idle air control valve
Code 59 Heated oxygen sensor (rear)
Code 61 Transaxle and ECM interlink
Code 62 Warm-up valve position sensor
One long pulse ECM
Continuous pulsing System normal

1991-92 Premier (late)
Code 11 Ignition reference circuit
Code 13 MAP sensor vacuum circuit
Code 14 MAP sensor electrical circuit
Code 15 Speed/distance sensor circuit
Code 17 Engine running too cool
Code 21 Oxygen sensor circuit
Code 22 Engine coolant temperature sensor circuit
Code 23 Charge temperature circuit
Code 24 Throttle position sensor circuit
Code 25 Automatic idle speed control circuit
Code 26 Peak injector current not reached
Code 26 Injector circuit
Code 27 Fuel injection circuit control
Code 32 EGR system
Code 33 Air conditioner clutch relay
Code 34 Speed control solenoid driver circuit
Code 35 Fan control relay circuit
Code 42 Automatic shutdown relay circuit
Code 43 Ignition coil circuit
Code 51 Oxygen sensor lean
Code 52 Oxygen sensor rich
Code 53 Internal engine controller fault
Code 54 Fuel sync pick-up circuit
Code 55 End of message
Code 63 EEPROM write denied
Code 77 Speed control power relay

SENSORS, INPUT
TEMPERATURE SENSORS

Engine	Year	Sensor	Resistance Ohms @ deg. F/C
1.5L, 1.6L, 1.8L, 2.0L, 2.4L	1989-98	Coolant	5100-6300 @ 32/0
			2100-2700 @ 68/20
			900-1300 @ 104/40
			260-360 @ 176/80
		Intake Air[1]	5300-6700 @ 32/0
			2300-3000 @ 68/20
			300-420 @ 176/80
2.0L Talon ex. Turbo	1995-98	Coolant, Intake Air	9000-11,000 @ 77/25
			600-800 @ 212/14

EAGLE

1989-98 Medallion, Premier, Summit, Talon, Vista
Eagle Vision — See Chrysler, Dodge, Plymouth

UNDERHOOD SERVICE SPECIFICATIONS

SENSORS, INPUT Continued

Engine	Year	Sensor	Resistance Ohms @ deg. F/C
2.5L, 3.0L	1989-91 (early)	Coolant, Intake Air	13,500 @ 20/-7 7500 @ 40/4 3400 @ 70/20 1600 @ 100/38 450 @ 160/70 185 @ 212/100
3.0L	1991 (late)-92	Coolant, Intake Air	7000-13,000 @ 70/21 700-10,000 @ 200/93

1 Measured between terminals 4 & 6 or 6 & 8 (bottom left and right) of airflow sensor connector.

MANIFOLD ABSOLUTE PRESSURE SENSOR

Engine	Year	Voltage @ Condition
1.5L	1993-94	0.9-1.5 @ idle
2.2L, 2.5L, 3.0L	1989-91 (early)	4-5 @ ign. on 1.5-2.1 @ idle
2.0L Turbo	1995-98	0.8-2.4 @ idle

MASS AIRFLOW SENSOR

Measured between terminals 3 & 6 (upper and lower left) of airflow sensor connector.

Engine	Year	Frequency (HZ) Idle	@ 2000 RPM
1.8L Talon	1993-94	25-40	67-88
1.8L Summit	1993-95	23-49	51-91
	1996	20-46	68-108
2.0L	1993-94	25-50	70-90
Turbo	1993-94	25-50	60-85
2.0L Turbo	1995-98	25-50	60-85
2.4L	1993-96	18-44	43-83

THROTTLE POSITION SENSOR

Engine	Year	Voltage Idle	WOT
1.5L	1989-92	.48-.52	4.5-5.5
	1993-96	0.3-1.0[1]	4.5-5.5
1.6L, 1.8L Talon, 2.0L	1989-94	.48-.52	—
	1995-98	0.4-1.0[1]	4.5-5.5
1.8L, 2.4L Wagon	1992-96	0.4-1.0[1]	—
2.5L	1989	—	4.6-4.7
3.0L	1989-91 (early)	0.5-1.0	—

1 Not adjustable.

IDLE AIR CONTROL POSITION SENSOR

Engine	Year	Resistance (ohms)
1.5L, 1.8L, 2.4L, as equipped	1989-94	4,000-6,000

SENSORS, INPUT Continued

CRANKSHAFT POSITION SENSOR

Measured between brown and blue terminals of crankshaft position sensor.

Engine	Year	Resistance (ohms)
2.2L, 2.5L, 3.0L	1989-91 (early)	125-275

ACTUATORS, OUTPUT

IDLE SPEED CONTROL SOLENOID

At 68°F (20°C)

1.6L: Measured between middle and either left or right cavities in both rows of 6-terminal ISC connector.

Engine	Year	Resistance (ohms)
1.5L, 1.8L, 2.0L Vista, 2.4L	1989-96	5-35
1.6L, 2.0L Talon	1989-94	28-33[1]
2.0L Talon ex. Turbo	1995-98	38-52
Turbo	1995-98	28-33[1]

1 Measured between all three pairs of terminals on six-row connector.

FUEL INJECTORS

Engine	Year	Resistance (ohms)	Temperature (deg. F/C)
1.6L, 1.8L, 2.0L, 2.4L	1989-96	13-16	68/20
2.0L Talon ex. Turbo	1995-98	11-15	68/20
2.0L Turbo	1990-98	2-3	68/20

COMPUTER TIMING ADVANCE

With engine at operating temperature, check advance at idle and 2000 rpm.

Engine	Year	Advance (Degrees) Idle	2000 rpm
1.5L	1993-95	2-18	20-40
	1996	2-18	25-45
1.8L Talon	1993-94	8-12	26-34
1.8L Summit	1993-95	0-13	20-40
	1996	0-13	22-42
1.8L Wagon	1993-95	0-13	10-30
	1996	0-13	22-42
2.0L Talon	1993-94	5-15	33-41
Turbo	1993-94	5-15	30-40
	1995-98	0-13	20-40
2.4L	1993-95	2-18	24-44
	1996	2-18	27-47

FORD, LINCOLN, MERCURY
1989-2000 Ford, Lincoln, Mercury, Merkur Including FWD Vans
Mercury Mountaineer & Lincoln Navigator—See Ford Trucks

ENGINE IDENTIFICATION

To identify any engine by the manufacturer's code, follow the four steps designated by the numbered blocks.

1 MODEL YEAR IDENTIFICATION: Refer to illustration of the Vehicle Identification Number (V.I.N.). The year is indicated by a code letter which is the 10th character of the V.I.N.

2 ENGINE CODE LOCATION: Refer to illustration of V.I.N. plate for location and designation of engine code.

3 ENGINE CODE: In the "CODE" column, find the engine code determined in Step 2.

4 ENGINE IDENTIFICATION: On the line where the engine code appears, read to the right to identify the engine.

V.I.N. PLATE LOCATION:

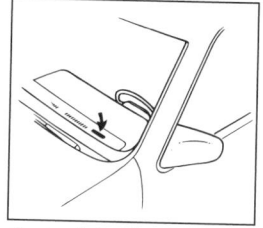

On top left side of instrument panel

Model year of vehicle:
2000 — Y
1999 — X
1998 — W
1997 — V
1996 — T
1995 — S
1994 — R
1993 — P
1992 — N
1991 — M
1990 — L
1989 — K

MODEL YEAR AND ENGINE IDENTIFICATION:

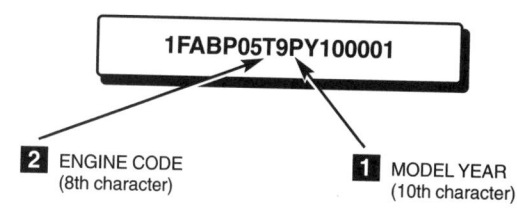

1FABP05T9PY100001

2 ENGINE CODE (8th character)

1 MODEL YEAR (10th character)

4 ENGINE IDENTIFICATION (left table)

YEAR	CODE	CYL.	liters	cu. in.	Fuel System	HP
2000	P	4	2.0	121	MFI	110, 114[1]
	3, Z	4	2.0	121	MFI	125, 130[1]
	L	6	2.5	153	MFI	165, 170[1]
	G	6	2.5 HO	153 HO	MFI	200
	2	6	3.0 EFF	182 EFF	MFI	145-150[1]
	U	6	3.0	182	MFI	150, 155[1]
	S	6	3.0	182	MFI	200, 210[1]
	T	6	3.3	200	MFI	170
	4	6	3.8	232	MFI	190, 200[1]
	A	8	3.9	240	MFI	252
	W	8	4.6 R	281 R	MFI	200-215[1]
	X	8	4.6 W	281 W	MFI	260
	9	8	4.6 NG	281 NG	MFI	175
	V	8	4.6 R	281 R	MFI	275, 320[1]
1999	P	4	2.0	121	MFI	110
	3, Z	4	2.0	121	MFI	125, 130[1]
	L	6	2.5	153	MFI	170
	G	6	2.5 HO	153 HO	MFI	200
	2	6	3.0 EFF	182 EFF	MFI	145-150[1]
	U	6	3.0	182	MFI	145-150[1]
	S	6	3.0	182	MFI	200
	T	6	3.3	200	MFI	170
	N	8	3.4	207	MFI	235
	4	6	3.8	232	MFI	190, 200[1]
	W	8	4.6 R	281 R	MFI	200, 220[1]
	X	8	4.6 W	281 W	MFI	260
	9	8	4.6 NG	281 NG	MFI	175
	V	8	4.6 R	281 R	MFI	275-320[1]
1998	P	4	2.0	121	MFI	110
	3, Z	4	2.0	121	MFI	125, 130[1]
	L	6	2.5	153	MFI	170
	G	6	2.5	153	MFI	195
	1 (Villager)	6	3.0	181	MFI	151
	1 (Taurus)	6	3.0 MFF	182 MFF	MFI	145-155[1]
	2	6	3.0 EFF	182 EFF	MFI	145-150[1]
	U	6	3.0	182	MFI	145-150[1]
	S	6	3.0	182	MFI	200
	N	8	3.4	207	MFI	235
	4 (ex. Windstar)	6	3.8	232	MFI	150
	4 (Windstar)	6	3.8	232	MFI	200
	W	8	4.6 R	281 R	MFI	200, 220[1]
	X	8	4.6 R	281 R	MFI	225
	9	8	4.6 NG	281 NG	MFI	175
	V	8	4.6	281	MFI	260-305[1]
1997	H	4	1.3	81	MFI	63
	A	4	2.0	122	MFI	114, 118[1]
	3, Z	4	2.0	121	MFI	125
	P	4	2.0	121	MFI	110
	L	6	2.5	153	MFI	170

4 ENGINE IDENTIFICATION (right table)

YEAR	CODE	CYL.	liters	cu. in.	Fuel System	HP
1997 Cont'd.	B	6	2.5	152	MFI	160, 164[1]
	1 (Villager)	6	3.0	181	MFI	151
	1 (Taurus)	6	3.0 MFF	182 MFF	MFI	145-155[1]
	2	6	3.0 EFF	182 EFF	MFI	145-150[1]
	U	6	3.0	182	MFI	140-150[1]
	S	6	3.0	182	MFI	200
	N	8	3.4 SHO	207 SHO	MFI	235
	4 (ex. Windstar)	6	3.8	232	MFI	145-150[1]
	4 (Windstar)	6	3.8	232	MFI	200
	6	8	4.6 W	281 W	MFI	190-210[1]
	W	8	4.6 R	281 R	MFI	190-210[1]
	X	8	4.6	281	MFI	215
	9	8	4.6 NG	281 NG	MFI	175
	V	8	4.6	281	MFI	260-305[1]
1996	H	4	1.3	81	MFI	63
	8	4	1.8	112	MFI	127
	J	4	1.9	113	MFI	88
	A	4	2.0	122	MFI	114, 118[1]
	3, Z	4	2.0	122	MFI	125
	L	6	2.5	153	MFI	170
	B	6	2.5	152	MFI	160, 164[1]
	W (Villager)	6	3.0	181	MFI	151
	1	6	3.0 MFF	182 MFF	MFI	130-145
	2	6	3.0 EFF	182 EFF	MFI	130-145
	U	6	3.0	182	MFI	145-150[1]
	S	6	3.0	182	MFI	200
	N	8	3.4 SHO	207 SHO	MFI	235
	4 (ex. Windstar)	6	3.8	232	MFI	145-150[1]
	4 (Windstar)	6	3.8	232	MFI	200
	6	8	4.6 W	281 W	MFI	190-210[1]
	W (ex. Villager)	8	4.6 R	281 R	MFI	190-210[1]
	X	8	4.6	281	MFI	215
	9	8	4.6 NG	281 NG	MFI	178
	V	8	4.6	281	MFI	260-305[1]
1995	H	4	1.3	81	MFI	63
	8	4	1.8	112	MFI	127
	J	4	1.9	113	MFI	88
	A	4	2.0	122	MFI	114, 118[1]
	3	4	2.0	122	MFI	125
	L	6	2.5	153	MFI	170
	B	6	2.5	152	MFI	160, 164[1]
	W (Villager)	6	3.0	181	MFI	151
	1	6	3.0 FF	182 FF	MFI	130-145
	U	6	3.0	182	MFI	140-147[1]
	Y	6	3.0 SHO	182 SHO	MFI	220
	P	6	3.2 SHO	195 SHO	MFI	220
	4	6	3.8	232	MFI	140-160[1]
	R	6	3.8 S	232 S	MFI	230
	W (ex. Villager)	8	4.6	281	MFI	190-210[1]

Copyright 2000 by Chek-Chart Publications

315

FORD, LINCOLN, MERCURY
1989-2000 Ford, Lincoln, Mercury, Merkur Including FWD Vans
Mercury Mountaineer & Lincoln Navigator—See Ford Trucks

ENGINE IDENTIFICATION Continued

YEAR	**3** ENGINE CODE	CYL.	**4** ENGINE IDENTIFICATION DISPL. liters	cu. in.	Fuel System	HP
1995 Cont'd.	V	8	4.6	281	MFI	260-290[1]
	T	8	5.0 HO	302 HO	MFI	215
	D	8	5.0 SHP	302 SHP	MFI	240
1994	H	4	1.3	79	MFI	63
	Z	4	1.6	98	MFI	100
	6	4	1.6 T	98 T	MFI	132
	8	4	1.8	110	MFI	127
	J	4	1.9	113	MFI	88
	A	4	2.0	121	MFI	114, 118[1]
	X	4	2.3	140	MFI	96
	B	6	2.5	152	MFI	160, 164[1]
	W (Villager)	6	3.0	181	MFI	151
	1	6	3.0 FF	182 FF	MFI	130-145
	U	6	3.0	182	MFI	130-140[1]
	Y	6	3.0 SHO	182 SHO	MFI	220
	P	6	3.2 SHO	195 SHO	MFI	220
	4	6	3.8	232	MFI	140-160[1]
	R	6	3.8 S	232 S	MFI	230
	W (ex. Villager)	8	4.6	281	MFI	190-210[1]
	V	8	4.6	281	MFI	280
	T	8	5.0 HO	302 HO	MFI	215
	D	8	5.0 SHP	302 SHP	MFI	235
1993	H	4	1.3	79	MFI	63
	Z	4	1.6	98	MFI	100
	6	4	1.6 T	98 T	MFI	132
	8	4	1.8	110	MFI	127
	J	4	1.9	113	MFI	88
	A	4	2.0	121	MFI	118
	M[2]	4	2.3	140	MFI	105
	X	4	2.3	140	MFI	96
	B	6	2.5	152	MFI	164
	W (Villager)	6	3.0	181	MFI	151
	U	6	3.0	182	MFI	130-145[1]
	Y	6	3.0 SHO	182 SHO	MFI	220
	P	6	3.2 SHO	195 SHO	MFI	220
	4	6	3.8	232	MFI	140-160[1]
	R	6	3.8 S	232 S	MFI	210
	W (ex. Villager)	8	4.6	281	MFI	190-210[1]
	V	8	4.6	281	MFI	280
	E	8	5.0 HO	302 HO	MFI	225
	T	8	5.0 HO	302 HO	MFI	200
	G	8	5.0 SHP	302 SHP	MFI	235
1992	H	4	1.3	79	MFI	63
	Z	4	1.6	98	MFI	100
	6	4	1.6 T	98 T	MFI	132
	8	4	1.8	110	MFI	127
	J	4	1.9	113	MFI	88
	C	4	2.2	133	MFI	110
	L	4	2.2 T	133 T	MFI	145
	M[2]	4	2.3	140	MFI	105
	X	4	2.3	140	MFI	96
	U	6	3.0	182	MFI	135, 145[1]
	Y	6	3.0 SHO	182 SHO	MFI	220
	4	6	3.8	232	MFI	140, 160[1]
	R	6	3.8 S	232 S	MFI	210
	W	8	4.6	281	MFI	190-210
	E	8	5.0 HO	302 HO	MFI	225
	T	8	5.0 HO	302 HO	MFI	200
1991	H	4	1.3	79	MFI	63
	Z	4	1.6	98	MFI	100
	6	4	1.6 T	98 T	MFI	132

YEAR	**3** ENGINE CODE	CYL.	**4** ENGINE IDENTIFICATION DISPL. liters	cu. in.	Fuel System	HP
1991 Cont'd.	8	4	1.8	110	MFI	127
	J	4	1.9	113	MFI	88
	C	4	2.2	133	MFI	110
	L	4	2.2 T	133 T	MFI	145
	M[2]	4	2.3	140	MFI	105
	X	4	2.3	140	MFI	98
	S	4	2.3	140	MFI	100
	N	4	2.5	153	MFI	90
	U	6	3.0	182	MFI	145
	Y	6	3.0 SHO	182 SHO	MFI	200
	4	6	3.8	232	MFI	140, 155[1]
	R	6	3.8 S	232 S	MFI	210
	W	8	4.6	281	MFI	185-200[1]
	E	8	5.0 HO	302 HO	MFI	225
	F	8	5.0	302	MFI	150-160[1]
	T	8	5.0 HO	302 HO	MFI	200
	G	8	5.8	351	2V	180
1990	H	4	1.3	79	MFI	63
	9	4	1.9	113	TBI	90
	J	4	1.9	113	MFI	110
	C	4	2.2	133	MFI	110
	L	4	2.2 T	133 T	MFI	145
	A[2]	4	2.3	140	MFI	88
	X	4	2.3	140	MFI	98
	S	4	2.3 HO	140 HO	MFI	100
	D	4	2.5	153	TBI	90
	U	6	3.0	182	MFI	140
	Y	6	3.0 SHO	182 SHO	MFI	220
	4	6	3.8	232	MFI	140
	R	6	3.8 S	232 S	MFI	210
	E	8	5.0 HO	302 HO	MFI	225
	F	8	5.0	302	MFI	150-160[1]
	G	8	5.8	351	2V	180
1989	K	4	1.3	79	2V	58
	H	4	1.3	79	MFI	63
	5	4	1.6	98	MFI	82
	9	4	1.9	113	TBI	90
	J	4	1.9	113	MFI	110
	C	4	2.2	133	MFI	110
	L	4	2.2 T	133 T	MFI	145
	A[2]	4	2.3	140	MFI	88
	W[2]	4	2.3 T	140 T	MFI	145, 175[1]
	X	4	2.3	140	MFI	98
	S	4	2.3 HO	140 HO	MFI	100
	D	4	2.5	153	TBI	90
	V	6	2.9	179	MFI	144
	U	6	3.0	182	MFI	140
	Y	6	3.0 SHO	182 SHO	MFI	220
	4	6	3.8	232	MFI	140
	C[3], R	6	3.8 S	232 S	MFI	210
	F	8	5.0	302	MFI	150
	E	8	5.0 HO	302 HO	MFI	225
	G	8	5.8	351	2V	180

1 Varies with model installation.   2 Overhead cam 2.3L only.
3 Early production only.   HO—High Output.
SHP—Super High Performance.   S—Supercharged.
SHO—Super High Output.   T—Turbo.   FF—Flexible Fuel.
MFF—Methanol Flexible Fuel.   EFF—Ethanol Flexible Fuel.
NG—Natural Gas.   TBI—Throttle Body Injection.
MFI—Multiport Fuel Injection.   2V—Two Venturi Carburetor.
W—Windsor Engine.   R—Romeo Engine.

UNDERHOOD SERVICE SPECIFICATIONS

FDTU1   FDTU1

CYLINDER NUMBERING SEQUENCE

4-CYL. FIRING ORDER: 1 3 4 2

— **Front of car** —

1989-93 1.3L Festiva 1989 1.6L Tracer 1994-97 1.3L Aspire	1991-94 1.6L Capri	1991-96 1.8L	2000 2.0L SPI	1991-96 1.9L 1997-99 2.0L SPI

CHEK-CHART

FORD, LINCOLN, MERCURY
1989-2000 Ford, Lincoln, Mercury, Merkur Including FWD Vans
Mercury Mountaineer & Lincoln Navigator—See Ford Trucks

UNDERHOOD SERVICE SPECIFICATIONS

FDTU2   FDTU2

CYLINDER NUMBERING SEQUENCE
4-CYL. FIRING ORDER: 1 3 4 2

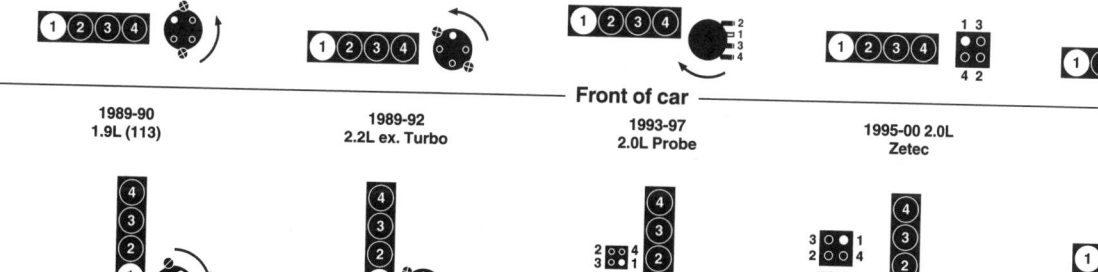

— Front of car —

| 1989-90 1.9L (113) | 1989-92 2.2L ex. Turbo | 1993-97 2.0L Probe | 1995-00 2.0L Zetec | 1989-92 2.2L Turbo |

 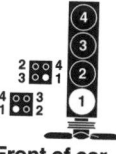 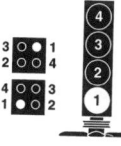 

— Front of car —

| 1989 2.3L (140) Turbo | 1989-90 2.3L (140) ex. Tempo/Topaz & Turbo | 1991-92 2.3L Mustang | 1993 2.3L Mustang | 2.3L (140) Tempo/Topaz 1989-91 2.5L (153) |

V6-CYL. FIRING ORDER: 2.5L Probe, 3.0L & 3.3L Villager, 1 2 3 4 5 6, Others 1 4 2 5 3 6

  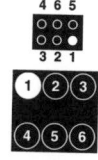 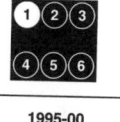  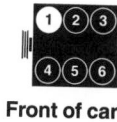

— Front of car —

| 1993-97 2.5L Probe | 1995-00 2.5L ex. Probe 1996-99 3.0L Duratec Code S | 1989-90 2.9L (179) | 2000 3.0L Duratec Code S FWD (coil-on-plug) | 2000 3.0L Lincoln LS (coil-on-plug) | 1989-95 3.0L ex. DOHC-SHO, Windstar & Villager | 1989-95 3.0L, 3.2L DOHC-SHO 1996-00 3.0L Taurus, Sable ex. Code S 1995-00 3.0L Windstar |

   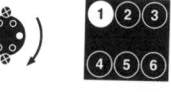

— Front of car —

| 1993-98 3.0L (181) Villager 1999-00 3.3L (200) | 1989-95 3.8L (232) FWD ex. Windstar | 1995 3.8L (232) Windstar | 1996-00 3.8L (232) Windstar | 1996-00 3.8L (232) RWD | 1989-95 3.8L (232) RWD ex. Supercharged | 1989-95 3.8L Supercharged |

8-CYL. FIRING ORDER 4.6L, 5.0L (302) HO; 5.8L (351) 1 3 7 2 6 5 4 8
3.9L 1 5 4 2 6 3 7 8

All Other 8-cyl.
1 5 4 2 6 3 7 8

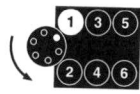  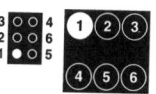 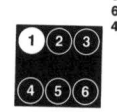 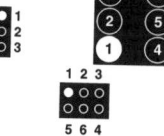  

— Front of car —

| 1996-99 3.4L SHO (Coil-on-plug) | 1995-97 4.6L Continental | 1998-00 4.6L Continental (Coil-on-plug) | 1991-93 4.6L 8-cyl. | 1994-98 4.6L ex. Continental, 1997-98 Mark VIII, & 1998 Crown Victoria, Grand Marquis, Town Car | 2000 3.9L 1997-98 4.6L Mark VIII, 1998-00 Crown Victoria, Grand Marquis, & Town Car 1999-00 Mustang (Coil-on-plug) | All Other 8-cyl. |

— TIMING MARK —

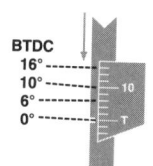 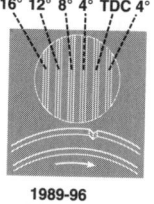 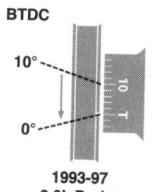  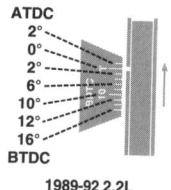 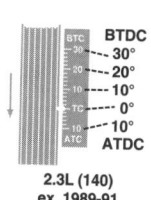

BTDC 16° 12° 8° 4° TDC 4°

BTDC
16° ----
10° ----
6° ----
0° ----

BTDC
10° ----
0° ----

No Timing Marks on Engine

ATDC
2° ----
0° ----
2° ----
6° ----
10° ----
12° ----
16° ----
BTDC

BTDC
30°
20°
10°
0°
10°
ATDC

| 1989-97 1.3L (79) 1989 1.6L (98) 1991-94 1.6L (98) 1991-96 1.8L (110) | 1989-96 1.9L (113) 1997-00 2.0L SPI | 1993-97 2.0L Probe | 2.0L Zetec | 1989-92 2.2L | 2.3L (140) ex. 1989-91 Tempo/Topaz |

FORD, LINCOLN, MERCURY

1989-2000 Ford, Lincoln, Mercury, Merkur Including FWD Vans
Mercury Mountaineer & Lincoln Navigator—See Ford Trucks

UNDERHOOD SERVICE SPECIFICATIONS

FDTU3

FDTU3

TIMING MARK

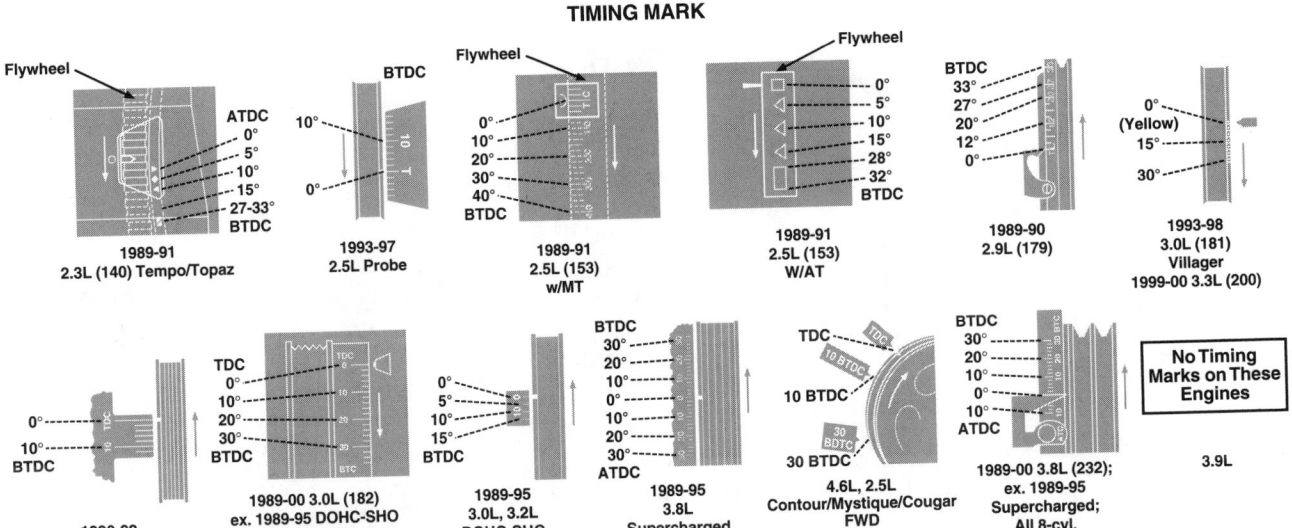

ELECTRICAL AND IGNITION SYSTEMS

BATTERY

Engine	Year	STANDARD BCI Group No.	STANDARD Crank. Perf.	OPTIONAL BCI Group No.	OPTIONAL Crank. Perf.
1.3L (81)	1989-93	35	390	—	—
	1994	35	355	—	—
	1995-97	35	460	—	—
1.6L (98)	1989	35	390	—	—
1.6L	1989	35	390	—	—
1.6L	1991-94	35	460	—	—
1.8L	1991-94	35	460	—	—
	1995	35	540	—	—
1.9L (113) TBI	1989-90	58	460	58	540
1.9L (113) FI	1989-90	58	540	—	—
1.9L	1991-95	35	460	—	—
2.0L Probe	1993-97	58R	580	—	—
	1996	35	505	58R	580
2.0L Contour, Mystique	1995-96	96R	590	40R	650
	1997	40R	650	—	—
	1998-00	40R	590	—	—
2.0L Escort, Tracer	1997-00	58	540	—	—
2.0L Focus	2000	96R	500	40R	540
2.2L	1989-92	56	505	—	—
2.3L (140) OHC ex. Turbo: MT	1989-93	58	460	58	540
AT	1989-93	58	540	—	—
2.3L (140) HSC w/MT	1989-93	58	460	58	540
2.3L (140) HSC w/AT	1989-93	58	540	—	—
2.3L	1994	58	540	—	—
2.3L	1989	58	540	65	850
2.5L (153) w/MT	1989	58	540	65	850
2.5L (153) w/AT	1989-91	65	650	65	850
2.5L Probe	1993-97	58R	580	—	—
	1996	35	505	58R	580
2.5L Contour, Mystique	1995-97	40R	650	—	—
	1998-00	40R	590	—	—
2.9L	1989	47	590	—	—
3.0L (182) ex. SHO: Taurus, Sable	1989-95	58	540	65	650
W/heated windshield	1989-93	65	850	—	—
3.0L LS	2000	66	650	66	750
3.0L Probe	1991-92	58R	540	—	—
3.0L Tempo	1992-94	58	460	—	—
3.0L Taurus, Sable DOHC	1996-00	58R	540	36R	650
	1996	36R	650	—	—
3.0L Windstar	1995-97	65	650	65	850
	1998-99	59	540	—	—

BATTERY Continued

Engine	Year	STANDARD BCI Group No.	STANDARD Crank. Perf.	OPTIONAL BCI Group No.	OPTIONAL Crank. Perf.
3.0L SHO, 3.2L SHO	1989-95	34	650	—	—
3.0L Villager	1993-98	35	460	24F	525
3.0L Windstar	1995	58	540	65	650
3.4L SHO	1996-99	36R	650	—	—
3.8L (232) RWD	1989-90	58	460	58	540
3.8L (232) FWD	1989-90	65	850	—	—
3.8L FWD	1991-95	65	650	65	850
3.8L RWD ex. Supercharged	1991	58	460	58	540
3.8L Thunderbird, Cougar ex. Supercharged	1992-96	58	540	65	650
	1997	59	540	65	650
3.8L Supercharged: MT	1991-95	58	540	65	650
AT	1991-95	65	650	—	—
Cold climate	1991-95	65	650	—	—
3.8L Mustang	1994-96	58	540	—	—
	1997-98	59	540	—	—
3.8L Windstar	1995-97	65	850	—	—
	1998-99	65	650	—	—
3.9L LS	2000	66	650	66	750
4.6L	1991	65	650	65	850
4.6L: Crown Victoria, Grand Marquis	1992-96	58	540	65	650
w/heated windshield	1992-96	65	850	—	—
	1997	59	540	65	650
	1998-00	65	650	65	750
Police or CNG	1997-00	65	850	—	—
Thunderbird, Cougar	1994-97	65	650	—	—
Continental, Town Car, Mark VIII	1992-98	65	650	65	850
	1999-00	65	650	65	750
Limousine	1995-98	65	850	—	—
	1999-00	65	750	—	—
Mustang	1996	58	540	—	—
	1997-00	59	540	—	—
5.0L (302): Mustang	1989-95	58	540	—	—
Crown Victoria, Grand Marquis Thunderbird	1989-91	58	540	65	650
	1991-93	65	650	—	—
Town Car	1989-90	65	650	65	850
All w/heated windshield	1989-90	65	850	—	—
5.8L (351)	1989-91	58	540	65	650

FORD, LINCOLN, MERCURY
1989-2000 Ford, Lincoln, Mercury, Merkur Including FWD Vans
Mercury Mountaineer & Lincoln Navigator—See Ford Trucks

UNDERHOOD SERVICE SPECIFICATIONS

FDTU4

FDTU4

GENERATOR

Ampere rating stamped on housing.

Application	Year	Rated Output	Test Output
All ex. Merkur	1989	40, 50, 60, 65, 70, 100	1
Merkur	1989	90	80-90 @ 2000
Aspire, Festiva	1990-95	50	35 @ 3000
	1996-97	—	54 @ 2000
Capri	1991-94	85	70 @ 3000
Contour, Mystique	1995-00	130	87 @ 2000
Probe	1990-92	70, 90	3
	1993-97	80, 90	3
Escort, Tracer	1990	60, 75, 80	2
	1991-96	65, 75	2
	1997-00	75	58 @ 2000
Tempo, Topaz	1990	65, 75	2
	1991	75, 95	2
	1992-94	90, 95	2
Taurus, Sable	1990-95	95, 100, 130	2
	1996-99	130	87 @ 2000
SHO	1990-93	90, 120	2
SHO	1994-95	120, 130	2
	1996-00	130	87 @ 2000
Thunderbird, Cougar	1990-93	65, 75, 95, 110	2
	1994-95	110, 130	2
	1996-97	130	87 @ 2000
Mustang	1990-93	75	2
	1994-95	130	2
	1996-00	130	87 @ 2000
Villager	1993-97	110	85 @ 2500
Continental	1990	100	2
	1991-95	130	2
	1996-00	—	87 @ 2000
Town Car, Crown Victoria, Grand Marquis	1990-91	65, 85, 100	2
	1992-95	95, 130	2
	1996-00	130	87 @ 2000
Mark VIII	1995-98	130	87 @ 2000

1 1989, if rated output cannot be obtained at 2000 rpm, eng. rpm may be increased to 2900 max. rpm.

2 Output at 2000 rpm must be near rated output or higher.

3 Output at 3000 rpm must be within 10% of rated output.

REGULATOR

Model	Year	Test Temp. (deg. F/C)	Voltage Setting
Festiva, Tracer, Probe	1989-90	68/20	14.4-15.0
Festiva, Capri, Probe ex. 3.0L; Escort, Tracer w/1.8L, Villager	1991-97	68/20	14.1-14.7
All others	1989-96	—	1
	1997-00	—	14.1-14.7[1]

1 Measure battery voltage and record figure. With engine operating off idle and all secondary electrical systems turned off, regulated voltage should be no greater than 3.0 volts above recorded figure. Turn on headlights and set heater blower to high. Regulated voltage off idle should be no less than 0.5 volts above recorded figure.

STARTER

Application	Year	Cranking Voltage (min. volts)	Ampere Draw @ Cranking Speed
Aspire, Festiva	1989-97	8.0	150-250
Capri	1991-95	8.0	—
Tracer	1989	8.0	—
Scorpio	1989	10.5	200-300
All Others	1989-91	9.6	150-250
All Others	1992-00	9.6	130-220

SPARK PLUGS

Engine	Year	Gap (inches)	Gap (mm)	Torque (ft-lb)
1.3L (81)	1989-97	.039-.043	1.0-1.1	11-17
1.6L (98)	1989-94	.039-.043	1.0-1.1	11-17
1.8L	1991-95	.039-.043	1.0-1.1	11-17
1.9L (113)	1989-90	.042-.046	1.07-1.17	10-15
1.9L	1991-96	.052-.056	1.32-1.42	10-20
2.0L Probe	1993-97	.039-.043	1.0-1.1	11-17
2.0L Contour, Mystique	1995-00	.048-.052	1.22-1.32	9-13
2.0L Escort, Tracer	1997-00	.052-.056	1.32-1.42	10-20
2.2L	1989-92	.039-.043	1.0-1.1	11-17
2.3L (140)	1989	.042-.046	1.07-1.17	10-15
2.3L HSC	1990-94	.052-.056	1.32-1.42	7-15
2.3L OHC	1990-93	.042-.046	1.07-1.17	5-11
2.5L	1989-90	.042-.046	1.07-1.17	5-11
2.5L Probe	1993-97	.039-.043	1.0-1.1	11-17
2.5L Contour, Mystique	1995-00	.052-.056	1.32-1.42	7-15
2.9L	1989	.042-.046	1.07-1.17	18-28
3.0L (182) ex. Villager	1989-00	.042-.046	1.07-1.17	7-15
DOHC	1996-00	.052-.056	1.32-1.42	7-14
3.0L Villager	1993-00	.031-.035	.8-.9	14-22
3.2L, 3.4L SHO	1993-99	.042-.046	1.07-1.17	7-15
3.8L (232)	1989-00	.052-.056	1.32-1.42	5-11
4.6L	1991-00	.052-.056	1.32-1.42	10-15
5.0L (302) HO	1989-95	.052-.056	1.32-1.42	10-15
Others	1989-91	.042-.046	1.07-1.17	10-15
5.8L (351)	1989-91	.042-.046	1.07-1.17	10-15

IGNITION COIL
FOR TESTING AND ADJUSTMENT DIAGRAMS, SEE APPENDIX A.

Application	Year	Windings	Resistance (ohms)
Dura-Spark ign.	1989-90	Primary	0.8-1.6
		Secondary	7700-10,500
1.3L	1994-97	Primary	0.5-0.7
		Secondary	20,000-31,000
1.3L, 1.6L, 1.8L	1989-93	Primary	0.8-1.6
		Secondary	6000-30,000
1.6L, 1.8L	1994-95	Primary	0.8-1.6
		Secondary	6000-30,000
2.0L w/AT	1993	Primary	.58-1.10
		Secondary	11,500-18,500
2.2L	1989-90	Primary	1.04-1.27
		Secondary	7100-9700
Turbo		Primary	.72-.88
		Secondary	10,300-13,900
2.2L	1991-92	Primary	0.8-1.6
		Secondary	6000-30,000
2.5L Probe	1993-97	Primary	.58-.86
		Secondary	11,500-18,500
2.9L	1989	Primary	0.3-1.0
		Secondary	8000-11,000
3.0L Villager	1993-00	Primary	1.4-1.6
		Secondary	9800-10,000
All w/coil pack	1994-00	Primary	0.50
		Secondary	12,000-14,500
All w/coil on plug	1996-00	Primary	0.3-0.8
		Secondary	4000-10,000

DISTRIBUTOR PICKUP
FOR TESTING AND ADJUSTMENT DIAGRAMS, SEE APPENDIX B.

Application	Resistance (ohms)	Air Gap (in./mm)
1989-90 1.6L, 1.9L w/TFI-1 ign.	650-1300	.017 min./.43 min.
1989-92 All others w/Dura-Spark ign.	400-1000[1]	.017 min./.43 min.
All w/EEC IV	—	—
1989-92 2.2L	900-1200	—
Turbo	210-260	—

1 With 250 watt heat lamp held 1 to 2 inches from coil for 5 to 10 minutes.

IGNITION RESISTOR
See UNDERHOOD SERVICE INSTRUCTIONS at the beginning of this section for test/adjustment diagrams.

Engine	Year	Type	Resistance (ohms)	Temperature (deg. F/C)
All w/Dura-Spark II, III	1989-91	Wire	0.8-1.6	—

FORD, LINCOLN, MERCURY

1989-2000 Ford, Lincoln, Mercury, Merkur Including FWD Vans
Mercury Mountaineer & Lincoln Navigator—See Ford Trucks

UNDERHOOD SERVICE SPECIFICATIONS

BASE TIMING

FOR TESTING AND ADJUSTMENT DIAGRAMS, SEE APPENDIX C.

Set timing at Before Top Dead Center and at slow idle unless otherwise specified.

Disconnect and plug distributor vacuum hose.

1989-95 with EEC IV & distributor: Disconnect single wire connector at distributor or remove shorting bar from double wire spout connector.

1989 1.3L 2V: Disconnect & plug distributor vacuum hose. At high altitude, disconnect barometric pressure sensor.

1989-93 1.3L FI: Ground one-pin self-test connector.

1989 1.6L: Disconnect distributor vacuum hose and black connector by distributor.

1989-94 1.6L, 2.2L ex. Turbo: Disconnect and plug distributor vacuum hoses.

1994-97 1.3L, 1989-97 1.8L, 2.2L Turbo, 2.5L Probe, 1993-97 2.0L Probe, ground STI cavity in Datalink connector.

1991-95: All w/o distributor, install EDIS checker and press SAW button. Timing should be at Set Value. When button is released, timing should advance to Check Value.

1996-00: Connect a Scan tool and access check timing function. Some models, timing is indexed from the crankshaft sensor and will not reflect the listed value when checking timing conventionally.

1993-98 3.0L Villager: Disconnect throttle position sensor.

Reset timing only if more than ±2 degrees from specification listed.

Timing must be set to specifications shown on emission decal if different from setting listed.

Engine	Year	Man. Trans. (degrees) @ RPM	Auto. Trans. (degrees) @ RPM
1.3L (81) 2V	1989	0±1	2±1
1.3L FI	1989-97	10±1	10±1
1.6L (98)	1989	2±2	2±2
1.6L	1991-94	2±1	2±1
Turbo	1991-94	12±1	12±1
1.8L	1991-96	10±1	10±1
1.9L (113) TBI & FI	1989-90	10	10
1.9L	1991-95	10±2[1]	10±2[1]
Check	1991-95	15 min.	15 min.
2.0L Probe	1993	10±1	12±1
	1994	12±1	12±1
	1995-97	10±1	10±1
2.0L Contour, Mystique	1995-00	10±2[1]	10±2[1]
Check	1995	15 min.	15 min.
2.0L Escort, Tracer	1997-00	10±2[1]	10±2[1]
2.2L	1989-92	6±1	6±1
Turbo	1989-92	9±1	—
2.3L (140) OHC FI	1989-90	10	10
2.3L OHC	1991-93	10[1]	10[1]
Check	1991-93	16 min.	16 min.
2.3L HSC	1989-94	15	15
2.5L (153)	1989-91	10	10
2.5L Probe	1993-97	10±1	10±1
Check	1993-97	6-18	6-18
2.5L Contour, Mystique	1995-00	—	10±2[1]
Check	1995	—	15 min.
2.9L	1989	10	10
3.0L (182) ex. Villager	1989-95	10	10
	1996-00	10±2[1]	10±2[1]
3.0L Villager	1993-00	—	15±2
3.0L SHO 3.2L SHO	1989-95	10[1]	10[1]
3.0L Flexfuel	1993-97	—	10±2[1]
Check	1993-95	—	15 min.
3.0L Windstar	1995-97	—	10±2[1]
Check	1995-96	—	15 min.
3.8L (232) FI	1989-95	10	10
California	1995	—	10±2[1]
Check	1995	—	15 min.
Supercharged	1989-95	10[1]	10[1]
Check	1993-95	15 min.	15 min.
3.8L	1996-00	10±2[1]	10±2[1]
4.6L	1991-95	—	10[1]
Check	1993-95	—	15 min.
4.6L	1996-00	10±2[1]	10±2[1]
5.0L (302)	1989-95	10	10
5.8L (351)	1989-91	—	14 @ 600 N

1 Timing not adjustable.

DISTRIBUTOR TIMING ADVANCE

Engine degrees at engine rpm, no load, in addition to basic timing setting.

Mechanical advance distributors only.

Engine	Transmission	Year	Distributor Number	Degrees @ 2500 RPM	
				Total	Centrifugal
1.3L (81) 2V	MT	1989	—	30.9-39.9[1]	6.9-10.9
1.3L FI	AT	1989	—	24-32[1]	6-10
1.6L (98)	MT & AT	1989	E8GY-A	43.3-53.3[1]	12.3-16.3
1.6L	MT & AT	1991-94	—	12-16	38-46
Turbo	MT & AT	1991-94	—	7-11	20-28[2]
2.2L ex. Turbo	MT & AT	1989-90	—	28.4-36.4[2]	10.4-14.4

1 Both vacuum chambers activated.
2 Vacuum retard, 4-8.

FUEL SYSTEM

FUEL SYSTEM PRESSURE

FOR TESTING AND ADJUSTMENT DIAGRAMS, SEE APPENDIX D.

Carbureted, pinch off fuel return line, if equipped.

All w/TBI, fuel pressure measured at inlet fitting on unit.

All w/FI, fuel pressure measured at fitting on fuel rail.

Engine	Year	Pressure	
		PSI	RPM
Carbureted:			
1.3L (81)	1989	3-6	idle
Fuel Injected: TBI			
1.9L (113)	1989-90	13-17	idle
2.5L (153)	1989-90	13-17	idle
	1989-90	35-55	idle

Engine	Year	Pressure		
		PSI[1]	PSI[2]	Fuel Pump
MFI:				
1.3L	1989-93	35-40	25-31	69-85
	1994-97	38-46	30-38	50 min.
1.6L	1991-94	37-42	37-41	64-85
1.8L	1991-95	38-46	30-37	64-85
1.9L, 2.3L OHC, 2.9L	1989-93	35-45	30-45	—
	1994-96	35-40	30-45	—
2.0L MT	1993	35-40	30-45	64-92
2.0L AT	1993	37-46	30-38	64-92
2.0L	1994-97	35-40	30-45	—
2.0L: Escort, Tracer	1998-00	—	55-85	—
Contour, Mystique	1998-00	—	30-45	—
2.2L	1989-92	34-40	37-41	64-85
2.3L HSC	1989-94	50-60	45-60	—
2.5L	1989-91	50-60	45-60	—
2.5L Probe	1993-95	37-46	30-38	64-92
2.5L Contour, Mystique	1995-97	35-40	30-45	—
	1998-00	—	45-60	—
3.0L Villager	1993-94	40-43	36-38	58-62
	1995-00	43	34	58-62
3.0L ex. SHO, 3.8L ex. S/C	1989-93	35-45	30-45	—
	1994-97	35-40	30-45	—
	1998-00	—	30-45	—
3.0L SHO, 3.2L SHO	1989-93	30-40	28-33	—
3.4L SHO	1996-97	35-40	30-45	—
	1998-00	—	30-45	—
3.8L S/C	1989-93	35-40	30-40	—
	1994-97	35-45	28-54	—
4.6L	1991-93	35-40	30-45	—
	1994-95	35-45	28-54	—
	1996-97	35-40	30-45	—
	1998-00	—	30-45	—
Continental	1998-00	—	45-60	—
5.0L	1989-93	35-45	30-45	—
	1994-95	35-40	30-45	—

1 Ignition on, fuel pump running.
2 Idle.

FORD, LINCOLN, MERCURY
1989-2000 Ford, Lincoln, Mercury, Merkur Including FWD Vans
Mercury Mountaineer & Lincoln Navigator—See Ford Trucks

UNDERHOOD SERVICE SPECIFICATIONS

FDTU6

FDTU6

FUEL SYSTEM PRESSURE Continued

Engine	Year	Pressure PSI[1]	Pressure PSI[2]	Fuel Pump
1.6L	1989	28-32	36-42	—

1 Vacuum hose connected to fuel pressure regulator.
2 Vacuum hose disconnected from fuel pressure regulator.

IDLE SPEED W/O COMPUTER CONTROL

1989-91:
5.8L (351) engine, disconnect the VOTM vacuum hose (A/C only). Set idle speed to spec. Apply manifold vacuum to the VOTM and set speed-up speed to spec. To set fast idle, disconnect and plug the EGR vacuum hose.

1989:
1.3L (81) 2V, set idle to specified value with cooling fan off. To set fast idle, disconnect fast idle pull-off solenoid vacuum hose and plug. Set fast idle cam on specified step and adjust to specified value. Electrically disconnect electric load vacuum solenoid and race engine momentarily. Set electric load speed-up to specified value. Electrically disconnect A/C speed-up solenoid, race engine momentarily, and set A/C speed-up to specified value.

1.6L (98), set idle to specified value with cooling fan off.

Engine	Year	SLOW Man. Trans.	SLOW Auto. Trans.	FAST Man. Trans.	FAST Auto. Trans.	Step of Cam
1.3L (81) 2V	1989	700-750	—	1650-2150	—	Second
1.6L (98)	1989	800-900	800-900 N	—	—	—
5.8L (351) Police	1989-91	—	600 D	—	1650 P	Kickdown
A/C speed-up	1989-91	—	700 D	—		

IDLE SPEED W/COMPUTER CONTROL
FOR TESTING AND ADJUSTMENT DIAGRAMS, SEE APPENDIX E.
Note: w/FI, if idle speed is higher than the specified checking speed, perform a system check before attempting to adjust the idle speed.

1989-97 1.3L: Jumper test connector (black, 1-pin) to ground.

1989-90 1.9L (113) MFI: With engine at operating temperature, disconnect and plug both EGR solenoid vacuum lines. Disconnect ISC electrical lead. Run engine at 2000 rpm for 60 seconds and return to idle. Adjust speed to specified setting speed within two minutes with engine cooling fan on. Repeat if two minutes is exceeded.

1991-94 1.6L Capri: Ground the self-test connector (white, 1-pin).

1991-92 1.8L: Jumper terminal 10 of diagnostic connector to ground. Canada models, apply parking brake to turn off headlights.

1993-97 1.8L, 2.0L Probe, 2.5L: Ground the STI terminal in the Datalink connector.

1989-90 1.9L (113) TBI, 2.3L (140) HSC TBI, 2.5L (153): Idle engine for two minutes (AT in drive) and check idle speed. To adjust, set system in self test mode (see Computer Diagnostic Codes), turn key to run position. When ISC plunger fully retracts, turn key off and disconnect diagnostic mode. Electrically disconnect ISC and gain access to throttle stop screw. Start engine and set idle to specified setting speed.

1991 1.9L: Disconnect ISC air bypass solenoid. Run engine at 2000 rpm for one minute and check/set idle to specified value.

1989-92 2.2L: Ground STI (black, 1-pin) and set idle to specified setting speed.

1989-91 2.3L HSC: Disconnect SPOUT connector. Remove PCV valve and install special tool with .020 orifice. Disconnect ISC and run engine at 2500 rpm for 30 seconds. Set idle to specified value.

1989-91 2.3L (140) OHC & Turbo, 2.9L: With engine at operating temperature, disconnect ISC electrical connector. Disconnect cooling fan electrical connector. Run engine at 2000 rpm for two minutes (1989-90) or 1500 rpm for 30 seconds (1991). Return to idle and adjust speed to specified setting speed. Reconnect leads and verify that checking speed is at specified value.

1993-94 2.5L w/MT, 3.0L Villager: Disconnect idle air control valve.

1991 2.5L
1991-94 3.0L, 3.8L, 4.6L
1992-95 1.9L, 2.3L, 5.0L ex. Mustang & Mark VII:
Connect a Scan tool and follow the tool manufacturer's instructions on Ford Idle Speed Setting. A constant pulse from the tool means that the idle speed is within limits. A pulse of 8 times per second indicates that the throttle position sensor is out of range due to over adjustment. A pulse of 4 times per second indicates that the base idle is too fast. A pulse of 1 per second indicates that the base idle speed is too slow.

If the idle is slow, inspect for a plate orifice plug. Remove it and turn the idle screw. Make adjustment until a steady pulse is indicated.

IDLE SPEED W/COMPUTER CONTROL Continued
If the idle is too fast: V6, V8 RWD, turn the idle speed screw. 4-cyl. RWD & all FWD, inspect the throttle plate orifice. If there is a plug in it, diagnosis of the system is needed. If there is no plug, block the orifice with tape, start the engine and check the idle speed. If it is still too fast, diagnosis of the system is needed. Once repairs have been made to the system, the idle speed can be adjusted. All models, turn the idle speed screw until the Scan tool pulse is constant.

1989-90 3.0L (182) ex. SHO: Disconnect timing SPOUT and air bypass valve connectors. Remove PCV valve and install PCV tool (.20" orifice). Run engine at 2000 rpm for 30 seconds (1989-90 only). Set idle to specified setting value. Reconnect connectors and verify checking value is correct.

1993-98 3.0L Villager: Disconnect IAC connector and set idle to specified value.

3.0L SHO: Remove PCV hose from intake manifold. Remove canister purge hose from intake manifold. Connect a vaccum hose between the two manifold open parts. Disconnect ISC electrical connector. Adjust idle to specified setting value.

1989-90 3.8L (232), 5.0L (302): With engine off, back out throttle plate stop screw enough to clear throttle lever pad. Insert a .070" feeder gauge between the screw and pad. Turn screw until contact is made, then turn in an additional: 5.0L ex. HO, 1⅞ turns; 3.8L & 5.0L HO, 1½ turns.

1991-95 5.0L Mustang, Mark VII: Insert a .025 feeler gauge between stop screw and throttle level. Set idle to specified value and remove feeler.

1994-95 Mustang 3.8L, Thunderbird & Cougar 4.6L
1995 All 4.6L
1996-98 All ex. 1.3L, 1.8L, 2.5L Probe, 3.0L Villager: If idle is not at specified value, remove cables from throttle body and inspect throttle return screw. If the throttle screw does not contact the throttle linkage lever arm, remove the clean air tube and verify that throttle plate is not obstructed and rotates fully closed. If the screw still does not make contact, place a .002-inch feeler gauge between the screw and lever arm. Turn the screw until it just touches the feeler gauge. Remove the gauge and adjust the screw clockwise ½ turn. Start the engine. If idle is still not at specified checking speed, further diagnosis of the system is needed.

1999-00: Check idle speed against specified value. If idle is not within the range listed, further diagnosis of the system is needed.

ALL FUEL INJECTED
Checking speed is the computer controlled idle speed value.

Engine	Year	Transmission	Setting Speed	Checking Speed
1.3L	1989	AT	800-900 N	—
1.3L	1990-92	MT	680-720	800-900
		AT	830-870 N	800-900 N
1.3L	1993	MT	680-720	—
		AT	830-870 N	—
1.3L	1994-97	MT	650-750	—
		AT	700-800 N	—
1.6L	1991-94	MT	800-900	—
		AT	800-900 N	—
1.8L	1991-95	MT	700-800	—
		AT	700-800 N	—
1.9L (113) TBI	1989-90	MT	550-650	760-840
		AT	550-650 N	760-840 D
1.9L (113) MFI	1989-90	MT	975	900-1100
1.9L	1991	MT	650	730-930
		AT	650 N	730-930 N
	1992	MT	1	800-900
		AT	1	800-900 N
	1993-95	MT	1	800-900
		AT	1	780-950 N
	1996	MT	—	700-750
		AT	—	755-805 N
2.0L	1993-94	MT	650-750	690-910
		AT	650-750 N	690-740 N
2.0L Probe	1995	MT	650-750	720-910
		AT	650-750 N	740-830 N
	1996-97	MT	650-750	720-770
		AT	650-750 N	855-905 N
2.0L Contour, Mystique, Cougar	1995	MT	—	780-980
		AT	—	700-900 N
	1996-98	MT	—	855-905
		AT	—	775-825 N
	1999-00	MT	—	790-900
		AT	—	790-900 N
2.0L Escort, Tracer	1997-98	MT	—	700-750
		AT	—	755-805 N
	1999-00	MT	—	750-820
		AT	—	730-790 N

FORD, LINCOLN, MERCURY
1989-2000 Ford, Lincoln, Mercury, Merkur Including FWD Vans
Mercury Mountaineer & Lincoln Navigator—See Ford Trucks

UNDERHOOD SERVICE SPECIFICATIONS

IDLE SPEED W/COMPUTER CONTROL Continued
ALL FUEL INJECTED Continued

Engine	Year	Transmission	Setting Speed	Checking Speed
2.2L	1989-92	MT	750	725-775
		AT	750 N	725-775 N
2.3L (140) HSC	1989-90	MT	1575	810-890
		AT	1050 D	690-750 D
2.3L HSC	1991	MT	1525-1575	810-890
		AT	925-975 D	680-760 D
2.3L HSC	1992-94	MT	1	840-950
		AT	1	840-950 N
2.3L OHC	1989-90	MT	600	770-830
		AT	650 N	770-830 D
2.3L OHC	1991	MT	575-625	780
		AT	625-675 N	720 D
	1992-93	MT	1	750-820
		AT	1	750-820 N
2.5L (153)	1989-90	MT	675-725	775-825
		AT	625-675 D	675-725 D
2.5L	1991	AT	1	750 D
2.5L Probe	1993	MT	600-700	—
		AT	600-700 N	—
	1994	MT	550-750	—
		AT	550-750 N	—
	1995-97	MT	600-700	—
		AT	600-700 N	—
2.5L Contour, Mystique, Cougar	1995	MT	—	790-820
		AT	—	920-965 N
	1996-98	MT	—	700-750
		AT	—	720-770 N
	1999-00	MT	—	700-760
		AT	—	700-760 N
2.9L	1989	AT	675-725 N	800-900 N
3.0L	1989-90	AT	760 D	—
SHO	1989-90	MT	770-830	—
3.0L	1991	MT	1	800
3.0L ex. Probe, Windstar	1992-95	MT	1	840-880
3-speed	1992-95	AT	1	800-870 N
4-speed	1992-95	AT	1	870-920 N
3.0L Probe	1992	MT	1	750-850
		AT	1	670-740 N
3.0L SHO	1991-95	MT	770-830	750-900
3.0L Villager	1993-98	AT	650-750 N	700-800 N
3.0L Windstar	1995-98	AT	—	675-725 N
	1999-00	AT	—	680-800 N
3.0L Taurus, Sable	1996-98	AT	—	875-925 N
3.0L Taurus, Sable	1999-00	AT	—	760-900 N
Flexfuel	1999-00	AT	—	840-900 N
3.2L SHO	1993-94	AT	—	720-780 N
	1995	AT	—	740-840 N
3.4L SHO	1996-99	AT	—	875-925 N
3.8L RWD	1989-90	AT	—	550-650 D
Supercharged	1989-90	MT	—	700-800
	1989-90	AT	—	550-650 D
3.8L FWD	1989-90	AT	—	650-750 D
Continental	1989-90	AT	—	620-720 D
3.8L Continental	1991	AT	1	625 D
Taurus, Sable	1991	AT	1	640 D
Police	1991	AT	1	700 D
Thunderbird, Cougar ex. S/C	1991	AT	1	600 D
3.8L: Taurus, Sable	1992-95	AT	1	690-770 N
Police	1992-94	AT	1	750-850 N
Thunderbird, Cougar	1992-95	AT	1	740-840 N
Supercharged	1992-95	MT	1	760-860
		AT	1	770-830 N
Mustang	1994-95	MT	—	695-745
		AT	—	675-725 N
Continental	1992-94	AT	1	700-750 N
3.8L Windstar	1995-98	AT	—	675-725 N
	1999-00	AT	—	700-730 N
Thunderbird, Cougar	1996-97	AT	—	680-730 N
Mustang	1996-98	MT	—	695-745 N
		AT	—	675-725 N
	1999-00	MT	—	700-780
		AT	—	700-730 N

IDLE SPEED W/COMPUTER CONTROL Continued
ALL FUEL INJECTED Continued

Engine	Year	Transmission	Setting Speed	Checking Speed
4.6L	1991	AT	1	560 D
4.6L SOHC	1992-94	AT	1	750-810 N
Thunderbird, Cougar	1994	AT	—	745-795 N
Town Car	1992-94	AT	1	690-750 N
4.6L Mark VIII	1993-95	AT	1	685-790 N
4.6L: Town Car	1995	AT	—	775-825 N
Crown Victoria, Grand Marquis	1995	AT	—	775-825 N
Continental	1995	AT	—	775-825 N
Thunderbird, Cougar	1995	AT	—	745-795 N
4.6L Mustang	1996-98	MT	—	630-680
		AT	—	630-680 N
Thunderbird, Cougar	1996-97	AT	—	745-795 N
Mark VIII	1996-98	AT	—	875-925 N
Others	1996-98	AT	—	775-825 N
CNG	1996-98	AT	—	775-825 N
4.6L SOHC Mustang	1999-00	MT	—	660-700
		AT	—	660-700 N
Crown Victoria, Grand Marquis, Town Car	1999-00	AT	—	790-815 N
CNG	1999-00	AT	—	790-815 N
4.6L DOHC Mustang	1999-00	MT	—	630-750
		AT	—	630-750 N
Continental	1999-00	AT	—	695-760N
5.0L: Mustang	1989-90	MT	—	625-775
	1989-90	AT	—	575-725 D
Mark VII	1989-90	AT	—	550-675 D
All others	1989-90	AT	—	525-650 D
5.0L: Mustang	1991-94	MT	625-725	
		AT	625-725 N	
	1995	MT	730-750	650-750
	1995	AT	630-650	650-750 N
Mark VII	1991-92	AT	625-725 N	
T-Bird, Cougar	1991	AT	1	610 D
	1992-93	AT	700-750 N	
Others	1991	AT	1	525-650 D

1 Idle speed is only adjustable with a Scan tool, see procedure.

ENGINE MECHANICAL

TIGHTENING TORQUES
FOR CYLINDER HEAD TORQUE SEQUENCES AND DIAGRAMS, SEE APPENDIX F.
Some fasteners are tightened in more than one step.
Some values are specified in inches.

		TORQUE FOOT-POUNDS/NEWTON METERS				
Engine	Year	Cylinder Head	Intake Manifold	Exhaust Manifold	Crankshaft Pulley	Water Pump
1.3L (81) Festiva, Aspire 1.6L (98) Tracer	1989-97	35-40/ 50-60, 56-60/ 75/81	14-20/ 19-26	12-17/ 16-23	109-152"/ 12-17	14-19/ 19-26
1.6L Capri	1991-94	14-25/ 20-34, 56-60/ 75/81	14-19/ 19-25	28-34/ 38-46	109-152"/ 12-17	14-19/ 19-25
1.8L	1991-95	56-60/ 76-81	14-19/ 19-25	28-34/ 38-46	69-152"/ 12-17	14-19/ 19-25
1.9L (113)	1989	44/60[1], +90°, +90°	12-15/ 16-20	15-20/ 21-27	74-90/ 100-121	5-8/ 7-10
1.9L	1990-95	44/60[1], +90°, +90°	12-15/ 16-20	15-20/ 21-27	81-96/ 110-130	5-8/ 7-10
2.0L Contour, Mystique	1995-00	18/25, 33/45, +105°	13/18	12/16	88/115	13/18

CHEK-CHART

FORD, LINCOLN, MERCURY
1989-2000 Ford, Lincoln, Mercury, Merkur Including FWD Vans
Mercury Mountaineer & Lincoln Navigator—See Ford Trucks

UNDERHOOD SERVICE SPECIFICATIONS
FDTU8   FDTU8

TIGHTENING TORQUES Continued

Engine	Year	Cylinder Head	Intake Manifold	Exhaust Manifold	Crankshaft Pulley	Water Pump
2.0L Probe	1993-97	13-16/18-22, +90°, +90°	14-19/19-25	14-21/20-28², 12-17/16-23³	116-123/157-167	14-19/19-25
2.0L Escort, Tracer	1997-00	11	15-22/20-30	15-20/21-27	81-96/110-130	15-22/20-30
2.2L	1989-92	57-64/80-86	14-22/19-30	16-21/22-28	9-13/12-17	14-19/19-25
2.3L (140) OHC: Ex. Turbo	1989-93	50-60/68-81, 80-90/108-122	20-29/26-38	15-17/20-23, 20-30/27-41	103-133/140-180	14-21/19-28
Turbo	1989	50-60/68-81, 80-90/108-122	14-21/19-28	16-23/22-31	100-120/136-162	14-21/19-28
2.3L (140) HSC, 2.5L (153) HSC	1989-94	51-59/70-80, 70-76/95-103	15-23/20-30	5-7/7-10, 20-30/27-41	140-170/190-230	15-23/20-30
2.5L Contour, Mystique, Cougar	1995-99	31/40 +90°¹²	8/10 upper 8 lower	15/20	37/50	89"/10 +90°
2.5L Probe	1993-97	17-19/23-26, +90°, +90°	14-18/19-25	14-18/19-25	116-122/157-167	14-18/19-25
2.9L Scorpio	1989	22/30, 51-55/70-75, +90°	3-6/4-8, 6-11/8-15, 11-15/15-21, 15-18/21-25⁴	20-30/27-41	85-96/115-130	7-9/9-12
3.0L Villager	1993-97	22/29⁵, 43/59	13-16/18-22	13-16/18-22	90-98/123-132	12-15/16-21
3.0L (182) ex. O.H.C.	1989-95	37/50, 68/92⁶	11/15, 18/25, 24/33	19/25	107/145	6-8/8-12
	1996-00	33-41/45-55⁶, 62-73/85-99	15-22/20-30, 19-24/26-32	15-18/20-25	30-40/40-55	76-106"/8-12
		20-24/27-33 +90° +90°	15-22/20-30, upper 18/25, 22-29, lower	15-18/20-25	93-121/125-165	76-106"/8-12, small 15/22, 20-30, large
3.0L SHO, 3.2L SHO	1989-95	37-50/49-69, 62-68/83-93	11-17/15-23	26-38/35-52	113-126/152-172	5-16/6-9
3.0L DOHC	1996-00	27-32/37-43, +90°	71-106"/8-12	13-16/18-22	77-87/95-105	16-18/22-25
3.4L SHO	1996-99	20-23/27-32, +90°	14-20/18-28	30-44/40-60	13	14-20/18-28
3.8L (232)	1989-94	37/50, 45/60, 51/70, 59/80⁷	7.5/10, 15/20, 24/32	15-22/20-30	93-121/125-165	15-22/20-30
	1995-00	15/20, 29/40, 37/50¹⁴	8/11, 15/20, 24/32	15-22/20-30	103-132/140-180	15-22/20-30

TIGHTENING TORQUES Continued

Engine	Year	Cylinder Head	Intake Manifold	Exhaust Manifold	Crankshaft Pulley	Water Pump
4.6L	1991-92	15-22/20-30, +85-95°, +85-95°	15-22/20-30	15-22/20-30	114-121/155-165	15-22/20-30
4.6L	1993-00	27-32/37-43, +85-95°, +85-95°	15-22/20-30⁸	15-22/20-30	114-121/155-165	15-22/20-30
5.0L (302)	1989-93	55-65/76-88, 65-72/88-98¹⁰	23-25/31-34⁹	18-24/24-32	70-90/95-122	12-18/16-24
5.0L (302)	1994-95	25-35/34-47, 45-55/61-75, +85-95°	8/11, 16/22, 23-25/31-34	26-32/32-43	35-50/42-68	15-21/20-28
5.8L (351)	1989-92	85/115, 95/129, 105-112/142-151	23-25/31-34⁹	18-24/24-32	70-90/95-122	12-18/16-24

1 Back off bolts and retorque to 44/60.
2 Nuts.
3 Studs.
4 Warm up engine and retorque to final specification.
5 Loosen all bolts. Then tighten to 22/29, and then 40-47/54-64.
6 First, tighten all bolts to 60/80, then back off 1 turn.
7 Back off bolts 2-3 turns and repeat tightening procedures.
8 DOHC, 7-13/10-18 +85-95°.
9 Retorque hot.
10 With flanged bolts: 25-35/34-47, 45-55/61-75, +90°.
11 Tighten all bolts to 30-44/40-60. Back off 1 turn. Retorque to 30-44/40-60, +90°, +90°.
12 Loosen one turn. Retorque to 31/40, +90°, +90°.
13 Tighten to 72-99/105-135. Back off one turn. Tighten to 35-39/49-53, +90°.
14 One at a time: Back bolts off 2-3 turns. Tighten long bolts to 29-37/40-50, +180°. Tighten short bolts to 11-18/15-25, +180°.

COMPRESSION PRESSURE
At cranking speed, engine temperature normalized, throttle open.

Engine	Year	PSI	Maximum Variation PSI
All	1989-00	Lowest cylinder pressure must be more than 75% of highest cylinder pressure.	

BELT TENSION
A belt in operation for 10 minutes is considered a used belt.
Deflection method: Table lists deflection at midpoint of belt segment.
Strand Tension method: Use a strand tension gauge. Measurements are in pounds.
With automatic tensioner: Inspect indicator marks and replace belt if index mark is not between reference marks.

Application	Year	Generator	Power Steering	Air cond.	Thermactor
Deflection method					
2.2L (inches)	1989-92	¼-5/16	¼-5/16	¼-5/16	—
2.2L (mm)	1989-92	6-12	6-12	6-12	—
USED BELTS					
Strand Tension method					
V-belts ex. AP	1989-90	80-100	80-100	80-100	—
V-belts AP	1989-90	—	—	—	40-60
Cogged	1989-90	110-130	110-130	110-130	110-130
V-ribbed (5 ribs)	1989-90	110-130	110-130	110-130	110-130
V-ribbed (6 ribs)	1989-90	140-160	140-160	140-160	140-160
Serpentine w/tensioner¹	1989-90	100-180	—	—	—
1.3L	1991-97	95-110	90-110	90-110	—
1.6L	1991-95	110-132	110-132	110-132	—
1.8L	1991-96	68-85	95-110	95-110	—
2.0L Probe	1993-97	110-150	110-150	110-150	—
2.5L Probe	1993-97	110-150	100-120	110-150	—
3.0L Villager	1993-97	145-165	125-145	125-145	—

FORD, LINCOLN, MERCURY
1989-2000 Ford, Lincoln, Mercury, Merkur Including FWD Vans
Mercury Mountaineer & Lincoln Navigator—See Ford Trucks

UNDERHOOD SERVICE SPECIFICATIONS

FDTU9   FDTU9

BELT TENSION Continued

Application	Year	Generator	Power Steering	Air cond.	Therm-actor
3.0L Others ex. SHO w/o tensioner	1991-92	110-130	110-130	110-130	—
3.0L Others ex. SHO	1994-95	130-160[1]	—	—	—
3.0L SHO, 3.2L SHO	1991-95	148-192	112-157	112-157	—
3.8L FWD	1994-95	130-160[1]	—	—	—
3.8L	1996-97	74 min.[1]	—	—	—
4.6L	1993-95	110-120[1]	—	—	—
	1996-97	74 min.[1]	—	—	—
5.0L Mustang	1991-95	100-150[1]	—	—	—
NEW BELTS					
Strand Tension method					
V-belts ex. AP	1989-90	90-130	90-130	90-130	—
V-belts AP	1989-90	—	—	—	50-90
Cogged	1989-90	120-160	120-160	120-160	120-160
V-ribbed (6 ribs)	1989-90	150-190	150-190	150-190	150-190
Serpentine w/tensioner[1]	1989-90	100-130			
1.3L	1991-97	110-130	110-125	110-125	—
1.6L	1991-95	110-132	110-132	110-132	—
1.8L	1991-96	86-103	110-132	110-132	—
2.0L Probe	1993-97	170-180	140-170	140-170	—
2.5L Probe	1993-97	160-190	130-150	160-190	—
3.0L Villager	1993-97	170-190	150-170	150-170	—
3.0L Others ex. SHO w/o tensioner	1991-92	140-160	140-160	140-160	—
3.0L Others ex. SHO	1994-95	160-190[1]	—	—	—
3.0L SHO, 3.2L SHO	1991-94	220-265	148-192	148-192	—
3.8L FWD	1994-95	160-190[1]	—	—	—
3.8L	1996-97	74 min.[1]	—	—	—
4.6L	1993-95	110-120[1]	—	—	—
	1996-97	74 min.[1]	—	—	—
5.0L Mustang	1991-95	100-150[1]	—	—	—

1 Checking figure, not adjustable.

SERPENTINE BELT DIAGRAMS

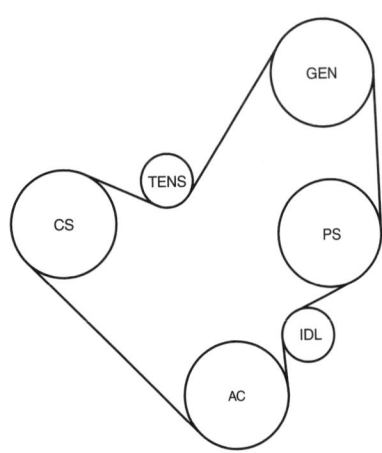

1991-96 1.9L w/PS & AC
1997-00 2.0L SOHC

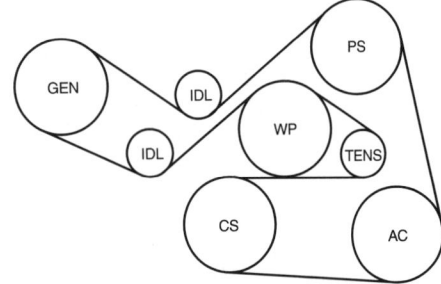

1997-00 Escort 2.0L DOHC

SERPENTINE BELT DIAGRAMS Continued

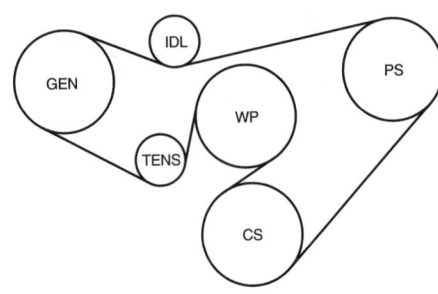

1995-00 2.0L Contour, Mystique, Cougar w/o AC

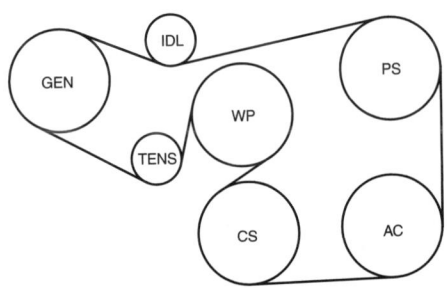

1995-00 2.0L Contour, Mystique, Cougar w/AC

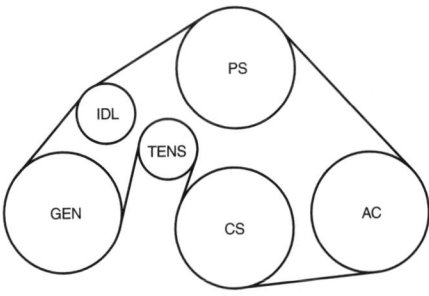

1995-00 2.5L Contour, Mystique, Cougar w/AC

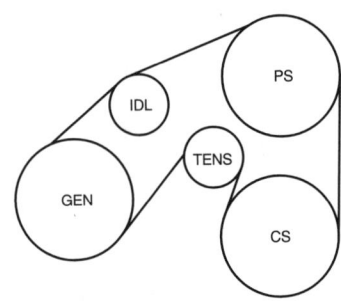

1995-00 2.5L Contour, Mystique, Cougar w/o AC

FORD, LINCOLN, MERCURY
1989-2000 Ford, Lincoln, Mercury, Merkur Including FWD Vans
Mercury Mountaineer & Lincoln Navigator—See Ford Trucks

UNDERHOOD SERVICE SPECIFICATIONS

FDTU10

FDTU10

SERPENTINE BELT DIAGRAMS Continued

SERPENTINE BELT DIAGRAMS Continued

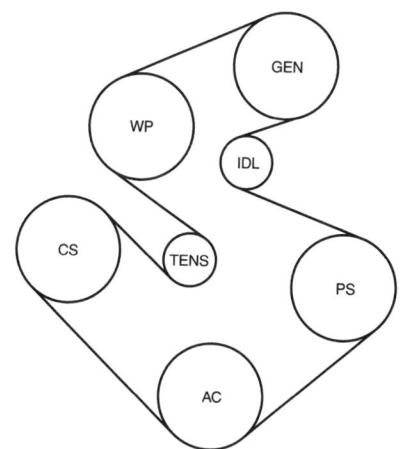

1996-00 3.0L ex. DOHC

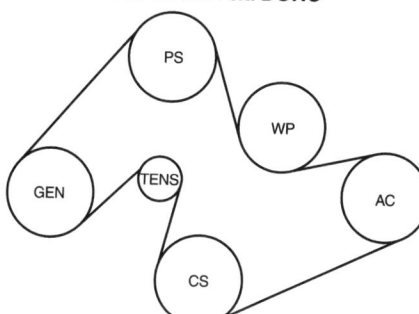

1996-00 3.0L DOHC

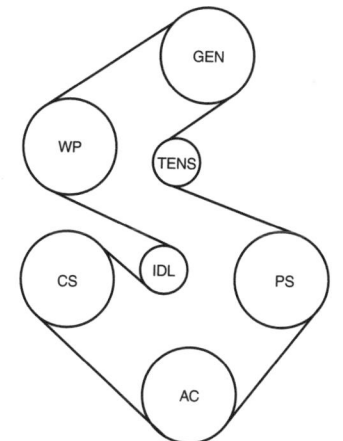

1993-95 3.0L Taurus, Sable

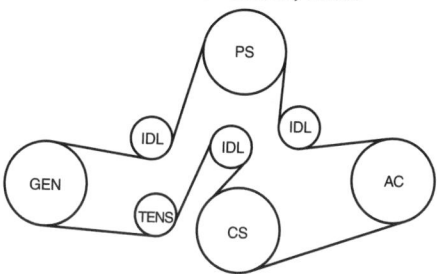

1996-00 3.4L SHO

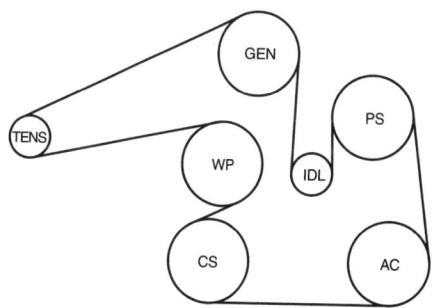

1989-96 3.8L FWD

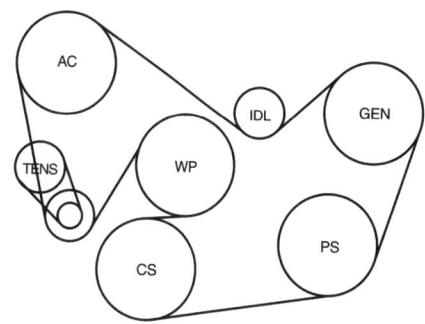

1989-00 3.8L RWD ex. Supercharged

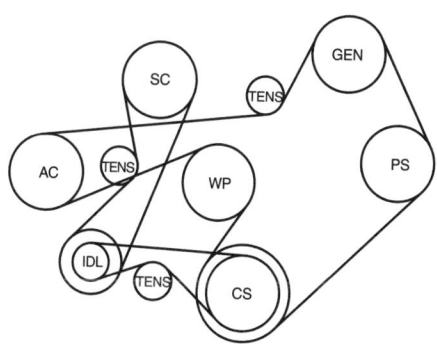

1989-95 3.8L Supercharged

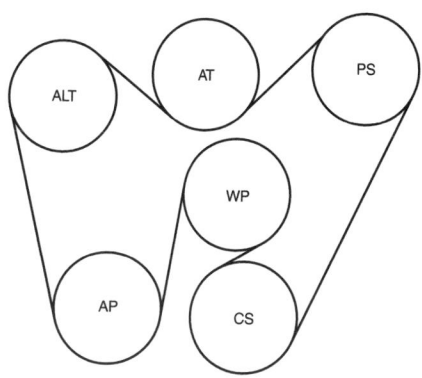

1989-93 5.0L Mustang, Mark VII w/o AC

FORD, LINCOLN, MERCURY
1989-2000 Ford, Lincoln, Mercury, Merkur Including FWD Vans
Mercury Mountaineer & Lincoln Navigator—See Ford Trucks

UNDERHOOD SERVICE SPECIFICATIONS

FDTU11

FDTU11

SERPENTINE BELT DIAGRAM Continued

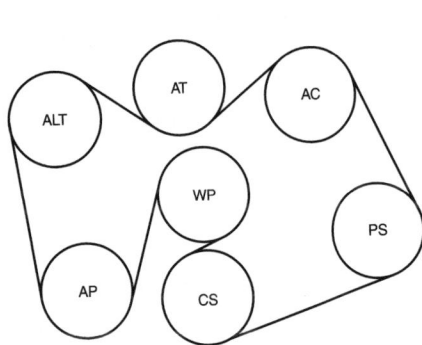

1989-93 5.0L Mustang, Mark VII w/AC

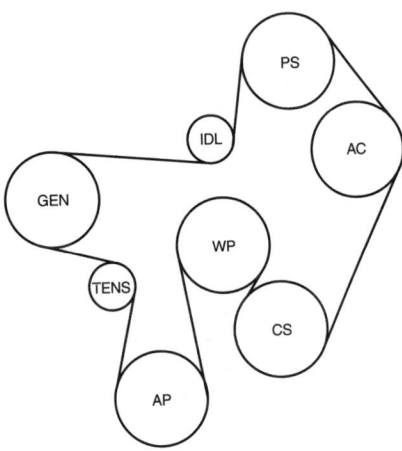

1991-93 5.0L Thunderbird, Cougar

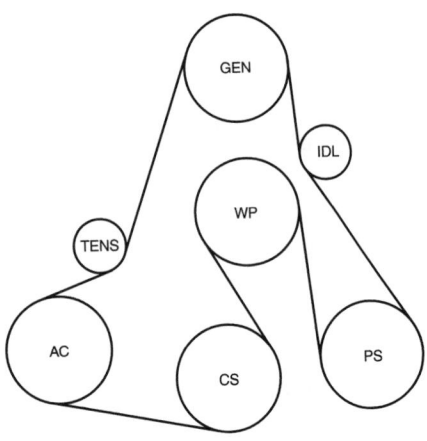

1991-93 4.6L All

SERPENTINE BELT DIAGRAM Continued

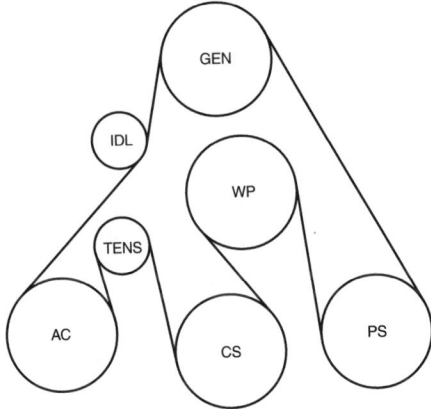

1994-00 4.6L ex. Continental

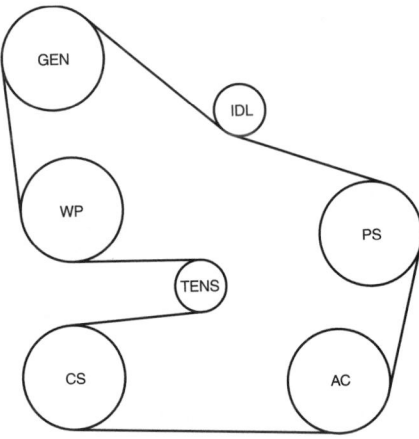

1995-96 4.6L Continental

ENGINE COMPUTER SYSTEM

DIAGNOSTIC TROUBLE CODES
FOR TESTING AND ADJUSTMENT DIAGRAMS, SEE APPENDIX G.
1989 Tracer
Ground two-pin test connector yellow terminal (near right strut tower). Connect an analog voltmeter between the green/black terminal on the six-pin self test connector under dash (-) and battery power (+). Voltmeter will sweep in long pulses indicating tens; or short pulses indicating ones.
Disconnect battery negative terminal for ten seconds to clear codes.

1989-92 Probe 4-cyl.
1989-93 Festiva
1991-94 Capri
Ground the single STI connector (black, 1-pin) to activate self-test system.
Disconnect battery negative terminal for ten seconds to clear codes.

1991-95 Escort, Tracer w/1.8L DOHC
1993-95 Probe
1994-95 Aspire
Ground the STI terminal of the Data Link connector.
Disconnect battery negative terminal for ten seconds to clear codes.

1993-95 Villager
Locate diagnostic test connector in engine compartment and disconnect it. Jumper the black/white and green-yellow/black wires. Wait two seconds and remove the jumper. Codes will be displayed on the malfunction indicator lamp.
Disconnect battery negative terminal for ten seconds to clear codes.

1989-91 MCU:
Complicated procedure required to obtain valid codes. See shop manual.
With key off, locate self-test connector. Connect a jumper wire from the upper right cavity to the second lower cavity from left. Connect an analog VOM from battery (+) to lower second from right cavity (-). Disconnect PCV valve vacuum line of EVAP canister control valve (4- & 6-cyl.). Remove PCV valve from valve cover and uncap restrictor in secondary air injection vacuum control line (8-cyl. as equipped).

FORD, LINCOLN, MERCURY

1989-2000 Ford, Lincoln, Mercury, Merkur Including FWD Vans
Mercury Mountaineer & Lincoln Navigator—See Ford Trucks

UNDERHOOD SERVICE SPECIFICATIONS

FDTU12   FDTU12

DIAGNOSTIC TROUBLE CODES Continued

1989-95 EEC IV w/2 or 3-digit codes:
Complicated procedure required to obtain valid codes. See shop manual.
Continental w/message center: Hold "Select," "Check Out," and "Reset" down. Turn ignition switch on.

All others: With engine at operating temperature and ignition off, locate SELF-TEST connector under hood. Connect a jumper wire between input connector (single terminal) and upper right cavity on connector. Connect an analog VOM to battery (+) and second bottom right cavity on connector. On some models, the "CHECK ENGINE" light will flash codes. A four-second delay separates individual codes. On Continental with message center, hold "SELECT," "CHECK OUT," and "RESET" buttons down to activate memory. SELF-TEST codes are revealed in a series of three separate test procedures (key on engine off, engine running, and continuous) and must be accessed in order.

Key on engine off: Place transmission in park or neutral, set parking brake, turn off all electrical equipment, place octane switch (2.3L SVO Turbo) in premium position. Activate SELF-TEST and place ignition key in run position, do not depress throttle. Observe and record service codes.

Engine running: Deactivate SELF-TEST. Start engine and run at greater than 2000 rpm for 2 minutes. Turn engine off, wait ten seconds & reactivate SELF-TEST. Start engine without depressing throttle. An engine ID code will be displayed (**Code 2**—4-cyl., **Code 3**—6-cyl., **Code 4**—8-cyl.), depress and release brake pedal once. Observe and record service codes.

Continuous: Allow engine to run at idle after all codes have been displayed. After approximately 2 minutes, continuous codes will be displayed. System will remain in continuous mode until ignition is switched off or SELF-TEST is deactivated.

1994-95 Mustang 3.8L;
Thunderbird, Cougar 4.6L
1995 All 4.6L
1996-00 All Models
A Scan tool must be used to retrieve codes and code definitions.

1989 Tracer
1989-90 Festiva, Probe
01 Ignition pulse
02 Crankshaft position sensor
03 Cylinder I.D. sensor
04 Cylinder I.D. sensor
05 Knock sensor circuit
08 Airflow meter vane
09 Engine coolant temperature sensor
10 Intake air temperature sensor
12 Throttle position sensor
13 MAP sensor
14 Barometric pressure sensor
15 Oxygen sensor
16 EGR position sensor
17 Fuel control circuit
18 Carburetor feedback system
19 Carburetor feedback system
20 Carburetor feedback system
21 Carburetor feedback system
22 Fuel shutoff solenoid
25 Pressure regulator control
26 Canister purge solenoid
27 Canister purge regulator
28 EGR control solenoid
29 EGR vent solenoid
31 Pulse air control solenoid
34 Idle speed control solenoid (FI)
34 Electrical load control solenoid (2V)
35 AC load solenoid
38 EFE heater
42 Turbo boost control solenoid
70 Wide open throttle switch
71 Throttle position sensor

Escort & Tracer 1.8L, Festiva, Capri, Probe ex. 3.0L
01 Crankshaft position sensor #1 circuit open or shorted (2.5L)
01 Ignition pickup circuit failure (2.2L Turbo)
01 Loss of ignition diagnostic module input to processor (others)
02 No crankshaft position sensor signal from crank angle sensor
03 No cylinder identification sensor TDC signal (2.0L)
03 Cylinder identification #1 circuit failure in the sensor input signal (others)
04 No crankshaft position sensor #1 signal from crank angle sensor
04 Cylinder identification #2 circuit failure in the sensor input signal (others)
05 Knock control circuit open or shorted
06 Insufficient input from vehicle speed sensor
08 Mass airflow sensor circuit open or shorted (2.0L)
08 Measuring core volume airflow sensor circuit shorted (2.5L)

DIAGNOSTIC TROUBLE CODES Continued

08 Volume air flow higher or lower than expected (others)
09 Engine coolant temperature higher or lower than expected
10 Intake air temperature higher or lower than expected
11 Intake air temperature circuit open or shorted
12 Throttle position sensor's rotational setting higher or lower than expected (1991-92)
12 Throttle position sensor circuit open or shorted (1993)
14 Barometric pressure sensor circuit open or shorted (1.6L)
14 Barometric pressure sensor higher or lower than expected. If cannot be erased, replace processor (others)
15 Oxygen sensor voltage always below .55V (left on V6)
16 EGR temperature sensor circuit open or shorted (2.5L)
16 EGR valve position higher or lower than expected (others)
17 Lack of oxygen sensor switch, system rich (1991-93)
17 Oxygen sensor does not switch (1993)
23 Oxygen sensor voltage always below .55V (right on V6)
24 Oxygen sensor does not switch (right on V6)
25 Fuel pressure regulator control circuit open or shorted
26 Canister purge solenoid circuit open or shorted
28 EGR control circuit open or shorted (2.2L Turbo, 2.5L)
28 EGR solenoid vacuum valve circuit open or shorted (others)
29 EGR vent solenoid circuit
34 Idle air control circuit open or shorted
41 High speed inlet air control circuit open or shorted (1.8L)
41 Variable resonance induction system #1 solenoid circuit (2.5L)
42 Turbocharger boost control circuit open or shorted
46 Variable resonance induction system #2 solenoid circuit
55 Pulse signal generator circuit failure
56 Transaxle oil temperature sensor circuit
57 Down shift signal circuit failure (1991-92)
57 Reduce torque signal #1 circuit (1993-95)
58 Reduce torque signal #2 circuit (1993-95)
59 Torque reduce/coolant temperature sensor signal circuit
60 1-2 shift error (1991-92 1.6L & 1993-95 all)
60 Shift solenoid #1 circuit failure (1991-92 others)
61 2-3 shift error (1991-92 1.6L & 1993-95 all)
61 Shift solenoid #2 circuit failure (1991-92 others)
62 3-4 shift error (1991-92 1.6L & 1993-95 all)
62 Shift solenoid #3 circuit failure (1991-92 others)
63 Converter clutch control circuit failure
64 Down shift solenoid circuit
65 Torque converter clutch solenoid circuit
66 Line pressure solenoid circuit
67 Low cooling fan relay circuit
68 High cooling fan relay circuit
69 Cooling fan coolant temperature sensor circuit

Villager
01 Pulse signal generator sensor circuit
02 Vehicle speed sensor circuit
03 Throttle position sensor circuit
04 Shift solenoid A circuit
05 Shift solenoid B circuit
06 Coasting clutch solenoid circuit
07 Torque converter clutch solenoid circuit
08 Transaxle oil temperature sensor
09 Engine RPM signal circuit
10 Line pressure solenoid circuit
11 Crankshaft position signal (PCM)
11 Memory backup fail (TCM)
12 Mass airflow sensor circuit (PCM)
12 Transaxle control module RAM circuit failure (TCM)
13 Engine coolant temperature circuit failure (PCM)
13 Transaxle control module ROM circuit failure (TCM)
14 Vehicle speed sensor circuit
21 Ignition signal in primary circuit
31 PCM failure
32 EGR control solenoid circuit
33 Oxygen sensor circuit
34 Knock sensor circuit
35 EGR temperature sensor circuit
43 Throttle position sensor circuit
45 Injector leak
51 Injector signal circuit
55 System pass

1989-91 V8 w/MCU
Code 11 System OK
Code 12 RPM out of spec.
Code 25 Knock sensor

FORD, LINCOLN, MERCURY
1989-2000 Ford, Lincoln, Mercury, Merkur Including FWD Vans
Mercury Mountaineer & Lincoln Navigator—See Ford Trucks

UNDERHOOD SERVICE SPECIFICATIONS

FDTU13

FDTU13

DIAGNOSTIC TROUBLE CODES Continued

Code 41 Fuel mixture lean
Code 42 Fuel mixture rich
Code 44 Secondary air injection
Code 45 Secondary air injection always upstream
Code 46 Secondary air injection not bypassing
Code 51 Hi-low vacuum switch
Code 53 Dual temperature switch
Code 54 Mid-temperature switch
Code 55 Mid-vacuum switch
Codes 61 & 65 Mid-vacuum switch closed
Code 62 Barometric switch

1989-90 All w/EEC IV
1991 1.9L, 2.3L, 3.0L SHO, 5.0L
1992 5.0L Mustang, Mark VII
1993-95 5.0L Mustang

Code Displayed	Test Condition	Results
10	R	Cylinder #1 low, cylinder balance test
11	I, R, C	Pass
12	R	RPM not within self test upper limit
13	R	RPM not within self test lower limit
13	I	D.C. motor did not move
13	C	D.C. motor does not follow dashpot
14	I, C	Ignition pickup circuit fault
15	I, C	ROM test failed or keep alive memory in continuous (1989)
15	I	ECM ROM test failed (1990-93)
15	C	ECM keep alive memory test failed (1990-93)
16	I	Ignition diagnostic module signal not received
16	R	ISC rpm exceeds self test range (1989 1.9L, 2.5L)
16	R	Idle high with ISC retracted (1990 1.9L, 2.5L)
16	R	RPM too low to perform oxygen sensor test (others)
17	R	ISC rpm below self test range (1989)
17	R	Idle high with ISC retracted (1990 1.9L, 2.5L)
18	C	Loss of tach input to processor, spout circuit grounded
18	C	Erratic input to processor (1989-90 2.3L w/o distributor)
18	C	1, 2, 3, 4 primary coil circuit failure (1991-92 2.3L)
18	R	Spout circuit open
19	R	RPM for idle EGR test not achieved (1.9L TBI)
19	I	Failure in EEC reference voltage (others)
19	C	CID circuit failure (3.0L SHO, 3.8L Supercharged)
19	R	Engine stumble during hard idle test
20	R	Cylinder #2 low, cylinder balance test
21	I, R	Coolant temperature sensor out of range
22	I, R, C	MAP/BARO sensor out of range
23	I, R	Throttle position sensor out of range
24	I, R	Intake air temperature sensor out of range
24	C	Coil #1 primary circuit failure
25	R	Knock not sensed during dynamic response test
26	I, R	Volume airflow sensor out of range (2.3L Turbo, 3.0L SHO)
27	R	Speed control servo leaks down during test
27	C	Insufficient input from vehicle speed sensor (1989)
27	C	Coil #2 primary circuit failure (1990-93)
28	C	Loss of tach, right side
28	I, R	Intake air temperature at volume airflow sensor out of range
28	I, R	Intake air temperature out of self test range (1990-93)
28	R	Speed control servo leaks up during test (others)
29	C	Insufficient input from vehicle speed sensor
30	R	Cylinder #3 low, cylinder balance test
31	I, R, C	EVP voltage out of range (2.3L OHC, 3.8L TBI)
31	I, R, C	EPT/EVP below minimum voltage (others)
32	R	EGR not controlling (2.3L OHC, 3.8L TBI)
32	I, R, C	EGR valve not seated (1.9L TBI, 2.9L, 3.0L)
32	I, R, C	EPT/EVP voltage below closed limit (others, sonic EGR)
33	R, C	EGR valve not seated (2.3L OHC, 3.8L TBI)
33	R, C	EGR valve not opening (others, sonic EGR)
34	R	Insufficient EGR flow (2.3L OHC & Turbo, 3.8L TBI)
34	I, R, C	Exhaust pressure high/defective EPT sensor (1.9L TBI, 2.3L HSC MFI, 3.0L)
34	R, C	EVP voltage above closed limit (others, sonic EGR)
35	R	RPM too low to perform EGR test (2.3L OHC, 3.8L TBI)
35	I, R, C	EPT/EVP circuit above maximum voltage (others)
36	R	Insufficient RPM increase during speed control test
37	R	Insufficient RPM decrease during speed control test
38	C	Idle tracking switch circuit open
39	C	AXOD lockup failed

DIAGNOSTIC TROUBLE CODES Continued

Code Displayed	Test Condition	Results
40	R	Cylinder #4 low, cylinder balance test
41	R	Oxygen sensor circuit, system lean
41	C	No oxygen sensor switch detected
42	R	Oxygen sensor circuit, system rich
42	C	No oxygen sensor switch detected
43	C	Oxygen sensor lean at WOT
44	R	Secondary air injection system inoperative
45	C	Coil #1 primary circuit failure
45	R	Secondary air upstream during self test
46	C	Coil #2 primary circuit failure
46	R	Secondary air not bypassed during self test
47	C	Spark timing error
47	R	Measured airflow low at base idle (1.9L MFI)
47	I	Speed control command switches circuit
48	C	Coil #3 circuit failure (3.0L SHO, 3.8L Supercharged)
48	C	Loss of secondary tach, left side (2.3L)
48	I	Speed control command switches circuit not functioning
48	R	Measured airflow high at base idle (1.9L MFI)
49	C	Default spark error (3.0L SHO, 3.8L Supercharged)
49	I	Speed control ground circuit open
49	R	Cylinder #5 low, cylinder balance test
51	I, R, C	Engine coolant temperature sensor circuit open
52	I	Power steering pressure switch circuit open
52	R	Power steering pressure switch did not change states
53	I, C	Throttle position sensor circuit above maximum voltage
54	I, R, C	Intake air temperature circuit open
55	R	Key power circuit low or open
56	I, R, C	Volume airflow circuit above maximum voltage
56	I, C	Transmission oil temperature circuit open
57	I	Octane adjust service pin in use/circuit grounded
57	C	Transmission neutral pressure switch circuit open
58	I	Crank fuel delay service pin in use/circuit grounded
58	R	Idle tracking switch circuit grounded (All w/TBI)
58	I	Idle tracking switch circuit open (1.9L TBI, 2.3L TBI)
58	I, C	Vane air flow circuit above maximum voltage (2.3L Turbo)
59	I	Idle adjust service pin in use/circuit grounded
59	I, C	Low speed fuel pump circuit (3.0L SHO)
59	I	AXOD 4-3 circuit closed
59	C	AXOD 4-3 circuit open
60	R	Cylinder #6 low, cylinder balance test
61	I, R, C	Engine coolant temperature circuit grounded
62	I, R	AXOD 3-2, 4-3 circuit grounded
63	I, R, C	TPS below minimum voltage
64	I, R, C	Intake air temperature sensor circuit grounded
65	C	Never went to closed loop
66	I, C	Volume airflow circuit input voltage below minimum
67	I, R, C	Transmission neutral pressure switch circuit failed closed/AC on during self test (3.0L, 3.8L FWD)
67	C	Clutch switch failed (1.9L MFI)
67	I, C	NDS circuit open/AC on during self test (others)
68	I, R	Idle tracking switch failed/circuit grounded or open (All TBI)
68	I, C	Intake air temperature circuit grounded (2.3L Turbo)
68	I, R, C	Transmission temperature switch circuit failed open (3.8L)
69	I, C	AXOD 3-2 circuit failed closed
70	C	Data communications link or ECM circuit failure
70	R	Cylinder #7 low, cylinder balance test
71	C	Idle tracking switch circuit shorted to ground (1.9L TBI, 2.3L TBI)
71	C	Software reinitialization detected (1.9L MFI)
71	C	Data communications link or CCA circuit failure (3.8L)
72	C	Power interrupt detected (1.9L MFI, 2.3L Turbo)
72	R	Insufficient MAP change during dynamic response test (others)
73	I, R	Insufficient throttle position sensor change during dynamic response test
74	R	Brake switch circuit open
75	R	Brake switch circuit closed
76	R	Insufficient volume air flow change during dynamic response test
77	R	Operator error during dynamic response test
78	R	Power interrupt detected
79	I	AC on during self test
80	R	Cylinder #8 low, cylinder balance test
81	I	BOOST circuit failure (2.3L Turbo)
81	I	Speed control vent failure (2.5L, 3.0L, 3.8L FWD)

FORD, LINCOLN, MERCURY
1989-2000 Ford, Lincoln, Mercury, Merkur Including FWD Vans
Mercury Mountaineer & Lincoln Navigator—See Ford Trucks

UNDERHOOD SERVICE SPECIFICATIONS

FDTU14

FDTU14

DIAGNOSTIC TROUBLE CODES Continued

Code Displayed	Test Condition	Results
81	I	Inlet air control solenoid (3.0L SHO)
81	I	Air management circuit #2 failure (others)
82	I	Speed control vacuum failure (2.5L, 3.0L, 3.8L FWD)
82	I	Electric fan circuit failure (2.3L Turbo)
82	I	Supercharger boost solenoid circuit (3.8L Supercharged)
82	I	Air management circuit #1 failure (others)
83	I	EGR control circuit (2.3L OHC, 3.8L TBI)
83	I, C	Low speed primary fuel pump (3.0L SHO)
83	I	Electric fan circuit failure (others)
84	I	EGR shut off circuit failure (2.3L Turbo)
84	I, R	EGR vent circuit failure (2.3L OHC, 3.8L TBI)
84	I, R	Electronic vacuum regulator circuit failure (others)
85	C	Adaptive lean limit reached (1.9L MFI)
85	C	3-4 solenoid circuit failure (2.3L Turbo)
85	I	Canister purge circuit (others)
86	C	Adaptive rich limit reached
86	R	4-3 shift solenoid circuit failure
87	I, C	Fuel pump circuit failure
88	I	Electric fan circuit failure
88	C	Loss of dual plug input control
89	I	Lockup solenoid circuit failure (3.0L, 3.8L FWD)
89	I	Exhaust heat crossover circuit failure (3.8L TBI)
89	I	Clutch converter override circuit failure (others)
90	R	PASSED (cylinder balance test)
91	R, C	Oxygen sensor input indicates system lean
92	R, C	Oxygen sensor input indicates system rich
93	I	Throttle position sensor circuit input low at max. D.C. motor extension
94	R	Secondary air system inoperative
95	I, C	Fuel pump circuit open, ECM to motor ground
96	I, C	Fuel pump circuit open, ECM to battery
98	R	Hard fault present
99	R	Idle not learned, ignore codes 12, 13

1991 2.3L OHC, 3.0L ex. SHO, 3.8L, 4.6L, 5.0L ex. Mustang, Mark VII
1992 All ex. 5.0L Mustang, Mark VII
1993 All ex. 5.0L Mustang
1994 All ex. 3.8L Mustang, 4.6L Thunderbird, Cougar
1995 All ex. 3.8L Mustang, 4.6L SOHC

10 Cylinder #1 low (cylinder balance test)
20 Cylinder #2 low (cylinder balance test)
30 Cylinder #3 low (cylinder balance test)
40 Cylinder #4 low (cylinder balance test)
50 Cylinder #5 low (cylinder balance test)
60 Cylinder #6 low (cylinder balance test)
70 Cylinder #7 low (cylinder balance test)
80 Cylinder #8 low (cylinder balance test)
90 Passed cylinder balance test
111 System PASS
112 Intake air temperature sensor circuit grounded
113 Intake air temperature sensor circuit open
114 Intake air temperature sensor out of range
116 Engine coolant temperature sensor out of range
117 Engine coolant sensor temperature circuit grounded
118 Engine coolant sensor temperature circuit open
121 Throttle position sensor out of range
122 Throttle position sensor circuit grounded
123 Throttle position sensor circuit open
124 Throttle position sensor voltage higher than expected
125 Throttle position sensor voltage lower than expected
126 MAP/BARO sensor out of range
128 MAP sensor vacuum hose damaged or disconnected
129 Insufficient MAP/MAF change during dynamic response test
136 System indicates lean (bank #2, driver side)
137 System indicates rich (bank #2, driver side)
138 Cold start injector
139 No oxygen sensor switches detected (bank 2, driver side)
141 Fuel system lean
144 No oxygen sensor switch detected
157 MAF sensor circuit below minimum voltage
158 MAF sensor circuit above maximum voltage
159 MAF higher or lower than expected
167 Insufficient throttle position change during dynamic response test
171 Oxygen sensor unable to switch, adaptive fuel at limit (bank #1 passenger side)
172 System indicates lean (bank #1, passenger side)
173 System indicates rich (bank #1, passenger side)

DIAGNOSTIC TROUBLE CODES Continued

174 Slow oxygen sensor switching
175 Fuel system at adaptive limits, oxygen sensor unable to switch (bank #2, driver side)
176 No oxygen sensor switch detected, system lean (bank #2, driver side)
177 No oxygen sensor switch detected, system rich (bank #2, driver side)
179 Adaptive fuel lean limit reached at part throttle, system rich (bank #1, passenger side)
181 Adaptive fuel rich limit reached at part throttle, system lean (bank #1, passenger side)
182 Adaptive fuel lean limit reached at idle, system rich (bank #1, passenger side)
183 Adaptive fuel rich limit reached at idle, system lean (bank #1, passenger side)
184 Mass airflow higher than expected
185 Mass airflow lower than expected
186 Injector pulsewidth higher than expected (models w/barometric pressure sensor)
186 Injector pulsewidth higher or MAF lower than expected (models w/o barometric pressure sensor)
187 Injector pulsewidth lower than expected (models w/barometric pressure sensor)
187 Injector pulsewidth lower or MAF lower than expected (models w/o barometric pressure sensor)
188 Adaptive fuel lean limit reached at part throttle, system rich (bank #2, driver side)
189 Adaptive fuel rich limit reached at part throttle, system lean (bank #2, driver side)
190 Adaptive fuel lean limit reached at idle, system rich (bank #2, driver side)
191 Adaptive fuel rich limit reached at idle, system lean (bank #2, driver side)
193 Flexible fuel sensor circuit failure
211 Profile ignition pickup circuit failure
212 Loss of ignition diagnostic module input to processor/spout circuit grounded
213 Spout circuit open
214 Cylinder identification circuit failure
215 Powertrain control module detected coil #1 primary circuit failure
216 Powertrain control module detected coil #2 primary circuit failure
217 Powertrain control module detected coil #3 primary circuit failure
218 Loss of ignition diagnostic module signal, left side
219 Spark timing defaulted to 10 degrees, spout circuit open
221 Spark timing error
222 Loss of ignition diagnostic module signal, right side
223 Loss of dual plug inhibit control
224 Powertrain control module detected coil 1, 2, 3, or 4 primary circuit failure
225 Knock not sensed during dynamic response test
226 Ignition diagnostic module signal not received
227 Crankshaft position sensor
232 Powertrain control module detected coil 1, 2, 3, or 4 primary circuit failure
233 Spark angle pulsewidth error
238 Powertrain control module detected coil #4 primary circuit failure
239 Crankshaft position signal received with engine off
241 EDIS to EEC processor ignition diagnostic module pulsewidth transmission error
242 Operating in DIS failure mode
243 Secondary circuit failure
244 CID circuit fault present when cylinder balance test requested
311 Secondary air system inoperative (right side with dual O_2 sensors)
312 Secondary air misdirected during self test
313 Secondary air not bypassed during self test
314 Secondary air system inoperative (left side with dual O_2 sensors)
326 EGR circuit voltage lower than expected
327 EVP/EPT circuit below minimum voltage
328 EGR closed valve voltage lower than expected
332 Insufficient EGR flow detected
334 EGR closed valve voltage higher than expected
335 EGR sensor voltage higher or lower than expected
336 Exhaust pressure high/EGR circuit voltage higher than expected
337 EVP/EPT circuit above maximum voltage
338 Engine coolant temperature lower than expected
339 Engine coolant temperature higher than expected
341 Octane adjust service pin in use
381 Frequent A/C clutch cycling
411 Cannot control RPM during self test, idle low
412 Cannot control RPM during self test, idle high
415 Idle speed control system at minimum learning limit
416 Idle air control system at maximum learning limit
452 Insufficient input from vehicle speed sensor
453 Servo leaking down during test
454 Servo leaking up during test
455 Insufficient RPM increase during test
456 Insufficient RPM decrease during test
457 Speed control command switches circuit not functioning
458 Speed control command switches stuck or circuit grounded
459 Speed control ground circuit open
511 Powertrain control module read only memory test failed
512 Powertrain control module keep alive memory test failed
513 Failure in powertrain control module internal voltage
519 Power steering pressure switch circuit open
521 Power steering pressure switch circuit did not change states
522 Vehicle not in Park or Neutral during test
524 Low speed fuel pump circuit open, battery to PCM

FORD, LINCOLN, MERCURY
1989-2000 Ford, Lincoln, Mercury, Merkur Including FWD Vans
Mercury Mountaineer & Lincoln Navigator—See Ford Trucks

UNDERHOOD SERVICE SPECIFICATIONS

FDTU15
FDTU15

DIAGNOSTIC TROUBLE CODES Continued

525 Vehicle in gear/AC on
527 Park/neutral switch circuit open
528 Clutch switch circuit failure
529 Data communications link or EEC processor circuit failure
532 Cluster control assembly circuit failure
533 Data communications link or electronic instrument cluster circuit failure
536 Brake switch circuit failure
538 Insufficient RPM change during dynamic response test or invalid cylinder balance test due to throttle movement during test or CID sensor failure
539 AC/Defrost on during test
542 Fuel pump circuit open, EEC processor to motor ground
543 Fuel pump circuit open, EEC processor to battery
551 Inlet air control circuit failure
552 Air management circuit 1 failure
553 Air management circuit 2 failure
554 Fuel pressure regulator control circuit failure
555 Supercharger bypass solenoid circuit failure
556 Fuel pump relay primary circuit failure
557 Low speed fuel pump primary circuit failure
558 EGR vacuum regulator circuit failure
559 Air conditioning on relay circuit failure
562 Auxiliary electric fan circuit failure
563 High speed electric fan circuit failure
564 Electric fan circuit failure
565 Canister purge circuit failure
566 3-4 shift solenoid circuit failure
567 Speed control vent circuit failure
568 Speed control vacuum circuit failure
569 Auxiliary canister purge circuit failure
571 EGR A solenoid circuit failure
572 EGR V solenoid circuit failure
578 A/C pressure sensor circuit shorted
579 Insufficient A/C pressure charge
581 Power to fan circuit over current
582 Fan circuit open
583 Power to fuel pump over current
584 Variable control relay module power ground circuit open
585 Power to A/C clutch over current
586 A/C clutch circuit open
587 Variable control relay module communications failure
617 1-2 shift error
618 2-3 shift error
619 3-4 shift error
621 Shift solenoid circuit #1 failure
622 Shift solenoid circuit #2 failure
623 Transmission control indicator light circuit failure
624 Electronic pressure regulator control circuit failure
625 Electronic pressure regulator control driver open in PCM
626 Coast clutch solenoid circuit failure
627 Converter clutch control solenoid circuit failure
628 Excessive converter clutch slippage
629 Converter clutch solenoid circuit failure
631 Overdrive cancel indicator light circuit failure
632 Overdrive cancel switch circuit did not change states
633 4WD switch closed during test
634 Manual lever position sensor voltage higher or lower than expected
636 Transmission oil temperature higher or lower than expected
637 Transmission oil temperature sensor circuit open
638 Transmission oil temperature sensor circuit grounded
639 Insufficient input from turbine speed sensor
641 Shift solenoid #3 circuit failure
643 Shift solenoid #4 circuit failure
645 Incorrect gear ratio obtained for first gear
646 Incorrect gear ratio obtained for second gear
647 Incorrect gear ratio obtained for third gear
648 Incorrect gear ratio obtained for fourth gear
649 Electronic pressure control higher or lower than expected
651 Electronic pressure control circuit failure
652 Modulated lock up solenoid circuit failure
653 Transmission control switch did not change states
654 Transmission range sensor not indicating park
656 Torque converter clutch continuous slip error
657 Transmission over temperature condition occurred
667 Transmission range sensor circuit voltage below minimum
668 Transmission range circuit voltage above maximum
675 Transmission range circuit voltage out of range
998 Hard fault present

SENSORS, INPUT

TEMPERATURE SENSORS
See UNDERHOOD SERVICE INSTRUCTIONS at the beginning of this section for test/adjustment diagrams.
1.3L IAT: Measured between upper terminal (GN/BK wire) of airflow sensor and ground.
1.6L IAT: Measured between terminal 25 (upper terminal on airflow connector) and ground.
2.2L IAT: Measured between first (R wire) and fifth (LG/W wire) of airflow sensor.
All others with EEC IV IAT: Measured between upper terminal (LG/P wire) of airflow sensor and ground.

Engine	Year	Sensor	Resistance Ohms @ deg. F/C
1.3L (81), 1.6L Capri, Tracer; 1.8L, 2.2L, 2.5L Probe	1989-96	Coolant	14,600-17,800 @ -4/-20 2200-2700 @ 68/16 1000-1300 @ 104/40 500-640 @ 140/60 290-355 @ 176/80
1.3L	1989-93	Intake Air	10,000-20,000 @ -4/-20
1.3L	1994-96	Intake Air	72,000-79,400 @ 32/0 54,300-58,600 @ 55/13 29,700-36,300 @ 77/25 17,900-19,300 @ 110/43 3300-3700 @ 185/85
1.6L, 1.8L, 2.2L, 2.5L Probe	1989-95	Intake Air	4000-7000 @ 32/0 2000-3000 @ 68/20 900-1300 @ 104/40 400-700 @ 140/60
All domestic models with EEC IV, EEC V	1989-00	Coolant, Intake Air, Transmission Fluid, Engine Fuel, Engine Oil	31,700-42,900 @ 68/20 13,650-18,650 @ 104/40 6500-8900 @ 140/60 3240-4440 @ 176/80 1770-2370 @ 212/100 980-1380 @ 248/115
	1997-00	Cylinder Head	96,255,000@ 32/0 37,387,000 @ 68/20 16,043,000 @ 104/40 7,987,000 @ 140/60 3,775,000 @ 176/80 2,034,000 @ 212/100 1,155,000 @ 248/120 689,000 @ 284/140 430,100 @ 320/160 279,100 @ 356/180
3.0L Villager	1993-97	Coolant	8000-12,000 @ 14/-10 2100-2900 @ 68/20 680-1000 @ 122/50 300-330 @ 176/80
1.3L	1989	Volume Air	3000-6000 @ 40/4 2000-3000 @ 68/20 500-2000 @ 90/32
1.6L (98)	1989	Volume Air	5800 @ 32/0 2700 @ 65/18 300 @ 185/85 180 @ 220/105
1.6L (98) FI, 1.9L (119) MFI, 2.3L (140) Turbo	1989-90	Volume Air	2100-2900 @ 68/20 1100-1350 @ 104/40 500-700 @ 140/60 280-380 @ 176/80 120-160 @ 212/100 110-120 @ 248/115
3.0L Villager	1993-00	EGR	225,000-255,000 @ 68-120/20-49 175,000-225,000 @ 130-148/55-65 140,00-175,000 @ 150-165/66-74 100,000-140,000 @ 168-190/76-88

MANIFOLD ABSOLUTE AND BAROMETRIC PRESSURE SENSORS
1.3L: Measured between lower right terminal (BR/BK wire) and ground.
1.6L: Measured between terminals 45 and 46 (lower right and upper left).
2.2L: Measured between upper right (LG/Y wire) and lower left (Y wire).
All others with EEC IV: Measured between center terminal of unit and ground.
MAP sensor valves based on 30" (102kPa) barometric pressure.

CHEK-CHART

FORD, LINCOLN, MERCURY
1989-2000 Ford, Lincoln, Mercury, Merkur Including FWD Vans
Mercury Mountaineer & Lincoln Navigator—See Ford Trucks

UNDERHOOD SERVICE SPECIFICATIONS

FDTU16

FDTU16

SENSORS, INPUT Continued
MANIFOLD ABSOLUTE AND BAROMETRIC PRESSURE SENSORS Continued

Engine	Year	Voltage @ in.Hg./kPa
1.3L FI	1989	3.5-4.5 @ 0/0
		2.5-3.5 @ 5/17
		2.5 max. @ 30/101

Engine	Year	Sensor	Frequency HZ @ in.Hg./kPa
1.6L, 2.2L	1989	MAP	0 @ 0/0
			3.5-4.5 @ 30/101
All ex. 1.3L, 1.6L, 1.8L, 2.2L, 2.5L Probe, 3.0L Villager	1989-00	MAP	159 @ 0/0
			141 @ 6/20
			125 @ 12/41
			109 @ 18/61
			95 @ 24/81
			80 @ 30/102
		BARO	116-128 @ 17/58
			122-134 @ 20/66
			129-141 @ 22/74
			136-148 @ 24/82
			143-155 @ 27/90
			150-162 @ 29/98
			156-168 @ 31/105

Engine	Year	Sensor	Voltage @ in.Hg./kPa
1.6L	1991-94	MAP, BARO	3.26-4.42 @ 0/0
			2.86-3.86 @ 5/17
			2.26-3.06 @ 10/34
			1.64-2.22 @ 15/51
			1.07-1.45 @ 20/68
			.49-.67 @ 25/85
2.0L w/AT	1993	MAP	3.9 @ 0/0
			3.6 @ 4/14
			2.5 @ 12/40
			1.5 @ 20/68
			0.4 @ 28/95
All Gas	1997-00	Fuel Oil, Pressure	0.5 @ 0/0
			1.1 @ 10/69
			1.6 @ 20/138
			2.2 @ 30/207
			2.8 @ 40/275
			3.4 @ 50/344

MASS OR VOLUME AIRFLOW SENSOR
Engines with multi-port injection.
1.6L MFI, 1.9L MFI, 2.3L MFI: Volume Airflow Sensors, measured between second upper terminal (W/BK wire) and ground.
3.0L SHO, 3.8L Supercharged, 5.0L MFI HO: Mass Airflow Sensors, measured between terminal D (uppermost) and ground.

Engine	Year	Voltage Ign. On	Idle
1.9L, 2.3L	1989-91	.17-.50	1.10-1.70
3.0L SHO, 3.8L Supercharged, 5.0L HO	1989-91	.70 max.	.20-1.50

Engine	Year	Vane Position Closed	Vane Position Open
1.3L	1989-91	.34-.46	3.6-4.4
	1992-93	4.5-5.0	0.5-1.5
	1994	3.0-3.3	7.0-8.0
1.6L	1991	1.9-2.1	7.8-8.0
	1992-94	3.0-3.3	7.0-8.0
1.8L	1991	3.6-4.4	0.4-1.1
	1992-95	4.5-5.0	0.5-1.5
2.2L	1989-91	3.0-3.3	5.0-7.0
2.2L	1992	3.0-3.3	7.0-8.0
2.5L Probe	1993-95	3.5-4.5	.35-.45

Engine	Year	Voltage @ MPH/KPH
All ex. 1.3L, 1.6L, 1.8L, 2.2L, 2.5L Probe	1992-95	0.8 @ idle
		1.0 @ 20/32
		1.7 @ 40/64
		2.1 @ 60/96

SENSORS, INPUT Continued
THROTTLE POSITION SENSOR (TPS)

Engines with EEC IV: Connect positive (+) probe of DVOM along terminal "A" (upper) of TPS. Connect negative (-) probe along terminal "B" (middle, LG/DG wire) and turn ignition on but do not start engine. Adjust TPS to specified value.

Engine	Year	TPS Voltage Idle	TPS Voltage WOT
1.3L	1992-93	0.9 max.	4.0 min.
	1994-97	.43-.57	3.2-4.2
1.6L, 1.8L	1992-93	0.9 max.	4.0 min.
	1994-95	.43-.57	3.2-4.2
1.9L TBI	1989-90	.39	4.84
1.9L MFI	1989-90	.24	4.84
1.9L	1991	.34	4.84
1.9L	1992-94	.43-.57	3.6-4.8
	1995-96	.65-1.25	4.2-4.6
2.0L MT	1993	.43-.57	3.6-4.8
2.0L AT	1993	.43-.57	3.2-4.2
2.0L	1994	.43-.57	3.2-4.2
	1995-98	.65-1.25	4.2-4.6
	1999-00	.53-1.27	4.65
2.2L	1989-90	.36-.66	4.30
2.3L	1989-90	.20	4.84
2.3L OHC	1991	.34	4.84
2.3L HSC	1991	.20	9.84
2.3L	1994	.43-.57	3.6-4.8
2.5L	1989-91	.39	4.84
2.5L Probe	1993-97	.43-.57	3.2-4.2
2.5L Contour, Mystique, Cougar	1995-98	.65-1.25	4.2-4.6
	1999-00	.53-1.27	4.65
2.9L	1989	1.0 max.[1]	3.8-4.2
3.0L ex. SHO	1989-91	.34	4.84
3.0L SHO	1989-91	.23	4.89
3.0L, 3.3L Villager	1993-00	.34-.46	3.5-4.7
3.0L Others	1992-94	.43-.57	3.6-4.8
	1995-98	.65-1.25	4.2-4.6
	1999-00	.53-1.27	4.65
3.2L SHO, 3.4L SHO	1995-98	.65-1.25	4.2-4.6
	1999-00	.53-1.27	4.65
3.8L, 4.6L, 5.0L	1989-91	.39	4.84
3.8L, 4.6L, 5.0L	1992-94	.43-.57	3.6-4.8
	1995-98	.65-1.25	4.2-4.6
	1999-00	.53-1.27	4.65

1 Not adjustable.

CRANKSHAFT POSITION SENSOR

Engine	Year	Resistance (ohms)
1.3L	1996-97	520-580
1.9L	1991-95	2300-2500
	1996	300-800
2.0L Probe	1996-97	520-580
Others	1996-00	300-800
2.3L	1990-91	300-750
2.5L ex. Probe	1996-00	300-800
2.5L Probe	1996-97	520-580
3.0L SHO	1989-91	300-750
3.0L Flexfuel	1993-95	2300-2500
3.0L Windstar	1995-96	2750-2850
	1997-00	300-800
3.0L ex. Windstar	1996-00	300-800
3.8L	1989-91	300-750
3.8L Calif.	1994-95	2300-2500
3.8L	1996-00	300-800
4.6L	1991	300-750
4.6L	1992-95	2300-2500
	1996-00	300-800

KNOCK SENSOR

Engine	Year	Resistance (ohms)
All	1996-00	4,390,000-5,350,000

FORD, LINCOLN, MERCURY
1989-2000 Ford, Lincoln, Mercury, Merkur Including FWD Vans
Mercury Mountaineer & Lincoln Navigator—See Ford Trucks

UNDERHOOD SERVICE SPECIFICATIONS

FDTU17   FDTU17

SENSORS, INPUT Continued
VEHICLE SPEED SENSOR

Engine	Year	Resistance (ohms)
All w/EEC IV, V	1989-97	190-250
	1998-00	170-270

TRANSMISSION RANGE SENSOR

Engine	Year	Resistance Ohms @ Position
All w/EECV	1996-00	4152-4568 @ P
		1368-1512 @ R
		696-770 @ N
		380-420 @ D
		200-220 @ 2
		77-85 @ 1

ACTUATORS, OUTPUT
IDLE SPEED CONTROL

All FI engines with ISC.

Engine	Year	Resistance (ohms)
All w/EEC IV, V	1989-99	6-13
1.3L	1994-97	7.7-9.3
1.8L	1995-96	6-14
2.0L Probe	1995-97	10.7-12.3
2.5L Probe	1995-97	10.7-12.3
3.0L, 3.3L Villager	1993-00	10.0

FUEL INJECTORS

Engine	Year	Resistance (ohms)	Temperature (deg. F/C)
1.3L	1996-97	12-16	
1.9L: TBI	1989	1-2	
MFI	1989	2.0-2.7	—
2.3L OHC	1989	15-19	—
2.3L HSC	1989	13.5-16	—
2.3L OHC, 3.0L	1990-91	13-16	—
2.5L	1989	1-2	—
2.5L Probe	1996-97	12-16	—
3.0L ex. SHO	1989	15-18	—
3.0L SHO, 3.8L, 5.0L	1989	13.5-19	—
3.0L Villager	1996-98	10-14	—
3.8L	1999-00	9-16	—
4.6L CNG	1997-00	4-6	—
All ex. 2.3L OHC, 3.0L	1990-91	15-18	—
All	1992	13-16	—
All Others	1993-00	11-18	—

COMPUTER TIMING ADVANCE

1989-91 specifications are in addition to base timing.

Activate system test procedure. See "DIAGNOSTIC TROUBLE CODES" section. Check advance against specifications.

1992-98 degrees of advance are measured at indicated vehicle speed. Measurement requires a road test using Ford's EEC-IV Monitor Box (Rotunda 007-00018) or EC-IV Monitor Recorder (Rotunda 007-00021), or equivalent test equipment.

Test with engine at operating temperature.

COMPUTER TIMING ADVANCE Continued

Year	Engine	Advance
1989-91	All w/EEC IV	17-23

Engine	Year	Idle	Degrees of Advance 30 MPH/50 KPH	Degrees of Advance 55 MPH/90 KPH
2.0L Probe w/MT	1993-95	10-14	26-30	28-32
2.0L w/AT	1994-95	14-22	26-30	28-32
2.0L Probe	1996-97	15-20	25-35	28-33
Contour, Mystique, Cougar	1996-00	10-15	19-30	25-36
Escort, Tracer	1997-98	15-22	28-35	25-35
	1999-00	15-25	19-30	25-36
2.3L HSC	1992-94	15-20	35-39	41-45
2.3L Mustang MT	1992-93	18-20	22-28	22-32
AT	1992-93	12-18	22-28	28-31
2.5L Contour, Mystique, Cougar	1995-00	4-7	19-30	25-36
3.0L ex. SHO MT	1992-95	22-26	38-42	42-46
AT	1992-95	22-26	36-48	47-51
3.0L ex. DOHC Taurus, Sable	1996-99	24-30	34-42	33-46
Flexfuel	1996-99	24-30	34-45	33-43
Windstar	1996-99	15-20	20-35	20-44
Villager	1996-98	15	36	25-35
3.0L DOHC	1996-00	12-27	25-42	20-40
3.0L SHO	1992-95	10-15	26-34	33-38
3.2L SHO	1993-95	16-21	32-36	30-36
3.4L SHO	1996-99	5-10	31-39	29-41
3.8L FWD	1992-95	25-30	34-38	40-45
Police	1992-93	21-25	36-40	38-42
RWD Ex. Mustang	1992-95	16-21	32-36	30-36
Supercharged MT	1992-94	18-22	32-34	31-35
AT	1992-94	18-23	28-33	28-33
3.8L Mustang	1994-95	18-25	28-32	30-35
3.8L Windstar	1996-00	15-20	25-35	27-36
Thunderbird, Cougar	1996-97	15-20	25-35	31-40
Mustang: MT	1996-98	15-20	20-35	20-40
AT	1996-98	15-20	25-35	31-40
Mustang: MT	1999-00	17-23	20-35	20-40
AT	1999-00	17-23	25-35	31-40
4.6L Thunderbird, Cougar	1994-95	22	20-31	28-30
4.6L Mustang	1996-00	15-20	29-38	25-35
DOHC	1996-00	11-15	17-20	19-24
Thunderbird, Cougar	1996-97	15-20	30-41	29-40
Continental	1996-00	8-10	20-28	22-32
Town Car	1996-00	18	33-36	32-38
Mark VIII	1996-98	13-19	19-32	25-36
Crown Victoria, Grand Marquis	1996-00	15-18	33-36	32-35
CNG	1996-99	5-10	20-31	20-28
5.0L Mustang	1992-95	16-20	32-36	36-42
T-Bird, Cougar	1992-93	19-23	33-37	40-44
Mark VII	1992-93	22-26	32-36	34-38

ENGINE IDENTIFICATION

To identify any engine by the manufacturer's code, follow the four steps designated by the numbered blocks.

1 **MODEL YEAR IDENTIFICATION:** Refer to illustration of the certification label.

2 **ENGINE CODE LOCATION:** Refer to illustration of the certification label.

3 **ENGINE CODE:** In the "CODE" column, find the engine code determined in Step 2.

4 **ENGINE IDENTIFICATION:** On the line where the engine code appears, read to the right to identify the engine.

MODEL YEAR DESIGNATION:

Stated on Emission Control Information label in the engine compartment. Also indicated from 10th character of V.I.N.

2000—Y	1999—X	1998—W
1997—V	1996—T	1995—S
1994—R	1993—P	1992—N
1991—M	1990—L	1989—K

MODEL YEAR AND ENGINE IDENTIFICATION:

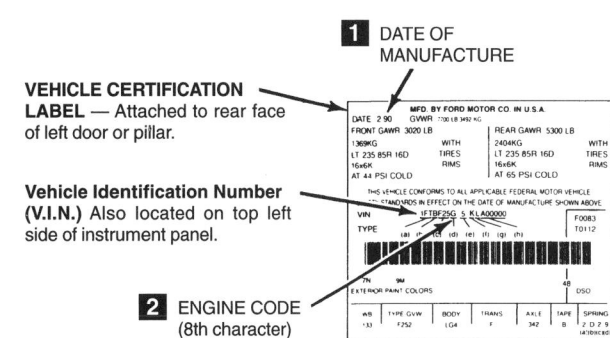

1 DATE OF MANUFACTURE

VEHICLE CERTIFICATION LABEL — Attached to rear face of left door or pillar.

Vehicle Identification Number (V.I.N.) Also located on top left side of instrument panel.

2 ENGINE CODE (8th character)

YEAR	CODE	CYL.	DISPL. liters	DISPL. cu. in.	Fuel System	HP
2000	C	4	2.5	152	MFI	119
	V	6	3.0 EFF	182 EFF	MFI	150
	U	6	3.0	182	MFI	150
	X	6	4.0	241	MFI	160
	E	6	4.0	241	MFI	210
	K	6	4.0 FF	241 FF	MFI	N/A
	2	6	4.2	256	MFI	195, 205[1]
	6	8	4.6 W	281 W	MFI	215
	W	8	4.6 R	281 R	MFI	215, 220[1]
	P	8	5.0	302	MFI	215
	L, Z	8	5.4	330	MFI	235-260[1]
	A	8	5.4	330	MFI	300
	3	8	5.4 SC	330 SC	MFI	360
	M	8	5.4 NG	330 NG	MFI	200
	S	10	6.8	415	MFI	265-310[1]
	F	8	7.3 TD	445 TD	MFI	215, 235[1]
1999	C	4	2.5	152	MFI	119
	V	6	3.0 EFF	182 EFF	MFI	152
	U	6	3.0	182	MFI	150
	X	6	4.0	241	MFI	160
	E	6	4.0	241	MFI	210
	2	6	4.2	256	MFI	195, 205[1]
	6	8	4.6 W	281 W	MFI	240
	W	8	4.6 R	281 R	MFI	215, 220[1]
	P	8	5.0	302	MFI	215
	L, Z	8	5.4	330	MFI	235, 260[1]
	A	8	5.4	330	MFI	300
	3	8	5.4 SC	330 SC	MFI	N/A
	M	8	5.4 NG	330 NG	MFI	195-200[1]
	S	10	6.8	415	MFI	265, 275[1]
	F	8	7.3 TD	445 TD	MFI	215, 235[1]
1998	C	4	2.5	152	MFI	119
	U	6	3.0	182	MFI	150
	X	6	4.0	241	MFI	160
	E	6	4.0	241	MFI	205
	2	6	4.2	256	MFI	200, 210[1]
	6	8	4.6 W	281 W	MFI	215, 220[1]
	W	8	4.6 R	281 R	MFI	215, 220[1]
	P	8	5.0	302	MFI	215
	L, Z	8	5.4	330	MFI	230, 235[1]
	M	8	5.4 NG	330 NG	MFI	190-200[1]
	H	8	5.8	351	MFI	205, 210[1]
	S	10	6.8	415	MFI	265
	F	8	7.3 TD	445 TD	MFI	215
	G	8	7.5	460	MFI	242-255[1]

YEAR	CODE	CYL.	DISPL. liters	DISPL. cu. in.	Fuel System	HP
1997	A	4	2.3	140	MFI	112
	U	6	3.0	182	MFI	140, 147[1]
	X	6	4.0	241	MFI	152, 160[1]
	E	6	4.0	241	MFI	205
	2	6	4.2	256	MFI	200-210[1]
	6	8	4.6 W	281 W	MFI	215, 220[1]
	W	8	4.6 R	281 R	MFI	215, 220[1]
	P	8	5.0	302	MFI	215
	L, M	8	5.4	330	MFI	230, 235[1]
	H	8	5.8	351	MFI	205, 210[1]
	S	10	6.8	415	MFI	265
	F	8	7.3 TD	445 TD	MFI	215
	G	8	7.5	460	MFI	242-255[1]
1996	A	4	2.3	140	MFI	112
	U	6	3.0	182	MFI	140-147[1]
	X	6	4.0	241	MFI	155-160[1]
	Y, 9, Z	6	4.9	300	MFI	145-150[1]
	N	8	5.0	302	MFI	199
	P	8	5.0	302	MFI	210
	H	8	5.8	351	MFI	205-210[1]
	F	8	7.3 TD	445 TD	MFI	210
	G	8	7.5	460	MFI	242-255[1]
1995	A	4	2.3	140	MFI	112
	U	6	3.0	182	MFI	135-145[1]
	X	6	4.0	241	MFI	155-160[1]
	Y, 9, Z	6	4.9	300	MFI	145-150[1]
	N	8	5.0	302	MFI	195-205[1]
	H	8	5.8	351	MFI	205-210[1]
	R	8	5.8 HP	351 HP	MFI	240
	F	8	7.3 TD	445 TD	MFI	210
	G	8	7.5	460	MFI	245-255[1]
1994	A	4	2.3	140	MFI	98, 100[1]
	U	6	3.0	182	MFI	135, 145[1]
	X	6	4.0	241	MFI	145-160[1]
	Y, 9, Z	6	4.9	300	MFI	145, 150[1]
	N	8	5.0	302	MFI	185
	H	8	5.8	351	MFI	200
	R	8	5.8 HP	351 HP	MFI	240
	M	8	7.3 D	445 D	MFI	165, 185[1]
	K	8	7.3 TD	445 TD	MFI	190
	F	8	7.3 TD	445 TD	MFI	200-210[1]
	G	8	7.5	460	MFI	230, 245[1]
1993	A	4	2.3	140	MFI	100
	U	6	3.0	182	MFI	135-145[1]

ENGINE IDENTIFICATION Continued

4 ENGINE IDENTIFICATION

YEAR	3 ENGINE CODE	CYL.	DISPL. liters	DISPL. cu. in.	Fuel System	HP
1993 Cont'd.	X	.6	4.0	241	MFI	145-160[1]
	Y	.6	4.9	300	MFI	145-160[1]
	N	.8	5.0	302	MFI	185
	H	.8	5.8	351	MFI	200
	R	.8	5.8 HP	351 HP	MFI	240
	M	.8	7.3 D	445 D	MFI	160-185[1]
	C	.8	7.3 TD	445 TD	MFI	190
	G	.8	7.5	460	MFI	230
1992	A	.4	2.3	140	MFI	100
	T	.6	2.9	179	MFI	140
	U	.6	3.0	182	MFI	145
	X	.6	4.0	241	MFI	145, 160[1]
	Y	.6	4.9	300	MFI	145, 160[1]
	N	.8	5.0	302	MFI	185
	H	.8	5.8	351	MFI	200
	M	.8	7.3 D	445 D	MFI	160, 180[1]
	G	.8	7.5	460	MFI	230
1991	A	.4	2.3	140	MFI	100
	T	.6	2.9	179	MFI	140
	U	.6	3.0	182	MFI	145
	X	.6	4.0	241	MFI	155, 160[1]
	Y	.6	4.9	300	MFI	145, 150[1]
	N	.8	5.0	302	MFI	185
	H	.8	5.8	351	MFI	200

4 ENGINE IDENTIFICATION

YEAR	3 ENGINE CODE	CYL.	DISPL. liters	DISPL. cu. in.	Fuel System	HP
1991 Cont'd.	M	.8	7.3 D	445 D	MFI	160, 180[1]
	G	.8	7.5	460	MFI	230
1990	A	.4	2.3	140	MFI	100
	T	.6	2.9	179	MFI	140
	U	.6	3.0	182	MFI	145
	X	.6	4.0	244	MFI	155, 160[1]
	Y	.6	4.9	300	MFI	145, 150[1]
	N	.8	5.0	302	MFI	185
	H	.8	5.8	351	MFI	210
	M	.8	7.3 D	445 D	MFI	160, 180[1]
	G	.8	7.5	460	MFI	230
1989	A	.4	2.3	140	MFI	100
	T	.6	2.9	179	MFI	140
	U	.6	3.0	182	MFI	145
	Y	.6	4.9	300	MFI	145, 150[1]
	N	.8	5.0	302	MFI	185
	H	.8	5.8	351	MFI	210
	M	.8	7.3 D	445 D	MFI	160, 180[1]
	G	.8	7.5	460	MFI	230

1 Engine horsepower varies with model installation.
D—Diesel.   MFI—Multiport Fuel Injection.   TD—Turbo Diesel.
HP—High Performance.   2V—Two Venturi Carburetor.   FF—Flexible Fuel
4V—Four Venturi Carburetor.   W—Windsor engine.   R—Romeo engine.
NG—Natural Gas.   SC—Supercharged.   EFF—Ethanol Flexible Fuel.

UNDERHOOD SERVICE SPECIFICATIONS

FDTTU1   CYLINDER NUMBERING SEQUENCE   FDTTU1

4-CYL. FIRING ORDER: 1 3 4 2

V6-CYL. FIRING ORDER: 1 4 2 5 3 6

— Front of car —

1989-92 2.3L (140)	1993-97 2.3L (140) 1998-00 2.5L (152)	2.9L (179)	1989-94 3.0L (182)	4.0L (241) ex. SOHC 1995-00 3.0L (182) 1997-00 4.2L (256)	1997-00 4.0L (241) SOHC Explorer, Mountaineer

6-CYL. FIRING ORDER: 1 5 3 6 2 4

8-CYL. FIRING ORDER: 4.6L, 5.0L (Code P), 5.4L, 5.8L 1 3 7 2 6 5 4 8

All Other 8-cyl. 1 5 4 2 6 3 7 8

10-CYL. FIRING ORDER: 1 6 5 10 2 7 3 8 4 9

— Front of car —

1989-96 4.9L (300)	1997-99 4.6L (281)	2000 4.6L (281), 5.4L (330) (Coil-on-plug)	1996-00 5.0L (302) Explorer, Mountaineer	All Other 8-cyl.	6.8L (415) V-10 (Coil-on-plug)

TIMING MARK

No Timing Marks on These Engines

4.2L (256)

BTDC 30° 20° 10° 0° / ATDC 10°

2.0L (122), 2.3L (140), 2.5L (152)

BTDC 33° 27° 20° 12° 0°

2.9L (179)

TDC 0° 10° 20° 30° BTDC

3.0L (182)

FORD TRUCKS
1989-2000 Includes Mercury Mountaineer, Lincoln Navigator,
Mazda Navajo, B2300, B2500, B3000, B4000 Trucks

UNDERHOOD SERVICE SPECIFICATIONS

FDTTU2   FDTTU2

TIMING MARK

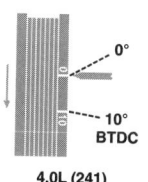

4.0L (241)

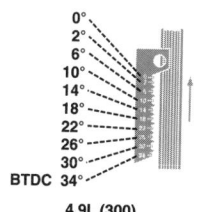

4.9L (300)

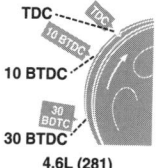

4.6L (281)
5.4L (330)
6.8L (415)

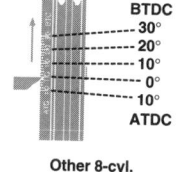

Other 8-cyl.

ELECTRICAL AND IGNITION SYSTEMS

BATTERY

Engine	Year	STANDARD BCI Group No.	STANDARD Crank. Perf.	OPTIONAL BCI Group No.	OPTIONAL Crank. Perf.
Ranger, Bronco II, Explorer, Mountaineer					
4-cyl.					
2.3L	1989-96	58	540[2]	65	650
	1997	59	540	65	650
2.5L	1998-00	59	540	—	—
V-6					
2.9L (177) Ranger	1989-92	58	540	65	650
Bronco II	1989-90	65	650	—	—
2.9L Explorer	1991-92	65	650	65	850
3.0L	1991-96	58	540[2]	65	650
	1997	59	540	65	650
2.5L	1998	59	540	—	—
4.0L	1991-96	65	650	65	850
	1997-98	65	650	—	—
F-Series: 6-cyl., V-6					
All	1989-96	65	650	65	850
	1997-00	59	540	65	750
8-cyl.					
All Gas	1989-96	65	650	65	850
	1997-00	59	540	65	750
All Diesel	1989-96	65	850	—	—
	1997-00	65[1]	750	—	—
Aerostar					
3.0L, 4.0L	1989-97	65	650	—	—
Econoline					
7.5L (460), all					
passenger vans	1989	64	535	—	—
6 cyl., V8 Gas	1989-91	64	535	—	—
	1992-96	65	650	65	850
	1997-00	65	650	65	750
6.9L (421), 7.3L Diesel	1989-91	27[1]	700	—	—
7.3L Diesel: Left	1992-96	65	850	—	—
Right	1992-96	50	600	—	—
7.3L Diesel	1997-00	65[1]	750	—	—
Auxiliary	1989-91	24F	350	—	—
	1992-96	50	400	—	—
	1997-00	65	625	—	—
Bronco, Expedition, Navigator					
All	1989-96	65	650	65	850
	1997-00	65	650	65	750

1 Requires two batteries.
2 Super Cab, 65 650.

GENERATOR

Ampere rated output is stamped on housing.

Application	Rated Output	Test Output
1989 Rear term.	40, 60	1
Side term.	70, 100	1
Int. regl.	40, 60, 65	1
1990-91 Ranger, Aerostar	75, 80	2
Bronco II	80	2
E-series	70, 100	2
F-series	60, 70, 75	2
Bronco	70, 75	2

GENERATOR Continued

Application	Rated Output	Test Output
1992-94 F-series	40, 60, 70, 75, 80, 95, 100, 130	2
1992-95 Aerostar, Ranger, Explorer	95, 130	2
Bronco	75, 95, 130	2
E-series	95, 130, 165	2
1995 F Series	60, 75, 80, 95, 130, 165	2
1996-00 Gasoline	95	76 @ 2000
	130	87 @ 2000
Diesel	130	87 @ 2000
	215	1600 @ 1750
1997-00 Explorer, Mountaineer	90	45 @ 2000
	110	60 @ 2000
1998-00 Expedition, Navigator	130	87 @ 2000

1 If rated output cannot be obtained at 2000 rpm, engine speed may be increased to a maximum of 2900 rpm.
2 Output at 2000 rpm should be near or over the rated output.

REGULATOR

1989-95: Measure battery voltage and record figure. With engine operating off idle and all secondary electrical systems turned off, regulated voltage should be no greater than 3.0 volts above recorded figure. Turn on headlights and set heater blower to high. Regulated voltage off idle should be no less than 0.5 volts above recorded figure.

1996-00: Voltage averages between 14.1-15.1. Measure battery voltage with engine above idle speed, voltage should be no less than 0.5 volts (loaded) and 2.5 volts (unloaded).

STARTER

Application	Year	Cranking Voltage (min. volts)	Ampere Draw @ Cranking Speed	Engine RPM
4-cyl., V6	1989-90	9.6	150-200	180-250
4.0L	1990	9.6	140-200	170-220
4-cyl., V6	1991-92	9.6	140-200	170-250
4-cyl., V6	1993-00	9.6	130-220	140-220
6-cyl., V8:				
4" or 101.60 mm dia.	1989-91	9.6	150-200	180-250
4½" or 114.3 mm dia.	1989-91	9.6	150-180	150-290
6-cyl. V6, V8	1992	9.6	140-200	200-250
6-cyl. V6, V8	1993-00	9.6	130-220	140-220
8-cyl. Diesel	1989-91	—	430-530	170-230

SPARK PLUGS

Engine	Year	Gap (inches)	Gap (mm)	Torque (ft-lb)
2.3L (140)	1989-97	.042-.046	1.07-1.17	10-15
2.5L	1998-00	.042-.046	1.07-1.17	10-15
3.0L	1989-00	.042-.046	1.07-1.17	10-15
4.0L	1990-00	.052-.056	1.22-1.32	10-15
4.2L, 4.6L	1997-00	.052-.056	1.22-1.32	7-15
4.9L (300)	1989-96	.042-.046	1.07-1.17	15-20
5.0L	1995-00	.052-.056	1.07-1.17	7-15
5.4L, 6.8L	1997-00	.052-.056	1.22-1.32	7-15
5.8L, 7.5L	1989-98	.042-.046	1.07-1.17	10-15

FORD TRUCKS
1989-2000 Includes Mercury Mountaineer, Lincoln Navigator, Mazda Navajo, B2300, B2500, B3000, B4000 Trucks

IGNITION COIL

For testing and adjustment diagrams, see Appendix A.

Winding Resistance (ohms at 75°F or 24°C)

Application	Year	Windings	Resistance (ohms)
All w/coil pack	1995-00	Primary	0.50
		Secondary	12,000-14,500
All w/coil on plug	1997-00	Primary	0.3-0.8
		Secondary	5500

BASE TIMING

FOR TESTING AND ADJUSTMENT DIAGRAMS, SEE APPENDIX C.

Set timing at Before Top Dead Center unless otherwise specified. Set timing below rpm setting listed or at idle if not specified.

Only reset timing if more than ±2 degrees from specifications listed.

Disconnect and plug distributor vacuum hose as equipped.

Engines with EEC IV, V, disconnect single wire, connector or shorting bar from two-wire connector at distributor. 1996, when shorting bar is replaced, timing should be at check value.

1989-95 2.3L:

1991-95 4.0L: Connect EDIS checker and press SAW key. Timing should heat set valve. With button released, timing should be at check value.

1996-97: Connect a Scan tool and access check timing function.

Engine	Year	Man. Trans. (degrees) @ RPM	Auto. Trans. (degrees) @ RPM
2.3L: Set	1989-95	10[1]	10[1]
Check	1992-95	16 min.	16 min.
2.3L	1996-97	10±2[1]	10±2[1]
2.5L	1998-00	10±2[1]	10±2[1]
2.9L (177)	1989-92	10	10
3.0L (182)	1989-95	10	10
	1996-00	10±2[1]	10±2[1]
4.0L: Set	1990-95	10[1]	10[1]
Check	1992-95	15 min.	15 min.
4.0L	1996-00	10±2[1]	10±2[1]
4.2L, 4.6L	1997-00	10±2[1]	10±2[1]
4.9L (300)	1989-95	10	10
	1996	10±3	10±3
Check	1996	18 min.	18 min.
5.0L (302)	1989-95	10	10
	1996	10±3	10±3
Check	1996	18 min.	18 min.
5.4L	1997-00	10±2[1]	10±2[1]
5.8L (351)	1989-95	10	10
	1996-97	10±3	10±3
Check	1996-97	18 min.	18 min.
6.8L	1997-00	10±2[1]	10±2[1]
7.5L (460) FI	1989-95	10	10
	1996-97	10±3	10±3
Check	1996-97	18 min.	18 min.

1 Timing not adjustable.

FUEL SYSTEM

FUEL SYSTEM PRESSURE

FOR TESTING AND ADJUSTMENT DIAGRAMS, SEE APPENDIX D.

Engine	Year	Pressure PSI	Pressure RPM
Fuel Injected:			
2.3L (140)	1989-97	35-45	ign. on
		30-45	idle
2.5L	1998-00	56-72	ign. on
2.9L (179), 3.0L (182), 4.0L	1989-97	35-45	ign. on
		30-45	idle
Ranger	1998-00	56-72	ign. on
Flexfuel	1998	47-63	ign. on
	1999	55-75	ign. on
Others	1998-00	30-45	ign. on
4.2L	1997	35-45	ign. on
		30-45	idle
	1998-00	30-45	ign. on

FUEL SYSTEM PRESSURE Continued

Engine	Year	Pressure PSI	Pressure RPM
4.9L (300)	1989-94	50-60	ign. on
		45-60	idle
	1995-96	35-45	ign. on
		30-45	idle
V8, V10	1989-97	35-45	ign. on
		30-45	idle
	1998-00	30-45	ign. on

IDLE SPEED W/COMPUTER CONTROL

FOR TESTING AND ADJUSTMENT DIAGRAMS, SEE APPENDIX E.

Note: W/FI, if idle speed is higher than the specified checking speed, perform a system check before attempting to adjust the idle speed.

Midpoint of range given is the preferred setting speed.

1989-95 2.9L, 7.5L FI:
1990-91 4.0L:
1989-94 2.3L: With engine at operating temperature and not running, disconnect air bypass valve electrical lead. Start engine, run at 2500 rpm for 30 seconds and check setting speed against specifications.

1989-94 3.0L (182): Disconnect spout connector and install PCV special tool. Disconnect air bypass valve electrical lead and adjust idle to specified setting speed.

1989-90 4.9L, 5.0L, 5.8L:
1991 5.0L, 5.8L HD early, 1992-95 5.0L ex. w/ E4OD trans.: Install a .050 (4.9L, 5.0L w/AT) or .030 (5.0L w/MT, 5.8L) feeler gauge between throttle plate stop screw and throttle lever. Disconnect ISC electrical lead and spout connector, start engine. Adjust idle to specified setting value.

1991-95 5.0L w/E4OD trans., 5.8L LD, 5.8L HD (Some), 1992-95, 4.9L: Connect a Scan tool and follow the tool manufacturer's instructions on Ford Idle Speed Setting. A constant pulse from the tool means that the idle speed is within limits. A pulse of 8 times per second indicates that the throttle position sensor is out of range due to over adjustment. A pulse of 4 times per second indicates that the base idle is too fast. A pulse of 1 per second indicates that the base idle speed is too slow.

If the idle is slow, inspect for a plate orifice plug. Remove it and turn the idle screw. Make adjustment until a steady pulse is indicated.

If the idle is too fast, inspect the throttle plate orifice. If there is a plug in it, diagnosis of the system is needed. If there is no plug, block the orifice with tape, start the engine and check the idle speed. If it is still too fast, diagnosis of the system is needed. Once repairs have been made to the system, the idle speed can be adjusted. Turn the idle speed screw until the Scan tool pulse is constant.

1995 2.3L, 3.0L Ranger, 4.0L:
1995 Ranger, Explorer:
1996-98 All:
If idle is not at specified value, remove cables from throttle body and inspect throttle return screw. If the throttle screw does not contact the throttle linkage lever arm, remove the clean air tube and verify that throttle plate is not obstructed and rotates fully closed. If the screw still does not make contact, place a .002-inch feeler gauge between the screw and lever arm. Turn the screw until it just touches the feeler gauge. Remove the gauge and adjust the screw clockwise ½ turn. Start the engine. If idle is still not at specified checking speed, further diagnosis of the system is needed.

1999-00 All:
Check idle speed against specified value. If idle is not within the range specified, further diagnosis of the system is needed.

ALL FUEL INJECTED
1991-94 Others, when no specifications appear in Setting Speeed column: Idle speed is adjustable only when using special tester.

Engine	Year	Transmission	Setting Speed	Checking Speed
2.3L	1989-90	MT	575[1]	645-795
		AT	575 N[1]	575-725 D
2.3L	1991	MT	475-575	645-795
		AT	475-575 N	575-725 D
2.3L	1992	MT	450-750	750-900
		AT	500-800 N	680-880 N
2.3L	1993-94	MT	450-750	750-900
		AT	500-800 N	680-880 N
2.3L, 2.5L	1995-98	MT	—	695-745
		AT	—	745-795 N
	1999-00	MT	—	760-830
		AT	—	760-820 N
2.9L	1989-90	MT	725	850
		AT	725 N	800 N

FORD TRUCKS
1989-2000 Includes Mercury Mountaineer, Lincoln Navigator, Mazda Navajo, B2300, B2500, B3000, B4000 Trucks
UNDERHOOD SERVICE SPECIFICATIONS
FDTTU4

FDTTU4

IDLE SPEED W/COMPUTER CONTROL Continued
ALL FUEL INJECTED Continued

Engine	Year	Transmission	Setting Speed	Checking Speed
2.9L	1991	MT	700	850
		AT	700 N	800 D
2.9L	1992	MT	700	810-890
3.0L	1989-90	MT	725	760-830
		AT	625 D	620-720 D
3.0L	1991	MT	550-650	—
		AT	550-650 N	—
3.0L	1992-94	MT	550-650	780-880
		AT	550-650 N	710-810 N
3.0L Aerostar	1995	AT	550-650 N	710-810 N
	1996-97	AT	—	725-775 N
3.0L Ranger, B3000	1995-98	MT	—	825-875
		AT	—	875-925 N
	1999-00	MT	—	760-800
		AT	—	880-920 N
4.0L	1990-91	MT	675	—
		AT	675 N	—
4.0L	1992-94		2	730-830
			2	730-830 N
4.0L ex. OHC	1995-98	MT	—	725-775
Ranger		AT	—	800-850 N
Others		AT	—	725-775 N
4.0L ex. OHC Ranger	1999-00	MT	—	760-800
		AT	—	760-830 N
Others		MT	—	715-810
		AT	—	750-830 N
4.0L SOHC	1997-98	AT	—	725-775 N
	1999-00	AT	—	750-830 N
4.2L	1997-98	MT	—	725-775
		AT	—	800-850 N
	1999-00	MT	—	680-830
		AT	—	680-830 N
4.6L	1997-98	MT	—	725-775
		AT	—	800-850 N
	1999-00	MT	—	680-830
		AT	—	680-830 N
4.9L w/calibr. 7-52ER, JR, KR, MR, QR, RR, ZR; 9-72JR	1989	MT	750	—
4.9L	1989	MT	650	—
	1989	AT	750 N	—
4.9L w/calibr. 7-52ER, JR, KR, MR, QR, RR, ZR; 9-72JR	1989	AT	650 N	—
4.9L	1990	MT	700	650-750
w/decal DEN	1990	MT	700	625-725
w/decal DES, DEY, DEZ	1990	MT	700	590-690
4.9L	1990	AT	675 N	550-650 D
w/E40D trans.	1990	AT	675 N	525-625 D
4.9L	1991	MT	2	700
		AT	2	600 D
w/decal G5A, G5D, G5H, G5L		AT	2	575 D
w/decal GHZ, GFJ, G5J		AT	2	640 D
4.9L	1992-95	MT	2	700-800
3-speed	1992-95	AT	2	600-700 N
4-speed	1992-94	AT	2	670-770 N
	1995		2	640-740 N
4.9L	1996	MT	—	725-775
		AT	—	800-850 N
5.0L (302)	1989-90	MT	700	—
		AT	675 N	—
5.0L	1991	MT	550-850	—
3-speed	1991	AT	525-825 N	—
4-speed	1991	AT	2	640-740
5.0L	1992-94	MT	550-850	660-760
3-speed	1992-94	AT	525-825 N	700-750 N
4-speed	1992-94	AT	2	640-740 N
5.0L	1995	MT	650-750	760-870
Ex. E40D	1995	AT	625-725	700-750 N
E40D	1995	AT	2	640-740 N
5.0L	1996-97	MT	—	725-775
	1996	AT	—	800-850 N
	1997-98	AT	—	725-775 N
	1999	AT	—	700-750 N
5.4L	1997-98	MT	—	800-850 N
		AT	—	800-850 N

IDLE SPEED W/COMPUTER CONTROL Continued
ALL FUEL INJECTED Continued

Engine	Year	Transmission	Setting Speed	Checking Speed
5.4L SOHC 4R70W	1999-00	MT	—	760-830
		AT	—	720 N
4R100		AT	—	760-830 N
5.4L DOHC Lightning		AT	—	760 N
Expedition, Navigator		AT	—	690-710 N
5.8L (351)	1989-90	MT	730	—
5.8L (351)	1989-90	AT	780 N	—
w/4-speed AT	1989-90	AT	730 N	—
5.8L: LD	1991	MT	2	750-850
		AT	2	750-850 N
HD, early	1991	MT	730	—
3-speed		AT	730 N	—
4-speed		AT	780 N	—
HD, late	1991	MT	2	750-850
		AT	2	750-850 N
5.8L	1993-95	MT	2	750-850
		AT	2	750-850 N
5.8L LD	1996	MT	—	725-775
		AT	—	800-850 N
5.8L HD	1996-97	MT	—	750-850
		AT	—	750-850 N
6.8L	1997-00	AT	—	750-800 N
7.3L DI Diesel	1994-96	MT	—	650
		AT	—	650 D
7.5L (460)	1989-94	MT	650	—
		AT	650 N	—
7.5L ex. 1996 Calif.	1995-96	MT	2	650-750
3-speed	1995-96	AT	2	770-870 N
4-speed	1995-96	AT	2	800-840 N
7.5L Calif.	1996-97	MT	—	725-775
	1996-97	AT	—	800-850 N

1 Reset to 600-650 N if carbon build-up problems in engine are encountered.
2 Idle speed is only adjustable with a Scan tool, see procedure.

ENGINE MECHANICAL

TIGHTENING TORQUES
FOR CYLINDER HEAD TORQUE SEQUENCES AND DIAGRAMS, SEE APPENDIX F.
Some fasteners are tightened in more than one step.
Some values are specified in inches.

		TORQUE FOOT-POUNDS/NEWTON METERS				
Engine	Year	Cylinder Head	Intake Manifold	Exhaust Manifold	Crankshaft Pulley	Water Pump
2.3L (140)	1989-93	50-60/ 68-81, 80-90/ 108-122	5-7/ 7-9, 14-21/ 19-28	178-204"/ 20-23, 20-30/ 27-41	103-133/ 140-180	15-22/ 19-29
2.3L, 2.5L	1994-00	51/70[3], +90-100°	19-28/ 26-38, 60-80	22/30, 45-59/ 60-80	103-133/ 140-180	15-22/ 19-29
2.9L (179)	1989-92	22/30, 51-55/ 70-75, +90°	6-11/ 8-15, 15-18/ 21-25	20-30/ 27-40	85-96/ 115-130	7-9/ 9-12
3.0L (182)	1989-93	37/50, 68/92	11/15, 18/24	19/25	93-121/ 125-165	7/10
4.0L ex. OHC	1990-93	24/32, +90°	6-11/ 8-15, 15-18/ 21-25	19/25	30-37/ 40-50, +80-90°	6-9/ 9-12
	1994-98	22-26/ 30-35, 52-56/ 70-75, +90°	6-8, 11/15, 15/21	20-27	30-37/ 40-50, +80-90°	6-9/ 9-12
	1999-00	48/65, 59-62/ 80-85, +90°	11/15	15-18/ 18-25	30-37/ 40-50, +85°	6-81 8-11
4.0L OHC	1997-00	25/35, +90°, +90°	9-10/ 10-14	15-18/ 18-25	44/60, +90°	6-81 8-11
4.2L	1997-00	14/20, 29/40, 36/50[5]	44"/5, 71-101"/ 8-12	15-22/ 20-30	20-28/ 28-36	15-22/ 20-30

FORD TRUCKS
1989-2000 Includes Mercury Mountaineer, Lincoln Navigator, Mazda Navajo, B2300, B2500, B3000, B4000 Trucks

CHEK-CHART

UNDERHOOD SERVICE SPECIFICATIONS

FDTTU5

FDTTU5

TIGHTENING TORQUES Continued

Engine	Year	Cylinder Head	Intake Manifold	Exhaust Manifold	Crankshaft Pulley	Water Pump
		TORQUE FOOT-POUNDS/NEWTON METERS				
4.6L, 5.4L, 6.8L	1997-00	27-31/ 32-43, +90°, +90°	18"/2, 6-8/ 8-12	13-17/ 18-22	34-39/ 47-53, +90°	15-22/ 20-30
4.9L (300)	1989-95	50-55/ 67-75, 60-65/ 82-88, 70-85/ 94-115	22-32/ 30-43	22-32/ 30-43	130-150/ 177-203	12-18/ 17-24
5.0L (302)	1989-97	55-65/ 75-88, 65-72/ 88-97⁴	23-25/ 32-33¹	18-24/ 25-32	70-90/ 95-122	12-18/ 17-24
	1998-99	25-35/ 37-47, 45-55/ 61-75, +90°	5-10/ 6-14 23-25 31-34	26/32	110-130/ 149-177	15-21/ 20-28
5.8L (351)	1989-97	85/115, 95/129, 105-112/ 143-151	23-25/ 32-33¹	18-24/ 25-32	70-90/ 95-122	12-18/ 17-24
7.3L (445) Diesel ex. DI	1989-94	65/88, 90/122, 100/135	24/33	35/47²	90/122	14/19
7.3L DI Diesel	1994-00	65/88, 85/115, 105/142	18/24	45/61	212/287	15/20
7.5L (460)	1989-97	70-80/ 95-108, 100-110/ 136-149, 130-140/ 177-189	8-12/ 11-16, 12-22/ 16-30, 22-35/ 30-47	22-30/ 30-48	70-90/ 95-122	12-18/ 16-24

1 With FI, upper to lower manifold, 12-18/17-24.
2 Retorque, again, to same specification.
3 Loosen all bolts and retighten to this specification.
4 With flanged bolts: 25-35/34-47, 45-55/61-75, +90°.
5 One bolt at a time: loosen 3 turns, torque short bolts to 15-22/20-30; long bolts to 30-36/40-50, then tighten all bolts 175-185°.

COMPRESSION PRESSURE

At cranking speed, engine temperature normalized, throttle open.

Engine	Year	PSI	Maximum Variation PSI
All	1989-00	Lowest reading cylinder must be more than 75% of the highest cylinder pressure.	

BELT TENSION

Without Automatic Tensioner
A belt in operation for 10 minutes is considered a used belt.
1989-95 Automatic tensioner used.
Deflection method: Table lists deflection at midpoint of belt segment.
Strand Tension method: Use a strand tension gauge. Measurements are in pounds.

Application	Year	Generator	Power Steering	Air Cond.	Air Pump
USED BELTS					
Strand Tension method					
Ranger, Bronco II: 4-cyl.	1989-92	140-160	—	—	—
V6	1989-92	110-130	—	—	—
Aerostar 3.0L	1989-94	110-130	80-100	140-160	—
7.5L	1989-95	—	—	—	110-130
NEW BELTS					
Strand Tension method					
Ranger, Bronco II: 4-cyl.	1989-92	150-190	—	—	—
V6	1989-92	120-160	—	—	—
Aerostar 3.0L	1989-94	120-160	110-140	150-190	—
7.5L	1989-95	—	—	—	160-200

BELT TENSION Continued

With Automatic Tensioner
Tension should be at specified value with index mark on pulley aligned with marks on tensioner. If marks are outside of range, replace the belt.

Engine	Year	Tension
2.3L, 3.0L ex. Aerostar	1993-95	—
4.0L	1991-95	108-132
4.9L	1989-93	90 min.
w/100A alt.	1989-93	117 min.
5.0L, 5.8L	1989-92	75 min.
w/100A alt.	1989-92	117 min.
5.0L, 5.8L	1993-96	51 min.
7.3L	1989-92	104 min.
Vac pump	1989-92	72 min.
7.3L	1993-94	70 min.
	1995	85 min.
7.5L PS & AC	1989-96	94 min.
All	1996-97	—

SERPENTINE BELT DIAGRAMS

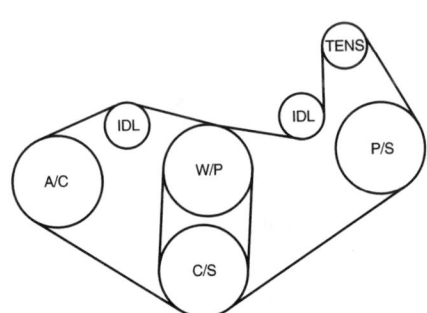

1989-91 2.3L

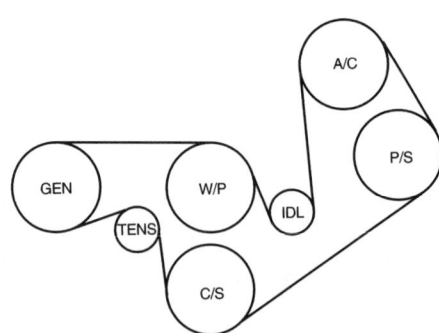

1992-00 2.3L, 2.5L w/PS

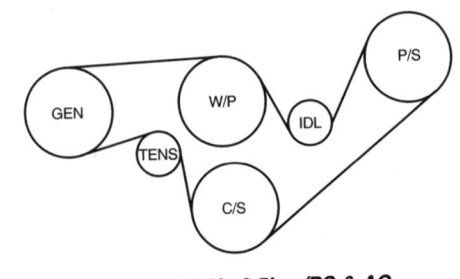

1992-00 2.3L, 2.5L w/PS & AC

FORD TRUCKS
1989-2000 Includes Mercury Mountaineer, Lincoln Navigator, Mazda Navajo, B2300, B2500, B3000, B4000 Trucks

SERPENTINE BELT DIAGRAMS Continued

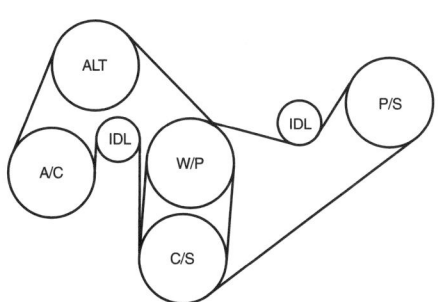

1990-94 3.0L Ranger
1992-94 3.0L Aerostar

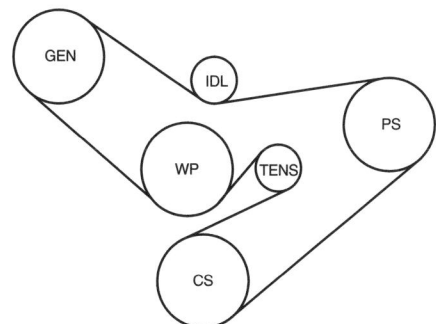

1995-00 3.0L Ranger w/o AC

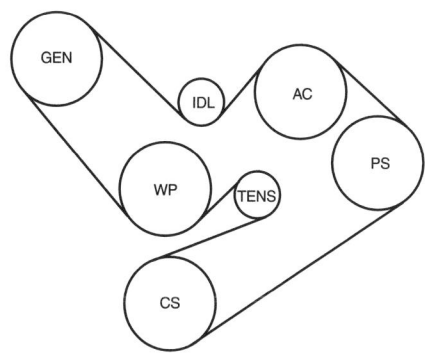

1995-00 3.0L Ranger w/AC

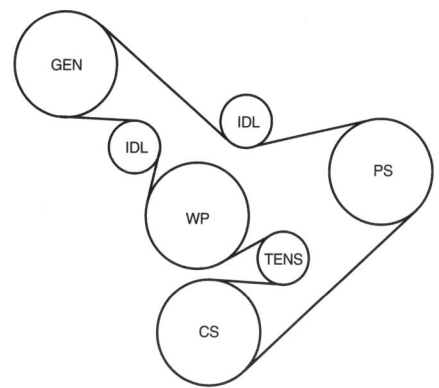

1995-97 3.0L Aerostar w/o AC

SERPENTINE BELT DIAGRAMS Continued

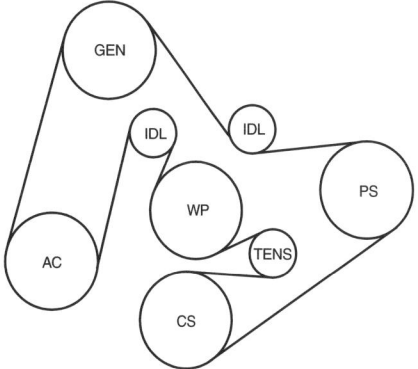

1995-97 3.0L Aerostar w/AC

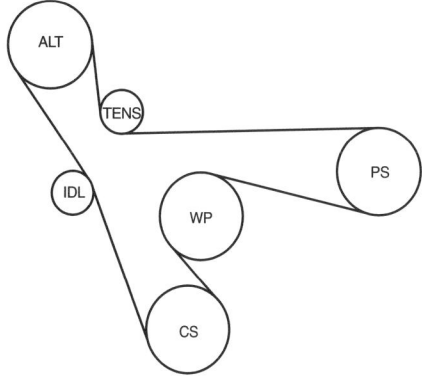

1990-94 4.0L w/o AC

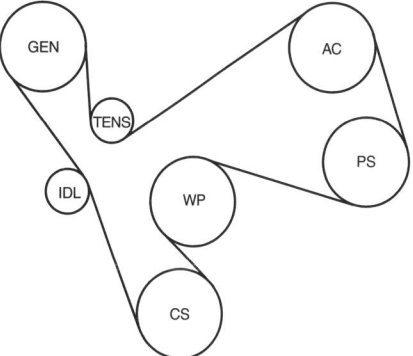

1990-94 4.0L w/AC

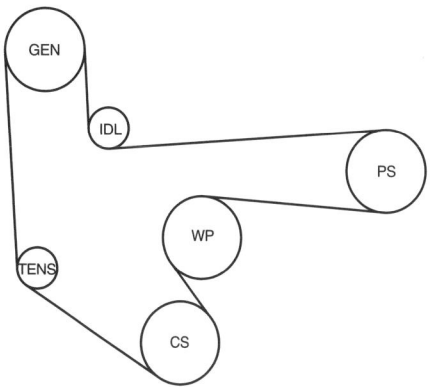

1995-00 4.0L ex. SOHC w/o AC

FORD TRUCKS
1989-2000 Includes Mercury Mountaineer, Lincoln Navigator, Mazda Navajo, B2300, B2500, B3000, B4000 Trucks

UNDERHOOD SERVICE SPECIFICATIONS

FDTTU7

FDTTU7

SERPENTINE BELT DIAGRAMS Continued

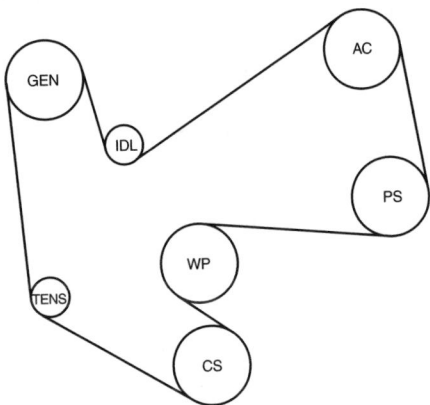

1995-00 4.0L ex. SOHC w/AC

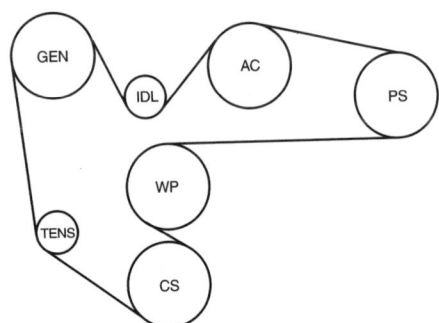

1996-00 4.0L SOHC

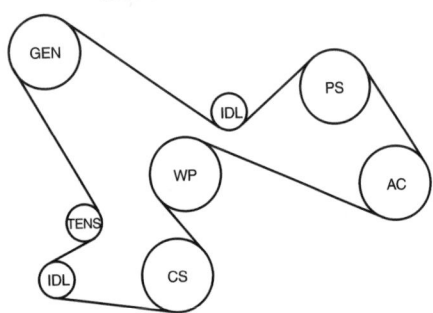

1995-00 5.0L Explorer, Mountaineer

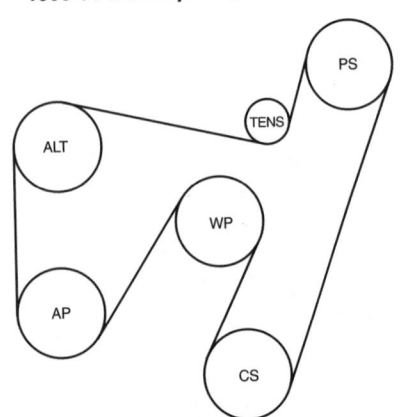

1989-97 4.9L w/o AC

SERPENTINE BELT DIAGRAMS Continued

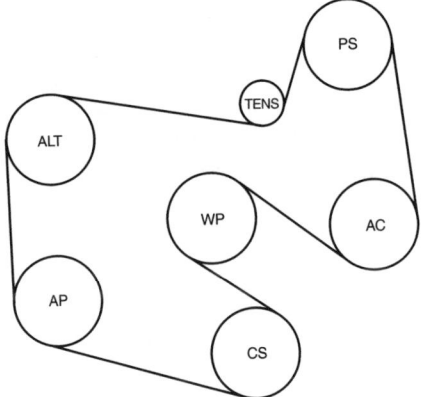

1989-97 4.9L w/AC

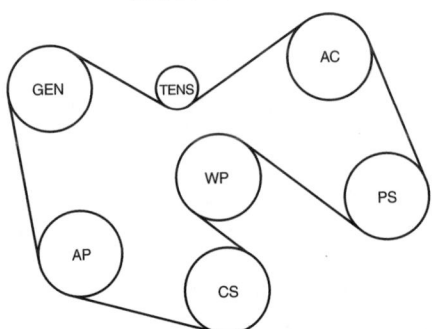

1989-92 5.0L, 5.8L

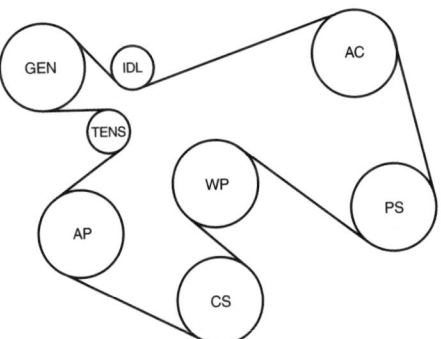

1993-97 5.0L, 5.8L

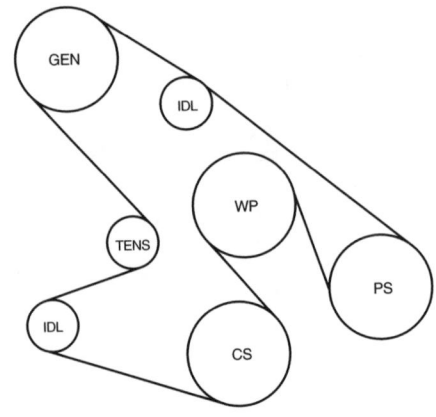

1997-00 4.2L w/o AC

FORD TRUCKS
1989-2000 Includes Mercury Mountaineer, Lincoln Navigator, Mazda Navajo, B2300, B2500, B3000, B4000 Trucks

UNDERHOOD SERVICE SPECIFICATIONS

FDTTU8   FDTTU8

SERPENTINE BELT DIAGRAMS Continued

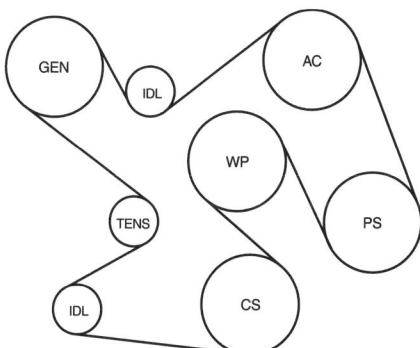

1997-00 4.2L w/AC

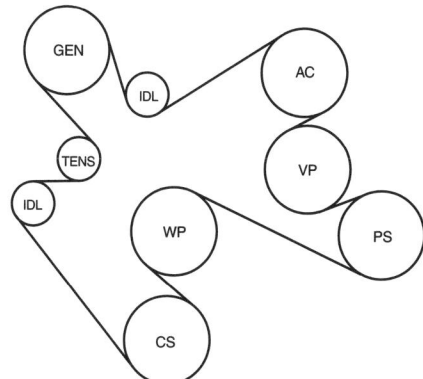

1994-98 7.3L DI Diesel

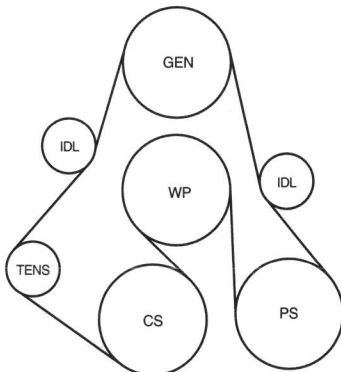

1997-00 4.6L, 5.4L, 8.0L w/o AC

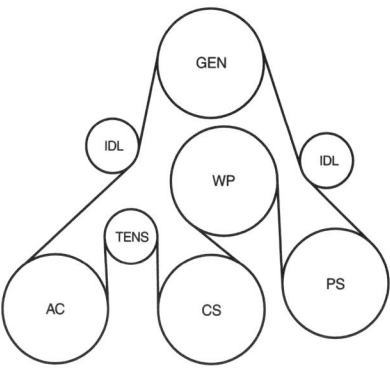

1997-00 4.6L, 5.4L, 8.0L w/AC

ENGINE COMPUTER SYSTEM

FOR TESTING AND ADJUSTMENT DIAGRAMS, SEE APPENDIX G.

DIAGNOSTIC TROUBLE CODES

1995 Ranger, Explorer
1996-00 All ex. 5.8L HD, 7.5L Calif: OBD-II system used. Connect a Scan tool and follow the manufacturer's instructions to retrieve codes.

MCU: Complicated procedure required to achieve valid codes. See shop manual. With key off, locate self-test connector. Connect a jumper wire from the upper right cavity to the second lower cavity from left. Connect an analog VOM from battery positive (+) terminal to lower second from right cavity (–). Remove PCV valve from valve cover and uncap restrictor in Secondary air injection vacuum control line (8-cyl. as equipped).

1989-94 EEC IV
1995 All ex. Ranger, Explorer
1996 5.8L HD, 7.5L ex. Calif.
Complicated procedure required to obtain valid codes. See shop manual. With engine at operating temperature and ignition off, locate SELF-TEST connector under hood. Connect a jumper wire between input connector (single terminal) and upper right cavity on connector. Connect an analog VOM to battery (+) and second bottom right cavity on connector. On later models w/3-digit codes, the MIL will flash codes. A four-second delay separates individual codes. SELF-TEST codes are revealed in a series of three separate test procedures (key on engine off, engine running, and continuous) and must be accessed in order.

Key on engine off: Place transmission in park or neutral, set parking brake, turn off all electrical equipment, place octane switch (2.3L SVO Turbo) in premium position. Activate SELF-TEST and place ignition key in run position, do not depress throttle. Observe and record service codes.

Engine running: Deactivate SELF-TEST. Start engine and run at greater than 2000 rpm for 2 minutes. Turn engine off, wait ten seconds & reactivate SELF-TEST. Start engine without depressing throttle. An engine ID code will be displayed (**Code 2**—4-cyl., **Code 3**—6-cyl., **Code 4**—8-cyl.), depress and release brake pedal once. Observe and record service codes.

Continuous: Allow engine to run at idle after all codes have been displayed. After approximately 2 minutes, continuous codes will be displayed. System will remain in continuous mode until ignition is switched off or SELF-TEST is deactivated.

1989 All w/EEC IV
1990 All ex. 5.0L w/E4OD transmission
1991 All ex. some with E4OD transmission
1992 2.9L, 5.0L & 5.8L w/o E4OD transmission, 7.3L & 7.5L w/E4OD
1993 7.3L w/E4OD transmission
Test condition: I—ignition on/engine off, R—engine running, C—continuous

Code Displayed	Test Condition	Results
10	R	Cylinder #1 low, cylinder balance test
11	I, R, C	Pass
12	R	RPM not within self test upper limit
13	R	RPM not within self test lower limit
13	I	D.C. motor did not move
13	C	D.C. motor does not follow dashpot
14	I, C	Ignition pickup circuit fault (Gas)
14	C	Engine RPM sensor circuit (Diesel)
15	I, C	ROM test failed or keep alive memory in continuous (1989)
15	I	ECM ROM test failed (1990-95)
15	C	ECM keep alive memory test failed (1990-95)
16	I	Ignition diagnostic module signal not received
16	R	RPM too low to perform oxygen sensor test
17	R	ISC RPM below self test range (1989)
18	C	Loss of tach input to processor, spout circuit grounded
18	C	Erratic input to processor (2.3L w/o distributor)
18	C	1, 2, 3, 4 primary coil circuit failure (1991-92 2.3L)
18	R	Spout circuit open
19	I	Failure in EEC reference voltage
19	C	CID circuit failure (4.0L)
19	R	Engine stumble during hard idle test
20	R	Cylinder #2 low, cylinder balance test
21	I, R	Coolant temperature sensor out of range
22	I, R, C	MAP/BARO sensor out of range
23	I, R	Throttle position sensor out of range (Gas)
23	I, R	Fuel injector pump lever out of range (Diesel)
24	I, R	Intake air temperature sensor out of range
24	C	Coil #1 primary circuit failure
25	R	Knock not sensed during dynamic response test
26	I, R	Transmission oil temp out of range (E4OD Trans)
27	R	Speed control servo leaks down during test
27	C	Insufficient input from vehicle speed sensor (1989)
27	C	Coil #2 primary circuit failure (1990-95)
28	C	Loss of tach, right side
28	I, R	Intake air temperature out of self test range (1990-95)
28	R	Speed control servo leaks up during test (others)
29	C	Insufficient input from vehicle speed sensor

FORD TRUCKS

DIAGNOSTIC TROUBLE CODES Continued

Code Displayed	Test Condition	Results
30	R	Cylinder #3 low, cylinder balance test
31	I, R, C	EPT/EVP below minimum voltage
32	I, R, C	EGR valve not seated (2.9L, 3.0L)
32	I, R, C	EPT/EVP voltage below closed limit (others, sonic EGR)
33	R, C	EGR valve not opening
34	R, C	EVP voltage above closed limit
35	I, R, C	EPT/EVP circuit above maximum voltage
36	R	Insufficient RPM increase during speed control test
37	R	Insufficient RPM decrease during speed control test
38	C	Idle tracking switch circuit open
39	C	AXOD lockup failed
40	R	Cylinder #4 low, cylinder balance test
41	R	Oxygen sensor circuit, system lean
41	C	No oxygen sensor switch detected
42	R	Oxygen sensor circuit, system rich
42	C	No oxygen sensor switch detected
43	C	Oxygen sensor lean at WOT
44	R	Secondary air injection system inoperative
45	C	Coil 1, 2, or 3 failure (4.0L)
45	C	Coil #1 primary circuit failure (others)
45	R	Secondary air upstream during self test
46	C	Coil #2 primary circuit failure
46	R	Secondary air not bypassed during self test
47	C	Spark timing error
47	I	4WD switch closed (E4OD)
47	I	Speed control command switches circuit (others)
48	C	Loss of secondary tach, left side (2.3L)
48	I	Speed control command switches circuit not functioning
49	C	1-2 shift error (E4OD)
49	I	Speed control ground circuit open
50	R	Cylinder #5 low, cylinder balance test
51	I, R, C	Engine coolant temperature sensor circuit open
52	I	Power steering pressure switch circuit open
52	R	Power steering pressure switch did not change states
53	I, C	Throttle position sensor circuit above maximum voltage (Gas)
53	I, R, C	Fuel injector pump lever circuit above maximum voltage (Diesel)
54	I, R, C	Intake air temperature circuit open
55	R	Key power circuit low or open
56	I, R, C	Volume air flow circuit above maximum voltage (Ex. w/E4OD)
56	I, C	Transmission oil temperature circuit open
57	I	Octane adjust service pin in use/circuit grounded
57	C	Transmission neutral pressure switch circuit open
58	I	Crank fuel delay service pin in use/circuit grounded
59	I	Idle adjust service pin in use/circuit grounded
59	C	E4OD 2-3 shift error
60	R	Cylinder #6 low, cylinder balance test
61	I, R, C	Engine coolant temperature circuit grounded
62	C	Converter clutch error (E4OD)
63	I, R, C	TPS below minimum voltage (Gas)
63	I, R, C	Fuel injector pump lever circuit below minimum voltage (Diesel)
64	I, R, C	Intake air temperature sensor circuit grounded
65	C	Never went to closed loop
65	R	Overdrive cancel switch (E4OD)
66	I, C	Volume air flow circuit input voltage below minimum (Ex. w/E4OD)
66	I, C	Transmission oil temperature circuit grounded (E4OD)
67	I, C	NDS circuit open/AC on during self test (Gas)
67	I, C	Manual lever position sensor out of range (Diesel)
68	I, R	Idle tracking switch failed/circuit grounded or open (All TBI)
69	C	E4OD 3-4 shift error
69	I, C	AXOD 3-2 circuit failed closed
70	C	Data communications link or ECM circuit failure
70	R	Cylinder #7 low, cylinder balance test
72	R	Insufficient MAP change during dynamic response test
73	I, R	Insufficient throttle position sensor change during dynamic response test
74	R	Brake switch circuit open
75	R	Brake switch circuit closed
76	R	Insufficient volume air flow change during dynamic response test
77	R	Operator error during dynamic response test
78	R	Power interrupt detected
79	I	AC on during self test
80	R	Cylinder #8 low, cylinder balance test
81	I	Air management circuit #2 failure
82	I	Air management circuit #1 failure
83	I	Electric fan circuit failure (others)
84	I, R	Electronic vacuum regulator circuit failure
85	I	Canister purge circuit

DIAGNOSTIC TROUBLE CODES Continued

Code Displayed	Test Condition	Results
86	C	Adaptive rich limit reached
86	R	4-3 shift solenoid circuit failure (E4OD)
87	I, C	Fuel pump circuit failure
88	I	Electric fan circuit failure
88	C	Loss of dual plug input control
89	I	Lockup solenoid circuit failure (4.0L)
89	I	Clutch converter override circuit failure
90	R	PASSED (cylinder balance test)
91	I	Shift solenoid #1 (E4OD)
91	R, C	Oxygen sensor input indicates system lean
92	I	Shift solenoid #2 (E4OD)
92	R, C	Oxygen sensor input indicates system rich
93	I	Coast clutch solenoid circuit (E4OD)
93	I	Throttle position sensor circuit input low at max. D.C. motor extension (others)
94	I	Converter clutch solenoid circuit (E4OD)
94	R	Secondary air system inoperative
95	I, C	Fuel pump circuit open, ECM to motor ground
96	I, C	Fuel pump circuit open, ECM to battery
97	I	Overdrive cancel indicator light circuit (E4OD)
98	I	Electronic pressure control drive open in ECM (E4OD)
98	R	Hard fault present
99	I, C	Electronic pressure control circuit (E4OD)
99	R	Idle not learned, ignore codes 12, 13

1990 5.0L w/E4OD transmission
1991-92 All models w/three-digit codes
1993-94 All ex. Diesel with E4OD transmission
1995 All ex. Ranger, Explorer; Diesel w/E4OD transmission
1996-97 5.8L HD, 7.5L ex. Calif.

Code Displayed	Results
10	Cylinder #1 low, cylinder balance test
20	Cylinder #2 low, cylinder balance test
30	Cylinder #3 low, cylinder balance test
40	Cylinder #4 low, cylinder balance test
50	Cylinder #5 low, cylinder balance test
60	Cylinder #6 low, cylinder balance test
70	Cylinder #7 low, cylinder balance test
80	Cylinder #8 low, cylinder balance test
90	Passed cylinder balance test
111	System PASS
112	Intake air temperature sensor circuit grounded
113	Intake air temperature sensor circuit open
114	Intake air temperature sensor out of range
116	Engine coolant temperature sensor out of range
117	Engine coolant sensor temperature circuit grounded
118	Engine coolant sensor temperature circuit open
121	Throttle position sensor out of range
122	Throttle position sensor circuit grounded
123	Throttle position sensor circuit open
124	Throttle position sensor voltage higher than expected
125	Throttle position sensor voltage lower than expected
126	MAP/BARO sensor out of range
128	MAP sensor vacuum hose damaged or disconnected
129	Insufficient MAP/MAF change during dynamic response test
136	System indicates lean (bank #2, driver side)
137	System indicates rich (bank #2, driver side)
138	Cold start injector
144	No oxygen sensor switch detected
157	MAF sensor circuit below minimum voltage
158	MAF sensor circuit above maximum voltage
159	MAF higher or lower than expected
167	Insufficient throttle change during dynamic response test
171	Oxygen sensor unable to switch, adaptive fuel at limit (bank #1, passenger side)
172	System indicates lean (bank #1, passenger side)
173	System indicates rich (bank #1, passenger side)
174	Slow oxygen sensor switching
175	Fuel system at adaptive limits, oxygen sensor unable to switch (bank #2, driver side)
176	No oxygen sensor switch detected, system lean (bank #2, driver side)
177	No oxygen sensor switch detected, system rich (bank #2, driver side)
179	Adaptive fuel lean limit reached at part throttle, system rich (bank #1, passenger side)
181	Adaptive fuel rich limit reached at part throttle, system lean (bank #1, passenger side)
182	Adaptive fuel lean limit reached at idle, system rich (bank #1, passenger side)

DIAGNOSTIC TROUBLE CODES Continued

Code Displayed	Results
183	Adaptive fuel rich limit reached at idle, system lean (bank #1, passenger side)
184	Mass air flow higher than expected
185	Mass air flow lower than expected
186	Injector pulsewidth higher than expected (models w/barometric pressure sensor)
186	Injector pulsewidth higher or MAF lower than expected (models w/o barometric pressure sensor)
187	Injector pulsewidth lower than expected (models w/barometric pressure sensor)
187	Injector pulsewidth lower or MAF lower than expected (models w/o barometric pressure sensor)
188	Adaptive fuel lean limit reached at part throttle, system rich (bank #2, driver side)
189	Adaptive fuel rich limit reached at part throttle, system lean (bank #2, driver side)
190	Adaptive fuel lean limit reached at idle, system rich (bank #2, driver side)
191	Adaptive fuel rich limit reached at idle, system lean (bank #2, driver side)
193	Flexible fuel sensor circuit failure
211	Profile ignition pickup circuit failure
212	Loss of ignition diagnostic module input to processor/spout circuit grounded
213	Spout circuit open
214	Cylinder identification circuit failure
215	Powertrain control module detected coil #1 primary circuit failure
216	Powertrain control module detected coil #2 primary circuit failure
217	Powertrain control module detected coil #3 primary circuit failure
218	Loss of ignition diagnostic module signal, left side
219	Spark timing defaulted to 10 degrees, spout circuit open
221	Spark timing error
222	Loss of ignition diagnostic module signal, right side
223	Loss of dual plug inhibit control
224	Powertrain control module detected coil 1, 2, 3, or 4 primary circuit failure
225	Knock not sensed during dynamic response test
226	Ignition diagnostic module signal not received
227	Crankshaft position sensor
232	Powertrain control module detected coil 1, 2, 3, or 4 primary circuit failure
233	Spark angle pulsewidth error
238	Powertrain control module detected coil #4 primary circuit failure
239	Crankshaft position signal received with engine off
241	EDIS to EEC processor Ignition diagnostic module pulsewidth transmission error
242	Operating in DIS failure mode
243	Secondary circuit failure
244	CID circuit fault present when cylinder balance test requested
311	Secondary air system inoperative (right side with dual O_2 sensors)
312	Secondary air misdirected during self test
313	Secondary air not bypassed during self test
314	Secondary air system inoperative (left side with dual O_2 sensors)
326	EGR circuit voltage lower than expected
327	EVP/EPT circuit below minimum voltage
328	EGR closed valve voltage lower than expected
332	Insufficient EGR flow detected
334	EGR closed valve voltage higher than expected
335	EGR sensor voltage higher or lower than expected
336	Exhaust pressure high/EGR circuit voltage higher than expected
337	EVP/EPT circuit above maximum voltage
338	Engine coolant temperature lower than expected
339	Engine coolant temperature higher than expected
341	Octane adjust service pin in use
411	Cannot control RPM during self test, idle low
412	Cannot control RPM during self test, idle high
415	Idle speed control system at minimum learning limit
416	Idle air control system at maximum learning limit
452	Insufficient input from vehicle speed sensor
453	Servo leaking down during test
454	Servo leaking up during test
455	Insufficient RPM increase during test
456	Insufficient RPM decrease during test
457	Speed control command switches circuit not functioning
458	Speed control command switches stuck or circuit grounded
459	Speed control ground circuit open
511	Powertrain control module read only memory test failed
512	Powertrain control module keep alive memory test failed
513	Failure in powertrain control module internal voltage
519	Power steering pressure switch circuit open
521	Power steering pressure switch circuit did not change states
522	Vehicle not in Park or Neutral during test
524	Low speed fuel pump circuit open, battery to PCM
525	Vehicle in gear/AC on
528	Clutch switch circuit failure
529	Data communications link or EEC processor circuit failure
532	Cluster control assembly circuit failure

DIAGNOSTIC TROUBLE CODES Continued

Code Displayed	Results
533	Data communications link or electronic instrument cluster circuit failure
536	Brake switch circuit failure
538	Insufficient RPM change during dynamic response test or invalid cylinder balance test due to throttle movement during test or CID sensor failure
539	AC/Defrost on during test
542	Fuel pump circuit open, EEC processor to motor ground
543	Fuel pump circuit open, EEC processor to battery
551	Inlet air control circuit failure
552	Air management circuit 1 failure
553	Air management circuit 2 failure
554	Fuel pressure regulator control circuit failure
555	Supercharger bypass solenoid circuit failure
556	Fuel pump relay primary circuit failure
557	Low speed fuel pump primary circuit failure
558	EGR vacuum regulator circuit failure
559	Air conditioning on relay circuit failure
562	Auxiliary electric fan circuit failure
563	High speed electric fan circuit failure
564	Electric fan circuit failure
565	Canister purge circuit failure
566	3-4 shift solenoid circuit failure
567	Speed control vent circuit failure
568	Speed control vacuum circuit failure
569	Auxiliary canister purge circuit failure
617	1-2 shift error
618	2-3 shift error
619	3-4 shift error
621	Shift solenoid circuit #1 failure
622	Shift solenoid circuit #2 failure
624	Electronic pressure regulator control circuit failure
625	Electronic pressure regulator control driver open in PCM
626	Coast clutch solenoid circuit failure
627	Converter clutch control solenoid circuit failure
628	Excessive converter clutch slippage
629	Converter clutch solenoid circuit failure
631	Overdrive cancel indicator light circuit failure
632	Overdrive cancel switch circuit did not change states
633	4WD switch closed during test
634	Manual lever position sensor voltage higher or lower than expected
636	Transmission oil temperature higher or lower than expected
637	Transmission oil temperature sensor circuit open
638	Transmission oil temperature sensor circuit grounded
639	Insufficient input from turbine speed sensor
641	Shift solenoid #3 circuit failure
643	Shift solenoid #4 circuit failure
645	Incorrect gear ratio obtained for first gear
646	Incorrect gear ratio obtained for second gear
647	Incorrect gear ratio obtained for third gear
648	Incorrect gear ratio obtained for fourth gear
649	Electronic pressure control higher or lower than expected
651	Electronic pressure control circuit failure
652	Modulated lock up solenoid circuit failure
654	Manual lever position sensor not indicating Park during test
656	Converter clutch control continuous slip error
998	Hard fault present

SENSORS, INPUT

TEMPERATURE SENSORS

Engine	Year	Sensor	Resistance Ohms @ deg. F/C
All FI	1989-00	Coolant,	31,700-42,900 @ 68/20
		Intake air,	13,650-18,650 @ 104/40
		Transmission oil,	6500-8900 @ 140/60
		Diesel engine oil,	3240-4440 @ 176/80
		Fuel temp.	1770-2370 @ 212/100
			980-1380 @ 248/115

MANIFOLD ABSOLUTE AND BAROMETRIC PRESSURE SENSORS

With EEC IV, measured between center terminal of unit and ground with ignition on and engine off. MAP sensor values based on 30" (102 kPa) barometric pressure.

Engine	Year	Sensor	Frequency Hz @	Vacuum In Hg/kPa
All, Gasoline	1989-94	MAP	159	0/0
All ex. Ranger, Explorer	1995-96	MAP	141	6/20
			125	12/40
			109	18/60
			95	24/80
			80	30/100

FORD TRUCKS
1989-2000 Includes Mercury Mountaineer, Lincoln Navigator, Mazda Navajo, B2300, B2500, B3000, B4000 Trucks

UNDERHOOD SERVICE SPECIFICATIONS

FDTTU11

FDTTU11

SENSORS, INPUT Continued

MANIFOLD ABSOLUTE AND BAROMETRIC PRESSURE SENSORS Continued

Engine	Year	Sensor	Frequency Hz @	Vacuum In Hg/kPa
All DI Diesel	1994-96	MAP	94	10/70
			111	15/100
			130	20/140
			145	25/170
			167	30/205
			181	35/235
			203	40/275
All	1989-94	BARO	116-128	17/58
All	1995-00		122-134	20/66
			129-141	22/74
			136-148	24/82
			143-155	27/90
			150-162	29/98
			156-168	31/105

Engine	Year	Voltage		Pressure PSI (kPa)
All	1996-00	Fuel	0.5	0 (0)
		Rail	1.1	10 (69)
		Pressure	1.6	20 (138)
			2.2	30 (207)
			2.8	40 (275)
			3.4	50 (344)
			3.9	60 (413)
			4.5	70 (482)

MASS AIRFLOW SENSOR

Voltage is measured at indicated vehicle speed.

Measurement requires a road test using Ford's EEC-IV Monitor Box (Rotunda 007-00018) or EC-IV Monitor Recorder (Rotunda 007-00021), or equivalent test equipment.

Engine	Year	Voltage @	Speed MPH/KPH
All	1991-95	.80 @	0/0
		1.00 @	20/32
		1.70 @	40/64
		2.10 @	60/96

CRANKSHAFT POSITION SENSOR

Engine	Year	Resistance (ohms)
4.0L	1990-95	2300-2500
All	1996-00	300-800

VEHICLE SPEED SENSOR

Engine	Year	Resistance (ohms)
All w/EEC	1989-97	190-250
	1998-00	170-270

KNOCK SENSOR

Engine	Year	Resistance Ohms
All	1996-00	4,390,000-5,350,000

TRANSMISSION RANGE SENSOR

Engine	Year	Resistance Ohms @ Position
All	1996-00	4152-4568 @ P
		1368-1512 @ R
		696-770 @ N
		380-420 @ D
		200-220 @ 2
		77-85 @ 1

THROTTLE POSITION SENSOR (TPS)

Engines with EEC IV: Connect positive probe of DVOM along terminal A (upper) of TPS and connect negative probe along terminal B (middle). Turn ignition on but do not start vehicle. Adjust TPS to specified value.

SENSORS, INPUT Continued

THROTTLE POSITION SENSOR (TPS)

		TPS Voltage	
Engine	Year	Minimum	Maximum
2.3L, 2.5L	1989-90	.34	4.84
	1991	.20	4.84
	1992-94	.43-.57	3.6-4.8
	1995-98	.65-1.25	4.2-4.6
	1999-00	.53-1.27	4.65
2.9L	1989-91	.34	4.84
	1992	.43-.57	3.6-4.8
3.0L	1989-90	.34	4.84
	1991	.20	4.84
	1992-94	.43-.57	3.6-4.8
	1995-98	.65-1.25	4.2-4.6
	1999-00	.53-1.27	4.65
4.0L	1990	.34	4.84
	1991	.20	4.84
	1992-94	.43-.57	3.6-4.8
	1995-98	.65-1.25	4.2-4.6
	1999-00	.53-1.27	4.65
4.2L, 4.6L	1997-00	.65-1.25	4.2-4.6
4.9L	1989-90	.20	4.84
	1991	.34	4.84
	1992-94	.43-.57	3.6-4.8
	1995-96	.65-1.25	4.2-4.6
5.0L	1989-90	.20	4.84
	1991	.34	4.84
	1992-94	.43-.57	3.6-4.8
	1995-98	.65-1.25	4.2-4.6
	1999	.53-1.27	4.65
5.4L, 6.8L	1997-98	.65-1.25	4.2-4.6
	1999-00	.53-1.27	4.65
5.8L, 7.5L	1989-90	.20	4.84
w/4-speed AT	1989-90	.34	4.84
5.8L, 7.5L	1991	.34	4.84
	1992-94	.43-.57	3.6-4.8
	1995-97	.65-1.25	4.2-4.6
7.3L DI Diesel	1994-97	.37 min.	4.50 max.

EGR VALVE POSITION SENSOR

Engine	Year	Voltage	Position
All, as equipped	1990-94	0.40	closed
All ex. Ranger, Explorer	1995-96	1.25	25%
		2.15	50%
		3.02	75%
		3.90	full open

ACTUATORS, OUTPUT

IDLE AIR CONTROL

Engine	Year	Resistance (ohms)
All w/EEC IV, V	1989-00	6-13

FUEL INJECTORS

Engine	Year	Resistance (ohms)	Temperature (deg. F/C)
3.0L	1989	15-18	—
All others	1989	13.5-18	—
2.3L, 3.0L	1990-91	15-18	—
All others	1990-91	13-16	—
4.0L	1992	14-17	—
All others	1992	13-16	—
4.0L	1993-94	12-19	—
4.2L	1999	9-16	—
CNG	1996-00	4-6	—
All others	1993-94	11-18	—
All Others	1995-00	11-18	—

ACTUATORS, OUTPUT Continued

COMPUTER TIMING ADVANCE

1992-97, specifications include initial timing.
1989-91, specifications are in addition to basic timing.
Test with engine at operating temperature.

1989-91, activate system test procedure. See "Diagnostic Trouble Codes" section. Check advance against specifications.
1992-97, degrees of advance are measured at indicated vehicle speed.

Year	Engine	Advance
1989-91	All w/EEC IV	17-23

Engine	Year	Idle	Degrees of Advance 30 MPH/50 KPH	55 MPH/90 KPH
2.3L	1992-94	18-22	28-32	30-34
	1995	22	22-30	18-30
2.3L, 2.5L: MT	1996-00	8-15	20-33	15-35
AT	1996-00	15-22	25-35	15-30
2.9L: MT	1992	24-28	28-34	30-36
AT	1992	24-28	30-36	32-36
3.0L: MT	1992	24-28	33-37	34-38
AT	1992	24-28	28-35	28-34
3.0L Aerostar: MT	1993-95	24-28	33-37	34-38
AT	1993-95	24-28	28-35	28-34
3.0L Ranger: MT	1993-94	20-28	28-37	28-38
AT	1993-94	20-28	28-35	28-34
3.0L Ranger, B3000	1995	22	20-30	28-30
3.0L Aerostar	1996-97	15-22	29-39	25-32
3.0L Ranger: MT	1996-99	10-18	25-30	19-35
AT	1996-99	11-15	26-31	25-35
4.0L Aerostar	1996-97	15-22	25-29	19-25
4.0L Explorer: MT	1996-00	10-12	20-25	19-25
AT	1996-00	11-20	26-31	20-32
4.0L Ranger, B4000:				
MT	1996-00	10-18	25-30	19-35
AT	1996-00	11-18	26-35	25-35

ACTUATORS, OUTPUT Continued

Engine	Year	Idle	Degrees of Advance 30 MPH/50 KPH	55 MPH/90 KPH
4.0L SOHC	1997-00	11-20	26-31	20-32
4.2L: MT	1997-00	11-20	20-35	10-16
AT	1997-00	11-20	15-35	20-39
4.6L: MT	1997-00	11-20	15-35	20-39
AT	1997-00	11-20	15-35	20-39
4.9L	1992-94	17-20	24-28	24-30
w/4-speed AT	1992-94	20-24	28-32	24-30
w/4-speed AT	1995	10-13	12-16	14-17
5.0L: MT	1992-95	12-14	26-30	38-42
3-speed AT	1992-93	14-20	28-36	30-40
4-speed AT	1992	18-22	36-40	36-42
4-speed AT, AODE	1993-94	20-22	42-48	42-48
4-speed AT, 4R70W	1995	20-22	30-37	30-38
4-speed AT, E40D	1993-95	18-22	36-40	36-42
5.0L Explorer	1996-97	12-17	32-40	25-37
Others: MT	1996	12-17	44-48	28-45
AT	1996	12-17	35-40	28-37
5.4L	1997-98	12-17	35-40	28-37
5.4L LD	1999-00	12-17	32-40	28-37
HD	1999-00	17-24	35-40	28-37
CNG	1999-00	15-25	20-35	20-30
5.8L	1992-94	16-20	32-36	36-42
5.8L: MT	1995	16-20	15-27	28-35
AT	1995	16-20	32-36	26-32
5.8L	1996-97	15-18	23-29	26-32
6.8L	1997-00	15-20	23-34	26-34
7.5L	1992-94	20-24	38-42	42-48
w/4-speed AT	1992-94	22-28	36-40	36-40
7.5L	1995	17-22	28-42	28-40
3-speed AT	1995	17-19	26-38	30-38
4-speed AT	1995	22-28	26-35	36-40
7.5L: MT	1996-97	22-26	25-32	22-40
AT	1996-97	22-26	25-28	27-32

GEO-ASUNA, CHEVROLET—PONTIAC

1989-93 Metro, Firefly, Sprint, Prizm, Storm, Sunfire, Tracker, Sunrunner
1994-2000 Metro, Firefly, Prizm, Tracker, Sunrunner

ENGINE IDENTIFICATION

To identify any engine by the manufacturer's code, follow the four steps designated by the numbered blocks.

1 MODEL YEAR IDENTIFICATION: Refer to illustration of the Vehicle Identification Number (V.I.N.). The year is indicated by a code letter which is the 10th character of the V.I.N.

2 ENGINE CODE LOCATION: Refer to illustration of V.I.N. plate for location and designation of engine code.

3 ENGINE CODE: In the "CODE" column, find the engine code determined in Step 2.

4 ENGINE IDENTIFICATION: On the line where the engine code appears, read to the right to identify the engine.

V.I.N. PLATE LOCATION:

On top left side of instrument panel

Model year of vehicle:
2000 — Y
1999 — X
1998 — W
1997 — V
1996 — T
1995 — S
1994 — R
1993 — P
1992 — N
1991 — M
1990 — L
1989 — K

MODEL YEAR AND ENGINE IDENTIFICATION:

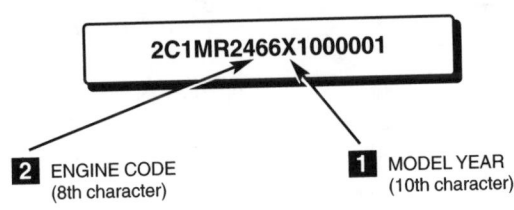

2C1MR2466X1000001

2 ENGINE CODE (8th character)

1 MODEL YEAR (10th character)

4 ENGINE IDENTIFICATION

YEAR	3 ENGINE CODE	CYL.	DISPL. liters	cc	Fuel System	HP
2000	6 (Metro)	3	1.0	993	TBI	55
	2 (Metro)	4	1.3	1291	MFI	79
	8 (Prizm)	4	1.8	1787	MFI	125
	6 (Tracker)	4	1.6	1986	MFI	97
	C (Tracker)	4	2.0	2483	MFI	127
1999	6 (Metro)	3	1.0	993	TBI	55
	2 (Metro)	4	1.3	1291	MFI	79
	8 (Prizm)	4	1.8	1787	MFI	120
	6 (Tracker)	4	1.6	1986	MFI	97
	C (Tracker)	4	2.0	2483	MFI	127
1996-98	6 (Metro)	3	1.0	993	TBI	55
	2 (Metro)	4	1.3	1291	TBI	70
	6 (Prizm)	4	1.6	1588	MFI	105
	8 (Prizm)	4	1.8	1787	MFI	115
	6 (Tracker)	4	1.6	1590	MFI	95
1995	6 (Metro)	3	1.0	993	TBI	55
	9 (Metro)	4	1.3	1291	TBI	70
	6 (Prizm)	4	1.6	1588	MFI	105
	8 (Prizm)	4	1.8	1787	MFI	115
	U (Tracker)	4	1.6	1590	TBI	80
	6 (Tracker)	4	1.6	1590	MFI	95
1994	6 (Metro)	3	1.0	993	TBI	55
	9 (Metro)	4	1.3	1291	TBI	70
	6 (Prizm)	4	1.6	1588	MFI	105
	8 (Prizm)	4	1.8	1787	MFI	115
	U (Tracker)	4	1.6	1590	TBI	80
	6 (Tracker)	4	1.6	1590	MFI	95
1993	6 (Metro)	3	1.0	993	TBI	55
	9 (Metro)	4	1.3	1291	MFI	70
	6 (Prizm)	4	1.6	1588	MFI	108
	8 (Prizm)	4	1.8	1787	MFI	115

4 ENGINE IDENTIFICATION

YEAR	3 ENGINE CODE	CYL.	DISPL. liters	cc	Fuel System	HP
1993 Cont'd.	6 (Storm)	4	1.6	1588	MFI	95
	8 (Storm)	4	1.8	1787	MFI	140
	U (Tracker)	4	1.6	1590	TBI	80
1992	6 (Metro)	3	1.0	993	TBI	52
	5 (Prizm)	4	1.6	1588	MFI	130
	6 (Prizm)	4	1.6	1588	MFI	102
	6 (Storm)	4	1.6	1588	MFI	95
	8 (Storm)	4	1.8	1787	MFI	140
	U (Tracker)	4	1.6	1588	TBI	80
1991	6 (Metro)	3	1.0	993	TBI	55
	2	3	1.0 T	993 T	MFI	70
	5 (Prizm)	4	1.6	1588	MFI	130
	6 (Prizm)	4	1.6	1588	MFI	102
	5 (Storm)	4	1.6	1588	MFI	130
	6 (Storm)	4	1.6	1588	MFI	95
	U (Tracker)	4	1.6	1588	TBI	80
1990	6 (Metro)	3	1.0	993	TBI	49
	2	3	1.0 T	993 T	MFI	N/A
	5 (Prizm)	4	1.6	1588	MFI	130
	6 (Prizm)	4	1.6	1588	MFI	102
	6 (Storm)	4	1.6	1588	MFI	95
	5 (Storm)	4	1.6	1588	MFI	125
	U	4	1.6	1590	TBI	80
1989	6 (Metro)	3	1.0	993	TBI	49
	2	3	1.0 T	993 T	MFI	70
	7	4	1.5	1471	2V	70
	6 (Prizm)	4	1.6	1588	MFI	102
	U	4	1.6	1590	TBI	80

TBI—Throttle Body Injection.   MFI—Multiport Fuel Injection.
T—Turbo.   2V—Two Venturi Carburetor.

UNDERHOOD SERVICE SPECIFICATIONS

CYLINDER NUMBERING SEQUENCE

GOITU1   GOITU1

4-CYL. FIRING ORDER: 1 3 4 2

1993-97 Metro 1.3L Code 9
1994-97 Firefly 1.3L Code 9

1998-00 Prizm 1.8L Code 8

1989-97 Prizm 1.6L Code 6
1.8L Code 8

1989-91 Metro, Sprint, Firefly
1992-00 Metro, Firefly 1.0L Code 6

1998-00 Metro, Firefly 1.3L Code 2

1989 Spectrum, Sunburst 1.5L ex. Turbo

1989-92 Prizm 1.6L Code 5

1990-93 Storm, Sunfire 1.6L Code 5, 6; 1.8L Code 8

Front of car

1989-95 Tracker, Sunrunner 1.6L 8-valve

1994-97 Tracker, Sunrunner 1.6L 16-valve

GEO-ASUNA, CHEVROLET—PONTIAC
1989-93 Metro, Firefly, Sprint, Prizm, Storm, Sunfire, Tracker, Sunrunner
1994-2000 Metro, Firefly, Prizm, Tracker, Sunrunner

UNDERHOOD SERVICE SPECIFICATIONS

GOITU2   **TIMING MARK**   GOITU2

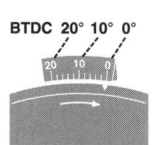

1989-91
Firefly, Sprint 1.0L
1989-97
Metro, Firefly Code 6
1993-97
Metro, Firefly Code 9

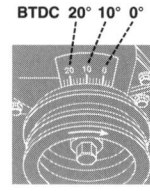

1989
Spectrum 1.5L

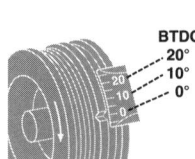

1989-92
Prizm Code 6
1990-92 Storm, Sunfire
Codes 5, 6, 8

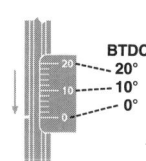

1990-92
Prizm Code 5

1989-98
Tracker, Sunrunner

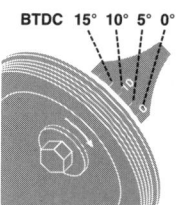

1993-97
Prizm 1.6L Code 6
Prizm 1.8L Code 8

ELECTRICAL AND IGNITION SYSTEMS

BATTERY

Engine	Year	STANDARD BCI Group No.	STANDARD Crank. Perf.	OPTIONAL BCI Group No.	OPTIONAL Crank. Perf.
1.0L	1989	45	410	—	—
1.0L	1990	26	440	—	—
1.0L, 1.3L	1991-94	26	390	—	—
	1995-00	26R	390	—	—
1.5L	1989	21R	410	—	—
1.6L Prizm	1989-92	35	370	—	—
1.6L, 1.8L Prizm	1993-00	35	310	—	—
1.6L, 1.8L Storm, Sunfire	1990-93	35	370	—	—
1.6L Tracker, Sunrunner	1989	45	470	—	—
	1990-94	26	525	—	—
	1995-98	26R	390	—	—

GENERATOR

Application	Year	Rated Output (amps)	Test Output (amps)
1.0L	1989-91	50, 55	40 @ 2000
1.0L, 1.3L	1992-00	50, 55	1
1.5L	1989	45, 60	30 @ 2000
1.6L Prizm	1989-92	60	1
1.6L Prizm	1993-94	70	1
1.6L Storm, Sunfire	1990	61	30 @ 2000
	1990	85	30 @ 2000
1.6L, 1.8L Storm, Sunfire: 1.6L	1991-92	75	2
1.8L	1992	85	2
1.6L, 1.8L Storm, Sunfire	1993	55	2
1.6L Tracker, Sunrunner	1989-97	55	1
1.8L Prizm	1993-97	70	1
	1993-95	77	1
	1998-00	55	1

1 Output at 2000 rpm must be within 10 amps of rated output.
2 Output at 2000 rpm must be within 15 amps of rated output.

REGULATOR

Engine	Year	Test Temp. (deg. F/C)	Voltage Setting
1.0L, 1.5L	1989-91	Cold	14.2-14.8
1.0L, 1.3L: 50A alt.	1992-95	77/25	14.2-14.8
55A alt.	1992-00	77/25	14.7-15.0
1.6L Prizm	1989-92	77/25	14.2-14.8
1.6L, 1.8L Prizm	1993-94	—	13.5-16.0
	1995-97	—	13.5-15.1
	1998-00	—	14.4-15.0
1.6L, 1.8L Storm, Sunfire	1990-93	—	13.5-16.0
1.6L Tracker, Sunrunner	1989-94	—	13.5-16.0
	1995-96	—	14.7-15.0
	1997-98	—	14.4-15.0

STARTER

Engine	Year	Cranking Voltage (min. volts)	Ampere Draw @ Cranking Speed
1.0L, 1.3L: MT	1992-94	9.5	270 max.
AT	1992-94	8.7	230 max.
1.0L, 1.3L: MT	1995-00	9.0	150 max.
AT	1995-00	7.7	300 max.
1.6L, Storm, Sunfire: MT	1990-93	8.7	230 max.
AT, SOHC	1990-93	8.0	280 max.
AT, DOHC	1990-91	8.5	300 max.
1.6L Tracker, Sunrunner	1989-98	7.7	300 max.
1.8L Prizm	1998-00	7.7	300 max.
1.8L Storm, Sunfire: MT	1992-93	8.0	230 max.
AT	1992-93	8.5	250 max.

SPARK PLUGS

Engine	Year	Gap (inches)	Gap (mm)	Torque (ft-lb)
1.0L	1989-00	.039-.043	1.0-1.1	21
1.3L	1993-00	.039-.043	1.0-1.1	21
1.5L	1989	.039-.043	1.0-1.1	14
1.6L, 1.8L Prizm	1989-97	.031	0.8	13
	1998-00	.043	1.1	21
1.6L, 1.8L Storm, Sunfire	1990-93	.041	1.05	14
1.6L Tracker, Sunrunner	1989-98	.028-.032	0.7-0.8	21

IGNITION COIL
FOR TESTING AND ADJUSTMENT DIAGRAMS, SEE APPENDIX A.
Winding Resistance (ohms at 75°F, or 24°C)

Engine	Year	Windings	Resistance (ohms)
1.0L	1989-92	Primary	1.33-1.55
		Secondary	10,700-14,500
1.0L	1993-94	Primary[1]	1.35-1.65
		Secondary	22,100-29,900
Convertible	1993	Primary	1.33-1.55
		Secondary	10,700-14,500
1.0L, 1.3L	1995	Primary	1.08-1.32
		Secondary	22,100-29,900
	1996-00	Primary	1.35-1.65
		Secondary	22,100-29,900
1.5L 2V	1989	Primary	1.1-1.8
		Secondary	11,200-20,500
1.5L Turbo	1989	Primary	0-2
		Secondary	6,000-30,000
1.6L Prizm Code 6	1989-91	Primary	1.3-1.6
		Secondary	10,400-14,000
1.6L Prizm Code 5	1990-91	Primary	0.4-0.5
		Secondary	10,200-13,800
1.6L Prizm	1992	Primary	1.3-1.6
		Secondary	10,400-14,000
1.6L, 1.8L Prizm	1993-94	Primary	1.41-2.05
		Secondary	11,400-18,400

GEO-ASUNA, CHEVROLET—PONTIAC
1989-93 Metro, Firefly, Sprint, Prizm, Storm, Sunfire, Tracker, Sunrunner
1994-2000 Metro, Firefly, Prizm, Tracker, Sunrunner

UNDERHOOD SERVICE SPECIFICATIONS

GOITU3   GOITU3

IGNITION COIL Continued

Engine	Year	Windings	Resistance (ohms)
1.6L Prizm	1994-95	Primary	1.41-2.05
		Secondary	11,400-18,400
	1996-97	Primary	.36-.55
		Secondary	9,000-15,400
1.8L Prizm	1994-95	Primary	.45-.65
		Secondary	11,400-18,400
	1996-97	Primary	.36-.55
		Secondary	9,000-15,400
1.6L, 1.8L Prizm	1998-00	Primary	.45-.65
		Secondary	11,400-18,400
1.6L Storm, Sunfire	1990	Primary	0-2
		Secondary	6,000-30,000
1.6L, 1.8L Storm, Sunfire	1991-92	Primary	1.2-1.5
		Secondary	10,200-13,800
1.6L, 1.8L Storm, Sunfire	1993	Primary	0.7-1.4
		Secondary	10,200-14,500
1.6L Tracker, Sunrunner	1989-90	Primary	1.35-1.65
		Secondary	11,000-14,500
	1991	Primary	0.7-1.2
	1992	Primary	.72-.88
	1991-92	Secondary	10,200-14,000
	1993-94	Primary	1.08-1.32
		Secondary	22,100-29,900
	1995	Primary	1.08-1.32
		Secondary	10,100-22,000
	1996-98	Primary	0.7-1.1
		Secondary	13,000-18,000

1 1994 Base models with MT and Calif. with AT, 1.08-1.32.

DISTRIBUTOR PICKUP
FOR TESTING AND ADJUSTMENT DIAGRAMS, SEE APPENDIX B.

Engine	Year	Resistance (ohms)	Air Gap (in./mm)
1.0L, 1.3L	1989-95	130-190	.008-.016/.2-.4
	1996-97	185-275	—
	1998-00	185-325	.008-.016/.2-.4
1.5L 2V	1989	140-180	.008-.016/.2-.4
1.6L Nova, Prizm	1989-92	140-180	.008-.016/.2-.4
1.6L, 1.8L Prizm:	1993-95	—	.008-.016/.2-.4
Terminals 3 & 6, 1.6L		240-325	—
Terminals 1 & 2, 1.8L		240-325	—
Terminals 2 & 5, 1.6L		475-650	—
1.6L, 1.8L Prizm	1996-97	185-275	—
1.6L, 1.8L Storm, Sunfire	1990-93	500-1500	—
1.6L Tracker, Sunrunner	1989-91	—	.008-.016/.2-.4

BASE TIMING
FOR TESTING AND ADJUSTMENT DIAGRAMS, SEE APPENDIX C.

1989-91, 1.0L TBI ex. LSI, 1991-93 Tracker, Sunrunner: Jumper terminals C and D of diagnostic connector by ignition coil (Metro) or battery (Tracker, Sunrunner).

1992-00 1.0L, 1.3L: Jumper terminals D & E of 6-terminal diagnostic connector by left strut tower.

1.6L, 1.8L Nova, Prizm FI: Jumper terminals T and E1 (1989-early 90) or TE1 and E1 (1990-late 99) of diagnostic connector under hood.

2000: Connect a Scan tool and access base timing function

1.6L, 1.8L Storm, Sunfire: Jumper far left and far right terminals of 3-terminal DLC connector under dash.

1994-98 1.6L TBI Tracker, Sunrunner: Jumper terminals C & D of 4-terminal DLC located by battery. 1.6L MFI jumper terminals 4 & 5 of 6-terminal DLC located by battery.

1989-91, all others: Disconnect and plug distributor vacuum hoses. 1.0L LSI, when vacuum hose is connected, timing will increase to Check specification.

Engine	Year	Man. Trans. (degrees) @ RPM	Auto. Trans. (degrees) @ RPM
1.0L: Set, all	1989-91	6	6
Check, LSI only	1989-91	12±1	12±1
1.0L	1992-00	5±1	5±1

BASE TIMING Continued

Engine	Year	Man. Trans. (degrees) @ RPM	Auto. Trans. (degrees) @ RPM
1.3L	1993-00	5±1	5±1
1.5L 2V	1989	15	10
1.6L, 1.8L FI Nova, Prizm	1989-96	10	10
	1997	10[1]	10[1]
	1998-00	8-10[1]	8-10[1]
1.6L, 1.8L Storm, Sunfire	1990-93	10	10
1.6L Tracker, Sunrunner: TBI	1989-95	8±1	8±1
MFI	1993-98	5±1	5±1

1 Not adjustable.

DISTRIBUTOR TIMING ADVANCE
Engine degrees at engine rpm, no load, in addition to basic timing setting.
Mechanical advance distributors only.

Engine	Trans-mission	Year	Distributor Number	Degrees @ 2500 RPM Total	Degrees @ 2500 RPM Centrifugal
1.5L 2V	MT	1989	94419559	30.5-38.5	4.5-8.5
1.5L 2V	AT	1989	94178219	28.5-36.5	4.5-8.5
1.6L Tracker, Sunrunner	MT & AT	1989	96058488	19.8-27.8	7.3-11.3

FUEL SYSTEM

FUEL SYSTEM PRESSURE
FOR TESTING AND ADJUSTMENT DIAGRAMS, SEE APPENDIX D.
At idle unless otherwise indicated.

Engine	Year	PSI	RPM
Carbureted & TBI:			
1.0L, 1.3L	1989-00	23-31	ign. on
		13-20	idle
1.6L Tracker, Sunrunner	1989-95	34-41	idle
		57 min.[1]	—

Engine	Year	Pressure PSI[2]	Pressure PSI[3]	Fuel Pump[1]
MFI:				
1.0L Turbo	1989-91	25-33	35-43	—
1.3L	1994-00	28.5-34	38.5-44	—
1.6L Nova, Prizm	1989-92	30-37	38-44	57 min.
1.6L, 1.8L Prizm	1993-97	31-37	38-44	—
	1998-00	—	44-50	—
1.6L Storm, Sunfire	1990-91	25-30	35-42	65 min.
1.6L, 1.8L Storm, Sunfire	1992	25-30	41-47	60 min.
1.6L Storm, Sunfire	1993	30-36	30-46	60 min.
1.6L Tracker, Sunrunner	1993-98	29-37	35-43	60 min.
1.8L Storm, Sunfire	1993	41-44	41-47	60 min.

1 Fuel pump pressure with return line briefly restricted.
2 Vacuum hose connected to fuel pressure regulator.
3 Vacuum hose disconnected from fuel pressure regulator.

IDLE SPEED W/O COMPUTER CONTROL

1.0L Turbo: Set idle to specified speed. To set electrical speed-up (1.0L), turn headlights on and adjust screw on solenoid. To set A/C speed-up (1.0L), turn A/C on and adjust screw on solenoid.

1.5L 2V: Disconnect and plug distributor vacuum, canister purge, EGR, ITC, vacuum hoses.

Air-conditioned models equipped with idle speed-up solenoid, turn A/C on and with solenoid fully extended, adjust solenoid to obtain specified rpm.

GEO-ASUNA, CHEVROLET—PONTIAC
1989-93 Metro, Firefly, Sprint, Prizm, Storm, Sunfire, Tracker, Sunrunner
1994-2000 Metro, Firefly, Prizm, Tracker, Sunrunner

UNDERHOOD SERVICE SPECIFICATIONS

GOITU4   GOITU4

IDLE SPEED W/O COMPUTER CONTROL Continued

Engine	Year	SLOW Man. Trans.	SLOW Auto. Trans.	FAST Man. Trans.	FAST Auto. Trans.	Step of Cam
1.0L Turbo	1989	700-800	—	—	—	—
Elect. speed-up	1989	750-850	—			
A/C speed-up	1989	950-1050	—			
1.5L 2V	1989	750	1000 N	—	—	—
A/C speed-up		850	980 N			

IDLE SPEED W/COMPUTER CONTROL
FOR TESTING AND ADJUSTMENT DIAGRAMS, SEE APPENDIX E.

1.0L TBI: 1989-93, 1994 XFI & Fed AT: Install a fuse into diagnostic connector in fuse block. Set idle to specified value. Turn A/C on and adjust speed-up to specified value.

1994 All MT ex. XFI and Calif AT; 1995-98 1.0L, 1.3L: Connect a Scan tool and run through idle speed checking procedure. Compare to specified value.

1.6L, 1.8L Prizm, 1989-92: Jumper terminals TE1 and E1 of diagnostic connector. Set idle to specified value. Turn A/C on and verify that speed increases to speed-up speed.

1989-91 1.6L Tracker, Sunrunner: Set idle to specified value.

1992-98 1.6L Tracker, Sunrunner: Ground diagnostic connector terminal #2, located by battery.

Engine	Year	Transmission	Checking Speed	Setting Speed	AC Speed-up
1.0L	1989-90	MT	—	700-800	850-950
1.0L	1989	AT	—	650-750 N	800-900 N
1.0L LSI	1990	AT	—	650-750 N	850-950
Others	1990	AT	—	800-900 N	800-900 N
1.0L XFI	1991-93	MT	—	650-750	650-750[1]
Convertible	1991-93	MT	—	800-900	800-900[1]
	1991-93	AT	—	800-900 N	800-900 N[1]
Others	1991-93	MT	—	750-850	750-850[1]
	1991-93	AT	—	800-900	800-900 N[1]
1.0L: XFI	1994	MT	—	650-750	850-950
Ex. XFI: Fed, Can.	1994	AT	—	800-900 N	850-950 N
Calif.	1994	AT	800-900 N	—	—
All	1994	MT	750-850	—	—
1.0L	1995-96	MT	750-850	—	—
	1997-00	MT	800-900 N	—	—
	1995-98	AT	800-900 N	—	—
1.3L	1993-94	MT	850	—	—
		AT	850 N	—	—
	1995-96	MT	750-850	—	—
	1997-00	MT	800-900 N	—	—
	1995-00	AT	800-900 N	—	—
1.6L Prizm code 6	1989-92	MT	—	800	900-1000
	1989-92	AT	—	800 D	900-1000 N
1.6L Prizm code 5	1990-92	MT	—	700	900-1000
	1990-92	AT	—	700 D	900-1000 N
1.6L, 1.8L Prizm	1993-00	MT	650-750	—	900-1000
	1993-00	AT	650-750 N	—	900-1000 N
1.6L Storm, Sunfire	1990-91	MT	800 max.	—	—
	1990-91	AT	800 N max.	—	—
1.6L Tracker, Sunrunner	1989-91	MT	750-850	800	950-1050
	1989-91	AT	750-850 N	800 N	950-1050 N
1.6L Tracker, Sunrunner	1992-98	MT	—	750-850	950-1050
	1992-98	AT	—	750-850 N	950-1050 N

1 Late 1992-93 models, 850-950 (N).

ENGINE MECHANICAL

TIGHTENING TORQUES
FOR CYLINDER HEAD TORQUE SEQUENCES AND DIAGRAMS, SEE APPENDIX F.
Some fasteners are tightened in more than one step.

TIGHTENING TORQUES Continued

		TORQUE FOOT-POUNDS/NEWTON METERS				
Engine	Year	Cylinder Head	Intake Manifold	Exhaust Manifold	Crankshaft Pulley	Water Pump
1.0L, 1.3L	1989-00	54/73	17/23	17/23	12/16	115"/13
1.5L	1989	29/40, 58-79	17/23	17/23	108/147	17/23
1.6L Prizm	1989-92	44/60	20/27[1]	18/25	87/118	11/15
1.6L, 1.8L Prizm	1993-97	22/29, +90°, +90°	14/19	25/34	87/118	124"/14
	1998-00	18/25, 36/49, 52/69, +90°	13/18	36/48	105/142	106"/12
1.6L Storm, Sunfire	1990-93	29/40, 58/79	17/23	30/39	87/118	18/24
1.6L Tracker, Sunrunner: 8-valve	1989-95	54/73	17/23	17/23	12/16	106"/12
16-valve	1993-94	48-51/65-70	14-20/18-28	14-20/18-28	10-13/14-18	7-9/10-13
	1995-98	26/35, 41/55, 52/70	17/23	17/23	12/16	106"/12
1.8L Storm, Sunfire	1992-93	29/40, 58/79	17/23	30/39	108/147	18/24

1 Code 6 engine, 14/19.

VALVE CLEARANCE
Engine cold, unless otherwise specified.

Engine	Year	Intake (inches)	Intake (mm)	Exhaust (inches)	Exhaust (mm)
1.5L 2V Hot	1989	.006	.15	.010	.25
1.6L FI Nova, Prizm	1989-92	.006-.010	.15-.25	.008-.012	.20-.30
1.6L, 1.8L Prizm	1993-97	.006-.010	.15-.25	.010-.014	.25-.35
	1998-00	.005-.007	.13-.17	.005-.007	.13-.17
1.6L, Storm, Sunfire: SOHC	1990-93	.004-.008	.10-.20	.008-.012	.20-.30
DOHC	1990-91	.006	.15	.010	.25
1.6L Tracker, Sunrunner	1989-98	.005-.007	.13-.17	.006-.008	.15-.19

COMPRESSION PRESSURE
At cranking speed or specified rpm, engine temperature normalized, throttle open.

Engine	Year	PSI @ RPM	Maximum Variation PSI
1.0L, 1.3L	1989-00	156-199	14
1.5L	1989	128-179	1
1.6L, 1.8L Prizm	1989-97	142-191	14
	1998-00	170-199	14
1.6L Storm, Sunfire	1990-91	142-191	14
1.6L Storm, Sunfire	1992-93	159	14
1.6L Tracker, Sunrunner	1989-98	170-199	14
1.8L Storm, Sunfire	1992-93	170	14

1 Lowest cylinder must be 65% of highest.

BELT TENSION

Engine	Year	Generator	Power Steering	Air Conditioning
Deflection method				
1.0L, 1.3L (inches)	1989-00	3/16-1/4	3/16-1/4	3/16-1/4
(mm)	1989-00	5-7	5-7	5-7
1.6L Tracker, Sunrunner (inches)	1989-98	3/16-5/16	3/16-5/16	5/16-1/2
(mm)	1989-98	5-8	5-8	8-12

GEO-ASUNA, CHEVROLET—PONTIAC
1989-93 Metro, Firefly, Sprint, Prizm, Storm, Sunfire, Tracker, Sunrunner
1994-2000 Metro, Firefly, Prizm, Tracker, Sunrunner

UNDERHOOD SERVICE SPECIFICATIONS

GOITU5

GOITU5

BELT TENSION Continued

Engine	Year	Generator	Power Steering	Air Conditioning
1.6L, 1.8L Prizm				
(inches)	1993-00	1/4-5/16	3/16-5/16	3/16-5/16
(mm)	1993-00	6-9	5-8	5-8
Strand Tension method				
1.5L	1989	70-110	70-110	70-110
1.6L Nova, Prizm	1989-92	110-150	60-100	60-100
1.6L Storm, Sunfire	1990-93	70-110	70-110	130-160

ENGINE COMPUTER SYSTEM

DIAGNOSTIC TROUBLE CODES
FOR TESTING AND ADJUSTMENT DIAGRAMS, SEE APPENDIX G.

1989 Spectrum, 1990-93 Storm, Sunfire
To activate diagnostic check, connect a jumper wire from terminals A & C of the DLC connector (the two outer cavities of the three-terminal connector) located under the dash near the ECM. To clear memory, remove the ECM fuse for a minimum of ten seconds.8

1989-95 Prizm
Jumper terminals T and E1 (1989-90) TE1 and E1 (1990-95) of diagnostic connector in engine compartment.

1989-93 Tracker, Sunrunner
Turn ignition on and jumper both terminals of the underhood check engine connector (blue/yellow and black wires).

1994-95 Tracker, Sunrunner
Turn ignition switch on and ground terminal B of the DLC by the battery.

1989-95 Metro
Install a fuse in diagnostic cavity of fuse block. Codes will be displayed on "CHECK ENGINE."

1996-00 All
OBD-II system used. Connect a Scan tool and follow manufacturer's instructions to retrieve codes.

1989 Spectrum 2V
Code 12 No tach signal to ECM
Code 13 Oxygen sensor circuit
Code 14 Shorted engine coolant sensor circuit
Codes 15 & 16 Open engine coolant sensor circuit
Code 21 Idle switch out of adjustment, or circuit open
Code 22 Fuel cut off relay, or open circuit
Code 23 Open or grounded M/C solenoid circuit
Code 25 Open or grounded vacuum switching valve
Code 42 Fuel cut-off relay, or circuit grounded
Code 44 Lean oxygen sensor
Code 45 Rich system
Code 51 Faulty PROM, or improper installation
Code 53 Shorted switching unit, or faulty ECM
Code 54 Shorted M/C solenoid, or faulty ECM
Code 55 Faulty ECM

1989-95 Metro, Tracker, Sunrunner, Storm, Sunfire
Code 12 Diagnostic function working
Code 13 Oxygen sensor
Code 14 Open engine coolant temperature sensor circuit
Code 15 Shorted engine coolant temperature sensor circuit
Code 21 Throttle position sensor circuit open
Code 22 Shorted throttle position sensor circuit
Code 23 Intake air temperature sensor circuit open
Code 24 Vehicle speed sensor
Code 25 Shorted intake air temperature circuit
Codes 31 & 32 MAP or barometric pressure sensor (1989-92)
Code 33 Airflow sensor (Turbo)
Code 33 MAP sensor (1990-92)
Code 41 Ignition signal circuit
Code 42 Crankshaft position sensor (ex. Storm, Sunfire)
Code 42 Ignition control circuit (Storm, Sunfire)
Code 44 ECM idle switch circuit (1989)
Codes 44 & 45 Idle switch circuit (1992 Tracker, Sunrunner)
Codes 44 & 45 Oxygen sensor (others)
Code 46 Idle speed control motor
Code 51 EGR system (ex. Storm, Sunfire)
Code 51 ECM (Storm, Sunfire)
Code 53 ECM ground circuit
On Steady ECM

DIAGNOSTIC TROUBLE CODES Continued

1989-95 Prizm
Continuous Flashing System normal
Codes 12 & 13 RPM signal
Code 14 Ignition signal
Code 16 PCM control circuit
Code 21 Oxygen sensor
Code 22 Coolant temperature sensor
Code 24 Intake air temperature sensor
Code 25 Air/fuel ratio lean
Code 26 Air/fuel ratio rich
Code 27 Sub oxygen sensor
Code 31 Mass airflow sensor
Code 41 Throttle position sensor
Code 42 Vehicle speed sensor
Code 43 Starter signal
Code 51 A/C Switch signal
Code 52 Knock sensor circuit
Code 53 ECM failure
Code 71 EGR system

SENSORS, INPUT
TEMPERATURE SENSORS
1.0L Turbo: Intake air temperature sensor measured between terminals 1 & 5 (first and last) of airflow sensor.

1.6L Prizm DOHC: Intake air temperature sensor measured between terminals E2 & THA (first and last) of airflow sensor.

Engine	Year	Sensor	Resistance Ohms @ deg. F/C
1.0L Turbo	1989-91	Coolant	5600 @ 32/0
			2500 @ 68/20
			1200 @ 104/40
			600 @ 140/60
			320 @ 176/80
			180 @ 212/100
		Intake Air	4000-7000 @ 32/0
			2000-3000 @ 68/20
			900-1300 @ 104/40
1.0L TBI, 1.6L Tracker, Sunrunner, 1.6L Storm, Sunfire	1989-90	Coolant, Intake Air	13,500 @ 20/-7
			7500 @ 40/4
			1800 @ 100/38
			450 @ 160/71
			185 @ 210/100
1.6L, 1.8L Storm, Sunfire	1991-93	Coolant, Intake Air	13,500 @ 20/-7
			7500 @ 40/4
			1800 @ 100/38
			450 @ 160/71
			185 @ 210/100
1.0L TBI, 1.3L, 1.6L Tracker, Sunrunner	1991-97	Coolant, Intake Air	14,650 @ 0/-18
			8100 @ 20/-7
			4800 @ 40/4
			2500 @ 70/21
			1250 @ 100/38
			400 @ 160/71
			190 @ 210/99
		EGR	214,000-314,000 @ 68/20
			91,000-126,000 @ 104/40
			42,000-55,500 @ 140/60
			21,000-26,500 @ 176/80
			11,000-13,500 @ 212/100
	1998-00	Coolant, Intake Air	9420 @ 32/0
			5670 @ 50/10
			3520 @ 68/20
			1459 @ 104/40
			667 @ 140/60
			332 @ 176/80
			177 @ 212/100
1.5L 2V	1989	Coolant	2100-2900 @ 68/20
			1000 max. @ operating temp.

GEO-ASUNA, CHEVROLET—PONTIAC
1989-93 Metro, Firefly, Sprint, Prizm, Storm, Sunfire, Tracker, Sunrunner
1994-2000 Metro, Firefly, Prizm, Tracker, Sunrunner

UNDERHOOD SERVICE SPECIFICATIONS

GOITU6   GOITU6

SENSORS, INPUT Continued

Engine	Year	Sensor	Resistance Ohms @ deg. F/C
1.6L FI, 1.8L Nova, Prizm	1989-97	Intake Air, Coolant	10,000-20,000 @ -4/-20
			4000-7000 @ 32/0
			2000-3000 @ 68/20
			900-1300 @ 104/40
			400-700 @ 176/80
			200-400 @ 212/100
		EGR	69,000-88,000 @ 122/50
			11,000-15,000 @ 212/100
			2000-4000 @ 302/150
	1998-00	Coolant, Intake Air	9420 @ 32/0
			5670 @ 50/10
			3520 @ 68/20
			1459 @ 104/40
			667 @ 140/60
			332 @ 176/80
			177 @ 212/100

MANIFOLD ABSOLUTE AND BAROMETRIC PRESSURE SENSORS
See UNDERHOOD SERVICE INSTRUCTIONS at the beginning of this section for test/adjustment diagrams.

Measure voltage with ignition on and engine off. With 10 in. Hg/34 kPa Hg applied to unit, voltage will be 1.5-2.1 less.

Engine	Year	Ign. On	Idle	WOT
		Voltage		
1.5L Turbo	1989	—	1.0-1.5	4.0-4.5
1.0L	1991-92	—	1.0-1.5	3.0-4.0
1.6L Tracker, Sunrunner	1991-92	—	1.0-1.5	4.0-4.5
1.6L, 1.8L Prizm	1989-93	3.2-3.7	1.4-1.8	—
	1996-00	—	1.0-1.5	4.5-4.8

Engine	Year	Voltage @ Altitude (feet)
1.0L, 1.6L Storm, Sunfire	1989-90	3.6-4.4 @ 0
1.6L Tracker, Sunrunner	1989-91	3.5-4.2 @ 1000
		3.4-4.1 @ 2000
		3.2-4.0 @ 3000
		3.1-3.8 @ 4000
		3.0-3.7 @ 5000
		2.9-3.6 @ 6000
		2.5-3.4 @ 7000

CRANKSHAFT POSITION SENSORS

Engine	Year	Resistance (ohms)	Temperature degrees F/C
1.0L, 1.3L	1996-00	360-460	68/20
		1630-2740	86/50
		2065-3225	212/100
1.6L, 1.8L Prizm	1996-97	1630-2740	86/50
		2065-3225	212/100
	1998-00	985-1670	50/122
		1265-1890	10/212
1.6L Tracker, Sunrunner	1996-98	360-460	68/20

VEHICLE SPEED SENSOR

Engine	Year	Resistance (ohms)
1.0L, 1.3L	1996-97	100-300
1.3L	1998-00	100-300

SENSORS, INPUT Continued

THROTTLE POSITION SENSOR
See UNDERHOOD SERVICE INSTRUCTIONS at the beginning of this section for test/adjustment diagrams.

1.6L DOHC: Resistance measured between terminals E2 & VTA (first and third) of TPS.

Engine	Year	Idle	WOT
		Voltage	
1.0L TBI AT	1989-91	.54	4.9
1.0L TBI	1992-94	.45-.65	—
1.0L, 1.3L	1995-97	.98-.102[1]	—
	1998-00	0.2-1.1	2.8-4.8

Engine	Year	Idle	WOT
		Resistance (ohms)	
1.5L 2V	1989	0.8 max.	4.5
1.6L Prizm code 5	1990-92	0.6 max.	4.5
1.6L, 1.8L Storm, Sunfire	1990-92	.20-1.25	4.0 min.
1.6L, 1.8L Prizm	1993	0.3-1.0	—
	1996-00	0.3-0.8	3.2-4.9
1.6L Tracker, Sunrunner	1989-90	.54	4.9
1.6L Tracker, Sunrunner	1991	.70 max.	4.9 min.
1.6L Tracker, Sunrunner: TBI	1992-95	.85-.95	—
MFI	1993-97	.5-1.2	—
	1998	.72-1.04	—

1 With a 0.14 inch (.35 mm) feeler gauge between the throttle stop screw and throttle lever.

ACTUATORS, OUTPUT

IDLE SPEED CONTROL
See UNDERHOOD SERVICE INSTRUCTIONS at the beginning of this section for test/adjustment diagrams.

1.5L Turbo, 1.6L Storm, Sunfire: Measured between terminals A & B and C & D of ISC.

Engine	Year	Resistance (ohms)
1.0L, 1.3L	1993-95	30-35
1.6L Tracker, Sunrunner	1989-90	5-10
1.6L Tracker, Sunrunner	1991-98	11-14
1.6L, 1.8L Storm, Sunfire	1990-93	40-80

FUEL INJECTORS

Engine	Year	Resistance (ohms)	Temperature (deg. F/C)
1.0L, 1.3L	1989-97	0.5-1.5	68/20
1.0L	1998-00	0.5-1.5	68/20
1.3L	1998-00	12-13	—
1.6L Prizm	1989-92	11-17	—
1.6L, 1.8L Prizm	1993-96	12-15	—
	1997-00	11.8-12.6	—
1.6L Tracker, Sunrunner: TBI	1989-94	1-2	68/20
MFI	1993-95	12-17	—
	1996-98	11.8-12.6	—

MIXTURE CONTROL SOLENOID

Engine	Year	Resistance (ohms)
1.5L 2V	1989	10 min.

HONDA
1989-2000 Includes Isuzu Oasis
Passport—See Isuzu

ENGINE IDENTIFICATION

To identify any engine by the manufacturer's code, follow the four steps designated by the numbered blocks.

V.I.N.
PLATE LOCATION:

Left side of hood support member.
Also top left side of instrument panel.

1 MODEL YEAR IDENTIFICATION:

10th character of V.I.N.

2000—Y	1999—X	1998—W
1997—V	1996—T	1995—S
1994—R	1993—P	1992—N
1991—M	1990—L	1989—K

2 ENGINE CODE LOCATION:

First 5 characters of engine number stamped on right top side of engine block or on decal by left hood hinge.

YEAR	3 ENGINE CODE	CYL.	4 ENGINE IDENTIFICATION DISPL. liters	cc	Fuel System	HP
1998-00	D16Y7	4	1.6	1590	MFI	106
	D16Y5	4	1.6	1590	MFI	115
	D16Y8	4	1.6	1590	MFI	127
	B16A2	4	1.6	1595	MFI	160
	B20B4	4	2.0	1972	MFI	126
	F23A1	4	2.3	2254	MFI	190
	F23A4, A5	4	2.3	2254	MFI	156
	H22A4	4	2.2	2157	MFI	190, 195
	J30A1	6	3.0	2997	MFI	200
	J35A1	6	3.5	3474	MFI	210
1997	D16Y7	4	1.6	1590	MFI	106
	D16Y5	4	1.6	1590	MFI	115
	D16Y8	4	1.6	1590	MFI	127
	B16A2	4	1.6	1590	MFI	160
	B20B4	4	2.0	1972	MFI	126
	F22B2	4	2.2	2165	MFI	130
	F22B6	4	2.2	2165	MFI	140
	F22B1	4	2.2	2165	MFI	145
	H22A4	4	2.2	2157	MFI	190, 195[1]
	C27A1	6	2.7	2675	MFI	170
1996	D16Y7	4	1.6	1590	MFI	106
	D16Y5	4	1.6	1590	MFI	115
	D16Y8	4	1.6	1590	MFI	127
	D16A2	4	1.6	1590	MFI	160
	F22B2	4	2.2	2165	MFI	130
	F22A1	4	2.2	2165	MFI	135
	F22B6	4	2.2	2165	MFI	140
	F22B1	4	2.2	2165	MFI	145
	H22A1	4	2.2	2165	MFI	190
	H23A1	4	2.3	2259	MFI	160
	C27A1	6	2.7	2675	MFI	170
1995	D15B8	4	1.5	1493	MFI	70
	D15Z1	4	1.5	1493	MFI	92
	D15B7	4	1.5	1493	MFI	102
	D16Z6	4	1.6	1590	MFI	125
	B16A3	4	1.6	1595	MFI	160
	F22A1	4	2.2	2156	MFI	135
	F22B2	4	2.2	2156	MFI	130, 135[1]
	F22B1	4	2.2	2156	MFI	145
	F22B6	4	2.2	2156	MFI	140
	H22A1	4	2.2	2156	MFI	190
	H23A1	4	2.3	2259	MFI	160
1994	D15B8	4	1.5	1493	MFI	70
	D15Z1	4	1.5	1493	MFI	92
	D15B7	4	1.5	1493	MFI	102
	D16Z6	4	1.6	1590	MFI	125
	B16A3	4	1.6	1595	MFI	160
	F22A1	4	2.2	2156	MFI	130, 135[1]
	F22B2	4	2.2	2156	MFI	130, 135[1]

YEAR	3 ENGINE CODE	CYL.	4 ENGINE IDENTIFICATION DISPL. liters	cc	Fuel System	HP
1994 Cont'd.	F22B1	4	2.2	2156	MFI	145
	H22A1	4	2.2	2156	MFI	190
	H23A1	4	2.3	2259	MFI	160
1993	D15B8	4	1.5	1493	MFI	70
	D15Z1	4	1.5	1493	MFI	92
	D15B7	4	1.5	1493	MFI	102
	D16Z6	4	1.6	1590	MFI	125
	F22A1	4	2.2	2156	MFI	125, 135[1]
	F22A6	4	2.2	2156	MFI	140[1]
	H22A1	4	2.2	2156	MFI	190
	H23A1	4	2.3	2259	MFI	160
1992	D15B8	4	1.5	1493	MFI	70
	D15Z1	4	1.5	1493	MFI	92
	D15B7	4	1.5	1493	MFI	102
	D16Z6	4	1.6	1590	MFI	125
	F22A1	4	2.2	2156	MFI	125
	F22A6	4	2.2	2156	MFI	135, 140[1]
	H23A1	4	2.3	2259	MFI	160
1991	D15B6	4	1.5	1493	MFI	62
	D15B1	4	1.5	1493	TBI	70
	D15B2	4	1.5	1493	TBI	93
	D16A6	4	1.6	1590	MFI	105
	B20A5	4	2.0	1958	MFI	135
	B21A1	4	2.1	2056	MFI	140
	F22A1	4	2.2	2156	MFI	125
	F22A4	4	2.2	2156	MFI	130
	F22A6	4	2.2	2156	MFI	140
1990	D15B6	4	1.5	1493	MFI	62
	D15B1	4	1.5	1493	TBI	70
	D15B2	4	1.5	1493	TBI	93
	D16A6	4	1.6	1590	MFI	105
	B20A3	4	2.0	1958	2-1V	104
	B20A5	4	2.0	1958	MFI	135
	B21A1	4	2.1	2056	MFI	140
	F22A1	4	2.2	2156	MFI	125
	F22A4	4	2.2	2156	MFI	130
1989	D15B6	4	1.5	1493	MFI	62
	D15B1	4	1.5	1493	TBI	70
	D15B2	4	1.5	1493	TBI	92
	D16A6	4	1.5	1590	MFI	105
	A20A1	4	2.0	1955	2V	98
	A20A3	4	2.0	1955	MFI	120
	B20A3	4	2.0	1958	2-1V	104
	B20A5	4	2.0	1958	MFI	135

1 Engine horsepower varies with model installation.
MFI—Multiport Fuel Injection.
TBI—Throttle Body Injection.   **1V—One Venturi Carburetor.**
2V—Two Venturi Carburetor.   **3V—Three Venturi Carburetor.**

UNDERHOOD SERVICE SPECIFICATIONS

HAITU2   HAITU2

CYLINDER NUMBERING SEQUENCE
4-CYL. FIRING ORDER: 1 3 4 2

— Front of car —

| 1989-91 Civic, CRX, 1493cc, 1950cc | 1992-00 Civic, Del Sol 1493cc, 1590cc, 1595cc 1994 Accord, Prelude 2156cc SOHC ex. VTEC 1995 Accord 2156cc | 1989-90 Prelude 1958cc 2 x 1V; 1989 Prelude, Accord 1955cc | 1997-00 1972cc CR-V | 1989-91 Prelude 1998cc FI, 2056cc FI |

V6 FIRING ORDER:
1 4 2 5 3 6

4-CYL. FIRING ORDER: 1 3 4 2

— Front of car —

1990-00 Accord, Prelude, Odyssey 2156cc, 2254cc SOHC	1993-00 Prelude 2156cc, 2157cc VTEC DOHC, 2259cc 1994-00 Accord 2156cc DOHC, VTEC

— Front of car —

| 1995-97 Accord 2675cc | 1998-99 Accord 2977cc | 2000 Accord 2977cc 1999-00 Odyssey 3474cc |

— TIMING MARK —

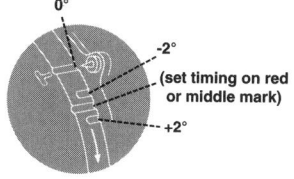 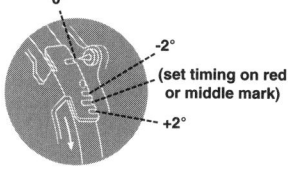 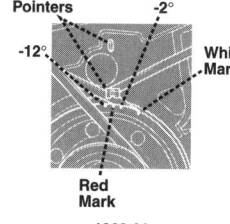 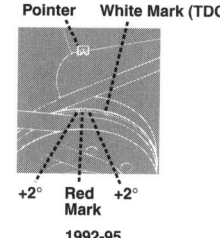

| 1989-93 Accord, 1989-98 Prelude w/MT | 1989-93 Accord, 1989-98 Prelude w/AT | 1989-91 Civic, CRX | 1992-95 Civic, Del Sol |

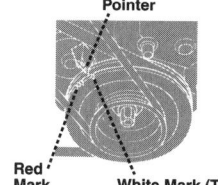 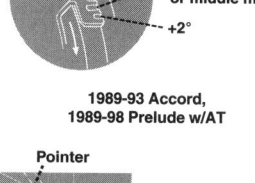 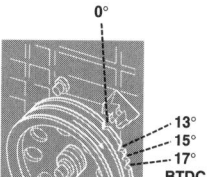 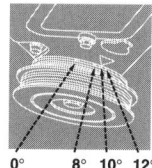

| 1996-99 Civic, Del Sol | 1994-99 Accord, Odyssey 4-cyl. | 1995-97 2675cc Accord | 1998-99 2977cc Accord |

ELECTRICAL AND IGNITION SYSTEMS

BATTERY
BCI equivalent shown, size may vary from original equipment.
Check clearance before replacing, holddown may need to be modified.

Engine	Year	STANDARD BCI Group No.	STANDARD Crank. Perf.	OPTIONAL BCI Group No.	OPTIONAL Crank. Perf.
Accord	1989	26	405	—	—
	1990-93	24	550	—	—
	1994-97	24F	550	—	—
	1998-00	35	455	—	—
Civic: U.S. prod.	1989	52	405	—	—
Japan prod.	1989	51	410	—	—
Civic	1990-91	51	405	—	—
	1992-00	51R	405	—	—
CR-V	1997-00	51R	405	—	—
CRX	1989-91	51	410	—	—
Del Sol	1992-97	51R	405	—	—
Odyssey	1995-00	24F	550	—	—
Prelude	1989	26	405	—	—
	1990-91	24	585	—	—
	1992-00	24F	550	—	—

GENERATOR

Application	Year	Rated Output	Test Output (amps @ eng. rpm)
Accord	1989	70	75-86 @ 2000
Accord	1990-91	80	78-95 @ 2000
Accord	1992-93	80	40 min. @ 2000
	1994-00	80	65 min. @ 2000
	1994-00	90	70 min. @ 2000
	1997-00	100	75 @ 2000
Civic, CRX	1989	60	38-48 @ 2000
Civic, CRX	1990-91	60	38-48 @ 2000
Civic	1992-95	70	40 min. @ 2000
Civic	1996-00	75, 80	50 min. @ 2000
CR-V	1997-00	100	75 min. @ 2000
Del Sol	1992-95	70	40 min. @ 2000
	1994-00	80	40 min. @ 2000
Del Sol	1996-97	75	50 min. @ 2000
		80	50 min. @ 2000
Odyssey	1995-97	95	75 min. @ 2000
Odyssey	1998	100	75 min. @ 2000
	1999-00	105	75 min. @ 2000
Prelude	1989	65	63-68 @ 2000

HAITU3

GENERATOR Continued

Application	Year	Rated Output	Test Output (amps @ eng. rpm)
Prelude	1990-91	70	70-80 @ 2000
Prelude	1992-96	80	55 min. @ 2000
		90	60 min. @ 2000
		95	65 min. @ 2000
	1997-99	100	75 min. @ 2000

REGULATOR

Application	Year	Test Temp. (deg. F/C)	Voltage Setting
All	1989-91	—	12.5-14.5
All	1992-00	—	13.5-15.1

STARTER

Engine	Year	Cranking Voltage (min. volts)	Max. Ampere Draw @ Cranking Speed
1493cc, 1590cc:			
0.8 kw	1989-91	8.0	200
1.0 kw	1989-91	8.5	230
1.2 kw	1989-91	8.0	280
1.4 kw	1989-91	8.0	350
1493cc, 1590cc, 1595cc	1992-95	8.0	400
1590cc	1996-00	8.5	350
1595cc: Mitsuba	1996-00	8.5	350
Nippondenso	1996-00	8.0	280
1955cc, 1958cc,			
2056cc, 2156cc	1989-94	8.5	350
Accord	1995	8.5	350
Prelude	1995-99	8.5	380
Accord: Mitsuba	1996-00	8.5	380
Nippondenso	1996-00	8.0	360
V6	1996-00	8.5	380
Odyssey	1995-98	8.5	350
CR-V	1997-00	8.5	380

SPARK PLUGS

1992-96 Prelude & 1997-00 all as equipped w/platinum tipped plugs; gap should be at specified value. Maximum gap is .051 in. (1.3 mm). Do not regap.

Engine	Year	Gap (inches)	Gap (mm)	Torque (ft-lb)
All	1989-93	.039-.043	1.0-1.1	13
1595cc	1994-97	.047-.051	1.2-1.3	13
All others	1994-00	.039-.043	1.0-1.1	13

IGNITION COIL
FOR TESTING AND ADJUSTMENT DIAGRAMS, SEE APPENDIX A.

Resistance (ohms @ 70°F or 21°C)

1990-91 1958cc, 2056cc: Primary windings measured between terminals A & D of coil connector. Secondary windings measured between terminal A of coil connector and high voltage terminal.

Engine	Year	Windings	Resistance (ohms)
1493cc, 1590cc	1989	Primary	0.3-0.5
		Secondary	9440-14,160
1493cc, 1590cc	1990-91	Primary	0.6-0.8
		Secondary	9760-14,640
1493cc, 1590cc, 1595cc	1992-95	Primary	0.6-0.8
		Secondary	12,800-19,200
1590cc, 1595cc TEC	1996-00	Primary	.45-.55
		Secondary	22,400-33,600
Hitachi	1996-00	Primary	.63-.77
		Secondary	12,800-19,200
1955cc	1989	Primary	1.2-1.5
		Secondary	11,074-11,526
1958cc	1989	Primary	1.2-1.5
		Secondary	9040-13,560

IGNITION COIL Continued

Engine	Year	Windings	Resistance (ohms)
1972cc	1997-00	Primary	.63-.77
		Secondary	12,800-19,200
1958cc, 2056cc	1990-91	Primary	0.3-0.4
		Secondary	9040-13,560
2156cc	1990-91	Primary	0.6-0.8
		Secondary	12,880-19,320
2156cc Odyssey	1995-97	Primary	0.4-0.6
		Secondary	22,000-34,000
2156cc others, 2259cc	1992-95	Primary	0.6-0.8
		Secondary	14,000-22,000
2156cc VTEC	1994-95	Primary	0.4-0.6
		Secondary	22,400-33,600
2156cc Accord	1996-97	Primary	.64-.78
		Secondary	14,400-21,600
VTEC	1996-97	Primary	.45-.55
		Secondary	16,800-25,200
2156cc, 2259cc Prelude	1996	Primary	0.6-0.8
		Secondary	14,000-22,000
2157cc	1997-99	Primary	.64-.78
		Secondary	14,400-21,600
2254cc	1998-99	Primary	.63-.77
		Secondary	12,800-19,200
VTEC	1998-99	Primary	.45-.55
		Secondary	16,800-25,200
2675cc	1995-97	Primary	0.3-0.4
		Secondary	14,000-22,000
2997cc	1998-99	Primary	.34-.42
		Secondary	17,100-20,900
3474cc	1999-00	Primary	.34-.42
		Secondary	17,100-20,900

DISTRIBUTOR PICKUP
FOR TESTING AND ADJUSTMENT DIAGRAMS, SEE APPENDIX B.

Includes TDC, camshaft and crankshaft position sensors mounted in distributor.

Application	Year	Resistance (ohms)	Air Gap (in./mm)
1493cc, 1590cc	1989-91	350-550[2]	—
1493cc, 1590cc, 1595cc	1992-95	350-700	—
1590cc Civic	1996-00	350-700	—
Del Sol	1996-97	500-1000	—
1595cc	1996-00	500-1000	—
1955cc FI, 1958cc 2×1V	1989-90	650-850	[1]
1958cc FI, 2056cc	1990-91	700-1100	—
1972cc	1997-00	350-700	—
2156cc	1990-91	350-700[2]	—
2156cc	1992-93	260-500	—
2156cc Accord ex. VTEC, Odyssey	1994-95	700-1300	—
Others	1994-95	350-700	—
2156cc Accord	1996-97	800-1500	—
Prelude	1996	350-700	—
2157cc	1998-99	260-460	—
2259cc	1992-96	350-700[2]	—

1 Equal space between pickup and reluctor on each side.

2 On 5 terminal connectors, measured between two low, or two center terminals. On 7 terminal connectors, measured between each of three adjacent pairs of terminals.

BASE TIMING
FOR TESTING AND ADJUSTMENT DIAGRAMS, SEE APPENDIX C.

1989: Leave distributor vacuum hoses, as equipped, connected.

1989: On models w/o vacuum advance (EST), remove yellow cap from timing connector (located in left rear engine compartment or by coil) and jumper the two terminals.

1990-00: Jumper terminals of 2-pin timing connector located on right side under dash.

UNDERHOOD SERVICE SPECIFICATIONS

BASE TIMING Continued

Engine	Year	Man. Trans. (degrees)	Auto. Trans. (degrees)
1493cc	1989-91	18±2	18±2
1493cc HF	1989-91	14±2	14±2
1493cc: D15B8	1992-95	12±2	12±2
Others	1992-95	16±2	16±2
1590cc	1989-91	18±2	18±2
	1992-95	16±2	16±2
	1996-00	12±2	12±2
1595cc	1994-97	16±2	—
	1999-00	12±2	—
1955cc 2V	1989	24±2[1]	15±2 D[1]
California	1989	20±2[1]	15±2 D[1]
1958cc 2×1V	1989	20±2[1]	15±2[1]
California	1989	15±2[1]	10±2[1]
1958cc FI, 2056cc, 2156cc, 2259cc	1989-97	15±2	15±2
1972cc	1997-00	16±2	16±2
2157cc	1997-99	15±2	15±2
2254cc	1998-99	12±2	12±2
2675cc	1995-97	—	15±2
2997cc	1998-00	—	10±2
3474cc	1999-00	—	10±2

1 With vacuum hoses disconnected and plugged, 4° BTDC.

DISTRIBUTOR TIMING ADVANCE
Engine degrees at engine rpm, no load, in addition to base timing setting.
Mechanical advance distributors only.

Engine	Transmission	Year	Distributor Number	Degrees @ 2500 RPM Total	Degrees @ 2500 RPM Centrifugal
1955cc 2V	MT	1989	D4R85-55/TD-41K	—	—
1955cc 2V	MT	1989	D4R84-57/TD-43K	34.8-42.8	12.8-16.8
1955cc 2V	AT	1989	D4R84-58/TD-42K	29.5-37.5	11.5-15.5
1955cc FI	MT	1989	TD-06N/9N	19.5-23.5[1]	12-16
1958cc FI	AT	1989	TD-07N/10N	17.5-21.5[1]	10-14

1 Subadvance, 11-15 @ 12".

FUEL SYSTEM

FUEL PUMP
FOR TESTING AND ADJUSTMENT DIAGRAMS, SEE APPENDIX D.
With fuel injection; pressure measured at fitting on fuel filter.

Engine	Year	Pressure PSI[1]	Pressure PSI[2]
Carbureted:			
1958cc 2×1	1989-90	2.6-3.3 ign. on	—
Fuel Injected:			
1493cc, 1590cc	1989-91	35-41	35-37
1493cc, 1590cc	1992-95	40-47	30-38
1590cc Civic	1996-00	38-46	28-36
1595cc	1999-00	40-47	30-37
Del Sol	1996-97	40-47	31-36
1955cc, 1958cc, 2056cc, 2156cc	1989-90	35-41	35-37
1972cc	1997-99	38-46	30-37
1972cc	1997-98	38-46	30-37
	1999-00	40-47	31-38
2156cc Accord, SOHC, Odyssey	1991-93	40-47	30-38
	1994-97	38-46	30-37
2156cc SOHC Prelude, 2259cc	1992-96	36-43	28-35
2156cc DOHC	1993-96	33-40	24-31
2157cc	1997-99	40-47	30-37
2254cc	1998-99	40-47	30-37
2675cc	1995-97	44-51	36-43
2997cc	1998-00	41-48	32-40
3474cc	1999-00	41-48	32-40

1 With pressure regulator vacuum hose disconnected.
2 With pressure regulator vacuum hose connected.

IDLE SPEED W/O COMPUTER CONTROL
Preferred setting is the midpoint of range given.

1989 1830cc, 1955cc 2V MT:
Disconnect and plug intake air control vacuum hose, with engine warm, set idle speed to specification.

Turn A/C on and adjust speed-up speed to specified value.

1955cc 2V AT:
Disconnect and plug intake air control vacuum hose. Remove filter from frequency solenoid valve and plug opening in valve. Lower idle speed as much as possible by adjusting throttle stop screw. Set base idle speed to specified value by adjusting screw on throttle cable linkage. Readjust throttle stop screw to idle speed specification. Place transmission in gear and adjust screw on boost diaphragm linkage to idle speed A. Place transmission in neutral and turn A/C on. Set speed-up speed to specified value by adjusting screw on boost diaphragm.

Engine	Year	SLOW Man. Trans.	SLOW Auto. Trans.	FAST Man. Trans.	FAST Auto. Trans.	Step of Cam
1955cc 2V	1989	750-850	650-750 N	2000-3000	2000-300 N	High
idle control A	1989	—	650-750 D			
speed-up	1989	750-850	650-750 N			
base idle	1989	—	580-680 N			
1958cc 2×1	1989-90	750-850	700-800 D	1600-2000	1600-2000 N	Third
speed-up		750-850	700-800 D			

IDLE SPEED W/COMPUTER CONTROL
FOR TESTING AND ADJUSTMENT DIAGRAMS, SEE APPENDIX E.

1998-00 2997cc, 3474cc; 1996-00 All 1590cc ex. D16Y5 & D16Y8 w/MT: Adjust as necessary by turning idle speed screw ½ turn at a time. Turn A/C on and verify that idle increases to specified value.

1989-00 All others: Electrically disconnect idle air control valve. 1998-00, disconnect FVAP purge control solenoid valve. Set idle to set speed. Remove HAZARD or BACKUP or CLOCK fuse for 10 seconds to reset ECM. Verify that idle is at checking speed. Turn headlights and A/C on separately to check speed-up speeds.
Canada, pull up on hand brake to turn headlights off.

Engine	Year	Trans-mission	Set Speed	Checking Speed	Speed-up Speed	Fast Idle (Cold)
1493cc	1989-91	MT	575-675	700-800	750-850	1000-2000
1493cc	1989-91	AT	575-675 N	700-800 N	750-850 N	1000-2000 N
Canada	1990-91	MT	575-675	750-850	750-850	1000-2000
	1990-91	AT	575-675 N	750-850 N	750-850 N	1000-2000 N
1493cc HF	1989-91	MT	450-550	550-650	600-700	1000-1800
Calif., High Alt.	1989-91	MT	450-550	600-700	600-700	1000-1800
1493cc D15B8	1992-95	MT	370-470	620-720	700-800[1]	—
1493cc D15Z1	1992-95	MT	370-470	550-650	650-750[1]	—
1493cc D15B7	1992-95	MT	370-470	620-720	700-800[1]	—
		AT	370-470 N	650-750 N	700-800 N[1]	—
1590cc	1989	MT	500-600	700-800	730-830 N	1000-1800 N
1590cc	1989	AT	500-600 N	700-800 N	770-870 N	1000-2000 N
1590cc	1990-91	MT	500-600	700-800	730-830[2]	1000-2000
		AT	500-600 N	700-800 N	730-830 N[2]	1000-2000 N
1590cc	1992-95	MT	370-470	620-720	700-800[1]	—
		AT	370-470	650-750 N	700-800[1]	—
1590cc D16Y7 US	1996-00	MT	620-720	—	760-860	—
		AT	650-750 N	—	760-860 N	—
Canada	1996-00	MT	700-800	—	760-860	—
		AT	700-800 N	—	760-860 N	—
D16Y5 US	1996-00	MT	400-500	620-720	700-800[1]	—
		AT	650-750 N	—	760-860 N	—
Canada	1996-00	MT	400-500	700-800	700-800[1]	—
		AT	700-800 N	—	760-860 N	—
D16Y8 US	1996-00	MT	400-500	620-720	700-800[1]	—
		AT	650-750 N	—	760-860 N	—
Canada	1996-00	MT	400-500 N	700-800 N	700-800 N[1]	—
		AT	700-800 N	—	760-860 N	—
1595cc	1994-95	MT	370-470	650-750	700-800[1]	—
1595cc	1996-00	MT	400-500	650-750	700-800[1]	—
		AT	400-500 N	650-750 N	700-800 N[1]	—

HONDA
1989-2000 Includes Isuzu Oasis
Passport—See Isuzu

UNDERHOOD SERVICE SPECIFICATIONS

IDLE SPEED W/COMPUTER CONTROL Continued

Engine	Year	Trans-mission	Set Speed	Checking Speed	Speed-up Speed	Fast Idle (Cold)
1955cc, 1958cc FI	1989	MT	600-700	700-800	700-800	1100-1900
		AT	600-700 N	700-800 N	700-800 N	1100-1900 N
1958cc, 2056cc	1990-91	MT	600-700	720-820	720-820	1100-1900
		AT	600-700 N	720-820 N	720-820 N	1100-1900 N
1972cc AC	1997-00	MT	430-530	700-800	700-800	1300-1700
	1997-00	MT			730-830	
	1997-00	AT	430-530N	700-800	700-800N	1300-1700N
AC	1997-00	AT			730-830N	
1972cc AC	1999-00	MT	430-530	680-780	680-780	1400-1800
	1999-00	MT			720-820	
	1999-00	AT	430-530N	680-780N	680-780N	1400-1800N
AC	1999-00	AT			720-820N	
2156cc SOHC	1990-93	MT	500-600	650-750	720-820	1400
		AT	500-600 N	650-750 N	720-820 N	1400 N
2156cc DOHC	1992-93		450-550	650-750	740-840	—
2156cc Accord	1994-97	MT	500-600	650-750	720-820	1400
		AT	500-600 N	650-750 N	720-820 N	1400 N
2156cc Odyssey	1995-97	AT	500-600 N	650-750 N	720-820 N	1600
2156cc Prelude SOHC	1994-96	MT	500-600	650-750	720-820	400
		AT	500-600 N	650-750 N	720-820 N	400
2156cc Prelude DOHC	1994-96	MT	500-600	650-750	740-840	400
2157cc	1997-99	MT	500-600	650-750	740-840	1200-1600
		AT	500-600 N	650-750 N	740-840 N	1200-1600 N
2254cc	1998-99	MT	650-750	720-820	—	1100-1500
		AT	650-750N	720-820N	—	1100-1500
2259cc	1992-96	MT	500-600	650-750	730-830	400
		AT	500-600 N	650-750 N	730-830 N	400
2675cc	1995	AT	500-600 N	650-750 N	720-820 N	720-820 N
	1996-97	AT	550-650 N	700-800 N	720-820 N	720-820 N
2997cc	1998-00	AT	630-730N	—	630-730N	—
3474cc	1999-00	AT	680-780N	—	680-780N	—

1 Electrical speed-up listed; A/C speed-up, 760-860.
2 A/C speed-up, 760-860 (N). Wagon, 760-860 (N).

ENGINE MECHANICAL

TIGHTENING TORQUES
FOR CYLINDER HEAD TORQUE SEQUENCES AND DIAGRAMS, SEE APPENDIX F.

Some fasteners are tightened in more than one stage.

		TORQUE FOOT-POUNDS/NEWTON METERS				
Engine	Year	Cylinder Head	Intake Manifold	Exhaust Manifold	Crankshaft Pulley	Water Pump
1493cc, 1590cc	1989-91	22/30, 47/65	16/22	23/32	119/165	9/12-short 33/45-long
1493cc D15B7, B8	1992-95	22/30, 47/65	17/23	23/32	134/185	9/12
1493cc D15Z1, 1590cc	1992-95	22/30, 53/73	17/23	23/32	134/185	9/12
1590cc	1996-00	14/20, 32/49, 49/67, 49/67	17/23	23/32	134/185	9/12
1595cc	1994-00	22/30, 61/85	17/23	23/32	134/185	9/12
1955cc	1989	22/32, 49/68	16/22	23/32	108/150	9/12
1958cc, 2056cc	1989-91	22/32, 49/68	16/22	23/32	108/150	9/12
1972cc	1997-00	22/29, 63/85	17/23	23/31	130/177	9/12

TIGHTENING TORQUES Continued

		TORQUE FOOT-POUNDS/NEWTON METERS				
Engine	Year	Cylinder Head	Intake Manifold	Exhaust Manifold	Crankshaft Pulley	Water Pump
2156cc Accord, Odyssey	1990-93	29/40, 51/70, 78/108	16/22	23/32	159/220	9/12
	1994-97	29/39, 51/70, 72/98	16/22,	23/32	181/245	9/12
2156cc Prelude, 2259cc	1992-96	29/40, 51/70, 72/100	16/22	23/32	159/220	16/22
2157cc	1997-99	29/39, 51/70, 72/98	16/22	23/32	181/245	9/12
2254cc	1998-99	22/29, +90° +90°	16/22	23/32	181/245	9/12
2675cc	1995-97	29/39, 56/76	16/22	22/30	181/245	16/22
2997cc	1998-00	29/39, 51/69, 72/98	16/22	22/30	181/245	9/12

VALVE CLEARANCE
Engine cold.

Engine	Year	Intake[1] (inches)	Intake[1] (mm)	Exhaust (inches)	Exhaust (mm)
1342cc, 1488cc, 1493cc ex. HF, 1590cc	1989-91	.007-.009	.17-.22	.009-.011	.22-.27
1493cc HF	1989-91	.005-.007	.12-.17	.007-.009	.17-.22
1493cc, 1590cc	1992-00	.007-.009	.17-.22	.009-.011	.22-.27
1595cc	1994-00	.006-.007	.15-.17	.007-.008	.17-.21
1830cc, 1955cc, 1958cc ex. FI	1989	.005-.007	.13-.17	.010-.012	.25-.30
1958cc FI, 2056cc	1989-91	.003-.005	.08-.12	.006-.008	.16-.20
1972cc	1997-00	.003-.005	.08-.12	.006-.008	.16-.20
2156cc SOHC	1990-97	.009-.011	.24-.28	.011-.013	.28-.32
2156cc DOHC	1993-96	.006-.007	.15-.19	.007-.008	.17-.21
2157cc	1997-99	.006-.007	.15-.17	.007-.008	.17-.21
2254cc	1998-99	.009-.011	.24-.28	.011-.013	.28-.32
2259cc	1992-96	.003-.004	.07-.11	.006-.007	.15-.19
2997cc	1998-00	.008-.009	.20-.24	.011-.013	.28-.32

1 Includes auxiliary air valve where applicable.

COMPRESSION PRESSURE
At 400 rpm, unless otherwise specified, engine temperature normalized, throttle open.

Engine	Year	PSI	Maximum Variation PSI
1493cc	1989-95	135-185	28
1590cc	1989-00	135-185	28
1595cc	1994-95	135-220	28
	1996-97	135-242	28
	1998-00	135-220	28
1955cc 2V	1989	135-171	28
1955cc FI, 1958cc, 2056cc, 2156cc, 2259cc	1989-97	135-178	28
1972cc	1997-00	135-178	28
2156cc DOHC	1993-96	135-185	28
2157cc	1997-99	135-185	28
2254cc	1998-99	135-178	28
2675cc	1995-97	142-171	28
2977cc	1998-00	135-178	28

UNDERHOOD SERVICE SPECIFICATIONS

BELT TENSION
Deflection method: Deflection midway between pulleys with an applied load of 22 pounds on longest belt segment.

Engine	Year	Generator	Power Steering	Air cond.	Air Pump
Civic, CRX (inches)	1989-91	3/8-7/16	3/8-1/2	3/8-7/16	
(mm)	1989-91	9-11	9-12	9-11	—
Prelude ex. FI (inches)	1989	9/32-3/8	3/4-7/8	3/8-1/2	
(mm)	1989	7-10	18-22	10-12	—
Accord, Prelude FI (inches)	1989	1/4-3/8	3/4-7/8	3/8-1/2	
(mm)	1989	6-10	18-22	10-12	—
Accord, Prelude (inches)	1990-93	3/8-7/16	1/2-5/8	3/8-7/16	—
(mm)	1990-93	10-12	12.5-16	10-12	—

Model	Year	Generator	Power Steering	Air Cond.
Strand Tension method				

Use a strand tension gauge. Measurements are in pounds.

NEW BELTS:				
CR-V	1997-00	170-200	165-198	170-200
Civic, Del Sol	1992-95	121-165	110-154	132-176
	1996-00	121-165	143-176	159-187
Accord: 4-cyl.	1994-00	120-170	165-198	209-254
V6	1995-00	154-200	165-198	209-254
Odyssey	1995-98	231-254	170-200	231-254
Prelude	1994-96	110-154	154-198	209-254
	1997-00	200-231	170-200	198-231
USED BELTS:				
CR-V	1997-00	88-120	88-120	88-120
Civic, Del Sol	1992-95	77-110	77-110	77-110
	1996-00	77-110	77-110	77-110
Accord: 4-cyl.	1994-00	66-99	88-121	99-132
V6	1995-00	77-110	88-121	110-143
Odyssey	1995-00	110-132	88-120	110-132
Prelude	1994-96	66-99	77-110	99-132
	1997-00	88-120	88-120	88-120

ENGINE COMPUTER SYSTEM

DIAGNOSTIC TROUBLE CODES
FOR TESTING AND ADJUSTMENT DIAGRAMS, SEE APPENDIX G.

1989-91 Civic, CRX, Prelude, Accord
When MFI dash light is on consistently, access ECM under passenger side carpet under dash or kick panel and turn ignition on. LED will flash in short (ones) or long (tens) durations corresponding to each code with two-second intervals between separate codes. After making repairs, remove battery negative cable for 10 seconds to reset ECM.

1992-00
OBD-II systems can still retrieve codes on MIL. Locate 2- and 3-pin connectors by passenger side kick panel or under dash. Jumper the terminals of the 2-pin connector only. Codes will be displayed on "Check" engine light. Remove "Hazard" or "Back Up" or "Clock" fuse in fuse block to erase codes.

Civic, CRX, Del Sol, Accord, Prelude w/FI
Code 0 ECM
Codes 1, 2 Oxygen content
Codes 3, 5 Manifold absolute pressure
Code 4 Crankshaft position sensor
Code 6 Engine coolant temperature
Code 7 Throttle position sensor
Code 8 TDC position
Code 9 Camshaft position sensor
Code 10 Intake air temperature
Code 12 EGR system
Code 13 MAP or BARO sensor
Code 14 Idle air control valve
Code 15 Ignition output signal
Code 16 Fuel Injector
Code 17 Vehicle speed sensor
Code 19 Torque converter clutch solenoid valve
Code 20 Electric load detector
Code 21 Spool solenoid valve
Code 22 Valve timing oil pressure switch
Code 23 Knock sensor
Codes 30, 31 AT-FI signal
Code 41 Oxygen sensor heater
Code 43 Fuel supply system
Code 48 Heated oxygen sensor
Code 50 Mass air flow sensor
Code 61 Primary oxygen sensor slow response
Code 63 Secondary oxygen sensor slow response
Code 65 Secondary oxygen sensor heater
Code 67 Catalyst efficiency low

DIAGNOSTIC TROUBLE CODES Continued
Code 70 Transaxle problem
Code 71 Cylinder 1 misfire
Code 72 Cylinder 2 misfire
Code 73 Cylinder 3 misfire
Code 74 Cylinder 4 misfire
Code 75 Cylinder 5 misfire
Code 76 Cylinder 6 misfire (6-cyl.)
Code 76 Random misfire (ex. 6-cyl.)
Code 80 EGR flow insufficient
Code 86 Engine coolant out of range
Code 91 EVAP system leak or fuel tank pressure sensor
Code 92 EVAP system purge

Prelude 2×1V
Code 1 Oxygen content
Code 2 Vehicle speed sensor
Codes 3, 5 Manifold absolute pressure
Code 4 Vacuum switch signal
Code 6 Engine coolant temperature sensor
Code 8 Ignition coil signal
Code 10 Intake air temperature
Code 14 Electronic air control

SENSORS, INPUT
TEMPERATURE SENSORS

Engine	Year	Sensor	Resistance Ohms @ deg. F/C
All FI	1989-00	Coolant, Intake Air	15,000-20,000 @ -4/-20
			5000-7000 @ 32/0
			2000-4000 @ 68/20
			900-1200 @ 104/40
			300-400 @ 176/80
			100-300 @ 248/115

MANIFOLD ABSOLUTE AND BAROMETRIC PRESSURE SENSORS

Engine	Year	Sensor	Voltage @ in. Hg./kPa
All FI	1989-00	MAP, Barometric	2.7-2.9 @ 0/0
			2.3-2.5 @ 5/17
			1.8-2.0 @ 10/34
			1.4-1.6 @ 15/51
			0.9-1.1 @ 20/68
1958cc 2×1V	1989-90	MAP	2.7-2.9 @ 0/0
			2.3-2.5 @ 5/17
			1.8-2.0 @ 10/34
			1.4-1.6 @ 15/51
			0.9-1.1 @ 20/68

THROTTLE POSITION SENSOR

Engine	Year	Resistance (ohms)	Voltage Idle	Voltage WOT
All FI	1989-00	—	0.5 max.	4.5

CRANKSHAFT POSITION SENSOR
Unit mounted at front of engine. Other ignition sensors, see Distributor Pickup.

Engine	Year	Resistance (ohms)
4-cyl. as equipped	1996	500-1000
4-cyl.: Civic, Del Sol, CR-V	1997-00	1600-3200
Accord, Odyssey	1997	1850-2450
Prelude	1997-99	1200-3200
V6: Crankshaft	1996-97	1800-2500
TDC, Cyl. position	1996-97	1500-3000

ACTUATORS, OUTPUT
IDLE SPEED CONTROL SOLENOID

Engine	Year	Resistance (ohms)
All FI	1989-90	8-15

FUEL INJECTORS

Engine	Year	Resistance (ohms)	Temperature (deg. F/C)
All MFI	1989-91	1.5-2.5	—
All TBI: Main injector	1989-91	0.8-1.6	—
Auxiliary injector	1989-91	6-10	—
All Civic	1992-95	10-13	—
All Accord, Prelude	1992-95	1.5-2.5	—

HYUNDAI
1989-2000

ENGINE IDENTIFICATION

To identify any engine by the manufacturer's code, follow the four steps designated by the numbered blocks.

V.I.N.
PLATE LOCATION:

Top of instrument panel visible through windshield.

1 MODEL YEAR IDENTIFICATION:

10th character of V.I.N.

2000—Y	1999—X	1998—W
1997—V	1996—T	1995—S
1994—R	1993—P	1992—N
1991—M	1990—L	1989—K

2 ENGINE CODE LOCATION:

8th character of V.I.N.

---

4 ENGINE IDENTIFICATION

YEAR	3 ENGINE CODE	CYL.	DISPL. liters	cc	Fuel System	HP
2000	G	4	1.5	1495	MFI	92
	F	4	2.0	1975	MFI	140
	S	4	2.4	2351	MFI	137
	V	4	2.5	2493	MFI	142
1999	N	4	1.5	1495	MFI	92
	M	4	1.8	1795	MFI	130
	F	4	2.0	1998	MFI	140
	D	4	2.4	2351	MFI	NA
	E	6	2.5	2493	MFI	NA
1997-98	N	4	1.5	1495	MFI	92, 105
	M	4	1.8	1795	MFI	130
	F	4	2.0	1975	MFI	140
	F	4	2.0	1997	MFI	137
	T	6	3.0	2972	MFI	142
1995-96	N	4	1.5	1495	MFI	92
	N	4	1.5 T	1495 T	MFI	115
	F	4	2.0	1997	MFI	137
	T	6	3.0	2972	MFI	142
1993-94	J	4	1.5	1468	MFI	81
	N	4	1.5	1495	MFI	92

YEAR	3 ENGINE CODE	CYL.	DISPL. liters	cc	Fuel System	HP
1993-94 Cont'd.	N	4	1.5 T	1495 T	MFI	115
	R	4	1.6	1597	MFI	105, 113
	M	4	1.8	1836	MFI	124
	F	4	2.0	1997	MFI	128
	T	6	3.0	2972	MFI	142
1992	J	4	1.5	1468	MFI	81
	R	4	1.6	1597	MFI	105, 113
	F	4	2.0	1997	MFI	128
	T	6	3.0	2972	MFI	142
1991	J	4	1.5	1468	MFI	81
	S	4	2.4	2351	MFI	116
	T	6	3.0	2972	MFI	142
1990	J	4	1.5	1468	MFI	81
	S	4	2.4	2351	MFI	116
	T	6	3.0	2972	MFI	142
1989	J	4	1.5	1468	2V	68
	S	4	2.4	2351	MFI	116
	T	6	3.0	2972	MFI	142

MFI—Multiport Fuel Injection. **2V—Two Venturi Carburetor.**
T—Turbo.

UNDERHOOD SERVICE SPECIFICATIONS

HIITU1   HIITU1

CYLINDER NUMBERING SEQUENCE

4-CYL. FIRING ORDER: 1 3 4 2

— Front of car —

1989-94 Excel, Scoupe 1468cc	1993-early 94 Scoupe 1495cc	1994 late-00 Accent, Scoupe 1495cc	1992-95 Some Elantra 1597cc, 1836cc, 1992-96 Sonata 1997cc

V6 FIRING ORDER:
1 2 3 4 5 6

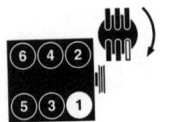

— Front of car —

1999-00 Sonata 2493cc	1989-98 Sonata 2972cc

— Front of car —

1994-95 Other Elantra 1597cc, 1836cc 1994-98 Sonata 1997cc	1996-00 Elantra, Tiburon 1795cc, 1975cc	1989-91 Sonata 2351cc	1999-00 Sonata 2351cc

HYUNDAI
1989-2000

UNDERHOOD SERVICE SPECIFICATIONS

TIMING MARK

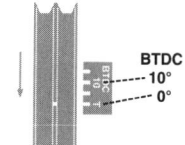

1989-94
Excel, Scoupe 1468cc,
Elantra 1597cc,1795cc, 1839cc
1989-98
Sonata 1997cc, 2351cc
1997-00
Tiburon 1795cc, 1975cc

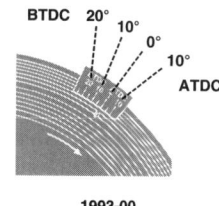

1993-00
1495cc

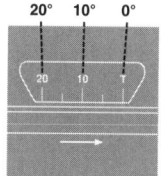

1989-98
Sonata 2972cc

ELECTRICAL AND IGNITION SYSTEMS

BATTERY

BCI equivalent shown, size may vary from original equipment.
Check clearance before replacing, holddown may need to be modified.

Engine	Year	STANDARD BCI Group No.	STANDARD Crank. Perf.	OPTIONAL BCI Group No.	OPTIONAL Crank. Perf.
1468cc	1989-94	25[1]	420[1]	—	—
Canada	1989-91	24	580	—	—
1495cc	1993-97	25	380	25	420
	1998-00	25	420	—	—
1597cc, 1836cc Elantra	1992-95	25	420	—	—
1795cc, 1975cc	1996-00	25	435	—	—
1997cc Sonata	1992-97	25	420	24	540
2351cc	1989-91	25	420	—	—
Canada	1989-91	24	580	—	—
2493cc	1999-00	24	540	—	—
2972cc	1990-98	24	540	—	—
Canada	1990-91	24	580	—	—

1 Some models use a Group 35.

GENERATOR

Engine	Year	Rated Output (amps)	Test Output (amps)
1468cc	1989	60	42 @ 2500
1468cc	1990-94	75	53 @ 2500
1495cc	1993-99	75	53 @ 2500
	1996-97	90	63 @ 2500
	2000	80	56 @ 2500
1597cc, 1836cc	1992-95	75	53 @ 2500
1795cc, 1975cc	1996-00	90	63 @ 2500
1997cc	1992-98	75, 90	53 @ 2500
2351cc	1989-91	75	53 @ 2500
	1999-00	95	630 @ 2500
2493cc	1999-00	95	63 @ 2500
2972cc	1990-98	90	53 @ 2500

REGULATOR

Engine	Year	Voltage Setting	Test Temp. (deg. F/C)
1468cc	1989	14.4-15.6	-4/-20
		14.2-15.2	68/20
		13.8-15.1	140/60
		13.6-15.0	176/80
All others	1989-00	14.2-15.4	-4/-20
		13.9-14.9	68/20
		13.4-14.6	140/60
		13.1-14.5	176/80

SPARK PLUGS

Engine	Year	Gap (inches)	Gap (mm)	Torque (ft-lb)
1468cc	1989-94	.039-.043	1.0-1.1	15-21
1495cc	1993-00	.039-.043	1.0-1.1	15-21
Turbo	1993-96	.031-.035	0.8-0.9	15-21

SPARK PLUGS Continued

Engine	Year	Gap (inches)	Gap (mm)	Torque (ft-lb)
1597cc, 1836cc	1992-95	.039-.043	1.0-1.1	15-21
1795cc, 1975cc	1996-00	.039-.043	1.0-1.1	15-21
1997cc	1992-98	.039-.043	1.0-1.1	15-21
2351cc	1989-91	.039-.043	1.0-1.1	15-21
	1999-00	.039-.043	1.0-1.1	15-21
2493cc	1999-00	.039-.043	1.0-1.1	15-21
2972cc	1990-98	.039-.043	1.0-1.1	15-21

IGNITION COIL
Winding resistance (ohms @ 68°F or 20°C)

1992 1597cc, 1997cc: Primary windings are measured between terminals 1 & 3 and 2 & 3 (diagonally) of 4-terminal coil connector. Secondary windings are measured between adjoining coil high tension towers.

Engine	Year	Windings	Resistance (ohms)
1468cc	1989	Primary	1.1-1.3
		Secondary	11,600-15,800
1468cc	1990-94	Primary	.72-.88
		Secondary	10,300-13,900
1495cc	1993-00	Primary	.45-.55
		Secondary	10,300-13,900
1597cc, 1836cc	1992-95	Primary	.77-.95
		Secondary	10,300-13,900
1795cc, 1975cc	1996-00	Primary	.45-.55
		Secondary	10,300-13,900
1997cc	1992-98	Primary	.77-.95
		Secondary	10,300-13,900
2351cc	1989-91	Primary	.72-.88
		Secondary	10,890-13,310
	1999-00	Primary	.78
		Secondary	20,000
2493cc	1999-00	Primary	.67-.81
		Secondary	11,300-15.300
2972cc	1990-98	Primary	.72-.88
		Secondary	10,300-13,900

DISTRIBUTOR PICKUP

Engine	Year	Resistance (ohms)	Air Gap (in./mm)
1468cc	1989	—	.030/.80

IGNITION RESISTOR

Engine	Year	Type	Resistance (ohms)	Temperature (deg. F/C)
1468cc	1989	Unit	1.2-1.6	68/20

BASE TIMING
Set timing at slow idle and Before Top Dead Center, unless otherwise specified.
Carbureted:
U.S. models except high altitude, leave vacuum hoses connected.
High altitude and Canadian models, disconnect and plug distributor vacuum hose.

BASE TIMING Continued

Fuel Injected:

1468cc, 2350cc, ground ignition timing connector.

1597cc, 1836cc, 1997cc, 2972cc, jumper terminals of ignition timing connector.

All models, when ignition timing connector is ungrounded or not jumpered, timing should be at Check value.

1495cc, 1795cc, 1975cc; 1999-00 All: Check timing with a timing light or scan tool. If timing is not within specified range, further diagnosis of the engine management system is necessary.

Engine	Year	Man. Trans. (degrees)	Auto. Trans. (degrees)
1468cc: Set	1989	5±2	5±2
1468cc: Set	1990-94	5±2	5±2
Check	1990-94	10±2	10±2
1495cc, thru 3/94	1993-94	9±5[1]	9±5[1]
1495cc Scoupe, from 4/94	1994-95	10±5[1]	10±5[1]
1495cc Accent	1995-00	9±5[1]	9±5[1]
DOHC	1996-97	11±5[1]	11±5[1]
1597cc, 1836cc: Set	1992-95	5±2	5±2
Check, 1597cc	1992-95	8±2	8±2
Check, 1834cc	1993-95	14±2	14±2
1795cc, 1975cc	1996-00	10±5[1]	10±5[1]
1997cc: Set	1992-93	5±2	5±2
Check	1992-93	8±2	8±2
1997cc	1994-98	5±2[1]	5±2[1]
2351cc: Set	1989-91	5±2	5±2
Check	1989-91	10±2	10±2
2351cc	1999-00	5±2[1]	5±2[1]
2493cc	1999-00	12±5[1]	12±5[1]
2972cc: Set	1989-98	—	5±2
Check	1989-98	—	15±2

1 Not adjustable, checking figure only.

DISTRIBUTOR TIMING ADVANCE

Engine degrees at engine rpm, no load, in addition to base timing setting.

Engine	Trans-mission	Year	Distributor Number	Degrees @ 2500 RPM Total	Degrees @ 2500 RPM Centrifugal
1468cc Fed.	MT	1989	21430	24-32	3-7
1468cc Fed.	AT	1989	21440	21-29	3-7
1468cc Calif.	MT & AT	1989	21410, 20	21-29	3-7

FUEL SYSTEM

FUEL SYSTEM PRESSURE

At idle

Engine	Year	Pressure PSI[1]	Pressure PSI[2]
Fuel Injected:			
All	1989-92	46-49	39 approx.
1495cc	1993-96	44.3	37 approx.
1495cc	1997-99	43.5	36 approx.
	2000	—	50 approx.
1795cc, 1975cc	1996-00	44.3	37 approx.
2351cc, 2493cc	1999-00	46-49	37 approx.
Others	1993-98	46-49	39 approx.

1 Vacuum hose connected to fuel pressure regulator.

2 Vacuum hose disconnected from fuel pressure regulator.

IDLE SPEED W/O COMPUTER CONTROL

To set idle speed, turn idle speed screw to obtain specified value. Adjust solenoids, as equipped, to obtain specified speed-up speed.

Midpoint of range given is the preferred setting speed.

Engine	Year	SLOW Man. Trans.	SLOW Auto. Trans.	FAST Man. Trans.	FAST Auto. Trans.	Step of Cam
1468cc	1989	700-900	700-900 N	2800	2700 N	Second
PS, Elec. speed-up	1989	750-950	750-950 N			
A/C speed-up	1989	850-900	850-900 N			

IDLE SPEED W/COMPUTER CONTROL

1468cc, 2350cc: Turn ignition on for 20 seconds. Disconnect ISC and start engine. Adjust to specified setting speed.

1597cc, 1836cc, 1997cc, 2972cc: Jumper ignition timing connector terminals, and Self Diagnostic check terminal (10 and ground of DLC).

Engine	Year	Setting Speed	Checking Speed	AC Speed-up
1468cc to 3/93 MT	1990-93	600-800	—	—
AT	1990-93	600-800 N	—	—
1468cc from 3/93: MT	1993-94	725-925	—	—
AT	1993-94	725-925 N	—	—
1495cc MT	1993-00	—	700-900	720-920
AT	1993-00	—	700-900 N	720-920 N
1597cc MT	1992-95	650-850	—	—
AT	1992-95	650-850 N	—	—
1795cc, 1975cc MT	1996-00	—	700-900	750-950
AT	1996-00	—	700-900 N	750-950 N
1836cc MT	1993-95	600-800	—	—
AT	1993-95	600-800 N	—	—
1997cc MT	1992-93	700-800	650-850	—
AT	1992-93	700-800 N	650-850 N	—
1997cc MT	1994-98	650-850	—	—
AT	1994-98	650-850 N	—	—
2351cc MT	1989-91	650-850	650-850	—
AT	1989-91	650-850 N	650-850 N	—
2351cc MT	1999-00	—	700-900	—
AT	1999-00	—	700-900 N	—
2493cc	1999-00	—	600-800 N	—
2972cc AT	1989-93	650-750 N	600-800 N	—
	1994-98	600-800 N	—	—

ENGINE MECHANICAL

TIGHTENING TORQUES

Engine	Year	TORQUE FOOT-POUNDS/NEWTON METERS Cylinder Head[1]	Intake Manifold	Exhaust Manifold	Crankshaft Pulley	Water Pump
1468cc	1989-94	51-54/ 69-74	12-14/ 16-19	12-14/ 16-20	9-11/ 12-15, small 51-72/ 70-100, large	9-11/ 12-15, short 14-20/ 20-27, long
1495cc	1993-99	51-54/ 69-74	11-14/ 15-20	11-14/ 15-20	9-10/ 13-14, small 140-148/ 190-200, large	9-11/ 12-15
	2000	17-20/ 23-27, +60°, +60°	11-15/ 15-20	11-15/ 15-20	103-111/ 140-150	9-11/ 12-15
1597cc	1992	65-72/ 90-100	11-14/ 15-20	18-22/ 25-30	14-22/ 20-29, small	9-11/ 12-15, short 14-20/ 20-26, long
1597cc, 1836cc	1993-95	76-83/ 105-115	11-14/ 15-20	18-22/ 25-30	14-22/ 20-29	9-11/ 12-15, short 14-20, 20-26, long
1795cc, 1975cc	1996-00	2	13-18/ 18-25	22-30/ 30-40	125-133/ 170-180	9-11/ 12-15
1997cc	1992-93	76-83/ 105-115	11-14/ 15-20	11-14/ 15-20	14-22/ 20-29, small 80-94/ 110-130, large	9-11/ 12-15, small 14-20/ 20-29, long
	1994-98	65-72/ 90-100	11-14/ 15-20	11-14/ 15-20	14-22/ 20-29, small 80-94/ 110-130, large	9-11/ 12-15, short 14-20/ 20-26, long
2350cc	1989-91	65-72/ 90-100	11-14/ 15-19	11-14/ 15-19	14-22/ 20-30	9-11/ 12-15, short 14-20/ 20-27, long

UNDERHOOD SERVICE SPECIFICATIONS

TIGHTENING TORQUES Continued

Engine	Year	TORQUE FOOT-POUNDS/NEWTON METERS				
		Cylinder Head[1]	Intake Manifold	Exhaust Manifold	Crankshaft Pulley	Water Pump
2350cc	1999-00	14/20, +90°[3]	[4]	22-29/ 30-40	80-94	11-15/ 15-22
2493cc	1999-00	18/25 +45°	13-15 19-21	18-22/ 25-30	130-138/ 180-190	11-16/ 15-22
2972cc	1990-91	65-72/ 88-98	11-14/ 15-20	11-14/ 15-20	108-116/ 147-157	14-20/ 20-26
	1992-93	76-83/ 105-115	11-14/ 15-20	11-16/ 15-22	108-116/ 147-157	14-20/ 20-26
	1994-98	65-72/ 90-100	11-14/ 15-20	11-16/ 15-22	108-116/ 147-157	14-20/ 20-26

1 Engine cold.
2 M10 bolts: 22/30,
 +60°,
 +60°
 M12 bolts: 26/35,
 +60°,
 +60°
3 Back off all bolts one turn then tighten to 14/20, +90°, +90°.
4 M8 bolts: 11-14/15-20;
 M6 bolts: 13-18/18-22;
 nuts: 25/40

VALVE CLEARANCE
Engine hot, measured at valve stem.

Engine	Year	Intake (inches)	Intake (mm)	Exhaust (inches)	Exhaust (mm)
1437cc, 1468cc, 1597cc, 1997cc SOHC	1989-94	.006	.15	.010[1]	.25[1]
1495cc thru 3/94	1993-94	.010	.25	.012	.30
2350cc	1989-91	[2]	[2]	—	—

1 2V engines, includes jet valve.
2 Jet valve, .010 in./.25 mm.

COMPRESSION PRESSURE
At cranking speed, engine warm, throttle open.

Engine	Year	PSI	Maximum Variation PSI
1468cc	1989	164 @ 250	—
1468cc	1990-94	171-192	14
1495cc	1993-95	171-192	14
Turbo	1993-95	135-149	14
1495cc SOHC	1996-00	220-234	14
DOHC	1996-97	199-213	14
1597cc, 1836cc	1992-95	171-192	14
1795cc, 1975cc	1996-00	199-213	14
1997cc	1992-98	171-192	14
2350cc	1999-00	178	14
2493cc	1999-00	149-170	14
2972cc	1990-98	149-170	14

BELT TENSION
Deflection method: With 22 pounds of pressure applied midway between pulleys on longest belt segment.

Engine	Year	Generator	Power Steering	Air Cond.	Air Pump
Deflection:					
All (mm)	1989-96	7-9	7-9	7-9	7-9
All (inches)	1989-96	1/4-3/8	1/4-3/8	1/4-3/8	1/4-3/8
Strand Tension Method:					
1495cc: New	1993-00	40	38-48	32-40	—
Used	1993-00	65-75	55-70	65-70	—
1795cc, 1975cc: New	1996-00	110-154	—	—	—
Used	1996-00	88	—	—	—
1997cc: New	1994-98	110-155	—	—	—
Used	1994-98	80	—	—	—

SERPENTINE BELT DIAGRAMS

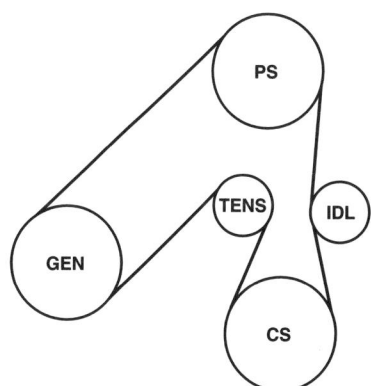

1990-00 V6 2493cc w/o AC

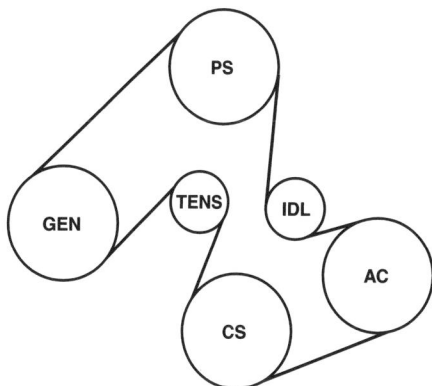

1990-00 V6 2493cc w/AC

ENGINE COMPUTER SYSTEM

DIAGNOSTIC TROUBLE CODES
1993-95 1495cc
Access the self diagnostic connector in driver side kick panel. Ground the L-wire (#10±) for 3 seconds. 4-digit codes will be displayed on malfunction indicator lamp.

1989 Sonata, 1990-95 All Others
Access diagnostic connector in glove box or driver's side kick panel and connect on analog voltmeter to the upper right (+) and lower left (-) cavities. Turn ignition on. Voltmeter will sweep in long pulses, indicating tenths; and short pulses, indicating ones.

1996-00 All
OBD-II system used. Connect a Scan tool and follow manufacturer's instructions to retrieve codes.

1993-95 1495cc
Code 1233 ECM failure, ROM
Code 1234 ECM failure, RAM
Code 1122 ECM failure, ROM/RAM
Code 3233 ECM failure, knock control
Code 3224 ECM failure, knock evaluation circuit
Code 3241 ECM failure, injector or purge control solenoid
Code 3242 ECM failure, idle speed control or A/C relay
Code 4155 ECM failure, injector PCV, ISC, A/C relay
Code 3128 O_2 sensor
Code 3117 Mass airflow sensor
Code 3145 Engine coolant temperature sensor
Code 3222 Phase sensor
Code 3232 Crankshaft position sensor
Code 3153 Throttle position sensor
Code 3211 Knock sensor
Code 3137 Generator
Code 3149 Compressor A/C
Code 3152 Turbo boost, too high

DIAGNOSTIC TROUBLE CODES Continued

Code 4156 Turbo boost, control deviation
Code 2121 Turbo boost, control valve
Code 3121 Turbo boost, pressure sensor
Code 3112 No. 1 injector
Code 3234 No. 2 injector
Code 3116 No. 3 injector
Code 3235 No. 4 injector
Code 3135 Purge control solenoid
Code 3114 Idle speed actuator, opening failure
Code 3122 Idle speed actuator, closing failure
Code 4151 Air/Fuel control
Code 4153 Air/Fuel adaptive failure, multiplicative
Code 4152 Air/Fuel adaptive failure, A/N
Code 4154 Air/Fuel adaptive failure, additive
Code 4444 System normal
Code 3333 End of message
1989 Sonata, 1990-95 Others
Code 11 Oxygen sensor
Code 12 Airflow sensor
Code 13 Intake air temperature sensor
Code 14 Throttle position sensor
Code 15 Motor position sensor
Code 21 Engine coolant temperature sensor
Code 22 Crankshaft position sensor
Code 23 TDC sensor
Code 24 Vehicle speed sensor
Code 25 Barometric pressure sensor
Code 41 Injector
Code 42 Fuel pump
Code 43 EGR
Code 44 Ignition coil
One long sweep ECM
Continuous pulsing System normal

SENSORS, INPUT

TEMPERATURE SENSORS

Engine	Year	Sensor	Resistance Ohms @ deg. F/C
1495cc, 1795cc, 1975cc, 2493cc	1993-00	Coolant	5180-6600 @ 32/0 2270-2730 @ 68/20 1059-1281 @ 104/40 298-322 @ 176/180 219-243 @ 194-190
All others	1989-00	Coolant	5900 @ 32/0 2500 @ 68/20 1100 @ 104/40 300 @ 176/80
1468cc	1989	Intake Air	2450 @ 68/20
2351cc	1989	Intake Air[1]	5900 @ 32/0 2500 @ 68/20 1100 @ 104/40 300 @ 176/80
1468cc, 1997cc, 2351cc, 2978cc	1990-00	Intake Air[2]	5400-6600 @ 32/0 2300-3000 @ 68/20 310-430 @ 176/80

1 Measured between terminals 2 & 4 of airflow sensor.
2 Measured between terminals 4 & 6 (lower right & left) of airflow sensor.

Engine	Year	Sensor	Voltage @	Temperature degrees F/C
1495cc, 1795cc, 1975cc, 2493cc	1996-00	Intake Air[3]	3.3-3.7 2.4-2.8 1.6-2.0 0.5-0.9	32/0 68/20 104/40 176/80

3 Measured between terminals 1 & 3 of MAF sensor.

PRESSURE SENSORS

Engine	Year	Sensor	Voltage @ in. Hg./kPa
All FI	1989-91	Barometric[1]	.79 @ 2.8/9 1.84 @ 7/24 4.00 @ 14.2/48

1 Measured between terminals 5 & 6 (lower middle & lower left) of airflow sensor.

SENSORS, INPUT Continued

THROTTLE POSITION SENSOR

1989 1468cc: Back out speed screws enough to close throttle valve. Connect DVOM between two lower horizontal blades of TPS. Adjust screw on linkage to specified voltage.
1989-91 early 1468cc, 2350cc: Measure voltage along single upper (-) and lower left (+) terminals of TPS.
1991 late-97 1468cc, 1597cc, 1836cc, 1997cc: Measure voltage between first and third terminals of TPS connector.
2972cc: Measured between upper and lower right terminals of TPS connector.

Model	Year	TPS Voltage	
		Idle	WOT
1468cc	1989	.25	—
1468cc	1990-94	.48-.52	4.5-5.5
1495cc	1993-95	.25-.60	4.2-4.6
	1996	.25-.80	4.2-4.8
	1997-00	.10-.875	4.2-4.8
1597cc, 1836cc	1992-95	.48-.52	4.5-5.5
1795cc, 1975cc	1996-97	.25-.80	4.2-4.8
	1998-00	.10-.875	4.2-4.8
1997cc	1989	.50	—
1997cc	1992-96	.48-.52	4.5-5.5
1997cc	1996-98	.40-1.0[1]	4.5-5.5
2351cc	1989-91	.48-.52	—
	1999-00	.30-.90	4.25-4.7
2493cc	1999-00	.25-.80	4.25-4.7
2972cc	1989-93	.48-.52	4.5-5.5
	1994-98	.40-1.0[1]	—

1 Not adjustable.

MASS AIRFLOW SENSOR

1989-93, measured between terminals 3 & 6 (upper and lower left) of airflow sensor.

Engine	Year	Volts @ Condition
2351cc	1989	2.2-3.2 @ idle
All	1990-91	2.7-3.2 @ idle
1495cc, 1795cc, 1975cc	1993-95	.94-.98 @ idle 1.76-1.79 @ 3000 rpm
	1996-00	0.7-1.1 @ idle 1.3-2.0 @ 3000 rpm
1495cc Turbo	1993-95	2.0-2.6 @ idle 2.66-3.3 @ 3000 rpm
2351cc, 2493cc	1999-00	0.5 @ idle 1.0 @ 2000 rpm
1468cc, 1597cc, 1836cc	1992-95	27-33 @ idle 60-80 @ 2000
1997cc	1992-93	25-50 @ idle 70-90 @ 2000
	1994	28-33 @ idle 60-80 @ 2000
	1995-98	25-50 @ idle 70-90 @ 2000
2972cc	1992-98	30-45 @ idle 85-105 @ 2000

CRANKSHAFT SENSOR

Engine	Year	Resistance (ohms) @ 68°F (20°C)
1495cc, 1795cc, 1975cc	1996-00	486-594

KNOCK SENSOR

Engine	Year	Resistance (ohms) @ 68°F (20°C)
1495cc, 1795cc, 1975cc	1996-00	5,000,000 approx.

ACTUATORS, OUTPUT

IDLE SPEED CONTROL SOLENOID

1468cc, 2350cc: Measured between two upper terminals of ISC connector.
1597cc, 1836cc, 1997cc, 2972cc: Measured between center and either left or right terminals on both rows of 6-terminal ISC connector.

UNDERHOOD SERVICE SPECIFICATIONS

ACTUATORS, OUTPUT Continued

IDLE SPEED CONTROL SOLENOID Continued

Engine	Year	Resistance (ohms) @ 68°F (20°C)
1468cc, 2351cc	1989-94	5-35
1495cc Scoupe	1993-95	13-14
1495cc Accent, 1795cc, 1975cc, 2493cc		
Term. 1 & 2	1996-00	10.5-14
Term. 2 & 3	1996-00	10-12.5
1597cc, 1836cc, 1997cc, 2972cc	1990-00	28-33

MIXTURE CONTROL SOLENOID

Engine	Year	Resistance (ohms)
1468cc	1989	54-66

ACTUATORS, OUTPUT Continued

COMPUTER TIMING ADVANCE

With engine at operating temperature, check advance at idle and 2000 rpm. Specifications include initial timing. At high altitudes, add 5°.

Engine	Year	Degrees	
		Idle	2000
1468cc	1990-94	8-12	26-34
1597cc, 1836cc	1992-95	5-15	32-40
1997cc	1992-98	5-15	33-41
2351cc	1989-91	5-15	30-40
2972cc	1990-92	5-15	30-40
	1993-98	5-15	32-40

FUEL INJECTORS

Engine	Year	Resistance (ohms)	Temperature (deg. F/C)
All	1989-95	13-16	68/20
1495cc, 1795cc, 1975cc	1996-00	15.55-16.25	68/20
1997cc, 2351cc, 2493cc, 2972cc	1996-00	13-16	68/20

ENGINE IDENTIFICATION

To identify any engine by the manufacturer's code, follow the four steps designated by the numbered blocks.

V.I.N.
PLATE LOCATION:

Chassis number appears on plate attached to instrument panel visible through windshield.

1 MODEL YEAR IDENTIFICATION:

10th character of V.I.N.

2000—Y	1999—X	1998—W	1997—V
1996—T	1995—S	1994—R	1993—P
1992—N	1991—M	1990—L	

2 ENGINE CODE LOCATION:

4th Character of V.I.N.

4 ENGINE IDENTIFICATION

YEAR	3 ENGINE CODE	CYL.	DISPL. liters	cc	Fuel System	HP
1999-00	B	4	2.0	1998	MFI	140
	C	6	3.0	2998	MFI	190
	A	6	3.3	3275	MFI	168
	B	8	4.1	4130	MFI	266
1998-97	A	6	3.0	2960	MFI	210
	C	6	3.0	2988	MFI	190
	A	6	3.3	3275	MFI	168
	B	8	4.1	4130	MFI	266
1996-95	B	4	2.0	1998	MFI	140
	A	6	3.0	2960	MFI	210
	C	6	3.0	2988	MFI	190
	N	8	4.5	4495	MFI	278

4 ENGINE IDENTIFICATION

YEAR	3 ENGINE CODE	CYL.	DISPL. liters	cc	Fuel System	HP
1994-93	C	4	2.0	1998	MFI	140
	A	6	3.0	2960	MFI	210
	N	8	4.5	4494	MFI	278
1992	C	4	2.0	1998	MFI	140
	H	6	3.0	2960	MFI	162
	N	8	4.5	4494	MFI	278
1991	C	4	2.0	1998	MFI	140
	H	6	3.0	2960	MFI	162
	N	8	4.5	4494	MFI	278
1990	H	6	3.0	2960	MFI	162
	N	8	4.5	4494	MFI	278

MFI—Multiport Fuel Injection.

UNDERHOOD SERVICE SPECIFICATIONS

IIITU1   **CYLINDER NUMBERING SEQUENCE**   IIITU1

4-CYL. FIRING ORDER:
1 3 4 2

V6 FIRING ORDER:
1 2 3 4 5 6

— Front of car —

1991-94 1998cc G20	1995-99 1998cc G20	1990-92 2960cc M30	1992-97 2960cc J30	1995-00 2988cc I30

V6 FIRING ORDER:
1 2 3 4 5 6

V8 FIRING ORDER:
1 8 7 3 6 5 4 2

— Front of car —

1997-00 QX4 3275cc   **1990-00 4130cc, 4494cc Q45**

ATDC 5° 0° 5° 10° 15° 20° BTDC

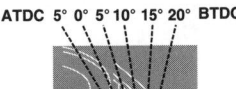
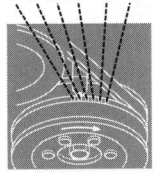

1990-00 1998cc G20, 2960cc M30 4130cc, 4494cc Q45 1997-00 QX4 3275cc

TIMING MARK

BTDC 30° 20° 10°   ATDC 0°

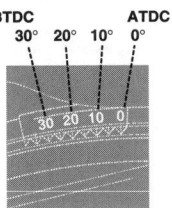

1993-97 2960cc J30

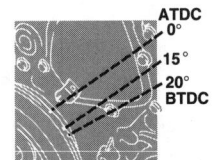

ATDC 0° / 15° / 20° BTDC

1995-00 2988cc I30

ELECTRICAL AND IGNITION SYSTEMS

BATTERY

BCI equivalent shown, size may vary from original equipment. Check clearance before replacing, holddown may need to be modified.

		STANDARD		OPTIONAL	
Engine	Year	BCI Group No.	Crank. Perf.	BCI Group No.	Crank. Perf.
G20	1991-94	24F	585	—	—
California	1991-94	35	350	—	—
G20	1995-96	24F	585	—	—
G20	1999	24F	550	—	—
I30	1995-99	85	350	24F	585
Canada	1995-99	24F	585	—	—
M30	1990-91	24	415	—	—
M30	1992	24	415	—	—
Convertible	1992	25	360	—	—
J30	1993-95	24	585	—	—
	1996-97	24	490	24	585
Canada	1996-97	24	585	—	—

BATTERY Continued

		STANDARD		OPTIONAL	
Engine	Year	BCI Group No.	Crank. Perf.	BCI Group No.	Crank. Perf.
Q45	1990-96	27	625	—	—
	1997-00	24	580	—	—
QX4	1997-99	25	355	27	445
Canada	1997-99	27	445	—	—

GENERATOR

Application	Year	Rated Output (amps)	Test Output (amps @ eng. rpm)
G20	1991-00	80	63 @ 2500
I30	1995-97	125	94 @ 2500
	1997-00	110	85 @ 2500
M30, J30	1990-97	90	65 @ 2500
Q45	1990-00	110	82 @ 2500
QX4	1997	90	65 @ 2500
	1998-00	100	78 @ 2500

UNDERHOOD SERVICE SPECIFICATIONS

IIITU2

IIITU2

REGULATOR

Application	Year	Test Temp. (deg. F/C)	Voltage Setting
All	1990-00	—	14.1-14.7

SPARK PLUGS

Application	Year	Gap (inches)	Gap (mm)	Torque (ft-lb)
All	1990-00	.039-.042	1.0-1.1	14-22

G20 without platinum-tipped spark plugs, .031-.035 (0.8-0.9).

IGNITION COIL
Resistance (ohms @ 68°F or 20°C).

Engine	Year	Windings	Resistance (ohms)
1998cc	1991-95	Primary	1.0[1]
		Secondary	10,000[1]
	1996-99	Primary	0.5-1.0
		Secondary	25,000[1]
2960cc	1990-92	Primary	1.0[1]
		Secondary	10,000[1]
2960cc	1993-97	Primary	0.9[1]
		Secondary	8,000[1]
3275cc	1997-00		1.0[1]
			10,000[1]
4494cc	1990-96	Primary	0.7[1]
		Secondary	8,000[1]

[1] Approximately.

BASE TIMING
Set timing at slow idle and Before Top Dead Center, unless otherwise specified.

All Models: Race engine at 2000 rpm for two minutes. Disconnect throttle position sensor harness. On models with coils connected to spark plugs, remove coil from #1 spark plug and connect a high tension wire between the two. Connect timing light inductive clamp to the high tension wire.

2960cc, 3275cc, 4494cc: Rotate camshaft sensor or distributor to adjust.

2988cc, 4130cc: Timing not adjustable.

Engine	Year	Man. Trans. (degrees)	Auto. Trans. (degrees)
1998cc	1991-99	15 ± 2	15 ± 2
2960cc	1990-95	—	15 ± 2
	1996-97	—	10 ± 2
2988cc	1995-00	15 ± 2[1]	15 ± 2[1]
3275cc	1997-00	15 ± 2	15 ± 2
4130cc	1997-00	—	15 ± 2[1]
4494cc	1990-96	—	15 ± 2

[1] Not adjustable.

FUEL SYSTEM

FUEL SYSTEM PRESSURE
Values are approximate pressure.

Engine	Year	Pressure[1] (PSI)	Pressure[2] (PSI)	RPM
1998cc	1991-96	36	43	idle
	1999-00	34	43	idle
2960cc	1990-92	34	43	idle
2960cc	1993-98	36	43	idle
2988cc	1995-00	34	43	idle
3275cc	1997-00	34	43	idle
4130cc	1997-00	34	43	idle
4494cc	1990-96	34	43	idle

[1] Vacuum hose connected to fuel pressure regulator.
[2] Vacuum hose disconnected from fuel pressure regulator.

IDLE SPEED W/COMPUTER CONTROL
1990-92 M30, 1990-95 Q45, 1992-95 J30: Disconnect idle air control valve electrical lead.

1992-96 G20, 1996-00 I30, J30, Q45, QX4: Disconnect throttle position sensor electrical lead.

All Models: Set idle speed. Reconnect electrical lead and verify that idle is at Checking Speed. Turn A/C on and verify that speed increases to Speed-up value.

IDLE SPEED W/COMPUTER CONTROL Continued

Engine	Year	Transmission	Checking Speed	Setting Speed	Speed-up Speed
1998cc	1991-94	MT	750-850	700-800	800-900
		AT	750-850N	700-800N	800-900N
	1995-00	MT	750-850	700-800	850 min.
		AT	750-850N	700-800N	850N min.
2960cc	1990-92	AT	750-850N	700N	750-850N
	1993-95	AT	670-770N	645-695N	750-850N
	1996-97	AT	670-770N	620-720N	800N min.
2988cc	1995-00	MT	575-675	525-625	850 min.
		AT	650-750N	600-700N	850N min.
3275cc	1997-00	MT	700-800	650-750	800 min.
		AT	700-800N	650-750N	800N min.
4130cc	1997-98	AT	600-700N	575-625N	700N min.
	1999-00	AT	600-700N	550-650N	700N min.
4494cc	1990	AT	700-800N	645-695N	700-800N
	1991-94	AT	600-700N	575-625N	700-800N
	1995-96	AT	600-700N	575-625N	700-700N

ENGINE MECHANICAL

TIGHTENING TORQUES
Some fasteners are tightened in more than one step.

Engine	Year	TORQUE FOOT-POUNDS/NEWTON METERS				
		Cylinder Head	Intake Manifold	Exhaust Manifold	Crankshaft Pulley	Water Pump
1998cc	1991-99	29/39, 58-78[1]	13-15 18-21	27-35 37-48	105-112 142-152	12-15 16-21
2960cc	1990-92	22/29, 43/59[2]	12-14 16-20	13-16/ 18-22	90-98/ 123-132	12-15/ 16-21
2960cc	1993-96	29/39, 90/123[3]	13-16/ 16-20	13-16/ 18-22	159-174/ 216-235	12-15/ 16-21
2988cc	1995-99	72/90[5]	13-16/ 18-27	21-24/ 28-32	29-36/ 39-49, +65°	63-85[5]/ 7-10
3275cc	1997-00	22/29, 43/59[2]	13-16/ 18-22	21-25/ 28-33	141-156/ 191-211	12-15/ 16-21
4130cc, 4494cc	1990-00	22/29, 69/89[4]	12-15/ 16-21	20-23/ 27-31	260-275/ 353-373	12-15/ 16-21

[1] Loosen fasteners, retorque to 25-33/34-44, then turn an additional 90-100° and again 90-100°.
[2] Loosen fasteners, retorque to 22/29, then turn an additional 60-65° (or 40-47/54-65).
[3] Loosen fasteners, retorque to 25/33, then turn an additional 70°.
[4] Loosen fasteners, retorque to 18-25/25-33, then turn an additional 90-95° (or 69-72/93-98).
[5] Loosen fasteners, retorque to 25-33/34-44 then turn 90° and, again, 90°.

COMPRESSION PRESSURE
At cranking speed, engine warm, throttle open.

Engine	Year	PSI	Maximum Variation PSI
1998cc	1991-00	149-178	14
2960cc	1990-92	128-173	14
2960cc	1993-97	142-186	14
2988cc	1990-00	142-185	14
3275cc	1997-00	128-173	14
4130cc	1997-00	144-186	14
4494cc	1990-96	142-185	14

VALVE CLEARANCE
Set with engine cold.

Engine	Year	Intake (inches)	Intake (mm)	Exhaust (inches)	Exhaust (mm)
2988cc I30	1995-00	.010-.013	.26-.34	.011-.015	.29-.37

BELT TENSION
Deflection midway between pulleys with an applied force of 22 lb.

Engine	Year	Generator	Power Steering	Air Cond.
Deflection method:				
1998cc(inches)	1991-96	1/4-9/32	1/8-3/16	9/32-5/16
(mm)	1991-96	7-8	3.5-4.5	6.5-7.5
2960cc(inches)	1990-92	1/4-5/16	1/2-9/16	3/8-7/16
(mm)	1990-92	6.5-7.5	12-14	8-9
2960cc(inches)	1993-98	1/4-5/16	9/16-1/2	5/16-5/8
(mm)	1993-98	6.5-7.5	11-13	8.5-9.5

Copyright 2000 by Chek-Chart Publications

UNDERHOOD SERVICE SPECIFICATIONS

IIITU3   IIITU3

BELT TENSION Continued

Engine	Year	Power Generator	Steering	Air Cond.
2988cc(inches)	1995-98	5/32	1/4	5/16
(mm)	1995-98	4.5	6.5	7.5
3275cc(inches)	1997-98	1/4	7/16	15/32
(mm)		6.5	11	12
4130cc(inches)	1997-98	3/16	15/32	7/16
(mm)		4.5	12	11
4494cc(inches)	1990-96	5/16-3/8	3/8-7/16[1]	5/16-3/8
(mm)	1990-96	7.5-8.5	8-9[1]	7.5-8.5

Strand Tension method:

Engine	Year	Power Generator	Steering	Air Cond.
NEW				
1998cc	1999-00	150-170	150-170	170-190
2998cc	1999-00	180-200	170-190	200-220
4130cc	1999-00	190-210	100-120	135-155
USED				
1998cc	1999-00	125-145	125-145	145-165
2998cc	1999-00	165-185	110-130	165-185
4130cc	1999-00	165-185[2]	80-100	110-130

1 With Super HICAS, 3/16-1/4" (5.5-6.5mm).
2 Water pump: 150-165, new; 120-140, used.

ENGINE COMPUTER SYSTEM

DIAGNOSTIC TROUBLE CODES

1990-95: To obtain codes, access ECU and locate LED's and mode selector switch cavity. Turn mode selector switch fully clockwise. After two seconds, turn switch counterclockwise. Again, turn switch clockwise, wait for two seconds, and then turn counterclockwise. The red LED will flash in long bursts (tens) or short bursts (ones) corresponding to codes.

To erase codes, disconnect battery terminal.

1996-00: To obtain codes, access ECU and locate mode selector switch cavity. Turn male selector switch fully clockwise. After two seconds, turn switch counterclockwise. Again turn switch clockwise, wait two seconds and then turn counterclockwise. The MIL will flush long bursts (tens) or short bursts (ones) corresponding to codes.

Code 11 Crankshaft position sensor
Code 12 Mass airflow meter circuit
Code 13 Engine coolant temperature sensor
Code 14 Vehicle speed sensor
Code 21 Ignition signal circuit
Code 22 Fuel pump
Code 25 IAC system
Code 28 Cooling fan
Code 31 ECM
Code 32 EGR
Code 33 Oxygen sensor circuit
Code 34 Knock sensor circuit
Code 35 Exhaust gas temperature sensor
Code 38 Closed loop control (left side)
Code 40 EGR system
Code 41 IAT sensor
Code 42 EGR vacuum valve (1996)
Code 42 Fuel temperature sensor (1990-95)
Code 43 Throttle sensor circuit
Code 45 Injector leak
Code 51 Injector circuit
Code 53 Oxygen sensor (right side)
Code 54 Automatic transmission to ECU interface circuit
Code 55 No malfunction
Code 63 Cylinder 6 misfire
Code 64 Cylinder 5 misfire
Code 65 Cylinder 4 misfire
Code 66 Cylinder 3 misfire
Code 67 Cylinder 2 misfire
Code 68 Cylinder 1 misfire
Code 72 Catalytic converter, right side
Code 73 Catalytic converter, left side
Code 76 Fuel injection system
Codes 77 & 78 Rear oxygen sensor
Code 82 Crankshaft sensor
Code 84 AT diagnosis com. line
Code 87 EVAP system
Code 91 Front oxygen sensor
Code 95 Crankshaft sensor
Code 98 Coolant temperature sensor

SENSORS, INPUT

TEMPERATURE SENSORS
Fuel temperature sensors are attached to fuel pressure regulator.

SENSORS, INPUT Continued

Engine	Year	Sensor	Resistance Ohms @ deg. F/C
All	1990-00	Coolant, Fuel	7000-11,000 @ 14/-10
			2100-2900 @ 68/20
			680-1000 @ 122/50
			300-330 @ 176/80
			736-260 @ 194/90
			140-150 @ 230/110

Engine	Year	Sensor	Resistance Ohms @ deg. F/C
2988cc, 4130cc	1999-00	EGR	6,800,000-11,100,000 @ 32/0
			900,000-1,200,000 @ 122/50
			17,000-24,000 @ 212/100
All others, as equipped	1990-00	EGR	77,000-94,000 @ 212/100
			7,900,000-9,700,000 @ 32/0
			570,000-700,000 @ 122/50
			80,000-100,000 @ 212/100
			10,000-20,000 @ 302/150

THROTTLE POSITION SENSOR

Engine	Year	Voltage Idle	Voltage WOT
1998cc	1991-94	.45-.55 min	4.0 max.
	1995-00	.35-.65	4.0 max.
2960cc, 2988cc	1990-95	0.4-0.5 min	4.0 max.
	1996-00	.35-.65	4.0 max.
3275cc	1997-00	0.3-0.7	4.0
4130cc #1	1997-00	.35-.65	4.0
#2	1997-00	.60-1.15	4.3-4.7
4494cc	1990-96	0.4-0.5	4.0 max.

MASS AIRFLOW SENSOR

Engine	Year	Voltage @ Idle	Voltage @ 2000 rpm
1998cc	1991-94	1.3-1.7	1.7-2.1
	1995-96	1.3-1.7	1.7-2.1
	1999-00	1.3-1.7	1.8-2.4
2960cc, 4494cc	1990	1.0-1.4	1.4-1.7
	1991-95	1.0-1.5	1.4-1.9
	1996-97	1.0-1.7	1.5-2.1
2988cc	1995-00	1.0-1.7	1.5-2.1
3275cc	1997-00	1.3-1.7	1.7-2.3
4130cc	1997-00	1.0-1.7	2.1 approx.

CRANKSHAFT & CAMSHAFT SENSORS

Engine	Year	Sensor	Resistance Ohms	Temperature (deg F/C)
1998cc, 2960cc	1996-00	Crankshaft	166-204	@ 68/20
2988cc	1996-00	Crankshaft	166-204	@ 68/10
Hitachi	1996-00	Camshaft	1440-1760	@ 68/20
Mitsubishi	1996-00	Camshaft	2090-2550	@ 68/20
3275cc, 4130cc	1997-00	Crankshaft	166-204	@ 68/20

FUEL INJECTORS

Engine	Year	Resistance (ohms)	Temperature (deg. F/C)
All	1990-00	10-14	—

ACTUATORS, OUTPUT

IDLE SPEED CONTROL

Engine	Year	Resistance (ohms)
2988cc, 4130cc	1995-00	30.0 approx.
All others	1990-00	10.0 approx.

AIR REGULATOR VALVE
Controls fast idle.

Engine	Year	Resistance (ohms)
1998cc	1995-96	70-80
2960cc	1993-97	70-80

COMPUTER TIMING ADVANCE

Engine	Year	Idle	Advance @ 2000 rpm
1998cc	1991-94	15	25 min.
	1995-00	13-15	25 min.
2960cc	1993-97	15	25 min.
2988cc	1995-00	15	25 min.
3275cc	1997-00	10	25 min.
4130cc	1997-00	15	25 min.
4494cc	1990-96	15	25 min.

ISUZU

ENGINE IDENTIFICATION

To identify any engine by the manufacturer's code, follow the four steps designated by the numbered blocks.

V.I.N. PLATE LOCATION:

Top of instrument panel visible through windshield.

1 MODEL YEAR IDENTIFICATION:

10th character of V.I.N.

2000—Y	1999—X	1998—W
1997—V	1996—T	1995—S
1994—R	1993—P	1992—N
1991—M	1990—L	1989—K

2 ENGINE CODE LOCATION:

8th character of V.I.N.

3 ENGINE — 4 ENGINE IDENTIFICATION

YEAR	CODE	CYL.	DISPL. liters	cc	Fuel System	HP
1998-00	D	4	2.2	2198	MFI	129
	W	6	3.2	3165	MFI	205
	X	6	3.5	3494	MFI	230
1996-97	E	4	2.6	2559	MFI	120
	V	6	3.2	3165	MFI	190
1995	L	4	2.3	2254	2V	96
	L	4	2.3	2254	MFI	100
	E	4	2.6	2559	MFI	120
	V	6	3.2	3165	MFI	175
	W	6	3.2	3165	MFI	190
1994	L	4	2.3	2254	2V	96
	L	4	2.3	2254	MFI	100
	E	4	2.6	2559	MFI	120
	Z	6	3.1	3137	TBI	120
	V	6	3.2	3165	MFI	175
	W	6	3.2	3165	MFI	190
1993	6	4	1.6	1588	MFI	96
	8	4	1.8	1809	MFI	140
	L	4	2.3	2254	MFI	96
	E	4	2.6	2559	MFI	120
	Z	6	3.1	3137	TBI	120
	V	6	3.2	3165	MFI	190
	W	6	3.2	3165	MFI	190
1992	6	4	1.6	1588	MFI	96
	4	4	1.6 T	1588 T	MFI	160
	8	4	1.8	1809	MFI	140

YEAR	CODE	CYL.	DISPL. liters	cc	Fuel System	HP
1992 Cont'd.	L	4	2.3	2254	2V	96
	E	4	2.6	2559	MFI	120
	Z	6	3.1	3137	TBI	120
	V	6	3.2	3165	MFI	175
	W	6	3.2	3165	MFI	190
1991	6	4	1.6	1588	MFI	96
	5	4	1.6	1588	MFI	130
	4	4	1.6 T	1588T	MFI	160
	L	4	2.3	2254	2V	96
	E	4	2.6	2559	MFI	120
	R	6	2.8	2827	TBII	120
	Z	6	3.1	3137	TBI	120
1990	6	4	1.6	1588	MFI	96
	5	4	1.6	1588	MFI	125
	L	4	2.3	2254	2V	96
	E	4	2.6	2559	MFI	120
	R	6	2.8	2827	TBI	120
1989	7	4	1.5	1471	2V	70
	9	4	1.5 T	1471 T	MFI	110
	5	4	1.6	1588	MFI	125
	F	4	2.0 T	1994 T	MFI	140
	L	4	2.3	2254	2V	96
	L	4	2.3	2254	MFI	110
	E	4	2.6	2559	MFI	120
	R	6	2.8	2827	TBI	120

TBI—Throttle Body Injection.   MFI—Multiport Fuel Injection.
2V—Two Venturi Carburetor.   D—Diesel.   T—Turbo.
TD—Turbo Diesel.

UNDERHOOD SERVICE SPECIFICATIONS

IUITU1

CYLINDER NUMBERING SEQUENCE

IUITU1

4-CYL. FIRING ORDER: 1 3 4 2

 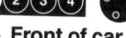

1989-93 I-Mark, Impulse, Stylus 1471cc, 1588cc DOHC	1990-93 Stylus 1588cc SOHC	1989 Impulse 1994cc Turbo, 1989-97 Amigo, Pickup, Trooper, Rodeo 2254cc, 2559cc

Front of car

6-CYL. FIRING ORDER: 1 2 3 4 5 6

   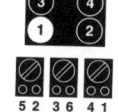  

Front of car

1989-95 Pickup, Trooper, Rodeo 2.8L, 3.1L	1993-95 Rodeo	1992-95 Trooper SOHC	1992-95 Trooper DOHC	1996-99 Rodeo, Trooper 3165cc, 3494cc

ISUZU

1989-2000 All Models Includes Acura SLX & Honda Passport
Hombre—See Chevrolet S10; Oasis—See Honda Odyssey

UNDERHOOD SERVICE SPECIFICATIONS

IUITU2IUITU2   IUITU2

TIMING MARK

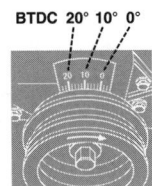

**1989 I-Mark 1471cc,
1989 Impulse 1994cc Turbo,
1989-93
I-Mark, Impulse, Stylus 1588cc**

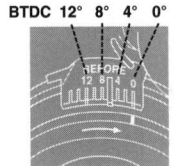

**1989-97
Impulse, Trooper, Amigo, Pickup
2254cc, 2559cc**

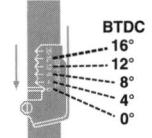

**1989-95
Pickup, Trooper, Rodeo
2.8L, 3.1L**

ELECTRICAL AND IGNITION SYSTEMS

BATTERY

BCI equivalent shown, size may vary from original equipment. Check clearance before replacing, holddown may need to be modified.

	STANDARD		OPTIONAL	
Engine	**BCI Group No.**	**Crank. Perf.**	**BCI Group No.**	**Crank. Perf.**
1989 I-Mark	21R	320	—	—
1989-94 Amigo Pickup: MT	25	430	—	—
AT	24	600	—	—
1989-91 Trooper: MT	25	360	—	—
AT	24	585	—	—
1992-94 Trooper: MT	24	490	27	620
AT	24	580	27	620
1991-92 Rodeo: 4-cyl., V6 MT	25	380	24	610
V6 AT	24	610	—	—
1993-97 Rodeo: 4-cyl.	86	430	—	—
V6 MT	86	430	—	—
V6 AT	24	600	—	—
1989 Impulse: MT	25	360	—	—
AT	24	490	—	—
1990-93 Stylus, Impulse	35	350	—	—
1995-97 Trooper: MT	24	490	27	625
AT	27	625	—	—
1998-00 All	24	490	24	580
			27	620

GENERATOR

Application	**Rated Output (amps @ eng. rpm)**	**Test Output (amps @ eng. rpm)**
1989 Impulse	60	30 @ 2000
Turbo	75	30 @ 2000
I-Mark	45,60	30 @ 2000
1990-93 Stylus, Impulse	75	1
1989-00 Amigo, Pickup, Trooper, Vehicross, Rodeo: 4-cyl.	50,60	1
V6 2.8L, 3.1L	85	1
V6 3.2L, 3.5L	60	20 min.
	75	25 min.

1 Output at 2000 rpm must be within 15 amps of rated output.

REGULATOR

Application	**Test Temp. (deg. F/C)**	**Voltage Setting**
1989 Impulse	—	14.05-15.03
Trooper V6	—	13.0-16.0
Others	—	14.2-14.8
1990-91 Trooper, 4-cyl.	—	14.2-14.8
V6	—	13.0-16.0
1990-97 Amigo, Pickup	—	13.0-16.0
Rodeo, 4-cyl., V6 3.2L	—	13.0-15.0
V6 3.1L	—	13.0-16.0
Stylus, Impulse	—	13.0-16.0
1992-97 Trooper	—	13.0-16.0
1998-00 All	—	13.0-16.0

STARTER

Model	**Cranking Voltage (min. volts)**	**Maximum Ampere Draw**
1989 I-Mark: MT	9.5	150
AT, Turbo	9.5	270
DOHC	8.0	280
Impulse, Trooper 4-cyl.	8.0	230
Trooper V6	9.0	—
1990-93 Stylus, MT	8.7	230
AT	8.0	280
Impulse, MT	8.7	230
AT	8.5	330
Turbo	8.0	280
1990-97 Amigo, Pickup, Trooper. Vehicross:		
4-cyl.	8.0	230
V6 2.8L, 3.1L	9.0	—
V6 3.2L, 3.5L	8.4	250
Rodeo, 4-cyl.	8.0	280
V6 3.1L	9.0	—
V6 3.2L	8.4	250

SPARK PLUGS

Engine	**Gap (inches)**	**Gap (mm)**	**Torque (ft-lb)**
1989-90 2.8L	.045	1.14	—
Others	.039-.043	1.0-1.1	—
1991-93 1.6L, 1.8L	.040	1.05	14
Turbo	.030	0.75	14
1991-95 2.3L, 2.6L	.040	1.05	14
2.8L, 3.1L	.045	1.14	14
3.2L	.039	0.43	1.0-1.1
1996-97 2.6L	.040	1.05	14
3.2L	.039-.043	1.0-1.1	14
1998-00 2.2L	.039-.043	1.0-1.1	14
3.2L, 3.5L	.039-.043	1.0-1.1	13

IGNITION COIL

Engine	**Year**	**Windings**	**Resistance (ohms)**
1471cc 2V	1989	Primary	1.2-1.5
		Secondary	10,200-13,500
1471cc Turbo, 1588cc	1989	Primary	0-2
		Secondary	6000-30,000
1588cc ex. Turbo, 1.8L	1990-93	Primary	1.2-1.5
		Secondary	10,200-13,800
1817cc, 1949cc, 1994cc, 2254cc FI	1989	Primary	1.13-1.53
		Secondary	10,200-13,800
2198cc	1998-00	Primary	0.8-1.8
		Secondary	9,000-12,000
2254cc 2V	1989-95	Primary	0.4-0.6
		Secondary	8600-13,000
2254cc FI	1994-98	Primary	.81-.99
		Secondary	7500-11,300
2559cc	1989-95	Primary	.81-.99
		Secondary	7500-11,300
	1996-97	Primary	0.8-1.3
V6 2.8L, 3.1L	1989-94	Primary	0.6-1.0
		Secondary	6500-10,200
3165cc, 3494cc	1996-00	Primary	0.8-1.3

Copyright 2000 by Chek-Chart Publications

DISTRIBUTOR PICKUP

Model	Resistance (ohms)	Air Gap (in./mm)
1471cc 2V	140-180	.008-.016/.2-.4
1471cc Turbo, 1588cc, 2.8L, 3.1L	500-1500	—
2156cc	800-1500	—
2254cc 2V	—	.012-.020/.3-.5

BASE TIMING

1471cc 2V, 2254cc 2V: Disconnect and plug distributor vacuum hose.

1588cc, 1809cc: Jumper first and third terminals of DLC connector by passenger side kick panel.

2156cc: Locate 2 & 3-terminal connectors under dash. Jumper the 2-terminal connector.

2.8L, 3.1L: Disconnect set timing connector by distributor.

Others: Set timing to specified value.

Engine	Year	Man. Trans. (degrees)	Auto. Trans. (degrees)
1471cc: Set	1989	3 @ 600-700	3 @ 850-950 N
Check[1]	1989	15 @ 750	10 @ 1000
1588cc, 1809cc	1989-93	10±1	10±1
1994cc FI, 2254cc FI	1989	12	12
2254cc 2V	1989-95	6	6
2254cc FI	1994-95	12	12
2559cc	1989-97	12	12
2.8L, 3.1L	1989-94	10	10
3165cc	1992-95	5[2]	5[2]
	1996-00	16[2]	16[2]
3494cc	1998-00	20[2]	20[2]

1 With vacuum hose connected.
2 Checking value, not adjustable.

DISTRIBUTOR TIMING ADVANCE

Engine degrees at engine rpm, no load, in addition to basic timing setting.

Mechanical advance distributors only.

Engine	Trans-mission	Year	Distributor Number	Degrees @ 2500 RPM Total	Degrees @ 2500 RPM Centrifugal
1471cc 2V	MT	1989	0401	30.5-38.5	4.5-8.5
1471cc 2V	AT	1989	0410	28.5-36.5	4.5-8.5

FUEL SYSTEM

FUEL SYSTEM PRESSURE

Engine	Year	Pressure PSI	RPM
Carbureted & TBI:			
1471cc 2V	1989	3.8-4.7	idle
2254cc 2V	1992-95	3.5	idle
2.8L, 3.1L	1989-94	9-13	idle
		13-18[1]	idle

1 With fuel return hose briefly restricted.

Engine	Year	Pressure PSI[1]	Pressure PSI[2]	Fuel Pump PSI
MFI:				
1471cc Turbo	1989	35.6	28.4	—
1588cc ex. Turbo	1989-91	35-38	25-30	—
1588cc Turbo	1991-92	—	40-47	65
1588cc ex. Turbo, 1809cc	1992-93	35-42	30-59	65 min.
2198cc	1998-00	42-55, ign. on	27-52, idle	55 min.
2254cc, 2559cc	1989-97	42	35	43
3165cc, 3494cc	1992-95	41-46	25-30	65 min.
	1996-00	42-55, ign. on	27-52, idle	55 min.

1 Pressure regulator vacuum hose disconnected.
2 Pressure regulator vacuum hose connected.

IDLE SPEED W/O COMPUTER CONTROL

1471cc 2V, 2254cc 2V: Disconnect and plug distributor, EVAP canister purge, and EGR vacuum hoses. Set idle to specified value. With A/C, turn A/C to maximum and adjust speed-up speed to specified value with solenoid fully extended.

2254cc FI: Disconnect wiring connector of vacuum solenoid valve and adjust idle speed by turning screw on throttle body.

2559cc: Disconnect and plug EVAP canister purge and EGR vacuum hoses. Disconnect pressure regulator vacuum solenoid valve electrical connector.

Midpoint of range given is the preferred setting.

Engine	Year	SLOW Man. Trans.	SLOW Auto. Trans.	FAST Man. Trans.	FAST Auto. Trans.	Step of Cam
1471cc 2V	1989	750	1000 N	3700	4100	High
speed-up	1989	850	980 N			
2254cc 2V	1989-95	850-950	850-950 N	2700-3000	2700-3000 N	High
2254cc FI	1989-95	850-950	850-950 N	—	—	—
2559cc	1989-95	850-950	850-950 N	—	—	—

IDLE SPEED W/COMPUTER CONTROL

1989-90 1471cc, 1588cc: Ground test terminal on DLC connector. Race engine over 2000 rpm and set idle to specified value.

Engine	Year	Setting Speed MT	Setting Speed AT	Checking Speed MT	Checking Speed AT
1471cc Turbo	1989	950	—	900-1000	—
1588cc	1989	900	—	—	—
1588cc	1990	950	950 N	—	—
1588cc	1991-93	—	—	800-900	890-990 N
Turbo	1991-93	—	—	850-950	—
1809cc	1992-93	—	—	800-900	800-900 N
2198cc	1998-00	—	—	750-900	750-900N
2.8L, 3.1L	1989-94	—	—	550-750	550-750 N
3.2L, 3.5L	1992-95	—	—	650-850	700-800 N
	1996-00	—	—	650-850	650-850 N

ENGINE MECHANICAL

TIGHTENING TORQUES

Some fasteners are tightened in more than one step.

Engine	Year	TORQUE FOOT-POUNDS/NEWTON METERS Cylinder Head	Intake Manifold	Exhaust Manifold	Crankshaft Pulley	Water Pump
1471cc	1989	29/39, 58/79	17/22	—	108/147	17/23
1588cc, 1809cc	1989-93	29/39, 58/79	17/22	30/39[1]	108/147	17/23
1994cc	1989	58/79, 72/98	16/21	16/21	86/117	14/19
2198cc	1998-00	18/25 +90°[1] +90°[1] +90°[1]	16/22	16/22	14/20	18/25
2254cc	1989-95	58/79, 72/98	16/21-nut 14/19-bolt	16/21	86/117	14/19
2559cc	1989-97	58/79, 72/98	16/21	33/44	86/117	14/19
2.8L, 3.1L	1989-94	40/55, +90°	19/26	25/34	70/95	7/10[2] 18/25[3]
3165cc, 3494cc	1992-00	47/64 72/98[4]	17/24	42/57	123/67	13/18

1 Turbo, 43/59.
2 Small bolts.
3 Large bolts.
4 Small bolts at front of head, 15/21.

ISUZU

1989-2000 All Models Includes Acura SLX & Honda Passport
Hombre—See Chevrolet S10; Oasis—See Honda Odyssey

VALVE CLEARANCE

Engine cold.

Model	Intake (inches)	Intake (mm)	Exhaust (inches)	Exhaust (mm)
1989-94 4-cyl. 2559cc	.006	.15	.010	.25
1989-92 2559cc	.008	.20	.008	.20
1993-97 2559cc	.006	.15	.010	.25
1998-00 3165cc	.011	.28	.012	.30
1998-00 3494cc	.011	.28	.015	.38

COMPRESSION PRESSURE

At cranking speed, engine warm, throttle open.

Engine	Year	PSI	Maximum Variation PSI
1471cc	1989	128-179	1
1588cc	1989-93	128 min.	1
1949cc FI, 1994cc	1989	125-178	1
2254cc 2V, 2559cc	1989-90	119-171	8.5
2254cc, 2559cc	1991-94	142-170[2]	—
	1995-97	128 min.	—
2254cc FI	1989	125-178	14
2.8L, 3.1L	1989-94	100 min.	3
3165cc, 3494cc	1992-00	128 min.	—

1 Lowest cylinder pressure must be within 6.5% of average cylinder pressure.
2 114 PSI minimum.
3 Lowest cylinder pressure must be within 75% of highest.

BELT TENSION

Model	Year	Generator	Power Steering	Air Cond.	Air Pump
Tension method					
I-Mark	1989	70-110	70-110	70-110	70-110
Stylus, Impulse	1990-93	70-110	120-150	120-150	—
Rodeo, Trooper					
V6 3.2L: New	1992-00	170-190	70-110	100-140	—
Used	1992-00	110-120	70-110	80-120	—
Deflection method					
All others (in.)	1989-00	3/8	3/8	3/8	3/8
(mm)	1989-00	10	10	10	10

SERPENTINE BELT DIAGRAMS

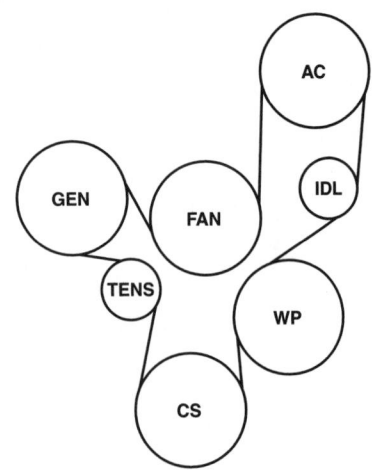

1998-99 4-cyl. 2198cc
w/oPS & w/AC

SERPENTINE BELT DIAGRAMS Continued

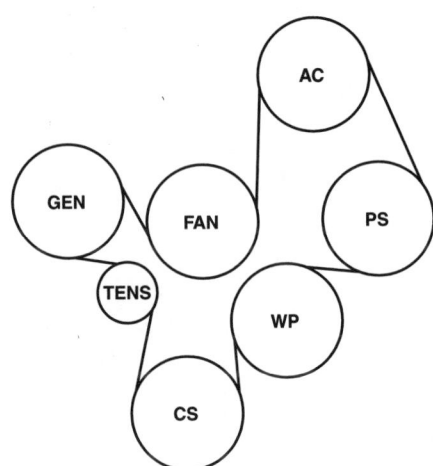

1998-99 4-cyl. 2198cc
w/PS & AC

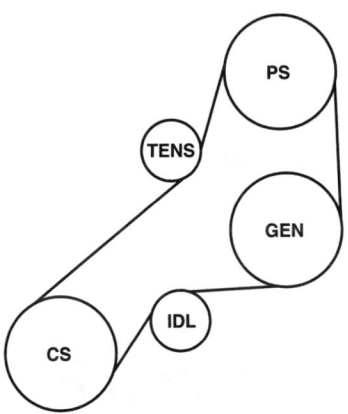

1991-93 4-cyl. 1809cc ex. Turbo
w/o AC

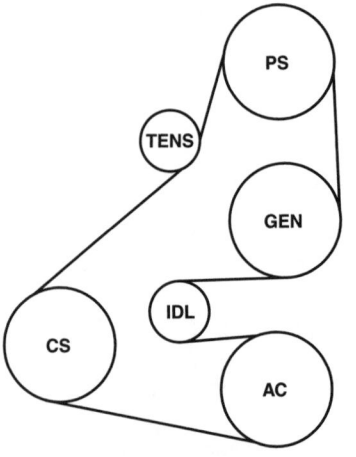

1991-93 4-cyl. 1809cc ex. Turbo
w/AC

ISUZU

1989-2000 All Models Includes Acura SLX & Honda Passport
Hombre—See Chevrolet S10; Oasis—See Honda Odyssey

UNDERHOOD SERVICE SPECIFICATIONS

IUITU5

IUITU5

SERPENTINE BELT DIAGRAMS Continued

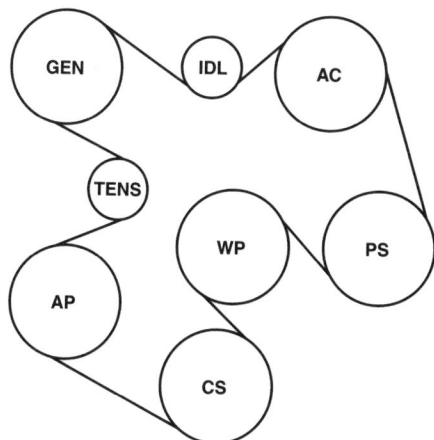

1990-95 V6 2.8L, 3.1L

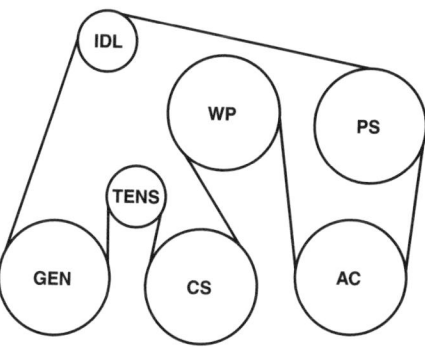

1998-99 V6 3.2L

ENGINE COMPUTER SYSTEM

DIAGNOSTIC TROUBLE CODES

1989-91 Trooper, 1989-95 Amigo, Pickup, Rodeo 4-cyl.

1989 Impulse ex. 1989 Turbo: To activate, ground diagnostic connector under dash or, when equipped with two leads, connect them together. To erase codes, remove ECM fuse for 10 seconds minimum.

1989 Impulse Turbo: Access ECM, turn ignition on and observe that codes 2 & 6 are displayed on LED on ECM body. Depress accelerator pedal and see that code 6 is erased. Start engine and observe that code 2 is erased. If LED continues to flash, there is a failure in the system.

To decode LED pulses, pulse cycle is 11 seconds long; LED will flash 7 times, once each second with a 4 second delay between cycles. During any of the 7 flashes, if the LED flashes 4 times quickly within a second a failure is indicated. Decode problem in following chart.

1989 I-Mark FWD:

To activate diagnostic check, connect a jumper wire from terminals "A" & "C" of the DLC connector (the two outer cavities of the three terminal connector) located under the dash near the ECM. Code 12 will flash, indicating the system has been activated, remove jumper wire before starting engine. To clear memory, remove the ECM fuse for a minimum of 10 seconds.

1989-91 Trooper, 1991-92 Rodeo V6, 1992-94 Pickup V6:
Jumper terminals "A" and "B" of DLC connector under dash. Codes will be displayed on Check Engine light. Remove ECM fuse for 10 seconds to clear codes.

1992-95 Trooper, 1993-95 Rodeo V6:
Jumper terminals 1 & 3 of three-cavity DLC connector under dash on passenger side kick panel.

I-Mark 2V, 1989-95 Amigo, Pickup 2V, 1989-94 V6 2.8L, 3.1L Trooper, Rodeo, Pickup:
Code 12 No tach signal to ECM
Code 13 Oxygen sensor circuit

DIAGNOSTIC TROUBLE CODES Continued

Code 14 Shorted engine coolant sensor circuit
Codes 15, 16 Open coolant sensor circuit
Code 21 Idle switch out of adjustment, or circuit open
Code 22 Fuel cutoff relay, or open circuit
Code 23 Open or grounded M/C solenoid circuit
Code 24 Vehicle speed sensor
Code 25 Open or grounded vacuum switching valve
Code 33 MAP sensor, signal voltage high
Code 34 MAP sensor, signal voltage low
Code 42 Fuel cut-off relay, or circuit grounded (2V)
Code 42 Ignition control circuit (FI)
Code 43 Ignition control circuit
Code 44 Lean oxygen sensor
Code 45 Rich system
Code 51 Shorted fuel cut solenoid (4-cyl.)
Code 51 Faulty PROM, or improper installation
Code 52 Faulty ECM or ROM (4-cyl.)
Code 52 CALPAK error (V6)
Code 53 Shorted switching solenoid
Code 54 Shorted M/C solenoid (4-cyl.)
Code 54 Fuel pump circuit
Code 55 Faulty ECM or oxygen sensor

Impulse ex. 1989 Turbo, 1989-94 4-cyl. FI Amigo, Pickup, Trooper, Rodeo:
Code 12 No tach signal to ECM
Code 13 Oxygen sensor circuit
Code 14 Shorted engine coolant sensor circuit
Code 15 Engine coolant sensor signal low
Code 16 Open engine coolant sensor circuit
Code 21 Idle and full-throttle switch activated
Code 22 Starter signal
Code 23 Power transistor circuit
Code 24 Pressure regulator vacuum switching valve
Code 26 EVAP canister purge vacuum switching valve
Code 26 EVAP canister purge driver transistor
Codes 32, 34 EGR temperature sensor
Code 33 FI output terminal shorted or open
Code 35 Power transistor circuit open
Code 41 Crankshaft position sensor signal erratic
Code 43 Idle contact switch always closed
Code 44 Lean oxygen sensor
Code 45 Rich system
Codes 51, 52, 55 Faulty ECM
Code 53 Pressure regulator driver transistor
Code 54 Power transistor or ground
Code 61 Airflow sensor hot wire broken or harness open
Code 62 Airflow sensor cold wire broken
Code 63 Vehicle speed sensor signal not received
Code 64 FI driver transistor or ground
Code 65 Full throttle switch always activated
Code 66 Knock sensor
Code 71 TPS signal abnormal
Code 72 EGR vacuum switching valve output terminal shorted or harness open
Code 73 EGR vacuum switching valve transistor or ground
1989 1471cc Turbo
1989-95 1588cc, 1809cc, 3165cc:
Code 12 No tach signal to ECM
Code 13 Oxygen sensor circuit
Code 14 Engine coolant sensor circuit (high temperature indicated)
Codes 15, 16 Open coolant sensor circuit (low temperature indicated)
Code 21 TPS voltage high
Code 22 TPS voltage low
Code 23 Intake air temperature sensor (signal voltage high)
Code 24 Vehicle speed sensor
Code 25 Intake air temperature sensor (signal voltage high)
Code 31 Wastegate control
Code 32 EGR failure
Code 33 MAP sensor voltage high
Code 34 MAP sensor voltage low
Code 42 Ignition control circuit
Code 43 Knock sensor
Code 44 Lean oxygen sensor
Code 45 Rich oxygen system
Code 51 Faulty PROM, or installation. Faulty MEMCAL

ISUZU

1989-2000 All Models Includes Acura SLX & Honda Passport
Hombre—See Chevrolet S10; Oasis—See Honda Odyssey

UNDERHOOD SERVICE SPECIFICATIONS

SENSORS, INPUT
TEMPERATURE SENSORS

Engine	Year	Sensor	Resistance Ohms @ deg. F/C
1471cc, 2254cc 2V	1989	Coolant	5600 @ 32/0
			2500 @ 68/20
			1200 @ 104/40
			600 @ 140/60
			320 @ 176/80
			180 @ 212/100
1588cc, 1809cc, 2198cc 2.8L, 3.1L, 3.2L, 3.5L	1989-93	Coolant Intake Air	13,500 @ 23/-7
			7500 @ 40/4
			3400 @ 70/21
			1800 @ 100/38
			450 @ 160/71
			185 @ 210/100
	1994-00	Coolant Intake Air	12,300 @ 23/-7
			7280 @ 41/5
			3520 @ 68/20
			1460 @ 104/40
			470 @ 160/70
			180 @ 212/100
1994cc, 2254cc FI, 2559cc	1989-96	Coolant	7000-12,000 @ 14/-10
			3000-5000 @ 50/10
			2000-3000 @ 68/20
			700-1000 @ 122/50
			200-400 @ 176/80
2254cc 2V	1990-95	Coolant	4100-4750 @ 59/15
			78-84 @ 265/128
1471cc Turbo	1989	Intake Air	9423 @ 32/0
			3515 @ 68/20
			1459 @ 104/40
			667 @ 140/60
			332 @ 176/80
			177 @ 212/100
1588cc, 1809cc, 2254cc, FI Impulse, 2559cc	1989-96	EGR	200,000 @ -40/-40
			28,000 @ 32/0
			5800 @ 104/40
			1000 @ 212/100
			135 @ 392/200

MANIFOLD ABSOLUTE PRESSURE SENSOR
Measure output voltage with vacuum hose disconnected. Apply 10 in. Hg/34 kPa to unit and voltage should be 1.5-2.1 less.

Engine	Year	Volts @ Altitude
1588cc, 1809cc	1989-93	3.8-5.5 @ 1000 max.
		3.6-5.3 @ 1000-2000
		3.5-5.1 @ 2000-3000
		3.3-5.0 @ 3000-4000
		3.2-4.8 @ 4000-5000
		3.0-4.6 @ 5000-6000
		2.9-4.5 @ 6000-7000
		2.5-4.3 @ 7000 or over

Engine	Year	Sensor	Voltage @ in. Hg./kPa
2.8L, 3.1L, 3.2L, 3.5L	1989-98	MAP	1-2 @ idle
			4.0-4.8 @ WOT

Engine	Year	Volts @ in./mm Hg.
2254cc 2V	1989-95	.12-.38 @ 5/17
		1.5-1.7 @ 12/41
		4.4-4.6 @ 28/95

SENSORS, INPUT Continued
CRANKSHAFT POSITION SENSOR
Resistance measured at room temperature.

Engine	Year	Resistance (ohms)
3165cc	1992-95	900-1200

THROTTLE POSITION SENSOR
1471cc Turbo, measured between red wire in TPS and ground.
2156cc, measured between left and right terminals of TPS connector.

Model	Year	TPS Idle	Voltage WOT
1471cc 2V	1989	[1]	—
1471cc Turbo	1989	0.35±0.04	4.0
1588cc, 1809cc	1989-93	1.25 max	4.0 min.
1994cc, 2254cc FI, 2559cc	1989-95	[2]	—
	1996-97	.22-1.0	—
2198cc	1998-00	.22 min.	4.88 max.
2.8L, 3.1L	1989-94	.48	—
3165cc, 3494cc	1992-95	.20-1.0 max.	4.0 max.
	1996-00	.22-1.0	4.88 max.

1 3000-6000 ohms at idle decreasing as throttle is opened. Measured between terminals 4 and 12 of carburetor connector.
2 2.6-4.6 volts difference between idle and WOT.

ACTUATORS, OUTPUT
IDLE SPEED CONTROL SOLENOID

Engine	Year	Resistance (ohms)
1471cc Turbo, 2.8L, 3.1L	1989-94	20 min.[1]
1588cc, 1809cc, 2198cc 3165cc, 3494cc	1989-00	40-80

1 Measured between terminals 1 & 2 and 3 & 4 of ISC.

AIR REGULATOR
Controls fast idle.

Engine	Year	Resistance (ohms)
2254cc FI, 2559cc	1989-97	45-50

MIXTURE CONTROL SOLENOID

Engine	Year	Resistance (ohms)
1471cc 2V	1989	10 min.
2254cc 2V	1989-95	20 min.

FUEL INJECTORS

Engine	Year	Resistance (ohms)	Temperature (deg. F/C)
All	1989	2-3	—
1588cc	1990	2 min.	—
Stylus	1991-93	2 min.	—
Impulse	1991-92	1.2-2.2	—
2198cc	1998-00	11.8-12.6	—
2559cc	1990-91	2-3	—
Pickup, Amigo	1991	13.8	—
2559cc	1992-97	13.8	—
2.8L, 3.1L	1990-94	1.2 min.	—
3165cc Trooper	1992-95	1.2-3.0	—
Rodeo	1993-95	11.8-12.6	—
3165cc, 3494cc	1996-00	11.8-12.6	—

ENGINE IDENTIFICATION

To identify any engine by the manufacturer's code, follow the four steps designated by the numbered blocks.

1 MODEL YEAR IDENTIFICATION: Refer to illustration of the Vehicle Identification Number (V.I.N.). The year is indicated by a code letter which is the 10th character of the V.I.N.

2 ENGINE CODE LOCATION: Refer to illustration of V.I.N. plate for location and designation of engine code.

3 ENGINE CODE: In the "CODE" column, find the engine code determined in Step 2.

4 ENGINE IDENTIFICATION: On the line where the engine code appears, read to the right to identify the engine.

V.I.N. PLATE LOCATION:

Under hood or top left side of instrument panel

Model year of vehicle:	
2000 — Y	1994 — R
1999 — X	1993 — P
1998 — W	1992 — N
1997 — V	1991 — M
1996 — T	1990 — L
1995 — S	1989 — K

1 MODEL YEAR IDENTIFICATION:

10th character of V.I.N.

2 ENGINE CODE LOCATION:

8th character of V.I.N.

Left table

YEAR	3 ENGINE CODE	CYL.	DISPL. liters	DISPL. cu. in.	Fuel System	HP
2000	P	4	2.5	150	MFI	120, 125[1]
	S	6	4.0	242	MFI	181-195[1]
	N	8	4.7	287	MFI	230, 235[1]
1999	P	4	2.5	150	MFI	120, 125[1]
	S	6	4.0	242	MFI	181-195[1]
	N	8	4.7	287	MFI	230
1998	P	4	2.5	150	MFI	120, 125[1]
	S	6	4.0	242	MFI	181-190[1]
	Y	8	5.2	318	MFI	220
	Z	8	5.9	360	MFI	245
1997	P	4	2.5	150	MFI	120, 125[1]
	S	6	4.0	242	MFI	181-190[1]
	Y	8	5.2	318	MFI	220
1996	P	4	2.5	150	MFI	125
	S	6	4.0	242	MFI	185, 190[1]
	Y	8	5.2	318	MFI	220

Right table

YEAR	3 ENGINE CODE	CYL.	DISPL. liters	DISPL. cu. in.	Fuel System	HP
1993-95	P	4	2.5	150	MFI	123, 130[1]
	S	6	4.0	242	MFI	180, 190[1]
	Y	8	5.2	318	MFI	220
1992	P	4	2.5	150	MFI	123, 130[1]
	S	6	4.0	242	MFI	180, 190[1]
1991	P	4	2.5	150	MFI	126, 128[1]
	S	6	4.0	242	MFI	180, 190[1]
	7	8	5.9	360	2V	144
1990	E	4	2.5	150	TBI	117, 121[1]
	L	6	4.0	242	MFI	177
	T	6	4.2	258	2V	112
	7	8	5.9	360	2V	144
1989	E	4	2.5	150	TBI	117, 121[1]
	L	6	4.0	242	MFI	177
	M	6	4.2	258	2V	112
	7	8	5.9	360	2V	144

TBI—Throttle Body Injection. MFI—Multiport Fuel Injection.
2V—Two Venturi Carburetor.
1 Engine horsepower varies with model installation.

UNDERHOOD SERVICE SPECIFICATIONS

JPTU1

CYLINDER NUMBERING SEQUENCE

JPTU1

4-CYL. FIRING ORDER:
1 3 4 2

L-6 FIRING ORDER: 1 5 3 6 2 4

8-CYL. FIRING ORDER:
1 8 4 3 6 5 7 2

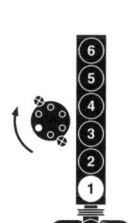

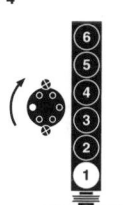

— Front of car —

| 1989-90 2.5L (150) | 1991-00 2.5L | 1989-99 4.0L (242) ex. 1999 G. Cherokee | 2000 4.0L 1999 4.0L G. Cherokee (coil rail) coils paired: cyl.1 & 6, 2 & 5, 3 & 4 | 1989-90 4.2L (258) | 4.7L (coil-on-plug) | 1989-91 5.9L (360) | 1993-98 5.2L, 5.9L |

TIMING MARK

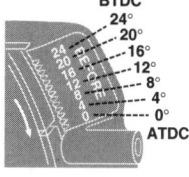

**2.5L (150)
4.0L (242)
1989-90 4.2L (258)**

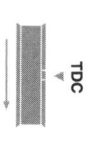

4.7L

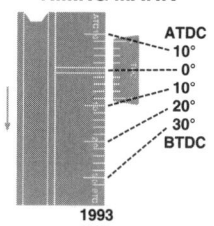

**1993
5.2L**

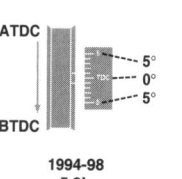

**1994-98
5.2L
1998
5.9L**

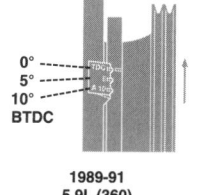

**1989-91
5.9L (360)**

UNDERHOOD SERVICE SPECIFICATIONS

ELECTRICAL AND IGNITION SYSTEMS

BATTERY

Engine	Year	STANDARD BCI Group No.	STANDARD Crank. Perf.	OPTIONAL BCI Group No.	OPTIONAL Crank. Perf.
Cherokee, Wagoneer, Comanche	1989-91	58	390	58	475
	1992-97	58	430	58	500
	1998-00	34	500	—	—
Wrangler, YJ	1989-90	55	420	56	450
	1991	58	390	58	475
	1992-95	58	430	58	500
	1997-00	34	500	36	600
Grand Wagoneer	1989-91	58	475	—	—
Grand Cherokee, Grand Wagoneer	1993-98	34	600	—	—
	1999-00	65	625	—	—

GENERATOR

Application	Rated Output (amps)	Test Output (amps @ 2500 rpm)
1989-90		
4.2L, 5.9L	56, 66, 78, 94	1
2.5L, 4.0L	61, 74, 85, 100	1
1991-92 Grand Wagoneer	78	1
Others	75, 90	2
1993-95 All	75, 90	2
1996 All	75, 90, 120	2
	117	90
	136	120
1997-00 Cherokee, Wrangler	81	75
	117	90
1997-98 Grand Cherokee	117	90
	136	120
1999-00 Grand Cherokee	136	100

1 Output at 2000 rpm must be within 10 amps of rated output.
2 Output at 2000 rpm must be at rated output.

REGULATOR

Application	Test Temp. (deg. F/C)	Voltage Setting
1989-91 4.2L, 5.9L	0-50/ -18 to 10	14.3-15.3
	50-100/ 10-38	13.9-14.9
	100-150/ 50-66	13.4-14.4
	150-200/ 66-93	13.0-14.1
1989-90 2.5L, 4.0L	—	13.5-16.0
1991-95 2.5L, 4.0L, 5.2L	-40 to 20/ -40 to -7	14.5-15.0
	20-80/ -7 to 27	13.9-15.0
	80-140/ 27-60	13.2-14.4
	140-160/ 60-71	13.2-13.8

STARTER

Engine	Year	Cranking Voltage (min. volts)	Ampere Draw @ Cranking Speed
4-cyl.	1989-94	9.6	160
	1995-00	9.6	130
6-cyl.	1989-91	9.6	160
	1992-94	9.6	130
	1995-00	9.6	160
8-cyl.	1989-91	9.6	160
	1993-96	9.6	130
	1997-00	9.6	160

SPARK PLUGS

Engine	Year	Gap (inches)	Gap (mm)	Torque (ft-lb)
All	1989-96	.035	.89	27
2.5L, 4.0L	1997-00	.035	.89	30
4.7L, 5.2L, 5.9L	1997-00	.040	1.01	30

IGNITION COIL
FOR TESTING AND ADJUSTMENT DIAGRAMS, SEE APPENDIX A.
Resistance (ohms at 75°F or 24°C)

Engine	Year	Windings	Resistance (ohms)
2.5L FI	1989	Primary	0.4-0.8
		Secondary	2500-5500
2.5L, 4.0L, 5.2L, 5.9L: Diamond	1991-00	Primary	.97-1.18
		Secondary	11,300-15,300
Toyodenso	1991-00	Primary	.95-1.20
		Secondary	11,300-13,300
4.0L (242)	1989-90	Primary	0.4-0.8
		Secondary	2500-5500
4.0L Grand Cherokee	1999-00	Primary	.71-.88
		Secondary	—
4.7L	1999-00	Primary	0.6-0.9
		Secondary	6000-9000
All others	1989-91	Primary	1.11-1.25
		Secondary	7700-9300

DISTRIBUTOR PICKUP
FOR TESTING AND ADJUSTMENT DIAGRAMS, SEE APPENDIX B.

Application	Resistance (ohms)	Air Gap (in./mm)
1989-91 4.2L (258), 5.9L (360)	400-800	0.17/.28 min

IGNITION RESISTOR

Engine	Year	Type	Resistance (ohms)	Temperature (deg. F/C)
4.2L, 5.9L	1989-91	Wire	1.3-1.4	—

BASE TIMING
Set timing at slow idle and Before Top Dead Center, unless otherwise specified. Disconnect and plug distributor vacuum line.

4.7L: TDC, notch on crankshaft. Must line up with arrow on timing chain cover.

5.2L, 5.9L: timing is not adjustable. Set timing marks to TDC and verify that rotor blade is aligned with notch on switch plate.

Engine	Year	Man. Trans. (degrees)	Auto. Trans. (degrees)
4.2L (258)	1989-90	9±2[1]	9±2[1]
High Altitude	1989-90	16±2[1]	16±2[1]
4.7L	1999	TDC[2]	TDC[2]
5.2L	1993-97	TDC[2]	TDC[2]
5.9L (360)	1989	12±2	12±2
High Altitude	1989	19±2	19±2
5.9L (360)	1990-91	—	10±2
High Altitude	1990-91	—	17±2

1 At 1600 rpm.
2 Not adjustable.

DISTRIBUTOR TIMING ADVANCE
Engine degrees at engine rpm, no load, in addition to basic timing setting.
Mechanical advance distributors only.

Engine	Transmission	Year	Distributor Number	Degrees @ 2500 RPM Total	Degrees @ 2500 RPM Centrifugal
4.2L (258)	MT & AT	1989-90	8933002353	23.5-31.5	6.5-10.5
5.9L (360)	MT & AT	1989-90	3233174	29.5-38.5	8-12
5.9L	AT	1990	53006450	27.5-37.5	7-12

UNDERHOOD SERVICE SPECIFICATIONS

FUEL SYSTEM

FUEL SYSTEM PRESSURE
FOR TESTING AND ADJUSTMENT DIAGRAMS, SEE APPENDIX D.

Engine	Year	Pressure PSI	Pressure RPM
Carbureted & TBI			
4-cyl. w/FI	1989-90	14-15	—
6-cyl. 2V	1989	4-5	idle
8-cyl.	1989-91	5.0-6.5	idle

Engine	Year	Pressure[1]	Pressure[2]
MFI			
2.5L, 4.0L, 5.2L	1989-95	31	38-42
	1996	47-51	—
2.5L	1997-00	47-51	—
4.0L	1997-00	47-51	—
Grand Wagoneer	1997-00	44-54	—
4.7L, 5.2L, 5.9L	1997-00	44-54	—

1 With pressure regulator vacuum hose connected.
2 With pressure regulator vacuum hose disconnected.

IDLE SPEED W/O COMPUTER CONTROL
The midpoint of the ranges given is the preferred setting.

On all models disconnect decel valve and canister purge hoses. Do not allow vehicle to idle for more than three minutes.

6-cyl. eng.: Disconnect and plug solenoid vacuum line. Disconnect solenoid electrical lead. Adjust idle speed. Apply vacuum to solenoid and set speed to specification. Apply battery voltage to solenoid and turn A/C on. Set speed-up to specification.

8-cyl. eng.: Adjust idle speed with solenoid fully extended. Electrically disconnect the solenoid and set shutdown speed to specification.

To set fast idle, disconnect and plug EGR vacuum hose.

Preferred setting is the midpoint of range given.

Engine	Year	SLOW Man. Trans.	SLOW Auto. Trans.	FAST Man. Trans.	FAST Auto. Trans.	Step of Cam
4.2L (258)	1989-91	630-730[1]	550-650 D[2]	1600-1800	1750-1950 P	Second
high altitude	1989-91	650-750[1]	600-700 D[2]	1600-1800	1750-1950 P	Second
5.9L (360)	1989-91	550-650	550-650 D	1400-1600	1500-1700 P	Second
shutdown idle	1989-91	450-500	450-500 N			

1 With Sole-Vac Vacuum actuator energized, 900±50. Holding solenoid, 1100±50.
2 With Sole-Vac Vacuum actuator energized, 900 D±50. Holding solenoid, 800 D±50.

IDLE SPEED W/COMPUTER CONTROL
FOR TESTING AND ADJUSTMENT DIAGRAMS, SEE APPENDIX E.

2.5L, 1989-90: Disconnect ISC and fully extend plunger with special tool. Adjust plunger head screw to specified value.

4.0L, 1989: Set idle to specified value by adjusting stop screw.

1993-98 5.2L; 1999-00 2.5L, 4.0L: Disconnect vacuum line at PCV valve and install special tool (0.185" orifice) in hose. Disconnect purge vacuum hose at throttle body and cap the vacuum source. Connect a Scan tool and access Minimum Airflow first. If idle is outside the value given, replace the throttle body.

Engine	Year	Checking Speed Man. Trans.	Checking Speed Auto. Trans.	Setting Speed Man. Trans.	Setting Speed Auto. Trans.
2.5L (150) FI	1989-90	750 min.	750 N min.	3500	3500 N
2.5L	1991	800	800 N	—	—
	1999-00	500-900	500-900 N	—	—
4.0L (242)	1989	—	—	700	700 N
4.0L	1990-91	550-650	550-650 N	—	—
	1999-00	500-900	500-900 N	—	—
5.2L, 5.9L	1993-98	—	500-900 N	—	—

ENGINE MECHANICAL

FOR CYLINDER HEAD TORQUE SEQUENCES AND DIAGRAMS, SEE APPENDIX F.

TIGHTENING TORQUES

Engine	Year	TORQUE FOOT-POUNDS/NEWTON METERS Cylinder Head	Intake Manifold	Exhaust Manifold	Crankshaft Pulley	Water Pump
2.5L (150)	1989-00	110/149[2]	23/31	23/31	80/108	22/30
4.0L (242)	1989-00	110/149[3]	23/31	30/41, outer 23/31, center	80/108	22/30
4.2L (258)	1989-90	85/115	23/31	23/31	80/108	13/18
4.7L	1999-00	15/20 35/47 +90°	105"/12	18/25	130/175	40/54
5.2L, 5.9L	1993-98	50/68, 105/143	72"/8, 12/16	15/20, nuts 20/27, bolts	135/183	30/41
5.9L (360)	1989-91	110/149	43/58	15/20, outer 25/34, center	90/122	4/5

1 Bolt number 8 (first bolt on left front), 75/102.
2 Bolt number 8 (1989) or 7 (1990-97) (first bolt on left front), 100/136.
3 Bolt number 11 (first bolt on right front), 100/136.

COMPRESSION PRESSURE
At cranking speed or specified rpm, engine temperature normalized, throttle open.

Engine	Year	PSI	Maximum Variation PSI
2.5L (150)	1989	155-185	30
2.5L	1990-00	120-150	30
4.0L	1991-00	120-150	30
4.2L (258)	1989-90	120-150	30
4.7L	1999-00	100 min.	25
5.2L, 5.9L	1993-98	100 min.	25
5.9L (360)	1989-91	120-140	30

BELT TENSION
A belt is considered used once it has been pretensioned and run. Use a strand tension gauge. Measurements are in pounds.

1993-99 4.7L, 5.2L, 5.9L: Automatic tensioner used. Replace belt if index marks are outside the inspection window.

Engine	Year	Generator	Power Steering or Idler	Air Cond.	Air Pump
USED BELTS					
4-cyl. Gas	1989	90-115	90-115	90-115	90-115
V8	1993-00	—	—	—	—
All Others	1989-97	90-115	90-115	90-115	90-115
Serpentine	1989-00	140-160	—	—	—
NEW BELTS					
4-cyl. Gas	1989	120-160	120-140	120-160	—
V8	1993-00	—	—	—	—
All Others	1989-97	125-155	125-155	125-155	125-155
Serpentine	1989-00	180-200	—	—	—

ENGINE COMPUTER SYSTEM

FOR TESTING AND ADJUSTMENT DIAGRAMS, SEE APPENDIX G.

DIAGNOSTIC TROUBLE CODES
1991-00 2.5L, 4.0L, 5.2L: Cycle ignition switch on-off-on-off-on. Codes will be displayed on malfunction indicator lamp.

1996-00 OBD-II systems still indicate codes on MIL

1991-00 2.5L, 4.0L, 5.2L:
Code 11 Ignition
Code 12 Battery disconnected in last 50 cycles
Code 13 MAP sensor vacuum
Code 14 MAP sensor electrical
Code 15 Vehicle speed sensor
Code 17 Engine running too cool

DIAGNOSTIC TROUBLE CODES Continued

Code 21 Oxygen sensor
Code 22 Engine coolant temperature sensor
Code 23 Intake air temperature circuit
Code 24 Throttle position sensor
Code 25 ISC control
Code 27 Fuel injector control
Code 31 EVAP purge solenoid circuit
Code 32 EGR system failure
Code 33 Air conditioning clutch relay
Code 34 Speed control solenoid driver
Code 35 Fan control relay (1991-94)
Code 35 Torque converter clutch solenoid (1997)
Code 37 Torque converter clutch solenoid circuit
Code 41 Generator field
Code 42 Automatic shutdown relay
Code 43 Multiple cylinder misfire
Code 44 Battery temperature sensor
Code 45 Overdrive solenoid (1989-94)
Code 45 Transmission temperature circuit (1997)
Code 46 Battery over voltage
Code 47 Battery under voltage
Code 51 Oxygen sensor lean
Code 52 Oxygen sensor rich
Code 53 Internal ECU fault
Code 54 Distributor or com sync pickup
Code 55 End of message
Code 62 SRI mileage accumulator
Code 63 Controller failure EEPROM write denied
Code 64 Catalytic converter efficiency
Code 65 Power steering switch
Code 72 Catalytic converter efficiency failure
Code 76 Fuel pump resistor bypass relay
Code 77 Speed control power relay

SENSORS, INPUT
TEMPERATURE SENSORS

Engine	Year	Sensor	Resistance Ohms @ deg. F/C
4.2L	1989-90	Coolant	continuity @ 100/38 max. no continuity above 100/38
2.5L FI, 4.0L	1989-90	Coolant, Intake Air	13,500 @ 20/-7 7500 @ 40/4 3400 @ 70/20 1600 @ 100/38 450 @ 160/70 185 @ 212/100
2.5L, 4.0L, 5.2L, 5.9L	1991-00	Coolant, Intake Air	85,850-108,390 @ -4/-20 49,250-61,430 @ 14/-10 17,990-21,810 @ 50/10 4900-5750 @ 104/40 1630-1870 @ 160/70 640-720 @ 212/100

SENSORS, INPUT Continued
PRESSURE SENSORS

Engine	Year	Sensor	Voltage Condition
2.5L	1989-99	Barometric	4.0-5.0, ign. on 1.5-2.1, idle
4.0L, 4.7L, 5.2L, 5.9L	1989-99	Barometric	4.0-5.0, ign. on 1.5-2.1, idle

CRANKSHAFT POSITION SENSOR

Engine	Year	Resistance (ohms)
2.5L FI, 4.0L	1989-91	125-275

THROTTLE POSITION SENSOR

2.5L, 1989: Connect DVOM across terminals A (+) and B (-) of TPS connector. Turn ignition on and fully open throttle plate. Check voltage against specified value.

4.0L, 1989-90: Connect DVOM between terminals C (+) and B (-). Measure voltage with throttle closed.

Engine	Year	Voltage	
		Idle	WOT
2.5L (150) FI	1989	—	4.6-4.7
2.5L	1991-97	.20 min.	4.8 max.
	1998	.35 min.	4.5 max.
	1999-00	.26-.95	4.5 max.
4.0L	1989	0.8	—
4.0L MT	1990	0.85	—
4.0L AT	1990	4.15	—
4.0L	1991-96	.20 min.	4.8 max.
4.0L	1997	.20 min.	4.8 max.
Grand Cherokee	1997	.35 min.	4.5 max.
	1998	.35 min.	4.5 max.
	1999-00	.26-.95	4.5 max.
4.7L	1999-00	.26-.95	4.5 max.
5.2L, 5.9L	1993-96	.20 min.	4.8 max.
	1997-98	.35 min.	4.5 max.

ACTUATORS, OUTPUT
FUEL INJECTORS

Engine	Year	Resistance (ohms)	Temperature (deg. F/C)
2.5L	1991-97	13.3-15.7	68/20
	1998-00	10.8-13.2	68/20
4.0L	1989-90	16	68/20
4.0L	1991-97	13.3-15.7	68/20
	1998-00	10.8-13.2	68/20
4.7L	1998-00	10.8-13.2	68/20
5.2L, 5.9L	1993-97	13.3-15.7	68/20
	1998-00	10.8-13.2	68/20

MIXTURE CONTROL SOLENOID

Engine	Year	Resistance (ohms)
Carbureted: 4.2L (258), 5.9L (360)	1989-91	50-95

ENGINE IDENTIFICATION

To identify any engine by the manufacturer's code, follow the four steps designated by the numbered blocks.

V.I.N. PLATE LOCATION:

Attached to top of instrument panel visible through windshield.

1 MODEL YEAR IDENTIFICATION:

10th character of V.I.N.

2000—Y	1999—X	1998—W
1997—V	1996—T	1995—S
1994—R	1993—P	1992—N
1991—M	1990—L	

2 ENGINE CODE LOCATION:

Prefix to engine number on engine block.

4 ENGINE IDENTIFICATION

YEAR	3 ENGINE CODE	CYL.	DISPL. liters	cc	Fuel System	HP
1998-00	IMZ-FE	6	3.0	2995	MFI	210, 220
	2JZ-GE	6	3.0	2997	MFI	225
	1UZ-FE	8	4.0	3969	MFI	290, 300
	2UZ-FE	8	4.7	4669	MFI	230
1996-97	IMZ-FE	6	3.0	2995	MFI	188
	2JZ-GE	6	3.0	2997	MFI	200-225
	1UZ-FE	8	4.0	3969	MFI	250, 260
	1FZ-FE	6	4.5	4477	MFI	212
1994-95	IMZ-FE	6	3.0	2995	MFI	188
	2JZ-GE	6	3.0	2997	MFI	220-225
	1UZ-FE	8	4.0	3969	MFI	250, 260

4 ENGINE IDENTIFICATION

YEAR	3 ENGINE CODE	CYL.	DISPL. liters	cc	Fuel System	HP
1993	3V-ZE	6	3.0	2958	MFI	185
	2JZ-GE	6	3.0	2997	MFI	220, 225
	1UZ-FE	8	4.0	3969	MFI	250
1992	3V-ZE	6	3.0	2958	MFI	185
	2JZ-GE	6	3.0	2997	MFI	225
	1UZ-FE	8	4.0	3969	MFI	250
1991	2V-ZE	6	2.5	2507	MFI	156
	1UZ-FE	8	4.0	3969	MFI	250
1990	2V-ZE	6	2.5	2507	MFI	156
	1UZ-FE	8	4.0	3969	MFI	250

MFI—Multiport Fuel Injection.

UNDERHOOD SERVICE SPECIFICATIONS

LXITU1   LXITU1

CYLINDER NUMBERING SEQUENCE

V6 FIRING ORDER:
1 2 3 4 5 6

6-CYL. FIRING ORDER:
1 5 3 6 2 4

TIMING MARK

V8 FIRING ORDER:
1 8 4 3 6 5 7 2

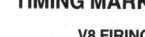

28C35   46C71

Front of car

| 1990-93 2507cc, 2958cc ES250, ES300 | 1994-00 2995cc ES300, RX300 | 1992-96 2997cc GS300, SC300 | 1997-00 2997cc GS300, SC300 | 1996-97 4477cc LX450 | 1990-96 3969cc LS400, SC400 | 1997-00 3969cc,4669cc GS400, LS400, SC400, LX470 |

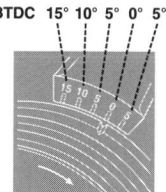

BTDC 15° 10° 5° 0° 5°

1990-00
2507cc, 2958cc, 2995cc
ES250, ES300, RX300

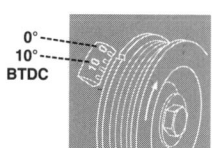

0°
10°
BTDC

1990-00
2997cc, 3969cc, 4669cc
GS300, SC300, LS400, SC400,
LX470

1996-97
4477cc
LX450

ELECTRICAL AND IGNITION SYSTEMS

BATTERY

BCI equivalent shown, size may vary from original equipment. Check clearance before replacing, holddown may need to be modified.

Engine	Year	STANDARD BCI Group No.	STANDARD Crank. Perf.	OPTIONAL BCI Group No.	OPTIONAL Crank. Perf.
ES250	1990-91	35	360	—	—
ES300	1992-97	35	350	24F	585
	1998-00	24F	585	—	—
GS300	1994-97	24F	585		

BATTERY Continued

Engine	Year	STANDARD BCI Group No.	STANDARD Crank. Perf.	OPTIONAL BCI Group No.	OPTIONAL Crank. Perf.
	1998-00	24F	585	—	—
GS400	1998-00	24	585	—	—
LS400	1990-94	27F	580	—	—
	1995-00	24F	585	—	—
SC300	1992-96	27F	450	—	—
	1997-00	24F	585	—	—
SC400	1992	27F	450	27F	625
	1993-00	27F	625	—	—

LEXUS
1990-2000

GENERATOR

Application	Year	Rated Output (amps)	Test Output (amps @ rpm)
ES250	1990-91	70	30 min. @ 2000
ES300	1992-00	80	30 min. @ 2000
GS300	1993-99	80	30 min. @ 2000
GS400	1998	100	30 min. @ 2000
LS400	1990-93	100	30 min. @ 2000
	1994-95	110	30 min. @ 2000
	1996-97	80	30 min. @ 2000
	1998-00	100	30 min. @ 2000
LX450	1997-98	80	30 min. @ 2000
LX470	1998-00	80, 100	30 min. @ 2000
RX300	1999	100	30 min. @ 2000
	2000	120	30 min. @ 2000
SC300	1992-93	120	30 min. @ 2000
	1994-96	110	30 min. @ 2000
	1997-00	80	30 min. @ 2000
SC400	1992-93	100	30 min. @ 2000
	1994-96	110	30 min @ 2000
	1997-00	100	30 min. @ 2000

REGULATOR

Application	Year	Test Temp. (deg. F/C)	Voltage Setting
All	1990-91	77/25	14.0-15.0
		239/115	13.5-14.3
	1992-93	77/25	14.0-14.3
		239/115	13.2-14.0
ES300	1994-96	77/25	14.0-15.1
		239/115	13.5-14.3
	1997	—	13.5-15.1
	1998-00	—	13.2-14.8
GS300, G5400, SC300	1994-96	77/25	13.6-14.8
		239/115	13.2-14.0
	1997-99	—	13.2-14.8
LS400, SC400	1994-00	77/25	13.7-14.7
		239/115	13.2-14.0
LX450	1997	—	13.5-15.1
LX470, RX300	1998-00	—	13.2-14.8

SPARK PLUGS
Do not regap platinum-tipped plugs. Replace when worn to .051" (1.3mm)

Application	Year	Gap (inches)	Gap (mm)	Torque (ft-lb)
SC400	1996	.031	0.8	13
LX450	1997	.031	0.8	13
LX470	1998-00	.043	1.1	13
All others	1990-00	.043	1.1	13

IGNITION COIL
Resistance (ohms @ 68°F or 20°C).

Engine	Year	Windings	Resistance (ohms)
All	1990-91	Primary	0.41-0.50
		Secondary	10,200-13,800
2958cc	1992-93	Primary	0.30-0.60
		Secondary	9000-15,000
2995cc	1994-95	Primary	.54-.84
	1996-97	Primary	.70-.94
		Secondary	10,800-14,900
2995cc Aisan	1998	Primary	.70-.94
		Secondary	10,800-14,900
Diamond	1998	Primary	.70-.94
		Secondary	6,800-11,700
2997cc	1992-94	Primary	0.20-0.30
		Secondary	6000-11,000
	1995-97	Primary	.21-.33
		Secondary	6400-11,100
	1998-99	Primary	.33-.52
		Secondary	8,500-14,700
3969cc LS400	1992-93	Primary	0.30-0.60

IGNITION COIL Continued
Resistance (ohms @ 68°F or 20°C).

Engine	Year	Windings	Resistance (ohms)
3969cc SC400	1992-93	Secondary	9000-15,000
		Primary	0.40-0.50
		Secondary	10,000-14,000
3969cc	1994-96	Primary	.36-.55
		Secondary	9000-15,400
4477cc	1997	Primary	.36-.55
		Secondary	9000-15,400

DISTRIBUTOR PICKUP

Application	Year	Resistance (ohms)	Air Gap (in./mm)
2507cc	1990	140-180	.008/0.2 min.
2507cc	1991	205-255[1]	.008/0.2 min.
2958cc	1992-93	125-190	.008/0.2 min.
2997cc	1992-96	125-200[1]	.008/0.2 min.
4477cc	1997	185-275	.008/0.2 min.

[1] NE pickup coil, 155-250

BASE TIMING
Set timing at slow idle and Before Top Dead Center, unless otherwise specified.

All Models: Jumper terminals TE1 and E1 of diagnostic connector under hood. When jumper is removed, timing should be at Check specification.

Engine	Year	Man. Trans. (degrees) @ RPM	Auto. Trans. (degrees) @ RPM
2507cc	1990-91	10	10
Check	1991	13-27	13-27
2958cc	1992-93	10	10
Check	1992-93	10-20	10-20
2995cc	1994-00	10[1] ± 2	10[1] ± 2
Check	1994-95	7-17	7-17
Check	1996-98	7-24	7-24
Check	1999-00	10-25	10-25
2997cc	1992-95	10	10
Check, SC300	1992-93	9-11	9-11
Check, SC300	1994-95	7-19	7-19
Check, GS300	1993-94	—	8-12
Check, GS300	1995	—	7-19
2997cc	1996	10± 2	10± 2
	1997-99	10[1] ± 2	10[1] ± 2
Check	1996-97	7-19	7-19
Check	1998-00	6-16	6-16
3969cc	1990-00	—	10[1] ± 2
4477cc	1997	—	3
Check	1997	—	2-13
4669cc	1998-00	—	5-15[1]

[1] Checking figure, timing not adjustable

FUEL SYSTEM

FUEL SYSTEM PRESSURE
Values are approximate pressure.

Engine	Year	Pressure[1] (PSI)	Pressure[2] (PSI)	RPM
2507cc, 2958cc	1990-93	33-37	38-44	idle
2995cc	1994-96	33-38	38-44	idle
	1997-99	44-50	—	—
2997cc, 3969cc	1990-97	28-34	38-44	idle
	1998-00	44-50	—	—
4669cc	1998-99	28-34	38-44	idle
	2000	38-44	—	idle

[1] Vacuum hose connected to fuel pressure regulator
[2] Vacuum hose disconnected from fuel pressure regulator

UNDERHOOD SERVICE SPECIFICATIONS

IDLE SPEED W/COMPUTER CONTROL

Verify that idle is at specified Checking speed. Turn A/C on and verify that speed increases to specified Speed-up speed with compressor clutch engaged.

Engine	Year	Trans.	Setting Speed	Checking Speed	Speed-up Speed
2507cc	1990-91	MT	—	650-750	780-820
	1990-91	AT	—	650-750N	780-820N
2958cc	1992-93	MT	—	650-750	700
	1992-93	AT	—	650-750N	700N
2995cc	1994-96	MT	—	650-750	700
	1994-96	AT	—	650-750N	700N
	1997-00	MT	—	650-750	650-750
		AT	—	650-750 N	650-750 N
2997cc SC300	1992-94	MT	—	650-750	900
	1992-94	AT	—	600-700N	800N
2997cc GS300	1993-94	AT	—	650-750N	800N
2997cc	1995-97	MT	—	650-750	900
	1995-97	AT	—	650-750N	800N
2997cc	1998-00	MT	—	650-750	850-950
	1998-00	AT	—	650-750N	750-850N
3969cc	1990-92	AT	—	600-700N	900N
3969cc LS400	1993-95	AT	—	650-750N	900N
	1996-97	AT	—	600-700N	700N
3969cc SC400	1993-97	AT	—	650-750N	700N
3969cc	1998-00	AT	—	700-800N	750-850N
4669cc	1998-00	AT	—	650-750N	750-850N

ENGINE MECHANICAL

TIGHTENING TORQUES

Some fasteners are tightened in more than one step.

Engine	Year	TORQUE FOOT-POUNDS/NEWTON METERS				
		Cylinder Head	Intake Manifold	Exhaust Manifold	Crankshaft Pulley	Water Pump
2507cc, 2958cc	1990-93	25/34, +90°, +90°[1]	13/18	29/39	181/245	14/20
2995cc	1994-99	40/54, +90°[1]	11/15	36/49	159/215	69¹/8
2997cc	1992-00	25/35, +90°, +90°[1]	21/28	30/40	239/324	15/21
3969cc	1990-00	29/39, +90°	13/18	33/44	181/245	14/20
4477cc	1997	29/39, +90°, +90°	15/21	29/39	304/412	15/21
4669cc	1998-00	24/32 +90° +90°	13/18	33/44	181/245	15/21

1 Small recessed head bolt, 13/18

COMPRESSION PRESSURE

At cranking speed, engine warm, throttle open

Engine	Year	PSI	Maximum Variation PSI
All	1990-93	142-178	14
2995cc	1994	142-178	14
	1995-00	145-218	14
2997cc	1994-97	156-185	14
	1998-00	156-192	14
3969cc	1994-00	142-178	14
4477cc	1997	128-171	14
4669cc	1998-00	142-192	14

BELT TENSION

Engine	Year	Generator	Power Steering	Air Cond.
USED BELTS				
2507cc	1990-91	95-135	60-100	95-135
2958cc, 2995cc	1992-00	95-135	95-135	95-135

BELT TENSION Continued

Engine	Year	Generator	Power Steering	Air Cond.
2997cc, 3969cc, 4669cc	1990-99	1	—	—
4477cc	1997	44-88	44-88	60-100
NEW BELTS				
2507cc	1990-91	170-180	100-150	170-180
2958cc, 2995cc	1992-99	170-180	150-185	170-180
2997cc, 3969cc, 4669cc	1990-99	1	—	—
4477cc	1997	88-132	88-132	100-150

1 Automatic tensioner. Inspect index marks on tensioner pulley; replace belt if outside these marks.

SERPENTINE BELT DIAGRAMS

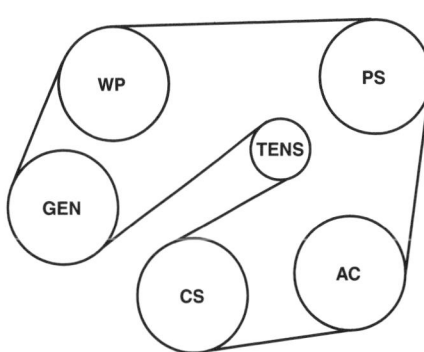

1992-99 V6 2997cc

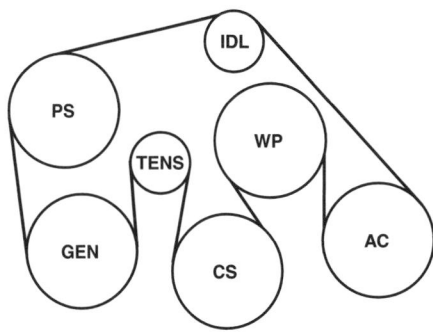

1990-99 V8 3969cc, 4669cc

ENGINE COMPUTER SYSTEM

DIAGNOSTIC TROUBLE CODES

1990-93 All
1994-95 2997cc, 3969cc
To obtain codes, jumper terminals TE1 and E1 of the Check connector in engine compartment.
To erase codes, remove EFI fuse from fuse block.
1994-95 2995cc
1996-00 All
Connect a Scan tool and run through diagnostic sequence according to manufacturer's instructions.

1990-95 All ex. 2995cc
Code 12, 13 RPM signal
Code 14, 15 Ignition signal circuit
Code 16 Automatic transmission to ECM interface circuit
Code 17, 18 Camshaft position sensor, V8 only
Code 21 Oxygen sensor, left or front side
Code 22 Engine coolant temperature sensor
Code 24 Intake air temperature sensor
Code 25 Fuel mixture lean
Code 26 Fuel mixture rich
Code 27 Sub-oxygen sensor, 6-cyl. or V8 left or front side
Code 28 Sub-oxygen sensor, right or rear side

UNDERHOOD SERVICE SPECIFICATIONS

DIAGNOSTIC TROUBLE CODES Continued

Code 29 Sub-oxygen sensor, V8 right side
Code 31, 32 Vacuum airflow sensor
Code 35 Barometric pressure sensor, ex. V6
Code 41 Throttle position sensor
Code 42 Vehicle speed sensor, 6-cyl.
Code 43 Starter signal
Code 47 Sub-throttle position sensor
Code 51 A/C neutral, TPS or accelerator switches
Code 52 Knock sensor signal, left or front side
Code 53 Knock control signal
Code 55 Knock sensor signal, right or rear side
Code 71 EGR system
Code 78 Fuel pump control signal

SENSORS, INPUT
TEMPERATURE SENSORS

Intake air temperature resistance measured between terminals THA & E2 of airflow sensor.

Engine	Year	Sensor	Resistance Ohms @ deg. F/C
All	1990-00	Coolant, Intake Air	10,000-20,000 @ -4/-20
			4000-7000 @ 32/0
			2000-3000 @ 68/20
			400-700 @ 140/60
			200-400 @ 176/80
			100-300 @ 212/100
All	1990-00	EGR Temp.	64,000-97,000 @ 122/50
			11,000-16,000 @ 212/100
			2000-4000 @ 302/150

THROTTLE POSITION SENSOR

Engine	Year	Resistance (ohms) Idle	Resistance (ohms) WOT
2958cc, 2995cc	1992-96	280-6400	2000-11,600
	1997	200-5700	2000-10,200
	1998-00	200-6300	2000-10,200
2997cc SC300	1992-93	200-800	3300-10,000
2997cc GS300	1993	340-6300	2400-11,200
2997cc	1994-00	340-6300	2400-11,200
3969cc	1990-92	200-12,000	3300-10,000
3969cc LS400	1993	340-6300	2400-11,200
SC400	1993	200-800	3300-14,000
3969cc	1994-97	340-6300	2400-11,200
	1998-00	1250-2350	—
4477cc	1997	200-5700	2000-10,200
4669cc	1998-00	1250-2350	—

MASS AIRFLOW SENSOR

Engine	Year	Resistance (ohms) Idle	Resistance (ohms) 2000 rpm
2507cc, 2958cc	1990-93	200-600	200-1200

SENSORS, INPUT Continued
CRANKSHAFT & CAMSHAFT POSITION SENSOR
Engine cold.

Engine	Year	Sensor	Resistance (ohms)
2995cc	1994-00	Camshaft	835-1400
		Crankshaft	1630-2740
2997cc	1996-97	Crankshaft	1630-2740
2997cc	1998-00	Camshaft	835-1400
		Crankshaft	1630-2740
3969cc	1990-91	Camshaft	950-1250
3969cc	1992-95	Camshaft, Crankshaft	835-1400
3969cc: LS400	1996	Camshaft, Crankshaft	835-1400
SC400	1996	Camshaft, Crankshaft	1630-2740
3969cc	1997	Camshaft, Crankshaft	835-1400
3969cc, 4669cc	1998-00	Camshaft	835-1400
		Crankshaft	1630-2740
4477cc	1996	Crankshaft	1630-2740
4669cc	1998-00	Crankshaft	835-1400
		Camshaft	1630-2740

ACTUATORS, OUTPUT
FUEL INJECTORS

Engine	Year	Resistance (ohms)	Temperature (deg. F/C)
All	1990-00	13.4-14.2	68/20

IDLE SPEED CONTROL
With three-terminal connector, measured between either left or right terminals and center terminal.
1998-99 ex. 2995cc, values given are for throttle control motor.

Engine		Year	Resistance (ohms)
All		1990-93	10-30
2995cc		1994	19.3-22.3
		1995-00	17-24.5
2997cc		1994	10-30
		1995	37-44
		1996-97	15-25
2997cc	Motor	1998-00	3-100
	Clutch	1998-00	4.2-5.2
3969cc		1994-95	34-54
		1996-97	31-61
3969cc	Motor	1998-99	3-100
	Clutch	1998-99	4.2-5.2
4477cc		1997	15-25
4669cc	Motor	1998-00	3-100
	Clutch	1998-00	4.2-5.2

ENGINE IDENTIFICATION

To identify any engine by the manufacturer's code, follow the four steps designated by the numbered blocks.

V.I.N.
PLATE LOCATION:

On engine bulkhead or on top left side of instrument panel visible through windshield.

1 MODEL YEAR IDENTIFICATION:

10th character of V.I.N.

2000—Y	1999—X	1998—W
1997—V	1996—T	1995—S
1994—R	1993—P	1992—N
1991—M	1990—L	1989—K

2 ENGINE CODE LOCATION:

8th character of V.I.N.

3 ENGINE ROTORS / **4** ENGINE IDENTIFICATION

YEAR	CODE or CYL.	liters	cc	Fuel System	HP
1999-00	2 4	1.6	1598	MFI	NA
	1, 3 4	1.8	1839	MFI	122, 125
	C 4	2.0	1991	MFI	125
	2 6	2.3	2255	MFI	210
	D 6	2.5	2497	MFI	170
1996-98	1 4	1.5	1468	MFI	90, 92
	2 4	1.8	1839	MFI	122
	3 4	1.8	1839	MFI	133
	C 4	2.0	1991	MFI	114, 118
	2 4	2.3 S	2255 S	MFI	210
	D 6	2.5	2497	MFI	160, 164
	2, 3 6	3.0	2954	MFI	155
1995	3 2	1.3 T	1308 T	MFI	225
	1 4	1.5	1468	MFI	90, 92
	5 4	1.6	1597	MFI	105
	2 4	1.8	1839	MFI	122
	C 4	2.0	1991	MFI	114, 118
	1 6	2.3 S	2255 S	MFI	210
	D 6	2.5	2497	MFI	160, 164
	2 6	2.5	2497	MFI	170
	2, 3 6	3.0	2954	MFI	155
	1 6	3.0	2954	MFI	193
1993-94	1, 2 2	1.3 T	1308 T	MFI	225
	2 4	1.6	1597	MFI	82
	1 4	1.6	1597	MFI	88
	1 4	1.6	1597	MFI	105, 116
	4 4	1.8	1839	MFI	103
	6 4	1.8	1839	MFI	125
	2 6	1.8	1844	MFI	130
	A 4	2.0	1991	MFI	118
	1 4	2.2	2187	2V	85
	2 4	2.2	2187	MFI	91
	B 6	2.5	2497	MFI	164
	1 4	2.6	2606	MFI	121
	1, 2, 3 6	3.0	2954	MFI	155
	2 6	3.0	2954	MFI	195
1992	1, 3 2	1.3	1308	MFI	160
	2, 4 2	1.3 T	1308 T	MFI	200
	2, 4 4	1.6	1597	MFI	82, 88
	1 4	1.6	1597	MFI	105, 116[1]
	4 4	1.8	1839	MFI	103
	6 4	1.8	1839	MFI	125
	2 6	1.8	1844	MFI	130
	1 4	2.2	2187	2V	85
	2 4	2.2	2187	MFI	91
	1, 2, A, B 4	2.2	2187	MFI	110
	3, 4, C, D 4	2.2 T	2187 T	MFI	145

3 ENGINE ROTORS / **4** ENGINE IDENTIFICATION

YEAR	CODE or CYL.	liters	cc	Fuel System	HP
1992 Cont'd.	1 4	2.6	2606	MFI	121
	1, 2, 3 6	3.0	2954	MFI	155
	2 6	3.0	2954	MFI	195
1991	1, 3 2	1.3	1308	MFI	160
	2, 4 2	1.3 T	1308 T	MFI	200
	2 4	1.6	1597	MFI	82
	1, 2 4	1.6	1597	MFI	105, 116[1]
	4, 8 4	1.8	1839	MFI	103
	6 4	1.8	1839	MFI	125
	1, 2, A, B 4	2.2	2187	MFI	110
	3, 4, C, D 4	2.2 T	2187 T	MFI	145
	3 4	2.2	2187	2V	85
	3 4	2.2	2187	MFI	91
	1, 4 4	2.6	2606	MFI	121
	1, 2, 3 6	3.0	2954	MFI	150, 158[1]
	2 6	3.0	2954	MFI	190
1990	1, 3 2	1.3	1308	MFI	160
	2, 4 2	1.3 T	1308 T	MFI	200
	2 4	1.6	1597	MFI	82
	1, 2 4	1.6	1597	MFI	116
	4, 8 4	1.8	1839	MFI	103
	6 4	1.8	1839	MFI	125
	3 4	2.2	2187	2V	85
	3 4	2.2	2187	MFI	91
	1, 2, A, B 4	2.2	2187	MFI	110
	3, 4, C, D 4	2.2 T	2187 T	MFI	145
	1, 4 4	2.6	2606	MFI	121
	2, 3 6	3.0	2954	MFI	150
	1 6	3.0	2954	MFI	158
	2 6	3.0	2954	MFI	190
1989	1, 3 2	1.3	1308	MFI	160
	2, 4 2	1.3 T	1308 T	MFI	200
	2 4	1.6	1597	MFI	82
	3 (2WD) 4	1.6 T	1597 T	MFI	132
	4 (2WD) 4	1.6 T	1597 T	MFI	132
	3 4	2.2	2187	2V	85
	1, 2, A, B 4	2.2	2187	MFI	110
	3, 4, C, D 4	2.2 T	2187 T	MFI	145
	1 4	2.6	2606	MFI	121
	2 4	2.6	2606	MFI	121
	1 6	3.0	2954	MFI	158
	2 (2WD) 6	3.0	2954	MFI	150
	3 (4WD) 6	3.0	2954	MFI	150

T—Turbo.   MFI—Multiport Fuel Injection.
2V—Two Venturi Carburetor.   S—Supercharged.
1 Engine horsepower varies with model installation.

UNDERHOOD SERVICE SPECIFICATIONS

CYLINDER NUMBERING SEQUENCE
Piston engine
4-CYL. FIRING ORDER: 1 3 4 2

———— Front of car ————

1995-97	1998-00	1989-94	1989	1990-00
Protegé 1468cc	Protegé 1468cc, 1597cc	323, MX-3, Precidia 1597cc ex. Turbo 1990-98 Protegé, MX-3, Precidia 1839cc	323 1597cc Turbo	Miata 1597cc, 1839cc

  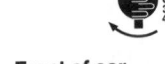 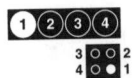 

———— Front of car ————

1999-00	1992-94 MX-3, Precidia 1844cc	1993-97 626, MX-6	1998-00	1989-94
Protegé 1839cc	1993-97 626, MX-6 1995-99 Millenia 2497cc	1991cc	626 1991cc	B2200, B2600, MPV 2184cc, 2555cc, 2606cc

V6 FIRING ORDER: 1 2 3 4 5 6

———— Front of car ————

1989-92 626, MX-6 2184cc ex. Turbo	1989-92 626, MX-6 2184cc Turbo	1995-99 Millenia 2255cc	1998-00 626 2497cc

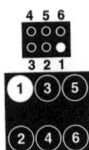  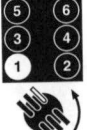

———— Front of car ————

2000 MPV 2497cc	1989-98 MPV, 929 2954cc SOHC	1990-95 929 2954cc DOHC

———— **TIMING MARK** ————

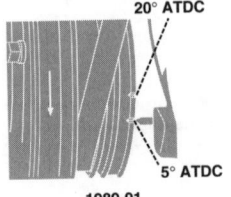 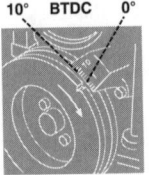 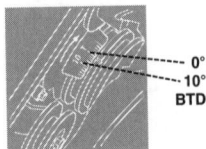

1989-91 1308cc	1989-92 626, MX-6, 1998cc, 2184cc 1989-92 B2200 2184cc	1989-94 323, 1597cc 1990-00 Protegé 1468cc, 1597cc	1989-97 MPV, B2600, 929 2606cc, 2954cc 1992-00 Protegé, Miata, MX-3, Precidia 1839cc, 1844cc MX-6, 626 Millenia, MPV, 1991cc, 2497cc

UNDERHOOD SERVICE SPECIFICATIONS

MAITU2

MAITU2

ELECTRICAL AND IGNITION SYSTEMS

BATTERY

BCI equivalent shown, size may vary from original equipment. Check clearance before replacing, holddown may need to be modified.

Engine	Year	STANDARD BCI Group No.	STANDARD Crank. Perf.	OPTIONAL BCI Group No.	OPTIONAL Crank. Perf.
RX-7	1989-90	21R	320	35	405
Canada	1989-90	35	405	—	—
RX-7	1991-92	35	350	35	420
Canada	1991-92	35	420	—	—
RX-7	1993	35	350	24F	495
RX-7: MT	1994-95	35	405	—	—
AT	1994-95	24F	490	—	—
323, Protegé	1989-90	21R	320	35	380
323, Protegé	1991	35	350	—	—
Calif.	1991	21R	310	—	—
323, Protegé	1992-94	35	350	—	—
	1995-00	21R	310	35	350
626, MX-6	1989-92	21R	320	35	360
626, MX-6	1993-99	58R	580	—	—
929	1989-91	21R	320	24F	585
929, Serenia	1992-95	35	350	24F	585
Canada	1992-95	24F	585	—	—
Pickup: B2200	1989-93	21	310	24	490
B2600	1989-93	21	310	24	585
Millenia: 2.3L	1995-99	35	450	24F	565
2.5L	1995-99	35	350	35	450
MPV	1989-95	21R	310	24F	585
	1996-98	35	350	24F	490
	2000	24F	350	24F	515
MX-3, Precidia: 4-cyl.	1992-95	21R	310	35	350
V6	1992-93	35	420	—	—
V6	1994	35	420	—	—
Calif.	1994	21R	310	—	—

GENERATOR

Engine	Year	Rated Output (amps)	Test Output (amps @ rpm)
1308cc	1989-92	80	60 @ 2500
	1993-95	100	100 @ 2500
1489cc	1995-98	65	55 @ idle
		70	70 @ 2000
1597cc FI	1989	60	60 @ 3000
1597cc Miata: MT	1990-93	60	60 @ 3000
AT	1990-93	65	65 @ 2500
1597cc MX-3	1992-95	70	70 @ 3000
1597cc Others	1990-92	65	65 @ 2500
1597cc	1999	—	77 max. @ 2000
1839cc Protegé	1990-94	65	65 @ 2500
	1995-98	—	55 @ idle
		—	70 @ 2000
1839cc Miata: MT	1994-97	65	65 @ 3000
AT	1994-97	70	70 @ 3000
1839cc Protegé	1999-00	—	81 max. @ 2000
Miata	1999-00	—	68 max. @ 2000
1844cc	1992-95	90	90 @ 3000
1991cc	1993-97	80	80 @ 3000
	1998-00	80	77 max. @ 2000
2184cc FI	1989	70	65 @ 3000
2184cc 626, MX-6	1990-92	70	65 @ 3000
Turbo w/MT	1990-92	70	65 @ 3000
Turbo w/AT	1990-92	80	60 @ 2500
2184cc Pickup, 2555cc	1989-93	55	50 @ 2500
2255cc Millenia	1995-00	110	78 @ 2000
2497cc 626, MX-6	1993-99	90	90 @ 3000
2497cc Millenia	1995-00	90	81 @ 2000
2497cc MPV	2000	—	98 @ 2000
2606cc: Pickup	1989-93	60	55 @ 3000
MPV	1989-93	70	70 @ 3000

GENERATOR Continued

Engine	Year	Rated Output (amps)	Test Output (amps @ rpm)
2954cc	1989-91	70	60 @ 3000
2954cc MPV	1992-98	70	70 @ 3000
2954cc 929	1992-95	90	90 @ 3000

REGULATOR

Application	Year	Voltage Setting	Test Temp. (deg. F/C)
323, 626, RX-7, MPV, Miata	1989	14.1-14.7	68/20
Pickup	1989	14.2-15.2	68/20
All Others	1989	14.4-15.0	68/20
Miata	1996-97	14.3-14.9	65/20
	1999-00	13.0-15.0	—
Millenia	1995-96	13.0-14.0	77/25
	1997-00	14.0-15.0	77/25
Protegé	1999-00	13.0-15.0	—
MPV	2000	13.0-15.0	—
All Others	1990-00	14.1-14.7	68/20

STARTER

Engine	Year	Cranking Voltage (min. volts)	Ampere Draw @ Cranking Speed
All	1989-90	8.0	—

SPARK PLUGS

Application	Year	Gap (inches)	Gap (mm)	Torque (ft-lb)
Rotary Engines:				
All	1989-92	.043-.067	1.1-1.7	9-13
	1993-95	.044-.066	1.1-1.7	13-17
Piston Engines:				
1998cc 2V, 2184cc 2V	1989-93	.030-.033	.75-.85	11-17
2255cc Millenia	1995-99	.028-.031	0.7-0.8	11-16
2497cc 626	1998-00	.028-.031	0.7-0.8	11-16
2497cc MPV	2000	.052-.055	1.3-1.4	9-13
All Others	1989-00	.039-.043	1.0-1.1	11-17

IGNITION COIL

Winding resistance (ohms @ 68°F, or 20°C)

1308cc, 1993-95: Secondary resistance is measured between both high tension terminals of leading side of coil.

1597cc, 1839cc Miata: Primary resistance measured between terminals 1 & 2 and 1 & 3 of coil connector. Secondary resistance measured between two left- or two right-side high tension terminals of coils with spark plug wires removed.

1844cc: Primary resistance measured between first and third terminals of 3-terminal coil connector. Secondary resistance measured between terminal C (closest to coil tower) of 3-terminal coil connector and high tension terminal of coil with spark plug wire removed.

All with remote coil, distributorless ignition: Primary resistance measured between both pairs of terminals on coil.

Application	Year	Windings	Resistance (ohms)
1308cc	1989-92	Primary	0.2-1.0
1308cc	1993-95	Primary	1.0 max.
		Secondary	9600-16,000
1489cc	1995-97	Primary	.49-.73
		Secondary	20,000-31,000
	1998	Primary	—
		Secondary	20,000-31,000
1597cc	1989	Primary	1
		Secondary	6000-30,000
1597cc Miata	1990-93	Primary	.78-.94
		Secondary	11,200-15,200
1597cc MX-3, Precidia	1994	Primary	.49-.73
		Secondary	20,000-31,000
1597cc, 1839cc, Others	1990-94	Primary	.81-.99
		Secondary	10,000-16,000
1597cc	1999-00	Primary	—
		Secondary	7000-12,000

MAZDA
1989-2000 All Models
1991-2000 Navajo, B2300, B2500, B3000, B4000—See Ford Trucks

UNDERHOOD SERVICE SPECIFICATIONS

MAITU3

MAITU3

IGNITION COIL Continued

Application	Year	Windings	Resistance (ohms)
1839cc Miata	1994-97	Primary	—
		Secondary	8700-12,900
	1998-00	Primary	—
		Secondary	8240-12,360
1839cc Protegé	1995-97	Primary	.49-.73
		Secondary	20,000-31,000
		Primary	—
		Secondary	20,000-31,000
1839cc All	1999-00	Primary	—
		Secondary	8000-14,000
1844cc	1992-93	Primary	.58-.86
		Secondary	11,500-18,500
	1994	Primary	.49-.73
		Secondary	20,000-31,000
1991cc	1993	Primary	.58-.86
		Secondary	11,500-18,500
1991cc: w/MT	1994-97	Primary	.49-.73
		Secondary	20,000-31,000
w/AT	1994	Primary	0.7 approx.
		Secondary	8530 approx.
w/AT	1995-97	Primary	0.4
		Secondary	8700
1991cc	1998-00	Primary	.45-.55
		Secondary	11,500-15,500
2184cc FI	1989-90	Primary	1.04-1.27
		Secondary	7100-9700
2184cc FI	1991-92	Primary	.77-.95
		Secondary	10,300-13,900
2184cc FI	1993	Primary	.77-.95
		Secondary	6000-30,000
2184cc Turbo	1989-92	Primary	.72-.88
		Secondary	10,300-13,900
2184cc 2V	1989-93	Primary	1.0-1.3
		Secondary	6000-30,000
2255cc	1999	Primary	.58-.72
		Secondary	20,000-31,000
2497cc	1993-94	Primary	.58-.86
		Secondary	11,500-18,500
	1995-97	Primary	.49-.73
		Secondary	20,000-31,000
2497cc Millenia	1998-00	Primary	.49-.73
		Secondary	20,000-31,000
2497cc 626, MPV	1998-00	Primary	.45-.55
		Secondary	11,500-15,500
2606cc	1989-90	Primary	.77-.95[2]
		Secondary	6000-30,000
	1991-92	Primary	.81-.99[2]
		Secondary	6000-30,000
	1993-94	Primary	.77-.95[2]
		Secondary	6000-30,000
2954cc 929	1989-91	Primary	.72-.88
		Secondary	10,000-30,000
	1992-95	Primary	.70-1.1
		Secondary	9000-17,000
2954cc MPV	1989-92	Primary	.81-.99
		Secondary	6000-30,000
	1993-95	Primary	.72-.88
		Secondary	10,000-30,000
	1996-98	Primary	.49-.74
		Secondary	20,000-31,000

1 Coil is defective if there is no continuity.
2 Measured between two terminals on right side of high tension tower. When measured on left side, 0.9-1.1.

DISTRIBUTOR PICKUP

Application	Year	Resistance (ohms)	Air Gap (in./mm)
2184cc FI	1990-92	900-1200	—
2606cc, mech. distr.	1989-90	900-1200	—
2954cc 929	1989-91	140-180[1]	—
2954cc MPV	1989-92	900-1200	—
	1993-95	205-255	—

1 Measured between all three left and right terminals individually.

TIMING PROCEDURE

Both leading and trailing ignition systems must be timed on rotary engines.

Rotary engine:

1989-90, rotate crankshaft position sensor to adjust.

Piston engines:

1989-91 626 Turbo, 929, MPV 6-cyl., 1992-93 626 Turbo, MPV 6-cyl.: Ground test connector (green connector, 1 wire).

1990-98 323, Protegé, Miata

1992-97 MX-3, 929, MPV, MX-6 & 626 ex. 1991cc w/AT: Ground diagnostic test terminal #10. Miata, turn crankshaft sensor to adjust. Some models, with terminal ungrounded, timing should be at check value.

1993-95 1991cc w/AT: Disconnect spout shorting bar from connector.

1998-00: Connect a scan tool and access ignition timing function. Timing should be at specified value. After exiting ignition timing mode, timing should be at check value. If not, further diagnosis of the system is needed.

All w/mechanical advance distributor: Disconnect and plug distributor vacuum hose(s). Loosen distributor lock nut and rotate to obtain specified timing.

Some models: When test terminal is ungrounded, verify that timing is at Check value.

BASE TIMING

Set timing at slow idle and Before Top Dead Center, unless otherwise specified.

Application	Year	Man. Trans. (degrees)	Auto. Trans. (degrees)
Rotary Engines:			
1308cc:			
Leading	1989-92	5 ATDC±1	5 ATDC±1
Trailing	1989-92	20 ATDC±2	20 ATDC±2
1308cc:			
Leading	1993-95	5 ATDC[1]	5 ATDC[1]
Trailing	1993-95	20 ATDC[1]	20 ATDC[1]
Piston Engines:			
1489cc	1995	0±1	0±1
	1996-97	10±1	10±1
	1998	10±1[1]	10±1[1]
Check	1995-98	6-18	6-18
1597cc	1989	2±1	2±1
Turbo	1989	12±1	12±1
1597cc, 323	1990-94	7±1	7±1
1597cc Miata	1990	8±1	8±1
1597cc Miata	1991-93	10±1	8±1
1597cc MX-3	1992-95	10±1	10±1
Check	1995	6-18	6-18
1597cc	1999-00	10±1[1]	10±1[1]
Check	1999-00	—	—
1839cc	1990-94	5±1	5±1
DOHC	1990-94	10±1	10±1
Check, Miata	1994	6-18	6-18
1839cc Protegé	1995-98	0±1	0±1
Check	1995-98	6-18	6-18
1839cc Miata	1995-97	10±1	10±1
Check	1995-97	6-18	6-18
1839cc All	1999-00	10±1[1]	10±1[1]
Check	1999-00	6-18	6-18
1844cc	1992-94	10±1	10±1
Check	1992-94	6-18	6-18
1991cc	1993	12±1	12±1
Check	1993	6-18	6-18
1991cc	1994-97	12±1	10±1
Check	1994-97	6-18	—
1991cc	1998-00	12±6[1]	12±6[1]
2184cc FI	1989-93	6±1	6±1
Turbo	1989-92	9±1	9±1
2184cc 2V	1989-93	6±1	6±1
2255cc Millenia	1995-99	—	7±1[1]
Check	1998-99	5-15	5-15
2497cc	1993-97	10±1	10±1
Check, 626, MX-6	1993-97	6-18	6-18
Check, Millenia	1995-97	—	1-16
2497cc 626, MPV	1998-00	10±6[1]	10±6[1]
2497cc Millenia	1998-00	10±1	10±1
Check	1998-00	6-18	6-18
2606cc	1989-94	5±1	5±1
2954cc 929	1989-91	15±1	15±1
DOHC	1990-91	—	8±1
2954cc 929	1992	—	10±1
Check	1992	—	7-20

UNDERHOOD SERVICE SPECIFICATIONS

MAITU4

MAITU4

BASE TIMING Continued

Application	Year	Man. Trans. (degrees)	Auto. Trans. (degrees)
2954cc 929	1993-95	—	12±1
Check	1993-95	—	7-20
2954cc MPV	1989-97	11±1	11±1
2954cc MPV	1998	11±1	11±1
Check	1998	-2–34	-2–34

1 Not adjustable.

DISTRIBUTOR TIMING ADVANCE

Engine degrees at engine rpm, no load, in addition to base timing setting.

Mechanical advance distributors only.

Engine	Trans-mission	Year	Distributor Number	Degrees @ 2500 RPM Total	Centrifugal
1597cc FI	MT & AT	1989	—	34-42	8-12
1597cc Turbo	MT & AT	1989	—	17.8-25.8	4.8-8.8
2184cc FI	MT & AT	1989-90	—	30.2-38.2	12.2-16.2
2184cc 2V	MT & AT	1989-93	—	25-33	9-13
2606cc[1]	MT & AT	1989-90	—	38-46[2]	24-28
2954cc MPV	MT & AT	1989-91	—	31-38	38-46

1 Late 1990 MPV has IC.
2 Vacuum retard, 4-8.

FUEL SYSTEM

FUEL PUMP

Engine	Year	Pressure (PSI) Fuel Line[1]	Fuel Line[2]	Fuel Pump
1308cc	1989-92	27-33	—	71-92
Turbo	1989-92	28.4	34-40	71-92
1308cc	1993-95	28-32	36-38	71-107
1489cc	1995-97	29-34	40-45	72-93
1489cc	1998	29-34	40-45	64-92
1597cc FI	1989	24.6-31.3	34-41	64-85
1597cc, 1839cc, 1844cc	1990-93	30-38	38-46	64-92
1597cc 323, 1839cc, 1844cc	1994	30-38	38-46	64-92
1597cc MX-3 Precidia	1994	28-37	37-47	70-95
1597cc	1999-00	30-38	38-46	64-92
1839cc Protegé, Miata	1995	29-34	40-45	72-93
1839cc Miata	1996-97	30-38	38-46	64-92
Protegé	1996-97	29-34	40-45	72-93
1839cc Protegé	1998	29-34	40-45	64-92
	1999-00	30-38	38-46	64-92
1839cc Miata	1999-00	53-61	—	64-92
1991cc	1993-98	30-38	38-46	64-92
2184cc 2V Mech.	1989-92	—	—	3.7-4.7
Elect.	1989-92	—	—	2.8-3.6
2184cc FI	1989-92	27-33	34-40	64-85
2255cc	1995-00	30-41	41-48	92-116
2497cc	1993-97	30-38	38-46	64-92
2497cc 626	1998-00	30-36	39-45	64-92
2497cc MPV	2000	55-61	—	86-110
2497cc Millenia	1998-00	30-38	38-46	64-92
2606cc, 2954cc	1989-98	28-38	38-46	64-85

1 Vacuum hose connected to pressure regulator.
2 Vacuum hose disconnected from pressure regulator.

IDLE SPEED W/O COMPUTER CONTROL

Midpoint of range given is the preferred setting.

1989-91 Rotary engine: Ground test connector (single wire, green connector) by battery.

1989-93 Gasoline piston engines: To set idle speed, turn idle speed screw to obtain specified idle. To set fast idle, set cam on specified step and adjust to specified value. To set speed-up speed, activate vacuum ports on vacuum solenoid that correspond to each speed-up system. Adjust vacuum ports on solenoid to specified value.

IDLE SPEED W/O COMPUTER CONTROL Continued

Engine	Year	SLOW Man. Trans.	SLOW Auto. Trans.	FAST Man. Trans.	FAST Auto. Trans.	Step of Cam
Rotary Engines:						
1308cc FI	1989-92	725-775	725-775 N	—	—	—
Speed-up	1989-92	800	750 D			
Piston Engines:						
2184cc 2V	1989-93	800-850	800-850 N	3000-4000	3000-4000 N	High
Speed-up: A/C	1989-93	1300-1500	1300-1500 N			
Elect. load, PS	1989-93	—	920-970 N			

IDLE SPEED W/COMPUTER CONTROL

Midpoint of range given is the preferred setting speed.

Canada models, apply parking brake to turn off headlights.

1991cc w/AT: If Scan tool indicates idle out of limits, remove timing shorting bar and set idle to specified value.

1989-95 All other models:
Ground test terminal 10 of DLC and set idle to specified value. Set idle to specified value. Turn on headlights and set heater blower to high. Electrical speed-up should be at specified value. Turn AC on and verify that idle increases to AC speed-up speed.

1996-99: Connect a Scan tool and access idle speed function. Set idle to specified value. Turn on headlights and set heater blowerd to high. Electrical speed-up should be at specified value. Turn AC on and verify that idle increases to AC speed-up speed.

Engine	Year	Transmission	Setting Speed	Electrical Speed-up	AC Speed-up
1308cc	1993-95	MT	700-750	—	875-925
		AT	700-750 N		775-825 N
1489cc	1995-98	MT	650-750	650-750	650-750
		AT	700-800 N	700-800 N	700-800 N
1597cc FI	1989	MT	800-900	—	—
		AT	800-900 N		
1597cc Miata	1990-93	MT	800-900	—	—
		AT	800-900 N		
1597cc 323	1990-94	MT	700-800	—	—
		AT	700-800 N		
1597cc MX-3	1992-93	MT	700-800	—	800-900
		AT	700-800 N		750-850 N
	1994-95	MT	650-750	—	—
	1994-95	AT	700-800 N		—
1597cc	1999-00	MT	650-750	650-750	700-800
		AT	650-750 N	650-750 N	700-800 N
1839cc Protegé	1990-94	MT	700-800	—	—
		AT	700-800 N	—	—
	1995-98	MT	700-800	—	700-800
		AT	700-800 N	—	700-800 N
1839cc Miata	1994-95	MT	800-900	—	—
		AT	750-850	—	—
	1996-98	MT	800-900	850	1000
		AT	750-850 N	800 N	800 N
	1999-00	MT	750-850	750-850	950-1050
		AT	750-850 N	750-850 N	750-850 N
1839cc Protegé	1999-00	MT	650-750	650-750	700-800
		AT	650-750 N	650-750 N	700-800 N
1844cc	1992-94	MT	640-700	—	720-780
		AT	640-700 N	—	720-760 N
1991cc	1993-95	MT	650-750	—	—
		AT	650-750 N	—	—
	1996-97	MT	650-750	725-825	725-825
		AT	650-750 N	675-775 N	725-825 N
	1998-00	MT	550-850	625-925	625-925
		AT	500-800 N	525-825 N	500-800 N
2184cc FI	1989	MT	750	—	800
		AT	750 N	—	800 N
2184cc FI, 626, MX-6	1990-92	MT	725-775	—	800
		AT	725-775 N	—	850 N
2184cc FI Pickup	1991-93	MT	730-770	—	—
		AT	750-790 N	—	—

MAZDA
1989-2000 All Models
1991-2000 Navajo, B2300, B2500, B3000, B4000—See Ford Trucks
UNDERHOOD SERVICE SPECIFICATIONS

MAITU5

MAITU5

IDLE SPEED W/COMPUTER CONTROL Continued

Engine	Year	Transmission	Setting Speed	Electrical Speed-up	AC Speed-up
2255cc	1995-00	AT	600-700 N	—	—
2497cc	1993-97	MT	600-700	—	775-875
		AT	600-700 N	—	775-875 N
2497cc Millenia	1998-00	AT	600-700 N	—	775-875 N
2497cc 626	1998-00	MT	550-750[1]	550-750	700-900
		AT	550-750 N[1]	550-750 N	700-900 N
2497cc MPV	2000	AT	700-800 N[1]	700-800 N	700-900 N
2606cc	1989-93	MT	730-770	—	—
		AT	750-790 N	—	—
	1994	MT	750-790	—	—
		AT	750-790 N	—	—
2954cc	1989-91	MT	630-670	—	—
		AT	630-670 N	—	—
DOHC	1990-91	AT	680-720 N	—	900 N
2954cc 929	1992-95	AT	680-720 N	—	—
2954cc MPV	1989-98	MT	780-820	—	—
		AT	780-820 N	—	—

1 Check valve only, not adjustable

ENGINE MECHANICAL

TIGHTENING TORQUES
FOR CYLINDER HEAD TORQUE SEQUENCES AND DIAGRAMS, SEE APPENDIX G.
Some fasteners are tightened in more than one step.
Some values are specified in inches.

Engine	Year	TORQUE FOOT-POUNDS/NEWTON METERS				
		Cylinder Head	Intake Manifold	Exhaust Manifold	Crankshaft Pulley	Water Pump
1308cc	1989-92	—	14-19/19-25	23-34/31-46	69-95"/7-11	13-20/18-26
	1993-95	—	12-16/16-22	48-57/65-78	70-95"/8-11	16-22/22-30
1489cc	1995-98	13-16/17-22, +90°, +90°	14-19/19-25	12-17/16-23	115-122/157-167	14-19/19-25
1597cc, 1839cc, SOHC	1989-95	56-60/76-81	14-19/19-25	12-17/16-23	109-152"/12-17	14-19/19-25
1597cc, 1839cc, DOHC	1989-98	56-60/76-81	14-19/19-25	29-42/39-57	109-152"/12-17	14-19/19-25
1597cc	1999-00	13-16/17-22, +90°, +90°	14-19/19-25	12-17/16-23	9-12/12-17	14-19/19-25
1839cc Protege	1999-00	13-16/17-22, +90°, +90°	14-19/19-25	28-34/16-23	9-12/12-17	14-19/19-25
1839cc Miata	1999-00	56-60/76-81	14-19/19-25	28-34/38-48	9-12/12-17	14-19/19-25
1844cc	1992-95	17-19/23-26, +90°, +90°	14-19/19-25	14-19/19-25	116-123/157-167	14-19/19-25
1991cc	1993-00	12-17/17-22, +90°, +90°	14-18/19-25	15-20/20-28	116-123/157-167	14-19/19-25
2184cc FI	1989-93	59-64/80-86	14-22/19-30	25-36/34-49	109-152"/12-17	14-19/19-25
2184cc 2V	1989-93	59-64/80-86	14-22/19-30	16-21/22-28	9-13/12-17	9-13/12-17
2255cc	1995-00	17-19/23-26, +90°, +90°	14-18/19-25	15-20/20-28	116-122/157-166	—
2497cc	1993-00	17-19/23-26, +90°, +90°	14-18/19-25	16-21/22-28	116-123/157-167	14-19/19-25

TIGHTENING TORQUES Continued

Engine	Year	TORQUE FOOT-POUNDS/NEWTON METERS				
		Cylinder Head	Intake Manifold	Exhaust Manifold	Crankshaft Pulley	Water Pump
2606cc	1989-94	60-63/80-86	14-22/19-30	16-21/22-28	130-145/173-196	14-19/19-25
2954cc	1989-98	14/20 +90°, +90°	14-19/19-25	16-21/22-28	116-123/157-167	14-19/19-25

1 Then back off 1 turn.
2 Back off bolt and retorque to this spec.

VALVE CLEARANCE
1995-00 Engine cold.

Engine	Year	Intake (inches)	Intake (mm)	Exhaust (inches)	Exhaust (mm)
1489cc	1995-98	.010-.012	.25-.31	.010-.012	.25-.31
1597cc	1999-00	.010-.012	.25-.31	.010-.012	.25-.31
1839cc	1997-98	.008-.009	.18-.24	.012-.013	.28-.34
1839cc Protegé	1999-00	.009-.011	.22-.27	.009-.011	.22-.27
Miata	1999-00	.008-.009	.18-.24	.012-.013	.28-.34
1991cc	1998-00	.009-.012	.22-.29	.009-.012	.22-.29
2255cc	1995-00	.011-.012	.27-.31	.011-.012	.25-.31
2497cc 626	1998-00	.010-.012	.25-.31	.010-.013	.27-.33

COMPRESSION PRESSURE
At cranking speed, engine warm, throttle open.

Application	Year	PSI	Maximum Variation PSI
Rotary Engines:			
All	1989-92	85 min.	21
	1993-95	100 min.	21
Piston Engines:			
1489cc	1995-98	146-195	28
1597cc 8 valve	1989-94	135-192	28
Calif.	1993-94	142-185	28
16 valve	1992-94	142-186	28
1597cc	1999-00	142-199	28
1839cc Protegé	1990-91	128-182	28
	1992-94	121-173	28
1839cc Miata	1994-97	128-182	28
	1999-00	146-209	28
1839cc Protegé	1994-98	139-185	28
	1999	156-199	28
1844cc	1992-94	142-193	28
1991cc	1993-00	119-171	28
2184cc FI	1989-93	114-162	28
Turbo	1989-92	98-139	28
2184cc 2V	1989-93	121-173	28
2255cc	1995-97	143-185	28
	1998-00	121-164	28
2497cc	1993-98	142-203	28
2497cc 626	1998-00	141-202	28
Millenia	1998-00	132-189	28
2606cc	1989-94	142-185	28
2954cc	1989-91	114-164	28
2954cc MPV	1992-98	121-164	28
929, Serenia	1992-95	156-213	28

1 Lowest cylinder pressure should be within 75% of highest.

BELT TENSION
With 22 pounds of pressure applied midway between pulleys on longest belt segment.
Navajo, B2300, B3000, B4000 use automatic tensioner. Replace belt if inlet marks on tensioner are outside the range.

Engine	Year	Generator	Power Steering	Air Cond.	Air Pump
Deflection Method:					
USED BELTS					
1308cc (inches)	1989-92	½-5/8	7/16-1/2	1/4-5/16	3/8-7/16
(mm)	1989-92	12-15	11-13	6-8	9-11

MAZDA
1989-2000 All Models
1991-2000 Navajo, B2300, B2500, B3000, B4000—See Ford Trucks
UNDERHOOD SERVICE SPECIFICATIONS
MAITU6

MAITU6

BELT TENSION Continued

Engine	Year	Generator	Power Steering	Air Cond.	Air Pump
2184cc FI (inches)	1989-92	5/16-3/8	5/16-3/8	5/16-3/8	—
(mm)	1989-92	7-9	7-9	7-9	—
2184cc 2V (inches)	1989-92	7/16-3/8	7/16-3/8	5/8-9/16	7/16-3/8
(mm)	1989-92	8-9	8-9	12-14	8-9
2954cc 929 (inches)	1989-90	3/8-7/16	3/8-7/16	3/8-7/16	—
(mm)	1989-90	10-12	9-11	9-11	—
Strand Tension Method:					
USED BELTS					
1308cc	1993-95	140-150	130-140	130-140	—
1489cc	1995-98	110-150	95-110	95-110	—
1597cc, 1839cc 323,					
Protegé	1989-94	68-85	95-110	95-110	—
1597cc Miata	1990-93	95-110	95-110	95-110	—
1597cc MX-3, Precidia	1992-95	110-158	95-110	95-110	—
1597cc	1999	110-158	95-110	95-110	—
1839cc Miata	1994-99	110-158	95-110	95-110	—
1839cc Protegé	1995-98	110-150	95-110	95-110	—
	1999	110-154	110-154	110-154	—
1844cc	1992-94	110-150	80-120	110-150	—
1991cc	1993-99	110-150	110-150	110-150	—
2255cc	1995-99	1	—	—	—
2497cc	1993-99	110-150	88-120	110-150	—
2606cc	1989-94	103-123	93-106	126-143	—
2954cc 929, Serenia	1991-95	92-110	92-110	92-110	—
2972cc MPV	1989-93	103-123	106-123	79-90	—
	1994-98	104-123	80-90	106-123	—
NEW BELTS					
1308cc	1993-95	160-170	170-190	170-190	—
1489cc	1995-98	110-160	110-130	110-130	—
1597cc, 1839cc					
323, Protegé	1989-94	85-103	110-132	110-132	—
1597cc Miata	1990-96	110-132	110-132	110-132	—
1597cc MX-3, Precidia	1992-95	110-167	110-132	110-132	—
1597cc	1999	110-167	132-154	132-154	—
1839cc Miata	1994-96	110-167	110-132	110-132	—
1839cc Protegé	1995-98	110-160	110-130	110-130	—
	1999	165-187	132-176	132-176	—
1844cc	1992-94	160-190	130-150	160-190	—
1991cc	1993-98	170-180	140-170	140-170	—
2255cc	1995-99	1	—	—	—
2497cc	1993-98	160-190	130-150	160-190	—
2606cc	1989-94	123-143	92-105	99-121	—
2954cc 929, Serenia	1991-95	110-125	110-125	110-125	—
2972cc MPV	1989-93	123-143	125-143	92-106	—
	1994-98	104-123	80-90	106-123	—

1 Automatic tensioner.

SERPENTINE BELT DIAGRAMS

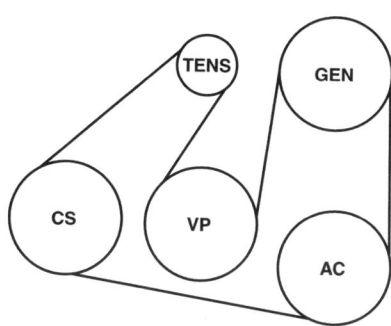

1995-99 2255cc outer belt

SERPENTINE BELT DIAGRAMS Continued

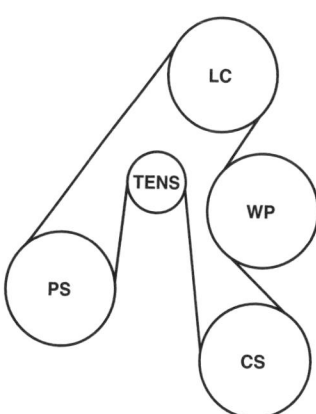

1995-99 V6 2255cc inner belt

ENGINE COMPUTER SYSTEM

DIAGNOSTIC TROUBLE CODES

1989-92 RX-7 FI Connect digital code checker (Tool #49 G018 9A0) to check connector located by battery (RX-7), or control unit (626).

1989-93 B2200 Connect system checker (Tool #49 H018 9A1) to connector above right-side wheel housing. Ground check connector (yellow/black) and turn ignition on.

1989-94 B2600, Miata,

1989-94 323, 626, MX-6, MX-3 929, MPV Connect system checker (Tool #49 H018 9A1) to DLC located by battery and ground green single wire connector, if equipped.

1993-94 RX-7, 626, MX-6 1991cc w/AT: Connect a Scan tool to the DLC and follow tool manufacturer's instructions to retrieve codes. (See three-digit codes under Ford section.)

1995 1489cc, 1839cc Protegé, 2255cc, 2497cc Millenia; 1996-99 All: OBD-II system check. Connect a Scan tool and follow the tool manufacturer's instructions to retrieve codes.

1989-91 RX-7
Code 1 Ignition coil, trailing side
Codes 2, 3 Crankshaft position sensor
Code 8 Mass airflow sensor
Code 9 Engine coolant temperature sensor
Code 10 Intake air temperature sensor, airflow meter
Code 11 Intake air temperature sensor, engine
Codes 12, 18 Throttle position sensor
Code 13 MAP sensor
Code 14 Barometric sensor
Code 15 Oxygen sensor
Code 17 Feedback system
Codes 20, 27, 37 Metering oil pump
Code 25 Pressure regulator solenoid
Code 26 Step motor, metering oil pump
Code 30 Split air solenoid valve
Code 31 Relief solenoid
Code 32 Switch solenoid
Code 33 Port air solenoid
Code 34 Air bypass valve solenoid
Code 38 Warm-up solenoid
Code 40 Auxiliary port valve
Code 41 Intake control solenoid
Code 51 Fuel pump resistor
Code 71 Injector, front
Code 73 Injector, rear
1989-95 323, 626, 929, MPV, Miata, MX-3
1993-95 RX-7
Code 1 Ignition pulse
Codes 2, 3, 4 Distributor pickups or crankshaft position sensor
Code 5 Knock sensor
Code 6 Speed sensor
Code 7 Knock sensor (right side, 929 DOHC)
Code 8 Mass airflow sensor

DIAGNOSTIC TROUBLE CODES Continued

Code 9 Engine coolant temperature sensor
Code 10 Intake air sensor in airflow meter
Code 11 Intake air sensor in intake manifold
Code 12 Throttle position sensor
Code 13 Barometric pressure sensor
Code 14 Barometric pressure sensor
Code 15 Oxygen sensor (left side, DOHC 929)
Code 16 EGR position sensor
Code 17 Feedback system (left side, DOHC 929)
Code 18 Throttle position sensor
Code 20 Metering oil pump position sensor
Code 23 Fuel temperature sensor (RX-7)
Code 23 Oxygen sensor (right side, DOHC 929)
Code 24 Feedback system (right side, DOHC 929)
Code 25 Pressure regulator solenoid
Codes 26, 27 Metering oil pump (RX-7)
Codes 26, 27 Purge central solenoids (others)
Code 28 EGR vacuum solenoid
Code 29 EGR vent solenoid
Codes 30 Split air bypass solenoid
Codes 31 Secondary air bypass valve
Codes 32 Secondary air switching solenoid
Codes 33 Port air bypass solenoid
Code 34 IAC valve
Code 36 Oxygen sensor heater, right side
Code 37 Metering oil pump, low voltage (RX-7)
Code 37 Oxygen sensor heater, left side (others)
Code 38 Accelerated warm-up solenoid (RX-7)
Code 40 Relief solenoid (RX-7)
Codes 40, 41 Induction control solenoid valves (others)
Code 43 Wastegate control solenoid
Code 44 Turbo control solenoid
Code 45 Charge control solenoid
Code 46 Charge relief solenoid
Code 46 VRIS solenoid (V6)
Code 50 Double throttle control solenoid
Code 51 Fuel pump relay
Code 54 Air pump relay
Code 55 Pulse generator
Code 60 AT solenoid, 1-2 shift
Code 61 AT solenoid, 2-3 shift
Code 62 AT solenoid, 3-4 shift
Code 63 AT solenoid, lock-up
Code 65 A/C signal
Code 67 Fan relay
Code 69 Fan coolant temperature sensor
Code 71 Front secondary injector
Code 73 Rear secondary injector
Code 76 Slip lock-up off signal
Code 77 Torque reduced signal

SENSORS, INPUT

TEMPERATURE SENSORS
Intake air temperature sensor.
1989-97 Measured between terminals E2 and THA of MAF sensor.
1998-99 1489cc, 1597cc: Measured between terminals D & E of MAF sensor.

Engine	Year	Sensor	Resistance Ohms @ deg. F/C
1308cc, 1597cc, 1839cc, 1844cc, 1991cc w/MT, 1998cc, 2184cc, 2497cc, 2606cc, 2954cc	1989-00	Coolant	14,500-17,800 @ -4/-20 2200-2700 @ 68/20 1000-1300 @ 104/40 500-640 @ 140/60 280-350 @ 176/80
		Intake Air[1]	10,000-20,000 @ -4/-20 4000-7000 @ 32/0 2000-3000 @ 68/20 900-1300 @ 104/40 400-700 @ 140/60

SENSORS, INPUT Continued

TEMPERATURE SENSORS Continued

Engine	Year	Sensor	Resistance Ohms @ deg. F/C
1308cc, 1597cc, 1839cc, 1844cc, 1991cc w/MT, 1998cc, 2184cc, 2497cc, 2606cc, 2954cc	1989-00	Intake Air[2]	29,000-37,000 @ 77/25 3100-3900 @ 185/85
	1994-00	Transmission Oil	33,000-108,000 @ 50/10 14,000-37,000 @ 90/30 4500-16,000 @ 130/50 2300-5000 @ 170/70 1300-2700 @ 210-100 700-1500 @ 250/120
1991cc w/AT	1993-97	Coolant, Intake Air	35,473-39,207 @ 68/20
1991cc, 2497cc 626	1998-00		7171-7925 @ 140/60 1131-1251 @ 176/80

1 Sensor contained in airflow meter.
2 Sensor located on intake manifold or air cleaner housing.

MANIFOLD ABSOLUTE PRESSURE SENSORS
1308cc: Measured between terminal D of pressure sensor and ground.
1597cc FI, 2184cc FI, 2606cc, 2954cc: Measured between L/O wire of sensor and ground with 4.5-5.5 volts reference.

Engine	Year	Sensor	Voltage @ Elevation
1597cc FI, 2184cc FI, 2606cc, 2954cc	1989-90	Barometric	3.5-4.5 @ 0 ft 2.5-3.5 @ 6500 ft

Engine	Year	Sensor	Voltage @ in./KPa
1308cc	1989-92	Pressure	2.8-3.2 @ 3.9/14
Turbo	1989-92	Pressure	1.9-2.1 @ 3.9/14
1305cc	1993-95	MAP	1.25-1.55 @ -20/-66 2.38-2.78 @ 0/0 4.35-4.65 @ 29/99
2184cc 2V	1989-93	Pressure	1.4 min. @ 0/0 4.9 max. @ 30/102

THROTTLE POSITION SENSOR

Engine	Year	Voltage Idle	Voltage WOT
1308cc	1990-92	.25-1.25	4.1-4.4
	1993-95	.75-1.25	4.8-5.0
	1995-97	0.3-0.7	3.4-5.3
1489cc ?8cc ?	1998	0.1-0.7	3.4-4.9
1597cc, 1839cc 323 Protegé w/AT	1990-94	0.1-1.0	3.0-4.6
1597cc MX-3, Precidia	1992-95	0.1-1.1	3.0-4.6
1597cc	1999-00	0.1-1.1	3.0-4.6
1839cc Miata	1994-99	0.1-1.1	3.0-4.6
1839cc Protegé	1995-97	0.5-0.6	2.8-4.5
	1998	0.5-0.6	2.8-4.8
	1999-00	0.1-1.1	3.0-4.6
1844cc	1992-95	0.1-1.1	2.8-4.5
1991cc	1993	1.0 max.	5.0
1991cc w/MT	1994	0.5	4.1
1991cc	1995-97	0.3-0.7	3.4-5.3
	1998-99	0.3-0.7	3.4-5.3
2184cc FI 626, MX-6	1990-92	.37-.66	3.58-5.17
2184cc FI Pickup	1990-92	.37-.66	4.5-5.5
2187cc	1993	.37-.66	3.58-5.17
2255cc	1995-99	0.1-1.1	2.8-4.5
2497cc	1992-94	0.1-1.1	3.0-4.6
	1995-97	0.1-1.1	2.8-4.5
2497cc 626	1998-00	0.3-1.0	2.8-4.5
Millenia	1998-00	0.1-1.1	2.8-4.5
MPV	2000	0.7-1.2	4.0-5.0
2606cc MPV	1989-92	0.5	4.3
	1993-94	.37-.66	3.56-5.17

MAZDA
1989-2000 All Models
1991-2000 Navajo, B2300, B2500, B3000, B4000—See Ford Trucks
UNDERHOOD SERVICE SPECIFICATIONS
MAITU8

MAITU8

SENSORS, INPUT Continued
THROTTLE POSITION SENSOR

Engine	Year	Voltage	
		Idle	WOT
2606cc Pickup	1990-92	.37-.66	4.5-5.5
	1993	.37-.66	3.56-5.17
2954cc MPV	1989-95	0.1-1.0	3.6-5.0
	1996-98	0.1-1.0	2.8-4.5
2954cc 929, Serenia	1989-91	0.1-1.0	3.6-5.0
	1992-95	0.1-1.1	2.8-4.5

CAMSHAFT & CRANKSHAFT POSITION SENSOR
Measured at 68°F (20°C).
1308cc, measured between both right or both left cavities on unit.
All others, measured between terminals A & B at sensor on front of engine.

Engine	Sensor	Year	Resistance (ohms)
1308cc	Crankshaft	1989-92	110-210
		1993-95	950-1250
1489cc	Crankshaft	1995-98	500-600
1597cc	Crankshaft	1999-00	550 approx.
1839cc	Crankshaft	1995-00	500-600
1844cc	Crankshaft	1992	950-1250
		1993-94	520-580
1991cc	Crankshaft	1998-00	550 approx.
	Camshaft	1998-99	950-1250
2255cc	Crankshaft	1995-97	520-580
		1998-00	950-1250
2497cc	Crankshaft	1993-97	520-580
2497cc 626	Crankshaft	1998-00	550 approx.
	Camshaft	1998-00	550 approx.
Millenia	Crankshaft	1998-00	520-580
MPV	Crankshaft	2000	315-385
	Camshaft	2000	292-385
2954cc 929, Serenia	Crankshaft	1994-95	950-1250
2954cc	Crankshaft	1996-98	300-800

MASS AIRFLOW SENSOR

Engine	Year	Resistance @ Ohms	Throttle Position
1308cc	1990-92	20-800	idle
		200-1000	WOT
1597cc 323, 1839cc Protegé, 2184cc Fl, 2497cc, 2954cc	1990-94	20-600	idle
		20-1200	WOT
2497cc	1995	20-600	idle
		20-1200	WOT
1844cc	1992-95	200-1000	idle
		20-800	WOT

Engine	Year	Voltage	
		Ign. on	Idle
1489cc	1996-97	1.0 max.	1.0-2.5
	1998	.64-1.5	0.8-2.2
1839cc	1996-97	1.0 max.	1.0-2.0
	1998-00	0.2-1.0	0.2-2.0
1991cc w/MT	1996-97	1.0-1.5	1.5-5.0
w/AT	1996-97	.15-.20	0.6-1.1
1991cc	1998-99	0.02	0.6-1.1

SENSORS, INPUT Continued
MASS AIRFLOW SENSOR Continued

Engine	Year	Voltage	
		Ign. on	Idle
2255cc, 2497cc ex. MPV	1996-97	1.0-1.5	1.5-2.5
	1998-00	1.3-1.5	1.5-3.0
2497cc MPV	2000	0-1.0	0.5-0.8
2954cc	1996-98	1.0	1.0-2.0

KNOCK SENSOR

Engine	Year	Resistance @ Ohms	Temperature F/C
1991cc, 2497cc	1998-00	560,000	68/20
2255cc	1998-00	560,000	68/20

ACTUATORS, OUTPUT
IDLE SPEED CONTROL
At 68°F (20°C).

Engine	Year	Resistance (ohms)
1308cc	1990-92	10-13
	1993-94	9.3-13.3
	1995	10.7-12.3
1489cc	1995-98	7.7-9.3
1597cc	1989	5-20
1597cc, 1839cc, 1844cc	1990-94	10-13
	1995-00	10.7-12.3
1991cc	1993-99	7.7-9.3
2184cc Fl	1989-93	6.3-9.9
2497cc	1993-94	10-13
	1995-97	10.7-12.3
2497cc 626	1998-00	8.7-10.5
Millenia	1998-00	10.7-12.3
2606cc	1989-94	7.7-9.3
2954cc	1989-94	10-13
	1995-98	10.7-12.3

FUEL INJECTORS

Engine	Year	Resistance (ohms)	Temperature (deg. F/C)
1308cc	1989-92	12-16	—
	1993-95	13.8 approx.	68/20
1489cc, 1597cc, 1839cc, 1844cc	1989-94	12-16	68/20
	1995-98	13.8 approx.	68/20
	1999-00	12-16	—
1991cc	1993-99	12-16	68/20
1998cc, 2187cc	1989-92	12-16	—
Turbo	1989	11-15	—
2255cc	1995-99	13.8 approx.	68/20
2497cc	1993-95	13.8 approx.	68/20
	1996-00	12-16	—
2606cc	1989-95	12-16	—
2954cc	1989-98	12-16	—

ENGINE IDENTIFICATION

To identify any engine by the manufacturer's code, follow the four steps designated by the numbered blocks.

1 **MODEL YEAR IDENTIFICATION:** Refer to illustration of the Vehicle Identification Number (V.I.N.). The year is indicated by a code letter which is the 7th character of the V.I.N.

3 **ENGINE CODE:** In the "CODE" column, find the engine code.

4 **ENGINE IDENTIFICATION:** On the line where the engine code appears, read to the right to identify the engine.

V.I.N. PLATE LOCATION:

On left front pillar post visible through windshield; or left side of instrument panel, visible through windshield.

1 **MODEL YEAR IDENTIFICATION:**

Seventh character of V.I.N., first character of emissions control label.

1999—X	1998—W	1997—V
1996—T	1995—S	1994—R
1993—P	1992—N	1991—M
1990—L	1989—K	

2 **ENGINE CODE LOCATION:**

Prefix to engine number, stamped on block.

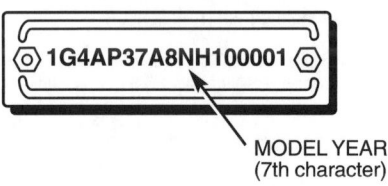

1G4AP37A8NH100001

MODEL YEAR
(7th character)

Left Table

YEAR	CODE	CYL.	liters	cc	Fuel System	HP
1999	111.973, 5	4	2.3 S	2295 S	FI	185
	112.920	6	2.8	2799	FI	194
	606.962	6	3.0 D	2996 D	FI	174
	112.940, 942	6	3.2	3199	FI	215
	112.941	6	3.2	3199	FI	221
	104.994	6	3.2	3199	FI	228
	119.981	8	4.2	4196	FI	275
	113.940, 944	8	4.3	4265	FI	275, 302
	113.942	8	4.4	4366	FI	268
	113.961	8	5.0	4966	FI	302
	119.980.982	8	5.0	4973	FI	315
	113	8	5.5	5499	FI	349
	190.982, 983	12	6.0	5987	FI	389
1998	111.974	4	2.3	2295	FI	148
	111.973	4	2.3 S	2295 S	FI	185
	112.920	6	2.8	2799	FI	194
	606.962	6	3.0 D	2996 D	FI	174
	112.940, 942	6	3.2	3199	FI	215
	112.941	6	3.2	3199	FI	221
	104.994	6	3.2	3199	FI	228
	119.981	8	4.2	4196	FI	275
	113.940	8	4.3	4265	FI	275
	119.980, 982	8	5.0	4973	FI	315
	120.982, 983	12	6.0	5987	FI	389
1997	111.974	4	2.3	2295	FI	148
	104.941	6	2.8	2799	FI	194
	606.912	6	3.0 D	2996 D	FI	134
	104.995	6	3.2	3199	FI	217
	104.991, 994	6	3.2	3199	FI	228
	104.941	6	3.6	3606	FI	276
	119.985, 981	8	4.2	4196	FI	275
	119.980, 982	8	5.0	4973	FI	315
	120.982, 983	12	6.0	5987	FI	389
1996	111.961	4	2.2	2199	FI	148
	104.941	6	2.8	2799	FI	194
	606.912	6	3.0 D	2996 D	FI	134
	104.995	6	3.2	3199	FI	217
	104.991, 994	6	3.2	3199	FI	228
	104.941	6	3.6	3606	FI	268
	119.975, 981	8	4.2	4196	FI	275
	119.980, 982	8	5.0	4973	FI	315
	120.982, 983	12	6.0	5987	FI	389
1995	111.961	4	2.2	2199	FI	148
	104.941	6	2.8	2799	FI	194
	606.910	6	3.0 D	2996 D	FI	134
	104.992	6	3.2	3199	FI	217
	104.991, 994	6	3.2	3199	FI	228
	603.971	6	3.5 TD	3449 TD	FI	148
	104.941	6	3.6	3606	FI	268
	119.971, 975	8	4.2	4196	FI	275
	119.970, 972	8	5.0	4973	FI	315
	120.980, 981	12	6.0	5987	FI	389
1994	111.961	4	2.2	2199	FI	147
	104.941	6	2.8	2799	FI	194
	104.992	6	3.2	3199	FI	217
	104.991, 104.994	6	3.2	3199	FI	228
	603.971	6	3.5 TD	3449 TD	FI	148

Right Table

YEAR	CODE	CYL.	liters	cc	Fuel System	HP
1994 Cont'd.	119.971, 119.975	8	4.2	4196	FI	275
	119.970, 119.972,					
	119.974	8	5.0	4973	FI	315
	120.980, 120.981	12	6.0	5987	FI	389
1993	102.985	4	2.3	2299	FI	130
	602.962	5	2.5 TD	2497 TD	FI	121
	103.942	6	2.6	2599	FI	158
	104.942	6	2.8	2799	FI	194
	103.985	6	3.0	2960	FI	177
	104.981	6	3.0	2960	FI	228
	104.992	6	3.2	3199	FI	217
	104.990	6	3.2	3199	FI	228
	603.971	6	3.5 TD	3449 TD	FI	148
	119.971, 119.975	8	4.2	4196	FI	275
	119.970, 119.974,					
	119.972	8	5.0	4973	FI	315
	120.980, 120.981	12	6.0	5987	FI	389
1992	102.985	4	2.3	2299	FI	130
	602.962	5	2.5 TD	2497 TD	FI	121
	103.942, 103.940	6	2.6	2599	FI	158
	103.983, 103.985	6	3.0	2960	FI	177
	104.980, 104.981	6	3.0	2960	FI	217, 228[1]
	104.990	6	3.2	3199	FI	228
	603.971	6	3.5 TD	3449 TD	FI	148
	119.975, 119.971	8	4.2	4196	FI	268, 282[1]
	119.960	8	5.0	4973	FI	322
	119.970, 119.974	8	5.0	4973	FI	322
	117.968	8	5.6	5547	FI	238
	120.980	12	6.0	5991	FI	402
1991	102.985	4	2.3	2299	FI	130
	602.962	5	2.5 TD	2497 TD	FI	121
	103.940, 103.942	6	2.6	2599	FI	158
	103.983	6	3.0	2962	FI	177
	104.980, 104.981	6	3.0	2962	FI	217, 228[1]
	603.970	6	3.5 TD	3449 TD	FI	134
	116.965	8	4.2	4196	FI	201
	119.960	8	5.0	4973	FI	322
	117.968	8	5.6	5547	FI	238
1990	602.962	5	2.5 TD	2497 TD	FI	120
	103.940, 103.942	6	2.6	2599	FI	158
	103.983	6	3.0	2962	FI	177
	124.050	6	3.0	2962	FI	217
	104.981	6	3.0	2962	FI	228
	603.970	6	3.5 TD	3449 TD	FI	133
	117.965	8	4.2	4196	FI	201
	119.960	8	5.0	4973	FI	322
	117.968	8	5.6	5547	FI	238
1989	602.911	5	2.5 D	2497 D	FI	90
	103.940, 103.942	6	2.6	2599	FI	158
	103.983	6	3.0	2962	FI	177
	117.965	8	4.2	4196	FI	201
	117.967	8	5.6	5547	FI	227
	117.968	8	5.6	5547	FI	238

**D—Diesel.   TD—Turbo Diesel.   FI—Fuel Injection.
S—Supercharged.
1 Engine horsepower varies with emission equipment package.**

UNDERHOOD SERVICE SPECIFICATIONS

CYLINDER NUMBERING SEQUENCE

4-CYL. FIRING ORDER:
1 3 4 2

5-CYL. FIRING ORDER:
1 2 4 5 3

L-6-CYL. FIRING ORDER:
1 5 3 6 2 4

V6-CYL. FIRING ORDER:
1 4 3 6 2 5

8-CYL. FIRING ORDER:
1 5 4 8 6 3 7 2

12-CYL. FIRING ORDER:
1 12 5 8 3 10 6 7 2 11 4 9

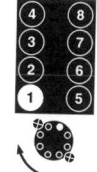

— Front of car —

2.3L 1989-93 190	2.6L, 3.0L 1989-93 190, 260, 280, 300, 320, 350	3.2L 1998 CLK320, E320, ML 320	4.2L, 5.6L 1989-97 400, 420, 560	6.0L 1992-97 600

TIMING MARK

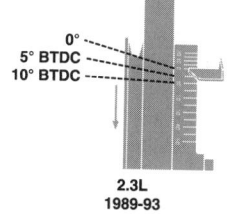

0°
5° BTDC
10° BTDC

2.3L
1989-93
190

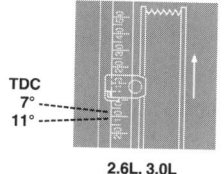

TDC
7°
11°

2.6L, 3.0L
1989-93
190, 260, 280,
300, 320, 350

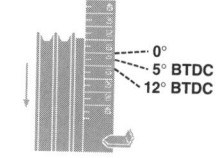
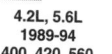

0°
5° BTDC
12° BTDC

4.2L, 5.6L
1989-94
400, 420, 560

40 30 20 10 T T 10 20 30 40

All Engines
1995-97
All Models

ELECTRICAL AND IGNITION SYSTEMS

BATTERY

BCI equivalent shown, size may vary from original equipment. Check clearance before replacing, holddown may need to be modified.

Engine/Model	Year	STANDARD BCI Group No.	STANDARD Crank. Perf.	OPTIONAL BCI Group No.	OPTIONAL Crank. Perf.
4-cyl.					
2.2L	1994	48	550	48	660
	1995-96	49	825	—	—
2.3L Gasoline	1989-93	48	495	—	—
SLK230	1997-98	48	690	—	—
C230	1997-98	49[1]	825	—	—
5-cyl.					
2.5L Diesel	1989-91	49	740	—	—
6-cyl.					
2.6L Gasoline	1989-93	48	495	—	—
2.8L	1994	48	660	—	—
	1995-98	49	825	—	—
3.0L Gasoline	1989	48	495	—	—
Roadster	1992-93	49	810	—	—
Sedan, Coupe	1990-92	48	495	—	—
Roadster	1990-91	49	740	—	—
Diesel	1995	49	825	—	—
	1996	49	690	—	—
	1997-98	49[1]	825	—	—
3.2L Coupe, Sedan	1992-93	49	810	—	—
E320	1995	48	660	—	—
	1996	49	690	—	—
	1997-98	48	690	—	—
S320, SL320	1994-98	49	825	—	—
CLK320, ML320	1997-98	49	825	—	—
3.5L Turbo Diesel	1991	49	740	—	—
	1993	49	810	—	—
	1994-95	49	825	—	—
8-cyl.					
4.2L Sedan	1989-91	49	740	—	—
	1992-93	49	810	—	—
E420, S420	1994-98	49	825	—	—
4.3L E430	1997-98	48	690	—	—
5.0L Roadster	1990-91	49	740	—	—
All models	1992-93	49	810	—	—
	1994-98	49	825	—	—
5.6L	1989-91	49	740	—	—
12-cyl.					
6.0L All	1992-93	49	810	—	—
	1994-98	49	825	—	—

1 Battery is vented to outside of vehicle.

GENERATOR

Application	Year	Rated Output (amps)	Test Output (amps @ rpm)
190 D	1989	70	70 @ 2480
190 E 2.3	1991-93	70	70 @ 2500
190 E 2.6	1990-93	70	70 @ 2250
w/AC	1990-93	80	80 @ 2250
260 E	1989	70	70 @ 2500
300 CE	1989-91	80	80 @ 2250
	1992-93	80	80 @ 2200
	1993	90	90 @ 2200
300 D	1991-93	70	70 @ 2200
300 E	1990-92	70	70 @ 2250
w/AC	1990-92	80	80 @ 2250
300 E 2.8L	1993	90	90 @ 2200
300 E 3.2L	1993	120	120 @ 2200
300 E 4MATIC	1990-93	80	80 @ 2160
300 SD	1992-93	80	80 @ 2200
300 SE	1990-91	80	80 @ 2250
	1992-93	120	120 @ 2200
300 SEL	1990-91	80	80 @ 2250
300 SL	1989-90	100	90 @ 2200
	1992-93	100	100 @ 2200
		110	110 @ 2250
300 TE ex. 4MATIC	1990-92	70	70 @ 2250
w/AC	1990-92	80	80 @ 2250
300 TE ex. 4MATIC	1993	120	120 @ 2200
300 TE, 4MATIC	1990-93	80	80 @ 2250
350 SD, SDL	1990-91	80	80 @ 2200
400 E	1992-93	110	110 @ 1950
400 SE	1992	120	120 @ 1950
400 SEL	1993	120	120 @ 1950
420 SEL	1989-91	80	80 @ 2250
500 E	1992-93	110	110 @ 1950
500 SEC	1993	120	120 @ 1950
500 SEL	1992-93	120	120 @ 1950
500 SL	1990-91	80	80 @ 2200
	1992-93	100	100 @ 2250
560 SEC, SEL	1990-92	80	80 @ 2200
560 SL	1989	70	70 @ 2230
600 SEC	1993	120	120 @ 1950
600 SEL	1992-93	120	120 @ 1950
600 SL	1993	110	110 @ 1950
C220	1994-96	70	70 @ 2200
w/AC	1994-96	90	80 @ 2200
C230	1997-99	90	90 @ 2200
C280	1994-97	90	90 @ 2200
C280	1998-99	90/115[1]	90/115[1] @ 2200
C36 AMG	1995-97	90	90 @ 2200
E300 Diesel, C43 AMG	1998-99	150	—
CLK320	1998	90/115	90/115 @ 2200

UNDERHOOD SERVICE SPECIFICATIONS

GENERATOR Continued

Application	Year	Rated Output (amps)	Test Output (amps @ rpm)
CLK320	1999	115	115 @ 2200
CLK430	1999	150	150 @ 2200
CL500	1998	143	143 @ 1950
CL600	1998	143	143 @ 1950
E300 Diesel	1995	90	90 @ 2200
	1996-97	90	90 @ 2500
	1998	90/120	90/120 @ 2500
	1999	120	120 @ 2500
	1994-96	90	90 @ 2200
	1997-99	90/115	90/115 @ 2300
E420	1994-96	110	110 @ 1950
	1997	115	115 @ 2300
E430	1998	115/150	115/150 @ 2200
	1999	150	150 @ 2200
E500	1994	110	110 @ 1950
E55 AMG	1999	150	150 @ 2200
ML320	1998-99	115	115 @ 2200
ML430	1999	150	150 @ 2200
S320	1994-98	120	120 @ 2200
S350 Turbo Diesel	1994-95	80	80 @ 2200
S420	1994	120	120 @ 1950
	1995-98	143	143 @ 1950
S500	1994	120	120 @ 2200
	1995-98	143	143 @ 1950
S600	1994	120	120 @ 2200
	1995-98	143	143 @ 1950
SL320	1994-97	110	110 @ 2200
SL500	1994	100	100 @ 2200
	1995-98	143	143 @ 1950
	1999	150	150 @ 2200
SL600	1994	110	110 @ 2200
	1995-98	143	143 @ 1950
	1999	150	150 @ 2200
SLK230	1998	90	90 @ 2100

1 Refer to sticker on generator for output rating.

REGULATOR

Application	Year	Test Temp. (deg. F/C)	Voltage Setting
All models	1989-99	Normal	13.0-14.5

STARTER

Engine	Year	Cranking Voltage (min. volts)
4-cyl. gas	1989-96	8.0
6-cyl.	1989-96	8.0
V8	1989	7.5
	1990-94	8.0
V12	1992-96	7.8
Diesel engines	1989-96	7.8

SPARK PLUGS

Engine	Year	Gap (inches)	Gap (mm)	Torque (ft-lb)
2199cc	1994-96	.032	.80	15-22
2295cc	1997-98	.032	.80	15-22
2295cc	1999	.039	1.0	15-22
2299cc	1989	.032	.80	8-14
	1991-93	.032	.80	8-14
2599cc	1989-93	.032	.80	8-14
2799cc	1993	.032	.80	—
	1994-98	.032	.80	15-22
2799cc	1999	.039	1.0	15-22
2960cc	1989-93	.032	.80	18-22
3199cc	1992-98	.032	.80	15-22
ML320, CLK320, E320	1998	.032	.80	15-22
CLK320, E320, ML320	1999	.039	1.0	15-22
3606cc	1995-98	.032	.80	15-22
4196cc, 5547cc	1989-93	.032	.80	19-24
4196cc	1994-97	.032	.80	15-22
4266cc	1998	.032	.80	15-22
4265cc	1999	.039	1.0	15-22
4366cc	1999	.039	1.0	15-22
4966cc	1999	.039	1.0	15-22

SPARK PLUGS Continued

Engine	Year	Gap (inches)	Gap (mm)	Torque (ft-lb)
4973cc	1990-93	.032	.80	18-22
	1994-98	.032	.80	15-22
5499cc	1999	.039	1.0	15-22
5547cc	1991	.032	.80	18-22
5987cc	1992-98	.032	.80	15-22
	1999	.039	1.0	15-22

IGNITION COIL
Winding Resistance (ohms at 68°F or 20°C)

Engine	Year	Windings	Resistance (ohms)
4-cyl.	1991-93	Primary	.50-.90
		Secondary	6000-16,000
	1994-96	Primary	.30-.60
		Secondary	5200-8500
6-cyl.	1989	Primary	.30-.60
		Secondary	7000-13,000
	1990-92	Primary	.30-.60
		Secondary	8000-13,000
3.0L SOHC	1993	Primary	.30-.60
		Secondary[1]	8000-13,000
2.8L, 3.0L DOHC, 3.2L	1991-97	Primary	.30-.60
		Secondary	5200-8500
8-cyl.	1990	Primary	.20-.40
		Secondary	8000-13,000
	1991-96	Primary	.30-.60
		Secondary[1]	8000-13,000
12-cyl.	1992-98	Primary	.30-.60
		Secondary[1]	8000-13,000

1 1996-98 Secondary resistance unreadable due to diode installation.

DISTRIBUTOR PICKUP

Application	Year	Resistance (ohms)
190E 2.3L	1991-93	500-700

BASE TIMING
Checking figures only, timing not adjusted
Before Top Dead Center with engine idling and vacuum hose connected to the ignition control one

Engine	Year	Man. Trans. (degrees)	Auto. Trans. (degrees)
2.3L	1991-93	10±2	10±2
2.6L	1989-93	9±2	9±2
3.0L	1989-94	8±2	8±2
3.0L DOHC	1990-93	—	8±2
4.2L SOHC	1989-91	—	12±2
5.0L	1990-92	—	12±2
5.6L	1989-91	—	12±2
6.0L	1993-94	—	0±2

FUEL SYSTEM

FUEL PRESSURE
With engine at operating temperature, and idling.

Engine	Year	PSI[1]	PS2[2]
2.2L	1994-96	46-52	54-61
3.0L DOHC, 3.2L, 3.6L	1990-97	46-52	54-61
4.2L	1992-96	46-52	54-61
5.0L	1990-94	46-52	54-61
6.0L	1992-95	46-52	54-61

1 W/vacuum to fuel pressure regulator.
2 W/o vacuum to fuel pressure regulator.

UNDERHOOD SERVICE SPECIFICATIONS

MZITU3

MZITU3

IDLE SPEED

Engine	Year	Man. Trans.	Auto. Trans.
2.2L	1994-96	—	650-850 N
2.3L	1991-93	700-800	700-800 N
2.5L Turbo Diesel	1991-94	720-760	660-760 N
2.6L	1989-93	650-750	650-750 N
2.8L	1993-97	—	600-800 N
3.0L SOHC	1989-93	650-750	650-750 N
3.0L DOHC	1991-94	650-750	650-750 N
3.0L Diesel	1995-97	—	580-680 N
3.2L	1991-98	—	550-700 D
3.5L Turbo Diesel	1991-95	—	610-650 N
3.6L	1995-97	—	650-750 N
4.2L	1989-96	—	600-750 N
5.0L	1990-96	—	600-750 N
5.6L	1989-91	—	600-750 N
6.0L	1992-95	—	600-750 N

ENGINE MECHANICAL

TIGHTENING TORQUES

Engine	Year	TORQUE FOOT-POUNDS/NEWTON METERS				
		Cylinder Head	Intake Manifold	Exhaust Manifold	Crankshaft Pulley	Water Pump
DIESEL ENGINES						
5-cyl.:						
2.5L	1989	18/25	—	—	236/320	7/10
2nd stage		30/40				
3rd stage[1]		90°, +90°				
2.5L	1990-93	11/15	—	—	236/320	7/10
2nd stage		26/35				
3rd stage[1]		90°, +90°				
6-cyl.:						
3.0L	1995-97	11/15	—	—	—	7/10
2nd stage		26/35				
3rd stage[1]		90°, +90°				
3.5L	1991-95	11/15	—	—	236/320	7/10
2nd stage		26/35				
3rd stage[1]		90°, +90°				
GASOLINE ENGINES						
4-cyl.:						
2.2L	1994-96	40/55	—	—	—	3
		+90°, +90°				
2.3L	1991-93	40/55	—	—	147/200	7/10
2nd stage		90°, +90°			90°, +90°	
3rd stage					221/300	
6-cyl.:						
2.6L	1989-93	52/70	—	—	221/300	17/23
2nd stage		90°, +90°				
2.8L, 3.2L	1992-97	40/55	—	—	295/400	18/25
2nd stage		90°, +90°				
3.0L SOHC	1989-93	52/70	—	—	221/300	18/25
2nd stage		90°, +90°				
3.0L DOHC	1989-93	40/55	—	—	295/400	18/25
		90°, +90°				
V8:						
4.2L	1989-91	22/30	—	—	295/400	15/21
2nd stage		44/60				
3rd stage[1]		44/60				
4.2L	1992-96	40/55	—	—	—	15/21
		+90°, +90°				
5.0L	1990-96	40/55	—	—	295/400	15/21
2nd stage		90°, +90°				
5.6L	1989-91	22/30	—	—	221/300	18/25
2nd stage[2]		44/60				
12-cyl.:						
5987cc	1992-97	40/55	—	—	295/400	15/21
2nd stage		90°, +90°				

1 Allow cylinder head to settle 10 minutes before final torque.
2 Tighten head to specification, allow to settle 10 minutes and retorque.
3 M6 bolts, 7/9; M8 bolts, 15/21.

COMPRESSION PRESSURE

At cranking speed, engine temperature normalized, throttle open.

Engine	Year	PSI @ RPM	Max. Variation PSI	Min. Allowable PSI
Diesel	1989-92	319-435	43	260
	1993-94	377-464	43	260
Gasoline	1989	145-174	22	123
2.2L	1995	176-205	22	—
2.3L, 2.6L, 3.0L SOHC, 4.2L, 5.6L	1990-94	145-174	43	123
3.0L DOHC, 3.2L, 4.2L, 5.0L, 6.0L	1990-94	195-224	43	174

BELT TENSION

All w/o Automatic Tensioner.
A belt in operation immediately after running is considered a used belt.
Strand Tension method: Measured in pounds with a strand gauge.

Engine	Year	New	Used
All V8:			
9.5mm belts	1989-92	66	44-45
12.5mm belts	1989-92	110	88-99

Deflection method: Table lists deflection at midpoint of longest belt segment under a 13 pound load.

Engine	Year	Generator	Power Steering	Air Cond.	Air Pump
USED BELTS					
All 4-, 5-, & 6-cyl.:					
(inches)	1989-92	3/8[1]	3/16	3/8[1]	3/8[1]
(mm)	1989-92	10[1]	5	10[1]	10[1]
All V8:					
(inches)	1989-92	3/8	3/8	3/16	3/8
(mm)	1989-92	10	10	5	10

1 Special tensioning tool required.

SERPENTINE BELT DIAGRAMS

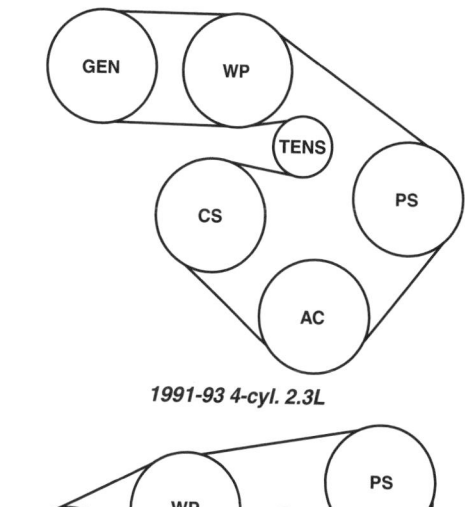

1991-93 4-cyl. 2.3L

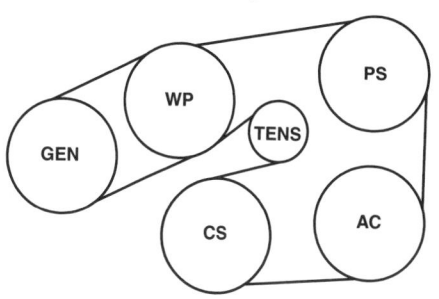

1994-98 2.2L, 2.3L ex. Supercharged

UNDERHOOD SERVICE SPECIFICATIONS

SERPENTINE BELT DIAGRAMS Continued

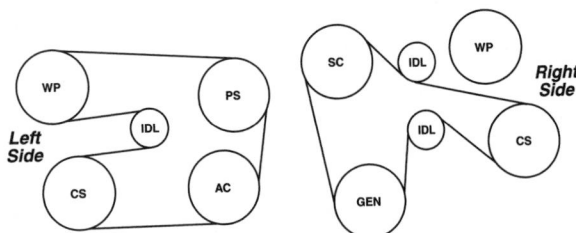

1998-00 4-cyl. 2.3L
Supercharged

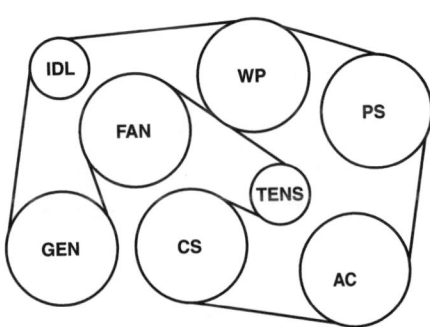

1989-97 6-cyl. 2.6L, 2.8L, 3.6L

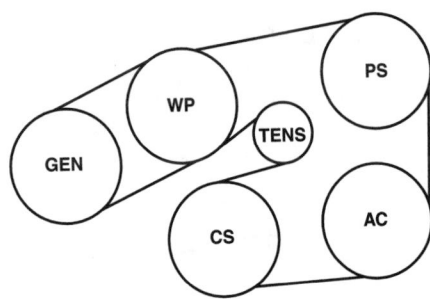

1995-00 6-cyl. 3.0L Diesel
E300

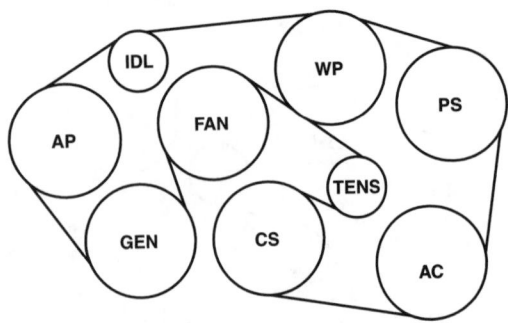

1991-98 6-cyl. 3.0L, 3.2L E Series
1992-99 V12 6.0L

SERPENTINE BELT DIAGRAMS Continued

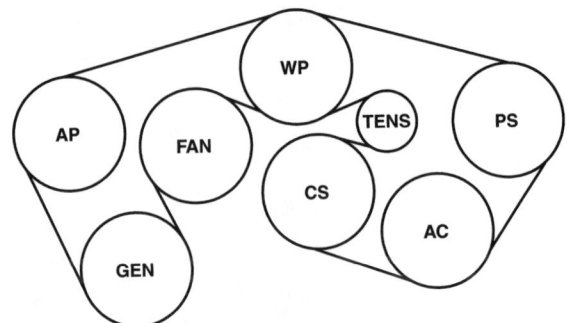

1990-98 V8 5.0L
1992-98 V8 4.2L
1990-98 6-cyl. 3.2L S Series

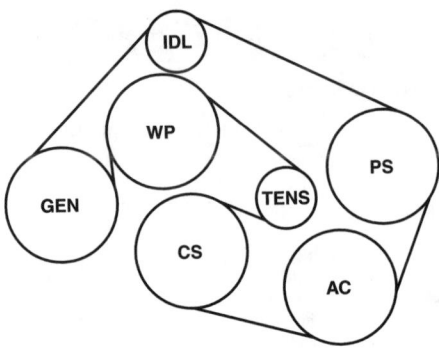

1998-00 V6 2.8L, 3.2L
1998-00 V8 4.3L, 5.0L

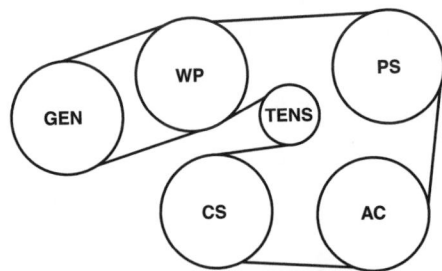

1990-93 6-cyl. 3.5L Diesel

ENGINE COMPUTER SYSTEM

DIAGNOSTIC TROUBLE CODES

Start engine and run until oil temperature reaches operating range, 140°-168°F (60°-80°C). Connect an "on-off ratio tester" (Bosch model KDJE-P600) to the diagnostic socket in the engine compartment. Allow engine to run at idle, failure codes will be displayed as a percentage on the meter.

1990-92 2960cc:

0%	Open circuit at socket 2 and 9-pole diagnostic connector.
	Open circuit in wire to socket 3 or 6 of 9-pole diagnostic connector or on-off ratio tester defective.
	Mixture adjustment rich.
10%	Volume air flow sensor position indicator polarity reversed or defective
	Terminals of wide open throttle/closed throttle position switch connector (idle/full load) reversed or short circuit, full load contact closed with insufficient air flow.
20%	Full load contact defective or wide open throttle/closed throttle position switch polarity reversed. 20% only indicated if wide open throttle/closed throttle position switch is activated.

DIAGNOSTIC TROUBLE CODES Continued

30% Short circuit or open circuit between CFI control module and 4-pole engine coolant temperature sensor, or 4-pole engine coolant temperature sensor defective or greater deviation of temperature values as compared with ignition control module.

40% Wire to volume air flow sensor position indicator has open circuit or short, or sensor defective.

50% Heated oxygen sensor not operational or defective, open circuit.

60% Speed signal at CFI control module implausible.

70% TNA-signal (rpm signal) at CFI control module implausible.

80% Data exchange between ignition control module and CFI control module defective.

90% Current to electrohydraulic actuator implausible.

95% Deceleration shut-off active.

100% Current or ground at CFI control module not present or CFI control module defective.
On-off ratio tester defective.
Lambda adjustment lean.
Heated oxygen sensor defective (short to circuit 31) (ground).

Oscillates No malfunction of monitored signals.

2960cc:
CFI control module

Code	Definition
1	No malfunctions in system
2	Full load contact, wide open throttle/closed throttle position switch implausible
3	Engine coolant temperature in CFI control module implausible
4	Volume air flow sensor position indicator potentiometer current implausible
5	Heated oxygen sensor signal implausible
7	TN-signal (rpm signal) at CFI control module implausible
8	Barometric correction signal from ignition control module
9	Current to electrohydraulic actuator implausible
10	Closed throttle position contact, wide open throttle/closed throttle position switch implausible
11	Secondary air injection system, open/short circuit
12	Absolute pressure values from ignition control module implausible
13	Intake air temperature implausible
14	Speed signal at CFI control module implausible
16	EGR switchover valve, open/short circuit
17	Heated oxygen sensor signal wire shorted to positive or ground
18	Current to idle air control valve implausible
22	Heated oxygen sensor heater voltage implausible
23	Short to positive in purge switchover valve circuit
25	Short to positive in start valve
26	Short to positive in upshift delay solenoid valve circuit
27	Data exchange between CFI control module and ignition control module
28	Intermittent contact in engine coolant temperature sensor circuit
29	Difference in engine coolant temperatures between CFI control module and ignition control module
31	Intermittent contact in intake air temperature sensor circuit
34	Engine coolant temperature from ignition control module implausible

Engine systems (MAS) control module

Code	Definition
1	No malfunctions in system
2	Fuel pump relay not functioning
3	TN signal (rpm) interrupted
4	Output for oxygen sensor heater control defective
5	Output for secondary air injection pump control defective
6	Output for kickdown switch control defective
9	Oxygen sensor heater open circuit
11	A/C compressor engagement signal missing
12	Output for A/C compressor control defective
13	Excessive A/C compressor belt slippage
14	Speed signal implausible
15	Short circuit detected in fuel pump circuit

Ignition control module

Code	Definition
1	No malfunctions in system
2	Maximum retard setting on at least one cylinder has been reached
3	Engine coolant temperature sensor defective
4	Load sensor in ignition control module defective
5	Knock sensors 1 and/or 2 defective
6	Camshaft position sensor defective

DIAGNOSTIC TROUBLE CODES Continued
Ignition control module Continued

Code	Definition
7	Knock control-output switch in ignition control module defective
8	Transmission overload protection switch does not close
9	Transmission overload protection switch does not open
10	Data exchange from ignition control module to CFI control module defective
11	Reference resistor defective
12	TN engine speed signal is outside the tolerance range
13	Wide open throttle contact does not open
14	Closed throttle position contact does not open
15	Ignition coil 1 output from ignition control module defective
17	Crankshaft position sensor defective

1992 3199cc:
10%	Closed throttle position recognition applied constantly
20%	Output of fuel injectors or one or more fuel injectors have open circuit
30%	Engine coolant temperature sensor
40%	Hot wire mass air flow sensor
50%[1]	Oxygen sensor not operational or defective, open circuit
60%	Camshaft position sensor
70%	TN-signal (rpm signal)
80%	CAN data exchange defective
90%	Vehicle speed signal
95%	Deceleration shut-off active

[1] Needle oscillates if all monitored signals are okay.

LH-SFI control module

Code	Definition
1	No malfunctions in system
2	Engine coolant temperature sensor circuit 1, open/short circuit
3	Engine coolant temperature sensor circuit 2, open/short circuit
4	Voltage at hot wire mass air flow sensor insufficient or too high
7	TN-signal (rpm signal) incorrect or open/short circuit
8	Camshaft position sensor signal, open/short circuit
9	Starter signal missing, open/short circuit
10	Closed throttle position recognition from electronic accelerator/cruise control/idle speed control module, short circuit
11	Secondary air injection system, open/short circuit
12	Burn-off control for hot wire mass air flow sensor, open/short circuit
13	Intake air temperature sensor, open/short circuit
16	EGR switchover valve, open/short circuit
17	No data transmission from electronic accelerator/cruise control/idle speed control module
18	No data transmission from ignition control module
20	No data transmission from LH-SFI control module
21	Heated oxygen sensor, open circuit
22	Heated oxygen sensor heater, open/short circuit
23	Purge switchover valve, open/short circuit
25	Adjustable camshaft timing solenoid, open/short circuit
27	Fuel injector, open/short circuit

Base module

Code	Definition
1	No malfunctions in system
5	Maximum permissible temperature in module box exceeded
6	Electromagnetic A/C compressor clutch blocked
7	Poly V-belt slipping
9	Voltage supply for LH-SFI control module interrupted
10	Voltage supply for LH-SFI control module interrupted
	Voltage supply for fuel injectors interrupted
11	Voltage supply for accessory equipment control modules interrupted
12	Voltage supply for ABS control module or ABS/ASR control module, or Automatic locking differential (ASD) control module interrupted
15	Voltage supply for automatic transmission kickdown valve interrupted
16	Voltage supply for electromagnetic A/C compressor clutch interrupted
17	Voltage supply for module box blower control interrupted

Diagnostic module

Code	Definition
1	No malfunctions in system
2	Heated oxygen sensor inoperative
3	Lambda control inoperative
4	Secondary air injection inoperative
5	Exhaust gas recirculation (EGR) inoperative

DIAGNOSTIC TROUBLE CODES Continued

Diagnostic module Continued

Code	Definition
6	Idle speed control inoperative
7	Ignition system defective
8	Engine coolant temperature sensor, open/short circuit
9	Intake air temperature sensor, open/short circuit
10	Voltage at mass air flow sensor too high/low
11	TN-signal (rpm) defective
12	Heated oxygen sensor heater, open/short circuit
13	Camshaft position sensor signal from ignition control module defective
14	Intake manifold pressure too low when starting
15	Wide open throttle information defective
16	Closed throttle information defective
17	Data exchange malfunction between individual control modules
18	Adjustable camshaft timing solenoid, open/short circuit
19	Fuel injectors open/short circuit or emission control system adaptation at limit
20	Speed signal missing
21	Purge switchover valve, open/short circuit
22	Camshaft position sensor signal defective
23	Intake manifold pressure with engine running too low
24	Starter ring gear segments defective
25	Knock sensors defective
26	Upshift delay switchover valve, open/short circuit
27	Engine coolant temperature sensor deviation between sensor circuit 1 and sensor circuit 2
28	Engine coolant temperature sensor (coolant temperature change monitor)

Ignition control module

Code	Definition
1	No malfunctions in system
2	Maximum retard setting on at least one cylinder has been reached
4	Load sensor in ignition control module defective
5	Knock sensors 1 and/or 2 defective
6	Camshaft position sensor defective
7	Knock control-output switch in ignition control module defective
8	Transmission overload protection switch does not close
9	Transmission overload protection switch does not open
11	Reference resistor defective
12	TN engine speed signal is outside of tolerance range
15	Ignition coil output from ignition control module defective
17	Crankshaft position sensor defective
20	Ignition control module DTC memory defective
21	Load sensor in ignition control module defective (recognized with engine running)
26	Ignition control module data exchange malfunction
27	LH-SFI control module data exchange malfunction
28	Electronic accelerator control/cruise control/idle speed control module data exchange malfunction

Electronic accelerator/cruise control/idle speed control module

Code	Definition
1	No malfunctions in system
2	Electronic accelerator/cruise control/idle speed control module
3	Electronic accelerator/cruise control/idle speed control actuator
4	Cruise control switch
5	Stop lamp switch
6	Starter lock-out/backup lamp switch
7	Data bus (CAN)
8	Left front axle vehicle speed sensor
9	Left rear axle vehicle speed sensor
10	Engine speed signal (TNA)
11	Fuel safety shut-off to LH-SFI control module
12	Electronic accelerator/cruise control/idle speed control module voltage supply
14	Closed throttle position switch

SENSORS, INPUT

TEMPERATURE SENSORS
Tolerance of 5%

Engine	Year	Sensor	Resistance Ohms @ deg. F/C
2.2L	1994-98	Intake Air	9,670 @ 50/10
			6,060 @ 68/20
			3,900 @ 86/30
			2,600 @ 100/40
			1,760 @ 122/50
			1,220 @ 140/60
			860 @ 158/70
			6,200 @ 176/80
All others	1989-98	Coolant, Intake Air	15,700 @ -4/-20
			10,000 @ 14/-10
			5,900 @ 32/0
			3,700 @ 50/10
			2,500 @ 68/20
			1,700 @ 86/30
			1,170 @ 100/40
			830 @ 122/50
			600 @ 140/60
			435 @ 160/70
			325 @ 176/80
			245 @ 194/90
			185 @ 212/100

CAMSHAFT POSITION SENSOR

Engine	Year	Resistance (ohms)
All	1989-98	900-1,600

CRANKSHAFT POSITION SENSORS

Engine	Year	Position Sensor Resistance (ohms)	Reference Sensor Resistance (ohms)
4-cyl. 2.3L			
SOHC	1989-93	680-1200	750
6-cyl. 2.6L	1989-93	680-1200	750
3.0L SOHC	1989-93	730-910	750
3.0L DOHC, 3.2L	1990-98	680-1200	—
V8 4.2L, 5.6L	1989	730-910	750
4.2L, 5.0L	1990-98	680-1200	—
12-cyl. 6.0L	1992-95	680-1200	—

ACTUATORS, OUTPUT

FUEL INJECTORS

Engine	Year	Resistance (ohms)
4-cyl.	1994-96	14-16
6-cyl.	1993-96	14-16
8-cyl.	1992-95	14-16
	1996-97	14-17
12-cyl.	1992-95	14-16
	1996	14-17

COMPUTER TIMING ADVANCE

Specifications include base timing.
Perform with engine at normal operating temperature.

Engine	Year	Degrees @ RPM Without Vacuum	Degrees @ RPM With Vacuum
2.3L	1991-93	24±2 @ 3200	41±2 @ 3200
2.6L	1989-93	27±2 @ 3200	42±2 @ 3200
3.0L	1989	29±2 @ 3200	42±2 @ 3200
3.0L SOHC	1990-93	29±2 @ 3200	42±2 @ 3200
DOHC	1990-93	23±2 @ 3200	36±2 @ 3200
3.2L	1992-93	23±2 @ 3200	36±2 @ 3200
4.2L	1989-91	30±2 @ 3500	43±2 @ 3500
5.0L	1990-92	1±2 @ Idle	16±2 @ Idle
5.6L	1989-91	26±2 @ 3500	42±2 @ 3500

ENGINE IDENTIFICATION

To identify any engine by the manufacturer's code, follow the four steps designated by the numbered blocks.

V.I.N. PLATE LOCATION:

Left side of instrument panel, visible through windshield.

1 MODEL YEAR IDENTIFICATION:

10th character of V.I.N.

2000—Y	1999—X	1998—W
1997—V	1996—T	1995—S
1994—R	1993—P	1992—N
1991—M	1990—L	1989—K

2 ENGINE CODE LOCATION:

8th character of V.I.N.

4 ENGINE IDENTIFICATION

YEAR	3 ENGINE CODE	CYL.	DISPL. liters	cc	Fuel System	HP
2000	A	4	1.5	1468	MFI	92
	C	4	1.8	1834	MFI	111, 113[1]
	G	4	2.4	2350	MFI	140, 145[1]
	H	6	3.0	2972	MFI	190, 195[1]
	L	6	3.0	2972	MFI	190, 195[1]
	P	6	3.5	3496	MFI	210
	R	6	3.5	3496	MFI	197, 200[1]
1999	A	4	1.5	1468	MFI	92
	C	4	1.8	1834	MFI	111, 113[1]
	Y	4	2.0	1996	MFI	140
	F	4	2.0	1997	MFI	205, 210[1]
	G	4	2.4	2350	MFI	132, 145[1]
	H, L	6	3.0	2972	MFI	151-195[1]
	J	6	3.0	2972	MFI	202-222[1]
	K	6	3.0	2972	MFI	320
	P	6	3.5	3496	MFI	210
	R	6	3.5	3496	MFI	197, 200[1]
1995-98	A	4	1.5	1468	MFI	92
	C	4	1.8	1834	MFI	113
	Y	4	2.0	1976	MFI	140
	F	4	2.0 T	1997 T	MFI	205, 210
	G	4	2.4	2350	MFI	116, 141[1]
	L	4	2.4	2350	MFI	160
	—	6	2.5	2497	MFI	155
	H	6	3.0	2972	MFI	151-175[1]
	J	6	3.0	2972	MFI	202-222
	K	6	3.0 T	2972 T	MFI	320
	M	6	3.5	3496	MFI	197, 200[1]
	P	6	3.5	3496	MFI	210, 214[1]
1994	A	4	1.5	1468	MFI	92
	B	4	1.8	1755	MFI	92
	C	4	1.8	1834	MFI	113
	E	4	2.0	1997	MFI	135
	F	4	2.0 T	1997 T	MFI	195
	G	4	2.4	2350	MFI	116, 141[1]
	L	4	2.4	2350	MFI	160
	H	6	3.0	2972	MFI	151-175[1]
	J	6	3.0	2972	MFI	202, 222[1]
	K	6	3.0 T	2972 T	MFI	320
	M	6	3.5	3496	MFI	215
1993	A	4	1.5	1468	MFI	92
	B	4	1.8	1755	MFI	92
	C	4	1.8	1834	MFI	113
	D	4	2.0	1997	MFI	121
	E	4	2.0	1997	MFI	135
	F	4	2.0 T	1997 T	MFI	180, 195[1]
	G	4	2.4	2350	MFI	116, 136
	H	6	3.0	2972	MFI	151

4 ENGINE IDENTIFICATION

YEAR	3 ENGINE CODE	CYL.	DISPL. liters	cc	Fuel System	HP
1993 Cont'd.	J	6	3.0	2972	MFI	202, 222[1]
	K	6	3.0 T	2972 T	MFI	300
1992	J	4	1.5	1468	MFI	81
	A	4	1.5	1468	MFI	92
	Y	4	1.6	1597	MFI	123
	T	4	1.8	1755	MFI	92
	D	4	1.8	1834	MFI	113
	V	4	2.0	1997	MFI	102
	R	4	2.0	1997	MFI	135
	U	4	2.0 T	1997 T	MFI	190
	W	4	2.4	2350	MFI	116
	S	6	3.0	2972	MFI	143, 151[1]
	B	6	3.0	2972	MFI	222
	C	6	3.0 T	2972 T	MFI	300
1991	J	4	1.5	1468	MFI	81
	A	4	1.5	1468	MFI	92
	Y	4	1.6	1597	MFI	123
	T	4	1.8	1755	MFI	92
	V	4	2.0	1997	MFI	102, 105[1]
	R	4	2.0	1997	MFI	135
	U	4	2.0 T	1997 T	MFI	190
	W	4	2.4	2350	MFI	116
	S	6	3.0	2972	MFI	143, 151[1]
	B	6	3.0	2972	MFI	222
	C	6	3.0 T	2972 T	MFI	300
1990	J	4	1.5	1468	MFI	81
	X	4	1.5	1468	MFI	81
	Y	4	1.6	1597	MFI	113
	T	4	1.8	1755	MFI	92
	V	4	2.0	1997	MFI	102
	R	4	2.0	1997	MFI	135
	U	4	2.0 T	1997 T	MFI	190
	W	4	2.4	2350	MFI	107, 116[1]
	E	4	2.6	2555	2V	109
	S	6	3.0	2972	MFI	142, 143[1]
1989	J	4	1.5	1468	2V	70
	X	4	1.5	1468	MFI	81
	Z	4	1.6 T	1597 T	MFI	135
	D	4	2.0	1997	2V	88, 90
	V	4	2.0	1997	MFI	102
	R	4	2.0	1997	MFI	135
	L	4	2.4	2350	MFI	107
	E	4	2.6	2555	2V	109
	N	4	2.6 T	2555 T	TBI	188
	S	6	3.0	2972	MFI	NA

TBI—Throttle Body Injection. **MFI**—Multiport Fuel Injection.
2V—Two Venturi Carburetor. **T**—Turbo. **FI**—Fuel Injection.
1 Engine horsepower varies with model installation.

UNDERHOOD SERVICE SPECIFICATIONS

CYLINDER NUMBERING SEQUENCE

4-CYL. FIRING ORDER: 1 3 4 2

1991-93 Precis 1468cc, 1989-90 Mirage, Precis 1468cc, 1989-92 Galant 1997cc SOHC

1991-96 Mirage 1468cc

1997-00 Mirage 1468cc

1989-92 Mirage 1597cc, 1989-93 Galant, Eclipse 1997cc DOHC 1995-98 Eclipse 1997cc Turbo

1990-94 Eclipse 1755cc, 1992 Expo 2350cc

1992-96 Expo, Mirage 1834cc, 1993-96 Expo 2350cc

1997-00 Mirage 1834cc

1993-98 Galant 1997cc, 2350cc SOHC 1995-97 Eclipse 2350cc

Front of car

UNDERHOOD SERVICE SPECIFICATIONS

MIITU2   MIITU2

CYLINDER NUMBERING SEQUENCE

4-CYL. FIRING ORDER: 1 3 4 2   **V6 FIRING ORDER: 1 2 3 4 5 6**

   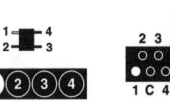   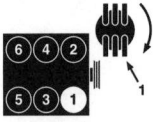 

— **Front of car** —

1989-90 Van 2351cc, 1989 Pickup 1997cc, 1990-96 Pickup 2350cc	**1994-98 Galant 2350cc DOHC**	**1999-00 Galant 2350cc 2000 Eclipse 2350cc**	**1995-99 Eclipse 1996cc**	**1997-99 Montero Sport 2350cc**	**1989-90 Pickup, Montero, Starion 2555cc**	**1989-00 V6, Eclipse, Galant, Sigma, Diamante, 3000GT SOHC**	**1989-96 Montero, Pickup 2972cc**

V6 FIRING ORDER: 1 2 3 4 5 6   ——— **TIMING MARK** ———

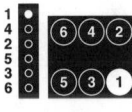      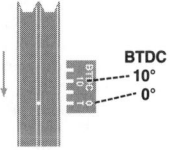 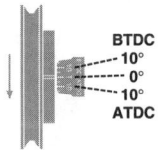 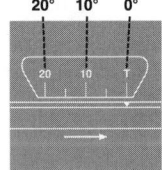

1991-99 3000GT, Diamante DOHC	**1991-99 3000GT, Diamante 2972cc DOHC**	**1997-00 Diamante 3497cc**	**1994-00 Montero 3497cc 1997-00 Montero Sport 2972cc, 3497cc**	**1989-00 Mirage, Precis, 1989-90 Galant, Van, 1989-00 Galant, Eclipse, 1990-96 Pickup 4-cyl., 1992-96 Expo**	**1989 Pickup, Montero, Starion 1997cc, 2555cc**	**1989-00 V6 Galant, Sigma, Montero, Pickup, Diamante, 3000GT**

ELECTRICAL AND IGNITION SYSTEMS

BATTERY

BCI equivalent shown, size may vary from original equipment. Check clearance before replacing, holddown may need to be modified.

Engine	Year	STANDARD BCI Group No.	STANDARD Crank. Perf.	OPTIONAL BCI Group No.	OPTIONAL Crank. Perf.
Diamante	1992-00	24	490	—	—
Eclipse	1990-94	86	430	—	—
	1995-99	86	430	86	525
	2000	86	525	—	—
Expo: 1.8L	1992-96	25	355	—	—
2.4L	1992-96	24	490	—	—
Galant	1989-93	51	430	—	—
	1994-96	25	585	—	—
	1997-98	25	490	—	—
	1999-00	86	525	—	—
Galant Sigma	1989-90	24	490	—	—
Mirage	1989	51	390	—	—
	1990-92	25	355	—	—
	1993-96	51	430	—	—
	1997-00	51R	435	—	—
Precis	1989-90	21	400	—	—
Starion	1989	45	455	—	—
3000GT	1991-93	24	490	—	—
	1994-99	25	520	—	—
2.4L	1990-96	51	430	—	—
Pickup 2.6L	1989	51	405	—	—
3.0L	1990-94	24	490	—	—
Montero	1989-91	51	405	—	—
	1992-00	24	490	—	—
Van	1989-90	51	405	—	—
Montero Sport	1997-98	25	490	—	—
	1999-00	25	520	24	580

GENERATOR

Engine	Year	Rated Output	Min. Test Output (amps. @ eng. rpm)
1468cc Precis	1989	55	55 @ 3000
	1989	60	60 @ 3000
1468cc Precis	1990-94	75	52 @ 2500
1468cc Mirage	1989-94	75	52 @ 2500
	1995-96	70	63 @ 2500
	1997-99	80	56 @ 2500
	1999-00	90	63 @ 2500
1597cc	1989	75	52 @ 2500
1597cc: MT	1990-92	65	46 @ 2500
AT	1990-92	75	52 @ 2500
1755cc, 1997cc Eclipse	1990-94	65	45 @ 2500
	1990-98	75	52 @ 2500
	1992-99	90	63 @ 2500
1834cc Expo	1992-96	60	42 @ 2500
	1992-93	65	46 @ 2500
	1995	75	53 @ 2500
1834cc Mirage	1992-95	65	46 @ 2500
	1992-95	70	49 @ 2500
	1995-96	75	52 @ 2500
	1997-99	80	56 @ 2500
	1999-00	90	63 @ 2500
1996cc Eclipse	1995-99	90	63 @ 2500
1997cc Galant	1989-93	75	53 @ 2500
		90	63 @ 2500
1997cc, 2555cc Pickup	1989	45	31 @ 2500
2350cc Eclipse	1996-00	90	63 @ 2500
2350cc Expo	1992-96	75	53 @ 2500
2350cc Galant: DOHC	1994-96	75	52 @ 2500
SOHC	1994-99	90	63 @ 2500
	2000	85	60 @ 2500
2350cc Montero Sport	1997-99	60	43 @ 2500
2350cc Van	1989-90	75	52 @ 2500
2350cc Pickup	1990-96	40	28 @ 2500
	1990-93	45	31 @ 2500
	1990-93	60	42 @ 2500

MITSUBISHI
1989-2000

UNDERHOOD SERVICE SPECIFICATIONS

GENERATOR Continued

Engine	Year	Rated Output	Min. Test Output (amps. @ eng. rpm)
2555cc Starion	1989	65	45 @ 2500
	1989	75	52 @ 2500
2555cc Montero	1989-91	50	31 @ 2500
	1989-91	55	38 @ 3000
2972cc Galant, Eclipse	1999-00	85	60 @ 2500
2972cc Pickup	1990-94	65	46 @ 2500
2972cc Montero	1989-93	75	52 @ 2500
	1997-00	85	59 @ 2500
2972cc Sigma	1989-90	75	52 @ 2500
2972cc 3000GT	1991-99	90	63 @ 2500
	1991-99	110	77 @ 2500
2972cc Diamante	1992-95	90	63 @ 2500
Wagon	1995	90	50 @ 2500
3497cc Montero, Montero Sport	1994-96	90	63 @ 2500
	1997-00	100	70 @ 2500
3497cc Diamante	1997-00	110	77 @ 2500

REGULATOR

Application	Year	Test Temp. (deg. F/C)	Voltage Setting
Precis	1989	—	14.4-15.0
1996cc Eclipse	1995-99	-4/-20	14.07-15.09
		32/0	13.89-14.89
		68/20	13.58-14.58
		104/40	13.15-14.15
		144/62	12.84-13.84
All others	1989-00	-4/-20	14.2-15.4
		68/20	13.9-15.9
		140/60	13.4-14.6
		175/80	13.1-14.5

STARTER

Engine	Year	Cranking Voltage (min. volts)	Ampere Draw @ Cranking Speed
All	1989	8.0	—

SPARK PLUGS

Engine	Year	Gap (inches)	Gap (mm)	Torque (ft-lb)
1597cc	1989	.028-.032	.7-.8	15-21
1996cc	1995-99	.048-.053	1.2-1.4	15-21
1997cc DOHC Turbo	1990-99	.028-.032	.7-.8	15-21
All others	1989-00	.039-.043	1.0-1.1	15-21

IGNITION COIL

Ignition system without distributor, primary windings are measured between terminals 1 & 4 and 2 & 3 (diagonally) of 4-terminal coil connector. Secondary windings are measured between adjoining coil high tension towers.

Engine	Year	Windings	Resistance (ohms)
1468cc 2V	1989	Primary	1.1-1.3
		Secondary	11,600-15,800
1468cc FI	1989-90	Primary	.72-.88
		Secondary	10,300-13,900
1468cc Precis	1991-94	Primary	.72-.88
		Secondary	10,300-13,900
1468cc Mirage	1991-96	Primary	0.9-1.2
		Secondary	20,000-29,000
	1997-00	Primary	0.5-0.7
		Secondary	15,000-21,000
1597cc DOHC	1989-92	Primary	.77-.95
		Secondary	10,300-13,900
1755cc	1990-94	Primary	0.9-1.2
		Secondary	19,000-27,000

IGNITION COIL Continued

Engine	Year	Windings	Resistance (ohms)
1834cc	1992-96	Primary	0.9-1.2
		Secondary	20,000-29,000
	1997-00	Primary	—
		Secondary	14,000-21,000
1996cc	1995-99	Primary	.51-.61
		Secondary	11,500-13,500
1997cc, 2555cc Pickup	1989	Primary	1.1-1.3
		Secondary	22,100-29,900
1997cc SOHC	1989-93	Primary	.72-.88
		Secondary	10,900-13,300
1997cc DOHC Eclipse	1991-92	Primary	.72-.95
		Secondary	10,300-13,900
1997cc DOHC Eclipse	1992-99	Primary	.70-.86
		Secondary	11,300-15,300
1997cc DOHC Galant	1989-93	Primary	.77-.95
		Secondary	10,300-13,900
2350cc	1989-92	Primary	.72-.88
		Secondary	10,300-13,900
2350cc Eclipse	1997-99	Primary	.74-.90
		Secondary	20,100-27,300
Eclipse	2000	Primary	—
		Secondary	8500-11,500
2350cc Expo, Galant SOHC	1993-98	Primary	0.9-1.2
		Secondary	20,000-29,000
2350cc Galant	1999-00	Primary	—
		Secondary	15,300-20,700
2350cc Galant DOHC	1994-96	Primary	.67-.81
		Secondary	11,300-15,300
2350cc Montero Sport	1997-99	Primary	.67-.81
		Secondary	11,300-15,300
2350cc Truck	1993-96	Primary	.72-.88
		Secondary	10,300-13,900
2555cc Montero	1989-90	Primary	1.1-1.3
		Secondary	14,500-19,500
2555cc Starion	1989	Primary	1.12-1.38
		Secondary	9400-12,700
2972cc SOHC	1989-99	Primary	.72-.88
		Secondary	10,300-13,900
Montero Sport, Eclipse, Galant	1995-96	Primary	.67-.81
		Secondary	13,300-15,300
	1997-00	Primary	.56-.68
		Secondary	9400-12,800
2972cc DOHC	1991-99	Primary	.67-.81
		Secondary	11,300-15,300
3497cc Montero	1994-96	Primary	.69-.85
		Secondary	15,300-20,700
	1997-99	Primary	.74-.90
		Secondary	20,100-27,300
3497cc Montero Sport	1999	Primary	.74-.90
		Secondary	20,100-27,300
3497cc Diamante	1997-00	Primary	.50-.70
		Secondary	9000-13,000

DISTRIBUTOR PICKUP

Engine	Year	Resistance (ohms)	Air Gap (in./mm)
1468cc, 2555cc 2V	1989-90	—	.030/.80
1595cc, 1795cc, 2555cc Turbo	1989	920-1120	—
1997cc Pickup, Tredia, Cordia	1989	130-190	.008/.015/.2-.4

IGNITION RESISTOR

Engine	Year	Type	Resistance (ohms)	Temperature (deg. F/C)
All, as equipped	1989	Unit	1.20-1.50	68/20

BASE TIMING

1989-90 All others, disconnect and plug distributor vacuum hoses.

1989-95 All w/FI: Ground ignition timing connector. When ungrounded, timing should advance to "Check" Specification. At high altitudes, timing may be advanced further than the Check value listed.

MITSUBISHI
1989-2000

UNDERHOOD SERVICE SPECIFICATIONS

BASE TIMING Continued

1996-00: Connect a scan tool and access ignition timing function. Timing should be at base value. When function is exited, timing should be at check value. If timing is not at specified value, further diagnosis of the system is necessary.

Engine	Year	Man. Trans. (degrees) @ RPM	Auto. Trans. (degrees) @ RPM
1468cc Precis	1989	5²±2	5±2
1468cc Precis	1989	5±2	5±2
1468cc 2V Mirage	1989	5¹±2	5¹±2
1468cc FI	1989-95	5±2	5±2
	1996-98	5±3⁴	5±3⁴
Check	1989-93	10±2	10±2
High Alt.	1989-93	15±2	15±2
Check	1994-97	10±7	10±7
1468cc	1996-00	5±3	5±3
Check	1996-00	10±7	10±7
1597cc	1989-92	5±2	5±2
Check	1989-92	8±2	8±2
High Alt.	1989-92	13±2	13±2
1755cc	1990-94	5±2	5±2
Check	1990-94	10±2	10±2
1834cc	1992-95	5±2	5±2
Calif.	1995	5±3⁴	5±3⁴
Check	1992-93	5±2	5±2
Check	1994-95	5±7	5±7
1834cc	1996-00	5±3⁴	5±3⁴
Check	1996-00	5±7	5±7
1996cc	1995-99	12⁴	12⁴
1997cc 2V	1989	8±2	8±2
1997cc FI: SOHC	1989-93	5±2	5±2
Check	1989-93	10±2	10±2
High Alt.	1989-93	15±2	15±2
1997 DOHC	1989-94	5±2	5±2
Check	1989	12±2	—
High Alt.	1989	17±2	—
Check	1990-94	8±2	8±2
1997cc Turbo	1990-94	5±2	5±2
Check Eclipse	1990-94	8±2	8±2
Check Galant	1990-92	12±2	12±2
1997cc Turbo	1995-99	5±3⁴	5±3⁴
Check	1995-99	8±7	8±7
2350cc SOHC	1989-94	5±2	5±2
Check	1989-93	8±2	8±2
High Alt.	1989-92	13±2	13±2
Check, Pickup	1994	8±7	8±7
Check, Expo, Galant	1994	10±7	10±7
2350cc Expo	1995	5±2	5±2
Calif.	1995	5±3⁴	5±3⁴
Check	1995	8±7	8±7
Truck	1995	5±2	5±2
Check	1995	8±7	8±7
2350cc Pickup	1996	5±2	5±2
Check	1996	8±7	8±7
2350cc Eclipse, Galant, Montero	1996-00	5±3⁴	5±3⁴
Check	1996-00	10±7	10±7
2350cc Expo	1996-97	5±3⁴	5±3⁴
Check	1996-97	15±7	15±7
2350cc DOHC	1994-96	5±3⁴	5±3⁴
Check	1994-96	8±7	8±7
2555cc 2V	1989-90	7±2	7±2
2555cc Turbo	1989	10±2	10±2
2972cc	1989-92	5±2	5±2
Check	1989-92	15±2	15±2
High Alt.	1989-92	—	20±2
2972cc SOHC Diamante	1993-95	5±2	5±2
Check	1993-95	15±2	15±2
High Alt.	1993-95	—	20±2
2972cc SOHC Montero	1993-94	5±2	5±2
Check	1993-94	15±2	15±2
2972cc SOHC Montero	1995-00	15±3⁴	15±3⁴
Check	1995-00	15±7	15±7
2972cc SOHC 3000GT, Galant, Eclipse	1997-00	5±3⁴	5±3⁴
Check	1997-00	15±7	15±7
2972cc DOHC	1993-98	5±3⁴	5±3⁴
Check	1993-98	15±7	15±7
High Alt.	1993-98	20±7	20±7
3497cc	1994-00	5±3⁴	5±3⁴
Check	1994-00	15±7	15±7

BASE TIMING Continued

1 With vacuum hose connected, high altitude, 10°.
2 Models without vacuum regulator valve, 7°.
3 With pressure sensor connected, high altitude, 15°.
4 Not adjustable.

DISTRIBUTOR TIMING ADVANCE

Engine degrees at engine rpm, no load, in addition to basic timing setting.
Mechanical advance distributors only.
1989 2555cc Turbo, Vacuum retard, 7° @ 9" Hg.

Engine	Trans-mission	Year	Distributor Number	Degrees @ 2500 RPM Total	Degrees @ 2500 RPM Centrifugal
1997cc Pickup	MT & AT	1989	MD110418	25.8-33.8	7.8-11.8
	MT & AT	1989	MD110419, 40	28.8-36.8	7.8-11.8
	MT & AT	1989	MD125103	25.8-33.8	7.8-11.8
2555cc 2V	MT & AT	1989	T3T65572	22.8-30.8	4.8-8.8
	MT & AT	1989-90	T3T65571	25.8-33.8	4.8-8.8
	MT & AT	1989	T3T65474, 76	22.8-30.8	4.8-8.8
2555cc Turbo	MT & AT	1989	T4T63372, 73	31.6-39.6	10.6-14.6

1 Pressure retard 6° @ 6 PSI.

FUEL SYSTEM

FUEL SYSTEM PRESSURE

Engine	Year	Pressure PSI¹	Pressure PSI²
1597cc Turbo SOHC, 2555cc Turbo	1989	35-38³	—
Montero V6 DOHC		—	47-50
All others ex. Turbo	1989-96	47-50	38
	1997-00	47-50	38
4-cyl. Turbo MT	1989-94	36-38	27
4-cyl. Turbo AT	1992-94	41-46	33
4-cyl. Turbo	1995-99	42-45	33
V6 Turbo	1991-99	43-45	34

1 Vacuum disconnected from fuel pressure regulator.
2 Vacuum connected to fuel pressure regulator.
3 Measured at TBI unit.

IDLE SPEED W/O COMPUTER CONTROL

Midpoint of range given is the preferred setting.

1468cc, Cordia w/MT: Set idle speed to specified value.

To set PS/Elect. speed-up, apply 12 volts to throttle opener solenoid and adjust to specified value. To set A/C speed-up, turn A/C on and adjust vacuum actuator to specified value.

All others: Set idle speed to specified value. Turn A/C on and adjust speed-up speed as needed.

Engine	Year	SLOW Man. Trans.	SLOW Auto. Trans.	FAST Man. Trans.	FAST Auto. Trans.	Step of Cam
1468cc Precis	1989	700-900	700-900 N	2800	2700 N	2nd High
PS, Elect. speed-up	1989	750-950	750-950 N			
A/C speed-up	1989	850-900	850-900			
1997cc Pickup	1989	650-850	650-850 N	2500	2450 N	2nd High
A/C speed-up	1989	850-900	850-900 N			
2555cc 2V	1989-90	700-900	700-900 N	2350	2300 N	2nd High
A/C speed-up, Pickup	1989	850-900	850-900 N			
A/C speed-up, Montero	1989-90	900-950	900-950 N			

UNDERHOOD SERVICE SPECIFICATIONS

MIITU5

IDLE SPEED W/COMPUTER CONTROL

Midpoint of range given is the preferred setting speed.

1989-93 1597cc, 1834cc, 1997cc DOHC, 2972cc;
1993 1997cc SOHC, 2350cc Expo & 2WD California Pickup;
1994 1997cc, 2350cc, 2WD California Pickup;
1995 2350cc Pickup 2WD Calif.:
Disconnect and ground female end of ignition timing connector. Ground terminal 10 of self-diagnostic connector (under dash). Set idle speed. Reinstate system, turn A/C on and verify the speed-up is at specified value.

1989-93 All Others;
1994-95 1755cc, 2350cc Pickup ex. Calif 2WD:
Verify that TPS voltage is at proper value. Turn ignition on for 20 seconds and turn off. Disconnect ISC servo. Ground red wire in connector (computer side of harness) (2.6L Turbo) and start engine. Set idle speed to specified value. Turn A/C on and verify that A/C speed-up speed is at specified value. This is not adjustable.

1994-95 1468cc, 1834cc, 2350 Expo, Galant; 2972cc, 3497cc;
1995 1997cc:
1996 All:
Ground the ignition timing connector and terminal 1 (upper left) of the 16 terminal self-diagnostic connector under dash. Set ideal to specified setting value. Turn A/C on and verify that speed-up speed is at specified value.

1995-99 1996cc:
Remove PCV valve from PCV hose and install special tool (.0125" orifice). Connect a Scan tool and access "Minimum Idle Speed." If checking speed is not 500-1100 (N), replace the throttle body.

1997-00: Connect a scan tool and access idle speed functions.

Engine	Year	Trans-mission	Setting Speed	Checking Speed	AC Speed-up
1468cc FI Mirage	1989-96	MT	700-800	650-850	800-900
	1989-92	AT	700-800 N	650-800 N	750 D
	1993-96	AT	700-800 N	650-850 N	800-900 N
1468cc Mirage	1997-98	MT	700-800	600-800	800-900
		AT	700-800 N	600-800 N	800-900 N
	1999-00	MT	650-750	600-800	750-950
		AT	650-750N	600-800N	750-950N
1468cc FI Precis: to 3/93	1990-93	MT	600-800	—	—
		AT	600-800 N	—	—
1468cc FI Precis: from 3/93	1993-94	MT	725-925	—	—
		AT	725-925 N	—	—
1597cc	1989-92	MT	700-800	650-850	850
		AT	700-800 N	650-850 N	700 D
1755cc	1990-94	MT	650-750	600-800	850
		AT	650-750 N	600-800 N	650 D
1834cc	1992-93	MT	700-800	650-850	830
		AT	700-800 N	650-850 N	830 N
California Expo	1993	MT	650-750	600-800	830
		AT	650-750 N	600-800 N	830 N
1834cc Mirage	1994-96	MT	700-800	650-850	800-900
		AT	700-800 N	650-850 N	800-900 N
	1997-99	MT	700-800	600-800	800-900
		AT	700-800 N	600-800 N	800-900 N
	1999-00	MT	650-750	600-800	750-950
		AT	650-750N	600-800N	750-950N
1834cc Expo	1994-96	MT	650-750	600-800	800-900
		AT	650-750 N	600-800 N	800-900 N
1996cc	1995-99	MT	—	700-900	—
		AT	—	700-900 N	—
1997cc SOHC	1989-92	MT	700-800	650-850	900
		AT	700-800 N	650-850 N	700 D
1997cc SOHC	1993	MT	650-750	600-800	850
		AT	650-750 N	600-800 N	650 D
1997cc DOHC	1990-99	MT	700-800	650-850	750-950
		AT	700-800 N	650-850 N	750-950 D
Turbo, Galant	1990-92	MT	750-850	700-900	850
2350cc Trucks	1989-91	MT	700-800	650-850	900
	1992	MT	700-800	650-850	1000
	1989-92	AT	700-800 N	650-850 N	700 D
2350cc Expo	1992-96	MT	700-800	650-850	800-900
		AT	700-800 N	650-850 N	800-900 N
2350cc SOHC Galant, Montero	1994-98	MT	700-800	650-850	800-900
		AT	700-800 N	650-850 N	800-900 N
2350cc Montero	1999	MT	700-800	650-850	750-950
		AT	700-800 N	650-850 N	750-950 N

IDLE SPEED W/COMPUTER CONTROL Continued

Engine	Year	Trans-mission	Setting Speed	Checking Speed	AC Speed-up
2350cc Galant, Eclipse	1999-00	MT	650-750	650-850	750-950
		AT	650-750 N	650-850 N	750-950 N
2350cc DOHC Galant	1994-96	MT	750-850	700-900	800
		AT	750-850 N	700-900 N	800 N
2350cc Truck	1993-96	MT	700-800	650-850	1000
		AT	700-800 N	650-850 N	700 D
2555cc Turbo	1989	MT	850	750-950	900
		AT	850 N	750-950 N	650 D
2972cc Galant, Eclipse	1999-00	AT	650-750 N	600-800N	750-950N
2972cc Others	1989-00	MT	650-750	600-800	900
		AT	650-750 N	600-800 N	650 D[1]
3497cc	1994-00		650-750	600-800	800-1000
			650-750 N	600-800 N	800-1000 N

1 Truck, 900 (N).

ENGINE MECHANICAL

TIGHTENING TORQUES

Specifications for cylinder head bolts are for cold engine.

		TORQUE FOOT-POUNDS/NEWTON METERS				
Engine	Year	Cylinder Head	Intake Manifold	Exhaust Manifold	Crankshaft Pulley	Water Pump
1468cc	1989-92	53/73	12-14/ 16-19	12-14/ 16-19	9-11/ 12-15	9-11/ 12-15[1]
thru 5/95	1993-95	53/73	13/18	13/18	62/85[2] 10/13[3]	10/14[3] 17/24[2]
from 6/95	1995-00	35/49[4], 14/20, +90°, +90°	13-18	12/17[3] 24/29[2]	76/103	9/13
1597cc	1989-92	80/110	11-14/ 15-19[3] 22-30/ 30-42[2]	18-22/ 25-30	14-22/ 20-30	9-11/ 12-15, short 14-20/ 20-27, long
1755cc	1990-94	53/73	12-14/ 16-19	12-14/ 16-19	11-13/ 15-18	9-11/ 12-15[1]
1834cc	1992-00	54/75[4], 14/20, +90°, +90° 7	13/18	22/30	134/185	18/24
1996cc 1997cc Pickup	1995-99 1989	80/110	17/23 11-14/ 15-19	17/23 11-14/ 15-19	105/142 15-21/ 20-30	9/12 9-11/ 12-15
1997cc SOHC ex. Pickup	1989-92	80/110	11-14/ 15-19	11-14/ 15-19	15-21/ 20-30	9-11/ 12-15[1]
1997cc DOHC	1989-92	80/110	11-14/ 15-19[3] 22-30/ 30-42[2]	18-22/ 25-30	14-22/ 20-30	9-11/ 12-15[1]
1997cc	1993-99	58/78[4] 14/20, +90° +90°	11-14/ 15-20[3] 22-30/ 30-42[2]	18-22/ 25-30	14-22/ 20-30	9-11/ 12-15[1]
2350cc ex. Expo	1989-92	80/110	11-14/ 15-20	11-14/ 15-20	15-21/ 20-30	9-11/ 12-15[1]
2350cc Expo	1992	80/110	13/18	13/18	18/25	10/14
2350cc Expo, Pickup	1993-96	58/78[4], 14/20, +90° +90°	13/18	22/30/	18-25	10/14
2350cc Galant, Eclipse, Montero	1994-00	58/78[4], 15/20, +90° +90°	15/20[5]	21/29, M8 36/49, M10	18/25	9-11/ 12-15
2555cc	1989-90	80/110[6]	11-14/ 15-19	11-14/ 15-19	80-95/ 110-130	9-11/ 12-15

MIITU6

TIGHTENING TORQUES Continued

Engine	Year	TORQUE FOOT-POUNDS/NEWTON METERS				
		Cylinder Head	Intake Manifold	Exhaust Manifold	Crankshaft Pulley	Water Pump
2972cc SOHC ex. Diamante	1989-93	80/110	11-14/ 15-19	11-15/ 15-21	109-115/ 150-160	14-19/ 20-27
2972cc SOHC Diamante	1992-99	80/110	13/18	14/19	108-116/ 150-160	17/24
2972cc DOHC Diamante	1992-95	80/110	13/18	21/30	130-137/ 180-190	17/24
2972cc DOHC 3000GT	1991-99	90/125[4], 90/125	13/18	22/30	130-137/ 180-190	17/24
2972cc DOHC Montero, 3497cc Montero	1994-00	80/108	16/21	22/29	136/185	17/24
3497cc Diamante	1997-00	80/108	13/17	36/49	134/181	17/23[3] 30/41[2]

1 Short bolts. Long bolts, 14-20/20-27.
2 Long bolts.
3 Short bolts.
4 Then fully loosen.
5 DOHC, 26/35.
6 Small bolts forward of cam gear, 11-15/15-22.
7 Tighten short bolts to 20/27 three times. Tighten long bolts to 25/33, 50/67, then 50/67 again. Turn all bolts 90°.

VALVE CLEARANCE
Engine hot.

Application	Year	Intake (inches)	Intake (mm)	Exhaust (inches)	Exhaust (mm)
Pickup, Gas	1989	1	1	1	1
Jet valve	1989	.010	.25	—	—
Mirage, Precis	1989-92	.006	.15	.010	.25
Jet valve, 2V	1989-92	.010	.25	—	—
Mirage: 1468cc	1993-97	.008	.20	.010	.25
1834cc	1993-97	.008	.20	.012	.30
Starion	1989	1	1	1	1
Jet valve	1989	.010	.25	—	—
Expo, 1834cc	1993-96	.008	.20	.012	.30

1 Hydraulic lifters except Jet valve.

COMPRESSION PRESSURE
At cranking speed, engine temperature normalized, throttle open.

Engine	Year	PSI @ 250 RPM	Maximum Variation PSI
1468cc Precis	1989	164	—
1468cc Precis	1990-92	171-192	14
1468cc Mirage	1989-96	137 min.	14
	1997-98	137-142	14
	1999-00	133-188	14
1597cc	1989	149 min.	14
	1990-91	171 min.	14
	1992	145 min.	14
1755cc	1990-94	131 min.	14
1834cc Mirage	1992-96	151 min.	14
	1997-00	151-199	14
Expo	1992-96	142 min.	1
1996cc	1995-99	170-225/100min.	
1997cc SOHC	1989-92	125 min.	14
	1993	139 min.	14
1997cc: DOHC, Eclipse	1989-91	137 min.	14
DOHC, Eclipse	1992-94	145 min.	14
	1995-96	133 min.	14
	1997-99	133-178	14
DOHC, Galant	1990-94	159 min.	14
Turbo	1990-91	114 min.	14
Turbo	1992-93	121 min.	14
2350cc	1989-92	119 min.	14

COMPRESSION PRESSURE Continued

Engine	Year	PSI @ 250 RPM	Maximum Variation PSI
2350cc Truck	1993-96	127 min.	14
Expo	1993-96	139 min.	14
2350cc Galant: SOHC	1994-96	145 min.	14
DOHC	1994-96	157 min.	14
2350cc	1997-98	145-192	14
2350cc Galant	1999-00	139-185	14
Eclipse	1999	145-192	14
	2000	139-185	14
Montero	1999-00	145-192	14
2555cc	1983-87	140	—
2555cc 2V	1989-90	119 min.	14
2555cc Turbo	1989	97 min.	14
2972cc SOHC Pickup, Montero	1989-92	119 min.	14
2972cc Pickup	1993-94	127 min.	14
2972cc Montero	1993-96	127 min.	14
	1997-00	127-171	14
2972cc SOHC Diamante[1]	1992-96	149 min.	14
3000 GT	1995-99	127-171	14
Galant	1999-00	83-119	14
2972cc DOHC	1991-96	139 min.	14
	1997-99	139-185	14
Turbo	1991-96	115 min.	14
	1997-99	115-156	14
3497cc	1994-96	139 min.	14
	1997-00	127-171	14

1 Lowest cylinder must be 75% of highest.

BELT TENSION
With 22 lbs. of force applied at midpoint of belt.

Engine	Year	Generator	Power Steering	Air Cond.	Air Pump
Deflection method:					
1997cc Pickup (inches)	1989	1/4-3/8	7/32-3/8	1/4-11/32	1/4-3/8
(mm)	1989	7-10	7-10	6-9	7-10
2555cc Pickup (inches)	1989	1/4-3/8	3/8-7/16	11/16-13/16	1/4-3/8
(mm)	1989	7-10	9-12	17-20	7-20
2555cc Montero (inches)	1989-90	11/32-3/8	11/32-3/8	11/16-1/2	11/32-3/8
(mm)	1989-90	9-12	9-12	17-20	9-12
2555cc Starion (inches)	1989	1/4-3/8	11/32-1/2	1/4-3/8	—
(mm)	1989	7-10	9-12	7-10	—
1468cc Precis (inches)	1989-90	1/4-3/8	1/4-3/8	5/16-3/8	1/4-3/8
(mm)	1989-90	7-9	7-9	8-10	7-9
2350cc (inches)	1989	1/4-3/8	1/4-3/8	1/4-3/8	—
(mm)	1989	7-10	7-10	7-10	—
2350cc Pickup (inches)	1992-96	7/32-3/8	5/16-3/8	1/4-5/16	—
(mm)	1992-96	7-10	8-10	6-9	—
2972cc Sigma (inches)	1989	1/4-3/8	1/4-3/8	5/32-3/16	—
(mm)	1989	7-10	7-10	4-5	—
2350cc Pickup (inches)	1990-95	7/32-3/8	1/4-5/16	5/16-3/8	—
(mm)	1990-95	7-10	6-9	8-10	—
2350cc Galant (inches)	1994-95	5/16-3/8	3/16-7/32	7/32-1/4	—
(mm)	1994-95	7.5-9	4.5-5.5	5.5-6	—
2972cc DOHC (inches)	1991-95	5/32-3/16	13/32-7/16	5/32-3/16	—
(mm)	1991-95	9-5	9-11	4-5	—
Strand Tension method:					
NEW					
1468cc FI	1989-96	110-155	110-190	80-95	—
	1997-00	143-187	143-187	143-187	—
1597cc	1989-92	110-155	110-155	80-95	—
1755cc, 1997cc	1989-95	110-155	110-155	104-126	—
1834cc: PS w/o A/C	1992-96	110-155	145-190	—	—
PS w/A/C	1992-96	110-155	165-175	165-175	—
1834cc	1997-00	110-154	143-187	143-187	—
1996cc	1995-99	110-160	137-159	137-159	—
1997cc	1995-99	110-155	110-155	86-99	—
2350cc Expo	1992-96	110-155	110-155	120-145	—
2350cc Galant, Eclipse	1994-96	110-154	110-154	55-118	—
	1997-98	110-154	110-154	110-154	—

UNDERHOOD SERVICE SPECIFICATIONS

BELT TENSION Continued

Engine	Year	Generator	Power Steering	Air Cond.	Air Pump
2350cc Galant	1999-00	176-220	143-187	143-187	—
2350cc Eclipse	1999-00	110-154	110-154	110-154	—
2350cc Montero	1997-99	110-154	110-154	121-143	—
2972cc SOHC	1989-00	110-155	110-155	104-126	—
2972cc DOHC	1992-99	145-200	145-200	110-155	—
3497cc	1994-00	140-185	110-154	110-154	—
USED					
1468cc FI	1989-96	90	65-110	55-70	—
	1997-00	99-121	99-121	99-121	—
1597cc	1989-92	90	90	55-70	—
1755cc, 1997cc	1989-95	55-110	55-110	71-88	—
1834cc: PS w/o A/C	1992-96	55-110	90-130	—	—
PS w/A/C	1992-96	55-110	110-140	110-140	—
1834cc	1997-00	77-99	99-121	99-121	—
1996cc	1995-99	90-100	93-115	93-115	—
1997cc	1995-99	55-110	55-110	57-75	—
2350cc Expo	1992-96	55-110	75-100	75-110	—
2350cc Galant, Eclipse	1994-96	55-118	55-118	57-75	—
	1997-98	55-110	77-99	57-75	—
2350cc Galant	1999-00	99-121	99-121	99-121	—
2350cc Eclipse	1999-00	55-110	77-99	77-99	—
2350cc Montero	1997-99	77-100	77-100	85-100	—
2972cc SOHC	1989-00	55-110	55-110	71-86	—
2972cc DOHC	1992-99	110-130	110-130	80-90	—
3497cc	1994-00	110-120	77-100	77-100	—

ENGINE COMPUTER SYSTEM

DIAGNOSTIC TROUBLE CODES

1989-93 All; 1994 Pickup, Eclipse:
Access diagnostic connector in or under glove box or by fuse block. Connect an analog voltmeter to upper right (+) and lower left (-) cavities. Turn ignition on with engine off.

1994 Mirage:
Access connector by fuse block. Connect an analog voltmeter (+) to terminal 25 (upper left) of 12 terminal male connector and (-) to terminal four or five (upper middle two) of 16 terminal female connector. Turn ignition on. Codes will be displayed as sweeps of the voltmeter needle. Disconnect battery negative terminal to erase codes.

1994 Galant, Diamante, Expo, 3000GT; 1995 Diamante, Expo 2.4L ex. Calif.:
Ground terminal 1 (upper left) of 16 terminal connector under dash. Turn ignition on. Codes will be displayed on CHECK ENGINE light. Disconnect battery negative terminal to erase codes.

1995 Eclipse, Expo 1.8L & 2.4L Calif.; 1996-00 All Models:
OBD-II system used. Connect a Scan tool and follow tool manufacturer's instructions to retrieve codes.

All models ex. OBD-II, remove ECM fuse for 15 seconds minimum to clear codes.

All, Van, codes will be displayed as sweeps of the voltmeter needle. Needle will sweep only if a problem in the system has been detected by the ECM.

1989 Starion, voltmeter needle will sweep to indicate short or long durations every two seconds for a 10-second cycle. If the needle does not sweep, the ECM has not detected a failure in the system.

The following deciphers each code:

0 = short sweep, 1 = long sweep

```
00000 = 0
10000 = 1
01000 = 2
11000 = 3
00100 = 4
10100 = 5
01100 = 6
11100 = 7
00010 = 8
```

1989 All, voltmeter needle will sweep in long durations indicating the number of tens, or short durations, indicating the number of ones.

1989 Starion:
Code 1 Oxygen sensor and/or computer
Code 2 Ignition signal or crankshaft position sensor
Code 3 Mass airflow sensor
Code 4 Manifold absolute pressure sensor
Code 5 Throttle position sensor

DIAGNOSTIC TROUBLE CODES Continued

Code 6 ISC motor position sensor
Code 7 Engine coolant temperature sensor
Code 8 Car speed signal or TDC sensor
1989-94 All others:
Code 9 No failure
Code 11 Oxygen sensor (front)
Code 12 Volume airflow sensor
Code 13 Intake air temperature sensor
Code 14 TPS
Code 15 Idle air control position sensor
Code 21 Coolant temperature sensor
Code 22 Crankshaft position sensor
Code 23 Camshaft position sensor
Code 24 Vehicle speed sensor
Code 25 Barometric pressure sensor
Code 31 Knock sensor
Code 32 MAP sensor
Code 36 Ignition timing adjustment
Code 39 Oxygen sensor (front on Turbo)
Code 41 Injector
Code 42 Fuel pump
Code 43 EGR
Code 44 Ignition coil (ex. V6 DOHC)
Code 44 1-4 coil power transistor (V6 DOHC)
Code 52 2-5 coil power transistor (V6 DOHC)
Code 53 3-6 coil power transistor (V6 DOHC)
Code 55 Idle air control position sensor
Code 59 Heated oxygen sensor (rear)
Code 61 Transmission & ECM interlink
Code 62 Induction control valve position sensor
Code 71 Traction control vacuum solenoid valve
Code 72 Traction control vent solenoid valve

1 long sweep ECM
Rapid pulsing Normal state

SENSORS, INPUT
TEMPERATURE SENSORS

Engine	Year	Sensor	Resistance Ohms @ deg. F/C
All	1989-93	Coolant	5900 @ 32/0
			2500 @ 68/20
			1100 @ 104/40
			300 @ 176/80
All ex. 1996cc	1994-00	Coolant	5100-6500 @ 32/0
			2100-2700 @ 68/20
			900-1300 @ 104/40
			200-360 @ 176/80
1996cc	1995-99	Coolant	7000-11,000 @ 77 (25)
			600-800 @ 212 (100)
1468cc FI, 1597cc, 2350cc, 2555cc Turbo, 2972cc	1989-93	Intake Air[1]	6000 @ 32/0
			2700 @ 68/20
			400 @ 176/80
All ex. 1966cc	1994-00	Intake Air[1]	5300-6700 @ 32/0
			2300-3000 @ 68/20
			1000-1500 @ 104/40
			300-420 @ 176/80
1996cc	1995-99	Intake Air	9000-11,000 @ 77/25
			600-800 @ 212/100

1 Measured between terminals 2 & 4 of airflow sensor.

MANIFOLD ABSOLUTE PRESSURE SENSORS
Precis, measured between terminals 5 & 6 (lower middle and lower left) of airflow connector.

Engine	Year	Sensor	Voltage @ in. Hg./@ kPa or Condition
1468cc Precis	1990-93	Barometric	0.79 @ 3/10
			1.84 @ 7/24
			4.00 @ 15/51
1468cc	1997-00	MAP	3.7-4.3 ign. on @ 0 alt.
			3.2-3.8 @ 4000 ft/1200 m
			0.9-1.5 @ idle

MIITU8

SENSORS, INPUT Continued
MANIFOLD ABSOLUTE PRESSURE SENSORS Continued

Engine	Year	Sensor	Voltage @ in. Hg./@ kPa or Condition
1997cc	1995-96	MAP	0.8-2.40 idle
	1997-99	MAP	3.7-4.3 ign. on @ 0 alt.
			3.2-3.8 ign. on @ 4000 ft/1200 m
			0.9-1.5 @ idle
2350cc, 2972cc Galant, Eclipse	1999-00	MAP	0.8-2.4 @ idle
2555cc Turbo	1989	Barometric	.79 @ 2.8/9
			1.84 @ 7/24
			4.00 @ 14.2/48
2972cc 3000 GT	1996-99	MAP	0.8-2.4 @ idle
		Barometric	3.7-4.30 0/0
			3.2-3.8 @ 4000 ft/1200 m

MASS AIRFLOW SENSOR
Except Precis, measured between red and black wire leads at idle.

Engine	Year	Volts
1468cc Precis	1990-91	2.7-3.2

Measured between terminals 3 & 6 (upper and lower left) of airflow sensor connector.

Engine	Year	Idle	Frequency (HZ) @ 2500 RPM
1468cc Mirage	1990	24-40	63-83
	1991-92	30-45	80-110
1597cc Mirage	1990-92	27-33	60-80
1755cc	1990-94	25-40	67-88
1834cc	1992-94	23-49	51-91
1834cc	1995	23-49	51-91
Calif.	1995	20-46	68-108
1834cc	1996	20-46	68-108
	1997-00	18-44	68-108
1997cc SOHC	1990-92	25-50	70-130
	1993	18-44	64-104
1997cc DOHC	1990-94	25-50	70-90
1997cc Turbo	1990-94	25-50	50-85
	1995	22-48	60-100
	1996-98	25-50	60-85
	1999	22-48	60-100
2350cc Van	1990	40-60	120-140
2350cc Pickup	1990-91	45-65	100-130
	1992-96	40-60	85-105
2350cc Eclipse	1997-99	18-44	43-83
	2000	22-51	80-120
2350cc Expo, Galant	1992	34-60	70-110
	1993-96	18-44	43-83
	1997-98	18-44	43-83
2350cc Galant	1999-00	22-51	80-120
2350cc Montero	1997-99	25-51	80-120
2972cc Pickup, Montero	1990	24-45	80-105
	1991	40-60	85-105
	1992-95	25-45	70-90
	1997-99	25-51	74-114
2972cc Sigma	1990	30-45	85-105
2972cc 3000GT	1991	25-50	70-100
2972cc DOHC 3000GT	1992-99	22-48	50-90
Turbo	1992-99	22-48	68-108
2972cc Diamante	1992-95	25-51	74-114
DOHC	1993-96	21-47	57-97
2972cc Galant, Eclipse	1999-00	—	—
3497cc Montero	1994-96	29-55	91-131
	1997-00	25-51	80-120
3497cc Montero Sport	1999-00	18-44	58-98
3497cc Diamante	1997-00	18-44	43-83

THROTTLE POSITION SENSOR (TPS)

All FI: Insert digital voltmeter probes along GW or blue lead (+) and B lead (-) (4-cyl.) on TPS connector. With ignition switch on and engine not running, check reading against specification at speed indicated. Rotate unit to adjust.

All 2V: Back off speed adjusting screw enough to fully close throttle valve. Connect digital voltmeter probes between two bottom terminals of TPS. With ignition on and engine not running, check reading against specifications at speed indicated. Rotate unit or turn TPS linkage screw to adjust.

SENSORS, INPUT Continued
THROTTLE POSITION SENSOR (TPS) Continued

Engine	Year	Setting Speed	TPS Idle	Voltage WOT
1468cc 2V	1989	—	.25	—
1468cc FI	1989-92	—	.48-.52	—
	1993-95	—	.30-1.0[1]	4.5-5.5
	1996-00	—	.40-1.0[1]	4.5-5.5
	1989-92	700	.48-.52	—
1755cc	1990-94	700	.48-.52	4.5-5.5
1834cc	1992-93	—	.30-1.0[1]	4.5-5.5
	1994-00	—	0.4-1.0[1]	4.5-5.5
1996cc	1995-99	—	0.4 min.	3.8 max.
1997cc FI	1989-92	—	.48-.52	4.5-5.5
1997cc SOHC	1993	—	.30-1.0[1]	4.5-5.5
1997cc DOHC	1993-94	—	.48-.52	4.5-5.5
	1995-99	—	.40-1.0[1]	4.5-5.5
1997cc Pickup, 2555cc 2V	1989	—	.25	—
2350cc Galant, Van, Pickup	1989-93	750	.48-.52	—
2350cc Pickup	1994-95	750	.48-.52	—
Calif. 2WD	1994-95	—	0.3-1.0[1]	4.5-5.5
2350cc Pickup	1996	—	.40-1.0[1]	4.5-5.5
2350cc Galant, Eclipse	1994-95	—	0.3-1.0[1]	4.5-5.5
	1996-98	—	.40-1.0[1]	4.5-5.5
2350cc Eclipse	1999	—	.40-1.0	4.5-5.5
2350cc Galant, Eclipse: Check	1999-00	—	.40-1.0	4.5-4.5
Set	1999-00	—	.535-.735	—
2350cc Expo, Montero	1992-93	—	.30-1.0[1]	4.5-5.5
	1994-99	—	.40-1.0[1]	4.5-5.5
2555cc Turbo	1989	750	.48-.52	—
2972cc Sigma	1989-90	—	.48-.52	4.5-5.5
2972cc 3000GT, Montero	1989-93	—	.30-1.0[1]	4.5-5.5
	1994-00	—	.40-1.0[1]	4.5-5.5
2972cc Galant, Eclipse: Check	1999-00	—	.40-1.0	4.5-5.5
Set	1999-00	—	.535-.735	—
2972cc Diamante	1992-96	—	.40-1.0[1]	4.5-5.5
w/Traction Control	1992-96	—	.58-.69	4.5-5.5
3497cc	1994-00	—	.40-1.0[1]	4.5-5.5

[1] Not adjustable

IDLE AIR CONTROL VALVE POSITION SENSOR

Engine	Year	Resistance (ohms)
All 4-cyl. SOHC ex. Turbo	1989-93	4000-6000
1755cc, 2350cc Pickup	1994-95	4000-6000

ACTUATORS, OUTPUT
IDLE SPEED CONTROL SOLENOID

Engine	Year	Resistance (ohms)
1468cc FI, 1755cc	1989-96	5-35
	1997-00	28-33[1]
1597cc DOHC	1989-92	28-33[1]
	1990-96	5-35
1834cc, 1997cc SOHC	1997-00	28-33[1]
1996cc	1995-99	38-52
1997cc, DOHC	1990-96	28-33[1]
2350cc SOHC	1989-96	5-35
	1997-00	28-33[1]
2350cc DOHC	1994-96	28-33[1]
2555cc Turbo	1989	5-35[2]
2972cc, 3497cc	1989-00	28-33[1]

[1] Measured between middle and either left or right cavities in both rows of ISC.
[2] Measured between terminals 1 & 4 of ISC.

FUEL INJECTORS

Engine	Year	Resistance (ohms)	Temperature (deg. F/C)
All FI ex. 1996cc & 1997cc Turbo, 2972cc Turbo	1989-00	13-16	68/20

UNDERHOOD SERVICE SPECIFICATIONS

ACTUATORS, OUTPUT Continued
FUEL INJECTORS Continued

Engine	Year	Resistance (ohms)	Temperature (deg. F/C)
1996cc	1995-99	11-15	68/20
1997cc Turbo	1989-99	2-3	68/20
2972cc Turbo	1991-99	2-3	68/20

MIXTURE CONTROL SOLENOID

Engine	Year	Resistance (ohms)	Temperature (deg. F/C)
1468cc 2V	1989	54-66	—
1795cc 2V, 1997cc	1989	54-66	—
2555cc 2V	1989-90	54-66	—

COMPUTER TIMING ADVANCE

With engine at operating temperature, check advance at idle and 2000 rpm. Specifications include initial timing. At high altitudes, add 5°.
1995 1834cc & 2350cc Calif. Expo and all Montero, higher advance is measured at 2500 rpm.

Engine	Year	Degrees	
		Idle	2000 RPM
1468cc FI	1989-90	8-12	26-34
	1991-92	7-13	13-38
	1993-96	2-18	25-45
	1997	2-18	36-56
	1998-00	2-18	30-50
1597cc	1989	5-15	30-38
	1990-92	5-15	32-40
1755cc	1990-94	8-12	26-34
1834cc: Expo	1992-95	0-13	10-30
Calif.	1995	0-13	22-42
Mirage	1993-95	0-13	20-40
Calif.	1995	0-13	22-42
1834cc	1996-00	0-13	22-42
Calif.	1996-00	2-18	30-50
1997cc: SOHC	1989-92	5-15	30-40
	1993	2-18	24-44

ACTUATORS, OUTPUT Continued
COMPUTER TIMING ADVANCE Continued

Engine	Year	Degrees	
		Idle	2000 RPM
1997cc DOHC	1989-94	5-15	33-41
Turbo	1990-94	5-15	30-40
	1995-99	0-13	20-40
2350cc Eclipse	1996-99	2-18	27-47
2350cc Galant	1994-99	2-18	27-47
	1999-00	2-18	15-35
2350cc Van	1989	5-15	35-43
2350cc Pickup	1990-96	6-12	36-42
2350cc Expo	1992	0-16	33-53
	1993-94	2-18	24-44
	1995	0-16	33-53
Calif.	1995	0-18	27-47
2350cc Expo	1996	2-18	24-44
2350cc Montero Sport	1997-99	2-18	15-35
2972cc Sigma	1989-90	13-20	27-31
Montero	1989	13-20	38-42
2972cc Montero, Pickup	1990-94	13-20	25-31
	1995-96	2-18	19-39
	1997-00	7-23	27-47
2972cc Diamante	1992-96	7-23	18-38
DOHC	1992-96	7-23	30-50
2972cc Galant, Eclipse	1999-00	7-23	28-48
2972cc 3000GT:			
SOHC	1997-99	7-23	13-39
DOHC	1991-92	7-23	30-40
	1993-95	7-23	30-50
	1996-99	7-23	32-52
Turbo	1991-92	7-23	28-35
	1993-95	7-23	23-43
	1996-99	7-23	25-45
3497cc Montero	1994-96	2-18	18-38
	1997-00	7-23	30-50
3497cc Montero Sport	1999-00	2-18	27-47
3497cc Diamante	1997-00	2-18	15-35

ENGINE IDENTIFICATION

To identify any engine by the manufacturer's code, follow the four steps designated by the numbered blocks.

V.I.N. PLATE LOCATION:

V.I.N. number appears on plate attached to instrument panel visible through windshield.

1 MODEL YEAR IDENTIFICATION:

10th character of V.I.N.

2000—Y	1999—X	1998—W
1997—V	1996—T	1995—S
1994—R	1993—P	1992—N
1991—M	1990—L	1989—K

2 ENGINE CODE LOCATION:

1989-92 All — 4th character of V.I.N.
1993-00 Villager — 8th character of V.I.N.
1993-00 Others — 4th character of V.I.N.

4 ENGINE IDENTIFICATION

YEAR	3 ENGINE CODE	CYL.	DISPL. liters	DISPL. cc	Fuel System	HP
1999-00	A (GA16)	4	1.6	1597	MFI	115
	B (SR20)	4	2.0	1998	MFI	140
	D (KA24)	4	2.4	2389	MFI	150
	C (VQ30)	6	3.0	2988	MFI	190
	T (VG33)	6	3.3	3275	MFI	170
	A (VG33)	6	3.3	3275	MFI	170
1998	A (GA16)	4	1.6	1597	MFI	115
	B (SR20)	4	2.0	1998	MFI	140
	D (KA24)	4	2.4	2389	MFI	150
	A (KA24)	4	2.4	2389	MFI	155
	1 (VG30)	6	3.0	2960	MFI	151-153[1]
	C (VQ30)	6	3.0	2988	MFI	190
	A (VG33)	6	3.3	3275	MFI	168
1997	A (GA16)	4	1.6	1597	MFI	115
	B (SR20)	4	2.0	1998	MFI	140
	S (KA24)	4	2.4	2389	MFI	134
	B (KA24)	4	2.4	2389	MFI	150
	A (KA24)	4	2.4	2389	MFI	155
	W (VG30)	6	3.0	2960	MFI	151-153[1]
	C (VQ30)	6	3.0	2988	MFI	190
	A (VG33)	6	3.3	3275	MFI	168
1995-96	A (GA16)	4	1.6	1597	MFI	115
	B (SR20)	4	2.0	1998	MFI	140
	S (KA24)	4	2.4	2389	MFI	134
	B (KA24)	4	2.4	2389	MFI	150
	A (KA24)	4	2.4	2389	MFI	155
	W (VG30)	6	3.0	2960	MFI	151
	H, I (VG30)	6	3.0	2960	MFI	160
	R (VG30)	6	3.0	2960	MFI	222
	C (VG30ET)	6	3.0[1]	3960 T	MFI	300
	C (VQ30)	6	3.0	2988	MFI	190
	A (VG33)	6	3.3	3275	MFI	168
1993-94	E (GA16)	4	1.6	1597	MFI	110
	G (SR20)	4	2.0	1998	MFI	140
	S (KA24)	4	2.4	2389	MFI	134
	B (KA24)	4	2.4	2389	MFI	150
	M (KA24)	4	2.4	2389	MFI	155
	W (VG30)	6	3.0	2960	MFI	151

4 ENGINE IDENTIFICATION

YEAR	3 ENGINE CODE	CYL.	DISPL. liters	DISPL. cc	Fuel System	HP
1993-94 Cont'd.	H, I (VG30)	6	3.0	2960	MFI	155, 160
	E (VE30)	6	3.0	2960	MFI	190
	R (VG30)	6	3.0	2960	MFI	222
	C (VG30ET)	6	3.0	2960	MFI	280, 300
1992	E (GA16)	4	1.6	1597	MFI	110
	G (SR20)	4	2.0	1998	MFI	140
	F (KA24)	4	2.4	2389	MFI	138, 140[1]
	S (KA24)	4	2.4	2389	MFI	134
	M (KA24)	4	2.4	2389	MFI	155
	H, I (VG30)	6	3.0	2960	MFI	153, 160
	E (VG30)	6	3.0	2960	MFI	190
	R (VG30)	6	3.0	2960	MFI	222
	C (VG30ET)	6	3.0 T	2960 T	MFI	300
1991	E (GA16)	4	1.6	1597	MFI	110
	G (SR20)	4	2.0	1998	MFI	140
	F (KA24)	4	2.4	2389	MFI	138
	M (KA24)	4	2.4	2389	MFI	155
	S (KA24)	4	2.4	2389	MFI	134
	H, I (VG30)	6	3.0	2960	MFI	153
	R (VG30)	6	3.0	2960	MFI	222
	C (VG30)	6	3.0 T	2960 T	MFI	300
1990	G (GA16)	4	1.6	1597	TBI	90
	C (CA18)	4	1.8	1809	MFI	125
	F (KA24)	4	2.4	2389	MFI	138
	H (KA24)	4	2.4	2389	MFI	140
	S (KA24)	4	2.4	2389	MFI	134
	H, I (VG30)	6	3.0	2960	MFI	153
	H, I (VG30)	6	3.0	2960	MFI	165
	R (VG30)	6	3.0	2960	MFI	222
	C (VG30ET)	6	3.0 T	2960 T	MFI	300
1989	G (GA16)	4	1.6	1577	TBI	90
	C (CA18)	4	1.8	1809	MFI	125
	H, I (CA20)	4	2.0	1974	MFI	94
	N (Z24)	4	2.4	2389	TBI	106
	H (KA24)	4	2.4	2389	MFI	140
	H, I (VG30)	6	3.0	2960	TBI or MFI	145-160[1]
	C (VG30ET)	6	3.0 T	2960 T	MFI	205

D—Diesel.   T—Turbo.   TBI—Throttle Body Injection.
MFI—Multiport Fuel Injection.   2V—Two Venturi Carburetor.
1 Engine horsepower varies with model installation.

UNDERHOOD SERVICE SPECIFICATIONS

DNITU1   DNITU1

CYLINDER NUMBERING SEQUENCE

4-CYL. FIRING ORDER: 1 3 4 2

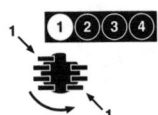

— Front of car —

| 1989-90 Sentra, Pulsar 1597cc | 1991-99 1597cc Sentra, NX | 1991-99 1998cc Sentra, NX | 1995-99 1988cc Sentra, 200SX | 1989 8-plug 200SX, Pickup, Pathfinder, Van 1809cc, 1952cc, 1974cc, 2389cc | 1989-90 Stanza, Multi 1974cc |

UNDERHOOD SERVICE SPECIFICATIONS

CYLINDER NUMBERING SEQUENCE

4-CYL. FIRING ORDER: 1 3 4 2   **V6 FIRING ORDER: 1 2 3 4 5 6**

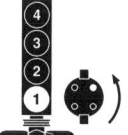    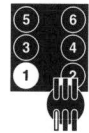 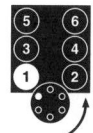

— Front of car —

1990-00 Pickup, Frontier, Xterra 2389cc	**1989-98** 240SX 2389cc	**1990-96** Altima, Axxess, Stanza 2389cc	**1997-00** Altima 2389cc	**1989** 300ZX, Pickup, Pathfinder 2960cc	**1990-96** Pickup, Pathfinder 2960cc

V6 FIRING ORDER: 1 2 3 4 5 6

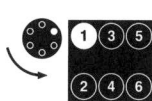  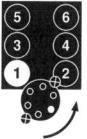

— Front of car —

1993-00 Quest 2960cc, 3275cc	**1989-94** Maxima 2960cc SOHC	**1995-00** Maxima 2988cc	**1996-00** Pathfinder, Frontier, Xterra 3275cc

— TIMING MARK —

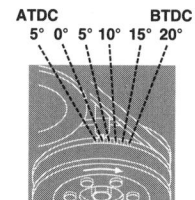 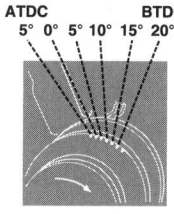 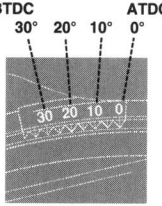 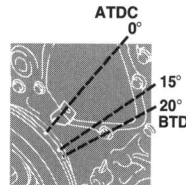 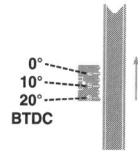

1989 Pulsar 1598cc, 1809cc DOHC; 1989 Stanza 1809cc, 1974cc; 1989-99 Sentra, Pulsar, 200SX 1597cc, 1998cc; 1989-98 240SX 2389cc; 1990-00 Stanza, Axxess, Pickup, Frontier 2389cc; 1993-00 Altima 2389cc; 1996-00 Pathfinder, Frontier, Xterra 3275cc	**1989-98** 2960cc SOHC	**1992-94** 2960cc DOHC Maxima **1990-96** 2960cc DOHC 300ZX	**1995-00** 2988cc Maxima	**1989 Pickup, Pathfinder** 1952cc, 2389cc

ELECTRICAL AND IGNITION SYSTEMS

BATTERY

Specifications given are for the manufacturer's recommended replacement and may vary from the battery supplied as original equipment.

		STANDARD		OPTIONAL	
Engine	Year	BCI Group No.	Crank. Perf.	BCI Group No.	Crank. Perf.
Altima	1993-95	35	350	—	—
Canada	1993-95	24F	585	—	—
Altima	1996-97	24F	550	—	—
Altima	1998-00	25	360	—	—
Canada	1998-00	24	415	—	—
Axxess	1990	35	350	—	—
Axxess					
Canada	1990-92	24F	415	—	—
Frontier: U.S.	1998-00	25	360	—	—
Canada	1998-00	24	415	—	—
Maxima	1989-94	35	355	24F	580
Canada	1989-94	24F	580	27F	620
Maxima: U.S.	1995	35	355	24F	580
Calif.	1995	24	415	—	—
Canada	1995	24F	580	—	—
Maxima: U.S.	1996-00	35	355	24F	580
Canada	1996-00	24F	580	—	—

BATTERY Continued

		STANDARD		OPTIONAL	
Engine	Year	BCI Group No.	Crank. Perf.	BCI Group No.	Crank. Perf.
Pickup, Pathfinder: U.S.	1992-95	25	350	—	—
Canada, 4-cyl.	1992-95	24	415	—	—
Canada, V6	1992-95	27	450	—	—
Pickup: U.S.	1996-97	21R	490	—	—
Canada	1996-97	24F	550	—	—
Pathfinder: U.S.	1996-00	25	355	27	445
Canada	1996-00	27	445	—	—
Pulsar	1989-90	35	380	—	—
Canada	1989-90	24F	435	—	—
Quest: U.S.	1993-95	35	350	—	—
Canada	1993-95	24F	585	—	—
Quest: U.S.	1996-00	35	450	—	—
Canada	1996-00	24F	525	—	—
Sentra	1989-90	35	350	24F	415
Canada	1989-90	24F	415	—	—
Sentra, NX: 1.6L	1991-94	35	350	—	—
Canada	1991-94	24F	415	—	—
2.0L	1991-94	35	350	24F	415
Canada	1991-94	24F	585	—	—
Sentra, 200SX: 1.6L	1995	35	350	—	—
2.0L	1995	35	490	—	—
Sentra, 200SX: U.S.	1996-99	21R	490	—	—
Canada	1996-99	24F	550	—	—

NISSAN
1989-2000

BATTERY Continued

Engine	Year	STANDARD BCI Group No.	STANDARD Crank. Perf.	OPTIONAL BCI Group No.	OPTIONAL Crank. Perf.
Stanza	1989-92	35	350	24F	415
Canada	1989-92	24F	415	—	—
240SX	1989-98	25	350	24	415
Canada	1989-98	24	415	—	—
300ZX	1989	25	380	—	—
Canada	1989	27	470	—	—
300ZX: MT	1990-96	24F	415	—	—
AT	1990-96	24F	580	—	—
AT, Convertible	1993-96	35	355	—	—
Pickup, Pathfinder: 4-cyl.	1989-91	25	380	25	435
V6	1989-91	25	380	27	470
Canada: 4-cyl.	1989-91	25	435	—	—
V6	1989-91	27	470	—	—

SPARK PLUGS

Application	Year	Gap (inches)	Gap (mm)	Torque (ft-lb)
Pickup	1989	.031-.035	.80-.90	14-22
Pulsar DOHC	1989	.043[1]	1.1[1]	14-22
Pickup V6	1990-95	.031-.035	.80-.90	14-22
NX, Sentra, 200SX 1998cc w/o platinum spark plugs	1991-99	.031-.035	.80-.90	14-22
Quest	1993-00	.031-.035	.80-.90	14-22
All Others	1989-00	.039-.043	1.0-1.1	14-22

1 Do not adjust.

IGNITION COIL
FOR TESTING AND ADJUSTMENT DIAGRAMS, SEE APPENDIX A.

Resistance (ohms @ 68°F or 20°C).

Engine	Year	Windings	Resistance (ohms)
1597cc	1989-90	Primary	0.84-1.02
		Secondary	8200-12,400
	1991-94	Primary	0.9 approx.
		Secondary	13,000 approx.
	1995-99	Primary	1.0 approx.
		Secondary	10,000 approx.
1998cc	1991-94	Primary	1.0 approx.
		Secondary	10,000 approx.
	1995-99	Primary	0.5-1.0
		Secondary	25,000 approx.
2389cc Altima, Frontier, Xterra	1992-00	Primary	1.0 approx.
		Secondary	10,000 approx.
2389cc 240SX	1990-94	Primary	1.0 approx.
		Secondary	10,000 approx.
	1995-98	Primary	1.0 approx.
		Secondary	26,000 approx.
2389cc Axxess, Pickup, Pathfinder, Stanza	1990-96	Primary	0.7 approx.
		Secondary	8000 approx.
2389cc Pickup	1997	Primary	1.0 approx.
		Secondary	7000-13,000
2960cc Maxima SOHC	1990-94	Primary	1.0 approx.
		Secondary	8200-12,400
2960cc Maxima DOHC	1992-94	Primary	0.8 approx.
2960cc Pickup, Pathfinder, Quest	1990-98	Primary	1.0 approx.
		Secondary	10,000 approx.
2960cc 300ZX	1990-95	Primary	0.7 approx.
		Secondary	8000 approx.
	1996	Primary	0.9 approx.
		Secondary	8000 approx.
3275cc	1996-00	Primary	1.0 approx.
		Secondary	10,000 approx.
All Others	1989	Primary	0.8-1.0
		Secondary	7600-11,400

GENERATOR

Application	Year	Rated Output (amps)	Test Output (amps @ eng. rpm)
Altima	1993-97	80	63 @ 2500
	1998-00	100	71 @ 2500
Axxess	1990-92	70	50 @ 2500
Frontier	1998-00	70	54 @ 2500
Maxima	1989-94	90	63 @ 2500
DOHC	1992-94	95	80 @ 2500
Maxima	1995	125	94 @ 2500
Maxima	1996	125	94 @ 2500
California	1996	110	82 @ 2500
Maxima	1997-00	100	83 @ 2500
		110	85 @ 2500
Micra	1989-91	50	42 @ 2500
NX: 1.6L	1991-93	70	50 @ 2500
2.0L	1991-93	80	63 @ 2500
Pathfinder	1996-98	90	65 @ 2500
	1999-00	100	78 @ 2500
Pickup, Pathfinder	1989	60	50 @ 2500
Pickup, Pathfinder	1990-95	60	48 @ 2500
V6		70	50 @ 2500
Pickup	1996-97	60	48 @ 2500
Quest	1993-98	110	85 @ 2500
	1999-00	125	90 @ 2500
Sentra, Pulsar	1989	60	50 @ 2500
		70	50 @ 2500
Sentra, Pulsar	1990	65	50 @ 2500
Canada	1990	70	50 @ 2500
Sentra, 200SX: 1.6L	1991-96	70	50 @ 2500
2.0L	1991-96	80	63 @ 2500
Sentra, 200SX	1997-99	80	65 @ 2500
Stanza, Multi	1989	70	50 @ 2500
Stanza	1990-92	70	50 @ 2500
		80	60 @ 2500
Xterra	2000	70	54 @ 2500
240SX	1989-94	80	60 @ 2500
	1995-98	80, 90	65 @ 2500
300ZX	1989	70	50 @ 2500
300ZX	1990-96	80	65 @ 2500
Turbo	1990-96	90	65 @ 2500

REGULATOR

Application	Year	Test Temp. (deg. F/C)	Voltage Setting
1974cc 200SX, Pickup	1989	68/20	14.4-15.0
All Others	1989	68/20	14.1-14.7
All	1990-00	68/20	14.1-14.7

DISTRIBUTOR PICKUP

Engine	Year	Resistance (ohms)	Air Gap (in./mm)
1237cc	1989-91	970-1170	—

UNDERHOOD SERVICE SPECIFICATIONS

TIMING PROCEDURE
FOR TESTING AND ADJUSTMENT DIAGRAMS, SEE APPENDIX C.

1989-95 1597cc FI: Check timing against specified value. Disconnect throttle position sensor harness before adjusting.

1989-90 1598cc, 1809cc DOHC: Remove spark plug/coil cover. Connect inductive clamp to wire between #1 coil and spark plug. Rotate crankshaft position sensor to adjust.

1990-95 1998cc, 2389cc
1996-00 All:
Disconnect throttle position sensor harness before adjusting.

1990-96 2960cc 300ZX: Remove #1 coil from mount and install a longer high tension wire. Connect inductive clamp to high tension wire. Rotate crankshaft position sensor to adjust.

1989 All Others: Set timing to specified value.

BASE TIMING
Set timing at slow idle and Before Top Dead Center, unless otherwise specified.

Application	Year	Man. Trans. (degrees) @ RPM	Auto. Trans. (degrees) @ RPM
1597cc FI: Checking	1989-90	7±5	7±5
Adjusting	1989-90	7	7
1597cc	1991-94	10±2	10±2
	1995-99	8±2	8±2
1598cc, 1809cc DOHC	1989-90	15±2	15±2
1974cc	1989	15±2	15±2
1998cc	1991-99	15±2	15±2
2389cc Pickup, Pathfinder	1989-98	10±2	10±2
2389cc Others	1989-90	15±2	15±2
2389cc Altima, 240SX, Frontier, Xterra	1991-00	20±2	20±2
2389cc Stanza	1991-92	15±2	15±2
2960cc Pickup, Pathfinder	1989	12±2	12±2
2960cc Maxima	1989	15±2	20±2
2960cc 300ZX	1989	15±2	20±2
Turbo	1989	10±2	15±2
2960cc Maxima, Pickup, Pathfinder	1990-95	15±2	15±2
2960cc Quest	1993-98	15±2	15±2
2960cc 300ZX	1990-95	15±2	15±2
2960cc 300ZX	1996	10±2	10±2
Turbo	1996	15±2	15±2
2988cc	1995-99	15[1]±2	15[1]±2
3275cc	1996-00	15±2	15±2

1 Not adjustable.

FUEL SYSTEM

FUEL SYSTEM PRESSURE
FOR TESTING AND ADJUSTMENT DIAGRAMS, SEE APPENDIX D.

All carbureted & TBI, measured at fuel inlet fitting on unit.

All MFI, measured between fuel filter and metal pipe. Values are approximate pressure.

Engine	Year	Pressure PSI	RPM
Carbureted & TBI:			
1597cc	1989-90	43[1]	idle
		34[2]	idle
2389cc	1989	36	idle
2960cc TBI	1989	36	idle
Fuel Injected (MFI):			
1597cc, 1998cc	1991-94	43	36	idle
	1995-99	43	34	idle
1809cc DOHC	1989-90	43	36	idle
1974cc	1989	43	37	idle
2389cc	1989-00	43	34	idle
2960cc Maxima	1989-94	43	36	idle
2960cc 300ZX	1989	37	30	idle
Turbo	1989	44	30	idle
2960cc 300ZX	1990-96	43	36	idle

FUEL SYSTEM PRESSURE Continued

Engine	Year	Pressure[1] (approx.)	Pressure[2] (approx.)	RPM
2960cc Pickup, Quest Pathfinder, Altima	1990-98	43	34	idle
2988cc	1995-00	43	34	idle
3275cc All	1996-00	43	34	idle

1 Without vacuum applied to fuel pressure regulator.
2 With vacuum applied to fuel pressure regulator.

IDLE SPEED W/O COMPUTER CONTROL
Preferred setting is the midpoint of ranges given.

With engine warm, turn idle speed adjusting screws to obtain specified rpm.

Allow engine to warm up, race engine several times. With FI, disconnect fast idle control device (FICD). Adjust throttle screw to obtain specified rpm.

Engine	Year	SLOW Man. Trans.	SLOW Auto. Trans.	FAST Man. Trans.	FAST Auto. Trans.	Step of Cam
2389cc Pickup, Pathfinder	1989	750-850	600-700 D	—	—	—
A/C speed-up	1989	850-950	850-950 N			
2960cc Pickup	1989	750-850	650-750 D	—	—	—
A/C speed-up	1989	850-950	850-950 D			
2960cc 300ZX	1989	650-750	650-750 D	—	—	—
High Altitude	1989	600-700	600-700 D	—	—	—
A/C speed-up, all	1989	750-850	750-850 D			

1 Checking figure, cannot be adjusted.

IDLE SPEED W/COMPUTER CONTROL
FOR TESTING AND ADJUSTMENT DIAGRAMS, SEE APPENDIX E.
Midpoint of range given is the preferred setting speed.

1989-00 1597cc FI, 1998cc, 2389cc, 1993-94 2960cc 300ZX ex. Turbo, 1995-96 2960cc 300ZX, Trucks; 1996-99 2960cc Quest 2988cc Maxima, 3275cc all:
With engine at operating temperature disconnect throttle position sensor harness connector. Start engine and set idle to specified setting speed. Turn engine off, reconnect harness and restart engine. Verify that idle speed is within checking speed. Turn on A/C and verify that idle increases to specified value.

1989 2960cc Turbo, 1989 1598cc, 1809cc DOHC:
With engine at operating temperature, turn ignition off and disconnect automatic air control (AAC) valve harness. Start engine and set idle to specified value. Switch engine off and reconnect harness. Restart engine and check idle speed against specified value. Turn A/C on and verify that speed-up is at specified value. All engines, turn A/C on and verify that speed-up speed is at specified value.

1989 1974cc Stanza:
Disconnect throttle valve and automatic air control valve harness. Start engine and adjust idle to specified setting speed. Turn engine off, reconnect harness and restart engine. Verify that idle is at specified checking speed.

1989-94 2960cc Maxima SOHC:
Turn diagnostic selector screw on ECM fully clockwise. Adjust idle to specified value. Turn selector screw fully counterclockwise and verify that idle is at specified checking value. Turn A/C on and verify that idle increases to specified value.

1990-94 2960cc Trucks
1990-92 2960cc 300ZX; 1993-94 2960cc 300XZ Turbo; 1993-95 2960cc Quest:
Disconnect IACV and set idle to specified value.

1990-96 2960cc 300ZX:
Attach inductive clamp to loop wire on power transistor behind upper radiator hose. Disconnect IAC and set idle to specified value.

All models: After checking/adjusting idle speed, reinstate connections and turn A/C on. Verify that speed increases to specified value.

IDLE SPEED W/COMPUTER CONTROL Continued

Engine	Year	Transmission	Setting Speed	Checking Speed	Speed-up Speed
1597cc 2WD	1989-90	MT	675-775	700-900	950-1150
Sentra	1989	AT	575-675 D	600-800 D	950-1150 N
Sentra	1990	AT	750-850 N	800-1000 N	950-1150 N
Pulsar	1989-90	AT	575-675 D	650-850 D	900-1100 N
1597cc 4WD	1989-90	MT	675-775	700-900	900-1100
	1989	AT	575-675 D	600-800 D	900-1100 N
	1990	AT	750-850 N	800-1000 N	900-1100 N
1597cc U.S.	1991-94	MT	550-650	600-700	600-700
Canada	1991-94	MT	550-650	700-800	700-800
All	1991-94	AT	675-775 N	750-850 N	750-850 N
1597cc	1995-99	MT	575-675	625-725	900 min.
Canada	1995-99	MT	575-675	700-800	900 min.
All	1995-99	AT	675-775 N	750-850 N	900 N min.
1809cc DOHC	1989-90	MT	700-800	750-850	950-1050
		AT	600-700	650-750 D	950-1050 N
1809cc Turbo	1989	MT	700	700-800	1000-1050
1974cc Stanza	1989	MT	650-750	700-800	950-1050
		AT	550-650 D	650-750 D	950-1050 N
1998cc	1991-94	MT	700-800	750-850	800-900
		AT	700-800 N	750-850 N	800-900 N
	1995-99	MT	700-800	750-850	850 min.
		AT	700-800 N	750-850 N	850 N min.
2389cc 240SX	1989	MT	650-750	700-800	950-1050
From eng. KA24-012039	1989-90	MT	600-700	650-750	950-1050
	1989-90	AT	650-750 N	700-800 N	950-1050 N
2389cc 240SX	1991-94	MT	600-700	650-750	950-1050
		AT	600-700 N	650-750 N	950-1050 N
	1995-96	MT	600-700	650-750	1000 min.
		AT	600-700 N	650-750 N	1000 N min.
	1997-98	MT	600-700	650-750	800 min.
		AT	600-700 N	650-750 N	800 N min.
2389cc Altima	1993-94	MT	600-700	650-750	750-850
		AT	600-700 N	650-750 N	750-850 N
	1995-00	MT	600-700	650-750	800 min.
		AT	600-700 N	650-750 N	800 N min.
2389cc Axxess, Stanza: U.S.	1990-92	MT	600-700	650-750	—
		AT	600-700 N	650-750 N	—
Canada	1990-92	MT	600-700	700-800	—
		AT	600-700 N	700-800 N	—
2389cc Frontier, Xterra	1998-00	MT	700-800	750-850	875 min.
		AT	700-800 N	750-850 N	875 N min.
2389cc Pickup, Pathfinder	1990-92	MT	700-800	750-850	800-900
		AT	700-800 N	750-850 N	800-900 N
2389cc Pickup, Pathfinder	1993-95	MT	700-800	750-850	—
	1993-95	AT	700-800 N	750-850 N	—
	1996-97	MT	700-800	750-850	900 min.
		AT	700-800 N	750-850 N	900 N min.
2960cc 300ZX Turbo	1989	MT	650	650-750	750-850
		AT	600 D	600-700 D	750-850 D
2960cc Maxima SOHC	1989-91	MT	700	700-800	750-850
	1989-94	AT	700 N	700-800 N	750-850 N
2960cc Maxima DOHC	1992-94	MT	650-750	700-800	750-850
	1992-93	AT	650-750 N	700-800 N	750-850 N
	1994	AT	650-750 N	740-840 N	750-850 N
2960cc Trucks	1990-95	MT	700	700-800	750-850
		AT	700 N	700-800 N	750-850 N
2960cc 300ZX	1990-94	MT	650	650-750	750-850
		AT	720 N	720-820 N	750-850 N
Turbo	1990-94	MT	650	650-750	800-900
		AT	700 N	700-800 N	800-900 N
2960cc 300ZX	1995-96	MT	600-700	650-750	800 min.
		AT	670-770 N	720-820 N	800 N min.
Turbo: U.S.	1995-96	MT	600-700	650-750	850 min.
Canada		MT	650-750	700-800	850 min.
		AT	650-750 N	700-800 N	800-900 N
2960cc Quest	1993-95	AT	650-750 N	700-800 N	750-850 N
	1996-98	AT	650-750 N	700-800 N	800 N min.
2988cc Maxima	1995-99	MT	550-650	600-700	850 min.
		AT	600-700 N	650-750 N	850 N min.
3275cc All	1996-00	MT	650-750	700-800	850 min.
		AT	650-750 N	700-800 N	850 N min.

ENGINE MECHANICAL

TIGHTENING TORQUES
FOR CYLINDER HEAD TORQUE SEQUENCES AND DIAGRAMS, SEE APPENDIX F.
Some fasteners are tightened in more than one step.

		TORQUE FOOT-POUNDS/NEWTON METERS				
Engine	Year	Cylinder Head	Intake Manifold	Exhaust Manifold	Crankshaft Pulley	Water Pump
1597cc	1989-90	22/29, 47/64[1]	12-15/16-21	12-15/16-21	98-112/132-155	4-6/6-8
1597cc	1991-99	22/29, 43/59[2]	12-15/16-21	12-15/16-21	98-112/132-152	5-6/6-8
1598cc, 1809cc DOHC	1989-90	22/29 76/103[3]	14-19/20-25	27-35/37-48	105-112/142-152	12-14/16-20
1809cc Turbo, 1974cc 200SX, Stanza	1989	22/29, 58/78[4]	14-19/19-25	14-22/20-29	90-98/123-132	12-14/16-20
1998cc	1991-99	29/39, 58/78[6]	13-15/15-21	27-35/37-48	105-112/142-152	12-15/16-21
2389cc	1989-90	22/29, 58/78[7]	12-14/16-20, 17-20/24-27	12-14/16-20	105-112/142-152	12-15/16-21
2389cc Axxess, Stanza, Pickup	1991-95	22/29, 58/78[3]	12-15/16-21	12-15/16-21	87-116/118-157	12-14/16-19
2389cc, Altima, 240SX, Frontier, Xterra	1991-00	22/29, 58/78[3]	12-15/16-21	27-35/37-48	105-112/142-152	12-14/16-19
2960cc Maxima 300ZX SOHC, 200SX	1989-94	22/29, 43/59[8]	13-16/18-22	13-16/18-22	90-98/123-132	12-15/16-21
2960cc 300ZX DOHC	1990-96	29/39, 90/123[9]	12-14/16-20	17-20/24-27	159-174/216-235	12-14/16-19
2960cc Maxima DOHC	1992-94	29/39, +70°[10]	17-20/24-27	17-20/24-27	123-130/167-177	12-15/16-21
2960cc Pickup, Pathfinder, Quest	1989-96	22/29, 43/59[8]	12-14/16-20 17-20/24-27	13-16/18-22 17-20/24-27	90-98/123-132	12-15/16-21
2988cc Maxima	1995-99	72/98[11]	13-16/18-22	22-24/30-32	14/22, +60°	5-7/7-10
3275cc All	1996-00	22/29, 43/59[8]	13-16/18-22	21-25/28-33	141-156/181-211	12-15/16-21

1 Loosen fasteners, retorque to 22/29, then 51-54/69-74.
2 Loosen fasteners, retorque to 22/29, then turn an additional 50°. Small bolts outside of valve cover torque to 4-6/6-8.
3 Loosen fasteners, retorque to 22/29, then turn an additional 85-90°.
4 Loosen fasteners, retorque to 22/29, then 54-61/74-83.
5 Loosen fasteners, retorque to 22/29, then turn an additional 90-95°.
6 Loosen fasteners, retorque to 29/39, then turn an additional 90°, and again turn 90°.
7 Loosen fasteners, retorque to 22/29, then turn an additional 80-85°(or 54-61/74-83).
8 Loosen fasteners, retorque to 22/29, then turn an additional 60-65°.
9 Loosen fasteners, retorque to 25-33/34-44, then turn bolts an additional 70° (or 90/123).
10 Loosen fasteners, retorque to 29/39, then turn an additional 70° (or 87-94/ 118-127).
11 Loosen fasteners, retorque to 22-24/30-32, then turn 90°, then another 90°.

UNDERHOOD SERVICE SPECIFICATIONS

VALVE CLEARANCE
Set with engine hot.

Engine	Year	Intake (inches)	Intake (mm)	Exhaust (inches)	Exhaust (mm)
1597cc	1991-94	.015	.37	.016	.40
	1995-99	.013-.016	.32-.40	.015-.018	.37-.45
1809cc Turbo, 2389cc	1989	.012	.30	.012	.30
2389cc, Altima, Frontier, Xterra	1993-00	.012-.015	.31-.39	.013-.016	.33-.41
2389cc 240SX	1991-97	.012-.015	.31-.39	.013-.016	.33-.41
2988cc Maxima	1995-96	.012-.013	.30-.34	.011-.015	.30-.37

COMPRESSION PRESSURE
At cranking speed, engine warm, throttle open.

Engine	Year	PSI	Maximum Variation PSI
1237cc Micra, 1597cc Sentra, Pulsar	1989-90	142-181	14
1597cc	1991-94	164-192	14
	1995-99	171-199	14
1598cc, 1809cc DOHC	1989-90	156-185	14
1809cc Turbo, 1974cc ex. Pickup	1989	128-171	14
1974cc, 2389cc Pickup	1989	128-171	1
1998cc	1991-99	149-178	14
2389cc Altima, Frontier, Xterra	1993-00	149-178	14
2389cc 240SX	1989-90	142-192	14
2389cc 240SX	1991-98	151-179	14
2389cc Pickup, Pathfinder	1990-97	142-192	14
2389cc Axxess, Stanza	1989-92	146-175	14
2960cc ex. Turbo	1989	128-179	14
Turbo	1989	121-169	14
2960cc 300ZX ex. Turbo	1990-96	142-186	14
Turbo	1990-96	128-171	14
2960cc Maxima DOHC	1992-95	142-185	14
2960cc Trucks, Quest	1990-98	128-173	14
2988cc	1995-99	142-185	14
3275cc	1996-00	128-173	14

1 Lowest cylinder pressure must be more than 80% of highest cylinder pressure.

BELT TENSION
A belt in operation 20 minutes is considered a used belt.
Deflection midway between pulleys with an applied load of 22 lb.

Engine	Year	Generator	Power Steering	Air Cond.
Deflection Method:				
1597cc Sentra (inches)	1989	11/32-3/8	9/32-11/32	11/32-3/8
(mm)	1989	8.5-9.5	7-9	9-10
1597cc Pulsar (inches)	1989	11/32-3/8	13/32	1/2
(mm)	1989	8.5-9.5	10.5	12.5
1597cc Pulsar (inches)	1989	11/32-3/8	9/32-11/32	11/32-3/8
(mm)	1989	8.5-9.5	7-9	9-10
1597cc (inches)	1990-98	9/32-5/16	5/32-1/4	5/32-1/4
(mm)	1990-98	7-9	4-6	4-6
1598cc, 1809cc DOHC (inches)	1989-90	1/4-5/16	9/32-11/32	1/8-5/32
(mm)	1989-90	6-8	7-9	3-4
1974cc Stanza (inches)	1989	7/32-9/32	9/32-11/32	1/8-5/32
(mm)	1989	5-7	7-9	3-4
1998cc (inches)	1991-98	9/32-5/16	9/32-5/16	5/32-7/32
(mm)	1991-98	7-8	7-8	4-5
2389cc Pickup (inches)	1989-96	7/32-9/32	3/8-7/16	3/8-7/16
(mm)	1989-96	5-7	9-11	11-13

BELT TENSION Continued

Engine	Year	Generator	Power Steering	Air Cond.
2389cc 240SX (inches)	1989-92	9/32-5/16	5/16-3/8	9/32-5/16
(mm)	1989-92	7-8	8-9	7-8
2389cc 240SX (inches)	1993-98	1/4-9/32	1/4-9/32	1/4-9/32
(mm)	1993-98	6-7	6-7	6-7
2389cc Altima (inches)	1993-98	1/4-9/32	1/4-9/32	1/4-5/16
(mm)	1993-98	6-7	6-7	7-8
2389cc Axxess (inches)	1990-92	7/32-5/16	7/32-5/16	5/32-7/32
(mm)	1990-92	5-6	5-6	4-5
2389cc Stanza (inches)	1990-92	1/4-9/32	1/4-9/32	3/16-1/4
(mm)	1990-92	6-7	6-7	5-6
2960cc, 300ZX (inches)	1989-96	5/16-3/8	1/2-5/8	3/8-7/16
(mm)	1989-96	7-9	13-16	9-11
2960cc, Quest, Maxima (inches)	1989-98	5/16-3/8	7/16-5/32	7/32-5/16
(mm)	1989-98	7-9	10-12	5-7
2960cc Pickup (inches)	1989-95	7/32-9/32	3/8-7/16	9/32-3/8
(mm)	1989-95	5-7	9-11	7-9
2988cc (inches)	1995-98	1/4-9/32	9/32-9/16	5/32-3/16
(mm)	1995-98	6-7	7-8	4-5
3275cc (inches)	1996-98	1/4-5/32	11/32-7/16	11/32-3/8
(mm)	1996-98	6-7	9-11	9-10
Strand Tension Method:				
NEW:				
1597cc	1999	150-165	135-155	150-165
1998cc	1999	150-170	150-170	170-190
2389cc Altima	1999-00	170-190	170-190	150-170
Frontier	1999-00	110-130	110-130	110-130
2988cc	1999-00	180-200	100-120	135-155
3275cc Quest	1999-00	170-190	150-170	150-170
Pathfinder	1999-00	—		
USED:				
1597cc	1999	120-140	110-130	120-140
1998cc	1999	125-145	125-145	145-165
2389cc Altima	1999-00	145-165	145-165	125-145
Frontier	1999-00	80-100	80-100	80-100
2988cc	1999-00	165-185	165-185	110-130
3275cc Quest	1999-00	145-165	125-145	125-145
Pathfinder	1999-00	—	—	—

ENGINE COMPUTER SYSTEM

DIAGNOSTIC TROUBLE CODES
FOR TESTING AND ADJUSTMENT DIAGRAMS, SEE APPENDIX G.

1989 All ex. Maxima:

1989 Pickup, Pathfinder, Van: With engine running, access ECM and turn diagnostic mode switch on. After LEDs flash three times, turn switch off. After obtaining codes, turn mode switch on. After LEDs flash four times, turn mode switch and ignition switch off.

1991-98 All ex. Trucks & Maxima SOHC 1995 300ZX, Quest: With ignition on, access ECM under dash. Turn mode selector clockwise, after two seconds turn counterclockwise. Repeat procedure. Codes will be displayed on LEDs similar to other models.

1990 Others, 1991-98 Trucks & Maxima SOHC: With engine running, access ECM and turn mode switch screw fully clockwise. After LEDs flash three times, turn switch fully counterclockwise.

All models: Codes will be displayed on LED and/or "Check" engine light, if equipped. Red LED flashes tens, green LED flashes ones.

1990 300ZX, Stanza; 1991-98 All ex. Trucks & Maxima SOHC: After obtaining codes, turn mode switch clockwise and, after two seconds, counterclockwise.

1990 Others, 1991-98 Trucks & Maxima SOHC: After obtaining codes, turn mode switch fully clockwise. After LEDs flash four times, turn mode switch counterclockwise and turn ignition switch off.
OBD-II system still displays codes on ECM LED or MIL.

UNDERHOOD SERVICE SPECIFICATIONS

DNITU7   DNITU7

DIAGNOSTIC TROUBLE CODES Continued

Code 11 Crankshaft position sensor
Code 12 Mass airflow sensor
Code 13 Engine coolant temperature sensor
Code 14 Vehicle speed sensor
Code 15 Mixture ratio control
Code 21 Ignition signal
Code 22 Fuel pump circuit
Code 23 Idle switch
Code 24 Neutral/clutch switch
Code 25 IAC valve
Code 26 Turbo boost
Code 28 Cooling fan
Code 29 Fuel system rich
Code 31 ECM
Code 32 EGR
Code 33 O_2 sensor 1989 (1989-91 300ZX left side)
Code 33 EGR sensor, 1990-91 others
Code 33 Front oxygen sensor (1996)
Code 34 Knock sensor
Code 36 EGR transducer
Code 37 Closed loop control
Code 41 Intake air temperature sensor
Code 42 TPS (4-cyl.) or fuel temperature sensor (V6)
Code 43 Throttle position sensor
Code 44, 55 System OK
Code 45 Injector leak
Code 51 Injector circuit
Code 53 O_2 sensor (300ZX right side)
Code 54 AT control unit to ECM problem
Code 55 No malfunction
Code 63 Cylinder 6 misfire
Code 64 Cylinder 5 misfire
Code 65 Cylinder 4 misfire
Code 66 Cylinder 3 misfire
Code 67 Cylinder 2 misfire
Code 68 Cylinder 1 misfire
Code 71 Random misfire
Code 72 Catalyst function
Code 74 EVAP pressure sensor
Code 75 EVAP leak
Code 76 FI system
Code 77 Rear oxygen sensor
Code 81 Vacuum cut bypass valve
Code 82 Crankshaft sensor
Code 84 AT to FI communication
Code 85 VTC solenoid
Code 87 EVAP canister purge control
Code 91 Front oxygen sensor
Code 95 Crankshaft sensor
Code 98 Coolant temp. sensor
Code 101 Camshaft sensor
Code 103 P/N switch
Code 105 EGR and canister control valve
Code 108 EVAP volume control
Code 111 EVAP purge
Code 115 Fuel injection system lean
Code 127 Engine speed signal
Code 132 MAP, BARO switch solenoid
Code 138 Cooling fan

SENSORS, INPUT
TEMPERATURE SENSORS

Air temperature sensor, all models with FI, measured between first and last terminal of airflow sensor.

Fuel temperature sensors are attached to the fuel pressure regulator.

Engine	Year	Sensor	Resistance Ohms @ deg. F/C
All	1989-00	Coolant	7000-11,400 @ 14/-10
			2100-2900 @ 68/20
			680-1000 @ 122/50
			300-330 @ 176/80
			235-260 @ 194/90
			140-150 @ 230/110

SENSORS, INPUT Continued
TEMPERATURE SENSORS Continued

Engine	Year	Sensor	Resistance Ohms @ deg. F/C
2389 FI, 2960cc	1989	Cylinder Head	8000-10,000 @ 14/-10
			2300-2700 @ 68/20
			700-900 @ 122/50
			300-330 @ 176/80
2960cc 300ZX 1809cc Turbo,	1989-96	Fuel	8000-10,000 @ 14/-10
1974cc FI	1989	Intake Air	8000-10,000 @ 14/-10
			2300-2700 @ 68/20
			700-900 @ 122/50
			300-330 @ 176/80
1597cc 2V Fed.,			
2389cc SOHC	1989-94	Intake Air	7000-11,400 @ 14/-10
2389cc 240SX	1995		2100-2900 @ 68/20
All	1996-00		680-1000 @ 122/50
			250-400 @ 176/80
2389cc Altima,	1999-00	EGR	6,800,000-11,100,000@32/0
2988cc			900,000-1,200,000@122/50
			17,000-24,000 @ 212/100
All others, as equipped	1989-98	EGR	79,000-97,000 @ 32/0
			5700-7000 @ 212/50
			800-1000 @ 212/100
			100-200 @ 302/150

THROTTLE POSITION SENSOR
5 volts reference.

Engine	Year	Voltage Idle	WOT
1597cc	1989-92	.45-.55	4.0
1597cc	1993-94	.40-.60	4.0
	1995-99	.35-.65	4.0
1598cc, 1809cc DOHC	1989-90	0.5	4.0
1998cc	1991-94	.45-.55	4.0
	1995-99	.35-.65	4.0
2389cc 240SX	1989-90	0.5	4.0
	1991-94	0.4-0.5	4.0
	1995-98	0.3-0.7	4.0
2389cc Stanza, Axxess	1990-92	0.4-0.5	5.0
2389cc Altima	1993-00	0.3-0.7	4.0
2389cc Frontier, Xterra	1998-00	0.2-0.8	3.5-4.5
2389cc Trucks	1989-92	0.4	4.0
2389cc Trucks	1993-97	0.4-0.6	4.0
2960cc Trucks	1989-92	0.5	4.0
	1993-94	0.4	4.0
2960cc 300ZX	1989	0.4	4.0
2960cc 300ZX	1990-95	0.4-0.5	4.0
	1996	.35-.65	4.0
2960cc Maxima SOHC	1989-94	0.5	4.2
DOHC	1992-94	0.4-0.5	4.0
2960cc Quest	1993-98	0.3-0.7	4.0
2960cc Trucks	1990-95	0.4	4.0
2988cc	1995-99	.35-.65	4.0
3275cc	1996-00	0.3-0.7	4.0

MASS AIRFLOW SENSOR
1995-98 Maxima: Connect voltmeter between ECM terminal 54 and ground.
1995-98 Sentra, 200SX, Quest: Connect voltmeter between ECM terminal 47 and ground.

Engine	Year	Voltage @ Idle	Voltage @ 2500 rpm
1597cc	1989-90	1.0 approx.	—
1597cc	1991-94	0.7-1.1	1.1-1.5
	1995-96	0.7-1.1	1.5-2.1
	1997-99	1.0-1.7	1.5-2.1
1598cc, 1809cc DOHC	1989-90	1.5 approx.	—
1998cc	1991-98	1.3-1.7	1.7-2.1
	1999	1.3-1.7	1.8-2.4
2389cc 240SX, Axxess	1989-90	1.0 approx.	—
2389cc 240SX	1991-94	1.0-1.5	1.4-1.9
	1995-98	1.3-1.7	1.7-2.1
2389cc Altima	1993-94	0.85-1.35	1.3-1.8
	1995-97	1.0-1.7	1.5-2.1
	1998-00	1.2-1.5	1.9-2.3
2389cc Frontier, Xterra	1998-00	0.9-1.8	1.9-2.3
2389cc Stanza	1990	0.8-1.5	—
2389cc Stanza	1991-92	1.3-1.8	1.8-2.2
2389cc Trucks	1991-97	1.0-3.0	—
2960cc Maxima SOHC	1989-94	1.0-1.3	1.8-2.0
DOHC	1992-94	0.8-1.5	1.4-1.8
2960cc 300ZX	1989	2.0 approx.	—

UNDERHOOD SERVICE SPECIFICATIONS

DNITU8

DNITU8

SENSORS, INPUT Continued

MASS AIRFLOW SENSOR Continued

Engine	Year	Voltage @ Idle	Voltage @ 2500 rpm
2960cc Trucks	1990-92	1.5-2.0	
2960cc Trucks	1993-97	1.0-3.0	—
2960cc 300ZX	1990-92	0.8-1.5	1.4-1.8
Turbo	1990-92	0.9-1.4	1.4-1.8
2960cc 300ZX	1993-96	0.8-1.5	1.4-1.8
2960cc Quest	1993-95	1.0-1.7	1.4-2.2
	1996-98	1.0-1.7	1.7-2.1
2988cc	1995-00	1.0-1.7	1.5-2.1
3275cc All	1996-00	1.0-1.7	1.7-2.3

CRANKSHAFT & CAMSHAFT POSITION SENSORS

At 77°F (25°C)

Engine	Year	Sensor	Resistance (ohms)
1597cc: MT	1995-99	Crankshaft	430-530
AT	1995-99	Crankshaft	165-205
1998cc	1995-99	Crankshaft	165-205
2389cc: Altima	1996-00	Crankshaft	430-530
240SX	1996-98	Crankshaft	165-205
2960cc Quest	1996-98	Crankshaft	430-530
2960cc 300ZX	1996	Crankshaft	165-205
2988cc Maxima	1995-99	Crankshaft	470-570
Hitachi		Camshaft	1440-1760
Mitsubishi		Camshaft	2090-2550
3275cc All	1996-00	Crankshaft	165-205

ACTUATORS, OUTPUT

IDLE SPEED CONTROL

1995-98 Sentra, 200SX 1597cc: Measure resistance between terminals 2 & 3 and 3 & 4.
1995-98 Maxima: Measure resistance between terminals 2&1 and 2&3, then terminals 5 & 4 and 5 & 6.

Engine	Year	Resistance (ohms)
1597cc; 1598cc, 1809cc DOHC	1989-94	10 approx.
1597cc	1995-98	50-100
	1999	138-238
1974cc	1989	30-40[3]
1998cc	1991-99	10 approx.
2389cc Pickup	1989	30-40
2389cc ex. Pickup	1989	10 approx.
2389cc	1990-97	10 approx.
2389cc 240SX	1998	10 approx.
Altima	1998-00	9.3-9.9
2960cc Maxima: SOHC	1989-94	27-40
DOHC	1991-94	10 approx.
2960cc 300ZX	1989	40
2960cc Pickup, Pathfinder	1989	30-40
2960cc All ex. Maxima	1990-98	10 approx.
2988cc	1995-00	30 approx.
3275cc All	1996-00	10 approx.

1 Measured between terminals A & B.
2 Measured between terminals C & D.
3 Measured between terminals A & B and B & C.

ACTUATORS, OUTPUT Continued

FUEL INJECTORS

Engine	Year	Resistance (ohms)	Temperature (deg. F/C)
1597cc	1989-90	1-2	—
	1991-94	10 approx.	—
	1995-98	10-14	—
1809cc DOHC	1989-90	10-15	—
	1989	2.5	—
1998cc	1991-98	10-14	—
2389cc TBI	1989	1.5	—
2389cc SOHC MFI	1989-94	10-15	—
2389cc DOHC	1991-94	11	—
2389cc ex. Trucks	1995-00	10-14	—
2389cc Trucks	1995-97	10-15	—
	1995-00	10-14	—
2960cc TBI	1989	1.5	—
	1989-98	10-14	—
2988cc, 3275cc	1995-00	10-14	—

AIR REGULATOR CONTROL VALVE

Controls fast idle on FI engines.

Engine	Year	Resistance (ohms)
1597cc, 1998cc	1991-94	70-80
1974cc, 2960cc	1989	30-50
2389cc 240SX	1989-92	70-80
2960cc Pickup, 300ZX, Quest	1990-98	70-80

COMPUTER TIMING ADVANCE

Includes initial timing.

Engine	Year	Advance @ Idle	Advance @ 2000 rpm
1597cc	1991-94	10	20 min.
	1995-96	6-10	25 min.
	1997-99	0-10	25 min.
1998cc	1991-94	15	25 min.
	1995-99	13-15	25 min.
2389cc: Stanza	1991-92	15	25 min.
240SX, Frontier	1991-00	20	25 min.
Altima	1993-97	20	25 min.
	1998-00	12	25 min.
2960cc 300ZX	1990-96	15	25 min.
2960cc Maxima DOHC	1992-94	15	25 min.
2960cc Quest	1993-98	15	25 min.
2988cc	1995-00	15	25 min.
3275cc	1996-00	10	25 min.

OLDSMOBILE
1989-2000
All Models Except Bravada, Silhouette

ENGINE IDENTIFICATION

To identify any engine by the manufacturer's code, follow the four steps designated by the numbered blocks.

1 MODEL YEAR IDENTIFICATION: Refer to illustration of the Vehicle Identification Number (V.I.N.). The year is indicated by a code letter which is the 10th character of the V.I.N.

2 ENGINE CODE LOCATION: Refer to illustration of V.I.N. plate for location and designation of engine code.

3 ENGINE CODE: In the "CODE" column, find the engine code determined in Step 2.

4 ENGINE IDENTIFICATION: On the line where the engine code appears, read to the right to identify the engine.

V.I.N. PLATE LOCATION:

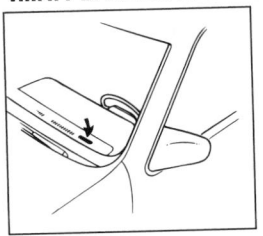

On top left side of instrument panel

Model year of vehicle:
2000 — Y
1999 — X
1998 — W
1997 — V
1996 — T
1995 — S
1994 — R
1993 — P
1992 — N
1991 — M
1990 — L
1989 — K

MODEL YEAR AND ENGINE IDENTIFICATION:

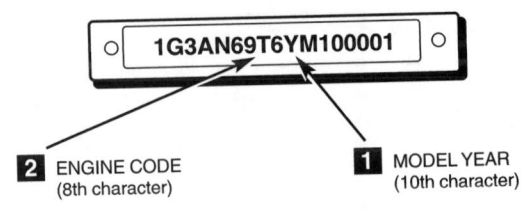

2 ENGINE CODE (8th character)   **1** MODEL YEAR (10th character)

YEAR	**3** ENGINE CODE	CYL.	**4** ENGINE IDENTIFICATION DISPL. liters	cu. in.	Fuel System	HP
2000	T	4	2.4	146	MFI	150
	E	6	3.4	207	MFI	170
	H	6	3.5	212	MFI	215
1999	T	4	2.4	146	MFI	150
	J	6	3.1	191	MFI	170
	M	6	3.1	191	MFI	150
	E	6	3.4	207	MFI	170
	H	6	3.5	212	MFI	215
	K	6	3.8	231	MFI	205
	1	6	3.8	231	MFI	240
	C	8	4.0	243	MFI	250
1998	T	4	2.4	146	MFI	150
	M	6	3.1	191	MFI	155, 160[1]
	K	6	3.8	231	MFI	195, 205[1]
	1	6	3.8	231	MFI	240
	C	8	4.0	243	MFI	250
1997	4	4	2.2	133	MFI	120
	T	4	2.4	146	MFI	150
	M	6	3.1	191	MFI	160
	X	6	3.4	207	MFI	215
	K	6	3.8	231	MFI	205
	1	6	3.8 S	3.8 S	MFI	240
	C	8	4.0	243	MFI	250
1996	4	4	2.2	133	MFI	120
	T	4	2.4	146	MFI	150
	M	6	3.1	191	MFI	160
	X	6	3.4	207	MFI	215
	K	6	3.8	231	MFI	205
	1	6	3.8 S	231 S	MFI	245
	C	8	4.0	243	MFI	250
1995	4	4	2.2	133	MFI	120
	D	4	2.3	138	MFI	150
	M	6	3.1	191	MFI	155, 160[1]
	X	6	3.4	206	MFI	210
	K	6	3.8	231	MFI	205
	1	6	3.8 S	231 S	MFI	225
	C	8	4.0	243	MFI	250
1994	4	4	2.2	133	MFI	120
	3	4	2.3	138	MFI	115
	D	4	2.3	138	MFI	155
	A	4	2.3 HO	138 HO	MFI	170
	M	6	3.1	191	MFI	160
	X	6	3.4	206	MFI	210
	1	6	3.8 S	231 S	MFI	225
	L	6	3.8	231	MFI	170
1993	4	4	2.2	133	MFI	110
	3	4	2.3	138	MFI	115
	D	4	2.3	138	MFI	155

YEAR	**3** ENGINE CODE	CYL.	**4** ENGINE IDENTIFICATION DISPL. liters	cu. in.	Fuel System	HP
1993 Cont'd.	A	4	2.3 HO	138 HO	MFI	175
	T	6	3.1	191	MFI	185
	N	6	3.3	204	MFI	160
	X	6	3.4	207	MFI	200
	1	6	3.8 S	231 S	MFI	205
	L	6	3.8	231	MFI	175
1992	3	4	2.3	138	MFI	120
	D	4	2.3	138	MFI	160
	A	4	2.3 HO	138 HO	MFI	180
	R	4	2.5	151	TBI	110
	T	6	3.1	191	MFI	140
	N	6	3.3	204	MFI	160
	X	6	3.4	207	MFI	200, 210
	1	6	3.8 S	231 S	MFI	205
	L	6	3.8	231	MFI	170
	E	8	5.0	305	TBI	170
	7	8	5.7	350	TBI	180
1991	D	4	2.3	138	MFI	160
	A	4	2.3 HO	138 HO	MFI	180
	R, U	4	2.5	151	TBI	110
	T	6	3.1	191	MFI	140
	N	6	3.3	204	MFI	160
	X	6	3.4	207	MFI	200, 210[1]
	C	6	3.8	231	MFI	165
	L	6	3.8	231	MFI	160
	E	8	5.0	305	TBI	170
1990	D	4	2.3	138	MFI	160
	A	4	2.3 HO	138 HO	MFI	180
	R, U	4	2.5	151	TBI	110
	T	6	3.1	191	MFI	135
	D	6	3.1	191	TBI	120
	N	6	3.3	204	MFI	160
	C	6	3.8	231	MFI	165
	Y	8	5.0	307	4V	140
1989	D	4	2.3	138	MFI	150
	A	4	2.3 HO	138 HO	MFI	180
	R	4	2.5	151	TBI	98
	U	4	2.5	151	TBI	110
	W	6	2.8	173	MFI	130
	T	6	3.1	191	MFI	140
	N	6	3.3	204	MFI	160
	C	6	3.8	231	MFI	165
	Y	8	5.0	307	4V	140

TBI—Throttle Body Injection.   **MFI**—Multiport Fuel Injection.
2V—Two Venturi Carburetor.   **4V**—Four Venturi Carburetor.
HO—High Output.   **S**—Supercharged.
1 Engine horsepower varies with model installation.

UNDERHOOD SERVICE SPECIFICATIONS

CYLINDER NUMBERING SEQUENCE
4-CYL. FIRING ORDER: 1 3 4 2

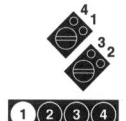

— Front of car —

1989 2.0L (122) 1993-97 2.2L CODE 4	1989-95 2.3L Code A, D 1993-94 2.3L Code 3 1996-00 2.4L Code T	1989-92 2.5L (151)

6-CYL. FIRING ORDER: 2.8L, 3.1L, 3.4L
1 2 3 4 5 6

All Others
1 6 5 4 3 2

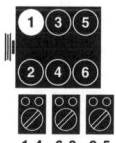

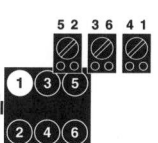

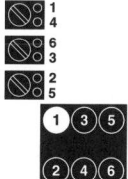

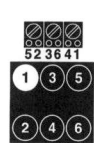

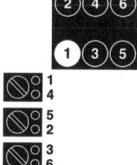

— Front of car —

1989 2.8L (173) 1989-93 3.1L Code T 1991-93 3.4L Code X	1994-99 3.1L Code M 1999 3.1L Code J	1994-95 3.4L Code X	1996-97 3.4L Code X	1999-00 3.4L Code E	1989-92 3.3L Code N

8-CYL. FIRING ORDER:
4.0L Code C 1 2 7 3 4 5 6 8
All Others 1 8 4 3 6 5 7 2

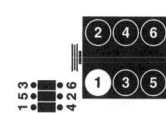

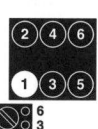

— Front of car —

1999-00 3.5L Code H	1989-91 3.8L Code C 1991-92 3.8L Code L Some	1991-92 3.8L Code L Some 1992-99 3.8L Code 1 1993 3.3L Code N 1993-94 3.8L Code L 1995-99 3.8L Code K	1995-99 4.0L Code C	1991-92 5.0L Code E 1992 5.7L Code 7	1989-90 5.0L (307)

TIMING MARK

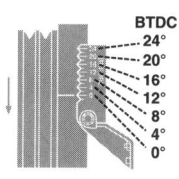

1989-90
5.0L (307)

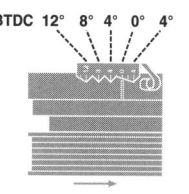

1991-92
5.0L Code E
1992
5.7L Code 7

OLDSMOBILE
1989-2000 All Models
Bravada, Silhouette—See Chevrolet/GMC Trucks

UNDERHOOD SERVICE SPECIFICATIONS

ELECTRICAL AND IGNITION SYSTEMS

BATTERY

Engine	Year	STANDARD BCI Group No.	STANDARD Crank. Perf.	OPTIONAL BCI Group No.	OPTIONAL Crank. Perf.
2.2L	1993-96	75	525	—	—
2.3L	1989-92	75	630	—	—
	1993-95	75	600	—	—
2.4L	1996-00	75	600	—	—
2.5L (151)	1989-92	75	630	—	—
2.8L (173): Ciera	1989	75	525	75	570
Firenza, Calais	1989	75	630	—	—
Cutlass	1989	75	525	—	—
3.1L	1989-93	75	525	—	—
3.1L: Achieva	1994-98	75	600	—	—
Ciera, Cutlass	1994-97	75	525	—	—
	1998-99	75	600	—	—
3.1L Cutlass	1997-98	75	600	—	—
3.3L	1989-92	75	630	—	—
3.3L: Achieva	1993	75	600	—	—
Ciera	1993	75	630	—	—
3.4L DOHC	1991-96	78	690	—	—
	1997	78	690	—	—
3.5L	1998-00	78	690	—	—
3.8L: 88, 98	1989-90	75	630	78	730
Toronado	1989-90	78	730	—	—
3.8L: 88	1991-94	75	630	78	770
	1995-96	78	600	78	770
98	1991-93	75	630	78	770
	1994-96	78	600	78	770
Toronado	1991-92	78	770	—	—
3.8L 88, Regency	1997-98	78	690	78	770
Intrigue	1998	78	690	—	—
4.0L Aurora	1995-97	76	970	—	—
	1998-99	79	880	—	—
5.0L (307) Custom Cruiser	1989	70	525	75	570
5.0L, 5.7L	1990-93	75	525	—	—

GENERATOR
See UNDERHOOD SERVICE INSTRUCTIONS at the beginning of this section for test/adjustment diagrams.

Application	Rated Output (amps)	Test Output (amps)	Field Current Draw (amps @ 12V)
1989-91	74, 85, 100, 105, 108, 120, 124, 140	1	—
1992-00	100, 105, 124, 140	1	—

1 Run engine at moderate speed; output must be within 15 amps of rated output.

REGULATOR

Application	Test Temp. (deg. F/C)	Voltage Setting
1989-95	Warm	13.5-16.0
1996-00	Warm	13.0-16.0

STARTER

Engine	Year	Cranking Voltage (min. volts)	Ampere Draw @ Cranking Speed
All	1989-00	9.0	—

SPARK PLUGS

Engine	Year	Gap (inches)	Gap (mm)	Torque (ft-lb)
2.2L	1993	.045	1.14	11
	1994-96	.060	1.52	11
2.3L	1989-94	.035	.89	17
	1995	.060	1.52	17
2.4L	1996-00	.060	1.52	13

SPARK PLUGS Continued

Engine	Year	Gap (inches)	Gap (mm)	Torque (ft-lb)
2.5L (151)	1989-92	.060	1.52	15
2.8L (173)	1989	.045	1.14	7-15
3.1L Code T, D	1989-94	.045	1.14	11
Code M	1994-99	.060	1.52	15
3.3L	1989-91	.060	1.52	20
	1992-93	.060	1.52	11
3.4L DOHC	1991-97	.045	1.14	11
3.8L Code C, K, L, 1	1989-99	.060	1.52	11
4.0L	1995-99	.060	1.52	11
5.0L, 5.7L	1991-92	.035	.89	11
5.0L (307)	1989-90	.060	1.52	25

IGNITION COIL
FOR TESTING AND ADJUSTMENT DIAGRAMS, SEE APPENDIX A.

Without distributor, primary resistance measured between the two coil primary power wires on each coil.

Secondary resistance, measured across each coil's two towers with coil removed from vehicle.

Application	Year	Resistance (ohms) Primary	Resistance (ohms) Secondary
All w/distributor	1989-92	0-2	6,000-30,000
2.0L, 2.5L, 2.8L, 3.1L, 3.4L	1989-95	—	5,000-10,000
2.2L	1993	—	5,000-10,000
	1994-96	—	5,000-8,000
2.3L	1989-95	—	10,000 max.
2.4L	1996-00	—	5,000-8,000
3.0L, 3.8L: Type I coils[1]	1989-91	.5-.9	10,000-13,000
Type II coils[1]	1991-92	.3-.5	5,000-7,000
3.1L	1996-98	—	5.000-7,000
3.3L	1989-93	.5-.9	5,000-8,000
3.4L	1996-97	—	5,000-8,000
3.8L	1993-99	.5-.9	5,000-8,000
4.0L	1995	.5-.9	—
	1996-99	—	5,000-8,000

1 Type I coils, 3 coil towers on each side of coil pack.
Type II coils, 6 coil towers on one side of coil pack.

DISTRIBUTOR PICKUP
FOR TESTING AND ADJUSTMENT DIAGRAMS, SEE APPENDIX B.

Application	Year	Resistance (ohms)	Air Gap (in./mm)
All	1989-92	500-1500	—

BASE TIMING
FOR TESTING AND ADJUSTMENT DIAGRAMS, SEE APPENDIX C.

Set timing at slow idle and Before Top Dead Center, unless otherwise specified.

All FI w/distributor: disconnect IC bypass connector (single connector, tan/black wire).

5.0L (307), ground diagnostic terminal of DLC

All others w/carburetor, disconnect 4-wire connector at distributor.

Timing MUST be set to specifications on emission label, if different from setting listed. If "Check Engine" light comes on during procedure, remove ECM fuse to clear.

Engine	Year	Man. Trans. (degrees) @ RPM	Auto. Trans. (degrees) @ RPM
5.0L, 5.7L	1991-93	—	0 @ 500 D
5.0L (307)	1989-90	—	20 @ 1100 P

FUEL SYSTEM

FUEL SYSTEM PRESSURE
FOR TESTING AND ADJUSTMENT DIAGRAMS, SEE APPENDIX D.

Carbureted models, pinch off fuel return line.

All models with TBI, pressure measured at fuel inlet of TBI.

All models with MFI, pressure measured at fuel rail.

UNDERHOOD SERVICE SPECIFICATIONS

FUEL SYSTEM PRESSURE Continued

Engine	Year	PSI	RPM
Carbureted, TBI:			
2.0L (122) FI	1989	9.0-13.0	ign. on
		13.0 min.[1]	ign. on
2.5L (151) FI	1989-92	9.0-13.0	ign. on
		13.0 min.[1]	ign. on
5.0L, 5.7L	1991-92	9-13	idle
		13.0 min.[1]	idle
5.0L (307)	1989-90	5.5-6.5	idle

1 Fuel pump pressure with return line briefly restricted.

Engine	Year	Pressure (PSI) Ign. On	Idle	Fuel Pump[1]
Fuel Injected (MFI):				
2.2L, 2.3L, 2.4L	1989-00	40-47	30-44	47 min.
2.8L (173)	1989	40-47	30-44	60 min.
3.1L	1989-99	40-47	30-44	47 min.
3.3L	1989	40-44	32-36	50 min.
	1990-93	40-47	30-44	47 min.
3.4L DOHC	1991-95	40-47	30-44	47 min.
	1996	48-55	38-52	55 min.
	1997	41-47	31-44	47 min.
3.8L (231) Code C	1989-91	40-47	31-43	75 min.
3.8L Code L, 1	1991-95	40-47	30-44	47 min.
3.8L Code K	1995-99	48-55	38-52	55 min.
4.0L	1995-97	48-55	38-52	55 min.
	1998-99	40-47	30-44	47 min.

1 With fuel return line briefly restricted.

IDLE SPEED W/COMPUTER CONTROL
FOR TESTING AND ADJUSTMENT DIAGRAMS, SEE APPENDIX E.

Midpoint of range given is the preferred setting speed.

Idle speed is adjustable only if specifications are shown in the "Minimum Speed" column.

All w/MFI & TBI (when specifications appear in "Minimum Speed" column): Ground diagnostic lead and turn ignition on for 30 seconds.

Remove IAC electrical lead and remove ground from diagnostic connector. Start engine and set minimum speed to specified value.

All carbureted w/ILC: Disconnect and plug vacuum hoses at EGR and canister purge valves. With engine at operating temperature, remove vacuum hose from ILC and plug. Set maximum speed to specified value by holding hex nut and turning plunger shaft. Reconnect ILC vacuum hose and check that minimum speed is at specified value. To adjust, remove rubber and metal plugs from rear center outlet tube, insert a 3/32" Allen wrench. Remove ILC hose and plug. Connect a remote vacuum source and apply vacuum to the unit. Adjust carb base screw to obtain specified base value.

ALL FUEL INJECTED

Engine	Year	Minimum Speed Man. Trans.	Minimum Speed Auto. Trans.	Checking Speed Man. Trans.	Checking Speed Auto. Trans.
2.2L	1993	—	—	—	725-875 N
2.3L	1990-92	—	—	800 max.[1]	800 N max.[1]
2.5L (151)	1989-92	550-650	550-650 N	800 max.[1]	800 N max.[1]
2.8L (173)	1989	—	—	750-950	650-750 D
3.1L MFI	1989-91	—	—	750-950	650-750 D
3.1L MFI Code T	1992-93	—	—	800-900	700-800 N
3.1L Code M	1993	—	—	—	600-700 D
3.3L	1989	—	—	—	650-750 N
3.3L Calais	1990	—	—	—	675-750 D
Ciera	1990	—	—	—	650-750 N
3.3L	1991-93	—	—	—	650-750 N
3.4L DOHC	1991-93	—	—	800-900	700-800 N
	1994-95	—	—	650-750	650-750 N
3.8L Code C	1989	—	—	—	650-750 N
	1990-91	—	—	—	650-850 N
3.8L Code K, L	1991-95	—	—	—	650-750 N
	1996-99	—	—	—	600-700 N
4.0L	1995-99	—	—	—	550-675 N
5.0L	1991	—	—	—	500-600 D

1 With ISC fully seated.

IDLE SPEED W/COMPUTER CONTROL Continued

ALL CARBURETED

Engine	Year	Trans.	Min. Speed	Max. Speed	Fast	Step of Cam
5.0L (307)	1989-90	AT	450 D	700 D	550 D	Low
base idle	1989-90	AT	450 D	—		

ENGINE MECHANICAL

TIGHTENING TORQUES
FOR CYLINDER HEAD TORQUE SEQUENCES AND DIAGRAMS, SEE APPENDIX F.

Some fasteners are tightened in more than one step.

Some values are specified in inches.

Engine	Year	Cylinder Head	Intake Manifold	Exhaust Manifold	Crankshaft Pulley	Water Pump
		TORQUE FOOT-POUNDS/NEWTON METERS				
2.2L	1993-96	46/63[1], 43/58[2], +90°, all	22/30[10]	115"/18	77/105	18/25
2.3L	1989-95	3	18/25	31/42, nuts 106"/12, studs	79/100, +90°	106"/12, cover 19/26, others
2.4L	1996-00	8	17/24	110"/13	129/178, +90°	10/14, cover 19/26, others
2.5L (151)	1989-92	18/25, 26/35[7], +90°	25/34	25/43[4], 37-50[6]	162/220	25/34
2.8L, 3.1L ex. Cutlass	1989	33/45, +90°	15/20, 24/33	20-30/ 15-22	76/103	7/10, short 18/24, long
2.8L, 3.1L Code T Cutlass	1989-93	33/45, +90°	16/22, 23/32	21/28	77/105	84"/10
3.1L Code M	1993-97	33/45, +90°	115"/13, lower 18/25, upper	12/16	76/103	89"/10
	1998-99	37/50, +90°	115"/13, lower 18/25, upper	12/16	76/103	89"/10
3.3L	1989-90	35/47, +130°[9]	88"/10	30/41	219/297	8/10, short 22/30, long
	1991-93	35/47, +130°[9]	88"/10	38/52	111/150, +76°	29/39
3.4L DOHC	1991-97	44/60, +90°	18/25, upper 116"/13, lower	116"/13, nut 13/17, stud	37/50[2], 75/108[1]	88"/10
3.8L Code C	1989-90	35/47, +130°[9]	88"/10	41/55	219/297	8/10
3.8L Code K, L	1990-97	35/47, +130°[9]	11	38/52	110/150, +76°	84"/10, short 29/39, long
	1998-00	37/50 +120°	11/15 lower 89"/10, upper	22/30	110/150, +76°	11/15 +80°
4.0L	1995-97	30/40, +70°, +60°, +60°	89"/10	18/25	105/145	—
	1998-00	30/40, +70°, +60°, +60°	89"/10	12/25	37/50, +120°	—
5.0L, 5.7L	1991-93	68/92	35/47	20/27, studs 26/35, bolts	70/95	30/41
5.0L (307)	1989-90	40/54, +95°, first and last bolts on exhaust manifold side +120°, all others	40/54	25/34	200-310/ 270-400	11/14

TIGHTENING TORQUES Continued

1 Long bolts.
2 Short bolts.
3 Tighten bolts 1-8 (long bolts), 30/40. Tighten bolts 9-10 (short bolts), 26/35. Then, turn all bolts 90°.
4 Four outer bolts.
5 Turn last bolt on left (number nine) to 29/40. Then, turn all except number nine 120°, turn number nine 90°.
6 Three inner bolts.
7 Turn last bolt on left (number nine) to 18/25.
8 Tighten bolts 1-8, 40/65. Tighten bolts 9-10, 30/40. Then tighten all bolts 90°.
9 Tighten four center bolts an additional 30°.
10 Upper manifold. Lower manifold: studs, 89"/10, nuts, 24/33.
11 1991-92: upper to lower, 21/29; lower to block, 89"/10. 1993-97: upper to lower & lower to block, 11/15.

COMPRESSION PRESSURE

At cranking speed or specified rpm, engine temperature normalized, throttle open.

Engine	Year	PSI	Maximum Variation PSI
All	1989-00	100 min.	1

1 Lowest cylinder pressure must be more than 70% of highest cylinder pressure.

BELT TENSION

All Except With Automatic Tensioner.

Use a strand tension gauge. Measurements are in pounds.

1989-92, a belt in operation 3 minutes is considered a used belt.

Engine	Year	Generator	Power Steering	Air Cond.	Air Pump
Used Belts					
2.3L	1989-94	—	110	—	—
2.5L Code U	1989-91	90	90	90	—
5.0L (307)	1989-90	110	110	110	55
Cogged or 3/8" belt	1989-90	90	—	—	90
New Belts					
2.3L	1989-94	—	110	—	—
2.5L Code U	1989-91	165	180	165	—
5.0L (307)	1989-90	150	165	165	135
Cogged	1989-90	135	—	—	—

1 Vacuum pump belt: used, 55; new, 125.

All With Automatic Tensioner

If index marks on tensioner are outside the range, replace the belt. If marks are within range and belt tension is below specified value, replace tensioner.

Engine	Year	Tension
2.2L	1993-96	50-70
2.3L, 2.4L	1989-96	50 min.
2.5L Ciera	1989-91	50-70
2.8L	1989	50-70
3.1L	1989-97	50-70
3.1L Achieva	1996	50-70
Ciera, Cutlass	1996	30-50
3.4L	1996-97	35-55
3.3L	1989-93	67 min.
3.8L Code C	1989-90	67 min.
3.8L	1995	50-70
5.0L, 5.7L	1991-95	105-125

SERPENTINE BELT DIAGRAMS

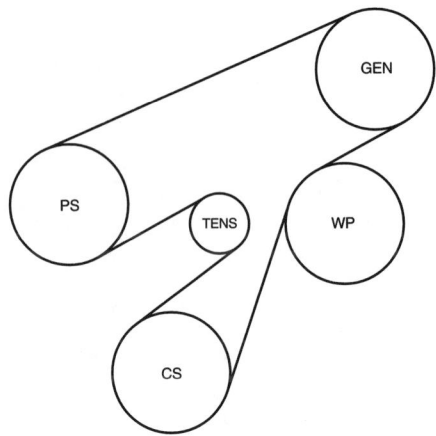

1989-92 2.5L
Code R w/o AC

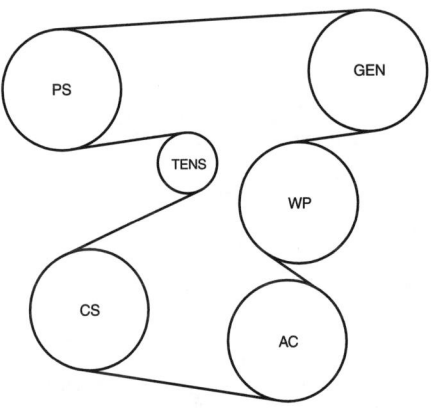

1989-92 2.5L
Code R w/AC

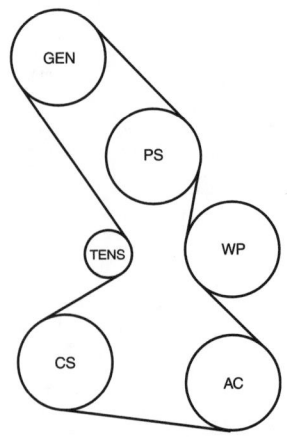

1989-98 2.8L, 3.1L FWD
Code W, T, M, D
1996-00 3.4L

OLDSMOBILE
1989-2000 All Models
Bravada, Silhouette—See Chevrolet/GMC Trucks

UNDERHOOD SERVICE SPECIFICATIONS

OETU5

OETU5

SERPENTINE BELT DIAGRAMS Continued

SERPENTINE BELT DIAGRAMS Continued

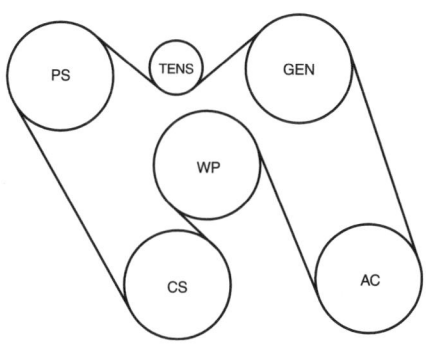

1989-94 3.3L Code N
3.8L Code C, L FWD

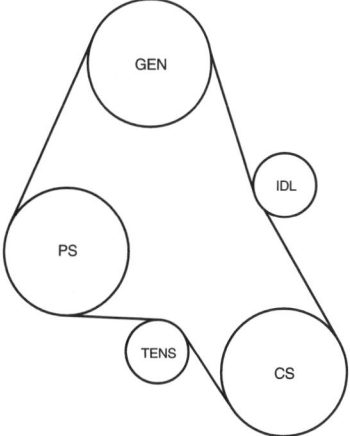

1991-95 3.8L
Supercharged Outer Belt

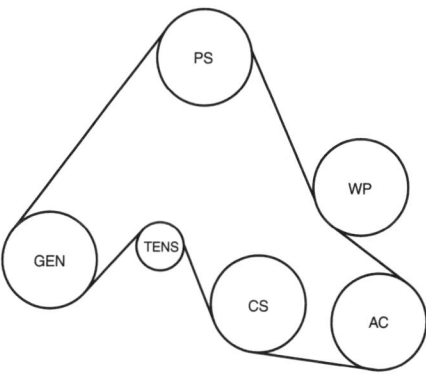

1991-97 3.4L DOHC

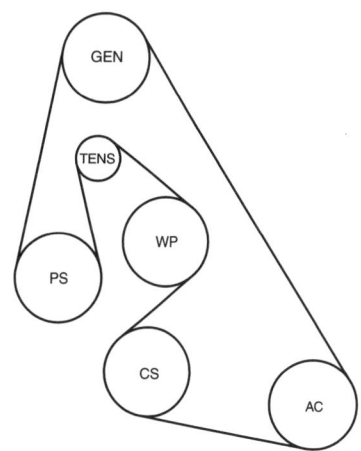

1995-98 3.8L FWD Code K
1995-98 3.8L Supercharged Outer Belt

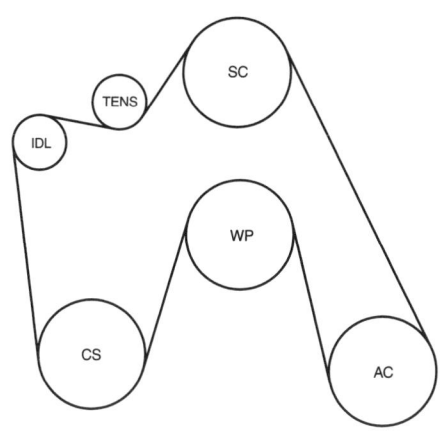

1991-95 3.8L
Supercharged Inner Belt

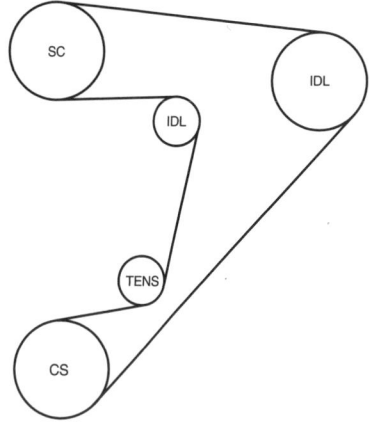

1995-98 3.8L
Supercharged Inner Belt

OLDSMOBILE
1989-2000 All Models
Bravada, Silhouette—See Chevrolet/GMC Trucks

SERPENTINE BELT DIAGRAMS Continued

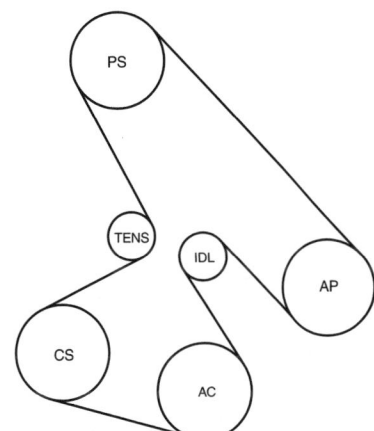

1995-98 4.0L

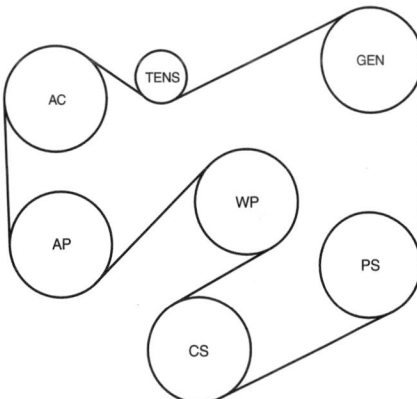

1989-92 5.0L, 5.7L
Code E, 7

ENGINE COMPUTER SYSTEM

DIAGNOSTIC TROUBLE CODES
FOR TESTING AND ADJUSTMENT DIAGRAMS, SEE APPENDIX G.

1989-95 All w/12-pin DLC ex. 1989-90 Toronado, Troféo with CRT
Connect a jumper between terminals A and B on under dash connector (identified by a slot between the terminals or in two upper right cavities on a two row connector). Turn ignition switch on. Code 12 will flash three times, then codes in memory will be displayed. Do not run engine with jumper connected.

Remove ECM fuse for a minimum of ten seconds to clear memory.

1989-90 Toronado, Troféo with CRT
To enter diagnostic mode, turn ignition switch on and push "off" and "warm" buttons simultaneously for three seconds and release. Any stored codes will be displayed.
To clear ECM code, press the "HI" switch after the ECM message is displayed. After accessing the ECM system, continually press the "LO" switch after each message until "CLEAR CODES" is displayed. Press the "BI LEVEL" button to exit diagnostics.

The computer system monitors other systems and functions besides the ECM trouble codes. See Service Manual for details.

1994-00 All w/16-pin DLC, OBD-II
A Scan tool is required to retrieve codes and code definitions.

1989-95 All w/12-pin DLC ex. 1989-90 Toronado, Troféo with CRT
Code 12 No tach reference to ECM
Code 13 Oxygen sensor circuit
Code 14 Engine coolant sensor circuit shorted

DIAGNOSTIC TROUBLE CODES Continued
Code 15 Engine coolant sensor circuit open
Code 16 System voltage high
Code 17 Spark reference circuit
Code 18 Cam and crank sensor sync signal
Code 19 Intermittent 7X circuit
Code 21 Throttle position sensor circuit open
Code 22 Throttle position sensor circuit shorted
Code 23 Open or ground MC solenoid (carbureted)
Code 23 Intake air temperature circuit open
Code 24 Vehicle speed sensor circuit
Code 25 Intake air temperature circuit shorted
Code 26 Quad driver circuit
Codes 27 & 28 Gear switch circuit (3.3L)
Codes 27 & 28 Quad driver circuit (2.3L)
Code 29 Fourth gear switch circuit open
Code 31 EVAP canister purge solenoid (carbureted)
Code 31 Park/Neutral switch, MFI; EGR circuit, TBI
Code 32 Barometric or altitude sensor (carbureted)
Code 32 EGR system failure (FI)
Code 33 MAP sensor circuit open (ex. 3.3L, 3.8L)
Code 33 MAF sensor circuit open (3.3L, 3.8L)
Code 34 MAP sensor circuit shorted (ex. 3.3L, 3.8L)
Code 34 MAF sensor circuit shorted (3.3L, 3.8L)
Code 34 MAP sensor circuit (carbureted)
Code 35 Idle speed or idle air control circuit
Code 36 MAF burnoff circuit (1989)
Code 36 Transaxle shift control (1990-91)
Code 37 Transmission brake switch error
Code 38 Brake switch circuit (1989-90)
Code 39 Torque converter clutch circuit
Code 40 Power steering pressure switch open
Code 41 Ignition control timing circuit problem (Camaro V6, all V8)
Code 41 No distributor reference pulses to ECM (1989-90 carbureted)
Code 41 Camshaft position sensor circuit (3.3L, 3.8L Code 3, C, L)
Code 41 Cylinder select error (ex. 3.3L, 3.8L)
Code 42 IC or IC bypass circuit grounded or open
Code 43 Knock sensor signal
Code 44 Air/fuel mixture lean
Codes 44 & 45 Faulty oxygen sensor
Code 45 Air/fuel mixture rich
Code 46 Power steering pressure switch circuit
Code 47 A/C clutch and cruise circuit
Code 48 Misfire
Code 51 Faulty PROM or installation, faulty Memcal or ECM
Code 52 CALPAK error
Codes 53, 54, 55 EGR system (3.3L, 3.8L)
Code 53 EGR vacuum sensor vacuum incorrect (carbureted)
Code 53 Generator voltage out of range (MFI, others)
Code 54 Shorted MC solenoid or faulty ECM (carbureted)
Code 54 Fuel pump circuit (FI)
Code 55 Grounded V-REF, faulty oxygen sensor or ECM
Code 56 Quad driver B circuit (3.8L)
Code 56 PASS key fuel enable circuit (others)
Code 58 PASS key fuel enable circuit (1990-93)
Code 58 Transmission fluid temperature sensor circuit shorted
Code 59 Transmission fluid temperature sensor circuit open
Code 61 Degraded Oxygen sensor (ex. 3.8L Code L)
Code 61 Cruise vent solenoid (3.8L Code L)
Code 62 Transmission gear switch (ex. 3.8L Code L)
Code 62 Cruise MDP solenoid (3.8L Code L)
Code 63 Cruise system problem
Code 65 Fuel injector circuit (ex. 3.8L Code L)
Code 65 Cruise servo position (3.8L Code L)
Code 66 A/C pressure sensor
Code 67 Cruise switches
Code 68 Cruise system problem
Code 69 A/C head pressure switch
Code 74 Traction control system circuit
Code 75 Digital EGR #1 solenoid
Code 76 Digital EGR #2 solenoid
Code 77 Digital EGR #3 solenoid
Code 79 Transmission fluid over temperature
Code 80 Transmission converter clutch slippage excessive
Code 81 Transmission 2-3 shift
Code 82 Ignition control 3X circuit
Code 83 Reverse inhibit system
Code 84 Transmission 3-2 control
Code 85 Faulty or incorrect PROM

DIAGNOSTIC TROUBLE CODES Continued

Code 86 A/D chip error
Code 87 EEPROM error
Code 90 Transmission clutch solenoid circuit error
Code 91 Skip shift lamp circuit
Code 93 Transmission pressure control solenoid
Code 95 Change oil lamp circuit
Code 96 Transmission system voltage low
Code 97 Vehicle speed sensor output circuit
Code 98 Invalid PCM program
Code 99 Invalid PCM program (1994-95)
Code 99 Power management, cruise system (1991-92)

1989-90 Toronado, Troféo w/CRT
Code 013 Open Oxygen sensor circuit
Code 014 Engine coolant sensor circuit, high temperature
Code 015 Engine coolant sensor circuit, low temperature
Code 016 System voltage out of range
Code 021 TPS circuit, signal voltage high
Code 022 TPS circuit, signal voltage low
Code 023 Intake air temperature, low temperature indicated
Code 024 Vehicle speed sensor circuit
Code 025 Intake air temperature, high temperature indicated
Code 026 Quad driver error
Code 027 Second gear switch circuit
Code 028 Third gear switch circuit
Code 029 Fourth gear switch circuit open
Code 031 Park/Neutral switch circuit
Code 034 Mass airflow sensor circuit
Code 038 Brake switch circuit
Code 039 Torque converter clutch circuit
Code 041 Camshaft position sensor circuit
Code 042 IC or bypass circuit
Code 043 IC system
Code 044 Lean exhaust
Code 045 Rich exhaust
Code 046 Power steering switch circuit (A/C clutch)
Code 047 ECM-BCM communication error
Code 048 Misfire
Code 051 PROM error
Code 063 EGR flow problem, small
Code 064 EGR flow problem, medium
Code 065 EGR flow problem, large

SENSORS, INPUT
TEMPERATURE SENSORS

Engine	Year	Sensor	Resistance Ohms @ deg. F/C
All	1989-90 1989-91	Coolant Intake Air[1]	13,500 @ 20/-7 7500 @ 40/4 3400 @ 70/20 1800 @ 100/38 450 @ 160/70 185 @ 210/100
All	1991-00 1992-00	Coolant Intake Air	28,700 @ -4/-20 12,300 @ 23/-5 7200 @ 41/5 3500 @ 68/20 1460 @ 104/40 470 @ 158/70 180 @ 210/100
All	1994-00	Transmission Oil[1]	25,809-28,677 @ -4 (-20) 14,558-16,176 @ 14 (-10) 8481-10,365 @ 0 (32) 3164-3867 @ 68 (20) 1313-1605 @ 104 (40) 420-514 @ 158 (70) 159-195 @ 212 (100) 69-85 @ 266 (130)

1 As equipped, not used on all engines.

MANIFOLD ABSOLUTE, VACUUM, AND BAROMETRIC PRESSURE SENSORS

Engines may use one, or a combination of these sensors. All sensors appear the same. Manifold Absolute Pressure sensors have vacuum line connected between the unit and manifold vacuum. On Barometric Pressure sensors, the line is not used and the connector is either open or has a filter installed over it. Pressure sensors also have a vacuum line between the sensor and intake manifold and only appear on carbureted models.

Barometric Pressure Sensors: Measure voltage with ignition on and engine off.

SENSORS, INPUT Continued

Manifold Absolute Pressure Sensors: Measure voltage with ignition on and engine off. Start engine and apply 10 in./250 mm Hg to unit, voltage should be 1.5 volts minimum less.
Pressure Sensors: Measure voltage as indicated.
5 volts reference.

MANIFOLD ABSOLUTE, VACUUM, AND BAROMETRIC PRESSURE SENSORS Cont.

Engine	Year	Sensor	Voltage @ Altitude/Condition
All, as equipped	1989-90	Barometric	3.8-5.5 @ 0-1000 3.6-5.3 @ 1000-2000 3.5-5.1 @ 2000-3000 3.3-5.0 @ 3000-4000 3.2-4.8 @ 4000-5000 3.0-4.6 @ 5000-6000 2.9-4.5 @ 6000-7000 2.5-4.3 @ 7000-

Engine	Year	Sensor	Voltage @ Condition
All	1989-00	MAP	1.0-1.5 @ idle 4.0-4.8 @ WOT

Engine	Year	Sensor	Voltage @ Altitude
2.5L 2V, 2.8L 2V, 4.3L (260), 5.0L	1989-91	Vacuum	.50-.64 @ ign. on 1.7-3.0[1]

1 10 in. Hg/34 kpa applied to unit.

CRANKSHAFT POSITION SENSORS

Air gap is measured between crankshaft sensor and interrupter rings.

Resistance is measured at room temperature.

Engine	Year	Resistance (ohms)	Air Gap (in./mm)
2.0L ex. OHC	1989-92	900-1200	—
2.2L	1993-95	800-1200	—
2.3L, 2.4L	1989-00	500-900	—
2.8L, 3.1L, 3.4L	1989-95	900-1200	—
2.5L	1989-92	800-900	—
3.0L, 3.3L, 3.8L w/FI	1989-93	—	.025/.65

THROTTLE POSITION SENSOR (TPS)

Verify that minimum idle is at specified value.

Make all checks/adjustments with engine at operating temperature.

Carbureted Models: Remove aluminum plug covering the adjustment screw. Remove the screw and connect a digital voltmeter from the TPS black wire (-) and either of the two other colored wires (+). If voltage is approximately 5 volts, this is the reference voltage lead. Connect DVOM to other wire in this case. Apply thread locking compound to the screw and with ignition on and engine not running (as applies), quickly adjust screw to obtain specified voltage at indicated condition.

Fuel Injected Models: Disconnect harness connector from TPS. Using three six-inch jumper wires, reconnect harness to TPS. With ignition on and engine not running (as applies), connect a digital voltmeter to black wire (-) and either of the two other colored wires (+). If voltage is approximately 5 volts, this is the reference voltage lead. Connect DVOM to other wire in this case. Check reading against specified value. If TPS is adjustable, loosen the unit retaining screws and rotate the unit to reach specified value.

Engine	Year	TPS Voltage Idle[1]	TPS Voltage WOT (approx.)
2.0L (122)	1989	.33-1.33[2]	5.0
2.2L	1993-94	.33-1.33[2]	4.0 min.
	1995-96	.20-.90[2]	4.0-4.7
2.3L	1989	.54	4.7 min.
	1990-93	.40-.90[2]	4.7 min.
	1994-95	.36-.96[2]	4.0 min.
2.4L	1996	.36-.96[2]	4.0 min.
	1997-00	.20-.90	4.0 min.
2.5L (151)	1989-90	.20-1.25[2]	5.0
2.5L	1991-92	.35-1.33[2]	5.0
2.8L	1989	.29-.98[2]	5.0
3.1L MFI	1989-95	.29-.98[2]	4.0 min.
	1996-99	.20-.74[2]	4.0 min.

OLDSMOBILE

1989-2000 All Models

Bravada, Silhouette—See Chevrolet/GMC Trucks

UNDERHOOD SERVICE SPECIFICATIONS

SENSORS, INPUT Continued

THROTTLE POSITION SENSOR (TPS) Continued

Engine	Year	TPS Voltage Idle[1]	TPS Voltage WOT (approx.)
3.3L	1989-92	.40	4.5 min.
	1993	.20-.74[2]	4.0 min.
3.4L DOHC	1991-94	.29-.98[2]	4.0 min.
	1995-97	.20-.74[2]	4.0 min.
3.8L (231) FI	1989-92	.40	5.1
3.8L	1993-99	.20-.74[2]	4.0 min.
4.0L	1995-99	.20-.74[2]	4.0 min.
5.0L, 5.7L	1991-92	.20-.95[2]	5.0
5.0L (307)	1989-90	.41[3]	5.0

1 ±.10 carbureted engines. ±.05 fuel injected engines.
2 Not adjustable.
3 Idle Speed or Load Compensator (ISC, ILC) retracted.

KNOCK SENSOR

Engine	Year	Resistance (ohms)
2.2L, 2.3L, 2.4L	1994-00	90,000-110,000
3.1L, 3.4L, 3.8L	1992-95	3300-4500
	1996-99	90,000-110,000
5.7L	1994-95	3300-4500
	1996	90,000-110,000

ACTUATORS, OUTPUT

IDLE SPEED CONTROL

All engines with ISC.

Measured between terminals A & B and C & D.

Engine	Year	Resistance (ohms)
2.8L, 3.1L Ciera, Cutlass	1989	48-58
3.8L Code C	1989	48-58

ACTUATORS, OUTPUT Continued

IDLE SPEED CONTROL Continued

Engine	Year	Resistance (ohms)
All others, TBI & MFI	1989	20 min.
All ex. Toronado	1990-91	40-80
3.8L Toronado	1990-91	48-58
All	1992-00	40-80

FUEL INJECTORS

Engine	Year	Resistance (ohms)	Temperature (deg. F/C)
2.0L, 2.5L	1989	1.2 min.	—
	1990-92	1.6 min.	
2.2L	1993-95	11.6-12.4	68/20
	1996	11.8-12.6	—
2.3L	1989-93	1.95-2.15	140/60
2.4L	1996-00	1.95-2.30	—
2.8L, 3.1L:			
Cutlass	1989-95	12-12.4[1]	—
Others	1989-93	8 min.	—
3.1L, 3.4L	1994-99	11.4-12.6	—
3.3L	1989-93	11.8-12.6[1]	68/20
3.8L	1991-93	14.5	68/20
	1994-95	14.3-14.7	—
	1996	11.4-12.6	—
4.0L	1995-99	11.8-12.6	—
5.0L, 5.7L	1991-93	1.2 min.	—

1 Values for all injectors should be within a range of 0.8 ohms at room temperature.

MIXTURE CONTROL SOLENOID-CARBURETED ENGINES

On some engines, the ECM will be damaged if the resistance of the mixture control solenoid is less than specified.

Engine	Year	Resistance (ohms)
All	1989-90	10 min.

ENGINE IDENTIFICATION

To identify any engine by the manufacturer's code, follow the four steps designated by the numbered blocks.

1 **MODEL YEAR IDENTIFICATION:** Refer to illustration of the Vehicle Identification Number (V.I.N.). The year is indicated by a code letter which is the 10th character of the V.I.N.

2 **ENGINE CODE LOCATION:** Refer to illustration of V.I.N. plate for location and designation of engine code.

3 **ENGINE CODE:** In the "CODE" column, find the engine code determined in Step 2.

4 **ENGINE IDENTIFICATION:** On the line where the engine code appears, read to the right to identify the engine.

V.I.N. PLATE LOCATION:

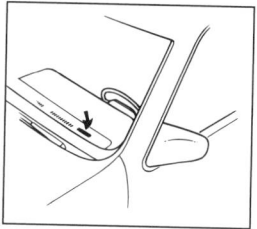

On top left side of instrument panel

Model year of vehicle:
2000 — Y
1999 — X
1998 — W
1997 — V
1996 — T
1995 — S
1994 — R
1993 — P
1992 — N
1991 — M
1990 — L
1989 — K

MODEL YEAR AND ENGINE IDENTIFICATION:

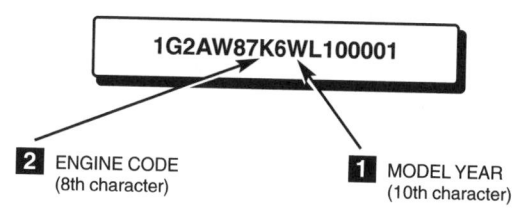

1G2AW87K6WL100001

2 ENGINE CODE (8th character)

1 MODEL YEAR (10th character)

ENGINE IDENTIFICATION

YEAR	CODE	CYL.	DISPL. liters	DISPL. cu. in.	Fuel System	HP
2000	4	4	2.2	133	MFI	115
	T	4	2.4	146	MFI	150
	J	6	3.1	191	MFI	175
	E	6	3.4	207	MFI	170, 175
	K	6	3.8	231	MFI	200, 205[1]
	1	6	3.8	231	MFI	240
	G	8	5.7	350	MFI	305, 320
1999	4	4	2.2	133	MFI	115
	T	4	2.4	146	MFI	150
	M	6	3.1	191	MFI	160
	E	6	3.4	207	MFI	180
	K	6	3.8	231	MFI	200, 205[1]
	1	6	3.8	231	MFI	240
	G	8	5.7	350	MFI	305, 320
1998	4	4	2.2	133	MFI	115
	T	4	2.4	146	MFI	150
	M	6	3.1	191	MFI	155, 160[1]
	K	6	3.8	231	MFI	195-205[1]
	1	6	3.8 S	231	MFI	240
	G	8	5.7	346	MFI	305
1997	4	4	2.2	133	MFI	120
	T	4	2.4	146	MFI	150
	M	6	3.1	191	MFI	155, 160[1]
	K	6	3.8	231	MFI	195-205[1]
	1	6	3.8 S	231 S	MFI	240
	P	8	5.7	350	MFI	285
1996	4	4	2.2	133	MFI	120
	T	4	2.4	146	MFI	150
	M	6	3.1	191	MFI	155, 160[1]
	X	6	3.4	207	MFI	210
	K	6	3.8	231	MFI	195-205[1]
	1	6	3.8 S	231 S	MFI	240
	P	8	5.7	350	MFI	280
1995	4	4	2.2	133	MFI	120
	D	4	2.3	138	MFI	150
	M	6	3.1	191	MFI	155, 160[1]
	S	6	3.4	207	MFI	160
	X	6	3.4	207	MFI	210
	K	6	3.8	231	MFI	171, 205[1]
	1	6	3.8 S	231 S	MFI	225
	P	8	5.7	350	MFI	275
1994	H	4	2.0	121	MFI	110
	3	4	2.3	138	MFI	115
	D	4	2.3	138	MFI	155
	A	4	2.3 HO	138 HO	MFI	175

ENGINE IDENTIFICATION

YEAR	CODE	CYL.	DISPL. liters	DISPL. cu. in.	Fuel System	HP
1994 Cont'd.	T	6	3.1	191	MFI	140
	M	6	3.1	191	MFI	155, 160[1]
	S	6	3.4	207	MFI	160
	X	6	3.4	207	MFI	210
	L	6	3.8	231	MFI	170
	1	6	3.8	231 S	MFI	225
	P	8	5.7	350	MFI	275
1993	6	4	1.6	97	TBI	74
	H	4	2.0	121	MFI	110
	3	4	2.3	138	MFI	115
	D	4	2.3	138	MFI	155
	A	4	2.3 HO	138 HO	MFI	175
	T	6	3.1	191	MFI	140
	N	6	3.3	204	MFI	160
	S	6	3.4	207	MFI	160
	X	6	3.4	207	MFI	200, 210[1]
	L	6	3.8	231	MFI	170
	1	6	3.8 S	231 S	MFI	205
	P	8	5.7	350	MFI	280
1992	6	4	1.6	97	TBI	74
	H	4	2.0	121	MFI	111
	3	4	2.3	138	MFI	120
	D	4	2.3	138	MFI	160
	A	4	2.3 HO	138 HO	MFI	180
	T	6	3.1	191	MFI	140
	N	6	3.3	204	MFI	160
	X	6	3.4	207	MFI	210
	L	6	3.8	231	MFI	170
	1	6	3.8 S	231 S	MFI	205
	E	8	5.0	305	TBI	170
	F	8	5.0	305 HO	MFI	205
	8	8	5.7	350	MFI	240
1991	6	4	1.6	97	TBI	74
	K	4	2.0	121	TBI	96
	D	4	2.3	138	MFI	160
	A	4	2.3 HO	138 HO	MFI	180
	R, U	4	2.5	151	TBI	110
	T	6	3.1	191	MFI	140
	V	6	3.1 T	191 T	MFI	205
	X	6	3.4	207	MFI	200, 210[1]
	E	8	5.0	305	TBI	170
	F	8	5.0	305	MFI	205, 225[1]
	8	8	5.7	350	MFI	240
1990	6	4	1.6	97	TBI	74
	K	4	2.0	121	TBI	96
	M	4	2.0 T	121 T	MFI	165
	D	4	2.3	138	MFI	160
	A	4	2.3	138 HO	MFI	180
	R, U	4	2.5	151	TBI	110
	T	6	3.1	191	MFI	135, 140

ENGINE IDENTIFICATION Continued

YEAR	**3** ENGINE CODE	CYL.	**4** ENGINE IDENTIFICATION DISPL. liters	cu. in.	Fuel System	HP
1990 Cont'd.	V	6	3.1 T	191 T	MFI	205
	D	6	3.1	191	TBI	120
	C	6	3.8	231	MFI	165
	E	8	5.0	305	TBI	170
	F	8	5.0	305	MFI	190, 225[1]
	Y	8	5.0	307	4V	140
	8	8	5.7	350	MFI	235
1989	6	4	1.6	97	TBI	74
	K	4	2.0	121	TBI	96
	M	4	2.0 T	121 T	MFI	165
	D	4	2.3	138	MFI	150
	R	4	2.5	151	TBI	98
	U	4	2.5	151	TBI	110
	W	6	2.8	173	MFI	125-130[1]

YEAR	**3** ENGINE CODE	CYL.	**4** ENGINE IDENTIFICATION DISPL. liters	cu. in.	Fuel System	HP
1989 Cont'd.	S	6	2.8	173	MFI	135
	T	6	3.1	191	MFI	140
	V	6	3.1	191 T	MFI	205
	C	6	3.8	231	MFI	165
	7	6	3.8	231 T	MFI	N/A
	E	8	5.0	305	TBI	170
	F	8	5.0	305	MFI	195
	Y	8	5.0	307	4V	140
	8	8	5.7	350	MFI	225-235[1]

[1]TBI—Throttle Body Injection. MFI—Multiport Fuel Injection.
2V—Two Venturi Carburetor. 4V—Four Venturi Carburetor.
HO—High Output. S—Supercharged. T—Turbocharged.
1 Engine horsepower varies with model installation.

UNDERHOOD SERVICE SPECIFICATIONS

PCTU1   PCTU1

CYLINDER NUMBERING SEQUENCE

4-CYL. FIRING ORDER: 1 3 4 2

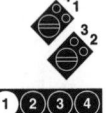

— Front of car —

1989-93 1.6L LeMans	1989-91 2.0L (122) OHC	1989-91 2.0L (122) ex. OHC, 2.2L Tempest Canada 1995-98 2.2L Code 4

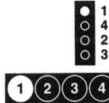

— Front of car —

1992-94 2.0L Code H	1989-95 2.3L Code A, D 1992-94 2.3L Code 3 1996-00 2.4L Code T	1989-91 2.5L (151)

6-CYL. FIRING ORDER:
2.8L, 3.1L, 3.4L 1 2 3 4 5 6
All Others
1 6 5 4 3 2

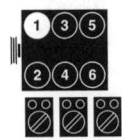

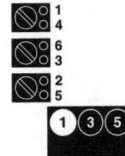

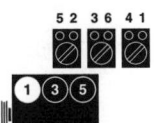
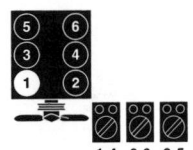

— Front of car —

1989 2.8L (173) ex. Firebird, Fiero 1989-94 3.1L Code T FWD 1990 3.1L Code V FWD 1991-93 3.4L Code X	1994-95 3.4L Code X	1996 3.4L Code X	1989 2.8L (173) Firebird 1990-92 3.1L Code T Firebird	1994-97 3.1L Code M	1993-95 3.4L Code S

UNDERHOOD SERVICE SPECIFICATIONS

PCTU2   PCTU2

CYLINDER NUMBERING SEQUENCE

6-CYL. FIRING ORDER:
2.8L, 3.1L, 3.4L 1 2 3 4 5 6
All Others
1 6 5 4 3 2

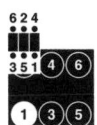

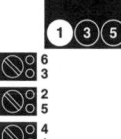
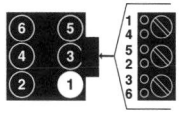

Front of car

1992 3.3L Code N	**1999-00** 3.4L Code E	**1989-90** 3.8L (231) FI Code C **1992** 3.8L Code L Some	**1992** 3.8L Code L Some, 3.8L Code 1 **1993** 3.3L Code N **1993-94** 3.8L Code L, 1 **1995-00** Code K, 1 ex. Firebird	**1995-00** 3.8L Code K Firebird

8-CYL. FIRING ORDER:
All except code G
1 8 4 3 6 5 7 2
Code G
1 8 7 2 6 5 4 3

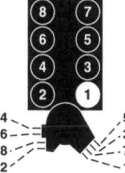

Front of car

1989-90 5.0L (307)	**1989-91** 5.7L Code 8	**1989-92** 5.0L (305) Codes E, F **1992** 5.7L (350) Code 8	**1993-97** 5.7L Code P	**1998-00** 5.7L Code G

TIMING MARK

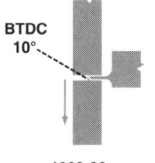

1989-93
LeMans 1.6L Code 6

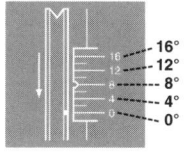

1989-91
2.0L (122) OHC

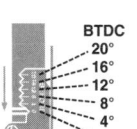

1992-94
2.0L Code H

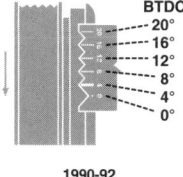

1989
2.8L (173) Firebird

1990-92
3.1L FI Code T
RWD

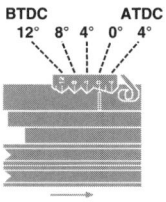

1989-92
5.0L (305)

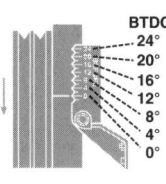

1989-90
5.0L (307)

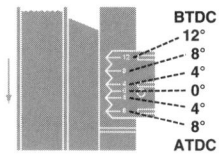

1989-92
5.7L (350) FI

PONTIAC
1989-2000 All Models
Firefly—See Geo/Chevrolet-Pontiac; Trans Sport—See Chevrolet/GMC Trucks

UNDERHOOD SERVICE SPECIFICATIONS

PCTU3

PCTU3

ELECTRICAL AND IGNITION SYSTEMS

BATTERY

Engine	Year	STANDARD BCI Group No.	STANDARD Crank. Perf.	OPTIONAL BCI Group No.	OPTIONAL Crank. Perf.
1.6L LeMans	1989-93	85	550	—	—
2.0L (122) Sunbird	1989-94	75	630	—	—
2.0L (122) Tempest: MT	1989	70	525	75	630
AT	1989	75	630	—	—
2.2L Tempest: MT	1990-91	75	525	75	570
AT	1990-91	75	570	—	—
2.2L	1995-00	75	525	—	—
2.3L (138)	1989-92	75	630	—	—
	1993-95	75	600	—	—
2.4L	1996-00	75	600	—	—
2.5L (151)	1989-91	75	630	—	—
2.8L (173) 6000	1989	75	525	75	570
Fiero, Tempest	1989	75	525	75	630
Grand Prix	1989	75	525	—	—
Canada	1989	75	630	—	—
3.1L Grand Prix	1991-96	75	525	—	—
	1997-99	78	600	—	—
Grand Am	1994-00	75	600	—	—
Firebird	1991-92	75	525	—	—
Sunbird	1992-94	75	525	—	—
Tempest	1991-92	75	525	75	630
6000	1991	75	525	75	570
3.3L	1992	75	630	—	—
	1993	75	600	—	—
3.4L Firebird	1993-95	75	525	—	—
3.4L DOHC	1991-96	75	690	—	—
3.8L (231)	1989-94	75	630	78	730
3.8L: Bonneville	1995-96	78	600	78	770
	1997-99	78	690	78	770
Firebird	1995-00	75	690	—	—
Grand Prix	1997-99	78	690	—	—
Supercharged	1998-99	78	770	—	—
5.0L (305)	1989	70	525	75	570
5.0L: MT	1990-91	75	525	75	570
AT	1990-91	75	570	—	—
5.0L	1992	75	525	75	570
5.0L (307)	1989	70	525	75	570
5.7L (350)	1989-92	75	630	—	—
	1993-00	75	525	—	—

GENERATOR

Application	Rated Output (amps)	Test Output (amps)
1989-91	74, 80, 85, 100, 105, 108, 120	1
1992-93 LeMans	60, 72	1
1992-97 Others	80, 100, 105, 124, 140	1
1998-00 Sunfire, Grand Am, Grand Prix	105	73 @ 2000
All others	105, 124	1

1 Output at 2000 rpm must be within 15 amps of rated output.

REGULATOR

Application	Test Temp. (deg. F/C)	Voltage Setting
1989-95	Warm	13.5-16.0
1996-00	Warm	13.0-16.0

STARTER

Engine	Year	Cranking Voltage (min. volts)	Ampere Draw @ Cranking Speed
All	1989-00	9.0	—

SPARK PLUGS

Engine	Year	Gap (inches)	Gap (mm)	Torque (ft-lb)
4-cyl.				
1.6L (98) LeMans	1989	.060[1]	1.52[1]	7-15
	1990-93	.045	1.14	7-15
2.0L OHC ex. Turbo	1989-94	.045	1.14	7-15
2.0L OHC Turbo	1989-90	.035	.89	15
2.2L	1995-00	.060	1.52	13
2.3L	1989-94	.035	.89	17
	1995	.060	1.52	17
2.4L	1996-00	.060	1.52	13
2.5L (151)	1989-91	.060	1.52	7-15
6-cyl.				
2.8L (173)	1989	.045	1.14	7-15
3.1L Code T, D	1989-94	.045	1.14	11
Code M, J	1994-00	.060	1.52	11
3.3L	1992-93	.060	1.52	11
3.4L	1991-96	.045	1.14	11
3.8L (231) Code C, L	1989-91	.060	1.52	20
3.8L	1992-00	.060	1.52	11
8-cyl.				
5.0L (305)	1989-91	.035	.89	22
	1992	.035	.89	11
5.0L (307)	1989	.060	1.52	20
5.7L (350)	1989-91	.035	.89	20
	1992	.035	.89	11
	1993-97	.050	1.24	11
	1998-00	.060	1.52	15

1 When AC R45XLS or equivalent plugs are used, .045 inch (1.14 mm).

IGNITION COIL
FOR TESTING AND ADJUSTMENT DIAGRAMS, SEE APPENDIX A.

Application	Year	Resistance (ohms) Primary[1]	Resistance (ohms) Secondary[2]
All w/distributor	1989-92	0-2	6,000-30,000
1.6L	1993	Primary	0.5 approx.
		Secondary	8,300 approx.
2.0L, 2.5L, 2.8L, 3.1L, 3.4L	1989-95	—	5,000-10,000
2.2L, 2.4L	1995-00	—	5,000-8,000
2.3L	1989-95	—	10,000 max.
3.0L, 3.8L: Type I coils[3]	1989-92	.5-1.0	10,000-13,000
Type II coils[3]	1992	.3-.5	5,000-7,000
3.1L, 3.4L	1996-00	—	5,000-7,000
3.3L	1992	.5-.9	5,000-8,000
3.3L, 3.8L	1993-95	.5-.9	5,000-8,000
	1996-00	—	5,000-8,000

1 Without distributor, measured between the two coil primary power wires on each coil.

2 Without distributor, measured across each coil's two towers with coil removed from vehicle.

3 Type I coils, 3 coil towers on each side of coil pack.
Type II coils, 6 coil towers on one side of coil pack.

DISTRIBUTOR PICKUP
FOR TESTING AND ADJUSTMENT DIAGRAMS, SEE APPENDIX B.

Engine	Year	Resistance (ohms)	Air Gap (in./mm)
All w/distributor	1989-93	500-1500	—

BASE TIMING
FOR TESTING AND ADJUSTMENT DIAGRAMS, SEE APPENDIX C.

Set timing at slow idle and Before Top Dead Center, unless otherwise specified.

Disconnect and plug distributor vacuum hose at distributor.

1989-91 2.0L (122) OHC.

Jumper terminals A & B of DLC under dash.

1989-93 1.6L LeMans: Ground the diagnostic test terminal. Line up pointer with notch on crankshaft pulley.

1989-92 All other FI w/distributors, disconnect timing bypass connector, single lead in engine harness between distributor and ECM.

5.0L (307), ground diagnostic terminal of DLC

PONTIAC
1989-2000 All Models
Firefly—See Geo/Chevrolet-Pontiac; Trans Sport—See Chevrolet/GMC Trucks
UNDERHOOD SERVICE SPECIFICATIONS
PCTU4

PCTU4

BASE TIMING Continued

Engine	Year	Man. Trans. (degrees) @ RPM	Auto. Trans. (degrees) @ RPM
1.6L LeMans	1989-93	10	10 N
2.0L (121) OHC	1989-91	8	8 D
2.8L (173) Firebird, Fiero	1989	10	10 D
3.1L Firebird	1990-92	10	10 D
5.0L TBI	1989-92	0	0 D
5.0L MFI	1989-92	6	6 D
5.0L (307)	1989	—	20 @ 1100 P
5.7L (350)	1989-92	—	6 D

FUEL SYSTEM

FUEL SYSTEM PRESSURE
FOR TESTING AND ADJUSTMENT DIAGRAMS, SEE APPENDIX D.

Carbureted models, pinch off fuel return hose.

All models with TBI, pressure measured at fuel inlet of TBI unit.

All models with MFI, pressure measured at fuel rail.

All ex. MFI

Engine	Year	PSI	RPM
4-cyl.			
1.6L (98)	1989-93	9.0-13.0	idle
		13 min.[1]	idle
2.0L (122)	1989	9.0-13.0	ign. on
		13 min.[1]	idle
2.5L (151)	1989-91	9.0-13.0	idle
		13 min.[1]	idle
8-cyl.			
5.0L (305) TBI	1989-92	9.0-13.0	idle
		13 min.[1]	idle
5.0L (307)	1989	5.5-6.5	idle

MFI

Engine	Year	Pressure (PSI) Ign. On	Pressure (PSI) Idle	Fuel Pump[1]
2.0L	1992-94	40-47	30-44	47 min.
2.0L (122) Turbo	1989-90	35-38	25-30	65 min.
2.2L	1995-00	40-47	30-44	47 min.
2.3L (138), 2.4L	1989-00	40-47	30-44	47 min.
3.1L	1989-99	40-47	31-44	47 min.
3.3L	1992-93	40-47	31-44	47 min.
3.4L	1991-95	40-47	31-44	47 min.
	1996-97	48-55	38-52	55 min.
3.8L (231) Code C	1989	40-47	37-43	75 min.
3.8L Code C, L, 1	1990-95	40-47	30-44	47 min.
3.8L Code K	1995-00	48-55	38-52	55 min.
5.0L (305), 5.7L (350)	1989-00	40-47	30-44	47 min.

1 With fuel return line briefly restricted.

IDLE SPEED W/COMPUTER CONTROL
FOR TESTING AND ADJUSTMENT DIAGRAMS, SEE APPENDIX E.

Midpoint of range given is the preferred setting speed.

If no specifications are listed under "Minimum Speed," the idle is not adjustable.

All w/FI & TBI when specifications are listed in Minimum Speed column: Ground diagnostic lead and turn ignition on for 30 seconds. Remove IAC lead and remove ground from diagnostic connector. Start engine and set minimum speed to specified value.

All carbureted w/ILC: Disconnect and plug vacuum hoses at EGR and canister purge valves. With engine at operating temperature, remove vacuum hose from ILC and plug. Set maximum speed to specifications by holding hex nut and turning plunger shaft. Reconnect ILC vacuum hose and check that minimum speed is correct. To adjust, remove rubber and metal plugs from rear center outlet tube, insert a 3/32" Allen wrench. Remove ILC hose and plug. Connect a remote vacuum source and apply vacuum to the unit. Adjust carb base screw to obtain minimum speed.

IDLE SPEED W/COMPUTER CONTROL Continued
ALL FUEL INJECTED

Engine	Year	Minimum Speed Man. Trans.	Minimum Speed Auto. Trans.	Checking Speed Man. Trans.	Checking Speed Auto. Trans.
1.6L (98)	1989-93	550-650	450-550 N	—	—
2.0L (122) ex. OHC	1989	450-650	450-650 N	—	—
2.0L (122) OHC	1989-91	450-600	450-600 N	800[1] max.	800[1] N max.
2.0L OHC	1992-93	—	—	800-950	775-925 N
2.0L (122) OHC Turbo	1989-90	550-650	550-650 N	—	—
2.0L	1992-94	—	—	800-950	775-925 N
2.2L	1990-91	450-650	450-650 N	—	—
	1992	—	—	525-675	525-675 N
2.5L (151)	1989-91	550-650	550-650 N	750-850	750-850 N
2.8L (173), 3.1L Firebird	1989			750-950	650-750 D
	1989	600-700	500-600 D		
3.1L MFI	1990-91	—	—	800[1] max.	800 N[1] max.
3.1L MFI FWD	1992-93	—	—	800-900	700-800 N
3.1L Firebird	1992	—	—	800[1] max.	800 N[1] max.
3.3L	1992-93	—	—	—	650-750 N
3.4L DOHC	1991-93	—	—	800-900	700-800 N
	1994-95	—	—	650-750	650-750 N
3.4L Firebird	1993-95	—	—	800[1] max.	800 N[1] max.
3.8L Code C	1989	—	—	—	650-750 N
3.8L	1990-91	—	—	—	650-850 N
	1992-95	—	—	—	650-750 N
	1996-97	—	—	—	600-700 N
5.0L (305) MFI	1989	400-450	400-450 N	—	—
	1990-92	—	—	600-800	600-800 N
5.0L (305) TBI	1989	400-450	400-450 N	—	—
	1990-92	—	—	550-750	500-600 D
5.7L (350)	1989	—	400-450 N	—	—
	1990-92	—	—	—	600-800 N

1 With ISC fully retracted.

ALL CARBURETED

Engine	Year	Trans.	Min. Speed	Max. Speed	Fast	Step of Cam
5.0L (307)	1989	AT	450 D	700 D	550 D	Low
base idle	1989	AT	450 D			

ENGINE MECHANICAL

TIGHTENING TORQUES
FOR CYLINDER HEAD TORQUE SEQUENCES AND DIAGRAMS, SEE APPENDIX F.

Some fasteners are tightened in more than one step.

Some values are specified in inches.

Engine	Year	TORQUE FOOT-POUNDS/NEWTON METERS Cylinder Head	Intake Manifold	Exhaust Manifold	Crankshaft Pulley	Water Pump
1.6L LeMans	1989-91	18/25, +60°, +60°, +60°, plus 30°-50° eng. warm	16/22	10/13	40/55	6/8
1.6L LeMans	1992-93	18/25, +60°, +60°, +30°	16/22	16/22	41/55	6/8
2.0L (122) ex. OHC	1989	73-83/ 99-113[1], 62-70/ 85-95[2]	15-22/ 20-30	6-13/ 8-18	66-89/ 90-120	15-22/ 20-30
2.0L (122) OHC	1989-94	18/25, +60°, +60°, +60°, plus 30°-50° eng. warm	16/22	16/22	15/21	18/25
2.2L	1990	41/55, +45°, +45°, +20°[1], +10°[2]	18/25	88"/13, studs 10/13, nuts	85/115	18/25

UNDERHOOD SERVICE SPECIFICATIONS

TIGHTENING TORQUES Continued

Engine	Year	Cylinder Head	Intake Manifold	Exhaust Manifold	Crankshaft Pulley	Water Pump
		TORQUE FOOT-POUNDS/NEWTON METERS				
2.2L	1991-00	43/58[2], 46/63[1], +90°	22/30[12]	115"/13	77/105	22/30[2], 18/25[1]
2.3L	1989-94	3	18/25	31/42	74/100 +90°	10/12, cover 19/26, others
2.4L	1996-00	14	17/24	110"/13	129/178, +90°	124"/14, cover 19/26, others
2.5L	1989-91	18/25, 26/35[7], +90°	25/34	25/43[4], 37-50[6]	162/220	25/34
2.8L, 3.1L MFI Code T	1989-94	33/45, +90°	15/20, 24/33	25/34	76/103	89"/10, short 18/24, long
2.8L, 3.1L Firebird	1989	33/45, +90°	13-18/ 18-24	25/34	66-84/ 90-115	15/21, short 27/37, long
3.1L Firebird	1990-92	40/55, +90°	15/21[8], 19/26[9]	25/34	70/95	88"/10, small 15/21, med. 25/34, large
3.1L Code M	1994-97	33/45, +90°	115"/13, lower 18/25, upper	12/16	75/102	89"/10
	1998-99	37/50, +90°	115"/13, lower 18/25, upper	12/16	75/102	89"/10
3.3L	1992-93	35/47, +130°[10]	88"/10, upper 22/30, lower	38/52	110/150, +76°	90"/19, short 22/30, long
3.4L DOHC	1991-94	37/50	18/25	116"/13, nuts 13/17, studs	78/105[1], 37/50[2]	89"/10
	1995-96	44/60, +90°	18/25	116"/13, nuts 13/17, studs	78/105, large bolt 37/50, small bolt	89"/10
3.4L Firebird	1993-94	33/45, +90°	18/25, upper 22/30, lower	18/25	50/79	88"/10[2], 33/45[1]
3.8L	1989-90	35/47, +130°[11]	88"/10, lower 19/26, upper 13	41/55	219/297	84"/10[2], 29/39[1]
	1991-95	35/47, +130°[10]		38/52	110/150, +76°	84"/10[2], 29/39[1]
	1996-97	37/50, +130°[10]	11/15, upper 89"/10, lower	107"/12	110/150, +76°	11/15, +80°
	1998-00	37/50 +120°	11/15 upper 89"/10, lower	22/30	110/150 +76°	11/15 +80°
4.3L, 5.0L, 5.7L	1989-92	68/93	35/47, 26/35[6]	20/27[4]	70/95	30/40
5.0L (307)	1989	40/54 +95°, first and last bolts on exhaust manifold side +120°, all others	40/54	25/34	200-310/ 270-400	11/14
5.7L	1993-95	65/88	71"/8, 35/48	26/35	75/102	31/42
	1996-97	22/30, 15	89"/10, 37/50	30/40	75/112	33/45
	1998-00	22/30 +76° +76°[16]				

1 Long or large bolts.
2 Short bolts. Medium bolts, if equipped, 16/21.
3 Tighten bolts 1-8 (long bolts), 30/40. Tighten bolts 9-10 (short bolts), 26/35. Then, turn all bolts 90°.

TIGHTENING TORQUES Continued

4 Four outer bolts.
5 Turn last bolt on left (number nine) to 29/40. Then, turn all except number nine 120°, turn number nine 90°.
6 Three inner bolts.
7 Turn last bolt on left (number nine) to 18/25.
8 Center two.
9 Others.
10 Turn four inner bolts an additional 30°.
11 To 60/81 maximum.
12 Upper manifold. Lower manifold: studs, 89"/10; nuts, 24/33.
13 1991-92: upper to lower, 21/29; lower to block, 89"/10. 1993-97: upper to lower & lower to block, 11/15.
14 Tighten bolts 1-8, 40/65. Tighten bolts 9-10, 30/40. Then, turn all bolts 90°.
15 After tightening all bolts to initial value, turn small bolts 67°. Turn medium and large bolts 80°.
16 Tighten medium bolts at front and rear of each cylinder an additional 34°.

COMPRESSION PRESSURE

At cranking speed or specified rpm, engine temperature normalized, throttle open.

Engine	Year	PSI	Maximum Variation PSI
All	1989-00	100 min.	1

1 Lowest cylinder pressure must be more than 70% of highest cylinder pressure.

BELT TENSION
All Except With Automatic Tensioner

A belt is considered used after one engine revolution.

Use a strand tension gauge. Measurements are in pounds.

Engine	Year	Generator	Power Steering	Air Cond.	Air Pump
Used Belts					
1.6L	1989-90	77	—	80	—
	1991	71	—	80-100	—
2.0L OHC	1989	—	—	80	—
2.0L OHC Turbo	1989	—	—	115	—
2.3L	1989-94	—	110	—	—
2.5L Code U	1989-91	90	90	90	—
5.0L (307)	1989	80	90	90	45
Cogged or ⅜" belt	1989	55	—	—	70
New Belts					
1.6L	1989-90	90	—	155	—
	1991	90	—	80-100	—
2.0L OHC	1989	—	—	155	—
2.0L OHC Turbo	1989	—	—	225	—
2.3L	1989-94	—	110	—	—
2.5L Code U	1989-91	165	180	165	—
5.0L (307)	1989	160	170	170	80
Cogged or ⅜" belt	1989	145	—	—	145

All With Automatic Tensioner
If index marks on tensioner are outside the range, replace the belt. If marks are within range and belt tension is below specified value, replace tensioner.

Engine	Year	Tension
2.0L OHC	1989-94	36-44
wA/C	1992-94	112-124
2.2L	1995-96	63-77
2.3L, 2.4L	1989-96	50 min.
2.5L 6000	1989-91	50-70
2.8L FWD	1989	50-70
2.8L Firebird	1989	116-142
w/A/C	1989	103-127
3.1L FWD	1989-95	50-70
3.1L Firebird	1990	116-142
w/A/C	1990	103-127
3.1L Firebird	1991-92	95-140
w/A/C	1991-92	85-110
3.1L Grand Am	1996	50-70
Grand Prix	1996	35-55
3.1L FWD	1997	50-70
3.3L	1992-93	67 min.
	1996	35-55
3.4L		67 min.
3.8L FWD	1989-90	50-70
	1995-96	50-70
5.0L, 5.7L Firebird	1989-92	99-121

PONTIAC
1989-2000 All Models
Firefly—See Geo/Chevrolet-Pontiac; Trans Sport—See Chevrolet/GMC Trucks
UNDERHOOD SERVICE SPECIFICATIONS
PCTU6

PCTU6

SERPENTINE BELT DIAGRAMS

SERPENTINE BELT DIAGRAMS Continued

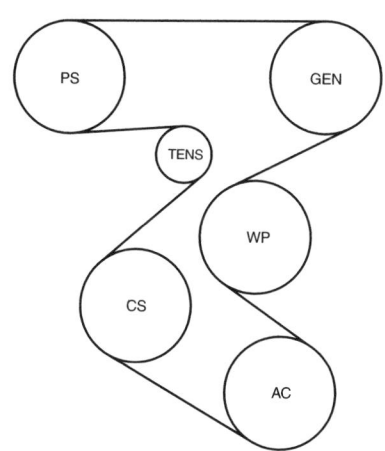

1989 2.0L Code 1
1990-00 2.2L Code G, 4 w/o AC

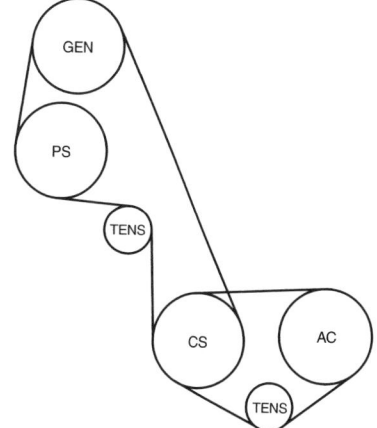

1989-91 2.0L OHC
Code K,M w/AC

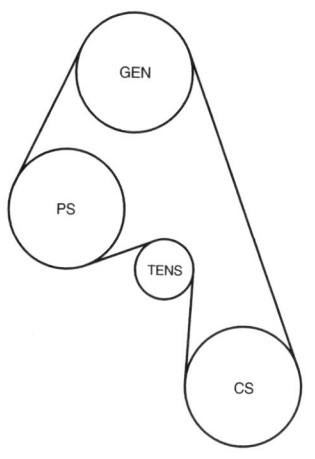

1989 2.0L Code 1
1990-00 2.2L Code G, 4 w/AC

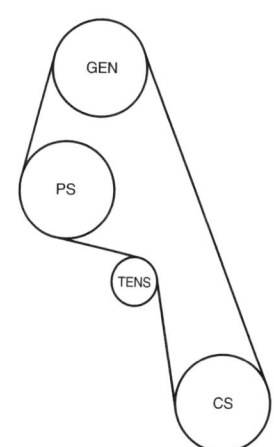

1992-94 2.0L OHC
Code H w/o AC

1989-91 2.0L OHC
Code K,M w/o AC

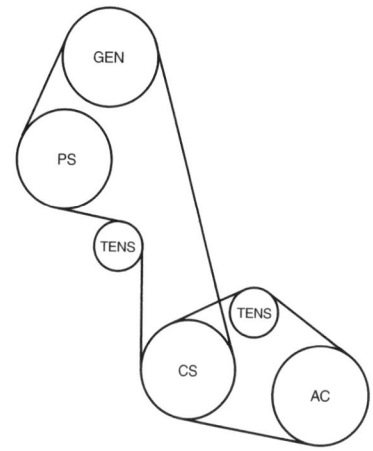

1992-94 2.0L OHC
Code H w/AC

PONTIAC
1989-2000 All Models
Firefly—See Geo/Chevrolet-Pontiac; Trans Sport—See Chevrolet/GMC Trucks

UNDERHOOD SERVICE SPECIFICATIONS

PCTU7

PCTU7

SERPENTINE BELT DIAGRAMS Continued

SERPENTINE BELT DIAGRAMS Continued

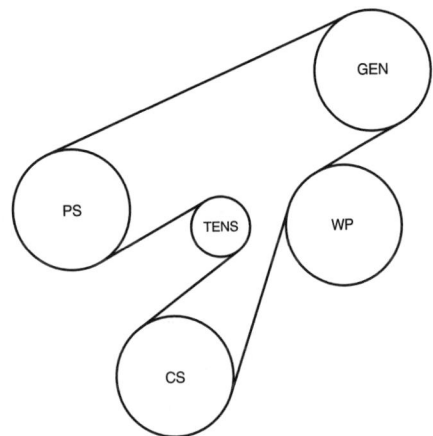

1989-92 2.5L
Code R w/o AC

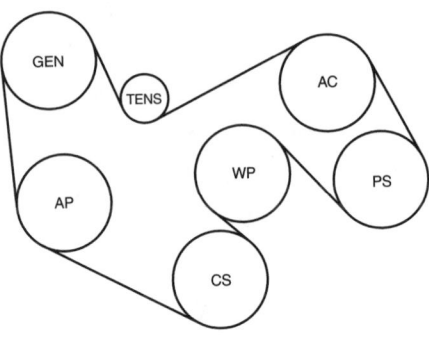

1989 2.8L
Firebird w/AT, w/o AC

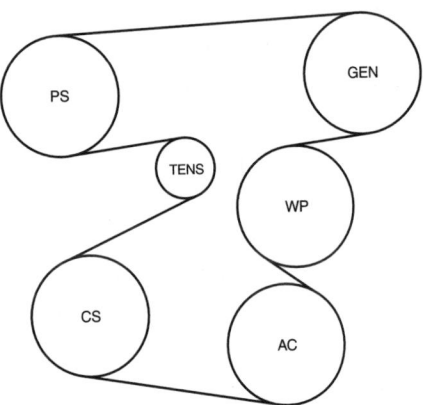

1989-92 2.5L
Code R w/AC

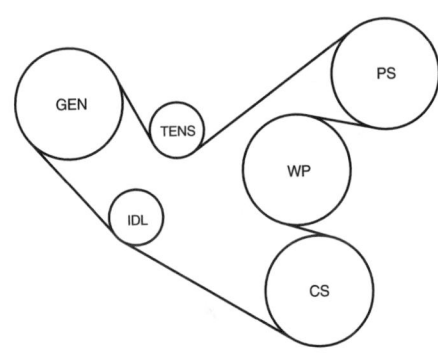

1989 2.8L
Firebird w/MT, w/o AC

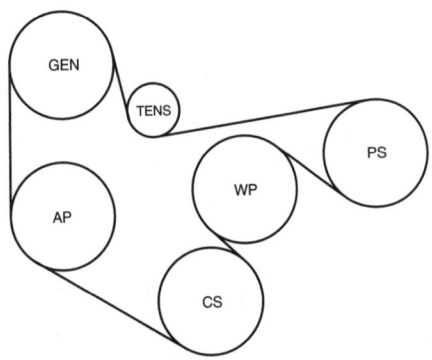

1989 2.8L
Firebird w/MT, w/o AC

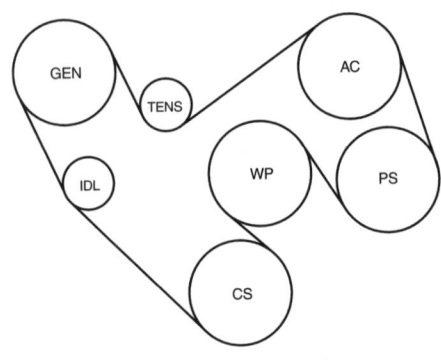

1989
Firebird w/MT & AC

SERPENTINE BELT DIAGRAMS Continued

SERPENTINE BELT DIAGRAMS Continued

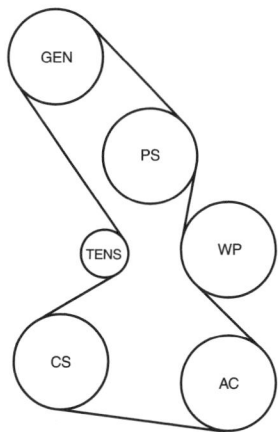

1989-98 2.8L, 3.1L FWD
Code W, T, M, D
1996-00 3.4L

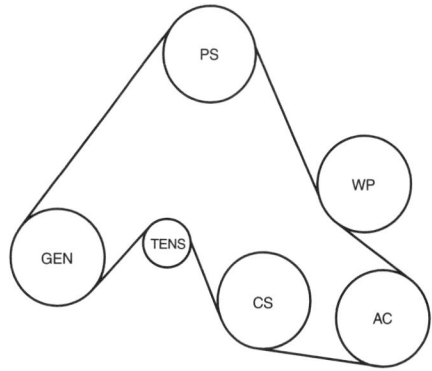

1991-97 3.4L DOHC

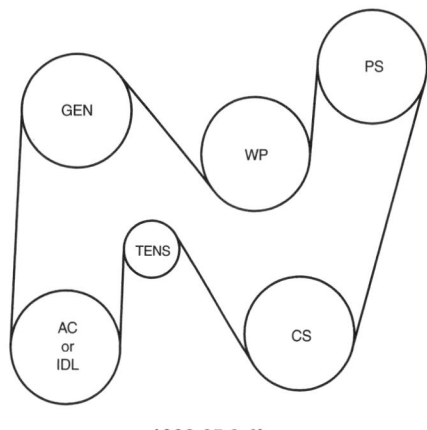

1990-92 3.1L
Firebird w/AC

1993-95 3.4L
Firebird

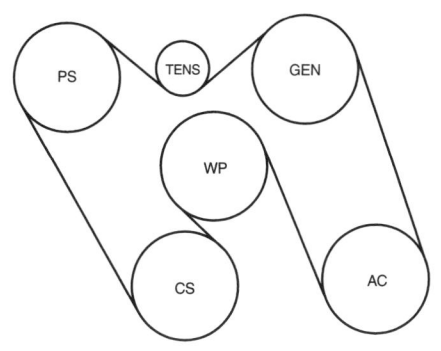

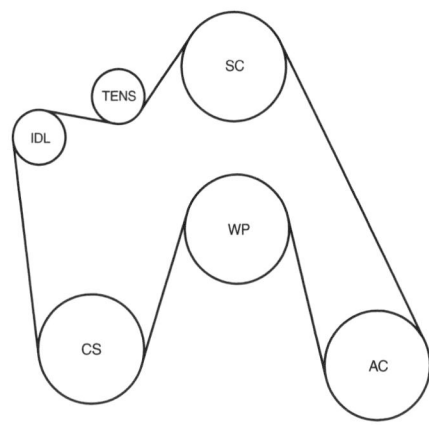

1989-94 3.3L Code N
3.8L Code C, L FWD

1991-95 3.8L
Supercharged Inner Belt

PONTIAC
1989-2000 All Models
Firefly—See Geo/Chevrolet-Pontiac; Trans Sport—See Chevrolet/GMC Trucks

UNDERHOOD SERVICE SPECIFICATIONS

PCTU9

PCTU9

SERPENTINE BELT DIAGRAMS Continued

SERPENTINE BELT DIAGRAMS Continued

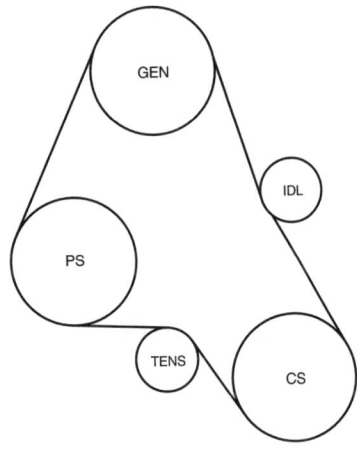

1991-95 3.8L
Supercharged Outer Belt

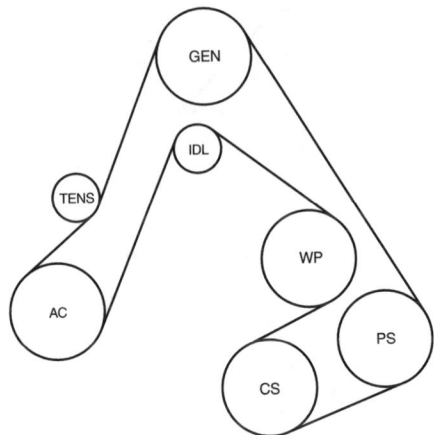

1995-00 3.8L
Firebird

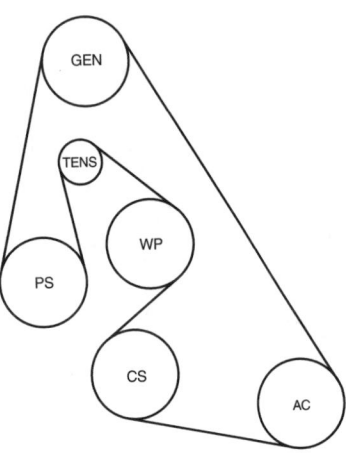

1995-00 3.8L FWD Code K
1995-00 3.8L Supercharged Outer Belt

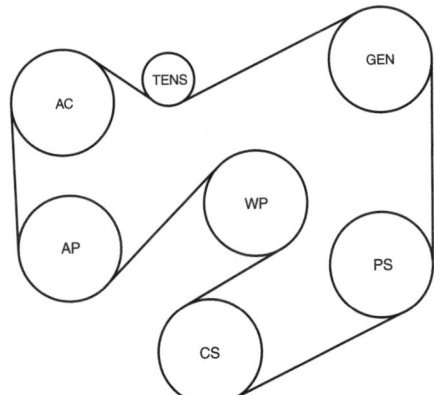

1989-93 5.0L, 5.7L
Code E, F, 7, 8

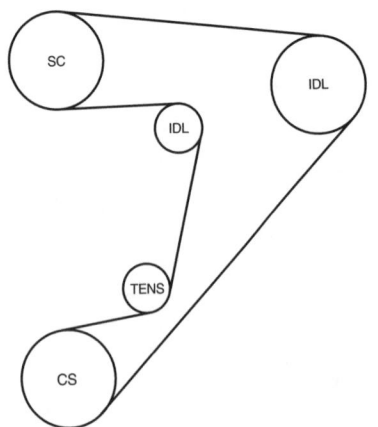

1995-00 3.8L
Supercharged Inner Belt

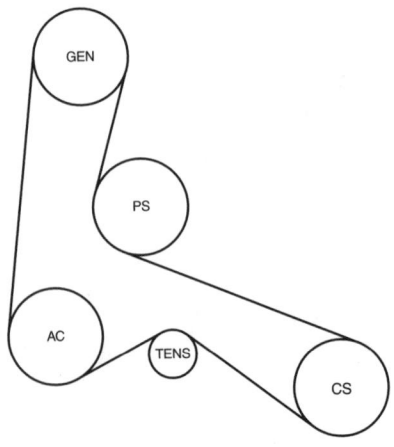

1993-97 5.7L Code P

PONTIAC
1989-2000 All Models
Firefly—See Geo/Chevrolet-Pontiac; Trans Sport—See Chevrolet/GMC Trucks
UNDERHOOD SERVICE SPECIFICATIONS
PCTU10

PCTU10

SERPENTINE BELT DIAGRAMS Continued

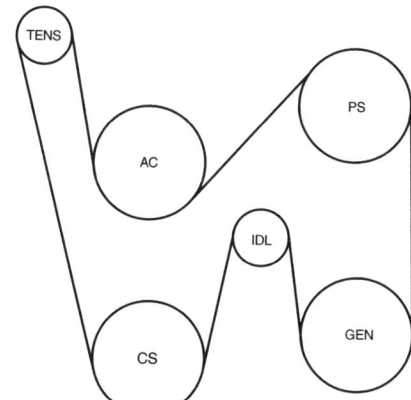

*1997-00 5.7L Code G
Firebird-Outer Belt*

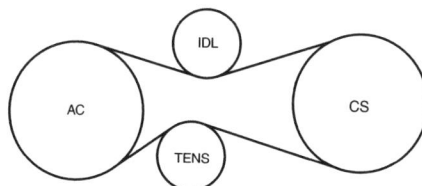

*1997-00 5.7L Code G
Firebird-Inner Belt*

ENGINE COMPUTER SYSTEM

DIAGNOSTIC TROUBLE CODES
FOR TESTING AND ADJUSTMENT DIAGRAMS, SEE APPENDIX G.

1989-95 All w/12-pin DLC
Connect a jumper between A and B terminals on under dash connector (identified by a slot between the terminals or on two upper right-hand cavities of the two-row connector). Turn ignition on. Code 12 will flash three times, then codes in memory will be displayed. Do not run engine with jumper connected.

1994-00 All w/16-pin DLC, OBD-II
A Scan tool is required to retrieve codes and code definitions.

1989-95 All w/12-pin DLC
Code 12 No tach reference to ECM
Code 13 Oxygen sensor circuit
Code 14 Engine coolant sensor circuit shorted
Code 15 Engine coolant sensor circuit open
Code 16 Missing 2X reference circuit (1992-95 2.3L)
Code 16 System over voltage (others)
Code 17 Camshaft sensor (Firebird V6)
Code 17 Spark reference circuit (others)
Code 18 Cam and crank sensor sync error (1989-95)
Code 18 Injector circuit (V8)
Code 19 Crankshaft position sensor (1989-91)
Code 19 Intermittent 7x or 58x reference circuit (1992-95)
Code 22 Throttle position sensor circuit shorted
Code 23 Open or grounded MC solenoid (carbureted)
Code 23 Intake air temperature circuit open
Code 24 Vehicle speed sensor circuit
Code 25 Intake air temperature (IAT) circuit (high temperature indicated)
Code 26 Canister purge solenoid (1994-95 V8)
Code 27 EGR vacuum control solenoid circuit (1994-95 V8)
Code 28 Transmission range pressure switch (1994-95 V8)
Codes 26, 27, 28 Quad driver error (others)
Code 29 Secondary air pump circuit
Codes 27, 28, 29 Transaxle gear switches (1989-93 3.3L, 3.8L)
Code 31 Wastegate solenoid (FI Turbo)

DIAGNOSTIC TROUBLE CODES Continued
Code 31 EVAP canister purge solenoid (carbureted)
Code 31 Park/Neutral switch (FI others)
Code 32 Barometric or altitude sensor (carbureted)
Code 32 EGR system fault (FI)
Code 33 MAP, MAF sensor circuit open
Code 34 MAP, MAF sensor circuit shorted
Code 34 Vacuum sensor circuit (carbureted)
Code 35 Idle speed or idle air control circuit
Code 36 MAF burn off circuit (1989-90)
Code 36 Transaxle shift control problem (1992-93 others)
Code 36 24x signal circuit (1993-94 Firebird)
Code 37 Transmission brake switch error
Code 38 Brake switch
Code 39 Torque converter clutch (3.3L, 3.8L)
Code 39 Clutch switch circuit (Firebird)
Code 41 Ignition control timing circuit problem (Camaro V6, all V8)
Code 41 No distributor reference pulses to ECM (carbureted)
Code 41 Ignition reference circuit (2.3L)
Code 41 Camshaft sensor circuit (3.8L Code C)
Code 41 Cylinder select error (others)
Code 42 IC or IC bypass circuit grounded or open
Code 43 Knock sensor signal
Code 44 Air/fuel mixture too lean (left side, with dual sensors)
Codes 44 & 45 Faulty oxygen sensor
Code 45 Air/fuel mixture rich (left side, with dual sensors)
Code 46 Vehicle anti-theft system (Firebird)
Code 46 Power steering pressure switch (others)
Code 47 Knock sensor module missing
Code 48 Mass airflow sensor circuit
Code 48 Misfire
Code 50 System voltage low
Code 51 EEPROM programming error (V8)
Code 51 Faulty PROM, MEM-CAL, ECM or installation
Code 52 Fuel CALPAK
Codes 53, 54, 55 EGR system (1993-95 3.3L, 3.8L)
Code 53 EGR vacuum sensor incorrect (carbureted)
Code 53 Vehicle anti-theft system (5.0L TBI)
Code 53 System over voltage (FI, others)
Code 54 Shorted MC solenoid or faulty ECM (carbureted)
Code 54 Fuel pump circuit voltage low (FI)
Code 55 Fuel lean monitor (1993-95 Firebird V8)
Code 55 Grounded V-REF, faulty oxygen sensor or ECM (others)
Code 56 Quad driver B circuit
Code 58 PASS fuel enable circuit (1990-95)
Code 58 Transmission fluid temperature sensor circuit shorted
Code 59 Transmission fluid temperature sensor circuit open
Code 61 A/C system (1993-95 Firebird)
Code 61 Cruise vent solenoid circuit (1992 3.8L)
Code 61 Degraded oxygen sensor (others)
Code 62 Transmission gear switch signal (others)
Code 62 Cruise vac circuit (3.8L)
Code 63 MAP sensor voltage high (others)
Code 63 Right oxygen sensor, circuit open (1993-95 Firebird)
Code 64 MAP sensor voltage low (others)
Code 64 Right oxygen sensor lean (1993-95 Firebird)
Codes 63, 64 EGR flow problem (1992-93 3.8L)
Code 65 EGR flow problem (1989-91 3.8L)
Code 65 Cruise servo position sensor (1992-95 3.8L)
Code 65 Right oxygen sensor rich (1993-95 Firebird)
Code 65 Fuel injector circuit (others)
Code 66 A/C pressure switch
Code 67 A/C pressure sensor (1993-95 Firebird)
Code 67 Cruise switch circuit (others)
Code 68 A/C relay circuit (1993-95 Firebird)
Code 68 Cruise system problem (others)
Code 69 A/C head pressure switch circuit (others)
Code 69 A/C clutch circuit (1993-95 Firebird)
Code 70 A/C clutch relay driver (V8)
Code 70 A/C pressure sensor (Camaro V6)
Code 72 Vehicle speed sensor
Code 73 A/C evaporator temperature sensor circuit shorted (Camaro V6)
Code 73 Transmission pressure control solenoid circuit (V8)
Code 74 Traction control system circuit
Code 75 Transmission system voltage low (V8)
Code 75 Digital EGR #1 solenoid (others)
Code 76 Digital EGR #2 solenoid (others)
Code 77 Cooling fan relay (V8)
Code 77 Digital EGR #3 solenoid (others)
Code 78 Secondary cooling fan relay
Code 79 Transmission fluid over temperature

PONTIAC
1989-2000 All Models
Firefly—See Geo/Chevrolet-Pontiac; Trans Sport—See Chevrolet/GMC Trucks

UNDERHOOD SERVICE SPECIFICATIONS

DIAGNOSTIC TROUBLE CODES Continued

Code 80 Transmission converter clutch slippage excessive
Code 81 Transmission 2-3 shift
Code 82 Transmission 1-2 shift (V8)
Code 82 Ignition control 3X circuit (others)
Code 83 Reverse inhibit system
Code 84 Transmission 3-2 control
Code 85 Transmission converter clutch locked on (V8)
Code 85 Faulty or incorrect PROM (others)
Code 86 A/D chip error
Code 87 EEPROM error
Code 90 Transmission clutch solenoid circuit error
Code 91 Skip shift lamp circuit
Code 93 Vehicle speed sensor output circuit (Camaro V8)
Code 93 Transmission pressure control solenoid (others)
Code 95 Change oil lamp circuit
Code 96 Low oil lamp circuit (Impala, Caprice)
Code 96 Transmission system voltage low (others)
Code 97 Vehicle speed sensor output circuit
Code 98 Invalid PCM program
Code 99 Invalid PCM program (1994-95, others)
Code 99 Tach output circuit (Camaro V8)
Code 99 Power management, cruise system (1991-95)

SENSORS, INPUT
TEMPERATURE SENSORS

Engine	Year	Sensor	Resistance Ohms @ deg. F/C
All	1989-90 1989-91	Coolant, Intake Air[1]	13,500 @ 20/-7 7500 @ 40/4 3400 @ 70/20 1800 @ 100/38 450 @ 160/70 185 @ 210/100
All	1991-00 1992-00	Coolant Intake Air	28,700 @ 4/-20 12,300 @ 23/-5 7280 @ 41/-5 3500 @ 68/20 1460 @ 104/40 470 @ 160/70 1800 @ 210/100
All	1994-00	Transmission Oil[1]	25,809-28,677 @ -4 (-20) 14,558-16,176 @ 14 (-10) 8481-10,365 @ 32 (0) 3164-3867 @ 68 (20) 1313-1605 @ 104 (40) 420-514 @ 158 (70) 159-195 @ 212 (100) 69-85 @ 266 (130)

1 As equipped, not used on all engines.

MANIFOLD ABSOLUTE, VACUUM, AND BAROMETRIC PRESSURE SENSORS

Engines may use one, or a combination of these sensors. All sensors appear the same. Manifold Absolute Pressure sensors have a vacuum line connected between the unit and manifold vacuum. On Barometric Pressure sensors, the line is not used and the connector is either open or has a filter installed over it. Pressure sensors also have a vacuum line between the sensor and intake manifold and appear only on carbureted models.

Barometric Pressure Sensors: Measure voltage with ignition on and engine off.

Manifold Absolute Pressure Sensors: Measure voltage with ignition on and engine off. Start engine and apply 10 in. Hg./34 kPa to unit, voltage should be 1.5 volts minimum less.

Pressure Sensors: Measure voltage as indicated.

5 volts reference.

Engine	Year	Sensor	Voltage @ Altitude
All, as equipped	1989-90	Barometric	3.8-5.5 @ 0-1000 3.6-5.3 @ 1000-2000 3.5-5.1 @ 2000-3000 3.3-5.0 @ 3000-4000 3.2-4.8 @ 4000-5000 3.0-4.6 @ 5000-6000 2.9-4.5 @ 6000-7000 2.5-4.3 @ 7000+

SENSORS, INPUT Continued
MANIFOLD ABSOLUTE, VACUUM, AND BAROMETRIC PRESSURE SENSORS Cont.

Engine	Year	Sensor	Voltage @ Condition
All	1989-00	MAP	1.0-1.5 @ idle 4.0-4.8 @ idle

CRANKSHAFT POSITION SENSORS
Resistance is measured at room temperature.

Engine	Year	Resistance (ohms)	Air Gap in./mm
2.0L	1989-91	900-1200	—
	1992-93	480-680	—
2.2L	1993-96	900-1200	—
	1997-00	700-1300	—
2.3L, 2.4L	1989-00	500-900	—
2.5L	1989-91	800-900	—
2.8L, 3.1L, 3.4L	1989-95	900-1200	—
3.0L, 3.3L, 3.8L FI	1989-93	—	.035/.65

THROTTLE POSITION SENSOR (TPS)
Verify that minimum idle is at specified value.

Make all checks/adjustments with engine at operating temperature.

Carbureted Models: Remove aluminum plug covering the adjustment screw. Remove the screw and connect a digital voltmeter to black wire (-) and either of the two other colored wires (+). If voltage is approximately 5 volts, this is the reference voltage lead. Connect DVOM to other wire in this case. Apply thread locking compound to the screw and with ignition on and engine not running (as applies), quickly adjust screw to obtain specified voltage at indicated condition.

Fuel Injected Models: Disconnect harness connector from TPS. Using three six-inch jumper wires, reconnect harness to TPS. With ignition on and engine not running (as applies), connect a digital voltmeter to black wire (-) and either of the two other colored wires (+). If voltage is approximately 5 volts, this is the reference voltage lead. Connect DVOM to other wire in this case. Check reading against specified value. If TPS is adjustable, loosen the unit retaining screws and rotate the unit to reach specified value.

Model	Year	TPS Voltage[1] Idle	TPS Voltage[1] WOT (approx.)
1.6L	1989-90	.20-1.25[3]	—
	1991-93	.40-1.25[3]	4.5
2.0L (122)	1989	.33-1.33[3]	5.0
	1990-91	.35-1.28[3]	4.5
	1992-94	.33-1.33[3]	4.5
2.2L	1990-94	.33-1.33[3]	4.0 min.
	1995-00	.20-.90[3]	4.0 min.
2.3L (138)	1989	.54	—
2.3L, 2.4L	1990-93	.40-.90[3]	4.9
	1994	.36-.96	4.0 min.
	1995-00	.20-.90[3]	4.0 min.
2.5L (151)	1989	.20-1.25[3]	4.5
	1990-91	.33-1.33[3]	4.8
2.8L Tempest, 6000	1989	.29-.98[3]	—
2.8L Firebird	1989	.55	—
3.1L	1989-95	.29-.98[3]	4.0 min.
	1996-00	.20-.74[3]	4.0. min.
3.3L	1992	.40	4.0 min.
	1993	.20-.74[3]	4.0 min.
3.4L	1991-94	.29-.98	4.0 min.
	1995-96	.20-.74	4.0-4.7
3.8L (231) FI	1989-92	.40	4.0 min.
3.8L	1993-00	.20-.74[3]	4.0 min.
5.0L (305) MFI, 5.7L	1989	.54	—
5.0L MFI, 5.7L	1990-91	.36-.96 max.[3]	5.0
	1992	.36-.62[3]	4.0 min.
5.0L (305) TBI	1989-90	.20-1.25[3]	5.0
	1991	.45-1.25[3]	5.0
	1992	.20-.95[3]	5.0
5.7L	1993-97	.36-.96	4.0 min.
	1998-00	.40-.90	4.0 min.

1 ± .10, carbureted engines; ± .05 FI engines.
2 High step of fast idle cam.
3 Not adjustable.

SENSORS, INPUT Continued
KNOCK SENSOR

Engine	Year	Resistance (ohms)
2.2L, 2.3L, 2.4L	1994-00	90,000-110,000
3.1L, 3.4L, 3.8L	1992-95	3300-4500
	1996-00	90,000-110,000
5.7L	1994-95	3300-4500
	1996-00	90,000-110,000

ACTUATORS, OUTPUT
IDLE SPEED CONTROL
All engines with ISC.
Measured between terminals A & B and C & D.

Engine	Year	Resistance (ohms)
2.8L, 3.1L Grand Prix, 6000	1989	48-58
All Other TBI & MFI	1989	20 min.
All carbureted	1989	10 min.
LeMans	1990-91	20 min.
All Others	1990-00	40-80

FUEL INJECTORS

Engine	Year	Resistance (ohms)	Temperature (deg. F/C)
2.0L TBI	1989	1.2 min.	—
	1990-91	1.6 min.	—
2.0L Turbo	1989-91	2.0 min.	—

ACTUATORS, OUTPUT Continued
FUEL INJECTORS Continued

Engine	Year	Resistance (ohms)	Temperature (deg. F/C)
2.0L MFI	1992-94	5.9-7.3	—
2.2L	1995-97	11.4-12.6	68/20
	1998-99	1.95-2.30	68/20
2.3L	1989-94	1.95-2.15	140/60
2.4L	1996-98	1.95-2.30	68/20
2.5L	1989	1.2 min.	—
	1990-92	1.6 min.	—
2.8L, 3.1L:			
Grand Prix	1989-93	12-12.4	—
Firebird	1993	11.8-12.6	—
All others	1989-93	8 min.	—
	1994-99	11.4-12.6	—
3.3L	1991-93	11.8-12.6	68/20
3.4L	1992-93	12-12.4	—
	1994-97	11.8-12.6	—
3.8L	1991-93	14.5	68/20
	1994-95	14.3-14.7	—
	1996-99	11.4-12.6	—
5.0L TBI	1989-92	1.2 min.	—
5.0L, 5.7L MFI	1989-92	10 min.	—
	1993-99	11.8-12.6	—

MIXTURE CONTROL SOLENOID-CARBURETED ENGINES
On some engines, the ECM will be damaged if the resistance of the mixture control solenoid is less than specified.

Engine	Year	Resistance (ohms)
All	1989	10 min.

PORSCHE
1989-99

ENGINE IDENTIFICATION

To identify any engine by the manufacturer's code, follow the four steps designated by the numbered blocks.

1 **MODEL YEAR IDENTIFICATION:** Refer to illustration of the Vehicle Identification Number (V.I.N.). The year is indicated by a code letter which is the 10th character of the V.I.N.

3 **ENGINE CODE:** In the "CODE" column, find the engine code.

4 **ENGINE IDENTIFICATION:** On the line where the engine code appears, read to the right to identify the engine.

V.I.N. PLATE LOCATION:

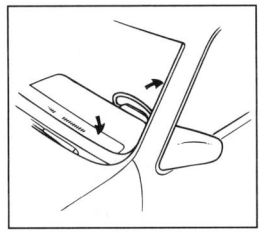

Driver's side windshield pillar, visible through windshield

1 MODEL YEAR IDENTIFICATION:

10th character of V.I.N.

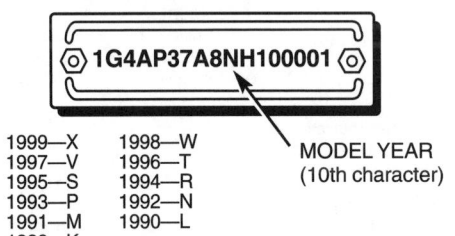

MODEL YEAR
(10th character)

1999—X	1998—W
1997—V	1996—T
1995—S	1994—R
1993—P	1992—N
1991—M	1990—L
1989—K	

2 ENGINE CODE LOCATION:

Prefix to engine number.
4-cyl. — 1989-98: Passenger's side of engine block, next to clutch housing.
6-cyl. — Boxster: Underneath crankcase; All others: Passenger's side of crankcase, next to fan housing.
8-cyl. — Top of front crankcase reinforcing rib.

ENGINE IDENTIFICATION (left table)

YEAR	3 ENGINE CODE	CYL.	DISPL. liters	cc	Fuel System	HP
1999	—	6	2.5	2480	DME	201
	M96	6	3.4	3387	DME	296
1998	—	6	2.5	2480	DME	201
	64T	6	3.6	3600	DME	282
1997	—	6	2.5	2480	DME	201
	64T	6	3.6	3600	DME	282
	—	6	3.6 T	3600 T	DME	400
1996	64T	6	3.6	3600	DME	282
	—	6	3.6 T	3600 T	DME	400
1995	42S	4	3.0	2990	DME	236
	64S	6	3.6	3600	DME	270
	85S	8	5.4	5397	LH	345
1994	42R	4	3.0	2990	DME	236
	—	6	3.6 T	3598 T	—	355
	63R	6	3.6	3600	DME	247
	81R, 85R	8	5.4	5397	LH	345
1993	42P	4	3.0	2990	DME	236
	62P	6	3.6	3600	DME	247
	85P, 81P	8	5.4	5397	LH	345
1992	42N	4	3.0	2990	DME	236
	68N	6	3.3 T	3299 T	CIS	315
	62N	6	3.6	3600	DME	247

ENGINE IDENTIFICATION (right table)

YEAR	3 ENGINE CODE	CYL.	DISPL. liters	cc	Fuel System	HP
1992 Cont'd.	81N	8	5.0	4957	LH	315
	85N	8	5.0	4957	LH	326
	—	8	5.4	5397	—	350
1991	42M	4	3.0	2990	DME	208
	68M	6	3.3 T	3299 T	CIS	315
	62M	6	3.6	3600	DME	247
	81M	8	5.0	4957	LH	315
	85M	8	5.0	4957	LH	326
1990	42L	4	3.0	2990	DME	208
	62L	6	3.6	3600	DME	247
	81L	8	5.0	4957	LH	316
	85L	8	5.0	4957	LH	326
1989	47K	4	2.5 T	2479 T	DME	247
	46K	4	2.7	2681	DME	162
	42K	4	3.0	2990	DME	208
	64K	6	3.2	3164	LH	214
	68K	6	3.3 T	3299 T	CIS	282
	62K	6	3.6	3600	DME	247
	81K	8	5.0	4957	LH	309

CIS—Continuous Injection System. **DME**—Digital Motor Electronics.
LH—LH-Jetronic. **T**—Turbo.

UNDERHOOD SERVICE SPECIFICATIONS

CYLINDER NUMBERING SEQUENCE

4-CYL. FIRING ORDER: 1 3 4 2

6-CYL. FIRING ORDER: 1 6 2 4 3 5

8-CYL. FIRING ORDER: 1 3 7 2 6 5 4 8

— Front of car —

944 1989 2681cc 944 1990-95 2990cc 944, 968	1989 911 3164cc, 911 3299cc	1989-92 4957cc 928

UNDERHOOD SERVICE SPECIFICATIONS

TIMING MARK

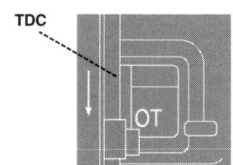

4-cyl. 2479cc
944
1989
4-cyl. 2681cc 944
1990
4-cyl. 2990cc 944

1989-96
6-cyl. 3164cc,
3600cc, 3299cc Turbo
911

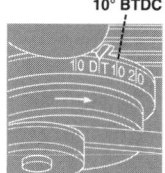

1989-95
V8 4957cc, 5397cc
928

ELECTRICAL AND IGNITION SYSTEMS

BATTERY
BCI equivalent shown, size may vary from original equipment. Check clearance and polarity before installing, holddown may need to be modified. Battery may be vented to outside of vehicle.

Model	Year	BCI Group No.	Crank. Perf.
911, 911 Turbo	1989	49	650
911 Carrera 4	1990-98	48	650
911 Carrera 2, Turbo Carrera	1991-98	48	650
928 S/4	1989	49	730
928 S/4, 928 GT, GTS	1990-95	48	650
944, 944 Turbo	1989	41	500
944 S2	1990-91	41	500
968	1992-95	91	600
Boxster	1997-98	48	650

GENERATOR

Engine	Year	Rated Output (amps)	Test Output (amps @ rpm)
2479cc	1989	115	98 @ 3000
2480cc	1997-99	120	120 @ 3000
2681cc	1989	115	98 @ 3000
2990cc	1989-95	115	98 @ 3000
3164cc, 3299cc	1989	90	74 @ 3000
3299cc	1991-92	115	98 @ 3000
3387cc	1999	115/120	115/120 @ 3000
3598cc Turbo	1994	115	98 @ 3000
3600cc	1989-98	115	98 @ 3000
4957cc	1989-92	115	98 @ 3000
5397cc	1993-95	115	115 @ 3000

STARTER

Engine	Year	Cranking Voltage (min. volts)
All	1989-95	8.0

SPARK PLUGS
Lubricate threads with anti-seize compound.

Engine	Year	Gap (inches)	Gap (mm)	Torque (ft-lb)
Turbo	1989	.028-.032	.70-.80	18-22
2480cc	1997-98	.031-.035	.80-.90	15-21
2681cc	1989	.028-.032	.70-.80	18-22
2990cc	1989-93	.028	0.7	18-22
	1994	.028-.032	.70-.80	18-22
3164cc	1989	.024-.032	.60-.80	22
3299cc	1989	.024-.032	.60-.80	22
	1991-93	.024-.032	.60-.80	15-22
3387cc	1999	.028-.032	.70-.80	—
Optional plugs		.05-.07	1.4-1.8	—
3598cc	1994	.031	.80	1.8
3600cc	1989-92	.031	0.8	22
	1993-98	.026-.030	0.7-0.8	16-22
4957cc	1989-92	.024-.032	.60-.80	22
5397cc	1992-94	.027-.035	0.7-0.9	18-22

IGNITION COIL

Engine	Year	Windings	Resistance (ohms)
4957cc	1989-92	Primary	0.4-0.7
		Secondary	5000-8700

BASE TIMING
Before Top Dead Center, unless otherwise specified.

1989 911 Turbo, disconnect and plug distributor vacuum hoses.

All others: Timing is not adjustable.

Engine	Year	Man. Trans. (degrees) @ RPM	Auto. Trans. (degrees) @ RPM
2681cc	1989	5±3	5±3
2990cc	1989-91	5±3	5±3
	1992-95	10±3	10±3
3164cc	1989	3±3	—
3299cc	1989	26±1	—
	1991-92	10±3	—
3598cc Turbo	1994	0±3	—
3600cc	1990-96	0±3	0±3
4957cc	1989-92	10±2	10±2
5397cc	1992-95	10±2	10±2

FUEL SYSTEM

FUEL INJECTION SYSTEM PRESSURE PROCEDURE
CIS System:
1. Connect appropriate fuel pressure gauge between the control pressure line of the fuel distributor and the outlet line of the warm-up regulator.
2. Energize fuel pump with jumper wire.
3. Bleed pressure gauge and set valve to open position, read control pressure.
4. Set valve to closed position, read line pressure.

DME System:
1. Connect pressure tester to fuel pipe.
2. Start engine and read pressure at idle.

LH-Jetronic System:
1. Connect appropriate fuel pressure gauge to inlet of fuel injection manifold.
2. Energize fuel pump: 944: remove DME relay and bridge cavities 30 & 87b, 911: connect fuses 16 & 17 with a jumper wire, 928: remove fuel pump relay and bridge cavities 30 & 87b.
3. Read line pressure.
4. Disconnect jumper wire, pressure should immediately drop to residual specification and maintain pressure for 20 minutes.

FUEL PRESSURE: DME, LH-JETRONIC, MOTRONIC

Engine	Year	System Pressure Not Running PSI (bar)	System Pressure At Idle PSI (bar)	Residual Pressure PSI (bar)
2479cc				
Turbo	1989	33-39 (2.3-2.7)	29 (2.0)	15 (1.0)

PEITU3

FUEL INJECTION SYSTEM PRESSURE PROCEDURE
Continued
FUEL PRESSURE: DME, LH-JETRONIC, MOTRONIC Continued

Engine	Year	System Pressure Not Running PSI (bar)	System Pressure At Idle PSI (bar)	Residual Pressure PSI (bar)
2681cc	1989	52-58 (3.6-4.0)	48 (3.3)	44 (3.0)
2990cc	1989-95	52-58 (3.6-4.0)	46-51 (3.1-3.5)	44 (3.0)
3164cc	1989	33-39 (2.3-2.7)	29 (2.0)	29 (2.0)
3600cc	1989-96	52-58 (3.6-4.0)	46-51 (3.1-3.5)	39 (2.7)
4957cc	1989-92	52-58 (3.6-4.0)	48 (3.3)	44 (3.0)
5397cc	1993-95	52-58 (3.6-4.0)	—	—

FUEL PRESSURE: CIS

Engine	Year	Control Pressure[1] PSI (bar)	Line Pressure PSI (bar)	Residual Pressure[2] PSI (bar)
3299cc	1989	51-57 (3.5-3.9)	87-97 (6.0-6.7)	22 (1.5)
	1991-92	51-57 (3.5-3.9)	87-97 (6.0-6.7)	22 (1.5)

1 With engine running at normal operating temperature.
2 Minimum pressure after 20 minutes.

COLD CONTROL PRESSURE: CIS

Model & Warm-up Regulator Part Number	Pressure[1] PSI (bar) @ 50°F (10°C) Ambient Temp.	Pressure[1] PSI (bar) @ 68°F (20°C) Ambient Temp.	Pressure[1] PSI (bar) @ 86°F (30°C) Ambient Temp.
911:			
0438140045	23-29 (1.6-2.0)	29-35 (2.0-2.4)	35-40 (2.4-2.8)
0438140069	17-23 (1.2-1.6)	26-32 (1.8-2.2)	35-40 (2.4-2.8)
0438140072	22-29 (1.5-2.0)	30-38 (2.1-2.6)	39-46 (2.7-3.2)
0438140090	20-26 (1.4-1.8)	29-35 (2.0-2.4)	38-45 (2.6-3.1)
911 Turbo:			
0438140016, 022	6-12 (0.4-0.8)	15-20 (1.0-1.4)	25-30 (1.7-2.1)
0438140054	15-22 (1.0-1.5)	23-30 (1.6-2.1)	33-39 (2.3-2.7)
0438140112	9-17 (0.6-1.2)	17-23 (1.2-1.6)	23-29 (1.6-2.0)
0438140153	13-23 (0.9-1.6)	22-26 (1.5-1.8)	32-36 (2.2-2.5)

1 With vacuum applied.

IDLE SPEED
911 ex. Turbo: Disconnect both cases of the Idle Speed Stabilizer (I.S.S.).
944, 968: Disconnect the Idle Speed Stabilizer (I.S.S.).
All models with adjustable idle speed, adjust idle to specified Setting Speed.

Model	Year	Checking Speed	Setting Speed
Boxster	1997-98	790N	—
911 All	1999	660-740	—
911 ex. Turbo	1989	—	860-900 (N)
911 Carrera 4	1989	840-920 (N)	—
911 Carrera 2 & 4	1990-96	840-920 (N)	—
W/MT	1994-96	760-840 (N)	—
W/Tiptronic	1994-96	710-790 (D)	—
W/AC	1996	840-920	—
911 Turbo	1989-92	—	850-950 (N)
	1993-94	—	900-1000 (N)
928 ex. GT	1989	650-700 (N)	—
GT	1989	750-800 (N)	—
	1990-95	650-700 (N)	—
944	1989-91	800-880 (N)	—
968 W/MT	1992-95	800-880 (N)	—
W/Tiptronic	1992-95	840-920 (N)	—

IDLE MIXTURE
Measured upstream of the catalytic converter, disconnect oxygen sensor and/or secondary air supply where applicable.

Engine	Year	CO% Low	CO% High
2479cc ex. DOHC	1989	0.4	0.8
2681cc	1989	0.4	0.8

IDLE MIXTURE Continued

Engine	Year	CO% Low	CO% High
2990cc	1989-94	0.4	0.8
3164cc	1989	0.4	0.8
3299cc	1989	0.4	0.8
3598cc Turbo	1994	0.8	1.2
3600cc	1989-96	0.4	1.2
4957cc	1989-92	0.4	1.2
5397cc	1993-94	0.4	1.2

1 Measured at tailpipe with air pump hose disconnected & plugged.

ENGINE MECHANICAL

TIGHTENING TORQUES

Engine	Year	Cylinder Head	Intake Manifold	Exhaust Manifold	Crankshaft Pulley	Water Pump
4-cyl.						
2.5L	1989	14/20	14/20	14/20	—	6/8[1]
2nd stage		36/50				
3rd stage		65/90				
3.0L	1989-91	14/20	—	—	—	6/8[1]
2nd stage		+60°				
3rd stage		+90°				
3.0L	1992-95	15/20	14/20			7/10[1]
2nd stage		+60°				
3rd stage		+90°				
6-cyl.						
3.2L	1989	14/20	—	—	58/80	—
2nd stage		+90°				
3.3L Turbo	1989-93	11/15	18/25	14/20	58/80	—
2nd stage		+90°				
3.6L	1989-95	14/20	—	17/23	173/235	—
2nd stage		+90°				
	1996	15/20			125/170	—
		+90°				
V8						
5.0L SOHC:	1989-91	14/20	11/15	—	218/195	—
2nd stage		36/50				
3rd stage		61/85				
4th stage		30 minutes				
5th stage		−90°				
6th stage		65/90				
5.0L DOHC, 5.4L DOHC:						
W/studs	1989-95	14/20	11/15	—	218/195	—
2nd stage		90°, +90°, +90°				
W/bolts	1989-95	14/20	11/15	—	218/195	—
2nd stage		90°, +90°				
5.4L SOHC	1993-95	14/20	11/15	—	218/195	—
2nd stage		36/50				
3rd stage		61/85				
4th stage		30 minutes				
5th stage		−90°				
6th stage		65/90				

1 Threads sealed with Loctite 270 or equivalent.

VALVE CLEARANCE

Engine	Year	Intake (inches)	Intake (mm)	Exhaust (inches)	Exhaust (mm)
Cold Setting:					
3164cc	1989	.004	.10	.004	.10
3299cc	1989	.004	.10	.004	.10
	1991-92	.004	.10	.004	.10
3600cc	1989-96	.004	.10	.004	.10

UNDERHOOD SERVICE SPECIFICATIONS

PEITU4

PEITU4

BELT TENSION

Model	Year	Alternator	Power Steering	Air Cond.
All ex. serpentine (inches)	1989	3/8	3/16	3/16
(mm)	1989	10	5	5
Serpentine belt	1989	9.2-9.8[1]	—	—

1 Porsche special tool No. 9201 required.

ENGINE COMPUTER SYSTEM

DIAGNOSTIC TROUBLE CODES

911 Carrera 4:

1. Connect Porsche Tester No. 9288 or 9268 using adapter No. 9268/2 to diagnostic connector in passenger footwell.

2. Read codes on tester. The second digit of a code may be displayed as a "2." This indicates the code was stored prior to the last operation of the vehicle.

944 S2:

1. Connect Porsche Tester to diagnostic connector.

2. Read codes on tester. The second digit of a code may be displayed as a "2." This indicates the code was set by a sporadic fault.

Code	Fault
1000	End of output
1111	System voltage out of range
1112	Idle switch contact grounded
1113	Full load switch contact grounded
1114	Engine temperature sensor circuit
1121	Airflow sensor signal
1122	Idle control circuit
1123	Oxygen sensor signal out of range
1124	Oxygen sensor circuit
1125	Intake air temperature sensor circuit
1131	Knock sensor No. 1 signal
1132	Knock sensor No. 2 signal
1133	Knock control regulation circuit
1134	Hall sender signal
1141	DME control unit
1142	Fuel pump relay circuit
1143	Tank venting valve circuit
1151	Fuel injector No. 1 circuit
1152	Fuel injector No. 2 circuit
1153	Fuel injector No. 3 circuit
1154	Fuel injector No. 4 circuit
1155	Fuel injector No. 5 circuit
1156	Fuel injector No. 6 circuit
1500	No faults in memory

928 S/4:

1. Connect Porsche Tester No. 9268 to diagnostic connector.

2. Switch ignition on and activate tester to access codes.

EZK Code	LH Code	Fault
2000	1000	End of output
—	1111	System voltage out of range
2112	1112	Idle switch contact grounded
2113	1113	Full load switch contact grounded
2114	1114	Engine temperature sensor circuit
2115	—	Throttle position sensor signal
—	1121	Mass airflow sensor signal
2121	—	Engine control module signal
—	1122	Idle control circuit
—	1123	Oxygen sensor signal rich
—	1124	Oxygen sensor signal lean
—	1125	Oxygen probe
2126	—	Transmission switch circuit
2131	—	Knock sensor No. 1 signal
2132	—	Knock sensor No. 2 signal
2133	—	Knock control regulation circuit
2134	—	Hall sender signal
2141	—	Engine control module
2500	1500	No faults in memory

DIAGNOSTIC TROUBLE CODES Continued

1995 911 Carrera:

Code	Fault
11	Supply voltage
14	Engine temperature sensor 2
15	Throttle potentiometer
18	Rpm signal
19	Speed signal <- speedometer
21	Hot film mass air flow sensor
22	Oxygen sensor (signal)
23, 24	Oxygen regulation/Oxygen sensor
25	Intake temperature sensor
26	Ignition timing change
27	Opening winding of idle stabilizer
28	Closing winding of idle stabilizer
31	Knock sensor 1
32	Knock sensor 2
33	Control unit faulty
34	Hall signal
36	Idle CO potentiometer
41	Control unit faulty
42	Fuel pump relay (DME-relay)
43	Tank ventilation relay
44	Air pump
45	Check Engine warning lamp
51	Injection valve cylinder 1
52	Injection valve cylinder 6
53	Injection valve cylinder 2
54	Injection valve cylinder 4
55	Injection valve cylinder 3
56	Injection valve cylinder 5
67, 69	Ground and plug connections

911 W/Tiptronic Transmission:

Code	Fault
11	Supply voltage. Emergency operation, no display
13	Supply voltage, drive links. Emergency operation
14	Supply voltage, sensor 5 V. Emergency operation
21	Rpm signal (engine). Emergency operation
22	Load signal. Emergency operation
24	Change of ignition timing. Emergency operation
25	Throttle potentiometer. Emergency operation
31	Solenoid valve 1. Emergency operation
32	Solenoid valve 2. Emergency operation
33	Solenoid valve, torque conv. clutch. Emergency operation
34	Pressure regulator. Emergency operation
35	Selector lever switch. Emergency operation
36	Speed sensor, transmission. Emergency operation
37	Transmission temperature sensor. Replacement value 60°C
38	Selector lever switch (for starting). Emergency operation
42	Control unit faulty. Emergency operation
43	Control unit faulty. Emergency operation
44	Control unit faulty. Emergency operation
45	Downshift protection. Emergency operation
46	Rev. limiter. Emergency operation
51	Manual program switch. No manual program
52	Up/down shift tip switch. No manual program
53	Kickdown switch. No kickdown
54	Transverse acceleration sensor. No upshift prevention
55	Speed signal 1 (ABS). No upshift prevention, no manual program, no downshift during braking
56	Combi-instrument input. No diagnosis
59	R-position switch. Emergency operation
60	Reverse light relay. No diagnosis
XX	Unknown fault code. Fault memory

PORSCHE
1989-99

UNDERHOOD SERVICE SPECIFICATIONS

SENSORS, INPUT
TEMPERATURE SENSORS

Engine	Year	Sensor	Resistance Ohms @ deg. F/C
4-cyl. 3.0L	1993-95	Coolant	4400-6800 @ 32/0 160-210 @ 212/100
3.0L	1990-95	Intake Air	4400-6800 @ 32/0 1400-3600 @ 60-85/15-30 100-130 @ 104/40
6-cyl. 3.2L	1989	Cylinder Head	3300-4100 @ 50/10 2200-2800 @ 68/20 1000-1300 @ 104/40 250-390 @ 176/80 160-200 @ 212/100
		Intake Air[1]	4400-6800 @ 32/0 1400-3600 @ 59-86/15-30 900-1300 @ 104/40
3.3L	1991-93	Cylinder Head	4400-6800 @ 32/0 160-210 @ 212/100
3.3L	1991-93	Intake Air	4400-6800 @ 32/0 100-130 @ 104/40
3.3L	1993	Coolant	4400-6800 @ 32/0 160-210 @ 212/100
3.6L	1993-95	Coolant	4400-6800 @ 32/0 160-210 @ 212/100
3.6L	1990-95	Cylinder Head	4400-6800 @ 32/0 160-210 @ 212/100
3.6L	1990-95	Intake Air	4400-6800 @ 32/0 1400-3600 @ 60-85/15-30 100-130 @ 104/40
V8 5.0L	1989-92	Coolant	4400-6800 @ 32/0 1400-3600 @ 59-86/15-30 900-1300 @ 104/40 480-720 @ 140/60 250-390 @ 176/80
5.0L	1990-92	Intake Air	4400-6800 @ 32/0 1400-3600 @ 60-85/15-30 100-130 @ 104/40
5.4L	1993-95	Coolant	4400-6800 @ 32/0 160-210 @ 212/100

SENSORS, INPUT Continued
TEMPERATURE SENSORS Continued

Engine	Year	Sensor	Resistance Ohms @ deg. F/C
V8 5.4L	1993-95	Intake Air	4400-6800 @ 32/0 1400-3600 @ 60-85/15-30 100-130 @ 104/40

1 Measured at terminals 1 & 4 of the airflow meter.

MASS AIRFLOW SENSOR

Engine	Year	Resistance (ohms) @ Terminal	Voltage @ Terminal
4-cyl. 3.0L	1992-95	—	10-13.8 @ 2 & 5
6-cyl. 3.2L	1989	—	4.5-5.5V @ 3 260mV @ 2[1] 4.6V @ 2[2]
V8 5.0L	1989-92	0-1000 @ 3 & 6 3600-4100 @ 3 & 5	4.5-5.5V @ 3 260mV @ 2[1] 4.6V @ 2[2]

1 With sensor plate in the closed position.
2 With sensor plate in the open position.

RPM & REFERENCE SENSORS

Engine	Year	Resistance (ohms)
6-cyl. 3.2L	1989	600-1600

ACTUATORS, OUTPUT
FUEL INJECTORS

Engine	Year	Resistance (ohms)
All	1993-94	2-3
911	1996	16

ENGINE IDENTIFICATION

To identify any engine by the manufacturer's code, follow the four steps designated by the numbered blocks.

1 MODEL YEAR IDENTIFICATION: Refer to illustration of the Vehicle Identification Number (V.I.N.). The year is indicated by a code letter which is the 10th character of the V.I.N.

2 ENGINE CODE LOCATION: Refer to illustration of V.I.N. plate for location and designation of engine code.

3 ENGINE CODE: In the "CODE" column, find the engine code determined in Step 2.

4 ENGINE IDENTIFICATION: On the line where the engine code appears, read to the right to identify the engine.

V.I.N. PLATE LOCATION:

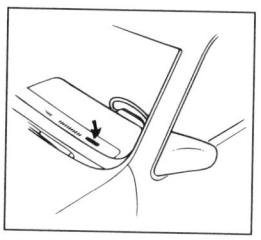

Driver's side of instrument panel, visible through windshield

1 MODEL YEAR IDENTIFICATION:

10th character of V.I.N.

1999—X	1998—W	1997—V
1996—T	1995—S	1994—R
1993—P	1992—N	1991—M
1990—L	1989—K	

2 ENGINE CODE LOCATION:

1989-98—8th character of V.I.N.

MODEL YEAR AND ENGINE IDENTIFICATION:

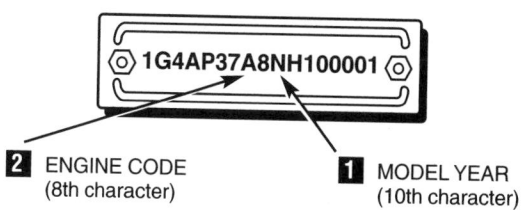

2 ENGINE CODE (8th character) **1** MODEL YEAR (10th character)

4 ENGINE IDENTIFICATION

YEAR	3 ENGINE CODE	CYL.	DISPL. liters	DISPL. cc	Fuel System	HP
1999	N, P	4	2.0 T	1985 T	FI	185, 200
	E	4	2.3	2290	FI	170
	Z	6	3.0	2962	FI	200
1998	N	4	2.0 T	1985 T	FI	185
	B	4	2.3	2290	FI	150
	R	4	2.3 T	2290 T	FI	225
1996-97	N	4	2.0 T	1985 T	FI	185
	B	4	2.3	2290	FI	150
	U	4	2.3 T	2290 T	FI	170
	M	4	2.3 T	2290 T	FI	200
	R	4	2.3 T	2290 T	FI	225
	V	6	2.5	2498	FI	170
	W	6	3.0	2962	FI	210
1995	J	4	2.0	1985	—	130
	N	4	2.0 T	1985 T	LH	185
	B	4	2.3	2290	LH, TR	150
	U	4	2.3 T	2290 T	—	170
	M	4	2.3 T	2290 T	TR	200
	R	4	2.3 T	2290 T	TR	225
	V	6	2.5	2498	LH	170
	W	6	3.0	2962	—	210
1994	N	4	2.0 T	1985 T	LH	185
	B	4	2.3	2290	LH, TR	150

4 ENGINE IDENTIFICATION

YEAR	3 ENGINE CODE	CYL.	DISPL. liters	DISPL. cc	Fuel System	HP
1994 Cont'd.	M	4	2.3 T	2290 T	TR	200
	R	4	2.3 T	2290 T	TR	225
	V	6	2.5	2498	LH	170
1993	L	4	2.0 T	1985 T	LH	160
	E	4	2.1	2119	LH	140
	B	4	2.3	2290	LH	150
	M	4	2.3 T	2290 T	TR	200
	R	4	2.3 T	2290 T	TR	225
1992	L	4	2.0 T	1985 T	LH	160
	E	4	2.1	2119	LH	140
	B	4	2.3	2290	LH	150
	M	4	2.3 T	2290 T	LH	200
1991	L	4	2.0 T	1985 T	LH	175
	E	4	2.1	2119	LH	140
	B	4	2.3	2290	LH	150
	M	4	2.3 T	2290 T	LH	200
1990	D	4	2.0	1985	LH	128, 130[1]
	L	4	2.0 T	1985 T	LH	160, 175[1]
	B	4	2.3	2290	LH	200
1989	D	4	2.0	1985	LH	128, 130[1]
	L	4	2.0 T	1985	LH	160, 165[1]

1 Engine horsepower varies with model installation and emissions equipment. T—Turbo. LH—LH-Jetronic.
TR—Trionic. CIS—Continuous Injection System.

UNDERHOOD SERVICE SPECIFICATIONS

SBITU1

CYLINDER NUMBERING SEQUENCE

4-CYL. FIRING ORDER: 1 3 4 2
V6-CYL. FIRING ORDER: 1 2 3 4 5 6

SBITU1

TIMING MARK

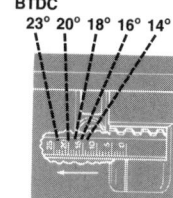

BTDC
23° 20° 18° 16° 14°

1989-90
1985cc
900, 9000

— Front of car —

1989-93
1985cc 16 Valve 900

1989-90
1985cc 16 Valve 9000

1991-99
2290cc 900, 9-5

SAAB
1989-99

CHEK-CHART

UNDERHOOD SERVICE SPECIFICATIONS

SBITU2

SBITU2

ELECTRICAL AND IGNITION SYSTEMS

BATTERY

Manufacturer's recommended BCI replacement shown, may vary from original equipment battery. Check clearance and polarity before installing, holddown may need to be modified.

Engine	Year	STANDARD BCI Group No.	STANDARD Crank. Perf.	OPTIONAL BCI Group No.	OPTIONAL Crank. Perf.
9-3	1999	47	580	—	—
9-5	1999	91	650	—	—
900 ex. Turbo	1996-98	47	520	—	—
Turbo	1996-98	47	600	—	—
	1994-95	47	520	—	—
	1993	26	405	—	—
	1989-92	26	530	—	—
9000	1994-98	41	570	—	—
	1993	47	450	34R	450
	1989-92	47	450	—	—

GENERATOR

Application	Manufacturer	Year	Rated Output (amps)	Test Output (amps @ rpm)
900	Bosch	1989-93	80	54 @ 1900
900 1985cc, 2299cc	Bosch	1994-98	90	45 @ 1800
2498cc	Bosch	1994-97	120	60 @ 1800
2962cc	—	1995-96	120	—
9000 MT	Bosch	1989-94	80	54 @ 1900
AT	Bosch	1989-94	115	—
9000 Aero	—	1993	115	—
9000 4-cyl.	—	1995-98	110	—
V6	—	1995-97	120	—
9000 2290cc	—	1998	90	—
9-3, 9-5	—	1999	130	—

REGULATOR

Integrated type, not adjustable.

Application	Year	Brush Wear Limit in. (mm)	Voltage Output Max.
All	1989-92	3/16 (5)	14.0

STARTER

Application	Year	Cranking Voltage (min. volts)	Maximum Ampere Draw @ RPM
All	1989-95	9.0	315 @ 1700
900 4-cyl.	1996-98	7.8	—
V6	1996-97	7.0	—

SPARK PLUGS

Engine/Model	Year	Gap (inches)	Gap (mm)	Torque (ft-lb)
9-3 2.0L	1999	.035-.039	.90-1.0	—
9-5, 2.3L, 3.0L	1999	.039-.043	1.0-1.1	—
900 2.0L	1989-97	.039	1.0	18
	1998	.039-.043	1.0-1.1	—
2.3L	1991-97	.024	.60	18
	1998	.024-.026	.60-.70	—
2.5L	1994-97	.031	.80	18
9000 4-cyl.	1989-95	.039-.047	1.0-1.2	18
	1996	.036-.043	0.9-1.1	18.5-21.5
	1997	.039-.043	1.0-1.1	20
	1998	.039-.047	1.0-1.2	—
V6	1994-96	.031	.80	18
	1997	.027-.035	.70-.90	20

IGNITION COIL

Application	Year	Windings	Resistance (ohms)
900 4-cyl.	1996-98	Primary	0.6-.8
		Secondary	7200-8200
V6	1996-97	Primary	0.4-.6
		Secondary	10,200-13,800
9000 4-cyl.	1996-98	Primary	0.5-.8
		Secondary	7200-8200
V6	1996-97	Primary	0.4-.6
		Secondary	10,200-13,800
All	1995	Primary	0.4-.6
		Secondary	10,000-14,000
All	1989-90	Primary	.52-.76
		Secondary	7200-8200
900 1985cc, 2290cc	1994	Primary	.62-.82
		Secondary	7200-8200
2498cc	1994	Primary	.42-.58
		Secondary	10,200-13,800
9000 w/Direct Ignition	1991-92	Primary	0.3
		Secondary	800-900

BASE TIMING

Before Top Dead Center, unless otherwise specified.

Disconnect and plug distributor vacuum hose.

Engine	Year	Man. Trans. (degrees) @ RPM	Auto. Trans. (degrees) @ RPM
16-Valve Turbo	1989-90	16 @ 850	16 @ 850
16-Valve Non-Turbo	1989-90	14 @ 850	14 @ 850
1985cc Turbo	1991-92	16 @ 850	16 @ 850
2119cc	1991-93	14 @ 850	14 @ 850
2290cc	1990-98	10[1] @ 850	10[1] @ 850

1 Not adjustable.

FUEL SYSTEM

FUEL SYSTEM PRESSURE

FUEL PRESSURE PROCEDURE

LH—Jetronic System:
1. Connect appropriate fuel pressure gauge to inlet of fuel injection manifold.
2. Energize fuel pump by connecting jumper wire from fuse #14 to fuse #22.
3. Read system pressure.
4. Disconnect jump wire, pressure should immediately drop to residual specification and maintain pressure for 10 minutes.

CIS System:
1. Connect appropriate fuel pressure gauge between the control pressure line of the fuel distributor and the outlet line of the warm-up regulator.
2. Remove fuel pump relay and energize pump by bridging cavities 30 & 87.
3. Bleed pressure gauge and set valve to open position, read control pressure.
4. Set valve to closed position, read line pressure.

FUEL PRESSURE: LH-JETRONIC

Engine	Year	System Pressure PSI (bar)	Residual Pressure PSI (bar)
1985cc Non-Turbo	1989-90	43.0 (3.06)	39 (2.8)
	1989-92	36.0 (2.5)	33 (2.3)
1985cc Turbo	1994-98	43 (3.0)	29 (2.0)
2119cc	1991-92	43 (3.0)	39 (2.8)
2290cc	1991-98	43 (3.0)	29 (2.0)
2498cc	1994-97	43 (3.0)	29 (2.0)

COLD CONTROL PRESSURE: CIS

Pressure Regulator Part Number	Pressure PSI (bar) @ 50°F (10°C) Ambient Temp.	Pressure PSI (bar) @ 68°F (20°C) Ambient Temp.	Pressure PSI (bar) @ 86°F (30°C) Ambient Temp.	Pressure PSI (bar) @ 104°F (40°C) Ambient Temp.
0438140020, 085, 070, 102, 111	8-21 (0.6-1.4)	21-24 (1.4-1.6)	24-30 (1.6-2.1)	30-36 (2.1-2.5)

UNDERHOOD SERVICE SPECIFICATIONS

SBITU3   SBITU3

IDLE SPEED
Idle speed is not adjustable unless otherwise noted.

Engine	Year	Manual Trans.	Auto. Trans.
9-3 1985cc	1999	900	900
9-5 2290cc	1999	825	825
2962cc	1999	700	700
900 16-Valve Turbo	1989	775-925[1]	775-925 N[1]
w/o Turbo	1989	775-925[1]	775-925 N[1]
All	1990-93	800-900	800-900 N
1985cc, 2290cc	1994-98	800-900	800-900 N
2498cc	1994-97	750-850	750-850 N
9000	1989-94	775-925[1]	775-925 N[1]
2290cc	1996-98	800-900	800-900
2962cc	1995-98	700-800	700-800 N

1 If equipped with idle speed screw, adjust to 850 N.

IDLE MIXTURE

Engine	Year	CO% Minimum	CO% Maximum
1985cc Turbo	1992-93	1.0	1.6
2119cc	1992	0.5	1.5
2290cc	1991-99	0.5	1.5

ENGINE MECHANICAL

TIGHTENING TORQUES

Engine	Year	TORQUE FOOT-POUNDS/NEWTON METERS				
		Cylinder Head	Intake Manifold	Exhaust Manifold	Crankshaft Pulley	Water Pump
2.0L	1989	44/60	14/18	19/25	140/190	15/20
2nd stage		59/80				
3rd stage		+90°				
2.0L	1990-93	44/60	16/22	19/25	140/190	15/20
2nd stage		59/80				
3rd stage		+90°				
1985cc	1994-99	44/60	16/22	18.5/25	140/190	16/22
2nd stage		59/80				
3rd stage		+90°				
2119cc	1991-93	44/59	16/22	18.5/25	129.5/175	—
2nd stage		60/80				
3rd stage		+90°				
2290cc	1994-99	44/60	16/22	18.5/25	129/175	18/25
2nd stage		59/80				
3rd stage		+90°				
2498cc	1994-97	18.5/25	15/20		185/250	
2nd stage		+90°			+45°	
3rd stage		+90°				
4th stage		+90°				
2962cc	1995-97	18.5/25	—	15/20	—	18.5/25
2nd stage		+90°				
3rd stage		+90°				
4th stage		+90°				

COMPRESSION PRESSURE
All models: Lowest cylinder must be within 10% of highest cylinder.

BELT TENSION

Model	Year	Generator	Power Steering	Air Cond.
USED BELTS				
Strand Tension method				
9000 w/serpentine	1989-93	110-130	—	75-85
900 w/single belt	1991-93	65-75	65-75	75-85
w/double belt	1991-93	140-150	—	—
Deflection method				
900 (inches)	1989-90	3/16[1]	3/16[2]	3/16[1]
(mm)	1989-90	5[1]	5[2]	5[1]

1 With 10 lb. of force at midpoint between pulleys.
2 With 15 lb. of force at midpoint between pulleys.

SERPENTINE BELT DIAGRAMS

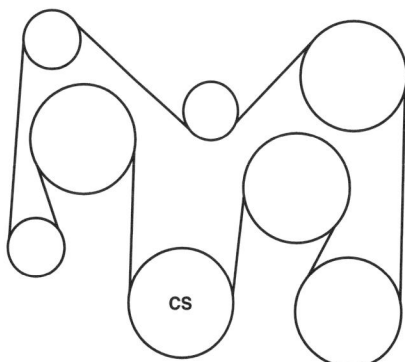

1993-99 4-cyl. 2.0L, 2.3L
900, 9-5

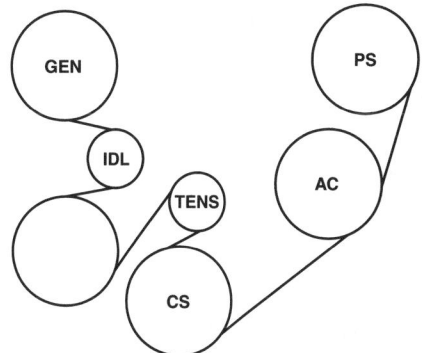

1989-97 4-cyl. 2.3L
9000

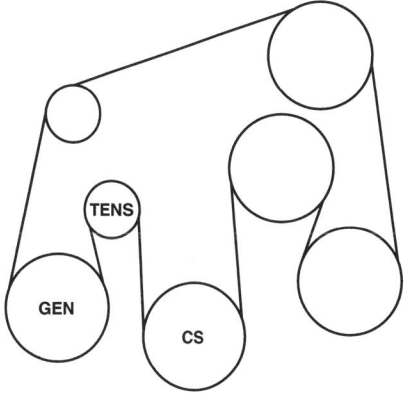

1998-99 4-cyl.
9-3

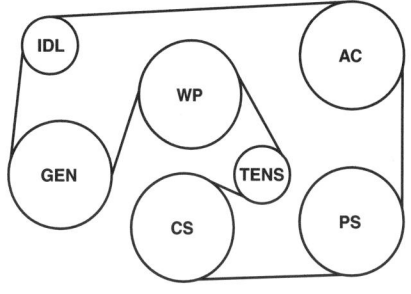

1995-99 V6 2.5L, 3.0L

UNDERHOOD SERVICE SPECIFICATIONS

SERPENTINE BELT DIAGRAMS Continued

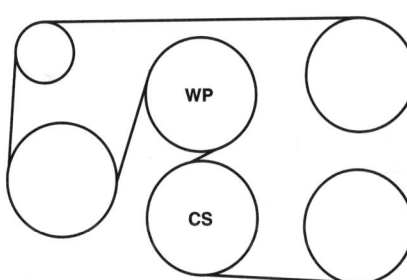

1999 V6 9-5

ENGINE COMPUTER SYSTEM

DIAGNOSTIC TROUBLE CODES

1989-90 All engines:

1. 900 models: Connect switched jumper lead (Part No. 83 93 886) in line between the pin No. 3 of the test socket on the passenger's side of engine compartment and ground. 9000 models: Connect switched jumper lead (Part No. 83 93 886) in line between the test socket on the driver's side of engine compartment and negative battery terminal.
2. Switch on ignition, CHECK ENGINE light will come on, turn jumper switch on and light will go out.
3. When CHECK ENGINE light flashes, immediately turn jumper switch off.
4. The primary error code will now be displayed by the CHECK ENGINE light as a series of short flashes. A long flash of the light will start and end each code; these are not part of the code.
5. To display additional codes, turn jumper switch on, after a brief flash of the light immediately turn switch off. Second code will now be displayed, repeat procedure for third code, 9 series of long flashes indicates no additional codes.
6. To erase memory, turn jumper switch on, after three short flashes of light turn switch off. Memory erased code will be displayed.

Code	Light[1]	Fault
00000	—	No more faults
12111	off	Oxygen adaptation, air-fuel mixture, throttle open
12112	off	Oxygen adaptation, air-fuel mixture, throttle closed
12113	off	Idle control adaptation, pulse ratio low
12114	off	Idle control adaptation, pulse ratio high
12211	off	Incorrect battery voltage (engine running)
12212	off	Throttle position sensor, idling contacts
12213	off	Throttle position sensor, full throttle contacts
12214	on	Temperature sensor signal out of range
12221	on	Mass airflow sensor signal absent, system in limp-home mode
12222	off	Idling control (AIC), no pulse switching, defective ECM
12223	on	Lean fuel mixture
12224	on	Rich fuel mixture
12225	on	Oxygen sensor signal, engine in limp-home mode
12231	off	No RPM signal[2]
12232	off	Open memory circuit to ECM
12233	off	Auto diagnostic program error
12444	—	Memory erased

1 Indicates condition while operating vehicle prior to testing.

2 If displayed as first fault with engine off, hold ignition key in start position until CHECK ENGINE light flashes, additional codes can now be accessed.

1991-92 All engines: Special test equipment required. Connect tester according to manufacturer's instructions. Faults will be displayed as a five-digit code. Intermittent faults are indicated by a first digit "2" or "3"; permanent faults are indicated by a "4," "5," or "6" first digit. Read remaining four digits from table.

Code	Application	Definition
2241	Engine Control Module	Signal to unit over 16 volts
2251	Engine Control Module	Signal to pin "4" below 1 volt
2252	Engine Control Module	Signal to unit below 10 volts
2291	System Voltage	Battery voltage out of range

DIAGNOSTIC TROUBLE CODES Continued

2440	Fuel Mixture	System rich, no oxygen sensor control
2441	Fuel Mixture	System rich at idle
2442	Fuel Mixture	System rich at speed
2450	Fuel Mixture	System lean, no oxygen sensor control
2451	Fuel Mixture	System lean at idle
2452	Fuel Mixture	System lean at speed
2460	Oxygen Sensor	Faulty sensor signal
2491	Fuel Mixture	Out of range at idle
2492	Fuel Mixture	Out of range at speed
4221	Vehicle Speed Sensor	No speed signal recorded
4261	Vehicle Speed Sensor	Faulty signal from road speed sensor
5641	Mass Airflow Sensor	Reference signal too high
5651	Mass Airflow Sensor	Reference signal too low
5691	Mass Airflow Sensor	Reference signal out of range
5723	Drive Sensor	Faulty transmission signal
5771	Throttle Sensor	Sensor signal shorted
5772	Throttle Sensor	Sensor signal open
6221	Temperature Sensor	Coolant sensor circuit open
6271	Temperature Sensor	Coolant sensor circuit shorted
6391	EGR System	Function faulty, temperature low
7192	Engine Control Module	Internal defect
8121	Mass Airflow Sensor	Burn-off not functioning
8321	Idle Control	Air control valve malfunction
8322	EVAP Canister Valve	Purge valve malfunction
8371	Fuel Injector	Faulty fuel injector
8372	EVAP Canister Valve	Purge valve circuit malfunction
8382	EVAP Canister Valve	Purge valve circuit shorted

SENSORS, INPUT

ENGINE COOLANT TEMPERATURE SENSOR

Engine	Year	Resistance Ohms @ deg. F/C
All	1989-94	14000 @ -4/-20
		5800 @ 32/0
		2600 @ 68/20
		320 @ 176/80
All	1995	5,700 @ 32 (0)
		3,700 @ 50 (10)
		2,300 @ 68 (20)
		1,600 @ 86 (30)
		1,000-1,300 @ 104 (40)
		565-670 @ 140 (60)
		295-365 @ 176 (80)
		180 @ 212 (100)
		140 @ 230 (110)
		110 @ 248 (120)
1985cc Turbo, 2290cc Turbo	1996-98	20,000-30,000 @ -22/-30
		7,000-11,400 @ -14/-10
		2,100-2,900 @ 68/20
		1,000-1,300 @ 104/60
		365-670 @ 140/60
		295-365 @ 176/80
		24-26 @ 194/90
		14-16 @ 230/110

INTAKE AIR TEMPERATURE SENSORS

Engine	Year	Ohms	Resistance Ohms @ deg. F/C
2290cc	1993	20-30	4.5 @ -22/-30
		8.3-10.6	3.9 @ 14/-10
		2.3-2.7	3.2 @ 68/20
		1.0-1.3	1.5 @ 104/40
		565-670	0.9 @ 140/60
		295-365	0.7 @ 176/80
All	1995	8,300-10,600	— @ 14/-10
		2,300-2,700	— @ 68/20
		1,000-1,300	— @ 104/40
		565-670	— @ 140/60
1985cc Turbo, 2290cc Turbo	1996-98	20,000-30,000	4.5 @ -22/-30
		7,000-11,400	3.9 @ -14/-10
		2,100-2,900	2.4 @ 68/20
		1,000-1,300	1.5 @ 104/40
		565-670	0/9 @ 140/60
		295-365	0.5 @ 176/80
		240-260	0.4 @ 194/90

UNDERHOOD SERVICE SPECIFICATIONS

SENSORS, INPUT Continued
MANIFOLD ABSOLUTE PRESSURE SENSOR

Engine	Year	Volts @ in./kPa
1985cc Turbo, 2290cc Turbo	1993-98	0.5 @ 25
		0.9 @ 50
		1.9 @ 100
		2.4 @ 125
		2.8 @ 150
		3.3 @ 175

IDLE AIR CONTROL VALVE

Engine	Year	Resistance Ohms @ deg. F/C
1985cc	1995	6-10 @ 68/20
1985cc Turbo	1996-98	6.7-8.7 @ 68/20
2290cc	1993-98	6-10 @ 68/20
2290cc Turbo	1996-98	6.7-8.7 @ 68/20
2962cc	1995-97	7.6-7.8 @ 68/20
900, all	1994	7.7 @ —

THROTTLE POSITION SENSOR

Engine/Application	Year	Resistance Ohms @ Terminal	Throttle Position
1985cc, 2498cc	1994-97	700-1000 @ 1 & 3	open
		2300-3400 @ 1 & 3	closed
1985cc Turbo, 2290cc Turbo	1996-98	2,000-3,000 @ 1 & 3	open
		800-1,200 @ 1 & 3	closed
2119cc, 2290cc	1991-92	1100-1500 @ 1 & 3	open
		2600-3000 @ 1 & 3	closed
2290cc	1993-94	700-1000 @ 1 & 3	open
		2300-3400 @ 1 & 3	closed

CRANKSHAFT SENSOR

Application	Year	Resistance (ohms)
All	1995-98	485-595

CAMSHAFT SENSOR
Air gap measured between sensor & cam.

Application	Year	Gap (inches/mm)	Output (volts)
All	1995-98	.059/1.5 max	5

SENSORS, INPUT Continued
MASS AIRFLOW SENSOR

Application	Year	Grams per sec.	Volts
9000 2962cc	1995-97	0	.15
		3.3	.75
		4.2	.85
		8.3	1.20
		17	1.65
		33	2.25
		69	3.05
		103	3.60
		133	4.05
		178	4.60

ACTUATORS, OUTPUT
FUEL INJECTORS

Engine	Year	Resistance (ohms)	Temperature (deg. F/C)
1985cc, 2290cc	1994	14.1-14.8	—
1985cc Turbo	1996-98	11.6-12.3	68/20
2290cc	1995	15.4-16.4	68/20
	1996-98	11.6-12.3	68/20
2498cc	1994-97	15.9	—
2962cc	1995-97	15.4-16.4	68/20

IDLE CONTROLLER

Engine	Fuel System	Year	Resistance (ohms)
2.0L	LH-Jetronic	1989-92	18-22[1]
2.1L	LH-Jetronic	1991-92	10-15[2]
2.3L	LH-Jetronic	1990-92	10-15[2]

1 Measured between terminals 3 & 4 and 4 & 5.
2 Measured between terminals 1 & 2 and 2 & 3.

COMPONENT AND SIGNAL TEST
1989-90 All engines:
1. Connect switched jumper lead between diagnostic socket and ground.
2. Set jumper switch to "ON" and switch ignition to run position, after a short flash of the "check engine" light, immediately set jumper switch to "off."
3. Listen for fuel pump to run as "check engine" begins to flash (no code).
4. Set jumper switch to "on" after a short flash of the "check engine" light, move switch to "off" position.
5. Read code displayed by "check engine" light and take action indicated below.
6. Repeat steps 4 & 5 until all components have been tested.

Code	Component	Action
None	Fuel pump	Listen, pump runs for less than 1 second
12411	Injection valves	Listen for operation
12412	Idle air control valve	Listen, valve switches once per second
12413	EVAP Canister purge valve	Listen, valve switches once per second
12421	Drive signal, AT	Shift from D to N, flashing should stop
12424	Throttle position sensor (idle signal)	Depress accelerator, flashing should stop
12424	Throttle position sensor (full throttle signal)	Floor accelerator, flashing should stop

ENGINE IDENTIFICATION

To identify any engine by the manufacturer's code, follow the four steps designated by the numbered blocks.

1 MODEL YEAR IDENTIFICATION: Refer to illustration of the Vehicle Identification Number (V.I.N.). The year is indicated by a code letter which is the 10th character of the V.I.N.

2 ENGINE CODE LOCATION: Refer to illustration of V.I.N. plate for location and designation of engine code.

3 ENGINE CODE: In the "CODE" column, find the engine code determined in step 2.

4 ENGINE IDENTIFICATION: On the line where the engine code appears, read to the right to identify the engine.

**V.I.N.
PLATE LOCATION:**

On top left side of instrument panel.

Model year of vehicle:
2000 — Y
1999 — X
1998 — W
1997 — V
1996 — T
1995 — S
1994 — R
1993 — P
1992 — N
1991 — M

MODEL YEAR AND ENGINE IDENTIFICATION:

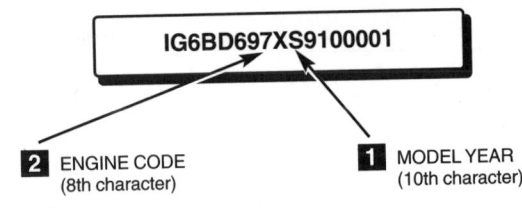

2 ENGINE CODE (8th character) **1** MODEL YEAR (10th character)

YEAR	**3** ENGINE CODE	CYL.	**4** ENGINE IDENTIFICATION DISPL. liters	cu. in.	Fuel System	HP
2000	8	4	1.9	1.6	MFI	100
	7	4	1.9	1.6	MFI	124
	F	4	2.2	134	MFI	137
	R	6	3.0	182	MFI	182
1995-99	8	4	1.9	116	MFI	100
	7	4	1.9	116	MFI	124

YEAR	**3** ENGINE CODE	CYL.	**4** ENGINE IDENTIFICATION DISPL. liters	cu. in.	Fuel System	HP
1993-94	9	4	1.9	116	TBI	85
	7	4	1.9	116	MFI	124
1991-92	9	4	1.9	116	TBI	85
	7	4	1.9	116	MFI	123

TBI—Throttle Body Injection.   **MFI—Multiport Fuel Injection.**

UNDERHOOD SERVICE SPECIFICATIONS

SNTU1   SNTU1

CYLINDER NUMBERING SEQUENCE

1.9L 4-CYL. FIRING ORDER: 1 3 4 2   **2.2L 4-CYL. FIRING ORDER: 1 4 3 2**   **3.0L V6 FIRING ORDER: 1 2 3 4 5 6**

4 1 2 3

1.9L

2.2L Code F

3.0L Code R

ELECTRICAL AND IGNITION SYSTEMS

BATTERY

Model	Year	BCI Group No.	Crank. Perf.
S-Series	1991-00	75[1]	525

[1] Requires special height battery of 7¼" (184 mm) maximum.

GENERATOR

Engine	Year	Rated Output (amps)	Test Output (amps)
1.9L	1991-94	85	[1]
	1995-00	96	[1]
2.2L, 3.0L	2000	—	20-60 @ idle

[1] Output at 2000 rpm must be within 15% of rated output.

REGULATOR

Year	Test Temp. (deg. F/C)	Voltage Setting
1991-00	—	13.0-16.0

STARTER

Engine	Year	Cranking Voltage (min. volts)	Ampere Draw @ Cranking Speed
All	1991-00	9.5	70-110[1] @ 250 90-130[2] @ 250

[1] Engine hot.
[2] Engine cold.

SPARK PLUGS

Engine	Year	Gap (inches)	Gap (mm)	Torque (ft-lb)
1.9L	1991-00	.040	1.0	20
2.2L	2000	.045	1.10	15
3.0L	2000	.035-.043	0.9-1.1	19

UNDERHOOD SERVICE SPECIFICATIONS

SNTU2

SNTU2

IGNITION COIL

Secondary resistance measured at each coil's high voltage terminals with spark plug wires removed.

Application	Year	Windings	Resistance (ohms)
1.9L	1991-96	Primary	—
		Secondary	7000-10,000
	1997-00	Primary	—
		Secondary	8000-15,000
3.0L	2000	Primary	—
		Secondary	8000-15,000

FUEL SYSTEM

FUEL SYSTEM PRESSURE

Engine	Year	Pressure PSI	Condition
1.9L SOHC	1991-94	26-31	idle
		46-94[1]	
1.9L DOHC	1991-94	38-44	ign. on
		31-36	idle
		46-94[1]	
1.9L	1995-00	38-44	ign. on
		31-36	idle
		46-94[1]	
2.2L	2000	50-60	ign. on
		65 min.[1]	
3.0L	2000	38-44	ign. on
		65 min.[1]	

[1] Fuel pump pressure.

IDLE SPEED W/COMPUTER CONTROL

1991-94: With IAC fully seated, install plug in air bypass port. Set idle to specified value.
1995-97: Check idle speed only.

Engine	Year	Transmission	Checking Speed	Setting Speed	AC Speed up
1.9L SOHC	1991-94	MT	700-800	400-600	700-800
		AT	600-700 D	400-600 N	725-825 D
1.9L DOHC	1991-94	MT	800-900	400-600	825-925
		AT	700-800 D	400-600 N	725-825 D
1.9L SOHC	1995-00	MT	700-800	—	—
		AT	600-700 D	—	725-825 D
1.9 DOHC	1995-00	MT	800-900	—	825-925
		AT	700-800 D	—	725-825 D

ENGINE MECHANICAL

TIGHTENING TORQUES

		TORQUE FOOT-POUNDS/NEWTON METERS				
Engine	Year	Cylinder Head	Intake Manifold	Exhaust Manifold	Crankshaft Pulley	Water Pump
1.9L SOHC	1991-00	22/30, 33/45, +90°	15/20	16/22	159/215	22/30
1.9L DOHC	1991-00	22/30, 37/50, +90°	22/30	23/31	159/215	22/30
2.2L	2000	22/30, +155°	7/10	13/18	74/100, +75°	18/25
3.0L	2000	18/25, +90°, +90°, +90°, +15°	15/20	15/20	—	19/25

COMPRESSION PRESSURE

With engine at normal operating temperature.

Engine	Year	Normal Range PSI	Maximum Variation PSI
1.9L	1991-94	180 min.	—
	1995-00	185-205/180 min.	—
2.2L	2000	185-225/100 min.	1

[1] Lowest cylinder must be 70% of highest.

BELT TENSION

Automatic tensioner used. The marking on the tensioner arm must be between the two marks on the tensioner body.

		Tension	
Engine	Year	Controlled	Minimum
All	1991-00	50-65	45 min.

ENGINE COMPUTER SYSTEM

DIAGNOSTIC TROUBLE CODES

1991-95: Connect a jumper between terminals A & B of diagnostic connector (two upper right-hand cavities of two-row connector).

Code 11 Transmission diagnostic codes present
Code 12 Diagnostic check only
Code 13 Oxygen sensor
Code 14, 15 Engine coolant temperature sensor
Code 17 PCM pull-up resistor
Code 19 6× signal fault
Code 21, 22 Throttle position sensor
Code 23, 25 Intake air temperature sensor
Code 24 Vehicle speed sensor
Code 26, 27 Quad driver error
Code 32 EGR system
Code 33, 34 MAP sensor
Code 35 Idle air control out of range
Code 41 IC circuit
Code 41 & 42 IC bypass
Code 42 Ignition bypass circuit
Code 43 Electronic spark control
Code 44 Oxygen sensor, lean
Code 45 Oxygen sensor, rich
Code 49 RPM - high idle (vacuum leak)
Code 51 PCM memory error
Code 55 A/D error
Code 46 Power steering pressure circuit
Code 80 ABS message fault
Code 82 PCM internal communication fault
Code 83 Low engine coolant

SENSORS, INPUT
TEMPERATURE SENSORS

Engine	Year	Sensor	Resistance Ohms @ deg. F/C
All	1991-00	Coolant	21,000-27,000 @ 0/-18
			11,000-15,000 @ 20/-7
			6,600-8,400 @ 40/4
			3,900-4,500 @ 60/16
			2,400-2,700 @ 80/27
			1,500-1,700 @ 100/38
			980-1,100 @ 120/49
			650-730 @ 140/60
			430-480 @ 160/72
			302-334 @ 180/83
			215-235 @ 200/94
All	1991-00	Intake Air	11,000-15,000 @ 20/-7
			6,600-8,400 @ 40/4
			3,900-4,500 @ 60/16
			2,400-2,700 @ 80/27
			1,500-1,700 @ 100/38
			980-1,100 @ 120/49
			650-730 @ 140/60
			430-480 @ 160/72
			302-334 @ 180/83
			215-235 @ 200/94
			159-172 @ 220/105

SNTU3

SENSORS, INPUT Continued
MANIFOLD ABSOLUTE PRESSURE SENSOR

Engine	Year	Voltage @ Condition
All	1991-00	1.0-1.5 @ idle
		4.0-4.8 @ WOT

VEHICLE SPEED SENSOR

Engine	Year	Resistance (ohms)
All	1991-96	700-900
	1997-00	800-1000

CRANKSHAFT POSITION SENSOR

Engine	Year	Resistance (ohms)
1.9L	1991-00	700-900
2.2L	2000	500-900

SENSORS, INPUT Continued
THROTTLE POSITION SENSOR

Engine	Year	TPS Voltage[1] Idle	WOT
1.9L	1991-94	.20-.60	4.5-4.9
	1995-00	.35-.70	4.5-4.9
2.2L	2000	.35 approx.	4.65 min.

1 Not adjustable.

ACTUATORS, OUTPUT
IDLE SPEED CONTROL

Engine	Year	Resistance (ohms)
1.9L	1996-00	40-80

FUEL INJECTORS

Engine	Year	Resistance (ohms)	Temperature (deg. F/C)
1.9L TBI	1991-94	1-2	—
MFI	1991-95	1.5-2.5	—
	1996-00	11.5-12.5	—
2.2L	2000	12-13	—
3.0L	2000	11-13	—

ENGINE IDENTIFICATION

To identify any engine by the manufacturer's code, follow the four steps designated by the numbered blocks.

1 MODEL YEAR IDENTIFICATION: Refer to illustration of the Vehicle Identification Number (V.I.N.). The year is indicated by a code letter which is the 10th character of the V.I.N.

2 ENGINE CODE LOCATION: Refer to illustration of V.I.N. plate for location and designation of engine code.

3 ENGINE CODE: In the "CODE" column, find the engine code determined in Step 2.

4 ENGINE IDENTIFICATION: On the line where the engine code appears, read to the right to identify the engine.

V.I.N. PLATE LOCATION:

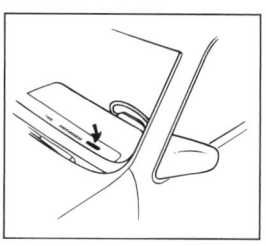

Left side of instrument panel, visible through windshield; also under hood on engine bulkhead

1 MODEL YEAR IDENTIFICATION:

10th character of V.I.N.

1999—X	1998—W	1997—V
1996—T	1995—S	1994—R
1993—P	1992—N	1991—M
1990—L	1989—K	

2 ENGINE CODE LOCATION:

1990-98, 6th character of V.I.N.
1989:
3-cyl.: On top of crankcase, flywheel end
4-cyl. & 6-cyl.: On right side of crankcase, front of vehicle.

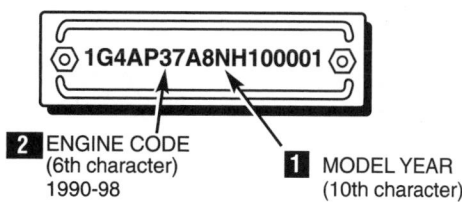

2 ENGINE CODE (6th character) 1990-98

1 MODEL YEAR (10th character)

4 ENGINE IDENTIFICATION

YEAR	3 ENGINE CODE	CYL.	DISPL. liters	cc	Fuel System	HP
1999	3, 4 4		2.2	2212	MFI	142
	6 4		2.5	2457	MFI	165
1998	3, 4 4		2.2	2212	MFI	137
	6 4		2.5	2457	MFI	165
1997	2 4		1.8	1820	MFI	115
	3, 4 4		2.2	2212	MFI	137
	6 4		2.5	2457	MFI	165
	3 6		3.3	3318	MFI	230
1996	2 4		1.8	1820	MFI	110
	3, 4 4		2.2	2212	MFI	135
	6 4		2.5	2457	MFI	155
	3 6		3.3	3318	MFI	230
1995	2 4		1.8	1820	MFI	110
	6 4		2.2	2212	MFI	135
	3 6		3.3	3318	MFI	230
1994	7, 8 3		1.2	1189	MFI	73
	4, 5 4		1.8	1781	TBI	90
	2 4		1.8	1820	MFI	110
	6 4		2.2	2212	MFI	130
	6 4		2.2 T	2212 T	MFI	160
	3 6		3.3	3318	MFI	230
1993	7, 8 3		1.2	1189	MFI	73
	4, 5 4		1.8	1781	TBI	90
	2 4		1.8	1820	MFI	110
	6 4		2.2	2212	MFI	130

4 ENGINE IDENTIFICATION

YEAR	3 ENGINE CODE	CYL.	DISPL. liters	cc	Fuel System	HP
1991 Cont'd.	6 4		2.2 T	2212 T	MFI	160
	3 6		3.3	3318	MFI	230
1992	7, 8 3		1.2	1189	2V	66
	7, 8 3		1.2	1189	MFI	73
	4, 5 4		1.8	1781	TBI	90
	6 4		2.2	2212	MFI	130
	6 4		2.2 T	2212 T	MFI	160
	3 6		3.3	3318	MFI	230
1991	7, 8 3		1.2	1189	2V	66
	4, 5 4		1.8	1781	TBI	90
	6 4		2.2	2212	MFI	130
	6 4		2.2 T	2212 T	MFI	160
	ER27 6		2.7	2672	MFI	145
1990	7, 8 3		1.2	1189	2V	66
	7, 8 3		1.2	1189	MFI	73
	4, 5 4		1.8	1781	TBI	90
	4, 5 4		1.8 T	1781 T	MFI	115
	6 4		2.2	2212	MFI	130
1989	EA12 3		1.2	1189	2V	66
	EA81 4		1.8	1781	2V	73
	EA82 4		1.8	1781	TBI	90
	EA82 4		1.8	1781	MFI	97
	EA82 4		1.8 T	1781 T	MFI	115
	ER27 6		2.7	2672	MFI	145

MFI—Multiport Fuel Injection.   **TBI—Throttle Body Injection.**
T—Turbocharged.   **2V—Two Venturi Carburetor.**

UNDERHOOD SERVICE SPECIFICATIONS

SUITU1   SUITU1

CYLINDER NUMBERING SEQUENCE

3-CYL. FIRING ORDER: 1 3 2

4-CYL. FIRING ORDER: 1 3 2 4

6-CYL. FIRING ORDER: 1 6 3 2 5 4

  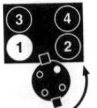 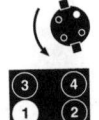  

Front of car

1989-91	1990-94	1989	1989-94	1990-99	1989-91
3-cyl. 1189cc 2V, Justy	3-cyl. 1189cc FI, Justy	4-cyl. 1781cc OHV Hatchback, 3 & 4-Door	4-cyl. 1781cc OHC	4-cyl. 1820cc, Impreza, Loyale, XT 2212cc, Legacy, Impreza 2457cc Impreza, Legacy, Forester	6-cyl. 2672cc, XT

─ TIMING MARK ─

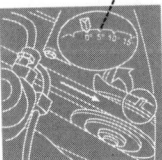

5° BTDC

**1989-94
3-cyl. 1189cc,
Justy**

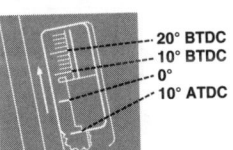

20° BTDC
10° BTDC
0°
10° ATDC

**1989-94
4-cyl. 1781cc,
Hatchback, 3 & 4-Door,
XT, Loyale**

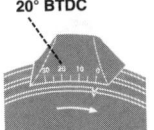

20° BTDC

**1989-91
6-cyl. 2672cc,
XT
1990-99
4-cyl. 1820cc, 2212cc, 2457cc,
Impreza, Loyale, XT, Legacy, Forester
1992-97
6-cyl. 3318cc,
SVX**

ELECTRICAL AND IGNITION SYSTEMS

BATTERY

BCI equivalent shown, size may vary from original equipment. Check clearance before replacing, holddown may need to be modified.

Engine	Year	BCI Group No.	Crank. Perf.
3-cyl.	1989-94	35	420
4-cyl. 1781cc MT	1989-94	21	310
1781cc AT ex. Turbo	1989-94	25	420
Turbo	1989-90	24	490
1820cc MT	1993-97	35	355
AT	1993-94	35	520
	1995-97	35	490
2.2L MT	1990-94	35	355
	1995	85	420
AT	1990-95	35	490
2.2L	1996-98	35	490
MT	1999	35	430
AT	1999	35	490
2457cc	1996	35	490
2457cc MT	1996-98	35	355
	1999	35	430
AT	1996-99	35	490
6-cyl. 2.7L: MT	1989-91	25	350
AT	1989-91	24	490
3.3L	1992-97	24	585

GENERATOR

Application	Year	Rated Output (amps)	Test Output (amps @ rpm)
All ex. OHC	1989	55	55 @ 5000
XT Coupe 4-cyl.	1989-91	65	53 @ 3000
3-cyl. 1189cc	1989-94	55	30 @ 2500

GENERATOR Continued

Application	Year	Rated Output (amps)	Test Output (amps @ rpm)
4-cyl. 1781cc OHC ex. XT Coupe	1989-94	60	49 @ 2500
1820cc	1993-97	75	64 @ 2500
2212cc	1990	85	66 @ 3000
	1991-94	70	60 @ 3000
Impreza	1995-99	75	62 @ 2500
Legacy	1995-99	85	62 @ 2500
2457cc Legacy	1996-99	85	62 @ 2500
Impreza, Forester	1998-99	75	64 @ 2500
6-cyl. 2672cc	1989-91	90	62 @ 3000
3318cc	1992-97	95	73 @ 2500

REGULATOR

Year	Test Temp. (deg. F/C)	Voltage Setting
1989-98	68/20	14.1-14.8

STARTER

Engine	Year	Cranking Voltage (min. volts)	Ampere Draw @ Cranking Speed
All 3-cyl.	1989-94	8.0	200
4-cyl. 1781cc, 2212cc MT	1989-99	8.0	280
AT	1989-99	8.0	370
1820cc MT	1993-97	8.0	280
AT	1993-97	7.7	300
2457cc MT	1998-99	7.5	300
AT	1998-99	7.7	400
6-cyl. MT	1989	8.0	280
AT	1989	8.0	370
6-cyl.	1992-97	8.0	300

UNDERHOOD SERVICE SPECIFICATIONS

SUITU3   SUITU3

SPARK PLUGS

Engine	Year	Gap (inches)	Gap (mm)	Torque[1] (ft-lb)
All	1989-99	.039-.043	1.0-1.1	13-17

1 With dry threads.

IGNITION COIL

Engine	Year	Windings	Resistance (ohms)
3-cyl. 1189cc	1989-94	Primary	0.8-1.0
		Secondary	8500-11,500
1781cc, 2672cc, all	1989-90	Primary	0.84-1.02
		Secondary	8000-12,000
1781cc	1991-93	Primary	0.1-1.0
		Secondary	8000-12,000
1820cc w/MT	1993-95	Primary	0.62-0.76
		Secondary	17,900-24,500
w/AT	1993-95	Primary	0.63-0.77
		Secondary	10,400-15,600
1820cc	1996-98	Primary	0.63-0.77
		Secondary	10,400-15,600
2212cc w/MT	1990-95	Primary	0.62-0.76
		Secondary	17,900-24,500
w/AT	1990-95	Primary	0.63-0.77
		Secondary	10,400-15,600
2212cc	1996-99	Primary	0.6-0.8
		Secondary	10,880-14,720
2457cc	1997-98	Primary	0.6-0.8
		Secondary	10,880-14,720
3318cc	1992-94	Primary	0.68-0.83

IGNITION PICKUP

Application	Year	Air Gap (in./mm)
3-cyl. 1189cc	1989	.012-.016/.3-.4

BASE TIMING

1989 Set timing at Before Top Dead Center, unless otherwise specified. Disconnect and plug vacuum hose(s). Turbo disconnect knock sensor under airflow meter.
1989-94 1189cc FI connect together the green, two pole test mode converters.
1990-99 4-cyl., 6-cyl. timing is not adjustable.

Engine	Year	Man. Trans. (degrees)	Auto. Trans. (degrees)
1189cc	1989-93	5±2	5±2
1781cc 2V	1989	8±2	8±2
1781cc	1989-93	20±2	20±2
1820cc	1993-97	20±2[1]	20±8[1]
2212cc ex. Turbo	1990-91	20±2[1]	20±8[1]
	1992-94	20±8[1]	20±8[1]
	1995-98	14±8[1]	20±8[1]
Impreza	1999	14±8[1]	20±8[1]
Legacy Calif.	1999	15	15
Federal	1999	10	15
Turbo	1991	15±2[1]	15±2[1]
	1992-94	15±8[1]	15±8[1]
2457cc	1996-98	15±8[1]	15±8[1]
	1999	10[1]	15[1]
2672cc	1989-91	20±2	20±2
3318cc	1992-97	20±8[1]	20±8[1]

1 Checking value only.

DISTRIBUTOR TIMING ADVANCE

Engine degrees at engine rpm, no load, in addition to base timing setting.

Engine	Transmission	Year	Distributor Number	Degrees @ 2500 RPM Total	Degrees @ 2500 RPM Centrifugal
1189cc	MT	1989	100291-A080	39-47	11-15

FUEL SYSTEM

FUEL PUMP

Engine	Year	Pressure PSI	Pressure RPM
1189cc 2V	1989-91	1.25-2.0	idle
1781cc 2V	1989	2.6-3.3	idle
MPFI	1989-90	26-30	idle
SPFI	1989-94	20-24	idle
1820cc	1993-94	26-30	idle
	1997-98	36.3	idle
2212cc	1990-95	26-30	idle
	1996-98	36.5	idle
	1999	43.4	idle
2457cc	1996-98	26-30	idle
	1999	43.4	idle
2672cc	1989	26-30	idle
3318cc	1992-94	36.3	idle

CARBURETOR CHOKE

Engine	Year	Make	Choke (notches) Man. Trans.	Choke (notches) Auto. Trans.
3-cyl. 1189cc	1989	Hitachi DFC328	high	high

IDLE SPEED W/O COMPUTER CONTROL

Disconnect and plug EVAP canister purge hose at carburetor or throttle body.
With FI, ensure that auxiliary air valve is closed.

Engine	Year	Manual[1] Trans.	Auto.[1] Trans.
3-cyl. 1189cc 2V	1989-93	750-850	—
Speed-up	1989-93	850-950	—
All 1595cc	1989	600-800	—
All 1781cc	1989-91	600-800	700-900 N
AC speed-up, 2V	1989	900-1000	900-1000 N
AC speed-up, FI	1989	800-900	800-900 N

1 Preferred setting is midpoint of range given.

IDLE SPEED W/COMPUTER CONTROL

1781cc TBI: Disconnect air valve control connector and set to specified setting speed.

Engine	Year	Setting Speed	Checking Speed	Speed-up
1189cc	1990-94	—	650-750	—
1781cc TBI	1989-90	500-600	600-800	800-900
Turbo	1989-90	—	700-900	—
1820cc	1993-94	—	600-800	800-900
	1995-98	—	600-800 N	750-850 N
2212cc	1990-99	—	600-800 N	800-900 N
2457cc	1996-99	—	600-800 N	800-900 N
2672cc	1989-91	—	650-850	800-900
3318cc	1992-97	—	510-710	750-850 N

ENGINE MECHANICAL

TIGHTENING TORQUES

Engine	Year	TORQUE FOOT-POUNDS/NEWTON METERS Cylinder Head	Intake Manifold	Exhaust Manifold	Crankshaft Pulley	Water Pump
3-cyl.						
1.2L:	1989	29/39	14-22/	14-22/	58-72/	6.9-7.3/
2nd stage		54/73	20-29	20-29	78-98	9.3-10.3
3rd stage[1]		57/77				
4-cyl.						
1781cc OHC:	1989-91	22/30	13-16/	19-22/	66-79/	—
2nd stage		43/60	18-22	25-29	89-107	—
3rd stage[2]		47/65				

SUBARU
1989-99

TIGHTENING TORQUES Continued

Engine	Year	Cylinder Head	Intake Manifold	Exhaust Manifold	Crankshaft Pulley	Water Pump
		TORQUE FOOT-POUNDS/NEWTON METERS				
1820cc	1993-96	22/29	6/8	25/34	—	—
2nd stage		51/69				
3rd stage		-180°				
4th stage		-180°				
5th stage						
center 2		25/34				
6th stage						
outer 4		11/15				
7th stage		+90°				
8th stage		+90°				
	1997	22/29	16.5-19.5/ 23-27	19-26/ 25-35	87-101/ 117-137	7-10/ 10-14
2nd stage		51/69				
3rd stage		-180°				
4th stage		-180°				
5th stage						
center 2		25/34				
6th stage						
outer 4		11/15				
7th stage		+90°				
8th stage		+90°				
2.2L DOHC	1990-91	51/69	—	19-26/ 25-35	66-79/ 86-107	6.5-8.0/ 9-11
2nd stage[3]						
center 2		25/34				
outer 4		14/20				
3rd stage		+90°				
4th stage		+90°				
2.2L	1995-96	22/29	17/19	19-26/ 25-35	69-76/ 93-103	7-10/ 10-14
2nd stage		51/69	23-27			
3rd stage		-180°				
4th stage		-180°				
5th stage						
center 2		25/34				
6th stage						
outer 4		11/15				
7th stage		+90°				
8th stage		+90°				
2.2L	1997-99	22/29	16.5-19.5/ 23-27	19-26/ 25-35	87-10/ 117-137	7-10/ 10-14
2nd stage		51/69				
3rd stage		-180°				
4th stage		-180°				
5th stage						
center 2		25/34				
6th stage						
outer 4		11/15				
7th stage		+90°				
8th stage		+90°				
2457cc	1996	22/29	19/26	25/34	—	—
2nd stage		51/69				
3rd stage		-180°				
4th stage		-180°				
5th stage						
center 2		25/34				
6th stage						
outer 4		11/15				
7th stage		+90°				
8th stage		+90°				
2457cc	1997-99	22/29	16.5-19.5/ 23-27	26/35	123-137/ 167-187	10/12 10/12
2nd stage		51/69				
3rd stage		-180°				
4th stage		-180°				
5th stage						
center 2		25/34				
6th stage						
outer 4		11/15				
7th stage		+90°				
8th stage		+90°				
6-cyl.						
2.7L	1989-91	22/30	13-16/ 18-22	19-22/ 25-29	66-79/ 89-107	—
2nd stage		47/64				—
3rd stage[1]		50/68				
3318cc	1996	—	19/26	32/43	—	—

1 Back off 90° before bringing to final torque.

2 Tighten to specification, run engine to operating temperature and allow to cool, back off and retorque one bolt at a time.

3 Back off 180° before bringing to 2nd stage torque.

VALVE CLEARANCE
Engine cold.

Engine	Year	Intake (inches)	Intake (mm)	Exhaust (inches)	Exhaust (mm)
3-cyl.	1989-93	.005-.007	.13-.17	.009-.011	.23-.27
4-cyl. ex. OHC	1989	.010	.25	.014	.35
4-cyl. all	1997-99	.007-.009	.18-.22	.009-.016	.23-.27

No adjustment on 1990-96 (hydraulic).

COMPRESSION PRESSURE
At cranking speed, engine warm, throttle open.

Engine	Year	PSI	Maximum Variation PSI
11890cc	1989-94	135-156	14
1781cc 2V	1989	132-161	28
	1989-91	117-145	28
TBI	1989-94	139-168	28
1820cc	1993-97	156-185	28
2212cc	1990-99	156-185	28
Turbo	1990-94	142-171	28
2457cc	1996-99	137-176	7
2672cc	1989-91	139-168	28
3318cc	1992-94	171-206	28

BELT TENSION

Deflection method: Table lists deflection at midpoint of longest belt segment under a 22-pound load.

Model	Year	Generator	Power Steering	Air Cond.
USED BELTS:				
Forester (inches)	1998-99	11/32-7/16	11/32-7/16	11/32-13/32
(mm)		9-11	9-11	9-10
Impreza (inches)	1993-96	11/32-7/16	11/32-7/16	11/32-13/32
(mm)		9-10	9-10	9-10
Impreza (inches)	1997	11/32-13/32	11/32-13/32	11/32-7/16
(mm)		9-10	9-10	9-11
Impreza (inches)	1998-99	11/32-7/16	11/32-7/16	11/32-13/32
(mm)		9-11	9-11	9-10
(mm)		13-15	9-11	11-13[1]
Justy (inches)	1989-94	5/16-3/8	—	7/16-1/2
(mm)		9-10	—	11-12
Ex. Justy (inches)	1989	3/8-7/16	1/4-3/8	3/8-1/2[1]
(mm)		9-11	7-9	10-12[1]
Legacy (inches)	1990-96	3/8-7/16	3/8-7/16	3/8-7/16
(mm)		9-11	9-11	9-10
Legacy (inches)	1997-98	11/32-13/32	11/32-13/32	11/32-7/16
(mm)		9-10	9-10	9-11
Legacy (inches)	1998-99	11/32-7/16	11/32-7/16	11/32-13/32
(mm)		9-11	9-11	9-10
Loyale (inches)	1990-94	1/2-9/16	3/8-7/16	7/16-1/2
(mm)		13-15	9-11	11-12[1]
SVX (inches)	1992-97	3/16-1/4	3/16-1/4	9/32-5/16
(mm)		5-6	5-6	7-8
XT (inches)	1990-91	3/8-7/16	5/16-7/16	5/16-7/16
(mm)		9-11	7-9	7-9

1 With both AC & PS; inches—5/16-11/32, mm—7.5-8.5.

UNDERHOOD SERVICE SPECIFICATIONS

ENGINE COMPUTER SYSTEM

DIAGNOSTIC TROUBLE CODES

To activate codes, connect male and female connectors under steering wheel to left of module. Turn ignition on but do not start car. Codes will be displayed as pulses on LED mounted on module. Long pulses indicate tens, short pulses indicate ones.

1989-91 3-cyl. 1189cc Justy
Code 14 Duty solenoid valve control
Code 15 Coasting fuel cut system
Code 21 Engine coolant temperature sensor
Code 22 Vacuum line charging solenoid control
Code 23 Pressure sensor system
Code 24 Idle-up solenoid control
Code 25 Fuel chamber vent solenoid control
Code 32 Oxygen sensor
Code 33 Vehicle speed sensor
Code 35 Purge control solenoid control
Code 52 Clutch switch
Code 62 Idle-up system
Code 63 Idle-up system

1989-94 All 4-cyl. 1781cc, 1989-91 6-cyl. 2672cc
Code 11 Crankshaft position sensor
Code 12 Starter switch
Code 13 Crankshaft position sensor or engine stalled
Code 14 Injectors 1 & 2
Code 15 Injectors 3 & 4
Code 21 Engine coolant temperature sensor
Code 22 Knock sensor
Code 23 Mass airflow sensor
Code 24 Secondary air control valve
Code 31 Throttle position sensor
Code 32 Oxygen sensor
Code 33 Vehicle speed sensor
Code 34 EGR solenoid
Code 35 Purge control solenoid
Code 41 Lean fuel mixture
Code 42 Idle switch
Code 44 Duty solenoid valve (wastegate control)
Code 45 Kick-down control relay
Code 51 Neutral switch continuously in on position
Code 54 Neutral switch
Code 55 EGR temperature sensor
Code 61 Parking switch

1990-94 4-cyl. 1820cc, 2212cc, 1992-93 6-cyl. 3318cc
Code 11 Crankshaft position sensor
Code 12 Starter switch
Code 13 Camshaft position sensor or engine stalled
Code 14 Injector, cylinder 1
Code 15 Injector, cylinder 2
Code 16 Injector, cylinder 3
Code 17 Injector, cylinder 4
Code 18 Injector, cylinder 5
Code 19 Injector, cylinder 6
Code 21 Engine coolant temperature sensor
Code 22 Knock sensor, right side
Code 23 Mass airflow sensor
Code 24 By-pass air valve
Code 28 Knock sensor, left side
Code 29 Crankshaft position sensor
Code 31 Throttle position sensor
Code 32 Oxygen sensor, right side
Code 33 Vehicle speed sensor
Code 34 EGR solenoid valve
Code 35 EVAP canister purge valve
Code 36 Air suction solenoid valve
Code 37 Oxygen sensor, left side
Code 38 No engine to transmission
Code 41 Air fuel ratio control
Code 42 Idle switch
Code 44 Wastegate control
Code 45 Barometric pressure sensor
Code 49 Mass airflow sensor
Code 51 Neutral switch
Code 52 Parking switch
Code 55 EGR temperature sensor
Code 56 EGR system

SENSORS, INPUT
TEMPERATURE SENSORS

Engine	Year	Sensor	Resistance Ohms @ deg. F/C
3-cyl. 1.2L	1989-94	Coolant	134-179 @ 122/50
			47-57 @ 176/80
			26-29 @ 212/100
			15-17 @ 248/120
4-cyl. 1781cc	1989-94	Coolant	7000-11,500 @ 14/-10
			2000-3000 @ 68/20
			700-1000 @ 122/50
Turbo 1820cc, 2212cc	1990-94	Wastegate Coolant	17-21 @ 68/20
			2500 @ 68/20
			400 @ 176/80
1820cc, 2212cc	1996-98	Transmission Oil	2100-2900 @ 68/20
			275-375 @ 176/80
6-cyl. 2.7L	1989-91	Coolant	7000-11,500 @ 14/-10
			2000-3000 @ 68/20
			700-1000 @ 122/50
3.3L	1992-94	Coolant	2500 @ 68/20
			400 @ 176/80

MASS AIRFLOW SENSOR

Engine	Year	Resistance Ohms @ Terminal	Voltage @ Terminal
4-cyl. 1781cc TBI	1989-90	10 max. @ B & ground	10 min. @ R
			0.1-0.5 @ W & B
Turbo	1989-90	10 max. @ B & BR	10 min. @ SA
			1-2 @ SA & BR
1820cc	1993-97	—	0.8-1.2
2212cc	1996-97	—	0.8-1.2
6-cyl. 2672cc	1989-91	10 max. @ B & BR	10 min. @ SA
			1-2 @ SA & BR

BAROMETRIC PRESSURE SENSOR

Engine	Year	Resistance (ohms)
3-cyl. 1.2L 2V	1989	32.7-39.9

CAMSHAFT & CRANKSHAFT SENSORS

Engine	Year	Resistance (ohms)
3318cc both	1997	1000-4000

THROTTLE POSITION SENSOR

Engine	Year	Resistance Ohms @ Terminal
1781cc TBI	1989-90	3500-6500 @ B & D
		1000 max. @ B & C[1]
		2400 min. @ B & C[2]
1781cc Turbo	1989-90	6-18 @ 1 & 3
		5.8-17.8 @ 1 & 2[1]
		1.5-5.1 @ 1 & 2[2]
2212cc	1990-94	12,000 @ 2 & 3
		4300 @ 2 & 4[1]
		1000 @ 2 & 4[2]
2672cc	1989-91	3-7 @ 1 & 4
		1000-11,000 @ 2 & 4[1]
		4200-15,000 @ 2 & 4[2]
3318cc	1992-94	5000 @ 1 & 3
		12,000 @ 2 & 3[2]
		5000 @ 2 & 3[1]

1 With throttle plate open.
2 With throttle plate closed.

UNDERHOOD SERVICE SPECIFICATIONS

SENSORS, INPUT Continued

SECONDARY AIR INJECTION CONTROL VALVE

Engine	Year	Resistance (ohms)
4-cyl. 1781cc SPFI	1989-90	7.3-13
2212cc w/MT	1990	9.6
w/AT	1990	9.0

ACTUATORS, OUTPUT

BY-PASS AIR CONTROLLER

Engine	Year	Resistance Ohms @ Terminal
6-cyl. 2.7L	1989-91	9500-11,500 @ 1 & 2
		8500-10,500 @ 2 & 3

ACTUATORS, OUTPUT Continued

IDLE UP SOLENOID

Engine	Year	Resistance (ohms)
All 2V	1989	32.7-39.9

FUEL INJECTORS

Engine	Year	Resistance (Ohms)
1781cc DL, GL	1989	0.5-2
Loyale	1990	0.5-2
XT	1989-91	2-3
Turbo GL	1989	2-3
Turbo Loyale	1990	2-3
2212cc Legacy	1990-92	11-12
SVX	1992	11-12
2457cc	1996-98	5-20
2672cc XT	1989-91	13.8

ENGINE IDENTIFICATION

To identify any engine by the manufacturer's code, follow the four steps designated by the numbered blocks.

V.I.N.
PLATE LOCATION:

Attached to top of instrument panel visible through windshield.

1 MODEL YEAR IDENTIFICATION:

10th character of V.I.N.

2000—Y	1999—X	1998—W
1997—V	1996—T	1995—S
1994—R	1993—P	1992—N
1991—M	1990—L	1989—K

2 ENGINE CODE LOCATION:

Prefix to engine number on side of engine block.

YEAR	3 ENGINE CODE	CYL.	4 ENGINE IDENTIFICATION DISPL. liters	cc	Fuel System	HP
2000	1NZ-FE	4	1.5	1497	MFI	108
	1ZZ-FE	4	1.8	1794	MFI	125
	2ZZ-GE	4	1.8	1796	MFI	180
	3S-FE	4	2.0	1998	MFI	127
	5S-FE	4	2.2	2164	MFI	133-136[1]
	2RZ-FE	4	2.4	2438	MFI	142
	3RZ-FE	4	2.7	2693	MFI	150
	1MZ-FE	6	3.0	2995	MFI	192-210[1]
	5VZ-FE	6	3.4	3378	MFI	183-190[1]
	2VZ-FE	8	4.7	4669	MFI	230-245[1]
1999	5E-FE	4	1.5	1497	MFI	93
	1ZZ-FE	4	1.8	1794	MFI	120
	3S-FE	4	2.0	1998	MFI	125, 127[1]
	5S-FE	4	2.2	2164	MFI	130, 133[1]
	2RZ-FE	4	2.4	2438	MFI	142
	3RZ-FE	4	2.7	2693	MFI	150
	IMZ-FE	6	3.0	2995	MFI	194-200[1]
	5VZ-FE	6	3.4	3378	MFI	183-190[1]
	2UZ-FE	8	4.7	4669	MFI	225, 245[1]
1998	5E-FE	4	1.5	1497	MFI	93
	1ZZ-FE	4	1.8	1794	MFI	120
	3S-FE	4	2.0	1998	MFI	125, 127[1]
	5S-FE	4	2.2	2164	MFI	130, 133
	2RZ-FE	4	2.4	2438	MFI	142
	3RZ-FE	4	2.7	2693	MFI	150
	IMZ-FE	6	3.0	2995	MFI	194-200[1]
	2JZ-GE	6	3.0	2997	MFI	225
	2JZ-GTE	6	3.0 T	2997T	MFI	320
	5VZ-FE	6	3.4	3378	MFI	183-190[1]
1996-97	5E-FE	4	1.5	1497	MFI	93
	4A-FE	4	1.6	1587	MFI	100
	7A-FE	4	1.8	1762	MFI	105
	3S-FE	4	2.0	1998	MFI	120
	5S-FE	4	2.2	2164	MFI	125-130[1]
	2RZ-FE	4	2.4	2438	MFI	142
	2TZ-FTE	4	2.4	2438	MFI	161
	3RZ-FE	4	2.7	2693	MFI	150
	IMZ-FE	6	3.0	2995	MFI	188, 192[1]
	2JZ-GE	6	3.0	2997	MFI	220
	2JZ-GTE	6	3.0 T	2997 T	MFI	320
	5VZ-FE	6	3.4	3378	MFI	190
	1FZ-FE	6	4.5	4477	MFI	212
1995	5E-FE	4	1.5	1497	MFI	93, 100
	4A-FE	4	1.6	1587	MFI	100, 105
	7A-FE	4	1.8	1762	MFI	105, 110
	3S-GTE	4	2.0 T	1998 T	MFI	200
	5S-FE	4	2.2	2164	MFI	125-135[1]
	22R-E	4	2.4	2366	MFI	116
	2TZ-FE	4	2.4	2438	MFI	138
	2TZ-FTE	4	2.4 S	2438 S	MFI	161
	3RZ-FE	4	2.7	2693	MFI	150
	3VZ-FE	6	3.0	2958	MFI	150
	IMZ-FE	6	3.0	2995	MFI	188, 192
	2JZ-GE	6	3.0	2997	MFI	220
	2JZ-GTE	6	3.0 T	2997 T	MFI	320
	5VZ-FE	6	3.4	3378	MFI	190
	1FZ-FE	6	4.5	4477	MFI	212

YEAR	3 ENGINE CODE	CYL.	4 ENGINE IDENTIFICATION DISPL. liters	cc	Fuel System	HP
1994	3E-E	4	1.5	1456	MFI	82
	5E-FE	4	1.5	1497	MFI	100
	4A-FE	4	1.6	1587	MFI	100, 105[1]
	7A-FE	4	1.8	1762	MFI	110, 115[1]
	3S-GTE	4	2.0 T	1998 T	MFI	200
	5S-FE	4	2.2	2164	MFI	125-135[1]
	22R-E	4	2.4	2366	MFI	116
	2TZ-FE	4	2.4	2438	MFI	138
	2TZ-FTE	4	2.4 S	2438 S	MFI	161
	3RZ-FE	4	2.7	2694	MFI	150
	3VZ-E	6	3.0	2958	MFI	150
	1MZ-FE	6	3.0	2995	MFI	188
	2JZ-GE	6	3.0	2997	MFI	220
	2JZ-GET	6	3.0 T	2997 T	MFI	320
	1FZ-FE	6	4.5	4477	MFI	212
1993	3E-E	4	1.5	1456	MFI	82
	5E-FE	4	1.5	1497	MFI	100
	4A-FE	4	1.6	1587	MFI	103, 105[1]
	7A-FE	4	1.8	1762	MFI	115
	3S-GTE	4	2.0 T	1998 T	MFI	200
	5S-FE	4	2.2	2164	MFI	130-145[1]
	22-RE	4	2.4	2366	MFI	116
	2TZ-FE	4	2.4	2438	MFI	138
	3VZ-FE	6	3.0	2958	MFI	150, 185[1]
	2JZ-GE	6	3.0	2997	MFI	220
	2JZ-GET	6	3.0 T	2997 T	MFI	320
	1FZ-FE	6	4.5	4477	MFI	212
1992	3E-E	4	1.5	1456	MFI	82
	5E-FE	4	1.5	1497	MFI	100
	4A-FE	4	1.6	1587	MFI	102, 103[1]
	3S-GTE	4	2.0 T	1998 T	MFI	200
	5S-FE	4	2.2	2164	MFI	130, 135[1]
	22R-E	4	2.4	2366	MFI	116
	2TZ-FE	4	2.4	2438	MFI	138
	7M-GE	6	3.0	2954	MFI	190, 200[1]
	7M-GET	6	3.0 T	2954 T	MFI	232
	3VZ-E	6	3.0	2958	MFI	150
	3VZ-FE	6	3.0	2958	MFI	185
	3F-E	6	4.0	3955	MFI	155
1991	3E-E	4	1.5	1456	MFI	82
	4A-FE	4	1.6	1587	MFI	102, 103[1]
	4A-GE	4	1.6	1587	MFI	130
	3S-FE	4	2.0	1998	MFI	115
	3S-GTE	4	2.0 T	1998 T	MFI	200
	5S-FE	4	2.2	2164	MFI	130, 135[1]
	22R-E	4	2.4	2366	MFI	116
	2TZ-FE	4	2.4	2438	MFI	138
	2V-ZE	4	2.5	2507	MFI	156
	7M-GE	6	3.0	2954	MFI	190, 200[1]
	7M-GET	6	3.0 T	2954 T	MFI	232
	3V-ZE	6	3.0	2958	MFI	150
	3F-E	6	4.0	3955	MFI	155
1990	3E	4	1.5	1456	2V	78
	3E-E	4	1.5	1456	MFI	82
	4A-FE	4	1.6	1587	MFI	101, 103[1]
	4A-GE	4	1.6	1587	MFI	130
	3S-FE	4	2.0	1998	MFI	115
	3S-GTE	4	2.0 T	1998 T	MFI	200
	5S-FE	4	2.2	2164	MFI	130
	22R	4	2.4	2366	2V	102
	22R-E	4	2.4	2366	MFI	116
	2VZ-FE	6	2.5	2507	MFI	156
	7M-GE	6	3.0	2954	MFI	190, 200[1]
	7M-GET	6	3.0 T	2954 T	MFI	232
	3V-ZE	6	3.0	2958	MFI	150
	3F-E	6	4.0	3955	MFI	155

ENGINE IDENTIFICATION Continued

YEAR	**3** ENGINE CODE	CYL.	**4** ENGINE IDENTIFICATION DISPL. liters	cc	Fuel System	HP
1989	3E	4	1.5	1546	2V	78
	4A-F	4	1.6	1587	2V	90
	4A-FE	4	1.6	1587	MFI	100
	4A-GE	4	1.6	1587	MFI	115
	4A-GELC	4	1.6	1587	MFI	115
	4A-GZE	4	1.6 S	1587 S	MFI	145
	3S-FE	4	2.0	1998	MFI	115
	3S-GE	4	2.0	1998	MFI	135
	3S-GTE	4	2.0 T	1998 T	MFI	190
	4Y-EC	4	2.2	2237	MFI	101
	22R	4	2.4	2366	2V	103

YEAR	**3** ENGINE CODE	CYL.	**4** ENGINE IDENTIFICATION DISPL. liters	cc	Fuel System	HP
1989 Cont'd.	22R-E	4	2.4	2366	MFI	116
	2V-ZE	6	2.5	2507	MFI	153
	7M-GE	6	3.0	2954	MFI	190, 200[1]
	7M-GET	6	3.0 T	2954 T	MFI	230
	3V-ZE	6	3.0	2958	MFI	150
	3F-E	6	4.0	3955	MFI	155

1 Engine horsepower varies with model installation.
T—Turbocharged.   S—Supercharged.
MFI—Multiport Fuel Injection.
2V—Two Venturi Carburetor.

UNDERHOOD SERVICE SPECIFICATIONS

TAITU1   TAITU1

CYLINDER NUMBERING SEQUENCE

4-CYL. FIRING ORDER:
1995 1497cc: 1 4 2 3
Others: 1 3 4 2

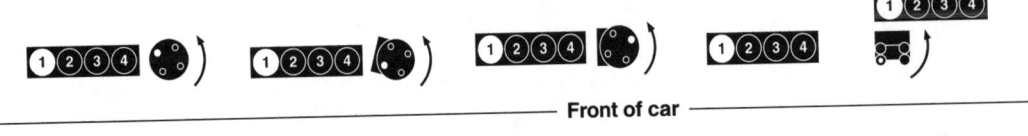

— Front of car —

| 1989-90 Tercel 1456cc 2V | 1990-94 Tercel 1456cc FI | 1992-95 Paseo 1497cc FI | 1997-00 1497cc | 1989 MR2 1587cc FI | 1989-97 Corolla, Celica 1587cc 4AF, FE 1762cc 7A-FE |

     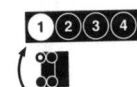 

— Front of car —

| 1989-91 Corolla 1587cc 4 AGE | 2000 Celica, Corolla 1794cc, 1796cc | 1989-98 Celica, Camry 1998cc DOHC ex. Turbo, 2164cc DOHC | 1997-00 RAV4 1998cc 1998-00 Camry, Solara 2164cc | 1989-93 Celica 1998cc Turbo | 1990-95 MR2 1998cc Turbo | 1989-90 Van 2237cc |

4-CYL. FIRING ORDER:
1995 1497cc: 1 4 2 3
Others: 1 3 4 2

6-CYL. FIRING ORDER: 1 5 3 6 2 4
V6 FIRING ORDER: 1 2 3 4 5 6

— Front of car —   — Front of car —

| 1990-95 MR2 2164cc | 1989-95 Pickup, 4-Runner 2366cc | 1994-98 Tacoma, T100, 4-Runner 2438cc, 2693cc (some) | 1994-00 Tacoma, 4-Runner 2438cc, 2693cc (others) | 1989-93 Camry 2507cc, 2958cc | 1989-98 Supra 2954cc, 2997cc ex. Turbo | 1989-95 Pickup, 4-Runner, T100 2958cc |

UNDERHOOD SERVICE SPECIFICATIONS

TAITU2   TAITU2

CYLINDER NUMBERING SEQUENCE

6-CYL. FIRING ORDER:
1 5 3 6 2 4
V6 FIRING ORDER:
1 2 3 4 5 6
V8 FIRING ORDER:
1 8 4 3 6 5 7 2

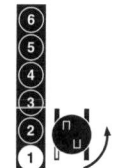
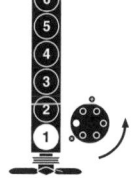

Front of car

| 1994-00 Avalon, Camry, Sienna, Solara 2995cc | 1995-00 Tacoma, T100, Tundra 4-Runner 3378cc | 1989-95 Land Cruiser 3955cc | 1993-97 Land Cruiser 4477cc | 1998-00 Landcruiser, Tundra 4669cc |

TIMING MARK

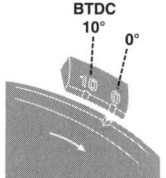

1989-00 Paseo, Tercel, Echo 1456cc, 1497cc 2000 Celica, Corolla 1794cc, 1796cc

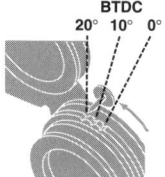

1989 MR2 1587cc

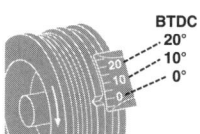
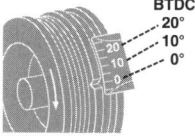

1989-92 Corolla, Celica 1587cc FWD

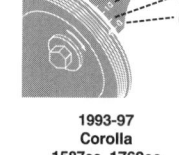

1993-97 Corolla 1587cc, 1762cc

1989-00 Camry, Celica, MR2, RAV4 1995cc, 1998cc 3S-FE, 2164cc 1994-00 Avalon, Camry, Solara, Sienna 2995cc

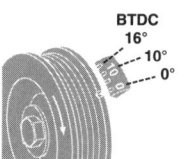

1989-95 Celica, MR2 1998cc 3S-GE, 1998cc Turbo

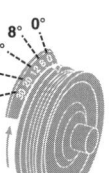

1989-90 Van 2237cc

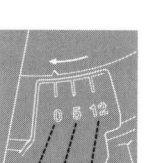

1989-95 Pickup 2366cc

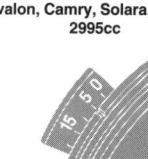

1991-97 Previa 2438cc

1994-00 Tacoma, T100, 4-Runner 2438cc, 2693cc

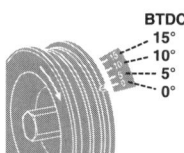

1989-92 Supra, Cressida 2759cc, 2954cc

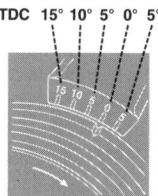

1989-93 Camry 2507cc, 2958cc; 1989-95 Pickup 2958cc

1993-98 Supra 2997cc 1998-00 Landcruiser, Tundra 4669cc

1995-00 Tacoma, T100, 4-Runner, Tundra 3378cc

1989-97 Land Cruiser 3955cc, 4477cc

ELECTRICAL AND IGNITION SYSTEMS

BATTERY

BCI equivalent shown, size may vary from original equipment. Check clearance before replacing, holddown may need to be modified.

Engine	Year	STANDARD BCI Group No.	STANDARD Crank. Perf.	OPTIONAL BCI Group No.	OPTIONAL Crank. Perf.
1456cc Tercel: MT	1989	21R	320	—	—
AT & Canada	1989	35	350	—	—
1456cc	1990	35	350	—	—
1456cc, 1497cc	1991-92	21	310	35	350
Canada	1991-92	35	350	—	—
1456cc, 1497cc	1993-99	21	310	25	350
Canada	1993-99	25	350	—	—
1587cc Corolla	1989-92	21R	320	35	350
Canada	1989-92	35	350	—	—

BATTERY Continued

Engine	Year	STANDARD BCI Group No.	STANDARD Crank. Perf.	OPTIONAL BCI Group No.	OPTIONAL Crank. Perf.
1587cc MR2	1989	35	350	—	—
1587cc Celica	1990-91	35	350	—	—
1587cc Celica	1992	24F	490	—	—
1587cc Corolla	1993-97	35	350	—	—
1762cc	1993-97	35	350	—	—
1794cc Corolla	1998-99	35	350	—	—
1995cc, 1998cc Celica	1989-91	35	350	—	—
1998cc Celica	1992	24F	490	—	—
1998cc Camry	1989	21R	320	35	380
Canada	1989	35	380	—	—
1998cc Camry:					
U.S. Prod.	1990-91	21R	330	—	—
Japan Prod.	1990-91	35	350	—	—
1998cc MR2	1991-92	35	350	—	—
	1993	35	350	24F	420

BATTERY Continued

Engine	Year	STANDARD BCI Group No.	STANDARD Crank. Perf.	OPTIONAL BCI Group No.	OPTIONAL Crank. Perf.
1998cc RAV4	1997-99	35	350	—	—
2164cc	1990-91	35	350	—	—
2164cc: Camry	1992	35	350	24F	585
Celica	1992	24F	490	—	—
MR2	1992	35	350	—	—
2164cc: Camry	1993-96	35	350	24F	490
MR2	1993-95	35	350	24F	490
Celica	1993	35	350	24F	490
	1994-96	35	350	35	405
2164cc Celica	1997-99	35	350	35	405
2164cc Camry, Solara	1997-99	35	350	24F	585
2237cc	1989	25	380	—	—
2366cc: Pickup, 4-Runner	1989-90	21	320	25	350
2366cc	1991-92	25	350	24	585
Canada	1991-92	24	585	—	—
2366cc	1993-95	25	350	—	—
2438cc Previa	1991-97	35	350	24F	585
Canada	1991-97	24F	585	—	—
2438cc Tacoma	1995-99	35	350	24F	585
2507cc Camry	1989	21R	320	35	350
Canada	1989	35	350	—	—
2507cc Camry:					
U.S. Prod.	1990-91	21R	330	—	—
Japan Prod.	1990-91	35	350	—	—
2693cc T100	1993-98	24F	585	—	—
Tacoma	1995-99	35	350	24F	585
4-Runner	1996-99	35	350	24F	585
2954cc	1989-91	27F	450	—	—
2958cc Pickup, 4-Runner	1989	25	380	—	—
4WD	1989	24	585	—	—
2958cc Pickup, 4-Runner	1989-92	24	585	—	—
2958cc Pickup, 4-Runner	1993-94	25	380	24	610
Canada	1993-94	24	585	—	—
2995cc Camry, Sienna	1994-99	24F	585	—	—
2995cc Avalon, Solara	1995-99	35	350	24F	585
2997cc MT	1994-96	24F	490	—	—
AT	1994-96	24F	585	—	—
2997cc	1997-98	24F	585	—	—
3378cc	1995-99	24F	585	—	—
3956cc Land Cruiser	1989-92	27	450	—	—
4477cc	1993-97	27F	470	27F	655
4669cc	1998-99	24F	585	—	—

GENERATOR

Application	Rated Output (amps)	Test Output (amps @ rpm)
1989-93	50, 55, 60, 70, 80, 100	30 min. @ 2000
1994-00	60, 70, 80, 90, 100	30 min. @ 2000

REGULATOR

Application	Year	Test Temp. (deg. F/C)	Voltage Setting
1587cc Supercharged	1989	77/25	13.7-14.8
2997cc	1993-98	77/25	13.6-14.8
		239/115	13.2-14.0
3956cc	1989-92	77/25	13.8-14.4
All others	1989-96	77/25	13.9-15.1
		239/115	13.5-14.3
2438cc Tacoma,			
2693cc, 3378cc	1997	—	13.2-14.7
2997cc	1997	—	13.2-14.8
All others	1997	—	13.5-15.1
Camry, Avalon, Sienna, Tercel,			
Echo, Corolla, Solara	1998-00	77/25	13.5-15.1
All others	1998-00	77/25	13.2-14.8

SPARK PLUGS

Engine	Year	Gap (inches)	Gap (mm)	Torque (ft-lb)
1456cc, 1497cc	1989-00	.043	1.1	11-15
1587cc 2WD	1989	.043	1.1	11-15
Others	1989	.031	.80	11-15
1587cc GTS	1990	.043	1.1	11-15
Others	1990	.031	.80	11-15
1587cc	1991-97	.031	.80	11-15
1762cc	1993-97	.031	.80	13
1794cc, 1796cc	1998-00	.043	1.1	13
1998cc ex. Turbo	1989-00	.043	1.1	11-15
1998cc Turbo	1989-95	.031	.80	11-15
2164cc	1990-00	.043	1.1	13
2366cc Trucks	1989-95	.031	.80	11-15
2438cc Previa	1991-97	.043	1.1	18
2438cc Tacoma	1995-00	.031	.80	13
Calif.	2000	.043	1.1	13
2507cc	1989-91	.043	1.1	18
2693cc	1994-00	.031	.80	13
Calif.	2000	.043	1.1	13
2954cc ex. Turbo	1989-92	.043	1.1	11-15
Turbo	1989-90	.031	.80	11-15
2958cc Trucks	1989-95	.031	.80	18
2958cc Camry	1992-93	.043	1.1	18
2995cc	1994-00	.043	1.1	13
2997cc	1993-98	.043	1.1	13
3378cc	1995-00	.043	1.1	13
3956cc	1989-90	.031	.80	11-15
3956cc	1991-92	.043	1.1	13
4477cc	1993-97	.031	.80	13
4669cc	1998-00	.043	1.1	13

IGNITION COIL
FOR TESTING AND ADJUSTMENT DIAGRAMS, SEE APPENDIX A.
1994-99 Tercel & Paseo with coil on plug: Measure primary resistance between the two adjoining terminals on coil connector. Measure secondary resistance between the + terminal on the connector and spark plug cavity.
1997-99 2164cc Camry, 1998cc RAV4, 2438cc & 2693cc Trucks; 1998-99 Corolla w/coil pack: Measure secondary resistance between the two high voltage terminasl of each coil.

Engine	Year	Windings	Resistance (ohms)
1456cc U.S.	1989	Primary	1.3-1.5
		Secondary	10,200-13,800
Canada	1989	Primary	0.4-0.5
		Secondary	10,200-13,800
1456cc	1990-91	Primary	0.4-0.5
		Secondary	10,200-13,800
1456cc, 1497cc Paseo	1992-95	Primary	.36-.55
		Secondary	9000-15,400
1497cc Tercel	1995	Primary	.67-1.05
		Secondary	9300-16,000
1497cc	1996-99	Primary	.67-1.05
		Secondary	9300-16,000
1587cc 2V	1989	Primary	1.3-1.5
		Secondary	10,200-13,800
1587cc FI 2WD:			
Corolla, FX	1989	Primary	0.4-0.5
		Secondary	10,200-13,800
Corolla 4WD	1989	Primary	0.3-0.5
		Secondary	7700-10,400
MR2	1989	Primary	0.5-0.7
		Secondary	11,000-16,000
1587cc (4A-FE)	1990-91	Primary	1.28-1.56
		Secondary	10,400-14,000
1587cc (4A-GE)	1990-91	Primary	0.4-0.5
		Secondary	10,200-13,800
1587cc, 1762cc	1992-95	Primary	1.11-1.75
		Secondary	9000-15,700
	1996-97	Primary	.36-.55
		Secondary	9000-15,400
1794cc	1998-99	Primary	—
		Secondary	9700-16,700
1998cc (3S-FE)	1989-91	Primary	0.4-0.5
		Secondary	7700-10,400

UNDERHOOD SERVICE SPECIFICATIONS

TAITU4   TAITU4

IGNITION COIL Continued

Engine	Year	Windings	Resistance (ohms)
1998cc (3S-GE, GTE)	1989-91	Primary	0.4-0.5
		Secondary	10,000-14,000
1998cc	1992-93	Primary	0.3-0.6
		Secondary	9000-15,000
1998cc	1994-96	Primary	.36-.55
		Secondary	9000-15,400
1998cc	1997-00	Primary	—
		Secondary	9700-16,700
2164cc	1990-91	Primary	0.4-0.5
		Secondary	10,000-14,000
2164cc Camry	1992	Primary	0.4-0.5
		Secondary	10,200-14,300
Others	1992	Primary	0.3-0.6
		Secondary	9000-15,000
2164cc	1993-96	Primary	.36-.55
		Secondary	9000-15,400
2164cc Celica	1997-99	Primary	.36-.55
		Secondary	9000-15,400
2164cc Camry, Solara	1997-00	Primary	—
		Secondary	9200-16,700
2237cc	1989	Primary	1.2-1.5
		Secondary	7700-10,400
2366cc 2V	1989-90	Primary	0.4-0.5
		Secondary	8500-11,500
2366cc FI & Turbo	1989-91	Primary	0.5-0.7
		Secondary	11,400-15,600
2366cc	1992	Primary	.40-.69
		Secondary	10,100-16,700
2366cc	1993-95	Primary	.36-.55
		Secondary	9000-15,400
2438cc	1991-97	Primary	.36-.55
		Secondary	9000-15,400
2438cc	1998-00	Primary	—
		Secondary	9700-16,700
2507cc	1989-91	Primary	0.4-0.5
		Secondary	10,200-13,800
2693cc	1994-96	Primary	.36-.55
		Secondary	9000-15,400
2693cc T100	1997	Primary	.36-.55
		Secondary	9000-15,400
2693cc Others	1997-00	Primary	—
		Secondary	9700-16,700
2954cc	1989-92	Primary	0.2-0.3
		Secondary	9000-12,500
Turbo	1989-92	Primary	0.3-0.6
		Secondary	—
2958cc	1989-91	Primary	0.4-0.5
		Secondary	10,200-13,800
2958cc Camry	1992	Primary	.21-.32
		Secondary	6400-10,700
2958cc Trucks	1992-95	Primary	.36-.55
		Secondary	9000-15,400
2995cc	1994-95	Primary	.54-.84
		Secondary	—
2995cc: Aisan	1996-00	Primary	.70-.94
		Secondary	10,800-14,900
Diamond	1998-00	Primary	.70-.94
		Secondary	6800-11,700
2997cc	1993-96	Primary	.21-.33
		Secondary	6400-11,100
	1997-98	Primary	.33-.52
		Secondary	8500-14,700
2997cc Turbo	1993-98	Primary	.54-.84
		Secondary	—
3378cc	1995-00	Primary	.67-1.05
		Secondary	9300-16,600
3956cc	1989-90	Primary	.52-.64
		Secondary	11,500-15,500
3956cc	1991	Primary	0.4-0.5
		Secondary	10,200-13,800
3956cc	1992	Primary	0.3-0.6
		Secondary	9000-15,000
4477cc	1993-97	Primary	.36-.55
		Secondary	9000-15,400

DISTRIBUTOR PICKUP

FOR TESTING AND ADJUSTMENT DIAGRAMS, SEE APPENDIX B.
Measured with engine cold.

Application	Year	Resistance (ohms)	Air Gap (in./mm)
All	1989	130-190	.008-.016/.20-.40
All ex. 2164cc, 2958cc	1990	130-190	.008-.016/.20-.40
1456cc	1991	370-530	.008-.016/.20-.40
1456cc Tercel	1992-94	370-530	.008-.016/.20-.40
1497cc Paseo	1992-95	185-275	.008-.016/.20-.40
NE Pickup	1992-95	370-530	.008-.016/.20-.40
1587cc, 1998cc	1991	185-265	.008-.016/.20-.40
NE Pickup	1991	140-180	.008-.016/.20-.40
1587cc, 1762cc	1992-97	185-275	.008-.016/.20-.40
NE Pickup	1993-95	370-530	.008-.016/.20-.40
1998cc	1991	125-190	.008-.016/.20-.40
NE Pickup	1991	155-240	.008-.016/.20-.40
1998cc Turbo	1991-95	125-200	.008-.016/.20-.40
NE Pickup	1991-95	155-240	.008-.016/.20-.40
1998cc	1996-97	135-220	.008-.016/.20-.40
2164cc	1990-91	125-190	.008-.016/.20-.40
NE Pickup	1990-91	155-240	.008-.016/.20-.40
2164cc Celica, Camry	1992-93	185-265	.008-.016/.20-.40
NE Pickup	1992-93	370-530	.008-.016/.20-.40
2164cc Celica, Camry	1994-95	185-275	.008-.016/.20-.40
California	1994-95	125-200	.008-.016/.20-.40
NE Pickup, all	1994-95	370-530	.008-.016/.20-.40
2164cc MR2	1992	150-230	.008-.016/.20-.40
2164cc MR2	1993-95	185-275	.008-.016/.20-.40
NE Pickup	1993-95	370-530	.008-.016/.20-.40
2164cc	1996-98	135-220	.008-.016/.20-.40
2366cc	1991-95	185-275	.008-.016/.20-.40
2438cc Previa	1992-97	125-200	.008-.016/.20-.40
NE Pickup	1992-95	155-250	.008-.016/.20-.40
2438cc Tacoma	1995-98	185-275	.008-.016/.20-.40
2507cc, 2954cc	1991	125-190	.008-.016/.20-.40
NE Pickup	1991	155-240	.008-.016/.20-.40
Turbo	1991	205-255	.008-.016/.20-.40
2693cc	1994-96	185-275	.008-.016/.20-.40
2954cc	1992	125-190	.008-.016/.20-.40
NE Pickup	1992	155-240	.008-.016/.20-.40
2958cc	1990	205-255	.008-.016/.20-.40
	1991	185-265	.008-.016/.20-.40
2958cc, 2997cc ex. Turbo	1992-97	125-200	.008-.016/.20-.40
NE Pickup	1992-97	155-250	.008-.016/.20-.40
3956cc	1991	130-210	.008-.016/.20-.40
	1992	185-265	.008-.016/.20-.40
4477cc	1993-96	185-275	.008-.016/.20-.40

TIMING PROCEDURE

FOR TESTING AND ADJUSTMENT DIAGRAMS, SEE APPENDIX C.

Carbureted models: Value cited is at 950 RPM maximum.

1989-90 1456cc, 1587cc 2V: Disconnect and plug distributor vacuum advance inner diaphragm vacuum hose only.

1989-90 2366cc 2V: Leave all hoses connected.

1989-00 All w/EST: Can be identified by the absence of a vacuum advance unit on the distributor. Place a jumper wire between the check connector cavities TE1 & E1 (4-, 6-cyl.) or TC & E1 (V8).

With jumper removed, timing should advance to Check specification.

2000 Corolla, Celica, Echo: Connect a scan tool and access ignition timing function.

BASE TIMING

Set at slow idle and Before Top Dead Center, unless otherwise specified.

Engine	Year	Man. Trans. (degrees)	Auto. Trans. (degrees)
1456cc 2V	1989-90	3	3
1456cc FI, 1497cc	1990-94	10	10
Check, Tercel	1991-94	7-17	7-17
Check, Paseo	1992-94	6-18	6-18
1497cc Tercel	1995	8-12[1]	8-12[1]
1497cc Paseo	1995	10	10
Check	1995	7-17	7-17
1497cc	1996-00	8-12[1]	8-12[1]
Check	1996-97	7-17	7-17

BASE TIMING Continued

Engine	Year	Man. Trans. (degrees)	Auto. Trans. (degrees)
1587cc 2V	1989	5	5
1587cc FI	1989-96	10	10
Check, 4A-FE	1989	10 min.	10 min.
Check, 4A-FE, Corolla	1990-96	5-15	5-15
Check, 4A-FE, Celica	1991-93	0-20	0-20
Check, 4A-GE: MT	1989-91	16 min.	16 min.
AT	1989	12 min.	12 min.
1762cc	1993-95	10	10
Check	1993-95	5-15	5-15
1762cc Celica	1996-97	10	10
Check	1996-97	5-15	5-15
1762cc Corolla	1996-97	10±2[1]	10±2[1]
1794cc Corolla	1998-00	8-12[1]	8-12[1]
Check	1998-99	6-15	6-15
1794cc Celica	2000	10-18[1]	10-18[1]
1796cc	2000	8-12[1]	8-12[1]
1998cc	1989-95	10	10
Check, 3S-FE	1989-91	13-22	13-22
Check, 3S-GE	1989	14-19	14-19
Check, Turbo	1989	14-19	14-19
Check, Turbo	1990-95	12-21	12-21
1998cc	1996-00	10±2[1]	10±2[1]
Check	1996-00	0-10	0-10
2164cc	1990-93	10	10
Check	1990-93	13-22	13-22
2164cc	1994	10	10
Check Camry, Celica	1994	0-10	0-10
Check MR2	1994	13-22	13-22
2164cc	1995	10	10
Check	1995	0-10	0-10
2164cc	1996	10±2	10±2
Check	1996	0-10	0-10
2164cc Celica	1997-99	10±2	10±2
Check	1997-99	0-10	0-10
2164cc Camry, Solara	1997-00	8-12[1]	8-12[1]
Check	1997-00	0-10	0-10
2237cc	1989	12	12
2366cc 2V	1989-90	0	0
2366cc FI & Turbo	1989-95	5	5
Check	1989-95	10-14	10-14
2438cc Previa	1991-97	5	5
Check	1991-95	12 approx.	12 approx.
Check	1996-97	—	7-17
2438cc Tacoma	1995-97	5±2	5±2
Check	1995-97	7-18	7-18
2438cc	1998-00	3-7[1]	3-7[1]
Check	1998-00	4-17	4-17
2507cc	1989-91	10	10
Check	1989-91	13-27	13-27
2693cc	1994-96	5±2	5±2
Check	1995-96	7-18	7-18
2693cc T100	1997	5±2	5±2
Check	1997	7-18	7-18
2693cc Others	1997-00	3-7[1]	3-7[1]
Check	1997-98	7-18	7-18
Check	1999-00	4-17	4-17
2954cc	1989-92	10	10
Check	1989-90	10-13	10-13
Check	1991-92	9-11	9-11
Check, Turbo	1989-92	12 min.	12 min.
2958cc	1989-95	10	10
Check, Trucks	1989-95	8 approx.	8 approx.
Check, Camry	1992-93	10-20	10-20
2995cc	1994-00	—	8-12[1]
Check	1994	—	10-20
Check	1995-98	—	7-24
Check, Sienna	1999-00	—	7-24
Check, Others	1999-00	10-25	10-25
2997cc	1993-98	10	10
Check	1993-98	7-19	7-19
2997cc Turbo	1993-98	8-12[1]	8-12[1]
Check	1993-98	10-20	10-20
3378cc	1995-98	8-12[1]	8-12[1]
Check	1995-98	12-22	12-22

BASE TIMING Continued

Engine	Year	Man. Trans. (degrees)	Auto. Trans. (degrees)
3378cc	1997-00	8-12[1]	8-12[1]
Check, 4-Runner	1997-98	3-19	3-19
Check, Others	1997-98	12-22	12-22
Check, All ex. Tundra	1999-00	3-19	3-19
Check, Tundra	2000	12-22	12-22
3956cc	1989-92	—	7
4477cc	1993-97	—	3
Check	1993-97	—	2-13
4669cc	1998-00	—	5-15

1 Not adjustable.

DISTRIBUTOR TIMING ADVANCE

Engine degrees at engine rpm, no load, in addition to base timing setting.

Mechanical advance distributors only.

Engine	Trans-mission	Year	Distributor Number	Degrees @ 2500 RPM Total	Degrees @ 2500 RPM Centrifugal
1456cc	MT & AT	1989-90	11010	35.1-43.1	7.1-11.1
1587cc 2V	MT & AT	1989	16120	24.5-32.5	2.5-6.5
2366cc	MT & AT	1989-90	35140	25.2-33.2	7.2-11.2

FUEL SYSTEM

FUEL SYSTEM PRESSURE
FOR TESTING AND ADJUSTMENT DIAGRAMS, SEE APPENDIX D.

Engine	Year	Pressure PSI	Pressure RPM
Carbureted:			
1456cc	1989-90	3.0	idle
1587cc	1989	2.5-3.5	idle
2366cc	1989-90	2.8-4.3	idle

Engine	Year	Pressure PSI[1]	Pressure PSI[2]
Fuel Injected:			
1456cc, 1497cc	1990-96	41-42	33-37
1497cc	1997-00	—	44-50
1587cc 2WD	1989	38-44	30-33
1587cc 4WD	1989	33-40	23-30
1587cc Supercharged	1989	33-40	20-27
1587cc, 1762cc	1990-97	38-44	30-37
1794cc, 1796cc	1998-00	—	44-50
1998cc, 2164cc, Camry, Celica	1989-91	38-44	33-37
1998cc, 2164cc MR2	1991	33-38	27-31
1998cc	1992-95	33-38	27-31
	1996-00	—	44-50
2164cc	1992-95	38-44	30-37
2164cc Celica	1996	38-44	30-37
Camry	1996	38-44	33-38
2164cc Celica	1997-99	38-44	33-38
Camry, Solara	1997-99	—	44-50
2237cc	1989	38-44	30-33
2366cc	1989-95	38-44	33-37
2438cc	1991-00	38-44	30-37
Supercharged	1994-97	33-40	24-31
2507cc	1989-91	38-44	33-37
2693cc	1994-00	38-44	31-37
2954cc	1989-91	38-44	33-37
Turbo	1989-91	33-40	23-30
2958cc	1989	38-44	33-37
	1990-95	38-44	30-37
2995cc	1994-96	38-44	33-38
	1997-00	—	44-50
2997cc	1993-97	38-44	28-34
Turbo	1993-98	33-38	27-31
3378cc	1995-00	38-44	33-38
4477cc	1993-99	38-44	31-37
4669cc	1998-00	38-44	28-39

1 Measured with pressure regulator vacuum disconnected.
2 Measured with pressure regulator vacuum connected.

UNDERHOOD SERVICE SPECIFICATIONS

IDLE SPEED W/O COMPUTER CONTROL

1989-90: 1995cc, 1998cc, 2237cc, 2366cc FI, with cooling fan off and air cleaner installed, race engine for two minutes and set idle to specified rpm. Turn A/C on and verify that idle increases to speed-up speed. Speed-up can be adjusted if adjustment screw is found on idle up device.

1452cc, 1456cc, 1587cc, with cooling fan off and air cleaner installed, set idle to specified rpm.

2366cc 2V, disconnect and plug hoses for HAI, MC, EGR, and choke opener. Adjust idle to specified rpm.

Fast idle adjustment:

1452cc, 1587cc, disconnect and plug vacuum hoses for AS and HIC systems. Remove air cleaner, disconnect vacuum hose from TVSV "M" port, and plug port. Set cam to specified step and adjust to specified rpm.

1456cc, 2366cc, disconnect and plug EGR vacuum hose(s) and adjust speed with cooling fan off.

1991-95 FI: Set idle speed to specified value. Turn A/C on and verify that speed increases to specified speed-up value.

THROTTLE POSITIONER: All years, disconnect and plug vacuum hose on end of unit. Allow step to move into position and adjust linkage screw.

Engine	Year	SLOW Man. Trans.	SLOW Auto. Trans.	FAST Man. Trans.	FAST Auto. Trans.	Step of Cam
1456cc 2V	1989-90	700	900 N	3000	3000 N	High
Throttle positioner	1989-90	1100[1]	1100 N[1]			
A/C speed-up	1989-90	900-1000	900-1000 N			
1456cc FI Tercel	1990-93	750	800 N	—	—	—
A/C speed-up	1990-93	900-1000	900-1000 N			
1456cc Tercel	1994	750	800 N	—	—	—
A/C speed-up	1994	1400-1500	1400-1500 N			
1587cc 2V	1989	650	750 N	3000	3000 N	High
Thrtl. pos., Corolla	1989	900	900 N			
Thrtl. pos., FX	1989	800	800 N			
A/C speed-up	1989	900-1000	900-1000 N			
1587cc FI	1989	800	800 N	—	—	—
A/C speed-up	1989	900-1000	900-1000 N			
1587cc, Corolla 2WD	1990-92	700	700 N	—	—	—
California	1991-92	800	800 N	—	—	—
4WD, GTS	1990-92	800	800 N			
A/C speed-up	1990-92	900-1000	900-1000 N			
1998cc (3S-GE)	1989	750	750 N	—	—	—
2237cc	1989	700	750 N	—	—	—
A/C speed-up	1989	900-1000	900-1000 N			
2366cc 2V	1989-90	700	700 N	3000	3000 N	High
A/C speed-up	1989-90	900-1000	900-1000 N			
2366cc FI: 2WD	1989-95	750	750 N	—	—	—
4WD	1989-95	750	800 N			
A/C speed-up, all	1989-95	900-1000	900-1000 N			
2958cc	1989-92	800	800 N	—	—	—
A/C speed-up	1989-92	900-1000	900-1000 N			

[1] Inner diaphragm; outer diaphragm, 1800-2200 (N).

IDLE SPEED W/COMPUTER CONTROL
FOR TESTING AND ADJUSTMENT DIAGRAMS, SEE APPENDIX E.

2000 Celica, Corolla, Echo: Connect a scan tool and access idle speed function.

All others: Jumper terminals E1 of check connector under hood. Race engine at 1000-1300 rpm for five seconds. Set idle to specified value if specifications are listed in Checking Speed column. Turn A/C on and verify that speed increases to Speed-up value with compressor running.

Engine	Year	Transmission	Checking Speed	Setting Speed	Speed-up
1497cc Paseo	1992-93	MT	—	750	900-1000
		AT	—	750 N	900-1000 N
	1994-95	MT	—	750	1400-1500
		AT	—	750 N	1400-1500 N

IDLE SPEED W/COMPUTER CONTROL Continued

Engine	Year	Transmission	Checking Speed	Setting Speed	Speed-up
1497cc Tercel	1995	MT	700-800	—	800-900
		AT	700-800 N	—	800-900 N
1497cc	1996-97	MT	700-800	—	800-900
		AT	700-800 N	—	800-900 N
	1998-99	MT	700-800	—	850-950
		AT	700-800 N	—	850-950 N
	2000	MT	600-700	—	825-925
		AT	650-750 N	—	825-925 N
1587cc Supercharged	1989	MT	800	800	850-950
		AT	800 N	800 N	850-950 N
1587cc Celica	1990-93	MT	—	800	900-1000
		AT	—	800 N	900-1000 N
1587cc, 1762cc	1993-97	MT	650-750	—	900
		AT	650-750 N	—	900 N
1794cc Corolla	1998-00	MT	650-750	—	850-950
		AT	650-750 N	—	850-950 N
1794cc Celica	2000	MT	650-750	—	850-950
		AT	700-800 N	—	850-950 N
1796cc	2000	MT	750-850	—	800-900
		AT	700-800 N	—	800-900 N
1998cc (3S-FE)	1989-91	MT	650-750	600-700	900-1000
		AT	650-750	600-700 N	900-1000 N
1998cc Turbo	1989-90	MT	700-800	—	900-1000
1998cc Turbo	1991-95	MT	750-850	—	900-1000
1998cc	1996-00	MT	700-800	—	850-950
		AT	700-800 N	—	850-950 N
2164cc Celica: U.S.	1990-91	MT	650-750	600-700	900-1000
		AT	650-750 N	600-700 N	900-1000 N
Canada	1990-91	MT	750-850	600-700 N	900-1000
		AT	700-800 N	600-700 N	900-1000 N
2164cc MR2: U.S.	1991-93	MT	700-800	650 min.	900-1000
		AT	650-750 N	650 N min.	900-1000 N
Canada	1991-93	MT	800-900	650 min.	900-1000
		AT	700-800 N	650 N min.	900-1000 N
2164cc MR2: U.S.	1994-95	MT	700-800	—	900-1000
		AT	700-800 N	—	900-1000 N
Canada	1994-95	MT	800-900	—	900-1000
		AT	700-800 N	—	900-1000 N
2164cc Camry	1992-95	MT	700-800	—	850
		AT	700-800 N	—	850 N
2164cc Celica: U.S.	1992-93	MT	650-750	—	900-1000
		AT	650-750 N	—	900-1000 N
Canada	1992-93	MT	700-800	—	900-1000
		AT	700-800 N	—	900-1000 N
2164cc Celica	1994-95	MT	700-800	—	850
		AT	700-800 N	—	850 N
2164cc	1996	MT	700-800	—	850
		AT	700-800 N	—	850 N
2164cc Celica	1997	MT	700-800	—	900
		AT	700-800 N	—	900 N
	1998-99	MT	650-750	—	800-900
		AT	650-750 N	—	800-900 N
2164cc Camry, Solara	1997-00	MT	650-750	—	650-750
		AT	650-750 N	—	650-750 N
2438cc	1991-93	MT	650-750	—	900-1000
		AT	700-800 N	—	900-1000 N
2438cc Previa	1994-97	MT	700-800	—	900-1000
		AT	700-800 N	—	900-1000 N
2438cc Tacoma	1995-00	MT	650-750	—	850-950
		AT	650-750 N	—	850-950 N
2507cc	1989-90	MT	650-750	650 min.	780-820
		AT	650-750 N	650 N min.	780-820 N[1]
2507cc	1991	MT	700	—	780-820
		AT	700 N	—	780-820 N
2693cc	1994-95	MT	650-750	—	900-1000
		AT	650-750 N	—	900-1000 N
	1996-00	MT	650-750	—	850-950
		AT	650-750 N	—	850-950 N
2954cc	1989-92	MT	700	—	900
		AT	700 N	—	650 D

IDLE SPEED W/COMPUTER CONTROL Continued

Engine	Year	Transmission	Checking Speed	Setting Speed	Speed-up
2954cc Turbo	1989-92	MT	650	—	900
		AT	650 N	—	700 D
2958cc Camry	1992	AT	650-750 N	—	700 N
2958cc Camry	1993	MT	700-800	—	850
		AT	700-800 N	—	850 N
2958cc Trucks	1993-95	MT	—	750-850	900-1000
		AT	—	750-850 N	900-1000 N
2995cc	1994-00	MT	650-750	—	650-750
		AT	650-750 N	—	650-750 N
2997cc	1993-98	MT	650-750	—	900-1000
		AT	650-750 N	—	900-1000 N
2997cc Turbo	1993-98	MT	600-700	—	900-1000
		AT	600-700 N	—	900-1000 N
3378cc	1995-00	MT	650-750	—	800-900
		AT	650-750 N	—	800-900 N
3956	1989-92	AT	650	—	900-1000 N
4474cc	1993-97	MT	600-700 N	—	800 N
4669cc	1998	AT	700-800 N	—	750-850 N
	1999-00	AT	650-750 N	—	750-850 N

1 With T-top, 950-1050 N.

ENGINE MECHANICAL

TIGHTENING TORQUES
FOR CYLINDER HEAD TORQUE SEQUENCES AND DIAGRAMS, SEE APPENDIX F.

Some fasteners are tightened in more than one step.

Some values are specified in inches.

		TORQUE FOOT-POUNDS/NEWTON METERS				
Engine	Year	Cylinder Head	Intake Manifold	Exhaust Manifold	Crankshaft Pulley	Water Pump
1456cc Tercel	1989-94	22/29, 36/49, +90°	15/19	38/51	112/152	13/17
1497cc	1992-99	33/45, +90°	14/19	35/47	112/157	13/17
	2000	22/29, +90°, +90°	22/30	20/27	96/128	8/11
1587cc (4A-GE)	1989-91	22/29, +90°, +90°	20/27	29/39	101/137	11/15
1587cc (4A-F, FE)	1989-92	44/60	15/19	18/25	87/118	11/15
1587cc, 1762cc	1993-97	22/29, +90°, +90°	15/19	25/34	87/118	11/15
1794cc	1998-00	36/49 90°	14/19	27/37	102/138	8/11
1796cc	2000	26/35, +90°	25/34	37/50	87/120	7/9
1998cc	1989	47/64	15/19	31/42	80/108	11/15
1998cc	1990-00	36/49, +90°	15/19	38/52	80/108	82"/9, 10mm 20/27, 12mm
2164cc	1990-00	36/49, +90°	15/19	36/49	80/108	82"/9
2237cc	1989	65/88[1]	36/49	36/49	116/157	13/18
2366cc	1989-95	58/78	15/19	33/44	116/157	14/20
2438cc, 2693cc	1991-99	29/39, +90°, +90°	22/29	36/49	192/260	21/28[1]
2507cc	1989-91	25/34, +90°, +90°	13/18	29/39	181/145	73"/8
2759cc, 2954cc	1989	58/78	13/18	29/39	195/265	78"/9
2954cc	1990-92	58/78	13/18	29/39	195/265	78"/9, 10 mm 14/20, 12 mm
2958cc Truck	1989-95	33/44, +90°, +90°	13/18	29/39	181/145	13/18

TIGHTENING TORQUES Continued

		TORQUE FOOT-POUNDS/NEWTON METERS				
Engine	Year	Cylinder Head	Intake Manifold	Exhaust Manifold	Crankshaft Pulley	Water Pump
2958cc Camry	1992-93	25/34, +90°, +90°	13/18	29/39	181/145	14/20
2995cc	1994-00	40/54[1], +90°	11/15	36/49	159/215	69 11/8
2997cc	1993-98	25/34, +90°, +90°	20/27	29/39	239/324	15/21
3378cc	1995-00	25/34, +90°, +90°	13/18	30/40	184/250	—
3956cc	1989-92	90/123	[2]	[2]	253/343	23/37
4477cc	1993-97	29/39, +90°, +90°	15/21	29/39	304/412	15/21
4669cc	1998-00	24/32 90° 90°	13/18	33/44	181/245	15/21

1 Small bolts, 14/17.
2 14 mm bolt, 37/50; 17 mm bolt, 51/69; nut, 41/56.

VALVE CLEARANCE
1456cc SOHC, 1587cc (4A-C), 2366cc, 3956cc, 4230cc, engine hot. All others, engine cold.

Engine	Year	Intake (inches)	Intake (mm)	Exhaust (inches)	Exhaust (mm)
1456cc Tercel	1989-94	.008	.20	.008	.20
1497cc	1992-99	.006-.010	.15-.25	.012-.016	.30-.40
	2000	.006-.010	.15-.25	.010-.014	.25-.35
1587cc FI, 1762cc	1989-97	.006-.010	.15-.25	.008-.012	.20-.30
1587cc, 1762cc Celica Corolla	1993	.006-.010	.15-.25	.008-.012	.20-.30
1587cc, 1762cc	1994-97	.006-.010	.15-.25	.010-.014	.25-.35
1794cc	1998-00	.006-.010	.15-.25	.010-.014	.25-.35
1796cc	2000	.006-.010	.15-.25	.014-.018	.35-.45
1998cc (3S-GE, GTE)	1989-91	.006-.010	.15-.25	.008-.012	.20-.30
1998cc Turbo Celica	1992-93	.006-.010	.15-.25	.011-.015	.28-.38
1998cc Turbo MR2	1992-93	.006-.010	.15-.25	.008-.012	.20-.30
	1994-95	.006-.010	.15-.25	.011-.015	.28-.38
1998cc (3S-FE)	1989-93	.007-.011	.19-.29	.011-.015	.28-.38
1998cc	1996-00	.007-.011	.19-.29	.011-.015	.28-.38
2164cc	1990-00	.007-.011	.19-.29	.011-.015	.28-.38
2366cc	1989-95	.008	.20	.012	.30
2438cc	1991-00	.006-.010	.15-.25	.010-.014	.25-.35
2507cc	1989-91	.005-.009	.13-.23	.011-.015	.27-.37
2693cc	1994-00	.006-.010	.15-.25	.010-.014	.25-.35
2954cc	1989-92	.006-.010	.15-.25	.008-.012	.20-.30
2958cc Truck	1989-95	.007-.011	.18-.28	.009-.013	.22-.32
2958cc Camry	1992-93	.005-.009	.13-.23	.011-.015	.28-.38
	1994-95	.007-.011	.18-.28	.009-.013	.22-.32
2995cc, 2997cc	1993-00	.006-.010	.15-.25	.010-.014	.25-.35
3378cc	1995-99	.006-.009	.13-.23	.011-.014	.28-.35
3956cc	1989-92	.008	.20	.014	.35
4477cc	1993-97	.006-.010	.15-.25	.010-.014	.25-.35
4669cc	1998-00	.006-.009	.13-.23	.011-.014	.28-.35

COMPRESSION PRESSURE
At cranking speed, engine temperature normalized, throttle open.

Engine	Year	PSI	Maximum Variation PSI
1456cc, 1497cc	1989-99	142-185	14
1587cc (4A-F, FE)	1989-97	142-191	14
1587cc (4A-GE)	1989-91	142-179	14
1587cc Supercharged	1989	121-156	14
1762cc	1993-97	142-191	14
1794cc	1998-00	145-215	14
1998cc	1989-91	142-178	14
1998cc Turbo	1989-93	128-178	14
	1994-95	128-164	14
1998cc	1996-00	128-178	14
2164cc	1990-00	142-178	14
2237cc	1989	128-178	14

UNDERHOOD SERVICE SPECIFICATIONS

TAITU8

TAITU8

COMPRESSION PRESSURE Continued

Engine	Year	PSI	Maximum Variation PSI
2366cc	1989-95	142-171	14
2438cc	1991-00	128-178	14
2507cc	1989-91	142-178	14
2693cc	1994-00	128-178	14
2954cc ex. Turbo	1989-92	128-156	14
Turbo	1989-92	128-142	14
2958cc Truck	1989-95	142-171	14
2958cc Car	1992-94	142-178	14
2995cc	1994-00	145-218	14
3956cc	1989-92	114-149	14
2997cc	1993-98	156-185	14
Turbo	1993-98	128-156	14
3378cc	1995-00	145-174	14
4477cc	1993-97	128-171	14
4669cc	1998-00	142-192	14

BELT TENSION

A belt in operation for 20 minutes is considered a used belt.

Deflection method: Measured with an applied load of 22-pounds at the midpoint of the longest segment.

Strand Tension method: Use belt tension gauge. Measurements are in pounds.

Models With Automatic Tensioner

Inspect index marks on tensioner, replace belt if marks are outside the range.

Engine	Year	Generator	Power Steering	Air Cond.	Air Pump
USED BELTS					
Strand Tension Method					
1456cc, 1497cc	1989-94	80-120	90-130	90-130	—
	1995-00	80-120	80-120	80-120	
1587cc 2V FWD	1989	110-150	60-100	60-100	110-150
1587cc FI	1989-92	110-150	60-100	110-150	—
1587cc MR2	1989	95-135	95-135	95-135	—
Supercharged	1989	95-135	95-135	95-135	—
1587cc, 1762cc	1993-97	170-180	100-150	140-180	—
1794cc	1998-99	1	—	—	—
1995cc, 1998cc (3S-GE)	1989-90	75-115	120-140	60-100	—
1998cc, 2164cc MR2	1991-93	85-125	85-125	80-120	—
	1994-95	85-125	—	75-125	—
1998cc (3S-FE) Celica, Camry	1989-93	75-115	120-140	60-100	—
1998cc	1996-00	75-115	75-115	100-120	—
2164cc Celica	1990-00	75-115	75-115	120-140	—
w/A/C	1990-00	120-140	120-140	170-180	—
2164cc Camry, Solara	1992-00	75-115	60-100	120-140	—
2237cc	1989	95-135	60-100	60-100	—
2366cc	1989-95	60-100	60-100	80-120	—
2438cc	1991-00	115-135	115-135	100-140	—
2693cc	1994-00	75-125	80-120	80-120	—
2954cc	1989	95-135	90-120	80-100	—
2958cc Truck	1989-95	80-120	60-100	60-100	—
2958cc Camry, 2995cc	1992-00	95-135	95-135	95-135	—
2997cc	1993-98	1	—	—	—
3378cc	1995-00	80-120	60-100	60-100	—
3956cc, 4477cc	1989-93	80-120	80-120	60-100	—
	1994-97	60-100	60-100	60-100	—
4669cc	1998-00	1	—	—	—
NEW BELTS					
Strand Tension Method					
1452cc, 1587cc RWD	1989-92	100-150	100-150	100-150	100-150
1456cc, 1497cc	1989-94	140-180	150-180	150-180	—
	1995-00	140-180	140-180	140-180	—
1587cc 2V FWD	1989	140-180	100-150	100-150	140-180
1587cc FI	1989-92	140-180	100-150	140-180	—
1587cc MR2	1989	170-180	170-180	140-180	—
Supercharged	1989	170-180	170-180	170-180	—
1587cc, 1762cc	1993-97	95-135	60-100	80-120	—
1794cc	1998-00	1	—	—	—
1995cc, 1998cc (3S-GE)	1989-90	100-150	170-180	100-150	—
1998cc (3S-FE) Celica, Camry	1989-93	100-150	170-180	115-135	—
1998cc, 2164cc MR2	1991-93	100-140	100-140	135-185	—
	1994-95	100-140	—	135-185	—

BELT TENSION Continued

Engine	Year	Generator	Power Steering	Air Cond.	Air Pump
1998cc	1996-00	100-150	100-150	140-190	—
2164cc Celica	1990-00	100-150	100-150	—	—
w/A/C	1990-00	170-180	170-180	115-135	—
2164cc Camry, Solara	1992-00	100-150	100-150	170-180	—
2237cc	1989	170-180	100-150	100-150	—
2366cc	1989-95	100-150	100-150	140-180	—
2438cc	1991-00	160-180	160-180	120-160	—
2693cc	1994-98	155-175	135-185	135-185	—
2954cc	1989	170-180	135-190	120-140	—
2958cc Truck	1989-95	135-185	100-150	100-150	—
2958cc Camry, 2995cc	1992-00	170-180	170-180	150-185	—
2997cc	1993-98	1	—	—	—
3378cc	1995-00	140-180	100-150	100-150	—
3956cc, 4477cc	1989-93	120-170	120-170	100-150	—
	1994-97	100-150	100-150	100-150	—
4669cc	1998-00	1	—	—	—

1 Automatic tensioner.

SERPENTINE BELT DIAGRAMS

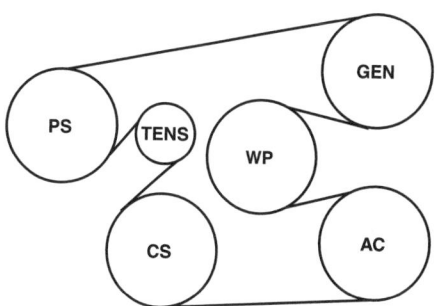

1998-00 4-cyl. 1794cc

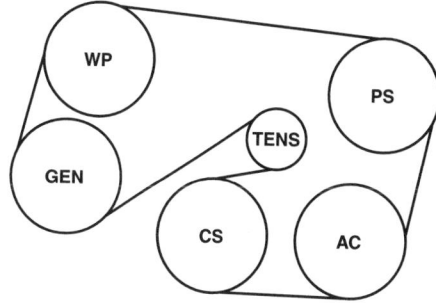

1993-98 V6 2997cc

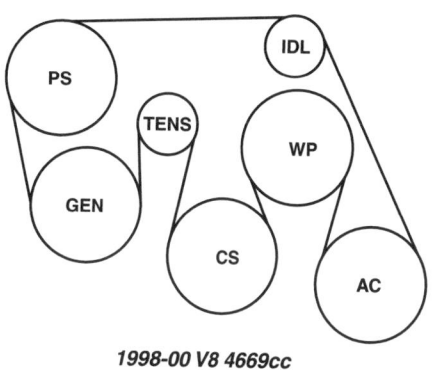

1998-00 V8 4669cc

UNDERHOOD SERVICE SPECIFICATIONS

ENGINE COMPUTER SYSTEM

DIAGNOSTIC TROUBLE CODES
FOR TESTING AND ADJUSTMENT DIAGRAMS, SEE APPENDIX G.

1989-95 All ex. Van & OBD-II systems
With engine at operating temperature, turn ignition switch on and place a jumper between cavities TE1 and E1 (1989-95) on the Check Engine connector located by the airflow sensor or the strut tower. Turn ignition on. "Check Engine" light will flash codes.

All models
To clear memory, remove STOP or FI fuse from fuseblock for 30 seconds.

1994-95 2438cc Supercharged, 2438cc Tacoma, 2693cc, 2995cc, 3378cc, 4477cc: 1996-00 All:
A scan tool is required to retrieve codes and code definitions.
Code 1 System OK
Codes 2, 3 Mass airflow sensor signal
Code 4 Engine temperature sensor circuit
Code 5 Oxygen sensor
Code 6 Ignition signal circuit
Code 7 Throttle position circuit

1989-95 All ex. OBD-II systems
Code — System OK
Code 11 ECM circuit
Codes 12, 13 RPM signal circuit
Code 14 Ignition signal
Code 16 Transmission electronic control
Code 21 Oxygen sensor circuit (left side, 2958cc)
Code 22 Engine temperature sensor circuit
Codes 23 & 24 Intake air temperature circuit
Code 25 Air/fuel ratio lean
Code 26 Air/fuel ratio rich
Codes 28 Oxygen sensor circuit (right side, 2958cc)
Code 31 Vacuum switches (1989 1.6L 2V Calif.)
Code 31 Vacuum sensor (1989-95 1.5L FI, 1.6L FI, 2.2L)
Codes 31, 32 Airflow meter circuit (others)
Code 34 Turbocharger pressure signal
Code 35 Barometric pressure sensor (1993-95 Supra)
Code 35 Turbocharger pressure signal (others)
Code 35 HAC sensor signal (ex. Turbo)
Code 41 Throttle position sensor circuit
Code 42 Vehicle speed sensor circuit
Code 43 Starter signal
Code 47 Sub throttle position sensor
Code 51 Neutral start or AC switch
Code 52 Knock sensor circuit (front side on Supra)
Code 53 Knock sensor circuit in ECU
Code 55 Knock sensor circuit (rear side on Supra)
Code 71 EGR
Code 72 Fuel cut solenoid
Code 72 Fuel pump control

SENSORS, INPUT

TEMPERATURE SENSORS
See UNDERHOOD SERVICE INSTRUCTIONS at the beginning of this section for test/adjustment diagrams.

All FI: Intake air temperature sensor when mounted in mass airflow sensor is measured between terminals E2 & THA (first and last) of mass airflow sensor electrical connector.

Engine	Year	Sensor	Resistance Ohms @ deg. F/C
All FI	1989-00	Coolant, Intake Air	10,000-20,000 @ -4/-20
			4000-7000 @ 32/0
			2000-3000 @ 68/20
			200-400 @ 176/80
			100-300 @ 212/100
All, as equipped	1990-00	EGR	64,000-97,000 @ 122/50
			11,000-15,000 @ 212/100
			2000-4000 @ 302/150

MANIFOLD ABSOLUTE PRESSURE SENSOR
Measure output voltage with vacuum hose disconnected. Apply vacuum to unit and compare voltage drop with those listed.

Engine	Year	Volts @ in. Hg./kPa
1456cc FI, 1497cc, 1587cc (4A-FE), 1762cc, 2164cc	1989-00	0.3-0.5 @ 4/14
		0.7-0.9 @ 8/28
		1.1-1.3 @ 12/42
		1.5-1.7 @ 16/56
		1.9-2.1 @ 20/70

SENSORS, INPUT Continued

MANIFOLD ABSOLUTE PRESSURE SENSOR Continued

Engine	Year	Volts @ in. Hg./kPa
1998cc Turbo	1989-95	.15-.35 @ 4/14
		0.4-0.6 @ 8/28
		.65-.85 @ 12/42
		0.9-1.1 @ 16/56
		1.15-1.35 @ 20/70

CRANKSHAFT & CAMSHAFT SENSORS
Resistance measured with engine cold.

Engine	Sensor	Year	Resistance (ohms)
1497cc	Both	1995-99	985-1600
1497cc	Camshaft	2000	1630-2740
	Crankshaft	2000	985-1600
1587cc	Crankshaft	1996-97	1630-2740
1762cc	Crankshaft	1995-97	1630-2740
1794cc	Camshaft	1998-99	835-1400
	Crankshaft	1998-99	985-1600
1794cc, 1796cc	Camshaft	2000	835-1400
	Crankshaft	2000	1630-2740
1998cc	Crankshaft	1996-97	985-1600
1998cc	Camshaft	1998-00	835-1400
	Crankshaft	1998-00	985-1600
2164cc	Both	1995-96	985-1600
2164cc: Celica	Both	1997-99	985-1600
Camry	Camshaft	1997-00	835-1400
	Crankshaft	1997-00	985-1600
2438cc	Crankshaft	1994-97	1630-2740
2438cc	Camshaft	1998-00	835-1400
	Crankshaft	1998-00	1630-2740
2693cc	Crankshaft	1994-96	1630-2740
2693cc	Camshaft	1997	835-1400
	Crankshaft	1997	985-1600
2693cc	Camshaft	1998-00	835-1400
	Crankshaft	1998-00	1630-2740
2995cc	Camshaft	1994-99	835-1400
	Crankshaft	1994-99	1630-2740
2995cc Denso	Camshaft	1998-00	835-1400
Wabash	Camshaft	1998-00	1690-2560
	Crankshaft	1998-00	1630-2760
2997cc Turbo:			
Nippondenso	Camshaft	1993-98	835-1400
Asian	Camshaft	1993-98	985-1600
	Crankshaft	1995-98	835-1400
3378cc	Camshaft	1995-00	835-1400
	Crankshaft	1995-00	1630-2740
4477cc	Crankshaft	1995-97	1630-2740
4669cc	Camshaft	1998-00	835-1400
	Crankshaft	1998-00	1630-2740

THROTTLE POSITION SENSOR
Resistance measured between terminals E2 & VTA (first and third) of TPS.

Engine	Year	Resistance (ohms) Idle	Resistance (ohms) WOT
1456cc Tercel	1992-94	200-800	3300-10,000
1497cc Paseo	1992-94	200-6000	2000-10,000
1497cc	1995-00	200-5700	2000-10,000
1587cc (4A-GE, GZE)	1989-91	200-800	3300-10,000
1587cc, 1762cc	1993-97	200-5700	3300-10,000
1794cc, 1796cc	1998-00	200-5700	2000-10,200
1998cc (3S-GE, GTE)	1989-91	200-800	3300-10,000
1998cc Celica	1992-93	470-610	3100-12,100
1998cc MR2	1992-94	200-600	2000-10,200
	1995	200-5700	2000-10,200
1998cc	1996-00	200-5700	2000-10,200
2164cc Camry, Celica	1990-93	200-600	2000-10,200
2164cc MR2 w/AT	1991-93	200-800	3300-10,000
2164cc	1994-00	200-5700	2000-10,200
2366cc (22R-E, RET)	1989-93	200-800	3300-10,000
2366cc	1994-95	470-6100	3100-12,100
2438cc	1991-93	300-6300	3500-10,300
	1994	470-6100	3100-12,100
	1995-00	200-5700	2000-10,200
2507cc	1989-91	300-6300	3500-10,300
2693cc	1994-00	200-5700	2000-10,200
2954cc (7M-GE, GTE)	1989-92	200-1200	3500-10,300

SENSORS, INPUT Continued
THROTTLE POSITION SENSOR Continued

Engine	Year	Resistance (ohms) Idle	Resistance (ohms) WOT
2958cc Truck	1989-92	200-800	3300-10,000
	1993-95	470-6100	3100-12,100
2958cc Camry, 2995cc	1992-96	280-640	2000-11,600
	1997-00	200-5700	2000-10,200
2997cc	1993-98	340-6300	2400-11,200
3378cc	1995-00	280-6400	2000-11,600
3956cc	1989-92	300-6300	3500-10,300
4477cc	1993	340-6300	2000-11,600
	1994-97	200-5700	2000-10,200
4669cc	1998-00	1250-2350	—

MASS AIRFLOW SENSOR

Resistance measured between terminals E2 & VS of airflow meter while moving measuring plate.

Engine	Year	Resistance (ohms) Closed	Resistance (ohms) Open
1587cc (4A-GE)	1989-92	20-400	20-3000
1587cc (4A-GZE)	1989	20-600	20-1200
1998cc (3S-FE, GE, GTE)	1989-94	20-600	20-1200
2366cc (22RE, RET)	1989-94	20-400	20-1200
2438cc, 2507cc	1989-94	20-600	20-1200
2759cc	1989	20-400	20-1200
2954cc, 2958cc, 3956cc	1989-93	20-600	20-1200
2958cc	1992-95	200-600	20-1200
4477cc	1993-95	200-600	20-1200

ACTUATORS, OUTPUT
IDLE SPEED CONTROL

With three-terminal connector, measured between either left or right terminals and center terminal.
4669cc: Specifications given are for throttle control motor.

Engine	Year	Resistance (ohms)
1497cc	1992-93	30-33
	1994	38.5-43.5
	1995-99	17-24.5
1587cc (4A-GZE)	1989	16-17
1587cc Celica	1990-93	27-37
1587cc Corolla, 1762cc all	1993-94	19.3-22.3
	1995-97	17-24.5
1998cc (3S-GE, GTE)	1989-91	16-17
1998cc	1991-93	19.3-22.3
MR2	1991-93	18-24
1998cc	1994-95	19.3-22.3
	1996-00	17-24.5
2164cc	1990-95	19.3-22.3
2164cc Camry	1996	17-24.5
Celica	1996	19.3-22.3
2164cc	1997-00	17-24.5
2438cc	1991-93	19.3-22.3
	1994	18.8-22.8
	1995-00	17-24.5
2507cc	1989-91	10-30
2693cc	1995-99	17-24.5
2759cc, 2954cc, 3956cc	1989-92	10-30
2995cc	1994-95	19.3-22.3
	1996-00	17-24.5
2997cc	1993-95	18-24
	1996-98	15-25

ACTUATORS, OUTPUT Continued
IDLE SPEED CONTROL Continued

Engine	Year	Resistance (ohms)
3378cc	1995-00	17-24.5
4477cc	1993-95	10-30
	1996-97	15-25
4669cc: motor	1998-00	3-100
clutch	1998-00	2.5-4.2

FUEL INJECTORS

Engine	Year	Resistance (ohms)	Temperature (deg. F/C)
Camry, Avalon, Solara	1989-94	13.8	—
	1995-00	13.4-14.2	—
Celica	1989-93	13.8	—
	1994-00	13.4-14.2	—
Turbo	1989-93	2-4	—
Corolla	1989-91	13.8	—
4WD Wagon	1992-94	13.8	68/20
	1995-00	13.4-14.2	—
Cressida	1989-92	13.8	—
Echo	2000	13.4-14.2	—
FX	1989	13.8	—
Land Cruiser	1989-92	13.8	—
	1993-94	12-16	—
	1995-99	13.4-14.2	—
MR2	1989-94	13.8	—
	1995	13.4-14.2	—
Supercharged	1989	2.9	—
Turbo	1991-95	2-4	—
Previa	1992-95	13.4-14.2	—
RAV4	1996-00	13.4-14.2	—
Sienna	1998-00	13.4-14.2	—
Supra	1989-92	13.8	—
	1993-97	13.4-14.2	—
Turbo	1989-92	2-3.8	—
Turbo	1993-97	1.95	—
Tercel, Paseo	1990-94	13.8	68/20
	1995-99	13.4-14.2	—
Tacoma: 4-cyl.	1995-97	12-16	—
	1998-00	13.4-14.2	—
V6	1995-00	13.4-14.2	—
Trucks	1989-00	13.4-14.2	—
T100: 4-cyl.	1994-97	12-16	—
	1998	13.4-14.2	—
V6	1993-98	13.4-14.2	—
Van	1989	1.1-2.2	—
4-Runner	1989-00	13.4-14.2	—

Cold Start Injector

Engine	Year	Resistance (ohms)	Temperature (deg. F/C)
Corolla & MR2 4A-GE, Van, Celica 3S-GE	1989-91	3-5	—
All others	1989-91	2-4	—
All, as equipped	1992-95	2-4	—

IDLE AIR VALVE

Provides high idle speed at cold start.
Measured with engine at operating temperature and idle air valve closed.

Engine	Year	Resistance (ohms)
1998cc 3Y, 2237cc 4Y	1989	40-60
1998cc (3S-FE)	1989-91	40-60
2366cc FI	1989-95	40-60

VOLKSWAGEN
1989-99

To identify any engine by the manufacturer's code, follow the four steps designated by the numbered blocks.

1 MODEL YEAR IDENTIFICATION: Refer to illustration of the Vehicle Identification Number (V.I.N.). The year is indicated by a code letter which is the 10th character of the V.I.N.

2 ENGINE CODE: In the "CODE" column, find the engine code.

3 ENGINE IDENTIFICATION: On the line where the engine code appears, read to the right to identify the engine.

V.I.N.
PLATE LOCATION:

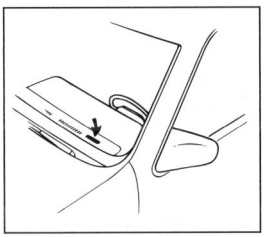

Left side of instrument panel,
visible through windshield

1 MODEL YEAR IDENTIFICATION:

10th character of V.I.N.

1999—X	1998—W	1997—V
1996—T	1995—S	1994—R
1993—P	1992—N	1991—M
1990—L	1989—K	

2 ENGINE CODE LOCATION:

Prefix to engine number.

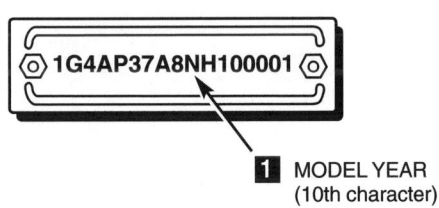

1 MODEL YEAR
(10th character)

YEAR	CODE	CYL.	liters	cc	Fuel System	HP
1999	AEB, APH	4	1.8T	178IT	MFI	150
	ALH	4	1.9TD	1896	MFI	90
	ABA, AEG	4	2.0	1984	MFI	115
	AHA	6	2.8	2771	MFI	190
	AES	6	2.8	2792	MFI	140
	AAA, AFP	6	2.8	2792	MFI	172
1998	AEB	4	1.8T	178IT	MFI	150
	AAZ, 1Z	4	1.9TD	1896TD	MFI	89
	ABA	4	2.0	1984	MFI	115
	AES	6	2.8	2792	MFI	139
	AAA	6	2.8	2792	MFI	172
1997	AAZ, 1Z	4	1.9 TD	1896 TD	MFI	89
	ABA	4	2.0	1984	MFI	115
	—	5	2.4 D	2370 D	MFI	77
	AES	6	2.8	2792	MFI	139
	AAA	6	2.8	2792	MFI	172
	—	6	2.9	2861	MFI	184
1996	AAZ, 1Z	4	1.9 TD	1896 TD	MFI	89
	ABA	4	2.0	1984	MFI	115
	AAF	5	2.5	2459	MFI	109
	AAA	6	2.8	2792	MFI	172
	—	6	2.9	2861	MFI	184
1995	AAZ, 1Z	4	1.9 TD	1896 TD	MFI	89
	ABA	4	2.0	1984	MFI	115
	AAB, ACV	5	2.4	2370	MFI	77
	AAF	5	2.5	2459	MFI	109
	AAA	6	2.8	2792	MFI	172
1994	ACC	4	1.8	1780	MFI	90
	AAZ, 1Z	4	1.9 D	1896 D	MFI	75
	ABA	4	2.0	1984	MFI	115
	9A	4	2.0	1984	MFI	134
	AAF	5	2.5	2461	MFI	109
	AAA	6	2.8	2792	MFI	172[1], 178[1]
1993	ABG	4	1.8	1780	MFI	81
	JH	4	1.8	1780	MFI	94
	ACC	4	1.8	1780	MFI	90
	AAZ	4	1.9 D	1896 D	MFI	75
	ABA	4	2.0	1984	MFI	115

YEAR	CODE	CYL.	liters	cc	Fuel System	HP
1993 Cont'd.	9A	4	2.0	1984	MFI	134
	AAB	5	2.4 D	2370	MFI	76
	AAF	5	2.5	2451	MFI	108
	AAA	6	2.8	2792	MFI	172, 178[1]
1992	1V	4	1.6 D	1590 D	MFI	59
	JN	4	1.8	1780	MFI	94
	2H	4	1.8	1780	MFI	81
	RV	4	1.8	1780	MFI	100
	PF	4	1.8	1780	MFI	105
	PG	4	1.8 S	1780 S	MFI	158
	9A	4	2.0	1984	MFI	134
	VR	6	2.8	2792	MFI	172
1991	ME	4	1.6 D	1588 D	MFI	52
	2H	4	1.8	1780	MFI	93
	JN	4	1.8	1780	MFI	81
	RV	4	1.8	1780	MFI	100
	PF	4	1.8	1780	MFI	105
	PG	4	1.8 S	1780 S	MFI	158
	9A	4	2.0	1984	MFI	134
	MV	4	2.1	2109	MFI	90
1990	ME	4	1.6 D	1588 D	MFI	52
	JH	4	1.8	1780	MFI	93
	JN	4	1.8	1780	MFI	81
	RV	4	1.8	1780	MFI	100
	PF	4	1.8	1780	MFI	105
	PG	4	1.8 S	1780 S	MFI	158
	9A	4	2.0	1984	MFI	134
	MV	4	2.1	2109	MFI	90
1989	JN	4	1.8	1780	MFI	81
	JH	4	1.8	1780	MFI	90
	RV	4	1.8	1780	MFI	100
	PF	4	1.8	1780	MFI	105
	PL	4	1.8	1780	MFI	123
	PG	4	1.8 S	1780 S	MFI	145
	MV	4	2.1	2109	MFI	95

D—Diesel. **S—Supercharged.** **TD—Turbo Diesel.**
1 Engine horsepower varies with model installation.

VOLKSWAGEN
1989-99

UNDERHOOD SERVICE SPECIFICATIONS

VNITU1

VNITU1

CYLINDER NUMBERING SEQUENCE

Vanagon
FIRING ORDER: 1 4 3 2

— Front of car —
1989-91
2109cc
Vanagon

All Other 4-cyl. Models FIRING ORDER: 1 3 4 2

— Front of car —

1989-93
1780cc
Fox

1989-99
1780cc, 1984cc SOHC
Cabriolet, Corrado,
Golf, GTI, Jetta

1990-94
1984cc
Passat, GTI DOHC

5-cyl. FIRING ORDER: 1 2 4 5 3

6-cyl. FIRING ORDER: 1 5 3 6 2 4

— Front of car —

1993-94
2461cc EuroVan

1992-94
2792cc
Corrado, Golf,
Jetta, Passat

1995-99
2792cc
GTI, Jetta, Passat

— TIMING MARK —

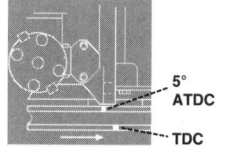

5°
ATDC

TDC

1989-91
2109cc
Vanagon

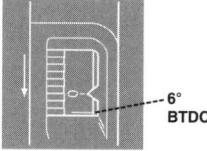

6°
BTDC

1989-93
1780cc
Fox

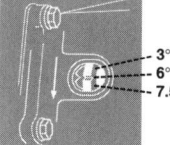

3° ATDC
6° BTDC
7.5° BTDC

1989-92
1780cc
ex. Fox

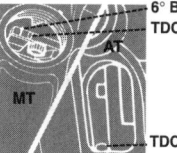

6° BTDC
TDC
AT

MT

TDC

1993-99
17980cc, 1984cc
Beetle, Cabriolet,
Fox, Golf,
Jetta, Passat

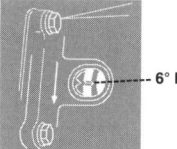

6° BTDC

1990-92
1984cc
Jetta, Passat

ELECTRICAL AND IGNITION SYSTEMS

BATTERY

BCI equivalent shown, size may vary from original equipment. Check clearance before replacing, holddown may need to be modified.

Engine	Year	STANDARD BCI Group No.	STANDARD Crank. Perf.	OPTIONAL BCI Group No.	OPTIONAL Crank. Perf.
1588cc Diesel	1989-92	41	650	—	—
1780cc All models	1989	41	435	41	500
	1990-91	41	575	—	—
	1992-93	41	500	—	—
1781cc Beetle	1998-99	47	480	—	—
1781cc Passat	1998	94R	640	—	—
	1999	48	570	—	—
1896cc Turbo Diesel	1995	41	650	—	—
Beetle, Passat	1998	98R	620	—	—
Golf, Jetta	1996	41	650	—	—
Golf, Jetta ex. Canada	1997-99	98R	620	—	—
Canada	1997-98	41	650	—	—
Passat	1996	42	460	41	650
Beetle	1998	99	360	—	—
	1999	48	640	—	—
1984cc All models	1990-91	41	575	—	—
	1992	41	500	—	—
	1993-94	41	575	—	—
Cabrio	1995-97	42	460	41	650
Cabrio, GTI	1998	99	360	—	—
Golf, Jetta, GTI	1995-96	41	575	41	650
Golf, Jetta	1997	42	460	—	—
Golf, Jetta	1998-99	97R	575	—	—
Passat	1996-97	42	460	41	650
Beetle	1998	99	360	—	—
	1999	47	480	—	—

BATTERY Continued

Engine	Year	STANDARD BCI Group No.	STANDARD Crank. Perf.	OPTIONAL BCI Group No.	OPTIONAL Crank. Perf.
2109cc Vanagon	1989	41	500	—	—
	1990-91	41	575	—	—
2370cc ex. Canada	1997	98R	620	—	—
Canada	1997	41	650	—	—
2771cc Passat	1998	94R	640	—	—
	1998	48	570	—	—
2792cc	1992	41	500	—	—
	1993-94	41	575	—	—
	1995	42	460	41	650
Passat	1996-97	42	460	41	650
GTI, Jetta	1996	41	575	41	650
GTI, Jetta	1997	42	460	—	—
GTI, Cabrio, Jetta	1999	97R	575	—	—
2861cc	1997	42	460	—	—

GENERATOR

See UNDERHOOD SERVICE INSTRUCTIONS at the beginning of this section for test/adjustment diagrams.

Engine	Year	Rated Output (amps @ eng. rpm)	Test Output (amps @ eng. rpm)
1588cc w/o AC	1989-91	65	49 @ 3000
w/AC	1989-92	90	74 @ 3000
1590cc w/o AC	1992	65	49 @ 3000
w/AC	1992	90	74 @ 3000
1780cc w/o AC	1989-93	65	49 @ 3000
w/AC	1989-93	90	74 @ 3000
1781cc w/o AC	1994	70	—
w/AC	1994	90	—

UNDERHOOD SERVICE SPECIFICATIONS

GENERATOR Continued

Engine	Year	Rated Output (amps @ eng. rpm)	Test Output (amps @ eng. rpm)
1781cc Turbo	1998-99	90	—
1896cc w/o AC	1994	70	—
w/AC	1994	90	—
1896cc w/o AC	1993	65	49 @ 3000
	1994-99	70	—
w/AC	1993-99	90	74 @ 3000
Passat	1997	120	—
1915cc w/o AC	1994	70	—
w/AC	1994	90	—
1984cc	1990-92	90	74 @ 3000
	1993	120	75 @ 3000
1984cc w/o AC	1994-99	70	—
w/AC	1994-99	90	—
All GLX	1994	120	—
2109cc	1989-91	90	74 @ 3000
2459cc	1992-93	90	74 @ 3000
2461cc w/o AC	1993	90	74 @ 3000
w/AC	1993-95	120	—
2771cc	1998-99	90	—
2792cc	1992-95	120	—
Jetta, GTI, Golf	1996-99	90	—
Passat	1996-98	120	—
EuroVan Camper	1999	120	—
EuroVan GLS, MV	1999	150	—
2861cc	1996	90	—

REGULATOR

Application	Year	Test Temp. (deg. F/C)	Voltage Setting
All	1989-93	68/20	13.5-14.5

STARTER

Engine	Year	Cranking Voltage (min. volts)	Ampere Draw @ Cranking Speed
All	1989-92	8.0	260
	1993-98	8.0	—

SPARK PLUGS

Engine	Year	Gap (inches)	Gap (mm)	Torque (ft-lb)
1780cc: Code ACC	1993-94	0.28-0.36	.7-.9	18
Code ABG	1993	.024-.031	.60-.80	15
Code JH	1989-93	.024-.032	.60-.80	15
Code JN, Fox	1989-92	.024-.032	.60-.80	17
Code PF	1989-92	.024-.032	.60-.80	15
Code PG	1989-91	.028-.032	.70-.80	15
	1992	.024-.028	.60-.70	15
Code PL	1989	.028-.036	.70-.90	15
Code RV	1989-92	.024-.032	.60-.80	15
Code 2H	1991-92	.028-.035	.70-.90	15
1781cc turbo	1998	.035-.043	.90-1.1	22
1984cc: Code ABA	1993-95	.031	.80	22
Code 9A	1990-94	.028-.036	.70-.90	15
2109cc: Code MV	1989-92	.024-.032	.60-.80	15
2461cc	1993	.028-.036	.70-.90	18
2792cc	1993-98	.028-.031	.7-.8	18

IGNITION COIL
FOR TESTING AND ADJUSTMENT DIAGRAMS, SEE APPENDIX A.

Engine	Year	Windings	Resistance (ohms @ 68°F or 20°C)
1780cc: Code ACC	1993-94	Primary	0.5-0.7
		Secondary	3000-4000
		Secondary	6900-8500
Code JH	1989-90	Primary	.52-.76
		Secondary	2400-3500
	1992	Primary	.70-.80
		Secondary	6900-8500

IGNITION COIL Continued

Engine	Year	Windings	Resistance (ohms @ 68°F or 20°C)
1780cc: Code JN	1989-91	Primary	.52-.76
		Secondary	2400-3500
Code PF, RV	1989-92	Primary	.65-.79
		Secondary	6900-8500
Code PG	1989-92	Primary	.60-.80
		Secondary	2400-3500
Code PL	1989	Primary	.65-.79
		Secondary	6900-8500
1984cc	1990-92	Primary	.60-.80
		Secondary	6500-8500
	1993-97	Primary	.50-1.2
		Secondary	3000-4000
2109cc	1989-92	Primary	.50-.80
		Secondary	2400-3500
2451cc	1993	Primary	0.5-0.7
		Secondary	3000-4000
2792cc	1993-94	Primary	0.5-0.7
		Secondary	7400-9400
	1995-98	Secondary	3500-4400

BASE TIMING
FOR TESTING AND ADJUSTMENT DIAGRAMS, SEE APPENDIX C.
Set at slow idle and Before Top Dead Center, unless otherwise specified.

All Engines: Connect tachometer and timing light; check idle speed, observe timing mark.

1780cc Supercharged, 1780cc Cole PF, RV, 2109cc: Disconnect engine coolant temperature sensor, check at 2000-2500 rpm.

All ex. Vanagon: Align mark on flywheel with pointer on bellhousing. Some models, remove TDC sensor to access mark.

Vanagon: Align notch on pulley with split in degree markings.

Engine	Year	Man. Trans. (degrees)	Auto. Trans. (degrees)
1780cc	1989-92	6±2	6±2
	1993-94	6±1[2,3]	6±1[2,3]
1984cc	1990-92	6±1[2,3]	6±1[2,3]
	1993-98	12[1]	12[1]
2109cc	1989-92	5±2	5±2
2461cc	1993	6±2	6±2
2792cc	1992-98	6[1,2]	6[1,2]

1 Not adjustable.
2 Connect a ST & access basic adj. Engine warm, electrical accessories & AC off.
3 Then rotate distributor to adjust.

DISTRIBUTOR TIMING ADVANCE
Engine degrees at engine rpm, no load, in addition to base timing.

Engine	Trans-mission	Year	Distributor Number	Total	Centrifugal
				Degrees @ 2500 RPM	
1780cc	MT & AT	1989-90	026905205B	24-33	14-19

FUEL SYSTEM

FUEL PRESSURE PROCEDURE
FOR TESTING AND ADJUSTMENT DIAGRAMS, SEE APPENDIX D.

CIS Systems:
1. With engine at operating temperature, connect appropriate pressure gauge between fuel distributor and warm-up regulator.
2. Set gauge valve to open position, start engine and run at idle, allow pressure to stabilize, read control pressure.
3. Set gauge valve to closed position, allow pressure to stabilize, read system pressure.
4. Set gauge to open position, switch off ignition, after 10 minutes read residual pressure.

CIS-E Systems:
1. With engine at operating temperature, connect appropriate pressure gauge between cold start line and lower chamber test fittings of the fuel distributor.
2. Disconnect electrical connector from the differential pressure regulator.
3. Set gauge valve to open position, remove fuel pump relay and bridge terminals to energize pump, allow pressure to stabilize, read system pressure.
4. Set gauge valve to closed position, energize fuel pump, read differential pressure.
5. Set gauge valve to open position, energize fuel pump for 30 seconds, after 10 minutes read residual pressure.

VOLKSWAGEN
1989-99

UNDERHOOD SERVICE SPECIFICATIONS

FUEL PRESSURE PROCEDURE Continued

Digijet, Digifont Systems:
1. Connect appropriate pressure gauge to test port of fuel rail.
2. Disconnect vacuum hose from pressure regulator, start engine and run at idle, allow pressure to stabilize and take reading.
3. Reconnect vacuum to pressure regulator and check gauge reading.
4. Switch ignition off, after 10 minutes read residual pressure.

FUEL PRESSURE: CIS, CIS-E

Engine	System	Year	System PSI	Control PSI	Differential PSI	Residual PSI
1780cc	CIS	1989-91	68-78	49-55	—	35-38
	CIS-E	1989-91	75-82	—	68-79	38
1984cc	CIS-E	1990-92	88-96	—	81-91	48

FUEL PRESSURE: Digijet, Digifont

		System Pressure		
Engine	Year	W/O Vacuum PSI	W/Vacuum PSI	Residual Pressure PSI
1780cc	1989-94	44	36	29
1984cc	1993-97	44	36	29
2109cc	1989-91	36	33	29
2451cc	1993	44	36	29
2792cc	1993-94	58	51	36
	1995-97	44	36	29

IDLE SPEED W/O COMPUTER CONTROL

All engines: Must be at operating temperature, all electrical equipment switched off, cooling fan not running. If equipped with ISS (idle speed stabilizer), disconnect both electrical plugs and connect them together.

		Slow		Maximum	
Engine	Year	Man. Trans.	Auto. Trans.	Man. Trans.	Auto. Trans.
1588cc Diesel	1989-92	920-980	—	5300-5400	—
1896cc Diesel	1993-94	870-930	—	4950-5150	—

IDLE SPEED W/COMPUTER CONTROL

FOR TESTING AND ADJUSTMENT DIAGRAMS, SEE APPENDIX E.

All engines: Must be at operating temperature, all electrical equipment switched off, cooling fan not running.

1989-91 1780cc w/CIS: Disconnect crankcase breather hoses from valve cover and intake air boot, position hoses to draw in fresh air. Disconnect canister vent hose at intake air boot. Clamp off hose to idle speed boost valve.

1989-91 1780cc w/CIS-E: Disconnect crankcase breather hoses from valve cover and intake air boot, position hoses to draw in fresh air. Remove "T" fitting for EVAP canister from intake air boot, rotate fitting 90 degrees and install restricted end into boot. Clamp off hose to idle speed boost valve.

1989-91 1780cc w/Digifont: Disconnect crankcase breather hoses. Run engine at idle for one minute, disconnect coolant temperature sensor. Rev engine to 3000 rpm several times, allow idle to stabilize before adjusting.

1990-91 1984cc: Disconnect crankcase breather hose, disconnect EVAP canister vent hose at purge valve.

Engine	Code	Year	Checking Speed	Adjusting Speed
1780cc	JH	1989	850-1000	—
	JN	1989-91	800-1000	840-880
	PF, RV	1989-92	750-850	—
	PG	1989-92	750-850	770-830
	PL	1989	—	800-900
	UM	1989-91	800-1000	840-880
	ACC	1993-94	750-1000[1]	—
1896cc Diesel	AAZ	1993-94	870-930[1]	—
1984cc	9A	1990-94	800-1000[1]	—
	ABA	1993-98	800-880	—
2109cc	MV	1989-91	830-930	—
2451cc	AAF	1993	775-825	—
2792cc	AAA, AES	1992-98	650-750[1]	—

1 Connect a ST & access basic adj. Engine warm, electrical accessories & AC off.

IDLE MIXTURE

Engine	Year	CO% Minimum	CO% Maximum
1780cc	1989	0.3	1.2
	1990-92	—	1.2
	1993-94	0.2	1.2
1982cc Code 9A	1990-94	0.2	1.2
1984cc	1993-95	0.3	1.2
2109cc	1989	0.3	1.2
2451cc	1993	0.3	1.2
2792cc	1993-94	0.3	1.5

ENGINE MECHANICAL

TIGHTENING TORQUES

FOR CYLINDER HEAD TORQUE SEQUENCES AND DIAGRAMS, SEE APPENDIX F.

		TORQUE FOOT-POUNDS/NEWTON METERS				
Engine	Year	Cylinder Head	Intake Manifold	Exhaust Manifold	Crankshaft Pulley	Water Pump
DIESEL ENGINES						
4-cyl.						
1.6L	1989-91	30/40	18/25	18/25	15/20	7/10
2nd stage		44/60				
3rd stage		+180°				
Warm retorque			+90°			
1.9L	1993-94	30/40,	33/45	18/25	18/25	7/10
2nd stage		44/60,				
3rd stage		+90°				
4th stage		+90°				
1.9L	1998	30/40,	—	—	66/90	—
		44/60,			+90°	
		+90°, +90°				
5-cyl.						
2.4L	1993	30/40	—	(M6)7/10	—	—
2nd stage		44/60		(M8)18/25		
3rd stage		+180°		(M10)30/40		
4th stage		+90°,+90°				
5th stage		+90°[1]				
2.4L	1994-95	30/40	—	—	—	—
2nd stage		44/60				
3rd stage		+90°[3]				
4th stage		+90°[3]				
GASOLINE ENGINES						
4-cyl.						
1.8L SOHC						
Ex. supercharged	1989-94	30/40	18/25	18/25	15/20	7/10
2nd stage		44/60				
3rd stage[2]		+180°				
Supercharged	1990-92	30/40	11/15	18/25	18/25	7/10
2nd stage		44/60				
3rd stage[2]		+180°				
1.8L DOHC	1989-92	30/40	15/20	18/25	15/20	7/10
2nd stage		44/60				
3rd stage[2]		+180°				
2.0L	1990-99	30/40	15/20	18/25	18/25	7/10
2nd stage		44/60				
3rd stage[2]		+180°				
2.1L	1989-91	37/50	15/20	18/25	43/60	15/20
2.5L	1993	30/40,	18/25	30/40	340/460	—
		44/60,				
		+90°, +90°				
6-cyl.						
2.8L	1993-98	30/40,	18/25	18/25	74/100	15/20
2nd stage		40/60,			+90°	
3rd stage		+180°				

1 With engine at operating temperature.
2 Two at 90° is permissible, must be in one even motion.
3 With soft head gasket 1995.

VOLKSWAGEN
1989-99

UNDERHOOD SERVICE SPECIFICATIONS

COMPRESSION PRESSURE
At cranking speed, throttle open, engine at operating temperature.

Engine	Year	PSI	Maximum Variation PSI
1588cc Diesel	1989-91	406-493	73
1590cc Diesel	1992	406-493	73
1780cc SOHC	1989-92	131-174	44
Supercharged	1990-92	116-174	44
DOHC	1989-92	145-189	44
1896cc	1993-99	377-493	73
1984cc	1990-99	145-189	44
2109cc	1989-91	145-189	44
2.4L Diesel	1993-95	377-493	72
2451cc	1993	130-175	44
2792cc	1993-99	145-188	44

BELT TENSION
A belt in operation 20 minutes is considered a used belt.

Engine	Year	Generator	Power Steering	Air Cond.
USED BELTS				
1780cc (inches)	1989-92	3/16	3/8	3/8
(mm)	1989-92	5	10	10
1984cc (inches)	1990-92	3/16	3/8	3/8
(mm)	1990-92	5	10	10
2109cc (inches)	1989-91	3/16	—	3/8
(mm)	1989-91	5	—	10
NEW BELTS				
1780cc (inches)	1989-92	5/64	3/8	3/8
(mm)	1989-92	2	10	10
1984cc (inches)	1990-92	5/64	3/8	3/8
(mm)	1990-92	2	10	10
2109cc (inches)	1989-91	5/64	—	3/8
(mm)	1989-91	2	—	10

SERPENTINE BELT DIAGRAM

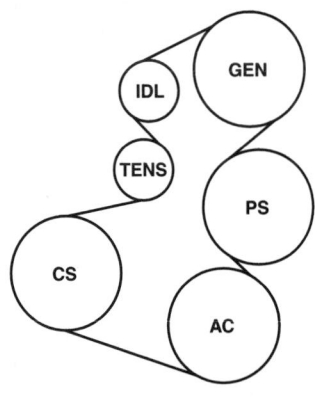

1993-99 V6

ENGINE COMPUTER SYSTEM

FOR TESTING AND ADJUSTMENT DIAGRAMS, SEE APPENDIX G.

DIAGNOSTIC TROUBLE CODES
Using Onboard Diagnostic System
1989-93 1780cc Golf, GTI, Jetta:
To activate: Turn ignition on but do not start engine, press and hold "CHECK" light rocker switch for at least 4 seconds. Codes will be displayed by light as a series of four digit codes with a 2.5 second pause between digits. Depress and hold switch for 4 seconds to access additional codes. When all codes have been displayed, code 0000 will flash, light on 2.5 seconds, light off 2.5 seconds.
To clear memory: Turn ignition switch off. Depress and hold rocker switch, turn ignition switch to on position, continue to hold rocker switch for at least 5 seconds, turn ignition off and release rocker switch.

Using External Diagnostic Tester
1989-93 1780cc Code RV, 1989-93 1780cc Code PG, 1990-91 1984cc:
Special tool required. Connect tester, VW Part No. VAG1551, and access codes.

DIAGNOSTIC TROUBLE CODES Continued
1993-95 1984cc Code ABA
Using External Diagnostic Tester
1993 2461cc EuroVan
1993-95 2792cc

Code	Application	Definition
1111	Control Module	Defective control module
1231	Vehicle Speed Sensor	No automatic transmission signal
1232	Throttle Position Actuator	Defective actuator or circuitry
2111	Engine Speed Sensor	Open circuit, sensor malfunctioning, RPM sensor rotor loose or malfunctioning, sensor loose
2112	Reference Sensor	No signal, out of range signal
2113	Hall Sensor	Defective sensor or circuitry
2113	Camshaft Position Sensor	Sensor malfunctioning or camshaft timing out of adjustment, open circuit or short circuit to positive, short circuit to ground
2121	Throttle Position Switch	Defective switch or circuitry
2141	Knock Sensor I	Excessive detonation detected
2142	Knock Sensor	Defective sensor or circuit
2142	AT Control Module	Defective wiring or connectors
2144	Knock Sensor II	Defective sensor or circuit
2212	Throttle Position Sensor	Defective sensor or circuitry
2214	RPM upper limit exceeded	Engine enters governed speed range, signal from (RPM) sensor disrupted
2222	Manifold Differential Pressure Sensor	Defective control unit, no vacuum supply
2231	Idle Speed Control	Idle out of regulation limit
2231	Idle Air Control regulation	Valve sticking or dirty, air leak between mass air flow sensor and engine
2232	Mass Air Flow Sensor	Defective sensor or circuit
2234	Supply Voltage	Battery voltage exceeds 15.5 volts, or below 6.1 volts
2242	CO Sensor	Defective sensor, open circuit
2243	Consumption signal	Short circuit to battery positive
2312	Engine Coolant Temperature Sensor	Defective sensor or circuit
2314	Engine/trans. electrical connection	Short circuit to ground
2322	Intake Air Temperature Sensor	Defective sensor or circuit
2323	Mass Air Flow Sensor	Defective sensor, open circuit
2324	Mass Air Flow Sensor	Sensor malfunctioning, open circuit or short circuit to battery positive, short to ground, unmetered air between sensor and engine
2341	Oxygen Sensor Control	Defective sensor heater, fuel pressure, evaporator emission frequency valve leaking, or exhaust leak
2342	Oxygen Sensor	Defective sensor or circuit
2411	EGR Temperature Sensor	No signal, system restricted
2412	Intake Air Temperature Sensor	Sensor malfunctioning, short circuit to ground, corrosion in connector, open circuit or short circuit to battery positive
2413	Mixture Control	Incorrect fuel pressure, check fuel pressure regulator
4311	Secondary Air Injection Pump Relay	Relay malfunctioning, short to battery positive, open circuit or short circuit to ground
4312	EGR Vacuum Regulator Solenoid Valve	Valve malfunctioning, open circuit or short circuit to ground, short circuit to battery positive
4313	Secondary Air Injection Solenoid Valve	Valve malfunctioning, short to battery positive, open circuit or short circuit to ground
4332	Final stage in control module	Loose wiring contacts to control elements or motronic engine control module malfunctioning
4343	EVAP Canister Purge Regulator Valve	Short circuit to battery positive, open circuit or short circuit to ground, valve malfunctioning
4411	Fuel Injector cyl. 1	Defective injector, open circuit
4412	Injector, cyl. 2	Fuel injector
4413	Injector, cyl. 3	Fuel injector
4414	Injector, cyl. 4	Fuel injector
4421	Injector, cyl. 5	Fuel injector

UNDERHOOD SERVICE SPECIFICATIONS

VNITU5

VNITU5

DIAGNOSTIC TROUBLE CODES Continued

Code	Application	Definition
4422	Injector, cyl. 6	Fuel injector
4431	Idle Air Control Valve	Short circuit to battery positive, open circuit or short circuit to ground, valve malfunctioning
4431	Idle Stabilizer	No signal, out of range signal
4433	Fuel Pump Relay	Relay malfunctioning, short circuit in wiring to battery positive
4444	No Faults	Memory clear
0000	End of Sequence	All fault codes have been displayed

SENSORS, INPUT

TEMPERATURE SENSORS

Engine	Year	Sensor	Resistance Ohms @ deg. F/C
All	1989-98	Coolant, Intake Air	5000-6500 @ 32/0
			1500-2000 @ 86/30
			500-650 @ 140/60
			200-300 @ 194/90
2109cc	1989-91	Intake Air	2300-2700 @ 68/20

MASS AIRFLOW SENSOR

Engine	Year	Resistance Ohms @ Terminal
1780cc		
Code PF, RV	1989-92	500-1000 @ 3 & 4
Code PG	1990-91	0-2000 @ 1 & 3
2109cc	1989-91	500-1000 @ 3 & 4
		500-1000 @ 6 & 9
		2300-2700 @ 1 & 4

THROTTLE POSITION SENSOR

Engine	Year	Resistance (ohms) Idle	WOT
1780cc	1993-94	520-1300	—
1984cc	1993-97	1,000-2,000	—
2792cc	1993-98	700-13,000	—

Engine	Year	Voltage @ Idle	Voltage @ WOT
2451cc	1993-95	0.3-1.7	3-5

ENGINE SPEED SENSOR

Engine	Year	Resistance (ohms)
1780cc, 2872cc	1993-98	500-700

ACTUATORS, OUTPUT
FUEL INJECTORS

Engine	Year	Resistance (ohms)
1780cc		
Cabriolet, Corrado	1990-91	15-20
Fox	1991	15-20
1984cc	1993-97	14-21.5
2109cc		
Vanagon	1989-91	15-20
2451cc	1993-95	15-20
2792cc	1993-98	15-21.5

CONTROL PRESSURE REGULATOR

Engine	Year	Resistance (ohms)
1780cc w/CIS		
Canada code JN	1989	16-22
1984cc DOHC	1990-94	15-25

DIFFERENTIAL PRESSURE REGULATOR

Engine	Year	Resistance (ohms)
1780cc w/CIS-E	1989-90	17.5-21.5

FREQUENCY VALVE

Engine	Year	Resistance (ohms)
All w/CIS	1989	2-3

IDLE AIR CONTROL VALVE

Engine	Year	Resistance (ohms)
1451cc	1993-95	2-10
1984cc	1993-98	7-10
2792cc	1993-98	10-20

COMPUTER TIMING ADVANCE

1780cc Engine: With engine at operating temperature, remove vacuum hose from control unit. Increase engine speed to specified rpm and compare to specified value.

2109cc Engine: With engine at operating temperature, disconnect Temperature Sensor II. Increase engine speed to 2000-2500 rpm and record timing. Reconnect Temperature Sensor II and increase engine speed to 3000 rpm, read timing and subtract previously recorded value. Compare with specified value. Values given are in addition to base timing.

Engine/Model	Year	Engine Code	Timing Advance Degrees @ RPM
1780cc:			
Corrado	1990-92	PG	25±5 @ 2500
Golf, Jetta	1989-92	RV, PF	30±3 @ 2300
Scirocco 16-valve	1989	PL	13 @ 2500
1984cc	1993-95	ABA	29-34 @ 3000
	1993-94	9A	29-34@3000
2109cc Vanagon	1989-90	MV	35±3 @ 3000
2451cc Calif.	1993	AAF	15-38 @ 2300
Others	1993	AAF	26-36 @ 2300

ENGINE IDENTIFICATION

To identify any engine by the manufacturer's code, follow the four steps designated by the numbered blocks.

1 **MODEL YEAR IDENTIFICATION:** Refer to illustration of the Vehicle Identification Number (V.I.N.). The year is indicated by a code letter which is the 10th character of the V.I.N.

2 **ENGINE CODE LOCATION:** Refer to illustration of V.I.N. plate for location and designation of engine code.

3 **ENGINE CODE:** In the "CODE" column, find the engine code determined in Step 2.

4 **ENGINE IDENTIFICATION:** On the line where the engine code appears, read to the right to identify the engine.

V.I.N.
PLATE LOCATION:

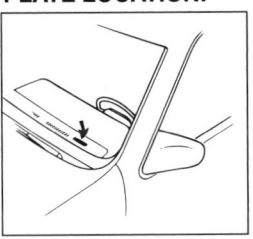

Top of instrument panel or left windshield post visible through windshield.

1 **MODEL YEAR IDENTIFICATION:**

10th character of V.I.N.

1999—X	1998—W	1997—V
1996—T	1995—S	1994—R
1993—P	1992—N	1991—M
1990—L	1989—K	

2 **ENGINE CODE LOCATION:**

6th and 7th characters of V.I.N.

MODEL YEAR AND ENGINE IDENTIFICATION:

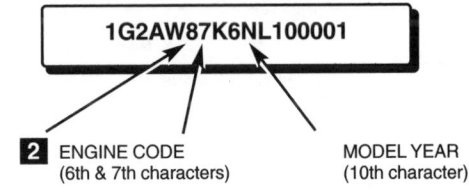

2 ENGINE CODE (6th & 7th characters)   MODEL YEAR (10th character)

4 ENGINE IDENTIFICATION

YEAR	**3** ENGINE CODE CYL.	DISPL. liters	cc	Fuel System	HP
1999	B5234T3 5	2.3T	2319T	MFI	236
	B5234T 5	2.3T	2319T	MFI	246
	B5254S 5	2.4	2435	MFI	162
	B5254T 5	2.4	2435	MFI	190
	B5254T 5	2.5	2473	MFI	190
	B6284T 6	2.8T	2783T	MFI	268
	B6304S 6	2.9	2922	MFI	201
1998	—(B5254FT) ...5	2.3T	2319T	MFI	236
	55 (B5254S) ...5	2.4	2435	MFI	168
	56 (B5254T) 5	2.4	2435	MFI	190
	— 5	2.5	2473	MFI	190
	95,96 (B6304S) ..6	2.9	2922	MFI	181
1997	57 (B5234T) 5	2.3 T	2319 T	MFI	222
	—(B5254FT) ...5	2.3 T	2319 T	MFI	240
	56 (B5254T) 5	2.4	2435	MFI	190
	55 (B5254S) ...5	2.4	2435	MFI	168
	95,96 (B6304S) ..6	2.9	2922	MFI	181
1996	57 (B5234T) 5	2.3 T	2319 T	MFI	222
	—(B5234T-SR) .5	2.3 T	2319 T	MFI	240
	51 (B5252S) ...5	2.4	2435	MFI	142
	55 (B5254S) ...5	2.4	2435	MFI	168
	93 (B6254FS) ..6	2.5	2473	MFI	170
	95, 96 (B6304FS)6	2.9	2922	MFI	181
1995	88 (B230FD) ...4	2.3	2316	MFI	114
	86, 87 (B230FT) 4	2.3	2316	MFI	162
	—(B5234) 5	2.3	2319	MFI	222
	— 5	2.3	2319	MFI	240
	51 (B5252S) ...5	2.4	2435	MFI	142
	55 (B5254S) ...5	2.4	2435	MFI	168
	93 (B6254FS) ..6	2.5	2473	MFI	168
	95, 96 (B6304FS)6	2.9	2922	MFI	181
1994	88 (B230F) 4	2.3	2316	MFI	114
	88 (B230F) 4	2.3	2316	MFI	114
	86, 87 (B230FT) 4	2.3 T	2316 T	MFI	162
	57 (B5234T) 5	2.3 T	2319 T	MFI	228
	41 (B5202S) ...5	2.4	2435	MFI	126

4 ENGINE IDENTIFICATION

YEAR	**3** ENGINE CODE CYL.	DISPL. liters	cc	Fuel System	HP
1994 Cont'd.	51 (B5252S) ...5	2.4	2435	MFI	140
	55 (B5254S(F) ..5	2.4	2435	MFI	140
	95 (B6304S(F) ..6	2.9	2922	MFI	204
1993	88 (B230F) 4	2.3	2316	MFI	114
	88 (B230F) 4	2.3	2316	MFI	114
	87 (B230FT) ...4	2.3 T	2316 T	MFI	162
	41 (B5202S) ...5	2.4	2435	MFI	126
	51 (B5252S) ...5	2.4	2435	MFI	140
	55 (B5254F) 5	2.4	2435	MFI	168
	95 (B6304) 6	2.9	2922	MFI	204
1992	82 (B230F) 4	2.3	2316	MFI	114
	88 (B230F) 4	2.3	2316	MFI	114
	88 (B230F) 4	2.3	2316	MFI	114
	87 (B230FT) ...4	2.3 T	2316 T	MFI	162
	89 (B234F) 4	2.3	2316	MFI	153
	95 (B6304) 6	2.9	2922	MFI	204
1991	88 (B230F) 4	2.3	2316	MFI	114
	88 (B230F) 4	2.3	2316	MFI	114
	87 (B230FT) ...4	2.3 T	2316 T	MFI	162, 188[1]
	89 (B234F) 4	2.3	2316	MFI	153
1990	88 (B230F) 4	2.3	2316	MFI	114
	88 (B230F) 4	2.3	2316	MFI	114
	89 (B234F) 4	2.3	2316	MFI	153
	87 (B230FT) ...4	2.3 T	2316 T	MFI	162, 188[1]
	69 (B280F) 6	2.8	2849	MFI	145
1989	88 (B230F) 4	2.3	2316	MFI	114
	88 (B230F) 4	2.3	2316	MFI	114
	89 (B234F) 4	2.3	2316	MFI	153
	87 (B230FT) ...4	2.3 T	2316 T	MFI	160, 175[1]
	69 (B280F) 6	2.8	2849	MFI	144

1 Engine horsepower varies with model installation.
T—Turbo.

UNDERHOOD SERVICE SPECIFICATIONS

VOITU1

CYLINDER NUMBERING SEQUENCE

VOITU1

4-CYL. FIRING ORDER:
1 3 4 2

5-CYL. FIRING ORDER:
1 2 4 5 3

6-CYL. FIRING ORDER:
1 5 3 6 2 4

V6-CYL. FIRING ORDER:
1 6 3 5 2 4

TIMING MARK

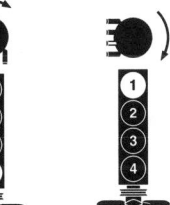

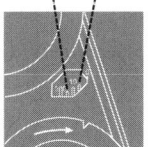

BTDC 15°   5° BTDC

— Front of car —

1989-93	1989-95	1989-92	1993-99	1992-99	1989-90	1989-95
2316cc	2316cc	2316cc	2435cc	2922cc	2849cc	2316cc
200-Series	700-Series	700-Series	850	960		
	SOHC	DOHC				
	900-Series					

ELECTRICAL AND IGNITION SYSTEMS

BATTERY

BCI equivalent shown, size may vary from original equipment. Check clearance before replacing, holddown may need to be modified.

Engine	Year	BCI Group No.	Crank. Perf.
4-cyl. 2316cc: 240	1989	47	450
740 ex. DOHC	1989	47	450
DOHC	1989	48	500
760 Turbo	1989	47	450
780 Turbo	1989	48	500
2316cc Ex. DOHC, Turbo	1990-93	47	450
DOHC, Turbo	1990	48	500
2316cc 940	1993-95	47	520
5-cyl. 2319cc, 2435cc 850	1993-97	47	520
2319cc, C70, S70, V70	1998-99	47	520
2435cc, C70, S70, V70	1998-99	47	520
2473cc V70	1998	47	520
6-cyl.	1989-90	48	500
2473cc 960	1995-96	48	600
2922cc 960	1993-97	48	600
S90, V90	1998	48	600

GENERATOR

Application	Year	Rated Output (amps)	Test Output (amps @ eng. rpm)
2316cc ex. Turbo	1989-92	80	46 @ 2000
Turbo	1989-92	100	34 @ 1500
2316cc	1993-94	80	31 @ 1500
	1993-95	100	31 @ 1500
2319cc Turbo 850	1994-96	100	31 @ 1800
	1997	80/100	45 @ 1800
2319cc	1998	80	—
C70, S70, V70	1998	100	—
S70, V70	1999	80	—
C70	1999	100	—
2319cc	1993-94	80	55 @ 1800
		100	52 @ 2000
2435cc	1993-96	100	30 @ 1800
	1997-99	80	45 @ 1800
2473cc	1996	120	—
	1998	80	—
2783cc	1999	120	—
2849cc	1989-90	100	34 @ 1500
2922cc	1992-97	120	60 @ 1800
	1998	100	—
		120	60 @ 1800
	1999	120	—

REGULATOR

Voltage measured at battery terminals.

Application	Year	Test Temp. (deg. F/C)	Voltage Setting
All	1989-99	77/25	13.8-14.6

STARTER

Manufacturer	Year	Cranking Voltage (min. volts)	Ampere Draw @ Cranking Speed
Bosch: 1.1 kW	1989-90	7.4	480-560
1.4, 2.0 kW	1989-92	9.0	185-220
1.4 kW	1993-97	4.5	625-800
1.4 kW	1998-99	4.0	650-750
1.7 kW	1993-97	3.8	650-840
	1998-99	4.0	650-750
2.2 kW	1993-95	3.0	720-950
2.2 kW	1996-98	4.0	1200-1300
	1999	4.0	650-750
Hitachi: Gas	1989-92	10.3	200

SPARK PLUGS

Engine	Year	Gap (inches)	Gap (mm)	Torque (ft-lb)
2316cc	1989-95	.028-.032	.70-.80	15-22
2319cc, 2435cc	1993-99	.028-.032	.70-.80	15-22
2473cc	1995-99	.024-.028	.60-.70	17-20
2783cc	1999	.028-.032	.70-.80	18
2849cc	1989-90	.024-.028	.60-.70	7-11
2922cc	1992-96	.028-.032	.70-.80	17-20
	1997-98	.024-.028	.60-.70	18
	1999	.028-.032	.70-.80	18

IGNITION COIL

Resistance (ohms @ 68°F or 20°C)

Engine	Year	Windings	Resistance (ohms)
2316cc			
w/Bendix injection	1989-92	Primary	0.5
		Secondary	5000
w/Bendix injection	1993-95	Primary	0.5-0.6
		Secondary	5000-7000
w/Bosch injection	1989-95	Primary	0.6-0.9
		Secondary	6900-8500
2319cc Turbo	1993-97	Primary	0.5-1.5
		Secondary	8000-9000
2435cc	1993-97	Primary	0.5-1.5
		Secondary	8000-9000
2473cc	1995	Primary	0.5
	1996	Primary	0.5-1.5
		Secondary	8000-9000
2849cc	1989-90	Primary	0.6-0.9
		Secondary	6500-9000
2922cc	1992-95	Primary	0.5
	1996	Primary	0.5-1.5
		Secondary	8000-9000
Bosch	1997-98	Primary	0.6-0.9
		Secondary	7000-8500
Bendix	1997-98	Primary	0.5-0.6
		Secondary	5000-7000

BASE TIMING
Before Top Dead Center, unless otherwise specified.

Engine	Year	Man. Trans. (degrees) @ Idle	Auto. Trans. (degrees) @ idle
2316cc SOHC:			
Bendix injection	1989-95	10±2[1]	10±2[1]
Bosch injection	1989-92	12±2[1]	12±2[1]
DOHC	1989-92	15±2[1]	15±2[1]
Turbo	1989-95	12±2	12±2
2319cc Turbo	1993-97	—	6±2[1]
2435cc	1993-94	10±2[1]	10±2[1]
Motronic	1995-96	5±2[1]	5±2[1]
	1997-98	6±2[1]	6±2[1]
Fenix	1995-98	10±2[1]	10±2[1]
2473cc	1995	5±2	5±2
	1996	9±2	9±2
2849cc	1989-90	—	16[1]
2922cc	1992-94	—	5±2[1]
	1995	10±2[1]	10±2[1]
	1996-98	—	9±2

1 For reference only, timing not adjustable.

FUEL SYSTEM

FUEL PRESSURE
With engine warm and running at idle.

Engine	Fuel System	Year	Control Pressure PSI	Line Pressure PSI	Residual Pressure PSI
2316cc	LH	1989-92	36	43	28-43
2319cc Turbo, 2435cc	LH	1993-97	—	43	29 min.
2435cc	M	1998	—	43	29 min.
2473cc	M	1995-96	—	43	—
2849cc	LH	1989-90	36	43	—
2922cc	M	1992-97	—	43	—

IDLE SPEED
Midpoint of range given is the preferred setting speed.

Models with CIS & 1989-95 All: Idle speed is not adjustable.

Turn on A/C to verify specified A/C speed-up.

Disconnect fuel system temperature sensor and verify specified cold idle speed.

Engine	Year	Checking Speed	Setting Speed	Cold Idle	AC Speed-up
2316cc					
SOHC ex. Turbo	1989-95	725-825 N	—	—	—
Turbo	1989-95	700-800 N	—	—	—
DOHC	1989-92	800-900 N	—	—	—
2319cc Turbo	1994-98	800-900 N	—	—	—
2435cc	1993	750-850 N	—	—	—
	1994-98	800-900 N	—	—	—
2473cc	1995-96	700-800 N	—	—	—
2849cc	1989-90	730-770 N	—	—	—
2922cc	1992-98	700-800 N	—	—	—

IDLE MIXTURE
1991-94 Measured at slow idle with oxygen sensor connected. Take sample from access port upstream of catalytic converter. Mixture not adjustable.
1989-90 Measured at slow idle with air pump or oxygen sensor disconnected. Take sample from access port upstream of catalytic converter.

Engine	Year	CO% Minimum	CO% Maximum
2316cc ex. DOHC	1989-90	0.4	0.8
DOHC	1989-90	0.2	1.0

IDLE MIXTURE Continued

Engine	Year	CO% Minimum	CO% Maximum
Turbo	1991-95	0.4	0.8
Turbo	1991-92	0.2	1.0
	1993-95	0.4	0.8
2319cc Turbo	1994-95	0.2	1.0
	1996	0.4	0.8
	1997	0.2	1.0
2435cc US	1993-98	0.2	1.0
Canada	1993-95	0.4	0.8
2473cc (F)	1995-96	0.4	0.8
(G)		0.5	2.0
2849cc	1989	0.2	1.0
2922cc (F)	1992-97	0.4	0.8
(G)	1992-97	0.5	2.0

ENGINE MECHANICAL

TIGHTENING TORQUES

		TORQUE FOOT-POUNDS/NEWTON METERS				
Engine	Year	Cylinder Head	Intake Manifold	Exhaust Manifold	Crankshaft Pulley	Water Pump
4-cyl.						
2.3L SOHC	1989-92	15/20	15/20	15/20	120/165	—
2nd stage		44/60				
3rd stage		+90°				
2.3L SOHC	1993-95	14/20	15/20	15/20	43/60, +60°	
2nd stage		43/60				
3rd stage		+90°				
2.3L DOHC	1989-95	15/20	15/20	15/20	120/165	—
2nd stage		30/40				
3rd stage		+115°				
5-cyl.						
2319cc, 2435cc	1993-95	15/20	15/20	18/25	133/180[1]	15/20
2nd stage		44/60				
3rd stage		+130°				
2319cc, 2435cc	1996-98	15/20	12/17	17/23	132/180[1]	12/17
2nd stage		44/60			18/25[4]	
3rd stage		+130°			+30°[4]	
V6						
2.5L	1995	15/20	15/20	18/25	222/300[1]	13/17
2nd stage		44/60			26/35	
3rd stage		+130°			+60°[4]	
2.8L	1989	43/60	—	—	177-206/ 240-280	—
2nd stage[3]		15/20, +106°				
Warm retorque[2]		+45°				
2.8L	1990	43/60	—	—	177-206/ 240-280	—
2nd stage[3]		30/40				
3rd stage		+180°				
2.9L	1992-98	14/20	15/20	18/25	220/300[1]	13/17
2nd stage		43/60			26/35	
3rd stage		+130°			+60°[4]	

1 Center bolt.
2 Run engine to operating temperature and allow to cool 2 hours before bringing to torque, repeat procedure after 1000 miles of service.
3 Back off and torque to specification one bolt at a time.
4 Flange bolts.

VALVE CLEARANCE

Engine	Year	Intake (inches)	Intake (mm)	Exhaust (inches)	Exhaust (mm)
2316cc SOHC:					
Cold	1989-90	.012-.016	.30-.40	.014-.016	.35-.40
Hot	1989-90	.014-.018	.35-.45	.016-.018	.40-.45
SOHC, Turbo:					
Cold	1991-95	.016	.40	.016	.40
Hot	1991-95	.018	.45	.018	.45
2849cc:					
Cold	1989-90	.004-.006	.10-.15	.010-.012	.25-.30
Hot	1989-90	.006-.008	.15-.20	.012-.014	.30-.35

UNDERHOOD SERVICE SPECIFICATIONS

VOITU3

VOITU3

COMPRESSION PRESSURE

At cranking speed, engine at operating temperature, throttle open.

Engine	Year	PSI	Maximum Variation PSI
2316cc	1989-92	128-156	28
2319cc Turbo	1994-95	156-185	28
	1996-99	160-188	28
2435cc	1993-99	184-218	28
2473cc	1995	184-213	28
	1996	174-203	28
2849cc	1989-90	114-156	28
2922cc	1992-95	184-213	28
	1996	174-203	28
	1997-98	188-218	28

BELT TENSION

A belt in operation for 20 minutes is considered a used belt.

Deflection method: Models without automatic tensioner, applied pressure of 15-20 lbs. at midpoint of longest belt segment.

Engine	Year	Generator	Power Steering	Air Cond.
All (inches)	1989-92	3/16-5/16	3/16-5/16	3/16-5/16
All (mm)	1989-92	5-10	5-10	5-10

SERPENTINE BELT DIAGRAMS

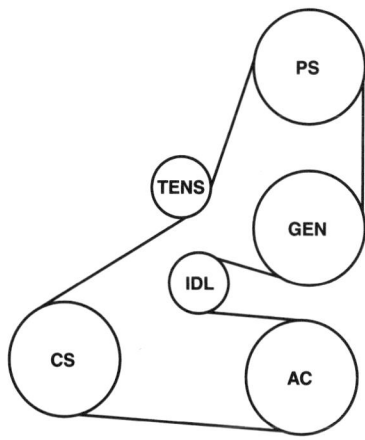

1992-98 960, S90, V90
1993-94 850

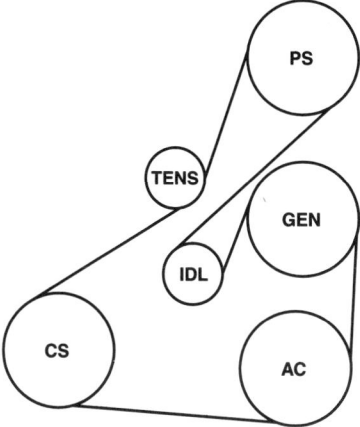

1995-99 850, C70, S70, V70

ENGINE COMPUTER SYSTEM

DIAGNOSTIC TROUBLE CODES
1993-95 2316cc, 2922cc

DTC	Fault Text
1-1-3	Injector group 1
	Injector group 2 (earlier models)
2-2-1	Long-term fuel trim, part load
2-3-1	Long-term fuel trim, part load
2-3-2	Long-term fuel trim, idle
2-3-3	Long-term idle air trim

Code	Application	Definition
115	Fuel Injector	Faulty injector (cyls. 3, 5, 6)
122	Air Temp.	Sensor signal absent or faulty
125	Fuel Injector	Signal to cyl. 2 injector signal
143	Knock Sensor	Front knock sensor signal absent or faulty
145	Fuel Injector	Signal to cyl. 4 injector faulty
154	EGR	EGR flow too high
155	Fuel Injector	Signal to cyl. 5 injector faulty
211	CO Potentiometer	Signal absent or faulty
212	Oxygen Sensor	Signal absent
214	RPM Sensor	Signal absent intermittently
243	Throttle Position	Signal absent or faulty
244	Knock Control	Knock control at limit
313	EVAP Valve	EVAP valve signal absent or faulty
314	Camshaft Position	Signal absent or faulty
323	Malfunction Lamp	Malfunction indicator lamp-signal faulty
324	EWP Relay	EWP relay signal absent or faulty
342	A/C Relay	A/C relay control signal faulty
344	Exhaust Gas Temp.	Signal absent or faulty

Code	Indicated Fault
242	Turbo control valve (TCU) signal absent or faulty
411	Throttle position sensor signal outside voltage range
412	Short-circuit in full-throttle switch
413	EGR temperature sensor signal absent or faulty
421	Boost pressure signal in control module faulty
423	Throttle position sensor signal outside voltage range
424	Load signal from fuel system absent or faulty
433	Rear knock sensor signal absent or faulty
511	Adaptive Lambda control too rich at idling
512	Lambda control too rich
514	Electric cooling fan half-speed operation faulty
515	Electric cooling fan full-speed operation faulty
521	Heated oxygen sensor (HO_2S) heating faulty
523	Signal to cooling fan in control module box faulty
524	Torque control signal to transmission faulty

1993-96 2319cc 5-cyl. engine; 2435cc, 1995-96 6-cyl. 2473cc

Code	Indicated Fault
1-1-1	No faults
1-1-2	ECM
1-1-3	Heated oxygen sensor (HO_2S) integrator at maximum enrichment limit
1-1-5	Injector 1
1-2-3	Engine coolant temperature sensor signal absent
1-3-1	Engine speed signal absent
1-3-2	Battery voltage too high/too low
1-3-5	Injector 3
1-4-4	Load signal from MFI control module absent/faulty
1-5-3	Rear HO_2S signal
2-2-1	Adaptive HO_2S control, engine running too rich at part-load
2-2-3	IAC valve signal absent/faulty
2-2-5	A/C pressure sensor, signal
2-3-1	Adaptive HO_2S control, engine running too lean at part-load
2-3-2	Long term fuel trim, idling
2-3-3	Long term idle air trim
2-4-5	IAC valve closing signal
3-1-1	Speedometer signal absent
3-1-5	EVAP system
3-2-4	Camshaft position sensor (CMP) signal intermittent
3-2-5	Memory failure
3-3-3	Rear knock sensor signal absent/faulty
3-3-5	Fault in lead
4-1-4	Boost pressure regulation
4-1-6	Boost pressure reduction from TCM

DIAGNOSTIC TROUBLE CODES Continued

Code	Indicated Fault
4-2-5	Rear HO$_2$S, regulating
4-3-2	High temperature (T>85°C) in control module box
4-3-5	Front HO$_2$S slow response
4-3-6	Rear HO$_2$S, compensation
4-4-3	TWC efficiency
4-4-4	Acceleration sensor, signal
4-5-1	Misfire cyl. 1
4-5-2	Misfire cyl. 2
4-5-3	Misfire cyl. 3
4-5-4	Misfire cyl. 4
4-5-5	Misfire cyl. 5
5-1-2	Heated oxygen sensor (HO2S) integrator at maximum lean-running limit
5-1-3	High temperature (T>95°C) in control module box
5-2-2	Rear HO$_2$S, preheating
5-3-1	Power stage group A
5-3-2	Power stage group B
5-3-3	Power stage group C
5-3-4	Power stage group D
5-3-5	TC control valve, signal
5-4-1	EVAP-valve, signal
5-4-2	Misfire more than 1 cylinder
5-4-3	Misfire at least 1 cylinder
5-4-4	Misfire more than 1 cylinder. TWC damage
5-4-5	Misfire at least 1 cyl. TWC damage
5-5-1	Misfire cyl. 1. TWC damage
5-5-2	Misfire cyl. 2. TWC damage
5-5-3	Misfire cyl. 3. TWC damage
5-5-4	Misfire cyl. 4. TWC damage
5-5-5	Misfire cyl. 5. TWC damage

1989-92 4-cyl. engines:

Remove cover from diagnostic unit, located behind the left front strut tower. Insert test probe into socket #2 to access injection codes, socket #6 for ignition codes. Depress button and read codes.

Code	Indicated Fault
1-1-3	Faulty fuel injector or wiring, fuel mixture rich/lean
1-2-1	Mass airflow sensor signal absent
1-3-3	Throttle switch, idle position
2-1-3	Throttle switch, full load position
2-2-1	Emission control system malfunction, fuel compensation out of range
2-3-1	Adaptive emission control malfunction at speed
2-3-2	Adaptive emission control malfunction at idle
2-3-3	Closed idle valve or unmetered air leakage
2-4-1	EGR system malfunction
3-1-2	Knock enrichment signal absent
3-2-1	Cold start valve signal absent
3-2-2	No mass airflow sensor hot wire burn-off
4-3-1	EGR temperature sender

SENSORS, INPUT

TEMPERATURE SENSORS

Engine	Year	Sensor	Resistance Ohms @ deg. F/C
All 4-cyl.	1989-95	Coolant	8100-10,800 @ 14/-10 2300-2700 @ 68/20 290-364 @ 176/80
5-cyl., 6-cyl.	1992-98	Coolant	7300 @ 32/0 2800 @ 68/20 1200 @ 104/40 560 @ 140/60 300 @ 176/80 206 @ 194/90 150 @ 212/100
V6 2.8L	1989-90	Coolant	8100-10,800 @ 14/-10 2300-2700 @ 68/20 290-364 @ 176/80
2316cc, 2435cc	1993-96	Intake Air	15,000 @ -4/-20 5800 @ 32/0 2500 @ 68/20 330 @ 176/80
2319cc Turbo	1994	EGR	500,000 @ 32/0 18,000 @ 212/100 2200 @ 392/200 580 @ 572/800

SENSORS, INPUT Continued

TEMPERATURE SENSORS Continued

Engine	Year	Sensor	Resistance Ohms @ deg. F/C
2319cc, 2435cc	1993-98	Transmission Oil	23-31 @ 303/150 1700-2300 @ 32/0
2922cc	1992-98	Transmission Oil	17.8-23.6 @ 320/160 1671-2463 @ 32/0

THROTTLE POSITION SENSOR

Engine	Year	Resistance Ohms Idle	WOT
2316cc	1991-94	2500-5000	300-500
2319cc	1993-97	900-1100	2300-2900
2435cc US	1993-95	900-1100	2300-2900
	1996-98	700-1400	1600-2400
Canada	1993-95	800-1200	2000-3000
2473cc	1995	1000	2500
	1996	700-1400	1600-2400
2922cc	1992-95	1000	2600
	1996	700-1400	1600-2400
	1997-98	1000	2600

MASS AIRFLOW SENSOR

Engine	Fuel System	Year	Resistance Ohms @ Terminal
4-cyl. 2316cc			
SOHC	LH-2.4	1989-90	3.5-4.0 @ 2 & 3 0-1000 @ 2 & 6
DOHC	LH-2.4	1989-90	2.5-4.0 @ 2 & 3 0-1000 @ 2 & 6
All		1991-95	2.5-4.0 @ 2 & 3
5-cyl. 2319cc Turbo	—	1992-95	110 @ 1 & 4
2435cc	LH-3.2	1993-95	110 @ 1 & 4
	M-4.3	1996-97	110 @ 1 & 4
V6 2473cc	M-1.8	1995	2-4 @ 2 & 3
2849cc	LH-2.2	1989-90	2.5-4.0 @ 2 & 3 0-1000 @ 2 & 6
2922cc	M-1.8	1992-97	2.5-4.0 @ 2 & 3

ACTUATORS, OUTPUT

RPM SENSOR

Engine	Year	Resistance (ohms)
2319cc Turbo	1992	215-265
	1993-98	260-340
2435cc	1993-98	260-340
2473cc	1996	260-340
2922cc	1996	260-340
	1997-98	240-400

FUEL INJECTORS

Engine	Year	Resistance (ohms)
2316cc Bendix inj.	1991-94	4
Volvo inj.	1991-95	14-17
Bosch inj.	1991-95	5.5-6.6
2319cc	1993-95	10-14
	1996-97	15.5-16.3
2435cc US	1993-95	10-14
Canada	1993-95	14-18
2435cc	1996-98	15.1-16.7
2473cc	1995	16
	1996	15.5-16.3
2922cc	1992-94	10-14
	1996-98	15.5-16.3

ACTUATORS, OUTPUT Continued

SECONDARY AIR INJECTION CONTROL VALVE

Engine	Fuel System	Year	Resistance Ohms @ Terminal
4-cyl. 2316cc	Bendix	1989-93	4
	LH-2.4	1989-92	8
5-cyl. 2435cc	LH-3.2	1993	9-14 @ 1 & 3
V6 2849cc	LH-2.2	1989-90	20 @ 3 & 4
			20 @ 4 & 5
2922cc	M-1.8	1992-93	25 @ 1 & 3

COMPUTER TIMING ADVANCE

Engine	Year	Transmission	Advance Vacuum Hose Disconnected	W/16 in. Hg Vacuum Applied
2316cc LH-FI ex. Turbo	1989	MT & AT	22-24	48-54

ACTUATORS, OUTPUT Continued

IDLE AIR CONTROL VALVE

Engine	Year	Resistance (ohms)	@	Terminal Number
2316cc	1991-95	4		—
2319cc Turbo	1991-97	10-14		1 & 2
2435cc Canada	1993-95	7.5-8.5		1 & 2
US	1993-97	10-14		1 & 2
2473cc Bosch	1995	25		—
Volvo	1995-96	10-14		1 & 2
2922cc Bosch	1992-97	25		—
Volvo	1992-97	10-14		1 & 2

THIS SECTION CONTAINS:

- COOLING SYSTEM CAPACITIES
- AIR-CONDITIONING SYSTEM REFRIGERANT CAPACITIES
- COOLING SYSTEM AIR-BLEED CHART
- TIRE SIZES & PRESSURES WHEEL RIM SIZES, WHEEL NUT TORQUE

COOLING SYSTEM CAPACITIES

(Includes heater. *Indicates with air conditioning)

Capacities are rounded off to the nearest half unit

MAKE, YEAR & MODEL	LITERS	QUARTS
PASSENGER CARS		
ACURA		
2000-98 2.3CL	7.0	7.5
3.0CL	7.5	8.0
2000-96 3.2TL	7.5	8.0
3.5RL	8.5	9.0
2000-95 SLX	9.0	9.5
2.5TL	7.0	7.5
NSX	12.0	12.5
2000-94 Integra	6.5	7.0
1997-96 2.2CL	7.0	75
1995-91 Legend	7.5	8.0
HD system	8.0	8.5
1994 NSX: W/MT	16.0	17.0
W/AT	16.5	17.5
1994-92 Vigor	6.0	6.5
1993 Integra: All W/AT	5.0	5.5
1.7L W/MT	6.0	6.5
1.8L W/MT	5.0	5.5
NSX: W/MT	12.0	12.5
W/AT	16.5	17.5
1992-91 NSX	12.0	12.5
1992 Integra	5.0	6.0
1991-90 Integra: W/MT	5.0	5.5
W/AT	5.5	6.0
1990-89 Legend: W/MT	9.0	9.5
W/AT	8.5	9.0
1989 Integra	5.5	6.0
AUDI		
1999 A4, 1.8L, 2.8L	6.5	6.9
TT	5.0	5.3
1999-98 A8	9.0	9.5
1999-96 V6, 5V	6.0	6.3
1999-95 A6	8.0	8.4
1998-96 A4, 4-cyl.	7.5	8.0
V6, 2V	8.5	9.0
1997-94 Cabriolet, 100	11.0	12.0
1996-95 S4 Quattro	8.5	9.0
1995 90, Sport90	11.0	11.5
1994-93 90S, 90CS, 90 Quattro	11.0	12.0
1994-92 S4	9.0	10.0
V8 Quattro	8.5	9.0
1993-92 100	12.0	12.5
1992 90, 90 Quattro	8.0	8.5
1991-90 Coupe Quattro	8.0	8.5
V8 Quattro	10.5	11.0
1991-89 100, 200, Quattro	8.0	8.5
80, 90, Quattro: 4-cyl.	7.0	7.5
5-cyl.	8.0	8.5
BMW		
1999 M3, M roadster & coupe	10.7	11.4
740i, iL	12.5	13.2
1999-91 316i, 318i, -iS, ti	6.5	7.0
323, 325; 328i, -iS	10.5	11.0
1999-96 Z3, 1.9L	6.5	7.0
2.8L	10.5	11.1
528i	10.5	11.1
540i	12.0	12.7
1999-93 750iL	13.0	13.5
1998-96 740i, -iL	12.0	12.5
M3	11.0	11.5
1997-94 840Ci	12.5	13.0
1997-91 850 Series	13.0	13.5
1995 320i; 325i, -iS; M3	11.0	11.5
1995-94 525i, -iT	10.5	11.0
530i, -iT; 540i	12.5	13.0
1994 320i	10.5	11.0
1994-93 740i, -iL	12.5	13.0
1993-91 535i	12.0	12.5
M3	9.5	10.0
M5	13.5	14.0
1992-89 750 Series	15.0	16.0
1990-89 325 Series, 535i, 635CSi, 735 Series	12.0	13.0
BUICK		
Century, Regal		
2000-97 All: V6 3100	11.0	11.5
All: V6 3.8L	11.5	12.0
1996-94 Century: 4-cyl.	10.0	10.5
V6	12.5	13.0

MAKE, YEAR & MODEL	LITERS	QUARTS
BUICK Continued		
2000-94 Regal: V6 3.1L	11.0	11.5
V6 3.8L	10.5	11.0
1993 Century: 4-cyl.	8.0	8.5
V6	10.0	10.5
1993-90 Regal: V6 3.1L	12.0	12.5
V6 3.8L	10.5	11.0
1992-89 Century: 4-cyl.	9.0	9.5
V6 2.8L	12.0	12.5
V6 3.3L	12.5	13.0
1989 Regal	12.0	12.5
Electra, Estate Wagon, LeSabre, Park Avenue, Reatta, Riviera, Roadmaster		
2000 LeSabre	9.5	10.0
Park Ave.	12.3	13.0
1999 LeSabre, Park Ave.		
Riviera	12.3	13.0
1998-95 Riviera	12.5	13.0
1998-97 Park Avenue	12.5	13.0
1997-89 Electra, LeSabre	12.5	13.0
1996 Roadmaster: V8 4.3L	17.0	18.0
V8 5.7L	16.0	17.0
1995-94 Roadmaster	13.5	14.0
W/HD radiator	14.0	14.5
1993-91 Roadmaster	16.0	17.0
W/HD radiator	16.5	17.5
1993-89 Reatta, Riviera	12.5	13.0
1990-89 Estate Wagon	15.5	16.0
Skyhawk		
1989 All	7.5	8.0
Skylark, Somerset		
1998-92 4-cyl.	10.0	10.5
V6	12.5	13.0
1991-89 4-cyl.	10.0	10.5
V6	12.0	12.5
CADILLAC		
Allanté		
1993 All	11.5	12.5
1992-91 All	10.0	11.0
1990-89 All	11.5	12.0
Catera		
2000-97 All	10.0	10.5
DeVille, Fleetwood FWD		
2000 DeVille	10.1	10.7
1998 DeVille	10.0	10.5
1997-95 DeVille	12.0	12.5
1994 DeVille: V8 4.6L	12.0	12.5
V8 4.9L	10.5	11.0
1993 DeVille	10.0	10.5
1992-90 All	11.5	12.0
1989 All	12.5	13.5
Eldorado, Seville		
2000-94 All	12.0	12.5
1993-89 All	11.5	12.0
Fleetwood Brougham RWD, Limousine		
1995 Fleetwood	13.0,14.5*	14.0,15.0*
W/HD system	16.0	17.0
1994 Fleetwood	16.5	17.5
1993 Fleetwood	14.5	15.0
W/HD radiator	15.0	15.5
1992-91 All	16.0	16.5
1990-89 V8 5.0L	14.5	15.0
V8 5.7L	16.0	16.5
CHEVROLET		
Beretta, Corsica		
1996-94 4-cyl.	10.0	10.5
V6	12.5	13.0
1993-90 4-cyl. 2.2L	9.0	9.5
4-cyl. 2.3L	10.0	10.5
V6: W/MT	11.0	12.0
W/AT	11.5	12.5
1989 V6: W/MT	15.0	16.0
W/AT	15.5	16.5
4-cyl.	12.5, 13.5*	13.0, 14.0*
Camaro		
2000-99 V6: W/MT	11.0	16.6
W/AT	10.8	11.4
V8: W/MT	11.3	11.9
W/AT	11.2	11.8

MAKE, YEAR & MODEL	LITERS	QUARTS
CHEVROLET Continued		
1998-93 V6: W/MT	12.0	12.5
W/AT	11.5	12.3
V8: W/MT	14.5	15.3
W/AT	14.3	15.1
1992 V6	14.0	15.0
V8 5.0L TBI	16.5, 17.0 *	17.5, 18.0*
V8 5.7L	16.0	16.5
1992-91 V8 5.0L MFI	17.0	18.0
1991-90 V6	13.5	14.5
V8 5.0L TBI	16.5, 17.0*	17.5, 18.0*
V8 5.7L	15.0, 15.5*	16.0, 16.5*
1990 V8 5.0L MFI	16.0, 16.5*	17.0, 17.5*
1989 V6	11.5	12.5
V8 5.0L (305) ex. MFI	14.5	15.5
V8 5.0L (305) MFI	16.0	17.0
V8 5.7L (350)	16.0	17.0
Caprice, Impala SS		
1996 Impala SS: V8 4.3L	17.0	18.0
V8 5.7L	16.0	17.0
1995-94 Caprice, Impala SS	13.5	14.0
W/HD radiator	14.0	14.5
1993 V8 5.0L	16.0	16.5
W/HD radiator	16.5	17.5
V8 5.7L	13.5	14.5
W/HD radiator	14.0	14.5
1992 All	16.5	17.5
1991 V8	15.5	16.5
1990 V8 5.0L (305): Sedan	15.5	16.5
Wagon	15.0	16.0
W/HD radiator	16.5	17.5
V8 5.7L (350)	14.0	15.0
1990-89 V6	11.5	12.0
1989 V8	16.0	17.0
Cavalier		
2000-99 2.2L	9.7	10.3
2.4L	10.1	10.7
1998-95 All	10.0	10.5
1994-92 V6	13.5	14.0
1994-90 4-cyl.	11.0	11.5
1991 V6	12.5	13.0
1990 V6	10.5	11.0
1989 4-cyl.	9.0	9.5
V6	10.5	11.0
Celebrity		
1990 4-cyl.	9.0, 9.5*	9.5, 10.0*
V6	12.5	13.0
1989 4-cyl.	9.0	9.5
V6 Gas	12.0	12.5
Corvette		
2000 MT	11.9	12.6
AT	11.6	12.3
1999 MT	12.2	12.9
AT	11.9	12.6
1998-97 MT	12.5	13.0
AT	12.0	12.5
1996 All	17.0	18.0
1995-91 All: ex. ZR-1	14.0	14.5
ZR-1	17.0	18.0
1990 All	15.5	16.5
1989 All	13.5	14.0
El Camino, GMC Caballero, Malibu, Monte Carlo		
2000 Monte Carlo, Impala: 3.4L	10.7	11.3
3.8L	11.0	11.7
Malibu: 2.4L	10.7	11.3
3.1L	12.9	13.6
1998 Monte Carlo: 3800	11.0	11.5
1998-97 Malibu: 2.4L	10.5	11.5
3100	13.0	13.5
Monte Carlo: 3100	11.0	11.5
1997 Monte Carlo: 3.4L	11.5	12.5
1996-95 All	11.5	12.5
Lumina		
2000 3.1L	10.9	11.6
1999 3.1L	10.9	11.6
3.8L	11.0	11.7
1998-94 V6 3.1L	11.0	11.5
V6 3.4L	11.5	12.5
1993 4-cyl.	11.0	12.0
1993-92 V6 3.1L	12.0	12.5
V6 3.4L: W/AT	12.0	12.5
W/MT	12.5	13.0
1992 4-cyl.	9.0	9.5

COOLING SYSTEM CAPACITIES

Capacities are rounded off to the nearest half unit

(Includes heater. *Indicates with air conditioning)

MAKE, YEAR & MODEL	LITERS	QUARTS
CHEVROLET Continued		
1991-90 4-cyl.	9.0	9.5
V6: Euro	12.0	12.5
Z34: W/MT	12.5	13.0
W/AT	12.0	12.5
Spectrum		
1989 All: ex. Turbo	6.5	7.0
Turbo	7.0	7.5
Sprint		
1991-89 All	4.0	4.5
CHRYSLER		
300 M		
2000-99 3.5L	9.0	9.5
Cirrus		
2000-95 4-cyl. 2.0L	8.0	8.5
4-cyl. 2.4L	8.5	9.0
V6 2.5L	10.0	10.5
Concorde, Conquest, Laser		
2000-99 2.7L, 3.2L	9.0	9.5
1998 All	8.0	8.0
1997-93 V6 3.3L	10.0	11.0
V6 3.5L	12.0	12.5
1989 All	9.0	9.5
E Class, LHS, New Yorker		
2000-99 3.5L	9.0	9.5
1997-94 3.3L	10.0	11.0
3.5L	12.0	12.5
1993-90 All	9.0	9.5
1989 All	9.0	9.5
Turbo	8.5	9.0
Fifth Avenue, Imperial		
1993-90 All	9.0	9.5
1989 All	14.5, 15.5*	15.5, 16.5*
LeBaron, TC		
1995 All	8.5	9.0
1994-89 4-cyl.	8.5	9.0
V6	9.0	9.5
Sebring		
2000-96 Ex. Convertible	7.0	7.5
Convertible:		
4-cyl. 2.4L	8.5	9.0
V6 2.5L	10.0	10.5
DAEWOO		
1999-98 Lanos	7.0	7.5
Nubira	7.0	7.5
Leganza	7.0	7.5
DAIHATSU		
1992-89 Charade:		
3-cyl.	4.0	4.5
4-cyl.	5.5	6.0
DODGE		
600, Aries, Daytona, Dynasty, Lancer, Shadow, Spirit		
1995-89 4-cyl.	8.5	9.0
V6	9.0	9.5
Avenger		
2000-96 All	7.0	7.5
Charger, Omni		
1990-89 All	8.5	9.0
Colt, Colt Vista		
1996-92 1.5L	5.0	5.5
1.8L	6.0	6.5
2.4L	6.5	7.0
1991-89 Colt:		
1.5L, 1.8L	5.0	5.5
1.6L DOHC	6.0	6.5
Vista	7.0	7.5
Diplomat		
1989 All	14.5, 15.5*	15.5, 16.5*
Intrepid		
2000-99 2.7L, 3.2L	9.0	9.5
1998 All	7.5	8.0
1997-93 V6 3.3L	10.0	11.0
V6 3.5L	12.0	12.5
Monaco		
1992-90 All	8.0	8.5

MAKE, YEAR & MODEL	LITERS	QUARTS
DODGE Continued		
Neon		
2000 All	6.0	6.5
1999-95 All	6.0, 6.5*	6.5, 7.0*
Stealth		
1996-91 All	8.0	8.5
Stratus		
2000-95 4-cyl. 2.0L	8.0	8.5
4-cyl. 2.4L	8.5	9.0
V6 2.5L	10.0	10.5
Viper		
2000-99 All	16.5	17.5
1997 8.0L	12.0	13.0
1996 8.0L	17.0	18.0
1995-92 8.0L	15.0	16.0
EAGLE		
1998-97 Talon	7.0	7.5
1997-93 Vision: V6 3.3L	10.0	11.0
V6 3.5L	12.0	12.5
1996-92 Summit Wagon: 1.8L	6.0	6.5
2.4L	6.5	7.0
1996-91 Summit: 1.5L	5.0	5.5
1.8L	6.0	6.5
Talon: 1.8L	6.0	6.5
2.0L	7.0	7.5
1993-89 2000 GTX	7.0	7.5
1992-89 Premier	8.0	8.5
1991-89 Vista	7.0	7.5
1990 Talon	7.0	7.5
1990-89 Summit: 1.5L	5.0	5.5
1.6L	6.0	6.5
1989 Medallion	6.5	7.0
FORD		
Aspire, Festiva		
1997 MT	5.0	5.5
AT	6.0	6.5
1996-94 All	6.0	6.5
1993-89 All	5.0	5.5
Contour		
2000-99 2.5L	9.5	10.0
2000-95 2.0L: W/MT	6.5	7.0
W/AT	7.0	7.5
1998-95 2.5L	8.5	9.0
Crown Victoria, LTD		
2000-99 4.6L	15.0	16.0
1998-92 All	13.5	14.0
1991-89 All	13.5	14.0
Escort, EXP		
2000-99 W/AT	6.0	6.5
W/MT	5.0	5.5
1998 2.0L Zetec w/AT	7.0	7.5
w/MT	6.6	7.0
2.0 SPI w/AT	7.5	8.0
w/MT	5.5	6.0
1997-91 W/MT	5.0	5.5
W/AT	6.0	6.5
1990-89 W/MT	8.0, 6.5*	8.5, 7.0*
W/AT	8.0, 7.0*	8.5, 7.5 *
Focus		
2000 All	5.5	6.0
Mustang		
2000-94 V6	11.0	12.0
V8	13.5	14.0
1993 4-cyl.	8.0	8.5
W/AC	9.0	9.5
V8	13.0	14.0
1992-89 4-cyl.	9.5	10.0
V8 5.0L (302)	13.5	14.0
Probe		
1997-93 4-cyl.	7.0	7.5
V6	7.5	8.0
1992-89 All	7.5	8.0
Taurus		
2000-99 3.0L Vulcan	11.0	11.5
3.0L Duratec, 3.4L	10.0	10.5
1998-93 V6 3.0L: ex. SHO	10.5	11.0
SHO & 3.2L	11.0	11.5
V6 3.8L	11.5	12.0

MAKE, YEAR & MODEL	LITERS	QUARTS
FORD Continued		
1992-89 4-cyl.	8.0	8.5
V6 3.0L: ex. SHO	10.5	11.0
SHO	11.0	11.5
V6 3.8L	12.0	12.5
Tempo		
1994-92 W/MT	7.5	8.0
W/AT	8.0	8.5
1991 All	7.5	8.0
1990-89 W/MT	7.0	7.5
W/AT	7.5	8.0
Thunderbird		
1997-93 V6	12.0	12.5
V8	13.5	14.0
1992 V6 3.8L	12.0	12.5
1992-91 V8 5.0L	13.5	14.0
1991 V6 3.8L	11.5	12.0
1990-89 V6 3.8L (232): FI	11.0	11.5
Supercharged	11.5	12.0
GEO		
2000 Metro: 3-cyl.	3.9	4.1
4-cyl. W/MT	4.5	5.0
W/AT	5.0	5.5
2000-97 Prism: w/MT	6.2	6.6
w/AT	6.1	6.4
1996-93 Prizm	6.0	6.5
1994-89 Metro	4.0	4.5
1993-92 Storm: W/MT	7.0	7.0
W/AT	7.5	7.5
1992-91 Prizm	5.5	6.0
1991-90 Storm: 4-cyl. SOHC	7.0	7.5
4-cyl. DOHC: W/MT	7.0	7.5
W/AT	7.5	8.0
1990-89 Prizm	6.0	6.5
1989 Spectrum	6.5	7.0
HONDA		
Accord		
2000-98 V6	7.5	8.0
4 cyl.	7.0	7.5
1997-94 All	7.0	7.5
1993-89 W/MT	6.5	7.0
W/AT	7.0	7.5
Civic, CR-V, CRX, Del Sol		
2000-98 Ex. CVT	4.0	4.5
CVT	4.5	4.5
2000-97 CR-V	4.0	4.5
1997-96 Civic	3.0	3.5
1997-94 Del Sol: 1.6L VTEC	4.0	4.5
Others	3.5	4.0
1993-92 All	3.5	4.0
1991-89 Civic, CRX	5.5	6.0
Odyssey		
2000-99	8.5	9.0
1998-95 V6	6.5	7.0
Prelude		
2000-97 All	7.0	7.5
1996-91 2.0L, 2.2L	7.0	7.5
2.2L VTEC, 2.3L	7.5	8.0
1990-89 Ex. FI: W/MT	7.0	7.5
W/AT	7.5	8.0
FI	8.0	8.5
S2000		
2000 All	7.5	8.0
HYUNDAI		
2000 Accent	6.5	7.0
Elantra, Tiburon	6.0	6.5
2000-99 Sonata	5.5	6.0
1999-92 Accent, Elantra, Tiburon	6.0	6.5
1997-95 Sonata: DOHC	7.5	8.0
V6	8.5	9.0
1995 Scoupe	6.5	7.0
1994 Scoupe	5.5	6.0
1994-92 Sonata: 4-cyl.	7.5	8.0
V6	9.0	9.5
1994-89 Excel	5.0	5.5
1993-91 Scoupe	5.0	5.5
1991-89 Sonata: 4-cyl.	7.0	7.5
V6	9.0	9.5

(Includes heater. *Indicates with air conditioning)

Capacities are rounded off to the nearest half unit

MAKE, YEAR & MODEL	LITERS	QUARTS
INFINITI		
2000 I30	7.5	8.0
2000-99 G20	6.0	6.5
2000-97 QX4	10.5	11.0
Q45	11.5	12.5
1999-96 I30	8.5	9.0
1997-93 J30	9.0	10.0
1996-91 G20: W/MT	6.0	6.5
W/AT	6.5	7.0
1995-90 Q45	10.5	11.0
1994-92 M30	9.0	9.5
1991-90 M30	8.5	9.0
ISUZU		
1999 Oasis	9.0	9.5
1998-95 Oasis	6.5	7.0
1993-90 Stylus: W/MT	7.0	7.5
W/AT	7.5	8.0
Impulse: SOHC: W/MT	7.0	7.5
W/AT	7.5	8.0
1993-90 Impulse: DOHC	7.5	8.0
1989 I-Mark: ex. Turbo	6.5	7.0
Turbo	7.0	7.5
Impulse	9.0	9.5
JAGUAR		
2000 S-Type: V6	10.5	11.1
V8	10.0	10.6
1999 XK8	11.6	12.3
XJ8, XJ8L, XJR	10.1	10.7
1998 XJ8, XJ8L, XJR-8,		
VandenPlas: ex. SC	10.0	10.5
XK8	9.5	10.0
1997 XJ6: 4.0L, ex. SC	5.0	5.5
4.0L Supercharged	7.5	7.5
6.0L	14.5	15.5
1996-95 XJ12	14.5	15.5
XJ6	8.0	8.5
XJR	9.0	9.5
1996-93 XJS: 6-cyl. 4.0L	10.0	10.5
12-cyl. 6.0L	20.0	21.0
1994 XJ12	15.5	16.0
1994-93 XJ6	9.0	9.5
1992 XJS: 6-cyl. 4.0L	11.5	12.5
12-cyl. 5.3L	20.0	21.0
1992-91 XJ6	12.5	13.0
1990 XJ6	9.5	10.0
KIA		
2000-95 Sportage	7.5	8.0
2000-93 Sephia	6.0	6.5
LEXUS		
2000-98 GS400	9.5	10.0
2000-97 ES300	9.0	9.5
2000-94 LS400	11.0	11.5
2000-93 GS300	7.5	8.0
2000-92 SC300	8.5	9.0
SC400	11.5	12.0
1996-92 ES300	8.5	9.0
1993-90 LS400	10.5	11.0
1991-90 ES250	9.5	10.0
LINCOLN		
2000 LS w/V6	10.5	11.0
W/V8	11.5	12.0
2000-99 Town Car	15.0	16.0
2000-98 Continental	15.0	16.0
1998-94 Mark VIII	15.0	16.0
1998-89 Town Car	13.5	14.0
1997 Continental	11.5	12.0
1996-95 Continental	13.5	14.0
1994-89 Continental	11.5	12.0
1993-89 Mark VIII, Mark VII	13.5	14.0
MAZDA		
Miata		
2000-90 All	6.0	6.5
Millenia		
2000-95 All	7.5	8.0
RX-7		
1995-93 All	8.5	9.0
1992-89 Ex. Turbo	7.5	8.0
Turbo	8.5	9.0

MAKE, YEAR & MODEL	LITERS	QUARTS
MAZDA Continued		
323, GLC, MX-3, Precidia, Protegé		
2000-99 1.6L	6.0	6.5
1.8L	7.5	8.0
1998-95 Protegé	6.0	6.5
1995-92 MX-3, Precidia: 4-cyl	6.0	6.5
V6	7.5	8.0
1994-89 323, Protegé: ex. Turbo:		
W/MT	5.0	5.5
W/AT	6.0	6.5
Turbo	6.0	6.5
626, MX-6		
2000-98 All	7.5	8.0
1997-93 4-cyl.	7.0	7.5
V6	7.5	8.0
1992-89 All	7.5	8.0
929, Serenia		
1995 W/heater	9.5	10.0
W/o heater	9.0	9.5
1994-90 All	9.5	10.0
1989 W/MT	9.0	9.5
W/AT	9.5	10.0
MERCEDES-BENZ		
1999 SL500	12.5	13.2
SL600	20.0	21.1
ML430	14.0	14.7
1999-98 CLK43	11.1	11.7
CL500	15.5	16.4
CL600	20.0	21.1
CLK320	9.0	9.5
E300, E320	10.0	10.6
E420, E430, E55	11.2	11.8
ML320	12.0	12.7
S320	11.5	12.1
S420, S500	15.5	16.4
SLK230	8.3	8.8
1998-94 C-Class: C220, C230	9.5	10.0
C280, C36AMG	10.0	10.5
C43 AMG	11.2	11.8
E-Class: E420, E500	15.5	16.5
E300 Diesel, E320	9.5	10.0
S-Class: S320	14.5	15.5
S350 Turbo Diesel	11.0	11.5
1998-94 S600	20.0	21.0
SL-Class: SL320	11.5	12.0
SL500	15.5	16.5
1997-94 SL600	20.0	21.0
1993-92 300D, -SD	11.0	11.5
300SE	14.5	15.5
400E, -SEL	15.5	16.5
500E, -SEC, -SEL, -SL	15.5	16.5
600SEC, -SEL, -SL	20.0	21.0
1993-91 190E	9.5	10.0
300CE, -E, -TE -4MATIC,		
SE, -SEL	9.5	10.0
300SL	11.5	12.0
350SD, -SDL	10.0	10.5
1991 500SL	15.0	16.0
1991-89 420SEL, 560SEC, -SEL	13.0	13.7
1990-89 190E	10.0	10.5
300 Series	10.0	10.5
1989-88 190D 2.5 & Turbo	8.5	9.0
MERCURY		
Capri		
1994-93 W/MT ex. Turbo	5.0	5.5
W/AT or Turbo	6.0	6.5
1992-91 All: ex. Turbo	5.0	5.5
Turbo	6.0	6.5
Cougar		
2000-99 2.0L	6.5	7.0
2.5L	9.5	10.0
1997-91 V6	12.0	12.5
V8	13.5	14.0
1990-89 V6 3.8L (232): FI	11.0	11.5
Supercharged	11.5	12.0
Grand Marquis, Marquis		
2000-99 4.6L	15.0	16.0
1998-94 All	13.5	14.0
1993-92 All	13.0	13.5
1991-89 All	13.5	14.0

MAKE, YEAR & MODEL	LITERS	QUARTS
MERCURY Continued		
Mystique		
2000-99 2.5L	9.5	10.0
2000-95 2.0L: W/MT	6.5	7.0
W/AT	7.0	7.5
1998-95 2.5L	8.5	9.0
Sable		
2000-98 3.0L 2V	11.0	11.5
3.0L 4V	10.0	10.5
1997-89 V6 3.0L	10.5	11.0
3.0L 4V, 3.4L SHO	11.0	11.5
V6 3.8L	11.5	12.0
Topaz		
1994 4-cyl.	7.5	8.0
V6	11.0	12.0
1993 4-cyl.	8.0	8.5
V6	9.5	10.0
1992 W/MT	7.5	8.0
W/AT	8.0	8.5
1991 All	7.5	8.0
1990-89 W/MT	7.0	7.5
W/AT	7.5	8.0
Tracer		
1999-89 W/MT	5.0	5.5
W/AT	6.0	6.5
Villager		
2000-99	10.5	11.0
1998-93 W/Trailer Tow	11.5	12.5
W/rear heater	13.0	14.0
W/o Trailer Tow	10.5	11.5
W/rear heater	12.0	12.5
MERKUR		
1989 Scorpio	8.5	9.0
MITSUBISHI		
2000 Eclipse: 2.4L	7.0	7.5
3.0L	8.0	8.5
2000-99 Galant: 2.4L	7.0	7.5
3.0L	8.0	8.5
2000-90 Mirage: 1.5L	5.0	5.5
1.8L	6.0	6.5
2000-98 Diamante	9.5	10.0
2000-90 Mirage: 1.5L	5.0	5.5
1.8L	6.0	6.5
1999-95 Eclipse	7.0	7.5
1999-91 3000GT	8.0	8.5
1998-89 Galant	7.0	7.5
1997-95 Diamante Wagon	9.5	10.0
1997-92 Diamante	8.0	8.5
1996-92 Expo: 1.8L	6.0	6.5
2.4L	6.5	7.0
1994-90 Eclipse: 1.8L	6.0	6.5
2.0L	7.0	7.5
1994-89 Precis	5.5	6.0
1989 Mirage: 1.5L	5.0	5.5
1.6L	6.0	6.5
Sigma	9.0	9.5
Starion	9.0	9.5
NISSAN		
200SX, 240SX		
1998 200SX	5.0, 5.5*	5.5, 6.0*
1998-95 240SX	7.0	7.5
1997 200SX: 1.6L	5.5	6.0
2.0L	6.0	6.5
1995 200SX: 1.6L	5.0	5.5
2.0L	5.5	6.0
1994-89 All	6.5	7.0
300ZX		
1996-90 All	9.0	9.5
1989 Ex. Turbo	10.5	11.0
Turbo	11.0	11.5
Altima, Axxess, Multi, Stanza		
2000-98 All	7.0	7.5
1997-93 All	8.0	8.5
1992-89 All	7.5	8.0
Maxima		
2000 All	7.5	8.0
1999-98 All	8.5	9.0
1997-95 All	9.0	9.5
1994-91 SOHC	8.5	9.0
DOHC	10.5	11.0
1990-89 All	9.0	9.5

COOLING SYSTEM CAPACITIES

Capacities are rounded off to the nearest half unit

(Includes heater. *Indicates with air conditioning)

MAKE, YEAR & MODEL	LITERS	QUARTS
NISSAN Continued		
Micra		
1991-89 All 4.5		5.0
NX, Sentra, 200SX		
1999-98 W/MT 5.0		5.5
W/AT 5.5		6.0
1997-91 1.6L 5.5		6.0
2.0L 6.0		6.5
1990-89 Pulsar:		
SOHC W/MT 5.5		6.0
SOHC W/AT & DOHC . 6.0		6.5
Sentra: 2WD 5.5		6.0
4WD 6.0		6.5
Quest		
2000-99 . . . . 10.5		11.0
1998-93 W/Trailer Tow 11.5		12.5
W/rear heater 13.0		14.0
W/o Trailer Tow 10.5		11.5
W/rear heater 12.0		12.5
OLDSMOBILE		
Achieva, Calais		
1998-95 4-cyl. 10.0		10.5
V6 . . . . 12.5		13.0
1994-91 4-cyl. ex. HO. 10.0		10.5
HO 10.5		11.0
V6 . . . . 10.5		11.0
1990-89 4-cyl. 10.0		10.5
V6 . . . . 12.0		12.5
Alero		
2000-99 2.4L 9.5		10.0
3.4L 11.8		12.5
Aurora		
1999-95 All 12.5		13.0
Cutlass, Ciera, Cutlass Supreme		
1998-97 Cutlass: 2.4L 11.0		11.5
3100 . . . . 13.0		13.5
1998-95 Cutlass Supreme:		
V6 3.1L 11.0		11.5
V6 3.4L 11.5		12.5
1996 Ciera: 4-cyl. 10.0		10.5
V6 . . . . 12.5		13.0
1994-93 Cutlass Ciera, Cutlass Cruiser:		
4-cyl. 8.0		8.5
V6 . . . . 11.0		11.5
1994-90 Cutlass Supreme 12.0		12.5
1992 Cutlass Ciera, Cutlass Cruiser:		
4-cyl. 2.5L 7.5		8.0
V6 3.3L 9.0		9.5
1991-90 Ciera, Cutlass Cruiser:		
4-cyl. 2.5L 7.5		8.0
V6 3.3L 9.5, 10.0*		10.0, 10.5*
1989 Cutlass Supreme 11.5, 12.0*		12.0, 12.5*
Ciera, Cutlass Cruiser:		
4-cyl. 2.5L (151) 9.0		9.5
W/HD cooling 11.5		12.0
V6 2.8L (173) 11.5		12.0
W/HD cooling 12.0		12.5
V6 3.8L 11.5, 12.0*		12.0, 13.0*
Intrigue		
2000-98 . . . . 9.5		10.
88, Ninety-Eight, Regency, Toronado, Troféo		
1999 Eighty-Eight, LSS 12.3		13.0
1998-97 All 12.5		13.0
1996-91 Eighty-Eight, Ninety-Eight 12.5		13.0
Custom Cruiser 16.0		17.0
W/HD Cooling 16.5		17.5
1992-89 Toronado, Troféo 12.0		13.0
W/HD Cooling 12.5		13.5
1990-89 Custom Cruiser . . . 14.5, 15.5*		15.5, 16.5*
Eighty-Eight 12.0		12.5
Ninety-Eight 12.0		12.5
PLYMOUTH		
Acclaim, Caravelle, Duster, Reliant, Sundance		
1995-89 4-cyl. 8.5		9.0
V6 . . . . 9.0		9.5
Breeze		
2000-95 4-cyl. 2.0L 8.0		8.5
4-cyl. 2.4L 8.5		9.0

MAKE, YEAR & MODEL	LITERS	QUARTS
PLYMOUTH Continued		
Colt, Colt Vista		
1996-92 1.5L 5.0		5.5
1.8L 6.0		6.5
2.4L 6.5		7.0
1991-89 Colt: 1.5L, 1.8L 5.0		5.5
1.6L DOHC 6.0		6.5
Vista 7.0		7.5
Caravelle Salon, Gran Fury		
1989 All 14.5, 15.5*		15.5, 16.5*
Horizon, Turismo		
1990-89 All 8.5		9.0
Laser		
1994-90 1.8L 6.0		6.5
2.0L 7.0		7.5
Neon		
2000 All 6.0		6.5
1999-95 All 6.0,6.5*		6.5,7.0*
Prowler		
2000-97 3.5L 10.5		11.0
PONTIAC		
6000, Grand Am, Le Mans		
2000-99 2.2L 9.7		10.3
2.4L 10.1		10.7
1998-94 Grand Am: 4-cyl. . . . 10.0		10.5
V6 . . . . 12.5		13.0
1993-92 Grand Am 10.0		10.5
1993-89 LeMans 7.5		8.0
1991 Grand Am:		
4-cyl. 2.3L		
ex. H.O., 2.5L 10.0		10.5
4-cyl. 2.3L H.O. 10.5		11.0
1991-90 6000: 4-cyl. . . . 9.0, 1 2.5*		9.5, 13.0*
V6 . . . . 11.5		12.5
1990 Grand Am:		
4-cyl. 2.3L ex. H.O . . . 7.0		7.5
4-cyl. 2.3L H.O., 2.5L . . 7.5		8.0
1989 6000: 4-cyl. 9.0		9.5
V6 ex. MFI 11.0		11.5
V6 W/MFI & Diesel . . . 12.0		12.5
Grand Am 7.5		8.0
Bonneville, Parisienne, Safari		
2000-92 Bonneville 12.5		13.0
1991-89 Bonneville 12.5		13.0
1989 Safari V8 . . . . 16.0		17.0
Firebird		
1998-93 V6: W/MT 12.0		12.5
W/AT 11.5		12.5
V8 . . . . 14.5		15.5
1992-91 V6 3.1L (191) 14.0		14.5
V8 5.0L (305) MFI 17.0		18.0
V8 5.7L (350) 15.5		16.5
1992-90 V8 5.0L (305) TBI . . 16.5, 17.0*		17.5, 18.0 *
1990 V6 3.1L (191) 13.5		14.5
V8 5.0L (305) MFI . . . 16.0, 16.5*		17.0, 17.5*
V8 5.7L (350) 15.0, 15.5*		16.0, 16.5*
1989 V6 2.8L (173) 11.5		12.5
V8 5.0L (305) ex. MFI . 14.5		15.5
V8 5.0L (305) MFI,		
5.7L (350) 16.0		17.0
Firefly		
1996-89 All 4.0		4.5
Grand Prix		
1998 V6 3100 . . . . 10.5		11.0
V6 3800 . . . . 11.5		12.5
1996-95 V6 3.1L 11.0		11.5
V6 3.4L 11.5		12.0
1994 V6 3.1L: W/OD 11.5		13.0
W/o OD 11.0		12.5
V6 3.4L 11.5		13.0
1993-91 4-cyl. 2.3L 9.0		9.5
V6 3.1L 12.0		12.5
V6 3.4L: W/AT 12.0		12.5
W/MT 12.5		13.0
1990 4-cyl. 2.3L 8.5		9.0
V6 3.1L: ex. Turbo . . 12.0		12.5
Turbo 12.5		13.0
1989 V6 2.8L, 3.1L 12.0		12.5

MAKE, YEAR & MODEL	LITERS	QUARTS
PONTIAC Continued		
Sunbird		
1994-91 Sunbird: 4-cyl. 11.0		11.5
V6 . . . . 13.5		14.0
1990-89 Sunbird 7.5		8.0
Sunfire		
1998-95 All 10.0		10.5
Tempest		
1991-90 4-cyl. 9.0		9.5
V6: W/MT 11.0		12.0
W/AT 11.5		12.5
1989 4-cyl. 12.5, 13.0*		13.5, 14.0*
V6: W/MT 15.0		16.0
W/AT 15.5		16.5
PORSCHE		
1999-98 911 . . . . 22.5		23.5
1998-97 Boxster 17.0		18.0
1995-89 928 . . . . 16.0		17.0
1995-94 968 . . . . 8.0		8.5
1993-90 944, 968 . . . . 8.0		8.5
1989 944 . . . . 8.5		9.0
SAAB		
1999 9-3 1985cc 8.5		8.7
9-5 2290cc 7.4		7.6
2962cc 7.2		7.4
1998-97 9000: 2.3L 9.0		9.5
V6 3.0L 8.5		9.0
900: 2.3L, 2.3L Turbo . 8.5		9.0
V6 2.5L 8.0		8.5
1994 900 . . . . 8.5		9.0
V6 . . . . 8.0		8.5
1994-89 9000 . . . . 9.0		9.5
1993-89 900 . . . . 10.0		10.5
SATURN		
2000 L-Series		
2.2L w/MT 7.0		7.4
2.2L w/AT 6.9		7.3
3.0L 7.4		7.8
2000-91 S-Series 6.5		7.0
SUBARU		
1999 Forester: MT 5.5		5.8
AT 5.7		6.0
1999-98 Impreza: 2.2L 5.8		6.2
2.5L 6.0		6.3
1999-96 Legacy: 2.2L 5.5		6.0
2.5L 6.0		6.5
1998 Forester 6.0		6.3
1997 Impreza 6.0		6.5
1997-95 SVX 7.5		8.0
1996-94 Impreza 6.0		6.5
1995-94 Justy 5.0		5.5
Legacy: Ex. Turbo . . . 6.0		6.5
Turbo 7.0		7.5
1993-92 SVX 7.0		7.5
1993-90 Justy: FWD, W/MT W/carb 4.5		5.0
Others W/FI 5.0		5.5
Legacy: FWD 6.0		6.0
4WD 7.0		7.5
Loyale: Ex. Turbo . . . 5.5		6.0
Turbo 6.0		6.5
1991-89 XT: 4-cyl. 5.5		6.0
V6 . . . . 7.0		7.5
1989 1800: Ex. Turbo 5.5		6.0
Turbo 6.0		6.5
Justy 4.5		5.0
SUZUKI		
2000 Esteem 5.0		5.5
2000-89 Swift 4.5		5.0
1999-95 Esteem 4.0		4.5
TOYOTA		
Avalon		
2000 All 9.0		9.5
1999-95 All 9.5		10.0
Camry, Solara		
2000-97 4-cyl. 7.0		7.5
V6 . . . . 9.0		9.5
1996-92 4-cyl. 6.0		6.5
V6 . . . . 8.5		9.0
1991-89 4-cyl. 6.5		7.0
V6 . . . . 9.5		10.0

(Includes heater. *Indicates with air conditioning)

Capacities are rounded off to the nearest half unit

MAKE, YEAR & MODEL	LITERS	QUARTS
TOYOTA Continued		
Celica		
2000 All	5.5	6.0
1999-94 1.8L: W/MT	6.0	6.5
W/AT	6.5	7.0
2.2L: W/MT	6.5	7.0
W/AT	7.0	7.5
1993-90 1.6L: W/MT	5.0	5.5
W/AT	5.5	6.0
2.0L Turbo	6.5	7.0
2.2L	6.0	6.5
1989 Ex. Turbo	6.0	6.5
Turbo	6.5	7.0
Corolla		
2000 All	5.5	6.0
1999-97 All	6.0	6.5
1996-95 1.6L W/Toyo radiator	5.0	5.5
1996-94 AT: All	6.0	6.5
MT: 1.6L W/Harrison radiator	6.0	6.5
1.6L W/Nippondenso radiator	5.0	5.5
1.8L W/Harrison radiator	6.0	6.5
1.8L W/Nippondenso radiator	5.5	6.0
1993-90 All	6.0	6.5
1989 Ex. FI	5.5	6.0
FI	6.0	6.5
Cressida		
1992-89 All	8.5	9.0
Echo		
2000 All	4.0	4.5
MR2		
1995-91 2.0L Turbo	13.5	14.5
2.2L	13.0	13.5
1989 W/MT	12.5	13.0
W/AT	13.0	13.5
Paseo, Tercel		
1999-89 All	5.0	5.5
Sienna		
2000-89 W/o rear heater	9.5	10.0
W/rear heater	10.5	11.0
Supra		
1998 Ex. Turbo	8.0	8.5
Turbo	9.0	9.5
1997-93 Ex. Turbo: W/MT	7.5	8.0
W/AT	8.5	9.0
Turbo	9.5	10.0
1992-89 All	8.0	8.5
VOLKSWAGEN		
1999-98 Passat: 1.8L Turbo: MT	5.6	5.9
AT	6.2	6.5
2.8L	10.0	10.4
Others w/2.8L	9.0	9.5
All 2.0L	5.0	5.3
All 1.9L	6.0	6.3
Cabrio	6.3	6.7
1997-96 Golf: GL	6.0	6.5
GTI	6.0	6.5
GTI VR6	8.0	8.5
Jetta: GL, GLS	6.0	6.5
GLX	8.0	8.5
Passat: GLX, TDI	9.0	9.5
1997-95 Cabrio	6.0	6.5
1996 Passat: GLS	6.5	7.0
1995 GTI, Jetta GLX	9.0	9.5
Passat	9.0	9.5
1995-94 Golf, Jetta	6.0	6.5
1994 Corrado, Passat	8.5	9.0
1993-91 Corrado	7.0	7.5
Cabriolet	5.0	5.0
1993-90 Passat	7.0	7.5
1993-89 Golf, GTI, Jetta	7.0	7.5
Fox: W/o AC	6.0	6.5
W/AC	6.5	7.0
1990 Corrado, Jetta	6.5	7.0
1990-89 Cabriolet	4.5	5.0

MAKE, YEAR & MODEL	LITERS	QUARTS
VOLVO		
1999 S80 2922cc	8.8	9.3
2783cc	9.6	10.1
1999-98 C70, S70, V70	7.0	7.4
S90, V90	10.0	10.5
1997-96 850 2.3L	7.0	7.4
2.4L	7.2	7.6
1995-93 850GLT	7.0	7.5
1995-92 960	10.0	10.5
1995-91 940	9.5	10.0
1993-92 240: W/MT	9.5	10.0
W/AT	9.0	9.5
1993-89 740 Gasoline, Coupe	9.5	10.0
1991-89 200 Series: W/MT	9.5	10.0
W/AT	9.0	9.5
1990 760, 780: 4-cyl. Turbo	10.0	10.5
V6	9.5	10.0
1989 760, 780: 4-cyl.	9.5	10.0
V6	10.0	10.5

LIGHT TRUCKS, UTILITY VEHICLES, VANS

MAKE, YEAR & MODEL	LITERS	QUARTS
ACURA		
1999-98 SLX: MT	9.0	9.5
AT	9.5	10.0
1997 SLX	9.0	9.5
1996-95 SLX: MT	8.5	9.0
AT	9.0	9.5
ASUNA		
1993-92 Sunrunner	5.0	5.5
CADILLAC TRUCKS		
2000-99 Escalade	16.5	17.5
CHEVROLET/GMC TRUCKS		
Astro, Safari		
2000-98 W/o rear heater	12.8	13.5
W/rear heater	15.6	16.5
1997-96 V6	13.5	14.5
W/rear heater	15.5	16.5
1993-89 4-cyl	9.5	10.0
W/rear heater	12.0	13.0
V6	13.0	13.5
W/rear heater	15.5	16.5
Blazer, Jimmy, Tahoe, Yukon		
2000-99 Yukon Denali	16.5	17.5
Yukon, Tahoe, w/Code R	16.5	17.5
W/Code R w/rear heater	19.0	20.0
W/Code J	23.5	25.0
W/Code J w/rear heater	26.0	27.5
1995 V8 5.7L	16.5	17.5
W/rear heater	19.0	20.0
V8 6.5L Diesel	22.0	23.5
W/rear heater	26.0	27.5
V8 7.4L	23.5	25.0
W/rear heater	26.0	27.5
1995-93 V6 4.3L	11.5	12.0
1994-93 V8 5.7L	16.5, 17.0*	17.5, 18.0*
V8 7.4L	22.0, 23.5*	23.0, 25.0*
1991 V8 5.7L	16.5, 17.5*	17.5, 18.5*
V8 6.2L Diesel	22.5, 23.5*	24.0, 25.0*
V8 7.4L	21.5, 22.5*	23.0, 24.0*
1990-89 6-cyl. 4.8L	14.5, 15.5*	15.5, 16.5*
V8 5.7L	16.5, 17.5*	17.5, 18.5*
V8 6.2L Diesel	23.5	25.0
Chevrolet Lumina Minivan, Venture, GMC APV		
1999 W/o rear heater	9.1	9.6
W/rear heater	11.3	11.9
1998-96 All	11.5	12.0
W/rear heater	13.0	13.5
1995-92 V6 3.1L	11.5, 12.0*	12.0, 13.0*
W/rear AC	13.5	14.5
W/rear heater	13.0	14.0
V6 3.8L	11.0	11.5
W/rear AC or heater	12.5	13.5
1991 All	12.5	13.5
W/rear AC	14.0	15.0
1990 All	12.5	13.5

MAKE, YEAR & MODEL	LITERS	QUARTS
CHEVROLET/GMC TRUCKS Continued		
GMT800 (Silverado, Sierra)		
1999 Code W W/MT	12.2	12.9
W/AT	11.9	12.6
Code V W/MT	13.0	13.7
W/AT	12.7	13.4
Code T W/AT	12.7	13.4
W/AT	14.1	14.9
With optional air cond.		
Code U W/AT	14.4	15.2
W/MT	14.0	14.8
With optional eng oil cooler		
W/AT	14.0	14.8
W/AT	13.6	14.4
With optional eng oil cooler		
6.5L Diesel w/rear heater	26.0	27.5
W/o rear heater	22.2	23.5
GMT400 (C/K Pickup, Sierra)		
1999 Code M, R	16.6	17.5
Code J	23.5	25.0
Code J (C3500HD)	27.0	28.5
6.5L Diesel w/rear heater	26.0	27.5
W/o rear heater	22.0	23.5
C, K, R, V Series Pickups, Suburban		
1997-95 4.3L	12.5	13.0
5.0L	16.5, 17.0*	17.5, 18.0*
5.7L	16.5, 19.0*	17.5, 20.0*
HD 3500	25.0, 25.5*	26.5, 27.0*
6.5L	26.0	27.5
7.4L	23.5, 26.0*	25.0, 27.5*
HD 3500	25.0, 27.0*	26.5, 28.5*
1994-89 V6 4.3L	10.5	11.0
6-cyl. 4.8L	14.5, 15.5*	15.5, 16.5*
V8 5.0L, 5.7L	16.5, 17.0*	17.5, 18.0*
HD 3500, 1994-92	25.0, 25.5*	26.5, 27.0*
V8 6.2L Diesel	23.5	25.0
V8 6.5L Diesel, LD	23.5	25.0
V8 6.5L Diesel, HD	25.0	26.5
V8 7.4L	22.0, 23.5*	23.5, 25.0*
HD 3500, 1994-92	25.0, 27.0*	26.5, 28.5*
G Series Vans		
2000-98 Express/Van Savana		
Code W r/rear heater	13.2	14.0
Code W others	10.4	11.0
Code M, R w/rear heater	18.9	20.0
Code M, R others	16.0	17.0
Code J w/rear heater	24.6	26.0
Code J others	21.8	23.0
6.5L Diesel w/rear heater	26.0	27.5
w/o rear heater	22.2	23.5
1997-90 V6 4.3L	10.5	11.0
W/rear heater	13.0	14.0
V8 5.0L, 5.7L	16.0	17.0
W/rear heater	19.0	20.0
V8 6.2L (C) Diesel	22.5	24.0
W/rear heater	25.5	27.0
V8 6.2L (J) Diesel	24.0	25.5
W/rear heater	27.0	28.5
1997-90 V8 6.5L Diesel	24.0	25.5
W/rear heater	27.0	28.5
V8 7.4L	22.0	23.5
W/rear heater	24.5	26.0
1989 V6 4.3L	10.5	11.0
V8 5.0L, 5.7L	16.0	17.0
W/rear heater	18.5	20.0
V8 6.2L Diesel	22.5	24.0
V8 7.4L	22.0	23.5
S Series Pickups, Sonoma, S Blazer & S Jimmy, Syclone, Typhoon		
2000-99 Envoy	11.1	11.7
Pickup 4.3L	11.5	12.1
2000-98 Blazer, Jimmy: W/AT	11.3	11.9
W/MT	11.3	11.9
Pickup: 2.2L	11.0	11.5
4.3L: W/MT	11.3	11.9
W/AT	11.1	11.7
1997-96 2.2L	11.0	11.5
4.3L: W/MT	11.5	12.0
W/AT	11.0	11.5
1995-89 4-cyl.	11.0	11.5
V6 2.8L	10.0	10.5
V6 4.3L, 1995-90	11.5	12.0
V6 4.3L, 1989	13.0	13.5

COOLING SYSTEM CAPACITIES

Capacities are rounded off to the nearest half unit

(Includes heater. *Indicates with air conditioning)

MAKE, YEAR & MODEL	LITERS	QUARTS
CHRYSLER, DODGE & PLYMOUTH TRUCKS		
B Series/Ram Van & Wagon		
2000 V6 3.9L	17.0	18.0
V8 W/o rear heater	19.0	20.0
W/rear heater	20.0	21.0
1999-92 V6 3.9L	14.0*	14.5*
V8 5.2L	15.5*	16.5*
V8 5.9L	14.5*	15.0*
W/rear heater	15.0	16.0
1991-89 V6 3.9L	13.5	14.5
V8 5.2L	15.5	16.5
V8 5.9L Gas	14.5	15.5
Caravan FWD, Mini Ram Van, Town & Country, Voyager		
2000 2.4L	10.5	11.0
V6 W/o rear heater	12.5	13.0
W/rear heater	15.0	16.0
1999 2.4L	9.0	9.5
3.0L, 3.3L, 3.8L	9.5	10.5
1998-96 4-cyl. 2.4L	10.5	11.0
W/rear heater	12.5	13.0
V6 3.0L, 3.3L, 3.8L	12.5	13.0
W/rear heater	15.0	16.0
1995-92 4-cyl	9.0	9.5
V6	9.5	10.0
1991-89 4-cyl. 2.2L, 2.5L	8.0	8.5
4-cyl. 2.6L	9.0	9.5
V6 3.0L, 3.3L	9.5	10.0
D, W Series Pickups; Ramcharger		
1993-92 V6 3.9L	14.0	15.0
6-cyl. 5.9L Diesel:		
MT	15.0	16.0
AT	16.0	17.0
V8 5.2L: 2WD	16.0	17.0
4WD	15.5	16.5
V8 5.9L Gas:		
2WD	15.0	15.5
4WD	14.0	15.0
1991-89 V6 3.9L	14.0	15.0
6-cyl. 5.9L Diesel:		
MT	15.5	16.5
AT	16.5	17.5
V8 5.2L	16.0	17.0
V8 5.9L gas	14.5	15.5
Dakota		
2000-89 4-cyl.: 2.2L, 2.5L	9.5	10.0
V6 3.9L	13.0	14.0
V8 4.7L	16.0	17.0
V8 5.2L, 5.9L	13.5	14.5
Durango		
2000-98 3.9L	13.0	14.0
V8 4.7L	16.0	17.0
5.2L, 5.9L	13.5	14.5
Raider, Ram 50		
1993-90 4-cyl. 2.4L	6.0	6.5
V6 3.0L	8.5	9.0
1989 Ram 50:		
2.0L	7.0	7.5
2.6L	8.0	8.5
Raider: 4-cyl.	8.0	8.5
V6	9.0	9.5
Ram 1500-3500 Pickup		
2000-94 V6, V8 gas	19.0	20.0
6-cyl. Diesel	23.0	24.0
V10	25.0	26.0
FORD, LINCOLN, MERCURY TRUCKS		
Aerostar		
1997-89 V6 3.0L	11.0	11.5
V6 4.0L	12.0	12.5
Bronco, Excursion, Expedition, F Series Pickup, Navigator		
2000 Excursion		
5.4L	18.5	19.5
W/rear heater	20.0	21.0
6.8L	29.0	30.5
W/rear heater	31.0	32.5
7.3L Diesel	31.0	32.5
2000-99 Expedition, Navigator		
4.6L W/1 row radiator	20.5	21.5
W/1 row radiator & rear heat	21.5	23.0
W/2 row radiator	22.0	23.0
W/2 row radiator & rear heat	23.5	25.0
5.4L W/1 row radiator	22.5	24.0
W/1 row radiator & rear heat	25.0	26.5
W/2 row radiator	24.0	25.5

MAKE, YEAR & MODEL	LITERS	QUARTS
FORD, LINCOLN, MERCURY TRUCKS Cont.		
W/2 row radiator & rear heat	26.5	28.0
F-150,1999 F-250 LD		
4.2L W/1 row radiator	19.0	20.0
W/2 row	20.5	21.5
4.6L W/1 row radiator	19.5	20.5
W/2 row	22.0	23.0
5.4L W/2 row radiator	22.5	24.0
F-250 HD, -350, -450, -550		
5.4L	17.0, 18.5*	18.0, 19.5*
6.8L	29.0	30.5
7.3L Diesel	31.0	32.5
1998-97 V6 4.2L	15.0, 16.5*	15.5, 17.5*
V8 4.6L, 5.4L	17.0, 18.5*	18.0, 19.5*
V8 7.3L Diesel	21.0	22.0
V8 7.5L	17.0, 17.0*	18.0, 18.0*
V10 6.8L	29.0, 29.0*	30.5, 30.5*
1996-94 Bronco, V8 5.0L: W/MT	12.0, 13.0*	13.0,14.0*
W/AT	13.0, 14.0	14.0,15.0*
V8 5.8L	15.0	16.0
Heavy duty	16.0	17.0
Pickup: 6-cyl.: W/MT	12.0, 13.0*	13.0, 14.0*
HD.	13.0, 14.5*	14.0, 15.5*
W/AT	13.0, 15.0*	14.0, 15.5*
V8 5.0L, 5.8L: W/MT	15.0, 15.5*	15.5, 16.5*
W/AT	15.5	16.5
Heavy duty	17.5	18.5
V8 7.3L Diesel	27.0	29.0
V8 7.5L	19.0	20.0
1993-89 6-cyl.: W/MT	12.0,13.0*	13.0,14.0*
W/AT	13.0,15.0*	14.0,15.5*
V8 5.0L: W/MT	12.0,13.0*	13.0,14.0*
W/AT	13.0,14.0*	14.0,15.0*
V8 5.8L: W/MT	14.0,15.0*	15.0,16.0*
W/AT	15.0,16.0*	16.0,17.0*
V8 6.9L Diesel	27.0	29.0
V8 7.3L Diesel	27.0	29.0
V8 7.5L	17.0	18.0
Bronco II, Explorer, Mountaineer, Ranger		
2000 Ranger		
2.5L w/manual	10.0	10.5
W/auto	9.5	10.0
3.0L	14.0	15.0
4.0L w/manual	13.0	13.5
W/auto	12.5	13.0
2000-98 Explorer, Mountaineer		
4.0L ex. SOHC	11.5	12.0
4.0L SOHC	13.0	14.0
5.0L	15.0	15.5
1999-98 Ranger		
2.5L	6.0, 6.5*	6.5, 7.0*
3.0L	9.0, 9.5*	9.5, 10.0*
4.0L	7.5, 8.0*	8.0, 8.5*
1997-93 4-cyl. 2.3L, 2.5L	6.5	7.0
V6 3.0L	9.0, 9.5*	9.5, 10.0*
W/XC	9.5, 9.5*	10.0, 10.0*
V6 4.0L	7.5, 8.0*	8.0, 8.5*
V8 5.0L	13.0	13.5
1992-90 4-cyl. 2.3L	6.0, 6.5*	6.5, 7.0*
V6 2.9L	6.5, 7.5*	7.0, 8.0*
V6 3.0L	9.0, 9.5*	9.5, 10.0*
V6 4.0L Explorer	7.0, 8.0*	7.5, 8.5*
V6 4.0L Ranger	7.5, 8.0*	8.0, 8.5*
1989 4-cyl. 2.0L	6.0	6.5
4-cyl. 2.3L Gas	6.0, 6.5*	6.5, 7.0*
4-cyl. 2.3L Diesel	11.5, 12.5*	12.0, 13.0*
V6 2.8L, 2.9L	7.0, 7.5*	7.5, 8.0*
E-Series Vans		
2000-98 4.2L	22.0	23.0
W/rear heater	24.0	25.5
4.6L	24.0	25.0
W/rear heater	25.5	27.0
5.4L	27.5	29.0
W/rear heater	29.5	31.0
6.8L	29.0	30.5
W/rear heater	31.0	33.0
7.3L Diesel	28.5	30.0
W/rear heater	31.0	32.5
1997-95 6-cyl. 4.9L	15.0,17.0*	16.0,19.0*
Heavy duty	17.0	19.0
V8 5.0L	17.5	18.5
Heavy duty	18.5	19.5
V8 5.8L	20.0,21.0*	21.0,22.0*
Heavy duty	21.0	22.0
V8 7.5L	27.0	29.0

MAKE, YEAR & MODEL	LITERS	QUARTS
FORD, LINCOLN, MERCURY TRUCKS Cont.		
1997-89 V8 7.3L Diesel	29.0	31.0
1994 6-cyl. 4.9L	16.0	17.0
V8 5.0L, 5.8L	18.5,19.0*	19.5,20.0*
V8 7.5L	22.5	23.5
1993-89 6-cyl. 4.9L	14.0,17.0*	15.0,18.0*
V8 5.0L	16.5,17.5*	17.5,18.5*
V8 5.8L	19.0,20.0*	20.0,21.0*
V8 6.9L	29.0	31.0
V8 7.5L	26.0	28.0
Windstar		
2000 W/o rear heater	14.0	15.0
W/rear heater	15.0	16.0
1999-95 W/o rear heater	11.5	12.0
W/rear heater	13.5	14.0
GEO TRACKER		
2000-99 1.6L	5.5	5.8
2.0L	6.5	6.9
1998 W/MT	5.3	5.6
W/AT	5.2	5.5
1997-90 All	5.2	5.5
1989 All	5.5	6.0
HONDA TRUCKS		
1997-94 Passport	9.0	9.5
ISUZU TRUCKS		
1999-98 Rodeo: 2.2L	7.0	7.5
3.2L	11.0	11.5
Trooper: MT	9.0	9.5
AT	9.5	10.0
1999-96 Hombre: 2.2L	11.0	11.5
4.3L w/MT	11.0	11.5
4.3L w/AT	11.5	12.0
1997-91 Rodeo:		
4-cyl. 2.6L	9.0	9.5
V6 3.1L	11.0	11.5
V6 3.2L	9.0	9.5
1997-92 Trooper: W/MT	8.5	9.0
W/AT	9.0	9.5
1995-89 Pickup, Amigo:		
4-cyl.	6.0	6.5
V6	11.0	11.5
1991-89 Trooper: 4-cyl.	8.0	8.5
V6	10.0	10.5
JEEP		
2000 Grand Cherokee 4.0L	14.0	15.0
4.7L V8	13.5	14.5
2000-89 Cherokee, Wagoneer:		
4-cyl.	9.5	10.0
6-cyl.	11.5	12.0
Wrangler, TJ, YJ: 4-cyl.	8.5	9.0
6-cyl.	10.0	10.5
1999 Grand Cherokee 4.0L, 4.7L	12.0	13.0
1998-97 Grand Cherokee: 6-cyl.	11.5	12.0
V8	14.0	15.0
1996-93 Grand Cherokee, Grand Wagoneer:		
6-cyl.	9.0	9.5
V8	14.0	15.0
1994-89 Comanche:		
4-cyl.	9.5	10.0
6-cyl.	11.5	12.0
1991-89 Grand Wagoneer, J Series Truck:		
6-cyl. 4.2L (258)	10.0	10.5
V8 5.9L (360)	13.0	14.0
LAND ROVER/RANGE ROVER		
1999 Discovery	8.0	8.4
Range Rover	11.3	12.0
1994 Defender 90	13.0	13.5
Discovery	11.5	12.0
LEXUS TRUCKS		
2000-98 LX470	15.0	16.0
W/rear heater	15.5	16.5
RX300	9.0	9.5
1997 LX450	13.5	14.5
W/rear heater	14.5	15.5

COOLING SYSTEM CAPACITIES

MAKE, YEAR & MODEL	LITERS	QUARTS
MAZDA TRUCKS		
2000 MPV	10.0	10.5
W/rear heater	12.0	12.5
2000-94 B2300, B2500	6.5	7.0
B3000	9.0, 9.5*	9.5, 10.0*
B4000	7.5, 8.0*	8.0, 8.5*
1998-96 MPV	9.5	10.5
1995-93 MPV: 4-cyl.	7.0	7.5
V6	10.0	10.5
1994 B2300	6.5	7.0
B3000	9.0, 9.5*	9.5, 10.0*
1994-93 Navajo	7.5, 8.0*	8.0, 8.5*
1993 B2200, B2600	7.5	8.0
1992-91 Navajo	8.0	8.5
1992-89 MPV: 4-cyl.	7.0	7.5
V6 W/MT	9.5	10.0
V6 W/AT	10.0	10.5
B2200, B2600 2WD	7.5	8.0
B2600 4WD	7.0	7.5
MITSUBISHI TRUCKS		
2000-92 Montero	9.5	10.0
2000-97 Montero Sport: 4 cyl.	8.0	8.5
W/rear heater	9.0	9.5
V6	9.0	9.5
W/rear heater	10.0	10.5
1996-92 Expo LRV:		
1.8L	6.0	6.5
2.4L	6.5	7.0
1996-90 Pickup:		
4-cyl	6.0	6.5
V6	8.5	9.0
1991-89 Montero:		
4-cyl	9.0	9.5
V6	9.5	10.0
1990-89 Van	8.0	8.5
W/rear heater	8.5	9.0
1989 Pickup: 2.0L	7.0	7.5
2.6L	8.0	8.5
NISSAN TRUCKS		
2000-99 Xterra: 4-cyl.	9.0	9.5
V6	11.0	11.5
2000-97 Pathfinder	10.0	10.5
1999-98 Frontier: 4-cyl.	9.0	9.5
V6	10.5	11.0
1997-90 Pickup, Pathfinder:		
4-cyl.: 2WD	8.0	8.5
4WD	9.0	9.5
V6: 2WD	10.5	11.5
4WD	11.5	12.5
1990-89 Van: W/front heater	8.5	9.0
W/front & rear heater	9.0	9.5
W/o heater	7.0	7.5
1989 D21 Pickup, Pathfinder:		
4-cyl.: Gas	8.0	8.5
Diesel	12.0	13.0
V6	10.0	10.5
Van	9.0	9.5

MAKE, YEAR & MODEL	LITERS	QUARTS
OLDSMOBILE TRUCKS		
2000-98 Silhouette	9.1	9.6
W/rear heater	11.3	11.9
Bravada	11.1	11.7
1997-96 Silhouette	11.5	12.0
W/rear heater	12.5	13.5
1995-94 Silhouette 3.1L	11.5, 12.0*	12.0, 12.5*
Silhouette 3.8L	11.0	11.5
W/rear AC	12.5	13.5
1994-91 Bravada	11.0	12.0
1993-92 Silhouette 3.1L:		
Copper-Brass rad	12.0	12.5
Aluminum rad	11.0	11.5
W/rear AC:		
Copper- Brass rad	13.5	14.5
Aluminum rad	12.5	13.5
Silhouette 3.8L	11.0	11.5
W/rear AC	12.5	13.5
1991 Silhouette	12.5	13.5
1990 Silhouette	10.0	12.0
PONTIAC TRUCKS		
2000-99 Montana, TransSport		
W/AT	9.1	9.6
W/rear heater	11.3	11.9
1998-96 TransSport	11.5	12.0
W/rear heater	12.5	13.5
1997-94 Sunrunner	5.0	5.5
1995-94 Trans Sport: V6 3.1L	11.5, 12.0*	12.0, 12.5*
W/rear heater	13.0	14.0
V6 3.8L	11.0	11.5
W/rear heater	12.0	13.0
1993-92 Trans Sport: 3.1L:		
W/o rear AC:		
Copper-Brass rad	12.0	12.5
Aluminum rad	11.0	11.5
W/rear AC:		
Copper-Brass rad	13.5	14.5
Aluminum rad	12.5	13.5
3.8L	11.0	11.5
W/rear AC	12.5	13.5
1991 Trans Sport	13.0	13.5
W/rear AC	14.0	15.0
1990 Trans Sport	10.0	10.5
RANGE ROVER: See LAND ROVER		
SUBARU		
1998 Forester	6.0	6.5
SUZUKI		
2000-99 Vitara: 1.6L	5.5	6.0
1.8L	6.5	7.0
Grand Vitara	8.0	8.5
W/rear heater	15.5	16.5
1998-93 Sidekick, X90	5.5	5.5
1995-89 Samurai	5.0	5.5
1992-89 Sidekick	5.0	5.5

MAKE, YEAR & MODEL	LITERS	QUARTS
TOYOTA TRUCKS		
2000 Tundra: V6	10.0	10.5
V8	11.5	12.0
2000-98 Land Cruiser	15.0	16.0
W/rear heater	15.5	16.5
2000-97 4Runner: 2.7L	10.0	10.5
W/rear heater	11.0	11.5
3.4L	8.0	8.5
W/rear heater	9.0	9.5
RAV4 w/MT	8.0	8.5
W/AT	7.5	8.0
2000-95 Tacoma: 2.4L	8.0	8.5
2.7L	8.0	8.5
3.4L: 2WD	9.5	10.0
4WD	10.0	10.5
1998 T100 2WD: 2.7L	9.0	9.5
3.4L	10.0	10.5
T100 4WD	10.0	10.5
1997 Land Cruiser	13.5	14.5
W/rear heater	14.5	15.5
1997-95 T100: 4-cyl.	8.5	9.0
1997-93 Previa	12.0	13.0
T100: V6	10.0	10.5
1996-95 Land Cruiser	12.5	13.0
W/rear heater	13.5	14.0
1994-93 Land Cruiser	14.0	15.0
T100: 4-cyl.	7.5	8.0
1994-92 4-Runner: 2.4L: MT	8.5	9.0
AT: W/o rear heater	9.0	9.5
W/rear heater	9.5	10.0
3.0L	10.0	10.5
Pickup: 4-cyl.	8.5	9.0
V6	10.5	11.0
1992-91 Previa	11.5	12.0
W/towing opt	12.5	13.0
Land Cruiser	18.5	19.5
1991-89 4-Runner & Pickup:		
4-cyl. W/MT	8.5	9.0
4-cyl. W/AT	9.0	9.5
V6	10.5	11.0
1990-89 Land Cruiser	19.5	20.5
1989 Van: 2WD	8.5	9.0
4WD	7.5	8.0
VOLKSWAGEN TRUCKS		
1999-98 EuroVan base	9.0	9.5
w/2 heat exchangers	10.8	11.4
w/2 heat exchangers & water heater	11.4	17.8
1997-96 EuroVan	11.6	12.2
1995 EuroVan: camper pkg.	11.5	12.0
1992-89 Vanagon	16.0	17.0

AIR CONDITIONING SYSTEM REFRIGERANT CAPACITIES*

*Factory installed, or factory supplied systems only

ACURA

MAKE, YEAR & MODEL	Kg.	Oz.
2000-99 3.5RL	0.8	27
3.2TL	0.7	25
2000-98 2.3CL	0.6	23
SLX	0.6	21
2000-97 3.0CL	0.6	23
2000-95 NSX	0.8	29
2000-94 Integra	0.7	24
1998-96 3.2TL	0.7	25
3.5RL	0.7	25
1997 2.2CL	0.6	22
1997-95 2.5TL	0.7	25
SLX	0.7	25
1995-92 Legend	0.7	26
Vigor	0.8	27
1993-92 Integra	0.9	32
w/R134a system	0.7	24
NSX	0.9	32
1991-86 All models	0.9	33

AUDI

MAKE, YEAR & MODEL	Kg.	Oz.
2000-99 TT	0.8	27
1999 A6	0.8	27
1999-97 A8	0.8	27
1999-96 A4	0.7	24
A4 (11-18-98 to 12-1-98)	0.6	21
(VIN 8D_XA065253 to XA077026)		
1998-97 Cabriolet	0.7	24
1998-96 A6	0.6	21
1995-93 90, 90 Quattro	0.7	25
100, S4 w/R134a system	0.6	21
V8 w/R134a system	0.8	30
1992 100	1.1	39
1991-89 100, 200, V8 Quattro	1.1	38
1990-88 80, 90, Coupe, Quattro	1.0	36
1989-84 5000	1.1	39
1986-81 4000, Coupe, Quattro	1.0	34
1983-81 5000	1.4	49

AMERICAN MOTORS

MAKE, YEAR & MODEL	Kg.	Oz.
1989-81 All models	0.9	34

AMC/RENAULT

MAKE, YEAR & MODEL	Kg.	Oz.
1989-84 Medallion, Alliance, Encore	0.8	28
1988 Eagle Wagon	0.9	34

BMW

MAKE, YEAR & MODEL	Kg.	Oz.
1998-95 7-Series	1.2	43
1997 Z3	0.9	32
3-Series	0.8	30
540	1.2	43
1997-93 8-Series	1.5	51
1995-94 3-Series	1.0	34
1995-93 5-Series:		
Flat pipe condenser	1.5	51
Round pipe condenser	1.6	54
1994-93 7-Series	1.6	53
w/rear AC	1.7	55
1993-92 318, 325 ex. convertible:		
R12 system	1.2	42
R134a system	1.0	36
318, 325 convertible:		
R12 system	1.0	34
R134a system	0.8	30
1993-91 5-Series: R12 system	1.9	68
R134a system:		
Flat pipe condenser	1.5	51
Round pipe condenser	1.6	54
1992-91 8-Series: R12 system	1.9	68
R134a system	1.5	51
7-Series:		
R12 system	1.9	68
w/rear AC	2.1	75
R134a system	1.6	53
w/rear AC	1.7	55
1991-88 3-Series	1.0	34
M3	0.9	30
1990-88 5-Series	1.9	68
M5	1.5	51
7-Series	1.9	68
w/rear AC	2.1	75
6-Series	1.1	38
w/rear AC	1.8	60
1989-85 5-Series	1.0	34
1989-83 3-Series	1.1	38
325	1.3	45
All others	1.3	45
1984-81 5-Series	1.3	45

BUICK

MAKE, YEAR & MODEL	Kg.	Oz.
2000-99 LeSabre, Park Ave., Riviera	1	1
2000-98 Century, Regal	0.8	30
1997-94 Century: 4-cyl	0.8	28
V6	0.9	32
LeSabre, Park Avenue	0.9	32
Regal, Riviera	0.9	32
Roadmaster	0.8	28
Skylark	1.0	36
1993 LeSabre: w/R12 system	1.1	38
w/R134a system	0.9	32
1993-92 Park Ave	1.1	38
Skylark	1.2	42
1993-91 Roadmaster	1.4	50
w/rear system	1.6	55
1993-89 Reatta	1.1	38
1993-88 Regal (FWD)	1.0	36
Electra	1.1	38
1993-86 Century, Riviera	1.1	38
1992-86 LeSabre	1.1	38
1991-86 Skyhawk: 1.8L	1.1	38
2.0L	1.0	36
Skylark, Somerset	1.0	36
1990-81 Estate Wagon, Regal (RWD)	1.6	54
1987-85 Electra	1.3	44
1985-81 LeSabre, Riviera	1.6	54
1985-81 Century, Skyhawk, Skylark	1.3	44
1984-81 Electra	1.6	54

1 Varies, see charge label under hood.

CADILLAC

MAKE, YEAR & MODEL	Kg.	Oz.
2000 Catera	1.0	2.1
DeVille, Eldorado, Seville	0.9	2.0
2000-96 Eldorado	0.9	32
1999-97 Catera	0.9	32
1998-96 Seville	0.9	32
1999-95 DeVille	0.9	32
1997 Fleetwood	0.9	32
1996-95 Fleetwood Concours	0.9	32
1995-88 Eldorado, Seville	1.1	38
1994 DeVille: 4.6L	1.1	38
4.9L	0.9	32
Fleetwood	1.4	50
1993-92 DeVille, Fleetwood, Sixty Special, FWD	1.1	36
1993-85 Fleetwood Brougham RWD	1.6	54
1991-85 DeVille, Fleetwood (FWD)	1.3	44
1990-87 Allanté	1.1	38
1988-87 Cimarron	1.0	36
1987-86 Eldorado, Seville	1.3	44
1985-82 Cimarron	1.3	44
1984-82 DeVille, Eldorado, Fleetwood, Seville	1.5	54
1981 All models	1.7	60

CHEVROLET

MAKE, YEAR & MODEL	Kg.	Oz.
2000 Impala, Monte Carlo	1.3	44
Corvette	0.7	22
2000-99 Camaro	1	1
Cavalier, Malibu	1	1
Lumina	0.9	1.9
1999 Corvette	1	1
1998 Camaro	0.7	24
1998-94 Cavalier	0.7	24
Lumina, Monte Carlo	0.8	30
1997-96 Camaro: V6 3.8L	0.8	28
V8 5.7L	0.9	32
1997 Malibu	0.8	28
1997-94 Beretta, Corsica	1.0	36
Caprice, Impala SS	0.8	28
1997-93 Camaro	0.9	32
1996-95 Corvette	0.9	32
1994-88 Corvette	1.0	36
1994-86 Cavalier	1.0	36
Rear only	0.4	16
1993-92 Beretta, Corsica	1.2	42
1993-91 Caprice	1.4	50
1993-90 Lumina	1.0	36
Rear only	0.4	16
1992-88 Camaro	1.0	36
1991-89 Beretta, Corsica	1.3	44
Sprint	0.5	18
1990-81 Caprice	1.6	54
1990-86 Celebrity	1.1	40
1989-87 Spectrum	0.8	28
1988-87 Beretta, Corsica, Corvette	1.0	36
1988-81 Monte Carlo, El Camino	1.6	54
1988-85 Sprint	0.7	24

CHEVROLET Continued

MAKE, YEAR & MODEL	Kg.	Oz.
1987-82 Camaro	1.4	48
Chevette	1.0	36
1986-82 Corvette	1.3	44
1986-85 Spectrum	0.7	24
1986-81 Impala, Malibu	1.6	54
1985-82 Cavalier, Celebrity	1.3	44
1985-80 Citation	1.3	44
1981-80 Camaro	1.6	54
Corvette	1.4	48

1 See charge label under hood.

CHEVROLET/GMC TRUCKS

MAKE, YEAR & MODEL	Kg.	Oz.
2000 Chevrolet Venture; Oldsmobile Silhouette; Pontiac TransSport & Montana: Front	0.9	32
Rear	1.3	48
2000-99 Envoy, S-Blazer, S-Jimmy	0.8	28
C, K-3500 Pickup	1.0	30
Crew Cab, Suburban, 4-Door Utility: Front	0.9	32
Rear	1.5	48
C, K Cierra, Silverado: Front	0.9	32
Rear	1.5	48
2000-98 Express & Savana Vans:		
Front only	1.4	48
Front & Rear	2.0	72
1998 S-Series Pickup, Sonoma	0.8	30
1997 Express & Savana Vans:		
Front only	1.3	48
Front & rear	2.2	78
1997-94 Chevrolet Lumina APV & Venture; Oldsmobile Silhouette; Pontiac TransSport: Front	1.0	36
Rear	1.4	48
1998-95 S-Blazer, S-Jimmy	0.9	30
1998-94 Astro, Safari: Front	0.9	32
Front & Rear	1.4	48
C-, K-Series: Pickup, Sierra	0.9	32
Crew Cab & Utility	1.0	36
Suburban: Front	1.0	36
w/Auxiliary Unit	1.8	64
1997-94 Lumina, Venture Minivan:		
Front only	1.0	36
Front & rear	1.4	48
Rear only	0.4	16
S-Series Pickup, Sonoma	0.9	32
Tahoe, Yukon	1.0	36
1997-93 G-Series Van: Front	1.4	48
Front & Rear	1.9	68
1994-91 S Blazer, S Jimmy	1.1	40
1993 Chevrolet Lumina APV		
Front	1.4	42
Rear	1.6	56
Lumina APV:		
Front	1.2	42
Rear	1.6	56
Rear only	0.4	16
1993-92 Astro, Safari:		
Front	1.4	48
Rear	1.7	60
C-, K-Series:		
Blazer, Jimmy, Yukon:		
Front	1.4	48
Front & Rear	1.9	68
Pickup	1.1	40
Crew Cab & Utility	1.4	48
Suburban: Front	1.4	48
w/Auxiliary Unit	1.9	68
1993-91 S-Series: Pickup, Sonoma, Syclone, Typhoon	1.1	40
1992 Chevrolet Lumina APV		
Front	1.4	48
Rear	1.6	65
G-Series Van, Rally, Vandura:		
Front	1.4	48
Front & Rear	1.7	60
Lumina APV:		
Front	1.4	50
Rear	1.8	65
Rear only	0.4	16
1991-90 Chevrolet Lumina APV	1.4	48
1991-89 Astro, Safari:		
Front	1.0	36
Rear	1.7	60
1991-88 C-, K-Series	1.1	40

AIR CONDITIONING SYSTEM REFRIGERANT CAPACITIES*

*Factory installed, or factory supplied systems only

MAKE, YEAR & MODEL	Kg.	Oz.
CHEVROLET/GMC TRUCKS Continued		
1991-87 G-Series Van:		
w/roof-mounted		
unit	2.0	69
Others	1.4	48
R-, V-Series: Pickup & Suburban		
w/roof-mounted unit	2.4	92
Others	1.4	48
1990-86 S-Series:		
Blazer, Jimmy,		
Pickup	1.6	56
1988-85 Astro, Safari: Front	0.9	32
Rear	1.4	48
1987-83 C-, G-, K-Series, Blazer, Jimmy		
Trucks & Van w/roof-mounted		
unit: G-Series Van	2.0	69
Others	2.4	94
1985-82 S-Series	1.1	37
1982-81 All w/roof-mounted unit	2.4	94
Ex. roof-mounted units:		
Vans	1.4	48
Others	1.7	60
CHRYSLER/DODGE/PLYMOUTH		
2000 Cirrus, Stratus, Breeze,		
Sebring Convertible	0.5	19
Neon	0.7	27
2000-99 Concorde, Intrepid, LHS,		
300M	0.7	25
2000-95 Avenger, Sebring	0.7	25
1999 Cirrus, Stratus, Breeze,		
Sebring Convertible	0.6	20
Neon	0.8	28
1998-95 Sebring Convertible	0.8	28
Breeze, Neon	0.8	28
1998-94 Concorde, Intrepid	0.8	28
1997-94 Acclaim, LeBaron, Spirit	0.7	26
Cirrus, LHS, New Yorker,		
Stealth, Stratus	0.8	28
Viper	0.9	33
1996-93 Breeze, Colt, Colt Wagon, Vista	0.8	28
1994 Duster, Shadow, Sundance	0.7	26
Laser	0.9	33
1993 Concorde, Intrepid	0.8	28
1993-92 All Other FWD: w/o rear AC	0.9	32
w/rear AC	1.2	43
1993-90 Laser	0.9	33
1992-91 Stealth	1.0	34
1992-90 Monaco	1.0	36
1992-89 Colt	1.0	36
1992-84 Vista	0.9	30
1991 Dynasty, New Yorker,		
Fifth Ave., Imperial	1.0	34
Others	0.9	32
1990-88 All other FWD models	1.1	38
1989-82 All RWD models	1.2	41
1989-84 Conquest	0.9	32
1988-81 Colt	0.9	32
1987-82 Omni, Horizon, Charger,		
Turismo	1.0	34
All other FWD models	1.1	38
1981 Gran Fury, St. Regis	1.3	46
All other RWD models	1.2	40
Omni, Horizon	1.0	34
CHRYSLER/DODGE/PLYMOUTH TRUCKS		
2000 Dakota	0.9	32
Durango w/single unit	0.8	28
W/dual unit	0.9	32
Ram 1500-3500	0.9	32
2000-93 Caravan, Town & Country,		
Voyager:		
Front	1.0	34
Front & Rear	1.3	46
1999-98 Ram Van & Wagon		
w/Single unit	1.0	34
w/Dual unit	1.3	46
Durango		
w/Single unit	0.8	28
w/Dual unit	0.85	30
1999 Ram Truck Pickup, Dakota		
w/Single unit	0.8	28
w/Dual unit	0.85	30
1998-94 Ram -1500, -2500, -3500		
Pickups	0.9	32
Dakota	0.9	32
1997-95 Ram Van, Wagon	1.1	40
w/rear AC	1.7	60
1994-91 B-Series Van, wagon	1.3	44
w/rear AC	1.8	62
1993-92 Ramcharger	1.3	44
1993-91 Dakota	1.2	40

MAKE, YEAR & MODEL	Kg.	Oz.
CHRYSLER/DODGE/PLYMOUTH TRUCKS Continued		
1993-90 Ram 50	0.9	30
1993-88 D-, W-Series Pickup	1.3	44
1992-90 Caravan, Mini Ram,		
Town and Country, Voyager	0.9	32
w/rear unit	1.2	43
1992-83 B-Series Van	1.4	48
w/rear unit	1.8	62
1990-87 Dakota	1.3	44
1989-84 Caravan, Mini-Ram,		
Town and Country, Voyager	1.1	38
w/rear AC	1.3	44
1989-81 Ram 50	0.9	32
1988-81 D-, W-Series Pickup	1.1	40
1982-81 B-Series van	1.5	54
w/rear unit	1.4	48
DAEWOO		
1999-98 Lanos	0.7	24
Nubria	0.8	26
Leganza	0.8	26
EAGLE		
1997-95 Talon	0.7	25
1997-93 Summit	0.8	27
Vision	0.8	28
1994-90 Talon	0.9	32
1992-88 Summit, Premier	1.0	36
FORD/MERCURY		
2000-99 Villager: Front	0.9	32
Front & rear	1.6	56
2000-98 Crown Victoria,		
Grand Marquis	1.1	38
2000-94 Escort, Tracer	0.8	28
1999-97 Sable, Taurus	0.9	34
1998-94 Mustang	0.9	34
Villager: Front	0.9	32
Front & rear	1.5	52
1997-95 Cougar, Thunderbird	1.0	36
Contour, Mystique	0.7	26
Windstar: Front	1.3	44
Front & rear	1.6	56
1997-94 Crown Victoria, Grand Marquis	0.9	34
1997-93 Probe	0.8	28
1996-95 Sable, Taurus	1.0	36
1995-94 Aspire	0.7	25
Capri	0.6	20
1994 Cougar, Sable, Taurus, Tempo,		
Thunderbird, Topaz	0.9	32
1993 Cougar, Mustang, Sable, Taurus,		
Thunderbird	1.1	40
Crown Victoria, Grand Marquis	1.1	38
Villager	1.0	36
w/rear AC	1.5	56
1993-92 Capri	0.7	25
1993-91 Escort, Tracer	1.0	34
1993-88 Festiva	0.7	25
Tempo, Topaz	1.0	36
1992 Crown Victoria,		
Grand Marquis	1.1	41
Sable, Taurus	1.1	40
1992-88 Cougar, Probe, Thunderbird	1.1	40
Mustang	1.1	40
1991 Capri	0.6	22
1991-88 Sable, Taurus	1.3	44
3.8L engine	1.1	40
Crown Victoria, Marquis	1.4	48
1990-88 Escort, EXP	1.0	36
1989-88 Tracer	0.9	31
1988-82 Escort, EXP, Lynx, Tempo,		
Topaz, Taurus, Sable	1.1	40
Crown Victoria,		
Grand Marquis	1.5	54
Capri, Cougar, LTD, Marquis,		
Mustang, Thunderbird	1.1	38
1982 Fairmont, Granada, Zephyr	1.1	38
1981 Fairmont, Granada, Zephyr	1.6	54
Capri, Cougar, LTD, Marquis		
Mustang, Thunderbird	1.6	54
FORD/MERCURY TRUCKS		
2000 Excursion, F-Super Duty		
W/o auxiliary	1.1	40
W/auxiliary	1.9	68
Expedition	1.0	37
W/auxiliary	1.7	62
2000-99 Explorer, Mountaineer	0.8	30
2000-99 Windstar, front	0.9	32
Front & rear	1.6	56

MAKE, YEAR & MODEL	Kg.	Oz.
FORD/MERCURY TRUCKS Continued		
2000-98 F-Series: F150,		
1999-98 F250 LD	0.9	32
Ranger	0.8	30
E-Series Van: Front	1.2	44
Front & rear	1.8	64
1999 F-250 HD, -350	0.9	32
1998 Windstar: Front	1.2	44
Front & rear	1.6	56
1998-94 Explorer, Mountaineer	0.6	22
1997 E-Series Van: Front	1.4	52
Front and rear	1.9	64
Ranger	0.6	22
1997-96 F-Series Pickup	1.1	38
1997-95 Aerostar: Front	0.7	24
Front & rear	1.0	36
1996 Bronco	1.1	38
1996-94 E-Series Van: Front	1.3	44
Front & rear	1.9	64
Ranger	0.7	26
1995-94 Bronco, F-Series Pickup	0.9	33
1994-93 Aerostar: Front	1.3	46
Front & rear	1.7	61
1993-91 Bronco, F-Series Pickup	1.3	44
1993-90 Bronco II, Explorer, Ranger	0.9	32
1993-81 E-Series Van: Front	1.6	54
Front & rear	2.0	70
1992-86 Aerostar	1.6	56
1990-84 Bronco, F-Series Pickup	1.5	52
1989-84 Bronco II, Ranger	1.1	40
1983-81 Bronco, F-Series Pickup	1.6	54
GEO		
2000-98 Metro, Prizm	1	1
1997 Metro	0.6	22
1997-89 Prizm	0.7	24
1997-91 Tracker	0.6	21
w/rear AC	0.7	24
1996-89 Metro	0.5	18
1994-91 Storm	0.6	21
1990-89 Tracker	0.7	25
1 See refrigerant charge label under hood.		
HONDA		
2000 Accord	0.8	27
S2000	0.6	22
2000-97 CR-V	0.7	24
Prelude	0.8	27
2000-96 Civic	0.6	22
2000-95 Odyssey: Front	0.6	23
Front & Rear	0.8	30
1999-94 Accord	0.6	22
1997-94 Civic, DelSol	0.5	18
Passport	0.7	23
1996-92 Prelude	0.6	23
1993 Accord	0.8	29
DelSol	0.6	22
1993-92 Civic	0.6	22
1992-88 Accord	0.9	32
1991-88 Civic, CRX, Prelude	0.9	32
1987-84 Civic, CRX	0.8	28
1987-83 Prelude	0.8	28
1987-82 Accord	0.7	25
1983-81 Civic	0.7	25
1982-81 Prelude	0.7	25
HYUNDAI		
2000 Accent	0.6	22
Elantra, Tiburon, Sonata	0.7	24
1999-96 All	0.7	24
1995-94 All ex. Sonata	0.7	24
Sonata	0.9	32
1993-87 All	0.9	32
INFINITI		
1999 G20	0.7	22
1999-97 Q45	0.7	24
QX4	0.7	24
1999-96 I30	0.7	24
1996-94 Q45	0.8	28
1997-93 J30	0.7	24
1996-91 G20	0.8	28
1993-90 Q45	1.2	41
M30	0.9	32
ISUZU		
1999-98 Hombre	0.8	28
1999-96 Oasis: Front	0.6	23
Front & Rear	0.8	30
1999-94 Amigo, Pickup, Rodeo,		
Trooper	0.7	26
1997-96 Hombre	0.9	32

*Factory installed, or factory supplied systems only

MAKE, YEAR & MODEL	Kg.	Oz.
ISUZU Continued		
1993-92 Stylus	0.6	22
Trooper	0.9	30
Impulse	0.6	22
1993-90 Amigo, Pickup	0.9	30
1993-91 Rodeo	1.0	35
1991-90 Impulse, Stylus	0.7	26
1991-87 Trooper	0.9	33
1989-88 Amigo, Pickup	1.0	33
1989-87 I-Mark (FWD)	0.8	28
1988-83 Impulse	1.0	35
1987-81 Pickup, I-Mark (RWD)	0.9	30
JAGUAR		
1998 XJ8, XJR-8, Vanden Plas	0.7	24
1997 XJ6	1.1	39
JEEP		
2000 Grand Cherokee	0.6	24
2000-97 Cherokee	0.5	20
Wrangler, TJ	0.5	20
1999 Grand Cherokee	0.7	24
1998-93 Grand Cherokee, Grand Wagoneer	0.8	28
1996-95 Cherokee	0.9	32
1995-88 Wrangler, YJ	0.9	32
1994-89 Cherokee	1.1	38
1992-89 Comanche, Wagoneer	1.1	38
1991-89 Grand Wagoneer	0.9	32
1988-84 Cherokee, Comanche, Wagoneer	0.9	32
Grand Wagoneer, J10, J20	1.0	36
1987-81 CJ5, CJ7	1.1	40
1983-81 Cherokee, Wagoneer, J10, J20	1.0	36
KIA		
2000-93 Sephia	0.7	25
2000-95 Sportage	0.7	25
LAND ROVER		
1999 Discovery, Range Rover		
Front	0.9	32
Front & Rear	1.1	40
LEXUS		
2000-99 RX300	0.6	21
2000-98 LX470	1.1	37
LS400	0.7	25
GS300, GS400	0.6	21
ES300	0.8	28
2000-95 SC300, SC400	0.9	34
1997-96 ES300, GS300, LX450	0.8	30
1997-95 LS400	0.8	30
1995-93 ES300, GS300	0.8	30
1994-93 LS400	0.9	34
SC300, SC400	0.8	30
1992 ES300, SC300, SC400	1.0	33
1992-90 LS 400	1.0	36
ES 250	0.7	27
LINCOLN		
2000 Navigator	1.0	37
W/auxiliary	1.7	62
LS	0.8	28
2000-98 Town car	1.1	38
Continental	1.0	38
Mark VIII	0.9	34
1997-95 All	0.9	34
1994 Continental	0.9	34
1994-93 Mark VIII	0.9	34
Town Car	1.0	36
1993-88 Continental	1.1	40
1992-91 Town Car	1.1	40
1992-85 Mark VII	1.1	40
1990-81 Town Car	1.4	48
1987-81 Continental, Mark VI	1.1	38
MAZDA		
2000 MPV	0.6	23
W/rear AC	0.8	30
2000-99 Protegé	0.6	19
2000-98 626	0.8	27
Millenia	0.8	28
Miata	0.6	19
2000-97 B2300, B2500, B3000, B4000	0.6	22
1997-95 Millenia	0.7	26
MPV: Single system	0.9	31
Twin system	1.0	34
Protegé	0.6	21
RX-7	0.5	17
1997-95 Miata, MX-5	0.6	19
1997-93 626, MX-6	0.7	25
1996-94 B2300, B3000, B4000	0.7	26
1995-92 929, Serenia	0.8	28

MAKE, YEAR & MODEL	Kg.	Oz.
MAZDA Continued		
1995-88 MX-3, Precida	0.8	27
1994 MPV: Single system	1.0	34
Twin system	1.2	45
Navajo	0.6	22
1994-93 RX-7:		
R12 system	0.6	21
R134a system	0.5	18
1994-90 323, Protegé	0.8	27
1993-89 MPV:		
Single system	1.1	37
Twin system	1.4	49
Navajo	0.8	28
1993-86 Pickup	0.8	27
1993-90 Miata	0.8	28
1992-88 626, MX-6	0.9	32
1991-90 929	1.0	35
1991-86 RX-7	0.8	27
1990-86 929	1.1	39
1989-86 323	0.8	28
1987-86 626	0.8	28
MERCEDES-BENZ		
1999 C43 AMG	0.8	30
E55 AMG, E320	1.0	35
SL500	0.8	28
ML430	0.7	27
E430	1.0	35
CLK430	0.8	30
C230	0.9	30
1999-98 ML320	0.7	27
C280, CLK320, SLK230	0.8	30
SL500	0.9	33
E300TD	1.0	35
CL600	1.1	40
w/rear AC	1.2	44
S320, S420	1.2	44
1997-94 C220, C230, C280: 1994-95	1.0	34
1996-97	0.9	30
E300, E320, E420, E500	1.0	34
SL320, SL500, SL600	1.0	34
S320, S350, S420, S500, S600	1.2	40
w/rear AC	1.4	48
1993-92 190D, E	1.0	34
300D, E, CE, TE; 400E, 500E	1.0	34
300SL, 500SL, 600SL	1.0	34
300SD, SE; 400SE, 500SEC, SEL; 600 SEC, SEL	1.2	40
w/rear AC	1.4	48
1991-90 300SL, 500SL	1.0	36
1991-89 190D, 190E	1.0	34
1991-86 260E, 300CD, D, E, TE	1.1	38
1991-86 300SE, SEL; 350D, SDL; 400SE, 420SEL, 500SEC, SEL; 560SEC, SEL	1.3	44
w/rear AC	1.5	54
1989-86 560SL	1.0	36
1988-84 190D, E,	1.1	38
16V	0.8	30
1985-84 500SEC, SEL	1.5	54
1985-81 380SE, SEC, SEL	1.5	54
380SL, SLC	1.0	36
300D, CD, TD	1.2	40
300SD	1.5	54
1984-81 240D	1.2	40
1981 280E, CE	1.2	40
MITSUBISHI		
2000 Eclipse	0.5	16
Diamante	0.6	22
Montero Sport	0.7	24
2000-99 Galant	0.6	23
2000-97 Montero	0.6	22
1999-97 Diamante	0.7	24
Montero Sport	0.7	24
1999-94 3000GT	0.8	28
1999-97 Eclipse	0.7	25
Mirage	0.5	20
1998-94 Galant	0.7	27
Montero	0.6	22
1996-95 Eclipse	0.6	23
Mirage	0.7	27
1996-94 Expo, Pickup	0.7	27
1994 Mirage	0.8	28
Precis	0.7	25
1996-92 Diamante, ex. wagon:		
R12 system	1.0	36
R134a system	0.7	27
Diamante Wagon	0.8	28
1994-90 Eclipse	0.9	33
1993 Mirage	0.8	28

MAKE, YEAR & MODEL	Kg.	Oz.
MITSUBISHI Continued		
1993-92 Expo, Precis	0.8	30
Montero	0.8	28
Pickup	0.8	30
1993-91 3000GT	0.9	34
1993-90 Pickup	0.8	30
1993-89 Galant	0.9	33
1992-90 Mirage	1.0	36
1991-87 Sigma	0.9	32
Montero	0.9	32
Precis	0.8	30
1990-87 Van/wagon: w/single unit	0.9	32
w/dual units	1.5	51
1989-86 Cordia, Galant, Tredia, Sigma	0.9	32
Mirage	0.9	32
1989-83 Starion, Pickup, Montero	0.9	32
1986-85 Mirage	0.7	25
1985-93 Cordia, Tredia	0.7	25
1985 Galant	0.7	25
NISSAN		
1999-98 Frontier	0.7	24
1999-97 Pathfinder	0.7	24
1999-95 240SX	0.7	24
Maxima, 200SX, Sentra	0.7	24
Quest:	0.9	32
w/rear AC	1.5	52
1999-93 Altima	0.8	28
1996-95 300ZX	0.6	21
1996-93 Pickup	0.8	28
1995-93 Pathfinder	0.8	28
1994 300ZX	0.7	23
1994-93 Quest	1.0	36
w/rear AC	1.6	56
1994-91 Maxima	0.9	33
Sentra	0.7	25
1993-91 NX	0.7	25
240SX	0.9	32
300ZX, Stanza	0.8	28
1992-80 Pickup, Pathfinder	0.9	32
1992-90 Axxess	0.9	32
1990 300ZX:		
Turbo	0.8	30
Ex. Turbo	0.9	32
1989-83 Pulsar	0.9	32
1990-89 240SX	1.0	36
1990-82 Sentra, Stanza	0.9	32
1990-81 Maxima	1.0	36
1989-84 300ZX	1.0	36
Van	1.5	53
1988-81 200SX	0.9	32
1983-81 280ZX	1.0	36
1982-81 210, 310	0.9	32
OLDSMOBILE		
2000 Intrigue	0.9	2.0
Alero	1	1
1999 Alero, Cutlass	0.8	1.8
Eighty-Eight, LSS	0.9	2.0
1999-98 Intrigue	0.8	30
1998-95 Aurora, Bravada	0.9	32
1998-94 Achieva	1.0	30
Cutlass Ciera: 2.2L	0.8	28
3.1L	0.9	32
Cutlass Supreme	0.8	30
1997-94 Eighty-Eight, Ninety-Eight	0.9	32
1994-91 Bravada	1.1	38
1993 Eighty-Eight, Ninety-Eight	1.1	38
1993-92 Achieva	1.2	42
Cutlass Ciera, Cutlass Cruiser	1.1	38
1993-88 Cutlass (FWD)	1.0	36
1992-91 Custom Cruiser	1.4	50
Toronado, Trofeo	1.1	38
1992-88 Ninety-Eight	1.1	38
1992-86 Delta 88	1.1	38
1991-86 Calais	1.0	36
Ciera	1.1	38
1990-81 Custom Cruiser	1.6	54
1989-86 Toronado, Trofeo	1.1	38
1988-86 Firenza:		
1.8L	1.1	38
2.0L	1.0	36
1988-81 Cutlass (RWD)	1.6	54
1987-85 Ninety-Eight	1.3	44
1985-81 Delta 88	1.6	54
1985-82 Ciera, Firenza	1.3	44
1985-81 Omega	1.3	44
Toronado	1.6	54
1984-81 Ninety-Eight	1.6	54

1 See refrigerant charge label under hood.

AIR CONDITIONING SYSTEM REFRIGERANT CAPACITIES*

*Factory installed, or factory supplied systems only

MAKE, YEAR & MODEL	Kg.	Oz.
PEUGEOT		
1992-81 405, 505	1.0	35
PONTIAC		
2000 Grand Prix	0.9	1.9
Bonneville	1	1
2000-99 Firebird, Sunfire	1	1
Grand Am	0.8	28
1999-98 Bonneville, Grand Prix	0.8	30
Firebird	0.7	24
1998-95 Sunfire	0.7	24
1998-94 Grand Am	1.0	35
Trans Sport: Front	0.9	32
Front & rear	1.3	46
1997-96 Firebird:		
V6 3.8L	0.8	28
V8 5.7L	0.9	32
1997-94 Bonneville	0.9	32
1996-94 Grand Prix	0.9	32
Sunrunner	0.6	21
1995-93 Firebird	0.9	32
1994-87 Sunbird	1.0	35
1993 Trans Sport	1.2	42
w/rear AC	1.6	56
1993-91 Grand Am	1.2	42
1993-88 LeMans	1.0	36
1993-88 Grand Prix	1.0	36
1993-87 Bonneville	1.1	38
1992-90 Trans Sport	1.4	50
w/rear AC	1.8	65
1992-88 Firebird	1.0	36
Grand Prix	1.0	36
1991-86 6000	1.1	40
1990-87 Safari	1.6	54
1990-85 Grand Am	1.0	36
1988-84 Fiero	1.1	38
1987-82 Firebird	1.4	48
1987-81 Parisienne, Safari	1.6	54
Grand Prix	1.5	52
1987-81 1000	1.0	36
1985-82 6000	1.3	44
Sunbird, (J)2000	1.2	40
1985-81 Bonneville, LeMans, Catalina	1.6	54
Phoenix	1.3	44
1981 Firebird	1.6	54

1 See refrigerant charge label under hood.

MAKE, YEAR & MODEL	Kg.	Oz.
PORSCHE		
1998 Boxster	0.8	29
1998-95 911	0.8	29
1995-94 928 w/basic system	0.8	30
w/M570 High Output Unit	1.0	37
968	0.9	33
1994-89 911 Carrera 4	0.9	33
1990-89 944S2	0.9	33
1989 928S4 w/rear evaporator	1.1	40
1989-84 911	1.3	47
944 from 2-85	0.9	33

MAKE, YEAR & MODEL	Kg.	Oz.
PORSCHE Continued		
1988-84 928 w/rear evaporator	1.2	42
924S	0.9	33
1985-83 944 to 2-85	1.1	40
1984-81 928	1.0	37
1983-81 911	1.2	44
1982-81 924	0.8	30
SAAB		
1999 9-3	0.8	28
9-5	0.9	33
1998 9000	0.8	28
1998-94 900	0.8	28
1997-92 9000 w/o rear AC	1.0	36
1992 9000 w/rear AC	1.4	48
1992-81 900	1.0	36
1990-86 9000	1.1	38
SATURN		
1999-98 All	0.7	24
1996-91 All	0.9	34
SUBARU		
1999-97 All	0.6	23
1996-94 All	0.7	25
1993 Impreza	0.7	26
1993-92 SVX	0.6	22
1993-90 Legacy	0.9	32
Loyale	0.8	30
1991-86 XT Coupe	0.7	27
1989-87 Sedan, Wagon: Hitachi	0.7	27
Panasonic	0.8	29
1986-83 All	0.7	27
SUZUKI		
1997-89 Esteem, Sidekick, X90	0.6	21
Swift	0.5	18
TOYOTA		
2000 Tundra	0.6	21
Celica	0.5	15
Echo	0.5	16
Avalon	0.6	21
Tacoma	0.6	21
Corolla	0.7	23
2000-99 Camry, Solara	0.8	28
2000-98 Land Cruiser	0.8	28
w/Dual AC	1.1	39
2000-96 Sienna	0.8	28
Dual AC, 4-dr	1.3	44
Dual AC, 5-dr	1.4	48
RAV 4	0.7	25
4-Runner	0.7	23
1999-98 Tercel	0.5	16
Celica, Corolla	0.7	23
1999-95 Avalon	0.8	30
Tacoma	0.6	21
1998-94 Camry	0.8	30
1997 Land Cruiser	0.8	30
Paseo, Tercel	0.6	21

MAKE, YEAR & MODEL	Kg.	Oz.
TOYOTA Continued		
1997-94 Celica, Supra, T100	0.7	24
1997-92 Corolla	0.7	25
1997-91 Previa	0.9	31
w/rear AC	1.2	41
1996-92 Land Cruiser	0.9	32
Paseo, Tercel	0.7	25
1995-94 MR2	0.7	25
1995-92 Pickup, 4-Runner	0.8	27
1993-92 Camry	1.0	35
Celica, Supra	0.7	25
1993-90 MR2	0.8	30
1992-90 Cressida	0.8	30
1991-90 Camry, Celica, Corolla, Supra, Tercel	0.7	25
Pickup, 4-Runner, Land Cruiser	0.8	28
1989-84 Van: w/dual AC	1.4	50
w/single AC	0.7	25
1989-81 Others	0.7	25
VOLKSWAGEN		
1999-98 Passat	0.7	24
Beetle	0.7	26
Jetta, Golf, Cabrio	0.8	27
EuroVan w/one evap.	1.0	35
w/two evap.	1.4	49
1998-96 Golf	0.8	28
1997-96 Cabrio	0.8	28
Passat	0.9	33
1995-93 Cabrio, Golf, GTI, Jetta	0.8	28
Corrado	1.0	35
1995-90 Passat	1.1	40
1993 Eurovan: Front	1.0	34
Front & rear	1.4	48
1992-90 Corrado	1.1	38
1992-85 Cabriolet, Scirocco	1.1	40
Golf, GTI, Jetta	1.1	38
1992-86 Vanagon	1.5	51
1988-87 Fox	1.2	42
1988-82 Quantum	1.0	34
1985-81 Vanagon	1.2	43
1984-81 Jetta, Rabbit	0.9	33
Scirocco	1.0	34
1981 Dasher	0.9	33
VOLVO		
1999 S80	1.0	34
1999-98 70 Series	0.7	26
1998 90 Series	0.9	31
1995-93 240 Series	0.7	26
740, 960	0.9	33
850 GLT	0.8	28
1995-91 940	0.9	33
1992-88 760	1.1	38
1992-81 240 Series	1.1	38
740, 780	1.2	40
1987-83 760	1.2	40

COOLING SYSTEM AIR BLEED CHART

A number of models have cooling systems that cannot be completely filled with coolant through the radiator filler. The result can be air pockets that restrict coolant flow which may result in engine overheating and damage. The manufacturers provide air bleeds or procedures to purge the air from the system. When servicing a cooling system, refer to the following chart. In most cases, briefly run the engine with HVAC controls set to warmest setting. This will aid in purging air from the heater core. If the model you are servicing is shown on the chart, bleed air from the system by loosening the air bleed and filling the system until coolant runs from the air bleed with no bubbles in it. Some systems require special procedures aside from or in addition to this. These will be reflected in the chart along with the type of bleeder, its location, coolant fill point, and whether or not the engine needs to be running.

MAKE, YEAR, MODEL, ENGINE	BLEEDER TYPE	LOCATION	FILL POINT	BLEED W/ENGINE @ RPM	SPECIAL NOTICE
ACURA 1989-95 Integra, Legend	screw	water outlet off of upper radiator hose	radiator	off	—
1992-94 Vigor	bolts	1. thermostat housing 2. near EGR valve	radiator	off	Fill until coolant flows from bleeders, then close bleeders. Close radiator cap to first stop. Run engine until warm. Recheck coolant level. Top off radiator.
1991-00 NSX	1. bolt 2. plug 3. cap 4. bolt	1. thermostat housing 2. radiator 3. heater pipe 4. water pipe at firewall	expansion tank	off	Tighten bleeders in order listed as bubbles cease. Refill expansion tank to MAX line. Loosen bleeder at thermostat housing to bleed excess air.
1995-98 2.5TL	bolt	thermostat housing intake manifold	radiator	off	Fill until coolant flows from bleeders, then close bleeders and fill radiator until full.
1996-98 3.2TL	bolt	thermostat housing	radiator	off	Fill until coolant flows from bleeders. Close bleeders.
1996-00 3.5RL	bolt	next to ECT sensor on water passage	radiator	off	Remove engine cover. Loosen bleed bolt. Fill at radiator until coolant flows from bleeder without bubbles. Fill to base of filler neck. Run engine with radiator cap off, until cooling fan comes on twice. Top up as necessary.
1997 2.2CL, 1998-00 2.3CL	bolt	thermostat housing	radiator	off	Fill until coolant flows from bleeder, without bubbles. Run engine with radiator cap off, until cooling fan comes on twice. Top up as necessary.
AUDI 1993-95 90 2771cc	screws	1. heater hose at firewall 2. water pipe next to temperature sensor, front of engine	expansion tank	off	—
1992-94 100 2771cc	screws	1. under water tray next to temperature sensor, front of engine	expansion tank	off	—
1996-98 A4 2771cc	screws	1. radiator hose 2. coolant pipe below expansion tank	radiator	off	Loosen hose clamp, pull back hose to expose vent hole. Open bleed screw at coolant pipe below expansion tank. Fill until coolant flows from bleeder hole then tighten screw. Fill again until coolant flows from vent hole, then push on coolant hose and tighten clamp.
BMW 1993-96 3-, 5-, 7-series	screws	1. radiator 2. thermostat housing (some models)	expansion tank	fast idle	Maintain coolant level at MAX throughout bleed procedure. Recheck cold.
8-series	bolt	expansion tank	expansion tank	off	Start engine briefly. Recheck level.
All SOHC 6-cyl.	screw	thermostat housing	radiator	fast idle	—
CHRYSLER/DODGE/ PLYMOUTH 1990-92 Monaco	valve	thermostat housing	reservoir	off	Bleed twice, before & after running.
1992-96 1.8L Vista, Colt wagon	bolt	thermostat housing	thermostat housing & radiator	off	Fill through housing until full. Replace washer, install bolt and top off radiator. With engine warm, rev 3 times. Recheck cold.
1989-94 4-cyl. 2.2L, 2.5L	vacuum valve or plug	thermostat housing	radiator	off	Recheck cold.
1990-97 V6 3.3L, 3.8L transverse engine	sending unit or plug	cylinder head	radiator	off	Recheck cold.
1991-93 2.2L Turbo III	sending unit	thermostat housing	radiator	off	Recheck cold.
1991-94 3.0L Stealth	—	—	radiator	—	With engine warm, race to 3000 RPM several times. and recheck coolant level when cold.
1996-99 2.4L Caravan, Voyager	sending unit	water outlet	radiator	—	Install when coolant flows freely.

COOLING SYSTEM AIR BLEED CHART

MAKE, MODEL, ENGINE	BLEEDER TYPE	LOCATION	FILL POINT	BLEED W/ENGINE @ RPM	SPECIAL NOTICE
CHRYSLER/DODGE/ PLYMOUTH Continued					
1997-00 Concorde, LHS, Intrepid, 300M	valve	3.3L, 1997 3.5L, thermostat housing; 2.7L, water outlet connector; 1998-00 3.2L/3.5L, intake manifold	expansion tank pressure bottle	off	Use 4 ft (1200mm) clear tubing to direct coolant from bleed valve to a clean catch basin. Fill until steady flow is established. Gently squeeze upper radiator hose until bubbles stop. Close valve.
1993-96 3.3L, 3.5L longitudinal engine	COMPLICATED PROCEDURE: SEE SERVICE MANUAL			—	—
EAGLE 1989 Medallion	screw	1. upper hose 2. heater hose 3. AT oil cooler	reservoir	off	—
1989-92 Premier: V6	valve	thermostat housing	reservoir	off	Bleed twice, before & after running.
1992-94 1.8L Summit wagon	bolt	thermostat housing	thermostat housing & radiator	—	Fill through housing until full. Install bolt and top off radiator. With engine warm, rev 3 times.
1997 Vision	valve	thermostat housing	expansion tank pressure bottle	off	Use clear tubing to direct coolant fron bleeder valve to a clean catch basin. Fill until steady flow is established. Gently squeeze upper radiator hose until bubbles stop. Close valve.
1993-96 Vision	COMPLICATED PROCEDURE: SEE SERVICE MANUAL			—	—
FORD, LINCOLN, MERCURY 1989-93 Taurus, Sable: 4-cyl.	plug	thermostat housing	radiator	off	Reinstall plug after filling radiator before starting engine.
1989-93 4-cyl. 2.3L OHC	heater hose	thermostat housing	radiator	—	Disconnect hose at water outlet connection and fill radiator until coolant is visible at the connection or reaches radiator cap filler neck.
1989-97 Thunderbird: 3.8L	plug	water bypass elbow	radiator	off	Reinstall plug after filling radiator before starting engine.
1993-97 Probe: 2.5L	—	—	filler port on water outlet	idle	Open both radiator & filler cap. Top off at filler with engine at idle. Stop engine & recheck at filler port. Fill reservoir to F-mark on dipstick.
1993-95 Mark VIII	—	—	Cap on top of engine pipes	—	Fill through engine cap until coolant reaches fill mark on reservoir. Install reservoir cap and fill until full at engine pipes.
1996-97 Continental, Mark VIII	plug	bypass tube	—	—	Fill to top of neck at bypass tube, allowing air to escape. Torque fill plug (12 ft-lbs/17 Nm). Set heater to MAX., blower HIGH through dash vents. Run engine to normal operating temperature. Recheck level when cool.
Villager, Lincoln LS	COMPLICATED PROCEDURE: SEE SERVICE MANUAL			—	—
GENERAL MOTORS 1995-00 2.2L Cavalier, Sunfire	valve	heater return pipe	surge tank	off	Close bleeder when coolant flows & bubbles cease— *before* starting engine. Warm engine, with HVAC set to "Heater" & "Full Hot." If no warm air within 5 minutes, turn off engine, allow to cool, recheck level.
1989-92 All 4-cyl. 1.8L, 2.0L OHC; 2.5L w/thermostat twist cap	caps	radiator & thermostat housing	thermo	—	Fill through thermostat housing until coolant reaches top of radiator neck. Recheck cold.
1989 V6 2.8L FWD ex. Century, Celebrity, Ciera, 6000	valve	thermostat housing	radiator	off	With high-mounted bypass hose (above radiator), also remove hose from pipe.
1998-94 Sunbird 2.0L	cap	thermostat housing	thermostat housing	off	Fill surge tank to FULL COLD mark. With engine off, fill through thermostat housing until coolant reaches housing cap seat. With both pressure caps closed, warm engine & allow to cool. Recheck level at surge tank.
2000 3.0L V6 Code R	hose connection	throttle body coolant return hose	surge tank	off	Reconnect throttle body coolant return hose when cooling system is filled to 80% of capacity.
1989-99 V6 3.1L Regal, Lumina, Monte Carlo, Cutlass Supreme, Grand Prix, Malibu	valves	1. thermostat housing 2. throttle body return pipe, 1989-97	radiator	off	Close valve when coolant flows from vent. Continue filling. Idle engine to operating temperature and top off.

COOLING SYSTEM AIR BLEED CHART

MAKE, MODEL, ENGINE	BLEEDER TYPE	LOCATION	FILL POINT	BLEED W/ENGINE @ RPM	SPECIAL NOTICE
GENERAL MOTORS **Continued** 2000 3.1L	valve	thermostat bypass pipe/heater pipe assembly	radiator	off	Close valve when coolant flows from vent. Continue filling. Idle engine to operating temperature and top off.
1991-97 V6 3.4L	valves	1. thermostat housing 2. heater inlet pipe	radiator	off	Fill through radiator neck until full. Allow system to stabilize and add coolant as needed. Install radiator cap and close air bleeds. Fill coolant reservoir to proper level.
1999-00 3.4L	valve	thermostat bypass pipe/heater pipe	surge tank	off	Close valve when coolant flows from vent. Run engine until upper hose is near hot. Top off surge tank.
3.5L	valve	on radiator above trans cooler pipe connection	surge tank	off	Fill through surge tank. Close valve when coolant starts to flow from valve.
1989-91 V6 3.8L Code C, 1989-93 V6 3.3L	—	—	radiator	—	Turn AC on Low, temp. on High. Rev engine to 3000 RPM at least five times to purge trapped air.
1991-96 3.8L Code L, 1 ex. Riviera	plug	thermostat housing	radiator	idle	Turn AC on Low, temp. on High. Cycle engine to 3000 RPM five times and slowly open air bleed.
1991-99 Riviera 1997-99 LeSabre, 88, Regency, Bonneville	valve	thermostat housing	radiator	idle	Fill radiator. Warm engine. With engine at idle, top off as needed. Cycle engine to 3000 RPM, five times. Open bleed valve for about 15 seconds to expel trapped air.
Cadillac 4.1L, 4.5L, 4.6L, 4.9L	—	—	radiator	—	Run engine at 2000 RPM for 10 minutes with cap off.
1992-97 5.7L Code P Corvette	screw	1. thermostat housing 2. throttle body	surge tank	off	—
1994-96 All RWD ex. Corvette	screw	upper radiator hose outlet	recovery reservoir	idle	Remove knock sensors when draining system.
1996-98 3.8L Camaro, Firebird	valve	water outlet	radiator	off	—
HONDA 1996-00 Accord 4-cyl, Prelude, Odyssey, Oasis	valve	thermostat housing	radiator	off	Fill to bottom of filler neck. Tighten bolt when coolant flows freely from bleeder, without bubbles.
1988-95 All	valve	thermostat housing	radiator	off	—
INFINITI G20	bolt pipe cap housing	thermostat housing & heater hose	radiator	off	Fill until coolant flows from bleeders, then close bleeders. Jam open cap valve with a U-shaped wire. Run engine to purge air through the coolant reservoir.
M30	bolt	cylinder head	radiator	off	Bolt on boss by PCV hose.
QX-4	bolt	on hose coupling above EBR valve	radiator	off	none
ISUZU – see Honda					
JEEP 1999-00 4.7L Grand Cherokee	plug	coolant outlet (upper radiator hose)	radiator	off	Fill until coolant flows from coolant bleed bore. 1999 repeat process after starting engine and running at 3000 RPM for 10 seconds.
LEXUS 1990-91 ES 250	valve	thermostat housing	radiator	off	—
1990-97 SC400, LS400	bolt	thermostat housing	thermostat housing	off	Fill through housing until full. Install bolt and fill reservoir.
1998-99 LS400	plug	throttle body	throttle body		Fill through throttle body housing until system is full. Install plug and fill reservoir.
MITSUBISHI 1997-00 Mirage 1994-98 Galant	bolt	water outlet fitting	radiator	off	Fill at radiator until coolant flows from bleed bolt. Tighten bolt. Warm engine. Rev to 3000 RPM 3 times. Recheck when cool.
1992-00 Montero, Montero Sport	bolt	water outlet fitting	radiator	off	Fill at radiator until coolant flows from bleed bolt. Tighten bolt. Warm engine. Rev to 3000 RPM 3 times. Recheck when cool.
1992-96 Expo 1.8L	bolt	thermostat housing	thermostat housing	off	1.8L only: Fill through bleeder bolt hole, until it overflows. Replace bolt & fill radiator.

COOLING SYSTEM AIR BLEED CHART

MAKE, MODEL, ENGINE	BLEEDER TYPE	LOCATION	FILL POINT	BLEED W/ENGINE @ RPM	SPECIAL NOTICE
NISSAN 1991-99 Sentra, NX, 200SX, 1.6L	bolts (2)	thermostat housing heater hose coupling	radiator	off	Remove both bolts when draining. Replace when coolant flows while filling.
2.0L	bolt	thermostat housing	radiator	off	Replace bolt when coolant flows while filling.
1993-98 240SX	valve	cylinder head near heater hose	radiator	off	Race warm engine 3 times. Recheck cold.
1993-00 Altima	plug	beneath distributor	radiator	off	With ignition ON, set HVAC to hottest setting. Note: Automatic AC—See Service Manual. Race warm engine 3 times. Recheck cold.
1996-00 Pathfinder	bolt	on hose coupling above EGR valve	radiator	off	none
1998-99 Frontier	bolt	on intake manifold by coolant sensor	radiator	off	none
1999 Quest	(draining) bolt	on hose by EBR valve	radiator		Remove bolt when draining, replace before filling.
1998-93 Quest	COMPLICATED PROCEDURE: SEE SERVICE MANUAL		—	—	
1989-90 Sentra, Pulsar	plug	cylinder head	radiator	off	Recheck cold.
1991-94 Sentra, NX: 1.6L	bolts (2)	1. cylinder head 2. heater hose outlet			1.6L & 2.0L: Fill until coolant flows from bleeders, then close bleeders. Jam open cap valve with a U-shaped wire. Run engine to purge air through the coolant reservoir.
2.0L	1. bolt 2. pipe cap, 1991-93	engine block below upper radiator hose & heater hose	radiator	off	(See above.)
1989-92 Axxess, Stanza	bolt	intake manifold plenum	radiator	off	Bolt located next to PCV valve. Recheck cold.
1989-90 240SX	bolt	thermostat housing	radiator	off	Recheck cold.
1990-94 300ZX	plug	radiator top tank	radiator	off	Recheck cold.
1989-94 Maxima: SOHC	bolt	intake manifold plenum	radiator	off	Bolt located next to PCV valve. Recheck cold.
DOHC	bolt	water inlet by throttle body	radiator	off	—
1989 Pickup V6	plug	heater pipe	radiator	off	Plug is by battery.
1990-96 Pickup: 4-cyl.	bolt	#1 intake manifold runner	radiator	off	Recheck cold.
V6	bolt	intake manifold plenum	radiator	off	Bolt located next to IAC valve. Recheck cold.
PORSCHE 1989 944, 924S	screw	thermostat housing	tank	fast idle	—
SAAB 1989-93 900	screw	thermostat housing	tank	off	—
SUBARU 1990-94 Legacy ex. Turbo	plug	radiator top tank	radiator	off	Run engine at 2000 to 3000 RPM for 5 minutes. Recheck cold.
w/Turbo	cap	coolant filler tank	coolant filler tank	off	Run engine at 2000 to 3000 RPM for 5 minutes. Recheck cold.
1995-98 Legacy	plug	radiator upper tank	radiator	fast idle	—
TOYOTA 1989-96 MR2	valves	1. radiator 2. heater 3. water inlet, 1985-89	engine compartment filler cap	off	Fit hoses to bleeders to allow level to rise to height of filler cap at engine until water flows from bleeders.
1989-91 Camry V6	valve	thermostat housing	radiator	off	—
VOLKSWAGEN 1993-97 EuroVan 2.5L	screw	heater hose	—	—	Remove cap from expansion tank. Run engine at fast idle. Recheck. Close expansion tank. Idle engine until cooling fans start. Recheck cold.
1989-91 Vanagon	valve	radiator	tank	fast idle	Raise front of vehicle 16" (40 cm). Open bleed connection in the engine compartment.
1989-94 Fox	thermo switch	cylinder head	tank	off	

Tire sizes and tire pressures represent the car manufacturer's recommendations (for normal speeds).
*For minimum load pressure, refer to tire decal.
•Cars equipped with Trailer Tow Option, refer to tire decal.

WHEEL NUT-TIGHTENING SEQUENCE

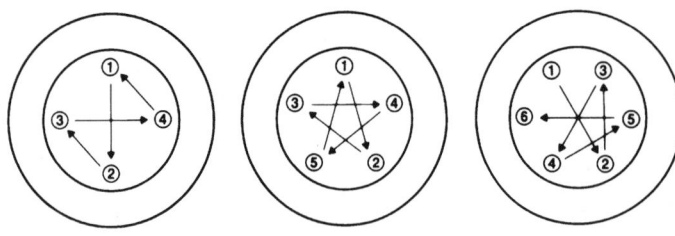

4-nut wheel　　　**5-nut wheel**　　　**6-nut wheel**

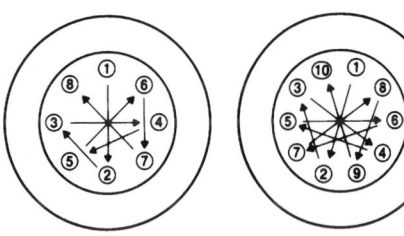

8-nut wheel　　　**10-nut wheel**

IMPORTANT:
Careless installation of wheels on a vehicle is a major cause of tire, wheel, and brake problems. Check all parts, including wheels, studs, and mounting faces of hub and wheels, for dirt, rust, or damage. Use a wire brush to remove dirt and rust. Replace any damaged parts.

Proper installation, including nut torque, is essential to safe, economical, trouble-free service. Use only the specified sizes and types of studs and nuts. Never use oil or grease on lug nuts or studs.

Tighten the nuts a quarter turn at a time following the criss-cross sequence shown at left. This is very important. Failure to tighten nuts in the criss-cross sequence will cause misalignment of the wheel and/or rotor damage.

Continue until all nuts are tightened to the torque specified in the table. Caution: Improper torque can cause distortion, fatigue cracks, or alignment problems. After running the vehicle for a short distance, check the nuts for tightness. Retighten all nuts to specified torque, as needed.

MAKE	MODEL	YEAR	ORIGINAL EQUIPMENT SIZE Standard	Optional	RECOMMENDED INFLATION PRESSURE Front - Rear	LUG NUT TORQUE Ft.-Lbs	RIM WIDTH
ACURA							
2.2CL							
	1998-97	All	205/55VR16		32-29	80	6-JJ
2.3CL							
	2000-98	All	205/55VR16		32-29	80	6-JJ
2.5TL							
	1999-95	All	205/60HR15		30-29	80	6-JJ
3.0CL							
	2000-96	All	205/55VR16		32-29	80	6-JJ
3.2TL							
	2000-99	All	P205/60VR16		32-32	80	6.5-JJ
	1998-95	All	205/65VR15		29-29	80	6.5-JJ
3.5RL							
	2000-95	All	P215/60VR16		29-29	80	6.5-JJ
Integra							
	2000-94	2-door	P195/60HR14		29-29	80	5.5-JJ
				P195/55VR15	35-33	80	5.5-, 6-JJ
		4-door	P195/55VR15		35-33	80	6-JJ
	1993-92	Ex. GS-R.	195/60R14		29-29	80	5.5-JJ
		GS-R	P195/60VR14		29-29	80	5.5-JJ
	1991-90	GS	P195/60R14		35-35	80	5.5-JJ
		RS & LS	195/60R14		32-32	80	5.5-JJ
	1989-86	All	195/60R14		32-32	80	5.5-JJ
Legend							
	1995-94	Ex GS & LS	205/60VR15		32-32	80	6.5-JJ
		GS & LS	215/55VR16		33-30	80	6.5-JJ
	1993-92	All	205/60VR15		32-30	80	6.5-JJ
	1991-90	Coupe	205/60VR15		32-30	80	5.5-JJ
		Sedan	205/60R15		32-32	80	5.5-JJ
	1989-86	All	205/60R15		32-32	80	5.5-JJ
NSX							
	2000-95	Front	215/45ZR16		33 —	80	7-JJ
		Rear	245/40ZR17		— 40	80	8.5-JJ
	1994-91	Front	205/50ZR15		35 —	80	6.5-JJ
		Rear	225/50ZR16		— 35	80	8-JJ
SLX							
	2000-96	All	245/70R16		30-35	80	7-JJ
Vigor							
	1994-92	All	205/60R15		30-28	80	6-JJ
					20-24	85	5-, 6-JJ
ASUNA (CANADA)							
Sunfire							
	1993-92	All	P185/60HR14		30-30	87	5.5-JJ
Sunrunner							
	1993	2WD	P195/75R15		23-23	60	5.5-JJ
		4WD		P205/75R15	23-23	60	5.5-JJ
AUDI							
100							
	1994-92	All	195/65HR15		34-34	80	6-J
	1991	All	195/65HR15		32-32	80	6-J
	1990	All	205/60VR15		30-30	80	6-J
	1989	Ex. E	205/60VR14		30-30	80	6-J
		E	185/70HR14		32-32	80	5.5-J
100 Quattro							
	1993	All	195/65VR15		34-34	80	7-J
	1991	All	195/65HR15		32-32	80	6-J
	1990-89	All	205/60VR15		30-30	80	6-J
200							
	1991	All	205/60VR15		32-32	80	6-J
	1990-89	All	205/60VR15		30-30	80	6-J
200 Quattro							
	1991	All	215/60HR15	215/60VR15	35-35	80	7.5-J
	1990-89	All	205/60VR15		30-30	80	6-J
80							
	1991	All	175/70VR14		32-32	80	5.5-J
				205/50VR15	34-34	80	7-J
	1990-89	All	175/70R14		32-32	80	5.5-J
80 Quattro							
	1991	All	175/70VR14		34-34	80	6-J
				205/50VR15	34-34	80	7-J
	1990-89	All	195/60VR14		34-34	80	6-J
90							
	1996-92	All	195/65HR15		32-32	80	7-J
	1991	All	175/70TR14		34-34	80	6-J
				205/50VR15	34-34	80	7-J
	1990-89	All	195/60VR14		34-34	80	6-J
90 Quattro							
	1996-92	All	205/65VR15	195/65VR15	32-32	80	7-J
	1991	All	175/70TR14		34-34	80	6-J
				205/50VR15	34-34	80	7-J
	1990-89	All	195/60VR14		34-34	80	6-J

AUDI Continued

MAKE	MODEL	YEAR	Standard	Optional	Front - Rear	Ft.-Lbs	RIM WIDTH
A4							
	1999	All	205/60HR15	205/55ZR16	N/A	90	7-J
	1998-95	All	195/65VR15	205/55HR16	32-32	80	7-J
A6, A6 Quattro							
	1999	All	195/65HR15		N/A	90	6-J
				205/55HR16	N/A	90	7-J
	1998-94	All	195/65HR15		34-34	80	7-J
A8							
	1999-98	All	225/60HR16		32-32	90	7-J
				225/55HR17	32-32	90	8-J
	1997	All	225/60HR16		32-32	80	7-J
				225/55HR17	32-32	80	8-J
Cabriolet							
	1999-97	All	195/65HR15	205/55HR16	32-32	80	7-J
	1996-94	All	195/65HR15		32-32	80	7-J
Coupe							
	1991-90	All	205/60VR15		32-32	80	7-J
S4							
	1994-92	All	225/50ZR16		35-35	80	8-J
S6 Quattro							
	1995-92	All	225/50ZR16		35-35	80	8-J
				215/60VR15	35-35	80	7.5-J
Sport 90							
	1997-94	All	195/65HR15		35-35	80	7-J
V8 Quattro							
	1994-91	All	215/60ZR15		35-35	80	7.5-J
	1990	All	215/60ZR15		30-30	80	7-J

BMW

MAKE	MODEL	YEAR	Standard	Optional	Front - Rear	Ft.-Lbs	RIM WIDTH
316i, 316ti, 318i, 318is, 318ti, 320i, 323is							
	1999	323i	185/65QR15		29-35	72	6.5-J
			195/65HR15		—	72	6.5-J
			205/55HR16		—	72	7-J
			205/60HR15		29-32	72	7-J
			225/55VR15		29-32	72	7-J
			225/50WR16		29-32	72	7-J
	1999-98	318i	185/65R15		29-34	72	6-J
		318i, -is, -ti Sedan, Convertible	205/60HR15		29-32	72	6.5-, 7-J
				225/55VR15	29-32	72	6.5-, 7-J
				225/50ZR16	29-32	72	7-J
	1997	316i	185/65HR15		32-29	72	6-J
				205/60HR15	29-34	72	6.5-, 7-J
	1997-94	318i, -is, -ti: Sedan	185/65R15		29-35	65-79	6-J
				205/60HR15	29-32	65-79	6.5-, 7-J
		Coupe, Convertible	205/60HR15		29-32	65-79	6.5-, 7-J
		320i	205/60HR15		29-32	65-79	6.5-, 7-J
	1993	All	185/65HR15	205/60HR15	29-32	81	6-J
	1992	All	195/65HR15		30-36	81	6-J
	1991	All	195/65HR14		30-36	81	5.5-J
				205/55R15	33-39	81	7-J
325i, 325ic, 325is, 328i, 328is							
	1999	328i	205/55HR15		—	72	—
			205/60HR15		29-33	72	7-J
			225/55WR16		29-33	72	7-J
			225/45WR17		—	72	8-J
	1998	328i: Coupe	205/60VR15		29-34	72	6.5-, 7-J
				225/55VR15	29-34	72	
				225/50ZR16	29-32	72	7-J
		Convertible	205/60HR15		29-32	72	6.5-, 7-J
				225/50ZR16	29-32	72	7-J
	1997	328i, -is	205/60HR15		29-34	72	6.5-, 7-J
				225/50ZR16	29-34	72	7-J
	1996-93	325i, is, ic	205/60HR15		29-32	65-79	6.5-, 7-J
	1992	Convertible	195/65HR14		33-39	81	6-J
		Ex. Conv.	205/60HR15		30-38	81	7-J
				225/55VR15	30-38	81	7-J
	1991-90	All	195/65R14		33-39	81	6-, 6.5-J
	1989	All	195/65R14	195/65VR14	33-39	81	5.5-, 6-J
325ix							
	1991-89	All	205/55VR15		33-41	81	7-J
525i							
	1996-94	Ex. Touring	205/65HR15	225/60R15	33-41	65-79	6.5-, 7-J
		Touring	225/60HR15		36-44	81	7-J
	1994-93	Ex. Touring	205/60HR15	225/60HR15	33-41	81	6.5-, 7-J
				240/45ZR415	33-41	81	195mm
		Touring	225/60HR15		36-44	81	6.5-, 7-J
				240/45ZR415	36-44	81	195mm

BMW Continued

MAKE	MODEL	YEAR	Standard	Optional	Front - Rear	Ft.-Lbs	RIM WIDTH
525i Continued							
	1992-91	All	205/65HR15	225/60HR15	33-41	81	6.5-, 7-J
				240/45ZR415	33-41	81	195mm
	1990	All	205/65VR15		33-41	81	7-J
	1989	All	205/65VR15	225/60VR15	33-41	81	6.5-, 7-J
				220/55R390	36-44	81	165mm
				240/45VR415	33-41	81	195mm
528, 528i							
	1999	528i	225/60HR15		33-41	72	7-J
				225/55HR16	33-41	72	7-J
				235/45WR17	33-41	72	8-J
	1998-97	528i	205/65R15		33-41	72	6.5-, 7-J
			225/60R15		33-41	72	6.5-, 7-J
				235/45R17	33-41	72	8-J
				255/40R17	33-41	72	9-J
530i							
	1996-94	All	225/60HR15		36-44	65-79	7-J
				240/45ZR415	33-41	81	195mm
533i, 535i							
	1993-92	All	225/60VR15		29-33	81	7-J
				225/60VR15	29-35	81	7-J
				240/45ZR415	29-35	81	195mm
	1991-90	All	205/65R15		35-44	81	6.5-, 7-J
				225/60ZR15	35-44	81	7-J
	1989	All	225/60VR15		35-44	81	6.5-, 7-J
				220/55R390	35-44	81	165mm
				240/45VR415	35-44	81	195mm
540i							
	1999-97	All	225/55R16		35-42	72	7-J
		Front		235/45R17	35-42	72	8-J
		Rear		255/40R17	35-42	72	9-J
633CSi, 635CSi, L6							
	1989	All	195/70R14		33-36	81	6-, 6.5-J
				200/60R390	33-36	81	165mm
733i, 735i, L7							
	1992-91	All	225/60ZR15		35-44	81	7-J
	1990	All	225/60VR15		35-44	81	7-J
	1989	All	205/65VR15	225/60R15	32-39	81	6.5-, 7-J
				220/55R390	32-39	81	165mm
				240/45VR415	32-39	81	195mm
740i, 740iL, 750iL							
	1999	740i	235/60HR16		33-41	72	8-J
				235/50ZR18	33-41	72	8-J
				255/45ZR18	33-41	72	8-J
		750i	235/60HR16		33-41	72	7.5-J
				235/50ZR18	33-41	72	7.5-J
				255/45ZR18	33-41	72	7.5-J
	1998-97	All	235/60WR16		32-29	72	7.5-J
				245/55WR16	32-29	72	8-J
	1996-95	All	235/60R16		32-39	81	7.5-J
	1994-93	All	225/60ZR15		35-39	81	7-J
				240/45ZR415	35-39	81	195mm
	1992-91	All	225/60ZR15		35-44	81	7-J
	1990	All	225/60VR15		35-44	81	7-J
	1989	All	225/60ZR15		32-36	81	7-J
				240/45ZR415	32-36	81	195mm
840Ci, 850Ci							
	1997-93	All	235/50ZR16		33-36	81	7.5-J
				235/45WR17	33-39	81	8-J
850CSi							
	1997-93	Front	235/45ZR17		33 —	81	8-J
		Rear	265/40ZR17		— 36	81	9-J
850i							
	1992	All	235/50ZR16		32-32	81	7.5-J
	1991	All	235/50ZR16	225/55R16	30-36	81	7.5-J
M3							
	1999-98	M3: Front	225/45ZR17		41—	72	7.5-J
		Rear	245/40ZR17		—48	72	8.5-J
		M Roadster: Front	225/45ZR17		35—	72	7.5-J
		Rear	245/40ZR17		—38	72	8.5, 9-J
	1997	All: Front	225/45ZR17		33 —	72	7.5-J
		Rear	245/45ZR17		— 45	72	8-J
	1996-95	All	235/40ZR17		33-36	65-79	7.5-J
	1991-89	All	205/55VR15		33-41	81	7-J
M5							
	1993	All	235/45ZR17		38-41	81	8-J
	1992	All	235/45ZR17		41-44	81	8-J
	1991	All	225/50R16		36-44	81	7-J
				235/45ZR17	41-44	81	8-J

MAKE / MODEL / YEAR	ORIGINAL EQUIPMENT SIZE Standard	Optional	RECOMMENDED INFLATION PRESSURE Front - Rear	LUG NUT TORQUE Ft.-Lbs	RIM WIDTH
BMW Continued					
M6					
1989 All	240/45VR415		36-41	81	195mm
	220/55R390		36-41	81	165mm
Z3					
1999-96 All	225/50ZR16		29-29	72	7-J
	205/60R15		29-29	72	6.5-, 7-J
All: Front	225/45RZ17		29-29	72	7.5-J
Rear	245/40ZR17		—32	—	8.5, 9-J
BUICK					
Century					
2000-97 All	P205/70R15		30-30	100	6-J
1999-97 All	P205/70R15		30-30	100	6-J
1996-92 All	P185/75R14		32-32	100	5.5-JJ
	P195/75R14		30-30	100	5.5-JJ
1991-89 Ex. GT	P185/75R14	P195/75R14	35-35	100	5.5-JJ
GT	P215/60R14		35-35	100	6.5-JJ
Electra					
1991-89 T-Type	P215/65R15		30-30	100	6-JJ
Limited	P205/75R14		30-30	100	6-JJ
	P215/65R15		30-30	100	6-JJ
Ultra	P205/70R15		30-30	100	6-JJ
1989 All	P205/75R14		30-30	100	6-JJ
T-Type	P215/65R15		30-30	100	6-JJ
Estate Wagon					
1990-89 All	P225/75R15		30-35	100	7-JJ
LeSabre					
2000 All	P215/70R15		33-33	—	—
	P225/60R16		30-30	—	—
1999-97 All	P205/70R15		30-30	100	6-JJ
	P215/60R16		30-30	100	6.5-JJ
1996-92 All	P205/70R15		30-30	100	6-JJ
	P215/60R16		30-30	100	6.5-JJ
1991-89 All	P205/75R14	P215/65R15	30-30	100	6-JJ
Park Avenue					
2000-97 All	P225/60R16		30-30	100	6.5-JJ
1996-93 Ex. Ultra	P205/70R15		30-30	100	6-JJ
	P215/60R16		30-30	100	6.5-JJ
Ultra	P215/70R15	P215/60R16	30-30	100	6-, 6.5-JJ
1992 All	P215/70R15		30-30	100	6-JJ
	P215/60R16		32-30	100	6.5-JJ
1991 All	P205/75R15	P215/65R15	30-30	100	6-JJ
Reatta					
1992-89 All	P215/65R15		30-30	100	6-JJ
Regal					
2000-97 LS	P215/70R15		30-30	—	6-J
GS	P225/60R16		30-30	—	6.5-J
1999-97 GS	P225/60R16		30-30	100	6.5-J
LS	P215/70R15		30-30	100	6.5-J
1996-93 Ex. GS	P205/70R15		30-30	100	6-JJ
	P215/70R15		30-30	100	6-JJ
	P225/60R16		30-30	100	6.5-JJ
GS	P225/60R16		30-30	100	6.5-JJ
1992 Ex. GS & GT	P205/70R14	P205/70R15	30-30	100	5.5-JJ
GS & GT	P225/60R16		30-30	100	6.5-JJ
1991-89 Ex. GT	P205/70R14		30-30	100	5.5-JJ
	P205/70R15		30-30	100	6-JJ
GT	P215/60R16		30-30	100	6.5-JJ
Riviera					
1999-95 All	P225/60R16		30-30	100	6.5-JJ
1993 All	P205/70R15		28-26	100	6-JJ
	P215/60R16		30-30	100	7-JJ
1992-90 All	P205/70R15		28-26	100	6.5-JJ
	P215/65R15		30-22	100	6.5-JJ
1989 All	P205/70R15	P215/65R15	30-30	100	6-JJ
Roadmaster					
1996-93 Sedan	P235/70R15	P225/70HR15	30-30	100	7-JJ
Wagon	P225/70R15		30-35	100	7-JJ
1992 Sedan	P225/70R15	P235/70R15	30-30	100	7-J
Wagon	P225/70R15	P235/70R15	30-35	100	7-J
1991 All	P225/75R15		30-35	100	7-J
Skyhawk					
1989 Ex. S/E	P185/80R14		35-35	100	5.5-JB
S/E	P215/60R14		30-30	100	6-JJ
Skylark					
1998-96 Ex. GS	P195/70R14		30-30	100	6-JJ
	P195/65R15		30-30	100	6-JJ
GS	P205/55R16		30-30	100	6-JJ
1995-93 Ex. GS	P185/75R14		35-35	100	6-JJ
	P195/65R15		30-30	100	6-JJ
GS	P205/55R16		35-35	100	6-JJ
1992 All	P185/75R14		35-35	100	6-JJ

MAKE / MODEL / YEAR	ORIGINAL EQUIPMENT SIZE Standard	Optional	RECOMMENDED INFLATION PRESSURE Front - Rear	LUG NUT TORQUE Ft.-Lbs	RIM WIDTH
BUICK Continued					
Skylark Continued					
1991 Ex. Gran Spt.	P185/75R14		35-35	100	6-JJ
	P195/70R14		30-30	100	6-JJ
Gran Sport	P215/60R14		30-30	100	6-JJ
1990-89 All	P185/80R13		35-35	100	5.5-JB
	P205/70R13		30-30	100	5.5-JB
	P215/60R14		30-30	100	6-JJ
CADILLAC					
Allante					
1993 All	P225/60ZR16		30-30	100	7-JJ
1992-89 All	P225/55VR16		28-24	100	7-JJ
Catera					
2000-97 All	P225/55R16		32-32	80	N/A
Concours					
2000 All	P225/60R16		30-30	100	—
DeVille					
2000 All	225/60R16		30-30	100	—
	P225/60R16		30-30	100	—
1998-97 All	P225/60R16		30-30	100	7-JJ
1996 Base	P225/60R15		30-30	100	7-JJ
Concours	P225/60HR16		30-30	100	7-JJ
1995-94 Base	P215/70R15		32-32	100	6-JJ
Concours	P225/60HR16		30-30	100	7-JJ
1993-92 Ex. Touring Sedan	P205/70R15		30-30	100	6-JJ
Touring Sedan	P215/60R16		32-30	100	6.5-JJ
1991-90 All	P205/70R15	P215/75R15	30-30	100	6-JJ
1989 All	P205/75R15		30-30	100	5.5-JJ
Eldorado					
2000-98 All	P235/60R16	P235/60ZR16	30-30	100	N/A
1997-93 W/Tour pkg	P225/60ZR16		29-29	100	7-JJ
W/o Tour pkg.	P225/60R16		28-26	100	7-JJ
1992 All	P225/60R16		28-26	100	7-JJ
STS & Touring	P225/60HR16		28-26	100	7-JJ
1991-90 Ex. STS	P205/70R15		28-26	100	6-JJ
	P215/65R15		28-26	100	7-JJ
STS	P215/60R16		28-26	100	7-JJ
1989 All	P205/75R14		30-30	100	5.5-JJ
	P215/65R15		32-32	100	6-JJ
Escalade					
2000-99 All	P265/70R16		35-35	N/A	7-JJ
Fleetwood (FWD)					
1992-91 All	P205/70R15		30-30	100	6-JJ
1990 All	P205/70R15	P215/75R15	30-30	100	6-JJ
1989 All	P205/75R15		30-30	100	5.5-JJ
Fleetwood Brougham (RWD)					
1997-95 All	P235/70R15	P235/75R15	35-35	100	7-JJ
1994-93 All	P235/70R15		35-35	100	7-JJ
1992-91 All	P225/75R15		30-30	100	7-JJ
1990-89 All	P225/75R15		30-30	100	6-JJ
Seville					
2000-98 All	P235/60R16	P235/60ZR16	30-30	100	N/A
1997-93 W/Touring pkg.	P225/60ZR16		29-29	100	7-JJ
W/o Tour pkg.	P225/60R16		28-26	100	7-JJ
1992 All	P225/60R16		28-26	100	7-JJ
STS & Touring	P225/60HR16		28-26	100	7-JJ
1991-90 Ex. STS	P205/70R15		28-26	100	6-JJ
	P215/65R15		28-26	100	7-JJ
STS	P215/60R16		28-26	100	7-JJ
1989 All	P205/75R14		30-30	100	5.5-JJ
	P215/65R15		32-32	100	6-JJ
CHEVROLET					
Beretta					
1996 Ex. Z26	P195/70R14	P205/60R15	30-30	100	6-JJ
Z26	P205/60R15	P205/55R16	30-30	100	8-JJ
1995 Ex. Z26	P185/75R14	P195/70R15	30-30	100	6-JJ
Z26	P205/60R15	P205/55R16	30-30	100	6-JJ
1994-93 Ex. GTZ	P185/75R14	P195/70R14	30-30	100	6-JJ
	P205/60R15		30-30	100	6-JJ
GTZ	P205/55VR16	P205/55R16	30-30	100	8-JJ
1992-91 Ex. GT & GTZ.	P185/75R14	P195/70R14	30-30	100	6-JJ
GTZ	P205/55VR16		30-30	100	7-JJ
GT	P205/60R15		30-30	100	7-JJ
1990-89 Ex. GT	P195/70R14		35-35	100	6-JJ
Convertible	P205/55R16		30-30	100	7-JJ
Camaro					
2000-99 Base	P215/60R16		30-30	100	8.0
Police	245/50ZR16		35-35	100	8.0
Z28	P235/55ZR16		30-30	100	8.0
W/SS Pkg.	P275/40ZR16		30-30	100	9.0

CHEVROLET Continued

MAKE	MODEL	YEAR	ORIGINAL EQUIPMENT SIZE Standard	Optional	RECOMMENDED INFLATION PRESSURE Front - Rear	LUG NUT TORQUE Ft.-Lbs	RIM WIDTH

Camaro Continued

Year	Model	Standard	Optional	Inflation	Torque	Rim Width
1998-94	Base	P215/60R16		30-30	100	7.5-J
		P235/55R16		30-30	100	8-J
	RS	P235/55R16		30-30	100	8-JJ
	Z28	P235/55R16	P245/50ZR16	30-30	100	8-J
	W/WS6 Susp	P275/40ZR17		30-30	100	9-J
1993	RS	P215/60R15		30-30	100	7.5-J
		P235/55R16		30-30	100	8-J
1993-91	Z28 Conv	P245/50ZR16		30-30	100	8-JJ
	Z28 coupe	P235/55R16	P245/50ZR16	30-30	100	8-J
1992	RS coupe	P215/65R15		30-30	100	7-JJ
		P235/55R16		30-30	100	8-JJ
1991-90	RS coupe	P215/65R15		30-30	100	7-JJ
1990	IROC: Conv	P245/50ZR16		30-30	100	8-JJ
	Ex. Convert	P215/65R15		35-35	100	7-JJ
		P245/50ZR16		30-30	100	8-JJ
1989	Ex. IROC	P215/65R15		30-30	100	7-JJ
	IROC	P215/65R15		35-35	100	7-JJ
		P245/50ZR16		30-30	100	8-JJ

Caprice

Year	Model	Standard	Optional	Inflation	Torque	Rim Width
1996-93	Sedan	P215/75R15	P225/70R15	30-30	100	7-JJ
			P235/70VR15	30-30	100	7-JJ
	Wagon	P225/75R15		30-35	100	7-JJ
1992	Sedan:					
	Ex. LTZ	P215/75R15		30-30	100	7-JJ
	LTZ	P235/70VR15		30-30	100	7-JJ
	Wagon	P225/75R15		30-35	100	7-JJ
1991	Sedan	P205/75R15	P215/75R15	30-30	80	7-JJ
			P225/70R15	30-30	80	7-JJ
	Wagon	P225/70R15		30-35	100	7-JJ
1990-89	Sedan	P205/75R15		35-35	80	6-JJ
			P225/70R15	30-30	80	7-JJ
	Wagon	P225/75R15		30-35	100	7-JJ

Cavalier

Year	Model	Standard	Optional	Inflation	Torque	Rim Width
2000-97	Base	P195/70R14		30-30	100	6-JJ
	LS, RS	P195/65R15		30-30	100	6-JJ
	Convertible	P195/65R15		30-28	—	6
	Z24	P205/55R16		30-30	100	6-JJ
1996-91	Base	P185/75R14		35-35	100	6-JJ
		P195/70R14		30-30	100	6-JJ
	RS, Wagon	P195/70R14		30-30	100	6-JJ
	Z24	P205/60R15		30-30	100	6-JJ
1990-89	Ex. Z24	P185/80R13		35-35	100	5.5-JB
	Z24	P215/60R14		35-35	100	6-JJ

Celebrity

Year	Model	Standard	Optional	Inflation	Torque	Rim Width
1990	Eurosport	P195/75R14		25-35	100	6.5-JJ
			P195/70R14	30-30	100	6.5-JJ
	Ex. Eurosport	P185/75R14		35-35	100	5.5-JJ
			P195/75R14	35-35	100	6.5-JJ
1989	Eurosport	P195/75R14	P195/70R14	30-30	100	5.5-, 6.5-JJ
	Ex. Eurosport	P185/75R14		35-35	100	5.5-JJ
			P195/75R14	35-35	100	6.5-JJ
	Diesel	P195/75R14		35-35	100	5.5-JJ

Corsica

Year	Model	Standard	Optional	Inflation	Torque	Rim Width
1996-95	All	P195/70R14		30-30	100	6-JJ
1994-91	All	P185/75R14	P205/60R15	30-30	100	6-JJ
1990-89	Ex. LTZ	P185/75R14	P195/70R14	30-30	100	6-JJ
	LTZ	P205/60R15		30-30	100	6-JJ

Corvette

Year	Model	Standard	Optional	Inflation	Torque	Rim Width
2000-97	Front	P245/45ZR17		30-30	100	8.5
	Rear	P275/40ZR18		30-30	100	9.5
1996-93	5.7L Code P, 5:					
	W/Adj Handling pkg	P275/40ZR17		35-35	100	9.5-JJ
	W/o Adj Handling pkg.:					
	Front	P255/45ZR17		35 —	100	8.5-JJ
	Rear	P285/40ZR17		— 35	100	9.5-JJ
1995-89	5.7L DOHC:					
	Front	P275/40ZR17		35 —	100	9.5-JJ
	Rear	P315/35ZR17		— 35	100	11-JJ
1992	5.7L Code P:					
	Coupe	P275/40ZR17		35-35	100	9.5-JJ
	Convertible	P275/40ZR17		30-30	100	9.5-JJ
1991-89	5.7L ex. DOHC:					
	Convertible	P275/40ZR17		30-30	100	9.5-JJ
	Ex. Conv.	P275/40ZR17		35-35	100	9.5-JJ

El Camino, Caballero
Impala SS

Year	Model	Standard	Optional	Inflation	Torque	Rim Width
2000	All	P225/60R16		30-30[1]	—	—
1996-94	All	P255/50ZR17		30-30	100	7-JJ

Lumina

Year	Model	Standard	Optional	Inflation	Torque	Rim Width
2000	Lumina	P205/70R15		30-30[1]	—	—
		P225/60R15		30-30[1]	—	—

CHEVROLET Continued

Lumina Continued

Year	Model	Standard	Optional	Inflation	Torque	Rim Width
1999	LS, LTZ	P225/60R16		30-30	100	6.5
	Police	P215/65R15		35-35	100	6.0
	Sedan	P205/70R15		30-30	100	6.0
1998-95	V6 3.1L	P205/70R15		30-30	100	6-JJ
			P215/65R16	30-30	100	N/A
			P225/60R16	30-30	100	6.5-JJ
	V6 3.4L	P225/60R16		30-30	100	6.5-JJ
1994-92	Eurosport:					
	V6 3.1L	P205/70R15		30-30	100	6-JJ
	V6 3.4L	P225/60R16	P215/60R16	30-30	100	6.5-JJ
	Z34	P225/60R16		30-30	100	6.5-JJ
1994-90	Ex. Eurospt	P195/75R14		30-30	100	5.5-JJ
1991	Eurosport	P205/75R15		30-30	100	6-JJ
			P225/60R16	30-30	100	6.5-JJ
1990	Eurosport	P205/65R15		35-35	100	6-JJ
			P215/60R16	35-35	100	6-JJ

Lumina APV, Venture, GMC APV

Year	Model	Standard	Optional	Inflation	Torque	Rim Width
2000-99	All	P215/70R15		35-35	100	6.0
1998-97	All	P205/70R15	P215/70R15	32-32	100	N/A
1996-94	All	P205/70R15		32-32	100	6-JJ
1993-92	All	P205/70R14	P205/70R15	35-35	100	6-JJ
1991-90	All	P205/70R14	P195/70R15	35-35	100	6-JJ

Malibu

Year	Model	Standard	Optional	Inflation	Torque	Rim Width
1999-97	All	P215/60R15		29-26	100	6-JJ

Metro

Year	Model	Standard	Optional	Inflation	Torque	Rim Width
1998	All	P155/80R13		32-32	45	4.5-B

Monte Carlo

Year	Model	Standard	Optional	Inflation	Torque	Rim Width
2000	Monte Carlo	P225/60R15		30-30[1]		
1998-95	Monte Carlo:					
	Ex. Z34	P205/70R15		30-30	100	6-JJ
			P215/65R15	30-30	100	N/A
			P225/60R16	30-30	100	6.5-JJ
	Z34	P225/60R16		30-30	100	6.5-JJ

1 Police tire pressure 35-35

Prizm

Year	Model	Standard	Optional	Inflation	Torque	Rim Width
1998	All	P175/65R14	P185/65R14	30-30	76	5.5-J

Sprint

Year	Model	Standard	Optional	Inflation	Torque	Rim Width
1991-89	All	P145/80R12		32-32	45	4-B
		P165/70R12		26-26	45	4.5-B

CHEVROLET/GMC TRUCKS
Astro, Safari Van

Year	Model	Standard	Optional	Inflation	Torque	Rim Width
2000-95	All	P215/75R15		35-35	100	6-, 6.5-JJ
			P235/65R15	35-35	100	6.5-JJ
1994	2WD Base	P205/75R15		35-35	90	6-JJ
	2WD XT, 4WD	P215/75R15		35-35	90	6-JJ
1993-90	Regl van	P205/75R15	P215/75R15	35-35	90	6-JJ
			P245/60HR15	35-35	90	6.5-JJ
	Ext van	P215/75R15		35-35	90	6-JJ
			P245/60HR15	35-35	90	6.5-JJ
1989	All	P205/75R15	P245/60HR15	35-35	90	6-JJ

Blazer, Jimmy

Year	Model	Standard	Optional	Inflation	Torque	Rim Width
1994-92	All	LT225/75R16C		—[1]	120	6.5-JJ
1991	2WD	P235/75R15		35-35	100	6-JJ
		31x10.5R15		—[1]	100	7-, 8-JJ
	4WD	P235/75R15		35-35	120	6-Adj
		31x10.5R15		—[1]	120	7-, 8-JJ
1990	All	P235/75R15		35-35	120	6-JJ
		31x10.5R15		—[1]	120	7-, 8-JJ
1989	All	P235/75R15		35-35	120	6-JJ
		P235/75R15XL		41-41	120	6-JJ

1 Tire pressure varies with different loads; refer to owner's manual or tire decal for proper inflation.

C10, C1500 2WD Pickup

Year	Model	Standard	Optional	Inflation	Torque	Rim Width
1999-96	All	P235/75R15		35-35	120	7-JJ
		LT225/75R16C		—[2]	120	6.5-JJ
		LT245/75R16C		—[2]	120	6.5-JJ
		LT265/75R16C		—[2]	120	6.5-JJ
1995	All	P235/75R15		35-35	120	7-JJ
		LT225/75R16C		—[2]	120	6.5-JJ
		LT265/75R16C		—[2]	120	6.5-JJ
1994-92	All	P225/75R15	P235/75R15	35-35	120	7-JJ
			P225/70R15	35-35	120	7-JJ
			P275/60R15	35-35	120	8-JJ
1991-89	Regl cab	P225/75R15	P235/75R15	35-35	120	6-JJ
	Ext cab	P235/75R15		35-35	120	6-JJ

MAKE	MODEL	YEAR	ORIGINAL EQUIPMENT SIZE Standard	Optional	RECOMMENDED INFLATION PRESSURE Front - Rear	LUG NUT TORQUE Ft.-Lbs	RIM WIDTH

CHEVROLET/GMC TRUCKS Continued
C20 2WD Pickup
C2500 2WD Pickup

YEAR	MODEL	Standard	Optional	Inflation	Torque	Rim Width
1999	All ex. HD	LT225/75R16D	LT245/75R16D	—[2]	160	N/A
1998-96	Crew Cab:					
	SRW	LT245/75R16E		—[2]	100	N/A
	DRW	LT225/75R16D	LT215/85R16D	—[2]	100	N/A
1998-95	All	LT225/75R16D	LT245/75R16E	—[2]	120	6.5-JJ
1994-92	All	LT225/75R16C	LT225/75R16D	—[2]	120	6.5-JJ
			LT245/75R16E	—[2]	120	6.5-JJ
1991-89	All	LT225/75R16D		—[2]	120[1]	6.5-JJ
			LT245/75R16C	—[2]	120[1]	6.5-JJ
			LT245/75R16E	—[2]	120[1]	6.5-JJ

1 With dual rear wheels, 140.
2 Tire pressure varies with different loads; refer to owner's manual or tire decal for proper inflation.

Express, Savana

YEAR	MODEL	Standard	Optional	Inflation	Torque	Rim Width
2000-97	All	P215/75R15	P235/75R15XL	30-30	140	N/A
			LT225/75R16D,E	—[1]	140	N/A
			LT245/75R16E5	—[1]	140	N/A

G10, G1500 Van

YEAR	MODEL	Standard	Optional	Inflation	Torque	Rim Width
2000-97	All	P215/75R15	P235/75R15	35-35	140	6-JJ
		P205/75R15	P215/75R15	35-35	140	6-JJ
			LT235/75R15	—[1]	140	N/A
1996-93	All	P215/75R15	P235/75R15	35-35	100	6-JJ
		P205/75R15	P215/75R15	35-35	100	6-JJ
			LT235/75R15	—[1]	100	N/A
1992	All	P205/75R15	P215/75R15	35-35	100	6-JJ
1991-89	All	P195/75R15	P205/75R15	35-35	100	6-, 6.5-JJ
			P215/75R15	35-35	100	6-, 6.5-JJ

G20, G2500 Van

YEAR	MODEL	Standard	Optional	Inflation	Torque	Rim Width
2000-97	All	P215/75R15	P235/75R15	35-35	140	6-JJ
		P205/75R15	P215/75R15	35-35	140	6-JJ
			LT225/75R15E	—[1]	140	N/A
1996-93	All	P215/75R15	P235/75R15	35-35	100	6-JJ
		P205/75R15	P215/75R15	35-35	100	6-JJ
			LT225/75R15E	—[1]	100	N/A
1992	All	P225/75R15	P235/75R15	35-35	100	6-JJ
1991-89	All	P225/75R15	P235/75R15	35-35	100	6-, 6.5-JJ

1 Tire pressure varies with different loads; refer to owner's manual or tire decal for proper inflation.

K10 4WD Pickup,
K1500 4WD Pickup

YEAR	MODEL	Standard	Optional	Inflation	Torque	Rim Width
1999	All	P245/75R16	P265/75R16C	35-35	140	6.5
			LT245/75R16C	—[1]	140	N/A
1998-97	All	P245/75R16		35-35	120	7-JJ
			LT265/75R16C	—[1]	120	6.5-JJ
1996-95	All	LT225/75R16C	LT245/75R16C	—[1]	120	6.5-JJ
			LT265/75R16C	—[1]	120	6.5-JJ
1994-92	All	P225/75R15	P235/75R15	35-35	120	7-JJ
			P225/70R15	35-35	120	7-JJ
			P275/60R15	35-35	120	7-JJ
1991-89	Regl cab	P225/75R15	P235/75R15	35-35	120	6-JJ
	Ext cab	P235/75R15		35-35	120	6-JJ

1 Tire pressure varies with different loads; refer to owner's manual or tire decal for proper inflation.

K20 4WD Pickup,
K2500 4WD Pickup

YEAR	MODEL	Standard	Optional	Inflation	Torque	Rim Width
1999	All	LT245/75R16D		—[1]	140	N/A
1998-96	Crew Cab:					
	SRW	LT245/75R16E		—[1]	140	N/A
	DRW	LT225/75R16D	LT215/85R16D	—[1]	140	N/A
1998-95	All	LT225/75R16D	LT245/75R16C	—[1]	140	6.5-JJ
			LT245/75R16E	—[1]	140	6.5-JJ
1994-92	All	LT225/75R16C	LT225/75R16D	—[1]	120	6.5-JJ
			LT245/75R16E	—[1]	120	6.5-JJ
1991	All	LT225/75R16D		—[1]	120	6.5-JJ
			LT245/75R16C	—[1]	120	6.5-JJ
			LT245/75R16E	—[1]	120	6.5-JJ
1990	All	LT225/75R16D		—[1]	105	6.5-JJ
			LT245/75R16C	—[1]	105	6.5-JJ
			LT245/75R16E	—[1]	105	6.5-JJ
1989	All	LT225/75R16D		—[1]	1205	6.5-JJ
			LT245/75R16C	—[1]	1205	6.5-JJ
			LT245/75R16E	—[1]	1205	6.5-JJ

1 Tire pressure varies with different loads; refer to owner's manual or tire decal for proper inflation.

CHEVROLET/GMC TRUCKS Continued
R10 2WD Pickup,
R1500 2WD Pickup

YEAR	MODEL	Standard	Optional	Inflation	Torque	Rim Width
1991-89	All	P235/75R15		32-35	100[1]	6-, 7-, 8-JJ
			P235/75R15XL	35-41	100[1]	6-, 7-, 8-JJ

1 5 9/16" lugs, 120 ft-lbs.
6 steel lug nuts, 90 ft-lbs.
SRW w/8 lug nuts, 140 ft-lbs.
DRW w/8 lug nuts, 125 ft-lbs.

R20 2WD Pickup,
R2500 2WD Pickup

YEAR	MODEL	Standard	Optional	Inflation	Torque	Rim Width
1991-89	All	LT225/75R16D		—[1]	100[1]	6.5-JJ
			LT245/75R16C	—[1]	100[1]	6.5-JJ
			LT245/75R16E	—[1]	100[1]	6.5-JJ

1 Tire pressure varies with different loads; refer to owner's manual or tire decal for proper inflation.

S10 Pickup, Syclone
S15 Pickup, Sonoma

YEAR	MODEL	Standard	Optional	Inflation	Torque	Rim Width
2000-95	2WD: Base	P205/75R15		35-35	95	6-JJ
	Sport pkg	P215/65R15		35-35	95	6-JJ
	4WD: R-cab, 117" WB	P235/70R15	P235/75R15	35-35	95	7-JJ
	Others	P205/75R15		35-35	95	6-JJ
			P235/75R15	35-35	95	7-JJ
1994-92	2WD	P205/75R14	P205/75R15	35-35	95	6-JJ
	4WD	P235/75R15		35-35	95	7-JJ
1992-91	Syclone	P245/50R16		35-35	100	7-JJ
1991	2WD	P205/75R14	P205/75R15	35-35	80	6-JJ
	4WD	P235/75R15		35-35	100	7-JJ
1990	2WD	P195/75R14	P205/75R15	35-35	80	6-JJ
			P215/75R15	35-35	80	7-JJ
	4WD	P195/75R15	P205/75R15	35-35	100	6-JJ
			P235/75R15	35-35	100	7-JJ
1989	2WD	P195/75R14	P205/75R15	35-35	73[1]	6-JJ
			P215/75R15	35-35	73[1]	7-JJ
	4WD	P195/75R15	P205/75R15	35-35	73[1]	6-JJ
			P235/75R15	35-35	73[1]	7-JJ

S-Series Blazer, Jimmy, Typhoon

YEAR	MODEL	Standard	Optional	Inflation	Torque	Rim Width
2000-97	All	P205/75R15		35-35	95	6-JJ
		P235/70R15		32-32	95	N/A
		P235/70R15		32-32	95	7-JJ
		31x10.5R15LT		30-30	N/A	N/A
1996-92	2WD	P205/75R15	P205/70R15	35-35	95	6-JJ
	4WD	P235/70R15		35-35	95	7-JJ
1993-92	Typhoon	P245/50R16		35-35	100	N/A
1991	2WD	P205/75R14	P205/75R15	35-35	70[1]	6-JJ
	4WD	P235/75R15		35-35	70[1]	7-JJ
1990	2WD	P195/75R14	P205/75R15	35-35	80	6-JJ
			P215/65R15	35-35	80	7-JJ
	4WD	P195/75R15	P205/75R15	35-35	100	6-JJ
			P235/75R15	35-35	100	7-JJ
1989	2WD	P195/75R14	P205/75R15	35-35	73[1]	6-JJ
			P215/65R15	35-35	73[1]	7-JJ
	4WD	P195/75R15	P205/75R15	35-35	73[1]	6-JJ
			P235/75R15	35-35	73[1]	7-JJ

1 With aluminum wheels, 90

Suburban

YEAR	MODEL	Standard	Optional	Inflation	Torque	Rim Width
2000-97	C1500	P235/75R15XL		35-35	—	7-
	K1500	P245/75R16		35-35	—	6.5-
	C2500	LT245/75R16C		1	—	6.5-
	K2500	LT245/75R16E		1	—	6.5-
1996-92	C1500	P235/75R15XL		35-35	—	7-JJ
	K1500	P245/75R16C		35-35	—	7-JJ
	C/K1500		LT245/75R16E	1	—	—
	C/K2500		LT245/75R16E	1	—	—
1998-92	C1500	P235/75R15XL	LT245/75R16E	35-35	120[5]	7-JJ
	C, K2500	LT245/75R16E		35-35	120[5]	6.5-JJ
	K1500	P245/75R16C	LT245/75R16E	35-35	120[5]	6.5-JJ
1991-89	R, V1500	P235/75R15		—[2]	N/A	6,7,8-JJ
			P235/75R15XL	—[2]	N/A	6,7,8-JJ
	R, V2500	LT235/75R16E		—[2]	N/A	6.5-JJ

1 Because of various chassis/loading combinations, see tire/certification label on driver's door.
2 Tire pressure varies with different loads; refer to owner's manual or tire decal for proper inflation.

Tahoe, Yukon

YEAR	MODEL	Standard	Optional	Inflation	Torque	Rim Width
2000-99	Tahoe Z71	LT265/75R16		—[1]	N/A	N/A
2000	Yukon Denali	P265/70R16		35-35	—	7-JJ

MAKE	MODEL	YEAR	ORIGINAL EQUIPMENT SIZE Standard	Optional	RECOMMENDED INFLATION PRESSURE Front - Rear	LUG NUT TORQUE Ft.-Lbs	RIM WIDTH

CHEVROLET/GMC TRUCKS Continued

Tahoe, Yukon Continued

		YEAR	Standard	Optional	Press.	Torque	Rim
	Tahoe, Yukon:	1999-98					
	Denali....		P265/70R16		35-35	N/A	7-JJ
	Police....		P235/70R15		35-35	N/A	7-JJ
	2WD....		P235/75R15		35-35	N/A	7-JJ
	4WD....		P245/75R16		35-35	N/A	6.5-, 7-JJ
	2WD.....	1997-96	P235/75R15		35-35	120	7-JJ
			LT235/75R16		—[1]	120	7-JJ
	4WD....		P245/75R16	LT245/75R16C	35-35	120	6.5-JJ
			LT265/75R16C		35-35	120	6.5-JJ
	2WD....	1995	P235/75R15		35-35	120	6.5-JJ
	4WD....		P235/75R15	P245/75R16	35-35	120	6.5-JJ
			LT245/75R16C		35-35	120	6.5-JJ
			LT265/75R16C		35-35	120	6.5-JJ
	All......	1994-92	LT225/75R16C		35-35	120	6.5-JJ

1 Because of various chassis/loading combinations, see tire/certification label on driver's door.

Tracker

		YEAR	Standard	Optional	Press.	Torque	Rim
	2WD.....	2000	P195/75R15		23-23	60	5.5-JJ
	4WD.....		P205/75R15		23-23	60	5.5-JJ
	2WD.....	1991	P195/75R15		23-23	37-58	5.5-JJ
	4WD.....		P205/75R15		23-23	37-58	5.5-JJ
	All.....	1990-89	P205/75R15		23-23	37-58	5.5-JJ

V10, V1500 4WD Pickup

		YEAR	Standard	Optional	Press.	Torque	Rim
	All......	1991-89	LT225/75R16D		—[2]	100[1]	6.5-JJ
			LT245/75R16C		—[2]	100[1]	6.5-JJ
			LT245/75R16E		—[2]	100[1]	6.5-JJ

1 5 9/16" lugs, 120 ft-lbs.
  6 steel lug nuts, 90 ft-lbs.
  SRW w/8 lug nuts, 140 ft-lbs.
  DRW w/8 lug nuts, 125 ft-lbs.
2 Tire pressure varies with different loads; refer to owner's manual or tire decal for proper inflation.

V20, V2500 4WD Pickup

		YEAR	Standard	Optional	Press.	Torque	Rim
	Regl cab....	1991	LT225/75R16D		—[2]	1001	6.5-JJ
			LT245/75R16E		—[2]	1001	6.5-JJ
	Ext cab....		LT245/75R16C		—[2]	1001	6.5-JJ
	Regl cab....	1990-89	LT225/75R16D		—[2]	1001	6.5-JJ
			LT245/75R16E		—[2]	1001	6.5-JJ
	Ext......		LT245/75R16C		—[2]	1001	6.5-JJ

1 5 9/16" lugs, 120 ft-lbs.
  6 steel lug nuts, 90 ft-lbs.
  SRW w/8 lug nuts, 140 ft-lbs.
  DRW w/8 lug nuts, 125 ft-lbs.
2 Tire pressure varies with different loads; refer to owner's manual or tire decal for proper inflation.

CHRYSLER

300 M

		YEAR	Standard	Optional	Press.	Torque	Rim
	All......	2000-99	P225/55R17		N/A	100	7.0
			225/60VR16		N/A	100	7.0

Cirrus

		YEAR	Standard	Optional	Press.	Torque	Rim
	All....	2000	P195/65R15		N/A	100	6.0
	All....	1999-98	P195/65HR15		31-31	100	6-J
	All....	1997	P195/70R14		N/A	100	N/A
			P195/65HR15		31-31	100	6-J
	All....	1996-95	P195/65HR15		31-31	100	6-J

Concorde

		YEAR	Standard	Optional	Press.	Torque	Rim
	All......	2000	P225/60R16		N/A	100	7.0
	All......	1999	P205/70R15		N/A	100	6.0
			P225/60R16		N/A	100	7.0
	All......	1998-97	P225/60R16		35-35	85-115	7-JJ
	All......	1996	P205/60R16		35-35	85-115	7-JJ
	All......	1995	P205/70R15		35-35	85-115	6-JJ
			P225/60R16		35-35	85-115	7-JJ
	All......	1994-93	P205/70R15		35-35	95	6-JJ
			P225/60R16		35-35	95	7-JJ

Conquest

		YEAR	Standard	Optional	Press.	Torque	Rim
	Front.....	1989	205/55VR16		27 —	65-80	7-JJ
			225/50VR16		27 —	65-80	8-JJ
	Rear.....		225/50VR16		— 27	65-80	8-JJ
			245/45VR16		— 27	65-80	9-JJ

Fifth Avenue

		YEAR	Standard	Optional	Press.	Torque	Rim
	All......	1993-90	P195/75R14		32-32	95	5.5-JJ
	All......	1989	P205/75R15		35-35	90	7-JJ

Imperial

		YEAR	Standard	Optional	Press.	Torque	Rim
	All......	1993-90	P195/75R14		32-32	95	5.5-JJ

CHRYSLER Continued

LeBaron Continued

		YEAR	Standard	Optional	Press.	Torque	Rim
	Sedan.....	1995-91	P195/70R14		29-29	95	5.5-JJ
			P205/60R15		32-32	95	6-JJ
	Coupe & convertible..		P205/60R15	P205/55R16	29-29	95	6-JJ
	GTC & LX ex. Sedan..	1993-91		P205/60R15	29-29	95	6-JJ
	Coupe & convertible.		P195/70R14		29-29	95	5.5-JJ
			P205/60R15		29-29	95	6-JJ
	All ex. GTC....	1990-89	P195/70R14		29-29	95	5.5-JJ
	GTC......		P205/55R16		29-29	95	6-J

LHS

		YEAR	Standard	Optional	Press.	Torque	Rim
	All......	2000-99	P225/55R17		N/A	100	7.0
	All......	1997-94	P225/60R16		32-32	85-115	7-JJ

New Yorker, Newport

		YEAR	Standard	Optional	Press.	Torque	Rim
	All......	1997-94	P225/60R16		32-32	85-115	7-JJ
	All......	1993-89	P195/75R14		32-32	95	5.5-JJ

TC by Maserati

		YEAR	Standard	Optional	Press.	Torque	Rim
	All......	1991-89	P205/60VR15		35-35	95	6-JJ

Sebring

		YEAR	Standard	Optional	Press.	Torque	Rim
	LXi......	2000-97	P215/50HR17		32-29	65-80[1]	6.5-JJ
	JX......	2000-96	P205/65R15		32-29	100	6.0
	JXi......		P215/55R16		32-29	100	6.5
			P215/55R16		32-29	100	6.5
	All......	2000	P195/65R15		N/A	100	6.0
	LX......	1999-95	P205/55HR16		N/A	65-80[1]	6.0-JJ
			P205/55HR16		N/A	65-80[1]	6.0
	LXi......	1996-95	P205/55HR16		32-29	100	6-JJ

1 1998 & earlier, torque to 100 ft. lbs.

Town & Country Van

		YEAR	Standard	Optional	Press.	Torque	Rim
	AWD......	2000	P215/70R15		N/A	100	6.5
	LX:/Limited..		P215/65R16		N/A	100	6.5
	LX FWD....		P215/65R15		N/A	100	6.5
	All......	1999-96	P215/65R16		35-35	85-115	6.5-JJ
	All......	1995	P205/70R15		35-35	85-115	6-JJ
	All......	1994-91	P205/70R15		35-35	95	6-JJ
	All......	1990-89	P205/70R15	P195/75R15	35-35	95	6-JJ

DAEWOO

Lanos

		YEAR	Standard	Optional	Press.	Torque	Rim
	All......	2000-98	185/60R14		32-32	66	5.5-J

Leganza

		YEAR	Standard	Optional	Press.	Torque	Rim
	All......	2000-98	205/60R15		29-29	66	6-J

Nubria

		YEAR	Standard	Optional	Press.	Torque	Rim
	All......	2000-98	185/65R14		30-28	66	5.5-J

DAIHATSU

Charade

		YEAR	Standard	Optional	Press.	Torque	Rim
	SE: Hatchback.	1992-91	P145/80R13		29-26	65-87	4.5-J
	Sedan....		P155/80R13		29-26	65-87	4.5-J
	SX: Hatchback.		P155/80R13		29-26	65-87	4.5-J
			P165/70R13		29-26	65-87	5-J
	Sedan....		P165/80R13		29-26	65-87	5-J
	SE: Hatchback.	1990	P145/80R13		29-26	65-87	4.5-J
	Sedan....		P155/80R13		29-26	65-87	4.5-J
	SX: Hatchback.		P155/80R13		29-26	65-87	4.5-J
			P165/70R13		29-26	65-87	5-J
	Sedan....		P165/80R13		29-26	65-87	5-J
	CES......	1989	P145/80R13		29-26	65-87	4.5-J
	CLS, CLX....		P155/80R13		29-26	65-87	4.5-J
			P165/80R13		29-26	65-87	5-J

Rocky

		YEAR	Standard	Optional	Press.	Torque	Rim
	All......	1992-90	P205/75R13	P225/75R15	35-35	65-87	6-J

DODGE

Aries

		YEAR	Standard	Optional	Press.	Torque	Rim
	Sedan.....	1989	175/80R13		35-35	95	5-JB
				185/70R14	35-35	95	5.5-JJ
	Wagon....		P175/70R14		35-35	95	5.5-JJ

Avenger

		YEAR	Standard	Optional	Press.	Torque	Rim
	Base.....	2000	P205/55HR16		N/A	65-80	6.0-JJ
	ES.....		P215/50R17		N/A	65-80	6.5-JJ
	Base.....	1999-98	P195/70R14		32-29	65-80[1]	5.5-J
	ES.....		P215/50R17		32-29	65-80[1]	6.5-JJ
	Base.....	1997-95	P195/70R14		32-29	95	5.5-J
	ES......		P205/55R16		32-29	95	6-JJ

1 1998, torque to 100 ft. lbs.

DODGE Continued

Caravan

MODEL YEAR	Standard	Optional	Front-Rear	Torque	Rim
2000 AWD: LE	P215/70R15		N/A	100	6.5
Others . . .	215/65R16		N/A	100	6.5
SE/LE FWD . .	P215/65R15		N/A	100	6.5
ES FWD	215/60R17		N/A	100	6.5
Others	P205/75R14		N/A	100	6.0
1999-96 Base	P205/75SR14		35-35	95	6-JJ
SE & LE . .	P215/65SR15	P215/65R16	35-35	95	6.5-JJ
ES . . .	P215/65R16		35-35	95	6.5-JJ
1995-91 Passenger van: 2WD:					
Long WB.	P205/70R15		35-35	95	6-JJ
Short WB.	P195/75R14	P205/70R14	35-35	95	5.5-, 6-JJ
4WD	P205/70R15		35-35	95	6-JJ
Cargo Van . . .	P195/75R14		35-35	95	5.5-JJ
	LT195/75R15		35-35	95	6-JJ
	P205/70R15		35-35	95	5.5-, 6-JJ
1990-89 All	P195/75R14	P205/70R14	35-35	95	5.5-JJ
	P205/70R15		35-35	95	5.5-, 6-JJ

Colt

MODEL YEAR	Standard	Optional	Front-Rear	Torque	Rim
1996-93 Ex. Wagon:					
1.5L	P145/80R13		31-31	N/A	4.5-B
	P155/80R13		31-31	N/A	5-B
1.8L	P175/70R13		31-31	N/A	5-B
	P185/65R14		29-26	N/A	5.5-JJ
1996-92 Wagon: FWD	P205/70SR14		26-26	N/A	5.5-JJ
	P185/75SR14		28-26	N/A	5.5-JJ
4WD	P205/70SR14		26-26	65-80	5.5-JJ
1992-91 Ex. Wagon . .	P155/80R13		29-29	N/A	4.5-, 5-JJ
1991-89 Wagon: FWD.	P175/70R13		26-26	N/A	5-JJ
4WD	P185/70R14		26-29	65-80	5.5-JJ

Daytona

MODEL YEAR	Standard	Optional	Front-Rear	Torque	Rim
1993 Ex. ES & IROC.	P185/70R14		32-32	95	5.5-JJ
	P205/60R15		32-32	95	6-JJ
IROC R/T . . .	P205/55ZR16		32-32	95	N/A
1993-89 ES . . .	P205/60R15		32-32	95	6-JJ
IROC ex. R/T.	P205/55VR16		32-32	95	6-JJ
1992-91 Ex. ES & IROC.	P185/70R14		32-32	95	5.5-JJ
	P205/55VR16		32-32	95	6-JJ
	P205/60R14		32-32	95	6-JJ
1990-89 Ex. ES & Shelby	P185/70R14		32-32	95	5.5-JJ
	P205/60R15		32-32	95	6-JJ
	P225/50R15		32-32	95	6.5-JJ

Diplomat

MODEL YEAR	Standard	Optional	Front-Rear	Torque	Rim
1989 All	P205/75R15		35-35	90	7-JJ

Dynasty

MODEL YEAR	Standard	Optional	Front-Rear	Torque	Rim
1993-89 All	P195/70R14		32-32	95	5.5-JJ

Intrepid

MODEL YEAR	Standard	Optional	Front-Rear	Torque	Rim
2000 R/T	P225/55R17		N/A	100	7.0
Others	P225/60R16		N/A	100	7.0
1999 Base	P205/70R15		N/A	100	6.0
	P225/60R16		N/A	100	7.0
ES	P225/60R16		N/A	100	7.0
1998-96 All	P225/60R16		35-35	85-115	7-JJ
1995-94 All	P205/70R15		35-35	85-115	6-JJ
	P225/60R16		35-35	85-115	7-JJ
1993 All	P205/70R15		35-35	85-115	6-JJ

Lancer

MODEL YEAR	Standard	Optional	Front-Rear	Torque	Rim
1989 ES	P195/70R14		29-29	95	5.5-JJ
	P205/60R15		29-29	95	6-JJ
Ex. Shelby . . .	P195/70R14		29-29	95	5.5-JJ
	P205/60R15		29-29	95	6-JJ
Shelby	P205/60R15		29-29	95	6-JJ

Monaco

MODEL YEAR	Standard	Optional	Front-Rear	Torque	Rim
1992 ES	P205/60R15		30-30	90	6-JJ
LX	P205/70R14		30-30	90	5.5-JJ
	P205/60R15		30-30	90	6-JJ
1991 ES	P205/70R14		32-32	90	5.5-JJ
LE	P195/70R14		32-32	90	5.5-JJ
1990 ES	P205/70R14		32-32	63	5.5-JJ
LE	P195/70R14		32-32	63	5.5-JJ

Neon

MODEL YEAR	Standard	Optional	Front-Rear	Torque	Rim
2000 Sedan	P185/65R14		N/A	100	5.5
	P185/60R15		N/A	100	6.0
ES	P185/60R15		N/A	100	6.0
1999 Base	P185/65R14		N/A	100	5.5
Competition . .	P175/65HR14		N/A	100	6.0
1998-97 Base	P175/70R14		32-32	100	6-J
Highline	P185/65R13		32-32	100	5.5-J
1996 All	P185/65R14		32-32	100	5.5-J
Sedan		P175/65HR14	32-32	100	6-J
Coupe		P185/60HR14	32-32	100	6-J

DODGE Continued

Neon Continued

MODEL YEAR	Standard	Optional	Front-Rear	Torque	Rim
1995 Base	P165/80R13		32-32	100	5-J
		P175/65HR14	32-32	100	6-J
Highline	P185/70R13		32-32	100	5-J
		P185/65R14	32-32	100	5.5-J
		P185/60HR14	32-32	100	6-J
Sport	P185/65R14		32-32	100	6-J

Omni

MODEL YEAR	Standard	Optional	Front-Rear	Torque	Rim
1990-89 All	P165/80R13		35-35	95	5-JB

Shadow

MODEL YEAR	Standard	Optional	Front-Rear	Torque	Rim
1994-93 Base	P185/70R14		32-32	95	5.5-JJ
ES:					
Convertible .	P185/70R14		32-32	95	5.5-JJ
Hatchback . .	P195/60HR15	P205/60R14	32-32	95	6-JJ
1992 Ex. ES & America . . .	P185/70R14		32-32	95	5.5-JJ
		P205/60R14	32-32	95	6-JJ
America	P185/70R14		32-32	95	5.5-JJ
ES	P195/60R15	P205/60R14	32-32	95	6-JJ
1991 Ex. ES	P185/70R14		32-32	95	5.5-JJ
ES	P195/60HR15		35-35	95	6-JJ
1990 All	P185/70R14		32-32	95	5.5-JJ
	P195/60R15		35-35	95	6-JJ
1989 H-Series . . .	P185/70R14		35-35	95	5.5-JJ
	P195/60R15		35-35	95	6-JJ
L-Series	P175/80R13		35-35	95	5-JB

Spirit

MODEL YEAR	Standard	Optional	Front-Rear	Torque	Rim
1995-93 Base	P185/70R14	P185/70R14	32-32	95	5.5-, 6-JJ
ES	P205/60R15		32-32	95	6-JJ
1992-90 Ex. ES, LE, R/T	P185/70R14		32-32	95	5.5-JJ
		P205/60R15	32-32	95	6-JJ
LE	P195/70R14		32-32	95	5.5-JJ
		P205/60R15	32-32	95	6-JJ
R/T	P205/60R15		32-32	95	6-JJ
1989 Ex. ES . . .	P195/70R14		32-32	95	5.5-JJ
ES	P205/60R15		32-32	95	6-JJ

Stealth

MODEL YEAR	Standard	Optional	Front-Rear	Torque	Rim
1996-91 Ex. ES, R/T . . .	P205/65R15		29-26	87-101	6.5-JJ
ES, R/T, 4WD. .	P245/45ZR17		32-29	87-101	8.5-JJ
ES, R/T, FWD. .	P225/55VR16		32-29	87-101	8-JJ

Stratus

MODEL YEAR	Standard	Optional	Front-Rear	Torque	Rim
2000 SE	P195/70R14		N/A	100	6.0
ES	P195/65R15		N/A	100	6.0
1999-97 All	P195/70R14		31-31	100	N/A
		P195/65HR15	31-31	100	6-J
1996-95 All	P195/65HR15		31-31	85-115	6-J

Viper

MODEL YEAR	Standard	Optional	Front-Rear	Torque	Rim
2000-99 Front	P275/35ZR18		N/A	N/A	10.0
Rear	P335/30ZR18		N/A	N/A	13.0
1998-93 Front	P275/40ZR17		35 —	N/A	10.0
Rear	P335/35ZR17		— 35	N/A	13.0

Vista

MODEL YEAR	Standard	Optional	Front-Rear	Torque	Rim
1994-93 All	P185/75R14		28-26	65-80	5.5-JJ
		P205/70R14	26-26	65-80	5.5-JJ
1992 2WD: W/AT . .	P205/70R14		26-26	65-80	5.5-JJ
W/MT . . .	P185/75R14		28-28	65-80	5.5-JJ
4WD	P205/70R14		26-26	65-80	5.5-JJ
1991-89 2WD	P165/80R13	P185/70R13	29-29	51-58[1]	5-J
4WD	P185/70R14		29-35	51-58[1]	5.5-JJ

1 With aluminum wheels, 65-80

DODGE TRUCKS

1500 Pickup

MODEL YEAR	Standard	Optional	Front-Rear	Torque	Rim
2000-98 2WD:					
6400 GVWR .	P225/75R16	P245/75R16	35-35	95	7.0
		P275/60R17	35-35	95	9.0
4WD: 6400/6600 GVWR . . .	P225/75R16XL		41-41	95	7.0
	P245/75R16STD		35-35	95	7.0
	P265/75R16STD		35-35	95	7.0
	LT275/70R17C		35-35	95	8.0
1997 2WD	P225/75R16	P245/75R16C	35-35	95	7.0
		LT265/75R16C	35-35	95	7.0
4WD	LT225/75R16C		45-35	95	7.0
		LT245/75R16C	40-35	95	7.0
		LT265/75R16C	35-35	95	7.0
1996-94 2WD	P225/75R16	P245/75R16C	35-35	80-110[1,2]	7.0
		LT265/75R16C	35-35	80-110[1,2]	7.0
4WD	LT225/75R16C		45-35	80-110[1,2]	7.0
		LT245/75R16C	40-35	80-110[1,2]	7.0
		LT265/75R16C	35-35	80-110[1,2]	7.0

1 Cone type nut, 9/16-18, 120-150.
2 Flanged type nut, 9/16-18, 130-160.

MAKE MODEL YEAR	ORIGINAL EQUIPMENT SIZE Standard	Optional	RECOMMENDED INFLATION PRESSURE Front - Rear	LUG NUT TORQUE Ft.-Lbs	RIM WIDTH

DODGE TRUCKS Continued

2500 Pickup

	Standard	Optional	Inflation	Torque	Rim
2000-98 2WD:					
6400 GVWR .	P225/75R16	P245/75R16	35-35	135[3]	7.0
		P275/60R17	35-35	135[3]	9.0
4WD:					
6400/6600					
GVWR . . .	P225/75R16XL		41-41	135[3]	7.0
	P245/75R16STD		35-35	135[3]	7.0
	P265/75R16STD		35-35	135[3]	7.0
	LT275/70R17C		35-35	135[3]	8.0
1997 2WD.	LT225/75R16D	LT245/75R16E	40-40	135	6.5
4WD.	LT225/75R16D		50-40	135	6.5
		LT245/75R16E	40-40	135	6.5
1996-94 2WD.	LT225/75R16D	LT245/75R16E	40-40	80-110[1,2]	6.5
4WD.	LT225/75R16D		50-40	80-110[1,2]	6.5
		LT245/75R16E	40-40	80-110[1,2]	6.5

1 Cone type nut, 9/16-18, 120-150.
2 Flanged type nut, 9/16-18, 130-160.
3 8 Lug wheel torque shown. Torque 5 lug wheel to 95 ft. lbs.

B150, 1500 Ram Van & Wagon

	Standard	Optional	Inflation	Torque	Rim
2000-99 1500. . .	P235/75R15	P235/75R15	35-41	85-110	6.5, 7-JJ
1998-96 All.	P235/75R15		35-35	85-110[1,2]	6.5-, 7-JJ
		P235/75R15XL	35-41	85-110[1,2]	6.5-, 7-JJ
1995-91 All.	P205/75R15	P225/75R15	35-35	85-110[1,2]	6.5-, 7-JJ
		P235/75R15XL	35-41	85-110[1,2]	6.5-, 7-JJ
1990-89 GVWR 4700-					
5100#. . . .	P195/75R15	P205/75R15	35-35	85-110[1,2]	5.5-JJ
		P225/75R15	35-35	85-110[1,2]	6.5-, 7-JJ
		P235/75R15XL	35-35	85-110[1,2]	6.5-, 7-JJ
GVWR 5300-					
6010#. . . .	P205/75R15		35-35	85-110[1,2]	5.5-JJ
		P235/75R15XL	35-41	85-110[1,2]	6.5-, 7-JJ

1 Cone type nut, 9/16-18, 120-150.
2 Flanged type nut, 9/16-18, 130-160

B250, 2500 Ram Van & Wagon

	Standard	Optional	Inflation	Torque	Rim
2000-99 All.	LT225/75R16D		50-65	135[3]	6.5
		LT225/75R16E	50-65	135[3]	6.5
1998-96 All.	P235/75R15		35-35	85-110[1,2]	6.5-, 7-JJ
		P235/75R15XL	41-41	85-110[1,2]	6.5-, 7-JJ
1995-91 All.	P225/75R15	P235/75R15XL	35-35	85-110[1,2]	6.5-, 7-JJ
1990-89 GVWR 4700-					
5100#. . . .	P225/75R15	P235/75R15	35-35	85-110[1,2]	6.5-, 7-JJ
		P235/75R15XL	41-41	85-110[1,2]	6.5-, 7-JJ

1 Cone nut 5/8"-18, 175-225
2 Flange nut 5/8"-18, 300-350
3 8 Lug wheel torque shown

D100 2WD Pickup

	Standard	Optional	Inflation	Torque	Rim
1993-90 D100S.	P205/75R15	P235/75R15XL	35-35	85-110[1,2]	6-, 6.5-JJ
		P235/75R15XL	35-35	85-110[1,2]	6,7-JJ
Regl cab . . .	P215/75R15		35-35	85-110[1,2]	6-, 6.5-JJ
		P235/75R15XL	35-35	85-110[1,2]	7-JJ
Ext cab	P235/75R15XL		35-35	85-110[1,2]	6,7-JJ
1989 All.	P205/75R15		35-35	85-110[1,2]	5.5-JJ
		P235/75R15XL	35-41	85-110[1,2]	6.5-JJ

1 Cone nut 5/8"-18, 175-225
2 Flange nut 5/8"-18, 300-350

D150 2WD Pickup

	Standard	Optional	Inflation	Torque	Rim
1993-90 D150S.	P205/75R15		35-35	85-110[1,2]	6-, 6.5-JJ
		P235/75R15XL	35-35	85-110[1,2]	6-, 7-JJ
Regl cab. . . .	P215/75R15		35-35	85-110[1,2]	6-, 6.5-JJ
		P235/75R15XL	35-35	85-110[1,2]	6-, 7-JJ
Ext cab. . .	P235/75R15XL		35-35	85-110[1,2]	6-, 7-JJ
1989 All.	P205/75R15		35-35	85-110[1,2]	5.5-JJ
		P235/75R15XL	35-41	85-110[1,2]	6.5-JJ

1 Cone nut 5/8"-18, 175-225
2 Flange nut 5/8"-18, 300-350

D250 2WD Pickup

	Standard	Optional	Inflation	Torque	Rim
1993-90 All.	LT215/85R16D		50-65	85-110[1,2]	6.0
		LT235/85R16E	40-80	85-110[1,2]	6.0
1989 GVWR 6600-					
6900#. . . .	LT215/85R16C		45-50	85-110[1,2]	6.0
		LT215/85R16D	45-65	85-110[1,2]	6.0
		LT235/85R16E	45-80	85-110[1,2]	6.0
		7.50-16LT/D	50-60	85-110[1,2]	6.0
GVWR 8510#. .	LT235/85R16E		45-80	85-110[1,2]	6.0

1 Cone nut 5/8"-18, 175-225
2 Flange nut 5/8"-18, 300-350

DODGE TRUCKS Continued

Dakota, Durango

	Standard	Optional	Inflation	Torque	Rim
2000-98 Durango. . . .	P235/75R15XL		35-41	85-110	6.0, 7.0
		31x10.5R15	35-41	85-110	8.0
2000-97 Dakota: 2WD. .	P215/75R15		35-35	85-110	6.0, 7.0
		P235/75R15	35-41	85-110	6.0, 7.0
		P235/70R15	35-35	85-110	8.0
2000 Option. . . .	P255/65R15		35-35	85-110	8.0
		P255/55R17	35-35	85-110	9.0
4WD.	P215/75R15		35-35	85-110	6.0, 7.0
		P235/75R15	35-35	85-110	6.0, 7.0
		31x10.5R15LT	35-41	85-110	8.0
1996 WS &					
Base:					
2WD	P205/75R15	P215/75R15	30-35	85-110	6-JJ
		LT215/75R15	30-40	85-110	6.5-JJ
4WD	P215/75R15	P235/75R15XL	35-35	85-110	6-JJ
Sport: 2WD . .	P215/75R15		30-35	85-110	6-JJ
		LT215/75R15	30-40	85-110	6.5-JJ
4WD . .	P235/75R15		35-35	85-110	6-JJ
1995-94 Reg. cab:					
2WD, 124" WB.	P195/75R15		30-35	85-110	6-JJ
4WD, 124" WB.	P205/75R15		30-35	85-110	6-JJ
Sport 2WD . .	P215/75R15		30-35	85-110	6-JJ
Sport 4WD .	P235/75R15		35-35	85-110	6-JJ
Regl cab					
112" WB. .	P195/75R15		30-35	85-110	6-JJ
Club cab:					
Base 2WD . .	P195/75R15		30-35	85-110	6-JJ
Base 4WD . .	P215/75R15		30-35	85-110	6-JJ
Sport 2WD. .	P215/75R15		30-35	85-110	6-JJ
Sport 4WD. .	P235/75R15XL		35-35	85-110	6-JJ
1993-92 2WD.	P195/75R15	P205/75R15	30-35	85-110	6-JJ
		P215/75R15	30-35	85-110	6-JJ
		LT215/75R15D	30-40	85-110	6.5-JJ
4WD: Regl cab	P195/75R15	P205/75R15	35-35	85-110	6-JJ
		P235/75R15XL	35-35	85-110	6-JJ
Ext cab	P235/7515XL		35-35	85-110	6-JJ
1991-90 2WD.	P195/75R15	P205/75R15	30-35	95	6-JJ
		P215/75R15	30-35	95	6-JJ
		LT215/75R15D	30-40	95	6.5-JJ
4WD: Regl cab	P195/75R15	P205/75R15	35-35	95	6-JJ
		P235/75R15XL	35-35	95	6-JJ
Ext cab. . . .	P235/7515XL		35-35	95	6-JJ
1989 2WD.	P195/75R15	P205/75R15	30-35	85	6-JJ
		P215/75R15	30-35	85	6-JJ
		LT215/75R15D	30-40	85	6.5-JJ
4WD: Regl cab	P195/75R15	P205/75R15	35-35	85	6-JJ
		P235/75R15XL	35-35	85	6-JJ
Ext cab. . . .	P235/7515XL		35-35	85	6-JJ

Raider

	Standard	Optional	Inflation	Torque	Rim
1989 4-cyl	P225/75R15		35-35	72-87	6-JJ
V6.	P235/75R15		35-35	72-87	6-JJ

Ram 50 Pickup

	Standard	Optional	Inflation	Torque	Rim
1993 2WD.	P195/75R14		26-35	87-101	6-JJ
4WD.	P225/75R15		26-35	87-101	6-JJ
1992-89 2WD.	P195/75R14	P205/75R14	26-35	87-101	6-JJ
		LT195/75R14	35-65	87-101	6.00
4WD.	P225/75R15		26-35	87-101	6-JJ

Ramcharger

	Standard	Optional	Inflation	Torque	Rim
1993 All.	P235/75R15XL		35-35	85-110[1,2]	6-, 7-JJ
		31X10.5R15LT	35-35	85-110[1,2]	7-JJ
1992-89 W/o					
rally whls. . .	P235/75R15XL		35-35	85-110[1,2]	6.5-JJ
W/rally whls. .	P235/75R15XL		35-35	85-110[1,2]	8-JJ

1 Cone nut 5/8"-18, 175-225
2 Flange nut 5/8"-18, 300-350

W100, W150 4WD Pickup

	Standard	Optional	Inflation	Torque	Rim
1993-90 All.	P235/75R15XL	31X10.5R15LT	35-35	85-110[1,2]	7-JJ
1991-90 GVWR 6200-					
6400#. . . .	P235/75R15XL		35-41	85-110[1,2]	6-JJ
GVWR 6400#.	P235/75R15XL		35-41	85-110[1,2]	6.5-JJ
1989 All.	P235/75R15XL		35-41	85-110[1,2]	6.5-JJ

W250 4WD Pickup

	Standard	Optional	Inflation	Torque	Rim
1993-90 All.	LT215/85R16D		40-40	85-110[1,2]	6.0
		LT215/75R16D	45-65	85-110[1,2]	6.0
		LT235/85R16E	35-35	85-110[1,2]	6.0
1989 GVWR 6600-					
6900#. . . .	LT215/85R16C		45-50	85-110[1,2]	6.0
		LT215/85R16D	45-65	85-110[1,2]	6.0
		LT235/85R16E	45-80	85-110[1,2]	6.0
		7.50-16LT/D	50-60	85-110[1,2]	6.0
GVWR 7500#. .	LT215/85R16D		55-65	85-110[1,2]	6.0
		LT235/85R16E	45-80	85-110[1,2]	6.0
GVWR 8510#. .	LT235/85R16E		45-80	85-110[1,2]	6.0

1 Cone nut 5/8"-18, 175-225
2 Flange nut 5/8"-18, 300-350

EAGLE

Medallion

1989	All		P185/65R14	P195/60R14	33-33	63	5.5-JJ

Premier

1992-91	ES	P205/60R15		30-30	90	6-JJ
	LX	P195/70R14		30-30	90	5.5-JJ
			P205/60R15	30-30	90	6-JJ
1990	ES	P205/60R15		30-30	63	6-JJ
	LX	P195/70R14		30-30	63	5.5-JJ
			P205/60R15	30-30	63	6-JJ
1989	All	P195/70R14		30-30	63	5.5-JJ
			P205/70R14	30-30	63	5.5,6-JJ
			P215/60R15	30-30	63	6-JJ

Summit

1996-95	2WD wagon	P185/70R13		30-30	65-80	5.5-JJ
	4WD wagon	P205/70R15		30-30	65-80	5.5-JJ
	DL Coupe	P145/80R13		31-31	65-80	4.5-B
			P175/70R13	31-31	65-80	5-B
	ESi: Coupe	P155/80R13		31-31	65-80	5-B
			P185/65R14	29-26	65-80	5.5-JJ
	Sedan	P185/65R14		29-26	65-80	5.5-JJ
	LX sedan	P175/70R13		31-31	65-80	5-B
1994-93	Base: Coupe	P145/80R13		31-31	65-80	4.5-JB
	Sedan	P155/80R13		31-31	65-80	5-JB
	ES: Coupe	P155/80R13		31-31	65-80	5-JB
	Sedan	P175/70R13		31-31	65-80	5-JB
	ESi	P205/70R15		35-35	65-80	6-JJ
			P225/60R16	35-35	65-80	7-JJ
	TSi	P225/60R16		35-35	65-80	7-JJ
1992	3-door: ES	P175/70R13		29-29	65-80	4.5-JB
	Ex. ES	P155/80R13		29-29	65-80	4.5-JB
	4-door: ES	P175/70R13		29-29	65-80	5-JB
	Ex. ES	P155/80R13		29-29	65-80	5-JB
	4WD wagon	P205/70R14		30-30	65-80	5.5-JJ
	FWD wagon:					
	W/AT	P205/70R14		30-30	65-80	5.5-JJ
	W/MT	P185/75R14		30-30	65-80	5.5-JJ
1991	Ex. ES	P155/80R13		30-30	65-80	5-JB
	ES	P175/70R13		30-30	65-80	5-JB
1990	DL	P155/80R13		30-30	65-80	5-JB
	ES	P195/60R14		29-29	65-80	5.5-JJ
	LX	P175/70R13		29-29	65-80	5.5-JB
1989	DL	P155/80R13		30-30	65-80	4.5-, 5-JB
			P155/80R13	30-30	65-80	5-JB
	LX	P175/70R13		29-29	65-80	5-JB
			P195/60R14	29-29	65-80	5.5-JJ

Talon

1998-97	Base, ESi	P195/70HR14		32-29	100	5.5-JJ
	TSi: 2WD	P205/55VR16		32-29	100	6-JJ
	4WD	P215/50R17		32-29	100	6.5-JJ
1996-95	Base, ESi	P195/70HR14		32-29	87-100	5.5-JJ
	TSi: 2WD	P205/55VR16		32-29	87-100	6-JJ
	4WD	P215/55VR16		32-29	87-100	6-JJ
1994-93	DL	P185/70R14		32-29	87-100	5.5-JJ
	ES	P205/55HR16		32-29	87-100	6-JJ
	TSi	P205/55VR16		32-29	87-100	6-JJ
1992	4WD	P205/55VR16		32-29	87-100	6-JJ
	FWD	P205/55R16	P205/55VR16	29-26	87-100	6-JJ
1991-90	Ex. Turbo	P205/55R16		30-30	87-100	6-JJ
	Turbo	P205/55VR16		30-30	87-100	6-JJ

Vision

1997-96	All	P225/60R16		35-35	95	6-JJ
	TSi		P225/60VR16	35-35	95	7-JJ
1995	ESi	P195/70HR14		35-35	95	6-JJ
	TSi: 2WD	P225/60HR16		35-35	95	7-JJ
	4WD	P215/55VR16		35-35	95	7-JJ
1994-93	ESi	P205/70R15		35-35	95	6-JJ
			P225/60R16	35-35	95	7-JJ
	TSi	P225/60R16		35-35	95	7-JJ

FORD

Aspire

1997-94	All	165/70R13		32-32	65-87	4.5-J

Contour

2000-99	LX	P185/70R14	P195/65R14	31-35	94	5.5
	SE	P185/70R14	P195/65R14	31-35	94	5.5
			P205/60R15	31-35	94	6.0
2000	SVT	215/50ZR16		N/A	N/A	N/A
1998-95	GL & LX	P185/70R14	P195/65R14	34-34	85-105	5.5
	SE	P205/60R15		31-34	85-105	6.0

Crown Victoria, Custom 500

2000-98	Base	P225/60SR16	P225/60TR16	N/A	85-104	7.0
	NGV	P225/60VR16		N/A	85-104	7.0
1997-93	W/o Perf & Hdlg pkg	P215/70R15	P225/70VR15	31-35	85-105	6.5-JJ
	W/Perf & Handling pkg	P225/60R16		31-35	85-105	6.5-, 7-JJ

FORD Continued

Crown Victoria, Custom 500 Continued

1992	All	P215/70R15	P225/70R15	31-35	85-105	6.5-JJ
1991-89	Sedan	P215/70R15		31-35	85-105	6-, 6.5-JJ
	Wagon	P215/70R15		27-35	85-105	6.5-JJ

Escort

2000-98	All	P185/65R14		32-32	66-86[1]	5.5
			P185/60R15	32-32	66-86[1]	5.5
2000	ZX2 option	P205/55R15		N/A	66-86[1]	N/A
1997	All	P185/65SR14		32-32	65-86	5.5-JJ
1996-91	GT	P185/60R15		32-32	85-105	5.5-JJ
	LX sedan	P175/65R14		32-32	85-105	5-JJ
	LX-E	P185/60R14		32-32	85-105	5.5-JJ
	All others	P175/70R13		32-32	85-105	5-JJ
1990-89	Ex. GT	P175/70R14		30-30	85-105	5-JJ
			P175/70R14	30-30	85-105	5.5-JJ
	GT	P185/60HR15		32-32	85-105	6-JJ
			P195/60R15	30-30	85-105	6-JJ

1 Aluminum wheels, 72-100

Festiva

1993-92	GL	165/70SR12		32-32	65-87	4.5-J
1991-90	L-Plus & LX	165/70SR12		29-29	65-87	4.5-B
1990-89	L	145SR12		32-29	65-87	4-B
			165/70SR12	32-29	65-87	4.5-J
	LX	165/70SR12		32-29	65-87	4.5-J

Focus

2000	ZX3	P195/60R15		N/A	N/A	N/A
	LX	P185/65R14		N/A	N/A	N/A
	SE, ZTS	P195/60R15		N/A	N/A	N/A

Mustang

2000-99	Ex. GT & Cobra	P205/65R15		N/A	95	7.0
			P225/55HR16	N/A	95	7.5
	Cobra	P245/45ZR17			95	8.0
	GT	P225/55HR16		N/A	95	7.5
	Option		P245/45ZR17		95	8.0
1998-94	Ex. GT or Cobra	P205/65TR15		35-35	85-105	6.5-, 7-JJ
	GT	P225/55TR16		30-30	85-105	7.5-JJ
			P245/45ZR17	30-30	85-105	8.0
	Cobra	P245/45ZR17		30-30	85-105	8.0
1993-91	4-cyl	P195/75R14		35-35	85-105	7-JJ
			P205/65R15	35-35	85-105	7-JJ
	V8	P225/55ZR16		30-30	85-105	7-JJ
1990-89	4-cyl	P195/75R14		35-35	85-105	5-, 5.5-JJ
	V8	P225/60VR15		30-30	85-105	7-JJ

Probe

1997-93	Base	P195/65SR14		32-26	65-87	5.5-JJ
			P205/55SR15	32-26	65-87	6-JJ
	GT	P225/50VR16		32-26	65-87	7-JJ
1992-91	GT	P205/60VR15		32-26	65-87	6-JJ
	LX	P195/70SR14		32-26	65-87	5.5-JJ
			P205/60HR15	32-26	65-87	6-JJ
	GL	P195/70VR14		32-26	65-87	6-JJ
1991-90	GL	P185/70SR14		32-26	65-87	5.5-JJ
			P195/70SR14	32-26	65-87	6-JJ
1990-89	GT	P195/60VR15		32-26	65-87	6-JJ
1989	GL & LX	P185/70SR14		32-26	65-87	5.5-JJ

Taurus

2000	All	P215/60R16		N/A	N/A	6
1999	LX, SE	P205/65R15		N/A	85-104	6.0
	SHO	P225/55ZR16		N/A	85-104	6.5
1998-96	GL, LX, LXE	P205/65R15		35-35	85-105	6-JJ
	SHO	P225/55VR16		N/A	85-105	7-JJ
			P225/55ZR16	N/A	85-105	7-JJ
1995-94	All	P205/65R15		35-35	85-105	6-JJ
	SHO 3.0L	P215/60VR16		35-35	85-105	6-JJ
	SHO 3.2L	P215/60ZR16		35-35	85-105	6-JJ
1993-92	GL	P205/70R14		35-35	85-105	5.5-JJ
			P205/65R15	35-35	85-105	6-JJ
	LX	P205/65R15		35-35	85-105	6-JJ
	Police pkg	P215/70HR14		35-35	85-105	5.5-JJ
	SHO	P215/60R16		35-35	85-105	6-JJ
1991-89	All	P205/70R14	P205/65R15	35-35	85-105	5.5-JJ
			P205/65R15	35-35	85-105	6-JJ
	SHO	P215/60R16		35-35	85-105	7-JJ

Tempo

1994	All	P185/70R14		30-30	85-105	5.5-JJ
1993-92	GLS	P185/60R15		30-30	85-105	6-JJ
	LX & GL	P185/70R14		30-30	85-105	5.5-JJ
1991-90	All	P185/70R14		30-30	85-105	5.5-JJ
1989	Ex. GLS	P185/70R14		30-30	85-105	5.5-JJ
	GLS	P185/70R14		30-30	85-105	6-JJ

FORD Continued

Thunderbird

Year	Model	Standard	Optional	Inflation (F-R)	Lug Nut Torque	Rim Width
1997-89	Ex. Super Coupe	P205/70R15		30-30	85-105	6-JJ
			P215/70R15	30-30	85-105	6.5-JJ
1995-91	Super Coupe..	P225/60ZR16		30-30	85-105	7-JJ
1990-89	Super Coupe..	P225/60VR16		30-30	85-105	7-JJ
1989	All ex. Super Coupe	P205/70R15		35-35	85-105	6-JJ
			P215/70R15	35-35	85-105	6.5-JJ

FORD TRUCKS

Aerostar

Year	Model	Standard	Optional	Inflation (F-R)	Lug Nut Torque	Rim Width
1997-89	All......	P215/70R14	P215/75R14	32-35	100	6-JJ

Bronco

Year	Model	Standard	Optional	Inflation (F-R)	Lug Nut Torque	Rim Width
1996-92	All......	P235/75R15XL		35-41	100	6-, 7-JJ
			P265/75R15SL	30-30	100	7.5-J
1991-89	All.....	P235/75R15XL		35-41	100	6-JK
			31x10.50/R15C	40-40	100	8-JJ

Bronco II

Year	Model	Standard	Optional	Inflation (F-R)	Lug Nut Torque	Rim Width
1990-89	All......	P205/75R15		35-35	100	6-JJ

E150 Van & Wagon

Year	Model	Standard	Optional	Inflation (F-R)	Lug Nut Torque	Rim Width
2000	All......	P235/75R15XL		N/A	74-133	6-J
		LT225/75R16Z		N/A	74-133	N/A
1999	E150: Wagon..	P235/75R15XL		N/A		6-J
	Van	P225/75R15XL		N/A		N/A
1998	Cargo Van...	P225/75R15SL	P235/75R15XL	35-35	100	N/A
		LT225/75R16E		35-35	100	N/A
	Club Wagon: Base	P215/75R15	P225/75R15S	35-35	100	6-J
	Heavy Duty..	P215/75R15	P225/75R15S	35-35	100	6-J
	Super ..	P215/75R15	P225/75R15S	35-35	100	6-J
1997-92	GVWR 5500#..	P215/75R15	P225/75R15S	35-35	100	6-J
	GVWR 6500-6700#	P235/75R15XL		41-41	100	6,7-J
1991-89	Long whlbs .	P235/75R15XL		41-41	100	6-JK
	Short whlbs..	P215/75R15	P225/75R15	35-35	100	6-JK
			P235/75R15XL	41-41	100	6-JK

E250/350 Van & Wagon

Year	Model	Standard	Optional	Inflation (F-R)	Lug Nut Torque	Rim Width
2000-99	Van	LT245/75R16E	LT225/75R16E	N/A	126-170	7K
	Wagon (Reg.) .	LT225/75R16E		N/A	126-170	7K
	(Extended). .	LT245/75R16E		N/A	126-170	7K
1998	Cargo Van...	LT225/75R16D	LT225/75R16E	35-35	100	N/A
	Club Wagon: Base....	P215/75R15	P225/75R15S	35-35	100	6-J
	Heavy Duty..	P215/75R15	P225/75R15S	35-35	100	6-J
	Super ..	P215/75R15	P225/75R15S	35-35	100	6-J
1997-92	GVWR 7200#..	LT225/75R16D		50-55	140	7-J,K
			LT225/75R16E	50-55	140	7-K
	GVWR 7300#..	LT215/85R16E		50-60	140	7-J,K
			LT225/75R16E	50-60	140	7-K
1991-89	LD......	LT215/85R16D,E		51-58	140	6-K

Expedition

Year	Model	Standard	Optional	Inflation (F-R)	Lug Nut Torque	Rim Width
2000	XLT.....	P2555/70R16			Torque All	7-J
			P265/60R17			7.5-J
	Eddie Bauer 2WD....	P275/60R17			100 (12mm bolt)	7.5-J
	4WD...	P265/70R17			150 (14mm bolt)	7.5-J
1999-97	All......	P255/70R16		30-35	83-112	7-, 7.5-J
	4WD Only...		P265/70R17	30-35	83-112	7-, 7.5-J

Explorer

Year	Model	Standard	Optional	Inflation (F-R)	Lug Nut Torque	Rim Width
2000	All......	P235/75R15SL		N/A	100	7-J
			P255/70R16	N/A	100	7-J
1999-91	All.....	P225/70R15SL		30-35	100	6.5-, 7-JJ
			P235/75R15SL	26-26	100	6.5-, 7-JJ
	Opt. 1999-95 .		P255/70R16	30-30	100	6.5-, 7-JJ

F150 Pickup

Year	Model	Standard	Optional	Inflation (F-R)	Lug Nut Torque	Rim Width
2000	Lariat 2WD..	P275/60R17		N/A	Torque All	
	4WD....	P265/70R17		N/A	100 (12mm bolt)	
		LT265/75R16D		N/A	150 (14mm bolt)	
		LT245/75R16D		N/A		
	Others....	P235/70R16SL	P255/70R16SL	N/A		
		LT265/70R17		N/A		
		LT245/75R16D		N/A		
		LT265/70R17		N/A		
1999-97	All.....	P235/70R16SL	P255/70R16SL	35-35	100	7-J
		LT245/75R16		35-35	100	7-J
	STX.....		P275/60R17	35-35	100	7.5-JJ
1996-92	4WD....	P235/75R15XL		35-41	100	6-, 7-JJ
			P265/75R15SL	30-30	100	7.5-J

FORD TRUCKS Continued

F150 Pickup Continued

Year	Model	Standard	Optional	Inflation (F-R)	Lug Nut Torque	Rim Width
1996-89	2WD.....	P215/75R15SL		35-35	100	6-J
			P235/75R15XL	35-41	100	6-, 7.5-JJ
1995-93	Lightning...	P275/60HR17		30-30	100	8-J
1991-89	4WD.....	P235/75R15XL		35-41	100	6-JK
			31x10.5R15C	40-40	100	8-JJ
1998-97	2WD.....	P255/70R16	LT245/75R16	35-35	140	7-J
	4WD.....	LT245/75R16		35-35	140	7-J
1996-92	4WD.....	P235/75R15XL		35-41	100	6-, 7-JJ
			P265/75R15SL	30-30	100	7.5-J
1996-89	2WD.....	LT215/85R16D		51-58	140	6.00
	....		LT235/85R16D,E	44-44	140	6.00
	....		7.50-LT/D	45-50	140	6.00
1991-89	4WD.....	LT235/85R16E		51-80	140	7-, 7.5-K

Ranger

Year	Model	Standard	Optional	Inflation (F-R)	Lug Nut Torque	Rim Width
2000	2WD.....	P225/70R15SL		N/A	100	N/A
			P245/75R16SL	N/A	100	N/A
	4WD: XL..	P215/75R15SL		N/A	100	N/A
	XLT.....	P235/75R15SL		N/A	100	N/A
			P245/75R16SL	N/A	100	N/A
			P245/75R16	N/A	100	N/A
1999-98	2WD: XL..	P205/75R14SL	P225/70R14SL	35-35	100	N/A
	XLT..	P205/75R14SL	P225/70R14SL	35-35	100	N/A
	Splash..	P235/60R15SL		35-35	100	N/A
	4WD..	P215/75R15SL	P235/75R15SL	35-35	100	N/A
	XLT..	P215/75R15SL	P235/75R15SL	35-35	100	N/A
			P235/75R16SL	35-35	100	N/A
			P265/75R15SL	35-35	100	N/A
	Splash..	P235/75R15SL		35-35	100	N/A
1997-93	2WD.....	P195/70R14SL		35-35	100	5.5-J
			P215/70R14SL	35-35	100	6-J
			P225/70R14SL	35-35	100	6-J
	4WD..	P215/75R15SL		35-35	100	6-J
			P235/75R15SL	30-35	100	7-J
			P265/75R15SL	30-35	100	7-J
	Splash: 2WD.....	P235/60R15		35-35	100	7-J
	4WD.....	P235/75R15		30-35	100	7-J
1992-89	2WD.....	P195/70R14	P215/70R14	35-35	100	5.5-JJ
	4WD.....	P235/75R15		35-35	100	6,7-JJ
			P235/75R15	30-35	100	7-JJ

Windstar

Year	Model	Standard	Optional	Inflation (F-R)	Lug Nut Torque	Rim Width
2000-99	3.0L & LX 3-dr	P205/70R15		N/A	100	6-JJ
	LX 4-dr & SE..	P215/70R15		N/A	100	6.5-JJ
	SEL.....	P225/60R16		N/A	100	6.5-JJ
	Van	P215/70R15		N/A	100	N/A
1998-95	All	P215/70R15	P205/70R15	35-35	85-105	5.5-, 6-JJ
			P225/60R16	35-35	85-105	5.5-, 6-JJ

GEO

Metro

Year	Model	Standard	Optional	Inflation (F-R)	Lug Nut Torque	Rim Width
2000-95	All	P155/80R13		32-32	45	4.5-B
1994-91	Conv.....	P165/65R13		30-30	45	4.5-JB
	Hardtop....	P145/80R12		32-32	45	4-B
1990-89	All	P145/80R12		32-32	45	4-B

Prizm

Year	Model	Standard	Optional	Inflation (F-R)	Lug Nut Torque	Rim Width
2000-93	All	P175/65R14	P185/65R14	30-30	76	5.5-J
1992-91	GSi	P185/60R14		30-30	76	5-J
1992	Ex. GSi & LSi.....	P155/80R13		30-30	76	5-JJ
	LSi.....	P175/70R13		29-25	76	5-JJ
1991	Hatchback ex. GSi....	P155/80R13		35-35	76	4.5-JB
			P175/70R13	29-25	76	5-J
1990	Ex. GSi	P175/70R13		29-25	76	5-J
	GSi	P185/60HR14		30-30	76	5.5-JJ
1989	All	P175/70R13		29-25	76	5-J

Spectrum

Year	Model	Standard	Optional	Inflation (F-R)	Lug Nut Torque	Rim Width
1989	W/Alum whls .	P155/80R13		35-35	87	4.5-JB
	W/o Alum whls .	P155/80R13		35-35	65	4.5-JB

Storm

Year	Model	Standard	Optional	Inflation (F-R)	Lug Nut Torque	Rim Width
1993-91	GSi	P205/50VR15		35-35	87	6-JJ
	Ex. GSi	P185/60HR14		30-30	87	5.5-JJ
1990	GSi	P185/60VR14		35-35	87	5.5-JJ

Tracker

Year	Model	Standard	Optional	Inflation (F-R)	Lug Nut Torque	Rim Width
1999-95	2WD.....	P195/75R15		24-26		5.5-JJ
	4WD.....	P205/75R15		24-26		5.5-JJ
1994-92	2WD.....	P195/75R15		23-23	60	5.5-JJ
	4WD.....	P205/75R15		23-23	60	5.5-JJ
1991	2WD.....	P195/75R15		23-23	37-58	5.5-JJ
	4WD.....	P205/75R15		23-23	37-58	5.5-JJ
1990-89	All	P205/75R15		23-23	37-58	5.5-JJ

HONDA

Make / Model / Year	Standard	Optional	Inflation (Front-Rear)	Lug Nut Torque (Ft.-Lbs)	Rim Width
Accord					
2000-98 Sedan: DX	P195/70SR14		32-32	80	5.5-JJ
EX, LX 4-cyl.	P195/65HR15		32-32	80	5.5-JJ
V6.	P205/65VR15		30-30	80	6-JJ
Coupe: EX	P205/60VR16		32-32	80	6-JJ
LX.	P205/65VR15		30-30	80	6-JJ
1997-96 DX	P185/70R14		32-32	80	5-J
EX: USA	195/60HR15		32-32	80	5.5-J
Canada	185/65R15		32-32	80	5-JJ
EX-R, Wagon	195/60HR15		32-32	80	5.5-JJ
LX, LXE: USA	185/65R15		32-32	80	5-J
Canada	185/70R14		32-32	80	5.5-J
V6-2.7L	205/60VR15		32-29	80	5.5-, 6-JJ
1995-90 DX, EX Can, LX	P185/70R14		32-32	80	5-J
EX USA, EX-R, S	195/60R15		32-32	80	5.5-JJ
V6.	205/60VR15		32-29	80	5.5-, 6-JJ
1989 Ex. LXi	P185/70R13		26-26	80	5-J
LXi.	195/60R14		26-26	80	6-J
Civic					
2000-99 Ex. Si & LX V6.	P185/65SR14		30-29	80	5-J
Si	P195/55VR15		N/A	80	N/A
1998-97 All	P185/65SR14		30-29	80	N/A
1996 DX: USA	P175/70SR13		32-32	80	N/A
EX	P185/65SR14		30-29	80	N/A
LX: USA	P185/65SR14		30-29	80	N/A
Canada	P175/70SR13		32-32	80	N/A
1995 CX: USA	P165/70R13		35-35	80	4.5-J
Canada	P175/70R13		32-32	80	5-J
DX, LX Canada	P175/70R13		32-32	80	5-J
EX: USA	P175/65R13	P185/60R14	29-29	80	5.5-J
Canada	P175/65R13		29-29	80	5-J
LX USA	P175/65R13		29-29	80	5-J
Si	P185/60R14		29-29	80	5-J
VX	P165/70R13		35-35	80	4.5-J
1994-93 2-dr:1.5L	P165/70R13		32-32	80	5-J
1.6L SOHC.	P185/60R14		29-29	80	5-J
3-dr: 1.5L (70 hp)	P165/70R13		35-32	80	4.5-J
1.5L (102 hp)	175/70R13		32-32	80	5-J
1.6L	P185/60R14		29-29	80	5-J
4-dr:1.5L	P175/70R13		32-32	80	5-J
1.6L	P175/65R14		29-29	80	5-J
1992 3-door	P165/70R13		35-32	80	4.5-J
		P185/60HR14	28-32	80	5-J
		P175/70SR13	32-32	80	5-J
4-door	P175/70SR13	P175/65HR14	32-32	80	5-J
1991-89 2WD Wagon	P175/70R13		32-32	80	4.5-J
4WD wagon	P175/70R14		32-32	80	4.5-J
DX sedan & hatchbk	P175/70R13		32-32	80	4.5-J
LX sedan	175/70R13		32-32	80	4.5-J
Si hatchback.	185/60R14		28-26	80	4.5-J
Std hatchback.	P165/70R13		35-32	80	4.5-J
1991-90 EX Sedan	175/65R14		32-32	80	5-J
CRX					
1991-89 DX & 1.5L Coupe	P175/70R13		28-28	80	4.5-J
HF	P165/70R13		35-32	80	4.5-J
Si	185/60R14		24-24	80	5-J
CR-V					
1999-97 All	P205/70R15		26-26	80	N/A
Del Sol					
1995-93 1.5L	P175/70SR13		32-32	80	5-J
1.5L: SOHC.	P185/60HR14		29-29	80	5-J
DOHC, VTEC.	P195/60VR14		29-29	80	5.5-JJ
Odyssey					
2000-99 All	P215/65R16		32-32	N/A	6.5-JJ
1998-95 All	P205/65R15		32-32	80	6-JJ
Passport					
1999 2WD	P235/75R15		29-29	87	6.5-JJ
4WD: 4-cyl	P235/75R15		29-29	87	6.5-JJ
		P245/70R16	26-26	87	7-JJ
V6.	P245/70R16		26-26	87	7-JJ
1998 2WD	P215/75R15		29-29	87	6.5-JJ
4WD: LX	P235/75R15		29-29	87	6.5-JJ
		P245/70R16	26-26	87	7-JJ
EX.	P245/70R16		26-26	87	7-JJ
1997-96 2WD	P225/75R16		29-32	80	6-JJ
4WD	P245/70R16		26-26	80	7-JJ
1995-94 All	225/75R15		26-26	80	6-JJ
LX 4WD		245/70R16	29-29	80	7.5-JJ
EX	P245/70R16		29-29	80	7.5-JJ

HONDA Continued

Make / Model / Year	Standard	Optional	Inflation (Front-Rear)	Lug Nut Torque (Ft.-Lbs)	Rim Width
Prelude					
2000-97 All	P205/50VR16		32-32	80	6.5-JJ
1996-92 S	185/70HR14		30-30	80	5.5-J
Others	205/55VR15		32-32	80	6.5-JJ
1991 All	195/60R14		28-26	80	5.5-JJ
1990-89 S	185/70HR13		28-26	80	5-J
Si	195/60R14		28-26	80	6-J
S2000					
2000 Front	P205/55WR16		—	—	—
Rear	P225/50WR16		—	—	—

HYUNDAI

Make / Model / Year	Standard	Optional	Inflation (Front-Rear)	Lug Nut Torque (Ft.-Lbs)	Rim Width
Accent					
2000 All	P155/80R13	P175/70R13	30-30	65-80	4.5, 5-J
		P185/60HR14	30-30	65-80	5-J
1999-97 All	P155/80R13	P175/70R13	30-30	65-80	4.5-, 5-J
		P175/65R14	30-30	65-80	4.5-, 5-J
1996-95 All	P155/80R13	P175/70R13	30-30	65-80	4.5-,5-J
Elantra					
2000 All	P195/60R14		30-30	65-80	5, 5.5-JJ
1999-96 All	P195/65R14	P195/60R14	30-30	65-80	5-J, 5.5-JJ
1995-94 All	P175/70R14	P185/60HR14	29-29	65-80	5.5-J
1993-92 All	P175/65R14	P185/60R14	32-32	65-80	5.5-,6-J
Excel					
1994-93 Base	P155/80R13		28-28	65-80	4.5-JJ
GL	P155/80R13		28-28	65-80	4.5-JJ
		P175/70R13	28-28	65-80	5-JJ
GS	P175/70R13		28-28	65-80	5-JJ
1992-91 GL	P155/80R13		28-28	65-80	4.5-JJ
		P175/70R13	28-28	65-80	5-JJ
GS, GLS	P175/70R14		28-28	65-80	5-J
1990 All	P155/80R13		30-30	65-80	4.5-J
		P175/70R13	30-30	65-80	5-J
1989 W/Alum whls.	P155/80R13		30-30	65-72	4.5-J
		P175/70R13	30-30	65-72	5-J
W/Steel whls.	P155/80R13		30-30	50-57	4.5-J
		P175/70R13	30-30	50-57	5-J
Scoupe					
1995-94 All	P175/65R14	P185/60HR14	28-28	65-80	5-JJ
1993 Base	P175/70R13		28-28	65-80	5-JJ
LS	P185/60HR14		28-28	65-80	5-J
1992 Ex. LS	P175/70R13		28-28	65-80	5-J
LS	P185/60R14		28-28	65-80	5-J
1991 Ex. LS	P175/70R13	P185/60R14	25-25	65-80	5-J
LS	P185/60R14		25-25	65-80	5-J
Sonata					
2000-93 W/Alum whls.	P205/60R15		30-30	65-80	6-J
W/Steel whls.	P195/70R14		30-30	65-80	5.5-JJ
1992-91 All	P195/70SR14		30-30	65-80	5-J
		P205/60HR15	30-30	65-80	6-JJ
1990 All	P185/70R14		30-30	65-80	5.5-JJ
		P195/70R14	30-30	65-80	5.5-JJ
1989 W/Alum whls.	P185/70R14		30-30	65-72	5-J
		P195/70R14	30-30	65-72	5.5-J
W/Steel whls.	P185/70R14		30-30	50-57	5-J
		P195/70R14	30-30	50-57	5.5-J
Tiburon					
2000-98 All	P195/60R14		30-30	65-80	5-J, 5.5-JJ

INFINITI

Make / Model / Year	Standard	Optional	Inflation (Front-Rear)	Lug Nut Torque (Ft.-Lbs)	Rim Width
G20					
1999 All	P195/65HR15	P195/60HR15	35-35	72-87	6-JJ
1996-95 All	P195/65HR14		35-35	72-87	6-JJ
1994 All	195/65HR14		35-35	72-87	6-JJ
1993-91 All	195/60HR14		35-35	72-87	6-JJ
I30					
2000 All	P215/55HR16		35-35	72-87	6.5-JJ
		P225/50VR17	35-35	72-87	7-JJ
1999-98 All	P205/65R15		35-35	72-87	6.5-JJ
		P225/50R16	N/A	72-87	6.5-JJ
1997-96 All	P205/65R15	P215/60HR15	35-35	72-87	6-, 6.5-JJ
J30					
1997-93 All	P215/60HR15		35-35	72-87	6.5-JJ
M30					
1991-90 All	P215/60R15		35-35	76-90	6.5-JJ
Q45					
2000-99 All	P215/60VR16		35-35	72-87	7-JJ
		P225/50VR17	35-35	72-87	7.5-JJ
1998-97 All	P215/60VR16		35-35	72-87	7-JJ
1996-90 All	P215/65VR15		35-35	72-87	6.5-JJ
QX4					
2000 All	P255/65SR16		35-35	87-108	7-JJ
1999-97 All	P245/70R16		35-35	87-108	7-JJ

MAKE MODEL YEAR	ORIGINAL EQUIPMENT SIZE Standard	Optional	RECOM-MENDED INFLATION PRESSURE Front - Rear	LUG NUT TORQUE Ft.-Lbs	RIM WIDTH
ISUZU					
Amigo					
1999-98 All	P235/75R15		29-29	N/A	6.5-JJ
		P245/70R16	26-26	N/A	7-JJ
1994 W/Alum whls.	P245/70R16		26-29	86-86	7-J
W/Steel whls.	P245/70R16		26-29	66-66	7-J
1993-92 All	P225/75R15		26-26	86-86	6-JJ
		31x10.5R15	29-29	86-86	7-JJ
1991-90 W/Alum whls.	P225/75R15		26-26	86-86	6-JJ
W/Steel whls.	31X10.5R15		29-29	58-87	7-JJ
1989 All	P225/75R15		26-26	58-87	6-JJ
Hombre					
1999-98 2WD	P205/75R15		35-35	100	N/A
4WD	P235/75R15		35-35	100	N/A
		31x10.5R15	35-35	100	N/A
1997 All	P205/75R15		N/A	95	N/A
I-Mark					
1989 LSS & RS:					
Alum whls . .	P185/60R14		29-26	87	5-J
Steel whls . .	P185/60R14		29-26	65	5-J
S: W/Alum whls	P155/80R13		30-30	87	4.5-J
W/Steel whls	P155/80R13		30-30	65	4.5-J
XS:					
W/Alum whls	P175/70R13		30-30	87	5-J
W/Steel whls	P175/70R13		30-30	65	5-J
Impulse					
1992-90 RS	205/50VR15		29-29	87	6-JJ
XS	P185/60HR14		29-29	87	5.5-JJ
1989 All	205/60R14		29-29	87	6-JJ
Oasis					
1998-95 All	P205/65R15		32-32	80	6-JJ
Pickup					
1995-94 2WD	P195/75R14		29-35	66[1]	5-J
4WD	P225/75R15		26-26	66[1]	6-J
		31x10.5R15	29-29	66[1]	7-J
1993-92 2WD 1/2-ton . .	P195/75R14		29-35	72[1]	5-J
	P205/75R14		29-35	72[1]	5.5-JJ
4WD 1/2-ton. .	P225/75R15		26-26	72[1]	6-JJ
		31x10.5R15	29-29	72[1]	7-JJ
1991-89 2WD: 1/2-ton .	P195/75R14		29-35	72[1]	5-J
	P205/75R14		29-35	72[1]	5.5-JJ
1-ton	185/R14/8		26-65	72[1]	5-J
4WD 1/2-ton. .	P225/75R15		26-26	72[1]	6-JJ
		31x10.5R15	29-29	72[1]	7-JJ

[1] With aluminum wheels, 87

MAKE MODEL YEAR	ORIGINAL EQUIPMENT SIZE Standard	Optional	RECOM-MENDED INFLATION PRESSURE Front - Rear	LUG NUT TORQUE Ft.-Lbs	RIM WIDTH
Rodeo					
1999-98 2WD	P215/75R15	P235/75R15	29-29	87	6.5-JJ
4WD	P235/75R15		29-29	87	6.5-JJ
		P245/70R16	26-26	87	7-JJ
1997-94 All	P225/75R15		29-32	87	6-J
		P245/70R16	26-26	87	7-JJ
1993-91 Ex. XS	P225/75R15		26-26	66[1]	6-JJ
		31x10.5R15	29-29	66[1]	7-JJ
XS	31x10.5R15		29-29	66[1]	7-JJ

[1] With aluminum wheels, 87

MAKE MODEL YEAR	ORIGINAL EQUIPMENT SIZE Standard	Optional	RECOM-MENDED INFLATION PRESSURE Front - Rear	LUG NUT TORQUE Ft.-Lbs	RIM WIDTH
Stylus					
1993-91 S	P175/70R13		30-30	87	5-J
RS	P175/70R13		29-26	87	5.5-JJ
1992-91 XS	P185/60HR14		29-26	87	5-J
1990 All	P175/70R13		30-30	87	5-J
Trooper					
1999-98 All	P245/70R16		26-26	N/A	7-JJ
1997-92 All	P245/70R16		30-35	87	7-JJ
1991-89 All	P235/75R15		35-35	58-87[1]	6-JJ
		31x10.5R15	28-28	58-87[1]	7-JJ

[1] With aluminum wheels, 80-94

MAKE MODEL YEAR	ORIGINAL EQUIPMENT SIZE Standard	Optional	RECOM-MENDED INFLATION PRESSURE Front - Rear	LUG NUT TORQUE Ft.-Lbs	RIM WIDTH
JAGUAR					
XJ12					
1998-95 Base	225/60ZR16		32-34	65-75	7-J
Sport	225/55ZR16		32-34	65-75	7-J
1994-93 All	225/60ZR16		34-34	65-75	7-J
XJ6 Series					
1998 Base	225/60ZR16		32-34	65-75	7-J
Sport		225/60ZR16	32-34	65-75	8-J
1997-95 Base	225/60ZR16		32-34[1]	65-75	7-J
Sport	225/55ZR16		32-34[1]	65-75	7-J
1994-93 All	225/60ZR16		34-34	65-75	7-J
1992-91 All	205/70VR15		27-30	65-75	7-J
1990-89 All	205/70VR15		27-30	65-75	6-JK

[1] With Supercharged 4.0L, Front tires: add 2 psi.

MAKE MODEL YEAR	ORIGINAL EQUIPMENT SIZE Standard	Optional	RECOM-MENDED INFLATION PRESSURE Front - Rear	LUG NUT TORQUE Ft.-Lbs	RIM WIDTH
JAGUAR Continued					
S-Type					
2000 All	225/55HR16		32-34	75	7, 7.5 in.
		235/50ZR17	32-34	75	—
XJ8 Series					
1999-97 XJ8-L	225/60ZR16		32-34	N/A	7-J
V8 XJ Sedan. .	225/55ZR16	225/60ZR16	32-34	N/A	N/A
		255/40ZR18	32-34	N/A	N/A
XJR					
1999 All	255/40ZR18		—	—	8-J
1998 All	225/40ZR18		32-34	N/A	8-J
1997-95 All	225/45ZR17		34-34	65-75	8.0
XJS Series					
1997 All	225/60ZR16		34-36	N/A	7-J
1996 All	225/60ZR16	225/55ZR16	34-36	65-75	7-J
1994-92 All	235/60ZR15	235/60VR15	36-36	65-75	6.5-J
		215/65R15	28-28	65-75	6.5-J
		225/55ZR16	26-28	65-75	7-J
1989 All	235/60VR15		27-30	65-75	6.5-J
XK8					
1999-98 All	245/50ZR17		32-34	N/A	8-J
JEEP					
Cherokee					
2000 SE	P215/75R15		N/A	85-110	7.0
Sport	P225/75R15		N/A	85-110	7.0
Others	P225/70R16		N/A	85-110	7.0
1999-93 All	P215/75R15	P225/75R15	30-30	85-110	7-JJ
		P225/70R15	30-35	85-110	7-JJ
1992 All	P195/75R15		33-33	85-110	6-, 7-JJ
		P215/75R15	30-30	85-110	7-JJ
		P225/70R15	30-30	85-110	7-JJ
1991-90 All	P195/75R15		33-33	75	6-JJ
		P205/75R15	30-30	75	6-, 7-JJ
		P215/75R15	30-30	75	7-JJ
		P225/75R15	30-30	75	7-JJ
		P225/70R15	30-35	75	7-JJ
1989 All	P195/75R15		33-33	75	6-JJ
		P205/75R15	30-30	75	6-, 7-JJ
		P215/65R15	30-30	75	6-JJ
		P215/75R15	30-30	75	6-JJ
		P225/70R15	30-30	75	7-JJ
		P225/75R15	30-30	75	7-JJ
Comanche					
1992 All	P195/75R15		30-30	85-110	6-JJ
	P205/75R15	P225/75R15	30-30	85-110	7-JJ
	P225/70R15	P215/75R15	30-30	85-110	7-JJ
1991-90 All	P195/75R15		33-33	75	6-, 7-JJ
		P205/75R15	30-30	75	6-, 7-JJ
		P215/75R15	30-30	75	7-JJ
		P225/75R15	30-30	75	7-JJ
		P225/70R15	30-35	75	7-JJ
1989 All	P195/75R15		33-33	75	6-JJ
		P205/75R15	30-30	75	6-JJ
		P215/65R15	30-30	75	6-JJ
		P215/75R15	30-30	75	6-, 7-JJ
		P205/75R15	30-30	75	7-JJ
		P225/75R15	30-30	75	7-JJ
		P225/70R15	30-30	75	7-JJ
Grand Cherokee, Grand Wagoneer					
2000-99 Laredo	P225/75R16	P245/70R16	N/A	85-110	7.0
Limited	P245/70R16		N/A	85-110	7.0
1998 All	P215/75R15	P225/75R15	36-36	86-110	7-J
		P235/75R15	36-36	85-110	7-J
		P245/70R15	36-36	85-110	7-J
1995-93 All	P215/75R15	P225/75R15	33-33	85-110	6-, 7-JJ
		P225/70R16	33-33	85-110	6-, 7-JJ
		P235/75R15	33-33	85-110	6-, 7-JJ
		P245/70R15	33-33	85-110	7-JJ
1991-89 All	P235/75R15		35-35	75	6-, 7-JJ
Wagoneer					
1990 All	P195/75R15		33-33	75	6-, 7-JJ
		P205/75R15	30-30	75	6-, 7-JJ
		P215/75R15	30-30	75	7-JJ
		P225/75R15	30-30	75	7-JJ
		P225/70R15	30-35	75	7-JJ
1989 All	P205/75R15		30-30	75	6-, 7-JJ
Wrangler, YJ, TJ					
2000 SE	P205/75R15		N/A	85-110	6.0
		P225/75R15	N/A	85-110	7.0
Sport	P215/75R15		N/A	85-110	7.0
		P225/75R15	N/A	85-110	7.0
Sahara	P225/60R16		N/A	85-110	7.0

MAKE MODEL YEAR	ORIGINAL EQUIPMENT SIZE Standard	Optional	RECOMMENDED INFLATION PRESSURE Front - Rear	LUG NUT TORQUE Ft.-Lbs	RIM WIDTH
JEEP Continued					
Wrangler, YJ, TJ Continued					
1999-97 All	P205/75R15	P215/75R15	30-30	85-110	7-JJ
		P225/75R15	30-35	85-110	7-JJ
		30x9.5R15LT	30-30	85-110	7-JJ
1996-92 All	P205/75R15	P215/75R15	30-30	85-110	7-JJ
		P225/75R15	30-35	85-110	7-JJ
		30x9.5R15LT	30-30	85-110	7-JJ
1991-90 All	P205/75R15	P215/75R15	30-30	80	7-JJ
		29x9.5R15LT	30-30	80	7-JJ
1989 All	P205/75R15	P215/75R15	30-30	75	7-JJ
		P225/75R15	30-30	75	7-JJ
KIA					
Sephia					
2000-98 All	P175/70R13		29-29	65-87	5-J
		P185/65HR14	29-29	65-87	5.5-JJ
1997-95 All	P175/70SR13		29-29	65-87	5-JJ
		P185/60R14	29-29	65-87	5.5-, 6-JJ
1994-93 All	P175/70SR13		29-29	65-87	5-JJ
Sportage					
2000-95 All	P205/75R15		26-26	72	6-JJ
LAND ROVER					
County Classic					
1995 All	205XR16		28-38	N/A	7.0
Discovery					
1999 All	255/65HR16	255/55HR18	28-46	103	8
1998-95 All	P235/70HR16		26-36	96	N/A
Defender 90					
1995 All	LT265/75R16		28-35	N/A	7.0
1994 All	205SR16	205TR16	28-35	N/A	7-JJ
1993 All	7.50R16		28-35	N/A	N/A
Range Rover					
1999-96 4.0 SE	255/65HR16		28-38	80	8.0
4.6 HSE	255/55HR18		28-38	80	8
1995-93 4.0 SE	255/65HR16		28-38	N/A	8.0
LWB	LT265/75R16		28-38	N/A	7.0
1992-89 All	205R16		28-38	90-95	7-JJ
LEXUS					
ES250					
1991-90 All	195/60VR15		32-29	76	5-JJ
ES300					
2000 All	P205/65VR15		26-26	76	6-JJ
		P215/60VR16	26-26	76	6.5-JJ
1999-92 All	P205/65VR15		26-26	76	6-JJ
GS300					
2000-93 All	P215/60VR16		30-30	76	7.5-JJ
		225/55VR16	32-32	76	8-JJ
GS400					
2000-98 All	225/55VR16		32-32	76	7.5-JJ
		235/45ZR17	33-33	76	8-JJ
LS400					
2000-93 All	P225/60VR16		29-29	76	7-JJ
1992-90 All	205/65VR15		30-30	76	6.5-JJ
LX450					
1997-96 All	P275/70HR16		32-32	76	6-, 6.5-JJ
LX470					
2000-98 All	P275/70R16		32-32	97	6.5-JJ
RX300					
2000-99 All	P225/70R16		30-30	76	6.5-JJ
SC300					
2000-95 All	225/55VR16		32-32	76	6-, 6.5-JJ
1994-93 All	P215/60VR15		32-32	76	6-, 6.5-JJ
1992 All	225/55VR16		32-32	76	7-JJ
SC400					
2000-95 All	225/55VR16		32-32	76	6-, 6.5-JJ
1994-93 All	P215/60VR15		32-32	76	6-, 6.5-JJ
LINCOLN					
Continental					
2000 All	P225/60HR16		N/A	95	7
		P225/60VR16	N/A	95	7
1999-95 All	P225/60HR16		30-30	80-105	7-JJ
		P225/60VR16	30-30	80-105	6.5
1994-89 All	P205/70R15		30-30	80-105	6.5-JJ
LS					
2000 V8 w/o Sport pkg	P215/60R1694V		30-30	100	7-J
w/Sport pkg	P235/50R1795V		30-30	100	7.5-J
		245/45R1795W	N/A	100	7.5-J
V6 w/auto	P215/60R1694H		30-30	100	7-J
w/manual	P235/50R1795V		30-30	100	7.5-J
		245/45R1795W	N/A	100	7.5-J

MAKE MODEL YEAR	ORIGINAL EQUIPMENT SIZE Standard	Optional	RECOMMENDED INFLATION PRESSURE Front - Rear	LUG NUT TORQUE Ft.-Lbs	RIM WIDTH
LINCOLN Continued					
Mark VI					
1983-80 All	P205/75R15		30-34	80-105	6-, 6.5-JJ
Mark VII					
1994-91 All	P225/60R16		30-30	80-105	7-JJ
1990-89 Ex. LSC	P215/70R15		30-30	80-105	6-JJ
LSC	P225/60R16		30-30	80-105	7-JJ
Mark VIII					
1998-93 All	P225/60R16		30-30	80-105	7-JJ
Navigator					
2000 4 x 2	P275/60R17		N/A	100 (12mm bolt) 150 (14mm bolt)	7.5-J
4 x 4	P255/75R17		N/A	100 (12mm bolt) 150 (14mm bolt)	7.5-J
1999 All	P245/75R16		N/A	83-112	N/A
		P255/75R17	N/A	83-112	N/A
1998-97 All	P255/70R16		35-35	N/A	N/A
		P265/70R17	35-35	N/A	N/A
Town Car					
2000 All	P225/60SR16		N/A	85-105	7
		P235/60TR16	N/A	85-105	7
1999-93 All	P215/70R15	P225/70R15	30-30	80-105	6.5-JJ
		P225/60R16	30-30	80-105	7-JJ
1992-90 All	P215/70R15		30-34	80-105	6-, 6.5-JJ
1989 All	P215/70R15		30-34	80-105	6-, 6.5-JJ
MAZDA					
323					
1994-92 All	P155/80SR13		32-32	65-87	5-J
		P175/70SR13	32-32	65-87	5-J
1991-90 Ex. SE	P155/80R13		32-32	65-87	4.5-J
SE	P175/70R13		32-32	65-87	5-J
1989 Base	155SR13		29-26	65-87	4.5-J
GT	185/60R14		29-26	65-87	5.5-J
LX	175/70SR13		29-26	65-87	5-J
SE	155SR13		29-26	65-87	4.5-J
Wagon	175/70SR13		29-26	65-87	5-J
626					
2000 2.0L	P185/70R14		32-26	65-87	5.5-JJ
		P205/60HR15	32-26	65-87	6-JJ
2.5L	P205/60HR15		32-26	65-87	6-JJ
		P205/55HR16	32-29	65-87	6.6-JJ
1999-98 2.0L	P185/70R14		32-26	65-87	5.5-JJ
2.5L	P205/60HR15		32-26	65-87	6-JJ
1997-95 DX, LX 4-cyl.	P195/65SR14		32-26	65-87	5.5-, 6-JJ
ES, LX-V6	P205/55VR15		32-26	65-87	6-, 6.5-JJ
1994-93 Base	P195/65SR14		32-26	65-87	6-JJ
ES, LS	P205/55VR15		32-26	65-87	6-JJ
1992-90 DX & LX	185/70SR14		32-26	65-87	5.5-J
GT	195/60VR15		32-26	65-87	6-JJ
1989 All	185/70SR14		28-26	65-87	5.5-JJ
		195/60HR15	28-26	65-87	6-JJ
929, Serenia (Canada)					
1995-92 All	P205/65HR15		28-28	65-87	6-JJ
1991-90 Ex. S	P195/65R15		30-30	65-87	6-JJ
S	P205/60R15		32-32	65-87	6-JJ
1989 All	P195/65R15		30-30	65-87	6-JJ
B2000, B2200 Pickup					
1993-91 All	P205/75R14		28-35	65-87[1]	5.5-JJ
1990 All	P205/75R14		32-32	65-87[1]	5.5-JJ
1989 All	P205/75R14		26-34	65-87[1]	5.5-JJ
		P225/70HR14	26-34	65-87[1]	6-JJ
B2300, B2500, B3000, B4000					
2000 2WD	P225/70R15		35-35	100	6-J
		P245/75R16	35-35	100	7-J
4WD	P215/75R15		35-35	100	6-J
		P235/75R15	35-35	100	7-J
		P265/75R15	35-35	100	7.5-J
		P245/75R15	35-35	100	7-J
1999 2WD	P205/75R14	P225/70R14	35-35	100	6-J
		P225/70R15	35-35	100	6-J
4WD	P215/75R15		35-35	100	6-J
		P235/75R15	35-35	100	7-J
		P265/75R15	30-35	100	7-J
1998 2WD	P205/75R14	P225/70R14	35-35	65-87	6-J
		P225/70R15	35-35	65-87	6-J
1996-94 2WD	P195/70R14	P215/70R14	35-35	65-87	5.5-J
		P225/70R14	35-35	65-87	6-J
4WD	P215/75R15		35-35	65-87	6-, 7-J
		P235/75R15	30-35	65-87	7-J
		P265/75R15	30-35	65-87	7-J

MAZDA Continued

B2600 Pickup

YEAR		Standard	Optional	INFL. PRESS.	LUG NUT TORQUE	RIM WIDTH
1993	2WD	P205/75R14		28-35	65-87	5.5-JJ
	4WD	P215/75R15	P235/75R15	28-31	65-87	6-JJ
1992-91	2WD	P205/75R14		28-35	65-87[1]	5.5-JJ
	4WD	P215/75R15	P235/75R15	28-31	65-87	6-JJ
1990	2WD	P205/75R14		32-32	65-87[1]	5.5-JJ
	4WD	P215/75R15		26-34	65-87[1]	6-JJ
			P235/75R15	26-34	65-87[1]	6-JJ
1989	2WD	P205/75R14		26-34	65-87[1]	5.5-JJ
			P225/70HR14	26-34	65-87[1]	6-JJ
	4WD	P215/75R15		26-34	65-87[1]	6-JJ
			P235/75R15	26-34	65-87[1]	6-JJ

1 With styled wheels, 87-108

Miata

YEAR		Standard	Optional	INFL. PRESS.	LUG NUT TORQUE	RIM WIDTH
2000-99	All	P185/60HR14		26-26	65-87	5.5-JJ
			195/50VR15	26-26	65-87	6-JJ
1998-96	All	P185/60HR14		26-26	65-87	5.5-JJ
1995	All	P185/60HR14	195/55VR15	26-26	65-87	6-JJ
1994-93	All	P185/60HR14		26-26	65-87	5.5-JJ
1992-90	All	P185/60HR14		26-26	65-87	5.5-J
			P205/60R15	32-26	65-87	6-JJ

Millenia

YEAR		Standard	Optional	INFL. PRESS.	LUG NUT TORQUE	RIM WIDTH
2000-99	All	P205/65HR15		32-29	65-87	6-JJ
			P215/55VR16	32-29	65-87	6.5-JJ
	2.3L Opt		P215/50VR17	32-29	65-87	6.5-J
1998-95	All	P205/65HR15		32-29	65-87	6-JJ
			P215/55VR16	32-29	65-87	6.5-JJ

MPV

YEAR		Standard	Optional	INFL. PRESS.	LUG NUT TORQUE	RIM WIDTH
2000	All	P205/65R15		35-35	65-87	5.5-JJ
			P215/60HR16	32-32	65-87	6-JJ
1999-94	4WD	P215/70R15		32-32	65-87	6-JJ
	2WD	P195/75R15	P215/65R15	32-35	65-87	6-JJ
1998	All	P225/70VR15		32-32	65-87	N/A
1993	2WD	P205/75R14	P205/70R14	35-35	65-87	5.5-JJ
			P215/65R15	35-35	65-87	6-JJ
	4WD	P215/65R15		32-32	65-87	6-JJ
1992	2WD	P205/75R14	P205/70R14	35-35	65-87[1]	5.5-JJ
			P215/65R15	35-35	65-87[1]	6-JJ
	4WD	P215/65R15		32-32	65-87[1]	6-JJ
1991	2WD	P205/70R14		35-35	65-87[1]	5.5-JJ
			P215/65R15	32-32	65-87[1]	6-JJ
	4WD	P215/65R15		35-35	65-87[1]	5.5-JJ
			P205/75R15	35-35	65-87[1]	6-JJ
1990	2WD	P205/70R14		32-32	65-87[1]	5.5-JJ
			P215/65R15	30-30	65-87[1]	6-JJ
	4WD	P215/65R15		30-30	65-87[1]	6-JJ
			P205/75R14	32-32	65-87[1]	5.5-JJ
1989	All	P205/70R14		35-35	65-87[1]	5.5-JJ
			P215/65R15	32-32	65-87[1]	6-JJ

1 With styled wheels, 87-108

MX-3, Precidia (Canada)

YEAR		Standard	Optional	INFL. PRESS.	LUG NUT TORQUE	RIM WIDTH
1995-94	4-cyl	P185/65SR14		32-32	65-87	5.5-JJ
1994-93	V6	P205/55VR15		28-28	65-87	6-JJ
1993	4-cy.	P185/65SR14		32-32	65-87	5.5-JJ
1992	Ex. GS	P185/65SR14		32-32	65-87	5.5-JJ
	GS	P205/55VR15		28-28	65-87	6-JJ

MX-6

YEAR		Standard	Optional	INFL. PRESS.	LUG NUT TORQUE	RIM WIDTH
1997-93	Base	P195/65SR14		32-26	65-87	5.5-, 6-JJ
	LS	P205/55VR15		32-26	65-87	5.5-, 6-JJ
1992-90	Ex. Turbo	P185/70SR14		32-26	65-87	5.5-J
			P195/60HR15	32-26	65-87	6-JJ
	Turbo	P195/60VR15	P205/60VR15	32-26	65-87	6-JJ

Navajo

YEAR		Standard	Optional	INFL. PRESS.	LUG NUT TORQUE	RIM WIDTH
1994-91	All	P225/70R15		35-35	85-115	7-JJ
			P235/75R15	26-26	85-115	7-JJ

Protege

YEAR		Standard	Optional	INFL. PRESS.	LUG NUT TORQUE	RIM WIDTH
2000-99	1.6L	P185/65R14		32-32	65-87	5.5-JJ
	1.8L	P185/65R14		32-32	65-87	5.5-JJ
			P195/55VR15	32-32	85-87	6-JJ
1998-95	DX, LX, LXE	P175/70SR13		32-32	65-87	5-J
	ES	P185/60SR14	P185/65SR14	32-32	65-87	5.5-JJ
1994-93	DX	P175/70SR13		32-32	65-87	5-J
	LX	P185/60HR14		32-32	65-87	5.5-JJ
1992	All	P175/70SR13		32-32	65-87	5-J
			P185/60HR14	32-32	65-87	5.5-JJ
1991-90	DX & SE	P175/70SR13		32-32	65-87	5-J
	LX	P185/60HR14		32-32	65-87	5.5-JJ
	4WD	P185/65R14		32-32	65-87	5.5-JJ

RX-7

YEAR		Standard	Optional	INFL. PRESS.	LUG NUT TORQUE	RIM WIDTH
1995-92	Type R	P225/50ZR16		32-32	65-87	8-JJ
	Others	225/50VR16		32-32	65-87	8-JJ

1 With styled wheels, 87-108

MAZDA Continued

RX-7 Continued

YEAR		Standard	Optional	INFL. PRESS.	LUG NUT TORQUE	RIM WIDTH
1991-89	Ex. Turbo	205/60VR15		32-32	65-87	6-JJ
		205/55VR16		32-32	65-87	7-JJ
	Turbo	205/55VR16		32-32	65-87	7-JJ

MERCEDES-BENZ

MODEL / YEAR		Standard	Optional	INFL. PRESS.	LUG NUT TORQUE	RIM WIDTH
190D, 190E						
1989	All	185/65R15		28-32	80	6-J
190E 2.3						
1993	All	185/65R15		27-29	110	6-J
1992	All	185/65R15		29-33	110	6-J
1991	All	185/65R15		29-33	80	6-J
190E 2.6						
1993	All	185/65R15		32-33	110	6-J
			205/55R15	35-41	110	7-J
1992	All	185/65VR15		29-33	110	6-J
1991-89	All	185/65VR15		29-33	80	6-J
260E						
1989	All	195/65VR15		29-35	80	6.5-J
300CE, 300E						
1993	All	195/65R15	195/65ZR15	26-26	80	6.5-J
1992	All	195/65R15		26-26	80	6.5-J
			205/65R15	26-26	80	7-J
1991-89	All	195/65VR15		29-35	80	6.5-J
300D						
1993-92	All	195/65HR15		N/A	80	6.5-J
300SD						
1993-92	All	225/60VR16		27-27	110	7.5-J
300SE						
1993-92	All	225/60VR16		27-27	110	7.5-J
1991-90	All	205/65R15		30-35	80	6.5-JJ
300SEL						
1991-90	All	205/65R15		30-35	80	6.5-JJ
1989	All	205/65VR15		30-35	80	6.5-J
300SL						
1992	All	225/55ZR16		27-27	80	8-J
1991-90	All	225/55ZR16		30-35	80	8-J
300TE						
1993	All	195/65R15	195/65ZR15	29-32	80	6.5-J
1992	All	195/65VR15		26-30	80	6.5-J
1991-89	All	195/65VR15		29-35	80	6.5-J
350SD, 350SDL						
1991	All	205/65R15		30-35	80	6.5-J
380SE						
1985-83	All	205/70HR14		28-30	80	6.5-J
1982-81	All	205/70HR14		28-30	66-81	6.5-J
400E						
1993	All	195/65R15	195/65ZR15	26-26	110	6.5-J
1992	All	195/65VR15		26-26	110	6.5-J
400SE						
1993-92	All	235/60ZR16		27-27	110	7.5-J
420SEL						
1991-89	All	205/65VR15		30-35	80	6.5-J
500E						
1993-92	All	225/55ZR16		30-33	110	8-J
500SEC, 500SEL						
1993-92	All	235/60ZR16		27-27	110	7.5-J
500SL						
1992-90	All	225/55ZR16		30-35	80	8-J
560SEC, 500SEL						
1991-89	All	205/65VR15		30-35	80	6.5-J
560SL						
1989	All	205/65VR15		29-35	80	7-J
600SEC						
1993	All	235/60ZR16		27-27	110	7.5-J
600SEL						
1993-92	All	235/60ZR16		27-27	110	7.5-J
C220, C230, C280						
1999-98	All	205/60R15		30-33	80	7.0
1997-94	All	195/65R15		30-33	110	6.5-J
C36AMG						
1999-98	All	P325/45ZR17		N/A	N/A	N/A
1997-94	Front	225/45ZR17		N/A	110	7.5-J
	Rear	245/40ZR17		N/A	110	8.5-J

MERCEDES-BENZ Continued

MODEL / YEAR		Standard	Optional	Inflation F-R	Torque	Rim
C43AMG						
1999-98	Front	225/45ZR17		33-36	80	7.5-J
	Rear.....	245/40ZR17		41-45	80	8.5-J
CL500, CL600						
1999-98	Front	235/60R16		N/A	N/A	7.5
	Rear.....	235/60R16		N/A	N/A	8.0
CLK320						
1999-98	All......	205/55R16		32-36	80	7.0
CLK430						
1999	Front	225/45ZR17		32-32	80	7.5-J
	Rear.....	245/40ZR17		33-33	80	8.5-J
E300, E320, E420						
1999-96	All......	215/55HR16		29-32	80	7.5-J
1995-94	All......	195/65HR15		N/A	80	6.5-J
E55AMG						
1999	Front	245/40ZR18		41-41	80	8-J
	Rear.....	275/35ZR18		48-48	80	9-J
E430						
1999	Front	215/55R16		32-32	80	7.5-J
	Rear.....	235/45R17		33-33	80	8-J
E500						
1999-96	All......	215/55HR16		N/A	80	7.5-J
1995-94	All......	225/55ZR16		30-33	80	8-J
ML320						
1999-98	All......	255/65HR16		32-32	110	8-J
ML430						
1999	All......	275/55HR17		32-32	110	8.5-J
S320, S350 Turbo Diesel						
1998-94	All......	225/60HR16		27-27	110	7.5-J
S420						
1998-94	All......	235/60HR16		27-27	110	7.5-J
S500						
1998-94	Front	235/60HR16		27 —	110	7.5-J
	Rear.....	235/60HR16		— 27	110	8-J
S600						
1998-94	All......	235/55ZR16		N/A	80	8-J
SL320, SL500, SL600						
1998-97	Base....	225/55ZR16		N/A	80	8-J
	Sport Pkg:					
	Front	245/40ZR18		N/A	80	8.5-J
	Rear.....	275/35ZR18		N/A	80	9.5-J
1996-94	All......	225/55ZR16		30-33	80	8-J
SL500, SL600						
1999	Base....	245/455WR17		33-36	80	8.25-J
	Sport Pkg.:					
	Front	245/40ZR18		N/A	80	8.5-J
	Rear.....	275/35ZR18		N/A	80	9.5-J
SLK Class						
1999-98	Front	205/55VR16		N/A	80	7-J
	Rear.....	225/50VR16		N/A	80	8-J

MERCURY

MODEL / YEAR		Standard	Optional	Inflation F-R	Torque	Rim
Capri						
1994-92	Ex. Turbo ...	P185/60R14		32-29	65-87	5.5-JJ
	Turbo	P195/50VR15		32-32	65-87	6-JJ
1991	All......	P185/60R14		32-29	65-87	5.5-JJ
Cougar						
2000-99	All......	P205/60R15		N/A	94[1]	6.0
			P215/50R16	N/A	94[1]	N/A
1997-93	All......	P205/70R15		30-30	85-105	6-JJ
			P215/70R15	30-30	85-105	6.5-JJ
1992-89	Ex. XR7	P205/70R15		30-30	85-105	6-JJ
			P215/70R15	30-30	85-105	6.5-JJ
	XR7	P225/60ZR16		30-30	85-105	7-JJ
			P225/60VR16	30-30	85-105	7-JJ

1 Steel alloy wheels, only.

MODEL / YEAR		Standard	Optional	Inflation F-R	Torque	Rim
Grand Marquis						
2000-98	All...	P225/60SR16	P225/60TR16	N/A	85-105	7.0
1997-92	W/o Adj					
	Handling pkg	P215/70R15	P225/70R15	31-35	85-105	6.5-JJ
	W/Handling Pkg.	P225/60R16		31-35	85-105	6.5-JJ
1991-89	Sedan....	P215/70R15		31-35	85-105	6-, 6.5-JJ
	Wagon....	P215/70R15		27-35	85-105	6.5-JJ
Mountaineer						
2000	Ex. AWD....	P225/70R15		N/A	100	7-J
	AWD....	P235/75R15		N/A	100	7-J
1999-98	All......	P225/70R15		N/A	100	7-J

MERCURY Continued

MODEL / YEAR		Standard	Optional	Inflation F-R	Torque	Rim
Mountaineer Continued						
1997	All......	P235/70R15SL		30-35	N/A	6.5-, 7-JJ
		P235/75R15SL		26-26	N/A	6.5-, 7-JJ
		P255/70R16		30-30	N/A	N/A
Mystique						
2000-95	GS......	P185/70R14	P195/65R14	31-35	94	5.5
	LS......	P205/60R15		31-35	94	6.0
Sable						
2000	All......	P215/60R16		N/A	N/A	6
1999	All......	P205/65R15		35-35	85-105	6-JJ
			P225/55ZR16	N/A	85-105	6.5
1998-92	All......	P205/65R15		35-35	85-105	6-JJ
1991-89	All......	P205/70R14		35-35	85-105	5.5-JJ
			P205/65R15	35-35	85-105	6-JJ
Topaz						
1994-93	All......	P185/70R14	P205/70R14	30-30	85-105	5.5-, 6-JJ
1992	GS & LS....	P185/70R14		30-30	85-105	5.5-JJ
	LTS & XR5.	P185/60R15		30-30	85-105	6-JJ
1991-89	All......	P185/70R14		30-30	85-105	5.5-JJ
Tracer						
1999-98	All......	P185/65R14		N/A	N/A	5.5
			P185/60R15	N/A	N/A	5.5
1997	All......	P185/65SR14		32-32	65-87	N/A
1996-95	Base....	P175/65R13		32-32	65-87	5-JJ
	LTS....	P185/60R14		32-32	65-87	5.5-JJ
1994-92	Sedan:					
	Ex. LTS ...	P175/70R13		32-32	65-87	5-JJ
	LTS ...	P185/60R14		32-32	65-87	5.5-JJ
1994-91	Wagon....	P175/65R14		32-32	65-87	5-JJ
1991	Ex. Wagon...	P175/70R13	P175/65R14	32-32	65-87	5-JJ
	LTS	P185/60HR14		32-32	65-87	5-JJ
1989	All......	P175/70R13		29-29	65-87	5-JJ
Villager						
2000-99	Base.....	P215/70R15		35-35	80	N/A
	Others....	P225/60R16		N/A	80	N/A
1998-93	All......	P205/75R15		35-35	79-87	5.5-JJ

MERKUR

MODEL / YEAR		Standard	Optional	Inflation F-R	Torque	Rim
Scorpio						
1989	All......	205/60HR15		32-32	52-73	6-J
XR4ti						
1989	All......	195/60HR15		32-32	75-101	5.5-J

MITSUBISHI

MODEL / YEAR		Standard	Optional	Inflation F-R	Torque	Rim
3000 GT						
1999	Base.....	225/55VR16		32-29	87-101	8-JJ
	SL.....	225/55VR17		32-29	87-101	8.5-JJ
	VR-4....	245/40VR18		32-29	87-101	8.5-JJ
1998-97	Base....	225/55VR16		32-29	87-101	8-JJ
	SL.....	245/45VR17		32-29	87-101	8.5-JJ
	VR-4....	245/40VR18		32-29	87-101	8.5-JJ
1996-95	Turbo & Spyder ..	245/40ZR18		32-29	87-100	8.5-JJ
	Others....	225/55VR16		32-29		8-J
1994	Ex. Turbo ...	255/55VR16		32-29	87-100	8-J
	Turbo ...	245/45ZR17		32-29	87-100	8.5-J
1993-91	Ex. Turbo ...	225/55VR16		32-29	87-100	8-J
	Turbo ...	245/45ZR17		32-29	87-100	8.5-J
Diamante						
2000	All......	P205/65R15		32-26	65-80	6-JJ
			P215/60R16	32-29	65-80	6-JJ
1998-92	Sedan....	205/65VR15		32-26	65-80	6-JJ
	Wagon....	P205/65HR15		33-29	65-80	6-JJ
Eclipse						
2000	RS......	195/65R15		32-29	65-80	6-JJ
	GS......	205/55R16		32-29	65-80	6-JJ
	GT......	215/50R17		32-29	65-80	6.5-JJ
1999-97	RS, GS....	P195/70R14		32-29	87-100	5.5-JJ
	GS-T, GS-X..	P205/55HR16		32-29	87-100	6.5-JJ
			P215/50R17	32-29	87-100	6.5-JJ
	GS Spyder..	P215/50VR17		32-29	87-100	6.5-JJ
1996-95	2WD: GS....	P205/55HR16		32-29	87-100	6-JJ
	GS-T....	P205/55VR16		32-29	87-100	6-JJ
	RS......	P195/70HR14		32-29	87-100	5.5-JJ
	AWD: W/AT..	P205/55VR16		32-29	87-100	6-JJ
	W/MT ..	215/55VR16		32-29	87-100	6-JJ
1994-93	1.8L	P185/70R14		29-26	87-100	5.5-JJ
			P205/55VR16	29-26	87-100	6-JJ
	2.0L	P205/55VR16		32-29	87-100	6-JJ
1992-91	All......	185/70R14		29-26	87-100	5.5-JJ
			205/55R16	32-29	87-100	6-JJ
1990	All......	185/70R14		29-26	65-80	5.5-JJ
			205/55R16	32-29	65-80	6-JJ

MITSUBISHI Continued

MAKE	MODEL	YEAR	Standard	Optional	Inflation Front-Rear	Lug Nut Torque	Rim Width
Expo							
	1996-92	Ex. LRV 205/70R14		26-26	65-80	5.5-JJ
		LRV: 4WD... 205/70R14		26-26	65-80	5.5-JJ
		FWD.... 185/75R14		28-26	65-80	5.5-JJ
Galant							
	2000	DE, ES 4-cyl. . 195/65R15		32-29	65-80	6-JJ
		ES V6, GT-Z, LS . 205/55R16		32-29	65-80	6-JJ
	1999	DE, ES 4-cyl. . 195/60R15		32-29	65-80	6-JJ
		ES V6, GT-Z, LS . 205/55R16		32-29	65-80	6-JJ
	1998-94	S, ES, DE ... P185/70HR14		29-26	65-80	5.5-JJ
		LS P195/60HR15		30-26	65-80	6-JJ
	1993	Ex. Turbo ... P185/70SR14		29-26	65-80	5.5-JJ
		Turbo: FWD .. 195/65HR15		30-26	65-80	6-JJ
		AWD.... 195/65HR14		32-29	65-80	5.5-JJ
		195/60HR15	195/60VR15	32-29	65-80	6-JJ
	1992-91	GS 195/65R14		30-26	65-80	5.5-JJ
		GSR, GSX, VR-4.. 195/60R15		32-29	65-80	6-JJ
		Others.... 185/70SR14		29-26	65-80	5.5-JJ
	1990-89	All P185/70R14		32-32	65-80	5.5-JJ
Mirage							
	2000	DE..... P175/60R14		31-31	65-80	5.5-JJ
		LS..... P185/65R14		31-31	65-80	5.5-JJ
	1999-97	DE..... P175/65R14		31-31	65-80	5.5-JJ
		LS..... P185/70HR14		32-29	65-80	6-JJ
	1996-94	1.5L.... P145/80R13	P155/80R13	31-31	65-80	4.5-, 5-B
			P175/70R13	31-31	65-80	4.5-, 5-B
		1.8L.... P175/70R13		31-31	65-80	5-J
			P185/65R14	29-26	65-80	5-J
	1993	2-door.... P145/80R13	P155/80R13	31-31	65-80	4.5-, 5-B
			P165/80R13	31-31	65-80	4.5-, 5-B
			P175/70R13	31-31	65-80	5-J
		4-door.... P155/80R13	P175/70R13	31-31	65-80	5-J
			P185/70R13	31-31	65-80	5-J
	1992-91	Ex. GS P155/80R13		32-32	65-80	4.5-J
			P175/70R13	32-32	65-80	5-J
		GS...... 195/60R14		29-29	65-80	5.5-JJ
	1990	All P155/80R13		32-32	65-80	4.5-J
			P175/70R13	32-32	65-80	5-J
	1989	All P155/80R13	P175/70R13	32-32	65-80	5-J
			P195/60R14	32-32	65-80	5.5-J
Montero							
	2000-98	All P265/70HR15		26-26		7-JJ
	1997-92	All P235/75SR15		26-35	72-87	6-JJ
			P265/70HR15	26-29	72-87	7-JJ
			LT31X10.5R15	30-40	72-87	7-JJ
	1991	All P225/75R15		26-35	72-87	6-JJ
			LT195/75R14	35-35	72-87	6-JJ
	1990-89	4-door.... P235/75R15		26-35	72-87	6-JJ
		2-door:				
		4-cyl.... P225/75R15		26-35	72-87	6-JJ
		V6.... P235/75R15		26-35	72-87	6-JJ
Montero Sport							
	2000	ES, LS..... P235/75R15		26-26	72-87	6-JJ
		XLS, Limited.. P255/70R16		26-26	72-87	7-JJ
	1999-97	All P225/75R15		26-26	72-87	6-JJ
			P265/70R15	26-26	72-87	7-JJ
Pickup							
	1996-89	2WD:				
		Ex. 1-ton... P195/75R14		26-35	87-10[1]	5-JJ
			P205/75R14	26-35	87-10[1]	6-JJ
		1-ton.... LT195/75R14		35-35	87-10[1]	5-JJ
		4WD.... P225/75R15		26-35	87-10[1]	6-JJ

1 With aluminum wheels, 65-80

MAKE	MODEL	YEAR	Standard	Optional	Inflation Front-Rear	Lug Nut Torque	Rim Width
Precis							
	1994-89	All P155/80R13		28-28	65-80	4.5-J
			175/70R13	32-32	65-80	5-J
Sigma							
	1989	All 195/60R15		32-32	65-80	6-JJ
Starion							
	1989	Front 205/55VR16		32 —	65-80	7-JJ
			225/50VR16	32 —	65-80	8-JJ
		Rear.... 225/50VR16		— 32	65-80	8-JJ
			245/45VR16	— 32	65-80	9-JJ
Van							
	1990-89	All P205/75R14		29-29	87-101	5.5-JJ

NISSAN/DATSUN

MAKE	MODEL	YEAR	Standard	Optional	Inflation Front-Rear	Lug Nut Torque	Rim Width
200SX							
	1998-95	Base.... P175/70R13		33-29	72-87	5-JJ
		SE.... P175/65R14		33-29	72-87	5.5-JJ
		SE-R.... P195/55R15		33-29	72-87	6-JJ

NISSAN/DATSUN Continued

MAKE	MODEL	YEAR	Standard	Optional	Inflation Front-Rear	Lug Nut Torque	Rim Width
240SX							
	1998-95	All P195/60HR15		—[2]	72-87	6-JJ
			P205/55VR16	—[2]	72-87	6.5-JJ
	1994-89	All 195/60R15	P205/60R15	29-29	72-87	6-JJ
300ZX							
	1996-90	Ex. Turbo ... P225/50VR16		—[2]	72-87	7.5-JJ
		Turbo:				
		Front.... P225/50ZR16		—[2]	72-87	7.5-JJ
		Rear.... P245/45ZR16		—[2]	72-87	8.5-JJ
	1989	Ex. Turbo .. P215/60R15		—[2]	72-87	6.5-JJ
		Turbo... 225/50VR16		—[2]	72-87	7-JJ
Altima							
	2000-98	All P195/65R15	P205/60R15	—[2]	72-87	6-JJ
	1997-93	All P205/60HR15		—[2]	72-87	6-JJ
Axxess							
	1990	All P195/70R14		—[2]	72-87	5.5-JJ
Frontier							
	2000	XE...... P215/65R15		—[2]	87-108	6-JJ
			P235/70R15	—[2]	87-108	7-JJ
			P265/70R15	—[2]	87-108	7-JJ
		SE...... P255/65R16		—[2]	87-108	7-JJ
	1999	2WD.... P215/65R15		—[2]	87-108	6-JJ
		4WD.... P235/70R15		—[2]	87-108	7-JJ
	1998	2WD.... P195/75R14		—[2]	87-108	5-JJ
			P215/65R15	—[2]	87-108	6-JJ
		4WD.... P215/75R15	P235/70R15	—[2]	87-108	7-JJ
Maxima							
	2000-97	All P205/65SR15	P205/60HR15	—[2]	72-87	6-, 6.5-JJ
			P215/55R16	—[2]	72-87	6.5-JJ
	1996-95	GXE..... 205/65R15		—[2]	72-87	6-JJ
		SE..... P215/60R15		—[2]	72-87	6-JJ
		GLE..... P205/60HR15		—[2]	72-87	6-JJ
	1994-93	SOHC.... P205/65HR15		—[2]	72-87	6-, 6.5-JJ
	1993-92	DOHC:				
		W/AT ... P205/65HR15		—[2]	72-87	6-, 6.5-JJ
		W/MT ... P205/65VR15		—[2]	72-87	6-, 6.5-JJ
	1992-89	SOHC: GXE .. P205/65R15		—[2]	72-87	6-JJ
		SE .. P205/65R15		—[2]	72-87	6.5-JJ
NX							
	1993-91	1.6L..... 175/70R13		—[2]	72-87	5-JJ
		2.0L..... 195/55VR14		—[2]	72-87	5.5-, 6-JJ
Pathfinder							
	2000	XE...... P245/70R16		—[2]	87-108	7-JJ
		SE, LE, Wider. P255/65R16		—[2]	87-108	7-JJ
	1999	All P235/70R15		—[2]	87-108	6.5-JJ
			P265/70R15	—[2]	87-108	7-JJ
	1997	2WD.... P235/70R15		—[2]	87-108	6.5-JJ
		4WD.... P235/70R15	P265/70R15	—[2]	87-108	6.5-JJ
	1996-95	2WD XE.... P215/75R15		—[2]	87-108	5.5-K
			P235/75R15	—[2]	87-108	6-JJ
		4WD: E P235/75R15		—[2]	87-108	6-JJ
		SE..... P215/75R15		—[2]	87-108	5.5-K
			P235/75R15	—[2]	87-108	6-JJ
		XE..... P235/75R15		—[2]	87-108	6-JJ
			31x10.5R15LT	—[2]	87-108	7-JJ
	1994-92	2WD.... P215/75R15	P235/75R15	—[2]	87-108	6-JJ
		4WD:				
		E & XE.. P215/75R15	P235/75R15	—[2]	87-108	6-JJ
			P215/75R15	—[2]	87-108	5.5-K
		SE .. P235/75R15		—[2]	87-108	6-JJ
			31x10.5R15LT	—[2]	87-108	7-JJ
	1991-90	2WD.... P215/75R15	P235/75R15	—[2]	87-108	6-JJ
		4WD:				
		E & XE.. P215/75R15		—[2]	87-108	6-JJ
			P215/75R15	—[2]	87-108	5.5-K
		SE P235/75R15		—[2]	87-108	6-JJ
			31x10.5R15LT	—[2]	87-108	7-JJ
	1989	All P215/75R15		—[2]	87-108	5.5-K
			P235/75R15	—[2]	87-108	6-JJ
			31x10.5R15	—[2]	87-108	7-JJ

2 See tire inflation label in glove box or on driver door pillar.

MAKE	MODEL	YEAR	Standard	Optional	Inflation Front-Rear	Lug Nut Torque	Rim Width
Pickup							
	1997	2WD..... P195/75R14		—[2]	87-108	5-J
			P215/70R14	—[2]	87-108	6-JJ
		4WD..... P235/75R15		—[2]	87-108	6-, 7-JJ
	1996-95	2WD Reg & K-cab Std . P195/75R14		—[2]	87-108	5-, 6-JJ
		2WD Reg & K-cab XE:				
		4-cyl. ... P215/75R14		—[2]	87-108	6-JJ
		V6..... P195/75R14		—[2]	87-108	5-, 6-J

NISSAN/DATSUN Continued

Pickup Continued

MAKE MODEL YEAR	ORIGINAL EQUIPMENT SIZE Standard	Optional	RECOMMENDED INFLATION PRESSURE Front - Rear	LUG NUT TORQUE Ft.-Lbs	RIM WIDTH
1996-95 King cab,					
SE 31x10.5R15LT			—[2]	87-108	7-JJ
2WD Regl cab					
HD . . . LT195/75R14			—[2]	87-108	5-J
4WD Reg &					
K-cab XE . . . P235/75R15			—[2]	87-108	6-JJ
1994-92 2WD: E ex.					
HD 195/75R14			—[2]	87-108	5-, 6-JJ
E HD LT195/75R14			—[2]	87-108	5-J
SE P215/75R15			—[2]	87-108	6-JJ
4WD: E & XE . P215/75R15			—[2]	87-108	5.5-, 6-JJ
		P235/75R15	—[2]	87-108	6-JJ
SE P235/75R15			—[2]	87-108	6-JJ
		31x10.5R15LT	—[2]	87-108	7-JJ
1991-90 2WD E ex. HD:					
W/SRW . . . P195/75R14			—[2]	87-108	5-, 6-JJ
W/DRW . . . P195/75R14			—[2]	166-203	5-, 6-JJ
2WD E HD:					
W/SRW . . . LT195/75R14			—[2]	87-108	5-J
W/DRW . . . LT195/75R14			—[2]	166-203	5-J
2WD SE:					
W/SRW . . . P215/75R14			—[2]	87-108	6-JJ
W/DRW . . . P215/75R14			—[2]	166-203	6-JJ
4WD E & XE:					
W/SRW . . . P215/75R15	P235/75R15	—[2]	87-108	6-JJ
		P215/75R15	—[2]	87-108	5.5-K
W/DRW . . . P215/75R15	P235/75R15	—[2]	166-203	6-JJ
		P215/75R15	—[2]	166-203	5.5-K
4WD SE:					
W/SRW . . . P235/75R15			—[2]	87-108	6-JJ
		31x10.5R15LT	—[2]	87-108	7-JJ
W/DRW . . . P235/75R15			—[2]	166-203	6-JJ
		31x10.5R15LT	—[2]	166-203	7-JJ
1989 2WD: W/SRW.. P185/75R14	P195/75R14	24-24	87-108	5-J
		P215/75R14	—[2]	87-108	5-J
W/DRW . . . P185/75R14	P195/75R14	24-24	166-203	5-J
		P215/75R14	28-28	166-203	6-JJ
HD cab-chassis:					
SRW LT195/75R14			35-35	87-108	5-J
DRW LT195/75R14			35-35	166-203	5-J
4WD: W/SRW P215/75R15			28-28	87-108	5.5-K
		P235/75R15	28-28	87-108	6-JJ
		31x10.5R15	28-28	87-108	7-JJ
W/DRW . . . P215/75R15			28-28	166-203	5.5-K
		P235/75R15	28-28	166-203	6-JJ
		31x10.5R15	28-28	166-203	7-JJ

2 See tire inflation label in glove box or on driver door pillar.

Pulsar

MAKE MODEL YEAR	Standard	Optional	INFLATION Front - Rear	LUG NUT TORQUE	RIM WIDTH
1990 All 185/70R13			29-26	72-87	5-JJ
1989 Ex. SE . . . 185/70R13			29-26	72-87	5-J
SE 195/60R14			29-26	72-87	6-JJ

Quest

2000-99 All P215/70R15			—[2]	72-87	5.5-, 6-JJ
		P225/60R16	—[2]	72-87	6-JJ
1998-96 All P205/75R15			—[2]	72-87	5.5-, 6.5-JJ
		P215/55R16	—[2]	72-87	6.5-JJ
1995-93 W/Extra					
Perf pkg . . . P215/70R15			—[2]	72-87	6-JJ
W/o Extra					
Perf pkg . . . P205/75R15			—[2]	72-87	5.5

Sentra

1998-95 Base P155/80R13			—[2]	72-87	5-J
XE P175/70R13			—[2]	72-87	5-J
GLE, GXE . . . P175/65R14			—[2]	72-87	5.5-JJ
SE P195/55R15			—[2]	72-87	6-JJ
1994-91 E: W/AT . . . P175/70R13			—[2]	72-87	5-JJ
W/MT . . . P155/80R13	P175/70R13	—[2]	72-87	5-JJ
SE-R P185/60R14			—[2]	72-87	5.5-JJ
XE, GXE, ST . . P175/70R13			—[2]	72-87	5-JJ
1990 All P155/80R13	P175/70R13	29-26	72-87	5-J
1989 SE Coupe . . . 185/60R14			29-26	72-87	5.5-JJ
XE P175/70R13			29-26	72-87	5-JJ
Others P155SR13			29-26	72-87	5-JJ

Stanza

1992-93 All P195/65HR14			—[2]	72-87	5.5-, 6-JJ
1991-90 All 195/65R14			—[2]	72-87	5.5-JJ
1989 Ex. wagon . . . P185/70R14			29-26	72-87	5-, 5.5-J

Van

1990-89 All P195/75R14	P205/70R14	24-24	72-87	5.5-JJ

Xterra

2000-99 All P235/70R15	P265/70R15	35-35	87-108	7-JJ

2 See tire inflation label in glove box or on driver door pillar.

OLDSMOBILE

88

MAKE MODEL YEAR	ORIGINAL EQUIPMENT SIZE Standard	Optional	RECOMMENDED INFLATION PRESSURE Front - Rear	LUG NUT TORQUE Ft.-Lbs	RIM WIDTH
2000-99 Ex.Touring					
Pkg P205/70R15			30-30	100	6.0
W/Touring					
Pkg P215/65R16			30-30	100	6.0
		P225/60R16	30-30	100	7.0
1998-97 All P205/70R15			30-30	100	6-JJ
		P225/60R16	30-30	100	7-JJ
		P215/65R15	30-30	100	N/A
1996-92 All P205/70R15			30-30	100	6-JJ
		P225/60R16	30-30	100	7-JJ
1991 All P205/70R15	P215/65R15	30-30	100	6-JJ
		P215/65R15	30-30	100	6-JJ
1990-89 All P205/75R14	P215/65R15	30-30	100	6-JJ

98, Regency

1998-97 All P205/70R15			30-30	100	6-JJ
1998-92 Touring Sedan . P225/60R16			30-30	100	7-JJ
1998-91 Regency . . . P205/70R15			30-30	100	6-JJ
1991 Touring Sedan . P215/65R16			30-30	100	7-JJ
1990-89 All P205/75R14	P215/65R15	30-30	100	6-JJ

Achieva

1998-97 All P195/70R14			30-30	100	6-J
		P195/65R15	30-30	100	6-J
1996-95 All P195/60R16	P195/65R15	30-30	100	6-J
1994 S P185/75R14	P195/65R15	30-30	100	6-J
SC, SL & SLE.. P205/55R16			30-30	100	6-J
1993-92 S P185/75R14			35-35	100	6-JJ
S W/SC pkg . P205/55R16			30-30	100	6-JJ
S W/SCX pkg.. P215/60VR16			30-30	100	6-JJ
SL P195/70R14	P195/65R15	30-30	100	6-JJ

Alero

2000-99 All P215/60R15	P225/50R16	30-30	100	N/A

Aurora

1999-95 All P235/60R16	P235/60VR16	30-30	100	7-J

Bravada

2000-95 All P235/70R15			32-32	100	7-JJ
1994-91 All P235/75R15			35-35	100	7-JJ

Calais

1991-90 Ex. S & SL.. P185/75R14			35-35	100	5.5-JJ
SL P195/70R14			35-35	100	6-JJ
		P215/60R14	30-30	100	6-JJ
1990 S P185/75R14			35-35	100	5.5-JJ
		P215/60R14	30-30	100	6-JJ
1989 Base model . . P185/80R13			35-35	100	5.5-JB
S . . P185/75R14			35-35	100	6-JJ
		P205/60R15	35-35	100	6-JJ
		P185/80R13	35-35	100	5.5-JB
		P195/70R14	30-30	100	6-JJ
		P215/60R14	30-30	100	6-JJ
SL P195/70R14	P215/70R14	30-30	100	6-JJ
Int'l Series. . . P205/55R16			35-35	100	6-JJ

Ciera

1996-92 All P185/75R14			32-32	100	5.5-JJ
		P195/75R14	30-30	100	6-JJ
1992 Optional P195/75R14			30-30	100	6-JJ
1991-89 Ex. Int'l					
Series P185/75R14	P195/70R14	35-35	100	5.5-JJ
		P215/60R14	35-35	100	6-JJ
Int'l Series. . . P215/60R14			35-35	100	6-JJ
Wagon. . . . P185/75R14			35-35	100	5.5-JJ
		P195/75R14	30-35	100	6-JJ

Custom Cruiser

1992-89 All P225/75R15			30-35	100	7-JJ

Cutlass, Cutlass Supreme

1999-98 Cutlass P215/60R15			29-26	—	—
1999-97 Cutlass P215/60R15			29-26	100	N/A
1997 Cutlass					
Supreme.. P215/60R16			30-30	100	6.5-JJ
1996-94 Conv. P215/60R16	P225/60R16	30-30	100	6.5-JJ
Hardtop P205/70R15			30-30	100	6-, 6.5-JJ
		P215/60R16	30-30	100	6.5-JJ
		P225/60R16	30-30	100	6.5-JJ
1993-92 Cruiser					
Wagon. . . . P185/75R14			30-35	100	5.5-JJ
		P195/70R14	30-35	100	6-JJ
Int'l					
Series P225/60R16			30-30	100	6-JJ
Supreme: S.. P205/70R15	P225/60R16	30-30	100	6-, 6.5-JJ
SL. P215/60R16	P225/60R16	30-30	100	6.5-JJ
1991-90 Supreme:					
Ex. SL P195/75R14			30-30	100	5.5-JJ
		P215/65R15	30-30	100	6-JJ
SL P205/70R15			35-35	100	6-JJ

MAKE	MODEL	YEAR	ORIGINAL EQUIPMENT SIZE Standard	Optional	RECOMMENDED INFLATION PRESSURE Front - Rear	LUG NUT TORQUE Ft.-Lbs	RIM WIDTH

OLDSMOBILE Continued

Cutlass, Cutlass Supreme Continued

MODEL/YEAR	Standard	Optional	Inflation	Torque	Rim Width
1989 Ex. Int'l Series	P195/75R14		30-30	100	5.5-JJ
		P215/65R15	30-30	100	6-JJ
Int'l Series..	P215/60R16		35-35	100	6-JJ

Intrigue

| 2000-98 All...... | P225/60R16 | | 30-30 | 100 | 7-JJ |

LSS

2000-99 All......	P225/60R16		30-30	100	7.0
All......	P205/70R15		30-30	100	6-JJ
		P215/65R15	30-30	100	6.5-JJ
		P225/60R16	30-30	100	7-JJ
1996-94 All......	P225/60R16		30-30	100	7-JJ

Silhouette Van

2000-99 All......	P215/70R15		35-35	100	6.0
1998-97 All......	P205/70R15	P215/70R15	35-35	100	6-JJ
1996-91 All......	P205/70R15	P205/65R15	35-35	100	6-JJ
1990 All......	P205/70R14	P195/70R15	35-35	100	6-JJ

Toronado

1992-91 All......	P215/65R15		30-30	100	6-JJ
1990-89 All......	P205/75R15		30-30	100	6-JJ
		P205/70R15	28-26	100	6-JJ
		P215/65R15	30-30	100	6-JJ

Trofeo

1992-91 All......	P215/60R16		30-30	100	7-JJ
1990 All......	P215/60R16		30-30	100	6-JJ
1989 All......	P215/65R15		30-30	100	6-JJ

PEUGEOT

405

1992-89 S & DL....	185/65R15		30-32	55-66	5.5-J
1991 Mi16.....	195/55VR15		33-33	55-66	6-J
1990-89 Mi16.....	195/60VR14		28-31	55-66	6-J

505

1992-90 Sedan....	185/65R15		29-32	41-48[1]	6-J
1992-89 Wagon....	195/65R15		28-32	41-48[1]	6-J
1989 S Sedan...	185/65HR15		29-32	41-48[1]	6-J
		205/60HR15	29-32	41-48[1]	6-J
STX.....	205/60HR15		29-32	41-48[1]	6-J

1 With alloy wheels, 59-66

PLYMOUTH

Acclaim

1995-92 All......	P185/70R14		35-35	95	5.5-JJ
		P195/70R14	32-32	95	5.5-JJ
1991-89 Ex. LE & LX..	P185/70R14		35-35	95	5.5-JJ
		P195/70R14	32-32	95	5.5-JJ
LE.....	P195/70R14		29-32	95	5.5-JJ
LX.....	P205/60R15		29-32	95	5.5-JJ

Breeze

2000-97 All......	P195/70R14		31-31	100	6
		P195/65HR15	31-31	100	6-J
1996 All......	P195/65HR15		31-31	100	6-J

Caravelle

| 1989 All...... | P185/70R14 | | 35-35 | 90 | 5.5-JJ |
| | | P205/75R15 | 35-35 | 90 | 7-JJ |

Colt

1996-93 1.5L.....	P145/80R13		31-31	65-80	4.5-B
		P155/80R13	31-31	65-80	5-B
1.8L.....	185/65R14		29-26	65-80	5.5-JJ
1992-91 Ex. GL....	P155/80R13		35-35	65-80	4.5-JB
GL.....	P175/70R13		35-35	65-80	5-JJ
1990-89 2WD wagon..	P175/70R13		26-26	65-80	5-J
4WD wagon:					
1.5L.....	P185/70R14		26-29	65-80	5.5-JJ
1.6L.....	195/60R14		29-29	65-80	5.5-JJ
Base.....	P145/80R13		29-29	65-80	4.5-J
Optional....	P185/80R13		29-29	65-80	4.5-J
		P175/70R13	29-29	65-80	5-J
1989 Hatchback:					
E, GT....	P155/80R13		29-29	65-80	5-JB
Ex. E, GT...	145/80R13		32-32	65-80	4.5-JB

Duster

| 1994-93 All...... | P195/60R15 | P205/60R14 | 35-35 | 95 | 6-JJ |
| 1992 All...... | P195/60R15 | | 35-35 | 95 | 6-JJ |

Gran Fury

| 1989 All...... | P205/75R15 | | 35-35 | 90 | 7-JJ |

Horizon

| 1990-89 All...... | P165/80R13 | | 35-35 | 95 | 5-JB |

PLYMOUTH Continued

Laser

1994-93 1.8L.....	P185/70R14		29-26	87-100	5.5-JJ
2.0L.....	P205/55HR16		29-26	87-100	6-JJ
2.0L Turbo..	P205/55VR16		32-29	87-100	6-JJ
1992-90 1.8L.....	P185/70R14		35-35	87-100	5.5-JJ
2.0L.....	P205/55VR16	205/55VR16	35-35	87-100	6-JJ
2.0L Turbo..	P205/55VR16		32-29	87-100	6-JJ

Neon

2000 Sedan.....	P185/65R14		N/A	100	5.5-J
		P185/60R15	N/A	100	6.0-J
LX.....	P185/60R15		N/A	100	6.0-J
1999-98 All......	P185/65R14		N/A	100	5.5-J
		175/65HR14	N/A	100	6-J
		P185/HR14	N/A	100	6-J
1997 Base.....	P175/70R14		32-32	100	N/A
Highline...	P185/65R14		32-32	100	5.5-J
1996-95 Base.....	P165/80R13		32-32	100	5-J
		P175/65HR14	32-32	100	6-J
Highline...	P185/70R13		32-32	100	5-J
		P185/65R14	32-32	100	5.5-J
		P185/60HR14	32-32	100	6-J
Sport....	P185/65R14		32-32	100	6-J

Prowler

2000 Front....	P225/45HR17		N/A	N/A	7.5
Rear....	P295/40VR20		N/A	N/A	10.0
1999 Front....	P225/40HR17		N/A	N/A	7.5
Rear....	P295/49HR20		N/A	N/A	10.0
1997 Front....	225/45R17		—	—	—
Rear.....	295/40R20		—	—	—

Reliant

1989 Ex. wagon...	P175/80R13		35-35	95	5-JB
		P185/70R14	35-35	95	5.5-JJ
Wagon....	P185/70R14		35-35	95	5.5-JJ

Sundance

| 1994-89 All...... | P185/70R14 | | 35-35 | 95 | 5.5-JJ |

Vista

1994-93 All......	P185/75R14		28-26	65-80	5.5-JJ
		P205/70R14	26-26	65-80	5.5-JJ
1992 2WD: W/AT..	P205/70R14		26-26	65-80	5.5-JJ
W/MT..	P185/75R14		28-28	65-80	5.5-JJ
4WD.....	P205/70R14		26-26	65-80	5.5-JJ
1991-89 2WD.....	P165/80R13	P185/70R13	29-29	51-58[1]	5-J
4WD....	P185/70R14		29-35	51-58[1]	5.5-JJ

1 With aluminum wheels, 65-80

Voyager

2000 Ex. SE....	P205/75R14		N/A	100	6.0
		P215/65R15	N/A	100	6.5
SE.....	P215/65R15		N/A	100	6.5
1999-96 Base.....	P205/75SR14		35-35	95	6-J
SE & LE..	P215/65SR15	P215/65R16	35-35	95	6.5-JJ
ES.....	P215/65R16		35-35	95	6.5-JJ
1995-91 2WD:					
Long WB..	P205/70R15		35-35	95	6-JJ
Short WB..	P195/75R14	P205/70R14	35-35	95	5.5-JJ
		P205/70R14	35-35	95	6-JJ
4WD....	P205/70R15		35-35	95	6-JJ
Cargo Van..	P195/75R14		35-35	95	5.5-JJ
		LT195/75R15	35-35	95	6-JJ
		P205/70R15	35-35	95	6-JJ
1990-89 All......	P195/75R14	P205/70R14	35-35	95	5.5-JJ
		P205/70R15	35-35	95	5.5-, 6-JJ

PLYMOUTH TRUCKS

6000

1991-90 LE.....	P185/75R14		35-35	100	5.5-JJ
SE.....	P195/70R15		30-30	100	6-JJ
1989 SE.....	P195/70R15		30-30	100	6-JJ
STE.....	P195/70R15		35-35	100	6-JJ

Bonneville, Catalina

2000 SE.....	P225/60R16		30-30	100	—
SLE, SSEi...			30-30	100	—
1999-92 SE.....	P215/65R15		30-30	100	6-JJ
		P225/60R16	30-30	100	7-JJ
SSE.....	P225/60R16		30-30	100	7-JJ
1994-92 SSEi.....	P225/60ZR16		30-30	100	7-JJ
1991-90 LE.....	P205/75R14		35-35	100	6-JJ
		P215/65R15	30-30	100	6-JJ
		P215/60R16	30-30	100	7-JJ
SE & SSE..	P215/60R16		30-30	100	7-JJ
1989 LE.....	P205/75R14	P205/70R15	35-35	100	6-JJ
		P215/65R15	30-30	100	6-JJ
SE.....	P215/65R15		30-30	100	6-JJ
SSE.....	P215/60R16		30-30	100	7-JJ

PLYMOUTH TRUCKS Continued

Firebird

MODEL/YEAR	Standard	Optional	Inflation	Torque	Rim Width
2000-99 Base	P215/60R60	P235/55R16	30-30	100	8-JJ
Coupes, Formula, Trans Am		P245/50ZR16	30-30	100	8-JJ
W/WS6 Pkg		P275/40ZR17	30-30	100	9-JJ
1998-94 V6	P215/60R16		30-30	100	7.5-J
		P235/55R16	30-30	100	8-J
Formula	P235/55R16	P245/50ZR16	30-30	100	8-J
Trans Am:					
Hardtop	P235/55ZR16		30-30	100	8-JJ
Convertible	P245/50ZR16		30-30	100	8-JJ
W/WS6	P275/40ZR17		30-30	100	9-J
1995-94 Formula Firehawk	P275/40ZR17		30-30	100	8-JJ
1994 Trans Am:					
ex. GT	P245/50ZR16		30-30	100	8-JJ
GT	P235/55R16		30-30	100	8-JJ
1993 V6	P215/60R16		30-30	100	7.5-JJ
Formula	P235/55R16		30-30	100	8-JJ
Trans Am	P245/50ZR16		30-30	100	8-JJ
1993-91 Formula Firehawk	P275/40ZR17		30-30	100	8-JJ
1992-90 Base	P215/65R15		30-30	100	7-JJ
Trans Am	P215/60R16	P245/50ZR16	30-30	100	8-JJ
Formula & GTA	P245/50ZR16		30-30	100	8-JJ
1989 Formula	P245/50ZR16		30-30	100	7-JJ
Trans Am:					
Ex. GTA	P215/65R15	P245/50ZR16	30-30	100	7-JJ
GTA	P245/50ZR16		30-30	100	7-JJ

Firefly

MODEL/YEAR	Standard	Optional	Inflation	Torque	Rim Width
1999-95 All	P155/80R13		32-32	100	4.5-B
1994 Convertible	P165/65R13		30-30	100	4.5-B
Others	P145/80R12		32-32	100	4-B
1991 Convertible	P165/65R13		30-30	100	4.5-B
1991-89 Turbo	P165/70R12		26-26	45	4.5-B
Others	P145/80R12		32-32	45	4-B

Grand Am

MODEL/YEAR	Standard	Optional	Inflation	Torque	Rim Width
2000 SE, SE1	P215/60R15		30-30	—	—
SE2, GT, GT1	P225/50R15		30-30	—	—
1998-92 GT, GTE	P205/55R16		35-35	100	6-JJ
1994-93 SE	P185/75R14	P205/55R16	35-35	100	6-JJ
		P195/65R15	30-30	100	6-JJ
1992 SE	P195/70R14		30-30	100	6-JJ
		P195/65R15	30-30	100	6-JJ
1991-90 LE	P185/75R14		35-35	100	5.5-JJ
		P195/70R14	30-30	100	6-JJ
SE	P205/55R16	P195/70R14	30-30	100	6-JJ
1989 Ex. SE	P185/80R13		35-35	100	5.5-JB
		P195/70R14	30-30	100	6-JJ
		P215/60R14	30-30	100	6-JJ
SE	P215/60R14		30-30	100	6-JJ

Grand Prix

MODEL/YEAR	Standard	Optional	Inflation	Torque	Rim Width
2000 SE	P205/70R15		30-30	100	6.5
GT	P225/60R16		30-30	100	6.5
1999-97 All	P205/70R15		30-30	100	6.5
		P225/60R16	30-30	100	6.5
1996-94 Coupe	P215/60R16		30-30	100	6.5-JJ
		P225/60R16	30-30	100	8-JJ
Sedan	P205/70R15		30-30	100	6-JJ
		P215/60R16	30-30	100	6.5-JJ
		P225/60R16	30-30	100	8-JJ
1993 LE, SE coupe	P205/70R15		30-30	100	6-JJ
		P215/60R16	30-30	100	6.5-JJ
		P225/60R16	30-30	100	8-JJ
SE sedan	P215/60R16		30-30	100	6.5-JJ
		P225/60R16	30-30	100	8-JJ
1993-92 STE, GT	P225/60R16		30-30	100	8-JJ
GTP	P245/50ZR16		30-30	100	8-JJ
1992-91 LE, SE sedan	P205/70R15		30-30	100	6-JJ
		P215/60R16	30-30	100	6.5-JJ
SE coupe	P205/70R15		30-30	100	6-JJ
		P215/60R16	30-30	100	6.5-JJ
		P225/60R16	30-30	100	8-JJ
1991 STE, GT	P215/60R16		30-30	100	6.5-JJ
		P225/60R16	30-30	100	8-JJ
GTP	P225/60R16		30-30	100	8-JJ
1990 LE coupe	P205/65R15		30-30	100	6.5-JJ
LE sedan	P195/75R14		30-30	100	5.5-JJ
		P205/65R15	30-30	100	6-JJ
1990-89 SE, STE	P215/60R16		30-30	100	6.5-JJ
Turbo	P245/50ZR16		30-30	100	8-JJ
1989 All ex. SE, STE, Turbo	P195/75R14	P195/70R15	30-30	100	6-JJ
		P215/60R16	30-30	100	7-JJ

PLYMOUTH TRUCKS Continued

LeMans

MODEL/YEAR	Standard	Optional	Inflation	Torque	Rim Width
1993-91 All	P175/70R13		35-35	65	5-JB
1990-89 Base	P175/70R13		35-35	65	5-JB
SE & GSE	185/60R14		35-35	65	6-JJ

Safari Wagon

MODEL/YEAR	Standard	Optional	Inflation	Torque	Rim Width
1989 All	P225/75R15		30-35	100	7-JJ

Sunbird

MODEL/YEAR	Standard	Optional	Inflation	Torque	Rim Width
1994 Conv	P195/65R15		30-30	100	5.5-JJ
		P195/70R14	30-30	100	6-JJ
Hardtop	P185/75R14		35-35	100	6-JJ
		P195/65R15	30-30	100	5.5-JJ
		P195/70R14	30-30	100	6-JJ
1993-92 SE	P185/75R14		35-35	100	6-JJ
		P195/65R15	30-30	100	5.5-JJ
		P195/70R14	30-30	100	6-JJ
GT	P195/65R15		30-30	100	5.5-JJ
1992-91 Base & LE	P185/75R14		35-35	100	5.5-JJ
		P195/70R14	30-30	100	6-JJ
1991-89 GT	P215/60R14		30-30	100	6-JJ
SE	P195/70R14		30-30	100	6-JJ
1990 GT	P215/60R14		30-30	100	6-JJ
LE & SE	P185/75R14		35-35	100	5.5-JJ
		P195/70R14	30-30	100	6-JJ
Turbo	P215/60R14		30-30	100	6-JJ
1989 LE	P185/80R13		35-35	100	5-JB
		P195/70R14	30-30	100	5.5-JJ
SE	P195/70R14		30-30	100	5.5-JJ
		P215/60R14	30-30	100	6-JJ

Sunfire

MODEL/YEAR	Standard	Optional	Inflation	Torque	Rim Width
2000-95 SE	P195/70R14		30-30	100	6-JJ
		P195/65R15	30-30	100	6-JJ
GT	P205/55R16		30-30	100	6-JJ

Trans Sport Van, Montana

MODEL/YEAR	Standard	Optional	Inflation	Torque	Rim Width
2000-99 All	P215/70R15		35-35	100	6.0
1998-97 Regl length	P205/70R15		35-35	100	6-J
		P215/70R15	35-35	100	N/A
Ext length	P215/70R15		35-35	100	N/A
1996-92 All	P205/70R15		35-35	100	6-JJ
1991 Ex. SE	P205/70R14		30-30	100	5.5-JJ
		P205/65R15	30-30	100	6-JJ
SE	P205/65R15		30-30	100	6-JJ
1990 Ex. SE	P205/70R14		35-35	100	6-JJ
SE	P195/70R15		35-35	100	6-JJ

PORSCHE

911

MODEL/YEAR	Standard	Optional	Inflation	Torque	Rim Width
1999-96 Carrera 2WD:					
Front	205/50ZR16		36 —	96	7-J
		205/50ZR17	36 —	96	7-J
		225/40ZR18	36 —	96	8-J
Rear	245/45ZR16		— 44	96	9-J
		255/40ZR17	— 36	96	9-J
		285/30ZR18	— 44	96	10-J
Carrera Coupe 4S 4WD:					
Front	225/40ZR18		36 —	96	8-J
Rear	285/30ZR18		— 44	96	10-J
		265/35ZR18	— 44	96	10-J
Cabriolet 4WD, Targa:					
Front	205/50ZR17		36 —	96	7-J
		225/40ZR18	— 44	96	7-J
Rear	255/40ZR17		36 —	96	8-J
		265/35ZR18	— 44	96	10-J
		285/30ZR18	— 44	96	10-J
911 Turbo:					
Front	P225/40ZR18		36 —	96	8-J
Rear	P285/30ZR18		— 44	96	10-J
1995-94 Front: 4WD	205/50ZR17		36 —	96	7-J
Cabriolet	205/55ZR16		36 —	96	6-J
Coupe	205/55ZR16		36 —	96	6-J
RS America	205/55ZR16		36 —	96	7-J
Speedster	205/50ZR17		36 —	96	7-J
Targa	205/55ZR16		36 —	96	6-J
Rear: 4WD	255/40ZR17		— 36	96	9-J
Cabriolet	225/50ZR16		— 44	96	8-J
Coupe	225/50ZR16		— 44	96	8-J
RS America	255/40ZR17		— 36	96	8-J
Speedster	255/40ZR17		— 36	96	8-J
Targa	225/50ZR16		— 44	96	8-J
911 Turbo:					
Front	225/40ZR18		36 —	96	8-J
Rear	265/35ZR18		— 43	96	10-J
1993-90 Ex. Turbo:					
Front	205/55ZR16		36 —	96	6-J
Rear	225/50ZR16		— 43	96	8-J
Turbo: Front	205/50ZR17		29 —	96	7-J
Rear	255/40ZR17		— 43	96	9-J

PORSCHE Continued

Make / Model / Year	Standard	Optional	Inflation Front–Rear	Lug Nut Torque Ft.-Lbs	Rim Width
911 Continued					
1989 Ex. Turbo:					
Front	205/55ZR16		29 —	96	6-J
Rear	225/50ZR16		— 36	96	8-J
Turbo: Front	205/55ZR16		29 —	96	7-J
Rear	245/45ZR16		— 43	96	9-J
928					
1995-92 Front	225/45ZR17		36 —	96	7.5-J
Rear	255/40ZR17		— 36	96	9-J
1991-90 Ex. GT: Front	225/50ZR16		29 —	96	7-J
Rear	245/45ZR16		— 43	96	8-J
GT: Front	225/50ZR16		29 —	96	7.5-J
Rear	245/45ZR16		— 43	96	9-J
1989 Front	225/50VR16		36 —	96	7-J
Rear	245/45VR16		— 43	96	8-J
944					
1991-90 Front	205/55ZR16		29 —	96	7-J
Rear	225/50ZR16		— 36	96	8-J
1989 Ex. Turbo	215/60ZR15		29-36	96	7-J
Turbo: Front	225/50ZR16		36 —	96	7-J
Rear	245/45ZR16		— 36	96	9-J
968					
1995-94 Front: Sport chassis	225/45ZR17		36 —	96	7.5-J
Ex. Sport chassis	205/55ZR16		36 —	96	7-J
		225/45ZR17	36 —	96	7.5-J
Rear: Sport chass.	245/40ZR17		— 36	96	9-J
Ex. sport chassis	225/50ZR16		— 36	96	8-J
		245/40ZR17	— 36	96	9-J
1993-92 Front	205/55ZR16		36 —	96	7-J
Rear	225/55ZR16		— 36	96	8-J
Boxster					
1999-97 Front	205/55ZR16	205/55ZR16	29—	95	6-J
		205/50ZR17	29—	95	7-J
Rear	225/50ZR16	205/50R16	—36	95	7-J
		255/40ZR17	—36	95	8.5-J

SAAB

Make / Model / Year	Standard	Optional	Inflation Front–Rear	Lug Nut Torque Ft.-Lbs	Rim Width
9-3					
1999 Base	195/60VR15		36-36	80	6.5
SE	205/50ZR16		41-41	80	6.5
9-5					
1999 Viggen	215/45ZR17		—	80	7.5
All	215/55VR16		39-39	80	6.5
900					
1998-95 S, SE	195/60VR15		32-32	80-90	6.0
SE Turbo	205/50ZR16		30-30	80-90	6.5
1994 SE	195/60VR15		32-32	77-96	6-J
Base & S	185/65HR15		30-30	77-96	5.5-J
	195/60VR15		32-32	77-96	6-J
Turbo	205/50ZR16		33-33	77-96	6.5
1993-92 Ex. Turbo	185/65R15		35-35	80-90	5.5-J
Turbo	195/60VR15		35-35	80-90	5.5-J
1991-90 Ex. SPG	185/65R15		35-36	80-90	5.5-J
Convertible	185/65R15		35-36	80-90	5.5-J
SPG	195/60VR14		38-39	80-90	5.5-J
1990 Ex. SPG	185/65R15		32-33	80-90	5.5-J
SPG	195/50ZR16		38-39	80-90	6.5-J
1989 Ex. Turbo	185/65R15		32-33	70-90	5.5-J
Turbo	185/65R15	195/60VR15	35-36	70-90	5.5-J
9000					
1998 CSE	205/55ZR16		32-32	80-90	6.5
1997-95 CS, CSE, CDE	195/65VR15		30-30	80-90	6-J
CSE Turbo	205/60VR15		32-32	80-90	6-J
Aero	205/55ZR16		32-32	80-90	6.5
1994 Aero	205/55ZR16		32-32	80-90	6.5
CDE, CS; CSE, Ex. Turbo.	195/65TR15	195/65VR15	30-30	80-90	6-J
CSE Turbo		205/60ZR15	32-32	80-90	6-J
1993-92 Ex. Turbo	195/65TR15		33-33	80-90	6-J
Turbo: Ex. 5-door	195/65VR15		33-33	80-90	6-J
5-door	205/50ZR16		38-38	80-90	6.5-J
1991 Ex. Turbo	195/65R15		32-32	80-90	6-J
Turbo: Ex. 5-door	205/50ZR16		35-35	80-90	6.5-J
5-door	195/65VR15		35-35	80-90	6-J
1990 Ex. Turbo	195/65R15		38-38	80-90	6-J
Turbo	195/65R15		35-35	80-90	6-J
1989 Ex. Turbo	185/65R15		32-33	75-90	6-J
		195/65R15	35-35	75-90	6-J
Turbo	205/55VR15		35-35	75-90	6-J

SATURN

Make / Model / Year	Standard	Optional	Inflation Front–Rear	Lug Nut Torque Ft.-Lbs	Rim Width
Coupe					
1999 All	P175/70R14		30-26	100	5-JJ
		P195/60R15	30-26	100	5-JJ
1998-97 SC2	P195/60R15		30-28	100	5-JJ
1998-96 SC1	P175/70R14		30-28	100	5-JJ
1996-92 SC2	P195/60R15		30-28	100	6-JJ
		P185/65R15	30-28	100	5-JJ
1995-93 SC1	P175/70R14		30-28	100	5-JJ
1992-91 SC	P195/60R15		30-28	100	6-JJ
Sedan, Sport Touring					
1999 All	P175/70R14		30-26	100	5-JJ
		P185/60R15	30-26	100	5-JJ
1998-97 SL, SL1	P175/70R14		30-28	100	5-JJ
SL2	P185/65R15		30-28	100	5-JJ
1996 SL2	P185/65R15		30-28	100	6-JJ
1996-91 SL1	P175/70R14		30-28	100	5-JJ
SL	P175/70R14		30-28	100	5-JJ
1995-91 SL2	P195/60R15		30-28	100	6-JJ
Wagon					
1999 All	P175/70R14		30-26	100	5-JJ
		P185/60R15	30-26	100	5-JJ
1998-97 SW1	P175/70R14		30-28	100	5-JJ
SW2	P185/65R15		30-28	100	5-JJ
1996 SW2	P185/65R15		30-28	100	6-JJ
1996-93 SW1	P175/70R14		30-28	100	5-JJ
1995-93 SW2	P195/60R15		30-28	100	5-JJ

SUBARU

Make / Model / Year	Standard	Optional	Inflation Front–Rear	Lug Nut Torque Ft.-Lbs	Rim Width
3-Door, 4-Door					
1989 Ex. Turbo:					
2WD DL	155SR13		28-28	58-72	4.5-J
2WD GL	175/70SR13		28-28	58-72	5-J
2WD GL-10	175/70HR13		28-28	58-72	5-J
4WD DL	165SR13		28-28	58-72	4.5-J
4WD GL	175/70SR13		28-28	58-72	5-J
Turbo: 2WD	175/70HR13		28-28	58-72	5-J
4WD	185/70HR13		28-28	58-72	5-J
Forester					
1999-98 All	P205/70R15		29-41	58-72	6-JJ
		P215/60R16	29-41	58-72	6.5-JJ
Hatchback					
1989 2WD: DL	155SR13		28-28	58-72	4.5-J
GL-10	175/70HR13		28-28	58-72	5-J
4WD DL	165SR13		28-28	58-72	4.5-J
GL, all	175/70SR13		28-28	58-72	5-J
Impreza					
1999-98 L	195/60HR15		32-29	58-72	6-JJ
2.5RS	P205/55HR16		32-29	58-72	7-JJ
Outback	P205/60R15		32-29	58-72	6-JJ
1997 Base	P175/70R14		32-29	58-72	5.5-JJ
		P195/60R15	32-29	58-72	6-JJ
Outback	P205/60R15		32-29	58-72	6-JJ
1996 Base, Sedan FFL	P165/80R13		32-29	58-72	5-B
1.8L AWD, Coupe FFL	P175/70R14		32-29	58-72	5.5-JJ
2.2L Outback	P185/70R14		32-29	58-72	N/A
LX, ex. Outback wagon	P195/60R15		32-29	58-72	6-JJ
1995-93 FWD	165/80HR13		31-25	65	5.0
AWD/FWD Coupe		175/70HR14	31-25	65	5.5
Justy					
1994-91 Ex. GL	145SR12		28-28	58-72	4-JB
GL	P165/65SR13		28-28	58-72	5-J
1990-89 FWD: DL	145SR12		28-28	58-72	4-JB
GL	165/65R13		28-28	58-72	5-JB
4WD	165/65R13		28-28	58-72	5-JB
Legacy					
1999-98 All	P185/70R14		32-30	58-72	5.5-JJ
		P195/60R15	32-30	58-72	6-JJ
		P205/55R16	32-30	58-72	6.5-JJ
		P205/70R15	32-30	58-72	6-JJ
1997 GT	P205/55HR16		32-29	58-72	6-JJ
Brighton, L	185/70SR14		32-30	58-72	5.5-JJ
LS, LSi	P195/60HR15		32-30	58-72	6-JJ
Outback, SUV	P205/70SR15		29-28	58-72	6-JJ
1996 GT	P195/60R15		32-30	58-72	6-JJ
1995-93 L, LS, LSi	185/70HR14		32-32	58-72	5-, 5.5-JJ
Sport Sedan	195/60HR15		32-32	58-72	6-JJ
Touring Wagon	195/60HR15		32-32	58-72	6-JJ
1992-91 Ex. Turbo: Sedan, FWD	P185/70HR14		30-29	58-72	5-, 5.5-JJ
Sedan, 4WD	P185/70HR14		32-32	58-72	5-, 5.5-J

SUBARU Continued

MAKE MODEL YEAR	ORIGINAL EQUIPMENT SIZE Standard / Optional	RECOMMENDED INFLATION PRESSURE Front - Rear	LUG NUT TORQUE Ft.-Lbs	RIM WIDTH
Legacy Continued				
1992-91 Turbo: Sedan, FWD P185/70HR14		30-29	58-72	5-, 5.5-JJ
Sedan, 4WD. P195/60HR15		32-32	58-72	6-J
Wagon, FWD. P185/70HR14		30-32	58-72	5-, 5.5-JJ
Wagon, 4WD. P185/70HR14		32-35	58-72	5-, 5.5-JJ
1990 FWD P175/70R14		30-29	58-72	5-J
4WD P185/70R14		32-32	58-72	5.5-J
Loyale				
1995-93 FWD 175/70SR13		28-28	58-72	5-J
4WD 165/70SR13		28-32	58-72	5-J
1992 FWD: Sedan .. 175/70SR13		28-28	58-72	5-J
Wagon .. 175/70SR13		28-32	58-72	5-J
4WD Wagon.. 165SR13		28-32	58-72	5-J
1991-90 Ex. Turbo:				
Sedan, FWD wagon. 175/70SR13		28-28	58-72	5-J
Wagon 4WD. 165SR13		28-32	58-72	5-J
Turbo: FWD. 175/70R13		28-28	58-72	5-J
4WD. 185/70HR13		28-28	58-72	5-J
SVX				
1997 All P215/55VR16		33-29	98-118	7.5-JJ
1996 All P225/50VR16		33-29	98-118	7.5-JJ
1995-92 All P225/50VR16		33-28	72-87	7.5-JJ
Wagon				
1989 Ex. Turbo: 2WD P155/80R13		28-32	58-72	5-J
4WD 185/70SR13		28-32	58-72	5-J
Turbo: 2WD.. 175/70HR13		28-32	58-72	5-J
4WD 185/70HR13		28-32	58-72	5-J
XT				
1991-90 4-cyl 185/70HR13		28-28	58-72	5-J
6-cyl: FWD. 195/60HR14		33-28	58-72	5.5-JJ
4WD 205/60HR14		33-28	58-72	5.5-JJ
1989 4-cyl: DL.. 165SR13		28-28	58-72	5-J
GL... 185/70HR13		28-28	58-72	5-J
6-cyl: FWD.. 195/60R14		33-28	58-72	5.5-JJ
4WD 205/60R14		33-28	58-72	5.5-JJ

SUZUKI

MAKE MODEL YEAR	ORIGINAL EQUIPMENT SIZE Standard / Optional	RECOMMENDED INFLATION PRESSURE Front - Rear	LUG NUT TORQUE Ft.-Lbs	RIM WIDTH
Esteem				
2000-98 All 175/70R13		29-29	61.5	4.5-J
P185/60R14		29-29	61.5	5-J
1997-95 All P155/80R13		29-29	61.5	4.5-J
P175/70R13		29-29	61.5	5-J
Samurai				
1996-90 2WD P195/75R15		20-26	58-80	5.5-J
4WD P205/70R15		20-26	58-80	5.5-J
1989 All P205/70R15		20-26	58-80	5.5-J
Sidekick				
1998-91 2WD P195/75R15		26-26	58-80	5.5-JJ
4WD P205/75R15		23-23	58-80	5.5-JJ
1990-89 All 205/75R15		23-23	58-80	6-JJ
Swift				
2000-99 All P155/80R13		29-29	37-51	4.5-J
1998-97 All P155/70R13		29-29	37-51	4.5-J
1996-95 All P155/80R13		29-29	37-51	4.5-J
1994-92 4-door Can. P165/65R13		26-26	37-51	4.5-J
1994-91 Ex. GT.. P155/70R13		29-29	37-51	4.5-J
GT P175/60R14		26-26	37-51	5-J
1990-89 GLX P155/70R13		28-28	37-51	5-J
GTI P175/60R14		26-26	37-51	5-J
Vitara				
2000-99 2-dr. 1.6L 2WD P195/75R15		29-29	58-80	5.5-JJ
2-dr. 1.6L 4WD P205/75R15		29-29	58-80	5.5-JJ
2-dr. 2.0L 2WD P215/65R16		29-29	58-80	6.5-JJ
4-dr. P215/65R16		29-29	58-80	6.5-JJ
Grand Vitara				
2000-99 All P235/60R15		29-29	58-80	7-JJ
X90				
1998-96 All P195/65R15		23-23	69	5.5-JJ

TOYOTA

MAKE MODEL YEAR	ORIGINAL EQUIPMENT SIZE Standard / Optional	RECOMMENDED INFLATION PRESSURE Front - Rear	LUG NUT TORQUE Ft.-Lbs	RIM WIDTH
4-Runner				
1999-96 All P225/75R15		29-29	76	N/A
P265/70R16		32-32	76	N/A
1995-89 4-cyl: 2WD P195/75R14		29-35	76	5-JJ
4WD P225/75R15		26-29	76	6-, 7-JJ
6-cyl: 2WD P205/75R14 / P215/65R15		29-35	76	6-JJ
4WD P225/75R15		26-29	76	6-, 7-JJ
31x10.5R15		26-29	76	7-JJ
Avalon				
2000 All P205/65HR15		31-31	76	6-JJ
P205/60HR16		32-32	76	6-JJ
1999-95 All ... P205/65HR15		32-32	76	6-JJ

TOYOTA Continued

MAKE MODEL YEAR	ORIGINAL EQUIPMENT SIZE Standard / Optional	RECOMMENDED INFLATION PRESSURE Front - Rear	LUG NUT TORQUE Ft.-Lbs	RIM WIDTH
Camry ex. Solara				
2000-98 4-cyl P195/70R14		30-30	76	5.5-JJ
V6 ...... P205/65R15 / P205/60R16		32-32	76	6-JJ
1997-93 4-cyl P195/70SR14		32-35	76	5.5-JJ
6-cyl ..... P205/65HR15 / P205/65VR15		32-35	76	6-JJ
1992 4-cyl P195/70HR14		29-29	76	5.5-JJ
6-cyl P205/65HR15		32-32	76	6-JJ
1991-89 4-cyl ..... 185/70SR14 / P185/70R14		30-30	76	5.5-JJ
6-cyl 195/60R15		32-28	76	5.5-JJ
Celica				
2000 Std. engine .. 195/60R15		29-29	76	6.5-JJ
..... P195/60HR15		29-29	76	6.5-JJ
H.O. engine .. 205/655VR15		32-32	76	6.5-JJ
P205/55VR15		32-32	76	6.5-JJ
205/50VR16		32-32	76	6.5-JJ
1999-98 All 203/55VR15		33-33	76	6.5-, 7-JJ
P205/55VR15		33-33	76	6.5-, 7-JJ
1997-94 1.8L P185/70R14		29-29	76	6-JJ
2.2L P205/55R15		33-33	76	6.5-, 7-JJ
1993-92 1.6L 185/65R14		29-29	76	6-JJ
2.0L Turbo.. 215/50VR15		32-30	76	6.5-JJ
2.2L 205/60R14		29-29	76	6-JJ
205/55VR15		32-32	76	6-JJ
215/50VR15		32-32	76	6.5-JJ
1991-90 1.6L 165SR13		30-29	76	5-JJ
185/70R13		28-26	76	5.5-JJ
2.0L Turbo.. 215/50VR15		30-28	76	6.5-JJ
2.2L 185/65R14		32-29	76	5.5-JJ
215/50VR15		30-28	76	6.5-JJ
1989 Ex. ST 185/70SR13		28-26	76	5.5-J
205/60R14		26-26	76	6-J
ST 165SR13		30-26	76	5-J
2.0L Turbo... 205/60R14		26-26	76	6-JJ
205/60VR14		30-30	76	6-JJ
Corolla				
2000-98 CE & VE .. P175/65R14		30-30	76	5.5-J
LE P185/65R14		30-30	76	5.5-J
1997-93 Base P175/65R14		30-30	76	5.5-J
DX & LE .. P185/65R14		30-30	76	5.5-J
1992-90 2WD: GTS .. 185/H60R14		26-26	76	5.5-JJ
Ex. GTS ... 155SR13 / 175/70SR13		28-28	76	5-J
P155/80R13		28-28	76	5-J
175/70R13		28-28	76	5-J
P175/70SR13		28-28	76	5-J
1992-89 4WD 165SR13		32-32	76	5-J
185/70SR13		26-26	76	5-J
1989 FWD ..... 155SR13 / P155/80R13		28-28	76	4.5-J
175/70SR13		26-26	76	5-J
P175/70HR13		32-32	76	5.5-J
P185/60HR14		32-32	76	5.5-J
Cressida				
1992-89 All 195/65HR15		32-32	76	6-JJ
Echo				
2000 All 155/80R13		32-32	76	5-J
P175/65R14		32-32	76	5.5-J
Land Cruiser				
2000-98 All P275/70R16		29-32	97	8-JJ
1997 All P275/70R16		32-32	109[1]	8-JJ
1996-93 All P275/70R16		32-32	116	8-JJ
1992-91 All P235/75R15XL		29-29	116	6-JJ
31x10.5R15LT		29-35	116	7-JJ
1990-89 All P225/75R15XL		26-34	116	6-JJ

[1] Aluminum wheels, 76

MAKE MODEL YEAR	ORIGINAL EQUIPMENT SIZE Standard / Optional	RECOMMENDED INFLATION PRESSURE Front - Rear	LUG NUT TORQUE Ft.-Lbs	RIM WIDTH
MR2				
1995-93 Front 195/55VR15		29 —	76	6-JJ
Rear 225/50VR15		— 33	76	7-JJ
1992-91 2.0L Turbo:				
Front 195/60VR14		29 —	76	6-JJ
Rear 205/60VR14		— 33	76	7-JJ
2.2L: Front.. 195/60HR14		29 —	76	6-JJ
Rear 205/60HR14		— 33	76	7-JJ
1989 All 185/60R14		30-30	76	5.5-JJ
Paseo				
1997-96 All P185/60R14		26-26	76	5.5-JJ
1995-92 All ..... 175/65HR14 / 185/60HR14		26-26	76	5.5-JJ
Pickup				
1995 4-cyl:				
2WD w/SRW P195/75R14		29-35	101	5-JJ
2WD w/DRW P195/75R14		29-35	170	5-JJ
4WD P225/75R15		26-29	76	6-, 7-JJ

TOYOTA Continued

MODEL / YEAR	Standard	Optional	INFLATION Front-Rear	LUG NUT TORQUE Ft.-Lbs	RIM WIDTH
Pickup					
1995 6-cyl:					
2WD w/SRW	P205/75R14	P215/65R15	29-35	101	6-JJ
2WD w/DRW	P205/75R14	P215/65R15	29-35	170	6-JJ
4WD	P225/75R15		26-29	76	6-, 7-JJ
		31x10.5R15	26-29	76	7-JJ
1994-89 4-cyl:					
2WD w/SRW	P195/75R14		29-35	101	5-J
2WD w/DRW	P195/75R14		29-35	170	5-JJ
4WD	P225/75R15		26-29	76	6-, 7-JJ
6-cyl:					
2WD w/SRW	P205/75R14	P215/65R15	29-35	101	6-JJ
2WD w/DRW	P205/75R14	P215/65R15	29-35	170	6-JJ
2WD w/DRW C&C		185R14LT6PR	32-32	170	5.5-J
2WD 1-ton w/DRW		185R14LT8PR	29-65	170	5.5-J
2WD 1-ton w/SRW		185R14LT8PR	29-65	101	5.5-J
4WD	P225/75R15		26-29	76	6-, 7-JJ
		31x10.5R15	26-29	76	7-JJ
Previa Van					
1997-95 All	P215/65R15		35-35	76	6-JJ
1994-91 All	P205/75R14	P215/65R15	35-35	76	6-JJ
RAV4					
2000-96 All	215/70R16		28-26	76	6-J, 6.5-JJ
		235/60HR16	25-25	76	6.5-JJ
Sienna					
2000-99 CE & VE	P205/70R15		35-35	76	6.5-JJ
XLE	P215/65R15		35-35	76	6.5-JJ
Solara					
2000-99 All	P205/65R15		29-29		6-JJ
		P205/60R16	32-32		6-JJ
Supra					
1998-97 Ex. Turbo:					
Front	225/50VR16		33 —	76	N/A
Rear	245/45VR16		— 33	76	N/A
1998-93 Turbo: Front	P235/45R17		36 —	76	8-JJ
Rear	P255/40ZR17		— 36	76	9.5-JJ
1996-93 Ex. Turbo:					
Front	P225/50ZR16		36 —	76	8-JJ
Rear	P245/50ZR16		— 36	76	9-JJ
1992-90 All	205/55R16	225/50ZR16	33-36	76	7-J
1989 All	225/50VR16		32-32	76	7-JJ
T100 Pickup					
1998-97 2WD	P215/75R15		33-35	76	6-JJ
		P235/75R15	26-28	76	7-JJ
		P265/70R16	26-29	76	7-JJ
1996-93 2WD	P215/75R15		33-35	76	6-JJ
		P235/75R15	26-28	76	7-JJ
4WD	P225/75R15	P265/70R16	26-29	76	7-JJ
		31X10.5 R15	26-29	76	7-JJ
Tacoma					
2000-95 2WD:					
Ex. Xtracab	P195/75R14		29-35	83	5-J
Xtracab	P215/70R14		29-29	83	6-J, 6-JJ
4WD & Prerunner	P225/75R15		26-29	83	6-JJ
		P265/75R15	26-26		7-J, 7-JJ
		31x10.5 R15	26-29	83	7-J, 7-JJ
Tercel					
1997 All	155SR13		34-32	76	N/A
		175/65R14	28-28	76	N/A
		185/60R14	26-26	76	N/A
1996-95 All	155/80R13		32-32	76	4.5-J
1994-92 USA	P145/80R13	155SR13	32-32	76	4.5-J
Canada	P155/80R13		32-32	76	4.5-J
1991-89 All	P145/80R13		32-32	76	4.5-J
		155SR13	28-28	76	5-J
		P155/80R13	28-28	76	5-J
Tundra					
2000 2WD, std. cab	P245/70R16		26-35	110	7-JJ
2WD, ext. cab	P245/70R16		26-35	110	7-JJ
		P265/70R16	26-29	110	7-JJ
4WD	P245/70R16		26-35	110	7-JJ
		P265/70R16	26-29	110	7-JJ
Off-road pkg.		P265/70R16	26-29	110	7-JJ
Van					
1989 2WD:					
Cargo Van	P175R14/6		40-40	76	5-J
Ex. Cargo Van	P195/75R14		35-35	76	5.5-JJ
4WD	P205/75R14		35-35	76	5.5-JJ

VOLKSWAGEN

MODEL / YEAR	Standard	Optional	INFLATION Front-Rear	LUG NUT TORQUE Ft.-Lbs	RIM WIDTH
Beetle					
1999-98 All		205/55R16	N/A	87	6.5-J
Cabrio					
1999-94 All		P195/60HR14	30-30	87	6-J
Cabriolet					
1993 All		185/60HR14	29-29	80	6-J
1992-91 All		185/60R14	29-26	80	6-J
1990 All		185/60R14	28-28	80	6-J
1989 All		185/60R15	28-28	80	6-J
Corrado					
1994-93 All		205/50HR15	30-28	80	6.5-J
1992-91 All		205/50VR15	33-29	80	6.5-J
1990 All		195/50VR15	41-36	80	6-J
EuroVan					
1999 All		205/65CR15	—	116	6, 7-J
Fox					
1993 All		175/70SR13	26-26	80	5.5-J
1992-91 2-door		155/80SR13	24-26	80	5-J
4-door		175/70SR13	24-28	80	5-J
1990-89 2-door		155SR13	24-26	80	5-J
4-door		175/70SR13	24-26	80	5.5-J
Wagon		175/70SR13	24-28	80	5.5-J
Golf					
1999-97 All		195/60HR14	30-28	87	6-J
1996-93 GL		185/60HR14	195/60HR14 30-28	80	6-J
1995-94 CL		175/70SR13	27-27	80	5.5
1993 CL		185/60HR14	32-29	80	6-J
1992 GL		175/70R13	29-25	80	5.5-J
1991 GL		175/70SR13	29-25	80	5.5-J
1990-89 GL		175/70SR13	29-25	80	5.5-J
1989 GLI		185/60HR14	29-25	80	6-J
GT		185/60HR14	29-25	80	6-J
GLI		205/55VR14	29-25	80	6-J
GT		205/55VR14	29-25	80	6-J
GTI					
1999-95 All		205/50HR15	30-28	87	6.5-J
1994 All		205/50VR15	30-28	80	6.5-J
1993 All		185/60HR14	32-29	80	6-J
1992-91 All		185/60R14	29-25	80	6-J
		195/50VR15	29-29	80	6.5-J
1990 All		175/70SR13	29-25	80	6-J
		195/50VR15	29-25	80	6.5-J
1989 All		185/60HR14	29-26	80	6-J
		205/55VR14	29-25	80	6-J
Jetta					
1999-97 GL, GT, GLS		195/60HR14	32-32	88	6-J
GLX		205/50HR15	30-28	88	6.5-J
1996-94 GL, GLS		185/60HR14	32-32	80	6-J
GLX		205/50HR15	30-28	80	6.5-J
1993 GL, GLS		185/60HR14	33-30	80	6-J
GLX		205/50VR15	36-33	80	6.5-J
1992-91 Carat, GL		185/60R14	32-32	80	6-J
		185/55VR15	33-33	80	6-J
1990 All		185/60VR14	29-29	80	6.5-J
		185/55VR15	29-29	80	6-J
		185/60R14	29-29	80	6-J
1989 Carat		185/60HR14	29-29	80	6-J
GLI		185/60HR14	29-29	80	6-J
Passat					
1999-98 All		195/65R15	32-32	87	6-J
1997-94 GLS		195/60HR14	32-32	80	6-J
GLX		215/50HR15	32-32	80	6-J
1993 GL & GLS		195/60HR14	32-32	80	6-J
GLX		215/50VR15	31-31	80	6-J
Synchro Canada		205/50VR15	30-33	80	6-J
1992-90 ex. GLX		195/60VR14	33-33	80	6-J
GLX		215/50VR15	31-31	80	6-J
Vanagon					
1991-89 All		185/R14C	40-48	130	5.5-J
		205/70R14	30-40	130	6-J
Camper GL		185/R14C	40-48	130	5.5-J
		205/70R14	30-40	130	6-J
Syncro		195/60HR14	30-33	130	6-J
		205/70R14	36-40	130	6-J
7-seat ex. GL		185/70R14C	43-53	130	5.5-JK
		185/70R14C	43-53	130	6-JK
GL Syncro		205/70R14	30-40	130	5.5-JK

VOLVO
70 Series

MODEL / YEAR	Standard	Optional	INFLATION Front-Rear	LUG NUT TORQUE Ft.-Lbs	RIM WIDTH
1999 C70:					
Convertible	205/55R16		N/A	N/A	7-J
Coupe	225/45ZR17		N/A	N/A	7.5-J

VOLVO Continued

70 Series Continued

MAKE MODEL YEAR	Standard	Optional	INFLATION PRESSURE Front - Rear	LUG NUT TORQUE Ft.-Lbs	RIM WIDTH
1999 S70, V70	195/60R15	205/55ZR16	N/A	N/A	6.5-J
W/AWD	195/65R15		N/A	N/A	6.5-J
V70:					
XC AWD	205/65R15		N/A	N/A	6.5-J
R AWD	205/55R16		N/A	N/A	7-J
1998 S70	185/65HR15		36-36	81	6-, 6.5-J
		195/60VR15	38-41	81	6-, 6.5-J
		205/55ZR15	42-42	81	6-, 6.5-J
V70	195/65VR15		36-41	81	6-, 6.5-J
		205/55VR16	41-46	81	6-, 6.5-J
		205/55VR15	35-41	81	6-, 6.5-J
		205/55ZR16	38-45	81	6.5-J
		205/45WR17	48-48	81	7-J

80 Series

MAKE MODEL YEAR	Standard	Optional	INFLATION PRESSURE Front - Rear	LUG NUT TORQUE Ft.-Lbs	RIM WIDTH
S80 2.9L	215/55R16		N/A	N/A	7-J
T6	225/55R16		N/A	N/A	7-J

90 Series

MAKE MODEL YEAR	Standard	Optional	INFLATION PRESSURE Front - Rear	LUG NUT TORQUE Ft.-Lbs	RIM WIDTH
1998 Sedan	205/55VR16		32-32	81	N/A
Wagon	195/65HR15		32-32	81	N/A

240

MAKE MODEL YEAR	Standard	Optional	INFLATION PRESSURE Front - Rear	LUG NUT TORQUE Ft.-Lbs	RIM WIDTH
1993-92 Sedan	185/70R14		35-35	85	5.5-J
Wagon	185/R14		35-35	85	5.5-J
1991 Sedan	185/70R14		35-35	63	5.5-J
Wagon	185/R14		35-35	63	5.5-J
1990-89 Canada	P185/75R14		35-35	63	5.5-J
USA: Sedan	185/70R14		35-35	63	5.5-J
Wagon	185SR14		35-35	63	5.5-J

VOLVO Continued

740

MAKE MODEL YEAR	Standard	Optional	INFLATION PRESSURE Front - Rear	LUG NUT TORQUE Ft.-Lbs	RIM WIDTH
1992-90 All	185/65R15		35-35	63	6-J
		195/60R15	35-35	63	6-J
1989 GL	185/70R14		30-36	63	6-J
GLE	185/70R14		30-36	63	6-J
		195/60R15	35-35	63	6-J

760

MAKE MODEL YEAR	Standard	Optional	INFLATION PRESSURE Front - Rear	LUG NUT TORQUE Ft.-Lbs	RIM WIDTH
1989 GLE	185/65R15		35-35	63	6-J
		195/60R15	35-35	63	6-J

780

MAKE MODEL YEAR	Standard	Optional	INFLATION PRESSURE Front - Rear	LUG NUT TORQUE Ft.-Lbs	RIM WIDTH
1990 All	195/65HR15		35-35	63	7-J
1989 All	205/60R15		35-35	63	6-JJ
		205/60R15	35-35	63	7-JJ

850

MAKE MODEL YEAR	Standard	Optional	INFLATION PRESSURE Front - Rear	LUG NUT TORQUE Ft.-Lbs	RIM WIDTH
1997 Ex. R Edition & Turbo	195/60VR15		N/A	N/A	N/A
R Edition	P105/45ZR17	P205/50ZR16	N/A	N/A	N/A
Turbo	205/50ZR16		33-32	N/A	6.5-J
1996-93 Ex. Turbo	195/60VR15		32-30	81	6-, 6.5-J
Turbo	205/50ZR16		33-32	81	6.5-J

940

MAKE MODEL YEAR	Standard	Optional	INFLATION PRESSURE Front - Rear	LUG NUT TORQUE Ft.-Lbs	RIM WIDTH
1995-93 Ex. Turbo	185/65R15		36-36	63	6-J
Turbo	195/65R15		28-28	63	6-J
1992-91 All	185/65R15		35-35	63	6-J
		205/55VR16	35-35	63	6.5-J
1991 SE	195/65R15		35-35	63	6-J
Turbo	205/55VR16		35-35	63	6.5-J

960

MAKE MODEL YEAR	Standard	Optional	INFLATION PRESSURE Front - Rear	LUG NUT TORQUE Ft.-Lbs	RIM WIDTH
1997-95 Sedan	205/55VR16		36-36	63	6.5-J
Wagon	195/65HR15		36-36	63	6-J
1994 All	195/65R15		36-36	63	6-J
1993-92 All	195/65VR15		36-36	63	6-J

THIS SECTION CONTAINS:

CHRYSLER, CHRYSLER IMPORTS, and EAGLE Coil Testing

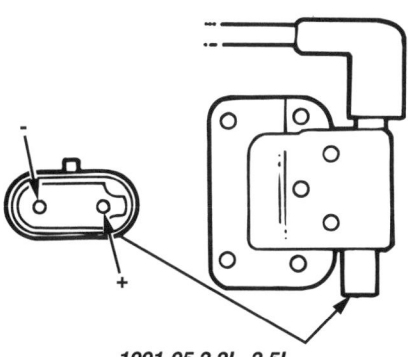

1991-95 2.2L, 2.5L.

PRIMARY RESISTANCE

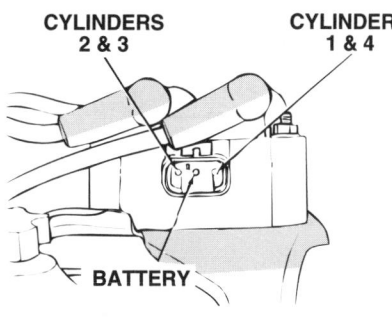

CYLINDERS 2 & 3

CYLINDERS 1 & 4

BATTERY

1995-99 2.0L Neon; 1995-98 2.0L non-Turbo Laser, Talon; 1995-98 2.0L, 2.4L Cirrus, Stratus, Breeze, Sebring Convertible; 2.4L Minivans. Measure primary resistance between battery & pin and pin corresponding for given cylinder.

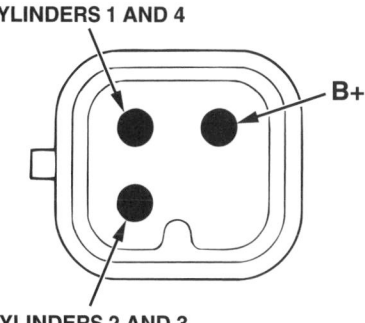

CYLINDERS 3 AND 6   B+

CYLINDERS 1 AND 4

CYLINDERS 2 AND 5

1993-97 3.5L, 1990-99 3.3L, 3.8L DIS, coil.

PRIMARY RESISTANCE

CYLINDERS 1 AND 4

B+

CYLINDERS 2 AND 3

1992 2.2L Turbo III.

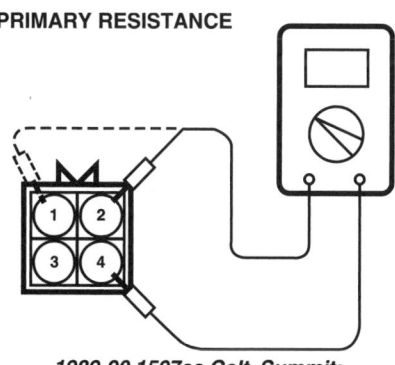

1989-90 1468cc, 1997cc Colt, Summit, Vista w/FI;
1992 2350cc Vista, Summit Wagon;
1991-96 2972cc SOHC.

PRIMARY RESISTANCE

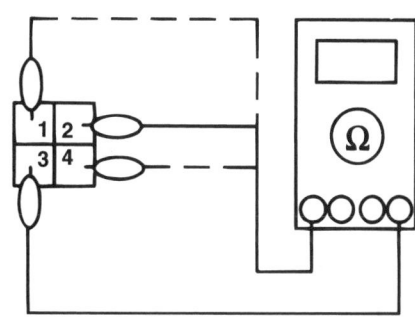

1991-96 2972cc DOHC Stealth.

PRIMARY RESISTANCE

1989-90 1597cc Colt, Summit;
1990 1997cc Laser, Talon.

PRIMARY RESISTANCE

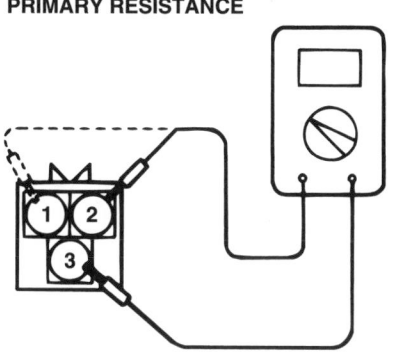

1991-94 1755cc Laser, Talon;
1991-94 1997cc Laser, Talon;
1995-98 2.0L Turbo, Talon.

PRIMARY RESISTANCE

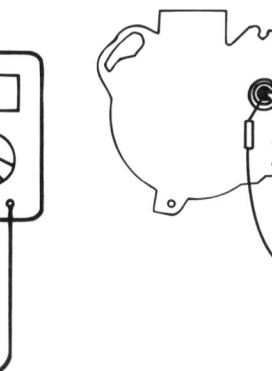

1992-96 1834cc Vista, Summit Wagon;
1993-96 2350cc;
1991-96 1468cc, 1834 cc Colt, Summit.

FORD Coil Testing

HIGH VOLTAGE TERMINAL

1989 Tracer, 1989-92 Probe Turbo,
1991-94 Capri, 1993-98 Villager;
1991-96 Escort, Tracer w/1.8L

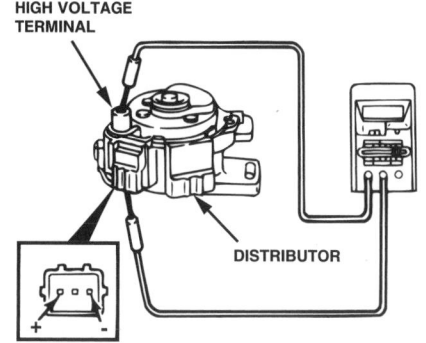

HIGH VOLTAGE TERMINAL

DISTRIBUTOR

1994-97 1.3L Aspire;
1993-97 2.5L Probe.

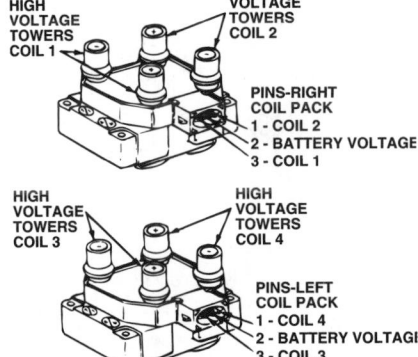

HIGH VOLTAGE TOWERS

COIL 2   COIL 3   COIL 1

PIN 4 - BATTERY VOLTAGE
PIN 3 - COIL 1
PIN 2 - COIL 3
PIN 1 - COIL 2

1989-95 3.8L Supercharged Thunderbird, Cougar; 1995-99 3.0L Taurus and Sable; 2.5L Contour/Mystique; 3.0L Windstar, and 3.8L Mustang, Thunderbird, Cougar coil connectors

HIGH VOLTAGE TOWERS COIL 1

HIGH VOLTAGE TOWERS COIL 2

PINS-RIGHT COIL PACK
1 - COIL 2
2 - BATTERY VOLTAGE
3 - COIL 1

HIGH VOLTAGE TOWERS COIL 3

HIGH VOLTAGE TOWERS COIL 4

PINS-LEFT COIL PACK
1 - COIL 4
2 - BATTERY VOLTAGE
3 - COIL 3

Four-Tower Coil Packs for 1.9L Escort/Tracer, 2.0L Contour/Mystique, 4.6L Mustang/Thunderbird/ Cougar/Crown Victoria/ Continental/Town Car/Mark VIII, 2.3L Ranger, 5.0L Explorer, 4.6L, 5.4L F-Series.

GM Coil Testing

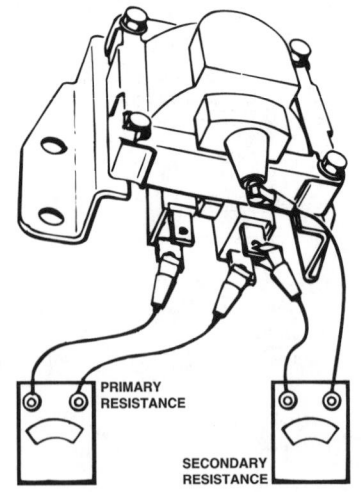

PRIMARY RESISTANCE

SECONDARY RESISTANCE

1989-90 HEI ignition, remote coil. Connect the ohmmeter according to the illustration and measure primary and secondary resistance.

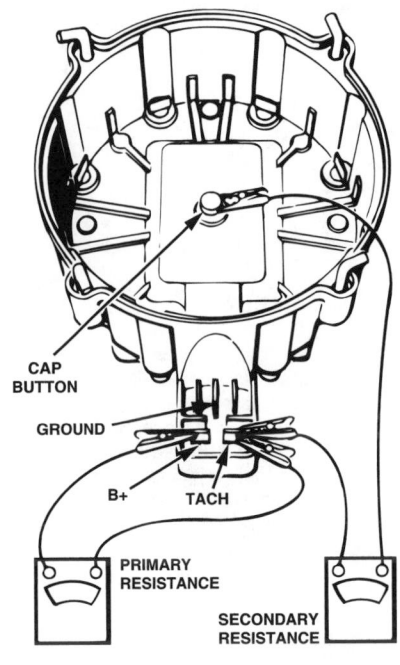

CAP BUTTON

GROUND

B+   TACH

PRIMARY RESISTANCE

SECONDARY RESISTANCE

HEI ignition, coil in cap. Connect the ohmmeter according to the illustration and measure primary and secondary resistance.

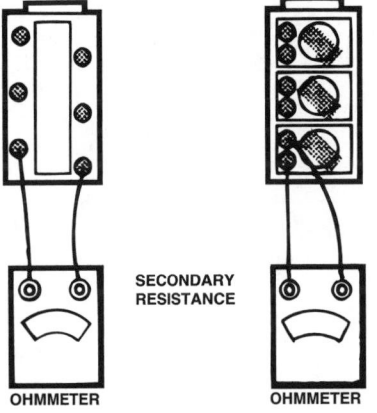

SECONDARY RESISTANCE

OHMMETER   OHMMETER

To check primary resistance on **Types I and II coils**, lift the coil cover, remove the wires from the primary terminals, and measure the resistance between the two terminals. Do the same for the remaining coils. Check secondary resistance as illustrated.

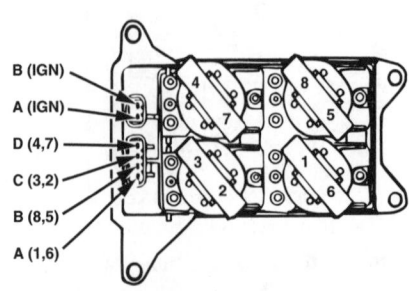

B (IGN)
A (IGN)
D (4,7)
C (3,2)
B (8,5)
A (1,6)

1990-95 5.7L DOHC, coil connectors.

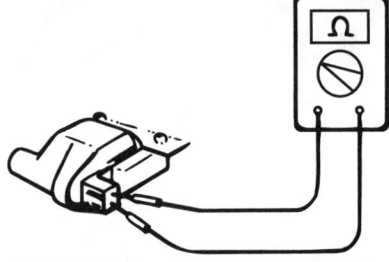

1991-95 TBI Geo Tracker, 1993-98 Metro.

*For **Geo Prizm** and **Chevrolet Nova**, see **Toyota***

HONDA Coil Testing

HIGH VOLTAGE TERMINAL

D   B

C   A

1989 Accord, Prelude w/FI. Measure primary resistance between terminals A and D. Measure secondary resistance between A and the high voltage terminal.

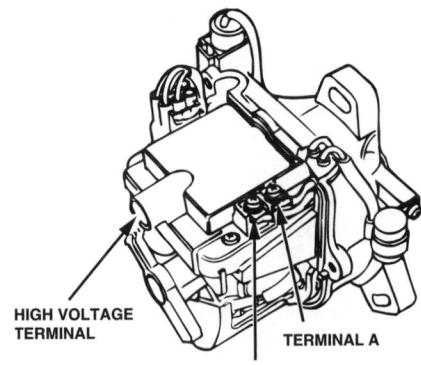

HIGH VOLTAGE TERMINAL

TERMINAL A

TERMINAL B

1989-91 Civic, CRX. Measure primary resistance between terminals A and B. Measure secondary resistance between A and the high voltage terminal.

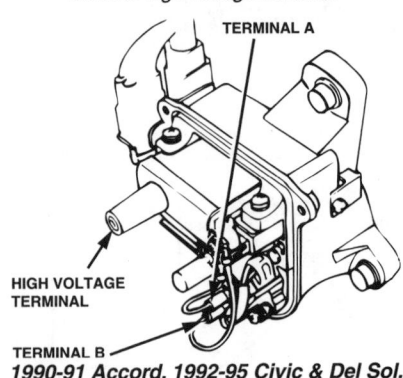

TERMINAL A

HIGH VOLTAGE TERMINAL

TERMINAL B

1990-91 Accord, 1992-95 Civic & Del Sol. Measure primary resistance between terminals A and B. Measure secondary resistance between A and the high voltage terminal.

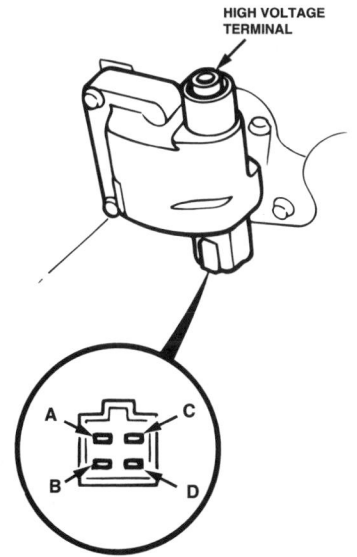

HIGH VOLTAGE
TERMINAL

1992-97 Accord w/F22B2 engine, C27A4 engine, 1992-98 Prelude. *Measure primary resistance between terminals A and B. Measure secondary resistance between terminal A and the high voltage terminal.*

NISSAN Coil Testing

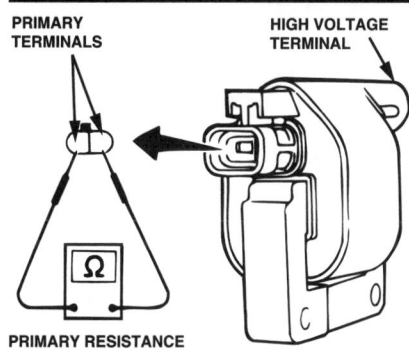

PRIMARY
TERMINALS

HIGH VOLTAGE
TERMINAL

PRIMARY RESISTANCE

1989-94 Sentra, Pulsar, NX; 1993-98 Quest; 1989-92 Stanza; 1989 300 ZX; 1989-94 Maxima SOHC; 1989-94 240SX; 1989-95 Pathfinder; 1989-97 Pickup
Check for more than one coil. Disconnect the coil power transistor(s). Measure primary resistance as illustrated. Measure secondary resistance between the high voltage terminal and each of the primary terminals. Compare the lowest reading with manufacturer's specifications for secondary resistance. Coil connectors may vary slightly between models.

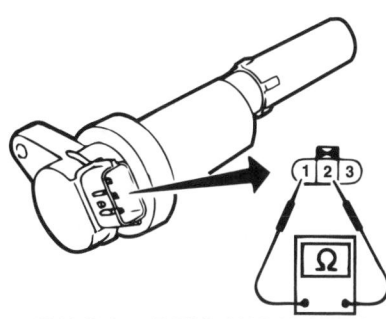

1989 Pulsar DOHC, 1990-96 300ZX, 1992-94 Maxima DOHC.
Disconnect coil and measure primary resistance between terminals 1 and 2.

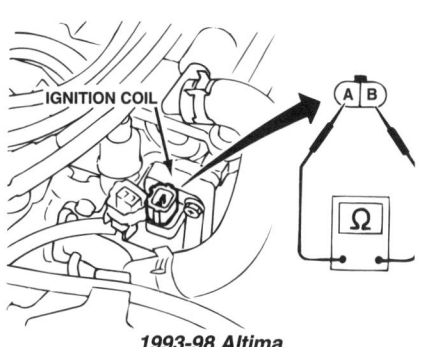

IGNITION COIL

1993-98 Altima

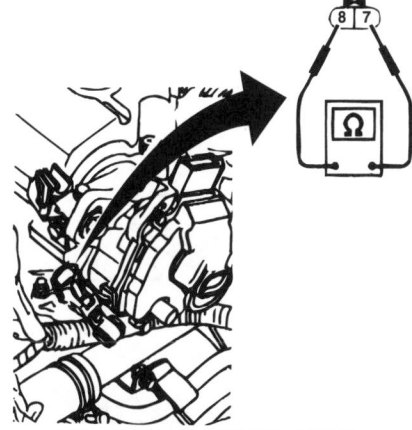

**1995-98 Sentra, 200SX, 240SX
1996-98 Pathfinder
1998 Frontier**

TOYOTA Coil Testing

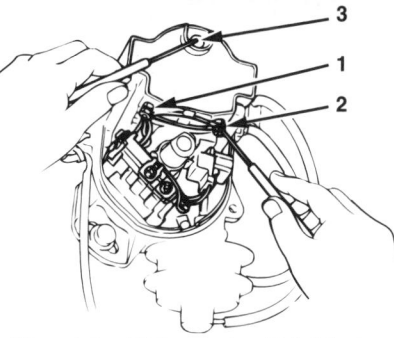

All models with integral coil/distributor.
Check primary resistance between points 1 and 2. Check secondary resistance between points 2 and 3.

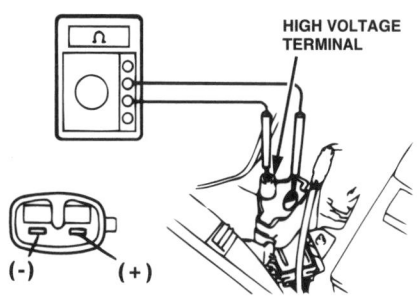

HIGH VOLTAGE
TERMINAL

(-)   (+)

SECONDARY RESISTANCE
All models with remote coil.
Check primary resistance between positive (+) and negative (-) connector terminals. Check secondary resistance between the positive and high voltage terminals as shown.

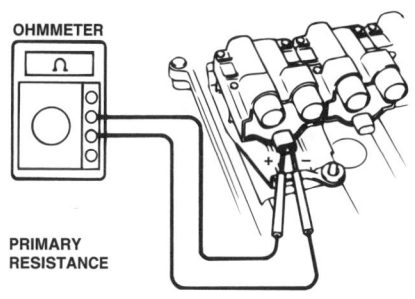

OHMMETER

PRIMARY
RESISTANCE

1989-92 Supra Turbo with coil pack. *With this coil, you cannot measure the secondary resistance.*

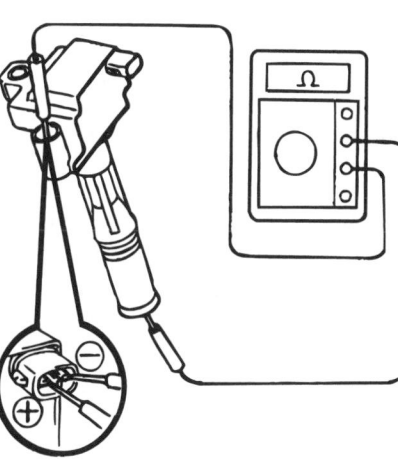

1994-99 Tercel, Paseo; 1995-99 5VZ-FE Trucks, V6 Camry, Avalon, Sienna

VOLKSWAGEN Coil Testing

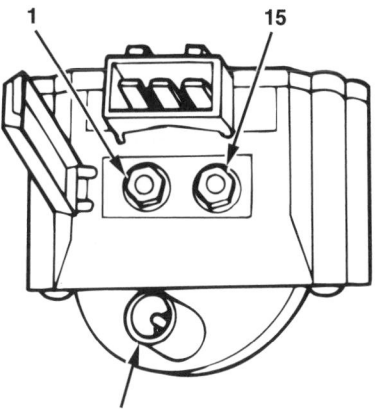

1   15

HIGH VOLTAGE
TERMINAL

1991-99 All 4-cyl. models with solid-state coil. *Check primary resistance between terminals 1 and 15, check secondary resistance between terminal 15 and the high voltage terminal.*

Procedures apply to distributors with magnetic reluctance pickup coils. Distributors with Hall effect or optical sensors are not covered.

CHRYSLER Pickup Coils

Check and adjust the pickup air gap as follows:

1. Align a tooth on the reluctor with the pickup coil.

2. Use non-magnetic feeler gauges to check the air gap.

3. To adjust the gap, align one reluctor blade with the pickup coil.

4. Loosen the pickup coil adjustment lock screw.

5. With a screwdriver blade inserted in the adjustment slot, shift the distributor plate so the correct size feeler gauge contacts the reluctor blade and the pickup coil.

6. Tighten the lock screw. No force should be required to remove the feeler gauge.

7. Apply vacuum to the distributor vacuum advance unit, and move the pickup plate through its range of travel. Watch the pickup coil to be sure it does not hit the reluctor. Recheck the air gap. If the pickup plate is loose, overhaul the distributor.

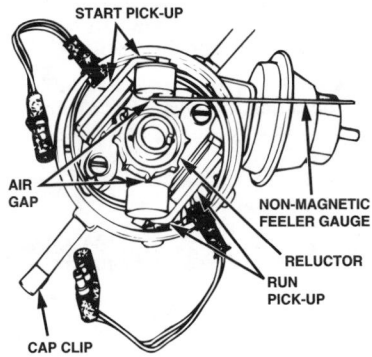

1989 V8. Use a non-magnetic feeler gauge to check the pickup air gap. Measure pickup coil resistance at two-terminal connector(s).

FORD Pickup Coils

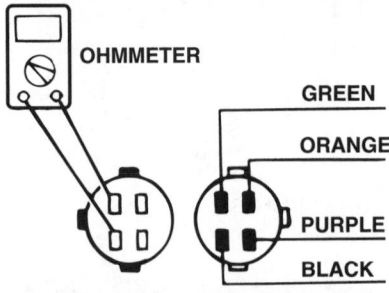

OHMMETER

GREEN
ORANGE
PURPLE
BLACK

1989-90 Dura-Spark ignition. Disconnect the distributor harness. Measure resistance between the orange and purple wire sockets at the connector.

1989-92 Probe 4-cylinder. With the distributor cap and rotor removed, measure the resistance between the points indicated.

E C A
F D B

1989-92 Probe Turbo. At the distributor connector, measure the resistance between terminals A and B, C and D, and E and F.

GM Pickup Coils

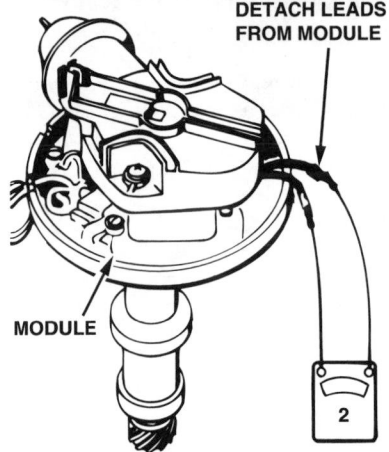

DETACH LEADS FROM MODULE

MODULE

2

1989-90. Connect the ohmmeter as shown in the illustration, and measure pickup coil resistance.

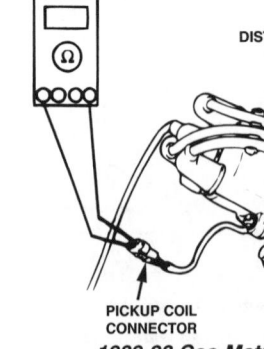

DISTRIBUTOR

PICKUP COIL CONNECTOR

1989-98 Geo Metro.

For **Geo Prizm** and **Chevrolet Nova**, see **Toyota**

HONDA Pickup Coils

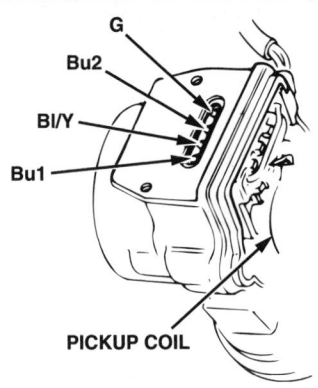

G
Bu2
Bl/Y
Bu1

PICKUP COIL

1989 w/FI Accord, Prelude. Remove igniter cover and pull igniter out. Check resistance between terminals G and Bu2.

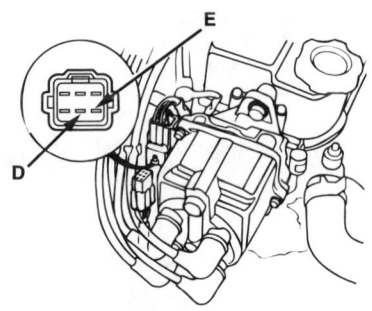

E
D

1989-91 CRX, Civic. Measure resistance between terminals D and E.

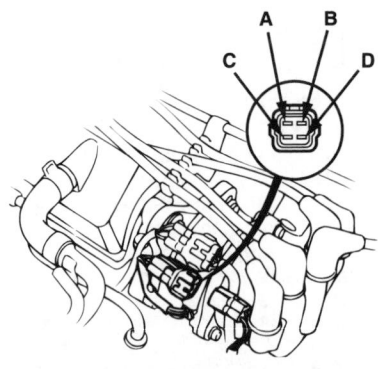

A   B
C   D

1990-91 Prelude FI. Disconnect the 4-pin connector and measure resistance between terminals C and D.

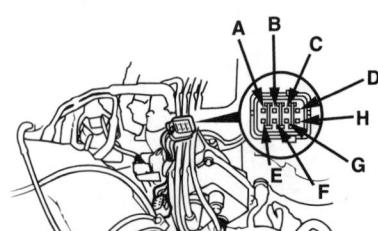

A B
C
D
H
G
E
F

1990-95 Accord, 1992-95 Civic, Prelude, 1993-95 Del Sol. Disconnect the TDC/CRANK/CYL 8-pin connector, and check resistance between terminals: F & B, crankshaft; C & G, TDC; D & H, camshaft.

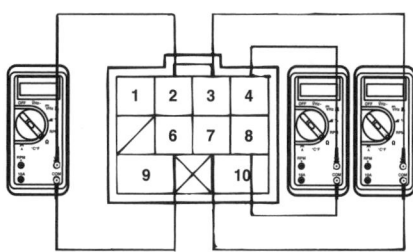

1996-99 Civic, Del Sol. Measure resistance between terminals: 2 & 6, 3 & 7, 4 & 8.

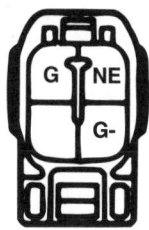

1989-90 Celica 3S-FE, 1989-91 Camry 3S-FE, 1989-92 Land Cruiser. Disconnect the connector and check the resistance between terminals G and G-, and NE and G-.

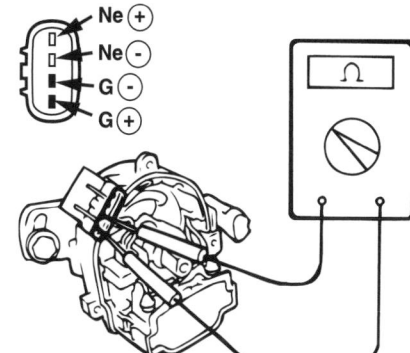

1992-95 Camry ex. 1994-95 California, 1993-95 MR2 5S-FE, 1994-96 Tacoma, 4-Runner, T100 2RZ-FE, 3RZ-FE. Disconnect the connector, and check the resistance between terminals G+ and G-, Ne+ and Ne- (ex. Trucks).

TOYOTA Pickup Coils

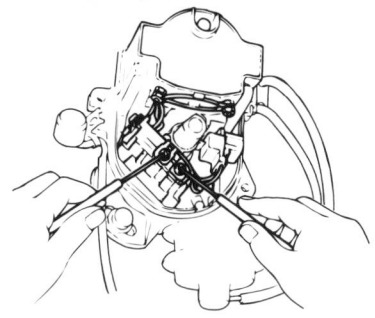

Most Toyota 4-cyl. models with integral coil/distributor. *Check primary resistance between the points indicated. When placing left probe on high tension terminal, secondary resistance is measured.*

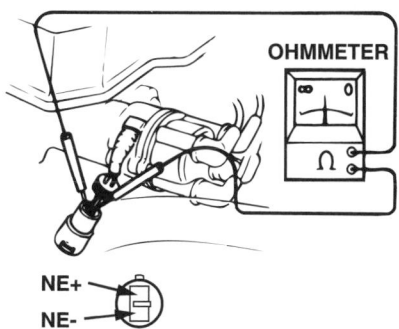

1989-94 Pickup, 4Runner 4-cyl., 1991-94 Paseo, Tercel. Check the resistance between the two terminals.

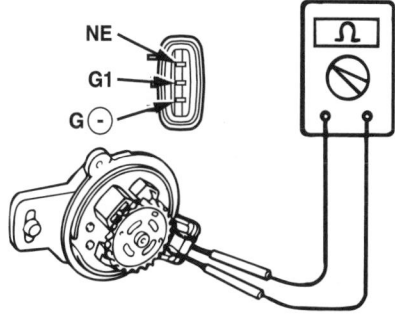

1991-92 MR2 5S-FE. Disconnect the connector, and check the resistance between terminals G1 and G-, NE and G-.

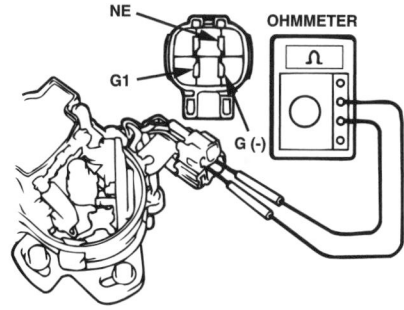

1989-92 Corolla, 1990-93 Celica 4A-FE. Disconnect the distributor connector and check the resistance between terminals G1 and G(-), and NE and G(-).

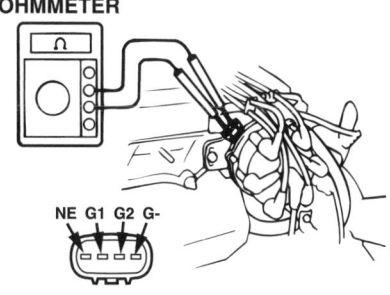

1989-94 Supra except Turbo, 1989-92 Cressida, 1991-95 Celica & MR2 3S-GTE, 1991-95 Previa, 1992-95 Pickup & 4Runner, 3VZ-E, 1992-93 Camry 3VZ-FE, 1993-97 Land Cruiser, 1994-95 5S-FE California. Disconnect the connector, and check the resistance between terminals G1 and G-, G2 and G-, and NE and G-.

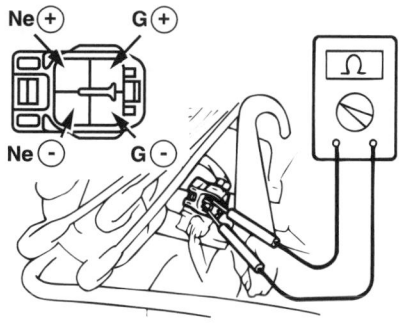

1992-94 Paseo, 1996-97 Corolla. Disconnect the connector, and check the resistance between terminals G+ and G-, Ne+ and Ne- (ex. Corolla).

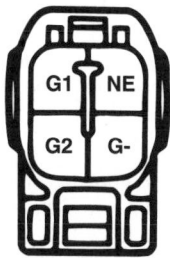

1989 Celica 3S-GE, 1989-92 Supra 7M-GTE, 1989-91 Pickup, 4Runner 3VZ-E, 1989-91 Camry 2ZV-FE. Disconnect the connector and check the resistance between terminals G1 and G-, G2 and G-, and NE and G-.

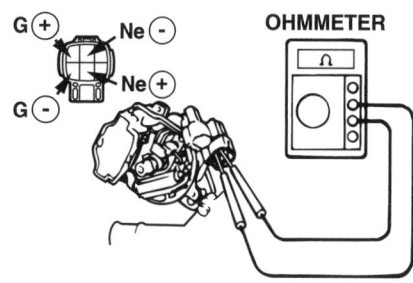

1993-94 Corolla, Celica 4A-FE, 7A-FE. Disconnect the distributor multi-plug and check resistance between terminals G+ and G-, and terminals Ne+ and Ne-.

CHRYSLER Ignition Timing

Domestic Models:

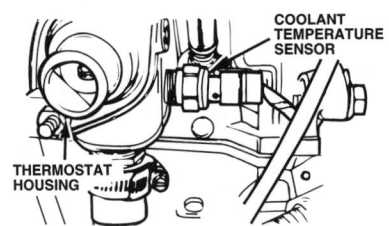

Import Models:

For engines with EST, connect a jumper wire to the ignition timing adjustment terminal and ground it.

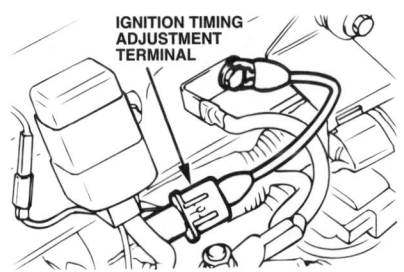

For Chrysler vehicles with EST and distributor, ground the ignition timing adjustment terminal.

For engines without EST, disconnect the white-striped vacuum hose from the vacuum diaphragm at the distributor, and plug the hose end.

On later models with mechanical and vacuum advance, as well as rudimentary computer-timing controls, disconnect the high altitude pressure sensor and ground it.

For 1990-96 imports with distributorless ignition systems (DIS):

Connect a jumper wire to the ignition timing adjustment terminal and ground it.

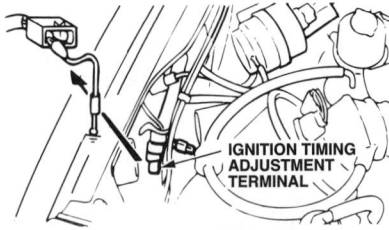

For Chrysler imports with distributorless ignition systems, ground the ignition timing adjustment terminal.

To adjust the timing, loosen the nut securing the crank angle sensor and rotate it.

FORD Ignition Timing

For non-EEC systems, remove the vacuum hoses from the distributor vacuum advance, and plug the hoses. If the car has a barometric pressure switch, disconnect the switch from the ignition module and jumper the connector pins (yellow and black wires).

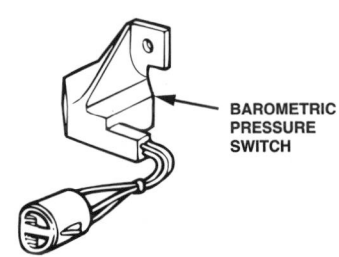

Ford non-EEC system with a barometric pressure switch.

For EEC-IV systems (except DIS and EDIS), remove the shorting bar from the double-wire spout connector.

On some GM fuel-injected engines with HEI, jumper across two terminals of the diagnostic connector.

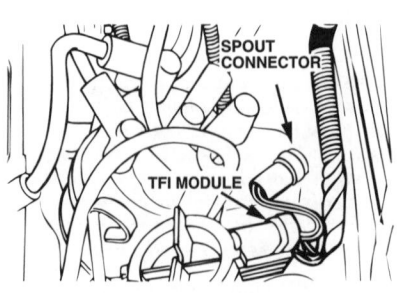

For Ford EEC-IV systems (except some DIS and EDIS), disconnect the connector near the distributor.

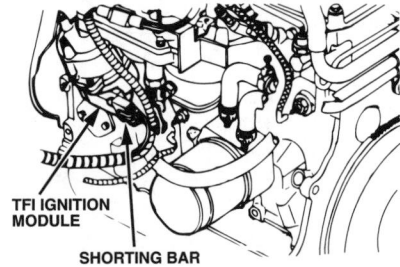

On some other EEC-IV systems (except DIS and EDIS), remove the shorting bar from the double-wire spout connector.

GM Ignition Timing

To check the base timing on most carbureted engines, you must disconnect the four-wire connector at the distributor, or ground the test terminal of the diagnostic connector. Note, however, that grounding the test terminal on some engines will put the system into a fixed-timing setting that is *not* base timing.

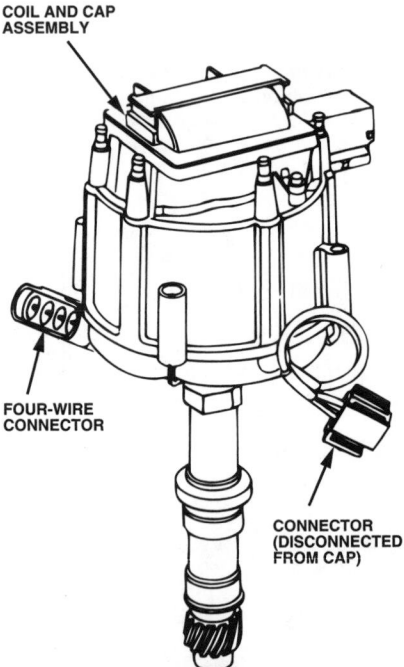

To check the base timing on most GM carbureted engines with HEI, disconnect the four-wire connector at the distributor.

On fuel-injected engines, you cannot disconnect the four-wire distributor connector to check the base timing because the computer needs a trigger signal to time the injector(s). On these engines, you must open a bypass connector in the distributor wiring harness, jumper across two terminals of the diagnostic connector, or ground a special connector in the engine compartment.

HONDA Ignition Timing

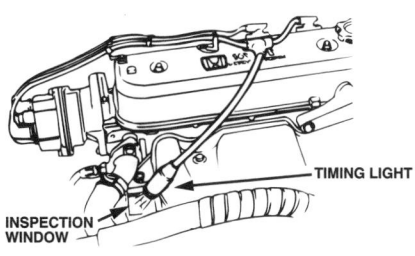

On Honda vehicles, you must remove the rubber cover from the inspection window to reveal the timing marks.

On fuel-injected vehicles, locate the service connector.

— On 1990 and later vehicles, the connector is located under the dashboard on the passenger side. Jumper the terminals of the 2-pin connector.

— On earlier fuel-injected vehicles, the connector is located behind the ignition coil. Remove the yellow rubber cover and jumper the terminals.

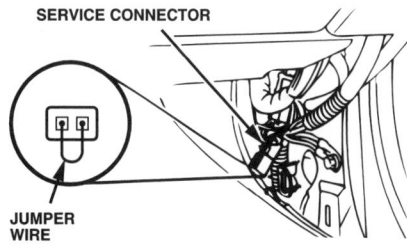

On 1990 and later Honda vehicles, the service connector is located in the far right corner under the dashboard. On earlier Honda vehicles, the connector is behind the coil.

NISSAN Ignition Timing

Use the notes on the Underhood Service Specifications page and the information below as a guide:

For vehicles with dual ignition coils, connect the timing light inductive clamp to the high tension wire between the number 1 coil and spark plug.

For vehicles with a throttle sensor, check the timing with the sensor connected, but disconnect the sensor before adjusting the timing.

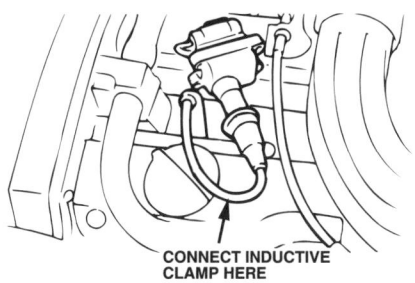

1989 Pulsar DOHC, connect the timing light inductive clamp to the high tension wire between the #1 coil and spark plug.

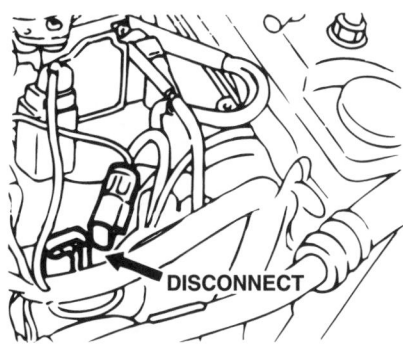

All models, disconnect the throttle position sensor before adjusting the timing.

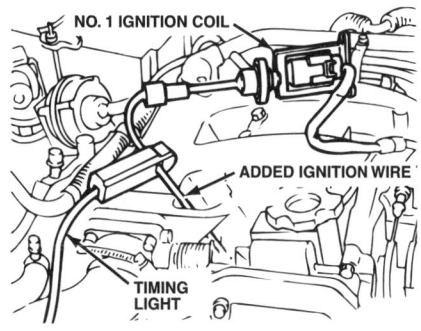

1990-96 300ZX, 1995-98 Maxima

TOYOTA Ignition Timing

Vehicles that do not have a vacuum advance diaphragm on the distributor have EST (electronic spark timing). Use a jumper wire to connect terminals TE1 and E1, or T and E1 (depending on the model), at the check connector.

For Toyota vehicles with EST, jumper terminals TE1 and E1, or T and E1 (depending on the model) at the Data Link Connector 1.

On some vehicles with vacuum advance, you must disconnect and plug the vacuum hose at the inner diaphragm, but leave other hoses connected, as mentioned in the notes on the Underhood Service Specifications page. Unless otherwise specified, for all other vehicles with vacuum advance, disconnect and plug the vacuum hoses at the distributor.

VOLKSWAGEN Ignition Timing

Use the notes on the Underhood Service Specifications page and the information below as a guide:

1989 **Scirocco, Cabriolet**
— CIS: Disconnect and plug vacuum hose.
— CIS-E: Leave hoses connected.
1989-92 **Golf, Jetta, GTI**
— CIS: Disconnect and plug vacuum hose.
— CIS-E: Check the idle or throttle switch to be sure that it is closed.
— Digifant II: Remove cap from CO tap tube and connect special tester.
1989-91 **Vanagon**
— Digijet: Disconnect plugs from idle stabilization unit and connect them together.
— Digifant: Disconnect temperature sensor II.
1989 **Fox**
— CIS/CIS-E: Disconnect vacuum hoses.
1989-92 **All models with Digifant**
Disconnect coolant temperature sensor.

CHRYSLER Fuel Pressure Tests

Pressure Test Gauge Connections

Use the following illustrations to locate test ports in various fuel-injected systems.

Domestics

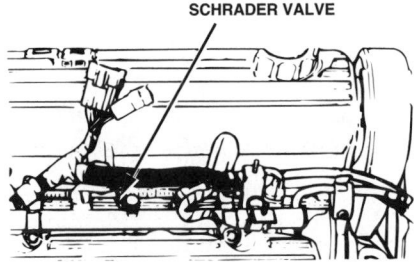

For Chrysler domestic engines with multi-point fuel injection, the Schrader valve is on the fuel rail.

For engines with throttle-body injection, measure the pressure using a tee connector at the fuel supply hose.

Imports

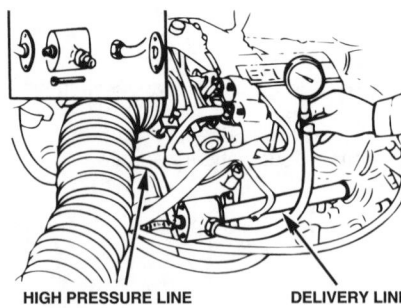

Connect the fuel pressure gauge between the fuel delivery line and the high pressure line. You will need an adapter to do this.

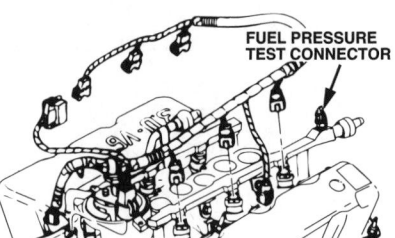

For models with multi-point injection, the test connector is on the fuel rail. On some 1996 models, the test connector is located on the fuel tank-mounted fuel pump module.

FORD Fuel Pressure Tests

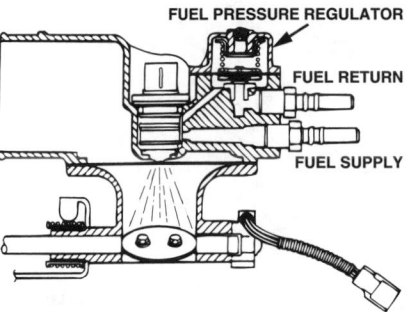

For Ford's throttle body injection system, measure the pressure at the fuel supply line with a tee connector and pressure gauge.

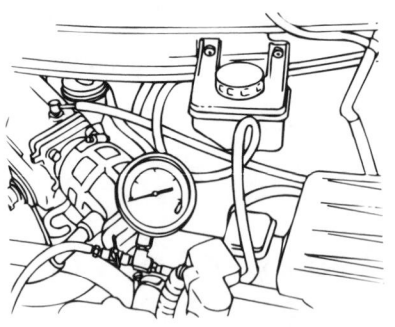

For Ford MFI test, measure pressure in fuel line between fuel filter and fuel rail with main valve open and drain valve closed.

Some CFI systems have a test connector similar to the one used on multi-point injected systems.

GM Fuel Pressure Tests

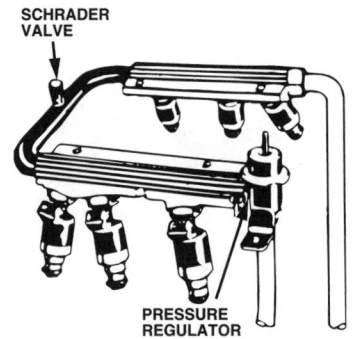

For GM vehicles with multi-point injection, use the Schrader valve connector on the fuel rail.

For GM vehicles with TBI, remove the section of hose between the fuel line and the throttle body, and connect the adapter and gauge.

HONDA Fuel Pressure Tests

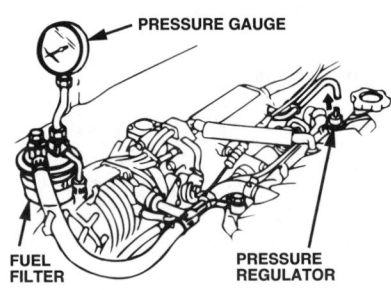

1989 Accord; 1989-91 Prelude; 1989-99 Civic, CRX, Del Sol; 1997-99 CR-V. Remove the bolt from the outlet line on top of the fuel filter. Thread an adapter in its place, and connect the pressure gauge. Disconnect and plug the fuel pressure regulator vacuum hose.

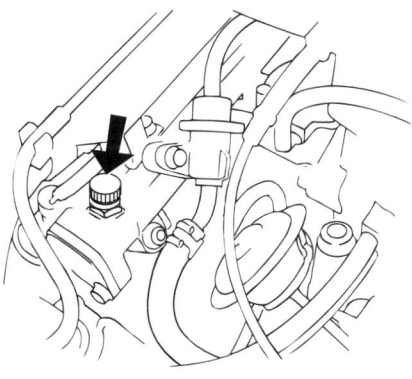

1992-96 Prelude.
Remove service bolt and attach guage.

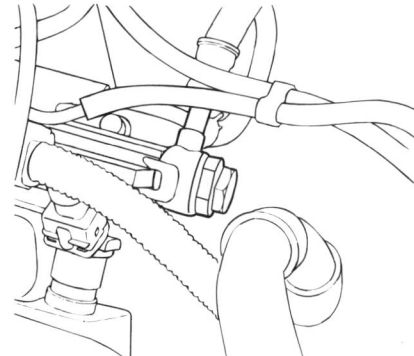

1990-99 Accprd 4-cyl.
Remove plug and install adapter and guage.

NISSAN Fuel Pressure Tests

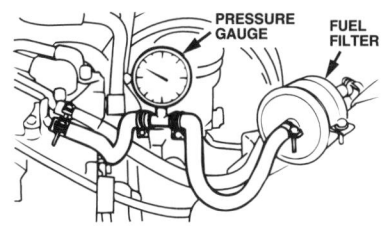

Remove the fuel outlet line at the fuel filter, and connect the gauge inline between the fuel filter outlet port and the fuel outlet line.

TOYOTA Fuel Pressure Tests

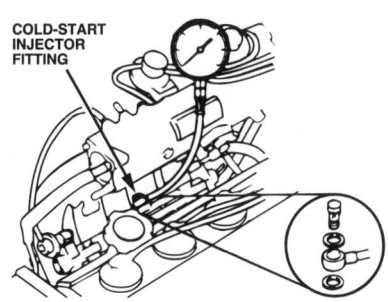

For Toyota, check the fuel pressure at the cold-start injector, fuel filter, or delivery pipe, depending on model. You will need a pressure gauge with a banjo fitting or an adapter.

VOLKSWAGEN Fuel Pressure Tests

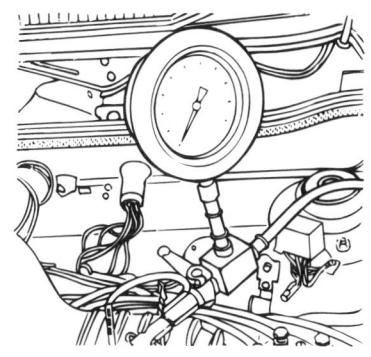

For the Bosch K-Jetronic or KE-Jetronic systems, you need a gauge with an adapter and an inline valve, so that you can shut off pressure when needed. Connect the adapter inline between the fuel distributor and the control pressure regulator.

CHRYSLER Idle Speed Adjustment

Domestic Models

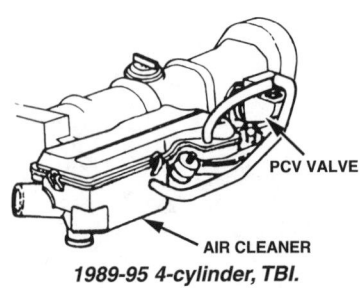

1989-95 4-cylinder, TBI.

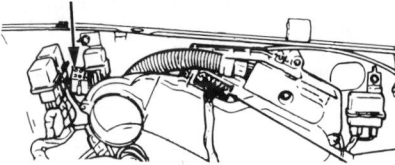

DIAGNOSTIC CONNECTOR

1989-92 4-cylinder except 1.8L, 2.0L,
with computer control.

Import Models

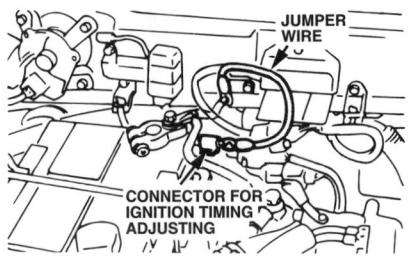

JUMPER WIRE

CONNECTOR FOR IGNITION TIMING ADJUSTING

All Models

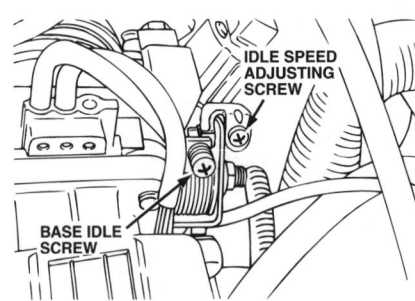

IDLE SPEED ADJUSTING SCREW

BASE IDLE SCREW

1989-92 1.5L, 1.6L, 1.8L, 2.0L

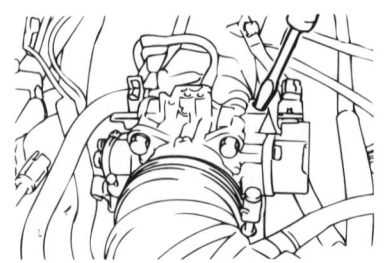

1993-96 1.5L, 1.8L, 2.4L.

FORD Idle Speed Adjustment

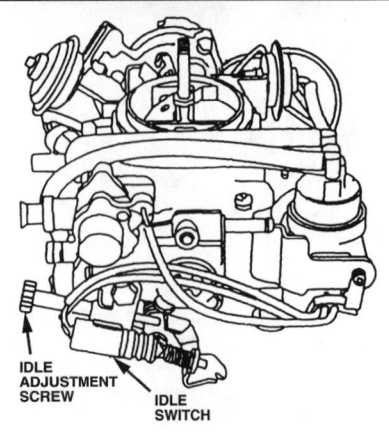

IDLE ADJUSTMENT SCREW
IDLE SWITCH

1989 1.3L 2V.

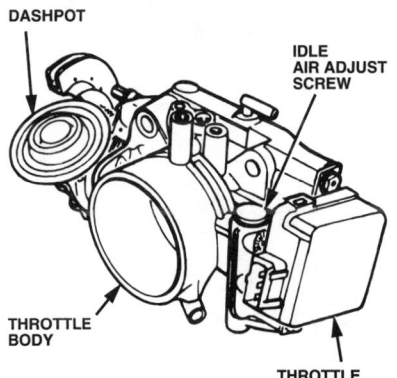

DASHPOT
IDLE AIR ADJUST SCREW
THROTTLE BODY
THROTTLE POSITION (TP) SENSOR

1989-93 1.3L MFI, 1989-94 1.6L MFI.

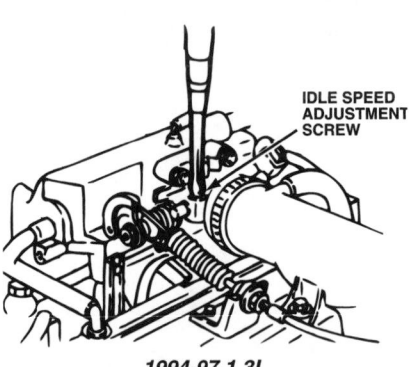

IDLE SPEED ADJUSTMENT SCREW

1994-97 1.3L

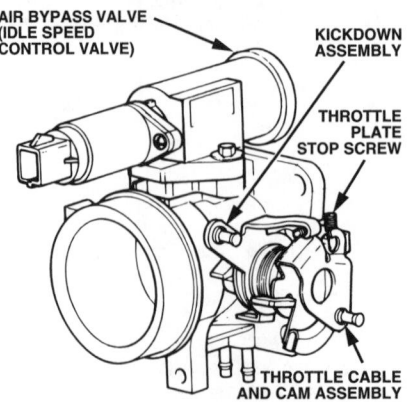

AIR BYPASS VALVE (IDLE SPEED CONTROL VALVE)
KICKDOWN ASSEMBLY
THROTTLE PLATE STOP SCREW
THROTTLE CABLE AND CAM ASSEMBLY

1989-90 1.9L MFI.

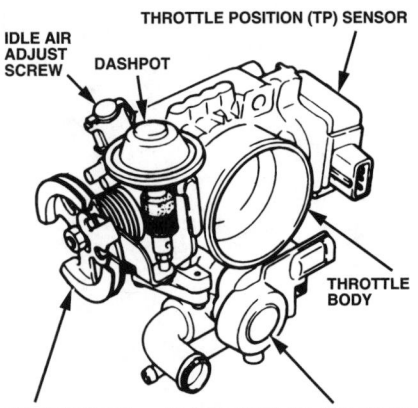

IDLE AIR ADJUST SCREW
DASHPOT
THROTTLE POSITION (TP) SENSOR
THROTTLE BODY
THROTTLE CAM
IDLE AIR CONTROL (IAC) VALVE

1991-96 1.8L DOHC.

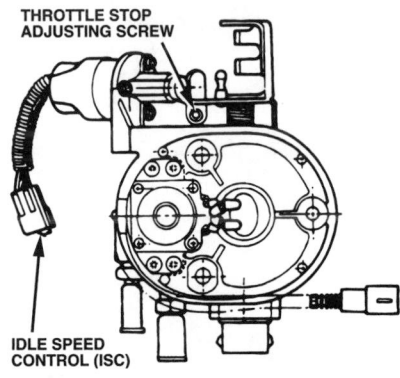

THROTTLE STOP ADJUSTING SCREW
IDLE SPEED CONTROL (ISC)

1989-90 1.9L TBI, 1989-90 2.5L TBI.

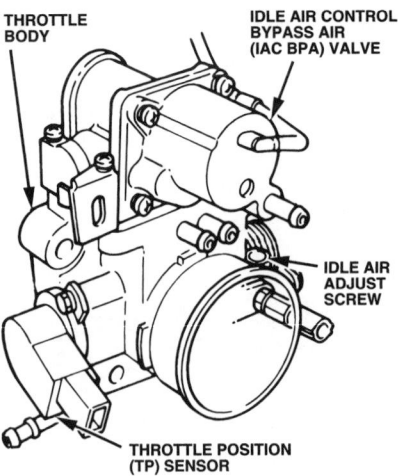

THROTTLE BODY
IDLE AIR CONTROL BYPASS AIR (IAC BPA) VALVE
IDLE AIR ADJUST SCREW
THROTTLE POSITION (TP) SENSOR

1993-97 2.0L Probe

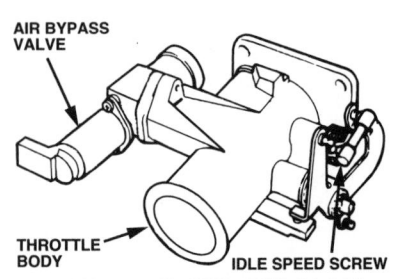

AIR BYPASS VALVE
THROTTLE BODY
IDLE SPEED SCREW

1989-91 2.3L OHC, 1989-91 2.9L.

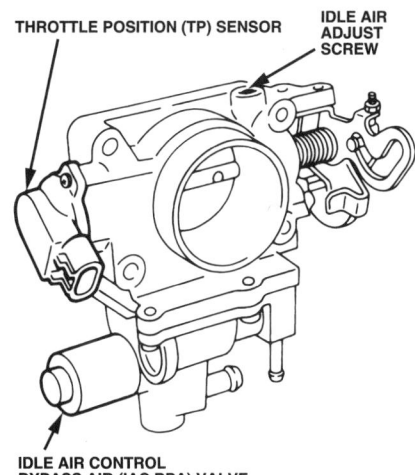

THROTTLE POSITION (TP) SENSOR

IDLE AIR ADJUST SCREW

IDLE AIR CONTROL BYPASS AIR (IAC BPA) VALVE

1993-97 V6 2.5L Probe

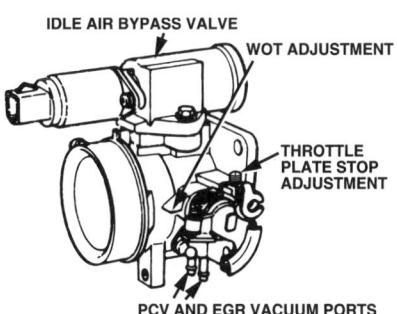

IDLE AIR BYPASS VALVE

WOT ADJUSTMENT

THROTTLE PLATE STOP ADJUSTMENT

PCV AND EGR VACUUM PORTS

1989-90 3.0L except SHO, 3.8L MFI,
1989-90 5.0L MFI, 1989-90 4.0L MFI.

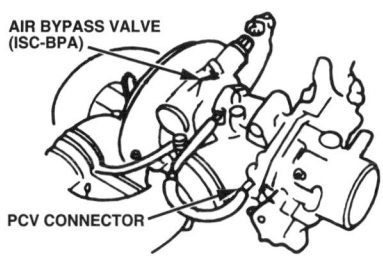

AIR BYPASS VALVE (ISC-BPA)

PCV CONNECTOR

1989-95 3.0L SHO.

IDLE AIR SET SCREW

1989-90 4.9L MFI, 5.0L MFI,
5.8L MFI.

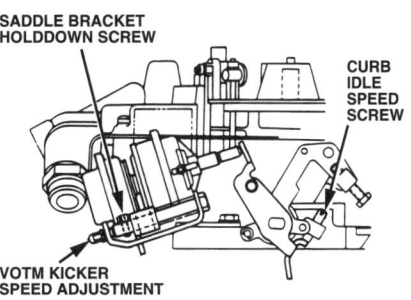

SADDLE BRACKET HOLDDOWN SCREW

CURB IDLE SPEED SCREW

VOTM KICKER SPEED ADJUSTMENT

1989-91 5.8L 2V.

GM Idle Speed Adjustment

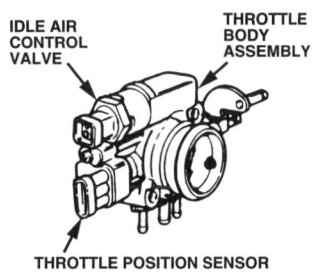

IDLE AIR CONTROL VALVE

THROTTLE BODY ASSEMBLY

THROTTLE POSITION SENSOR

1989 with TBI or MFI.

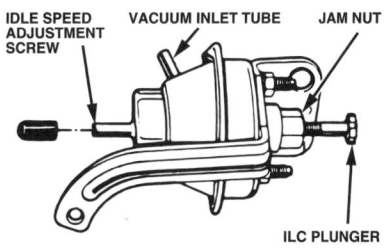

IDLE SPEED ADJUSTMENT SCREW

VACUUM INLET TUBE

JAM NUT

ILC PLUNGER

All carbureted engines with ILC, with
computer controls.

HONDA Idle Speed Adjustment

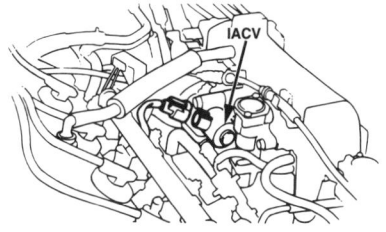

IACV

1989-99, All w/Fl.
Disconnect the 2-pin connector from
the IAC valve before checking and
adjusting the idle.

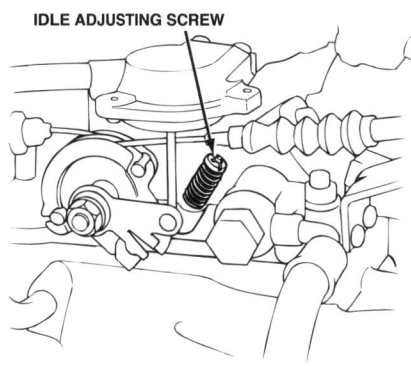

PLUG

1989 Accord 1955cc 2V.
Remove the air filter from the frequency
solenoid valve, and plug the opening in
the frequency solenoid valve.

IDLE ADJUSTING SCREW

1989-91 Civic, CRX

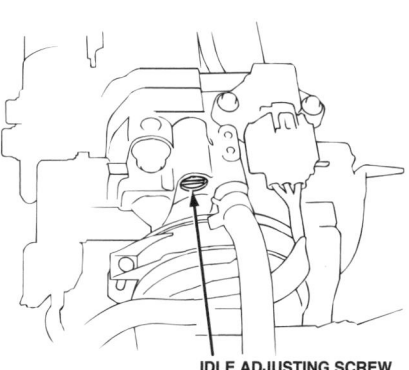

IDLE ADJUSTING SCREW

1992-95 Civic, CRX, Del Sol
1992-96 Prelude

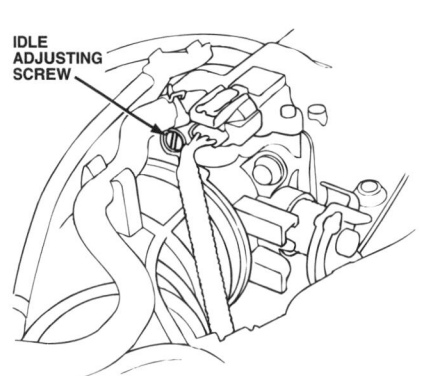

IDLE ADJUSTING SCREW

1996-99 Civic, Del Sol, CR-V,
Accord 4-cyl.; 1997-98 Prelude

NISSAN Idle Speed Adjustment

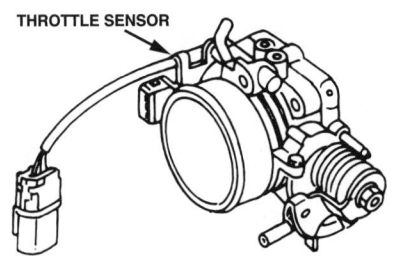

1989-92 GA16, disconnect throttle position sensor.

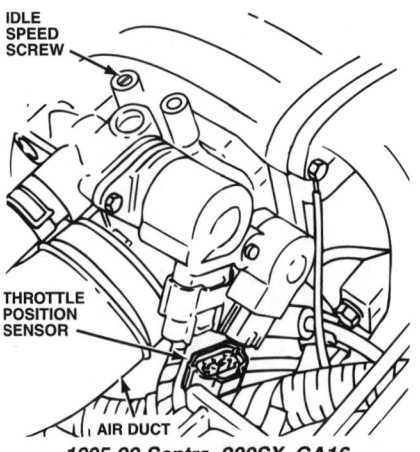

1995-99 Sentra, 200SX, GA16

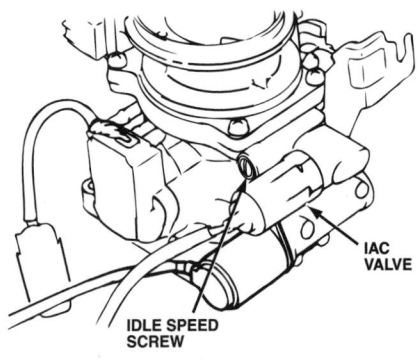

1990-95 Pathfinder KA24
1990-98 Pickup, Frontier KA24

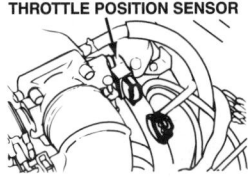

1991-94 Sentra, NX, GA16

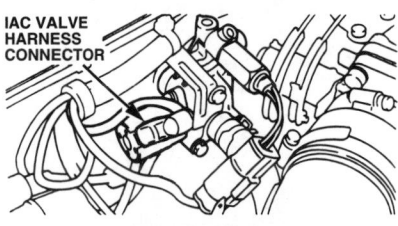

1989 VG30 Turbo,
1989 CA16, CA18 DOHC.

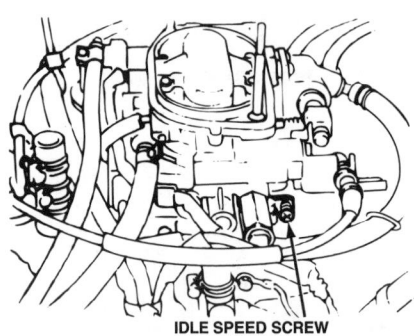

IDLE SPEED SCREW
1989 Pickup, Pathfinder

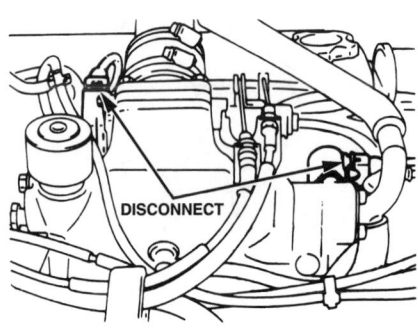

1989 CA20 Stanza.

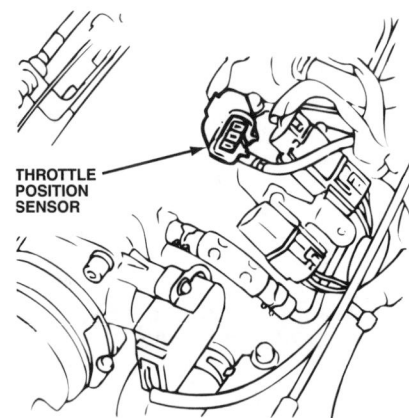

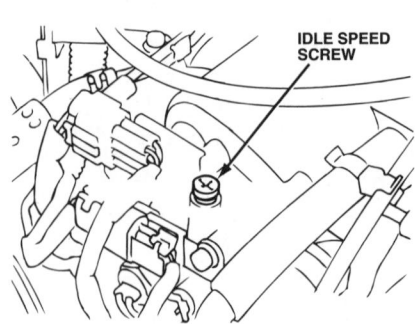

1991-99 Sentra, NX, 200SX, SR20

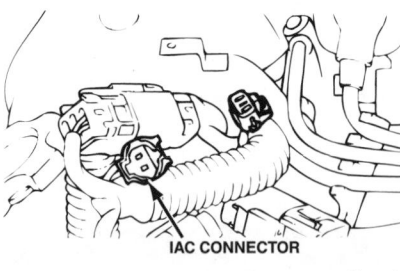

IAC CONNECTOR

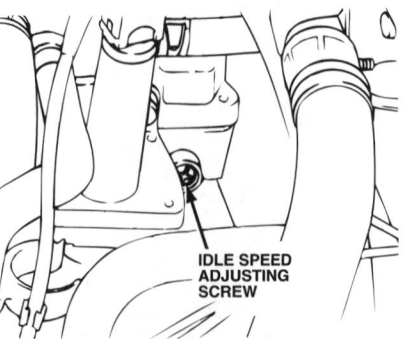

IDLE SPEED ADJUSTING SCREW

1990-95 Pathfinder VG30
1990-98 Pickup, Frontier VG30

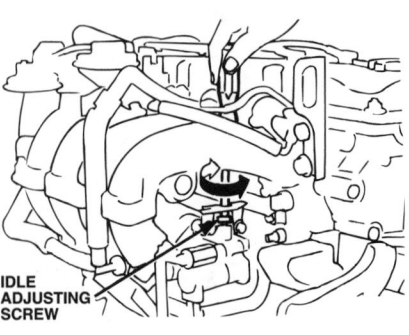

1993-98 Altima

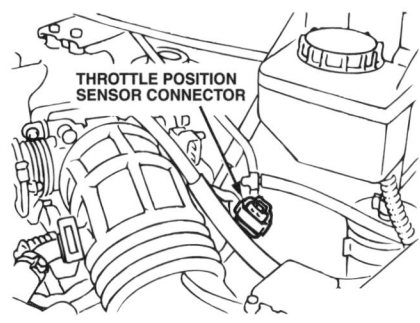

THROTTLE POSITION SENSOR CONNECTOR

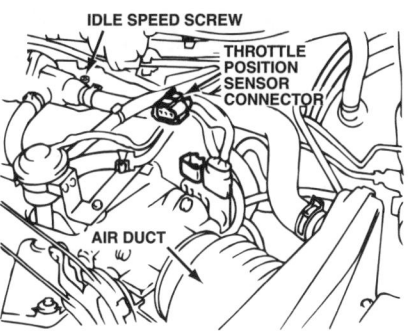

IDLE SPEED SCREW
THROTTLE POSITION SENSOR CONNECTOR
AIR DUCT

1995-98 Maxima DOHC

TOYOTA Idle Speed Adjustment

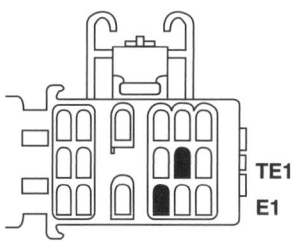

TE1
E1

For vehicles with FI and computer controls, jumper terminals T and E1 or TE1 and E1 before checking and adjusting the idle speed.

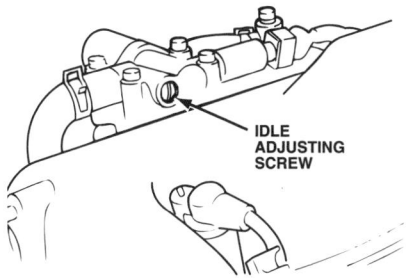

IDLE ADJUSTING SCREW

1993-99 Quest

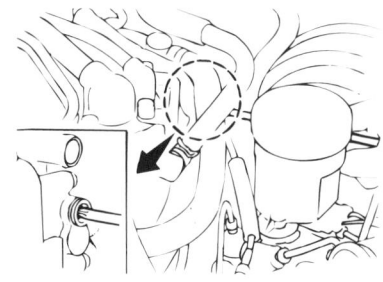

1990-96 300ZX, disconnect the IAC valve harness.

TO HAI TO MC
PLUG
PLUG

1989-90 2366cc 2V, without computer controls.

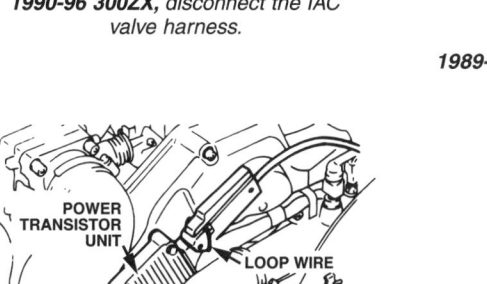

FULLY CLOCKWISE
DIAGNOSTIC MODE SELECTOR

1989-94 VG30 SOHC Maxima.

POWER TRANSISTOR UNIT
LOOP WIRE

1990-96 300ZX. Connect tachometer clamp to loop wire by power transistor.

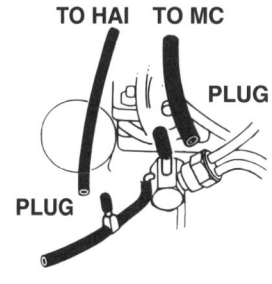

IDLE SPEED ADJUSTING SCREW

1989-91 All FI, without computer controls.

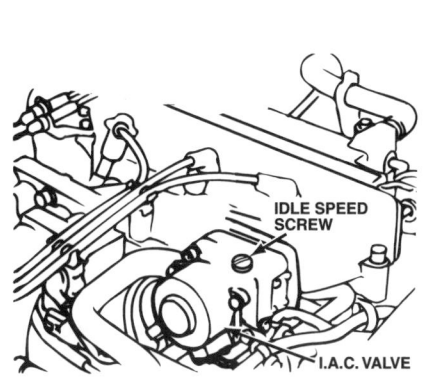

IDLE SPEED SCREW
I.A.C. VALVE

1989-94 Maxima SOHC

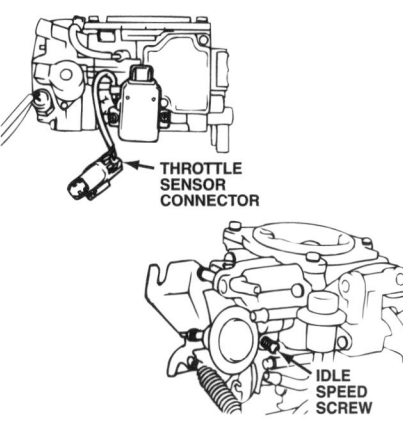

THROTTLE SENSOR CONNECTOR
IDLE SPEED SCREW

1989-90 Sentra, Pulsar GA16, E16

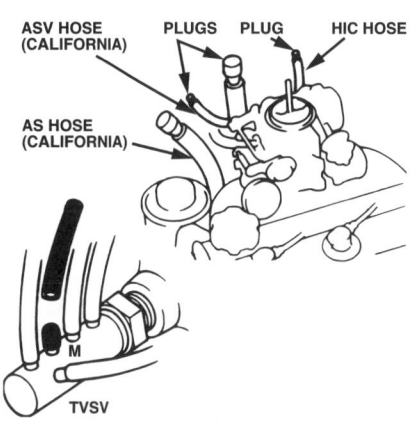

ASV HOSE (CALIFORNIA)
PLUGS PLUG HIC HOSE
AS HOSE (CALIFORNIA)
M
TVSV

1989-90 1452cc, 1587cc, 2V.

CHRYSLER CORP., JEEP, EAGLE

Note: "F" is used to designate front of engine or location of drive belts. "L" and "R" designate left or right cylinder heads on V engines. See below.

Displ.	Code	Years
1.5	A	91-96
1.5	X	89-90
1.6	Y	89-90
1.6 T	Z	89
1.8	B	93-94
1.8	C	93-96
1.8	T	89-92
1.8	D	92
2.0	E	93-94
2.0 T	F	93-98
2.0	R	90-92
2.0 T	U	90-92
2.4	G	93-94
2.4	W	90-92

Displ.	Code	Years
2.0	C	95-98
2.0	Y	95-98
2.4	X	95-98

Displ.	Code	Years
2.0	V	89-91

Displ.	Code	Years
2.0	D	89

Displ.	Code	Years
2.2 T	A	89-92
2.2 T	C	90
2.2	D	89-94
2.5	G	95
2.5 T	J	89-92
2.5	K	89-95
2.5	P	91-97

Displ.	Code	Years
2.6	E	89
2.6 T	N	89

Displ.	Code	Years
2.7	R	98-99

RF / LF bolt sequence diagrams:

Displ.	Code	Years
3.0	U	90-92
3.3	T	93-97

Displ.	Code	Years
3.2	J	98
3.5	D	97
3.5	F	93-97

Displ.	Code	Years
3.9	X	89-98

Displ.	Code	Years
3.3	R	90-97
3.3	J	95
3.3	U	95-97
3.8	L	91-97

Displ.	Code	Years
4.0	S	89-98

Displ.	Code	Years
5.2	P	89
5.2	S	89
5.2	T	95-97
5.2	Y	89-98
5.9	W	91
5.9	Z	90-98
5.9	5	89-98

Displ.	Code	Years
5.9	7	89-91

Displ.	Code	Years
5.9 TD	D	97-98
5.9 TD	C	94-96
5.9 TD	8	89-93

FORD

Displ.	Code	Years
8.0	W	94-98

Displ.	Code	Years
1.6	5	89
1.9	J	89-94
1.9	9	89-90
2.0	P	97-98

Displ.	Code	Years
1.3	H	89-97
1.3	K	89
1.6	Z	91-94
1.6 T	6	91-94
1.8	8	91-96

Displ.	Code	Years
2.0	Z	95-98
2.0	3	96-98

Displ.	Code	Years
2.0	A	93-97
2.2	C	89-92
2.2 T	L	89-92
2.3 HO	S	89-91
2.3	X	89-94
2.5	D	89-90
2.5	N	91

Displ.	Code	Years
2.5	B	93-97

Displ.	Code	Years
2.5	L	95-98

Displ.	Code	Years
2.3	A	89-97
2.3	M	91-92
2.3	W	89
4.6	W	91-92

Displ.	Code	Years
2.9	V	89
2.9	T	91-92

Displ.	Code	Years
3.0	W	93-98

Displ.	Code	Years
5.0	P	96-98
5.0	D	94
5.0 HO	E	89-92
5.0	F	89-91

Displ.	Code	Years
3.0	1	96-97
3.0	U	89-97

Displ.	Code	Years
3.0	S	96-97
3.0 HO	Y	89-95
3.2	P	93-96

Displ.	Code	Years
3.8	C	89
3.8	R	89-95
3.8	4	89-97
4.2	2	97-98

Displ.	Code	Years
4.0	X	91-97

Displ.	Code	Years
4.6	9	96-98
		Cars
4.6	6	96-97
4.6	X	96-98
4.6	W	91-98
4.6	V	93-98
		Trucks
4.6	6	97-98
4.6	W	97-98
5.4	L	97-98
5.4	M	97-98

Displ.	Code	Years
4.9	Y	89-96

Displ.	Code	Years
5.0	N	89-96
5.0 HO	T	91-94
5.8	G	89-91
5.8	H	89-97
5.8	R	94
7.5	G	89-97

Displ.	Code	Years
7.3 D	M	89-94
7.3 D	K	94

Initial stages / Final stage diagrams

Displ.	Code	Years
7.3 D	F	94-98

GM

Displ.	Code	Years
1.0	6	89-98
1.0	2	89-91

Displ.	Code	Years
1.3	9	95-97

Displ.	Code	Years
1.3	9	98

Displ.	Code	Years
1.6	6*	90-92
1.8	8	92-93

*Isuzu engine

Displ.	Code	Years
1.6	5	89-92
1.6	6*	89-97
1.8	8	94-97

*Toyota engine

Displ.	Code	Years
1.3	9	96
1.6	U	89-95

Displ.	Code	Years
1.6	6*	94-98

*Suzuki engine

Displ.	Code	Years
1.6	6*	89-92
1.9	7	91-92
1.9	9	91-92
2.0	H	92-94
2.0	K	89-91
2.0 T	M	89-90
2.0	1	89
2.0	6	91
2.2	G	90-91
2.2	4	92-97

*Daewoo engine

Displ.	Code	Years
1.8	8	98

Displ.	Code	Years
2.3	A	94
2.3	D	94-95
2.3	3	94
2.4	T	96-98

Displ.	Code	Years
2.3	A	90-93
2.3	D	89-93
2.3	3	92-93

Displ.	Code	Years
2.5	A	91-92
2.5	E	89-91
2.5	R	89-92
2.5	U	89-91

Displ.	Code	Years
2.8	B	89
2.8	R	89-92
2.8	S	89
2.8	W	89
3.0	R	97-98
3.1	D	90-95
3.1	M	94-98
3.1	T	89-94
3.4	E	96-98
3.4	S	93-94
3.4	X	91-97

LF ⑥ ① ③ ⑦ RF
⑧ ④ ② ⑤

3.3	N	89-92
3.8	C	89-91
3.8	K	95-98
3.8	L	91-95
3.8	1	91-98

⑧ ⑤ ⑨
LF ⑫ ④ ① ⑬ RF
⑪ ⑦ ③ ② ⑥ ⑩

4.3	B	90-92
4.3	W	92-98
4.3	Z	89-94
4.3	X	96-98

LF ⑥ ③ ① ④ ⑤ RF
⑩ ⑦ ② ⑧ ⑨

4.5	3	90
4.5	5	89-90
4.5	8	90-92
4.9	B	91-95

LF ⑦ ③ ① ⑤ ⑨
⑩ ⑥ ② ④ ⑧

⑨ ⑤ ① ③ ⑦
⑧ ④ ② ⑥ ⑩ RF

4.0	C	95-98
4.6	9	93-98
4.6	Y	93-98

F ⑬ ⑨ ⑤ ① ④ ⑧ ⑫
⑭ ⑩ ⑥ ② ③ ⑦ ⑪

4.8	T	89

LF ⑦ ⑤ ① ③ ⑨ RF
⑧ ⑥ ② ④ ⑩

5.0	Y	89-90

⑬ ⑤ ② ⑩
LF ⑰ ⑨ ① ⑥ ⑭ RF
⑯ ⑫ ⑧ ④ ③ ⑦ ⑪ ⑮

4.3	W	94-96
5.0	E	89-92
5.0	F	89-92
5.0	H	89-96
5.7	K	89-96
5.7	M	89-91, 96-98
5.7	P	92-96
5.7	R	96-98
5.7	7	91-92
5.7	8	89-92

LF ⑧ ⑥ ② ④ ⑩
⑨ ③ ① ⑤ ⑦

RF ⑨ ③ ① ⑤ ⑦
⑧ ⑥ ② ④ ⑩

5.7	J	89-94

⑭ ⑩ ⑥ ② ③ ⑦ ⑪ ⑮
LF ⑰ ⑨ ① ⑧ ⑯ RF
⑬ ⑤ ④ ⑫

6.2 D	C	89-93
6.2 D	J	89-93
6.5 D	F	92-98
6.5 D	P	94-96
6.5 D	S	94-98
6.5 D	Y	94-96

⑮ ⑬ ⑪ ⑫ ⑭
LF ⑥ ③ ① ⑤ ⑨ RF
⑦ ⑥ ② ④ ⑧

5.7	G	97-98

⑫ ③
LF ⑯ ⑨ ① ⑥ ⑬ RF
⑮ ⑧ ② ⑦ ⑭
⑪ ⑤ ④ ⑩

7.4	J	96-98
7.4	N	89-96
7.4	W	89

HONDA

⑨ ⑤ ① ③ ⑦
⑧ ④ ② ⑥ ⑩ F

1.6	B16A3	94-95
2.2	H22A1	93-96
2.2	H22A4	97-98
2.3	H23A1	92-96

⑧ ⑥ ② ④ ⑩
⑨ ③ ① ⑤ ⑦ F

1.5	D15B1	89-91	2.0	B20A3	89
1.5	D15B2	89-91	2.0	B20A5	89-91
1.5	D15B6	89-91	2.1	B21A1	90-91
1.5	D15B7	92-95	2.2	F22A1	90-95
1.5	D15B8	92-95	2.2	F22A4	90-91
1.5	D15Z1	92-95	2.2	F22A6	91-93
1.6	D16A6	89-91	2.2	F22B1	96-97
1.6	D16Y5	96-98	2.2	F22B2	96-97
1.6	D16Y7	96-98	2.2	F22B6	95-97
1.6	D16Y8	96-98	2.3	F23A1	98
1.6	D16Z6	92-95	2.3	F23A4	98
2.0	A20A1	89	2.3	F23A5	98
2.0	A20A3	89			

⑦ ③ ① ⑤ ⑨
⑧ ④ ② ⑥ ⑩ F

2.6	E	97

⑪
⑥ ② ③ ⑦
LF ⑩ RF
⑤ ① ④ ⑧
⑨

3.2	V	97

RF & LF ⑧ ② ④ ⑥
⑤ ③ ① ⑦

2.7	C27A4	97

RF & LF ⑥ ① ③ ⑦
⑤ ② ④ ⑧

3.2	W	98

RF & LF ⑥ ④ ② ⑧
⑦ ① ③ ⑤

3.0	J30A1	98

MAZDA

F ⑧ ④ ① ⑤ ⑨
⑦ ③ ② ⑥ ⑩

1.5	1	95-98
1.6	1,2,3,4	89-95
1.8	2,3,4,6,8	90-98

RF ③ ⑦ ⑥ ②
④ ⑧ ⑤ ①

LF ① ⑤ ⑧ ④
② ⑥ ⑦ ③

2.3	1,2	95-98

F ⑩ ⑥ ② ③ ⑦
⑨ ⑤ ① ④ ⑧

2.2	1,2,3,A,B	89-94

RF & LF ⑥ ② ③ ⑦
⑤ ① ④ ⑧

2.5	2,B,D	93-98
3.0	1,2,3	89-98

NISSAN

F ⑨ ③ ① ⑥ ⑧
⑦ ⑤ ② ④ ⑩

2.4	KA24E	89-94
2.4	KA24DE	91-98

RF ⑥ ④ ② ⑧
⑦ ① ③ ⑤

LF ⑦ ① ③ ⑤
⑥ ④ ② ⑧

3.0	VE30DE	92
3.0	VG30DE	90-96
3.0	VG30DETT	90-96
3.0	VQ30E	95-98

⑪
F ⑬ ⑨ ③ ① ⑥ ⑧
⑭ ⑦ ⑤ ② ④ ⑩
⑫ ⑮

1.6	GA16	89-98

⑪ ⑦ ③ ① ⑥ ⑩
RF ⑬ ⑤ ④ ⑫
⑨ ② ⑧

⑧ ② ⑨
LF ⑫ ④ ⑤ ⑬
⑩ ⑥ ① ③ ⑦ ⑪

3.0	VG30E	89-98
3.0	VG30i	89

F ⑨ ③ ① ⑤ ⑦
⑧ ⑥ ② ④ ⑩

1.8	CA18DE	89

F ⑦ ③ ① ⑤ ⑨
⑧ ④ ② ⑥ ⑩

2.0	CA20E	89
2.4	Z24i	89

⑩ ⑤ ② ③ ⑥ ⑪
RF ⑨ ④ ⑦ ⑫
⑧ ① ⑬

⑧ ① ⑬
LF ⑨ ④ ⑦ ⑫
⑩ ⑤ ② ③ ⑥ ⑪

3.3	VG33E	96-98

F ⑦ ③ ① ⑤ ⑨
⑧ ④ ② ⑥ ⑩

2.0	SR20DE	91-98

TOYOTA

F ⑧ ⑥ ① ③ ⑨
⑩ ④ ② ⑤ ⑦

1.5	5E-FE	92-98
1.6	4A-FE	89-92
2.0	3S-FE	89-98
2.0	3S-GE	89
2.0 T	3S-GTE	89-96
2.2	5S-FE	90-97
2.4	2TZ-FE	91-97
2.4	2TZ-FTE	94-97
2.4	2RZ-FE	94-98
2.7	3RZ-FE	94-98

RF ⑦ ② ④ ⑥
⑤ ③ ① ⑧

LF ⑧ ① ③ ⑤
⑥ ④ ② ⑦

2.5	2VZ-E	89
2.5	2VZ-FE	90-91
3.0	3VZ-FE	92-95
3.4	5VZ-FE	95-98

F ⑨ ③ ① ⑥ ⑧
⑦ ⑤ ② ④ ⑩

1.5	3E	89-90
1.5	3E-E	90-94

RF ⑧ ② ④ ⑥
⑤ ③ ① ⑦

LF ⑦ ① ③ ⑤
⑥ ④ ② ⑧

3.0	3VZ-E	89-95
3.0	3VZFE	92-95

F ⑦ ③ ① ⑥ ⑩
⑨ ⑤ ② ④ ⑧

1.6	4A-GE	89-91
1.6	4A-GELC	89
1.6 S	4A-GZE	89

RF ⑦ ② ④ ⑥
⑤ ③ ① ⑧

LF ⑤ ③ ① ⑧
⑦ ② ④ ⑥

3.0	1MZ-FE	94-98

F ⑧ ④ ② ⑤ ⑨
⑩ ⑥ ① ③ ⑦

1.6	4A-F	89
1.8	1ZZ-FE	98

F ⑫ ⑧ ④ ② ⑤ ⑨ ⑬
⑭ ⑩ ⑥ ① ③ ⑦ ⑪

3.0	7M-GE	89-92
3.0	7M-GET	89-92
3.0	2JZ-GE	93-98
3.0	2JZ-GTE	93-98
4.5	1FZ-FE	93-97

F ⑧ ⑦ ① ③ ⑨
⑩ ④ ② ⑤ ⑥

1.5	4A-FE	93-97
1.8	7A-FE	93-97

F ⑮ ⑨ ⑤ ① ④ ⑧ ⑫
⑬ ⑪ ⑦ ③ ② ⑥ ⑩ ⑭

4.0	3F-E	89-92

⑬ ⑫ ⑪
⑧ ⑥ ① ③ ⑨
⑩ ④ ② ⑤ ⑦

2.2	4Y-EC	89

RF ⑩ ④ ② ⑤ ⑦
⑧ ⑥ ① ③ ⑨

LF ② ③ ① ⑥ ⑧
⑦ ⑤ ② ④ ⑩

4.7	2UZ-FE	98

F ⑩ ④ ② ⑤ ⑦
⑧ ⑥ ① ③ ⑨

2.4	22R	89-90
2.4	22R-E	89-95

VOLKSWAGEN

F ⑦ ① ③ ⑤
⑥ ④ ② ⑧

2.1	MV	89-91

F ⑩ ④ ② ⑥ ⑧
⑦ ⑤ ① ③ ⑨

1.8	All	89-94
1.9 D	AAZ, 1Z	93-98
2.0	9A	90-94
2.0	ABA	93-98

F ⑨ ⑤ ③ ① ⑦ ⑪
⑫ ⑧ ② ④ ⑥ ⑩

2.5	AAF	92-93

F ⑱ ⑭ ⑧ ② ⑦ ③ ⑳
⑯ ⑩ ④ ① ⑤ ⑪ ⑰
⑫ ⑥ ③ ⑨ ⑮ ⑲

2.8	AAA	92-98

CHRYSLER Engine Computers

DIAGNOSTIC TESTS:

For Chrysler domestics, you must use a special diagnostic tester or the CHECK ENGINE, POWER LOSS, or POWER LIMITED light on the dash board when retrieving trouble codes. To activate the diagnostics system, rapidly turn the ignition switch ON-OFF-ON-OFF-ON. Leave the ignition switch ON, and watch the warning lamp on the dash or the LED on the logic module. Either indicator will flash the 2-digit trouble codes. Code 55 signals the end of the test.

Chrysler domestics. If you use the Chrysler test meter attached to the diagnostic connector in the engine compartment, follow the manufacturer's instructions.

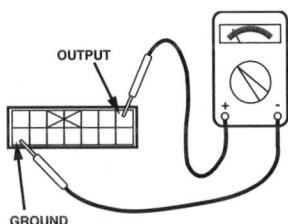

Chrysler imports and some Eagle models. Connect a voltmeter to the diagnostic connector. Count the needle sweeps on the voltmeter to obtain trouble codes.

SENSOR TESTS:

Chrysler Domestics. Set the special diagnostic tester to the "Read Sensor Values" mode.

Chrysler Imports and some Eagle models. You must use the ECI checker to test some sensors, such as the barometric pressure sensor and the motor position sensor without disconnecting it from the wiring harness. However, some sensors can be checked with a volt-ohm-meter.

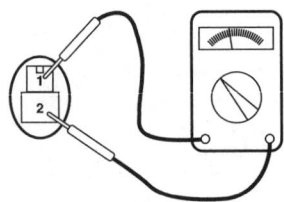

Coolant temperature sensor. Measure the resistance between the two terminals.

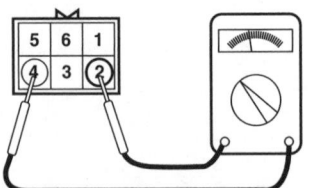

1989-92 Intake air temperature sensor, 4-cylinder engines with FI. ex. Turbo. Measure the resistance between terminals 2 and 4 of the airflow connector.

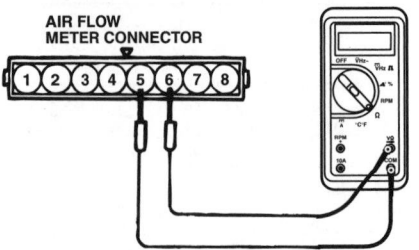

1993-96 Colt, Summit. Intake air temperature sensor. Measure resistance between terminals 5 and 6.

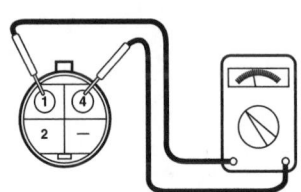

1989-91 Motor position sensor. Measure the resistance between terminals 1 and 4 of the ISC motor connector for motor position sensor resistance.

FORD Engine Computers

DIAGNOSTIC TESTS:

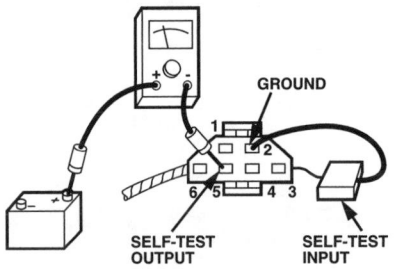

1989-95 All Domestics. Attach a voltmeter to the self-test connector, and use a jumper wire to connect the self-test input lead to the number 2 slot of the connector.

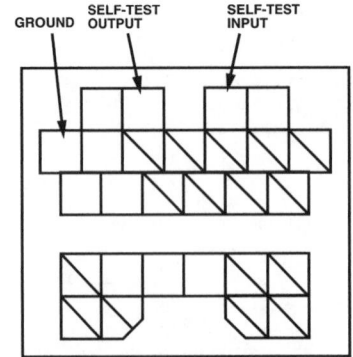

1991-95 1.8L Escort, Tracer, 1993-95 2.0L, 2.5L Probe, 1994-95 1.3L Festiva. Connect the positive lead of an analog voltmeter to the self-test output terminal, connect the negative meter lead to engine ground. Jump the self-test input terminal to ground.

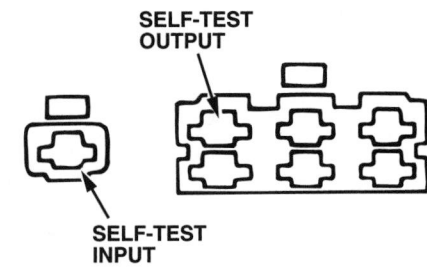

1989-93 1.3L Festiva, 1991-94 1.6L Capri. Connect the positive lead of an analog voltmeter to the self-test output terminal, connect the negative meter lead to engine ground. Jump the self-test input terminal to ground.

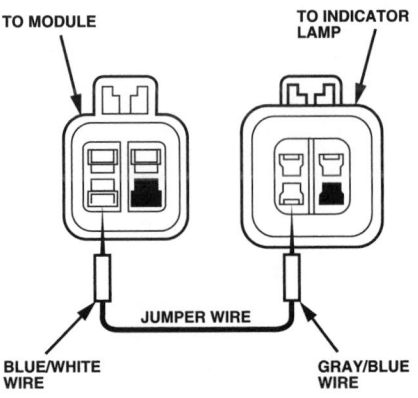

1993-95 3.0L Villager. When using a scan tool, connect to the diagnostic terminal in the fuse box. To actuate the indicator lamp, locate and disconnect the four-position, three-wire diagnostic test connector on top of the transaxle. Install a jumper wire between the blue/white and gray/blue wires as shown. Wait two seconds, remove the jumper wire, and reconnect the multi-plug.

SENSOR TESTS:

DOMESTICS:

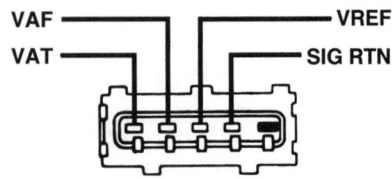

1989-90 Vane air temperature sensor. Measure the resistance between the VAT terminal and a good ground. Also, measure the voltage of the vane airflow sensor between terminal VAF and ground.

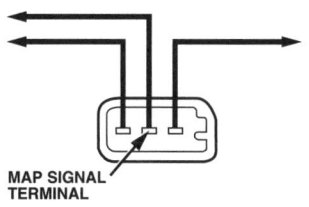

1989-95 MAP sensor. Measure the voltage between the center terminal and ground.

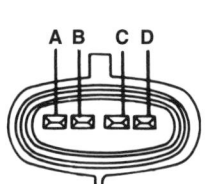

1989-95 Mass airflow sensor. Measure the voltage between terminal D and ground.

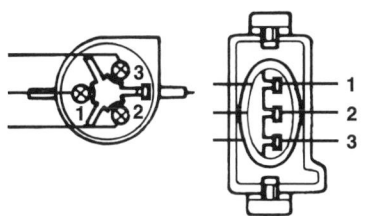

1989-98 Throttle position sensor. Measure the voltage between terminal 2 and 3.

GM Engine Computers

DIAGNOSTIC TESTS:

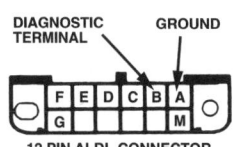

Most 1989-95 domestic vehicles without CRT diagnostic displays DTC retrievals. Connect a jump wire between the ground terminal (A) and the diagnostic terminal (B).

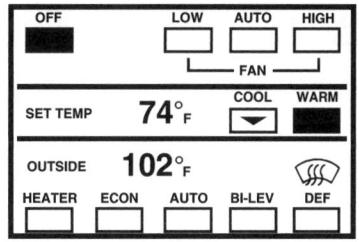

CLIMATE CONTROL KEYPAD

1989-95 Vehicles with CRT diagnostic displays. To activate the self diagnostic system, simultaneously press the OFF and WARM buttons on the climate control keypad.

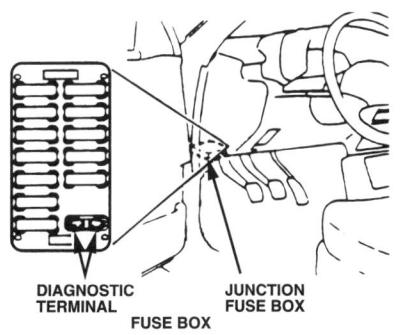

1989-95 Metro and Tracker. Insert the spare fuse into the vacant diagnostic terminal. Data can also be accessed at the under hood data link connector.

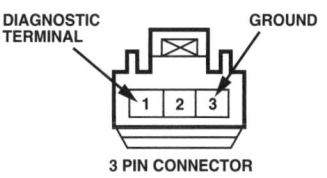

3 PIN CONNECTOR

1990-93 Storm. Connect a jumper wire between the diagnostic terminal (1) and the ground terminal (3).

1992-95 Tracker, except 1994-95 California models. Connect a jumper wire between the diagnostic terminal (2) and the ground terminal (3).

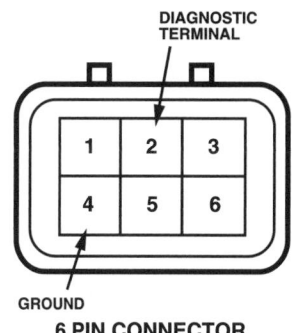

6 PIN CONNECTOR

1992-95 Metro, 1994-95 California Tracker. Connect a jumper wire between the diagnostic terminal (2) and the ground terminal (4).

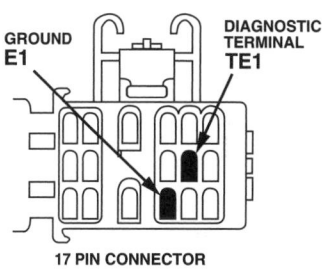

17 PIN CONNECTOR

1989-95 Prizm. Connect a jumper wire between the diagnostic terminal (TE1) and the ground terminal (E1).

SENSOR TESTS:

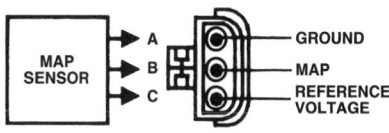

MAP sensor. Test at the three terminal connectors. One terminal has reference voltage. Check voltage between terminals A and B.

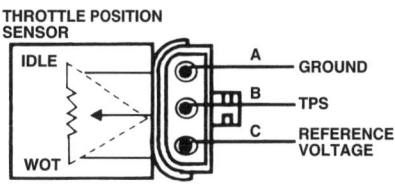

Throttle position sensor. Test the throttle position sensor voltage between terminals A and B.

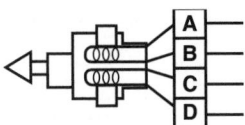

Idle speed controller. *Test the resistance between terminals A and B, and between terminals C and D.*

HONDA Engine Computers

DIAGNOSTIC TESTS:

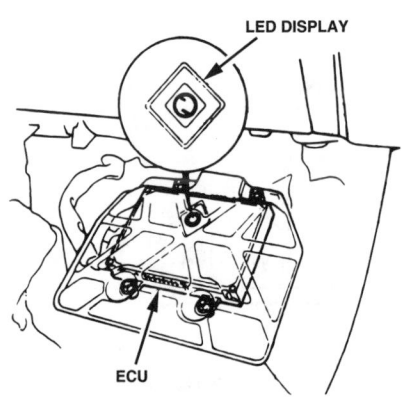

1989-90 Civic, CRX, Prelude, Accord.

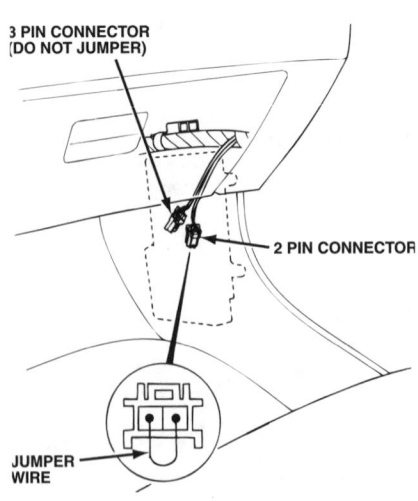

1992-98 All ex. Passport.

NISSAN Engine Computers

DIAGNOSTIC TESTS:

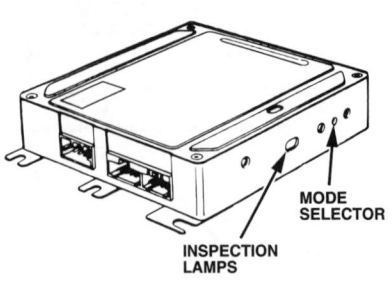

1990 Some, 1991-98 All.
Select the troubleshooting mode using the screw on the side of the ECU.

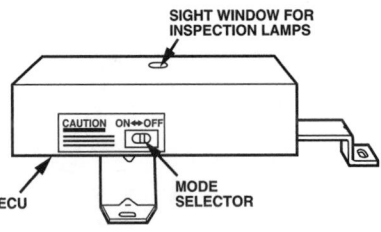

1989 All, 1990 Some. *Use the toggle switch on the side of the ECU to activate the troubleshooting mode.*

SENSOR TESTS:

1989 300 ZX.
Fuel temperature sensor. *Measure resistance between the single terminal and a good ground.*

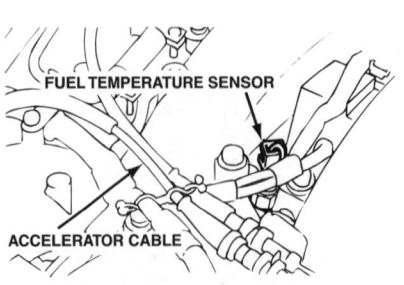

1990-96 300ZX.
Fuel temperature sensor.

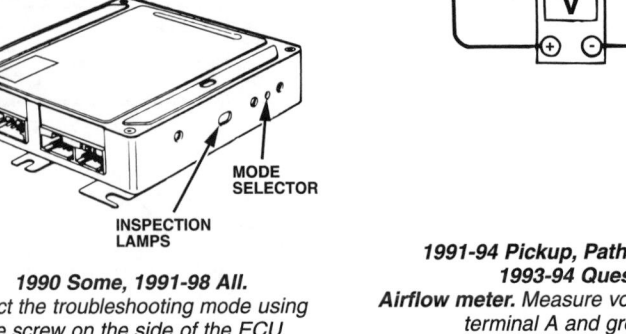

1991-94 Pickup, Pathfinder V6
1993-94 Quest
Airflow meter. *Measure voltage between terminal A and ground.*

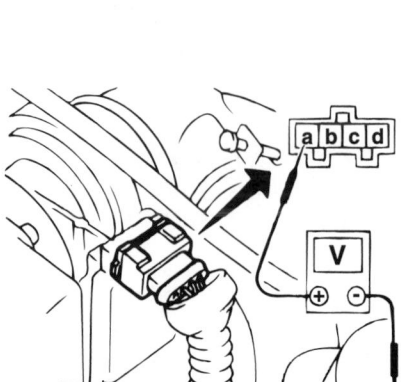

1991-98 Sentra, NX, 200SX. **Airflow meter.** *Measure between terminal A and ground.*

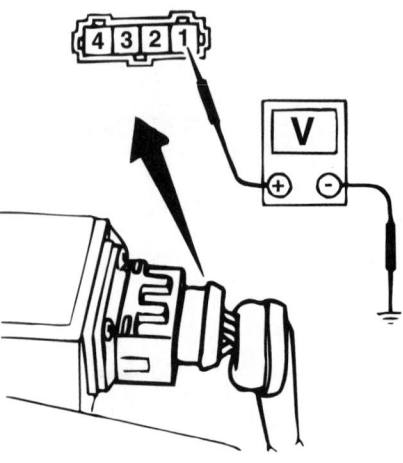

1991-98 240 SX, Pickup, Frontier 4-cyl.;
1993-98 Altima; 1996-98 Pathfinder.
Airflow meter. *Measure voltage between terminal 1 and groove.*

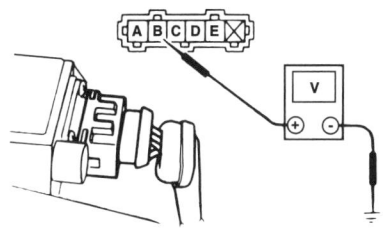

1990-96 300ZX, 1989-94 Maxima. Airflow meter. *Measure the voltage between terminal B and a good ground.*

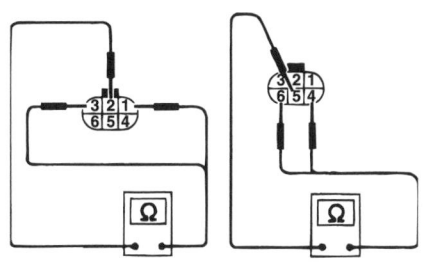

1995-98 Maxima. Idle air control. *Measure resistance between terminals 2 and 1, 2 and 3; 5 and 4, 5 and 6.*

SENSOR TESTS:

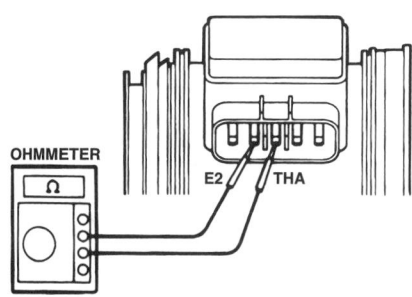

1993-97 Supra, Land Cruiser; 1995-97 Previa; 1995-98 Tacoma, T100; 1996-98 4-Runner. Intake air temperature sensor. *Measure resistance between terminals E2 and THA.*

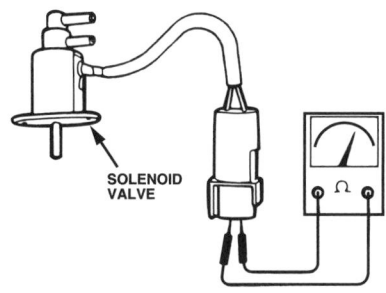

Idle speed control actuator, Sentra, Pulsar. *Measure resistance between terminals A and B, and between terminals B and C.*

TOYOTA Engine Computers

DIAGNOSTIC TESTS:

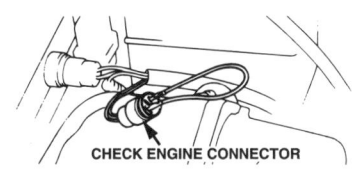

CHECK ENGINE CONNECTOR

1989 Van.

1991-94 Previa; 1991-95 MR2 Turbo; 1989 Celica; 1989-91 Camry; 1989-95 Pickup, 4-Runner V6; T100. Intake air temperature sensor. *Measure resistance between terminals E2 and THA.* **Airflow meter:** *Measure resistance between terminals E2 and VS while moving the plate.*

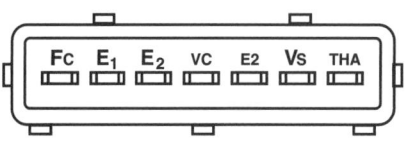

Fc E₁ E₂ VC E2 VS THA

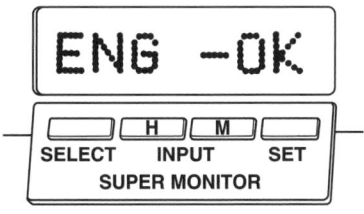

ENG –OK

SELECT INPUT SET
SUPER MONITOR

1989-92 Cressida, Supra with Super Monitor.

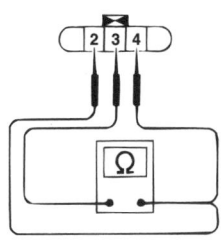

1995-98 Sentra, 200SX, GA16. Idle air control. *Measure resistance between terminals 2 and 3, 3 and 4.*

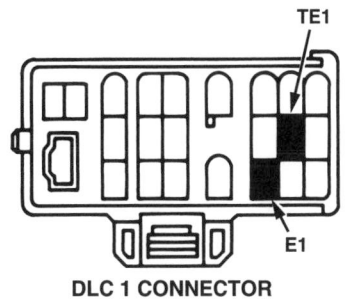

DLC 1 CONNECTOR

TE1
E1

1989-95 All models with DLC Connector. *Connect a jumper wire between terminals TE1 and E1 to display codes on the malfunction indicator lamp.*

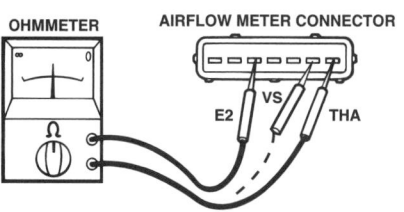

OHMMETER **AIRFLOW METER CONNECTOR**

E2   VS   THA

1989 4A-GZE MR2; 1989-91 4AGE Corolla & MR2; 1989-95 Pickup, 4-Runner 4 Cyl.; 1989-92 Supra ex. Turbo, Cressida, Land Cruiser. Intake temperature sensor. *Measure resistance between terminals E2 and THA of the airflow meter connector.* **Airflow meter:** *Measure resistance between terminals E2 and VS while moving the plate.*

1991-94 Sentra & NX 1597cc, 1998 Maxima. Idle speed control actuator. *Measure resistance at the two-terminal connector.*

SOLENOID VALVE

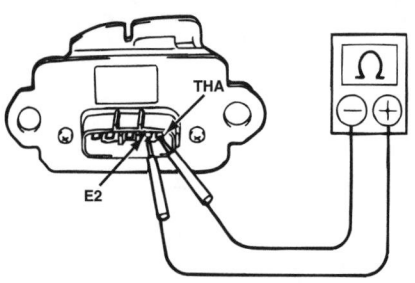

1989-92 Supra Turbo; 1995-98 Camry V6, Avalon, Sienna. Intake air temperature sensor. Measure resistance between terminals E2 and THA.

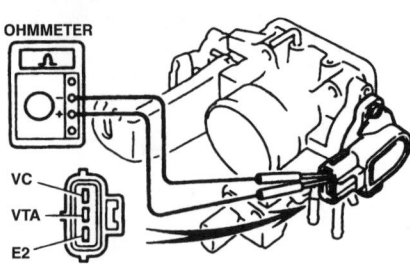

1997-98 Tercel, Paseo. Throttle position sensor. Measure resistance between terminals E2 and VTA.

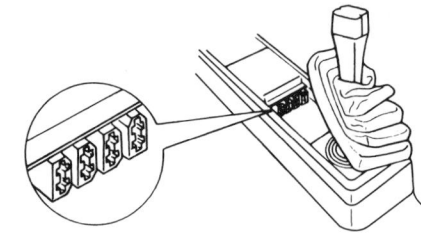

For some 1989-95 Volkswagens, use a diagnostic tester to obtain trouble codes. The tester hook-ups are located in a variety of places, depending on the model.

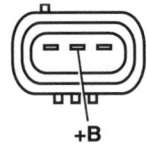

Idle speed control actuator, with three terminals. Measure the resistance between the center terminal and either the left or right terminal.

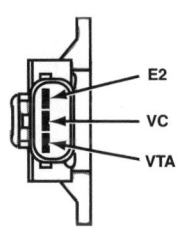

1997-98 3RZ-FE, 5VZ-FE, Tacoma, 4-Runner, T100. Throttle position sensor. Measure resistance between terminals E2 and VTA.

SENSOR TESTS:

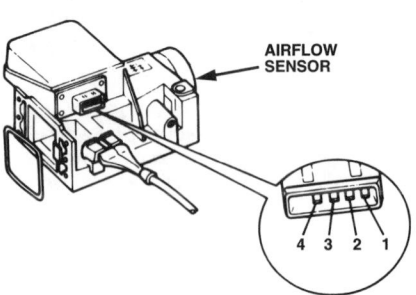

1989-92 Intake air temperature sensor and airflow sensor. Measure the intake air temperature and flow sensor resistance at the same connector.

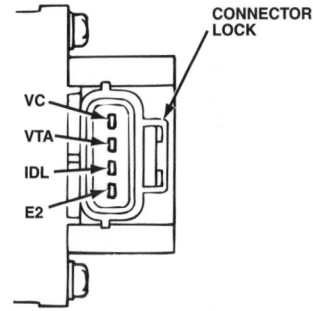

1989-92 Cressida, Supra, Corolla 4A-GE; 1989-94 Camry; 1989-95 MR2; 1989-97 Land Cruiser; 1989-98 Celica; 1990-96 Tercel, Paseo; 1993-97 Corolla; 1993-98 Supra; 1994-96 3RZ-FE, 5VZ-FE Tacoma, 4-Runner, T100; 1995-98 RAV4. Throttle position sensor. Measure resistance between terminals E2 and VTA.

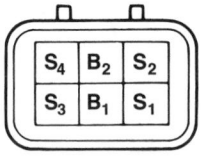

Idle speed control actuator, with six terminals. Measure the resistance between B1 and S1 & S3, and between B2 and S2 & S4.

VOLKSWAGEN Engine Computers

DIAGNOSTIC TESTS:

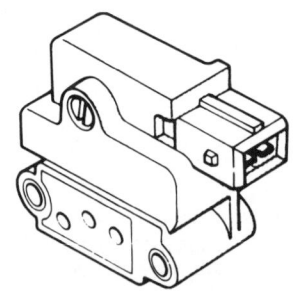

1989-90 Differential pressure regulator. Check resistance at the two terminal connectors.

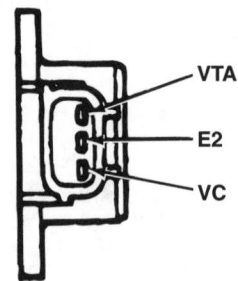

1995-98 Camry V6, Avalon, Sienna; 1998 Corolla. Throttle position sensor. Measure resistance between terminals E2 and VTA.

This is the rocker switch used to obtain codes in some 1989-92 VW vehicles.

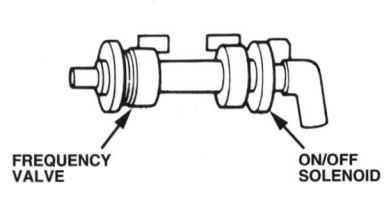

1989 Frequency valve. Test resistance at the spade terminal on the frequency valve.

LIST OF ABBREVIATIONS

Excluding lubricant and footnote symbols, and model nomenclature. These abbreviations may be punctuated.

AC	Air Conditioning		ILC	Idle Load Compensator
AIR	Air Injection Reactor		ISC	Idle Speed Control
AIS	Automatic Idle Speed		ISS	Integrated Idle Stabilization System
AT	Automatic Transmission		LD	Light Duty (emissions package)
ATDC	After Top Dead Center (same as ATC)		LED	Light Emitting Diode
BARO	Barometric Pressure (sensor)		LH	L-Jetronic system with Heated air flow sensor
BCDD	Boost Control Deceleration Device			
BCI	Battery Council International (battery group number)		MAF	Mass Air Flow (sensor)
			MAP	Manifold Absolute Pressure (sensor)
BTDC	Before Top Dead Center (same as BTC)		MAT	Manifold Air Temperature (sensor)
BVSV	Bi-metal Vacuum Switching Valve		MC	Mixture Control
Calpak	Device on FI systems to allow fuel delivery in event of PROM or ECM malfunction		MCU	Microprocessor Control Unit (computer)
			MFI	Multi-Point Fuel Injection
			MPFI	Multi-Point Fuel Injection
CC	Catalytic Converter		MT	Manual Transmission
CCC	Computer Command Control		OD	Overdrive (transmission)
CFI	Central Fuel Injection (Ford)		O_2	Oxygen (sensor)
CFI	Cross Fire Injection (GM dual throttle body)		PCV	Positive Crankcase Ventilation
			PGM-FI	Programmed Fuel Injection
CO	Carbon Monoxide		PROM	Programmable Read-Only Memory (computer chip)
CV	Constant Velocity (joint)			
CVCC	Compound Vortex Controlled Combustion (engine design)		PSI	Pounds per Square Inch
			PVS	Ported Vacuum Switch
CYL	Cylinders		RAM	Random Access Memory
C^3I	Computer Controlled Computer Ignition (no distributor)		RPM	Revolutions Per Minute
			RWD	Rear-Wheel Drive
C-4	Computer-Controlled Catalytic Converter		SOHC	Single Overhead Cam
			SCC	Spark Control Computer
DIS	Direct or Distributorless Ignition System (no distributor)		SFI	Sequential Fuel Injection
			TAC	Thermal Air Control
DOHC	Double Overhead Cam		TAD	Thermactor Air Diverter (valve)
DVOM	Digital Volt-Ohmmeter		TBI	Throttle-Body (fuel) Injection
ECA	Electronic Control Assembly (computer)		TCC	Transmission/Transaxle Converter Clutch
ECI	Electronic Control Injection		TDC	Top Dead Center
ECM	Electronic Control Module (computer)		TFI	Thick Film Integrated (ignition system)
ECS	Evaporative Control System		TPS	Throttle Position Sensor
EEC	Electronic Engine Control includes EEC-II, EEC-III, EEC-IV		TPT	Throttle Position Transducer
			TWC	Three-Way Catalyst
EFC	Electronic Fuel Control		TVS	Thermal Vacuum Switch
EFE	Early Fuel Evaporation		TVSV	Thermal Vacuum Shutoff Valve
EFI	Electronic Fuel Injection (system)		VCV	Vacuum Control Valve
EGR	Exhaust Gas Recirculation		VIN	Vehicle Identification Number
EI	Electronic Ignition		VOM	Volt-Ohmmeter
ESC	Electronic Spark Control		WOT	Wide Open Throttle
EST	Electronic Spark Timing		VOTM	Vacuum Operated Throttle Modulator
FI	Fuel Injected or Fuel Injection		V-REF	Voltage Reference
FWD	Front-Wheel Drive		VSS	Vehicle Speed Sensor
HAI	Heated Air Intake		VV	Variable Venturi (carburetor)
HC	Hydrocarbons		1V	One barrel (carburetor)
HD	Heavy Duty (emissions package)		2V	Two barrel (carburetor)
HEI	High Energy Ignition		2x1	Two one-barrel (carburetors)
HF	High Fuel economy (engine)		3V	Three barrel (carburetor)
HIC	Hot Idle Compensation		2WD	Two-Wheel Drive
HO	High Output		4V	Four barrel (carburetor)
HSC	High Swirl Combustion		4WD	Four-Wheel Drive
H_2O	Water Column (manometer)			
IAC	Idle Air Control			
IDI	Integrate Direct Ignition			

NOTES

NOTES

NOTES